ENGLISH PUBLIC LAW

Edited by
PROFESSOR DAVID FELDMAN
Rouse Ball Professor of English Law, University of Cambridge

Oxford English Law Series Editor
PROFESSOR PETER BIRKS
Regius Professor of Civil Law, University of Oxford

OXFORD
UNIVERSITY PRESS

OXFORD

UNIVERSITY PRESS

Great Clarendon Street, Oxford OX2 6DP

Oxford University Press is a department of the University of Oxford.
It furthers the University's objective of excellence in research, scholarship,
and education by publishing worldwide in

Oxford New York

Auckland Bangkok Buenos Aires Cape Town Chennai
Dar es Salaam Delhi Hong Kong Istanbul Karachi Kolkata
Kuala Lumpur Madrid Melbourne Mexico City Mumbai Nairobi
São Paulo Shanghai Taipei Tokyo Toronto

Oxford is a registered trade mark of Oxford University Press
in the UK and in certain other countries

Published in the United States
by Oxford University Press Inc., New York

© The Editor and Contributors 2004

The moral rights of the authors have been asserted
Database right Oxford University Press (maker)

First published 2004

Crown copyright material is reproduced under Click Licence Number with the permission of the
Controller of Her Majesty's Stationery Office

British Library Cataloguing in Publication Data

Data available

Library of Congress Cataloging in Publication Data

Data available

ISBN 0–19–876551–7

1 3 5 7 9 10 8 6 4 2

Typeset in Garamond by
Cambrian Typesetters, Frimley, Surrey

Printed in Italy
on acid-free paper by
Legoprint S.p.A

EDITOR

Professor David Feldman
Downing College Cambridge

CONTRIBUTORS

Professor Andrew Ashworth QC FBA
All Souls College Oxford

Professor S. H. Bailey
University of Nottingham

Professor Eric Barendt
University College London

Professor A. W. Bradley
*Institute of European and Comparative
Law, University of Oxford*

Professor Paul Craig QC FBA
St John's College Oxford

Professor Evelyn Ellis
University of Birmingham

Professor Sandra Fredman
Exeter College Oxford

Professor L. H. Leigh
*Commission Member, Criminal Cases
Review Commission*

Professor Andrew Le Sueur
University of Birmingham

Professor Christopher McCrudden
Lincoln College Oxford

Professor Dawn Oliver
University College London

Professor Michael Purdue
The City University

Professor Tony Prosser
University of Bristol

Professor Genevra Richardson
*Queen Mary, University of
London*

Professor A. T. H. Smith
Gonville and Caius College Cambridge

Professor Maurice Sunkin
University of Essex

Professor Martin Wasik
University of Keele

OXFORD ENGLISH LAW

SERIES EDITOR'S FOREWORD

Oxford English Law is an ambitious project. It aims to overcome two reproaches to the common law. One is that, good as it may be at micro-rationality, it is chronically indifferent to macro-rationality. It makes lists. It gives no time to asking how the subjects in its lists fit together, how for instance contract relates to tort and both to the law of property. This indifference leads it to make mistakes more often than it should. The other reproach is that it is enormously long-winded. Judgments of the higher courts have become immensely long, often now reaching seventy or even a hundred pages. A textbook on a single subject is likely to cite two thousand or more, and a good lawyer's knowledge of such a subject will be built upon first-hand study of about five hundred. And of course statutes proliferate as never before.

Against this background *Oxford English Law* stands for intellectual order, and for allowing the wood to show through the constantly multiplying leaves. A Law Lord remarked to me on one occasion that their Lordships did not really need help with the fine detail of the law. They were there to sort that out themselves. What they needed, like all common lawyers, was help in keeping a grip on the less rapidly evolving network of principle which provides the rational structure of the law. *Oxford English Law* aims to meet that need. It gives an ordered, accurate, and economical account of the common law, not indeed of all of it, but of all parts of its core subjects, rationally inter-related.

The Emperor Justinian confidently declared in the sixth century, 'This study has two aspects, public and private. Public law deals with the structure of the Roman state, and private law is concerned with the aspirations of individuals' (J *Inst* 1.1.4). This project started with *English Private Law*, which was published in two volumes in 2000 and has now been twice supplemented. We were lucky at that time to be able to put together a team each of whom was a leading authority in his field. Although English law, ever since Dicey, has had some difficulty with the line between public law and private law, from the inception of the project the intention was always that once we had brought *English Private Law* successfully to birth, *English Public Law* should follow. With its appearance the profession and the universities will for the first time be able to see the nature of the project as a whole. It is a brand new way of presenting the common law. It is different but reliable. It is a sure guide to the network of principle from which disputes of detail always arise. We hope that judges, practitioners, and professors will look on it and find it good.

It will be seen that for these purposes public law breaks down into constitutional law, administrative law, and criminal law. Into this trio in recent years the law of human rights, certainly the greatest juridical achievement in the history of the western legal tradition, has burrowed ever deeper and more rapidly. Those who qualified a quarter of a century ago hardly recognize the landscape. We were incredibly lucky, therefore, to be able to persuade Professor David Feldman to become editor of *English Public Law*. In human rights and civil liberties there is no greater authority. In this highly specialized world, there is as it turns out no author common to both volumes. But the project has again been fortunate in securing the commitment of the very best lawyers in each field. We are extremely grateful to them, for their standing will turn out to have been indispensable in proving that relatively brief treatments need lack nothing in authority.

Early on we made a conscious decision to omit, at least for the moment, one important slice of public law, namely public international law or, from the standpoint of this series, foreign relations law. There cannot and should not be an English international law, but there is a great deal of English law about relations with foreign governments and nationals. The question whether to take the project forward into that field is for the moment suspended. When second editions come into consideration, it will become live again.

It needs to be said that the role of the General Editor in the making of this great book has been vanishingly small. Someone had to fire the starting gun. Thereafter, success belonged entirely to the learning and stamina of Professor Feldman and his very distinguished collaborators. In this kind of project, General Editors can nag and make a nuisance of themselves. For any success in that negative role, this one now has an opportunity to apologize.

Peter Birks
All Souls
1.1.04

EDITOR'S PREFACE

This volume is intended to provide a clear, principled, authoritative, up-to-date account of English public law, complementing *English Private Law*,[1] the first volume of the Oxford University Press project *Oxford English Law*, of which Professor Peter Birks is Series Editor. Its purpose, like that of *English Private Law*, is to offer a structured overview of its field in which the principles are clearly identified, leading to more understanding by reducing the dominance of the excessively detailed information which is now available from the Internet and other sources. Too often this detail represents a barrier to understanding. We hope that this volume will counteract that, by providing an account of public law in which the principles dominate and the details are chosen to clarify rather than obscure the systematic overview, in a manner reminiscent of *Gloag and Henderson's Law of Scotland*.[2]

The book is designed principally for lawyers, public servants, politicians and political scientists in England who seek a first point of reference when they need to know how the public sector is affected by law, and for lawyers and political scientists in other jurisdictions who want a convenient general account of the slightly unusual working of the system of public law in England. We also hope that practitioners, judges, academics and students of law and political science in England will find answers to at least some of their more specialized questions in the book.

For the purpose of this book, English public law is treated as including both the rules governing the allocation of power and responsibility between different tiers and agencies of government and those controlling the relationship between the institutions of government and private citizens. It thus encompasses criminal law, sentencing and procedure alongside constitutional and administrative law, human rights law, and systems for providing remedies in public law.

There are three reasons for undertaking this project, and for its particular focus on England. First, the United Kingdom's constitution is at a stage of unusually rapid and fundamental change. The second half of the twentieth century saw the rapid development of the European Communities and Union, of devolution and human rights; of privatization of public assets, regulation, and provision of services

---

[1] P Birks (ed), *English Private Law* (Oxford: Oxford University Press, 2000).

[2] WA Wilson and A Forte (eds), *Gloag and Henderson The Law of Scotland* (10th edn, 1995). See P Birks, 'Preface', in *English Private Law*, above, xxix-xxx.

through public-private partnerships; of new ways of dealing with grievances. Judicial review grew in scope and importance. Criminal law, procedure and sentencing were put on an increasingly principled footing. Parliament began, however uncertainly, to modernize itself. Central government came to be dominated by the so-called 'new public management', and the role and performance of local government were increasingly put in the spotlight. In all these spheres, the pull of principle frequently struggles against short-term political expediency and pragmatism. It is a suitable moment to ask how far the traditional principles of the constitution—the sovereignty and legislative supremacy of Parliament, the rule of law, and representative and responsible government—still dominate public law, and whether they mean the same as they once did.

Secondly, it is a propitious moment to examine the United Kingdom's public law system as a whole from a distinctively English perspective. The three separate legal systems in the United Kingdom—England and Wales, Scotland and Northern Ireland—have always had different traditions in administrative law and criminal law and procedure, although the nature and degree of the differences varies from place to place. Recent constitutional history, including the move towards devolution, has made it possible to speak of distinctive constitutional arrangements in Scotland, Wales and Northern Ireland. It is now appropriate to consider how England fares, without undervaluing the contribution of the other parts of the United Kingdom or international influences from Europe and beyond. While England and Wales still form a single unit for many legal purposes, devolution has made Welsh public law sufficiently different from that in England to justify the focus and title of this volume.

Thirdly, English public law is interesting because the relationship between public law and politics is not obscured in the way that it is in some other constitutional systems. The interplay of constitutional and political theory and practical politics is not moderated by any need to accommodate solutions within a constitutional text. It works itself out through a mixture of statute, political practices and case law which operate against a background of more or less malleable principles. The principles are important, but are constantly under challenge. The way in which this affects constitutional law, administrative law, human rights law and criminal law and procedure can be a valuable study for public lawyers and political scientists in many different systems.

The structure of the volume is as follows. The book is divided into four parts, dealing respectively with constitutional law, standards for legal accountability in public law, remedies in public law, and criminal law, procedure and sentencing. The contributors have tried, in each field, to make clear the underlying principles governing their subjects, and to bring out the common features (especially constitutional principles) which shape them.

Part I of the book, comprising chapters 1 to 6, deals with constitutional law. In chapter 1, Professor Barendt provides a sketch of the fundamental principles on which the constitution is based, its institutions and its influences, and Professor Ellis explains the sources of English public law. Chapters 2 to 6 examine in greater detail the operation of those principles in the main institutions of the state. In chapter 2, Professor Oliver examines Parliament and its work, and Professor Ellis provides an account of the doctrine of parliamentary sovereignty and the effect of the primacy of European Community law. Professor Le Sueur looks at central government and its evolving structures in chapter 3, and Professor Bailey does the same for local government in chapter 4. Professor Prosser addresses the powers and accountability of the increasingly important range of agencies and regulators in chapter 5. In chapter 6, Professor Bradley looks at the position of the judiciary, taking account of the Government's recent reform proposals.

Part II is concerned with the standards which are used to secure the accountability of public bodies to the judiciary for the legality of their activities. These include the traditional principles of judicial review of administrative action, and, since the Human Rights Act 1998 came fully into force, the Convention rights which became part of English law under that Act. Chapter 7 briefly explains the nature of the standards used, and explores the general principles governing the use of Convention rights in English law. Chapters 8 to 12 examine the current and potential effect of a number of particular Convention rights. Chapter 8 covers basic civil and personal rights: the right to life; freedom from torture, inhuman and degrading treatment and punishment, slavery and servitude; the right to liberty of the person; and the rights to respect for private and family life, to marry and found a family, and to freedom of thought, conscience and religion. Chapter 9 looks at the political rights: the freedoms of expression, peaceful assembly and association; and the right to free elections. In chapter 10, Professor Fredman examines the background to and the growing importance of social and political rights in English law, and in chapter 11 Professor McCrudden does the same for rights to equality and non-discrimination. Professor Bailey deals with due process rights derived from the European Convention on Human Rights in chapter 12.

In chapters 13 to 16 the contributors turn their attention to principles of judicial review. Professor Craig draws attention to the way in which judicial review is shaped by fundamental constitutional rules and principles in chapter 13, then the next three chapters provide a more detailed survey of particular grounds of review, based on the tripartite division into illegality, irrationality and procedural impropriety. Professor Sunkin examines review for illegality in chapter 14; Professor Bailey deals with natural justice, fairness and procedural legitimate expectations in chapter 15; and in chapter 16 Professor Craig explains the principles on which courts review executive acts and decisions for defects going to the merits, including rationality, proportionality, and substantive legitimate expectations.

In Part III of the book we turn our attention to the remedies available in public law. We use the word 'remedies' loosely. Some of them are purely remedial, including those judicial remedies available in the Administrative Court for breaches of principles of judicial review. Others involve the making or application of policies, including the use of certain tribunals and inquiries, or aim to improve administration as much as to remedy wrongs, including ombudsman systems. In chapter 17, Professor Craig examines the principles and procedures governing access to judicial review of administrative action, including locus standi, the range of cases which are amenable to judicial review, and relationship between judicial review and other forms of redress. Professor Sunkin then explains in chapter 18 the different remedies available in judicial review proceedings. Chapter 19 describes the remedies which are available for violations of Convention rights under the Human Rights Act 1998. Professor Richardson surveys the operation of the complex collection of tribunals in chapter 20, and Professor Purdue does the same for public sector ombudsmen and public inquiries in the system of administration in chapters 21 and 22.

Part IV of the book covers criminal law, procedure and sentencing. In chapter 23, Professor Leigh provides a detailed account of the institutions which are responsible for the criminal justice process, and of procedures for investigating crimes, prosecuting suspected offenders, and appealing against or reviewing the decisions of the courts in criminal matters. Professor Ashworth analyses the general principles which apply (or ought to apply) throughout English criminal law in chapter 24, including the different elements in criminal offences (such as capacity, criminal conduct, fault, and defences). Chapters 25 to 27 then look at the operation of those principles in relation to particular offences. There is a discussion of homicide (Professor Ashworth), and assaults and sexual offences (Professor Smith), in chapter 25. Professor Smith then covers offences against property, including offences of dishonesty, criminal damage and computer misuse, in chapter 26, and offences against the state (including treason and official secrets), public order and public morality (both under statute and at common law), in chapter 27. In chapter 28, Professor Wasik rounds off Part IV by drawing out a number of general principles of sentencing and showing how they apply to people who have been convicted of offences in England.

Naturally, there have been difficult decisions about what to include and exclude, and how much space to devote to those matters which are included. There is no examination of particular fields of public administration, such as housing, prisons or social security. Such treatment would be interesting and, in its own way, useful, but it would have distorted the structure, which is based on the premise that there are general principles of public law which apply across the board. Not everyone will agree with the resulting structure, and there are certainly matters which could have been included: for example, there is no extended treatment of public sector procurement, which is undoubtedly important. It may be possible to make some changes in future editions if we are persuaded that they are desirable. In the meantime, I hope that readers will find the present arrangement useful, illuminating and coherent.

On my own behalf and that of my fellow contributors, I take this opportunity to acknowledge the efforts of the many people who have helped us to bring the project to fruition. First, I must mention some personal debts. While working on the book, I was employed by two institutions which generously allowed me the freedom to continue the work: the University of Birmingham, where I was Dean of Law from 1997 until 2000; and the two Houses of Parliament, where I was Legal Adviser to the Joint Committee on Human Rights from 2000 until 2004. Although I will have moved on again by the time the book is published, it is fair to record the fact that credit is due to those institutions for its completion. During the summer of 2002, Veronica Daly lent valuable research assistance, which particularly improved chapter 9. Less direct but equally important has been the moral and material support of my family—Jill, Becky and Jonathan, not to mention the two dogs, two cats (one of which sadly died during the production process), horse and three sheep—who with a good grace tolerated a long-term interference with the right to a normal family life.

Next, there are debts which I share with the other contributors. A number of people besides the authors have contributed directly to the preparation of the book. The team which Oxford University Press brought together has believed strongly in the project from the outset, and has devoted itself to its success. Chris Rycroft has been a constant source of advice, enthusiasm, practical help and encouragement. David Stott and Rebecca Allen successively provided great support and responded constructively to difficulties and annoyances with unfailing good humour. Chris, Rebecca, Katarina Wihlborg, and Louise Kavanagh have seen the book through its production stages with utter unflappability and attention to detail, while the copy-editor, Nicola Freshwater, and the proof-reader, Sandra Sinden, have performed wonders to enhance the accuracy, consistency and clarity of the finished product. It has been a pleasure to work with them all, and my fellow contributors and I greatly appreciate their efforts.

Professor Peter Birks has done far more than provide the book with a Series Editor's Foreword. He is the driving force behind the whole *Oxford English Law* project. When he and Chris Rycroft first invited me to join the project, Peter's enthusiasm and clarity of vision were inspirational. *English Private Law*, which he edited, then provided a template for the work of our contributors and set a high standard for us to try to maintain. I hope that the present volume will help to fulfil Peter's aspirations for the series, and that he will find in it at least a reasonable approximation to the subject-matter, approach and qualities which he originally envisaged.

My greatest debt, of course, is owed to the contributors. It has been a privilege to work with such outstanding authorities on their various fields. Their contribution to the project has gone well beyond writing their chapters. From an early stage, they gave generously of their time and expertise, helping to devise a coherent structure for the volume and advising on the relationship between different sections. Their ready cooperation with each other, the team at the Press and me, and their expertise and skill in overcoming problems, have made the lengthy gestation of the book far smoother than I could reasonably have hoped that it would be. So far as the book succeeds in achieving its objectives, it will be the result of their commitment and abilities. All defects should be laid at my door.

David Feldman
Yieldingtree, 2 January 2004

CONTENTS—SUMMARY

CONTENTS

I CONSTITUTIONAL LAW

1. Constitutional Fundamentals

2. The Law of Parliament

III REMEDIES IN PUBLIC LAW

Contents

TABLE OF CASES

TABLES OF LEGISLATION

UK Statutes

Statutory Instruments

Australia

Canada

France

Germany

India

New Zealand

South Africa

Sweden

USA

TABLE OF TREATIES AND CONVENTIONS

LIST OF ABBREVIATIONS

AC	Law Reports, Appeal Cases
ACD	Administrative Court Digest
Ad & E	Adolphus & Ellis's Reports, King's Bench and Queen's Bench
Admin LR	Administrative Law Reports
AG	Advocate General
A-G	Attorney-General
All ER	All England Law Reports
App Cas	Law Reports, Appeal Cases 1875–1890
Beav	Beavan's Reports, Rolls Court
Bing	Bingham's Reports, Common Pleas
BLGR	Butterworths Local Government Reports
BOT	British Overseas Territory
Burr	Burrow's Reports, King's Bench
C & P	Carrington & Payne's Reports, Nisi Prius
CAT	Competition Appeal Tribunal
CC	County Council
CCLR	Community Care Law Reports
Ch	Law Reports, Chancery Division
CICB	Criminal Injuries Compensation Board
Cl & Fin	Clark & Finnelly's Reports, House of Lords
CLP	Current Legal Problems
CMLR	Common Market Law Reports
Co Rep	Coke's Reports, King's Bench
COD	Crown Office Digest
Con LR	Construction Law Reports
CPLR	Civil Practice Law Reports
Cr & J	Crompton & Jervis's Reports, Exchequer
Cr & Ph	Craig & Phillips's Reports, Chancery
Cr App R	Criminal Appeal Reports
Cr App R (S)	Criminal Appeal Reports (Sentencing)
Crim LR	Criminal Law Review
CSMC	Civil Service Management Code
DDA	Disability Discrimination Act
DPP	Director of Public Prosecutions

DR	Decisions and Reports of the EComHR from 1975 onwards
DRC	Disability Rights Commission
East	East's Term Reports, King's Bench
EC	European Community
ECA	European Communities Act
ECHR	European Convention on Human Rights
ECJ	European Court of Justice
EComHR	European Commission on Human Rights
ECR	European Court Reports
ECtHR	European Court of Human Rights
Ed CR	Education Case Reports
Ed LR	Education Law Reports
EHLR	Environmental Health Law Reports
EHRR	European Human Rights Reports
EIP	Examination in Public
ELR	European Law Review
EMLR	Entertainment and Media Law Reports
Env LR	Environmental Law Reports
EOC	Equal Opportunities Commission
ESC	European Social Charter
ETMR	European Trade Marks Reports
Ex D	Law Reports, Exchequer Division
F & F	Foster & Finlason's Reports, Nisi Prius
FCR	Family Court Reporter
FLR	Family Law Reports
HLC	Clark's Reports, House of Lords
HLR	Housing Law Reports
HRA	Human Rights Act
HRLR	Human Rights Law Reports
HSC	Health Service Commissioner
ICCPR	International Covenant on Civil and Political Rights
ICESCR	International Covenant on Economic, Social and Cultural Rights
ICR	Industrial Case Reports
ILJ	Industrial Law Journal
ILM	International Legal Materials
Imm AR	Immigration Appeal Reports
INLR	Immigration and Nationality Law Reports

IR	Irish Reports
IRLR	Industrial Relations Law Reports
J	Journal
JCHR	Joint Committee on Human Rights
JCSI	Joint Committee on Statutory Instruments
JJ	Justices
JP	Justice of the Peace Reports
JP Jo	Justice of the Peace and Local Government Review
JPL	Journal of Planning and Environment Law
KB	Law Reports, King's Bench Division
L	Law
LBC	London Borough Council
LCA	Local Commissioner for Administration
Ld Raym	Lord Raymond's Reports, King's Bench and Common Pleas
LGLR	Local Government Law Reports
LGR	Local Government Reports
LJMC	Law Journal, Magistrates' Cases
LJQB	Law Journal, Queen's Bench
LQR	Law Quarterly Review
LR (vol) CP	Law Reports, Common Pleas
LS	Legal Studies
LT	Law Times
MBC	Metropolitan Borough Council
Med LR	Medical Law Reports
MLR	Modern Law Review
MP	Member of Parliament
My & Cr	Mylne & Craig's Reports, Chancery
NDPB	non-departmental public body
NHS	National Health Service
NI	Northern Ireland Law Reports
NLJ	New Law Journal
NPC	New Property Cases
OAPA	Offences Against the Person Act
ODPM	Office of the Deputy Prime Minister
OJ	Official Journal of the European Communities
OJLS	Oxford Journal of Legal Studies

P & CR	Property, Planning & Compensation Reports
PCA	Parliamentary Commissioner for Administration
PHA	Protection from Harassment Act
PL	Public Law
PLCR	Planning Law Case Reports
Plowd	Plowden's Reports
PLR	Estates Gazette Planning Law Reports
Q	Quarterly
QB	Law Reports, Queen's Bench Division
QBD	Law Reports, Queen's Bench Division 1875–1890
RA	Rating Appeals
Rev	Review
RRA	Race Relations Act
RTR	Road Traffic Reports
RVR	Rating and Valuation Reporter
Salk	Salkeld's Reports, King's Bench
SDA	Sex Discrimination Act
SLT	Scots Law Times
SO	Standing Order
St Tr	State Trials
Str	Strange's Reports
TEC	Treaty Establishing the European Community
Term Rep	Term Reports
TEU	Treaty on European Union
TLGR	Transport, Local Government and the Regions
TLR	Times Law Reports
UDC	Urban District Council
UKCLR	United Kingdom Competition Law Reports
UKHRR	United Kingdom Human Rights Reports
WLR	Weekly Law Reports

PART I

CONSTITUTIONAL LAW

1

CONSTITUTIONAL FUNDAMENTALS

A. Fundamental Principles

(1) Introduction

(a) Constitutions

Like many other organizations, countries have a constitution. Usually this takes **1.01** the form of a single document which sets out the functions of the state's principal political institutions—the legislature, the executive and the courts. Constitutions often set out the basic rights of citizens and they may empower the courts to strike down legislation or executive acts which infringe them—the procedure known as judicial review. Further, the text of the constitution will usually provide how it may be amended, although a few provisions may be regarded as so fundamental that they cannot be repealed or altered. Some constitutions also include general provisions about the character of the state—that it is a democracy promoting the welfare of its citizens—which contain political aspirations rather than legally binding rules.

There is no single constitutional document for the United Kingdom or for **1.02** England, one of the countries which, together with Scotland, Wales, and Northern Ireland, make up the United Kingdom. However, politicians, lawyers, and others in the United Kingdom frequently refer to its constitution. A broader meaning of the term 'constitution' is that it refers to the collection of rules prescribing the powers of the principal political institutions—Parliament, the government, and the courts—and the rights and liberties of individuals, whether or not they are incorporated in a single document (or in a limited collection of texts).

In so far as this broader meaning of the term is acceptable, the United Kingdom has a constitution.

(b) What is constitutional law?

1.03 It is relatively easy to determine the contours of constitutional law in a jurisdiction with a constitutional text. Any issue concerning the interpretation of the provisions of the documentary constitution is a question of constitutional law, though a court may decide that a particular provision is not intended to be legally binding and is to be understood as only a statement of political aims. It may be more difficult to identify what counts as constitutional law in the United Kingdom, as it is impossible to resort to the formal test: what is in the authoritative constitutional text?

1.04 In a classic work, *Introduction to the Study of the Law of the Constitution*, Dicey stated that 'constitutional law . . . appears to include all rules which directly or indirectly affect the distribution or the exercise of the sovereign power in the state'.[1] He distinguished those rules which are 'laws' in the strict sense from those practices and understandings dealing with the exercise of sovereign power which should be regarded as principles of constitutional morality or constitutional conventions. The difference, in his view, is that constitutional law is enforced by the courts, while constitutional conventions are not.[2]

1.05 Many examples can be given of rules of constitutional law in England, as Dicey defined that term. The common law rule that Parliament has unlimited legal authority to make or repeal any law it likes is a rule of constitutional law, the most important in English law. Courts also decide what counts as a valid Act of Parliament and determine the relationship of parliamentary legislative supremacy to the principle of the primacy of EC law.[3] For a long time judges have determined the scope of the Crown's prerogative powers. All these matters raise questions of constitutional law. In contrast, courts do not claim authority to enforce constitutional conventions, such as the rule that the monarch must assent to Bills passed by the House of Commons and the House of Lords or the convention that he should dissolve Parliament when requested by the Prime Minister. Political life in England could not be conducted unless conventions such as these were observed; therefore, any outline of fundamental constitutional principles must discuss them and their relationship to constitutional law.

1.06 Although it is clear that some principles of English law are rules of *constitutional law*, it may be difficult to characterize others. For example, there is general agree-

---

[1] AV Dicey, *The Law of the Constitution* (10th edn, London: Macmillan, 1959) 23.
[2] ibid 24; see paras 1.38–1.39 below.
[3] See paras 1.81–1.87 below.

ment that the rights to freedom of expression and to a fair trial, protected in other countries by the written constitution, are aspects of constitutional law; indeed, in recent cases judges have explicitly referred to such rights as 'constitutional'.[4] It is much less clear whether statutory rights to adequate housing or to social security benefits should be treated in the same way. There is similar uncertainty whether it is appropriate to regard rules concerning the funding and organization of political parties as constitutional law. Obviously these rules are crucial to the conduct of political and public life. Elections and political parties are often covered, to some extent, in modern constitutions, so reference is made to these topics later in this exposition of the fundamental principles of the constitution in England.[5]

(c) Constitutional law, administrative law and public law

Traditionally English law, like other legal systems, distinguishes constitutional   **1.07**
from administrative law. Again, this distinction may be drawn easily in jurisdictions with a written constitution; legal principles for the control of government and its agencies, not developed from the constitutional text, constitute a distinct system of administrative rather than constitutional law. This line cannot be drawn in England. Instead, a crude functional distinction may be made. Constitutional law concerns the distribution of powers between the branches of government, the general principles governing their relationships and those guaranteeing the fundamental rights of citizens. Administrative law consists of the detailed rules for the control of government. But in so far as they rest on constitutional principles, administrative law may be regarded as an aspect of constitutional law.[6]

In the last two decades courts in England have often referred to 'public law', con-   **1.08**
trasting it with the principles of private law. The distinction was initially drawn in the context of the procedure for challenging administrative decisions; the House of Lords held that decisions of public authorities infringing public law rights may only be challenged by the procedure known as the application for judicial review rather than by the ordinary civil procedure used to assert private law rights.[7] Subsequently judges have on occasion used the term 'public law' more generally. In effect they treat it as a broad concept embracing both principles of administrative and constitutional law.[8]

---

[4] See para 1.97 below.
[5] See paras 1.45–1.48 below.
[6] Sir W Wade, *Administrative Law* (7th edn, Oxford: Clarendon, 1994) 6.
[7] *O'Reilly v Mackman* [1983] 2 AC 237: see paras 17.61–17.68 below.
[8] See the speeches of Lords Diplock and Roskill in *Council of Civil Service Unions v Minister for Civil Service* [1985] AC 374, HL. The latter referred to the 'branch of public or administrative law' concerned with the control of executive action.

(2) The UK Constitution

1.09   The following paragraphs outline prominent characteristics of the UK constitution. It should be emphasized that these constitutional arrangements are now undergoing a period of change as radical as any since the resolution of the constitutional struggles between Stuart monarchs and Parliament at the end of the 17th century. The transfer of power from London to a Scottish Parliament is one major development. Others have resulted from the United Kingdom's membership of the European Union and the incorporation of the European Human Rights Convention into UK law. These developments have encouraged the courts recently to formulate novel constitutional principles which would have astonished commentators only 20 or 30 years ago.

(a) Is there a constitution?

1.10   Distinguished writers have doubted whether England (or for that matter the United Kingdom of which England is a part) has a constitution. The most famous of these sceptics was the French scholar Alexis de Tocqueville. As Parliament is always free to modify the constitution, which could therefore change continually, it would be better, in his view, to conclude that in reality it did not exist at all.[9] For de Tocqueville, it would be appropriate to use the term 'constitution' only with reference to higher laws unamendable by the normal legislative process.

1.11   This conclusion should be rejected. The better view is that the United Kingdom does have a constitution, though it is dissimilar from almost every other constitution in the world in that it is not set out in a single text or even in a limited set of documents. Moreover, there is no sharp distinction between general legislation and constitutional legislation; laws such as Magna Carta 1215, the Bill of Rights 1689, and the European Communities Act 1972, all of which deal with fundamental constitutional matters, may in principle be repealed as easily as a statute regulating a profession or the Animals Act 1971. (Whether a constitution, or constitutional arrangements, of this kind is as satisfactory as the more usual documentary constitution, with special rules for its amendment, is another matter.) It would be rather paradoxical to conclude that, while there are constitutional rules and laws in England, as there clearly are, there is nevertheless no constitution.[10]

---

[9] *Democracy in America* (1835) i, ch VI. See also Thomas Paine, *Rights of Man* (1791–92, Penguin Classics edn, 1985) 193 and FF Ridley, 'There is no British Constitution: A Dangerous Case of the Emperor's Clothes' (1988) 41 Parliamentary Affairs 340.

[10] But see S Sedley, 'The Sound of Silence: Constitutional Law without a Constitution' (1994) 110 LQR 270.

(b) A written, but uncodified constitution

It is sometimes said that the constitution is unwritten, or at least partly unwritten.[11] This is misleading. Constitutional law in the United Kingdom (or England) in the strict sense of rules enforced by the courts is written. Obviously, statutes and decisions of the courts on points of constitutional and administrative law are all written. Many constitutional conventions are also written, perhaps in published statements by politicians or by constitutional experts or in authoritative books on the constitution. However, unlike statutes and court rulings, they are rarely formulated in an authoritative text, so there is ample room for disagreement about their scope and application.

1.12

What is characteristic of the constitutional arrangements in the United Kingdom is that they are uncodified. They are not reduced to a single text or series of documents which can be identified as the constitution. This reflects the point that the constitution is a *common law* constitution, in the sense that its fundamental principles such as the principles of parliamentary supremacy and of the rule of law are expressed in judicial decisions. Like the rulings of the courts on contract and tort, these decisions have not been set out in a code.[12]

1.13

(c) A flexible constitution

The constitution is flexible in the sense that there is no sharp difference between ordinary and constitutional legislation; statutes dealing with constitutional matters are not subject to any special procedure for amendment and may in principle be as easily repealed as other statutes by express words. A contrast may be drawn with written rigid constitutions,[13] where there are special procedures for amendment, while some provisions cannot be amended at all.[14]

1.14

It is doubtful whether much importance should be ascribed to this distinction. The UK constitution is almost unique in its complete flexibility in theory. But in practice it may be as difficult to change its fundamental rules as those of some rigid constitutions. The principle of parliamentary supremacy, it has been said, is a political fact which can only be changed by revolution;[15] it has perhaps been modified by

1.15

---

[11] Dicey (n 1 above) 32, and Sir WI Jennings, *The Law and the Constitution* (5th edn, London: University of London Press, 1959) 36.

[12] O Dixon, 'The Common Law as an Ultimate Constitutional Foundation' (1957) 31 Australian LJ 240; S Sedley, 'The Common Law and the Constitution' in Lord Nolan and Sir Stephen Sedley (eds), *The Making & Remaking of the British Constitution* (London: Blackstone, 1997) ch 2.

[13] J Bryce, *Studies in History and Jurisprudence* (Oxford: Clarendon Press, 1901), Essay III.

[14] Art V of the US Constitution sets out a procedure which broadly requires amendments to be proposed by two thirds of both Houses of Congress and ratified by the legislatures of three quarters of the states; but no amendment may deprive a state of its equal representation in the Senate without its consent.

[15] HWR Wade, 'The Basis of Legal Sovereignty' [1955] CLJ 172.

UK membership of the European Community, but it is difficult to point to other instances where it has been amended.[16] On the other hand, the German Basic Law—a rigid constitution—has been amended as many as 40 times since its adoption in 1949. The distinction between flexible and rigid constitutions is perhaps of more theoretical than practical significance.

(d) A monarchical constitution

1.16   It is debatable how much importance should now be attached to the fact that the United Kingdom has a monarchical, not a republican constitution.[17] During the great constitutional struggles of the 17th century the monarch claimed to exercise a wide range of legal powers, known as prerogative power, without the consent of Parliament. But the scope of these powers has been considerably cut down by judicial rulings,[18] and by the Bill of Rights 1689 heralding the victory of Parliament over the monarchical claims. That statute made it clear that the monarch had no authority to suspend the enforcement of general laws or to dispense individuals from the obligation to obey them. Further, the consent of Parliament was necessary to raise taxation.

1.17   The continued existence of the monarchy has not prevented the development of parliamentary democracy in England and of the constitutional principle of the legislative supremacy of Parliament. But the monarch is head of state. She is also Supreme Governor of the established Church of England (and head of the established Presbyterian Church of Scotland).[19] Moreover, the Queen continues to enjoy significant legal powers. For example, as a matter of constitutional *law*, she must assent to Bills for them to become valid Acts of Parliament, though by constitutional *convention* she is required to give assent. No monarch has in fact withheld Royal Assent since Queen Anne refused in 1708 to agree to a Bill to institute a Scottish militia.[20]

(i) The residual constitutional powers of the monarch

1.18   Although it is now clear that the monarch must generally act on the advice of ministers, in some circumstances she may retain personal discretion how to exercise her legal powers; in other words, the exercise of these powers may not always be regulated by established constitutional conventions.[21] For example, it is possible

---

[16] But its weight with respect to other principles has perhaps lessened recently: see paras 1.114–1.117 below.

[17] See V Bogdanor, *The Monarchy and the Constitution* (Oxford: Clarendon Press, 1995).

[18] See paras 1.25–1.28 below.

[19] Under controversial, but still unrepealed provisions of the Act of Settlement 1701, the monarch may not be, or marry, a Roman Catholic.

[20] In 1913–14 George V considered refusal of Royal Assent to the Home Rule Bill; most constitutional experts considered he could properly exercise his legal power: see Bogdanor (n 17 above) 122–135.

[21] ibid ch 4.

that on some occasions the monarch retains a residual discretion in the choice of Prime Minister. Admittedly, when a political party commands a majority in the House of Commons, a well-established convention requires the Queen to invite the leader of that party to become Prime Minister and form an administration. But there may be occasions when no party enjoys a majority after a general election; there is a 'hung Parliament'. In this situation there might be disagreement between the leaders of the two main political parties about the appropriate course of action. Further, it might be clear that the leader of a third party would be prepared to form a coalition government with the leader of the second strongest party, but not with the leader of the party with most members of Parliament. In the event of a 'hung Parliament' the monarch does, it seems, enjoy some discretion how to act, though it would be prudent for her to encourage discussions between the political leaders before issuing a firm invitation to one of them to form a government.

Related to the predicament of the monarch in the case of a 'hung Parliament' is the question how much discretion she enjoys whether to refuse a request for a dissolution of Parliament and a general election. Normally, as a matter of constitutional convention she must grant a Prime Minister's request. But she would be entitled to exercise her legal power to refuse a request (in defiance of the general convention that she must act in accordance with the advice of ministers) if a Prime Minister, defeated at an election, were to advise dissolution of the newly elected Parliament in an attempt to reverse the result. It would not generally be constitutional for her to refuse the dissolution request of a Prime Minister who was (in his view) unable to govern effectively with a tiny parliamentary majority or who was defeated on a vote of no confidence. However, in the latter situation, a monarch might be entitled to refuse the request, if it were clear that the opposition parties were prepared to form a coalition government. This would be particularly true if the country faced a genuine political or economic emergency, when the holding of a general election could be considered undesirable.[22] **1.19**

In some circumstances, therefore, the monarch probably retains a degree of discretion how to exercise important constitutional powers. The existence of these residual powers is politically controversial. A monarch's discretion to refuse a dissolution may be defended as a check on the possible abuse of power by a Prime Minister, just as arguably it would be constitutionally appropriate for the Queen to refuse to give Royal Assent to a Bill, which without good reason extended the life of a Parliament beyond five years (and so delayed an election) or a Bill which disenfranchised a class of voters thought likely to vote for opposition parties. In either of these circumstances, the monarch would be acting as a guardian of the democratic constitution, so it would be appropriate for her to act independently in disregard of ministerial advice. **1.20**

---

[22] ibid 157–62.

(ii) The Crown in the monarchical constitution

1.21   The legal character and status of the Crown have given rise to considerable diffi-culties.[23] To some extent they derive from English constitutional history. The concept of 'the Crown' may be used to refer either to the powers and immunities of the monarch acting in her personal capacity or to powers and immunities be-longing to the government and its ministers. In previous centuries when the monarch still effectively controlled government, there was no sharp difference be-tween the two meanings. For example, it was impossible to bring an action in con-tract or in tort against the monarch personally; neither could such an action be brought against the Crown as a corporation.

1.22   This position could not be sustained in the context of a modern democracy com-mitted to the rule of law and the protection of the rights of citizens. The legal po-sition was transformed when the courts recognized that ministers and officials could incur liability in their personal capacity. A Secretary of State could, there-fore, be sued in the courts for trespass, if he ordered officials to search someone's property without legal authority.[24] Moreover, legislation generally confers statu-tory powers on a Secretary of State or minister, rather than the Crown. The deci-sions of a central government minister may be challenged in the courts under the principles of administrative law, in the same way as those of a local authority or other body or tribunal set up by statute.

1.23   However, it was only in 1947 that the immunities of the Crown itself from legal proceedings for breach of contract and in tort were abolished by statute.[25] The leg-islation abolishing these immunities did provide that injunctions and orders for specific performance could not be granted against the Crown itself,[26] as distinct from its officers such as government ministers. In *M v Home Office,* Lord Woolf explained that, where a statute imposes a duty on a specific minister, rather than on the Crown in general, there is no reason why an injunction should not be granted to restrain him from acting in breach of that duty.[27] The House of Lords held in this leading case that a finding of contempt of court can lawfully be made against a minister acting in his official capacity or against a government depart-ment. Contempt proceedings could, therefore, be taken against the Home Secretary, when he had wrongly, albeit in good faith, failed to comply with an earl-ier court order to bring back to England an applicant for asylum who had been

---

[23] See M Sunkin and S Payne (eds), *The Nature of the Crown: A Legal and Political Analysis* (Oxford: OUP, 1999).
[24] *Entick v Carrington* (1765) 19 St Tr 1030, Ct of Common Pleas; *Wilkes v Wood* (1769) 19 St Tr 1406, Ct of Common Pleas.
[25] Crown Proceedings Act 1947, ss 1–2.
[26] ibid s 21(1)(a).
[27] [1994] 1 AC 377.

sent back to Zaire improperly. But the Lords maintained the distinction of legal principle between the government department or minister acting officially on the one hand, and the Crown, on the other; a finding of contempt could be made against the former, but not against the Crown directly.

It is questionable whether these nice distinctions make much sense today, or in- **1.24** deed whether they are really necessary in the context of contemporary constitutional arrangements.[28] Nothing would be lost if the Crown as government lost its historic privileges and immunities, though the reigning monarch should perhaps retain some personal immunity from legal action.[29] Arguably, a more realistic view was taken by the House of Lords in *Town Investments Ltd v Department of the Environment*.[30] It held that a lease held by the Minister of Works, the head of the government department responsible for the accommodation of all civil servants, was in effect taken by the government or, to use the public law term of art, by the Crown. In a striking, though controversial passage, Lord Diplock said:

> But to continue nowadays to speak of 'the Crown' as doing legislative or executive acts of government, which, in reality as distinct from legal fiction, are decided on and done by human beings other than the Queen herself, involves risk of confusion.

In his view, it would be less confusing to speak of the government, including within the term all ministers and parliamentary secretaries under whose direction the work of government was conducted. On this approach the traditional distinction between the Crown and a minister acting in his official capacity would become immaterial; either could be held criminally or civilly liable in appropriate circumstances.

(iii) The royal prerogative

Although the Crown's powers were significantly curtailed in the 17th century, the **1.25** scope of its non-statutory authority remains considerable. In law this authority still belongs to the monarch, but in practice what are termed prerogative powers are exercisable by the government in general or by a specific minister. In addition to the powers already discussed, such as the power to appoint the Prime Minister and to dissolve Parliament, the royal prerogative includes the power to make treaties, to declare and conduct war, to make dispositions for the armed services, to pardon offences (the prerogative of mercy), and to stop a criminal prosecution.

There is disagreement concerning the exact character and definition of the royal **1.26** prerogative. For Blackstone, it is the special or extraordinary authority which the

---

[28] However, see HWR Wade's defence of the distinction as a compromise, 'The Crown, Ministers and Officials: Legal Status and Liability' in *The Nature of the Crown* (n 23 above) 23–32.
[29] S Sedley (n 10 above) 288–289.
[30] [1978] AC 359.

Crown enjoys beyond the powers which all people have at common law.[31] This definition has been adopted by Lord Parmoor: 'Royal Prerogative implies a privilege in the Crown of a special and exclusive character'.[32] Dicey, however, regarded the prerogative as '[t]he residue of discretionary or arbitrary authority, which at any given time is legally left in the hand of the Crown'.[33] This definition suggests that any decision or conduct of the government, not taken under statutory powers, may be regarded as the exercise of a prerogative power.

1.27 Although Dicey's definition is open to criticism for being merely descriptive and unacceptably broad, it has frequently been cited with approval.[34] Moreover, it has been held that the Criminal Injuries Compensation Board (CICB) was set up by the executive (or the Crown) under the prerogative power and was liable to judicial review, although any person is free to establish a scheme for compensating the victims of crime.[35] The establishment of the CICB could not be regarded as a prerogative act under Blackstone's definition. In *Council for Civil Service Unions v Minister for Civil Service* (GCHQ case) Lord Diplock appeared indifferent whether the residual common law powers of the Crown—in that case, to bar civil servants working at Government Communications Headquarters from membership of trades unions—should be characterized as prerogative powers.[36] What was more important was the capacity of the courts to review the exercise of executive power.

1.28 Since the 17th century the courts have established that it is for them to determine the scope of the royal prerogative, or what should now be termed the government's common law powers. They held, for example, in leading cases in English constitutional history that the monarch could not himself sit in the courts[37] and that he could not change the law, in particular create new criminal offences, by proclamation.[38] Lord Diplock has said that the courts will not now broaden the scope of prerogative powers,[39] but it is hard to ascribe much significance to these remarks, given the general nature of the powers which have been recognized. In *R v Secretary of State for the Home Department, ex p Northumbria Police Authority*,[40] the Court of Appeal was prepared to accept that the government is entitled to distribute CS gas to a chief constable, without the consent of the local

---

[31] 1 *Commentaries on the Laws of England* 238.
[32] *A-G v De Keyser's Royal Hotel* [1920] AC 508, 571, HL.
[33] *Introduction to the Study of the Law of the Constitution* (n 1 above) 424.
[34] Lord Reid in *Burmah Oil v Lord Advocate* [1965] AC 75, 99, HL; Lord Roskill in *Council of Civil Service Unions v Minister for Civil Service* [1985] AC 374, 416, HL.
[35] *R v Criminal Injuries Compensation Board, ex p Lain* [1967] 2 QB 864, DC.
[36] [1985] AC 374, 409, HL.
[37] *Prohibitions del Roy* (1607) 12 Co Rep 63.
[38] *Case of Proclamations* (1611) 12 Co Rep 74.
[39] In *BBC v Johns* [1965] Ch 32, 79, CA.
[40] [1989] 1 QB 26.

police authority, in the exercise of the traditional prerogative power to keep the Queen's peace. The judges were unconcerned by the absence of earlier judicial authority delineating the scope of this power.[41]

The courts used to disclaim entitlement to review the exercise of a prerogative power, whatever its character.[42] Their reluctance to intervene contrasted sharply with their willingness to review the exercise by a minister of his statutory powers on the grounds of abuse or gross unreasonableness. In the GCHQ case, however, the House of Lords held that the exercise of prerogative power should in principle no longer be immune from review.[43] The question for the courts should be instead whether the subject matter of the prerogative power made it suitable for judicial review. It would be inappropriate for judges to determine, for instance, whether a treaty should be concluded or Parliament dissolved. But the Lords would have been prepared to review the decision in that case—the imposition without consultation of a ban on staff at GCHQ belonging to national trades unions—if the minister had not argued that it had been taken for reasons of national security.

1.29

Subsequent to the GCHQ ruling, courts have upheld challenges to a refusal to grant a passport[44] and to a refusal to exercise the prerogative of mercy.[45] On the other hand, they remain unwilling to consider challenges to the making of treaties and the conduct of foreign policy,[46] and, more surprisingly, to the discharge from the armed forces of servicemen with homosexual orientation.[47] A broad line is drawn between those decisions which involve a significant element of policy, where it would be inappropriate for the courts to intervene, and those which pose more justiciable issues, where the courts can more easily formulate standards of reasonableness.[48]

1.30

The prerogative now is less significant than it used to be. It remains, however, relatively important in the context of foreign affairs, where traditionally the executive is unconstrained by legislation. With regard to domestic affairs, governmental powers are almost entirely based on statute, rather than on the Crown's common law authority. Moreover, a prerogative power is abrogated by the enactment of a statute which grants the government a power equivalent to

1.31

---

[41] See AW Bradley, 'Police Powers and the Prerogative' [1988] PL 298, and S Payne in *The Nature of the Crown* (n 23 above) 102–106.
[42] See *Chandler v DPP* [1964] AC 763, HL; *Blackburn v A-G* [1971] 1 WLR 1037, CA.
[43] *Council of Civil Service Unions v Minister for Civil Service* [1985] AC 374, HL.
[44] *R v Secretary of State for Foreign and Commonwealth Affairs, ex p Everett* [1989] 1 QB 811, CA.
[45] *R v Secretary of State for the Home Department, ex p Bentley* [1994] QB 349, DC.
[46] *Ex p Molyneaux* [1986] 1 WLR 331, DC; *R v Secretary of State for Foreign and Commonwealth Affairs, ex p Rees-Mogg* [1994] QB 552, DC.
[47] *R v Ministry of Defence, ex p Smith* [1996] QB 517, CA.
[48] See B Hadley in *The Nature of the Crown* (n 23 above) 219–229.

that it enjoyed at common law.[49] Nevertheless, the royal prerogative remains a notable feature of the constitution, even though it has largely become divorced from its origins in the monarchical constitution under which the reigning monarch exercised considerable independent authority.

(e) Constitutional conventions

(i) The constitutional significance of conventions

1.32 Constitutional conventions may be defined as principles of political or constitutional morality which are regarded as binding, but which are not legally enforceable. Many of them limit the legal powers of the Crown, in effect transforming the royal prerogative exercisable by the monarch in person into governmental authority exercised by ministers. Indeed, the most important single constitutional convention is that requiring the King or Queen to act on the advice of ministers.[50] Other conventions concern the collective responsibility of ministers and their individual responsibility to Parliament.

1.33 In the absence of these conventions English constitutional law would still appear much as it did towards the end of the 17th century, when the monarch chose his ministers. They were accountable to him, rather than to the House of Commons. The present position and authority of the Prime Minister and other members of the Cabinet are attributable to convention and not law. The purpose of constitutional conventions is, therefore, to ensure that the legal structure of the constitution operates in conformity with the values of parliamentary democracy.[51] As Sir Ivor Jennings wrote, 'constitutional conventions . . . provide the flesh which clothes the dry bones of the law; they make the legal constitution work . . .'.[52] Conventions admittedly influence the development of other areas of English law and are to be found in other constitutions.[53] But their role in the UK constitution is peculiarly significant; they have the effect of revising it to bring it into line with political and social developments.

(ii) Establishing constitutional conventions

1.34 It is much harder to determine the existence and scope of a constitutional convention than to identify a rule of constitutional law. First, rules of law almost always

---

[49] *A-G v De Keyser's Royal Hotel* [1920] AC 508, HL. There are nice questions, however, whether the statute covers the same ground as the prerogative, and also whether a prerogative power revives if the statute is repealed.

[50] Sometimes it might still be constitutional for a monarch to exercise legal powers without, or in disregard of, ministerial advice: paras 1.18–1.20 above.

[51] *Reference re Amendment of the Constitution of Canada* (1982) 125 DLR (3d) 1, 84 (Sup Ct Canada).

[52] Jennings (n 11 above) 81.

[53] CR Munro, *Studies in Constitutional Law* (2nd edn, London: Butterworths, 1999), 59–60.

have a clear source in legislation or in a judicial decision or a series of decisions. Secondly, the courts provide authoritative rulings on the interpretation and application of rules of constitutional law, such as the principle of parliamentary legislative supremacy and its relationship to EC law. In contrast, there is no hierarchy of sources for establishing constitutional conventions; more importantly, there is no tribunal to determine their scope nor to enforce them if their application is contested. These questions may be explored in books on constitutional law or politics, among politicians and civil servants, and in the correspondence columns of newspapers.[54] But they can rarely, if ever, be definitively resolved.

It is sometimes said that conventions are standards found in previous political practice, or precedents, which are accepted as binding by the persons whom the standards purport to govern.[55] For instance, the convention requiring the Queen to assent to legislation which has passed properly through the Commons and Lords is evidenced by the uniform practice of monarchs for nearly 300 years and their acceptance now that they must comply with the principle. But a convention may be created by a political statement or by the agreement of all the persons concerned without any prior practice to point to its existence.[56]   **1.35**

If prior practice is unnecessary to establish a convention, neither is it sufficient. What is crucial is that it is accepted as binding. Difficulties, however, arise when politicians decide that a particular convention does not bind them, as happened to the principle of *collective* Cabinet responsibility in 1975–77; two Prime Ministers, Wilson and Callaghan, decided to allow members of their Cabinets to express personal views with regard to the role of the United Kingdom in Europe. There is probably still a convention of collective Cabinet responsibility, though it may be suspended by a Prime Minister when he considers it expedient. It may be hard to distinguish a weak convention of this kind from a statement of general political practice which does not impose constitutional obligations.   **1.36**

Similar uncertainties have existed with regard to the principle of *individual* ministerial responsibility to Parliament. On a traditional view, the convention required ministers to resign if they were personally at fault in the conduct of policy or there had been serious maladministration in their department. On occasion a minister did resign because he considered he was under a constitutional   **1.37**

---

[54] The scope of the convention limiting the monarch's power to refuse a Prime Minister's request for dissolution of Parliament was vigorously discussed in letters to *The Times* in April–May 1950.

[55] Jennings (n 11 above) 136.

[56] The Balfour Declaration of 1926 announcing that the UK Parliament would not legislate for the Dominions without their consent has been treated as a convention. The ministerial code of conduct, issued by the Prime Minister's office, arguably creates constitutional conventions binding on ministers.

obligation to do so following such a failure.[57] But the existence of a strong convention imposing such an obligation was often disputed.[58] It was not consistently observed. Following a resolution of the House of Commons, proposed by the government, it was replaced in 1997 with a weaker requirement that a minister should offer his resignation to the Prime Minister, if he knowingly misleads the House.[59] This probably amounts to a reformulation of the convention by agreement between the persons affected.

(iii) Conventions and constitutional law

1.38   On the orthodox view, a sharp line can be drawn between principles of constitutional law and conventions. The former may be enforced by the courts, while the latter may not.[60] Adopting that approach, the Privy Council rejected an argument that constitutional convention imposed limits on the entitlement of the Westminster Parliament to enact legislation for Southern Rhodesia without its consent.[61]

1.39   It is more accurate, however, to say that questions of constitutional law may in principle always be resolved by the courts, although the judge may rule that in the case before him there is no legally enforceable obligation.[62] On the other hand, courts will not pronounce on constitutional conventions, unless they are specifically authorized to do this by statute.[63] Another qualification to the orthodox view is that a convention may provide the foundation for the application of a principle of common law. That happened in *A-G v Jonathan Cape*,[64] when the judge ruled, on the basis of the principle of collective Cabinet responsibility, that there was a relationship of confidence between its members. In appropriate cases, that could be enforced under the well-established jurisdiction to restrain a breach of confidence. With these reservations, the orthodox view should be accepted as correct.

---

[57] In 1956 Sir Thomas Dugdale resigned as Minister for Agriculture following maladministration in that department, and in 1982 Lord Carrington resigned after the Foreign Office failed to anticipate invasion of the Falklands Islands.

[58] SE Finer, 'The Individual Responsibility of Ministers' (1956) 34 Public Administration 377.

[59] See D Woodhouse, 'Ministerial Responsibility: Something Old, Something New' [1997] PL 262.

[60] Dicey (n 1 above) 24; Munro (n 53 above) 60–72.

[61] *Madzimbamuto v Lardner-Burke* [1969] 1 AC 645, 723, PC, *per* Lord Reid.

[62] This may be because enforcement would interfere with the privilege of a House of Parliament to regulate its own affairs (*Bradlaugh v Gossett* (1884) 12 QBD 271, DC), or because a statute is interpreted not to impose a legally enforceable obligation.

[63] In *Reference re Amendment of the Constitution of Canada* (n 51 above), the Supreme Court of Canada considered whether there was a convention requiring the consent of the Provinces before the federal Parliament presented proposals for constitutional amendment, because legislation gave it jurisdiction to determine the issue.

[64] [1976] QB 752, Lord Widgery CJ.

(f) A unitary constitution

The United Kingdom of Great Britain and Northern Ireland comprises four **1.40**
countries: England, Wales, Scotland, and Northern Island. Its constitution is unitary. As a matter of constitutional law Parliament in Westminster has ultimate authority to enact laws for all parts of the United Kingdom, although recently
substantial legislative or executive power has been devolved to Scotland, Northern
Ireland, and Wales. The unitary constitution may be contrasted with federal constitutions, such as those of the United States of America, Germany, and Canada.
Under a federal constitution, legislative and executive power is divided between
the federal (or central) and state (or provincial) authorities, the powers of which
cannot be unilaterally altered by the federal Parliament (or for that matter by the
state parliaments acting together).

From an historical perspective, the United Kingdom may be characterized as a **1.41**
union of four countries which have earlier been independent, albeit to different
degrees. Wales was in effect absorbed into England by the Statute of Wales (1284),
though it is unclear whether it was really an independent country before that
time.[65] For over 200 years before the enactment of the Welsh Language Act 1967
the word 'England' in legislation was deemed to include Wales. England and
Wales constitute a single jurisdiction for the purposes of public as well as private
law.

Although James VI of Scotland became King of England as James I in 1603, **1.42**
England and Scotland only merged their Parliaments in 1707. The Acts of Union,
enacted by the Scottish and then by the English Parliaments in that year, merged
them into a single Parliament of the United Kingdom of Great Britain. The legislation, however, provided that the positions of the Presbyterian Church of
Scotland as the established church and of the courts and Scots private law were
fundamental and could not be altered. These provisions have been respected;
Scots law remains distinct from English law. But the usual view is that under the
principle of legislative supremacy, the Westminster Parliament could repeal any
provision in the Act of Union.[66]

Ireland became fully united with Great Britain on 1 January 1801.[67] After a long **1.43**
period of both constitutional and armed struggle, the Government of Ireland Act
1920 partitioned the country, establishing Parliaments in Belfast for the six counties of Ulster and in Dublin for the rest of Ireland. In fact, the latter obtained full
independence in 1922. The Ulster Parliament in Stormont continued to exercise
substantial, though not unlimited, legislative powers under the 1920 legislation

---

[65] Munro (n 53 above) 19–20.
[66] See para 1.84 below.
[67] Act of Union with Ireland 1800.

until 1972. Following years of growing civil unrest between the Protestant and Catholic communities, the powers of the Stormont Parliament were transferred to the Secretary of State for Northern Ireland; direct rule by London was imposed.[68]

1.44 The dominant position of England within the United Kingdom is evidenced by the assumption at different periods of legislative power by the Westminster Parliament over Wales, Scotland, and Ireland. Moreover, it was only towards the end of the 19th century that the special position of Scotland was recognized with the institution of the Scottish Office and the appointment of a Secretary with executive responsibilities. It was natural, therefore, in that period for writers on constitutional law to speak of the English Constitution[69] or of the constitutional law of England,[70] when it would have been accurate to refer to constitutional law in the United Kingdom. Modern writers do not make the same mistake. Ironically, with the devolution of legislative powers to Edinburgh and Belfast, it makes some sense to refer now to the constitutional law of Scotland or of Northern Ireland as distinct areas of study; in contrast, it remains difficult to distinguish the fundamental principles of English constitutional law from those of the United Kingdom as a whole.

(g) A democratic constitution

1.45 The United Kingdom is a parliamentary democracy. A general election must be held every five years,[71] though in practice Prime Ministers usually request a dissolution of Parliament a year before the end of that period at a time favourable to the government party. All citizens over the age of 18, with a few exceptions, are entitled to vote to elect a member of Parliament.[72] Elections for the Parliament in Westminster are conducted in single member constituencies under the simple majority system, often known as first-past-the-post. A member of Parliament may, therefore, be elected with well under 40 per cent, let alone 50 per cent, of the votes cast in the constituency. Moreover, constituencies vary significantly in their size; a rural constituency covering a large geographical area has fewer voters than those in city centres.

1.46 Questions may be raised whether these arrangements are fair or satisfy the fundamental principle that all citizens have an *equal* right to vote. It is now taken for

---

[68] Northern Ireland (Temporary Provisions) Act 1972. Direct rule remained until 1998, with the exception of a few months in 1973 when there was an unsuccessful attempt to devolve power to an Assembly and Executive in which power was shared between the two communities.

[69] The title of Bagehot's celebrated essays, first published in book form in 1867. The term was also used by De Tocqueville (n 9 above).

[70] Dicey (n 1 above) 6 et passim.

[71] Parliament Act 1911, s 7.

[72] For details, see Munro (n 53 above) 92–97.

granted that each citizen has one vote, but entitlement to vote in a marginal city centre constituency has arguably greater value than the right to vote in a large rural constituency where one party has a large majority. The US Supreme Court has ruled that the Equal Protection Clause of the Constitution requires states to draw up congressional districts with approximately equal numbers of voters.[73] In contrast, the UK Parliamentary Constituencies Act 1986 gave Boundary Commissions significant discretion in formulating proposals for the number and size of parliamentary constituencies. They are directed to take a number of factors into account; geographical and other factors are given the same importance as the desirability of avoiding disparity in the size of constituencies. The courts are reluctant to interfere with this process in order to establish a right to vote of equal value.[74] Further, though there has been considerable discussion concerning the merits of the first-past-the-post electoral system, it is likely to survive for the foreseeable future for the Westminster Parliament. (In contrast, elections for the Scottish Parliament and the Assemblies in Northern Ireland and Wales set up under the measures devolving power to these bodies are conducted under electoral systems designed to achieve greater proportionality between the votes for each party and the seats it wins.)

Political parties play a crucial role in the functioning of modern democracies. **1.47** However, constitutional and legal arrangements in the United Kingdom have hitherto paid little regard to them, in contrast with their recognition and regulation in many post-war documentary constitutions. It was only in 1969 that the law allowed the party affiliation of candidates for election to be indicated on ballot papers. In 1998 legislation enabled parties to register to protect their candidates against use of the party's name or a similar name by other candidates likely to confuse voters.[75] This legislation has now been replaced by the Political Parties, Elections and Referendums Act 2000. This is a major constitutional reform. It imposes accounting requirements on political parties, the registration of which is mandatory; it also regulates donations to them, expenditure on election campaigns and the conduct of referendums. An Electoral Commission is established for these purposes; it also assumes the functions of the Boundary Commissions in reviewing the number and size of constituencies.[76]

The purpose of this reform was to reduce two principal risks: first, the improper **1.48** influence on the political process which might be exercised by rich donors making undisclosed donations to a party's funds, and secondly, the distortion of the

---

[73] *Baker v Carr* 369 US 186 (1962).
[74] *R v Boundary Commission for England, ex p Foot* [1983] 1 QB 600, CA. See Munro (n 53 above) 97–106.
[75] Registration of Political Parties Act 1998.
[76] See KD Ewing, 'Transparency, Accountability and Equality: The Political Parties, Elections and Referendums Act 2000' [2001] PL 542.

electoral process from massive expenditure by a party or candidate which rivals cannot afford. Its general significance is that the legal arrangements for political parties in the United Kingdom are now similar to those which exist under documentary constitutions. In this respect, as in others, the constitution is going through a period of rapid change.

(3) Devolution

(a) General

1.49   Over the last 30 to 40 years there has been pressure from nationalist political parties and others in Scotland and Wales to transfer political power from London to Edinburgh and Cardiff. Nationalist fervour has been joined by a more widespread feeling, to some extent shared in parts of England, that it is better for decisions over certain matters to be taken locally. The political factors leading to devolution in Northern Ireland were different. The Province had enjoyed considerable autonomy before the imposition of direct rule in 1972; most Unionist politicians were keen to regain that freedom, while Nationalist politicians and communities saw devolution as a possible step towards a break with the United Kingdom and integration with the Republic of Ireland.

1.50   Unlike the previous Conservative administration which had been in power since 1979, the Labour government which took office in May 1997 was committed to devolution. Laws enacted in 1998 have conferred wide legislative powers on elected bodies in Scotland and in Northern Ireland; other legislation has transferred executive power to an elected Assembly in Wales. These developments compromise the character of the unitary constitution; there are now significant differences in the constitutional arrangements under which the four nations forming the United Kingdom are governed.[77] Indeed, the arrangements are so diverse that one commentator has rightly said that their common description as 'asymmetrical devolution' is inaccurate; that term assumes variations on, or departures from, a clear pattern. In her view the devolution arrangements should be regarded as 'haphazard'.[78]

1.51   The enactments provide explicitly that the power of the UK Parliament in Westminster to enact legislation for Scotland and Northern Ireland is unaffected by the grant of legislative authority to discrete institutions in those countries;[79] an equivalent provision was unnecessary in the measure for Wales, as it did not transfer legislative power. The courts, and in particular the Judicial Committee of the

---

[77] See N Burrows, *Devolution* (London: Sweet & Maxwell, 2000); AJ Ward, 'Devolution: Labour's Strange Constitutional "Design"' in J Jowell and D Oliver (eds), *The Changing Constitution* (4th edn, Oxford: Clarendon, 2000) 111.

[78] Burrows (n 77 above) 91.

[79] Scotland Act 1998, s 28(7); Northern Ireland Act 1998, s 5(6).

Privy Council, have power to determine whether measures of the Scottish Parliament and Executive, and of the Assemblies in Northern Ireland and Wales have been taken within the competence conferred on them by the devolution enactments. In contrast, courts do not have any authority to entertain a challenge to any future Act of Parliament in Westminster which legislates for a matter over which competence has been devolved; in these circumstances, it must be accepted that Parliament has exercised its unlimited authority to make laws for Scotland or Northern Ireland, as the case may be. In terms of legal theory, therefore, Parliament has retained its legislative supremacy and the constitution remains unitary rather than federal. (In a federal constitution, it is usual for a court to have jurisdiction to review the validity of both federal and state (or provincial) legislation.)[80] However, in so far as a convention may develop that the UK Parliament refrains from legislation over a devolved matter, without the consent of the representative body in Scotland or Northern Ireland, the constitution may begin to assume quasi-federal characteristics.

The Acts of Parliament devolving power to Scotland and to Northern Ireland cre- **1.52** ate in effect textual constitutions for those countries. (The same is true to a much lesser extent for Wales; the Government of Wales Act 1998 is almost entirely concerned with matters of executive government and public administration, rather than fundamental constitutional principles.) It may now be appropriate in some contexts to refer to Scots or Northern Ireland constitutional (or public) law. This book is, however, concerned with English public law, so it deals only in outline with the division of powers between the UK Parliament and government in London and the bodies in Edinburgh, Belfast, and Cardiff to which powers have been transferred. Nevertheless, the devolution measures will certainly influence the development of English public law.

(b) Scotland Act 1998

The Scotland Act 1998 is the most significant of the three measures. It sets up a **1.53** Scottish Parliament and provides for a Scottish Executive (or government) with a First Minister at its head. The choice of the term 'Parliament' perhaps has more emotive than legal significance. But it is clear that the Parliament in Edinburgh has legislative power over all matters, subject to a number of exceptions set out in the 1998 enactment, principally concerning specified 'reserved matters'.[81] In the first place these matters concern fundamental constitutional issues, the registration and funding of political parties, foreign affairs, defence, and the civil service in Scotland which remains a UK public service. Secondly, a number of specific policy areas are reserved for the UK Parliament: among them are fiscal, economic

---

[80] See EM Barendt, *An Introduction to Constitutional Law* (Oxford: OUP, 1998) 55–56.
[81] Scotland Act 1998, Sch 5.

and monetary policy, company, insolvency, and competition law, energy, transport matters, social security, employment and industrial relations. Despite these substantial reservations, the Scottish Parliament has competence to enact legislation over such matters as education, housing, local government, law and order, and indeed over all other areas not specifically reserved for the UK Parliament. Further, the Parliament has limited competence to vary the standard rate of income tax fixed at Westminster.[82]

1.54 The competence of the Parliament in Edinburgh to legislate within the scope of its powers may be controlled in a number of ways. On the introduction of a Bill both the member of the Scottish Executive with responsibility for it and the Parliament's Presiding Officer must separately determine that it is within its legislative competence. That competence may be challenged by the reference of a Bill, or any provision in a Bill, to the Judicial Committee of the Privy Council;[83] its decisions are binding on all courts.[84] Alternatively, the validity of Scottish legislation may be challenged after its enactment as a 'devolution issue'; a challenge may be made before any court, though it may refer the matter to a higher court or, in the case of the Court of Appeal or the House of Lords, to the Judicial Committee.[85]

1.55 The Scotland Act 1998 contains detailed provisions for the appointment of the First Minister, of the other ministers and of the two law officers who together constitute the Executive.[86] The Parliament must nominate one of its members to be First Minister within 28 days of an election or of a vacancy in the office created by a previous incumbent's resignation or death in office.[87] Formally the First Minister is appointed by the monarch. She also appoints the other ministers and the law officers whose nomination by the First Minister has been approved by Parliament.[88] All members of the Executive must resign if Parliament resolves that it no longer has confidence in the government.[89] While these provisions preserve the monarchical constitution in so far as they require the Crown to appoint ministers, in effect they put into statute the convention that a government must enjoy the confidence of Parliament. Further, the right of the Scottish Parliament not to approve the nomination of a minister (or the dismissal of a law officer) gives it an authority which the UK Parliament does not enjoy. Further, the First Minister

---

[82] Scotland Act 1998, ss 73–78.
[83] ibid s 33. A reference may be made by the Lord Advocate (law officer of the Scottish government), or the Advocate General (law officer for Scotland of the UK government) or the Attorney-General for England and Wales.
[84] ibid s 103(1).
[85] ibid Sch 6. In some cases a reference *must* be made to the Judicial Committee: ibid para 33.
[86] ibid s 44.
[87] ibid s 46.
[88] ibid ss 47(1) and 48(1).
[89] ibid ss 45(2), 47(3) and 48(2).

cannot request the monarch to dissolve Parliament. The Scottish Parliament may only be dissolved before the lapse of its fixed term of four years if two-thirds of its members vote for that step or if it fails to nominate a First Minister within the required 28 days.[90] Therefore, unlike a Prime Minister in London, the First Minister cannot issue a threat to call an election as a means of disciplining members of his party who have withdrawn support from the government. Moreover, under the Scotland Act itself, Parliament consists of members chosen by majority vote in one member constituencies and regional members chosen by a proportional system. As a result, it is very unlikely that an Executive will be drawn from one party; coalition government is likely to be the rule rather than the exception, as it has been in the United Kingdom. In conjunction with the statutory provisions discussed in this paragraph, the electoral system gives individual members of the Scottish Parliament a stronger voice than members of Parliament in Westminster usually enjoy.

(c) Northern Ireland Act 1998

The Northern Ireland Act 1998 was introduced in the wake of the historic Good Friday agreement. It provides for the institution of an Assembly with legislative powers and an Executive Committee chosen from its members. However, the Assembly has no competence to legislate on a range of 'excepted matters', to some extent similar to those reserved for the UK Parliament under the Scotland Act; there is also a range of 'reserved matters',[91] notably criminal law and the courts, public order and police, emergency powers, and the civil service, over which the Assembly will enjoy competence only when the Secretary of State for Northern Ireland has conferred it by Order in Council.[92] (Equally, he may withdraw legislative competence from the Assembly by Order.[93]) The Attorney-General for Northern Ireland, a minister of the UK government, may refer a Bill to the Judicial Committee for it to review the Assembly's competence to enact it; it is then for the Secretary of State for Northern Ireland, not the Presiding Officer of the devolved legislature as with Scotland, to present a Bill for Royal Assent. **1.56**

The First Minister and Deputy First Minister are elected together; they must enjoy the support of a majority of the Assembly as a whole and of both Unionist and Nationalist members. If either resigns, both must stand down. They jointly decide the number and functions of the members of the Executive Committee,[94] but (in contrast to the arrangements for Scotland and Wales) do not appoint them. Instead, members are nominated by officers of each party and are chosen by **1.57**

---

[90] ibid s 3.
[91] Northern Ireland Act 1998, Sch 3.
[92] ibid s 8.
[93] ibid s 4(2).
[94] ibid s 17.

proportional election.[95] Further, they may only be dismissed by the appropriate officer of the party, not by the First or Deputy First Ministers or by the Assembly as a whole. These extremely complex arrangements reflect the need to achieve a compromise between the sectarian communities, rather than the standard features of ministerial responsibility.

1.58   Section 1 of the Northern Ireland Act 1998 repeats a provision in earlier legislation declaring that it remains part of the United Kingdom and will not cease to be so without the consent of a majority of its people. It remains doubtful whether this is of more than political importance, given that the UK Parliament is always free to repeal its earlier legislation, at least if it does this clearly by express language.[96] Other provisions of largely political importance concern the establishment of the North-South Ministerial Council, the British-Irish Council, and the British-Irish Intergovernmental Conference, all of them mechanisms to diffuse tension between the communities in Northern Ireland.[97]

(d) Government of Wales Act 1998

1.59   This measure, unlike the other two statutes, does not confer legislative power. The Welsh Assembly enjoys only the administrative functions transferred under the 1998 legislation itself or by subsequent enactments. As in the other devolution measures, there are a number of provisions concerning the election of the Assembly and the choice of its First Secretary and Executive Committee. The former is elected by the Assembly, but he then appoints other members of the Committee without reference to the Assembly as a whole.[98] The Committee is, however, accountable to it.[99]

1.60   The sole concession of the Government of Wales Act 1998 to a legislative role for the Assembly is in the requirement imposed on the Secretary of State for Wales to undertake consultation with it on the UK government's legislative programme as soon as reasonably practicable after the start of the parliamentary session.[100] This is not an absolute duty. The Secretary is only required to undertake such consultation as appears to him appropriate; moreover, there is no duty to consult if there are considerations relating to a particular Bill, such as a Finance Bill, making it inappropriate. On the other hand, the broad freedom recognized in the statute for the Assembly to make representations about any matter concerning Wales is treated as embracing a right to formulate legislative proposals.[101]

---

[95] Northern Ireland Act 1998 (n 91 above) s 18.
[96] See paras 1.85–1.87 below.
[97] Northern Ireland Act 1998, ss 52–56.
[98] Government of Wales Act 1998, s 53.
[99] For details, see Ward (n 77 above) 121–122.
[100] s 31.
[101] Burrows (n 77 above) 80–81.

In practice the significance of administrative devolution to Wales depends on how **1.61**
UK statutes are drafted. Framework legislation leaving much detail to be filled in
by administrative rules and decisions will give the Assembly substantial discretion
to determine policy in areas such as education and agriculture. In contrast, detailed legislation would leave it little more room for policy formation than that enjoyed by a local authority.

(e) The significance of devolution for constitutional law

The devolution of power to Scotland, Northern Ireland, and Wales does not have **1.62**
any direct impact on the constitutional arrangements applicable in England.
Subject only to the primacy of incompatible EC law, the UK Parliament will continue to exercise unlimited legislative authority over England. However, devolution will probably have long term repercussions.

The first point concerns the courts. 'Devolution issues' concerning the legality of **1.63**
measures of the legislative and executive bodies set up by the devolution enactments may ultimately be resolved on appeal by the Judicial Committee of the
Privy Council; even the House of Lords must refer such an issue to the Judicial
Committee, unless the House considers it more appropriate that it should determine the question.[102] It was considered undesirable for devolution issues generally
to be resolved by the Appellate Committee of the House of Lords, because it has
formed part of the Westminster Parliament. As decisions of the Judicial
Committee on such issues are binding on other courts (including the House of
Lords), the former has assumed to some extent the role of a constitutional
court.[103] (Its unique importance is underlined by the fact that there may be an appeal to it on devolution issues in criminal cases from the High Court of Justiciary
in Scotland, although there is no appeal in Scottish criminal cases to the House of
Lords on other grounds.) This enhanced role for the Judicial Committee might,
however, be reconsidered when the Supreme Court replaces the House of Lords as
the highest appellate court under changes announced by the government in June
2003.

Secondly, some features of the devolved arrangements, in particular under the **1.64**
Scotland Act 1998, may highlight possible drawbacks in the constitutional
arrangements for the United Kingdom as a whole. For instance, both the rule confining early dissolution of the Scottish Parliament before lapse of the four years'
term to unusual circumstances and that requiring ministers nominated by the First
Minister to be approved by Parliament give its individual members a significant

---

[102] See, eg, Scotland Act 1998, Sch 6, paras 23 & 32.
[103] But it is only a constitutional court for 'devolution issues': *Hoekstra v Lord Advocate* [2001] 1
AC 216, 221, PC. For discussion, see A O'Neill QC, 'Judicial Politics and the Judicial Committee:
the Devolution Jurisprudence of the Privy Council' (2001) 64 MLR 603, 615–618.

role which members of the Westminster Parliament may envy. There is a better balance of power between legislature and executive in Scotland than there is under the UK constitution.

1.65 The third point is the most obvious one. The transfer of power to Scotland and to the other nations in the United Kingdom has prompted calls for devolution to the regions of England, which the present government intends to meet, albeit to a limited extent. Further, there is the related difficulty that members of the Westminster Parliament from Scotland may vote on legislation, say, concerning education in England, while English members have no voice on such a matter in Scotland. Their votes could overturn a majority among English members on a Bill which only concerned England; indeed England could conceivably be governed by a political party which owed its majority at Westminster to Scottish and Welsh members. These are among the reasons why the devolution arrangements introduced a few years ago may not remain stable.

(4) The European Union

(a) Membership of the European Community and Union

1.66 European economic and political integration has developed over the last 50 years to encourage the spread of democracy on the continent and to avoid repetition of the tragedies of the two world wars. After an initial reluctance to participate in the enterprise, in January 1973 the United Kingdom joined the European Communities established by the Treaty of Paris (1951) and the Treaty of Rome (1957).[104] Under the Treaty of Rome wide powers were given by the participating states to the European Economic Community, as the European Community was then known, for it to regulate trade, competition, company law, and many other matters; in these areas, English law is substantially influenced by both the provisions of the Treaty and by rules made by the Community institutions under its authority.

1.67 In 1992 the member states of the Community agreed the Maastricht Treaty on European Union (TEU), which has been amended by the Treaties of Amsterdam (1997) and Nice (2001). All these treaties mark further stages in the gradual process of European integration. The European Union uses the institutions which had been set up by the earlier treaties: the European Parliament, Council, Commission and the Court of Justice (ECJ), all of which continue to exercise their powers under the Treaty of Rome, as amended by the TEU and subsequent agreements. As interpreted by the ECJ, EC law is on some occasions directly enforceable within the legal systems of the member states. In these circumstances it

---

[104] The former established the European Coal and Steel Community, the latter the European Economic Community and Euratom. See further paras 1.155 et seq, below.

prevails over inconsistent national law in much the same way as federal law prevails over the law of a state or province under a federal constitution. The implications of membership of the Community for constitutional law in the United Kingdom (and in other member states) are, therefore, considerable.

In contrast with the terms of the EC Treaty (which forms the first pillar of the   **1.68**
European Union), those provisions of the TEU concerned with the Common Foreign and Security Policy and with Police and Judicial Co-operation in Criminal Matters (the second and third pillars) bear more resemblance to those of a standard international agreement than those of a supra-national constitution. For example, the Council has less legislative power than it enjoys under the Treaty of Rome, while the role of the ECJ to make binding rulings is relatively limited. For these reasons, the term 'Community law' is often used in this book, although it is usual now for politicians and commentators to refer to the European Union, rather than to the longer established European Community. This usage would no longer be appropriate, if all three pillars of the TEU were drafted in similar terms.

(b) General principles of Community law

Three related legal principles show the distinctive character of the European   **1.69**
Community, differentiating it from other international organizations in which the United Kingdom participates. They have been formulated by the ECJ which has authority to make binding rulings when legal questions are referred to it by national courts and tribunals.[105] First, under the Treaty of Rome, a regulation (issued by the European Parliament acting jointly with the Council, by the Council, or by the Commission) 'shall be binding in its entirety and directly applicable in all Member States'.[106] This principle of direct applicability means that regulations become part of the law of each state on the date they enter into force under the rules set out in the Treaty itself;[107] there is no need for Parliament at Westminster (or other national legislatures) to implement them by national legislation.

The second fundamental principle is that of direct effect. Under this doctrine, pro-   **1.70**
visions of Community law may create directly effective rights, which individuals and organizations are entitled to enforce in their national courts. The principle was first formulated by the ECJ in the *Van Gend en Loos* case,[108] when a company was able to resist an action in the Netherlands courts for the payment of customs duties with the argument that imposition of the duty was contrary to the Treaty of Rome. The ECJ ruled that a provision which is clear and precise, is unconditional, and does not leave room for the exercise of discretion in its application, creates enforceable

---

[105] EC Treaty, Art 234.
[106] ibid Art 249.
[107] ibid Art 254.
[108] Case 26/62 [1963] ECR 1.

rights; national courts must protect these rights. The principle has been applied to provisions in Community directives,[109] despite the fact that this type of legislative measure, unlike regulations, gives national authorities choice with regard to the form and method of implementation.[110]

1.71   Flowing from this doctrine is the third fundamental principle: the supremacy of Community law over inconsistent national law. It would make no sense for individuals to be able to enforce a directly effective right, say, to equal pay in one member state, but for that right not to be protected in another member state because its court applied a national law which, in its view, should prevail over Community law. The principle of Community supremacy precludes that possibility; national courts must enforce directly effective Community rights, notwithstanding any inconsistent rule of national law. Moreover, as the ECJ pointed out in its seminal decision in *Costa v ENEL*,[111] the principle of direct applicability would be meaningless if member states were free to negative the effect of a regulation by enacting incompatible legislation. It concluded:

> The transfer by the states from their domestic legal system to the Community legal system of the rights and obligations arising under the Treaty carries with it a permanent limitation of their sovereign rights, against which a subsequent unilateral act incompatible with the concept of the Community cannot prevail.

The ECJ has held that Community law prevails over incompatible national law, even when the latter has been enacted subsequent to the EC measure,[112] and over provisions in a national constitution.[113]

(c) European Communities Act 1972

1.72   The Treaty of Accession under which the United Kingdom joined the European Communities was made under the royal prerogative power exercisable nominally by the Crown, but in effect by the government. Legislation was necessary, because of the principle of English law that treaties are not enforceable by the courts, unless their terms are incorporated in legislation. The European Communities Act 1972 (ECA) was, therefore, enacted to give effect to Community law and to ensure that the rights created by that law are respected in the United Kingdom.

1.73   ECA 1972, s 2(1) provides that all rights and obligations created by or arising under the Community treaties are enforceable in the United Kingdom without further enactment. In effect, the provision incorporates in legislation the Community principles of direct applicability and direct effect. This is reinforced

---

[109] See Case 41/74 *Van Duyn v Home Office* [1974] ECR 1137.
[110] EC Treaty, Art 249.
[111] Case 6/64 [1964] ECR 585.
[112] Case 106/77 *Simmenthal* [1978] ECR 629.
[113] Case 11/70 *Internationale Handelsgesellschaft* [1970] ECR 1125.

by s 3 which requires the courts to determine questions concerning the meaning and effect of the Treaties and Community legislation in accordance with the decisions of, and the principles formulated by, the ECJ. Among those principles are those of direct effect and Community supremacy.

An aspect of the principle of the legislative supremacy of Parliament, as traditionally understood, has been that it cannot bind its successors; Parliament is always free to repeal or amend earlier legislation and it may do this impliedly as well as explicitly.[114] That principle has been modified by the provision in the ECA 1972 that 'any enactment passed or to be passed . . . shall be construed and have effect subject to the foregoing provisions of this section',[115] which includes s 2(1) providing for the enforcement of Community law rights. This opaque provision means that the courts in England must give effect to Community law rights, notwithstanding inconsistent national legislation, even though that legislation is enacted subsequent to the ECA and to the issue of the Community measure. The principle of Community supremacy has been recognized by the House of Lords. In the *Factortame* case,[116] it refused to apply the Merchant Shipping Act 1988 in so far as it infringed the Community law rule, prohibiting discrimination on the basis of nationality. (The 1988 legislation required British fishing vessels to be owned and controlled by UK citizens.) **1.74**

(d) Constitutional implications of the European Union

Whether or not the European Union is already akin legally to a federation, membership of the Union has considerable implications for constitutional law in England. In the first place, the courts will no longer apply legislation inconsistent with directly effective provisions of Community law, incorporated into English law by the ECA 1972. The terms of that Act are not impliedly repealed by legislation such as the Merchant Shipping Act 1998, although it is likely that the court would apply legislation expressly repealing the 1972 Act, in the event of withdrawal from the Union. The ECA 1972 has become a constitutional statute, immune from implicit amendment or repeal.[117] **1.75**

Secondly, the courts are required by the ECA 1972 to comply with the principles of Community law. In addition to the principles already discussed, Community law imposes an obligation on courts of last resort to refer questions about the meaning and validity to the ECJ. These questions include disputes about the relationship of Community and national law. It follows that the ECJ now has the **1.76**

---

[114] See paras 1.85–1.87 and 2.142–2.155 below.

[115] ECA 1972, s 2(4).

[116] *Factortame Ltd v Secretary of State for Transport (No 2)* [1991] 1 AC 603. See also *Equal Opportunities Commission v Secretary of State for Employment* [1994] 1 WLR 409, HL.

[117] See Laws LJ in *Thoburn v Sunderland City Council* [2002] EWHC 195; [2003] QB 151; but cf para 1.120 below.

last word on questions of ultimate constitutional authority in the United Kingdom (and other member states), at least as far as Community law is involved.

1.77 A third point is that membership of the Union has implications for the constitutional principle of ministerial responsibility to Parliament. Ministers cannot be held responsible for matters in which the Community exercises effective control in the same way as they can be in respect of matters entirely outside Community competence or for which substantial discretion is left to domestic authorities. Moreover, it is difficult effectively to hold a minister responsible for a Community measure which has been decided by a majority vote in the Council of Ministers. The minister can argue that the United Kingdom was outvoted.[118] The effect is to alter the balance of power between the executive and the legislature in favour of the former.

(5) *Principles of the Constitution*

1.78 Constitutional law in the United Kingdom, or (if the term is preferred) English constitutional law, is dominated by three principles: the legislative supremacy of Parliament, the rule of law, and the separation of powers. Traditionally, the first of these has been regarded as much the most important, at least since the end of the 19th century when the doctrine of parliamentary sovereignty was formulated by Dicey. (In this exposition the term 'legislative supremacy' is preferred to Dicey's 'parliamentary sovereignty', because it is easy to confuse the latter with political or national sovereignty.) More recently, some scholars and judges have attached relatively more weight to the other two principles; this development has itself been encouraged by legislation such as the ECA 1972, giving priority to EC law over inconsistent legislation, and the Human Rights Act 1998 (HRA) which strengthens the protection of civil liberties.

(a) **Legislative supremacy of Parliament**

(i) *The traditional doctrine*

1.79 Under the doctrine Parliament has unlimited legislative authority. Negatively, it asserts that no other institution enjoys independent legislative capacity. The Crown cannot amend the law by its prerogative power; rulings of the courts are often reversed by legislation. More positively, it has been implicit in the doctrine that there is no distinction between ordinary and constitutional legislation. Traditionally Parliament has been free to repeal any earlier enactment; even a statute of fundamental constitutional importance such as the Triennial Act 1694 limiting the duration of a parliament to three years was repealed by ordinary legislation.[119]

---

[118] Munro (n 53 above) 209–214.
[119] Septennial Act 1716; see Dicey (n 1 above) 44–48.

This principle was described by Dicey as 'the dominant characteristic of our po- **1.80** litical institutions' from a legal perspective, and 'the very keystone of the law of the constitution'.[120] It assumes the role in English law played by the documentary constitution in other jurisdictions, in that it is the ultimate source of other legal rules, whether they emanate from the legislature itself, from central government or other public authorities. Unlike a documentary constitution, it is not possible to give the principle a precise date. Rather, it has emerged from political history. The Bill of Rights 1689 clearly constituted a seminal stage in this development. That statute, enacted at the culmination of the struggles between the Stuart monarchs and successive Parliaments in the Glorious Revolution, abolished several prerogative powers: the Crown was no longer entitled to tax without parliamentary consent, nor to suspend the application of statutes. Subsequently, the courts no longer vacillated between the competing claims of monarch and Parliament, but accepted the latter's claim to unlimited legislative authority.

The unlimited legislative supremacy of Parliament is a legal principle formulated **1.81** and applied by the courts. They have ruled, for example, that parliamentary legislation is not limited by international law[121] or by common law rights.[122] Nor as a matter of law is it limited by the existence of any convention that Parliament should not legislate. In *Madzimbamuto v Lardner-Burke* the Privy Council denied that Parliament's legislative capacity was limited by a well-established convention that it should not legislate for Southern Rhodesia without its consent. Lord Reid added:[123]

> It is often said that it would be unconstitutional for the United Kingdom Parliament to do certain things, meaning that the moral, political and other reasons against doing them are so strong that most people would regard it as highly improper if Parliament did these things. But that does not mean that it is beyond the power of Parliament to do such things. If Parliament chose to do any of them the courts could not hold the Act of Parliament invalid.

What this means is that the courts in England would uphold the validity of a statute, even if it departed from practical reality. For instance, English courts would, as far as possible, enforce a statute which banned smoking on the streets of Paris.[124]

---

[120] ibid 39, 70.
[121] *Cheney v Conn* [1968] 1 WLR 242, Ungoed-Thomas J.
[122] *R v Jordan* [1967] Crim LR 483, DC.
[123] [1969] 1 AC 645, 723.
[124] See WI Jennings (n 11 above) 171, pointing out that such a law could be enforced against a Frenchman visiting England for a few hours.

(ii) What is an Act of Parliament?

1.82   One consequence of the *legal* character of the principle is that the courts determine what counts as an Act of Parliament. Normally this is a formality. But questions may be raised whether a measure is a valid enactment. Traditionally, an enactment is valid only if it appears to have been passed by the House of Commons and the House of Lords and to have received the Royal Assent.[125] It is the Queen in Parliament which exercises parliamentary supremacy, not the House of Commons. A resolution of the House is not equivalent to an Act of Parliament.[126]

1.83   However, what counts as a valid Act of Parliament has been amended by statute itself. The Parliament Acts 1911–1949 provide that a Bill may be presented for Royal Assent if certain conditions are satisfied. These are in brief that the Speaker certifies that it is a Money Bill which has not been passed by the House of Lords within a month after it had been sent to the House, or that it is a Public Bill (other than one extending the duration of Parliament beyond five years) which has been rejected by the Lords in two successive sessions.[127] In these circumstances the common law definition of the Queen in Parliament has been changed. Parliamentary legal supremacy means in reality the supremacy of the House of Commons.

(iii) Legislative supremacy and the Acts of Union

1.84   It has been suggested that the Act of Union with Scotland 1707 and the Act of Union with Ireland 1800 contained unamendable fundamental provisions.[128] The latter contained provisions explicitly stated to stay permanently in force, but they have all been repealed; a challenge to the repeal of the provision guaranteeing the establishment of the Anglican church in Ireland was easily rejected.[129] The position with regard to the Scottish Act of Union may be less clear. It has been said that the principle of unlimited parliamentary sovereignty was an aspect of English constitutional law, which had never formed part of the constitutional law north of the border.[130] But other Scottish judges, notably Lord Reid in the House of Lords,[131] have accepted the principle. Whatever doubts have been expressed with regard to the status of the principle in Scotland, they have not been shared in

---

[125] See Lord Campbell in *Edinburgh & Dalkeith Railway Co v Wauchope* (1842) 8 Cl & F 710, 724, HL, discussed by RFV Heuston, *Essays in Constitutional Law* (2nd edn, London: Stevens, 1964) 17–21.

[126] *Stockdale v Hansard* (1839) 9 Ad & E 1, QB.

[127] See para 2.48 below.

[128] TB Smith, 'The Union of 1707 as Fundamental Law' [1957] PL 99; N MacCormick, 'Does the United Kingdom have a Constitution: Reflections on *MacCormick v Lord Advocate*' (1978) 29 Northern Ireland Legal Q 1.

[129] *Ex p Canon Selwyn* (1872) 36 JP Jo 54, QB.

[130] Lord Cooper in *MacCormick v Lord Advocate* 1953 SC 396, 411 (Ct of Session, Inner House).

[131] *British Railways Board v Pickin* [1974] AC 765, 782.

England. Moreover, the Scotland Act 1998 provides that the Act of Union is to take effect subject to it, which suggests that the 1707 Act should not be regarded as a fundamental, unalterable measure.[132]

(iv) Can Parliament bind its successors?

Parliament cannot bind later Parliaments simply by enacting that provisions in its legislation are intended to last 'for ever' or that inconsistent provisions in subsequent enactments are of no effect.[133] The legislative supremacy of Parliament has meant that each Parliament is free to repeal or amend the legislation of its predecessors, whether it does this explicitly or impliedly. A subsequent enactment impliedly repeals earlier provisions inconsistent with it.   **1.85**

But it might be possible for a Parliament to make it more difficult for subsequent Parliaments to enact legislation on some subjects. For example, a law guaranteeing protection for fundamental human rights might provide that future legislation infringing them should not be presented for Royal Assent unless it had previously been approved at a referendum or had been passed by a two-thirds majority of the House of Commons. It is not clear whether the courts in England should accept a restriction of this kind on the 'manner and form', rather than the simple content, of the legislation of successor Parliaments.[134]   **1.86**

(v) Implications for legislative supremacy of the ECA 1972

The House of Lords has held that EC law must be applied in England, notwithstanding the terms of legislation enacted subsequent to the Community measure. Under the traditional doctrine of parliamentary supremacy that legislation should have been interpreted as impliedly repealing the ECA 1972 incorporating Community law into English law.[135] The ECA may be regarded as a 'constitutional statute', which is not subject to implied repeal.[136] This amounts to a significant modification of the traditional principle of parliamentary supremacy, although it does not directly affect its weight outside that context.   **1.87**

(b) The rule of law

(i) Conceptions of the rule of law

If the rule of law means little more than a principle of legality, it seems rather commonplace to say that it is an important aspect of constitutional law in England.   **1.88**

---

[132] Scotland Act 1998, s 37.

[133] *Vauxhall Estates Ltd v Liverpool Corp* [1932] 1 KB 733, DC; *Ellen Street Estates Ltd v Minister of Health* [1934] 1 KB 590, CA.

[134] See paras 2.152–2.155 below for full discussion.

[135] *Factortame Ltd v Secretary of State for Transport (No 2)* [1991] 1 AC 603; see paras 1.74–1.75 above, and paras 2.177–2.188 below for fuller treatment.

[136] *Thoburn v Sunderland City Council* [2002] EWHC 195; [2003] QB 151 at [63].

For any legal system can be contrasted with a state of anarchy or with arbitrary totalitarian rule where the police and ad hoc tribunals act in a wholly unregulated and unpredictable manner. However, it may be possible to ascribe more significance to the concept. The fundamental questions are: what does the rule of law mean and what does it entail for constitutional law in England? Another issue concerns its significance for the protection of civil liberties, which until recently have not been explicitly guaranteed in English law.

1.89   The classic exposition of the rule of law is that of Dicey.[137] In his view, it was, together with the principle of parliamentary sovereignty, the principal feature of the constitution. It meant first, the absence of arbitrary power on the part of the government. In particular nobody could be punished at the whim of an official or court; a breach of the law had to be established before the ordinary courts. Secondly, everyone, including an official, is subject to the same law; the rule of law means 'equality before the law, or the equal subjection of all classes to the ordinary law of the land administered by the ordinary courts . . .'.[138] On this point Dicey contrasted, controversially, English law with the law in France (and other civil law jurisdictions) where the conduct of public authorities and officials is governed by a separate body of legal principles enforced by special tribunals. A third aspect of the rule of law, according to Dicey, was that the general principles of the constitution, in particular the liberties of individuals, are not set out in a text, but have emerged from the decisions of the courts in actions brought on particular facts. For that reason, he thought that individual liberties are more secure in England than they are in other countries where constitutional guarantees may not be enforced effectively by the courts and where they may be suspended during an emergency.

1.90   It is easy to dispute aspects of this account.[139] Many statutes in England confer wide discretionary powers on public authorities and officials; it may sometimes be hard to distinguish such powers from the arbitrary authority incompatible with adherence to the rule of law. Secondly, statutes sometimes in effect protect officials, for example, the police from the liability to which they, like ordinary citizens, would otherwise be exposed. Indeed, until the Crown Proceedings Act 1947 the government could not be held vicariously liable for the carelessness or other wrongdoing of its employees; the monarch still enjoys personal immunity from tort liability.[140] Further, Dicey was wrong to argue that civil liberties are more securely protected in English law merely because they emerge from the decisions of the courts in particular cases. In principle they may be guaranteed as strongly by

---

[137] Dicey (n 1 above) ch IV.
[138] ibid 202.
[139] See Jennings (n 11 above) 54–62.
[140] Crown Proceedings Act 1947, s 40(1).

written constitutions; in practice, of course, their effective protection depends on the interpretation and application of the constitution by the courts, but the same point can be made with regard to the common law.

Other commentators now argue for a richer conception of the rule of law than Dicey's understanding. The rule of law, it has been argued, requires at least the law to be sufficiently certain to provide citizens with clear guidance; retrospective laws are therefore incompatible with the rule of law. Moreover, it must be enforced by independent and impartial judges.[141] Otherwise it would be difficult sharply to distinguish a constitutional order from arbitrary government. Even this perspective may be too unambitious. The rule of law may be understood as protecting the autonomy and dignity of individuals. It requires government decisions to be rational and justifiable by reference to an understanding of the common good. Consequently, fundamental rights of conscience, expression and association are implicit in commitment to the rule; without them citizens would be unable to understand or criticize government.[142] On this approach, the rule of law is a substantive principle with real content.   **1.91**

These arguments are of immense constitutional significance. If the rule of law is equated, as it was on the traditional Diceyan account, with adherence to the requirements of formal legality, an official act or decision which has been authorized by Parliament cannot be effectively challenged in the courts. A fortiori, under the principle of legislative supremacy the courts must apply enactments of Parliament, no matter how oppressive or arbitrary their content. If, however, the rule of law has substantive content, challenges to administrative decisions, and perhaps even Acts of Parliament, should be upheld where there has been a clear violation of fundamental rights.   **1.92**

Some recent judgments provide support for these richer conceptions of the rule of law. Lord Steyn has said that the rule 'enforces minimum standards of fairness, both substantive and procedural'.[143] It was therefore unlawful for the Home Secretary to increase the tariff—the part of a mandatory life sentence which must be served in prison to satisfy the requirements of retribution and deterrence—which had been fixed by a previous Home Secretary. The increase amounted to a retrospective increase in the sentence in violation of fundamental principles of fairness. Lord Steyn has also held that it would be as much of an abdication of the rule of law for a Home Secretary, as it would be for a judge, to take a newspaper   **1.93**

---

[141] J Raz, 'The Rule of Law and its Virtue' (1977) 93 LQR 195.

[142] TRS Allan, 'The Rule of Law as the Rule of Reason: Consent and Constitutionalism' (1999) 115 LQR 221, and the same author, *Constitutional Justice: a Liberal Theory of the Rule of Law* (Oxford: OUP, 2001). But see P Craig, 'Formal and Substantive Conceptions of the Rule of Law: an Analytical Framework' [1997] PL 467.

[143] *R v Secretary of State for the Home Department, ex p Pierson* [1998] AC 539, 575, HL.

campaign and public petitions into account when determining a tariff.[144] Elsewhere he has suggested the right to freedom of expression was implicit in the rule of law; without it the rule would be ineffective.[145] The House of Lords invoked the rule of law as justification for its decision that English courts should refuse to try someone who had been brought back to the country in disregard of the extradition process and in breach of international law.[146] But no decision suggests that an Act of Parliament would be invalid for infringement of the rule of law.

(ii) The rule of law and civil liberties

1.94 The protection by the ordinary courts of civil liberties, such as the right to personal freedom from arbitrary arrest, search and seizure and the right to freedom of expression, is usually regarded as an important aspect of the rule of law. As Dicey pointed out, in English law these rights have emerged from judicial rulings such as the famous decision that a general warrant to seize papers issued by a Secretary of State was illegal in the absence of any legal basis for such an infringement of the right to property.[147] Fundamental rights have not been formulated in England by a constitution or a Bill of Rights, as they have been in other jurisdictions such as the United States of America, Canada, and Germany.

1.95 While the existence and scope of fundamental rights in England has largely been a matter for the common law, statute has played an increasingly significant role in modifying or adding to them. For example, the Police and Criminal Evidence Act 1984, the Criminal Justice and Public Order Act 1994, and the Anti-terrorism, Crime and Security Act 2001 have all increased the powers of the police to stop and search individuals, to search their property after arrest, and to detain them for questioning. On the other hand, the rights not to suffer discrimination on the basis of race, colour or sex have been formulated by statute, notably the Race Relations Act 1976 and the Sex Discrimination Act 1975. The common law by comparison rarely provided protection against such discrimination.[148]

1.96 Under a conception of the rule of law such as Dicey's, individuals are free to speak or do those things which the law does not forbid. Rights are purely residual. But that provides an unsatisfactory and incomplete account of civil liberties in English law. First, public authorities and the police may enjoy the same residual freedoms

---

[144] *R v Secretary of State for the Home Department, ex p Venables* [1998] AC 407, 526, HL.

[145] *R v Secretary of State for the Home Department, ex p Simms* [1999] 3 All ER 400, 407–408, HL.

[146] *R v Horseferry Road Magistrates' Court, ex p Bennett* [1994] AC 42.

[147] *Entick v Carrington* (1776) 19 St Tr 1030. The decision instantiates all three aspects of the rule of law: hostility to arbitrary powers, subjection of officials to the ordinary courts, and the formulation of rights in concrete litigation.

[148] See Lord Simon in *Applin v Race Relations Board* [1975] AC 259, 286, HL.

as private individuals. That explains why the common law has failed to protect privacy against telephone-tapping and other interceptions of communications by the police and other authorities.[149] Secondly, the traditional account of the rule of law underestimates the part played by statute in formulating and defining rights, such as the right to privacy and the right not to suffer discrimination on the basis of race, colour or sex.

The third point is the most important. Courts often treat fundamental human rights as covered by positive principles of the common law. Judges protect the rights against legislative infringement by invoking a presumption that, in the absence of express language clearly indicating a contrary intention, Parliament does not intend to restrict them. Legislation has, for example, been narrowly construed not to interfere with a right of peaceful protest,[150] a right of access to the courts,[151] or a right to a fair hearing before an administrative decision is taken affecting individual interests.[152] The use of presumptions in these cases suggests the rule of law gives strong protection to fundamental liberties and has a much richer content than that suggested by Dicey. The right to freedom of expression and the right of access to the courts, for example, are regarded as more than residual liberties; they are constitutional rights of crucial importance in a liberal democratic society.[153] Otherwise, the courts could not invoke them to justify a restrictive interpretation of the terms of legislation.   **1.97**

(iii) Impact of the HRA 1998

Civil liberties have now been given stronger protection in England (and in Scotland and Northern Ireland) by the HRA 1998. The Act incorporates rights guaranteed by the European Convention on Human Rights and Fundamental Freedoms into UK law. Since 2 October 2000 when the measure took effect, it has been 'unlawful for a public authority to act in a way which is incompatible with a Convention right'.[154] The HRA expands, therefore, the scope of judicial review of administrative acts and decisions.[155] Further, as the courts are 'public   **1.98**

---

[149] See Sir R Megarry V-C in *Malone v Metropolitan Police Commissioner* [1979] Ch 344, 367. The restriction was held incompatible with the right to respect for private life guaranteed by the European Human Rights Convention, as it was not 'prescribed by law': *Malone v UK* (1984) 4 EHRR 14, ECtHR. The interception of communications has been authorized by statute, now Regulation of Investigatory Powers Act 2000.

[150] *Cozens v Brutus* [1973] AC 854, HL; *DPP v Jones* [1999] 2 AC 240, HL.

[151] *Raymond v Honey* [1983] 1 AC 1, HL; *R v Secretary of State for the Home Department, ex p Leech (No 2)* (1994) QB 198, CA.

[152] *Ridge v Baldwin* [1964] AC 40, HL.

[153] See *R v Secretary of State for the Home Department, ex p Simms* [2000] 2 AC 115, 131 *per* Lord Hoffmann, and *R (on the application of ProLife Alliance) v BBC* [2002] EWCA Civ 297; [2002] 2 All ER 756, 773 *per* Laws LJ.

[154] HRA 1998, s 6(1).

[155] See paras 17.44–17.46 below.

authorities',[156] the common law must be developed in conformity with the Convention rights set out in Sch 1 to the Act.

1.99   Under s 3(1) of the 1998 Act Parliamentary legislation must, so far as possible, 'be read and given effect in a way which is compatible with the Convention rights'. If, however, such an interpretation is not possible, a court may declare a provision in an Act of Parliament incompatible with a Convention right;[157] but the HRA does not authorize a court to invalidate the provision or to hold it inapplicable in so far as it infringes the right. The Act preserves parliamentary legislative supremacy, although a government may come under political pressure after a declaration of incompatibility to amend its legislation to remove the inconsistency with the Convention right.

1.100   The HRA 1998 is constitutionally significant. Clearly, it strengthens the capacity of the courts to protect fundamental human rights—at least the Convention rights incorporated into UK law. Courts must now interpret apparently unambiguous legislation, perhaps even through the implication of terms, to give it a meaning compatible with respect for the Convention.[158] To that extent, the weight of parliamentary legislative supremacy has been reduced, and that of the rule of law with a rich content has been increased. On the other hand, the decision of the House of Lords in *Re S (children: care plan)*[159] establishes that the 1998 Act has not brought about a radical shift in the respective weight of these two constitutional principles. The Lords held that courts should not, under the guise of interpretation, amend legislation in an attempt to render it compatible with Convention rights. It should not be forgotten that the HRA 1998 preserves the principle of legislative supremacy.

(c) Separation of powers

1.101   The principle of the separation of powers has been of immense importance in constitutional theory. It underpins many written constitutions, notably that of the United States of America which vests legislative, executive, and judicial powers in different institutions: Congress, the President, and the courts. Its role in English constitutional law is less clear. Many commentators either ignore it, or consider it to be of little significance. On the other hand, some judges regard it as the basis of the constitution and have used it to justify their decisions.[160]

---

[156] HRA 1998, s 6(3)(a).
[157] ibid s 4(2).
[158] *R v A* [2001] UKHL 25; [2002] 1 AC 45.
[159] [2002] UKHL 10; [2002] 2 All ER 192.
[160] See Lords Diplock and Scarman in *Duport Steels v Sirs* [1980] 1 WLR 142, 157, 169, HL, and Sir John Donaldson MR in *R v HM Treasury, ex p Smedley* [1985] QB 657, 666, CA.

(i) Theories of the separation of powers

Under the pure theory of the separation of powers, associated with Montesquieu's **1.102**
The Spirit of the Laws, there are three distinct functions of government—legislative, executive, and judicial—which should be exercised by separate persons or institutions, each independent of the others.[161] If the same person exercised two or
more powers, there would be a risk of tyranny. The theory requires both a separation of functions and a separation of persons exercising these functions. The
Constitution of the Fifth French Republic (1958) reflects this pure theory in so far
as the ordinary courts may not question the validity of administrative acts, let
alone primary legislation of the National Assembly. Ministers may not sit in the
Assembly; to that extent there is a strict separation of persons exercising legislative
and executive functions.

Other constitutions adopt a modified or partial theory, under which two or more **1.103**
persons or institutions may share the exercise of a particular function. For example, under the US Constitution, the President may veto a Bill passed by Congress,
though the veto may be overridden by a two-thirds majority in both Houses of
Congress. The courts are entitled to invalidate unconstitutional Acts of Congress
or presidential orders.[162] The partial theory reflects the underlying value of the
separation of powers principle, the avoidance of concentrations of power, but
achieves this by a complex system of checks and balances. Each institution participating, say, in the legislative function, is able to control abuses of power by the
other institutions.

(ii) Separation of powers in the English constitution

The constitution in England does not strictly observe the separation of powers in **1.104**
either version of the theory. Indeed, it has been written that 'the efficient secret of
the English Constitution may be described as the close union, the nearly complete
fusion, of the executive and legislative powers'.[163] As the government is drawn
from members of the legislative body, mostly the House of Commons, there is
clearly no separation of persons exercising the legislative and executive (or governmental) functions.[164] The most extreme violation of this aspect of the principle was the position of the Lord Chancellor. He has been a member of the
Cabinet, as Speaker of the House of Lords he has sat in the legislature, and he was
able to sit as a judge in the Appellate Committee of the House, thereby potentially

[161] See MJC Vile, *Constitutionalism and the Separation of Powers* (Oxford: Clarendon Press, 1967),
and E Barendt, 'Separation of Powers and Constitutional Government' [1995] PL 599.
[162] *Marbury v Madison* 1 Cranch 137 (1803), US Sup Ct.
[163] W Bagehot, *The English Constitution* (London: Collins, 1963, Introd by RHS Crossman).
[164] House of Commons Disqualification Act 1975, s 2 does provide that no more than 95 ministers may sit in the House of Commons, but that amounts to about 15% of its composition.

exercising all three functions.[165] In June 2003 the government announced its intention to abolish the position of Lord Chancellor.

1.105 Further, the courts may not control the constitutionality of legislation in England, with the single exception of incompatibility with EC law.[166] Senior judges have been appointed by the Prime Minister or the Lord Chancellor. (An independent Judicial Appointments Commission is likely to assume this role of the Lord Chancellor under the reforms proposed in 2003.) These appointments do not require parliamentary approval, so there is no constitutional control over their selection. The constitution in England, therefore, lacks some of the checks and balances to the abuse of legislative or executive power found in the US Constitution and post-war constitutions in Europe, such as the Basic Law of Germany.

1.106 Although the constitution does not observe the separation of powers principle strictly, it would be wrong to conclude it is entirely absent.[167] It may be seen at work in the following sets of circumstances. Moreover, it may be taken into account by the courts; it amounts then to a principle of constitutional law, the scope and application of which is determined judicially.

1.107 **Independence of the judiciary.** This has two aspects. First, statutory provisions insulate judges from political pressure. The most important protects senior judges from summary dismissal by the executive; they hold office during good behaviour and may only be removed on the presentation of an address passed by both Houses of Parliament to the Crown.[168] Other legislation precludes full-time judges from sitting in the House of Commons.[169]

1.108 The Law Lords are fully entitled to speak and vote in the House of Lords, but some choose not to do this on the ground that participation in the work of the legislature compromises their independence. The position of the Lord Chancellor was increasingly considered anomalous, in that a government minister could sit as a judge in the House of Lords. These defects will be remedied by the establishment of a Supreme Court under the reforms announced by the government in June 2003. It is unlikely that Supreme Court judges will be members of the House of Lords.[170]

[165] D Woodhouse, 'The Office of Lord Chancellor' [1998] PL 617.
[166] See paras 1.74–1.75 above and paras 2.158–2.161 below.
[167] C Munro, 'The Separation of Powers: Not such a Myth' [1981] PL 19.
[168] The provision, dating back to Act of Settlement 1701, is now in Supreme Court Act 1981, s 11.
[169] House of Commons Disqualification Act 1975, s 1(1).
[170] A Le Sueur, 'New Labour's next (surprisingly quick) steps in constitutional reform' [2003] PL 368.

Secondly, concern for judicial independence underlies decisions protecting the **1.109**
right of access to the courts against attempts by the executive or Parliament to oust
their jurisdiction. These rulings also reflect the separation of powers which requires decisions affecting the life, liberty, and other vital interests of individuals to
be taken by courts independent of the legislative and executive powers. There
would be no point in protecting the independence of the judiciary, if its jurisdiction over such decisions were curtailed. The courts have therefore held there is a
strong presumption that legislation does not authorize exclusion of their jurisdiction.[171] The Privy Council has even invalidated a statute in Ceylon (now Sri
Lanka) setting up a special court for the trial of the leaders of an insurrection on
the ground that the legislature was in effect usurping the role of the ordinary
courts.[172] It is unlikely that an English court would take the same approach, which
would entail a departure from the fundamental principle of parliamentary supremacy.[173]

Judicial review of the executive. It has been common to explain judicial review **1.110**
of executive acts as resting on the principle that government must act within the
powers conferred by legislation, often referred to as the ultra vires principle. That
explanation is generally seen as too simple. It does not justify the resort of the
courts to strong presumptions that Parliament does not intend to authorize restrictions of civil liberties or other departures from the rule of law, unless it uses explicit language that makes it plain beyond doubt that the legislation does permit
them. A better justification for judicial review is that the separation of powers requires the courts to check the abuse of power by government, particularly evident
when it infringes civil liberties.

The separation of powers principle also explains judicial review in circumstances **1.111**
where it seems artificial to place reliance on the ultra vires principle. First, it justifies the courts' jurisdiction to check the abusive exercise of prerogative powers (ex
hypothesi not conferred by statute); it also explains why it is inappropriate for
judges to exercise judicial power when the issue in the particular case, for instance,
a challenge to the making of a treaty, has a high political content.[174] Secondly, the
courts insist that the executive should not attempt to exercise legislative power
and so usurp the functions of Parliament. This principle goes back to the 17th
century,[175] but has recently been applied by the House of Lords. In *R v Secretary of*

---

[171] *Anisminic v Foreign Compensation Commission* [1969] 2 AC 147, HL; *Commissioners for Customs and Excise v Cure and Deeley Ltd* [1962] 1 QB 340, Sachs J.

[172] *Liyanage v The Queen* [1967] 1 AC 259.

[173] See, however, TRS Allan, *Constitutional Justice* (n 142 above) 148–157, who argues that Acts of Attainder should be invalidated for infringing both separation of powers and the rule of law.

[174] *Council of Civil Service Unions v Minister for the Civil Service* [1985] AC 374, discussed in paras 1.27–1.29 above.

[175] *Case of Proclamations* (1611) 12 Co Rep 74.

State for the Home Department, ex p Fire Brigades Union,[176] a majority of the House held it was illegal for the Home Secretary to introduce a scheme for the compensation of the victims of criminal injuries under his common law prerogative powers, rather than implement a more generous scheme which had been established by legislation. The government should legislate through Parliament; it would have been a clear infringement of the separation of powers for the executive to by-pass the legislature altogether, as it attempted to do in this case. The separation of powers principle explains the ruling more satisfactorily than the ultra vires principle, for the government did not even pretend to act under statute.

1.112 **Ministerial responsibility to Parliament.**   Although there is no strict separation of persons between members of the legislature and executive, the separation of powers principle does influence their relationship. The underlying value of the principle is the avoidance of absolute power. It therefore requires government to be responsible to Parliament; that means that, if it is defeated on a vote of confidence, it must resign. That happens less often than it used to do in the 19th century because the party system ensures that usually a government can rely on the loyal support of the members of Parliament forming the majority of the House of Commons from which it is drawn. But the principle of ministerial responsibility was evident in 1979 when the minority Labour government was defeated by one vote on a confidence motion and the Prime Minister was compelled to advise the Queen to dissolve Parliament for a general election.

1.113 The principle of ministerial responsibility is a constitutional convention, rather than a rule of constitutional law. The courts may not enforce it against a government which refused to resign after it had been defeated on a confidence motion. But it remains an aspect of the separation of powers principle which has both a legal and political dimension. Some judges, however, have wrongly regarded the separation of powers as merely a political doctrine, requiring the courts to abstain from judicial review, purely because ministers are responsible to Parliament. The dissenting Law Lords in the *Fire Brigades Union* case, Lords Keith and Mustill, argued that it was inappropriate for the courts to review the Home Secretary's decision to replace the statutory compensation scheme with the less generous common law scheme, because he was responsible to Parliament. This view is wrong. Under the separation of powers principle, ministers are politically responsible to Parliament, but are legally answerable to the courts if they claim to exercise powers they do not enjoy.

(d) Balancing the principles of the modern constitution

1.114 At the end of the 19th century when Dicey wrote his account of constitutional

---

[176] [1995] 2 AC 513.

principles, the primacy of parliamentary legislative supremacy was not in doubt. The rule of law provided a weak constraint. The courts generally applied properly enacted statutes, even if their plain meaning was to restrict the exercise of a fundamental right. Little attention was paid to the principle of the separation of powers as a check on the abuse of power by Parliament or the government.

Whatever its merits a century ago, this account is now clearly inaccurate. Although parliamentary legislative supremacy remains a fundamental aspect of the constitution, its application is restricted when courts invoke as a competing constitutional principle a rich conception of the rule of law or the separation of powers. Courts do not interpret legislation to allow the violation of constitutional rights such as the right to freedom of expression or of access to the courts; the decision of a minister, apparently authorized by the terms of legislation, may be invalidated because it infringes the rule of law or flouts an aspect of the separation of powers. **1.115**

Additionally, some statutes, notably the ECA 1972, but also the HRA 1998 and the devolution measures have been described as 'constitutional', in contradiction of the traditional view that there is no distinction in English law between ordinary and constitutional legislation. Unlike ordinary legislation, the latter is not subject to implied repeal; express language indicating that Parliament intended this consequence is required for the repeal of constitutional legislation.[177] Whether this radical approach would be upheld by the House of Lords, it reflects political reality. It is very unlikely that the Westminster Parliament will repeal any of the constitutional legislation discussed in these pages. **1.116**

The most important point is this. The courts always have the last word on the application of legislation, as well as the development of the common law. For that reason, judges have sometimes referred to the shared sovereignties of Parliament and the courts; the former in making the law, the latter in interpreting and applying it.[178] Any account of the constitution which gives undisputed primacy to parliamentary legislative supremacy is inevitably too simple. The courts as custodians of the common law constitution must also give due weight to the values of the rule of law and the separation of powers. They are right to do this, as unlimited deference to parliamentary supremacy may put liberty at peril. **1.117**

---

[177] Laws LJ in *Thoburn v Sunderland City Council* [2002] EWHC 195; [2003] QB 151 at [62]–[64].

[178] Lord Bridge in *X Ltd v Morgan Grampian (Publishers) Ltd* [1991] 1 AC 1, 48, HL; S Sedley (n 12 above) 26.

B. Sources of Law and the Hierarchy of Norms

(1) The Constitutional Framework

1.118   Since there is no single written or codified constitution in the United Kingdom, there is no formal document to which to turn for an authoritative indication of the sources from which spring those rules which come to be treated as binding laws. Indeed, the very absence of such a document has contributed to a rich jurisprudential debate about the nature of law and how it is to be identified. For some so-called 'realists', there is no such thing as law on a purely theoretical plane. For others, theoretical law not only exists but is in nature different from other rules and can be identified only by means of criteria which are laid down by a 'rule of recognition'.[179]

1.119   Whichever polarity lies closer to the truth, it is nevertheless the case that, without a written constitution, the practical identification of what society at any given time treats as its laws has to be achieved by the courts in order for them to carry out their primary function of settling disputes. As Bell explains in *English Private Law*, judges have to support their decisions by recourse to legal reasons or justifications and, to do this, must pinpoint their sources.[180] The evolution of the sources of the law and the relationships between those sources has thus been effectively under the exclusive control of the judiciary. However, judges are of course themselves the products of the political and social times in which they live and such contexts are amply reflected in their evolving view of the ways in which laws are created and the importance to be ascribed to each source. This fact alone accounts for an important part of the dynamic of the law-making process.

(2) Sources of Law

(a) **Statutory sources**

(i) Primary

1.120   **The evolution of the present position.**   A further consequence of the lack of a written constitution in the United Kingdom is that no formal hierarchy is ascribed to the different sources of law which are recognized by the courts.[181] This is

---

[179] See HLA Hart, *The Concept of Law* (2nd edn, Oxford: Clarendon Press, 1994).

[180] P Birks (ed), *English Private Law* (Oxford: OUP, 2000) paras 1.01–1.04.

[181] However, there is a somewhat heterodox view, already noted (paras 1.75 and 1.87 above), that some statutes have special status on account of their constitutional significance. As Laws LJ said in *Thoburn v Sunderland City Council* [2002] EWHC 195; [2003] QB 151 at [62] and [63]: 'We should recognise a hierarchy of Acts of Parliament: as it were "ordinary" statutes and "constitutional" statutes. The two categories must be distinguished on a principled basis. In my opinion a constitutional statute is one which (a) conditions the legal relationship between citizen and State in some

in sharp contrast to most other jurisdictions, in which the national constitution not only sets out such an order of priority but also often proclaims certain rules as unalterable or as alterable only by a specially stringent process.[182] The flexibility of the British system has the advantage of facilitating change in response to new social, political, economic or other demands but, conversely, results in an inability to protect fundamental rights, freedoms or other interests. The latter defect has been especially evident in modern times and, as will be discussed below, has been partially mitigated in relation to the European Union and the European Convention on Human Rights through the adoption of essentially pragmatic legislative measures.

All law, from whatever source it springs, is therefore of equal weight. However, if a legal system acknowledges a number of different sources of law, as does the UK legal system, it is obvious that there will be chaos unless some rule is adopted to indicate which is to prevail. The current rule is that Acts of Parliament take precedence over all other sources of law and that it is only in their absence that such sources will be given legal recognition and effect; this principle is usually referred to as the legislative supremacy of the Westminster Parliament.[183] Nevertheless, this position was only reached after prolonged confrontation, in particular between the Monarch and Parliament.   **1.121**

The Parliament of today is usually acknowledged by historians as having its origins in the reign of Edward I at the end of the 13th century.[184] The recognition of the existence of a higher authority than the King appears to date from a similar period, Bracton writing in the 13th century that the King ought to be subject to God and the law because the law made him King.[185] Magna Carta, signed in 1215, articulated the balance of powers which was sought by the feudal barons between the King, themselves and their feudal subjects; most famously, it proclaimed: **1.122**

---

general, overarching manner, or (b) enlarges or diminishes the scope of what we would now regard as fundamental constitutional rights ... Ordinary statutes may be impliedly repealed. Constitutional statutes may not.'

[182] eg, the Federal US Constitution can only be altered by a specially strict legislative process: having been proposed by a two-thirds majority of both Houses of Congress, an amendment must be approved by the legislatures of three-quarters of the states; alternatively, following initiation by two-thirds of the states, the amendment must be ratified by conventions in three-quarters of the states. The fundamental rights provisions of the Federal German Constitution are expressed to be unalterable.

[183] Although this is the formal legal position, in practice today English law yields to contradictory provisions of EU law, and a statute which conflicts with the European Convention on Human Rights can be made the subject of a declaration of incompatibility; however, as will be seen below, these results are themselves the consequence of Acts of the Westminster Parliament.

[184] See TFT Plucknett, *Taswell-Langmead's English Constitutional History* (11th edn, London: Sweet & Maxwell, 1960).

[185] *De Legibus et Consuetudinibus Angliae*, f 5b. See also WS Holdsworth, *A History of English Law* (3rd edn, London: Methuen, 1923) vol II.

No freeman shall be taken, or imprisoned, or disseised, or outlawed, or exiled, or in any way destroyed, nor will we go upon him, except by the legal judgment of his peers or by the law of the land.[186]

1.123   Magna Carta also contained the seed from which sprang the principle that the levying of taxation required the consent of Parliament, a principle which was of vital practical as well as theoretical importance since it limited the ability of the Monarch to raise the necessary money to support his or her policies.[187] However, monarchs for over 300 succeeding years asserted rights to interfere substantially with the legislative process, to summon and prorogue Parliament as of right, and to levy taxation. It was the middle years of the 17th century which witnessed the most profound changes in the constitutional balance between the monarch, Parliament and the courts, and on which the modern system of 'constitutional' or 'limited' monarchy is based. The courts began, though not through a uniform linear process, to exert their jurisdiction over the King. The vital principle was established that the courts had power to determine and enforce the limits of the royal prerogative; furthermore, whatever else the monarch might be permitted to do by means of prerogative powers, it was established that such powers could never extend to legislating:

1. The King by his proclamation cannot create any offence which was not one before; for then he might alter the law of the land in a high point; for if he may create an offence where none is, upon that ensues fine and imprisonment.
2. The King hath no prerogative but what the law of the land allows him.
3. But the King for the prevention of offences may by proclamation admonish his subjects that they keep the laws and do not offend them upon punishment to be inflicted by law; the neglect of such proclamation aggravates the offence.
4. If an offence be not punishable in the Star Chamber,[188] the prohibition of it by proclamation cannot make it so.[189]

1.124   A more modern statement of the principle is to be found in *The Zamora*[190] where Lord Parker of Waddington stated:

---

[186] Clause 39.

[187] In particular, clause 12 provided that no scutage or aid was to be taken without the consent of the common council, the feudal council of tenants in chief, except for the ransoming of the King's body, the knighting of his eldest son, and the first marriage of his eldest daughter.

[188] The Court of Star Chamber was probably created in 1487. It had criminal jurisdiction, in particular over offences alleged to be against the state. It did not use juries and was widely feared because of its use of torture.

[189] *Case of Proclamations* (1611) 12 Co Rep 74. Sir Edward Coke, Chief Justice of the King's Bench, had been asked by the Council whether the King could use his power to make proclamations to prohibit the building of new houses in London (in an early attempt to prevent urban sprawl) and to prohibit making wheat into starch. Coke conferred with Chief Justice Fleming, Chief Baron Tanfield and Baron Altham and together they delivered their judgment in front of the Privy Council. Plucknett comments: 'By their firmness on this occasion the judges rendered an important service to their country. A check was given to the exercise of arbitrary power in this direction . . .': (n 184 above) 343.

[190] [1916] 2 AC 77.

The idea that the King in Council, or indeed any branch of the Executive, has power to prescribe or alter the law to be administered by courts of law in this country is out of harmony with the principles of our Constitution. It is true that, under a number of modern statutes, various branches of the Executive have power to make rules having the force of statutes, but all such rules derive their validity from the statute which creates the power, and not from the executive body by which they are made.[191]

Over the next few decades battles nevertheless continued between Parliament and the absolutist Charles I, in particular over the extent of the royal prerogative and its relationship with the raising of taxes;[192] the ensuing Civil War of 1642–49 ended with Charles's execution and there followed the only period of non-monarchist government in the recorded history of this country. The monarchy was restored in 1660 and the new King's first Parliament gave its retrospective blessing to the activities of the previous Convention Parliament, an event of considerable significance since it underlined that henceforth it was the combination of monarch and Parliament which were to exert supreme legal power. The Restoration did not, however, mark the end of the constitutional conflict. James II (1685–88) asserted the rights to 'suspend' the general operation of statutes[193] and to 'dispense' with their consequences in particular circumstances.[194] He was driven from the throne in the 'Glorious Revolution' of 1688 and succeeded by William and Mary of Orange. An assembly was summoned, consisting of peers, members of the Commons who had sat during the reign of Charles II, and the Alderman of the City of London. This advised the summoning of a convention of peers and representatives of the shires and the boroughs which speedily declared itself to be the lawful new Parliament and enacted the Bill of Rights of 1688.

1.125

The Bill of Rights is the single most important document in the evolution of the modern constitutional balance between monarch and Parliament.[195] In particular, it established beyond any further doubt the principle that Parliament has the supreme right to legislate for the country, stating in its first substantive Articles:

1.126

---

[191] ibid 90.

[192] In *Darnel's Case* (1627) 3 St Tr 1, five knights were imprisoned for refusing to pay a forced loan. Although the Petition of Right of 1627, which was assented to by the King and considered to be a statute, subsequently forbade taxation 'without common consent by Act of Parliament', this did not prevent Charles I from continuing to assert a right to impose taxes in support of his foreign policy and in the exercise of his prerogative powers: see *R v Hampden (The Case of Ship-Money)* (1637) 3 St Tr 825.

[193] A practice which was disapproved by the courts in *The Case of the Seven Bishops* (1688) 12 St Tr 133.

[194] This was afforded grudging approval by the judges in *Godden v Hales* (1686) 11 St Tr 1166.

[195] Plucknett described it as 'the coping-stone of the constitutional building': (n 184 above) 449. 'Henceforth the theory of divine hereditary right, destroyed by the expulsion of James II and the negation of the rights of his innocent son, lived on only in the imaginations of those who mingled politics with romance. The Crown became the official representative of the community, to carry out its wishes so far as they are expressed or can be ascertained': Sir WR Anson, *The Law and Custom of the Constitution* (4th edn, Oxford: Clarendon Press, 1935) 46.

> That the pretended power of suspending laws or the execution of laws by regal authority without consent of Parliament is illegal; that the pretended power of dispensing with laws or the execution of laws by regal authority as it hath been assumed and exercised of late is illegal.[196]

In addition, it clearly refuted any lingering notion that the monarch could control taxation, even those taxes connected with the prerogative power to conduct foreign policy. In Article 4, it laid down that:

> Levying money for or to the use of the Crown by pretence of prerogative without grant of Parliament for longer time or in other manner than the same is or shall be granted is illegal.[197]

1.127   The framework of the modern system of parliamentary supremacy was thus put in place and it has not been substantially disturbed since the 17th century, despite union with Scotland in 1707, union with Ireland in 1800 and its subsequent dissolution in 1922, the conferring of independence on numerous former colonies of the Crown, accession to the European Communities in 1972, devolution of government to Northern Ireland, Scotland and Wales, and the enactment of the Human Rights Act (HRA) in 1998.

1.128   **The characteristics of primary legislation.**[198]   If primary legislation enjoys such an exalted status amongst the sources of law, it is clearly crucial to be able to identify it with certainty and to distinguish it from lesser forms of creation.[199] By far the most important instruments of primary legislation today are Acts of the Westminster Parliament.

1.129   The basic rule is that a valid Act of Parliament must have been passed by the House of Commons and the House of Lords and must thereafter have received the

---

[196] The conditional prohibition of the power of dispensation, restricted only to the way in which it had been exercised 'of late', preserves the prerogative power to pardon convicted criminals. This power is today exercised by the Home Secretary on behalf of the Crown.

[197] Attempts by central and local government to collect taxes without express statutory authorization are therefore invariably struck down by the courts: see *A-G v Wilts United Dairies* (1922) 37 TLR 884, *Congreve v Home Office* [1976] QB 629 and *McCarthy and Stone (Developments) Ltd v Richmond upon Thames LBC* [1992] 2 AC 48.

[198] See F Bennion, *Bennion on Statute Law* (3rd edn, London: Longman, 1990).

[199] For the purposes of the HRA 1998, s 21 states that '"primary legislation" means any: (a) public general Act; (b) local and personal Act; (c) private Act; (d) Measure of the Church Assembly; (e) Measure of the General Synod of the Church of England; (f) Order in Council—(i) made in exercise of her Majesty's Royal Prerogative; (ii) made under s.38(1)(a) of the Northern Ireland Constitution Act 1973 or the corresponding provision of the Northern Ireland Act 1998; or (iii) amending an Act of a kind mentioned in paragraph (a), (b) or (c); and includes an order or other instrument made under primary legislation (otherwise than by the National Assembly for Wales, a member of the Scottish Executive, a Northern Ireland Minister or a Northern Ireland Department) to the extent to which it operates to bring one or more provisions of that legislation into force or amends any primary legislation'.

Royal Assent.[200] However, the courts are wary of confrontation with Parliament over the way in which Parliament organizes its affairs.[201] They are therefore reluctant to inquire into the provenance of any instrument which purports to be a true Act of Parliament. The position stated in 1842 by Lord Campbell in *Edinburgh and Dalkeith Rly v Wauchope*[202] remains accurate today:

> All that a Court of Justice can do is to look to the Parliament roll: if from that it should appear that a Bill has passed both Houses and received the Royal Assent, no Court of Justice can enquire into the mode in which it was introduced into Parliament, nor into what was done previous to its introduction, or what passed in Parliament during its progress in its various stages through both Houses.[203]

In addition to the need to avoid jurisdictional contretemps between the legislature and the judiciary, the rationale for such a rule might also be thought to lie in a desire to reinforce the certainty of the legal system for the benefit of the general public and to discourage possible mischief-makers from undermining that certainty. However, the approach taken by the courts is not mitigated even where the Act of Parliament concerned is a private one, in other words, one dealing with a local or personal matter, which therefore affects the rights of only a section of the population and not the population at large. Parliamentary procedure in such cases seeks to protect those whose interests might be at risk, yet the courts will enforce legislation even where it appears to have been procured in disobedience to such parliamentary safeguards. Thus, in *Pickin v British Rlys Board*,[204] despite allegations that Parliament had been misled by the British Railways Board into treating a Bill as an unopposed one, the resultant legislation was treated as valid by a unanimous House of Lords with the consequence that Mr Pickin was divested of land of which he would otherwise have been the undisputed owner. **1.130**

There is one exception to the rule that primary legislation requires the assent of both Houses of Parliament and the monarch. This is under the conditions stipulated by the Parliament Acts 1911 and 1949.[205] These Acts were passed in order to **1.131**

---

[200] Michael Zander in *The Law-Making Process* (5th edn, London: Butterworths, 1999) points out that 'one of the most remarkable features of the procedure is that Her Majesty does not have the texts of the bills to which she signifies her assent. She only has the short title!' (p 73).

[201] There were bruising battles over this issue in *Ashby v White* (1703–04) 2 Ld Raym 938, 3 Ld Raym 320, 14 St Tr 695 and *Stockdale v Hansard* (1839) 9 Ad & E 1.

[202] 8 Cl & F 710. See also *Lee v Bude and Torrington Rly* (1871) LR & CP 576 in which Willes J stated (at 582): 'Are we to act as regents over what is done by Parliament with the consent of the Queen, Lords, and Commons? I deny that any such authority exists. If an Act of Parliament has been obtained improperly, it is for the legislature to correct it by repealing it: but, so long as it exists as law, the courts are bound to obey it. The proceedings here are judicial, not autocratic, which they would be if we could make laws instead of administering them.'

[203] 8 Cl & F 710, 725.

[204] [1974] AC 765.

[205] There is, however, a contrary view that Acts passed by means of this procedure enjoy only the status of delegated legislation, and should thus be discussed in the next section; see in particular Jackson and Leopold (eds), *O Hood Phillips and Jackson: Constitutional and Administrative Law* (8th

resolve differences which had arisen between the two Houses, and in order to give the democratically elected Commons the upper hand in the legislative process. Their effect is that the House of Lords no longer has power to reject Money Bills and can delay their passage by only one month; the power of the House in relation to other Public Bills is reduced to the ability to delay their passage over two successive sessions.[206] Thus, some effective primary legislation may bear the imprimatur of only the House of Commons and the monarch.[207]

1.132 Orders in Council issued under the royal prerogative are treated by the HRA 1998 as primary legislation, and they are so referred to on some occasions in judicial statements.[208] Such Orders in Council, however, are merely the formal manifestation of the exercise of the sovereign's common law powers which, since the Case of Proclamations of 1611,[209] cannot be used to change the law of this country.[210] They would therefore only be truly 'legislative' in the sense of creating new general law in circumstances in which the royal prerogative itself still extended this far, for example if the Crown were to conquer new territory and to seek to impose its own laws there.

(ii) Secondary

1.133 The number of matters on which governments today wish to procure legislation, coupled with the detail and technicality of many of the issues addressed,

---

edn, London: Sweet & Maxwell, 2001) 79–80 : 'The Parliament Acts do not alter the composition of Parliament. When an Act is passed by the Queen and the Commons under the provisions of the Parliament Acts, the enacting formula must state that this is done in accordance with the provisions of those Acts (which include the sending of the Bill to the Lords), and so it may best be regarded as a kind of subordinate or delegated legislation.' See also HWR Wade in his review of Keir and Lawson's *Cases in Constitutional Law* in [1954] CLJ 263, 265, and in 'The Basis of Legal Sovereignty' [1955] CLJ 172, 193.

[206] In the case of a Bill to extend the life of Parliament beyond five years, one year must elapse between the date of the Bill's second reading in the Commons in the first session and the date of its third reading in the second session.

[207] The use of the Parliament Acts procedure has not, however, proved popular, at least until recent times. The Parliament Act 1911 was used to ensure the enactment of the Parliament Act 1949, a fact which leads the editors of *O Hood Phillips and Jackson: Constitutional and Administrative Law* (n 205 above) to conclude that the 1949 Act is not a true Act of Parliament because it 'offended against the general principle of logic and law that delegates (the Queen and Commons) cannot enlarge the authority delegated to them' (p 80). The War Crimes Act 1991, the European Parliamentary Elections Act 1999 and the Sexual Offences (Amendment) Act 2000 were enacted under the Parliament Acts procedure, without the consent of the House of Lords. The increasing tendency to side-step the Lords today may reflect a growing respect for the principle of democracy, together with confidence that democracy is guaranteed by the Commons; an alternative interpretation might be that governments of the late 20th and early 21st centuries have become more authoritarian than their predecessors.

[208] See eg *Council of Civil Service Unions v Minister for Civil Service* [1984] 3 WLR 1174, 1185 *per* Lord Fraser.

[209] Discussed above.

[210] In *Council of Civil Service Unions v Minister for Civil Service* [1984] 3 WLR 1174, the Order in Council regulated the conduct of members of the Civil Service, a matter more akin to contract than legislation.

mean that Parliament itself is unable to enact all the legislation which is demanded. Since, as was seen in the preceding section, the monarchy (and thus today the executive) has not enjoyed any independent legislative power[211] since the 17th century, Parliament finds itself obliged to delegate a great deal of power to legislate; by far the greater part of the legislation produced in any one year in the United Kingdom now takes the form of secondary or 'delegated' legislation.[212]

However, it is important to bear in mind that the process is merely one of delegation, not out-and-out transfer of legislative power. It follows that the person enjoying delegated legislative power cannot exceed the mandate conferred by Parliament in the relevant enabling Act. Any purported exercise of delegated power which exceeds the authority conferred, either because it is substantively outside the limits stated, or because it neglects the procedures stipulated, or because it is exercised for a purpose not contemplated by the parent Act, is liable to be struck down by the courts as ultra vires.

1.134

Whenever legislative power is delegated, the process of law-making takes a step away from the democratic ideal.[213] In 1992, the House of Lords therefore established a Delegated Powers and Deregulation Committee which examines all government Bills with a view to seeing whether they delegate power appropriately.[214] The proper role of democracy also probably accounts, at least in part, for a series of strict rules adopted by the judiciary in relation to the permissible scope of delegated legislation. Of course, in a system unbounded by formal written constitutional guarantees, Parliament may delegate whatever powers it sees fit. However, there are a number of matters which the courts will not presume to be contained in delegated legislation and for which clear express words are required. An example is the so-called 'Henry VIII clause' (an allusion to that King's autocratic character) which confers a power to amend primary legislation, either with or without

1.135

---

[211] cf the position in France, where the executive enjoys an inherent power to legislate in order to elaborate the details of statutes.

[212] To the rationales mentioned in the text for the existence of delegated legislation, the Committee on Ministers' Powers (the 'Donoughmore Committee') added that it is sometimes difficult to include all necessary details in a single instrument, that flexibility and experimentation are facilitated by delegated legislation, and that it provides a quick way to respond to crises; see Cmnd 4060, 1932.

[213] Fear that rapidly increasing amounts of delegated legislation threatened democracy in the early part of the twentieth century were voiced by Lord Hewart CJ in *The New Despotism* (London: Ernest Benn Ltd, 1929). In more recent times, the claim has been made that governments use delegated legislation for the impermissible function of legislating over matters of principle, as distinct from detail; see in particular the *Report of the Inquiry into the Export of Defence Equipment and Dual-Use Goods to Iraq and Related Prosecutions* ('the Scott Report') (1995–96 HC 115).

[214] Ganz points out that it is 'paradoxical that it is the unelected House of Lords rather than the House of Commons which set up this committee which functions as "the constitutional conscience of the House in relation to delegated powers"': *Understanding Public Law* (3rd edn, London: Sweet & Maxwell, 2001) 54.

any further parliamentary scrutiny;[215] such clauses are disapproved of in principle because they enable the executive to undo what Parliament (the instrument of democracy) has willed.[216]

1.136 Nevertheless, exceptional cases are encountered, such for example as s 2(4) of the European Communities Act 1972 (ECA), which expressly permits the amendment of primary law by delegated legislation wherever necessary for the implementation of EU law, and s 10(2) of the HRA 1998, which permits the amendment of primary legislation by delegated legislation in order to render domestic law compatible with the European Convention on Human Rights and Fundamental Freedoms.[217] A far-reaching example of a Henry VIII clause, albeit one which is restricted by special consultative procedures, is contained in the Deregulation and Contracting Out Act 1994. Section 1 enables a minister of the Crown to amend or repeal primary legislation which imposes a burden on trade or business. Before making such an order, the minister must consult with representative organisations; after doing so, the minister can lay a draft order before Parliament but this must be accompanied by information on a number of matters prescribed by the statute, such as the estimated savings which will result from the order.

1.137 Although it is highly unlikely that any court would ever imply a Henry VIII clause into a statute, the judges give effect to such terms when they are expressly incorporated in an enabling Act. In *Thoburn v Sunderland City Council*,[218] the Divisional Court also roundly rejected the assertion that a Henry VIII clause could only be valid where it was limited to the amendment of pre-existing legislation.

1.138 For similar reasons of democracy, the courts also insist that delegated legislation must be very clear before it will be interpreted to authorize the raising of taxation[219] or to permit sub-delegation.[220]

---

[215] As seen above, it is argued in *O Hood Phillips and Jackson: Constitutional and Administrative Law* (n 205 above) that the Parliament Act 1949 offends against this principle.

[216] Similarly, where specific rights have been conferred by statute, the courts will not permit them to be cut down by subordinate legislation passed under the authority of another Act: *R v Secretary of State for Social Security, ex p Joint Council for the Welfare of Immigrants* [1997] 1 WLR 275.

[217] See also Juries Act 1974, s 21.

[218] [2002] EWHC 195; [2003] QB 151.

[219] As discussed above, the power to levy taxes has long been regarded as the preserve of Parliament itself; see *A-G v Wilts United Dairies Ltd* (1921) 39 TLR 781. Nevertheless, the Excise Duties (Surcharges or Rebates) Act 1979 and the Value Added Tax Act 1994 permit variations in tax rates to be imposed by delegated legislation; similarly, in order for effect to be given at once to tax changes proposed in the annual Budget by the Chancellor of the Exchequer, some taxes can be collected for a transitional period pursuant merely to a resolution of the House of Commons under the Provisional Collection of Taxes Act 1968. See also Scotland Act 1998, s 73, discussed below.

[220] See *R v Burah* (1878) 2 App Cas 889 and *Hodge v R* (1883) 9 App Cas 117.

Particularly suspect in the eyes of the judges are clauses in enabling Acts which **1.139** purport to oust the jurisdiction of the courts to review the use to which the power has been put.[221] This is hardly surprising since such a provision could have the effect of seriously imbalancing the relationship between the executive and the courts. Such provisions are encountered on rare occasions, particularly where finality is an important public concern, and they are upheld by the judiciary provided they are clearly expressed by Parliament. However, their use is rare in the sphere of delegated legislation, as distinct from other areas of administrative decision-making.[222]

Since intra vires delegated legislation has the blessing of Parliament, so long as it **1.140** remains in force it has precisely the same effects as primary legislation. Thus, for example, it is no defence to a criminal charge of breaching delegated legislation that it lacks the potency of primary legislation.[223]

Delegated legislative power may be conferred by Parliament on any person. The **1.141** following section describes the most commonly encountered types of delegated legislation, but the list is not, and cannot be, exhaustive.

Legislative acts of devolved parliaments. In the closing years of the 20th cen- **1.142** tury, legislation was enacted to provide for devolved government in Northern Ireland, Scotland and Wales.[224] Only in Northern Ireland had there previously been any attempt at such a system of government; from the creation of the Province in 1921 until the imposition of direct rule by Westminster during the 'Troubles' in 1972, Northern Ireland possessed its own devolved Parliament and Executive. The new devolution arrangements have had a profound effect upon the balance of powers in the United Kingdom and radically altered the effective sources of law.

The powers devolved are different in the three regions concerned[225] and each **1.143** must therefore be examined in turn. However, since the term 'devolution' nec- essarily implies delegation rather than a passing of ownership, it should be stressed that in no case was legislative power transferred outright to any of the

---

[221] Perhaps the most famous example of a judicial refusal to accept an ouster clause occurred in *Anisminic Ltd v Foreign Compensation Commission* [1969] 2 AC 147, where s 4(4) of the Foreign Compensation Act 1950 stated that a decision of the Commission could not be called into question in any court of law; the House of Lords ruled that this only applied to intra vires decisions.

[222] But an example is to be found in Scotland Act 1998, s 28(5), discussed below.

[223] See eg *Hodge v R* (1883) 9 App Cas 117 and *Kruse v Johnson* [1898] 2 QB 91.

[224] This is relevant to this book since it denotes, at least in practice, a diminution in the powers of the Westminster Parliament and government.

[225] Burrows has observed that 'the most striking feature of the three Acts of Parliament enacted in 1998 is the extent of the differences between the devolution settlements for Scotland, Wales and Northern Ireland' which she argues avoided insurmountable political obstacles for a government which was attempting to achieve constitutional reform as quickly as possible: see N Burrows, *Devolution* (London: Sweet & Maxwell, 2000).

regional assemblies.[226] Furthermore, Parliament at Westminster remains competent to legislate for the regions even on devolved matters. Each assembly owes its existence and authority to the enabling Act of the Westminster Parliament; each would therefore be extinguished with the repeal of the relevant constitutive Act. Moreover, HRA 1998, s 21 defines 'subordinate legislation' to include Acts of the Scottish Parliament, Acts of the Parliament of Northern Ireland, measures of the Assembly established under s 1 of the Northern Ireland Assembly Act 1973, and Acts of the Northern Ireland Assembly. The consequence of this is that such measures may be quashed by the courts if they breach the Convention rights.[227]

1.144   In the case of Northern Ireland, the Northern Ireland Act 1998 sets out a sophisticated scheme for devolved government in that Province. The Act was a product of the Belfast Agreement of April 10, 1998[228] and it made provision for a staged transition towards devolution. Section 3 permitted the Secretary of State to lay a draft Order in Council before Parliament bringing the new system into effect, 'if it appears to the Secretary of State that sufficient progress has been made in implementing the Belfast Agreement'; the draft Order required approval by resolution of each House of Parliament and was eventually made in December 1999.[229] Under the scheme, the new Northern Ireland Assembly has power to make laws, known as 'Acts', which are subject to the Royal Assent.[230] Its legislative competence is limited,[231] in particular with regard to a number of 'excepted matters' set out in Sch 2. In addition, it is expressly provided that the Assembly cannot legislate contrary to the Convention rights protected by the HRA or contrary to EC law; neither may such legislation discriminate on the ground of religious belief or political opinion. Certain pieces of primary legislation of the UK Parliament, in particular the ECA 1972 and the HRA 1998, are expressed to be entrenched and therefore not susceptible to modification by the Assembly.[232]

1.145   The Scotland Act 1998 set up a Scottish Parliament, the first to have existed since the Union of Scotland with England in 1707. Devolution in Scotland has been functional since 1999. The Scottish Parliament has power to make laws, known as

---

[226] The White Paper *Scotland's Parliament* (Cm 3658, 1998) made this clear in para 42: 'The United Kingdom Parliament is and will remain sovereign in all matters'. The contrary view is that the devolved legislatures possess power to enact primary legislation within the fields of their jurisdiction and that power to legislate has been transferred to them. For arguments in support of such a position, see Burrows (n 225 above).

[227] s 3(2)(b), subject to s 3(2)(c).

[228] Cm 4292, 1998.

[229] The devolved institutions have subsequently been suspended for temporary periods due to political difficulties.

[230] Northern Ireland Act 1998, s 5.

[231] ibid s 6.

[232] ibid s 7.

'Acts of the Scottish Parliament', which are subject to the Royal Assent.[233] In a cautious provision reflective of the existing case law discussed above in relation to the Westminster Parliament, the Act provides that the validity of an Act of the Scottish Parliament is not affected by any invalidity in the proceedings of the Parliament leading to its enactment.[234] In so providing, the Act extends a force to Acts of the Scottish Parliament exceeding that of other types of secondary legislation since the latter may be quashed in judicial review proceedings if the procedures stipulated for their enactment have not been complied with. Disputes as to the effect of this provision can, however, be anticipated where a procedural irregularity is so fundamental as to undermine the whole nature of an instrument as a true Act of the Scottish Parliament.

Despite the legislative authority of the new Parliament, the power of the UK Parliament to legislate for Scotland is expressly preserved.[235] Although technically unnecessary because of the sovereignty of the Westminster Parliament,[236] this provision formally emphasizes the subordinate status of the Scottish Parliament. The Act goes on to set out limits to the powers of the Scottish Parliament, stating somewhat ambiguously that an Act is not law 'so far as' any provision of it is outside the legislative competence of the Parliament.[237] The major fetters on the Parliament's powers are the restricted and reserved matters set out in Schs 4 and 5, together with legislation which would be incompatible with the Convention rights protected by the HRA or incompatible with EC law.[238] In addition, in deference to Scotland's historic criminal system, the Scottish Parliament is disempowered from legislating so as to remove the Lord Advocate from his position as head of the systems of criminal prosecutions and investigation of deaths in Scotland.[239] However, unusually for a subordinate body, the Scottish Parliament has been entrusted with a tax-varying power; it can alter the basic rate of income tax for Scottish taxpayers either upwards or downwards by up to three points for a year of assessment.[240]

1.146

---

[233] Scotland Act 1998, s 28(1) and (2). CMG Himsworth and CR Munro, in their Annotations to the Act in Sweet & Maxwell's *Current Law Statutes*, offer the interesting observation that, since Her Majesty is part of the UK Parliament but not part of the Scottish Parliament, the function of the Royal Assent is even more formal in this situation than in relation to Westminster legislation. In addition, there is the potential for conflicting advice (by the Scottish First Minister or others) to be offered to the sovereign as to whether or not to give the Royal Assent.

[234] s 28(5).

[235] s 28(7).

[236] Discussed in paras 2.173–2.175 below.

[237] Scotland Act 1998, s 29(1). Cf the clearer drafting of s 6(1) of the Northern Ireland Act 1998, which states: 'A provision of an Act is not law if it is outside the legislative competence of the Assembly'.

[238] Scotland Act 1998, s 29(2)(b), (c) and (d).

[239] ibid s 29(2)(e).

[240] ibid s 73. Scottish taxpayers are defined in s 75 as those resident in the UK for whom Scotland is the part of the UK with which they have the closest connection during the relevant year. The tax-varying power is exercisable via a resolution of the Scottish Parliament.

1.147 The borderline between matters within and without the competence of the Scottish Parliament is necessarily an extremely difficult one both to define in theory and to determine in practice. Provision is therefore made for the Advocate General, the Lord Advocate or the Attorney-General to refer the question of whether a Bill or any provision of a Bill would be within the legislative competence of the Parliament to the Judicial Committee of the Privy Council.[241] In addition, where a provision of an Act of the Scottish Parliament could be read in such a way as to be outside the Parliament's legislative competence, it is provided that the provision must be read as narrowly as is required for it to be within competence, if such a reading is possible.[242] The Lord Advocate explained when the Scotland Bill was in the House of Lords that this section was intended to enable the courts to give effect to legislation, rather than invalidating it; the example he gave was of legislation of the Scottish Parliament permitting the holding of a referendum on any matter in Scotland. This could be interpreted as extending to a referendum on reserved matters, such as independence or the monarchy, in which case the Act would be pro tanto ultra vires; however, the section requires the judges to read the legislation as narrowly as necessary for it to be intra vires, and this would enable the power to be interpreted to extend only to referendums on issues within competence.[243] He added that this is 'thought to be the normal rule of construction which the courts would apply in construing legislation from parliaments with limited powers. They would seek to give effect to that legislation rather than to invalidate it. This is called the principle of efficacy.'[244]

1.148 Devolution in Wales is a matter of less theoretical legal significance in the present context than devolution to Northern Ireland and Scotland. This is because the scheme set up, though in operation since 1999, does not directly delegate law-making power, with the consequence that no new source of law was created. The Government of Wales Act 1998 established a National Assembly for Wales whose functions are limited to administering Wales. The Assembly nevertheless possesses the kinds of delegated legislative powers which would formerly have been possessed by a Minister of the Crown and it may exercise delegated legislative power to implement EC obligations pursuant to ECA 1972, s 2(2).[245] It can also promote and oppose private Bills in Parliament.[246]

1.149 **Statutory instruments.** An important type of delegated legislation in practice is known as the 'statutory instrument'. Statutory instruments constitute statistically the largest category of domestic delegated legislation. They are regulated as to

---

[241] Scotland Act 1998, s 33.
[242] ibid s 101(1) and (2).
[243] *Hansard*, HL vol 593, cols 1952–1956.
[244] ibid col 1953.
[245] Government of Wales Act 1998, s 29.
[246] ibid s 37.

their surrounding procedural requirements by the Statutory Instruments Act 1946.[247] Section 1(1) of this Act defines statutory instruments as follows:

> Where by this Act or any Act passed after the commencement of this Act power to make, confirm or approve orders, rules, regulations or other subordinate legislation is conferred on His Majesty in Council or on any Minister of the Crown then, if the power is expressed—
> (a) in the case of a power conferred on His Majesty, to be exercisable by Order in Council;
> (b) in the case of a power conferred on a Minister of the Crown, to be exercisable by statutory instrument,
> any document by which that power is exercised shall be known as a 'statutory instrument' . . .

It can be seen from this definition that Orders in Council are only statutory instruments where power to make them is delegated by Parliament; thus, Orders in Council made under the authority of the royal prerogative[248] are not within the scope of the Statutory Instruments Act. Statutory Orders in Council are the most formal type of delegated legislation and are therefore usually reserved for the most important functions, such as bringing legislation into effect or acting under emergency powers. It is also evident from s 1 of the Statutory Instruments Act that there are a number of sub-species of statutory instrument; in practice, the expression 'regulation' is usually used to describe legislation which has wide general effect and 'rules' reserved for procedural matters, but the nomenclature used is of no formal legal significance.   **1.150**

Bye-laws. 'Bye-law' is the term adopted to describe law created where power is delegated to a local authority or statutory enterprise; such powers are typically confined to legislation affecting the particular area covered by the authority or enterprise in question.   **1.151**

Rules of court. Rules of court determine matters of procedure and are enacted in most areas of the civil law by the Civil Procedure Rule Committee under the authority of s 1 of the Civil Procedure Act 1997.[249] In criminal cases they are made by the Crown Court Rule Committee pursuant to s 86 of the Supreme Court Act 1981.   **1.152**

Other domestic delegated legislation. As already indicated, delegated legislation may take an unlimited variety of forms which cannot therefore be comprehensively listed. However, mention must be made of a number of bodies of rules which are commonly made today and which occupy a grey area which is difficult   **1.153**

---

[247] As amended by the Statutory Instruments (Production and Sale) Act 1996.
[248] Discussed at para 1.132 above.
[249] The rules of court so made must be laid before Parliament and are subject to annulment by negative resolution.

to categorize, somewhere between legislation and exhortation. Particularly difficult to classify are rules made under express statutory authority, such as the
Immigration Rules[250] and various so-called 'codes of practice'. A typical example
of the latter is provided by s 56A of the Sex Discrimination Act 1975, which provides that the Equal Opportunities Commission may issue codes of practice containing such guidance as the Commission thinks fit for the elimination of
discrimination and the promotion of equality of opportunity. Subsection (10)
goes on to state that a failure on the part of any person to observe any provision of
such a code shall not of itself render the person liable to legal proceedings; however the theoretical and practical significance of the code lies in the fact that it is
admissible in evidence before an employment tribunal and, if any provision of it
appears relevant, the tribunal must take it into account.[251]

1.154 Nevertheless, definitely not to be classified as true delegated legislation are the
numerous techniques used by government departments in practice and without
specific statutory authorization in order to impose their will; examples include
ministerial statements of policy and circulars to local government and others.
Notwithstanding their persuasive and other indirect influences, such tools have
no formal statutory power to create new law. If, for example, a government department issues in a non-statutory form advice which is incorrect as to a matter of
law, the courts will intervene to restrain publication.[252] However, the intrusive
reach of such instruments is revealed by the words of Lord Bridge of Harwich in
Gillick v Department of Health and Social Security where he stated that:

> the occasions of a departmental non-statutory publication raising . . . a clearly defined
> issue of law, unclouded by political, social or moral overtones, will be rare. In cases
> where any proposition of law implicit in a departmental advisory document is inter-
> woven with questions of social and ethical controversy, the court should . . . exercise its
> discretion with the utmost restraint, confine itself to deciding whether the proposition
> of law is erroneous and avoid either expressing *ex cathedra* opinions in areas of social
> and ethical controversy in which it has no claim to speak with authority or proferring
> answers to hypothetical questions of law which do not strictly arise for decision.[253]

1.155 **EU law.** Whatever may be the current direction which the political configura-
tion of the European Union is taking, there can be no doubt that the drafters of
the original Treaty of Rome intended to create, at the very least, an embryonic federal partnership.[254] Since a federation requires its own laws and legal system, the

---

[250] Made pursuant to the Immigration Act 1971.
[251] See further G Ganz, *Quasi-legislation* (London: Sweet & Maxwell, 1987) and R Baldwin and J
Houghton, 'Circular Arguments: The Status and Legitimacy of Administrative Rules' [1986] PL
239.
[252] *Royal College of Nursing v Department of Health and Social Security* [1981] AC 800.
[253] [1986] AC 112, 193–194.
[254] See the Schuman Declaration of 9 May 1950. Also U Kitzinger, *The Politics and Economics of
European Integration* (Westport, Connecticut: Greenwood Press, 1963).

European Communities were born with both law-making powers and the beginnings of a law enforcement system which centred upon the European Court of Justice (ECJ) and the local courts in the member states.

The United Kingdom became subject to the legal system and the law enforcement mechanisms of the European Communities when it acceded to the Treaty of Rome in 1972. Provision was made by the ECA 1972 for EC law to enter into the United Kingdom's own legal system on the terms provided for by the Community system. In particular, s 2(1) of the 1972 Act provides:

> All such rights, powers, liabilities, obligations and restrictions from time to time created or arising by or under the Treaties, and all such remedies and procedures from time to time provided for by or under the Treaties, as in accordance with the Treaties are without further enactment to be given legal effect or used in the United Kingdom shall be recognised and available in law, and be enforced, allowed and followed accordingly . . .

The European Union is thus a source of law in the United Kingdom to which statutory authority has been given. Moreover, in both theory and practice, it is an extremely important source.

The original Treaty of Rome provided in 1957 for there to be primary and secondary tiers of European law and this remains broadly true in the European Union of the 21st century. The main primary source of EU law is the founding treaties, together with the amendments made to them over the intervening years. The original treaties created three separate communities, the European Coal and Steel Community, the European Economic Community, and EURATOM. In practice, by far the most important was the Economic Community. This has today been subsumed into the European 'Union' which was created by the Treaty of Maastricht in 1991. Since the Treaty of Amsterdam in 1997,[255] the Union has consisted of three so-called 'pillars': the European Communities, the Common Foreign and Security Policy, and Police and Co-operation in Criminal Matters. The most important legislative powers are to be found in the Economic Treaty, although there are also some significant ones under the third pillar.

Secondary legislation in the European Union has to be made on the authority of an enabling provision contained in one of the constituent treaties, since the law-making institutions possess no inherent powers.[256] Such enabling provisions are usually specific to the area of law covered;[257] there are, however, also a few more

1.156

1.157

1.158

---

[255] The Treaty of Amsterdam renumbered the articles of the original Treaty. The numbers referred to in the present work follow the Treaty of Amsterdam.

[256] Secondary legislation not based on a relevant enabling provision is liable to be annulled by the ECJ in proceedings under Art 230 TEC.

[257] eg, Art 13 TEC which permits anti-discrimination legislation, Art 40 which permits legislation to facilitate the free movement of workers, and Art 83 which permits competition legislation.

generalized ones, such as Article 94 authorizing secondary legislation for the approximation of the laws of the member states which directly affect the establishment or functioning of the common market and Article 308 authorizing such legislation where it is necessary to attain one of the objectives of the Community but the Treaty has not provided the necessary powers. The treaties provide for a bewildering array of different procedures for the making of secondary legislation.[258] The chief players in the legislative process are, however, the Commission, which usually instigates legislation by issuing a 'proposal', the Council, and the European Parliament. In a reflection of the underlying federalist ideals of the Treaty drafters, the Commission's function is to represent the Community interest,[259] whilst the Council consists of representatives of the governments of the member states,[260] and the Parliament represents the people of the Union.[261]

1.159   There are three instruments of EU secondary legislation. Their characteristics are defined by Article 249 of the Treaty Establishing the European Community (TEC). Regulations are expressed to have 'general application' which means that they create binding obligations for all legal persons within the jurisdiction of the Union; although they may in practice deal with a highly specialized area and therefore be of interest to a relatively small group, they create general law and possess the potential to affect the legal position of anyone who comes within their reach. Regulations are also stated to be 'binding in their entirety' and 'directly applicable in all Member States'. The meaning of this latter phrase is not immediately evident but becomes clear by comparison with what the Article proceeds to say about the second type of legal instrument, the directive; regulations are intended to take automatic legal force and to require no further implementing measures on the part of the legislative or other authorities in the member states.[262] Their automatic admission into the legal system of the United Kingdom is achieved by ECA 1972, s 2(1), quoted above; the constitutional significance of this process should not be underestimated since it results in the creation of new law, enforceable before the courts of the United Kingdom, which emanates from a source outside this country yet does not require any further legitimation by Parliament at Westminster. It follows from their nature as immediately applicable law that regulations are the appropriate instrument for achieving uniformity of legal provision in all the member states of the Union.

1.160   The second type of instrument referred to by Article 249 is the directive. This is expressed to be 'binding, as to the result to be achieved, upon each Member State

---

[258] Chief amongst them are the procedures set out in Arts 251 and 252 TEC.
[259] ibid Art 213
[260] ibid Art 203.
[261] ibid Art 189.
[262] Confirmation of this view is also provided by the decision of the ECJ in Case 93/71 *Leonesio v Italian Ministry of Agriculture and Fisheries* [1972] ECR 287.

to which it is addressed'; however, it leaves to the national authorities 'the choice of form and methods'. Directives are, therefore, addressed to the member states rather than to legal persons generally; furthermore, they do not take effect within the legal systems of the member states as they stand, but require domestic implementing legislation to be enacted within a stipulated period. They are of use when harmonized, rather than identical, laws are required on a particular matter. Power to implement directives in the United Kingdom is conferred by ECA 1972, s 2(2) which authorizes the making of Orders in Council and ministerial regulations for this purpose;[263] contrary to the usual principle described in para 1.121 above, since it may be necessary to amend the primary law of the United Kingdom in order to comply with this country's EU obligations, such Orders in Council and ministerial regulations are expressly permitted to override parliamentary legislation.[264] There are, however, statutory limitations on the substantive scope of s 2(2) delegated legislation; it may not impose or increase taxation, be retroactive, sub-delegate legislative authority, or create new criminal offences other than minor ones.[265] In addition, s 2(2) delegated legislation must be subject to either the negative or positive resolution procedure in Parliament.[266] Neither the substantive limitations nor the requirement for negative or positive parliamentary resolution can be dispensed with without primary legislation.[267]

Decisions constitute the third instrument of secondary legislation. A decision is, according to Article 249, 'binding in its entirety upon those to whom it is addressed'. Decisions are, thus, addressed to particular persons or groups of persons. They create legal obligations for such persons but are incapable of creating more generalized legal duties. **1.161**

The legal and practical significance of EU law has become clear largely as a consequence of decisions of the ECJ, in particular, where it has given preliminary rulings at the request of national courts seeking guidance on the meaning or effect of a particular piece of EU law.[268] EU law is enforceable in such national courts and **1.162**

---

[263] More precisely, ECA 1972, s 2(2) authorizes delegated legislation '(a) for the purpose of implementing any Community obligation of the United Kingdom, or enabling any such obligation to be implemented, or of enabling any rights enjoyed or to be enjoyed by the United Kingdom under or by virtue of the Treaties to be exercised; or (b) for the purpose of dealing with matters arising out of or related to any such obligation or rights . . .'. In *R v Secretary of State for Trade and Industry, ex p Unison* [1997] 1 CMLR 459, it was held that (b) is to be given its natural, everyday meaning, with the result that it confers power to legislate over a matter related to one governed by EU law though not itself a direct consequence of EU law.

[264] ECA 1972, s 2(4) provides: 'The provision that may be made under subsection (2) above includes . . . any such provision (of any such extent) as might be made by Act of Parliament'.

[265] ibid Sch 2, para 1(1).

[266] ibid Sch 2, para 2(2).

[267] This is the consequence of the closing words of the ECA 1972, s 2(4): 'except as may be provided by any Act passed after this Act, Schedule 2 shall have effect in connection with the powers conferred by this and the following sections of this Act to make Orders in Council and regulations'.

[268] Jurisdiction to give such preliminary rulings is conferred by Art 234 TEC.

the preliminary rulings procedure is intended to ensure that they all adopt a relatively uniform construction of its provisions. In giving preliminary rulings, the ECJ has significantly advanced the federalist goals of the Union since it has emphasized that individual people are as much the subjects of the law of the Union as are its member states;[269] traditional international law, by contrast, concerns itself primarily with regulating relations between states.

1.163   The chief vehicle by means of which EU law is enabled to operate as a source of law within the member states of the Union, including the United Kingdom, is the doctrine which has become known as 'direct effect'.[270] A provision of EU law is said to take direct effect where it creates rights for individual legal persons without the need for further implementing legislation. The genesis of the doctrine of direct effect can be found in one of the earliest decisions on the Treaty of Rome by the ECJ, *Van Gend en Loos*,[271] in which the Court stated:

> The objective of the EEC Treaty which is to establish a Common Market, the functioning of which is of direct concern to interested parties in the Community implies that this Treaty is more than an agreement creating only mutual obligations between the contracting parties. This view is confirmed by the Preamble to the Treaty which refers not only to governments but to peoples. It is also confirmed more specifically by the establishment of institutions endowed with sovereign rights, the exercise of which affects Member States and also their citizens. Furthermore, it must be noted that the nationals of the States brought together in the Community are called upon to co-operate in the functioning of this Community, through the intermediary of the European Parliament and the Economic and Social Committee. In addition, the task assigned to the Court of Justice under Article 177,[272] the object of which is to secure uniform interpretation of the Treaty by the national courts and tribunals, confirms that the States have acknowledged that Community law has an authority which can be invoked by their nationals before those courts and tribunals. The conclusion to be drawn from this is that the Community constitutes a new legal order in international law for the benefit of which the States have limited their sovereign rights, albeit within limited fields, and the subjects of which comprise not only the Member States but also their nationals. Independently of the legislation of Member States, community law therefore not only imposes obligations on individuals but is intended to confer upon them rights which become part of their legal heritage.[273]

---

[269] A vocal body of academic and other opinion takes the view that the ECJ has exceeded the permissible boundaries of its jurisdiction and asserted an unacceptably political role; see in particular TC Hartley, *Constitutional Problems of the European Union* (Oxford: Hart, 1999).

[270] It is also sometimes referred to as 'direct applicability' but this usage is confusing because it confounds the concept presently under discussion with the automatic legal effect conferred on regulations by Art 249, discussed above. In public international law, treaty provisions which are enforceable in national courts are described as 'self-executing' provisions.

[271] Case 26/62 *Van Gend en Loos v Nederlandse Tariefcommissie* [1963] ECR 1.

[272] Now Art 234.

[273] [1963] ECR 1, 12–13.

In addition to relying on this theoretical and essentially political foundation for **1.164**
the concept of direct effect, the ECJ has also resorted to the more pragmatic justification that the concept aids the enforcement of the law of the Union; although the Treaty provides for the direct prosecution of member states which
flout their Community obligations,[274] such procedures cannot be used in all instances because of a lack of time and resources on the part of the main institution involved, the Commission. An individual directly enforcing his or her
rights under EU law puts pressure on the recalcitrant member state to remedy
its breach of the law since the effect of a successful action is to place the individual in the situation which would have followed from compliance by the member state.

The principle that the primary law of the Union can create rights for individuals **1.165**
was established early in the life of the Economic Community and it is clear today
that many articles in the TEC are directly enforceable by individuals in their national courts. There are four conditions which an article must satisfy in order for
it to take direct effect.[275] They are that it must be clear (since judges across the
Union must be able to understand and apply it without great variation), unconditional, non-discretionary,[276] and final; 'final' means that the provision in question is legally complete and does not require legislative intervention, by either the
EU institutions or the member states, in order for it to be applied.

Once the principle of direct effect for primary law was established, the ECJ pro- **1.166**
ceeded to hold in an important series of cases that the secondary law of the Union
was also capable of direct enforcement by individuals. This was a relatively
straightforward step in the case of regulations since, as seen above, such instruments are expressed by the Treaty to be 'directly applicable', in other words, automatically the law in all the member states without a need for implementation. The
Court therefore held that, provided that they satisfy the four criteria for the direct
effect of Treaty provisions, regulations may be directly enforceable.[277]

---

[274] Arts 226, 227 and 228 TEC.
[275] These conditions were first articulated in Case 26/62 *Van Gend en Loos v Nederlandse Tariefcommissie* [1963] ECR 1.
[276] The ECJ originally required a provision to be negative if it was to take direct effect, but this condition has evolved over the years into a requirement of non-discretion; see Case 28/67 *Molkerei-Zentrale Westfalen/Lippe GmbH v Hauptzollamt Munchen* [1968] ECR 143, Case 57/65 *Lutticke Hauptzollamt Saarlouis* [1966] ECR 205 and Case C-271/91 *Marshall v Southampton and South-West Hampshire Area Health Authority (No 2)* [1993] ECR I-4367. The fact that a provision is ex-pressly addressed to the member states does not mean that it necessarily confers any element of discretion on them and so is not sufficient to preclude its direct effect: Case 43/75 *Defrenne v Sabena* [1976] ECR 455.
[277] Case 93/71 *Leonesio v Italian Ministry of Agriculture and Forestry* [1972] ECR 287, Case 43/71 *Politi Sas v Minister of Finance* [1971] ECR 1039 and Case 41/74 *Van Duyn v Home Office* [1974] ECR 1337.

1.167   It was, however, a much bigger step to hold that directives could take direct effect; since a directive is defined as an instrument which requires legislative implementation by the member states, it follows that, until such implementation, a directive has not penetrated into the legal order of the member state concerned and should not therefore be capable of enforcement by a court. The same is true of decisions, which create obligations only for their addressees. The policy advantage of holding directives, in particular, to be directly effective was clearly attractive to the ECJ; member states are frequently tardy in their implementation of directives and the consequence of the direct enforcement of the instruments is to render such tardiness irrelevant from the viewpoint of the individual. The following discussion relates mainly to directives rather than decisions, since directives are in practice of much greater importance than decisions because of the scope of the obligations which they contain; in addition, the majority of decisions by the ECJ in this area have been concerned with directives.

1.168   It is arguable that the Court became carried away by its enthusiasm for the policy objective of maximizing the effectiveness of directives and that this led it to a number of unprincipled decisions during the 1970s. Thus, it held in *Grad v Finanzampt Traunstein*[278] that a decision combined with a Treaty provision and two directives took direct effect; in *SACE v Italian Ministry of Finance*[279] it held that a Treaty article together with a directive took direct effect; and in *Van Duyn v Home Office*[280] it upheld the direct effect of Article 3 of Directive 64/221[281] on the exceptions to the principle of the free movement of workers. In none of these cases, despite argument by the litigants directed to the defining qualities of directives, did the Court even attempt to explain how an unimplemented instrument could be enforced in the courts of a member state; instead, it confined the rationalization of its decision to the useful results which would follow from such direct enforceability. It proceeded to build up a substantial body of case law on the enforceability of directives,[282] holding in particular that a sufficiently precise directive could take direct effect even where it was authorized by a non-directly effective Treaty provision.[283]

---

[278] Case 9/70 [1970] ECR 825.
[279] Case 33/70 [1970] ECR 1213.
[280] Case 41/74 [1974] ECR 1337.
[281] [1963–64] OJ Sp Ed 117.
[282] Case 67/74 *Bonsignore v City of Cologne* [1975] ECR 297; Case 48/75 *State v Royer* [1976] ECR 497; Case 30/77 *R v Bouchereau* [1977] 2 CMLR 800; Case 36/75 *Rutili v Minister of the Interior* [1975] ECR 1219; and Case 38/77 *Enka BV v Inspecteur der Invoerrechten en Accijnzen* [1977] ECR 2203.
[283] Case 51/76 *Verbond v Inspecteur der Invoerrechten en Accijnzen* [1977] ECR 113. Cf *Van Duyn* (n 277 above) in which the Directive was supported by the directly effective Art 48 (now Art 39) of the Treaty.

It seems likely that it was only goaded into more disciplined thinking by the threat   **1.169**
of mutiny on the part of national courts; in a noteworthy assertion of independence, the French Conseil d'Etat[284] in *Cohn-Bendit v Minister of the Interior*[285] refused on the ground of the wording of Article 249 to accept the possibility of the direct effect of Article 6 of Directive 64/221. It is hardly likely to be coincidental that the ECJ very soon afterwards explained how it justified its conclusion that unimplemented directives could indeed take direct effect. The explanation lies in a procedural, rather than a substantive, rule of law. The procedural mechanism involved is the well-known legal principle that a person may not rely on his or her own wrong in order to assert legal rights; thus, the ECJ held in *Pubblico Ministero v Ratti*[286] that a 'Member State which has not adopted the implementing measures required by the directive in the prescribed periods may not rely, as against individuals, on its own failure to perform the obligations which the directive entails'.[287] In the circumstances of the case, the consequence was that criminal proceedings could not be maintained against the head of an undertaking who had not complied with Italian legislation on the packaging of industrial products when that legislation fell short of the requirements of a directive whose implementation period had expired.

In *Becker v Finanzampt Munster-Innenstadt*,[288] the ECJ summarized the law on   **1.170**
the circumstances in which directives take direct effect:

> [W]herever the provisions of a directive appear, as far as their subject matter is concerned, to be unconditional and sufficiently precise, those provisions may, in the absence of implementing measures adopted within the prescribed period, be relied upon as against any national provision which is incompatible with the directive[289] or in so far as the provisions define rights which individuals are able to assert against the state.[290]

The consequences of this ruling can be seen to be both positive and negative. On the plus side, a convincing reason was now available to convince national courts to follow the decisions of the ECJ. However, the down-side was that the mechanism can be of use only where the relevant proceedings are against a member state; since only a member state can be at fault in failing to implement a directive by means of national legislation within the period stipulated in the instrument, it follows that a directive can only be enforceable against a member state. The enforcement of a provision of the European Union against a member state is usually

---

[284] The Conseil d'Etat is the top court in the hierarchy of French administrative courts.
[285] [1980] 1 CMLR 543.
[286] Case 148/78 [1979] ECR 1629.
[287] ibid 1642.
[288] Case 8/81 [1982] ECR 53.
[289] This principle of the supremacy of EU law over incompatible national legislation is discussed at paras 2.177 et seq below.
[290] [1982] ECR 53, 71.

referred to a 'vertical direct effect', whilst enforcement against another individual is known as 'horizontal direct effect'. Since it is clear that primary EU law and, by the same logic, regulations may take horizontal as well as vertical direct effect,[291] directives thus suffer from an important shortcoming by comparison with these other instruments of EU law. That directives cannot be enforced by one individual against another was, however, confirmed by subsequent decisions of the ECJ.[292]

1.171 The inability of directives to take horizontal direct effect is perceived by the ECJ as a gap in the legal protection of individuals under EU law and also as a threat to the full and proper application of that law.[293] Accordingly, it has taken three important steps to mitigate this shortcoming. In the first place, it has given a generous construction to 'the state' for the purpose of explaining against whom an unimplemented directive is enforceable. Thus, in *Foster v British Gas plc*,[294] it held that:

> [A] body, whatever its legal form, which has been made responsible, pursuant to a measure adopted by the state, for providing a public service under the control of the state and has for that purpose special powers beyond those which result from the normal rules applicable in relations between individuals is included in any event among the bodies against which the provisions of a Directive capable of having direct effect may be relied upon.[295]

1.172 Secondly, as will be discussed below, the ECJ demands special rules of statutory interpretation where these can aid the effectiveness of a directive. Thirdly, the lack of horizontal direct effect of directives has provided the catalyst for the development of the doctrine of state liability, the so-called *Francovich* principle.[296] This holds a member state liable in damages to an individual where loss has been caused to that individual by the state's failure to implement a directive within the time

---

[291] Case 43/75 *Defrenne v Sabena* [1976] ECR 455.

[292] See in particular Case 152/84 *Marshall v Southampton and South-West Hampshire Area Health Authority* [1986] ECR 723 and Case C-91/92 *Faccini Dori v Recreb Srl* [1994] ECR I-3325. For the exceptional circumstances in which an incidental form of horizontal direct effect can be accorded to a directive, see Case C-194/94 *CIA Security v Signalson* [1996] ECR I-2201, Case C-129/94 *Bernaldez* [1996] ECR I-1829, Case C-441/93 *Panagis Pafitis v TKE* [1996] ECR I-1347 and Case C-443/98 *Unilever Italia SpA v Central Food SpA* [2000] ECR I-7535.

[293] cf the remarks of AG Van Gerven in Case C-271/91 *Marshall v Southampton and South-West Hampshire Area Health Authority (No 2)* [1993] ECR I-4367, of AG Lenz in Case C-91/92 *Faccini Dori v Recreb Srl* [1994] ECR I-3325 and of AG Jacobs in Case C-316/93 *Vaneetveld v SA Le Foyer* [1994] ECR I-763. For academic criticism of the ECJ's position, see T Tridimas, 'Horizontal Effect of Directives: A Missed Opportunity?' (1994) 19 ELR 621; J Coppel, 'Horizontal Effect of Directives' (1997) 26 ILJ 69 and R Mastroianni, 'On the Distinction Between Vertical and Horizontal Direct Effects of Community Directives: What Role for the Principle of Equality?' (1999) 5 European Public L 417.

[294] Case C-188/89 [1990] ECR I-3313.

[295] [1990] ECR I-3313, 3348-3349.

[296] From Cases C-6 & 9/90 *Francovich and Bonifaci v Italy* [1991] ECR I-5357.

stipulated, provided that the instrument requires the grant of rights to individuals, that the content of those rights is identifiable on the basis of the provisions of the directive itself, and that there is a causal link between the breach of the state's obligation and the loss suffered by the individual.[297]

In addition to the statutory rules of EU law which provide a source of UK law **1.173** through the doctrine of direct effect, there are also unwritten general principles of EU law which equate to the common law and act as a source of law on which individuals in the United Kingdom may rely.[298] In some instances, the TEC expressly directs the ECJ to have recourse to such principles.[299] The ECJ has placed special reliance on general principles in its formulation of fundamental human rights[300] and has developed a substantial body of case law on the protection of such rights as legal certainty,[301] legitimate expectation,[302] proportionality,[303] and equal treatment.[304]

European Convention on Human Rights and Fundamental Freedoms 1950. **1.174** Since the HRA 1998 came into operation on 2 October 2000, the European Convention on Human Rights has been a formal statutory source of the law of this country. This is the consequence of s 3(1) which requires that legislation must be read and given effect in a way which is compatible with Convention rights.[305] This obligation is not limited to legislation enacted after the HRA but applies to prior legislation as well.[306]

---

[297] The *Francovich* principle was extended by later cases to state liability for loss caused to an individual by any sufficiently serious breach by a member state of its obligations under EU law; see Joined Cases C-46 & 48/93 *Brasserie du Pecheur v Germany* and *R v Secretary of State for Transport, ex p Factortame* [1996] ECR I-1029; Case C-392/93 *R v HM Treasury, ex p British Telecommunications plc* [1996] ECR I-1631; Case C-5/94 *R v Ministry of Agriculture, Fisheries and Food, ex p Hedley Lomas (Ireland) Ltd* [1996] ECR I-2553 and Joined Cases C-178, 179, 188, 189 & 190/94 *Dillenkofer v Germany* [1996] ECR I-4845.

[298] See A Arnull, *The General Principles of EEC Law and the Individual* (London: Leicester University Press, 1990) and T Tridimas, *General Principles of EC Law* (Oxford: OUP, 1999).

[299] See in particular Art 220: 'The Court of Justice shall ensure that in the interpretation and application of this Treaty the law is observed'; Art 230: the ECJ has jurisdiction to annul acts 'on grounds of lack of competence, infringement of an essential procedural requirement, infringement of this Treaty or of any rule of law relating to its application, or misuse of powers'; and Art 288(2): 'In the case of non-contractual liability, the Community shall, in accordance with the general principles common to the laws of the Member States, make good any damage caused by its institutions or by its servants in the performance of their duties'.

[300] See Opinion 2/94 On the Accession by the Community to the European Convention on the Protection of Human Rights and Fundamental Freedoms [1996] ECR I-1759.

[301] eg Joined Cases 212–217/80 *Salumi* [1981] ECR 2735.

[302] eg Case C-331/88 *Fedesa* [1990] ECR I-4023.

[303] eg Case 66/82 *Fromançais v Forma* [1983] ECR 395.

[304] Case 149/77 *Defrenne v Sabena* [1978] ECR 1365. See further A Arnull, *The European Union and Its Court of Justice* (Oxford: OUP, 1999).

[305] This subsection is discussed in detail in paras 1.216 et seq below.

[306] HRA 1998, s 3(2)(a). See further ch 7 below.

1.175 HRA 1998, s 1, together with Sch 1, sets out those rights under the Convention and its Protocols which are transformed into UK law and which are known as 'the Convention rights'. They are the rights to: legal protection of life (Article 2), protection from torture and inhumane or degrading treatment or punishment (Article 3), protection from slavery and forced labour (Article 4), liberty and security of person except in prescribed cases and in accordance with legal procedures (Article 5), fair trial in both civil and criminal cases (Article 6), no punishment without its sanction by national or international law at the time of commission (Article 7), respect for private and family life, home and correspondence (Article 8), freedom of thought, conscience and religion (Article 9), freedom of expression (Article 10), freedom of peaceful assembly and association, including the right to form and join trade unions (Article 11), to marry and found a family (Article 12), enjoyment of the rights and freedoms set out in the Convention without discrimination (Article 14), peaceful enjoyment of possessions (Protocol 1, Article 1), education (Protocol 1, Article 2), free elections by secret ballot (Protocol 1, Article 3), and abolition of the death penalty apart from in respect of acts committed in time of war or of imminent threat of war (Protocol 6, Article 1).

(b) Case law

1.176 Despite the fact that law deriving from a statutory source takes precedence over that emanating from any other source, it is a distinctive feature of the British constitution that law can be, and frequently is, also made by the judiciary. Such case law, or 'common law', is in no sense inferior to statutory law. Unless or until it is repealed or amended by statute, it has full force.

1.177 This characteristic of both the public and the private law of this country has a profound impact on the way in which English law is conceptualized. For countries such as France and Germany which have written constitutions and largely codified bodies of law, the function of the judge is to fit the case before him or herself into the relevant prescribed statutory framework; this job having been done, the reasoning of the court is of no formal significance, though it may in practice suggest the outcome of future similar cases. The 'law' in such a system is contained in the constitution or statute; the judge's role is confined merely to its application. In this country, however, the law itself is conceived of in terms of the way in which it is applied in concrete situations. The words and reasoning of the judge therefore assume a fundamental importance and are literally themselves sources of law.[307]

1.178 On one view, this lower level of abstraction at which law is defined in England has an important consequence in terms of democracy since, whatever their other

---

[307] Although for many years the fiction was maintained that the judges, in deciding cases, were merely revealing the pre-existing common law. This was the so-called 'declaratory theory' of the common law which was postulated by Blackstone: 'the decisions of courts of justice are the evidence of what is common law' (*Commentaries*, 13th edn, vol i, 88–89).

qualifications or attributes, the judges are in no sense democratically accountable. On the other hand, whenever a judge decides that the law applies in a particular way in particular circumstances, whether that law is statutory or common law in origin, he or she exercises a function which is one step away from the democratic statutory process and which operates as the final say as to the effect of the law on the litigant concerned. However the concept of law is articulated, therefore, the judiciary in a sense always possesses the upper hand in comparison with the legislature.

Despite the ever-increasing quantity of statutory material, there are important areas of public law which remain exclusively or largely the province of the common law. The rules about the substantive content of the doctrines of ultra vires and natural justice are examples in point. In other areas, the law today consists of a statutory base, onto which has been built an edifice of more detailed judicial decisions, a clear example being the HRA 1998 and the growing body of case law pursuant to it; as Bell observes in *English Private Law*, the task of the lawyer in such circumstances is 'to integrate rules from these different sources into a coherent whole'.[308]   **1.179**

In order to develop by a rational, iterative process, case law must be classified according to its importance and this is achieved by reference to a formal hierarchy between the courts of this country. This is the subject matter of the doctrine of precedent which is discussed below.   **1.180**

(c) Parliamentary privilege

Parliamentary privilege is defined by Erskine May as 'the sum of the peculiar rights enjoyed by each House collectively as a constituent part of the High Court of Parliament, and by members of each House individually, without which they could not discharge their functions, and which exceed those possessed by other bodies or individuals'.[309] The most important of these rights in practice are the right to freedom of speech unconstrained by the threat of any legal proceedings in the courts and the right of each House to regulate its own proceedings.   **1.181**

The privileges of Parliament have their origins in a mixture of custom, precedent and statute, the most important statutory provision being Article 9 of the Bill of Rights of 1688, guaranteeing 'freedom of speech and debates or proceedings in Parliament'. Whatever their precise source, the privileges of Parliament are usually regarded as a part of the common law in the sense that the courts recognize their existence and claim that it is within the judicial power to ensure that Parliament only acts within the limits of its jurisdiction. As Lord Browne-Wilkinson explained in   **1.182**

---

[308] Birks (n 180 above) para 1.22.
[309] Sir T Erskine May, *Treatise on the Law, Privileges, Proceedings and Usage of Parliament* (22nd edn, London: Butterworths, 1997) 65.

Pepper v Hart,[310] 'it is for the courts to decide whether a privilege exists and for the House to decide whether such privilege has been infringed'.[311]

(d) Custom

1.183 To the list of sources of law which have already been discussed there should, for the sake of completeness, be added custom. There can be little doubt that custom informs the general policies pursued by the judges and thus constitutes an indirect source of law. As Zander explains:

> In a multitude of ways the courts are constantly referring to the actions and practices of the community as a point of reference in order to determine either rules or the application of existing rules. Thus in the whole field of negligence, which forms the staple diet of many judges, the court has to determine whether the conduct of the parties fell above or below the reasonable standard of performance required at any given time in the field in question. If the issue, for example, is whether a surgeon is negligent, the court hears expert evidence as to the practice of surgeons in regard to the procedure in question. It then decides that what was done by the defendant surgeon is acceptable and therefore free from liability, or not acceptable and therefore subject to liability. In making that judgment the court will bear in mind amongst other things the state of development of medical knowledge, the difficulty and cost of taking the precautions that were not taken in that case, the differences that may exist between the level of practice to be expected in a London teaching hospital as against a small provincial one and a host of similar considerations. The practice of the community will be fed into the process of decision-making as one of the factors to be taken into account . . . Custom in the sense of what the community does is therefore a potent living source of law in the sense that the courts draw upon it and rework it into the daily application of the common law.[312]

However, local customs occasionally play a more direct part in the law-making process and operate as exceptions to the general common law; this is so where they have existed continuously since 'time immemorial' (which actually means since 1189[313]), and where in addition they are reasonable, sufficiently precise and regarded as binding by those whom they affect.[314]

1.184 Customary laws do not play a major role in the field of public law, their chief manifestation in that area being in relation to the privileges of Parliament. Nevertheless, isolated cases occasionally occur in other public law areas.[315]

---

[310] [1993] AC 593.
[311] ibid 645. See paras 2.106 et seq below.
[312] Zander (n 200 above) 399.
[313] *Simpson v Wells* (1872) LR 7 CP 592.
[314] *New Windsor Corp v Mellor* [1974] 2 All ER 510.
[315] See, eg, the case quoted by Zander (n 200 above) in which the High Court held that anglers have a customary common law right to dig on the foreshore for worms for use as their own fishing-bait: The Guardian, 12 December 1992.

(e) Other influential sources of law

There are, no doubt, many other indirect contributors to the ultimate product **1.185**
which we call the law. Two of the most noteworthy in public law are the rules of
international law and the writings of those learned in the law.

(i) International law

Much of international law is today contained in treaties. Since the power to enter **1.186**
into treaties on behalf of the United Kingdom is a matter which remains within
the royal prerogative and since, as already discussed, the Crown has no power by
means of the prerogative to change the law of the land,[316] it follows that treaties
cannot act as a direct source of the law of the United Kingdom.[317] They may nevertheless act as an important indirect source where legislation is passed to give
effect to their terms, such as (albeit belatedly) in the case of the European
Convention on Human Rights.

The remaining part of international law, 'customary international law', derives **1.187**
like the common law from long usage and judicial decisions. There has been, and
still is,[318] some debate about the precise way in which such customary international law influences the content of English law. The original view was that customary international law was automatically incorporated into English law.[319] This
theory owed much to the notion of 'natural law' which was considered in medieval
times to be the ultimate source of both the common law and the law governing relations between one sovereign and another; each was a manifestation in its own
sphere of the law of nature. However, during the 19th and 20th centuries, this approach gave way to a more reluctant admission of customary international law by
the English courts. International law was by that date regarded as requiring transformation into English law, which meant that it required an act of positive acceptance by the courts or by Parliament.[320] Lord Atkin encapsulated this view in
Chung Chi Cheung v R:[321]

> [S]o far, at any rate, as the Courts of this country are concerned, international law
> has no validity save in so far as its principles are accepted and adopted by our own
> domestic law. There is no external power that imposes its rules upon our own code
> of substantive law or procedure. The Courts acknowledge the existence of a body of

---

[316] *Case of Proclamations* (1611) 12 Co Rep 74.
[317] *Amies v Inner London Education Authority* [1977] ICR 308; *Blackburn v A-G* [1971] 1 WLR 1037.
[318] See in particular the remarks of Lord Denning MR in *Trendtex Trading v Central Bank of Nigeria* [1977] 1 QB 529, 553–554.
[319] *Buvot v Barbut* (1736) 3 Burr 1481, 4 Burr 2016; *Triquet v Bath* (1764) 3 Burr 1478 and *De Wutz v Hendricks* (1824) 2 Bing 314.
[320] *R v Keyn* (1876) 2 Ex D 63; *R v Secretary of State for the Home Department, ex p Thakrar* [1974] QB 684.
[321] [1939] AC 160.

rules which nations accept amongst themselves. On any judicial issue they seek to ascertain what the relevant rule is, and, having found it, they will treat it as incorporated into the domestic law, so far as it is not inconsistent with rules enacted by statutes or finally declared by their tribunals.[322]

1.188 The problem presented by this second view is that, if followed slavishly, it could embed in English law an outdated version of an international rule.[323] The approach therefore taken today appears to be that adopted by the majority of the Court of Appeal in *Trendtex Trading v Bank of Nigeria,*[324] namely to acknowledge that the rules of customary international law change with the times and that it is the modern manifestation of an old rule which is to be applied by the courts. In the words of Lord Denning MR: 'Seeing that the rules of international law have changed— and do change—and that the courts have given effect to the changes without any Act of Parliament, it follows to my mind inexorably that the rules of international law, as existing from time to time, do form part of our English law'.[325]

1.189 Whatever the mechanism by which international law, whether customary or treaty-based, finds its way into the substantive content of English law, as Lord Atkin pointed out it is certain that it can always be ousted by an Act of Parliament.[326]

(ii) Academic legal writing

1.190 It will be evident from earlier passages in this section that a considerable part of modern public law has its footings in the past, sometimes the very distant past. Records relating to such times are often fragmentary and this, amongst other factors, has led courts to the use of academic legal writing as evidence of the law in previous eras. The view a century ago was that a writer could only be treated as 'authoritative' if he or she was already dead (since that precluded the writer from changing his or her opinion). Thus, the works of constitutional writers such as Coke, Bracton, Blackstone and, of less antiquity, Dicey can be found cited with relative frequency by the courts.

1.191 In sharp distinction to continental European legal practice, the writings of scholars who are still alive used not to be regarded as in any sense authoritative. However, this view has now changed and it would in practice be unusual in a difficult case decided today by a higher court not to find reference both in the arguments of counsel and the decision of the judge to the relevant academic literature. The difference between such citations and those of the early constitutional writers lies in the purpose to

---

[322] *Chung Chi Cheung v R* [1939] AC 167–168.
[323] This is a consequence of the doctrine of precedent, discussed in paras 1.234 et seq below.
[324] [1977] 1 QB 529.
[325] ibid 554.
[326] *Chung Chi Cheung* n 321 above, at 167–168; *Mortensen v Peters* (1906) 14 SLT 227; *Macarthys Ltd v Smith* [1979] 3 CMLR 44.

which they are put. Rather than providing evidence as to the existing state of the law, modern academic writings are usually relied upon to support the logic of the argument for reaching a particular decision or favouring a particular policy objective.

The changed judicial attitude towards the use of academic writing is probably a re-   **1.192**
flection of two related phenomena: the growth in the respectability of law as an academic discipline and the increased recourse of modern judges to theory and principle, as distinct from pure pragmatism.

(3) Principles of Statutory Interpretation[327]

The principle of the legislative supremacy of Parliament at Westminster formally   **1.193**
deals the trump card in the law-making process to the legislature. Nevertheless, since it is the judiciary which actually has to apply even parliamentary law to the facts of cases, the judges retain an ace up their sleeves. All words possess a spectrum of possible meanings. The process of assigning a meaning to a statutory provision, in other words the process of interpretation, is necessarily in some part a subjective one in which the interpreter's own values and perspectives are bound to play a role. This phenomenon was particularly pronounced for Lord Halsbury LC when, in *Hilder v Dexter*,[328] he was called upon to decide a case based on a statute for whose drafting he himself had been responsible:

> [I]n construing a statute I believe the worst person to construe it is the person who is responsible for its drafting. He is very much disposed to confuse what he intended to do with the effect of the language which in fact has been employed. At the time he drafted the statute, at all events, he may have been under the impression that he had given full effect to what was intended, but he may be mistaken in construing it afterwards just because what was in his mind was what was intended, though, perhaps, it was not done. For that reason I abstain from giving any judgment in this case myself . . .[329]

Conceding that some element of subjectivity will always remain in the interpreta-   **1.194**
tive process, the best which can probably be hoped for is that the judiciary will be ever-alert to this factor and will actively strive to minimize any bias to which it might lead. That this can be far from easy to achieve was evidenced by the first Court of Appeal decision on the Sex Discrimination Act of 1975. The innate conservatism of the judiciary surfaced on this occasion and had the effect of substantially rewriting the statutory text. *Peake v Automotive Products Ltd*[330] concerned an

---

[327] See F Bennion, *Statutory Interpretation* (3rd edn, London: Butterworths, 1997); J Bell and G Engle (eds), *Cross on Statutory Interpretation* (3rd edn, London: Butterworths, 1995) and C Manchester, D Salter, P Moodie and B Lynch, *Exploring the Law: The Dynamics of Precedent and Statutory Interpretation* (2nd edn, London: Sweet & Maxwell, 2000).
[328] [1902] AC 475.
[329] ibid 477.
[330] [1977] ICR 968.

employer's practice of allowing women employees to leave a factory five minutes before men, to avoid their being jostled in the general rush at the end of the day. A male employee complained that this constituted unlawful discrimination against him on the ground of his sex but, for three reasons, the Court of Appeal disagreed. First, in the words of Lord Denning MR (though nowhere in the Act itself), it would be very wrong:

> if this statute were thought to obliterate the differences between men and women or to do away with the chivalry and courtesy which we expect mankind to give to womankind. The natural differences of sex must be regarded even in the interpretation of an Act of Parliament . . . instances were put before us in the course of argument, such as a cruise liner which employs both men and women. Would it be wrong to have a regulation 'Women and children first'? Or in the case of a factory in case of fire? As soon as such instances are considered the answer is clear. It is not discrimination for mankind to treat womankind with the courtesy and chivalry which we have been taught to believe is right conduct in our society.[331]

1.195 Yet a rethinking of the relationship between men and women was precisely what this statute sought to achieve, at least in the sphere of the workplace. Secondly, the Court of Appeal held that arrangements made in the interests of safety and good administration did not infringe the Act; this conclusion was highly subjective in view of the fact that the Act contained numerous exceptions and these matters were not included amongst them. Thirdly, the court was so far prepared to dispense with the statutory words as to dismiss the claim as de minimis.[332]

1.196 A genuinely difficult and subtle balance has also to be maintained in the interpretation of statutes between respect for democracy in the law-making process and common sense or purpose in the application of law. The dilemma which presents itself to the judges is whether to choose simply what it appears that Parliament has said or, alternatively, what Parliament appeared to wish to say. The formulation usually resorted to by the British judiciary is to attempt to derive 'the intention of Parliament'. This is, clearly, an elusive concept since every member of Parliament who voted for a particular provision of a Bill may have had in mind a slightly different view of the effect of that provision. 'Parliament' itself is an amorphous body which cannot in truth be said to have the ability to arrive at 'an intention'. Thus, as Lord Reid explained in a famous *dictum*:

> We often say that we are looking for the intention of Parliament, but that is not quite accurate. We are seeking the meaning of the words which Parliament used. We are seeking not what Parliament meant but the true meaning of what they said.[333]

---

[331] *Peake v Automotive Products Ltd* [1977] ICR 973.
[332] In other words, of trifling importance: de minimis non curat lex.
[333] *Black Clawson International Ltd v Papierwerke Waldhof-Aschaffenburg AG* [1975 AC 591, 613.

The British judiciary has, in general, approached this problem by adopting a style   **1.197**
which pays considerable deference to the precise words used by Parliament and by
a marked reluctance to look to any guide to meaning beyond the formulation used
in the statute itself.[334] In the words of Lord Oliver of Aylmerton:

> A statute is, after all, the formal and complete intimation to the citizen of a par-
> ticular rule of the law which he is enjoined, sometimes under penalty, to obey and
> by which he is both expected and entitled to regulate his conduct. We must,
> therefore, I believe, be very cautious in opening the door to the reception of
> material not readily or ordinarily accessible to the citizen whose rights and duties
> are to be affected by the words in which the legislature has elected to express
> its will.[335]

However, the courts have also devised some mechanisms to avoid the worst infelicities to which such an approach can sometimes lead and, as will be seen below,
they have begun in recent years to favour a more purposive interpretation of
statutes.

(a) The approach of the British judiciary

(i) *Literal rule*

The literal rule is the first of three traditional so-called 'rules' of statutory inter-   **1.198**
pretation, the others being the 'Golden rule' and the 'Mischief rule'. In reality,
since words never have fixed meanings, all these 'rules' are better regarded as general approaches. Statutory interpretation is not an 'exact science'.[336]

The literal rule is usually defined as meaning that the first task for a court which is   **1.199**
construing a statutory provision is to give the words used their ordinary literal
meaning in the relevant context but without recourse to any extrinsic materials,
including the legislative history of the provision:

> Where the meaning of the statutory words is plain and unambiguous it is not for the
> judges to invent fancied ambiguities as an excuse for failing to give effect to its plain
> meaning because they themselves consider that the consequences of doing so would
> be inexpedient, or even unjust or immoral.[337]

---

[334] *Davis v Johnson* [1979] AC 264; *Hadmor Productions Ltd v Hamilton* [1983] 1 AC 191. In
Beswick v Beswick [1968] AC 58, Lord Reid explained: 'For purely practical reasons we do not permit debates in either House to be cited: it would add greatly to the time and expense involved in
preparing cases involving the construction of a statute if counsel were expected to read all the debates
in Hansard, and it would often be impracticable for counsel to get access to at least the older reports
of debates in Select Committees of the House of Commons; moreover, in a very large proportion of
cases such a search, even if practicable, would throw no light on the question before the court' (p 74).
Cf Lord Reid's speech in *R v Warner* [1969] 2 AC 256, 279. For the modern approach to this question, see *Pepper v Hart* [1993] AC 593, discussed below.
[335] *Pepper v Hart* [1992] AC 593, 619–620.
[336] See Glanville Williams, 'The Meaning of Literal Interpretation—II' [1981] NLJ 1149.
[337] *Per* Lord Diplock in *Duport Steels Ltd v Sirs* [1980] 1 All ER 529, 541.

This apparently unassailable statement in truth masks sleight of the judicial hand, since what may seem 'plain and unambiguous' to one person may not seem so to another. In addition, the primary meaning of words may be nuanced by their context so that they acquire a secondary meaning. As Professor Glanville Williams observed, judges differ in their willingness to recognize such secondary meanings:

> [T]hey may mask their real motivations by speaking of literal interpretation and of words being plain and unambiguous; but such language is not controlling. Some judges tend to be of a formalistic, legalistic turn of mind while others are more socially conscious. Then again a judge may have strong social or moral views in relation to one type of activity but not in relation to another. If the judge is sufficiently convinced that it was the intention of Parliament to cover the situation (or would have been its intention if it had thought of it), or else that this situation ought socially or morally to be covered, he will strive to find a secondary meaning (or to imply words into the statute) in order to cover it; if he either believes that it ought not to be covered or is not satisfied that Parliament intended it to be covered he will be disposed to say that it cannot be brought within the statutory words.[338]

1.200 If all the judges concerned in a case agree about the 'plain and unambiguous' meaning to be assigned to the words of a statute, there will clearly be no difficulty in applying the statute. The problems of course arise where the words appear ambiguous or result in consequences which give rise to doubt as to whether this was really what the legislature intended. At this point, the balance has to be addressed between preserving democracy and reaching a sensible result, a situation in which many judges feel exposed to allegations of inappropriate partiality:

> I should like to have a good definition of what is such an absurdity that you are to disregard the plain words of an Act of Parliament. It is to be remembered that what seems absurd to one man does not seem absurd to another . . . I think it is infinitely better, although an absurdity or injustice or other objectionable result may be evolved as the consequence of your construction, to adhere to the words of an Act of Parliament and leave the legislature to set it right than to alter those words according to one's notion of an absurdity.[339]

(ii) Golden rule

1.201 Despite this understandable reluctance on the part of judges to interfere with the apparently ordinary meaning of an Act of Parliament, the 'Golden rule' steps in where absurdity reaches a proportion which is unacceptable to the members of a court, albeit that it is impossible to predict with certainty when this will occur:

> I believe that it is not disputed that what Lord Wensleydale used to call the Golden rule is right, viz., that we are to take the whole statute together, and construe it all together, giving the words their ordinary signification, unless when so applied they produce an inconsistency, or an absurdity or inconvenience so great as to convince

---

[338] Glanville Williams, 'The Meaning of Literal Interpretation—I' [1981] NLJ 1128, 1129.
[339] *Hill v East and West India Dock Co* (1884) 9 App Cas 448, 464–465 *per* Lord Bramwell.

the Court that the intention could not have been to use them in their ordinary signification, and to justify the Court in putting on them some other signification, which, though less proper, is one which the Court thinks the words will bear.[340]

In modern times, the place of the 'Golden rule' has been taken by a generally   **1.202**
more purposive approach to statutory interpretation, as discussed below. However, the principle was effectively applied in 2000 in *Inco Europe Ltd v First Choice*.[341] The question was whether the Court of Appeal possessed jurisdiction to hear an appeal from an arbitration decision. The matter was governed by s 18(1) of the Supreme Court Act 1981, as amended by the Arbitration Act 1996, which stated: 'no appeal shall lie to the Court of Appeal'. However, both the Court of Appeal and the House of Lords unanimously held that such an appeal was nevertheless available. The reason for this rejection of the literal words of the statute was that it appeared that there had been no legislative intent to change from the previous situation, in which recourse to the Court of Appeal was possible. Lord Nicholls explained:

> I freely acknowledge that this interpretation of s.18(1)(g) involves reading words into the paragraph. It has long been established that the role of the courts in construing legislation is not confined to resolving ambiguities in statutory language. The court must be able to correct obvious drafting errors. In suitable cases, in discharging its interpretative function the court will add words, or omit words or substitute words.[342]

(iii) Mischief rule

An alternative, and arguably less subjective, method of resolving an interpretative   **1.203**
problem in a statute is to rely on the principle established in *Heydon's Case*,[343] usually known as the 'Mischief rule':

> And it was resolved by them, that for the sure and true interpretation of all statutes in general (be they penal or beneficial, restrictive or enlarging of the Common Law), four things are to be discerned and considered:
> 1st. What was the Common Law before the making of the Act.
> 2nd. What was the mischief and defect for which the Common Law did not provide.
> 3rd. What remedy the Parliament hath resolved and appointed to cure the disease of the commonwealth.
> And, 4th. The true reason of the remedy; and then the office of all the Judges is always to make such construction as shall suppress the mischief, and advance the remedy and to suppress subtle inventions and evasions for continuance of the mischief, and *pro privato commodo*, and to add force and life to the cure and remedy, according to the true intent of the makers of the Act, *pro bono publico*.

---

[340] *River Wear Commissioners v Adamson* (1877) 2 App Cas 743, 764–765 *per* Lord Blackburn.
[341] [2000] 1 WLR 586.
[342] ibid 592.
[343] *Heydon's Case* (1584) 3 Co Rep 7a.

1.204 In ascertaining the mischief which the statute was designed to cure, courts today (though not in the time of *Heydon's Case*) have recourse to evidence outside the words of the statute itself. In particular, they frequently examine the report of an official body, such as the Law Commission or a Royal Commission, or a White Paper which preceded the enactment of the legislation in question.[344] They are usually careful to stress, however, that their quest is not for the intention of those individuals who drafted the relevant report but rather for the defect in the pre-existing law which the new legislation was designed to remedy.[345]

(iv) Statutes implementing a treaty obligation

1.205 The courts when construing statutes which were intended to implement treaty obligations of the United Kingdom will normally adopt an interpretation which favours the purposes of the relevant treaty.[346] This explicitly purposive approach reflects the demands of international comity. As in other areas, however, the warmth with which the judges espouse this principle varies from one individual to another. Lord Denning MR took a generous view in *Saloman v Commissioners of Customs and Excise*,[347] stating that courts 'ought always to interpret our statutes so as to be in conformity with international law, whether or not the statute expressly refers to the treaty'.[348] Diplock LJ, on the other hand, was more guarded:

> [T]he court must in the first instance construe the [domestic] legislation, for that is what the court has to apply. If the terms of the legislation are clear and unambiguous, they must be given effect to, whether or not they carry out Her Majesty's treaty obligations, for the sovereign power of the Queen in Parliament extends to breaking treaties (see *Ellerman Lines v Murray*[349]), and any remedy for such a breach of an international obligation lies in a forum other than Her Majesty's own courts. But if the terms of the legislation are not clear but are reasonably capable of more than one meaning, the treaty itself becomes relevant, for there is a *prima facie* presumption that Parliament does not intend to act in breach of international law, including therein specific treaty obligations; and if one of the meanings which can reasonably be ascribed to the legislation is consonant with the treaty obligations and another or others are not, the meaning which is consonant is to be preferred. Thus, in case of lack of clarity in the words used in the legislation, the terms of the treaty are relevant to enable the court to make its choice between the possible meanings of these words by applying the presumption.[350]

---

[344] *Black-Clawson International Ltd v Papierwerke Waldhof-Aschaffenburg AG* [1975] AC 591.
[345] cf *R v Secretary of State for Transport, ex p Factortame Ltd* [1990] 2 AC 85.
[346] See further R Gardiner, 'Interpreting Treaties in the United Kingdom' in M Freeman (ed), *Legislation and the Courts* (Aldershot: Dartmouth, 1997) 115 and R Gardiner, 'Air Law's Fog: The Application of International and English Law' (1990) 43 CLP 159.
[347] [1967] 2 QB 116.
[348] ibid 141.
[349] [1931] AC 126.
[350] [1967] 2 QB 116, 143–144.

Provided that the material concerned is public and accessible, and provided that it clearly points towards a definitive legislative intention, the courts will turn to *travaux préparatoires* to ascertain the intention behind a treaty which has a bearing on the meaning of a domestic statute; this is because this practice is adopted by courts in other states and in international fora[351] and also because the style of drafting of international instruments usually differs markedly from that of UK legislation.[352]

Where the international instrument concerned emanates from the European Union, the courts adopt an especially purposive approach: **1.206**

> [E]ven if the obligation to observe the provisions of Article 119 [of the EC Treaty] were an obligation assumed by the United Kingdom under an ordinary international treaty or convention and there were no question of the treaty obligation being directly applicable as part of the law to be applied by the courts in this country without need for any further enactment, it is a principle of construction of United Kingdom statutes, now too well established to call for citation of authority, that the words of a statute passed after the Treaty has been signed and dealing with the subject matter of the international obligation of the United Kingdom, are to be construed, if they are reasonably capable of bearing such a meaning, as intended to carry out the obligation, and not to be inconsistent with it. *A fortiori* is this the case where the Treaty obligation arises under one of the Community Treaties to which section 2 of the European Communities Act 1972 applies.[353]

The generosity of the judges towards EU law of course reflects the specially compelling qualities of that law and the high degree of political integration within the European Union. These qualities have led to a relaxation in the approach to the interpretation of domestic implementing legislation, to an extent not generally discernible in other fields. For example, in *Litster v Forth Dry Dock Co Ltd*,[354] the House of Lords implied a phrase into domestic delegated legislation which had been enacted for the express purpose of implementing a directive; without the relevant phrase, the domestic legislation would not have given full effect to the directive as it had been interpreted by the ECJ. Similarly, in *Pickstone v Freemans plc*,[355] the House of Lords implied words into the Equal Pay (Amendment) Regulations of 1983, without which they would have failed to achieve their object and the United Kingdom would have remained in breach of its EU obligations as had been determined in an earlier prosecution before the ECJ; furthermore, in order to ascertain the purpose of the domestic Regulations, the House took account of the Minister's statement to Parliament, on the express ground that the Regulations (as delegated legislation) were not subject to the full parliamentary **1.207**

---

[351] See Art 32 of the Vienna Convention on the Law of Treaties 1969.
[352] *Fothergill v Monarch Airlines Ltd* [1981] AC 251.
[353] *Garland v British Rail Engineering Ltd* [1983] 2 AC 751, 771 *per* Lord Diplock.
[354] [1990] 1 AC 546.
[355] [1989] AC 66.

process for primary legislation which would have afforded opportunities for its amendment.

(v) Criminal and tax statutes

1.208 It is often said to be a well-established principle that, if a court encounters an ambiguity or a doubt in a statute imposing a penalty or a tax, the uncertainty will be resolved in favour of the citizen.[356] However, modern commentators have observed that the principle only operates as a long-stop where doubt remains after all other avenues have been exhausted,[357] and numerous examples can be found of situations in which the courts have proved willing to give a broad and purposive reading in particular to statutes imposing criminal liability.[358] Likewise, courts in modern times are awake to the multiplicity of devices devised to avoid tax liability and will interpret legislation robustly in order to prevent the worst excesses.[359]

(vi) Teleological interpretation

1.209 Despite the leaning of the English judiciary towards the literal interpretation of statutory words in the context of the times in which they were enacted, there are occasions on which the judges have taken a more dynamic view of their role. In such cases, they have attempted to read legislation in the way in which they believe Parliament would have wished to phrase it in order to achieve its desired end, had Parliament known of later developments; this is usually known as 'teleological' interpretation. It is, of course, well nigh impossible to predict when the judiciary will prove itself prepared to take this approach, daring as it does to play a part in the process whereby legislation is amended and brought up to date. Sometimes, however, a court proves so enthusiastic to read legislation teleologically that it will permit this approach to prevail even in the face of other so-called 'rules' of statutory interpretation.

1.210 A famous example occurred in *Corkery v Carpenter*,[360] where the defendant was charged with being drunk in charge of a bicycle contrary to s 12 of the Licensing Act 1872. The section penalized '[e]very person who . . . is drunk while in charge on any highway or other public place of any carriage, horse, cattle or steam engine . . .'. Counsel for the defence had four powerful arguments for the contention that a 'carriage' could not be construed to include a bicycle. First, the word 'bicycle' did not appear in the statutory section and, although *Stone's Justices Manual* took the view that a bicycle would be covered by the Act, the cases used in support of this

---

[356] See eg *Tuck and Sons v Priester* (1887) 19 QBD 629; *Fisher v Bell* [1961] 1 QB 394 and *Vestey v IRC* [1980] AC 1148.

[357] See A Ashworth, 'Interpreting Criminal Statutes: A Crisis of Legality?' (1991) 107 LQR 419.

[358] See eg *Smith v Hughes* [1960] 2 All ER 859 and *A-G's Reference (No 1 of 1988)* [1989] 2 All ER 1.

[359] *Ensign Tankers (Leasing) Ltd v Stokes* [1992] 2 All ER 275.

[360] [1951] 1 KB 102.

proposition were all concerned with different statutes. Secondly, it was a 'cardinal' principle of statutory interpretation that, in statutes concerning matters relating to the general public, words are presumed to be used in their popular sense; it was clear from the old song 'Daisy, Daisy' that the popular meaning of 'carriage' did not embrace 'bicycle' since the singer asserts:

> It won't be a stylish marriage,
> I can't afford a carriage.
> But you'll look sweet upon the seat
> Of a bicycle made for two.

Thirdly, and perhaps most persuasively, s 12 was a penal section which should therefore be interpreted narrowly. Finally, the common denominator of the things listed in s 12 was force, motive power independent of the muscular efforts of the person in charge, which was plainly not a feature of a bicycle.

Notwithstanding the intellectual force of these arguments, the Divisional Court **1.211** called for no argument from the prosecution and gave s 12 a teleological interpretation, with the consequence that the word 'carriage' was held to include a bicycle. Lord Goddard CJ stated that the first thing to do when construing a statute of this sort was to ascertain its purpose. Here, it was clear that the Act had been passed for the protection of the public and the preservation of public order. An analogy was drawn with *Taylor v Goodwin*,[361] which involved s 78 of the Highway Act 1835; this prohibited the furious driving of 'any sort of carriage' and was interpreted as covering a bicycle, even though bicycles had not been known in 1835, since the legislature had 'clearly' desired to outlaw the use of any sort of carriage in a manner dangerous to the life or limb of a passenger. In remarkably extreme terms, Lord Goddard concluded:

> Applying that case, nothing can be more dangerous than a drunken man with a bicycle on a highway: he is dangerous whether he is riding the bicycle or pushing it, because even if he is pushing it he has not proper control over it, and can be a danger to others and himself.[362]

It is sometimes said that the older a statutory provision is, the more likely it is to **1.212** be given a teleological interpretation.[363] However, *Royal College of Nursing v Department of Health and Social Security*[364] demonstrated that it is not so much the lapse of time as the pace of contextual development which urges a teleological approach upon the judiciary.[365] The issue was whether the termination of a pregnancy

---

[361] (1878–79) LR 4 QBD 228.
[362] [1951] 1 KB 102, 106.
[363] 'The interpretation of a statutory provision is not necessarily the one which the original legislature would have endorsed, and as the distance between enactment and interpretation increases, a pure originalist inquiry becomes impossible and/or irrelevant': WN Eskridge, *Dynamic Statutory Interpretation* (Cambridge, Massachusetts: Harvard University Press, 1994) 5–6.
[364] [1981] AC 800.
[365] See also *R (on the application of Quintavalle) v Secretary of State for Health* [2002] 2 WLR 550.

by medical induction using an abortifacient substance constituted 'termination by a registered medical practitioner' within the wording of s 1(1) of the Abortion Act 1967, where it was a nurse rather than a doctor who actually gave the drug to the patient albeit that a doctor attached the equipment by which the drug was administered. Only 14 years had elapsed between the passing of the Abortion Act and the action; however, medical developments had progressed fast during this time. In 1967, and for the following five years, all methods of abortion were surgical and therefore of practical necessity required to be performed by a medical practitioner. However, since 1972, a new, non-surgical procedure had been developed and was in widespread use by the time of the case.

1.213   The unpredictability of when teleological interpretation will be resorted to by the English judiciary was highlighted by the conclusions arrived at by the three courts which heard the case. At first instance, Woolf J was prepared to take a teleological approach and he therefore held the new method of abortion to be within the terms of the statute. His decision was reversed by a unanimous Court of Appeal, where Sir George Baker proclaimed:

> [I]t is not for judges 'to read words into an Act of Parliament unless clear reason for it is to be found within the four corners of the Act itself' *per* Lord Loreburn in *Vickers, Sons & Maxim Ltd v Evans*,[366] cited by Viscount Dilhorne in *Stock v Frank Jones (Tipton) Ltd*.[367] Nor is a judge entitled to read an Act differently from what it says simply because he thinks Parliament would have so provided had the situation been envisaged at that time.[368]

For Lord Denning MR, also in the Court of Appeal, the controversy surrounding the subject of abortion was sufficient to signal to the judges that they should not take a proactive view:

> Abortion is a subject on which many people feel strongly . . . Emotions run so high on both sides that I feel that we as judges must go by the very words of the statute— without stretching it one way or the other—and writing nothing in which is not there.[369]

1.214   However, the House of Lords, by a majority of three to two favoured the teleological reading of the Abortion Act, saying that its provisions were satisfied where the treatment for the termination of a pregnancy was prescribed by a registered medical practitioner and carried out in accordance with that doctor's directions, provided that the doctor remained in charge throughout.[370] The desire to advance the purpose of the Act emerged most clearly from Lord Keith's speech:

---

[366] [1910] AC 444, 445.
[367] [1978] 1 WLR 231, 235A.
[368] [1981] AC 800, 813.
[369] ibid 805.
[370] There were therefore, in total, more judges in favour of a holding of illegality than of legality, despite the final outcome of the case.

I . . . conclude that termination of pregnancy by means of the procedures under consideration is authorised by the terms of section 1 subsection 1. This conclusion is the more satisfactory as it appears to me to be fully in accordance with that part of the policy and purpose of the Act which was directed to securing that socially acceptable abortions should be carried out under the safest conditions attainable.[371]

(vii) Linguistic techniques which aid construction

The courts have developed a series of linguistic techniques to assist in the process of statutory interpretation. These are in the main based on common sense. The most frequently encountered are: (a) the maxim ejusdem generis, by which where a general category follows a more specific list, the general category is restricted to things of the class listed specifically (unless the statute expressly provides otherwise); and (b) the maxim that expressio unius est exclusio alterius. This second means that where specific things of a given type are referred to expressly, the implication is that others of that type which are not so mentioned are intended to be excluded.

1.215

(viii) Human Rights Act

The HRA 1998 creates a new rule of statutory interpretation in areas governed by the European Convention on Human Rights.[372] This is the consequence of s 3(1):

1.216

> So far as it is possible to do so, primary legislation and subordinate legislation[373] must be read and given effect in a way which is compatible with the Convention rights.

The most important result of this subsection as far as substantive English public law is concerned is that it drives courts towards a rights-based interpretation of all relevant legal rules, rather than the less principled approach taken before the HRA. Thus, for example, where a patient is detained under s 3 of the Mental Health Act 1983, Article 5(4) of the Convention now means that the routine use of a target date for a hearing is unlawful and that every application by a patient should be heard as soon as reasonably practicable.[374] Similarly, where a mother is

1.217

---

[371] [1981] AC 800, 835.

[372] According to David Steel J, the 'tentacles of the Human Rights Act 1998 reach into some unexpected places', eg the procedures adopted by the Commercial Court when exercising its supervisory jurisdiction as regards arbitration: see *Mousaka Inc v Golden Seagull Maritime Inc* [2002] 1 WLR 395, 397. See further paras 7.55 et seq below; Lord Lester of Herne Hill, 'The Art of the Possible—Interpreting Statutes under the Human Rights Act 1998' [1998] European Human Rights L Rev 665. For a quantitative assessment of the early impact of the HRA, see F Klug and K Starmer, 'Incorporation through the "front door": the first year of the Human Rights Act' [2001] PL 654.

[373] The subsection applies to such primary and subordinate legislation 'whenever enacted': s 3(2). However, the Act does not have retrospective effect where a criminal trial took place before it came into operation, even where an appeal occurs after this date: *R v Lambert* [2001] 3 WLR 206; *R v Kansal (No 2)* [2001] 3 WLR 1562.

[374] *R (on the application of C) v London South and West Region Mental Health Review Tribunal* [2002] 1 WLR 176.

serving a prison sentence, the Prison Service may have a general policy that her children should cease to live with her once they reach the age of 18 months, but the requirement of respect for family life pursuant to Article 8 of the Convention means that this policy must not be operated rigidly.[375]

1.218   The interpretative obligation to which s 3 gives rise is similar to that in relation to directly effective EU law, whose supremacy over conflicting provisions of domestic law must be guaranteed.[376] In the case of the HRA, however, where it proves impossible to read domestic law so as to comply with Convention rights, only secondary domestic law can be struck down by the courts of the United Kingdom;[377] primary legislation can at most be made the subject of a 'declaration of incompatibility'.[378] It is inevitable that this formulation will exert pressure on domestic courts to temper their previous approach to statutory interpretation in an attempt to shoe-horn primary legislation in particular into compatibility with Convention rights. The intellectual legitimacy of this process is fortified at least in the case of post-HRA legislation by s 19, which requires a minister in charge of a Bill before either House of Parliament to make a statement that the Bill is compatible with the Convention rights. (However, if unable to do so, the minister may state that the government nevertheless wishes the House to proceed with the Bill.)

1.219   A clear illustration of the kinds of dilemmas faced by the courts since the enactment of the HRA came in *Re S*.[379] The Court of Appeal had made two major adjustments to the Children Act 1989 in an effort to construe it as compatible with the HRA, in particular as regards the Convention right to respect for private and family life. The House of Lords rejected these amendments on the ground that they disrupted the balance which Parliament had intended between the role of local authorities and the courts in relation to children: the Children Act envisaged that local authorities would have full responsibility for children subject to care orders, whilst the amendments would give the courts a new supervisory role. Lord Nicholls of Birkenhead made an important statement of principle:

> Section 3(1) [of the Human Rights Act] . . . is a powerful tool whose use is obligatory. It is not an optional canon of construction. Nor is its use dependent on the existence of ambiguity. Further, the section applies retrospectively. So far as it is possible to do so, primary legislation 'must be read and given effect' to in a way which is compatible with Convention rights. This is forthright, uncompromising language. But the reach of this tool is not unlimited. Section 3 is concerned with interpretation . . . In applying section 3 courts must be ever mindful of this outer limit. The Human Rights Act reserves the amendment of primary legislation to

---

[375] *R (on the application of P) v Secretary of State for the Home Department* [2001] 1 WLR 2002.
[376] See discussion in paras 2.177 et seq below.
[377] HRA 1998, s 3(2)(b). See eg *R (on the application of Daly) v Secretary of State for the Home Department* [2001] 2 WLR 1622.
[378] ibid s 4, discussed further in paras 2.160–2.161 below.
[379] [2002] 2 WLR 720.

Parliament. By this means the Act seeks to preserve parliamentary sovereignty. The Act maintains the constitutional boundary. Interpretation of statutes is a matter for the courts; the enactment of statutes, and the amendment of statutes, are matters for Parliament. Up to this point there is no real difficulty. The area of real difficulty lies in identifying the limits of interpretation in a particular case . . . For present purposes it is sufficient to say that a meaning which departs substantially from a fundamental feature of an Act of Parliament is likely to have crossed the boundary between interpretation and amendment.[380]

Similarly, in *R (on the application of Anderson) v Home Secretary*,[381] the House of Lords faced the boundary between interpretation and amendment. The issue was the compatibility with Article 6(1) of the Convention of the Home Secretary's power pursuant to s 29 of the Crime (Sentences) Act 1997 to fix a convicted murderer's tariff to be served as a minimum sentence. It was argued that, since the Home Secretary is a member of the executive, the claimant's right to a fair hearing by an independent and impartial tribunal was breached by s 29. In upholding this argument, Lord Bingham of Cornhill stated:

1.220

> To read section 29 as precluding participation by the Home Secretary, if it were possible to do so, would not be judicial interpretation but judicial vandalism: it would give the section an effect quite different from that which Parliament intended and would go well beyond any interpretative process sanctioned by section 3 of the 1998 Act.[382]

On the other hand, in *R v A*,[383] the House of Lords relied on s 3 to interpret s 41(3) of the Youth Justice and Criminal Evidence Act 1999 so as to permit the admission of evidence as to a previous sexual relationship in a rape trial where, without the influence of Article 6 of the Convention and on a purely literal interpretation of s 41(3), such evidence would have been inadmissible. The degree of judicial angst to which this process gave rise is clear. Lord Hope of Craighead considered that this decision overstepped the dividing line between interpretation and legislation since it was at odds with the whole structure of s 41. However, Lord Steyn, expressing the view adopted by the majority, said:

1.221

> In accordance with the will of Parliament as reflected in section 3 it will sometimes be necessary to adopt an interpretation which linguistically may appear strained.

---

[380] ibid 731. In *R (on the application of H) v London North and East Region Mental Health Review Tribunal* [2001] 3 WLR 512, Lord Phillips of Worth Matravers MR said: 'It is of course the duty of the court to strive to interpret statutes in a manner compatible with the Convention and we are aware of instances where this has involved straining the meaning of statutory language. We do not consider however that such an approach enables us to interpret a requirement that a tribunal must act if satisfied that a state of affairs does not exist as meaning that it must act if not satisfied that a state of affairs does exist' (at 519–520). See also *Poplar Housing Association Ltd v Donoghue* [2002] QB 48 and *Wilson v First County Ltd (No 2)* [2001] 3 WLR 42.

[381] [2002] 3 WLR 1800.

[382] ibid 1814.

[383] [2001] 3 All ER 1.

The techniques to be used will not only involve the reading down of express language in a statute but also the implication of provisions. A declaration of incompatibility is a measure of last resort. It must be avoided unless it is plainly impossible to do so. If a *clear* limitation on Convention rights is stated in *terms*, such an impossibility will arise (*R v Secretary of State for the Home Department, Ex p. Simms*[384]). There is, however, no limitation of such a nature in the present case.[385]

1.222 A court which is determining a question relating to a Convention right is required by HRA 1998, s 2 to take into account, wherever relevant, any judgment, decision, declaration or advisory opinion of the European Court of Human Rights, any opinion or decision of the Commission, and decision of the Committee of Ministers.[386] This has resulted in large numbers of cases, especially decisions of the European Court of Human Rights, being cited in English cases; in *R (on the application of Al-Hasan) v Home Secretary*,[387] Lord Woolf CJ cautioned that restraint should be exercised since it is 'the principles which are relevant and important'.[388]

(b) The impact of the European Court of Justice

1.223 Even a cursory glance at the text of a piece of EU legislation, whether primary or secondary, reveals that its drafting is of a wholly different style from that used in UK legislation. The more general EU formulation reflects continental traditions and is partly a consequence of the need for multi-lingual texts.[389] Its interpretation requires a different approach from the judiciary from that adopted in relation to more precise wording. Where principles are expressed at a relatively high level of abstraction, judges are clearly required to exercise more creativity and imagination when applying the law to factual situations. The ECJ has responded with enthusiasm to the challenge presented to it and, relying in the main on purposive and teleological methods of interpretation,[390] has quite frequently created a large and sophisticated body of law from apparently sparse beginnings.[391]

---

[384] [2000] 2 AC 115, 132 *per* Lord Hoffmann. For a further example of a difference of judicial opinion as to the latitude afforded to the judiciary by s 3, see *Adan v Newham LBC* [2002] 1 All ER 931.

[385] [2001] 3 All ER 1, 17. See also *Cachia v Faluyi* [2001] 1 WLR 1966, where the Court of Appeal expressly gave a non-literal construction to s 2(3) of the Fatal Accidents Act 1976 in order to guarantee a Convention right; Brooke LJ said (at 1972): 'This is a very good example of the way in which the enactment of the Human Rights Act 1998 now enables English judges to do justice in a way which was not previously open to us'.

[386] This is discussed further below, in relation to the doctrine of precedent.

[387] [2002] 1 WLR 545.

[388] ibid 565.

[389] For discussion of the consequences of multi-lingual texts in EU law, see Case 238/81 *CILFIT v Ministry of Health* [1982] ECR 3415.

[390] cf the more literal approach displayed by the ECJ in Case 152/84 *Marshall v Southampton and South-West Hampshire Area Health Authority* [1986] ECR 723 and Case C-91/92 *Faccini Dori v Recreb Srl* [1994] ECR I-3325 on the non-horizontal direct effect of directives, discussed above.

[391] eg, in the fields of equal pay and the free movement of goods. For further discussion of the ECJ's methods of interpretation of EU law, see A Arnull (n 304 above) especially ch 14.

The ECJ has not, however, restricted itself to adopting principles regarding its own interpretation of EU law. It has also developed important principles governing the methods of construction to be adopted by national courts when applying their own law in circumstances in which EU law is also influential. As discussed above, the ECJ has been concerned to mitigate as far as possible the inability of directives to take horizontal direct effect, that is to say, to create rights enforceable by one individual against another. This has led it to create an interpretative principle often referred to as the principle of 'indirect effect'.

1.224

The principle of indirect effect means that the intention of a directive[392] must be taken into account by a national court whenever it is interpreting a provision of national law which deals with the same subject matter. The principle is of considerable assistance to individuals because, even where they are unable to enforce the terms of a directive directly because the other party to the litigation is not the state,[393] they can demand that the national court tries to give effect to the intention of the directive in its application of parallel national law. Putting this slightly differently, the national court is required to resolve any ambiguities or infelicities in the domestic statute in favour of the meaning contained in the directive. The notion of indirect effect was first advanced in the situation where the relevant national legislation was enacted after the directive and in an apparent attempt to implement that directive.[394] However, it was later, and somewhat controversially,[395] extended to the reverse scenario, in which the national law precedes the directive and cannot thus be regarded as an attempt to implement that instrument.[396] The so-called *Marleasing* principle establishes that when a national court is applying national law, whether statute or common law and whether prior to or subsequent to a relevant directive, the national court must interpret its own law so far as possible in the light of the wording and purpose of the directive. Moreover, when interpreting and applying national law, 'every national court must presume that the state had the intention of fulfilling entirely the obligations arising' from a directive.[397] The *Marleasing* principle has become accepted and is enforced by the English courts, as evidenced for example by the decision of the House of Lords in

1.225

---

[392] Or indeed a non-binding instrument of EU law, such as a recommendation: Case 322/88 *Grimaldi v Fonds des Maladies Professionelles* [1989] ECR 4407.

[393] Even given the broad interpretation given by the ECJ to the concept of the state for this purpose, discussed above.

[394] Case 14/83 *Von Colson and Kamann v Land Nordrhein Westfalen* [1984] ECR 1891. The principle applies even when the implentation period for the directive has not yet elapsed: Case 80/86 *Public Prosecutor v Kolpinghuis Nijmegen BV* [1987] ECR 3969.

[395] See the remarks of AG Slynn in Case 152/84 *Marshall v Southampton and South-West Hampshire Area Health Health Authority* [1986] ECR 723, 733, and of AG Mischo in Case 80/86 *Public Prosecutor v Kolpinghuis Nijmegen BV* [1987] ECR 3969, 3980.

[396] Case C-106/89 *Marleasing SA v La Comercial Internacional de Alimentacion SA* [1990] ECR I-4135.

[397] Case C-334/92 *Wagner Miret v Fondo de Garantia Salarial* [1993] ECR I-6911, 6932.

Webb v EMO (Air Cargo) Ltd,[398] where the Sex Discrimination Act of 1975 was given a fairly tortured interpretation in order to ensure its compliance with the Equal Treatment Directive of 1976.[399]

1.226　Nevertheless, the usual principle of strict interpretation in penal cases must also be respected. Thus, a directive 'cannot, of itself and independently of a national law adopted by a Member State for its implementation, have the effect of determining or aggravating the liability in criminal law of persons who act in contravention of the provisions of that directive'.[400] The ECJ has also held that the obligation to have regard to a directive in the interpretation of national law 'is limited by the general principles of law which form part of Community law and in particular by the principles of legal certainty and non-retroactivity'.[401] It summed up the position in *Criminal Proceedings Against X*:[402]

> More specifically, in a case such as that in the main proceedings, which concerns the extent of liability in criminal law arising under legislation adopted for the specific purpose of implementing a directive, the principle that a provision of the criminal law may not be applied extensively to the detriment of the defendant, which is the corollary of the principle of legality in relation to crime and punishment and more generally of the principle of legal certainty, precludes bringing criminal proceedings in respect of conduct not clearly defined as culpable by law. That principle, which is one of the general legal principles underlying the constitutional traditions common to the Member States, has also been enshrined in various international treaties.[403]

(c) The interpretation of UK legislation in the 21st century

1.227　Perhaps at least partly in consequence of having a different approach to statutory interpretation thrust upon them by the United Kingdom's membership of the European Union, the judiciary in the closing years of the 20th century began to take a somewhat more confident and freer approach to their role in the construction of legislation. Their quest for Parliament's intention has today ceased to be confined to that of the strict literal constructionist and become instead a more purposive search for what Parliament would wish to achieve in the factual circumstances which present themselves in the case in hand.

1.228　The defining moment came with the decision of a specially-convened seven-man Appellate Committee of the House of Lords in *Pepper v Hart*.[404] The case presented a dilemma which was remarkable for its clarity: a conventional interpretation of s 63 of the Finance Act 1976 rendered the taxpayers liable to income tax on

---

[398] [1995] 4 All ER 577.
[399] Directive 76/207 [1976] OJ L39/40.
[400] Case 14/86 *Pretore di Salo v Persons Unknown* [1987] ECR III-2545.
[401] Case 80/86 *Public Prosecutor v Kolpinghuis Nijmegen BV* [1987] ECR 3969, 3986.
[402] Joined Cases C-74 & 129/95 [1996] ECR I-6609.
[403] ibid 6637.
[404] [1993] AC 593.

the full market value of the benefit which they, as teachers at an independent school, received when their children were educated at the school at a special concessionary rate. On the other hand, recourse to material extrinsic to the statute itself, in particular debates in Parliament as recorded in *Hansard*, clearly revealed that Parliament had proceeded on the understanding that these benefits should not be taxable on this basis but rather that they should be assessed on the basis of the marginal cost which they imposed on the employer (which in the circumstances of the case was very small). The issue was whether the judges should regard themselves as obliged by the former exclusionary rule to 'wear blinkers which . . . conceal the vital clue to the intended meaning of an enactment'?[405]

There were four main arguments in favour of retaining the exclusionary rule. The   **1.229** chief 'constitutional' argument was that to rely on a ministerial statement in Parliament would be to elevate the minister's view above what Parliament itself had enacted, and that this would be especially unwise since the ministerial statement might have been made 'to satisfy the political requirements of persuasion and debate, often under pressure of time and business'.[406] Secondly, in order to establish the significance to be attached to a statement, it would be necessary to understand its context and this might entail alterations to parliamentary procedures. Thirdly, it was argued that the use of parliamentary material would give rise to practical difficulties, particularly in terms of cost and time. Fourthly, it was asserted that to use what was said in Parliament as an aid to interpretation would constitute a breach of Article 9 of the Bill of Rights of 1688 because it would amount to an impeachment or questioning of 'freedom of speech and debates or proceedings in Parliament'.

The House nevertheless concluded that the old rule should be modified, albeit   **1.230** under strict conditions. In the words of Lord Browne-Wilkinson:

> [M]y main reason for reaching this conclusion is based on principle. Statute law consists of the words that Parliament has enacted. It is for the courts to construe those words and it is the court's duty in so doing to give effect to the intention of Parliament in using those words. It is an inescapable fact that, despite all the care taken in passing legislation, some statutory provisions when applied to the circumstances under consideration in any specific case are found to be ambiguous. One of the reasons for such ambiguity is that the members of the legislature in enacting the statutory provision may have been told what result those words are intended to achieve. Faced with a given set of words which are capable of conveying that meaning it is not surprising if the words are accepted as having that meaning. Parliament never intends to enact an ambiguity. Contrast with that the position of the courts. The courts are faced simply with a set of words which are in fact capable of bearing two meanings. The courts are ignorant of the underlying Parliamentary purpose.

---

[405] ibid 617 *per* Lord Bridge of Harwich.
[406] ibid 634.

Unless something in other parts of the legislation discloses such purpose, the courts are forced to adopt one of the two possible meanings using highly technical rules of construction. In many, I suspect most, cases references to Parliamentary materials will not throw any light on the matter. But in a few cases it may emerge that the very question was considered by Parliament in passing the legislation. Why in such a case should the courts blind themselves to a clear indication of what Parliament intended in using those words? The court cannot attach a meaning to words which they cannot bear, but if the words are capable of bearing more than one meaning why should not Parliament's true intention be enforced rather than thwarted?[407]

1.231 The practical difficulties were also dismissed by the House, not least because their Lordships did not consider them to have been manifested in those jurisdictions which permit the use of parliamentary material. As to Article 9 of the Bill of Rights, it was enacted to insulate members of Parliament from pressure by the monarch but there was no question of any criticism of members in the present context; '[f]ar from questioning the independence of Parliament and its debates, the courts would be giving effect to what is said and done there'.[408] The precise circumstances in which a court should therefore henceforth have recourse to the legislative history of a provision in order to tease out its meaning were set out by Lord Browne-Wilkinson:

> [T]he exclusionary rule should be relaxed so as to permit reference to Parliamentary materials where (a) legislation is ambiguous or obscure, or leads to an absurdity; (b) the material relied upon consists of one or more statements by a minister or other promoter of the Bill together if necessary with such other Parliamentary material as is necessary to understand such statements and their effect; (c) the statements relied upon are clear.[409]

1.232 The decision in *Pepper v Hart* has been subjected to swingeing criticism, in particular by Lord Steyn. In addition to substantially increasing the cost of litigation with no accompanying advantage, he believes that it is profoundly detrimental to the constitution:

> The basis on which the exclusionary rule was relaxed ignores constitutional arguments of substance. Lord Bridge described the rule as 'a technical rule of construction'.[410] And implicitly that is how the majority approached the matter. Surely, it was much more. It was a rule of constitutional importance which guaranteed that only Parliament, and not the executive, ultimately legislates; and that the courts are obliged to interpret and apply what Parliament has enacted, and nothing more or less. To give the executive, which promotes a Bill, the right to put its own gloss on

---

[407] *Pepper v Hart* [1993] AC 634–635.
[408] ibid 638. Furthermore, the courts had for a number of years before *Pepper v Hart* made use of *Hansard* in judicial review proceedings in order to decide whether a statutory power had been exercised in an ultra vires manner. For discussion of the use of *Hansard* in this context, see A Bradley, 'The Use of Hansard in Judicial Review Proceedings—A Further Note', Memorandum to the Joint Committee on Parliamentary Privilege, 9 April 1999.
[409] ibid 640.
[410] [1992] AC 593, 616.

the Bill is a substantial inroad on a constitutional principle, shifting legislative power from Parliament to the executive. Given that the ministerial explanation is *ex hypothesi* clear on the very point of construction, *Pepper v Hart* treats qualifying ministerial policy statements as canonical. It treats them as a source of law. It is in constitutional terms a retrograde step: it enables the executive to make law. It is to be noted that the objection is not to the idea of a judge looking at *Hansard*. For example, it may be unobjectionable for a judge to identify the mischief of a statute from *Hansard*. What is constitutionally unacceptable is to treat the intentions of the government as revealed in debates as reflecting the will of Parliament.[411]

As Lord Steyn also observes, the effect of *Pepper v Hart* has been to alter the be-   **1.233**
haviour of ministers since it encourages them to explain the effect of proposed legislation in the way in which the government would like it to be understood, again enhancing the powers of the executive at Parliament's expense. As evidence of this tendency, he cites the Lord Chancellor's parliamentary response when asked about the omission to incorporate Article 13 of the European Convention on Human Rights: 'One always has in mind *Pepper v Hart* when one is asked questions of that kind. I shall reply as candidly as I may.'[412]

(4) The Doctrine of Precedent

As Bell explains in *English Private Law*, the concept of 'precedent' covers two   **1.234**
ideas:

> In the broad sense, precedent involves treating previous judicial decisions as authoritative statements of the law which can serve as good legal reasons for subsequent decisions. In the narrow sense, precedent (often described as stare decisis) requires judges in specific courts to treat certain previous decisions, notably of superior courts, as a binding reason. In this sense, the precedent offers a sufficient reason for the decision.[413]

(a) Precedent in its broad sense

The broad sense of precedent is common to most legal traditions, even those of   **1.235**
countries such as France and Germany in which all or at least the greater part of the law is codified and legal decisions must be formally justified by reference to a statutory source; civilian courts frequently in practice follow their own decisions, albeit that the technical legal authority for a subsequent case is not expressed to be its predecessor. The ECJ, in particular, endeavours to build up bodies of case law which proceed on a rational basis from one decision to the next.[414] There are

---

[411] J Steyn, '*Pepper v Hart*: A Re-Examination' (2001) 21 OJLS 59, 68.

[412] *Hansard*, HL vol 583, col 476.

[413] P Birks (n 180 above) para 1.64.

[414] The ECJ also possesses power to reverse its own previous decision, a power which it exercises occasionally. See eg Case C-208/90 *Emmott v Minister for Social Welfare* [1991] ECR I-4269 and Case 188/95 *Fantask v Industriministeriet* [1997] ECR I-6783.

several reasons for this practice: once a court has made up its mind on a particular point, after reasoned argument and critical analysis, it will usually have no wish to change its mind, at least unless or until relevant surrounding circumstances alter; the judiciary will strive to treat like cases in the same way, to ensure that justice is administered evenly; the substantive content of the law is also rendered more certain by this practice; and, in addition, it saves judicial time and cost to litigants if they can rely on previous decisions rather than having to relitigate.

(b) The principle of stare decisis

1.236   Under the system of stare decisis which operates in the English courts, it is not the whole of a previous judgment which is binding on a court which subsequently hears a similar case. Only the central core, the ratio decidendi, constitutes the precedent; the remaining parts of the judgment, which have a persuasive influence in later litigation, are known as the obiter dicta. Although these expressions are in common legal usage, there is no exact, agreed, judicial definition of them. Zander's definition of the ratio is nonetheless widely accepted: 'a proposition of law which decides the case, in the light or in the context of the material facts'.[415] This formulation immediately reveals the inherent elusiveness of the concept: the extent of the binding proposition is delimited by the facts which are considered material. The ratio of a decision can therefore often be expressed in different ways, depending upon the level of abstraction focused upon. If a large number of facts are regarded as material, then the ratio of the case will be correspondingly narrow. On the other hand, if few facts are regarded as material, the case may stand for a wide proposition of law which will govern a broad range of subsequent cases.

1.237   To take a single example from an incalculable pool of cases, in *R v Miller*,[416] a court wished to determine the ratio of *R v Clarke*[417] in which a man had been charged with raping his wife after she had obtained a non-cohabitation order. In *Miller*, the alleged rape took place after the wife had filed for divorce but before any order had been made. The question in *Miller* was therefore whether the existence of a court order had constituted a material fact in *Clarke*. Byrne J had held in *Clarke*:

> The position, therefore, was that the wife, by process of law, namely, by marriage, had given consent to the husband to exercise the marital right during such time as the ordinary relations created by the marriage contract subsisted between them, but by a further process of law, namely the justices' order, her consent to marital intercourse was revoked. Thus, in my opinion, the husband was not entitled to have intercourse with her without her consent.[418]

---

[415] Zander (n 200 above) 263.
[416] [1954] 2 QB 282.
[417] [1949] 2 All ER 448.
[418] ibid 449.

As counsel in *Miller* observed, this formulation could either support the narrow proposition that consent to marital intercourse could only be revoked by a court order or the broader proposition that it was withdrawn on the cessation of 'ordinary relations' between the spouses.

The ratio of a case may also be obscured by the practice of English courts of giving a number of judgments, rather than a single concurring one. Although the judges concerned may all arrive at the same ultimate decision as to how to dispose of the case, each may reach this conclusion by a different logical and verbal route. In such situations, even where the judges purport to agree with one another, it can prove very difficult to determine which facts were material to all, or at least the majority, and how the ratio should therefore be expressed. A well-known example of this is provided by *Thomas v Sawkins*.[419] A meeting was held to protest against the Incitement to Disaffection Bill (then before Parliament) and to demand the dismissal of a local chief constable. The meeting was open to the public and some police officers attended. The police officers were asked by the organizers to leave and a police officer then assaulted one of them, thinking that the organizer was about to use force to eject the police. The police officer was charged with assault but magistrates dismissed the charge on the grounds that the police had reasonable grounds for thinking that if they were not present seditious speeches, incitement to violence and breaches of the peace would occur and that they were therefore entitled to enter and remain at the meeting. **1.238**

The Divisional Court upheld this conclusion, but each of the three judges involved used substantially different language. Lord Hewart CJ held that the police had powers to enter and remain on private premises when they had reasonable grounds to believe an offence was imminent or likely to be committed. However, Avory J, although professing himself as of the same opinion as Lord Hewart, restricted his judgment to the case where the police had reasonable grounds for believing that if they were not present seditious speeches would be made and or that a breach of the peace would take place; the police were entitled to enter and remain on the premises to prevent any such offence or breach of the peace. The third judge, Lawrence J, effectively frustrated the hunt for the ratio of the case by saying that he agreed with its conclusion on its 'particular facts' but without stating which facts he regarded as material. **1.239**

These types of problems which are endemic to the principle of stare decisis mean that the system is by no means as rigid or predictable in practice as it might seem in theory. A judge who wishes to reach a different opinion from one contained in a case which apparently creates a binding precedent will often be tempted to 'distinguish' the earlier case, in other words, to hold that there is a material factual **1.240**

---

[419] [1935] 2 KB 249.

difference between the two. The scope for manipulation of the system provides the life blood of the adversarial process.

1.241 The system of stare decisis which operates in the English courts depends upon a hierarchy of those courts. At the apex stands the ECJ and the Court of First Instance whose decisions bind all English courts in accordance with s 3 of the European Communities Act 1972. This provides:

> (1) For the purposes of all legal proceedings any question as to the meaning or effect of any of the Treaties, or as to the validity, meaning or effect of any Community instrument, shall be treated as a question of law (and, if not referred to the European Court, be for determination as such in accordance with the principles laid down by and any relevant decision of the European Court or any court attached thereto).

1.242 The House of Lords is the highest court in the domestic hierarchy and its decisions bind all other courts in the land. For many years, the House regarded itself as bound by its own decisions[420] but in 1966 it announced that it was abandoning this view, in the interests of justice and in order to aid development of the law.[421] In practice, it has not made extensive use of its power to change its mind and those cases in which it has done so have generally involved strikingly changed social or economic mores in the intervening years.[422] Despite some celebrated rebellions instigated by Lord Denning,[423] the Court of Appeal is bound by decisions of the House of Lords. It is also bound, as regards its Civil Division, by its own decisions. The rule was set out in *Young v Bristol Aeroplane Co Ltd*[424] where Lord Greene MR explained that the only exceptions are (1) where there are two conflicting Court of Appeal decisions and the Court has to decide which one to follow; (2) where its previous decision, though not expressly overruled, cannot stand with a decision of the House of Lords; and (3) where its previous decision was *per incuriam*, in other words, given in ignorance of a material piece of law.

1.243 The Court of Appeal, Criminal Division, is likewise bound by its own decisions, but the rule is less rigidly applied in relation to criminal cases because personal liberty is often at stake. As to lower courts, although there is some dispute in relation to the Divisional Court, it appears to be bound by decisions of the Court of Appeal (and, of course, of the House of Lords) and also to be subject to the rule in *Young v Bristol Aeroplane*.[425] The decisions of trial courts (whether the High

---

[420] *Beamish v Beamish* (1861) 9 HLC 274; *London Tramways v London County Council* [1898] AC 375.

[421] *Practice Statement (Judicial Precedent)* [1966] 1 WLR 1234.

[422] For examples of refusals to depart from earlier decisions even where those earlier decisions were regarded as wrong, see *R v Knuller Ltd* [1973] AC 435 and *R v Kansal (No 2)* [2001] 3 WLR 1562.

[423] *Broome v Cassell* [1971] 2 QB 354; *Schorsch Meir GmbH v Henin* [1975] QB 416.

[424] [1944] KB 718. Cf *Davis v Johnson* [1979] AC 317.

[425] But see *R v Greater Manchester Coroner, ex p Tal* [1984] 3 All ER 240 and *Hornigold v Chief Constable of Lancashire* [1985] Crim LR 792.

Court, county court or magistrates' court) are not binding upon one another[426] but decisions of the High Court and above are binding on county and magistrates' courts. Decisions of the Judicial Committee of the Privy Council are not binding on any English courts, except in devolution cases.[427]

However, even decisions which are not technically binding may be persuasive, **1.244** sometimes very strongly so.[428] English courts pay special attention to the decisions of the higher courts in comparable Anglo-American jurisdictions, particularly those in Commonwealth countries.[429] Similarly, obiter dicta from English courts may in practice be of weighty authority.[430] A very important source of persuasive authority today is the European Court of Human Rights. Pursuant to HRA 1998, s 2, any judgment, decision, declaration or advisory opinion of the European Court of Human Rights, any opinion or decision of the Commission, and any decision of the Committee of Ministers must, wherever relevant, be taken 'into account' by a UK court determining a matter related to a Convention right.[431] The Strasbourg jurisprudence was not elevated to the status of a binding precedent in part at least because the Strasbourg organs themselves operate no formal system of stare decisis and it would have made no sense to give them a greater authority in domestic law. However, Lord Slynn of Hadley observed in *R (on the application of Alconbury Ltd) v Secretary of State for the Environment, Transport and the Regions*[432] that, in the absence of special circumstances, an English court 'should follow any clear and constant jurisprudence of the European Court of Human Rights. If it does not do so there is at least a possibility that the case will go to that court, which is likely in the ordinary case to follow its own constant jurisprudence.'[433]

In practice, Strasbourg decisions on the scope of Convention rights are likely to **1.245** exert more influence than those dealing with justified interference with rights

---

[426] But Nourse J held in *Colchester Estates v Carlton Industries plc* [1984] 2 All ER 601 that, where a second High Court decision has fully reviewed but not followed an earlier one, the second case should effectively settle the matter for the High Court.

[427] See Scotland Act 1998, s 103; Government of Wales Act 1998, Sch 8, para 32; and Northern Ireland Act 1998, s 82.

[428] Perhaps the most famous example is that of the Privy Council decision in *The Wagon Mound (No 1)* [1961] AC 388 which has been far more influential on the development of the law of negligence than the Court of Appeal's decision in *Re Polemis* [1921] 3 KB 560.

[429] *Practice Direction (Citation of Authorities)* [2001] 1 WLR 1001 acknowledges at para 9.1 that '[c]ases decided in other jurisdictions can, if properly used, be a valuable source of law in this jurisdiction'. McGoldrick has observed that, since the entry into force of the HRA in October 2000, there has been a significant increase in the use by English courts of comparative jurisprudence, with Canadian materials having the strongest influence: see 'The United Kingdom's Human Rights Act 1998 in Theory and Practice' (2001) 50 ICLQ 901, 919.

[430] eg, the modern law on negligent misstatement is based on what were actually obiter dicta of the House of Lords in *Hedley Byrne v Heller & Partners* [1964] AC 465.

[431] Since November 1999, only the Court has rendered such decisions.

[432] [2001] 2 WLR 1389.

[433] ibid 1399.

since the latter category of cases are uniquely dependent on surrounding factual circumstances. In cases concerning the scope of Convention rights there is nothing to prevent a UK court from going further than the Strasbourg jurisprudence requires. As David Feldman has explained, 'Convention rights as applied in the United Kingdom will be ECHR rights in terms of their phraseology, but not necessarily in their content. Convention rights in domestic law will derive their authority from Parliament, and will be inspired by, but not validated by, the ECHR.'[434] Since other states which are party to the European Convention on Human Rights have developing bodies of jurisprudence on the scope and applicability of the Convention rights, the decisions of courts in these countries may today also prove a useful source to which a UK court may turn.

1.246   The obligations imposed on all English courts by HRA 1998, s 3 are discussed in paras 1.216 et seq above and paras 7.55 et seq below. It will be recalled that all English courts must today read and give effect to primary and subordinate legislation in a way which is compatible with the Convention rights, so far as this is possible. This provision has consequences for the doctrine of stare decisis which is little short of revolutionary. It renders all pre-existing precedents liable to be re-opened even at the behest of the lowest courts, on the ground that the relevant decision is incompatible with the Convention rights. Thus, a magistrates' court today might refuse to follow a pre-2000 decision of the House of Lords if that House of Lords decision did not respect one of the Convention rights.

---

[434] D Feldman, 'Proportionality and the Human Rights Act 1998' in E Ellis (ed), *The Principle of Proportionality in the Laws of Europe* (Oxford: Hart Publishing, 1999) 119. See further paras 7.28–7.31 and 7.35–7.46 below.

2

THE LAW OF PARLIAMENT

A. The Constitution of Parliament and its Role in Government Formation

(1) Introduction

Unlike the legislatures of almost all other democracies, the Parliament of the **2.01** United Kingdom does not derive its existence or its powers from a written constitution. There is little statutory regulation applicable to the Parliament. There are nevertheless a number of rules of a broadly legal nature governing the ways in which Parliament operates. These are together known as the law and custom of Parliament (lex et consuetudo parliamenti). The courts recognize the existence of these rules, and accept the claims of the Houses of Parliament to be self-regulating. The courts thus concede that the two Houses have 'exclusive cognizance' of their own proceedings, that they enjoy parliamentary privilege, and they have the legal right to punish for contempt. Much of what follows in the first two sections of this chapter is, then, an account of rules relating to the Parliament of the United Kingdom, many of which might not be recognized as laws in a positivist's sense in many other jurisdictions. The principal focus will be on the dominant chamber, the House of Commons. Consideration of particular arrangements in the second chamber will concentrate on the ways in which they differ in significant respects from those in the House of Commons.

(2) The UK Parliament as a Creature of the Royal Prerogative

2.02 As Erskine May puts it 'The legal existence of Parliament results from the exercise of royal prerogative'.[1] The Queen in Parliament (commonly known as Parliament) is the supreme legislature (subject to the primacy of European Community law) for the whole of the United Kingdom.[2] There being no written constitution for the United Kingdom, there is no basic instrument establishing Parliament and granting it powers and authority. It was originally a creature of the royal prerogative and thus of the monarch. The summoning, prorogation and dissolution of Parliament[3] are performed by the sovereign in the exercise of royal prerogative powers[4] expressed in Orders in Council. The exercise of these powers is governed by conventions requiring the sovereign to act only on advice.[5] In comparison the Scottish Parliament owes its existence to the Scotland Act 1998.

(a) The summoning and dissolution of Parliament

2.03 Once summoned, a Parliament continues in existence until dissolution. Parliament is dissolved by effluxion of time five years after its first meeting.[6] This five-year period runs from the date specified for the first meeting of a new Parliament in the Order in Council summoning it. Subject to this five-year limit, dissolution of Parliament may take place by royal proclamation under the Great Seal at any time. Thus, unlike most legislatures, the UK Parliament has a maximum duration determined by statute but an election can be called before the end of that period at the discretion of the Prime Minister.

---

[1] Sir T Erskine May, *Treatise on the Law, Privileges, Proceedings and Usage of Parliament* (22nd edn, London: Butterworths, 1997) 11. The two seminal works on the Parliament are Erskine May, and R Blackburn, A Kennon and Sir Michael Wheeler-Booth, *Griffith and Ryle on Parliament. Functions, Practice and Procedures* (2nd edn, London: Sweet & Maxwell, 2003). Note from Dawn Oliver: I am grateful to Andrew Kennon for comments on an earlier draft of this and the next section of this chapter. Any defects are my responsibility.

[2] See generally Erskine May (n 1 above).

[3] See R Blackburn, *The Meeting of Parliament: The Law and Practice Relating to the Frequency and Duration of the UK Parliament* (Aldershot: Dartmouth, 1990).

[4] On the royal prerogative see paras 1.25–1.31 above.

[5] See G Marshall, *Constitutional Conventions* (Oxford: Clarendon, 1984); R Brazier, *Constitutional Practice* (2nd edn, Oxford: Clarendon, 1994).

[6] Septennial Act 1715, as amended by Parliament Act 1911, s 7. See B Markesinis, *The Theory and Practice of the Dissolution of Parliament* (Cambridge: CUP, 1972).

Dissolution is granted to the Prime Minister by the sovereign with the advice of   **2.04**
the Privy Council. This is a formality. By convention dissolution is granted following a request from the Prime Minister. There may be some residual discretion
on the part of the sovereign to refuse a dissolution that has been requested by the
Prime Minister[7] if, for instance, the Prime Minister does not have the support of
his Cabinet or his party for such a request[8] or there has been a recent general election, but the occasion has not arisen for such a refusal. A Prime Minister will feel
compelled to resign if the government is defeated on a motion of confidence on a
matter central to its administration or if it becomes apparent that the government
can no longer command a majority in the House of Commons. In those circumstances it will be evident that Her Majesty's Government can no longer be carried
on, as it will not be able to get its legislative measures (including, most importantly, financial measures necessary to keep the government machine working)
passed. Subject to a conventional requirement that a dissolution will be granted
after the loss of a motion of confidence in the House of Commons, a Prime
Minister may choose what seems to him or her to be the most favourable time for
a dissolution.

Upon dissolution the government continues in office, in effect as a caretaker gov-   **2.05**
ernment, until the result of the general election is known, when a new administration may be formed.

The statutory requirement is that writs for the election of a new Parliament should   **2.06**
be issued within three years of the ending of a Parliament.[9] However, in practice a
new Parliament will be summoned within a matter of weeks of the dissolution of
the previous Parliament. This is because certain measures, notably the authorization of income taxes and the need for appropriation of money for the use of the
Crown or government are subject to annual statutory authorization by
Parliament. In practice, therefore, Parliaments must be held annually. Upon dissolution the sovereign formally issues the order for the issue of writs for the election of a new Parliament and the summoning of the new Parliament, specifying
the date on which it shall first meet.

(b) Parliamentary sessions

Parliament sits in sessions which normally have a duration of about a year. If a gen-   **2.07**
eral election takes place in the spring the first session of that Parliament will probably run until the October of the following year. The sovereign opens each session
in the House of Lords, the Commons are summoned by Black Rod to attend, and

---

[7] See Marshall (n 5 above); Brazier (n 5 above); V Bogdanor, *The Monarchy and the Constitution*
(Oxford: Clarendon Press, 1995).
[8] See eg Sir WI Jennings, *Cabinet Government* (3rd edn, Cambridge: CUP, 1959) 86.
[9] 16 Cha 2 c1 and 6 & 7 Will & Mary c 2.

the sovereign reads the 'Queen's speech' (the Speech from the Throne), written by the government, in which the legislative programme for the session and the government's policies are set out.

2.08   Parliament is prorogued at the end of each session, formally by order of the sovereign, but at the discretion of the government. Although there is no statutory requirement that parliamentary sessions commence almost immediately after prorogation, in practice sessions need to follow closely upon one another. Prorogation usually takes place in late October, and the new session commences within a few days thereafter. The effect of prorogation is to terminate all legislative proceedings in each House. (However, the business of the Appellate Committee of the House of Lords is not interrupted by prorogation.) All bills not completed by that time fall. In late 2002 the House of Commons and the House of Lords each agreed, as part of the modernization process that was undertaken after the 1997 general election, to permit the carry over of some bills from one session to the next.

(3) The House of Commons: Composition, Pay and Rations

(a) Elections

2.09   Parliament is bicameral, consisting of the House of Commons and the House of Lords.

2.10   The House of Commons is regarded as the lower (though predominant) chamber. The House that was elected in 2001 consists of 659 members elected for single member constituencies by the 'first past the post' (or plurality) method of election. The number of members of the House is reviewed periodically by the Boundary Commissions for England, Wales, Scotland and Northern Ireland, which are to be subsumed in the Electoral Commission that was created in 2001. The boundaries of constituencies and redistribution where population movements so require are governed by the Parliamentary Constituencies Act 1986.[10] Under the electoral system the candidate who receives more votes than any other candidate is declared elected. In constituencies in which more than two candidates are standing for election, this will commonly mean that the winning candidate has fewer than 50 per cent of the votes cast.

2.11   Despite the fact that individual members of Parliament (MPs) may well not receive a majority of the votes cast in their constituencies, the system is sometimes known as a majoritarian one. This is because it normally operates so as to produce a one party majority in the House of Commons and thus a one party government. Under this electoral system it is hard for parties with thinly spread support to win

---

[10]   See *Griffith and Ryle* (n 1 above) paras 2-003–2-009.

seats. Parties with support concentrated in particular constituencies are better able to win seats, though in numbers disproportionate to the level of their electoral support.

In the general election in 2001 the voting figures and results were as follows.[11]   **2.12**

	Seats	*% votes*	*% share of seats*
Conservative	166	32	25.2
Liberal Democrat	52	18	7.9
Labour	412	41	62.5
Scottish National Party	5	2	0.8
Other	24	7	3.6
Total	**659**	**100**	**100**

(b) Representation

It is the House of Commons which gives the UK constitution its characteristic of a   **2.13** representative democracy. Members of the House of Commons are representatives of their constituencies and their constituents. They are not delegates of their parties, and they may not be mandated by outside interests. Although under the doctrine of parliamentary privilege (discussed below) the courts do not have jurisdiction over the official activities of MPs, it is clear that it would be regarded as contrary to the law and the constitution for either the extra-parliamentary parties or other outside interests to seek to mandate MPs—or any elected representatives.[12] Any attempt to mandate them would be regarded as a contempt of Parliament.[13]

MPs make themselves available to all their constituents, regardless of political af-   **2.14** filiation, to give advice, to ask parliamentary questions and generally to act as voices for interests in their constituencies. They are also expected to exercise their judgment independently of outside pressures in their parliamentary activities and to concern themselves for the general public good. In 1947 the House of Commons resolved that the duty of an MP was 'to his constituents and to the country as a whole, rather than to any particular section thereof'.[14] In particular it would be improper for an MP to enter into any contractual agreement with any outside body, controlling or limiting the MP's complete independence and freedom of action in Parliament or stipulating that he shall act in any way as the

---

[11] See Electoral Commission, *Election 2001. The Official Results* (2001).

[12] See eg *Bromley LBC v Greater London Council* [1983] AC 768, 829 *per* Lord Diplock (elected representatives must not treat themselves as irrevocably bound to carry out policies in an election manifesto); *Conservative Central Office v Burrell* [1982] 1 WLR 522, 525; *Amalgamated Society of Rly Servants v Osborne* [1910] AC 87, 111, 114–115.

[13] Erskine May (n 1 above) ch 8; the case of WJ Brown, *Hansard,* HC Deb col 284 (15 July 1947); (HC 118 1946–47).

[14] The case of WJ Brown, ibid.

representative of such outside body in regard to any matters to be transacted in Parliament.[15] The operation of party discipline and the whip system in the House of Commons is not regarded as incompatible with their duties, however.

2.15   It is clear from the table above that the overall composition of the House of Commons is not 'representative' in the sense of reflecting the balance of electoral support for each party. Nor is it representative or reflective of the composition of the electorate: women and members of the ethnic minorities are disproportionately few in number: after the 2001 general election there were only 118 women MPs, 17.9 per cent of the House; and there were 12 MPs from ethnic minorities, 1.8 per cent of the House. (In the electorate overall the proportion of members of ethnic minorities is some 7 per cent). By the Sex Discrimination (Election Candidates) Act 2002 the constituency parties are permitted to require all-women shortlists for the selection of candidates and this may in due course lead to an increase in the number of women MPs.

(c) Parties in the House of Commons and the payroll vote

2.16   Although candidates may stand for election as independents, under the first past the post system it is rare for an independent to be elected. On the ballot paper candidates are entitled to include a five-word description, which candidates for political parties use to indicate their party affiliation. Those standing for election on a party ticket are selected according to the rules of the party selecting them, normally by the local or constituency party. There is no statutory regulation of these rules (although by the Sex Discrimination (Election Candidate) Act 2002 the parties are permitted, though not required, to take positive action measures to reduce inequality in the number of women members elected for a party[16]). Each party has provision in its rules for the 'deselection' of candidates, including the sitting members in certain circumstances.

2.17   Party discipline and loyalty are central features of the operation of the House of Commons. The whip system there is strong. Since by convention members of the government must be members of one or other House of Parliament, and since the Prime Minister has the right to determine who shall hold government office, MPs with governmental ambitions may feel constrained in the exercise of their functions to follow the party line. It is not uncommon for a backbench MP to defy a party whip, but it is rare for a government to lose a vote in the House of Commons as a result of abstention by backbenchers or of backbenchers voting against the government.

---

[15] The case of WJ Brown, ibid; see also Committee of Privileges Report (1974–75 HC 634); Committee of Privileges Report (1990–91 HC 420);

[16] This provision was passed to reverse the position under the case of *Jepson and Dyas-Elliott v Labour Party* [1996] IRLR 116 that a policy in favour of all-women shortlists was unlawful as being discriminatory.

There are up to 95 holders of ministerial office in the House of Commons.[17] The salaries paid to them[18] are in addition to their parliamentary salaries. In addition there are a number of unpaid parliamentary private secretaries. The convention of collective ministerial responsibility requires that all members of the government support the policy of the government of the day, on pain of being dismissed from ministerial office by the Prime Minister for dissent. This natural group of support for the government is known as 'the payroll vote'.
2.18

Thus although the House of Commons is the representative chamber, and the United Kingdom is a representative democracy in the special sense that MPs are elected representatives of their constituents, in practice the parliamentary activity of MPs is largely governed by party influences. There is very little sense of a corporate House of Commons identity separate from party in the chamber.
2.19

If an MP crosses the floor of the House (ie, relinquishes the whip of the party on whose label he or she was elected and takes another party whip) there is no power of recall in the constituency or the constituency party, and the MP is under no legal duty to resign or stand for re-election in a by-election.
2.20

(d) Pay and rations in the House of Commons

Members of the House of Commons receive salaries of some £55,000 as of spring 2003. Each MP may also claim allowances as follows:
2.21

- Annual staffing (secretarial and research assistance, for instance) of between £62,000 and £72,000 per annum. Staff salaries are paid centrally by the House.
- Incidental expenses provision of £18,000 may be claimed for expenses such as office rent (with computer equipment and training, etc, now funded centrally).
- Travel expenses.

Up to 83 members of the House of Commons who are ministers also receive ministerial salaries, which are additional to their parliamentary salaries and allowances.

Special financial provision is made for opposition party activity in Parliament. No such provision is made for independent members. Funds are paid for the running costs of the office of the Leader of the Official Opposition. For 2002–2003 this amounted to some £531,000. The Leader of the Official Opposition, the chief whip and two opposition assistant whips also receive salaries in addition to their salaries as MPs. In case of doubt the Speaker designates the official opposition, currently the Conservative Party. The official opposition is sometimes referred to as 'Her Majesty's Opposition', indicating the importance of opposition to the system.
2.22

---

[17] House of Commons Disqualification Act 1975, s 2.
[18] Ministerial and Other Salaries Act 1975.

2.23 All opposition parties with two or more MPs or one MP and 150,000 votes in the preceding general election, receive sums towards their parliamentary activities, known as 'Short money'. The sum is not to be spent by or on the business of the extra-parliamentary party organizations. The sum payable to each opposition party is calculated by reference to the number of seats won and the number of votes cast for the party at the preceding general election. Allocations to the two main opposition parties for 2002–2003 were as follows: Conservatives £3.5 million; Liberal Democrats £1.2 million. The opposition parties also receive reimbursement of travel and associated expenses of their parliamentary activity.

2.24 Opposition parties are further entitled to policy development grants under the Political Parties, Elections and Referendums Act 2000, s 12. These are designed to assist in the development of policies for inclusion in any election manifesto, and are administered by the Electoral Commission.

(4) The House of Lords: Composition, Pay and Rations

2.25 The House of Lords is the upper chamber, sometimes (paradoxically) referred to as the second chamber. It consists of some 700 members in all (there is no legal cap on the number of members), none of whom are popularly elected. Most members take a party whip, but there is a substantial body of independent members, including the Bishops,[19] the Lords of Appeal and retired Lords of Appeal,[20] and a number of others who do not take a party whip and sit on the crossbenches. There is no legally enforceable or political or moral obligation on any member to attend or participate in the business of the House, although the parties make efforts to secure that sufficient numbers of those taking their party whip attend to enable the parties to fulfil their functions in the House. A token distinction between a 'working peers list' and an honours list grew up in the 1980s and in practice nowadays most appointees are expected to be 'working peers'.

(a) Appointment to the House of Lords

2.26 The present position, as of September 2003, on appointment to the House of Lords is that the Prime Minister (on whose advice the Queen acts) decides how many new members should be appointed to the House, how many new members each party should have and consequently the party balance, and how many new crossbenchers there should be. There is no statutory or other formal regulation of

---

[19] These are Bishops and Archbishops of the Church of England, the established church for England (but not for Scotland, Wales or Northern Ireland). They are sometimes referred to as 'the Lords Spiritual' (as in the words of enactment of statutes). They sit on the Bishops' Benches in the chamber.

[20] The Lords of Appeal and retired Lords of Appeal up to age 75 sit in the Appellate Committee of the House of Lords, which is the highest court of appeal for England and for Scotland except in relation to Scottish criminal matters. See further discussion in para 2.37 below and ch 6.

this prime ministerial or royal power. As a matter of practice when appointing peers from other parties, the Prime Minister does so on the nomination of the leader of that party. These party nominees are granted peerages and are expected to take their party whip. There is no legal regulation of the ways in which the parties select these members. Nor are there any other formal (eg, merit-based or based on the needs of the House for particular experience or expertise in its membership) criteria for these appointments. Before nominees are appointed they are subject to scrutiny for propriety only, by the Appointments Commission (see below).

In 2000 an Appointments Commission was appointed by the Prime Minister to bring forward nominations for appointment of a specified number of independent members. This advisory body is not statutory. The public expectation was that those they nominated would be 'people's peers', the implication being that those nominated would not necessarily be people of distinction, but 'ordinary people'. The first nominations were made in 2001. They were for the most part people who would have been appointed in any event, and the Appointments Commission was derided by the press as being elitist. The Appointments Commission required of those it nominated that they agree to be 'working peers', despite the fact that a peerage has historically been an honour. In practice those it nominated have not attended regularly. **2.27**

The Appointments Commission is still in existence although it had, as of December 2003, brought forward no further nominations. The Commission does not appoint the Lords of Appeal in Ordinary (who are appointed under the Appellate Jurisdiction Act 1876 by the Queen on the advice of the Prime Minister who will have consulted the Lord Chancellor), nor the Lords Spiritual. **2.28**

Despite the existence of the Appointments Commission, charged with nominating independent members of the House of Lords, the Prime Minister reserves the right to appoint some independent members. For instance, the retiring Speaker of the House of Commons, Cabinet Secretary and Chief of Defence Staff. **2.29**

(b) Composition of the House of Lords and party affiliation

As of November 2003 the membership of the House of Lords was as follows: **2.30**

- 554 life peers, appointed by the Queen on the advice of the Prime Minister, to be members of the House for life. These include:
  - 183 members taking the Labour whip;
  - 160 members taking the Conservative whip;
  - 59 members taking the Liberal Democrat whip;
  - 146 crossbenchers who take no party whip. The crossbenchers include 27 Lords of Appeal in Ordinary and retired Lords of Appeal, who have been granted life peerages under the Appellate Jurisdiction Act 1876;
  - 7 others.

- 92 hereditary peers. By the House of Lords Act 1999 all hereditary peers were removed from membership of the House save for:
  - 75 who were elected by the body of hereditary peers in proportion to the then party allegiance or crossbench membership of all hereditary peers;
  - 15 hereditary peers elected to membership by all the then members of the House to serve as office holders, for example as deputy speakers (the Lord Chancellor, appointed by the government, is ex officio Speaker of the House of Lords, but the government proposed in July 2003 to abolish the office. When this is effected, other arrangements will have to be made for choosing the Speaker of the House of Lords).

  When one of the 75 hereditary members elected by hereditary peers dies, runners up from the 1999 election take their place. When one of the 15 holders of office dies (as happened in 2003) the whole house elects a replacement from among the hereditary peers who wish to stand for election. The Clerk of the Parliaments maintains a register of those peers.[21]
- Two hereditary Great Officers of State, the Earl Marshall (the Duke of Norfolk) and the Lord Great Chamberlain, also retained their membership of the House.
- Up to 26 archbishops and bishops of the Church of England. These become members of the House of Lords by seniority of appointment as bishops, and they serve until retirement, normally at 70. They are not life peers. They sit on the Bishops Benches in the House as Lords Spiritual.

There is no provision for life peers or hereditary peers to resign, though they may take leave of absence. As of July 2003 13 peers were on leave of absence.

2.31 The allegiance of members of the House of Lords (including hereditary peers) as of April 2003 was as follows:

Conservative	210
Labour	186
Liberal Democrat	64
Independents[22]	179

These figures excluded seven 'others' and 12 peers on leave of absence.

2.32 Thus no one party has a majority in the House of Lords. Party affiliation is not proportionate to the level of support for the parties in the 2001 election; nor indeed is it related to any other measure. The Prime Minister announced in 1999 that he would seek broad parity between the Conservative and Labour membership, and a

---

[21] Lord Weatherill introduced the House of Lords (Amendment) Bill (HL 32) in the House of Lords in February 2003, which if enacted would end the system of replacing hereditary peers by election. The number of hereditary peers in the House of Lords would thus, over time, diminish.

[22] Including crossbenchers, Law Lords and retired Law Lords, but excluding Archbishops and Bishops.

large number of life peerages have been awarded since 1997 to bring up the numbers sitting on the government benches, but parity has not yet been achieved.

(c) Pay and rations in the House of Lords

Members of the Second Chamber do not receive salaries, save for the leader of the **2.33** official opposition, the opposition chief whip, the chairman of committees, his deputies, and ministers in the House of Lords (who receive ministerial salaries). Members are entitled to claim a per diem tax-free allowance for expenses incurred for the purposes of attendance. These are, as of February 2003, £124 for overnight accommodation, £62 for travel and subsistence, and £52 for general office expenses and secretarial or research assistance.

The first two opposition parties in the House of Lords receive 'Cranborne money' **2.34** on principles similar to the 'Short money' paid to parties in the House of Commons, to be spent on parliamentary activity. The allocations for 2002–2003 were: Conservatives £231,000; Liberal Democrats £69,000.

(5) Reform of the Composition of the House of Lords

The government's stated intention when the House of Lords Act 1999 was **2.35** passed was that the removal of most hereditary peers was to be the first step in a process of reform of the composition and functions of the House of Lords.[23] A Royal Commission on Reform of the House of Lords was appointed to make recommendations on the role, functions and composition of the second chamber, in early 1999. In its report[24] the Royal Commission recommended, on composition, that there be a relatively small proportion of directly elected members (either 87 or 195) and that all other members should be appointed by an independent statutory Appointments Commission working to statutory criteria and published policies designed to enable the House to fulfil its functions.[25] However, there has been no consensus either within the government or within either House about what further reforms should be made, and in particular about what, if any, proportion of its members should be elected, on what system they should be elected, and how, by whom and on what terms appointed members should be appointed.[26]

---

[23] See *Modernising Parliament—Reforming the House of Lords* (Cm 4183, 1999).

[24] *A House for the Future* (Cm 4534, January 2000).

[25] These functions are primarily those of revision of legislation, scrutiny of the executive and consideration of matters of public interest. The legal powers of the second chamber include the right to refuse consent to much primary and secondary legislation and thus to impose delay on government to cause it to think again before pressing forward with legislation.

[26] The two Houses debated a number of options for reforming the composition of the House of Lords on 4 February 2003. There was no majority for any of the options in the House of Commons; in the House of Lords there was majority support for a wholly appointed chamber. See the following

2.36   The Queen's Speech of November 2003 included a proposal for legislation to remove the remaining hereditary peers from the House of Lords. The omission of a commitment to election of a proportion of members of the House proved controversial and as of December 2003 it was uncertain whether a measure to remove the hereditary peers without provision for election of at least some members of the second chamber would pass. The Government's other proposals for reform of the second chamber included that there should be a statutory, independent Appointments Commission which would: determine numbers and timing of appointments, ensuring that the balance of party members had regard to the outcome of the previous general election and that the Government of the day should not have an overall majority in the House; select independent members of the House (except Law Lords and the Bishops), having regard to the make-up of society and ensuring that the appointment of non-party members averaged twenty per cent of new appointments over each Parliament; and oversee party nominations, vetting them for propriety.

(a) The Law Lords

2.37   The presence of the Law Lords (and, in his capacity as head of the judiciary, of the Lord Chancellor) in the second chamber raises issues to do with the separation of powers and compliance with Article 6 of the European Convention on Human Rights (ECHR). The European Court of Human Rights (ECtHR) decided in *Procola v Luxembourg*[27] that the Luxembourg Conseil d'Etat was not an independent and impartial tribunal for the purposes of Article 6 of the European Convention on Human Rights (to which the United Kingdom is signatory), since its members had an advisory function in relation to the passage of legislation. In the case of *McGonnell v UK*,[28] the ECtHR decided that it was incompatible with the requirement in Article 6 ECHR that the Deputy Bailiff of Guernsey, who was the sole judge in the case in issue, should also have been President of the Parliament (the States of Deliberation) when it adopted the legislation in issue in the case. The ECtHR held that '. . . any direct involvement in the passage of legislation, or of executive rules, was likely to be sufficient to cast doubt on the judicial impartiality of a person subsequently called on to determine a dispute over whether reasons existed to permit a variation from the wording of the legislation or rules at issue'. The Lord Chancellor presides in the House of Lords, and the Lords of Appeal in Ordinary, as well as sitting in the Appellate Committee, may also sit in the Lords when it is exercising its legislative functions. The *McGonnell*

---

reports of the Joint Committee on House of Lords Reform: First Report (2002–03 HL 17; HC 171); Second Report (2002–03 HL 97; HC 668); see Government Response (2002–03 HL 155; HC 1027).

[27] (1995) 22 EHRR 193.
[28] (2000) 30 EHRR 289.

decision suggests that these arrangements may not be compatible with Article 6 ECHR. When the government's decisions to abolish the office of Lord Chancellor and establish a Supreme Court (see para 2.38 below) are implemented (they will require legislation) these problems will be resolved.

In response to concerns about these matters, and in particular to a recommenda- **2.38** tion from the Royal Commission on Reform of the House of Lords,[29] the Senior Law Lord, Lord Bingham of Cornhill, set out the conventions that the Law Lords would observe regarding their participation in the non-judicial work of the second chamber: the Lords of Appeal in Ordinary do not think it appropriate to engage in matters where there is a strong element of party political controversy; and they bear in mind that they might render themselves ineligible to sit judicially if they were to express an opinion on a matter which might later be relevant to an appeal to the House.[30] The effect of these principles is that the Law Lords' role in the legislative business of the second chamber and in general debates there is much reduced, rendering their membership increasingly anomalous, and reducing some of the perceived benefits of having Law Lords in the chamber (such as their ability to bring their expertise to bear in debates, committee work, etc, and the appreciation of the realities of politics that their contact with the political world in the second chamber brings). In July 2003 the government proposed the abolition of the office of Lord Chancellor and the establishment of a new Supreme Court to take the place of the Appellate Committee of the House of Lords. The Lords of Appeal would sit in the new court, and they would no longer be members of the House of Lords.[31]

(6) Parliament and Government Formation

(a) The parliamentary executive

By convention all members of the government must be members of one or other **2.39** of the two Houses of Parliament. There is a statutory limit of 95 holders of ministerial office in the House of Commons.[32] Appointment of the Prime Minister and other ministers is done by the sovereign under the royal prerogative, and is governed by convention.

The persons appointed to be Prime Minister and Chancellor of the Exchequer **2.40** must by convention be members of the House of Commons. These requirements are linked to the convention that the Prime Minister must be a person who commands the support of a majority in the House of Commons, so that Her Majesty's

---

[29] Cm 4534, 2000, recommendation 26.
[30] *Hansard*, HL vol 614, col 419 (22 June 2000).
[31] See consultation paper from the Department for Constitutional Affairs, *Constitutional Reform: a Supreme Court for the UK*, CP11/03, July 2003, and ch 6.
[32] House of Commons Disqualification Act 1975, s 2.

Government may be carried on, and acceptance of the House of Commons' financial privileges (noted below). These conventions are the sources of the parliamentary executive and of the expression 'Her Majesty's Government' to indicate the executive.

2.41 The Prime Minister is required by convention to offer his resignation and that of his administration to the Queen in certain circumstances. These include where the Prime Minister can no longer command the support of a majority in the House of Commons after a general election, normally because another party has an overall majority in the House. Where a government loses a vote of confidence in the House of Commons the Prime Minister should either offer his resignation or ask for a dissolution. The latter has been the normal practice in recent years.

(b) Appointment of the Prime Minister and members of the government

2.42 The House of Commons does not have any formal or statutory procedural role in the actual appointment of ministers. There is no provision for the House of Commons itself to nominate a Prime Minister, unlike the position in the Scottish Parliament, for instance, which by s 46 of the Scotland Act 1998 elects its First Minister who is then formally appointed by the monarch.[33] However, the choice of Prime Minister will depend upon House of Commons support.

2.43 The Queen appoints a Prime Minister, and such other ministers as the Prime Minister advises the monarch to appoint. The procedure for and conventions governing the appointment of a government are as follows.

- If after a general election the incumbent government retains a majority in the House of Commons, the Prime Minister will be entitled to remain in post. Generally there will be a reshuffle and the Queen will appoint to the government those people whom the Prime Minister recommends for appointment.
- If after a general election another party has won a majority in the House of Commons, the incumbent Prime Minister is required by convention to resign, and the Queen invites the leader of the majority party to form a government. The identity of the leader of the majority party will be clear, as the party itself will have elected its leader before the election and the Queen will not need to exercise discretion. The election of a party leader is not regulated by statute and each political party has its own procedure for electing a leader. Whereas formerly each parliamentary party elected its own leader, the strong trend since the 1980s has been towards allowing the members of the extra-parliamentary parties to participate in the election of the party leader.

---

[33] The Irish Prime Minister (the Taoiseach) is elected by the Dail. The election is preceded by negotiations between the parties.

- If after a general election there is a hung Parliament (ie, one in which no party in the House of Commons has a majority), then by convention the incumbent Prime Minister is entitled to attempt to form a government, for instance by inviting another party to join a coalition or by negotiating a pact with another party according to which the other party will refrain from bringing the government down on a vote on the Queen's speech.[34] If in such a situation the incumbent Prime Minister finds that he or she is unable to command a majority in the House (as was the case after the first election in 1974, when the incumbent Prime Minister, Edward Heath, tried unsuccessfully to negotiate a pact or coalition with the Liberals, led at that time by Jeremy Thorpe) the Queen will invite another person to see if he or she can form a government. This person may be the leader of the largest or next largest party in the House of Commons apart from that of the previously incumbent government. However, if another person can command a majority in the House, for instance through a coalition or a pact formed from two or more smaller parties, the sovereign may invite that person to form a government. The sovereign has a discretion in such cases, and may be in a difficult constitutional position, as the largest or next largest party may well claim to be entitled to form a government. However, the basic convention being that the sovereign should invite the person who can command a majority in the House to form a government, if that person is not the leader of the largest or next largest party there would be nothing unconstitutional in the sovereign inviting the person who can form a government that commands the support of a majority in the House of Commons to do so. The underlying principle is that government must be carried on, and a leader who cannot command the support of a majority would be brought down on the debate on the Queen's speech or soon thereafter if there is another person in the House who can command a majority.

(c) Removal or resignation of ministers

The House of Commons may in effect dismiss a Prime Minister through a vote of no confidence. By convention a Prime Minister will be expected to resign or ask for a dissolution in such an event. This happened most recently in 1979, when the Labour government under James Callaghan was defeated on a vote of confidence. The Prime Minister requested and was granted a dissolution. The Conservative Party under Mrs Thatcher won a majority, Callaghan resigned and Margaret Thatcher was appointed Prime Minister. **2.44**

The House of Commons may have a role in the dismissal of a member of the government if, exceptionally, there were to be a vote of no confidence in a particular **2.45**

---

[34] The Queen's speech sets out the government's programme for the first session of the Parliament and is delivered at the first meeting of the new Parliament.

minister. In such a case the minister would be expected to offer his resignation to the Prime Minister. The House of Commons itself however has no direct power to dismiss a minister. In the absence of culpability in decisions taken by him personally or his own acts or omissions (in which case resignation may be expected[35]) the obligation of a minister is limited to giving an account of the matter in issue, undertaking to put matters right and make amends to those who have been affected. If there were some degree of culpability an apology may also be expected.

2.46 Ministers will be expected to offer their resignation to the Prime Minister in certain circumstances. First, if they have misled the House. This long-established position was reasserted in the resolutions of the two Houses shortly before the dissolution of Parliament in March 1997.[36] The requirement is now incorporated in the Ministerial Code, for which the Prime Minister is responsible. The Prime Minister may be asked to account for his responsibilities under the Code by the House of Commons Liaison Committee, consisting of select committee chairmen. Prime Minister Blair agreed in 2002 to meet that Committee twice a year. Further, ministers may be driven to resign if criticism of their conduct by MPs (or by the press) causes embarrassment to the government or damages their credibility or authority.[37]

B. The Powers and Privileges of Parliament

(1) Legislative Powers

(a) Primary legislation for the United Kingdom, England and Wales

2.47 While Scotland and Northern Ireland have devolved legislatures with power to pass Acts—primary legislation[38] (respectively the Scottish Parliament and the Northern Ireland Assembly)—there is no separate legislature for England and Wales. Thus Parliament is both the supreme legislative body for the United Kingdom, and the sole body with power to enact statutes for England and Wales.

---

[35] See the Crichel Down affair, report of the inquiry (Cmd 9176, 1954), discussed at *Griffith and Ryle* (n 1 above) para 1-056.

[36] *Hansard*, HC cols 1046–1047 (19 March 1997); *Hansard*, HL cols 1055–1062 (20 March 1997). See further paras 2.80–2.83 below.

[37] On ministerial resignations and individual ministerial responsibility generally see SE Finer, 'The Individual Responsibility of Ministers' (1956) 34 Public Administration 377; G Marshall, *Ministerial Responsibility* (Oxford: OUP, 1989); D Woodhouse, *Ministers and Parliament. Accountability in Theory and Practice* (Oxford: Clarendon Press, 1994) and 'Ministerial responsibility: Something old, something new' [1997] PL 262; *Report of the inquiry into the Export of Defence-related Equipment and Dual-use Goods to Iraq and Related Prosecutions* (the Scott Report) (1995–96 HC 115).

[38] But note that there is some debate as to whether Acts of the Scottish Parliament or the Northern Ireland Assembly are, technically, primary legislation; see N Burrows, *Devolution* (2000) ch 3. This debate need not detain us here.

Acts that apply to the whole of the United Kingdom, and those that apply only to England and/or Wales are passed by the UK Parliament. All members of each House of Parliament are entitled to participate in the legislative process, including, in relation to legislation for England and Wales, members of the House of Commons sitting for constituencies in Scotland and Northern Ireland.

The passing of Acts of Parliament, the principal form of primary legislation for England,[39] normally requires the consent of the House of Commons and the House of Lords, followed by Royal Assent. However, exceptions to this principle are provided by the Parliament Acts 1911 and 1949, as follows: **2.48**

- Any Bill first introduced in the House of Commons, other than a Bill to extend the maximum duration of Parliament beyond five years, may be presented for Royal Assent in the following session of Parliament without the consent of the Lords a year after its first second reading in the Commons.[40] The duration of Parliament was extended by Acts of Parliament during the first and second world wars.
- The House of Lords may consent to, but is not entitled to amend, Money Bills. A Bill may be certified a Money Bill by the Speaker of the House of Commons if it contains *only* provisions dealing with taxation or the appropriation of moneys to the use of the Crown.[41] A Money Bill which has been passed by the House of Commons but has not yet been passed by the Lords may receive royal assent one month after it was sent to the House of Lords.

The procedure for the passage of Bills is laid down by the standing orders of the two Houses. These require in principle three readings, a committee stage[42] for detailed scrutiny and possible amendment of each Bill, and a report stage at which further amendment is permitted. The committee stage of Bills or parts of Bills that are regarded as being of first class constitutional importance will be taken by a Committee of the whole House, so that all members may participate.   **2.49**

The two Houses must agree on the terms of the Bill before Royal Assent can be given (subject to the government invoking the Parliament Acts 1911 and 1949) and they communicate by message.   **2.50**

The scrutiny at committee stage in each House takes place after second reading. The committee stage scrutiny is by debate, and is not done according to any explicit   **2.51**

---

[39] Orders in Council made by the Queen in Council under the royal prerogative or under powers granted by statutes, such as the European Communities Act 1972, are also regarded as primary legislation, though in many respects they resemble more closely secondary legislation made by statutory instrument under statutory power. Orders in Council are treated as primary legislation under HRA 1998, s 21. See further discussion of Orders in Council at paras 2.61–2.62 below.

[40] Parliament Act 1911, s 2 as amended by Parliament Act 1949.

[41] See Parliament Act 1911, ss 1, 3.

[42] Apart from the normal standing committee, other possibilities include special standing committees, select committees and Committee of the Whole House.

criteria, such as compatibility with the United Kingdom's international obligations (for instance, the ECHR or international treaty obligations[43]). Scrutiny is done at large, as if on the floor of the House, and forms part of the process of giving or refusing consent to legislation on behalf of the electorate, which is a core function of the House of Commons and a representative democracy. In practice the government uses the committee stage to propose its own amendments to the Bill; the committee stage provides opportunities to improve the Bill, to draw attention to weaknesses in the Bill and to harass the government.[44] At this stage it is not permitted to oppose the overall principle of the Bill, which will have been debated at second reading, before the Bill was sent to committee.

2.52   Since 1998, as part of the modernization process in Parliament, other options for considering legislation have been introduced. Some Bills will be published by the government as draft Bills and will be subjected to pre-legislative scrutiny by evidence-taking select committees of one or other House or joint committees of both. For instance the draft Financial Services and Markets Bill was examined by a joint committee of both Houses. Its recommendations for bringing the proposals on penalties for market abuse into compliance with the Convention rights incorporated into UK law by the Human Rights Act 1998 (HRA) were accepted by the government,[45] and incorporated into the Bill which became the Financial Services and Markets Act 2000. The draft Local Government Organization and Standards Bill (1998–1999) was also examined by a joint committee. And a draft Freedom of Information Bill (1998–1999) was examined by separate committees in each House. Only one Bill was subject to pre-legislative scrutiny in the 1999–2000 session. There were nine draft Bills in the 2002–2003 session. All draft Bills are also examined by the Joint Committee on Human Rights. The publication of Bills in draft for scrutiny is a matter for government, not for Parliament itself.

2.53   In its Second Report, *A Reform Programme*[46] the Modernization Committee of the House of Commons[47] recommended that the government continue to increase with each session the publication of Bills in draft and that where this was

---

[43] Bills may be scrutinized for these issues in the Joint Committee on Human Rights and the House of Lords Constitution Committee.

[44] See the Second Report of the Select Committee on Procedure, *Public Bill Procedure* (1984–85 HC 49–1) para 30.

[45] See First Report of the Joint Committee on the Draft Financial Services and Markets Bill (1998–99 HC 50, HL 328), Second Report (1998–99 HC 465, HL 66).

[46] 2001–02 HC 1168.

[47] A Modernization Committee was appointed after the 1997 general election, under the chairmanship of successive Leaders of the House. Its reports have persuaded the House of Commons to introduce, among other reforms, new more family friendly sitting hours in the House, to remove certain archaic traditions, to rationalize the legislative process and provide more resources for select committees.

not possible the government should submit a detailed statement of policy for pre-legislative scrutiny. The House of Commons accepted these recommendations in principle in late 2002.

The Joint Committee on Human Rights scrutinizes bills for compatibility with **2.54** Convention rights and reports to each House. The Delegated Powers and Deregulation Committee of the House of Lords scrutinizes bills for the inappropriate delegation of legislative power, and reports to the House. The House of Lords Constitution Committee scrutinizes bills for any constitutional issues they may raise and reports to the House.

Thus some of the functions that are performed in other systems by bodies exter- **2.55** nal to the legislature, for instance by a Supreme Court with powers to strike down legislation that is incompatible with a constitutional provision (as in the United States) or by a Constitutional Council or Council of State with powers to report on Bills that fail to meet constitutional requirements (like the Conseil constitutionnel or the Conseil d'etat in France) are internalized in the UK Parliament, particularly in the second chamber. In the absence of a written constitution it would be problematic for the United Kingdom to establish independent external institutions such as a constitutional court or council charged with such 'watchdog' responsibilities, but the fact that these internal scrutiny arrangements are in place is recognition of the importance of scrutiny against criteria other than party political ones in a democratic system. The relatively apolitical second chamber with members having appropriate legal and other expertise seems better suited than the more party political and partisan House of Commons to this form of scrutiny.

(b) Secondary legislation

Certain secondary legislation is made by the responsible government minister, **2.56** usually in the form of regulations made under statutory powers. These 'statutory instruments' or drafts of them are laid before Parliament. By the Statutory Instruments Act 1946 they are subject either to affirmative or negative procedure—in practice, the difference between active and tacit consent. The parent Act may specify the procedure to be followed. There is normally no power in Parliament to amend these instruments.

If the instrument is subject to negative procedure, it is laid before Parliament and **2.57** unless a motion is tabled for it to be debated and time is found for debate, it will come into effect automatically after the prescribed period. Very few of these orders are considered by the House—only four out of a total of 1,241 laid before the House in 1999–2000, for instance.[48] If a statutory instrument or a draft one is subject to the affirmative procedure, the order or draft order is laid before

---

[48] See *Griffith and Ryle* (n 1 above) paras 6-162–6-167; see also para 5.40 below.

Parliament and the minister moves a motion for its approval. Only after such approval can a draft order come into effect. Once the motion is tabled, but before it is passed, the instrument stands referred to a standing committee on delegated legislation for debate on the merits. It is also considered by the Joint Committee on Statutory Instruments, for consideration whether it is within the powers of the minister to make it, whether it imposes a financial charge, whether its drafting is defective, and various other matters.[49]

2.58   Under the Regulatory Reform Act 2001 (which superseded the provisions originally found in the Deregulation and Contracting Out Act 1994) a new and elaborate procedure was introduced for the making of orders to amend primary legislation by statutory instrument so as to remove unnecessary regulatory burdens.[50] Statutory provisions enabling such orders to be made are often referred to as 'Henry VIII' clauses, since that monarch was given to claiming the right to amend Acts by order. The procedure under the Regulatory Reform Act 2001 involves the minister producing a draft order for consultation and scrutiny by the House of Commons Select Committee on Regulatory Reform and the House of Lords Delegated Powers and Regulatory Reform Committee. The latter committee advises whether the draft should be amended, and whether it should be made or not made. The minister may then lay the instrument before Parliament for debate and approval.

2.59   Normally a simple resolution in Parliament is not regarded as effective to change or make the law,[51] and thus the powers under this Act for the House to approve such an order and thus to enable provisions in a previous Act to be amended or repealed represent an erosion of the legislative supremacy of Parliament. In return these measures are subject to closer parliamentary scrutiny than other secondary legislation. In effect under the Regulatory Reform Act a proposal by a minister endorsed by votes of the two Houses, not as part of the normal legislative procedure required for passing Acts, authorizes the repeal of statutory provisions.[52]

2.60   Under HRA 1998, s 10 and Sch 2, a minister may lay a remedial order before Parliament to remove an incompatibility with the ECHR in certain circumstances. These orders are subject to scrutiny by the Joint Committee on Human Rights, discussed at paras 7.119 et seq below. They represent a further erosion of the primacy of Acts of the UK Parliament.[53]

---

[49] See Standing Order 151, House of Commons.
[50] For an assessment of this procedure see D Miers, 'The deregulation procedure: An expanding role' [1999] PL 477.
[51] See *Bowles v Bank of England* [1913] 1 Ch 57.
[52] The Provisional Collection of Taxes Act has a similar, but temporary, effect; see below.
[53] See further discussion in ch 7.

(i) Orders in Council: a note

Many executive orders (including orders making certain public appointments) **2.61**
may be made by Order in Council under the royal prerogative and under some
statutory powers. Statutory powers to make Orders in Council are included in
the Emergency Powers Act 1920, exercisable once a state of emergency has been
declared. There are also powers, under European Communities Act 1972, s 2(2),
to make Orders in Council to implement Community obligations and for other
purposes to do with European law.[54] By s 1(3) European treaties may be designated by Order in Council. Remedial orders under the HRA 1998 are also made
as Orders in Council.[55] When made under statutory powers, these orders are subject to the Statutory Instruments Act 1946 and they count as delegated legislation.

Orders in Council made under the prerogative are technically primary legislation. **2.62**
They are not however subject to parliamentary consent or scrutiny, unless this is
explicitly provided for. A royal proclamation is issued when publicity needs to be
given to such orders. These orders are approved by the sovereign at a meeting of
the Privy Council attended normally only by four members. There is no formal
parliamentary participation.

(2) Scrutiny of European Legislation and Policy

The two Houses of the UK Parliament have complementary arrangements for the **2.63**
scrutiny of documents and proposals for EU legislation. The House of Commons
has imposed a requirement on ministers that they should not, other than in exceptional circumstances, enter into any new commitments in the Council until
the Commons scrutiny process has been completed (this is known as the scrutiny
reserve). A similar resolution applies to the House of Lords' scrutiny process. But
these resolutions do not prevent ministers, once the scrutiny process is complete,
from consenting to new commitments even in the face of reservations expressed
by the committees of either House to proposed directives, regulations or decisions. There is however considerable political pressure on ministers to respond to
the findings of parliamentary committees and account for their conduct of negotiations in the Council and the directives that result.

In the House of Commons two types of committees are responsible for scrutiny **2.64**
of European legislation. The House of Commons' European Scrutiny
Committee, via its advisers, rapidly sifts all proposals, such as draft proposals for
legislation, under consideration in the Council of Ministers, may take evidence

---

[54] See para 1.136 above.
[55] See paras 7.119 et seq below.

and reports to the House on the legal and political importance of each document, and recommends to one of the three European Standing Committees of the Commons which ones should be subject to debate.

2.65 These committees are hampered by the fact that the time available for their consideration of documents is often short as they receive them not long before the Council is due to make a decision on them. Also the task requires considerable expertise and dedication of time and it is not always possible to find backbenchers willing to make the commitment to the work of the committee.

2.66 The House of Lords' activity in relation to European draft legislation complements that of the Commons. Its work is highly regarded in the other member states[56] and in the Community institutions themselves. The House of Lords' Select Committee on the European Communities, chaired by a salaried officer and member of the House, considers any Community proposal which it believes should be drawn to the attention of the House. The Committee has six subject based committees, on Agriculture, Fisheries and Food; Economic and Financial Affairs, Trade and External Relations; Social Affairs, Education and Home Affairs; Energy, Industry and Transport; Environment, Public Heath and Consumer Protection; Law and Institutions. These subcommittees and the committee identify some 30 or 40 items of EU business each year for in-depth study and analysis, and produce their own valuable, detailed reports.[57] The European Union Committee is particularly effective, and has a high reputation among member states for the quality of its scrutiny of legislation.

2.67 The combined activities of these House of Commons and House of Lords committees produce one of the most highly developed systems in the European Union for considering proposed European legislation and other proposals and for ensuring that ministers are aware of the balance of opinion within Parliament before they commit the country to any significant new position.

(3) Taxation and Spending

(a) Statutory authorization of taxation

2.68 By Article 4 of the Bill of Rights 1688 '[t]he levying Money for or to the use of the Crowne by ptence of Prerogative without Grant of Parliament for longer time or in other manner than the same is or shall be granted is Illegall'. The modern rendering would be that there shall be no taxation without representation. This is taken to mean that taxation must be clearly authorized by Act of Parliament. Any

---

[56] See Thirty-third Report of the House of Commons European Scrutiny Committee, *Democracy and Accountability in the EU and the Role of National Parliaments* (2001–02 HC 152).

[57] See eg the report on *EU Charter of Fundamental Rights* (1999–2000 HL 67), a highly regarded report on the draft charter.

attempt to impose taxation without such authorization will be regarded as unlawful.[58]

Special arrangements are in place in relation to the annual budget statement and Finance Bill. Income tax is an annual tax which is authorized by the annual Finance Act. By the Provisional Collection of Taxes Act 1968, the collection of taxes at new rates is permitted under a resolution of the House of Commons pending the passing of the Finance Act, but conditional on that Act receiving Royal Assent and becoming law within four months of the resolution. Thus the resolution has to be confirmed by statute.

2.69

The imposition of tax is within the privileges of the House of Commons. The House of Lords may not amend a Money Bill or any financial provision in another Bill. This position is based upon two resolutions of the House of Commons. The first, of 1671, maintained '[t]hat in all aids given to the King by the Commons, the rate or tax ought not to be altered by the Lords'. The second resolution, in 1678, stated '[t]hat all aids and supplies, and aids to his Majesty in Parliament, are the sole gift of the Commons; and all bills for the granting of any such aids and supplies ought to begin with the Commons; and that it is the undoubted and sole right of the Commons to direct, limit, and appoint in such bills the ends, purposes, considerations, conditions, limitations, and qualifications of such grants, which ought not to be changed or altered by the House of Lords'.[59]

2.70

A fundamental rule of procedure is that no charge on public funds or on the people may be incurred except on the initiative of the Crown. A Bill imposing a tax, must be supported by a financial resolution in the House of Commons. A Bill imposing a new charge on public funds must be supported by a 'money resolution'. These resolutions may be passed only on the initiative or recommendation of the government. Thus it is not possible for a private member's Bill or a Bill originating in the House of Lords to propose a tax or a new charge on public funds without the consent of the government.

2.71

In a Report from the Leader's Group appointed to consider how the working practices of the House can be improved, and to make recommendations[60] it was proposed that a new ad hoc committee for finance bills should be established in the House of Lords, that would look at issues to do with taxation (other than those within the financial privilege of the Commons such as rates of tax). The government rejected the proposal, maintaining that this would in fact trespass on the Commons' privileges.

2.72

---

[58] See eg *Congreve v Home Office* [1976] QB 629; *Bowles v Bank of England* [1913] 1 Ch 57.
[59] (1667–87) CJ 235, 509.
[60] 2001–02 HL 111; see also Fifth Report of the Select Committee on the Procedure of the House (2001–02 HL 148).

(b) The requirement for parliamentary authority for public expenditure

2.73 In principle money provided by Parliament may only be spent on statutorily authorized objects. There are some exceptions to this principle. For instance, the Criminal Injuries Compensation Scheme, by which payments were made out of public funds to victims of crime, ran for some 30 years without statutory authority, and the legality of these payments was not challenged. The legality of the scheme was accepted by the courts in *R v Secretary of State for the Home Department, ex p Fire Brigades Union.*[61]

2.74 According to a concordat reached originally in 1932 between the Treasury and the House of Commons, and which is set out in *Government Accounting*, 'while it is competent to Parliament, by means of an annual vote embodied in the Appropriation Acts, in effect to extend powers specifically limited by statute, constitutional propriety requires that such extensions should be regularized at the earliest possible date by amending legislation, unless they are of a purely emergency or non-continuing character'.

(c) The grant of supply to government

2.75 The revenues raised by taxation are paid into the Exchequer Account at the Bank of England, forming the Consolidated Fund.[62] Money may not be withdrawn from this fund save in accordance with parliamentary authority, certified by the Comptroller and Auditor General, an officer of Parliament. Exceptionally funds may be applied direct from the Consolidated Fund, and not subject to a vote, notably payments to the European Communities, the Civil List (paid to the sovereign), and salaries of certain holders of office whose position is required for constitutional reasons to be insulated from the political pressures that could be imposed if the House of Commons, controlled by the government, were to refuse a vote. These include salaries of the Speaker of the House of Commons, the Comptroller and Auditor General, the Parliamentary Commissioner for Administration, the Leader of the Opposition, and of judges, all of which are charged directly on the Consolidated Fund.

2.76 The grant of supply to the Crown—the government—is given by voting the Supply Estimates submitted by government to the House of Commons, followed by passage of one or more Consolidated Fund Acts each year and the annual Appropriation Act. These Acts authorize the Treasury to issue money from the Consolidated Fund to defray the costs of providing the public service in question. Some of these estimates may be selected for debate on Estimates Days. The

---

[61] [1995] 2 AC 513.
[62] Exchequer and Audit Departments Act 1866, s 10.

Appropriation Act appropriates money vote by vote to the services for which they were granted. This process has become something of a formality and the House of Commons does not in practice refuse supply requested by the government. These Bills are passed by an accelerated procedure with no debate on second and third reading and no committee stage. The House of Commons' Procedure Committee commented in 1999 that the House's power over expenditure was 'if not a constitutional myth, very close to one'.[63]

Historically the right of the House of Commons to grant or refuse supply was exercised subject to the convention that there should be no grant of supply to the Crown before the redress of grievances. This gave rise to the right of opposition parties to determine the business of the house on a number of 'Supply Days' before the approval of the Supply Estimates. These are now known as 'Opposition Days', currently 20 per session, shared between the official opposition and other opposition parties, and no longer taking place at the time of the approval of the Supply Estimates.   **2.77**

(d) Parliamentary scrutiny of public expenditure

The House of Commons is responsible for ensuring that money, once granted to the government, is properly spent. Sums appropriated to a particular service may not be spent on another service, and in principle such sums should be spent on costs incurred in the year in which they are granted. Government departments must submit appropriation accounts to Parliament. These are audited on its behalf by the Comptroller and Auditor General, an officer of Parliament, and the staff of the National Audit Office. They report to Parliament, in particular to the Committee for Public Accounts.[64]   **2.78**

(4) Scrutiny of the Executive

A, perhaps the, major function of Parliament, given the dominance of the executive in its legislative activity, is the scrutiny of government, its policy and its administration. Both Houses exercise these functions, though their institutional arrangements for doing so are different. While ministers in each House are accountable in the sense that they are expected to answer questions asked on the floor of each House and written questions, and to speak in debates, in practice detailed scrutiny of the executive takes place in the select committees of each House. *Griffith and Ryle* stress that Parliament is primarily a responsive body rather than one that takes initiatives, and the scrutiny function is the primary way in which this function is performed.   **2.79**

---

[63] Report of the Procedure Committee (1998–99 HC 295) para 1.
[64] It should be noted that the Treasury also conducts strict audits of public expenditure. And the courts may rule expenditure that has not been statutorily authorized to be unlawful: *R v Secretary of State for Foreign Affairs, ex p World Development Movement* [1995] 1 All ER 611.

Ministerial responsibility is discussed at length in chapter 3 below and will be considered in outline only here, where our focus is on the arrangements in the two Houses of Parliament for imposing ministerial responsibility.

(a) Individual ministerial responsibility to Parliament

2.80 Scrutiny of the executive depends to a large extent on the willingness of the executive to submit to scrutiny and to provide the House with the information that it seeks. A central convention of the British constitution is that ministers are individually responsible to Parliament for all that happens in their departments, and for their own policies. This convention is discussed in some detail in chapter 3 below. This means that they are expected to answer questions about those matters—they are accountable. Accountability is enforced through a range of procedures in Parliament, including debates, questions for oral or written answer, and select committee investigations. In each of these ministers will be expected to present their policies and justify them or to respond to criticisms and comments made by parliamentarians. In practice there are a number of questions which ministers will not answer. However, no coercive or penal parliamentary sanctions are available against ministers who decline to answer questions.

2.81 Shortly before the general election in 1997, in response to criticisms of the doctrines of ministerial responsibility to Parliament that had been made by the Scott inquiry into the Export of Defence-related Equipment and Dual-use Goods to Iraq and Related Prosecutions,[65] both Houses of Parliament passed resolutions on ministerial responsibility, asserting the Houses' position.[66]

2.82 The House of Commons' resolution[67] reads as follows:

> That, in the opinion of this House, the following principles should govern the conduct of Ministers of the Crown in relation to Parliament:
>
> (1) Ministers have a duty to Parliament to account, and be held to account, for the policies, decisions and actions of their Departments and Next Steps Agencies;
>
> (2) It is of paramount importance that Ministers give accurate and truthful information to Parliament, correcting any inadvertent error at the earliest opportunity. Ministers who knowingly mislead Parliament will be expected to offer their resignation to the Prime Minister;
>
> (3) Ministers should be as open as possible with Parliament, refusing to provide information only when disclosure would not be in the public interest, which should be decided in accordance with relevant statute and the Government's Code of Practice on Access to Government Information (Second Edition, January 1997);

---

[65] 1995–96 HC 115.

[66] *Hansard*, HC cols 1046–1047 (19 March 1997); *Hansard*, HL cols 1055–1062 (20 March 1997).

[67] The House of Lords resolution was slightly differently phrased.

(4) Similarly, Ministers should require civil servants who give evidence before Parliamentary Committees on their behalf and under their directions to be as helpful as possible in providing accurate, truthful and full information in accordance with the duties and responsibilities of civil servants as set out in the Civil Service Code (January 1996).

These resolutions focus on the duty of ministers to account. They say nothing about what a minister should do if something has gone wrong in his department.

There has as yet been no evaluation of whether the 1997 resolutions on minister- **2.83** ial responsibility have in practice made any difference to ministerial account- ability, but it is worth noting that the Speaker of the House of Commons from 1997 to 2001, Betty Boothroyd MP, protested from time to time about the unwillingness of ministers to be accountable to Parliament in various ways. For instance, many policy statements were (and still are) made, outside Parliament, to the Press or the BBC on the *Today* programme. Her objection was that Parliament's role was downgraded if ministers could avoid facing the House. In December 2001 the government undertook, in response to pressure from the Public Administration Select Committee, that ministers would be required to make policy announcements first to Parliament. The Select Committee ex- pressed the hope that this explicit acceptance of what was in fact a long under- stood requirement would 'help to tackle one of the main sources of public cynicism about politicians—the accusations of media manipulation, leak and spin that have been leveled at recent governments of both parties'.[68] It is under- standable that ministers should wish to obtain media coverage of their state- ments. As part of the modernization process that it has been undergoing since the 1997 general election, the House of Commons accepted a change to sitting hours so that ministerial statements made in Parliament could catch radio and television—and press-coverage.

(b) The Prime Minister's accountability to the House of Commons

There has been some disagreement about the Prime Minister's role in relation to **2.84** ministerial conduct and his own accountability to the Commons. Generally it is the departmental minister responsible for matters who has to answer questions and is responsible to Parliament. The Prime Minister does not himself have re- sponsibilities for matters for which other departmental ministers are accountable. The Prime Minister is Minister for the Civil Service, and has responsibility for various departments and teams from time to time, such as the Cabinet Office, the Office for Public Services Reform and the Forward Strategy Unit, but in the past Prime Ministers have been reluctant even to answer questions about these, leaving it to junior ministers in those departments or offices to do so.

---

[68] Public Administration Select Committee Second Report (2001–02 HC 439) para 5.

2.85 The position taken by recent Prime Ministers has been that it would breach an alleged constitutional convention set by their predecessors, that Prime Ministers do not appear before select committees, and it would blur ministerial accountability if a Prime Minister strayed into his Cabinet colleagues' responsibilities. Eventually, Prime Minister Blair agreed in a written answer in early 2002 to meet the Liaison Committee twice a year.[69] The first of these meetings took place on 16 July 2002.

2.86 The Prime Minister has sole responsibility for the Ministerial Code (previously known as *Questions of Procedure for Ministers*), which is revised by each new Prime Minister and, since 1992, has been republished after each general election. The revised version of the Code that was published in July 1997 incorporated the resolution on ministerial responsibility passed by the House of Commons in 1997, stressed that it was for the Prime Minister to determine whether a minister had acted in conformity with the Code in particular circumstance and drew out and made explicit the ethical principles and rules governing Cabinet government to form a separate section within the Code.

(c) Civil servants, ministers and ministerial responsibility

2.87 The civil service forms part of the Crown, and technically and from a legal point of view it has no separate existence from the government of the day.[70] Civil servants owe their duties to the Crown (in reality the Administration or executive of the day) and not to the minister for whom they work.[71]

2.88 Civil servants may be called before select committees, but they appear on behalf of and at the direction of their minister.[72] A minister may therefore control how, and whether, civil servants in the department answer questions. If a civil servant does not answer a question it will be for the minister to do so. The rider to this rule is that accounting officers—the permanent secretary in departments and chief executives in executive (*Next Steps*[73]) agencies as agency accounting officers—have personal legal responsibility for the financing and expenditure of their departments, for which they are accountable to the Comptroller and Auditor General and the National Audit Office, and to the Public Accounts Committee of the House of Commons.[74] If he is in doubt about the regularity of

---

[69] *Hansard*, HC col 465W (26 April 2002). This concession was made by the Prime Minister after rejecting these proposals on various grounds, and under sustained pressure from the Liaison Committee and the Public Administration Committee: see 2001–02 HC 439.

[70] See *Civil Service Management Code* (1993), s 4, Annex A, para 3; see also *Carltona v Commissioners of Works* [1943] 2 All ER 560.

[71] See Civil Service Code, para 2 (to be found as Annex A to the Civil Service Management Code).

[72] See *Departmental Evidence and Response to Select Committees* (Cabinet Office) para 37.

[73] See ch 3 below; and Efficiency Unit, *Improving Management in Government: The Next Steps* (1998).

[74] Exchequer and Audit Departments Act 1866, s 22.

expenditure or safeguarding public funds the accounting officer may ask for written instructions from the minister before he will take action.[75]

Apart from the special position of accounting officers, it is accepted that it is not for civil servants to take in public a different view of the public interest from that of their minister.[76] The Ministerial Code (2001) now makes plain that ministers must uphold the political impartiality of the Civil Service, and not ask civil servants to act in any way which would conflict with the Civil Service Code.[77]

2.89

In recent years ministers have claimed that they are responsible—and therefore obliged to take the blame if things go wrong—only for their policies, and that others, notably the chief executives of agencies in their departments, are responsible for operational or administrative matters. Ministers accept a duty to give an account to Parliament of operational matters—indeed they assert the exclusive right to give such an account and deny civil servants the right to do so save on their behalf and at their direction.[78] They also accept that they are under a duty to put things right if they have gone wrong. But they have been reluctant to accept blame for operational errors in their departments or agencies for which they are accountable.[79] More recently however, with the government's emphasis on the importance of service delivery, ministers have been readier to take responsibility for operational shortcomings.

2.90

Ministers are regarded by the House of Commons as being responsible not only for policy (in the sense that the formulation of policy is their job), but also for securing that the implementation of their policy, including operational matters, is properly organized, funded, etc. It is part of their job to secure that

2.91

---

[75] This happens only rarely. In *R v Secretary of State for Foreign Affairs, ex p World Development Movement* [1995] 1 WLR 386, DC, it was held that the spending of money from the Overseas Aid vote on the Pergau Dam in Malaysia had been unlawful, and in that case the Permanent Secretary as Accounting Officer had expressed the view to the minister that the project was an abuse of the aid programme as being an uneconomic project and not a sound development project.

[76] This view was accepted by the court in *R v Ponting* [1985] Crim LR 318.

[77] Ministerial Code (2001) paras 1(ix), 58.

[78] See *Departmental Evidence and Response to Select Committees* (Cabinet Office).

[79] eg, after the escape of prisoners from the high security Parkhurst prison in January 1995 (see *Review of Prison Service Security in England and Wales and the Escape from Parkhurst Prison on Tuesday 3rd January 1995* (Cm 3020, 1995)) the Home Secretary, Michael Howard, maintained that he was not responsible for operational matters such as ensuring security at prisons, and that since nothing had gone wrong with the things he was responsible for—the things it was his job to do—he had no duty to resign (*Hansard*, HC col 40 (10 January 1995)). After the general election in May 1997 the new Home Secretary, Jack Straw, announced that 'as a first step towards restoring proper ministerial responsibility' all parliamentary questions about the Prison Service would be answered by ministers and not by the Director General, adding that 'I regard it as essential that Ministers should answer personally to the House for what is done in our prisons and not leave the matter to their civil servants' (*Hansard*, HC col 396 (19 May 1997)).

these matters are attended to and they will be considered blameworthy if they do not do so.[80]

2.92 There is no clear line between the area of personal responsibility (in the sense of 'job') of ministers and their mere duty to account—explain—to Parliament what has happened in their departments. This factor undermines accountability. There is no ministerial job specification. The minister-made distinction between policy and operational or administrative matters is hard to apply in practice, since policy can be made at all kinds of level, and operational matters may be very policy laden. The Treasury and Civil Service Committee[81] proposed in 1994 a more useful distinction than one between policy and administration to base the accountability of executive agencies (see para 2.93 below), a more tangible distinction between decisions made by the minister of a parent Department, for which the minister is responsible, and decisions made by the Agency, for which he is accountable. We have already noted that ministers are also regarded as responsible for seeing to it that agencies are properly established, staffed and financed.

(d) Ministerial responsibility for agencies

2.93 A question when executive agencies were being established in departments from 1989 was whether the chief executives would be directly accountable to Parliament for them, or whether they would be in the same position as permanent secretaries and other civil servants in departments, answering in Parliament 'on behalf of their ministers and under their direction'.[82] The *Next Steps* report on which the executive agency arrangements were based[83] was not specific on the forms of accountability, except that it proposed that in hearings by the Public Accounts Committee the departmental accounting officer (who would normally be the permanent secretary in the department) should be accompanied by the manager of the agency. The accounting officer would answer questions about the framework within which the agency operated while the manager would answer questions about operations within the framework.[84]

2.94 The position where an individual MP raises questions about the conduct of these agencies is not entirely clear. The government's position remains that '[i]t is ministers who are accountable to Parliament for all that their Departments do includ-

---

[80] See eg Third Report from the Select Committee on the Parliamentary Commissioner for Administration (1994–95 HC 199) para 27 (on the subject of complaints about the operation of the Child Support Agency).

[81] Fifth Report, *The Role of the Civil Service* (1993–94 HC 27-I).

[82] *Departmental Evidence and Response to Select Committees* (formerly *Memorandum of Guidance for Officials Appearing before Select Committees* (1988), or the Osmotherly rules).

[83] Efficiency Unit, *Improving Management in Government: The Next Steps* (1998).

[84] ibid, Annex A, para 7.

ing the work of executive agencies'.[85] Agency framework documents make provision for responsibility, and the position varies from agency to agency. Broadly, if the Secretary of State receives a question about an agency in the department, he or she has to decide whether it is a matter to do with strategy or resources, in which case he or she deals with it, or an operational matter in which case it is passed on to the Chief Executive. The Chief Executive's reply is placed in the House of Commons library so that it is accessible both to all MPs and to the public. If the MP asking the question is dissatisfied with the Chief Executive's reply, he or she may table a further question to the minister, who will press the Chief Executive on the matter and in due course give a ministerial reply that is published in *Hansard*.

(e) Select committees

In the House of Commons there has been, since 1979, a system of departmentally related select committees,[86] so that each of the major ministerial departments is subject to scrutiny as to its administration and policy. In addition there are a number of functional, cross-cutting select committees, including the Committee for Public Accounts and the Public Administration Select Committee (to which the Commissioner for Public Administration—known as the Parliamentary Ombudsman—reports); and domestic select committees, including the Committee of Standards and Privileges, the Committee of Selection, and the Procedure Committee. Select committees are established at the start of each Parliament and members are appointed for the duration of the Parliament. **2.95**

The membership of the committees reflects the balance of the parties in the House, so that the government of the day has a majority on each committee. Proposals for membership of the committees are put to the House of Commons by the Committee of Selection for approval. In practice the members from each party are selected according to the rules of the parties, subject to agreement by their whips. **2.96**

The chairs of these committees are elected by the committee members, but prior to election the chairmanships are shared out by agreement through the usual channels between the parties, in approximate proportion to their representation in the House. By convention certain committees, including the Committee for Public Accounts, are chaired by Opposition members. **2.97**

In 2002 the House of Commons rejected a proposal by the Leader of the House and the Modernization Committee, which had been preceded by a recommendation of the Liaison Committee,[87] that committee membership should be determined by a **2.98**

[85] *The Civil Service: Continuity and Change* (1994) xx.
[86] See *Griffith and Ryle* (n 1 above) ch 11; Erskine May (n 1 above) ch 26; G Drewry, *The New Select Committees* (2nd edn, Oxford: OUP, 1989).
[87] *Shifting the Balance: Select Committees and the Executive* (1999–2000 HC 300).

committee of senior members of the House. This would have undermined the influence of the party whips and of the parties' own rules governing the selection of members for committee membership. The parties and the party whips therefore have considerable influence over appointments to these committees. In 2003 the House of Commons resolved that chairs of committees should be paid additional salaries of £12,500 year annum in recognition of the additional workload they bear, and to provide an alternative to government appointment as a career path for MPs. As a result the patronage of the whips has in fact become greater.

2.99 These committees make large numbers of reports to the House, many of them critical of government policy or of the way in which government is conducted, notwithstanding the influence of the whips over their composition and chairmanships. The government agreed in 1978 that it would respond to select committee reports, normally within two months of their publication. Some of these reports are debated, either in the Chamber of the House of Commons, for instance on the three Estimates Days each year, or in Westminster Hall, the 'parallel' chamber.[88] Some of these committees have shown great persistence in pressing the government to be more accountable to Parliament. For instance, the Public Administration Committee extracted agreement from the government that full answers should be given to parliamentary questions[89] and that ministerial statements should be made first to the House and not to the press.[90]

2.100 In May 2002 the House of Commons approved a set of core tasks for the select committees, as follows:

- to consider major policy initiatives;
- to consider the government's response to major emerging issues;
- to propose changes where evidence persuades the Committee that present policy requires amendment;
- to conduct pre-legislative scrutiny of draft Bills;
- to examine and report on main Estimates, annual expenditure plans and annual resource accounts;
- to monitor performance against targets in the public service agreements;
- to take evidence from each responsible departmental minister at least annually;
- to take evidence from independent regulators and inspectorates;
- to consider the reports of executive agencies;

---

[88] In 1999 the House of Commons agreed, as part of its modernization programme, that debates could be held in the Grand Committee Room off Westminster Hall in the Palace of Westminster as well as in the Chamber of the House (see Modernization Committee, Second Report (1998–99 HC 194)). The House of Lords reached a similar decision about holding debates in their Moses Room to take the committee stage of less controversial Bills.

[89] See eg 2001–02 HC 464, 1086.

[90] See further discussion at para 2.83 above.

- to consider, and if appropriate report on, major appointments made by a Secretary of State or other senior ministers;
- to examine treaties within their subject areas.[91]

Select committees may call for persons and papers. If such a call is not complied with the House (not the Committee itself) may make orders for attendance and production of documents. Ministers and civil servants, and other witnesses such as regulators, chief executives of other non-departmental public bodies and those working in private bodies, also appear before these committees. Members of the House cannot however be ordered to attend. Since ministers are members of one or other House it follows that they may not be formally ordered to attend or produce papers. Thus there is no formal sanction for refusal of co-operation and these matters are governed by political processes. **2.101**

(f) The House of Lords and scrutiny of the executive

In principle the executive is subject to scrutiny in the House of Lords as in the House of Commons. There are however a number of differences in the machinery for holding the executive to account in the second chamber. These flow largely from the different composition, role and functions of the House of Lords. Its members are not elected; it is a relatively non-partisan chamber with some expertise among its membership that is lacking in the House of Commons. The differences in arrangements also result from acceptance of the financial privileges of the House of Commons. **2.102**

In the House of Lords there is no system of departmentally related select committees charged with scrutiny of the executive and of other matters of public interest. However, there are a number of committees with particular expertise. These include: **2.103**

- the Science and Technology Committee;
- the Economic Affairs Committee;
- the Constitution Committee;
- the European Union Committee with its six sub-committees (discussed above).

Ad hoc House of Lords' committees on specialist subjects or a matter of general interest or a particular Bill are established from time to time (for instance, in the session 2001–2002, committees on specialist subjects investigated Stem-Cell Research, Animals in Scientific Procedures, and Religious Offences). Ad hoc committees may also be established to deal with domestic matters, such as parliamentary privileges and broadcasting. **2.104**

---

[91] These tasks were recommended for approval by the Modernization Committee: *Select Committees*, First Report of the Select Committee on Modernization of the House of Commons (2001–02 HC 221). This recommendation was approved by the House (*Hansard*, HC cols 648–730 (14 May 2002)).

2.105   In addition there are joint committees, notably the Joint Committee on Human Rights and the Joint Committee on House of Lords Reform.

(5) The Privileges of Parliament, Exclusive Cognizance, and Self-regulation

2.106   Both Houses of Parliament claim 'exclusive cognizance' of their proceedings and enjoy certain 'privileges'. They are self-regulating as regards both their procedures, and their proceedings. The courts accept that they have no jurisdiction over these matters.[92] So for instance the courts will not inquire into whether, in the course of the legislative process, the standing orders of each House were complied with, or whether misleading statements were made in one or other House. All that the courts will do is look at the Parliament Roll to determine whether an Act has been passed.[93]

(a) The legal basis and rationale for privilege

2.107   Parliamentary privilege forms part of the law and custom of Parliament (the lex et consuetudo parliamenti) which as a matter of common law is recognized by the courts. The financial privileges of the Commons have already been noted. Privileges and 'exclusive cognizance' formally belong to each House of Parliament, which may choose not to insist upon a privilege.[94]

2.108   Privilege has never been regarded as a perquisite of individual membership of Parliament. Privileges were originally developed to enable each House and its members to discharge their functions properly, including the giving of advice to the monarch. Privilege later (in the 17th century) came to provide protection for members from interference by the monarch—the Crown—in an executive capacity. This later history is reflected in the fact that at the commencement of every Parliament the Speaker, in the name and on behalf of the Commons, claims from the monarch the 'ancient undoubted rights and privileges', in particular freedom of speech in debate, freedom from arrest,[95] freedom of access to Her Majesty whenever occasion shall require,[96] and that the most favourable construction should be placed upon all their proceedings. The position has now been reached, however, that the Crown—the executive—has virtual control of the House of Commons through its majority. The House does not regard this

---

[92] *Bradlaugh v Gosset* [1883–84] 12 QBD 271, 278–286.

[93] *Edinburgh and Dalkeith Rly v Wauchope* (1842) 8 Cl & F 710; *Pickin v British Rlys Board* [1974] AC 765.

[94] This does not apply to the privilege granted by Art 9 of the Bill of Rights, which may not be waived unless waiver is provided for by statute: *Prebble v Television New Zealand Ltd* [1995] AC 321, PC. The position would change if clause 12 of the draft Corruption Bill 2003 were to be enacted. See further discussion at para 2.134 below.

[95] This freedom is of little significance and does not extend to criminal arrest.

[96] This is of purely formal significance though it is the basis on which members attend state ceremonies at which the sovereign is present.

control as an interference with its privileges. The early justifications for these privileges have gone. The modern rationales for privilege are that, in accordance with the constitutional theory implicit in the United Kingdom's constitutional arrangements, members ought to exercise their functions and their judgments as to the public interest free from molestation by non-members, including the press and pressure groups, and from limitations on their freedom that might be imposed by the courts.[97]

(b) The existence of a privilege

Although the courts will inquire into whether a claimed privilege exists and if so what is its scope, if satisfied that a privilege covers the case in hand they accept that Parliament has 'exclusive cognizance' of the matter and will decline jurisdiction over it. **2.109**

Both Parliament and the courts recognize that neither has the power to create new privileges, except by statute.[98] There have been a number of clashes between Parliament and the courts over the existence of privilege and the exclusive cognizance of parliamentary procedures. Proposals have been made by parliamentary committees from time to time to clarify the scope of privilege but these have not been implemented by legislation.[99] In practice however the boundaries of privilege and exclusive cognizance are now fairly well settled. **2.110**

(c) Freedom of speech

The most important privilege in modern conditions is freedom of speech. By Article 9 of the Bill of Rights 1688 '. . . the freedom of speech and debates or proceedings in Parlyament ought not to be impeached or questioned in any Court or Place out of Parliament'. There is thus an additional statutory basis for the privilege of free speech. **2.111**

The scope of 'proceedings in Parliament' for the purpose of the privilege of free speech has not been authoritatively or formally defined. Erskine May states that it is 'some formal action, usually a decision, taken by the House in its collective capacity'.[100] This extends to the whole process leading up to a decision, including debates in which members participate. Proceedings in Parliament include the tabling of parliamentary questions, things done and said by a member in the **2.112**

---

[97] The two Houses of Parliament are specifically excluded from HRA 1998, s 6, which provides that it is unlawful for a public authority to act incompatibly with Convention rights. The courts may not therefore entertain an allegation that the House has acted in breach of Convention rights.

[98] *Stockdale v Hansard* (1839) 3 St Tr (NS) 723.

[99] eg, Report of the Commons Select Committee on Parliamentary Privilege (1967–68 HC 34) paras 80–92; Second Report of the Joint Committee on Parliamentary Publications of Proceedings in Parliament (1969–70 HL 109, HC 261) paras 12–34; Committee of Privileges (1976–77 HC 417) paras 7–8; Report of the Joint Committee on Parliamentary Privilege (1998–99 HC 214).

[100] Erskine May (n 1 above) 95.

exercise of his functions in a committee or in the house, or undertaken in the course of parliamentary business.[101]

(d) Regulation of free speech by the Houses of Parliament

2.113   The privilege of free speech protects members of the two Houses from outside control. It also protects witnesses giving evidence to parliamentary committees. But the House itself imposes certain limits on the freedom of speech of members. These include prohibition of the use of 'unparliamentary language'. Many of these restraints are informally enforced, through the power of the Speaker to control proceedings in the Chamber. Others are provided for in the MPs' Code of Conduct, adopted in 1996,[102] which prohibits, among other things, paid advocacy by MPs and the paid asking of parliamentary questions. These rules are formally enforced through the disciplinary procedures of the Committee for Standards and Privileges and the Chamber, assisted and advised by the Parliamentary Commissioner for Standards (see paras 2.131–2.132 below). For instance, paid advocacy on behalf of any outside body or individual is prohibited and breach of this prohibition would be subject to the House of Commons' own self-regulatory disciplinary procedures.[103]

(e) Privilege, free speech and the courts

2.114   The courts have had to interpret the phrase 'proceedings in Parliament' where Article 9 of the Bill of Rights is relied upon in litigation by a party seeking to have evidence excluded. The courts form their own view as to what is or is not a proceeding in Parliament and do not consider themselves bound by the opinions of either House on the matter.[104] They may therefore come into conflict with the Houses. In *Pepper v Hart*[105] the Appellate Committee of the House of Lords held by a majority that it had the power to look at reports of parliamentary debates to determine the meaning of a statutory provision if the words of the Act were ambiguous or absurd or, given a literal interpretation, produced a perverse meaning. The Attorney-General,[106] on behalf of the House of Commons, claimed that for

---

[101] See eg *Rivlin v Bilainkin* [1953] 1 QB 485; Report from the Select Committee on the Official Secrets Act (the Duncan Sandys case) (1938–39 HC 146).

[102] See para 2.123 below.

[103] (1994–95) CJ 551. A resolution to this effect was passed in response to the first report of the Committee on Standards in Public Life (Cm 2850, 1995).

[104] *Bradlaugh v Gosset* [1883–84] 12 QBD 271, 281–282.

[105] [1992] 2 WLR 1032.

[106] One of the anomalies of the system is that the Attorney-General acts not only as legal adviser to the government but also as legal adviser to Parliament. This can place the Attorney-General in a difficult position where his professional duties lie in conflicting directions. In *Pepper v Hart* the interests of the government, a party to the litigation, and Parliament could have been in conflict. If the House of Commons itself had taken the view that its interests lay in the courts giving effect to its in-

the court to do so would amount to a breach of the privilege of free speech. The Appellate Committee rejected this view, claiming instead that reference to *Hansard* would enable the courts to give effect to, rather than to frustrate or call in question, the intention of Parliament. In *Wilson v First County Trust Ltd (No 2)*[107] the Speaker of the House of Commons and the Clerk of the Parliaments intervened to raise the issue whether it would be contrary to Article 9 for the courts to refer to *Hansard* when determining whether a statutory provision was incompatible with the Convention rights set out in the HRA 1998. The Appellate Committee held that it would not be contrary to Article 9 for the courts to do so in order to obtain background information to enable them to determine whether there was a legitimate policy objective in a provision that was on the face of it an interference with a Convention right, or whether the provision in question satisfied the proportionality test.[108]

Clause 12 of the draft Corruption Bill that was published in March 2003 for pre-legislative scrutiny provided that 'no enactment or rule of law preventing proceedings in Parliament being impeached or questioned in any court or place out of Parliament is to prevent any evidence being admissible in proceeding for a corruption offence'. If this provision were to be enacted then the protection afforded by Article 9 and parliamentary privilege would no longer apply in such cases.   **2.115**

(f) Privilege in defamation cases

Article 9 and the law of parliamentary privilege extend to 'privilege' in defamation cases, in which MPs are immune from action for defamation for statements made in Parliament. This common law privilege in defamation cases extends beyond what would be regarded by the House of Commons itself as 'proceedings in Parliament' attracting privilege. For instance, it has been held that a communication by an MP to the Law Society of a constituent's complaint about a solicitor's firm was protected by qualified privilege when the solicitor in question sued the MP for defamation, because MPs have an interest in receiving and following up complaints about the conduct of a public official—solicitors being in some respects public officials.[109] The ECtHR held in *A v UK*,[110] in which an MP speaking in the House of Commons' chamber had accused a named person   **2.116**

---

tentions, then reference to *Hansard* would have been in the interests of House of Commons as it saw them. The interests of the taxpayer were in conflict with those of government. In the days before the start of the war in Iraq in March 2003 the Attorney-General presented a summary of his view as to the legality of any attack on Iraq to the House of Commons in his capacity as legal adviser to the government. Although there is a Legal Services Office headed by Speaker's Counsel in the House of Commons, this does not appear to be regarded as an authoritative source of advice on such matters.

[107] [2003] UKHL 40; The Times, 11 July 2003.
[108] See, eg, *per* Lord Nicholls, ibid at [62]–[67]; see further ch 7 below.
[109] *Beach v Freeson* [1972] QB 14.
[110] *A v UK* (2003) 13 BHRC 623.

of being 'a neighbour from hell', that the fact that Article 9 denies claimants the right to sue for defamation by a MP in the course of proceedings in Parliament does not constitute a breach of the right under Article 6 ECHR of access to an independent and impartial tribunal in the determination of a person's civil rights.[111] The ECtHR upheld the immunity on the ground that it pursued a legitimate aim of protecting free speech in Parliament and maintaining the separation of powers between the legislature and the judiciary,[112] and that it did not impose a disproportionate restriction on the right of access to courts under Article 6.[113]

2.117 By Defamation Act 1996, s 13, it was provided that where, in defamation proceedings, the conduct of a person[114] in or in relation to proceedings in Parliament is in issue, that person may waive the protection of Article 9 of the Bill of Rights of 1688 (or other parliamentary privilege) which prevents any proceedings in Parliament from being impeached or questioned outside of Parliament. Where this protection has been waived evidence may be given and findings made about the person's conduct, and this will not be regarded as infringing the privilege of either House. However, the waiver does not remove the member's protection from legal liability.[115] This provision was passed in response to a particular problem, and the amendment was moved in the House of Lords by one of the Law Lords, Lord Hoffmann, at the request of Lord Mackay of Clashfern, the Lord Chancellor at the time. There had been no consultation process or consideration of the constitutional implications of such a measure before this major departure from the principle of Article 9 of the Bill of Rights 1688 was made. The Joint Committee on Parliamentary Privilege recommended that s 13 be repealed and that it should be for the House and not for the MP to decide, in the interests of justice, whether the privilege should be waived.[116]

(6) Contempt and the Penal Jurisdiction of Parliament

2.118 The House has the power to punish those who offend it for contempt of Parliament,

---

[111] Parliament is excluded from the duty to respect Convention rights in UK domestic law by HRA 1998, s 6, so such a claimant could not succeed in an action in the UK courts.

[112] *A v UK* 13 BHRC 623 at [77].

[113] ibid at [83].

[114] The person will normally be a member of Parliament.

[115] This provision was passed to enable Neil Hamilton MP to sue The Guardian newspaper for defamation when the latter had stated that Hamilton had accepted money in return for asking parliamentary questions. The action had originally been struck out since parliamentary privilege would have prevented the defendant from relying on evidence of proceedings in Parliament to substantiate his defence and thus Hamilton would have been unable to vindicate himself. After s 13 was passed, Hamilton waived privilege and successfully applied for the trial of the action to be permitted. However the trial did not take place, for other reasons. Hamilton subsequently sued Mohammed Al Fayed for defamation, waiving parliamentary privilege under s 13 of the Defamation Act 1996. The jury found for the defendant.

[116] First Report of the Joint Committee on Parliamentary Privilege (HL Paper 43-1 and HC 214-1, 1998–99) paras 68, 69. See discussion of clause 12 of the draft Corruption Bill 2003, para 2.134 below.

and it defines for itself whether particular actions amount to contempts. Contempt has been defined as '. . . any act or omission which obstructs or impedes either House of Parliament in the performance of its functions or which obstructs or impedes any Member or Officer in the discharge of his duty'.[117]

The following have been found to amount to contempts:[118]

2.119

- Misconduct by members, including deliberately misleading the House, or acceptance of bribes.
- Premature disclosure of committee proceedings or of evidence given to a committee.
- Attempting to intimidate members, including by threatening to stop public investment in a constituency if the member opposes certain policies; or inciting members of the public to telephone a member and thus to harass him; molesting members and publishing material reflecting on members' conduct.
- Seeking to punish a member for his actions in Parliament, for instance by terminating a sponsorship agreement.

(a) Penalties for contempt, breach of privilege or breach of standards of conduct

The penalties that may be imposed by the House of Commons on those found to have acted in breach of privilege, in breach of the code of conduct, or in contempt of the House include suspension from the service of the House for a period, reprimand and admonition. The power to impose a penalty of imprisonment is obsolete. The Committee on Standards in Public Life recommended the introduction of a power to fine without suspension from the service of the House. This was accepted in principle by the Committee on Standards and Privileges,[119] but it has not yet been implemented. It may require legislation. The usual result of a finding that a member has breached the standards expected is an apology from the member. The member then withdraws from the House, and the report of the Committee for Standards and Privileges is debated. In serious cases the member is suspended, with loss of pay, from the service of the House for a period of several weeks.

2.120

By way of example of the operation of the penal system, in February 2003 an MP was found by the Committee on Standards and Privileges of the House of Commons to have claimed additional costs allowances totalling some £90,000 to which he was not entitled.[120] This was both an improper use of allowances and a breach of the Code of Conduct of the House of Commons. The MP repaid the sum, and apologized to the House, stating that the claim had been made negligently.

2.121

---

[117] Erskine May (n 1 above) ch 9.
[118] ibid ch 8; *Griffith and Ryle* (n 1 above) paras 3-024–3-025.
[119] Eighth Report of the Committee on Standards and Privileges (2002–03 HC 403) para 50.
[120] Third Report of the Select Committee on Standards and Privileges, *Complaints against Mr Michael Trend* (2002–03 HC 435).

The House imposed a two-week period of suspension from the services of the House. In a Memorandum[121] submitted to the Committee the Parliamentary Commissioner for Standards expressed the view that false claims for allowances could be criminal offences under ss 15 and 16 of the Theft Act 1968, for which a member could be prosecuted and which would not be covered by parliamentary privilege.

2.122   In general the House exercises its penal jurisdiction as sparingly as possible and only when satisfied that to do so is essential in order to provide reasonable protection for the House, its members or its officers from such improper obstruction or attempt at or threat of obstruction causing or likely to cause substantial interference with the performance of their respective functions.[122] To the extent that allegations are criminal in nature, as with bribery or false claims for parliamentary allowances, or that the penalties involve interferences with the civil rights or obligations of members (as where a member is suspended without the pay to which he would normally be entitled), the penal powers of the House do not appear to meet the requirements of Article 6 ECHR that a person should have access to an independent and impartial tribunal in such cases.

(7) Self-regulation, Standards of Conduct and Members' Interests

2.123   An aspect of the exclusive cognizance that each House asserts over its own proceedings is the setting and regulation of standards of conduct in each House. As we have noted, the courts decline jurisdiction over disputes relating to parliamentary proceedings and conduct.[123] The standards of conduct expected of members of the House of Commons were not codified until a Code of Conduct was adopted by the House in 1996. Standards had been elaborated over the years in the form of resolutions of the House, passed after reports from the Committee for Privileges on complaints about the conduct of members.[124] Thus, for instance, bribery of an MP has been regarded by the House of Commons as 'a high crime and misdemeanour' since the 18th century. Bribery of an MP or acceptance of a bribe by an MP has long been a contempt of Parliament punishable by the House. Bribery of an MP, or acceptance of a bribe by an MP, are not however crimes for which either a member or a person bribing a member can be prosecuted under the Public Bodies Corrupt Practices Act 1889 and the Prevention of Corruption Act 1906, because neither House is regarded as a public body and nor are members agents within the meaning in those Acts.[125] In some cases such a prosecution

---

[121] Third Report of the Select Committee on Standards and Privileges (n 120 above), Appendix.
[122] Report of the Privileges Committee (1976–77 HC 417); (1977–78) CJ 170.
[123] *Bradlaugh v Gosset* [1883–84] 12 QBD 271.
[124] See eg the WJ Brown case (1946–47 HC 118); *Hansard*, HC col 284 (15 July 1947); the National Union of Mineworkers case (1974–75 HC 634).
[125] See Joint Committee on Parliamentary Privilege (1998–99 HL 214) para 135.

would also call into question the freedom of speech and debates and proceedings, which are protected by Article 9 of the Bill of Rights and parliamentary privilege.[126]

Each House has devised its own system for the regulation of conduct. These include provisions for the registration and declaration of interests, prohibition of certain kinds of interest, and disqualification of members from participation in proceedings if they have certain interests. Many of these provisions have been introduced only in response to sustained pressure from the press, the Committee on Standards in Public Life, and other quarters. The House of Commons has not been willing to regulate standards of conduct without outside pressure. **2.124**

(a) Reforming self-regulation: the background

After a series of scandals about the offering of sums of money to MPs in exchange for their asking parliamentary questions, and other concerns about the standards of conduct of MPs and others in public life in the early to mid-1990s, a new stricter system of self-regulation was introduced in the House of Commons. This was done in response to recommendations made by the Committee on Standards in Public Life which had been appointed to inquire into standards and make recommendations in 1995. The Committee formulated 'Seven Principles of Public Life', namely selflessness, integrity, objectivity, accountability, openness, honesty, and leadership.[127] It recommended that the House of Commons should adopt a code of conduct, and that a person of independent standing should be appointed to investigate allegations of breach of standards of conduct and report to the Committee for Privileges. **2.125**

The House broadly accepted the recommendations. It replaced the Committee of Privileges and the Committee of Members' Interests with a new Committee on Standards and Privileges, adopted a code of conduct[128] which incorporated the seven principles, and appointed a Parliamentary Commissioner for Standards. The register of interests which had been in existence for some years was put on a formal basis and all MPs were required to register a wider range of interests. **2.126**

These reforms responded to a small number of cases of members accepting payment for parliamentary services, highlighted by some MPs accepting payment for asking questions in Parliament. **2.127**

---

[126] But cf *R v Greenaway* (Buckley J, Central Criminal Court, 25 June 1992, noted by AW Bradley at [1998] PL 356). Buckley J ruled that parliamentary privilege was no bar to a prosecution of an MP for taking a bribe under the common law.
[127] First Report of the Committee on Standards in Public Life (Cm 2850, 1995).
[128] 1995–96 HC 688.

(b) The Register of Interests

2.128 MPs were first required by resolutions of the House of Commons of 22 May 1974 to register their interests in the Commons' Register of Members' Interests, and to declare any interests they may have when speaking in debates or other proceedings in the House of Commons, or communicating with other members or ministers.[129] The obligation exists whether or not the interest in question has been registered.

2.129 In 1996 in the aftermath of allegations of sleaze and the first report of the Committee on Standards and Privileges,[130] a new Register of Members' Interests was introduced, imposing wider obligations of registration, including the depositing of consultancy contracts to which a member was a party and information about remuneration received for outside activities. The Parliamentary Commissioner for Standards was given responsibility, among other things, for advising MPs on their obligations in relation to registration of interests, maintaining the register, and investigating complaints of failure to register interests. Failure to declare or to register an interest may be regarded as a contempt of the House.

2.130 The formalization of the standards and the tightening up of registration requirements spawned a large number of complaints, mostly about failure by MPs, including some ministers, to register all the interests that they were required to register. Some of these complaints were trivial and were made for party political reasons in a tit for tat battle between the parties. The Committee for Standards and Privileges now requires members who have complaints to make them informally to the person alleged to have breached the rules before they are referred to the Parliamentary Commissioner for Standards. The hope is that the parties themselves and their whips will seek to stop such complaints being made by their members in a partisan spirit.

(c) The Parliamentary Commissioner for Standards

2.131 The first Parliamentary Commissioner for Standards was appointed in 1996 on the recommendation of the Committee on Standards in Public Life that 'a person of independent standing' should be appointed. The position is not statutory. The Commissioner is protected by parliamentary privilege. His role is to investigate the conduct of members and to report directly to the Standards and Privileges Committee, 'a part of Parliament's own process'.[131] The Parliamentary Commissioner for Standards advises members about the Register of Interests and

---

[129] See also the report of the Select Committee on Members' Interests (1969–70 HC 57).
[130] First Report of the Committee on Standards and Privileges, *Complaint of Alleged Improper Pressure Brought to Bear on the Select Committee on Members Interests in 1994* (1996–97 HC 88).
[131] *R v Parliamentary Commissioner for Standards, ex p Mohammed Al Fayed* [1998] 1 WLR 669.

makes findings of fact where complaints are referred to him, though these findings are not formally binding on the Committee or on the House of Commons. Nor are any views the Commissioner expresses, or conclusions he reaches about the guilt of members accused of breaching the code of conduct, binding on the Committee or on the House, though a finding of innocence is unlikely to be rejected by them.

There is a lack of clarity about the role of the Parliamentary Commissioner for Standards. The second Parliamentary Commissioner for Standards[132] was unpopular with many MPs, partly because of differing interpretations of the role. The Commissioner considered herself to be there in part to reassure the public that complaints were properly investigated and that standards were being upheld, whereas many MPs considered the Commissioner to be a servant of the House, advising and assisting MPs, the Committee for Standards and Privileges and the House as a whole. When her three-year period of office expired the post was advertised and she was invited to apply for it. She decided not to do so. The circumstances led to concern about the 'independence' of the position and proposals for reform, for instance that the Commissioner should be regarded as an office holder and not an employee of the House.[133] The Committee on Standards and Privileges accepted this proposal 'as representing a desirable clarification of what is already perceived to be the Commissioner's actual status'.[134] The House of Commons agreed in June 2003 that the Parliamentary Commissioner for Standards' independence should be enhanced by appointment for a non-renewable period of five years. However neither the Committee on Standards in Public Life nor the Standards and Privileges Committee has followed the GRECO recommendation (see para 2.141 below) that the Parliamentary Commissioner for Standards should be put on a statutory basis.

2.132

(d) Fairness issues

There have been concerns over the fairness of investigations of complex contested cases of breaches of standards of conduct by the Parliamentary Commissioner for Standards and about the role of the Committee for Standards and Privileges and the House of Commons in making findings of guilt. Some MPs under investigation have been unwilling to co-operate with the Commissioner and have complained that the procedure was not fair to them. These complaints have given rise to proposals for reform, for instance by giving a right of appeal to or review by a court or other independent tribunal against a finding by the House or the

2.133

---

[132] Mrs Elizabeth Filkin, Parliamentary Commissioner for Standards from 1999–2002.
[133] This was proposed by the Committee on Standards in Public Life in its Eighth Report (Cm 5663, 2002).
[134] 2002–03 HC 403, para 76.

Committee for Standards and Privileges.[135] Such proposals have not found favour either with the Committee on Standards in Public Life or with the House of Commons. In June 2003 the House of Commons decided that the Parliamentary Commissioner for Standards should have the power (and the duty, if so requested by the Committee for Standards and Privileges) to appoint an Investigatory Panel consisting of the Commissioner as chair, plus a legally qualified assessor and a member of the House appointed by the Speaker, to assist him in establishing the facts relevant to the investigation.[136]

(e) Bribery of MPs: removal of immunity from prosecution

2.134   A number of official reports have recommended that bribery of an MP, and acceptance of a bribe by an MP, should be criminalized.[137] In the 2002–2003 session of Parliament a draft Corruption Bill which would, among other things, bring bribery of an MP within the statutory offence of corruption, was published for pre-legislative scrutiny in Parliament.[138] (It has already been noted that clause 12 of the draft Corruption Bill 2003 would remove the bar on the giving of evidence of proceedings in Parliament in prosecutions for corruption.) The Bill proposed the replacing of the common law offence of bribery and existing statutory provisions on corruption with statutory offences. The corrupt conferring of an advantage or the corrupt obtaining of an advantage by any person would be criminalized.[139] Advantages (eg, payments) would be corrupt if they result in a person doing something in return for the advantage which should be done only for the public (which MPs are supposed to do). The present difficulty in prosecuting MPs for corruption would be removed if a Corruption Act were passed.

(f) Self-regulation in the House of Lords

2.135   The House of Lords enjoys broadly the same privileges (except the financial privileges) as the House of Commons, together with the power to deal with contempts and the right to exclusive cognizance of its own proceedings. There are however

---

[135] The procedures for dealing with parliamentary privilege and conduct have been considered by a number of parliamentary bodies (see Report of the Joint Committee on Parliamentary Privilege (1998–99 HL 43, HC 214); Fifth Report of the Committee on Standards and Privileges (2000–01 HC 267)) and the matter has been revisited by the Committee on Standards in Public Life, Sixth Report (Cm 4557, 2000), Eighth Report (Cm 5663, 2002).

[136] *Hansard*, HC col 1257 (26 June 2003).

[137] See Report of the Salmon Commission on standards of conduct in public life (Cmnd 6524, 1976); Law Commission, *Legislating the Criminal Code: Corruption* (Law Com No 248, 1997); Fifth Report of the Committee on Standards and Privileges (2000–01 HC 267); Committee on Standards in Public Life, Sixth Report (2000); Home Office, *Clarification of the law relating to the Bribery of Members of Parliament* (discussion paper, December 1996); Home Office, *Raising Standards and Upholding Integrity: The Prevention of Corruption* (Cm 4759, June 2000).

[138] See draft Corruption Bill, Home Office (March 2003). However, no Corruption Bill was promised in the Queen's Speech in November 2003 for the 2003–04 session of Parliament.

[139] Clauses 1 and 2.

few formal rules or sanctions in the second chamber: the House is said to thrive on self-discipline. Formally there is a power to imprison indefinitely, but this has not been used for 100 years and the Joint Committee on Parliamentary Privilege recommended that it should be abolished. There is also a power to fine, which has not been used for 200 years. The Joint Committee recommended that it should be confirmed as an available sanction. There appears to be no power to suspend or expel a member. In effect the possibility of 'naming and shaming' acts as an effective deterrent in the House of Lords and would be regarded as a strong penalty if a member were to be found in breach of the rules.

There have been very few problems to do with privilege, interests and conduct in the House of Lords compared to those in the House of Commons. This is no doubt to do with the relatively non-partisan ethos of the House, its lack of power in relation to financial matters, its relatively weak position in relation to government, and the ethos of personal honour. On the other hand, since the 1970s lobbyists have given increasing attention to the House of Lords as a chamber where minority interests may be given a voice, something which raises issues to do with the regulation of relations between outside bodies and individual members of the second chamber, the registration of interests and clarity about the role of that chamber. **2.136**

Historically conduct in the House has been ruled largely by the principles of personal honour and that members should not accept financial inducements in relation to their activities in the House. There was little formal regulation or articulation of standards of conduct until 1996. From 1996 a Register of Interests was established. In 2001, in response to a report of the Committee on Standards in Public Life,[140] the registration requirements were tightened. The Register of Interests is maintained by a Registrar appointed by the Clerk of the Parliaments. The Registrar reports to the Committee for Privileges' sub-committee on Lords' Interests, on which three Law Lords serve. **2.137**

The House of Lords' Code of Conduct came into force on 1 April 2002. It requires all members of the House in receipt of a writ of summons, who are not on leave of absence, to register all relevant interests. Members are further required to observe the seven principles of public life; to comply with the Code of Conduct; to act on their personal honour; not to accept any financial inducement as an incentive or reward for exercising parliamentary duties; and to comply with the 'no paid advocacy' rule.[141] The Code also provides that: 'In the conduct of their parliamentary duties, Members . . . shall resolve any conflict between their personal interest and the public interest in favour of the public interest.' **2.138**

---

[140] Seventh Report, *Standards of Conduct in the House of Lords* (Cm 4903). The Committee did not base its recommendations on concern about standards, but on the basis that regulation of standards was expected by the public.
[141] At para 4.

2.139   The second chamber has not appointed an equivalent of the House of Commons' Parliamentary Commissioner for Standards, or any independent adviser. Any potential complaints should normally be raised in a private communication with the member concerned, and if the complainant wishes to pursue a complaint he or she should refer it directly to the sub-committee on Lords' Interests, through its chairman, and not via the floor of the House. An appeal lies from decisions of the sub-committee to the full Committee for Privileges, and the conclusions of the sub-committee and the full committee are to be reported to the House.

2.140   Thus the procedures and mechanisms for dealing with complaints of breach of privilege or breaches of duties to register interests or comply with the code of conduct and the like are different in the House of Lords from those in the House of Commons. They are much lighter in touch and less formalized, and the fairness of procedures for dealing with any complaints is greater than in the Commons.

(g) The future of self-regulation

2.141   The system of self-regulation in the UK Parliament was criticized by the Council of Europe's Group of States against Corruption (GRECO) project in 1999. It expressed concern at the continuing self-regulation pursued by the UK Parliament and proposed that MPs should not be exempt from the law for corruption offences, that the registration of interests system should be tightened up, that the Parliamentary Commissioner for Standards and his powers should be put on a statutory basis with the power to compel the production of information and attendance, and that codes of conduct should also be put on a statutory basis.[142] The draft Corruption Bill, if passed, would deal with some of these concerns but there is as yet no move towards placing the Parliamentary Commissioner for Standards on a statutory footing, or introducing a similar position for the House of Lords.

C. The Legislative Supremacy of Parliament and its Limits

(1) The Principle of Parliamentary Supremacy

(a) Origins of the principle

2.142   Discussion of the legislative supremacy of Parliament[143] must begin with the distinction between the concepts of supremacy and sovereignty. The word 'supremacy'

---

[142] GRECO, *First Evaluation Round: Evaluation Report on the United Kingdom* (Council of Europe, 2001); see also A Doig, 'Sleaze Fatigue: An Inauspicious Year for Democracy' (2002) 55 Parliamentary Affairs 389.

[143] As to which see in particular AW Bradley and KD Ewing, *Constitutional and Administrative Law* (12th edn, London: Longman, 1997) ch 4; P Jackson and P Leopold (eds), *O Hood Phillips and Jackson: Constitutional and Administrative Law* (8th edn, London: Sweet and Maxwell, 2001) ch 2, and A Le Sueur and M Sunkin, *Public Law* (London: Longman, 1997) ch 5.

connotes a body which is hierarchically above all others or which has an authority greater than that of its rivals. 'Sovereignty', on the other hand, suggests omnipotence, the ability to do anything.[144] John Austin famously proclaimed the theory that in all developed legal systems there existed a sovereign institution which possessed an unlimited power to make law.[145] Although the truth of this statement may be challenged,[146] there is no doubt that it has over the ages stimulated informed discussion of the British constitution, especially the writings of Albert Venn Dicey, whose attention to and reverence for the principle earned him the reputation of father of the theory of the supremacy of Parliament at Westminster.[147]

According to classical legal theory enshrined in the, admittedly unwritten, consti- **2.143**
tution of the United Kingdom, its Parliament (which consists of the House of Commons, the House of Lords and the monarch) is legally both supreme and sovereign in the above senses. In other words, what Parliament at Westminster has enacted must always be obeyed by the courts; there is no power of judicial review over primary legislation.[148] In addition, Parliament can in theory make law on any subject which it pleases and there are no 'fundamental' laws which restrict its powers. The only negative aspect of these principles, although it has a positive side too, is that Parliament cannot fetter itself for the future and cannot bind its own successor Parliaments. This is the so-called 'continuing' theory of parliamentary supremacy. In Dicey's often-quoted words, Parliament possesses:

> [U]nder the English constitution, the right to make or unmake any law whatever;
> and further that no person or body is recognised by the law of England as having a
> right to override or set aside the legislation of Parliament.[149]

This is an unusual, perhaps unique, combination of qualities since the parlia- **2.144**
ments of most modern states are limited by the terms of the national constitution which gives them authority.[150] Yet, in the language of Kelsen it represents the 'grundnorm' of the legal system in the United Kingdom.[151] In a seminal article

---

[144] The concept of sovereignty is also applied to states as a matter of international law and refers to their freedom of action or independence.

[145] John Austin, *The Province of Jurisprudence Determined* (London: Weidenfeld and Nicholson, 1954). See also N MacCormick, 'Beyond the Sovereign State' (1993) 56 MLR 1.

[146] It is, for example, difficult to apply to a federal state.

[147] AV Dicey, *Law of the Constitution* (10th edn, London: Macmillan, 1959).

[148] This theory has had to be radically tempered in relation to EU law and is also becoming eroded in other situations, as discussed below. In the US, the Supreme Court asserted the power to declare federal legislation unconstitutional, and thus effectively to strike it down, in *Marbury v Madison* (1803) 1 Cranch 137.

[149] Dicey (n 147 above) 39–40.

[150] For illustrations, see *Bribery Commissioner v Ranasinghe* [1965] AC 172 and *Harris v Minister of the Interior* [1952] (2) AD 428.

[151] cf N MacCormick, 'Does the United Kingdom Have a Constitution? Reflections on MacCormick v Lord Advocate' (1978) 29 Northern Ireland Legal Q 1.

published in 1955, Wade explained that the rule of judicial obedience to Acts of Parliament:

> is in one sense a rule of common law, but in another sense—which applies to no other rule of common law—it is the ultimate *political* fact upon which the whole system of legislation hangs . . . What Salmond calls the 'ultimate legal principle' is therefore a rule which is unique in being unchangeable by Parliament—it is changed by revolution, not by legislation; it lies in the keeping of the courts, and no Act of Parliament can take it from them.[152]

2.145 There are today however a number of brakes on the sovereignty of the Parliament of the United Kingdom, many practical but also some potentially legal ones; legal theory and political reality therefore by no means continue to march in step with one another. As will be discussed below, some modern commentators now go so far as to believe that Wade's 'revolution' has now taken place. The extent to which the supremacy of Parliament has been abridged, and the question of whether this abridgement is legal or merely practical, are discussed at paras 2.158 et seq below.

2.146 The struggle for ascendancy between the King and Parliament during the Middle Ages was discussed in chapter 1. The defining moment as regards the evolution of today's constitutional settlement was the Bill of Rights of 1688. To this document can be ascribed the principle of constitutional monarchy and a formal acceptance of Parliament's powers over the Crown. The year 1688 therefore marks the birth of the doctrine of the supremacy of Parliament at Westminster.

(b) Evidence of the principle

2.147 For the principles of parliamentary supremacy and sovereignty to be logically demonstrable as part of the law, as Wade pointed out, they must be unconditionally accepted by the courts. It would be of no avail for Parliament itself simply to proclaim such rules if they were not applied both in theory and practice. In Dicey's words, a law 'may be defined as "any rule which will be enforced by the courts"'.[153] This is also a practical manifestation of Hart's 'Rule of Recognition'[154] and it provides another example of the delicate balance which must be achieved between legislature and judiciary; just as in the case of statutory interpretation, democracy demands that Parliament's will be done but only the courts possess the practical power to ensure this result.

2.148 In fact, judicial acceptance of the ultimate authority of Parliament at Westminster has been so complete that the issue has rarely even been argued in modern times

---

[152] HWR Wade, 'The Legal Basis of Sovereignty' [1955] CLJ 172, 188–189. See also HWR Wade, 'Sovereignty and the European Communities' (1972) 88 LQR 1.
[153] Dicey (n 147 above) 40.
[154] See HLA Hart, *The Concept of Law* (2nd edn, Oxford: Clarendon Press, 1994), especially ch 6.

in an English court.[155] Even a limited assault on the doctrine was repelled by the House of Lords in *Pickin v British Rlys Board*[156] where Lord Simon of Glaisdale proclaimed:

> The system by which, in this country, those liable to be affected by general political decisions have some control over the decision-making is parliamentary democracy. Its peculiar feature in constitutional law is the sovereignty of Parliament. This involves that, contrary to what was sometimes asserted in the eighteenth century, and in contradistinction to some other democratic systems, the courts in this country have no power to declare enacted law to be invalid.[157]

The status of the doctrine has, however, been raised indirectly in relation to the way in which Parliament manifests its intention to amend an existing statute. The principle adopted by the court is that the latest expression of the parliamentary will is the one which prevails; in other words, the latest Act in time is the one which the courts will apply.[158] This principle applies where a later Act expressly amends or repeals an earlier Act. It also applies where a later Act is simply inconsistent with an earlier Act but without making any express reference to it; to the extent of the inconsistency, the courts hold that the later Act takes effect and impliedly repeals its predecessor.[159]

2.149

This has led to the question of whether Parliament can fetter itself for the future as to the way in which it must repeal or amend a statute; can it effectively prescribe express rather than implied repeal? This matter was raised in *Vauxhall Estates Ltd v Liverpool Corp*.[160] The Acquisition of Land (Assessment of Compensation) Act 1919 provided a scheme for the assessment of compensation where land was compulsorily acquired for public purposes. Its s 7(1) was an unusual provision which stated: 'The provisions of the Act or order by which the land is authorised to be acquired . . . shall, in relation to the matters dealt with in this Act, have effect subject to this Act, and so far as inconsistent with this Act those provisions shall cease to have or shall not have effect . . .'. Six years later, the Housing Act 1925 provided for the assessment of compensation in these cases on a different basis. The question for the Divisional Court was which Act should be used for the purpose of determining compensation. Counsel for the claimants, HA Hill, suggested ingeniously that the wording of s 7(1) of the 1919 Act precluded the possibility of the implied repeal of that Act; he argued that the sub-section did not

2.150

---

[155] There were unsuccessful attempts to disprove the supremacy of Parliament in *R v Jordan* [1967] Crim LR 483 and *Cheney v Conn* [1968] 1 WLR 242. Cf *Thoburn v Sunderland City Council* [2002] EWHC 195; [2003] QB 151.

[156] [1974] AC 765.

[157] ibid 798.

[158] This principle is sometimes referred to by the judges by the Latin maxim: 'Leges posteriores priores contrarias abrogant'.

[159] *Dean of Ely v Bliss* (1842) 5 Beav 574.

[160] [1932] 1 KB 733.

purport to bind the legislature absolutely for the future but merely that it demanded express words for the repeal of the 1919 Act. Two members of the Divisional Court did not decide whether the words of s 7(1) were intended to govern future statutes and the third, Avory J, concluded that it was restricted to existing Acts. Nevertheless, the Court held that, even on the assumption that the 1919 Act did intend to govern future cases, it could not preclude its own implied repeal. Furthermore, because of the inconsistency between its own provisions and those of the 1919 Act, the 1925 Act did in fact impliedly repeal the relevant sections of the 1919 Act.

2.151 Mr Hill took the opportunity to try out his argument once more two years later when the same issue came before the Court of Appeal in *Ellen Street Estates Ltd v Minister of Health*.[161] The Court of Appeal unhesitatingly upheld the decision of the Divisional Court, Maugham LJ stating:

> The Legislature cannot, according to our constitution, bind itself as to the form of subsequent legislation, and it is impossible for Parliament to enact that in a subsequent statute dealing with the same subject-matter there can be no implied repeal. If in a subsequent Act Parliament chooses to make it plain that the earlier statute is being to some extent repealed, effect must be given to that intention just because it is the will of the Legislature.[162]

2.152 The question of whether Parliament can ever legally bind itself has also been raised in relation to the closely-related issue of the procedure which must be adopted for the enactment of valid legislation—the so-called 'manner and form'[163] of legislation. There is a real logical problem here since Parliament's authority cannot be assured unless the authenticity of its Acts can be verified; Parliament must therefore in some sense commit itself to a mandatory procedure.[164] On the other hand, if restrictions on manner and form are to be permitted, not only do they disobey the rule that one Parliament cannot bind its successor but they also provide a back door by which substantive restrictions on the legislative capacity of Parliament may enter: if legislation on a particular topic is made more difficult to enact than hitherto, Parliament's authority to pass it is pro tanto limited.

2.153 It was seen in chapter 1 that the British courts steadfastly refuse to question the procedure by which legislation has passed through the Westminster Parliament and that they will simply accept as Acts those which appear as such on their face.[165]

---

[161] [1934] 1 KB 590.
[162] ibid 597.
[163] This expression hails from the Colonial Laws Validity Act 1865, s 5. See also *A-G for New South Wales v Trethowan* [1932] AC 526 and *Harris v Minister of the Interior* [1952] 1 TLR 1245.
[164] For an outstandingly clear analysis of the conflicting views expressed on this matter, see PP Craig, 'Sovereignty of the United Kingdom Parliament after *Factortame*' (1991) 11 Ybk of Eur L 221.
[165] *Edinburgh and Dalkeith Rly v Wauchope* (1842) 8 Cl & F 71; *Lee v Bude and Torrington Rly* (1871) LR 6 CP 576; *Pickin v British Rlys Board* [1974] AC 765; see paras 1.129 et seq above.

However, this is an inherently reactionary approach to take, since it implies that Parliament could never decide, with legal effect, to change its own procedures. It would seem logical to suppose that, provided that the rule of recognition was satisfied—in other words, that the judges accepted whatever new procedure was provided for by statute—a new 'manner and form' for legislation could become effective.[166] This is sometimes referred to as the 'self-embracing' view of parliamentary sovereignty. It follows that serious controversy can be anticipated in the event that Parliament decides to change its procedures for the future by, for example, requiring a particularly stringent voting requirement or the consent of the public expressed through the medium of a referendum for legislation on a particular topic.

Perhaps the closest an English court has come to dealing with such a matter is to be found in *Manuel v A-G*.[167] Canadian Indian bands challenged the validity of the Canada Act 1982, on the ground that it breached s 4 of the Statute of Westminster 1931, which provides that no Act of the UK Parliament shall extend to a dominion unless it is expressly declared in that Act that that dominion has requested and consented to it. Although the Canada Act 1982 contained such a statement, it was alleged that this was insufficient to guarantee the Act's vires since the real consent of the dominion, pursuant to constitutional arrangements which had been in force for many years, required the consent of the Indian bands and this had not been obtained. The Court of Appeal proceeded on the assumption that Parliament 'can effectively tie the hands of its successors, if it passes a statute which provides that any future legislation on a specified subject shall be enacted only with certain specified consents' which it described as 'of great interest and fundamental importance to constitutional lawyers', but the Court emphasized that it was not purporting to decide the point.[168] It nevertheless went on to hold that the Canada Act 1982 did comply with s 4 of the Statute of Westminster and that its validity was therefore not in question. *Manuel* therefore contains a tiny judicial hint that English courts might consider a future UK Parliament bound by a stipulation as to manner and form, although under what conditions this might be so it is difficult to predict.[169]

2.154

Whether or not Parliament can go to the lengths of redefining itself, as opposed to merely altering its procedures, and where the dividing line is to be drawn between these two concepts, is a matter which is discussed below.[170]

2.155

---

[166] See Sir WI Jennings, *The Law and the Constitution* (5th edn, London: University of London Press, 1959); RFV Heuston, *Essays in Constitutional Law* (2nd edn, London: Stevens, 1964) and Lord Hailsham, *The Dilemma of Democracy* (London: Collins, 1978).

[167] [1983] 1 Ch 77.

[168] ibid 104 and 105.

[169] For further support for the idea that Parliament can limit itself as to manner and form, see also Dixon J in the Australian High Court in *A-G for New South Wales v Trethowan* (1931) 44 CLR 394, 426.

[170] See also G Winterton, 'The British Grundnorm: Parliamentary Supremacy Re-examined' (1976) 92 LQR 591.

(2) *Practical Limitations*

2.156 Practical matters often restrain or direct the subject matter and content of legislation, irrespective of any theoretical lack of limits to Parliament's powers. Of particular importance are the obligations binding the United Kingdom in international law. This is sometimes a matter of enlightened self-interest since the United Kingdom would not wish to undermine its ability to criticize other states for, for example, contravening international human rights treaties by itself failing to conform to the demands of international law. In similar vein, the United Kingdom could in theory continue to legislate for its many former dominions and colonies, but in practice such legislation would be politically unacceptable and would bring ridicule on the Westminster Parliament since it would undoubtedly be ignored in the independent country concerned. In the words of Lord Denning MR in *Blackburn v A-G*:[171]

> We have all been brought up to believe that, in legal theory, one Parliament cannot bind another and that no Act is irreversible. But legal theory does not always march alongside political reality. Take the Statute of Westminster 1931, which takes away the power of Parliament to legislate for the Dominions. Does anyone imagine that Parliament could or would reverse that Statute? Take the Acts which have granted independence to the Dominions and territories overseas. Can anyone imagine that Parliament could or would reverse these laws and take away their independence? Most clearly not. Freedom once given cannot be taken away. Legal theory must give way to practical politics.[172]

2.157 This inhibition upon the power of Westminster to legislate for its former colonies is frequently ascribed to constitutional convention. The political mandate given by the people at the last general election is also widely regarded as placing a constraint on any government's legislative agenda; for example, it would be politically non-feasible for the Labour government to renege on the promise it gave the electorate in 2001 to hold a referendum on whether or not the country should adopt the Euro. The public acceptability of legislation is also a factor to be weighed by Parliament; for example, the poll tax which was introduced by the Local Government Finance Act 1988 had eventually to be repealed because it failed to command the obedience of large sections of the population.[173]

(a) Parliamentary supremacy and the Human Rights Act 1998

2.158 The Human Rights Act 1998 (HRA) presents a classic example, albeit a modern one, of the practical or pragmatic limitation of Parliament's supremacy. Despite

---

[171] [1971] CMLR 784.

[172] ibid 790. See also *British Coal Corp v The King* [1935] AC 500.

[173] However, Le Sueur and Sunkin (n 143 above) comment wisely that it is 'dangerously complacent' to rely upon public opinion to restrain oppressive legislation 'in a constitutional system where the executive effectively controls Parliament and public opinion is often uncertain or easily influenced' (p 195).

being one of the original architects and signatories of the European Convention on Fundamental Rights and Freedoms of 1950, the United Kingdom had not incorporated this international instrument into domestic law until the passage of the HRA. A number of explanations were advanced for this legislative foot-dragging, amongst them the inability of Parliament to entrench and thus to protect the provisions of the Convention, the assertion that the United Kingdom's law anyway fully complied with the requirements of the Convention,[174] and the reluctance of successive governments to give the judiciary the added power which would flow from being able to measure domestic law up against the requirements of the Convention.

The incoming Labour administration in 1997 had pledged in its Manifesto to implement the Convention and this became one of its first constitutional achievements. The HRA adopts an artful compromise; it both formally and practically respects the supremacy of Parliament but it also provides principles by which conflicts between the Convention and the law of the United Kingdom can be avoided and procedures for the speedy remedying of any conflicts which are uncovered. **2.159**

Having set out the 'Convention rights' which are to be protected,[175] the Act requires courts and tribunals dealing with Convention rights to take into account relevant decisions of the European Court of Human Rights, the Commission and the Committee of Ministers.[176] The Act renders it unlawful for a public authority to act in a way which is incompatible with a Convention right.[177] All courts and tribunals are directed to read and give effect to both primary and subordinate legislation, so far as it is possible to do so, in a way which is compatible with the Convention rights.[178] The effect of s 3(2) of the Act is to permit courts and tribunals to strike down subordinate legislation[179] which is found to infringe the Convention rights, but—in deference to the supremacy of Parliament—this power does not extend to primary legislation or to subordinate legislation where primary legislation prevents removal of the incompatibility. By way of compromise, s 4 provides that any court from the High Court upwards which finds a piece of primary legislation to be incompatible with a Convention right may make a 'declaration of incompatibility'. Section 10 then goes on to empower a minister of **2.160**

---

[174] This latter justification was particularly unconvincing since the UK has on numerous occasions been found guilty by the European Court of Human Rights of breaches of the Convention. Examples include phone-tapping by the police, the ban on the publication of the memoirs of the former MI5 officer Peter Wright, and the use of corporal punishment in schools.

[175] In s 1 and Sch 1, discussed in ch 7 below.

[176] HRA 1998, s 2.

[177] ibid s 6.

[178] ibid s 3(1), discussed in ch 1 above and ch 7 below.

[179] 'Subordinate legislation' is defined by s 21 to include Acts of the Scottish Parliament.

the Crown by order to make such amendments as he considers necessary to re-move the incompatibility.[180]

2.161 The full practical consequence of these provisions will take some years to become plain. If the invariable reaction to a declaration of incompatibility proves to be an immediate remedial order, it might be concluded that the authority of Parliament has in fact been considerably diminished and its supremacy relinquished to the Convention and the courts. The effect of such a position would, in practice, be only slightly different from a power of judicial review over primary legislation. Furthermore, although the HRA itself is ordinary legislation enacted in the usual way by Parliament and thus theoretically capable of both express and implied re-peal, it is of course highly improbable, and would be politically well-nigh un-thinkable, that it would ever be removed from the statute book.

(3) Possible Legal Limitations to the Principle

(a) The law of nature

2.162 Before the modern constitutional settlement was arrived at, the judges of the com-mon law courts sometimes asserted a power to interfere with the application of a statute on the ground that it defied reason or common sense.[181] They based such a power on 'the law of nature'. The most famous example is *Dr Bonham's Case* of 1610,[182] where the Court of King's Bench held a doctor not liable to pay a fine ex-acted under the Charter of the Royal College of Physicians which had been con-firmed by an Act of Parliament. The Court found that the Charter did not anyway authorize the fine but Coke CJ also stated: 'when an Act of Parliament is against common right and reason, or repugnant, or impossible to be performed, the com-mon law will controul it, and adjudge such act to be void'. Hood Phillips has pointed out, however, not only that this statement was technically obiter, but that it was also inconsistent with what Coke said in his *Institutes*.[183]

2.163 The accepted modern position was stated by Lord Reid in *Pickin v British Rlys Board*:[184]

---

[180] Further requirements in relation to remedial orders are set out in Sch 2, including that a draft remedial order must have been laid before Parliament for 60 days and approved by a resolution of each House of Parliament unless the matter is an urgent one. See paras 7.107–7.130 below.

[181] See also Blackstone, *Commentaries* vol I, p 41.

[182] 8 Co Rep 114. See also *Day v Savadge* (1614) Hob 85 and *R v Love* (1653) 5 St Tr 825.

[183] See 4 Inst 36. Jackson and Leopold (eds) (n 143 above) add (p 45): 'Coke as a Law Officer sup-ported the prerogative, as a judge the supremacy of the common law (which he equated with reason), and as a parliamentarian the sovereignty of Parliament'. For a fascinating account of the historical role played by the concept of the law of nature, see TFT Plucknett, 'Bonham's Case and Judicial Review' (1926) 40 Harvard L Rev 30. The view has been expressed that *Dr Bonham's Case* was merely a robust example of statutory interpretation: see SE Thorne, 'Dr Bonham's Case' (1938) 54 LQR 543.

[184] [1974] AC 765.

In earlier times many learned lawyers seem to have believed that an Act of Parliament could be disregarded in so far as it was contrary to the law of God or the law of nature or natural justice but since the supremacy of Parliament was finally demonstrated by the revolution of 1688 any such idea has become obsolete.[185]

(b) The redefinition of Parliament

A logical and therefore plausible potential limitation of the concept of the supremacy of Parliament emerges from a thorough examination of what is meant by 'Parliament'. If 'Parliament' is taken to mean the supreme law-giver in society at a particular moment in history, then it becomes clear that the composition of Parliament has changed radically over the centuries. In the early Middle Ages, the supreme law-giver was undoubtedly the King. Yet, little by little, the King ceded this power to Parliament, in the sense of representatives of the people. Again, the Parliament of England and Wales changed its composition in 1706 when it merged with the Parliament of Scotland to become the Parliament of Great Britain. Some would also say that the same argument can be extended to the Parliament Acts of 1911 and 1949 so that, for the purposes of these Acts, Parliament today is composed simply of the House of Commons and the monarch.[186] In the future, it might be that Parliament's composition will change again, perhaps with the removal or complete reconstitution of the House of Lords, or with the disestablishment of the monarchy.

2.164

However this phenomenon is expressed in jurisprudential terms, whether as a change in the rule of recognition or as a shifting of the grundnorm, it seems likely that the judges and society at large would come to accept a possible evolution in the components of Parliament.[187] The really difficult issue is to know what the requirements are for the legal acceptance of such an evolution, and where the line is to be drawn between adjusting the manner and form of legislation (which may or may not be effective) and the full redefinition of Parliament. It seems clear from cases such as *Edinburgh and Dalkeith Rly v Wauchope*[188] and *Pickin v British Rlys Board*[189] that a mere matter of parliamentary procedure will not be investigated or pursued by a court; but what about a requirement that a particular piece of legislation is to require a special majority in the House of Commons or the consent of the population expressed in a referendum? The former might perhaps be regarded as a matter of parliamentary procedure, and thus not within the cognizance of a

2.165

---

[185] ibid 782. Nevertheless, it is not unknown even today to hear an echo of Coke's words; see eg Sir John Laws, 'Law and Democracy' [1995] PL 72 and Lord Woolf, '*Droit Public*—English Style' [1995] PL 57. Cf Sir Stephen Sedley, 'Human Rights: A Twenty-First Century Agenda' [1995] PL 386.

[186] cf Jackson and Leopold (eds) (n 143 above) 79–80 and P Mirfield, 'Can the House of Lords Lawfully be Abolished?' (1979) 95 LQR 36.

[187] See also Jennings (n 166 above).

[188] (1842) 8 Cl & F 710.

[189] [1974] AC 765.

court, but the holding of a referendum is arguably the addition of a new element to Parliament which might well be considered to have the effect of 'redefining' it. Until such a case is directly considered by a court against the particular social and political back-drop in which it arises, it is impossible to predict the outcome. The application of the redefinition theory to the problems posed by devolution and by the reception of EU law into the United Kingdom's legal system are considered below.

(c) The legal termination of Parliament

2.166 Another possible way in which the supremacy of Parliament might come to an end is with the legal termination of our existing Parliament. Even Dicey accepted that a sovereign parliament can bring its own authority to an end:

> Let the reader, however, note that the impossibility of placing a limit on the exercise of sovereignty does not in any way prohibit either logically, or in matter of fact, the abdication of sovereignty. This is worth observation, because a strange dogma is sometimes put forward that a sovereign power, such as the Parliament of the United Kingdom, can never by its own act divest itself of sovereignty. This position is however clearly untenable . . . To argue or imply that because sovereignty is not limitable (which is true) it cannot be surrendered (which is palpably untrue) involves the confusion of two distinct ideas. It is like arguing that because no man can, while he lives, give up, do what he will, his freedom of volition, so no man can commit suicide. A sovereign power . . . may simply put an end to its own existence. Parliament could extinguish itself by legally dissolving itself and leaving no means whereby a subsequent Parliament could be legally summoned . . .[190]

2.167 Considerable thought and insight was offered on the possible legal limitation of Parliament by Professor Owen Hood Phillips. His view was:

> It appears that the only way by which the legislature of this country could become legally limited would be for the United Kingdom Parliament to extinguish itself, after surrendering its powers to a new written constitution with entrenched provisions (eg. as to abolition of the Second Chamber, the life of Parliament, membership of EEC and a Bill of Rights) and judicial review—a constitution limiting the powers of the new legislature *and to which the new legislature would owe its existence.* The new constitution could either be drafted by the existing Parliament, or its drafting could be entrusted to a constituent assembly, the new constitution perhaps receiving the extra moral sanction of an inaugural referendum. In either case there would be a *breach of continuity* between the old and the new constitutions.[191]

---

[190] Dicey (n 147 above) 69–70, n 1.
[191] Jackson and Leopold (eds) (n 143 above) 82. See also O Hood Phillips, *Reform of the Constitution* (London: Chatto and Windus, 1970).

(d) Acts of Union

England has during the past 300 years sought to unite itself with two other countries,   **2.168**
Ireland and Scotland. The Union with Ireland was achieved, from the perspective of
British law, by the Union with Ireland Act of 1800. This provided that the two
kingdoms were to be united forever. In addition, it stated that the Churches of
England and Ireland were to be united and that this ecclesiastical union was to be
'an essential and fundamental part' of the union of the states. Notwithstanding
these clear words, the Church of Ireland was disestablished by the Irish Church
Act 1869 and, in *Ex p Canon Selwyn*,[192] a clergyman unsuccessfully challenged the
legality of this Act. Furthermore, the union of the two states was partially undone
in legislative terms by the Irish Free State (Constitution) Act 1922. The power, or
at any rate the de facto power, of Parliament was thus demonstrated and the difficulties encountered were seen to be political rather than legal.

In the case of Northern Ireland, s 1(2) of the Ireland Act 1949 declared that   **2.169**
Northern Ireland would not cease to be part of the United Kingdom without
the consent of the Northern Ireland Parliament. When the Northern Ireland
Constitution Act of 1973 abolished the Northern Ireland Parliament it nevertheless provided in s 1 that Northern Ireland would not cease to be part of the United
Kingdom without the consent of the majority of the people of Northern Ireland
voting in a poll held for this purpose. This position was preserved by the Northern
Ireland Act 1974 and is today protected by s 1(1) of the Northern Ireland Act
1998. If it were ever sought to detach Northern Ireland from the United Kingdom
without securing the consent of a majority of its people, the event would undoubtedly provide the most appropriate test yet seen for the redefinition theory
discussed above.

As regards the union with Scotland significant doubts have been expressed as to   **2.170**
the legal ability of the Westminster Parliament to dissolve the union. The Union
with Scotland Act of 1706 was preceded by a treaty[193] between the two kingdoms.
It was enacted by the English Parliament and provides for a single state and parliament. Article XVIII of the Act of Union provides that Scots law is alterable by
the Parliament of Great Britain but that no alterations can be made 'in laws which
concern private rights except for evident utility of the subjects within Scotland'.
The 1706 Act also guaranteed the Protestant religion and Presbyterian Church
government in Scotland, in addition requiring professors at Scottish universities
to subscribe to the Confession of Faith and stating that these aspects of the union
were fundamental and permanent. Once again, these instruments have proved

---

[192] (1872) 36 JP 54.
[193] For the anomalous nature of this treaty, see TB Smith, 'The Union of 1707 as Fundamental
Law' [1957] PL 99.

not to be entirely immune to change since the religious provisions were altered by the Church Patronage (Scotland) Act 1711 and by the Universities (Scotland) Act 1853;[194] nonetheless, the mere fact of their breach does not establish the legal validity of that breach.[195]

2.171   Article XVIII of the Act of Union has given rise to serious dispute. In *Gibson v Lord Advocate*,[196] a Scottish fisherman challenged s 2(1) of the European Communities Act 1972 (ECA)[197] in so far as it brought into legal effect a Community regulation which deprived Scottish fishermen of their pre-existing exclusive rights over Scottish waters. He argued that this was a matter of 'private rights' and that the change was not for the 'evident utility' of the Scottish people. In the Court of Session, Lord Keith held that this was a matter of public, not private, law and that Article XVIII was thus not applicable. He added that the question of whether legislation was of 'evident utility' was anyway not justiciable in the Court of Session, being an essentially political matter. However, he reserved his opinion on the position were an Act to purport to abolish the Court of Session or the Church of Scotland or to amend all Scots private law.[198]

2.172   Similar views were expressed about the possibly fundamental nature of the Act of Union and its consequences in *MacCormick v Lord Advocate*.[199] The present Queen adopted the title 'Elizabeth II' under power conferred by the Royal Titles Act 1953. The litigants disputed the legality of this usage in Scotland, where the Queen is not the second Elizabeth. The Court of Session held that the Treaty of Union did not prohibit the use of the title and that the litigants had no standing in the action. However, it added that it was not satisfied that the Royal Titles Act would have been conclusive if it had been repugnant to the Treaty though, like Lord Keith in *Gibson*, the Court considered that it would have no jurisdiction in such a case. Lord Cooper stated that:

> The principle of the unlimited sovereignty of Parliament is a distinctively English principle which has no counterpart in Scottish constitutional law . . . I have diffi-culty in seeing why it should have been supposed that the new Parliament of Great Britain must inherit all the peculiar characteristics of the English Parliament but none of the Scottish Parliament, as if all that happened in 1707 was that Scottish representatives were admitted to the Parliament of England.[200]

---

[194] cf JDB Mitchell, 'Sovereignty of Parliament—Yet Again' (1963) 79 LQR 196 and Smith (n 193 above).
[195] As Middleton observes in 'New Thoughts on the Union' (1954) 66 Juridical Rev 37, 49: 'The fact that Parliament has done something cannot prove that it was entitled to do it'.
[196] [1975] 1 CMLR 563.
[197] Discussed in ch 1 above.
[198] See JM Thomson, 'Community Law, the Act of Union and the Supremacy of Parliament' (1976) 92 LQR 36.
[199] 1953 SC 396.
[200] ibid 411.

There is therefore some quite persuasive evidence that at least the union with Scotland does indeed place legal fetters on the powers of Parliament at Westminster.[201]

(e) Devolution

It was seen in chapter 1 that devolved governments were set up in Northern **2.173** Ireland, Scotland and Wales by legislation enacted in 1998. Both the Northern Ireland Assembly and the Scottish Parliament were given law-making powers. As observed in chapter 1, the word 'devolution' implies that power was delegated to these regional parliaments, rather than being transferred outright; in addition, Parliament at Westminster is expressed to remain competent to legislate for the regions even on devolved matters.[202] It would therefore appear that the devolution legislation represents merely an exercise of the competence of Parliament at Westminster and that it does not erode its traditional legislative supremacy,[203] albeit that it is generally acknowledged that constitutional conventions will develop to restrain Westminster from legislating on devolved issues.

However, there is a contrary view that the devolution settlement will—at least **2.174** with the passage of time—become irreversible and that the devolved parliaments in reality possess a power to enact primary legislation which can rival that of Parliament at Westminster. This view is based on an analogy with the relationship between UK law and EU law, which is discussed in the following section; in essence, the argument is that devolution has produced a new constitutional legal order in the United Kingdom. In the words of Burrows, the objectives of this new legal order are:

> to modernise the United Kingdom constitution by decentralising power to bring government closer to the people and by transferring legislative competencies to newly created institutions. In areas covered by the legislation, Westminster has transferred its legislative powers to the Parliaments in Scotland and Northern Ireland and, so long as they operate within their own spheres, the primary legislation adopted by them must be applied within the relevant region. In case of a conflict, the courts should apply the primary legislation of the devolved legislature. This does not give the courts a power to review the legality of United Kingdom legislation, merely to set it aside in case of conflict in order to ground the devolution settlement in objective principles based on the rule of law.[204]

---

[201] See further MacCormick (n 151 above); Mitchell (n 194 above) and Smith (n 193 above). Cf *Sillars v Smith* [1982] SLT 539 and CR Munro, *Studies in Constitutional Law* (2nd edn, London: Butterworths, 1999) ch 5.

[202] Scotland Act 1998, s 28(7); Northern Ireland Act 1998, s 5(6).

[203] 'The United Kingdom has not become a federal system [as a consequence of the devolution legislation], but it is moving in at least a quasi-federal direction': Jackson and Leopold (eds) (n 143 above) 109.

[204] N Burrows, *Devolution* (London: Sweet and Maxwell, 2000) 65. Cf R Brazier, 'The Constitution of the United Kingdom' [1999] CLJ 96 and Munro (n 201 above) ch 5.

2.175   Although such an analysis of course conflicts with the orthodox view of the sovereignty of the Westminster Parliament, Burrows considers that it coincides with the political reality of what has occurred as a result of devolution. The legal explanations for how such a result might have come about are similar to those discussed below in relation to EU law.

(f) Membership of the European Union

2.176   Another very real threat which exists today, both theoretically and practically, to the supremacy of Parliament is posed by the United Kingdom's membership of the European Union. This is because it is a fundamental principle of EU law that it itself must prevail in all circumstances when it comes into conflict with the law of a member state. This doctrine's rivalry with the supremacy of Parliament is evident from its name alone, the 'supremacy of EU law'. The section of this chapter that follows examines the doctrine and its potential implications in more detail.

(4) The Doctrine of Supremacy of EU Law and its Implications

2.177   The supremacy of EU law is closely related to the doctrine of direct effect, which was discussed in chapter 1. Both notions were first articulated by the European Court of Justice (ECJ) early in the life of the Economic Community in *Van Gend en Loos v Nederlandse Tariefcommissie*.[205] Combined, they mean that an individual is entitled to rely in the courts of a member state on a provision of EU law which is formulated in clear and precise terms and to demand that that provision is enforced in preference to any contrary provision contained in national law. The power which this places in the hands of individuals and the significance which it ascribes to the law of the European Union strongly support the federal ambitions of the drafters of the Treaty.[206]

(a) Development of the doctrine of supremacy of EU law

2.178   The process by which the ECJ developed the doctrine of the supremacy of EU law reveals a growing self-confidence on the part of that court. In *Van Gend en Loos*, the supremacy of EU law was merely a conclusion to be drawn from the ECJ's general statements and from the fact that an individual was held to be entitled to have Article 12 of the Treaty enforced in preference to the law of the Netherlands. The ECJ's language was much stronger in its second decision on the subject, *Costa v ENEL*.[207] Here it stated:

> By contrast with ordinary international treaties, the EEC Treaty has created its own legal system which, on the entry into force of the treaty, became an integral part of

---

[205]   Case 26/62 [1963] ECR 1.
[206]   As to which see ch 1 above.
[207]   Case 6/64 [1964] 3 ECR 585.

the legal systems of the Member States and which their courts are bound to apply. By creating a Community of unlimited duration, having its own institutions, its own personality and its own legal capacity and capacity of representation on the international plane, and, more particularly, real powers stemming from a limitation of sovereignty or a transfer of powers from the States to the Community, the Member States have limited their sovereign rights, and, albeit within limited fields, have created a body of law which binds both their nationals and themselves. The integration into the laws of each Member State of provisions which derive from the Community, and more generally the terms and spirit of the Treaty, make it impossible for the Member State, as a corollary, to accord precedence to a unilateral and subsequent measure over a legal system accepted by them on a basis of reciprocity . . . The transfer by the States from their domestic legal system to the Community legal system of the rights and obligations arising under the Treaty carries with it a permanent limitation of their sovereign rights against which a subsequent unilateral act incompatible with the concept of the Community cannot prevail.[208]

This reasoning runs directly counter to the supremacy of the UK Parliament. It is based on the idea that member states curtailed their own sovereignty when they acceded to the European Union; they are supposed, in the view of the ECJ, to have transferred part of their power to legislate to the European Union and its institutions. This process is not described as a delegation, or any kind of temporary loan; it is an out and out 'transfer' and therefore irrevocable. The response of the United Kingdom to these demands is discussed below. **2.179**

In addition to justifying the supremacy of EU law on the basis that the member states restrict their sovereignty and their legislative powers on accession to the Union, the ECJ has also explained the supremacy of EU law on other, albeit related, grounds. In *Costa v ENEL*, it also asserted that it follows from the whole nature and spirit of the Community enterprise that its law must be of a different and higher kind than national law; the member states only undertake certain obligations and restrictions provided that all the other member states are placed in the same position;[209] if the states had general powers to contradict EU law by means of their own national legislation, then clearly the member states would not all be in the same position. In other words, the notion of reciprocity is vital to the Union and it could not exist without acknowledgement of the supremacy of EU law. **2.180**

A closely related reason expressed by the ECJ for the supremacy of EU law is that its *effet utile* would be compromised if its authority could be countermanded by national legislation.[210] There would be no way in which the uniform application of EU law could be guaranteed and without such application the Union could **2.181**

---

[208] ibid 593–594.

[209] This rationale has become compromised in modern times by the 'variable geometry' embraced by the Treaties of Maastricht and Amsterdam, permitting member states to opt out of specific aspects of EU law.

[210] See Case 14/68 *Walt Wilhelm v Bundeskartellamt* [1969] ECR 1.

not operate effectively. In addition, the ECJ has sometimes advanced other, less basic, reasons for the supremacy of EU law; in particular, in *Costa v ENEL*, it pointed out that the Treaty does permit the member states to legislate unilaterally in a few specific cases, but these cases are provided by way of exception and would be unnecessary if there was a general national right to legislate in defiance of EU law.[211]

2.182   The scope of the doctrine of supremacy of EU law has become clear from the case law of the ECJ. Both the *Van Gend en Loos* and *Costa* cases concerned the supremacy of Treaty provisions and both made it clear that the principle was not a simple application of the *lex posterior* rule since the national legislation impugned in each was enacted after the relevant Treaty provisions came into operation. In other words, EU law prevails over incompatible national law whether it is enacted before or after that law.[212] In addition, it prevails whether it takes the form of primary law (the Treaty) or of directly effective secondary law; thus, for example, in *Politi Sas v Minister of Finance*[213] a regulation was held to prevail over inconsistent national law and in *Enka BV v Inspecteur der Invoerrechten en Accijnzen*[214] a directive was relied upon by an individual to protect himself from having incompatible national law enforced against him.

2.183   Furthermore, the ECJ adheres to its principles even where the incompatible national law is contained in the constitution of a member state since to allow EU law to be judged according to the standards of national constitutions would threaten its coherent and uniform application throughout the Union;[215] however, the ECJ mitigated the apparent harshness of this decision by adding that 'respect for fundamental rights forms an integral part of the general principles of law protected by the Court of Justice' and that the 'protection of such rights, whilst inspired by the constitutional traditions common to the Member States, must be ensured within the framework of the structure and objectives of the Community'.[216]

---

[211] See Case 6/64 [1964] 3 ECR 585, 593–594.

[212] The only exception to this principle is contained in Art 307 of the Treaty Establishing the European Community: 'The rights and obligations arising from agreements concluded before 1 January 1958 or, for acceding States, before the date of their accession, between one or more Member States on the one hand, and one or more third countries on the other, shall not be affected by the provisions of this Treaty'.

[213] Case 43/71 [1971] ECR 1039.

[214] Case 38/77 [1977] ECR 2203.

[215] Case 11/70 *Internationale Handelsgesellschaft v Einfuhr- und Vorratsstelle Getreide* [1970] ECR 1125 and Case 44/79 *Hauer v Land Rheinland-Pfalz* [1979] ECR 3727. National courts may not be prepared to surrender absolutely to the supremacy of EU law over the national constitution; see in particular the remarks of the Federal German Constitutional Court in *Brunner v European Union Treaty* [1994] CMLR 57. See also F Hoffmeister, 'German Bundesverfassungsgericht: Alcan Decision of 17 February 2000; Constitutional Review of EC Regulation on Bananas, Decision of 7 June 2000' (2001) 38 CML Rev 791.

[216] [1970] ECR 1125, 1134.

The immediacy of the notion of the supremacy of EU law became evident in the   **2.184**
Simmenthal cases.[217] A company had imported meat into Italy from France, paying fees for health checks at the frontier. It challenged these fees, on the basis that
they constituted a disguised form of customs duties and were therefore contrary
both to the Treaty and to some EU regulations governing the meat market. The
domestic court agreed and ordered the government to pay back the fees. However,
it was met with the argument that the legislation imposing the fees, which had
been passed in 1970, was not invalidated until a decision to that effect had been
obtained from the Italian Constitutional Court. A preliminary ruling was sought
from the ECJ, asking essentially whether the effect of the supremacy of EU law
was to render the conflicting national law automatically void, or whether it did
not become void until annulled by the Constitutional Court. The ECJ replied in
unequivocal terms that EU law takes immediate precedence over existing and subsequent conflicting law and that no annulment by the Constitutional Court was
needed.

Difficult questions can arise where the precise meaning and direct effect of a par-   **2.185**
ticular piece of EU law have not yet been established, so that it is not yet clear
whether that law must be given effect to in preference to national law. However,
even in these circumstances, the ECJ emphasizes the importance which it attaches
to upholding the supremacy of EU law. In *R v Secretary of State for Transport, ex p
Factortame*,[218] the issue was the compatibility of the UK Merchant Shipping Act
1988 with EU law. The applicants were the owners of fishing vessels who had been
excluded by the Act from the right to fish against the British quota. They sought
interim protection of their alleged EU rights before the British courts; the matter
was of considerable urgency and importance to them since they were losing huge
sums whilst their fishing fleets were out of action. However, at the time of the action discussed here, the nature and scope of their rights in EU law had not been
established. The predicament faced by national courts in such a situation was
summed up in the House of Lords by Lord Bridge:

> If the applicants fail to establish the rights they claim before the ECJ, the effect of
> the interim relief granted would be to have conferred upon them rights directly con-
> trary to Parliament's sovereign will and correspondingly to have deprived British
> fishing vessels, as defined by Parliament, of the enjoyment of a substantial propor-
> tion of the UK quota of stocks of fish protected by the common fisheries policy.[219]

The House of Lords also faced the problem that to have granted interim relief in   **2.186**
these circumstances would have breached the rule which existed in UK law at that

---

[217] Case 35/76 *Simmenthal v Italian Minister of Finance* [1976] ECR 1871; Case 70/77
Simmenthal v Italian Minister of Finance [1978] ECR 1453 and Case 92/78 *Simmenthal v
Commission* [1979] ECR 777.
[218] Case C-213/89 [1990] ECR I-2433.
[219] [1989] 2 WLR 997, 1014.

date forbidding the grant of an injunction against the Crown. The House therefore referred the case to the ECJ for a preliminary ruling. The ECJ did not focus its attention on the tricky balance which a national court must achieve in such a case between upholding its own national law until that law is definitively shown to be inapplicable and respecting the supremacy of EU law. Instead, it held merely that, where a national court is faced with an issue of EU law and considers that the sole obstacle to its interim protection of that EU law is a rule of national law, it must set aside the rule of national law.[220] However, it returned to the matter in *Zuckerfabrik Süderdithmarschen AG v Hauptzollamt Itzehoe*.[221] It aligned the principles which apply to the suspension of national law which is alleged to conflict with Community rights with the suspension of national law implementing EU law which is alleged to be invalid:

> The interim legal protection which Community law ensures for individuals before national courts must remain the same, irrespective of whether they contest the compatibility of national legal provisions with Community law or the validity of secondary Community law, in view of the fact that the dispute in both cases is based on Community law itself.[222]

It went on to rule that suspension of enforcement of a national measure adopted in implementation of EU legislation may be granted by a national court only:

(i)   if that court entertains serious doubts as to the validity of the Community measure and, should the question of the validity of the contested measure not already have been brought before the Court, itself refers that question to the Court;

(ii) if there is urgency and a threat of serious and irreparable damage to the applicant;

(iii) and if the national court takes due account of the Community's interests.[223]

2.187   The vindication of the supremacy of EU law is usually achieved by a legal person, whether human or corporate, enforcing directly effective rights in a national court, notwithstanding the existence of incompatible national law. Thus for example in the *Marshall* cases, Ms Marshall enforced her directly effective EU right not to be obliged to retire at a younger age than her male colleagues and to receive adequate and substantial damages for breach of this right, in the face of provisions in the Sex Discrimination Act 1975 which denied her the right to claim discrimination in relation to her retirement age and which capped the damages receivable in such circumstances.[224]

---

[220] The ECJ relied on its earlier ruling in Case 106/77 *Amministrazione delle Finanze dello Stato v Simmenthal SpA* [1978] ECR 629. The House of Lords later made up its own mind to protect the alleged EU rights: [1990] 3 WLR 818.

[221] Joined Cases C-143/88 & C-92/89 [1991] ECR I-415.

[222] ibid 541.

[223] ibid 544.

[224] *Marshall v Southampton and South-West Hampshire Area Authority (No 2)* [1994] ICR 242.

However, there is also another route open in some circumstances where **2.188** Parliament legislates in contravention of EU law, as was demonstrated in *R v Secretary of State for Employment, ex p EOC*.[225] The Equal Opportunities Commission brought an action for judicial review of certain provisions contained in the Employment Protection (Consolidation) Act 1978. These provisions limited employment rights to those who had worked continuously either for two years at 16 or more hours per week or for five years in the case of those working between eight and 16 hours per week. The Commission was joined in the action by Ms Day who was unable to claim redundancy benefit because she could not satisfy these threshold provisions. The basis of the claim was that the legislation contravened what is now Article 141 of the Treaty, the Equal Pay Directive[226] and the Equal Treatment Directive[227] because it indirectly discriminated against women in the workforce, since many more women than men are in practice able to satisfy the thresholds. The House of Lords held that Ms Day's claim was a purely private law one and that it should therefore be brought against her former employer in an employment tribunal, not in proceedings for judicial review in the Divisional Court. However, the claim of the Equal Opportunities Commission was held to be admissible and, indeed, it proved ultimately successful. The Supreme Court Act 1981, s 31(3) and the Civil Procedure Rules, Pt 54 deem an applicant to have locus standi to seek judicial review on proof of 'a sufficient interest in the matter to which the application relates'.[228] The Equal Opportunities Commission's statutory duties include '(a) to work towards the elimination of discrimination, (b) to promote equality of opportunity between men and women generally . . .'.[229] A majority in the House of Lords accepted that this gave the Commission standing 'to agitate in judicial review proceedings related to sex discrimination which are of public importance and affect a large section of the population'.[230] The Secretary of State argued that the court had power to make a declaration in judicial review proceedings only if one of the prerogative orders would be available and that no such order could be made here because there was no quashable decision. The House of Lords dismissed this principle as too narrow both on the grounds of how the action for judicial review had evolved historically and because it would mean that a declaration would be available where subordinate legislation contravened EU law, since certiorari could be granted here, but not where primary legislation did so. On the substance of the matter, the Commission convinced the House of the existence of unjustified indirect discrimination and it was awarded a declaration

---

[225] [1994] 2 WLR 409.
[226] Directive 75/117 [1975] OJ L45/19.
[227] Directive 76/207 [1976] OJ L39/40.
[228] See further paras 17.33 et seq below.
[229] Sex Discrimination Act 1975, s 53(1).
[230] [1994] 2 WLR 409, 418 *per* Lord Keith of Kinkel.

that the relevant provisions of the Employment Protection (Consolidation) Act 1978 were incompatible with EU law. The crucial principle of English public law which emerges from the case is, therefore, that a person or body with a sufficient interest in the subject matter of the action may use judicial review proceedings to obtain a declaration that an Act of Parliament contravenes EU law. Whatever the legal status of the supremacy of Parliament in the light of the United Kingdom's membership of the European Union, which is discussed at paras 2.202 et seq below, there can be little doubt that this principle represents a sizeable dent in the de facto significance of the supremacy of Parliament.

(b) Practical responses in the United Kingdom to the supremacy of EU law

2.189 Around the time of the United Kingdom's accession to the European Communities (which occurred on 1 January 1973), there was much public and academic discussion about the relationship between the supremacy of Parliament at Westminster and the new legal system into which the country was entering. There appears to have been a widespread appreciation of the fundamental nature of the Communities and, in particular, of the concept of the supremacy of EU law, which had clearly been established by the ECJ by that date.

2.190 Amongst the many views expressed, there emerged a laissez-faire approach to this matter. This was to the effect that, as a matter of political reality, there never would be a clash between the law of the United Kingdom and that of the European Union. An analogy was drawn with the Statute of Westminster of 1931 and the many subsequent Acts which granted independence to Great Britain's former colonies; in theory, Parliament at Westminster could legislate but in practice it would not do so. This attitude was, perhaps surprisingly, adopted by the UK government itself; the White Paper on Community Accession in 1967 remarked: 'Within the fields occupied by Community law, Parliament would have to refrain from passing fresh legislation inconsistent with that law'.[231]

2.191 On closer analysis, such a view represents a wholly unsatisfactory response to the potential problem posed. There is a crucial difference between the independence situation and membership of the European Union and that difference consists in the likelihood of inadvertent conflicting legislation being enacted. Parliament is very unlikely ever inadvertently to pass legislation which extends to the territory of a former colony but it can quite easily inadvertently contravene EU law because EU law encroaches into many areas which were formerly the province of national Parliaments.[232] The laissez-faire response offered no solution to the judges who

---

[231] *Legal and Constitutional Implications of United Kingdom Membership of the European Communities* (Cmnd 3301) para 23.

[232] Indeed it has done so on numerous occasions, perhaps the best-known example being in the Merchant Shipping Act 1988 which resulted in the series of *Factortame* cases discussed above.

might be faced with such a problem and, with the benefit of hindsight, it can be seen to be little more than a head-in-the-sand attitude.

A more helpful approach was offered by Wade.[233] Proceeding from the assumption that Parliament could not limit its own supremacy as a matter of law, he suggested that Parliament could enact a European Communities Act each year in which it would proclaim the supremacy of EU law and lay to rest any conflicts between statutes and EU law which had arisen in the course of the past year. As an alternative, he suggested that a small change might be made in the wording of all Acts passed after the beginning of 1973; for example, they might all conclude with a formula such as: 'this Act conforms to the European Communities'. As will be seen below, neither of these solutions was in fact adopted by the legislature.

2.192

Another solution suggested around the same time was however taken up by government. Trinidade advocated the establishment of a Standing Committee in Parliament to examine all draft national and EU legislation with the object of spotting possible conflicts before they occurred.[234] Two parliamentary select committees exist today which have powers similar to those suggested by Trinidade. The House of Commons Select Committee on European Legislation examines draft EU legislative instruments with a view to determining whether they reveal questions of legal or political importance or whether they are likely to affect the existing law of the United Kingdom. The House of Lords Select Committee on the European Communities has somewhat wider powers, being permitted also to comment on the merits of proposed EU legislation; it reports on those proposals which raise important questions of policy or principle and on other questions to which it believes the attention of the House should be drawn. In practice, the work of both select committees undoubtedly goes a long way to reducing the possibility of conflict between the law of the United Kingdom and that of the European Union.

2.193

(c) The approach adopted by the European Communities Act 1972

The ECA 1972 adopts a subtle and complex approach to the supremacy of EU law. It contains no provision which purports to confer outright legislative authority on the European Union, nor one which expressly transfers legislative authority away from Parliament at Westminster. However, the combined effect of ss 2 and 3 is to respect the supremacy of EU law, at least for so long as the Act remains in force.

2.194

It was seen in chapter 1 that s 2(1) incorporates EU law into enforceable law in the United Kingdom. In particular, it provides that 'all such rights . . . created by or

2.195

---

[233] Wade, 'Sovereignty and the European Communities' (n 152 above).
[234] FA Trinidade, 'Parliamentary Sovereignty and the Primacy of European Community Law' (1972) 35 MLR 375.

arising under the Treaties . . . as in accordance with the Treaties are without further enactment to be given legal effect . . . shall be recognised and available in law . . .'. As discussed above, the right of a litigant to have EU law treated as supreme is an enforceable legal right. The supremacy of EU law is thus given legislative blessing by s 2(1). This on its own would not, however, be sufficient to protect an EU right which has been brought into effect by s 2(1) from being expressly or impliedly abrogated by a later Act of Parliament. Section 2(4) attempts to remedy this problem. Its relevant part in the present context provides:

> [A]ny enactment passed or to be passed . . . shall be construed and have effect subject to the foregoing provisions of this section . . .

This is a stealthy way of providing that, as of the beginning of 1973, all statutes, whether already enacted or yet to be enacted, must be read and given effect to with the enforceable principles of EU law in mind; since one of the enforceable principles of EU law is the right to have that law treated as supreme over national law, it follows that the sub-section is saying that all legislation must henceforth be read and given effect to subject to the principle that EU law is supreme over it.

2.196   This position is reinforced by s 3(1):

> For the purposes of all legal proceedings any question as to the meaning or effect of any of the Treaties, or as to the validity, meaning or effect of any Community instrument, shall be treated as a question of law (and, if not referred to the European Court, be for determination as such in accordance with the principles laid down by and any relevant decision of the European Court or any court attached thereto).[235]

This provision has the effect of elevating decisions of the ECJ to binding precedents for all UK courts and tribunals.[236] Since a consistent line of decisions of the ECJ has created the principle of the supremacy of EU law, it follows that that principle is binding law in the United Kingdom.

2.197   There is no question but that these statutory provisions have proved effective to guarantee the practical supremacy of EU law before the courts and tribunals of the United Kingdom. From an early stage of membership of the Communities, the judiciary expressed acceptance of the principle in a number of obiter dicta.[237] It soon became clear that they were also prepared to adopt what was effectively a new approach to statutory interpretation in cases where there was a risk that too literal

---

[235] As amended by the European Communities (Amendment) Act 1986, s 2(a).

[236] The doctrine of precedent is discussed in ch 1 above. It is unclear what quirk of legislative drafting led to the most important part of s 3(1) being put into parentheses.

[237] See eg *R v Secchi* [1975] 1 CMLR 383; *Shields v Coomes (Holdings) Ltd* [1978] ICR 1159; *Worringham v Lloyds Bank* [1982] 1 WLR 841 and *Garden Cottage Foods Ltd v Milk Marketing Board* [1982] 3 WLR 514 and [1983] 3 WLR 143.

a construction of a UK statute might jeopardize the supremacy of EU law.[238] Lord Denning MR, for example, stated in *Macarthys Ltd v Smith*[239] that a court dealing with a matter covered by both domestic and EU law should look first at the EU law. Then, he continued, 'we should look at our own legislation on the point—giving it, of course, full faith and credit—assuming that it does fully comply with the obligations under the Treaty. In construing our statute, we are entitled to look to the Treaty as an aid to its construction . . .'.[240] The defining moment probably came in *Garland v British Rail Engineering Ltd*.[241] A woman employee discovered, on retirement from British Rail, that she would no longer be entitled to receive travel concessions for her family as she had enjoyed during employment. Retired male employees continued to receive travel concessions for their families, so she complained of sex discrimination over pay. The relevant UK law was contained in the Equal Pay Act 1970, as amended by the Sex Discrimination Act 1975. The difficulty faced by Ms Garland was that s 6(4) of the Sex Discrimination Act provided that the rules forbidding employment discrimination did not apply 'to provision in relation to death or retirement'. The industrial tribunal hearing her case held that this precluded her claim. The Employment Appeal Tribunal disagreed, holding that the words of s 6(4) ought not to be construed widely so as to encompass a privilege which existed during employment and which was permitted by the employer to continue into retirement. The Court of Appeal restored the decision of the industrial tribunal on the grounds that the wording of s 6(4) was deliberately broad. When the matter reached the House of Lords, it was pointed out that EU law was also involved, in particular what is now Article 141 of the Treaty which requires equal pay for equal work without discrimination on the ground of sex; this provision had, moreover, been held to take direct effect in *Defrenne v Sabena*.[242] Delivering the judgment of the House of Lords, Lord Diplock stated:

> [T]he words of section 6(4) of the Sex Discrimination Act 1975 that fall to be construed, 'provision in relation to . . . retirement', without any undue straining of the ordinary meaning of the language used, are capable of bearing either the narrow meaning accepted by the Employment Appeal Tribunal or the wider meaning preferred by the Court of Appeal but acknowledged by that court to be largely a matter of first impression. Had the attention of the court been drawn to Article [141] of the EEC Treaty and the judgment of the European Court of Justice in *Defrenne v*

---

[238] This was a view strongly advocated by O Hood Phillips in 'Has the incoming tide reached the Palace of Westminster?' (1979) 95 LQR 167 and 'High tide in the Strand? Post-1972 Acts and Community law' (1980) 96 LQR 31. See also TRS Allan, 'Parliamentary sovereignty: Lord Denning's Dexterous Revolution' (1983) 3 OJLS 22.

[239] [1979] 3 CMLR 44.

[240] ibid 47. See also the remarks of Phillips J in *Charles Early v Smith* and *Snoxell v Vauxhall Motors* [1977] ICR 700.

[241] [1983] 2 AC 751.

[242] Case 43/75 [1976] ECR 455.

Sabena . . . I have no doubt that, consistently with statements made by Lord Denning MR in previous cases, they would have construed section 6(4) so as not to make it inconsistent with Article [141].²⁴³

Following a preliminary ruling from the ECJ that EU law did indeed forbid discrimination of the type which had occurred here, the House of Lords went on to rule that the construction of s 6(4) which had been adopted by the Employment Appeal Tribunal was the correct one, with the result that Ms Garland won her claim.

2.198   More recently, UK courts have also expressly accepted the interpretative principle laid down by the ECJ in *Marleasing SA v La Comercial Internacional de Alimentacion SA*,²⁴⁴ namely that domestic law must, so far as possible, be construed so as to accord with EU law (in particular, a directive), even when the domestic law chronologically pre-dates the relevant EU law. Thus, in *Webb v EMO (Air Cargo) Ltd*,²⁴⁵ the House of Lords held that the Sex Discrimination Act 1975 must be interpreted so as to accord with the meaning of the Equal Treatment Directive which was enacted one year later.²⁴⁶

2.199   Cases such as those so far discussed in this section, have arguably only a relatively insignificant impact—at least in legal terms—on the supremacy of Parliament, since the court ultimately enforces the terms of the relevant statute. It is clearly a much more radical step to disapply a statute of the Westminster Parliament in favour of EU law, yet the judiciary has demonstrated on a number of occasions that it is prepared to go this far. The first clear example came in *Macarthys Ltd v Smith*.²⁴⁷ The issue was whether a woman was entitled to claim equal pay with a male colleague who had performed her job before she was appointed to it. The Equal Pay Act 1970 appeared to preclude such a comparison, whereas EU law, at least arguably, permitted it. A majority of judges in the Court of Appeal refused to take the line advocated by Lord Denning MR, that is to say, to interpret the Equal Pay Act so as to accord with EU law. Instead, they took a traditional, literal view of the meaning of the Equal Pay Act and were driven to the conclusion that it embraced only simultaneous job comparisons. Aware that this might lead to a conflict with EU law, the court referred the case for a preliminary ruling to the ECJ, which held that EU law did indeed permit successive comparisons for this purpose. The net result of this approach was, therefore, that a conflict was indeed found to exist between the Equal Pay Act and EU law. The Court of Appeal nevertheless went on to apply the EU law in preference to the domestic statute. Before the reference to the ECJ, Lord Denning MR stated:

---

²⁴³ [1983] 2 AC 751, 771.
²⁴⁴ Case C-106/89 [1990] ECR I-4135, discussed at para 1.225 above .
²⁴⁵ .[1995] 4 All ER 577.
²⁴⁶ See n 227 above. See also *Coote v Granada Hospitality Ltd (No 2)* [1999] IRLR 452.
²⁴⁷ [1979] 3 CMLR 44 and [1980] 2 CMLR 217.

Under section 2(1) and (4) of the European Communities Act 1972 the principles laid down in the Treaty are 'without further enactment' to be given legal effect in the United Kingdom: and have priority over 'any enactment passed to be passed' by our Parliament. So we are entitled—and I think bound—to look at Article [141] of the Treaty because it is directly applicable here: and also any directive which is directly applicable here[248] . . . If on close investigation it should appear that our legislation is deficient—or is inconsistent with Community law—by some oversight of our draftsmen—then it is our bounden duty to give priority to Community law. Such is the result of section 2(1) and (4) of the European Communities Act 1972.[249]

On the return of the case from Luxembourg, he proclaimed in even more tren-chant terms:

It is important now to declare—and it must be made plain—that the provisions of Article [141] of the Treaty of Rome take priority over anything in our English statute on equal pay which is inconsistent with Article [141]. That priority is given by our own law. It is given by the European Communities Act 1972 itself. Community law is now part of our law: and, whenever there is any inconsistency, Community law has priority.[250]

Similar unconditional acceptance by the judiciary of the supremacy of EU law **2.200** where there is a direct conflict between it and UK law is evident in *R v Secretary of State for Transport, ex p Factortame Ltd.*[251] Lord Bridge held:

Some public comments on the decision of the European Court of Justice, affirming the jurisdiction of the courts of Member States to override national legislation if necessary to enable interim relief to be granted in protection of rights under Community law, have suggested that this was a novel and dangerous invasion by a Community institution of the sovereignty of the United Kingdom Parliament. But such comments are based on a misconception. If the supremacy within the European Community of Community law over the national law of Member States was not always inherent in the EEC Treaty it was certainly well established in the ju-risprudence of the European Court of Justice long before the United Kingdom joined the Community. Thus, whatever limitation of its sovereignty Parliament ac-cepted when it enacted the European Communities Act 1972 was entirely volun-tary. Under the terms of the Act of 1972 it has always been clear that it was the duty of a United Kingdom court, when delivering final judgment, to override any rule of national law found to be in conflict with any directly enforceable rule of Community law. Similarly, when decisions of the European Court of Justice have exposed areas of United Kingdom statute law which failed to implement Council directives, Parliament has always loyally accepted the obligation to make appropri-ate and prompt amendments. Thus there is nothing in any way novel in according

---

[248] Lord Denning's use of the term 'directly applicable' here reflects the usage sometimes adopted, particularly in the past, by the ECJ. It is clear from the context of Lord Denning's remarks that he is referring to the concept described in the present work, and more usually generally today, as 'direct effect'.

[249] [1979] 3 CMLR 44, 46–47.

[250] [1980] 2 CMLR 217, 218.

[251] [1990] 3 CMLR 375.

supremacy to rules of Community law in those areas to which they apply and to insist that, in the protection of rights under Community law, national courts must not be inhibited by rules of national law from granting interim relief in appropriate cases is no more than a logical recognition of that supremacy.[252]

2.201   A practical application of this principle is to be found in *Bossa v Nordstress Ltd.*[253] Mr Bossa had been rejected for a job offered in the United Kingdom on the ground of his Italian nationality. His claim for unlawful race discrimination was countered by the argument that s 8 of the Race Relations Act 1976 excepts from the operation of the Act jobs which are performed wholly or mainly outside Great Britain, and this appeared to be the situation in relation to Mr Bossa. The Employment Appeal Tribunal nevertheless held that s 8 must be disapplied because it conflicted with the directly effective Treaty provision[254] guaranteeing free movement of workers. Morison J held:

> It is possible to give effect to the supremacy of European law by simply disapplying, in this case, section 8. That means that the industrial tribunal will consider the complaint in the normal way and, if appropriate, make such orders with regard to remedy as lies within their competence under the Act.[255]

(d) Does the supremacy of EU law abridge the supremacy of Parliament?

2.202   Much has been written about the way in which the United Kingdom has made provision for the supremacy of EU law, although there remains considerable scope for further speculation on the matter. However, one thing which is tolerably clear is that the country has not chosen the path set out by the ECJ to achieve obedience to EU law. It has been seen above that that Court believes that accession to the Communities must carry with it an automatic limitation on the sovereign powers of the state and a consequential limitation of the legislative power of the state's parliament. Whether or not the United Kingdom could ever have achieved such a result depends on whether there are any ways in which it could bring to an end the rule by which its Parliament is recognized as supreme. It was suggested in the analysis of the possible ways in which a future Parliament might limit itself that there is potential for Parliament at Westminster either to extinguish itself completely, which would result in a break in the legal continuum, or else for Parliament to redefine itself; in the present context, if Parliament were to redefine itself, it would have to make provision for the supreme law-maker in matters within the jurisdiction of the European Union to become the European institutions. Whatever else can be concluded about the current arrangements, it is incontrovertible that Parliament neither brought its own life to an end nor formally and expressly redefined itself in 1972.

---

[252] [1990] 3 CMLR 375 (n 251 above), 379–380. See also *R v Secretary of State for Employment, ex p EOC* [1994] 2 WLR 409, particularly the remarks of Lord Keith of Kinkel at 416.
[253] [1998] IRLR 284.
[254] Then Art 48 but today Art 39.
[255] [1998] IRLR 284, 287.

A range of views has been expressed on the legal fate of the doctrine of the supremacy of Parliament in the context of EU law. At one extreme lies the recent opinion expressed by Wade. It was seen at the beginning of this chapter that his original view was that the supremacy of Parliament was a 'political fact' which could only be changed by a 'legal revolution'; by 1996 he believed that such a revolution had actually taken place. Although acknowledging that Parliament still possessed the power to repudiate the ECA 1972 and take the United Kingdom out of the European Union altogether, he asserted that '[w]hile Britain remains in the Community we are in a regime in which Parliament has bound its successors successfully, and which is nothing if not revolutionary'.[256] He continued:

> [I]n *Factortame* the House of Lords elected to allow the Parliament of 1972 to fetter the Parliament of 1988 in order that Community law might be given the primacy which practical politics obviously required. This in no way implies that the judges . . . decided otherwise than for what appeared to them to be good legal reasons. The point is simply that the rule of recognition is itself a political fact which the judges themselves are able to change when they are confronted with a new situation which so demands . . . In *Factortame* it arose from the creation of new ties with Europe.[257]

Other commentators take a more moderate view, to the effect that the process of acceptance of the supremacy of EU law over UK parliamentary law is essentially a practical evolutionary one, achieved in large measure by sensitive judicial interpretative techniques. A notable example is provided by Allan, who considers that 'bold and creative statutory interpretation may at some point embrace acceptance of a limited degree of entrenchment . . . The importance of Lord Denning's judgment in *Macarthys Ltd v Smith* lies in the degree of strength of the principle of construction adopted: statutes will be presumed to be intended not to conflict (nor to be applied in case of conflict) with Community law unless Parliament states the contrary.'[258]

A third point of view posits that there has been no need for any change in the old rule of recognition since the artful wording of the ECA 1972 manages to guarantee the supremacy of EU law without altering the rule of recognition or causing any break in the legal continuum.[259] The devices employed by s 2(1) and (4), as has been seen, demand an approach by the judiciary to all existing and future statutes which acknowledges the supremacy of EU law. It can be argued that this is little more than an attempt to entrench the will of the Parliament which existed in 1972 and that this is impossible because, according to traditional British constitutional

2.203

2.204

2.205

---

[256] HWR Wade, 'Sovereignty—Revolution or Evolution?' (1996) 112 LQR 568, 571.
[257] ibid 574.
[258] Allan (n 238 above).
[259] See E Ellis, 'Supremacy of Parliament and European law' (1980) 96 LQR 511 and J Eekelaar, 'The Death of Parliamentary Sovereignty—A Comment' (1997) 113 LQR 185. For further discussion of this and related issues, see Craig (n 164 above).

law, no Parliament can bind its successors. Thus, the provision made in 1972 is open to repeal by a future Parliament. In the words of Lord Denning MR in *Macarthys Ltd v Smith*:[260]

> Thus far I have assumed that our Parliament, whenever it passes legislation, intends to fulfil its obligations under the Treaty. If the time should come when our Parliament deliberately passes an Act—with the intention of repudiating the Treaty or any provision in it—or intentionally of acting inconsistently with it—and says so in express terms—then I should have thought that it would be the duty of our courts to follow the statute of our Parliament. I do not however envisage any such situation.[261]

2.206   If repeal is possible, then it follows as a matter of logic that such repeal may occur either expressly or impliedly. It is suggested that, when Lord Denning referred to 'express terms' in the passage quoted above, he was not restricting his remarks to the express repeal of the ECA 1972 but, rather, was referring to clear words being required to indicate an intention to depart from the Act.

2.207   The most acute difficulties in this context are associated with the concept of implied repeal. As *Vauxhall Estates Ltd v Liverpool Corp*[262] and *Ellen Street Estates Ltd v Minister of Health*[263] demonstrate, an Act which seeks to entrench itself can be repealed impliedly merely by the enactment of later legislation which is inconsistent with it. This, it can be postulated, is what would happen if Parliament were to legislate in a way which conflicted with EU law; to the extent of the inconsistency, the later statute should take effect and should impliedly repeal ECA 1972, s 2(1) and (4) because it demonstrates a new intent to depart from the principle that EU law is supreme.

2.208   However, this is in reality an unsound analysis because the parallel between a potential conflict between EU and domestic law and the *Vauxhall/Ellen Street* situation is inexact. In the *Vauxhall* and *Ellen Street* cases, the earlier statute set out substantive rules on the assessment of compensation. Even if it could be interpreted as intended to govern future situations notwithstanding new legislation, it was contradicted as to the substance of its provisions by a later Act, which therefore impliedly repealed it. In the case of the ECA 1972, the rule which s 2(1) and (4) attempts to apply to future legislation is that such legislation should 'be construed and have effect' subject to the principle that EU law is supreme over it. When a conflict arises between substantive domestic law and substantive EU law, for example between the EU common fisheries rules and the Merchant Shipping Act 1988, nothing occurs which can be said in any sense to contradict, or even to

---

[260] [1979] 3 CMLR 44.
[261] ibid 47.
[262] [1932] 1 KB 733, discussed at para 2.150 above.
[263] [1934] 1 KB 590, discussed at para 2.151 above.

diverge from, the ECA 1972. The only conflict is between the substantive rules of law on the given matter. If there is no conflict with the ECA, there can be no question of its being impliedly repealed.[264] In fact, far from being repealed in such a situation, the ECA is actually being applied. The very situation for which it provides has occurred and the direction it contains to the judges to apply EU law rather than domestic law springs into action.[265] High level judicial support for this view is to be found in the speech of Lord Bridge in *R v Secretary of State for Transport, ex p Factortame*:[266]

> By virtue of section 2(4) of the [ECA] of 1972 Part II of the [Merchant Shipping] Act of 1988 is to be construed and take effect subject to directly enforceable Community rights and those rights are, by section 2(1) of the Act of 1972, to be 'recognised and available in law, and . . . enforced, allowed and followed accordingly . . .' This has precisely the same effect as if a section were incorporated in Part II of the Act of 1988 which in terms enacted that the provisions with respect to the registration of British fishing vessels were to be without prejudice to the directly enforceable Community rights of nationals of any Member State of the EEC. Thus it is common ground that, in so far as the applicants succeed before the ECJ in obtaining a ruling in support of the Community rights which they claim, those rights will prevail over the restrictions imposed on registration of British fishing vessels by Part II of the Act of 1988 . . .[267]

If the view expressed here does indeed represent a correct understanding of the operation of the ECA 1972, important consequences must be noted. First, the basis on which the supremacy of EU law rests in the United Kingdom is a statute and, moreover, the statute of a Parliament which appears to continue to possess theoretically unlimited powers at least in this field.[268] This means that the supremacy of EU law is guaranteed but only for as long as Parliament chooses it to be so. In effect, Parliament has delegated its authority to legislate on matters within the jurisdiction of the European Union to the Community institutions; EU law in the United Kingdom is therefore a form of subordinate legislation. It follows that, should the Community institutions act outside the powers conferred by the ECA 1972, the courts could quash any resulting domestic legislation on the ground that it was ultra vires its enabling Act.

2.209

Secondly, since the supremacy of EU law rests on the flimsy constitutional footing of an ordinary statute, it could be repealed. The issue of express repeal of the whole ECA 1972 is a highly theoretical one, since presumably this would signify

2.210

---

[264] See also *Thoburn v Sunderland City Council* [2002] EWHC 195; [2003] QB 151.
[265] It is submitted that a very similar analysis can be applied to Human Rights Act 1998, s 3(1) which provides: 'So far as it is possible to do so, primary legislation and subordinate legislation must be read and given effect in a way which is compatible with the Convention rights'.
[266] [1990] 2 AC 85.
[267] ibid 140.
[268] As already noted, its legislative competence may already be limited in relation to the Union with Scotland, Northern Ireland and devolution.

the departure of the United Kingdom from membership of the European Union and the political consequences would overwhelm any theoretical legal position. However, there remain two further possibilities. The first is that a future Parliament might unilaterally decide to opt out of a particular provision of EU law, albeit continuing to support the supremacy of EU law as a general proposition; if Parliament remains supreme, this appears legally possible although not in keeping with the spirit of EU law. In addition, there would appear to be the possibility of the implied repeal of ECA 1972, s 2(1) and (4), in the event that a future Parliament were to make different provision governing the relationship between domestic and EU law; even if such a later statute made no reference to the ECA 1972, to the extent of its inconsistency with it, it would impliedly repeal it.[269]

2.211   All this, however, exists in the realms of legal and jurisprudential theory. The practical truth of the matter is that Parliament's hands are well and truly bound by the demands of EU law, as it seems likely that in future years they will also be constrained by the HRA and by the devolution statutes.

---

[269] cf *Thoburn v Sunderland City Council* [2002] EWHC 195; [2003] QB 151.

3

THE NATURE, POWERS AND ACCOUNTABILITY OF CENTRAL GOVERNMENT

A. The Nature of Central Government in the United Kingdom

(1) The Characteristics of Central Government

(a) Models of central government—Crown, Westminster and multi-level governance

The term 'central government' is widely used in the United Kingdom but it does **3.01** not have any exact legal meaning. Nor is there any precise legal concept of 'the executive' or 'executive power' in the constitutional arrangements of the United Kingdom.[1] Central government in the United Kingdom is 'more plural than

---

[1] cf the US Constitution, Art II.1 ('the Executive Power shall be vested in the President . . .') and the Scotland Act 1998, where powers are vested in the Scottish Executive rather than individual Scottish ministers (discussed at paras 1.53 et seq, above). There is, though, a broad *political* concept of whole government, in the form of 'Her Majesty's Government', and the constitutional *convention* (not law) of collective ministerial responsibility: see below.

173

unitary'.[2] It is best understood as a set of office-holders, public authorities,[3] and other institutions:

- Ministers.[4] In September 2003, there were 89 ministers in office. Together with the Law Officers[5] and the government 'whips',[6] they constitute 'Her Majesty's Government'. In the UK system of parliamentary government, all ministers are required to be members of either the House of Commons (MPs) or House of Lords (peers).
- The Cabinet and its committees.[7] The Cabinet has no formal legal powers and is established by convention rather than law. The size of the Cabinet can vary; in September 2003, it comprised 21 ministers. Many Cabinet decisions are made not at the short weekly meeting of the full Cabinet but in one of the 50 or so Cabinet committees.
- The Privy Council, one of the most ancient parts of the central government machine which now has a range of executive, legislative and judicial functions.[8]
- Departments.[9] The policy-making work of central government is carried out principally through departments of state. Work is re-allocated between them from time to time under the direction of the Prime Minister. In 2003, there were 17 departments headed by ministers.
- Executive agencies, bodies headed by a chief executive and staffed by civil servants, work in conjunction with particular departments to deliver practical government services (such as the issue of passports, payment of welfare benefits and the administration of criminal records).[10]
- Several hundred non-departmental public bodies (NDPBs) of various kinds exist, carrying out a range of policy-making, regulatory, advisory and implementation functions.[11]

---

[2] T Daintith and A Page, *The Executive in the Constitution: Structure, Autonomy and Internal Control* (Oxford: OUP, 1999) 6. See also P Dunleavy, 'The Architecture of the British Central State, Part I: Framework for Analysis' (1989) 67 Public Administration 249; Martin J Smith, 'Reconceptualizing the British State: Theoretical and Empirical Challenges to Central Government' (1998) 76 Public Administration 45.

[3] The term 'public authority' has only relatively recently become a technical legal one, in part defined by the HRA 1998, s 6(3) and in part by the body of law relating to judicial review (Civil Procedure Rules 54.1). Lacking any formal legal powers, the Cabinet is not a public authority. The Civil Service has no constitutional status separate from ministers and departments.

[4] See para 3.35 below.

[5] See para 3.92 below.

[6] MPs and peers appointed by the Prime Minister to manage the voting by governing the party's members in Parliament.

[7] See para 3.45 below.

[8] See para 3.49 below.

[9] See para 3.56 below.

[10] See para 3.62 below. They are also known as 'Next Steps agencies'.

[11] See para 3.67 and ch 5, below.

- The Home Civil Service and Diplomatic Service is composed of approximately 500,000 professional, permanent, politically neutral officials employed in departments, executive agencies and NDPBs.[12]
- The Armed Forces, the Intelligence Service, the Security Service and national police organizations[13] responsible for defence, national security and combating crime.
- The Head of State.[14]
- The Law Officers.[15]

In the absence of a codified constitution, attempts to draw up a list of the institu- **3.02**
tions and offices of central government must be approached with a little caution, as the use of the adjective 'central' in relation to some governmental activities may be open to debate. For instance, the National Health Service is under the overall political leadership of a Secretary of State and the direction of the Department of Health, and is funded by central government, but a radical programme is being implemented to shift the balance of power within the NHS away from Whitehall[16] and towards front line clinical staff and their patients through new Strategic Health Authorities, Primary Care Trusts, NHS Trusts, an independent Chief Inspector of Healthcare, and so on.[17]

The United Kingdom's main constitutional arrangements are not the product of **3.03**
a purposive design, but of incremental development. A simple list of the office-holders and institutions of central government, such as the one set out above, cannot provide much by way of an understanding of the theory and practice of central government in the United Kingdom. Scholars have therefore sought to give accounts of the essence of the system. Three main narratives may be distinguished: ones based on (i) the Crown; (ii) the Westminster model; and (iii) more

---

[12] See para 3.69 below.

[13] See para 3.78 below. Generally in the UK, policing is not a matter for central government. There are 52 separate constabularies covering all geographical areas in the UK and five non-geographical police forces (eg, the British Transport Police).

[14] See para 3.87 below.

[15] See para 3.92 below.

[16] A term meaning 'any of the government offices situated in Whitehall, London' or, figuratively, 'the British government generally' (*Oxford English Dictionary*). See further, Peter Hennessey, *Whitehall* (London: Fontana Press, 1990) 17.

[17] Department of Health, *The NHS Plan: A Plan for Investment, A Plan for Reform* (Cm 4818, 2000) para 7.1: 'For fifty years the NHS has been subject to day-to-day running from Whitehall. A million strong service cannot be run in this way. If it is to better respond to the needs of patients the NHS can no longer be run as a monolithic, top-down, monopoly provider. Instead within a framework of clear national standards, subject to common inspection, power needs to be devolved to locally run services with the freedom to innovate and improve care for patients.' The Government's aim, as the NHS Plan sets out, is for, 'the centre to do only what it needs to do: then there will be maximum devolution of power to local doctors and other health professionals'. See Health and Social Care Act 2001 and National Health Service Reform and Health Care Professions Act 2002.

recent accounts of fragmented and multi-level governance. These models are not mutually exclusive and textbook accounts often interweave all three into their descriptions.

(i) The Crown model

3.04   First, the main organizing theme may be said to be 'the Crown', which still today can provide a unifying view of UK central government.[18] The starting point for a Crown-based account is the constitutional monarchy and Head of State. Executive power was once vested in the king or queen; and in modern conditions, the monarch still participates in formal conduct of day-to-day government business. Sometimes this is through the Queen in Council (the Privy Council), at other times through the Queen in person. The terminology of the central government machine is replete with references to the Crown: Her Majesty's Government; the royal prerogative; litigation is conducted in the Queen's Bench Division of the High Court; criminal prosecutions are brought in the name of the Crown (not the State); minors and mentally ill people convicted of serious crimes may be detained at 'Her Majesty's pleasure'.

3.05   Constitutional convention requires the Queen always to act on the advice of ministers. In relation to parliamentary legislation, Royal Assent to Bills follows the advice from the House of Commons and the House of Lords.[19] The Crown still possesses important, inherent non-statutory powers (the prerogative); these too are exercised on the advice of ministers.[20] In the absence of any other single source of executive power,[21] the Crown also provides a way of explaining, or emphasizing, the underlying continuity of government when ministers change after a general election[22] and major constitutional reform occurs.[23]

---

[18] See paras 1.16 et seq above; Joseph M Jacob, *The Republican Crown* (Aldershot: Dartmouth, 1996) 1: 'At the heart of Britain, law does not rule. The Crown is at this centre'; M Sunkin and S Payne (eds), *The Nature of the Crown: A Legal and Political Analysis* (Oxford: OUP, 1999); Tony Benn, *Arguments for Democracy* (London: Cape, 1981) 8–9; Ferdinand Mount, *The British Constitution Now* (London: Heinemann, 1992) ch 3.

[19] See the words of enactment: 'BE IT ENACTED by the Queen's most Excellent Majesty, by and with the advice and consent of the Lords Spiritual and Temporal, and Commons, in this present Parliament assembled, and by the authority of the same, as follows . . .'.

[20] See paras 1.18–1.20, 1.25, 2.13 et seq and 2.43.

[21] See n 2 above.

[22] eg, all government records, past and present, are the property of the Crown (see Lord Hunt of Tanworth, 'Access to a Previous Government's Papers' [1982] PL 514; and the UK's permanent and politically objective civil servants are 'servants of the Crown'.

[23] eg, following devolution in 1998, the newly established Scottish Executive comprises ministers of the Crown and the First Minister assumed responsibility for advising the Queen on the exercise of prerogative powers relating to Scottish affairs. The exercise of functions by the National Assembly for Wales 'is to be regarded as done on behalf of the Crown' (Government of Wales Act 1998, s 1(3)).

While the Crown may continue to have some use in describing the structures and   **3.06**
functions of central government, it has limitations. One is that the legal concept
of the Crown does not provide a useful working tool for lawyers; the legal nature
of the Crown is still remarkably underdeveloped and little understood.[24] Another
limit is that the Crown does not provide a basis for the whole of central government. As a leading scholar wrote in the 1930s, though the 'uninitiated might perhaps, not inexcusably, imagine that all public power is exercised in England in the
name of the Crown and by the servants of the Crown . . . nothing could be further
from the fact'.[25]

(ii) The Westminster model

A second strand in accounts of UK central government puts ministers and   **3.07**
Parliament, rather than the Crown, at the heart of things. The Westminster model
emphasizes the parliamentary character of central government. The institutions
of central government, notably individual ministers and the Cabinet collectively,
derive their democratic legitimacy from the fact that ministers are members of
Parliament, and in their ministerial capacity are accountable to Parliament for the
conduct of government. Ministers remain in power only so long as they retain the
confidence of the House of Commons.[26] Through debates, select committee inquiries and parliamentary questions, ministers are called to account for the conduct of government affairs. The UK Parliament thus has two roles: sustaining the
government of the day and also scrutinizing its actions. These tasks do not sit easily with each other.[27]

The United Kingdom's first-past-the-post electoral system and the dominance   **3.08**
over national politics by two parties (Conservative and Labour) since 1945 has
led to single party rather than coalition governments. The reality of the
Westminster model has been that the governing party controls Parliament,
rather than vice versa. The principle of parliamentary sovereignty,[28] the absence
of a codified constitution,[29] the lack of entrenched constitutional rights for individuals,[30] and the possibility of central government action based on prerogative rather than statutory powers, cleared the way for far-reaching changes to be

---

[24] See paras 1.21 et seq above. For two *causes celebres* in which the courts have had to grapple with
questions of the legal status of the Crown, see *Town Investments Ltd v Department of the Environment*
[1978] AC 359 and *M v Home Office* [1994] 1 AC 377.

[25] Sir Maurice Amos, *The English Constitution* (London: Longman, 1930) 110.

[26] On the constitutional conventions of collective and individual ministerial responsibility, see
paras 3.48 and 3.132 below.

[27] See Part C below. For an historical perspective, see Matthew Flinders, 'Shifting the Balance?
Parliament, the Executive and the British Constitution' (2002) 50 Political Studies 23.

[28] See paras 1.79 et seq and 2.142 et seq above.

[29] See paras 1.12 et seq above.

[30] Until enactment of the HRA 1998 (but even Convention rights cannot be said to be 'entrenched' as the UK Parliament may still enact legislation contrary to them).

implemented by governments to the structure,[31] functions,[32] ethos,[33] and management techniques[34] of central government.[35] Some changes, such as the creation of executive agencies to carry out operational activities previously undertaken directly by departments, were achieved without new legislation and remarkably little prior debate within Parliament.

3.09   Before becoming Prime Minister, Tony Blair was able to describe the United Kingdom has having 'the most centralised government of any State in the Western World'.[36] A generation before, a Conservative politician diagnosed an 'elective dictatorship'.[37] Moreover, there is a perennial debate as to whether the United Kingdom has or is moving towards having 'Prime Ministerial government', that is whether despite the absence of formal legal authority in the hands of a single chief executive officer, the powers of successive Prime Ministers have grown and, perhaps, become presidential in substance if not in form.[38]

(iii) Multi-level, fragmented governance model

3.10   A third strand in accounts of the United Kingdom's central government is emerging. Most political scientists now reject the Westminster model as a realistic portrayal of the United Kingdom's system of government. The claim that ministers are at the heart of government is questioned on two fronts: the emergence of multi-level government; and the phenomenon of the fragmentation or 'hybridization' of internal central government structures associated with a range of reforms collectively known as 'new public management'.[39]

---

[31] eg, the creation of executive agencies and devolution.

[32] Between 1979 and 1990, Conservative governments privatized inter alia British Telecom, British Gas, British Airways, British Aerospace, British Airports Authority, British Steel, British Shipbuilders, regional water and electricity companies and British Rail.

[33] eg, Citizen's Charter programme (now 'Service First'). Gavin Drewry, 'Whatever happened to the Citizen's Charter?' [2002] PL 9.

[34] In particular, the set of approaches to the role of the public sector known as 'new public management' (n 39 below).

[35] cf administrative culture in Germany. British political scientists carrying out a comparative study found that '[w]henever we walked into a German civil servant's office, the relevant legal texts were piled on the table and he or she gave answers to most questions about the relationship between ministries and agencies while leafing through them', N Elder and EC Page, 'Culture and Agency: Fragmentation and Agency Structures in Germany and Sweden' (1998) 13 Public Policy and Administration J 28, 43.

[36] John Smith Memorial Lecture, 7 February 1996, quoted in Samuel H Beer, 'Strong Government and Democratic Control' (1999) 70 Political Q 146.

[37] Lord Hailsham, *The Dilemma of Democracy: Diagnosis and Prescription* (London: Collins, 1978) ch 20.

[38] See para 3.40 below.

[39] New public management includes 'market testing' (where possible, government tasks are tested with accounting devices to discover whether they could be provided more cheaply by the private sector), the Fundamental Expenditure Review (whereby each department must review its work and resources to make savings), the Financial Management Initiative (systematic efficiency audits to improve management of resources), the Next Steps programme (which led to the creation

From this perspective, the bodies enumerated above[40] are 'central' in so far as they may be differentiated from other levels of government—namely, (i) local authorities, (ii) the devolved executive institutions established in Scotland, Wales and Northern Ireland in 1998, and also (iii) the institutions of the European Union. The creation of new institutions exercising executive and law-making powers at sub-national and supra-national level has resulted in multi-level governance.[41] Many areas of policy-making that were once within the exclusive domain of UK central government are now transferred to, or are shared with, devolved government and/or the European Union. Questions of division of powers, which were once seen as the exclusive preserve of federal constitutions, now arise in relation to the United Kingdom. Multi-level governance also embraces the interdependence of states through international organizations, including the Commonwealth of Nations,[42] the World Trade Organization,[43] the United Nations,[44] and the

3.11

---

of executive agencies separate from departments), 'value for money' within specified cash limits, and the creation of business plans for departments. There have been a series of programmes and initiatives seeking to improve efficiency and effectiveness, including the Financial Management Initiative (1982), Improving Management in Government: the Next Steps (1988), Competing for Quality Programme (1991), The Citizen's Charter (1991), The Civil Service: Continuity and Change (1994). See Diana Woodhouse, *In Pursuit of Good Administration: Ministers, Civil Servants, and Judges* (Oxford: OUP, 1997) 5: 'Public administration has therefore developed a hybrid form. It may be undertaken by traditional civil servants within departments of government, by temporary civil servants, still within government departments but operating under private-sector controls and incentives adopted by executive agencies, and by private sector contractors. Alternatively, it may be undertaken by quangos or non-departmental bodies, established to operate at arm's length from the minister in a regulatory, advisory or executive capacity.'

[40] See para 3.01 above.

[41] See further N Douglas Lewis, *Law and Governance* (London: Cavendish, 2001); L Hooghe and G Marks, *Multi-Level Governance and European Integration* (Maryland: Rowan & Littlefield, 2001); A Chayes and AH Chayes, *The new sovereignty: compliance with international regulatory regimes* (Cambridge, Massachusetts: Harvard University Press, 1995).

[42] The Commonwealth was established in 1949 and now has 54 members, almost all being former dominions and colonies of the UK. The Queen is Head of the Commonwealth. It is a voluntary association of independent sovereign states, consulting and co-operating in the common interests of their peoples and in the promotion of international understanding and world peace. There are regular Commonwealth Heads of Government meetings. The Commonwealth has produced a number of declarations relating to principles of constitutionalism and good government, including the Declaration of Commonwealth Principles (Singapore, 1971), the Harare Commonwealth Declaration (1991), and the Bangalore Principles (1988) set out by a colloquium of Commonwealth judges.

[43] The free trade rules are made and enforced under the auspices of the WTO. The Agreement Establishing the World Trade Organization was signed on 15 April 1994 by the EC, its member states and many other states. That Agreement is a 'Community treaty' for the purposes of the European Communities Act 1972 (see European Communities (Definition of Treaties) (The Agreement Establishing the World Trade Organisation) Order 1995, SI 1995/265). The UK negotiates in the WTO as part of the EU. Membership of the WTO requires modifications to UK law to ensure compatibility with WTO treaties (see eg Patents and Trade Marks (World Trade Organisation) Regulations 1999, SI 1999/1899).

[44] The United Nations Act 1946 empowers 'His Majesty' to make secondary legislation (in the form of an Order in Council) to give effect to decisions of the UN Security Council taken under Art 41 of the UN Charter. Such secondary legislation has been made to give effect to sanctions and to recognize UN tribunals on war crimes.

Council of Europe[45] (especially through enforcement of international human rights norms by the European Court of Human Rights).

3.12   A second reason why the Westminster model is ceasing to be a realistic portrayal of how executive power is organized and public policy made and implemented is that over the past 20 years there has been a fragmentation of government bodies, methods of regulation and other governmental functions. Although ministers and departments still exert control over resources and have important powers to direct, complex networks of office-holders and bodies in the public, private and voluntary sectors tackle most social needs and problems. Many activities that were once under the direct control of central government, or carried out by wholly state-owned corporations, have been sold to private sector enterprises that are regulated by a range of different kinds of institution.[46] Within the remains of the public sector, there has been a disaggregation: some functions have been 'contracted out'; 'compulsory competitive tendering' processes are in place; there are 'internal markets' whereby providers and purchasers of goods and services within government act at arm's length; the setting of objectives or standards against which performance is measured. There is also currently a vogue for 'public/private partnerships' in which privately owned capital or management expertise is used by government to achieve its ends.[47] The policy-advice function of the civil service has been separated from the managerial task of delivering services with the creation of executive agencies separate from departments. In short, the range of activities carried out by central government has changed, methods of working have altered and a broader range of institutions are involved in formulating and implementing public policy than was the case 30 years ago.[48]

3.13   Political scientists now prefer the terminology of 'governance' rather than 'government' as this signifies better the 'interaction and linkages between the state, the market and civil society'.[49] The emphasis is on networks and processes rather than institutions. The operation of central government institutions needs to be set into the context of 'a much wider array of public, private and voluntary organizations

---

[45] There are currently 45 members of the Council of Europe. The Council of Europe aims: 'to protect human rights, pluralist democracy and the rule of law; to promote awareness and encourage the development of Europe's cultural identity and diversity; to seek solutions to problems facing European society (discrimination against minorities, xenophobia, intolerance, environmental protection, human cloning, Aids, drugs, organised crime, etc.); to help consolidate democratic stability in Europe by backing political, legislative and constitutional reform'. Care must be taken to differentiate the Council of Europe from the entirely separate supra-national organization, the European Union!

[46] See ch 5 below.

[47] Thus, people may be incarcerated in privately owned prisons and modernization of the London Underground is to be funded by private capital.

[48] See Public Administration Committee, *Making Government Work: The Emerging Issues*, 7th Report (2000–01 HC 94).

[49] Matthew Flinders, 'Governance in Whitehall' (2002) 80 Public Administration 51, 52.

than would traditionally be included with in the "governmental" framework'.[50] A problem for constitutional law and practice is that innovations in forms of accountability have not always kept pace with developments in the nature of UK government.[51]

With the advent of multi-level government and the internal disaggregation of central government, questions arise as to the status and role of the core bodies of UK central government. It has been said that there is a 'hollowing out' of the central state, such that the capacity of ministers and departments to 'steer the system'—to govern—has been greatly diminished.[52] There is, however, some evidence that this view is mistaken.[53]

3.14

(b) Division of powers in the UK constitution

Devolution of executive power within the United Kingdom and membership of the European Union have important repercussions for central government. In a system of multi-level government, 'central government' needs now to be defined in terms of the legal powers possessed by the actors at that level in distinction to supra- and sub-national institutions.

3.15

In countries with federal systems of government, one of the functions of a codified constitution is to set out which fields of policy-making belong to federal level government and which belong to the constituent parts ('states', 'provinces', 'länder', etc). This may be done either by reserving general powers to central government and enumerating the policy areas over which the constituent parts have jurisdiction (as in Canada and Australia) or vice versa (as in the USA). The concepts and practices of federalism cannot be used in relation to the United Kingdom, either in relation to central government's relations with the devolved institutions in Scotland, Northern Ireland and Wales or the institutions of the European Union. This is because parliamentary sovereignty enables central government (assuming it has a majority in Parliament) to amend its relationship to local government and the devolved institutions by means of ordinary legislation. The powers of sub-national levels of government have no constitutional protection within the United Kingdom. Political realities may, however, make it difficult to amend the devolution Acts without consent of the nations—but formal power to do so is expressly reserved to the UK Parliament.[54] Nor is federalism apt

3.16

---

[50] ibid.

[51] See Part C below.

[52] RAW Rhodes, 'The Hollowing Out of the State: The Changing Nature of the Public Service in Britain' (1994) 65 Political Q 138.

[53] Ian Holliday, 'Is the British State Hollowing Out?' (2000) 71 Political Q 167 and below.

[54] See para 1.51 above. The UK government has already exercised its powers to suspend devolved government in Northern Ireland on more than one occasion.

to describe the constitutional relationship between the United Kingdom and the European Union, as the European Union is not itself a state.[55]

3.17 Even if the concept of federalism is inapplicable to the UK constitution, there remains a practical need to define the division of powers between different levels of government and to map out the legal nature and extent of the areas of policy-making that belong to central government.

3.18 Central government can, first, be distinguished from local government throughout the United Kingdom.[56] Local authorities always have been, and remain, subordinate institutions in the sense that they have little autonomy from central government. In many respects, they are to be regarded as the agents of central government in relation to their main fields of responsibility. Local authorities have no protected status in the constitution and have been subject to almost constant reorganization instigated by central government. As between central government and local authorities, the allocation of functions is to be found in Acts of Parliament. The main policy fields in which local authorities are involved include: education; social services; transport; town and country planning; fire services; consumer protection; refuse collection and disposal; public libraries; public housing and advice to homeless people; local highways; building regulation; environmental health; recreation and cultural matters. Legal disputes about the division of powers between central and local government are determined by the Administrative Court (part of the High Court of England and Wales) in claims for judicial review.

3.19 Central government can, secondly, be differentiated from the executive bodies in Scotland, Northern Ireland and Wales created by the devolution Acts in 1998.[57] The asymmetrical or 'haphazard' form of devolved powers results in England, by far the largest part of the United Kingdom, not itself having any executive separate from that of the United Kingdom as a whole.[58] Any dispute between a devolved executive body and central government about the allocation of functions ultimately falls to be determined by the Judicial Committee of the Privy Council.[59]

3.20 Thirdly, the functions of central government must be set in the context of the United Kingdom's membership, since 1973, of the European Community and the European Union.[60] The European Court of Justice ultimately determines division of powers disputes in this context.

[55] This is of course to simplify. See further Hooghe and Marks (n 41 above).
[56] See ch 4 below.
[57] See paras 1.55, 1.57 and 1.59 et seq above.
[58] See para 3.27 below.
[59] Judicial Committee (Powers in Devolution Cases) Order 1999, SI 1999/1320.
[60] On development of EC and EU, see paras 1.66 et seq above.

In the United Kingdom's multi-layered system of government many broad fields **3.21** of governmental policy-making—such as environmental protection, the regulation of building development and transport—engage the responsibilities of government at all levels: local, devolved, central and European Union. Relatively few fields of central government policy-making are unaffected by shared decision-making and laws made by the European Union. The allocation of functions as between these levels has been criticized as overly complex and lacking transparency: provisions dividing competence as scattered throughout the treaties and regard must also be had to the European Court of Justice's judgments relating to the demarcation of power between the European Union and member states.[61] The current arrangements can be represented in a diagram:

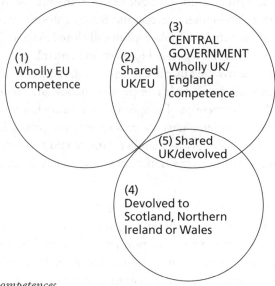

(i) Wholly EU competences

Several fields of policy-making vitally important to the operation of the European **3.22** Union fall within its exclusive competence. As in other member states, central government in the United Kingdom has no power to develop policy and initiate national legislation on these topics except to give effect to EC policy (though ministers will participate in the EC's decision-making on them). Ministers may participate in the decision-making process in the Council that leads to the adoption of EC legislation, but qualified majority voting can lead to EC legislation being made contrary to the wishes of the United Kingdom. The main fields in which the European Community has exclusive competence are: the 'four freedoms' of the single market—free movement between member states of goods, services, capital

---

[61] One of the aims of the Convention on the Future of the EU is to consider how better to delimit the competences of the EU and its member states.

and people; the common agriculture and fisheries policies; trade with non-EU states; sex discrimination; and the single currency and monetary policy (for those member states which are participating in this).

(ii) Shared EU and UK competences

3.23 Responsibility over some fields of policy is shared between member states and the European Union. Such shared competencies may be 'complementary' or 'concurrent'. In relation to complementary competencies, the role of the European Community is limited to supplementing, supporting or co-ordinating action of member states; member states retain the power to make legislation covering the field. These fields include: employment; customs co-operation; education; vocational training and youth; culture; public health; trans-European network; industry; research and development; economic policy co-ordination.[62] Concurrent competencies are those fields of policy specifically listed in the EC Treaty; once the European Community has legislated in those areas member states can no longer legislate on the issues covered by the EC legislation, except to implement it. Such concurrent competencies include competition policy and environmental management. In all fields where the European Community has non-exclusive competence, whether complementary or concurrent, the principle of subsidiarity operates: what the lesser entity (ie member state) can do adequately should not be done by the greater entity (ie the European Union) unless it can do it better.[63]

(iii) Competences exclusive to the United Kingdom

3.24 The fields of policy over which the central government in the United Kingdom and England has exclusive competence are nowhere enumerated. Specific powers granting legal authority to take executive action and make policy to ministers and other public authorities comprising central government are found in Acts of Parliament and delegated legislation. In relation to England, they include education, health services, and legal regulation of the family. In relation to the whole United Kingdom, they include income tax (though the Scottish Parliament may vary the rate of income tax by two pence in the pound in Scotland) and social security. Ministers may also obtain legal authority in the form of prerogative power: as the Prime Minister has recently conceded: 'The exercise of powers under the prerogative has evolved over many years, and a precise list is not possible'.[64] An attempt will, however, be made below to set out some of the principal prerogative powers.[65] The conduct of international relations was once, par excellence, a function of central government

---

[62] CONV 75/02 (31 May 2002).
[63] See further Antonio Estella, *The EU principle of subsidiarity and its critique* (Oxford: OUP, 2002).
[64] *Hansard*, HC col 292W (24 October 2001) (Mr Blair).
[65] See para 3.109 below and paras 1.25–1.28 above.

but in many situations this is no longer so as the European Community has exclusive competence in relation to trade agreements with any non-EU state.

(iv) Competences of the devolved governments

The schemes for division of powers between central government and the devolved executive bodies over fields of policy differ in the Scotland Act, Northern Ireland Act and Government of Wales Act 1998. Under the Scotland Act, the Scottish Executive has all those powers that are not specifically 'relating to' the enumerated list of policy fields reserved to the United Kingdom. Reserved powers are, however, substantial in nature and number.[66] The fields over which the Scotland Executive and Scottish Parliament have jurisdiction are not expressly enumerated in the Scotland Act, but they include: education; economic and industrial development; tourism; health; agriculture and food (in the context of EC policy); criminal justice; policing (in partnership with the police constabularies in Scotland); culture and sport; tourism; housing; and town and country planning. In contrast to Scotland, the policy areas over which the National Assembly for Wales has jurisdiction are explicitly enumerated as the Welsh devolution scheme defines devolved, rather than 'reserved', matters: agriculture, fisheries and food; education and training; health and social services; highways; and housing.[67] The devolution scheme for Northern Ireland has three categories of policy area: 'excepted' matters that are intended to remain matters for the United Kingdom for the foreseeable future;[68] matters 'reserved' to the United Kingdom which are retained by the United Kingdom for the time being but which may be transferred to Northern Ireland at some point in the future;[69] and 'transferred' matters[70] being areas of policy that are neither 'excepted' nor 'reserved'. These matters are not specifically enumerated in the Act. The Secretary of State for Northern Ireland[71] may, from time to time, decide what areas of policy in the 'reserved' list shall be transferred. Once transferred, they may be recalled into the field of competence of the United Kingdom. Devolution has resulted in there being important differences between the policies pursued by the UK government (in relation to England and

3.25

---

[66] See para 1.53 above.

[67] Government of Wales Act 1998, Sch 2, and ss 27–28; see para 1.59 above.

[68] Northern Ireland Act 1998, Sch 2; see para 1.56 above. This includes matters relating to the Crown, international relations, defence, nationality and immigration, the appointment of judges and elections in Northern Ireland.

[69] ibid Sch 3. These include: navigation; civil aviation; domicile; postal services; disqualification from the Northern Ireland Assembly; criminal law; public order and prisons; organization of the police force; firearms and explosives; civil defence; the courts; many aspects of import and export controls and trade with places outside the UK, and business competition.

[70] ibid s 4(1).

[71] The minister in the UK government with responsibility for Northern Ireland, see para 3.57 below.

Wales) and those operating in Scotland, Northern Ireland and Wales, especially in relation to matters such as schools, hospitals and rural and economic development.[72]

(v) Competences shared between UK and devolved governments

3.26 There are areas of policy over which jurisdiction is shared between devolved institutions and central government.[73] In relation to Scotland, 'Joint powers are those where it is a legal requirement for Scottish Ministers and UK Ministers to act in agreement and together, or for UK Ministers to act only after consultation with the Scottish Ministers (or vice versa). Concurrent powers are those which either UK or Scottish Ministers or both are able to exercise in Scotland.'[74] The UK government has drawn up a series of documents known as 'concordats' with the devolved executive bodies to provide a framework for intergovernmental relations within the United Kingdom.[75] Concordats cover such topics as how executive bodies in Scotland, Northern Ireland and Wales participate in deciding the United Kingdom's stance on agenda items before the EU Council, regulation of regional incentives promoting inward investment, and UK ministerial meetings with the fishing industry in Scotland.

(c) Asymmetrical devolution: distinction between all-UK and English matters

3.27 It will be apparent that asymmetrical devolution has resulted in a situation whereby 'central government'—ministers and departments—are sometimes concerned with matters relating to the whole of the United Kingdom and at other times are confined to matters relating to England only (which has no executive government separate from that of the United Kingdom as a whole). Thus, some central government departments—such as HM Treasury, the Ministry of Defence, the Department for International Development and the Foreign and Commonwealth Office—have all-UK functions, whereas much of the work of ministers and civil servants in some other departments—for example, the Department for Environment, Rural Affairs and Food, the Department of Health and Department for Education and Skills—relates mainly to England. The following table indicates some of the policy areas falling on each side of the divide.

[72] See John Adams and Peter Robinson, *Devolution in Practice: Public Policy Differences within the UK* (London: IPPR, 2002).
[73] In relation to Wales, see David Miers and David Lambert, 'Law making in Wales: Wales Legislation on-line' [2002] PL 663.
[74] Concordat between the Scottish Executive and the Lord Chancellor's Department, para 7.
[75] See R Rawlings, 'Concordats and the Constitution' (2000) 11 LQR 257.

'Central government' relating to whole UK *	'Central government' relating to England only
Defence	Education
Foreign and Commonwealth relations	Rural affairs, fishing and food
Tax and economic policies	Housing
Immigration and nationality	Health
Constitutional reform	Tourism
Human rights and equality issues	Aspects of trade and industry
Energy	Town and country planning
Aviation	Highways
Regulation of political parties	

* These are some of the main areas of policy that are 'reserved matters' under the Scotland Act; and 'exempted' or (currently) reserved under the Northern Ireland Act; and which are not enumerated as functions of the National Assembly for Wales in the Government of Wales Act.

In some respects the all-UK/England divide in central government may appear to **3.28** be an awkward one; thus, the Department for Environment, Rural Affairs and Food is responsible for English agriculture (agriculture being a devolved area of policy-making in Scotland, Wales and Northern Ireland) but also for the all-UK dimension to agriculture when a UK minister attends a meeting of the EU Council to determine EC law and policy relating to agriculture. It cannot always be assumed that the 'English' view of what is desirable fits easily with the views of executive bodies in other parts of the United Kingdom.

(d) The finance of central government

In history, controversies about the funding of government led to constitutional **3.29** conflict between the Crown and Parliament.[76] As late as 1911, the first attempt to reform the hereditary House of Lords was sparked off by its refusal to pass legislation giving effect to the Liberal Government's 'People's Budget' which sought to introduce redistributive taxation.

The functions of central government—including the provision of welfare benefits, **3.30** the National Health Service, education and defence[77]—are funded by direct and indirect taxation of the annual incomes of individuals and corporations, capital

[76] See paras 1.16, 1.125 et seq and 2.68 et seq above.
[77] UK government expenditure according to sector in 1996–97 was: 32% on welfare benefits and pensions; 17% on health and social services; 12% on education; 7% on defence; and 5% on law and order (The Economist, 28 March 1998, 36).

gains, inheritance, etc;[78] customs and excise duties[79] levied on goods and services (including value added tax); government borrowing in the capital markets and the levy of miscellaneous charges.

3.31 It is a constitutional principle of great importance that central government may only raise such taxes, and spend such sums for specified purposes, as are authorized annually by Parliament. A major financial and economic statement ('the Budget') is made to the House of Commons each spring by the Chancellor of the Exchequer.[80] The purpose of the Budget is to provide a survey on the economic health of the United Kingdom and its public finances and to outline proposed changes in tax. The Budget statement is accompanied by publication to the House of Commons of 'Estimates'—detailed statements for each government department of anticipated expenditure in the forthcoming year. In the weeks that follow, legal authority is given to tax changes in the form of one or more Finance Acts.

3.32 Public revenues, including tax and duties, are paid into the Consolidated Fund, an account kept at the Bank of England.[81] Government spending from the Consolidated Fund is authorized by Parliament on an annual basis by one or more Appropriation Acts and Consolidated Fund Acts. An Appropriation Act lists sums to be spent under various heads of expenditure and authorizes HM Treasury to borrow money. The Consolidated Fund Acts authorize the transfer of funds from the Bank of England to the account of the Paymaster-General (a government minister) who, in turn, allocates funds to departments in accordance with parliamentary approval.

3.33 In each department and executive agency, a senior civil servant is the 'accounting officer', personally responsible to Parliament for the proper expenditure of funds in accordance with the annual parliamentary 'vote' (ie, the funds voted by Parliament under the Consolidated Fund Acts and the Appropriation Acts). Accounting officers are answerable to the House of Commons' Public Accounts Committee, established in 1861, which investigates both formal propriety of government spending and also its 'value for money'. The committee's work is aided by the National Audit Office (headed by the Comptroller and Auditor General, an officer of the House of Commons), the function of which is to report to Parliament on the economy, efficiency and effectiveness with which government bodies have used public money.

---

[78] The principal statutes are the Taxes Management Act 1970 and the Income and Corporation Taxes Act 1998. On the role of the Inland Revenue Commissioners, see below.

[79] The main statute is the Customs and Excise Management Act 1979. Customs duties, payable on imports of goods, are levied only on goods arriving from outside the EU. These are now an EU tax, with revenue being paid by the UK government to the EU. The EC Treaty has abolished all duties on trade between member states.

[80] See para 3.43 below.

[81] On its constitutional status, see Bank of England Act 1998.

(2) The Machinery of Government

This section describes, in turn, the main institutions and office-holders with central government. **3.34**

(a) Ministers

Even in an era of multi-level and fragmented governance,[82] an account of the constitutional and legal role of ministers is an appropriate starting point. Legally and politically, government ministers are at the core of central government, even if the scope and nature of their political authority has altered in recent years. Most legal power to conduct the business of central government lies in the hands of individual government ministers, conferred on them by Acts of Parliament or the prerogative.[83] As party politicians, ministers often have a decisive impact on the direction of public policy and the fact of their membership of Parliament helps to confer democratic legitimacy on government action. **3.35**

In the UK system of parliamentary government, all ministers are required to be a member of the House of Commons or the House of Lords. No more than 95 MPs may hold ministerial office, a statutory restriction designed to hold in check the patronage powers of the Prime Minister.[84] In recent years, there have typically been between 80 and 90 ministers. Ministers are chosen by the Prime Minister[85] to provide political leadership to one of the departments. The formalities of ministerial appointments occur in a variety of ways.[86] The most senior minister in each department normally carries the title 'one of Her Majesty's Principal Secretaries of State';[87] more junior ministers are styled 'Minister of State' and 'Parliamentary-under-Secretary'.[88] Ministers may appoint 'Parliamentary Private Secretaries', MPs **3.36**

---

[82] See para 3.10 above.
[83] See paras 3.102 and 3.109 below.
[84] House of Commons Disqualification Act 1975, s 2, Sch 2.
[85] See para 3.40 below.
[86] Rodney Brazier, *Constitutional Practice* (Oxford: Clarendon, 1988) 61. The methods of appointment, varying according to the ministerial office, include: taking an oath of office before the Queen in Council (on which, see below); taking an oath of office before a more senior minister; and/or receiving three seals of office (which are returned upon the minister ceasing to hold office).
[87] Interpretation Act 1978, s 5, Sch 1.
[88] Departures from this standard terminology are: the Chancellor of the Exchequer is the ministerial head of HM Treasury, where the junior ministers are the Chief Secretary to the Treasury (which carries with it membership of the Cabinet), the Paymaster General, the Economic Secretary, and the Financial Secretary; the President of the Council is the ministerial head of the Privy Council Office; and the Chancellor of the Duchy of Lancaster (which is an ancient Crown estate, providing private income which, by convention, is used by the monarch to meet some costs associated with public duties; the duties associated with administration of the Duchy by the 'Chancellor' are not onerous and, by convention, this post is combined with a flexible Cabinet position, by which a Prime Minister is able to deploy a minister to deal with cross-departmental issues).

who act as unpaid aides.[89] In law, there is just a single office of Secretary of State[90] and it is possible for one Secretary of State to act for any other (unless, which is rare, legislation confers powers on a specific named Secretary of State).

3.37 Some Secretaries of State have their broad public duties and functions set out in an Act of Parliament, as, for instance, in s 1(1) of the National Health Service Act 1977:

> It is the Secretary of State's duty to continue the promotion in England and Wales of a comprehensive health service designed to secure improvement—(a) in the physical and mental health of the people of those countries, and (b) in the prevention, diagnosis and treatment of illness, and for that purpose to secure the effective provision of services in accordance with this Act.

3.38 Some, but not all, Secretaries of State have the legal personality of a corporation sole for the purposes of owning property and making contracts; others do so in the name of the Crown. The Deputy Prime Minister, also styled 'First Secretary of State', deputizes for the Prime Minister and is the political head of his own department.[91] Some Prime Ministers have appointed a Minister without Portfolio to the Cabinet. One person may occupy two distinct ministerial offices.[92]

3.39 Ministers are said to perform four main generic roles.[93] First, they set and direct the policy agenda of central government. Here, the principles and manifesto commitments of the political party that forms the government will often be decisive, though in some policy areas (such as criminal justice) there have been significant continuities between recent Labour and Conservative governments' policies. Secondly, ministers have political functions in representing the interests of their departments in Cabinet, Parliament, the EU Council, and their political party. Ministers answer oral questions in Parliament (typically every three to five weeks) and written questions about the conduct of their department; this is a central principle of the parliamentary system of government.[94] In every parliamentary

---

[89] Though not part of the government, Parliamentary Private Secretaries are bound by the convention of collective responsibility and must refrain from criticism of government policy (for discussion on whether this is justified, see David L Ellis, 'Collective Ministerial Responsibility and Collective Solidarity' [1980] PL 367).

[90] AJC Simcock, 'One and Many—The Office of Secretary of State' (1992) 70 Public Administration 535.

[91] There is no formal constitutional post of Deputy Prime Minister. See V Bogdanor, *The Monarchy and the Constitution* (Oxford: Clarendon Press, 1995) 87.

[92] eg, in the 2003 Labour government, Patricia Hewitt MP combined the roles of Secretary of State for Social Security with that of Minister for Women and Alistair Darling MP was Secretary of State for Transport and Secretary of State for Scotland. By convention, the Prime Minister also holds the posts of First Lord of the Treasury and Minister for the Civil Service.

[93] D Marsh, D Richards and MJ Smith, 'Re-Assessing the Role of Departmental Cabinet Ministers' (2000) 78 Public Administration 305. For a more personal account, see Gerald Kaufman, *How to be a Minister* (London: Faber and Faber, 1997).

[94] See Part C below.

session, many ministers will, if their departments are seeking new legislation to cover areas for which they are responsible, steer Bills through the legislative procedures of Parliament; here too ministers are answerable for the department's plans. They also often appear in the news media to defend departmental policies. Constitutional propriety demands that major policy announcements are made first to Parliament, rather than to the news media, but this is not always observed.[95] Thirdly, ministers have high-level managerial tasks in relation to the running of their departments[96] and also make executive decisions.[97] Ministers spend on average two years in a ministerial post before being 'reshuffled' by the Prime Minister to another department, or out of the government. The constitutional relationship between ministers and civil servants is considered below.[98] Many ministers appoint 'special advisers' to assist them.[99]

The most senior minister in status is the Prime Minister, by convention the leader of **3.40** the largest political party in the House of Commons, who is the United Kingdom's Head of Government.[100] Political scientists and constitutional scholars have spilt much ink on the nature of the office of Prime Minister (rather to the neglect of other ministers). Debates have centred on the question whether the Prime Minister should be regarded as primus inter partes (first among equals in relation to his or her ministerial colleagues) or whether a presidential style is emerging (in which there is a concentration of de facto executive power in the hands of the Prime Minister, at the expense of other ministers).[101] From a strictly legal point of view, the Prime Minister has very few statutory powers compared to those in the hands of other ministers. It has recently been suggested that the powers of the Prime Minister ought to be codified in an Act of Parliament, though as the following written exchange between an MP and the Prime Minister indicates, such reform is very unlikely to take place.[102]

Prime Minister's Powers

Mr. Allen: To ask the Prime Minister (1) if he will introduce legislation to give statutory definition to the powers of the Prime Minister; and if he will make a statement;

---

[95] Ministers may, of course, also be keen to keep stories out of the media spotlight!

[96] Though ministers tend not to regard themselves as the chief executive of the department; that is the function of the Permanent Secretary (the most senior civil servant in the department): see Hennessey (n 16 above) 607.

[97] Until November 2002, the Home Secretary determined the minimum number of years to be served by people given mandatory sentences of life imprisonment by the courts; in *R v Secretary of State for the Home Department, ex p Anderson* [2002] UKHL 46; [2002] 3 WLR 1800 the House of Lords held this power to be incompatible with Convention rights.

[98] See para 3.69 below.

[99] See para 3.76 below.

[100] The head of state of the UK is Her Majesty The Queen; see para 3.87 below.

[101] See D Kavanagh and A Seldon, *The Powers behind the Prime Minister* (London: Harper Collins, 1999); Peter Hennessey, 'The Blair Style of Government: An Historical Perspective and an Interim Audit' (1998) 33 *Government and Opposition* 3.

[102] *Hansard*, HC col 818W (15 October 2001).

(2) if he will list those of his powers (a) granted to him by statute and (b) which can be exercised (i) without statutory authority and (ii) under royal prerogative.

The Prime Minister: In addition to general references to the Prime Minister, there are more than 50 specific powers conferred on the office by statute, most in relation to appointments. The Prime Minister also holds the titles and duties of the Minister for the Civil Service and the First Lord of the Treasury. The Prime Minister's roles as the head of Her Majesty's Government, her principal adviser and as Chairman of the Cabinet are not, however, defined in legislation. These roles, including the exercise of powers under the royal prerogative, have evolved over many years, drawing on convention and usage, and it is not possible precisely to define them. The Government have no plans to introduce legislation in this area.

3.41 The powers relating to appointments in the hands of the Prime Minister are, as indicated, many and various but four main functions can be identified. First, the Prime Minister has powers of patronage. After assuming office after a general election, and in periodic Cabinet reshuffles, the Prime Minister appoints other ministers.[103] The Prime Minister also decides on the appointment of the United Kingdom's most senior judges (in consultation with the Lord Chancellor)[104] and bishops of the Church of England. Secondly, the Prime Minister is the personal face of collective government: he or she is answerable to the House of Commons, to the general public through the news media, and to his or her political party, for the overall conduct of government policy. Thirdly, the Prime Minister has important functions in co-ordinating the central government machine. The setting of overall priorities for a government, and the co-ordination of work of different departments, is also crucial. This is achieved in part through the Prime Minister's chairmanship of the Cabinet and many Cabinet committees, and also through the work of 'the New Centre'.[105] The United Kingdom has never established a formal 'Prime Minister's Department'; the Prime Minister's Office is a flexible and relatively small group of special advisers and permanent civil servants.[106] The Ministerial Code[107] requires all

---

[103] Formally, the appointment as minister is carried out by the Queen on the advice of the Prime Minister. See below.

[104] An independent Judicial Appointments Commission for England and Wales was established in 2001 following Sir Leonard Peach's Report, *An Independent Scrutiny of the Appointment Processes of Judges and Queen's Counsel in England & Wales* (London: LCD, 2000). Its function is to carry out an on-going audit of appointments procedures and to hear complaints from individuals and organizations about their operation. Although in law it is the Prime Minister who is responsible for making senior judicial appointments (to the rank of Lords of Appeal in Ordinary—the 'Law Lords'—and Lords Justices of Appeal—judges of the Court of Appeal in England and Wales), reliance is placed on the views of the Lord Chancellor and a team of politically neutral civil servants in the Lord Chancellor's Office. The Lord Chancellor is in law responsible for recommending appointments of all judges below the rank of Law Lord. In June 2003, the government announced that it proposed to establish new arrangements for judicial appointments and a new UK Supreme Court.

[105] A term apparently coined by the House of Commons Select Committee on Public Administration. See below.

[106] See para 3.76 below.

[107] This is a non-statutory document published from time to time by the Cabinet Office; see further n 120 below.

ministerial interviews and appearances in the news media to be 'cleared' beforehand with the Prime Minister's Office. It is possible to point to the increasing power of the New Centre—the Prime Minister, the expanding Prime Minister's Office, the Cabinet Office[108]—and to suggest that a single executive office 'in all but name' is emerging in the UK constitutional system. Precedent suggests that though Prime Ministers may consult Cabinet colleagues, the decision to request a dissolution of Parliament (so that a general election is held) is that of the Prime Minister alone.

Fourthly, Prime Ministers may choose to become involved in particular policy de- **3.42** cisions. Especially in relation to international affairs, the Prime Minister possesses prerogative powers that, legally, he may exercise without reference to Cabinet, let alone Parliament.[109] Over recent years, a great deal of the Prime Minister's time has been taken up with decision-making over international matters, including British military action in Kosovo in 1999, reaction to the terrorist events on 11 September 2001, and military action in Iraq in 2003.

The Prime Minister's relationship with the Chancellor of the Exchequer has **3.43** proved to be important in recent governments. Relatively little attention is paid to the office of Chancellor of the Exchequer in the constitutional law textbooks, yet it seems clear that the powers of this office are of such significance as almost to rival those of the Prime Minister. The Chancellor of the Exchequer is the ministerial head of HM Treasury, a department that exerts a controlling influence on not only the scale but also the content of policies pursued by other departments. A House of Commons select committee recently reported that:[110]

> We believe that the Treasury has become more powerful in two significant respects in recent years. Firstly, its influence over the strategic direction of the Government has grown. The Treasury's role in leading the welfare reform programme and introducing stakeholder pensions and tax credits has led to the Treasury taking a greater role in social security policy. Secondly, Public Service Agreements have substantially increased the Treasury's influence over the affairs of spending departments . . . We are concerned that the Treasury as an institution has recently begun to exert too much influence over policy areas which are properly the business of other departments and that this is not necessarily in the best interests of the Treasury or the Government as a whole.

The power of HM Treasury is such that both the Chancellor of the Exchequer and **3.44** the Prime Minister ought jointly to be regarded as primus inter partes in relation to other ministers. By convention the Prime Minister and Chancellor of the

---

[108] See paras 3.59 and 3.76 below.
[109] For illustrations, see Patrick Gordon-Walker, *The Cabinet* (London: Jonathan Cape, 1970): 'Atlee decided to make the atom bomb and Eden to invade Suez without consulting the Cabinet' (p 86) and 'In September 1938 Chamberlain sent a telegram to Hitler to arrange a meeting and later signed the Munich declaration before informing the Cabinet' (p 87).
[110] Treasury Committee, Third Report 1999/2000 (HC 492).

Exchequer sit next to each other at Cabinet meetings. Institutional and personal rivalries between the Treasury and the Prime Minister/Cabinet Office have not gone unnoticed. There is bipolar administration centred on 10 Downing Street and HM Treasury.[111]

(b) The Cabinet and its committees

3.45   Like the office of Prime Minister, the Cabinet is a creature of constitutional convention rather than formal law.[112] It is the gathering of senior ministers, typically 20 in number, normally once a week at 10 Downing Street, though it may meet at any time and location. Much work is done through a plethora of committees, some of which include officials as well as ministers. The Cabinet Secretariat, part of the department called the Cabinet Office, supports the work of the Cabinet. Ministers often meet each other outside the formal structures of Cabinet. Although the Cabinet is composed entirely of members of the House of Commons and House of Lords, more particularly the leading members of the majority party in the Commons,[113] it is not a committee of Parliament.[114] Decisions taken in Cabinet and its committees nevertheless exert significant control over Parliament, as it is a Cabinet committee that decides upon and manages the legislative agenda in each annual session of Parliament.[115] The organization of the forthcoming week's business in Parliament is discussed at the preceding Thursday's Cabinet meeting.

3.46   The relative powers of the Prime Minister and the Cabinet have been the subject of much analysis and debate. For some, the 'central directing instrument of government, in legislation as well as in administration, is the Cabinet . . . It is the Cabinet which controls Parliament and governs the country.'[116] For another, the 'post-war epoch has seen the final transformation of Cabinet Government into Prime Ministerial Government'.[117] Still others relate the role and importance of the Cabinet to the leadership styles of particular Prime Ministers.[118] What is in-

---

[111] Peter Hennessey, *The Prime Minister: The Office and its Holders since 1945* (London: Penguin, 2000).

[112] See further Gordon-Walker (n 109 above); Peter Hennessey, *Cabinet* (Oxford: Basil Blackwell, 1996).

[113] Between 1997 and 2002, there was a joint Labour-Lib Dem Cabinet committee, originally set up to oversee the government's programme of constitutional reform and later expanded to cover European common foreign and security policy.

[114] Nor, for that matter, is it a committee of the Privy Council, though all members of the Cabinet are Privy Counsellors.

[115] See para 3.106 below.

[116] LS Amery, *Thoughts on the Constitution* (Oxford: OUP, 1947) 70.

[117] RHS Crossman, Introduction to Walter Bagehot's *The English Constitution* (London: Collins, 1963).

[118] For a survey, see Chris Brady, 'Collective responsibility of the Cabinet: an ethical, constitutional or managerial tool?' (1999) 53 Parliamentary Affairs 214; Ellis (n 89 above).

disputable is that the Prime Minister has considerable control over the agenda of the Cabinet itself and the number, membership and terms of reference of Cabinet committees. The Prime Minister presides over the Cabinet and any Cabinet committees of which he is a member. The Prime Minister may also exercise prerogative powers without prior reference to Cabinet.[119] It is equally clear, however, that the Cabinet is the source of a Prime Minister's political authority: without the support of Cabinet colleagues, a Prime Minister cannot continue in power for long.

Decisions made or ratified by Cabinet and its committees are given legal effect through the statutory or prerogative powers of individual ministers.   **3.47**

All ministers are bound by the convention of collective ministerial responsibility,[120] which comprises three sets of principles.[121] First, the government must resign from office if ministers no longer command the support of a majority of the House of Commons. From time to time, government Bills are defeated but this does not trigger a need for collective resignation; rather, the defeat has to be on a motion of confidence.[122] Secondly, an obligation of solidarity means that a minister who disagrees with a decision taken in Cabinet, or Cabinet committee, or a decision of another minister, is nevertheless obliged to accept it and if needs be defend it in public, even if he or she disagrees with it and regardless of whether he or she was involved in making it. A minister must resign from government if he or she feels unable to do this.[123] Naturally, political realities and interpersonal dynamics may complicate this basic rule. In exceptional circumstances, a Cabinet may 'agree to differ' on a vital issue of national importance, and allow ministers to dissent from the majority view in public.[124] Thirdly, collective responsibility in the past implied an obligation of confidentiality, so that ministers were expected to refrain from disclosing information about Cabinet business in their autobiographies; this is now more honoured in the breach. The demands of open government have also led to information that was once regarded as secret, such as the composition of Cabinet committees, now being routinely published.   **3.48**

---

[119] See para 3.109 above.

[120] *Ministerial Code: A Code of Conduct and Guidance for Ministers on Procedures* (London: Cabinet Office, 2001), foreword: 'Ministers must uphold the principle of collective responsibility' and ss 16–18.

[121] Geoffrey Marshall (ed), *Ministerial Responsibility* (Oxford: OUP, 1989) 3.

[122] Philip Norton, 'Government Defeats in the House of Commons: Myth and Reality' [1978] PL 360.

[123] The same principle applies to Parliamentary Private Secretaries, the significant number of backbench MPs of the governing party who volunteer their services as aides to ministers. The position may be different in Scotland: see Barry Winetrobe, 'Collective responsibility in devolved Scotland' [2002] PL 24.

[124] Arthur Silkin, 'The "Agreement to Differ" of 1975' (1977) 46 Political Q 65.

(c) The Privy Council

3.49   The Privy Council is one of most ancient yet least known institutions of the central government machine. In the distant past, the Privy Council was the main advisory body to the Crown (as monarch), but its political importance came to be eclipsed by the rise of Cabinet. Its continuing formal significance is attested to by the requirement that if a minister is called to attend the Privy Council this takes precedence over any other official engagement, even a meeting of the Cabinet.[125] Whether its methods of work are an efficient use of the time of busy ministers is surely open to question. [126]

3.50   The Privy Council as a whole consists of the Queen and about 400 others (there is no limit on the number) who are 'invariably chosen by the Crown from amongst noblemen of high rank, persons who have held or hold high political office, persons eminent in science or letters or very senior civil servants'.[127] By convention, all Cabinet ministers—and most other ministers also—become Privy Councillors. Appointment to the Privy Council is for life.

3.51   In practice, the work of the Privy Council is carried out by Her Majesty in Council (the regular, formal meetings of the monarch and selected Cabinet ministers), and the Privy Council acting without the Queen (in which form miscellaneous regulatory and executive decisions are made, usually then confirmed by Her Majesty in Council).

3.52   There are several standing committees of the Privy Council.[128] The work of the Privy Council is supported by a secretariat in the Privy Council Office (a department led by a Cabinet minister who is styled 'President of the Council', a post normally combined with that of Leader of the House of Commons).

3.53   Unlike other departments, the Privy Council Office and its ministerial head have no policy programmes of their own;[129] where the Privy Council is involved in making legislation, in matters such as the regulation of health care professions and universities, it does so in conjunction with the department and any statutory body

---

[125] Ministerial Code, s 2.

[126] This may require ministers to travel considerable distances for a very short formal meeting: see Anthony Howard (ed), *The Crossman Diaries: Selections from the diaries of a Cabinet Minister 1964–1970* (London: Methuen, 1979) 31.

[127] *Halsbury's Laws* (4th edn) vol 8(2), para 5.22. Privy Counsellors are entitled to use the title 'Right Honourable' before their name.

[128] The Judicial Committee (see below), the Universities Committee, the Scottish Universities Committee, the Committee for the Purposes of the Crown Office Act 1877, the Committee for the Affairs of Jersey and Guernsey, the Baronetage Committee, and the Political Scrutiny Committee (*Hansard*, HC col 174 (13 January 1998)).

[129] Though the minister, in his or her capacity as Leader of the House of Commons, may have important policy programmes in relation to reform of Parliament.

responsible for the policy field in question.[130] It also approves legislation made by the legislatures of Jersey and Guernsey[131] and approves changes to the internal governance of the Church of England.

The Queen in Council has no deliberative or consultative function. Cabinet ministers meet the Queen at Privy Council meetings to confer formal legal validity on instruments which have already been agreed upon in Cabinet or a department. Meetings take place at a venue of the Queen's choosing, often at Buckingham Place, but also at her other residences such as Balmoral, Windsor Castle and Sandringham. The Privy Council met 12 times during 2001. The Privy Council has legislative power. Some is in the form of delegated legislation, where an Act of Parliament confers law-making power on 'Her Majesty'.[132] The Privy Council still retains some legislative power authorized not by Parliament, but the royal prerogative.[133] Confusingly, both forms of legislation—delegated by Parliament and arising from the prerogative—are known as Orders in Council.[134] Proclamations, made under various Acts, are also issued to regulate matters such as coinage and public holidays. Some ministers regard Privy Council meetings as a waste of time.

3.54

The Judicial Committee of the Privy Council is a court, now established by statute.[135] Although served by the same secretariat as the rest of the Privy Council, it is an independent judicial body. It acts as the final court of appeal for 17 independent states (former UK dominions or colonies), the British Overseas Territories and the Bailiwicks of Jersey and Guernsey, and the Isle of Man. Its jurisdiction to hear appeals relating to registration decisions of certain professional bodies, such as the General Medical Council, was transferred to the High Court in 2002.[136] In 1998, the Judicial Committee acquired the important new jurisdiction to determine 'devolution issues'. Altogether, it hears approximately 70 cases a year. Most cases are determined by panels of the 12 Lords of Appeal in Ordinary (who also sit as judges of the Appellate Committee of the House of

3.55

---

[130] Whereas once the participation of the Privy Council might have been viewed as an anachronistic hangover from the past, today '[t]he allocation of responsibility for these matters to the Privy Council rather than to the Secretary of State with the major policy interest builds in wider cross-Government participation. In this, as in other ways, the Privy Council is an important part of "joined-up Government"' (www.privy-council.org.uk, September 2002).

[131] The Channel Islands (the Bailiwicks of Jersey and Guernsey) are not part of the UK; nor are they parts of the EU.

[132] See eg Ministry of Agriculture, Fisheries and Food (Dissolution) Order 2002, SI 2002/794. The preamble explains that this was made: 'At the Court at Buckingham Palace, the 26th day of March 2002, Present, The Queen's Most Excellent Majesty in Council'. Such Orders in Council are also statutory instruments and are published by HMSO as such.

[133] Most notably the Civil Service Orders in Council, regulating the civil service (see n 71 below). Such Orders in Council are now published at www.privy-council.org.uk. See also paras 1.132 and 1.150 above.

[134] See para 1.150 above.

[135] Judicial Committee Acts 1833 and 1844.

[136] See National Health Service Reform and Health Professionals Act 2002, Pt 2.

Lords), but judges (and retired judges up to the age of 75) of the Court of Appeal of England and Wales, and appellate judges from Northern Ireland, Scotland and some Commonwealth states are also entitled to sit. Strictly speaking, the Lord President of Council, and former Lords President, are also eligible to sit on a 'Board' of the Judicial Committee,[137] but by convention do not do so. In July 2003, the government began consultations on whether the devolution jurisdiction of the Judicial Committee should be transferred to the proposed new UK Supreme Court.

(d) Departments

3.56 For more than 150 years, the basic units of central government for developing and implementing policy have been departments (also once known as 'ministries').[138] The allocation of responsibilities between central government departments, and the names of government departments, are altered from time to time. Departmental reorganization is a matter for the Prime Minister and legal effect is given to it by delegated legislation made under the Ministers of the Crown Act 1975.[139] Most departments lack formal legal personality; their private law relations, such as contracting, are generally carried out in the name of 'the Crown'; their public law functions most often in the name of 'the Secretary of State'. Because of the unitary character of the office of Secretary of State, in whom most formal legal powers are vested, reorganization of departments can be carried out with relative ease. In 2003, the principal departments included:

- Department for Culture, Media and Sport (DCMS)[140]
- Ministry of Defence
- Department for Education and Skills (DfES)
- Department for the Environment, Food and Rural Affairs (DEFRA)
- Foreign and Commonwealth Office (FCO)
- Department of Health

---

[137] *Hansard*, HC col 224 (28 January 1998) (Mr Hoon MP).

[138] For historical accounts, see Hennessey (n 16 above) and B Schaffer, 'The Idea of the Ministerial Department: Bentham, Mill and Bagehot' (1957) 3 The Australian J of Politics and History 60. All departments now have websites containing information about their internal organization and responsibilities. See also Smith, Marsh and Richards, *The Changing Role of Central Government Departments* (Basingstoke: Macmillan, 2001).

[139] eg Ministry of Agriculture, Fisheries and Food (Dissolution) Order 2002, SI 2002/794. The functions previously carried out under the auspices of MAFF were reorganized following criticisms relating to BSE and the foot and mouth disease outbreak in the UK. Article 2(2) provided that '. . . the functions of the Minister of Agriculture, Fisheries and Food are hereby transferred to the Secretary of State'. The new Secretary of State is the Secretary of State for Environment, Food and Rural Affairs. This change abolishes one of the last major departments in which functions were carried on by specified 'minister' rather than the all-encompassing 'Secretary of State'.

[140] Responsibilities include licensing of gambling, alcohol sales; censorship of film and video; horseracing; tourism; the National Lottery; heritage and museums.

- Home Office[141]
- Department for International Development (DFID)
- Department for Constitutional Affairs (DCA)[142]
- Privy Council Office[143]
- Department for Trade and Industry (DTI)[144]
- Department for Transport[145]
- Department for Work and Pensions
- Her Majesty's Treasury[146]
- Office of the Deputy Prime Minister[147]
- Cabinet Office[148]

Following the transfer of executive powers to new bodies in Scotland, Northern **3.57** Ireland and Wales under the devolution Acts of 1998, some of the above mentioned departments have responsibility mainly for matters arising in England only, whereas others retain a remit for the whole of the United Kingdom.[149] The Secretaries of State for Scotland, for Wales and for Northern Ireland represent the interests of the devolved parts of the United Kingdom in Cabinet. The Secretary of State for Northern Ireland is the ministerial head of a freestanding department, the Northern Ireland Office. Following a government reorganization in June 2003, the Secretary of State for Scotland and Secretary of State for Wales are part-time appointments (each minister having another ministerial post) and the

---

[141] Community policy (including family policy), crime reduction and criminal justice (including police and prisons), drug misuse, immigration and nationality, passports, race equality.

[142] Created in June 2003 to replace the Lord Chancellor's Department, the DCA has responsibility for policy on courts in England and Wales and (until such time as this function is transferred to the Northern Ireland Executive) Northern Ireland; freedom of information; data protection; human rights issues arising from the UK's international obligations and overseeing implementation of the HRA 1998; constitutional reform; the Channel Islands (the Bailiwicks of Jersey and Guernsey) and the Isle of Man; electoral law; referendums; regulation of funding of political parties. On the abolition of the post of Lord Chancellor, see Andrew Le Sueur, 'New Labour's next (surprisingly quick) steps in constitutional reform' [2003] PL 368.

[143] The ministerial head is styled 'President of the Council' and the post is usually combined with Leader of the House of Commons (with responsibility for planning the legislative and other business of Parliament). Chartered bodies, universities and professional discipline. The Judicial Committee of the Privy Council is a court.

[144] Science, engineering and technology resources; energy; consumer protection; competition policy; overseas trade; regulation of utilities and other national industries; Women and Equality Unit.

[145] Including regulation of railways; aviation; and highways.

[146] The Treasury's overall aim is 'to raise the rate of sustainable growth, and achieve rising prosperity, through creating economic and employment opportunities for all'.

[147] Created in May 2002, this department deals with regional policy, local government, planning, housing, urban policy and social exclusion.

[148] This has four main roles: to support the Prime Minister in leading the government; to support the government in transacting its business; to lead and support the reform and delivery programme; to co-ordinate security and intelligence (Sir Andrew Turnbull, 'Cabinet Office Reform and Delivery in the Civil Service, Paper to the Civil Service Management Board', 24 June 2002).

[149] See para 3.27 above.

Scotland Office and Wales Office, while retaining their identities, have been incorporated within the new Department for Constitutional Affairs.[150] Generally it is notable that the work of some departments is more dominated by EU concerns than others.[151]

3.58 As already noted, there is no department attached to the office of Prime Minister, who relies upon the Cabinet Office for administrative support and policy advice. There is however a growing number of staff in the Prime Minister's Office at 10 Downing Street (the official residence and office of the Prime Minister), both permanent civil servants and special advisers,[152] and the Prime Minister's Office is regarded by some as a Prime Minister's department in all but name.[153]

3.59 The overall co-ordination of central government policy-making and implementation is clearly of vital importance. The Cabinet Office, HM Treasury,[154] the Prime Minister's Office, and the Office of the Deputy Prime Minister[155] all contribute to this task, though their relationships are not always clear. For many years, it has been recognized that the allocation of policy responsibilities to separate departments creates problems of 'departmentalism', a disorder that includes: an over-focus on the specific objectives of a particular department at the expense of the general social problem in hand; neglecting complicated problems that do not fit easily within a single department's portfolio of responsibility; and a reluctance of ministers and officials to engage in cross-departmental initiatives because of weak or perverse financial incentives (budgets are allocated on a departmental basis).[156] Like governments before it,[157] the Blair administration, in power since 1997, has sought to promote 'joined-up government' or 'holistic governance'. Several specialist units responsible for cross-cutting social problems were created,

---

[150] See R Hazell, 'Merger, what merger? Scotland, Wales and the Department for Constitutional Affairs' [2003] PL 650 and *Three into One Won't Go: the Future of the Territorial Secretaries of State* (London: UCL Constitution Unit, 2001). For a historical account, see R Brazier, 'The Constitution of the United Kingdom' (1999) 58 CLJ 96.

[151] Thus, most areas of policy handled by HM Treasury and DEFRA involve EU considerations.

[152] In February 2000, there were 149 staff. On special advisers, see para 3.76 below.

[153] Martin Burch and Ian Holliday, 'The Prime Minister's and Cabinet Office: an Executive Office in all but Name' (1999) 52 Parliamentary Affairs 32; Dennis Kavanagh and Anthony Seldon, *The Powers Behind the Prime Minister: the Hidden Influence of No. 10* (London: HarperCollins, 1999).

[154] In relation to the control and priority setting of government expenditure. Also has views on social policy

[155] See n 147 above.

[156] See further the Cabinet Office's White Paper, *Modernising Government* (Cm 4310, 1999); Flinders (n 49 above); Dennis Kavanagh and David Richards, 'Departmentalism and Joined-Up Government: Back to the Future' (2001) 54 Parliamentary Affairs 1; T Ling, 'Delivering Joined-Up Government in the UK: Dimensions, Issues and Problems' (2002) 80 Public Administration 615.

[157] eg the approach of the Heath government in 1970 to reduce the number of departments, create 'super-departments' such as the Department of the Environment and the Department for Trade and Industry, and reduce the size of the Cabinet: see *The Reorganisation of Central Government* (Cmd 4506, 1970).

for example the Social Exclusion Unit set up to promote policies to combat poverty and deprivation (originally it was located within the Cabinet Office and later in the Office of the Deputy Prime Minister). While encouraging departments to work co-operatively with one another, where appropriate, may have benefits in terms of efficiency and effectiveness,[158] from the constitutional perspective caution is needed: joined-up government may result in less defined lines of accountability for policy and delivery if a single minister is not answerable to Parliament for a matter.[159] The structures put in place since 1997, collectively known as 'the New Centre', in this latest attempt to co-ordinate departments is complex—the Policy and Innovation Unit, the Strategic Communications Unit (both in the Prime Minister's Office), various task forces and review groups,[160] the Prime Minister's Chief Adviser on Delivery, the Strategy Unit, the Prime Minister's Chief Adviser on Public Services Reform, the revised remit of the Minister for the Cabinet Office—have, on one analysis, 'themselves become locked in to a struggle for ascendancy'[161] and it is arguable that the main consequence has been to 'strengthen the centre'.

The management of departments has been the subject of almost constant reform **3.60** initiatives in recent years under successive governments. The working practices of many departments have been altered, and made more complex, by new public management approaches.[162] During the 1990s, reorganization led to almost all the practical service delivery functions once directly dealt with by departments being hived off to newly created executive agencies (sometimes referred to as Next Steps agencies).[163] The Citizen's Charter programme sought to inculcate a greater customer focus on government dealings with people.[164] In short, 'Departments are no longer whole units but the sum of various and varied parts'.[165]

The Blair Government has continued to pursue reforms aimed at improving im- **3.61** plementation of policy and delivery of services.[166] The overall aim of changes over the past 20 years or so appears to be to make departments and executive agencies adopt methods of work, and an ethos, borrowed from industry and commerce. It seems, however, that ministers and senior civil servants may have misunderstood

---

[158] For an early assessment of some attempts, see Report by the Comptroller and Auditor General, *Joining Up to Improve Public Services* (2001–02 HC 383).
[159] See para 3.140 below.
[160] This is a loose term. For discussion see (Neill) Committee on Standards in Public Life, *Reinforcing Standards* (Cm 4557, 2000) paras 10.5–10.6.
[161] Kavanagh and Richards (n 156 above) 17.
[162] See above.
[163] See below.
[164] Now called the 'Service First programme' run by the Cabinet Office. See Drewry (n 33 above).
[165] Woodhouse (n 39 above) 46.
[166] A 'Delivery Unit' was established within the Office of the Deputy Prime Minister.

those methods and ethos and it is questionable whether, in any event, they are appropriate models for the public sector.[167]

(e) Executive agencies

3.62 Executive agencies (sometimes referred to as Next Steps agencies) were created during the 1990s as part of the bundle of new techniques known as 'new public management'.[168] The main impetus was a belief that efficiency and effectiveness of central government would be improved if there was a formal separation between (i) the civil service function of advising ministers on policy and (ii) the practical delivery of services to the pubic (for example, calculating and paying social security benefits, issuing passports, running prisons). Departments retained the policy advice function, but the number of civil servants here was drastically reduced. Operational matters were hived off to executive agencies, where specialist management skills could be developed at arm's length from the department.

3.63 Most departments now have several executive agencies attached to them.[169] Today, almost all service delivery functions of central government are carried out by executive agencies. The relationship between a department and an executive agency is regulated by a 'framework document'. This typically sets out the agency's budget, the responsibilities of the executive agency, the results to be achieved and targets against which its performance will be measured. Departments retain overall budgetary control. Some bodies that have the status of executive agencies are not directly connected to a department.[170]

3.64 Agencies are headed by chief executives. In several agencies, people from outside the career civil service have been appointed as chief executives with backgrounds in the business or voluntary sectors. When operational problems arise, the chief executive may appear in the news media to answer criticisms and defend the agency in question, either with or without the responsible minister doing the

---

[167] See Cabinet Office (Efficiency Unit), *Career Management and Succession Planning Study* ('the Oughton Report') (1993) and Vernon Bogdanor, 'Civil Service Reform: A Critique' (2001) 72 Political Q 291.

[168] PN Leopold, 'Letters to and from "next steps" agency chief executives' [1994] PL 214; Norman Lewis and Diane Longley, 'Ministerial responsibility: the next steps' [1996] PL 490; Norman Lewis, 'Reviewing change in government: new public management and next steps' [1994] PL 105; Gavin Drewry, 'The civil service: from the 1940s to "Next Steps" and beyond' (1994) 47 Parliamentary Affairs 583; Patricia Greer, *Transforming central government: the next steps initiative* (Open University Press, 1994). For comparative studies, see Peter Leyland and Daniele Donati, 'Executive accountability and the changing face of government: UK and Italy compared' (2001) 7 European Public L 217; Elder and Page (n 35 above) (by comparison with Sweden, UK next steps reforms are not radical, they argue).

[169] Thus, in 2003, the Department for Transport's executive agencies included: the Driving Standards Agency; the Driver and Vehicle Licensing Agency; the Highways Agency; the Maritime and Coastguard Agency; the Vehicle Certification Agency; and the Vehicle Inspectorate.

[170] eg, the Treasury Solicitor's Department and the Strategic Rail Authority.

same. The chief executive is expected to avoid discussion of policy matters. When a chief executive does speak in public, it is now accepted that he does so not as a mere mouthpiece of the minister (the long-established constitutional convention applying to other civil servants), but directly as an office-holder in his own right.

There is significant variation in size, function and political sensitivity of the work **3.65** carried out by executive agencies. As with departments, some caution is needed in making generalizations about them. Recent research suggests that one benefit flowing from the creation of executive agencies has been to bring concern for operational matters into the policy-making stage (at departmental level): the 'British Next Steps initiative is best characterised as an elaborate and effective programme of delegation within the existing constitutional framework'.[171] Whatever the overall assessment of the success of executive agencies, the work of a very small number of executive agencies has notably been the subject of sustained controversy and criticism by Parliament and in the news media: the Prison Service;[172] the Child Support Agency (which seeks to ensure that absent parents give financial support to their children);[173] the Benefits Agency, and the Qualifications Authority.

The advent of executive agencies inevitably leads to questions about their legal **3.66** and constitutional status. In an early case, the court held that as a matter of law decisions taken by officials within executive agencies were regarded as decisions of the Secretary of State[174]—the same rule as applied to decisions by officials within departments.[175] The broader constitutional questions of accountability have proved more difficult, not least because the distinction between policy and operational matters is not always easy to make.[176] Before the creation of executive agencies, ministers answered questions from MPs about the operational work within their departments and any problems that arose. For a period of time, a practice emerged that some written questions to a minister were passed to the Chief Executive of the Agency concerned and his reply was printed in *Hansard*—though in 1997 the Home Secretary announced that he personally would answer all parliamentary questions relating to the Prison Service.[177]

---

[171] Elder and Page (n 35 above).

[172] Including the controversial dismissal of Derek Lewis, the Chief Executive, by the Home Secretary in 1996; for Mr Lewis's own account, see *Hidden Agendas: Politics, Law and Disorder* (London: Hamish Hamilton, 1997).

[173] See Carol Harlow, 'Accountability, New Public Management, and the Problems of the Child Support Agency' (1999) 26 J of L and Society 150; Peter Barberis, 'The New Public Management and a New Accountability' (1998) 76 Public Administration 451.

[174] *R v Secretary of State for Social Security, ex p Sherwin* (1996) 32 BMLR 1; Mark Freedland, 'The rule against delegation and the Carltona doctrine in an agency context' [1996] PL 19.

[175] *Carltona Ltd v Commissioners of Works* [1943] 2 All ER 560, discussed below.

[176] See para 3.139 below.

[177] The Ministerial Code provides that 'Ministers are accountable to Parliament for the policies, decisions and actions of their departments *and agencies*' (emphasis added). See further paras 5.19–5.22 below.

(f) Non-departmental public bodies[178]

3.67 More than 1,000 NDPBs, formerly called quangos,[179] exist and can appropriately be described as part of the machinery of central government. These are bodies which have a 'role in the process of national Government but is not a Government Department or part of one and which accordingly operates to a greater or lesser extent at arm's length from Ministers'.[180] A minister will, however, be answerable to Parliament, for the work of each such body. Some NDPBs often take the form of 'advisory committees' of academic and other experts, supported by a small secretariat of civil servants.[181] Others have important executive functions including the distribution of public funds, allocation of licences or enforcement of law and policy (eg, relating to the environment). NDPBs include: Advisory Council on Libraries; Animal Welfare Advisory Committee; the Arts Council for England; English Heritage; the Environment Agency; Equal Opportunities Commission; Commission for Racial Equality; Regional Development Agencies; Civil Aviation Authority; Competition Commission; Countryside Agency; and the Criminal Cases Review Commission.

3.68 Of particular importance are the Commissioners of Inland Revenue and the Commissioners of Customs and Excise. The Commissioners of Inland Revenue are appointed by the Crown to advise Treasury ministers on tax questions and make an annual report to Parliament. In relation to their function of collecting tax in individual cases, they are independent of ministerial control. They appoint tax inspectors and collectors. The Commissioners of Customs and Excise have a similar role in relation to collecting and managing duties (including value added tax).

(g) The Civil Service

3.69 The UK Civil Service is not, itself, an institution; it 'has no constitutional personality or responsibility separate from the duly constituted government of the day'.[182] In broad terms, the Civil Service may be defined as the permanent official staff of departments and executive agencies. Approximately 2 per cent of the United Kingdom's work force is civil servants: in October 2002 there were a little under 500,000 civil servants (a reduction of some 40 per cent compared to staffing levels in the 1970s). Three-quarters work within executive agencies; most of the remainder within departments.

---

[178] See generally ch 5 below.
[179] Quasi-non-governmental organizations.
[180] Cabinet Office website (www.cabinet-office.gov.uk), on which a directory of NDPBs is published.
[181] Stuart Weir and Wendy Hall, *Behind Closed Doors: Advisory Quangos in the Corridors of Power* (London: Channel 4, 1995).
[182] HM Treasury, *Civil Service Management Code* (1993), s 4, annex A, para 3.

Three features are said to set apart the senior UK civil servants from their coun-   **3.70**
terparts elsewhere in Europe and in the USA: they are accountable to Parliament
only through ministers; they are selected and promoted on merit; and they are required to be politically neutral in their work.[183] Political neutrality, or objectivity,
of senior civil servants manifests itself in several senses: their employment continues when a new political party forms the government after a general election; the
personal political activities of senior civil servants are also restricted;[184] and appointments and promotions of civil servants are not directly in the hands of ministers.[185] The independent Civil Service Commissioners, established in 1855,
oversee appointments in the Civil Service (which are made by particular departments in the name of the Crown) to ensure that they are on merit on the basis of
fair and open competition; the Commissioners also hear and determine appeals in
cases of concerns about propriety and conscience raised by civil servants under the
Civil Service Code that are not resolved through internal procedures.

With justification it can be said that 'the status and role of the civil service are mat-   **3.71**
ters which are somewhat shrouded in constitutional convention, royal prerogative,
unwritten assumption, and outmoded precedent'.[186] The desirability of having a
Civil Service Act, placing the civil service on a statutory footing for the first time, is
widely recognized as necessary.[187] The Home Civil Service and the Diplomatic
Service work under somewhat different conditions and each has its own head.
Currently, terms and conditions of employment for civil servants are set out in the
Civil Service Order in Council 1995 (as amended) and the Diplomatic Service
Order in Council 1991 (as amended), prerogative legislation made by the Privy
Council without parliamentary involvement, the Civil Service Management Code
(CSMC), and the Civil Service Code.[188] A Minister for the Civil Service is ac-
countable to Parliament for questions relating to the civil service; by convention
this is a ministerial post held by the Prime Minister him or herself.

---

[183] Oonagh Gay, *Advisers to Ministers*, House of Commons Library Research Paper 00/42, 1.
[184] But see para 3.76 below on special advisers.
[185] In 2002, the Civil Service Commissioner rejected plans by government for ministers to be involved in interviewing candidates for senior Civil Service posts (The Times, 27 June 2002, 12).
[186] Adam Tomkins, *The Constitution After Scott: Government Unwrapped* (Oxford: OUP, 1998)
75; and see Gavin Drewry, 'The Civil Service' in R Blackburn and R Plant (eds), *Constitutional
Reform: the Labour Government's Constitutional Reform Agenda* (London: Longman, 1999) ch 7.
[187] For a debate in the House of Lords calling for such legislation to be expedited, see *Hansard*, HL
col 691 (1 May 2002). In July 2002, the government indicated the proposed Civil Service Bill will
be delayed for at least 18 months as the government has other priorities and wishes to consider two
on-going inquiries on the issue before introducing legislation (The Times, 3 July 2002, 10). This
delay has led the House of Commons Select Committee on Public Administration to announce that
it will draw up its own Civil Service Bill.
[188] There is, in addition, various statutory legislation, eg Civil Service (Management Functions)
Act 1992. For a cause celebre relating to the exercise of power under the Civil Service Order in
Council by the Minister for the Civil Service, see *Council of Civil Service Unions v Minister for the
Civil Service* [1985] AC 374.

3.72   Civil servants are employed by the Crown. The legal status of their contracts of employment (if any) has been subject to considerable debate.[189] The Head of the Home Civil Service is also Secretary to the Cabinet, is the chief official in the Cabinet Office and attends Cabinet meetings. The most senior civil servant in each department is normally styled the 'Permanent Secretary'.[190] Officials working for the Scottish Executive, National Assembly for Wales and Northern Ireland Executive are part of the Home Civil Service.

3.73   Statutory and prerogative powers and duties are conferred on the Secretaries of State.[191] English law recognizes the practical necessity for most such powers to be exercised not by ministers personally, but by officials acting on behalf of ministers and without ministers being aware of the particular case (though some decisions will be taken by ministers personally). Ministerial powers may generally therefore be lawfully delegated to civil servants acting in the name of the Secretary of State within departments[192] and executive agencies.[193] This is not, strictly speaking, delegation of power to civil servants as in law the decision is still that of the minister.[194]

3.74   For several years, the Civil Service has been 'undergoing substantial management and cultural reform'.[195] Several challenges face the Civil Service. First, doubts have arisen about the capacity of the organization to cope with the demands of modern government: 'the key problems identified by critics of the Civil Service have been the perceived slowness of its reaction, poor performance in providing policy advice, an inattention to policy delivery, inadequate understanding of risk management issues, and bad project management'.[196] Whether new public management

---

[189] See Jack Beatson, 'Crown Service: Contract or Status?' (1988) 104 LQR 182; Mark Freedland, 'Contracting the Employment of Civil Services—a Transparent Exercise?' [1995] PL 224; S Fredman and G Morris, *The State as Employer: Labour Law in the Public Services* (London: Mansell, 1989).

[190] Not to be confused with the Secretary *of State* (the senior minister) or *Parliamentary* Secretary of State (a junior minister).

[191] See para 3.36 above.

[192] *Carltona v Ministry of Works* [1943] 2 All ER 560; *Woollett v Minister of Agriculture and Fisheries* [1955] 1 QB 103; *R v Secretary of State for the Home Department, ex p Oladehinde* [1991] 1 AC 254. In relation to the status of planning inspectors working (now) in the Office of the Deputy Prime Minister to determine appeals against the refusal of planning permission by local authorities and the grant of development permission by ministers, see *R v Secretary of State for the Environment, Transport and the Regions, ex p Holdings & Barnes Plc* ('the Alconbury case') [2001] UKHL 23; [2001] 2 WLR 1389.

[193] *R v Secretary of State for Social Security, ex p Sherwin* (1996) 32 BMLR 1 (relating to the Benefits Agency).

[194] *R v Skinner (Edward George)* [1968] 3 All ER 124.

[195] Sir Richard Wilson (Head of the Home Civil Service), 'The Civil Service in the New Millennium' (May 1999). On recent changes, see RAW Rhodes, 'New Labour's civil service: summing-up joining-up' (2000) 71 Political Q 151; S Richards, 'New Labour—New Civil Service' (1997) 67 Political Q 311.

[196] Public Administration Committee, Seventh Report, *Making Government Work: the Emerging Issues, Report and Proceedings of the Committee* (2000–01 HC 94) para 20.

techniques,[197] and the creation of 'the New Centre' to achieve joined-up government[198] will redress these problems remains to be seen.

Secondly, there is a need for greater clarity about accountability for policies and programmes.[199] The creation of executive agencies, some headed by high-profile chief executives, has called into question the traditional assumption underlying the Westminster model, that the prime mechanism for ensuring constitutional accountability is that ministers are answerable to Parliament.[200] So too with the practice of senior civil servants appearing before parliamentary select committees to answer questions about the work of their departments.[201]

3.75

A third set of concerns relates to the appropriate relationships between ministers, permanent civil servants and the increasing number of 'special advisers' employed within departments. There are now over 80 special advisers, 26 of them in 10 Downing Street.[202] These are political appointees, made directly by ministers, and are either policy advisers (experts with political views) or public relations practitioners ('spin doctors').[203] Their use, though viewed with alarm by some commentators, reflects the constitutional position that: 'The Civil Service has no monopoly of policy analysis and advice. The Government takes account of views from many sources of which the Government Party is legitimately one.'[204] Special advisers are 'temporary civil servants'[205] and are generally bound by the same terms as permanent civil servants, with the exception of the rules on political activities. A Code of Conduct for Special Advisers explains:[206]

3.76

> Special advisers are employed to help Ministers on matters where the work of Government and the work of the Government Party overlap and it would be inappropriate for permanent civil servants to become involved. They are an additional resource for the Minister providing advice from a standpoint that is more politically

---

[197] See para 3.08 above.

[198] See para 3.59 above.

[199] See generally Part C below.

[200] See para 3.140 above. As the Public Administration Committee put it (n 196 above) para 27: 'This new profile for civil servants has implications not only for accountability (is the Minister or the civil servant accountable?) but also for the role of junior Ministers (if a named civil servant is identified with a particular policy, what is the Minister for?)'.

[201] See para 3.147 below.

[202] *Hansard*, HC col 526W (31 March 2003); *Hansard*, HL col 705 (1 May 2002); *Hansard*, HC col 825W (11 November 1999); *Hansard*, HL col 72WA (5 July 1999). There were 38 in post when the Labour government took office in 1997. Two special advisers became well-known to the informed public—Alastair Campbell was the Prime Minister's Official Spokesman between 1997–2002 (responsible for twice daily briefings to the news media) and subsequently Director of Communications and Strategy; and Jonathan Powell is the Prime Minister's Chief of Staff.

[203] *Code of Conduct for Special Advisers*, para 8: 'Special advisers are able to represent Ministers' views on Government policy to the media with a degree of political commitment that would not be possible for the permanent Civil Service' (available from www.cabinet-office.gov.uk).

[204] ibid para 12.

[205] Civil Service Order in Council, Art 3.

[206] *Code of Conduct for Special Advisers*, para 2.

committed and politically aware than would be available to a Minister from the Civil Service.

At the time of writing, the role of special advisers is under consideration.[207]

3.77   Fourthly, questions have been raised about the general issue of ethics in public service. The fragmentation of the Civil Service—through creation of executive agencies, civil servants working for the separate governments of Scotland, Northern Ireland and Wales, contracting out of departmental functions to the private and voluntary sectors, the increasing use of special advisers, different pay and grading structures—has led some commentators to argue that there is no longer a core set of values shared by all who devise and implement central government policy.[208] In response to this new pluralism, attempts are being made to 'develop a strong sense of "corporacy", or commitment to shared objective, across the service, in part to compensate for the fragmentation of departments'.[209]

(h) The Armed, Security and Intelligence Services

3.78   One of the core functions of central government is to protect the security of the realm. Defence and national security are par excellence policy fields subject to multi-level governance and needing joined-up government.[210] Examination of this falls outside the scope of this chapter, save to say that the United Kingdom is a member of the United Nations, NATO, the Western European Union, and the European Union has a role in relation to defence.

3.79   There are three separate armed services in the United Kingdom: the British Army; the Royal Navy; and the Royal Air Force.[211] They 'contribute to the UK's defence and security principally through their deployments overseas, although they retain a responsibility for the security of UK airspace and waters'.[212] The government takes the view that '[t]he security and defence of the UK . . . [rests] on the UK's membership of NATO and our willingness and ability to participate in operations and tasks abroad with partner countries in mutual self-defence'.[213] British armed

---

[207] By the Committee on Standards in Public Life (a standing committee responsible for investigating and reporting on questions of ethics) in its Ninth Report, *Defining the Boundaries with the Executive: Ministers, Special Advisors and the Permanent Civil Service* (Cm 5775, 2003) and the House of Commons Select Committee on Public Administration.

[208] See Woodhouse (n 39 above) 32. And see Gordon-Walker (n 109 above) 68: 'Until 1919 civil servants tended to remain all their working life in one department: in that year a single service was created within which officials could be freely transferred between departments . . . The consequence of these developments has been a gradual rise of a collective view of the Civil Service, particularly among leading officials.'

[209] Kavanagh and Richards (n 156 above) 14.

[210] See para 3.59 above.

[211] See C Dandeker and L Freedman, 'The British Armed Services' (2002) 73 Political Q 465.

[212] Defence Committee, Sixth Report, *Defence and Security in the UK* (2001–02 HC 518-I).

[213] *The Strategic Defence Review: A New Chapter* (Cm 5566, 1998), discussed at *Hansard*, HC col 44 (31 October 2002).

service personnel also participate in multinational peacekeeping forces and emergency aid initiatives abroad. As a subsidiary task, the armed services, especially the Army, may also be deployed within the United Kingdom at times of national emergency, as happened in 2001 when troops were used to kill and dispose of farm animals during a foot-and-mouth disease epidemic and in 2002 to man fire-engines during a strike of civilian fire-fighters.

The formulation, conduct and resourcing of UK defence policy is under the political control of the Secretary of State for Defence, the member of the Cabinet who is the ministerial head of the Ministry of Defence (MOD).[214] The mission statement of the MOD is to: 'Deliver security for the people of the United Kingdom and the Overseas Territories, by defending them, including against terrorism, and act as a force for good by strengthening international peace and security'. Ministers in the MOD are supported at the highest level by senior non-military civil servants and a serving officer of the armed forces—the Chief of Defence Staff—who is the principal military adviser to the government. Statutes and letters patent (legal instruments made by the Crown) confer legal authority for the conduct of defence on to the Defence Council, which consists of the four MOD ministers and ten senior officials, including the Chief of Defence Staff and the permanent secretary to the MOD. Like other departments, many of the MOD's operations are carried out through executive agencies. In the event of a major emergency involving a threat to the security of the realm, the national crisis centre would be the Cabinet Office Briefing Room, from which the central government response would be co-ordinated. The Cabinet Office Briefing Room is responsible for determining the government's overall political strategy towards any specific terrorist incident.[215] **3.80**

The Bill of Rights 1688 prohibits the raising or keeping of a standing army within the United Kingdom in time of peace, unless with the consent of Parliament. Since the 1960s, the necessary parliamentary authority to maintain the Armed Forces in peacetime is given annually each spring by a vote in the House of Commons and an Armed Forces Act is re-enacted every five years.[216] Similar arrangements apply to the statutes establishing the Royal Navy and RAF. The quinquennial Bills are scrutinized by a House of Commons select committee on the Armed Forces, which takes oral and written evidence and reports to the House. A separate select committee on defence examines the expenditure, administration and policy of the MOD and its associated public bodies. **3.81**

The UK armed services consist of full-time and part-time professional personnel: there is no conscription of civilians to perform a period of national service. **3.82**

[214] See para 3.56 above.
[215] See n 212 above, para 7.
[216] At the time of writing, the last such was the Armed Forces Act 2001.

Members of the armed services are subject to a separate system of disciplinary laws administered by service courts (the most senior of which is the Courts-Martial Appeal Court), modified recently following findings by the European Court of Human Rights that some aspects of the system breached Convention rights.[217]

3.83 In addition to the armed services, several other government bodies are responsible for defending the realm and protecting national security.

3.84 The Security Service (colloquially known as 'MI5') is the UK security intelligence agency. It collects and disseminates intelligence; investigates, assesses and counters threats; and advises government on protection. Its existence and work was placed on a statutory basis by the Security Service Act 1989.[218] Before this, it had operated on the basis of prerogative powers. It is a civilian organization and its employees are civil servants; they have no legal authority to detain or arrest people, or any other executive powers. The police or HM Customs and Excise take any necessary steps to bring prosecutions. The Home Secretary has ministerial responsibility for the work of the Security Service.

3.85 The Secret Intelligence Service ('MI6') and the Government Communication Headquarters (GCHQ) have the principal responsibility for gathering overseas intelligence. Again, these agencies have no executive powers. The Foreign Secretary has ministerial responsibility.

3.86 Policing in the United Kingdom has not, historically, been a matter for central government but rather some 52 separate geographical constabularies, each accountable to local institutions, and a further five non-geographical police forces.[219] The National Crime Squad was established in 1998 to tackle serious or organized crime within England and Wales; it is a NDPB and its objectives are determined by the Home Secretary.[220] The National Criminal Intelligence Service was set up in 1992 to provide law enforcement agencies with intelligence on major criminals.[221]

(i) The head of state

3.87 In the United Kingdom, the offices of head of government and head of state are separate; the Prime Minister occupies the former; the monarch (currently Her Majesty Queen Elizabeth II who ascended to the throne in 1952) the latter.[222] The

---

[217] *Morris v UK* (2002) 34 EHRR 52. See further GR Rubin, 'UK military law: autonomy, civilianisation, juridification' (2000) 65 MLR 36 and *Boyd v Army Prosecuting Authority* [2003] UKHL 31; [2003] 1 AC 734.

[218] Amended in 1996. The work of all the intelligence agencies is affected by the Regulation of Investigatory Powers Act 2000.

[219] eg, the British Transport Police.

[220] National Crime Squad (Secretary of State's Objectives) Order 1999, SI 1999/821.

[221] Police Act 1996.

[222] See paras 1.16 et seq above and Bogdanor (n 91 above).

hereditary nature of the office of head of state results from a mix of common law rules regulated by Acts of Parliament.[223] The basic rule for the descent of the Crown is that male heirs take precedence over females, with children representing their deceased ancestors.[224] As a result of laws passed amidst the 17th and 18th century religious struggles between factions of the Christian church in Britain, a person of Roman Catholic faith is expressly barred from inheriting or occupying the throne and the sovereign must be in communion with the Church of England, the established church in England.[225] (The United Kingdom shares its head of state with 15 other Commonwealth nations,[226] including Australia, Canada and New Zealand). As well as her role as head of state(s), the sovereign is Head of the Commonwealth and Supreme Governor of the Church of England. Members of the Royal Family apart from the sovereign have no formal constitutional function as such, though many are appointed as Privy Counsellors.[227]

The Queen appoints a Private Secretary (following some consultation with the Prime Minister and senior civil servants), a post that has been said to be 'one of the most important posts in the British system of government, for it forms the mainstay of the institution of constitutional monarchy'.[228] The Private Secretary is the channel of communication between the Queen and the governments of the United Kingdom and the other states of which she is sovereign. According to some commentators, 'the Queen and her heir apparent are still to a large extent cocooned in a private working environment with reactionary and subservient sycophancy to ancient tradition'.[229] **3.88**

The Royal Household receives funding for its public work from a variety of sources: the Civil List (a grant from Parliament out of the Consolidated Fund to **3.89**

---

[223] Coronation Oath Act 1689; Act of Settlement 1701; Royal Marriages Act 1772; Accession Declaration Act 1910; Declaration of Abdication Act 1936; Regency Act 1937 (as amended in 1943, 1953); J Jaconelli, 'Regency and Parliamentary Sovereignty' [2002] PL 449; Rodney Brazier, 'Skipping a Generation in the Line of Succession' [2000] PL 568 and 'The Constitutional Position of the Prince of Wales' [1995] PL 501.

[224] The current line of succession is: HRH The Prince of Wales (Prince Charles); HRH Prince William (Prince Charles' elder son); HRH Prince Harry (Prince Charles' younger son); HRH The Duke of York (Prince Andrew, the Queen's second son); HRH Princess Beatrice (Prince Andrew's elder daughter); HRH Princess Eugenie (Prince Andrew's younger daughter); HRH Prince Edward (the Queen's youngest son); Lady Louise Windsor (Prince Edward's daughter); HRH The Princess Royal (Princess Anne, the Queen's daughter); Peter Phillips, Esq (Princess Anne's son); Miss Zara Phillips (Princess Anne's daughter); Viscount Linley (David Armstrong-Jones, son of Princess Margaret, the Queen's deceased sister); etc.

[225] Act of Settlement 1701. Three members of the extended royal family have excluded themselves from the line of succession by marrying Roman Catholics.

[226] On the Commonwealth, see n 42 above.

[227] See para 3.49 above.

[228] Bogdanor (n 91 above) 214.

[229] R Blackburn and R Plant, 'Monarchy and the Royal Prerogative' in Blackburn and Plant (eds), *Constitutional Reform: the Labour Government's Constitutional Reform Agenda* (London: Longman, 1999) ch 6.

cover official expenditure); income from visitors to royal palaces; grants from government departments (eg, the Department for Culture, Media and Sport for the upkeep of royal palaces and from the Department for Transport for travel); and the Privy Purse (primarily income from the Duchy of Lancaster). Since 1993, the Queen has voluntarily paid tax on the Privy Purse and her private income.

3.90   The distant historical roots of the sovereign's status reveal themselves in several features of the United Kingdom's constitutional practices that can sit uneasily with modern values. A wide range of oaths of office in the United Kingdom requires office-holders to swear loyalty to the Queen (rather than, as in some other states, the constitution).[230] British citizens who acquire nationality through naturalization similarly have to swear allegiance to the Queen. Acts of Parliament do not apply to the sovereign and the Royal Household is, accordingly, exempt from anti-discrimination laws and other legal provisions designed to protect the interests of workers. The appropriateness of the priority of male heirs over female ones in the succession has also been called into question.[231] Doubts have also arisen as to whether in a modern multi-cultural society there should be such a direct link between the United Kingdom's head of state and the Church of England; many within and outside the Church favour disestablishment (as has happened with churches in Wales, Scotland and Ireland). Most fundamentally, the idea of a hereditary head of state seems, to a few, anachronistic[232]—and 'in the longer term there is little doubt the monarch is doomed'.[233]

3.91   The main executive tasks[234] of the sovereign are as follows.

• To appoint the Prime Minister, inviting him or her to form a government.[235] After a general election (or resignation or death of a Prime Minister), the sovereign summons the leader of the largest party in the House of Commons and appoints him or her Prime Minister. The appointment is signified by the Prime Minister kissing the sovereign's hands. If there is a 'hung' Parliament, in which no one party in the House of Commons has an outright majority, it

---

[230] These include: MPs, judges, Privy Counsellors, members of the armed services and bishops of the Church of England.

[231] See the unsuccessful Succession to the Crown Bill, *Hansard*, HL col 909 (27 February 1998).

[232] Rodney Brazier, 'A British Republic' (2002) 61 CLJ 351. For a reform agenda, see Fabian Society Commission on the Future of the Monarchy, *The Future of the Monarchy* (London: Fabian Society, 2003).

[233] Blackburn and Plant (n 229 above) 152.

[234] The legislative role of the sovereign in Parliament is to grant royal assent passed by both Houses of Parliament, or in accordance with the Parliament Acts 1911–47. The sovereign is also formally associated with judicial functions: criminal prosecutions are brought in the name of the Crown (not 'the People' or 'the State' as in other constitutional systems).

[235] See para 2.43 above. Brazier (n 86 above) chs 2–3. The Queen also appoints the Scottish First Minister and has regular audiences with him or her.

may not be clear which party leader should be summoned to form the government. The constitutional conventions relating to such a situation are far from certain.[236]

- To appoint other ministers, on the advice of the Prime Minister.[237] Here the Queen's role is entirely formal, the real power of patronage belonging to the Prime Minister.

- To dissolve Parliament. The United Kingdom does not have fixed term Parliaments. A general election is required to be held at least every five years, the Prime Minister deciding the timing of a general election. It is the Queen who formally makes a proclamation of dissolution, and there is some speculation about the circumstances in which it might be constitutionally proper for a sovereign to refuse a request from a Prime Minister for a dissolution.[238]

- To preside over the annual State Opening of Parliament and deliver the Queen's Speech, drafted by the government setting out the Bills it intends to introduce during the forthcoming session.

- To preside at meetings of the Privy Council.[239]

- The sovereign has 'the right to be consulted, the right to encourage and the right to warn' the government.[240] As one minister put it, these 'do not amount to much: they are the attributes of a Head of State without power'.[241] During parliamentary sessions, the Prime Minister has a weekly audience with the sovereign, who also receives a substantial number of state papers and briefing documents, including all Cabinet papers and minutes and Foreign and Commonwealth Office communications. She also has less frequent meetings with other members of the UK Cabinet and occasional informal meetings with senior politicians of opposition parties.[242]

- The monarch is Head of the Armed Forces 'and it is the monarch alone who can declare war and peace'[243]—on the advice of the 'responsible ministers'.[244]

---

[236] Robert Blackburn, 'The dissolution of Parliament: the Crown Prerogatives (House of Commons Control) Bill 1988' (1989) 52 MLR 837; and para 2.43 above.

[237] On the formalities of appointment, see n 86 above.

[238] Brazier (n 86 above) 151.

[239] See para 3.49 above.

[240] W Bagehot, *The English Constitution* (London: Collins, 1963) 111.

[241] Gordon-Walker (n 109 above) 72.

[242] In relation to the devolved executive bodies: *Wales*—the Queen does *not* appoint, but does hold audiences from time to time with the First Secretary of the National Assembly of Wales, 'however, the formal advice on which Her Majesty acts in relation to Wales is provided by her UK ministers' (www.royal.gov.uk). The subordinate legislation made by the National Assembly does not require royal assent; *Scotland*—the Queen appoints and holds regular audiences with the Scottish First Minister who advises the monarch on the exercise of prerogative powers relating to Scotland (see above); the Queen grants Royal Assent to Scottish Bills.

[243] See www.royal.gov.uk (accessed July 2003). On the somewhat uncertain practice, see C Gearty, 'How We Declare War' (2002) 24 London Review of Books, 3 October.

[244] See para 3.80 above.

- To hold formal audiences, including those at which she receives letters of credence from ambassadors and Commonwealth High Commissioners; and with newly appointed bishops of the Church of England.
- To grant honours. Some honours are entirely at the personal disposal of the sovereign, but most are made on the recommendation of the Prime Minister (having first been approved by a scrutiny committee).[245]
- To grant (or perhaps, in extraordinary circumstances, to refuse) royal assent to Bills.[246] By convention, the Queen assents to Bills that have passed though the legislative process of both Houses of Parliament, or are presented for Royal Assent in accordance with the Parliament Acts 1911 and 1947 (when the House of Lords has three times rejected a Bill approved by the Commons). A monarch has not refused royal assent to a Bill since 1708.

(j) The Law Officers

3.92 If the rule of law is conceived as a 'principle of institutional morality',[247] practical arrangements should exist within central government to ensure the adherence to law and ethics of constitutionalism. As with the whole central government machine, the provision of legal advice and legal services takes place in a plural, fragmented structure rather than through a single, unified corps of professional advisers.[248] The Government Legal Service contains over 1,600 lawyers working with particular departments or in the Treasury Solicitor's Department (which provides litigation services and legal advice to other departments). In addition, the professional lawyers are employed as Parliamentary Counsel (specialist legislative draftsmen), in the corps of Foreign and Commonwealth Office Legal Advisers, and the Crown Prosecution Service.

3.93 In addition to legal advice from professional lawyers employed by government, legal advice functions are carried out by political appointees—the UK Law Officers.

3.94 The Prime Minister is required to appoint Law Officers. These posts include that of Attorney-General and Solicitor-General. They are the principal legal advisers to the government and are chosen from among those MPs or peers of the governing party who are qualified as barristers or solicitors. Their work is supported by the Legal Secretariat to the Law Officers. The work of the Law Officers falls

[245] See para 3.41 below.
[246] R Blackburn, 'The Royal Assent to legislation and the monarch's fundamental human rights' [2003] PL 205.
[247] See generally paras 1.88 et seq above and J Jowell, 'The Rule of Law' in Jowell and Oliver (eds), *The Changing Constitution* (Oxford: OUP, 2000) ch 1.
[248] Daintith and Page (n 2 above) 297.

into three main categories. First, they act as lawyers for the government. They provide high-level legal advice to the Cabinet and departments.[249] The Attorney-General is not a member of Cabinet, but may be invited to attend. The Law Officers occasionally appear in court as counsel representing a department in high profile and politically sensitive cases. Under the Human Rights Act 1998 (HRA), the Attorney-General must be given notice of any case in which a party seeks a declaration that a statutory provision is incompatible with a Convention right.

Secondly, the Law Officers occupy what are effectively ministerial positions. They have 'superintendence' over several parts of the central government machinery—the Crown Prosecution Service; the Serious Fraud Office; the Treasury Solicitor's Department; and the Solicitor to HM Customs and Excise—and are accountable to Parliament for the work of these bodies. **3.95**

Thirdly, the Law Officers act as 'guardians of the public interest'. In relation to this work, the Law Officers act in a 'wholly independent and quasi-judicial capacity and not as a member of the Government'.[250] The functions of the Law Officers in relation to individual criminal cases fall within this category. The Law Officers have statutory powers to refer cases to the Court of Appeal where a sentence appears to be unduly lenient and to bring prosecutions for contempt of court. They also devise policy guidelines on a range of matters, mostly relating to prosecutions, and have functions in relation to charities. The Attorney-General is ex officio head of the Bar of England and Wales. **3.96**

The Attorney-General and Solicitor-General are appointed in relation to the legal system of England and Wales. The Northern Ireland Constitution Act 1973 provides that the Attorney-General for England and Wales also holds the post of Attorney-General for Northern Ireland. The Advocate-General for Scotland, a post created by the Scotland Act 1998, advises the UK government on Scottish law matters;[251] as with the other UK Law Officers, the post-holder must be an MP or peer. **3.97**

More informally, until 2003 the Cabinet was also able to seek, or be given, legal advice by the Lord Chancellor. Any advice tendered to Cabinet by the Lord Chancellor did not have the formal constitutional status of that from the Law Officers.[252] The constitutional status of the post of Lord Chancellor was the **3.98**

---

[249] Ministerial Code, para 22. This stipulates that the advice to government from the Law Officers is not made public; but for a discussion of the A-G's advice on the legality under international law of UK military action in Iraq, see *Hansard*, HL col 68 (17 March 2003).
[250] *Attorney-General's Review of the Year 2001/2002*, para 19.
[251] Within the Scottish Executive, the Scottish Law Officers (the Lord Advocate and the Solicitor-General for Scotland) advise on legal matters. The National Assembly for Wales is advised by the Counsel-General to the Welsh Assembly.
[252] For discussion of situations in which the Lord Chancellor has tendered legal advice to Cabinet colleagues, see Daintith and Page (n 2 above) 298.

subject of much critical comment in the United Kingdom[253] and had long perplexed overseas observers. The Lord Chancellor had three main roles. He was the ministerial head of a major government department,[254] and he sat in Cabinet and participated in the work of Cabinet committees.[255] Secondly, the Lord Chancellor was the presiding officer of the House of Lords, the upper chamber of the UK Parliament. Thirdly, the Lord Chancellor was entitled to sit as the presiding judge (and did so from time to time) in the United Kingdom's two highest courts—the Appellate Committee of the House of Lords and the Judicial Committee of the Privy Council. With the retirement from office of Lord Irvine of Lairg LC in June 2003, the government announced its intention to abolish the post. The Lord Chancellor's Department was restyled the Department for Constitutional Affairs, the ministerial head of which is the newly established Secretary of State for Constitutional Affairs. The government also plans to establish a new UK Supreme Court to which the jurisdiction of the Appellate Committee of the House of Lords will be transferred.

B. The Domestic and International Legal Powers of Central Government

(1) Introduction

3.99   The rule of law[256] requires central government action to be based on legal authority. As Laws LJ noted in relation to local authorities:

> . . . any action to be taken must be justified by positive law. A public body has no heritage of legal rights which it enjoys for its own sake; at every turn, all of its dealings constitute the fulfilment of duties which it owes to others; indeed, it exists for no other purpose . . . Under our law, this is true of every public body. The rule is necessary in order to protect people from arbitrary interference by those set in power over them.[257]

3.100   The same broad proposition applies to the office-holders and institutions of central government, though caveats are needed. First, ministers have at their disposal a source of legal authority not possessed by other public authorities in the United Kingdom—prerogative powers. Secondly, it needs to be recalled that there is a disjuncture between political influence and legal power at the core of

---

[253] See eg Diana Woodhouse, *The Office of Lord Chancellor* (Oxford: Hart, 2001); R Cornes, '*McGonnell v UK*, the Lord Chancellor and the Law Lords' [2000] PL 166; Lord Steyn, 'The Case for a Supreme Court' (2002) 118 LQR 382; cf Lord Cooke of Thorndon, 'The Law Lords: an Endangered Heritage' (2003) 119 LQR 49.

[254] See n 142 above.

[255] See para 3.45 above.

[256] See paras 1.88 et seq above.

[257] *R v Somerset CC, ex p Fewings* [1995] 1 All ER 513, 524.

central government: the Prime Minister has few statutory powers at his disposal, and the Cabinet none at all. Thirdly, central government stands in a unique relation with Parliament. Whereas other levels of government within the United Kingdom—local authorities and devolved institutions—are the subjects of legislation, central government is both a subject and the controller of primary legislation.[258]

The Westminster model of the UK constitution takes as its paradigm ministers   **3.101**
and Acts of Parliament: ministers initiate Bills, which are subjected to parliamentary scrutiny, receive approval, and the Acts provide a legal foundation for the executive action taken by central government.[259] The Westminster model is now rejected by most political scientists as a realistic view of how the UK constitution operates.[260] The arrangements for the acquisition and use of legal power by central government provide evidence to support this view.

- There is widespread delegation of legislative powers to ministers. Rules made in this way are subject to only relatively cursory parliamentary scrutiny. Central government has very considerable legal rule-making capacity.
- Acts of Parliament often confer on ministers the power to determine if and when provisions of Acts of Parliament come into force, through the making (in the form of delegated legislation) of 'appointed day orders'.
- The use of 'Henry VIII clauses' in Acts of Parliament, whereby ministers are empowered to repeal or amend Acts, appears to be increasing.[261]
- Perhaps most significantly, UK ministers sitting in the EU Council have important powers to adopt EC legislation—in the form of directives and regulations—often with little or no prior involvement by the UK Parliament.

In all these ways, the central government can be seen to have greater control over legislation than might be implied by the classic Westminster model of the UK constitution.

(2) Acquisition and Use of Statutory Powers

The statute book is replete with examples of ministers being conferred with statu-   **3.102**
tory power to take action, either in the form of a legal duty or a legal discretionary power. One illustration is s 3 of the International Development Act 2002: 'The Secretary of State may provide any person or body with assistance for the purpose of alleviating the effects of a natural or man-made disaster or other emergency on the population of one or more countries outside the United Kingdom'.[262]

---

[258] See para 3.07 above.
[259] On the legislative process, see paras 2.48–2.55 above.
[260] See para 3.10 above.
[261] See paras 1.135 et seq above.
[262] On the constitutional status of 'the Secretary of State', see para 3.36 above.

3.103   If a minister needs to acquire new legal authority for a proposed policy, a decision needs to be taken as to whether a new Act of Parliament is required or whether a provision enabling delegated legislation to be made covers the desired action. The pros and cons of each method will need to be carefully considered. To obtain a new Act of Parliament, a minister will first have to argue for time to be made available for his or her department's Bill in the annual legislative timetable. Parliamentary time is limited. Typically, between 35 and 50 government Bills can be presented to Parliament during an annual session. Competition between departments for inclusion of their Bills in the Queen's Speech at the State Opening of Parliament, in which the government announces its legislative agenda for the forthcoming year, can be intense. Co-ordination of the government's legislative programme is undertaken by a Cabinet committee.[263] Specialist lawyers known as Parliamentary Counsel draft government Bills. Bills which have not received Royal Assent by the end of the parliamentary session in which they are introduced may fall and have to be re-introduced afresh in the following session if the government wishes to persist with them.[264] Steering a major Bill through the legislative procedures of both Houses of Parliament is a time-consuming and arduous activity for a minister and departmental advisers.

3.104   One significant advantage of obtaining legal authority in the form of an Act of Parliament is that its provisions will be relatively immune from legal challenge. In the absence of a codified constitution in the United Kingdom, primary legislation cannot be held by a court to be 'unconstitutional', though provisions may be declared to be incompatible with Convention rights[265] and, if found to be incompatible with EC law, disapplied.[266] The exercise of a statutory power by a minister may, however, be subject to judicial review[267]—though some statutory powers and duties are so broad in nature as not to be justiciable.

(3) Acquisition and Use of Powers to Make Delegated Legislation

3.105   Acts of Parliament often confer power on ministers to make delegated legislation.[268] An illustration can be found in the Export Control Act 2002. Section 1(1) provides that: 'The Secretary of State may by order make provision for or in connection with

---

[263] The Ministerial Committee on the Legislative Programme, the terms of reference of which are: 'To prepare and submit to Cabinet drafts of the Queen's speeches to Parliament and proposals for the legislative programme; to monitor and progress of Bills in preparation and during their passage through Parliament; to review the programme as necessary; to examine all draft Bills; to consider the Parliamentary handling of Government Bills; EC documents, and Private Members' business, and such other related matters as may be necessary; and to keep under review the Government's policy in relation to issues of Parliamentary procedures'.

[264] During the 2002–03 parliamentary session, a limited reform was introduced to permit Bills in the House of Commons to be carried over to a new session.

[265] See chs 1 and 2 above.

[266] See chs 1 and 2 above.

[267] See chs 1 and 2 above.

[268] See ch 1 above. On 'remedial orders' made under the HRA 1998, see paras 7.119 et seq below.

the imposition of export controls in relation to goods of any description'. Section 13 stipulates that: '(1) The power to make an order under this Act is exercisable by statutory instrument' and '(2) A statutory instrument containing a control order . . . shall be laid before Parliament after being made but, unless it is approved by a resolution of each House before the end of the period of 40 days beginning with the day on which it is made, shall cease to have effect at the end of that period'. It is common for there to be statutory requirements placed on the minister (or other promoter of delegated legislation) to consult with specified bodies or, more generally, people likely to be affected by the regulation.

A minister will often be advised to obtain legal authority for a proposed policy by making delegated legislation. The parliamentary timetable enables a far larger quantity of delegated legislation to proceed through Parliament than Bills: in a typical year, over 3,000 such instruments are made. Delegated legislation, in the form of a 'statutory instrument'[269] or less commonly an 'Order in Council', often receives relatively little detailed scrutiny by Parliament.[270] A committee of MPs and peers, the Joint Committee on Statutory Instruments, advised by lawyers, scrutinizes draft delegated legislation on a number of grounds,[271] but cannot comment on the merits of the policy sought to be pursued by the minister. Only a small proportion of the delegated legislation laid by ministers before Parliament is debated. Such debates, when they occur, are normally limited to 90 minutes and MPs or peers are not permitted to move amendments to the draft, only to affirm or reject the legislation as a whole. A standing committee of the House of Lords considers provisions in Bills that confer delegated powers. Delegated legislation is drafted by lawyers within the department concerned, not by Parliamentary

3.106

---

[269] Statutory Instruments Act 1946.

[270] See JD Hayhurst and P Wallington, 'The Parliamentary Scrutiny of Delegated Legislation' [1988] PL 547; G Alderman, 'The Parliamentary Delegated Legislation' [1989] PL 38; T St J N Bates, 'The Future of Parliamentary Scrutiny of Delegated Legislation: Some Judicial Perspectives' (1998) 19 Statute L Rev 155.

[271] Standing Orders of the House of Commons, para 151. The criteria are: (1) that it imposes a charge on the public revenues or contains provisions requiring payments to be made to the Exchequer or any government department or to any local or public authority in consideration of any licence or consent or of any services to be rendered, or prescribes the amount of any such charge or payment; (2) that it is made in pursuance of any enactment containing specific provisions excluding it from challenge in the courts, either at all times or after the expiration of a specific period; (3) that it purports to have retrospective effect where the parent statute confers no express authority so to provide; (4) that there appears to have been unjustifiable delay in the publication or in the laying of it before Parliament; (5) that there appears to have been unjustifiable delay in sending a notification under the proviso to s 4(1) of the Statutory Instruments Act 1946, where an instrument has come into operation before it has been laid before Parliament; (6) that there appears to be a doubt whether it is intra vires or that it appears to make some unusual or unexpected use of the powers conferred by the statute under which it is made; (7) that for any special reason its form or purport calls for elucidation; (8) that its drafting appears to be defective; 'or on any other ground which does not impinge on its merits or on the policy behind it; and to report its decision with the reasons thereof in any particular case'.

Counsel. A disadvantage of delegated legislation, from a minister's point of view, is that its lawfulness is open to challenge before the courts on a range of grounds, though such challenges are relatively rare.[272]

(4) Ministerial Power to Bring Acts of Parliament into Force

3.107 It is a function of central government to decide if and when to bring statutory provisions contained in Acts of Parliament into force. Many provisions in Acts are stipulated to come into force on the day Royal Assent to the Bill is granted; alternatively, a specified date may be set down. If neither of these methods is used, an Act may confer power on a minister to determine when the 'appointed day' for the Act's coming into force will be. For example, s 55(2) of the Employment Act 2002 provides that:

> This Act, except sections 45, 46, 51 and 52 and this section, shall come into force on such day as the Secretary of State may by order made by statutory instrument appoint, and different days may be so appointed for different purposes.

3.108 The rationale for appointed day orders is obvious: especially where complex schemes are involved, resources may need to be put in place before practical implication is possible. The constitutional danger is that a minister may use the power to delay unduly provisions approved by Parliament and effectively put them into abeyance. The minister does, however, have a legal duty to keep the question of when to bring a provision into force and may not lawfully announce that a provision will never be brought into force.[273]

(5) Prerogative Powers

3.109 In some situations, government ministers may be able to take action based on prerogative powers.[274] These are the common law powers of Crown, recognized as such by the courts.[275] They 'remain in existence to the extent that Parliament has not expressly or by implication extinguished them'.[276] Prerogative powers are

---

[272] For a case study, see A Le Sueur and M Sunkin, *Public Law* (London: Longman, 1997) ch 11 (on the Board and Lodgings Regulations); the scope for judicial review of delegated legislation was considered by the Court of Appeal in *R (on the application of Javed) v Secretary of State for the Home Department* [2001] EWCA Civ 789; [2002] QB 129.
[273] *R v Secretary of State for the Home Department, ex p Fire Brigades Union* [1995] 2 AC 513. TRS Allan, 'Parliament, ministers, courts and prerogative: criminal injuries compensation and the dormant statute'(1995) 54 CLJ 481; Ian Leigh, 'The prerogative, legislative power, and the democratic deficit: the Fire Brigades Union case' [1995] Web JCLI 3.
[274] See paras 1.25 et seq above for further discussion of the definition of prerogative powers; and Blackburn and Plant (n 229 above).
[275] See paras 1.25 et seq above for further discussion of the scope and definition of royal prerogative.
[276] Lord Browne-Wilkinson, *R v Secretary of State for the Home Department, ex p Fire Brigades Union* [1995] 2 AC 513, 552.

unique to the Crown; other non-statutory legal powers of central government are best regarded as a separate category.[277] An immediate problem in describing the range of government functions that are authorized by prerogative power is that no comprehensive list of such powers exists, as is demonstrated by the following parliamentary question to the Home Secretary:

> Mr. Corbyn: To ask the Secretary of State for the Home Department if he will introduce legislation to bring the exercise of the Royal Prerogative under parliamentary scrutiny.
>
> Mr. Mike O'Brien: No. With very few exceptions, the Royal Prerogative is exercised only on the advice of Ministers. This provides accountability to Parliament for its exercise.[278]

And:

> Mr. Carmichael: To ask the Secretary of State for the Home Department what decisions have been made by his Department in the last year under authority from the royal prerogative.
>
> Mr. Blunkett: Records are not kept of the individual occasions on which powers under the royal prerogative are exercised, nor would it be practicable to do so.[279]

What does seem tolerably clear is that the prerogative is not a general power in the hands of central government to take action in the national interest.[280] Rather, it is a collection of specific powers relating to particular areas of policy: 'The limits within which the executive government may impose obligations or restraints upon citizens of the United Kingdom without any statutory authority are now well settled and incapable of extension'.[281] Prerogative powers are exercised by 'the Crown'—which, according to the context, may mean a minister, the Queen in Council (ie, the Privy Council) or the monarch personally. Since devolution in 1998, the First Minister in Scotland may be the person who advises the Queen on the exercise of prerogative powers relating to wholly Scottish matters.[282]   **3.110**

In the absence of any codified list of prerogative powers, the following should be treated only as indicative of the principal ones.   **3.111**

---

[277] See para 3.118 below.
[278] *Hansard*, HC col 865W (22 February 2000).
[279] *Hansard*, HC col 1068W (27 June 2002).
[280] C Vincenzi, *Crown Powers, Subjects and Citizens* (London: Pinter, 1998).
[281] *BBC v Johns (Inspector of Taxes)* [1965] Ch 32, 79 *per* Diplock LJ.
[282] *Hansard*, HL col WA51 (1 July 1999) (Baroness Jay); and for a similar statement, *Hansard*, HC col 215 (30 June 1999) (The Prime Minister). Scotland Act 1998, s 53. Cf Northern Ireland Act 1998, s 23.

(a) Treaties

3.112   To sign and ratify treaties.[283] Parliamentary debates may be held before or during the period of negotiation of a treaty, but this is more of an exception than a norm.[284] The minister responsible for formally concluding treaties is the Secretary of State for Foreign and Commonwealth Affairs, who will sign the agreed treaty at a ceremony, though occasionally the Prime Minister or another minister signs. After signature, the text of the treaty is published as a Command Paper. Before the United Kingdom ratifies a treaty, the treaty is laid before both Houses of Parliament, along with an explanatory memorandum, for 21 sitting days (the so-called 'Ponsonby rule').[285] Special arrangements exist where a treaty seeks to increase the powers of the European Parliament; here the government may not ratify such a treaty unless it has been approved by the UK Parliament.[286]

3.113   In the United Kingdom's legal systems, treaties are not self-executing, ie they do not have direct effect. If treaty commitments entered into by the government require change to UK laws, legislation must be made—in the form of an Act of Parliament or delegated legislation—to incorporate the treaty into national law or otherwise modify national law. It is the practice of the government to seek parliamentary assent to such legislation before the treaty is ratified. Treaty-making by the government is subject to relatively little judicial control: the courts have tended to view it as 'non-justiciable'[287] though have been called on to consider claims for judicial review relating to the validity of government action relating to treaties.[288]

(b) Passports

3.114   The issue and withdrawal of passports also takes place under prerogative power (exercised by the Home Secretary within the United Kingdom, and the Foreign Secretary at overseas ports). The possibility of introducing a statutory right to passports has been debated in Parliament in the past but successive governments have taken the view that the current system has worked well and change is not required.[289] The legality of a refusal to issue a passport, or the withdrawal of one,

---

[283]   cf HWR Wade, *Constitutional Fundamentals* (Oxford: OUP, 1980) 46 (where it is argued that such powers are not prerogative in that they do not alter people's rights, duties or status in domestic law. Colin Warbrick, 'International law and domestic law: ministerial powers' (1989) 38 ICLQ 965.

[284]   eg, before the Rome conference on establishing the International Criminal Court.

[285]   For comparative perspectives, see New Zealand Law Commission Report No 45 (December 1997) and E Jurgens, 'Parliaments and Treaty-Making' (1995) 1 J of Legislative Studies 175.

[286]   European Parliamentary Elections Act 1978, s 6(1). Richard Rawlings, 'Legal politics: the United Kingdom and ratification of the Treaty on European Union: Part 2' [1994] PL 367.

[287]   *Council of Civil Service Unions v Minister for the Civil Service* [1985] AC 374, 410.

[288]   eg, *R v Secretary of State for Foreign and Commonwealth Affairs, ex p Rees-Mogg* [1994] QB 552; L Collins, 'Foreign relations and the judiciary' (2002) 51 ICLQ 485.

[289]   *Hansard*, HC col WA107 (25 July 2002).

where it affects an individual and has no foreign policy implications, is subject to judicial review[290] but not to investigation by the Parliamentary Commissioner for Administration ('the Parliamentary Ombudsman') in cases of alleged maladministration.[291]

(c) Other prerogative powers

(1) To recognize foreign governments.   **3.115**

(2) To conduct diplomatic relations.[292]

(3) To appoint UK ambassadors.[293]

(4) To ensure the peace and good government of the British Overseas Territories,[294] the Bailiwicks of Jersey and Guernsey, and the Isle of Man.

(5) Immigration control is now regulated by statute, but s 33(5) of the Immigration Act 1971 expressly states that 'this Act shall not be taken to supersede or impair any power exercisable by Her Majesty in relation to aliens by virtue of Her Prerogative'.

(6) To declare war and commit UK armed forces.[295] The Prime Minister and Foreign Secretary, in consultation with others, make decisions about the

---

[290] *R v Secretary of State for Foreign and Commonwealth Affairs, ex p Everett* [1989] QB 811.

[291] Parliamentary Commission Act 1967, Sch 3 (Matters not subject to investigation).

[292] Current disputes over territory include: Gibraltar with Spain; Argentina claims Falkland Islands, South Georgia and the South Sandwich Islands; Mauritius and the Seychelles claim the Chagos Archipelago (the UK-administered British Indian Ocean Territory, in relation to which note *R v Secretary of State for the Foreign and Commonwealth Office, ex p Bancoult* [2001] QB 1067; Stephanie Palmer, '"They made a desert and called it peace": banishment and the royal prerogative' (2001) 60 CLJ 234; Adam Tomkins, 'Magna Carta, Crown and colonies' [2001] PL 571); the Rockall continental shelf dispute involving Denmark and Iceland; a territorial claim in Antarctica (British Antarctic Territory) overlaps an Argentine claim and partially overlaps a Chilean claim; and there are disputes with Iceland, Denmark, and Ireland over the Faroe Islands continental shelf boundary.

[293] Ambassadors are generally (but not invariably) career diplomats.

[294] The UK has responsibility under international law for a number of colonies and other entities that may broadly be described as dependent territories. Many of these have an importance beyond their size because their favourable tax regimes have encouraged the growth of off-shore finance industry. Two groups should be distinguished. Fourteen British Overseas Territories (BOTs), known until 2002 as 'British Dependent Territories'. The link between the UK and the BOTs is regulated in the constitution of each territory. Unlike some other colonial powers, such as France, the BOTs are not and have never been part of UK territory. Inhabitants did not have full British citizenship until conferred by the British Overseas Territories Act 2002. BOTs have a substantial measure of responsibility for the conduct of their own affairs. Governors or Commissioners, representing the Crown, are appointed by the UK government and are responsible for the external affairs and, in some cases, the internal security and public service. Other British islands have a somewhat different constitutional relationship with the UK. The Bailiwicks of Jersey and Guernsey (the Channel Islands) lie off the coast of France. They are neither members nor associate members of the EU but have a special relationship set out in Protocol 3 of the UK's Treaty of Accession. Legislation passed by the States in each Bailiwick (the legislatures) require the sanction of the Queen in Council. The UK government is responsible for their defence and international relations. Officials within the DCA are responsible for UK-island relationships.

[295] See further M Supperstone (ed), *Brownlie's Law of Public Order and National Security* (2nd edn, London: Butterworths, 1981).

deployment of British armed forces abroad in military operations. There is no constitutional convention that Parliament debate, let alone vote upon, such decisions before they are made. No such debate was held prior to the United Kingdom's military intervention in Kosovo in 1999. When a debate was eventually held a backbench MP stated:[296]

> The debate says much about democracy in this country in that, 60 days into the bombardment, there has been no substantive vote in the British Parliament on the authority of the Government to proceed with the bombardment of Yugoslavia. There has been no vote on whether there is to be a declaration of war, nor on the appropriation of vast amounts of money for this programme and there will not be a substantive vote either today, or, I suspect, on any other day. It ill behoves us to lecture the rest of the world on the rule of law and democracy when we have the archaic system of the royal prerogative handled by the Prime Minister and the Foreign Secretary to decide whether this country is at war.

(7) To requisition ships needed by the government in times of war.[297]

(8) To destroy property to prevent it falling into enemy hands.[298]

(9) To declare a state of emergency and take steps to preserve the 'Queen's peace' and maintain law and order during times of non-emergency.[299]

(10) To appoint judges in England and Wales. This is done by the Queen on the advice of the Prime Minister or Lord Chancellor. In 2003, a new system for making judicial appointments was proposed by the Government.

(11) To establish Royal Commissions and other committees.[300]

(12) To grant the prerogative of mercy. This permits convicted prisoners in England and Wales to be released on the order of the Home Secretary. It has traditionally been exercised in three ways: a free pardon, a conditional pardon or the remission, or partial remission, of the penalty imposed by a court.[301] It is necessarily reserved for the most exceptional of circumstances. It is rarely exercised;[302] a secret government review in 2001 did not lead to any significant change of policy.[303] Each case is considered on its own merits. The main

---

[296] *Hansard*, HC col 923 (18 May 1999) (Jeremy Corbyn MP).

[297] See *The Broadmayne* [1916] P 64.

[298] D Bonner, *Emergency Powers in Peacetime* (London: Sweet & Maxwell, 1985) 8–10.

[299] *R v Secretary of State for the Home Department, ex p Northumbria Police Authority* [1989] QB 26; AW Bradley, 'Police Powers and the Prerogative' [1988] PL 298; David Feldman, 'The King's peace, the royal prerogative and public order: the roots and early development of binding over powers' (1988) 47 CLJ 101.

[300] eg, Committee on Standards in Public Life (see para 3.133 below).

[301] *Hansard*, HL col 164WA (17 April 2002).

[302] In the years 1988–94, the annual number of pardons granted ranged from 12 to 50: *Hansard*, HC col 307 (9 March 1995). Between 1979 and 1995, 1,253 free and three conditional pardons were granted under the exercise of the royal prerogative of mercy: *Hansard*, HC col 217 (2 February 1995).

[303] *Hansard*, HC col 181W (1 July 2002).

reasons for granting the prerogative of mercy are where '(a) the sentencing court were unaware or misinformed about matters which may have affected the sentence, no avenue of appeal exists and it is not possible or appropriate to refer the matter to the Court of Appeal; and (b) where developments subsequent to the sentence and unconnected with the circumstances of the conviction suggest that special remission should be granted as an act of mercy, for example where a prisoner suffers from a terminal illness or gives valuable assistance to the authorities'.[304]

(13) To dissolve Parliament before the five year period laid down by statute.[305]

(14) To create peers (ie, members of the upper house of the legislature). The current reforms to the House of Lords do not envisage the removal of all life peers.[306]

(15) To appoint (and dismiss) the Prime Minister.[307]

(16) To appoint (and dismiss) other ministers.[308]

(17) To appoint bishops of the Church of England.[309]

(18) The grant of honours, awards or privileges within the gift of the Crown, including the grant of Royal Charters and the status of City.

(19) To regulate the Civil Service. The terms and conditions of employment for civil servants are regulated by an Order in Council (primary prerogative legislation made by the Privy Council).[310]

(20) To grant Royal Assent to Bills approved by both Houses of Parliament or in accordance with the Parliament Acts 1911 and 1947.[311]

As well as possessing discretionary powers and duties pursuant to prerogative powers, the Crown also enjoys certain immunity from legal action. Acts of Parliament do not bind the Crown unless they do so expressly.[312] Moreover, the

3.116

---

[304] *Hansard*, HC col 7 (15 April 1991).

[305] Exercised by the Queen on the advice of the Prime Minister, see above.

[306] This power remains in the hands of the Prime Minister who advises the Queen. Since 2000, the House of Lords Appointments Commission (itself established under prerogative powers) has functioned (1) to recommend people for appointment as non-party political life peers and (2) to vet all nominations for membership of the House, including those made by political parties, to ensure the highest standards of propriety.

[307] See para 3.40 above.

[308] See para 3.35 above.

[309] On 8 July 2002, the Church of England's general synod (its governing body, exercising powers delegated to it by the UK Parliament) voted in favour of allowing the Prime Minister and the Queen to continue having the ultimate say in choosing its bishops. Twenty four bishops sit as members of the House of Lords during the term of the Episcopal office. A Crown Appointments Commission, the chair of which is appointed by the Prime Minister, oversees the process and sends two names to the Prime Minister who, in turn, selects one to recommend to the Queen for appointment to the vacant See; he may also request further names to be nominated if he disapproves of the two suggested candidates.

[310] See para 3.54 above.

[311] See para 3.91 above.

[312] *Lord Advocate v Dumbarton DC* [1990] 2 AC 580.

courts do not grant certain types of coercive orders directly against the Crown, though in most instances declaratory relief will achieve the desired effect.[313]

3.117 There are two perspectives on the continued existence of prerogative powers. One, taken by successive governments, is that all executive bodies need discretionary powers in relation to various sensitive issues (including the conduct of foreign relations). The prerogative powers provide this and are subject to parliamentary oversight and appropriate judicial control. An alternative view is that prerogative powers are an outmoded and dangerously unaccountable source of government power and ought to be replaced with statutory powers.

(6) Residual Freedom to Act Without Specific Legal Authority

3.118 The proposition put forward by Laws LJ in *R v Somerset CC, ex p Fewings*[314]—that in contrast to private individuals, the decisions and actions of public authorities 'must be justified by some positive law'—may be subject to exceptions in relation to central government departments and ministers. In the well-known case of *Malone v Metropolitan Police*,[315] Sir Robert Megarry VC articulated the proposition that a public authority (there, the police) could lawfully take action without specific legal authority, in so far as it did not interfere with a person's property rights or constitute a tortious act: 'If the tapping of telephones by the Post Office at the request of the police can be carried out without any breach of the law, it does not require any statutory or common law power to justify it: it can lawfully be done simply because there is nothing to make it unlawful'. As a general approach to the question of the legality of governmental action, this needs to be treated with extreme caution and is better viewed as applicable (if at all) only to central government departments and ministers.

3.119 First, it cannot apply to any public authority created by an Act of Parliament: in these circumstances, statute law provides a comprehensive catalogue of all the legal rights possessed by such a body—though some such rights to take action may be implied or framed in very broad terms. In the absence of express or implied legal authorization, the action will be ultra vires. The principle in *Malone* can therefore apply only to non-statutory public authorities. The 'Ram doctrine' asserts:[316]

---

[313] Crown Proceedings Act 1947 and *M v Home Office* [1994] 1 AC 377.

[314] See para 3.99 above.

[315] [1979] Ch 344. The law relating to telephone tapping in the UK has been reformed and is now subject to specific statutory regulation, prompted in part by the European Court of Human Rights' ruling in *Malone v UK* (1987) 7 EHRR 14.

[316] So named after the government lawyer who articulated it in an internal government memorandum written in 1945 but made public only in 2003: see *Hansard*, HC col WA12 (25 February 2003). See Lord Lester of Herne Hill and Matthew Weait, 'The use of ministerial powers without parliamentary authority: the Ram doctrine' [2003] PL 415.

A Minister of the Crown is not in the same position as a statutory corporation. A statutory corporation . . . is entirely a creature of statute and has no powers except those conferred upon it by or under statute, but a Minister of the Crown, even though there may have been a statute authorising his appointment, is not a creature of statute and may, as an agent of the Crown, exercise any powers which the Crown has power to exercise, except in so far as he is precluded from doing so by statute. In other words, in the case of a Government Department, one must look at statutes to see what it may not do, not as in the case of a company to see what it may do.

In other words, 'ministers and their departments have common law powers which derive from the Crown's status as a corporation sole',[317] distinct from prerogative powers.

It is therefore conceivable that a Secretary of State may have some 'freedom to act' **3.120** in the absence of specific statutory or prerogative power, though the ambit of such action will necessarily be limited. The implementation of government policy normally requires either the alteration of people's existing legal rights or the spending of public money, or both. A Secretary of State is 'free to act' only in so far as this does not infringe any other person's existing legal rights. Moreover, if the action involves the spending of a significant amount of public money, especially if it is to recur annually, then parliamentary approval for this expenditure will be needed (even if not for the action itself).[318] Moreover, since the HRA 1998, any interference with the qualified Convention rights, such as respect for privacy (Article 8 ECHR) and freedom of expression (Article 10 ECHR), will require to be done in a manner 'prescribed by' or 'in accordance with' the law and this is likely to require positive and relatively certain legal authority.[319]

(7) Powers of Central Government Derived from EC Law

Central government has acquired important new policy and law-making powers **3.121** since the United Kingdom's accession to the European Community in 1973. It is widely accepted that a 'democratic deficit' exists: the executive's powers have increased and the capacity of the UK Parliament (like the legislatures of other member states) has not been sufficiently adapted to suit the new constitutional framework. National parliaments have no formal role in the EC legislative process, though the UK Parliament is amongst the most effective of all the member states' legislatures.[320] British ministers, meeting behind closed doors with ministers from other member states, have power to adopt EC legislation which is binding on the United Kingdom and has primacy over any conflicting national

---

[317] See Baroness Scotland of Asthal, ibid.
[318] See para 3.31 above.
[319] See paras 7.158 and 7.162 below.
[320] For an overview, see Adam Jan Cygan, *National Parliaments in an Integrated Europe: An Anglo-German Perspective* (The Hague: Kluwer International, 2001).

law. The need for greater democratic legitimacy and more effective accountability is currently the subject of debate in the European Convention on the Future of Europe,[321] and is recognized by UK ministers[322] and the EU institutions themselves.[323]

3.122 The powers of UK central government relating to the European Union, including the European Community,[324] may be analysed according to traditional categories of English law. The periodic revision of the international treaties that form the framework for the European Union—as at Maastricht, Amsterdam and Nice— are assented to by the UK government using prerogative powers to sign and ratify treaties, though parliamentary approval is needed if the treaty enlarges the powers of the European Parliament.[325] Treaties are not self-executing or directly effective within the United Kingdom's legal systems until they are incorporated by Act of Parliament (the much amended European Communities Act 1972). Neither UK law nor convention creates a general requirement for national referendums to be held, no matter how sweeping the innovations being introduced. There is, however, a specific obligation to hold a referendum on adopting the Euro as the UK currency. Nevertheless, the practice of ensuring that an Act of Parliament implementing a treaty is in place before the UK government ratifies a treaty at least ensures parliamentary debate. The same arrangements apply to the two inter-governmental pillars of the European Union, dealing with common foreign and security policy, and police and judicial co-operation on criminal matters.

3.123 Like treaty making, the regular attendance by UK ministers at Council meetings is authorized by prerogative power relating to the conduct of international affairs. The extensive powers of the Council to adopt laws has therefore, from the UK viewpoint, led to a considerable increase in law-making by the executive at the expense of the UK Parliament. As a former minister has noted:

> . . . all the laws in Europe are made by the royal prerogative of treaty making. I was on the Council of Ministers for four years. Every time that I agreed to something, I was using the royal prerogative of treaty making. Indeed, since we joined the European Community as it was, the power to make laws by prerogative has returned for the first time since 1649 . . .[326]

---

[321] And see House of Commons Select Committee on European Scrutiny, 33rd report, *Democracy and Accountability in the European Union and the Role of National Parliaments* (2001–02 HC 1257).

[322] eg, Peter Hain MP (Minister for Europe), 'meeting in private is both objectionable in principle and makes it much more difficult for national Parliaments to hold Ministers to account', *Hansard*, HC col 217WH (9 July 2002).

[323] eg, the Inter-Governmental Conference in Nice in December 2000 acknowledged 'the need to improve and to monitor the democratic legitimacy and transparency of the Union and its institutions, in order to bring them closer to the citizens of the Member States'. Treaty of Nice, Declaration 23.

[324] On the distinction between the EU and EC, see para 1.68 above.

[325] See para 3.112 above.

[326] *Hansard*, HC col 1038 (9 November 1999).

The fact that the Council does not meet in public exacerbates the difficulty facing the UK Parliament, and other national parliaments, in holding ministers to account. There are eight to ten meetings of the Council each month.

Since 1973, each House of the UK Parliament has established a system of com-   **3.124**
mittees to scrutinize legislative proposals and other developments emanating from the EC institutions, and the UK government's stance in relation to them. The basic approach is that there is a 'scrutiny reserve':[327]

> No Minister of the Crown should give agreement in the Council or in the European Council to any proposal for European Community legislation or for a common strategy, joint action or common position under Title V or a common position, framework decision, decision or convention under Title VI of the Treaty on European Union—(a) which is still subject to scrutiny (that is, on which the European Scrutiny Committee has not completed its scrutiny) or (b) which is awaiting consideration by the House (that is, which has been recommended by the European Scrutiny Committee for consideration pursuant to Standing Order No. 119 (European Standing Committees) but in respect of which the House has not come to a Resolution).
>
> . . . The Minister concerned may, however, give agreement—(a) to a proposal which is still subject to scrutiny if he considers that it is confidential, routine or trivial or is substantially the same as a proposal on which scrutiny has been completed; (b) to a proposal which is awaiting consideration by the House if the European Scrutiny Committee has indicated that agreement need not be withheld pending consideration.
>
> The Minister concerned may also give agreement to a proposal which is still subject to scrutiny or awaiting consideration by the House if he decides that for special reasons agreement should be given; but he should explain his reasons—(a) in every such case, to the European Scrutiny Committee at the first opportunity after reaching his decision; and (b) in the case of a proposal awaiting consideration by the House, to the House at the first opportunity after giving agreement.
>
> In relation to any proposal which requires adoption by unanimity, abstention shall, for the purposes of paragraph (4), be treated as giving agreement.

The scrutiny reserve is a matter of parliamentary practice, not law. It has been suggested that the arrangement should be turned into a statutory obligation and enforceable in the courts.[328]

Some scrutiny committees in national parliaments (notably those in Denmark,   **3.125**
Finland and Sweden) 'concentrate on questioning Ministers before Council meetings and establishing a negotiating mandate'.[329] The House of Commons has

---

[327] Resolution of the House of Commons, 17 November 1998; Resolution of the House of Lords, 6 December 1999.

[328] The Conservative Party's Commission to Strengthen Parliament (under Lord Norton's chairmanship), *Strengthening Parliament* (London: Conservative Party, 2000).

[329] House of Commons European Scrutiny Committee, 30th report, *European Scrutiny in the Commons* (2001–02 HC 1256) para 7.

adopted a rather different approach, with a strong emphasis on a comprehensive analysis of EU documents and written explanatory memoranda from the UK government[330] (though ministers are sometimes questioned before and after Council meetings). The European Scrutiny Committee, consisting of 16 MPs from the main political parties, receives all documents and assesses their legal and/or political importance and whether they should be subject to further scrutiny in one of the two Standing Committees (of 13 MPs, nominated for the duration of the Parliament) which typically meet 14 times during each annual parliamentary session, or in exceptional cases subject to debate on the floor of the House. The European Scrutiny committee does not focus on the merits of proposals; the two European Standing Committees do and may call ministers and others to answer questions.

3.126 Once EC legislation is adopted, it either is directly applicable (regulations) or needs to be transposed into national law within a set time (directives). Most directives are given effect in the United Kingdom by means of delegated legislation,[331] though some are the subject of Acts of Parliament. Either way, the UK Parliament has no power to alter the content of the EC obligation. No House of Commons committee has responsibility for overseeing EU legislation implemented by statutory instruments and most are subject to the negative resolution procedure (whereby they come into force unless an MP objects), with the result that there may be no parliamentary scrutiny at all, save for the technical oversight of the Joint Committee on Statutory Instruments. Select committees monitoring the expenditure, administration and policy of the main government departments may, in the course of their inquiries, consider questions of EU law and policy.[332]

3.127 The House of Lords has a vital role in scrutinizing EU matters. Over 70 peers are involved in the European Union Committee and its six sub-committees (which cover areas of EU policy). Its terms of reference are to examine 'EU documents and other matters relating to the EU'. A scrutiny reserve, in broadly similar terms to that of the House of Commons, is in place.[333] It remains to be seen how the EU scrutiny work of the House of Lords is affected by reform of the upper chamber.[334]

---

[330] These include legislative proposals such as draft regulations, directives and decisions and other documents such as Green and White Papers and Commission reports. Documents are deposited in Parliament within two working days of an English text reaching the Foreign and Commonwealth Office. Each document is accompanied by an Explanatory Memorandum written by a government department. Over 1,000 documents are deposited in Parliament each year.

[331] About one-sixth of the statutory instruments made each year in the UK relate to EU matters: see Edward C Page, 'The Impact of European Legislation on British Public Policy Making: A Research Note' (1998) 76 Public Administration 803, 805.

[332] See para 3.146 below.

[333] *Hansard*, HL col 1020 (6 December 1999).

[334] See paras 2.63–2.67 above.

C. Accountability of Central Government

(1) Introduction

The final part of this chapter examines aspects of how the office-holders and insti-   **3.128**
tutions of central government are held to account for their actions (or inaction). A
parliamentary select committee in 1997 lamented that '[a]ccountability is an elusive concept and trying to find an accurate and comprehensive definition is correspondingly difficult'.[335] Academics complain that accountability is a 'complex and
chameleon-like term'.[336] The pragmatic definition adopted here is to regard accountability as the formal processes by which actors within central government are
called to explain their action (or inaction) to another office-holder or institution
and, if needs be, to accept sanctions for serious fault.[337]

As in all parliamentary democracies, the ultimate form of accountability for   **3.129**
central government is at a general election prompted either by timing (one must
be held every five years) or because the Cabinet has lost the support of the
majority of MPs in the House of Commons.[338] In British constitutional thinking, electoral accountability has formed the justification for parliamentary
supremacy[339]—which in reality normally means the supremacy of ministers
who control the legislative agenda and much else about the work of the House
of Commons. Electoral accountability is a blunt instrument in the United
Kingdom. Competition between political parties is limited in so far as the
United Kingdom has been governed by single-party governments for relatively
long periods,[340] voter turnout at general elections has been lower than politicians wish,[341] and there is evidence of public disillusionment with political
parties generally.

Between elections, central government is called upon to explain its actions, in-   **3.130**
action and failures in several different ways.

---

[335] Treasury Committee, *Accountability of the Bank of England* (1997–98 HC 282) para 7.
[336] Richard Mulgan, ' "Accountability": an Ever-expanding Concept?' (2000) 78 Public
Administration 555.
[337] There is an extensive literature on 'accountability' by constitutional lawyers, political scientists
and others, including: Adam Tomkins (n 186 above); Dawn Oliver and Gavin Drewry, *Public
Service Reforms: Issues of Accountability and Public Law* (London: Pinter, 1996); Dawn Oliver,
Constitutional Reform in the UK (Oxford: OUP, 2003); Robert Pyper (ed), *Aspects of Accountability
in the British System of Government* (Eastham: Tudor, 1996); Diana Woodhouse, 'The
Reconstruction of Constitutional Accountability' [2002] PL 73.
[338] On the convention of collective Cabinet responsibility, see above.
[339] See chs 1 and 2 above.
[340] The Conservatives were in government 1979–97 and the Labour party has formed governments since 1997.
[341] Less than 60% in 2001.

- Parliamentary inquiries, questions and debates require ministers to justify their conduct and the work of their departments. A minister who loses the confidence of the House of Commons, either because of personal fault or a failure within a department, may in the last resort be compelled to resign and return to the backbenches. The rules governing parliamentary accountability of these kinds are constitutional conventions (rather than law) and the Standing Orders of Parliament.

- Departments, and other institutions of central government, are subject to investigation by the Parliamentary Commissioner for Administration (colloquially called the Parliamentary Ombudsman).[342] The focus here is on instances of 'maladministration' where individuals and organizations have suffered injustice in consequence of official action. The Parliamentary Commissioner for Administration is an officer of the House of Commons.

- The legality of central government action may be challenged in the courts,[343] most notably by claims for judicial review in the Administrative Court.[344]

- A wide variety of adjudicative tribunals hear appeals from individuals aggrieved by decisions of central government departments (and other public authorities).[345]

- Ad hoc committees of inquiry into scandals and disasters, often chaired by a judge, may be established to find facts and recommend action.[346] The legal basis and form of inquiries, for example whether public hearings are held, may be controversial.[347] The findings of such inquiries may be debated in Parliament.[348]

- The managerial efficacy and propriety of central government spending is subject to a range of accountability mechanisms, including investigations by the National Audit Office (under the control of the Auditor and Comptroller General)[349] and inquiries by the Public Accounts Committee in the House of Commons.

---

[342] See ch 21 below.

[343] That legal and political accountability are distinct is illustrated by the Court of Appeal decision in *R (on the application of Javed) v Secretary of State for the Home Department* [2001] EWCA Civ 789; [2002] QB 129 where the court rejected the government's argument that a ministerial decision debated and approved in Parliament should not be subject to judicial review challenge on grounds of unreasonableness.

[344] See ch 17 below.

[345] See ch 20 below.

[346] eg, Sir Richard Scott's Inquiry into the Export of Defence Equipment and Dual-use Goods to Iraq and Related Prosecutions (1995–96 HC 115), and Lord Phillips's Inquiry into the emergence and identification of Bovine Spongiform Encephalopathy (BSE) and variant Creutzfeldt-Jakob Disease (vCJD) and the action taken in response to it (HC Paper (1999–2000) no 887-XV).

[347] See eg *R (on the application of Persey) v Secretary of State for the Environment, Food and Rural Affairs* [2002] EWHC 371; [2003] QB 794 where a court held there was no right to a public inquiry into the government's response to the foot-and-mouth disease epidemic that blighted the UK in 2001; cf *R v Secretary of State for Health, ex p Wagstaff* [2001] 1 WLR 292 where it was held that a committee of inquiry into multiple murders by Dr Shipman should be held in public.

[348] See further ch 22 below.

[349] Like the Parliamentary Ombudsman, an officer of the House of Commons.

Most of these mechanisms of accountability will be considered in detail elsewhere   **3.131**
in this book; the present chapter therefore focuses on the role of Parliament in calling ministers and officials within central government to account.

(2) The Convention of Individual Ministerial Responsibility to Parliament

The Westminster model of the constitution[350] takes as the paradigm form of ac-   **3.132**
countability the practice that ministers are answerable to Parliament—individual
ministerial responsibility.[351] The basic rules of individual ministerial responsibility have the status of constitutional conventions, not law.[352] They are recognized
by central government in its Ministerial Code, a document published for ministers by the Cabinet Office from time to time,[353] and in resolutions passed by each
House of Parliament.[354] The Ministerial Code states:

- Ministers have a duty to Parliament to account, and be held to account, for the
  policies, decisions and actions of their departments and 'next steps' [ie execu-
  tive] agencies;
- it is of paramount importance that Ministers give accurate and truthful information to Parliament, correcting any inadvertent error at the earliest opportunity. Ministers who knowingly mislead Parliament will be expected to offer
  their resignation to the Prime Minister;
- Ministers should be as open as possible with Parliament and the public,
  refusing to provide information only when disclosure would not be in the
  public interest which should be decided in accordance with the relevant
  statutes and the Government's Code of Practice on Access to Government
  Information;[355]
- Ministers should similarly require civil servants who give evidence before
  Parliamentary Committees on their behalf and under their direction to be as
  helpful as possible in providing accurate, truthful and full information in accordance with the duties and responsibilities of civil servants as set out in the
  Civil Service Code;
- Ministers must ensure that no conflict arises, or appears to arise, between their
  public duties and their private interests;

---

[350] See para 3.07 above. For comparative perspectives on 'officers of Parliament', see Oonagh Gay,
'The fall of Canada's privacy czar: institutionalising officers of Parliament' [2003] PL 632.

[351] To be distinguished from the convention of collective ministerial responsibility, discussed at
para 2.41 above.

[352] On conventions, see paras 1.32 et seq above.

[353] See n 120 above.

[354] *Hansard*, HC cols 1046–1047 (19 March 1997) and HL col 1057 (20 March 1997).

[355] Note: this is a reference to the non-statutory arrangements for access to official information in
force at the time of writing. The Freedom of Information Act 2000, expected to be fully in force by
2005, will bring about changes and place rights to information (for the public and MPs) from central government on a statutory footing for the first time.

- Ministers should avoid accepting any gift or hospitality which might, or might reasonably appear to, compromise their judgement or place them under an improper obligation;
- Ministers in the House of Commons must keep separate their roles as Minister and constituency Member;
- Ministers must not use government resources for Party political purposes. They must uphold the political impartiality of the Civil Service and not ask civil servants to act in any way which would conflict with the Civil Service Code.

3.133 These precepts of public accountability and appropriate conduct in public life reflect long-established expectations of desirable government practice, but were given renewed attention in the wake of two significant reports by committees during the 1990s. In 1994, the Prime Minister of the day (John Major) established a standing Committee on Standards in Public Life. The main impetus for this was the 'cash for questions' scandal, in which it emerged that a small number of MPs had accepted money to ask parliamentary questions about matters relating to the interests of some businesses and individuals.[356] The committee's terms of reference are:[357]

> To examine current concerns about standards of conduct of all holders of public office, including arrangements relating to financial and commercial activities, and make recommendations as to any changes in present arrangements which might be required to ensure the highest standards of propriety in public life.
>
> For these purposes, public office should include: Ministers, civil servants and advisers; Members of Parliament and UK Members of the European Parliament; Members and senior officers of all non-departmental public bodies and of national health service bodies; non-ministerial office holders; members and other senior officers of other bodies discharging publicly-funded functions; and elected members and senior officers of local authorities

3.134 In its early work, the Committee on Standards of Public Life set out 'seven principles of public life'—selflessness, integrity, objectivity, accountability, openness, honesty and leadership—and recommended revisions to what is now known as the Ministerial Code and the arrangements for investigating cases of alleged misconduct by ministers, civil servants and others in public life.[358] A Parliamentary Commissioner for Standards was appointed by the House of Commons with the role to investigate complaints against MPs (including ministers).

3.135 The second influential report was that made by Sir Richard Scott following a three-year long inquiry set up in 1992 into events surrounding the unsuccessful prosecution of executives of a company called Matrix Churchill for allegedly

---

[356] On parliamentary questions, see paras 3.143–3.144 below.

[357] *Hansard*, HC col 758 (25 October 1994); these were subsequently expanded to include the task of investigating the funding of political parties. See further www.public-standards.gov.uk.

[358] First Report of the Committee on Standards in Public Life (Cm 2850, 1995).

breaching export controls to Iraq in relation to machine tools with dual civilian and military uses.[359] The Scott report raised serious questions about the efficacy of ministerial accountability[360] and prompted Parliament to pass resolutions (referred to above) on ministerial accountability.

Much of the debate on individual ministerial responsibility surrounds the question when ministers should accept blame (and ultimately resign) for the failures of civil servants within their departments and executive agencies—or whether the ultimate requirement of resignation operates only for personal errors of judgment, failures of leadership, or misconduct by the minister.[361] Identifying clear principles is difficult because ministerial resignations are rare events and largely dictated by political realities:[362]   **3.136**

> . . . in the end the 'convention' turns out to be the truism that if a minister is not supported by Cabinet colleagues and/or members of his parliamentary party in the course of debate censuring his conduct, it is highly probable that he or she will face a majority of MPs demanding resignation, and in those circumstances would have little option but to comply.

Before turning to the mechanisms of accountability provided within Parliament, it is necessary to consider who may be the subject of scrutiny when a problem within central government arises. They may be: (1) one or more ministers within a department; (2) senior civil servants within a department; (3) the chief executive of an executive agency.   **3.137**

In the past, even senior civil servants were excluded from the equation: according to the traditional formulation of individual ministerial responsibility, 'ministers are accountable to the public, via Parliament, for their own decisions and for the work of their departments; civil servants are accountable internally—and only internally— to their political chiefs'.[363] Two main weaknesses are inherent in this approach. First, within departments, the 'classic doctrine of individual ministerial responsibility is based on the twin fiction that a minister delegates power to civil servants (the so-called "Carltona" doctrine) and that she or he is in charge of their department'.[364] The reality is that a minister will probably know little about points of detail on policy and is often highly dependent on the advice and knowledge of senior civil servants. A second weakness with the traditional understanding of individual   **3.138**

---

[359] Report of the Inquiry into the Export of Defence Equipment and Dual-use Goods to Iraq and Related Prosecutions (HC Paper (1995–96) no 115).
[360] For analysis, see further Adam Tomkins (n 186 above).
[361] See R Brazier, 'It is a constitutional issue: fitness for ministerial office in the 1990s' [1994] PL 431; D Woodhouse, 'Ministerial responsibility in the 1990s: when do ministers resign? (1993) 46 Parliamentary Affairs 297.
[362] SE Finer, V Bogdanor and B Rudden, *Comparing Constitutions* (Oxford: OUP, 1995) 83.
[363] Barberis (n 173 above).
[364] Harlow (n 173 above).

ministerial responsibility is that it fails to take account of the executive agencies created since the 1980s,[365] headed by chief executives, which are now responsible for the practical implementation of almost all central government action.

3.139   In recent years, two adaptations to the convention of individual ministerial responsibility have therefore emerged. First, a distinction has grown up between ministerial 'responsibility' (connoting the acceptance of blame by a minister) and 'accountability' (signifying only a duty to explain in the absence of blame attaching to a minister)[366]—a dichotomy 'widely rejected as spurious' outside government.[367] A minister is expected to explain, justify and defend all matters falling under the auspices of his or her department in Parliament; but a minister is unlikely to accept that he or she is at fault where the blame can be attached to senior civil servants within the department or an executive agency. A second, connected, adaptation has been the emergence of a distinction between 'policy' matters (for which a minister may be both responsible and accountable) and 'operational' or 'administrative' problems (for which a minister is only accountable where the failure has arisen in an executive agency). The operation of the modified version of individual ministerial responsibility is best seen in the context of the various parliamentary processes of accountability and it is to these that we now turn.

(3) Mechanisms and Methods of Government Accountability to Parliament

3.140   The convention of individual ministerial responsibility is premised on the existence of formal channels of communication between the government and Parliament through which ministers (and, to an extent, senior civil servants and chief executives of executive agencies) explain their personal conduct and, more importantly, the work of the government. It is widely accepted, including by the government itself, that parliamentary procedures are in need of reform.[368] Several different processes may usefully be distinguished.

3.141   First, the legislative process requires a minister introducing a Bill to defend departmental policy and aspirations, and provides MPs and peers with opportunities to question and veto government plans for new law.[369] Government defeats are however relatively rare and most successful amendments to Bills are actually proposed by government itself.

---

[365] See para 3.62 above.

[366] See Woodhouse (n 337 above).

[367] Harlow (n 173 above) 152.

[368] At the time of writing, a number of reforms are proposed, or are being implemented, including changes to the structure of the House of Commons' working week and daily sitting hours. Concern about the ability of the Commons to exert influence over the government is nothing new: for a historical account, see Flinders (n 27 above).

[369] See paras 2.49 et seq above.

Secondly, ministers make statements to Parliament announcing government **3.142**
policy and explaining failures—though in recent years, governments have been
criticized for making important announcements to the news media before the
Commons.

Thirdly, ministers answer oral and written questions in both Houses. Parlia- **3.143**
mentary questions 'should either press for action or seek information'[370] and must
relate to the work of the minister's department. MPs and peers seeking answers to
oral questions must submit their questions at least ten sitting days (or two weeks)
before the relevant ministerial question session is scheduled[371]—a procedural requirement that may prevent topical questions being put to the minister.[372] Prime
Minister's questions are taken every Wednesday when Parliament is in session:
they are 'an excellent way of holding the Prime Minister to account but . . . it is 80
per cent about theatre as well'.[373]

Ministers are required to answer written questions within three to seven days, **3.144**
though delays are endemic—partly explained by the sheer volume of questions[374]—and answers are sometimes evasive or incomplete.[375] Written answers
may be 'blocked' on the grounds of excessive cost involved and a number of other
factors (such as commercial confidentiality) set out in the code on access to information (soon to be replaced by the Freedom of Information Act 2000). Where a
matter falls within the remit of an executive agency (rather than a department),
MPs may ask formal written questions to the chief executive and since 1992 the
answers to these questions have been published in *Hansard* (the official record of
parliamentary proceedings).

Fourthly, debates on the floor of chambers of both Houses of Parliament— **3.145**
including adjournment and 'Opposition day' debates—provide further opportunities for MPs and peers to question and debate government policy and
conduct.

Fifthly, since 1979, a system of select committees has been established in the House **3.146**
of Commons.[376] Each committee consists of between 11 and 17 backbench MPs

---

[370] See Public Administration Select Committee, *Ministerial Accountability and Parliamentary Questions* (2000–01 HC 61) para 4.
[371] See para 3.39 above.
[372] On the frequency of ministerial question times, see ibid.
[373] Tony Blair, giving evidence to the Liaison Committee (a House of Commons select commit-tee): (2002–03 HC 1095) para 2. This was the first time that a serving Prime Minister had given evidence to a select committee since the 1930s.
[374] In 2001, over 16,700 written answers were tabled.
[375] See *Hansard*, HC col 137WH (21 March 2002). See further Barry Hough, 'Ministerial re-sponses to parliamentary questions' [2003] PL 211.
[376] See G Drewry (ed), *The New Select Committees* (2nd edn, Oxford: OUP, 1989).

and has the task of examining 'the expenditure, administration and policy'[377] of one of the main government departments. They are therefore scrutiny committees.[378] The aim in setting them up was to enable more detailed and considered scrutiny than is possible on the floor of the House. There is general consensus that departmental select committees have been successful in their overall goal. MPs themselves recently reported:[379]

> These have proved successful vehicles for scrutiny in the twenty years or so since they were set up. They enable Members to develop an expertise and authority in specialised areas of public policy. They provide a forum for detailed examination of Ministers at length which is not always practical in the full Chamber. At their best they enable Members from both sides of the House to examine the issues in a non-partisan environment and to assess what is in the interest of the public not the advantage of the party.

3.147   Select committees have powers to send for 'persons, papers and records' relating to their field of inquiry. Senior civil servants are often called by select committees to give evidence on the topic under investigation; they 'do so on behalf of their Ministers and under their directions'.[380] This also applies broadly to civil servants who are chief executives of executive agencies: 'While Agency Chief Executives have managerial authority to the extent set out in their Framework Documents, like other officials they give evidence on behalf of the Minister to whom they are accountable and are subject to that Minister's instruction'.[381] A priority in the House of Commons modernization programme is now to 'strengthen the independence, status and resources of Parliament's committees of scrutiny'.[382] From a comparative perspective, weaknesses are apparent: the Commons select committees 'are much poorer in the resources they can command than in other parliaments and they have a weak record of stability of membership. They also have a much more marginal role in scrutinising

---

[377] It has recently been suggested that committees should be given a clearer remit: 'It shall be the duty, where appropriate, of each select committee: to consider major policy initiatives; to consider the Government's response to major emerging issues; to propose changes where evidence persuades the Committee that present policy requires amendment; to conduct pre-legislative scrutiny of draft bills; to examine and report on main Estimates, annual expenditure plans and annual resource accounts; to monitor performance against targets in the public service agreements; to take evidence from each Minister at least annually; to take evidence from independent regulators and inspectorates; to consider the reports of Executive Agencies; to consider, and if appropriate report on, major appointments by a Secretary of State or other senior ministers; to examine treaties within their subject areas'. See Select Committee on Modernization of the House of Commons, *First Report* (6 February 2002), para 34.

[378] It is proposed to change their name to better reflect their work. Select Committee on Modernization of the House of Commons, *First Report*, para 37.

[379] ibid para 2.

[380] Cabinet Office, *Departmental Evidence and Response to Select Committees*, para 37.

[381] ibid para 43.

[382] ibid.

legislation, which is the principal function of the parallel committees in some other parliaments.'[383]

Sixthly, a 'parallel chamber' has recently been set up. Inspired by practices in the Australian House of Representatives, the idea is to hold debates away from the House of Commons in the Grand Committee Room of Westminster Hall. Reports of select committees have been debated, along with other topics chosen by backbench MPs.

3.148

[383] Democratic Audit's report, *The Challenge for Parliament: Making Government Accountable* (2001), quoted ibid.

4

THE STRUCTURE, POWERS AND ACCOUNTABILITY OF LOCAL GOVERNMENT

A. Introduction and Background

(1) Introductory Outline[1]

It is of course possible for a state to adopt arrangements for government whereby all responsibilities are exercised by centralized institutions. For a state of any significant size, however, it is wholly impracticable for those centralized institutions to have a physical presence only in the state's capital. There is bound, at the very least, to be a network of local and regional offices through which citizens can more easily interact with the institutions that regulate their lives or provide services.

4.01

---

[1] The main general works on local government law are: SH Bailey et al, *Cross on Local Government Law* (London: Sweet & Maxwell); SH Bailey (ed), *Encyclopedia of Local Government Law* (London: Sweet & Maxwell); P Elias and J Goudie (eds), *Butterworths Local Government Law* (London: Butterworths); A Arden, J Manning and S Collins, *Local Government Constitutional and Administrative Law* (London: Sweet & Maxwell, 1999). Historical perspectives are provided by Sir Ivor Jennings, *Principles of Local Government Law* (4th edn by JAG Griffith, London: University of London Press, 1960) and Sir William O Hart and JF Garner, *Hart's Introduction to the Law of Local Government and Administration* (9th edn, London: Butterworths, 1973). Important academic monographs are M Loughlin, *Legality and Locality: The Role of Law in Central-Local Government Relations* (Oxford: Clarendon, 1996) and I Leigh, *Law, Politics, and Local Democracy* (Oxford: OUP, 2000).

Most states go further than this and entrust some functions to directly or indirectly elected local authorities or to non-elected local agencies. An increasing number of functions have been transferred to the private sector, commonly but not necessarily subject to detailed regulation by the state. Such authorities and agencies enjoy an element of autonomy in that they, ex hypothesi, are not part of the central institutions of the state. However, the nature and extent of that autonomy can vary widely, as can the number of tiers of government. In most states, the structure and powers of the institutions of government are established by the (written) constitution. Many adopt a federal structure whereby there is a formal division of functions between the different layers of government.

4.02 The United Kingdom, as a unitary state without a formal written constitution, enjoys the widest legal flexibility in the design of its arrangements for local or regional government. The pattern that has emerged contains all the elements outlined above. First, many important functions are performed by central government departments or by agencies sponsored and effectively controlled by them. For example, the provision of social security benefits is managed by the Department of Work and Pensions and the Benefits Agency, the latter having a large network of local offices. The discharge of those functions of a range of central government departments that have particular impact locally or regionally has since 1994 been co-ordinated through the nine Government Offices for the Regions. Secondly, many functions have been removed from the direct control or even influence of elected bodies and entrusted to a whole series of agencies both inside and outside the public sector. Obvious examples are, respectively, the National Health Service and the police, and the public utilities (gas, electricity, telecommunications, water and sewerage). Thirdly, a range of functions has remained with (and some new functions have been allocated to) elected local authorities. The whole of England and Wales is divided into areas, each with one or more tiers of elected local government.

4.03 The 19th century saw the progressive establishment of elected local authorities to cover all areas of England and Wales. For much of the 20th century there has been uncertainty as to the proper structure and role of local government, with regular and probably too frequent changes to both structure and function. Some of these changes reflect changes in view as to the proper role of the state and the most appropriate ways in which state functions can be performed. Here, change has a similar impact on elected authorities and non-elected agencies. Others are focused more directly on the particular role of *elected* authorities outside Parliament. Here it is notable (and perhaps to be expected) that the big changes to the structure and functioning of local authorities in England and Wales in the second half of the 20th century have tended to be driven as a matter of party-political policy rather than consensus based upon the recommendations of a Royal Commission.

The pattern of local authorities in England and Wales in 2003 is as follows. In **4.04** England, outside London, there are 'principal councils' for each 'principal area'. These may be 'single tier' or unitary authorities (exercising all local authority functions) or 'two-tier'. These unitary authorities are (1) the 36 metropolitan district councils, which became unitary by virtue of the Local Government Act 1985, and (2) 46 new unitary authorities established by orders under the Local Government Act 1992. Where two-tier arrangements are in place, functions are divided between a (non-metropolitan) county council and a number of district councils. In London, there are 32 unitary London borough councils and the City of London Corporation, with some specific strategic functions exercised by the Greater London Authority established by the Greater London Authority Act 1999. In Wales there are 22 unitary county or county borough councils established by the Local Government (Wales) Act 1994; here, most of the functions of central government relating to local authorities are now exercised by the National Assembly for Wales set up by the Government of Wales Act 1998. Below the level of principal councils there may be parish councils or parish meetings (in England) and community councils or community meetings (in Wales). Above the level of principal councils there are at present no directly elected bodies, but the government has proposed that it should be open to people in a region to adopt arrangements for an elected regional assembly.

This variegated position has been reached piecemeal through a succession of **4.05** processes that have both significantly reduced the number of authorities[2] and increased the proportion of unitary authorities. The main functions currently performed by local authorities lie in the areas of town and country planning, public health and the environment, highways, housing, education, social services, licensing and registration, and the recreational services with a host of other more minor powers and duties.

(2) The History of Structural Reforms

(a) The 19th century

The establishment of elected local authorities across England and Wales was es- **4.06** sentially a process of the 19th century. At the start of the century, functions that today would be regarded as functions of local government were exercised by boroughs incorporated by charter granted by the Crown, by justices of the peace and by other ad hoc bodies. The Poor Law Amendment Act 1834 provided for the election (with a limited franchise) of local boards of guardians as part of a reformed structure for the poor law that involved significant central control. The

---

[2] In England, from 1,246 before 1974–75, to circa 410 between 1974–75 and 1996–98, to 387 under the current structure. In Wales the corresponding figures are 181, 45 and 22: D Wilson and C Game, *Local Government in the United Kingdom* (3rd edn, Basingstoke: Palgrave, 2002) 73.

Municipal Corporations Act 1835 introduced significant reforms in the boroughs, including the introduction of the elective principle (on a broader franchise than for the poor law guardians) and the conferment of powers in relation to such matters as police, street lighting and bye-laws, and of the right to raise money by levying a rate. Specific legislation in responding to concerns about public health saw the introduction of local boards of health in some areas[3] and then 'sanitary authorities' throughout England and Wales,[4] the law being consolidated in the landmark Public Health Act 1875.

4.07 The introduction of elected, multi-function, local authorities across the whole of England and Wales was effected by the Local Government Act 1888. This established county councils throughout England and Wales, and conferred the status of county borough on boroughs with a population of 50,000 or more. County boroughs were effectively unitary authorities, independent of the county council; some were also formally constituted as counties. Outside county boroughs, functions were divided between the county council and smaller authorities including borough councils and sanitary authorities. The urban and rural sanitary authorities became urban and rural district councils by virtue of the Local Government Act 1894, which Act also provided for the establishment of parish councils and parish meetings. All these authorities (except those boroughs that were charter corporations and parish meetings, which were not incorporated) were statutory corporations. In the case of charter corporations, the corporations acted through the agency of its council; statutory powers were, however, normally conferred on the council rather than the corporation and it was the council that was for the purposes of local government law the 'local authority'. In the case of statutory corporations, the council itself was the corporate body.[5]

(b) The 20th century

4.08 The legislation concerning the constitution and general powers of local authorities was consolidated by the Local Government Act 1933.[6] The broad structure established by the 19th century legislation, however, remained in place outside London, until 1 April 1974, when a new pattern introduced by the Local Government Act 1972 came into effect. The 1972 Act also restated the law concerning the constitution, administration and finance of local authorities and remains as the foundation Act, although much amended and supplemented since.

---

[3] Public Health Act 1848.
[4] Public Health Act 1872.
[5] See further paras 4.38–4.40.
[6] In the same period, housing, public health, and food and drugs legislation was consolidated by the Housing Act 1936, the Public Health Act 1936 and the Food and Drugs Act 1938. Other landmark postwar Acts were the Education Act 1944 and the Town and Country Planning Act 1947. Highways legislation was consolidated as late as 1959 by the Highways Act of that year.

(i) The Local Government Act 1972

The 1972 Act followed a fundamental review of local government in England by **4.09**
a Royal Commission set up by the Labour government and chaired by Lord
Redcliffe-Maud.[7] The Act sought to address the four basic defects in the existing
structure identified by the Royal Commission. These were: (1) that local government areas did not fit the pattern of life and work in modern England; (2) that the
fragmentation of England into 79 county boroughs and 45 counties, dividing
town from country, had made the proper planning of development and transportation impossible; (3) that the division of responsibility within the areas of
county councils and between such councils and county borough councils involved the fragmentation of services; and (4) that many local authorities were too
small in size and revenue.[8] However, the Conservative government that took office in 1972 did not accept the proposal of the majority of the Royal Commission[9]
that England outside London should be divided into 61 new local government
areas, 58 with unitary authorities and three metropolitan areas with functions
divided between a metropolitan authority and metropolitan district councils.
Instead, the 1972 Act extended the two tier principle across the whole of England
and Wales, with different arrangements for the allocation of functions in metropolitan and non-metropolitan areas.[10] In six metropolitan areas,[11] most functions
were to be exercised by metropolitan district councils, with strategic responsibilities concerning such matters as planning, transportation and waste regulation exercised by metropolitan county councils. Elsewhere, the county councils would
deal with such matters as education and social services and the district council
with such matters as housing and public health, with other functions divided between the two tiers. Proposals by the Royal Commission for the establishment of
provincial councils were not taken up. There was also a substantial reduction in
the number of authorities at both county and district level, largely through amalgamation. In three areas, however, (Avon, Cleveland and Humberside) new non-
metropolitan counties were established that cut across existing historical patterns.

(ii) Subsequent structural changes

The pattern established by the 1972 Act did not prove stable and has been subject **4.10**
to a series of modifications. The main steps were these. First, the Conservative

---

[7] *Royal Commission on Local Government in England 1966–1969* (Cmnd 4040, 1969).
[8] ibid para 6.
[9] There was an extended dissent by Mr Derek Senior, who proposed a two-level structure based
on 35 city-regions and 148 districts: (Cmnd 4040–I) vol II.
[10] See the White Paper, *Local Government in England: Government Proposals for Reorganisation*
(Cmnd 4584, 1971) and the Consultative Document, *The Reform of Local Government in Wales*
(1971).
[11] Greater Manchester, Merseyside, South Yorkshire, Tyne and Wear, West Midlands, West
Yorkshire.

government in 1985 secured the abolition of the (Labour-dominated) metropolitan county councils.[12] Functions were transferred either to the metropolitan district councils or to new joint authorities for police, fire and civil defence and transport.

4.11 Secondly, the Conservative government's new-found enthusiasm for unitary authorities was carried forward with a process of structural reorganization conducted by the Local Government Commission established by the Local Government Act 1992. Here, the reorganization was effected not by primary legislation but by structural change orders made under the 1992 Act. The process was for the Commission to make recommendations following extensive local consultation as to the preferred model for local authorities in the area; recommendations were then implemented, with or without modification, by an order made by the Secretary of State.[13] The process ran into some legal and political difficulty, largely because of a difference of emphasis on the desirability of unitary authorities between the government and the Commission.[14] The eventual outcome involved (1) the abolition of the unfavoured new counties of Avon, Cleveland and Humberside, with their constituent districts (or combinations of districts) becoming unitary authorities; (2) the abolition of the county of Hereford and Worcester, with the old county of Herefordshire established as a unitary authority and Worcestershire remaining two-tier; (3) the establishment of unitary authorities for many large urban areas within non-metropolitan counties, commonly the former county boroughs, with two-tier arrangements remaining elsewhere;[15] and (4) the establishment of unitary authorities for the Isle of Wight and Berkshire.[16] The overall pattern now has a large number of unitary authorities (as favoured by the Redcliffe-Maud Commission); the return of awkward divisions between adjacent unitary and two-tier areas; and the restoration of some of the old historical boundaries and associations that had not been forgotten in the 20 years following the 1972 Act.

4.12 Thirdly, the structure of local government in Wales was reformed by primary legislation, the Local Government (Wales) Act 1994, driven through following a process of consultation that began with apparent consensus and ended in

---

[12] Local Government Act 1985. See the White Paper, *Streamlining the Cities* (Cmnd 9063, 1983).

[13] Local Government Act 1992, s 17, as amended.

[14] See Leigh (n 1 above) 16–22; M Grant, 'Progress and transition: the work of the Local Government Commission for England' [1999] J of Local Government L 23. One sentence in the government's original guidance, giving a steer that two-tier arrangements should be the exception, was held to be unlawful: *R v Secretary of State for the Environment, ex p Lancashire CC*; *R v Secretary of State for the Environment, ex p Derbyshire CC* [1994] 4 All ER 165.

[15] Although not a large urban area, the pre-1974 county of Rutland was re-established as a unitary authority.

[16] See *Cross on Local Government Law* (n 1 above) para 3–14.

disagreement.[17] The two-tier pattern established by the Local Government Act 1972 was replaced by one with only unitary authorities.

Fourthly, the structure of local government in London has followed a separate path. **4.13** The London Government Act 1963, following the recommendations of the Royal Commission on London Government,[18] abolished the London County Council, the Middlesex County Council, 28 metropolitan borough councils and all other local authorities (except the Corporation of the City of London and the Temples) within Greater London. It established the Greater London Council and the London borough councils. The Greater London Council had responsibility for metropolitan roads, traffic management, refuse disposal, the fire service and, in the inner London area, education (through the Inner London Education Authority) and building control. It shared responsibility for housing and planning with the London borough councils and the Common Council of the City of London. Following a period of highly visible political and litigious opposition to the Conservative government, the Greater London Council was abolished, at the same time as the metropolitan county councils, by the Local Government Act 1985.[19] The Inner London Education Authority continued as a separate authority, but was in turn abolished, on 1 April 1990, by the Education Reform Act 1988. The London borough councils thus became unitary authorities. By virtue of the Greater London Authority (Referendum) Act 1998, promoted by the Labour government, a referendum was held on a proposal to establish a Greater London Authority comprising an elected assembly and a separately elected mayor.[20] The result was favourable (72 per cent to 28 per cent) and the new body established by the Greater London Authority Act 1999. The Authority's principal purposes are to promote economic development and wealth creation, social development and improvements of the environment in Greater London. It has power to do anything which it considers will further any one or more of these purposes, subject to restrictions that prevent expenditure on things that may be done by specified bodies.[21]

(c) Central government responsibility

While local authorities have to interact with a number of central government departments, one department always has lead responsibility for local government. **4.14**

---

[17] See P Griffiths and C Crawford, *Current Law Statutes Annotated 1994* (Sweet & Maxwell) 19-3–19-5; White Paper, *Local Government in Wales: A Charter for the Future* (1993).
[18] Cmnd 1164, 1960. Chairman: Sir Edwin Herbert.
[19] With effect from 1 April 1986.
[20] See White Paper, *A Mayor and Assembly for London* (Cm 3897, 1998).
[21] 1999 Act, ss 30, 31. The restrictions apply in respect of things that may be done by Transport for London, the Metropolitan Police Authority and the London Fire and Civil Defence Authority, and the provision of housing, education and social or health services where such provision may be made by a London borough council, the Common Council or any other public bodies; they do not prevent expenditure in co-operating with or facilitating or co-ordinating the activities of the named bodies.

The line effectively began with the Local Government Board[22] and continued with the Ministry of Health, the Ministry of Housing and Local Government, the Department of the Environment, the Department of the Environment, Transport and the Regions, the Department for Transport, Local Government and the Regions and currently (2003), following the separate establishment of a separate Department of Transport, the Office of the Deputy Prime Minister.[23]

(3) The Purposes and Role of Local Government

(a) Changes in role

4.15 The transformation of the structure of local government over the course of the 20th century has been matched by significant changes in its purposes and role. The key changes have been (1) the transfer of a number of important functions from local authorities to other agencies; (2) a change of emphasis across a number of services from being the direct provider of the service to being an enabler or facilitator, in some cases securing the provision of the service through a contracting process involving private sector organizations; (3) subjection, along with other public sector agencies, to the tenets of 'new public management'; and (4) the fundamental reorganization of the way in which councils (other than parish and community councils) do their business, effected by the Local Government Act 2000.

4.16 A context for these changes has been provided by continuing debate over the reasons that justify the continued existence of a network of multi-function local authorities, as distinct from other, non-elected, forms of local governance. It is notable that while there is general agreement that these should be a tier of elected local authorities, there is no such general consensus on the justifications for that position.[24] The traditional position, advocated by John Stuart Mill and others, was that local government provided an opportunity for political participation and the education of the citizen in the practice of politics and government, helped to ensure efficient service delivery and reflected a tradition of opposition to an overly centralized government.[25] Later writers attached greater weight to the promotion of efficiency and the role of the local authority as a co-ordinator of services and in the balancing of priorities and less on the notion of local government as a 'bulwark against central tyranny', or as a vehicle for political participation.[26] The increases in central control over local government under the Conservative government in

---

[22] This was established by the Local Government Act 1871, and inherited (inter alia) the public health functions of the Privy Council and Home Office, and the functions of the Poor Law Board.

[23] A title that is both opaque and inevitably time-limited.

[24] See G Stoker, 'Normative Theories of Local Government and Democracy' in D King and G Stoker (eds), *Rethinking Local Democracy* (Basingstoke: Macmillan/ESRC, 1996) ch 1.

[25] ibid 5–7.

[26] ibid 7–11, citing LJ Sharpe, 'Theories and Values of Local Government' (1970) 18 Political Studies 153.

office from 1979 were met by arguments that the concentration of power in central hands was a danger to a free society.[27] It was also argued that the allocation of a range of functions to one body facilitated the setting of priorities.[28] There are difficulties with all these arguments. First, the argument based on political participation becomes increasingly difficult to sustain as the turnout at local elections continues to decline.[29] Secondly, it has been difficult for local authorities to demonstrate that services are more efficiently delivered by them or under their superintendence, than by or through other central or local bodies. Indeed, the clear view of central government, under both Conservative and Labour administrations, has been that there has been considerable room for improvement in service delivery across the whole of the public sector, including elected local authorities. Thirdly, the notion that local authorities can protect individual liberty against the actions of central government is both itself problematic[30] and unsupported by evidence. It has been recognized that:

> there can be no simple presumption that 'local democracy' is necessarily superior to other forms or levels of political decision-making, particularly where localism may undermine equity.[31]

Nevertheless, a case can be made to see local authorities as campaigning bodies, empowering groups and individuals to make decisions or to act, and providing a framework within which locally-based groups can operate.[32] Something of this can be seen in the Labour government's approach to the role of local government.[33]

(b) Transfer of functions away from local government

There are many illustrations of functions which have been transferred away from elected local authorities. They include responsibility for hospitals and public utilities,[34] public transport, higher education institutions and further education colleges. Particular powers have been reallocated (and new powers allocated) at

4.17

---

[27] ibid 11–14, citing G Jones and J Stewart, *The Case for Local Government* (2nd edn, London: Allen & Unwin, 1985).

[28] ibid 12–13, citing K Young, 'The Justification of Local Government' in M Goldsmith (ed), *Essays on the Future of Local Government* (West Yorkshire Metropolitan County Council, 1986).

[29] From over 40% for most classes of local authority in England through the 1980s and most of the 1990s to 29% (unitaries), 32% (non-metropolitan districts) and 26% (metropolitan districts) in 2000 (elections by thirds): Wilson and Game (n 2 above) 222; and this at a time when the proportion of uncontested elections has been falling (ibid 223–224).

[30] See Stoker (n 24 above) 15: 'local government *is* government and, as such, might have as damaging an effect on individual liberty as could central government'.

[31] A Cochrane, 'From Theories to Practices; Looking for Local Democracy in Britain' in King and Stoker (n 24 above) 194.

[32] See generally Cochrane, ibid.

[33] See further paras 4.21–4.23.

[34] The loss of these responsibilities forms part of WA Robson's view of 'local government in crisis' in *The Development of Local Government* (3rd edn, London: George Allen & Unwin, 1954).

different times to such bodies as new town and urban development corporations, housing action trusts, police authorities, training and enterprise councils and the governing bodies of grant-maintained schools.

(c) The move from service provider to enabler

4.18 One key aspect of Conservative government policy for local government was the reduction of the role of local authorities as the direct provider of services. Illustrations included the Compulsory Competitive Tendering regime established by the Local Government, Planning and Land Act 1980 and the Local Government Act 1988, which required a range of services[35] to be opened to competitive tendering from the private sector. Others were the possibility for council tenants to opt for the local authority to be replaced as landlord, and for the parents of children in state schools to vote for their school to become grant-maintained by the Department for Education. There has been little evidence of any significant wish by the Labour government to restore responsibilities for direct service provision, although some of the mechanisms have changed.[36]

(d) New public management

4.19 Local authorities, as are other public bodies, have increasingly been required by central government explicitly to adopt approaches originally designed for use in the private sector, generally grouped under the label of 'new public management'. Aspects include increased reliance on market forces; greater emphasis on the public as customer and on customer choice; the development of techniques for the measurement of performance, with an emphasis on economy (using fewer resources), efficiency (using no more resources than necessary to meet objectives) and effectiveness (the extent to which objectives are actually achieved); developed arrangements for audit extending well beyond matters of financial probity to include organizational efficiency and effectiveness; and the construction of league tables and the concomitant 'naming and shaming' of those that underperform.[37] Operationally, it is becoming increasingly difficult to distinguish local authorities from other kinds of public sector body.

(e) New constitutional arrangements

4.20 The Local Government Act 2000 required most councils (other than parish and

---

[35] Including construction and maintenance work, refuse collection, cleaning, catering for school and welfare purposes, vehicle maintenance and management, housing management and a range of services (legal, construction and property, financial, IT and personnel).

[36] eg, the replacement of Compulsory Competitive Tendering by a Best Value regime under the Local Government Act 1999.

[37] See generally, J Greenwood, R Pyper and D Wilson, *New Public Administration in Britain* (3rd edn, London: Routledge, 2002) ch 1.

community councils) to adopt radically new arrangements for the conduct of their business. The new 'executive arrangements' require each council to establish a small executive (possibly with an elected mayor) to be responsible for many (although not all) decisions, complemented by arrangements for 'overview and scrutiny' by those councillors who are not members of the executive. These are examined in more detail below.[38]

(f) A new role: community leadership

The Labour government's programme for the reform and modernization of local government in England sees councils, in partnership with central government, business, the voluntary sectors and others as having a 'vital role to play in improving the quality of people's lives'; they 'need to provide vision and leadership for their local communities, and to deliver high quality services to their local people'.[39] This has been taken forward with new legal powers to promote community well-being, a duty to prepare a community strategy for promoting or improving the economic, social and environment well-being of its area, and the development of local strategic partnerships.[40] Effective local democracy is seen as essential to both strong community leadership and improved service delivery. Democratically elected councils provide the means for expressing and resolving conflicts within communities as to their view and priorities, and are responsible for:

> ensuring that differing points of view are heard and understood, for promoting understanding, and for making tough choices.

They are accountable to the local electorate for these choices.[41] The government's stated policy is to create the conditions that enable councils to make a success of this leadership role, bolstering democratic legitimacy by the modernization of electoral arrangements; promoting new constitutional arrangements to ensure sound governance; the encouragement of effective partnerships; the promotion of effective community engagement and empowerment through the building of community capacity, improved involvement of citizens in decision-making and civic education; the provision of new legal powers; continuous improvement in the delivery of services; and the removal of central controls.[42]

The articulation of the new general purpose for local government of providing community leadership, alongside the delivery of public services, is significant. It is a role that can only properly be performed by democratically elected institutions. It certainly has the potential of improving the democratic accountability of

4.21

4.22

4.23

---

[38] See paras 4.66–4.74.
[39] White Paper, *Local Leadership, Local Choice* (Cm 4298, 1999) para 1.2.
[40] See paras 4.52–4.58.
[41] White Paper, *Strong Local Leadership—Quality Public Services* (Cm 5327, 2001) paras 2.2–2.4.
[42] ibid ch 2.

the whole network of contributors to local governance. It remains to be seen how effectively this new role can be discharged, and how helpful the new legal structures will prove to be.

B. Local Authorities in English Law

(1) The Constitutional Context of Local Government

(a) Status of local authorities in English law

4.24 The starting point is that local authorities today owe their existence and powers entirely to statute. One consequence of the absence of a written constitution is that there is no mechanism whereby, as a matter of law, the existence of a tier of elected local government can be entrenched against removal by the ordinary process of the enactment of primary legislation. There are many examples of local councils that have been legislated out of existence.[43] It is, however, submitted that the democratic character of local government, that makes it unique among other institutions for local governance, provides a basis for an argument that it does enjoy a constitutional position that makes it necessary, if its powers are to be curtailed, for this to be done expressly and not by implication.[44]

4.25 Notwithstanding the fact that the status of local government is not legally entrenched, the current political consensus is strongly supportive of its contribution.

(b) Relationship between local authorities and central government

4.26 Central government's ability to secure the passage of primary legislation naturally gives it the upper hand in its dealings with local government. The relationship between the two levels of government is expressed both in law and in the practice of the conduct of business between central and local institutions. There are many mechanisms that can be enshrined in statute through which the responsible central government departments can assert varying measures of control or influence. These include the making of regulations governing particular activities; control through inspection; detailed conditions attached to specific grants; powers to act in default; controls over the appointment and dismissal of officers; the need for bye-laws to be confirmed by a minister; specific powers to give directions or guidance

---

[43] eg, urban and rural district councils, metropolitan county councils, the Greater London Council and the Inner London Education Authority.

[44] Developing the position expressed by Laws LJ in *Thoburn v Sunderland City Council* [2002] EWHC 195; [2003] QB 151 under which 'constitutional statutes' are immune from implied repeal. One of Laws LJ's criteria for the identification of such a statute was that it 'conditions the legal relationship between citizen and state in some general overarching manner'; his Lordship's examples included the devolution legislation, but the existence of elected local government cannot sensibly be distinguished.

and to hear and determine appeals; requirements of consent to particular acts; and statutory audit requirements.[45] More significant in practice than any of these has been the progressive strengthening of central controls over both capital and recurrent expenditure.[46]

The working relationship between central and local government cannot be understood simply from an examination of the legislative framework, and has seen significant changes over time.[47] In practice, in the 19th and for most of the 20th centuries, the central departments were in no position to assume 'a strategic directive responsibility over local government',[48] lacking both staff and other resources and significant legal powers to give directions. Their default powers covered only a small part of the range of statutory functions and were very infrequently exercised. However, their supervisory powers led to close involvement with the activities of local government, without the local authorities becoming mere agents: **4.27**

> The central authority . . . saw itself as a checking agency to ensure that the interests of individuals and sectional groups were properly considered and that local majorities did not abuse their powers.[49]

The relationship was one of interdependence, buttressed by the 'shared assumptions and values of local and national politicians' and professional networks of local authority officers and civil servants.[50] This position survived the structural reforms of the 1960s and 1970s but not the advent of the Conservative government in 1979.

The Conservative government took steps to respond to the facts that both the proportion of national expenditure undertaken by local authorities and the proportion of that expenditure met by central government had increased over the century. This led to the introduction of a series of measures, of increasing complexity, designed to control both revenue and capital expenditure. These, and government's determination to change the role of local government away from that of service provider, aroused significant opposition (and non-compliance) from local authorities, especially but not only those controlled by the Labour party. The territory was increasingly 'juridified' with both the creation of a vast complex of statutory constraints and duties, much poorly drafted, and the development of a significant body of case law in which the courts, with some reluctance, took on the role of umpire.[51] **4.28**

---

[45] See generally *Cross on Local Government Law* (n 1 above) ch 9.
[46] See further paras 4.80–4.84.
[47] A fascinating account is provided by Loughlin (n 1 above).
[48] ibid 41.
[49] ibid 52.
[50] ibid 69, 70–71.
[51] ibid chs 3, 5–7.

4.29 The position from the mid-1990s has seen the rebuilding of relations, with the improvement in the country's economy, general acceptance through local government of its changed role, the dismantling of some of the legal controls by the Labour government,[52] and the establishment of new consultative machinery at the national level.[53] The government, indeed, has indicated its intention to transform the relationship between local and central government in England, moving:

> to a partnership based on clear standards, common priorities, greater freedoms for councils to deliver, and effective action where they do not.[54]

Service priorities for local government in England have been agreed through the Central/Local Partnership framework.[55] Proposed reforms of local government finance are also designed to change the balance of control.[56]

(c) The European Charter of Local Self-Government

4.30 A statement of the principles according to which local government should be established is found in the European Charter of Local Self-Government, originally promulgated by the Council of Europe in 1985.[57] The Conservative government refused to sign the Charter, maintaining that local government was a matter for national rather than international decision. The Labour government, however, signed it on 3 June 1997, and ratified it with effect from 1 August 1998, on the basis that the United Kingdom accepted (and complied with) all the principles set out therein.[58] In the

---

[52] The Local Government Act 1999 introduced more flexible arrangements for the 'capping' of the setting of council tax where budgets are in the view of the Secretary of State excessive. The government celebrated the end of 'crude and universal' capping but the powers remain extensive: see Leigh (n 1 above) 112–113. Steps have been taken from time to time to remove detailed controls over specific acts: see eg, Local Government Act 1974, s 35 and Local Government Planning and Land Act 1980, s 1. The 1974 Act, s 35(3) gives the Secretary of State a general power to remove or relax controls. The government has announced plans to halve the number of plans it requires councils to develop and to deregulate 84 consent regime powers: ODPM News Releases 034, 11 July 2002, and 065, 3 September 2002.

[53] A Central/Local Partnership Meeting programme has been established for ministers and the Local Government Association.

[54] White Paper, *Strong Local Leadership—Quality Public Services* (Cm 5327, 2001) para 7.2.

[55] These are: raising standards across our schools; improving the quality of life of children, young people and families at risk and of older people; promoting healthier communities and narrowing health inequalities; creating stronger and safer communities; transforming our local environment; meeting local transport needs more effectively; and promoting the economic vitality of localities. There are associated performance targets agreed by ministers as part of the Spending Review process: ODPM News Release 049, 29 July 2002.

[56] Cm 5327, 2001, Pt II.

[57] European Treaty Series No 122 (1985).

[58] DETR Press Notice 155/ENV, 2 March 1998. The UK stated that it intended to confine the scope of the Charter to county, district and London borough councils and the Council of the Isles of Scilly in England, county and county borough councils in Wales, and the equivalent in Scotland. It also declared its understanding that the term 'local authority' in the Charter 'does not include local or regional bodies such as police authorities which, by reason of the specialist functions for which they are responsible, are composed of both elected and appointed members'.

Preamble, the signatory states note that local authorities are one of the main foundations of any democratic regime; that the right of citizens to participate in the conduct of public affairs is one of the democratic principles shared by all member states; that it is at the local level that this right can be most directly exercised; that the safeguarding and reinforcement of local self-government in the different European countries is an important contribution to the construction of a Europe based on the principles of democracy and the decentralization of power. They assert that:

> this entails the existence of local authorities endowed with democratically constituted decision-making bodies and possessing a wide degree of autonomy with regard to their responsibilities, the ways and means by which those responsibilities are exercised and the resources required for their fulfilment.

The detailed principles are set out in ten articles. A key provision is that the: **4.31**

> principle of local self-government shall be recognised in domestic legislation, and where practicable in the constitution.[59]

Local self-government:

> denotes the right and the ability of local authorities, within the limits of the law, to regulate and manage a substantial share of public affairs under their own responsibility and in the interests of the local population.[60]

Members are to be freely elected by secret ballot on the basis of direct, equal, uni **4.32**
versal suffrage.[61] Basic powers and responsibilities are to be prescribed by the constitution or by the state, although this is not to prevent 'the attribution to local authorities of powers and responsibilities for specific purposes in accordance with the law'. Local authorities are, within the law, to have full discretion to exercise their initiative with regard to any matters which are not excluded from their competence nor assigned to any other authority. Public responsibilities are 'generally to be exercised, in preference, by those authorities which are closest to the citizen'. Powers given to local authorities are normally to be full and exclusive, and may not be 'undermined or limited by another, central or regional, authority except as provided for by the law'.[62] Changes in local authority boundaries are not to be made without prior consultation of the local communities concerned.[63] Any administrative supervision of local authorities may only be exercised according to such procedures and in such cases as are provided for by the constitution or by statute; shall normally aim only at ensuring compliance with the law and constitutional principles but may be exercised 'with regard to expediency by higher-level authorities' in respect of tasks the execution of which is delegated to local authorities; and

---

[59] Art 2.
[60] Art 3(1).
[61] Art 3(2).
[62] Art 4.
[63] Art 5.

shall be exercised in such a way as to ensure that the intervention of the controlling authority is kept in proportion to the importance of the interests which it is intended to protect.[64]

4.33 As to finance, local authorities are to be:

> entitled, within national economic policy, to adequate financial resources of their own, of which they may dispose freely within the framework of their powers.

The resources must be commensurate with responsibilities and part at least must derive from local taxes and charges of which 'within the limits of statute, they have the power to determine the rate'. As far as possible, grants are not to be earmarked for specific projects and local authorities shall have access to national capital markets within the limits of the law.[65] Local authorities are to have the right to associate and the right of recourse to a judicial remedy in order to secure free exercise of their powers and respect for such principles of local self-government as are enshrined in the constitution or domestic legislation.[66]

4.34 These principles, freely accepted by the government in signing and ratifying the charter, provide a framework for the evaluation of arrangements in England and Wales. It is argued that current arrangements fall short in a number of respects, in particular those relating to administrative supervision.[67] Thus there is no express recognition of the principle of local self-government in that there is no succinct legislative statement of the principles of local democracy. Until the enactment of the general well-being powers in s 2 of the Local Government Act 2000, there was nothing approaching a power of general competence. Some at least of the powers conferred on non-elected local bodies might more suitably be allocated to local authorities. Consultation on boundary changes might need to be more proactive. Some reduction in detailed central controls (as proposed by the government in its White Paper, *Strong Local Leadership—Quality Public Services*) would be necessary for compliance; it was not clear that the proposed structure for performance measurement and assessment would be compliant, in the light of the express requirement of proportionality. The proposed changes in local government finance proposed in Pt II of the 2001 White Paper would make compliance with Article 8 more secure. Given the opacity of the drafting of the Charter's provisions, some of these points are not, however, clear-cut. In any event, even demonstrated non-compliance would be a matter of political rather than legal significance. There is, however, no reason why the principles set out in the Charter should not be cited as part of the context in which local government legislation is to be interpreted by

---

[64] Art 8.
[65] Art 9.
[66] Arts 10, 11.
[67] J Smith, 'The European Charter of Local Self-Government: Does the UK Government Comply?' [2002] J of Local Government L 90.

the courts, given the general presumption that Parliament does not intend to legislate in breach of its international obligations.[68]

A report to the Congress of Local and Regional Authorities of Europe on local and regional democracy in the United Kingdom[69] welcomed the United Kingdom's devolution measures and the enhancement of local government's role in community leadership but expressed concerns at the 'serious setbacks in the financial field' with over 80 per cent dependence on national funding (which was incompatible with Article 9) and the 'capping' of local taxes (incompatible with Article 8) and at the (possibly) excessive role of the Audit Commission in supervision. The Charter principles should be incorporated into domestic law and considered as binding, and the principle of local self-government should be given formal legal and quasi-constitutional recognition.   **4.35**

(d) EU law and local authorities

EU law has had a significant impact on the activities of local authorities. A number of areas of substantive law falling within the responsibilities of local authorities have been reformed in consequence of EC legislation implemented by directives. These include environmental law,[70] requirements for environmental impact assessments for specified classes of development,[71] waste management,[72] and food safety.[73] Local authorities, as other public bodies, are subject to the European public procurement regime.[74] Unimplemented, but directly effective directives can be relied upon against a local authority as an 'emanation of the state'.[75] Conversely, an unimplemented directive cannot be enforced by a local authority against a private individual.[76]   **4.36**

---

[68] *Garland v British Rail Engineering Ltd* [1983] 2 AC 751, 771, *per* Lord Diplock.

[69] Recommendation 49 (1998) on the situation of local and regional democracy in the UK. Adopted by the Congress of 28 May 1998. See www.coe.fr/cplre/textad/rec/1998/rec49(98)e.htm.

[70] eg, Urban Waste Water Treatment (England and Wales) Regulations 1994, SI 1994/2841, as amended, implementing Directive (EEC) 91/271 [1991] OJ L135/312; Pollution Prevention and Control (England and Wales) Regulations 2000, SI 2000/1973), implementing Council Directive (EC) 96/61 on Integrated Pollution Prevention and Control [1996] OJ L257/26.

[71] eg, Town and County Planning (Environmental Impact Assessment) (England and Wales) Regulations 1999, SI 1999/293, as amended.

[72] Controlled Waste Regulations 1992, SI 1992/588, as amended; Waste Management Licensing Regulations 1994, SI 1994/1056, as amended; Waste Framework Directive (EEC) 75/442 [1975] OJ L194/39, as amended.

[73] Many regulations made under the Food Safety Act 1990, ss 16,17, as amended.

[74] Public Works Contracts Regulations 1991, SI 1991/2680, as amended; Public Supply Contracts Regulations 1995, SI 1995/201, as amended; Public Services Contracts Regulations 1993, SI 1993/3228, as amended; implementing Directives 93/97 [1993] OJ L199/54, 93/36 [1993] OJ L199/1, 92/50 [1992] OJ L209/1, as amended.

[75] Case 152/84 *Marshall v Southampton and South West Hampshire Area Health Authority* [1986] QB 401 (provision of Equal Treatment Directive (EEC) 76/207 [1996] OJ L39/40 directly effective against health authority in its capacity as employer); *R v London Boroughs Transport Committee, ex p Freight Transport Association Ltd* [1990] 1 CMLR 229 (Committee held to be an 'emanation of the state').

[76] *Wychavon DC v Secretary of State for the Environment* [1994] Environmental LR 239.

(e) The European Convention on Human Rights

4.37   The European Convention on Human Rights (ECHR), and now the Human Rights Act 1998, have had an increasing impact on local authorities, although the effect on substantive law has not been as great as that of EU law. A local authority is clearly a 'public authority' for the purpose of the 1998 Act. The impact to date has perhaps been greatest in the area of child care, where Articles 6 and 8 ECHR have been held to be applicable to local authority decision-making.[77] A large number of challenges to local authorities on Convention grounds have been unsuccessful.[78]

(2) Powers and Duties of Local Authorities

(a) Corporate status

4.38   Local authorities are constituted as corporate bodies, and so are legal persons distinct from their members. Some (boroughs outside London) were established by charter under the royal prerogative; all today are statutory corporations. It was argued that a body established by royal charter (broadly speaking) had all the powers of a natural person; a body established by statute has only those powers conferred expressly or impliedly by statute. The latter principle has in the past operated as a significant constraint on local authority activity although much of its limiting effect has been removed, in particular by Pt I of the Local Government Act 2000.

4.39   The possibility that the old boroughs established by charter had broader powers than those local authorities that were established by statute was certainly mooted.[79] Such a proposition would have been of limited practical effect given a separate rule[80] that payments from the borough fund had to be for specified purposes (including payments made with statutory authority), but the repeal of that provision by the Local Government Act 1933 opened up the possibility that this possibility had become of some practical value to chartered boroughs.[81] However,

---

[77] *W v UK* Series A No 121 (1987) 10 EHRR 29, 74, 87 (right to respect for family life in Art 8 requires parental participation in procedures by which public authorities take decisions concerning children in care); *R v UK* Series A No 121 (1987) 10 EHRR 28, 29, 74, 87 (breach of Art 6 because parents were unable, while their children were in care, to have questions of their access to their children determined by an impartial tribunal); *TP and KM v UK* [2001] 2 FLR 549 (breach of Art 8 through failure adequately to involve parent in decision-making process concerning child in care).

[78] The political restrictions placed on local government officers under the Local Government and Housing Act 1989 (para 4.65) have been held not to infringe Arts 10 or 11 ECHR or Art 3 of Protocol 1: *Ahmed v UK* Application 22954/93 (2000) 29 EHRR 1; challenges to planning decisions on the ground that civil rights and obligations have not been determined by an 'independent and impartial tribunal' have generally failed: paras 12.29–12.34 below.

[79] *A-G v Manchester Corp* [1906] 1 Ch 643, 651, *per* Farwell J, obiter.

[80] Municipal Corporations Act 1882, s 140.

[81] This was accepted, obiter, by Bennett J in *A-G v Leicester Corp* [1943] 1 Ch 86.

the point was never settled.[82] In any event, statutory authority would have been necessary for the exercise of powers that interfered with the legal rights of others.

The London Government Act 1963[83] provided that the London boroughs could **4.40** be incorporated either by charter granted by the Crown or by an order of the minister. It was held in *Hazell v Hammersmith and Fulham LBC*[84] that the borough, which had been granted a royal charter under the Act, was to be regarded as a statutory corporation.[85] It would have been possible for the Crown to establish it solely under the royal prerogative apart from the Act, in which case it would have had the powers of a natural person, but this had not been done. It could not have been intended that London boroughs constituted through the two routes were to have different powers. Furthermore, it was the council and not the corporation that was the 'local authority' for the purposes of the Local Government Act 1972:

> . . . the council cannot ignore their statutory constraints and lawfully exercise in the name of the borough a power which on the true construction of the statutory powers was not open to the council.[86]

All the local authorities established by the Local Government Act 1972[87] are statutory corporations.

(b) The ultra vires doctrine

As bodies set up by statute, local authorities are subject to the ultra vires doctrine. **4.41** The basic principle is that they may only exercise such powers as are conferred expressly by or derived by reasonable implication from statute.[88] Two kinds of issue can arise: first, whether a council has positive authority to undertake a particular activity; secondly, the extent to which, in pursuing an authorized activity, the council is constrained by limitations that require it to act with procedural fairness and not to fetter or abuse its discretion. The principles of judicial review that govern the latter kind of issue are dealt with at length elsewhere in this work.[89] The former has received particular attention in local government law.

The general tendency has (until recently) been for Parliament to confer powers on **4.42** local authorities that are specific rather than general. There has been no power of general competence enabling an authority, for example, to take any action it considers to

---

[82] See generally Jennings (n 1 above) 143–149.
[83] s 1(2), (3).
[84] [1992] 2 AC 1.
[85] ibid 39–43 *per* Lord Templeman.
[86] ibid 43 *per* Lord Templeman.
[87] s 2(3) (county and district councils in England); s 14(2) (parish councils in England); s 21(2), substituted by Local Government (Wales) Act 1994, s 2 (county and county borough councils in Wales); s 33(1), substituted by 1994 Act, s 13 (community councils in Wales).
[88] *Baroness Wenlock v River Dee Co* (1885) 10 App Cas 354, 362 *per* Lord Watson.
[89] See chs 14–16 below.

be in the interests of its area or its inhabitants. Furthermore, local government has been unique in that the possible consequences of a council's acting ultra vires have included, in addition to legal challenge in the courts, that individual councillors who had authorized ultra vires action could be required to reimburse any ensuing losses to the authority from their own pockets and disqualified from membership.[90] It is not surprising that there have been recurrent arguments that the ultra vires doctrine (certainly as interpreted and applied by the courts) has had an unduly constraining effect upon local authorities.[91]

4.43 It should, however, be noted that there are a number of relevant factors that tend to have a liberating rather than a restrictive effect. First, there is the recognition that powers can be conferred by 'reasonable implication',[92] although any powers that are coercive in the sense of interfering with the legal rights of others will have to be conferred either expressly or by necessary (not merely reasonable) implication.[93] Secondly, the common law recognized that the doctrines of ultra vires:

> ought to be reasonably, and not unreasonably, understood and applied, and that whatever may fairly be regarded as incidental to, or consequential upon, those things which the legislature has authorised ought not (unless expressly prohibited) to be held by judicial construction to be *ultra vires*.[94]

This doctrine was put into statutory form in s 111 of the Local Government Act 1972. Thirdly, a number of general powers have been enacted, the most significant step being taken with the conferral by Pt I of the Local Government Act 2000 of a general power to act for the community well-being.

(c) Case law

4.44 A number of the leading cases concern the broad theme of the extent to which local authorities could engage in 'municipal trading'. Such activities might earn profit for benefit of the local community, but might well also be seen as unfair (probably subsidized) competition by local businesses. Accordingly, the establishment of a laundry service was held not to be authorized by a power to establish a

---

[90] These possibilities have been removed by Local Government Act 2000, s 90.

[91] See C Crawford et al, *Law relating to local government: Research report* (DETR, 2000), which found that the ultra vires doctrine (notwithstanding the modifications discussed in the following paragraphs) 'is now generally seen as inhibiting innovation', given the increasingly narrow approach of the courts and its complexity and uncertainty (pp 2–3).

[92] See n 88 above.

[93] cf Lord Hoffmann in *R v Secretary of State for the Home Department, ex p Simms* [2000] 2 AC 115, 131: 'In the absence of express language or necessary implication to the contrary, the courts . . . presume that even the most general words were intended to be subject to the basic rights of the individual'. Whether this approach in the case of local authorities has survived the enactment of s 111 of the Local Government Act 1972 is considered below.

[94] *per* Lord Selborne LC in *A-G v Great Eastern Rly Co* (1880) 5 App Cas 473, 478.

wash-house (where people come to wash their own clothes);[95] and a power for a council to use its tramways 'for the purpose of conveying animals goods minerals and parcels' was held not to authorize the establishment of a general parcels delivery service within and beyond the area covered by the tramway system, not confined to goods and parcels carried on the tramways.[96] Conversely, a council could set up a printing, bookbinding and stationery works for the purpose of executing work for it as this was incidental to or consequential upon the carrying out of its functions.[97] Over the years there have been many matters for which express permission has had to be made by statute following negative decisions by the courts.[98]

(d) Incidental powers

Section 111 of the Local Government Act 1972 provides: **4.45**

(1) Without prejudice to any powers exercisable apart from this section but subject to the provisions of this Act and any other enactment passed before or after this Act, a local authority shall have power to do any thing (whether or not involving the expenditure, borrowing or lending of money or the acquisition or disposal of any property or rights) which is calculated to facilitate, or is conducive or incidental to, the discharge of any of their functions . . .

(3) A local authority shall not by virtue of this section raise money, whether by means of rates, precepts or borrowing, or lend money except in accordance with the enactments relating to those matters respectively . . .

According to DOE Circular 121/72,[99] this proposition had long represented the law and had been included 'for the avoidance of any doubt which might hamper local initiative'. Its parameters were, however, tested in a series of cases in the 1980s and 1990s as local authorities sought to find ways (some of them imaginative) to avoid restrictions on local activity and expenditure imposed by central government.

One clear feature is that the s 111 powers must be ancillary to a 'function' of a local **4.46** authority conferred by some other provision. In this context, 'function':

refers to the multiplicity of specific statutory activities the council is expressly or impliedly under a duty to perform or has power to perform.[100]

---

[95] *A-G v Fulham Corp* [1921] 1 Ch 440.
[96] *A-G v Manchester Corp* [1906] 1 Ch 643.
[97] *A-G v Smethwick Corp* [1932] 1 Ch 562. See also *A-G v Crayford UDC* [1962] Ch 575.
[98] See HM Fox, 'Judicial Control of the Spending Powers of Local Authorities' (1956) 72 LQR 237, 241–246, noting examples concerning the payment of the travelling and subsistence expenses of councillors, the payment of gratuities, pensions and bonuses to staff, meeting the costs of celebrating events of local and national importance such as the Coronation, and contributing to charities.
[99] para 16.
[100] *per* Woolf LJ in *Hazell v Hammersmith and Fulham LBC* [1990] 2 QB 697, 722–723, approved by the Court of Appeal and the House of Lords: [1990] 2 QB 697, 785; [1992] 2 AC 1, 29.

The function must of course itself be intra vires. It is not necessary to link the claimed ancillary power to another expressly conferred power, but sufficient that it can be linked to a function.[101] However, the authorities diverge on the question whether the 'function' can be conferred impliedly. It is submitted that the better view is that they can; the principle that statutory powers can be conferred both expressly and impliedly is well established, and it would be strange if local authorities were the only statutory bodies to which this did not apply. There is, moreover, no suggestion that the enactment of s 111(1) was intended to narrow the powers of local authorities.[102] This position has been supported in a number of cases.[103]

4.47   However, the decision in *R v Richmond upon Thames LBC, ex p McCarthy and Stone (Developments) Ltd*[104] can be regarded as an authority the other way. Here it was held that the giving of pre-planning application advice facilitated and was conducive and incidental to the function of determining planning applications and was not itself a 'function' of the council. Accordingly, a power to charge for such advice could not be justified by reference to s 111(1), as that would be something 'incidental to the incidental'. It was accepted in argument that the giving of pre-application advice was justified by reference to s 111(1), and Lord Lowry regarded it as clear that this was 'not itself a function of the council'.[105] The question whether there can be such a thing as an 'implied function' was not reached and *McCarthy and Stone* is therefore not authority for the proposition that there is not. The distinction between an 'implied function' and an 'incidental power' is admittedly one of some subtlety, turning on the degree to which an activity is either self-standing or subordinate to some other function. Furthermore, it is submitted that, whatever the view on the last point, the automatic exclusion of anything 'incidental to the incidental' operates as an unnecessarily crude limitation to the ambit of s 111(1). The decision in *McCarthy and Stone* can amply be justified on the alternative ground specified by Lord Lowry, namely that s 111(1) could not be construed as conferring a general power to charge for services, even apart from the

---

[101]   *R v DPP, ex p Duckenfield* [2000] 1 WLR 55 (police authority entitled under s 111(1) to fund legal representation of officers in legal proceedings as ancillary to the authority's general function of securing the maintenance of an efficient and effective force).

[102]   See C Crawford in C Crawford and C Grace (eds), *'Conducive or Incidental To?' Local Authority Discretionary Powers in the Modern Era* (University of Birmingham, 1992) 5–6.

[103]   Woolf LJ in *Hazell v Hammersmith and Fulham LBC* [1990] 2 QB 697: Nourse LJ in *R v Eden DC, ex p Moffat*, The Times, 24 November 1988, CA; Watkins LJ in *Allsop v North Tyneside MBC* (1992) 90 LGR 462, 480–481; *R (on the application of A) v Hertfordshire CC* [2001] EWHC Admin 211; [2001] BLGR 435 (power of social services department to communicate to education department and school governors the conclusion, after inquiries under s 47 of the Children Act 1989, that a head teacher presents a risk of significant harm to children available by implication from the authority's responsibilities for the welfare and protection of children; this did not rest on s 111(1) of the 1972 Act).

[104]   [1992] 2 AC 48.

[105]   ibid 70.

general requirement that a power to charge can only be conferred by statute expressly or by necessary implication.[106]

It has also been suggested that the enactment of s 111(1) is to be taken as super- **4.48**
seding the common law,[107] although the latter was arguably wider,[108] and there is
no indication that this was Parliament's intention.[109]

The courts have tended to uphold reliance on s 111(1) in respect of matters that **4.49**
facilitate the internal working of local authorities,[110] and to reject it in cases where
Parliament has made detailed provision as to how certain statutory powers are
to be carried out and an authority is claiming additional powers outside that code
by reference to s 111(1),[111] or where the authority is seeking a power to make
charges.[112]

(e) General powers

The impact of the ultra vires doctrine has been modified by the enactment over **4.50**
time of a series of more general powers. These include general powers to make
agreements with other public bodies for the supply of goods, materials, services,

---

[106] ibid 75, citing *A-G v Wilts United Dairies Ltd* (1921) 37 TLR 884, 886 as authority for the latter proposition.
[107] *per* Slade LJ, obiter in the Court of Appeal in *McCarthy and Stone* [1980] 2 All ER 852, 858.
[108] By extending to 'consequential' matters: see J Bennett and S Cirell, *Municipal Trading* (London: Longman, 1992) 61.
[109] Note the introductory words to s 111(1).
[110] *R v Greater London Council, ex p Westminster City Council (No 1)*, The Times, 27 December 1984 (decision to release one member of staff to joint committee of trade unions in interest of maintaining good staff relations lawful under s 111(1)); *R v Eden DC, ex p Moffat*, The Times, 24 November 1988 (council entitled to set up working party of councillors and officers to consider council's structure and efficiency); *Islington LBC v Camp* (QBD, 29 July 1999) (secondment of officer to joint committee); *Newbold v Leicester City Council* (1999) 2 LGLR 303 (contractual scheme to buy out additional payments to street cleansing drivers for emergency work); *R (on the application of Lashley) v Broadland DC* (2001) 3 LGLR 474 (consideration of councillor's conduct by standards committee, prior to Local Government Act 2000); *Grubb v PriceWaterhouse Coopers* (2000) 3 LGLR 244 (payment to third parties to cover councillors' accommodation and subsistence at conference); *R v Westminster City Council, ex p Legg* (2000) 2 LGLR 961 (indemnity granted to members or officers in respect of their legal costs incurred in responding to objections made to auditor).
[111] *Hazell v Hammersmith and Fulham LBC* [1992] 2 AC 1 (comprehensive code concerning borrowing in Local Government Act 1992, Sch 13 inconsistent with any incidental power to conduct interest rate swap transactions); *Allsop v North Tyneside MBC* (1992) 90 LGR 462 (enhanced voluntary severance scheme inconsistent with express provision made for severance payments by regulations); *Credit Suisse v Allerdale BC* [1997] QB 302 (guarantee in respect of sums borrowed by company established by the council to carry out timeshare residential development which the council could not carry out itself because of government limits on borrowing held unlawful).
[112] *R v Richmond upon Thames LBC, ex p McCarthy and Stone (Developments) Ltd* [1992] 2 AC 48; *R v Liverpool City Council, ex p Barry* [2001] EWCA Civ 384, (2001) 3 LGLR 40 (no power to charge fees in respect of doorman registration scheme); but cf *R v Greater Manchester Police Authority, ex p Century Motors (Farnworth Ltd)*, The Times, 31 May 1996 (power to charge in respect of vehicle recovery scheme arose by necessary implication).

transport and equipment and to carry out maintenance work;[113] where the authority considers it expedient for the promotion or protection of the interest of the inhabitants of its area to prosecute or defend or appear in any legal proceedings and, in the case of civil proceedings, to institute them in its own name;[114] to spend up to a prescribed limit for any purpose which is in the interests of the area or its inhabitants;[115] and to promote economic development.[116] Also important was the Local Government (Contracts) Act 1997,[117] which provided that certain ('certified') contracts should be presumed to be legal for private law purposes, although subject to public law challenge by judicial review or audit. This was designed to facilitate Private Finance Initiative arrangements.

4.51   There have also been proposals for the enactment of a general power for a local authority to spend money for the benefit of its area or inhabitants, subject to control by the electorate and by central government in the interests of national economic or financial policy.[118] This change has not been implemented, although Pt I of the Local Government Act 2000 belatedly comes near to it.

(f) Community well-being

4.52   A new general power was introduced by Pt I of the Local Government Act 2000 to support local authorities in the discharge of their newly articulated role as community leaders. Section 2 provides that every local authority is to have power to do anything which it considers is likely to achieve any one or more of the following objects:

    (a) the promotion or improvement of the economic well-being of its area;
    (b) the promotion or improvement of the social well-being of its area;
    (c) the promotion or improvement of the environmental well-being of its area.[119]

4.53   The power may be exercised in relation to or for the benefit of:

---

[113] Local Authorities (Goods and Services) Act 1970.

[114] Local Government Act 1972, s 222. This power has been used, for example, to seek injunctions restraining unlawful Sunday trading (*Stoke-on-Trent City Council v B & Q (Retail) Ltd* [1984] AC 754); a public nuisance caused by pigeon droppings (*Wandsworth LBC v Railtrack plc* [2001] 1 WLR 308) or the activities of a drug dealer (*Nottingham City Council v Z (a child)* [2002] 1 WLR 607). The council must consider whether proceeding is in the interests of the inhabitants, but there is a rebuttable presumption that this is so: the *Stoke-on-Trent* case, above.

[115] Local Government Act 1972, s 137. This power originated in s 6 of the Local Government (Financial Provisions) Act 1963 (expenditure up to a 0.4p rate); s 137 raised the limit to 2p, replaced by a (small) prescribed sum per head of the population on the abolition of domestic rates.

[116] Local Government and Housing Act 1989, Pt III (ss 33–38).

[117] See A Arden and S Cirell, 'Safe harbours for some; others still at sea? The Local Government (Contracts) Act 1997 and indemnities for officers and members' [1998] J of Local Government L 13.

[118] Royal Commission on Local Government in England (Cmnd 4040, 1969) vol I, para 323.

[119] s 2(1).

(a) the whole or any part of the authority's area; or

(b) all or any of persons resident or present in its area.[120]

In determining whether or how to use this power, the authority must have regard   **4.54**
to its 'community strategy' prepared under s 4.[121] The power includes power to:

(a) incur expenditure (there being no spending limits);

(b) give financial assistance to any person,

(c) enter into arrangements or agreements with any person,

(d) co-operate with, or facilitate or co-ordinate the activities of, any person,

(e) exercise on behalf of any person the functions of that person,

(f) provide staff, goods, services or accommodation to any person.[122]

It also includes power to do anything in relation to, or for the benefit of, any person or area situated outside its area if it considers that it is likely to achieve any one or more of the objects in s 2(1).[123] The power is subject to the general duty of best value.[124] It will, for example, enable local authorities to form or participate in companies, trusts or charities, including joint venture companies.[125]

The general power is subject to limitations set out in s 3. Accordingly, it does not   **4.55**
enable an authority to do anything that it is unable to do by virtue of any prohibition, restriction or limitation of its powers which is contained in any enactment, including one comprised in subordinate legislation (whenever passed or made).[126] Unlike the case with s 137 of the 1972 Act, the mere existence of another power under which an activity could be undertaken is not a bar to the use of s 2(1). Another limitation is that the s 2(1) power does not enable an authority to raise money, whether by precepts, borrowing or otherwise; this is intended to exclude charging but not the incidental receipt of income.[127] The power cannot be used as authority to make a bye-law.[128]

The Secretary of State is also given a general power to amend or repeal enactments   **4.56**
that obstruct the exercise of the s 2(1) power, or requirements to produce a plan or strategy.[129] The general power under s 137 of the 1972 Act is now restricted to

---

[120] s 2(2). 'Person' includes 'a body of persons corporate or unincorporate': Interpretation Act 1978, Sch 1. Persons 'present' would include tourists, commuters and travellers: *DETR Guidance* (March 2001) para 30.

[121] s 2(3).

[122] s 2(4).

[123] s 2(5).

[124] See para 4.87.

[125] *DETR Guidance*, paras 42, 43.

[126] s 3(1), (8). This is intended to mean prohibitions, etc, spelt out explicitly in the face of the 'legislation': *DETR Guidance*, para 63.

[127] s 3(2); *DETR Guidance*, paras 66, 67, 68 (giving as examples of incidental income, a dividend from shares bought to support a struggling local enterprise, interest on a loan, an indemnity for costs incurred, and the receipt of voluntary contributions from partner organizations).

[128] *DETR Guidance*, para 72.

[129] ss 5, 6.

parish and community councils, other than a power to make charitable donations which remains for all. The economic development powers in ss 33 to 35 of the Local Government and Housing Act 1989 have been repealed.[130]

4.57   The early case law on the new power has adopted a broad approach to its interpretation. In *R (on the application of J) v Enfield LBC*[131] Elias J held that the council had power to provide financial assistance under s 2 to the claimant (a person who had overstayed the period permitted on her visa to remain in the United Kingdom and was seeking leave to remain) and her child. Section 2(4)(b) expressly covered the provision of financial assistance and such provision would be capable of promoting the social well-being of the area by benefiting two persons resident there. There were 'restrictions' preventing the provision of accommodation given the claimant's status as an overstayer,[132] but not the provision of financial assistance. In an important passage, Elias J noted that:

> [Section 2] is drafted in very broad terms which provide a source of power enabling authorities to do many things which they could not hitherto have done. In my view, a 'prohibition, restriction or limitation' is one which will almost always be found in an express legislative provision. I do not discount the possibility that such might arise by necessary implication, but I would have thought that would be very rare. (I note that the Guidance . . . assumes that any restriction, prohibition or limitation must be expressly spelt out in the legislation: see paras. 62 and 63. However, Mr Sales did not adopt that position, and I doubt whether it must always do so as a matter of construction of section 3.) Of course, where Parliament has conferred a positive power to do X, it will by implication have denied the right for that power to be exercised to do Y, but that is merely saying the Parliament has defined a clear boundary for marking out the scope of the power. In my view it would be inapt to describe the area where no power has been conferred as constituting a prohibition, restriction or limitation on the power which is contained in an enactment.

A further point was that if a refusal to exercise the s 2 power would infringe the claimant's rights under Article 8 ECHR (by separating her from her child for no good reason), then the authority would come under an obligation to exercise the power in her favour.

4.58   It remains the case, however, that there have been relatively few exercises of the s 2 power in the period immediately following its implementation. It has been suggested that councils have been preoccupied with introducing the new executive

---

[130] s 8, Sch 6.

[131] [2002] EWHC 432; [2002] 2 FLR 1. Elias J's general approach was endorsed, obiter, by the Court of Appeal in *R (on the application of W) v Lambeth LBC* [2002] EWCA Civ 613; [2002] 2 All ER 901.

[132] Housing Act 1996, ss 159–161, 185; Immigration and Asylum Act 1999, s 118. Another example is the National Assistance Act 1948, s 21(1A) which provides that a person excluded from benefits by s 115 of the Immigration and Asylum Act 1999 may not be provided with residential accommodation if the need for care and attention has arisen solely because he or she is destitute: *R (on the application of Khan) v Oxfordshire CC* [2002] EWHC 2211; (2002) 5 CCLR 611.

arrangements under Pt II of the 2000 Act and so have not had the resources to explore imaginative use of its new powers.[133] A further obvious limitation is that local authorities must still operate within the financial resources available to them.

(g) Specific powers and duties

Specific powers and duties are conferred or imposed on local authorities under a wide variety of enactments.[134] In addition, specific powers may be obtained by securing the passage of a local Act of Parliament[135] although, outside London, it has become relatively uncommon for this device to be used. In addition, local authorities have a number of powers to make bye-laws, both generally for 'good rule and government and the suppression of nuisances'[136] and to regulate a range of specific activities.[137] Bye-laws must be confirmed by a minister. A local Act is not open to challenge on any ground, including an argument that Parliament has been misled;[138] a bye-law, by contrast, is open to challenge, directly or collaterally,[139] on the grounds that it is ultra vires,[140] uncertain,[141] inconsistent with the general law[142] or unreasonable.[143]

4.59

(3) The Constitution of Local Authorities

(a) Constitution

A principal council[144] comprises the chairman and councillors or, where there is an elected mayor, the elected mayor, chairman and councillors.[145] The members

4.60

---

[133] Transport, Local Government and the Regions Committee, *How the Local Government Act 2000 is working: 14th report* (2001–02 HC 602–I) paras 9–11.

[134] See generally, *Cross on Local Government Law* (n 1 above) Pt III (Services).

[135] A power to promote or oppose a local Bill is available to all local authorities except that a parish or community council can only oppose such a Bill: Local Government Act 1972, s 239.

[136] 1972 Act, s 235 (unitary, district and London borough councils).

[137] See *Cross on Local Government Law* (n 1 above) Appendix E.

[138] *Pickin v British Rlys Board* [1974] AC 765.

[139] *Boddington v British Transport Police* [1999] 2 AC 143.

[140] *R v Wood* (1855) 5 E & B 49 (bye-law requiring occupiers to clear snow from the footpath opposite their premises held not to fall within a power to make bye-laws with respect to the removal by the occupier of dust, ashes, rubbish, filth, manure, dung and soil).

[141] *Percy v Hall* [1997] QB 924 (see discussion in *Cross on Local Government Law* (n 1 above) para 6–08).

[142] *Powell v May* [1946] KB 330.

[143] *Kruse v Johnson* [1898] 2 QB 91 (upholding validity of bye-laws prohibiting any person from playing music or singing within 50 yards of any dwelling-house after being requested to desist; Lord Russell of Killowen CJ noted that bye-laws made by elected bodies should be supported if possible and only struck down as unreasonable if they were 'partial and unequal in their operation as between classes' or 'manifestly unjust'; if they 'disclosed bad faith' or if they 'involved such oppressive or gratuitous interference with the rights of those subject to them as could find no justification in the minds of reasonable men').

[144] ie, a council elected for a non-metropolitan county, a district or a London borough in England, or a county or county borough in Wales: 1972 Act, s 270(1).

[145] 1972 Act, ss 2, 8, 21, Sch 2, as amended.

and (if there is one) elected mayor are elected at local elections.[146] The chairman is elected by the members. The council must also appoint a vice-chairman.[147] Elections for county councils in England and county and county borough councils in Wales take place every four years. Elections for metropolitan district councils take place every year (except every fourth year) and the members retire by thirds. Non-metropolitan district councils may request the Secretary of State to provide for simultaneous elections or elections by thirds.[148] However, Pt IV of the Local Government Act 2000 enables elections to be held more often to promote accountability. Three options are available for the scheme for the ordinary elections of councillors of a principal council: (1) simultaneous elections of all councillors every four years; (2) elections every two years with half of the councillors retiring in each election year; (3) elections in three years in every four, with councillors retiring by thirds. The scheme for any specified council or description of councils is to be made by order by the Secretary of State.[149] The government has indicated a preference in England for elections by thirds as the standard pattern for all unitary councils and a pattern in two-tier areas in which the county and district councils would elect by halves in alternate years.[150] Similar arrangements apply in respect of parish and community councils[151] and the Greater London Authority.[152] Joint authorities established in the metropolitan areas in England, to discharge functions in respect of (1) fire and civil defence, (2) passenger transport; and (originally) (3) police, are not directly elected but comprise elected members of the specified constituent councils appointed by each council to membership of the joint authority.[153]

(b) The committee system

4.61 The traditional way in which local authorities have conducted their business has been through a hierarchy of committees and sub-committees of councillors, commonly mapping on to a series of service departments headed and run by professional officers. Each council would have arrangements whereby decision-making responsibilities would be delegated to specified committees and sub-committees;

---

[146] See generally *Cross on Local Government Law* (n 1 above) ch 11.

[147] 1972 Act, ss 3–5, 22–24.

[148] ibid s 7, as amended.

[149] Local Government Act 2000, ss 84–86.

[150] White Paper, *Modern Local Government: In Touch with the People* (Cm 4014, 1998) paras 4.9–4.13.

[151] The council consists of the chairman and members and is a corporate body; the members are elected: Local Government Act 1972, ss 14–16, 33–35. Provision is made for parish and community meetings of local government electors in parishes and communities where there is no council: ibid ss 9(1), 13, 27(1), 32. In England, the chairman of the parish meeting and the proper officer of the district council are a corporate body, as 'parish trustees'.

[152] A corporate body comprising the Mayor of London and the London Assembly; the Mayor and the Assembly members are all elected: Greater London Authority Act 1999, ss 1, 2.

[153] Local Government Act 1985, Pt IV and Schs 10–12.

this could be a full delegation of the power to decide, which once exercised would be binding on the council,[154] or the reference of a matter for consideration and a report back to the council (or committee) as the case might be. There were also statutory requirements for each council to have committees to discharge specified functions.[155] With certain exceptions, all decisions had to be made by councillors, acting on the advice of professional officers. A series of measures, beginning with the Local Government Act 1972, has moved local authority decision-making away from this model. First, the 1972 Act introduced a new general power for a council to arrange for its functions to be discharged by an officer.[156] The intention was for councillors to concentrate more on policy issues and less on detail.[157] Increasing use was also in practice made of a central policy committee that cut across departmental boundaries and it was increasingly common for the most senior professional officer to be a chief executive (who might come from a range of professional backgrounds, including legal) rather than the (legally-qualified) 'Town Clerk' (or the equivalent). The interests of minority parties were subsequently strengthened by the introduction of a general requirement that committees and sub-committees be politically balanced, reflecting the proportions of political groups within the overall membership of the council.[158]

The Labour government in 1999 expressed the view that the committee system **4.62** did not work. It was inefficient and opaque, and weakened accountability. In reality, major decisions were often taken outside formal local authority meetings at meetings of the ruling majority group or in consultation across political groups where there was a 'hung' council. There was a lack of clarity as to who took decisions and councillors complained that they spent too much time on committee work.[159] Accordingly, the government introduced legislation (Pt II of the Local Government Act 2000) that required principal councils, after consultation and in some circumstances a referendum, to choose one of three prescribed models for 'executive arrangements'. The purpose was to confine the decision-making role in respect of many, but not all, functions to a small executive, with the councillors not appointed to the executive undertaking an 'overview and scrutiny' role.

---

[154] *Battelley v Finsbury BC* (1958) 56 LGR 165.

[155] Before 1 April 1974 this list included (1) education, police, sea fisheries, social services and superannuation; and (2) health, finance, allotments, diseases of animals, public health and housing and youth employment. The requirements in group (2) were removed by the 1972 Act; those in group (1) (1992 Act, s 101(9)) have since been reduced, leaving only the references to sea fisheries and social services.

[156] 1972 Act, s 101(1), (2). A committee may arrange for its functions to be discharged by an officer (unless the council directs otherwise); a sub-committee may do so (unless the council or parent committee directs otherwise).

[157] Bains Report, *The New Local Authorities: Management and Structure* (HMSO, 1972).

[158] Local Government and Housing Act 1989, ss 15, 16, 17, Sch 1; Local Government (Committees and Political Groups) Regulations 1990, SI 1990/1553, as amended.

[159] White Paper, *Local Leadership, Local Choice* (Cm 4298, 1999) 8–10.

4.63 The resulting legal structure is highly complex. The basic legal provisions governing decision-making remain in place. There is, accordingly, a general power to arrange for functions to be discharged by committees, sub-committees and officers[160] and general powers for a local authority to appoint (and for two of more local authorities jointly to appoint) committees and for committees to appoint sub-committees.[161] There is, however, no general power to arrange for a function to be discharged by a single councillor.[162] Detailed provision is made for the calling and conduct of meetings[163] and for access to information by both members[164] and the public.[165]

4.64 An examination of the legal structure for decision-making established by the Local Government Act 1972 does not provide a complete picture to the extent that its operation in practice is heavily influenced by party politics. The politicization of local government has been a steady, long-term trend; by 2001–02, only 3 per cent of principal councils had 60 per cent or more of seats held by independents, and 13 per cent with 20–59 per cent. However, across England and Wales there has been considerable variation in the extent to which individual councils have been dominated by one party or there has been fragmentation among a range of parties, and how this has changed over time.[166] The consequence has been that in many cases the real forum in which decisions have effectively been made has been in meetings of councillors of the ruling party group (or coalition) rather than in formal meetings of the council or its committees. The realities were to an extent

---

[160] 1972 Act, s 101, as amended.

[161] ibid s 102, as amended.

[162] No provision for this is made in s 101 and there cannot be a committee or sub-committee comprising a single member: *R v Secretary of State for Education and Science, ex p Birmingham City Council* (1984) 83 LGR 79; *R v Secretary of State for the Environment, ex p Hillingdon LBC* [1986] 1 WLR 967. Power can, however, be delegated to an officer who is required to act in consultation with a member (such as a committee chairman), provided the former's discretion is not on the facts fettered: *R v Port Talbot BC, ex p Jones* [1988] 2 All ER 207; *Fraser v Secretary of State for the Environment* (1987) 56 P & CR 386. Compare the position under executive arrangements: para 4.71.

[163] 1972 Act, Sch 12, as amended, which includes a general power to make standing orders for the regulation of the authority's proceedings and business (para 42). The chair may exercise a second and casting vote if there is no majority on a particular point: *R v Bradford Metropolitan City Council, ex p Corris* [1990] 2 QB 363.

[164] A member has a common law right of access to such documents as are reasonably necessary to enable him or her properly to perform his or her duties: *R v Barnes BC, ex p Conlan* [1938] 3 All ER 226; *R v Lancashire CC Police Authority, ex p Hook* [1980] QB 603; *R v Hackney LBC, ex p Gamper* [1985] 1 WLR 1220 (principle extends to access to meetings). A member of a principal council also has a statutory right of access to documents concerning any business before the council, a committee or sub-committee, subject to specified categories of exempt information: 1972 Act, s 100F, inserted by the Local Government (Access to Information) Act 1985, s 1.

[165] Public Bodies (Admission to Meetings) Act 1960 (originally a private member's Bill promoted by M Thatcher MP); Local Government (Access to Information) Act 1985, inserting Pt VA (ss 100A–100K) in the 1972 Act, and replacing the provisions of the 1960 Act in respect of principal councils and other specified bodies. New rights are conferred by the Freedom of Information Act 2000.

[166] Wilson and Game (n 2 above) 276–285.

recognized by the judges in deciding that in exercising the right to vote a councillor may be influenced by, but his or her discretion may not be fettered by, party
loyalty and party policy[167] and that support for the party line does not enable a decision to be challenged on the ground that there was a real possibility of bias, provided, again, that the discretion has not been fettered.[168]

Some modifications were also made by statute, following the recommendations of **4.65**
the Widdicombe Committee of Inquiry into the Conduct of Local Authority
Business.[169] These included a requirement that committees and sub-committees
be politically balanced;[170] the prohibition of 'twin-tracking' (preventing persons
holding a politically restricted post[171] from standing for election as or otherwise
becoming or remaining a member of any local authority), and the placing of further restrictions on the political activities of persons holding such posts;[172] the introduction of restrictions on political influence over the appointment and
removal of officers;[173] and the introduction of a general rule (subject to exceptions) that only elected members on committees and sub-committees were to
have voting rights.[174]

(c) Executive arrangements

Part II of the Local Government Act 2000 has in the case of most principal coun- **4.66**
cils introduced a new structure for decision-making that is superimposed on the
existing system in relation to many, but not all, classes of business. The arrangements are prescribed in great detail in the primary legislation, in a series of regulations (one set for England and another for Wales) and very full codes of guidance

---

[167] *R v Waltham Forest LBC, ex p Baxter* [1988] QB 419; cf *R v Local Commissioner for
Administration in North and North-East England, ex p Liverpool City Council* (2000) 2 LGLR 603.
See C Crawford, 'Rule of law, lawyers or ombudsmen?' [2001] J of Local Government L 73.
[168] *R v Amber Valley DC, ex p Jackson* [1985] 1 WLR 298. See further paras 15.88–15.90.
[169] Cmnd 9797, 1986.
[170] Local Government and Housing Act 1989, ss 5–16; Local Government (Committees and
Political Groups) Regulations 1990, SI 1990/1553.
[171] ie, those specified in 1989 Act, s 2, which include the head of paid service, chief officers, deputy
chief officers, officers earning more than a specified salary, and officers who give advice directly to
the authority or its executive or committees or who exercise delegated powers. Exemptions can be
granted under s 3.
[172] 1989 Act, ss 1–3; Local Government Officers (Political Restrictions) Regulations 1990, SI
1990/851. The validity of the regulations was upheld in *NALGO v Secretary of State for the
Environment* (1993) 5 Administrative LR 785 and the restrictions held not to violate the ECHR in
Ahmed v UK (1998) 1 LGLR 94. For reform proposals, see GS Morris, 'Local government workers
and rights of political participation: time for a change' [1998] PL 25.
[173] The 1989 Act established a requirement to appoint a head of paid service and a monitoring officer, each with specified statutory responsibilities (ss 4, 5, 5A); required all staff to be appointed on
merit (ss 7, 8), with separate arrangements for the appointment of a limited number of political as-
sistants (s 9).
[174] 1989 Act, s 13; Local Government (Committees and Political Groups) Regulations 1990, SI
1990/1553, as amended.

(again different as between England[175] and Wales). Both the regulations and guidance have been the subject of regular modification as the new system has been introduced.

4.67 Each principal council, other than councils for 'small shire districts',[176] was required to introduce 'executive arrangements' by 2002. These involve the establishment of an executive conforming to one of three specified models and a series of overview and scrutiny committees. The three models currently permitted[177] are (1) a *mayor and cabinet executive*, with an elected mayor and two or more councillors of the authority appointed to the executive by the mayor; (2) a *leader and cabinet executive*, with a councillor elected as the executive leader by the authority and two or more councillors appointed to the executive by either the executive leader or the council;[178] and (3) a *mayor and council manager executive*, with an elected mayor and an officer of the authority (the 'council manager') appointed to the executive by the authority. Separate provision was not made for a leader and council manager executive but model (2) can come close to that with extensive delegation to the chief executive.[179] The executive under models (1) and (2) may not exceed ten in number. No member of the executive may be a member of an overview and scrutiny committee.[180]

4.68 The requirements of the Local Government and Housing Act 1989 as to political balance do not apply to the executive (which can accordingly be one-party) or a committee of the executive,[181] but continue to apply to overview and scrutiny committees. The intention is that the executive will have wide-ranging leadership roles, including leading the community planning process and the search for best value, leading the preparation of the authority's policies and budget, taking in-year decisions on resources and priorities and being the focus for forming partnerships with other organizations.[182]

4.69 It was for each council to determine its preferred model for executive arrangements, except that it was required to hold a referendum where it proposed a model that included an elected mayor,[183] and it could be required to hold a referendum

---

[175] ODPM (formerly DETR), *Local Government Act 2000 Guidance to English Local Authorities* (2000).

[176] ie, the council for a district in an area for which there is a county council and where the resident population on 30 June 1999 was less than 85,000.

[177] These are set out in the legislation: 2000 Act, s 11(2)–(4) may be, but have not yet been prescribed in regulations: 2000 Act, ss 11(5), 12.

[178] Which of these is to apply is to be specified by the council in drawing up the executive arrangements.

[179] *ODPM Guidance*, paras 4.76–4.79.

[180] 2000 Act, s 21(9).

[181] ibid s 24.

[182] *ODPM Guidance*, para 4.20.

[183] 2000 Act, ss 25(2), 27; Local Authorities (Conduct of Referendums) (England) Regulations 2001, SI 2001/1298, as amended.

as to whether there should be an elected mayor by a petition signed by at least 5 per cent of the local electorate, or by a direction from the Secretary of State.[184] Small shire districts could opt for executive arrangements or instead adopt 'alternative arrangements' which do not involve an executive but do include arrangements for the appointment of committees and sub-committees to review or scrutinize decisions, and that are likely to ensure that decisions are taken in an efficient, transparent and accountable way.[185] Such arrangements may also be adopted as fall-back proposals where the main proposals put to a referendum by any council are rejected.[186]

In practice a large majority of councils (317) have adopted the leader and cabinet model; eight the mayor and cabinet; one the mayor and council manager; and 59 alternative arrangements. The consultation exercises conducted by councils aroused little interest, and only eight out of 23 referenda supported an elected mayor model.[187] **4.70**

The decision-making processes to be followed under executive arrangements are prescribed in great detail. First, there are lists of functions that (1) are not to be an executive responsibility;[188] (2) may be (but need not be) an executive responsibility; and (3) are not to be the sole responsibility of an executive.[189] All other functions are to be an executive responsibility.[190] Secondly, the method by which executive functions are to be discharged depends on the model. Under model (1) they may be discharged by the elected mayor or he or she may arrange for their discharge by the executive, another executive member, a committee of the executive or an officer of the authority. Under model (2), the executive arrangements themselves allocate functions among the executive, any members or committees of the **4.71**

---

[184] ibid ss 34, 35; Local Authorities (Referendums) (Petitions and Directions) (England) Regulations 2000, SI 2000/2852, as amended; Local Authorities (Referendums) (Petitions and Directions) (Wales) Regulations 2001, SI 2001/2292. The government adopted a policy not to direct the holding of a referendum on whether to have an elected mayor where that was not the council's preference: ODPM News release 019, 25 June 2002.

[185] ibid, ss 31, 32; Local Authorities (Alternative Arrangements) (England) Regulations 2001, SI 2001/1299). These provide that specified functions (including the making of plans and strategies) cannot be delegated; limit the number of members on committees and sub-committees; and require the appointment of one or more overview and scrutiny committees. See also *ODPM Guidance*, ch 9. For Wales, see the Local Authorities (Alternative Arrangements) (Wales) Regulations 2001, SI 2001/2284, as amended.

[186] 2000 Act, s 27(2). This occurred in the case of Brighton and Hove Council.

[187] TLGR Committee Report (n 133 above) paras 48–50.

[188] Broadly speaking, functions relating to town and country planning, licensing and registration functions, functions relating to health and safety, elections, the name and status of areas and individuals, bye-laws, local Bills, pensions, rights of way and other miscellaneous functions.

[189] ie, the making of specified plans and strategies.

[190] 2000 Act, s 13; Local Authorities (Functions and Responsibilities) (England) Regulations 2000, SI 2000/2853, as amended; Local Authorities Executive Arrangements (Functions and Responsibilities) (Wales) Regulations 2001, SI 2001/2291, as amended.

executive and any officers of the authority. Under model (3), the council manager may discharge the functions or arrange for them to be discharged by the executive or an officer of the authority. Provision can be made for the discharge of executive functions by area committees or by or jointly with another authority.[191] Thirdly, while in general meetings of the executive may be held in public or in private, written records must be made of all executive decisions and meetings where 'key decisions' are to be made or other specified matters to be discussed must be held in public.[192] A 'key decision' is an executive decision which is likely to result in significant[193] expenditure or savings or to be significant in terms of its effects on communities living or working in an area comprising two or more wards or electoral decisions.[194] A rolling 'forward plan' setting out key decisions to be made over the following four months must be published. There are extensive requirements as to public access to meetings or information, and all members of the council have rights of access to documents additional to their other rights.[195]

4.72   The decisions made through the processes just outlined are subject to review by one or more overview and scrutiny committees. These have power to review or scrutinize decisions (both executive and non-executive); and to make reports or recommendations to the authority or the executive concerning the discharge of executive and non-executive functions and any other matter which affects the authority. This should involve both the development and review of policy and holding the executive to account. The political balance requirements do apply to these committees.[196]

4.73   The aim of executive arrangements is to improve transparency and accountability in decision-making by reducing the number of, but making readily identifiable, the individuals and bodies who make the decisions, and improving the arrangements for scrutiny. It is of course too early to assess their effectiveness, but the early indications are not uniformly promising. While decision-making may have become faster, there are indications that the changes have left the councillors

---

[191] 2000 Act, ss 14–20; Local Authorities (Arrangements for the Discharge of Functions) (England) Regulations 2000, SI 2000/2851, as amended; Local Authorities (Executive Arrangements) (Discharge of Functions) (Wales) Regulations 2002, SI 2002/802, as amended. The power to delegate to an individual executive member has to date been relatively little used: Audit Commission, *Developing new political arrangements: a snapshot* (District Audit, 2002) 6.

[192] Local Authorities (Executive Arrangements) (Access to Information) (England) Regulations 2000, SI 2000/3272, regs 4, 7.

[193] Having regard to the local authority's budget for the service or function in question.

[194] The council must have regard to guidance issued by the Secretary of State: see *ODPM Guidance*, paras 7.16–7.21.

[195] 2000 Act, s 22; Local Authorities (Executive Arrangements) (Access to Information) (England) Regulations 2000, SI 2000/3272, as amended; Local Authorities (Executive Arrangements) (Decisions, Documents and Meetings) (Wales) Regulations 2001, SI 2001/2290, as amended.

[196] 2000 Act, s 21; *ODPM Guidance*, ch 3; S Snape, S Leach and C Copus, *The Development of Overview and Scrutiny in Local Government* (ODPM, September 2002).

who are not executive members less well informed and less enthusiastic about their role; the definition of 'key decisions' is uncertain; many decisions continue effectively to be made in private and 'rubber stamped' or justified in public; the role of the full council has been weakened; attendance by councillors at meetings may actually have increased; and overview and scrutiny committees have had only a marginal effect, and can be subject to informal party political influence, notwithstanding the Secretary of State's recommendation that whipping should not take place.[197]

These may prove to be transitional problems, but the fact remains that there is **4.74** likely to be a close correlation between the ability of an individual councillor to influence actual outcomes and satisfaction in the performance of the role.[198] There are concerns that the more limited role for councillors outside the executive may make it more difficult to attract able new candidates into local politics; conversely, the additional demands on the time of executive members may make it more difficult for that role to be combined with full time employment. The extent of the detail set out by and under Pt II of the 2000 Act has rightly been characterized as 'the antithesis of trust and confidence in local government to act responsibly'.[199]

(d) The conduct of members

The law relating to the conduct of members has been remodelled by Pt III of the **4.75** Local Government Act 2000. Previously, the position of local authority members was unusual in that (1) they were subject to criminal law penalties if they failed to disclose direct and indirect pecuniary interest in matters under consideration at a meeting at which they were present, and to refrain from discussion and voting;[200] and (2) were subject to the sanctions of surcharge and disqualification where they authorized expenditure that was 'contrary to law', or they had failed to bring into account a sum which ought to have been included, or where there was a loss or deficiency due to wilful misconduct.[201] Non-pecuniary interests were the subject of

---

[197] TLGR Committee Report (n 133 above) paras 8, 20, 22–24, 25, 27, 28–29, 33, 37. The biggest single issue identified in a survey of 201 chief executives was backbench members feeling left out of the decision-making process: Audit Commission, *Developing new political arrangements: a snapshot* (District Audit, 2002) 4.

[198] The TLGR Committee received evidence that the arrangements were most successful where the split between executive and scrutiny was blurred and proposals fully discussed across political groups before formally being made: ibid para 31.

[199] RJB Morris, in evidence to the TLGR Committee, ibid para 14. The Committee recommended that local authorities should be given the freedom to develop constitutions that respond to local needs: para 15. Notwithstanding the detailed regulations and guidance, there has been considerable variation in how arrangements have been implemented, in the light of differences in the capacity for change and the attitude of members: Audit Commission, *Developing new political arrangements: a snapshot* (District Audit, 2002) 1.

[200] Local Government Act 1972, ss 94–98.

[201] Audit Commission Act 1998, ss 17, 18.

the National Code of Local Government Conduct, [202] breach of which could lead to a finding of maladministration by the Local Government Ombudsman.[203] These arrangements were strongly criticized by the Nolan Committee on Standards in Public Life[204] as unclear and inconsistent.

4.76 Part III of the 2000 Act introduced new arrangements built on (with some differences) the recommendations of the Nolan Committee. The principles that govern the conduct of members and co-opted members of local authorities in England are specified by an order of the Secretary of State.[205] The Secretary of State has also issued model codes of conduct setting out a series of general obligations and requirements to disclose personal interests and, where such interests are also prejudicial, (normally) to leave the room where a meeting is being held at which the matter is being considered, not to exercise executive functions in relation to that matter and not to seek improperly to influence a decision about that matter. Prescribed interests must be registered.[206] Each authority must adopt its own code of conduct, which must incorporate mandatory provisions of the model code, may incorporate optional provisions of that code and may incorporate other provisions that are not inconsistent with the model code. Each member must give a written undertaking that he or she will comply with the code.[207] On adoption of the code, the former provisions concerning interests and disallowance and surcharge are disapplied.

4.77 Each authority other than a parish or community council must appoint a standards committee, which in England must have at least one independent member (and at least 25 per cent independent members where it comprises three or more members). This is to promote and maintain high standards of conduct and to assist members to observe the code of conduct.[208] Allegations of non-compliance with an authority's code are investigated in England by an ethical standards officer of the Standards Board for England, and in Wales by the Local Government Ombudsman for Wales.

---

[202] Originally a non-statutory code (DoE Circular 94/75); subsequently a statutory code made under ss 30 and 31 of the Local Government and Housing Act 1989 (DoE Circular 8/90).

[203] See para 4.89.

[204] *Third Report on Standards of Conduct in Local Government in England, Scotland and Wales* (Cm 2702, 1997).

[205] 2000 Act, s 49; Relevant Authorities (General Principles) Order 2001, SI 2001/1401. These are selflessness, honesty and integrity, objectivity, accountability, openness, personal judgment, respect for others, duty to uphold the law, stewardship and leadership. In Wales, the National Assembly has made the Conduct of Members (Principles) (Wales) Order 2001, SI 2001/2276.

[206] 2000 Act, s 50; Local Authorities (Model Code of Conduct) (England) Order 2001, SI 2001/3575, providing for separate codes for authorities that are and that are not operating executive arrangements. There are also separate codes for parish councils, National Park and Broads Authorities and Police Authorities. In Wales the National Assembly has made the Conduct of Members (Model Code of Conduct) Wales) Order 2001, SI 2001/2289.

[207] 2000 Act, ss 51, 52.

[208] ibid s 53; Relevant Authorities (Standards Committees) Regulations 2001, SI 2001/2812; Standards Committees (Wales) Regulations 2001, SI 2001/2283.

Decisions as to whether there has been a breach are determined by independent case tribunals, which have the power to order suspension or partial suspension for a period not exceeding one year, or disqualification from office for a period not exceeding five years, and to make recommendations to the authority.[209]

These arrangements are clearly more appropriate than reliance on the criminal law. **4.78** It is to be expected that the case law of the tribunals will bring further clarity into the detailed requirements of the ethical framework. It is particularly appropriate that the extraordinary powers of disallowance and surcharge, which have involved the imposition of (uninsurable) obligations to repay substantial sums of money on individual councillors, commonly of limited means, have been abolished. Liability here was not confined to cases of wilful misconduct[210] and was controversial even in cases where such misconduct was established given that sums could become payable that were much larger than the likely level for a fine had the matter constituted and had been dealt with as a criminal offence.[211] The lack of any corresponding liabilities arising out of unlawful decisions at the level of central government pointed up the unfairness of the special regime applicable to local councillors.

(e) Finance

Local authorities can only take action where they have the financial resources to do **4.79** so. The greater the extent that their functions take the form of duties rather than powers, the less their freedom to exercise such specific and general powers as are available to them. This position is to an extent modified by the willingness of the courts in some contexts, but not others, to hold that the availability of resources can be a relevant factor in determining the scope of a statutory duty.[212] The position

---

[209] 2000 Act, ss 57–80; Local Government Investigations (Functions of Monitoring Officers and Standards Committees (Wales) Regulations 2001, SI 2001/2281; Local Commissioner in Wales (Standards Investigations) Order 2001, SI 2001/2286.

[210] In cases of expenditure 'contrary to law': eg the paying of a minimum wage of £4 to all employees, male and female, to the extent that this exceeded what was reasonable by reference to considerations properly regarded as relevant in fixing wage rates: *Roberts v Hopwood* [1925] AC 578; cf *Pickwell v Camden LBC* [1983] 1 QB 902 (settlement with manual workers higher than national settlement not 'contrary to law').

[211] See eg *Asher v Lacey* [1973] 1 WLR 1412 (councillors' failure to increase council house rents as required by the Housing Finance Act 1972); *Smith v Skinner* (1986) 26 RVR 45, DC; *Lloyd v McMahon* [1987] AC 625 (delay in the making of rates for 1985–86 in Lambeth and Liverpool); *Porter v Magill* [2002] 2 AC 357 (losses caused by policy of council house sales directed towards electoral advantage, a deliberate, blatant and dishonest use of public power); summary judgment was subsequently given in favour of the council for some £26m: *Westminster City Council v Porter and Weeks* [2002] EWHC 1589 and 2179; [2003] Ch 436.

[212] *R v Gloucestershire CC, ex p Barry* [1997] AC 584 (where the House of Lords, by a strained process of interpretation, held that the availability of resources was a relevant consideration when assessing an applicant's need for a service for the purposes of the Chronically Sick and Disabled Persons Act 1970; *R v Sefton MBC, ex p Help the Aged* [1997] 4 All ER 532, following *Barry* but holding that once the level of the duty was established, lack of resources was no justification for failing to perform that duty; cf *R v Bristol City Council, ex p Penfold* [1998] COD 210 and *R v East Sussex CC,*

today is that the ability of local authorities to raise finance for both capital and revenue expenditure is heavily constrained. Traditionally, capital expenditure was financed by borrowing, which required the consent of central government; revenue expenditure was met by a combination of rates and central government grants. The rates were a local tax based on an estimate of the net annual value of the property rated.[213] The balance between grants and rates, and the balance between central government grants that were general or for specific purposes, varied over time.

4.80   The Local Government Finance Act 1988 confined the rating system to non-domestic property and centralized its operation, the level of rate being set by central government. Domestic rates were replaced by the community charge, a controversial tax on individuals that was not related to income. This was in turn replaced by the council tax, a domestic property charge based on a valuation of the value of premises, introduced by the Local Government Finance Act 1992. Central government secured the introduction of powers to limit (directly ('cap') or indirectly) the levels of, successively, rates, community charge and council tax that could be set by individual councils or groups of councils. A variety of mechanisms was used, that involved much complexity and controversy and varying degrees of effectiveness.[214] The position today is that only some 19 per cent of local authority net expenditure is locally determined.[215]

4.81   The current regime for capital finance is set out in Pt IV of the Local Government and Housing Act 1989.[216] Local authorities have a general power to borrow, and may enter other forms of credit arrangements; permission to do so is given by the Secretary of State in England and the National Assembly in Wales through basic and supplementary credit approvals for each authority. Each authority must remain within its aggregate credit limit. Capital expenditure may also be financed from capital receipts from the sale of assets (within prescribed limits), and from capital grants arising from central government or EU programmes.

4.82   The government White Paper, *Strong Local Leadership—Quality Public Services*[217] contains proposals for the reform of local government finance, to be carried forward

---

ex p Tandy [1998] AC 714, where a different view was taken in respect of other statutory provisions. See J Howell, 'Public duties and resources: "Won't pay—Won't do"' [1998] J of Local Government L 49.

[213] ie, the rateable value, being an estimate of the rent at which the property might reasonably be expected to be let from year to year, free of all tenant's rates and taxes and deducting therefrom the probable annual average cost of repairs, insurance and other expenses necessary to maintain the property in a state fit to command such rent: *Cross on Local Government Law* (n 1 above) para 15-01.

[214] See generally Loughlin (n 1 above) ch 5.

[215] Wilson and Game (n 2 above) 208 (2001–02 figures: council tax 19%; non-domestic rates 22%; service specific grants 28%; revenue support grant 31%). Comparative figures for locally determined expenditure in 1975–76, 1989–90 and 1992–93 were 35%, 53% and 15%.

[216] See *Cross on Local Government Law* (n 1 above) paras 12-19–12-37.

[217] Cm 5327, 2001.

into a Local Government Bill in the 2002–03 session. While there is no quick and easy way of shifting the balance between locally and centrally-determined funding, a proportion of grant will be targeted to support individual local public service agreements that set out specific service improvements; apart from this, new formulae will be developed for the distribution of the general grant. The system of credit approvals will be replaced by a 'new prudential regime' under which each authority sets 'prudential limits' for its borrowing, in accordance with guidance in a code developed by CIPFA, and must keep within those limits. Central government will retain a reserve power to set a limit on the rate at which local authorities can increase their borrowings. This will be used to ensure there is no short-term surge in borrowing following abolition of credit approvals, and in respect of individual authorities which fail to set a prudential limit or which breach the limit, and could be used to set a limit to meet a risk to the national economy. The balance in central support for capital investment between the revenue support grant (providing a revenue stream to support borrowing) and capital grants will be reviewed. For the better performing councils, the balance between general and ring-fenced support will be adjusted in favour of the former.

Authorities will continue to be encouraged to explore Private Finance Initiative arrangements. The council tax has been widely accepted by taxpayers and is generally well understood; there will be a general revaluation in time for the council tax bills issued in 2007. The Local Government Act 1999 introduced 'capping' powers that were more selective than those previously in place; these will not be used against higher-performing authorities. The power to set the level of business rate will not be returned to local authorities, although there will be a scheme for business improvement districts under which district, borough and unitary councils will be able to take forward schemes that benefit the local community, financed by an additional levy on the rates, subject to the agreement of local ratepayers. Finally, local authorities will be permitted to trade in any service in which they have a strong performance in delivery and given a general power to charge for discretionary services. **4.83**

The draft Local Government Bill has been subject to pre-legislative scrutiny by the Transport, Local Government and the Regions Committee, which regarded it as making some 'small steps in the right direction' while increasing the powers of the Secretary of State.[218] It proposed the removal of powers to limit the borrowing of individual authorities and to determine the minimum level of reserves held by local authorities, and the dropping of what was a new proposal to merge the revenue support grant and national non-domestic rates. The latter recommendation was accepted.[219] **4.84**

---

[218] *Draft Local Government Bill: 15th Report* (2001–02 HC 981-I).
[219] *Government Response* (Cm 5638, November 2002).

(4) The Accountability of Local Authorities

4.85   Local authorities are accountable for their actions (and failures to act) through a variety of mechanisms. They are accountable politically to the local electorate; and indeed, steps are being taken to encourage more people to vote at local elections.[220] They are accountable to central government through the wide variety of devices whereby central government may exert control or influence, including requirements to submit plans and strategies for approval and to submit reports and information.[221] They are subject to audit by an auditor appointed by the Audit Commission. The auditor must be satisfied that the accounts are prepared in accordance with regulations, that proper practices have been observed in the compilation of the accounts, that the body has made proper arrangements for securing economy, efficiency and effectiveness in its use of resources, and that it has made required arrangements for the collecting, recording and publishing of performance information.[222]

4.86   Some safeguards against improper action are provided by the conferral of particular statutory responsibilities on the 'head of paid service' and the 'monitoring officer'.[223] The former must, where he or she considers it appropriate, prepare a report on the co-ordination of the authority's functions and staffing matters; the monitoring officer must prepare a report where it appears to him or her that any proposal, decision or omission by the authority or one of its committees, subcommittees or officers constitutes or may give rise to a contravention of any enactment or rule of law, or maladministration under Pt III of the Local Government Act 1974. These reports must be considered by the authority but are not binding.

4.87   Finally, local authorities are under a duty to make arrangements to secure continuous improvement in the way in which functions are exercised, having regard to a combination of economy, efficiency and effectiveness. This 'duty of Best Value' involves the specification by the Secretary of State of performance indicators against which each authority's performance is to be measured and performance standards to be met by authorities in relation to performance indicators; rolling programmes of reviews of all its functions; an annual Best Value performance plan to be audited by the external auditor; the periodic inspection of functions by the Audit Commission; and extensive powers of direction, including that a specified function of a Best Value authority be exercised for a period by the Secretary of

---

[220] See Electoral Commission, *The shape of elections to come: A strategic evaluation of the 2003 electoral pilot scheme* (2003).
[221] See paras 4.26–4.29.
[222] Audit Commission Act 1998, s 5; Code of Audit Practice 2002; Accounts and Audit Regulations 2003, SI 2003/533; *Cross on Local Government Law* (n 1 above) ch 13.
[223] To be appointed under the Local Government and Housing Act 1989, ss 4, 5, as amended.

State or a person nominated by the Secretary of State.[224] This last power provides a significant new weapon to the armoury of the Secretary of State.[225]

The White Paper, *Strong Local Leadership—Quality Public Services*[226] proposed a **4.88** framework for Comprehensive Performance Assessments (CPAs), under which local authority performance would be measured against BVPI (Best Value Performance Indicator) performance levels, inspection and audit reports, corporate governance assessment and self-assessment by the local authority. The process would be led by the Audit Commission, with support from other inspectorates, and each council would be given an overall assessment (originally proposed as 'high-performing', 'striving', 'coasting' and 'poor-performing'). Serious corporate failure may lead to the transfer of functions to other bodies, the appointment of an administrator to restore solvency or franchising management.

The acts and omissions of local authorities are subject to scrutiny by the Local **4.89** Commissioners for Administration (Local Government Ombudsmen) established by Pt III of the Local Government Act 1974. Complaints may be made through an elected member or directly and the Ombudsman reports on whether the complainant has suffered injustice as the result of maladministration.[227]

Finally, local authorities are accountable in law for their torts and for breaches of **4.90** contract,[228] are subject to judicial review in respect of their public functions,[229] and

---

[224] Local Government Act 1999, ss 1–17; Local Government (Best Value), Performance Plans and Reviews Order 1999, SI 1999/3251, as amended; Local Government (Best Value) (Reviews and Performance Plans) (Wales) Order 2000, SI 2000/1271; Local Government (Best Value) Performance Indicators and Performance Standards Order 2003, SI 2003/530; Local Government (Best Value Performance Indicators) (Wales) Order 2002, SI 2002/757. See P Vincent-Jones, 'Central-local relations under the Local Government Act 1999: a new consensus?' (2000) 63 MLR 84.

[225] There is a range of levels of intervention: see Audit Commission, *A Force for Change: Central government intervention in failing local government services* (2002). For example, following an adverse Corporate Governance Inspection report by the Audit Commission on Hull Council in 2002 the minister stated that he expected the council to submit an action plan and liaise closely with ODPM officials; following submission of the action plan he stated that he expected the council to establish a Partnership Liaison Board to give strategic direction, including four places for government nominees, and other steps. The case for intervention would be kept under review: ODPM News Release 082, 20 September 2002.

[226] Cm 5327, 2001, ch 3; see also *Tackling Poor Performance in Local Government: A Consultation Paper* (ODPM, August 2002). The patronizing terminology proposed in the White Paper appears from the Consultation Paper to have been replaced by the labels 'excellent', 'good', 'fair', 'weak', and 'poor' (with or without the capacity to improve). CPAs have been carried out by the Audit Commission under existing powers; express provision is made for them in the Local Government Bill 2002–03. Recent legislation has added further powers of intervention: eg Police Reform Act 2002, National Health Service Reform and Health Care Professions Act 2002.

[227] See further, ch 21 below.

[228] See *Cross on Local Government Law* (n 1 above) ch 8.

[229] The line can be difficult to draw; eg, decisions to sell or not to sell land will be seen as a private law matter unless some additional public law element is present, such as a change in policy or a failure to comply with statutory requirements: *R v Bolsover DC, ex p Pepper* (2000) 3 LGLR 337.

are public authorities for the purposes of the Human Rights Act 1998,[230] and so subject to its requirements for all purposes. Case law concerning local authorities provides many illustrations of the application of the conventional grounds for judicial review. Three general points are worthy of note.

4.91 First, it has been said that the views of the elected representatives of the people are entitled to considerable respect, both where it is alleged that an act of a local authority is ultra vires[231] and where an appeal lies on the merits against a local authority's decision.[232] However, as regards the former, this consideration can only properly have weight where the issue is one of irrationality or proportionality rather than illegality; the views of elected members cannot confer power that is not otherwise present.[233] Similarly, while the existence of an electoral mandate may help support a decision against an argument that it is unreasonable,[234] a manifesto commitment cannot justify an illegal act[235] and the treatment of such a commitment as binding may constitute an unlawful fetter on discretion.[236]

4.92 Secondly, there are authorities that state that local authorities in exercising discretionary powers to spend are subject to a fiduciary duty owed to ratepayers.[237] There are many difficulties and uncertainties. The doctrine is controversial in so far as it may go further than ordinary *Wednesbury* principles in constraining the freedom of local authorities by prioritizing the interests of ratepayers. It is uncertain in scope. It apparently involves not only (and at the least) a requirement that the interests of ratepayers as the contributors of funds be taken into account, but also a duty to act on business principles[238] and not thriftlessly[239] and a duty fairly

---

[230] See paras 7.138 et seq below.
[231] Lord Russell of Killowen CJ in *Kruse v Johnson* [1898] 2 QB 91, 99.
[232] *Sagnata Investments Ltd v Norwich Corp* [1971] 2 QB 614, 636–637, *per* Edmund Davies LJ and 640, *per* Phillimore LJ.
[233] See Laws J in *R v Somerset CC, ex p Fewings* [1995] 1 All ER 513, 528–529.
[234] *Secretary of State for Education and Science v Tameside MBC* [1977] AC 1014.
[235] *Bromley LBC v Greater London Council* [1983] 1 AC 768. See de Smith, Woolf and Jowell, *Judicial Review of Administrative Action* (5th edn, London: Sweet & Maxwell, 1995) paras 13-064–13-066.
[236] *per* Lord Diplock and Brandon in *Bromley*, ibid 830–831, 853; cf Lord Wilberforce at 815.
[237] *Roberts v Hopwood* [1925] AC 578, 595–596 *per* Lord Atkinson: a body administering funds contributed in whole or in part by persons other than its members stands towards those persons 'somewhat in the position of trustees or managers of the property of others'; *Bromley LBC v Greater London Council* [1983] 1 AC 768, 815, *per* Lord Wilberforce. See generally Loughlin (n 1 above) ch 5; Leigh (n 1 above) 131–139.
[238] *Prescott v Birmingham Corp* [1955] Ch 210 (where the Court of Appeal held that a travel concessions scheme for the benefit of certain categories of old people was unlawful); *Bromley LBC v Greater London Council* [1983] 1 AC 768, 815, 819 *per* Lord Wilberforce, 831, 839 *per* Lord Keith, 842 *per* Lord Scarman, and 851 *per* Lord Brandon (the House, Lord Diplock dissenting on this point, held that the fiduciary duty confined the scope of the relevant legislation; this view has been widely criticized: see Loughlin (n 1 above)).
[239] *Bromley LBC v Greater London Council* [1983] 1 AC 768, 829 *per* Lord Diplock.

to balance the interests of different groups.[240] The duty was formulated as one owed to ratepayers. This would now cover domestic council tax payers, and presumably businesses who pay non-domestic rates notwithstanding that the money is now only collected by local authorities on behalf of the government. It has not been suggested that the fiduciary duty is owed to central government, notwithstanding that it provides most of the funding for local government.[241] Confined (in any of its manifestations) to the status of a legally relevant consideration, the fiduciary duty is relatively harmless as it is for the authority to determine the weight to be given to all relevant considerations, subject to challenge only where the ultimate decision is irrational. At any higher status it is of doubtful validity and would be better quietly forgotten.[242] Nevertheless, references to this additional dimension are still found,[243] although it has been emphasized that the reference to business principles does not require revenue to be maximized on ordinary business principles of profit and loss.[244] A separate principle enables a local authority to recover, through proceedings for breach of trust, losses caused to it by the wilful misconduct of a councillor.[245]

Thirdly, the courts have indicated that in applying the principles of *Wednesbury*   **4.93**
unreasonableness, a low intensity of review is to be applied to decisions in the

---

[240] ibid 815, 819–820 *per* Lord Wilberforce, 829–830 *per* Lord Diplock, and 838–839, 842 *per* Lord Scarman; *R v Newcastle-upon-Tyne City Council, ex p Dixon* (1995) 92 LGR 168, 178–179; in *Bromley* the GLC in introducing a substantial subsidy for London Transport fares had failed fairly to balance the respective interests of the travelling public and the ratepayers.

[241] It has been suggested that it might extend to national taxpayers (Arden, Manning and Collins (n 1 above) para 2.3.51), although the relationship is arguably too remote.

[242] This was essentially the approach of the Divisional Court in *Pickwell v Camden LBC* [1983] QB 962, in holding that a wage settlement in excess of a national agreement was not contrary to law; it was clearly stated to be the proper approach in *R v Greenwich LBC, ex p Cedar Transport Group Ltd* [1983] RA 173, and other cases discussed by Loughlin (n 1 above) 253–254. Cf, however, Elias J in *R (on the application of Structadene) v Hackney LBC* [2001] 2 All ER 225, who held that breach of fiduciary duty and *Wednesbury* unreasonableness were separate grounds for holding a sale of council land at less than best value, with neither ministerial consent nor any explanation of other benefits arising from the sale, was unlawful.

[243] *per* Elias J in *R (on the application of Molinaro) v Kensington and Chelsea RLBC* [2001] EWHC Admin 896; [2002] BLGR 336: 'the doctrine . . . can sometimes be used to enable the court to consider the weight afforded to the relevant factors, and to ensure that the fiduciary obligation is given proper significance' (at [40]). However, the doctrine was not engaged in any significant way here as the effect on local taxpayers of the decision was minimal. If the first proposition is right there are echoes of the principle of proportionality and the protection of substantive legitimate expectations.

[244] *R v London Transport Executive, ex p Greater London Council* [1983] 1 QB 484, where the Divisional Court upheld the legality of a 'balanced plan' revised after consultation for a 25% cut in London Transport fares, which had been doubled after *Bromley LBC v Greater London Council* [1983] 1 AC 768, avoiding or evading some of the reasoning in *Bromley* as to the proper interpretation of the governing legislation.

[245] *Westminster City Council v Porter and Weeks* [2002] EWHC 1589 and 2179; Ch 436, following *A-G v Aspinall* (1837) 2 My & Cr 613 and *A-G v Wilson* (1840) Cr & Ph 1. This remedy was not superseded by the statutory audit machinery now found in the Audit Commission Act 1998, and the remedies are cumulative rather than alternative.

general area of social and economic policy, such as the exercise by central government of powers to control local authority expenditure.[246]

C. Other Institutions for Local Governance

4.94 As mentioned above,[247] there is a wide range of non-elected bodies that discharge functions for local governance. Of growing importance are the nine regional development agencies established in England by the Regional Development Agencies Act 1998.[248] Each agency comprises between eight and 15 members appointed by the Secretary of State (or, in London, by the Mayor of London). Its purposes are to further the economic development and regeneration of the area, to promote business efficiency, investment and competitiveness and employment, to enhance the development and application of skills relevant to employment and to contribute to the achievement of sustainable development in the United Kingdom where relevant to its area. The Secretary of State may designate a representative body as the regional chamber for the purposes of consultation. He provides grants and loans and may authorize borrowing. The White Paper, *Your Region, Your Choice*[249] set out proposals for consultation within the regions as to whether there should be elected regional assemblies; there would be a consultation within at least one region during the present Parliament, and it would be for each region to decide whether it wanted such a body.[250]

4.95 Other bodies of note include the hierarchy of bodies within the National Health Service (strategic health authorities; Acute Hospitals and Primary Care NHS Trusts) and police authorities. The former include non-executive directors appointed by the NHS Appointments Commission.[251] Police authorities[252] normally comprise 17 members, including nine who are members of relevant councils for the area,[253] five 'independent members' appointed by the other members from a short-list prepared by the Secretary of State from a list of names

---

[246] *R v Secretary of State for the Environment, ex p Nottinghamshire CC* [1986] AC 240; *R v Secretary of State for the Environment, ex p Hammersmith and Fulham LBC* [1991] 1 AC 521. On the application of *Wednesbury* to local government, see Sir Robert Carnwath, 'The reasonable limits of local authority powers' [1996] PL 244, arguing that the principle required refinement and that the courts should adopt a positive role in helping to shape and protect the role of local government in the constitution.

[247] See para 4.17.

[248] Following the White Paper, *Building Partnerships for Prosperity* (Cm 3814, 1997).

[249] Cm 5511, May 2002.

[250] ODPM News Release 054, 31 July 2002.

[251] National Health Service and Community Care Act 1980.

[252] Police Act 1996, s 3 and Sch 1.

[253] ie, councils for a county, district, county borough or London borough except for district councils in areas having a county council. If there is more than one relevant council, appointments are made by a joint committee.

nominated by a selection panel constituted under Sch 3 to the Police Act 1996, and three magistrates. The authority appoints its chairman from among its members. It must secure the maintenance of an efficient and effective police force for its area, having regard to any *policing objectives* determined by the Secretary of State,[254] any *local policing objectives* determined by the authority, any *performance targets* established by the authority (whether or not by direction of the Secretary of State) and any *local policing plan* issued by it.[255] The police force is under the direction and control of the chief constable.[256] Both NHS Trusts and police forces are subject to developed regimes for audit, inspection performance measurement, and are subject to a measure of scrutiny by local authorities.[257]

---

[254] The Police (Secretary of State's Objectives) Order 2002, SI 2002/695, was revoked by SI 2003/830; strategic objectives are now set out in the National Policing Plan 2003–2006, made by the Secretary of State under the 1996 Act, s 36A.

[255] Police Act 1996, s 6.

[256] ibid s 10. See further *Cross on Local Government Law* (n 1 above) ch 24.

[257] Every relevant council must make arrangements for enabling questions on police matters to be put at council meetings for answer by a person nominated by the police authority: Police Act 1996, s 20; in an interesting move, matters relating to the health service have been made subject to scrutiny by overview and scrutiny committees: Health and Social Care Act 2001, ss 7–10, amending Local Government Act 2000, s 21. See the Local Authority (Overview and Scrutiny Committees Health Scrutiny Functions) Regulations 2002, SI 2002/3048.

5

THE POWERS AND ACCOUNTABILITY OF AGENCIES AND REGULATORS

A. Introduction

(1) The Scope and Scheme of the Chapter

The key defining feature of the bodies covered by this chapter is that they are not   **5.01**
part of central or local government but nevertheless perform regulatory functions,
the latter including both constituting markets through competition law and intervening in markets for social reasons. There is some overlap between the bodies
covered here and the official concept of non-departmental public bodies but the
correspondence is by no means exact; non-ministerial government departments
would not fall within this category, and many bodies within it do not regulate but
are, for example, merely advisory.[1] One type of body has been excluded; the 'Next
Steps' agencies to which service delivery by central government has been delegated.[2] Those regulators which take the form of non-ministerial government departments have been included, however, on the ground that they have an effective

---

[1] See Cabinet Office, *Public Bodies Directory* (2000).
[2] See ch 3 above.

independence from direct government control. In addition, it is inevitable that no attempt will be made to cover in any detail the large variety of bodies which perform the task of professional self-regulation; examples would be the Law Society and the General Medical Council.[3] There will however be discussion of some general issues of self-regulation in Part B and selected examples of self-regulation will be described in Part D.

5.02   Even after these exclusions, the legal form of the bodies to be discussed is immensely varied, many having a statutory basis but others lacking this, such as the Board of Governors of the BBC, established by Royal Charter, and the Panel on Take-overs and Mergers which was established privately and performs its functions 'without visible means of legal support'.[4] As these two examples indicate, there is also a complex relationship between public regulation and private self-regulation.

5.03   The picture is complicated further by the absence in English public law of an overarching statement of principle, either procedural or substantive, to give a coherent structure to the operation of these institutions. By contrast, US Federal Law has the Administrative Procedure Act setting procedural principles for rule-making and adjudication by federal agencies,[5] whilst French administrative law has a developed body of law on the substantive principles of *service public.*[6]

5.04   In the absence of similar organizing principles in English law, this chapter will follow two approaches. In Part B it will attempt to distil some general principles from existing law and practice. In Parts C and D it will proceed by exemplification, examining key regulatory bodies performing economic and non-economic functions. It is only by combining some general principles and examining particular agencies in more detail that a reasonably representative account of their powers and accountability can be given.

(2) The Development of Regulatory Institutions

(a) Early history

5.05   Regulation has a long history in the United Kingdom and has been implemented by a very large variety of different types of institution.[7] Some early regulatory principles were implemented by the courts;[8] Parliament took an important role

---

[3] Solicitors Act 1974; Medical Act 1983.
[4] Lord Donaldson MR in *R v Panel on Take-overs and Mergers, ex p Datafin plc* [1987] QB 815, 824.
[5] 5 USC §§ 551 et seq.
[6] For a summary see Conseil d'Etat, *Etudes et Documents No 46, Rapport Public 1994, Le Service Public* (1995).
[7] See T Prosser, *Law and the Regulators* (Oxford: Clarendon, 1997) ch 2.
[8] See eg *Allnutt v Inglis* (1810) 12 East 527.

through the use of private Acts, especially in the case of railway regulation. However, a large number of other regulatory institutions could be identified by the 19th century, including, notoriously, the Poor Law Commission of 1834.[9] A mixture of courts, government departments and commissions continued to perform regulatory functions into the 20th century; an example of the latter was the creation of the Electricity Commissioners by the Electricity Supply Act 1919.

(b) Post-war agencies

However, nationalization in the 20th century in general replaced independent regulation with direct governmental regulation through public ownership.[10] Although new institutions in the form of consumer councils were set up, these were weak and there was little concern with principles of institutional design in doing so. Nevertheless, alongside public ownership, some important regulatory commissions were established where private as well as public enterprise was active in the market. The first example was that of civil aviation where in 1938 an Air Transport Licensing Authority had been set up, licensing services through formal hearings. In 1960 it became the Air Transport Licensing Board and in 1972 the Civil Aviation Authority which still carries out licensing and other regulatory functions.[11]   **5.06**

A further example was that of independent television, where the Independent Television Authority was set up by the Television Act 1954 with licensing and enforcement responsibilities. It later became the Independent Broadcasting Authority and, under the Broadcasting Act 1990, the Independent Television Commission; its operation will be examined below.[12] A large number of other agencies were established during the late 1960s; for example, the Race Relations Board (1965), the Monopolies Commission (1965), the Community Relations Commission (1968), and they were followed by the Equal Opportunities Commission in 1975 and the Commission for Racial Equality in 1977. It is noticeable that several of these agencies had strong social or rights-based remits rather than specializing in economic regulation. However, the major source of the growth of British regulatory agencies came through the primarily economic process of privatization.   **5.07**

(c) Privatization and the regulators

The agencies discussed above were in the form of commissions under which a group of members reaches a collective decision, supported by a specialist staff.   **5.08**

---

[9] HW Arthurs, *'Without the Law': Administrative Justice and Legal Pluralism in Nineteenth-Century England* (Toronto: University of Toronto Press, 1985).
[10] For more details see T Prosser, *Nationalised Industries and Public Control* (Oxford: Blackwell, 1986).
[11] Civil Aviation Act 1971.
[12] See paras 5.93–5.95.

However, a different form of agency had also begun to emerge in which legal powers were granted to an individual, also supported by administrators; the body was given the status of a non-ministerial government department. The first important example was that of the Director General of Fair Trading and the Office of Fair Trading.[13]

5.09 This model was also adopted for the utility regulators during the privatization programme from 1984 onwards. The first example was that of the Director General of Telecommunications supported by the Office of Telecommunications (OFTEL).[14] This was followed by the Director General of Gas Supply and the Office of Gas Supply (OFGAS)[15] to which was added the Director General of Electricity Supply and the Office of Electricity Regulation (OFFER).[16] With the increased interdependence of the gas and electricity markets the two offices were later merged administratively into the Office of Gas and Electricity Markets (OFGEM), and the two regulators have been replaced from 1 October 2001 by a commission, the Gas and Electricity Markets Authority.[17] The Director of Water Services and the Office of Water Services (OFWAT) were created in 1989.[18] The Rail Regulator and the Office of the Rail Regulator (ORR) followed, in this case alongside a second agency more closely linked to government, initially the Office of the Franchising Director but more recently the Strategic Rail Authority.[19] Finally, a similar model, though this time in the form of a commission, has been adopted to regulate the Post Office even whilst it remains in public ownership. This is the Postal Services Commission (Postcomm).[20] As is apparent from these examples, the preferred model since the change of government in 1997 has become that of a commission; the Communications Act 2003 and the Railways and Transport Safety Act 2003 will create commissions for communications and rail regulation, and the Enterprise Act 2002 replaces the Director General of Fair Trading with a corporate Office of Fair Trading.

(d) European liberalization

5.10 At this stage a further influence in the establishment of agencies should be mentioned; that of the liberalization of certain utility services within the European Union. A central theme of such liberalization has been to require a separation of regulatory and operational functions. Previously these had been carried out together in

---

[13] Fair Trading Act 1973, Pt I; for the background see I Ramsay, 'The Office of Fair Trading: Policing the Consumer Marketplace' in R Baldwin and C McCrudden (eds), *Regulation and Public Law* (London: Weidenfeld & Nicolson, 1987).

[14] Telecommunications Act 1984, Pts I–III.

[15] Gas Act 1986, Pt I.

[16] Electricity Act 1989, Pt I.

[17] Utilities Act 2000, Pt I.

[18] Water Act 1989, Pt I, consolidated in Water Industry Act 1991, Pt I.

[19] Railways Act 1993, Pt I; Transport Act 2000, Pt IV.

[20] Postal Services Act 2000, Pt I.

many member states by an integrated public enterprise. Although the separation of functions does not inevitably require the establishment of regulatory commissions as regulatory functions may be carried out by government, in practice liberalization has been a major factor in encouraging their establishment.[21] Thus in the most advanced area of liberalization, that of telecommunications, national regulatory authorities have been established in each member state, and the Commission regularly monitors their independence, powers and operation.[22] Similar, but less well-advanced, processes are taking place in energy and postal services.

B. General Principles

(1) The Legal Basis for Agencies

(a) Statute

As will be apparent from the discussion above, the major commissions and the individual utility regulators have been established by the use of statute. This has a number of advantages in terms of accountability: it sets a clear definition of the powers of the body and makes challenge for ultra vires easier; it makes it clear that judicial review is available against decisions of the agency; it permits a clearer allocation of power as between the agency and, for example, bodies representing consumers also created by the statute; and it permits full parliamentary debate about the nature of the agency when it is being established.

5.11

One example of the use of statute will be given here; that for the Postal Services Commission. The Postal Services Act 2000 establishes the Commission as a body corporate performing its functions on behalf of the Crown, and it is to consist of a Chairman, a Chief Executive, and at least three other members appointed by the Secretary of State; members can only be removed for incapacity or misbehaviour.[23] The Act sets out the duties of the Commission, notably to secure the provision of a universal postal service and to further the interests of users of postal services.[24] It has the power to license providers of postal services and is given the power to enforce the conditions of licences and to impose financial penalties for breach, in both cases after complying with procedural requirements.[25]

5.12

---

[21] See for background G Majone, *Regulating Europe* (London: Routledge, 1996) esp chs 4 and 12.
[22] See the Commission's *Annual Report on the Implementation of the Telecommunications Regulatory Package*, most recently the Eighth Report at http://europa.eu.int/information_society/topics/telecoms/implementation/annual_report/8threport/index_en.htm, consulted 11 March 2003.
[23] Postal Services Act 2000, s 1, Sch 1.
[24] ibid ss 3–5.
[25] ibid ss 11–13, 22–37.

(b) Other public sources of authority

5.13 A slight variant on the use of statute referred to above occurs in the case of the Financial Services Authority. In this case the Authority is actually a company limited by guarantee under the Companies Act 1985.[26] However, the Financial Services and Markets Act 2000 confers functions upon it and requires it to comply with requirements as to its constitution and procedures.[27] In this case, the Authority is expressed not to be acting on behalf of the Crown. The origins of this unusual status lie in the previous system of partial self-regulation of financial services. However, statute also sets out an unusually detailed legislative mandate for the operation of the Authority, including a framework of regulatory objectives and principles.[28] Perhaps paradoxically, but due to the need to inspire market confidence in the regulator, statute here provides fuller criteria for accountability than in the case of bodies created directly by statute.

5.14 A marked contrast is that of the BBC Board of Governors. Whilst private broadcasters are regulated under statute,[29] the BBC operates through a Royal Charter and an Agreement between the Corporation and the Secretary of State.[30] The Charter establishes the BBC as a Corporation of 12 governors appointed by the Queen in Council, each for a period of five years. It requires broadcasting services to be provided 'as public services' and the Agreement imposes content requirements similar to those of private broadcasters. Nevertheless, the role of the governors is much less well defined than that of regulators established by statute and this led to criticism of a lack of clarity of roles and lack of transparency both by the BBC's competitors and supporters of public service broadcasting.[31] Revocation is for the monarch on the advice of the Secretary of State that provisions of the Charter or Agreement have been broken.[32]

(c) Regulatory bodies established other than under public law

5.15 There have been many bodies established by contract or other agreement which have assumed regulatory functions. The most extensive system was that of financial services, where the system of so-called 'self-regulatory organizations' was supervised by the Securities and Investments Board, itself a non-statutory company

---

[26] Companies Act 1985, s 6.
[27] Financial Services and Markets Act 2000, s 1, Sch 1.
[28] ibid s 2.
[29] Broadcasting Acts 1990 and 1996; Communications Act 2003.
[30] Department of National Heritage, *Copy of Royal Charter for the Continuance of the British Broadcasting Corporation* (Cm 3248, 1996) and *Copy of the Agreement Dated the 25th Day of January 1996 Between her Majesty's Secretary of State for National Heritage and the British Broadcasting Corporation* (Cm 3152, 1996).
[31] See paras 5.89–5.92 below.
[32] For the availability of judicial review see paras 5.27–5.29 below.

limited by guarantee to which powers were delegated by government.[33] As mentioned above,[34] this has now been superseded by more direct forms of statutory regulation after problems of the effectiveness and legitimacy of this form of so-called self-regulation.

An existing example of a regulatory body established without the use of public law   **5.16**
or statutory techniques, and indeed with no direct use of private law, is the Take-overs Panel (Panel on Take-overs and Mergers), which is an unincorporated association with no legal personality, and which has no contractual relationship with those it monitors. It is concerned with take-overs of companies the shares of which are owned by the public and protects the interests of shareholders. It was set up by the Stock Exchange in 1968 on the recommendation of the governor of the Bank of England. Given the failure of the European Union to agree on the Thirteenth Company Law Directive, which would have imposed a loose legal regulatory framework on these aspects of takeovers, it remains in effect a private regulatory body. It does however also issue an annual report and is subject to judicial review, as discussed below.[35]

(d) Self-regulation

It is increasingly common to suggest some form of self-regulation as an alternative   **5.17**
to direct regulation by agencies. This has been particularly so in relation to the press with the role of the Press Complaints Commission, in financial services and more recently in broadcasting and the internet. However, the relationship between self-regulation and other forms of regulation is extremely complex, and almost invariably self-regulation is accompanied by more direct interventions on the part of public authorities, including the use of civil or criminal sanctions. Recognizing this, recent attention has shifted to 'co-regulation' or 'enforced self-regulation' rather than positing self-regulation as an alternative to more formal regulatory techniques.[36]

In addition to the academic interest in these more complex forms of self-regula-   **5.18**
tion, a government White Paper has distinguished formal regulation where government or a regulator define and enforce detailed requirements, self-regulation where there is no regulatory involvement or schemes are created by government but develop their own rules and sanctions, and co-regulation. In this latter case there is a more active involvement of government or regulator in seeking a solution to an emerging concern or problem, for example by setting objectives or providing

---

[33] Financial Services Act 1986, s 114 and Sch 9.
[34] See para 5.13 above.
[35] *R v Panel on Take-overs and Mergers, ex p Datafin plc* [1987] QB 815, CA.
[36] See notably I Ayres and J Braithwaite, *Responsive Regulation: Transcending the Deregulation Debate* (Oxford: OUP, 1992) and J Black, 'Constitutionalising Self-Regulation' (1996) 59 MLR 24.

support for sanctions.[37] It seems likely that further combinations of formal regulation and self-regulation will emerge, and more details will be given below.[38]

(2) Agency Accountability

(a) **Parliamentary accountability**

5.19   Although the agencies discussed in this chapter are all distanced from central government, parliamentary accountability has had an important role to play in many cases. The least important form is that of parliamentary questions to ministers. Controversy has arisen around the responsibility of ministers to answer directly in relation to the 'Next Steps' executive agencies which form part of central government, but in the case of the agencies here it is highly unlikely that a minister would answer a parliamentary question, except one relating to his or her own direct actions taken in relation to the agencies.[39] Examples of the latter would include appointments or those relatively rare situations where an agency investigates only as a preliminary to a ministerial decision, such as in monopoly and merger control.[40]

5.20   Much more important in practice has been the role of parliamentary select committees, in particular the subject committees of the House of Commons. In a number of areas, committees have undertaken wide-ranging inquiries in which the operation of regulatory bodies has been central; examples would include broadcasting, financial services and transport.[41] In addition, select committees have looked directly at the work and operation of a number of agencies. The most far-reaching example is the detailed scrutiny of the Bank of England's Monetary Policy Committee by the Treasury Committee of the House of Commons. This includes holding (non-statutory and non-binding) confirmation hearings of new ministerial appointees to the Committee and publishing an annual end of term report on the Committee's work.[42] Other committees have also examined in detail the work of utility regulators.[43]

---

[37] Department of Trade and Industry (DTI) and Department for Culture, Media and Sport, *A New Future for Communications* (Cm 5010, 2000) s 8.11.

[38] See paras 5.97–5.98 and 5.101–5.103 below.

[39] See Erskine May, *Treatise on the Law, Privileges, Proceedings and Usage of Parliament* (22nd edn, London: Butterworths, 1997) 299–300.

[40] See *R v Secretary of State for Trade, ex p Anderson Strathclyde plc* [1983] 2 All ER 233, DC. The ministerial role in monopoly and merger cases is reduced dramatically with the passage of the Enterprise Act 2002.

[41] For examples from many inquiries see Culture, Media and Sport Committee, *The Multi-Media Revolution* (1997–98 HC 520); Treasury Committee, *Financial Services Regulation* (1998–99 HC 73); Transport, Local Government and the Regions Committee, *Passenger Rail Franchising and the Future of Railway Infrastructure* (2001–02 HC 239).

[42] eg, Treasury Committee, *The Monetary Policy Committee of the Bank of England: Confirmation Hearing* (2000–01 HC 449); *The Monetary Policy Committee: An End of Term Report* (2000–01 HC 42).

[43] See eg Trade and Industry Committee, *Local Loop Unbundling* (2000–01 HC 90). The Committee also took general evidence on the work of OFTEL and of OFGEM during the 1999–2000 session.

A further source of scrutiny of growing importance is the work of the National   **5.21**
Audit Office and the Committee of Public Accounts, in particular their value for
money audit.[44] Once more the statutory regulators have been subject to detailed
scrutiny by both of them; most importantly, perhaps, two detailed studies have
been carried out into the work of the utility regulators as a group.[45] Studies have
also been carried out into particular areas of their work.[46] Alongside the work of the
select committees, these studies provide the most rigorous assessment and the best
source of information currently available relating to the work of these regulators.

The status of the utility regulators as non-ministerial government departments   **5.22**
secures audit access for the Office and Committee. The position is more complex, and less satisfactory, with regard to other regulatory bodies, where access
will depend on individual statutes or agreements. Thus, for example, the
Financial Services Authority is excluded from scrutiny by the Office and
Committee, despite support from them for its inclusion. There were two models
for the audit of non-departmental public bodies which are not companies. In
some cases the minister appoints an external auditor; in other cases the legislation establishing the body appoints the Comptroller and Auditor-General auditor, thus opening up National Audit Office and Public Accounts Committee
scrutiny. Recent legislation permits the Treasury to provide by order for such
audit, although companies legislation precludes this for bodies in the form of
companies.[47] The government announced in spring 2002 that it planned to extend audit by the Comptroller and Auditor-General to all non-departmental
public bodies, including the (previously excluded) Environment Agency and the
Housing Corporation. Powers would also be given for such audit of several bodies in the form of companies, and to extend statutory rights of access.[48] Orders to
this effect were made in February 2003.[49] In addition to audit rights, the

---

[44] For general information on their work see paras 2.93–2.105 above.

[45] National Audit Office, *The Work of the Directors General Telecommunications, Gas Supply, Water Services and Electricity Supply* (1995–96 HC 645); Public Accounts Committee, same title (1996–97 HC 89); National Audit Office, *Pipes and Wires* (2001–02 HC 723); Public Accounts Committee, same title (2002–03 HC 831).

[46] eg, National Audit Office, *Opening the Post: Postcomm and Postal Services* (2001–02 HC 521); Public Accounts Committee, *Postcomm: Opening the Post* (2001–02 HC 632); National Audit Office, *Giving Domestic Consumers a Choice of Electricity Supplier* (2000–01 HC 85) and Public Accounts Committee, same title (2001–02 HC 446); National Audit Office, *Office of Gas and Electricity Markets: Giving Customers a Choice—the Introduction of Competition into the Domestic Gas Market* (1998–99 HC 403) and Public Accounts Committee, same title (1999–2000 HC 171).

[47] Government Resources and Accounts Act 2000, s 25(6)–(10) and Companies Act 1989, s 25; the position is reviewed in HM Treasury, *Holding to Account: The Review of Audit and Accountability for Central Government* (the Sharman Report) (2001).

[48] HM Treasury, *Audit and Accountability in Central Government* (Cm 5456, 2002).

[49] Government Resources and Accounts Act 2000 (Examinations by Comptroller and Auditor General) Order 2003; Government Resources and Accounts Act 2000 (Rights of Access of Comptroller and Auditor General) Order 2003.

Comptroller and Auditor-General has access by statute or agreement to a number of other bodies, and the National Audit Act 1983 permits him to undertake value for money studies of them; this also extends to any body appointed by or on behalf of the Crown which is mainly supported by public funds.[50] Thus we are witnessing a gradual extension of the powers of the National Audit Office and Public Accounts Committee in relation to those regulatory bodies not previously covered.

(b) Judicial review

5.23   Once more, there are several different issues which need to be untangled here; no attempt will be made to cover the general scope of judicial review in English law, which is discussed in paras 17.69 et seq below. The first question is the degree of scrutiny to which regulatory decisions will be subject where there is no doubt that a regulator's decisions are susceptible to judicial review; the second is whether judicial review is available in the case of bodies which are in some sense self-regulatory. Before discussing these, it should be noted that there has been a recent tendency to replace common law judicial review with statutory appeals on point of law. A very important example is that of the appeal right from the Competition Appeal Tribunal to the Court of Appeal in relation to decisions taken under the Competition Act 1998, and another is the similar appeal from the Financial Services and Markets Tribunal (itself an appellate body for the Financial Services Authority).[51] The move to statutory appeal rights may in itself create further use of the judicial machinery through by-passing the requirement to commence proceedings in the High Court and the remaining complexities of judicial review procedure.

(i) The intensity of review in economic regulation

5.24   It has not been unknown for there to have been challenges by judicial review of the economic regulators, and there are some grounds for believing that such challenges will increase in the future, even where judicial review rather than appeal on point of law is still the appropriate procedure.[52] In practice, the courts have granted agencies considerable latitude in matters of regulatory judgment. This has perhaps been most striking in relation to the Competition Commission, which, until 2001, had not lost a judicial review case despite regular challenges. Probably the most important challenge to a substantive issue

---

[50] National Audit Act 1983, ss 6(3)(c) and 7.
[51] Competition Act 1998, s 49; Financial Services and Markets Act 2000, s 137.
[52] For a comprehensive account of challenges to the utility regulators, see C Scott, 'The Juridification of Relations in the UK Utilities Sector' in J Black, P Muchlinski and P Walker (eds), *Commercial Regulation and Judicial Review* (Oxford: Hart, 1998) 19–61.

before it involved a matter of jurisdictional fact, but nevertheless the Commission's view was upheld and it is clear that the House of Lords was in favour of interpreting its powers widely and in favour of a flexible approach to its definition of the scope of investigations.[53] The Commission was also afforded considerable procedural flexibility provided that it complied with the basic rules of natural justice.[54] Similarly, in cases involving the economic powers of the Independent Television Commission in allocating broadcasting licences, the House of Lords, whilst accepting that the Commission was subject to the requirements of natural justice, was reluctant to impose any demanding standard of substantive review and, in a later case, the High Court emphasized that 'a very heavy burden falls on the party seeking to upset a qualitative judgment of the nature described and arrived at by the qualified and experienced body which is the Commission'.[55]

It is possible that the permissive approach of the courts may be changing. The first case to be lost by the Competition Commission or its predecessor was the *Interbrew* case in 2001.[56] This concerned procedural unfairness rather than the Commission's substantive judgment, the Commission having failed to raise with the company involved a remedy it was considering. In combination with the role of Article 6 of the European Convention on Human Rights (ECHR)[57] this suggests that procedural challenges are likely to be the most successful in future. Nevertheless, on matters of substance, the creation of the Appeal Tribunal under the Competition Act 1998 and the Enterprise Act 2002 and the creation of an appeal right on point of law to the Court of Appeal are likely to create a considerable body of case law in an area previously without much guidance from the courts.

5.25

The approach of the courts on judicial review from the utility regulators has in general been similarly restrained, with an acceptance of the breadth of the substantive discretion of the regulator together with a concern that the basic requirements of procedural fairness are observed.[58] In most of the cases where a lesser degree of deference has been adopted to decisions of substance, this can be explained by appeal to general principles of administrative law, for example equal

5.26

---

[53] *South Yorkshire Transport v Monopolies and Mergers Commission* [1993] 1 WLR 23, HL.

[54] *R v Monopolies and Mergers Commission, ex p Stagecoach Holdings plc*, The Times, 23 July 1996, DC.

[55] *R v Independent Television Commission, ex p TSW Broadcasting Ltd* [1996] EMLR 291; *R v Independent Television Commission, ex p Virgin Television Ltd* [1996] EMLR 318.

[56] *Interbrew SA v Competition Commission* [2001] EWHC Admin 367; [2001] UKCLR 954, QBD.

[57] See para 5.33 below.

[58] cf *R v Director General of Telecommunications, ex p British Telecommunications plc* (CO/3596/96, QBD), noted by Scott at (1997) 8 Utilities L Rev 120, and *R v Director General of Gas Supply, ex p Smith* (CRO/1398/88, QBD, 31 July 1989).

treatment and underlying principles of due process.[59] In this area recourse to judicial review will continue to be necessary, except in telecommunications where, as a result of the requirements of European law, a right of appeal on point of law to the High Court, and later to the Competition Appeal Tribunal on the merits, was created.[60] No appeal lies to the Competition Appeal Tribunal from utility regulators' licensing decisions, which will be discussed in more detail below.[61]

(ii) Availability of judicial review against non-statutory regulators

5.27 The general rules on the availability of judicial review against bodies exercising what may be seen as private functions are set out in paras 17.70 to 17.87 below, and need not be rehearsed here.[62] The starting point is still the *Datafin* case dealing with decisions of the Take-overs Panel.[63] Despite the lack of any legal basis for the Panel's decisions, the Court of Appeal held that review was available as the Panel was performing a public duty, its decisions affected the rights of citizens, and its powers were backed up by the statutory powers of government. In this case an alternative contractual remedy was not available. However, the court should be slow to intervene, such intervention should be by declaration (as it then was) and should be 'historic rather than contemporaneous' in order to maintain market confidence. These criteria are likely to apply to other regulators established by non-statutory means, so one can expect that their decisions will be reviewable in principle though that review will be limited in extent.[64] Thus the decisions of the so-called self-regulatory organizations in financial services regulation were clearly subject to judicial review.[65]

5.28 This expansive view of the scope of judicial review has not, however, permitted the review of other self-regulatory bodies which have been treated as more private in nature; thus the Jockey Club was held to be outside the scope of review as it did not exercise governmental powers and was in no sense a public body, and similar

---

[59] See *R v Director General of Electricity Supply, ex p Scottish Power* (QBCOF 95/1469/D, CA, 3 February 1997) noted at (1997) 8 Utilities L Rev 126; *R v Director General of Water Services, ex p Lancashire CC*, The Times, 6 March 1998.

[60] Telecommunications (Appeals) Regulations 1999, SI 1999/3180, inserting a new s 46B into the Telecommunications Act 1984; Electronic Communications Act 2000, s 12; Communications Act 2003, ss 192–196.

[61] See para 5.70 below.

[62] For a most useful analysis of the case law in this area see P Craig, *Administrative Law* (4th edn, London: Sweet & Maxwell, 1999) 774–778

[63] *R v Panel on Take-overs and Mergers, ex p Datafin plc* [1987] QB 815.

[64] For judicial reluctance to intervene even on procedural grounds see *R v Panel on Take-overs and Mergers, ex p Guinness* [1990] 1 QB 146, CA, and for a similar decision to *Datafin* in another context see *R v Advertising Standards Authority, ex p The Insurance Services plc* [1990] COD 42.

[65] See eg *R v Financial Intermediaries Managers and Brokers Regulatory Association, ex p Cochrane* [1990] COD 33.

exclusions for judicial review were applied to the Football Association and Lloyd's of London.[66]

A slightly different question is whether the procedure of judicial review is the most appropriate one, given the existence of private law remedies. The availability of a private law remedy has been accepted even in the case of a utility regulator where there are contractual issues involved though this did not necessarily preclude the use of judicial review.[67] If a relationship is perceived as wholly contractual (as was emphatically not the case in *Datafin*), the courts may consider a contractual remedy to be more appropriate.[68]

5.29

(c) Availability of damages from regulatory bodies

Once more, this is discussed in detail in paras 18.72 and 19.42 et seq below. In general the courts have been reluctant to impose liability in negligence on regulatory bodies.[69] In addition, in certain cases of statutory bodies, a degree of statutory immunity from claims for damages is afforded. For example, in the case of the Financial Services Authority, both the Authority itself and its members, officers or staff are exempted from liability in damages except in the case of bad faith or in respect of an act or omission unlawful by virtue of the Human Rights Act 1998 (HRA).[70] Largely as a result of the existence of such an exemption, we have seen a revival in one area of regulation of the tort of misfeasance in public office. In litigation against the Bank of England (as predecessor of the Financial Services Authority) in relation to its regulation of a defaulting bank, the House of Lords refused to strike out a claim based on this tort and so unprotected by the Bank's statutory exemption which did not extend to matters of bad faith.[71]

5.30

(d) The European Convention on Human Rights

Chapters 7 to 12 of this work examine the general principles and applicability of the ECHR and the effect of the HRA 1998. In relation to regulatory bodies, two issues arise; the definition of 'public authority' in the Act and which rights are likely to be most relevant in bringing a challenge.

5.31

---

[66] *R v Disciplinary Committee of the Jockey Club, ex p Aga Khan* [1993] 1 WLR 909; *R v Football Association Ltd, ex p Football League Ltd* [1993] 2 All ER 833; *R v Lloyd's of London, ex p Briggs* [1993] 1 Lloyd's Rep 176.

[67] *Mercury Communications v Director General of Telecommunications* [1996] 1 All ER 575, HL.

[68] *R v Lord Chancellor, ex p Hibbit and Saunders* [1993] COD 326.

[69] *Yuen Kun Yeu v A-G of Hong Kong* [1988] AC 175, PC; *Davis v Radcliffe* [1990] 1 WLR 821, HL.

[70] Financial Services and Markets Act 2000, Sch 1, para 19. For the possibly considerable implications of the HRA 1998 for the exemption see *Osman v UK* (2000) 29 EHRR 245, and A Page, 'Regulating the Regulator—A Lawyer's Perspective on Accountability and Control' in E Ferran and C Goodhart (eds), *Regulating Financial Services and Markets in the 21ˢᵗ Century* (Oxford: Hart, 2001) 127, 145–147.

[71] *Three Rivers DC v Bank of England (No 3)* [2001] UKHL 16; [2001] 2 All ER 513.

(i) The definition of a 'public authority'

5.32 Section 6 of the HRA 1998 makes it unlawful for a public authority to act in a way which is incompatible with a Convention right. This will be sufficient to include the statutory regulators covered in this chapter; indeed, much of the work in designing the Financial Services Authority involved making its procedures proof against challenge under the ECHR.[72] More complicated questions arise in relation to self-regulatory bodies and those established on a non-statutory basis. The Act specifies that 'public authority' includes bodies certain of whose functions are of a public nature unless the nature of the act in question is private.[73] The case law on the application of these provisions is not at the time of writing particularly clear. Thus the Chancery Division held that the Royal Society for the Prevention of Cruelty to Animals is not a public authority, at least in relation to regulation of its own membership.[74] On the other hand, a housing association was held to fall within the definition in relation to the service of a possession order as its role was so closely assimilated to that of a local authority that it was performing public functions.[75] However, the Leonard Cheshire Homes, a company registered by guarantee and registered charity, providing accommodation on behalf of local and health authorities, was not a public authority for the purposes of the HRA.[76] These cases should be treated with considerable caution as none of them concerned the exercise of regulatory functions over others by the body concerned; the *Cheshire Homes* case, for example, concerned the closure of a residential home owned by Cheshire Homes itself. Where a self-regulatory body takes what is clearly a regulatory decision affecting the operation of other market actors it is much more likely that it will be found to qualify as a public authority under the Act.[77]

(ii) The relevant Convention rights

5.33 The most important Convention right is clearly Article 6 providing the rights to a fair hearing before an independent tribunal in the determination of civil rights and obligations. It is well accepted that this is likely to require a considerable degree of procedural protection where regulatory bodies take decisions affecting, for

---

[72] See D Waters and M Hopper, 'Regulatory Discipline and the European Convention on Human Rights—A Reality Check' in Ferran and Goodhart (n 70 above) 95.

[73] HRA 1998, s 6(3)(b), (5).

[74] *Royal Society for the Prevention of Cruelty to Animals v A-G* [2002] 1 WLR 448.

[75] *Poplar Housing and Regeneration Community Association Ltd v Donoghue* [2001] EWCA Civ 595; [2002] QB 48.

[76] *R (on the application of Heather) v Leonard Cheshire Foundation* [2002] EWCA Civ 366; [2002] 2 All ER 936.

[77] 'This is analogous to the position in judicial review, where a regulatory body may be deemed public but the activities of the body which is regulated may be categorised private.' *Poplar Housing and Regeneration Community Association Ltd v Donoghue* [2001] EWCA Civ 595; [2002] QB 48 at [65]. See further paras 7.131 et seq below.

example, the right to trade in the marketplace or imposing financial sanctions. Thus a considerable effort in designing the procedures of the Financial Services Authority went into ensuring that its disciplinary powers and, in particular, its power to impose fines for 'market abuse', were Convention compliant. This was achieved through an internal separation between those responsible for investigation and recommending the institution of disciplinary proceedings and those responsible for deciding whether action would be taken, the latter task being that of a separate Enforcement Committee.[78] There is also a full appeal on the merits to the Financial Services and Markets Tribunal, with a further right of appeal on point of law to the courts.[79] Indeed, in the case of the market abuse provisions, it was accepted that there was a real possibility that these would be treated as imposing criminal liability and further procedural protections have been provided, such as the right to apply for legal assistance.[80] It remains to be seen whether other regulatory procedures, designed before the HRA, will be so compliant; examples of possible problems will be where the regulatory bodies have power to take enforcement action or to impose financial penalties on those regulated directly without full due process rights, including an independent element, as in the case of the Independent Television Commission and the utility regulators. The chief question at issue will be whether the right to apply to the courts to challenge such actions is sufficient to correct any lack of due process at the regulatory level.[81]

The other Convention right which may come into play in relation to regulatory **5.34** decisions, especially those by economic regulators, is Article 1 of Protocol 1. This provides a right to the peaceful enjoyment of possessions, and deprivation of possessions must be in the public interest and subject to conditions provided by law. However, this is expressed as not in any way to impair the right of a state to enforce such laws as it deems necessary to control property in the general interest or to secure the payment of taxes or other contributions on penalties. This provision corresponds to the right to property seen in many national constitutions, and may come into play not only where a regulatory body imposes penalties, but where it withholds or imposes conditions on the grant of a licence essential to an applicant's business.[82] However, it must be stressed that there is a very extensive margin of appreciation for states to act in the public or general interest, and this is likely to mean that few challenges based on this article are successful except in cases of

---

[78] Financial Services and Markets Act 2000, s 395(2) and see Page (n 70 above) 140–142.
[79] ibid s 208(4).
[80] ibid ss 134–136. On the question of what constitutes a criminal charge, see now *R (on the application of Fleurose) v Securities and Futures Authority Ltd* [2001] EWCA Civ 2015; [2002] IRLR 297.
[81] *R (on the application of Alconbury Developments) v Secretary of State for the Environment, Transport and the Regions* [2001] UKHL 23; [2001] 2 WLR 1389; *Begum (Runa) v Tower Hamlets LBC* [2003] UKHL 5; [2003] 2 WLR 388.
[82] *Tre Traktörer Aktiebolag v Sweden* (1991) 13 EHRR 309.

an unlawful expropriation of property going well beyond normal regulatory bounds.[83]

(e) Executive self-regulation and regulatory bodies

5.35 We now move into a less well-known set of principles which may in some circumstances provide a source of agency accountability. From the 1990s we have seen in the United Kingdom the development of executive self-regulation through the statement of principles of better government.[84] The effect has been to lay down an extensive (if not always coherent or precise) procedural code for the operation of central government, and in many cases the principles will extend to regulatory bodies other than central government. This may go some way to fill the absence, noted at the outset of this chapter, of any overarching legal framework for regulatory decision-making in the United Kingdom comparable to the US Administrative Procedure Act or the French jurisprudence of *service public*. It is important to stress that in the vast majority of cases these rules have not been given force of law, for example by statute. However, it may be possible to use the developing doctrine of legitimate expectation to ensure that public bodies keep to the principles set out in the various documents, although this has been largely untried so far.[85] Moreover, we can see the beginnings of a tendency to incorporate these principles into new legislation; for example, the Financial Services and Markets Act requires the Financial Services Authority to have regard to proportionality between benefits and burdens it imposes, and the Communications Act will require the Office of Communications to have regard to the principles that its activities should be transparent, accountable, proportionate, consistent and targeted only at cases in which action is needed; it is also to publish and meet promptness standards.[86] The following sections will set out briefly the key sources of the principles of executive self-regulation which may be relevant to regulatory bodies.

(i) The Citizen's Charter and Service First

5.36 The best known source of executive self-regulation is through the Citizen's Charter, now rebranded as Service First. Although the Charter is more a move-

---

[83] *Tre Traktörer Aktiebolag v Sweden* (n 82 above), and see *Lithgow v UK* (1986) 8 EHRR 329.

[84] For an excellent summary see T Daintith and A Page, *The Executive in the Constitution: Structure, Autonomy and Internal Control* (Oxford: OUP, 1999) ch 11. A major official summary of recent developments and plans is the Cabinet Office White Paper *Modernising Government* (Cm 4310, 1999).

[85] For the doctrine of legitimate expectation see paras 16.34 et seq below; *R v North and East Devon Health Authority, ex p Coughlan* [2001] QB 213, CA and *R v North Derbyshire Health Authority, ex p Fisher* [1997] 8 Med LR 327.

[86] Financial Services and Markets Act 2000, s 2(3)(c); Communications Act 2003, ss 3(3)(a) and 8.

Deregulation (Sunday Dancing) Order 2000 allows public dances held on Sundays to charge an admission fee, and the Deregulation (Sunday Licensing) Order 2001 allows extensions to liquor licences to be granted beyond 10.30 pm on Sundays.[97] In 2002 deregulation orders included those removing the 20 member limit for partnerships and extending entitlement to the vaccine damage payments scheme.[98] A substantial number of further measures is planned in the government's Regulatory Reform Action Plan.[99] There is thus considerable scope for substantive changes to regulatory requirements through the use of delegated legislation following this special process.

(v) Model appeal provisions

Yet another outcome of the deregulation and better regulation process has been the issue of model appeal provisions which can be incorporated into enactments in relation to appeals against enforcement action in relation to any matter.[100] They provide for the appointment of a registrar and tribunal to hear appeals, and set out the procedures to be adopted, including, for example, the right to a public hearing, the right to representation and a duty to give reasons. They have been incorporated into the Chemical Weapons Act 1996 in relation to licences for the holding of toxic chemicals.[101] Although their use has been limited so far, they form a rare example of the use of formal delegated legislation to provide procedural rights within the better regulation scheme.

5.41

(vi) The Enforcement Concordat

Of more general effect than the formal rules described in the previous paragraph is the Enforcement Concordat, also published by the Regulatory Impact Unit in the Cabinet Office.[102] In familiar style, this sets out principles of good enforcement policy, comprising:

5.42

- standard setting;
- openness;
- helpfulness;
- well-publicized, effective and timely complaints procedures;
- proportionality; and
- consistency.

---

[97] SI 2000/3372 and SI 2001/920.

[98] SI 2002/3203 and SI 2002/1592.

[99] Cabinet Office, *Regulatory Reform: The Government's Action Plan* (2002), available at www.cabinet-office.gov.uk/regulation/actionplan/docs/rrap.pdf, consulted 25 February 2003.

[100] Deregulation (Model Appeal Provisions) Order 1996, SI 1996/1678.

[101] Chemical Weapons (Licence Appeal Provisions) Order 1996, SI 1996/3030.

[102] Cabinet Office, *Enforcement Concordat* (1999), available at www.cabinet-office.gov.uk/regulation/PublicSector/Enforcement/Concordate.pdf, consulted 24 February 2003.

The Concordat also promises that advice will be confirmed in writing, an opportunity to make representations will be given before action is taken except in the case of urgency where a later written explanation will be given, and that advice on appeal rights will be given.

(f) The Parliamentary Commissioner for Administration

5.43 The general work of the Commissioner, and plans for reform, are covered in chapter 21 of this work. Although it mainly covers central government departments, the jurisdiction of the Commissioner does extend to certain regulatory bodies acting at arm's length from government. There is, however, no clear principle as to which regulators should be included; it will depend on inclusion within Sch 2 of the Parliamentary Commissioner Act 1967, as extensively amended by later statutes. All the utility regulators are so included, although it must be said that so far the Commissioner has played only a minimal role in providing a remedy in relation to their actions.[103] By contrast, the Financial Services Authority is excluded, although it is under a duty to make arrangements for the investigation of complaints arising out of the exercise of its functions, including appointing an independent complaints investigator in the form of the Financial Ombudsman Service.[104]

5.44 Having noted the lack of principle in determining the scope of the powers of the Parliamentary Commissioner, it must be added that recent moves have been in the direction of increasing the range of bodies within her jurisdiction. The Parliamentary and Health Service Commissioners Act 1987 provides for the extension of the jurisdiction to include specified non-departmental public bodies; these include, for example, the Equal Opportunities Commission, the Commission for Racial Equality and the Data Protection Registrar.[105] Further extensions of jurisdiction may be made by Order in Council, although an order may only extend to bodies established by statute or delegated legislation or by a minister or government department, and which receive half their revenues from public funds and are appointed by the Crown or a minister. Such an extension of jurisdiction may not cover a body regulating a profession. In 1999 jurisdiction was further extended to cover 158 more non-departmental public bodies, including the Broadcasting Standards Commission, the Civil Aviation Authority and consumer representation bodies for the utilities; further additions have included the Competition Commission.[106] Current plans for reform of ombudsmen do not propose further changes in jurisdiction.

---

[103] See C Graham, *Regulating Public Utilities—A Constitutional Approach* (Oxford: Hart, 2000) 75–76.
[104] Financial Services and Markets Act 2000, Sch 1, para 7; see also Page (n 70 above) 147–148.
[105] Parliamentary and Health Service Commissioners Act 1987, s 1 (inserting a new s 4 into the 1967 Act) and Sch 1 (inserting a new Sch 2).
[106] Parliamentary Commissioner Order 1999, SI 1999/277; Parliamentary Commissioner (No 2) Order 1999, SI 1999/2028.

(g) Access to information

In the case of individual statutory regulators, there are in some cases provisions re-   **5.45**
lating to the publication of information, and these will be considered below.[107]

In determining the coverage of the Freedom of Information Act 2000 a similar   **5.46**
approach has been adopted to that for the jurisdiction of the Parliamentary
Commissioner. The Act lists bodies which are public authorities and so fall within
the Act; most important are those set out in Pt VI of Sch 1 which will be public
authorities so long as they are established by government and appointed by the
Crown or a minister.[108] Other bodies may be added by order provided they satisfy
these conditions. The Utilities Regulators fall within the Act as non-ministerial
government departments.[109] Other bodies listed in the Schedule include the
Competition Commission (otherwise than as an appeal tribunal), and the Health
and Safety Commission and Executive. The Financial Services Authority has now
been added.[110] Other new regulatory bodies have been added to the list by the
statute setting them up; the Security Industry Authority, the Patient Information
Advisory Group and the Central Police Training and Development Authority.[111]
In addition, companies wholly owned by the Crown or by public authorities covered by the Act are also included within its scope.

Pending the full entry into force of the Freedom of Information Act 2000 in 2005,   **5.47**
reliance will have to be placed on individual statutory provisions for each regulator
and the non-statutory Code of Practice on Access to Government Information,
which applies to bodies under the jurisdiction of the Parliamentary Commissioner.[112]

C. Agencies for Economic Regulation

(1) The General Competition Authorities: The Office of Fair Trading and the Competition Commission

(a) The Office of Fair Trading: introduction

The Director General of Fair Trading and the Office of Fair Trading were established   **5.48**
by the Fair Trading Act 1973 with a number of different consumer protection and

---

[107] See eg Utilities Act 2000, s 21, relating to the Gas and Electricity Consumers Council, and para
5.76 below.
[108] Freedom of Information Act 2000, ss 3(1), 4(2–4).
[109] ibid Sch 1, Pt I.
[110] Freedom of Information (Additional Public Authorities) Order 2003, SI 2003/1882.
[111] Private Security Industry Act 2001, Sch 1, para 23; Health and Social Care Act 2001, Sch 5,
para 18; Criminal Justice and Police Act 2001, Sch 4, para 8.
[112] Lord Chancellor's Department, *Code of Practice on Access to Government Information* (revised
edn, 1998).

competition law functions.[113] The important consumer protection functions will not be covered here, and this chapter will instead concentrate on the competition law role of the Office. This has been fundamentally transformed by the Competition Act 1998 and the Enterprise Act 2002, considerably increasing both the direct decision-making powers of the Office and its investigatory powers. Accountability has been increased through the provision of appeal on the merits to the Competition Appeal Tribunal.

5.49   The 1973 Act vested powers directly in the Director General as an officer appointed by the Secretary of State.[114] The (non-statutory) Office was established as a non-ministerial government department, thereby creating a precedent for the other economic regulators to be considered below. The Director General's functions included keeping under review commercial activities with a view to becoming aware of monopoly situations or uncompetitive practices.[115] Of much greater current importance for competition law is, however, the Competition Act 1998. This conferred on the Director General the task of enforcing the two prohibitions in the Act, of anti-competitive agreements and abuse of a dominant position. The Act did not re-establish the Director General or the Office, but did give substantially increased powers of investigation to him, as will be considered in the next section. It also created a right of appeal from his decisions under the Act to the Competition Commission.[116]

5.50   Finally, however, the Enterprise Act 2002 re-establishes the Office of Fair Trading as a new corporate authority, abolishing the office of Director General of Fair Trading and transferring his functions to the Office, with effect from 1 April 2003. The Office is a body corporate consisting of a chairman and at least four other members, though it will remain a non-ministerial government department and will act on behalf of the Crown.[117] The Office will be obliged to have regard 'in addition to any relevant general guidance as to the governance of public bodies, to such generally accepted principles of good corporate governance as it is reasonable to regard as applicable . . .'.[118] It must also publish an annual plan setting out its main objectives and priorities for the year ahead, after consultation; the plan will be laid before Parliament.[119]

---

[113] For details of the establishment of the institutions see Ramsay (n 13 above). The Office's website is at www.oft.gov.uk.

[114] Fair Trading Act 1943, s 1 and Sch 1.

[115] ibid s 2(2).

[116] Competition Act 1998, s 46.

[117] Enterprise Act 2002, ss 1–2 and Sch 1.

[118] ibid s 1(4).

[119] ibid s 3.

(b) The Office of Fair Trading: investigatory powers

The investigatory powers of the Director General in competition matters were   **5.51**
considerably strengthened by the 1998 Act, and these powers will be transferred
to the new corporate Office of Fair Trading.[120] The Director General has produced
guidelines on the use of his investigatory powers.[121] The 1998 Act also widens
powers of investigation at the request of the European Commission in relation to
alleged breaches of Community law.[122]

In investigating an alleged breach of either of the Act's prohibitions, the Office has   **5.52**
power to require the production of specified documents or any other specified
information which it considers relevant to the conduct of the investigation; this
has been interpreted as including requiring the compilation of information not
yet in recorded form, for example relating to market share.[123] This requirement
to produce documents does not, however, apply to documents covered by legal
professional privilege, although confidentiality is not as such a ground for non-
disclosure.[124] The Director General has recognized that the EC law jurisprudence
on self-incrimination may also limit the extent to which information which might
involve the admission of an infringement can be required.[125]

In addition, the Office has, under the 1998 Act, new powers of entry to premises,   **5.53**
either with or without a warrant. Thus any authorized officer of the Office may
enter premises in connection with an investigation into the two prohibitions; two
days' notice must be given unless he reasonably suspects that the premises are occupied by a party in breach of one of the prohibitions.[126] The officer may require
information to be given and may take copies of documents; information held on
computer may be required in a 'visible and legible' form.[127] These provisions thus
permit 'dawn raids' of a kind familiar from European competition law enforcement.

With a High Court warrant, entry is permitted where there are reasonable   **5.54**
grounds to believe that documents required have not been produced, where
there is a suspicion that documents will be concealed, removed, tampered with

---

[120] For a detailed analysis of these powers see Iain MacNeil, 'Investigations Under the
Competition Act 1998' in B Rodger and A MacCulloch, *The UK Competition Act: A New Era for UK
Competition Law* (Oxford: Hart, 2000).
[121] Office of Fair Trading Guideline 404, *Powers of Investigation*.
[122] Competition Act 1998, ss 63–65.
[123] ibid s 26 and MacNeil (n 120 above) 80. For powers to obtain information in relation to
merger and market investigations, see Enterprise Act 2002, ss 109, 174.
[124] ibid s 30.
[125] *Powers of Investigation* (n 121 above) paras 6.3–6.4, citing Case 374/87 *Orkem v Commission*
[1989] ECR 3283, but cf MacNeil (n 120 above) 86–89.
[126] Competition Act 1998, s 27(1)–(2).
[127] ibid s 27(5).

or destroyed, or where it has not been possible to secure authorized entry without a warrant.[128]

5.55 Failure to comply with these requirements is an offence under the Act; it is also an offence to destroy or falsify documents.[129] Penalties include an unlimited fine and, in certain circumstances, up to two years' imprisonment.[130]

5.56 These are thus substantial powers for use in the conduct of investigations under the 1998 Act. It should also be added that the Office acquired under the Act substantial powers to impose penalties on companies in breach of the prohibitions. Thus as well as having power to order an infringement of the Act to be brought to an end, the Director General may impose a penalty of up to 10 per cent of the turnover of the company.[131] In marked contrast to the position before the passing of the 1998 Act, interim measures may also be issued.[132] The Enterprise Act 2002 goes even further than the 1998 Act, imposing criminal penalties for participation in cartels, the Office of Fair Trading having power to institute proceedings.[133] For this purpose it also extends investigatory powers, including giving the Office the power to require persons under investigation to answer questions, although the answers cannot be used directly as evidence in a cartel offence prosecution.[134] The Office also acquires access to surveillance powers under the Regulation of Investigatory Powers Act 2000, thus permitting, for example, the use of surveillance devices in residential premises (including hotels) and private vehicles.[135] Finally, the Enterprise Act gives the Office of Fair Trading new powers to apply to the court for an order disqualifying a person from serving as a company director.[136]

(c) The Competition Commission: introduction

5.57 The Competition Commission has a long history, in the form of the Monopolies and Mergers Commission, as the central investigatory body in UK competition law.[137] In this role it was notable for two characteristics; its role was essentially advisory, with decisions being taken by the Secretary of State who was partially free not to follow its advice, and the avoidance of anything resembling legal formality

---

[128] Competition Act 1998, s 28(1).
[129] ibid ss 42–43.
[130] For details see *Powers of Investigation* (n 121 above) para 7.7.
[131] Competition Act 1998, ss 32, 33, 36. Once more detailed guidelines have been issued here; OFT Guideline 423, *Guidance on the Appropriate Amount of a Penalty*.
[132] ibid s 35.
[133] Enterprise Act, Pt 6.
[134] ibid ss 193(1), 197.
[135] Regulation of Investigatory Powers Act 2000, s 199.
[136] Enterprise Act 2002, s 204.
[137] For an excellent detailed account see the official history, S Wilks, *In the Public Interest: Competition Policy and the Monopolies and Mergers Commission* (Manchester: Manchester University Press, 1999). The Commission's website is at www.competition-commission.org.uk.

in its procedures. Both these characteristics have been fundamentally changed as a result of the Competition Act 1998, with further changes made by the Enterprise Act 2002.

After the 1998 Act the Commission had two very different roles. The first is the **5.58** older one of being an investigative body through its reporting panel. This involved monopoly references under the Fair Trading Act 1973, merger control under the same Act, licence modification references from the utility regulators and (rare) efficiency audits of public sector organizations under the Competition Act 1980. The first two areas are, however, now substantially changed by the Enterprise Act, which replaces the monopolies regime with market investigation references based on a competition-oriented test and gives the Commission its own remedial powers; similar provision is made for mergers.[138] The role of the Commission under the 1998 Act was fundamentally different from its previous functions as it acted as an appellate authority from decisions of the Director General of Fair Trading in relation to breach of the Act's prohibitions. Thus a separate Appeal Tribunal system was established within the Commission; it is replaced by an independent Competition Appeal Tribunal under the Enterprise Act.[139] The reforms will lead to a considerable increase in the legal formality of competition procedures and substantive decisions.

(d) The Competition Commission: procedures

The Competition Commission itself was established by the 1998 Act and assumed **5.59** the functions of the former Monopolies and Mergers Commission as well as the new ones conferred by the Act.[140] In its reporting functions, little change was made to procedures which remain essentially investigatory and discretionary; the Commission was given power to determine its own procedure subject to directions from the Secretary of State (which have never been given).[141] The Commission has proceeded through gathering information by means of written questionnaires and holding public interest hearings, which are however held in private and which are non-competitive in the sense that they take place in the absence of other parties. The Commission has experimented with the use of public hearings in some recent cases, and the *Interbrew* decision[142] represented the first loss of a judicial review case in the Commission's history, for failure to raise with a party a remedy which it was considering. One can thus expect a more legally-shaped procedure to be adopted in future on the reporting side, and this is reinforced by the Enterprise Act which

---

[138] Enterprise Act 2002, Pts 3 and 4.
[139] ibid Pt 2 and Sch 2.
[140] Competition Act 1998, s 45(1).
[141] Fair Trading Act 1973, ss 81(2)–(3).
[142] *Interbrew SA v Competition Commission* [2001] EWHC Admin 367; [2001] UKCLR 954, QBD

requires the publication of procedural rules for reporting cases.[143] In addition, in a most important change, the Competition Appeal Tribunal will be able to review (on the same grounds as in judicial review) decisions by the Office of Fair Trading, Competition Commission or Secretary of State in relation to mergers or market investigations.[144] No doubt reflecting the role of the ECHR, we thus see a very marked move towards procedural fairness and judicial scrutiny in relation to the Commission's procedures.

(e) Competition appeals

5.60   The major institutional innovation introduced by the Competition Act 1998 was to give the Competition Commission a new role as an appellate body in relation to decisions by the Director General of Fair Trading on breaches of the Act's prohibitions. This, together with the creation of a right of appeal on point of law with leave from the Commission's appellate decisions to the Court of Appeal, represents a radical change from the traditional model of political responsibility for competition policy towards a more judicialized model.

5.61   The appeal provisions are set out in ss 46–49 of the Competition Act, and are supplemented by detailed Competition Appeal Tribunal Rules.[145] An appeal may be made against any decision relating to breach of one of the Act's prohibitions, to the granting of exemptions or the imposition or amount of any penalty imposed.[146] Unusually, provision is also made for third party appeals by a party with a sufficient interest, or a body representing such persons.[147]

5.62   The Act provided for the setting up of appeal tribunals to hear appeals under it.[148] The appellate system is headed by the President of the Appeal Tribunals; the first President is Sir Christopher Bellamy QC, former judge of the Court of First Instance of the European Communities, and he is responsible for constituting each tribunal. The tribunal rules stress the importance of active case management and exchange of information before the oral hearing, which is to be kept as short as possible and in which the tribunal is to 'seek to avoid formality'; the hearing is to be in public unless the tribunal is satisfied that confidential information is to be considered.[149]

5.63   Soon after the Act came into effect in March 2000 a number of important decisions were taken by the Tribunal, most notably granting interim relief pending an

---

[143] Enterprise Act 2002, s 187 and Sch 12.
[144] ibid ss 120 and 179.
[145] SI 2003/1372. The Commission has also issued *A Guide to Appeals Under the Competition Act 1998* (2000).
[146] Competition Act 1998, s 46.
[147] ibid s 47, as amended and simplified by Enterprise Act 2002, s 17.
[148] ibid s 48, now replaced by Enterprise Act 2002, Pt 2.
[149] rr 50–51.

appeal,[150] reducing fines imposed by the Director General,[151] setting aside the Director General's analysis of the product market on which his decision had been based,[152] and deciding that in certain circumstances a decision by the Director General of Fair Trading not to pursue a complaint was appealable to the Tribunal.[153] A further important substantive decision overturned the Director-General's decision that purchasing by public bodies was not covered by the Act's prohibition on abuse of a dominant position.[154]

Once more the appeal arrangements are subject to changes in the Enterprise Act. Apart from the new appeal on judicial review grounds in market investigation and merger cases referred to above, the Act creates a new Competition Appeal Tribunal independent of the Competition Commission and includes procedural rules for it. New provision is made for third party appeals, and, most unusually, claims for damages will be permitted before the Tribunal where a breach of competition law has been established, including representative claims by consumer groups.[155] A new Competition Service is also established to support the Appeal Tribunal.[156]   **5.64**

(2) The Utility Regulators

(a) Privatization and regulation

The United Kingdom was a pioneer in privatizing public utilities, and this led to the necessity of creating new regulatory institutions for them; as mentioned above, the key examples are the Director General of Telecommunications and the Office of Telecommunications (OFTEL), the Gas and Electricity Markets Authority and the Office of Gas and Electricity Markets (OFGEM), the Director General of Water Services and the Office of Water Services (OFWAT), the Rail Regulator and the Office of the Rail Regulator (ORR) and (regulating a public enterprise) the Postal Services Commission (POSTCOMM). In addition, the Civil Aviation Authority was given powers of economic regulation over major airports and (later) air traffic control. The model used for the new bodies was that of the Office of Fair Trading; thus they take the form of non-ministerial government departments and powers were vested in an individual Director General, although in the cases of gas and electricity and of postal services a commission model has now been preferred. Appointment is by the relevant minister for a five-year period, and removal is possible only   **5.65**

---

[150] *Napp Pharmaceuticals v Director General of Fair Trading* [2001] CAT 1.
[151] *Napp Pharmaceuticals v Director General of Fair Trading* [2002] CAT 1.
[152] *Aberdeen Journals Ltd v Director General of Fair Trading* [2002] CAT 4.
[153] *Bettercare Group Ltd v Director General of Fair Trading* [2002] CAT 6.
[154] *Bettercare Group Ltd v Director General of Fair Trading* [2002] CAT 7.
[155] Enterprise Act 2002, ss 17, 18–19.
[156] ibid s 13.

on the ground of incapacity or misbehaviour, thereby preventing dismissal on grounds of policy difference from the government.[157] Initially, at least in the areas where competition was seen as possible in the future, the regulators were viewed as temporary institutions; however, they have rapidly acquired a range of regulatory responsibilities, social as well as economic, and now seem a permanent presence.[158]

5.66   The tasks of the regulators have been varied, but can be summed up as enforcing the licences under which utility enterprises operate, modifying the licences and protecting consumers. These will be described in more detail below, but it should be noted that the initial licences were granted not by the regulators but by the government, and modification (which includes the all-important setting of price controls) may only take place with the consent of the regulated enterprise or after a reference to the Competition Commission. Further tasks include setting service standards for regulated enterprises[159] and resolving certain individual grievances, for example in relation to billing.[160]

(b) The original model of regulator

5.67   As will be apparent already, there was an initial model of regulator which has been subject to some change in more recent examples. It is still the model for water, although the latter may also be changed by the Water Bill published in spring 2003. A similar model was adopted for the Rail Regulator also, although his duties have been different in a number of respects due to the complexity of the privatized rail industry; for example, he works alongside another regulator in the form initially of the Franchising Director and then of the Strategic Rail Authority. This is also subject to change under the Railways and Transport Safety Act 2003.

5.68   The initial model involved vesting legal powers in the Director General who was subject to a number of complex and potentially conflicting duties. Thus, for example, under the Telecommunications Act 1984 two primary duties were imposed; to ensure that, so far as practicable, telecommunications services are provided throughout the United Kingdom which satisfy all reasonable demands and to ensure that providers of telecommunications services are able to finance them.[161] Secondary duties included the promotion of the interests of consumers and the maintenance and promotion of effective competition.[162] In later statutes

---

[157] See Telecommunications Act 1984, s 1(3); Utilities Act 2000, Sch 1, para 3(2); Water Industry Act 1991, s 1(4); Railways Act 1993, s 1(3); Postal Services Act 2000, Sch 1, para 2(3).

[158] For the most influential initial statement of regulatory philosophy see S Littlechild, *Regulation of British Telecommunications Profitability* (London: Department of Industry, 1983) and for the development of the regulators and their tasks see Prosser (n 7 above).

[159] See Competition and Service (Utilities) Act 1992, and Utilities Act 2000, ss 54–58, 89–94.

[160] See eg Telecommunications Act 1984, s 27G.

[161] ibid ss 3(1)(a)–(b).

[162] ibid ss 3(2)(a)–(b).

protecting the interests of consumers in rural areas and of pensioners were added as secondary duties.[163]

Varied patterns of consumer protection were also adopted in each case. For tele-   **5.69**
communications, the regulator was advised by six advisory committees on telecommunications and a network of some 160 local advisory committees. For gas, a separate Gas Consumers Council was established by statute, whilst for water the Director General established customer service committees under statutory powers, of which he appointed the members, also establishing a non-statutory National Consumer Council. For electricity the arrangements were similar to water, although the national council had a statutory base, and for rail, statutory regional and national committees were established; a statutory consumer protection body was also established for postal services. This apparent uncertainty as to how best to protect consumers has been partially remedied in the more recent model to be discussed below.

Finally, procedural duties were crude or non-existent in this early model. Most   **5.70**
notably, when the all-important licence amendments were made (including modification of price controls), where the amendment was made with the agreement of the regulated company (as in the vast majority of cases), all that was required was that notice of the proposed modification and reasons for it be published, and at least 28 days allowed for representations to be made.[164] This permitted the modification to be agreed as a fait accompli with the regulated company, with merely limited consultation after the event. In practice the regulators, in particular the Director General of Telecommunications, went far beyond this in their consultative procedures, but the legal requirements remained very weak.[165] It should be added that the enforcement powers of the regulators were also weak; for example, they were not able to impose fines on regulated enterprises but merely to make provisional and final orders to remedy breaches of a licence, breach of a final order creating civil liability to third parties.[166] This gap was partially remedied by later legislation, for example giving the power to require compensation for breach of services standards and giving the Rail Regulator the power to impose financial penalties of up to 10 per cent of turnover.[167]

---

[163] See eg Water Industry Act 1991, ss 2(3)(a)(i), 2(4).
[164] See eg Telecommunications Act 1984, s 12(2).
[165] For details of practice see Prosser (n 7 above) 83–86.
[166] See eg Telecommunications Act 1984, ss 16, 18(6).
[167] Competition and Service (Utilities) Act 1992, s 1, inserting a new s 27A(4) into the Telecommunications Act 1984; Transport Act 2000, s 225, inserting a new s 57A into the Railways Act 1993. See also para 5.77 below.

(c) The new regulatory model

5.71   In the more recent legislation establishing or modifying regulatory arrangements a different model has been adopted, one which owes its origins to the government's review of utilities regulation carried out in 1998.[168] The most developed example can be found in the Utilities Act 2000 establishing new arrangements for gas and electricity regulation, but in modified form it can also be found in the Postal Services Act 2000. The Communications Act 2003 creates a new Office of Communications in commission form for both telecommunications and broadcasting; a similar move to commissions is proposed also in the Water Bill (a Water Services Regulation Authority) and the Railways and Transport Safety Act (a corporate Office of Rail Regulation).

5.72   The first major difference is that regulatory powers are vested in a commission rather than in an individual director general.[169] Thus the Utilities Act establishes a new body corporate, the Gas and Electricity Markets Authority, to take over the powers formerly exercised by the Directors General of Gas Supply and of Electricity Supply. It is to consist of a chairman and at least two other members, appointed by the Secretary of State under similar terms to those of the Directors General.[170] OFGEM remains as a non-ministerial government department to assist the Commission.

5.73   The second major change is the clarification of the key duties applying to the new regulatory bodies. Gas and electricity are dealt with separately in the Utilities Act, but in both cases there is a new primary duty to protect the interests of consumers, wherever possible by promoting effective competition. The regulatory body is also to have regard to a number of secondary duties, including securing that all reasonable demands are met, that licence holders are able to finance their activities, and that it takes into account the interests of the disabled, the chronically sick, pensioners, those on low incomes and those in rural areas.[171] The duty is somewhat different for postal services, where the primary duty of the Commission is to secure the provision of a universal postal service and furthering the interests of users is made subject to this.[172]

---

[168] DTI, *A Fair Deal for Consumers: Modernising the Framework for Utility Regulation* (Cm 3898, 1998); *A Fair Deal for Consumers: The Response to Consultation* (1998).

[169] The Civil Aviation Authority, responsible for regulating airports and air traffic control, has always taken the form of a commission. However, its legal duties and procedures remain closer to those of the original regulatory model, with some differences such as a compulsory reference to the Competition Commission in setting airport charges. See Airports Act 1986, Pt IV and Transport Act 2000, Pt I.

[170] Utilities Act 2000, s 1 and Sch 1. See also Postal Services Act 2000, s 1 and Sch 1.

[171] Utilities Act 2000, s 9 (inserting a new s 4AA into the Gas Act 1996) and s 13 (inserting a new s 3A into the Electricity Act 1989).

[172] Postal Services Act 2000, ss 4–5.

A further development is the inclusion in the new model of a power for the   **5.74**
Secretary of State to issue guidance on social and environmental matters to which
the regulatory body must have regard.[173] This guidance is subject to the negative
resolution procedure in the House of Commons, and the intention is to separate
more clearly the economic duties of the regulator and the social duties to be imposed by ministers after a democratic process, an issue which had caused problems
in the earlier model of regulation. According to the government, it was not intended to use this model to impose financial burdens on the regulated industries.[174] Guidance has now been issued.[175] Similar arrangements apply in relation
to the Postal Services Commission, and here guidance has also been issued.[176]

The third major change in the new model is the adoption of a system of consumer   **5.75**
protection through the establishment of bodies independent of the regulator on a
statutory basis. Thus the Utilities Act provides for a new Gas and Electricity
Consumer Council (in practice known as Energywatch). It does not have Crown
status but is appointed by the Secretary of State, consisting of a chairman and at
least two other members.[177] Detailed provision for its functions is made in the
Act; these include obtaining and keeping under review information on consumer
matters, provision of information to public authorities and consumers, dealing
with consumer complaints and investigating other matters relating to the interests of consumers.[178] Similar provision is made in the Postal Services Act for the
establishment and functions of the Consumer Council for Postal Services
(Postwatch).[179]

A further distinction from the earlier regulatory model is a degree of procedural   **5.76**
sophistication in the design of the new institutions. The limited requirements of
transparency on the part of the early utility regulators were mentioned above.
Under the Utilities Act, this is partially remedied. For example, the new Authority
is under a duty to publish a forward work programme annually after public consultation; it is also under a duty to give reasons for a wide range of decisions, including revocation and modification of licences and enforcement action.[180]
Further powers are given to the consumer council to acquire information and to

---

[173] Utilities Act 2000, s 10 (inserting a new s 4AB into the Gas Act 1986) and s 14 (inserting a new
s 3B into the Electricity Act 1989). It should be added that the position of the Rail Regulator has
been somewhat special in this regard; he was originally subject to a temporary duty to have regard to
guidance from the Secretary of State; this was reintroduced as a permanent duty by Transport Act
2000, s 224(6).
[174] *A Fair Deal for Consumers: Response to Consultation* (n 168 above) para 14.
[175] DTI, *Social and Environmental Guidance to the Gas and Electricity Markets Authority* (2002).
[176] Postal Services Act, s 42; DTI, *Social and Environmental Guidance to the Postal Services
Commission* (2001).
[177] Utilities Act 2000, s 2, Sch 2.
[178] ibid ss 17–27.
[179] Postal Services Act 2000, ss 2, 51–58 and Sch 2.
[180] Utilities Act 2000, ss 4, 42, 87.

publish it.[181] These provisions are not emulated in the Postal Services Act with the exception of those relating to the provision of information.[182]

5.77 Finally, important modifications have been made to strengthen enforcement powers of the regulator under the new model. Thus the Utilities Act 2000 provides new powers for the Commission to impose financial penalties for breach of licence conditions or failure to achieve service standards; these are limited to 10 per cent of turnover and they must be reasonable in all the circumstances.[183] Appeal against penalties and their amount lie to the High Court on grounds similar to those in judicial review.[184] Similar provisions are set out in the Postal Services Act.[185]

(d) Concurrent powers under the Competition Act 1998

5.78 One role for the utility regulators of growing importance has been to act as specialist competition authorities in their sectors. This was hampered by fragmented powers under individual licences to take action, and a major reform was made by the Competition Act 1998 which gave them concurrent powers to enforce the Act's prohibitions of anti-competitive agreements and abuse of a dominant position.[186] The powers were conferred on the Directors General of Telecommunications, of Gas and Electricity Supply (and their successor Authority), of Water Services and the Rail Regulator, though not on the Postal Services Commission. The Act also gives the utility regulators in exercising these powers the wider investigative rights conferred on the Director General of Fair Trading under the Act and discussed above; appeal against a prohibition decision or a penalty lies to the Competition Appeal Tribunal. Regulations have been made permitting exchange of information between the regulators and with the Director General of Fair Trading and to avoid double jeopardy by setting out the arrangements for the division of responsibilities between the regulators and the general competition authorities.[187] The Enterprise Act 2002 also gives the sectoral regulators power to undertake market investigations under its provisions, as well as concurrent powers to apply for director disqualification

---

[181] Utilities Act 2000, ss 24–27 and see Utilities Act 2000 (Supply of Information) Regulations 2000, SI 2000/2956.

[182] Postal Services Act 2000, s 58. On the power of the Postal Services Commission to require the provision of information see ss 47–50; for the powers relating to other utility regulators see eg Electricity Act 1989 s 28, as amended by Utilities Act 2000, Sch 6. This is supplemented by provisions contained in individual licences.

[183] Utilities Act 2000, s 59, adding new ss 27A–F to the Electricity Act 1989; s 95, adding new ss 30A–F to the Gas Act 1986.

[184] ibid new ss 27E and 30E.

[185] Postal Services Act 2000, ss 30–37.

[186] Competition Act 1998, s 54 and Sch 10; for background and details see T Prosser, 'Competition, Regulators and Public Service' in Rodger and MacCulloch (n 120 above) 225. The Civil Aviation Authority later acquired concurrent powers for use in the regulation of air traffic control services: Transport Act 2000, Sch 8, para 14.

[187] Competition Act 1998 (Concurrency) Regulations 2000, SI 2000/260; see also Office of Fair Trading, *Concurrent Application to the Regulated Industries* (OFT 405).

and, when the Secretary of State has made the appropriate order, to investigate 'super-complaints' by designated consumer bodies.[188]

(e) Challenging decisions of the utility regulators

On the earlier model of utility regulator described above, challenge of decisions was **5.79** by judicial review, and the statutes establishing them set out certain procedural provisions affecting this, for example replicating the provisions more usually seen in land-use planning law providing a statutory right of review within 42 days and then that the validity of a final or provisional order 'shall not be questioned in any legal proceedings whatsoever'.[189] As described above,[190] in most cases judicial review has been relatively unintrusive and concerned with general principle rather than intervening on matters close to the merits of the case. Statutory appeal rights were remarkable by their absence. Although the power of the regulated industry to force a reference of a licence amendment which it refuses to accept to the Competition Commission is sometimes referred to as an appeal right, it is really sui generis, applying as it does to only one party and permitting the Commission to undertake a more general inquiry than one simply limited to the dispute in question.

As a more sophisticated model of regulation has developed, there has been some in- **5.80** crease in the availability of appeal rights. Thus in telecommunications licensing (including licence modification) a wider appeal right to the High Court was introduced as a result of the requirements of European law.[191] A right of appeal on the merits in telecommunications matters to the Competition Appeal Tribunal is now provided by the Communications Act.[192] As we have seen, the concurrent powers under the 1998 Act attract a right of appeal on the merits to the Competition Commission Appeal Tribunal. However other regulatory decisions can still be challenged only through judicial review, for example licence modification decisions by the regulators or by the Competition Commission after a reference from a utility regulator, and this is not due to change under the Enterprise Act.

(3) The Financial Services Authority

(a) Introduction and the nature of the Authority

If we have seen gradual development of procedural rights and more sophisticated **5.81** legal and institutional design in the cases of the competition authorities and of the

---

[188] Enterprise Act 2000, Sch 9, Pt 2; ss 204–205.
[189] eg Telecommunications Act 1984, s 18(1)–(3). For the effect of such a provision see *R v Secretary of State for the Environment, ex p Ostler* [1977] QB 122.
[190] See paras 5.24–5.26 above.
[191] Telecommunications (Appeals) Regulations 1999, SI 1999/3180, inserting a new s 46B into the Telecommunications Act 1984; see also the Electronic Communications Act 2000, s 12.
[192] ss 192–196.

utility regulators, the Financial Services Authority gives us an example of more radical change and far more highly developed procedures both in rule-making and in adjudication. This is no doubt due to the problems encountered with earlier models of self-regulation which failed to provide public reassurance as to the trustworthiness of the industry, to avoid major financial scandals such as that surrounding pensions mis-selling, or to incorporate adequate procedural protections for those affected. In this section I shall not deal with the complex substantive law of financial services but shall merely give a brief overview of the institutional arrangements and the procedures required under the Financial Services and Markets Act 2000.[193]

5.82 As mentioned earlier, the Financial Services Authority has the status of a company limited by guarantee under the Companies Act 1985. However, it is subject to much greater legal control than any other regulatory body discussed here. To quote the leading commentator on its work:

> In the arrangements that have emerged one can discern the outlines of an alternative model or theory of regulatory accountability, one that is not over-reliant on fictions about ministerial responsibility. Key elements of that model include the FSA's statutory objectives, which provide the basis for a 'positive' system of accountability, due process and oversight.[194]

5.83 To commence with the system of statutory objectives, the Financial Services and Markets Act 2000 sets out four regulatory objectives of market confidence, public awareness, the protection of consumers and the reduction of financial crime, and these are further defined in subsequent sections.[195] In addition, the Act establishes seven regulatory principles to which the Authority is to have regard; these include the economic and efficient use of resources, proportionality of restrictions imposed to the resulting benefits, and the need to minimize adverse effects on competition.[196] This statutory statement of the objectives of the authority did not appear in earlier financial services regulation and goes far beyond anything attempted for utilities regulation, even under the more recent model.

(b) The Financial Services Authority's procedures

(i) Rule-making

5.84 In addition, far more attention has been paid to creating a consultative structure for rule-making by the Authority than was the case for other regulatory bodies described earlier.[197] Thus when the Authority proposes to make any rules, it must

---

[193] For more detailed discussion see the essays in Ferran and Goodhart (n 70 above). The Authority's website is www.fsa.gov.uk.
[194] Page (n 70 above)128.
[195] Financial Services and Markets Act 2000, ss 2(2), 3–6.
[196] ibid s 2(3).
[197] For fuller details of the Authority's rule-making powers see Page (n 70 above)137–140.

first publish a draft accompanied by a cost benefit analysis and an explanation of the purpose of the proposed rules and must invite representations on them.[198] When the rules are published the Authority must also publish a general account of the representations received and its response to them; differences from the initial draft rules must be justified by cost benefit analysis.[199] Again we see here a move toward much more legally demanding procedures for rule-making which, in the case of the utility regulators, had been left to the discretion of individual Directors General. In addition to these general requirements, the Authority is obliged to maintain effective arrangements for consulting practitioners and consumers on the extent to which its general policies and practices are consistent with its general duties, and to establish, and to consider representations by, a Practitioner Panel and a Consumer Panel to represent those interests.[200] Membership is selected by the Authority, although Treasury consent is necessary for the dismissal of a Panel chairman.[201]

(ii) Adjudication

Much more structured arrangements are also provided for adjudication than has been the case for earlier regulatory bodies.[202] Thus in disciplinary and enforcement decisions, a separation is required between investigation and recommending disciplinary proceedings, and the actual decision whether to impose a penalty; the Act requires that a decision to issue a notice 'is taken by a person not directly involved in establishing the evidence on which that decision is based'.[203] Thus the decisions on such action are taken by a separate Enforcement Committee appointed by the Authority but with only the Chairman being an Authority employee, and various procedural rights are available in relation to the taking of disciplinary decisions, for example the rights to make representations, to have access to material relied on by the Authority and to reasons.[204] A full appeal right on the merits exists to the Financial Services and Markets Appeals Tribunal with further appeal on point of law to the Court of Appeal.[205] Appeal also lies to the tribunal in relation to proceedings taken for market abuse, which may result in fines. Unusually, but (as with so many other procedural requirements here) reflecting ECHR concerns, the Act empowers the Lord Chancellor to establish a legal assistance scheme for proceedings before the tribunal in these cases and there are limits

5.85

---

[198] Financial Services and Markets Act 2000 s 155(1)–(2).
[199] ibid s 155(5)–(6).
[200] ibid ss 8–11.
[201] ibid ss 9(3), 10(3).
[202] For fuller details see Page (n 70 above) 140–144.
[203] Financial Services and Markets Act 2000 s 395(2).
[204] ibid ss 387(2), 394, 388(1).
[205] ibid s 208(4), 137, 133(4).

on the admissibility of evidence which may be in breach of the rule against self-incrimination.[206]

5.86 It will be apparent, then, from this brief survey of the Financial Services Authority and its procedures, that we have here a far more sophisticated form of regulatory institution than those discussed earlier. The reasons for this are various; the lack of success of earlier attempts at self-regulation which proved both ineffective and without providing the benefits of flexibility which self-regulation is supposed to offer; an area of regulation in which litigation is more frequent than in, for example, utility regulation, and the all-powerful effect of the ECHR, especially given the uncertainty about whether some exercises of power by the Authority may amount to the determination of criminal charges.[207] What will be important over the next few years will be the extent to which these influences result in regulatory reforms elsewhere reflecting the Financial Services Authority model; experience of the interpretation of the human rights requirements by the UK courts so far suggests that there will be reluctance to require a major reassessment of other regulatory institutions on the basis of the procedural requirements of the Convention.[208]

D. Agencies for Non-Economic Regulation

5.87 The agencies discussed above have all been concerned with economic regulation as their main task; with maintaining open markets in the case of the competition authorities, with regulating monopoly and opening markets in the case of the utility regulators, and with consumer protection and maintaining the integrity of markets in the case of the Financial Services Authority. The regulatory bodies to be described in this section have a different focus. Although some of their tasks are economic, they are also responsible for implementing social policies; diversity and quality of content in broadcasting and the protection of health and safety.

(1) The Regulation of Broadcasting

5.88 Although the role of the marketplace in broadcasting is increasing rapidly with the growth in the number of channels available and the convergence of broadcasting with other media, there is still a commitment by government to maintain public

---

[206] Financial Services and Markets Act 2000, ss 134–6, 174 and see *Saunders v UK* (1997) 23 EHRR 313. For the scope of criminal charges in the context of disciplinary proceedings see *R (on the application of Fleurose) v Securities and Futures Authority* [2001] EWCA Civ 2015; [2002] IRLR 297.

[207] For more details of this human rights background see Waters and Hopper (n 72 above).

[208] See in particular *R (on the application of Alconbury Developments) v Secretary of State for the Environment, Transport and the Regions* [2001] UKHL 23; [2001] 2 WLR 1389.

service broadcasting alongside the market system.[209] In the United Kingdom this has been done in two ways; by the special role of the BBC as a distinctive public service broadcaster and by imposing statutory public service requirements on private broadcasters (including the special remit of Channel 4[210]), currently administered by the Independent Broadcasting Commission. These requirements have taken two forms. The first is that of 'positive' programming requirements seeking to secure high quality and diverse programming, for example by requiring programming to inform and educate as well as to entertain and to cover a wide range of subject matter in order to meet all interests in the population. The second comprises 'negative' requirements to prevent too graphic a portrayal of sex and violence and to ensure that audiences are not misled by advertising. It should be added that broadcasting regulation is subject to major reform under the Communications Act 2003, and this forms part of a general process of lifting regulatory constraints on private broadcasters.[211]

(a) The BBC

Regulation of the BBC is quite different from any of the earlier examples discussed in this chapter, and in some ways falls closer to private self-regulation than to the statutory regulation applying to private broadcasters. It was founded not by statute but by a Royal Charter as a Corporation of 12 governors appointed by the Queen in Council for a period of five years. The governors are trustees for the public interest through ensuring that the terms of Charter and other obligations are fulfilled whilst the management of the Corporation is left to the Director General and the Board of Management. The separation of regulatory and operational functions is thus by no means as clear as in other areas discussed in this chapter, including private broadcasting; this affects both the public service regulation discussed in this section and the supervision of the BBC's fair trading policies designed to avoid unfair competition.[212]

5.89

The Charter requires the BBC to provide broadcasting services 'as public services' and programmes of information, education and entertainment.[213] The major regulatory provisions are however contained in the Agreement between the Corporation and the Secretary of State, in which the former undertakes to maintain 'high general standards in all respects (and in particular in respect of their content, quality and editorial integrity' and to offer a wide range of subject

5.90

---

[209] See Department for Culture, Media and Sport and DTI, *A New Future for Communications* (Cm 5010, 2000) ch 5.

[210] Broadcasting Act 1990, s 25.

[211] For an excellent overview of broadcasting regulation see T Gibbons, *Regulating the Media* (2nd edn, London: Sweet & Maxwell, 1998).

[212] See G Born and T Prosser, 'Culture and Consumerism: Citizenship, Public Service Broadcasting and the BBC's Fair Trading Obligations' (2001) 64 MLR 657.

[213] Department of National Heritage, *Copy of Royal Charter* (n 30 above) Art 3(a).

matter.[214] Further requirements are imposed, inter alia, of due accuracy and impartiality in relation to controversial subjects and prohibiting offence to good taste and decency.[215]

5.91   There are strong reasons for doubting the adequacy of such a non-statutory basis for the regulation of a public service. First, due to the peculiar legal device of using an agreement between the Corporation and the Secretary of State, there has been legal doubt as to the enforceability of the undertakings made in it by anyone other than the government, and in particular, about the availability of judicial review in relation to such breach.[216] The strengthening of the Agreement in 1996 to impose requirements closer to those applying to private broadcasters, and the developing doctrine of legitimate expectation, now make it highly likely that the BBC is now subject to such enforceable obligations. However, a second problem is that the Charter may be revoked by the Crown where it appears to the Secretary of State that there is reasonable ground to believe that any of the provisions in it have been breached. Although it is probable that the decision would be subject to judicial review as an exercise of the royal prerogative,[217] the procedural protections are minimal, consisting only of giving the BBC the opportunity to satisfy the minister that there has been no breach. Not only is this in itself unsatisfactory, but it gives the impression that the only interested parties are the Corporation and the Secretary of State rather than including the viewing public.

5.92   The most heavily debated problem, however, has concerned the regulatory role of the Board of Governors. Under the Communications Act, the new Office of Communications is to have wide-ranging regulatory responsibilities over the rest of broadcasting and telecommunications. It will have certain powers over the BBC, notably setting basic standards on matters such as taste and decency, quotas for regional and independent production, and economic regulation including fair trading. The Governors have strongly opposed any further extension of OFCOM regulation to cover the Corporation's qualitative public service remit, preferring self-regulation and retaining their role as 'trustees of the public interest'. In response to criticism of this role, internal reforms have been introduced which will clarify the distinction between the role of the Governors and that of management, and to focus the former's responsibilities on implementing public

---

[214] Department of National Heritage, *Copy of the Agreement* (n 30 above) clause 3(1).

[215] ibid clause 5(1).

[216] See R Craufurd-Smith, *Broadcasting Law and Fundamental Rights* (Oxford: OUP, 1997) 73–78 and *Houston v BBC* 1995 SLT 1305, which does not provide a definitive answer either way. Provisions of the agreement were however accepted as sufficient to comply with the requirement that restrictions on freedom of expression be 'prescribed by law' under Art 10 ECHR; *R (on the application of ProLife Alliance) v BBC* [2002] EWCA Civ 297, [2002] 3 WLR 1080 at [24], [27] *per* Laws LJ, reversed on other grounds [2003] UKHL 23, [2003] 2 WLR 1403.

[217] It would appear to fall within the categories of reviewable prerogative powers set out in *Council of Civil Service Unions v Minister for the Civil Service* [1985] AC 374; see paras 1.28–1.30 above.

service priorities, including the publication of key objectives and increased transparency through the publication of annual 'Statements of Programming Policy'. There will also be more focused administrative support for the Governors.[218] It is yet to be seen whether these internal reforms will satisfy vociferous demands for more independent regulation of the BBC, emanating in particular from its private competitors.

(b) Regulating the commercial broadcasting sector

(i) *The Independent Television Commission*

Commercial broadcasting has a long history of regulation by commission, dating back to the establishment of the Independent Television Authority (later the Independent Broadcasting Authority) in 1954. The earlier institutions were seriously criticized for lack of transparency and of fair procedure.[219] The current regulatory body is the Independent Television Commission, established as a commission composed of a chairman, deputy chairman and eight to ten other members under the Broadcasting Act 1990.[220] Its functions include licensing the commercial broadcasting sector, including cable and satellite broadcasting, and enforcing quality standards and licence conditions. Both impose substantial requirements in relation to the public service broadcasters of Channels 3, 4 and 5, including positive programme requirements such as minimum percentages of original programming, of independent productions and of European programmes, although these vary from broadcaster to broadcaster. The Commission is also responsible for enforcing the currently complex rules limiting concentration of media ownership.[221] **5.93**

The Commission has an important code-making role; it is required to draw up, and from time to time review, a code of guidance on the rules relating to the inclusion of violence in programmes, on the inclusion in programmes of appeals for donations, and on other matters it considers appropriate.[222] It is also required to draw up and review a code relating to advertising and sponsorship, in this case after consulting licence holders and representatives of viewers, advertisers and professional organizations.[223] Finally, it is obliged to draw up a code relating to the preservation of due impartiality in programming.[224] The provisions of the codes are enforceable as licence conditions. Detailed codes have been issued, thereby **5.94**

---

[218] BBC, *BBC Governance in the Ofcom Age* (2002).
[219] N Lewis, 'IBA Programme Contract Awards' [1975] PL 317.
[220] Broadcasting Act 1990, s 1 and Sch 1. The website is www.itc.org.uk.
[221] Broadcasting Act 1996, Sch 2, amending Broadcasting Act 1990, Sch 2. Major change will be introduced by the Communications Bill.
[222] Broadcasting Act 1990, s 7.
[223] ibid s 9.
[224] ibid s 6(3), (5)–(7).

fleshing out the statutory obligations of the public service broadcasters.[225] The Commission has also set out guidance on its public consultation procedures for code-making and for other purposes.[226] This commits the Commission to providing cost-benefit analysis where appropriate, to giving a period of 12 weeks for responses in major and complex consultations, to the provision of the information necessary for those consulted to arrive at a view on proposals, and to publish responses on its website, allowing a further 14 days for further comments on them.

5.95 An issue of further importance is that of licence enforcement. Under the 1990 Act the Commission was given a range of sanctions, including for the first time financial penalties for breach of licence conditions.[227] Financial penalties have been imposed regularly and can be substantial; for example, in 1998 Carlton Television was fined £2 million for 'grave breaches' of the Programme Code where the content of a documentary had been fabricated. This clearly raises issues of due process and compatibility with Article 6 ECHR as no independent decision-maker is involved, leaving only scrutiny by judicial review; the 1990 Act merely requires the giving of notice and a reasonable opportunity to make representations about the matter complained of.[228] The Commission has itself published a procedure for the application of statutory sanctions, expressed inter alia as taking into account the coming into effect of the HRA 1998.[229] This procedure distinguishes between 'lesser sanctions' such as the requirement to broadcast an apology, and 'greater sanctions' such as financial penalties. In the case of the former, investigation is delegated to the Senior Management Group of the Commission's staff and reported to the Commission, although in exceptional cases the Commission may decide the issue itself. For the latter, the case will be delegated to a sub-committee of members of the Commission, though in some cases it may be considered by the full Commission. In all cases the licensee will be given the opportunity to request an oral hearing and all information will be disclosed subject to limited exceptions required by law. It remains to be seen whether this will satisfy the requirements of the Convention; however, more fundamental changes are to be introduced under the Communications Act and these will be considered below.

(ii) Negative content regulation and the Broadcasting Standards Commission

5.96 It will be apparent from the discussion above that the Independent Television Commission is engaged in both positive programme regulation through general

---

[225] Independent Television Commission, *The ITC Programme Code* (revised 2002); *The ITC Code of Advertising Standards and Practice* (1998); *The ITC Code of Programme Sponsorship* (revised 2000).
[226] Independent Television Commission, *Guidance on Public Consulation*.
[227] Broadcasting Act 1990, s 41.
[228] ibid s 41(1), (3). For the implications of the Convention, see para. 5.33 above.
[229] Independent Television Commission, *Outline Procedure for Application of Statutory Sanctions* (2001).

programming requirements and negative regulation through acting where licence conditions and codes have been breached. In the second role its work is supplemented by the Broadcasting Standards Commission, established under the Broadcasting Act 1996 to replace the former Broadcasting Complaints Commission and Broadcasting Standards Council.[230] Unlike the other regulator, the Standards Commission's jurisdiction extends to the BBC. It is required to draw up, after consultation, a code relating to avoidance of unjust or unfair treatment and a code relating to broadcasting standards generally.[231] The Commission also has the duty to monitor standards and to consider complaints relating to the above matters.[232] Procedural duties are set out in the Act relating to the consideration of complaints but they are limited in nature; for example there is a discretion to dispense with a hearing.[233] To a considerable extent the Standards Commission's work duplicates that of the Independent Television Commission (though the latter does not of course cover the BBC) and it will be incorporated into the new general regulatory arrangements in the Communications Act, which will now be considered.

(iii) Self-regulation and the Office of Communications

The Independent Television Commission has moved gradually towards a system of **5.97** 'light-touch' regulation involving the use of monitored self-regulation by the regulated companies; this will also form the basis of the new system to be introduced at the end of 2003 under the Communications Act 2003. The beginnings of this can be seen as early as 1993 with the move to annual performance reviews drawn up by the Commission to create an overview of the performance of each licensed company rather than dealing only with individual issues of enforcement.[234] In its 2000 Communications White Paper the government proposed establishing a new single regulator, the Office of Communications, to cover both telecommunications and broadcasting (though, as mentioned above, not extending fully to the BBC), and these proposals are included in the Act.[235] Three tiers of regulation will be used; the first setting out minimum content requirements for all broadcasters through codes and rules on advertising and sponsorship; the second setting out quantifiable public service obligations such as quotas for independent and original productions, applying only to public service broadcasters. The third tier is that of qualitative public service requirements. In the case of the BBC this will be a matter for the governors, but for commercial broadcasters the requirements will be set out in statute but

---

[230] Broadcasting Act 1996, ss 106–30.
[231] ibid ss 107–108.
[232] ibid ss 109–114.
[233] ibid ss 115–116.
[234] For a summary see Prosser (n 7 above) 263–264.
[235] *A New Future for Communications* (n 209 above) chs 5–8.

implemented through self-regulation, with each broadcaster developing statements of programming policy for the regulator setting out in detail how each broadcaster's public service remit has been implemented.[236]

5.98   The Independent Television Commission in fact anticipated the changes by replacing its performance reviews with 'statements of programming commitment' from regulated companies against which they will report annually. The Communications Act reinforces this approach, for example by requiring the new OFCOM to review regulatory burdens and by establishing the three tier system, including the preparation of statements of programme policy in accordance with guidance from OFCOM.[237] The future regulation of commercial broadcasting is thus likely to involve a shift to forms of self-regulation monitored by the statutory regulatory body. OFCOM will have a 'backstop' power to regulate, including the power to impose financial sanctions, though only a limited right of appeal is provided from it in broadcasting, as opposed to telecommunications, matters.

(2) Health and Safety Regulation

(a) Introduction and the institutions

5.99   In broadcasting a move towards some form of self-regulation within a statutory framework is currently taking place, but other forms of participation of the regulated in the regulatory process can been seen clearly in the case of health and safety regulation, the final area to be examined in this chapter. This will enable us to consider more fully the role of tripartism in regulation, rule-making and enforcement procedures.[238]

5.100   The current system of health and safety regulation has been much longer established than the other cases discussed here which have all been subject to recent change. It has its origins in the Robens Report of 1972 which recommended increased self-regulation with the involvement of employers, employees, local authorities and other interests.[239] Implementation was by the Health and Safety at Work Act 1974. The Act established two bodies; the Health and Safety Commission consisting of a Chair plus three members appointed after consulting employers' organizations and three members after consulting organizations representing employees; in addition up to three further members can be appointed to

---

[236] *A New Future for Communications*, paras 5.5–5.8.

[237] Communications Act, ss 6, 264–271.

[238] For a general introduction see Health and Safety Commission, *The Health and Safety System in Great Britain* (3rd edn, 2002), available at www.hse.gov.uk/pubns/ohsingb.pdf, consulted 24 February 2003.

[239] *Safety and Health at Work* (Cmnd 5034, 1972); for the history see R Baldwin, 'Health and Safety at Work: Consensus and Self-Regulation' in Baldwin and McCrudden (n 13 above).

represent the public interest after consulting local authority organizations.[240] Tripartism was thus built into the system from the beginning. The Commission has general oversight of the Health and Safety Executive, to which it may delegate its functions and to which it may issue directions.[241] The Executive is a three-person statutory board headed by a Director General and has chief responsibility for implementing health and safety law; it is appointed by the Commission with the approval of the Secretary of State.[242]

As Baldwin noted, 'it is the tripartism and consensual basis of health and safety regulation that is its most notable feature'.[243] This was particularly evident through the system of safety representatives and safety committees, the former appointed by trade unions and the latter established at the request of union representatives.[244] This clearly became problematic with the decline of unionized employment, and in 1996 further regulations were made to extend consultation rights beyond unionized workforces.[245] The regulations also provide rights of access to information in both cases.[246] The functions of the safety representatives include representing employees in consultation with employers, investigating hazards and complaints and carrying out inspections.[247] Safety committees are established at the request of union-recognized safety representatives and have the function of keeping under review the measures taken to ensure the health and safety of employees.[248]

5.101

This participative style of implementation is supplemented by wide-ranging consultation procedures. They make use of an extensive process of advisory committees; currently these comprise seven subject committees and 15 industry advisory committees. All include employer and employee representatives. The consultative process is not confined to the committees, however, and is of particular importance in the drafting of new regulations and approved codes of practice.[249] These are essential given the predominantly goal-setting nature of the law in this field;

5.102

---

[240] Health and Safety at Work Act 1974, s 10(3).

[241] ibid s 11(4).

[242] ibid s 10(5).

[243] See n 239 above, 136.

[244] Health and Safety at Work Act 1974, s 2(4); Safety Representatives and Safety Committee Regulations 1977, SI 1977/500.

[245] Health and Safety (Consultation with Employees) Regulations 1996, SI 1996/1513.

[246] Health and Safety at Work Act 1974, s 2(2)(c); Safety Representatives and Safety Committee Regulations, reg 7; Health and Safety (Consultation with Employees) Regulations, reg 5.

[247] Safety Representatives and Safety Committee Regulations, reg 4; for the more limited functions of non-union representatives see Health and Safety (Consultation with Employees) Regulations, regs 3, 6.

[248] Health and Safety at Work Act 1974, s 2(7).

[249] See Health and Safety at Work Act 1974, ss 15, 16. Regulations are made by the Secretary of State, but normally on the proposal of the Commission; codes of practice need the approval of the Secretary of State under s 16(2).

and are supplemented by non-binding guidance setting out good practice. They were designed to replace the previous complex and untidy body of health and safety law spread across a large number of different statutes.[250] The Executive has adopted the general principles of good regulation referred to above,[251] and issues two-stage consultations, involving both a discussion document and a more focused consultation document setting out the options. A regulatory impact assessment is also used.

5.103   What is thus apparent in this case is a very different form of regulatory design from that encountered earlier. Rather than regulation and self-regulation being conceived as separate spheres, strong elements of self-regulation have been built into the design of the statutory system, with stronger participative and consultative procedures than those of, for example, the utility regulators. This is not without its problems, notably the limited rights for non-unionized workforces, but has contributed to a remarkably stable regulatory system.

(b) Enforcement

5.104   In earlier discussion little has been said about the practice of enforcement by regulatory bodies, though it should be recalled that government has sought to make enforcement more transparent and proportional through its Enforcement Concordat.[252] In the case of health and safety, the major means of enforcement is through preventative inspection; inspectors have the power to issue improvement or prohibition notices.[253] The former requires a contravention to be remedied within a specified period; the latter is available only where there may be a 'risk of serious personal injury' and may have immediate effect. Appeal on the merits lies to an employment tribunal against both types of notice.[254] The Executive may also bring criminal proceedings. Over 17,000 notices were issued in 1999–2000, and some 2,500 criminal charges laid.[255]

5.105   The Commission has adopted a policy statement on enforcement, which will apply both to the Executive and to local authorities enforcing health and safety law.[256] The principles of enforcement are;

---

[250] For a detailed analysis of the rule-making process see R Baldwin, *Rules and Government* (Oxford: Clarendon, 1995) 129–41.

[251] See paras 5.35 et seq.

[252] See para 5.42 above.

[253] Health and Safety at Work Act 1974, ss 21–22. For details of enforcement practice see Baldwin (n 250 above) ch 6.

[254] ibid s 24.

[255] For an important decision on the ECHR and criminal enforcement proceedings see *Davies v Health and Safety Executive* [2002] EWCA Crim 2949; [2003] IRLR 170.

[256] *Enforcement Policy Statement* (HSC 15, 2002), available at www.hse.gov.uk/pubns/hsc15.pdf, consulted 24 February 2003.

- Proportionality, which is defined as relating enforcement action to the risks. This is of particular importance given the central legal test of securing health and safety 'so far as is reasonably practicable'.[257]
- Targeting, defined as making sure that action is targeted primarily on the most serious risks and those who are best placed to control them.
- Consistency, defined not as uniformity but as taking a similar approach in similar circumstances to achieve similar ends.
- Transparency, defined as helping duty holders to understand what is expected of them and what they should expect from enforcing authorities. This includes distinguishing between statutory requirements and mere advice and guidance.

The enforcement authorities are also stated to be subject to a general principle of accountability, requiring that they must have policies and standards against which they can be judged and an effective and easily accessible mechanism for dealing with comments and complaints. Guidance is also given in relation to decisions to prosecute.

The enforcement policies of the Executive have been criticized, for example for relying too much on a Robens-derived consensual approach assuming an identity of interest between employer and employee, and thus for placing too much stress on voluntarism.[258] Nevertheless, we do see in the experience of the regulator here many of the themes which are currently emerging in relation to the other regulatory bodies discussed earlier. These include the importance of structured arrangements for consultation of interest groups and a combination of public regulation and self-regulation in which regulatory tasks are delegated but within a statutory framework and are subject to monitoring by the public authorities. We can also see more flexible approaches to enforcement structured by published statements of policy reflecting the general principles of good regulation. It is probably these features which explain the unusually long life of the current system of health and safety regulation; they are now being shared in other regulatory institutions. **5.106**

E. Conclusions

Anyone reading this analysis of regulatory bodies in the United Kingdom cannot fail to be struck by the degree of inconsistency and pragmatism in the institutional arrangements described. Thus transparency and arrangements for consultation vary hugely, as do the structures of legal duties of the agencies and their appeal **5.107**

---

[257] Health and Safety at Work Act 1974, s 2(1).
[258] Baldwin (n 250 above) 172–173; see generally N Gunningham, *Safeguarding the Worker* (Sydney: The Law Book Company, 1984) and B Hutter, *Regulation and Risk: Occupational Health and Safety on the Railways* (Oxford: OUP, 2001) esp 312–317.

arrangements. Having said this, there does appear to be a process of institutional learning taking place; the more recent regulators have been subject to something beyond the minimal consultation requirements which existed earlier, and in the case of the Financial Services Authority both the structure of the legal duties and the rule-making procedures are relatively sophisticated. There has also been progress in developing better appeal procedures, especially in competition law, rather than relying on judicial review alone. Indeed, the Competition Appeal Tribunal could form a specialist regulatory court, at least in matters of economic regulation. The commission model rather than the individual director general, has now firmly taken its place as the preferred institution for regulation.

5.108   What this suggests is that there has been some acceptance that we need to learn and adopt the best practice from the wide range of different regulators which now exists in the United Kingdom. Alongside this, has been a gradual acceptance that principles of good regulation can be developed, and these have formed the core of the executive self-regulation initiatives discussed earlier. So far, the initiatives, whether of better regulation or of regulatory transparency and consultation, have been almost entirely in extra-legal form, dependent on goodwill and practice. What is surely now needed is a fuller development of best practice and of coherent principle with legal support. One means of implementing this would be a generic Regulatory Reform Act bringing best practice and principle together and providing the sort of over-arching legal structure so missing from the current arrangements described here.

6

THE CONSTITUTIONAL POSITION OF
THE JUDICIARY

A. Constitutional Role of the Judiciary

(a) The function of adjudication

Within the legal system in England and Wales, it is the duty of the judges acting **6.01** within the system of courts to provide authoritative settlements of disputes about legal rights and duties,[1] by determining disputed questions of fact and law in accordance with (1) the common law, as expounded in previous decisions of the courts, and (2) laws enacted by Parliament.[2]

The function of adjudication arises in two broad contexts: **6.02**

(1) where a person is charged with a criminal offence and pleads not guilty, the judge presides over the trial and, if the defendant is convicted (or if he pleaded guilty) imposes the sentence;
(2) where a dispute as to the civil rights and obligations of the parties comes to a court for decision, the judge conducts the trial and delivers judgment.

In English law, unlike many European legal systems, disputes as to civil rights and obligations include not only disputes in private law between two or more

---

[1] PH Russell, in PH Russell and DM O'Brien, (ed) *Judicial Independence in the Age of Democracy: Critical Perspectives from around the World* (Charlottesville: University Press of Virginia, 2001) 9.
[2] As to which, see paras 1.120 et seq above.

persons, but also disputes in public law between an individual and a public body or official.[3] Moreover, certain classes of dispute over civil rights and duties (for example, a claim by an employee that she has been unfairly dismissed by an employer; or a claim by an individual that social security benefits due to her have been wrongly withheld by the Benefits Agency) are adjudicated not in courts with a general civil jurisdiction but in specialized tribunals.[4]

6.03   In performing their central task of adjudication, the judges are required:

- to apply the common law in accordance with the doctrine of precedent (stare decisis), under which judges must observe prior decisions that are binding upon them; and
- to apply the laws made by Parliament and by other bodies with authority to legislate (including ministers with delegated powers, the National Assembly of Wales, organs of the European Union, and local authorities)[5] and for this purpose to determine the meaning of any relevant legislation; and, if necessary, to decide whether subordinate legislation has been validly made.[6]

It is a fundamental rule of constitutional law that the courts have no power to review the validity of an Act of Parliament, but this rule is subject to the obligations that follow from the United Kingdom's membership of the European Union and the European Communities Act 1972.[7] Under the Human Rights Act 1998 (HRA), the judges must give effect in English law to the rights protected by the European Convention on Human Rights (ECHR); for this purpose all courts and tribunals must take account of decisions by the European Court of Human Rights (ECtHR).[8] Depending on the status of a court or tribunal in the hierarchy of courts and tribunals, the task of adjudication involves the making of (1) decisions at first instance and (2) decisions on appeal from lower courts and tribunals. Where proceedings in judicial review are concerned, a jurisdiction which is exercised by the Administrative Court (as part of the High Court), the court

---

[3] On the extent to which the common law recognizes a distinction between private and public law, see JWF Allison, *A Continental Distinction in the Common Law: a Historical and Comparative Perspective on English Public Law* (rev edn, New York: OUP, 2000). See also JDB Mitchell, 'The Causes and Effects of the Absence of a System of Public Law in the United Kingdom' [1965] PL 95 and Lord Woolf, '*Droit Public*—English Style' [1995] PL 57.

[4] See ch 20 below.

[5] See ch 1 above.

[6] *Boddington v British Transport Police* [1999] 2 AC 143.

[7] See *R v Secretary of State for Transport, ex p Factortame Ltd* [1990] 2 AC 85; *R v Secretary of State for Transport, ex p Factortame Ltd (No 2)* [1991] 1 AC 603; and *R v Secretary of State for Employment, ex p Equal Opportunities Commission* [1995] 1 AC 1.

[8] The HRA 1998 has altered the powers of the courts in relation to legislation in several important respects (as to which see eg KD Ewing, 'The Human Rights Act and Parliamentary Democracy' (1999) 62 MLR 79) but the Act does not enable the superior courts to exercise the function of legislating. See paras 1.216–1.222 above, and 7.29–7.31 and 7.35–7.46 below, and eg *In re S (Minors) (Care Order: Implementation of Care Plan)* [2002] UKHL 10; [2002] 2 AC 291.

must review the legality of the acts and decisions of tribunals, public authorities and officials according to the principles of administrative law.[9]

(b) The structure of the civil and criminal courts in England and Wales

Accounts of the structure of the civil and criminal courts in England and Wales **6.04** may be found in many works on the legal system.[10] The table below lists the main courts in England and Wales, together with a note of those who adjudicate in them. Some courts make considerable use of part-time judges; thus recorders sit in the county court and the Crown Court, and deputy High Court judges sit in the High Court.[11] Subject to age limits, retired judges may sit in the High Court and Court of Appeal; those who are members of the House of Lords may sit in the Appellate Committee of the House; and those who are members of the Privy Council may sit in the Judicial Committee of the Privy Council. Full-time court officers (in particular, Masters of the High Court) perform judicial duties of a mainly procedural nature, but they are not included in the table. In the magistrates' courts, adjudication is mainly entrusted to lay magistrates, appointed from the community and trained as magistrates but without legal qualifications; in some courts, the magistrates' jurisdiction is exercised by legally qualified district judges and deputy district judges (magistrates' court).

County court (civil proceedings)	(1) Circuit judges (2) District judges and part-time deputy district judges (3) Recorders (part-time)
High Court: Queen's Bench, Chancery and Family Divisions (including the Administrative Court and other specialist courts, such as the Commercial Court)	(1) High Court judges assigned to the relevant Division (2) Deputy High Court judges (part-time)
Court of Appeal (Civil and Criminal Divisions)	Lords Justices of Appeal (sitting in certain cases with High Court judges)

[9] As to which, see chs 14–16 below.

[10] See eg M Zander, *Cases and Materials on the English Legal System* (7th edn, London: Butterworths, 1996).

[11] After the High Court of Justiciary in Scotland had decided *Starrs v Ruxton* 2000 JC 208 (and see n 13 below), the Scottish Parliament amended the law to authorize the appointment of part-time sheriffs, and to govern their tenure of the position and their removal: Bail, Judicial Appointments etc Act 2000 (Scotland), inserting ss 11A–11C into the Sheriff Courts (Scotland) Act 1971. In England and Wales the terms of appointment of part-time judges were changed to ensure that such judges meet the standards of independence required by Art 6(1) ECHR.

House of Lords (civil and criminal jurisdiction)	Lords of Appeal in Ordinary, together with the Lord Chancellor and other peers qualified to sit as Lords of Appeal
Judicial Committee of the Privy Council	Lords of Appeal in Ordinary together with the Lord Chancellor, other peers qualified to sit as Lords of Appeal, and other qualified members of the Privy Council (by reason of holding high judicial office)
Crown Court (criminal proceedings)	(1) High Court judges (of the Queen's Bench Division) (2) Circuit judges (3) Recorders (part-time)
Magistrates' courts (summary criminal cases, and also family proceedings courts and youth courts)	Lay magistrates; district judges and deputy district judges (magistrates' court)

6.05 The statutory basis for much of the foregoing may be found in the Supreme Court Act 1981, as amended by subsequent legislation, including the Courts Act 2003. Part I of the 1981 Act deals with the constitution of the Supreme Court of England and Wales. The Supreme Court is declared to consist of the Court of Appeal, the High Court and the Crown Court, and the Lord Chancellor is declared to be president of the Supreme Court (s 1), and thus the holder of the most senior judicial office in England and Wales. The Court of Appeal consists of several ex officio judges as well as 35 Lord and Lady Justices of Appeal (s 2); its work is conducted in a criminal division (whose president is the Lord Chief Justice) and a civil division (whose president is the Master of the Rolls) (s 3). The High Court comprises certain senior judges and not more than 106 puisne judges (s 4), who sit in the Court's three divisions (s 5). The Act permits the number of judges to be increased by Order in Council, and the divisional structure of the High Court may be altered by the same means (s 7). Other key provisions deal with the appointment of judges and the requisite qualifications (s 10), the tenure of judges of the Supreme Court, their retiring age and the procedure for removing them from office (s 11), payment of their salaries (s 12) and the order of precedence of the judges of the Supreme Court (s 13).[12]

6.06 The court structures in Northern Ireland and Scotland are distinct from those in England and Wales. In matters of constitutional principle, such as judicial

---

[12] The Courts Act 2003, s 64, empowers the Lord Chancellor to make delegated legislation amending the titles of the holders of judicial office (for example, if the need for this should arise for reasons of gender). See also s 63 of that Act.

independence, the position of the judiciary is in essence the same throughout the United Kingdom, but differences exist in the law relating to judges as between England and Wales, Scotland and Northern Ireland. An important example is found in the Scotland Act 1998, which placed the tenure of Court of Session judges on a new basis and created an elaborate procedure for their removal on stated grounds.[13] The present chapter is in principle limited to a discussion of English law.

(c) The role of tribunals in adjudication

In addition to the courts of civil and criminal jurisdiction, the adjudication of certain classes of dispute is entrusted to over 70 categories of tribunal (for example, employment tribunals, immigration adjudicators, mental health review tribunals and social security appeal tribunals).[14] Since 1957, it has been recognized that these tribunals provide machinery for adjudication within specific areas of law and government.[15] They are considered to be exercising judicial rather than executive functions, although the disputes that they determine often arise from the decisions made by executive bodies administering public services and schemes of regulation. Since the Tribunals and Inquiries Act was enacted in 1958, the constitutional position of these tribunals has been brought closer to that of the civil courts.[16] This trend has been reinforced by the HRA 1998, which increased the necessity of ensuring that courts and tribunals alike are compliant with Article 6(1) ECHR in respect of their independence and impartiality.[17] In practice, full-time judges may be seconded from their ordinary duties to preside over certain tribunals. In 2002, circuit judges acted as chief immigration adjudicator, president of the (social security) appeals service, and chief social security commissioner; and High Court judges were President of the Employment Appeal Tribunal and President of the Immigration Appeal Tribunal respectively.[18] Because a full account is given of tribunals in chapter 20 below, the present chapter concentrates on the civil and criminal courts of general jurisdiction, but the massive contribution that the tribunals make to the administration of justice must never be forgotten.

6.07

---

[13] Scotland Act 1998, s 95; and see CMG Himsworth, 'Securing the tenure of Scottish judges: a somewhat academic exercise?' [1999] PL 14. For the tenure of sheriffs in Scotland, see Sheriff Courts (Scotland) Act 1971 (and n 11 above); for the removal of a sheriff, see *Stewart v Secretary of State for Scotland* 1998 SC (HL) 81.

[14] See ch 20 below.

[15] See Report of Committee on Tribunals and Inquiries (Cmnd 218, 1957) 9.

[16] See now the Tribunals and Inquiries Act 1992, and the annual reports of the Council on Tribunals.

[17] See ch 12 below.

[18] Report of the Lord Chancellor's Department, *Judicial Appointments in England and Wales*, April 2003.

(d) The impact of European law on the system of courts

6.08　In this chapter, except where the context requires a different meaning, references to the judiciary are generally to the full-time professional judges, namely the circuit judges, High Court judges and those who sit in appellate courts. One result of the HRA 1998 has been to give prominence to Article 6(1) ECHR. The right of every person to a fair and public trial 'by an independent and impartial tribunal established by law' requires every court and tribunal to display minimum standards of independence and impartiality.[19] The use within the legal system of part-time judges must therefore achieve the requisite standards of independence and impartiality. The right to a fair trial under Article 6(1) was breached in Scotland when the deployment of part-time judges in the sheriff court was under the control of the Lord Advocate, who was also responsible for the system of public prosecutions.[20]

6.09　An account of the court system applying to England and Wales today is incomplete without a reference to the judicial institutions of the European Union (the European Court of Justice and the First Instance Court at Luxembourg),[21] which have played a vital role in developing uniform and autonomous rules of EC law, and to the ECtHR at Strasbourg, which adjudicates upon complaints by individual applicants that their Convention rights have been infringed and whose decisions have developed principles for the interpretation of Convention rights.[22] It is the existence of these European courts that has enabled the developing principles of European law to be identified and received into the national legal systems of Europe.

(e) Proposals for reform of the machinery of justice

6.10　In June 2003, the government took the occasion of a Cabinet reshuffle and the resignation of the Lord Chancellor (Lord Irvine of Lairg) to announce wide-ranging changes in the machinery of justice. These included the appointment with immediate effect of a Secretary of State for Constitutional Affairs, to head a Department of Constitutional Affairs that would take over many functions relating to the system of justice from the Lord Chancellor's Department; the Secretary of State was also to hold the position of Lord Chancellor for the time being until legislation was enacted to abolish the ancient office of Lord Chancellor; new procedures would be created for the appointment of judges, and legislation would be enacted to remove the function of hearing appeals from the Lords of Appeal in

---

[19] See n 28 below, and ch 12 below.
[20] *Starrs v Ruxton* 2000 JC 208.
[21] As to which, see eg S Douglas-Scott, *Constitutional Law of the European Union* (Harlow: Longman, 2002) ch 5.
[22] For the Court and its place in the Convention system, see M Janis, R Kay and AW Bradley, *European Human Rights Law: Text and Materials* (2nd edn, Oxford: OUP, 2000) chs 2, 3.

Ordinary sitting in the House of Lords as an Appellate Committee and to transfer this function to a new Supreme Court for the United Kingdom. The creation of the Department of Constitutional Affairs and the appointment of the Secretary of State could take effect at once, but primary legislation was needed to give effect to the proposed new procedure for the appointment of judges and the creation of a new Supreme Court. In this chapter, reference will be made where appropriate both to changes that had already taken effect by November 2003 and also proposals by the government that were subject to legislation.[23]

B. Independence of the Judiciary

(a) The judiciary and the Crown

The independence of the judiciary is fundamental to the operation of the legal system and it is often said that the rule of law depends on the ability of the judiciary to make 'independent' decisions. But it is not a concept with a single meaning and its content today is heavily influenced both by constitutional history and by the continuing evolution of political and social culture. According to Blackstone, the jurisdiction of all courts was 'either indirectly or immediately derived from the Crown'.[24] In the landmark case of *Prohibitions del Roy*,[25] the common law judges declared that the King was not entitled to sit with the judges to administer justice in person. But the 17th century constitutional conflicts often drew the judiciary into partisan decision-making, and it is from the Act of Settlement 1700 that the independence of the judges from the Crown arose in law.[26] That Act declared:

6.11

> That judges' commissions be made quamdiu se bene gesserint [during good behaviour], and their salaries ascertained and established, but upon the address of both Houses of Parliament it may be lawful to remove them.

Today, there are still many formal links between the judiciary and the Crown. In particular, judicial office is held under the Crown and a judge's commission of appointment comes from the Crown.[27] It is an established convention that High

---

[23] For the consultation papers on reform of the machinery of justice issued by the Department of Constitutional Affairs, see *Constitutional reform: a new way of appointing Judges* (CP 10/03, July 2003); *Constitutional reform: a Supreme Court for the United Kingdom* (CP 11/03); *Constitutional reform: reforming the office of the Lord Chancellor* (CP 13/03, September 2003); and *The Future of Queen's Counsel* (CP 08/03).

[24] Blackstone, 1 *Commentaries,* Book I, ch VII.

[25] (1607) 12 Co Rep 63.

[26] The significance of the Act of Settlement provision is assessed in RB Stevens, *The English Judges: their Role in the Changing Constitution* (Oxford: Hart, 2002).

[27] For the judicial oath, see Supreme Court Act 1981, s 10(4) and the Promissory Oaths Act 1868.

Court judges in England and Wales receive a knighthood (women judges become Dames) and that Lords Justices of Appeal should be appointed members of the Privy Council (entitling them to the style 'Right Honourable'). But the sovereign has long ceased to exercise any influence over the selection of persons to hold judicial office, nor does the sovereign exercise any part in the disciplining or dismissal of judges.

(b) Judicial independence and the separation of powers

6.12 The independence, or autonomy, of the judiciary is often said to express the doctrine of separation of powers so far as this is recognized in the constitutional structure of British government. Thus, the judges act independently of the executive and of Parliament, exercising their functions to the best of their capability without fear or favour, affection or ill will, as the judicial oath requires. The importance of judicial independence is reinforced by Article 6 ECHR:

> In the determination of his civil rights and obligations or of any criminal charge against him, everyone is entitled to a fair and public hearing within a reasonable time by an independent and impartial tribunal established by law.

Although the ECHR does not require compliance by a national constitution with any particular version of the separation of powers, the ECtHR must if necessary decide whether a particular court or tribunal satisfies the requirements of 'independence' and 'impartiality'.[28]

6.13 The importance of judicial independence has been recognized in many decisions of the courts, sometimes in the context of the separation of powers.[29] Lord Diplock said:

> . . . it cannot be too strongly emphasised that the British Constitution, though largely unwritten, is firmly based on the separation of powers: Parliament makes the laws, the judiciary interprets them.[30]

And Lord Mustill has said:

> It is a feature of the peculiarly British conception of the separation of powers that Parliament, the executive and the courts have each their distinct and largely exclusive

---

[28] See eg *Findlay v UK* (1997) 24 EHRR 221 (courts martial); *McGonnell v UK* (2000) 30 EHRR 289 (officer in Guernsey with both judicial and executive functions), discussed by R Cornes, 'McGonnell v. United Kingdom, the Lord Chancellor and the Law Lords' [2000] PL 166. And see paras 1.104–1.109 above and 12.29–12.36 below.

[29] The decisions include *Liyanage v R* [1967] 1 AC 259; *Duport Steels Ltd v Sirs* [1980] 1 All ER 529; *R v Secretary of State for the Environment, ex p Nottinghamshire CC* [1986] AC 240; and *R v Secretary of State for the Home Department, ex p Fire Brigades Union* [1995] 2 AC 513.

[30] *Duport Steels Ltd v Sirs* [1980] 1 All ER 529, 541. At 550, Lord Keith said: 'The one public interest which courts of law are properly entitled to treat as their concern is the standing of and the degree of respect commanded by the judicial system'. At 551, Lord Scarman said: 'the Constitution's separation of powers, or more accurately functions, must be observed if judicial independence is not to be put at risk'.

domain. Parliament has a legally unchallengeable right to make whatever laws it thinks fit. The executive carries on the administration of the country in accordance with the powers conferred on it by law. The courts interpret the laws, and see that they are obeyed.[31]

The independence of the judiciary is the subject of an extensive literature.[32] It is a doc-trine with many facets. Two major aspects of the doctrine are the ability of individual judges and courts to make their decision in an 'independent' manner, and the au-thority and respect afforded to the judiciary within the system of government.[33] In part the doctrine derives from legal rules, but no less importantly it is founded upon unwritten rules, constitutional conventions, understandings and common practice. The limits of independent decision-making are in a formal sense set by the law itself (independent decisions ought not to be arbitrary) but also depend upon sociological, cultural and economic factors.[34] In 2003, the government proposed that, upon the abolition of the office of Lord Chancellor, the Secretary of State for Constitutional Affairs would exercise the Lord Chancellor's former role of safeguarding judicial in-dependence, both within and outside government.[35] It remains to be seen whether a statutory duty of this kind would be able to maintain in being conventional rules and practices that had grown up over a long period of legal history. **6.14**

(c) Judicial independence and public law

Where the cases arising for adjudication are limited to disputes between private parties, it may be easier as a matter of constitutional law to achieve the ideal of an independent and impartial judge. But it is also necessary to ensure the indepen-dence of the judiciary from the executive if justice is to be done by the courts in disputes between private individuals and public authorities. Lord Steyn has said: **6.15**

---

[31] *R v Secretary of State for the Home Department, ex p Fire Brigades Union* [1995] 2 AC 513, 567.

[32] N Browne-Wilkinson, 'The Independence of the Judiciary in the 1980s' [1988] PL 44; DGT Williams, 'Bias; the judges and the separation of powers' [2000] PL 45; RB Stevens, *The Independence of the Judiciary: the View from the Lord Chancellor's Office* (Oxford: Clarendon, 1993); Stevens (n 26 above); Lord Ackner, 'The Erosion of Judicial Independence' (John Stuart Mill Institute, 1997); Lord Hope 2002 SLT (News) 105; Lord Steyn, 'The Case for a Supreme Court' (2002) 118 LQR 382; Russell and O'Brien (n 1 above); and S Shetreet and J Deschênes (eds), *Judicial Independence: the Contemporary Debate* (Dordrecht: Nijhoff, 1985). Contrast the approach of JAG Griffith, *The Politics of the Judiciary* (5th edn, London: Fontana, 1997) which, without discussing for-mal questions of judicial independence, argues that the judges in exercising their judicial duties cannot be expected to be neutral on social and political questions. See also *Parliamentary Supremacy, Judicial Independence: Latimer House Guidelines for the Commonwealth* (Commonwealth Secretariat, 1998).

[33] See eg S Shetreet in Shetreet and Deschênes (n 32 above) 590; Stevens, *The English Judges* (n 26 above) chs 6 and 7.

[34] See eg the remarkable homogeneity of judicial decision-making in the area of civil liberties early in the 20th century, analysed in KD Ewing and CA Gearty, *The Struggle for Civil Liberties: Political Freedom and the Rule of Law in Britain, 1914–1945* (Oxford: OUP, 2000) esp ch 8. See also Russell (n 1 above) ch 1.

[35] See *Constitutional reform: a new way of appointing judges* (n 23 above) para 114; and *Constitutional reform: reforming the office of the Lord Chancellor* (n 23 above) para 15.

Public law has been transformed over the last 30 years. The claim that the courts stand between the executive and the citizen, and control all abuse of executive power, has been reinvigorated and become a foundation of our modern democracy.[36]

The relationship between judiciary and executive should ideally be one of mutual respect, but if necessary the courts have power to order public authorities, including ministers and departments of government, to perform their legal duties.[37]

> The proper constitutional relationship of the executive with the courts is that the courts will respect all acts of the executive within its lawful province, and that the executive will respect all decisions of the courts as to what its lawful province is.[38]

Governmental bodies, no less than private individuals, must comply with decisions of the courts. The rule of law in this sense is not a static doctrine. Thus, it has been said that the role of the courts in relation to the administration now involves the task of ensuring respect for the principles of constitutional democracy.[39] Even if such a role is generally accepted, a separation of functions between judiciary and executive continues to be important. Jowell has stated:

> The respective roles of judges and administrators in a democratic society, and their competence, are fundamentally distinct and will remain so.[40]

It must not, however, be assumed that the maintenance of the distinction will always be achieved without controversy, particularly where government ministers disagree strongly with judicial decisions and express their criticisms publicly.[41] Moreover, there was in 2003 much expression of political concern in relation to the sentencing decisions made by judges sitting in the criminal courts. While it is for the legislature to determine the maximum penalties that may be imposed for particular offences and in some cases (more controversially) the minimum penalties, Parliament's legislative authority may be exercised in an intrusive way that indicates a lack of confidence in the exercise by judges of their sentencing powers.[42]

---

[36] Lord Steyn (n 32 above) 385.

[37] *M v Home Office* [1994] 1 AC 377; *Gairy v A-G of Grenada* [2001] UKPC 30; [2002] 1 AC 167.

[38] *M v Home Office* [1992] QB 270, 314, Nolan LJ, approving a formulation presented in argument by S Sedley QC. The liability of the Crown to observe the law is discussed in M Sunkin and S Payne (eds), *The Nature of the Crown: A Legal and Political Analysis* (Oxford: OUP, 1999) esp ch 3 (M Loughlin) and ch 9 (T Cornford).

[39] See para 6.21 below.

[40] J Jowell, 'Beyond the Rule of Law: Towards Constitutional Judicial Review' [2000] PL 671, 681 (cited by Lord Steyn in *R (on the application of Daly) v Secretary of State for the Home Department* [2001] UKHL 26; [2001] 2 AC 532 at [28]).

[41] See para 6.39 below

[42] See eg the legislative debates relating to the Criminal Justice Act 2003; and, on one aspect of the sentencing proposals contained in the Bill for that Act, see 9th Report, House of Lords Committee on the Constitution, *Criminal Justice Bill* (HL Paper 129, 2002–03).

(d) Judicial decision-making and the accountability of judges

An essential facet of judicial independence is that judges are not directly answer- **6.16**
able either to the executive or to Parliament for their decisions. Although the
judges as a body are (or ought to be) accountable for the manner in which the
courts serve the public at large in the administration of justice, methods of ensuring that accountability must not be such as to prejudice the core principle of judicial independence.[43]

The primary form of accountability applying to the judiciary derives from four **6.17**
vital aspects of the decision-making process: as a general rule, court hearings take
place in public (except where this would prejudice the cause of justice itself);
judicial proceedings are typically adversarial; judicial decisions must take account
of the submissions of the parties and be supported with reasons; and, except for
courts from which there is no further right of appeal or review, decisions may be
challenged by means of an appeal or review before a higher court in the hierarchy.[44] There is also a stress in the common law system on identifying the judge
who has taken the decision. Unlike some other European legal systems, English law
does not favour the concept of a collegial decision in which individual reasoning
and dissent are habitually suppressed.[45] Further, the fact that an appeal to a higher
court succeeds in itself implies no criticism of the first court's decision. On an appeal, new evidence may (under certain conditions)[46] be submitted or new arguments made that lead to a different outcome; or it may simply be that the appeal
court takes a different view of the relevant law or the facts. But sometimes an appellate hearing will show that something has gone wrong and the appeal court may
then criticize the trial judge—for example, for excessive delay in preparing and delivering judgment,[47] for failure to deal with the arguments presented by the parties,
or for having heard the case even when there was a real risk of bias.[48]

---

[43] The Courts Act 2003 contains many provisions that, without eroding judicial independence,
seek to improve the accountability of the courts as an essential part of the system for civil and criminal justice: see eg the general duty that the Act places on the Lord Chancellor to ensure that there is
an efficient and effective system of courts (s 1) and the creation of a new inspectorate of court administration (Pt 5).

[44] And see JJ Spigelman 'Judicial accountability and performance indicators' (2002) 21 CJQ 18.
Art 6(1) ECHR does not require that there be a right of appeal against judicial decisions, but where
there is a right of appeal, it must comply with the same requirements of due process that apply to first
instance decisions: *Delcourt v Belgium* (1970) 1 EHRR 355; *Monell and Morris v UK* (1987) 10
EHRR 205. Art 2 of Protocol 7 to the ECHR guarantees a right of appeal in criminal matters, but
Protocol 7 has not been ratified by the UK.

[45] In this respect, the practice of the European Court of Justice is markedly less attractive to an
English lawyer than that of the ECtHR.

[46] See eg *Ladd v Marshall* [1954] 1 WLR 1489.

[47] *Goose v Wilson Sandford & Co*, The Times, 19 February 1998: the Court of Appeal ordered a
new trial; the judge in question retired two months later.

[48] For the law relating to judicial bias, see paras 15.68–15.93 below.

(e) Accountability and final courts of appeal

6.18   In the case of a final court of appeal, such as the House of Lords, a dispute before the House may be subject to a reference to the European Court of Justice on a point of EC law. In other cases, the House's decision may cause the unsuccessful party to apply to the ECtHR, claiming that his or her Convention rights were infringed by the decision. In the first of the series of decisions relating to the proposed extradition of General Pinochet, one of the Law Lords (Lord Hoffmann) had sat in an Appellate Committee of the House of Lords to consider the proposed extradition, but did not disclose the close connection he had in a charitable organization that was linked with a campaigning body (Amnesty International) that had been permitted to argue in support of the extradition. Thereafter, when the link became known to Pinochet's lawyers, a differently constituted Appellate Committee held that the House had an inherent power to review its first decision, to decide whether the judge had been disqualified by his interest from sitting and, if necessary, to set the first decision aside and hear the appeal again. Lord Browne-Wilkinson said:

> In principle it must be that your Lordships, as the ultimate court of appeal, have power to correct any injustice caused by an earlier order of the House. [However,] the House will not reopen any appeal save in circumstances where, through no fault of a party, he or she has been subjected to an unfair procedure.[49]

(f) The limitations of accountability through procedures of appeal

6.19   The existence of a right of appeal to a higher court is plainly compatible with judicial independence, the guarantees of which apply also to the appellate court. But the right of appeal alone may not be sufficient to secure judicial accountability. The courts frequently make decisions or perform their functions in a manner which may adversely affect groups or individuals who have no right of appeal. Article 6(1) ECHR entitles the individual to a fair hearing before an independent and impartial court 'within a reasonable time', but not every instance of delay (for instance, an unnecessary adjournment that leads to additional costs) will give rise to a remedy. Further, judicial behaviour may be insensitive, rude or ill-judged in relation to a witness, an advocate or a third party, without giving rise to any right of appeal. Thus the right to appeal does not ensure that judges will in all instances carry out their duties in an acceptable manner. The question arises, whether it is possible to provide for additional means of accountability that will not adversely affect a judge's independence.[50] This question needs to be borne in mind in later sections of this chapter dealing with such matters as procedure for removing judges from office, means of dealing with complaints made against judges, and judicial immunity from liability.

---

[49] *R v Bow Street Metropolitan Stipendiary Magistrate, ex p Pinochet Ugarte (No 2)* [2000] 1 AC 119, 132. If the House had held that this jurisdiction did not exist, Pinochet would have been entitled to seek a remedy from the ECtHR, claiming a breach of Art 6(1) ECHR.

[50] See Russell (n 1 above) and Spigelman (n 44 above).

C. The Relationship of the Courts with Parliament

(a) Ultimate authority and the application of statutes

We have seen that there is a basic distinction to be drawn between the process of legislation by Parliament and the role of the judiciary in applying the law. The unwritten and evolutionary nature of the British constitutional structure does not provide a specific answer to the question, where does ultimate authority lie? On one view of parliamentary sovereignty, the courts are subordinate to Parliament because an Act of Parliament must prevail over any inconsistent judicial decision.[51] On another view, there are, or may be, constitutional fundamentals that lie in the keeping of the courts rather than with Parliament. In particular, it is the courts and not Parliament that decide in case of dispute the legal effect of an Act of Parliament and when it should be applied. In 1991, Lord Bridge said:

> The rule of law rests upon twin foundations: the sovereignty of the Queen in Parliament in making the law and the sovereignty of the Queens' courts in interpreting and applying the law.[52]

6.20

It is consistent with this statement that the courts have the inherent power of interpreting and applying legislation, and that they may through their decisions refine and develop their approach to these tasks. A recent instance of this power has been the approval given by the House of Lords to the principle that individuals have democratic rights against the state that must be maintained by the courts, except where there is a clear and unequivocal intention expressed by Parliament that such rights should be abrogated.[53] The exercise of this power reinforces the view that the authority of the courts in reviewing the acts of executive bodies is inherent in their common law jurisdiction, rather than being derived from the presumed intention of Parliament.[54] However, Parliament may legislate to modify the approach that the judiciary should take to statutory interpretation, and this

6.21

---

[51] Stevens (n 26 above) 96, refers to 'the apparently irreconcilable concepts of parliamentary sovereignty and judicial independence'.

[52] *X v Morgan-Grampian Ltd* [1991] 1 AC 1, 48. And see S Sedley, 'Human Rights: A Twenty-First Century Agenda' [1995] PL 386, 389 (referring to 'a bi-polar sovereignty of the Crown in Parliament and the Crown in its courts').

[53] The approach is summarized in Jowell (n 40 above) 674–676. The case law includes *R v Lord Chancellor, ex p Witham* [1997] 1 WLR 104; *R v Secretary of State for the Home Department, ex p Pierson* [1998] AC 539; *R v Secretary of State for the Home Department, ex p Sims* [2000] 2 AC 115; and *R (on the application of Daly) v Secretary of State for the Home Department* [2001] UKHL 26; [2001] 2 AC 532.

[54] On this broad area of dispute, see C Forsyth (ed), *Judicial Review and the Constitution* (Oxford: Hart, 2000); M Elliott, *The Constitutional Foundations of Judicial Review* (Oxford: Hart, 2001); PA Joseph, 'The demise of ultra vires—judicial review in the New Zealand courts' [2001] PL 354; and P Craig and N Bamforth, 'Constitutional analysis, constitutional principle and judicial review' [2001] PL 763.

was done in the HRA 1998.[55] It is also within the authority of Parliament to legislate to modify or in specific cases to exclude scope for judicial review.[56] But it does not follow that Parliament has unlimited authority to exclude the judicial interpretation of legislation altogether, to abrogate the entire process of judicial review or to substitute an extra-judicial process for the jurisdiction of the courts.[57]

(b) The judges and political activities

6.22 For the courts to exercise a legitimate role within a democracy, their decisions must (so far as possible) neither depend nor be seen to depend upon the judges' own political preferences. At the end of the 19th century, when Lord Halsbury was Lord Chancellor, judges were often appointed because of their support for the government of which Lord Halsbury was a member. Today, appointments depend on merit and not politics.[58] Active support for a political party ought not to be a disqualifying factor. But once appointed to a full-time judicial post, a judge is expected to sever any links with a political party that he or she may have. In 1968, a Scottish judge (Lord Avonside) ran into a political storm when he agreed to serve as member of a committee to consider the future of Scottish government that was appointed by the leader of the Conservative Opposition in Parliament: the controversy in Scotland subsided only when Lord Avonside resigned from the committee.[59]

(c) The place of the Law Lords in Parliament

6.23 The presence of the Law Lords (Lords of Appeal in Ordinary) in the House of Lords is a manifest departure from the principle of separation of powers. But is it merely a historical anomaly, or does it have adverse consequences? In practice, the Law Lords sit in the House of Lords on the cross-benches, and take part in legislative work only to a limited extent, for instance by assisting in the scrutiny of European legislation or by speaking in debates that affect reform of the law and the legal system.[60] In June 2000, giving effect to a recommendation of the Royal

---

[55] For which, see paras 1.216–1.222 above and 7.55–7.82 below. See also F Bennion, *Statutory Interpretation* (4th edn, London: Butterworths, 2002) 1127–1159.

[56] See eg Referendums (Scotland and Wales) Act 1997, s 4 and Regulation of Investigatory Powers Act 2000, s 67(8).

[57] In the debate on the constitutional foundations of judicial review that is mentioned above, even those who argue that the foundations of judicial review lie in the inherent jurisdiction of the courts and not in the presumed intention of Parliament accept that the law on judicial review may be modified by Parliament: see eg, Jowell (338) and Craig (381–386) in Forsyth (n 54 above) and cf Elliott (n 54 above) 145–157.

[58] *Judicial Appointments in England and Wales* (Lord Chancellor's Department, April 2003) foreword. But see JAG Griffith, *The Politics of the Judiciary* (n 32 above) 22, for the conclusion that the system of judicial appointments leads to too homogeneous a judiciary, in which there is a gross imbalance in the representation of women and those from ethnic minorities.

[59] See The Times and The Scotsman, 26 July to 6 August 1968.

[60] For an unfortunate departure from this policy into an acutely political matter, see the amendment to the Bill of Rights 1689, Art 9 made by the Defamation Act 1996, s 13. This change in the

Commission on Reform of the House of Lords,[61] it was stated on behalf of the currently serving Lords of Appeal in Ordinary that (1) they 'do not think it appropriate to engage in matters where there is a strong element of party political controversy' and (2) they 'bear in mind that they might render themselves ineligible to sit judicially if they were to express an opinion on a matter which might later be relevant to an appeal to the House'.[62] It has sometimes been argued that the presence of the senior judges in the House of Lords enables the House to receive authoritative legal advice from within its own membership. But if the second matter stated by the Law Lords in the statement of June 2000 is given full weight, the argument for their membership is deprived of virtually all its force. In 2002, the Court of Session held that participation by Lord Hardie in the legislative work of the House of Lords while holding the post of Lord Advocate, was such as to disqualify him on the ground of bias (after he had been appointed to the Court of Session) from sitting judicially to hear a dispute that related directly to matters on which he had expressed a definite view in the course of legislative debate.[63] In 2003, the government's decision to establish a Supreme Court for the United Kingdom to exercise the jurisdiction of the House of Lords in hearing appeals was supported by the argument that the senior judges' membership of the House of Lords raised questions as to whether their independence from the executive and the legislature was sufficiently transparent.[64] There can be no doubt that the separation of powers between the judiciary and the legislature will be much more clearly seen when a Supreme Court has been created.

(d) The Lord Chancellor and the decision of cases

The Lord Chancellor is in law the head of the judiciary in England and Wales,[65]   **6.24**
but he holds a senior Cabinet office as well as presiding over the House of Lords in

---

law was proposed (with the support of the government) by Lord Hoffmann (a Lord of Appeal in Ordinary), but the change was later criticized by the Joint Committee on Parliamentary Privilege (1998–99 HL Paper 43-I, HC 214-I) 23–29.

[61] Cm 4534, 2000, recommendation 59.

[62] *Hansard*, HL Deb col 419 (22 June 2000) (Lord Bingham of Cornhill). Lord Steyn's later observation goes much further: 'The privilege of serving Law Lords to participate in legislative business is no longer defensible': (n 32 above) 383. For argument to the contrary, see Lord Cooke of Thorndon, 'The Law Lords—an Endangered Heritage' (2003) 119 LQR 49.

[63] *Davidson v Scottish Ministers (No 2)* 2002 SLT 1231. It does not follow from this decision that lesser forms of participation in the legislative process would disqualify: disclosure of the involvement would at least have enabled the parties to consider whether the judge should hear the case.

[64] *Constitutional reform: a Supreme Court for the United Kingdom* (n 23 above) para 2.

[65] By the Supreme Court Act 1981, s 1(2), the Lord Chancellor is declared to be 'president of the Supreme Court'. In the British constitutional tradition, however, such a formal declaration is wholly compatible with the development of customary practice and conventions that would make the position of president 'dignified' rather than 'efficient', in at least those respects in which the exercise of actual power by the Lord Chancellor would conflict with other constitutional principles. For a full account of the office, see D Woodhouse, *The Office of Lord Chancellor* (Oxford: Hart, 2001).

its legislative capacity and seeing many government Bills through the House. This position conflicts with the need for a separation between the judiciary and the legislature. The judiciary are required individually and collectively to act impartially in matters of political controversy. The Lord Chancellor himself cannot be perceived as an independent and impartial judge when, as well as serving as head of the judiciary, he is also a Cabinet minister responsible for the administration of justice, and Speaker of the House of Lords. Recent Lord Chancellors have sat less frequently to hear appeals to the House. In 1999, the Lord Chancellor (Lord Irvine of Lairg) denied that there were any conventions restricting his participation in the judicial business of the House,[66] a denial which flew in the face of the practice of Lord Chancellors as it had become established before 1999. However, whatever the position may have been in the past, there were in 2003 overwhelming arguments against the Lord Chancellor continuing to sit as a judge.[67] Indeed, there is no need for him to have any responsibility for the operation of the judicial work of the Law Lords, in view of the appointment in 2000 of a named Law Lord as the senior judge in the House.[68] In June 2003, the government's proposals for constitutional reforms in the machinery of justice[69] included the decision to abolish the post of Lord Chancellor and to replace that position with a Secretary of State for Constitutional Affairs. Lord Falconer of Thoroton was in June 2003 appointed to the new office of Secretary of State and to the post of Lord Chancellor pending its abolition: upon his appointment, he stated that he did not propose to sit judicially, regarding this aspect of the Lord Chancellor's traditional office as 'anachronistic and questionable'.[70]

(e) Other aspects of the relationship between Parliament and the courts

(i) The removal of judges

6.25 The constitutional relationship between Parliament and the judiciary embodies several other matters. First, Parliament plays no part in appointing judges (save that of enacting the formal qualifications for appointment),[71] and no approval by Parliament is required before judicial appointments by the executive take effect. However, as we have seen, since the Act of Settlement 1700 senior judges have been protected from dismissal by the Crown except with the prior approval of each House of Parliament. Today, judges of the High Court and the Court of

---

[66] *Hansard*, HL Deb cols 77–78, written answers (22 June 1999) cited in Steyn (n 32 above) 386. For the reason given in the previous note, this denial cannot be accepted.

[67] See Steyn (n 32 above).

[68] See (2000) 19 CJQ 351, for a note on the formalities of the appointment, including a reference to HL Standing Order 87(4).

[69] See para 6.10 above.

[70] See *Constitutional reform: reforming the office of the Lord Chancellor* (n 23 above) foreword. Had the Lord Chancellor continued to sit as a judge to hear appeals, the practice would have been likely to attract the censure of the ECtHR as being in breach of Art 6(1) ECHR.

[71] For which, see Supreme Court Act 1981, s 10 (as amended). And see para 6.34 below (appointing the judges).

Appeal hold office during good behaviour, subject to a power of removal by the Queen on an address presented by both Houses of Parliament.[72] A similar provision applies to Lords of Appeal in Ordinary.[73] While the precise meaning of these provisions is not certain, it can be accepted that the two Houses would not be willing to pass an address for removal of a judge except if he or she had been guilty of serious misconduct. Inferior judges are not protected to the same extent as High Court judges: thus, circuit judges and district judges may be removed from office by the Lord Chancellor, if he thinks fit, for incapacity or misbehaviour.[74] Such decisions by the Lord Chancellor are subject to judicial review, for example on grounds of natural justice,[75] but do not require to be approved by Parliament. The Courts Act 2003, s 11(2), for the first time places on a statutory basis the Lord Chancellor's power to remove lay magistrates for misconduct or inability or failure to perform duties; the power may be exercised without any involvement of Parliament. In July 2003, the Lord Chancellor's functions in respect of the dismissal and disciplining of judges came under review in consequence of the decision by the government that the Lord Chancellor's post should be abolished.[76]

(ii) Parliamentary approval of judicial salaries

Giving effect to the provision in the Act of Settlement that the salaries of judges shall be 'ascertained and established', there is permanent statutory authority for charging judicial salaries on the Consolidated Fund;[77] thus provision for judicial salaries does not require the approval of Parliament each year. There is also authority for the Lord Chancellor, acting with the approval of the Prime Minister, to increase judicial salaries.[78] In practice, judicial salaries are examined regularly, along with the salaries of senior civil servants, members of the armed forces, ministers and MPs, by the advisory Senior Salaries Review Body.[79]

6.26

---

[72] ibid s 11(3).

[73] Appellate Jurisdiction Act 1876, s 6.

[74] Courts Act 1971, s 17(4). A contrast may be drawn with the procedure in Scotland for the removal of sheriffs: Sheriff Courts (Scotland) Act 1971, s 12, on which see *Stewart v Secretary of State for Scotland* 1998 SC (HL) 81. New provision was made for the removal of Court of Session judges in the Scotland Act 1998, s 95: see n 13 above.

[75] See eg *Ex p Ramshay* (1852) 21 LJQB 238.

[76] *Constitutional reform: a new way of appointing judges* (n 23 above) paras 100–107.

[77] Supreme Court Act 1981, s 12(5).

[78] ibid s 12(1), (3). See also the Judicial Pensions and Retirement Act 1993.

[79] The Senior Salaries Review Board's report for 2003 was published on 7 February 2003 and its recommendations for increasing judicial salaries were accepted by the government. One consequence of this report was a substantial increase in the salary of the Lord Chancellor, which is required by the Ministerial and Other Persons and Salaries Act 1991 (as amended by the Ministerial and Other Salaries Order 1998) to be £2,500 more than the salary for the time being paid to the Lord Chief Justice. The increase attracted political controversy and Lord Chancellor Irvine declined to accept it. On his appointment in June 2003 to the office of Lord Chancellor pending its abolition, Lord Falconer of Thoroton stated that he would accept only the salary that was paid to other members of the House of Lords who held Cabinet posts.

(iii) Freedom of debate in Parliament and attacks on the judges

6.27 The freedom of speech and debate in Parliament is the House of Commons' most important privilege. By Article 9 of the Bill of Rights, 'the freedom of speech and debates or proceedings in Parliament ought not to be impeached or questioned in any court or place out of Parliament'.[80] The purpose of the freedom is to protect freedom of speech within Parliament from external interference, and exercise of the freedom is regulated by the practice of the House. The administration of justice is a proper subject for parliamentary debate, but a long-standing rule of the House protects judges from certain forms of attack. Criticism of the conduct of a judge may not be expressed by members except on a substantive motion calling for his or her dismissal.[81] In 1973, when the National Industrial Relations Court and its president (Sir John Donaldson, a High Court judge) were the subject of political controversy, the Speaker ruled that it could be argued in debate on a motion calling for the abolition of the Court that a judge's decision was wrong, and the reasons for this view could be given. But no reflections on a judge's character or motive could be made except on a motion for his dismissal.[82] In the event, parliamentary time was not found for debate of a motion signed by over 180 Labour MPs calling for Sir John's dismissal. From time to time, MPs wish to raise in the House a controversial decision or sentence made or imposed by a judge. In 1987, the Speaker ruled: 'It is perfectly in order to criticise or to question a sentence, but it is not in order to criticise a judge. That has to be done by motion.'[83] Questions to ministers that reflect on a judge's character are not accepted by the Table Office.[84] The reason for these parliamentary rules is 'based on the need for comity and mutual respect between the legislature and the judiciary; and the requirement that judicial officers be protected from remarks that might needlessly undermine respect for the judiciary'.[85]

---

[80] For a comprehensive review of the operation of Art 9, see the report of the Joint Committee on Parliamentary Privilege (1998–99 HL 43-1, HC 214-1); and see PM Leopold, 'Report of the Joint Committee on Parliamentary Privilege' [1999] PL 604. See also paras 6.29–6.31 below regarding reference to parliamentary statements in the course of litigation.

[81] Erskine May, *Treatise on the Law, Privileges, Proceedings and Usage of Parliament* (22nd edn, London: Butterworths, 1997) 385.

[82] *Hansard*, HC Deb col 1092 (4 December 1973). See also *Hansard*, HC Deb, 10 December 1973, col 42; and Erskine May, p 385.

[83] *Hansard*, HC Deb col 641 (2 July 1987).

[84] Erskine May (n 81 above) 297. In March 2002, in the Australian Senate, a senator abused parliamentary privilege to mount a baseless personal attack on a member of the High Court of Australia: the speaker chose not to name the judge in question until the closing sentence of his speech; his subsequent apology was accepted by the judge. See E Campbell and M Groves, 'Attacks on judges under parliamentary privilege: a sorry Australian episode' [2002] PL 626.

[85] AR Browning (ed), *House of Representative Practice* (2nd edn, Canberra: Australian Government Publishing Service, 1989) 231, cited by Campbell and Groves (n 84 above) 634.

(iv) The sub judice rule

A further rule of the House of Commons that seeks to protect the integrity of the **6.28**
trial process and to exclude political pressure on judges hearing controversial cases
is the sub judice rule, whereby matters awaiting adjudication by a court may not
be raised in debate. The rule applies to both civil and criminal cases and, when notice of appeal has been given, it applies until the case is disposed of on appeal.[86]
However, in civil cases, the Speaker may permit reference to matters pending adjudication where they relate to ministerial decisions that may be challenged in
court by judicial review, or to issues of national importance, such as the national
economy, public order or the essentials of life.[87] If an MP were intentionally to
seek to interfere with a pending trial by making statements in debate in breach of
the sub judice rule, he or she would be protected by Article 9 of the Bill of Rights
from proceedings for contempt of court, but not from disciplinary proceedings
taken by Parliament itself.[88] The sub judice rule applies to tribunals appointed
under the Tribunals of Inquiry (Evidence) Act 1921, but not to ad hoc, informal
inquiries, even when they are conducted by a judge (such as the inquiry by Sir
Richard Scott into the Matrix-Churchill affair).[89]

(v) The use of parliamentary proceedings in litigation

In addition to the sub judice rule, there are other respects in which the law and **6.29**
practice of Parliament maintain a distance between legislative debate and the
process of adjudication. In earlier times, the House was anxious to retain control
over the reporting of debates within Parliament. This historic concern led to the
practice whereby the special leave of the House of Commons was needed before the
reports of debates or proceedings in Parliament could be given as evidence in judicial proceedings. In 1980, a change in practice occurred when the House permitted reference to be made in court to the record of debates in *Hansard* and to
published accounts of evidence given to parliamentary committees.[90] Alongside
the control that the House exercised over the use in court of its own proceedings,
the judges developed a firm rule of statutory interpretation (known as the exclusionary rule),[91] which excluded statements made in Parliament from being looked
at by the courts for the purposes of statutory interpretation. In 1993, a significant
change in the judicial use of *Hansard* occurred when the House of Lords held, as an
exception to the exclusionary rule, that the courts may use ministerial statements

---

[86] Erskine May (n 81 above) 333, 383–384.
[87] ibid 383.
[88] ibid 383.
[89] See para 6.43 below; and ch 22 below.
[90] *Hansard*, HC Deb col 167 (3 December 1979) and col 879 (31 October 1980); 1978–79 HC
102; and PM Leopold, 'References in Court to Hansard' [1981] PL 316. Also Bennion (n 55 above)
566–571.
[91] See Bennion (n 55 above) 545–552. For the history of the rule, see 552–566.

in *Hansard* to resolve ambiguities in legislation.[92] When a court is considering whether a statutory provision is compatible with a Convention right protected by the HRA 1998, the court may take account of statements in Parliament as background information tending to show the likely impact of the legislation and the nature of the social problem at which it is aimed, but the proportionality of the statutory provision is not to be judged by the quality of the reasons for it advanced in the course of debate.[93]

(vi) Reference to parliamentary statements in judicial review proceedings

6.30 Notwithstanding Article 9 of the Bill of Rights, ministerial statements in Parliament are often used as evidence in court in the judicial review of executive decisions, for example to show the motivation lying behind a ministerial decision or the findings of fact that a minister had made.[94] While it is uncertain whether the courts would permit a claimant to seek to show that a minister had made a lying or deceitful statement in Parliament,[95] the justification for allowing such statements to be admitted in judicial review proceedings is that it would be wrong for a minister (as a member of the executive) to make a statement in Parliament on a matter of public concern and for this to be excluded from consideration by the court when it might be directly relevant to issues of motive or intention that are in dispute. Such an exclusionary rule could seriously limit the effectiveness of judicial review and, at worst, might encourage ministers to protect dubious decisions from judicial scrutiny by justifying them only in Parliament. Against this, a situation of possible conflict between courts and Parliament would arise if a court were asked to make a finding that a minister had misled the House and the House had decided that the minister had not done so.

6.31 Developments in the law and practice of judicial review since 1980 have sometimes caused members of Parliament concern that the judges who sit in the Administrative Court are trespassing on legislative ground. One instance occurred in 1993, when those opposed to European integration applied for a judicial declaration that the United Kingdom could not lawfully ratify the Treaty on European Union, although the Treaty had for certain purposes already been approved by Parliament in the form of the European Communities (Amendment)

---

[92] *Pepper v Hart* [1993] AC 593; *R v Secretary of State for the Environment, ex p Spath Holme Ltd* [2001] 2 AC 349. For a critical re-assessment of the reasoning in *Pepper v Hart*, see J Steyn 'Pepper v Hart: A Re-examination' (2001) 21 OJLS 59.

[93] *Wilson v First CountyTrust Ltd* [2003] UKHL 40; [2003] 4 All ER 97.

[94] *R v Secretary of State for the Home Department, ex p Brind* [1991] 1 AC 696; *Pepper v Hart* [1993] AC 593, 639 (Lord Browne-Wilkinson); *Wilson v First CountyTrust Ltd* [2003] UKHL 40, [2003] 4 All ER 97 at [60]. Also Report of the Joint Committee on Parliamentary Privilege (n 80 above) paras 46–59 and see generally paras 2.114 et seq above.

[95] The Joint Committee on Parliamentary Privilege (n 80 above) considered that such statements could be used to question the minister's good faith; buf cf *Prebble v Television New Zealand Ltd* [1995] 1 AC 321, 333.

Act 1993.[96] Shortly before the hearing of the judicial review, the Speaker warned that the judges should not trespass on the proper functioning of Parliament, citing Article 9 of the Bill of Rights.[97] In the event, the arguments made in the case gave rise to no concern on this score, counsel for the applicant disclaiming any intention to question proceedings in Parliament.

(f) Parliamentary oversight of the Department of Constitutional Affairs

While judicial independence means that the judiciary are not responsible to Parliament for their acts and decisions in the way in which ministers are, the courts and the structure of justice itself would not exist if the system were not authorized and financed by Parliament. Issues as to the resources that the courts need to administer justice at an acceptable level inevitably raise questions about the competing claims being made on government for expenditure, and the views of the senior judiciary must be taken into account in the decision-making process.[98] Yet to the extent that the costs of justice are charged on funds provided by Parliament, the use of those funds must be subject to public accountability; in particular, the system of audit by the National Audit Office applies to the Department of Constitutional Affairs, that replaced the former Lord Chancellor's Department in June 2003.[99] When the present system of select committees to exercise oversight over government departments was established by the House of Commons in 1979, it did not initially extend to what was then the Lord Chancellor's Department: the view was taken by the government that the new Select Committee on Home Affairs should not be allowed to threaten the independence of the judiciary, and that the Lord Chancellor's functions were all deeply interwoven with judicial matters.[100] In 1991, the situation was modified to the extent that the remit of the Select Committee on Home Affairs was extended to include (with some important qualifications) the policy, administration and expenditure of the Lord Chancellor's Department and the

6.32

---

[96] *R v Secretary of State for Foreign and Commonwealth Affairs, ex p Rees-Mogg* [1994] QB 552.

[97] See *Hansard*, HC Deb col 353 (21 July 1993) (Betty Boothroyd MP); and R Rawlings, 'Legal politics: the United Kingdom and ratification of the Treaty on European Union: Part 2' [1994] PL 367, 377–381.

[98] A matter addressed in Lord Browne-Wilkinson, 'The Independence of the Judiciary in the 1980s' [1988] PL 44. See also DB Casson and IR Scott, in Shetreet and Deschênes (n 32 above) ch 14.

[99] See eg the following reports by the National Audit Office: *The Lord Chancellor's Department: Collection of fines and other financial penalties in the criminal justice system* (2001–02 HC 672); *The Community Legal Service: the introduction of contracting* (2002–03 HC 89); and *New IT Systems for Magistrates' Courts: the Libra project* (2002–03 HC 327).

[100] See *Hansard*, HC Deb col 38 (25 June 1979) (Norman St John-Stevas MP). Opposing views were expressed at 51 (Merlyn Rees MP), 112 (Michael English MP) and 117–122 (Peter Archer MP). An amendment to include the Lord Chancellor's Department and the Law Officers' Department in the remit of the Select Committee on Home Affairs was defeated by 186 to 87 (cols 229–232). Inclusion of these departments in the select committee system had been favoured by the Select Committee on Procedure (1977–78 HC 588-1).

Law Officers' Department.[101] In January 2003, in a decision that was long overdue, the House of Commons created a select committee to examine the expenditure, administration and policy of the Lord Chancellor's Department, including the work of the staff provided for the administrative work of courts and tribunals, but excluding consideration of individual cases and appointments.[102] The committee may thus (subject to this important exclusion) examine civil and criminal justice, legal services, courts and tribunals, judicial appointments, constitutional issues within the Lord Chancellor's responsibility, executive agencies for which he is responsible (including the Court Service, the Northern Ireland Court Service, the Land Registry and the Public Record Office) and other associated public bodies. In 2003, it was manifest that the Lord Chancellor's Department, and its successor the Department of Constitutional Affairs, could not be described as a 'small department', as it had been described in 1979.[103]

(g) Jurisdiction of the Parliamentary Ombudsman relating to the courts

6.33   Since 1967, MPs have been able to refer complaints against government departments to the Parliamentary Commissioner for Administration (Parliamentary Ombudsman) for investigation and report, where the complaint is of maladministration that has caused the complainant injustice and has occurred in the exercise of a department's administrative functions.[104] The Department for Constitutional Affairs (which succeeded the Lord Chancellor's Department in June 2003) is like other departments subject to investigation by the Ombudsman. However, the Ombudsman's jurisdiction does not apply to decisions by courts or tribunals, since they are not decisions taken in the exercise of a government department's administrative functions. In fact, many administrative actions are taken that relate to judicial proceedings, whether in courts or tribunals, by civil servants working within the Department or in a department responsible for servicing tribunals. Complex border-line decisions had to be made under the 1967 Act as originally enacted, distinguishing between those complaints against court officials that could be investigated (as relating to administrative functions) and those that could not be investigated because they related to judicial functions. The Act of 1967, as amended, now provides that the Parliamentary Commissioner may not investigate:

  (1) the commencement or conduct of civil or criminal proceedings before any court in the United Kingdom, court martial or international court;

---

[101] Hansard, HC Deb cols 576–605 (18 July 1991). The decision followed a recommendation made in the 2nd Report from the Select Committee on Procedure, 1989–90 (HC 19-I, 1989–90).
[102] See *Hansard*, HC Deb cols 644–688 (27 January 2003).
[103] *Hansard*, HC Deb col 38 (25 June 1979) (Norman St John-Stevas MP).
[104] Parliamentary Commissioner Act 1967, s 5. And see ch 21 below.

(2) action taken by persons appointed by the Lord Chancellor as the administrative staff of courts or tribunals, being action taken on the direction or by authority of persons acting in a judicial capacity.[105]

It follows from this that actions by the administrative staff of courts or tribunals may be investigated when they are *not* taken on the direction or by authority of a judge or other person (for example, a tribunal chairman) acting in a judicial capacity. Even when a complaint is within the jurisdiction of the Ombudsman, the Ombudsman has a discretion not to investigate a complaint where the complainant has or had a right of recourse to a tribunal or to proceedings in any court; but the Ombudsman may investigate such a complaint, if it is otherwise within his jurisdiction, if the complainant could not reasonably be expected to seek a remedy from the court or tribunal concerned.[106]

D. The Relationship of the Judiciary with the Executive

(a) Appointing the judges

The appointment of judges is entrusted to the executive. As we have seen, **6.34** Parliament plays no part in appointing judges,[107] other than enacting the qualifications that are required for someone to be eligible for appointment. Thus for appointment of a High Court judge, the individual must have had for at least ten years the right of audience in the High Court (whether as a barrister or a solicitor), or have been a Circuit judge for at least two years; for appointment to the Court of Appeal, he or she must have had the right of audience in the High Court for at least ten years or must be a High Court judge.[108] The selection of judges for appointment from those who are qualified to be appointed is in England and Wales, with few exceptions, a matter for the Lord Chancellor.[109] Appointments are made in the name of the Crown, but the Queen acts on the advice of the Lord

---

[105] ibid s 5(3) and Sch 3 (as amended). By the Parliamentary Commissioner Act 1994, acts of the Appeal Service (for social security appeals) may be investigated by the Ombudsman. For maladministration by staff of the Registrar of Criminal Appeals in implementing the decision of a judge, see *Quinland v Governor of Swaleside Prison* [2002] EWCA Civ 174; [2003] QB 306 (no compensation payable in law because of the Crown Proceedings Act 1947, s 2(5)): and see para 6.50 below.

[106] Parliamentary Commissioner Act 1967, s 5(2).

[107] See para 6.25 above.

[108] Courts and Legal Services Act 1990, s 71(1), amending Supreme Court Act 1981, s 10(3). For appointment as a Circuit judge, a person must have had (for at least ten years) the right of audience in the Crown Court or in county courts, or be a recorder or (for at least three years) have held a full-time judicial office such as that of a district judge: Courts Act 1971, s 16(3), as amended by the 1990 Act.

[109] For a recent critique of this position, see the Glidewell Report, prepared on behalf of the Bar Council (and see paras 6.36 and 6.37 below).

Chancellor, except when (as with the most senior appointments)[110] the nomination to the Queen is made by the Prime Minister. In practice, the greater part of the appointment process is carried out by civil servants within the Judicial Group of the Department of Constitutional Affairs, which succeeded to the functions of the Lord Chancellor's Department in June 2003. While the statutory requirements for appointment cannot be changed without legislation, the policies and practices surrounding the selection and nomination of judges by the Lord Chancellor may change without changes in the law. Thus the appointment of judges by the Lord Chancellor solely on party political grounds, which often occurred late in the 19th century when Lord Halsbury was Lord Chancellor, is today excluded by the emphasis on selection by merit and by the need for transparency in the selection process. The present overriding principle is that appointments are made on merit.[111] After 1997, a great deal was done by the Lord Chancellor's Department to make the process more transparent. The Department of Constitutional Affairs now regularly publishes information of the procedures followed,[112] which include extensive consultation, particularly within the judiciary. Except for appointments to the Court of Appeal and the House of Lords, all judicial appointments are advertised. In the case of High Court appointments, the practice of the Lord Chancellor is to select for appointment some who have not submitted applications as well as some who have done so.[113]

(b) The Commission for Judicial Appointments

6.35   In 1999, the procedures for appointing judges and for conferring the title of Queen's Counsel were reviewed by Sir Leonard Peach.[114] In response to recommendations in the Peach report, the Lord Chancellor created an advisory Commission for Judicial Appointments, with oversight of the selection procedure, including the task of investigating individual grievances and complaints relating to the appointment of judges and of Queen's Counsel.[115] The Commissioners 'shall, in the manner they consider best calculated to promote economy, efficiency, effectiveness and fairness in appointment procedures, exercise their functions with the object of maintaining the principle of selection on

---

[110] These include the Lords of Appeal in Ordinary, Lords Justices of Appeal, Lord Chief Justice, Master of the Rolls and President of the Family Division.

[111] See Lord Chancellor's Department, *Judicial Appointments in England and Wales*, April 2003.

[112] ibid.

[113] This practice was criticized by the Commission for Judicial Appointments, in its *Annual Report 2003* (April 2003) paras 5.16–5.21.

[114] See Report of the Independent Scrutiny of the Appointments Process of Judges and Queen's Counsel (December 1999).

[115] See the Judicial Appointments Order in Council, which took effect in March 2001, with the appointment of the first Commissioner. The Commission's remit does not include the appointment of the Lords of Appeal in Ordinary, the heads of Divisions of the High Court or the appointment of lay magistrates.

merit . . .'. The Commission's first report, published in 2002, stated that it had upheld three complaints made regarding the selection of Queen's Counsel in 2001, relating to the sifting of applications in the light of responses to the process of consultation. More generally, the Commission was not satisfied that the system yet did enough to promote diversity in the judiciary so as to reflect more closely the potential pool of applicants from which appointments were made. The Commission raised, without answering, the question of whether judicial appointments and the selection of Queen's Counsel should continue to be made by a government minister.[116] The Commission's second annual report upheld eight out of 12 complaints that had been investigated; the issues that arose related to such matters as concerns about reliance on automatic consultation in competitions for certain appointments, the need to clarify the criteria of 'merit' in relation to some posts, and the style and conduct of some appointment interviews.[117] The Commission also recommended the appointment of an independent Judicial Appointments Commission.

(c) The case against the executive power to appoint judges

The question of whether judicial appointments and the selection of Queen's **6.36**
Counsel should continue to be made by a government minister received a negative answer in March 2003, in a consultation paper prepared for the Bar Council by a committee chaired by Sir Ian Glidewell, a retired Lord Justice of Appeal. The committee recommended that judicial appointments should no longer be undertaken by the Lord Chancellor, but should be entrusted to a new, high calibre and independent High Court Appointments Board for England and Wales, on the lines of the Judicial Appointments Board in Scotland;[118] and that the selection of Queen's Counsel should be entrusted to an independent panel with a broad, diverse representation, chaired by a retired Law Lord or Lord Justice of Appeal, who would recommend a list of suitable persons to the Lord Chancellor, for formal recommendation to the Crown.[119]

In arguing the case for removing the power to appoint judges from the Lord **6.37**
Chancellor, the Glidewell committee referred to the changing constitutional functions of the judiciary, particularly in the light of devolution and the HRA 1998, and continued:

---

[116] Particular criticism was made of the process by which an official had, in the light of replies from those consulted, prepared lists of those applicants (1) who were strongly supported and those (2) who were less strongly supported but were considered to warrant the Lord Chancellor's consideration.

[117] Judicial Appointments Commission, *Annual Report 2003*.

[118] This Board, including both lawyers and lay persons, was created by the Scottish Executive to advise on the appointment of Court of Session judges and sheriffs, a matter devolved by the Scotland Act 1998, s 95.

[119] Consultation Document from the Bar Council Working Party on Judicial Appointments and Silk, March 2003.

These considerations lead to this very important consequence if the judiciary is to perform its proper role in the 21ˢᵗ century. It must be protected by constitutional safeguards from the risk or even the perception that its independence might be threatened by the Executive. Put simply, it has become constitutionally unacceptable in our view that the judges should be appointed by the government of the day. We will stress that this is not an attack on the present or any past or future Lord Chancellor. It is a matter of public perception. Appointments will increasingly come under public scrutiny and attack if an appointment is seen or suspected to be based on the belief that a candidate will favour the government line.[120]

In June 2003, the government announced that it had decided to legislate for the creation of a Judicial Appointments Commission that would be responsible for the selection for appointment of the great majority of judges in England and Wales. Among the issues that would be decided after consultation were whether the actual appointments would be made by the Commission or by a government minister on the advice of the Commission, the composition of the Commission, the means of securing the independence of the Commission, and possible measures for promoting greater diversity within the judiciary.[121]

(d) Judicial independence and the promotion of judges

6.38   From the viewpoint of maintaining judicial independence, it is indeed important that, leaving aside the manner in which appointments are made, judges when appointed should enjoy security of tenure. However, in performing his or her duties, a judge who knows that the possibility of removal from office is very small, may be more concerned about the possibility of being promoted from his or her present position to a more senior judicial position. England and Wales do not have a career judiciary in the sense in which, in other European systems, qualified lawyers may serve their entire professional career in judicial office. But deputy district judges may hope to become district judges, and some district judges may become circuit judges in due course. Circuit judges may be appointed to the High Court bench, opening up the possibility of further advancement in the judicial hierarchy (to the Court of Appeal or the House of Lords). For a practising barrister, a route that is commonly followed before his or her appointment to the High Court, with the possibility of further advancement to appellate positions, is (1) to secure appointment as a part-time recorder, (2) to have been appointed as a Queen's Counsel and (3) to sit as a Deputy High Court judge. These three stages were in 2003 all dependent on the decision of the Lord Chancellor. If advancement through all these stages depends on merit, as it is said to do, then the process of selection at every stage should be such as to exclude the

---

[120] Report of Bar Council Working Party on Judicial Appointments and Silk, para 10.14. For a more conservative view, see Sir S Kentridge, 'The Highest Court: Selecting the Judges' [2003] CLJ 55.

[121] *Constitutional reform: a new way of appointing judges* (CP 10.30); and see para 6.35 above.

possibility that parties affected by judicial decisions should be able to exercise improper influence. These considerations indicate that appointments by way of promotion to a more senior judicial position should be included within the tasks of a Judicial Appointments Commission, together with the making of initial appointments. Another consequence of a policy of basing appointments to more senior posts on merit is that the Prime Minister should no longer participate in the making of the most senior appointments, as is the case with the Lords of Appeal in Ordinary and the presidents of the divisions of the High Court.

(e) Executive criticism of the judges

Although the HRA 1998 and the devolution legislation in 1998 vested further constitutional tasks in the judiciary, those tasks built upon the functions of the judiciary in applying principles of administrative law to official decisions.[122] That jurisdiction is inherently likely to lead on occasion to decisions by the courts that are unwelcome to those holding executive office.[123] In particular, because of the range of its responsibilities, the Home Office is particularly vulnerable to adverse judicial decisions. When such decisions are made against government departments, whether by the Administrative Court or a higher court, ministers may always appeal and argue that the decision should have been different. But they ought not to display impatience with the judges and complain that they are intentionally seeking to reverse laws made by Parliament. This was the ill-tempered criticism made in February 2003 by the Home Secretary (Mr Blunkett) of a decision by Collins J quashing decisions that six asylum-seekers should be denied all support because they were considered not to have claimed asylum as soon as was reasonably practicable after entering the United Kingdom.[124] On appeal, the decision by Collins J was upheld, albeit on partly different grounds. Stressing that the task of any court 'when faced with issues of statutory construction, such as those which arise in this case, is to deduce and give effect to the intention of Parliament,' the Court of Appeal observed: 'The approach of Collins J to his task cannot be faulted and we commend the care with which, in his lengthy judgment, he addressed the difficult issues before him.'[125] While the Home Secretary's attack on the judge's decision in this case took an extreme form, the conduct of previous Home Secretaries in the 1990s had been similar.[126] The attack in 2003 coincided

6.39

---

[122] See chs 7 and 13–16 below.

[123] See eg *M v Home Office* [1994] 1 AC 377 (Home Secretary held to have acted in contempt of court by cancelling arrangements for return to the UK of a Nigerian asylum-seeker).

[124] AW Bradley, 'Judicial independence under attack' [2003] PL 397.

[125] *R (on the application of Q) v Secretary of State for the Home Department* [2003] EWCA Civ 364; [2003] 2 All ER 905, at [4] and [5]. The case concerned the interpretation of the Nationality, Immigration and Asylum Act 2002, s 55, which in subs (5) required the decision-maker to take into account the need to avoid breaching a person's Convention rights.

[126] See A Le Sueur, 'The Judicial Review Debate: from Partnership to Friction' (1996) 31 Government and Opposition 8.

with a period of evident tension between the Home Secretary and the senior judiciary in relation to the performance by the judges of their sentencing functions in criminal justice.[127]

6.40 Executive impatience with a judge was seen in a different context when during the period of 1991 to 1993, the Lord Chancellor (Lord Mackay of Clashfern) disagreed with the position taken up by a High Court judge (Wood J), the appointed President of the Employment Appeal Tribunal, relating to a procedure which Wood J regarded as necessary in the interests of justice but which the Lord Chancellor considered prevented the Tribunal from disposing of appeals efficiently. After extensive correspondence with Wood J, the Lord Chancellor wrote a letter in which he stated: 'If you do not feel that you can give me [an 'immediate assurance' that had been requested] I must ask you to consider your position'.[128] When the affair was debated in the House of Lords, Lord Oliver observed that the Lord Chancellor appeared to hold the view that the principle of judicial independence was infringed 'only if an attempt is made to dictate or influence the decision in a particular individual case'; in Lord Oliver's view, the pressure which was applied in this case 'constituted an attempt by the Executive—no doubt in the praiseworthy interests of economy and expedition—to overbear the conscience of a judge in the way in which he was to exercise his judicial duty and his judicial discretion'.[129] In reply, Lord Mackay denied that the letter had prejudiced judicial independence, but regretted that his intention had not been expressed more plainly.

(f) Complaints against the judges and judicial discipline

6.41 One responsibility exercised by the Lord Chancellor exists because of the lack of formal procedure for dealing with complaints against a judge or for exercising disciplinary powers over a judge. We have seen that in general members of the executive should refrain from criticizing a judge for his or her decisions. The Lord Chancellor's position is different in that he is also head of the judiciary. Except for High Court judges and above, the Lord Chancellor has the power to remove a judge from office for incapacity or misbehaviour.[130] Although such removal from office occurs very rarely, the Lord Chancellor is frequently called on to consider complaints against judges.[131] In 2001–02, he received 2,100 complaints against

---

[127] See para 6.15 above.
[128] See The Observer, 6 March 1994. Also F Purchas, 'Lord Mackay and the judiciary' [1994] NLJ 527; and Ackner (n 32 above) 16–18.
[129] *Hansard*, HL Deb col 751 (27 April 1994). Although many speakers in the debate regretted the need for it to have been held, the report of the debate is of absorbing interest for the illuminating views of judicial independence which were then expressed.
[130] See eg for circuit judges, Courts Act 1971, s 17(4).
[131] The details that follow are taken from Lord Chancellor's Department, *Judicial Appointments Annual Report 2001–02*, ch 6.

judges, most of which were complaints about their decisions, and were thus not considered. As many as 347 complaints were about the personal conduct of judges, not about their decisions, and these were investigated by officials in the Department acting for the Lord Chancellor. No dismissals occurred in the year in question, but in many cases further action was taken, in the form of a letter from the Lord Chancellor rebuking the judge for conduct falling below the expected standards of conduct or requesting that the judge should attend for interview with his or her presiding judge. The Lord Chancellor was particularly concerned to see that complaints of discriminatory conduct were dealt with. If the appointment of judges were in future to be taken from the Lord Chancellor and entrusted to a separate body, as was proposed by the government in 2003, the change would need to include provision for dismissal in serious cases and for enabling appropriate disciplinary measures to be taken in less serious cases. The exercise of disciplinary functions would seem to be a matter that in general should be entrusted to the senior judges.

(g) Judicial participation in the media

An example of the manner in which the Lord Chancellor has been concerned **6.42** with setting the standards of judicial conduct is provided by his role in determining the extent to which serving judges may take part in media discussion of current issues. The former restrictive policy, referred to as the 'Kilmuir rules', was based on a letter from Lord Chancellor Kilmuir in 1955 to the chairman of the BBC,[132] written after consultation with the Lord Chief Justice and other senior judges, disapproving a BBC proposal for a series of radio talks by judges on eminent judges of the past. Upon appointment as Lord Chancellor in 1987, Lord Mackay stated that these rules should be abolished; he considered that judges should be free to speak to the press or television, subject to their being able to do so without in any way prejudicing performance of their judicial work.[133] Soon after the HRA 1998 was enacted, the Scottish courts provided a notable example of the danger of a judge's published views on current issues disqualifying him or her from deciding cases that involved those issues.[134] A less dramatic illustration came from England when a decision made by a part-time recorder upholding a claim for personal injuries was set aside on appeal because of articles published by the recorder (and unknown to the defendant's lawyers)

---

[132] The text of the letter was not published until 1986: see [1986] PL 383. It included the memorable sentence: 'So long as a Judge keeps silent his reputation for wisdom and impartiality remains unassailable: but every utterance which he makes in public, except in the course of the actual performance of his judicial duties, must necessarily bring him within the focus of criticism.'

[133] The Times, 4 November 1988.

[134] *Hoekstra v HM Advocate* 2001 SLT 28 (newly retired High Court judge publishing newspaper article making strident criticism of the HRA 1998, but proceeding to take part in criminal appeal based on human rights grounds).

that were very critical of the practices of insurance companies in defending such claims.[135]

(h) Use of the judges for non-judicial purposes

6.43   Questions about the proper relationship between the judiciary and the executive arise in relation to the appointment by the government of judges to undertake ad hoc tasks for the executive that are outside the normal sphere of judicial duties. Judges are frequently called on by the executive to preside over royal commissions, departmental committees, tribunals of inquiry conducted under the Tribunals of Inquiry (Evidence) Act 1921 and other inquiries—whether conducted under statutes or without the benefit of statutory authority.[136] Some judges are particularly successful in the important task of discovering what caused a major public disaster causing loss of life (such as a railway accident or an explosion) and of making recommendations for the future.[137] But difficulties may well arise if the political element of an inquiry is substantial.

6.44   These difficulties were seen most acutely in the inquiry by Sir Richard Scott into the arms for Iraq affair involving the abortive prosecution of the Matrix Churchill company.[138] Although government departments co-operated with the Scott inquiry in providing documents and in supplying official witnesses, and Sir Richard Scott did not ask to have statutory powers conferred on the inquiry, the whole process proved highly controversial, much of the investigation being concerned with the propriety or otherwise of administrative decisions, ministerial letters and answers in Parliament. In particular, the arrangements made by the government for the publication of the Scott report were oppressive and one-sided.[139] Different procedures were adopted in August and September 2003 for the conduct of Lord Hutton's inquiry into the suicide of Dr David Kelly, a Minister of Defence scientist, against a highly political background of events relating to the preparation of the government's case for making war against Iraq.

6.45   Because of the difficulties that may arise where an inquiry has a high political content, there is a need for clearer principles than now exist as to the circumstances in

---

[135]   *Timmins v Gormley*, reported with *Locabail (UK) Ltd v Bayfield Properties Ltd* [2000] QB 451. And see paras 15.83 et seq below.

[136]   See also JAG Griffith (n 32 above) ch 2; and ch 22 below.

[137]   The senior judge in Scotland (Lord President Cullen) has had the distinction of conducting three major inquiries—into the Piper Alpha disaster (Cm 1310, 1990), the Dunblane primary school shooting (Cm 3386, 1996), and the Paddington rail disaster in 1999 (*The Ladbroke Grove Rail Inquiry: Parts 1 and 2*, Health and Safety Executive, 2001).

[138]   For the Scott report, see 1995–96 HC 115; the collection of articles at [1996] PL 357–507; and A Tomkins, *The Constitution after Scott: Government Unwrapped* (Oxford: Clarendon Press, 1998).

[139]   AW Bradley, 'Commissions of Inquiry and Governmental Accountability—Recent British Experience' in A Manson and D Mullan (ed), *Commissions of Inquiry—Praise or Reappraise?* (Toronto: Irwin Law, 2003) ch 2.

which a judge is relieved from his or her normal duties to undertake a major inquiry.[140] The use of retired judges[141] rather than serving judges avoids many such difficulties. Certainly, professional persons with experience in relevant fields may have strengths that make them preferable to judges for the conduct of some inquiries. Although the discussion so far has concerned ad hoc inquiries of various kinds, recent statutes (beginning with the Interception of Communications Act 1985) have empowered the government to appoint senior judges to conduct certain inquiries on a regular basis in matters affecting national security. Thus the commissioners appointed by the Prime Minister under the Regulation of Investigatory Powers Act 2000 to review the interception of communications and the intelligence services are required to be persons who hold or have held high judicial office.[142] Although the Commissioner reports annually to the Prime Minister, and the report is laid before Parliament, this practice raises questions as to the effect of such work for the executive on the outlook of the judges concerned. Such experience might well disqualify the judge in question from adjudicating in cases that turn upon considerations of national security or the work of the security services.

(i) Judicial training

One recent development in the administration of the courts that has been very marked in the last 25 years is the increasing attention that is paid to the training of judges and to such matters as the induction and orientation of newly appointed judges. It is today generally accepted that the fact that an individual is suitable for appointment as a judge by reason of his or her professional experience as a practising lawyer does not necessarily mean that he or she is immediately qualified to perform judicial duties. The Judicial Studies Board was created in 1979. Funded by the Department for Constitutional Affairs (formerly by the Lord Chancellor's Department), it provides a full programme of training and induction courses for all judges. It is fundamental to the work of the Board that its programme should be under the control and direction of the senior judiciary, as was the Board's major exercise in 2000 in introducing all judges in England and Wales to the essentials of the HRA.[143] This example illustrates the importance of ensuring that a scheme of judicial training is not structured so as to enable officials within the executive branch of government to train judges to make decisions that are acceptable to the executive.

6.46

---

[140] Such principles would include the ability of a judge to decide whether he or she wishes to undertake the task in question, the need for the president of the court in question to release the judge from ordinary duties, assurances about departmental co-operation in the inquiry and (in the light of what happened to the Scott report) the arrangements for publication of the report.

[141] See eg the report of the Stephen Lawrence Inquiry, chaired by Sir William Macpherson of Cluny (Cm 4262, 1999).

[142] Regulation of Investigatory Powers Act 2000, ss 57(5), 59(5).

[143] And see A Finlay, 'The Human Rights Act: the Lord Chancellor's Department's Preparations for Implementation' [1999] European Human Rights L Rev 512.

E. Liability for the Exercise of Judicial Power

(a) Judicial immunity from liability in damages

6.47   An important means of securing the accountability of many professional and occupational groups is the liability in tort that may ensue for individuals who in carrying out their duties fall below the accepted standards of the group concerned or
do not observe the legal rules that apply to them. Thus actions in negligence are
regularly brought against accountants, architects and doctors, and actions for excess or abuse of powers are brought against police officers. But the common law
has been firmly opposed to there being a remedy in tort for those who are injured
or suffer loss at the hands of a judge whose acts or decisions fall below a reasonable
standard of competence. Although other arguments for denying such a remedy
exist, a leading justification for the denial of a remedy has been the doctrine of judicial independence. As was said in 1868, judicial immunity 'is for the benefit of
the public, whose interest it is that the judges should be at liberty to exercise their
functions with independence and without fear of consequences'.[144] And in 1976,
Margaret Brazier wrote that 'at the core of the principle of judicial independence
lies the immunity of judges from civil actions'.[145] Today, it is not self-evident that
the doctrine of judicial independence depends on the judges having absolute immunity from liability for acts done or words said in the course of their office. A recent study of the subject concluded: 'the best explanation for the continued
existence of absolute judicial immunity is judicial self-protection'.[146]

6.48   The common law rule is that the judge of a superior court is not liable for anything
done or said in the exercise of judicial functions, however malicious, corrupt or
oppressive are the acts or words complained of.[147] Similar immunity attaches also
to words spoken by parties, counsel and witnesses in the course of judicial proceedings,[148] but advocates do not today have immunity for the negligent conduct

---

[144] *Scott v Stansfield* (1868) LR 3 Ex 220, 223 (Kelly CB).

[145] M Brazier, 'Judicial Immunity and the Independence of the Judiciary' [1976] PL 397. This
article remains valuable for its survey of the case law and its discussion of *Sirros v Moore* [1975]
QB 118.

[146] A Olowofoyeku, *Suing Judges: a Study of Judicial Immunity* (Oxford: Clarendon Press, 1993)
200; in support of his thesis, the author quotes from Cockburn CJ's dissenting judgment in
Dawkins v Paulet (1869) LR 5 QB 93, 110, to the effect that judges would not be deterred from performing their duties by any fear of being sued. The author argues that there should be qualified,
rather than absolute, immunity for all officers who exercise judicial functions.

[147] *Anderson v Gorrie* [1895] 1 QB 668: Lord Esher MR denied that there could be any liability
even where a judge was 'guilty of a gross dereliction of duty'. But he added a delphic qualification:
'If a judge goes beyond his jurisdiction, a different set of considerations arise' (671). For accounts of
judicial immunity, see AM Dugdale (ed), *Clerk &Lindsell on Torts* (18th edn, London: Sweet &
Maxwell, 2000) ch 17.1; M Brazier and J Murphy (eds), *Street on Torts* (10th edn, London:
Butterworths, 1999) 102.

[148] *Munster v Lamb* (1883) 11 QBD 588.

of a client's case in court.[149] There was formerly much complexity in the case law as to the liability of magistrates, since the jurisdiction of inferior courts is subject to limits that do not apply to superior courts; liability for magistrates could arise for acts outside their jurisdiction, even when they believed in good faith that they were acting within their jurisdiction.[150] In 1990, the liability of magistrates was placed on a clearer basis by legislation: (1) magistrates (and justices' clerks) are not liable for any acts that occur in the execution of their duty as such and that relate to any matter within their jurisdiction; (2) nor are they liable for any acts in the purported execution of their duty but which do not relate to any matter within their jurisdiction, unless the claimant can show that the defendant acted in bad faith.[151] This change in the law for magistrates brought their position nearer to that of superior court judges. Despite the proposition quoted above for which *Anderson v Gorrie* has long provided authority, it is difficult to justify absolute immunity for those holding judicial office 'however malicious, corrupt or oppressive' their conduct may be. There appears to be no reason, at least as a matter of law, why the developing tort of misfeasance in a public office[152] should not be applied to decisions by a corrupt and dishonest judge. Such a judge would be likely to know whom an adverse decision would injure and to know also that he or she was acting wrongly. A successful action would require clear proof of corruption or dishonesty (for instance, proof that a judge had accepted a bribe to favour one party). But miscarriages of justice may occur in many situations (for instance, to litigants who suffer an increased burden of costs because of unacceptable judicial conduct),[153] where misfeasance in this extreme sense could not be shown.

(b) Immunity of the Crown from liability for judicial acts

The Crown Proceedings Act 1947, s 2(1) made it possible to sue government departments as of right in tort, imposing vicarious liability upon the Crown for torts committed by its servants and agents as if the Crown were a private person of full age and capacity. Even if we assume that the holders of judicial office are the Crown's servants or agents for this purpose, the 1947 Act stated that the Crown was not vicariously liable where the individual servant or agent was not personally liable in tort.[154] Since judges were protected by the rule of absolute immunity, this would have prevented any vicarious liability arising in respect of the judiciary.

6.49

---

[149] *Hall (Arthur JS) & Co v Simons* [2002] 1 AC 615, HL, not following *Rondel v Worsley* [1969] 1 AC 191.

[150] Of recent decisions, see in particular *Sirros v Moore* [1975] QB 118 and *Re McC* [1985] AC 528.

[151] Courts and Legal Services Act 1990, s 108. See now Courts Act 2003, ss 31–32.

[152] For which, see *Three Rivers DC v Bank of England (No 3)* [2003] 2 AC 1, 187–237.

[153] See eg the burden of wasted costs in *Goose v Wilson Sandford & Co*, The Times, 19 February 1998, discussed by A Olowofoyeku, 'State Liability for the Exercise of Judicial Power' [1998] PL 444.

[154] Crown Proceedings Act 1947, s 2(1), proviso.

Moreover, to put the matter beyond any possible argument, s 2(5) of the 1947 Act stated that the Crown is not liable for the conduct of any person 'while discharging or purporting to discharge any responsibilities of a judicial nature vested in him, or any responsibilities which he has in connection with the execution of judicial process'. However, this provision did not affect the individual liability of any person (such as a magistrate or a law-enforcement officer) which might otherwise exist in law, since the aim of s 2(5) was solely to prevent any *vicarious* liability arising in relation to responsibilities of a judicial nature.

6.50   The plain intention expressed in the Crown Proceedings Act 1947, taken with the rule of absolute immunity at common law, excluded any possibility of the Crown being liable for the wrongful acts of judges and others acting in a judicial capacity. The meaning of 'judicial' used as an element in a rule of law is capable of widely differing meanings, depending on the purpose of the rule in question. In *Jones v Department of Employment*,[155] the Court of Appeal held that a civil servant employed as an 'adjudication officer' to decide claims for unemployment benefit in accordance with the legislation was not discharging responsibilities of a judicial nature for purposes of s 2(5), but was acting in an administrative capacity. However, this did not avail the claimant, since the court's primary reason for striking out the action was that no duty of care in private law was owed to the claimant to make the correct decision. In *Welsh v Chief Constable of Merseyside Police*,[156] the Crown Prosecution Service was sued because a mistake within the Service had led to the claimant being arrested and held in custody unnecessarily. Tudor Evans J held that s 2(5) of the 1947 Act was concerned with maintaining immunity for judicial functions, but what had occurred in the case was an administrative mistake (a failure to inform the court that certain of the claimant's offences had already been taken into consideration by the Crown Court) for which there was no immunity.

6.51   A different approach to s 2(5) was taken by the Court of Appeal in *Quinland v Governor of Swaleside Prison and the Lord Chancellor's Department*,[157] where a failure by the Criminal Appeal Office to process promptly the note of a judge granting the claimant leave to appeal had led to him spending six weeks longer in prison than the sentence imposed on him required. On the court's view, this was maladministration, but it was held that s 2(5) excluded any legal liability since the functions of the Criminal Appeal Office had arisen in connection with the execution of judicial process. Hale LJ said that the Court Service 'may be an agency of the executive but it exists, in part if not in whole, to facilitate and implement the workings

---

[155] [1989] QB 1; and see WJ Swadling, 'Liability for Negligent Refusal of Unemployment Benefit' [1988] PL 328.
[156] [1993] 1 All ER 692.
[157] [2002] EWCA Civ 174; [2003] QB 306.

of the judiciary. There are some of its activities over which the judiciary and not the executive must have the ultimate control. Whatever else these may include, they must include the putting into effect of the orders or directions of a court.'[158]

(c) State liability for miscarriages of justice

The facts in the *Quinland* case occurred several years before the HRA 1998, **6.52** and it is significant that Clarke and Hale LJJ expressly reserved their position on the possible effect of that Act upon s 2(5) of the Crown Proceedings Act 1947. Since 1947, it has been accepted that miscarriages of justice may occur and may cause loss and injury to an innocent person for which compensation should be provided.[159] The Criminal Appeal Act 1995 created a Criminal Cases Review Commission to investigate alleged miscarriages of justice and to refer cases to the Court of Appeal. Where it is established beyond reasonable doubt that there has been a miscarriage of justice, the individual is entitled to a payment of compensation from the Home Secretary, determined by an assessor.[160] The unjustified loss of an individual's liberty, particularly if it lasts for many years, is certainly a grave matter, and is a vivid illustration of the effect that the powers of the state (whether acting through executive officers or the judiciary) may have upon an individual's fundamental rights. Under many Commonwealth constitutions, it is accepted that the protection of fundamental rights may require a remedy to be provided where such rights have been violated, even if such a remedy does not exist at common law. In *Maharaj v A-G of Trinidad (No 2)*,[161] the Judicial Committee of the Privy Council held (Lord Hailsham dissenting) that the constitution of Trinidad and Tobago required the state to compensate a lawyer who had been committed to prison for contempt of court by the order of a judge which was later held to be unlawful. Nonetheless, the Judicial Committee also held that the constitution did not alter the rule of public policy that a judge should not be made liable for anything done by him in the exercise of his judicial functions. Accordingly, the claimant recovered compensation from the state, but the personal immunity of the judge was upheld. The decision in *Maharaj* confirms that a rule of immunity may be justified so far as the judge's position is concerned, but that this justification does not provide a sufficient reason for completely depriving an individual of a right to compensation.

(d) The effect of the Human Rights Act 1998 on immunity for judicial acts

Under Article 41 ECHR, a state may be liable to provide 'just satisfaction' to an **6.53** individual whose Convention rights have been breached but to whom national

---

[158] ibid at [41].
[159] See AW Bradley and KD Ewing, *Constitutional and Administrative Law* (13th edn, Harlow: Longman, 2001) ch 18F.
[160] See Criminal Justice Act 1988, s 133 and Criminal Appeal Act 1995, s 28.
[161] [1979] AC 385.

law allows only partial reparation to be made; it is no defence to a claim for violation of rights that the decision in question was made on behalf of the state by a court or tribunal.[162] By Article 5(5), the ECHR also confers an express entitlement to compensation upon anyone who is arrested or detained in breach of the main provisions of Article 5 (right to liberty and security). With the aim of enabling Convention rights to have effect within the United Kingdom, the HRA 1998 imposed new obligations of protecting Convention rights on all courts and tribunals in the United Kingdom.[163] The Act declared that courts and tribunals were 'public authorities' for the purposes of s 6(1), by which it is 'unlawful for a public authority to act in a way which is incompatible with a Convention right'. The Act (by s 7(1)) entitles any person who claims that a public authority has acted incompatibly with his or her Convention rights to bring proceedings against the authority in the appropriate court or tribunal, or to rely on the Convention rights concerned in any legal proceedings. In proceedings brought for this purpose before a civil court with power to award damages or order payment of compensation, the court may grant damages for the breach of a Convention right if this appears to the court to be a 'just and appropriate' remedy. The HRA makes further provision for the availability of a remedy when it is the decision of a court or tribunal that caused the violation of a Convention right. By s 9(3):

> In proceedings under this Act in respect of a judicial act done in good faith, damages may not be ordered otherwise than to compensate a person to the extent required by Article 5(5) of the Convention.

A judicial act is defined as 'a judicial act of a court and includes an act done on the instructions, or on behalf of, a judge' (s 9(5)).

6.54 It results from these provisions of the HRA 1998 that damages may be awarded in respect of a judicial act only if the act was done in bad faith, or if the individual is relying on his or her right to compensation under Article 5(5). The general scheme of the HRA is that if damages are awarded against a public authority for a violation of the claimant's Convention rights, they will be payable by the public authority in question (whereas if a successful claim is made at Strasbourg and 'just satisfaction' is ordered, payment must be made on behalf of the state). In the case of damages awarded in respect of a judicial act, the 1998 Act provides that the award is not to be made against the judge or the court, but against the Crown, which must be represented in the proceedings by the Minister responsible for the court 'or a person or government department nominated by him' (s 9(4),(5)). In England and Wales, the responsible minister for this purpose was in 2003 the Lord Chancellor. The result of these provisions is that in respect of judicial acts, compensation may be awarded in narrowly defined circumstances where a court

---

[162] See eg *Sunday Times Ltd v UK* (1979) 2 EHRR 245.
[163] See paras 7.139 and 19.61 et seq below.

or tribunal has violated an individual's Convention rights: such compensation will be borne by the executive, and not by the judge, court or tribunal in question. However, the restrictions on the individual's right to compensation may mean that the HRA does not in this respect go far enough in enabling individuals to obtain remedies in the national courts, compared with what the claimant might have obtained from taking the case to Strasbourg.

Part II

STANDARDS FOR LEGAL ACCOUNTABILITY IN PUBLIC LAW: HUMAN RIGHTS AND JUDICIAL REVIEW

7

STANDARDS OF REVIEW AND HUMAN RIGHTS IN ENGLISH LAW

A. The Nature of Legal Standards for Scrutinizing Official Action

The chapters in Part I of this work were mainly concerned with the structure and functions of public institutions and with the relationships between them. The chapters in Part II are directed to the standards by which public institutions and officials are held legally accountable for the discharge of their responsibilities. **7.01**

Standards for legal accountability fall into two broad types. First, there are standards which apply generally to the work of all public bodies. They amount to minimum standards of legally acceptable behaviour in the exercise of public functions, which apply regardless of the particular context in which a body is operating and the specific activity it is undertaking. Some, at least, of the standards must be sufficiently flexible to allow them to have effect in widely different situations without frustrating the beneficial functions of public policy or administration in that field. The principles of procedural fairness are of this kind: the elements in a fair decision-making process depend, to some extent, on the type of decision that is being made and the circumstances in which it must work.[1] But the **7.02**

---

[1] See chs 12 and 15.

basic principles must be capable of being applied in all situations to which they are relevant.

7.03   The second type of standard is one fashioned to a particular area of public administration or public function. Legislation establishing a public body for a particular purpose, or instituting a new legal regime to govern an area of activity, typically sets out in some detail the rules which are to govern the work of public bodies in that field. Sometimes primary legislation contains the rules, but more often it empowers another person or body (often a minister of the Crown) to lay down the detailed rules in subordinate legislation.

7.04   As this work is concerned with the general principles of English public law, the chapters in this Part of the work concentrate on standards of the first, generally applicable, kind. The main general standards are those originating in the European Convention on Human Rights (ECHR) as given effect in English law by the Human Rights Act 1998 (HRA), and the common law grounds of judicial review which can be grouped under the headings of illegality, procedural propriety, and irrationality. Together they provide the basis for securing the legal accountability of public authorities to ensure that they exercise their functions in a way that accords with the principles of the rule of law and respects fundamental values of human dignity and equality and parliamentary democracy. Particular, detailed rules governing specific areas of public administration are discussed only to the extent that they usefully illustrate more general issues or themes.

7.05   The arrangement of Part II is as follows. The remainder of this chapter provides a general account of the role of human rights in English law, including the structure of the HRA 1998 and general principles relating to the rights which the Act makes part of English law. Chapters 8 to 12 examine the impact of groups of rights on the law, including civil and political rights (chapters 8 and 9), social, economic and cultural rights (chapter 10), equality-related rights (chapter 11), and due process rights (chapter 12). Chapters 13 to 16 examine the effect of principles of judicial review, starting with an account of the fundamental principles of administrative law (chapter 13), then exploring the principle of legality (chapter 14), the common law principles of procedural propriety (chapter 15), and ending with review based on substantive values such as rationality of decisions (chapter 16).

B.   The Historical Background to and Use of Human Rights in English Law apart from the Human Rights Act 1998

(a) Early bills of rights

7.06   The protection of human rights in English law was, until quite recently, haphazard and indirect. A number of pieces of legislation had, over the centuries, encapsulated some rights. Magna Carta, imposed by the nobility on King John in 1215 and subsequently reaffirmed a number of times, reaching its current form in 1297, was described as the 'Great Charter of the Liberties of England, and of the Liberties of the Forest'. Many provisions have been repealed, but those remaining in force include confirmation of the freedom of the (then Roman Catholic, now Anglican) church of England, and of the grant of a number of particular liberties to freemen. The latter include the right of freemen not to be taken or imprisoned, or disseised of their freeholds, liberties or free customs; the right not to be outlawed, exiled, or otherwise destroyed; and their right not to be condemned except by lawful judgment of their peers or by the law of the land. Finally, there is an undertaking not to sell, deny or defer justice or right.[2] These provisions may be regarded as a cornerstone of the rule of law in England, with an impact that continues to shape modern constitutional thinking.[3] In 1688, the Bill of Rights (accepted by King William III and Queen Mary II on being offered the Crown after the departure of King James II) declared (among other things) the right to petition the monarch, the right of Protestants to have arms for their defence subject to conditions and as allowed by law, the right to free elections to Parliament, and the right to freedom of speech and debate in Parliament. It also included a ban on excessive bail, excessive fines, and the infliction of cruel and unusual punishments.[4]

(b) The common law and fundamental rights

In the 17th and 18th centuries, partly inspired by theories of natural law, common **7.07** lawyers developed the notion that some rights, embedded in the common law, were fundamental to the constitutional settlement. Early in the 17th century, Coke suggested (controversially) that even Parliament might not interfere with these rights, for example by making a man a judge in his own cause. Later in the century, parliamentarians used the idea of fundamental rights as a weapon in their attack on the royal prerogative.[5] In the 18th century, it was commonplace to regard rights to property and to liberty of the person as sufficiently fundamental to require clear legal authority for any purported interference with them.[6] The cases in which judges accepted and applied these principles came to be regarded as embodying a central plank in the constitution.

---

[2] Statute 25 Edw 1 (1297), preamble and cc 1 and 29.
[3] Lord Irvine of Lairg, 'The Spirit of Magna Carta continues to resonate in modern law' (2003) 119 LQR 227.
[4] 1 Will and Mar sess 2, c 2, confirmed by the Crown and Parliament Recognition Act 1689, 2 Will and Mar, c 1.
[5] For different views of the scope and impact of this, see JW Gough, *Fundamental Law in English History* (Oxford: Clarendon Press, 1955) chs 1–10; J Goldsworthy, *The Sovereignty of Parliament— History and Philosophy* (Oxford: OUP, 1999) chs 3–5.
[6] See, eg, *Entick v Carrington* (1765) 2 Wils 275; *Leach v Money* (1775) 19 St Tr 1001; *Somersett v Stewart* (1772) 20 St Tr 1.

(c) Lasting significance of these developments

7.08   The developments mentioned above were of considerable practical (and even greater symbolic) importance, but did not amount to a catalogue of people's fundamental rights. They were an expression of two ideas. First, they made it clear that officers were given power over people not absolutely but on condition that they used it in certain ways. There were limits to the circumstances in which powers would be regarded as being used justifiably. This was an aspect of feudal relationships, and the work of theorists like John Locke carried it forward into the period when rulers claimed absolute power. Secondly, it became a constitutional orthodoxy that all officials and bodies (with the exception of the monarch in person and Parliament) could be made legally accountable in the courts for their actions, by reference to objectively ascertainable legal standards. Embedding these two ideas in English constitutional law and practice was a key step in the development of the rule of law. Although much of Magna Carta and the Bill of Rights 1688 was a response to particular abuses, the response was framed in the light of these important, fundamental principles which in the fullness of time made possible a catalogue of people's fundamental rights.

(d) Utilitarianism, parliamentary sovereignty, democracy, and rights

7.09   Through the 19th and much of the 20th centuries, the idea of fundamental rights largely gave way to parliamentary sovereignty and representative democracy as the dominance of natural law gave way to utilitarian theories. Many statutes conferred specific rights on people. For example, Parliament removed many of the disqualifications which had excluded people of faiths other than that of the Church of England from many opportunities to participate in public life;[7] it steadily widened the electorate starting with the Reform Acts of 1832 and 1867; in the later 20th century it conferred a right to be free from discrimination on a growing range of grounds;[8] and it imposed, then relaxed, rules controlling abuse of rights in the criminal justice system.[9] However, there was no systematic attempt to use statutes to codify people's liberties or rights, or to identify some liberties and rights as being constitutionally fundamental.

7.10   Indeed, the constitutional structure and traditions in England were (and to some extent remain) inimical to any attempt to give certain liberties or rights higher status

---

[7] See, eg, the repeal of the Test and Corporation Acts in 1828, the passage of the Catholic Emancipation Act 1829, and in 1866 the removal of the words 'on the true faith of a Christian' from the oath to be taken by MPs, which had excluded Jews from sitting in Parliament.

[8] See, eg, Race Relations Act 1968, replaced by the Race Relations Act 1976; Sex Discrimination Act 1975; Disability Discrimination Act 1995. Further legislation is soon to outlaw discrimination on the grounds of age, religion and sexual orientation, to give effect to obligations under Community law: see further ch 11 below.

[9] See Police and Criminal Evidence Act 1984, and amendments in subsequent legislation.

than others, or to entrench them. Professor AV Dicey, writing late in the 19th century and early in the 20th, claimed to have identified two features of the British constitution as fundamental. First, the constitution was founded on people's liberty, embedded in and protected by common law. Secondly, Parliament could enact, amend or repeal any law whatsoever, including earlier statutes, regardless of the impact on liberty.[10] The assumption was that political, rather than judicial, controls would prevent excessive interference by statute with people's liberty.

Dicey himself recognized that the growth of collectivism in the 19th and early 20th centuries put these assumptions under pressure.[11] As the 20th century wore on, it was increasingly clear that parliamentary democracy was not an ideal means of protecting rights. Parliament was at least as likely to interfere with rights as to respect them, and had no systematic means of ensuring that it was aware of the human rights implications of its legislation.[12]   **7.11**

(e) International human rights treaties and parliamentary sovereignty

During the first half of the 20th century, and particularly in the thinking of the Allies during the Second World War, human rights gradually became a benchmark for the legitimacy of state action in the international sphere.[13] After the Second World War, the newly formed United Nations and the Council of Europe developed codes of fundamental rights. The United Kingdom was a leading contributor to the process that led to the European Convention for the Protection of Human Rights and Fundamental Freedoms, better known as the European Convention on Human Rights (ECHR).[14] As the British Empire turned into the Commonwealth, and a growing number of former dominions achieved full independence, it became commonplace to include in their new constitutions a set of fundamental rights, often similar to (but sometimes more extensive than) those contained in the ECHR, and to make them judicially enforceable as limits on legislative or executive competence.   **7.12**

Even while this was happening, the theory and practice of the constitution in the United Kingdom remained fundamentally unreceptive to any such restriction on Parliament's legislative power. There were several reasons for this. The doctrine of the legislative supremacy of Parliament was so well entrenched that it was difficult   **7.13**

---

[10] AV Dicey, *Lectures Introductory to the Study of the Law of the Constitution* (London: Macmillan, 1885), and subsequent revisions until the 7th edn (1908). (Dicey's 8th edn, in 1914, reprinted the text of the 7th edn with an introductory essay on developments after 1908.)

[11] AV Dicey, *Lectures on the Relation between Law & Public Opinion in England during the Nineteenth Century* (London: Macmillan, 1908).

[12] For an overview, see D Feldman, 'Civil Liberties' in V Bogdanor (ed), *The British Constitution in the Twentieth Century* (Oxford: OUP, 2003) ch 11.

[13] See AW Brian Simpson, *Human Rights and the End of Empire* (Oxford: OUP, 2001) chs 3–5.

[14] Simpson (n 13 above) chs 7–15; Lord Steyn, 'Human rights: the legacy of Mrs. Roosevelt' [2002] PL 473.

for constitutional lawyers to contemplate restricting it. The idea of allowing judges to enforce human rights against the executive was opposed by left-wing politicians, who considered the rights under the ECHR to be unduly individualistic and saw both the rights themselves and the judiciary as antagonistic to the collectivist programmes that the Labour Party historically espoused. Some parliamentarians in all parties were concerned about anything that could weaken the democratic structures of Parliament or the democratic responsiveness and accountability of the government, and an obligation to respect human rights could certainly produce that effect. Parliamentarians particularly opposed the idea of allowing the government, using the royal prerogative, to change the powers and freedoms of the legislature by entering into international human rights treaties.

7.14 Nevertheless, international human rights treaties increasingly had some impact in the law of England and Wales. Within government, legislative proposals were monitored for potential human rights violations. When the European Court of Human Rights decided that English law was incompatible with the ECHR, the UK government honoured its obligation under international law to introduce legislation, where necessary, to remove the incompatibility. Gradually a solid body of legislation built up which was shaped, wholly or partly, by European human rights law.

7.15 Alongside the growing influence of human rights in international law, from the beginning of 1973 English law came into the orbit of the European Economic Community (later the European Communities and, more recently still, the European Union). After some hesitation, the Court of Justice of the European Communities accepted that it, and national courts interpreting Community law, would have regard to the fundamental rights forming general principles of Community law when they become relevant to a question of Community law, either as grounds for judicial review of the action of Community institutions or as guides to the interpretation of Community law.[15] These 'general principles' are derived from the common constitutional traditions of the member states (where they can be identified), and from international treaties to which member states have contributed. They therefore include the rights under the ECHR. Although the Court of Justice has rarely struck down a legislative or executive act by a Community institution on the ground of an incompatibility with a Convention right, the ECHR has increasingly influenced the thinking of member states about the structures of the European Communities and the European Union.[16] The human rights standards recognized by the Court of Justice were finally given expression in the Treaties, in what is now Article 6(2) of the Amsterdam Treaty.[17]

---

[15] eg, see Case 4/73 *Nold v Commission* [1974] ECR 491; Case 36/75 *Rutili v Minister for the Interior* [1975] ECR 1219.

[16] See eg Case T-177/01 *Jégo-Quéré et Cie v Commission* [2003] QB 854, CFI; Case C-50/00P *Unión de Pequeños Agricultores v Council of the European Union* [2003] QB 893, ECJ.

[17] Formerly Art F2 of the Maastricht Treaty.

The Maastricht Treaty also saw the incorporation of the Treaties of a Social **7.16** Chapter, giving additional rights in employment and certain other rights. The United Kingdom initially secured an opt-out from the Social Chapter, although later the Labour government elected in 1997 acceded to it. The protection for human rights in EU law was then extended by the EU Charter of Fundamental Rights, proclaimed at the EU summit in Nice in December 2000. The Charter covers a wide range of social and economic rights alongside the core (mainly civil and political) rights derived from the ECHR, and is expressed to apply to EU institutions and to institutions in member states when implementing Community law. In the view of the UK government, the Charter has no binding legal force, but it is being used by the Court of Justice as an aid to interpreting EU law, including the human rights obligations recognized in Article 6(2) of the Amsterdam Treaty. Further developments are under discussion which might give additional force to the Charter. One of the most important is the work of a Convention established to draft a European Constitution. Such a constitution would be given effect in a further treaty between member states, and would be likely to include the Charter among its enforceable provisions.

For the moment, gaps remain in the protection offered to rights through the **7.17** Court of Justice. There is a lack of clarity as to the rights which can be protected. There is no clear statement of the acceptable grounds for interfering with rights. Finally, there is no guarantee that the Court of Justice will interpret rights as generously as the European Court of Human Rights would. This creates a risk that inconsistent decisions will emerge from the two courts. The European Union is not a party to the ECHR, and the European Court of Human Rights has no power to hold the European Union or its institutions (as distinct from the member states, which are all parties to the ECHR) to account for violations of rights under the ECHR.

Quite apart from international human rights law and Community law, in the **7.18** 1980s and 1990s the common law renewed its concern for fundamental rights. The theoretical framework was laid in a series of books and articles in which scholars and judges argued that certain fundamental rights could be found embedded in the common law, notably a right to equality before the law, a right to have access to courts, a right to fair procedures, and a right to dignity and bodily integrity.[18] Judges then began to rely on these rights in their decisions in judicial review proceedings in ways we will examine in subsequent chapters as they become relevant to particular rights and the grounds of judicial review.

---

[18] See, eg, Sir John Laws, 'Is the High Court the guardian of fundamental constitutional rights?' [1993] PL 59; TRS Allan, *Law, Liberty, and Justice: the Legal Foundations of British Constitutionalism* (Oxford: Clarendon Press, 1993).

(f) Judges and human rights treaties

7.19   As judges and practitioners became increasingly familiar with human rights, the courts increasingly accepted that human rights derived from international treaties can properly influence decision-making in domestic litigation.[19] Even without legislation to give effect to human rights treaties, courts relied on human rights in the following ways.

- When interpreting ambiguous legislative provisions, the courts assumed that Parliament intended to legislate in conformity with the United Kingdom's obligations in international law.[20]
- When legislation was intended to fulfil an obligation under international law, judges would interpret and apply it so far as possible to make it effective for that purpose.[21]
- Courts developed the common law as far as possible in conformity with human rights. To this end, they have established that the justification for administrative acts interfering with fundamental rights will be subjected to a more intense standard of judicial review (particularly anxious scrutiny) than other acts; a strong justification will be needed if they are not to be regarded as irrational.[22] It seems that not all the Convention rights under the ECHR will be treated as fundamental for this purpose. For example, it has been said that the right to respect for the home (Article 8 ECHR) does not require courts to subject decisions about the allocation of the public housing stock to anxious scrutiny.[23] Nor should courts apply any closer or more rigorous analysis of such administrative decisions than would ordinarily apply on an application for judicial review.[24]
- Where courts have to exercise discretion, for example in relation to sentencing and remedies, they use it in a way that is consistent with human rights whenever possible.[25]
- Courts treat the United Kingdom's international treaty obligations as a guide to what public policy requires when that becomes relevant to the determination of a case.[26]

---

[19] See M Hunt, *Using Human Rights Law in English Courts* (Oxford: Hart Publishing, 1997) esp chs 4–7.

[20] See, eg, *Waddington v Miah* [1974] 1 WLR 683, HL.

[21] See, eg, *R (on the application of Mullen) v Secretary of State for the Home Department* [2002] EWCA Civ 1882; [2003] 2 WLR 835, on the relationship between Art 14(6) ICCPR and s 133 of the Criminal Justice Act 1988 on compensation for defendants whose convictions have been quashed.

[22] See, eg, *Bugdaycay v Secretary of State for the Home Department* [1987] AC 514, HL.

[23] *Begum (Runa) v Tower Hamlets LBC* [2003] UKHL 5; [2003] 3 WLR 388 at [7] *per* Lord Bingham of Cornhill.

[24] ibid, disapproving a dictum of Laws LJ in the Court of Appeal in the same case, [2002] EWCA Civ 239; [2002] 1 WLR 2491 at [44].

[25] See, eg, *Rantzen v Mirror Group Newspapers (1986) Ltd* [1994] QB 670, CA; *John v MGN Ltd* [1997] QB 586, CA.

[26] See, eg, *Blathwayt v Baron Cawley* [1976] AC 397, HL.

- People sometimes have a legitimate expectation, enforceable in judicial review proceedings, that the government will act in accordance with human rights obligations binding on the United Kingdom in international law.[27]
- As noted above, general principles of EC law include those fundamental rights which are to be found in the common constitutional traditions of member states and the international treaties to which they have contributed, including for example the ECHR and the International Covenant on Civil and Political Rights (ICCPR). These rights find their way into English law when domestic courts are adjudicating on cases to which Community law applies, since the courts are bound to apply Community law by the European Communities Act 1972.

However, before the passage of the HRA 1998 nobody could bring an action in England to enforce a right under an international human rights instrument unless (1) legislation had made the right part of municipal law, (2) the right was indirectly part of domestic law because of its incorporation into Community law, or (3) the subject matter of the right was adequately protected by the private law of tort, contract, property and so on, or by a public law procedure such as judicial review. There were many cases in which people had to resort to the European Commission and Court of Human Rights to vindicate rights under the ECHR. This showed that the United Kingdom was not consistently discharging its duties, under Articles 1 and 13 ECHR, to secure the rights to everyone within the jurisdiction, and to provide an effective remedy before a national authority for any violation of a Convention right. The same applied to rights under other international treaties, with the additional difficulty that people in the United Kingdom had, and still have, no means of seeking redress for violations of those treaties from an international tribunal. **7.20**

A move to formalize the position of fundamental freedoms and human rights in English law gradually moved up the political agenda during the last quarter of the 20th century. This was not the result of a surge of popular or populist feeling in favour of rights. Instead, a steady trend in the thought of the legal and intellectual establishment slowly affected the thinking of some political leaders. Numerous private members' Bills had been introduced to Parliament over the years on one or other of two models: either to give effect in English law to some or all of the rights by which the United Kingdom was already bound in international law;[28] or to legislate for an indigenous Bill of Rights adapted to local needs and conditions, **7.21**

---

[27] *R v Secretary of State for the Home Department, ex p Ahmed and Patel* [1998] INLR 570; Lord Lester, 'Government Compliance with International Human Rights Law: A New Year's Legitimate Expectation' [1996] PL 187. On legitimate expectation, see paras 16.34 et seq below.

[28] See M Zander, *A Bill of Rights?* (4th edn, London: Sweet & Maxwell, 1997); Lord Lester, 'The mouse that roared: the Human Rights Bill 1995' [1995] PL 198; Lord Lester of Herne Hill QC, 'First steps towards a constitutional bill of rights' [1997] European Human Rights L Rev 124.

sometimes as part of a full-scale constitutional restatement.[29] Although none of these Bills succeeded in becoming law, they served to stimulate debate inside and outside Parliament.

7.22 When the Labour Party came to power after the 1997 general election, it was already committed to incorporating into municipal law at least some of the rights under the ECHR and its various Protocols. The government quickly introduced to Parliament a Bill based on the ECHR, but with some limitations and adaptations to make it acceptable in the constitutional traditions of the United Kingdom. This Bill became the HRA 1998.

C. The Human Rights Act 1998[30]

7.23 The architecture of the Act has six particularly important features.

- It makes specified rights under the ECHR (the 'Convention rights') part of municipal law, and explains the significance which the Strasbourg case law is to have (ss 1 and 2).
- It applies for most purposes only prospectively, not retrospectively, although this has caused some difficulties of interpretation and application in the courts.
- It requires that all legislation (whether primary or subordinate, and whenever enacted or made) is to be read and given effect in a manner compatible with Convention rights so far as it is possible to do so (s 3).
- It preserves parliamentary sovereignty. Parliament remains free to legislate in a manner incompatible with the Convention rights and has done so, although the terms on which it is constitutionally legitimate for Parliament to use this freedom are still being worked out. Furthermore, the Act is not entrenched, and is, in theory, liable to amendment in the usual way. Nevertheless, the way our courts approach fundamental human rights makes it very unlikely that any provision of the Act will be subject to implied repeal by subsequent legislation, and the enactment of subsequent legislation incompatible with Convention rights

---

[29] See, eg, Institute for Public Policy Research, *The Constitution of the United Kingdom* (London: IPPR, 1991); Liberty, *A People's Charter: Liberty's Bill of Rights* (London: Liberty, 1991); and Tony Benn MP's Commonwealth of Britain Bill, in Tony Benn and Andrew Hood, *Common Sense: A New Constitution for Britain* (London: Hutchinson, 1993).

[30] The Act has generated a large literature. For books combining authoritative introductions with excellent treatment of detailed aspects, see Lord Lester of Herne Hill QC and David Pannick QC, *Human Rights Law and Practice* (London: Butterworths, 1999, with 1st Supplement 2000); Keir Starmer, *European Human Rights Law* (London: Legal Action Group, 1999); Stephen Grosz, Jack Beatson QC, and Peter Duffy QC, *Human Rights: The 1998 Act and the European Convention* (London: Sweet and Maxwell, 1999); John Wadham and Helen Mountfield, *Blackstone's Guide to the Human Rights Act 1998* (2nd edn, London: Blackstone Press, 2000); Richard Clayton and Hugh Tomlinson, *The Law of Human Rights* (Oxford: OUP, 2000, with 2nd cumulative supplement, 2003).

will neither repeal nor limit the general scope of the Convention rights. But the courts cannot strike down or refuse to apply a provision in primary legislation on the ground that it is incompatible with a Convention right. Under s 4, they may make a declaration of incompatibility, but that does not affect either the validity or the legitimacy of the impugned provisions. Public authorities must continue to perform their duties under incompatible primary legislation, and s 6(2) makes it clear that they do not act unlawfully if their actions or decisions are authorized by the incompatible legislation.

- Subject to the special status of primary legislation, s 6(1) of the Act imposes a legal duty on public authorities (a term which is not fully defined, but includes courts and tribunals and people or bodies some of whose functions are of a public nature) to act in a manner compatible with Convention rights, and entitles the victim of a violation of such a right to a remedy. Subordinate legislation which is incompatible with a Convention right is liable to be quashed or declared invalid, unless it could not have been drafted to be compatible with the right because of the demands of primary legislation.

- The Act makes special provision for the remedies which may be awarded for a violation of Convention rights. The conditions for granting remedies (other than a declaration of incompatibility) are set out in ss 7, 8 and 9 of the Act.

This section of the chapter provides a fuller explanation of the first five features of the Act. The remedies available for a violation of a Convention right are examined in chapter 19, below.   **7.24**

(1) The Convention Rights and Their Authority in English Courts

(a) What are the Convention rights?

Section 1(1) of the HRA 1998 defines the 'Convention rights' as the rights and fundamental freedoms set out in the various articles of the ECHR, specified in s 1 of the Act. The rights apply as they have effect in international law 'for the time being in relation to the United Kingdom'.[31] Schedule 1 to the Act reproduces the English-language version of these rights, but as the Convention rights are those operating under the ECHR the French-language version of them is equally authentic and authoritative. The current list of rights is as follows: **7.25**

- the right to legal protection for life, and to legal limitations on circumstances in which intentional deprivation of life is permissible (Article 2);
- the right to be free of torture and inhuman or degrading treatment or punishment (Article 3);
- the right to be free of slavery, servitude, and forced or compulsory labour (Article 4);

---

[31] HRA 1998, s 21(1).

- the right not to be deprived of liberty and security of the person except in accordance with a procedure prescribed by law and with various safeguards (Article 5);
- the right to a fair and public hearing within a reasonable time by an independent and impartial tribunal established by law in determination of civil rights and obligations and criminal charges, with special procedural safeguards in criminal cases (Article 6);
- the right not to be punished for an action which did not constitute an offence under national or international law at the time of its commission (Article 7);
- the right to respect for private and family life, home and correspondence (Article 8);
- the right to freedom of thought, conscience and religion (Article 9);
- the right to freedom of expression, including receiving information, without interference by a public authority and regardless of frontiers (Article 10);
- the right to freedom of peaceful assembly and association, including the right to form and join a trade union (Article 11);
- the right to marry and found a family (Article 12);
- the right to have the other rights secured without discrimination (Article 14);
- the entitlement to peaceful enjoyment of possessions, and limitations on deprivation of property (Protocol 1, Article 1);
- the right to education, in relation to which the state is to respect the right of parents to ensure that children receive education in conformity with their religious and philosophical convictions (Protocol 1, Article 2);
- the right to free elections by secret ballot at reasonable intervals (Protocol 1, Article 3);
- the right not to be sentenced to death save in respect of acts committed in time of war or of imminent threat of war (Protocol 6, Articles 1 and 2).

The principles governing the interpretation of these rights are considered below.[32]

(i) Limitations on the Convention rights

7.26 Many of the rights are subject to qualifications, either expressly in the text of the Convention or impliedly as a result of judicial interpretation. The principles governing the application of these qualifications are considered below.[33] The rights are also subject to a number of general provisions in the Convention, as follows:

- Article 16, which provides that the rights of aliens to freedom of expression, freedom of peaceful assembly and association, and freedom from discrimination may be restricted by the state, as long as other rights are respected;

---

[32] See paras 7.152–7.157 below.
[33] See paras 7.158–7.168 below. The UK has ratified but not yet implemented in HRA 1998, Protocol 13 ECHR prohibiting the death penalty at any time.

- Article 17, providing that nothing in the ECHR permits any state, group or person to engage in any activity or perform any act aimed at the destruction of any of the rights and freedoms under the ECHR or at their limitation to a greater extent than is provided for in the ECHR itself;
- Article 18, which stipulates that restrictions to rights and freedoms which are permitted under the ECHR must not be applied for any purpose other than those for which they have been prescribed;
- any designated derogation (currently a derogation from Article 5 ECHR to allow the United Kingdom to detain foreign nationals who are suspected international terrorists without trial if they cannot be tried or deported for a legal or practical reason);[34] and
- any designated reservation (currently the United Kingdom's reservation to parents' right to have their children taught in conformity with their own religious and philosophical convictions).[35]

(ii) Amending the list of rights and qualifications having effect in domestic law

Schedules 1 and 3 may be amended by statutory instrument for certain purposes. At the time the Act was passed, a designated derogation was in force in relation to the period for which people arrested on suspicion of having committed terrorist offences could be held without being taken before a judicial officer under Article 5.4 ECHR. When the Terrorism Act 2000 changed the law, that derogation was withdrawn and Sch 3 to the Act was amended accordingly.[36] When ss 21 to 23 of the Anti-terrorism, Crime and Security Act 2001 were passed, authorizing the detention of suspected international terrorists who were not UK nationals and could not be deported for practical or legal reasons, a designated derogation from the right to liberty of the person under Article 5.1 ECHR was added.[37] In the same way, if the United Kingdom were to ratify Protocols 4, 7 or 12, containing rights which the United Kingdom has not yet accepted, it would not be necessary to pass primary legislation in order to amend the Act to include the new rights as 'Convention rights'. An order to make Protocol 13 ECHR one of the Convention rights is imminent.   **7.27**

(b) The authority of case law of the European Court of Human Rights and other Strasbourg institutions on the interpretation of Convention rights

Before Protocol 11 to the ECHR came into force, there were three bodies with decision-making functions in relation to alleged violations of Convention rights. First, there was the European Commission of Human Rights, which   **7.28**

---

[34] HRA 1998 (Designated Derogation) Order 2001, SI 2001/3641.
[35] See s 1(1) and (2). Articles 16 to 18 are set out in Sch 1 to the Act. The designated derogation and reservation are set out in Sch 3 to the Act as amended.
[36] HRA 1998 (Amendment) Order 2001, SI 2001/1216.
[37] HRA 1998 (Designated Derogation) Order 2001, SI 2001/3641.

received applications from states or victims of alleged violations, made a decision about admissibility, tried to broker a friendly settlement of admissible complaints, and if this was impossible reported its opinion on the merits of the case. Secondly, there was the European Court of Human Rights, a judicial body to which cases could be referred after the report of the Commission. The decision of the Court was final. Thirdly, there was the Committee of Ministers, a political body. By a special majority, this could find a violation of a Convention right in a case not referred to the Court after the report of the Commission. Where the Court or the Committee had decided that a violation had occurred, the Committee was then responsible for ensuring compliance with the judgment or decision. Under the new procedure put in place by Protocol 11, the Commission no longer exists, and the Committee of Ministers is restricted to overseeing compliance by states with judgments of the Court.

7.29 From all these sources, and particularly from the Commission and the Court, a considerable case law has built up on the interpretation of the Convention. The HRA 1998 provides that domestic courts and tribunals must 'take into account' any relevant decision of the Strasbourg institutions, which for practical purposes means the Commission and the Court, when interpreting a Convention right.[38] The case law is thus persuasive but not binding. There is no doctrine of stare decisis in the Strasbourg institutions, which treat the ECHR as a dynamic instrument, not a static one.

(i) When should Strasbourg case law be followed?

7.30 The absence of a system of stare decisis in Strasbourg has presented English courts with the problem of deciding when, and to what extent, they should follow Strasbourg case law, and when they should regard themselves as being free to diverge from it. In principle, national courts interpreting Convention rights under the HRA 1998 should be free to adopt a more liberal interpretation of Convention rights than the Strasbourg Court, and should not adopt a more restrictive interpretation. When it comes to deciding whether a public authority's act or decision constitutes an interference with a right, English courts should not refuse to treat behaviour as an interference if it would be treated as such by the Strasbourg organs. When assessing the justification for interfering with a right, the purposes for which it is permitted to interfere with Convention rights (for example, under Article 8(2), 'in the interests of national security, public safety or the economic well-being of the country, for the prevention of disorder or crime, for the protection of health or morals, or for the protection of the rights and freedoms of others') should not be given a wider meaning than the

---

[38] HRA 1998, s 2(1).

Strasbourg Court would have allowed.[39] This is considered further below at paras 7.35 et seq.

When it decides whether an interference is 'necessary in a democratic society' for   **7.31**
a permitted purpose, an English court should often allow less leeway to public authorities than the Strasbourg Court does. In Strasbourg, the Court has used the notion of the 'margin of appreciation' to allow an area of discretion to a state when deciding whether there is a pressing social need to interfere with a right and whether the measure taken is proportionate to the need. The 'margin of appreciation' does not apply in municipal law. It is entirely a creature of international, not national, law. As Lord Hope of Craighead said in *R v DPP, ex p Kebilene*,[40] the idea of the 'margin of appreciation' is premised on the greater ability of national than international authorities to make judgments about where there is a pressing social need and what is a proportionate response to it in the circumstances which obtain in a particular state. Courts which are national authorities cannot duck the issue in that way, although (as in current administrative law) courts may respect what Lord Lester and David Pannick have called a 'discretionary area of judgment' of decision-makers who are specially well qualified to make particular judgments or, in relation to political judgments, who are democratically accountable for their decisions.[41]

(c) Deference towards specially qualified decision-makers: a domestic version of the margin of appreciation?

At the same time, English courts recognize that they are constitutionally better   **7.32**
placed to make some assessments than others. In relation to some matters, therefore, they are willing to show a degree of deference to the decision-making of other institutions which appear to the courts to be better placed to make that decision. This is not a new idea. In the days before the HRA 1998 came into force, courts showed a relatively high degree of deference towards certain decision-makers in relation to particular kinds of issues, and accordingly applied a less intense standard of review to those decisions. For example, judges accepted that Parliament, or people accountable to Parliament, were particularly well placed to take political decisions about the allocation of public funds and the burden of taxation.

---

[39] See generally Sir Anthony Hooper, 'The Impact of the HRA on Judicial Decision-making' [1998] European Human Rights L Rev 676 at 682–683; David Pannick QC, 'Principles of Interpretation of the HRA and the Discretionary Area of Judgment' [1998] PL 545; Richard A Edwards, 'Generosity and the HRA: the Right Interpretation?' [1999] PL 400; Lord Irvine of Lairg LC, 'Activism and Restraint: Human Rights and the Interpretative Process' [1999] European Human Rights L Rev 350; David Feldman, 'Precedent and the European Court of Human Rights', in Law Commission Consultation Paper No 157, *Criminal Law: Bail and the HRA 1998*, Appendix C, 112–124.
[40] [2000] 2 AC 326, 380–381, HL, *per* Lord Hope of Craighead.
[41] Lester and Pannick (n 30 above) para 3.21.

Judges would therefore apply a light touch when asked to review the rationality of such decisions. Courts would also show respect for the judgments of expert bodies and individuals within the scope of their special expertise. When faced with a decision made in reliance on sources of information which could not be revealed to them (such as national security information derived from the Security and Intelligence Services), courts would apply a low intensity of review for rationality, even if it led to unsatisfactory decisions surviving scrutiny: whatever the short-comings of a minister's judgments on security matters, there was no reason to think that the courts would be better decision-makers on the basis of less evidence. Finally, some decisions were thought to be non-justiciable, on either constitutional or pragmatic grounds, although the number of such decisions was shrinking. On the other hand, where a decision is justiciable, judges are particularly well placed to decide questions of law, so they would still review the legality of those decisions in the usual way.

7.33 Since the courts began to grapple with Convention rights directly, there have been several judicial expressions of an opinion that judges should show a special degree of deference to Parliament or, sometimes, to the executive because of their particular status as democratically accountable bodies. This is said to be the domestic equivalent of the doctrine of the margin of appreciation.[42] However, it is important to bear in mind the limited effect of any deference in the process of judicial decision-making concerning Convention rights. As noted above,[43] courts had recognized before the HRA 1998 that an act or decision interfering with a fundamental right should be subjected to particularly intense scrutiny. The HRA 1998 cannot provide a reason for reducing the intensity of that scrutiny when Convention rights are in issue. Furthermore, deference applies only at a very late stage in the process of judicial decision-making. It would be constitutionally improper for courts to defer to a view of the legislature or executive, or any other non-judicial public body, as to the proper interpretation of a Convention right and the qualifications to it. Interpreting and applying legislation and giving effect to rights and duties is a quintessentially judicial task, and the judges cannot surrender it to another body without undermining a major element of the rule of law. Deference is proper, if at all, only after it is established to the court's satisfaction that a right has been interfered with, that the interference is in accordance with the law and serves a legitimate aim as understood in the context of the Convention, and that it does not deprive the victim of the very essence of the right. It then becomes necessary to decide whether

---

[42] See, eg, *R v DPP, ex p Kebilene* [2000] 2 AC 326, 380–381, HL, *per* Lord Hope of Craighead; *Brown v Stott* [2003] 1 AC 681, PC, at 703 *per* Lord Bingham of Cornhill and 710–711 *per* Lord Steyn. For cogent criticism of the English courts' extensive use of the idea of deference to limit protection for rights, see R Edwards, 'Judicial deference under the Human Rights Act' (2002) 65 MLR 859.

[43] See para 7.19 above.

the interference is justified as a proportionate response to a pressing social need. At this very late stage, a court may be justified in taking into account the view of the original decision-maker on matters particularly within his or her constitutional competence and expertise: the existence of a pressing social need to interfere with the right, and whether the measures adopted strike a fair balance between the competing rights and interests and are proportionate to the legitimate aim pursued. Even on these matters, the courts must ultimately be able to decide whether the legislature, executive or other decision-maker reached a correct judgment.

One of the most thorough examinations of the proper scope of deference to decision-makers is to be found in the dissenting judgment of Laws LJ in *International Transport Roth GmbH v Secretary of State for the Home Department*.[44] His Lordship drew attention to the supervisory nature of the court's jurisdiction: it cannot substitute its own view of what a decision-maker should do for that of the decision-maker originally entrusted with the duty of decision, but can only intervene if the original decision-maker failed to comply with the minimal standards imposed by the Convention rights. This led Laws LJ to suggest that four principles could be identified. They overlap the traditional grounds for deference in administrative law, but it is helpful to set them out, subject to certain caveats.

7.34

- Greater deference should be paid to an Act of Parliament than to a decision of the executive or to subordinate legislation.[45] This is acceptable on the basis that one House of Parliament is directly elected by the people, but courts should not defer unless it can be shown that the particular provision and its human rights implications were actually considered by the House of Commons. Because of parliamentary timetabling, too many provisions in statutes have not received any, or more than cursory, consideration at any stage in their passage through the House of Commons. Scrutiny of legislation in the House of Lords arguably does not deserve the same degree of deference as that in the Commons, as the Lords are not democratically accountable. Legislation pre-dating the HRA 1998 is particularly unlikely to have been subjected to parliamentary consideration of human rights implications.
- There is more scope for deference where the Convention itself requires a balance to be struck between competing interests than where a right is stated in unqualified terms.[46] But it would be wrong to suggest that there is any room for deference to the view of a non-judicial body as to the proper interpretation of

---

[44] [2002] EWCA Civ 158, [2003] QB 728 at [83]–[87].
[45] ibid at [83].
[46] ibid at [84].

the right, as opposed to the balance of interests when applying a qualification to it.[47]

- '[G]reater deference is due to democratic powers, including Parliament and the executive, when the subject-matter is peculiarly within their constitutional responsibility, and less when it lies within the constitutional responsibility of the courts.'[48]

- Greater deference is appropriate when the issue lies within the expertise of the democratic powers than when it lies within the judicial expertise of the courts.[49]

This approach was approved by Lord Walker of Gestingthorpe in *R (on the application of Prolife Alliance) v British Broadcasting Corp.*[50] However, in the same case Lord Hoffmann stressed that the fundamental question is whether the decision under review is within the special legal and constitutional competence of the primary decision-maker, so as to make it inappropriate for a reviewing court to substitute its view for that of the primary decision-maker.[51]

(d) Factors affecting the domestic authority of decisions of the Strasbourg bodies

7.35 Generally, the English courts give at least as much protection to rights as would be offered by the Strasbourg Court. To do otherwise would defeat one of the purposes of the HRA 1998, by making it necessary for people alleging violations of their Convention rights to have resort to Strasbourg instead of being able to obtain a satisfactory remedy in the United Kingdom. Thus English courts have tended to follow decisions of the European Court of Human Rights. But they do so as a matter of choice, not obligation. As with any system of case law without strict rules of stare decisis, decisions and judgments have weight rather than binding force. The English courts are gradually developing principles to guide them in deciding how much weight to attach to different decisions of the Strasbourg institutions. Some decisions are more likely to be followed than others.

7.36 The likelihood that a decision will be followed appears to depend on a number factors, including:

- the identity of the body which made the decision (whether it was decided by the Commission or the Court, and, if the Court, whether it was decided by a

---

[47] Laws LJ appeared to leave open such a possibility in his judgment in *International Transport Roth*, and in *Sheffield City Council v Smart* [2002] EWCA Civ 4; [2002] HLR 34 at [22]–[27] (margin of discretion possibly allowed to decision-maker in interpreting meaning of 'respect' in Art 8(1) ECHR). It is respectfully submitted that this would be constitutionally inappropriate, for the reasons outlined in para 7.33 above.
[48] *International Transport Roth GmbH v Secretary of State for the Home Department* [2002] EWCA Civ 158, [2003] QB 728 at [85].
[49] ibid at [87].
[50] [2003] UKHL 23; [2003] 2 WLR 1403 at [136].
[51] ibid at [75]–[76].

three-judge committee as an admissibility decision, by a seven-judge chamber on the merits, or by the Grand Chamber);

- the thoroughness of the discussion of the issue in the decision in question;
- the degree of similarity between the issue decided by the Strasbourg institution and the issue for decision in the English court;
- if the decision was made in an application against the United Kingdom, the extent to which the Strasbourg body appears to have understood the domestic factual and legal context;
- the time since the decision was made, and whether there has subsequently been a reasoned and principled development in the jurisprudence which might lead to a different conclusion; and
- whether the Strasbourg decision could lead to a result which the court finds unacceptable either in principle or on grounds of public policy.

For example, the House of Lords 'will not without good reason depart from the principles laid down in a carefully considered judgment of the court sitting as a Grand Chamber'.[52] A court will be particularly likely to follow a Strasbourg decision (even one which departs from a line of authority which was previously favourable to the United Kingdom) if it considers the views of domestic courts on the issue in question, particularly if (in the domestic court's view) the Strasbourg court properly understood the political, legal and administrative context.[53] It will also be likely to follow a decision it thinks is correct in principle, even if it represents a departure both from previous decisions of the European Court of Human Rights and national courts.[54]   **7.37**

However, it follows from those principles that there will be cases where English courts do not follow Strasbourg case law. If English judges think that the Strasbourg bodies have misunderstood the political, legal or institutional context in which a case arises, or have underestimated the ability of a trial court to secure a fair hearing, or have shown insufficient deference to a democratically accountable decision-maker, they may decide to go their own way, explaining their reasoning and hoping that the Strasbourg court will find it persuasive in any subsequent proceedings.   **7.38**

---

[52] *R (on the application of Anderson) v Secretary of State for the Home Department* [2002] UKHL 46; [2003] 1 AC 837 at [18] *per* Lord Bingham of Cornhill, referring to *R (on the application of Alconbury Developments Ltd) v Secretary of State for the Environment, Transport and the Regions* [2001] UKHL 23; [2001] 2 WLR 1389 at [26].

[53] *R (on the application of Anderson) v Secretary of State for the Home Department* [2002] UKHL 46; [2003] 1 AC 837.

[54] See, eg, *Ghaidan v Godin-Mendoza* [2002] EWCA Civ 1533; [2003] 2 WLR 478, in which the Court of Appeal followed the decision of the Strasbourg court in *Salgueiro da Silva Mouta v Portugal* Application 33290/96 (2001) 31 EHRR 47, holding discrimination on the ground of sexual orientation to be within the ambit of Arts 8 and 14 ECHR, to justify departing from the interpretation of 'living together as man and wife' in the Rent Act 1977 adopted by the House of Lords in *Fitzpatrick v Sterling Housing Association Ltd* [2001] 1 AC 27, HL. (The House of Lords has given leave to appeal in *Ghaidan v Godin-Mendoza*.)

7.39   This tendency has been particularly noticeable in cases concerning the right to a fair hearing. For example, in *Morris v UK*,[55] the European Court of Human Rights held that a court martial could not provide an independent and impartial hearing because the junior officers on the court were junior in status to the President of the court, and could objectively be thought to be subject to pressure to agree with the President, in view of the hierarchical system of discipline and the reporting system in the armed forces. The Ministry of Defence had accepted this, and was considering how best to change the structure of courts martial when the House of Lords, in *R v Spear*,[56] refused to follow the decision in *Morris v UK*, and held that the court martial system complied with the requirements of Article 6 ECHR. Their Lordships justified this step by saying that there was no factual evidence that junior members of courts martial were ever in fact subject to pressure to reach particular decisions, or ever had their career progression held back because of the way they decided cases. It was also said that the Strasbourg Court had not received as much help in understanding the court martial system as could have been expected. As a result, the Grand Chamber of the European Court of Human Rights has agreed to re-examine the issue in another case currently pending before it, and the government is waiting to see the result before amending the procedures.

7.40   Another example is the privilege against self-incrimination, which the Strasbourg Court treats as a fundamental element of a fair hearing in the determination of a criminal charge, closely related to the presumption of innocence, under Article 6(1) and (2) ECHR.[57] In a series of cases, courts in the United Kingdom have sought to treat the right as being of less than fundamental importance, so that it can be taken away if public-interest considerations are thought to outweigh it. This approach was bolstered by a claim that special deference is due to Parliament's decision to take away the privilege against self-incrimination by statute. This deference was, with respect, misplaced. Their Lordships seem to have given too little weight to the fact that the statutes in question were passed before the HRA 1998, so that Parliament was not required to carry out the balancing exercise, to which the courts claimed to defer, in terms of Article 6.[58] Nevertheless, there seems to be an underlying view that public policy considerations militate strongly against preventing self-incriminating statements ever being admissible in criminal proceedings against a person who was coerced into making them. More flexibility is thought to be needed. Similarly, the Court of Appeal has refused to

---

[55] Application 38784/97 (2002) 34 EHRR 52.

[56] [2002] UKHL 31; [2003] 1 AC 734.

[57] *Funke v France* Series A No 256-A (1993) 16 EHRR 297; *Saunders v UK* Application 19187/91 (1997) 23 EHRR 313; *Heaney and McGuinness v Ireland* Application 34720/97 (2001) 33 EHRR 12; *Allan v UK* Application No 48539/99 (2003) 36 EHRR 12.

[58] See, eg, *Brown v Stott* [2003] 1 AC 681, PC, a devolution case under the Scotland Act 1998, followed in England in *DPP v Wilson* [2001] EWHC Admin 198; [2002] RTR 37, DC.

follow a decision of the Strasbourg Court holding that convicting someone solely on the basis of a statement by a witness who failed to attend the hearing always violates a defendant's right to examine prosecution witnesses under Article 6(3). The English court regarded this as unacceptably inflexible, offering an incentive for defendants to intimidate prosecution witnesses into refusing to attend court.[59]

In some other cases under Article 6, courts have adopted a narrower view of the reach of rights or have provided lesser forms of redress than might have been expected in the light of the Strasbourg case law. In *Bunkate v Netherland*[60] the European Court of Human Rights decided that a conviction after excessively long criminal proceedings which violated Article 6(1) ECHR should not be sustained. However, in *Mills v HM Advocate*,[61] a Scottish devolution case, a defendant attempted to stop a criminal trial on the ground that it was outside the powers of the Lord Advocate (as a member of the Scottish Executive) to proceed with it when it would lead to an inevitable violation of Article 6(1) on the ground of delay. The Judicial Committee of the Privy Council, upholding the decision of the High Court of Justiciary, decided that the trial could not properly proceed, because the terms of the Scotland Act 1998 put it beyond the power of the Lord Advocate to pursue a prosecution if it would inevitably violate a Convention right. However, their Lordships expressed the view, obiter, that the position would be different in England and Wales, because in cases not involving devolution issues the trial court could ensure that delay did not compromise a fair hearing. There were a number of ways, other than staying the proceedings permanently, in which the court might provide redress for delay. For example, a significant reduction in sentence could be a way of giving just satisfaction. If this is followed, it would lead English law away from the way in which the European Court of Human Rights has given effect to Article 6. It is not clear how the right to a trial within a reasonable time can be made real and effective if a trial is allowed to continue after an unreasonable delay. **7.41**

Courts in the United Kingdom have also been reluctant to provide effective remedies for violations of Article 6 ECHR where the use of coerced self-incriminating evidence has led to a person's conviction in breach of Article 6(1) and (2). Even when the Strasbourg Court has held that defendants' convictions violated Article 6(1) because they were based on coerced self-incrimination, the English courts have refused to quash the convictions.[62] They have held that the conviction could not be said to be 'unsafe' within the meaning of the Criminal Appeal Act 1968 as amended when it was reached in accordance with the statutory rules in force at the **7.42**

---

[59] *R v M (Witness Statement)* [2003] EWCA Crim 357; The Times, 2 May 2003, CA.
[60] Series A No 248-B (1993) 19 EHRR 477.
[61] [2002] UKPC D2; [2002] 3 WLR 1597.
[62] *R v Lyons* [2002] UKHL 44; [2002] 3 WLR 1562.

time, and the trial as a whole did not appear to be unfair.[63] This outcome is to some extent the result of the primacy of the doctrine of parliamentary sovereignty over Convention rights, coupled with the non-retroactive operation of the HRA 1998.[64] The courts felt unable to say that defendants were entitled to have a conviction quashed for unfairness when it was obtained in accordance with statutes in force at the time of the trial. It leaves a significant gap in the structure of remedies for violations of Convention rights. However, the position might be different in relation to convictions post-dating the entry into force of the HRA 1998.

7.43 One more example will suffice. English judges have sometimes given a very narrow interpretation to the term 'criminal charge' in Article 6(1) ECHR, and to 'criminal offence' in Articles 6(1) and 7. For example, in *R (on the application of McCann) v Manchester Crown Court*[65] the House of Lords decided that the making of an anti-social behaviour order did not involve the determination of a criminal charge, despite the serious consequences for the defendant. In *R v H (Fitness to Plead)*,[66] the House of Lords held that an inquiry into whether the defendant, who was unfit to plead, did an act constituting the actus reus of the offence[67] was not the determination of a criminal charge, even though the decision had consequences for the disposal of the accused, the inquiry took place in a criminal forum, and the outcome of the procedure was in substance indistinguishable from a finding of guilt.

7.44 On the other hand, in *International Transport Roth GmbH v Secretary of State for the Home Department*[68] Simon Brown LJ in the Court of Appeal was prepared to hold that a decision by the Home Secretary to impose substantial fixed penalties on drivers of lorries on which illegal immigrants entered the United Kingdom involved the determination of a criminal charge. In another recent case, *R (on the application of U) v Commissioner of Police of the Metropolis*,[69] the Divisional Court approved a concession by counsel for the police that giving a final warning to a juvenile for a sexual offence amounted to the determination of a criminal charge, because of the automatic consequence that the juvenile was required to register in the Sex Offenders Register. The decision to administer the final warning without the informed consent of the juvenile or his parents or guardian, given after being informed of the consequences of accepting the warning, was unfair and violated Article 6(1) ECHR.

---

[63] *R v Kansal (No 2)* [2001] UKHL 62, [2002] 2 AC 69; *R v Lyons* [2002] UKHL 44, [2002] 3 WLR 1562.

[64] See paras 7.51–7.53 below.

[65] [2002] UKHL 39; [2003] 1 AC 787.

[66] [2003] UKHL 1; [2003] 1 WLR 411.

[67] Criminal Procedure (Insanity) Act 1964, s 4A as amended.

[68] [2002] EWCA Civ 158; [2003] QB 728.

[69] [2002] EWHC Admin 2486; [2003] 1 WLR 897, DC, at [35].

Furthermore, it seems that the English courts are sometimes willing to give a wider **7.45** meaning to the term 'civil rights and obligations' in Article 6(1) ECHR than the Strasbourg Court has so far done. For example, in *Begum (Runa) v Tower Hamlets LBC*,[70] the House of Lords was prepared to accept, without actually deciding, that the right of a homeless person to assistance with housing was a civil right within Article 6(1), despite the fact that the right arose in public law and the kinds of assistance available to a homeless person would often be subject to official discretion. Their Lordships regarded the Strasbourg case law on the subject as being unsettled, but were prepared in principle to say that there was a trend in Strasbourg towards adopting a meaning for 'civil rights and obligations' wide enough to encompass a right to public sector housing. In the continental tradition, this right would normally have been subject to review in administrative proceedings rather than courts, but it had economic value despite the fact that it was dependent on the allocation of public resources. The only reason for not deciding authoritatively that the right fell within Article 6(1) was that the House thought it important that the procedural requirements arising under Article 6(1) should be sufficiently flexible to take account of the needs of public administration in a field involving competing claims to public resources. As it was not clear how much flexibility the Strasbourg Court would allow, it was desirable to leave open the possibility of arguing that Article 6(1) does not apply to those decisions in the event that the Strasbourg Court later decides that inflexible procedural standards apply.[71]

Even where the courts accept the Strasbourg view of the relevant rights, the struc- **7.46** ture of UK legislation makes it difficult to provide a suitable remedy for the violation. For example, there might be difficulty in providing just satisfaction in national law where a public authority acts under national legislation which cannot be read or given effect in a manner compatible with Convention rights.[72]

(e) Use of other international human rights instruments

Courts remain free to refer to international instruments which are binding on the **7.47** United Kingdom but are not among the Convention rights when interpreting Convention rights, in the same way that they made use of the body of the ECHR itself before incorporation. Such instruments include Article 13 ECHR, the ICCPR, the UN Convention on the Rights of the Child, and a range of conventions dealing with discrimination and some social rights. They are used by the

---

[70] [2003] UKHL 5; [2003] 3 WLR 388.
[71] ibid, particularly at [69]–[70] *per* Lord Hoffmann, with whom the other Law Lords agreed.
[72] See eg *Re S (Minors) (Care Order: Implementation of Care Plan)* [2002] UKHL 10; [2002] 2 AC 291, refusing to read continuing control by court over implementation of care plan for child in local authority care into legislation which had placed responsibility squarely on local authorities. But cf *Adan v Newham LBC* [2001] EWCA Civ 1916; [2002] 1 WLR 2120 (extended powers for county court to review housing decisions).

Court in Strasbourg as an aid to interpreting rights under the ECHR, and can be used by our courts and tribunals for the same purpose. These instruments may also be used when interpreting ambiguous municipal legislation, developing the common law, or exercising discretion as to the grant of remedies. For example, in *R (on the application of Mullen) v Secretary of State for the Home Department*[73] the Court of Appeal used Article 14.6 ICCPR (concerning the right of a person whose conviction has been quashed or who has been pardoned on the ground that there has been shown to be a miscarriage of justice) when deciding whether s 133 of the Criminal Justice Act 1988 imposed a duty on the Secretary of State to compensate people only if they had been proved to be innocent. The Court of Appeal decided that the purpose of s 133 was to give effect to Article 14.6, and was limited to cases where a person had been proved to have been punished as a result of a miscarriage of justice. Section 133 was therefore interpreted as covering cases where there had been a miscarriage of justice (including cases where the bringing of the prosecution had amounted to an abuse of process), but not cases where a conviction had been quashed on grounds that did not amount to establishing a miscarriage of justice.

(f) Judgments of courts in other jurisdictions in the United Kingdom

7.48 Courts and tribunals in England and Wales have regard to decisions in other jurisdictions of the United Kingdom on the interpretation of Convention rights and the 1998 Act more generally. For example, the English courts have taken account of decisions of the Scottish courts and the Judicial Committee of the Privy Council in relation to the interpretation of Convention rights in cases raising devolution issues under the Scotland Act 1998. However, as *Mills v HM Advocate*[74] shows, it is important to take the devolution context into account when deciding how far a decision under the Scotland Act 1998 (or the Northern Ireland Act 1998 and the Government of Wales Act 1998) is applicable in a non-devolution context.

(g) Judgments of courts in jurisdictions outside the United Kingdom

7.49 Courts in England and Wales sometimes also consider judgments of courts in other countries, particularly in common law jurisdictions, which have a wealth of experience of interpreting constitutional or quasi-constitutional bills of rights. These decisions may be of considerable assistance. This is not because their conclusions are transferable directly to the British context. Different constitutional structures, institutional arrangements and socio-political traditions make it unlikely that rights will be the same, or identically interpreted, in different countries. For example, there are clear differences between the meaning of freedom of

---

[73] [2002] EWCA Civ 1882; [2003] 2 WLR 835.
[74] [2002] UKPC D2; [2002] 3 WLR 1597; see para 7.41 above.

expression, and the extent to which it is regarded as a qualified right, in Australia, the United States, Canada, and Council of Europe members: it is closest to being an absolute right in the United States than elsewhere, and where the freedom is qualified, the result of any balancing exercise depends heavily on assessments of the needs of different societies. Nevertheless, the case law of different countries can be instructive in helping to identify the matters which need to be considered—for instance, there is consensus on the special need to protect political expression in a democracy—and in suggesting legitimate methods of interpreting rights and conducting any balancing exercise. Decisions of the Supreme Court of India under that country's 1947 Constitution, those of the Canadian Supreme Court on the Charter of Rights and Freedoms, those of the Court of Appeal of New Zealand on the New Zealand Bill of Rights Act 1990, and those of the South African Constitutional Court on the rights under South Africa's 1993 and 1996 Constitutions, may all contain useful insights. The decisions of courts in other Council of Europe states on constitutional and international human-rights issues may also be very helpful.[75]

However, our courts should ensure that they understand the constitutional and **7.50** legal background to decisions of foreign courts before making use of their judgments, in order to minimize the twin risks of counsel 'cherry-picking' among authorities, and misusing for one purpose ideas developed for a different context or purpose. For example, the case law of the US Supreme Court is often likely to be unhelpful, in view of the very considerable differences between the constitutional structure and heritage of the United States and those of the United Kingdom. This will apply particularly to assessing justifications for interfering with rights, for example under Article 8(2). Again, unlike the United Kingdom, many European countries have a monist (rather than dualist) approach to the relationship between municipal and international law, and this can significantly affect the way in which they give effect to human rights, making their reasoning and assumption inapplicable in the United Kingdom. Even when examining decisions from other UK jurisdictions, it will be important to bear in mind that (as noted above) a decision made in the context of a 'devolution issue' under the Scotland Act 1998, the Northern Ireland Act 1998, or the Government of Wales Act 1998, establishing the legislative competence of a devolved legislature or executive, may not be directly applicable to a case arising out of an alleged violation of a Convention right by an ordinary administrative body or a limited-purpose public authority. The United Kingdom, and its constituent parts, is engaged on the

---

[75] The English-language literature on fundamental rights in other European jurisdictions is growing. See eg Conor Gearty (ed), *European Civil Liberties and the European Convention on Human Rights: A Comparative Study* (The Hague: Martinus Nijhoff, 1997); Robert Blackburn and Jörg Polakiewicz (eds), *Fundamental Rights in Europe: The ECHR and its Member States, 1950–2000* (Oxford: OUP, 2001).

task of developing a human rights jurisprudence that grows out of its particular constitutional traditions and is adaptable to the different needs of each part of the United Kingdom.

(2) The Temporal Effect of the Human Rights Act 1998

7.51 The general principle is that legislation does not apply retrospectively unless it is clearly intended to do so, either from express words or by necessary implication. Retroactive legislation tends to undermine the principle of legal certainty by preventing people from knowing their obligations at the time they decide how to act. This applies as much to human rights legislation as to any other. The HRA 1998 is expressly stated to operate retrospectively in only one situation. Section 22(4) provides that s 7(1)(b) applies to proceedings brought by or at the instigation of a public authority 'whenever the act in question took place'. Section 7(1)(b) allows a person claiming to be the victim of a violation of a Convention right to rely on the right in proceedings brought by or at the instigation of a public authority. The retrospective application of the rights does not extend to proceedings brought against a public authority under s 7(1)(a). In other words, the rights operate retrospectively as a shield, but not as a sword (although it is not clear whether a Convention right can be used retrospectively as the basis of a counter-claim in civil proceedings brought by a public authority).

7.52 There are thus three conditions which must be met before a Convention right can be relied on in proceedings in respect of an act that took place before the HRA 1998 came into force. First, the proceedings must be brought by or at the instigation of a public authority. This requirement is met in most prosecutions (other than private prosecutions), in actions for penalties brought by public authorities, and in ordinary litigation instigated by public authorities. But it excludes the application of the Act retrospectively in actions brought against, rather than by, public authorities.[76] Secondly, only the defendant may rely on the right. Thirdly, the defendant must claim to be the victim of a violation of a Convention right (a requirement considered further in chapter 19 below).

7.53 In both civil proceedings between private parties and criminal prosecutions, it has been held that a party cannot rely, in an appeal brought after the Act came into force, on the failure of a trial court or tribunal to act in a manner compatible with a Convention right.[77]

---

[76] See eg *Wainwright v Home Office* [2001] EWCA Civ 2081; [2002] QB 1334.
[77] *Wilson v First County Trust Ltd (No 2)* [2001] EWCA Civ 633, [2002] QB 74 (civil proceedings) and see also [2003] UKHL 40, [2003] 3 WLR 568; *R v Lambert* [2001] UKHL 37; [2002] 2 AC 545; para 7.80 below.

This may be subject to one exception.[78] When legislation is relevant to the disposition of a case concerning an act that took place before the HRA 1998 came
into force, the Court of Appeal in *Wilson v First County Trust Ltd (No 2)*[79] made
a declaration of incompatibility under s 4 of the Act, declaring a provision to
be incompatible with a Convention right but leaving the provision valid and
effective, in order to give effect to its duty under s 6 to ensure that its orders are
compatible with Convention rights. The Court of Appeal held that its own decision on the appeal was an act to which s 6 applied, and had to be compatible
with Convention rights. However, this decision did not sit entirely comfort-
ably with subsequent decisions of the House of Lords in criminal cases holding
that s 6 does not impose a duty on a court to give effect to Convention rights,
even by way of reinterpretation of legislation in pursuance of the duty under
s 3 of the Act (explained below), in cases relating to events occurring before
2 October 2000.[80] On appeal the House of Lords decided that the rights and
obligations of the parties to a pre-HRA agreement could not be reinterpreted
in the light of s 3 of the HRA 1998, because there is a presumption that legislation does not retrospectively interfere with people's rights and obligations
unless a contrary intention is expressed.[81] This seems to limit, and perhaps entirely exclude, the possibility of using s 3 to reinterpret legislation as it applies
to rights and obligations arising before 2 October 2000, although s 3 can be
used to reinterpret pre-HRA legislation as it applies to obligations and rights
arising after that date.

(3) The Interpretation of Legislation[82]

(a) General principle

Section 3 of the Act provides:

    (1) So far as it is possible to do so, primary legislation and subordinate legislation
        must be read and given effect in a way which is compatible with the
        Convention rights.

    (2) This section—
        (a) applies to primary legislation and secondary legislation whenever enacted;
        (b) does not affect the validity, continuing operation or enforcement of any in-
            compatible primary legislation; and
        (c) does not affect the validity, continuing operation or enforcement of any in-
            compatible subordinate legislation if (disregarding any possibility of revo-
            cation) primary legislation prevents removal of the incompatibility.

7.54

7.55

---

[78] See in addition para 7.57 below.
[79] [2001] EWCA Civ 633, [2002] QB 74.
[80] See eg *R v Lambert* [2001] UKHL 37, [2002] 2 AC 545; para 7.80 below.
[81] [2003] UKHL 40; [2003] 3 WLR 568.
[82] See the discussion by Professor Evelyn Ellis, paras 1.216–1.222 above.

7.56 As Lord Woolf CJ pointed out in *Poplar Housing and Regeneration Community Association v Donoghue*,[83] s 3 is mandatory in its terms, and applies when legislation would otherwise be in conflict with a Convention right. In such an event, the court must adopt a different approach to interpreting and applying the legislation from that which courts normally adopted before the HRA 1998 came into force. Instead of simply seeking to give effect to the intention of Parliament as expressed in any one statute, the court must now, so far as possible, also give effect to Parliament's intention, expressed in s 3 of the 1998 Act, that all legislation must be read and given effect in a manner compatible with Convention rights. The court cannot be relieved of its obligation by any agreement between the parties to the litigation, or by the views of the Crown if it is a party.[84] The obligation is not limited to situations in which there is an ambiguity in the legislation to be interpreted.[85]

(b) Temporal effect

7.57 The obligation under s 3 applies to reading of legislation passed before, as well as after, the 1998 Act, and also to the interpretation and implementation of the 1998 Act itself. When applied to previous legislation, the courts may have to depart from the interpretation established in earlier case law. For example, in *Fitzpatrick v Sterling Housing Association Ltd*,[86] decided after the HRA 1998 had been passed but before s 3 came into force, the House of Lords held that two men who had been living together in a loving homosexual relationship for 18 years could not be said to have been 'living together as husband and wife' so as to allow the survivor to succeed to the tenancy after the tenant had died. The words 'husband and wife' were said to be gender-specific (although a majority of the House decided that the survivor could succeed as a member of the deceased tenant's 'family'). In *Ghaidan v Godin-Mendoza*,[87] however, the Court of Appeal applied s 3 of the 1998 Act to interpret 'living together as husband and wife' in the 1977 Act as including a couple living together in a stable homosexual relationship, in order to avoid an incompatibility with the right to be free of discrimination, on the ground of one's sexuality, in the enjoyment of the right to respect for the home under Articles 8 and 14 ECHR.

7.58 In certain cases, the Court of Appeal has held that the court's duty under s 3 applies even when the events to which proceedings relate took place before 2 October 2000.[88] In *Wilson v First County Trust Ltd (No 2)*,[89] the court recognized

---

83 [2001] EWCA Civ 595; [2002] QB 48 at [75].
84 ibid.
85 *R v DPP, ex p Kebilene* [2000] 2 AC 326, 373 *per* Lord Cooke of Thorndon; *R v A (No 2)* [2001] UKHL 25; [2002] 1 AC 509, *per* Lord Steyn at [44] and Lord Hope of Craighead at [108].
86 [2001] 1 AC 27, HL.
87 [2002] EWCA Civ 1533; [2003] 2 WLR 478.
88 See *Wilson v First County Trust Ltd (No 2)* [2001] EWCA Civ 633; [2002] QB 74.
89 ibid.

that s 22(4) of the Act provides that people may not normally rely on Convention rights in respect of acts taking place before 2 October 2000. This was said to reflect a legislative policy of protecting public authorities against a large number of retrospective claims.[90] However, as noted in para 7.54, the House of Lords decided that s 3 does not require or permit the courts to reinterpret legislation as it applies to rights and obligations arising before the HRA came into force on 2 October 2000.[91]

7.59 Another circumstance in which s 3 has been applied to a claim arising out of events pre-dating 2 October 2000 is where Community law is relevant to the issue. In *Chief Constable of the West Yorkshire Police v A (No 2)*,[92] it was held that the Sex Discrimination Act 1975 had to be reinterpreted as covering discrimination against someone on the ground that he was a transsexual, using s 3 of the HRA 1998. The retrospective effect arose because Community law already treated the protection against sex discrimination in the EC Equal Treatment Directive as encompassing discrimination on the ground of gender reassignment.[93] The Sex Discrimination Act 1975 was subsequently amended to bring it into line with Community law, but the facts of *Chief Constable of West Yorkshire Police* arose before the amendments were made. Nevertheless, the Court of Appeal decided that it had a duty to apply s 3 retrospectively, relying both on *Wilson v First County Trust Ltd (No 2)*, above, and on the fact that Community law had applied with direct effect in the United Kingdom before the amendments, so reinterpreting the Sex Discrimination Act 1975 in reliance on s 3 of the HRA 1998 did not really produce a retrospective change to the law.

7.60 Fortunately, as time passes, the question of retrospectivity is likely to cause problems in progressively fewer cases.

(c) What are the limits to the court's duty under s 3?

7.61 The court's duty under s 3 extends only to reading and giving effect to the legislation. The interpretation adopted must be one which can legitimately be said to be a reading of the legislation, and must give effect to it. A court is not allowed to depart so far from the text of the legislation, when read together with s 3, that the result would be regarded as legislation (which is Parliament's role) rather than interpretation (which is the judges' role). But it is not always easy to decide where the borderline between interpretation and legislation comes. Drawing the boundary demands a judgment about the proper constitutional role of the judge in relation to each piece of legislation. A number of factors are relevant when deciding

---

[90] ibid at [21].
[91] [2003] UKHL 40; [2003] 3 WLR 568.
[92] [2002] EWCA Civ 1584; [2003] 1 All ER 255.
[93] Case C-13/94 *P v S and Cornwall CC* [1996] ECR I-2143.

whether a suggested reading of a legislative provision is one which it is legitimate for a judge to adopt in the light of s 3 of the HRA 1998, although sometimes the relevant factors pull in different directions.

(i) No radical alteration of the effect of a statutory provision

7.62 If a reading of the provision radically alters the effect of the legislation, it is likely to be regarded as going beyond interpretation.[94] Legislation containing clear and unequivocal words expressly contradicting the meaning it would have to be given in order to make it compatible with a Convention right would not be capable of being read in a compatible manner, even under s 3.[95]

7.63 However, sometimes courts are prepared to achieve a radically different outcome from the one indicated by the normal meaning of the words used in the legislation. For example, in *R v A (No 2)*,[96] the House of Lords had to construe s 41 of the Youth Justice and Criminal Evidence Act 1999. The section was designed to protect complainants alleging sexual offences against being cross-examined about their previous sexual conduct. Section 41(1) prohibited questions being asked, or evidence adduced, about the complainant's sexual behaviour without the leave of the court. Section 41(2) provided that the court might give leave only if satisfied that refusing leave might have the result of rendering unsafe the conclusion of the court or jury on a relevant issue, and that one of a number of conditions applied. The first condition, under s 41(3), was that the evidence related to a relevant issue (and was not adduced mainly for the purpose of impugning the complainant's credibility: s 41(4)), and the issue (1) was not an issue of consent, or (2) was an issue of consent and the behaviour to which it related was alleged to have taken place at or about the same time as the event which was the subject matter of the charge, or (3) was an issue of consent and the sexual behaviour of the complainant to which the evidence related was so similar to the behaviour of the complainant alleged by the defendant at time of the alleged offence or to other behaviour allegedly occurring at or about the same time that the similarity could not reasonably be explained as a coincidence. The second condition, under s 41(5), was that the evidence or question related to any evidence adduced by the prosecution about the complainant's sexual behaviour, and would go no further than necessary to rebut or explain the evidence adduced by the prosecution.

7.64 The House of Lords decided unanimously that evidence of a complainant's sexual behaviour on previous occasions, for example during a long-standing relationship with the defendant, might be relevant to the issue of whether the complainant had

---

[94] Lord Woolf CJ in *Poplar Housing and Regeneration Community Association v Donoghue* [2001] EWCA Civ 595; [2002] QB 48 at [75].

[95] *R v A (No 2)* [2001] UKHL 25; [2002] 1 AC 509 at [108] *per* Lord Hope of Craighead.

[96] ibid.

consented. Their Lordships also held that preventing a defendant from adducing such evidence on the issue of consent (while allowing it, for example, on the question whether the defendant had honestly believed that the complainant had been consenting) could deprive the defendant of a fair trial by denying him the opportunity to advance relevant evidence to rebut the complainant's evidence in respect of one of the elements of the offence. That would have violated the defendant's right to a fair hearing under Article 6(1) ECHR. While accepting the justification for Parliament's decision to restrict such questioning and evidence—in order to protect the complainant against humiliation and to prevent prejudicial evidence which was not probative in relation to the offence—the House decided that it could not simply defer to Parliament's judgment when interpreting s 41 in the light of Convention rights. It was for the judges to decide what amounted to a fair hearing within the meaning of Article 6(1). The content of a right was a question of law, and judges were in a particularly good position, by reference both to their special expertise and to their constitutional position, to assess what fairness required. While some individual elements in a fair trial might be restricted so long as the overall fairness of the hearing was maintained, and due weight should be given to Parliament's view that the mischief at which the legislation aimed should be corrected, there was limited scope for deference in relation to the proportionality of the interference with the right of a defendant in a criminal trial to offer a full defence.[97] Indeed, Lord Hutton referred to the right to make a full defence as an absolute right which was of the essence of a fair trial.[98]

7.65 For these reasons, a majority considered that the terms of s 41 might interfere in a disproportionate and unjustifiable way with the right to a fair hearing. Lord Hope deferred more extensively to Parliament's views of the appropriate balance in relation to prejudice to the wider interests of the community in a 'highly sensitive and carefully researched field',[99] and doubted whether it could be said that s 41 was a disproportionate response to the legitimate legislative objective.[100] But all agreed that there might be individual cases in which the section would, on its natural meaning, make it difficult to ensure a fair hearing, and were prepared to accept that in such a case the strong interpretative obligation under s 3 of the HRA 1998 could come into play.

7.66 That being so, the question was whether s 3 of the HRA could be used to read and give effect to s 41 of the 1999 Act in a way that would allow defendants a fair trial in accordance with their Article 6 rights. Their Lordships held that it was not possible, even using s 3 of the 1998 Act, to interpret s 41(3)(b) as covering evidence

---

[97] ibid at [36] *per* Lord Steyn.
[98] ibid at [161].
[99] ibid at [99].
[100] ibid at [108].

of sexual conduct more than a few hours before the events forming the basis of the complainant's allegation. On the other hand, s 41(3)(c) might be used to allow a defendant to bring in the evidence or put the questions, as long as s 3 was used to disable, so far as necessary, the requirement of s 41(3)(c) that the evidence or questions should only be admitted to show that previous (consensual) conduct was so similar to that alleged to constitute the offence that 'the similarity cannot reasonably be explained as a coincidence'. Evidence might be admitted under s 41(3)(c) even if there was no question of any similarity being coincidental, because the obligation of the court under s 3 applied even if there was no ambiguity in the legislation.

(ii) The reading must be consistent with the fundamental features of the structure of the legislation being interpreted

7.67   Another principle limiting the effect of s 3 is concerned with the architecture of the legislation being interpreted. If a reading introduces a feature which is antithetical to a fundamental feature of the design of the legislation, it is very likely to be regarded as legislative rather than interpretative. For example, in *Re S (Minors) (Care Order: Implementation of Care Plan)*[101] the House of Lords was invited to extend the powers of the courts to supervise the implementation by local authorities of final care plans previously approved under the Children Act 1989. This was said to be necessary in order to protect the children's right to respect for private and family life against violation through the subsequent failure or inability of a local authority to implement the care plan. The House of Lords, reversing the decision of the Court of Appeal, decided that this would have been inconsistent with a fundamental feature of the design of the 1989 Act. That Act had been designed to transfer responsibility for overseeing care plans from the courts (under the wardship jurisdiction) to local authorities. The structure of powers and obligations under the Act reflected that.[102] The courts can intervene in the exercise of those functions only if, on ordinary principles of judicial review, the local authority is acting in a way that is illegal, irrational, or procedurally improper.[103] Extending the powers of the court to supervise the work of local authorities more intrusively would have been inconsistent with that fundamental feature of the design of the legislation. Although this arguably left the children with inadequate protection for their Convention rights, the remedy would have to lie in legislative amendment to, rather than judicial reinterpretation of, the 1989 Act. In a similar way, in *Sheffield City Council v Smart*[104] the Court of Appeal was asked to refuse a local housing authority's application for possession of premises held on an unsecured

---

[101] [2002] UKHL 10; [2002] 2 AC 291.
[102] See SM Cretney, in Peter Birks (ed), *English Private Law* (Oxford: OUP, 2000) vol 2, paras 2.200–2.203.
[103] *Re M and H (Minors) (Local Authority: Parental Rights)* [1990] 1 AC 686, HL.
[104] [2002] EWCA Civ 4; [2002] HLR 34.

tenancy, because granting possession would, it was argued, be incompatible with the tenant's right to respect for the home under Article 8 ECHR. The Court of Appeal held that giving effect to the legislation in that way would be inconsistent with a fundamental part of its design, as it would effectively turn an unsecured tenancy into a secured tenancy.

This does not mean that courts will never use s 3 of the HRA 1998 to extend their **7.68** jurisdiction to supervise administrative decision-making beyond the normal grounds for judicial review. Everything depends on the nature of the legislation being considered, and the extent to which the extension would affect what is thought to be a fundamental part of the design of the legislation. For example, in *Adan v Newham LBC*[105] there was a statutory right for a person aggrieved by certain decisions of a local housing authority to appeal to the county court on a point of law. The Court of Appeal held that the county court could review questions of fact as well as law where the facts were relevant to the protection of the appellant's Convention rights. As an administrative decision which is incompatible with a Convention right is normally unlawful,[106] facts relevant to establishing such a violation can be regarded as jurisdictional facts which the primary decision-maker must decide correctly if he or she is to act lawfully. In accordance with long-standing principles of administrative law, such questions of 'jurisdictional fact' are to be regarded as questions of law for the purpose of establishing the review powers of courts.[107] In that way, it was possible to give effect to the legislation in a way that both protected the rights of the appellant and was consistent with the structure of the legislation itself.

Similarly it has been held that the compatibility with the right to peaceful enjoy- **7.69** ment of possessions (under Article 2 of Protocol 1 to the ECHR) of a decision by the Commissioners of Customs and Excise to forfeit vehicles in which dutiable goods were brought into the United Kingdom without paying the duty is a question of law, not discretion, even so far as it involves an assessment of the proportionality of the decision. The court is therefore required to make its own assessment of the proper balance between the rights of the owner of the vehicle and the public interest in deterring smuggling, rather than deferring to the view of the Commissioners. Instead, the Commissioners bore the burden of persuading the court that their decision was justified.[108]

---

[105] [2001] EWCA 1916; [2002] 1 WLR 2120.
[106] HRA 1998, s 6(1).
[107] See paras 14.17–14.19 below
[108] *Lindsay v Commissioners of Customs and Excise* [2002] EWCA Civ 267; [2002] 1 WLR 1766; *Commissioners of Customs and Excise v Newbury* [2003] EWHC 702; [2003] 2 All ER 964, DC; and cf *Gascoyne v Commissioners of Customs and Excise* [2003] EWHC 257; [2003] 2 WLR 1311, where a policy to return a vehicle to its owner only in exceptional circumstances was held to be proportionate when it applied only in cases of commercial smuggling rather than to people bringing goods into the country for their own use or that of friends.

(d) Techniques for reading legislation under s 3

7.70 When operating within the limits of s 3, a number of techniques may be used. These are sometimes referred to as 'reading in', 'reading out', and 'reading down'. These are only shorthand labels, and the techniques that they describe overlap rather than being entirely separate. Nevertheless, brief consideration of each of them can be instructive.

(i) Reading into the legislation

7.71 Reading words into legislation is always likely to be regarded as a legislative rather than an interpretative technique. It therefore requires justification. The clearest justification arises in relation to the interpretation of legislation passed before the HRA 1998. As the Court of Appeal observed, obiter, in *Poplar Housing and Regeneration Community Association Ltd v Donoghue*:[109] 'It is as though legislation which predates the HRA 1998 and conflicts with the Convention has to be treated as being subsequently amended to incorporate the language of section 3'. This is no more than an application of orthodox principles of constitutional law and statutory interpretation whereby a provision in a statute can be treated as impliedly amending inconsistent provisions in earlier legislation.

7.72 For obvious reasons, reading in will less often be justified when interpreting primary legislation passed after the 1998 Act, but there might be circumstances in which there are compelling reasons for using the technique even then, as s 3 of the 1998 Act operates as strong guidance to the interpretation of all legislation, and there is the usual presumption that Parliament does not intend to legislate in a manner inconsistent with the United Kingdom's international obligations, including those arising under human rights treaties. Subordinate legislation made after the passing of the 1998 Act can more readily be adjusted by reading words in to produce compatibility with Convention rights, since the alternative would be to invalidate the subordinate legislation to the extent of the incompatibility.

(ii) Reading out

7.73 Reading words or provisions out of legislation is a radical step, and (like reading in) is most likely to be justified when dealing with legislation passed or made before the 1998 Act, and subordinate legislation made subsequently.

(iii) Reading down or up

7.74 The most obviously interpretative, rather than legislative, of the techniques is adopting a restrictive (or, sometimes expansive) reading of words in legislation. It

---

[109] [2001] EWCA Civ 595; [2002] QB 48 at [75].

is a more easily justifiable technique for judges, because the words are not changed, but their meaning or their impact on a particular situation is selected to secure compatibility, so far as possible, with Convention rights. It has been used regularly when courts have decided that a different, perhaps more natural, reading of the words would produce a result that would threaten a Convention right.

For example, in *R v Offen*[110] the Court of Appeal gave an extended meaning to 'exceptional circumstances' in s 2(2) of the Crime (Sentences) Act 1997. The section required a court to pass a sentence of life imprisonment on any adult who had been convicted of a second serious offence, 'unless the court is of the opinion that there are exceptional circumstances relating to either of the offences or to the offender which justify its not doing so'. The category of 'serious offences' included some (such as robbery while in possession of an imitation firearm) which, on the facts of an individual case, might not appear to be particularly serious, but the Court of Appeal had previously decided that an 'exceptional circumstance' 'need not be unique, or unprecedented, or very rare; but it cannot be one that is regularly, or routinely, or normally encountered'.[111] As a result, the legislation was capable of leading to courts having to pass life sentences on people who could not be regarded as representing a continuing danger to the public. In *Offen*, it was argued that this threatened to violate two Convention rights. The Court of Appeal accepted that the imposition of a sentence which was disproportionate to the facts of the case and the threat posed by the offender could amount to inhuman or degrading punishment contrary to Article 3 ECHR, and the deprivation of liberty in pursuance of a disproportionate sentence could violate the right to liberty of the person under Article 5 ECHR.[112] To avoid these risks, the Court of Appeal decided that judges should have regard to the rationale for the legislation when deciding whether there were exceptional circumstances. The policy was to protect the public against people who had already committed two serious offences, because they were assumed to present a future threat against which the public should be protected by passing a life sentence. In that legislative context, the fact that a particular offender might not actually present a future risk could properly be regarded as an exceptional circumstance justifying the exercise of sentencing discretion.[113] Applying s 3 of the HRA 1998, the Court of Appeal decided that this was the approach that should be followed, giving effect to the intention of Parliament 'in a more just, less arbitrary and more proportionate manner'.[114]

7.75

Offen is an example of 'reading up' the scope of an exception to increase judicial discretion to sentence fairly. Another example of 'reading up', or extending the

7.76

---

[110] [2001] 1 WLR 253, CA.

[111] *R v Kelly (Edward)* [2000] QB 198, CA.

[112] [2001] 1 WLR 253 at [95], citing *R v Governor of Brockhill Prison, ex p Evans (No 2)* [2001] 2 AC 19, 38 *per* Lord Hope of Craighead.

[113] ibid at [79].

[114] ibid at [99].

scope of, a provision to increase the discretion of trial judges to admit evidence or allow questions to secure a fair trial is *R v A (No 2)*, the 'rape-shield' decision discussed earlier.[115]

7.77   Examples of 'reading down', or restricting the scope of duties imposed on people by legislation, include treating the word 'must' as meaning 'may'. Section 32(3) of the Immigration and Asylum Act 1999 provided that, if the Secretary of State decided a carrier was liable to a penalty for carrying illegal immigrants into the country, the carrier must pay the penalty within a set time, but s 34 provided for certain defences which were to be considered by the Secretary of State. When the Secretary of State decided that certain carriers were liable to a penalty, rejecting their defence, they applied for judicial review of his decision, assuming that the word 'must' meant that they had no other way of advancing a defence to an independent and impartial tribunal. The Divisional Court pointed out that, were that to be the case, the Secretary of State would always be acting as judge in his own cause, violating Article 6(1) ECHR. Without referring expressly to s 3 of the 1998 Act, the court decided that the carriers could, but need not, pay by the set date. Instead, they could wait for the Secretary of State to sue them for the penalty, and raise the defence before the court in those proceedings. It would be more appropriate to examine the evidence supporting a defence in the county court than to do so in judicial review proceedings.[116]

7.78   Provisions imposing a burden of proof on the defendant in criminal proceedings provide another example of the technique of 'reading down'. They potentially lead to a breach of the presumption of innocence in Article 6(2) ECHR. In a number of cases, such legislation has been read as imposing only an evidential burden (ie, the burden of leading sufficient evidence to put the matter in issue, leaving the prosecution to prove its case on the issue) rather than a legal or probative burden (the burden of proving the facts in issue to the appropriate standard of proof).[117] However, much depends on context. The defendant's right not to have to prove his or her case is implied from Article 6, not expressly stated in it. The courts have held that the right can be restricted, and a burden (legal as well as evidential) can be placed on the defendant, if there is a sufficiently compelling public interest in doing so and the measure is proportionate to it and does not deprive the defendant of a trial which is fair, all things considered. Section 3 of the HRA 1998 will

---

[115] [2001] UKHL 25; [2002] 1 AC 509. See above, paras 7.63 et seq.

[116] *R (on the application of Balbo B & C Auto Transporti Internazionali) v Secretary of State for the Home Department* [2001] EWHC Admin 195; [2001] 1 WLR 1556, DC.

[117] *R v Lambert* [2001] UKHL 37; [2002] 2 AC 545 (Misuse of Drugs Act 1971, s 28(2) and (3)); *R v Carass* [2001] EWCA Crim 2845, [2002] 1 WLR 1714 (Insolvency Act 1986, s 206: defence to charge of concealing debts of company in anticipation of winding up); *Sheldrake v DPP* [2003] EWHC 273; [2003] 2 All ER 497 (Road Traffic Act 1988, s 5(2): defence to a charge of being in charge of a vehicle with an excessive blood-alcohol level if the defendant proves that there was no likelihood of his driving while in that condition).

not be used to read down such reverse-onus provisions if these conditions are met.[118]

Furthermore, the obligation is to 'read and give effect to' the legislation in a compatible manner. Even if it is not possible to 'read' a provision in a manner which will guarantee compatibility in all circumstances, one may still be able to 'give effect to' it in order to avoid incompatibility in individual cases. This case-by-case approach is particularly likely to be appropriate when dealing with statutory provisions which confer discretions. Under s 6(1), any public authority within the meaning of s 6 is bound by the Convention rights, and acts unlawfully if it acts in a manner incompatible with a Convention right unless required to act in that way by primary legislation which cannot be interpreted so as to allow for Convention-compatible action. Public authorities (including courts and tribunals) therefore have a duty to exercise their discretion, whenever possible, in a Convention-compatible manner. As the House of Lords held in *R v A (No 2)*,[119] in relation to the discretion of judges to allow certain questions or admit certain evidence in trials for sexual offences, the duty to secure a fair hearing under Article 6 ECHR could best be achieved by the trial judge deciding, in each case, how best to proceed in the light of the obligation under s 3 to interpret the legislation conferring the discretion in a manner compatible with Convention rights so far as it was possible to do so. Another course might be to use judicial discretion as to the grant of remedies (since all civil remedies except damages are usually discretionary) in such a way as to avoid incompatible outcomes, although the importance of not frustrating the clear will of Parliament expressed in primary legislation makes it impossible to guarantee that this can always be achieved.

7.79

Courts are reluctant to do anything that would in effect frustrate valid, albeit incompatible legislation, and this constitutional constraint, flowing from the doctrine of Parliament's legislative supremacy, limits the use that they are prepared to make of s 3. In a number of cases they have refused remedies where granting them would thwart the will of Parliament. For example, in *R v Lambert*[120] the House of Lords by a majority (Lord Steyn dissenting) decided that the HRA 1998 did not apply retrospectively, so that a person convicted before the Act came into force could not subsequently appeal on the ground that the conviction violated Convention rights. Lord Slynn of Hadley denied that an appeal court had an obligation to quash a decision which was good as the law stood at the time it was

7.80

---

[118] *A-G's Reference (No 4 of 2002)* [2003] EWCA Crim 762; [2003] HRLR 15 (defence to charge of membership of proscribed organization under Terrorism Act 2000, s 11); *R v Matthews* [2003] EWCA Crim 813; The Times, 28 April 2003 (defence of good reason or lawful authority for having a bladed weapon in a public place under Criminal Justice Act 1988, s 139).

[119] [2001] UKHL 25, [2002] 1 AC 509. See paras 7.63 et seq, above.

[120] [2001] UKHL 37; [2002] 2 AC 545.

made.[121] Later, in *R v Kansal (No 2)*[122] a slightly differently constituted Appellate Committee of the House revisited the question. It decided by a three-two majority that the decision on non-retrospectivity in *Lambert* had been wrong, but went on to hold by a four-one majority that it would not be right to depart from it. In *R v Lyons*,[123] the House unanimously applied the ratio of the decision in *Lambert*. Former directors of Guinness plc had been convicted of offences in relation to the takeover by Guinness of Distillers. The European Court of Human Rights had decided that the use at the trial of self-incriminating statements obtained by coercion had rendered the trial unfair, in contravention of Article 6 ECHR. The case was referred back to the Court of Appeal in the light of that decision. The Court of Appeal and, on further appeal, the House of Lords refused to overturn the convictions, holding that they had been proper under the law in force at the time, and that it would be wrong for courts to disapply the relevant statutes retrospectively by quashing the convictions. Although this left the appellants without an effective remedy for the violation of their Article 6 rights, parliamentary sovereignty had to be respected.

(iv) Emerging judicial policy on the use of s 3

7.81   The shape of a judicial policy emerges from these decisions. Judges are most willing to use s 3 on legislation which affects people's right to have access to a court for a fair hearing of their cases. They are much less likely to use s 3 where legislation gives effect to the legislature's judgment on matters of social policy, or where a Convention-compatible interpretation of the legislation would have an impact in a wide range of social and legal contexts which the judges cannot easily foresee or cater for in a judgment in an individual case. The decision of the House of Lords in *Bellinger v Bellinger*[124] is an example of the latter point. The question was whether a marriage between a man and a post-operative male-to-female transsexual was valid. Section 11(c) of the Matrimonial Causes Act 1973 provided that marriages are valid only if the parties are respectively 'male and female'. English law had previously regarded a post-operative transsexual for legal purposes as retaining the sex with which he or she had been born, although certain inroads had been made on that principle by Community law in the context of sex discrimination law. The European Court of Human Rights had held that English law in this respect violated both the right to respect for private and family life and the right to marry, under Articles 8 and 12 ECHR.[125] The House of Lords accepted that s 11(c) as previously interpreted was incompatible with those rights. However, it decided that it could not use s 3 of the HRA 1998 to interpret 'male and female'

---

[121] *R v Lambert* (n 120 above) at [12]–[13].
[122] [2001] UKHL 62; [2002] 2 AC 69.
[123] [2002] UKHL 44; [2002] 3 WLR 1562.
[124] [2003] UKHL 21; [2003] 2 WLR 1174.
[125] See paras 8.63 and 8.80 below.

as referring to current gender rather than sex at birth. Changes to the status of transsexuals needed to be looked at comprehensively by the legislature in order to answer difficult questions. Should the law recognize only post-operative changes? If so, what surgical steps needed to have been taken before recognition should be given? If not, at what stage should a change of gender be recognized? How (if at all) should recognition be given in fields of law unrelated to marriage? What changes would be administratively feasible? Parliament was in a better position than the courts to make these decisions. Accordingly, the House declined to use s 3 of the 1998 Act to reinterpret s 11 of the 1973 Act. Instead, it granted a declaration of incompatibility in respect of s 11, leaving it in force until such time as legislation was passed to amend it.

This illustrates how decisions about the use of s 3 of the HRA 1998 are related to, **7.82** affect, and are affected by a number of other factors. These include:

- The availability of a declaration of incompatibility under s 4 of the Act, which can be granted in cases where judges decide that there is an incompatibility which cannot be avoided by interpretative means. Because judges have been given a way of drawing an incompatibility to the attention of the executive and Parliament, relying on them to amend the law in order to achieve compatibility, they are less inclined to stretch the words of legislation to achieve compatibility.
- The effect of s 6(1) of the Act on discretion. Essentially, unless primary legislation makes it absolutely clear that the discretion must be exercised incompatibly with a Convention right, administrative and judicial authorities must use their discretion in a way that is compatible with the rights. This makes it less important for courts to 'read down' statutory provisions granting discretion. Instead, they can stress that discretion must be exercised on a case-by-case basis in such a way as to protect Convention rights, taking account in respect of judicial discretion (as the House of Lords said in *R v A (No 2)*)[126] of the duty under s 3 of the Act. If this is not done in a particular case, the decision can be challenged by way of appeal or judicial review.
- The availability in some cases of alternative remedies, perhaps by applying traditional common law principles developed to take account of Convention rights.
- The notion of deference, including deference to the judgments made by Parliament about the need for and proportionality of legislative interference with Convention rights. It should be noted, however, that the idea of deference to legislation is properly applied only to legislation passed after the HRA 1998, when it can often be shown that Parliament assessed the measures in terms of the necessity for and proportionality of an interference with the right in question.

---

[126] [2001] UKHL 25; [2002] 1 AC 509. See paras 7.63 et seq above.

(4) The Impact of the Act on the Making and Validity of Legislation

(a) Making legislation: the duties of ministers and Parliament

7.83   People involved in the making of primary legislation are not bound, under national law, to act compatibly with the Convention rights. Section 6(6) of the Act provides that an act cannot fall within the duty imposed by s 6(1) if it is only a failure to introduce in, or lay before, Parliament a proposal for legislation, or to make any primary legislation or remedial order. Of particular relevance to Acts of Parliament and other legislation requiring parliamentary approval, s 6(3) excludes from the category of 'public authorities', which alone are subject to the duty to act compatibly, 'either House of Parliament or a person exercising functions in connection with proceedings in Parliament'.

7.84   Nevertheless, the freedom to propose, debate and pass or make legislation which is incompatible with Convention rights, and so with the United Kingdom's obligations in international law, carries with it certain responsibilities. One of them is to ensure that Parliament can consider whether the legislation in question would interfere with a Convention right, and, if it would, whether the interference would be justifiable.[127] This is partly to ensure that Parliament can properly discharge its responsibility when scrutinizing the human rights implications of proposed legislation. It is also partly because of the approach courts and tribunals should adopt to interpreting the legislation subsequently, and to deciding whether it is compatible with Convention rights. It has already been suggested[128] that courts should defer to Parliament's assessment of the justification for interfering with a Convention right, and accord a significant margin of discretion to Parliament in making that assessment, only if Parliament has actually considered the matter.

7.85   To facilitate the exercise of Parliament's function in considering the human rights implications of proposed legislation, various steps have been prescribed by Act of Parliament, provided for under resolutions or Standing Orders of each House, or laid down in administrative guidance issued for departments. Before the HRA 1998, there was no systematic way of alerting Parliament to the human rights implications of legislation proposed to it. Since the Act was passed, there have been two major advances intended to fill this gap: first, obligations imposed on ministers and departments (and the promoters of private Bills) to inform Parliament about their views of the compatibility of the proposed measures with Convention rights; secondly, the work of the Joint Committee on Human Rights within

---

[127]   See Anthony Lester QC, 'Parliamentary Scrutiny of Legislation under the HRA 1998] [2002] European Human Rights L Rev 432; David Feldman, 'Parliamentary Scrutiny of Legislation and Human Rights' [2002] PL 323.

[128]   See paras 7.40 and 7.82 above.

Parliament. The paragraphs following explain these steps as they apply to Government Bills, private members' Bills, private Bills, statutory instruments, and measures of the Church of England and its General Synod.

(b) Government Bills

(i) Action by ministers and departments

In relation to a government Bill introduced to either House of Parliament, s 19 of the 1998 Act requires the minister in charge of the Bill to state, before second reading, either that in his or her view the Bill is compatible with the Convention rights (a 'statement of compatibility' under s 19(1)(a)), or that he is unable to make a statement of compatibility but that nevertheless the government (not the individual minister) wishes the House to proceed with the Bill (under s 19(1)(b)). The statement must be in writing, and must be published 'in such manner as the Minister making it considers appropriate'. This section came into force in December 1998.

7.86

Since then, the printed version of every Bill published on first introduction to either House has carried, on its cover, a statement made by the responsible minister in one of two forms. The usual form is a printed statement under s 19(1)(a) that a named minister 'has made the following statement under section 19(1)(a)' of the HRA 1998: 'In my view the provisions of the [*title of Bill*] Bill are compatible with the Convention rights'. This statement covers the contents of the Bill on first introduction to that House. When the Bill, as amended, passes to the other House, the printed version of the Bill on first introduction to the second House carries a similar statement, made by the minister responsible for the Bill in that House. Naturally, the statement does not cover amendments made subsequently.

7.87

The alternative form, under s 19(1)(b), has been used only twice since December 1998. The most significant use was in relation to the Communications Bill, introduced to the House of Commons on 19 November 2002. That Bill included, in clause 309, provision for the continuation of the total ban on political advertising on television and radio that had always been applied to commercial broadcasting organizations in the United Kingdom. A decision of the European Court of Human Rights gave reason to think that such a ban might well be considered to be incompatible with the right to freedom of expression under Article 10 ECHR. The government had decided that there were overwhelming reasons for continuing the ban, and intended to argue, both in domestic courts and in the European Court of Human Rights if necessary, that the ban was actually justifiable under Article 10(2) ECHR. Nevertheless, the minister (Tessa Jowell MP) decided that she could not conscientiously make a statement of compatibility, and instead the following statement under s 19(1)(b) was printed: 'I am unable (but only because of clause 309) to make a statement that, in my view, the provisions of the Communications Bill are

7.88

compatible with the Convention rights. However, the Government nevertheless wishes the House to proceed with the Bill.' When it considered this statement, the Joint Committee on Human Rights decided that the minister was, in the circumstances, justified in making this statement and inviting the House of Commons to consider the Bill notwithstanding the possible incompatibility.[129]

7.89   The government's guidance to departments makes it clear that the responsible minister is expected to have taken legal advice before making a statement (whether of compatibility or possible incompatibility) under s 19(1).[130] The Guidance, as subsequently updated, makes it clear that the department in the published Explanatory Notes to the Bill should be prepared to describe in general terms the most significant Convention issues thought to arise, and where necessary refer to the policy justification for what is proposed, although it is not expected that they will cite case law. They are not to disclose legal advice. Similarly, when asked to do so during debate in Parliament the minister should be prepared to give a general outline of the arguments that led him or her to the conclusion reached on the compatibility of particular provisions in the Bill.[131]

(ii) Joint Committee on Human Rights

7.90   Every Bill introduced to either House (including private members' Bills and private Bills) is considered by the Joint Committee on Human Rights (JCHR).[132] Where it feels that a government Bill has significant implications for human rights, the Committee takes evidence (usually in written form) from the responsible minister. This can help to elucidate the government's reasons for thinking that a provision in the Bill does not engage a right, or that any interference with a right is justified in terms of human rights law. The Committee also invites evidence from non-governmental organizations and others. In the course of this process and in the light of the evidence as it emerges, it reports to each House its view of the human rights implications of the Bill.[133] The Committee's remit, to consider matters relating to human rights in the United Kingdom, includes, but is not limited to, Convention rights under the HRA 1998. The Committee's reports therefore

---

[129] JCHR, First Report of 2002–03, *Scrutiny of Bills: Progress Report* (HL Paper 24; HC 191) paras 11–16; Fourth Report of 2002–03, *Scrutiny of Bills: Further Progress Report* (HL Paper 50; HC 397) paras 40–41.

[130] *The HRA 1998 Guidance for Departments* (2nd edn, 2000) paras 32–37 and Annex A, available at www.lcd.gov.uk/hract/guidance.htm.

[131] ibid para 39, as replaced by *Human Rights Guidance: Section 19 Statements: Revised Guidance for Departments*, available at www.dca.gov.uk/hract/guidance/guide-updated.htm.

[132] The JCHR is a joint select committee of both Houses, first established in January 2001. Its remit and powers are set out in resolutions of each House. It has six members from each House. There is currently no government majority. It is required to consider matters relating to human rights, and (as will be explained below) it has specific responsibilities in relation to remedial orders.

[133] For the principles currently governing the JCHR's working practices in relation to government Bills, see its First Report of 2002–03 (n 129 above) paras 2–4.

include, but often go beyond, an assessment of the compatibility of the Bill with Convention rights. The Committee cannot block the passage of a Bill or a provision in it: the two Houses are responsible for deciding whether to accept the Committee's view, and, if they accept it, for deciding what (if anything) to do about it. Nevertheless, the Committee's reports frequently influence debates on Bills in both Houses, and are taken into account by the government when considering whether to propose amendments to the Bills.[134]

(c) Private members' Bills

A private member of either House who introduces a Bill is not required to make any statement about the compatibility of the Bill with Convention rights. However, where the Bill is a 'Government hand-out' (ie, a government-inspired Bill which a member has agreed to promote on the government's behalf), the government has accepted that the minister responsible for the policy should make an oral statement during the Second Reading debate expressing the government's view of the Bill's compatibility with Convention rights, as a matter of good practice.[135] This practice has since been extended to other private members' Bills: the minister whose responsibilities are most closely related to the subject matter of the Bill can be expected to make a statement about its Convention compatibility at some convenient point in the Bill's passage through the House. **7.91**

The JCHR will examine the Bill and report on its human rights implications more generally, giving the member responsible for introducing the Bill (and, where appropriate, the relevant minister) an opportunity to express views.[136] **7.92**

(d) Private Bills

Section 19 of the HRA 1998 does not apply to private Bills. There was, as a result, concern that there was insufficient assurance that Convention rights would be properly considered in the process of drafting private Bills. This led to arrangements being put in place under standing orders. The promoters of the Bill are now required to present their opinion of the compatibility of the Bill with Convention rights when presenting the Bill to Parliament.[137] This is done in the form of a statement on the printed version of the Bill, in a rather similar form to that used for a minister's s 19(1) statement on a government Bill. It gives little insight into the reasoning underlying the promoters' opinion. **7.93**

Thereafter, not later than the second sitting day after the First Reading of the Bill, **7.94**

---

[134] For fuller accounts, see Lester (n 127 above) at 435–451; Feldman (n 127 above) at 333–341, 347–348.
[135] *The HRA 1998 Guidance for Departments* (n 130 above) para 38.
[136] JCHR, First Report of 2002–03 (n 129 above) paras 5–7.
[137] HC Standing Order 38(3).

a minister must report to the House his or her opinion of the adequacy of the promoters' assessment of the Bill's Convention compatibility.[138] This task is undertaken, on the basis of legal advice, by the minister whose responsibilities are most closely related to the subject matter of the Bill. On at least one occasion, in relation to the Hereford Markets Bill in the 2002–03 session, the minister has formed the opinion that the promoters' assessment was inadequate, apparently because it did not explain why a provision that appeared to interfere with the right to the peaceful enjoyment of possessions under Article 1 of Protocol 1 to the ECHR was justified.[139] This does not necessarily mean that the provision is incompatible with a Convention right, but only that the promoters' assessment should have been fuller or more persuasive.

7.95   Every private Bill is considered by the JCHR, which reports on the Bill's human rights implications when appropriate. The JCHR's assessment, unlike that of the minister under standing orders, is concerned with the substantive impact of the Bill on human rights. Thus the Committee decided that the Hereford Markets Bill was likely to be compatible with Convention rights, despite the minister's reservations about the quality of the promoters' assessment.[140] On the other hand, despite the relevant minister's view that the promoters' assessment had been adequate, the JCHR suggested that provisions of the Nottingham City Council Bill dealing with investigative powers should be amended to provide additional protection for the right to respect for private life, the home and correspondence under Article 8 ECHR, and the promoters amended the Bill to take account of the suggestion.[141]

(e) **Statutory instruments**

7.96   Although s 19 of the HRA 1998 does not apply to secondary legislation, a minister who invites either House to approve a statutory instrument or draft statutory instrument which is subject to the affirmative resolution procedure is advised, as a matter of good practice, to volunteer his or her view regarding its compatibility with human rights during debate on the motion to approve it. The same applies to any statutory instrument which amends primary legislation (which itself counts as primary legislation under the 1998 Act). Where secondary legislation which amends primary legislation is not subject to the affirmative resolution procedure, the minister in charge of it should make the statement in writing in an appropriate form, such as a letter to the Joint Committee on Statutory Instruments (JCSI).[142]

---

[138] HC Standing Order 98a.

[139] See the report by the Parliamentary Under-Secretary of State, Office of the Deputy Prime Minister (Tony McNulty MP) on the Hereford Markets Bill, 28 January 2003, reproduced in JCHR Fourth Report of 2002–03 (n 129 above) Appendix 9, Ev 22.

[140] JCHR, Fourth Report of 2002–03 (n 129 above) paras 57–58.

[141] JCHR, Third Report of 2002–03, *Scrutiny of Bills: Further Progress Report* (HL Paper 41, HC 375) paras 70–76; Fourth Report (n 129 above) paras 59–60.

[142] *The HRA 1998 Guidance for Departments* (n 130 above) para 40.

The JCSI is required by standing orders to examine statutory instruments and **7.97** draft statutory instruments (other than remedial orders) laid before each House and to report to each House on a number of matters having nothing to do with the substantive merits of the instruments. These matters to be drawn to the attention of each House include 'that there appears to be a doubt whether it is *intra vires* . . .'.[143] Most statutory instruments are secondary legislation for the purposes of ss 3 and 6 of the HRA 1998, and would therefore be invalid to the extent of any incompatibility with a Convention right (unless an instrument is made under provisions of primary legislation to give effect to or enforce those provisions, and the provisions cannot be read or given effect in a way that is compatible with the Convention rights).[144] The JCSI therefore considers the Convention compatibility of these instruments under the heading of a risk of ultra vires. Although the government accepts no duty to express a view spontaneously on the human rights implications of secondary legislation which neither amends primary legislation nor is subject to the affirmative resolution procedure, the JCSI can in practice elicit such information by raising questions with the relevant department.

Where a statutory instrument is treated as primary legislation for the purposes of the **7.98** HRA 1998, or is made under provisions of primary legislation to give effect to or enforce those provisions which cannot be read or given effect in a way that is compatible with the Convention rights, an incompatibility with a Convention right would not make it ultra vires. The JCHR is therefore prepared to examine such an instrument if it is referred to the JCHR by the JCSI or by members of either House.

(f) Church of England legislation

The Church of England is governed by measures made by the Church of England **7.99** Assembly and the General Synod of the Church of England. These measures are primary legislation for the purposes of the HRA 1998, and so are valid and effective notwithstanding any incompatibility with human rights.[145] The General Synod has its own elaborate procedures for debating proposals for measures. The Church is self-governing: measures are made under its own inherent powers,[146] and so are not regarded as secondary legislation. Measures do not become effective until they have been approved by each House of Parliament and have received royal assent, but neither House of Parliament can amend a Church measure. The two Houses of Parliament decide whether or not to approve a measure in the light of a report by the Ecclesiastical Committee. This unusual body is a joint select committee of both Houses, established by statute under the Church of England Assembly (Powers) Act 1919. Under s 3, the Committee must report on the nature and legal effect of the

---

[143] House of Lords SO (Public Business) 70A; House of Commons SO 151, para (f).
[144] See HRA 1998, s 6(2)(b).
[145] HRA 1998, s 21(1).
[146] See Synodical Government Measure 1969.

measure, and its expediency particularly with relation to the constitutional rights of Her Majesty's subjects. The category of constitutional rights, interpreted in the light of the HRA 1998, is apt to include the Convention rights under the latter Act. The Ecclesiastical Committee can therefore report to each House of Parliament on the implications of the measure for Convention rights. Because of this, the JCHR has not so far found it necessary to examine a measure.

(5) The Validity of Legislation Which is Incompatible with Convention Rights

7.100 As noted above, s 3(2) of the HRA 1998 provides that incompatibility with a Convention right 'does not affect the validity, continuing operation or enforcement of any incompatible primary legislation'. It also makes similar provision in respect of incompatible secondary legislation 'if (disregarding any possibility of revocation) primary legislation prevents removal of the incompatibility'.

(a) Primary legislation

(i) Extended meaning of 'primary legislation'

7.101 'Primary legislation' includes, as one would expect, all public general, local, personal, and private Acts of the Westminster Parliament. In addition, s 21(1) of the HRA 1998 extends the category to include:

- any measure of the Church Assembly or the General Synod of the Church of England, which (as already noted) are made by those bodies under inherent powers, although they do not take effect unless they receive the royal assent after each House of Parliament has passed a resolution for the measures to be presented to Her Majesty for that purpose;
- any Order in Council made under s 38(1)(a) of the Northern Ireland Constitution Act 1973, or now under s 84(1) of the Northern Ireland Act 1998, which give power to provide for elections (other than the franchise) and constituencies in Northern Ireland;
- any Order in Council made under the royal prerogative;
- any Order in Council which amends an Act of Parliament. These include some remedial orders made under the HRA itself. However, other remedial orders may amend primary legislation which is not an Act of Parliament, such as Orders in Council under the royal prerogative or orders made under the Northern Ireland legislation. Remedial orders of this latter kind will not themselves be primary legislation within the meaning of the Act; and
- any order or other instrument which brings primary legislation into force (commencement orders).[147]

---

[147] HRA 1998, s 21(1).

There is an air of unreality about some of these provisions. Statutory instruments **7.102** made under the authority of Northern Ireland Constitution Act 1973, s 38(1)(a) or the Northern Ireland Act 1998, s 84(1) are not in any real sense 'primary'. It has been convenient to maintain the fiction that they are, in order to respect the political sensibilities of the different parts of the community in Northern Ireland. But when legislation by the Northern Ireland Assembly counts as subordinate legislation for the purposes of the HRA 1998,[148] it looks odd for statutory instruments made for Northern Ireland by the Secretary of State to be treated as primary legislation.

Orders in Council made under the royal prerogative are 'primary legislation' in **7.103** the sense that the power to make them has not been delegated by higher authority, but treating them as entitled to the same level of respect as Acts of Parliament, and as being equally legitimate even when incompatible with Convention rights, is inconsistent with modern constitutional theory. The principle of legality, which forms part of the rule of law, requires that the executive should be accountable to the courts for the legality of its use of prerogative powers. In *Council of Civil Service Unions v Minister for the Civil Service*,[149] the House of Lords held that the exercise of prerogative powers was in principle amenable to judicial review, as long as their subject matter was justiciable. Under the HRA 1998, Orders in Council made under the prerogative are liable to be quashed for breach of the traditional principles of judicial review, but not for incompatibility with a Convention right.

There is rather more constitutional justification for regarding Church measures as **7.104** primary legislation for the purposes of the HRA 1998. They have an independent source of legislative authority, despite needing the approval of Parliament and the Royal Assent; and the arrangements reflect a constitutional division of power between the religious and secular arms of the state. But while the Church of England remains established as an estate of the realm, it seems inappropriate and illegitimate that there should be any suggestion of allowing it to be a Convention-rights free zone. Yet that is the implication of denying an effective remedy to anyone whose Convention rights are violated by a Church measure: although one of the higher secular courts (but not a Church court) could in theory make a declaration of incompatibility, that would not provide just satisfaction for the victim of a violation unless the Church legislated to remove the incompatibility and provided redress for past victims.

(b) Subordinate legislation

Section 3(2)(c) of the HRA 1998 provides that the duty to read and give effect to **7.105** legislation in a way which is compatible with Convention rights, 'does not affect

---

[148] See sub-paras (c)–(e) of the definition of 'subordinate legislation' in HRA 1998, s 21(1).
[149] [1985] AC 374, HL.

the validity, continuing operation or enforcement of any incompatible subordinate legislation if (disregarding any possibility of revocation) primary legislation prevents the removal of the incompatibility'. It is implicit in this that subordinate legislation, as defined in s 21(1) of the Act, is invalid and ineffective to the extent that it cannot be interpreted so as to be compatible with any Convention right, unless primary legislation makes removal of the incompatibility impossible.

7.106   For this reason, it is possible for s 10(4) to refer to a 'provision . . . in subordinate legislation' which 'has been quashed, or declared invalid, by reason of incompatibility with a Convention right'. A public authority making a piece of subordinate legislation which is incompatible with a Convention right acts unlawfully by virtue of s 6(1).

(6) Declarations of Incompatibility, Adverse Rulings in Strasbourg,
and Remedial Orders

(a) Declarations of incompatibility

7.107   The drafters of the HRA 1998 set their faces against allowing courts to quash primary legislation which is held to be incompatible with a Convention right. In this way, parliamentary sovereignty was protected (although, as observed above, the absolute protection of primary legislation against invalidity as a result of incompatibility with a Convention right applies to a number of types of legislation other than Acts of Parliament, and thereby goes further than is necessary or is conformable to modern constitutional principles). However, the interpretation of Convention rights is essentially a judicial function rather than a legislative one. The Act therefore adopted a compromise between on the one hand full judicial review of primary legislation, including a power to strike down Acts which are incompatible with Convention rights, which would have weakened parliamentary supremacy in legislation; and on the other hand a complete absence of judicial review of primary legislation, which might have undermined belief in the importance of the Convention rights. The solution was to allow judges in some circumstances to decide whether primary legislation is compatible with Convention rights, drawing any incompatibility to the attention of Parliament and ministers, but not to allow judges to invalidate the legislation on that account.

7.108   The compromise is achieved in the following way. Certain courts have power under s 4 of the HRA 1998 to declare that provisions in legislation are incompatible with Convention rights (a 'declaration of incompatibility'). A court may make a declaration of incompatibility in respect of a provision in primary legislation if, in proceedings before it, the court is satisfied that the provision is incompatible.[150] It may also make a declaration of incompatibility in respect of either

---

[150] HRA 1998, s 4(1) and (2).

primary legislation or a provision in subordinate legislation made in pursuance of the primary legislation if, in proceedings before it, the court is satisfied: (1) that the provision in the subordinate legislation is incompatible with a Convention right; and (2) that (disregarding any possibility that the subordinate legislation might be revoked) the primary legislation prevents the removal of the incompatibility.[151]

A declaration of incompatibility does not affect the validity, continuing operation **7.109** or enforcement of the incompatibility provision, and (rather curiously) is not binding on the parties to the proceedings.[152] It is, therefore, of little immediate value to the victim of the incompatibility. Nevertheless, it may lead to remedial legislation, and to a remedy being given to the victim for past wrongs either under a new statutory scheme with retrospective operation or ex gratia.

Only certain courts may make a declaration of incompatibility. In England and **7.110** Wales, these are the House of Lords in its judicial capacity, the Judicial Committee of the Privy Council, the Courts-Martial Appeal Court, the High Court, and the Court of Appeal.[153] The High Court includes tribunals which have the status of superior courts of record, such as the Special Immigration Appeals Commission. Although Church measures are primary legislation and are principally enforced through ecclesiastical courts, no ecclesiastical court may make a declaration of incompatibility in respect of a measure.

A court which is considering making a declaration of incompatibility must invite **7.111** the Crown (in the person of the responsible minister, department, or executive) to intervene in the proceedings.[154] If the relevant person or body decides to intervene, it may adopt one of three stances. First, it can argue that the legislation as interpreted on normal principles of interpretation is compatible. To do this, it may be necessary to argue for an interpretation of the relevant right which is relatively narrow in scope, or for an expansive meaning to be given to any permitted exceptions to the right. Secondly, it might argue that the legislation is compatible by arguing for a non-traditional interpretation of it, making use of the duty of the court under s 3 to read and give effect to the legislation in a Convention-compatible way when it is possible to do so. This position might be adopted either alongside or instead of the first stance. However, the court might not be prepared to stretch the natural or literal meaning of a provision, even when invited to do so by a minister.[155] Thirdly, the body might accept that the legislation, as traditionally interpreted, is incompatible,

---

[151] ibid s 4(3) and (4).
[152] ibid s 4(6).
[153] ibid s 4(5).
[154] ibid ss 4, 5.
[155] See, eg, *R (on the application of H) v London North and East London Region Mental Health Review Tribunal* [2001] EWCA Civ 415; [2002] QB 1. On reasons for deciding not to make use of s 3, see paras 7.54 and 7.109 above.

but argue that an extended interpretation under s 3 should not be given to it, perhaps because the administrative, social or policy ramifications of any change in the way that the legislation operates make it desirable for any alteration to be made by Parliament after fully exploring the options, rather than by judicial decision. A body adopting this stance might (or might not) accept that the court should make a declaration of incompatibility.[156]

7.112   A declaration of incompatibility is a discretionary remedy. It has been suggested that the exercise of the discretion 'will be influenced by the usual considerations which apply to the grant of declarations'.[157] Generally, however, it has been accepted that there is value in ensuring that a domestic court can give an authoritative statement of the rights of the victim, even if the issue is already covered by a decision of the European Court of Human Rights.[158]

7.113   When a court makes a declaration of incompatibility in relation to an Act of Parliament, it is a form of judicial review of the Act, albeit one that leaves the Act fully effective and so cannot be said to represent a worthwhile remedy.[159] Although courts must sometimes disapply an Act of Parliament if it is incompatible with Community law,[160] s 4 of the HRA 1998 is the first statutory provision expressly to invite the judges to tell Parliament that it has acted wrongly when legislating. Yet Parliament is not bound by Convention rights because it is not a public authority within the meaning of s 6, and a minister who is a party to litigation in which the declaration is made is not bound by the declaration, because of s 4(6)(b). It seems to follow that the wrong which a court identifies when declaring an Act of Parliament to be incompatible with a Convention right is a nonlegal wrong. Making such a declaration takes the judges into new fields. They are implicitly criticizing Parliament, in a way that appears to be inconsistent with Article 9 of the Bill of Rights 1688. To that extent at least, it is submitted that Article 9 of the Bill of Rights is impliedly limited by s 4 of the HRA 1998. In addition, courts in this area are applying standards which are part of national law, but the judges are not straightforwardly adjudicating on legal wrongs.

---

[156] Compare *Bellinger v Bellinger* [2003] UKHL 21; [2003] 2 WLR 1174 (declaration of incompatibility made where incompatibility was accepted but minister argued that the declaration would serve no useful purpose) with *Tarbuck and Blood v Secretary of State for Health* (consent order, 3 March 2003), where a declaration of incompatibility was made by consent as part of the settlement of an action.

[157] *Poplar Housing and Regeneration Community Association Ltd v Donoghue* [2001] EWCA Civ 595; [2002] QB 48 at [75(e)].

[158] *Bellinger v Bellinger* [2003] UKHL 21; [2003] 2 WLR 1174; *R (on the application of M) v Secretary of State for Health* [2003] EWHC 1094; The Times, 25 April 2003.

[159] On the impact on parliamentary sovereignty and the effectiveness of a declaration of incompatibility as a remedy, see David Feldman, 'The Human Rights Act 1998 and Constitutional Principles' (1999) 19 LS 186; Ian Leigh and Laurence Lustgarten, 'Making Rights Real: The Courts, Remedies and the Human Rights Act' [1999] CLJ 509, esp 536–542.

[160] *R v Secretary of State for Transport, ex p Factortame Ltd (No 2)* [1991] 1 AC 603, HL.

(b) Responses to declarations of incompatibility

A declaration of incompatibility does not compel anyone to do anything. It is, in ef-   **7.114**
fect, an invitation to the relevant minister and Parliament to reconsider the incompatible legislation. When a declaration is made, the government has several options.

(i) Appeal

If the declaration was not made by a court of last resort, the obvious course is for   **7.115**
the government to appeal. This is frequently, though not invariably, done. In a
number of cases, a decision that a legislative provision is incompatible with a
Convention right has been reversed on appeal. If the declaration was made by a
court of last resort, or there is no appeal, other options must be considered.

(ii) Inaction

As a matter of domestic law, the minister need do nothing. The declaration does   **7.116**
not bind any party,[161] and failing to introduce corrective legislation or to make a remedial order does not amount to a breach of the duty in national law to act compatibly with Convention rights.[162] However, this course will rarely be followed.
During the passage of the Human Rights Bill, the Lord Chancellor said that 'the
declaration is very likely to prompt the Government and Parliament to respond',
and the Home Secretary said that they would be likely to do so rapidly.[163] Such
statements might give rise to a constitutional convention making a rapid response
obligatory, if backed by the development of a consistent practice. However, experience to date has been limited, because of the small number of declarations of
incompatibility to have survived appeal. Sometimes there have been speedy legislative responses, such as the remedial order in respect of the Mental Health Act
1983. At other times, the response may take longer, either because the legislation
needed has proved to be complex and difficult to draft, or because there has been
too little time available in the legislative programme. A powerful incentive to act is
the thought that failure to take appropriate remedial measures is likely to lead the
victim of the incompatibility to apply to the European Court of Human Rights.

(iii) Rectifying the incompatibility by primary legislation

The incompatible primary legislation may be amended by introducing a Bill to   **7.117**
Parliament if it is in the form of an Act, or by other means if it takes another form.
A Bill is likely to be used if a suitable Bill is already before Parliament, which can

---

[161] HRA 1998, s 4(6)(b).
[162] ibid s 6(6).
[163] *Hansard*, HL Deb vol 582, col 1231 (3 November 1997) (Lord Irvine of Lairg LC on second
reading); *Hansard*, HC Deb vol 307, col 780 (Jack Straw MP on second reading).

be amended to remedy the incompatibility. For example, in 2002 the Nationality, Immigration and Asylum Bill was amended by introducing provisions to correct the incompatibility between Article 6 ECHR and Article 1 of Protocol 1 and the fixed penalty of £2,000 per immigrant imposed by s 32 of the Immigration and Asylum Act 1999 on carriers on whose vehicles illegal immigrants enter the United Kingdom.[164] Alternatively, a short Bill can sometimes be introduced by the government, or by a back-bencher with government support, to remedy the incompatibility.[165] A Bill is likely to be needed where an incompatibility has wide-ranging implications for the law, or its correction requires important judgments to be made about social policy, application of resources, administrative procedures, or morality. Where the issue is very complex, it might take some time (years rather than months) to consult widely, draft an appropriate Bill, and steer it through Parliament. There is always a risk that the Bill will be rejected by Parliament, or amended in a way that prevents it from remedying the incompatibility effectively. In that event, there is likely to be recourse to Strasbourg.

7.118   A Bill may include provision for compensation to be paid, or other forms of redress provided, to earlier victims of the violation.

(c) Remedial orders

7.119   In limited circumstances, the responsible minister or Her Majesty in Council[166] may make a 'remedial order' under s 10 of and Sch 2 to the Act. These special statutory instruments can amend or repeal any primary legislation, and subordinate legislation if it is protected from invalidity by primary legislation, so far as the minister considers necessary to remove an incompatibility between the legislation and a Convention right, and may include appropriate incidental, supplemental, consequential and transitional provision.[167] However, no remedial order may be made to amend a measure of the Church Assembly or General Synod of the Church of England.[168]

7.120   It is usually of questionable constitutional legitimacy to allow a statutory instrument to amend or repeal a provision in an Act of Parliament, because of the risk that the executive will usurp the legislative authority of Parliament, weakening the

---

[164] See *International Transport Roth GmbH v Secretary of State for the Home Department* [2002] EWCA Civ 158; [2003] QB 728 (declaration of incompatibility); Nationality, Immigration and Asylum Act 2002, s 125 and Sch 8 (amending Immigration and Asylum Act 1999, s 32).

[165] See eg the Human Fertilization and Embryology (Deceased Fathers) Bill introduced to the House of Commons with support from the government to remove the incompatibility between Art 8 ECHR and the provisions of the Human Fertilization and Embryology Act 1990 preventing particulars of a widow's deceased husband being entered as the father's particulars in the register of births where a child is born after the father's death using the father's stored sperm without his written consent: *Tarbuck and Blood v Secretary of State for Health* (consent order, 3 March 2003).

[166] The power of Her Majesty in Council arises when the incompatible legislation is an Order in Council: HRA 1998, s 10(5).

[167] ibid s 10(2)–(4), and Sch 2, para 1.

[168] ibid s 10(6).

democratic protection for people's rights. Because of this, the making of remedial orders under the HRA 1998 is hedged about with conditions and stringent procedural requirements.[169] In the particular context of the human rights legislation these orders do not represent a major threat, since they can only be used to give added protection to rights, not to interfere with them.[170] The Act limits the risk that ministers will use the orders for improper ends, and maximizes the opportunity for parliamentary scrutiny.

(i) Circumstances in which a remedial order may be made

There are two events which may lead a minister to consider making a remedial order: a declaration of incompatibility being made under s 4 of the HRA 1998 by a court in the United Kingdom; and certain findings by the European Court of Human Rights.[171]

7.121

(ii) Following a declaration of incompatibility

A minister may make a remedial order only when: anyone who could appeal against the court's decision has stated in writing that they do not intend to do so; or the time for an appeal has expired without any appeal being brought; or any appeal has been determined or abandoned.[172] The minister must then have formed the view that there are compelling reasons for making a remedial order rather than introducing a Bill to Parliament or remedying the incompatibility in some other way.[173] As a court may only make a declaration of incompatibility in respect of a provision of the ECHR which has been made part of domestic law in the United Kingdom by s 1 of the HRA 1998, a remedial order made in these circumstances can only remedy an incompatibility with one of the Convention rights as defined in that section. It therefore cannot be used to remedy an incompatibility with (for example) the right to an effective remedy before a national authority for a violation of a Convention right (Article 13 ECHR), or the duty of the United Kingdom as a party to the ECHR not to hinder a person's effective exercise of the right to apply to the European Court of Human Rights (Article 34 ECHR).

7.122

(iii) Following a finding of the European Court of Human Rights

A remedial order may be made if it appears to a minister (or, in the case of an incompatible Order in Council, to Her Majesty in Council) that, having regard to

7.123

---

[169] These were recommended by the House of Lords Delegated Powers and Deregulation Committee when the Human Rights Bill was before the House of Lords in 1997.

[170] See *Hansard*, HL Deb vol 582, col 1231 (3 November 1997) (Lord Irvine of Lairg LC on second reading in the House of Lords).

[171] HRA 1998, s 10(1).

[172] ibid s 10(1)(a), (2).

[173] ibid s 10(2).

a finding by the European Court of Human Rights, made on or after 2 October 2000 in proceedings against the United Kingdom, a provision of legislation is incompatible with an obligation of the United Kingdom under the ECHR[174] which appears to the minister or to Her Majesty in Council to show that a provision of legislation is incompatible with an obligation of the United Kingdom arising from the ECHR. The obligations of the United Kingdom arising from the ECHR operate in international law, and may arise from any of the articles of the ECHR, not only those which were made part of domestic law by the HRA 1998. A remedial order made following a decision of the European Court of Human Rights may therefore remedy incompatibilities with a wider range of rights than one made after a declaration of incompatibility by a court in the United Kingdom. Nevertheless, there are limits: a judgment made against another state cannot trigger a remedial order, even if it gives the clearest indication that legislation in the United Kingdom is incompatible with an obligation under the ECHR.

(iv) Procedures

7.124   The remedial order was envisaged as a fast-track method of rectifying a violation.[175] However, except in cases of urgency, the process of making a remedial order is a long one to ensure that Parliament has a full opportunity to scrutinize a draft of the Order and the reasons for making it. The procedures are complex.[176] Only in an urgent case can the order be made quickly, coming into force speedily, and ceasing to operate after 120 days if it is not subsequently approved by both Houses of Parliament.[177] The HRA 1998 does not define 'urgency'. In its report on the first remedial order to be laid before Parliament, the Joint Committee on Human Rights expressed the view that the urgent procedure should always be used when the incompatibility is one which affects the liberty of the individual.[178]

(v) Non-urgent procedure

7.125   Initially a document must be laid before Parliament containing an explanation of the incompatibility which the draft order seeks to remove, details of the relevant declaration of incompatibility or finding of the European Court of Human Rights, a statement of the reasons for seeking to make a remedial order and for

---

[174] HRA 1998, s 10(1)(b), (2).

[175] *Rights Brought Home* (Cm 3782, 1997), para 2.18.

[176] The procedures are described in detail, and recommendations for improvement are made, in JCHR, Seventh Report of 2001–02, *Making of Remedial Orders* (HL Paper 58, HC 473). The recommendations were endorsed by the House of Commons Procedure Committee, First Report of 2001–02, *Making Remedial Orders: Recommendations by the Joint Committee on Human Rights* (2001–02 HC 626), but no action has yet been taken to give effect to them.

[177] See HRA 1998, s 10(7) and Sch 2, para 2.

[178] JCHR, Sixth Report of 2001–02, *Mental Health Act 1983 (Remedial) Order 2001* (HL Paper 57, HC 472) paras 30–35.

If it is possible to exercise a discretion in a manner compatible with Convention **7.133** rights, it is unlawful to choose a way of exercising it which is incompatible in its effect. Only if primary legislation, which cannot be interpreted under s 3 to allow compatible action, prevents any other outcome will it be lawful to act incompatibly. Section 6(2) provides that it is not unlawful for a public authority to act incompatibly with a Convention right if '(a) as the result of one or more provisions of primary legislation, the authority could not have acted differently; or (b) in the case of one or more provisions of, or made under, primary legislation which cannot be read or given effect in a way which is compatible with the Convention rights, the authority was acting so as to give effect to or enforce those provisions'. This protects parliamentary sovereignty, and particularly the capacity of Parliament to legislate to violate Convention rights so long as it does so clearly and unambiguously.

By virtue of s 6(6), 'act' normally includes 'omission' for the purpose of the duty **7.134** under s 6(1). However, it was desired to protect parliamentary sovereignty by avoiding the imposition of a legally enforceable duty to make or amend primary legislation. As noted earlier, s 6(6) therefore provides that 'a failure to (a) introduce in, or lay before, Parliament a proposal for legislation; or (b) make any primary legislation or remedial order' is not an unlawful act for the purpose of grounding liability under s 6(1).

(b) What is a public authority?

As s 6(1) imposes legal duties only on a 'public authority', it is important to know **7.135** which people or bodies fall into that category.

(i) Exclusion for Parliament and those exercising functions in connection with proceedings in Parliament

One group of bodies is expressly excluded: a proviso to s 6(3) provides that the **7.136** term 'does not include either House of Parliament or a person exercising functions in connection with proceedings in Parliament'. This is in line with the determination of the drafters of the Act to protect parliamentary privilege and the legislative sovereignty of Parliament from being hamstrung by Convention rights.

Beyond that exclusion, the Act does not offer a complete definition of 'public au- **7.137** thority'. Instead, in effect it creates three types of public authorities, which have been respectively called 'standard' public authorities, 'functional' public authorities, and courts and tribunals.[188]

(ii) 'Standard' public authorities

The first category consists of bodies which are so clearly public authorities that **7.138**

---

[188] Clayton and Tomlinson (n 30 above) vol 1, para 5.08.

they do not need to be identified. These include, for example, central government departments and ministers of the Crown, local authorities, health authorities, the police, Inland Revenue Commissioners and Customs and Excise Commissioners. It is hard to define the characteristics which bring a body into this category, but three important indications might be: that the body's activities are governed by public law; that it exercises powers allowing it to exercise lawful authority over people or other bodies who are not bound to it by a private law relationship; and that it has no private interests to advance. For example, in *Aston Cantlow and Wilmcote with Billesley Parochial Church Council v Wallbank*,[189] the Court of Appeal decided that a parochial church council is a 'standard' public authority. Relevant factors included: it is a statutory corporation which is part of the Church of England; the Church of England has a unique status, and the canon law of the Church has been part of the law of the land since the Anglican reformation in the 16th century; the parochial church council is responsible for enforcing aspects of canon law and applies it to all who are within the parish, whether or not they are members of the Church of England. This was said to make it 'inescapable' that the parochial church council was a public authority for the purposes of the HRA 1998.[190] However, on appeal the House of Lords decided that a parochial church council is not a 'standard' public authority, not least because it does not exercise authority in any normal sense. Nevertheless, it may be a 'functional' public authority in relation to some of its functions.[191] Bodies which are 'standard' public authorities are bound to act compatibly with the Convention rights in all their activities, including those governed by private law (such as entering into contracts), unless compelled by primary legislation to act incompatibly.

(iii) Courts and tribunals

7.139 Section 6(3)(a) provides that every court or tribunal is a public authority. These adjudicative bodies are therefore subject to all the duties which flow from s 6(1). This has a range of possible consequences. The main one is that the court's procedures and the exercise of any discretion must be compatible with Convention rights including particularly (but not solely) the due process rights under Article 6 ECHR. The extent to which it affects the way the court approaches substantive law will be considered below.[192]

(iv) 'Functional' public authorities

7.140 Functional public authorities acquire their special status and obligations from s 6(3)(b) and (5). Subsection (3)(b) provides that the term 'public authority' in s 6 includes 'any person certain of whose functions are functions of a public nature

---

[189] [2001] EWCA Civ 713; [2002] Ch 51.
[190] ibid at [28]–[36].
[191] [2003] UKHL 37; [2003] 3 WLR 283. See further paras 7.140 et seq below.
[192] See paras 19.61 et seq below.

...', but subs (5) qualifies this to the extent that 'in relation to a particular act, a person is not a public authority by virtue only of subsection (3)(b) if the nature of the act is private'. This means that the applicability of the Convention rights under s 6(3)(b) is limited. The fact that an act is of a public nature will not alone suffice to make the body a public authority and so subject to Convention rights. Even if a body is a functional public authority, it is not obliged to act compatibly with Convention rights in relation to acts of a private nature. This may seem to be a recipe for arid, technical arguments. In fact, it is a matter of principle, of great importance in English public law. Over the past 20 years or so, more and more governmental functions have been contracted out to private bodies. We now have privately run prisons, and housing associations and other social landlords have taken over responsibilities for discharging public sector housing obligations in many localities. Vital services such as the supply of clean water, electricity and gas have been privatized. Even services which remain under state control, such as the national health service and the state education system, have been commercialized to a greater or lesser extent through the private finance initiative and public–private partnerships, notably in the fields of health, education and housing. If the Convention rights of people who use a particular service depend on the identity of the person or body who happens to be providing them in a particular area, there is a danger that people who depend on public sector services will enjoy better protection in some areas (where a public authority provides the service) than others (where it has been contracted out to a private provider). It would be regrettable if people's rights depend on where they live, but that would be the result of failing to achieve a coherent set of criteria for identifying functional public authorities and requiring them to comply with Convention rights when providing a range of public services. The test for a functional public authority is therefore very important.

7.141 Before a person or body which is neither a standard public authority nor a court or tribunal is obliged to act compatibly with Convention rights, one must answer two questions. The first question is, 'Does the body perform a public function?' The second question, which arises only if an affirmative answer has been given to the first question, is, 'Is the particular act in issue an act of a private nature?' Only if the first question has been answered affirmatively and the second has been answered negatively will the court have to decide whether the body acted compatibly with Convention rights. The two questions are clearly different: the publicness or privateness of a body's functions are entirely different from the public or private nature of a particular act. The House of Lords made this clear in *Aston Cantlow and Wilmcote with Billesley Parochial Church Council v Wallbank*[193] when holding that a parochial church council was not exercising a public function when enforcing the obligation of a lay rector to pay for repairs to the roof of the

---

[193] [2003] UKHL 37; [2003] 3 WLR 283.

church's chancel. The obligation was in the nature of a private law charge on, or incident of, ownership of the lay rector's land. Enforcing it therefore was a private rather than a public function. The High Court in *Marcic v Thames Water Utilities Ltd* regarded a privatized public utility such as a water company as a functional public authority when performing the function of providing sewage services, so that it was bound by Convention rights when deciding whether to take action to prevent sewage escaping from its drains to flood private houses. For reasons of public health, sewage has long been regarded as a public function assigned to local government and special boards, and there was no reason why it should cease to be regarded as such when the business of providing the service was privatized.[194] The House of Lords seems to have accepted this, but held that this company had not violated a Convention right on the facts of the case.

7.142 Unfortunately, other early decisions on the classification of bodies as functional public authorities have not distinguished properly between the two questions and the issues that are relevant to them. As a result, some judgments have tended to be based on the impressionistic application of lists of indicators of publicness or privateness, rather than coherent analysis. A few examples will suffice. In *Poplar Housing and Regeneration Community Association Ltd v Donoghue*[195] the Court of Appeal entirely turned its back on a functional test. Instead of asking whether a housing association, which had taken over a local housing authority's housing stock and was managing it on behalf of the authority, was performing a public function, the court decided that case law on the bodies which are amenable to judicial review had inspired the approach adopted in s 6 of the HRA 1998 to identifying the bodies which were subject to Convention rights. The court identified a number of factors which were of particular importance. The housing authority was still subject to its statutory duties after transferring its housing stock to the housing association, which was merely the instrument by which the authority discharged its functions. Providing rented accommodation is not without more a public function. The fact that a body is motivated by its conception of the public interest does not make it a public authority, and its activities may remain of a private nature. An act may be public or private depending on a number of features which 'impose a public character or stamp on the act'. These include: statutory authority for the act; the extent to which the act is controlled by another body which is clearly a public authority; and the degree to which acts which could be of a private nature are enmeshed with the activities of a public body. The closer the relationship between a public body and the activity in question, the more likely it will

---

[194] [2001] EWHC Tech 421; [2002] QB 929; [2002] EWCA Civ 65; [2002] QB 929, CA; [2003] UKHL 66, HL.
[195] [2001] EWCA Civ 595; [2002] QB 48.

be that a court will regard it as a public function.[196] But there was no clear demarcation line. Overall and on balance, the court regarded the housing association's role as being so closely assimilated to that of the housing authority as to
make the association a public authority under s 6(3)(b).[197]

This was, with respect, a confusing way of approaching the issue. The court failed   **7.143**
to distinguish between the two issues it had to decide under s 6(3)(b), namely (1)
whether the housing association exercised a public function and (2) whether the
particular act in issue was of a private nature. It treated the nature of the act as relevant to the nature of the function, which should properly be considered on a
higher level of generality. As a result, having decided that the association was exercising a public function it never went on to consider whether the particular act
was of a private nature, and therefore one to which the Convention rights should
not apply. It is also unsatisfactory to apply the test for deciding whether a body is
amenable to judicial review to the very different task of deciding what a claimant's
substantive rights against the body are to be. The 'public body' test in judicial review was developed for purely procedural purposes, in order to push the generality of challenges to certain kinds of body into a procedure (the application for
judicial review) in which claimants have fewer procedural rights than in ordinary
civil litigation. The object was to protect public bodies. This is hardly a satisfactory approach to deciding what bodies are to be subject to the obligations arising
from substantive Convention rights. The HRA 1998 was not designed to give
special procedural protection to public bodies. It was intended to impose substantial additional obligations on them, to allow the state to discharge its obligation under Article 1 ECHR to secure the enjoyment of the rights to everyone
within its jurisdiction.

Even when judges have avoided the confusion between the test for amenability to   **7.144**
judicial review and the test for functional public authorities, and have managed to
distinguish the question whether a body is exercising a public function from the
question whether the body is a public body, further confusion may arise from a
misplaced emphasis on the idea of 'authority'. For example, in *R (on the application
of Heather) v Leonard Cheshire Foundation*[198] the Court of Appeal decided that the
Leonard Cheshire Foundation, a charitable foundation, was not a functional, limited-purpose public authority when providing accommodation in a care home for
residents with disabilities whose places were being funded by a local authority
under the National Assistance Act 1948. The charity was providing a means by
which the local authority could discharge its statutory responsibilities, but the nature of the facilities provided was the same as the nature of facilities provided for

---

[196] ibid at [65].
[197] ibid at [66].
[198] [2002] EWCA Civ 366; [2002] 2 All ER 936.

other residents who were not placed in the charity's homes by local authorities. The court also found it relevant that the charity, while performing a statutory function, was not exercising statutory powers; the idea of 'authority' was thought to carry with it the notion of an exercise of power. The court therefore decided that the charity's function with regard to the residents placed by local authorities was not a public function.

7.145   The two grounds for the decision that the charity was not a functional public authority (the similarity of the facilities being provided to publicly funded and other residents respectively, and the idea that an authority should exercise power) are both concerned with the body's functions rather than its institutional character or its relationship with other institutions. Nevertheless, both the reasoning and the outcome may be questioned. The fact that the charity provided similar services to residents, whether or not they fell within a statutory scheme for providing assistance, does not lead inexorably to the conclusion that the charity is not performing public functions, at least in relation to those who are entitled to the services by virtue of a statutory scheme. One can distinguish between the services provided and the function being discharged. A doctor who practises both in the NHS and privately offers the same service to both private patients and NHS patients, but is still performing a public function when working for the NHS. The *service* is the same, but the *function* is a public one only when working for the NHS (allowing the NHS to discharge its statutory obligations). Similarly a charity which does similar work, sometimes for its own purposes and sometimes to allow a statutory body to discharge statutory obligations, should be classified as a public authority for the purposes of the HRA 1998 when allowing a statutory body to discharge its statutory obligations. If this is not so, people statutorily entitled (as against public bodies) to receive particular services will have more extensive rights if the public body provides the service itself than if the service is provided by a contractor on behalf of the public body. As the recipient's entitlement is statutory and is similar in either case, there is no justification for making his or her entitlement depend on who actually delivers the service.

7.146   The idea that an authority is a body exercising power is equally unpersuasive in this context. The HRA 1998 says that a body with public functions is, for its purpose, a public authority, and so bound by the Convention rights. It does not say that a body with public functions is bound by the Convention rights only if it is exercising authority in the sense of power. 'Public authority' is a term of art in the Act. It is not an authority (in common parlance) which is exercising public functions. If it were, no body which had only duties and no powers could be bound by the Convention rights unless it were an 'all-purpose' public authority. That would not be consistent with the scheme of the Act. The House of Lords was therefore right to hold in *Aston Cantlow and Wilmcote with Billesley Parochial Church*

Council v Wallbank[199] that one must focus on a particular function a body is exercising, not the nature of the body, in order to decide whether it is exercising a public function so as to make it a 'functional' public authority for the purpose of s 6(3)(b) of the HRA 1998.

It might be said (and was said in the *Leonard Cheshire Foundation* case) that the **7.147** onus is on public authorities to ensure that they impose contractual requirements on contractors to comply with Convention rights. However, this would not allow the state to provide an adequate guarantee that everyone in the jurisdiction who dealt with that body would be equally able to enjoy their Convention rights, as required under international law by Articles 1 and 14 ECHR and in national law by Article 14. What is needed is an approach that concentrates properly on the *function* being exercised in relation to the person affected, rather than the *job* being done or the *service* being provided by the immediate provider.

To illustrate the correct approach, which is consistent with that adopted by the **7.148** House of Lords in *Aston Cantlow and Wilmcote with Billesley Parochial Church Council v Wallbank*,[200] one can look at two decisions of the Administrative Court. In the first, *R (on the application of A) v Partnerships in Care Ltd*,[201] a private mental health care provider was providing care for a compulsorily admitted patient, under an arrangement with her health authority. The private provider decided for commercial reasons to discontinue the specialist unit in which the claimant was cared for, without providing her with alternative care. Deciding a preliminary issue about the applicability of the right to be free of degrading treatment under Article 3 ECHR and the right to respect for private life under Article 8 ECHR, Keith J decided that the company was a functional public authority for the purposes of the HRA 1998. Keith J was influenced by the fact that reg 12(1) of the Nursing Homes and Mental Nursing Homes Regulations 1984[202] imposed a duty on the hospital itself to provide adequate professional staff and adequate treatment. His Lordship thought that this would make the hospital managers into a functional public authority for that purpose, and make them subject to judicial review (although, as suggested above, amenability to judicial review should not be seen as a necessary hallmark of a functional public authority under the HRA 1998).[203] He also accepted the relevance of the facts that mental health care is a matter of public interest, that the claimant was compulsorily rather than voluntarily detained and had had no opportunity to negotiate the company's obligations, and that failure to provide adequate care would be likely to prolong her

---

[199] [2003] UKHL 37; [2003] 3 WLR 283.
[200] [2003] UKHL 37; [2003] 3 WLR 283.
[201] [2002] EWHC Admin 529; [2002] 1 WLR 2610.
[202] SI 1984/1578.
[203] [2002] EWHC Admin 529; [2002] 1 WLR 2610 at [24], [25].

detention under the Mental Health Act 1983. These are all relevant factors when deciding whether a function is public, rather than whether the job being done or the body concerned is distinctively public.

7.149 The other case is *R (on the application of Beer) v Hampshire Farmers Market Ltd.*[204] Hampshire County Council had established a farmers' market to improve farmers' access to trading outlets. The Council set up a private company to run the market, with assistance from Council staff and with one of the Council managers as a director. The company had a virtual monopoly on weekend markets in the area. The company refused to allow the claimant, a farmer, to participate in the market, and the claimant sought judicial review alleging that the decision was incompatible with (inter alia) Convention rights to due process under Article 6 ECHR. Field J decided that the company was a functional public authority, because it was a not-for-profit organization promoting the public interest, and it had a virtual monopoly on weekend markets.

7.150 It is hard to distinguish the decisions in *R (on the application of A) v Partnerships in Care Ltd* and *R v Hampshire Farmers Market Ltd* from that in *R (on the application of Heather) v Leonard Cheshire Foundation*. On principled grounds and having regard to the purposes of the HRA 1998, the decisions in the former two cases are to be preferred to that in the *Leonard Cheshire* case. Furthermore, the approach adopted in the former two cases, concentrating on the nature of the function, is to be preferred to the approach in the *Poplar* case (which looked also at the nature of the body, the body's institutional ties to other bodies, and the nature of the job being undertaken).

D. General Principles Governing the Application of Convention Rights

7.151 When interpreting the Convention rights and their qualifications, the European Court of Human Rights (and, previously, the Commission) developed a number of important principles to guide their work. English courts must have regard to those principles when interpreting Convention rights for the purposes of the HRA 1998.[205]

(a) Fundamental values

7.152 The Court considers that the Convention was rooted in certain fundamental values, particularly human dignity, equality, and democracy. Democracy requires, as

---

[204] [2002] EWHC Admin 2559. Affirmed by the Court of Appeal [2003] EWCA Civ 1056; The Times, 25 August 2003.
[205] See paras 7.28–7.29 and 7.35 et seq above; Clayton and Tomlinson (n 30 above) ch 6.

the Court has often said,[206] a commitment to the values of tolerance, pluralism and broad-mindedness without which democracy would be impossible. Equality is a particularly pervasive value in the approach to the Convention. The right to equal enjoyment of rights is expressly protected by Article 14 ECHR. Although Article 14 appears to confer only a right not to be discriminated against in the enjoyment of other Convention rights,[207] the Strasbourg organs have drawn attention to the fact that Article 14 imposes a positive as well as negative obligation on states as to the way in which the enjoyment of Convention rights is secured.[208]

(b) Rights must be made real and effective

The Convention rights must not be merely theoretical or illusory. They must be made real and effective. This is required both by Article 1 ECHR, whereby each contracting party undertakes to guarantee the enjoyment of the Convention rights to everyone in its jurisdiction, and by Article 13, which requires states to ensure that a national authority provides an effective remedy for every violation of a Convention right. Neither Article 1 nor Article 13 is included among the rights which became part of English law by virtue of the HRA 1998, but they are central to the way that the Court, and formerly the Commission, have approached their task of interpreting and administering the Convention.[209] For example, they have influenced the imposition of positive obligations on states and the development of the notion of the autonomous meaning of certain Convention terms.[210] It also produced a general approach to interpreting the Convention (shared with the approach to interpreting bills of rights in many national constitutions) which stipulates that a generous meaning is to be given to the statements of rights, while the permitted restrictions of the rights are to be strictly construed. Similarly, where the Convention permits states to limit rights it is interpreted as not allowing a state to deprive anyone of the very essence of the right. In this way, the core values and integrity of the Convention rights can be upheld.

(c) Positive obligations of states

If rights are to be made real and effective, it is not always enough for the state to refrain from interfering with them. Sometimes the state must take positive action to protect people's rights against interference by others, or to protect people against circumstances which threaten their ability to enjoy rights. There are

7.153

7.154

---

[206] eg, in *Handyside v UK* Series A No 24 (1979–80) 1 EHRR 737.

[207] When Protocol 12 comes into force, it will create a free-standing right to be free of discrimination on a wide variety of grounds.

[208] See the Report of the Commission in the *Belgian Linguistic Case* Series B No 3, (1967) 305–306, 24 June 1965. For further discussion of equality and Art 14, see ch 11 below.

[209] See, eg, *Airey v Ireland (No 1)* Series A No 32 (1979–80) 2 EHRR 305.

[210] See paras 7.154–7.155 and 7.157 below.

several sources of express positive obligations. For example, Article 1 ECHR, as already noted, requires the contracting parties to secure to everyone within their jurisdiction the Convention rights. This obliges states to establish appropriate legal rules and procedures for those purposes. Article 13, giving a right to an effective remedy for violations of Convention rights, imposes an obligation on the state to ensure that it has appropriate rules and institutions in place to provide such a remedy. Article 2(1), by providing for everyone's right to life to be protected by law, requires the state to have appropriate legal rules and procedures in place to provide that protection.[211] Article 5(1) requires the state to provide legal rules and procedures to govern the circumstances in which people may lawfully be deprived of their liberty. Article 5(2)–(5) imposes obligations in respect of the treatment of people who have been lawfully deprived of their freedom, together with an obligation to compensate people for detentions which do not comply with the requirements of the Article. Article 6(1) requires the state to provide legal rules and procedures to permit fair trials and to comply with the positive obligations set out in Article 6 in relation to the conduct of hearings. Article 12 requires the state to provide legal rules to permit people to change their civil status through marriage.

7.155   Other positive obligations have been taken to be implied in the Convention having regard to its underlying values and purposes. For example:

- The right to life under Article 2 impliedly requires the state to protect people against threats to their lives in certain circumstances, to lay down procedures to ensure that proper care is taken when assessing the absolute necessity for taking life, and to ensure that there is an effective investigation of allegations of killing.[212]
- The right to be free of torture and inhuman or degrading treatment or punishment under Article 3 requires the state to take adequate steps to protect people effectively against such treatment at the hands of private as well as public bodies and persons, including a possibility of successfully prosecuting suspected offenders.[213]
- The right to respect for private and family life, home and correspondence under Article 8(1) carries with it positive obligations, since the idea of 'respect' is not a passive one. For instance, the responsible public authorities may have an obligation under Article 8 to use environmental and planning law to control polluters whose activities make it difficult or unhealthy for people to live in their homes in affected areas,[214] or to provide information about environmental hazards.[215] Article 8 impliedly confers a right to obtain information about one's own back-

---

[211] *McCann v UK* Series A No 324 (1995) 21 EHRR 97.

[212] ibid.

[213] See eg *A v UK* Application 25599/94 (1998) 27 EHRR 611.

[214] See *López Ostra v Spain* Series A No 303-C (1994) 20 EHRR 277, where the level of harm caused was insufficient to amount to a breach of Art 3 but the failure of the state to control it was nevertheless a violation of Art 8.

[215] See *Guerra v Italy* Application 14967/89 (1998) 26 EHRR 357 at [35].

ground and history when one has been in the care of a public authority.[216] States must meet standards of security, accuracy and accountability for the storage and dissemination of information about people.[217] The idea of family life has been interpreted as protecting the value of mutual enjoyment of a wide range of de facto relationships of personal intimacy and genetic closeness,[218] and as requiring fair procedural protections provided by law for parents when their children are in danger of being taken into care: the Court has held that an interference with family life, in order to be justifiable, must be regulated by procedures adequate to ensure that the various interests are taken fairly into account.[219] Even when a child is in care, public authorities must not normally place the children and manage their contacts so as to make a restoration of family relationships unlikely.[220]

• The right to freedom of assembly under Article 11 imposes an obligation on the state to take appropriate steps to ensure that counter-demonstrators do not make it impossible for demonstrators to assemble and protest peacefully.[221]

(d) The Convention as a living instrument

The Court treats the Convention as a living instrument. The scope and content of   **7.156**
the Convention rights are interpreted dynamically, constantly developing in reaction to events in the world, other international treaties, changing moral and social structures and beliefs, advances in standards in policy areas, and scientific and medical developments.[222] It follows that there is no doctrine of stare decisis such as would be familiar to common lawyers. Nonetheless, the Court values consistency,[223] and will depart from previous decisions only if they are plainly shown to have been wrongly decided or to have been superseded by relevant changes in social circumstances or values current among the contracting parties.

---

[216] *Gaskin v UK* Series A No 160 (1989) 12 EHRR 36. For an account of the international arrangements in relation to this, see James Michael, *Privacy and Human Rights* (Aldershot: Dartmouth, 1994); James Michael, in McCrudden and Chambers, *Individual Rights and the Law in Britain* (Oxford: Clarendon Press, 1994) ch 9. For the English law, as influenced by the EC Data Protection Directive, see Data Protection Act 1998, which will have to be (re)interpreted in the light of HRA 1998, s 3.

[217] *Leander v Sweden* Series A No 116 (1987) 9 EHRR 433.

[218] *Marckx v Belgium* Series A No 31 (1979) 2 EHRR 330; *Berrehab v Netherlands* Series A No 138 (1988) 11 EHRR 322.

[219] *W v UK* Series A No 121-A (1987) 10 EHRR 29, introducing due-process values to a range of decision-making functions which might not fall naturally within Art 6(1).

[220] *Olsson v Sweden* Series A No 130 (1988) 11 EHRR 259; *Hokkanen v Finland* Series A No 299-A (1994) 19 EHRR 139.

[221] *Plattform 'Ärzte für das Leben' v Austria* Series A No 139 (1988) 13 EHRR 204.

[222] See eg *Tyrer v UK* Series A No 31 (1978) 2 EHRR 1; P van Dijk and GJH van Hoof, *Theory and Practice of the European Convention on Human Rights* (3rd edn, The Hague: Kluwer, 1998) 77–80.

[223] For this reason, Art 30 ECHR allows a Chamber to relinquish a case to the Grand Chamber of the Court for an authoritative judgment 'where the resolution of a question before the Chamber might have a result inconsistent with a judgment previously delivered by the Court'.

(e) Autonomous and partially autonomous meanings of terms used in the ECHR

7.157 Many of the terms of the treaty are treated as having an 'autonomous meaning'. This means that those terms have a meaning which may be different from that which the same or similar terms have in the municipal law of any contracting party.[224] The objects are to ensure that, so far as possible, terms in the Convention have a consistent meaning when applied to any of the contracting parties, and to prevent states unilaterally denying the protection of the Convention to people within their jurisdictions by categorizing issues in such a way that the rights do not arise, or by giving terms a specially restricted or extended meaning. For example:

- in Article 6 (fair trial rights in the determination of criminal charges and civil rights and obligations), the concepts of 'determination', 'criminal charge', 'civil right' and 'civil obligation' have autonomous meanings, so a state cannot exclude the operation of Article 6 in a particular context by treating a matter as non-criminal, or defining a right or obligation as public rather than civil, for the purposes of municipal law;
- similarly in Article 7 (nulla poena sine lege), the concept of 'criminal offence' has an autonomous meaning;
- in Article 8 (right to respect for private and family life, home and correspondence), 'private life', 'family life', 'home' and 'correspondence' all have autonomous meanings.

These autonomous meanings will be explored further as and when they become relevant in relation to substantive rights.

(f) Interpreting grounds for interfering with rights

7.158 Most of the Convention rights are accompanied by express provision for their limitation in certain circumstances. Typically these limitations are themselves restricted by express requirements, such as those found in the second paragraphs of Articles 8 to 11. These include the following elements:

- Any interference with the right must be 'prescribed by law', or 'in accordance with a procedure prescribed by law', or 'lawful', or 'in accordance with the law'. All these formulations have been held to import similar requirements derived from two principles of the rule of law. First, the principle of legality requires that any interference with a right must have a sufficient basis in law. Secondly, the principle of legal certainty requires that people should be able to know with sufficient confidence when they are liable to interference with their rights.
- An interference must be directed to achieving one of a limited number of legitimate aims, often enumerated in the relevant article.

---

[224] See eg Van Dijk and Van Hoof (n 222 above) 77; *Engel v Netherlands* Series A No 22 (1976) 1 EHRR 647.

- An interference must be 'necessary in a democratic society' for that legitimate purpose. The principle of necessity in a democratic society, which could have been regarded as merely hortatory and lacking sufficient content to form part of a legal obligation, has been given substance by the European Court of Human Rights: the interference must be a response to a pressing social need, and must be proportionate to the aim pursued. The Court has adopted a model of democracy which is different from mere majority rule. In a democracy which respects Convention rights, minorities must be adequately protected against unfair treatment and the abuse by the majority of a dominant position.[225]

A court must apply those tests in that order. If an interference with a right does not meet the requirements of the principle of legality or that of legal certainty, it is unlawful, even if it is undertaken for a legitimate aim. If it satisfies the principle of legal certainty but does not pursue a legitimate aim, it is unlawful, even if it is proportionate to a pressing social need. And so on. The very last question to be addressed is that of proportionality: a disproportionate interference with a right is unlawful even if all the other tests have been met.

Even where the Convention allows the state to interfere with or deprive someone **7.159** of a right without expressly imposing those conditions on the exercise of the power, the Court has treated the power as being impliedly subject to similar conditions. For example, the state may interfere with (or even deprive people of) the right to peaceful enjoyment of possessions under Article 1 of Protocol 1 to the ECHR in the general interest, but the Court has insisted that the power must be used only in circumstances which strike a fair balance between the rights of the individual and the public interest. This idea of fair balance was developed to limit the state's widely expressed power of interference, and it incorporates the notion that the interference must serve a legitimate state aim and must be proportionate to it. Unfortunately, English courts have misunderstood the purpose of the idea of fair balance. Dicta of the European Court of Human Rights stressing the importance of fair balance in the structure of the Convention have been treated as justifying English courts in reading additional restrictions into Convention rights, such as the right to a fair hearing or the right to be presumed innocent until proved guilty.[226] This reverses the proper use of the 'fair balance' principle. Fair balance, or proportionality, cannot justify an interference which is otherwise unlawful, for the reasons outlined in the previous paragraph.

The principles of legality and legal certainty and the idea of necessity in a democ- **7.160** ratic society are now examined in more detail.

---

[225] *Handyside v UK* Series A No 24 (1976) 1 EHRR 737 at [49]; *Chassagnou v France* Applications 25088/94, 29331/95, 28443/95 (1999) 7 BHRC 151 at [112].
[226] See eg the use of dicta in *Sporrong and Lönnroth v Sweden* Series A No 52 (1982) 5 EHRR 35, in *Brown v Stott* [2003] 1 AC 681, PC.

(g) Principle of legality

7.161   The terms 'lawful', 'in accordance with a procedure prescribed by law', 'in accordance with the law', and 'prescribed by law' have partly autonomous meanings in the Convention. That is to say, an interference must be shown to be *both* (1) not unlawful in municipal law *and* (2) in compliance with European standards of legality. These standards require that, among other things:

- there must be a sound foundation in positive municipal law for the state's interference with the right, so that the interference can be said to be regulated by law in the jurisdiction concerned;[227] and
- the system of regulation must be adequate to ensure that the rights of all those people affected are taken into account (importing at least some Article 6 standards).[228]

(h) Principle of legal certainty

7.162   The municipal law which authorizes an interference with a right must be sufficiently clear and accessible to people to allow them to predict with reasonable certainty when and how their rights will be affected.[229] As the Court has regularly reiterated: 'A norm cannot be regarded as "law" unless it is formulated with sufficient precision to enable the citizen to regulate his conduct: he must be able—if need be with appropriate advice—to foresee, to a degree that is reasonable in the circumstances, the consequences which a given action may entail . . . .'.[230] This is why retrospective legislation, especially criminal legislation, is highly suspect, and is prohibited by Article 7 ECHR. Not only must the relevant law be expressed in sufficiently clear terms to allow people to understand their obligations, but it must be reasonably accessible to those who are affected by it, at the time when they have to decide how to act.

(i) Pressing social need

7.163   The Court usually allows states a wide latitude when deciding whether there is a pressing social need for action, but the onus is on the state to explain to the Court's satisfaction why there was thought to be a pressing social need for a particular measure that interferes with a Convention right.

(j) Proportionality

7.164   The principle of proportionality is a vehicle for conducting a balancing exercise.[231] It does not directly balance the right against the reason for interfering with

---

[227] *Malone v UK* Series A No 82 (1984) 7 EHRR 14; *Halford v UK* (1997) 24 EHRR 523.

[228] See, eg, *W v UK* Series A No 121-A (1987) 10 EHRR 29.

[229] *Malone v UK* Series A No 82 (1984) 7 EHRR 14.

[230] *Gaweda v Poland* Application 26229/95 [2002] ETMR 63 at [39], just one of many examples of the use of this formulation.

[231] See Van Dijk and Van Hoof (n 222 above) 80–82; Jeremy McBride, 'Proportionality and the European Convention on Human Rights', in Evelyn Ellis (ed), *The Principle of Proportionality in the Laws of Europe* (Oxford: Hart Publishing, 1999) 23–35.

it. Instead, it balances the nature and extent of the interference against the reasons for interfering. Proportionality is assessed mainly by asking whether the interference with the right is more extensive than is justified by the legitimate aim. This involves balancing the seriousness of the interference against the seriousness of the threat to the interests which are protected within the purposes for which it is legitimate to interfere with the right. Part of that balancing exercise requires the Court to consider whether the extent of the interference is greater than is reasonably necessary to achieve the legitimate aim. In a democratic society, there must also be proper safeguards against arbitrariness.

When assessing the proportionality of an interference with a Convention right, the court or tribunal must take into account a number of factors, including: **7.165**

- whether it would have been possible to achieve the legitimate aim by a less intrusive means;
- whether the interference is such as to deprive the right-holder of the very essence of the right;
- whether the right is of sufficient importance in the circumstances to warrant particularly strong reasons being required to justify any interference; and
- whether the interference causes harm to the right-holder which is serious enough to outweigh any benefit which that interference might achieve through furthering a legitimate aim.

The European Court of Human Rights allows a 'margin of appreciation', or area   **7.166**
of discretionary judgment, to states in relation to judgments about the existence of a pressing social need and the nature of an appropriate response. The notion of the 'margin of appreciation' is based on the fact that these judgments involve political assessments of social conditions, and national authorities are in a better position than an international tribunal to judge what is necessary under local conditions. In public international law, it offers a way of mediating the tension between the claims of state sovereignty in relation to international institutions and the need to universalize human rights standards so far as possible in international law. The doctrine has no application in English law, because the doctrine of subsidiarity cannot apply within a single legal system. However, the English courts have developed an idea of deference to the judgment of specially qualified decision-makers. This has already examined above.[232]

British judges have done a good deal to explain the proper use of the principle of   **7.167**
proportionality. In *De Freitas v Permanent Secretary of Ministry of Agriculture, Fisheries, Lands and Housing*,[233] a decision pre-dating the entry into force of the HRA 1998, the Privy Council had to consider the application of the principle to

---

[232] See paras 7.31–7.34.
[233] [1999] 1 AC 99, PC.

an interference with rights under a national constitution. Lord Clyde, delivering the opinion of the Board, said that in determining whether a limitation on a fundamental constitutional right was arbitrary or excessive, the court should ask itself three questions. First, was the legislative object sufficiently important to justify limiting the fundamental right? Secondly, were the measures interfering with the right rationally connected to the legislative objective? Thirdly, did the means used to pursue the objective impair the right no more than necessary to accomplish the objective? Subsequently, in *Samaroo and Sezek v Secretary of State for the Home Department*,[234] there was a challenge under the HRA to a deportation order made against a drug dealer. In the Court of Appeal, Dyson LJ added a fourth element to the inquiry: did the measure have an excessive or disproportionate effect on the interests of the people affected? Although the court would allow the Secretary of State a significant margin of discretion, the onus lay on the Secretary of State to establish the justification convincingly, showing the court that he had struck a fair balance, with the weight given to different factors being the subject of careful scrutiny by the court.[235] This makes it clear that the proportionality of a measure is ultimately a matter for the court, not for the primary decision-maker, notwithstanding any margin of discretion that may be allowed.[236]

7.168   There is a difference between disproportionality and irrationality. A power may be used in a disproportionate way even if it would not be stigmatized as irrational within the meaning that term has in judicial review proceedings (ie, so unreasonable that no reasonable decision-maker could properly have made that decision).[237] As Lord Steyn said in *R (on the application of Daly) v Secretary of State for the Home Department*,[238] there are at least three reasons for the difference between the two standards. First, while a court reviewing a decision for irrationality accepts that a decision is rational unless it is self-evidently irrational, the onus of establishing proportionality is on the decision-maker, and the court may be required to assess for itself the balance struck by the decision-maker. In other words, subject to the appropriate degree of deference being shown, there is no presumption of proportionality. Secondly, as part of the assessment, the court may have to decide the relative weight to be accorded to the different interests under consideration. Thirdly, even where a heightened level of scrutiny is applied to the rationality of

---

[234] [2001] EWCA Civ 1189; [2001] UKHRR 1150 at [19]–[20].

[235] ibid at [38].

[236] See eg *Lindsay v Commissioners of Customs and Excise* [2002] EWCA Civ 267; [2002] 1 WLR 1766; *International Transport Roth GmbH v Secretary of State for the Home Department* [2002] EWCA Civ 158; [2002] QB 728, *per* Simon Brown and Jonathan Parker LJJ; *R (on the application of Hoverspeed Ltd) v Commissioners of Customs and Excise* [2002] EWHC 1630; [2002] 3 WLR 1219, DC; *Commissioners of Customs and Excise v Newbury* [2003] EWHC 702; [2003] 2 All ER 964, DC, on the proportionality of the use of powers to impose penalties and forfeiture on people whose vehicles have been used for illegal immigration or evading customs duties.

[237] See paras 16.06–16.33 below.

[238] [2001] UKHL 26; [2001] 2 AC 532 at [27] et seq.

measures interfering with fundamental rights,[239] that will not necessarily be sufficient to protect human rights. Any attempt to collapse proportionality into irrationality, for example by saying that a decision or act will be proportionate unless no reasonable decision-maker could have come to the conclusion that it was proportionate, is illegitimate.

E. Conclusion

This chapter has sought to set the scene for discussion of standards of review, and 7.169 to introduce the historical and methodological background to the operation of the Convention rights under the HRA 1998. The next two chapters will examine the standards of review arising under particular Convention rights.

---

[239] See *Bugdaycay v Secretary of State for the Home Department* [1987] AC 514, HL; *R v Ministry of Defence, ex p Smith* [1996] QB 517, 554, CA; para 7.19 above and para 16.08 below.

8

RIGHTS TO LIFE, PHYSICAL AND MORAL INTEGRITY, FREEDOM OF LIFESTYLE AND RELIGION OR BELIEF

A. Introduction

This chapter and chapter 9 examine the standards provided under the Human **8.01**
Rights Act 1998 (HRA) to protect a set of rights, sometimes described as civil
and political rights, which allow an individual to survive and participate in society. The rights considered in this chapter are largely personal, and are concerned
with individual autonomy, dignity, and physical integrity. They include the
rights to physical and moral integrity: the right to life, the right to be free of torture and inhuman or degrading treatment or punishment, and the right to respect for home and correspondence. Also covered are rights to make important
personal choices: the right to respect for private life, the right to respect for family life, the right to marry and found a family, and the right to freedom of conscience, religion and belief. Chapter 9 deals with those rights which are largely

political, including freedom of expression, freedom of peaceful assembly and association, and the right to participate in public life.

8.02 These chapters examine the rights from a public law perspective. Many aspects of private law serve to protect the rights, including the law of tort and employment law, but they lie outside the scope of this volume.[1] The focus of these chapters is on the ways in which public law protects the rights, and the ways in which rights help to shape public law by providing standards governing decision-making and the other activities of public bodies.

8.03 Four general propositions provide the background to the discussion in these chapters. First, those Convention rights under the European Convention on Human Rights (ECHR) which form part of English law by virtue of the HRA 1998 bind public authorities, which act unlawfully if they behave in a manner incompatible with them unless they are compelled by primary legislation to act in that way. Secondly, other human rights instruments, binding the United Kingdom in international law but not yet made part of English law, may influence judicial decision-making in the ways discussed in chapter 7 above. In this chapter and the following one, we concentrate on the rights which are part of English law under the HRA 1998. Thirdly, most of the rights to be considered here are subject to qualifications: an interference with the right may be justified in certain circumstances, but the public authority must show that its behaviour is justified. Fourthly, most of the rights impose certain positive obligations on public authorities in some circumstances to advance or protect the rights, going beyond a negative obligation merely to avoid interfering with them. In relation to each right, we will examine both the negative and the positive obligations which arise.

B. The Right to Life

8.04 The right to life is protected by Article 2 ECHR. This provides:

1. Everyone's right to life shall be protected by law. No one shall be deprived of his life intentionally save in the execution of a sentence of a court following his conviction of a crime for which this penalty is provided by law.
2. Deprivation of life shall not be regarded as inflicted in contravention of this Article when it results from the use of force which is no more than absolutely necessary:
   (a) in defence of any person from unlawful violence;
   (b) in order to effect a lawful arrest or to prevent the escape of a person lawfully detained;
   (c) in action lawfully taken for the purpose of quelling a riot or insurrection.

---

[1] For an account of them, see Peter Birks (ed), *English Private Law* (Oxford: OUP, 2000) esp ch 2, 'Family' (Stephen Cretney), ch 12, 'Employment' (Mark Freedland), ch 14, 'Tort' (John Davies), and ch 18, 'Judicial Remedies' (Andrew Burrows).

The right is further protected by Protocol 6 to the ECHR, which is also part of English law by virtue of the HRA 1998. Article 1 of Protocol 6 provides that the death penalty is to be abolished, and that no one shall be condemned to such penalty or executed. Article 2 allows the death penalty in time of war or imminent threat of war, but the United Kingdom ratified Protocol 13 ECHR, which prohibits the death penalty in all circumstances, in October 2003. An order making Protocol 13 a Convention right under HRA 1998 is expected shortly. Following the passing of the HRA 1998, the death penalty for treason and piracy (the last offences for which a sentence of death could be passed in the United Kingdom) was replaced with a maximum sentence of life imprisonment by the Crime and Disorder Act 1998, s 36.

The obligations of the state under Article 2 ECHR are as follows. First, there is an obligation on public authorities under Article 2(1) not to deprive anyone of his or her life intentionally, unless the deprivation can be justified under Article 2(2). Secondly, there are positive obligations to protect people's lives in some circumstances, by such means as protecting people whose lives are known to be threatened, efficiently investigating suspicious deaths, and providing legal sanctions against private individuals who take other people's lives. The state cannot derogate from obligations under Article 2 or Protocol 6, even in circumstances of public emergency threatening the life of the nation.[2] Nor can the state enter any reservation to the obligation to abolish, and not to apply, the death penalty.[3] **8.05**

(1) Negative Obligations of Public Authorities

(a) The obligation to avoid depriving people of life

Where a person is killed by agents of the state, it self-evidently engages the negative obligation not to deprive anyone of life. The only question is whether the acts of the state can be justified under the terms of Article 2(2). But the negative obligation under Article 2(1) is wider than a duty merely to avoid intentional killing. It extends to a duty not to put anyone at significantly heightened risk of death through the intentional activities of the state. For example, if the state undertakes a programme of mass immunization, it has a responsibility to ensure that adequate precautions are taken to minimize the risk that death will result from the immunization.[4] The state may also violate a person's right to life by extraditing or deporting him to a country in which he is shown to be at risk of being killed, if either the public authorities in that country, their agents or people acting under their control are likely to be the aggressors, or the authorities there will be unable or unwilling to offer adequate legal and practical protection against the threat.[5] In **8.06**

---

[2] Art 15(2) ECHR; Protocol 6, Art 3.
[3] Protocol 6, Art 4.
[4] *Association X v UK* Application 7154/75 DR 14, 31, EComHR (measles).
[5] See, mutatis mutandis, *Chahal v UK* Application 22414/93 (1997) 23 EHRR 413.

the same way, it would violate Protocol 6 ECHR to deport or extradite someone to a jurisdiction where he or she is liable to be executed for a criminal offence.

(b) Justifications for depriving people of life

8.07   As noted in para 8.04, the death penalty has been abolished in the United Kingdom. We can therefore concentrate on the other situations in which deprivation of life may be justified under Article 2(2). These are deaths resulting from the use of force which is no more than absolutely necessary (1) to defend someone from unlawful violence, (2) to effect a lawful arrest or prevent the escape from custody of a person lawfully detained, or (3) in the course of lawful action to quell a riot or insurrection. The state may permit anyone to take another's life in those circumstances. These elements will be considered in turn.

(i) Use of force which is no more than absolutely necessary to defend someone from unlawful violence

8.08   This allows for killing not only in self-defence but also where necessary to rescue others from unlawful violence. It does not permit the use of lethal force to rescue people from lawful violence, natural hazards, or accidental disasters.

(ii) Use of force which is no more than absolutely necessary to effect a lawful arrest or prevent the escape from custody of a person lawfully detained

8.09   This exception covers any death resulting from the use of the necessary degree of force for one of the authorized purposes. If an innocent bystander is killed by accident, that death will not violate Article 2, as long as the level of force used is no more than absolutely necessary for one of the permitted purposes.

(iii) Use of force which is no more than absolutely necessary in the course of lawful action to quell a riot or insurrection

8.10   Like the previous exception, this covers the death of anyone, including innocent third parties, resulting from the use of absolutely necessary force when taking lawful action to quell a riot or insurrection. 'Insurrection' has no technical meaning in English law, but refers to an attempt to take over the government of the country by force. 'Riot' used to be an offence at common law, and is now a statutory offence under Public Order Act 1986, s 1. The statutory offence is committed where 12 or more people use or threaten unlawful violence (knowing that their behaviour is or may be violent), for a common purpose, and the violence is such as would cause a hypothetical person of reasonable firmness, were one to be present, to fear for his or her personal safety.

(iv) Meaning of 'absolutely necessary'

8.11   The force used must be 'no more than absolutely necessary'. This is a strict standard, but does not mean that the agents of the state must prove that no lesser degree of force could have accomplished the permitted objective. As interpreted by the European Court of Human Rights (ECtHR), the term allows a small amount of discretion to the state authorities, including those at the scene, to decide what level of force is needed, as long as adequate safeguards are in place to ensure that the decision is made in the light of the best possible assessment of the available information in the circumstances of the case. The test is one of proportionality, but the right to life is particularly important, so very strict standards must be applied (both by the original decision-maker and by a court reviewing the level of force used) when making the assessment. The right to life is particularly important, so the test of proportionality must be applied particularly stringently when people are at risk and lethal force is used deliberately. In *Gül v Turkey*,[6] the Court held unanimously that the Turkish security forces conducting an operation against the Kurdish separatist PKK organization had used disproportionate force when, without any reasonable belief that their own or anyone else's lives were in danger, they fired a long burst of machine-gun bullets through a door behind which Mehmet Gül was standing, killing him.

8.12 Article 2 is not concerned only with the act which causes death. It imposes standards on the whole process of planning and implementing operations in which lethal force may be used. In *McCann v UK*,[7] three people suspected of being about to plant a bomb were shot dead in an anti-terrorist operation by UK security forces in Gibraltar. The ECtHR accepted that the state could justify the use of lethal force if agents honestly believed, with good reason, that their lives or other people's lives were imminently at risk, even if it later turned out (as was the case) that the belief was mistaken. However, the state must ensure that the planning of the operation, the checking of information, and the command and control systems, are adequate to ensure a proper level of protection for the right to life, for example by ensuring that the risk was continuously assessed in the light of the most up to date information and the assessments were fed to the agents in the field. By a majority, the Court decided that the safeguards had been insufficient, so there had been a violation of Article 2.

8.13 The agents of the state owe duties to suspected criminals, their victims, and others who are in the vicinity. This can require very delicate judgments to be made where people have been kidnapped and are thought to be in danger from their captors. In such circumstances, the Court appears to accept that slightly more flexibility is needed in applying the test of proportionality. In *Andronicou and Constantinou v Cyprus*[8] a man was holding his fiancée at gun-point in their apartment. The woman was screaming that her life was in danger. The police burst into

---

[6] Application 22676/93 (2002) 34 EHRR 28.
[7] Series A No 324 (1996) 21 EHRR 97, esp at [147]–[150] and [200].
[8] Application 25052/94 (1998) 25 EHRR 491.

the apartment firing automatic weapons. Both the man and the woman were fatally injured. The evidence suggested that the police had failed to check some information about the weapons at the man's disposal, that insufficient lighting had been provided for the assault on the apartment, and that a great many rounds had been fired. On the other hand, the police had been told not to fire unless they believed that their lives or the woman's life were in danger, and their belief that she was in danger was reasonable in the circumstances. In those circumstances, the majority of the Court decided, 'it has not been shown that the rescue operation was not planned and organised in a way which minimised to the greatest extent possible any risk to the lives of the couple', and that the use of lethal force, 'however regrettable it may have been, did not exceed what was "absolutely necessary" for the purpose of defending the lives of Elsie Constantinou and the officers . . .'.[9]

(v) English law on the use of force

8.14   The use of force to effect an arrest, prevent the escape of people in custody, and control public disorder is governed by both statute and common law. Three sources of powers to use force are particularly important: the Criminal Law Act 1967, s 3; the Police and Criminal Evidence Act 1984, s 117; and the common law power to prevent or stop a breach of the peace. Section 3(1) of the Criminal Law Act 1978 states: 'A person may use such force as is reasonable in the circumstances in the prevention of crime, or in effecting or assisting in the lawful arrest of offenders or suspected offenders or of persons unlawfully at large'. A standard of pure reasonableness would not satisfy the 'strict necessity' requirement of Article 2 ECHR. Section 117 of the Police and Criminal Evidence Act 1984 allows the police to use reasonable force if necessary in order to exercise one of the powers conferred by that Act. The common law power to prevent or stop a reasonably apprehended and imminent breach of the peace also carries with it a power to use reasonable force if necessary for that purpose.[10] All these powers are subject to a requirement of necessity for deciding whether to use any force, but a standard of reasonableness when deciding how much force to use. The powers under s 117 of the 1984 Act and s 3(1) of the 1967 Act must be read and given effect so as to be compatible with the right to life under Article 2, because of s 3 of the HRA 1998. Lethal force is to be regarded as reasonable only if it meets the 'strict necessity' test of Article 2. Section 3 of the 1998 Act does not apply to the common law power in respect of breach of the peace. However, the courts, the police, armed forces, and security and intelligence services are all public authorities for the purposes of the HRA 1998, and so are subject to the requirements of Article 2. It follows that the standard of reasonableness at common law in relation to the use of lethal force must be treated as having the same Convention-compatible meaning as that under statute.

---

[9]   *Andronicou and Constantinou v Cyprus* (n 8 above) at [186], [194].
[10]   *Humphries v Connor* (1864) 17 Ir CLR 1; *O'Kelly v Harvey* (1883) 15 Cox CC 435.

(2) *Positive Obligations of Public Authorities*

Under Article 2 ECHR, state agencies have a number of positive obligations to-   **8.15**
wards people whose lives are at risk. These include: a duty to safeguard the lives of
those who are in the custody or care of public authorities; a duty to protect certain
other people against threats to their lives; a duty to conduct an efficient investigation of suspicious deaths; a duty to secure the legal accountability of those responsible; and a duty to provide information to those who are at risk from a threat
to their lives and to the relatives of those who have died. These positive obligations
have been developed in the case law of the ECtHR. Protecting people against
threats from third parties involves the use of public resources, so the Court has
made it clear that states will often be allowed more flexibility in deciding how to
perform the obligations than is permitted when a public authority itself creates
the threat to a person's life.

(a) Safeguarding those in the custody and care of public authorities

Under Article 2 ECHR, the state may be liable if people die in the custody of the   **8.16**
police, security forces, prisons, while compulsorily detained in a mental hospital,
or in analogous circumstances where the victims are in the care and custody of the
state and are not able to take independent steps to protect themselves against
threats. In principle, an applicant who alleges that the state, through its own
agents, is responsible for causing a death must prove the allegation beyond reasonable doubt. However, where a death occurs behind closed doors in prisons or
police stations, or in the course of secret operations by state forces, it is more or less
impossible for an outsider to provide direct evidence of that kind. The ECtHR has
therefore adjusted the burden of proof in such cases. The applicant must show
that the victim died while in the custody of an organization for which the state was
responsible. Even here, the Court will sometimes draw an inference of death from
the disappearance of a detainee where no body had been found.[11] Once the fact of
death in state custody has been established to the Court's satisfaction, the state
carries the burden of explaining how the death occurred, and showing that the
agents of the state were not responsible for it. The explanation must be credible,
and must be supported by convincing evidence.[12]

---

[11] *Tas v Turkey* Application 24396/94 (2001) 33 EHRR 15.
[12] *Çakici v Turkey* Application 23657/94 (2001) 31 EHRR 5; *Ertak v Turkey* (9 May 2000,
ECtHR); *Velikova v Bulgaria* Application 41488/98 (18 May 2000, ECtHR); *Timartas v Turkey* (13
June 2000, ECtHR). The same principles apply under Art 3 to non-fatal harm allegedly caused by
torture or inhuman or degrading treatment or punishment, sustained in state custody: *Tomasi v
France* Series A No 241-A (1993) 15 EHRR 1; *Ribitsch v Austria* Series A No 336 (1996) 21 EHRR
573; *Tekin v Turkey* Application 22496/93 (2001) 31 EHRR 4; *Selmouni v France* (2000) 29 EHRR
403.

8.17   This has the effect of transferring attention in international law from the acts or omissions of individuals to the responsibility of the state system to care for those in its custody. Under the HRA 1998, a cause of action will lie in tort under s 7 for breach of the statutory duty under s 6(1) of the Act to act compatibly with the victim's right to life. However, it is probably necessary to identify the body or individual who was responsible for securing the right before an action will lie. For example, if a person dies in prison as a result of violence the prison governor is likely to be the person responsible for any violation of the right to life. In a hospital, the governing body will be responsible. Only if someone can be identified as having responsibility for the acts or omissions which caused the violation will a cause of action be available.

(b) Protecting people against threats to their lives

8.18   The obligation to provide protection against risks arises in several ways, as the case law on Article 2 ECHR demonstrates.

8.19   First, public authorities' planning and implementing policies always have a duty to take account of threats to life which the policy may entail. It is possible that Article 2 and the right to injunctions and damages under the HRA 1998 will enlarge the range of legal remedies available. The European Commission of Human Rights took the view in *X v Federal Republic of Germany*[13] that allowing a sick person to be evicted from his home, endangering his life, may infringe Article 2. The Commission also declared admissible a complaint by a prisoner in *SimonHerold v Austria*[14] that the conditions and treatment which he suffered in prison had led to serious illness and breached Article 2. It seems, therefore, that Article 2 requires all public authority decision-makers to have regard in all cases (including applications for recovery of property) to the risk to health and life which might result from depriving a person of means of support or housing. At common law, too, public bodies have a legal obligation to protect people against a threat to health and dignity through destitution. Only clear words in a statute can authorize the withdrawal of publicly funded support from someone whose life and dignity depend on it.[15]

8.20   Secondly, public authorities have an obligation under Article 2 ECHR and the HRA 1998 to take reasonable steps to protect people against threats to their lives from the acts of others. This obligation attaches to all public authorities with relevant responsibilities. Other public authorities may also owe such duties. For example, the police

---

[13] Application 5207/71, CD 39, 99.

[14] Application 4340/69, CD 38, 18; a friendly settlement was later achieved: EComHR, report of 19 December 1972.

[15] *R v Secretary of State for Social Security, ex p Joint Council for the Welfare of Immigrants* [1997] 1 WLR 275, CA. See, eg, Nationality, Immigration and Asylum Act 2002, s 54, and *R (on the application of K) v Lambeth LBC* [2003] EWHC 871; The Times, 14 May 2003, Silber J.

and prison authorities must ensure that sufficient information about prisoners is provided to prevent dangerous people being put in cells with potential victims.[16] A local social services authority may be obliged by Article 2 to take appropriate steps to protect children who are at risk of suffering death at the hands of members of their families.[17] The ECtHR has held that the positive obligation under Article 2 arises where 'the authorities knew or ought to have known at the time of the existence of a real and immediate risk to the life of an identified individual or individuals from the criminal acts of a third party', and 'they failed to take measures within the scope of their powers which, judged reasonably, might have been expected to avoid that risk'.[18] A state has been held to be liable when it failed to take action to protect a journalist and a doctor against attacks. An official report to the government had warned that attacks were being launched on supporters of particular groups, and the victims were known to have been threatened. The government took no action to control its forces or to protect the victims.[19] On the other hand, if the police know that a person is harassing someone, but after making appropriate inquiries have good reason to believe that he does not represent an immediate threat to life so that they see no need, or have no power, to take him into custody, there will be no liability under Article 2 if he unexpectedly attacks members of the victim's family.[20]

Sometimes it will be necessary for public authorities to restrict the Convention rights of some people in order to protect the right to life of others. For example, in *Venables and Thompson v News Group Newspapers*[21] the applicants had been convicted of the murder of a young child when they were ten years old. As they approached their 18th birthdays, it became likely that they would shortly be released from custody. There was evidence that they would be at risk of revenge attacks after their release, and that the media would pursue them and publish their whereabouts if they had the opportunity. In order to protect their lives and allow them a reasonable chance of a normal life, it was intended to provide them with new identities on their release. The High Court made an order restraining the media from publishing their new identities or any details about their names or whereabouts after their release. While recognizing the importance of press freedom under Article 10(1) ECHR and s 12 of the HRA 1998, Dame Elizabeth Butler-Sloss P held that it was outweighed in that particular case, because of the strong evidence that the teenagers' lives would be immediately at risk on release if they were identified, that it would be a continuing threat, that publication of their new

8.21

---

[16] *Edwards v UK* Application 46477/99 (2002) 35 EHRR 19.
[17] See, eg, mutatis mutandis, *Z v UK* Application 29392/95 (2002) 34 EHRR 3.
[18] *Osman v UK* Application 23452/94 (2000) 29 EHRR 245 at [63].
[19] *Kılıç v Turkey* Application 22492/93 (2001) 33 EHRR 58; *Kaya v Turkey* Application 22535/93 (28 March 2000, ECtHR).
[20] *Osman v UK* Application 23452/94 (2000) 29 EHRR 245.
[21] [2001] Fam 430.

identities would substantially increase the risk and would make a normal life impossible for them, and that several media organizations would be likely to reveal their whereabouts and identities, notwithstanding the Press Complaints Commission Code of Practice, if they were allowed to do so.

(c) Efficiently investigating suspicious deaths

8.22   After a death, if there are reasonable grounds for suspecting homicide, the agencies of the state must ensure that an efficient and effective official investigation is conducted. There is a violation of Article 2 ECHR where the investigators are too ready to accept the account given by state agents, regardless of the credibility of their account in the light of other evidence. If the investigators drag their heels, fail to follow up leads or contact obvious sources of information, and do not adequately check apparent inconsistencies in the evidence or contradictory reports, so that no suspect can be identified and charged, they violate Article 2. Where agents of the state are implicated, the state has a special responsibility to investigate,[22] and the investigators must be independent of the agency or police force which is implicated.[23]

8.23   It is not sufficient for the inquiry merely to establish the cause of death. Any contributory failure in the available protective systems, such as the health service, social services, or the police or prison service, must be investigated so that lessons can be learned and accountability achieved. For this reason, coroners' inquests may be insufficiently far-reaching to meet the requirements of Article 2.[24] Where an inquest takes place, the selection of evidence to put before the jury and the directions to the jury must take account of the requirement of Article 2 for a full and effective inquiry leading to legal accountability.[25] Even a criminal prosecution will not always suffice, for example if the defendant pleads guilty so that there is no full, evidential hearing.[26] The inquiry must be effective to achieve the purposes of Article 2. This will often demand that witnesses should be compellable. The inquiry and its findings must be open to public scrutiny,[27] and the victims (who for this purpose include the close relations of the deceased person) must be sufficiently able to participate in it.

---

[22] *McCann v UK* Series A No 324 (1996) 21 EHRR 97; *Kaya v Turkey* (1999) 28 EHRR 1; *Jordan v UK* Application 24746/94 (2003) 37 EHRR 2.

[23] *Finucane v UK* Application 29177/95 (1 July 2003, ECtHR).

[24] See, eg, *Edwards v UK* Application 46477/99 (2002) 35 EHRR 19; *Finucane v UK*, ibid.

[25] *R (on the application of Stanley) v Coroner for Inner North London* [2003] EWHC 1180; The Times, 12 June 2003, Silber J.

[26] See *R (on the application of Amin) v Secretary of State for the Home Department; R (on the application of Middleton) v HM Coroner for West Somersetshire* [2003] UKHL 51, [2003] 3 WLR 1169, HL (order for independent inquiry into death, with representation for deceased's family).

[27] See *R v Secretary of State for Health, ex p Wagstaff* [2001] 1 WLR 292, DC (irrational not to permit the inquiry into the deaths of patients at the hands of Dr Harold Shipman to sit in public).

(d) Securing the legal accountability of those responsible for deaths

The right to life requires the state to provide effective legal means by which Article **8.24** 2 can be vindicated after an unlawful death. Because the right to life is fundamental, the ECtHR has held that the official inquiry which follows a suspicious death must be designed to result in criminal proceedings which are likely to lead to the punishment of the person responsible, not merely to a private action for compensation.[28] Where the Crown Prosecution Service decides not to bring a criminal prosecution before a coroner's inquest has been held, that decision must be regarded as provisional, to be reconsidered in the light of the verdict of the coroner's jury.[29] If the Crown Prosecution Service decides not to prosecute after a coroner's inquest has reached a verdict of unlawful killing, it should be prepared to give reasons for not proceeding.[30] Even then, it is usually possible for interested parties to launch a private prosecution or to bring an action for damages against the suspected offender.

Victims of an alleged violation of Article 2 rights, including indirect victims such **8.25** as surviving relations or a widow or widower, must be able to test the responsibility of state agencies for a death before an independent and impartial tribunal. This is an aspect of securing accountability for state action which is an essential part of the rule of law which is essential to securing respect for human rights in a democratic society. In other words, some aspects of the right to a fair trial under Article 6 ECHR and the right to an effective remedy for arguable violations of other Convention rights under Article 13 ECHR bolster legal protection for the right to life under Article 2. Where access to a tribunal is blocked, or the available tribunal is insufficiently independent and impartial because one of the judges is a member of the force which is under suspicion,[31] the state breaches one of its duties under Article 2.

In English law, there has historically been a general, public interest immunity **8.26** from liability for negligence in respect of discretionary and policy decisions made during investigations.[32] However, subsequent decisions of English courts

---

[28] See, eg, *Kaya v Turkey* (1999) 28 EHRR 1 at [105]; *Cakici v Turkey* Application 23657/94 (2001) 31 EHRR 5 at [112]–[113]; *Velikova v Bulgaria* Application 41488/98 (18 May 2000, ECtHR) at [89]. See also *Akkoc v Turkey* Application 22947/93 (2002) 34 EHRR 51 at [77]: the state's obligation under Art 2(1) 'involves a primary duty on the State to secure the right to life by putting in place effective criminal-law provisions to deter the commission of offences against the person backed up by law-enforcement machinery for the prevention, suppression and punishment of breaches of such provisions'.

[29] *R (on the application of Stanley) v Coroner for Inner North London* [2003] EWHC 1180; The Times, 12 June 2003, Silber J.

[30] *R v DPP, ex p Manning* [2001] QB 330, DC.

[31] See, eg, *Incal v Turkey* (2000) 29 EHRR 449 at [65]–[73].

[32] *Hill v Chief Constable of West Yorkshire* [1989] AC 53, HL; *Osman v Ferguson* [1993] 4 All ER 344, CA.

have established limits on the common law immunity of the police from liability for negligence in the exercise of their function to protect life.[33] Apart from liability for negligence, there is now a statutory cause of action for violating the right to life under HRA 1998, ss 6 and 7,[34] relying on the violation of Article 2, which involves considerations similarly to those relevant to an action for negligence.

(e) Providing information to people at risk and the relatives of deceased persons

8.27 Article 2 ECHR imposes various duties to provide information about threats to life. One reason for this is to let potential victims know that they are at risk. Where a person may have been put at risk by something done by or on behalf of a public authority, but may be unaware of the threat to his or her life and its implications, the public authority has a duty to give the fullest possible information to those who are likely to have been affected.[35] This is necessary both to allow the victims to take any steps that may be possible to protect themselves, and to treat them in accordance with their dignity and autonomy as individuals. For example, if a public authority knows that a man has been exposed to state-generated radiation, Article 2 may require it to provide advice of its own motion to the parents in relation to the man's daughter, conceived after the man's exposure, if it appears likely at the time that the father's exposure might have engendered a real risk to the daughter's health, and possibly whether or not the authority considers that the information would assist the daughter.[36] (The duty to disclose information which is not relevant to the daughter's treatment is likely to arise under Article 8 ECHR, the right to respect for private and family life, rather than the right to life under Article 2.)

8.28 After a death has occurred, the provision of information has other purposes. One is to allow the relations of the victim to understand and come to terms with the death. Another purpose is to allow the public to identify the underlying causes of the death, and satisfy itself that appropriate steps are being taken to remedy any systemic defect. This underlines the need for the relations of the deceased to be able to participate in the inquiry, and for the public at large to be given the most extensive possible access to it. For example, where a witness has

---

[33] See, eg, *Waters v Metropolitan Police Commissioner* [2000] 1 WLR 1607, 1618, HL, *per* Lord Hutton; and, most recently, *X v East Berkshire Community Health NHS Trust* (31 July 2003, CA) (children can sue for suffering caused by misdiagnosis of abuse leading to their separation from families).

[34] As victims within the meaning given to the word by the Court under Art 34, close relations or a widow or widower would have standing to sue under s 7 of the 1998 Act.

[35] It has been held that the duty to give this information operates only in public law, and does not give rise to a cause of action for damages: *Smith v Secretary of State for Health* [2002] EWHC 200; [2002] Lloyd's Rep Med 333.

[36] *LCB v UK* (1999) 27 EHRR 212 at [38], [40].

made a statement to the Police Complaints Authority for the purpose of the Authority's investigation of police action, the statement is usually confidential; but when the statement is made by an eye-witness to a death, the interest in disclosing the statement to victims and their relations, protected by Article 2, may outweigh the interest in maintaining the confidentiality of the statement so as to permit or require the disclosure, but only after the Authority has completed its investigation and reached its conclusion.[37]

In *McGinley and Egan v UK*,[38] servicemen exposed to radiation during tests of **8.29** nuclear weapons on Christmas Island claimed to have suffered illness as a result. They alleged violations of (inter alia) the right to respect for private and family life under Article 8 ECHR, because the state had not made available to them information about their exposure to radiation. The ECtHR decided that Article 8 imposed a positive obligation to make information available. As always in relation to positive obligations, there had to be a 'fair balance . . . between the general interest of the community and the competing interests of the individual, or individuals, concerned'.[39] In view of the level of harm which radiation can cause, and the anxiety and distress which uncertainty about the level of their exposure would have caused, the Court considered that the state ought to have made available information about the level of radioactivity on Christmas Island following the tests, particularly as there was no national security reason for withholding it.[40] Judges De Meyer, Valticos, and Morenilla, dissenting, favoured also a positive duty on the state to take active steps to monitor the condition of those at risk, although the existence of such a duty would depend on the state of scientific knowledge from time to time.

C. The Right to be Free of Torture and Inhuman and Degrading Treatment and Punishment

This right is protected by Article 3 ECHR: 'No one shall be subjected to torture **8.30** or to inhuman or degrading treatment or punishment'. Like the right to life, the right is non-derogable, and carries both negative and positive obligations. Unlike the right to life, there is no qualification to the right under Article 3: in no circumstances may torture, inhuman or degrading treatment, or inhuman or degrading punishment be justified.[41] The right protects against both physical and

---

[37] See *R (on the application of Green) v Police Complaints Authority* [2002] EWCA Civ 389; [2002] UKHRR 985.

[38] Applications 21825/93 & 23414/94 (1999) 27 EHRR 1.

[39] ibid at [98].

[40] ibid at [100]–[101].

[41] *Ireland v UK* Series A No 25 (1979–80) 2 EHRR 25 (report, 25 January 1976); *Tyrer v UK* Series A No 26 (1978) 2 EHRR 1; *Aksoy v Turkey* (1997) 23 EHRR 553 at [81].

mental suffering, and protects human dignity and autonomy as well as physical integrity.[42]

(1) Negative Obligations

8.31 The negative obligations are to avoid causing the prohibited forms of suffering: torture, inhuman treatment, degrading treatment, inhuman punishment, and degrading punishment. As the infliction of such suffering can never be justified, the scope of the negative obligations is determined by the definition of each of those forms of suffering.

(a) Torture

8.32 In *Ireland v UK* 13 of the 17 judges of the ECtHR adopted a strict test for torture based on the special intensity of the suffering caused, saying that torture was 'deliberate inhuman treatment causing very serious and cruel suffering'.[43] The majority of the Court said that the treatment must be applied by an agent of the state for the purpose of obtaining information, and must:

> attain a minimum level of severity if it is to fall within the scope of Article 3. The assessment of the minimum is, in the nature of things, relative; it depends on all the circumstances of the case, such as the duration of the treatment, its physical or mental effects and, in some cases, the sex, age and state of health of the victim, etc.[44]

8.33 Mental as well as physical assaults are capable of amounting to torture, and the definition has been widened beyond acts done to obtain information or confessions. In *Aydin v Turkey*,[45] the Court decided that being blindfolded, forcibly stripped and raped causes such a loss of dignity, degradation and sense of defilement and powerlessness that the combination of physical and mental violence inevitably amounted to torture.[46] The Court accepted evidence that international standards regarded the rape of a female detainee by an agent of the state as torture when done for purposes such as the extraction of information or confessions or the humiliation, punishment or intimidation of the victim.[47] It therefore seems that torture must be deliberate, cause very severe physical or mental suffering, and be inflicted for one of a number of purposes which include, but are not limited to, obtaining

---

[42] See, eg, *Pretty v UK* Application 2346/02 (2002) 35 EHRR 1; *R (on the application of S) v Secretary of State for the Home Department*, The Times, 6 August 2003, Maurice Kay J.

[43] *Ireland v UK* Series A No 25 (1979–80) 2 EHRR 25 at [167]; *Aksoy v Turkey* (1997) 23 EHRR 553 at [81].

[44] *Ireland v UK* Series A No 25 (1979–80) 2 EHRR 25 at [162].

[45] Application 23178/94 (1998) 25 EHRR 251.

[46] ibid at [48]–[51].

[47] The Court noted the decision of the Inter-American Court of Human Rights in *Fernando and Raquel Mejia v Peru*, 1 March 1996, Report No 5/96, Case 10,970, and other international legal standards on investigation of allegations of rape made by detainees, in particular UN Convention against Torture, Arts 11 and 12.

information or confessions. The characteristics and circumstances of the victim are relevant.

In the United Kingdom, the Criminal Justice Act 1988, s 134, makes it an offence **8.34** to inflict severe pain or suffering (thus including psychological torture) on another, where the offender is a public official or person acting in an official capacity, in the performance or purported performance of his official duties, or is acting at the instigation, or with the consent or acquiescence, of such a person performing or purporting to perform his official duties.[48] The definition of torture under the 1988 Act is wider than that adopted by the ECtHR. Section 134 is wide enough to encompass, for example, mistreatment of patients by nurses and medics in the prison medical service, as the purpose of the torturer is irrelevant: only the status of the offender as a public official (or someone under his instigation, etc), acting in purported performance of his official duties, is significant. However, there is a defence where the defendant had lawful authority, justification, or excuse under the law of the part of the United Kingdom where the torture took place, or (if it was inflicted abroad by a UK official) the law of the part of the United Kingdom under which the official was purporting to act, or (if it was inflicted abroad by an official of a foreign state) under the law of the country in which it was inflicted.[49] This defence may have the effect, in some cases, of preventing the section from providing adequate protection against torture as now understood in the light of the case law of the ECtHR on Article 3.

(b) Inhuman or degrading treatment

The ECtHR has been reluctant to define the term 'inhuman or degrading treat- **8.35** ment' too closely. In general, inhuman treatment is a form of treatment which inflicts severe physical or psychological harm on the victim, while degrading treatment seriously humiliates the victim, lowering him in his own estimation and that of others. In each case, the suffering or humiliation must reach a high threshold level of seriousness, which will vary according to the severity and duration of the suffering, the characteristics of the victim, and perhaps to some extent the degree of premeditation on the part of those responsible.[50] For example, children are more vulnerable than adults, and in particular need of protection through Article 3. In *A v UK*,[51] a nine-year-old boy had been repeatedly caned by his mother's partner; the beating was very painful, and left extensive bruising. The ECtHR decided that the level of suffering fell within the range forbidden by Article 3 because a garden cane had been used, with considerable force, on more than one occasion.

---

[48] Criminal Justice Act 1988, s 134(1), (2).
[49] ibid s 134(5).
[50] *Kudla v Poland* Application 30210/96 (2002) 35 EHRR 11 at [91]–[92].
[51] (1998) 27 EHRR 611.

This may signal that inflicting a certain level of physical pain on someone who is in one's power will now be treated as inherently humiliating for him.

8.36 Other examples of inhuman or degrading treatment can be given. It is possible that discriminatory treatment might be sufficiently degrading to violate Article 3 rights, as the European Commission of Human Rights held in the *East African Asians* case.[52] Although a type of interrogation which victimized homosexuals as such, prying into their private lives and sexual experiences, was not regarded as causing sufficiently severe suffering to constitute inhuman or degrading treatment in *Smith and Grady v UK (No 1)*,[53] the Court left open the possibility that such treatment could in principle violate Article 3 if shown to have been the result of bias based on sexual orientation. Withdrawing financial and other support from asylum-seekers, leaving them utterly destitute, can produce a violation of Article 3.[54] The list of circumstances which can give rise to a violation of Article 3 is not closed.

8.37 The Court has been particularly willing to hold that injury amounts to inhuman treatment where people are in the custody of the state, or are being arrested and are under the control of the police or security forces. Where violence is especially likely and independent monitoring is difficult, special protection is needed. Any recourse to physical violence against a person deprived of liberty diminishes his or her dignity and is in principle degrading treatment in violation of Article 3, unless the force has been made necessary by his or her own conduct.[55] The state is therefore required to provide a persuasive explanation, supported by credible evidence, to justify any injury which has been shown to have been inflicted on a person while in custody.[56]

8.38 When the state detains someone in custody under legal authority, Article 3 imposes positive obligations to ensure that the conditions of detention are decent and that medical attention of an appropriate standard is provided to those who need it. In *Kudla v Poland*[57] the Court wrote:

> . . . the State must ensure that a person is detained in conditions which are compatible with respect for his human dignity, that the manner and method of the

---

[52] (1973) 3 EHRR 76.

[53] (2000) 29 EHRR 493.

[54] *R (on the application of Q) v Secretary of State for the Home Department* [2003] EWCA Civ 364, [2003] 2 All ER 905; *R (on the application of S) v Secretary of State for the Home Department*, The Times, 6 August 2003, Maurice Kay J.

[55] *Tekin v Turkey* Application 22496/93 (2001) 31 EHRR 4 at [52], [53]; *Satik v Turkey* Application 31866/96 (10 October 2000) at [54].

[56] *Tomasi v France* Series A No 241-A (1993) 15 EHRR 1; *Ribitsch v Austria* Series A No 336 (1996) 21 EHRR 573; *Tekin v Turkey* Application 22496/93 (2001) 31 EHRR 4; *Satik v Turkey* Application 31866/96 (10 October 2000) at [54]; *Rehbock v Slovenia* Application 29462/95 (28 November 2000).

[57] Application 30210/96 (2002) 35 EHRR 11 at [93]–[94].

execution of the measure do not subject him to distress or hardship of an intensity exceeding the unavoidable level of suffering inherent in detention and that, given the practical demands of imprisonment, his health and well-being are adequately secured by, among other things, providing him with the requisite medical assistance . . .

A state often has an obligation to protect a person against the risk of being treated **8.39** in an inhuman or degrading way by another state. In *Soering v UK*,[58] it was held that extraditing a murder suspect to Virginia in the United States, where he would be liable to the death penalty, would violate Article 3, because the delays and conditions on death row would expose him to mental suffering ('death row phenomenon') of exceptional severity and duration, having regard to his youth and mental state at the time of the alleged offence.[59] It violates Article 3 to deport a person to a country where he or she is liable to suffer the requisite level of severe harm as a result of state action[60] or because it would be impossible to obtain treatment for a lethal disease.[61]

The International Covenant on Civil and Political Rights, Article 7 (which deals with **8.40** torture and inhuman or degrading treatment or punishment), provides: 'In particular, no one shall be subjected without his free consent to medical or scientific experimentation'. Such experimentation was held to be a crime against international law by the Nuremberg War Crimes Tribunal.[62] It is very likely that an experiment which presents a serious threat to life or health would be cognizable by the ECtHR or the English courts as an infringement of the right to life under Article 2 or a special form of torture or inhuman treatment under Article 3.[63]

Article 3 has significance for the conditions of detention, especially where a de- **8.41** tainee suffers from an illness or disability which is made worse by the conditions, or which requires treatment or the provision of special assistance which is not available. The ECtHR has held that it is degrading treatment to hold a person awaiting deportation in detention for an inordinate length of time in conditions

---

[58] Series A No 161 (1989) 11 EHRR 439.

[59] As a result, the UK government refused to extradite the applicant to the US on any charge for which the sentence might include the death penalty. The US, in a diplomatic note, confirmed that in the circumstances US law would prohibit the prosecution of the applicant in Virginia for the offence of capital murder, and the UK was prepared to extradite him on that understanding: Resolution DH(90)8 of the Committee of Ministers, adopted 12 March 1990, appendix.

[60] *Chahal v UK* Application 22414/93 (1997) 23 EHRR 413; *Ahmed v Austria* (1997) 24 EHRR 278; *Hilal v UK* Application 45276/99 (2001) 33 EHRR 2.

[61] *D v UK* Application 30240/96 (1997) 24 EHRR 423. Cf *Bensaid v UK* Application 44599/98 (2001) 33 EHRR 10, where there was some evidence that treatment for a psychotic illness would be available in Algeria, and it was held that it would not violate Art 3 to deport the would-be immigrant.

[62] See further NS Rodley, *The Treatment of Prisoners Under International Law* (2nd edn, Oxford: Clarendon Press, 1999) 297–301.

[63] See *McGinley and Egan v UK* Applications 21825/93 & 23414/94 (1999) 27 EHRR 1.

of overcrowding, without proper sleeping facilities.[64] Where conditions in prison have an effect on a person's health, they are still more likely to lead to a violation of Article 3. For example, there have been findings of violations of Article 3 where a prisoner was held for long periods in a cell without a toilet and with inadequate lighting, space and ventilation, exacerbating his eczema.[65] There was a violation when a severely disabled person was held in a cell without the facilities appropriate to her condition.[66] A mentally disordered offender held in seclusion in prison for disciplinary reasons, with inadequate medical treatment and insufficient monitoring given the risk of suicide, suffered a violation of Article 3.[67] And a mental patient, compulsorily detained in mental hospital under the Mental Health Act 1983, suffered degrading treatment when put in seclusion in circumstances which did not comply with the Code of Practice which was not legally binding but had been drawn up in part to protect people against the risk of inhuman or degrading treatment.[68]

(c) Inhuman or degrading punishment

8.42   The term 'punishment' imports the idea of a disagreeable experience inflicted as a consequence of conviction for a crime. As such, it is narrower than 'treatment', which is apt to cover anything done to a person in any circumstances. Since any punishment inevitably involves a degree of suffering and humiliation, in order for a punishment to violate Article 3, the humiliation must be different from and greater than the usual and inevitable element of humiliation. 'The assessment is, in the nature of things, relative: it depends on all the circumstances of the case and, in particular, on the nature and context of the punishment itself and the manner and method of its execution.'[69] For example, imprisonment in itself does not violate Article 3. Even a mandatory life sentence does not violate Article 3.[70] Nor does the imposition of a prison sentence of indeterminate length, at any rate while the prisoner can be regarded as serving the punitive part of the sentence rather than being detained for preventive purposes.[71] But being imprisoned for a long period in very bad conditions might do so.[72] A sentence of flogging (which is no longer permitted in English law) is inherently degrading.[73]

---

[64] *Dougoz v Greece* Application 40907/98 (2002) 34 EHRR 61 esp at [46]–[49].

[65] *Napier v Scottish Ministers* [2002] UKHRR 308, Outer House of Court of Session (Lord Macfadyen).

[66] *Price v UK* Application 33394/96 (2002) 34 EHRR 53.

[67] *Keenan v UK* Application 27229/95 (2001) 33 EHRR 38.

[68] *R (on the application of Munjaz) v Mersey Care NHS Trust* [2003] EWCA Civ 1036; The Times, 25 July 2003.

[69] *Tyrer v UK* Series A No 26 (1979–80) 2 EHRR 1 at [30] (judicial birching degrading).

[70] *R v Lichniak* [2002] UKHL 47; [2003] 1 AC 903.

[71] *Hussain and Singh v UK* (1996) 22 EHRR 1; *T and V v UK* Applications 24724/94 & 24888/94 (2000) 30 EHRR 121.

[72] See, mutatis mutandis, *Dougoz v Greece* Application 40907/98 (2002) 34 EHRR 61.

[73] *Tyrer v UK* Series A No 26 (1979–80) 2 EHRR 1; *Pinder v The Queen* [2002] UKPC 46, [2003] 1 AC 620.

(2) Positive Obligations

As interpreted by the ECtHR, Article 3 imposes positive obligations similar to **8.43**
those which arise under Article 2 (the right to life). Public authorities have a duty
to take reasonable steps in the circumstances, balancing the interests of the right-
holder against those of other people, to protect people against threats of torture or
inhuman or degrading treatment or punishment by state agencies or others.
Public authorities also have a duty to investigate alleged violations efficiently, a
duty to make provision for securing the legal accountability of people who inflict
torture or inhuman or degrading treatment or punishment on others, and a duty
to provide such information as is needed to allow people to protect themselves
against the risk of suffering. Sometimes the duty to protect people includes an
obligation to provide medical assistance, social security benefits or help with
housing, in order to provide a safety net against the kinds of destitution and un-
controlled disease which can cause very severe suffering.

(a) The duty to protect people

This duty arises in many different settings, and the content of the duty varies **8.44**
with the context. Social services departments have responsibilities towards children whom they know, or ought to know, are at risk of abuse in the family,[74]
although the role of courts in overseeing social services departments in implementing care plans is limited by the scheme of the Children Act 1989, which is
capable of leaving a gap in the scheme of protection for children's Article 3
rights.[75] There is also a duty to provide support for children who are destitute,
which is met under English law by s 17 of the Children Act 1989.[76] The duty to
protect against degrading levels of destitution also protects asylum seekers.[77] The
courts are increasingly protecting people who are incapable of making their own
decisions against unauthorized administration of medical treatment without
their consent.[78]

---

[74] See, eg, *Z v UK* Application 29392/95 (2002) 34 EHRR 3; *E v UK* Application 33218/96
(2003) 36 EHRR 31.
[75] *Re S (Minors) (Care Order: Implementation of Care Plan)* [2002] UKHL 10; [2002] 2 AC 291.
[76] See eg *R (on the application of W) v Lambeth LBC* [2002] EWCA Civ 613, [2002] 2 All ER 901;
R (on the application of Mani) v Lambeth LBC [2003] EWCA Civ 836, The Times, 23 July 2003.
[77] Nationality, Immigration and Asylum Act 2002, ss 54 and 55, and *R (on the application of
Kimani) v Lambeth LBC*, The Times, 6 August 2003, CA.
[78] On the operation of the Mental Health Act 1983 in relation to treatment without consent, see
eg *R (on the application of Wilkinson) v Broadmoor Special Hospital Authority* [2001] EWCA Civ
1545, [2002] 1 WLR 419; *R (on the application of Wooder) v Feggetter* [2002] EWCA Civ 554,
[2003] QB 219; *R (on the application of B) v Ashworth Hospital Authority* [2003] EWCA Civ 547,
The Times, 24 April 2003; and, somewhat less satisfactorily, *Re F (Mental Patient: Sterilisation)*
[1990] 2 AC 1, HL.

(b) The duty of efficient investigation

8.45   In English law, there is a duty on the police, and sometimes on other agencies, to investigate allegations of behaviour amounting to torture and inhuman or degrading treatment. Because of the fundamental nature of the obligations under Article 3, the ECtHR has held that Article 3 has been violated where state authorities fail to conduct an adequate investigation of an allegation that someone has been the victim of inhuman or degrading treatment. The adequacy of an investigation is assessed having regard to the speed with which it is instigated, the investigators' independence of the state agencies being investigated (when allegations implicated state officials), the vigour and efficiency with which it is pursued, and the thoroughness of the report of the findings. If something goes wrong (such as a file being mislaid) which undermines the effectiveness of the investigation and of any possibility of subsequent remedies in respect of the injury, the inadequacy of the investigation will itself amount to a violation of Article 3.[79] If the authorities adopt an unhelpful, obstructive and complacent attitude to somebody reporting a suspected death or disappearance, who is emotionally close to the primary victim and was present when he or she was taken away, the person making the report may also be a victim of a violation of Article 3 if she suffers long-drawn-out fear or apprehension for the primary victim.[80]

(c) The duty to secure legal accountability of wrongdoers

8.46   Article 3 ECHR imposes on state authorities a positive duty to secure an effective legal remedy for anyone who suffers assaults on their physical or mental well-being sufficiently serious to amount to inhuman or degrading treatment, and the legal accountability of those responsible. One purpose is to deter future infringements of Article 3 rights. While civil remedies may be adequate to secure some rights, people's physical and moral integrity and dignity are so fundamentally important that criminal penalties are needed to give adequate protection against serious violations, such as rape or sexual assault.[81]

8.47   The type and level of protection which is needed will vary depending on the circumstances and the characteristics of the victim. In *A v UK*,[82] the ECtHR held that the law of assault and battery provided insufficient protection for children against suffering because the pursuer or prosecutor must show that the treatment

---

[79] See, eg, the approach in *Kaya v Turkey* (12 February 1998, RJD 1998-I); *Yasa v Turkey* (1999) 28 EHRR 408; *Assenov v Bulgaria* Application 24760/94 (1999) 28 EHRR 652; *Satik v Turkey* Application 31866/96 (10 October 2000) at [58]–[60] (investigations ineffective: violation of Art 3); *Caloc v France* Application 33951/96 (2002) 35 EHRR 14 (no violation of Art 3).

[80] *Çiçek v Turkey* Application 25704/94 (27 February 2001).

[81] See *X and Y v Netherlands* Series A No 91 (1986) 8 EHRR 235 (decided under Art 8, but similar principles apply to Art 3).

[82] (1999) 27 EHRR 611.

meted out to the child had exceeded 'reasonable chastisement'. The law is now interpreted as requiring judges to instruct juries to take account of the factors identified as relevant by the ECtHR.[83] On the other hand, Article 3 does not at present require English law to provide a remedy against the agents of another state for torture if the defendants are entitled to state or diplomatic immunity.[84]

(d) The duty to provide information and involve the victims in the investigation

As under Article 2, the victims and their relatives must be given sufficient infor-   **8.48**
mation, and must be sufficiently involved in the investigation, to allow them to understand the causes of the violation of Article 3, although the extent of involvement may vary according to the nature of the inquiry and the stage it has reached.[85] The English courts may enforce these duties, which bind public authorities under s 6 of the HRA 1998. Enforcement may be undertaken in judicial review proceedings, through compensatory remedies under ss 7 and 8 of the Act, or through a combination of both types of remedies.

D. Freedom from Slavery and Forced Labour

Article 4 ECHR provides: **8.49**

1.   No one shall be held in slavery or servitude.
2.   No one shall be required to perform forced or compulsory labour.
3.   For the purpose of this article 'forced or compulsory labour' shall not include:
     (a)   any work required to be done in the ordinary course of detention imposed according to the provisions of article 5 of this Convention or during conditional release from such detention;
     (b)   any service of a military character or, in case of conscientious objectors in countries where they are recognised, service exacted instead of compulsory military service;
     (c)   any service exacted in case of an emergency or calamity threatening the life or well-being of the community;
     (d)   any work or service which forms part of normal civic obligations.

(a) Slavery and servitude

Slavery and servitude are a matter of an individual's legal status. A slave is some-   **8.50**
one over whom another person can exercise powers derived from a right of ownership. A state of servitude is one in which the serf is obliged to work for

---

[83]   *R v H* [2001] EWCA Crim 1024; [2002] 1 Cr App R 7.
[84]   *Al-Adsani v UK (merits)* Application 35763/97 (2002) 34 EHRR 11 (Grand Chamber, by a 9–8 majority).
[85]   See eg *R (on the application of Green) v Police Complaints Authority* [2002] EWCA Civ 389; [2002] UKHRR 985.

someone else and remain on that person's property, without the possibility of changing those conditions by his or her own acts.[86] Neither status exists in English law.

(b) Forced or compulsory labour

8.51 Forced labour is work undertaken under a physical or mental constraint. Compulsory labour is work of any kind, including professional work, undertaken against the worker's will and under a threat of a penalty, rather than merely compensatory or private law damages, for non-performance.[87] There was a violation of Article 4 (not saved by Article 4(3)(d)) where the state required its male citizens to serve in the fire brigade, with a financial payment being enforced for those who refused to serve.[88] However, a duty imposed on lawyers to spend part of their time providing free legal advice or participating in a legal aid programme does not violate Article 4.[89]

E. Liberty of the Person

8.52 Guarantees against arbitrary arrest and detention are offered by Article 5 ECHR, which provides:

> 1. Everyone has the right to liberty and security of person. No one shall be deprived of his liberty save in the following cases and in accordance with a procedure prescribed by law:
> (a) the lawful detention of a person after conviction by a competent court;
> (b) the lawful arrest or detention of a person for noncompliance with the lawful order of a court or in order to secure the fulfilment of any obligation prescribed by law;
> (c) the lawful arrest or detention of a person effected for the purpose of bringing him before the competent legal authority on reasonable suspicion of having committed an offence or when it is reasonably considered necessary to prevent his committing an offence or fleeing after having done so;
> (d) the detention of a minor by lawful order for the purpose of educational supervision or his lawful detention for the purpose of bringing him before the competent legal authority;
> (e) the lawful detention of persons for the prevention of the spreading of infectious diseases, of persons of unsound mind, alcoholics or drug addicts or vagrants;
> (f) the lawful arrest or detention of a person to prevent his effecting an unauthorised entry into the country or of a person against whom action is being taken with a view to deportation or extradition.

---

[86] See *Van Droogenbroeck v Belgium* Series A No 50 (1982) 4 EHRR 443; *Van der Mussele v Belgium* Series A No 70 (1983) 6 EHRR 363.

[87] *Van der Mussele v Belgium*, ibid.

[88] *Schmidt v Federal Republic of Germany* Series A No 291-B (1994) 18 EHRR 513.

[89] *Van der Mussele v Belgium* Series A No 70 (1983) 6 EHRR 363.

2. Everyone who is arrested shall be informed promptly, in a language which he understands, of the reasons for his arrest and of any charge against him.

3. Everyone arrested or detained in accordance with the provisions of paragraph 1(c) of this Article shall be brought promptly before a judge or other officer authorised by law to exercise judicial power and shall be entitled to trial within a reasonable time or to release pending trial. Release may be conditioned by guarantees to appear for trial.

4. Everyone who is deprived of his liberty by arrest or detention shall be entitled to take proceedings by which the lawfulness of his detention shall be decided speedily by a court and his release ordered if the detention is not lawful.

5. Everyone who has been the victim of arrest or detention in contravention of the provisions of this Article shall have an enforceable right to compensation.

(a) Meaning of 'deprivation of liberty'

There is a distinction between a deprivation of liberty and a restriction of liberty. **8.53** Only a deprivation engages Article 5(1). The difference is one of degree, not of kind. Relevant factors in deciding which has occurred include the type, duration, practical effect, and manner of the detention.[90] If there is a deprivation of liberty, it can be justified only in accordance with the list of permitted justifications in Article 5(1). That list is exhaustive, and the justifications are narrowly interpreted.[91]

Before the HRA 1998 came into force, the House of Lords held by a bare major- **8.54** ity that a mental patient, who had been taken to hospital without being told whether or not he was being held under a statutory power, and had not tried to leave when placed in an unlocked ward, had not been detained, despite the doctor's statement that he would have been compulsorily detained had he attempted to leave.[92] Under the HRA 1998 and Article 5(1), a court would now have to take account of the reality that the patient was not free to leave and probably felt constrained to remain.[93] This might lead to a different result. There are situations in which preventing someone from leaving a place is very unlikely to amount to a deprivation of liberty. Under Article 5(1) and the HRA 1998, a deprivation of liberty does not take place if someone is detained for a very limited time. Searches of the person falling short of arrest entail a detention for only a short period. They probably do not engage Article 5(1), either because the deprivation of liberty falls under a de minimis principle or because detaining someone to require them to

---

[90] See, eg, *Guzzardi v Italy* Series A No 39 (1981) 3 EHRR 333 (exile to a small island does amount to deprivation); *Amuur v France* (1996) 22 EHRR 533 (being held in international transit zone at airport, able to leave but not enter the country, was deprivation).

[91] *Ciulla v Italy* Series A No 148 (1991) 13 EHRR 346.

[92] *R v Bournewood Community and Mental Health NHS Trust, ex p L* [1999] 1 AC 458, HL (Lords Goff, Lloyd and Hope; Lords Nolan and Steyn dissented). The House overruled a unanimous Court of Appeal, [1998] 2 WLR 764. See further ch 7 above.

[93] See *De Wilde, Ooms and Versyp v Belgium* (the 'Vagrancy Cases') Series A No 12 (1979–80) 1 EHRR 373 (voluntary surrender to custody does not deprive people of the protection of Art 5) and the decision of the EComHR in *Walverens v Belgium*, report of 5 March 1980.

submit to a search under a legal power is within the exception in Article 5(1)(b), 'the lawful . . . detention of a person . . . in order to secure the fulfilment of any obligation prescribed by law'.[94]

8.55 A detention may be lawful where someone is imprisoned pursuant to a lawful sentence of a properly constituted court; or restrained for his or her own good by a parent,[95] guardian, or teacher; or detained in hospital according to procedures laid down in the Mental Health Act 1983; or detained in accordance with immigration legislation for as short a time as possible in order to allow immigration authorities to decide whether to authorize entry to the country.[96] Legislation may provide for people to be detained for specified purposes in connection with the investigation of crime. Detention need not be preceded by an arrest; it is lawful if it is authorized by law, and is carried out for a lawful purpose and in compliance with required procedures.

(b) Procedural rights under Article 5 ECHR

8.56 People who have been deprived of their liberty are entitled to two forms of legal protection. First, Article 5(4) provides that they must be able to take proceedings in which the legality of the deprivation can be tested, and release can be ordered if the detention is found not to be lawful. In English law, this requirement is met by means of procedures such as habeas corpus, judicial review of detention decisions, and in many cases the use of a specialized tribunal such as the Mental Health Review Tribunal to keep the justification for detention under review. Secondly, Article 5(5) requires that anyone arrested or detained in contravention of the article must have an enforceable right to compensation. In England, this right is usually restricted by judicial immunity from liability where a person is detained by an order of a court made in good faith, which later turns out to be unlawful. Generally, s 9(1) of the HRA 1998 maintains that immunity. To meet the requirements of Article 5(5), however, s 9(3) and (4) allows damages to be sought from the Crown for a judicial act done in good faith where it results in a detention which violates Article 5. Other immunities, such as that under the Mental Health Act 1983, s 139(1), must be read down whenever possible to secure compatibility with Article 5(5).[97]

---

[94] *McVeigh, O'Neill and Evans v UK* Applications 8022/77, 8025/77 & 8027/77 (1981) 5 EHRR 71 (detention to seek information under anti-terrorism legislation).

[95] In a much-criticized decision, *Nielsen v Denmark* Series A No 144 (1989) 11 EHRR 175, the Court held that a 12-year-old child had not been deprived of his liberty when compulsorily detained for over five months in a psychiatric hospital at his mother's request without any independent review of his detention on the basis of his medical condition. Children's liberty was necessarily restricted by properly exercised parental authority, and the Court found no evidence that the mother had acted improperly.

[96] *R (on the application of Saadi) v Secretary of State for the Home Department* [2002] UKHL 41; [2002] 1 WLR 3131.

[97] *R (on the application of W) v Doncaster MBC* [2003] EWHC 192; The Times, 12 March 2003, Stanley Burnton J.

F. Privacy, Lifestyle, and Related Rights

(1) Introduction

English law has traditionally not protected privacy as such, but a growing number **8.57** of privacy-related interests have been recognized as being entitled to legal protection in recent years. Sometimes these have been the subject of developments in the common law of breach of confidence or of property-related causes of action such as nuisance. In other respects statute has intervened, often in the light of adverse decisions in the ECtHR or of conventions and directives emanating from the Council of Europe and the European Communities and European Union respectively. Under the HRA 1998, Article 8 ECHR has for the first time introduced to English law a wide range of privacy-related rights, together with a set of systematic criteria for assessing claims that a public authority has violated or is threatening those rights. This section concentrates on the standards which Article 8 imposes on public authorities.

Article 8 ECHR provides: **8.58**

1. Everyone has the right to respect for his private and family life, his home and his correspondence.
2. There shall be no interference by a public authority with the exercise of this right except such as is in accordance with the law and is necessary in a democratic society in the interests of national security, public safety or the economic well-being of the country, for the prevention of disorder or crime, for the protection of health or morals, or for the protection of the rights and freedoms of others.

(2) The Interests Protected by Article 8(1) ECHR

The core purpose of Article 8 is to protect the individual against arbitrary inter- **8.59** ference by public authorities with certain interests which are particularly important to a person's ability to live a fulfilled and fulfilling life.[98] The interests singled out as particularly requiring respect are 'private and family life',[99] 'home' and 'correspondence'. These terms have been interpreted generously by the ECtHR, by reference to notions of dignity and personal autonomy which underpin privacy-related rights.[100] The interpretation of Article 8 is dynamic and continuous, and the field of protected interests is never closed. Furthermore, while the core purpose is to protect people against arbitrary interference by public authorities, the state's duty to 'respect' the interests sometimes carries with it positive obligations

---

[98] *Hokkanen v Finland* Series A No 299-A (1995) 19 EHRR 139 at [55].
[99] These words are doubtless to be read disjunctively, but they are closely linked. Sir JES Fawcett, *The Application of the European Convention on Human Rights* (2nd edn, Oxford: Clarendon Press, 1987) 211.
[100] See *Pretty v UK* Application 2346/02 (2002) 35 EHRR 1.

to take action to support and enhance people's ability to enjoy them. This could have major consequences for public expenditure and social resources, so the Court has stressed that the extent of any positive obligation will be set in such a way as to avoid imposing unreasonable burdens on the state.[101]

8.60 'Private and family life' takes place in various forms of private and public space, involving many different activities, and access to many types of information and communication. Physical and moral integrity are central to it, as are the enjoyment of personal relationships and respect for personal identity. The 'home' is extremely important, whether it is a castle, a hovel, or a caravan, and regardless of whether or not one has a legal right to occupy it. 'Correspondence' includes all forms of communication. The interests in private and family life, home and correspondence overlap and reinforce each other. Furthermore, it is not always possible or desirable to separate one's private interests from one's business activities. People increasingly conduct businesses from home, and have privacy-related interests even when at work. People often approach others for professional services affecting their private lives. The Court has therefore extended the protection of Article 8 to business premises.[102] The sections which follow outline the range of interests currently covered by Article 8(1).

(3) Private Life and Lifestyle Generally

8.61 Almost any activity forming part of private life is capable of engaging Article 8(1), although the more trivial it is, the easier it is likely to be to justify an interference, and the less likely it is to give rise to positive obligations. For example, the right of a doctor to choose to drink alcohol is a lifestyle choice protected by Article 8(1), but it is fairly easy to justify the relevant professional body in restricting the freedom by making the doctor give up alcohol and take random alcohol tests as a condition of continuing to practise medicine, in order to protect patients.[103]

(a) Personal status and identity

8.62 Where a person's birth affects his or her status, any legal disability resulting from it (for example, by reason of a legal status of illegitimacy) engages the right to respect for private and family life under Article 8(1). If the disability is not justified in terms of Article 8(2), it will violate that right. Furthermore, if the different treatment of a person by reason of birth does not serve a legitimate aim or is insufficiently rationally and objectively justified, it will violate the right to be free of

---

[101] See, eg, *Botta v Italy* Application 21439/93 (1998) 26 EHRR 241.
[102] See eg *Niemietz v Germany* Series A No 251-B (1993) 16 EHRR 97; *Halford v UK* Application 20605/92 (1997) 24 EHRR 523.
[103] *Whitefield v General Medical Council* [2002] UKPC 62; [2003] IRLR 39.

discrimination under Article 14 ECHR, taken together with Article 8.[104] Freedom to choose a name is also protected, because one's name is an aspect of one's private and family life. However, a public authority can justify preventing a person from choosing a new name if the restriction is in accordance with the law and, in the opinion of the authority, the person suffers little inconvenience from having the existing name and the proposed new name does not identify him or her particularly directly with his or her family. But restrictions on taking new names must not discriminate between people disproportionately, or without an objective, rational justification, or there will be a violation of Article 14 taken together with Article 8.[105] Identity cards must not identify a person in ways which cause unnecessary embarrassment, at any rate if they have to be produced on demand for the purposes of policing or, perhaps, access to services.[106]

(b) Sexual identity and gender

After long hesitation, the European Court of Justice, the ECtHR and the English courts have concluded that there is no sufficient justification for refusing to recognize for legal purposes the reassigned gender of a person who is being treated for gender dysphoria.[107] English law is in some respects incompatible with this conclusion. The government published for consultation in 2003 a draft Bill designed to remedy the incompatibility, and a Gender RecognitionBill has been introduced to Parliament in the 2003–04 session.

8.63

(c) Privacy and activities in public settings

Almost everyone must carry on life partly in public, and private interests need protection in public places as well as on private property. The duty to respect private life can apply in any place where people have to carry on their lives. Although being at work, in prison or at school necessarily limits one's privacy, aspects of Article 8 rights which are not inevitably and necessarily taken away will continue to operate.[108] Public authorities also have positive duties in respect of personal information and pictures which they hold, including material obtained from CCTV cameras and

8.64

---

[104] *Marckx v Belgium* Series A No 31 (1979–80) 2 EHRR 330.

[105] *Burghartz v Switzerland* Series A No 280-B (1994) 18 EHRR 101; *Stjerna v Finland* Series A No 299-B (1997) 24 EHRR 195; *Guillot v France* (decision of 24 October 1996, EComHR).

[106] See *B v France* Series A No 232-C (1993) 16 EHRR 1.

[107] See particularly *Goodwin v UK* Application 28957/95 (2002) 35 EHRR 18; *Bellinger v Bellinger* [2003] UKHL 21, [2003] 2 WLR 1174, and the discussion of the right to marry under Art 12 ECHR, paras 8.78 et seq below.

[108] See, eg, *Golder v UK* Series A No 18 (1979–80) 1 EHRR 524 (prison); *Costello-Roberts v UK* Series A No 247-C (1995) 19 EHRR 112 (school); *Niemietz v Germany* Series A No 251-B (1993) 16 EHRR 97; *Halford v UK* Application 20605/92(1997) 24 EHRR 523 (workplace); *Peck v UK* Application 44647/98 (2003) 36 EHRR 41 (inadequate control over use of CCTV material breached Art 8, and lack of remedy in English courts breached Art 13: cf *R v Brentwood BC, ex p Peck*, The Times, 18 December 1997, DC).

public records where the use to which the public authority puts the material affects people's private lives.[109] The question is whether the person has, in all the circumstances, a reasonable or legitimate expectation of privacy. On private premises, even drug dealers are entitled to the protection of Article 8.[110] However, this will not necessarily make evidence inadmissible merely because it was obtained in violation of Article 8,[111] and when in public places drug dealers have no legitimate expectation that public officials will respect the privacy of their business.[112]

(d) Personal integrity

8.65   This is a somewhat diffuse category, concerned with the people's abilities to carry on their lives in an autonomous and dignified way. In *Botta v Italy*,[113] the ECtHR wrote:

> Private life, in the Court's view, includes a person's physical and psychological integrity; the guarantee afforded by Article 8 of the Convention is primarily intended to ensure the development, without outside interference, of the personality of each individual in his relations with other human beings . . .

Physical integrity overlaps with rights considered in sections B and C above. Psychological integrity is about a person's ability to select values by which to live, and to pursue a chosen life-style or plan for life, so far as that is not protected by any of the other Convention rights, such as freedom of religion or the right to marry and found a family.

8.66   The right to personal integrity is capable of giving rise to positive obligations on a public authority, including obligations which are similar to those arising under treaties designed to protect economic and social rights, particularly in respect of people who have a disability, where there is:

> a direct and immediate link between the measures sought by an applicant and the latter's private and/or family life . . . In the instant case, however, the right asserted

---

[109] See *Rotaru v Romania* Application 28341/95 (2000) 8 BHRC 449; *Peck v UK*, App. No. 44647/98, judgment of 28 Jan 2003; *R (on the application of Ellis) v Chief Constable of Essex Police* [2003] EWHC 1321, The Times, 17 June 2003, DC (need for Art 8 rights of members of offender's family to be considered before releasing information about offender pursuant to 'offender naming scheme'); Katherine S Williams, Craig Johnstone and Mark Goodwin, 'Closed Circuit Television (CCTV) Surveillance in Urban Britain: Beyond the Rhetoric of Crime Prevention' in J Gold and G Revill (eds), *Landscapes of Defence* (London: Longman, 2000); Andrew von Hirsch, 'The Ethics of Public Television Surveillance' in Andrew von Hirsch, David Garland and Alison Wakefield (eds), *Ethical and Social Perspectives on Situational Crime Prevention* (Oxford: Hart Publishing, 2000) 59–76.

[110] *Khan v UK* Application 35394/97 (2001) 31 EHRR 45, where a violation was found of Art 8 because there was no legal authority for, or judicial regulation of, the placing of a microphone on the outside wall of a suspect's dwelling.

[111] *Khan v UK*, ibid.

[112] *Lüdi v Switzerland* Series A No 238 (1992) 15 EHRR 173. Cf *Kruslin v France* Series A No 176-A (199) 12 EHRR 547.

[113] Application 21439/93 (1998) 26 EHRR 241at [32].

by Mr. Botta, namely the right to gain access to the beach and the sea at a place distant from his normal place of residence during his holidays, concerns interpersonal relations of such broad and indeterminate scope that there can be no conceivable direct link between the measures the State was urged to take in order to make good the omissions of the private bathing establishments and the applicant's private life. Accordingly, Article 8 is not applicable.[114]

In such cases, public authorities can probably discharge their positive obligations by making provision which complies with relevant international obligations and recommendations.

(e) Personal information: data protection and access[115]

Public authorities have several kinds of obligations in respect of personal infor-   **8.67**
mation. The right to respect for private life is continuously engaged when a public authority seeks, collects, stores, processes, compares, or disseminates personal information or opinions about, or images of, a data subject, even if the information is concerned with the data subject's alleged acts in the public (or political) domain.[116] The state must justify any such treatment by reference to the principles of Article 8(2) ECHR. Certain types of information are regarded as particularly important or intimate, including information about health,[117] social security,[118] and sexuality.[119] Public authorities have particularly heavy obligations to ensure that such information is collected in ways which respect private life, is stored in ways which safeguard its security, and is kept for no longer than necessary for a legitimate purpose under Article 8(2). The public authority must also ensure that the information is not used for an improper purpose, is checked for accuracy, is made available to the data subject when possible, and is not disclosed without strong reasons and adequate checks on the appropriateness and legality of the disclosure.[120]

Public authorities have a positive obligation to give people access to informa-   **8.68**
tion about their own backgrounds and histories when they have been in the care of the public authority, unless it is decided that non-disclosure is justified under Article 8(2) after deploying decision-making procedures which ensure that the

---

[114] ibid at [34]–[35].

[115] For accounts of the international arrangements in relation to this, see James Michael, *Privacy and Human Rights* (Paris: Dartmouth/UNESCO Publishing, 1994); David Feldman, 'Information and Privacy', in Jack Beatson and Yvonne Cripps (eds), *Freedom of Expression and Freedom of Information: Essays in Honour of Sir David Williams* (Oxford: OUP, 2000) 299–324.

[116] *Rotaru v Romania* Application 28341/95 (2000) 8 BHRC 449.

[117] *Guerra v Italy* (1998) 26 EHRR 357; *McGinley and Egan v UK* Applications 21825/93 & 23414/94 (1999) 27 EHRR 1; *Z v Finland* (1998) 25 EHRR 371.

[118] *MS v Sweden* (1997) 3 BHRC 248.

[119] *Lustig-Prean v UK (No 1)* (2000) 29 EHRR 548.

[120] See, eg, *Leander v Sweden* Series A No 116 (1987) 9 EHRR 433.

requirements of Article 8(2) will be reliably applied.[121] In England, the standards of Article 8 in relation to information are amplified and bolstered by the provisions of the Data Protection Act 1998 and the Freedom of Information Act 2000.

(f) Sexuality

8.69 Sexual orientation and activity is an aspect of private life. The criminalization of homosexuality violated homosexuals' right to respect for private life.[122] However, not all sexual activity automatically attracts the protection of Article 8, and the majority of the ECtHR was not enthusiastic in accepting that the idea of private life extended to sado-masochism.[123] It is extremely unlikely, in the current state of European attitudes, that sexual activity between adults and children would engage Article 8(1). Even if it did, the state would have little difficulty in justifying legally restricting it under Article 8(2). While the state is entitled to impose restrictions on sexual freedom to protect vulnerable people, a discriminatory restriction which is not justified by reference to an objective and rational criterion, or is disproportionate to any legitimate, justifying objective, will violate Article 8. Thus there was a violation where English law made it an offence for male homosexual acts to take place when more than two men were present, but no such restriction was imposed on other types of sexual activity.[124] As well as engaging Article 8, sexuality is a 'suspect category' for the purpose of the anti-discrimination provision under Article 14, and discrimination on the grounds of sexuality (for example, in relation to child custody matters) will be hard to justify.[125]

(4) Family Life

8.70 Family life overlaps with the right to marry and found a family under Article 12 ECHR (see section G below). Respect for family life requires the state to respect the value of mutual enjoyment of a wide range of de facto relationships of personal intimacy and genetic closeness. The question is whether in fact a genuine, familial inter-relationship subsists between the parties.[126] The category of such relationships is not closed, and includes:

---

[121] *Gaskin v UK* Series A No 160 (1990) 12 EHRR 36.

[122] See *Dudgeon v UK (No 2)* Series A No 45 (1982) 4 EHRR 149; *Norris v Ireland* Series A No 142 (1991) 13 EHRR 186; *Modinos v Cyprus* Series A No 259 (1993) 16 EHRR 485; *Lustig-Prean v UK (No 1)* (2000) 29 EHRR 548.

[123] *Laskey, Jaggard and Brown v UK* (1997) 24 EHRR 39.

[124] *ADT v UK* Application 35765/97 (2001) 31 EHRR 33.

[125] *Salgueiro da Silva Mouta v Portugal* Application 33290/96 (2001) 31 EHRR 47; but cf *Fretté v France* Application 36515/97 [2003] 2 FCR 39. See ch 11 below.

[126] *Marckx v Belgium* Series A No 31 (1979–80) 2 EHRR 330; *Berrehab v Netherlands* Series A No 138 (1989) 11 EHRR 322.

- the mutual enjoyment by parent and child of each other's company;[127]
- relationships between members of the extended family, such as uncle and nephew, where there is a real tie between them;[128]
- the relationship between a man and his child, conceived when the man and the mother were unmarried but living together, following the break-up of the relationship;[129]
- the relationship between a man and his child conceived during an extra-marital affair between the mother and the man;[130]
- the right of a child to have his or her natural father recognized as such in the birth certificate.[131]

A decision to take a child into the care of a public authority always engages Article 8(1). When considering the compatibility of such a decision with Article 8, local authorities are allowed some leeway in making the assessment where there is an element of urgency, but when matters are less urgent the right to respect for family life requires fair procedural protections provided by law for parents and their children.[132]

8.71

Once the child is in care, there will be time for considered decision-making, and the standard of review will be more demanding. Whenever possible, the public authority must aim to re-establish family relationships as quickly as can safely be achieved.[133] However, the rights and interests of all parties must be taken into account, not just the person complaining to the Court.[134]

8.72

The right to respect for family life may affect deportation decisions and immigration rules, as it includes a right not to have the family broken up by a deportation

8.73

---

[127] *Andersson v Sweden* Series A No 226 (1992) 14 EHRR 615.

[128] *Boyle v UK* Series A No 282-B (1995) 19 EHRR 179 (uncle denied contact with child in care following abuse allegations, without legal process to determine issue—friendly settlement following determination on merits by Commission).

[129] *Keegan v Ireland* Series A No 290 (1994) 18 EHRR 342 (adoption of child without father's consent violated father's Art 8 rights).

[130] *Kroon v Netherlands* Series A No 297-C (1995) 19 EHRR 263 (legal presumption of the child's legitimacy, preventing real father from legally recognizing the child as his own, violated rights under Art 8; law of state must enable family ties to be developed, and legally recognized and safeguarded).

[131] This was accepted in a declaration of incompatibility made by consent in March 2003 in unreported litigation between Mrs Diane Blood and the Department of Health, in respect of provisions of the Human Fertilisation and Embryology Act 1990 which prevented her deceased husband's name being entered as the father in the birth certificate of a child conceived by Mrs Blood using her late husband's frozen sperm. A private Member's Bill, the Human Fertilisation and Embryology (Deceased Fathers) Bill (Mr Stephen McCabe MP), designed to remove the incompatibility, is currently before the House of Lords having completed its Commons stages. See Joint Committee on Human Rights, Eighth Report (2002–03 HL 90; HC 634) paras 31–36.

[132] *W v UK* Series A No 121-A (1988) 10 EHRR 29.

[133] *Olsson v Sweden (No 1* Series A No 130 (1989) 11 EHRR 259; *Hokkanen v Finland* Series A No 299-A (1995) 19 EHRR 139.

[134] *Glaser v UK* Application 32346/96 (2001) 33 EHRR 1.

decision unless the state has carefully struck a balance between the interests of members of the family and the interest in maintaining immigration control.[135]

(5) The Home and its Environment

8.74 'Home' includes any place which is in fact currently used (rather than intended for use) as a private home, even if the use as a home is unlawful,[136] as long as the public do not have access to the place otherwise than for private business.[137] Article 8 protects homes against unjustified destruction by or with the acquiescence of a public authority.[138] In relation to eviction from one's home, it requires the eviction to be subject to an appropriate judicial process in which the court can assess whether in the circumstances it would be justifiable under Article 8(2).[139] Public authorities have an obligation not to create a noise hazard or other environmental pollution interfering with rights under Article 8(1) unless it can be justified under Article 8(2). In English law, this is achieved through a combination of the law of nuisance and the HRA 1998, s 6.[140]

8.75 Article 8 also imposes a positive obligation on state agencies to take reasonable steps, using their legal powers of regulation and enforcement, to protect people's homes against pollution and similar hazards, created by private enterprises, which make it unsafe or excessively unpleasant to live in a particular area. While a failure to use a power may be justified, it will fall to be assessed by reference to the criteria in Article 8(2), including that of proportionality.[141] Where the state exercises a regulatory role, for example by setting maximum levels of noise and the maximum number of night flights landing and taking off at airports, the procedure for doing so must be adequate to take account of the rights of residents in the locality.[142] The state may also violate the right to respect for the home by failing to warn inhabitants of an area about a threat to their health from environmental factors known to a state agency.[143]

---

[135] See eg *Ahmut v Netherlands* (1997) 24 EHRR 62; *R v Secretary of State for the Home Department, ex p R*, The Times, 29 November 2000, Gage J.

[136] *Buckley v UK* Application 20348/92 (1997) 23 EHRR 101 at [54]; *Harrow LBC v Qazi* [2003] UKHL 43; [2003] 3 WLR 792, HL.

[137] See *Loizidou v Turkey* Application 15318/89 (1997) 23 EHRR 513; *Pentidis v Greece* Application 23238/94 (1997) 24 EHRR CD1, EComHR; struck out of list by Court (9 June 1997, RJD 1997-III, No 39) (refusal of permission to use building as place of worship for Jehovah's Witnesses does not engage Art 8, although it violated Art 9).

[138] *Akdivar v Turkey* (1997) 23 EHRR 143.

[139] See eg *Southwark LBC v St Brice* [2001] EWCA Civ 1138; [2002] 1 WLR 1537.

[140] See *Dennis v Ministry of Defence* [2003] EWHC 793; [2003] 19 EGCS 118, Buckley J. (training Harrier jet pilots).

[141] *López Ostra v Spain* Series A No 303-C (1995) 20 EHRR 277.

[142] *Hatton v UK* Application 36022/97, The Times, 10 July 2003, GC, reversing by a 12–5 majority a decision of a Section that English procedures failed to provide such an assessment, but nevertheless finding a violation of Art 13 because English law provided no means by which an arguable case of a violation of Art 8 in that context could be litigated.

[143] *Guerra v Italy* (1998) 26 EHRR 357.

The right to respect for the home extends to ensuring that people are not arbi-   **8.76**
trarily prevented from living in a place of their choice.[144] It is permissible to restrict the use of land in order to advance public interests in orderly development
and conservation. This has been held to justify refusing to allow a person to live in
a caravan on her own land, placed there without planning consent;[145] but before
enforcing planning controls, the various interests relevant to the balancing exercise required by Article 8(2) must be properly taken into account in the light of the
individual's own circumstances.[146]

(6) Communications

Under Article 8(1) ECHR, correspondence is specifically protected. The Court is   **8.77**
concerned to treat the various elements in Article 8(1) on an equal footing, contributing cumulatively to the protection of privacy interests. This has prompted
the Court to extend the ideas of private life and the home so as to cover the same
range of fields and activities that are protected as correspondence, including business premises. All forms of communications, including telephone and e-mail, are
now protected.[147]

G. The Right to Marry and Found a Family

(1) The Right to Marry

This right is guaranteed by Article 12 ECHR, which provides: 'Men and women   **8.78**
of marriageable age have the right to marry and to found a family, according to the
national laws governing the exercise of this right'. The limitation in the final clause
of Article 12 imposes on states a positive obligation to provide by law for marriage,
and to regulate its inception and its incidents, but leaves a wide discretion to the
state as to the kind of law which it puts in place to govern marriage, as long as the
law does not deny people the very essence of the right.

Thus the state is free to make rules preventing marriage on the basis of the current   **8.79**
marital status of the parties, and to make its own decision about whether or not to

---

[144] *Gillow v UK* Series A No 109 (1989) 11 EHRR 335. See also *Wiggins v UK* Application
7456/76 (report: 13 DR 40, EComHR).
[145] See, eg, *Chapman v UK* Application 27238/95 (2001) 33 EHRR 18.
[146] *South Buckinghamshire DC v Porter, Wrexham CBC v Berry, Chichester DC v Searle* [2003]
UKHL 26, [2003] 2 WLR 1547; *South Buckinghamshire DC v Secretary of State for Transport, Local
Government and the Regions* [2003] EWCA Civ 687, The Times, 23 May 2003.
[147] See eg *Malone v UK* Series A No 82 (1985) 7 EHRR 14; *Huvig v France* (1990) 12 EHRR 547;
Niemietz v Germany Series A No 251-B (1993) 16 EHRR 97; *Halford v UK* Application 20605/92
(1997) 24 EHRR 523 (unregulated interception of calls made by a serving police officer from work
violated Art 8). See also *Kopp v Switzerland* (1999) 27 EHRR 91; *Valenzuela Contreras v Spain*
(1999) 28 EHRR 483; *Amann v Switzerland* (2000) 30 EHRR 843.

make available a procedure to dissolve a marriage. The state must not exercise its power in such a way as to deprive a person of the very essence of the right to marry. Nevertheless, the right to marry does not imply a right to escape from marriage, and does not guarantee a right to marry more than once in a lifetime.[148] But there are limits to the state's discretion to prohibit remarriage. If a state allows divorce, and a divorce has been granted, the state is not permitted to impose on one of the parties a period of time during which he or she is not permitted to remarry. That would threaten the substance of the right to marry in countries where the state, by allowing a dissolution, has demonstrated that it does not intend to limit the parties to marriage on one occasion only.[149] Nor is a public authority allowed to prevent someone from marrying on public policy grounds, without clear legal authority, as this would devalue the right and deprive the person of its essence.[150]

8.80   In England, marriage traditionally meant the union of one woman and one man, for life, to the exclusion of all others. Although the provision for divorce by statute, and recognition of certain polygamous marriages celebrated abroad, has watered down the absolute nature of this commitment, the law still assumes that people are capable of having only one sex, which they retain throughout life, and which is identified exclusively by reference to the biological characteristics of genitalia, chromosomes, and hormones, at the time of birth.[151] This gives rise to special problems for transsexuals and people who cannot be unambiguously shown to be physically of either sex. Although English law does not impose any special impediments to obtaining gender reassignment therapy, neither has it so far been prepared to recognize therapy as changing a patient's legal status. A person who was registered as male at birth is not permitted to have that allocation of sex altered after treatment to replace the physical stigmata of manhood with those of womanhood, and vice versa. This can effectively prevent people from marrying the partners of their choice. Section 11 of the Matrimonial Causes Act 1973 provides that a marriage is void if the parties to it are not respectively 'male and female'. This is interpreted as referring to biological sex, not socially constructed gender.[152] Because this is likely to prevent people from marrying anyone whom they would like to marry, the ECtHR and the House of Lords have held that English law is incompatible with the right of transsexuals to marry.[153] The government has published a draft Bill for consultation in 2003, and has introduced remedial legislation to Parliament in the 2003–04 session (the Gender Recognition Bill).

---

[148] *Johnston v Ireland* Series A No 112 (1987) 9 EHRR 203.

[149] *F v Switzerland* Series A No 128 (1988) 10 EHRR 411.

[150] *R (on the application of Crown Prosecution Service) v Registrar-General of Births, Deaths and Marriages* [2002] EWCA Civ 1661, [2003] 2 WLR 504 (no power to prevent person charged with offence from marrying prosecution witness, despite this resulting in the witness no longer being compellable).

[151] *Corbett v Corbett (No 1)* [1971] P 83.

[152] *Bellinger v Bellinger* [2003] UKHL 21; [2003] 2 WLR 1174.

[153] *Goodwin v UK* Application 28957/95 (2002) 35 EHRR 18; *Bellinger v Bellinger*, ibid.

(2) The Right to Found a Family

The right to found a family under Article 12 ECHR is primarily one imposing a **8.81**
negative duty of non-interference on the state. If the right to found a family were
to be treated as giving rise to positive obligations on the state, it could impose significant economic, medical and social responsibilities on society. For example, if
founding a family is taken to include child-rearing, the right might in appropriate
circumstances include pre-natal, obstetric, neo-natal and post-natal care and support, from medical services, social services, and through the social security system.
For infertile couples, there might be a right to assisted reproduction, unless there
were Convention-compliant reasons for denying the service to them. This would
not be impossible, but would probably be best examined under Article 8 (the right
to respect for family life) which would provide express criteria in Article 8(2) for
deciding whether the state was acting properly. Already under Article 8 prison authorities have a duty to adopt a reasonable policy in relation to allowing male inmates to donate sperm for the purpose of artificially inseminating their partners
outside the prison, as well as the usual administrative law duty when applying a
policy to be willing to consider whether each case has individual circumstances
taking it outside the policy.[154]

Adoption provides one means of founding a family. At the same time, adoption **8.82**
brings to an end the parental responsibilities of the natural parents, bringing into
play their right to respect for family life under Article 8 where a child in the care
of a local authority is placed for adoption without the agreement of the natural
parents. The law must resolve potential conflicts between prospective adoptive
parents and natural parents. Article 12 does not require any particular system of
adoption, nor recognition of foreign adoption orders.[155] This is another area better dealt with in the light of the standards of Article 8 than under Article 12.

Founding a family by IVF is regulated by the Human Fertilisation and Embryology **8.83**
Authority under the Human Fertilisation and Embryology Act 1990. The Act sets
out the circumstances in which gametes or embryos may be stored or used for the
purpose of allowing a woman to give birth to a child. The Act is designed to protect
the interests of all those involved in the process, including the mother, the child,
other members of the family, and the sperm donor. In order to protect the interests
of the sperm donor in controlling the use to be made of his genetic material, licences for storing and using gametes and embryos under the Act require the user to
ensure that gametes are used only if their donor has consented in writing to their

---

[154] *R (on the application of Mellor) v Secretary of State for the Home Department* [2001] EWCA Civ
742; [2002] QB 13.
[155] *X and Y v UK* Application 7229/75 (1977) 12 DR 32; *X v Netherlands* Application 8896/80
(1981) 24 DR 176. However, the position might be different if the matter were relitigated now.

use after proper counselling, and has not withdrawn that consent.[156] The Human Fertilisation and Embryology Authority in its discretion under the Act imposes further requirements (which it is free to vary or waive in particular cases) as conditions of a licence.[157]

H. Freedom of Thought, Conscience and Religion

8.84   A number of provisions in the HRA 1998 and the ECHR protect freedom of belief. The primary source of protection is Article 9 ECHR, which provides:

1. Everyone has the right to freedom of thought, conscience and religion; this right includes freedom to change his religion or belief and freedom, either alone or in community with others and in public or private, to manifest his religion and belief, in worship, teaching, practice and observance.
2. Freedom to manifest one's religion or beliefs shall be subject only to such limitations as are prescribed by law and are necessary in a democratic society in the interests of public safety, for the protection of public order, health or morals, or for the protection of the rights and freedoms of others.

8.85   Article 9(1) contains a general freedom of thought, conscience and religion. The paragraph then specifies certain sub-sets of that general freedom: (a) the freedom to change one's religion or belief; and (b) the freedom to manifest one's religion or belief. The only part of the freedom which a public authority may be permitted to limit is subset (b), freedom to manifest a religion or belief. Limitation here is permitted because behaviour in the face of other people, or in circumstances which affect the community, may legitimately be regarded as bringing conflicting rights and interests into play. Even in that area, any limitation of the freedom must meet the requirements of Article 9(2).

8.86   Other rights which support the freedom include the right to respect for private life under Article 8 (outlined in section F of this chapter), the right to hold and express opinions under Article 10, freedom of peaceful association and assembly under Article 11, the right to educate one's children according to one's philosophical convictions under Article 2 of Protocol 1 to the ECHR, and the right under Article 14 to be free from discrimination in the enjoyment of those rights. In this section, we concentrate mainly on the rights and freedoms under Article 9. Nevertheless, it is noteworthy that this is a context in which the right not to be discriminated against, under Article 14 taken together with Article 9, may require people of different religions to be treated differently if the application of the same rule to all results in people of some religions being disadvantaged in a way that is

---

[156] Human Fertilisation and Embryology Act 1990, Sch 3.
[157] On this, see *R v Human Fertilisation and Embryology Authority, ex p Blood* [1999] Fam 151, CA.

not objectively and rationally justifiable.[158] As Professor Christopher McCrudden points out, this means that Article 14 confers a right to be free of indirect, as well as direct, discrimination here.[159]

(1) Freedoms Which are Unqualified and Cannot be Limited

As noted above, Article 9 ECHR permits no limitation of freedom of thought and conscience, or of freedom to change one's religion or belief. Only the freedom to manifest a religion or belief may be limited under Article 9(2). Thought, conscience and religion are broadly and inclusively interpreted, encompassing a wide range of belief and value systems going well beyond the major, recognized religions and philosophies.[160] The law and public authorities must ensure that people are not subject to religious indoctrination by the state.[161] People who are not members of a church must not be subject to a tax the revenue of which goes to support that church.[162] A person must not be required to manifest a religion or belief other than his or her own, for example by taking an oath, in order to qualify for public office.[163]

8.87

However, the range of matters of conscience falling under Article 9(1) is not infinite. It does not cover purely charitable or political opinions, beliefs, or activities,[164] which may instead fall to be assessed under Articles 10 and 11. Nor does it protect all individual judgments on moral matters, such as a belief in the desirability of euthanasia or assisted suicide.[165] It seems that a judgment must be an integral part of some ethical or religious system if it is to be protected by Article 9. Other ethical positions fall to be protected, if at all, by Article 8 or, in the context of education, Article 2 of Protocol 1. Furthermore, Article 9(1) does not prohibit all state involvement in religious affairs. It is permissible for a state to have an established religion,[166] such as the Church of England. The state may also take on a role in regulating religions more generally, in order to avoid the disorder which

8.88

---

[158] *Thlimmenos v Greece* Application 34369/97 (2001) 31 EHRR 15.

[159] See ch 11 below.

[160] See, eg, the EComHR decisions: *Arrowsmith v UK* (1978) 19 DR 5 (pacifism); *X and Church of Scientology v Sweden* (1979) 16 DR 68 (Scientology); *Omkarananda and the Divine Light Zentrum v Switzerland* (1981) 25 DR 105 (Divine Light Zentrum); *Chappell v UK* (1987) 53 DR 241 (Druidism); *H v UK* Application 18187/91 (1993) 16 EHRR CD44 (veganism), and *Iskcon v UK* (1994) 76A DR 90 (the Krishna consciousness movement).

[161] *Angelini v Sweden* (1986) 51 DR 1, EComHR.

[162] *Darby v Sweden (merits)* Application 11581/85, EComHR, report of 9 May 1989: violation of Art 9. There was legislative provision for exempting dissenters resident in Sweden from the tax. As the applicant was resident in Finland, he had also suffered discrimination in violation of Art 14 taken together with Art 9.

[163] *Buscarini v San Marino* Application 24645/94 (2000) 30 EHRR 208.

[164] See eg *McFeeley v UK* Application 8317/78 (1981) 3 EHRR 161, EComHR; *Socialist Party v Turkey* (1999) 27 EHRR 51.

[165] See *Pretty v UK* Application 2346/02 (2002) 35 EHRR 1.

[166] *Darby v Sweden (admissibility)* Application 11581/85 (decision of 11 April 1988, EComHR).

may follow from splits in or conflicts between religious groups. However, it would be incompatible with Article 9(1) for a public authority to try to determine which beliefs are valid when deciding which groups should benefit from legal recognition.[167] Such an interference with freedom of thought and religion, when it has nothing to do with the manifestation of religion or belief, would not be justifiable under Article 9(2). Public authorities need to exercise their functions in the same way in respect of the established and non-established religious groups alike if they are to avoid a charge of arbitrariness.[168] Even where the state's functions are limited to regulating the manifestation of religions and beliefs and have a legitimate aim under Article 9(2), the steps taken must be proportionate to the aim pursued if they are to be justifiable.[169]

(2) *Manifestation of Religion or Beliefs*

8.89   If the concepts of thought, conscience and religion have been given wide meanings, the idea of a manifestation of religion or belief is less extensively interpreted. An activity counts as a manifestation of religion or beliefs only if it is either an act of witness to the religion or beliefs (such as participating in an act of worship) or is actually required by the religion or beliefs in question (such as a member of an evangelical religion attempting to persuade others to accept its truth,[170] or a Jew eating kosher food[171]). Other decisions as to the best course of action, although taken in the light of religious or other beliefs, are not treated as a manifestation of them. For example, it does not violate Article 9 to discipline a school pupil for refusing to take part in a parade of which the pupil and his or her parents disapprove on grounds related to religion if participation is not prohibited by the religion.[172] Similarly, it has been denied that prohibiting corporal punishment in all schools, including religious schools, violates any right under Article 9 of members of a fundamentalist Christian sect to have their children educated in accordance with their belief, based on biblical texts, that corporal punishment is a desirable form of discipline,[173] although threatening a pupil with corporal punishment may violate the right of a parent, under Article 2 of Protocol 1, who disapproves of such discipline to have their child educated in accordance with the parent's philosophical convictions.[174]

---

[167]   *Manoussakis v Greece* (1997) 23 EHRR 387.

[168]   *Metropolitan Church of Bessarabia v Moldova* Application 45701/99 (2002) 35 EHRR 13.

[169]   *Serif v Greece* Application 38178/97 (2001) 31 EHRR 20.

[170]   *Kokkinakis v Greece* Series A No 260-A (1994) 17 EHRR 397 (Jehovah's Witness attempting to evangelize).

[171]   *Cha'are Shalom Ve Tsedek v France* Application 27417/95 (2000) 9 BHRC 27.

[172]   *Efstratiou v Greece, Valsamis v Greece* (18 December 1996, Reports 1996-V, ECtHR).

[173]   *R (on the application of Williamson) v Secretary of State for Education and Employment* [2002] EWCA Civ 1926; [2003] 1 All ER 385 *per* Buxton LJ; cf the judgments of Rix and Arden L JJ. The HL has given leave to appeal.

[174]   *Campbell and Cosans v UK* Series A No 48 (1982) 2 EHRR 293.

Even if there is a limitation of the right to manifest one's religion or beliefs, it may **8.90** be justifiable if it is prescribed by law and necessary in a democratic society (ie, a proportionate response to a pressing social need) to achieve one of the legitimate aims listed in Article 9(2). When assessing the need for a limitation, and its proportionality, the social and institutional context is significant. For example, in view of the need for strict discipline within an hierarchical structure in the armed forces it may be necessary and proportionate to prohibit members of the forces from trying to convert each other, yet be a disproportionate limitation of the right to manifest their religion to prevent them from evangelizing among civilians.[175]

However, even in those areas where the state is permitted to limit the freedom **8.91** under Article 9, the HRA 1998 gives special protection to the Article 9 rights of religious organizations, and their members when acting collectively rather than individually, against abridgement by courts when deciding questions relevant to litigation. Section 13 provides:

(1) If a court's determination of any question arising under this Act might affect the exercise by a religious organisation of the Convention right to freedom of thought, conscience and religion, it must have particular regard to the importance of that right.
(2) In this section 'court' includes a tribunal.

It is not clear what it means to 'have particular regard to the importance' of a right, but the same formulation appears in s 12 of the Act in relation to freedom of expression. It seems likely to mean that Article 9 must be very carefully considered and given great weight when interpreting legislation and scrutinizing the legality of administrative action, but not that it should necessarily have greater weight than other Convention rights if they conflict.

This provision covers all aspects of Article 9 rights. On the other hand, in some **8.92** ways it is very limited in its scope. It applies only in the course of litigation in courts and tribunals. It is concerned only with the exercise of Article 9 rights by 'religious organizations' and their members acting collectively, so it does not entitle them to be protected against being offended by other people's exercise of Article 9 rights (since it is not a natural use of language to speak of a right being 'exercised' passively). It does not attempt to elevate the rights under Article 9 above other Convention rights.

Despite its restricted scope, s 13 of the HRA 1998 may present significant prob- **8.93** lems of compatibility in one respect. If the exercise of Article 9 rights by a religious organization conflicts with the exercise of Article 9 rights by a non-religious organization or by an individual, s 13 might be regarded as requiring a court to give greater weight to the Article 9 rights of the religious organization than to those of

---

[175] *Larissis v Greece* (1999) 27 EHRR 329.

a secular belief-based organization or individual. If s 13 has that effect, it would be a clear example of discrimination on the ground of religion or belief. Unless the difference in treatment could be shown to be objectively and rationally justified, and proportionate to a legitimate state aim, it would give rise to a violation of Article 14 taken together with Article 9. This might result in the embarrassing spectacle of a court having to make a declaration of incompatibility, under s 4 of the HRA 1998, in respect of s 13 of the same Act. However, the terms of s 13 are sufficiently vague to make it possible for a court to read and give effect to it in a Convention-compatible way, avoiding unjustified discrimination, in reliance on s 3 of the Act.

9

POLITICAL RIGHTS

A. Introduction

This chapter examines the impact of a number of rights, particularly important for **9.01** conducting political activities, on public administration and policy-making. The rights in question are: the right to freedom of expression, guaranteed by ECHR Article 10 of the European Convention on Human Rights (ECHR); the right to freedom of peaceful assembly and association, guaranteed by Article 11; and the right to free elections, as recognized by Article 3 of Protocol 1 to the ECHR. Through common law, the Human Rights Act 1998 (HRA) and ordinary legislation, they provide standards against which public authorities' decision-making must be judged. These rights are special, for two reasons. First, they do not only restrict the discretion of public authorities. To a considerable degree, the legitimacy of the work of public authorities depends on their respect for these rights. Democratic approval and democratic accountability are two of the supports for the legitimacy of all public decision-making. For a democracy to function satisfactorily, people must be free to participate in politics, and must have access to information about the political process, public affairs, and society generally. They must also be free to express their views, and to join others to advance their aims. The rights examined in this chapter help to guarantee these necessary conditions.

9.02 The rights in question, and particularly freedom of expression, can be used in a large number of different settings and for many purposes. Expressing one's self is a part of most private, commercial and social activities, as well as public and political ones. The main foci of this chapter are positive protections for the rights in relation to public and political activities, and restrictions on the freedom of public authorities to interfere with the rights in any setting.

9.03 English law has a long tradition of protecting freedom of expression. At common law, the need to prevent the threat of actions for defamation producing an undue constraint on free discussion led the courts to take account of the standards of the ECHR before the HRA 1998. The importance of freedom of expression (particularly for political debate) has been well understood, although it has never been seen as an absolute right (except in Parliament). Parliament has made major incursions on the freedom through legislation intended to achieve a variety of purposes, including combating racist abuse, maintaining public order and morality, protecting national security, protecting consumers against misleading advertising or intrusive marketing techniques, and securing political impartiality and good taste in the broadcast media. The common law has also restricted the freedom in order to preserve public order, uphold standards of taste and decency, and limit offence to certain religious beliefs.

9.04 Freedoms of peaceful assembly and association have also been long recognized in English law, but have been even more prone to restriction in order to protect public order and commercial interests. The right to operate trade unions (which mainly concerns private law, and so lies outside the scope of this volume) was slow to be accepted. Freedom of assembly has been limited by the shortage of locations in England and Wales where people are entitled to gather publicly, coupled with the draconian nature of the private law of trespass (linked to the near-absolute nature of many real property rights). Legislation has further restricted freedom of assembly in order to maintain public order and control people's behaviour in spaces that are accessible to the public.

9.05 The right to free elections was the result of a long struggle, and is protected by statute, both under ordinary English law and under Article 3 of Protocol 1 to the ECHR. It guarantees the minimum formal conditions for the operation of the United Kingdom's system of representative, parliamentary democracy.

Section B of this chapter explains the scope of the interests protected in relation to   **9.06**
freedom of expression. Section C looks at a number of restrictions on the freedom
in English law. Section D deals with protected interests in relation to freedom of
peaceful assembly and association (imposing positive as well as negative obligations on public authorities), and section E outlines the permitted restrictions.
Section F looks at the way in which the right to free elections is protected.

B. The Protection of Freedom of Expression[1]

(1) Freedom of Expression at Common Law and Under the Human Rights Act 1998

In English law, people have always been free to express themselves as they wish,   **9.07**
unless the freedom has been abridged by a rule of law. The same could be said of
any other activity. But recently, courts have begun to see freedom of expression as
having a special status as a 'constitutional right' in English law. The idea of constitutional rights is hard to pin down, given the amorphous quality of much of the
constitution, but the special status of the right has been manifested in three ways.
First, the right is available to all, regardless of their legal status or disabilities. Even
prisoners can assert the right, although the way in which it is exercised may be regulated to accommodate competing interests in the secure and efficient operation
of prisons and other institutions. Secondly, the right must be respected whenever
it is relevant, so that restrictions can be imposed on expression only if a compelling
need exists to restrict it. For example, in judicial review proceedings the importance of the freedom has to be factored into a court's judgment as to whether the
interference with the freedom is reasonable. Thirdly, although Parliament may
take away the right (or authorize others to take it away), it can do so only by clear
and unambiguous provisions.[2]

These developments have been strengthened by the passing of the HRA 1998,   **9.08**
making Article 10 ECHR part of English law. One beneficial effect of Article 10
is to provide (in Article 10(2)) a set of criteria allowing systematic evaluation of
purported justifications for interfering with the freedom.

Article 10, which now forms part of national law by virtue of the HRA 1998, pro-   **9.09**
vides:

1. Everyone has the right to freedom of expression. This right shall include freedom to hold opinions and to receive and impart information and ideas without
   interference by public authority and regardless of frontiers. This Article shall not

---

[1] See Richard Clayton and Hugh Tomlinson, *The Law of Human Rights* (Oxford: OUP, 2000)
vol 1, ch 15.
[2] *R v Secretary of State for the Home Department, ex p Simms* [2000] 2 AC 115, HL.

prevent States from requiring the licensing of broadcasting, television or cinema enterprises.

2. The exercise of these freedoms, since it carries with it duties and responsibilities, may be subject to such formalities, conditions, restrictions or penalties as are prescribed by law and are necessary in a democratic society, in the interests of national security, territorial integrity or public safety, for the prevention of disorder or crime, for the protection of health or morals, for the protection of the reputation or rights of others, for preventing the disclosure of information received in confidence, or for maintaining the authority and impartiality of the judiciary.

9.10   The structure of Article 10 requires a public authority to decide, first, whether its activities or decisions affect freedom of expression as defined in Article 10(1). If they do, the authority must ensure that any interference with the right is justified by reference to the criteria set out in Article 10(2), unless (as provided by s 6(2) of the HRA 1998) primary legislation requires the authority to act in a way that cannot be justified under that paragraph.

(2)   The Interests Protected by Article 10(1) ECHR

9.11   The European Court of Human Rights (ECtHR) has always stressed the importance of freedom of expression to liberal-democratic society. Discussion and disagreement, even about fundamental values, is assumed to be healthy and in need of protection. The expression of both unpopular and popular ideas is protected.

> Subject to paragraph 2 of Article 10, it [Article 10(1)] is applicable not only to 'information' or 'ideas' that are favourably received or regarded as inoffensive but also to those that offend, shock or disturb the state or any sector of the population. Such are the demands of pluralism, tolerance and broadmindedness without which there is no 'democratic society'.[3]

(a)   What is 'expression'?

9.12   Article 10(1) encompasses any action or inaction intended to have expressive content. Communicative acts and publications clearly fall within Article 10(1). Artistic works, including films, are covered, although licensing of cinema is permitted under Article 10(1).[4] Membership of a political party and participating in a demonstration (even if it obstructs people who are going lawfully about their business) are expressive acts, because they allow people to identify themselves publicly with a viewpoint and to work to implement it. Without this, the freedom to hold and express opinions would be empty.[5] In protecting the incidental rights

---

[3] *Handyside v UK* Series A No 24 (1979–80) 1 EHRR 737 at [49].
[4] *Müller v Switzerland* Series A No 133 (1991) 13 EHRR 212; *Chorherr v Austria* Series A No 266-B (1994) 17 EHRR 358; *Otto-Preminger Institut v Austria* Series A No 295-A (1995) 19 EHRR 34.
[5] *Vogt v Germany* Series A No 323 (1996) 21 EHRR 205 (membership of, and acting as prospective candidate for, German Communist Party); *Steel v UK* (1999) 28 EHRR 603 (anti-road-building protesters); *Hashman and Harrap v UK* Application 25594/94 (2000) 30 EHRR 241 (hunt saboteurs).

necessary to make freedom of expression effective, Article 10(1) overlaps to some extent with freedom of peaceful assembly and association under Article 11 ECHR. The right to communicate coupled with the right to receive information and ideas mean that Article 10(1) protects the publication of material even if the government considers the publication to be prejudicial to national security.[6]

(b) The special value of scrutiny and criticism of public authorities and politicians

All these forms of expression are protected, whether the motivation of the person exercising the freedom is personal, commercial, or political.[7] The importance of allowing the news media to investigate possible miscarriages of justice, and to keep under scrutiny conditions in prisons and other closed institutions, is reflected in England in decisions holding that prisoners are entitled to contact journalists directly by way of an interview if they have a good reason for doing so, and a prison policy of allowing such contact only in exceptional circumstances gives insufficient weight to the right under Article 10(1) ECHR to be a justifiable intrusion on it under Article 10(2).[8] But, because of the importance of free expression in a democracy, political expression is particularly strongly protected, especially if the speaker is seeking elective office[9] or is already a member of a legislative body.[10] Criticism of government, even if expressed in insulting terms, is seen as part and parcel of democratic politics, so 'interferences with the freedom of expression of an opposition member of parliament, like the applicant, call for the closest scrutiny on the part of the Court'.[11] Political opposition to government in general deserves specially strong protection, because in a liberal democracy 'a person opposed to official ideas and positions must be able to find a place in the political arena'.[12] In addition, there is a strong public interest in openly debating many issues which are of public concern without being the subject of party-political controversy, and Article 10 protects contributions to the debate as extensively as purely political debate.[13] Scrutiny of the behaviour of politicians generally is regarded as sufficiently important to

9.13

---

[6] *Vereinigung Demokratische Soldaten Österreich and Gubi v Austria* Series A No 302 (1995) 20 EHRR 56; *Vereniging Weekblad Bluf! v Netherlands* Series A No 306-A (1995) 20 EHRR 189.

[7] On commercial expression, see eg *Markt intern Verlag v Germany* Series A No 165 (1990) 12 EHRR 161; *Casado Coca v Spain* Series A No 285-A (1994) 18 EHRR 1.

[8] *R v Secretary of State for the Home Department, ex p Simms* [2000] 2 AC 115, HL; *R (on the application of Hirst) v Secretary of State for the Home Department* [2002] EWHC 602, [2002] 1 WLR 2929, Elias J.

[9] *Vogt v Germany* Series A No 323 (1996) 21 EHRR 205.

[10] *Castells v Spain* Series A No 236 (1992) 14 EHRR 445; *A v UK* Application 35373/97 (2003) 36 EHRR 51.

[11] *Castells*, ibid at [42].

[12] *Piermont v France* Series A No 314 (1995) 20 EHRR 301 at [76].

[13] See, eg, *Thorgeirson v Iceland* Series A No 239 (1992) 14 EHRR 843 at [64] (allegations that police had mistreated people); *Hertel v Switzerland* Application 25181/94 (1999) 28 EHRR 534 (scientific information about possible dangers of cooking food in microwave ovens); *Bladet Tromsø and Stensaas v Norway* Application 21980/93 (2000) 29 EHRR 125 (reports of inhumane methods used in culling seals).

make it unjustifiable to prevent the media from publishing relevant details of politicians' activities, including photographs.[14] In English law, this is recognized in several ways. For example, public bodies such as local authorities are not entitled to sue for defamation, because of the overriding public interest in not inhibiting criticism of governmental bodies.[15] Individual politicians and other public figures can sue for libel, but may be met with a defence of qualified privilege if the defendant is a newspaper or media organization, the defamatory publication relates to the claimant's public role, the journalist and publisher act responsibly (for example by checking the reliability of information as far as possible) and fairly, the publication is appropriate in tone and timing, and so on. This common law defence, which is based on a 'need to know' on the part of the people who are informed and a duty to inform on the part of the publisher, is extended to journalists because of their special responsibility for informing the public about political, governmental and related matters and for scrutinizing the conduct of public figures in order to facilitate the maintenance of the conditions for democratic accountability.[16] In order to avoid imposing a disproportionate chill on investigative journalism and freedom of the press, the courts have also progressively extended their power to limit the damages awarded by juries in defamation actions in the light of the requirements of Article 10.[17]

(c) Limitations

9.14   The freedom under Article 10(1) has certain limitations contained in the ECHR itself. As Article 10(2) points out, the exercise of the freedom 'carries with it duties and responsibilities'. Apart from the balancing exercise required under Article 10(2) itself, Articles 16 and 17 ECHR are directly relevant to the limits on the scope of Article 10(1). Article 16 states: 'Nothing in Articles 10, 11 and 14 shall be regarded as preventing the High Contracting Parties from imposing restrictions on the political activities of aliens'. In other words, nationals of other states do not enjoy freedom of political expression under Article 10. Public authorities are permitted to restrict their freedom of political expression, and (it has been held) to exclude people from the country if the purpose of their proposed entry is to make political (not just party-political) speeches.[18] In addition, Article 17 provides:

---

[14] *Nilsen and Johnsen v Denmark,* ECHR 1999-VII at [52]; *Krone Verlag GmbH & Co KG v Austria* Application 34315/96 (2003) 36 EHRR 57 at [37].

[15] *Derbyshire CC v Times Newspapers Ltd* [1993] AC 534, HL.

[16] *Reynolds v Times Newspapers Ltd* [2001] 2 AC 127, HL; *Loutchansky v Times Newspapers Ltd (No 1)* [2001] EWCA Civ 536, [2002] QB 321.

[17] See *Tolstoy Miloslavsky v UK* Series A No 316-B (1995) 20 EHRR 442, and in English courts see eg *John v MGN Ltd* [1997] QB 586, CA; *Kiam v MGN Ltd* [2002] EWCA Civ 43, [2003] QB 281; and, on principles governing damages for defamation more generally, *Grobbelaar v News Group Newspapers Ltd* [2002] UKHL 40, [2002] 1 WLR 3024.

[18] *R (on the application of Farrakhan) v Secretary of State for the Home Department* [2002] EWCA Civ 606; [2002] QB 1391.

> Nothing in this Convention may be interpreted as implying for any State, group or person any right to engage in any activity or perform any act aimed at the destruction of any of the rights and freedom set forth herein or at their limitation to a greater extent than is provided for in the Convention.

This is relevant both to the application of Article 16 and to the exercise by public authorities of the power to interfere with freedom of expression in accordance with the criteria set out in Article 10(2), whereby the interference, to be justifiable, must by 'prescribed by law', pursue one of the legitimate aims for a restriction exhaustively listed in Article 10(2), and be 'necessary in a democratic society' for that purpose.[19]

(3) Special Protections for Freedom of Expression in English Law

English public law offers special protection to freedom of expression in several contexts. These include: (1) the provisions relating specifically to the right in s 12 of the HRA 1998; (2) the protection for proceedings in Parliament under Article IX of the Bill of Rights 1688; (3) assistance to those who want to express political views during election campaigns and at similar times; (4) protection against coerced disclosure of journalists' working materials and the identity of their sources; and (5) certain free-speech duties on the part of higher education institutions. This section will concentrate on those. There are, in addition, other public law provisions such as the right to petition the monarch, under the Bill of Rights 1688, which are now of only historical significance; and some private law protections, such as the defences of justification (truth) and fair comment to actions for defamation, which lie outside the scope of this volume.[20]

9.15

(a) Protecting freedom of expression against abridgment in the course of litigation: s 12 of the Human Rights Act 1998

Section 12 was designed to protect the news media against having their activities frustrated by the development of new private rights on the back of Convention rights. There was particular concern about the scope for any new private law right of privacy interfering with the freedom of the press to investigate and publish reports on misbehaviour by people in the public eye. Among other things, the provisions of s 12(4) require courts, when considering whether to grant any relief which might affect the exercise of a right under Article 10 ECHR, to:

9.16

> have particular regard to the importance of the right to freedom of expression and, where the proceedings relate to material which the respondent claims, or which

---

[19] For a general account of the meaning of these terms, see *Sunday Times v UK* Series A No 30 (1979–80) 2 EHRR 245, and ch 7 above. On their application to Art 10(2) in particular, see section C of this chapter.

[20] See John Davies, in Peter Birks (ed), *English Private Law* (Oxford: OUP, 2000) paras 14.288–14.299.

appears to the court, to be journalistic, literary or artistic material (or to conduct connected with such material), to—

(a) the extent to which—
    (i)   the material has, or is about to, become available to the public; or
    (ii) it is, or would be, in the public interest for the material to be published;
(b) any relevant privacy code.

The effect of this is examined in chapter 19 below. Here, we may simply note that the provisions are of general application to all legal proceedings (private law proceedings as well as public law proceedings), and do not seek to elevate rights under Article 10 above other Convention rights, but probably make it more difficult to justify interfering with the Convention right under Article 10 to advance social or public interests.

(b) Protection for proceedings in Parliament: Article IX of the Bill of Rights 1688

9.17 The Bill of Rights 1688, Article IX, provides 'that the freedom of speech and debate or proceedings in Parliament ought not to be impeached or questioned in any court or place out of Parliament'. The scope of this provision is more fully considered elsewhere in this volume,[21] but the main effect is that members of the House of Commons and the House of Lords are free to say anything in Parliament without being called to account in the courts for what they say. For present purposes, it is important to note that, by virtue of s 3 of the HRA 1998, Article IX of the Bill of Rights must now be read and given effect by courts in a manner compatible with Convention rights. Article IX must also be read in the light of other provisions of the HRA 1998. For example, the 1998 Act sometimes requires courts to decide whether legislation is compatible with Convention rights. For that purpose, a court might have to decide whether the legislation serves a legitimate purpose, and whether it represents a fair balance between competing rights and interests. On the unusual occasions when it is relevant to a matter the court has to decide, the judges may look to *Hansard*, the official report of proceedings in Parliament, for indications as to Parliament's purpose in enacting the legislation. This does not 'call in question' proceedings in Parliament, even if the court ultimately declares that the legislation is incompatible with a Convention right. It merely allows the judges to understand the intention of Parliament, and to give effect as fairly as possible to the court's obligations under the HRA 1998.[22]

(c) Assistance to political expression during election campaigns and at similar times

9.18 In order to facilitate participation in the democratic political process, a range of measures offer special assistance to election candidates, political parties and

---

[21] See paras 2.111–2.117 above.
[22] *Wilson v First County Trust Ltd (No 2)* [2003] UKHL 40; [2003] 3 WLR 568.

others who wish to express political views. The assistance relates to meetings, postal communications, and broadcasts. First, candidates in parliamentary and local government elections are entitled to use rooms on premises used by schools or local authorities free of charge for holding election meetings. This right may be exercised at reasonable times between the day on which the election writ is received and the day before polling day.[23] Secondly, candidates in parliamentary and European Assembly elections are entitled to send one free postal communication to each elector in the constituency, or to have one unaddressed communication delivered free to each registered delivery point in the constituency.[24] Thirdly, broadcasting organizations may permit a political party registered with the Electoral Commission[25] to make party election broadcasts during the election campaign, subject to the broadcasting organization's obligations to ensure its impartiality and to comply with legal requirements for broadcasts to avoid unfairness and offensiveness.[26] Similar provisions now apply to organizations designated by the Electoral Commission as permitted participants in referendums.[27] The codes for broadcasters promulgated by OFCOM under the Communications Act 2003 must provide for a duty to carry certain party political broadcasts in accordance as long as they comply with the Political Parties, Elections and Referendums Act 2000.[28]

Political broadcasting is generally hedged about with restrictions. No political advertising, or advertising by a body whose purposes are wholly or mainly political, is to be permitted on the broadcast media.[29] This total ban may be incompatible with the right to freedom of expression under Article 10,[30] but Parliament has taken the view that the risk of incompatibility is justified, and the government's view is that the arguments for compatibility are stronger than those against.[31] The main justification is that there is statutory provision for party political broadcasts, and that control of other political broadcasting is required to prevent certain views receiving a disproportionate amount of airtime because they are supported by wealthy interests.

9.19

---

[23] Representation of the People Act 1983, ss 95 and 96, as amended by the Representation of the People Act 1985, Sch 4.

[24] Representation of the People Act 1983, s 97.

[25] Political Parties, Elections and Referendums Act 2000, s 37. The Electoral Commission is established under Pt I of that Act.

[26] *R (on the application of Prolife Alliance) v BBC* [2003] UKHL 23; [2003] 2 WLR 1403.

[27] Political Parties, Elections and Referendums Act 2000, ss 108, 110 and Sch 12.

[28] Communications Act 2003, s 333.

[29] ibid ss 319(2)(g), 321(2).

[30] See *VgT Verein Gegang Tierfabriken v Switzerland* Application 24699/94 (2002) 34 EHRR 4; cf *R v Radio Authority, ex p Bull* [1998] QB 294, CA and *R (on the application of Prolife Alliance) v BBC* [2003] UKHL 23; [2003] 2 WLR 1403.

[31] See Joint Committee on Human Rights, First Report of 2002–03, *Scrutiny of Bills: Progress Report* (HL Paper 24; HC 191) 9–10, esp para 15; Fourth Report of 2002–03, *Scrutiny of Bills: Further Progress Report* (HL Paper 50; HC 397) paras 40–41.

9.20   In another effort to prevent wealth being used to give one party a major advantage in putting across its election message, there are strict restrictions on the
amount a party can spend on an election campaign,[32] and expenditure by third
parties in support of or opposition to a candidate or party is normally limited
to £5.[33] This was held to be an unjustifiable interference with the freedom of
expression of third parties in supporting their preferred candidate, violating
Article 10,[34] so the law was amended. Under the current law, a third party may
notify the Electoral Commission and become a 'recognised third party', entitled to spend very significant amounts of money (up to £793,500 during a general election campaign in England) as long as he or she complies with the
requirements of the legislation relating to the filing of accounts and related financial controls.[35]

**(d) Protection against coerced disclosure of journalists' working materials and
the identity of their sources**

9.21   The common law did not confer any privilege allowing journalists to refuse to
provide information or evidence in the course of legal proceedings or criminal investigations, even if it involved divulging the source of information obtained in
confidence.[36] However, s 10 of the Contempt of Court Act 1981 provides:

> No court may require a person to disclose, nor is any person guilty of contempt for
> refusing to disclose, the source of information contained in a publication for which
> he is responsible, unless it be established to the satisfaction of the court that disclo-
> sure is necessary in the interests of justice or national security or for the prevention
> of disorder or crime.

The section attempts to strike a balance between, on the one hand, the public interest in journalists and other authors being able to secure information by assur-
ing their sources of anonymity and freedom from reprisal, and, on the other hand,
competing public interests. It provides for the interest in freedom of information
to be overridden only in order to secure the public interests in justice, national security, and prevention of disorder or crime, and then only if it is *necessary* to override the source's anonymity in order to secure one of the specified objectives. The
exceptions were drafted to be consistent with Article 10(2), and are capable of
being applied in a compatible manner.

9.22   This proved prescient, as the ECtHR later decided that Article 10 requires protection for journalists' confidential sources, and further held that in at least one case

---

[32] Political Parties, Elections and Referendums Act 2000, ss 72–84 and Sch 9.
[33] Representation of the People Act 1983, s 75.
[34] *Bowman v UK* (1998) 26 EHRR 1.
[35] Political Parties, Elections and Referendums Act 2000, ss 88–100 and Schs 10 and 11.
[36] See *AG v Mulholland and Foster* [1963] 2 QB 477, CA; *British Steel Corp v Granada Television
Ltd* [1981] AC 1096, HL.

the section had not been applied in such a way as to comply with the obligations of Article 10, because too little weight had been given to the interest in a free press and too much to the interests of justice.[37] Now courts will order journalists to disclose sources only in exceptional cases, for example where all other methods of discovering the source of a leak have failed, there is a real danger of further leaks, there was an urgent need to act to protect an important interest, such as patient confidentiality, and the damage to the claimant from not stopping the leak would be very severe.[38]

In criminal investigations, procedural protection was given in the Police and Criminal Evidence Act 1984 (PACE). Sections 11 to 14 of the Act, and Sch 1, provide a partial shield against enforced disclosure of 'journalistic material' on a search under a warrant issued ex parte. Journalistic material is defined as material acquired or created for the purposes of journalism which is in the possession of a person who himself acquired or created it for that purpose.[39] All 'journalistic material' became either excluded material (if it is held in confidence and consists of documents or other records)[40] or special procedure material (if it is not held in confidence, or is in any other form).[41] No search warrant can normally be granted in respect of such material.[42] In relation to most investigations, the police now have to apply to a circuit judge for an order for access or production rather than a warrant, and the procedure requires notice of the application to be given to the person holding the material, who can argue at an inter partes hearing before a circuit judge that the access conditions are not met.[43]

9.23

There are three exceptions:

9.24

- cases where a warrant can properly be issued under PACE, Sch 1, para 12;
- investigations into terrorist offences and drugtrafficking offences, where a circuit judge may make an order for access to or production of material or issue a warrant ex parte even in respect of excluded material, without the need to comply with the special conditions under PACE, Sch 1, para 12;[44]

---

[37] *Goodwin v UK* Application 17488/90 (1996) 22 EHRR 123, arising out of the decision in *X Ltd v Morgan Grampian (Publishers) Ltd* [1991] 1 AC 1, HL.

[38] See *Ashworth Hospital Authority v MGN Ltd* [2002] UKHL 29, [2002] 1 WLR 2033, which was held to be such a case; *Interbrew SA v Financial Times Ltd* [2002] EWCA Civ 274, [2002] 2 Lloyd's Rep 229; and *Mersey Care NHS Trust v Ackroyd* [2003] EWCA Civ 663, The Times, 21 May 2003 (journalist should be given opportunity to assert privilege at a full hearing, and summary judgment should not be given on the claim for disclosure).

[39] PACE 1984, s 13(1), (2).

[40] ibid s 11(1)(c).

[41] ibid s 14(1)(b).

[42] ibid s 9.

[43] ibid Sch 1.

[44] See paras 9.25 et seq below.

- before the HRA 1998 came into force, it was held that warrants issued in Scotland, where the procedures for protecting journalistic material do not apply, and backed for execution in England and Wales,[45] allowed the police to evade the protection normally available in England and Wales under PACE.[46] This may sometimes fail to secure the protection for journalists' sources required by Article 10 ECHR. In such cases, an officer exercising his or her discretion to execute a warrant in that way would now be acting unlawfully under s 6 of the HRA 1998.

9.25 Disclosure of journalistic material will not be ordered, nor a warrant granted, unless one of the sets of access conditions is satisfied. Where the journalistic material is special procedure material (which is, in this context, journalistic material which does not consist of documents held in confidence), disclosure can be ordered under the 'first set of access conditions', ie those under Sch 1, para 2, in cases where before PACE no search warrant could have been obtained, because there was no provision for granting warrants in respect of the offences. For this purpose, it is necessary to show (inter alia) that the public interest would be served by an order requiring access to the material. (This is not necessary under the second set of access conditions, which apply where, before PACE, a search warrant could have been granted.) The case law under PACE before the HRA 1998 came into force made it seem likely that the public interest would nearly always be served by requiring access where it is likely (in the words PACE, Sch 1, para 1) to be relevant evidence of, or of substantial value to an investigation relating to, a serious arrestable offence. However, if the interest in bringing offenders to justice were absolute, the requirement to consider the public interest would be redundant, as adding nothing to the other access conditions. In addition, there would be a danger of violating the rights of media under Article 10 ECHR in a case where the order had a chilling effect on the gathering, imparting and receiving of information about current affairs. To give effect to Article 10 and the HRA 1998, the types of consideration which are relevant to s 10 of the Contempt of Court Act 1981, above, should be applied under the first set of access conditions under PACE, Sch 1.

9.26 The second set of access conditions, contained in PACE, Sch 1, para 3, applies to all journalistic material, whether held in confidence (thus qualifying as so-called 'excluded material' under the 1984 Act) or not. The second set of access conditions is satisfied if:

- there are reasonable grounds for believing that there is material which consists of or includes excluded material or special procedure material (but does not include items subject to legal privilege) on specified premises; and

---

[45] Summary Jurisdiction (Process) Act 1881, s 4.
[46] *R v Manchester Stipendiary Magistrate, ex p Granada Television Ltd* [2001] 1 AC 300, HL.

- but for the prohibition in PACE, s 9 on issuing search warrants for such material, a search of the premises for that material could have been authorized by a warrant issued to a constable under an enactment other than Sch 1 to the 1984 Act itself; and
- the issue of such a warrant would have been appropriate.

(e) Free-speech duties of higher-education institutions

The governing bodies of higher educational institutions maintained by, or substantially dependent on assistance from, the Higher Education Funding Council for England or the Further Education Funding Council for England (including colleges of education) are required to take 'such steps as are reasonably practicable to ensure that freedom of speech within the law is secured for members, students and employees of the establishment and for visiting speakers'.[47] The duty of the governing bodies of institutions is expressed to include, in particular, 'the duty to ensure, so far as is reasonably practicable, that the use of any premises of the establishment is not denied to any individual or body of persons on any ground connected with—(*a*) the beliefs or views of that individual or of any member of that body; or (*b*) the policy or objectives of that body'.[48] In *R v University of Liverpool, ex p Caesar-Gordon*,[49] the Divisional Court held that the duty was local to the University and its premises. The governing body need not take into consideration persons and places outside its control. It was therefore ultra vires for the university to take account of the risk of disorder elsewhere when imposing restrictions on a political meeting on campus. Such matters are the concern of the police, not educational institutions. **9.27**

On the other hand, the court in the same case decided that it was lawful to ban publicity until the morning of the meeting, to require that those attending should be able to produce a valid student or staff card, and to reserve the right to charge the organizers of the meeting for the cost of maintaining security at the meeting. Thus governing bodies have considerable discretion in order to secure the necessary conditions for free speech at the meeting and elsewhere on campus. **9.28**

A code of practice is to be issued and kept up to date by the governing body, setting out the procedures to be followed and standards of conduct to be observed in relation to the organization and conduct of meetings,[50] and every person and body concerned in the government of the establishment is under a duty to take such steps as are reasonably practicable to ensure that the code is complied with, including the institution of disciplinary measures where appropriate.[51] **9.29**

---

[47] Education (No 2) Act 1986, s 43(1).
[48] ibid s 43(2).
[49] [1991] 1 QB 124, DC.
[50] Education (No 2) Act 1986, s 43(3).
[51] ibid s 43(4).

(f) Freedom of information

9.30 The close link between access to information and the ability to safeguard one's welfare and identity, protected by Article 8 ECHR, has already been noted in chapter 8 above. But access to information also contributes to freedom of expression, and particularly to the maintenance of a democratically accountable system of government. The Freedom of Information Act 2000 embodies the principles that openness in government is to be pursued as a good, that restrictions on access to information need to be justified according to justiciable standards, and that enforcement procedures should be provided. The Act is currently undergoing a staged implementation process, and is overseen by the Information Commissioner, a public authority established under the Act.

9.31 The Act imposes a duty on public authorities to respond to requests for information. A person who, in writing, requests specified information from a public authority is entitled to be informed in writing whether the public authority holds the information ('the duty to confirm or deny'), and, if it does, to have the information communicated to him within 20 working days (unless a fee is due and has not been paid).[52] Despite the title of the Act, public authorities have no duty to be proactive in releasing information unless they are under a legal obligation to do so at common law or under another statute. The person requesting the information may be required to pay a fee set by regulations made by the Secretary of State, and if the estimated cost of complying with a request exceeds an 'appropriate limit' (also set by regulations made by the Secretary of State) the public authority may either refuse the request or charge a higher fee for complying, based on the cost of compliance, according to a formula set out in the regulations.[53] Public authorities subject to the duties under the Act are the bodies listed in Sch 1 to the Act, including all governmental bodies and various regulatory bodies such as the General Medical Council, together with 'publicly-owned companies' (ie government-owned companies).[54] Some of the listed public authorities are subject to the duties under the Act only in respect of certain information.[55]

9.32 The Act contains a large number of exemptions. Public bodies may refuse to comply with a request which is vexatious or which is the same as one that has already been dealt with.[56] Types of information exempted by Pt II of the Act include:

- information which is accessible to the applicant by other means, or is intended for publication at some (known or unknown) future date (ss 21 and 22);

---

[52] Freedom of Information Act 2000, ss 1(1), 8, 10.
[53] ibid ss 9, 12, 13
[54] ibid ss 3(1), 6. The Secretary of State may amend the list in Sch 1: s 4.
[55] ibid s 7 and Sch 1, Pt III, para 45.
[56] ibid s 14.

- information supplied directly or indirectly by, or relating to, security, intelligence and criminal intelligence services and the tribunals dealing with complaints about them, together with other information conclusively certified by a minister as requiring exemption in order to safeguard national security (ss 23, 24 and 25);
- information disclosure of which would, or would be likely to, prejudice defence, or the capability, effectiveness or security of relevant armed forces (s 26);
- information disclosure of which would, or would be likely to, prejudice relations with another state, international organization or court, or the United Kingdom's interests abroad (s 27) or relations with administrations in other parts of the United Kingdom (s 28);
- information disclosure of which would, or would be likely to, prejudice the economic interests of the United Kingdom or the financial interests of any administration in the United Kingdom;
- information relating to an investigation by a public authority which might lead to criminal proceedings (s 30);
- information which would be likely to prejudice the prevention or detection of crime, the administration of justice, immigration controls, etc (s 31) or court records (s 32);
- information disclosure of which would be likely to prejudice the audit functions of public authorities discharging such functions (s 33);
- information which must be exempted in order to avoid an infringement of the privileges of Parliament (s 34);
- information held by a government department or the National Assembly for Wales relating to the formulation of government policy, ministerial communications, advice by the Law Officers, or the operation of a ministerial private office (s 35), or which would be likely to prejudice the maintenance of collective ministerial responsibility, the work of the executive committee of the Northern Ireland Assembly, or the work of the National Assembly for Wales; or which would be likely to inhibit the provision of advice or exchange of views for the purposes of deliberation, or (widest of all) 'would otherwise prejudice, or would be likely otherwise to prejudice, the effective conduct of public affairs' (s 36);
- information relating to communications with members of the Royal Family or relating to the conferring by the Crown of any honour or dignity (s 37);
- information which, if disclosed, would be likely to endanger anyone's physical or mental health, or endanger an individual's safety (s 38);
- environmental information which the authority holding it is obliged to make available to the public, or has a statutory exemption from being made available (s 39);
- information covered by the Data Protection Act 1998, together with certain other personal information (s 40);

- information provided to the authority in confidence, disclosure of which would be an actionable breach of confidence (s 41);
- information subject to legal professional privilege (s 42);
- trade secrets, or information disclosure of which would be likely to prejudice any person's commercial interests (s 43);
- information disclosure of which is prohibited under any enactment, would be incompatible with a European Community obligation, or would constitute a contempt of court (s 44).

This means that the general entitlement set out in s 1 of the Freedom of Information Act 2000 is heavily qualified by public and governmental interests of which the government is itself sometimes to be the judge, as well as being subordinated to private interests in respect of commerce, confidentiality and personal data.

9.33 The Act provides for the promotion, monitoring and enforcement of the duties under it. Section 45 requires the Lord Chancellor to issue a code of practice guiding public authorities on desirable practices and procedures under the Act. Under s 47, the Information Commissioner has the task of promoting good practice by public authorities, informing and advising the public, and assessing an authority's practices (with its consent). The Commissioner is also the arbiter of most claims by public authorities to exemptions. If a public authority decides that the information sought is covered by an exemption, or that for any other reason there is no duty of disclosure, it must generally provide a written statement to that effect, unless the statement would have the effect of revealing the information in question.[57] The person who made the requests can then complain to the Commissioner, who has power under s 51 to require the authority to provide information so that the Commissioner can decide whether the claim to exemption is justified. If the Commissioner decides that the authority has failed to comply with its duties under the Act, she can issue a decision or enforcement notice requiring the authority to take appropriate action under s 52. The authority usually has to comply, on pain of court proceedings under s 53. However, a government department, the National Assembly for Wales, or another authority designated by a Secretary of State, can evade compliance by way of a certificate, issued by a Secretary of State under s 53, stating that the Secretary of State has formed the view on reasonable grounds that there has been no failure to comply with the duty in question. In addition, either the public authority or the applicant may appeal under Pt V of the Act to the Tribunal established under the Act against a notice served by the Commissioner, or against a Secretary of State's national security certificate. In a case not involving a certificate, either party can appeal to the High Court on a point of law against a decision of the Tribunal.

---

[57] Freedom of Information Act 2000, s 17.

C. Permitted Restrictions on Freedom of Expression

(1) The Human Rights Act 1998 and Permitted Interference with Freedom of Expression

Where the right to freedom of expression is engaged, any interference must be jus- **9.34**
tified in English law on one of two grounds. The first justification is that the interference is required by primary legislation within the meaning of the HRA
1998. In this case, a public authority acts lawfully (as a matter of English law, although not necessarily in international law under the ECHR) in acting in accordance with the legislation even if that results in a violation of a Convention right.[58]
Alternatively, the public authority may show that the interference is justified in accordance with the terms of Article 10(2) ECHR. To fall within Article 10(2), the
interference must be: (1) 'prescribed by law', meaning that it must have a legal
basis in English law and must be sufficiently clear in its scope to comply with the
principle of legal certainty; (2) in pursuit of one of the permitted aims listed in
Article 10(2); and (3) 'necessary in a democratic society' for that purpose, meaning that it must answer a pressing social need and be proportionate to the need,
and must not take away the very essence of the right from the person asserting it.[59]

The circumstances in which a restriction on freedom of expression is justifiable, **9.35**
and the types and level of safeguards which are demanded, depend on the type
of expression (including to some extent the content of the expression) and the
context in which it takes place. Because of the importance of robust political expression in a democracy, noted above, '[t]he limits of acceptable criticism are accordingly wider as regards a politician as such than as regards a private individual.
Unlike the latter, the former inevitably and necessarily lays himself open to close
scrutiny of his every word and deed by both journalists and the public at large, and
he must consequently display a greater degree of tolerance.'[60] By contrast, public
servants are generally expected to be politically neutral in their work. It is therefore easier to justify using law to restrict abuse of public servants than similar
abuse of politicians.[61] But by the same token the desirability of maintaining the
political neutrality of public servants makes it possible to justify restricting their
own participation in political activities.[62]

When considering whether interference with freedom of expression is justified, **9.36**
the ECtHR distinguishes to some extent between factual statements and value

---

[58] HRA 1998, s 6(2).
[59] See para 7.158 above.
[60] *Lingens v Austria* Series A No 103 (1986) 8 EHRR 407 at [42]. See to the same effect
Oberschlick v Austria Series A No 204 (1995) 19 EHRR 389 at [57]–[59].
[61] *Janowski v Poland* Application 25716/94 (2000) 29 EHRR 705.
[62] *Rekvényi v Hungary* Application 25390/94 (2000) 30 EHRR 519.

judgments. It is reasonably easy to justify imposing a penalty or requiring compensation, and restraining republication, where a person makes a false and damaging factual assertion, particularly if the speaker failed to take reasonable care to check the information. Article 10(2), in accepting that freedom of expression may be restricted to protect people's reputations, recognizes a right to protection against the publication of unfounded factual reproach.[63] Journalists in particular may be expected to support their assertions on a reasonable basis of investigation and information, since one of the duties and responsibilities of journalists to which Article 10(2) refers is the duty to abide by journalistic ethics.[64] As noted above, English law makes provision for this by allowing defamatory statements about politicians and similar public figures to be published without the protection of 'qualified privilege', providing a defence to civil liability, only if the publisher has acted responsibly in bringing the matter to the attention of the public.[65] But restrictions must not stifle fair comment on a matter of public interest.[66]

9.37 On the other hand, debate about values produces statements which are not demonstrably true or false, but are nevertheless central to political dialogue. Article 10 therefore requires particularly rigorous scrutiny of any attempt to restrict people's freedom to form, express or give effect to value judgments.[67] Yet even the expression of value judgments may be restricted or penalized to give effect to the responsibilities and duties which accompany the freedom. These include a responsibility to avoid making gratuitous personal attacks on people, even if they are politicians. For example, there was no violation of Article 10 when a journalist was convicted of publishing an insulting report on the private and family life of a former politician. The offensive words expressed a value judgment about aspects of the politician's life which related to no matter of real public concern or general importance. The attack was not a contribution to political discussion, and could in any case have been expressed without resorting to insulting expressions. When assessing the proportionality of the interference, it was relevant that the penalty imposed was a relatively minor fine.[68]

9.38 Even where an attack is not gratuitously personal, public authorities are permitted to impose restraints, penalties, or a duty to compensate if a journalist makes

---

[63] *Prager and Oberschlick v Austria* Series A No 313 (1996) 21 EHRR 1.

[64] *Barfod v Denmark* Series A No 149 (1991) 13 EHRR 493; *Thorgeirson v Iceland* Series A No 239 (1992) 14 EHRR 843; *De Haes and Gijsels v Belgium* Application 19983/92 (1998) 25 EHRR 1; *Fressoz and Roire v France* Application 29183/95 (2001) 31 EHRR 2 at [54]; *Bladet Tromsø and Stensaas v Norway* Application 21980/93 (2000) 29 EHRR 125.

[65] See para. 9.13 above.

[66] See *Unabhängige Initiative Informationsvielfalt v Austria* Application 22525/95 (26 February 2002, ECtHR).

[67] See, eg, *Lingens v Austria* Series A No 103 (1986) 8 EHRR 407; *Vogt v Germany* Series A No 323 (1996) 21 EHRR 205.

[68] *Tammer v Estonia* Application 41205/98 (2001) 10 BHRC 543.

damaging, value-based criticisms without any appropriate foundation of fact. If a value judgment depends on a factual premise, the state is entitled to insist on there being a sufficient evidential basis (such as original research, or material published in an official report) for the value judgment.[69]

It is easier to justify interference with freedom of expression in respect of some other kinds of expression. These include pornographic or blasphemous material. However, it should be borne in mind that decisions of the ECtHR in these areas are based on allowing states a wide margin of appreciation when assessing the needs of their own societies in respect of bolstering morality and religious sensitivities. Public authorities in England, including courts, are still required to assess the balance of interests under Article 10(2) in the light of local conditions.   **9.39**

Racist expression and the promulgation of racial hatred are categories of expression which are even less strongly protected by Article 10. The ECtHR interprets Article 10 in the light of Article 17 ECHR, Article 20 of the International Covenant on Civil and Political Rights (ICCPR) (which requires the prohibition of propaganda for war and advocacy of national, racial or religious hatred that constitutes incitement to discrimination, hostility or violence), and Article 4 of the International Convention on the Elimination of All Forms of Racial Discrimination (requiring, among other things, that dissemination of ideas based on racial superiority or hatred be made an offence punishable by law). This permits states to control, under Article 10(2) ECHR, publicity given to racist views and hate speech, as long as the controls satisfy the tests of legality, necessity and proportionality.[70]   **9.40**

(2) Protecting State Security

(a) Criminal law

A number of statutes are designed to protect state security, and in doing so can interfere with freedom of expression. These are examined in chapter 27 below. As will be seen there, the interference with freedom of expression is generally justifiable under Article 10(2) ECHR.   **9.41**

(b) Civil law

The law of breach of confidence has been pressed into service in recent years to allow some potentially damaging disclosures to be restrained before they occur, and to prevent people benefiting from making such disclosures after they have   **9.42**

---

[69] On what constitutes a sufficient evidential or factual basis for a value judgment, see *Castells v Spain* Series A No 236 (1992) 14 EHRR 445; *Jerusalem v Austria* Application 26958/95 (27 February 2001, ECtHR); *Bladet Tromsø and Stensaas v Norway* Application 21980/93 (2000) 29 EHRR 125.

[70] *Jersild v Denmark* Series A No 298 (1995) 19 EHRR 1.

occurred. Prior restraint of expression is likely to be more difficult to justify than subsequent legal action, because of the specially chilling effect it has on debate in a democracy. Breach of confidence is essentially a private law wrong, not a public law one.[71] Someone who seeks to restrain an alleged breach of confidence, or to obtain a remedy for a past breach, must show that the material or information in issue has the necessary quality of confidentiality, either because it is by its nature of a sensitive personal or business kind or because it was imparted subject to an express or implied obligation to keep it confidential. When the claimant is a public authority, it is assumed to have no private interests to protect. It must therefore also show that there is a recognized public interest in restraining the disclosure or publication, and that this public interest outweighs that in freedom of expression in the circumstances of the case.[72] No public authority, not even the Security Service, is entitled to be immune from public criticism,[73] and any restriction of publication which effectively immunizes a public authority is likely to be held to be a disproportionate interference with freedom of expression and, therefore, a violation of Article 10.

9.43 When an action for breach of confidence is pending, it is permissible to grant an injunction restraining, pending trial, publication of material not yet in the public domain if there is a real risk that it will damage a public interest and that the damage would be serious enough to outweigh the right to freedom of expression.[74] Although the court must ultimately decide whether material covered by an injunction may be published, an injunction may allow the appropriate public authority (usually the Attorney-General) to authorize publication after examining the proposed publication. This does not amount to state censorship, because the court has the final say.[75]

9.44 An interim injunction, preserving the confidentiality of the material pending trial of the action, may be made against the world at large, as long as it is drawn no more widely than necessary to preserve the confidential character of the material in issue pending trial and the injunction is expressed in terms sufficiently clear to allow people to know what is required of them. Anyone who knowingly breaches such an injunction is guilty of contempt of court.[76] By contrast, it has been said that a final injunction binds only the parties to it, and does not bind even those third parties who have notice of it,[77] although if correct this leaves a significant lacuna in the legal protection for confidential information.

---

[71] See William Cornish in Birks (n 20 above) paras 6.43–6.49.

[72] *A-G v Guardian Newspapers Ltd (No 2)* [1990] 1 AC 109, HL.

[73] *A-G v Punch Ltd* [2002] UKHL 50; [2003] 1 AC 1046 at [29] *per* Lord Nicholls of Birkenhead.

[74] *A-G v Guardian Newspapers Ltd (No 1)* [1987] 1 WLR 1248, HL, read in the light of *Observer and Guardian v UK* Series A No 216 (1992) 14 EHRR 153, and the HRA 1998.

[75] *A-G v Punch Ltd* [2002] UKHL 50; [2003] 1 AC 1046.

[76] *A-G v Times Newspapers Ltd* [1992] 1 AC 191, HL; *A-G v Punch Ltd* [2002] UKHL 50; [2003] 1 AC 1046.

[77] *Jockey Club v Buffham* [2002] EWHC 1866; [2003] QB 462, Gray J.

(3) Protecting Decency and Morality

English law contains a range of offences against decency and morality. These are ex- **9.45**
amined in chapter 27 below. Some of these may give rise to a risk of violating the
right to freedom of expression. For example, the common law offences of outraging
public decency and conspiring to outrage public decency are so uncertain in their
scope that they are in danger of failing the test of being 'prescribed by law' under
Article 10(2), because it is not sufficiently clearly foreseeable what conduct will lead
to criminal liability. Once an offence has been defined with sufficient particularity
to meet the 'prescribed by law' criterion, the ECtHR has accepted that it may be permissible to restrict freedom of expression to protect other people's right to be free
from outrage to their moral or religious sensibilities.[78] The Court also tends to allow
states a significant 'margin of appreciation' when deciding, in the light of local conditions, what steps are needed to safeguard that freedom from outrage.[79] The margin of appreciation is inapplicable in English courts, because it is not inappropriate
for local courts to make their own assessment of need and proportionality in the
light of local conditions. Although English courts may be willing to apply a reduced
intensity of scrutiny to Parliament's assessment of what is needed in the field of
morality,[80] that does not relieve them of their primary responsibility for reassessing
and, if necessary, adjusting the common law offences in the light of their duty as
public authorities to act compatibly with Convention rights when not compelled by
primary legislation to do otherwise, under s 6 of the HRA 1998.

(4) Protecting the Administration of Justice

The administration of justice is protected by the law of contempt of court.[81] There **9.46**
are two kinds of contempts. A civil contempt is committed when somebody dis-
obeys an order made by a court in the course of, or at the conclusion of, litigation.
This applies to both public and private law proceedings. Publishing information
or material in breach of an order not to do so is an example of a civil contempt.[82]
Despite being called 'civil', the court can impose a penalty for the contempt, including a large fine or imprisonment, so the law can be regarded as penal. This interferes with rights under Article 10(1), but will generally be justifiable under
Article 10(2) as being for the protection of the rights of litigants and to uphold the
authority and impartiality of the judiciary.

---

[78] See, eg, *Otto-Preminger Institut v Austria* Series A No 295-A (1995) 19 EHRR 34 at [47]–[48].
[79] See, eg, *Handyside v UK* Series A No 24 (1979–80) 1 EHRR 737.
[80] See paras 7.33 et seq, above.
[81] See generally CJ Miller, *Contempt of Court* (3rd edn, Oxford: OUP, 2000); D Eady and ATH
Smith, *Eady and Smith on Contempt* (London: Sweet and Maxwell, 2000); NV Lowe and BE Sufrin,
Borrie and Lowe: The Law of Contempt (3rd edn, London: Butterworths, 1995).
[82] See, eg, *A-G v Greater Manchester Newspapers Ltd*, The Times, 7 December 2001, Dame
Elizabeth Butler-Sloss P.

9.47 Criminal contempts fall into several classes. Contempt in the face of the court is committed by anyone who, in court, interferes with the proceedings, abuses the process of the court, or threatens, insults, or interferes with the judge, any witness, a juror, or a party. It includes refusal by a witness to answer questions, an assault on the judge, or casting aspersions on a juror. It also encompasses demonstrations in court.[83] In terms of human rights, the main problem arises from the procedure for dealing with alleged contempts in the face of the court. The judge sitting in the case is, under English law, entitled to try the alleged contemnor summarily. The judge is thus in danger of acting as witness, prosecutor and judge in a way that could deny the accused person a fair hearing before an independent and impartial tribunal, as required by Article 6(1) ECHR. In *Wilkinson v Lord Chancellor's Department*,[84] the Court of Appeal said that the summary procedure did not infringe the rule against bias, nemo iudex in causa sua, because the judge was acting to protect the administration of justice, not herself. The Court went on to hold that no fair-minded and informed observer would be led to conclude that there was a real possibility that the judge was biased, so there was no breach of the rule against bias or of Article 6(1).[85] This seems sustainable on the facts of the case: one party to the proceedings had used foul and abusive language towards another party and her solicitor in the courtroom, and had tried to attack them physically, being restrained by a police officer and two security guards after a protracted and violent struggle to which the judge had been a witness. But if the abuse and violence had been directed against the judge herself, rather than against one of the other parties, it is submitted that summary proceedings before that judge would breach the rule against bias and Article 6(1).

9.48 Another form of criminal contempt is 'scandalizing the court', defined as '[a]ny act done or writing published calculated to bring a Court or a judge of the Court into contempt, or to lower his authority . . .'.[86] This potentially represents a very extensive incursion into freedom of expression, and could erode the principle that public authorities (including courts) are not to be immune from public criticism. Nevertheless, it does not necessarily violate Article 10 ECHR. The ECtHR has held that it was justifiable under Article 10(2) to penalize an author for suggesting that lay judges in Greenland, who were employed by a council which was a party to a case before the court, had voted for a judgment in their employer's favour because of that link. The state was said to have had a legitimate interest in protecting the reputation of its judges, in order to uphold the authority of the judiciary without which public confidence in courts as the proper forum for deciding legal disputes would be undermined, and with it any possibility of a litigant being able to

---

[83] *Morris v Crown Office* [1970] 2 QB 114, CA.
[84] [2003] EWCA Civ 95, [2003] 1 WLR 1254, CA.
[85] ibid at [25]–[26].
[86] *R v Gray* [1900] 2 QB 36, 40 *per* Lord Russell CJ.

enjoy the benefits of winning a case after a hearing publicly recognized as being fair. That decision is probably explained by the very small population in Finland, which gives rise to particular social needs. It is clear from a subsequent case, *Prager and Oberschlick v Austria*,[87] that the Court recognizes a strong public interest in a democracy in ensuring that allegations of impropriety on the part of judges are aired and properly investigated. In that case, it was held that the state had been entitled to penalize authors for allegations about the behaviour of judges in Vienna when the authors had failed either to substantiate the claims at their trials or to show that the articles amounted to fair comment. The general principle seems to be that a state may penalize mere insults or allegations of judicial impropriety which strike at the legitimacy of the state's judicial process, but the interference with freedom of expression will be disproportionate, and hence not necessary in a democratic society, if the author is not allowed to establish the truth of the allegations or the fairness of any comment, or if the penalty is out of proportion to the seriousness of the offence.

The contempt power may be used to prevent or penalize an act which prejudices **9.49** or impedes legal proceedings. Examples of impeding proceedings include interfering with a prisoner's mail to prevent him from bringing legal proceedings against a prison officer,[88] and holding a person up to public ridicule in the hope of deterring him or her from suing the publisher for libel[89] or from continuing to defend a civil action.[90] Examples of prejudicing proceedings include publishing an article, before a pending trial, which assesses the evidence and concludes that the defendant must be liable,[91] and vilifying people suspected of criminal offences in such a way that it becomes difficult or impossible for them to receive a fair trial.[92] However, in order not to violate the right to freedom of expression under Article 10 it is important to limit these kinds of contempt to cases in which the publication is expressed in unbalanced terms rather than objectively informing the public about the case, and is likely to influence the tribunal.[93] Compatibility with Article 10 is assisted by the Contempt of Court Act 1981. Whereas previously these kinds of contempt had attracted strict liability, s 2 of the 1981 Act (enacted following an adverse decision of the ECtHR in *Sunday Times v UK*[94]) limited strict liability to publications in proceedings which are 'active',[95] and then only if

---

[87] Series A No 313 (1996) 21 EHRR 1.

[88] *Raymond v Honey* [1983] 1 AC 1, HL.

[89] *A-G v Hislop* [1991] 1 QB 514, CA.

[90] *A-G v Times Newspapers Ltd* [1974] AC 273, HL.

[91] ibid.

[92] See eg *A-G v News Group Newspapers plc* [1989] QB 110, DC.

[93] *Worm v Austria* Application 22714/93 (1998) 25 EHRR 454 at [44]–[50].

[94] Series A No 30 (1979–80) 2 EHRR 245.

[95] In first-instance criminal cases, this point is reached when a person is arrested without warrant, or summoned to appear, or charged. In first-instance civil cases, proceedings are active when arrangements for a hearing are made, or in other cases when the hearing begins: Contempt of Court Act 1981, s 2(4) and Sch 1.

there is a substantial risk that the proceedings will be seriously prejudiced.[96] The Act also provides that fair and accurate reports in good faith of legal proceedings held in public do not make anyone liable to strict liability contempt (although the court may in some circumstances order that publication of the account be delayed).[97] Nor does discussion in good faith of public affairs or other matters of public interest.[98]

(5) *Protecting Confidences*

9.50   As already noted,[99] courts may restrain a threatened breach of confidence, and may also give remedies where a breach has occurred. The remedies may include an account of profits at the suit of a public authority whose confidential material has been misused, depriving the defendant of the financial benefits of the disclosure.[100] (This is not a compensatory award, since the public authority is unlikely to have wished to exploit the commercial opportunity to disclose the material even if it has the power to do so.)

(6) *Regulation of the Media*

9.51   The ECHR gives no special authority to states to regulate print media. Any restraint on their freedom of expression must be fully justified by reference to the criteria in Article 10(2) if it is to be legitimate. English law makes no attempt to control these media. Ownership is regulated under the ordinary law relating to monopolies, with certain sector-specific adjustments, in ss 58 and 59 of the Fair Trading Act 1973.[101] The investigative methods used by print media, and the content of their publications, is subject to self-regulation by the Press Complaints Commission, a body established by the industry, which published its own codes of practice and can give decisions (but not remedies) on complaints against newspapers. But in relation to broadcast media, by contrast, the last sentence of Article 10(1) accepts that states are entitled to introduce a licensing system for cinemas and broadcasting. The United Kingdom has always regulated broadcasting particularly carefully. The regulatory scheme for media ownership and spectrum allocation is in the process of change, with a unified system of control being introduced under the auspices of OFCOM under the Communications Act 2003. The new scheme represents a significant relaxation

---

[96] Contempt of Court Act 1981, s 2(2).

[97] ibid s 4.

[98] ibid s 5.

[99] See para 9.42 above.

[100] *A-G v Guardian Newspapers Ltd (No 2)* [1990] 1 AC 109, HL; *A-G v Blake (Jonathan Cape Ltd, third party)* [2001] 1 AC 268, HL.

[101] Oversight is in the hands of the Office of Fair Trading and the Competition Commission established under the Competition Act 1998, and of the European Commission in relation to the enforcement of Community law.

of control as compared with the previous one.[102] Generally, the arrangements are likely to secure compatibility with Article 10 and other Convention rights, not least because OFCOM is a public authority and so required by s 6 of the HRA 1998 to act compatibly with Convention rights unless primary legislation makes that impossible.

A few specific provisions of the Communications Act 2003 give rise to a risk of in-compatibility with freedom of expression under Article 10.[103] One, already mentioned (see para 9.19 above) relates to the ban on political advertising on radio and television. Another is the prohibition on any religious body holding a television broadcasting licence or a national radio broadcasting licence (although religious bodies are not disqualified from holding local radio licences).[104] The previous, total ban on religious bodies holding any broadcasting licence for television or radio (whether national or local) was upheld by the ECtHR as a proportionate restriction for the purpose of promoting efficient use of scarce spectrum resources, thereby helping to guarantee pluralism in the media, to cater for a variety of tastes and interests, and to avoid discrimination between religious groups in the allocation of licences.[105] However, circumstances have changed. The advent of digital broadcasting has greatly eased the problem of spectrum scarcity, and the decision to allow religious broadcasters to apply for local radio licences might suggest that it is no longer necessary and proportionate to prevent them from applying for other licences, in view of the fact that the freedom to apply does not guarantee that a licence will be granted.

(7) Combating Racism

As noted in para 9.40 above, international human rights instruments oblige states parties to prohibit racist expression and the promulgation of racial hatred, and Article 10 ECHR is interpreted in the light of those instruments.[106] English law goes some way towards giving effect to this obligation through two provisions of the criminal law which restrict racist expression. Section 18 of the Public Order Act 1986 penalizes expression in order to protect people against being threatened, abused or insulted by words or behaviour, visible in public places, which are intended or likely to stir up racial hatred. 'Racial' here has the same meaning as in the Race Relations Act 1976, and includes race, colour, nationality, and ethnic or

9.52

9.53

---

[102] See paras 5.88–5.98 above.
[103] See Joint Committee on Human Rights, Nineteenth Report of 2001–02, *Draft Communications Bill* (HL Paper 149; HC 1002) paras 51–64; First Report of 2002–03, *Scrutiny of Bills: Progress Report* (HL Paper 24; HC 191) paras 9–26.
[104] Broadcasting Act 1990, Sch 2, Pt 2, para 2, as amended by Communications Act 2003, s 348.
[105] *United Christian Broadcasters v UK* Application 44802/98 (admissibility decision, 7 November 2000, ECtHR) (inadmissible).
[106] *Jersild v Denmark* Series A No 298 (1995) 19 EHRR 1.

national origin. It does not include religion.[107] This leaves the United Kingdom out of line with the obligations imposed by (for example) Article 20 ICCPR. Although the legislation is under-inclusive, the restriction which it imposes on freedom of expression is clearly justifiable under Article 10(2) ECHR.

9.54 The other significant piece of legislation which interferes with racist expression is aimed at racist chanting by crowds of supporters at soccer matches. The Football (Offences) Act 1991 makes it an offence to engage or take part in chanting of an indecent or racist nature, either alone or in concert with others, at designated football matches (mainly Football League and Premiership matches).[108] Unlike the offence under s 18 of the Public Order Act 1986, the offence is committed by chanting any term with a racial connotation or connection if it is intended to be derogatory. It is not necessary to use it in a way designed to stir up hatred.[109] In view of judgments of the ECtHR holding that the state is entitled (subject to certain conditions) to protect people against outrage to their sensibilities from gratuitously offensive words or behaviour,[110] there can be no doubt that the legislation is justifiable in terms of Article 10(2), as well as being laudable in terms of other international human rights provisions.

D. The Scope of Freedom of Peaceful Assembly and Association[111]

(1) General Principles

9.55 English law has not until recently given much weight to the freedom to assemble in public. People can always gather on private premises as long as the owner or occupier permits them to do so. But there are few, if any, places where people can gather as of right, unless they have an estate or interest in the land in question. In English law, historically, the field has been dominated by principles which limit rather than protect freedom of assembly: the desirability of maintaining public order and the Queen's peace; respect for rights of property; and respect for the discretion and judgment of the police. Under the HRA 1998, these principles have to operate compatibly with the right to freedom of peaceful assembly and

---

[107] See further paras 27.88–27.91 below. A provision to outlaw incitement to religious hatred was included in the Anti-terrorism, Crime and Security Bill in 2001, but was defeated in the House of Lords before the Bill was passed.

[108] Football (Offences) Act 1991, s 3, as amended by the Football (Offences and Disorder) Act 1999, s 9.

[109] *DPP v Stoke on Trent Magistrates' Court* [2003] EWHC 1593; The Times, 23 June 2003, DC.

[110] See, eg, para 9.45 above.

[111] See generally Clayton and Tomlinson (n 1 above) vol 1, ch 16.

association under Article 11 ECHR. There is also a growing sense of the social importance of public space.[112]

Article 11 provides: **9.56**

1. Everyone has the right to freedom of peaceful assembly and to freedom of association with others, including the right to form and join trade unions for the protection of his interests.
2. No restrictions shall be placed on the exercise of these rights other than such as are prescribed by law and are necessary in a democratic society in the interests of national security or public safety, for the prevention of disorder or crime, for the protection of health or morals or for the protection of the rights and freedoms of others. This Article shall not prevent the imposition of lawful restrictions on the exercise of these rights by members of the armed forces, of the police or of the administration of the state.

There are three particularly significant general characteristics of the rights under Article 11.

First, the right to freedom of peaceful assembly must now be recognized as being   **9.57**
of central importance in a functioning democracy, whether exercised in private or in public, and whether the assembly is moving or stationary.[113] Those who wish to restrict or interfere with a peaceful assembly accordingly carry a significant burden of providing legal justification. Instead of a presumption in favour of order, there is now a presumption in favour of freedom of peaceful assembly. As the ECtHR has said, freedom of peaceful assembly 'is of such importance that it cannot be restricted, even for an *avocat*, so long as the person concerned does not himself commit any reprehensible act on such an occasion'.[114]

Secondly, Article 11(1) imposes positive obligations on public authorities to take   **9.58**
reasonable and appropriate measures to enable people to exercise the right, providing protection against counter-demonstrators if necessary (for example, to allow anti-abortion campaigners to demonstrate despite a counter-demonstration by pro-abortion campaigners).[115] Demonstrations make demands on others. To be effective, there must be some form of communication between demonstrators and observers, so freedom to assemble for demonstrative purposes presupposes that the freedom of other people from annoyance is to be restricted at least so far as necessary to allow the protester to impart the nature of the protest and invite people to

---

[112] For recent analyses, see Helen Fenwick, *Civil Rights: New Labour, Freedom and the Human Rights Act* (London: Longman, 2000) 112–170; N Whitty, T Murphy and S Livingstone, *Civil Liberties Law: The Human Rights Act Era* (London: Butterworths, 2001) ch 2; D Feldman, *Civil Liberties and Human Rights in the UK* (2nd edn, Oxford: OUP, 2002) ch 18.
[113] *Rassemblement Jurassien and Unité Jurasienne v Switzerland* Application 8191/78 (1980) 17 DR 93, EComHR; *Christians against Racism and Fascism v UK* Application 8440/78 (1981) 21 DR 138, EComHR; *Ezelin v France* Series A No 202 (1992) 14 EHRR 362.
[114] *Ezelin v France*, ibid at [53].
[115] *Plattform 'Ärzte für das Leben' v Austria* Series A No 139 (1991) 13 EHRR 204 at [38].

join in protest or discussion. However, the effectiveness of such protection cannot be guaranteed, and public authorities have a good deal of discretion as to the resources and means employed when giving effect to a balance between the competing rights.[116]

9.59   Thirdly, Article 11 protects people against being disciplined or victimized on account of their participation in public, collective expressions of political views. Under the HRA 1998, bodies regarded as public authorities are directly bound by the duty to respect freedom of assembly and association under Article 11.[117] The right to freedom of association under Article 11 is infringed when people's freedom to choose when and with whom they do not wish to associate is seriously interfered with, either by imposing severe sanctions on them for refusing to associate (as where people lost their jobs for refusal to join a particular union under a closed-shop agreement) or by restricting people's range of choices so that they have no real choice.[118] It is possible that the appropriate public authorities (such as courts) also have a positive obligation to prevent private bodies, such as employers, from disciplining people on account of the exercise of freedom of peaceful assembly under Article 11. The strictly limited exceptions in Article 11(1) allowing restrictions on the freedom of members of the armed forces, police, and public administrators do not imply any restriction for members of other groups, and must themselves be narrowly construed.[119]

9.60   The statutory and common law on freedom of assembly must now be given effect in the light of these principles, unless it is impossible to do so because of primary legislation which cannot be interpreted in a manner compatible with Convention rights.[120]

(2) Freedom of Peaceful Assembly

(a) Assembly in public

9.61   As noted earlier, there are few, if any, places where people have the right to assemble on land which they do not own or lawfully occupy. However, English public law has imposed special constraints on the way in which a public body

---

[116] *Plattform 'Ärzte für das Leben' v Austria* (n 115 above), at [34].

[117] *Ezelin v France* Series A No 202 (1992) 14 EHRR 362.

[118] *Young, James, and Webster v UK* Series A No 44 (1982) 4 EHRR 38. See E Barendt, *Freedom of Speech* (Oxford: Clarendon Press, 1985) ch 10.

[119] *Vogt v Germany* Series A No 323 (1996) 21 EHRR 205; *United Communist Party of Turkey v Turkey* Application 19392/92 (1998) 26 EHRR 121; Alistair Mowbray, 'The Role of the European Court of Human Rights in the Promotion of Democracy' [1999] PL 703, 710–713. It is noteworthy that under the ICCPR, the limitation of the rights of the police and members of the armed forces applies only in relation to the freedom of association and the right to form and join a trade union (Art 22 ICCPR), not to freedom of peaceful assembly (Art 21 ICCPR).

[120] HRA 1998, ss 3, 6.

may exercise its control over access to land which it holds. The underlying notion is that public bodies hold property for public, not private, purposes, and so can be required to justify their use of the property by reference to public law principles: people must not be excluded from property in a way which is ultra vires, serves an improper purpose, or is irrational, arbitrary or discriminatory; and any decision to exclude people must be made fairly and after taking account of relevant, and not irrelevant, considerations.[121]

Public highways, including public roads and public rights of way, are also public   **9.62** for this purpose. The essence of a highway is that people have the right to pass and re-pass along it. While stationary assemblies on roads are always likely to be unlawful, constituting an obstruction of the highway and a public nuisance, people in groups proceeding along the highway are presumptively lawful, unless they do something which exceeds their rights. People are also entitled to do anything which is legitimately incidental to the right to pass and re-pass along the highway. This has been held to include not only resting where necessary or repairing broken vehicles, but also assembling in a peaceful and non-obstructive manner on land held by the highway authority adjoining the highway, to demonstrate.[122] This relatively recent development is likely to be strengthened by the application to public authorities of Articles 10 and 11 under the HRA 1998.

(b) Assembly on private property

In England and Wales, all land is owned by somebody and is subject to the private   **9.63** law of land ownership. Where it is in private ownership, the owners are not subject to public law duties, and usually have near-absolute powers to exclude others from the land. But many privately owned pieces of land are places to which people go, with the landowner's encouragement, in order to conduct business or other activities which redound to the landowner's commercial benefit. Shopping malls are typical of this kind of location. As shopping malls come to contain an increasing proportion of retail outlets, they increasingly take on the quality of a shopping centre in a town to which people are forced to resort. If the landowner can restrict the freedom of assembly of people who come to his or her commercial bazaar, it leaves even fewer places in which people can bring their message to large numbers of their fellow citizens, and restricts their ability to make effective use of their rights under Articles 10 and 11.

It would be possible to extend this to such places as private shopping centres, al-   **9.64** though there are indications that legal tribunals (both national and international) are

---

[121] See, eg, *R v Barnet LBC, ex p Johnson* (1990) 89 LGR 581, CA, affirming (1989) 88 LGR 73, DC; *Wheeler v Leicester City Council* [1985] AC 1054, HL; *R v Somerset CC, ex p Fewings* [1995] 1 WLR 1037, CA, affirming on different grounds Laws J, [1995] 1 All ER 513.

[122] *DPP v Jones (Margaret)* [1999] 2 AC 240, HL.

reluctant as yet to take this to the lengths of requiring private landowners to admit people or permit conduct against their wills. The ECtHR has decided, taking account of the property rights of landowners under Article 1 of Protocol to the ECHR, that it would impose an unreasonable burden on the state to impose a positive obligation on it under Articles 10 and 11 to prevent the owners of a private shopping mall in a town centre banning environmental campaigners from collecting signatures for a petition and conducting other expressive activities on its premises.[123]

(3) Freedom of Association

9.65 Freedom of association has both a positive and a negative aspect. In its positive aspect, it allows people to associate with people of their choice. Its negative aspect allows people to be free of being forced to associate with people against their wills. For example, it infringes Article 11 ECHR to require employees of a company to join a particular trade union in pursuit of a closed-shop agreement, unless that can be justified under Article 11(2).[124] An organization is usually entitled to protect itself, and its members, from being joined by members who are unsympathetic to its aims or policies, as long as the requirements of Article 11(2) are met.[125] The state has a positive obligation to take reasonable and appropriate steps to ensure that employment law does not permit private employers to interfere with the ability of trade unions to strive to advance their members' interests, for example by paying higher salaries to employees who accept individually negotiated contracts than to those who, as members of a trade union, seek collectively negotiated agreements.[126]

E. Permitted Restrictions on Freedom of Assembly and Association

(1) Justifying Interference with Article 11 Rights

9.66 Although little positive help is given under English law to people who wish to exercise the freedoms of peaceful assembly and association, no permission is usually required for people to exercise the freedoms as long as they find ways of doing it without infringing legal restrictions. English law on the subject therefore mainly consists of the restrictions. Under the HRA 1998, any restriction must be justifiable under Article 11(2) ECHR, unless it is contained in primary legislation which cannot be read or given effect compatibly with the freedom. As in relation to other

---

[123] *Appleby v UK* Application 44306/98, The Times, 13 May 2003 (Judge Maruste dissenting). See also *CIN Properties Ltd v Rawlins* [1995] 2 EGLR 130, CA, and K Gray and SF Gray, 'Civil Rights, Civil Wrongs and Quasi-Public Space' [1999] European Human Rights L Rev 46.
[124] *Young, James, and Webster v UK* Series A No 44 (1982) 4 EHRR 38.
[125] *Royal Society for the Prevention of Cruelty to Animals v A-G* [2002] 1 WLR 448, Lightman J.
[126] *Wilson and National Union of Journalists v UK* Application 30668/96 (2002) 35 EHRR 20.

rights, including Article 10, the justification for an interference must satisfy the following tests.

(a) Any restriction must be 'prescribed by law'

As that phrase has been interpreted by the ECtHR, it imports a dual test. First, the restriction must be lawful under national law. Secondly, it must be consistent with the principles of legality and legal certainty assessed from the standpoint of the ECHR, being sufficiently clear and predictable in its effects to allow people to know with reasonable confidence what conduct is required of them. A restriction may be lawful under English law, yet fail the 'prescribed by law' test if, for example, the criterion for imposing a restriction is insufficiently clear and objective to allow people to be reasonably clear about their obligations. Binding someone over to be 'of good behaviour' after a protest against hunting does not allow this, and so was not justifiable.[127] By contrast, a breach of the peace is a reasonably well understood legal concept, so binding over to keep the peace (as interpreted by English courts)[128] and prohibiting conduct causing 'a breach of the peace likely to cause annoyance' (as interpreted by Austrian courts)[129] imposed sufficiently precise obligations to pass the test of being 'prescribed by law'.

9.67

(b) Legitimate aim and 'necessary in a democratic society'

The interference must be shown to pursue one of the legitimate aims listed in Article 11(2). In addition, it must be necessary in a democratic society in support of that aim. That is, it must be a proportionate response to a pressing social need. Restrictions which interfere with the right more than necessary to achieve the purpose, or applied without regard to the peacefulness of an assembly and the importance of the right, will be incompatible with Article 11. There was a violation of this article, together with Article 10, where the police arrested demonstrators and a court sought to bind them over in circumstances where there had been no immediate threat to property, life or limb.[130]

9.68

(2) Powers to Prevent Breaches of the Peace

(a) Meaning of 'breach of the peace'

A breach of the peace is a positive act, in public or in private, which harms a person or damages his messuage[131] in his presence, or which is likely to cause such

9.69

---

[127] *Hasman and Harrup v UK* Application 25594/94 (25 November 1999, ECtHR).
[128] *Steel v UK* (1999) 28 EHRR 603. See para 9.68 below.
[129] *Chorherr v Austria* Series A No 266-B (1994) 17 EHRR 358.
[130] *Steel v UK* (1999) 28 EHRR 603.
[131] 'Originally, the portion of land intended to be occupied, or actually occupied, as a site for a dwelling-house and its appurtenances. In modern legal language, a dwelling-house with its outbuildings and curtilage and the adjacent land assigned to its use.' *Oxford English Dictionary*.

harm or puts someone in fear of such harm being done.[132] The act need not be unlawful in itself, but must give rise to a real risk, not a mere possibility, of violence.[133] Merely waving a handbag, albeit hysterically, in front of a police officer cannot give rise to a threat of violence, and so cannot be a breach of the peace.[134] A breach of the peace is not a criminal offence under English law, but it triggers various police powers, including a power to detain people if necessary to prevent or end the breach. Detention for this purpose has been said to be an offence for the purposes of Article 5(1) ECHR, so that arrest or detention in respect of a breach of the peace can be justified under Article 5(1)(c) if the other conditions laid down by that paragraph are met.[135]

(b) Permitted restrictions

9.70 In order to stop a breach of the peace which is in progress, or to prevent a reasonably apprehended breach of the peace which is imminent both in time and place, any person may use such force as is reasonable to restrain people or to remove the cause of the disturbance. Police officers are acting in the execution of their duty when giving instructions to people in order to defuse or prevent a breach of the peace.[136] Steps which may be taken include removing a provocative emblem from a person,[137] or physically restraining someone while dispersing a meeting which was threatened with disruption, even though the disruption was being threatened by other people.[138] The police are allowed considerable leeway in deciding what steps are reasonable and necessary, and when anticipated violence can reasonably be regarded as imminent.[139] The police have been held to be justified in requiring the organizers of a meeting to move it to another location, where there was thought likely to be a hostile audience at the original site.[140]

9.71 However, if anybody could stifle the expression of views by threatening violence, freedom of expression and freedom of protest would be worth little. The HRA 1998, s 6 requires public authorities, including the police, to give more weight to the rights of people holding assemblies under Articles 10 and 11. In the light of

---

[132] *R v Howell* [1982] QB 416, CA, discussed by ATH Smith, 'Breaching the Peace and Disturbing the Quiet' [1982] PL 212.

[133] See *R v Morpeth Ward Justices, ex p Ward* [1996] Crim LR 497, DC; *Percy v DPP* [1995] 1 WLR 1382, DC.

[134] *Jarrett v Chief Constable of West Midlands Police* [2003] EWCA Civ 397; The Times, 28 February 2003.

[135] *Williamson v Chief Constable of West Midlands Police* [2003] EWCA Civ 337; (2003) 167 JP 181.

[136] *Albert v Lavin* [1982] AC 546, HL.

[137] *Humphries v Connor* (1864) 17 Ir CLR 1.

[138] *O'Kelly v Harvey* (1883) 15 Cox CC 435.

[139] *Moss v McLachlan* [1984] IRLR 76, DC, probably the high water mark of police discretion.

[140] *Duncan v Jones* [1936] 1 KB 218, DC.

that, it will often be the case that, as O'Brien J said in *R v Londonderry Justices*:[141] 'If danger arises from the exercise of lawful rights resulting in a breach of the peace, the remedy is the presence of sufficient force to prevent the result, not the legal condemnation of those who exercise those rights'. This will not always be so: as the ECtHR held in *Plattform 'Ärzte für das Leben' v Austria*,[142] the positive obligation under Article 11 is only to take reasonable and appropriate steps to allow the peaceful demonstration to proceed, so there may be circumstances in which resource and safety considerations militate in favour of restricting freedom of peaceful assembly, or restricting people's freedom to go about their lawful business in the face of violent protest. Such an approach has been seen in English law before the HRA 1998.[143]

Nevertheless, both before the 1998 Act came into force and subsequently, it is not **9.72** appropriate to leave the matter entirely in the discretion of the police subject only to the public law test of *Wednesbury* unreasonableness or irrationality. The decision to interfere with a person's Article 11 rights must give appropriate weight to the rights, and must be justified by reference to the more exacting standards of Article 11(2), including a test of proportionality. Attaching weight to the freedom of peaceful assembly and freedom of expression is likely to limit the number of occasions on which it will be proper to intervene in an assembly merely to protect passers-by from annoyance or offence.[144] But the police still have discretion, as long as they properly balance all the interests, as shown by the fact that the European Court of Justice has reached a similar conclusion when free movement of goods under Community law was disrupted by a protest.[145]

(3) Powers to Ban or Impose Conditions

The Public Order Act 1986, Pt II, confers powers on the police going beyond the **9.73** common law powers to deal with a breach of the peace. At the same time, it imposes certain duties on people who organize public processions.

(a) Notice of processions

The legislation requires organizers of public processions to give written notice to **9.74** the police at least six clear days before the procession is to be held, or as early as is reasonably practicable, if it is intended to demonstrate support for or opposition

---

[141] (1891) 28 LR Ir 440, 450.
[142] Series A No 139 (1991) 13 EHRR 204 at [32]–[34].
[143] See *R v Chief Constable of Sussex, ex p International Trader's Ferry Ltd* [1999] 2 AC 418, HL; C Barnard and I Hare, 'Police Discretion and the Rule of Law: Economic Community Rights versus Civil Rights' (2000) 63 MLR 581.
[144] See eg *Redmond-Bate v DPP* (1997) 7 BHRC 375, DC.
[145] Case C-112/00 *Eugen Schmidberger, Internationale Transporte und Planzüge v Austria*, The Times, 27 June 2003, ECJ.

to the views or actions of any person or persons, or to publicize a cause or campaign, or to mark or commemorate any event.[146] There are exceptions for processions commonly or customarily held in that police area, and funeral processions organized by a funeral director acting in the ordinary course of his business.

(b) Imposing conditions on processions

9.75 The police can impose conditions on public processions (whether or not notice has been given or is required) under s 12 of the Public Order Act 1986.[147] The police can exercise the power if the chief officer for the police force, or the senior officer at the scene, reasonably believes, having regard to the time, place and route of the procession, that either (1) it may result in serious public disorder, serious damage to property, or serious disruption to the life of the community, or (2) the organizers' purpose is to intimidate others with a view to compelling them not to do or omit something which they have a right to do or omit.[148] The conditions are contained in directions to the organizers, and may be such as appear to the officer to be necessary to prevent the anticipated disorder, damage, disruption, or intimidation. Section 12(1) provides that they may include, but are not limited to, conditions as to the route of the procession, or prohibiting it from entering any specified public place. Conditions which are so demanding that they amount in effect to a ban are an improper use of the power, and so are unlawful on ordinary public law principles.[149] They may also violate Articles 10 and 11, failing the test of proportionality. However, the decision of the ECtHR in *Jersild v Denmark*[150] shows that a restriction is permitted in order to protect people against the corrosive effects of racist speech. The same may be true of other forms of hate-speech. It is therefore legitimate to require the officer exercising the discretion to consider the probable reaction of other groups to the views expressed by the procession. Nevertheless, the duty on public authorities to take reasonable steps to safeguard the right to assemble peacefully under Article 11 and the developing common law presumption in favour of protecting peaceful speakers or demonstrators against hostile reactions is likely to alleviate this risk that people whose views are unpopular with bottlethrowers will have a more restricted freedom than those whose views are more popular.

(c) Prohibiting processions

9.76 Section 13 of the Public Order Act 1986 provides a power to prohibit entirely public processions, or a class of public processions, in a specified location for a set

---

[146] Public Order Act 1986, s 11(1), (5), (6).
[147] ibid s 12(2).
[148] ibid s 12(1).
[149] See *DPP v Baillie* [1995] Crim LR 426, DC, a decision on the analogous power in respect of assemblies under s 14 of the Act.
[150] Series A No 298 (1995) 19 EHRR 1.

period. The chief officer of police may exercise the power if he or she reasonably believes that the powers to impose conditions under s 12 will be insufficient to prevent serious public disorder resulting from public processions held in a district or part of a district, because of the particular circumstances existing in that district or part.[151] Outside London[152] the chief officer must apply to the council for an order prohibiting the holding of all public processions, or a specified class of them, in the district or part of the district concerned, for a specified period not exceeding three months. The council may then make an order (though it has a discretion), with the consent of the Home Secretary, either in the terms requested in the chief officer's application or with such amendments to those terms as the Home Secretary is prepared to approve.[153] In London, the Commissioner of Police of the Metropolis, or (in the City) the Commissioner of Police for the City of London, may make a similar order with the consent of the Home Secretary.[154]

The power to prohibit processions operates in a much narrower band of circum- **9.77**
stances than the power to impose conditions. It does not apply to circumstances giving rise to a risk of serious damage to property, serious disruption to the life of the community, or intimidation, unless the chief officer reasonably believes that they will result in serious public disorder. In order to avoid discrimination against processions by particular groups or opinions, s 13(1) does not permit the banning of a single procession. Instead, the chief officer of police must apply to the council for an order prohibiting all public processions, or a specified class of processions, in the district or part of a district concerned, for a specified period not exceeding three months. The repercussions of applying for an order may therefore go well beyond the particular procession. The general chilling effect on freedom of expression and assembly, and the justification for such an effect under Article 11(2), must be properly considered by the chief officer, the local authority and the Home Secretary if a ban on processions is not to be unlawful by virtue of s 6 of the HRA 1998 as incompatible with Article 11.

(d) Imposing conditions on other public assemblies

Assemblies, in contrast to processions, are presumptively unlawful if not held in a **9.78**
place where the organizers have permission to hold it. Hyde Park Corner is vested in the Crown.[155] Highways are vested in the Crown or local authorities, subject to a right of members of the public to pass and re-pass on them.[156] An assembly on a highway may be a public nuisance and a contravention of s 137 of the Highways

---

[151] Public Order Act 1986 s 13(1).
[152] ibid s 13(3).
[153] ibid s 13(2).
[154] ibid s 13(4). Orders may be revoked or varied by further orders made in the same way: s 13(5).
[155] *Bailey v Williamson* (1873) LR 8 QB 118, DC. See Royal and Other Parks and Gardens Regulations 1977, SI 1977/217.
[156] *R v Graham and Burns* (1888) 16 Cox CC 420; *Ex p Lewis* (1888) 21 QBD 191, DC.

Act 1980 if passage along the highway is obstructed unreasonably. The police have a discretion as to how to deal with an unreasonable obstruction of the highway. The fact that other meetings have been held at the same place in the past will not prevent the next one from being prosecuted as an obstruction.[157] Trafalgar Square, a traditional venue for demonstrations, is a highway, and meetings there are controlled by the Secretary of State for Transport, the Environment and the Regions under powers conferred by statutory instrument which were held to be compatible in principle with Article 11 in *Rai, Allmond and 'Negotiate Now!' v UK*.[158] There are regulations covering the use of many public places.[159] The regulations are subject to judicial review if they are outside the powers conferred by the enabling legislation,[160] or are incompatible with freedom of assembly under Article 11(1) for example because they pursue an illegitimate aim, or restrict the freedom more than is proportionate to the pressing social need which has been identified as justifying the restriction.

9.79 There is a general power to impose conditions on public assemblies in certain circumstances, contained in s 14(1) of the Public Order Act 1986. The power may be exercised by the chief officer of police or the senior officer at the site of the meeting,[161] who may give directions imposing certain conditions on the assembly if both the following conditions apply:

- the meeting is a public assembly within the meaning of the Act. A public assembly consists of 20 or more people[162] in a public place;[163] and
- the officer reasonably believes that, having regard to the place or time of the assembly and the circumstances in which it is to be held (or being held), *either* it may result in serious public disorder, serious damage to property, or serious disruption to the life of the community, *or* the purpose of the organizers is to intimidate others with a view to compelling them to refrain from doing something which they have a right to do, or to do something which they have a right not to do.

9.80 The directions may include such conditions as appear to the officer to be necessary to prevent the anticipated serious public disorder, damage, disruption, or intimidation. However, they may relate only to the place at which the assembly may

---

[157] *Arrowsmith v Jenkins* [1963] 2 QB 561, DC.

[158] Application 25522/94 (1995) 19 EHRR CD93, EComHR (inadmissible).

[159] See M Supperstone (ed), *Brownlie's Law of Public Order and National Security* (2nd edn, London: Butterworths, 1981) 35–38; DGT Williams, *Keeping the Peace* (London: Hutchinson, 1967).

[160] *DPP v Hutchinson* [1990] 2 AC 783, HL.

[161] Public Order Act 1986, s 14(2). The chief officer may delegate the power to a deputy or assistant chief constable (in London, an assistant commissioner): s 15.

[162] The Anti-social Behaviour Act 2003 when in force will reduce the number of people from 20 to two.

[163] Public Order Act 1986, s 16.

be held or may continue, its maximum duration, or the maximum number of people who may attend. This gives the officer a very wide discretion, couched in subjective language, but it can be reviewed on ordinary public law principles. For instance, if the power appears to have been used for an improper purpose, if the conditions imposed amount virtually to a ban, they will be unlawful.[164] They must also comply with the duty under the HRA 1998, s 6 to act compatibly with Convention rights. The conditions will be incompatible if their nature or extent is not justified under Article 10(2) or Article 11(2).

(e) Prohibiting trespassory assemblies

A council may make an order, on the application of a chief constable and with the consent of the Home Secretary, prohibiting trespassory assemblies within a specified area not exceeding a radius of five miles, during a specified period not exceeding four days.[165] A trespassory assembly is an assembly of 20 or more people on land to which the public has no right of access or only a limited right of access, without or in excess of the limits of the occupier's permission.[166] The chief constable may apply to the council for an order if he reasonably believes that an assembly:

9.81

- is intended to be held on land to which the public have no right of access or only a limited right of access;
- is likely to be held without the occupier's permission or in excess of any such permission; and
- may result in serious disruption to the life of the community, or in significant damage to the land or a building or monument on it if the land, building or monument is of historical, architectural, archaeological or scientific importance.[167]

Within the area covered by an order, a constable in uniform may stop and redirect a person he reasonably believes to be on his way to a prohibited trespassory assembly.[168] It is an offence to organize or take part in a prohibited trespassory assembly, or to incite another person to do so.[169]

These provisions could have a decidedly chilling effect on free expression, and could be used in circumstances which would not fall within the legitimate purposes for interfering with freedom of expression under Article 10(2). The risk is

9.82

---

[164] *DPP v Baillie* [1995] Crim LR 426, DC.
[165] Public Order Act 1986, s 14A(2), (6).
[166] ibid s 14A(5). At present, the power relates only to assemblies in the open air. The Anti-social Behaviour Bill, currently before Parliament, would, if passed, make it possible to impose orders on trespassory assemblies taking place indoors.
[167] ibid s 14A(1). On the procedure in London, see s 14A(3), (4).
[168] ibid s 14C.
[169] ibid s 14B(1)–(3).

much reduced by two factors. First, the HRA 1998, s 6 makes it unlawful for a public authority to make or confirm an order if it would be incompatible with a Convention right, so the requirements of Article 10(2) are added to the preconditions for making an order expressed in s 14A. Secondly, the decision of the House of Lords in *DPP v Jones (Margaret)*[170] significantly limits the impact of the orders. The House of Lords was unanimous in holding that the trespassory nature of the anticipated assembly is a necessary precondition for the making of an order, not a result of it, so the making of an order does not make otherwise lawful assemblies into trespassory assemblies (although their Lordships divided on the extent of the people's entitlements incidental to their right to pass and re-pass on the highway).

(4) Power to Enter Private Premises

9.83 Generally, the state does not seek to regulate private meetings held on private premises with the occupier's consent. The only power which has been clearly asserted in relation to private meetings is a common law power to enter, or remain on, private premises in order to stop or prevent a breach of the peace. The police may enter or remain on premises to prevent or stop a breach of the peace which is reasonably apprehended as being imminent,[171] or is in progress, or to conduct a fresh pursuit of a person who has just been causing a breach of the peace. They may also stay for long enough to ensure that the breach is not likely to recur. However, they may not enter premises to arrest a person for a breach of the peace once it has ended and the risk of repetition has abated.[172] The use of this power must now be mediated by the need to act compatibly with Article 8 ECHR, alongside Articles 9, 10 and 11, by virtue of the HRA 1998.

(5) Restrictions on Freedom of Association

9.84 Generally, English law imposes no restriction on the people with whom one may associate. However, there are certain exceptions. Under the Race Relations Act 1976, a club with 25 or more members is required to offer any goods, facilities and services which it provides without discriminating on the ground of race.[173] This makes it unlawful for such clubs to operate a policy for selecting members which discriminates, directly or indirectly, on racial grounds. Clubs with fewer than 25 members do not constitute a section of the public if there is a genuine selection procedure for members, and so are not subject to the Race Relations Act 1976 in

---

[170] [1999] 2 AC 240, HL.

[171] *Thomas v Sawkins* [1935] 2 KB 249. For discussion and criticism, see AL Goodhart, 'Thomas *v* Sawkins: A Constitutional Innovation' (1936) 6 CLJ 22; Williams (n 159 above) ch 6, esp 142–144.

[172] *R v Marsden* (1868) LR 1 CCR 131; *Robson v Hallett* [1967] 2 QB 939, DC; *McConnell v Chief Constable of Greater Manchester Police* [1990] 1 WLR 364, CA.

[173] Race Relations Act 1976, s 28.

the provision of goods and services.[174] This ensures that people are free to choose, in pursuance of their right to respect for private life, those other people with whom they wish to associate in small groups in their social lives.

Some groups are, however, proscribed by law. Under s 3 of, and Sch 2 to, the **9.85** Terrorism Act 2000, certain organizations are proscribed as being concerned in terrorism as defined in s 1, and the Home Secretary has power by order to add other organizations to, or remove organizations from, the list of proscribed organizations. Under s 11, it is an offence to belong, or to profess to belong, to a proscribed organization. Under s 12, it is an offence to invite support for such an organization (not being limited to the provision of money or property), or to arrange, manage or address a meeting of three or more people to encourage support for it. Section 13 makes it an offence to wear in public a uniform which gives rise to a reasonable suspicion that he or she is a supporter of a proscribed organization. In addition, under s 21 of the Anti-terrorism, Crime and Security Act 2001, the Home Secretary may certify that a person is a suspected terrorist if he or she is a member of or belongs to, or has links with, an international terrorist group, and a person so certified may, if not a UK national, be removed from the country or held indefinitely until he or she can be safely and lawfully removed, under ss 22 and 23.

These provisions have the capacity to restrict people's right to freedom of associa- **9.86** tion under Article 11 ECHR. It is not clear that they are always justified under Article 11(2). In particular, the proscription of organizations under the Terrorism Act 2000 may not always clearly serve a legitimate aim and be proportionate to a pressing social need; and the certification of people under the Anti-terrorism, Crime and Security Act 2001 on the basis of 'links' with an international terrorist group may not be based on a legal provision of sufficient clarity and certainty to meet the 'prescribed by law' requirement of Article 11(2). In most cases, however, the restriction is likely to be held to be justifiable in order to combat crime and protect the rights of others. Where the people linked to the organization are not UK nationals, Article 16 ECHR, allowing the state to restrict the political activity of aliens notwithstanding anything in (among other provisions) Article 11, is likely to avoid the need to justify the restriction too rigorously under Article 11(2).

F. Free Elections

The last right covered in this chapter is the right to free elections. This is guaran- **9.87** teed by Article 3 of Protocol 1 to the ECHR, which provides:

---

[174] *Charter v Race Relations Board* [1973] AC 868, HL; *Dockers' Labour Club and Institute Ltd v Race Relations Board* [1976] AC 285, HL.

The High Contracting Parties undertake to hold free elections at reasonable intervals by secret ballot, under conditions which will allow the free expression of the
opinion of the people in the choice of the legislature.

9.88 Article 3 imposes a positive obligation on the state in respect of elections to 'the
legislature'. There may be more than one legislature in a state. The article appears
to apply to elections to legislative bodies with original, rather than delegated,
functions under the constitution.[175] In the United Kingdom, this means that it
applies to the Westminster Parliament, but certainly does not apply to local and
county councils, and may not apply to devolved legislatures in Wales, Scotland
and Northern Ireland. It also applies to elections to supra-national legislative bodies such as the European Parliament.[176]

9.89 Article 3 requires that people should be free to participate in the elections[177] and
to vote, but does not demand that any one system of voting should be used.[178] The
right to participate is not absolute. In the United Kingdom, there is a restriction
on voting by convicted prisoners, and this has been held to be acceptable both by
the European Commission on Human Rights and by English judges,[179] although
it is slightly surprising that there was no violation of Article 14 ECHR (non-discrimination) taken together with Article 3 of Protocol 1 in view of the difficulty
of finding an objective and rational justification for denying the vote to prisoners
as a category without regard to their circumstances. In the light of the decisions,
the denial of the vote in the United Kingdom to peers (at common law), people
under the age of 18, people compulsorily detained as a mental patient, people
convicted of corrupt or illegal practices at an election, and certain other categories
is likely to be held to be justifiable.[180] The categories of people who may not be
candidates for election is also probably justifiable under the ECHR. They include
peers, aliens, people under the age of 21, persons of unsound mind, judges, civil
servants, members of the regular armed forces, police officers, members of non-
Commonwealth legislatures, convicted prisoners, and various other categories of
people.[181]

9.90 It seems that constituencies are not required to contain the same number of voters in order to satisfy Article 3, but systematic discrimination against a particular
group, or gerrymandering, would be likely to violate Article 3 taken with Article

---

[175] See *Mathieu-Mohin v Belgium* Series A No 113 (1986) 10 EHRR 1; Clayton and Tomlinson
(n 1 above) vol 1, 1388–1389.
[176] *Matthews v UK* Application 24833/94 (1999) 28 EHRR 361.
[177] *Bowman v UK* Application 24839/94 (1998) 26 EHRR 1.
[178] *Liberal Party, Mrs R and Mr P v UK* (1980) 21 DR 211, EComHR.
[179] See *H v Netherlands* (1979) 33 DR 242, EComHR; *R (on the application of Pearson) v Secretary
of State for the Home Department* [2001] EWHC Admin 239, [2001] HRLR 39.
[180] Representation of the People Act 1983, ss 1, 3, 7, 160.
[181] Clayton and Tomlinson (n 1 above) vol 1, 1384–1385.

14. The size and shape of constituencies, previously the responsibility of the Boundaries Commission, is now under the control of the Electoral Commission established under the Political Parties, Elections and Referendums Act 2000.

We have already noted various ways in which participants in elections and referendums are assisted in getting their messages to the voters in English law.[182]   **9.91**

G. Conclusion

This chapter has outlined the relationship between the obligations and powers of public authorities in respect of essentially political rights in English law, taking account of the impact of the HRA 1998 on the legal standards which previously applied. Those standards have continued to develop alongside the Convention rights under the HRA 1998. The common law and the 1998 Act are likely to cross-pollinate for some time to come. It can be said that the Act will probably have the effect of underpinning the already growing respect of the common law for pluralist political participation and expression as an essential element in maintaining and enhancing the democratic pedigree of English law. At the same time, the need to balance individual rights and social interests, inherent in the structure of political rights under the ECHR, presents judges and legislators with a considerable challenge. As they face up to it, lawyers and politicians must begin to articulate some of the fundamental principles of the model of indirect, representative democracy which underpins English public law. These principles were previously largely implicit rather than explicit in the constitution, and as they are drawn out the model itself must respond to the modern trend for people to engage in political campaigning on particular issues alongside, rather than within, the structure of traditional political parties. The political rights outlined in this chapter should provide a framework within which these adjustments can be made in a reasonably coherent way.   **9.92**

---

[182] See paras 9.18 et seq above.

10

SOCIAL, ECONOMIC AND CULTURAL RIGHTS

A. Introduction[1]

The enactment of the Human Rights Act 1998 (HRA) marked a watershed in **10.01** the legal culture of human rights in Britain. In the course of bringing about this change, however, remarkably little attention was paid to the rights themselves. The oft-stated policy of 'bringing rights home' assumed without question that the rights to be incorporated were those found in the European Convention on Human Rights (ECHR). In making this choice, policy-makers were expressing an implicit preference for the type of rights contained within the ECHR, almost all of which fall within the category known as 'civil and political rights'. Incorporation of socio-economic rights was never on the agenda.[2]

---

[1] The author is indebted to David Feldman and Christopher McCrudden for their very helpful comments on earlier drafts of this chapter.

[2] Contrast the full discussion and recommendation to incorporate socio-economic rights in the consultation on a Northern Ireland Bill of Rights. See Northern Ireland Human Rights Commission, *Making a Bill of Rights for Northern Ireland* (September 2001) ch 14.

10.02   Yet the major international and regional codes of human rights to which the United Kingdom is a party come in pairs, one of which refers to civil and political rights, and the other to economic and social (and often cultural) rights.[3] While the ECHR avowedly contains the political and civil rights to which the Council of Europe states are committed, the European Social Charter (ESC) contains the equivalent economic and social rights. Similarly, the International Covenant on Civil and Political Rights (ICCPR) is paired with the International Covenant on Economic, Social and Cultural Rights (ICESCR).

10.03   Traditionally, civil and political rights have been understood to refer to rights which protect individuals against intrusion by the state, while socio-economic rights concern rights to protection by the state against want or need. The decision to incorporate the former rather than the latter reflects an assumption that socio-economic rights are quintessentially political, to be regulated by Parliament rather than the courts.

10.04   This is not to say that the United Kingdom ignores or neglects the substantive issues covered by social rights. Entitlements, being political questions, are regulated by statute as part of the welfare state or labour law. But since such entitlements are not considered as 'fundamental human rights', courts have not developed techniques of statutory interpretation appropriate to human rights, but have preferred strict construction of the words of the relevant legislation. In an era before the advent of human rights law, this was an entirely consistent approach. But now that civil and political rights have been incorporated into domestic law, the question arises whether socio-economic entitlements should also be given the status of fundamental human rights. The incorporation of socio-economic rights has already been recommended for the proposed Northern Ireland Bill of Rights.[4] Moreover, the EU Charter of Fundamental Rights contains a number of central socio-economic rights. If the EU Charter becomes binding at EU level, this question will become even more pressing.

10.05   The exclusion of socio-economic rights from the HRA 1998 has been premised on the assumption that rights fall into two different categories. In this chapter, however, it is argued that it is too simplistic to view civil and political rights as separate and distinct from socio-economic rights. The difficult questions confronting the courts do not follow the contours of the traditional divide. Instead, the real challenges arise when one or more of three factors are implicated: (1) significant resource implications; (2) a positive duty to perform, and (3) 'target' duties, or duties subject to 'progressive realization'. These challenges can arise in

---

[3] An important recent exception is the European Charter of Fundamental Rights, proclaimed in 2000, which incorporates the whole spectrum of rights in one document. This is discussed in detail at paras 10.70–10.76 below.

[4] *Making a Bill of Rights for Northern Ireland* (n 2 above) ch 14.

respect of both sets of rights, and have already been confronted in adjudication under the HRA 1998.

It is therefore more helpful to focus on the nature of the obligation generated by different rights. As recent analysis has shown, both sets of rights give rise to a cluster of obligations: a primary duty to respect, a secondary duty to protect, and a tertiary duty to fulfil.[5] It is the secondary and tertiary obligations which raise specific difficulties for the judiciary, whatever category the right itself falls into. Many civil and political rights have already been interpreted as giving rise to positive duties with resource implications. The case law shows the courts struggling to develop appropriate standards of review in these areas.

10.06

The challenge for English public law is to evolve appropriate standards to adjudicate these different sorts of obligations. Should courts approach these issues using ordinary techniques of statutory interpretation, or should there be an overriding requirement of conformity with fundamental human rights principles? And what standard of review should be adopted? The familiar debate as to whether *Wednesbury* unreasonableness or proportionality is appropriate may need further refinement in respect of resource intensive rights. On the one hand, the polycentric nature of the dispute and the clear political dimension argue for judicial deference. On the other hand, there should be appropriate and robust protection of fundamental rights, however they are categorized. Instead of the familiar dichotomy between autonomy of executive decision-making and judicial intervention, it is possible to insert a third dimension, in the form of democratic constraints. These could take the form of judicially enforced requirements of participation by affected parties, as well as accountability via transparency and the articulation of intelligible reasons. The rapid evolution of rights beyond the primary duty makes it essential to pay closer attention to such questions.

10.07

B. The Nature of Socio-Economic Rights

(1) Socio-Economic Rights: The Traditional Analysis

(a) The ideology of socio-economic rights

Socio-economic rights have tended to be set apart from civil and political rights because they embody a different philosophy of the relationship between the individual and the state. Traditional human rights theory posits the state as a potential threat to liberty. The role of human rights, therefore, is to protect individuals against the state. By contrast, socio-economic rights are based on a more positive

10.08

---

[5] H Shue, *Basic Rights: Subsistence, Affluence, and US Foreign Policy* (2nd edn, Princeton: Princeton University Press, 1996).

vision of the state. Instead of being a threat to liberty, the state is viewed as essential to the maintenance of liberty.

10.09   Underlying this difference are also two distinct versions of liberty. The traditional model posits liberty as freedom from interference. Socio-economic rights are founded on a different vision of freedom, the attempt to secure freedom from want and fear. As President Roosevelt put it in 1941: 'True individual freedom cannot exist without economic security and independence . . . We have accepted, so to speak, a second bill of rights, under which a new basis of security and prosperity can be established for all.'[6] Thus, instead of keeping the state at bay, the active participation of the state in moving towards this ideal is enlisted.

10.10   For some, these two notions of freedom are mutually exclusive. Kelley, for example, argues that liberty rights reflect a political philosophy that prizes freedom, while welfare rights reflect a philosophy that is willing to sacrifice freedom.[7] By contrast, there are many who argue that true freedom is impossible without social rights. The rights to freedom of speech, freedom of association, or freedom of religion are of little or no value to a starving or homeless person. In order properly to enjoy these freedoms, the basic needs of individuals must be met.

10.11   It is true that at first glance, some civic rights do not appear to depend on the means or social standing of the individual. Among these are the right not to be detained without trial, the right not to be tortured, or the right to freedom of conscience or religion. However, those with few means will find it much harder to redress the violation of such rights than those who are well off. Other rights depend directly on means. The right to a fair trial, the right to freedom of speech, the right to stand for Parliament all require certain minimum resources.

10.12   The interrelationship between the two sets of rights works in both directions. Political and civil rights, including freedom of speech, might be highly instrumental in preventing or ameliorating poverty. Trade unions can only flourish in a climate of civil and political liberties. As Sen has argued, if leaders are not accountable to the population, and are insulated from the effects of famine or drought, they have no incentive to take action to protect the population from such disasters. Freedom of the press, a free opposition and freedom of information 'spread the penalty of famine to the ruling groups'. They also contribute greatly to dissemination of information which can assist in the prevention of such disasters. Moreover, he argues, the conceptualization of what constitutes a 'need', from the many deprivations we suffer in life, is itself a product of debate, discussion and the

---

[6]   11th Annual Message to Congress (11 January 1944) in J Israel (ed), *The State of the Union Messages of the Presidents* (New York: Chelsea House Publishers, 1966) vol 3, 2881, cited in H Steiner and P Alston, *International Human Rights in Context* (2nd edn, Oxford: OUP, 2000) 243.

[7]   D Kelley, *A Life of One's Own: Individual Rights and the Welfare State* (Washington DC: Cato Institute, 1998) 1.

political process. 'Political rights, including freedom of expression and discussion, are not only pivotal in inducing political responses to economic needs, they are also central to the conceptualisation of economic needs themselves.'[8] Most importantly, measures taken to ameliorate need can only be legitimate and effective with democratic participation.

This interrelationship was recognized at the Vienna World Conference in 1993, **10.13** which declared that all rights are 'indivisible and interdependent and inter-related'. One of the fundamental principles of the International Labour Organization (ILO) is that 'freedom of expression and of association are essential to sustained progress'.[9] Similarly, the preamble of the ICCPR states: 'The ideal of free human beings enjoying civil and political freedom and freedom from fear and want can only be achieved if conditions are created whereby everyone may enjoy his [or her] civil and political rights, as well as his [or her] economic, social and cultural rights'. A parallel provision is found in the ICESCR.

(b) Types of socio-economic rights

The notion of the state as facilitating freedom from want receives expression in **10.14** two different kinds of social rights. The first entails direct provision by the state against poverty, ill health, old age or other economic misfortunes. The second requires the state to facilitate self-help by individuals. Individuals have a right to be in a position to provide for themselves through work, without exploitation and under decent terms and conditions.

In the first category fall such rights as the right of everyone to an adequate stan- **10.15** dard of living, including adequate food, clothing and housing; the right to the highest attainable standard of physical and mental health; the right to social security, and education. For example, the ESC includes rights to vocational training, health, social security, welfare and assistance. Special mention is made of protection of the family, especially of mothers before and after childbirth, and of children. Added to these are the rights of every elderly person to social protection; the right to protection against poverty and social exclusion; and the right to housing. In domestic law, these issues are not conceived of as rights per se, but instead as falling within the realms of social policy.[10]

In the second category of social rights, the state, instead of providing directly, fa- **10.16** cilitates self-help through work. This in turn covers two sub-categories. The first directly regulates terms and conditions at work. It includes not merely the right to

---

[8] Amartya Sen, 'Freedoms and Needs', The New Republic, 10 and 17 January 1994, 31, 32, cited in Steiner and Alston (n 6 above) 269.

[9] ILO, Declaration of Philadelphia, adopted by the International Labour Conference in 1944 and later incorporated into the ILO's constitution.

[10] 4th Report of the United Kingdom on the implementation of the ICESCR, 28 February 2001.

work, but also the right to just and favourable conditions of work, fair wages, safe and healthy working conditions, reasonable working hours, and paid holidays.[11] The revised ESC of 1996 also includes the right of workers to dignity at work, to equal opportunities regardless of sex or family responsibilities, to protection in cases of termination of employment and insolvency, and to information and consultation in collective redundancies. The second sub-category facilitates self-help through organizational rights: the right to form and join free trade unions, the right to strike,[12] the right to bargain collectively,[13] and the right to take part in the determination and improvement of working conditions in the undertaking. In domestic law, these rights are considered to be part of labour law.

10.17   These two categories (direct provision and facilitation) are not, of course, mutually exclusive. For example, the right to adequate food imposes, in the first instance, an obligation on the state to facilitate people's access to the means of ensuring their own livelihood. It also requires direct provision of food, for those who, for reasons beyond their control, are unable to provide for themselves.[14]

10.18   Thus far the discussion has proceeded as if social and economic rights formed a single, harmonious whole. In fact, it is possible to see social rights as not just distinct, but as in potential conflict with economic rights. This is particularly clear in the context of EU law. As will be seen below, in the European Union, economic rights such as freedom of movement of persons, capital and goods have been given the status of fundamental rights. These, in turn, have been used to limit both social rights and civil and political rights. It is for this reason that the European Court of Justice began to develop its own jurisprudence of fundamental rights, culminating in the drafting of the EU Charter itself.

10.19   The link between social and economic rights has also been exploited to advance a neo-liberal characterization of fundamental rights, which uses the terminology of 'social and economic rights' to subordinate the social to the economic. Thus, it has been argued, the ICESCR has failed to protect 'economic freedoms, property rights, non-discriminatory conditions of competition and the rule of law'.[15] On this view, it is necessary to assert the indivisibility of civil, political, economic, social and cultural human rights in order to reduce the risk that some 'inalienable' human rights will be left without protection—and these rights are those found in

---

[11] Art 7 ICSECR; Arts 1–4 ESC (1996).

[12] Art 8 ICSECR; Arts 5, 6 ESC.

[13] Art 6 ESC.

[14] Committee on Economic, Cultural and Social Rights (CESC), *General Comment 12 (1999)*, UN Doc E/C/12 1999/5, para 15.

[15] E Petersmann, 'Time for a United Nations Global Compact' (2002) 13 European J of International L 621, 639–640; and see the persuasive critiques by P Alston, 'Resisting the Merger and Acquisition of Human Rights by Trade Law' (2002) 13 European J of International L 815 and R Howse, 'Human Rights in the WTO' (2002) 13 European J of International L 651.

an economic constitution which protects the 'welfare-increasing effects of economic and political competition'.[16] Individuals should be empowered to pursue human rights values (such as the right to import and export goods and services) through decentralized 'market governance mechanisms', rather than through the 'authoritarian' regulatory functions of governments which cannot directly produce the economic resources needed for the protection of human rights.

To avoid this result, it is more appropriate to consider economic freedoms and social rights separately, and to focus expressly on how they can be reconciled,[17] rather than following the established practice of running them together as a package. It is for this reason that this chapter uses the terminology of socio-economic rights. However, the general assumption that social, economic and cultural rights form a logical bundle remains at the core of key human rights documents such as the ICESCR.   **10.20**

Less attention has been paid to the category of 'cultural' rights. The ICESCR recognizes the right of everyone to 'take part in cultural life' and the corresponding obligations on states parties 'include those necessary for the conservation, the development and the diffusion of . . . culture'.[18] However, cultural rights are not defined. More illuminating is the draft UNESCO Declaration of Cultural Rights,[19] according to which culture should be regarded as 'the set of distinctive spiritual, material, intellectual and emotional features of society or a social group, and that it encompasses, in addition to art and literature, lifestyles, ways of living together, value systems, traditions and beliefs'. Cultural rights therefore entail that 'all persons should be able to express themselves and to create and disseminate their work in the language of their choice, and particularly in their mother tongue; all persons should be entitled to quality education and training that fully respect their cultural identity; and all persons should be able to participate in the cultural life of their choice and conduct their own cultural practices, subject to respect for human rights and fundamental freedoms'.[20]   **10.21**

Cultural rights are closely associated with minority rights. The majority in a state takes its own culture for granted and is in a position to impose that culture on minorities, either through express assimilationist policies, or by failing to provide the appropriate opportunities or resources for minority cultural expression. Cultural rights can therefore fall on both sides of the traditional divide between civil and political rights and socio-economic rights. Freedom of speech, assembly,   **10.22**

---

[16] E Petersmann, 'Taking Human Dignity, Poverty and Empowerment of Individuals More Seriously' [2002] 13 European J of International L 845, 851.
[17] Alston (n 15 above) 843.
[18] Arts 15(1) and (2).
[19] UNESCO General Conference, session 31, Paris 2001: 31 C/44 Rev 2.
[20] Draft UNESCO declaration on cultural diversity, Art 5.

and religion are aspects of cultural rights which appear to fall squarely within the category of civil and political rights, establishing protection against intrusion by the state. But on closer inspection, it can be seen that for these to provide adequate protection for cultural rights, active intervention by the state is required. Thus freedom of speech is only useful to a minority if the state facilitates and provides for expression in the language of choice; as well as education in the language and religion of choice. In addition, it is necessary for the state to adjust majority cultural practices to accommodate minorities.

(c) Socio-economic rights and civil and political rights: blurring the boundaries

10.23   The incorporation of the civil and political rights under the ECHR and not socio-economic rights under sister conventions has been defended on the grounds that whereas the former are justiciable, the latter are not appropriately dealt with by courts. This is for three overlapping reasons. First, it is argued that socio-economic rights have significant resource implications. Judicial intervention would skew the process of resource allocation, which should be essentially political.

10.24   Secondly, socio-economic rights are said to give rise to positive duties on the state to take action. This is said to contrast with civil and political rights which impose a 'negative' duty on the state, ie a duty not to interfere with liberty. Suitability for judicial resolution has been considered to follow this cleavage. Whereas legislation to prevent interference can be, it is argued, relatively straightforward, aimed primarily at restraining the executive arm of government, positive rights require extensive regulation by courts of the executive.

10.25   Thirdly, socio-economic rights are said to be programmatic. While some rights, particularly the self-help rights, may be capable of immediate fulfilment, others, such as those requiring direct provision by the state, are dependent on the amount of resources available to the state. Shortage of resources may well make it impossible or extremely difficult for the state to make immediate provision. In recognition of this, the obligation placed on the state is often a programmatic one, demanding not immediate fulfilment, but progressive realization. Thus under Article 2 ICESCR, states parties undertake to 'take steps . . . to the maximum of its available resources, with a view to achieving progressively the full realisation of the rights recognised in the present Covenant'. By contrast, the obligations under the companion 'civil liberties' charters are mandatory and immediate. Thus Article 1 ECHR states that the parties 'shall secure to everyone within their jurisdiction the rights and freedoms' defined in the Convention. Similarly, states parties to the ICCPR undertake to give effect to the rights recognized in the Charter.

10.26   However, experience of the ECHR has already demonstrated that these three factors (the positive duty, resource implications and progressive realization) do not arise solely in respect of socio-economic rights. Even paradigmatic civil rights, such as the right not to be tortured, carry with them some element of positive duty on the part of the state. As well as refraining from torturing individuals directly, the state must protect individuals against interference by other, non-state actors.[21]

Nor are civil and political rights free of resource implications. The duty to secure **10.27** a fair trial (for example under Article 6 ECHR) requires significant expenditure in setting up courts which are sufficiently resourced to avoid unreasonable delay. What amounts to a 'reasonable delay' and 'reasonable resources' may well depend on the total available resources of a country and its political priorities. More resources are required to provide interpreters and legal aid in criminal proceedings. The very basic civic right to vote would not take place unless a government committed public funds to create fair electoral machinery.

Nor do such difficulties inevitably arise in the context of socio-economic rights. **10.28** In fact, socio-economic rights include a complex mix of different sorts of obligations. This is well illustrated by considering the ESC. Although this is a catalogue of economic and social rights, closer inspection shows that some rights do not necessarily impose positive duties, involve the state in resource allocation, or are programmatic. Examples of such rights are the rights to freedom of association, to strike and to collective bargaining. Others do, however, impose certain rules of social, economic or administrative organization. Provisions for vocational training, health, welfare, social security and social assistance are all of this nature.

The rights also differ in terms of their immediacy. Some of the obligations require **10.29** a state to take immediate action: to issue safety and health regulations, to set a minimum age of employment at 15, to afford leave of at least 12 weeks before and after childbirth, and to provide for equal pay for men and women doing work of equal value.[22] These are, in Kahn Freund's terms, obligations of result.[23] Other duties are more an obligation of means, whereby a state must aim to achieve a result by employing all the means reasonably available. For example, states undertake not to achieve, but to aim at a high and stable level of employment, progressively to reduce working hours, and to endeavour to raise progressively the system of social security to a higher level.[24]

(d) Redrawing the boundaries: the nature of the obligation

The above discussion has shown that the traditional categories of civil and political **10.30** rights on the one hand and socio-economic rights on the other are misleading. Far

---

[21] See para 10.33 below.
[22] See Arts 3(1), 7(1), 8(1) and 4(3) ICESCR.
[23] O Kahn Freund, 'The European Social Charter' in FG Jacobs (ed), *European Law and the Individual* (Amsterdam: North-Holland Publishing Co, 1976) 187.
[24] See Arts 1(1), 2(1), and 12(3) ICESCR.

more useful is to consider each right as giving rise to a cluster of obligations, some of which require the state to abstain from interfering, and others which entail positive action and resource allocation. It should be stressed at this point that the elucidation of different types of obligation does not mean that the obligation can exist independently of the right. The right remains primary; but greater analytic and practical clarity is achieved by a better understanding of the types of correlative obligations.

10.31   In his seminal work, Shue argues that rights can give rise to three types of correlative obligation: the primary obligation to respect, the secondary obligation to protect, and the tertiary obligation to promote.[25] *Primary* obligations require the state itself to refrain from infringing on a right. *Secondary* obligations require the state to protect the right against invasion by others. *Tertiary* obligations have been further sub-divided to include the duty to *facilitate* and the duty to *provide*. The obligation to *facilitate* means that the state must take active measures to strengthen people's access to resources, and to facilitate the effective use of resources. Finally, when an individual or group is unable to provide for themselves, states have an obligation to *provide* the right directly.[26]

10.32   Civil and political rights appear to be the paradigm example of rights giving rise to primary obligations: the state has a duty not to torture individuals, not to interfere with their bodily integrity, not to intrude on their homes or private lives, and not to interfere with their speech or religion. However, socio-economic rights frequently generate primary obligations too. Thus the right to a home gives rise to an obligation on the state not to carry out forced evictions; and the right to belong to a trade union requires the state to refrain from banning unions.

10.33   Secondary duties, by contrast, require the state to take positive steps, including the provision of a police force and criminal justice system, and the creation of legal prohibitions on private actors not to interfere with others' rights. Whereas such obligations have traditionally been associated primarily with socio-economic rights, it is clear that many civil and political rights also give rise to positive duties. In fact, as seen below, recent case law from the ECHR demonstrates the rapid evolution of positive duties generated by the rights contained therein.

10.34   It is the tertiary duties, to facilitate and provide, which pose the greatest challenges. These duties generally need only to be realized progressively and to the maximum of available resources. Thus some of the most oft-cited difficulties with socio-economic rights are in fact only associated with the tertiary obligation, and, as we have seen, the tertiary obligation is not inevitably triggered by socio-economic rights. But when tertiary duties are implicated, they do raise particular challenges for courts. These need to be confronted in their own right, rather than being used as a pretext for downgrading all socio-economic rights.

---

[25] Shue (n 5 above).
[26] *General Comment 12 (1999)* (n 14 above) para 13.

Thus the distinction between primary, secondary and tertiary obligations is a more precise and useful means of analysing different rights than the traditional categorization of civil and political rights and socio-economic rights. At the same time, it should be reiterated that the focus on obligations is merely a means of understanding and dealing with rights appropriately; it should not be regarded as an abandonment of the primary importance of rights themselves. **10.35**

(2) Justiciability and the Role of the Court

Critics of socio-economic rights frequently object, not to the ideal embodied in the right itself, but to the use of courts to interpret the right and provide remedies for individuals. The provision of socio-economic rights, on this argument, takes place through social policy delivery, in which the courts have an appropriately minor role. This is largely the approach in the United Kingdom, as reflected in its report to the UN Committee on its compliance with the socio-economic rights in the ICESCR.[27] **10.36**

There are two sorts of criticism of courts in this context. The first questions the legitimacy of the courts to deal with essentially political decisions about allocation of resources. Judges interpreting open-textured social rights could well draw on personal or institutional value judgments which upset the political balance. Alternatively, judges may not want to take responsibility for complex balancing of priorities when individual lives are at stake. **10.37**

The second criticism of courts is concerned with their competence. While courts have expertise in interpreting relatively determinate rules of law, it is argued, judges are not well equipped to deal with open-textured policy aims, to undertake cost-benefit analyses, to assess progress towards achieving objectives, or to examine spending priorities. The litigation process is particularly ill-suited for such tasks. Litigation is a bipolar process. It is initiated by an individual complainant, focuses on an individual grievance, is based only on information presented by the litigants, and requires individual resolution. Polycentric decisions, having ripple effects over a wide area of interests, are not effectively dealt with by resolving individual complaints in a piecemeal and ad hoc manner in the judicial arena. **10.38**

Redrawing the boundaries between civil and political rights and socio-economic rights to reflect different sorts of obligations makes it possible to examine the difficult questions of justiciability in a more focused manner. It is not so much the nature of the rights, as the type of obligation which gives rise to these problems. Primary obligations give rise to fewest problems of this sort, whether they are triggered by civil and political rights or socio-economic rights. This is because they are **10.39**

---

[27] UK report on Implementation of the ICESCR (4th periodic report submitted by states parties under Arts 16 and 17 of the Covenant), 30 January 2001.

generally negative, immediate, and determinate. But even in this area, there may, as we have seen, be resource implications.

10.40 More difficult questions arise in respect of secondary and tertiary obligations. First, it may be argued that it is impossible to define a minimum core content, and therefore the duties are indeterminate and non-justiciable. Asserting rights to social security, to protection against poverty, to the protection of health, or to housing does not, on its own, tell us what standard of living is the minimum commensurate with human dignity and freedom. This leads Kelley to argue that there is no appropriate role for the courts. Since there is 'no universal and non-arbitrary standard for distinguishing need from luxury', it is for the political process to draw the line.[28]

10.41 However, the indeterminacy of such rights can be overstated. The Committee on Economic, Social and Cultural Rights has set itself the task of developing the normative content of the rights. Although it recognizes the complexity of defining such a content given the wide variation in financial and administrative resources available to a state, the Committee has sought to develop a universal minimum standard while accepting that it may take some time to achieve.[29] An example is provided by the right to adequate housing. Thus it maintains 'while adequacy is determined in part by social, economic, cultural, climatic, ecological and other factors, the Committee believes that it is nonetheless possible to identify certain aspects of the right that must be taken into account. These include protection against forced eviction, harassment and other threats; access to safe drinking water, energy for cooking, heating and lighting, sanitation and washing facilities, site drainage and emergency services. In addition, housing must be affordable, habitable and in a location which allows access to jobs, schools and health-care.'[30] Although the minimum core may not be immediately realizable, a housing strategy must be adopted to achieve these ends.

10.42 The Committee has not defined a minimum core content to all the rights, but it is not difficult to identify the most blatant aspects. For example extreme poverty is defined as income or consumption of less than $1 a day; while relative poverty is defined as the poorest fifth of the population. The indicator for malnourishment is the proportion of children under five who are underweight.[31]

10.43 The second problem for the courts, arising specifically in respect of the tertiary obligation, concerns their programmatic nature. The traditional view defines a right as creating a corresponding obligation in another party, usually the state, to

---

[28] Kelley (n 7 above) 1.
[29] Steiner and Alston (n 6 above) 305.
[30] CESC, *General Comment 4 (1991)*, UN Doc E/1992/23, Annex III.
[31] UN Development Programme Poverty Report 1998, 15.

fulfil the right. But since tertiary rights are framed in terms of goals or targets, it is more difficult to locate such an obligation. Does the 'right' then evaporate into a mere aspiration?

It is, however, possible to demonstrate that the obligations generated by socio-economic rights can in fact be demarcated relatively precisely. This has been successfully achieved by the Committee on Economic, Social and Cultural Rights. 'The fact that realisation over time . . . is foreseen under the Covenant should not be misinterpreted as depriving the obligation of all meaningful content', it maintains. In order to demarcate the obligation more clearly, the Committee distinguishes between obligations of *conduct*, which are concrete and immediate, and obligations of *result*, which are more aspirational. The full realization of the relevant rights is an obligation of result. But the duty to take steps by all appropriate means is an obligation of conduct that is unqualified. The right therefore generates an immediate obligation to take steps towards the goal, and those steps should be 'deliberate, concrete and targeted as clearly as possible towards meeting the obligations recognised in the Covenant'.[32]

10.44

This is not to say that the judicial process is the sole or even inevitably the most appropriate means of enforcing socio-economic rights. A variety of other mechanisms may be better suited, ranging from tribunals, to ombudsmen, to audit bodies, to parliamentary scrutiny committees. A great deal of useful experience has been gained about the role of reporting mechanisms from the UN Committee, which has developed sophisticated techniques of monitoring compliance with the ICESCR.

10.45

But nor does it this mean that the courts should have no role. 'Courts are frequently involved in decision making on a considerable range of matters which have important resource allocation implications. The adoption of a rigid classification of economic, social and cultural rights which puts them, by definition, beyond the reach of the courts would thus be arbitrary . . . [and] drastically curtail the capacity of the courts to protect the rights of the most vulnerable and disadvantaged groups in society'.[33] The challenge is to define an appropriate role for the courts. It is to the role of the court that we now turn.

10.46

(3) Are Socio-Economic Rights Fundamental Rights?

In the United Kingdom, welfare has always been considered to lie in the domain of ordinary legislation and executive discretion. Indeed, welfare entitlements have always been labelled 'benefits', reflecting an ideology of concession and discretion, not one of rights. So far as labour law is concerned, until the 1970s, even legislative

10.47

---

[32] CESC, *General Comment 3 (1990)*, UN Doc E/199123, Annex III.
[33] CESC, *General Comment 9 (1998)*, UN Doc E/1999/22, Annex IV, para 10.

rights were eschewed, on the basis that courts could not be trusted to adjudicate collective matters. In the past three decades, the area has become largely statutory. This raises two sorts of questions for English public law. The first is whether socio-economic rights have been effectively delivered, whether by social policy, statute or other methods. The second is what the courts can do about a failure properly to do so. When the courts are implicated, a key further question of judicial approach arises. Should socio-economic rights be regarded as fundamental human rights, or subject to ordinary canons of statutory interpretation or review of executive discretion?

10.48   What difference would it make then for rights to be considered as fundamental? In the context of review of discretion, the current approach is to require no more than *Wednesbury* reasonableness; and where resource allocation is concerned the courts have articulated a particularly deferential standard, often requiring proof of abuse of power before intervention can be justified.[34] A fundamental rights approach, by contrast, would require the courts to take a more intrusive approach. On such an approach, the state is required to justify any infringement of a right to a high level. This is often expressed as a proportionality principle, entailing judicial scrutiny of both the end pursued, and the appropriateness of the means to the ends. In particular, the state would need to establish that it was pursuing a legitimate state interest, and that this purpose could not be achieved without infringing on the right. Even on a fundamental rights approach, the intensity of judicial review could vary. A more intense standard would require the state to establish a 'pressing' state interest, and to show 'minimal impairment' of the right. A less intensive standard would be content with a legitimate state interest, and proof that the infringement of the right was 'reasonably necessary' to achieve that aim.

10.49   The move from a deferential towards a fundamental rights approach has already been experienced in relation to ECHR rights. Even before the HRA 1998 came into force, the courts were generally in agreement with the well known dictum of Sir Thomas Bingham MR, when he said: 'The more substantial the interference with human rights, the more the court will require by way of justification before it is satisfied that the decision is reasonable . . .'.[35] Even this was held not to be sufficiently stringent to comply with the ECHR, which required a strict proportionality approach.[36] A move to a fundamental rights approach in the context of socio-economic rights would require a similar stiffening of the standard.

10.50   In the context of statutory interpretation, a fundamental rights approach has a similar impact. Instead of strict textual analysis, courts following a fundamental

---

[34] *R v Secretary of State for the Environment, ex p Nottinghamshire CC* [1986] AC 240, HL; *R v Secretary of State for the Environment, ex p Hammersmith and Fulham LBC* [1990] 1 AC 521, HL.
[35] *R v Ministry of Defence, ex p Smith* [1996] QB 517, 554.
[36] *Smith and Grady v UK (No 1)* (1999) 29 EHRR 493.

rights approach will draw on such rights as an interpretive and purposive resource. A particularly salient example of such an approach is found in the opinion of the Advocate General in the case of *R (on the application of BECTU) v Secretary of State for Trade and Industry*,[37] which was concerned with the right to paid annual leave granted by the EC Working Time Directive.[38] UK regulations only afforded the right to workers after they had been continuously employed for 13 weeks by the same employer, thus depriving workers on short-term contracts from enjoying the right. The Directive requires member states to ensure that every worker is entitled to paid annual leave of at least four weeks 'in accordance with the conditions for entitlement to, and granting of, such leave laid down by national legislation and/or practice'.[39] The question was whether these words went so far as to permit a member state to deprive some workers of the right altogether in specific circumstances such as that they did not work continuously for the same employer for more than 13 weeks at a time.

In interpreting this proviso, Advocate General Tesauro consciously took a funda-   **10.51**
mental rights approach. 'In order to give a helpful answer to the national court, it is appropriate to step back and, above all place entitlement to paid annual leave in the wider context of fundamental social rights.' He went on to show that the right to paid annual leave had been recognized as a fundamental human right in the Universal Declaration of Human Rights,[40] the ESC of 1961[41] and the ICESCR.[42] Most importantly, the EU Charter of Fundamental Rights declares expressly that every worker has a right to an annual period of paid leave.[43] Although he acknowledged that the Charter was not in itself legally binding, he took to the view that 'we cannot ignore its clear purpose of serving, where its provisions so allow, as a substantive point of reference for all those involved . . . in the Community context. Accordingly, I consider that the Charter provides us with the most reliable and definitive confirmation of the fact that the right to paid annual leave constitutes a fundamental human right.'[44]

This led him to a particular mode of interpretation of the relevant provisions.   **10.52**
Because paid leave is a fundamental social right, derogations must be applied restrictively. Therefore, whereas national laws or practice may lay down conditions and arrangements for the accrual and taking of leave, they may not go so far as to stop any entitlement from arising, by making it conditional upon completion of

---

[37] Case C-173/99 [2001] ECR I-4881.
[38] Directive (EC) 93/104 [1993] OJ 307/18.
[39] ibid Art 7(1).
[40] Art 24: 'Everyone has the right to . . . periodic holidays with pay'.
[41] Art 2(3).
[42] Art 7(d).
[43] Art 31(2).
[44] ECR I-4881 at [22]–[28].

a minimum qualifying period with the same employer. Any permissible limitations could be justified only if they were proved strictly necessary. In particular, and significantly, a limitation on the right could not in any circumstances be justified solely on the grounds that the right would be too costly for the employer.

10.53 The Court itself was less explicit in its reliance on a fundamental rights approach than the Advocate General. But it too drew on the Community Charter of Fundamental Social Rights of Workers adopted in 1989, and stated explicitly that the entitlement of every worker to paid annual leave must be regarded as a particularly important principle of Community social law from which there can be no derogations.

10.54 The domestic courts are still wrestling with the appropriate balance between deference and scrutiny, particularly in the areas in which civil and political rights clearly raise issues of resource allocation. This can be seen in the recent *ProLife* case, which concerned the duty of the BBC to provide free broadcasting time to registered political parties, subject to the general standards of taste and decency with which all programmes are required by law to comply. ProLife, a political party campaigning against abortion, complained that its right to free speech under Article 10 ECHR had been infringed when the BBC refused to transmit videos showing 'prolonged and deeply disturbing' images of aborted foetuses. Laws LJ in the Court of Appeal[45] made it clear that where fundamental rights were at issue, usual techniques of statutory interpretation needed radical revision. 'The court's duty in confronting the claims of free speech, and the claims that may be ranged against it, in a context like that of the present case is very far distant from any exercise of textual interpretation. We are dealing here with bedrock principles.'[46]

10.55 However, the House of Lords took a more complex view. As Lord Nicholls put it: 'Article 10 does not entitle ProLife Alliance or anyone else to make free television broadcasts. Article 10 confers no such right. But that by no means exhausts the application of article 10 in this context. In this context the principle underlying article 10 requires that access to an important public medium of communication should not be refused on discriminatory, arbitrary or unreasonable grounds. Nor should access be granted subject to discriminatory, arbitrary or unreasonable conditions. A restriction on the content of a programme, produced by a political party to promote its stated aims, must be justified. Otherwise it will not be acceptable. This is especially so where, as here, the restriction operates by way of prior restraint. On its face prior restraint is seriously inimical to freedom of political communication.'[47]

---

[45] *R (on the application of ProLife Alliance) v BBC* [2002] EWCA Civ 297; [2002] 3 WLR 1080.
[46] ibid at [34].
[47] [2003] UKHL 23; [2003] 2 WLR 1403 at [8].

Just as before its incorporation the ECHR was increasingly a source of interpretive principles by domestic courts in their construction of domestic law, so the ESC principles could perform this function. What is striking is that they have not. As will be seen below, domestic courts have been loath to use the same approach in the context of social rights, preferring strict statutory interpretation and marked deference to executive decision-making. **10.56**

C. Sources of Socio-Economic Rights

(1) International

There are several international treaties concerning socio-economic rights to which the United Kingdom is a party, most important of which is the ICESCR. Such treaties are not directly binding on domestic courts.[48] Despite being of persuasive authority, the ICESCR has played little if any role in domestic litigation.[49] The more direct obligation of the United Kingdom is to report to the Committee on Economic, Social and Cultural Rights on the measures it has adopted and the progress made in achieving the observance of the rights under the ICESCR.[50] **10.57**

Also an important source of socio-economic rights, specifically in the labour law field, is the ILO. The UK government has ratified 84 ILO conventions, (of which 65 are in force) including those on freedom of association,[51] and the right to organize.[52] Although these obligations are not directly enforceable as part of domestic law, until the 1980s successive governments sought to comply with their obligations. However, the Thatcher and Major governments saw the conventions as a spoke in the wheel of productivity and flexibility. Five ILO conventions were denounced between 1979 and 1987, and only one of 25 new ILO conventions adopted in this period was ratified by the United Kingdom. **10.58**

During this period, the UK government went even further and defied international standards. In particular, it refused to reinstate trade union rights for civil servants employed at the Government Communications Headquarters. This was despite the finding by the ILO Committee on Freedom of Association in 1984 that this violated ILO conventions. Annual condemnation by the ILO of the UK government met with equally determined resistance. It was only after the Labour government came into power in 1997 that the ban on trade unions at GCHQ was reversed, bringing the United Kingdom back into line with the ILO **10.59**

---

[48] They are of course binding in international law.
[49] See further paras 10.77 et seq below.
[50] See eg 4th Report (n 10 above).
[51] Convention No 87 (1948).
[52] Convention No 98 (1949).

Committee on Freedom of Association. However, since 1997, only two conventions have been ratified, one concerning child labour and the other related to the hours of work of seafarers.

(2) Council of Europe: The European Social Charter

10.60   As mentioned above, the social and economic counterpart of the ECHR is the ESC. First adopted in 1961, it was revised and revitalized in 1996 to include important modernizing measures such the right of workers to dignity at work, to equal opportunities regardless of sex or family responsibilities, and to participate in the determination and improvement of working conditions in the undertaking. This came into force in July 1999.

10.61   The Charter, as with other catalogues of socio-economic rights, demonstrates the importance of focusing on the different types of obligations imposed on the state. In the 1996 ESC, for example, the immediacy of the obligation of the contracting party varies widely according to the substance of the right. Several articles require the state to 'provide' that a right be guaranteed[53] or to 'ensure' that an individual has the right in question.[54] In other rights, the emphasis is far more on tertiary obligations. Thus the right to protection against poverty and social exclusion[55] requires states 'to take measures within the framework of an overall and co-ordinated approach to promote' the effective access of persons at risk of poverty to employment, housing, training, education, culture, and social and medical assistance. Similarly the right to housing[56] translates into an undertaking to 'take measures designed to promote access to housing of an adequate standard, to prevent and reduce homelessness with a view to its gradual elimination [and] to make the prices of housing accessible to those without adequate resources'.

10.62   In all, the United Kingdom has accepted only 60 of the Charter's 72 paragraphs. This is fewer than most EU member states: only Denmark has accepted fewer. Of the 28 'hard core' paragraphs, the United Kingdom has agreed to be bound by 25. Although the United Kingdom signed the revised ESC on 7 November 1997, it has not yet been ratified.

10.63   The ESC is expressly referred to in the Treaty of Amsterdam as a source of principles of EU social policy.[57] It should therefore in principle be an important source of fundamental principles of social rights. Nevertheless, as with the international

---

[53] Art 25 ESC: protection in case of insolvency.
[54] Unfair dismissal (Art 24 ESC); protection of workers' representatives (Art 28 ESC); right to information and consultation in collective redundancies (Art 29 ESC).
[55] Art 30 ESC.
[56] Art 31 ESC.
[57] See para 10.68 below.

documents, it has played very little part in the domestic jurisprudence.[58] Compliance is instead dependent on the effectiveness of the Council of Europe monitoring system which is based on the submission of biennial reports by contracting parties. The record of the United Kingdom on this score is far from perfect.

(3) EU Social Law[59]

Unlike the international obligations referred to above, EU law is directly enforceable in domestic law. It therefore has the most direct impact on English public law. Nevertheless, it is only recently that EU law has moved into the arena of social law. The EEC Treaty signed in 1957 contained no express provisions for the protection of human rights and its provisions on social policy were aspirational rather than taking the form of legally enforceable provisions.[60] Instead the purposes were limited to economic integration. Rights only warranted protection if they were necessary for the furtherance of this economic ideal. It was for this reason that social rights, with the exception of free movement of labour and equal pay for equal work, were excluded.[61] **10.64**

During the 1970s, the Heads of Government committed themselves to a community which gave equal priority to social policy as to the realization of economic union. However, there was no Treaty amendment giving the Community the power to legislate in the social field. The result was that outside the areas of equal pay and of health and safety only a trickle of directives emerged during the 1970s.[62] By the mid-1990s, this had resulted in a legislative log-jam, with the UK government exercising an effective veto over further developments in the protection of social rights. **10.65**

In the meanwhile, the European Court of Justice was struggling to resolve the clash between 'economic freedoms' and 'social standards'. The vocabulary of fundamental rights to characterize the free movement provisions[63] led to their wide-ranging use to limit public power, and protect free market competition. Any rule which had an impact on trade could be struck down even if it had its origins in social policy **10.66**

---

[58] See paras 10.77 et seq below.
[59] This section is drawn from Hepple and Fredman, 'Great Britain' in Blanpain (ed), *International Encyclopaedia of Labour Law* (Deventer: Kluwer). See S Fredman, C McCrudden and M Freedland, 'An EU Charter of Fundamental Rights' [2000] PL 178.
[60] See Art 117 Treaty of Rome.
[61] 'Social Aspects of European Economic Co-operation: Report of a Group of Experts' [1956] 74 Industrial L Rev 99, 104–105.
[62] Directive (EC) 75/120 [1975] OJ L48/29 (collective redundancies); Directive (EC) 80/987 [1980] OJ L283/23 (insolvency); and Directive (EC) 77/187 [1977] OJ L61/26 (transfer of undertakings).
[63] See M Maduro, 'Striking the Elusive Balance Between Economic Freedom and Social Rights in the EU' in P Alston (ed), *The EU and Human Rights* (Oxford: OUP, 1999) 449, 451–452.

concerns[64] unless it was necessary to attain an objective justified in regard to Community law.[65] The effect of this approach to social rights was witnessed in the decisions on Sunday trading.[66] In these cases, the Court held that limitations on Sunday trading, although based in social concerns, could be subjected to strict scrutiny because they reduced the sale of imported goods from other member states. This meant that national courts were left with the difficult task of deciding whether the social concerns behind Sunday trading restrictions could be justified as compatible with the exceptions set out in Community law.[67]

10.67   More recently, the focus on the free market has been somewhat tempered. In the *Keck*[68] decision in 1993, the Court recognized that traders had been given too powerful a weapon to challenge any rules whose effect was to limit their commercial freedom even where such rules were not aimed at products from other member states. This 'exploded the notion that there might be an individual "right to trade" capable of vindication via EC internal market law',[69] and made it possible for states to regulate some aspects of trade free of EC scrutiny. Nevertheless, there remains a tension between 'the image of the Community worker as a mobile unit of production . . . and the image of the worker as human being, exercising the personal right to move and to live in another State and to take up employment there without discrimination, to improve the standard of living of his or her family'.[70]

10.68   From 1986, a concerted effort was made to put social policy on an entirely new footing, culminating in the Treaty of Amsterdam. Article 2 states that the Community aims to promote, by means of the common market, not just a high degree of competitiveness and economic development, but also a high level of employment and social protection, equality between men and women, protection of the environment and the raising of the standard of living among member states. Article 136 refers specifically to 'fundamental social rights such as those set out in the European Social Charter signed at Turin on 18 October 1961 and in the 1989 Community Charter of the Fundamental Social Rights of Workers'.

---

[64] The *Cassis de Dijon* decision: Case 120/78 *Rewe-Zentrale AG v Bundesmonopolverwaltung für Branntwein* [1979] ECR 649.

[65] Art 30 EEC Treaty: 'Public morality, public policy or public security; the protection of health and life of humans, animals or plants, the protection of national treasures possessing artistic, historic or archaeological value; or the protection of industrial and commercial property'. This was augmented in the *Cassis de Dijon* decision to include the effectiveness of fiscal supervision, the protection of public health, the fairness of commercial transactions and the defence of the consumer: [1979] ECR 649 at [8].

[66] Case 145/88 *Torfaen BC v B & Q plc* [1989] ECR 3851.

[67] Cases C-306/88, 394/90 and 169/91 *Stoke-on-Trent City Council v B & Q plc* [1992] ECR I-6457. For a similar pattern in respect of competition law, see P Davies, 'Market Integration and Social Policy in the Court of Justice' (1995) 24 ILJ 49.

[68] Cases C 267 & 268/91 *Keck and Mithouard* [1993] ECR I-6097.

[69] S Weatherill, 'After *Keck*' [1996] CML Rev 885, 904-906.

[70] P Craig and G de Burca, *EU Law: Text, Cases and Materials* (3rd edn, Oxford: OUP, 2002) 665.

Most importantly, the Social Chapter[71] for the first time gives a proper mandate for the Community to legislate in respect of aspects of social law. Important socio-economic rights, however, are excluded. Most surprisingly, freedom of association, pay, and the right to strike or to impose lock-outs remain outside of the legislative competence of the European Union.

The result of the accumulation of new powers has been an acceleration of social **10.69** policy directives, including the right to maximum limits on working time and four weeks' paid holiday;[72] the right of pregnant workers to protection against dismissal and maternity leave;[73] the right to parental and family leave;[74] and the right to equal treatment for part-time workers.[75] The Treaty also includes a new title on employment designed to generate policies to combat unemployment.

However, by far the most sophisticated contribution to the field of socio-economic **10.70** rights is the EU Charter of Fundamental Rights, adopted in Nice in December 2000. This is because it expressly and self-consciously breaks out of the traditional distinction between civil and political rights, on the one hand, and social and economic on the other. Instead, the rights are arranged in chapters, based on several major concepts: human dignity, fundamental freedoms, equality, solidarity, citizenship and justice. The chapter on fundamental freedoms includes the right to freedom of association at all levels, including the right to form and to join trade unions; the right to education; and the right to engage in work. The equality rights include respect for cultural, religious and linguistic diversity, the rights of the child, of the elderly and of those with disabilities. Among the solidarity rights are found workers' rights to information and consultation, the right of collective bargaining, the right to strike, protection against unjustified dismissal and the right to fair and just working conditions. There is also a recognition of the right to social security, access to health care, and environmental and consumer protection.

Instead of the traditional distinction, the EU Charter specifically differentiates **10.71** between rights and principles. As explained by Vitorino, the drafters intended to distinguish between enforceable rights on the one hand, and principles that can be relied on against the authorities. 'Rights', which can be pleaded directly in a court in a particular dispute, can be identified by the fact that the holder is clearly designated. Thus Article 28 gives workers and employers the right to negotiate and to take collective action, and 'every worker' is given the rights to protection against dismissal, and to fair and just working conditions.

---

[71] Arts 136-143 EC.
[72] Working Time Directive (n 38 above).
[73] Pregnant Workers' Directive (EC) 92/85 [1992] OJ L348/1.
[74] Parental Leave Directive (EC) 96/34 [1996] OJ L145/4.
[75] Part-Time Workers Directive (EC) 97/81 [1998] OJ L14/9. For developments in sex discrimination at EU level, see paras 11.33 et seq below.

10.72   Principles, by contrast, give rise to a different sort of obligation. They are mandatory for the authorities, who must comply with them when exercising their powers. They must be observed, and may call for implementation through legislative or executive acts. Thus, they become significant for the courts when such acts are interpreted or reviewed.[76] But they cannot be used by private individuals to bring an action in court to enforce them. To make this absolutely clear, the 2002 Convention recommended the addition of a clause to the Charter stating as follows:

> The provisions of this Charter which contain principles may be implemented by legislative and executive acts taken by institutions and bodies of the Union, and by acts of Member States when they are implementing Union law, in the exercise of their respective powers. They shall be judicially cognisable only in the interpretation of such acts and in the ruling on their legality.[77]

This approach is strongly reminiscent of the distinction in the Indian Constitution between fundamental rights and directive principles.[78]

10.73   The 2002 Convention also reiterated that the wording of the Charter should make it very clear which sort of obligation was being referred to. Principles can be identified by the fact that the right-holder is not expressly designated, but instead, the Union is referred to as having to respect or recognize a specific value.[79] Thus Article 34, relating to the provision of social security, states: 'the union recognises and respects the entitlement to social security benefits and social services . . . the right to social and housing assistance'. Similarly, Article 38, on consumer protection states: 'Union policies shall ensure a high level of consumer protection'. Cultural rights, found in Article 22, are similarly phrased as: 'The Union shall respect cultural, religious and linguistic diversity'; while, in respect of disability, Article 26 states: 'The Union recognises and respects the right of persons with disabilities to benefit from measures designed to ensure their independence, social and occupational integration and participation in the life of the community'.[80]

10.74   It is arguable that the Charter stops too far short of creating a genuine set of socio-economic rights, indivisible from civil and political rights. This is partly because it does not include all the rights found in either the ESC or the EU's own Charter of Fundamental Social Rights of Workers of 1989, and partly because of the equivocal way in which many of these obligations are expressed.[81] Even rights giving rise

---

[76] Final report of Working Group II CONV 354/02, para 6, Brussels, 22 October 2002.

[77] Proposed clause 52 (5). Report of Working Group II, Annex.

[78] See para 10.139 below.

[79] Antonio Vitorino, 'The Charter of Fundamental Rights as a Foundation for the Area of Freedom, Security and Justice' Exeter Paper in European Law 4 (University of Exeter, May 2001) 25–26.

[80] ibid 25.

[81] KD Ewing, *The EU Charter of Fundamental Rights: Waste of Time or Wasted Opportunity?* (London: Institute of Employment Rights, 2002).

to primary obligations, such as the right of collective bargaining and the right to information and consultation, are subject to conditions provided for either by Community law or national law or both. Even more problematic is the fact that the 'principles', which clearly place positive duties on governments to take action, have no corresponding compliance mechanisms, comparable to the committees which scrutinize compliance with the ESC or the ICESCR.

Much controversy has, indeed, surrounded the extent to which the Charter should be binding. Because of the opposition of some member states, it was decided to issue the Charter in the form of a 'solemn proclamation'. Nevertheless, there is no doubt that it has legal effects. There are at least two ways in which these effects manifest themselves. First, the European Court of Justice may draw on the principles in the Charter in reaching the decision. As shown above, this has already been manifested in the opinion of Advocate General Tesauro in the recent case of *R (on the application of BECTU) v Secretary of State for Trade and Industry*.[82]   **10.75**

Secondly, the Commission has already decided to 'mainstream' the Charter, on the ground that its implications should be felt 'in every aspect of the Union's legislative activity and day-to-day management and in its negotiations with the outside world'.[83] A Communication[84] requires all legislative initiatives to be checked against the Charter. A recital is to be inserted into all instruments stating that the legislation has been reviewed in this way, thereby creating a visible link to the Charter. According to Commissioner Vitorino, by the time the status of the Charter is reconsidered in 2004, it will already have been confirmed in practice, and the impetus to incorporate it into the treaties will be unstoppable. [85]   **10.76**

D. Application of Social Rights in Domestic Law

(1) Domestic Provision in Statute and Policy

As suggested above, the primary means of providing socio-economic rights in domestic law has been through social policy and statute. Thus, when asked by the ICESCR Committee to elaborate the effect the United Kingdom intends to give to its obligations under the ICESCR, the UK government stated that the Convention is not directly applied as law. Instead, each article of the Convention is given effect by specific laws, policies and practices described in the paragraphs   **10.77**

---

[82]   Case C-173/99 ECR I-4881.
[83]   Vitorino (n 79 above) 16.
[84]   Communication of the Commission on the legal nature of the Charter of Fundamental Rights of the EU; Com (2000)644 final of 11 October 2000.
[85]   Vitorino (n 79 above) 16.

of the reports relating to that article.[86] This section therefore briefly describes the way in which the United Kingdom, through its reports on both the ICESCR and the ESC, perceives itself as providing the major socio-economic rights established in these two treaties. It is noteworthy that the approach in the UK reports is entirely descriptive, describing existing provision, rather than regarding the treaties as creating normative standards according to which active measures need to be taken to ensure compliance.

10.78   As will be seen, many rights are delivered through social policy, and do not create individual entitlements. Where individual entitlements do arise, they are either closely defined by the statute, or depend heavily on discretionary powers of public authorities. It is in this context that the question arises as to whether courts should be involved in any way in such delivery. If they are, should courts use ordinary techniques of statutory interpretation and principles of judicial review? Or should they adopt a fundamental rights approach, which entails a strong presumption in favour of the right, and a heavy onus on the state to justify encroachment?

(a) Work

10.79   The first major socio-economic right protected in both treaties is the right to work.[87] To ensure the effective exercise of the right to work, states must 'accept as one of their primary aims and responsibilities the achievement and maintenance of as high and stable a level of employment as possible'. At the same time they must effectively protect the right of the worker to earn a living in an occupation freely entered on, to maintain free employment services, and to provide vocational training and guidance.[88]

10.80   The right to work in domestic law is delivered primarily through labour market policies. The current government has concentrated on 'welfare to work' policies as the key to helping people to take up employment, combined with tax benefit reforms to make work pay.[89] Central to these policies have been the New Deal programmes, which aim to help unemployed people move from welfare into work. Notably, they go beyond the provision of a benefit payment, and instead provide positive assistance with skills and experience, the aim being to assist individuals to

---

[86] Implementation of the ICESCR: Issues to be taken up in connection with the consideration of the 4th Periodic Report of the United Kingdom of Great Britain and Northern Ireland (E/C.12/4Add.5, E/C.12/4/Add.7, E/C.12/4/Add.8): Response of the Government of the United Kingdom, A1.

[87] Art 6 ICESCR; Art 1 ESC.

[88] Art 1 ESC.

[89] ESC 21st Report on the Implementation of the ESC submitted by the Government of the United Kingdom, 4 September 2001, RAP/Cha/UK/XXII(2001) 3–61.

enter and remain in employment throughout their working lives.[90] However, they do not create individualized, justiciable rights. A further means of promoting work is through training, in particular, the 'Modern Apprenticeship' programme. As at December 2000, 225,500 young people had places in this scheme, while a further 53,500 were in other types of work-based training. The government claims a high degree of success for these policies, with over 95 per cent of young people on Advanced Modern Apprenticeships, and 84 per cent of those on Modern Apprenticeships were in employment six months after leaving.

(b) Working conditions

Allied to the right to work is the right to just and favourable conditions of work, including fair wages, a decent living, safe and healthy working conditions, equal opportunity for promotion, reasonable limitation of working hours, and paid holidays.[91] Until 1997, several major aspects of these rights were not catered for in legislation, but some of the gaps have subsequently been filled. Thus the right to reasonable working hours and paid holidays was not provided for in UK legislation until 1998, the idea being that collective bargaining was sufficient. This was remedied by the introduction of the Working Time Regulations in 1998.[92] Notably, the impetus for change was the mandatory legislation introduced in the European Union[93] rather than the ICESCR or the ESC. Unlike the policy measures on the right to work, the working hours legislation does create individual justiciable rights and therefore directly raises the question whether a court should draw on fundamental rights principles, or use ordinary techniques of statutory interpretation. As was seen above, the fundamental rights approach enabled the Advocate General in *BECTU*[94] to give an expansive definition of the right to paid holidays, as opposed to the much narrower statutory approach of the domestic courts.

10.81

Similarly, there were no systematic attempts to establish a national minimum wage[95] until the National Minimum Wage Act 1998, which, the government claims, has benefited more than a million workers. This gives an individual right, enforceable in the courts. It is also enforced by specialist compliance officers from the Inland Revenue, who undertake appropriate action to ensure that the minimum rate and any arrears of pay are paid. Here too, the question arises whether judges will regard the minimum wage as a fundamental right and interpret it accordingly, or whether it should be interpreted according to ordinary statutory

10.82

---

[90] ibid para 6.04.
[91] Art 7 ICESCR; Art 2 ESC (specifying inter alia two weeks' paid holiday).
[92] SI 1998/1833.
[93] Working Time Directive (n 38 above).
[94] See para 10.51 above.
[95] Wages Councils set minimum pay for specified categories of low paid workers until their abolition by Trade Union Reform and Employment Relations Act 1993, s 35. See Trades Boards Act 1909, Wages Councils Act 1945, Wages Act 1986.

construction. In a recent case, the domestic courts used a restrictive statutory approach to the enforcement powers of the Inland Revenue, denuding workers in many cases of an effective remedy.[96] Notably, the government responded by promising remedial legislation.[97]

10.83   In the 2001 reporting round, the Committee for Social, Economic and Cultural Rights specifically asked the UK government whether the minimum wage provided for a reasonable standard of living. In its response, the government stressed, not the standard of living provided, but the affordability to the employer. Thus, it stated, the minimum wage was set at a rate which was 'affordable by most employers and [did] not put at risk the very jobs the lower-paid need if they are to benefit from the minimum wage'.[98] It also argued that, with tax measures such as the Working Families Tax Credit and other benefits, the minimum wage provided a guaranteed minimum income of at least £225 a week (£11,700 per year) for families with someone in full-time work (which for this purpose is counted as 35 hours per week). Whether this provided a reasonable standard of living was not specifically dealt with.

(c) Trade unions

10.84   Article 8 ICESCR establishes the right to form and join trade unions and the right to strike. The ESC establishes, in addition, the right to bargain collectively.[99] These rights are provided for only tangentially by a set of complex statutory provisions,[100] augmented, since 2000, by the right to freedom of association incorporated through the HRA 1998. Although subject to repeated criticism from the international bodies in respect of its lack of compliance with these measures, the UK government has insisted that these provisions are justifiable.[101] In particular, there is no individual right to strike, since most industrial action will amount to either a breach of contract or the commission of a tort, and immunities available to trade unions do not extend to individuals.

(d) Social security

10.85   Article 9 ICESCR states simply that there is a right to social security, mirrored, in somewhat more detail, in Article 12 ESC. This right is met in domestic law by a comprehensive scheme of social security cash benefits, which includes provision

---

[96] *Inland Revenue Commissioners v Bebb Travel plc* [2003] EWCA Civ 563; The Times, 25 April 2003.

[97] National Minimum Wage (Enforcement Notices) Bill, see www.publications.parliament.uk/pa/ld200203/ldbills/008/2003008.htm.

[98] Response of the UK Government (n 86 above) A.15.

[99] Art 5 ESC (right to organize); Art 6 (right to collective bargaining, including right to strike).

[100] Trade Union and Labour Relations (Consolidation) Act 1992; Employment Rights Act 1996; Employment Relations Act 1999 on which see S Deakin and G Morris, *Labour Law* (3rd edn, London: Butterworths, 2001) chs 7–11.

[101] See eg ESC 21st report (n 89 above) paras 16–23.

for sickness, invalidity, maternity, old-age, survivors, employment injury, unemployment, and family benefits.[102] Although there is considerable discretion, particularly in the initial allocation of budgets for these rights, there is nevertheless scope for individualized claims. These have always been adjudicated, at least initially, by tribunals rather than courts, although in some cases, such as the social fund and housing benefit, decisions are subject only to internal review.[103] The reforms introduced in 1998 concentrated on establishing a new system for making decisions on cases and handling appeals. The tribunal system was considerably simplified, with a single unified appeal jurisdiction replacing Social Security, Medical, Disability, Child Support and Vaccine Damage Tribunals.[104] At the same time, there is a clear move towards greater executive control and away from judicial or quasi-judicial decision-making. Thus the Secretary of State is responsible for all decisions made,[105] and agency chief executives are responsible for guidance, monitoring and reporting on decision-making, in place of the Chief Adjudication Officer. Instead of the independent tribunal service, the Secretary of State is responsible for the administration of the appeals process, which is delivered by a new executive agency. In addition, the 1998 Act gives the Secretary of State the power to override a decision of an appeal tribunal, or even a social security commissioner.[106]

(e) Families and child welfare

Protection and assistance of the family is established under Article 10 ICESCR, including the right to paid maternity leave or leave with adequate social security benefits.[107] These are provided for by a range of different mechanisms, ranging from child benefit, to family law statutes, to provision for inheritance of tenancies to protection against domestic violence and the provision of paid maternity leave. **10.86**

Also included in Article 10 is the duty to take special protective measures for children and young persons. These duties are provided for under the Children Act 1989, which places a duty on every local authority to safeguard and promote the welfare of children within its area who are in need[108] and, so far as is consistent with that duty, to promote the upbringing of such children by their families.[109] For this purpose local authorities have a wide range of duties and powers which include the **10.87**

---

[102] See Social Security Act 1998 and comments in ESC 21st report (n 89 above) 94–102 .

[103] Social Security Administration Act 1992, ss 63, 64–66, 134–135.

[104] Social Security Act 1998, s 4.

[105] ibid s 1.

[106] ibid s 10(1)(b).

[107] See, correspondingly, Arts 8, 16 and 17 ESC .

[108] Defined as children who are unlikely to achieve or maintain a reasonable standard of health or development, or whose health or development is likely to be significantly impaired, without the provision of the local authority's services, and children who are disabled.

[109] Children Act 1989, s 17.

provision of services for disabled children, and the provision of accommodation and assistance to enable children to live with their families. Local authorities have a further duty towards children in need of protection.[110] A local authority may apply to the court for a care order where a child is suffering, or is likely to suffer, significant harm attributable to lack of parental care or the child's being beyond parental control. Finally, a local authority is required to provide accommodation for children in need who appear to require accommodation as a result of there being no person who has parental responsibility for them, or their being lost or abandoned, or the person who has been caring for them being prevented from providing them with suitable accommodation or care.[111] Where a local authority is looking after a child, it is responsible for his or her accommodation and maintenance. As will be seen below, the extent to which these duties create justiciable rights has been the subject of several important cases.

(f) Food and clothing

10.88   Article 11 ICESCR establishes the right to an adequate standard of living, including adequate food, clothing and housing, and to the continuous improvement of living conditions. Provision for this right, apart from housing, is almost entirely in the form of social policy rather than specific statutory entitlements. In the most recent reporting round on the ICESCR, the Committee was specifically concerned with what it perceived as the absence of a 'national anti-poverty strategy with goals and targets, which is structured and allows for participation of the poor, to provide coherence to its existing policies on poverty and "social exclusion"'. In its response, the government stressed that it did have an anti-poverty strategy, focusing on social exclusion, as set out in annual *Opportunity for All* reports. Its goals were both to prevent social exclusion happening in the first place; and to reintegrate those who become excluded, by using a variety of responses, including tackling failing communities and unfair discrimination. It emphasized too the participatory nature of these initiatives, For example, in England, the National Strategy Neighbourhood Renewal consultation exercise drew heavily on the views of those directly affected by poverty. For young people, the government is providing more opportunities for children and young people to get involved in the planning, delivery and evaluation of policies and services relevant to them.[112]

(g) Housing

10.89   So far as the right to adequate housing is concerned, this is dealt with by local authorities, acting under statutory powers, who have the discretion to decide who

---

[110]   Children Act 1989, s 47.
[111]   ibid s 20.
[112]   Response of the UK Government (n 86 above) A.25.

qualifies for social housing.[113] They are required to have a published allocation scheme which sets out their priorities and procedures for allocating social housing. If an authority is satisfied that an applicant is unintentionally homeless[114] and in priority need, it must either help the applicant to obtain accommodation or secure accommodation for the applicant. In either case, accommodation must be suitable for the applicant's household and available for two years.[115] If an applicant is intentionally homeless but in priority need, she must be provided with accommodation by the authority for a reasonable period, to allow her an opportunity to find accommodation for herself. The authority's allocation scheme must give 'reasonable preference' to certain categories of households, such as those in unsanitary, overcrowded or unsatisfactory housing; those with dependent children or a pregnant woman; those who need settled housing on medical or welfare grounds; people who would have difficulty in securing such accommodation because of their social or economic circumstances; and people who have been accepted as unintentionally homeless and in priority need. There is a right of appeal (after an internal review) to the county court on a point of law.[116]

10.90   Local authorities also have powers to evict tenants from social housing,[117] an issue which, as will be seen below, has been extensively litigated in domestic courts under the HRA 1998. Recently, the government has been:

> keen to ensure that social landlords have appropriate measures to deal effectively with tenants who cause problems to their neighbours, or who otherwise do not fulfil the responsibilities set out in their tenancy agreement. But the Government has also made it clear to social landlords that eviction should be regarded as a last resort after other, preventive, measures have failed to bring about an improvement in the tenant's behaviour. Such measures may include mediation to reduce the likelihood of neighbour disputes escalating; seeking an agreement with a tenant in arrears with his rent for repayment of manageable sums of arrears over an agreed period of time; and, for serious cases of nuisance, injunctions aimed at preventing further nuisance or anti-social behaviour whilst allowing the tenant to remain on the property.[118]

10.91   In order to promote tenant participation, the government has proposed that local authorities and tenants introduce compacts—local written agreements—setting out how tenants will be involved in decisions by the local authority on housing issues in ways which meet their needs and priorities. A National Framework for Tenant Participation Compacts was published in June 1999, which sets out the core standards to be incorporated in compacts. Local authorities were expected to

---

[113] Housing Act 1996, Pts VI and VII.
[114] A person is homeless in law if there is no accommodation she is legally entitled to occupy and which it is reasonable for her to occupy.
[115] Housing Act 1996, s 195.
[116] ibid s 201 and see *Begum (Nipa) v Tower Hamlets LBC* [2000] 1 WLR 306, CA.
[117] Housing Act 1985, as amended by ibid.
[118] 4th Report (n 10 above) para 11.68.

implement compacts by April 2000. By April 2002, at least 140 compacts were in existence, and almost all local authorities had an area-wide compact in place.

(h) Health

10.92 The National Health Service (NHS) is cited as meeting the obligation to provide for the highest possible standard of mental and physical health.[119] Medical services are provided on the basis of clinical need, not the ability to pay. In July 2000, the government published the NHS Plan, which sets out a ten-year programme to modernize the NHS. The NHS Plan, according to the government report, was developed following the most substantial consultation exercise ever undertaken within the health service. It tackles the systematic weaknesses which have held back the service and sets out a programme for a new relationship between the patient and the health service. The government has made a commitment to shape the NHS around the needs and preferences of individual patients, their families and their carers; to respond to different needs of different populations; continuously to improve quality services and to minimize errors; to help keep people healthy and work to reduce health inequalities.[120]

(i) Culture and scientific progress

10.93 So far as the right of everyone to take part in cultural life and to enjoy the benefits of scientific progress[121] is concerned, provision is almost entirely in the form of social policy rather than individualized rights. A government department is responsible for government policy and administration of expenditure on national museums and art galleries, the historic environment, the Arts Council, the British Library, the Government Art Collection and other national cultural bodies. It also has responsibilities in respect of public libraries, the media, tourism and the creative industries, including the arts, film, the music industry, and television and radio broadcasting. In its 2001 report, the government declared that its objective was to increase the appreciation of and participation in, the arts in the United Kingdom from one half to two-thirds of the population over the next ten years. As part of this policy, government funds were allocated to enable national museums and art galleries which had previously charged for admission to offer free admission for children from April 1999 and to pensioners from April 2000. The Department for Culture, Media and Sport is continuing its programme of increasing access.[122] Cultural diversity was also stressed as a significant factor in the cultural life of the United Kingdom and the government stated its intention to ensure that subsidized artistic activity reflects the full range of that diversity.

---

[119] Art 12 ICESCR; Art 11 ESC; 4th Report (n 10 above) para 9.01.
[120] ESC 21st report (n 89 above).
[121] Art 15 ICESCR.
[122] 4th Report (n 10 above) para 15.21.

(2) The European Court of Human Rights

(a) Introduction

Although the ECHR has been traditionally considered to include only civil and **10.94**
political rights, recent case law has demonstrated a robust evolution beyond primary duties to secondary duties. Frequently, this goes no further than requiring the state to prohibit private individuals from infringing on the rights. This is relatively straightforward, since it has few resource implications and is an immediately effective duty. But the European Court of Human Rights has also developed the duty to include the establishment of appropriate institutional mechanisms, with clear resource implications. This raises the question of what standard of scrutiny the Court has used to determine whether the state has met this obligation. In several cases, the Court has been relatively deferent to the state's determination of how resources should be allocated. As long as a decision to restrict a right by limiting the available resources is demonstrated to be rational, the state's action would be upheld. In a trilogy of cases in 2002, the Court went further and insisted that the state demonstrate that limiting a right because of available resources had to be justified as necessary to achieve a legitimate state aim, but the Court has since retreated from this robust position. These trends are expanded below.

(b) Positive duties and Article 11: freedom of association and assembly

Several important cases demonstrate the expansion from primary to secondary **10.95**
obligations in the form of imposing a duty to prohibit private individuals from infringing rights. The Article 11 right to belong to a trade union has been held to go further than protecting the individual against arbitrary interference by public authorities. It also imposes a positive duty on the state to secure the effective enjoyment of those rights by prohibiting private employers from infringing on the right.[123]
Similarly, in the *Costello-Roberts* case,[124] the Court held that although the act of administering corporal punishment was the act of a headmaster of an independent school, the United Kingdom would still be responsible if it proved to be incompatible with Article 3 (torture) or Article 8 (private and family life) or both.[125]

However, the ECHR case law has moved further still and interpreted Convention **10.96**
rights as giving rise to positive duties which have clear resource implications. Take as a start, the right to freedom of assembly in Article 11 ECHR. This has always been considered to be a paradigmatic civil and political right. But the Court has

---

[123] *Wilson v UK* (2002) 35 EHRR 20.
[124] *Costello-Roberts v UK* Series A No 247-C (1995) 19 EHRR 112.
[125] The obligation to secure to children their right to education under Art 2 of Protocol 1 meant that the state could not absolve itself from this responsibility by delegating its obligations to private bodies or individuals.

recently interpreted it, in the *Plattform* case, to include not just the primary obligation, to refrain from banning marches, but also the secondary obligation, to protect participants in a peaceful demonstration from disruption by a violent counter-demonstration. 'Genuine, effective freedom of peaceful assembly cannot be reduced to a mere duty on the part of the state not to interfere . . . Article 11 sometimes requires positive measures to be taken, even in the sphere of relations between individuals, if need be.'[126]

10.97   This has clear resource implications for the state, in the form of the cost of policing. In this respect, the standard developed by the court in *Plattform* was a deferent one. The obligation was 'an obligation as to measures to be taken and not as to results to be achieved'. The duty was therefore only to 'take reasonable and appropriate measures to enable lawful demonstrations to proceed peacefully'. States are not expected to guarantee this absolutely and they have a wide discretion in the choice of the means to be used.[127]

(c) Positive duties and Article 2: right to life

10.98   Similar developments have taken place in respect of Article 2, the right to life. Recent cases have shown that Article 2 does not merely restrain the state from taking life unlawfully, the primary obligation. It also imposes an express obligation on the state, to 'secure the right to life by putting in place effective criminal law provisions to deter the commission of offences against the person, backed up by law enforcement machinery for the prevention, suppression and sanctioning of breaches of such provisions . . .'.[128] This also includes, in certain well-defined circumstances, a positive obligation on the authorities to take preventive operational measures to protect an individual whose life is at risk from the criminal acts of another individual.[129] Notably, the duty is a proactive one: public authorities must do more than react after a breach of the right. They must scrutinize all their planning and policy to be sure that the right to life is not infringed, including appropriate training, instructions and briefing.[130]

10.99   In these cases too, there are clear resource implications. What standard, then, has the Court applied? In *Osman*,[131] it was expressly stated that, bearing in mind the difficulties involved in policing modern societies, the unpredictability of human conduct, and the operational choices which must be made in terms of priorities and resources, such an obligation must be interpreted in a way which does not

---

[126] *Plattform 'Ärzte für das Leben' v Austria* Series A No 139 (1988) 13 EHRR 204 at [32].
[127] ibid at [34].
[128] *Osman v UK* Application 23452/94 (1998) 29 EHRR 245 at [116].
[129] ibid.
[130] *McCann v UK* Series A No 324 (1995) 21 EHRR 97.
[131] *Osman v UK* Application 23452/94 (1998) 29 EHRR 245.

impose an impossible or disproportionate burden on the authorities. Accordingly, not every claimed risk to life can entail for the authorities a Convention requirement to take operational measures to prevent that risk from materializing. The standard is whether the authorities did all that could be reasonably expected of them to avoid a real and immediate risk to life of which they have or ought to have knowledge.

(d) Positive duties and Article 6: right to a fair trial

The Court has been less deferent in respect of the secondary obligations under **10.100** Article 6, the right to trial. As well as the duty to establish courts which operate within a reasonable time, there is a duty to provide legal aid in criminal proceedings. Legal aid is not automatic in civil proceedings, but failure to provide legal assistance may breach Article 6, where it is indispensable for effective access to court because of the complexity of the procedure or because the dispute entails an emotional involvement.[132] Despite its resource intensive nature, the Court has been recently been willing to apply a relatively intense standard of review to the denial of legal representation. Thus in *P v UK*,[133] the Court recognized that though it may not be easy to pursue proceedings as a litigant in person, the limited public funds available for civil actions render a procedure of selection a necessary feature of the system of administration of justice. However, it is necessary to demonstrate that any such procedure functions in a manner which is neither arbitrary nor disproportionate, nor impinges on the essence of the right of access to court.

(e) Positive duties and Article 3: right not to be subjected to torture or inhuman or degrading treatment

Similar points can be made in respect of Article 3, the right not to be subjected to **10.101** torture or inhuman or degrading treatment, again a right which has traditionally been thought to fall within the heartland of civil and political rights. Here too the ECHR has gone beyond the primary obligation of restraint, to consider the secondary obligation to prevent others from infringing the right.[134] This was particularly evident in the recent child abuse case of *Z v UK*[135] which concerned the extent of the responsibility of the state to protect children against abuse by their parents. The Court emphasized that Article 3 requires states to take measures designed to ensure that individuals within their jurisdiction are not subjected to torture or inhuman or degrading treatment, including such ill-treatment administered by private individuals. These measures should provide effective protection, in particular, of children and other vulnerable persons, and include reasonable steps to prevent ill-treatment of which the authorities had or ought to have had

---

[132] See *Airey v Ireland (No 1)* Series A No 32 (1979–80) 2 EHRR 305 at [26]–[28].
[133] *P v UK* Application 56547/00 (2002) 35 EHRR 31.
[134] *Chahal v UK* Application 22414/93 (1996) 23 EHRR 413.
[135] Application 29392/95 (2002) 34 EHRR 3.

knowledge. The Court acknowledged 'the difficult and sensitive decisions facing social services and the important countervailing principle of respecting and preserving family life'. The present case, however, left no doubt as to the failure of the system to protect these child applicants from serious, long-term neglect and abuse.

(f) Positive duties and Article 8: right to respect for private and family life, home and correspondence

10.102   This merging of the boundaries between civil and political rights and socio-economic rights has been most clearly demonstrated in respect of Article 8: the right to respect for private, family life, home and correspondence. The Court made the transition from the primary obligation to the secondary obligation as early as 1979. Thus, it stated, although 'the object of the Article is "essentially" that of protecting the individual against arbitrary interference by public authorities . . . it does not merely compel the state to abstain from such interference: in addition to this primarily negative undertaking, there may be positive obligations inherent in an effective "respect"'.[136]

10.103   Nevertheless, the Court has resisted several attempts to interpret the right to respect for home and family as a right to the provision of a home as such. It has thus refused to move beyond the secondary to the tertiary obligation, and thereby to transform a civil and political right into a social and economic one. Thus in *Chapman v UK*[137] the Court stated: 'It is important to recall that Article 8 does not in terms give a right to be provided with a home. Nor does any of the jurisprudence of the court acknowledge such a right. While it is clearly desirable that every human being has a place where he or she can live in dignity and which he or she can call home, there are unfortunately in the contracting states many persons who have no home. Whether the state provides funds to enable everyone to have a home is a matter for political not judicial decision.'[138] In the case in question, the result was that the positive obligation under Article 8 did not extend so far as to require contracting states to make available an adequate number of suitably equipped sites to the gypsy community.

10.104   Similarly, the Court has been reluctant to intervene too directly in decisions requiring governments to balance fairness to the individual with the interests of the community. This approach is clearly demonstrated in the 2003 case of *Hatton v UK*.[139] In this case, the applicants, who all lived in the vicinity of Heathrow airport, complained that the increase in night-time noise interfered with their

---

[136]   *Marckx v Belgium* Series A No 31 (1979) 2 EHRR 330.
[137]   Application 27238/95 (2001) 33 EHRR 18.
[138]   ibid at [99].
[139]   Application 36022/97, 8 July 2003, Grand Chamber; cf decision of Third Section of the Court (2002) 34 EHRR 1.

Article 8 right to respect for their private and family lives and their homes. At first instance, the Court appeared to be moving towards a more intensive form of scrutiny. In striking a fair balance between the competing interests of the individual and of the community as a whole, the Court insisted that states must seek to achieve their aims in the way that is least onerous as regards human rights. Because the UK government had not seriously attempted to find the least onerous solution as regards human rights, the Court refused to accept that the government had struck the right balance between the United Kingdom's economic well-being and the applicants' effective enjoyment of their Article 8 right.

However, the Grand Chamber took a very different view, stressing the subsidiary role of the Convention in the face of decisions by democratically elected authorities: 'The national authorities have direct democratic legitimation and are, as the Court has held on many occasions, in principle better placed than an international court to evaluate local needs and conditions. In matters of general policy, on which opinions within a democratic society may reasonably differ widely, the role of the domestic policy maker should be given special weight' (para 99). The result was that 'whilst the State is required to give due consideration to the particular interests the respect for which it is obliged to secure by virtue of Article 8, it must in principle be left a choice between different ways and means of meeting this obligation. The Court's supervisory function being of a subsidiary nature, it is limited to reviewing whether or not the particular solution adopted can be regarded as striking a fair balance' (para 123). Nor did it agree with the earlier Court's insistence on thorough research, being willing instead to assume that night flights 'contribute at least to a certain extent to the general economy' and asserting that it was difficult, if not impossible, to draw a clear line between the interests of the aviation industry and the economic interests of the country as a whole. **10.105**

The Grand Chamber did, however, accept that the obligations under Article 8 extended beyond the primary obligation to refrain from actively interfering, to the secondary obligation to take reasonable and appropriate measures to prevent others from interfering with that right. Thus, the Court held, the 'State's responsibility in environmental cases may also arise from a failure to regulate private industry in a manner securing proper respect for the rights enshrined in Article 8 of the Convention' (para 119). **10.106**

(g) Conclusion

The robust standard of the first decision in *Hatton*, put together with the similar standard in *P v UK* (legal aid) and *Z v UK* (protection against child abuse) yields a trilogy of 2002 cases in which the Court was prepared to apply a strict standard of review of secondary obligations. However, the decision of the Grand Chamber in *Hatton* signalled a retreat into deference, based on the Court's perception that decisions in this field are better made by democratically elected decision-makers. **10.107**

(3) Domestic Courts

(a) **Reliance on ESC and ICESCR**

10.108   There has been little direct reliance on the socio-economic rights in the ICESCR or ESC themselves. Thus the closest a court has come to relying directly on an article of the ICESCR is the case of *Stefan v General Medical Council*,[140] in which the right to work in Article 6 was cited in support of a duty on the part of the General Medical Council to give reasons for its decision to suspend a doctor from the medical roll. However, even in this case, the court found alternative methods to reach its decision.

10.109   In other cases, litigants have unsuccessfully attempted to rely on these rights.[141] Indeed, in several asylum cases, courts have held that socio-economic rights guaranteed under the ICESCR are 'third category' and weaker than traditional civil and political rights. In *Horvath v Secretary of State for the Home Department*,[142] an asylum seeker contended that discrimination against Roma in the field of employment, education and the right to marry amounted to persecution for the purposes of asylum law. Although the tribunal noted that deprival of such rights in extreme cases might amount to persecution, the Court of Appeal found it unnecessary to decide this point. Ward LJ took the preliminary view that 'breach of third category rights cannot be said as a matter of law to amount to persecution just as it cannot be said as a matter of law that breach of these rights could never amount to persecution. 'It is a matter of fact and degree and judgment in the individual case.'[143]

(b) **Implying socio-economic rights—a home-grown approach**

10.110   There are, nevertheless, many contexts in which it might have been possible for the courts to develop a 'home-grown' rights based approach to socio-economic rights. As is well known, prior to the incorporation of the ECHR, the courts gradually intensified the use of the ECHR as a background constraint on executive-decision making.[144] This approach stopped short of a proportionality approach, as required by the ECHR,[145] but at least signified a recognition of the fundamental nature of the rights therein.

---

[140] *Stefan v General Medical Council (No 1)* [1999] 1 WLR 1293, PC.

[141] *Associated Newspapers Ltd v Wilson; Associated British Ports v Palmer* [1995] 2 AC 454, HL; *UK Association of Professional Engineers (UKAPE) v Advisory, Conciliation and Arbitration Service (ACAS)* [1981] AC 424, HL; *Douglas v Clifford, Coppock & Carter* (CA, Civ Div); *Mensah v West Middlesex University Hospital NHS Trust* (EAT/424/99).

[142] *Horvath v Secretary of State for the Home Department* [2000] Imm AR 205.

[143] ibid. See also *R (on the application of Okere) v Immigration Appeal Tribunal* (CO/5067/1999, QBD).

[144] See generally M Hunt, *Using Human Rights Law in English Courts* (Oxford: Hart Publishing, 1997).

[145] *Smith and Grady v UK (No 1)* (2000) 29 EHRR 493.

However, the approach to socio-economic rights has been quite the opposite. As **10.111**
soon as resources appear to be implicated, the courts become more rather than less
deferent, paying little or no regard to the countervailing existence of a fundamental right.[146] This is particularly true in respect of discretionary powers.[147] But even
where statute has imposed explicit duties to provide, the courts have been quick
to find a flexible interpretation in order to relieve the financial burdens on a public authority. Where they have taken decisions which protected individuals, the
reasoning has been based less on a rights-based approach than on strict textual
statutory construction.

The reluctance to interpret discretionary powers in a rights-based fashion is most **10.112**
clearly evident in the well-known case of *R v Cambridge Health Authority, ex p B*.[148]
The case concerned the refusal of a health authority to provide further treatment
to a young girl with leukaemia on the grounds that the expenditure involved was
not an effective use of resources given the small prospect of success and its responsibility to ensure that it had sufficient funds for the treatment of other patients. The Court of Appeal decided unanimously that the court was not in a
position to decide on the correctness of the decision. 'Difficult and agonising
judgments have to be made as to how a limited budget is best allocated to the maximum advantage of the maximum number of patients. That is not a judgment
which the court can make.'[149]

This differed markedly from the judgment at first instance of Laws J. Although he **10.113**
acknowledged that the court should not make orders for the use of health service
funds in ignorance of the knock-on effect on other patients, he went on to say that
'where the question is whether the life of a 10-year old girl might be saved by however slim a chance, the responsible authorities . . . must do more than toll the bell
of tight resources'. The standard he imposed was therefore not one of substitution of judicial opinion, or even of proportionality. Instead, it was one of accountability. The authority must 'explain the priorities that have led them to decline to fund
the treatment' and they had not adequately done do. Nevertheless, Sir Thomas
Bingham in the Court of Appeal was not prepared even to go so far as to impose a
duty of accountability, regarding it as totally unrealistic.

The House of Lords has also been reluctant to take a rights-based approach in in- **10.114**
terpreting statutory duties to provide, even if the statute appears to impose a
mandatory duty. In *R v Gloucestershire CC, ex p Barry*[150] authorities were under a

---

[146] See generally E Palmer, 'Resource Allocation, Welfare Rights—Mapping the Boundaries of
Judicial Control in Public Administrative Law' [2000] 20 OJLS 63.
[147] *R v Cambridge Health Authority, ex p B* [1995] 1 WLR 898, CA.
[148] ibid.
[149] *per* Sir Thomas Bingham MR at 906.
[150] [1997] AC 584 .

statutory duty[151] to cater for the needs of disabled or chronically sick persons. On its face, the statute appeared to entail a strict duty to make provision once an individual's needs had been assessed. But the court was acutely aware of the high level of costs such an interpretation would entail for an authority already under severe budgetary constraints. As a result, the court decided that the statute could be interpreted to permit resources to be taken into account in the assessment of the needs themselves. Thus, in effect, a mandatory duty was interpreted as permitting wide discretion.

10.115   A different result was reached in *R v East Sussex CC, ex p Tandy*,[152] which concerned whether resources could be taken into account in fulfilling the statutory duty to provide suitable education at home for those unable to attend school.[153] In contrast to the decision in *Barry*, the House of Lords decided that they could not: suitability should be assessed according to educational needs only, irrespective of resources. Lord Browne-Wilkinson made it clear that in statutory interpretation, the court should not downgrade duties into discretions. However, the result was not reached on a fundamental rights approach, but on the basis of close attention to the wording of the statute itself, which made it clear that resources were relevant in other parts of the statute, but not in the provision in question.[154] As well as stressing the strict statutory wording rather than background principles, Lord Browne-Wilkinson specifically upheld the Court of Appeal's approach in *Ex p B*.[155]

(c) The influence of the ECHR

10.116   To what extent has this changed with the development of a human rights culture post-incorporation of the ECHR? The most frequent forum in which questions of socio-economic rights has arisen is in respect of Article 8, the right to respect for home and family life. Most often, these have concerned the provision of social housing. Litigants have frequently relied on Article 8 in order to persuade courts to impose some restraint on powers given to local authorities, particularly in respect of the power to evict.

(i) *Standard of review: eviction*

10.117   Courts have on the whole accepted that the eviction of a tenant falls within Article 8(1).[156] As Sedley LJ put it in *Lambeth LBC v Howard*, 'any attempt to

---

[151]   Chronically Sick and Disabled Persons Act 1970, s 2(1).
[152]   [1998] AC 714.
[153]   Education Act 1993 s 298.
[154]   See Palmer (n 146 above).
[155]   [1995] 1 WLR 898, CA
[156]   *Lambeth LBC v Howard* [2001] EWCA Civ 468, (2001) 33 HLR 58 at [30] and [32]; *Poplar Housing & Regeneration Community Association Ltd v Donoghue* [2001] EWCA Civ 595, [2002] QB 48 at [67]; *R (on the application of McLellan) v Bracknell Forest BC* [2001] EWCA Civ 1510, [2002] QB 1129.

evict a person, whether directly or by process of law, from his or her home would on the face of it be a derogation from the respect, that is the integrity to which the home is prima facie entitled'.[157] However, although at first sight, eviction appears to be a classic primary obligation of restraint, in fact, eviction is a key tool in the allocation of resources in accordance with predetermined housing priorities. Thus, in determining whether the breach is justified under Article 8(2), courts have been acutely aware of the resource implications. The overall trend in such cases has been for the courts to take a highly deferent approach, even when litigants are demanding no more than the minimal accountability criterion, namely that the authority give clear and intelligible reasons for decisions.

This can be demonstrated by referring to several recent cases which concerned the question of whether a tenant can be evicted from his or her home without scrutiny by the court making the order. In order to obtain possession expeditiously and therefore to allocate housing according to priority lists, several statutes oblige a court to give an order for possession as long as notice has been given, without further scrutiny. Such a procedure is found in s 21(4) of the Housing Act 1988, which requires a court to make an order for possession once notice to quit had been given. There is no requirement for the court to be satisfied that it was reasonable to make such an order. **10.118**

In *Poplar Housing & Regeneration Community Association Ltd v Donoghue*,[158] the tenant challenged the compatibility of this power with Article 8. In applying Article 8(2), the resource implications were foremost in the court's mind. Although he paid lip service to the proportionality test in Article 8(2), Woolf CJ did not genuinely apply it. Instead, he emphasized that supply of social housing was far outweighed by demand and legislative changes had been introduced specifically to increase the number of properties available for private renting. 'The economic and other implications of any policy in this area are extremely complex and far-reaching. This is an area where, in our judgement, the courts must treat the decision of Parliament as to what is in the public interest with particular deference.'[159] Instead of applying the necessity standard required by Article 8(2), he simply repeated that it was 'perfectly understandable that Parliament should have provided a procedure which ensured possession could be obtained expeditiously'. **10.119**

Yet, all the court was being asked to do was to require the authority to give reasons for its decision as a condition for the grant of an order. Such minimal accountability is consistent with the primary obligation to respect the rights of citizens, without drawing the court into complex decisions in the realms of secondary or tertiary obligations. If the judges had been clearer as to the structure of **10.120**

---

[157] *Lambeth LBC v Howard* [2001] EWCA Civ 468; (2001) 33 HLR 58 at [30].
[158] [2001] EWCA Civ 595; [2002] QB 48.
[159] ibid at [69].

the obligations entailed by socio-economic rights, they would have been able to see that the imposition of a duty of accountability—to give clear and intelligible reasons as suggested by Laws J in *Ex p B*—was not the thin end of the wedge to second-guess all local authority spending priorities.

10.121 Similarly, in the *McLellan* case,[160] a scheme was instituted permitting tenants during the first 12 months to be evicted 'without long battles in the county court'.[161] The scheme was aimed at tenants with anti-social behaviour or in arrears and did not require local authorities to be satisfied that breaches of the tenancy agreement had taken place. Provided the correct procedure had been followed, the county court was obliged to issue the order for possession and could not entertain a defence based on a denial of the allegations of breaches of the tenancy agreement.[162] There were quasi-judicial safeguards: the authority was required to inform the tenant of its reasons for applying for an order for possession, and the tenant had the right to a review of the decision by the authority.

10.122 Again the court articulated the proportionality test in Article 8(2), but its decision upholding the power again did not in practice apply the test. Instead, stressing as in *Poplar* that 'it is very much for Parliament to make relevant judgements in this area', the court simply held that the quasi-judicial and other safeguards available to the tenant were sufficient to comply with Article 8(2).

(ii) Programmatic or target duties

10.123 Domestic courts have also been required to consider programmatic duties. One such duty is the 'target' duty, so labelled by Woolf LJ (as he then was) in respect of the duty to provide education under the Education Act 1944.[163] Similarly, the duty under the Children Act 1989 to provide services for children has been characterized as a proactive provision, requiring authorities to take steps of a strategic, or community-wide, nature rather than giving rise to individual rights.[164] This approach is highly reminiscent of rights subject to progressive realization in the ICESCR or the ESC.

10.124 The question arises here whether the domestic courts have been able to translate this into any immediately enforceable obligation of *conduct*, as part of the means of achieving the ultimate obligation of *result*. This issue took the form of the question whether a target duty of this sort crystallizes into an immediate obligation in

---

[160] *R (on the application of McLellan) v Bracknell Forest BC* [2001] EWCA Civ 1510; [2002] QB 1129 concerning Housing Act 1996, s 127(2).

[161] ibid at [63].

[162] There was power to adjourn the possession proceeding pending judicial review if there was a real chance of permission to apply being granted. There was also power to postpone the giving up of possession for up to six weeks.

[163] *R v Inner London Education Authority, ex p Ali* (1990) 2 Admin LR 822 at 828C-E.

[164] *R (on the application of A) v Lambeth LBC* [2001] EWCA Civ 1624; [2002] 1 FLR 353.

respect of any particular individual.[165] Again, the courts have preferred techniques of strict statutory interpretation rather than the more principled human rights approach seen in the Advocate General's approach in *BECTU* or the judgment of Laws LJ in the *ProLife* case discussed above.

This is clear from *R (on the application of A) v Lambeth LBC*,[166] which concerned the interpretation of a local authority's duties under s 17 of the Children Act 1989 to 'safeguard and promote the welfare of children within their area who are in need ... by providing a range and level of services appropriate to those children's needs'. In marked contrast to his judgment on freedom of speech in *ProLife* case, Laws LJ in this case was at pains to make it clear that the arguments addressed to him were 'better addressed by a politician to the legislature than by counsel to a court of law. However vigorous the judicial review jurisdiction, we have to bear in mind that from first to last this case is about the construction of a statute; conditioned, certainly, by the Human Rights Act 1998 if a true Convention point arises, but yet no more nor less than the construction of the Act.'[167] Sir Phillip Otton went even further and stated that: 'In so far as a purposive approach is appropriate I consider that to accede to [counsel's] argument would be to impose an impossible burden upon the respondent Council'.[168] **10.125**

The absence of a rights-based approach in dealing with tertiary obligations is particularly clear in the 2002 case of *R (on application of W) v Lambeth*,[169] also a case under s 17 of the Children Act 1989. W was evicted with her two children for arrears of rent. This meant that she was 'intentionally' homeless and so not eligible for housing under the housing legislation. Instead, she asked the authority to house her under its power under s 17 to provide services for children in need and their families. The authority declined, and its decision was upheld by the Court of Appeal. **10.126**

For Brooke LJ, the fact that s 17 imposed on the court a 'target duty' meant that, in relation to individual children, it was only a power not a duty. The only immediate duty was to give intelligible and adequate reasons why it was not willing to exercise the power, given other pressures on its resources. He accepted that Article 8 imposed positive obligations. However, his version of Article 8(2) downgraded it from a proportionality standard to a mere requirement to take into account all relevant considerations. Thus he stated, Article 8(2) permits the authority and the government to take into account 'the economic well-being of the country', 'the protection of health or morals' and 'the protection of the rights and freedoms of **10.127**

---

[165] See, eg, *R v Kensington and Chelsea RLBC, ex p Kujtim* [1999] 4 All ER 161.
[166] *R (on the application of A) v Lambeth LBC* [2001] EWCA Civ 1624; [2002] 1 FLR 353.
[167] ibid at [22].
[168] ibid at [46].
[169] [2002] EWCA Civ 613; [2002] 2 All ER 901.

others' when deciding how public resources should be allocated. There was no recognition that Article 8(2) does far more—it requires proof that the aim is legitimate, that the means are necessary to achieve that aim and that the substance of the right is not thereby entirely denuded of value.

10.128 It is true that the case raised some of the most complex polycentric problems. The local authority had a severe budgetary deficit, and a very long waiting list for housing. There was a considerable shortage of social housing, meaning that the very expensive and unsatisfactory alternative of bed and breakfast accommodation had to be provided to meet short-term housing need. It also had a large number of families who had small children and no homes, but did not qualify for social housing because they were found to be intentionally homeless. In addition, an inquiry had recently found that Lambeth was not performing its statutory duties adequately in respect of child abuse, children with disabilities and other children in need. The result was that 30 per cent of resources usually spent on housing had been diverted to this area. It is true that resources are finite, often desperately so. However, this should not detract from the necessity to demonstrate, when individual rights have been curtailed, that the result was necessary and proportionate.

10.129 The case forms an interesting contrast to the *ProLife* case[170] itself, which, as we have seen, highlighted the interaction between civil and political rights, in the form of freedom of speech, and allocation of resources in the form of broadcasting time. As Lord Hoffman stated in the House of Lords: 'In general the citizen has no right to require the state to furnish him with the means of expressing his views, whether by publishing a book, or presenting a theatrical production, or broadcasting a television programme'.[171] Moreover, as he stressed, this was by no means a total ban on freedom of speech. 'The Alliance still had (and used) the opportunity to broadcast its chosen text, and it was still at liberty to use a variety of other means of communicating its message.' The role of the court was therefore primarily to ensure that 'access to an important public medium of communication should not be refused on discriminatory, arbitrary or unreasonable grounds. Nor should access be granted subject to discriminatory, arbitrary or unreasonable conditions. A restriction on the content of a programme, produced by a political party to promote its stated aims, must be justified'.[172]

(iii) Legitimate expectations and the right to be housed

10.130 Also a striking contrast to *W* is the case of *Coughlan*,[173] in which it was held that an authority must keep open a residential establishment because it had created a

---

[170] *R (on the application of ProLife Alliance) v BBC* [2002] EWCA Civ 297; [2002] 3 WLR 1080.
[171] ibid at [126].
[172] ibid at [8] *per* Lord Nicholls.
[173] *R v North and East Devon Health Authority, ex p Coughlan* [2001] QB 213. See also *R (on the application of Theophilus) v Lewisham LBC* [2002] EWHC 1371; [2002] 3 All ER 851.

legitimate expectation to that effect. The applicant, a severely disabled woman, had been promised that she would not be moved from Mardon House, where she currently resided. However, the local authority subsequently decided that, contrary to earlier expectations, Mardon House had become 'a prohibitively expensive white elephant, which the authority would need to support at excessively high cost and at the expense of resources for other services'. It therefore took steps to close the unit, while at the same time, in recognition of its promise to the residents, it committed itself to accept a continuing commitment to finance the care of the residents of Mardon House for whom it was responsible.

The Court of Appeal took a very different view of the resource implications from the cases above. This is because the central focus of the case was not the right to a home as such, but the authority's claimed right to renege on its promise. It was because the decision to move Miss Coughlan was in breach of the health authority's own promise, that the decision was held to be unfair and an abuse of power. In a striking departure from the deferent standard noted above, the court took upon itself the task of weighing the requirements of fairness against any overriding interest relied upon for the change of policy. Thus, Lord Woolf stated, 'where the court considers that a lawful promise or practice has induced a legitimate expectation of a *benefit which is substantive*, not simply procedural, authority now establishes that here too the court will in a proper case decide whether to frustrate the expectation is so unfair that to take a new and different course will amount to an abuse of power. Here, once the legitimacy of the expectation is established, the court will have the task of weighing the requirements of fairness against any overriding interest relied upon for the change of policy.'[174]

10.131

What is particularly striking about this case is the extent to which the court went in challenging the authority's decision on resources. Lord Woolf stressed that 'in drawing the balance of conflicting interests the court will not accept the policy change without demur but will pay the closest attention to the assessment made by the public body itself'. He went on to decide that the extent to which the public cost was going to be reduced by moving Miss Coughlan to local authority care was 'not dramatic . . . The saving would be in terms of economic and logistical efficiency in the use respectively of Mardon House and the local authority home. The price of this saving was to be not only the breach of a plain promise made to Miss Coughlan but, perhaps more importantly, the loss of her only home and of a purpose-built environment which had come to mean even more to her than a home does to most people . . . We accept, on what is effectively uncontested evidence, that an enforced move of this kind will be emotionally devastating and seriously anti-therapeutic.'[175] In reaching this conclusion, the court was also

10.132

---

[174] *Coughlan*, ibid at [57].
[175] ibid at [92].

influenced by a fundamental rights approach. Although the HRA 1998 had not yet come into force, the Court of Appeal held that the judge was justified in holding that health authority's conduct was in breach of Article 8 and was not justified by the provisions of Article 8(2).

10.133   It is difficult to see why the existence of an undertaking in *Coughlan* made it possible for the court to adopt an intensive standard of scrutiny, when breach of a socio-economic right on its own does not. The case demonstrates that such a standard is possible. At the same time, *Coughlan* did not adequately address the very complex issues raised by resource intensive obligations. Although it was prepared to find that the cost to the authority was 'not dramatic', it did not properly articulate what test should be used to decide the balance between the right and the cost to the public authority. Its only contribution on this score was to reiterate that the more substantial the interference with human rights, the more the court will require by way of justification before it is satisfied that the decision is reasonable[176] or fair.

(iv) Resource implications: intensity of review

10.134   A more sustained consideration of how to address the resource implications of positive rights is found in *Hooper v Secretary of State for Work and Pensions*.[177] Prior to reforms which came into effect in 2001, widows but not widowers were eligible for widow's payment and widow's pensions.[178] The applicants, who were widowers whose wives had died before the reforms came into effect, argued that the provisions breached the equality guarantee in Article 14 (equality) read with Article 8 (the right to respect for family life).[179] The court held that Article 8 was engaged, in that the availability of pecuniary support afforded by these payments formed a significant part of a family's plans for a secure future.[180] Since there was a clear differentiation on grounds of sex, Article 14 would be breached unless the differentiation could be justified. The case therefore depended on the standard of justification required.

10.135   The case is relevant for our purposes because it entailed positive provision by the state of a benefit. As Moses J put it, the claimant 'seeks to impose upon the Government a positive obligation to allocate resources to him'.[181] Moreover, such

---

[176] *R v Ministry of Defence, ex p Smith* [1996] QB 517, 554.
[177] *R (on the application of Hooper) v Secretary of State for Work and Pensions* [2003] EWCA Civ 813 (and see also [2002] EWHC 191; [2002] UKHRR 785).
[178] Social Security Contributions and Benefits Act 1992, ss 36–38. The provisions were amended by the Welfare Reform and Pensions Act 1999, but the claimants had lost their wives before the reforms came into force on 9 April 2001.
[179] It rejected the argument that Art 1 of Protocol 1 (the right to peaceful enjoyment of possessions) was engaged since these were non-contributory rights and were therefore not a 'possession'.
[180] *R (on the application of Hooper) v Secretary of State for Work and Pensions* [2002] EWHC 191; [2002] UKHRR 785 at [26].
[181] ibid at [114].

an obligation would have significant cost implications. Indeed, the government had argued that if the existing scheme was extended to men, it would cost £250 million a year. It was largely for this reason that the reforms introduced in 2001 did not extend the widow's pension to men. Instead, they achieved equality between men and women by a 'levelling down' option, in the form of the bereavement allowance, which was less favourable than the widow's pension because it was limited to a period of 52 weeks. (In *Hooper*, the claimants were seeking a 'levelling up' option, namely equality with widows who were bereaved before the reforms came into effect.) Thus the court was directly confronted with a right which, if fulfilled, would have significant cost implications.

The Court of Appeal held that 'a very considerable margin of discretion' should be accorded to the Secretary of State in this context, because 'difficult questions of economic and social policy were involved, the resolution of which fell within the province of the executive and the legislature rather than the courts'.[182] Nevertheless, the Court held that the burden lay with the Secretary of State to provide objective justification for the discrimination. Notably, the Court of Appeal was prepared to scrutinize the evidence for itself and come to the conclusion that the Secretary of State had not provided sufficient justification, despite the wide margin of discretion. To do this, the judges referred particularly to comments made in Parliament on behalf of the government.   **10.136**

How then were the considerable resource implications dealt with? The Court approached this issue in a manner which is strikingly similar to the notion of a programmatic right. 'The State is entitled not merely to a wide margin of appreciation when considering whether and when a change is required to the law in order to ensure it remains convention compliant in changing circumstances, but that, having so decided, it is entitled to such time as is reasonable to make the necessary change.'[183]   **10.137**

(4) Lessons from Abroad

(a) United States

Experience from other jurisdictions reveals a wide range of responses. At the least interventionist end of the spectrum lies the US Supreme Court, which has refused to make the transition from the primary obligation of restraint to the obligations to protect or fulfil, except in special circumstances. Thus, in *DeShaney*,[184] as in *Z v UK*,[185] the mother of a child severely abused by his father brought an action on the   **10.138**

---

[182] [2003] EWCA Civ 813 at [62] *per* Lord Phillips MR.
[183] ibid at [78].
[184] *DeShaney v Winnebago County Department of Social Services* 109 S Ct 998 (1989).
[185] Application 29392/95 (2002) 34 EHRR 3.

basis that social workers, despite receiving complaints of the abuse, had not removed him from his father's custody. The claim was brought under the Due Process Clause of the Fourteenth Amendment, which provides that '[n]o State shall . . . deprive any person of life, liberty, or property, without due process of law'. Rehnquist J, in a classic restatement of the traditional divide, stated: 'Nothing in the language of the Due Process Clause itself requires the State to protect the life, liberty, and property of its citizens against invasion by private actors. The Clause is phrased as a limitation on the State's power to act, not as a guarantee of certain minimal levels of safety and security.'[186] Not surprisingly, the Supreme Court has also refused to take the further step into creating an affirmative right to governmental aid.[187] 'Although the liberty protected by the Due Process Clause affords protection against unwarranted government interference . . . it does not confer an entitlement to such [governmental aid] as may be necessary to realize all the advantages of that freedom.'[188]

(b) India

10.139 At the other end of the spectrum is the Indian experience. The Indian Constitution of 1950 makes a distinction between 'fundamental rights' and 'directive principles'. Fundamental rights include most of the classic civil and political rights. The directive principles cover more 'socio-economic rights', such as the right to work, to education and nutrition, and are usually programmatic. For example, Article 41 states that the state shall 'within the limits of its economic capacity and development, make effective provision for securing the right to work, to education and to public assistance'. Fundamental rights can be enforced by individuals in court. Principles, by contrast, are not enforceable by the court, but 'are nevertheless fundamental in the governance of the country and it shall be the duty of the State to apply these principles in making laws'.[189] This is strongly reminiscent of the division in the EU Charter between rights and principles.

10.140 Despite the distinction between justiciable rights and non-justiciable directive principles, the Indian Supreme Court has synthesized the two, drawing on the directive principles in order to interpret fundamental rights. The result is that fundamental rights have been construed as giving rise to secondary and even tertiary duties.[190] Thus in a case in 1996, the court stated: 'Article 21 [the right to life] imposes an

---

[186] *DeShaney v Winnebago County Department of Social Services* 109 S Ct 998, 1003.

[187] *Harris v McRae,* 448 US 297, 317–318 (1980) (no obligation to fund abortions or other medical services) (discussing Due Process Clause of Fifth Amendment); *Lindsey v Normet,* 405 US 56, 74, (1972) (no obligation to provide adequate housing) (discussing Due Process Clause of Fourteenth Amendment).

[188] *Harris v McRae,* 448 US 297, 317–318.

[189] Art 37.

[190] See VD Mahajan, *Constitutional Law of India* (7th edn, Lucknow: Eastern Book Company, 1991) 230–234, and BL Hansaria, *Right to Life and Liberty under the Constitution (A Critical Analysis of Art 21)* (Bombay: NM Tripathi Private Ltd, 1993) 24–40.

obligation on the State to safeguard the right to life of every person . . . Failure on the part of a Government hospital to provide timely medical treatment to a person in need of such treatment results in violation of his right to life guaranteed under Article 21.'[191] In *Olga Tellis*,[192] thousands of pavement and slum dwellers challenged the attempt by the City of Bombay to evict and move them to areas far from the possibility of obtaining work. The right to life was interpreted, against the background of the directive principles, to include the right to livelihood, and the right to live in the vicinity of available work.

What standard has the court then used to scrutinize such decisions? It stressed in *Olga Tellis* that the Constitution did not place an absolute ban on the deprivation of livelihood: it required such deprivation to be according to a procedure established by law. It therefore insisted primarily on procedural protection, primarily in the form of notice of eviction. This was seen, however, not as a formal gesture, but an aspect of participatory democracy. Notice would give the opportunity for response and dialogue and with it a heightened chance of compromise, observance of the law, and accuracy of judgment of the state authority.

10.141

At the same time, the remedies for failure of procedure were substantive, including the duty to move the slum dwellers to pitches at a reasonable distance. Indeed, it is the remedies as much as the substance which have been radical in the hands of the Indian Supreme Court. Thus in a recent case, relating to child labour, the Supreme Court ordered employers to pay into a fund for the rehabilitation of child workers and requested the state to find jobs for adult members of families of child workers.[193] As one commentator has described it, these processes have at times 'led to a mini-takeover of the administrative regime' by the courts.[194]

10.142

(c) South Africa

Perhaps the most detailed scrutiny of the issues raised by socio-economic rights is found in the South African jurisprudence. The new Constitution, eschewing the notion of directive principles, gives express rights to housing, health care, food, water and social security. These rights are all justiciable by individuals in courts, although many of them are expressed in programmatic form. Thus in s 27 everyone has the right of access to health care, but s 27(2) states that the state must take reasonable measures, within its available resources, to achieve the progressive realization of the right.

10.143

---

[191] *Paschim Banga Khet Mazdoor Samity v State of West Bengal* AIR (1996) SC 2426.
[192] *Olga Tellis v Bombay Municipal Corp* AIR (1986) SC 180.
[193] *Mehta v State of Tamil Nadu* (1997) 2 BHRC 258.
[194] U Baxi, 'Judicial Discourse: The Dialectics of the Face and the Mask' (1993) 35 J of the Indian Law Institute 1, 7, and see Steiner and Alston (n 6 above) 285.

10.144 The justiciability of the rights was put beyond question in the certification proceedings before the South African Constitutional Court, which stated:

> [T]hese rights are, at least to some extent, justiciable . . . Many of the civil and political rights entrenched in the [constitutional text] will give rise to similar budgetary implications without compromising their justiciability. The fact that socio-economic rights will almost inevitably give rise to such implications does not seem to us to be a bar to their justiciability. At the very minimum, socio-economic rights can be negatively protected from improper invasion.[195]

10.145 At the same time, the Constitutional Court has insisted that the availability of resources is not a separate issue, but is integral to defining the reach of the right itself.[196] Rejecting the concept of an immediately enforceable minimum core content to the right, it has repeatedly stressed that 'courts are ill-suited to adjudicate upon issues where court orders could have multiple social and economic consequences for the community. The Constitution contemplates rather a restrained and focused role for the courts, namely, to require the state to take measures to meet its constitutional obligations and to subject the reasonableness of these measures to evaluation. Such determinations of reasonableness may in fact have budgetary implications, but are not in themselves directed at rearranging budgets. In this way the judicial, legislative and executive functions achieve appropriate constitutional balance.'[197] A key aspect of this is the need to protect democratic processes so as to ensure accountability, responsiveness and openness.

10.146 This approach has been applied in three major cases. The facts of the first, *Soobramoney*,[198] were similar to those of *Ex p B* above, and concerned a challenge by a patient of a decision to refuse him dialysis treatment, because he did not fit the priority criteria established by the hospital authority. The Court held that, in a world of highly limited resources, the authorities were permitted to ration health care. Indeed, according to Sachs J: 'In all the open and democratic societies based upon dignity, freedom and equality with which I am familiar, the rationing of access to life-prolonging resources is regarded as integral to, rather than incompatible with, a human rights approach to health care.'[199] However, emphasizing that the government could not merely 'toll the bell of scarce resources', he insisted that the lack of principled criteria for regulating such access could be more open to challenge than the existence and application of such criteria.

---

[195] *Ex p Chairperson of the Constitutional Assembly: In Re Certification of the Constitution of the Republic of South Africa*, 1996 (4) SA 744; 1996 (10) BCLR 1253 (CC) para 78.

[196] *Minister of Health v Treatment Action Campaign*, 5 July 2002; *Republic of South Africa v Grootboom*, 4 October 2000, '*Soobramoney*'.

[197] *Treatment Action Campaign* at [38].

[198] See n 196 above.

[199] *Soobramoney* at [52].

Two more recent cases have elicited a more interventionist response, although still **10.147** within the framework of reasonableness and balance articulated above. Thus in *Grootboom*, squatters on private land who had been forcibly evicted claimed that their rights to shelter had been violated. The Court stressed that the Constitution obliges the state to act positively to provide access to housing, health-care, sufficient food and water, and social security to those unable to support themselves and their dependants. These duties were not free-floating: those in need have a corresponding right to demand that they be fulfilled. Yacoob J emphasized the importance of the appropriate balance between fundamental rights and shortage of resources. 'I am conscious that it is an extremely difficult task for the state to meet these obligations in the conditions that prevail in our country. This is recognised by the Constitution which expressly provides that the state is not obliged to go beyond available resources or to realise these rights immediately. I stress however, that despite all these qualifications, these are rights, and the Constitution obliges the state to give effect to them. This is an obligation that courts can, and in appropriate circumstances, must enforce.'[200] This balance meant that individuals could not claim shelter or housing immediately upon demand. However, the state had a duty to devise and implement a coherent, co-ordinated programme designed to meet its obligations. The programme adopted fell short of the obligations in that it failed to provide for any form of relief to those desperately in need of access to housing.

Similarly, in the important *HIV-AIDS*[201] case, the refusal of the state to provide **10.148** anti-retroviral drugs to mothers and new-born babies except in restricted pilot schemes was struck down by the Constitutional Court. Most importantly, the Court was prepared to examine the state's reasons for the policy closely, and to come to its own conclusion that they did not reach the required standard of reasonableness. Thus the state was ordered not just to permit and facilitate the use of nevirapine for the purpose of reducing the risk of mother-to-child transmission of HIV, but also to make nevirapine available at hospitals and clinics.

E. Alternatives to Courts

The above discussion has concentrated on the role of the courts, as is appropriate **10.149** in a book of this nature. Many argue, however, that it is more appropriate for socio-economic rights to be monitored through a compliance mechanism, based on reporting requirements and scrutiny by a committee or other non-judicial mechanism. It is for this reason that the ESC is monitored by a committee, while

[200] ibid at [93]–[94] *per* Yacoob J.
[201] *Treatment Action Campaign*.

its civil and political sister, the ECHR, includes an individual right of complaint to a court. Similarly, the ICESCR is monitored by the Committee on Social, Economic and Cultural Rights.

10.150   There are some clear advantages to a non-judicial method of enforcement. Instead of focusing on the two parties only, a committee can look at the whole picture, with all its polycentric implications. It is also not limited to the provision of individual remedies, but can make more programmatic recommendations, to match programmatic duties. Thus the UN Committee has developed sophisticated techniques, first in formulating specific obligations, as seen above, and then in delineating performance standards and setting up monitoring systems.

10.151   However, this is a difficult task. Progressive realization requires measurement of both current and past performance, together with an evaluation of whether the state is moving expeditiously towards the goal. Many governments do not have the relevant data, and may be unwilling to collect it. Even if the data were all available, analysis requires a high level of statistical expertise, and the results are inevitably open to varying interpretations and subject to numerous caveats.[202]

10.152   The UN Committee has again developed innovative responses, in particular by moving away from externally imposed and technical standards to benchmarks set by governments on the basis of appropriate democratic consultation and participation from the social partners and civil society.[203] Participation by individuals and mechanisms of accountability are crucial both in deciding on the strategies to achieve goals and in monitoring compliance. Civil and political rights are therefore part of the process of achieving social rights.

10.153   Nevertheless, the reporting mechanism has had a woeful record in inducing compliance. This is particularly true of the ESC, which is monitored by the Social Rights Committee of the Council of Europe. The recently completed 15th cycle of supervision, covering national reports relating to 1995–98, found that, of the 17 non-core provisions examined, the United Kingdom had complied with nine, but was in breach of four and more information was needed on a further four. The 14th cycle, which examined compliance with the core provisions, found the United Kingdom in breach of several key provisions, including the right to work, the right to organize, the right to bargain collectively, the right to social and medical assistance, and the right of migrant workers and their families to protection and assistance.

---

[202] A Chapman, 'A New Approach to Monitoring the ICESCR', Review of the International Commission of Jurists, No 55, December 1995, 23.

[203] P Alston, 'International Governance in the Normative Areas' UN Development Programme, Background Papers: Human Development Report 1999, 15–18. Steiner and Alston (n 6 above) 317.

One way of strengthening compliance could be through a system of individual **10.154** complaints, similar to the individual right of complaint to the ECHR. Such a system has been proposed for the ICESCR, but little has come of discussions. The only such procedure to emerge is the recent addition to the ESC of a collective complaints procedure, permitting organizations such as specified trade unions, employers associations and non-governmental organizations to bring complaints against states who have ratified the Protocol.[204] However, the Protocol is limited by the lack of a remedial element.[205] Only nine states have ratified it, and the United Kingdom is not among them.

F. Conclusion

This chapter has argued that instead of the traditional classifications of rights into **10.155** civil and political or social and economic, a greater focus on the nature of the obligation is required. Secondary and tertiary obligations pose greater challenges for the courts than primary obligations. Although the polycentric nature of the dispute and the clear political dimension argue for a degree of judicial deference, there should be appropriate and robust protection of fundamental rights, however they are categorized. In achieving this balance, courts will need to do more than 'toll the bell of resources'. Instead they need to insist on accountability, transparency and appropriate participation by affected individuals and groups. In so doing, more attention needs to be paid to suitable modification of the court procedure itself, including wider rules of standing for both individuals and groups, a move away from a strictly bipolar decision-making process, better information gathering powers and more imaginative remedial structures.

---

[204] Additional Protocol to the ESC 1961 providing for a system of collective complaints.
[205] H Cullen, 'The Collective Complaints Mechanism of the European Social Charter' [2000] ELR 25.

11

EQUALITY AND NON-DISCRIMINATION

A. Introduction

This chapter[1] explores the extent to which English public law applies principles of equality and non-discrimination to the activities of public authorities in England, broadly defined to include Parliament, the executive, and the courts.   **11.01**

(1) Diversity of the Meaning and Functions of Equality and Non-Discrimination Norms

The difficulty in expressing the principles of equality and non-discrimination currently applicable in English public law derives from several different aspects of the   **11.02**

---

[1] Grateful thanks are due to several colleagues who commented on previous drafts, in particular: Trevor Allen, Dawn Oliver QC, Bob Hepple, Sandra Fredman, Peter Birks QC, David Pannick QC, Evelyn Ellis, Sacha Prechal, Stephen Weatherill, Christine Boch, Annick Masselot, Jeffrey Jowell QC, Lord Justice Sedley, Anne Peters and Robin Allen QC. Any remaining errors are mine.

way these principles have emerged and currently arise. There is no one legal meaning of equality or discrimination applicable in the different circumstances; the meanings of equality and discrimination are diverse. There is no consistency in the circumstances in which stronger or weaker conceptions of equality and discrimination currently apply. There is no one organizing principle or purpose underlying the principles of equality and non-discrimination currently applicable; the justifications offered for the legal principles of equality and non-discrimination are diverse. Equality in English public law is, then, essentially pluralistic in its sources, in its origins, in its meaning, in its application, and in its functions.

(2) Four Categories of Equality and Non-Discrimination in English Public Law

11.03 Equality and non-discrimination are complex concepts, with considerable debate on their meanings and justification. Four categories[2] of equality and non-discrimination applicable in English public law are identifiable in this chapter.[3]

(a) Equality as 'rationality'

11.04 The first meaning of equality is where the principle of non-discrimination (interpreted as the limited principle that likes should be treated alike, unless there is an adequate justification for not applying this principle) is a self-standing principle of general application, without specific limitation on the circumstances in which it is applicable (except that it be in the public realm, broadly defined), and without limitation on the grounds on which the difference of treatment is challengeable. In other jurisdictions, this approach to equality is particularly associated with constitutional guarantees. In the English public law context, it is judicially created. This meaning is essentially rationality-based.

(b) Equality as protective of 'prized public goods'

11.05 In the second meaning, the non-discrimination principle becomes an adjunct to the protection of particularly prized 'public goods', including human and other rights. The principle is essentially that such 'prized public goods' should

---

[2] I will use the term 'category' and 'meaning' interchangeably in this chapter. No significance should be attached to this.

[3] The first three meanings have echoes in the US Fourteenth Amendment context where, at the risk of oversimplification, the US Supreme Court distinguishes those legislative or governmental distinctions where the courts will be more deferential to political judgments (when the so-called 'rational relationship' test is adopted), from those the courts consider they should pay particular attention to where the distinctions are based on 'suspect classifications' (race is the paradigm) or where 'fundamental interests' (such as the right to travel) are at stake (when the so-called 'strict scrutiny' test is adopted). The reason why this example from the US is of some interest is because a similar approach has evolved in the UK, although this is only now becoming clear. The fourth meaning does not have any clear equivalent in the US constitutional context, although there are somewhat similar statutory requirements for government contractors.

in principle be distributed to everyone without distinction. In the distribution of the 'public good', equals should be treated on a non-discriminatory basis, except where differences can be justified. In this context, the focus is on the distribution of the public good, rather than the characteristics of the recipient. The courts will scrutinize public authorities' (less frequently, private bodies') actions in a more intense way than under the first meaning, when the actions of the public authority give rise to discrimination (defined essentially as treating someone differently) in these circumstances. This meaning is a mixture of judicial and statutory creation.

(c) Equality as preventing 'status-harms' arising from discrimination on particular grounds

In the third meaning of non-discrimination, almost entirely the creation of legislation, with some recent common law developments in support, the focus of attention shifts from the importance of the 'prized public good' (particularly the human right in issue) and turns instead to the association between a limited number of particular characteristics (such as race, gender, etc) and the discrimination suffered by those who have, or who are perceived to have, those characteristics. The courts will scrutinize public authorities' (and others') actions in a more intense way than under the first meaning, where the public authorities' actions discriminate against individuals with those particular characteristics. In this context, however, the meaning of discrimination expands beyond the principle that likes should be treated alike to embrace also the principle that unlikes should not be treated alike. This meaning is essentially aimed at preventing status-harms arising from discrimination on particular grounds. **11.06**

(d) Equality as proactive promotion of equality of opportunity between particular groups

In the fourth meaning, again almost entirely the creation of legislation, certain public authorities are placed under a duty actively to take steps to promote greater equality of opportunity and good relations (the legal meanings of which are yet to be fully articulated) for particular groups. In that sense, it is a further development of the third ('status-based') meaning. However, the concept of 'equality of opportunity' goes beyond any of the concepts of discrimination characteristic of the previous meanings. Under this fourth approach, a public authority to which this duty applies is under a duty to do more than ensure the absence of discrimination from its employment, educational, and other specified functions; it must also act positively to promote equality of opportunity and good relations between different groups throughout all its policy-making and in carrying out all its activities. **11.07**

11.08 Several caveats are necessary regarding these distinctions. First, the categories are constructed to try to make sense of a sometimes bewildering range of legal material; these categories have received no judicial approval. Secondly, these categories are not watertight, but porous, with developments in one category influencing approaches in others. Thirdly, in some respects, the principles underlying each category may be in tension with each other, and this may require decisions as to priority between the categories in the case of conflict. English public law has only just begun to explore these tensions. Fourthly, this chapter attempts to describe the current approaches to equality and non-discrimination in English public law, rather than to provide a normative analysis of these approaches. The fourfold distinction described may or may not be convincing philosophically.[4] It may or may not be satisfying politically. No arguments are introduced advocating changes that might usefully be introduced into public law the better to advance these, or other, meanings of equality and non-discrimination.

(4) Structure of the Chapter

11.09 The structure of the chapter is as follows. A brief history of the evolution of the principles of equality and non-discrimination in English public law will be offered in Part B. This will help to clarify also the sources of legal obligations and rights relevant for deriving non-discrimination and equality principles. The meanings of equality and non-discrimination applicable in different contexts will be considered in greater detail in Part C.

B. History and Sources

(1) Introduction

11.10 There are several principal sources from which legally binding equality and non-discrimination rights and obligations relevant to public authorities are derived. The way the non-discrimination and equality norms deriving from these sources are interpreted, and the vital issue of how these sources relate to each other, results in significant part from the way in which the norms of equality and non-discrimination in English public law have evolved historically. There is no consistent pattern of historical development in the common law or statute; the history of the

---

[4] For discussion of the varying philosophical conceptions of equality and their relationship to anti-discrimination law, see Christopher McCrudden, 'Editor's Introduction: Theorizing About Anti-Discrimination Law: A Review of Recent Literature' in Christopher McCrudden (ed), *Anti-Discrimination Law* (2nd edn, The International Library of Essays in Law and Legal Theory, Ashgate Publishing Ltd, forthcoming).

principles of equality and non-discrimination in English public law is a patch-work of historically contingent developments.

(2) Equality and Non-Discrimination in English Law Prior to Legislative Intervention

We begin with the place and significance of equality and non-discrimination in English common law prior to legislative intervention. Prior to the first race relations legislation in 1965, there was no *general* rule, policy, or principle in common law directly relevant to combating racial or other forms of discrimination.[5] There were several reasons why this was so.

11.11

Although the common law, as we shall see, contained legal norms that played a role in the evolution of a principle of non-discrimination, the common law was, first and foremost a source of discrimination itself, particularly for women. In 1889, Lord Esher MR could say: 'I take it that by neither the common law nor the constitution of this country from the beginning of the common law until now can a woman be entitled to exercise any public function'.[6] Women could not vote, nor work in certain professions.[7] Married women were under considerable legal disabilities due to their married status. Illegitimate children were under severe legal disadvantages. Infants were under certain legal disabilities.

11.12

Another significant reason delaying the development of common law principles of equality and non-discrimination was the importance attaching to freedom of contract and the right to property in the common law.[8] The common law, as a corollary of the notion of freedom of contract 'allows the freedom not to contract . . . Similarly, the common law recognizes the rights of private parties to do what they please with their property. Such a right necessarily guarantees the right to exclude.'[9] Non-discrimination and equality norms, therefore, not infrequently challenged freedom of contract and the right to property, and when the judiciary was faced with this challenge, it frequently held that freedom of contract and property rights prevented the emergence of a non-discrimination norm. Despite the decision by Lord Mansfield in *Sommersett's Case*,[10] in which slavery was declared 'so

11.13

---

[5] 'English law has very little to say about discrimination', wrote Griffith prior to the 1965 legislation: JAG Griffith et al, *Coloured Immigrants in Britain* (London: Oxford University Press, 1960) 171.

[6] Lord Esher MN in *Beresford-Hope v Lady Sandhurst* (1889) 23 QBD 79.

[7] Sandra Fredman, *Women and the Law* (Oxford: Clarendon Press, 1997) ch 2.

[8] 'When this freedom [of contract] came into conflict with the post-Second World War concept of "freedom from discrimination"', wrote Hepple, 'it is hardly surprising that the older and better appreciated freedom has prevailed.' B Hepple, *Race, Jobs and the Law in Britain* (2nd edn, Harmondsworth: Penguin, 1970) 155.

[9] Note, 'The Antidiscrimination Principle in the Common Law' (1993) 102 Harvard L Rev 1994.

[10] (1772) 20 St Tr 1.

odious that nothing can be suffered to support it except positive law', as late as 1859, an English court refused to invalidate a contract made by a British subject for the sale of slaves in Brazil.[11] In the context of employment discrimination, freedom of contract was supplemented by a tradition of legal abstention from industrial relations issues.

11.14 There were, however, several islands of non-discrimination in the common law.[12] English common law 'has traditionally placed ancient duties, requiring equality of treatment, upon common carriers, inn keepers and some monopoly enterprises such as ports and harbours, obliging them to accept all travelers'.[13] Some have seen in these developments an emerging common law duty of equal and adequate service.[14]

11.15 As equality between the races and between men and women became more important politically during the 20th century in Britain, the courts occasionally used the concept of 'public policy' as a basis on which to attack discrimination. Some century after the enactment of legislation abolishing slavery, public policy was used as the basis for refusing to give effect to foreign laws concerning slavery.[15] In 1966, in *Nagle v Feilden*[16] the refusal of the Jockey Club to provide a horse trainer's licence to a woman was held to be against public policy. In 1971, in *Edwards v SOGAT*,[17] Lord Denning held (although the case did not turn on allegations of discrimination) that the courts 'will not allow a power to be exercised arbitrarily or capriciously or with unfair discrimination, neither in the making of rules or in the enforcement of them'.

11.16 Thus far, we have been considering the role of equality and non-discrimination in the common law dealing with relations between private individuals. In Dicey's elaboration of the concept of the 'rule of law', which he regarded as a constitutional obligation applicable to the conduct of public authorities in England, equality was a significant (if narrowly defined) element: 'With us, every official, from the Prime Minister down to a constable or collector of taxes, is under the same responsibility for every act done without legal justification'.[18] This conception of the rule of law

---

[11] *Satos v Illidge* (1859) 6 CB (ns) 841; (1860) 8 CB (ns) 861. See further AP Lester and G Bindman, *Race and Law* (Penguin Books, 1972) 35–42.

[12] See eg *Constantine v Imperial Hotels Ltd* [1944] KB 693; *Re Dominion Students' Hall Trust* [1947] Ch 183; *Re Meres' Will Trust*, The Times, 4 May 1957; *Clayton v Ramsden* [1943] AC 320.

[13] De Smith, Woolf and Jowell, *Judicial Review of Administrative Action* (5th edn, London: Sweet and Maxwell, 1995) para 13-040.

[14] For a discussion of the early English cases which some have seen as the basis of such a duty at common law, see Charles M Haar and Daniel Wm Fessler, *The Wrong Side of the Tracks: A Revolutionary Rediscovery of the Common Law Tradition of Fairness in the Struggle Against Inequality* (New York: Simon and Schuster, 1986) chs 2 and 3.

[15] *Regazzoni v KC Sethia (1944) Ltd* [1956] 2 QB 490, CA.

[16] [1966] 2 QB 633, CA.

[17] [1971] Ch 354.

[18] AV Dicey, *Law of the Constitution* (10th edn, London: Macmillan, 1959) 193.

both reflects (and, to some extent) contributed to the further development of English public law in several important respects. So, for example, the development of resistance to claims of Crown and other executive powers was in part explained on the basis of a rule of law principle incorporating an equality dimension. This meant that public authorities had no greater inherent powers than the ordinary citizen at common law. Such powers needed specific statutory or other legal authority in order to be upheld.[19]

Some decisions reviewing local authority decision-making, beginning from the end of the 19th century, indicated that discrimination might be seen as unreasonable. In the 1898 decision in *Kruse v Johnson*,[20] it was held that bye-laws could be held unreasonable because of '[p]artial and unequal treatment in their operation as between different classes'. In 1911, in *Board of Education v Rice*,[21] which concerned the public body's power to fund church schools less favourably than other schools, it was said to be '. . . clear that the local authority ought to be as impartial as the rate collector who demands the rate without reference to the particular views of the ratepayer'. In *Prescott v Birmingham Corp*,[22] the decision of the local authority to award free travel to the elderly was unlawful because the discrimination breached the Corporation's fiduciary duty to the ratepayers, that is the duty to treat all the ratepayers equally in this case.   **11.17**

Beyond this limited understanding of equality, however, English public law was hardly fertile ground on which to develop robust equality or non-discrimination norms. Indeed, depending on how it is interpreted, the Diceyan rule of law might be seen as a barrier to the development of such principles. As we saw above, under this limited view of the rule of law, public authorities are not free to do anything that their constitutive powers do not expressly or by necessary implication include. It was because the courts saw many forms of discrimination (though not discrimination between ratepayers, hence *Prescott*) as impliedly within their powers that authorities were permitted for many years to engage in discrimination that would no longer be thought acceptable. Without specific legislative prohibitions against discrimination by public authorities, such discrimination appeared to be largely permitted. Indeed, legislation was more often the source of such discrimination and remnants of such discrimination continue to the present day.[23] The virtual abstention by the courts from effective substantive or procedural review of   **11.18**

---

[19] *Entick v Carrington* (1795) 19 St Tr 1029; *R v Somerset CC, ex p Fewings* [1995] 1 WLR 1037.

[20] [1898] 2 QB 291, *per* Lord Russell of Killowen CJ.

[21] [1911] AC 179.

[22] [1955] Ch 210.

[23] Act of Settlement 1700: '. . . all and every person and persons that . . . should be reconciled to or shall hold communion with the see or church of Rome or should professe the popish religion or marry a papist should be excluded and are . . . made for ever incapable to inherit, possess or enjoy the crown and government of this realm.'

the acts of public bodies by way of judicial review from the First World War until around the beginning of the 1960s also contributed to the absence of a non-discrimination principle becoming embedded in the common law. Prior to the enactment of domestic legislation, there were some attempts to argue that the common law provided protection to those discriminated against on grounds of sex, for example, but these were unsuccessful.[24] Discrimination on the basis of religion was also tolerated.[25] Where statutory or other powers were given to public authorities, these were not interpreted as limited by any equality or non-discrimination norm.[26] The Privy Council in particular was unwilling to strike down the most blatant discrimination by public bodies in Canada,[27] East Africa,[28] and South Africa.[29] The judicial view appeared to be that Parliament was the appropriate source of control of unfair discrimination by public authorities, and that it should be remedied politically, and not through the courts.[30] Indeed, in several infamous cases, such powers were interpreted as prohibiting public authorities from pursuing equality considerations.[31]

(3) Welfare State, Social Rights and Equality

11.19   A vital way in which equality guarantees are underpinned is by ensuring that basic social protections for the most vulnerable are secured, such as housing, food, and education. To the extent that such protections are provided to all, substantive equality will be furthered. This chapter mostly considers explicit legal requirements on public authorities not to discriminate and to further equality of opportunity, rather than attempting to set out a full account of the role of public authorities in furthering equality, particularly on the basis of class and wealth by providing social protections more generally. Much of the legislation emanating from the welfare state, essentially dating from the beginning of the 20th century but coming to fulfilment after the Second World War, attempts to further a substantive vision of equality in that context. These developments are considered elsewhere in this book.

11.20   The development of the welfare state illustrates, however, that there may be potential conflicts between the differing meanings of equality sketched out above.

---

[24] *Bebb v Law Society* [1914] 1 Ch 286, CA; *Price v Rhondda UDC* [1923] 2 Ch 372, Ch D; *Short v Poole Corp* [1926] 1 Ch 66, CA.

[25] *Weinberger v Inglis* [1919] AC 606.

[26] See the Privy Council decisions upholding racial discrimination in Canada and in East and South Africa: Lester and Bindman (n 11 above) 35–69.

[27] *Co-operative Committee on Japanese Canadians v A-G for Canada* [1947] AC 85, PC.

[28] *Commissioner for Local Government Lands and Settlement v Kaderbhai* [1931] AC 652, PC.

[29] *Madrassa Anjuman Islamia of Kholwad v Municipal Council of Johannesburg* [1922] 1 AC 500, PC.

[30] *R (ex p Zadig) v Halliday* [1917] AC 260, *per* Lord Dunedin.

[31] eg, *Roberts v Hopwood* [1925] AC 578. For a discussion of common law cases striking down attempts at securing equality for women, see Fredman (n 7 above) ch 2.

Not infrequently, in targeting resources to the most needy in order to secure equality in fact, others are excluded from the benefit. Equality conceived as formal equality may find troubling the pragmatic distinctions necessary in this context. The income tax provides a useful example. The tax system is one of the most important methods of funding the welfare state, and thus a conception of equality founded in distributive justice. However, income tax places a heavier tax burden on those who are wealthier through progressive tax rates—the more you earn, the higher the tax rate. How far should the progressive element be limited by a conception of formal equality?

There is, however, an additional important role that welfare state provisions play, **11.21** with a closer connection to anti-discrimination law. Some issues begin as anti-discrimination debates and become translated over time into claims for a particular substantive benefit in the form of welfare state-type social protections. For example, reliance on a traditional sex discrimination analysis to address the issues of how to treat pregnant women has proven much less important in practice than provisions giving pregnant women specific detailed rights relating to time off, rights of return, and pay during pregnancy.

(4) Development of Statutory Anti-Discrimination and Equality Legislation

In part as a reaction against the limited promise that the common law appeared to **11.22** hold, but more because of the political perceptions that there were serious social problems that needed to be addressed, there were several major legislative interventions explicitly designed to further equality and non-discrimination. These have tended to come in bursts of legislative activity relating to concerns about the status of particular groups. Thus, for example, statutes were passed in the late 19th century regarding married women's equality, entitling married women to retain their property (to some extent) and (subsequently) their wages. More general equality provisions, however, date from the 20th century. The first, rather limited, intervention derived from the movement for women's suffrage and women's equality in the early part of the 20th century. The Sex Disqualification (Removal) Act 1919, passed in response to the principle articulated by Lord Esher MR, and quoted above, provided, in part, and subject to several exceptions, that: '. . . a person shall not be disqualified by sex or marriage from the exercise of any public function, or from being appointed to or holding any civil or judicial office or post, or from entering or assuming or carrying on any civil profession or vocation, or from admission to any incorporated society . . .'.[32]

---

[32] A study of the Act concluded, however, that 'the most remarkable thing about [the Act] is how little it has been relied upon as a means of establishing the unlawfulness of sex discrimination in employment': WB Creighton, *Working Women and the Law* (London: Mansell, 1979) 68. The Act was cited in *Nagle v Feilden* [1966] 2 QB 633, CA as a source of public policy. For an unsuccessful attempt to rely on the Act, see *Hugh-Jones v St John's College, Cambridge* [1979] ICR 848, EAT.

11.23   Legislative intervention regarding discrimination dates primarily from the 1960s, however. The first area of discrimination to be tackled legislatively was racial discrimination, leading to the limited Race Relations Act 1965. Although limited in its ambit, the debate over the 1965 Bill was crucial in seeing a shift from a criminal model of enforcement to a civil-administrative model of enforcement, and in demonstrating the importance at that time of the US state and federal anti-discrimination legislation on the British model. An important omission from the 1965 Act was employment and this, together with the need to reformulate the enforcement procedures, led to the Race Relations Act 1968, which was somewhat more expansive in its coverage.[33]

11.24   Beginning with the Equal Pay Act in 1970, in part stimulated by future membership of the European Community, in part due to the growing feminist movement, Parliament increasingly tackled discrimination on the grounds of sex. In 1975, the Sex Discrimination Act was passed. Together with the Race Relations Act 1976, these significantly developed the institutional mechanisms available to individuals to seek redress against discrimination. The 1975 Act was the last major piece of gender discrimination legislation that was not enacted in reaction to EC law developments. Race discrimination legislation, however, has been substantially shaped by domestic political concerns, notably the reaction to the MacPherson report, published following the inquiry into the matters arising from the death of Stephen Lawrence.[34] The report identified 'institutional racism' within the police force.[35] So too, disability discrimination legislation derived essentially from political pressure from increasingly vocal domestic disability rights pressure groups. With the development of EC legislation dealing with these and other grounds of discrimination, however, it is likely that a somewhat similar Europeanization will take place in these areas as has already taken place with regard to gender equality. A final important influence in developing domestic anti-discrimination legislation was the devolution of power to the devolved legislatures and executives in Scotland, Wales and Northern Ireland. In many cases, primary and secondary legislation is supplemented by codes of practice. We will consider each of these developments in somewhat greater detail in the following paragraphs.

---

[33] See Christopher McCrudden, 'Racial Discrimination' in Christopher McCrudden and Gerald Chambers, *Individual Rights and the Law in Britain* (Oxford: Clarendon Press, 1994) 410–455.

[34] *The Stephen Lawrence Inquiry* (Cm 4262-I, 1999).

[35] The report defined 'institutional racism' as: 'The collective failure of an organization to provide an appropriate and professional service to people because of their colour, culture or ethnic origin. It can be seen or detected in processes, attitudes and behaviour which amount to discrimination through unwitting prejudice, ignorance, thoughtlessness and racist stereotyping which disadvantage minority ethnic people.'

(a) Race, sex, disability and human rights legislation

The principal statutes currently requiring non-discrimination in certain contexts **11.25**
by public authorities are: that dealing with sex discrimination, which is governed
by the Equal Pay Act 1970 and the Sex Discrimination Act 1975 (SDA) (as
amended); that dealing with race discrimination, which is governed by the Race
Relations Act 1976 (RRA) (as amended); and that dealing with disability discrimination, which is governed by the Disability Discrimination Act 1995
(DDA), and the Disability Rights Commission (DRC) Act 1999. Although disparate and with significant differences, they share many common concepts. One
important similarity is that, for the most part, with significant exceptions,[36] they
apply to both the public and private sectors. The Human Rights Act 1998 (HRA)
has added substantially to this legislation, and will be considered subsequently.

(i) *Racial discrimination*

The RRA 1976, as amended, prohibits discrimination on the grounds of race, **11.26**
colour, ethnic or national origin, and nationality in carrying out particular functions, such as when acting as an employer, in education, in providing housing, and
other services to the public. Although there have been several amendments of the
Act, the most important is the Race Relations (Amendment) Act 2000, which includes provisions that outlaw race discrimination in all public authority functions
not already covered by the RRA 1976, with certain exceptions. It also requires
certain public authorities to have due regard to the need to promote equality of
opportunity (which is a concept wider than non-discrimination[37]) and good
race relations in carrying out certain activities. The 1976 Act established the
Commission for Racial Equality (CRE), which oversees the implementation of the
legislation and is equipped with certain enforcement powers. There are several issues
related to racial discrimination that will not be considered further here; in particular, criminal offences of incitement to racial hatred and racially aggravated offences.

(ii) *Gender discrimination and equality*

There are two principal statutes prohibiting gender discrimination and equal- **11.27**
ity.[38] The Equal Pay Act 1970, as amended, requires employers to provide equal
pay between men and women employees. The SDA 1975, as amended, prohibits
discrimination on the grounds of sex by those carrying out particular functions,
such as when acting as an employer, and in providing education, housing, and

---

[36] The public sector has positive duties in the field of race. Negative duties do not apply to all
parts of the public sector, except for race, as a result of the Race Relations (Amendment) Act 2000.
[37] See para 11.187 below.
[38] On the relationship between 'gender' and 'sex', see paras 11.123 et seq, below.

other services to the public. These statutes have been extensively amended, notably by legislation implementing EC sex discrimination requirements. The 1975 Act established the Equal Opportunities Commission (EOC), which oversees the implementation of the 1970 and 1975 legislation and is equipped with certain enforcement powers. There are many separate pieces of legislation dealing with rights that are of particular significance to women and that may be regarded as helping to ensure a degree of substantive equality between men and women in the workplace that will not be further considered here, such as maternity rights.

(iii) Disability discrimination

11.28   The principal statute in the field of disability discrimination is the DDA 1995 which requires employers and certain other service providers not to discriminate on the grounds of disability in certain contexts, and establishes an obligation on a range of individuals and bodies to make 'reasonable adjustments' to accommodate those who are disabled. The DRC Act 1999 establishes a commission to oversee the implementation of the legislation and is equipped with certain enforcement powers.

(b) Devolved administrations

(i) Anti-discrimination and equality legislation regarding the devolved administrations

11.29   The devolved administrations in Scotland, Wales and Northern Ireland operate under the authority of legislation that contains non-discrimination and equality obligations, although of somewhat varying types. The Northern Ireland Act 1998 prohibits discrimination on the grounds of religious belief or political opinion by the Northern Ireland Assembly in carrying out its legislative functions, and by the Northern Ireland Executive in carrying out its administrative and executive functions. In addition, most public authorities in Northern Ireland are required to have due regard to the need to promote equality of opportunity between persons of different religious belief, political opinion, racial group, age, marital status or sexual orientation, between men and women, between persons with a disability and persons without, and between persons with dependants and persons without. Without prejudice to this obligation, public authorities must have regard to the desirability of promoting good relations between persons of different religious belief, political opinion, or racial group. The Welsh Assembly is required to make appropriate arrangements with a view to securing that its functions are exercised,[39] and its business conducted,[40] with due regard to the principle that there should be

---

[39] Government of Wales Act 1998, s 120.
[40] ibid s 48. See also Conduct of Members (Principles) (Wales) Order 2001, SI 2001/2276, Sch.

equality of opportunity for all people. In addition, the Welsh Language Act 1993 incorporates a principle of equality between the Welsh and English languages.[41] This chapter will not consider legislation regarding the devolved administrations in any detail.

(ii) Anti-discrimination and equality legislation in the devolved administrations

The legislation noted previously dealing with racial, gender and disability dis-   **11.30** crimination either applies directly in Scotland, Wales and Northern Ireland, or there is directly equivalent legislation applying in these areas, deriving from the legislative authority of the devolved governments. In addition, however, there is also legislation that is unique to particular jurisdictions. In particular, the Fair Employment and Treatment (Northern Ireland) Order 1998[42] in Northern Ireland prohibits discrimination by employers and other service providers (including public authorities) on grounds of religious belief or political opinion, as well as establishing a duty on employers to bring about 'fair participation' between Catholics and Protestants in employment, an example of the fourth meaning of equality sketched out above, applied to the private sector. This legislation will not be considered further in this chapter.[43]

(c) Codes and other domestic instruments

(i) Statutory codes of practice

Several of these anti-discrimination laws empower the bodies given responsibility   **11.31** for ensuring compliance with the legislation, to issue codes of practice to provide guidance for employers and service providers on how to avoid discrimination and promote equality of opportunity. The scope of the legislation varies somewhat. The RRA restricts such codes to employment, housing and the public sector statutory duty. The SDA restricts such codes to employment. The DDA empowers the DRC to prepare codes covering employment as well as goods, facilities and services. Codes of practice relating to employment have been issued dealing with race,[44] gender,[45] and disability.[46] In addition, there are codes of practice dealing

---

[41] See *Williams v Cowell (t/a The Stables) (No 1)* [2000] 1 WLR 187, CA.

[42] SI 1998/3162.

[43] See Christopher McCrudden, 'Affirmative Action and Fair Participation: Interpreting the Fair Employment Act 1989' (1992) 21 ILJ 170.

[44] CRE, *Code of Practice for the Elimination of racial discrimination and the promotion of equality of opportunity in employment* (1983).

[45] EOC, *Code of Practice on sex discrimination: equal opportunity policies, procedures and practices in employment* (1985); EOC, *Code of Practice on Equal Pay* (1997).

[46] *Code of Practice for the elimination of discrimination in the field of employment against disabled persons or persons who have had a disability* (1996). See also *Guidance on matters to be taken into account in determining questions relating to the definition of disability* (London: HMSO, 1996).

with race in housing,[47] and relating to the public authority statutory duty.[48] Codes of practice have also been issued dealing with disability discrimination in education,[49] goods, facilities and services,[50] and by trade organizations.[51] Lastly, under the Asylum and Immigration Act 1996 the Secretary of State has issued a code of practice as to the measures which an employer is to be expected to take, or not to take, with a view to securing that, while avoiding the commission of an offence under s 8 of the 1996 Act, the employer also avoids unlawful discrimination.[52] Section 8 of the 1996 Act provides that an employer who employs a person subject to immigration control who does not have the right to take employment shall be guilty of an offence. Like the other codes, a failure on the part of any person to observe a provision of the code does not of itself make him liable to any proceedings. However, the code is admissible in evidence in proceedings before industrial and employment tribunals.

(ii) Other domestic instruments

11.32 In addition to these codes of practice based on statutory authority, there are other instruments that have been developed that address discrimination. In 1998, the UK government issued 'Policy Appraisal for Equal Treatment' which specifies procedures for government departments to ensure that policy advice to ministers does not have unjustified disparate impact on certain groups, primarily on the basis of race, gender and disability. An equivalent policy in Northern Ireland has been held to be legally binding in certain respects to the extent that departments were bound to apply the guidelines and a failure to do so would result in the minister not taking into account a relevant consideration and disappointing a legitimate expectation that the policy would be properly implemented.[53] In addition, a non-statutory code of practice has been published dealing with age discrimination.[54]

---

[47] CRE, *Code of Practice in Rented Housing for the elimination of racial discrimination and the promotion of equal opportunities* (1991); CRE, *Code of Practice in Non-Rented Housing for the elimination of racial discrimination and the promotion of equal opportunities* (1992).

[48] CRE, *General Statutory Duty: Code of Practice* (2002).

[49] DRC *Code of Practice for Schools* (2002) and *DRC Code of Practice for providers of Post-16 education and related services* (2002).

[50] *Disability Discrimination Act 1995 Code of Practice on the Rights of Access to Goods, Facilities, Services and Premises* (2002).

[51] *Code of Practice on the Duties of Trade Organisations to their Disabled Members and Applicants* (1999).

[52] *Immigration and Asylum Act 1999—Section 22: Code of Practice for all employers on the avoidance of race discrimination in recruitment practice while seeking to prevent illegal working* (2001).

[53] *Casey v Department of Education for Northern Ireland* (QB, 16 October 1996).

[54] *Age Diversity in Employment: a Code of Practice* (DfEE, 1999). This Code is accompanied by 'Age Diversity in Employment—Guidance and Case Studies'. A revised code was issued subsequently: *Age Diversity at Work* (DfEE, 2002).

(5) *Growth of EC Law on Equality and Discrimination*

As a result of the European Communities Act 1972, the United Kingdom is **11.33** obliged as a matter of domestic law to implement the requirements of EC law. There are several different, but overlapping, sources of EC law that establish general equality and non-discrimination norms binding on EC institutions, and the member states 'where they implement, or act within the scope of, Community law'. In addition, EC law prohibits other natural and legal persons as well as EC institutions and the member states from discriminating in more limited circumstances, for example where their actions breach prohibitions of discrimination on grounds of nationality and sex discrimination.

(a) **Equality as a general principle of EC law**

The European Court of Justice (ECJ) has developed a jurisprudence that subjects **11.34** the exercise of Community competence to the requirement that it complies with 'general principles' of EC law.[55] This has implications for equality and discrimination in several principal ways.

Despite the existence of numerous provisions of the Treaty 'that provide for the **11.35** principle of equal treatment with regard to specific matters',[56] the ECJ has held that the principle of equality is one of the general principles of EC law. Within the sphere of EC law, this principle of equality precludes comparable situations from being treated differently, and different situations from being treated in the same way,[57] unless the treatment is objectively justified.[58] The ECJ has recognized, for example, that the principle that everyone is equal before the law is a basic principle of EC law.[59] Why did the Court find it necessary to hold that equality is a general principle of EC law? Tridimas observes: 'It may be that those [specific] provisions do not guarantee equal treatment in all cases so that the development of a general principle is necessary to cover the lacunae left in written law. The main reason for the development of a general principle, however, seems to be one of principle rather than one of practical necessity.'[60]

---

[55] See, in general, Takis Tridimas, *The General Principles of EC Law* (Oxford: OUP, 1999) ch 2. See also 'Equality' in AG Toth, *The Oxford Encyclopaedia of European Community Law* (Oxford: Clarendon Press, 1990) vol 1, 188–201.

[56] Tridimas (n 55 above) 40.

[57] Case 106/83 *Sermide SpA v Cassa Conguaglio Zucchero* [1984] ECR 4209 at [28]. See also, Opinion of AG Van Gerven delivered on 15 September 1993, Case C-146/91 *Koinopraxia Enoseon Georgikon Synetairismon Diacheir iseos Enchorion Proionton Syn. PE (KYDEP) v Commission* [1994] ECR I-4199.

[58] See, eg, Case C-189/01 *Jippes v Minister van Landbouw, Natuurbeheer en Visserij* [2001] ECR I-5689 at [129] and Case C-149/96 *Portugal v Council* [1999] ECR I-8395 at [91].

[59] Case 283/83 *Racke* [1984] ECR 3791; Case 15/95 *EARL* [1997] ECR I-1961; Case 292/97 *Karlson* (13 April 2000).

[60] Tridimas (n 55 above) 41

11.36   Secondly, the protection of fundamental rights is one of the general principles of EC law. The requirements flowing from the protection of fundamental rights in the Community legal order are binding on the EC institutions. They are also binding on member states when they implement EC rules.[61] The 'fundamental rights' identified by the ECJ are drawn from the constitutional traditions of the member states and, in particular, the European Convention on Human Rights (ECHR). Among the fundamental rights protected by the ECJ, particular aspects of equality have been identified. These include religious equality[62] and the prohibition of sex discrimination.[63] More broadly, the Court has held that fundamental rights 'include the general principle of equality and non-discrimination'.[64]

11.37   In this context, equality as an element of fundamental rights does have an autonomous, if uncertain, role in EC law.[65] Although in the third *Defrenne* case[66] the ECJ recognized that the elimination of sex discrimination formed part of fundamental rights, the Court declined to widen the scope of Article 119 (now 141), which provides for equal pay between men and women, to require equality in respect of other working conditions. In *Razzouk*, however, after reiterating that sex discrimination is a fundamental right, the Court held that it must, therefore, be upheld in the context of relations between the institutions and their employees. The Court held, therefore, that, in interpreting the Staff Regulations, the requirements of the principle of equal treatment 'are in no way limited to those resulting from Article 119 [now 141] of the EEC Treaty or from the Community directives adopted in this field'.[67] So too, equality as an aspect of fundamental rights played an important role in *P v S and Cornwall CC*,[68] regarding whether discrimination on the grounds of gender reassignment was prohibited under EC law. For Tridimas, the case 'provides a prime example of the way the Court views the principle of equality as a general principle of EC law transcending the provisions of Community legislation'. In other cases, however, such as *Grant* (regarding discrimination on grounds of sexual orientation), the Court has been cautious in drawing on the apparent logic of this position to reach conclusions that are, in the Court's view, beyond the existing European political consensus.[69]

---

[61] Case C-442/00 *Caballero v Fondo de Garantia Salarial (Fogasa)* [2003] IRLR 115 at [30].
[62] Case 130/75 *Prais v Council* [1976] ECR 1589.
[63] Case C-149/77 *Defrenne v Sabena* [1978] ECR I-1365 at [26], [27]. See C Docksey, 'The Principle of Equality between Women and Men as Fundamental Right under Community Law' (1991) 20 ILJ 258.
[64] Case C-442/00 *Caballero v Fondo de Garantia Salarial (Fogasa)* [2003] IRLR 115 at [32].
[65] Tridimas (n 55 above) 69.
[66] Case C-149/77 *Defrenne v Sabena* [1978] ECR I-1365.
[67] Joined cases 75 & 117/82 *Razzouk and Beydoun v Commission* [1984] ECR 1509 at [17]. See also Case C-37/89 *Michel Weiser v Caisse Nationale des Barreaux Francais* [1990] ECR I-2395.
[68] Case C-13/94 [1996] ECR I-2143.
[69] Case C-249/96 *Grant v South West Trains Ltd* [1998] ECR I-621.

(b) Equality obligations in the Community treaties and secondary legislation

We may turn now to consider the specific circumstances in which the principles **11.38** of equality and non-discrimination arise as legally enforceable. There are specific provisions of the Community and Union treaties that establish equality and non-discrimination obligations and, in some cases, rights.

(i) Equality of treatment in economic contexts

There are several EC Treaty provisions in which the principles of non-discrimination **11.39** or equality are expressly mentioned. These are regarded as specific enumerations of the general principle of equality.[70] The principal examples are Article 12 (ex 6) EC (discrimination on the grounds of being a national of one of the member states is prohibited), Article 18 (ex 8a) EC (every citizen of the Union has the right to move and reside freely within the territory of the member states, subject to certain limitations), Article 34(2) (ex 40(3)) EC (non-discrimination between producers and consumers in the context of the Common Agricultural Policy), Article 39 (ex 48) EC (non-discrimination as between workers who are nationals of the host state and those who are nationals of another member state), Article 43 (ex 52) EC (equal treatment as between nationals and non-nationals who are established in a self-employed capacity in a member state), Article 49 (ex 59) EC (equal treatment for providers of services), and Article 90 (ex 95) EC (non-discrimination in the field of taxation as between domestic and imported goods).[71] 'Probably the most obvious and central manifestation of the non-discrimination principle in EC law has been in the context of prohibiting discrimination on grounds of nationality or origin.'[72] A considerable body of secondary legislation has further supplemented these provisions.[73]

(ii) Equality and non-discrimination in the area of gender

Articles 2 and 3(2) EC impose the objective of promoting equality between men **11.40** and women in the Community. Article 141 EC provides for the right to equality between men and women in the context of pay. This also provides, however, that the principle of equal treatment does not prevent the maintenance or adoption of measures providing for specific advantages in order to make it easier for the under-represented sex to pursue a vocational activity or to prevent or compensate for disadvantages in professional careers.[74]

---

[70] Case 1/72 *Frilli v Belgium* [1972] ECR 457 at [19]; *Royal Scholten-Honig (Holdings) Ltd v Intervention Board for Agricultural Produce* [1978] ECR 2037 at [26].

[71] Art 18 EC.

[72] G de Búrca, 'The Role of Equality in European Community Law', in A Dashwood and S O'Leary, *The Principle of Equal Treatment in EC Law* (London: Sweet & Maxwell, 1997) 20.

[73] eg, Council Regulation (EEC) 1612/68 on the free movement of workers within the Community [1968] OJ L257/2.

[74] Art 141(4) EC.

11.41   In addition, there is a set of legislative provisions addressing gender inequality that sets a legal framework for women's equality in employment and working conditions more generally. These initially comprised three directives: one on equal pay (which incorporated the International Labour Organization concept of 'equal pay for work of equal value'),[75] one on equal treatment in other aspects of employment (such as hiring, promotions, and dismissals),[76] and the third on equal treatment in a limited number of social security matters.[77] During the 1980s, only two of several proposed directives on equality were adopted, both in 1986, and both of very limited scope: one on equality in occupational social security, and one on equality between self-employed men and women (the Occupational Social Security Directive[78] and the Self Employed Directive[79]). It was not until the late 1980s when the Council accepted the development of a new social dimension to complement the Single Market initiative, and the voting system in Council was modified to permit qualified majority voting in some areas, that further equality legislation was forthcoming.

11.42   Several pieces of legislation adopted since then are of importance. The first was the acceptance by the Council in 1992 of a directive providing certain rights to pregnant women, and those who are breast-feeding (Pregnant Workers Directive).[80] The second was the passage of the Working Time Directive in 1993.[81] The third was the agreement under the Social Protocol (and excluding the United Kingdom initially) of the Parental Leave Directive, providing for periods of time off work for mothers and fathers in certain circumstances).[82] The fourth was the acceptance of an Occupational Social Security Directive, amending the 1986

---

[75] Council Directive (EEC) 75/117 on the approximation of the laws of the Member States relating to the application of the principle of equal pay for men and women [1975] OJ L45/198.

[76] Council Directive (EEC) 76/207 on the implementation of the principle of equal treatment for men and women as regards access to employment, vocational training and promotion, and working conditions [1976] OJ L39/40.

[77] Council Directive (EEC) 79/7 on the progressive implementation of the principle of equal treatment for men and women in matters of social security [1979] OJ L6/24.

[78] Council Directive (EEC) 86/378 on the implementation of the principle of equal treatment for men and women in occupational social security schemes [1986] OJ L225/40.

[79] Council Directive (EEC) 86/613 on the application of the principle of equal treatment between men and women engaged in an activity, including agriculture, in a self-employed capacity, and on the protection of self-employed women during pregnancy and motherhood [1986] OJ L359/56.

[80] Council Directive (EEC) 92/85 on the introduction of measures to encourage improvements in the safety and health at work of pregnant workers who have recently given birth or are breast-feeding [1992] OJ L348/1.

[81] Council Directive (EC) 93/104 concerning certain aspects of the organization of working time [1993] OJ L307/18.

[82] Council Directive (EC) 96/34 on the framework agreement on parental leave concluded by UNICE, CEEP and the ETUC [1996] OJ L145/11, eventually agreed to by the UK in Council Directive (EC) 97/75 amending and extending, to the United Kingdom of Great Britain and Northern Ireland, Directive (EC) 96/34 on the framework agreement on parental leave concluded by UNICE, CEEP and the ETUC [1997] OJ L10/24.

Occupational Social Security Directive).[83] Fifthly, in 1997, the Council adopted the Burden of Proof Directive under the Social Protocol.[84] This included a legislative definition of indirect discrimination for the first time, and provisions aiming to adjust the rules on the burden of proof in sex discrimination cases. Sixthly, the Part-time Workers Directive prohibited discrimination between part-time and full-time workers in certain circumstances.[85] Most recently, significant amendments to the 1976 Equal Treatment Directive were introduced in 2002.[86]

In addition, there must also be added the promulgation of 'soft law' instruments. **11.43** These instruments, although not in the form of traditional legislation, and thus not directly enforceable, have set standards and raised expectations, whilst also having considerable indirect influence on the interpretation of the main 'hard law' instruments, particularly in the context of national legislation; they are not, therefore, devoid of legal effect. The Commission and Council have adopted such instruments in several areas of gender equality, in particular in such difficult areas as equal pay, positive action, sexual harassment, and women's representation.[87]

(iii) Equality and non-discrimination on other grounds

Article 13 EC enacts a general legislative power to tackle a broad range of types of **11.44** discrimination.[88] On the basis of Article 13 EC, the Community has now developed

---

[83] Council Directive (EC) 96/97 amending Directive (EEC) 86/378 on the implementation of the principle of equal treatment for men and women in occupational social security schemes [1997] OJ L14/13.

[84] Council Directive (EC) 97/80 on the burden of proof in cases of discrimination based on sex [1998] OJ L14/6, eventually accepted by the UK in Council Directive (EC) 98/52 on the extension of Directive (EC) 97/80 on the burden of proof in cases of discrimination based on sex to the United Kingdom of Great Britain and Northern Ireland [1998] OJ L205/66.

[85] Council Directive (EC) 97/81 concerning the Framework Agreement on part-time work concluded by UNICE, CEEP and the ETUC—Annex: Framework Agreement on part-time work [1998] OJ L14/9.

[86] Council Directive (EC) 2002/73 of the European Parliament and of the Council of 23 September 2002 amending Council Directive (EEC) 76/207 on the implementation of the principle of equal treatment for men and women as regards access to employment, vocational training and promotion, and working conditions [2002] OJ L269/15.

[87] The EC has put in place a series of action programmes aimed at promoting equal opportunities between men and women which promote the use of positive action measures, eg the Fourth Action Programme on Equal Opportunities for Men and Women (1996–2000). See also Commission Communication, 'Incorporating equal opportunities for women and men into all commission policies and activities' COM (2000) 334; Commission Communication on the consultation of management and labour on the prevention of sexual harassment at work COM (1996) 378; Council Resolution of 27 March 1995 on the balanced participation of men and women in decision-making [1995] OJ L168; Council Recommendation of 2 December 1996 on the balanced participation of men and women in the decision-making process [1996] OJ L319/11; Council Recommendation 84/635 on the promotion of positive action for women [1984] OJ L331/34.

[88] 'Without prejudice to the other provisions of this Treaty and within the limits of the powers conferred by it upon the Community, the Council, acting unanimously on a proposal from the Commission and after consulting the European Parliament, may take appropriate action to combat discrimination based on sex, racial or ethnic origin, religion or belief, disability, age or sexual

an important initial package of measures, in areas other than gender discrimination.[89] The Race Discrimination Directive[90] prohibits racial and ethnic origin discrimination in access to employment, vocational training, employment and working conditions, membership of and involvement in unions, and employer organizations, social protection, including social security and health care, 'social advantages', education, as well as goods and services, including housing. The Framework Directive[91] prohibits discrimination primarily in the employment context (access to employment, self-employment and occupations; vocational guidance and training; employment and working conditions, including dismissals and pay; membership of organizations), but across the rest of the Article 13 EC categories (disability, age, sexual orientation, religion and belief). A programme to promote action to combat discrimination completes this initial package. These directives lay down minimum requirements and give member states the option of introducing or maintaining more favourable provisions. The directives may not be used to justify any regression in the situation that already prevails in each member state. Member states were required to implement the Race Directive by July 2003. The provisions in the Framework Directive in relation to religion or belief and sexual orientation must be implemented by November 2003, and those on age and disability by November 2006.

(c) EU Charter of Fundamental Rights

11.45   Another source of the equality principle in EU law is the EU Charter of Fundamental Rights promulgated in 2000.[92] In part, this document sets out more systematically the fundamental rights already considered by the ECJ as arising from the general principles of EC law. The Charter goes further, however, in setting out a wider catalogue of rights that are considered to be fundamental in the Community/Union.

11.46   The Charter contains a chapter headed 'equality'. This includes a general provision setting out that everyone is equal before the law.[93] Discrimination based on

---

orientation.' For a discussion of the background to Art 13 EC, see M Bell and L Waddington, 'The 1996 Intergovernmental Conference and the Prospects of a Non-discrimination Treaty Article' (1996) 25 ILJ 320, (stressing the important role played by NGOs and the European Parliament in achieving Art 13 EC). M Bell, 'The New Article 13 EC Treaty: A Sound Basis for European Anti-Discrimination Law?' (1999) 6 Maastricht J of European L 5, 6–7, discusses further the background to the drafting of Art 13 EC.

[89]   The literature on equality and the Amsterdam Treaty, together with analysis of the new Art 13 EC directives (in draft and as enacted) is already voluminous; see Mark Bell, *Anti-discrimination Law and the European Union* (Oxford: OUP, 2002).

[90]   Council Directive (EC) 2000/43 implementing the principle of equal treatment between persons irrespective of racial or ethnic origin [2000] OJ L180/22.

[91]   Council Directive (EC) 2000/78 establishing a general framework for equal treatment in employment and occupation [2000] OJ 303/16.

[92]   [2000] OJ C 364/1.

[93]   Art 20.

any ground 'such as sex, race, colour, ethnic or social origin, genetic features, language, religion or belief, political or any other opinion, membership of a national minority, property, birth, disability, age or sexual orientation shall be prohibited'.[94] Discrimination on grounds of nationality is prohibited.[95] The Union is to respect cultural, religious and linguistic diversity.[96] Equality between men and women must be ensured in all areas, including employment, work and pay, but the principle of equality 'shall not prevent the maintenance or adoption of measures providing for specific advantages in favour of the under-represented sex'.[97] Certain rights of children are recognized, including the right to such protection and care as necessary for their well-being.[98] The rights of the elderly to lead a life of dignity and independence and to participate in social and cultural life is recognized and respected,[99] as is the right of persons with disabilities to benefit from measures designed to ensure their independence, social and occupational integration and participation in the life of the Community.[100]

The extent to which these provisions will be seen as giving rise to a legally en- **11.47** forceable principle of equality remains to be seen. The legal status of this document is much discussed, and will be subject to further consideration in 2004, but several Advocates General and the Court of First Instance have already referred to the Charter in their opinions and decisions.

(6) Equality and Human Rights

Equality and non-discrimination is, arguably, in the course of being subsumed **11.48** within a broader human rights discourse in English public law. In this context, the domestic reach of the law relating to equality is being expanded to encompass a more inclusive ideal of equality, one that encompasses race, ethnic origin, disability, religion and belief, sexual orientation, and age. It is notable that many of the international human rights treaty commitments that the United Kingdom has entered into since the end of the Second World War contain equality requirements of a broad-based inclusive type. Article 14 ECHR is merely one example of this trend. An important indication of this within the European Community is the development of the EU Charter of Fundamental Rights.[101] This is not, of

---

[94] Art 21(1).
[95] Art 21(2): '[w]ithin the scope of application of the Treaty establishing the European Community and of the treaty on European Union, and without prejudice to the special provisions of those Treaties.'
[96] Art 22.
[97] Art 23.
[98] Art 24.
[99] Art 25.
[100] Art 26.
[101] The Charter was jointly and solemnly proclaimed at Nice in December 2001 by the Council, Commission and Parliament. However, there is no reference to the Charter in the Treaty of Nice, and it does not yet have any legally binding effect. See further para 11.45 above. The equality clause

course, a development that is restricted to the Community. The Fourth World Conference on Women held in Beijing in September 1995 emphatically defined women's rights as human rights. The UN Conference on racial equality held in South Africa at the end of the summer of 2001 also placed policies against racial discrimination in a human rights context.[102] It may, however, be problematic to consider equality and non-discrimination merely as one among a number of human rights of the type included in the ECHR, deriving from the same principle. Lord Hoffmann has stressed, for example, in *Matthews v Ministry of Defence*, that 'distributive justice . . . is not a fundamental human right'.[103] Human rights 'certainly do not include the right to a fair distribution of resources or fair treatment in economic terms'. This view is controversial as an analysis of the principles underlying human rights protection generally. Leaving aside whether this is an accurate analysis of the principles underlying the substantive rights in the ECHR, we shall see that, at least in some of its guises, equality is closely linked to issues of distributive justice. To interpret it otherwise, because equality is also part of human rights discourse, would unduly limit the reach of these aspects of the equality principle.

(a) European Convention on Human Rights

11.49   The United Kingdom ratified the ECHR in 1951, accepted the right of individual petition for the first time in the mid-1960s, but did not incorporate the ECHR into UK law until the HRA 1998, coming into effect in 2000. Before incorporation, the ECHR had no direct application in British law, although it was increasingly referred to, for example, where there were ambiguities in domestic law that the courts considered should be resolved consistently with UK international obligations.[104]

11.50   Article 14 ECHR provides that 'the enjoyment of the rights and freedoms set forth in [the] Convention shall be secured without discrimination on any ground such as sex, race, colour, language, religion, political or other opinion, national or social origin, association with a national minority, property, birth or other status'. The Council of Europe has adopted a new equality provision (Protocol 12) that will go some way to remedying some of the deficiencies of Article 14 ECHR.[105] The Protocol, in effect, would add an additional provision to Article 14 that

---

in the Charter provides in Art 20, 'Everyone is equal before the law', while Art 21(1) reads: ' Any discrimination based on any ground such as sex, race, colour, ethnic or social origin, genetic features, language, religion or belief, political or any other opinion, membership of a national minority, property, birth, disability, age or sexual orientation shall be prohibited'.

[102] Declaration and Programme of Action, World Conference Against Racism, Racial Discrimination, Xenophobia and Related Intolerance, 8 September 2001.

[103] [2003] UKHL 4; [2003] 2 WLR 435 at [26].

[104] *R v Secretary of State for the Home Department, ex p Brind* [1991] 1 AC 696.

[105] Protocol 12 to the ECHR, adopted Rome, 4 November 2000.

would prohibit discrimination on any grounds such as those set out in Article 14 by a public authority in circumstances where other Convention rights are not engaged, whilst '[r]eaffirming that the principle of non-discrimination does not prevent States Parties from taking measures in order to promote full and effective equality, provided that there is an objective and reasonable justification for those measures'.[106] The United Kingdom has neither signed nor ratified this Protocol; nor has the Protocol yet secured sufficient ratifications for it to come into force for those that have ratified it.

(b) Other international and regional human rights instruments

In addition to the ECHR, the United Kingdom has ratified several international human rights instruments that contain non-discrimination requirements. These include the major general human rights instruments concluded under the auspices of the United Nations (the International Covenant on Economic, Social and Cultural Rights 1966, the International Covenant on Civil and Political Rights 1966, Convention on the Rights of the Child 1989). The United Kingdom has also ratified several treaties with a specific focus on discrimination and equality (Convention on the Political Rights of Women 1953, Convention on the Elimination of All Forms of Racial Discrimination 1966, and the Convention on the Elimination of All Forms of Discrimination Against Women 1979[107]). The United Kingdom has ratified several International Labour Organization instruments (the Equal Remuneration Convention 1951 (No 100) and the Discrimination (Employment and Occupation) Convention 1958 (No 111). The United Kingdom has ratified several Council of Europe conventions (on economic and social rights (European Social Charter 1961, but not the revised European Social Charter, 1996), national minorities (Framework Convention for the Protection of National Minorities 1995), and minority languages (European Charter for Regional or Minority Languages, 1992)). To some extent these instruments may come to be seen as reinforcing the HRA's incorporation of the ECHR; it is unclear whether they will be seen by the courts as supplementing the ECHR, particularly Article 14.[108]

11.51

(7) *Changing Approaches in the Domestic Courts*

Partly as a result of these developments, the common law has moved a long way from where it stood on issues of discrimination and equality at the beginning of the 20th century, before legislative intervention. By the end of the 20th century,

11.52

---

[106] Preamble, fourth indent.
[107] Convention on the Eradication of All Forms of Discrimination Against Women 1979 (1980) ILM 33.
[108] See Deirdre Fottrell, 'Reinforcing the Human Rights Act—the Role of the International Covenant on Civil and Political Rights' [2002] PL 485.

Oliver was able to identify this important trend. '[E]quality in the sense of non-discrimination,' she wrote, 'is creeping into the system . . . in both public and private law.'[109]

(a) Relationship between common law and anti-discrimination statutes

11.53   One of the early issues that the English courts needed to address after legislative intervention was the relationship between such statutes and the pre-existing common law. Initially, in several cases, the courts regarded the legislative intervention as limiting common law rights such as freedom of association. Such legislation should, therefore, be interpreted restrictively. This approach is illustrated in several cases that reached the House of Lords in the 1970s. In *Ealing LBC v Race Relations Board,*[110] the House of Lords held that to discriminate on grounds of nationality did not contravene the 1968 Act's prohibition on discrimination 'on grounds of national origin'. So too, in other cases, refusal on the grounds of ethnic origin to permit a person to become a member of a club was held not to be unlawful under the legislation, nor at common law.[111] These decisions required the intervention of legislation to overturn them.[112] So too, initially, the courts appeared hostile to the enforcement powers given to the CRE and the EOC.[113] More recently, the courts have proven more sympathetic to the idea that anti-discrimination norms should not be seen as limited by common law concepts of freedom of contract and property. In particular, Parliament was not assumed to desire a limited interpretation of the legislation, but one that would fulfil its purpose of tackling injustice.[114]

(b) EC law and domestic law

11.54   EC law also played a significant indirect role in influencing the interpretation of domestic legislation. This was due to the requirement under EC law that domestic legislation in the field where a directive operates, and which is considered as implementing that directive and satisfying the member state's obligations to implement the directive should be interpreted 'as far as possible' to conform to the directive's obligations. This was particularly influential in the context of gender discrimination, where this approach had a significant effect in expanding the interpretation

---

[109] Dawn Oliver, *Common Values and the Public–Private Divide* (London: Butterworths, 1999) 64.
[110] [1972] AC 342.
[111] *Charter v Race Relations Board* [1973] AC 868; *Dockers' Labour Club v Race Relations Board* [1976] AC 285.
[112] See Race Relations Act 1976, ss 3(1) and 25.
[113] See the cases discussed in Christopher McCrudden, 'The Commission for Racial Equality: Formal Investigations in the Shadow of Judicial Review' in Robert Baldwin and Christopher McCrudden, *Regulation and Public Law* (London: Weidenfeld & Nicolson, 1987) 222–266
[114] See, eg, *Zarczynska v Levy* [1979] 1 WLR 125; *Home Office v CRE* [1982] QB 385; *Savjani v Inland Revenue Commissioners* [1981] QB 458, CA; *Mandla v Dowell Lee* [1983] 2 AC 548, HL.

of domestic sex discrimination legislation. In addition, where British anti-discrimination legislation shared the same concepts, such as the concept of discrimination itself, EC approaches to the interpretation of that concept in the gender context significantly influenced the domestic interpretation of the concept in the race discrimination legislation, on the basis that domestic anti-discrimination legislation should be interpreted consistently across the different grounds.

(c) Effect of the unincorporated ECHR

Even before the HRA 1998 incorporated the ECHR, the equality dimensions of   **11.55**
the unincorporated ECHR also played a role in influencing the interpretation of legislation and the development of the common law.[115] The provisions of the ECHR and its Protocols were not incorporated by legislation into English law and therefore the ECHR could not be relied on or enforced directly in the English courts.[116] However, as Lord Slynn said, '[s]ome of the rights set out in the Convention may already be reflected in principles established by the common law or set out in specific statutes and the Convention may influence the development of the common law when rights are claimed under the latter'.[117] By 2002, Lord Woolf CJ was able to say: 'The right not to be discriminated against is one of the most significant requirements of the protection provided by the rule of law. It is now enshrined in Article 14 of the ECHR, but long before the HRA came into force the common law recognized the importance of not discriminating.'[118]

(d) Development of judicial review and private law

The common law continues to develop as a source for equality and non-discrimination   **11.56**
norms in English law both in public law and in private law. Equality and non-discrimination norms have been developed in areas of private law particularly applicable to public authorities, such as tort. More especially, however, in judicial review of administrative action, equality and non-discrimination norms have been held, although not consistently, to be relevant in the development of particular concepts, particularly aspects of '*Wednesbury* unreasonableness'. The existing parameters of these norms is increasingly hotly debated in the academic literature, in particular whether a general principle of equality or non-discrimination at common law can now be said to be in existence. How far, for example, English private common law may yet see the emergence of a right to equality of respect also remains debatable.[119]

---

[115] In some cases, the ECHR jurisprudence on equality also came in via EC law. *Chief Constable of West Yorkshire Police v A (No 2)* [2002] EWCA Civ 1584; [2003] 1 All ER 255 at [42].

[116] *R v Secretary of State for the Home Department, ex p Brind* [1991] 1 AC 696; *R v Ministry of Defence, ex p Smith* [1996] QB 517, CA.

[117] *Re Barony of Moynihan* [2000] 1 FLR 113, HL, Committee for Privileges.

[118] *A v Secretary of State for the Home Department* [2002] EWCA Civ 1502; [2003] 2 WLR 564.

[119] cf Peter Birks, 'Harassment and Hubris: The Right to an Equality of Respect' [1997] Irish Jurist 1.

(e) Judicial development of the common law in other jurisdictions

11.57 Judicial decisions from other jurisdictions have been drawn on as persuasive authority, on occasion, from which British courts interpreting equality and non-discrimination norms may derive assistance.[120] This has been the case, particularly, in the development of equality and non-discrimination norms in the common law,[121] in the interpretation of the ECHR by UK courts following its incorporation into UK law by the HRA 1998,[122] and in the interpretation of domestic anti-discrimination legislation. There is an extensive jurisprudence developing in several common law countries (New Zealand,[123] Australia,[124] Canada,[125] and the United States[126]) considering the extent to which the common law can be yet further developed to provide remedies for discrimination of particular types.[127]

---

[120] See generally, Christopher McCrudden, 'A Common Law of Human Rights? Transnational Judicial Conversations on Constitutional Rights' (2000) 20 OJLS 499, reprinted in K O'Donovan and G Rubin, *Human Rights and Legal History* (Oxford: OUP, 2000).

[121] See, eg the reference to the New Zealand decision of *Van Gorkom v A-G* [1979] 1 NZLR 535 in *R v Secretary of State for Health, ex p Richardson* [1995] COD 58, *per* Leggatt LJ.

[122] See, eg reference to the Canadian Supreme Court case of *Vriend v Alberta* [1998] 1 SCR 493, and the Committee on Civil and Political Rights decision in *Toonen v Australia* [1997] 1 HRR 97 in *Secretary of State for Defence v MacDonald* [2002] ICR 174, Ex Div, *per* Lord Prosser.

[123] For a discussion of the emergence of a non-discrimination principle in the context of public utility regulation in New Zealand, see M Taggart, 'Public Utilities and Public Law', in Philip A Joseph (ed), *Essays on the Constitution* (Wellington, NZ: Brookers, 1995) 214–264.

[124] Compare *Kruger v Commonwealth of Australia* (1997) 190 CLR 1, HC Aus, Brennan J, with the earlier case of *Leeth v Commonwealth of Australia* (1992) 174 CLR 455, HC Aus, Deane and Toohey JJ.

[125] Amnon Reichman, 'Professional Status and the Freedom to Contract: Towards a Common Law Duty of Non-Discrimination' (2001) 14 Canadian J of L and Jurisprudence 79; Amnon Reichman, 'Property Rights, Public Policy and the Limits of the Legal Power to Discriminate' in D Friedman and D Barak-Erez, *Human Rights in Private Law* (Oxford: Hart Publishing, 2001) 245; B Vizkelety, 'Discrimination, the Right to Seek Redress and the Common Law: A Century Old Debate' (1992) 15 Dalhousie LJ 306; HL Molot, 'The Duty of Business to Serve the Public: Analogy to the Innkeeper's Obligation' (1968) 46 Canadian Bar Rev 612.

[126] Note (n 9 above); Greenbaum, 'Toward a Common Law of Employment Discrimination' (1985) 58 Temple LQ 65; JW Singer, 'No Right to Exclude: Public Accomodations and Private Property' (1996) 90 Northwestern U L Rev 1283; CM Haar and D Wm Fessler, *The Wrong Side of the Tracks: A Revolutionary Rediscovery of the Common Law Tradition of Fairness in the Struggle Against Inequality* (New York: Simon and Schuster, 1986); Neil G Williams, 'Offer, Acceptance and Improper Considerations: A Common Law Model for the Prohibition of Racial Discrimination in the Contracting Process' (1994) 62 George Washington L Rev 183.

[127] However, Lord Hope has expressed a sceptical view of common law development of anti-discrimination law in *Rhys-Harper v Relaxion Group plc* [2003] UKHL 33 at [78]: 'It is a remarkable fact that, although discrimination on whatever grounds is widely regarded as morally unacceptable, the common law was unable to provide a sound basis for removing it from situations where those who were vulnerable to discrimination were at risk and ensuring that all people were treated equally. Experience has taught us that this is a matter which can only be dealt with by legislation, and that it requires careful regulation by Parliament.'

(8) Legislative Reform of Anti-Discrimination Law

We have seen above that the Amsterdam Treaty provided, in Article 13 EC, a gen-   **11.58**
eral legislative power to tackle a broader range of types of discrimination.[128] This
competence was the basis for the Race Directive and the Framework Directive discussed earlier. The United Kingdom's response to this package of measures was in
two parts. One part involved the enactment of a series of statutory rules implementing the directives under the European Communities Act 1972.[129] It remains
to be seen how far the domestic implementation measures are complete. A second
response involved initiating a debate on the appropriate institutional structures
for enforcing the whole range of anti-discrimination measures.[130] In particular,
should there be a single equality body established that would take over the functions of the existing separate commissions (the CRE, the EOC and the DRC)
enforcing the domestic race, sex and disability discrimination legislation respectively, whilst adding equivalent enforcement functions relating to the new prohibitions on age, sexual orientation and religious discrimination? A third possible
response was, however, rejected by the government (at least for Great Britain[131]),
namely the enactment of a single piece of legislation consolidating and harmo-
nizing the set of differing anti-discrimination obligations into a single Equality
Act. Reform proposals to this effect were, however, presented to Parliament early
in 2003,[132] following an examination of the issue.[133]

C. Conceptions of Equality and Non-Discrimination Applicable in English Public Law

Having considered the main developments in English public law relevant to   **11.59**
equality and non-discrimination, we turn in the remainder of this chapter to
consider in more detail the four conceptions of equality and non-discrimination sketched out in the introduction to this chapter. The four conceptions are:

---

[128] See para 11.44 above.
[129] Race Relations Act 1976 (Amendment) Regulations 2003, SI 2003/1626; Employment
Equality (Sexual Orientation) Regulations 2003, SI 2003/000; Employment Equality (Religion
and Belief) Regulations 2003, SI 2003/1660; Disability Discrimination Act 1995 (Amendment)
Regulations 2003, SI 2003/1673. At the time of writing, no proposals had been made regarding age
discrimination. See further *Equality and Diversity: The way ahead* (2002).
[130] *Equality and Diversity: Making it happen* (2002).
[131] In Northern Ireland, the devolved government announced in 2002 that it would proceed with
a Single Equality Bill. This work continued even after the suspension of that government in 2002.
[132] Equality Bill [HL], introduced in the House of Lords by Lord Lester of Herne Hill, 14 January
2003.
[133] Bob Hepple, Mary Coussey and Tufyal Choudhury, *Equality: a New Framework. The Report of
the Independent Review of the Enforcement of UK Anti-Discrimination Legislation* (Oxford: Hart
Publishing, 2000).

equality as 'rationality', equality as protective of prized public goods, equality as preventing status-harms, and equality as promoting equality of opportunity.

(1) Equality and Rationality

(a) Introduction

11.60 The principle that 'likes should be treated alike' has become generally accepted as part of English public law discourse. Lord Hoffmann, in *Arthur JS Hall v Simons*,[134] referred to, 'the fundamental principle of justice which requires that people should be treated equally and like cases treated alike'. The principle is commonly adverted to by English courts as both a background principle justifying judicial decision-making, and as giving rise to direct *legal* obligations and rights enforceable by an individual. In this context, the principle that likes should be treated alike is both a legal principle, and (in more limited circumstances) a legal rule. As a principle it is a consideration that will be taken into account, among others, in exercising the judicial function, but its weight and its relative importance vis-à-vis other considerations will vary depending on the circumstances. As a legal rule, it gives rise to legal *obligations* for the public authority enforceable by those individuals who have suffered the inequality of treatment.

(b) Equality and non-discrimination as principles of statutory interpretation

11.61 The most common situations in which the indirect effect of this non-discrimination principle occurs are when the courts are developing the common law, and when the courts are interpreting statutes.[135] Although, frequently, the use of equality and non-discrimination norms as interpretative principles takes place in cases where public authorities are involved, the courts have also adopted this interpretative principle in situations where only private parties are involved, as we shall see.

11.62 An important way in which the interpretative principle has been put into effect is by using principles of statutory interpretation that permit 'updating' a statute to conform to changed social circumstances. The classic statement of this principle is the speech of Lord Wilberforce in *Royal College of Nursing of the UK v Department of Health and Social Security*.[136]

> In interpreting an Act of Parliament it is proper, and indeed necessary, to have regard to the state of affairs existing, and known by Parliament to be existing, at the time. It is a fair presumption that Parliament's policy or intention is directed to that state of affairs. Leaving aside cases of omission by inadvertence, this being not such

---

[134] [2002] 1 AC 615.
[135] In addition to the cases cited, see also *Mendoza v Ghaidan* [2002] EWCA Civ 1533; [2003] 2 WLR 478 and *White v White* [2001] UKHL 9; [2001] 1 WLR 481.
[136] [1981] AC 800, 822.

a case when a new state of affairs, or a fresh set of facts bearing on policy, comes into existence, the courts have to consider whether they fall within the parliamentary intention. They may be held to do so if they fall within the same genus of facts as those to which the expressed policy has been formulated. They may also be held to do so if there can be detected a clear purpose in the legislation which can only be fulfilled if the extension is made. How liberally these principles may be applied must depend on the nature of the enactment, and the strictness or otherwise of the words in which it has been expressed.

(c) Equality and judicial review of administrative action

One of the principal ways in which this principle of rationality as equality is given   **11.63**
legal form in English public law is in judicial review of administrative action. The rule of law has been interpreted, for example, as including a right of access to the courts, which upholds an important element of the idea of equality before the law.[137] Inequality of treatment and discrimination are seen more generally, however, in the guise of 'unreasonableness'. There are different formulations of the unreasonableness standard. The formulation by Lord Greene in the *Wednesbury* case[138] that the courts can only intervene if a decision 'is so unreasonable that no reasonable authority could ever come to it' is the principal source of the *Wednesbury* test. In the *GCHQ* case,[139] Lord Diplock reformulated the test somewhat, allowing the courts to intervene where the public body's decision 'is so outrageous in its defiance of logic or accepted moral standards that no sensible person who had applied his mind to the question to be decided could have arrived at it'. The example of dismissing a teacher because of the colour of her hair has frequently been seen as the paradigmatic example of unreasonableness in these senses.

Equality is seen as the opposite, in these contexts, of relying on irrelevant cri-   **11.64**
teria. It is essentially a test of arbitrariness. Somewhat more broadly, 'equality in the sense of consistency'[140] has been a basis for judicial review on the grounds of *Wednesbury* unreasonableness. As we have seen earlier, decisions reviewing local authority decision-making indicated that discrimination might be seen as unreasonable.[141] This earlier line of authority has been developed as a means of

---

[137] *R v Lord Chancellor, ex p Witham* [1998] QB 575.
[138] *Associated Provincial Picture Houses Ltd v Wednesbury Corp* [1948] 1 KB 223.
[139] *Council of Civil Service Unions v Minister for the Civil Service* [1985] AC 374.
[140] De Smith, Woolf and Jowell (n 13 above) para 13-041.
[141] In *Kruse v Johnson* [1898] 2 QB 91, it was held that bye-laws could be held unreasonable, because of 'partial and unequal treatment in their operation as between different classes', *per* Lord Russell of Killowen CJ. In *Board of Education v Rice* [1911] AC 179, which concerned the public body's power to fund church schools less favourably than other schools it was said: '. . . it is clear that the local authority ought to be as impartial as the rate collector who demands the rate without reference to the particular views of the ratepayer'. In *Prescott v Birmingham Corp* [1955] Ch 210 the decision of the local authority to award free bus passes to the elderly was unlawful because it was discriminatory.

implementing this non-discrimination principle. In *R v Immigration Appeal Tribunal, ex p Manshoora Begum*,[142] the court held, citing *Kruse v Johnson*, that a requirement in immigration rules that a dependent relative seeking entry must have a standard of living substantially below that of her own country was ultra vires, in disqualifying from admission under the rule 'virtually all those from the poorer countries of the world, irrespective of whatever exceptional circumstances may surround their case, and yet allow most dependants from the more affluent countries to be considered on general compassionate grounds'. Jowell points to this decision as a clear 'articulation of equality as a substantive standard'.[143]

11.65   It has been held to be a 'cardinal principle of good public administration that all persons in a similar position should be treated similarly'.[144] The test for applicants for student grants should be consistently applied.[145] The Home Secretary should consider the time served by co-defendants in considering the remission of a prisoner's sentence.[146] *Inland Revenue Commissioners v National Federation of Self Employed and Small Businesses*[147] has been interpreted as indicating that the courts 'would intervene if satisfied that there was discrimination on the part of the IRC between different classes of taxpayer'.[148] In *R v Director General of Electricity Supply, ex p Scottish Power plc*,[149] a distinction drawn by regulation between two corporations in setting price controls was held not to be justified and 'irrational'. The principle of consistency creates a presumption that the government will follow its own policy and that there must be a good reason for any departure from such a policy.[150] In *Matadeen*,[151] Lord Hoffmann said that '. . . treating like cases alike and unlike cases differently is a general axiom of rational behaviour. It is, for example, frequently invoked by the courts in proceedings for judicial review as a ground for holding some administrative act to have been irrational'.[152] Such cases have led the authoritative de Smith, Woolf and Jowell to conclude that decisions taken in violation of the principle of equality ('which requires decisions to be consistently applied and prohibits measures which make unjustifiable or unfair distinctions between individuals'[153]) constitutes a common law or constitutional principle such

---

[142] [1986] Imm AR 385, QBD.

[143] Jeffrey Jowell QC, 'Is Equality a Constitutional Principle?' (1994) 47 CLP 1, 13.

[144] *R v Hertfordshire CC, ex p Cheung*, The Times, 4 April 1986, *per* Lord Donaldson MR.

[145] ibid.

[146] *R v Secretary of State for the Home Department, ex p Walsh* [1992] COD 240.

[147] [1982] AC 617, HL.

[148] Oliver (n 109 above) 105.

[149] CA, 3 February 1997; for an analysis of the equal treatment elements of the case, see Aileen McHarg, 'A Duty to be Consistent' [1998] MLR 93.

[150] *R v Secretary of State for the Home Department, ex p Urmaza* [1996] COD 479.

[151] [1999] 1 AC 98.

[152] Citing Jowell (n 143 above) 12–14 and de Smith, Woolf and Jowell (n 13 above) paras 13-036–13-045.

[153] ibid para 13-005.

that decisions taken in violation of it constitute a distinct way in which power may be improperly exercised for the purpose of *Wednesbury* review.[154] In *Colman v General Medical Council*,[155] an argument was put that, on the basis of *Nagle v Feilden*[156] and *Cummings v Birkenhead Corp*,[157] there was now 'a general principle of equality of treatment under the law, namely that administrative action should not, without an objective or rational justification, treat similar groups differently, or different groups similarly'. Auld J, however, held that 'equality of treatment in this context . . . is surely an aspect of rationality' and an 'example . . . of the *Wednesbury* approach'. The cases cited 'are authorities for the proposition that a decision which is so unreasonable as to be capricious is ultra vires', and that discrimination can be unreasonable.

This is not to say, however, that the approach taken by the courts in judicial review amounts to a particularly intense type of scrutiny, or that the test adopted is a model of clarity. Rather the contrary. The principle of consistency has not been welcomed judicially without reservation.[158] De Smith, Woolf and Jowell observe, 'the courts have to guard against . . . having to second guess administrators who are entitled to a "margin of appreciation" of the facts or merits of a case'.[159] Arguments concerning inequality in electoral boundaries were rejected, in part on the ground that review of the Boundary Commission for England should not interfere with tasks properly allocated to Parliament.[160] Discrimination by a local authority on the grounds of religion,[161] by the armed forces on the grounds of sexual orientation,[162] and by immigration authorities on grounds of sex,[163] have been held not to be *Wednesbury* unreasonable. It is unclear how decisions held to be unreasonable can be clearly distinguished from those that are held not to be unreasonable.

11.66

---

[154] See, in particular, the uses made of the principle of consistency by the Northern Ireland courts in *In the matter of an application by Wright and Fisher for Judicial Review* (QBD, 20 December 1996, Girvan J); *R v Northern Ireland Civil Service Commission, ex p Keleghan* (Girvan J); *Re Croft's Application* [1997] NI 457, 491 *per* Girvan J; *Re Morrison and Kinkead* (27 February 1998, Kerr J); *Re Colgan* [1996] NI 24 *per* Girvan J.

[155] The Times, 14 December 1988, QBD, Crown Office List.

[156] [1966] 2 QB 633, CA.

[157] [1972] Ch 12.

[158] The approach adopted in *R v Secretary of State for the Home Department, ex p Urmaza* [1996] COD 479 was criticized by Hurst J in *R v Secretary of State for the Home Department, ex p Gangadeen and Kahn* [1998] 1 FLR 762, which cited with approval the approach in *R v Secretary of State for the Home Department, ex p Ozminnos* [1994] Imm AR 287. *Gangadeen* was cited with approval in *R (on the application of Holub) v Secretary of State for the Home Department* [2001] 1 WLR 1359.

[159] De Smith, Woolf and Jowell (n 13 above) para 13-007.

[160] *R v Boundary Commission for England, ex p Gateshead BC* [1983] QB 600, 635–636, CA, *per* Sir John Donaldson MR.

[161] *Ahmad v Inner London Education Authority* [1978] QB 36, CA.

[162] *R v Ministry of Defence, ex p Smith* [1996] QB 517.

[163] *R v Entry Clearance Officer (Bombay), ex p Amin* [1983] 2 AC 818, 833, *per* Lord Fraser: '. . . not all sex discrimination is unlawful . . . Discrimination is only unlawful if it occurs in one of the fields in which it is prohibited in the [SDA 1975].'

11.67 What does appear clear, however, is that where Parliament could be regarded as having considered the matter and retained the discrimination, the courts will be even more hesitant about declaring administrative applications of that discrimination irrational on *Wednesbury* grounds. In *R v Secretary of State for the Home Department, ex p Kwapong (Kwaku Boateng),*[164] the fact that Parliament had not applied the SDA 1975 to the immigration rules meant that 'it is impossible' that the discriminatory rule could be considered as irrational (*per* Ralph Gibson LJ). In *R v Secretary of State for Health, ex p Richardson,*[165] a complaint was made that the arrangements for the provision of drugs without charge for those of pensionable age under the National Health Service discriminated against men on the ground of sex, because the state pension age was 65 for men but 60 for women. Leggatt LJ held that, despite *Kruse v Johnson*[166] and *R v Immigration Appeal Tribunal, ex p Manshoora Begum,*[167] it would be 'impossible to establish perversity where all that the Secretary of State has decided to do' was to follow Parliament's intention to allow the Secretary of State to apply a pensionable age test, as reflected in the SDA, and the Equal Treatment Directive, both of which contained exceptions for such discrimination.

(d) The academic debate: 'What does this amount to?'

11.68 There is considerable debate whether these developments amount to a separate meaning of equality in English public law, and what its status is if such a separate meaning does exist. Allan has argued that a suitably revised version of Dicey's rule of law embodies a constitutional principle of rationality and equality. Most importantly, this common law constitutional principle is applicable to governmental decision-making as a whole, including decision-making by Parliament. Therefore, he argues, in the absence 'of a written constitution which enjoys the status of fundamental law, the common law must serve as a constitutional framework and expression of the community's most important values. It therefore enjoys a superiority to legislation in the sense that a statute must be interpreted consistently with deep-rooted common law principles even where the consequence is some diminution in its efficacy. When an Act of Parliament contradicts "common right and reason", as Coke CJ expressed it, it must be appropriately "controlled".'[168] The implication, it seems, is that the courts should interpret legislation so as to comply with these principles. Indeed, Allan considers that existing principles of public law

---

[164] [1994] Imm AR 207, CA.
[165] [1995] COD 58.
[166] [1898] 2 QB 291, *per* Lord Russell of Killowen CJ.
[167] [1986] Imm AR 385, QBD.
[168] TRS Allan, 'The Rule of Law as the Rule of Reason: Consent and Constitutionalism' (1999) 115 LQR 221, 241–242, quoting *Bonham's Case* (1609) 8 Co Rep 107, 118. See also TRS Allan, 'Legislative Supremacy and the Rule of Law: Democracy and Constitutionalism' (1985) 44 CLJ 111.

embody this approach: 'Its principles of public law impose standards of procedural fairness and substantive rationality on government ministers and civil servants . . . In the circumstances of the modern administrative-regulatory state,
judicial review of executive action is required to ensure that governmental bodies
adhere to the general principles of fairness, equality and proportionality.'[169] This
'governing ideal' exerts 'a powerful discipline: every distinction between persons,
as regards their treatment by the state, must be capable of justification in accordance with one coherent, if controversial, vision of justice, consistently applied
and open to inspection and dissent'.[170]

For Jowell, however, who also argues that there is a general principle of equality in   **11.69**
English public law, the principle does not wholly derive from the rule of law.[171]
Although he agrees that the rule of law requires formal equality 'which prohibits
laws from being enforced unequally', and is based on the rule of law, this does not
sufficiently capture the breadth of the principle that he identifies.[172] In particular,
it does not 'require substantive equality'.[173] The conception of equality he identifies is one that 'requires government not to treat people unequally without justification'.[174] 'It forbids not only the unequal application of equal laws, but also
forbids unequal laws.'[175] Essentially, 'it prevents distinctions that are not properly
justified. Distinctions between individuals or groups must be reasonably related
to government's legitimate purposes. Under our system, equality may be expressly
violated if Parliament clearly so requires.'[176] However, 'its apparent violation will
provoke strong questioning and require rational justification'.[177]

In response, Stanton-Ife rejects the view that a principle of equality of the type   **11.70**
that Jowell identifies does or should exist as a constitutional principle in English
law.[178] In particular, he views the cases on which Jowell bases his principle as not
espousing a conception of equality at all, properly understood. His argument is
that *any* principle 'already contains the idea of generality, which itself contains the
idea of equality of application to a class'.[179] There is, he argues, 'nothing to be
gained from Jowell's two step test according to which we first assume that government must not treat people unequally unless secondly, some justification for

---

[169] ibid 244.
[170] ibid 244.
[171] Jowell (n 143 above).
[172] ibid 4.
[173] ibid 4.
[174] ibid 7.
[175] ibid.
[176] ibid.
[177] ibid.
[178] John Stanton-Ife, 'Should Equality be a Constitutional Principle?' (2000) 11 Kings College LJ
132.
[179] ibid 138.

doing so can be shown'.[180] 'The first idea can be excised without loss, which leaves us again with the notions of reasonableness, rationality and the rule of law that Jowell wishes to go beyond.'[181]

(e) Conclusion

11.71   Equality as rationality essentially requires that where the exercise of governmental power results in unequal treatment, it should be properly justified, according to consistently applied, persuasive and acceptable criteria. However, a general idea of equality as rationality cannot operate without criteria of likeness, difference, acceptability and justification. As Lord Hoffmann said in the important Privy Council decision in *Matadeen v Pointu*:[182]

> Their Lordships do not doubt that such a principle ['Equality before the law requires that persons should be uniformly treated, unless there is some valid reason to treat them differently'] is one of the building blocks of democracy and necessarily permeates any democratic constitution. Indeed, their Lordships would go further and say that treating like cases alike and unlike cases differently is a general axiom of rational behaviour ... But the very banality of the principle must suggest a doubt as to whether merely to state it can provide an answer to the kind of problem which arises in this case. Of course persons should be uniformly treated, unless there is some valid reason to treat them differently. But what counts as a valid reason for treating them differently? And, perhaps more important, who is to decide whether the reason is valid or not? Must it always be the courts? The reasons for not treating people uniformly often involve, as they do in this case, questions of social policy on which views may differ. These are questions which the elected representatives of the people have some claim to decide for themselves. The fact that equality of treatment is a general principle of rational behaviour does not entail that it should necessarily be a justiciable principle—that it should always be the judges who have the last word on whether the principle has been observed. In this, as in other areas of constitutional law, sonorous judicial statements of uncontroversial principle often conceal the real problem, which is to mark out the boundary between the powers of the judiciary, the legislature and the executive in deciding how that principle is to be applied.

11.72   We can regard this first meaning of equality in English public law as having two complementary functions. It is both a general principle underpinning the other categories to be discussed subsequently, as well as a residual category of scrutiny in its own right.

11.73   As regards the first function of this first meaning, it provides a starting point from which the more detailed meanings of equality that follow ultimately derive. In this sense, the necessary criteria of likeness, difference and justification are supplied in the second, third and fourth meanings of equality. In the second meaning these

---

[180]   John Stanton-Ife (n 178 above) 150.
[181]   ibid 152.
[182]   [1999] 1 AC 98.

criteria are supplied by an account of how particularly important interests should be distributed, and in the third and fourth meanings by referring to how particular characteristics of persons should affect the distribution of opportunities more generally. Where, for example, mal-distribution of constitutional rights is in issue, or the use of race as a criterion of exclusion is present, judgments of unreasonableness or irrationality have more on which to 'bite' and they induce more sceptical scrutiny. A greater effort is required to justify such decisions than where other decisions not involving these considerations are in issue.

As regards the second function of the first meaning, the courts stand ready to scrutinize decisions more generally, however weakly, on the basis of unequal treatment, even those decisions that do not involve situations in which particularly important interests, or where particular 'status-harms', are in issue. **11.74**

Will the common law development of a principle of equality in this first sense on the basis of *Wednesbury* unreasonableness be seen as less necessary now that the HRA has provided for the incorporation of Article 14? It was argued by counsel in *R (on the application of Montana) v Secretary of State for the Home Department*,[183] that in addition to Convention rights there was an equality duty at common law on which he could rely independently, as part of the 'principle of legality', relying on *Matadeen* and *Arthur JS Hall v Simons*.[184] Schiemann LJ, however, found that the 'common law principles . . . are broadly stated in the decisions . . . But on analysis we do not think they add much, if anything, to the . . . Convention rights.' Where Article 14 applies, then, the alternative ground of *Wednesbury* unreasonableness may not add much. Where it does not, however, this first ground still has a potentially important (if limited) role to play. **11.75**

(2) *Human Rights, Fundamental Interests, and Non-Discrimination*

(a) Introduction

In the second approach, the role of the non-discrimination principle is an adjunct to the protection of particularly prized 'public goods'. The principle is essentially that in the distribution of the 'prized public good', equals should be treated equally, except where differences can be justified. In this context, the focus is on the distribution of the prized public good, rather than the characteristics of the recipient, except for the purpose of justifying different treatment. A key issue, in this context, is what 'public goods' are to be regarded as of sufficient importance to attract heightened equality-based scrutiny. One example is to be found in the interpretation of Article 14 ECHR, where the 'prized public goods' in issue are fundamental human rights. Indeed, this is also a characteristic approach to the **11.76**

---

[183] [2001] 1 WLR 552, CA.
[184] [2002] 1 AC 615.

role sometimes accorded equality and non-discrimination in international human rights law more generally.[185] A second example is in the context of EC law, where the 'prized public goods' in issue are to be found in those provisions of the Treaty furthering the economic integration of the Community. Before turning to consider Article 14, and EC law, it is, however, important to note that this approach is also (arguably) found in other areas of English public law.

(b) Common law examples?

(i) Duty to serve of those engaged in public callings and non-discrimination

11.77   As we have seen, one of the islands of non-discrimination norms that the common law developed prior to legislative intervention beginning in the 1960s[186] was the English common law requirement that placed duties, requiring equality of treatment, on common carriers, inn-keepers and some monopoly enterprises such as ports and harbours, obliging them to accept all travellers.[187] Two interpretations of the duty to serve have been identified. One interpretation considers that the duty to serve arose in the 15th century 'in response to the monopoly power of private parties engaged in public callings'.[188] A second interpretation focuses rather on 'specific actions undertaken by the general entity' by which it undertook to offer goods and services to the general public.[189]

11.78   Support for the first interpretation may be derived from *Nagle v Feilden*,[190] where Lord Denning MR stressed that the sex discrimination exercised by the Jockey Club concerned 'an association which exercises a virtual monopoly in an important field of human activity'. Danckwerts LJ took an equivalent position: 'the courts have the right to protect the right of a person to work where it is being prevented by the dictatorial exercise of powers by a body which holds a monopoly'. So too Salmon LJ wrote that 'there are monopolistic associations, such as trade unions, the Stock Exchange and the Inns of Court which control certain trades or spheres of human activity in which no man can earn his living unless he is admitted to membership of the association . . . If it can be shown . . . that a candidate has been capriciously and unreasonably refused admission, it is certainly arguable that the law will intervene to protect him.' Essentially, the test is the forerunner of a *Wednesbury* unreasonableness test to a group of monopolistic service providers

---

[185] See M Bossuyt, *L'interdiction de la discrimination dans le droit international des droits de l'homme* (Bruxelles: Bruylant, 1976) 68–69.

[186] See, eg *Rothfield v North British Rly Co* (1920) 57 SLR 661; *Constantine v Imperial Hotels Ltd* [1944] KB 693; *Re Dominion Students' Hall Trust* [1947] Ch 183; *Re Meres' Will Trust*, The Times, 4 May 1957; *Clayton v Ramsden* [1943] AC 320.

[187] De Smith, Woolf and Jowell (n 13 above) para 13-040.

[188] Note (n 9 above) 1995. See eg *Allnutt v Inglis* (1810) 12 East 527, 104 ER 206, 210–211, *per* Lord Ellenborough CJ.

[189] Note (n 9 above) 1995.

[190] [1966] 2 QB 633, CA.

that might otherwise be regarded as outside the scope of judicial review of public authorities' actions. An equivalent approach can be seen in certain statutory requirements relating to some public bodies, particularly utility providers, to exercise their functions so as not to discriminate. For example, water providers must ensure that there is no undue discrimination against any class of customers when fixing or agreeing charges.[191]

(ii) 'Right to work'

An additional way of viewing *Nagle v Feilden* is available. This considers the case **11.79** as standing for the proposition that in the context of particularly important rights, discrimination is impermissible at common law. In this context, it was the 'right to work' which was in issue. Support for this interpretation comes from Lord Denning: 'The common law of England has for centuries recognised that a man has a right to work at his trade or profession without being unjustly excluded from it. He is not to be shut out from it at the whim of those having the governance of it. If they make a rule which enables them to reject his application arbitrarily or capriciously, not reasonably, that rule is bad. It is against public policy. The courts will not give effect to it . . . [A] man's right to work at his trade or profession is just as important to him as, perhaps more important than, his rights of property. Just as the courts will intervene to protect his rights of property, they will also intervene to protect his right to work.'

(iii) 'Public policy'

The role of public policy as a source from which this second conception of equal- **11.80** ity derives has been anything but straightforward. The courts occasionally have used the concept of 'public policy' as a basis on which to attack discrimination, when it occurred in the context of other rights. As we have seen, public policy was used as the basis for refusing to give effect to foreign laws concerning slavery.[192] In *Oppenheimer v Cattermole*,[193] Lord Cross considered that public policy required that racially discriminatory Nazi legislation should be disregarded: '. . . what we are concerned with here is legislation which takes away without compensation from a section of the citizen body singled out on racial grounds all their property on which the state passing the legislation can lay its hands and, in addition, deprives them of their citizenship. To my mind a law of this sort constitutes so grave an infringement of human rights that the courts of this country ought to refuse to recognize it as law at all.' The House of Lords decision in *Islam v Secretary of State*[194] may also be seen as an example of this approach. The House of Lords held

---

[191] See, eg, Water Industry Act 1991, s 143 (as amended).
[192] *Regazzoni v KC Sethia (1944) Ltd* [1956] 2 QB 490, CA.
[193] [1976] AC 249.
[194] *Islam v Secretary of State and R v Immigration Appeal Tribunal, ex p Shah* [1999] 2 AC 629.

that because, in Pakistan, women were discriminated against as a group in matters of fundamental human rights, and the state gave them no protection because they were perceived as not being entitled to the same human rights as men, women in Pakistan constituted a 'particular social group' for the purposes of Article 1A(2) of the Convention and Protocol relating to the Status of Refugees so as to entitle them to refugee status under the Convention.

11.81 In several cases, however, the courts rejected arguments that they should apply such an interpretative principle by using public policy, especially where it may come up against other rights that are seen to be in conflict with it. In *Re Lysaght*,[195] it was held that a gift by will to found a studentship for medical study, except for students 'of the Jewish or Roman Catholic faith' was not void as being contrary to public policy. Buckley J said: 'I accept that racial and religious discrimination is nowadays widely regarded as deplorable in many respects, and I am aware that there is a bill dealing with racial relations at present under consideration by Parliament, but I think it is going much too far to say that the endowment of a charity, the beneficiaries of which are to be drawn from a particular faith or are to exclude adherents to a particular faith, is contrary to public policy. The testatrix's desire to exclude persons of the Jewish faith or of the Roman Catholic faith from those eligible for the studentship in the present case appears to me to be un-amiable, and I would accept the suggestion of counsel for the Attorney-General that it is undesirable, but it is not, I think, contrary to public policy.' Similarly, in *Blathwayt v Lord Crawley*,[196] a forfeiture clause in a trust established by a will, which deprived the beneficiary of the benefits of the trust if he became a Roman Catholic, was held by the House of Lords not to be contrary to public policy on the ground of impermissible discrimination. Lord Wilberforce held that despite there being legislation against discrimination on other grounds, it would not be justifiable for the courts to introduce a rule of law against such discrimination: 'To do so would bring about a substantial reduction of another freedom, firmly rooted in our own law, namely that of testamentary disposition'.

(c) Enhanced *Wednesbury* test

11.82 Providing a role for the non-discrimination principle in ensuring that important substantive rights should be protected was not developed at common law beyond the right to work. However, in the context of developing judicial review of administrative action, the courts have developed a somewhat similar approach, what has been called the 'enhanced *Wednesbury* test'. This is applicable when judicial review is being sought of a decision that involves alleged breaches of human rights. This approach draws on decisions of the House of Lords in *Bugdaycay v Secretary*

---

[195] *Re Lysaght (decd)* [1966] 1 Ch 191, Ch D.
[196] [1976] AC 397.

of Article 14 has occurred by seeking answers to several interrelated questions. Brooke LJ's summary in *Wandsworth LBC v Michalak*[210] is becoming authoritative,[211] although subject to revision.[212] On the basis of these decisions, and taking into account the case law of the ECtHR and the recent case law of the British courts under Article 14, the following set of questions appears to capture the approach currently being adopted in practice by courts in England:

(i) Do the facts fall within the ambit of one or more of the substantive Convention provisions?

The non-discrimination requirement in Article 14 is not 'free-standing' but is **11.89** dependent on other rights in the ECHR being engaged. That does not mean that another right has to have been breached. As the ECtHR held in *Schmidt v Germany*:[213] 'Article 14 complements the other substantive provisions of the Convention and the Protocols. It has no independent existence since it has effect solely in relation to "the enjoyment of the rights and freedoms" safeguarded by those provisions. Although the application of Article 14 does not presuppose a breach of those provisions—and to this extent it is autonomous—there can be no reason for its application unless the facts at issue fall within the ambit of one or more of the latter.'

An example may help to illustrate the point. In the Schmidt case, although the **11.90** ECtHR found that there was no violation of Article 4(3)(d) prohibiting forced or compulsory labour, the Court went on to hold that an obligation imposed on men (and only on men) to serve in the fire brigade (or pay a financial contribution in lieu of this service) amounted to a breach of Article 14 taken in conjunction with Article 4(3)(d). There may be a violation of Article 14 considered together with another article in a case where there would be no violation of that other article taken alone.[214] It is sufficient that the facts of the case fall 'within the ambit' of the

---

[210] [2002] EWCA Civ 271; [2003] 1 WLR 617 at [20]: '(i) Do the facts fall within the ambit of one or more of the substantive Convention provisions . . . ? (ii) If so, was there different treatment as respects that right between the complainant on the one hand and other persons put forward for comparison (the chosen comparator) on the other? (iii) Were the chosen comparators in an analogous situation to the complainant's situation? (iv) If so, did the difference in treatment have an objective and reasonable justification: in other words, did it pursue a legitimate aim and did the differential treatment bear a reasonable relationship or proportionality to the aim sought to be achieved?'

[211] Accepted by Lord Woolf CJ in *A v Secretary of State for the Home Department* [2002] EWCA Civ 1502; [2003] 2 WLR 564 at [56]; Buxton LJ in *Mendoza v Ghaidan* [2002] EWCA Civ 1533; [2003] 2 WLR 478 at [6], and Burton J in *R (on the application of Smith) v Barking and Dagenham LBC* [2002] EWHC 2400; [2002] All ER (D) 266, QBD (Admin Ct) at [10].

[212] In *R (Carson) v Secretary of State for Work and Pensions* [2002] EWHC Admin 978; [2002] 3 All ER 994, Stanley Burnton J added an additional question: 'Is the basis for the different treatment of the complainant as against that of the chosen comparator based on "any ground such as . . ." within the meaning of art. 14?'

[213] Series A No 219-B (1994) 18 EHRR 513 at [22].

[214] *Abdulaziz v UK* Series A No 94 (1985) EHRR 471.

rights guaranteed by the Convention.[215] Where that is not the case, however, then a claim of discrimination will not succeed.[216] As Nowicki has written, Article 14 'is triggered . . . if the facts mentioned in the complaint belong to the sphere covered by one of those rights and freedoms in Article 14. While it is not always easy to define, that sphere is of paramount importance since it largely determines the extent of the protection against discrimination provided under the Convention.'[217]

11.91   One area that has given rise to difficulty in this regard in the British courts is how far Article 14 is engaged as regards rights that the state has voluntarily guaranteed over and above those required by the ECHR. It is clear that not all domestically generated rights fall within Article 14's ambit. In *Malekshad v Howard de Walden Estates Ltd*,[218] Sedley LJ doubted whether Article 14 'applies not only to the minimum of steps required of the state in the discharge of its positive obligations, but to the totality of steps that it decides to take to that end. I would want to be satisfied by clear jurisprudence or compelling argument of the much larger proposition, which is not apparent on the face of the Convention, that any domestic legislative measure that creates rights of any kind falls without more within the charmed circle of Article 14.'[219] Moses J in *R (on the application of Hooper) v Secretary of State for Work and Pensions*,[220] drew a distinction between two situations: where a right has been provided by the state which is greater than is necessary to satisfy an article of the ECHR (where Article 14 is engaged[221]), and where no benefits have been provided to anyone and the claimant asserts that the state is under an obligation to provide them in order to protect the rights enshrined under Article 14 (where Article 14 is not engaged).[222] Buxton LJ, in *Mendoza v Ghaidan*,[223] held that, with regard to Article 8, '. . . once the state has chosen to intervene in factual areas *characteristic* of those protected by article 8, article 14 is engaged if there is relevant discrimination in the mode of that intervention'.[224]

(ii) Have persons been treated differently to other persons in similar circumstances?

11.92   This question may appropriately be seen as comprising two elements: Was there different treatment as respects the substantive right in issue between the complainant

---

[215] *Belgian Linguistic Case (No 1)* Series A No 5 (1979–80) 1 EHRR 241.

[216] *R (on the application of Pretty) v DPP* [2001] UKHL 61; [2002] 1 AC 800 (inability to link Art 14 to another article defeated Mrs Pretty's claim of discrimination).

[217] MA Nowicki, 'Perspectives on Equal Protection—Part II: The European Convention of Human Rights: Prohibition on Discrimination' [1999] St Louis-Warsaw Transatlantic LJ 17, 20.

[218] [2001] EWCA Civ 761; [2002] QB 364.

[219] ibid at [54].

[220] [2002] EWHC 191; [2002] UKHRR 785, QBD (Admin Ct) at [17].

[221] Citing *Abdulaziz v UK* Series A No 94 (1985) EHRR 471 at [71].

[222] Citing *Botta v Italy* Application 21439/93 (1998) 26 EHRR 241.

[223] [2002] EWCA Civ 1533; [2003] 2 WLR 478.

[224] ibid at [12] (emphasis added).

on the one hand and other persons put forward for comparison (the chosen comparator) on the other? Were the chosen comparators 'in an analogous or relevantly similar situation'[225] to the situation of the complainant?

As regards persons being treated differently to other persons in similar circumstances, the Court of Appeal considered the issue of which comparison is appropriate under Article 14 in *Wandsworth LBC v Michalak*.[226] Mr Michalak was directed to give up possession of a flat that a distant relation of his had rented from the council before his death. He argued that the possession order was contrary to Article 14 read together with Article 8 (protecting private and family life). The relevant legislation provided that a member of the family of the tenant could succeed to the secured tenancy after the death of the previous tenant, but the definition of a member of the family was defined in a way that excluded Mr Michalak from benefiting from the provision. He argued, however, that the provision should be interpreted to include him in order to avoid discrimination. He argued that he was being denied a secure tenancy by succession in circumstances in which others would be entitled to a successor tenancy, that is between people in his position and people in relevantly similar situations. Two comparators were identified, the first being members of a tenant's family mentioned in the legislation (who would be entitled to a secure tenancy), the other being someone of a similar degree of relationship to a tenant as he had with the previous tenant (who would be entitled to Rent Act tenancy). The court held that the first comparison was appropriate, and therefore required consideration of 'objective and reasonable justification'. The second comparison was not appropriate because the significant differences between protected tenancies under the Rent Act, and secure tenancies under the Housing Act were too different for the chosen comparators to be regarded as in a relatively similar situation. The differences between the two schemes included differences relating to the assignment of tenancies, the succession of tenancies, rent levels, the right to allow others to reside, obligations on landlords to consult tenants, and rights to buy at a discount. **11.93**

(iii) *Was the difference in treatment attributable to the state?*

The primary addressee of the obligation to be found in Article 14 is the state. However, in certain circumstances, there is a positive duty element that attaches to Article 14, requiring the state to prevent discrimination by others. In *Pearce v Governing Body of Mayfield School*[227] Hale LJ considered (obiter) that Articles 8 and 14 ECHR required that homosexuals were entitled to the same respect as **11.94**

---

[225] *Stubbings v UK* Application 22083/93 (1996) 23 EHRR 213.
[226] [2002] EWCA Civ 271; [2003] 1 WLR 617. See also *R (on the application of Montana) v Secretary of State for the Home Department* [2003] 1 WLR 617 (those who acquired citizenship by birth were not true comparators with those who could apply for citizenship).
[227] [2001] EWCA Civ 1347; [2002] ICR 198.

heterosexuals. This involved being open about their sexuality, making public their commitment to their partner and displaying affection in a seemly way in public without being subjected to repeated abuse or bullying for doing so. Furthermore, effective respect for these rights potentially entailed a public authority's responsibility for promoting conditions in which a person was able to express their identity.

(iv) Was the difference of treatment on a ground set out in Article 14?

11.95 In several respects the prohibited grounds of discrimination are considerably broader than those to be found in domestic anti-discrimination legislation in Britain. Moses J in *Hooper* held that in order to establish a breach of Article 14, there needed to be established discrimination on the basis of 'personal characteristics' capable of founding the claim of discrimination.[228] Laws LJ in *R (on the application of Waite) v Hammersmith and Fulham LBC*[229] considered that there must be some limit on the type of grounds that could be considered: 'The Article lists potential grounds of discrimination prefaced by the words "on any ground such as". This is a formulation which at once calls for an application of what is known as the ejusdem generis principle. No less is this so because the context is not a conventional British statute, but a living instrument constituted by the European Convention on Human Rights. The Article does not prohibit any discrimination whatever in the enjoyment of Convention rights. The list of potential grounds sets out personal characteristics: sex, race and so forth. If a ground not listed is to be relied on, one would have thought that it must, broadly at least, be of the same kind.'[230]

11.96 The question of what can constitute 'any other status' for the purposes of Article 14 arose in *R (on the application of Carson) v Secretary of State for Work and Pensions*.[231] The issue was the distinction between persons ordinarily resident in Great Britain, and those not ordinarily resident as regards the application of UK pensions legislation. Only a person ordinarily resident was entitled to an uprated pension. Unless the person not ordinarily resident was present in the country, uprating did not apply. It was held that residence was a ground within the scope of Article 14. 'Like domicile and nationality, it is an aspect of personal status.'[232] In *Pretty*,[233] Lord Hope held that Article 14 was capable of extending to discrimination in the enjoyment of Convention rights on the ground of physical or mental capacity.[234]

---

[228] [2002] EWHC 191; [2002] UKHRR 785 at [145].
[229] [2002] EWCA Civ 482; [2003] HLR 3.
[230] ibid at [22].
[231] [2002] EWHC 978; [2002] 3 All ER 994, QBD (Admin Ct).
[232] ibid at [57] *per* Stanley Burnton J.
[233] *R (on the application of Pretty) v DPP* [2001] UKHL 61; [2002] 1 AC 800.
[234] ibid at [105].

(v) Has the difference in treatment a 'reasonable and objective justification'?

There are several elements in this test that need to be distinguished: (1) Has the **11.97** state established the justification?[235] (2) Does the difference in treatment have a legitimate aim or aims? (3) If it does have a legitimate aim, (a) is the objective sufficiently important to justify limiting a fundamental right; (b) are the measures designed to meet the objective rationally connected to it; and (c) are the means used to impair the right or freedom no more than is necessary to accomplish the objective?[236] The domestic courts have addressed several of these issues in interpreting the HRA 1998 in the context of Article 14 ECHR.

As Buxton LJ points out in *Mendoza v Ghaidan*,[237] the burden of proof on the **11.98** state to establish justification 'reflects the seriousness with which Convention jurisprudence views discrimination, and the limited extent to which such discrimination can be tolerated. In seeking to discharge that burden, it is simply not enough to claim that what has been done falls within the permissible ambit of Parliament's discretion: because all that that shows is that the decisions taken are not to be regarded as necessarily unjustified. A much more positive argument is required if the burden . . . is to be discharged.'

What is the difference between the intensity of this test, and that adopted in **11.99** judicial review under either the traditional *Wednesbury* test or the enhanced *Wednesbury* test? In *R (on the application of Mahmood) v Secretary of State for the Home Department*,[238] the Court of Appeal appeared to suggest that there might be little difference in practice between these tests. However, Lord Steyn in *R (on the application of Daly) v Secretary of State for the Home Department*[239] said:

> Clearly, these criteria are more precise and more sophisticated than the traditional grounds of review. What is the difference for the disposal of concrete cases . . .? First, the doctrine of proportionality may require the reviewing court to assess the balance which the decision maker has struck, not merely whether it is within the range of rational or reasonable decisions. Secondly, the proportionality test may go further than the traditional grounds of review in as much as it may require attention to be directed to the relative weight accorded to interests and considerations. Thirdly, even the heightened scrutiny test developed in *R v Ministry of Defence, ex p Smith*, [1996] QB 517 at 554 is not necessarily appropriate to the protection of human

---

[235] *Pine Valley Developments Ltd v Ireland* Series A No 222 [1992] 14 EHRR 319 at [64].
[236] *de Freitas v Permanent Secretary of Ministry of Agriculture, Fisheries, Lands and Housing* [1999] 1 AC 69, *per* Lord Clyde, adopted by Lord Steyn in *R (on the application of Daly) v Secretary of State for the Home Department* [2001] UKHL 26; [2001] 2 AC 532 at [27].
[237] [2002] EWCA Civ 1533; [2003] 2 WLR 478 at [18].
[238] [2001] 1 WLR 840.
[239] [2002] EWCA Civ 1533; [2003] 2 WLR 478 at [27]. For a pre-*Daly* discussion of the issue, see Mark Elliott, 'The Human Rights Act 1998 and the Standard of Substantive Review' (2001) 60 CLJ 301, 302–308. For a discussion of *Daly*, see Mark Elliott, 'Human Rights Review: Raising the Standard' (2001) 60 CLJ 455.

rights . . . In other words, the intensity of the review, in similar cases, is guaranteed by the twin requirements that the limitation of the right was necessary in a democratic society, in the sense of meeting a pressing social need, and the question whether the interference was really proportionate to the legitimate aim being pursued.[240]

11.100   The Court of Appeal has held that a parochial church council is debarred from enforcing a common law obligation on a lay rector to pay for the repairs of a parish church on the ground that the obligation is unlawful because it is incompatible with the lay rector's rights under Article 14 read together with Article 1 of Protocol 1 (peaceful enjoyment of possessions). The common law distinguished between owners of land that was formerly glebe land and owners of land that was not by making the former but not the latter liable for repairs. The distinction failed the test of 'reasonable and objective justification' because, although the common law liability served the legitimate need of maintaining historic buildings in the public interest, the liability to pay for the repairs was levied exclusively on the owners of land 'without any surviving reasonable and objective justification for distinguishing them from other freehold property owners whether locally or nationally'.[241]

11.101   In *Nasser v United Bank of Kuwait*,[242] the Court of Appeal held that the discretion, under CPR 25.13 and 25.15, to award security for costs against an individual claimant or appellant not resident in a contracting state of the Brussels and Lugano Conventions on the Jurisdiction and Enforcement of Judgments in Civil and Commercial Matters was to be exercised only on objectively justified grounds relating to obstacles to, or the burden of, enforcement in the context of the particular individual or country concerned. It would be both discriminatory and unjustifiable if the mere fact of residence outside a contracting state of the enforcement conventions could justify the exercise of the discretion to make orders for security for costs with the purpose or effect of protecting defendants or respondents to appeals against risks to which they would equally be subject, and in relation to which they would have no protection, if the claim or appeal had been brought by a resident of a contracting state of the enforcement conventions. Potential difficulties or burdens of enforcement in states not party to those conventions were the rationale for the existence of the discretion, and it should be exercised in a manner reflecting its rationale. It could not be used to discriminate against individuals resident in such states on grounds unrelated to enforcement. In that connection, there could be no inflexible assumption that any such person should provide security for costs. Enforcement was not necessarily more difficult

---

[240] Buxton LJ in *Mendoza* echoed this approach: '[O]nce it is accepted that we are not simply bound by whatever Parliament has decided . . . then we need to see whether the steps taken in implementation of the supposed policy are, not merely reasonable and proportionate, but also logically explicable as forwarding that policy.' [2002] EWCA Civ 1533; [2003] 2 WLR 478 at [20].

[241] *Aston Cantlow and Wilmcote with Billesley Parochial Church Council v Wallbank* [2001] EWCA Civ 713; [2002] Ch 51 at [51].

[242] [2001] EWCA Civ 556; [2002] 1 WLR 1868.

merely because a person was not resident in England or another contracting state of the enforcement conventions.

It is unclear, however, how far the domestic courts are committed to applying the heightened-scrutiny proportionality test, even when human rights are engaged. In *A v Secretary of State for the Home Department*,[243] the Special Immigration Appeals Commission held that the Home Secretary acted unlawfully under Article 14 ECHR, in holding in detention, without charge or trial, terrorist suspects under anti-terrorism legislation that permitted the detention of suspects who were not citizens of the United Kingdom. The Commission held that, although the government had entered a valid derogation under the Convention in respect of Article 5 ECHR, the detentions were unlawful under Article 14, applying a proportionality test, on the grounds that there was no reasonable relationship between the means employed (the detention only of non-UK citizens) and the aim sought to be achieved (countering the threat posed by international terrorists). If the detentions were necessary in the case of non-UK citizens who were suspected international terrorists, confining detention to the alien section of the population would be proper only if the threat stemmed 'exclusively or almost exclusively' from that alien section.[244] Although the government's conclusion as to how best to achieve its legitimate aim was entitled to 'a degree of deference' from the Commission,[245] the evidence demonstrated that the threat was not confined to non-UK citizens. The Court of Appeal, however, considered that the distinction between nationals and aliens in being subject to detention under anti-terrorism legislation was justified, because there is 'a *rational* connection between this detention and the purpose which the Secretary of State wishes to achieve. It is a purpose which cannot be applied to nationals, namely detention pending deportation, irrespective of when that deportation will take place', even if that deportation cannot take place immediately.[246] It is unclear whether the use of the term 'rational' in this context indicates a preference for the older, weaker *Wednesbury* test.

(vi) *Margin of discretion*

In applying the test of objective and reasonable justification, the ECtHR has made clear that states 'enjoy a margin of appreciation in assessing whether and to what extent differences in otherwise similar situations justify a different treatment in law'.[247] The British courts have distinguished their approach from that of the

11.102

11.103

---

[243] [2002] EWCA Civ 1502; [2003] 2 WLR 564.

[244] ibid at [94].

[245] ibid at [92].

[246] *per* Lord Woolf CJ in *A v Secretary of State for the Home Department* [2002] EWCA Civ 1502; [2003] 2 WLR 564 at [52] (emphasis added).

[247] *Stubbings v UK* Application 22083/93 (1996) 23 EHRR 213.

'margin of appreciation', as applied by the ECtHR. 'Judicial recognition and assertion of the human right defined in the Convention is not a substitute for the processes of democratic government but a complement to them. While a national court does not accord the margin of appreciation recognized by the European Court as a supra-national court, it will give weight to the decisions of a representative legislature and a democratic government within the discretionary area of judgment accorded to those bodies.'[248] The British courts have thus adopted a degree of 'deference' towards judgments made by political actors. As Buxton LJ said in *Mendoza v Ghaidan*,[249] 'the courts will exercise "deference" in relation to decisions of Parliament, even where Convention rights are potentially engaged'. The starting point is the speech by Lord Hope in *R v DPP, ex p Kebilene*,[250] in which he wrote: 'It will be easier for [deference] to be recognized where the issues involve questions of social or economic policy, much less so where the rights are of high constitutional importance or are of the kind where the courts are especially well placed to assess the need for protection'. In the discrimination context, several elements appear to come into play in deciding what degree of deference to accord.

11.104 When issues of social and economic policy are involved, the courts are more willing to extend a significant degree of deference to policy established by Parliament. So, for example, Burton J in *R (on the application of Smith) v Barking and Dagenham LBC*[251] said that 'the domestic courts . . . will give both respect and leeway to policy established by Parliament; particularly in an area of policy with competing social and economic considerations such as housing'. In *Wandsworth LBC v Michalak*[252] the Court of Appeal considered whether an objective and reasonable justification existed for treating some of those sharing a household differently from others in determining the ability to become a successor to a secured tenancy in respect of council housing under the Housing Act 1985. The Court held that there was an objective and reasonable justification based on the fact that secure tenancies were particularly valuable and that it was reasonable that the government wished to restrict the resources that it wanted to expend on providing these benefits to those who were particularly close relatives, which Mr Michalak was not. Brooke LJ held: 'It appears to me that this is pre-eminently a field in which the courts should defer to the decisions taken by a democratically elected Parliament, which has determined the manner in which public resources should be allocated for local authority housing on preferential terms. Parliament decided to continue to . . . introduce a measure of legal certainty . . . when explaining with precision the type of close relative who should be entitled to be the first (and only)

---

[248] Lord Bingham in *Brown v Stott* [2003] 1 AC 681, 703.
[249] [2002] EWCA Civ 1533; [2003] 2 WLR 478 at [16].
[250] [2000] 2 AC 326.
[251] [2002] EWHC 2400; [2002] All ER (D) 266, QBD (Admin Ct) at [12].
[252] [2002] EWCA Civ 271; [2003] 1 WLR 617.

successor to a secure tenancy. It is understandable why Parliament wished a home not to be broken up on the death of a secure tenant when his wife or other very close relative was living with him as a member of his family at that time. It is equally understandable why Parliament decided that this privilege should not be extended to a more distant relative like Mr. Michalak who was living at the secure tenant's house at the time of his death.'[253]

This deference extends to the question of how best to implement a policy where the issue is whether to make individualized judgments or to construct rules of general application. So, in *R (on the application of Hooper) v Secretary of State for Work and Pensions*,[254] Moses J held that 'In determining how to target resources to those in need, the legislature is entitled to impose "bright-line" rules which are easy to apply and which may not focus with precision on the merits of individual cases. No logic can indicate where the balance should be struck; evaluative judgments are required, based on experience . . . [S]uch bright line rules in the context of social and economic policy do not lead to incompatibility even if individual hardship is occasioned.'   **11.105**

So too, in *Hooper*, Moses J said, in considering whether other alternatives could have been adopted by government in that case: 'On the other hand, in relation to the issue as to whether an alternative could have been adopted, it seems to me that the court should adopt a restrained approach. That question directly engages questions of social and economic policy with which the court is ill equipped to deal. It concerns the appropriate allocation of resources. In so far as the justification is attacked on the basis that the solution was not the best which could have been devised, . . . I shall not substitute my view for that of the Government in relation to alternative solutions.'   **11.106**

When the court attaches high constitutional importance to the right to non-discrimination the court is less likely to exercise deference. '[I]ssues of discrimination . . . do have high constitutional importance, and are issues that the courts should not shrink from. In such cases deference has only a minor role to play.'[255] What is the appropriate balance to be drawn between exercising greater deference because the area involves social or economic policy, and exercising less deference because the complaint is one of discrimination and hence of high constitutional importance? Moses J, in *Hooper*, provided the appropriate answer: **11.107**

> I suspect that it is neither possible nor productive to determine with any precision the degree of deference to be paid to the legislature when the issues concern social and economic policy and the constitutionally important right not to be discriminated against on the ground of gender. It seems to me that the court can have regard to both

---

[253] ibid at [41].
[254] [2002] EWHC 191; [2002] UKHRR 785 at [115].
[255] Buxton LJ in *Mendoza v Ghaidan* [2002] EWCA Civ 1533; [2003] 2 WLR 478 at [19] (see also Keene LJ at [44]).

those features by . . . subjecting the reasons advanced by the Government to a degree of scrutiny commensurate with the importance of the right. In so doing the court is merely exercising judicial techniques with which it is familiar. Whatever expression is used ('are the reasons compelling? Do they stack up?') a court is unlikely to find justification where the reasons advanced do not support the conclusion . . . If the reasons advanced by the Defendant are insubstantial or, even if they are substantial, they do not persuade me, I shall decline to find any objective justification.[256]

11.108   When the factors that in the past provided an objective justification for discrimination have changed, the courts will test whether the state has acted reasonably and proportionately in failing to introduce changes to respond to the change of circumstances. In *Hooper*[257] Moses J considered that:

> Parliament was far better placed than the court to make an overall assessment of how limited resources should be allocated to meet need and when the time had arrived for removing an advantage afforded to women to compensate them for their historical disadvantage in the labour market. That the right to non-discrimination on the grounds of gender is fundamental to democracy cannot be gainsaid, but in the instant case objective justification for such discrimination in the past has been advanced. The reasons for not introducing change earlier have been, to my mind, substantiated. The time taken to make changes seems to me to have been a reasonable and proportionate response to the problem. At the heart of the issue lies the question of how resources, raised by taxation, should be allocated.

(vii)   Objective justification and 'status harms'

11.109   We noted earlier how the function of Article 14 appeared to be dual faceted: primarily protecting the meaning of equality in its second meaning, but in some respects furthering the third meaning of equality. The latter role occurs primarily in the context of considering whether an objective justification has been established. The ECtHR has developed an approach that requires the state in certain circumstances to present particularly convincing reasons justifying the difference in treatment in order to be acceptable. Some grounds of discrimination are considered to be particularly serious, requiring this higher degree of justification than others. The ECtHR appears to apply a two-level standard of scrutiny, with differentiations based on gender and race appearing to be given such heightened scrutiny. Thus the Court has stated that the advancement of gender equality is a major goal of states that are parties to the Convention, and very weighty reasons would need to be advanced to justify a difference of treatment on grounds of sex.[258] This approach has

---

[256] [2002] EWHC 191; [2002] UKHRR 785 at [106], *per* Moses J.
[257] ibid at [118]–[119].
[258] *Abdulaziz v UK* Series A No 94 (1985) EHRR 471 at [78]. See also *Schuler-Zgraggen v Switzerland* Series A No 263 (1993) 16 EHRR 405 at [67]; *Burghartz v Switzerland* Series A No 280-B (1994) 18 EHRR 101; *Schmidt v Germany* Series A No 291-B (1994) 18 EHRR 513 at [27]; *Van Raalte v Netherlands* Series A No 732 (1997) 24 EHRR 503 at [39]; *Wessels-Bergervoet v Netherlands* (4 June 2002) at [49].

also led to decisions by the European Commission on Human Rights that in some cases racial discrimination may amount to a breach of Article 3's prohibition of degrading treatment.[259] Other grounds of discrimination, such as religion,[260] nationality,[261] illegitimacy,[262] and sexual orientation[263] may also attract a similar high degree of justification to survive scrutiny.

(e) EC law

(i) Differing functions of equality in EC law

A rough and ready distinction can be made between two overlapping, but relatively separate, functions of EC equality law. First, there are those aspects of EC equality law, operating primarily in the economic sphere, where equality has particular importance in furthering the market-integration goals of the Community. As de Búrca explains: 'the principle can be seen as an *instrument* for the attainment of specific Community aims . . . promoting equal treatment as a means of eradicating obstacles to the completion of the single market'.[264] Advocate General Tesauro has pointed to the fundamental importance of equality in this context: '[T]he principle of equal treatment is fundamental not only because it is a cornerstone of contemporary legal systems but for a more specific reason: Community legislation chiefly concerns economic situations and activities. If, in this field, different rules are laid down for similar situations, the result is not merely inequality before the law, but also, and inevitably, distortions of competition which are absolutely irreconcilable with the fundamental philosophy of the common market.'[265] This function is often regarded as the dominant function of equality in EC law. 'The principle of equality', writes Tridimas, 'acquires particular importance in the field of economic law . . . Equality . . . is . . . a keystone of integration. The notion of distortions of competition is central to understanding its function in Community economic law.'[266] In this category, for example, we might place the provisions regarding non-discrimination between producers and consumers.

11.110

A second function of the principle of equal treatment in EC law has been identified, however. In this the principle of equal treatment is of particular importance

11.111

---

[259] *East African Asians v UK* (1973) 3 EHRR 76, EComHR; *East African Asians v UK* Application 4403/70 (1995) 19 EHRR CD1, EComHR.
[260] *Hoffmann v Austria* Series A No 255-C (1993) 17 EHRR 293.
[261] *Gaygusuz v Austria* (1997) 23 EHRR 364 (ECtHR indicated that it would require very weighty reasons to justify differential treatment based exclusively on nationality).
[262] *Marckx v Belgium* Series A No 31 (1979) 2 EHRR 330; but cf *McMichael v UK* Series A No 307-B (1995) 20 EHRR 205.
[263] *Smith and Grady v UK* (2000) 29 EHRR 493 at [90]; *Lustig-Prean and Beckett v UK* (2000) 29 EHRR 548 at [82], but see *Fretté v France* Application 36515/97 [2003] 2 FCR 39.
[264] de Búrca (n 72 above) 23–24.
[265] Case C-63/89 *Les Assurances du Credit SA v Council of Ministers* [1991] ECR I-1799, 1829.
[266] Tridimas (n 55 above) 45.

in demonstrating that the goals of the Community go beyond economic goals and extend to the protection of the European social model, defined to include equality considerations. In this context, equality is seen either as important intrinsically or (at least) as important for non-economic integration. As de Búrca explains, equality can be seen 'as a value which mediates and possibly constrains or redirects other specific Community measures or goals. Thus, for example, Community measures might be subject to challenge for failure to comply with the equal treatment, or legislation might be tempered by the requirement that there should be no discrimination on grounds such as race or religion in its application . . . [M]ore controversially, the principle could be viewed as an independent Community goal . . .'[267] In this second category, for example, we might place the provisions regarding sex discrimination. We shall consider this aspect of Community equality in the next section.

11.112   Drawing a sharp distinction between these two functions is, however, somewhat problematic. In part, the distinction is sometimes overdrawn because aspects of equality, which began within the first function, moved to fulfil the second function. Confining the discussion to the grounds of gender, we see that the motivations for introducing prohibitions in discrimination may change, and that they may differ significantly from the reasons why similar legislation is introduced in the United Kingdom. The Treaty of Rome of 1957, which included a single article on equality between women and men, namely Article 119 EC regarding equal pay, was included originally to counter what would now be identified as the problem of 'social dumping' (an economic integration function). For over a decade, this provision had no noticeable effect on the member states, and it was not until the path-breaking decisions by the ECJ in the *Defrenne* cases[268] in the 1970s that the provision began to be seriously considered as giving rise to enforceable legal rights. This judicial activism coincided with the rise of the women's movement in western Europe, and these two factors, combined with the decision of the Community to balance economic policy with a social dimension more generally, led to three main pieces of equality legislation being enacted in the latter half of the 1970s. Increasingly, gender equality became centrally concerned with that social dimension, as an aspect of fundamental rights, and thus an element in the second function of equality.

11.113   A second reason for being wary of too sharp a distinction being drawn is that particular instantiations of equality currently appear to fulfil both functions. The most prominent example is as regards discrimination on grounds of nationality. The dual faceted nature of Article 12 (ex 6) EC is addressed by Advocate General

---

[267] de Búrca (n 72 above) 23–24.
[268] See Case 80/70 *Defrenne v Sabena* [1971] ECR 445; Case 43/75 *Defrenne v Sabena (No 2)* [1976] ECR 455; Case 149/77 *Defrenne v Sabena (No 3)* [1978] ECR 1365.

Jacobs in *Collins v Imtrat Handelsgesellschaft mbH*, in which he stresses that the prohibition on discrimination on grounds of (EC member state) nationality both furthers economic integration of the Community, and demonstrates that the Community is not just economic, but a 'common enterprise in which all the citizens of Europe are able to participate as individuals . . .'.[269] As Tridimas writes: '. . . the ECJ has transformed Article 12[6] from a general, programmatic, provision to an autonomous source of rights and obligations *beyond the sphere of the internal market strictly understood* which encompasses a diverse range of situations and whose outer limits remain elusive'.[270]

A third reason for being cautious in drawing the distinction too sharply lies in the difficulty of attributing reasons to the EC institutions for the adoption of particular equality provisions. As regards the provisions of the Framework Directive, for example, there is much current academic debate. We can really only speculate on the reasons that led to the enactment of these provisions, and there is some disagreement in the academic commentary as to how much the Community was motivated by economic or social integration motives,[271] and how far the future enlargement of the Community was important.[272] It is quite possible, indeed likely, that different motives underpinned the inclusion of different grounds of discrimination.[273] It is also likely that the Commission was anxious to exploit the political opportunity it was offered to include as broad a range of grounds as possible in as few directives as possible, knowing that some grounds would be unlikely to be accepted if they were contained in separate instruments.

11.114

---

[269] Joined Cases C 92 & 326/92 [1993] ECR I-5145, 5163.

[270] Tridimas (n 55 above) 87 (emphasis added).

[271] L Waddington, 'Testing the Limits of the EC Treaty Art on Non-discrimination' (1999) 28 ILJ 133, 134: '. . . Art 13 EC's inclusion in the Treaty was not primarily prompted by the desire to combat discrimination for economic reasons or to complement the single market. Instead it is part of a trend which is arguably reflected more in rhetoric than in reality; to bring Europe "closer to the citizens"' (footnote omitted). In contrast, see S Fredman, 'Equality: A New Generation?' (2001) 30 ILJ 145, 149 (pointing to an economic rationale for Community responsibility, as set out in the recitals to the new directives); and S McInerney, 'Equal treatment between persons irrespective of racial or ethnic origin: a comment' (2000) 25 ELR 317, 322–323 (who points to the market-orientated rationale as providing a secondary rationale for the Race Directive).

[272] M Bell, 'Art 13 EC: The European Commission's Anti-discrimination Proposals' (2000) 29 ILJ 79, 84 (importance of new directives in the context of enlargement of the Community).

[273] Social integration, particularly in the context of far-Right electoral successes in some European countries, appears to have been influential in speeding the adoption of the Race Directive. The inclusion of age as one of the prohibited grounds, however, should perhaps be viewed, as McGlynn points out, as being part of a larger EC policy about addressing the economic need for 'labour market change to encourage older workers to remain employment active, to persuade employers to reduce the use of "early exit" and to make vocational training and lifelong learning available to all', although it subsequently took on a fundamental rights perspective. C McGlynn, 'Age Discrimination and European Union Law' (paper delivered to workshop organized by the Swedish National Institute for Working Life on *Discrimination and affirmative action on the labour market—legal perspectives*, Brussels, 6–7 November 2000) 4.

11.115   Equality in EC law is relevant for the second, third and fourth meanings of equality sketched out above. In this section, we concentrate on its importance for the second meaning. Where entitlements or interests provided for in the Treaty, etc, are being 'distributed', then the EC equality principle requires that likes should be treated alike, and differences treated differently, unless there are objectively justified reasons for departing from that principle. This is of particular importance with regard to economic relations. In this sense, the approach of the ECJ is to regard the Treaty requirements as of such importance for the functioning of the market that failure to ensure that they are applied equally requires heightened judicial scrutiny. It is as if each particular article in the Treaty has an additional equality clause that provides that that article has to be applied to conform to the equal treatment principle.[274] In this situation, there is no need to identify any specific prohibited ground of discrimination (such as nationality). It is sufficient to establish an unjustified difference in treatment. This is an application of the second meaning of equality.

(ii) Relationship between Wednesbury *review and review under EC law*

11.116   The standard of judicial review attaching to the application of the equal treatment principle in EC law is complex, and only the barest outline of some of the complexities will be provided here. First, according to Tridimas, in general, '[t]he principle of substantive equality endorsed by the Court of Justice entails a stricter degree of judicial scrutiny than the concept of Wednesbury unreasonableness . . . A prime difference between Community law and English law . . . lies in that the former requires the decision maker to demonstrate a substantive justification or, in other words, to "provide a fully reasoned case." The authority is not constrained merely by the requirement that the decision must be one which a reasonable authority might take.'[275] The quotation is taken from the judgment of Laws J, in *R v Ministry of Agriculture, Fisheries and Food, ex p First City Trading*,[276] which provides the most extensive judicial comparison between the *Wednesbury* unreasonableness test and the Community test. The relevant passage is worth quoting in full:

> The difference between Wednesbury and European review is that in the former case the legal limits lie further back . . . [A]t least as regards a requirement such as that of objective justification in an equal treatment case, the European rule requires the decision-maker to provide a fully reasoned case. It is not enough merely to set out the problem, and assert that within his discretion the Minister chose this or that solution, constrained only by the requirement that his decision must have been one which a reasonable Minister might make. Rather the court will test the solution arrived at, and pass it only if substantial factual considerations are put forward in its

---

[274] See, eg, Case C-309/89 *Codorniu SA v Council of Ministers* [1994] ECR I-1853 at [26].
[275] Tridimas (n 55 above) 42.
[276] [1997] 1 CMLR 250.

justification: considerations which are relevant, reasonable, and proportionate to the aim in view. But as I understand the jurisprudence the court is not concerned to agree or disagree with the decision; that would be to travel beyond the boundaries of proper judicial authority and usurp the primary decision-maker's function. This *Wednesbury* and European review are different models—one looser, one tighter—of the same judicial concept, which is the imposition of compulsory standards on decision-makers so as to secure the repudiation of arbitrary power.[277]

This general approach is subject to numerous caveats, however. One is of particular importance. As Tridimas observes, 'there are fundamental differences in the application of the principle of equality as a ground of review of *Community* measures and as a ground of review of *national* measures affecting the fundamental freedoms. In the first case, the application of the principle is qualified by the discretion of the Community legislature and the Court focuses more on the objectives of the measure in issue. In the second case, the Court applies the principle of equality as an instrument of integration, and focuses more on the effects of the measure.'[278] In practice, judicial scrutiny of Community acts often seems closer to *Wednesbury* unreasonableness than the heightened scrutiny generally characteristic of EC law, and thus comes closer to the first meaning of equality.

11.117

(f) Conclusion

In the second meaning of discrimination, then, the role of equality is to secure the availability of the 'prized public good', free from arbitrariness, such as that seen when access to that right is restricted for reasons that do not withstand objective scrutiny. The more important the right or public good in issue, the more intense is the scrutiny by the courts of the reasons for selective allocation. What constitutes such prized public goods to which equality is attached? So far, in English public law, two major groups of such goods can be identified with some degree of confidence: fundamental human rights (such as those particularly found in the ECHR) and fundamental economic principles (such as those found in EC internal market law). Essentially, in both contexts, the function of equality is the same: to ensure that the distribution of the prized public good is not restricted by the use of arbitrary or unjustified criteria of distribution.

11.118

(3) Non-Discrimination, Particular Characteristics and the 'Grounds' of Discrimination

(a) Introduction

The third approach differs from the second in being less concerned with the importance of the good being allocated, and more concerned with the use of actual

11.119

---

[277] ibid at 279.
[278] Tridimas (n 55 above) 47–48 (emphasis added).

or imputed identity in a wide range of situations. In the second meaning, the harm to be prevented lies in the arbitrary allocation of something that in principle all should have. In the third meaning, the harm lies in the use made of particular characteristics to affect the allocation of a wide range of opportunities, which may or may not reach the importance of rights, but where the use of those characteristics is unacceptable in such decisions. In the third approach to non-discrimination, the focus of attention shifts from the importance of the 'public good' (particularly the human right in issue) and turns instead to the association between a limited number of particular characteristics (such as race, gender, etc) and the discrimination suffered by those who have, or are perceived to have, those characteristics, where the public authorities' actions discriminate against individuals with those particular characteristics. Classically, this third approach is used in Britain to target particularly race and gender discrimination. We have seen this approach developing in the context of Article 14 (with the emphasis given to the greater need to justify distinctions on certain grounds). We shall see it also in the development of a limited anti-discrimination jurisprudence under Article 3 ECHR. We can also identify the emergence of a somewhat similar (although very much more limited) approach at common law in the development of the common law tort of misfeasance in public office, in the technique of 'updating' statutes by interpretation, in the (uncertain) influence of anti-discrimination law in influencing the development of conceptions of 'public policy', and in the development of the meaning of *Wednesbury* unreasonableness. The most developed examples of this approach, however, are to be found in domestic and EC legislation, to which we turn first.

(b) Three models of legislation

11.120 We can distinguish three distinct approaches adopted by the legislature in furthering this third meaning of discrimination.

(i) Piecemeal abolition of discrimination

11.121 First, in piecemeal legislation passed for over a century, Parliament has adopted provisions abolishing specific statutory or common law discrimination on particular grounds. Reference was made above to legislation relating to discrimination against married women in the area of property and participation in public life. Other examples include the abolition of discrimination on the basis of illegitimacy in certain property matters, abolition of discrimination in several criminal offences on the basis of sexual orientation,[279] and abolition of discrimination on the basis of religion in the exercise of certain civil rights.

---

[279] eg, Sexual Offences (Amendment) Act 2000 (age of consent).

(ii) Criminal law protections

Secondly, Parliament has legislated to provide certain criminal sanctions for particular types of actions closely related to racial discrimination, in particular. For example, the Public Order Act 1986[280] prohibits incitement to racial hatred. The Crime and Disorder Act 1998[281] created a new category of racially (and subsequently religiously[282]) aggravated criminal offences, where offences displaying racial or religious aggravation attract more severe punishment.[283] A criminal offence of harassment was enacted in the Protection from Harassment Act 1997, which was intended to be used, inter alia, to counter racial harassment.

11.122

(iii) Anti-discrimination legislation

Thirdly, this approach has been most developed in the context of domestic and European legislation providing for civil law prohibitions of discrimination on certain particular grounds, covering a range of situations and activities in both the private and public spheres. In particular, it is the legislation in Britain dealing with race, gender and disability, and in EC provisions dealing with gender equality, discrimination on the basis of race and nationality, and under the Framework Directive, that is more relevant here. In this legislation, domestic and EC law specify that particular characteristics of persons should not be used as the basis of the distribution of opportunities. Here, specific grounds of discrimination (gender, race, etc) are prohibited, unless there are objectively justified reasons for the difference in treatment based on these grounds. In EC law, the idea of 'status-harms' first begins with the prohibition of discrimination on the basis of gender, subsequently influences the judicial approach in cases of nationality discrimination, and is broadened considerably in the new Article 13 directives. In British domestic law, the prohibition of racial discrimination is first, followed by gender and disability. These are examples of the third meaning of equality. It is this legislative approach that is the primary focus of this section of the chapter.

11.123

(c) Contours of existing anti-discrimination legislation

(i) Grounds of discrimination subject to heightened degree of scrutiny

Existing British anti-discrimination legislation prohibits discrimination, in certain areas of activity, on a wide variety of specific grounds, including race, colour, ethnic or national origin, nationality, sex (including pregnancy), gender

11.124

---

[280] Pt III.
[281] ss 28–32.
[282] Anti-Terrorism, Crime and Security Act 2001, s 39.
[283] See Elizabeth Burney, 'Using the Law on Racially Aggravated Offences' [2003] Crim LR 28.

reassignment,[284] being married, trade union activity, fixed term working,[285] part-time working, and suffering under a disability. EC law now prohibits discrimination on the grounds of nationality, sex, race, disability, religion or belief, sexual orientation, and age.[286] These are the grounds that attract heightened scrutiny under domestic and EC law.

(ii) Common and divergent features of legislative approach

11.125 The legislative approaches that single out only particular grounds of discrimination as subject to scrutiny (particularly the UK domestic statutory requirements and the specific EC Treaty and secondary legislation requirements, leaving judicial review of administrative action, the ECHR and the EU Charter to one side), are all characterized, in contrast with those legal regimes discussed above, by the specificity and detail of the legislative provisions, and by the extent to which they require a much deeper level of scrutiny in the areas covered by the legislation. The English courts have been cautious about adopting a view that the legislation reflecting this third category of equality should be interpreted as based on a universal principle. As Lord Hope has written: 'The fact is that the principle of equal treatment is easy to state but difficult to apply in practice. In the result the legislation which is under scrutiny in these appeals is designed to be specific and particular rather than universal in its application, and it is still being developed incrementally . . .'[287]

11.126 There are many common features of the EC and domestic British statutory approaches and the interpretation of this legislation. This is hardly surprising, since they have influenced each other so considerably, and been (directly or indirectly) influenced by equivalent anti-discrimination legislation and judicial interpretation in other jurisdictions, particularly the United States. All focus on promoting a version of equality defined as the absence of 'discrimination'. All include a definition of discrimination that encompasses the need to go beyond the idea of discrimination as simply ensuring that likes are treated alike and encompasses the idea that in certain cases it is necessary to ensure that those differently situated are not necessarily treated the same. (We shall examine subsequently the different ways in which this element is conceptualized legally.) All include specific and general defences and exceptions to the non-discrimination principle (such as ones based on genuine occupational qualifications). All include provisions to ensure that some forms of positive or affirmative action are not to be regarded as unlawful. All provide a remedy for the resolution of individual grievances and

---

[284] Sex Discrimination (Gender Reassignment) Regulations 1999, SI 1999/1102.
[285] Fixed-term Employees (Prevention of Less Favourable Treatment) Regulations 2002, SI 2002/2034.
[286] See paras 11.38–11.44 above.
[287] *Relaxion Group v Rhys-Harper* [2003] UKHL 33 at [78].

protection for those involved in litigation; victimization is widely prohibited, for example. Many have provisions specifying the nature of the burden of proof in adversarial proceedings. Some have provisions allowing associations and organizations to pursue claims for equal treatment. All provide for sanctions to be imposed against those found to have discriminated.

The legislative and judicial approaches diverge, however, in several important respects. We shall examine some of these similarities and divergences in more detail in the following paragraphs.   **11.127**

(iii) Approach to coverage

Unlike under the first and second approaches discussed above, the third approach   **11.128**
has a significantly different approach to coverage. Unlike under the first approach, it does not apply to all public authorities in respect of all their activities, but only to those specified in the relevant legislation. Unlike under the second approach, it does not apply as a penumbra of all major areas of rights (indeed many fundamental rights are not included within the coverage of British anti-discrimination law), but (again) is limited only to those areas of activity (some of which would not be considered as involving rights under the ECHR) specifically included in the legislation. In another respect, of course the approach taken under this third approach is considerably broader in scope, covering both public and private sector actors operating in those areas covered, whereas to a considerable extent the first and second approaches apply only to the public sector.

In general, the approach taken to the question of coverage has been to begin with   **11.129**
a restricted list of activities subject to this non-discrimination principle, and gradually to expand the types of activities covered. Thus, the usual approach has often been to begin by including employment and then to add other areas of activity subsequently such as housing, education, and goods facilities and services. This practice is reflected in the pattern of areas included or excluded under currently applicable anti-discrimination law in England.

Existing anti-discrimination legislation applicable in England covers the area of   **11.130**
employment and related areas, education, and the provision of goods facilities and services and the disposal and management of property, but (again) not consistently. Protection from discrimination on grounds of gender reassignment only applies to the employment and training field, not discrimination in the areas of goods, facilities and services. The prohibition of discrimination against married persons applies in relation to employment only, but does not apply for the purposes of the Equal Pay Act 1970. As regards coverage of public sector functions, it has previously been the case that anti-discrimination legislation provisions concerned with the provision of goods facilities and services did not apply to functions performed by public bodies if they could not be undertaken by a private

body,[288] but this limit was removed by the Race Relations (Amendment) Act 2001 in relation to racial discrimination. In certain respects, the hitherto protected area of immigration is, for example, now subject to a non-discrimination norm in the context of a limited prohibition of racial discrimination.[289]

11.131   Both the Race Directive and the Framework Directive prohibit discrimination by 'all persons, as regards both the public and private sectors, including public bodies', in relation to employment, the conditions for access to employment, self-employment, and occupation; access to all types and to all levels of vocational guidance, vocational training, advanced vocational training, and retraining; employment and working conditions, including dismissals and pay; and membership of and involvement in an organization of workers or employers, or any other organization whose members carry on a particular profession, including the benefits provided for by such organizations. The Race Directive, in addition, prohibits discrimination in other areas such as social protection, including social security and health care; social advantages, education (including grants and scholarships), and access to and supply of goods and services, including housing.

11.132   EC law's specific prohibitions of discrimination on grounds of nationality apply to a wide variety of economic activity: non-discrimination between producers and consumers in the context of the Common Agricultural Policy, non-discrimination as between workers who are nationals of the host state and those who are nationals of another member state, equal treatment as between nationals and non-nationals who are established in a self-employed capacity in a member state, equal treatment for providers of services, and non-discrimination in the field of taxation as between domestic and imported goods.

11.133   EC law has had a major impact on the coverage of this approach to discrimination in another important respect. Prior to the development of EC anti-discrimination law, the areas covered by British anti-discrimination law excluded the ability to challenge discrimination in otherwise included areas of activity (such as employment) if that discrimination resulted from legislation, thus preserving parliamentary sovereignty. With the advent of EC anti-discrimination law, however, such legislation is now challengeable in domestic courts. This has resulted in more care being taken to ensure that policy advice leading up to legislation conforms to

---

[288] *R v Entry Clearance Officer (Bombay), ex p Amin* [1983] 2 AC 818.

[289] Race Relations (Amendment) Act 2000, s 65 gives a right of appeal to a person who alleges that an authority has, in taking any decision under the Immigration Acts relating to that person's entitlement to enter or remain in the UK, racially discriminated against him. These amendments also provide that where a person brings an appeal on race discrimination grounds, the Secretary of State may certify that appeal as manifestly unfounded. If the adjudicator agrees with the certificate, the person is prevented from appealing against the adjudicator's decision to the Immigration Appeal Tribunal. See also Immigration (European Economic Area) (Amendment) Regulations 2001, SI 2001/865, reg 6.

a non-discrimination approach, leading to the publication of internal guidance to departments on the issue.[290]

(iv) Enforcement

A clearly identifiable feature of this third approach, unlike under either the first or **11.134** second approaches, is the extent to which particular attention is given to devising methods of enforcement appropriate to implementing these non-discrimination goals. Cases of alleged discrimination in employment under sex, race and disability discrimination law are heard by the employment tribunals, which also have responsibility for hearing other types of employment disputes. The Race and Framework Directives reverse the burden of proof in civil cases. They provide that when complainants establish, before a court or other competent authority, facts from which it may be presumed that there has been direct or indirect discrimination, it is for the respondent to prove that there has been no breach of the principle of equal treatment. The Race and Framework Directives contain provisions on victimization. Member states must introduce into their national legal systems such measures as are necessary to protect individuals from any adverse treatment or adverse consequence as a reaction to a complaint or to proceedings aimed at enforcing compliance with the principle of equal treatment.

It is in the context of public enforcement mechanisms that the enforcement of the **11.135** third approach to discrimination most clearly differs from the second and third approaches. There are several public bodies with responsibilities for furthering the aims of the various different pieces of anti-discrimination legislation. (There is no such body operating in England for the enforcement of the HRA 1998, although there is such a body in Northern Ireland.) Over the three areas of existing domestic anti-discrimination legislation the various bodies have broadly similar functions, powers and duties, including working towards the elimination of unlawful discrimination, keeping the legislation under review, conducting research, and enforcement functions. Among their enforcement functions, each has the power to investigate, assist complainants, and initiate litigation in its own name in certain limited areas. The SDA, RRA and DDA all give powers to the various statutory bodies to conduct investigations in their respective areas. All three areas of existing anti-discrimination law contain provisions for the respective bodies to seek injunctions in cases of persistent discrimination, discriminatory advertisements, instructions to discriminate, and pressure to discriminate, except that under the DDA discriminatory advertisements are not unlawful. All three areas of existing anti-discrimination law give powers to the respective bodies to offer advice and assistance to individuals bringing a complaint before the tribunals and courts, with minor variations.

---

[290] Policy Appraisal for Equal Treatment (1998).

11.136 Both the Race and the Framework Directives require member states to ensure that associations, organizations or other legal entities which have, in accordance with the criteria laid down by their national laws, a legitimate interest in ensuring that the provisions of these directives are complied with, may engage, on behalf or in support of the complainant with his or her approval, in any judicial or administrative procedure provided for the enforcement of obligations under the directives. The Race Directive, but not the Framework Directive, requires member states to designate a body or bodies for the promotion of equal treatment of all persons without discrimination on grounds of different racial or ethnic origin. These bodies must have the functions of providing independent assistance to victims of discrimination in pursuing their complaints of discrimination, conducting independent investigations or surveys concerning discrimination, and publishing reports and making recommendations on issues relating to discrimination based on racial or ethnic origin.

(d) Common law

11.137 Although the law tackling status-discrimination on certain grounds derives primarily from legislation, whether EC or domestic, the common law has responded to these developments in several ways.

(i) Misfeasance in public office

11.138 The ingredients of the tort of misfeasance in public office were identified by the House of Lords in *Three Rivers DC v Bank of England (No 3)*.[291] The tort arises when the officer exercised a power specifically intending to injure the plaintiff, or when he or she acted in the knowledge of, or with reckless indifference to, the illegality of the official's act and in the knowledge of, or with reckless indifference to, the probability of causing injury to the plaintiff or persons of a class of which the plaintiff was a member.[292] It is this latter element that opens up the possibility of linking the tort with non-discrimination. There are, therefore, two different forms of liability for misfeasance in public office. 'First there is the case of targeted malice by a public officer, i.e. conduct specifically intended to injure a person or persons. This type of case involves bad faith in the sense of the exercise of public power for an improper or ulterior motive. The second form is where a public officer acts knowing that he has no power to do the act complained of and that the act will probably injure the plaintiff. It involves bad faith inasmuch as the public officer does not have an honest belief that his act is lawful.'[293] It was held in *Thomas*

---

[291] [2000] 2 WLR 1220. See also Mads Andenas and Duncan Fairgrieve, 'Misfeasance in Public Office, Governmental Liability and European Influences' (2002) 51 ICLQ 757.

[292] However, an action for misfeasance in public office is not excluded when the predictable victim was neither an identifiable individual nor an identifiable group of individuals: *Akenzua v Secretary of State for the Home Department* [2002] EWCA Civ 1470; [2003] 1 WLR 741.

[293] *Three Rivers DC v Bank of England (No 3)* [2000] 2 WLR 1220, HL, *per* Lord Steyn.

v Secretary of State for the Home Office[294] that if prison officers deliberately and dishonestly abused their positions by racially discriminating against and abusing prisoners, or at least encouraging, or deliberately failing to stop, such abuse by other inmates, this would satisfy the requirements of the tort. Indirectly, therefore, the common law incorporates what is legislatively regarded as abuse (racial harassment, a type of racial discrimination that is almost paradigmatically a status harm) into the developing area of misfeasance in order to provide a common law remedy.

(ii) Statutory interpretation

The courts have drawn on several principles of statutory interpretation to further the policy behind the third meaning of equality. In *R v Miah*,[295] for example, Lord Reid drew on the principle of statutory interpretation that Parliament did not intend, in the absence of express words, to infringe a fundamental principle of the British constitution or to act contrary to international treaty obligations of the United Kingdom, to inform his interpretation of the phrase 'ordinarily relevant' in the context of determining eligibility for a grant for higher education. Holding that it is a fundamental principle of the British constitution that all persons are equal before the law, and that that common law principle was also guaranteed by international human rights conventions binding on the United Kingdom, Lord Reid decided that if the term 'ordinarily resident' was ambiguous, the ambiguity should be resolved in favour of a construction in accordance with the principle of equality before the law and equal protection of the law, rather than in favour of a construction that involved discrimination on the basis of ethnic or national origins.

11.139

Without specifically adverting to the idea that the statute needs to be updated, the courts have been willing to apply the principle of 'updating', discussed earlier, particularly in cases dealing with sex discrimination. In *R v R*,[296] for example, the House of Lords held that the rule, deriving from Hale,[297] that a husband cannot be criminally liable for raping his wife if he has sexual intercourse with her without her consent no longer formed part of the law of England. A husband and wife are now to be regarded as equal partners in marriage and it is unacceptable that by marriage the wife submits herself irrevocably to sexual intercourse in all circumstances or that it is an incident of modern marriage that the wife consents to intercourse in all circumstances, including sexual intercourse obtained only by

11.140

---

[294] QBD, 31 July 2000, *per* Buckley J. See also *Anglin v Secretary of State for Foreign Affairs* (CA, 2 November 1995); *Harmon CFEM Facades (UK) Ltd v Corporate Officer of the House of Commons* 67 Con LR 1.

[295] *R v Miah* [1974] 1 WLR 683.

[296] [1992] 1 AC 599, HL.

[297] Sir Matthew Hale, *History of the Pleas of the Crown* (1736) 629.

force. In s 1(1) of the Sexual Offences (Amendment) Act 1976, which defines rape as having 'unlawful' intercourse with a woman without her consent, the word 'unlawful' is to be treated as mere surplusage and not as meaning 'outside marriage', since it is unlawful to have sexual intercourse with any woman without her consent. In his speech, Lord Keith of Kinkel said: 'The common law is . . . capable of evolving in the light of changing social, economic and cultural developments. Hale's proposition reflected the state of affairs in these respects at the time it was enunciated. Since then the status of women, and particularly of married women, has changed out of all recognition in various ways which are very familiar and upon which it is unnecessary to go into detail. Apart from property matters and the availability of matrimonial remedies, one of the most important changes is that marriage is in modern times regarded as a partnership of equals, and no longer one in which the wife must be the subservient chattel of the husband. Hale's proposition involves that by marriage a wife gives her irrevocable consent to sexual intercourse with her husband under all circumstances and irrespective of the state of her health or how she happens to be feeling at the time. In modern times any reasonable person must regard that conception as quite unacceptable.' He went on to consider whether the 1976 Act presented an obstacle to the House 'declaring that in modern times the supposed marital exception in rape forms no part of the law of England'. In concluding that it did not, and that the House of Lords should not leave the issue to be decided by Parliament, Lord Keith quoted Lord Lane in the Court of Appeal, with approval: 'The remaining and no less difficult question is whether . . . this is an area where the court should step aside to leave the matter to the parliamentary process. This is not the creation of a new offence, it is the removal of a common law fiction which has become anachronistic and offensive and we consider that it is our duty having reached that conclusion to act upon it.'[298]

11.141   In *Lambert v Lambert*[299] the Court of Appeal decided that, taking into account the importance of gender equality, s 25(2) of the Matrimonial Causes Act 1973 should not be interpreted to place greater value on the contribution of the breadwinner than that of the homemaker as a justification for dividing the product of the breadwinner's efforts unequally between the husband and the wife on divorce.

11.142   This approach has been used in several cases to allow the non-discrimination principle to be argued, although not always successfully, in cases other than sex discrimination. In *Fitzpatrick v Sterling Housing Association Ltd*,[300] two questions of interpretation were before the House of Lords. The first involved whether an extended meaning could be given to the word 'spouse' so that it applied to include

---

[298] [1991] 2 WLR 1065, 1074, CA.
[299] [2002] EWCA Civ 1685; [2003] 2 WLR 631.
[300] [2001] 1 AC 27.

same-sex partners. The House of Lords held that it did not. In the statutory context, the word meant a person who was legally the husband or wife of the original tenant, and the extended definition clearly applied to those persons who, though not legally husband and wife, lived as such without being married. However, such words were gender-specific, connoting a relationship between a man and a woman. Thus the man was required to show that the woman was living with him as 'his' wife, and the woman had to show that the man was living with her as 'her' husband.

However, on the second question of construction, the House held that a same-sex partner was capable of being a member of the original tenant's 'family'. Such a person would have to establish the necessary characteristics of the word 'family' as used in that provision, namely a mutual degree of inter-dependence, the sharing of lives in a single family unit living in one house, caring and love, commitment and support. Thus a transient superficial relationship would not be sufficient even though it was intimate; nor would mere cohabitation by friends as a matter of convenience. In his speech, Lord Nichols found that, regarding the second issue: 'A man and woman living together in a stable and permanent sexual relationship are capable of being members of a family for this purpose. Once this is accepted, there can be no rational or other basis on which the like conclusion can be withheld from a similarly stable and permanent sexual relationship between two men or between two women. Where a relationship of this character exists, it cannot make sense to say that, although a heterosexual partnership can give rise to membership of a family for Rent Act purposes, a homosexual partnership cannot.' He considered that it was legitimate, therefore, for him to view the word 'family' as used in the Rent Acts as having changed its meaning as ways of life and social attitudes had changed, so that it could legitimately be interpreted in 1999 as having a different and wider meaning than when it was first enacted in 1920. Lord Clyde, also, saw 'no grounds for treating the provisions with which we are concerned as being in the relatively rare category of cases where Parliament intended the language to be fixed at the time when the original Act was passed. The rule of contemporary exposition should be applied only in relation to very old statutes . . . The general presumption is that an updating construction is to be applied . . .'

11.143

(e) *Wednesbury* reasonableness and 'status-harms'

We saw above that *Wednesbury* unreasonableness has been developed to provide a basis for heightened protection of important substantive rights, and equal treatment in the delivery of these rights. Similarly, *Wednesbury* unreasonableness has more recently been developed to prevent public bodies from exercising their powers in such a way as to result in status-harms arising of a type similar to, but going beyond, the anti-discrimination legislation considered in this section.

11.144

11.145   This development may be seen to have been anticipated in *Cummings v Birkenhead Corp*,[301] where parents of children from Roman Catholic primary schools challenged circulars sent out by the local education authority that confined parents' choice to Roman Catholic secondary schools and denied their children the opportunity of being considered for non-Roman Catholic schools. Although the Court of Appeal held that there was no ground for saying that the authority had acted unreasonably. Lord Denning set out the test for discrimination-related claims under the *Wednesbury* reasonableness test as follows: 'if this education authority were to allocate boys to particular schools according to the colour of their hair *or, for that matter, the colour of their skin*, it would be so unreasonable, so capricious, so irrelevant to any proper system of education that it would be ultra vires altogether, and this court would strike it down at once. But, if there were valid educational reasons for a policy, as, for instance, in an area where immigrant children were backward in the English tongue and needed special teaching, then it would be perfectly right to allocate those in need to special schools where they would be given extra facilities for learning English. In short, if the policy is one which could reasonably be upheld for good educational reasons it is valid. But if it is so unreasonable that no reasonable authority could entertain it, it is invalid.'[302]

11.146   More recently, litigation arose concerning the criteria for qualification for payment from a fund established by the UK government to provide ex gratia payments to internees of the Japanese during the Second World War. Two separate cases challenging the criteria of eligibility illustrate the emerging state of the law, and the extent to which status-harms appear now to attract a different level of scrutiny than where such harms are not apparent. In the first case, a challenge was made to the decision that in order to qualify a civilian had to be a British subject who was born in the United Kingdom or whose parents or grandparents had been born in the United Kingdom. These criteria were, it was alleged, unlawful because they were 'irrational' and (separately) because they breached the 'common law principle of equality'. It was held, however, that the criteria were not irrational, because the government was entitled to take the view that the recipient had to have had strong links with the United Kingdom at the time of internment in order to benefit from the compensation. Nor were the criteria contrary to any common law principle of equality: 'if the decision assailed in the present case withstands attack on the ground of unreasonableness there is no basis for concluding that it falls on the ground of inequality'.[303]

---

[301] [1972] Ch 12.
[302] ibid, emphasis added.
[303] *R (on the application of Association of British Civilian Internees (Far East Region)) v Secretary of State for Defence* [2002] EWHC 2119; The Independent, 31 October 2002, QBD (Admin Ct), *per* Scott Baker J at [54]. Art 14 ECHR was not applicable because no substantive right was engaged. Ex gratia payments of the type in issue in this case, fell outside the scope of Art 1 of Protocol 1.

In the second case, however, several Nepalese nationals who had been members of the Gurkha rifle brigades as part of the (colonial) Indian Army and had been interned by the Japanese, successfully challenged the criteria of eligibility for compensation as irrational on *Wednesbury* grounds.[304] The relevant criteria challenged were those which limited eligibility to surviving former members of the UK armed forces, or surviving former servicemen who received payments under provisions of the 1951 Treaty of Peace with Japan, under the auspices of the UK government. The claimants did not fall within these categories, or any of the other categories laid down. The effect of the distinctions between those who qualified and those who did not was to make eligible 'European' officers in the Gurkhas because they had been included in the peace treaty, but not 'natives' in these regiments. The distinction was ostensible drawn on the basis that the two groups were subject to different disciplinary codes. The basis for the distinction, however, was found by the court to be 'a clear distinction drawn on "de facto" racial grounds (disguised as "de jure" Constitutional ones)'.[305] To apply that distinction to the new scheme 'undermines the rationality of the exclusion' of the Gurkhas.[306] The court distinguished this case from the previous case: 'The distinction drawn upon racial grounds was not present' in the former.[307] Even though the decision-makers did not appreciate the racial basis of the distinction, it was unlawful. The court adopted the extra-judicial argument of Lord Steyn regarding the development of *Wednesbury* unreasonableness in situations of status discrimination:

11.147

> The importance of the development of constitutional rights has not come to an end with the advent of the Human Rights Act. One illustration is sufficient. The anti-discrimination provision contained in Article 14 of the European Convention is parasitic in as much as it serves only to protect other Convention rights. There is no general or free-standing prohibition of discrimination. This is a relatively weak provision. On the other hand, the constitutional principle of equality developed domestically by English courts is wider. The law and the government must accord every individual equal concern and respect for their welfare and dignity. Everyone is entitled to equal protection of the law, which must be applied without fear or favour. Except where compellingly justified distinctions must never be made on the grounds of race, colour, belief, gender or other irrational ground. Individuals are therefore comprehensively protected from discrimination by the principle of equality. This constitutional right has a continuing role to play. The organic development of constitutional rights is therefore a complementary and parallel process to the application of human rights legislation.[308]

---

[304] *R (on the application of Gurung) v Ministry of Defence* [2002] EWHC 2463; The Times, 28 December 2002, QBD (Admin Ct).
[305] ibid at [56].
[306] ibid at [56].
[307] ibid at [56].
[308] Lecture given by Lord Steyn, 18 September 2002, 18, quoted ibid at [36].

11.148   Note, in particular, the emphasis given to distinctions on the grounds of race, colour, belief and gender, and the need for such distinctions to be 'compellingly justified', a strikingly similar requirement to that under the 'enhanced *Wednesbury*' test and even (possibly) the *Daly* tests discussed above. Note also that the legislative developments are seen as informing the common law developments. As a source of public policy, the use made of anti-discrimination legislation that is not legally determinative in the instant case as a source for the interpretative principle has a mixed history. In both *Re Lysaght (decd)*[309] and *Blathwayt v Lord Crawley*,[310] we have seen that arguments that anti-discrimination legislation, then in the course of passing through Parliament or having recently been passed, should have an influence on perceptions of 'public policy' in those cases were rejected. In *Nagle v Feilden*, however, Danckwerts LJ considered that the Sex Disqualification (Removal) Act 1919, 'whether it applies to the present case or not, shows the position of present-day thought', and was an appropriate source for the argument that sex discrimination by the Jockey Club was contrary to public policy.

11.149   The Gurkha case also illustrates that the grounds of unacceptability are likely to change over time. As Bingham MR said in *R v Ministry of Defence, ex p Smith*,[311] in the context of a discussion on the development of judicial review of administrative action at common law, after referring to changes of attitude in society towards same-sex relationships: 'I regard the progressive development and refinement of public and professional opinion at home and abroad, here very briefly described, as an important feature of this case. A belief which represented unquestioned orthodoxy in Year X may have become questionable by Year Y, and unsustainable by Year Z. Public and professional opinion are a continuum.'[312]

(f) Article 3 ECHR

11.150   Although, as we have seen, the approach under Article 14 ECHR is, substantially at least, one that promotes the second meaning of equality, we have also seen that in some respects an interpretation of Article 14 is emerging that supports the third approach to equality. Such an approach is even more clearly demonstrated in the approach taken to the application of Article 3 ECHR to discrimination. Article 3 prohibits 'torture or inhuman or degrading treatment or punishment'.

11.151   The application of Article 3 to discrimination issues began in the report by the European Commission on Human Rights in *East African Asians v UK*,[313] in which the Commission found that, in certain circumstances, discrimination based on

---

[309] [1966] 1 Ch 191, Ch D.
[310] [1976] AC 397.
[311] [1996] QB 517, 552–554.
[312] ibid 554.
[313] (1973) 3 EHRR 76, EComHR.

race could of itself amount to a breach of Article 3, as amounting to degrading treatment. Since then, the ECtHR has reiterated that discrimination may breach Article 3, under certain conditions.[314] In *Abdulaziz v UK*, there was no violation of Article 3 because the differences in treatment complained of (allegedly based on race) 'did not denote any contempt or lack of respect for the personality of the applicants and that it was not designed to, and did not, humiliate or debase . . . .'.[315] In *Smith and Grady v UK*, although the Court was willing to extend the coverage of Article 3 to include discrimination on the basis of sexual orientation,[316] it held that the discrimination must attain a minimum level of severity that will be assessed taking into account all the circumstances of the case, such as the duration of the treatment and its physical or mental effects. The Court continued: 'treatment may be considered degrading if it is such as to arouse in its victims feelings of fear, anguish and inferiority capable of humiliating and debasing them and possibly breaking their physical or moral resistance. Moreover, it is sufficient if the victim is humiliated in his or her own eyes.'[317]

(g) Meaning of equality and discrimination in these contexts

One of the most important developments characteristic of the third approach to equality has been the development of the meaning of unlawful discrimination. This is also one of the most conceptually difficult issues involving judicial interpretation. We have seen earlier that, under the EC conception of equal treatment, equality has two dimensions: treating likes alike, and treating differences differently. Failure to treat likes alike, or treating different situations the same are both breaches of the equal treatment principle, unless there are objective justifications demonstrated. **11.152**

(i) Treating likes alike: direct discrimination and equal pay

The approach that has been taken in legislation has been to include a prohibition of direct discrimination, which reflects the requirement that likes should be treated alike. A similar formula is used in the RRA and the SDA to describe direct discrimination: the treatment of a person on the grounds of a prohibited characteristic less favourably than another person. The Race Directive and the Framework Directive prohibit direct discrimination. This 'shall be taken to occur where one person is treated less favourably than another is, has been or would be treated' on the prohibited grounds. The RRA provides that segregation on the **11.153**

---

[314] *Abdulaziz v UK* Series A No 94 (1985) EHRR 471 at [90]–[91]; *Smith and Grady v UK* (2000) 29 EHRR 493 at [120]–[121].
[315] *Abdulaziz v UK* Series A No 94 (1985) EHRR 471 at [90]–[91].
[316] *Smith and Grady v UK* (2000) 29 EHRR 493 at [121].
[317] ibid at [120]. See also *Cyprus v Turkey* Application No 25781/94 (2002) 35 EHRR 30 at [302]–[311] (Greek Cypriots in Northern Cyprus subjected to discrimination amounting to degrading treatment).

basis of race constitutes direct discrimination for the purposes of the Act. There is no equivalent inclusion of a prohibition of segregation in any of the other anti-discrimination legislation.

11.154 A somewhat different approach is taken in the equal pay context. Equal pay legislation does not use the terms direct and indirect discrimination and a somewhat specialized conceptual scheme is established. The legislation provides for equal pay between men and women by giving a woman (or a man) the right to equality in the terms of her (his) contract of employment where she (he) is employed on like work to that of a man, or work rated as equivalent to that of a man, or work of equal value to that of a man. Any term of the woman's contract that is less favourable to her than the same term in the man's contract is improved so that they are equal. European law has also taken the concept of 'equal pay for work of equal value' to require an equal pay comparison between a man and a woman even where they are not doing the same, or similar jobs, but where they are said to be doing work of equal *value*, as measured under an analytical job-evaluation approach. This has allowed equal pay litigation to tackle such notorious problems as the under-valuation of women in female-dominated workforces, but problems of comparison have meant that it has been less effective in challenging the segregation of the labour market than is necessary.[318]

(ii) Differing domestic and EC approaches to 'treating differences differently'

11.155 The legislative approach taken to the requirement to treat differences differently has given rise to a set of additional approaches. Four approaches have been adopted to the problem of how to identify the criteria of difference that mean that different treatment should be accorded. These are: the development of the concept of indirect discrimination, the development of pregnancy discrimination, the development of the concept of 'reasonable accommodation' in disability discrimination law, and the development of positive action as lawful in limited circumstances where it would otherwise breach the prohibition of direct discrimination. These constitute, at least to some extent, somewhat different approaches to 'treating differences differently'. Where indirect discrimination has been established, in practice a respondent is required to alter the discriminatory practice for all comers. In the context of pregnancy, an approach is taken concentrating on permitting the pregnant woman to be treated differently, rather than generalizing the treatment that is accorded her to everyone else. Where the absence of a 'reasonable adjustment' in the disability context is established, the respondent is not required to alter the approach for everyone either, but only for the person adversely affected by that practice. Under positive action, the approach is to focus on the need to modify certain requirements only for members of the disadvantaged group. Each of these will be examined in turn.

---

[318] Case 170/84 *Bilka-Kaufhaus GmbH v Weber von Hartz* [1986] ECR 1607.

Development of indirect discrimination.   Considerable academic attention has   **11.156**
been given in several jurisdictions to explaining why the change from legislation
being concerned only with direct discrimination to being concerned with both
direct and indirect discrimination occurred. Without seeking to enter that debate
too deeply, we can identify several features of the approach to the definition
of direct discrimination that appear to have played a part in leading to the legislative development of indirect discrimination.

First, 'direct discrimination' in the British anti-discrimination legislative scheme   **11.157**
was, at least initially, largely confined to what might loosely be called 'intentional
discrimination'. (It was not until *James v Eastleigh BC*[319] that the concept of direct
discrimination was clearly interpreted as involving the broader 'but for' test, in
which attention is given, not to the intention of the perpetrator, but the causal
link between the action challenged and the protected characteristic, such as race
or gender.)

Secondly, the circumstances in which discrimination was unlawful were closely   **11.158**
defined legislatively. Most of the legislative scheme was taken up with identifying
the circumstances (such as employment relations, provision of goods and services,
etc) in which 'discrimination' was lawful or unlawful. There was no general self-
standing prohibition of discrimination; it was always linked to particular social
situations.

Thirdly, and crucially, the grounds on which discrimination was prohibited were   **11.159**
also narrow, and specifically identified as a closed list of categories. Initially, they
included only colour, race, and ethnic or national origin. As with the second feature identified previously, this meant that the prohibition was not a generalized
non-discrimination standard, but rather one that related to discrimination only
on some particular grounds, and in particular circumstances. All in all, the concept of direct discrimination, originally conceived, appeared a limited legislative
intervention to deal with particular perceived social problems, rather than an attempt to stake out a general principle of equality.

The direct discrimination model was prone to two problems: first, considerable   **11.160**
problems of proof of discrimination on these limited grounds were identified, with
perpetrators arguing, for example, that it was not on the grounds of 'race' that the
discrimination occurred, it was on some other grounds (for example, on the
grounds of religion, then a non-included ground); secondly, the social problems
that the discrimination legislation attempted to tackle proved more intractable
than had been supposed, leading to reconsideration whether an emphasis on those
with bad intentions was any longer appropriate in a situation where empirical evidence demonstrated that exclusion was as often institutional as personal.

---

[319] [1990] 2 AC 751, HL.

11.161   The features of the concept of direct discrimination came to be seen as too limiting to address the particular perceived social problems. Of the three features of direct discrimination identified, only one was substantially modified, however, that relating to 'intention'. The essence of the concept of indirect discrimination was the need to justify adverse effects, irrespective of the intention of the perpetrator. The introduction of the concept of indirect discrimination did not involve substantial change in either the second or the third features. The approach of adopting a closed list of circumstances (employment, etc) was retained. The approach of adopting a closed list of categories (race, etc) was also retained. Indeed, retention of these two features might be seen to have facilitated putting into operation the concept of indirect discrimination, because they limited the circumstances in which the need to justify adverse effects would legally arise.

11.162   **Meaning of indirect discrimination.**   Indirect discrimination arises for the purposes of the RRA where a 'requirement or condition' can be complied with only by a considerably smaller proportion of one group than another, where it is to the detriment of the person indirectly discriminated against because he or she cannot comply with it, and where it cannot be shown to be justifiable. The definition of indirect discrimination for the purposes of the SDA is somewhat different. The DDA does not include a prohibition of indirect discrimination. The Race and Framework Directives prohibit indirect discrimination. This occurs 'where an apparently neutral provision, criterion or practice would put persons (of racial or ethnic origin) (having a particular religion or belief, a particular disability, a particular age, or a particular sexual orientation) at a particular disadvantage compared with other persons, unless that provision criterion or practice is objectively justified by a legitimate aim and the means of achieving that aim are appropriate and necessary . . .'.

11.163   The adoption of the concept of indirect discrimination had two important consequences. First, it shifts attention from the perpetrator to the victim, and reduces the opportunities for techniques to be adopted to avoid successful challenge if the respondent was engaged in direct discrimination. Secondly, it shifted attention from the victim conceived as an individual to the victim conceived as part of a larger social group. Legally, these developments meant that an 'objective' view had to be taken by the courts and tribunals as to what the relevant social group consisted of, rather than being satisfied to rely on the perpetrator's subjective view of the social group which was all that was necessary in the context of direct discrimination.

11.164   Both direct and indirect discrimination involve a comparative exercise, as would be expected since 'to discriminate' in everyday language involves a preference for one thing over another, an essentially comparative approach. The comparisons involved in direct and indirect discrimination are, however, somewhat different in particular respects. First, as we have seen, the concept of direct discrimination, as originally conceived, involved the comparison that the perpetrator drew (or would have drawn) between one person and another on the basis of the *perpetrator's* view of the individual's race or gender. In the context of indirect discrimination, the comparison is, rather, between the effect of the requirement or condition on two (or more) *objectively* defined social groups. Secondly, whereas the approach to comparison in direct discrimination did not (at least at first) appear to be particularly problematic (the problem was, rather, with securing convincing evidence of the perpetrator's intention), the approach to comparison in indirect discrimination became a central issue, particularly in defining the group adversely affected and the comparator group less adversely affected. What constituted the relevant comparator groups gives rise to considerable dispute.

A final, crucial, contrast between direct and indirect discrimination is the approach taken to justification. In the context of direct discrimination, the approach taken in drafting the legislation is to specify as precisely as possible the particular situations in which direct discrimination is not unlawful by way of detailed exceptions.[320] In indirect discrimination, however, the possible justifications for adopting a condition or requirement that has an adverse effect on particular groups are next to impossible to list comprehensively. The alternative approach, then, was to draft a general justification provision allowing the user of the challenged requirement or condition to show that it was nevertheless 'justified'. This generalized justification approach was not adopted with regard to direct discrimination. **11.165**

Crucially, the British statutory approach to legislating anti-discrimination requirements was the one chosen in the EC context in secondary legislation when prohibitions of sex discrimination, and (much later) race and other forms of discrimination were adopted. Importantly, the list of categories of the grounds of prohibited discrimination was closed. Equally crucially, the ECJ (and subsequently the legislature) adopted the concepts of direct and indirect discrimination. **11.166**

The concept of indirect discrimination enables challenges to be made to practices or policies which, although apparently non-discriminatory between men and women, in fact have a greater adverse effect on individuals of one sex than of the other. Where such a differential impact is established, then it is for the person seeking to use such a policy or practice to justify it on acceptable grounds, and **11.167**

---

[320] But see DDA 1995, s 5(1)(b) and (4), where a general justification defence is available; Part-Time Workers (Prevention of Less Favourable Treatment) Regulations 2000, SI 2000/1551, reg 5(2)(b); Fixed-Term Employees (Prevention of Less Favourable Treatment) Regulations 2002, SI 2002/2034. See, in general, John Bowers and Elena Moran, 'Justification in Direct Sex Discrimination Law: Breaking the Taboo' (2002) 31 ILJ 307.

general assumptions or assertions of the contested policy's utility will not be enough. So, for example, there has been much litigation contesting differential treatment between part-time and full-time workers, in many cases leading to decisions striking down adverse treatment of part-time workers as indirectly discriminatory against women because in practice part-time workers in several member states are mostly women.[321] Although deriving from the American judicial interpretation of the statutory prohibitions of discrimination in employment, the approach now applicable in English law goes somewhat further than the US Supreme Court, allowing the concept of indirect discrimination to be used to contest legislative as well as employer-originated policies,[322] and indirect discrimination deriving from a provision in a collective agreement.[323]

11.168 The reach of indirect discrimination is limited by the development of the concept of 'justification'. The courts have interpreted this to allow arguments to be developed justifying unequal pay, or policies with an adverse impact, on the basis that one group was better organized than another, or on the basis that one group was more competitive in the market place than another.[324] On other occasions, the courts have held that a particular trend of decision should be limited to prevent it interfering in a sphere of social policy it considers to be legitimately left to government. We can see examples of this in some of the decisions upholding 'justifications' advanced for social security legislation alleged to be indirectly discriminatory.[325] The approach of the ECJ in the *Megner* case illustrates this.[326] The Court observed that, in the current state of EC law, social policy is a matter for the member states. 'Consequently, it is for the member states to choose the measures capable of achieving the aim of their social and employment policy. In exercising

---

[321] See Case 170/84 *Bilka-Kaufhaus GmbH v Karin Weber von Hartz* [1986] ECR 1607; Case C-243/95 *Hill v Revenue Commissioners* [1998] ECR I-3739; Case C-1/95 *Gerster v Freistaat Bayern* [1997] ECR I-5253; Case C-100/95 *Kording v Senator Fur Finanze* [1997] ECR I-5289; Case C-309/97 *Angestelltenbetriebsrat der Weiner Gebietskrankenkasse v Weiner Gebietskrankenkasse* [1999] ECR I-2865.

[322] See Case C-355/93 *Enderby v Frenchay Health Authority and Secretary of State for Health* [1993] ECR 673; Case C-400/93 *Dansk Industri* [1995] ECR I-1275.

[323] See Case C-317/93 *Nolte v Landesver-sicherungsanstalt Hannover* [1995] ECR I-4625; Case C-444/93 *Megner and Sheffel v Innungskrankenkasse Vorderpfalz* [1995] ECR I-4741; Case C-8/94 *Laperre v Bestvurcommissie Brevepsazken in de Provincie Zuid-Holland* [1996] ECR I-273; Case C-280/94 *Van Damme and Ozturk* [1996] ECR I-625; Case C-167/97 *Seymour-Smith and Perez* [1996] ECR I-623.

[324] Case 96/80 *Jenkins v Kingsgate (Clothing Productions) Ltd* [1981] ECR 911; Case 170/84 *Bilka-Kaufhaus GmbH v Karin Weber von Hartz* [1986] ECR 1607; Case C-355/93 *Enderby v Frenchay Health Authority and Secretary of State for Health* [1993] ECR 673; *Mandate v Penneys* [1999] ELR 89.

[325] Case C-317/93 *Nolte v Landesver-sicherungsanstalt Hannover* [1995] ECR I-4625; Case C-444/93 *Megner and Sheffel v Innungskrankenkasse Vorderpfalz* [1995] ECR I-4741; Case C-8/94 *Laperre v Bestvurcommissie Brevepsazken in de Provincie Zuid-Holland* [1996] ECR I-273; Case C-280/94 *Van Damme and Ozturk* [1996] ECR I-625.

[326] ibid.

that competence, the member states have a broad margin of discretion.' The Court continued: 'It should be noted that the social and employment policy aim relied on by the German Government is objectively unrelated to any discrimination on grounds of sex and that, in exercising its competence, the national legislature was reasonably entitled to consider that the legislation in question was necessary in order to achieve that aim.' This appears closer to the first meaning of equality.

Pregnancy discrimination. In the context of the third meaning of equality, the requirement to treat different situations differently is illustrated by the approach of the ECJ in *Brown v Rentokil Ltd*,[327] dealing with the lawfulness under EC law of dismissing a pregnant worker. After holding that '[i]t is well settled that discrimination involves the application of different rules to comparable situations or the application of the same rule to different situations',[328] the Court went on to hold that: 'Where it is relied on to dismiss a pregnant worker because of absences due to incapacity for work resulting from her pregnancy, such a contractual term, applying both to men and to women, is applied in the same way to different situations since, as is clear from the answer given to the first part of the first question, the situation of a pregnant worker who is unfit for work as a result of disorders associated with her pregnancy cannot be considered to be the same as that of a male worker who is ill and absent through incapacity for work for the same length of time'.[329]   **11.169**

Reasonable adjustment. The DDA, as well as prohibiting direct discrimination, provides that discrimination occurs as the result of an unjustified failure to comply with the duty of reasonable adjustment in relation to both employment and the provision of goods, facilities and services. Examples are given of what this might mean in practice in the case of employment. Subordinate legislation may define further what would be required for reasonable adjustment. How should we regard such provisions? Waddington regards the duty of reasonable adjustment in the Framework Directive as a 'third and separate form of discrimination, and aside from direct and indirect discrimination'.[330] In American academic discussions on the equivalent provisions in US law, Jolls argues that a sharp distinction between   **11.170**

---

[327] Case C-394/96 [1998] ECR I-4185.
[328] ibid at [30], citing Case C-342/93 *Gillespie v Northern Health and Social Services Board* [1996] ECR I-475 at [16].
[329] ibid at [31].
[330] L Waddington, 'Art 13 EC: Setting Priorities in the Proposal for a Horizontal Employment Directive' (2000) 29 ILJ 176, 178. See also R Whittle, 'The Concept of Disability Discrimination and its Legal Construction' (paper delivered to workshop organized by the Swedish National Institute for Working Life on *Discrimination and affirmative action on the labour market—legal perspectives*, Brussels, 6–7 November 2000) 12; P Skidmore, 'EC Framework Directive on Equal Treatment in Employment: Towards a Comprehensive Community Anti-Discrimination Policy?' (2001) 30 ILJ 126, 129.

the two legal forms is overblown as the two forms of legal intervention share many of the same characteristics.[331] They have the same sorts of economic consequences, and the parallels between the two are particularly strong when indirect discrimination is included within the scope of the core idea of the anti-discrimination principle. Kelman sees both as currently operating in existing anti-discrimination law, but views them as importantly distinct.[332] He contrasts a norm against 'simple discrimination' from a norm requiring 'accommodation'. The first, he argues, provides victims with a fairly strong right to be free from such treatment, while those seeking to benefit from accommodation mandates have the ability to claim to receive treatment that disregards some costs to the provider of that treatment. This claim is a *distributive* claim, meaning that those seeking accommodation are making claims to scarce resources that others are in competition for, and that it is a prima facie claim, meaning that the person only has the right to be accommodated provided the demands are not 'unreasonable'. Others argue,[333] however, that accommodation requirements are fundamentally distinct from anti-discrimination law traditionally conceived. Issacharoff and Nelson analyse the Americans With Disabilities Act and conclude that it is not just another anti-discrimination statute.[334] The failure to recognize this and provide a clearer and more workable set of directives as to how much redistribution is appropriate under the accommodation mandates provision of the statute has led to considerable difficulties of interpretation for the courts, which are essentially incapable of making the judgments required. It remains to be seen to what extent these issues cause problems for British courts.

11.171   **Positive action and unlawful discrimination.**   The RRA and the SDA both provide for limited positive action measures that may be taken, primarily in the employment context. Gender specific training, and race specific training are permitted in so far as the legislation permits the provision of training or encouragement confined to women or to men, or to persons of a particular racial group, to help fit them for, or to avail themselves of, the opportunities for doing particular work from which, when compared with the proportion of that group in the general population, or in a particular area, they have been either absent or under-represented in the previous 12 months. The provision of training or encouragement confined to a particular under-represented gender or racial group among

---

[331] C Jolls, 'Accommodation Mandates and Antidiscrimination Law' (2000) 53 *Stanford L Rev* 223.

[332] M Kelman, 'Market Discrimination and Groups', *Stanford Public Law and Legal Theory Working Paper Series No 8* (February 2000).

[333] P Karlen and G Rutherglen, 'Disabilities, Discrimination, and Reasonable Accommodation' (1996) 46 Duke LJ 1.

[334] S Issacharoff and J Nelson, 'Discrimination with a Difference: Can Employment Discrimination Law Accommodate the American With Disabilities Act?' (2001) 79 North Carolina L Rev 307.

employees and officials of a trade union, employers association, or trade or professional association is also permitted. The RRA also permits any act to afford persons of a particular racial group access to facilities or services to meet their special needs in regard to education, training or welfare, or any ancillary benefits. The Race and Framework Directives provide that the principle of equal treatment shall not prevent a member state from taking specific measures 'to prevent or compensate for disadvantages linked to [the grounds covered by the directives]'. Such action is permitted, not required. The objective of permitting these measures is 'ensuring full equality'.

Most recently, the Sex Discrimination (Election Candidates) Act 2002 enables political parties, if they wish, to adopt positive measures to reduce inequality in the numbers of men and women elected as representatives of their party, providing that such positive action is not unlawful sex discrimination. The legislation covers elections to the House of Commons, the Scottish Parliament, the National Assembly for Wales, the Northern Ireland Assembly, the European Parliament and local government elections (excluding directly elected mayors and community councils in Scotland.) The Act has a 'sunset clause' that would cause the provisions to expire at the end of 2015.   **11.172**

The ECJ has also recognized that to achieve equality of opportunity between women and men it will be necessary on occasion to go beyond the eradication of discrimination, and that positive action may be appropriate even where it results in the preferential treatment of the formerly disadvantaged group. Crucially, the ECJ seems to accept the importance of permitting member states the discretion to take positive action to redress the societal discrimination which women (in particular) face, in order to lead to genuine equality of opportunity in the future, although the exact parameters of when this is permissible and within what constraints are the subject of continuing consideration by the Court.[335]   **11.173**

(iii) Article 14 ECHR and treating differences differently

Basic approach.   In our consideration of Article 14 ECHR previously, we considered situations where complainants argue that they have been treated differently from those similarly situated. What of the situation where the complainant argues that he or she has been treated the same, but he or she should have been   **11.174**

---

[335] Case C-450/93 *Kalanke v Freie Hansestadt Bremen* [1995] ECR I-3051; Case C-409/95 *Marschall v Land Nordrhein-Westfalen* [1997] ECR I-6363; Case C-158/97 *Re Badeck's Application* [2000] ECR I-1875; Case C-407/98 *Abrahamsson v Fogelqvist* [2000] ECR I-5539; Case C-476/99 *Lommers v Minister van Landbouw Natuurbeheer en Visserij* [2002] IRLR 430. See further, D Schiek, 'Positive Action before the European Court of Justice—New Conceptions of Equality in Community Law? From Kalanke and Marschall to Badeck' (2000) 16 Int J of Comparative Labour L and Industrial Relations 251.

treated differently? A similar approach to that adopted in EC law is now identifiable in the Article 14 jurisprudence of the ECtHR, where both facets of the equality principle have now found support. It is, however, most often in the context of what we have termed 'status-harms' that the concept of equality requiring differences to be treated differently commonly arises in the Article 14 context.

11.175   The ECtHR has appeared to take somewhat different approaches over the course of its history, with two (arguably inconsistent) strands of case law being apparent. In one strand of the jurisprudence, in *Abdulaziz*,[336] the ECtHR rejected claims of discrimination based on an argument that immigration restrictions that had the effect of disadvantaging one racial group more than another amounted to racial discrimination. The Court appears to have adopted an approach to the meaning of discrimination under Article 14 that concentrates on the intention of the state, rather than the effect of the policy. On the basis of this case, commentators concluded that there was no claim available for indirect discrimination under Article 14.[337]

11.176   However, in another, more recent, strand of the case law, in *Thlimmenos v Greece*,[338] the applicant had been prevented from becoming a chartered accountant because he had been convicted of the offence of refusing to wear a military uniform. His refusal had been on the ground that he was a Jehovah's Witness. He complained that the law excluding persons convicted of such offences from appointment as chartered accountants did not distinguish between persons convicted as a result of their religious beliefs and persons convicted on other grounds. The ECtHR held that Article 14 was engaged and that Greece violated his right not to be discriminated against in the enjoyment of his right under Article 9 ECHR by failing to introduce appropriate exceptions to the rule barring persons convicted of a felony from the profession of chartered accountants. After noting that '[t]he court has so far considered that the right under art 14 not to be discriminated against in the enjoyment of the rights guaranteed under the convention is violated when states treat differently persons in analogous situations without providing an objective and reasonable justification', the Court went on to hold 'that this is not the only facet of the prohibition of discrimination in art 14. The right not to be discriminated against in the enjoyment of the rights guaranteed under the convention is also violated when states without an objective and reasonable justification fail to treat differently persons whose situations are significantly different.'

11.177   The full implications of this aspect of the case have yet to be fully explored; so far, although the ECtHR has reiterated the legitimacy of the approach adopted in

---

[336] *Abdulaziz v UK* Series A No 94 (1985) EHRR 471.
[337] Fredman (n 7 above) thinks not, citing *Abdulaziz*.
[338] Application 34369/97 (2001) 31 EHRR 15.

Thlimmenos,[339] few complaints based on this approach have been accepted by the Court.[340]

Indirect discrimination?   There is currently some discussion in domestic courts   **11.178**
as to how far the approach adopted by the ECtHR coincides with the 'indirect discrimination' test adopted in EC and domestic law. It is currently unclear to what
extent the ECtHR currently understands the concept of discrimination to encompass 'indirect discrimination', and with it the more technical aspects of 'comparators' and 'differential impact'. The issue has been raised in several UK cases of
whether ECtHR jurisprudence has a concept of indirect discrimination. In *R (on
the application of L (a child)) v Manchester City Council*[341] it was held that Article
14 'extends both to direct discrimination, that is discrimination which is directed
at the status of the victim, and to indirect discrimination, that which has a disproportionate effect on a particular group'. Lord Carswell CJ, in the Northern
Ireland Court of Appeal, has taken a more cautious approach. He was 'willing to
assume . . . that Article 14 prohibits indirect discrimination as well as direct discrimination, though we shall reserve our opinion on the point'.[342]

However, there is more extensive discussion in *R (on the application of S) v Chief*   **11.179**
Constable of South Yorkshire that is relevant to the issue.[343] The police had taken
fingerprints and DNA samples from the claimants after they had been arrested
and charged for certain offences. The Criminal Justice and Police Act 2001 empowered the police to retain these samples even after one claimant was acquitted
and the proceedings against the other claimant were discontinued, and the police
did in fact retain these samples. The claimants alleged that the retention infringed
their rights under Article 8 (protection of family life) and Article 14 read with
Article 8. As regards the Article 14 claim, the claimants argued that the retention
of the samples discriminated against them in comparison with other innocent
persons. They were therefore being discriminated against on the basis of their status of having been acquitted. The Court of Appeal held that the retention of the
samples was compatible with Articles 8 and 14 ECHR. Once fingerprints and
samples had been lawfully obtained, there was a clear objective distinction between individuals from whom such samples had been taken and individuals from
whom they had not been taken.

---

[339] But see *Fretté v France* Application 36515/97 [2003] 2 FCR 39, partly concurring opinion of
Judge Costa, joined by Judges Jungwiert and Traja: 'although in the Thlimmenos case, in which I sat,
the Court reached a unanimous decision, I do wonder whether it may have gone a little far on that
occasion, and I note that the judgment was delivered before the opening for signature of Protocol
No. 12—which I view as a key factor'.

[340] See *Coster v UK* Application 24876/94 (2001) 33 EHRR 20; *Chapman v UK* Application
27238/95 (2001) 33 EHRR 18; *Beard v UK* Application 24882/94 (2001) 33 EHRR 19.

[341] [2001] EWHC Admin 707; [2002] 1 FLR 43.

[342] *Re Applications by Noel Anderson and others for Judicial Review* (CA, NI).

[343] [2002] EWCA Civ 1275; [2002] 1 WLR 3223.

11.180   An issue arose between Waller LJ and Sedley LJ which is relevant to the issue of indirect discrimination under Article 14. In the course of his judgment, Waller LJ held that the way the claimants had identified the appropriate comparator was incorrect. Rather than the comparison being among those who were innocent, the comparison should have been seen as involving only persons from whom samples had been lawfully taken. 'Those persons are being treated alike and there is thus in my view no breach of art. 14.'[344] Sedley LJ, on the other hand, disagreed. For him, to 'confine the pool for testing its effect to other people in the identical position, as Waller LJ would do, and to conclude—inexorably—that they are all being treated alike' was incorrect. It is at this point that the issue of indirect discrimination arises, for Sedley LJ introduces the concept to demonstrate that a wider pool of comparison than that adopted by Waller LJ is appropriate. He argues that '[t]o take as your pool simply the group which asserts that it is being discriminated against and to find—as you practically always will—that they are all being treated the same is to defeat the rationale of indirect discrimination'.[345]

11.181   The relevance of the case for the purpose of this discussion lies not in the issue of pools of comparison (for Sedley LJ a central issue) but rather the assumption that indirect discrimination is a relevant issue in the context of Article 14 at all. In his judgment,[346] he drew on the concept of discrimination adopted in the EC and UK statutory contexts to derive the contours of a concept of indirect discrimination in the Article 14 context: 'There is a logical and consistent concept of indirect discrimination in the statutory formula contained in s.1(1)(b) of the SDA 1975 and s.1(1)(b) of the RRA 1976. It reappears, with adaptations, in the DDA 1995. It was derived from the exegetic concept of indirect discrimination developed by the United States Supreme Court in Griggs v Duke Power Co, 28 L.Ed.2d 158 (1971). It corresponds closely with the jurisprudence of the European Court of Justice (initially in relation to the free movement of goods: Ruhr v ECSC [1957] ECR 011; subsequently across the board in relation to gender equality); with a series of EU Council directives, including the recent Race Directive (2000/78/EC); and with the jurisprudence of the ECtHR (Belgian Linguistics Case (No.2) (1979–80) 1 EHRR 252). It is therefore of real importance that this court should not adopt a deviant approach [to the interpretation of Article 14, presumably].'

11.182   To the extent that a similar concept is used in similar contexts, they should be interpreted similarly, and so far as Sedley LJ's judgment was primarily about the appropriate approach to be taken to indirect discrimination, understandable. However, his understanding that indirect discrimination is part of the meaning of

---

[344] *R (on the application of S) v Chief Constable of South Yorkshire* (n 343 above), at [65].
[345] ibid at [91].
[346] ibid at [89].

Article 14 is more controversial. If the purpose of introducing the concept of indirect discrimination into the interpretation of Article 14 is to ensure that differences are treated differently, other approaches are also available.

Reasonable accommodation?   An alternative approach, for example, which is   **11.183**
closer to a 'reasonable accommodation' approach was adopted in *Clarke v
Secretary of State for Transport, Local Government and the Regions,*[347] Burton J held
that it was contrary to Article 14 read with Article 8 for a planning inspector to
take into account a 'gypsy's' refusal of conventional accommodation (on the
ground that his cultural identity was based on an itinerant lifestyle) in refusing to
overturn a local council decision to refuse him planning permission to use certain
land as a site on which to station a caravan for residential use. The availability of
'unsuitable' accommodation would not usually be taken into account in refusal of
planning permission. In failing to adopt a concept of unsuitability that included
the gypsy's cultural identity as itinerant, the inspector discriminated against the
gypsy.

In the domestic litigation in *Pretty*, Lord Hope held that the claimant 'can reason-   **11.184**
ably claim that her physical situation is significantly different from that of others
who wish to commit suicide, as she cannot take her own life without another person's assistance'[348] and appeared to agree that this could have provided the basis for
a challenge under Article 14 if another article had been engaged (which it was
not). Emerging from these cases, we can identify a looser, less technical approach
to understanding the requirement to treat differences differently in the context of
Article 14 interpretation than that which might emerge if the technicalities of the
domestic and European 'indirect discrimination' test were to be adopted in full.

Positive action.   Apart from the constraints of EC law, as discussed, there may   **11.185**
also be constraints on positive action arising from the ECHR. The Northern
Ireland High Court has, however, considered that there was an objective justification for a system of quotas in favour of Catholics in filling positions in the
Northern Ireland police force, giving a broad margin of discretion to domestic authorities in deciding whether such measures are necessary.[349] In upholding the
challenged provision under the HRA, Kerr J gave a detailed judgment concentrating on the issue of whether there was an objective justification for the measures.

> The need to correct the imbalance in the police force was undeniable. That had been
> recognised for a long time but earlier attempts to deal with it had foundered. It can-
> not seriously be disputed that a police force should be representative of the commu-
> nity that it serves . . . As to the proportionality of the provision it is significant that

---

[347] [2001] EWHC Admin 800; The Times, 9 November 2001.
[348] *R (on the application of Pretty) v DPP* [2001] UKHL 61; [2002] 1 AC 800 at [105].
[349] *Re Parsons' Application for Judicial Review* [2002] NI 378 at [34]–[35].

(i) various other initiatives have failed in the past; and (ii) no alternative method of achieving the aim could be suggested by the applicant. It is also of considerable importance that the measure was so firmly supported by the Equality Commission. Moreover all candidates must achieve a minimum standard of suitability and there is no reason to suppose that the calibre of police officer recruited in the way proposed by the legislation will be anything less than appropriate. Finally, the temporary nature of the arrangements and the opportunity to review them speak strongly in favour of the proposition that they are proportionate to the aim that they seek to fulfil.

(h) Conclusion

11.186 In several ways, the third category of discrimination and equality is more complex than the first and second categories discussed previously, and this greater complexity has resulted in the emergence of legal issues that are so far relatively underdeveloped in the context of discussions about the other categories. The development of EC legislation applying this third category to a wider set of grounds, and the need to interpret the HRA 1998 in the context of already existing anti-discrimination law, is likely to ensure that the third category remains the most complex meaning for some time to come.

(4) *Public Authorities and Duties to Promote Equality of Opportunity*

(a) Introduction

11.187 In the fourth meaning, entirely the creation of domestic statute and EC law so far, certain public authorities are placed under a duty actively to take steps to promote greater equality of opportunity (the legal meaning of which is yet to be fully articulated) for particular groups. The concept of 'equality of opportunity' goes beyond any of the concepts of discrimination characteristic of the previous meanings and involves not only a duty on the public authority to eliminate discrimination from its activities, which is seen as merely one example of where equality of opportunity is denied, but actively to take steps to promote greater equality of opportunity through its activities. Under this approach, a public authority to which this duty applies is under a duty to do more than ensure the absence of discrimination from its employment, educational, and other specified functions, but also to act positively to promote equality of opportunity between different groups throughout all policy-making and in carrying out all those activities to which the duty applies.

(b) Common law

11.188 Not only did the common law not oblige public authorities actively to promote equality in this way, it placed some limits in the way of particular authorities that chose to do so. In general, public authorities are prevented from doing anything not specifically authorized, particularly where it may be in tension with other more specific obligations. Several of the cases limiting local authorities' activities, discussed above, demonstrate this. So, more recently, do those cases considering how far the pursuit of ethical policies may be lawfully pursued by a local authority. In *Ex p Fewings*,[350] for example, a local authority sought to ban hunting on common land appropriated by the authority. It was held that the powers of the authority over the land were not wide enough to permit the decision. It is unclear how far these restrictions would be held to constrain public authorities from promoting equality of opportunity without statutory authorization and support.

(c) Local authority statutory duty

Some indications are given, however, in several cases dealing with an early (less elaborate) predecessor to the general public sector duty relating to racial equality (see below), which was imposed on local authorities by the RRA 1976. Section 71 provided that '[w]ithout prejudice to their obligation to comply with any other provision of this Act, it shall be the duty of every local authority to make appropriate arrangements with a view to securing that their various functions are carried out with due regard to the need (a) to eliminate unlawful racial discrimination and (b) to promote equality of opportunity, and good relations between persons of different racial groups'. **11.189**

In *Wheeler v Leicester City Council*,[351] the council banned a rugby football club from using city recreation grounds for 12 months for its failure to take sufficient action to persuade its members not to play in South Africa, then enforcing a policy of apartheid. The House of Lords held that the council had power under s 71 to consider the best interests of race relations when exercising its statutory discretion in the management of the recreation ground. However, in the absence of any infringement of the law or any improper conduct by the club, the ban was unreasonable, and a misuse of its statutory powers. However, Lord Roskill, delivering the leading speech, rejected the argument put forward on behalf of the club members that s 71 should be given a narrow construction so that its effect would be limited to the actions of the council as regards its own internal behaviour only. **11.190**

In *R v Lewisham LBC, ex p Shell UK Ltd*,[352] it was held, on the basis of *Wheeler*, that 'though the scope of s. 71 of the 1976 Act is wide and embraces all the activities of the council, a council cannot use its statutory powers in order to punish a body or person who has done nothing contrary to English law'.[353] The court held, given the multi-racial character of the borough, that the duty permitted the council to decide **11.191**

---

[350] *R v Somerset CC, ex p Fewings* [1995] 1 WLR 1037. See also *R v Liverpool City Council, ex p Secretary of State for Employment* [1989] COD 404 (imposing certain conditions on receipt of grants unlawful).
[351] [1985] AC 1054.
[352] [1988] 1 All ER 938.
[353] *per* Neill LJ.

that trade with a particular company should cease because of that company's links with South Africa. However, since the purpose of the boycott of the company by the council was broader, exerting pressure to sever all trading links between the company and South Africa, and was not therefore restricted to a wish to impose race relations in the borough, the actions of the council were unlawful.

(d) General equality duties for specific public bodies

11.192   In some cases, legislation applying to specific public authorities imposes a broad duty of equality of opportunity applying to several different groups. The Broadcasting Act 1990, for example, provides that certain television and sound broadcasting licences shall include conditions requiring the licence holder 'to make arrangements for promoting, in relation to employment by him, equality of opportunity between men and women and between different racial groups'.[354] The Greater London Authority is required to 'make appropriate arrangements with a view to securing that' in the exercise of its powers, in the formulation of its policies and proposals, and in their implementation, 'there is due regard to the principle that there should be equality of opportunity for all people'.[355] In addition, the Greater London Authority Act 1999 places the Greater London Authority, the Metropolitan Police Authority, and the London Fire and Emergency Planning Authority under a duty, in exercising their functions, 'to have regard to the need 'to promote equality of opportunity for all persons irrespective of their race, sex, disability, age, sexual orientation or religion', 'to eliminate unlawful discrimination', and 'to promote good relations between persons of different racial groups, religious beliefs and sexual orientation'.[356] The Learning and Skills Council for England is required, in exercising its functions, to 'have due regard to the need to promote equality of opportunity between persons of different racial groups, between men and women, and between persons who are disabled and persons who are not'.[357] Child-care providers need to provide information on their commitment to equality of opportunity.[358] The members of particular public bodies are under specific personal obligations to 'carry out their duties and responsibilities with due regard to the need to promote equality of opportunity for all people, regardless of their gender, race, disability, sexual orientation, age or religion, and show respect and consideration for others'.[359]

---

[354] Broadcasting Act 1990, ss 34, 38, and 68.
[355] Greater London Authority Act 1999, s 33.
[356] ibid s 404.
[357] Learning and Skills Act 2000, s 14.
[358] Tax Credit (New Category of Child Care Provider) Regulations 2002, SI 2002/1417, Sch 2, Pt I, para 1.
[359] Conduct of Members (Principles) (Wales) Order 2001, SI 2001/2276, Sch, para 7; Conduct of Members (Model Code of Conduct) (Wales) Order 2001, SI 2001/2289, Sch, Pt II, para 4; Local Government Act 2000 (Model Code of Conduct) (Amendment) Order 2002, SI 2002/1719; Relevant Authorities (General Principles) Order 2001, SI 2001/1401, Sch, para 7; Local Authorities

(e) Race Relations (Amendment) Act 2000 duty to promote equality of opportunity

In other cases, there is an equivalent duty applying to a wide group of public au-   **11.193**
thorities, but with the narrower focus of only applying in the racial context. In
particular, the Race Relations (Amendment) Act 2000 requires that each of a
specified list of public bodies must, in carrying out its functions, have due regard
to the need to eliminate unlawful racial discrimination; and to promote equality
of opportunity and good relations between persons of different racial groups.[360]

(i) Application to the public sector

These positive duties apply only to public sector bodies and not, unlike many as-   **11.194**
pects of the way in which the third meaning of equality is put into operation, to
the public and private sectors. This is not to say that a similar approach might not
be adopted for the private sector (the 'fair participation' duty of employers under
the Fair Employment and Treatment (Northern Ireland) Order 1998 has some
similarity), and this has been recommended, but at the time of writing there is no
equivalent private sector duty applicable in England.

The public authorities subject to these statutory duties include ministers of the   **11.195**
Crown and government departments (not including the Security Service, the
Intelligence Service or the Government Communications Headquarters); the
National Assembly for Wales and Assembly subsidiaries; the armed forces; health
authorities; special health authorities; primary care trusts; National Health
Service trusts; local authorities, the Greater London Authority; the Common
Council of the City of London in its capacity as a local authority or port health au-
thority; the Sub-Treasurer of the Inner Temple or the Under-Treasurer of the
Middle Temple, in his capacity as a local authority; the Council of the Isles of
Scilly; parish meetings; charter trustees; fire authorities; waste disposal authorities; port health authorities; licensing planning committees; internal drainage
boards; local probation boards established under the Criminal Justice and Court
Services Act 2000, s 4; the Broads Authority; joint committees; joint boards; passenger transport executives; Transport for London; the London Development
Agency; regional development agencies; national park authorities; magistrates'
courts committees; governing bodies of educational establishments maintained

---

(Model Code of Conduct) (England) Order 2001, SI 2001/3575, Sch 1, para 2 and Sch 2, para 2;
Parish Councils (Model Code of Conduct) Order 2001, SI 2001/3576; National Parks and Broads
Authorities (Model Code of Conduct) (England) Order 2001, SI 2001/3577; Police Authorities
(Model Code of Conduct) Order 2001, SI 2001/3578.

[360] s 71. See, in general, Colm O'Cinneide, 'The Race Relations (Amendment) Act 2000' [2001]
PL 220. In relation to the carrying out of immigration and nationality functions, however, the duty
is more limited: to have due regard to the need to eliminate unlawful racial discrimination and to
promote good relations between persons of different racial groups.

by local education authorities; governing bodies of institutions within the further and the higher education sectors; the Housing Corporation; housing action trusts; police authorities; the Metropolitan Police Authority; the Service Authority for the National Criminal Intelligence Service and the Service Authority for the National Crime Squad.

(ii) Duties involved

11.196 The Secretary of State has made an order that imposes certain more specific duties on certain bodies and other persons who are subject to the general duty.[361] The duties are imposed for the purpose of ensuring the better performance of the general duty. The Order imposes on specified bodies a duty to publish a Race Equality Scheme, that is a scheme showing how it intends to fulfil the general duty and its duties under this Order. The Order imposes on specified educational bodies duties to prepare a statement of their race equality policy, to have arrangements in place for fulfilling duties to assess and monitor the impact of their policies on different racial groups, and to fulfil those duties in accordance with such arrangements. The Order imposes on bodies a duty to have in place arrangements for fulfilling duties to monitor, by reference to racial groups, various aspects of education and employment at educational establishments, and to fulfil those duties in accordance with such arrangements. The Order also imposes on other specified bodies a duty to have in place arrangements for fulfilling duties to monitor, by reference to racial groups, various aspects of employment by those bodies, and to fulfil those duties in accordance with such arrangements. The Secretary of State has also approved the CRE Code of Practice relating to these statutory duties.

(iii) Relationship between the public sector duty and other statutory duties

11.197 The responsibility of the public body is to have '*due* regard' to the need to promote equality of opportunity and good relations. That appears to mean that it is to be regarded as expressing a strong public policy preference in favour of these policies. They are more than simply 'relevant considerations', which would have been expressed by using language such as 'regard'. This does not, of course, mean that the duties override other statutory duties, and when such duties stand in the way of taking the equal opportunity duty into account appropriately, then the other existing duty prevails. An example may be in the area of public procurement by local government bodies. Were such a body to conclude that the public sector race duty would be forwarded by inserting equality requirements into its procurement contracts, then it would have to be sure that it did not breach the limitations imposed by the Local Government Act 1988.[362]

---

[361] Race Relations Act 1976 (Statutory Duties) Order 2001, SI 2001/3458.
[362] ss 17 and 18.

(iv) *Enforcement*

As regards enforcement of the duty, the CRE has a central role. If the CRE is satis-   **11.198**
fied that a person has failed to comply with, or is failing to comply with, any duty it
may serve on that person a compliance notice, which requires the person concerned
to comply with the duty concerned and to inform the CRE of the steps that the person has taken, or is taking, to comply with the duty; and may also require the person
concerned to furnish the CRE with such other written information as may be reasonably required by the notice in order to verify that the duty has been complied
with. The CRE may apply to a designated county court for an order requiring an
authority subject to the statutory duties to furnish any information required by a
compliance notice if the person fails to furnish the information to the CRE in
accordance with the notice, or the CRE has reasonable cause to believe that the person does not intend to furnish the information. If the CRE considers that a person
has not, within three months of the date on which a compliance notice was served
on that person, complied with any requirement of the notice for that person to comply with a duty imposed by an order, it may apply to a designated county court for
an order requiring the person to comply with the requirement of the notice.

(f) EC obligation to promote gender equality

Barnard[363] rightly observes the gender, race and framework directives, 'do not   **11.199**
focus on the achievement of equality in the broader, more results-oriented, redistributive sense'. However, there is some evidence of the emergence of the fourth
meaning of equality in EC law. Thus, for example, we have seen that Articles 2 and
3(2) EC impose the objective of promoting equality between men and women in
the Community. Recently, Advocate General Stix-Hackl in *Dory*[364] has interpreted this as imposing an obligation on the Community actively to promote
equality between men and women. It remains to be seen how far this interpretation presages the development of a more fully worked out fourth meaning of
equality in EC law (at least with regard to women's equality).

(g) Positive/affirmative action

A characteristic of the third approach, discussed in the previous section, is that   **11.200**
positive/affirmative action is permitted, but not required. An emerging characteristic of the fourth approach is that, under this approach, positive/affirmative
action may be a requirement, where such action would be lawful. It would appear
to be the case that for those subject to this duty, there is now an obligation to

---

[363] Catherine Barnard, 'The Changing Scope of the Fundamental Principle of Equality?' (2001)
46 McGill LJ 955, 976.
[364] Case C-186/01 *Dory v Germany*, Opinion, 28 November 2002.

consider whether adoption by it of lawful affirmative action measures would further equality of opportunity and, if it would, to consider adopting such measures.

(h) Conclusion

11.201   The fourth meaning of equality in English public law is the least developed, not least because it is also the most recently developed. It has, however, the potential to be by far the most far reaching in its meaning, depending on its interpretation and enforcement. It also illustrates further the changing categories of equality and the relationship between them. We saw that in the first meaning of equality, formal equality required that divergence by public bodies such as local authorities in delivering services to the detriment of some classes of ratepayer was successfully challenged, leading on occasion to policies in favour of the disadvantaged to be held to be ultra vires. Under the fourth meaning of equality, some at least of these policies could well be seen as examples of how to put into effect the broader conception of equality of opportunity.

12

DUE PROCESS RIGHTS

A. Introduction[1]

The concept of procedural due process has for centuries been an established fea-   **12.01**
ture of the common law, albeit not commonly or necessarily under that label.[2]
The idea that every person is entitled to a fair hearing before decisions are taken
that adversely affect his or her interests, including in particular exercise of the coercive powers of courts of law in civil and criminal litigation, is firmly established,
although views have naturally varied over time as to what is and is not procedurally fair in different contexts. This principle is reflected in Article 6 of the
European Convention on Human Rights (ECHR), which gives rise to
'Convention rights' within the United Kingdom under the Human Rights Act
1998.[3]

---

[1] This chapter draws on and develops work previously found in SH Bailey, JPL Ching, MJ Gunn
and DC Ormerod, *Smith, Bailey and Gunn on the Modern English Legal System* (4th edn, London:
Sweet & Maxwell, 2002) 559–568.

[2] See paras 15.01–15.07 below.

[3] Procedural safeguards have also been found necessary for the protection of family life under Art
8 ECHR, particularly as regards decisions affecting the care and custody of children: see *McMichael
v UK* Series A No 308 (1995) 20 EHRR 205 at [91].

B. Article 6 ECHR[4]

12.02   Article 6 provides as follows:

Article 6—Right to a fair trial

1 In the determination of his civil rights and obligations or of any criminal charge against him, everyone is entitled to a fair and public hearing within a reasonable time by an independent and impartial tribunal established by law. Judgment shall be pronounced publicly but the press and public may be excluded from all or part of the trial in the interests of morals, public order or national security in a democratic society, where the interests of juveniles or the protection of the private life of the parties so require, or to the extent strictly necessary in the opinion of the court in special circumstances where publicity would prejudice the interests of justice.

2 Everyone charged with a criminal offence shall be presumed innocent until proved guilty according to law.

3 Everyone charged with a criminal offence has the following minimum rights:

a to be informed promptly, in a language which he understands and in detail, of the nature and cause of the accusation against him:

b to have adequate time and facilities for the preparation of his defence;

c to defend himself in person or through legal assistance of his own choosing or, if he has not sufficient means to pay for legal assistance, to be given it free when the interests of justice so require;

d to examine or have examined witnesses against him and to obtain the attendance and examination of witnesses on his behalf under the same conditions as witnesses against him;

e to have the free assistance of an interpreter if he cannot understand or speak the language used in court.

12.03   This chapter focuses on the general requirements of Article 6(1). The remaining paragraphs are dealt with, so far as relevant, in Part IV of this work. It should, however, be noted here that aspects at least of the provisions of Article 6(2) and (3) may be applied in other contexts on the basis that they are inherent in Article 6(1). Furthermore, while the overall fairness of a trial cannot be compromised:

the constituent rights comprised, whether expressly or implicitly, within Article 6 are not themselves absolute. Limited qualification of these rights is acceptable if reasonably directed by national authorities towards a clear and proper public objective and if representing no greater qualification than the situation calls for.[5]

---

[4] See J Simor and B Emmerson (eds), *Human Rights Practice* (London: Sweet & Maxwell, 2000); AR Mowbray, *Cases and Materials on the European Convention of Human Rights* (London: Butterworths, 2001) ch 6; C Overy and RCA White, *Jacobs & White, European Convention on Human Rights* (3rd edn, Oxford: OUP, 2002); S Stavros, *The Guarantees for Accused Persons Under Article 6 of the European Convention on Human Rights* (Dordrecht: Martinus Nijhoff, 1993).

[5] *per* Lord Bingham in *Brown v Stott* [2003] 1 AC 681, 704.

Key concepts that may give rise to issues under Article 6(1) include whether there **12.04** is (1) a 'determination of civil rights and obligations'; (2) a 'criminal charge'; (3) a 'fair and public hearing'; (4) 'within a reasonable time'; (5) 'by an independent and impartial tribunal.' The applicable principles are as follows.

(1) 'Determination of civil rights and obligations'

Here, a broad autonomous approach has been adopted, although the European **12.05** Court of Human Rights (ECtHR) has not developed detailed criteria. For this provision to apply to a case (or contestation[6]) it is not necessary that both parties be private persons. Furthermore, the character of the governing legislation, for example, as civil, commercial or administrative law, and whether the matter falls within the jurisdiction of an ordinary court or a specialist administrative body, are of little consequence.[7] It must be shown that there is a genuine and serious dispute[8] and that its resolution has a direct effect (is 'directly decisive for') a civil right or obligation.[9]

In *Ringeisen v Austria*[10] it was held that Article 6(1) applied to the decision of an **12.06** administrative commission, applying administrative law principles, whether to approve a contract for sale of agricultural land for building as being in the public interest, as this was 'decisive for relations in civil law' between the seller and buyer. It has now been held by the ECtHR that Article 6(1) does apply to decisions that affect public servants, although disputes are excluded where they are raised:

> by public servants whose duties typify the specific activities of the public service in so far as the latter is acting as the depository of public authority responsible for protecting the general interests of the State or other public authorities.[11]

The state has a legitimate interest in requiring of such public servants 'a special **12.07** bond of trust and loyalty'.[12] Examples of posts that entail 'direct or indirect

---

[6] The words phrase 'contestation sur' appears in the French text of Art 6 (rather than 'determination of') and thus has no direct counterpart in the English text. It should be given a substantive rather than a formal meaning: *Le Compte, Van Leuven and De Meyere v Belgium* Series A No 43 (1981) 4 EHRR 1 at [45].

[7] *Ringeisen v Austria (No 1)* Series A No 13 (1971) 1 EHRR 455 at [94].

[8] *Benthem v Netherlands* Application 8848/80 (1985) 8 EHRR 1 at [32].

[9] *Le Compte, Van Leuven and De Meyere v Belgium* Series A No 43 (1981) 4 EHRR 1 at [47].

[10] (1971) 1 EHRR 455. The ECtHR rejected the claim on the merits, holding that there was no evidence of a lack of impartiality. See also *König v Germany (No 1)* Series A No 27 (1978) 2 EHRR 170 (Art 6 applicable to decisions of administrative court to revoke authorizations to run clinic and to practise medicine; concept of 'civil rights and obligations' must be interpreted autonomously and not solely by reference to the domestic law of the respondent state and is not confined to private law disputes in the traditional sense).

[11] *Pellegrin v France* (2001) 31 EHRR 26 , Judgment of 8 December 1999, para at [66].

[12] ibid at [65].

participation in the exercise of powers conferred by public law and duties designed to safeguard the general interests of the State or of other public authorities'[13] include the armed forces and the police[14] and senior officials of a ministry of foreign affairs,[15] but not a school caretaker.[16] Disputes about pensions are, however, all covered by Article 6(1), as on retirement employees break the 'special bond'.[17]

12.08 'Civil rights' may include entitlements to social insurance and welfare benefits provided by the state,[18] and be engaged by issues concerning contributions to social insurance schemes,[19] but not situations where benefits may be provided by the state as a matter of discretion,[20] or, generally, to tax disputes,[21] or a decision to deport an alien.[22]

(a) Article 6 and planning decisions

12.09 In *R (on the application of Holding & Barnes plc) v Secretary of State for the Environment, Transport and the Regions, ex p Holding and Barnes plc*[23] the House of Lords considered the application of these principles to the planning system, in particular the power of the Secretary of State to determine directly whether planning permission should be granted, where a particular planning application was called in or an appeal 'recovered' from final determination by a planning inspector, or the Secretary of State was the statutory decision-maker. Lords Slynn, Hoffmann, Clyde and Hutton[24] rejected an argument, raised on an intervention by Scottish

---

[13] *Pellegrin v France* (n 11 above) at [66].

[14] ibid.

[15] *Martinez-Caro de La Concha Castaneda v Spain* (admissibility decision, 7 March 2000).

[16] *Procaccini v Italy* (30 March 2000).

[17] *Pellegrin v France* (2001) 31 EHRR 26 at [67].

[18] *Feldbrugge v Netherlands* Series A No 99 (1986) 8 EHRR 425 and *Deumeland v Germany* Series A No 120 (1986) 8 EHRR 448 (social insurance); *Salesi v Italy* Series A No 257-E (1993) 26 EHRR 187 (welfare benefits arising as a matter of right rather than discretion, even though no contributions were payable by the claimant); the ECtHR found in *Feldbrugge* that the private law features of the arrangements (effect on claimant in her personal, economic capacity; close connection with the contract of employment; affinities with insurance under the ordinary law) outweighed the public law features (relevant rules enshrined in legislation; compulsory nature of the insurance; assumption by the state of responsibility for social protection).

[19] *Schouten and Meldrum v Netherlands* Series A No 304 (1994) 19 EHRR 432.

[20] *Machatova v Slovak Republic* Application 27552/95 (1997) 24 EHRR CD44 (payment of a hardship allowance).

[21] *Ferrazzini v Italy* Application 44759/98 (2002) 34 EHRR 45[GC], at [29]. The imposition of tax penalties may, however, constitute determination of a 'criminal charge': see paras 12.15–12.18 below.

[22] *Maaovic v France* (2001) 33 EHRR 1057 (this conforms to the intention of the original parties to the ECHR; procedural standards are expressly applied in such cases by Protocol 7, Art 1, which has been ratified by a few states only, not including the UK).

[23] [2001] UKHL 23; [2003] 2 AC 295.

[24] ibid at [27]–[38], [131]–[135], [145]–[157], [181]–[184].

ministers, that these planning decisions did not involve the determination of civil rights and obligations but were simply the exercise of legal powers which affected, perhaps changed, such rights and obligations; a decision on judicial review whether a planning decision was lawful would, however, constitute the determination of a civil right to a lawful decision. It was held that a 'dispute' or 'contestation' arose at least from the time when a power was exercised and objection was taken to that exercise.[25] The members of the House were agreed that, in the light of the ECtHR's jurisprudence,[26] Article 6(1) clearly applied in this context.

Similarly, a decision to grant planning permission to X in respect of Y's land[27] and a decision to grant planning permission to X in respect of X's land for a development that will detrimentally affect both the enjoyment of Y of his home and its monetary value,[28] are determinations that affect Y's civil rights. **12.10**

These cases may be compared with the decision in *R (on the application of Vetterlein) v Hampshire CC*.[29] Here, the Council granted planning permission for an incinerator notwithstanding objections on environmental grounds from the claimants, who lived, respectively, 1.63, 1.79 and 2.14 miles from the centre of the application site. Sullivan J held that Article 6(1) did not apply. Even if it could be assumed that close proximity to and/or likelihood of significant impact from a proposed development 'may bring an objector's civil rights into play' there was no 'genuine and serious' dispute here: **12.11**

> The grant of permission was not 'directly decisive' of such rights as the claimants may have. The claimants' connection with the decision to grant planning permission is tenuous at best, and the environmental consequences for them . . . are remote in the extreme.[30]

Furthermore, a decision by a local authority to take steps required by an enforcement notice in default of compliance by the recipient of the notice does not engage Article 6(1); the 'civil right' in question will already have been **12.12**

---

[25] *per* Lord Clyde at [147].

[26] Including *Bryan v UK* Series A No 335-A (1995) 21 EHRR 342; *Chapman v UK* Application 27238/95 (2001) 33 EHRR 18, Judgment of January 18, 2001.

[27] *British Telecommunications plc v Gloucester City Council* [2001] EWHC Admin 1001; [2002] 2 P & CR 33.

[28] *R (on the application of Kathro) v Rhondda Cynon Taff County BC* [2001] EWHC Admin 527, [2002] Env LR 15; *R (on the application of Friends Provident Life Office) v Secretary of State for Transport, Local Government and the Regions* [2001] EWHC Admin 820, [2002] 1 WLR 1450 (civil rights of owner of shopping centre held to be directly affected by proposed new large retail development); *R (on the application of Adlard) v Secretary of State for the Environment, Transport and the Regions* [2002] EWHC 7, [2002] NPC 10 (this point did not arise on appeal: [2002] 1 WLR 2515).

[29] [2001] EWHC Admin 560; [2002] Env LR 8. See also *R (on the application of Cummins (a child)) v Camden LBC* [2001] EWHC Admin 1116 (effect of proposed development on view from claimant's flat and on playground associated with the block of flats too remote).

[30] [2001] EWHC Admin 560; [2002] Env LR 8 at [66], [67].

determined by the procedure that led to the valid and effective enforcement notice in question.[31]

(b) Other situations

12.13 Further examples of situations involving the determination of civil rights and obligations include a decision of the Crown Court hearing an appeal from licensing justices;[32] the decision of a professional disciplinary tribunal that a person was not fit to practise;[33] the determination under regulations whether a person was to be treated as possessing capital of which he had deprived himself for the purpose of decreasing the amount that he might be liable to pay for his residential care;[34] the decision of a review panel in respect of the termination of an introductory tenancy;[35] and decisions of the Secretary of State to withdraw support provided under Pt VI of the Immigration and Asylum Act 1999 from a destitute asylum-seeker[36] or to refuse support on the ground that he was not satisfied that asylum was claimed as soon as reasonably practicable after arrival in the United Kingdom.[37]

12.14 A person's right to express a preference as to which school his or her child should attend is not a 'civil right'.[38] Similarly, there is no private right for a person to receive education suitable to his or her needs, which would be engaged, for example, by a decision concerning exclusion of that person from a school.[39] Furthermore, the decision of an independent appeal panel whether to reinstate an excluded pupil does not engage Article 6(1) by virtue of its effect on the civil right to enjoy a fair reputation; the proceedings are not directly decisive of reputation and the potentiality for damage is recognized through the requirement that natural justice be observed in those proceedings.[40] Whether the duty

---

[31] *R (on application of M) v Horsham DC* [2003] EWHC 234.

[32] *R (on the application of Smith) v Lincoln Crown Court* [2001] EWHC Admin 928; [2002] 1 WLR 1332.

[33] *R (on the application of Fleurose) v Securities & Futures Authority* [2001] EWCA Civ 2015; [2002] IRLR 297.

[34] *R (on the application of Beeson) v Dorset CC* [2002] EWCA Civ 1812; [2003] HRLR 11.

[35] *McLellan v Bracknell Forest BC* [2001] EWCA Civ 1510; [2002] QB 1129.

[36] *R (on the application of Husain) v Asylum Support Adjudicator* [2001] EWHC Admin 852; [2002] ACD 10.

[37] *R (on the application of Q) v Secretary of State for the Home Department* [2003] EWCA Civ 364; [2003] 2 All ER 905.

[38] *R v Richmond upon Thames LBC Appeal Committee, ex p JC (A child)* [2001] Ed LR 21; cf *Simpson v UK* (1989) 64 DR 188.

[39] *R (on the application of B (a child)) v Alperton Community School Head Teacher and Governing Body* [2001] EWHC Admin 229; [2001] Ed LR 359, where it was held that the right to sue in negligence recognized in *Phelps v Hillingdon LBC* [2001] 2 AC 619 did not constitute such a private right.

[40] ibid, considering *Golder v UK* Series A No 18 (1975) 1 EHRR 524, *Helmers v Sweden* Series A No 212 (1993) 15 EHRR 285 and *Fayed v UK* Series A No 294-B (1994) 18 EHRR 393; followed

of a local housing authority, in specified circumstances, to secure accommodation for a homeless person gives rise to a 'civil right' has not been resolved.[41]

(2) 'Criminal charge'

This too must be given an autonomous interpretation and a matter may be classi- **12.15** fied as 'criminal' for the purposes of Article 6 that would not be so classified in domestic law.[42] Three criteria are applied: the legal classification of the offence in domestic law; the nature of the offence (in particular, whether the penalty has a 'deterrent and punitive purpose'); and the nature and degree of severity of the possible penalties.[43] Matters classified as criminal in domestic law will be so characterized for the purposes of Article 6; the converse is not necessarily the case. The other two criteria are alternative and not cumulative, and an offence may qualify as criminal either through its nature or through the severity of the penalty. However, a cumulative approach may be adopted where the separate analysis of each criterion does not make it possible to reach a clear conclusion on the question.[44]

Disciplinary proceedings[45] and the imposition of penalties for tax evasion[46] may **12.16** or may not fall within Article 6 according to the circumstances. For example, it

---

in *R (on the application of S (a child)) v C High School Head Teacher* [2001] EWHC Admin 513; [2002] Ed LR 73.

[41] This question was left open by the House of Lords in *Begum (Runa) v Tower Hamlets LBC* [2003] UKHL 5; [2003] 2 WLR 388, [2003] 2 WLR 388.

[42] *Engel v Netherlands (No 1)* Series A No 22 (1976) 1 EHRR 647; *A-G's Reference (No 2 of 2001)* [2001] EWCA Crim 1568; [2001] 1 WLR 1869 (in general the term 'charge' corresponds to the sense used in English criminal procedure, and does not in the ordinary way extend to interrogation or interview).

[43] *Öztürk v Germany* Series A No 73 (1984) 6 EHRR 409 at [50] (imposition of fine by court for minor motoring offence held to involve 'criminal charge'); *Lauko v Slovakia* Application 26138/95 (2001) 33 EHRR 40, at [56] (imposition of fine by administrative authority for minor offence against civil propriety held to involve 'criminal charge'; violation of Art 6(1) found as the decisions could not be reviewed by a court).

[44] *Lauko*, ibid at [57].

[45] *Engel v Netherlands (No 1)* Series A No 22 (1976) 1 EHRR 647: military disciplinary offences leading to liability only to light punishment not within Art 6; other, more serious, disciplinary offences were. Cf *Campbell and Fell v UK* Series A No 80 (1984) 7 EHRR 165 (prison disciplinary proceedings attracting serious loss of remission subject to Art 6); *R (on the application of Carroll, Al-Hasan and Greenfield) v Secretary of State for the Home Department* [2001] EWCA Civ 1224, [2002] 1 WLR 545 (proceedings for prison disciplinary offence where maximum penalty was 42 additional days not criminal); but cf now *Ezeh and Connors v UK* Applications 39665/98 and 40086/98 (2002) 35 EHRR 28, where it was held that the award of, respectively 40 and seven 'additional days' was 'appreciably detrimental' and that the presumption that such awards were criminal had not been rebutted; *R (on the application of Fleurose) v Securities & Futures Authority* [2001] EWCA Civ 2015, [2002] IRLR 297 (proceedings before the disciplinary appeal tribunal of the Securities & Futures Authority not criminal); *Official Receiver v Stern (No 1)* [2001] 1 WLR 2230 (proceedings for disqualification of a company director not criminal for the purposes of Art 6).

[46] *Benham v UK* Application 19380/92 (1996) 22 EHRR 293 (proceedings for non-payment of the community charge held to be criminal); *Janosevic v Sweden* (23 July 2002) (substantial tax

has been held that Article 6(1) does not apply to proceedings of an independent appeal panel appointed under the School Standards and Framework Act 1998 concerning exclusion of a pupil from a state school on disciplinary grounds, notwithstanding that the misconduct alleged constituted a criminal offence. Although expulsion was significant it did not lead to a denial of access to the educational system or constitute the determination of a criminal charge. The relevant provisions were not part of the general law, applicable to persons generally; the sanction was not criminal and not disproportionate to the disciplinarian objective it existed to achieve.[47] Similarly, Article 6 does not apply to internal disciplinary mechanisms whereby an employer decides whether or not to trust an employee and whether he or she has been guilty of a fundamental breach of contract.[48]

12.17   In some situations, it is clear that the proceedings are subject to Article 6(1) as involving the determination of a civil right, and the issue is whether the additional protections under Article 6(2) and (3) for those 'charged with a criminal offence' are applicable. Here, the position in respect of anti-social behaviour orders and sex offender orders under, respectively, ss 1 and 2 of the Crime and Disorder Act 1998[49] can be compared with the regime of fixed penalty fines for lorry drivers bringing clandestine entrants to the United Kingdom.[50] The former are civil, the latter criminal. Given the uncertainties at the borders of this distinction, 'the classification of proceedings between criminal and civil is secondary to the more directly relevant question of just what protections are required for a fair trial'.[51]

---

surcharges imposed on objective grounds, following provision of incorrect information, in order to exert pressure on taxpayers to comply with their legal obligations and to punish breaches held to involve determination of 'criminal charge'); *Han & Yau v Customs and Excise Commissioners* [2001] EWCA Civ 1048, [2001] 1 WLR 2253 (civil penalties for dishonest evasion of VAT held to involve determination of 'criminal charge'). It is not necessary for these purposes that the possible penalties include that of imprisonment: *Han & Yau*, ibid.

[47]   *R (on the application of B (a child)) v Alperton Community School Head Teacher and Governing Body* [2001] EWHC Admin 229; [2001] Ed LR 359. Neither was a civil right at stake: see para 12.14 above.

[48]   *R (on the application of H) v Hertfordshire CC* [2002] EWCA Civ 146.

[49]   *R (on the application of McCann) v Manchester Crown Court* [2002] UKHL 39, [2003] 1 AC 787 (anti-social behaviour order); *B v Chief Constable of Avon and Somerset* [2001] 1 WLR 340 (sex offender order); *Jones v Greater Manchester Police Authority* [2001] EWHC Admin 189, [2002] ACD 4 (sex offender order) (such orders were civil in form and were not designed to punish for past misconduct but to protect others in the future).

[50]   *International Transport Roth GmbH v Secretary of State for the Home Department* [2002] EWCA Civ 158, [2003] QB 728 (Simon Brown and Jonathan Parker LJJ, Laws LJ dissenting) (true nature of the scheme was to deter dishonesty and carelessness on the part of carriers; penalty not merely severe but fixed); cf *Goldsmith v Customs and Excise Commissioners* [2001] EWHC Admin 285, [2001] 1 WLR 1673 (proceedings for forfeiture of goods (26kg of tobacco) not proved to be for applicant's personal use held to be civil; only consequence for the applicant was the loss of the goods); approved in *R (on the application of Mudie) v Dover Magistrates' Court* [2003] EWCA Civ 237, [2003] 2 WLR 1344.

[51]   *International Transport*, ibid at [33], *per* Simon Brown LJ.

A 'charge' is 'the official notification given to an individual by the competent authority of an allegation that he has committed a criminal offence'[52] or 'other measures which carry the implication of such an allegation and which likewise substantially affect the situation of the suspect'.[53] Article 6 applies from the time of charge to the conclusion of appeal proceedings.[54]

12.18

(3) 'Fair and public hearing'

(a) Access to a court

This may, according to the circumstances, include a right of effective access to a court.[55] This right is not expressly conferred by the ECHR, but is regarded as inherent, having regard to the object and purpose of the ECHR and to general principles of law. It is this right which alone makes it in fact possible to benefit from the procedural guarantees expressly set out in Article 6(1): 'The fair, public and expeditious characteristics of judicial proceedings are of no value at all if there are no judicial proceedings'.[56]

12.19

The rights guaranteed by the ECHR are not 'theoretical or illusory' but rights that are 'practical and effective'. Accordingly, a state may be obliged to take positive steps to enable a person to be represented in court proceedings by a lawyer,[57] although there is no general entitlement to legal aid wherever the determination of civil rights and obligations is in issue.[58] A state is entitled to adopt rules setting a limitation period within which an action must be brought, provided that it 'does not restrict or reduce the access left to the

12.20

---

[52] *Eckle v Germany* Series A No 51 (1983) EHRR 1 at [73].
[53] *Foti v Italy* Series A No 56 (1983) 5 EHRR 313 at [52].
[54] *Wemhoff v Germany* Series A No 7 (1968) 1 EHRR 55 at [18], [20].
[55] *Golder v UK* Series A No 18 (1975) 1 EHRR 524 (rights of access to a court by prisoner for determination of civil claim); *Airey v Ireland (No 1)* Series A No 32 (1979) 2 EHRR 305 (rights of access must be practical and effective).
[56] *Golder*, ibid at [35], [36].
[57] *Airey v Ireland (No 1)* Series A No 32 (1979) 2 EHRR 305 (breach of Art 6(1) where there was no legal aid for judicial separation proceedings that had to be heard in the High Court, involved complicated points of law and the need to prove adultery, unnatural practices or cruelty, and given that marital disputes often entailed an emotional involvement scarcely compatible with the degree of objectivity required by advocacy in court); *P, C and S v UK* Application 56547/00 (2002) 35 EHRR 31 (breach of Art 6(1) where refusal of extended adjournment of applications for care and freeing for adoption orders following her lawyers' withdrawal left applicant to represent herself in complex and emotive proceedings). The same approach is adopted as a matter of the fairness of the hearing where the issue arises in respect of a respondent to proceedings: *McVicar v UK* Application 46311/99 (2002) 35 EHRR 22 (no breach of Art 6(1) arising from lack of legal aid for defamation proceedings where defendant was a 'well educated and experienced journalist . . . capable of formulating cogent argument' and the matter turned on the truth or otherwise of the allegations).
[58] *Airey*, ibid at [26].

individual in such a way or to such an extent that the very essence of the right is impaired'.[59]

12.21 Such a rule must pursue a legitimate aim and there must be a reasonable relationship of proportionality between the means employed and the aim sought to be achieved.[60] By way of contrast, provisions enabling ministers to issue (unreviewable) certificates denying access to ordinary legal processes, such as complaints of discrimination or unfair dismissal, on the grounds of national security, have been held to constitute a disproportionate restriction of the right of access.[61] The right of access may be held to have been denied where there is a broad blanket rule excluding civil liability where competing public policy arguments cannot be evaluated,[62] but not merely where domestic law after the proper and fair examination of the claim determines that no remedy is available in a given situation.[63] Similarly, the imposition of a fixed penalty regime disproportionate to the object to be achieved may be held to infringe the applicant's right to have the appropriate level of penalty determined by an independent tribunal.[64] The right of access may require the Civil Procedure Rules to be interpreted in such a way (via s 3(1) of the HRA 1998 Act) as to remove an unjustifiable hindrance to a litigant's right to proceed.[65]

(b) Fair hearings

12.22 The right to a fair hearing also requires equality of arms,[66] including adequate

---

[59] *Stubbings v UK* Application 22083/93 (1996) 23 EHRR 213 at [50].

[60] ibid. The ECtHR held that the English law of limitation, which allowed the applicants six years from their 18th birthday to commence proceedings (here in respect of alleged childhood sexual abuse), did not contravene Art 6(1). See also *Fogarty v UK* Application 37112/97 (2002) 34 EHRR 12 (application of international law doctrine of sovereign immunity through the State Immunity Act 1978 not disproportionate); *A v UK* Application 35373/97 (2003) 36 EHRR 51 (doctrine of absolute parliamentary privilege not disproportionate).

[61] *Tinnelly & Sons Ltd v UK* Application 20390/92 (1998) 27 EHRR 249.

[62] *Osman v UK* Application 23452/94 (2000) 29 EHRR 245.

[63] *Z v UK* Application 29392/95 (2002) 34 EHRR 3, Judgment of May 10, 2001; *TP and KM v UK* Application 28945/95 (2002) 34 EHRR 2. There may, however, be a breach of Art 13 (absence of effective remedy, see paras 19.01–19.02, 19.10–19.14, 19.31, 19.35 and 19.47 below). See also *Matthews v Ministry of Defence* [2003] UKHL 4; [2003] 1 AC 1163 (bar to tort claim by servicemen held to be a substantive not procedural limitation and so not in violation of Art 6(1)).

[64] *International Transport Roth GmbH v Secretary of State for the Home Department* [2002] EWCA Civ 158, [2003] QB 728 (Simon Brown and Jonathan Parker LJJ, Laws LJ dissenting).

[65] *Goode v Martin* [2001] EWCA Civ 1899; [2002] 1 WLR 1828.

[66] This involves 'a "fair balance" between the parties' and 'implies that each party must be afforded a reasonable opportunity to present his case—including his evidence—under conditions that do not place him at a substantial disadvantage vis-à-vis his opponent': *Dombo Beheer BV v Netherlands* Series A No 274-A (1993) 18 EHRR 213 at [33]. This applies in principle to both criminal and civil cases: ibid (application of Dutch procedural rule that a person who was a party to litigation could not be heard as a witness in his or her own case held to be violation of Art 6(1)). For

disclosure of relevant evidence,[67] the right not to incriminate oneself,[68] and the right of a defendant to participate effectively in his or her criminal trial.[69] Courts must give reasons for their judgments, although the extent of this obligation depends on the circumstances and a detailed answer to every argument is not necessarily required.[70] Article 6 is, however, concerned only with procedural fairness and not the fairness of the substantive law.[71]

(c) Public hearings

Where Article 6(1) applies there is a general right for a hearing to be held and for judgment to be pronounced in public, subject to specified exceptions.[72] The public character of such proceedings 'protects litigants against the administration **12.23**

---

example, a policy to refuse a dyslexic prisoner the use of a word processor to conduct his litigation would infringe the 'equality of arms' principle: *R (on the application of Ponting) v Governor of HM Prison Whitemoor* [2002] EWCA Civ 224 at [77] *per* Schiemann LJ, obiter (the court upheld the prison service arrangement that allowed such use subject to conditions).

[67] *Rowe v UK* Application 28901/95 (2000) 30 EHRR 1. The entitlement to disclosure is not absolute; restrictions can be imposed, where strictly necessary, to protect competing interests, such as national security, witnesses at risk of reprisals, or to preserve the fundamental rights of another individual or to safeguard an important public interest: ibid at [61]; on the facts there was a breach of Art 6(1) where evidence was withheld by the prosecution on public interest grounds without notifying the judge. New arrangements involving the review of non-disclosure decisions by the trial judge were introduced by the Criminal Procedure and Investigations Act 1996.

[68] *Funke v France* Series A No 256-A (1993) 16 EHRR 297 (imposition of daily fine for failure to produce foreign bank account details held to infringe F's right to remain silent and not to contribute to incriminating himself); *John Murray v UK* Application 18731/91 (1996) 22 EHRR 29 (application of provisions of Northern Irish law enabling 'common sense' inferences to be drawn from silence held not to violate Art 6(1); to base a conviction solely or mainly on silence would constitute a violation); *Saunders v UK* Application 19187/91 (1996) 23 EHRR 313 (use at trial of answers given to DTI inspector under legal compulsion held to violate Art 6(1)); *Condron v UK* Application 35718/97 (2001) 31 EHRR 1 (failure of trial judge to give appropriate direction to jury as regards inferences from silence held to violate Art 6(1)); *Allan v UK* Application 48539/99 (2003) 36 EHRR 12 (use of statements made to police informer placed in A's cell for the purpose of eliciting information from him held to violate Art 6(1)).

[69] *Stanford v UK*, The Times, 8 March 1994 (implicit right to hear and follow proceedings not violated by use of glass screens in front of the dock which caused a minimal loss of sound); *V v UK* Application 24888/94 (1999) 30 EHRR 121 (violation of Art 6(1) where 11-year old defendant was tried for murder in adult court (with modifications); the fact that he was represented by skilled counsel was not sufficient given his immaturity and disturbed emotional state).

[70] *Hiro Balani v Spain* Series A No 303-B (1995) 19 EHRR 566; *Garcia Ruiz v Spain* Application 30544/96 (2001) 31 EHRR 222. This does not require magistrates to give reasons for rejecting submissions of no case: *Moran v DPP* [2002] EWHC 89; [2002] ACD 49; professional judges must, however, give reasons: *Flannery v Halifax Estate Agencies Ltd* [2000] 1 WLR 377 (pre-HRA); *English v Emery Reimbold & Strick Ltd* [2002] EWCA Civ 605, [2002] 1 WLR 2409 (decisions concerning costs in civil cases); *R (on application of Cunningham) v Exeter Crown Court* [2003] EWHC 184, [2003] Crim LR 340 (decisions concerning costs in criminal cases).

[71] *R v Gemmell (Aaron Roy)* [2002] EWCA Crim 1992; [2003] 1 Cr App R 23 (appropriateness or otherwise of the *Caldwell* test for recklessness not a matter arising under Art 6), citing *Z v UK* Application 29392/95 (2002) 34 EHRR 3 at [87], [98], [100].

[72] See paras 6.16 and 12.02 above.

of justice in secret with no public scrutiny; it is also one of the means whereby confidence in the courts, superior and inferior, can be maintained'.[73]

12.24 The right to a public hearing can be waived, and it is, for example, permissible for disciplinary proceedings to be held in private if the respondent consents.[74] The exclusion of press and public by virtue of Article 6(1) exceptions has been held to be justified in respect of prison disciplinary hearings before Boards of Visitors[75] on grounds of public order and security, and in respect of family proceedings concerning the residence of children, to protect the child's privacy and to enable parents and other witnesses to 'express themselves candidly on highly personal issues without fear of public curiosity or comment'.[76]

(4) 'Within a reasonable time'

12.25 This requirement applies to civil and criminal proceedings. Each case must be assessed according to its circumstances, including the complexity of the case, the applicant's conduct and the manner in which the matter was dealt with by the administrative and judicial authorities.[77] The 'reasonable time' may begin to run before the formal launch of proceedings.[78] The issue has arisen in a very large number of cases before the ECtHR[79] and in domestic law. It is closely associated with the right of those arrested or detained to trial within a reasonable time or to release pending trial;[80] in these cases there must be 'special diligence in the conduct of the prosecution'.[81] The purpose of the reasonable time requirement of Article 6(1) is to protect the parties against 'excessive procedural delays' and 'in criminal matters especially . . . to avoid that a person charged should remain too long in a state of uncertainty about his fate'.[82] Each case very much turns on its

---

[73] *Pretto v Italy* Series A No 71 (1983) 6 EHRR 182 at 21.

[74] *Le Compte, Van Leuven and De Meyere v Belgium* Series A No 43 (1981) 4 EHRR 1 at [59] (violation of Art 6(1) established where medical disciplinary proceedings were conducted in private contrary to the respondents' wishes; a private hearing might have been justified under the Art 6(1) exceptions had there been a need to protect 'professional secrecy' or for 'protection of the private life' of the doctors or patients).

[75] *Campbell and Fell v UK* Series A No 80 (1984) 7 EHRR 165 at [86]–[88] (the disciplinary jurisdiction of Boards of Visitors has since been abolished); but cf *Riepan v Austria* [2001] Crim LR 230.

[76] *P and B v UK* Applications 35974/97 and 36337/97 (2002) 34 EHRR 19.

[77] *König v Germany (No 1)* Series A No 27 (1978) 2 EHRR 170 at [99] (delays of over 10 years in administrative proceedings that were still not concluded and a delay of over five years in separate proceedings each held to breach Art 6(1)).

[78] ibid at [98].

[79] The leading authorities are helpfully summarized by Lord Bingham in *Dyer (Procurator Fiscal, Linlithgow) v Watson* [2002] UKPC D1; [2002] 3 WLR 1488 at [30]–[55].

[80] Art 5(3) ECHR.

[81] *Stögmüller v Austria* Series A No 9 (1969) 1 EHRR 155, 191.

[82] ibid.

own facts, although a number of general points can be made.[83] First, 'the threshold of proving a breach of the reasonable time requirement is a high one, not easily crossed'.[84]

Unless the period on its face, and without more, gives ground for real concern, it **12.26** is almost certainly unnecessary to go further. Conversely, lengthy periods of time have been found not to be unreasonable in complex cases. Then, the applicant cannot complain of delays of which he or she is the cause. The general underfunding of the legal system in a particular state is no excuse; on the other hand the ECtHR will take account of the 'practical realities of litigious life even in a reasonably well-organised legal system'.[85]

An important point is that it is not necessary for breach of the reasonable time re- **12.27** quirement that there be any prejudice to the fairness of the trial itself; the right to trial within a reasonable time and the right to a fair hearing are independent rights.[86]

Violations of the reasonable time requirement by the United Kingdom have been **12.28** found in a number of cases before the ECtHR[87] and domestic courts.[88]

---

[83] *per* Lord Bingham in *Dyer v Watson* [2002] UKPC D1; [2002] 3 WLR 1488 at [48]–[55].
[84] ibid at [52].
[85] ibid at [55].
[86] ibid at [50]; *Eckle v Germany* Series A No 51 (1983) EHRR 1 at [66].
[87] *Darnell v UK* Series A No 272 (1994) 18 EHRR 205 (delay of nine years in civil proceedings); *Robins v UK* (1997) 26 EHRR 527 (took over four years to resolve a 'relatively straightforward dispute over costs'); *Howarth v UK* Application 38081/97 (2001) 31 EHRR 37 (period of two years in dealing with A-G's reference of an unduly lenient sentence to the Court of Appeal (Crim Div); there was 'no judicial activity' from the grant of leave in December 1995 to the hearing in March 1997); *Davies v UK* Application 42007/98 (2002) 35 EHRR 29 (5½ years to resolve proceedings, admittedly complex, for disqualification of a company director; evidence was served late, in December 1992, by the Secretary of State, whose application for leave to serve the evidence out of time was determined in January 1994 with an appeal determined in May 1996). See also *Somjee v UK* Application 42116/98 (2003) 36 EHRR 16; *Foley v UK* Application 39197/98 (2003) 36 EHRR 15; *Mitchell and Holloway v UK* Application 44808/98 (2003) 36 EHRR 52; *Obasa v UK* (16 January 2003).
[88] On the application of these principles to the domestic criminal process see *A-G's Reference (No 2 of 2001)* [2001] EWCA Crim 1568; [2001] 1 WLR 1869 (unreasonable delay in breach of Art 6(1) does not necessarily render a conviction unsafe, but may in appropriate circumstances be remedied by being taken into account in sentencing); *R v James (David John)* [2002] EWCA Crim 1119 (no violation of Art 6(1) following five-year delay in complex fraud case); *Dyer v Watson* [2002] UKPC D1; [2002] 3 WLR 1488 (Privy Council held that 20-month period between charge and trial for perjury did not violate Art 6(1), but that a 27–28 month overall period in the case of a defendant charged with serious sexual offences and aged 13 at the time the alleged offences were committed, which was neither explained nor justified, did; in the case of children, proceedings had to be prosecuted expeditiously and without any unnecessary delay: *per* Lord Bingham at [23], [61], referring to the UN Standard Minimum Rules for the Administration of Juvenile Justice (Beijing, 29 November 1985) r 20.1).

(5) 'Independent and impartial tribunal'

12.29 This requirement echoes the common law nemo judex principle.[89] 'Independent' and 'impartial' are separate, but closely related requirements. As to the former, regard must be had to the manner of the appointment of the tribunal members, their terms of office, the existence of guarantees against outside pressure and the question whether the tribunal presents an appearance of independence.[90] There are two aspects to the question of 'impartiality': first, 'the tribunal must be subjectively free of personal prejudice or bias'; secondly, 'it must also be impartial from an objective viewpoint, that is, it must offer sufficient guarantees to exclude any legitimate doubt in this respect . . .'.[91] These requirements have led to the reintroduction of an approach in applying the nemo judex principle that places more emphasis on the need to avoid the appearance of bias.[92] They have also led to the fundamental remodelling of arrangements for courts-martial in the United Kingdom[93] and the progressive elimination of the role of the Home Secretary in setting the tariff element of the life sentence for convicted murderers.[94]

---

[89] See paras 15.68–15.93 below.

[90] *Findlay v UK* Application 22107/93 (1997) 24 EHRR 221 at [73]. It is not necessary that the 'guarantees' 'must as a matter of law be formal, in some way cast in stone' (*per* Laws LJ in *R v Spear (John)* [2001] EWCA Crim 2; [2001] QB 804 at [35]); the question is whether a reasonable man apprised of the relevant facts available to the 'persistent, even dogged inquirer as a member of the public' would conclude that there was a real doubt as to the tribunal's impartiality or independence (*Scanfuture UK Ltd v Secretary of State for Trade and Industry* [2001] IRLR 416, EAT; *R (on the application of Husain) v Asylum Support Adjudicator* [2001] EWHC Admin 852, [2002] ACD 10).

[91] *Findlay*, ibid. See *McGonnell v UK* Application 28488/95 (2000) 30 EHRR 289 (sufficient doubt for breach of Art 6(1) as to Guernsey judge's impartiality when participating in planning appeal arose from his previous act in presiding over Guernsey's parliament when it considered the detailed development plan for the land in question); *V v UK* Application 24888/94 (1999) 30 EHRR 121 (breach of Art 6(1) in role of Home Secretary in determining tariff for juvenile murderers; independent means, inter alia, 'independent . . . of the executive').

[92] See para 15.84 below.

[93] See *Findlay v UK* Application 22107/93 (1997) 24 EHRR 221 (convening officer appointed the members of the court-martial and the prosecuting and defending officers, prepared the evidence and had power to vary the sentence). In *Morris v UK* Application 38784/97 (2002) 34 EHRR 52 the ECtHR held that the changes effected by the Armed Forces Act 1996 had mostly but not fully secured compliance, the role as members of the court-martial of junior officers who might be subject to influence and the role of the reviewing authority remaining problematic; the House of Lords subsequently found the arrangements to be compliant, and that the concerns expressed in *Morris* were based on a misunderstanding of the position of the junior officers and noting that the reviewing authority could not increase the sentence: *R v Spear (John)* [2002] UKHL 31; [2003] 1 AC 734.

[94] *V v UK* Application 24888/94 (1999) 30 EHRR 121; *R (on the application of Anderson and Taylor) v Secretary of State for the Home Department* [2002] UKHL 46; [2003] 1 AC 837 (HL held that the Home Secretary's role in relation to mandatory life sentence prisoners was incompatible with Art 6(1), following *Stafford v UK* Application 46295/99 (2002) 35 EHRR 32).

The absence of an independent and impartial tribunal may, however, be cured if **12.30** the proceedings before it are subject to 'subsequent control by a judicial body that has full jurisdiction and does provide the guarantees of Article 6(1)'.[95] It has been accepted that this does not require a full appeal on the merits of every administrative decision taken by the executive that affects private rights.[96] The extent to which judicial review or a statutory application to quash provides 'full jurisdiction' has been considered in a number of cases by the European Court and Commission.[97] In *Bryan v UK*[98] the ECtHR held that because the appointment of an inspector to hear an appeal against an enforcement notice could be revoked by the executive where the executive's own policies might be in issue, the inspector's appointment did not satisfy Article 6(1) requirements as to the appearance of independence. However, the High Court's powers of review were sufficient for compliance with Article 6(1) overall. The ECtHR stated that in making this assessment, it was necessary to have regard to matters such as the subject matter of the decision appealed against, the manner in which it was arrived at and the content of the dispute, including the desired and actual grounds of appeal. Here, the ECtHR noted the quasi-judicial character of the proceedings before the inspector, the inspector's duty to exercise independent judgment, the requirement that inspectors must not be subject to any improper influence, and the stated mission of the inspectorate to uphold the principle of openness, fairness and impartiality. Any shortcomings in these respects could have been reviewed by the High Court. The High Court was able to deal with most of the points in fact raised by the appellant. As to the facts and planning merits, the High Court did not have jurisdiction to substitute its view for that of the inspector, but could intervene if the inspector had taken into account irrelevant factors or had omitted to take account of relevant factors or if the evidence was not capable of supporting a finding of fact or if the decision was perverse or irrational. Such an approach by an appeal tribunal on questions of fact could reasonably be expected in specialized areas of the law such as this, particularly where the facts had already been established in the course of a quasi-judicial procedure governed by many of the Article 6(1) safeguards.[99]

---

[95] *Albert and Le Compte v Belgium* Series A No 58 (1983) 5 EHRR 533 at [29].
[96] *Kaplan v UK* Application 7598/96 (1980) 4 EHRR 64 at [161], EComHR.
[97] *Iskcon v UK* Application 20490/92 (1994) 18 EHRR CD133, EComHR (no violation of Art 6(1) in determination by inspector of appeal against enforcement notice); *Bryan v UK* Series A No 335-A (1995) 21 EHRR 342; *Chapman v UK* Application 27238/95 (2001) 33 EHRR 18 (no violation of Art 6(1) in determination by inspector of appeal against enforcement notice); *Howard v UK* Application 10825/84 (1987) 9 EHRR CD 116, EComHR; *Varey v UK* Application 26662/95 (EComHR, October 27, 1999) (no violation of Art 6(1) in determination of Secretary of State to dismiss appeals against refusal of planning permission, contrary to inspectors' recommendations).
[98] ibid.
[99] ibid at [40]–[47].

12.31   *Bryan v UK* was applied in respect of the decision of an inspector to dismiss an appeal against a discontinuance notice[100] and in determining a planning appeal.[101] However, in *R (on the application of Holding & Barnes plc) v Secretary of the State for the Environment, Transport and the Regions*[102] the Divisional Court granted a declaration that provisions enabling the Secretary of State to call in planning applications, to direct that a planning appeal should be determined by himself rather than his inspector (a 'recovered appeal'), and to approve compulsory purchase and highway orders were incompatible with Article 6(1). This was on the ground that the Secretary of State was not independent and impartial and that the processes in question were not saved by the possibility of challenge before the High Court by a statutory application to quash. The court held that *Bryan v UK* was distinguishable and that it was impossible to read the relevant provisions in such a way (for example by enlarging the permissible grounds of appeal) as to comply with Article 6(1). The House of Lords unanimously allowed an appeal[103] on the ground that, while the Secretary of State could not be seen objectively as independent and impartial (and this was accepted by him), the powers of the High Court were in fact sufficient.[104] Furthermore, this overall conclusion applied even to decisions where the financial interests of other government departments were engaged, although particular points might arise in subsequent proceedings. It was noted that decisions were taken by ministers who so far as possible had no connection with the area from which the case came, assisted by a decision officer who worked separately from other civil servants involved in casework. There would also have been an inquiry conducted by an inspector, who would report to the Secretary of State. The situation whereby, in practice in rare and controversial cases, decisions on planning policy could be made by a democratically accountable member of the executive was well entrenched in UK constitutional practice and the House expressed itself satisfied that this conformed to Article 6(1):

> To substitute for the Secretary of State an independent and impartial body with no central electoral accountability would not only be a recipe for chaos: it would be profoundly undemocratic.[105]

12.32   Lord Hoffmann noted[106] that a distinction was to be drawn between matters of fact and matters of planning policy or expediency. It was only in relation to the

---

[100]   *O'Brien v Department of the Environment, Transport and the Regions* (QBD, January 28, 2001).
[101]   *Bhamjee v Secretary of State for the Environment, Transport and the Regions* (QBD, January 23, 2001).
[102]   [2001] HRLR 102. See to the same effect the decision of the Court of Session in *County Properties Ltd v Scottish Ministers* [2000] HRLR 677.
[103]   [2001] UKHL 23; [2003] 2 AC 295.
[104]   Applying *Bryan v UK* Series A No 335-A (1995) 21 EHRR 342 and *Zumtobel v Austria* Series A No 268-A (1993) 17 EHRR 116.
[105]   [2001] UKHL 23; [2003] 2 AC 295 at [60] *per* Lord Nolan.
[106]   ibid at [98]–[117].

former that the additional safeguards identified in *Bryan v UK* in respect of the inspector's involvement were needed to justify the limited review of findings of fact by the High Court. It was separately accepted by the ECtHR in *Zumtobel v Austria* that 'respect must be accorded to decisions taken by administrative authorities on grounds of expediency'[107] and as regards these matters 'there has never been a single voice in the Commission or the European Court to suggest that our provisions for judicial review are inadequate to satisfy Article 6'.[108] For Lord Slynn, the powers of the High Court were already sufficient; however, the express recognition of proportionality and review for mistakes of fact as permissible grounds of challenge would be desirable and make the position even clearer.[109] This was left open by other members of the House.[110]

The distinction between matters of policy and matters of fact has been applied in subsequent cases, with, where the decision-maker is not independent and impartial, judicial review being recognized as an adequate remedy in respect of the former but not the latter.[111] The Court of Appeal has also held that, notwithstanding the dicta of Lord Slynn in *Alconbury Holding & Barnes*, mentioned above, it would not be a legitimate process of interpretation to enlarge the powers of a court with jurisdiction to consider appeal on points of law so as to enable it to redetermine

12.33

---

[107] (1993) 17 EHRR 116 at [32].

[108] [2001] UKHL 23; [2003] 2 AC 295 at [122].

[109] ibid at [51]–[54].

[110] ibid, *per* Lord Nolan at [62] and Lord Clyde at [169] (expressing some scepticism).

[111] *R (on the application of Vetterlein) v Hampshire CC* [2001] EWHC Admin 560, [2002] Env LR 8 (opportunity for objectors to a grant of planning permission to make detailed representations during the public consultation process and to address the committee where the issues were questions of professional judgment sufficient to constitute a fair hearing (although the right to a fair hearing did not in fact arise on the facts)); *British Telecommunications plc v Gloucester City Council* [2001] EWHC Admin 1001; [2002] 2 P & CR 33 (judicial review sufficient in respect of policy matters); *R (on the application of Kathro) v Rhondda Cynon Taff County BC* [2001] EWHC Admin 527, [2002] Env LR 15 (council not independent and impartial as regards grant of planning permission in respect of its own land, but judicial review adequate remedy as the primary facts and inferences from those facts were not in dispute); *R (on the application of Friends Provident Life Office) v Secretary of State for Transport, Local Government and the Regions* [2001] EWHC Admin 820, [2002] 1 WLR 1450 (assessment of likely impact of proposed development to be regarded for this purpose as planning judgment rather than 'an issue of fact and the evaluation of fact'); *McLellan v Bracknell Forest BC* [2001] EWCA Civ 1510, [2002] QB 1129 (review panel independent and impartial as regards decision to proceed with termination of introductory tenancy but judicial review adequate remedy where issue was reasonableness of termination decision); cf *Adan v Newham LBC* [2001] EWCA Civ 1916, [2002] 1 WLR 2120 (dicta that review officer not independent and impartial as regards review of homelessness application but appeal on point of law would be an adequate remedy unless there was a material dispute as to the primary facts; in such cases it would be necessary for an independent and impartial review officer to be appointed through use of statutory contracting out powers); *Begum (Runa) v Tower Hamlets LBC* [2002] EWCA Civ 239, [2002] 1 WLR 2491 (CA disapproved dicta in *Adan* that appeal on point of law (equivalent to judicial review) would not constitute an adequate remedy in all cases). There is no residual requirement in a case concerning judgment and discretion rather than fact finding for there to be an oral hearing at first instance: *R (on the application of Adlard) v Secretary of State for the Environment, Transport and the Regions* [2002] EWCA Civ 735; [2002] 1 WLR 2515.

questions of (non-jurisdictional) fact on the ground that this was necessary to secure compliance with Article 6(1).[112]

12.34 The significance of the distinction between policy and fact has, however, been reduced by the decision of the House of Lords in *Begum (Runa) v Tower Hamlets LBC*.[113] Here, the House held that the possibility of review by the county court of determinations, including decisions on matters of fact, by a local housing authority as to whether it owed a duty under Pt VII of the Housing Act 1996 to secure accommodation for a homeless person, was sufficient for compliance with Article 6(1). The review mechanism, an appeal under s 204 of the 1996 Act, applied conventional judicial review principles. The House held that there was no necessity for an appeal on the merits on factual issues, although it left open the question whether the county court should apply a greater intensity of review on factual issues. The House, furthermore, indicated that review on conventional judicial review grounds would generally be sufficient in cases of administrative decision-making, as in discharging regulatory functions (such as licensing or granting planning permission) or administering schemes of social welfare.[114] Accordingly, in a number of situations previously considered by the lower courts,[115] the distinction between policy and fact would not longer be significant, judicial review being sufficient in all cases. It should be noted, however, that the decision in *Begum* concerned a matter where it was assumed that a 'civil right' was engaged and recognized that a decision that it was so engaged would involve an extension of the Strasbourg jurisprudence. It is submitted that the more clearly a situation falls within the core of the 'civil right' concept, the less likely it is where facts are in issue that the right to an independent and impartial tribunal will be satisfied by recourse to a court equipped only with the conventional powers of judicial review.

12.35 Non-compliance overall with the requirement of access to an independent and impartial tribunal has been found in respect of housing benefit review boards;[116]

---

[112] *Adan v Newham LBC* [2001] EWCA Civ 1916; [2002] 1 WLR 2120 (Brooke LJ and David Steel J, Hale LJ dissenting on this point). The general views of the Court of Appeal in *Adan* on Art 6 were obiter, and were disapproved by the Court of Appeal in *Begum (Runa) v Tower Hamlets LBC* [2002] EWCA Civ 239, [2002] 1 WLR 2491. The court in *Begum* did not need to express a view on this specific point.

[113] [2003] UKHL 5; [2003] 2 WLR 388.

[114] See Lord Hoffmann, ibid at [42], [59]. At [41] his Lordship distinguished *Bryan v UK* Series A No 335-A (1995) 21 EHRR 342, on the ground that it concerned an appeal against an enforcement notice where the inspector's decision on an appeal would be binding in subsequent criminal proceedings.

[115] Including those summarized in n 111 above.

[116] *R (on the application of Bewry) v Norwich City Council* [2001] EWHC Admin 657, [2002] HRLR 2 (councillor membership of Board determining issue involving credibility; breach of common law requirement equivalent to that comprised in Art 6); distinguished in *R (on the application of Bibi) v Rochdale MBC Housing Benefit Review Board* [2001] EWHC Admin 967

part-time sheriffs in Scotland appointed by the Lord Advocate with a limited term of office;[117] the Crown Court when constituted (in accordance with the rules) to hear an appeal from licensing justices so as to include other members of the licensing committee to which those justices belonged;[118] and a panel including councillors appointed to determine a question arising under regulations made under the National Assistance Act 1948.[119]

The independent and impartial tribunal must itself be 'established by law'. The fact that one of the members of the court lacks the required qualifications does not necessarily involve an infringement of this requirement.[120]   **12.36**

(6) Other Requirements

Article 6(2) and (3) imposes particular requirements, including the presumption   **12.37**
of innocence, in respect of persons 'charged with a criminal offence'. These are
also applicable to disciplinary proceedings that fall within Article 6(1).[121]

(councillor membership of Board meant that it could not be independent or expert in the *Holding & Barnes* sense, but judicial review was a sufficient remedy given that most of the facts were not substantially in issue and that the councillors had no personal interest in their finding that a tenancy was not on a commercial basis and so did not enable a claim to be made for housing benefit).

[117] *Starrs v Ruxton* 2000 JC 208.

[118] *R (on the application of Smith) v Lincoln Crown Court* [2001] EWHC Admin 928; [2002] 1 WLR 1332 (judicial review of the Crown Court held to be an inadequate remedy).

[119] *R (on the application of Beeson) v Dorset CC* [2001] EWHC Admin 986; [2002] HRLR 15 (the panel had to comprise 'at least' one independent member and so a fully independent panel could actually be appointed; the key issue was one of credibility and so judicial review was an inadequate remedy). This decision was, however, reversed by the Court of Appeal: [2002] EWCA Civ 1812, [2003] HRLR 11, endorsed by the House of Lords in *Begum (Runa) v Tower Hamlets LBC* [2003] UKHL 5; [2003] 2 WLR 388: see Lord Hoffmann at [58], [59].

[120] *Tameside MBC v Grant* [2002] Fam 194 (only two of three members of a family proceedings court were members, as required, of the family panel; however, the court would have been composed of two (qualified) justices, the bench here was unanimous, there was no suggestion of bias or unfairness, specialist knowledge of child law was not required in respect of the issue determined by the bench); *Fawdry & Co v Murfitt* [2002] EWCA Civ 643, [2003] QB 104 (Hale and Ward LJJ; point left open by Sedley LJ) (common law doctrine upholding acts of de facto judge who acts in office under a general supposition of his or her competence to do so sufficiently accessible and foreseeable for compliance with Art 6(1)).

[121] *Albert and Le Compte v Belgium* Series A No 58 (1983) 5 EHRR 533 at [39].

13

FUNDAMENTAL PRINCIPLES OF ADMINISTRATIVE LAW

The object of this chapter should be made clear at the outset. Previous chapters of this book have considered the application of principles such as equality. The chapters that follow will focus on administrative law principles, both procedural and substantive. This chapter will not attempt to replicate these analyses. It will rather be concerned with the way in which these principles have been shaped by norms of a constitutional law nature. The discussion will focus on sovereignty, the rule of law and the separation of powers. **13.01**

A. Sovereignty

(1) General

Nineteenth century thinking about sovereignty was dominated by Dicey. His conclusions echoed those of earlier writers such as Blackstone. Sovereign power existed and was possessed by Parliament. Dicey's empirical argument in support of sovereignty was eclectic. It was based partly on the writings of jurists, such as Coke and Blackstone, partly on examples of parliamentary authority drawn from the past, as exemplified by the Acts of Union and the Septennial Act, and partly on instances where Parliament had exercised authority over private rights.[1] This **13.02**

---

[1] AV Dicey, *An Introduction to the Study of the Law of the Constitution* (10th edn, London: Macmillan, 1959) 41–50.

positive side of the argument was complemented by a negative, in which Dicey dismissed other possible sources of legislative power, such as the monarch; and in which he also dismissed the possibility of other institutions, such as the courts, placing limitations on what Parliament could do. The empirical analysis was complemented by a normative argument, which was designed to show that it was sound, in terms of principle, for Parliament to have this unlimited power. The essence of the argument was that a Parliament, duly elected on the extended franchise, represented the most authoritative expression of the will of the nation. The Parliament thereby elected should therefore be able to carry out any action. Moreover, Dicey believed that the Parliament would control the executive and that MPs would not pass legislation contrary to the interests of those who elected them. Constitutional protections against the exercise of parliamentary power were not therefore required, since the permanent wishes of the representative portion of Parliament would not differ in the long run from the wishes of the electors.

13.03 The modern debate over sovereignty has been perceived as a contest between the traditionalists, represented by Sir William Wade, and upholders of the new view, represented by Jennings/Heuston/Marshall. Sir William Wade argued[2] that there could be no substantive limits placed on a Parliament. No Act of the sovereign legislature could be judicially invalidated. It was always open to the legislature to repeal any previous legislation, and therefore no Parliament could bind its successors. Where there was a conflict between two Acts of Parliament, the later repealed the earlier. He also rejected the possibility of any procedural limits on Parliament. It was not possible to entrench legislation by requiring some specially safeguarded process before it could be repealed. Such legislation could be repealed by an ordinary Act of Parliament in the normal manner, thereby rendering the special safeguards legally futile. There was therefore only one limit to Parliament's legal power: it could not detract from its own continuing sovereignty.

13.04 The proponents of the new view challenged this thesis. They argued that manner and form provisions, enacted in a particular statute, would be binding: a later statute dealing with the same subject matter could only alter the earlier statute if passed in accordance with the provisions of that earlier statute.[3]

13.05 It should however be recognized that while assertions of parliamentary sovereignty are to be found over the preceding centuries, the form of argument used is not identical to that now characterized as the traditionalist view. The constitutional discourse of previous generations revealed an awareness of the need for

---

[2] HWR Wade, 'The Basis of Legal Sovereignty' [1955] CLJ 172, 174.
[3] Sir WI Jennings, *The Law of the Constitution* (5th edn, London: University of London Press, 1959) ch 4; RFV Heuston, *Essays in Constitutional Law* (2nd edn, London: Stevens, 1964) ch 1; G Marshall, *Constitutional Theory* (Oxford: Clarendon, 1971) ch 3.

principled justifications for the existence of sovereign power, in a way that has been largely forgotten.[4]

(2) The Human Rights Act

It is a generally accepted consequence of the sovereignty principle that the courts will not invalidate primary legislation. The Human Rights Act 1998 (HRA) has not formally changed this. The framers of the HRA were not in favour of what might be termed 'hard constitutional review' such as exists in some other countries where the courts can strike down legislation that is incompatible with fundamental rights. This degree of judicial power was felt to be unsuitable for the United Kingdom with its traditions of parliamentary sovereignty. The HRA does however impose on the courts an interpretative obligation. The HRA therefore encapsulates a 'softer' form of constitutional review in relation to the scrutiny of legislation. If legislation is challenged, s 3 of the HRA provides that 'so far as it is possible to do so, primary legislation and subordinate legislation must be read and given effect in a way which is compatible with the Convention rights'. Where a court is satisfied that primary legislation is incompatible with a Convention right then it can, pursuant to s 4 of the HRA, make a declaration of that incompatibility. While a declaration of incompatibility does not, in itself, affect the validity of the challenged legislation, it does, however, trigger s 10 of the HRA. This applies where a declaration of incompatibility has been made and any appeal rights have either been exhausted, attempted or are not intended to be used. A minister of the Crown is then empowered to amend the offending legislation through the passage of secondary legislation.

13.06

It is clear that the interpretation accorded by the courts to the key words of s 3 will be crucial. The courts are instructed by s 3 that 'so far as it is possible to do so' legislation must be read and given effect in a way which is compatible with the Convention rights. The more the courts are willing to construe legislation to be in conformity with Convention rights, the less they will need to issue declarations of incompatibility. There has been much academic discussion as to the limits of s 3.[5]

13.07

It is clear from the case law that judges accord somewhat differing interpretations to s 3. This is evident from *R v A*.[6] It was argued that s 41 of the Youth Justice and

13.08

---

[4] P Craig, 'Public Law, Political Theory and Legal Theory' [2000] PL 211.

[5] G Marshall, 'Two Kinds of Compatibility: More about Section 3 of the Human Rights Act 1998' [1999] PL 377; F Bennion, 'What Interpretation is "Possible" under Section 3(1) of the Human Rights Act 1998?' [2000] PL 77; Lord Lester, 'The Art of the Possible—Interpreting Statutes under the Human Rights Act' [1998] European Human Rights L Rev 665; Sir William Wade, 'Human Rights and the Judiciary' [1998] European Human Rights L Rev 520; R Clayton, 'The Limits of What's "Possible": Statutory Construction under the Human Rights Act' [2002] European Human Rights L Rev 559.

[6] *R v A (complainant's sexual history)* [2001] UKHL 25; [2002] 1 AC 45.

Criminal Evidence Act 1999 violated Article 6 of the European Convention on Human Rights (ECHR). Section 41 severely restricted the cross-examination of a rape victim about her sexual conduct, which might otherwise be of relevance to a defence based on consent. The House of Lords held that s 41 must be read subject to s 3 of the HRA. The test for the admissibility of such evidence should be whether it was so relevant to the issue of consent that to exclude it would endanger the fairness of the trial and thus be in breach of Article 6. Lord Steyn held that s 3 required the courts to 'subordinate the niceties of the language in section 41(3) to broader considerations of relevance'.[7] He reached that conclusion on certain assumptions about the meaning of s 3:[8]

> [T]he interpretative obligation under section 3 . . . is a strong one. It applies even if there is no ambiguity in the language in the sense of the language being capable of two different meanings . . . The White Paper made clear that the obligation goes far beyond the rule which enabled the courts to take convention rights into account in resolving any ambiguity in a legislative provision . . . Parliament specifically rejected the legislative model of requiring a reasonable interpretation. Section 3 of the 1998 Act places a duty on the court to strive to find a possible interpretation compatible with convention rights. Under ordinary methods of interpretation a court may depart from the language of the statute to avoid absurd consequences: s 3 goes much further. Undoubtedly, a court must always look for a contextual and purposive interpretation: s 3 is more radical in its effect. It is a general principle of the interpretation of legal instruments that the text is the primary source of interpretation: other sources are subordinate to it . . . Section 3 of the 1998 Act qualifies this general principle because it requires a court to find an interpretation compatible with convention rights if it is possible to do so . . . In accordance with the will of Parliament as reflected in s 3 it will sometimes be necessary to adopt an interpretation which linguistically may appear strained. The techniques to be used will not only involve the reading down of express language in a statute but also the implication of provisions. A declaration of incompatibility is a measure of last resort. It must be avoided unless it is plainly impossible to do so. If a *clear* limitation of convention rights is stated in *terms*, such an impossibility will arise . . . There is, however, no limitation of such a nature in the present case.

Lord Hope gave a somewhat more cautious reading of s 3, as is evident in the following quotation:[9]

> The rule of construction which s 3 lays down is quite unlike any previous rule of statutory interpretation. There is no need to identify an ambiguity or absurdity. Compatibility with convention rights is the sole guiding principle. That is the paramount object which the rule seeks to achieve. But the rule is only a rule of interpretation. It does not entitle the judges to act as legislators. As Lord Woolf CJ said in *Poplar Housing* . . . s 3 of the 1998 Act does not entitle the court to legislate; its task is still one

---

[7] *R v A (complainant's sexual history)* (n 6 above) at [45].
[8] ibid at [44]. Italics in the original.
[9] ibid at [108]. See also, *R v Lambert (Steven)* [2001] UKHL 37, [2002] 2 AC 545 at [79]–[81]; *Re S (children) (care order: implementation of care plan)* [2002] UKHL 10, [2002] 2 AC 291 at [40].

of interpretation. The compatibility is to be achieved only so far as this is possible. Plainly this will not be possible if the legislation contains provisions which expressly contradict the meaning which the enactment would have to be given to make it compatible. It seems to me that the same result must follow if they do so by necessary implication, as this too is a means of identifying the plain intention of Parliament.

The way in which the courts apply s 3 can be illuminated by considering decisions where they have saved legislation from incompatibility by using s 3, and by considering cases where they have not felt able to do so. **13.09**

There have been a number of instances in which the courts have saved legislation from incompatibility through s 3. They have 'read in' provisions, normally by implying words in a statute, or 'read down' legislation, by according it a narrower interpretation to ensure that it remains valid. The line between these two techniques may, however, be a fine one. In *R v A*,[10] the House of Lords in effect modified the test for the admissibility of evidence contained in the primary legislation, by reading words into the statute. In *R v Lambert (Steven)*[11] the House of Lords read down s 28 of the Misuse of Drugs Act 1971 that imposed a reverse burden of proof. The ordinary meaning of s 28 was that it imposed the legal burden of proof on the accused, but the House of Lords decided that it should be construed, pursuant to s 3, as imposing only an evidential burden, so as to render it compatible with Article 6(2) ECHR. **13.10**

There have been other decisions where the courts have felt unable to save the legislation through s 3 and have issued declarations of incompatibility. In *Wilson v First County Trust Ltd (No 2)*[12] the court held that s 127(3) of the Consumer Credit Act 1974 was incompatible with Article 6 and Article 1 of Protocol 1. Section 127(3) provided that an improperly executed consumer credit agreement could not be enforced by order of the court, unless the debtor signed a document containing all the prescribed terms of the agreement. The court found that this was a disproportionate interference with Convention rights, because the legislation prevented the court from having regard to prejudice or culpability. Morritt V-C held that s 127(3) could not be saved by s 3 of the HRA. The court was required 'to go as far as, but not beyond, what is legally possible',[13] and could not give the words a meaning that they could not bear. Morritt V-C felt unable to read down the legislation so as to render it compatible with Convention rights. On appeal, the House of Lords accepted this interpretation, but decided that it was compatible with Convention rights properly interpreted.[13a] **13.11**

---

[10] [2001] UKHL 25; [2002] 1 AC 45.
[11] [2001] UKHL 37; [2002] 2 AC 545.
[12] [2001] EWCA Civ 633; [2002] QB 74.
[13] ibid at [42].
[13a] [2003] UKHL 40, [2003] 3 WLR 568, HL.

13.12 A similar reluctance to read down legislative provisions is evident in *Matthews v Ministry of Defence*.[14] The court held that the Crown Proceedings Act 1947, s 10, which prevented in certain circumstances an action in tort against the Crown by a serviceman, did not infringe Article 6 ECHR, because a serviceman had no civil right that engaged this article. Counsel for the claimant argued, drawing on *R v A*,[15] that the court should read down s 10, by adding a sentence the effect of which was that the section would not be used unless the Secretary of State was satisfied that the injury occurred in warlike conditions. The court rejected this argument, in part because Convention rights were not engaged. Lord Phillips MR held moreover that it would be beyond the courts' power under s 3 of the HRA to imply such a clause, since the fundamental alteration of the scope of s 10 would amount to legislation by the court, which was not permissible.[16] The reluctance to rewrite legislation was evident once again in *International Transport Roth GmbH v Secretary of State for the Home Department*.[17] The court considered the Immigration and Asylum Act 1999, Pt II. It provided for fixed penalties on hauliers who intentionally or negligently allowed a person to gain illicit entry to the United Kingdom, and imposed a reverse burden of proof. The court found the scheme to be inconsistent with Convention rights. It could not be saved by s 3, since a radically different approach would be required to comply with the ECHR.[18] This would entail a fundamental re-orientation of the roles of the minister and the court under the scheme, such that the 'rewritten scheme would not be recognisable as the scheme which Parliament intended'.[19]

13.13 The limits to s 3 have also been apparent in cases where the court has not issued a declaration of incompatibility. The overall legislative scheme was decisive as to the limits of s 3 of the HRA in *Re S (children) (care order: implementation of care plan)*,[20] which was concerned with the Children Act 1989, s 38. The Court of Appeal had, pursuant to s 3 of the HRA, read into s 38 of the 1989 Act a wider discretion to make an interim care order. It also introduced a new procedure by which certain essential elements of a care plan would be identified and elevated to a starred status. It would then be open for a court to check whether the starred elements were being fulfilled. Lord Nicholls, giving judgment for the House of Lords, held that the introduction of the starring system could not be justified under s 3 of the HRA. Parliament had under the 1989 Act entrusted local authorities, not the courts, with the responsibility for looking after children who

---

[14] [2002] EWCA Civ 773; [2002] 1 WLR 2621.
[15] [2001] UKHL 25; [2002] 1 AC 45.
[16] [2002] EWCA Civ 773; [2002] 1 WLR 2621 at [76]. The point was not considered in the House of Lords, *Matthews v Ministry of Defence* [2003] UKHL 4; [2003] 2 WLR 435.
[17] [2002] EWCA Civ 158; [2003] QB 728.
[18] ibid at [66].
[19] ibid at [156].
[20] [2002] UKHL 10; [2002] 2 AC 291.

were subject to care orders. The starring system departed substantially from that system, and constituted an amendment of the 1989 Act, not its interpretation: a 'meaning which departs substantially from a fundamental feature of an Act of Parliament is likely to have crossed the boundary between interpretation and legislation'.[21] The boundary line between interpretation and legislation could be crossed even though a limitation on a Convention right was not stated in express terms in the legislation under scrutiny. Lord Nicholls stated that Lord Steyn's dictum in *R v A*[22] should not be taken to mean that a clear limitation on Convention rights was the only circumstance in which an interpretation incompatible with Convention rights could arise.[23]

(3) The Ultra Vires Debate

There has been an academic debate as to the foundations of judicial review, and the implications that this has for the sovereignty of Parliament.[24] Limits of space preclude detailed examination of the contending arguments, but the bare outlines of the debate can be conveyed here. It is important at the outset to be clear about a point that is often lost sight of. The magic phrase 'ultra vires' is indicative of action being beyond power. It does not, in and of itself, tell us whether an act is beyond power because the legislature has intended to place certain limits on an agency, or whether these limits are more properly regarded as a common law creation of the courts. It is this issue which divides the two camps in the debate about the foundations of judicial review.

13.14

The traditional ultra vires model, or specific legislative intent model, was based on the assumption that judicial review was legitimated on the ground that the courts were applying the intent of the legislature. The courts' function was to police the boundaries stipulated by Parliament. The ultra vires principle was regarded as both a necessary and sufficient basis for judicial intervention. It was necessary in the sense that any ground of judicial review had to be fitted into the ultra vires doctrine in order for it to be acceptable. It was sufficient in the sense that if such a ground of review could be so fitted into the ultra vires principle it obviated the need for further independent inquiry. On this view, the doctrines which make up

13.15

---

[21] ibid at [40].

[22] [2001] UKHL 25; [2002] 1 AC 45 at [44].

[23] *Re S (children) (care order: implementation of care plan)* [2002] UKHL 10; [2002] 2 AC 291 at [40].

[24] Many of the relevant articles are to be found in C Forsyth (ed), *Judicial Review and the Constitution* (Oxford: Hart, 2000). See also, M Elliott, *The Constitutional Foundations of Judicial Review* (Oxford: Hart, 2001); N Barber, 'The Academic Mythologians' (2001) 22 OJLS 369; P Craig and N Bamforth, 'Constitutional Analysis, Constitutional Principle and Judicial Review' [2001] PL 763; TRS Allan, 'The Constitutional Foundations of Judicial Review: Constitutional Conundrum or Interpretative Inquiry' [2002] CLJ 87; P Craig, 'Constitutional Foundations, the Rule of Law and Supremacy' [2003] PL 92.

administrative law derived their legitimacy and content from the fact that the legislature intended them to apply in a particular way in a particular statutory context.

13.16   Advocates of the common law model of illegality challenged these assumptions. They argued that the ultra vires principle as articulated above was indeterminate, unrealistic, beset by internal tensions, and unable to explain the application of public law principles to those bodies which did not derive their power from statute. It is of course important to keep bodies within their assigned spheres. It is moreover self-evident that the enabling legislation must be considered when determining the ambit of a body's powers. This is not, however, the same thing as saying that the heads of review, their meaning or the intensity with which they are applied can be justified by legislative intent. The central issue is therefore how far these relevant legal rules and their application can be satisfactorily explained by reference to legislative intent. Proponents of the common law model argue that the principles of judicial review are in reality developed by the courts. They are the creation of the common law. The legislature will rarely provide any indications as to the content and limits of what constitutes judicial review. When legislation is passed the courts will impose the controls which constitute judicial review which they believe are normatively justified on the grounds of justice and the rule of law. They will decide on the appropriate procedural and substantive principles of judicial review that should apply to statutory and non-statutory bodies alike. Agency action that infringes these principles will be unlawful. If the omnipotent Parliament does not like these controls then it is open to it to make this unequivocally clear. If it does so the courts will then adhere to such dictates. If Parliament does manifest a specific intent as to the grounds of review the courts will also obey this, in just the same way as they will obey such intent in other areas where the primary obligations themselves are the creation of the common law. There is, therefore, nothing odd or strange about a set of principles derived from the common law, which are then supplemented or complemented by specific legislative intent if and when this is to be found. This is the paradigm in areas such as contract, tort, restitution, and trusts.

13.17   There is also a modified ultra vires model, or general legislative intent model. Supporters of the ultra vires doctrine have accepted many of the criticisms voiced by proponents of the common law model. They have conceded that the legislature will rarely have any specific intent as to the content of the rules that make up judicial review. They have accepted that it is legitimate for the courts to impose judicial review directly on bodies that do not derive their power from statute. They maintain, however, that ultra vires must still be the central principle of judicial review. It is argued that legislative intent must be found in order to vindicate judicial review, since to discard the ultra vires principle would entail a strong challenge to Parliamentary sovereignty, and would also involve the exercise of untrammelled power by the courts. They further maintain that legislative intent can be found to legitimate the exercise of judicial power. They acknowledge that it is unrealistic to imagine that Parliament has any specific intent as to how the grounds of review should apply in any particular instance. The argument is now put in terms of general legislative intent. Parliament is taken to intend that its legislation conforms to the basic principles of fairness and justice which operate in a constitutional democracy. However, because Parliament itself cannot realistically work out the precise ramifications of this general idea it delegates power to the courts which then fashion the more particular application of this idea in accordance with the rule of law.

The modified ultra vires model, or general legislative intent model, is based on the assumption that the controls which constitute judicial review are only justified if we can find some positive, albeit implied, legislative intent to the effect that such controls should exist. We must find that Parliament intends to prohibit the making of vague regulations etc, in order for such judicial controls to be constitutionally acceptable. If we cannot do so then it is argued that the legislature must be taken to have authorized the making of, for example, vague regulations. It is this which is said to compel continued adherence to the ultra vires doctrine as the foundation of judicial review. Advocates of the common law model deny this causality. They maintain that unless Parliament has clearly authorized action inconsistent with the judicially created controls then such controls should be operative and the relevant action should be prohibited. There is no need to find any positive legislative intent to justify the imposition of the controls that constitute judicial review. The courts develop and impose the controls they believe are normatively justified. Agency action which infringes these controls is therefore illegal, unless Parliament clearly stipulates to the contrary. There is no difference in this respect between contract and tort, and judicial review. The core principles of all these subjects are the creation of the common law. They will apply unless Parliament has indicated otherwise. **13.18**

B. The Rule of Law

(1) General

In one sense the role played by the rule of law in judicial review is deceptively simple. It is frequently cited by the courts as the overarching justification for the principles that constitute judicial review at any one point in time. When used in this way it connotes the idea that government, and more generally the exercise of public power, is subject to constraints, both procedural and substantive. It is also common to find the courts citing the rule of law as justification for the particular **13.19** procedural or substantive constraint that is at issue in the instant case. The rule of law will be held to demand, justify or legitimate the imposition of the principle of judicial review.

13.20   It is rare for the courts to go beyond this and indicate a more specific or detailed vision of the rule of law, or to explicate in greater detail the nature of the connection between the rule of law and the principle of judicial review in the case at hand. This is unsurprising. Courts decide cases, and do not write theses on abstract constitutional concepts, even though they frequently employ them. It is clear moreover that when we move beyond the 'simple' usage of the rule of law adumbrated above, the territory rapidly becomes more complex and controversial. The literature is vast, and the debate intense. It is rather like going from the shallow to the deep end of the pool in one short step. What follows below is a brief guide to these difficult waters.

(2) Formal Conceptions

13.21   Formal conceptions of the rule of law address the manner in which the law was promulgated, (was it by a properly authorized person, in a properly authorized manner, etc); the clarity of the ensuing norm, (was it sufficiently clear to guide an individual's conduct so as to enable a person to plan his or her life, etc); and the temporal dimension of the enacted norm, (was it prospective or retrospective, etc). Formal conceptions of the rule of law are not concerned with whether the law was a good law or a bad law, provided that the formal precepts of the rule of law were met.

13.22   It may be helpful to make clear why those who subscribe to the formal conception of the rule of law insist that the concept should bear this meaning. Raz provides the clearest explanation:[25]

> If the rule of law is the rule of the good law then to explain its nature is to propound a complete social philosophy. But if so the term lacks any useful function. We have no need to be converted to the rule of law just in order to discover that to believe in it is to believe that good should triumph. The rule of law is a political ideal which a legal system may lack or possess to a greater or lesser degree. That much is common ground. It is also to be insisted that the rule of law is just one of the virtues which a legal system may be judged and by which it is to be judged. It is not to be confused with democracy, justice, equality (before the law or otherwise), human rights of any kind or respect for persons of for the dignity of man.

13.23   The essence of Raz's argument can be explained as follows. We may all agree that laws should be just, that their content should be morally sound and that substantive rights should be protected within society. If however the rule of law is taken to encompass the necessity for 'good laws' in this sense then the concept ceases to have an independent function. There is a wealth of literature devoted to the meaning of

---

[25]   J Raz, 'The Rule of Law and its Virtue' (1977) 93 LQR 195, 196.

a just society, the nature of the rights which should subsist therein, and the appropriate boundaries of governmental action. Political theory has tackled questions such as these from time immemorial. Raz's argument is that to bring these issues within the rubric of the rule of law would have the effect of robbing this concept of any function *independent* of such political theories. Laws would be condemned or upheld as being in conformity with, or contrary to, the rule of law in this substantive sense when the condemnation or praise would be reflective of attachment to one particular political theory. It is for this reason that Raz insists that the rule of law should be seen in formal terms. The consequence of this reading is, as Raz admits, that the rule of law could be met by regimes whose laws are morally objectionable, provided that they comply with the formal precepts which comprise the rule of law. It is equally the case, on this view, that a democratic regime will not necessarily always have laws which do measure up to the rule of law.

13.24 It is equally important to be clear as to what is entailed by the formal conception of the rule of law. Raz makes it clear that it cannot just mean that government action is authorized by law since the concept would then be thin indeed. Any law properly passed by Parliament would meet the rule of law defined in this manner. That laws should be passed in the correct legal manner is none the less a *necessary* facet of a formal conception of the rule of law. It is not however *sufficient*. The other important aspect of the rule of law is that the laws thus promulgated should be capable of guiding one's conduct in order that one can plan one's life. It is from this general precept that Raz then deduces a number of more specific attributes that laws should have in order that they could be said to be in compliance with the rule of law. All are related to this idea of enabling individuals to be able to plan their lives. The 'list' includes the following: that laws should be prospective, not retrospective; that they should be relatively stable; that particular laws should be guided by open, general and clear rules; that there should be an independent judiciary; that there should be access to the courts; and that the discretion which law enforcement agencies possess should not be allowed to undermine the purposes of the relevant legal rules. On this view the rule of law is essentially a negative value as Raz himself admits. Given that the law can empower the state to do all manner of things, the rule of law minimizes the danger created by the law itself. It does so by ensuring that whatever the content of the law, at least it should be open, clear, stable, general and applied by an impartial judiciary. It would however be mistaken not to recognize the more positive side of the rule of law when viewed in this manner. Even if the actual content of the law is morally reprehensible, conformity to the rule of law will often be necessary to ensure that individuals actually comply with the demands which the law imposes.

13.25 We must however be wary of common misapprehensions. Legal positivists who subscribe to a formal conception of the rule of law do not believe that the law is value neutral. They maintain that there is a distinction between the existing rules and their normative justification. The formal conception follows from their belief that in determining what the law is, there is no necessary link between law and moral precepts.[26] Inclusive legal positivists maintain, by way of contrast, that there can be instances where the determination of what the law is will entail moral considerations.[27] It is moreover accepted by positivists that courts can have recourse to moral considerations in determining what the law ought to be, when the existing sources of law run out.[28]

13.26   The implications for public law doctrine in liberal, democratic regimes are more 'open' than is commonly imagined. It is wrong to conclude that the formal rule of law only enables the courts to apply formal constraints on governmental power, or that it excludes all reference to moral considerations. There will be many source-based norms, whether derived from statute, precedent or the constitution, which the courts must, on the positivist thesis, faithfully apply. These norms will, in liberal polities, commonly enshrine a plethora of substantive rights. There is moreover nothing within the positivist thesis to prevent the courts interpreting such norms so as to require substantive constraints on the way in which power is exercised. It is the courts' task to interpret the source-based norms that exist. They may well conclude, as an interpretation of the existing law,[29] that the norms contain substantive limits, relating to, for example, the exercise of discretion. The conclusion will be reinforced where other source-based norms, such as precedent, require the imposition of such constraints. It is equally mistaken to think that positivism excludes all moral considerations from public law. This is in part because many of the source-based norms in liberal polities deal with issues of justice. It is in part because all positivists accept that regard can be had to moral considerations when the existing sources run out. The fact that a court has recourse to moral considerations does not therefore tell one whether it is reasoning in a positivist or non-positivist view manner. A positivist judge might decide, where the existing sources stop, that moral considerations provide a persuasive case for the imposition of proportionality.

13.27   It is also important to understand that, as Raz emphasizes, the formal conception of the rule of law is only one virtue of a legal system, and may have to be sacrificed to attain other desired ends. It might be felt that the rule of law virtues of having

---

[26] J Raz, *The Authority of Law, Essays on Law and Morality* (Oxford: OUP, 1979) 49–50; J Raz, *Ethics in the Public Domain, Essays on the Morality of Law and Politics* (Oxford: OUP, 1994) chs 10, 13; A Marmor, 'Exclusive Legal Positivism' in J Coleman and S Shapiro (eds), *The Oxford Handbook of Jurisprudence and the Philosophy of Law* (Oxford: OUP, 2002) ch 3.

[27] J Coleman, 'Negative and Positive Positivism' (1982) 11 J of Legal Studies 139; P Soper, 'Legal Theory and the Obligation of the Judge: The Hart/Dworkin Dispute' (1977) 75 Michigan L Rev 511; A Marmor (n 26 above); K Himma, 'Inclusive Legal Positivism' in Coleman and Shapiro (n 26 above) ch 4.

[28] Raz, *The Authority of Law* (n 26 above) 49–50, 181, 193–194; Raz, *Ethics* (n 26 above) chs 10, 13; Marmor (n 26 above).

[29] Raz, *Ethics* (n 26 above) ch 17.

clear, general norms must be sacrificed if the best or only way to achieve a desired goal is to have more discretionary, open textured legal provisions. This may be the case in circumstances when it is not possible to lay down in advance in the enabling legislation clear, prospective rules in sufficient detail to cover all eventualities. Modifications to the rule of law in this manner are not somehow forbidden or proscribed. Given that it is only one virtue of a legal system it should not prevent the attainment of other virtues valued by that system.

(3) Substantive Conceptions

It is not fortuitous that one of the principal advocates of the formal conception of the rule of law, Raz, is also a leading exponent of legal positivism. The formal conception of the rule of law, and the desire to keep legal questions separate from broader issues of political theory in deciding what the content of the law actually is, fit naturally together. **13.28**

The view of law and adjudication espoused by Dworkin is very different. It is central to this thesis that, subject to questions of fit, the courts should be deciding legal questions according to the best theory of justice.[30] On this view broader questions of political theory are central to the resolution of what rights people currently possess. Dworkin does not therefore conceive of the rule of law in purely formal terms.[31] He distinguishes between two different conceptions of the rule of law. **13.29**

The first, which he terms the rule book conception, is in effect a version of the formal rule of law discussed above. It says nothing about the content of the laws which exist within a legal system, but merely insists that the government should never exercise power against individuals except in accordance with rules which have been set out in advance and made available to all. As Dworkin recognizes, those who have this conception of the rule of law care about the content of the law, 'but they say that this is matter of substantive justice, and that substantive justice is an independent ideal, in no sense part of the ideal of the rule of law'.[32] **13.30**

The second conception of the rule of law is termed by Dworkin the rights conception. He defines it in the following manner.[33] **13.31**

> It assumes that citizens have moral rights and duties with respect to one another, and political rights against the state as a whole. It insists that these moral and political rights be recognized in positive law, so that they may be enforced *upon the demand of individual citizens* through courts or other judicial institutions of the familiar type, so far as this is practicable. The rule of law on this conception is the ideal of rule by an accurate public conception of individual rights. It does not

---

[30] R Dworkin, *Law's Empire* (London: Fontana, 1986).
[31] R Dworkin, *A Matter of Principle* (Cambridge, Mass: Harvard University Press, 1985) 11–12.
[32] ibid 11.
[33] ibid 11–12. Italics in the original.

distinguish, as the rule book conception does, between the rule of law and substantive justice; on the contrary it requires, as part of the ideal of law, that the rules in the book capture and enforce moral rights.

13.32 Proponents of a rights-based or substantive conception of the rule of law do have regard to the values enshrined in the formal conception of the rule of law. This is because such values feature in any serious theory of justice,[34] and because these values are relevant when deciding 'whether the plaintiff has a moral right to receive, in court, what he or she or it demands'.[35]

> The rule book is *relevant* to that ultimate question. In a democracy, people have at least a strong *prima facie* moral right that courts enforce the rights that a representative legislature has enacted. That is why some cases are easy cases on the rights model as well as on the rule book model. If it is clear what the legislature has granted them, then it is also clear what they have a moral right to receive in court. (That statement must be qualified in a democracy whose constitution limits legislative power. It must also be qualified, though it is a complex question how it must be qualified, in a democracy whose laws are fundamentally unjust.)[36]

13.33 Dworkin's argument serves to emphasize that the meaning of the rule of law will be inextricably linked with one's definition of law itself and with the proper adjudicative role of the judge. A positivist is likely to subscribe to the formal sense of the rule of law, and to keep this distinct from the content of particular laws. A rights-based analysis of the Dworkinian kind is diametrically opposed to this dichotomy between form and substance. The content of laws will be evaluated in order to determine whether they are compatible with the moral rights which individuals possess.

13.34 We can now summarize the implications of a substantive conception of the rule of law, of the kind articulated by Dworkin. Individuals have rights, both with respect to one another, and against the state. The rule of law is the ideal of rule by an accurate public conception of individual rights. It does not distinguish between the rule of law and substantive justice. It requires, as part of the ideal of law, that the rules in the book capture and enforce moral rights. There is no distinction between constitutional and administrative law rights that form part of the rule of law and those which do not. This does not mean that the substantive conception is consistent with only one theory of justice or freedom. It does mean that it is not independent of the particular theory or theories of justice, which constitute its content at any point in time. Dworkin regards a particular variant of liberalism as the best political theory. His conception of law and adjudication, based on fit and justification, can however

---

[34] R Dworkin (n 31 above) 12–13.
[35] ibid 16.
[36] ibid. Italics in the original.

perfectly well be used in support of other theories of justice, as Dworkin recognizes.[37] Writers have, for example, used Dworkin's theory to provide support for republicanism.[38] The implications for administrative law doctrine are not self-executing. They will depend upon the interpretation accorded to Dworkinian ideas of fit and justification. It would be possible to conclude, for example, either that the courts should substitute judgment on errors of law, or that they should adopt the two-part *Chevron* test.[39]

(4) Mixed Conceptions

There is, as stated above, a wealth of different theories of the rule of law. Limits of space preclude a detailed analysis of all such theories. Brief mention should however be made of two such theories.   **13.35**

Allan has argued that the rule of law should have the formal connotation outlined above, but he wishes to move beyond this and to imbue it with a more substantive content. He is unhappy with the purely formal version of the rule of law, but also mindful of the dangers of making the rule of law synonymous with some particular vision of substantive justice. He seeks, therefore, to incorporate within the rule of law some substantive rights, while at the same time trying to avoid tying these too closely to any specific conception of justice.[40] It is however extremely difficult to specify some particular rights, and not others, that would be agreed to by proponents of differing conceptions of liberalism or democracy. The chosen list reflects the principles which would be agreed to by those who subscribe to a particular version of liberalism and democracy, and does not include principles which advocates of other conceptions of liberalism and democracy would regard as equally, or more, important.[41]   **13.36**

Dyzenhaus proffers a process-based conception of the rule of law, in the sense that it accords pre-eminence to the values of accountability and participation. The focus is on public rational justification, and on the 'citizen as active participant in the legal order and not on the substance incorporated into law'.[42] This is however problematic. It is clear that any theory of justice will entail some notion of participation and accountability. The very meaning accorded to participation and accountability will however vary depending upon the more general democratic   **13.37**

---

[37] Dworkin (n 30 above) 410.

[38] See, eg, F Michelman, 'Traces of Self-Government' (1986–87) 100 Harvard L Rev 4.

[39] *Chevron USA Inc v NRDC* 467 US 837 (1984).

[40] eg TRS Allan, *Law, Liberty and Justice, The Legal Foundations of British Constitutionalism* (Oxford: Clarendon Press, 1993); TRS Allan, 'The Rule of Law as the Rule of Reason: Consent and Constitutionalism' (1999) 115 LQR 221; TRS Allan, *Constitutional Justice, A Liberal Theory of the Rule of Law* (Oxford: OUP, 2001).

[41] Craig (n 24 above).

[42] D Dyzenhaus, 'Form and Substance in the Rule of Law: A Democratic Justification for Judicial Review' in Forsyth (ed) (n 24 above) ch 7.

theory, or theory of justice, that is being espoused. It is equally clear that process and substance interact. The idea that the rule of law can be explicated principally or solely in terms of participation and accountability is untenable because the meaning accorded to such ideas will be dependent upon, and resonate with, substantive principles. It is for this reason that it has been convincingly argued that no ostensibly process-based theory can avoid making substantive value judgments.[43] This is in part because many constitutional and administrative law norms are manifestly substantive in nature. It is in part because even allegedly procedural norms necessitate substantive choices. This is true in relation to both process writ small, or adjudicative process, and process writ large, or representative process. If, for example, we decide that representative process is appropriate within a particular context, then we must determine who should be allowed to participate through the vote, and this will entail substantive judgments as to the nature of a political community. If, for example, we decide that certain discrete and insular minorities, that are likely to lose out in the political process, require special protection then we must have criteria to identify such groups. Given that not all groups that lose out in the political struggle can be so regarded, the criteria will inevitably require us to decide which of these groups is exercising fundamental rights.

(5) Dicey's Conception

13.38 Dicey's conception of the rule of law is perhaps the best known within the United Kingdom.[44] Dicey's first limb of the rule of law was that:[45]

> [N]o man is punishable or can be lawfully made to suffer in body or goods except for a distinct breach of law established in the ordinary legal manner before the ordinary courts of the land. In this sense the rule of law is contrasted with every system of government based on the exercise by persons in authority of wide, arbitrary, or discretionary powers of constraint.

13.39 There are a number of well-known critiques of this principle. It is generally accepted that Dicey underestimated both the existence of discretionary power which existed at the time when he was writing; and also the fact that such discretionary power was often a necessary and legitimate consequence of the growth of governmental power in the 19th century.

13.40 Dicey's second principle of the rule of law was concerned with equality. Dicey's formulation of the principle was as follows:[46]

13.41

[43] L Tribe, 'The Puzzling Persistence of Process-Based Constitutional Theories' (1980) 89 Yale LJ 1063; P Brest, 'The Substance of Process' (1981) 42 Ohio State LJ 131; R Dworkin, 'The Forum of Principle' (1981) 56 New York U L Rev 469.
[44] Dicey (n 1 above).
[45] ibid 188.
[46] ibid 193.

> We mean . . . when we speak of the 'rule of law' as a characteristic of our country,
> not only that with us no man is above the law, but (what is a different thing) that
> here every man, whatever be his rank or condition, is subject to the ordinary law of
> the realm and amenable to the jurisdiction of the ordinary tribunals.

There are also well-known critiques of Dicey's second principle. He misunderstood **13.41**
the French droit administratif, and misapprehended how much administrative law
existed in 19th century England, with adjudication through specialist tribunals
rather than the ordinary courts.[47]

Dicey's third limb of the rule of law was rather different in nature. The essence of **13.42**
this precept can be stated as follows:[48]

> We may say that the constitution is pervaded by the rule of law on the ground that
> the general principles of the constitution (as for example the right to personal lib-
> erty, or the right of public meeting) are with us the result of judicial decisions de-
> termining the rights of private persons in particular cases brought before the courts;
> whereas under many foreign constitutions the security (such as it is) given to the
> rights of individuals appears to result, from the general principles of the constitu-
> tion.

There has been a lively debate as to whether Dicey's rule of law was purely formal **13.43**
or whether he intended it to have a substantive dimension.[49] This can be exemplified in relation to Dicey's first limb of the rule of law. The first sentence of this limb
is clearly formal. It requires that laws under which people are condemned should
be passed in the correct legal manner and that guilt should only be established
through the ordinary trial process. It does not touch the content of the laws which
an individual will face when taken before the courts. The words used by Dicey in
his second sentence could bear a substantive meaning.[50] On this view a law properly enacted by Parliament, in compliance with all correct procedures, which was
pristinely clear in its application, and which was applied by an impartial judiciary,
might nonetheless be tainted as 'arbitrary' if it was thought to infringe certain fundamental rights, or if it entailed excessive punishment. It is equally clear that the
word arbitrary can have a formal meaning. When used in this latter sense the word
arbitrary would provide the foundation for criticism of two kinds of norm. One
category would comprise those allegedly legal rules that have no legal foundation.
They might not have been enacted in the proper manner because, for example,
they have not been passed through Parliament and do not come within the ambit
of the prerogative. The other category of formal arbitrariness would be for those

---

[47] HW Arthurs, '*Without the Law*', *Administrative Justice and Legal Pluralism in Nineteenth Century England* (Toronto: University of Toronto Press, 1985).

[48] Dicey (n 1 above) 195–196.

[49] P Craig, 'Formal and Substantive Conceptions of the Rule of Law: An Analytical Framework' [1997] PL 467; Allan, *Law, Liberty and Justice* (n 40 above) ch 2; Allan, 'The Rule of Law as the Rule of Reason' (n 40 above).

[50] See, eg, Allan, *Law, Liberty and Justice* (n 40 above) 46.

norms which have been passed in the correct legal manner, but where the resulting law was impossibly vague or unclear, with the result that individuals had no idea how to plan their lives in the light of the relevant legal rule. Formal arbitrariness in either of these senses is independent of whether the content of the legislation was good or bad, just or unjust.

13.44 The debate as to whether Dicey's rule of law was formal or whether it contained a substantive component can also be exemplified in relation to Dicey's third limb of the rule of law. A common error is to read this aspect of the rule of law as demanding that a society must possess certain individual rights if it is to conform to the rule of law. That is not however what Dicey actually said. His argument was not that the rule of law demanded adherence to certain specific substantive rights. It was that if you wished to protect such rights then the common law technique was better than that employed on the continent. He felt that the protection of rights on the continent through Bills of Rights was ineffective, since such constitutional documents could so easily be abrogated at the stroke of a pen. Under the common law, where individual rights were the result of numerous judicial decisions indicating when the individual was at liberty to speak freely, etc, it would be considerably more difficult for an authoritarian regime to sweep these rights aside.[51]

C. The Separation of Powers

(1) General

13.45 The separation of powers is regarded as a central construct in our constitutional structure. It should nonetheless be recognized that in historical terms it was not always of such importance. The dominant constitutional concept concerned with the relationship between the constituent parts of government was the republican concept of balanced constitutionalism. The constitutional order was perceived to be one of balance, in which the King, Commons and Lords each possessed important powers. Their respective powers were seen as justified in two complementary senses. They were perceived as representing different legitimate interests within society; and the division of power between them was seen as a bulwark against tyranny. Indeed, for writers such as Blackstone and de Lolme, the very essence of tyranny was a form of constitutional ordering in which power was not distributed and counterbalanced in this manner.[52] It was this conception of balanced constitutionalism, and not Montesquieu's vision of separation of powers, which captured the essence of the division of authority within the state.[53]

---

[51] Dicey (n 1 above) 200–202.
[52] Sir W Blackstone, *Commentaries on the Law of England* (16th edn, 1825) vol I, book 2, 146–156.
[53] B Kemp, *King and Commons 1660–1832* (London: Macmillan, 1957) 82–87.

We draw from the separation of powers precepts about the relationship between **13.46** the executive and the legislature. The 'lessons' from this aspect of the separation of powers have always been difficult for a parliamentary system, such as ours. This is reflected in the standard treatment, which indicates the plethora of ways in which the executive and the legislature interact, with the result that the former controls the latter.

The separation of powers also speaks to the relationship between the courts, the **13.47** legislature and the executive. The concept operates as a source of judicial legitimacy, with the courts defending their role as the rightful interpreters of legislation, and of the legality of executive action. It serves also as the foundation for judicial restraint, with the courts being mindful of not substituting their view on matters of discretion for that of the body to whom Parliament has granted the power.

The remainder of this discussion will be concerned with the separation of powers **13.48** so far as it affects the relationship between the courts, legislature and the executive. It should be recognized that the mere invocation of the phrase the 'separation of powers' does not in and of itself resolve the relationship between the courts, the legislature and the executive. This is because the concept operates both as a source of judicial legitimacy, and as a source of judicial restraint, in the manner described above. The 'tension' and 'interplay' between them underlie much of the case law on judicial review. This can be exemplified in relation to judicial review generally, and in relation to judicial review under the HRA 1998. These will be considered in turn.

(2) General Judicial Review

The foundational assumption underlying judicial review over discretion is that it **13.49** is not for the courts to substitute their choice as to how the discretion ought to have been exercised for that of the administrative authority. They should not intervene, reassess the matter afresh and decide, for example, that funds ought to be allocated in one way rather than another. Decisions as to political and social choice are made by the legislature, or by a person assigned the task by the legislature.[54] To sanction judicial intervention simply because the court would prefer a different choice to that of the administrator runs counter to this fundamental assumption, and would entail a reallocation of power from the legislature and executive to the courts.

The courts accept that it is not their task to substitute judgment. This is exempli- **13.50** fied by *R v Cambridge Health Authority, ex p B (No 1)*.[55] The applicant, B, was a

---

[54] *R v Ministry of Agriculture, Fisheries and Food, ex p First City Trading* [1997] 1 CMLR 250, 278.
[55] [1995] 1 WLR 898.

10-year-old girl who was extremely ill. She had received a bone marrow transplant, but the treatment had not proven to be effective. The hospital, acting on the advice of specialists, decided that B had only a short time to live and that further major therapy should not be given. B's father sought the opinion of two further specialists, who thought that a second bone marrow transplant might have some chance of success. Such treatment could, however, only be administered privately because there were no beds in the National Health Service within a hospital which could carry out such therapy. The proposed treatment would take place in two stages, the first of which would cost £15,000 and have a 10–20 per cent chance of success; the second stage would cost £60,000 with a similar 10–20 per cent chance of success. B's father requested the health authority to allocate the funds necessary for this therapy. It refused to do so, given the limited nature of the funds at its disposal and the small likelihood that the treatment would be effective. B's father then sought judicial review of this decision, but failed before the Court of Appeal. Sir Thomas Bingham MR recognized the tragic nature of B's situation, but stressed that the courts were not the arbiters of the merits in such cases. It was not for the courts to express any opinion as to the likely success or not of the relevant medical treatment.[56] The courts should, said the Master of the Rolls, confine themselves to the lawfulness of the decision under scrutiny. The basic rationale for the health authority's refusal to press further with treatment for B was scarcity of resources. The court's role in this respect was perforce limited:[57]

> I have no doubt that in a perfect world any treatment which a patient . . . sought would be provided if doctors were willing to give it, no matter how much it cost, particularly when a life was potentially at stake. It would however, in my view, be shutting one's eyes to the real world if the court were to proceed on the basis that we do live in such a world. It is common knowledge that health authorities of all kinds are constantly pressed to make ends meet. They cannot pay their nurses as much as they would like; they cannot provide all the treatments they would like; they cannot purchase all the extremely expensive medical equipment they would like; they cannot carry out all the research they would like; they cannot build all the hospitals and specialist units they would like. Difficult and agonising judgments have to be made as to how a limited budget is best allocated to the maximum advantage of the maximum number of patients. That is not a judgment which the court can make. In my judgment, it is not something that a health authority such as this authority can be fairly criticised for not advancing before the court.

13.51 While it is accepted that it is not for the courts to substitute judgment, it is also recognized that there should be some control over the rationality of the decisions made by the administration. The theme that runs throughout this area is the desire to fashion legal criteria to control discretionary decision-making, by emphasizing the aspect of the separation of powers that legitimizes judicial control,

---

[56] *R v Cambridge Health Authority, ex p B (No 1)* (n 55 above) 904–905.
[57] ibid 906.

without thereby leading to substitution of judgment or too great an intrusion on the merits, by according due weight to the aspect of the separation of powers that places emphasis on judicial restraint. This is exemplified by the debates, judicial and extra-judicial, about unreasonableness and proportionality as tests for review, and the meaning that should be accorded to these concepts.

(3) Judicial Review Under the Human Rights Act

Similar tensions are apparent in relation to adjudication under the HRA 1998. **13.52** It is clear that our courts recognize a domestic concept of deference within the HRA. Lord Hope in *R v DPP, ex p Kebilene*[58] held that the Strasbourg margin of appreciation doctrine was not available to national courts under the HRA, but that national courts should however recognize that difficult choices might have to be made between the rights of the individual and the needs of society. It followed that in some circumstances the courts should acknowledge an area of judgment 'within which the judiciary will defer, on democratic grounds, to the considered opinion of the elected body or person whose actual decision is said to be incompatible with the Convention'.[59] Such an area of judgment would more readily be found where the ECHR required a balance to be struck, or where the case raised issues of social and economic policy. It would be less likely to be found where the right was unqualified, or where the rights were of high constitutional importance which the courts were well placed to assess.[60] Similar themes were echoed forcefully by Lord Hoffmann in *R (on the application of Holding & Barnes plc) v Secretary of State for the Environment, Transport and the Regions*.[61] He stated that 'in a democratic country, decisions as to what the general interest requires are made by democratically elected bodies, or persons accountable to them'.[62] On some occasions Parliament would be able to lay down the general policy in advance through legislation. In other areas it was not possible to formulate general rules, and the question of what the general interest required would have to be decided on a case by case basis, as with planning. In these latter areas Parliament will delegate decision-making to ministers, or local authorities, thereby preserving the democratic principle. In such instances the 'only fair method of decision is by some person or body accountable to the electorate'.[63] The HRA 'was no doubt intended to strengthen the rule of law but not inaugurate the rule of lawyers'.[64] There were, however, limits to deference. Certain basic individual rights 'should not be capable in any circumstances of

---

[58] [2000] 2 AC 326, HL.
[59] ibid 380.
[60] ibid 380.
[61] [2001] UKHL 23; [2001] 2 WLR 1389.
[62] ibid at [69].
[63] ibid at [70].
[64] ibid at [129].

being overridden by the majority, even if they think that the public interest so requires'.[65] These were rights which belonged to individuals 'simply by virtue of their humanity, independently of any utilitarian calculation'.[66] The importance of deference has been emphasized in other cases.[67]

13.53 The courts have had to grapple with the limits of deference, or what is known as the discretionary area of judgment, in the HRA case law, in particular in cases arising under s 6. The leading authority on the test for review is *R (on the application of Daly) v Secretary of State for the Home Department*.[68] The applicant challenged the policy, made pursuant to s 47(1) of the Prison Act 1952, whereby a prisoner could not be present during a search of his cell, when prison officers examined legally privileged correspondence. He argued that this infringed his common law right to communicate confidentially with his legal adviser, and Article 8 ECHR. Lord Steyn clarified the test for review under the HRA, and this was reaffirmed by the House of Lords in *R v Shayler*.[69] Lord Steyn referred to the judgment in *R (on the application of Mahmood (Amjad)) v Secretary of State for the Home Department*[70] and observed[71] that this formulation was cast in terms of heightened scrutiny under the *Wednesbury* test. This level of scrutiny had been held to be insufficient by the European Court of Human Rights.[72] This was because it effectively excluded any consideration by the national court of whether the interference with the applicant's rights answered a pressing social need or was proportionate to national security or public order. Lord Steyn held[73] that there was a material difference between the heightened scrutiny test, and one framed in terms of proportionality. While Lord Steyn accepted that many cases would be decided the same way under either test, he acknowledged that the intensity of review would be greater under proportionality. This was so for two reasons. Proportionality could, said Lord Steyn, require the reviewing court to assess the balance struck by the decision-maker, not merely whether it was within the range of reasonable decisions. The proportionality test could, secondly, oblige the

---

[65] (n 61 above) at [70].

[66] ibid at [70].

[67] *Brown v Stott* [2003] 1 AC 681, HL; *R (on the application of Marper) v Chief Constable of South Yorkshire* [2002] EWCA Civ 1275, [2002] 1 WLR 3223; *A v Secretary of State for the Home Department* [2002] EWCA Civ 1502, [2003] 2 WLR 564. See, however, *R (on the application of ProLife Alliance) v BBC* [2003] UKHL 23, [2003] 2 WLR 1403 at [75–77] where L Hoffmann deprecated use of the word 'deference', preferring to express the matter in terms of the proper allocation of decision-making power as between courts and the legislative/executive.

[68] [2001] UKHL 26; [2001] 2 AC 532.

[69] [2002] UKHL 11; [2003] 1 AC 247 at [3].

[70] [2001] 1 WLR 840, 857, CA.

[71] *R (on the application of Daly) v Secretary of State for the Home Department* [2001] UKHL 26; [2001] 2 AC 532 at [26].

[72] *Smith and Grady v UK (No 1)* (1999) 29 EHRR 493 at [138].

[73] *R (on the application of Daly) v Secretary of State for the Home Department* [2001] UKHL 26; [2001] 2 AC 532 at [26].

court to pay attention to the relative weight accorded to relevant interests, in a manner not generally done under the traditional approach to review. The proper intensity of review was, said Lord Steyn, guaranteed by the twin requirements that the limitation of the right was necessary in a democratic society, in the sense of meeting a pressing social need, and really was proportionate to the legitimate aim being pursued.[74]

It is clear that the test in *Daly* has been accepted in subsequent cases. It is equally **13.54** clear that the application of the proportionality test has been affected by the discretionary area of judgment that the courts are willing to accord to the body being reviewed. The discretionary area of judgment/deference is the vehicle through which the courts bring into play that aspect of the separation of powers that is concerned with judicial restraint. This can be exemplified by considering briefly certain leading decisions.

In *R (on the applications of P and Q) v Secretary of State for the Home Department*,[75] **13.55** the court considered the policy of the Prison Service, which stipulated, inter alia, that children who accompanied their mothers to prison must leave a specialist prison unit for mothers and babies when they were 18 months old. It was argued that this policy interfered with family life and infringed Article 8. Lord Phillips MR accepted the approach to review laid down in *Daly*. He held that the intensity of review would nonetheless depend on the subject matter of the particular case, and that in applying the proportionality test within Article 8(2) deference should be accorded to the Prison Service as an expert body that had devised the relevant policy.[76] Lord Phillips held that the Prison Service policy must allow for some discretionary exceptions to the 18-month rule.[77] The court then proceeded to decide whether such an exception was warranted in the two cases before it, concluding that this was so in one case, but not the other.

In *R (on the application of Samaroo) v Secretary of State for the Home Department*,[78] **13.56** the court was faced with a different type of case based on Article 8. The claimant had lived in the United Kingdom since 1989, was married to a UK citizen, and they had a child. He was convicted of drug trafficking, imprisoned and the Home Secretary sought to deport him on his release from prison. It was recognized that the deportation would interfere with family life under Article 8, but the Home Secretary relied on the need to prevent crime within Article 8(2). Dyson LJ acknowledged that the *Daly* test applied, and accepted that the Home Secretary's response had to be proportionate, but there was a difference of view as to what that

---

[74] ibid at [27].
[75] [2001] EWCA Civ 1151; [2001] 1 WLR 2002.
[76] ibid at [61], [64].
[77] ibid at [100]–[101], [106].
[78] [2001] EWCA Civ 1139; [2001] UKHRR 1150.

meant on the facts of the case. The claimant argued that the issue was whether not deporting him, and hence preserving his family life, would undermine the Home Secretary's deterrence policy. Dyson LJ disagreed. He accepted that the prevention of crime through the deterrent impact of deportation was a legitimate aim within Article 8(2), and that there was no less restrictive alternative.[79] Dyson LJ held that the issue was as to whether the Home Secretary had struck a fair balance between the interest of the community in the prevention of crime, and the claimant's Article 8 rights,[80] and in this sense had a disproportionate impact on the claimant's rights. In deciding on that issue the Home Secretary had a discretionary area of judgment, the extent of which would depend, inter alia, on the nature of the Convention right, the extent to which the issues require consideration of social, political and economic factors, the extent to which the court has expertise, and whether the rights claimed are of especial importance.[81] The court's assessment of the weight accorded by the Home Secretary to the community's interest and that of the claimant would be searching, but would pay due regard to the Home Secretary's discretionary area of judgment.[82] The court found against the claimant.

13.57 The interplay between the *Daly* test, and the discretion left to the executive, is also apparent in *R (on the application of Farrakhan) v Secretary of State for the Home Department*.[83] Farrakhan was the leader of the Nation of Islam, and had, in the past, made various anti-Semitic statements. He wished to visit the United Kingdom, inter alia, to address a series of meetings. The Home Secretary defended his refusal to allow him entry on the ground that, even if this limited Farrakhan's speech rights under Article 10(1), it was nonetheless justified to prevent the risk of public disorder under Article 10(2). The claimant argued that the Home Secretary had not presented sufficient reasons to indicate that there was a risk of public disorder so as to come within Article 10(2). The court disagreed. Lord Phillips MR accepted that proportionality as set out in *Daly* provided the test for review. He also held that when applying proportionality 'the margin of appreciation or discretion accorded to the decision-maker is all important, for it is only by recognising the margin of discretion that the court avoids substituting its own decision for that of the decision-maker'.[84] Lord Phillips concluded that there were a number of reasons for according a wide measure of discretion in this case.[85] The reasons were as follows. The case was about immigration, and the European

---

[79] *R (on the application of Samaroo) v Secretary of State for the Home Department* (n 78 above) at [20].
[80] ibid at [25].
[81] ibid at [35].
[82] ibid at [39].
[83] [2002] EWCA Civ 606; [2002] QB 1391.
[84] ibid at [67].
[85] ibid at [71]–[77].

Court of Human Rights attached considerable weight to the right of a state to control entry into its territory. The contested decision was the personal decision of the Home Secretary. The Home Secretary was in a better position than the court to consider the likely consequence of admitting Farrakhan. The Home Secretary was democratically accountable for his decision. The contested decision only had a limited impact on Farrakhan's speech right, since the 'reality is that it was a particular forum that was denied to him rather than the freedom to express his views'.[86]

There is much academic debate as to the precise boundaries and application of **13.58** deference within the HRA.[87] While it is generally accepted that some conception of deference should operate within the HRA, there has been more debate as to the criteria that should trigger deference, and as to the degree of deference that should be accorded to the legislature or the executive. This is a complex issue that cannot be examined in detail here. It requires consideration of the relationship between courts and legislature in a constitutional democracy, combined with an appreciation of the different types of case in which the issue can arise.[88]

---

[86] ibid at [77].

[87] D Dyzenhaus, 'The Politics of Deference: Judicial Review and Democracy' in M Taggart (ed), *The Province of Administrative Law* (Oxford: Hart, 1997) ch 13; P Craig, 'The Courts, the Human Rights Act and Judicial Review' (2001) 117 LQR 589; R Edwards, 'Judicial Deference and the Human Rights Act' (2002) 65 MLR 859; J Jowell, 'Judicial Deference and Human Rights: A Question of Competence' in P Craig and R Rawlings (eds), *Law and Administration in Europe, Essays in Honour of Carol Harlow* (Oxford: OUP, 2003) ch 4; M Hunt, 'Sovereignty's Blight: Why Contemporary Public Law Needs the Concept of "Due Deference"' in N Bamforth and P Leyland (eds), *Public Law in a Multi-Layered Constitution* (Oxford: Hart, 2003) ch 13; TRS Allan, 'Common Law Reason and the Limits of Judicial Deference', forthcoming; P Craig, 'Deference, Democracy and Distinction', forthcoming.

[88] Craig, 'Deference, Democracy and Distinction' (n 87 above).

14

GROUNDS FOR JUDICIAL REVIEW: ILLEGALITY IN THE STRICT SENSE

A. Introduction

Judicial review is concerned with ensuring that actions of public bodies, including **14.01** the executive, are lawful. Public bodies possess no inherent legal authority. They can only do what the law authorizes[1] and must do what the law demands.[2] If an action

---

[1] *Entick v Carrington* (1765) 19 St Tr 1030.
[2] In *R v Somerset CC, ex p Fewings* [1995] 1 All ER 513, 524e–g Laws J (as he then was) said: 'For private persons, the rule is that you may do anything you choose which the law does not prohibit . . . But for public bodies the rule is opposite . . . It is that any action to be taken must

or inaction of a public body is not authorized in law it has no legal effect and may be found to be invalid.[3] Ultimately it is for the courts to determine what the law permits or demands. The courts undertake this task by interpreting the relevant legislation and by applying and developing the common law. These well known propositions are central to what might be called the basic principle of legality.[4]

14.02 In practice this principle is enforced by means of the various heads or grounds of judicial review. Many different formulations of these grounds are to be found in the cases and in the literature. However, the best known modern classification is that provided by Lord Diplock in *Council of Civil Service Unions v Minister for the Civil Service.*[5] Here he distinguished between three heads of review: 'illegality', 'irrationality' and 'procedural impropriety'. In this chapter we are concerned with 'illegality', by which Lord Diplock meant 'that the decision-maker must understand correctly the law that regulates his decision-making power and must give effect to it'.[6]

14.03 Before proceeding it is important to emphasize that terms such as 'illegality', 'irrationality' and 'procedural impropriety', are no more than aids for classifying and analysing various types of test that will be used by the courts in determining whether the actions of public bodies satisfy the principle of legality.[7] In this sense the heads indicate the variety of routes by which legality is ensured. Moreover, as Lord Diplock himself emphasized, these three heads are not exhaustive and new heads of review continue to be developed by the courts, the best known being proportionality. Nor should the heads of review be treated as water-tight divisions for, as we will see in a moment, there are inevitable overlaps between them.

14.04 As the above indicates, the nomenclature in this area sometimes appears more important than the substance and the terminology can be confusing, especially for those unfamiliar with the field. The relationship between what Lord Diplock referred to as

---

be justified by positive law. A public body has no heritage of legal rights which it enjoys for its own sake; at every turn, all of its dealings constitute the fulfilment of duties which it owes to others; indeed, it exists for no other purpose . . . a public body enjoys no rights properly so called . . .'

   [3] The courts, however, may exercise their discretion to treat such action as having practical effects where, for example, it is necessary to do so in order to protect the interests of good administration or third parties.

   [4] cf Lord Hoffmann's reference to the principle of legality in *R v Secretary of State for the Home Department, ex p Simms* [2000] 2 AC 115, 131.

   [5] [1985] AC 374.

   [6] ibid 410D. 'Illegality' carries a different meaning in public law to that used in private law where it is normally associated with tortious liability: see P Cane, *An Introduction to Administrative Law* (3rd edn, Oxford: Clarendon Press, 1998) 242–243.

   [7] eg, the term 'illegality' is not always expressly referred to. For instance, in *R (on the application of Holding & Barnes plc) v Secretary of State for the Environment, Transport and the Regions* [2001] UKHL 23; [2001] 2 WLR 1389 at [73], Lord Hoffman said that '[t]he principles of judicial review . . . ensure that administrative decisions will be taken rationally, in accordance with a fair procedure and within the powers conferred by Parliament'.

716

'illegality' and 'irrationality' on the one hand and what is often referred to as *Wednesbury* unreasonableness is often particularly unclear. Before commenting on this relationship, a word about discretion.

(1) Decisions, Discretion and Duties

Much judicial review litigation is concerned with whether public bodies have law-fully exercised discretionary powers. Where discretion has been conferred it is implicit that the body concerned has freedom to choose whether and how to act. How much freedom a body has will depend on the nature of the powers granted. Distinctions are often made, for example, between 'broad' and 'narrow' or 'strong' and 'weak' discretion or between 'subjective' or 'unfettered' discretion and 'objective' or 'fettered' discretion.[8] In practice public authorities will be given power to act in a particular context, say to grant licences or planning permission or to determine whether a person should be granted asylum. Within this context the power may appear unlimited, as when the legislation allows a planning authority to grant planning permission 'subject to such conditions as it thinks fit' or the Home Secretary to deport those who appear to him to constitute a threat to national security. Often powers will be more circumscribed. For example, the legislation may require the authority to take certain factors into account, or to act only when certain facts are established, or when there are reasonable grounds for doing so. The breadth of the discretion granted, and the freedom of choice permitted to the decision-maker will depend on the particular terms of its grant and ultimately on how these terms are construed by the courts. As a matter of general principle, even where no express limitations are imposed, discretionary power must be exercised in accordance with the object and policy of the legislation by which it is conferred and in accordance with the principles of judicial review. The courts therefore determine the legal parameters of discretionary power both by construing and applying the relevant legislation and by developing and applying the common law requirements of legality.

14.05

Judicial attitudes to discretionary power have changed over the years as the courts have become increasingly prepared to subject the exercise of discretion to legal scrutiny. The advent of the so-called human rights culture into our public law has added new techniques for such scrutiny, based on the proportionality principle. As is explained elsewhere, these techniques are not designed to abrogate discretion by allowing judges to replace decisions of public bodies with their own. Their purpose is to ensure that discretion is exercised in accordance with the law and compatibly with human rights requirements. Judges are sensitive to the need to maintain a proper constitutional balance between the courts and public bodies

14.06

---

[8] See generally, R Dworkin, *Taking Rights Seriously* (London: Duckworth, 1977) 32; DJ Galligan, *Discretionary Powers* (Oxford: Clarendon, 1986).

justified and proportionate, particularly where their actions impinge upon human rights.[15]

14.11 As used in this chapter the term 'illegality' is therefore one form of unlawfulness. It is essentially concerned with ensuring that decision-makers properly understand and give effect to the legislation that confers their powers and regulates their activities; it also involves ensuring that public bodies act in conformity with the common law. 'Illegality' may occur in a wide variety of forms that are impossible to list exhaustively, particularly given the dynamic nature of this area. Nonetheless, it may be safely said that action (or inaction) of a public body will be tainted by 'illegality' when the body misinterprets the law under which it purports to act and therefore:

- acts without legal authority;
- wrongly delegates its power or otherwise renders itself unable to exercise its powers;
- seeks to achieve purposes that are not in accordance with the objects and policy of that legislation;
- reaches a decision on the basis of legally irrelevant factors or without considering factors that the law requires to be considered;
- misunderstands or ignores established and relevant facts; or
- acts in a way which is incompatible with a Convention right under the provisions of s 6(1) of the Human Rights Act 1998 (HRA).

These matters will be considered later in this chapter, but before moving on several further introductory comments are required.

(3) Illegality and Procedural Impropriety

14.12 Under the head of 'illegality' the court is typically concerned with the legal power of the authority to take the decision that was taken. This situation may be contrasted with the typical challenge under the head of procedural propriety where the challenge focuses upon the propriety and fairness of the procedures adopted rather than the legality of the decision itself. For this reason it is sometimes said that illegality is concerned with matters of substance while procedural impropriety is concerned with matters of procedure. This may be a convenient distinction to keep in mind but is one that is not always easily maintained in practice. There are many situations, for example, where the events may give rise to arguments based both in illegality and procedural impropriety or unfairness. Failure to allow a party to present evidence or to cross-examine witnesses, for instance, may be both unfair and result in a decision that is tainted by illegality because it is taken

---

[15] See further paras 16.01–16.33 below.

without regard to relevant considerations. Similarly, the well-known principle that when public bodies are charged with exercising a discretion they must not rigidly adhere to a policy in such a way that prevents them from deciding individual cases on their merits may give rise to claims under both illegality and procedural fairness. It is illegal for an authority to abdicate discretion that has been conferred upon it by Parliament and it is also procedurally unfair to decide a matter without considering the merits of the case in hand.[16]

(4) Illegality and the Merits of Decision-making

It is said that judicial review is a supervisory process that is not concerned with the merits of decisions as such. However, like many of the terms used in the context of judicial review, what is meant by the 'merits' of decisions is not always clear. Traditionally the requirements of 'illegality' and legal rationality focus upon the factors that inform the making of the decision. In other words they are concerned with the *inputs* into the decision, but not with the actual making of the decision itself.[17] According to this traditional approach how the decision-maker weighs and balances factors such as the evidence, the various competing demands on resources, issues of policy, if any, and then arrives at the decision is not for a judicial review judge to adjudicate upon. If a discretion has been conferred this implies that at some point there is a core of choice that is beyond the reach of the court.[18] There may be an opportunity to appeal on the grounds that the decision was wrong. But, if no such appeal exists, it is to be assumed that the matter should be left to those upon whom discretionary power has been conferred, subject to the tests of illegality, irrationality, and procedural propriety. These propositions are commonly summarized by saying that judicial review is concerned with the process of decision-making rather than with the merits of the decision taken, save where the decision is patently irrational or absurd.[19]

14.13

This remains an accurate statement of principle, but in recent years the courts have refined and expanded the matters over which scrutiny extends in judicial review proceedings. This process has been further encouraged by Parliament under

14.14

---

[16] See paras 14.42–14.55 below.

[17] Cane (n 6 above).

[18] The size of this core will vary depending on the nature of the discretion conferred and the context.

[19] In *R v Chief Constable of the North Wales Police, ex p Evans* [1982] 1 WLR 1155, 1173–1174 Lord Brightman said: 'Judicial review is concerned, not with the decision, but with the decision-making process. Unless that restriction on the power of the court is observed, the court will . . . under the guise of preventing an abuse of power, be itself guilty of usurping power'. In *R (on the application of Holding & Barnes plc) v Secretary of State for the Environment, Transport and the Regions* [2001] UKHL 23; [2001] 2 WLR 1389 at [61] Lord Nolan said that 'a review of the merits of the *decision-making process* is fundamental to the courts' jurisdiction—the powers of review may even extend to a decision on a question of fact . . .' (emphasis added).

the provisions of the HRA 1998. The result is that while judicial review does not provide a 'complete rehearing on the merits of a decision',[20] the courts are now able to subject the process of decision-making to the closest scrutiny. The courts, in particular, have all but discarded their traditional reluctance to scrutinize whether decision-makers have given appropriate weight to relevant considerations[21] and, as we shall see in a moment, are prepared to accept that it may be appropriate to review the factual foundation of decisions. Whether the courts will employ their armoury to the full, however, will depend on the context and in particular on factors such as the expertise of the body being reviewed, the function being performed, and the human rights implications, if any.[22]

(5) Illegality and Error of Law

14.15   The relationship between the terms 'error of law' and 'illegality' deserves a mention. In orthodox theory it is technically possible for a body to commit an error of law that would not be illegal or unlawful in the judicial review sense of these terms. This is because according to that theory decisions of tribunals and inferior courts would only be impugned in judicial review proceedings if these bodies acted beyond their jurisdiction and bodies do not step beyond their jurisdiction every time they make an error of law.[23] In practice most errors of law would be rectified by way of appeal on a point of law rather than judicial review. However where no, or no adequate or suitable appeal exists, judicial review would be the only legal remedy. Recognizing this, the courts gradually accepted the possibility that errors of law may be reviewed. The first important step was in *R v Northumberland Compensation Appeal Tribunal, ex p Shaw*[24] where Lord Denning MR reinvented the possibility of certiorari being used to quash errors of law on the face of the record. Since the decision in *Anisminic v Foreign Compensation Commission*[25] it is

---

[20] *per* Lord Slynn in *R (on the application of Holding & Barnes plc) v Secretary of State for the Environment, Transport and the Regions* [2001] UKHL 23; [2001] 2 WLR 1389 at [52].

[21] See paras 14.00–14.00 below.

[22] In *Begum (Runa) v Tower Hamlets LBC* [2003] UKHL 5; [2003] 2 WLR 388 at [42]–[44] Lord Hoffman referred to certain relevant contextual matters by drawing a distinction between situations in which utilitarian principles do and do not have a place. He intimated that they have no place in relation to criminal law or private rights, but they do have a place when it comes to schemes of regulation or social welfare. Parliament, he said, is entitled to take the view that it is not in the public interest that an excessive proportion of the funds available for the welfare scheme should be consumed in administration and legal disputes. This appears to be a call to adopt a cautious approach to judicial review where litigation might undermine the efficiency of administration in the context of social welfare and housing disputes.

[23] When the term jurisdiction is used in this sense bodies do not lose jurisdiction simply by making mistakes: if they have jurisdiction to go right they also have jurisdiction to go wrong. See Lord Reid in *R v Governor of Brixton Prison, ex p Armah* [1968] AC 192, 234 and *Anisminic v Foreign Compensation Commission* [1969] 2 AC 147.

[24] [1952] 1 KB 338.

[25] [1969] 2 AC 147.

now accepted that in general any error of law is potentially reviewable even when not disclosed on the face of the record.[26] Of course, this does not mean that judges will quash a decision whatever the error. The courts, for instance, are unlikely to intervene where minor errors of law have been made or where the errors are purely technical and have had no material impact on the outcome. Nor does it imply that the courts will permit the use of judicial review where alternative appellate procedures exist.[27] Nonetheless, in general, it may now be assumed that errors of law are reviewable as an aspect of 'illegality' whenever judicial review proceedings are permissible.

(6) Illegality and Facts

The traditional view is that judicial review is concerned with law but not with **14.16** matters of fact. This view was summarized by Lord Brightman in the context of a challenge to a local housing authority's decision on homelessness:[28]

> Parliament intended the local authority to be the judge of fact . . . Where the existence or non existence of a fact is left to the judgment and discretion of a public body . . . it is the duty of the court to leave the decision of that fact to the public body to whom Parliament has entrusted the decision-making power save in a case where it is obvious that the public body, consciously or unconsciously, are acting perversely.

It is now well established, however, that the courts' supervisory jurisdiction does **14.17** extend to factual issues in the following circumstances. The first is where issues of precedent or jurisdictional fact are involved. That is to say, where the legal power of the public body depends on its making a correct factual determination on an issue: for example, where the immigration authorities only have power to deport someone who is, as a matter of fact, an 'illegal entrant'. [29] Secondly, the courts may impugn a discretionary decision if it is based on 'ignorance or misunderstanding of an established and relevant fact'.[30] The courts may also impugn a decision for which there is no supporting evidence.[31] It is also now clear that the courts may

---

[26] eg, see *O'Reilly v Mackman* [1983] 2 AC 237 (Lord Diplock) and *Boddington v British Transport Police* [1999] 2 AC 143 (Lord Irving LC). One exception is in relation to the jurisdiction of university visitors: *R v Hull University Visitor, ex p Page* [1993] AC 682.

[27] *R v Secretary of State for the Home Department, ex p Swati* [1986] 1 WLR 477; cf *R v Chief Constable of Merseyside, ex p Calveley* [1986] QB 424.

[28] *R v Hillingdon LBC, ex p Puhlhofer* [1986] AC 484, 518. See also *Secretary of State for Employment v ASLEF (No 2)* [1972] 2 QB 455, 493 *per* Lord Denning MR.

[29] *R v Secretary of State for the Home Department, ex p Khawaja* [1984] AC 74. See further paras 14.23–14.25 below.

[30] Lord Wilberforce in *Secretary of State for Education v Tameside MBC* [1977] 1 AC 1014, 1047; and more recently Lord Slynn in *R v Criminal Injuries Compensation Board, ex p A* [1999] 2 AC 330, 344–345 and *R (on the application of Holding & Barnes plc) v Secretary of State for the Environment, Transport and the Regions* [2001] UKHL 23; [2001] 2 WLR 1389 at [53]–[54].

[31] *Coleen Properties Ltd v Minister of Housing and Local Government* [1971] 1 WLR 433.

be required to review findings of fact where proportionality arguments are involved.[32]

14.18 Despite the views of some leading commentators,[33] however, it is not yet established that English courts can review a decision solely on the basis that the decision-maker has acted on a wrong factual basis. Subject to the caveat below, in principle there is nothing objectionable in the courts having this jurisdiction and support for them doing so has recently been given by Lord Slynn when in *Holding & Barnes* he cited the following statement by Wade and Forsyth with approval:[34]

> This ground of review has long been familiar in French law and is has been adopted by statute in Australia. It is no less needed in this country, since decisions based upon wrong facts are a cause of injustice which the courts should be able to remedy. If a 'wrong factual basis' doctrine should become established, it would apparently be a new branch of the *ultra vires* doctrine, analogous to finding facts based upon no evidence or acting upon a misapprehension of law.[35]

14.19 The caveat lies in the need to establish a way of reviewing on this basis without forcing the court to re-evaluate findings of fact reasonably made by the decision-maker. The Court of Appeal, for instance, has recently rejected the argument that the supervisory jurisdiction extends to situations in which it is claimed that the 'decision-maker got the facts wrong by preferring one version of the facts to another when it could reasonably have accepted either version'.[36] Brooke LJ said that, 'what is quite clear is that a court of supervisory jurisdiction does not, without more, have the power to substitute its own view of the primary facts for the view reasonably adopted by the body to whom the fact-finding power has been entrusted'.[37]

---

[32] See further paras 7.164–7.168 above and 16.89 below. Even prior to the HRA 1998, where the Secretary of State's decision in an Art 3 case was challenged in judicial review, while not a primary fact-finder, the court had the obligation to consider whether or not underlying factual material compelled a different conclusion to that reached by the Secretary of State: *R v Secretary of State for the Home Department, ex p Turgut* [2001] 1 All ER 719.

[33] eg Sir William Wade and Christopher Forsyth, *Administrative Law* (8th edn, Oxford: OUP, 2000) 282–283.

[34] *R (on the application of Holding & Barnes plc) v Secretary of State for the Environment, Transport and the Regions* [2001] UKHL 23; [2001] 2 WLR 1389 at [53].

[35] See now Wade and Forsyth (n 33 above) 283.

[36] Brooke LJ, in *Adan v Newham LBC* [2001] EWCA Civ 1916; [2002] 1 WLR 2120 at [35].

[37] ibid at [41]. The majority also rejected the argument that the court should interpret the words 'may appeal to the County Court on any point of law arising from the decision' in s 204(1) of the Housing Act 1996 as meaning 'any point of law, or if it is necessary to do so in order to ensure that an appellant's Convention Rights are not violated, any point of fact'. Hale LJ, in the minority, held that this interpretation should be adopted. See further the decision of the House of Lords in *Begum (Runa) v Tower Hamlets LBC* [2003] UKHL 5; [2003] 2 WLR 388.

B. The Body Must Have Legal Authority to Act

It is an elementary principle that a public body may only act when it has express **14.20**
or implied legal authority to do so. A committee of a local authority cannot, for
example, undertake disciplinary functions without the legal authority to do so.[38]
Likewise a tribunal or inferior court cannot deal with a matter that falls beyond its
permitted field of inquiry.

(1) Express and Implied Powers

Public bodies have legal authority to do what is expressly authorized and im- **14.21**
plied powers to do whatever is reasonably incidental to, or consequential upon,
what is expressly authorized.[39] A local authority, for example, was able to establish a printing, bookbinding and stationery works because the court regarded
this as being incidental to its express functions.[40] Likewise the power to detain
mentally ill offenders implied that a hospital had power to control what its
patients wore, thereby enabling a hospital to prevent male patients dressing in
female clothes.[41] On the other hand, a local authority authorized to operate a
tram service could not operate a bus service.[42] And an authority permitted to
provide facilities where people could wash their clothes could not establish a
municipal laundry.[43]

In the context of the powers of local government, this principle is now contained **14.22**
in s 111(1) of the Local Government Act 1972:

> . . . subject to the provisions of this Act and any other enactment . . . a local au-
> thority shall have power to do any thing . . . which is calculated to facilitate, or is
> conducive or incidental to, the discharge of any of their functions.

It seems that in order to justify action under s 111 local authorities have to establish that the action facilitates, or is conducive or incidental to the discharge
of, functions which are expressly authorized by legislation. It has been held, for
example, that s 111 does not permit local authorities to charge for giving developers advice before an application for planning permission was made.
Power exists to give advice because this facilitates the consideration of planning
permission (a function that is specifically authorized by legislation), however

---

[38] eg *R v Portsmouth City Council, ex p Gregory* [1990] 2 Admin LR 681
[39] *A-G v Great Eastern Rly Co* (1880) 5 App Cas 473, 478 *per* Lord Selborne LC.
[40] *A-G v Smethwick Corp* [1932] 1 Ch 562.
[41] *R (on the application of E) v Ashworth Hospital Authority* [2001] EWHC 1089; [2002]
ACD 23.
[42] *London County Council v A-G* [1902] AC 165.
[43] *A-G v Fulham Corp* [1921] 1 Ch 440.

an authority cannot charge for this advice because the imposition of the charge is only incidental to the giving of advice and not the consideration of planning permission. As one judge put it, the charges were 'incidental to the incidental'.[44]

(2) Precedent Fact

14.23 Where legislation requires certain conditions to be satisfied before a public body is able to act, it will be unlawful for it to act unless these conditions are satisfied. Where, for example, action can only be undertaken if certain facts exist, the facts must exist for the action to be lawful. Such issues are generally described as issues of 'precedent fact' or now less commonly, issues of 'jurisdictional fact'.[45] Despite the traditional antipathy towards being involved in factual issues in judicial review proceedings, the courts will not permit public bodies to have the final say on factual issues such as these. If they were to do so this would be tantamount to giving public bodies freedom to decide whether or not they have legal authority to act in a particular matter and this would offend the principle of legality.

14.24 The leading decision is that of the House of Lords in *R v Secretary of State for the Home Department, ex p Khawaja*.[46] Here the Secretary of State had power to detain and remove 'illegal entrants'.[47] Relying on the earlier decision of the House of Lords in *Zamir v Secretary of State for the Home Department*[48] the Secretary of State argued that this power permitted detention and removal where the authorities had 'reasonable grounds for believing a person to be an illegal entrant'. In *Khawaja* the House rejected this argument and reversed its decision in *Zamir* on this point. It held that draconian powers to arrest without trial as a first stage in the removal of someone from this country could only be given to the immigration authorities by clear statutory language. Here the legislation gave power only to detain people who were 'illegal entrants'; it did not give power to detain people whom the immigration authorities reasonably believed to be illegal entrants.[49] Before exercising this power the authorities

---

[44] *McCarthy & Stone (Developments) Ltd v Richmond upon Thames LBC* [1992] 2 AC 48. Also, *Hazell v Hammersmith and Fulham LBC* [1992] 2 AC 1 (a local authority had no power to speculate in interest rate swaps); *Credit Suisse v Allerdale BC* [1997] QB 306; *Credit Suisse v Waltham Forest LBC* [1997] QB 362.

[45] See para 14.17 above.

[46] [1984] AC 74. See also *White and Collins v Minister of Health* [1939] 2 KB 838 (a local authority had power to acquire land provided it was not part of a park and the court could review the authority's decision that the land was not part of a park); *R v Fulham, Hammersmith and Kensington Rent Tribunal, ex p Zerek* [1951] 2 KB 1 (whether the tribunal was dealing with accommodation that was furnished or unfurnished).

[47] Immigration Act 1971, s 33.

[48] [1980] AC 930.

[49] ibid 97, *per* Lord Fraser of Tullybelton.

had therefore to establish, on a balance of probabilities,[50] that the person is an illegal entrant.[51]

The courts may regard the *Khawaja* approach as being too blunt in situations   **14.25**
where they feel that decision-makers should be accorded some margin of appreciation. This issue recently arose in *R v Collins, ex p Brady*.[52] Brady had been convicted, with Myra Hindley, of the 'Moors Murders'. For many years he was detained in high security prisons but was later transferred to what became Ashworth Hospital. The question in this case was whether the hospital could lawfully force-feed Brady under the provisions of s 63 of the Mental Health Act 1983. The legality of force-feeding depended on whether the feeding was medical treatment given 'for the mental disorder from which [the patient] is suffering'. On behalf of Brady it was accepted that force-feeding could be medical treatment, but it was argued that because he had taken the decision to starve himself to death as a protest the force-feeding was not being administered as a treatment within s 63 for a mental disorder. In other words Brady was asking the courts to determine, as a precedent fact, whether the treatment was being administered for this reason. Maurice Kay J rejected the argument that the courts could decide this. He said that s 63 was about clinical judgments and that it 'would be wholly undesirable' if medical officers 'were challengeable in relation to s 63 on any basis other than the appropriate *Wednesbury* one'.[53]

C. Public Bodies Must Exercise the Discretionary Power that has been Conferred upon Them

As a general principle if decision-making power is conferred upon a person or   **14.26**
body it is for that person or body and no other to exercise the power. The body cannot, without express or implicit authorization, delegate its power to another. Nor can the body prevent itself from exercising its discretionary power by, for example, deferring to another, treating policy as if it were binding, or by entering into agreements that purport to prevent it from exercising its discretion.

---

[50] ibid 124C, *per* Lord Bridge.
[51] In *R v Secretary of State for the Home Department, ex p Oni* (CO/2863/98, 25 October 1999) Sullivan J held that whether a British citizen has been 'ordinarily resident' in this country under s 7 of the Immigration Act 1971 is a precedent fact to be determined by the court. This being so, since the respondent had failed to establish on a balance of probabilities that the applicant was not 'ordinarily resident' there was no legal power to deport. Cf *R v Secretary of State for the Home Department, ex p Onibiyo* [1996] QB 768; *R v Secretary of State for the Home Department, ex p Rahman* [1998] QB 136.
[52] (2001) 58 BLMR 173, (2000) Lloyd's Rep Med 355.
[53] ibid at [33].

(1) A Person or Body Cannot Delegate Decision-making Responsibility to Another, Unless Authorized to Do So

14.27 Given the highly centralized nature of legal and political power in the United Kingdom it is perhaps unsurprising that judges are sometimes said to have an antipathy to delegation.[54] Even if this is true, the courts accept that public administration would be impossible without delegation to and involvement of officers, experts, committees and other agencies. As in many areas of public law, the courts must therefore tread carefully when developing and applying legal principle to ensure that the law recognizes the day-to-day realities of administration.[55]

14.28 Most disputes turn on the wording of specific provisions and judicial attitudes to delegation in particular cases are likely to be influenced by the function being performed, the nature and scope of the powers involved and factors such as whether rights, reputations and significant interests of individuals are affected.

14.29 Nonetheless it is a general principle that if decision-making power is conferred upon a person or body it is for that person or body and no other to exercise the power. The body cannot, without express or implicit authorization, delegate its power to another. In effect there is a presumption against delegation so that in general powers should only be delegated where this is expressly or implicitly authorized.[56] It goes without saying that delegation will be unlawful if expressly (or implicitly) prohibited or if the decision to delegate 'was irrational in administrative terms'.[57] Where power has been lawfully delegated the delegate must act within the scope of the actual power that has been delegated.[58]

14.30 The prohibition of unauthorized delegation rests on several justifications. First, it flows from the traditional view that legal powers are delegated by Parliament to those it entrusts to act in the public interest. Further delegation is therefore not permissible unless approved by Parliament. Secondly, there is a corresponding principle that if Parliament has conferred responsibility to make decisions upon a

---

[54] This might suggest the existence of tension between the presumption against delegation and the process of devolution.

[55] Wade and Forsyth (n 33 above) 319 observe that: 'Sometimes the judicial aversion to delegation is carried to lengths which make administration difficult . . .'.

[56] In this respect there is no effective difference between delegation and creating an agency relationship, which also requires legal authority. Although, of course, there are situations where it is lawful for public authorities to appoint agents but not to delegate. Wade and Forsyth (n 33 above) 320 point out that occasionally courts may invoke the rules of agency to justify a questionable delegation, citing as an example *R v Chapman, ex p Arlidge* [1918] 2 QB 298 (where a committee was permitted to ratify an earlier decision of its chairman to institute proceedings for nuisance). On the relationship between delegation and agency see also de Smith, Woolf and Jowell, *Principles of Judicial Review* (London: Sweet & Maxwell, 1999) paras 5-108 and 5-109.

[57] Lord Donaldson MR in *R v Secretary of State for the Home Department, ex p Oladehinde* [1991] 1 AC 254, 282.

[58] *Blackpool Corp v Locker* [1948] 1 KB 349.

particular body that body cannot pass this responsibility to another. Both of these propositions indicate a link between the presumption against delegation and trust. That is to say, the notion that when power has been conferred upon a person 'trust is being placed in his individual judgment and discretion' and for this reason he must exercise that power personally unless he has been expressly authorized to delegate to another.[59] In the context of local government, for example, it has been said that where public powers are conferred on local authorities, it is the body of elected councillors who must exercise those powers, as if on trust. The body of councillors may, however, lawfully delegate the functions of the authority to a committee, an officer of the authority, or another local authority[60] under the provisions of s 101 of the Local Government Act 1972.[61] It may be noted that no similar provision exists to authorize delegation within central government.[62] Finally, unauthorized delegation may also offend obligations to act fairly and the requirements of procedural propriety.[63]

While rigid conceptual distinctions between administrative, judicial and quasi-judicial functions are no longer made, the courts are reluctant to permit delegation by judicial bodies[64] or those charged with making disciplinary decisions that might adversely affect the rights and reputation of individuals. A well-known illustration is provided by *Barnard v National Dock Labour Board*.[65] Here suspended dock-workers successfully challenged their suspension on the grounds that the London Dock Labour Board had unlawfully delegated its disciplinary powers to the London port manager. The Court of Appeal held that the Board could not delegate an important disciplinary matter such as this. Likewise, the House of Lords held that a dock-worker's dismissal was invalid because the Board **14.31**

---

[59] de Smith, Woolf and Jowell (n 56 above) para 5-102. See also Lord Bingham in *Porter v Magill* [2001] UKHL 67; [2002] 2 AC 357 at [12], quoting the Lord Chancellor of Ireland in *A-G ex rel Rea v Belfast Corp* (1855) 4 Ir Ch R 119, 160–161. This principle is said to be expressed in the maxim delegates non potest delegare. Cf Wade and Forsyth (n 33 above) 316 who say that the proper home for this maxim is in the law of agency.

[60] Delegation may need to be formally done, *R v St Edmundsbury BC, ex p Walton* [1999] Env LR 879.

[61] s 101 does not authorize the delegation of activities that are not the functions of an authority and nor does it permit delegation to bodies not mentioned, including the directors of a private company. See *Credit Suisse v Allerdale BC* [1997] QB 306; *Credit Suisse v Waltham Forest BC* [1997] QB 362. In *R v Servite Houses, ex p Goldsmith* (2001) 33 HLR 35 Moses J held that s 101 did not permit Wandsworth LBC to appoint Servite Houses as its agent to provide community care services.

[62] See para 14.35 below.

[63] See para 15.36 below.

[64] In *R v Brixton Prison Governor, ex p Enahoro* [1963] 2 QB 455, 481, Lord Parker CJ said that: 'It is settled that certainly no person made responsible for a judicial decision can delegate his responsibility'.

[65] [1953] 2 QB 18. In *Blackpool Corp v Locker* [1948] AC 488 Denning LJ drew a distinction between administrative functions, 'which can often be delegated' and a judicial function which 'rarely can be'. But this is not to imply that the courts are necessarily ready to accept the delegation of administrative functions, see Wade and Forsyth (n 33 above) 321.

had unlawfully delegated its functions to a disciplinary committee.[66] A disciplinary body may allow its individual members to do such things as investigate specific matters, interview witnesses, and hear submissions, but the body as a whole must retain final decision-making responsibility and to this end it must ensure that it has sufficient information to make a proper decision.[67] It must also ensure that it acts fairly to those subject to the proceedings.[68]

14.32 The courts will also be reluctant to permit the delegation of discretionary power, particularly where the exercise of the power impinges upon individual rights. As in disciplinary proceedings, a body with discretionary powers may allow others to undertake particular tasks provided always that it retains supervisory power and responsibility for making the final decision; and that it possesses the factual and other information necessary to enable it to do so.

14.33 By contrast, the courts may be willing to allow some degree of delegation, even where no specific authorization exists, if the tasks involved are purely administrative and no discretion is involved. *Allingham v Minister of Agriculture and Fisheries*[69] provides a well-known illustration of the line between permissible and impermissible delegation. Here the Minister of Agriculture had delegated to a war agricultural committee power to give directions with respect to the cultivation, management or use of land. The committee sub-delegated to its officer power to determine in which fields specified crops were to be grown and to issue directions to the farmer. This was held to be unlawful because the committee had not retained the final say on whether the officer's determination should be adopted or not. The task of the officer should have been limited to making recommendations that the committee was free to accept or reject.[70] As Wade and Forsyth emphasize, such a requirement is not simply a matter of form. In many situations it will be clear that real discretion will be exercised by those who make the recommendation, but the

---

[66] *Vine v National Dock Labour Board* [1957] AC 488; also *General Council of Medical Education and Registration of the UK v Dental Board of the UK* [1936] Ch 41.

[67] eg *Osgood v Nelson* (1872) LR 5 HL 636; *R v Commission for Racial Equality, ex p Cottrell and Rothon* [1980] 1 WLR 1580.

[68] The body must, for example, provide opportunities to see and test the evidence and any recommendations. See further de Smith, Woolf and Jowell (n 56 above) para 5-105, nn 72 and 73.

[69] [1948] 1 All ER 780.

[70] See also *High v Billings* (1903) 89 LT 550 (a local Board had unlawfully delegated power to grant permission for the laying of drains to their surveyor without retaining ability to decide the applications themselves); *R v Secretary of State for Education and Science, ex p Birmingham CC* (1984) 83 LGR 79 (local education authority could not leave it to its chairman to set the date for the closure of a school); *R v Monopolies and Mergers Commission, ex p Argyll Group Plc* [1986] 1 WLR 763 (the Commission could not leave it to its chairman to decide that a takeover proposal had been abandoned); *R v DPP, ex p Association of First Division Civil Servants*, The Times, 24 May 1988 (it was unlawful for the DPP to delegate to non-lawyers the decisions whether there was sufficient evidence to proceed with prosecutions); *R v Devon CC, ex p G* [1989] AC 573 (the education committee had unlawfully delegated to a school medical officer the decision whether the state of a child's health warranted the provision of free transport).

courts are willing to accept this situation if the legally responsible body genuinely applies its mind to the matter and makes a conscious choice. It would be unlawful for an authority simply to rubber-stamp its officers' recommendations.[71]

The courts will rarely permit delegation where statute has entrusted powers to a named officer, unless this is specifically permitted. In the context of sentencing, for example, the courts have drawn a distinction between the conferral of power upon the Home Secretary and conferral of power upon the Lord Chief Justice. Whereas Parliament is taken to assume that the former will rarely take decisions personally, it is assumed that power of the Lord Chief Justice will be exercised personally without delegation.[72]   **14.34**

(a) The 'Carltona' principle: decision-making within central government departments

It has just been observed that Parliament is taken to assume that ministerial powers are often exercised by decisions taken by others within the government department rather than by the minister personally.[73] It is misleading to regard this arrangement as involving a delegation of authority by the minister. This is because discretionary power is conferred upon ministers not as individuals but in their capacity as office holders who, while acting with the help of the collective expertise of the department and its officials, remain legally and politically responsible for the decision that is taken.[74] It is more appropriate, and now more common, to refer to power being devolved, rather than delegated, within a department.[75]   **14.35**

---

[71] *High v Billings* (1903) 89 LT 550; *Labour Relations Board of Saskatoon v Spears* [1948] 1 DLR 340 (the Board, charged with determining whether a trade union was supported by the majority of employees, could not simply leave this decision to an officer whose decision it adopted); *Cader v Commissioners for Mosques* (1963) 66 NLR 16 (Board charged with appointing trustees of a mosque could not simply adopt a list of names put forward by an outsider). For a discussion of the division of decision-making powers between officers and elected members of local authorities, see paras 4.66 et seq above, especially paras 4.71–4.74.

[72] *R v Secretary of State for the Home Department, ex p Doody* [1994] 1 AC 531, 567 *per* Lord Mustill. See also the judgment of Staughton LJ in the Court of Appeal adopted by Lord Mustill [1993] QB 157.

[73] In *Bushell v Secretary of State of State for the Environment* [1981] AC 75, 95, Lord Diplock said: 'To treat the minister in his decision-making capacity as someone separate and distinct from the department of government of which he is the political head and for whose actions he alone in constitutional theory is accountable to Parliament is to ignore not only practical realities but also Parliament's intention. Ministers come and go; departments, though their names may change from time to time, remain. Discretion in making administrative decisions is conferred on a minister not as an individual but as the holder of an office in which he will have available to him in arriving at his discretion the collective knowledge, experience and expertise of all those who serve the Crown in the department of which, for the time being, he is the political head.'

[74] In *R v Skinner* [1968] 2 QB 700, 707, Widgery LCJ said: 'If a decision is made on his behalf by one of his officials, then that constitutionally is the Minister's decision. It is not strictly a matter of delegation; it is that the official acts as the Minister himself and the official's decision is the Minister's decision.'

[75] For this reason no formal delegation of authority is needed: *Lewisham BC v Roberts* [1949] 2 KB 608; *R v Skinner* [1968] 2 QB 700.

14.36   The leading case, *Carltona Ltd v Commissioners of Works*,[76] arose when a requisitioning order made by an official on behalf of the Commissioners of Works was challenged. The Commissioners of Works, which was a ministry, were given power to requisition land, 'if it appears to that authority necessary or expedient to do so'. Although in practice the Commissioners did not meet as a body and their powers were exercised entirely by officials, the Court of Appeal held that this procedure was perfectly lawful. Lord Greene MR provided the classic statement of the doctrine, when he said that:[77]

> In the administration of government in this country the functions which are given to ministers . . . are functions so multifarious that no minister could ever personally attend to them. To take the example of the present case no doubt there have been thousands of requisitions in this country by individual ministries. It cannot be supposed that this regulation meant that, in each case, the minister in person should direct his mind to the matter. The duties imposed upon ministers and the powers given to ministers are normally exercised under the authority of the ministers by responsible officials of the department. Public business could not be carried on if that were not the case. Constitutionally, the decision of such an official is, of course, the decision of the minister. It is he who must answer before Parliament for anything that his officials have done under his authority . . .

It should be unnecessary to add that the minister will also be accountable to the courts for the legality of 'anything that his officials have done under his authority'. As will be seen shortly, it is now accepted that the courts may review action taken under the *Carltona* doctrine if, for example, the officials who actually make the decisions are insufficiently senior or inadequately qualified or otherwise unsuited for the task conferred upon them.[78]

14.37   The *Carltona* doctrine, which has been described as a 'common law constitutional power'[79] permits the performance of functions without ministers having personally to address their minds to the matter in question. It appears to extend to judicial and legislative functions.[80] The doctrine, however, does not apply where powers are expressly conferred upon an official, such as a planning inspector. Nor does it authorize a minister, or officials in one department, to exercise powers conferred upon a minister in another department.[81] It has been argued that the doctrine does not apply to authorize those within the recently established executive

---

[76] [1943] 2 All E.R. 560.

[77] ibid 563

[78] See Lord Donaldson MR in *R v Secretary of State for the Home Department, ex p Oladehinde* [1991] 1 AC 254, 284–285.

[79] ibid.

[80] de Smith, Woolf and Jowell (n 56 above) para 5-113, where it is pointed out that in certain government departments statutory instruments are signed by senior officials acting under a general grant of authority from the minister.

[81] *Lavender & Son Ltd v Minister of Housing and Local Government* [1970] 1 WLR 1231. Note, however, powers conferred upon the 'Secretary of State' may be exercised by any Secretary of State.

agencies to take decisions in the name of the minister.[82] This, however, was rejected by the Court of Appeal, upholding the Divisional Court, in *R v Secretary of State for Social Services ex p Sherwin*.[83] Here it was held that the creation of the Benefits Agency had no effect on the operation of the *Carltona* doctrine which continued to apply provided the minister retains responsibility for actions of the agency and decisions are taken by persons of sufficient seniority in the agency.[84]

The doctrine will not apply where statute expressly requires the minister to make **14.38** the decision in person or otherwise imposes limits on the involvement of others.[85] It appears, although it is not absolutely certain, that the doctrine may also be excluded by necessary implication.[86] In this context, commentators agree that certain matters are of such importance that the minister should deal with them in person, even though Parliament has not expressly prevented devolution to officials. The most obvious of these would be decisions affecting liberty or fundamental human rights.[87] While there are dicta to support this view,[88] the weight of recent authority seems to indicate that no such class of case exists.[89] De Smith, Woolf and Jowell say that 'there appears to be no English case in which the exercise of discretion has been held invalid on this ground and many of the dicta that

---

[82] Mark Freedland, 'The rule against delegation and the Carltona doctrine in an agency context' [1996] PL 19 and Mark Freedland, 'The Crown and the Changing Nature of Government' in Maurice Sunkin and Sebastian Payne (eds) *The Nature of the Crown* (Oxford: OUP, 1999).

[83] (1996) 32 BMLR 1, QBD. The Court of Appeal's decision (22 July 1996) is unreported.

[84] In the Divisional Court in *Sherwin*, ibid, Latham J indicated some agencies may not fall within the *Carltona* principle. They may not do so, he said, where '. . . an agency is established in such a way that a minister could no longer, in any sensible analysis, be accountable to Parliament for its decisions'.

[85] eg s 13(5) of the Immigration Act 1971 provides that a person shall not be entitled to appeal against a refusal of leave to enter, or against a refusal of an entry clearance, if the Secretary of State certifies that directions have been given by the Secretary of State (and not by a person acting under his authority).

[86] Lord Donaldson MR in *R v Secretary of State for the Home Department, ex p Oladehinde* [1991] 1 AC 254, 282 said: 'I have no doubt that there can be an implied limitation which can affect the Carltona principle'. He gave as an example the delegation by the Secretary of State of his duty to consider a petition by a prisoner under the prison rules or the prison department's standing orders or his disciplinary powers in respect of prison officers.

[87] See Lanham, 'Delegation and the Alter Ego Principle' (1984) 100 LQR 587.

[88] In *R v Chiswick Police Station Superintendent, ex p Sacksteder* [1918] 1 KB 578 it was held that a decision to deport an alien had to be taken by the minister and in *Liversidge v Anderson* [1942] AC 206 it was assumed that the decision to detain under wartime detention powers had to be taken by the minister. See also Staughton LJ in *R v Secretary of State for the Home Department, ex p Doody* [1994] 1 AC 531 quoting Mason J in *Minister for Aboriginal Affairs v Peko-Wallsend Ltd* (1986) 162 CLR 24, 38.

[89] However cf *R v Skinner* [1968] 2 QB 700 (minister not personally required to approve breath test equipment); *R v Secretary of State for the Home Department, ex p Doody* [1994] 1 AC 531 (decision concerning a life sentence prisoner's tariff period could be taken on behalf of the Home Secretary by a minister of state in the Home Office). Note also *Duncan v Cammell Laird & Co* [1942] AC 624 (decision to issue a public interest immunity certificate seeking to have documentary evidence withheld from legal proceedings may be taken by the permanent head of the department as well as the minister).

appear to support the existence of such an obligation are at best equivocal'[90] and Wade and Forsyth are equally cautious.[91] Certainly the decisions of the House of Lords in *R v Secretary of State for the Home Department, ex p Oladehinde*[92] and *R v Secretary of State for the Home Department, ex p Doody*[93] provide little or no support for the proposition that there is a class of decision that ministers cannot devolve to their officials. In the former decision the House of Lords and the Court of Appeal held that there was no legal impediment to the Home Secretary authorizing immigration inspectors to take the decision to deport immigrants who are in breach of their conditions of entry or who are overstayers.[94] In the latter case the House accepted that the Home Secretary's power to fix the penal element in a sentence imposed on a life prisoner could be entrusted to a junior minister in the Home Office.[95] In both cases the decisions involved rights to liberty and yet the judges stressed that Parliament must be taken to have assumed that such decisions will not be taken by ministers personally.[96]

14.39   The above discussion should not be assumed to imply that the *Carltona doctrine*, as it is now understood, provides a complete veil protecting decision-making arrangements within government departments from judicial scrutiny. These arrangements are subject to the normal principles of judicial review if, for example, authority is devolved upon those who are too junior or insufficiently qualified to make the decision, or where the arrangements are unsuitable in other ways. In *Carltona* itself Lord Greene MR said that the minister:

> must answer before Parliament for anything that his officials have done under his authority, and, if for an important matter he selected an official of such junior standing that he could not be expected competently to perform the work, the minister would have to answer for that in Parliament.

---

[90]   de Smith, Woolf and Jowell (n 56 above) para 5-113.
[91]   Wade and Forsyth (n 33 above) 239.
[92]   [1991] 1 AC 254.
[93]   [1994] 1 AC 531.
[94]   Lord Griffiths noted that the Immigration Act 1971 imposed three explicit limitations on the Secretary of State's power to devolve and for this reason he 'should be very slow to read into the statute a further implicit limitation'. He added that if the Secretary of State could not devolve decisions to deport, the Act would be unworkable: [1991] 1 AC 254, 303.
[95]   s 61(1) of the Criminal Justice Act 1967 confers power to release a life prisoner on the Secretary of State. In the Court of Appeal Staughton LJ said that: 'Mr. Scrivener points out that, in the days of capital punishment, it was the practice for the Home Secretary personally to decide whether to recommend a reprieve; and political memoirs record how seriously that responsibility was regarded. The fixing of a tariff period for life prisoners is likewise of great importance to the individuals affected. But so, no doubt, is the exercise of a great many other powers which are entrusted to the Secretary of State for the Home Department. Parliament must be well aware of the great burden that is imposed on senior ministers, who not only take charge of their departments but also speak for them in Parliament, attend meetings of the Cabinet and its committees, and see to their constituency affairs if they are members of the House of Commons.': [1993] QB 157, 196.
[96]   Arguably, the decision of the Home Secretary to consider the release of those detained during Her Majesty's pleasure must be taken by the Home Secretary personally.

Today arrangements of this sort may be treated as matters for the courts as well as **14.40** for Parliament. In *Oladehinde* the House of Lords accepted the application of the *Carltona* doctrine but only after the careful scrutiny of the legislative framework and decision-making context within the Home Office. Moreover, Lord Griffiths made it clear that not all arrangements would have been legally acceptable. He said, for example:

> I can . . . see no reason why he [the minister] should not authorize members of the [immigration service] to take decisions under the *Carltona* principle *providing they do not conflict with or embarrass them in the discharge of their specific statutory duties under the Act and that the decisions are suitable to their grading and experience.*[97]

If the arrangements were inappropriate for these or other reasons,[98] they, and any **14.41** decisions made, would be open to challenge on normal judicial review grounds. In the absence of statutory requirements to the contrary, judges may well expect departments to show that decisions which affect fundamental rights or other vital interests are subject to close supervision at the highest level within the department and in some cases it might be unlawful for there not to be a degree of substantive ministerial involvement.

(2) There Must be a Real Exercise of Discretion

In *Wednesbury* Lord Greene MR listed, as one of the requirements of the lawful ex- **14.42** ercise of power, the need for there to be a 'real exercise of the discretion'.[99] This implies that a body endowed with discretionary power must apply its mind to the matter in question and exercise the choice that is inherent in the nature of discretion. A public body cannot, for example, abdicate its responsibility for deciding something by relying on others, or by rigidly applying policies or contractual commitments. Each of these situations will be dealt with in turn.

(a) Abdicating discretionary power by relying on others or acting under another's dictation

We have seen that a body will have acted unlawfully if it delegates its power to an- **14.43** other without legal authority. Even if no formal delegation has occurred, it will also be unlawful for a body given discretion to regard itself as being bound by the views of others. In *Ellis v Dubowski*,[100] for example, a county council with responsibility for granting cinema licences was held to have acted unlawfully when it granted a licence subject to a condition that no film could be shown which had

---

[97] [1991] 1 AC 254, 303, emphasis added.

[98] Lord Griffiths said that 'it has been recognised that it would not be right to authorise an inspector to take a decision to deport in any case on which he had been engaged as an immigration officer . . .': ibid 303.

[99] Lord Greene MR in *Associated Provincial Picture Houses Ltd v Wednesbury Corp* [1948] 1 KB 223.

[100] [1921] 3 KB 621.

not been certified by the British Board of Film Censors. The court took the view that by this condition the council had in effect abdicated its responsibility to the Board.[101] There was, by contrast, no abdication of power when an authority reserved for itself the power to dispense with the requirement of certification.[102]

14.44   *Lavender & Son Ltd v Minister of Housing and Local Government*[103] provides an example of a similar approach being adopted by the courts in a case involving central government decision-making.[104] Lavender & Sons Ltd applied for planning permission to extract minerals from high quality agricultural land. The local planning authority refused planning permission and Lavender appealed to the Minister of Housing and Local Government, whose responsibility it was to consider appeals in such cases. The Minister rejected the appeal. His decision letter contained the following explanation:

> It is the Minister's present policy that land in the reservations should not be released for mineral working unless the Minister of Agriculture, Fisheries and Food is not opposed to the working. In the present case the agricultural objection has not been waived, and the Minister has therefore decided not to grant planning permission . . .

In allowing Lavender's challenge to the Minister's decision, Willis J said that:

> It seems to me that by adopting and applying his stated policy he has in effect inhibited himself from exercising a proper discretion . . . in any case where the Minister of Agriculture . . . [objects] . . . to mineral working . . . I think that the minister has fettered himself in such a way that in this case it was not he who made the decision which Parliament made him responsible.

14.45   The judge accepted that the Minister could have a policy on to how he would deal with cases of this type and that it was appropriate for him to consult with the Minister of Agriculture where agricultural land was involved. Here, however, the Minister had effectively given the Minister of Agriculture a veto on a matter that Parliament had expected him to decide. This does not, of course, prevent Ministers consulting, or taking into account the opinion of others when making decisions.[105]

(b) Fettering discretion by over rigid policies[106]

14.46   It is proper, and sometimes necessary,[107] for public authorities to adopt policies.

---

[101]   Wade and Forsyth (n 33 above) 326 cite this case as an example of a situation in which the courts 'condemn . . . administrative arrangements which must seem quite natural and proper to those who make them'.

[102]   *Mills v London CC* [1925] 1 KB 213.

[103]   [1970] 1 WLR 1231.

[104]   See also *Simms Motor Units Ltd v Minister of Labour* [1946] 2 All ER 201.

[105]   eg *Kent CC v Secretary of State for the Environment* (1977) 75 LGR 452.

[106]   See Chris Hilson, 'Judicial Review, Policies and the Fettering of Discretion' [2002] PL 111.

[107]   Auld LJ has said that 'it might well be irrational not to have' a policy: *R v North West Lancashire Health Authority, ex p A* [2000] 1 WLR 977, 991.

Policies will guide and inform decision-making. As well as being conducive to 'the coherent and consistent performance of administrative functions'[108] they may help to ensure fairness[109] and, if publicized, contribute to transparency.[110] However, while they may be used to guide a public authority, policies must not prevent an authority from lawfully exercising the discretionary power that has been conferred upon it.[111] If a policy purports to do this it will be unlawful, as will any decision applying that policy. This limitation on policy-making applies in addition to the requirements that policies be compatible with Convention rights,[112] that they pursue proper purposes,[113] and that they be formulated in accordance with the relevancy principle.[114] In passing it should be noted that while public authorities must not apply policies in a way that fetters their discretion, nor should they disregard policies where to do so is unfair or results in an abuse of power.[115]

The principles in this area of judicial review have evolved as judges have attempted **14.47** to reconcile the tension between the competing virtues of consistency and predictability on the one hand and flexibility and responsive decision-making on the other. Two main concerns underlie the approach of the judges. The first is to ensure that when discretion has been conferred upon public bodies these bodies do not prevent themselves from using that discretion to respond to change, or to unforeseen or exceptional situations. If they were to do so, this would frustrate the reason why discretionary power was conferred upon them. As Lord Browne-Wilkinson has explained:

> When Parliament confers a discretionary power exercisable from time to time over a period, such power must be exercised on each occasion in the light of the circumstances at that time. In consequence, the person on whom the power is conferred cannot fetter the future exercise of his discretion by committing himself now as to the way in which he will exercise his power in the future.

---

[108] *per* Lord Clyde in *R (on the application of Holding & Barnes plc) v Secretary of State for the Environment, Transport and the Regions* [2001] UKHL 23; [2001] 2 WLR 1389 at [143].

[109] See Staughton LJ in *R v Southwark LBC, ex p Udu* [1996] Ed LR 390, 391.

[110] It may be a breach of natural justice not to disclose the principles upon which a decision will be reached: *R v Criminal Injuries Compensation Board, ex p Ince* [1973] 1 WLR 1334, 1345.

[111] For a discussion of the advantages and disadvantages of policies, see J Jowell, 'The Legal Control of Administrative Discretion' [1973] PL 178. See also, DJ Galligan 'The Nature and Functions of Policy Within Discretionary Power' [1976] PL 332; Galligan (n 8 above).

[112] *R (on the application of Daly) v Secretary of State for the Home Department* [2001] 2 AC 532; *Smith and Grady v UK* (1999) 29 EHRR 493 and see further below paras 14.53–14.55.

[113] See paras 14.62–14.79 below.

[114] See paras 14.80–14.113 below. In *A-G ex rel Tilley v Wandsworth LBC* [1981] 1 WLR 854 Templeman LJ expressed the view obiter that a council policy not to house families with young children where the parents had become homeless intentionally would be unlawful, whether or not it provided for exceptional cases, because it was inimical to the aim of the housing legislation, namely that the interests of children should be considered in every case. See Hilson (n 106 above) 115.

[115] eg, because it breaches legitimate expectations. See further paras 16.34–16.89 below and *R v North and East Devon Health Authority, ex p Coughlan* [2001] QB 213.

14.48 The second concern is to ensure 'individualized justice'.[116] Where public authorities have discretion in the granting of licences, planning permission, applications
for housing, student grants and a multitude of other matters, they must deal with
these matters by applying their mind to the merits of each case that comes before
them. If they have been given discretionary power they cannot apply a policy as
if it were a binding rule mandating a particular outcome. The leading modern
decision is that of the House of Lords in *British Oxygen Co Ltd v Minister of
Technology*.[117] The Board of Trade had discretionary power to make grants for capital expenditure. It adopted a policy not to pay grants where individual items of
expenditure were less than £25. The British Oxygen Company (BOC) spent £4
million buying new gas cylinders and applied for a grant. Despite the overall expenditure, their application was refused on the ground that since each cylinder
cost less than £25 it would be contrary to the Board's policy to make a grant. The
BOC unsuccessfully challenged the decision arguing inter alia that the Board's
policy prevented it from considering the merits of their particular case. In the
House of Lords Lord Reid, applying principles earlier enunciated by Banks LJ in
R v Port of London Authority, ex Kynoch Ltd,[118] said:

> The general rule is that anyone who has to exercise a statutory discretion must not
> 'shut his ears' . . . a large authority may have had to deal already with a multitude of
> similar applications and then they will almost certainly have evolved a policy so pre-
> cise that it could well be called a rule. There can be no objection to this, provided
> the authority is always willing to listen to anyone with something new to say.[119]

If an authority refuses to listen to an argument that a policy should not be applied
in a particular case this will be open to challenge both on the ground of illegality
and procedural unfairness.

14.49 The above principles have been applied in a wide variety of contexts involving the
whole spectrum of public decision at both local and central levels. Litigation will normally be triggered by the way a policy has been applied in a particular case, although
in some circumstances the court will concentrate on the legality of the policy itself. In
each case, however, the key question will be whether the authority has shown itself
willing and able to exercise its discretionary power either in relation to the policy or
the way it has been applied in the instant case. The authority must, for example, be
prepared 'to listen to a substantial argument reasonably presented urging a change of
policy' or be 'willing to listen to anyone with something new to say'.[120] This does not

---

[116] See further KC Davis, *Discretionary Justice* (Urbana: University of Illinois Press, 1971). Note
that de Smith, Woolf and Jowell (n 56 above) para 10-001 deal with fettering of discretion under
procedural propriety,.

[117] [1971] AC 610. The litigation was originally initiated against the Board of Trade but by the
date of the court decision responsibility had been transferred to the Minister of Technology.

[118] [1919] 1 KB 176.

[119] ibid 183.

[120] See Lord Reid's speech in *British Oxygen Co Ltd v Minister of Technology* [1971] AC 610, 625.

imply that an authority must be ready to change its policy, 'but it does imply that the authority should not close its mind in advance, especially if a new or more detailed argument is drawn to its attention, or if circumstances change'.[121] Thus a policy not to permit the sale of literature in parks, even in the most deserving case, was struck down because its effect was to prevent an authority deciding whether or not to permit the sale of leaflets for the benefit of the blind.[122] Likewise, but in a very different age and context, it has been held unlawful for a local authority to treat itself as bound to fulfil a manifesto commitment.[123] More recently one of the reasons why the Home Secretary's policy in relation to children sentenced to be detained during Her Majesty's pleasure was unlawful was that, *even in exceptional circumstances*, it treated as irrelevant the progress and development of the child who had been detained.[124]

By contrast, in the *British Oxygen Co* case the company's challenge failed because there was no evidence that the Board had 'shut its ears' by refusing to consider the Company's representations as to why the policy should not be applied. As this case shows, bodies are not expected to retain completely open minds, but they must, as Lord Reid, put it, at least keep their mind ajar. It would have been different, for instance, had the Board resolved not to consider the application at all.[125] Likewise, a policy to discourage development that interfered with the operation of the Jodrell Bank radio telescope was not unlawful because the minister concerned satisfied the courts that he was willing to judge each application on its merits.[126] The Minister was unable to do this in *Lavender*.[127] Here the evidence indicated that as soon as the officials in the Ministry of Housing and Local Government saw that the application concerned first class agricultural land they closed the file and sent it off to the Minister of Agriculture to await his decision. Had there been evidence that they had themselves considered the case on its merits the outcome might have been different.

14.50

As these decisions indicate, the courts will look beyond the wording of the policy to examine the actual practice of the public authority. In so doing they will not accept a public authority's claim that it is willing to keep an open mind without supporting

14.51

---

[121] Sir Christopher Bellamy QC (sitting as a deputy judge of the High Court) in *R (on the application of H) v Ashworth Hospital Authority* [2001] EWHC Admin 872; [2002] 1 FCR 206 at [133].

[122] *R v London CC, ex p Corrie* [1918] 1 KB 68. See also *Re Findlay* [1985] AC 318, especially Lord Scarman at 336. Hilson (n 106 above) 117–118 notes a line of cases on taxi licences in which the courts have upheld policies that appear not to permit exceptions. Hilson suggests that these might fall beyond the general rule enunciated by Banks LJ in *Ex p Kynoch* [1919] 1 KB 176 and Lord Reid in *British Oxygen Co Ltd v Minister of Technology* [1971] AC 610.

[123] *R v GLC, ex p Bromley LBC* [1983] 1 AC 768.

[124] *R v Secretary of State for the Home Department, ex p Venables* [1998] AC 407.

[125] *R v Walsall JJ* (1854) 3 WR 69; *R v Barry DC, ex p Jones* (1900) 16 TLR 556.

[126] *Stringer v Minister of Housing and Local Government* [1970] 1 WLR 1281.

[127] [1970] 1 WLR 1231.

evidence of this. In *R (on the application of H) v Ashworth Hospital Authority*,[128] for example, the High Court held the hospital's no-condoms policy to be lawful, but only once a careful scrutiny of the evidence had satisfied it of the Authority's willingness to consider arguments that the policy should be changed. A policy may be upheld if, despite its wording, the general decision-making context indicates that exceptional cases will in fact be considered. On the other hand, a policy that appears to permit exceptions will be struck down if the authority fails to show that it would permit exceptions in practice. In *R v North West Lancashire Health Authority, ex p A*[129] the court considered the legality of a policy not to fund gender realignment surgery, save in cases of 'overriding clinical need'. Despite this wording, having examined the evidence of the way the policy was applied in practice, Auld LJ concluded that the authority was not genuinely willing to accept the existence of exceptional cases and thus in reality the Authority adopted a blanket policy not to fund this form of surgery. Statistics may help to determine the reality of the situation. In *R v Warwickshire CC, ex p Collymore*[130] Judge J decided the authority had applied its policy in relation to student grants far too rigidly in the light of evidence that in three years the authority had not made a single new discretionary award and not a single appeal out of 300 had succeeded.[131] A policy may also be struck down if the authority lacks a procedure for dealing with exceptional cases.[132]

14.52 More recently, in *Gunn-Russo v Nugent Care Society*,[133] Scott Baker J held that the Nugent Care Society had acted unlawfully when it refused to disclose adoption records to the claimant, a person in her fifties who was adopted as a child at the age of two. Here the Society was held to have applied its policy not to disclose information given in confidence without properly considering the claimant's particular circumstances and the fact that a long passage of time had passed since the claimant was adopted and that none of the key players except the claimant was still alive. The Society should have weighed up these factors and balanced them against the benefit of maintaining confidentiality. Instead, they adopted a policy '. . . which they are convinced is right and they are not going to change it. The maintenance of confidentiality trumps everything, regardless of the circumstances.'

---

[128] [2001] EWHC Admin 272; [2002] 1 FCR 206.
[129] [2000] 1 WLR 977.
[130] [1995] Ed LR 217.
[131] See Hilson (n 106 above) 124–126 for discussion of the way the courts are prepared to use statistics to determine whether authorities are genuinely keeping an open mind.
[132] *R v Bexley LBC, ex p Jones* [1995] COD 46.
[133] [2001] EWHC Admin 566; [2002] 1 FLR 1.

(c) Blanket policies and human rights

Blanket policies may now be challengeable on the traditional principles, includ- **14.53**
ing those discussed in this section, and on human rights grounds.[134] While the traditional principles relating to blanket policies may reinforce human rights claims,
there are indications that these principles may no longer be utilized by the courts
where it is alleged that human rights are violated. In *R (on the application of Daly)
v Secretary of State for the Home Department*,[135] for example, the House of Lords
held that the Secretary of State's policy always to examine prisoners' legal correspondence in the absence of the prisoner was a disproportionate infringement of
the common law right to confidentiality. This decision was reached without considering the traditional principles on blanket policies. More recently the Court
of Appeal in *R (on the application of P and Q) v Secretary of State for the Home
Department*[136] has indicated that in human rights cases the traditional approach of
the judges has been supplanted by the proportionality-based approach.

In this case two female prisoners challenged decisions to separate them from their **14.54**
children in accordance with a policy that babies could not remain with their
mothers in prison beyond the age of 18 months. The Court of Appeal held that
while the Prison Service was entitled to have such a policy, it could not be operated rigidly in the face of other considerations, including the catastrophic effect
that separation would have on the child. Speaking for the Court of Appeal, Lord
Phillips MR commented that, 'before the introduction of a rights-based culture
into English public law these applications for judicial review would have been
quite unarguable'.[137] Referring to the decision of the House of Lords in *Daly*, and
in particular to the speech of Lord Steyn, he said that the central question in the
case was whether the state can justify violating the right to respect for family life
(under Article 8 ECHR) 'that would be inherent not only in the separation of
these two mothers from their 18-month-old children, but also in the separation of
these children from their mothers'. He said that:[138]

> On the new Daly approach we have to determine in these appeals whether the in-
> terference proposed by the Prison Service in the application of its policy in each of
> these cases is really proportionate to the legitimate aim, sanctioned by article 8(2) of
> the Convention, which it seeks to pursue. In making this judgment we must be
> careful to show appropriate deference to the fact that the Prison Service is the expert
> body appointed to carry out this sensitive public function.

---

[134] Blanket policies may violate the spirit of human rights law in failing to provide a sufficient proportionality-based balancing between the general interest aims served by the policy and the merits
of the individual's case, see Hilson (n 106 above) 128.
[135] [2001] UKHL 26; [2001] 2 AC 532.
[136] [2001] EWCA Civ 1151; [2001] 1 WLR 2002.
[137] ibid at [56].
[138] ibid at [64].

14.55   Whether the Master of the Rolls was correct to say that these cases would have been unarguable prior to the introduction of what he calls the human-rights culture is questionable.[139] Nonetheless, it cannot be doubted that when human rights are engaged it is not sufficient for the courts simply to determine whether the authority has maintained a sufficient degree of genuine flexibility. The human rights culture requires more of public bodies than the requirement that they keep their minds ajar. They are now required to show that they have actively considered the impact of their policies on the human rights of those affected and that any infringement is justified as being necessary and proportionate, assuming that any infringement is permissible.[140]

(d) Fettering discretion by contractual obligations

14.56   Public authorities cannot fetter their discretion by policy. Nor can they do so by entering into contracts or other commitments. In *Birkdale District Supply Co Ltd v Southport Corp* the Earl of Birkenhead stated the principle in the following way:

> . . . if a person or public body is entrusted by the legislature with certain powers and duties expressly or impliedly for public purposes, those persons or bodies cannot divest themselves of these powers and duties . They cannot enter into any contract or take any action incompatible with the due exercise of their powers or the discharge of their duties.[141]

14.57   Contracting, like policy-making, is a vital aspect of public administration and public authorities have wide powers to enter into contracts in order to pursue their functions.[142] In so doing, public authorities will inevitably limit their freedom of action. This is generally acceptable and it goes without saying that public authorities will be held bound by obligations legally entered into.[143] However, public bodies have no legal authority to enter into agreements that are incompatible with their public functions and which prevent them from exercising their statutory powers. Such contracts will be ultra vires and invalid and, therefore,

---

[139]   cf Hilson (n 106 above) 127, who comments: 'With respect, the Court of Appeal misstated the position under pre-Human Rights Act administrative law . . . After all, the policy in the case allowed for no exceptions on its face and, although discretionary exceptions were occasionally made, these were not part of the formal system. On the basis of the [earlier case law] such an approach is clearly unlawful.' See also *R v Home Secretary, ex p Simms* [2000] 2 AC 115.

[140]   eg, the rights under Art 3 are absolute.

[141]   [1926] AC 355, 364.

[142]   An agreement will not be invalid if it may be reasonably regarded as furthering statutory functions: *R v Hammersmith and Fulham LBC, ex p Beddowes* [1987] 1 QB 1050.

[143]   Failure to respect agreements made may also give rise to challenge on grounds of abuse of power or unfairness. See, eg, *R v North and East Devon Health Authority ex p Coughlan* [2001] QB 213; *R v Liverpool Corp, ex p Liverpool Taxi Fleet Operators' Association* [1972] 2 QB 299 (the Court of Appeal held that a taxi licensing authority had acted unfairly by increasing the number of taxi cab licences without first consulting existing taxi drivers in accordance with its earlier agreement to do so). See also paras 15.29–15.34 below.

unenforceable by the public authority and any other party.[144] This situation is exemplified by the decision of the House of Lords in *Ayr Harbour Trustees v Oswald.*[145]

Here the harbour trustees had statutory power to acquire land compulsorily to be   **14.58**
used for the construction of works associated with the harbour. Using this power they acquired land but, in an attempt to reduce the compensation payable to the owner, agreed to grant the owner a perpetual covenant protecting his access to the harbour from adjoining land. The House of Lords held this covenant to be invalid because its effect was to prevent the trustees ever using the affected land, even where it might be necessary to do so in the public interest. Lord Blackburn said:[146]

> I think, that where the legislature confer powers on any body to take land compulsorily for a particular purpose, it is on the ground that the using of that land for that purpose will be for the public good . . . a contract, purporting to bind them and their successors not to use those powers, is void.

This principle has been applied to the powers of the Crown as well as other public authorities. Thus it has been held that a covenant limiting use of land to agriculture could not prevent the Crown using land for an airfield[147] and a grant of a lease could not prevent the Crown requisitioning the property under wartime legislation.[148] Similarly, a planning authority cannot bind itself by contract to exercise its statutory discretion to grant or refuse planning permission in any particular way.[149]

These decisions may be contrasted with that in *Birkdale District Supply Co Ltd v*   **14.59**
Southport Corp.[150] Here the House of Lords refused to hold ultra vires a contract entered into by the Birkdale Electricity Supply Co Ltd whereby it agreed that it would not increase the price of its electricity above that charged by Southport Corporation, the neighbouring electricity supplier. The House distinguished the *Ayr Harbour* case on the ground that the trustees had 'renounced a part of their statutory birthright'[151] by preventing themselves from ever exercising their statutory rights in respect to the land affected by the covenant. By contrast, here the agreement concerned trading profits, rather than the company's ability to undertake its basic responsibility to supply electricity.

---

[144] There is no right to damages or compensation in such a situation. Cf French law, see n 155 below.
[145] (1883) 8 App Cas 623.
[146] ibid 634.
[147] *Marten v Flight Refuelling Ltd* [1962] Ch 115.
[148] *Commissioners of Crown Lands v Page* [1960] 2 QB 274.
[149] *Stringer v Minister of Housing and Local Government* [1970] 1 WLR 1281; *Windsor and Maidenhead RBC v Brandrose Investments Ltd* [1983] 1 WLR 509.
[150] [1926] AC 355.
[151] On the use of this phrase (by Lord Sumner) see Lord Radcliffe in *British Transport Commission v Westmoreland CC* [1958] AC 126, 155–156.

14.60   In general, the courts are reluctant to find agreements invalid and will try to reconcile contractual obligations with the authority's functions, particularly when it appears that a public authority is seeking to escape obligations that have been willingly entered into and from which it has benefited. The *Ayr Harbour* case, for instance, was not applied in *Stourcliffe Estates Co Ltd v Bournemouth Corp*.[152] Here Bournemouth Corporation had purchased land from the plaintiff to be used as a public park and covenanted not to erect any buildings except summerhouses, a band stand or shelters. When the Corporation later wanted to use its powers to build public conveniences it argued that the covenant preventing it from doing so in the park was invalid. The Court of Appeal rejected this argument. The Corporation had voluntarily agreed to limit its power in relation to this particular land and could not now argue that one part of the agreement, by which it acquired the parkland, was invalid. In short, authorities cannot avoid agreements simply because these conflict with what they now want to do. It has been held, for example, that a local authority could dedicate a park for public use even though this would prevent the authority from letting the land in the future.[153] In another case it was held that because a corporation was bound by its agreement to permit land to be used as an airport it was unable to use its powers to build housing on the land. Pennycuick V-C commented that, 'obviously, where a power is exercised in such a manner as to create a right extending over a term of years, the existence of that right *pro tanto* excludes the exercise of other statutory powers in respect of the same subject-matter, but there is no authority and I can see no principle upon which the sort of exercise could be held invalid as a fetter upon the future exercise of powers . . .'. One difference between this situation and that in the *Ayr Harbour* case is that there the covenant prevented the trustees from exercising their powers in relation to the particular land for all time and this prohibition went to the heart of their responsibilities. Here the agreement did not go the heart of the corporation's responsibilities. After all, although the corporation could not, during the life of the agreement, build on this land, it could build elsewhere.

14.61   If express contractual terms cannot prevent public authorities performing their statutory powers, a fortiori implied terms cannot do so either. In *Cory (William) & Sons Ltd v London Corporation*[154] the London Corporation had contracted with the plaintiff company for the removal of waste by barge. The Corporation, in its capacity as port health authority, later introduced new bye-laws which imposed more stringent requirements on the transport of waste and made the contract uneconomic. The company argued that the contract implied an undertaking by the Corporation that it would not amend the bye-laws so as to impose more onerous

---

[152] [1910] 2 Ch 12.
[153] See *Blake v Hendon* [1962] 1 QB 283; *Dowty Boulton Paul Ltd v Wolverhampton Corp* [1971] 1 WLR 204.
[154] [1951] 2 KB 476.

burdens than were already imposed by the contract. The Court of Appeal rejected this argument on the grounds that the Corporation had statutory powers to make the bye-laws and these powers could not be fettered by contract. It has been observed that there would be no objection to a term, whether express or implied that the corporation would provide compensation if it amended the bye-laws.[155]

(e) Estoppel and discretion

The importance traditionally attached to the need to ensure that public bodies remain free to exercise their discretionary powers in the public interest is also reflected in the principle that public authorities cannot be estopped from exercising their public powers by statements made by their officers.[156] This principle may not apply where the officer concerned has ostensible or delegated authority in relation to the matter,[157] or where the statements create legitimate expectations. These are issues that are considered in detail elsewhere.[158]

14.61a

D. The Proper Purpose Principle

It is a fundamental principle of public law that public bodies can only use their powers for the purposes for which they have been expressly or implicitly conferred.[159] Where legal power is used for extraneous or improper purposes or on the

14.62

---

[155] Wade and Forsyth (n 33 above) 336. The authors comment that this result is achieved in French law by the doctrine of fait du prince, under which a contractor can claim an equitable adjustment if the government, by use of its powers, upsets the calculations on which the contract was made. They cite JDB Mitchell, *The Contracts of Public Authorities* (London: G Bell & Sons, 1954) 193 and cf P Rogerson, 'On Fettering of Public Power' [1971] PL 300.

[156] *Southend-on-Sea Corp v Hodgson (Wickford) Ltd* [1962] 1 QB 416. Here it was held that a statement made by a local authority's borough engineer that planning permission was not necessary in order to use land as a builders' yard did not prevent the authority serving an enforcement notice on a person who had relied on the statement when buying the land.

[157] *Lever Finance Ltd v Westminster LBC* [1971] 1 QB 222. Here the Court of Appeal held that an authority was bound by a decision of its planning officer that variations in a plan that had already been granted planning permission were not material and could therefore be made without being reconsidered. In fact the variations were material with the result that housing was built closer to neighbouring housing than the planning authority would have permitted had it considered the plans afresh. Lord Denning MR said that the planning officer had been given 'ostensible authority' because it was normal practice to allow officers to approve non-material variations in plans and the applicants assumed that the officer had been given this power and was acting properly. Sachs LJ said that there had been a lawful delegation to the officer. For a critique of the decision, see Wade and Forsyth (n 33 above) 341.

[158] See further paras 15.29–15.34 and 16.34–16.89 below.

[159] There are many judicial statements of this principle which is said to have been first developed in cases where public authorities were given powers compulsorily to acquire private property on payment of compensation (de Smith, Woolf and Jowell (n 56 above) para 5-063): *Galloway v London Corp* (1866) LR 1 HL 34, 43. See more recently Neil LJ in *Credit Suisse v Allerdale BC* [1997] QB 306, 333; *Hall & Co Ltd v Shoreham by Sea UDC* [1964] 1 WLR 240; *R v Tower Hamlets LBC, ex p Chetnik Developments Ltd* [1988] AC 858, 872 *per* Lord Bridge (with the concurrence of other

basis of legally irrelevant considerations, that power is abused and the consequential illegality may result in the decision being impugned by the courts. The ultimate decision as to whether illegality has occurred is for the courts and not the public body.[160]

(1) The Proper Purpose Principle and the Relevancy Principle

14.63   This section considers the proper purpose principle. The next section considers the relevancy principle. These two principles are closely related.[161] Indeed, it has been said that they are 'often inextricably linked'.[162] Certainly, commentators often differ as to the head under which a case should be considered.[163] The truth is that in many situations it is impossible to distinguish between them, particularly when improper purposes have been pursued and by implication the decision-making process is also tarnished by breach of the relevancy principle. Whether one or other issue predominates will tend to be a matter of emphasis and language. Having said this, more substantial reasons for drawing a distinction between these two heads of review may exist.

14.64   First, the evidence may necessitate concentration on one head rather than the other. The evidence may, for example, provide insight into the factors considered or neglected, but say little or nothing about the precise motives or purposes of the decision-maker, particularly where the decision is the product of several minds who may not have articulated their purpose and may not have a single purpose in mind. Secondly, in other cases there may be no dispute as to the legality of the ends to be achieved, but justifiable argument that during its deliberations the public body breached the relevancy principle. Thirdly, and more broadly, the two heads of review focus on different aspects of decision-making. The proper purposes principle looks at the ends to be achieved and asks whether these are legally compatible with the purposes for which the decision-making power was conferred. The relevancy principle asks a rather different question, namely whether

---

members of the House of Lords); Lord Bridge in *R v Secretary of State for the Environment, ex p Hammersmith and Fulham LBC* [1991] 1 AC 521, 597; Lord Ackner in *R v Secretary of State for the Home Department, ex p Brind* [1991] 1 AC 696, 761; *R (on the application of Spath Holme Ltd) v Secretary of State for the Environment* [2001] 2 AC 349.

[160]   eg, in *R v Secretary of State for Foreign and Commonwealth Affairs, ex p World Development Movement Ltd* [1995] 1 WLR 386, 401 Rose LJ commented: '. . . I am unable to accept Mr Richards' submission that it is the Secretary of State's thinking which is determinative of whether the purpose was within the statute . . . Whatever the Secretary of State's intention or purpose may have been, it is . . . a matter for the courts and not the Secretary of State to determine whether, on the evidence before the court, the particular conduct was, or was not, within the statutory purpose.'

[161]   GDS Taylor, 'Judicial Review of Improper Purposes and Irrelevant Considerations' [1976] CLJ 272.

[162]   de Smith, Woolf and Jowell (n 56 above) para 5-067.

[163]   eg, de Smith, Woolf and Jowell (n 56 above) treat the prison parole cases as improper purposes cases, whereas Wade and Forsyth (n 33 above) seem to regard them as irrelevant consideration cases.

the decision-maker has adopted the appropriate process of reasoning and whether the conclusions reached are supported by proper considerations. It is in this sense that relevancy tends to be more closely concerned with the rationality of the decision-making process whereas the proper purposes principle is more concerned with the substantive quality of the decision and its objectives.

(2) The Proper Purpose Principle Illustrated

The recent decision of the House of Lords in *Porter v Magill* provides a graphic illustration of the proper purposes principle.[164] Here it was held unlawful for Westminster City Council to use its public powers under the housing legislation to further the electoral interests of the Conservative Party. Lord Bingham expressed the 'overriding principle' in the following way:

14.65

> Elected politicians of course wish to act in a manner which will commend them and their party (when, as is now usual, they belong to one) to the electorate. Such an ambition is the life-blood of democracy and a potent spur to responsible decision-taking and administration. Councillors do not act improperly or unlawfully if, exercising public powers for a public purpose for which such powers were conferred, they hope that such exercise will earn the gratitude and support of the electorate and thus strengthen their electoral position. The law would indeed part company with the realities of party politics if it were to hold otherwise. But a public power is not exercised lawfully if it is exercised not for a public purpose for which the power was conferred but in order to promote the electoral advantage of a political party . . .[165]

Two types of situation exist: where the powers are conferred for purposes that are expressly identified and where the purposes are not expressly identified.

(3) Where the Purposes are Expressly Identified

The most straightforward situations occur where powers are conferred for purposes that are expressly stated and there is clear evidence showing that the authority has exercised its power in order to achieve other purposes.[166] *Sydney Municipal Council v Campbell*[167] provides a well-known example. Section 16 of the Sydney Corporation Amendment Act 1905 empowered the Council to purchase compulsorily any land for the purposes of 'carrying out improvements in or remodelling any portion of the city'. It was established that the Council had abused this power by using it to acquire land in order to benefit from an increase in land value

14.66

---

[164] [2001] UKHL 67; [2002] 2 AC 357.

[165] ibid at [21]–[25] (emphasis added).

[166] Whether an authority has acted for an improper purpose must be established by the evidence as a matter of fact, *per* Lord Loreburn in *Marquess of Clanricarde v Congested District Board for Ireland* (1914) 79 JP 481.

[167] [1925] AC 338.

that was likely to result from a proposed extension of a highway by the Council. Often cases are not this straightforward: the goals to be achieved by the public body may be difficult to identify or prove; the body might be acting in order to achieve several objectives, some of which might be proper, but others arguably not so. One of the most common problems arises, however, when the purposes for which the powers are conferred are not specifically expressed by the legislation.

(4) Where Legislation Does Not Expressly Identify the Purpose: the Policy and Objects Approach

14.67   The more difficult situation occurs where the legislation confers broad discretionary power, but makes no specific reference to the purpose for which that power is to be used. Here courts are required to discover the power's purpose by interpreting the language of the specific provisions in the context of the objects and policy of the legislation as a whole.[168] *Padfield v Minister of Agriculture, Fisheries and Food*[169] is the leading case.

14.68   Legislation establishing the Milk Marketing Scheme provided a system for dealing with complaints of milk producers arising from the operation of the scheme. If a complaint was made a complaints committee could be established to investigate the matter, but only 'if the Minister [of Agriculture] . . . so directs'. On its face this appeared to give the Minister unfettered discretion as to whether to direct the establishment of a complaints committee or not. Milk producers in the south east of England complained that the pricing policy operated by the scheme treated them unfairly because it meant that they were being paid less for their milk than were producers in other parts of the country. When they asked the Minister to establish a committee to examine their complaints he refused to do so. He said that the complaint was unsuitable for investigation by a committee because it raised wide issues going beyond the immediate concern of the complainants, indicating that he owed no duty to producers in particular regions. He also indicated that one of the factors that he considered was the possibility that if the committee did uphold the complaint he in turn would be expected to make a statutory order giving effect to the committee's recommendations.

14.69   The producers sought an order of mandamus to compel the Minister to establish a committee. He responded by arguing that the legislation gave him complete discretion for which he was politically accountable but with which the courts could not interfere. He also argued that since he was under no obligation to give reasons for his decision he could not be found to have acted improperly on the basis of reasons that

---

[168] See de Smith, Woolf and Jowell (n 56 above) para 5-076, n 56.
[169] [1968] AC 997. Also, *Congreve v Home Office* [1976] QB 629. The Court of Appeal held that the Minister could not use his powers to revoke TV licences so as to prevent licence-holders renewing their licences before they expired and before the licence fee was increased.

he had voluntarily given. The House of Lords, by a majority, rejected these arguments. Lord Reid said:

> It is implicit in the argument for the Minister that there are only two possible interpretations of [the Act]—either he must refer every complaint or he has an unfettered discretion to refuse to refer in any case. I do not think that is right.
>
> Parliament must have conferred the discretion with the intention that it should be used to promote the policy and objects of the Act; the policy and objects of the Act must be determined by construing the Act as a whole and construction is always a matter of law for the court . . . In a matter of this kind . . . if the Minister, by reason of his having misconstrued the Act of for any other reason, so uses his discretion as to thwart or run counter to the policy and objects of the Act, then our law would be very defective if persons aggrieved were not entitled to the protection of the court.[170]

Having construed the Act Lord Reid turned to the Minister's reasons for refusing to establish a committee. In relation to the first of these (that the complaint raised wide issues) Lord Reid said that this indicated that the Minister had clearly misdirected himself. The Act, he said, plainly contemplated that the widest issues could be investigated if the complaint was genuine and substantial. He likewise held that nothing in the Act indicated that the Minister owed no duty to producers in particular regions. He went on to say if the Minister's reasons indicated that he thought that he was entitled to refuse to refer a complaint to a committee, 'because, if he did so, he might later find himself in an embarrassing situation, that would plainly be a bad reason . . .'.[171] The argument that the Minister's decision could not be challenged on the basis of reasons voluntarily given was also rejected. The duty of the Minister is to act in accordance with the policy and objects of the Act and if it 'were to appear from all the circumstances of the case' that he has not done so, then the court must be entitled to act. On this point, Lord Pearce said that if all the prima facie reasons indicate that he should exercise his discretion in a certain way 'and he gives no reason whatever for taking a contrary course, the court may infer that he has no good reason and that he is not using the power given by Parliament to carry out its intentions'. **14.70**

Padfield provides a classical example of the basic proposition that however wide they appear on their face, discretionary powers must always be exercised in accordance with the law. In this instance, the Minister's reasons indicated to the court that he had misconstrued the Act and therefore the nature of his powers. He may also have acted in order to save himself political embarrassment, a factor that was **14.71**

---

[170] [1968] AC 997, 1030.
[171] Following the decision the Minister established a committee. In due course it upheld the complaint as the Minister had feared it would. The saga ended when the Minister told the House of Commons that he had refused to accept the committee's findings and that despite the report he had decided not to change the pricing structure of the milk marketing scheme.

clearly irrelevant to the Act. The decision also illustrates how arguments based on misconstruction of the law, improper purpose and irrelevant considerations may overlap and more importantly, how they inform the essential inquiry into whether discretion has been exercised lawfully.

14.72 The now elementary proposition that power must be used in accordance with the policy and object of the Act by which it is conferred has been applied in a wide variety of situations of which the following is merely a selection of examples. Even before *Padfield* the proposition was well established in English public law. For example, power to pay 'such wages as . . . [local authorities] . . . may think fit'[172] could not be used (in the now infamous words of Lord Atkinson) to further '. . . eccentric principles of socialist philanthropy, or . . . a feminist ambition to secure the equality of the sexes in the matter of wages and the world of labour . . .'[173] and power to deport could not be used to extradite.[174] Since the decision a local authority was held to be unable to use its statutory duty under s 71 of the Race Relations Act 1976 to promote race relations in its area in order to punish a rugby football club because three of its members had played in South Africa during the apartheid era;[175] a local authority was held to have abused its duty to 'provide a comprehensive and efficient library service' when it banned the provision of certain newspapers because it wanted to show support for workers who were in a long-running industrial dispute with their employers, the publishers of the papers.[176] In *R v Inner London Education Authority, ex p Brunyate*[177] it was held that school governors could not be removed in order to undermine their independence, despite the wide wording of the Act which said that a governor 'shall be removable by the authority by whom he was appointed'.[178] In *R v Secretary of State for Foreign and Commonwealth Affairs, ex p World Development Movement Ltd*,[179] the question was whether s 1(1) of the Overseas Development and Co-operation Act 1980 gave the Secretary of State power to pay grant aid for the purpose of supporting projects that were not economically sound. The section did not specifically provide that development projects had to be economically sound. Nonetheless, after reviewing the background to the legislation, including various policy statements, Rose LJ (with whom Scott Baker J agreed) concluded that the omission of the word 'sound' from

---

[172] Metropolis Management Act 1855, s 62.
[173] *Roberts v Hopwood* [1925] AC 578.
[174] *R v Brixton Prison Governor, ex p Soblen (No 2)* [1963] 2 QB 243.
[175] *Wheeler v Leicester City Council* [1985] AC 1054. Also, *R v Liverpoool City Council, ex p Secretary of State for Employment* [1988] COD 404: decisions to withdraw grant aid from organizations which might consider joining the government's employment training scheme held to be an abuse of power.
[176] *R v Ealing, ex p Times* (1986) 85 LGR 316.
[177] [1989] 1 WLR 542.
[178] Education Act 1944, s 21(1).
[179] [1995] 1 WLR 386.

the legislation did not mean that unsound projects could be supported: 'it seems to me that if Parliament had intended to confer a power to disburse money for unsound development purposes, it could have been expected to say so expressly'.[180] It has also been held that powers conferred by one Act cannot be used to achieve the aims of different statutory provisions. Discretionary power conferred by the planning legislation could not, for example, be used to achieve housing objectives,[181] and power to dismiss school teachers on 'educational grounds', for example, cannot be used to dismiss teachers in order to save money.[182] In one decision a local authority was held to have abused its powers when it imposed a ceiling on the number of remunerable hours guardians ad litem could spend on their cases.[183] The ceiling helped to save cost, but the decision conflicted with the principle that guardians ad litem are independent.

(5) Plurality of Purposes and Mixed Motives

Legislation is often complex and its objects and policies may be unclear. On occasion it may be arguable that the legislation is intended to achieve several, possibly incompatible objects. Moreover, policies and attitudes to the meaning of statutory provisions change over time.[184] For these and other reasons, discerning the objects and policies that it is appropriate for public bodies to pursue is potentially fraught with difficulty, both for the authorities concerned and for the courts. Discerning the meaning and purpose of legislation is not the only difficulty, however. Public bodies may act for a variety of reasons, only some of which may be legitimate. As Schiemann LJ has put it: **14.73**

> Frequently individual persons act for mixed motives. Further, group decisions may have multiple motivations—in part because there are many votes cast and in part because each voter may himself have several motivations . . .[185]

Given this reality, how do the courts approach mixed motive situations? It is not surprising that this area has been likened to 'a legal porcupine which bristles with difficulties as soon as it is touched'. De Smith, Woolf and Jowell identify six tests that have been used by judges in multiple purpose cases, 'none of which', they say, **14.74**

---

[180] ibid at 402.
[181] In *R v Hillingdon LBC, ex p Royco Homes* [1974] QB 740.
[182] *Hanson v Radcliffe UDC* [1922] 2 Ch 490; *Sadler v Sheffield Corp* [1924] 1 Ch 483.
[183] *R v Cornwall CC, ex p Cornwall and Isles of Scilly Guardians ad litem and Reporting Officers Panel* [1992] 1 WLR 427. See also the resource decisions under irrelevant considerations, paras 14.93–14.105 below.
[184] eg, de Smith, Woolf and Jowell (n 56 above) refer at para 5-080 to planning cases where the term 'material considerations' was once understood to refer essentially to considerations which were physical in nature and to exclude consideration of personal circumstances. More recently the 'human factor' has become more significant: *Westminster City Council v Great Portland Estates plc* [1985] AC 661; *Mitchell v Secretary of State for the Environment* (1994) JPL 916.
[185] *Porter v Magill* [2001] UKHL 67; [2002] 2 AC 357, 390.

'is entirely satisfactory'.[186] Once semantic distinctions are stripped away the main principles appear to be as follows.

14.75   If a 'primary', 'dominant' or 'true' purpose can be identified that is within the scope of the power conferred, the existence of other unauthorized goals that may also be achieved will not render the action unlawful.[187] The classic example was the decision of the House of Lords in *Westminster Corp v London & NW Rly*.[188] Here Westminster Corporation had power to build a public convenience but no power to build subways. This being so, could it lawfully build a lavatory beneath a street with access from either side so that a subway was effectively created? The House of Lords said that it was necessary to determine the primary object of the Corporation. This was a question of fact to be decided on the evidence that was available. In the event the majority of their Lordships held the Corporation's primary object was to build a public convenience with adequate access from both sides of the road. That the scheme also provided a subway was a secondary and permissible benefit.[189]

14.76   Where no primary or dominant purpose can be singled out, the court's task is more difficult. In *R v Inner London Education Authority, ex p Westminster City Council*[190] the Inner London Education Authority was opposed to the (then) Conservative government's policy to restrict local government expenditure. It decided to use its power to spend money on publishing information in its area 'on matters relating to local government',[191] to mount a media and poster campaign aimed at increasing public awareness of the implications of government policy. This decision was challenged on the grounds that it constituted an abuse of power. The Authority accepted that the decision involved both lawful purposes (to inform the public) and unlawful purposes (to persuade the public that government policies were wrong), but denied that its decision was for this reason an abuse of power.

14.77   Here it was difficult to discern a dominant goal and therefore Glidewell LJ could not rely exclusively on the approach outlined above. Instead, he asked whether the

---

[186] de Smith, Woolf and Jowell (n 56 above) para 5-082. In summary these involve asking the following questions: (1) what was the true purpose? (2) What was the dominant purpose test? (3) Would the power have been exercised if the decision-maker had not desired to achieve the unauthorized purpose? (4) Were any of the purposes pursued authorized? (If so, the existence of unauthorized purposes will not affect the legality of the action.) (5) Were any of the purposes pursued unauthorized? If so, and if the unauthorized purpose has materially affected the outcome of the action, the decision will be illegal. (6) Would the same decision have been reached had only relevant considerations been considered or only authorized purposes been pursued?

[187] Wade and Forsyth (n 33 above) 410.

[188] [1905] AC 426. Also *R v Brighton Corp, ex p Shoosmith* (1907) 96 LT 762; *R v Brixton Prison Governor ex p Soblen (No 2)* [1963] 2 QB 243.

[189] On this they disagreed with the Court of Appeal.

[190] [1986] 1 WLR 28.

[191] Local Government Act 1972, s 142(2).

desire to pursue the unlawful purpose had materially influenced the making of the decision. If it had, the decision was flawed because the Authority had been materially influenced by an irrelevant consideration.[192] He expressed his conclusion as follows:

> . . . I find that one of the sub committee's purposes was the giving of information. But I also find that it had the purpose of persuading members of the public . . . and indeed I believe that this was a, if not the, major purpose of the decision . . . I thus hold that ILEA's sub committee did . . . take into account an irrelevant consideration, and thus that the decision was not validly reached.[193]

Discerning a 'true purpose' or whether particular factors 'materially affected' decisions cannot be done scientifically. Unless the authority has made it obvious why it has acted and stated its priorities judges are forced, as Glidewell LJ was, to reach a decision on the facts as they appear to them. In the event, his judgment indicates that the existence of any unlawful consideration that exerts a material (or substantial) influence on the deliberations of the body may lead to a finding that the body has abused its powers, even when other lawful considerations may have been equally or even more influential.[194] **14.78**

R v Broadcasting Complaints Commission, ex p Owen[195] is an example of a case in which good and bad reasons for action could be disentangled in a way that showed that the bad reasons were unlikely to have materially affected the outcome. It indicates that the courts will not always intervene when public bodies have taken account of irrelevant factors or been partly motivated by a desire to further improper purposes. The Broadcasting Complaints Commission had given five reasons why it would not entertain a complaint. One of these was flawed as being irrelevant.[196] Nonetheless, the court was satisfied that since the same decision would have been reached on the basis of the valid reasons alone, the decision was not disturbed.[197] One way of understanding this case is to say that the improper consideration was insufficiently influential to the body in making its decision. The case also provides an illustration of the court using its discretion not to interfere where intervention **14.79**

---

[192] Following the approach of Megaw J in *Hanks v Minister of Housing and Local Government* [1963] 1 QB 999 at 1020.

[193] [1986] 1 WLR 28, 36c–f.

[194] See also *R v Lewisham LBC, ex p Shell UK Ltd* [1988] 1 All ER 938. Here the Council decided, in the interests of good race relations, to boycott Shell and to persuade other councils to do likewise. When Shell challenged the decision the Divisional Court held that the council was entitled to decide that the boycott was in the interests of good race relations, but that it was improper for the Council to put political pressure on Shell to procure its withdrawal from South Africa. Since 'the wish to achieve this purpose exerted a very substantial influence on the decision' the Council had acted illegally (*per* Neill LJ at 952).

[195] *R v Broadcasting Complaints Commission, ex p Owen* [1985] QB 1153.

[196] See para 14.80 below.

[197] cf *R v Rochdale MBC, ex p Cromer Ring Mill Ltd* [1982] 3 All ER 761.

would amount to overturning a conclusion that was sustainable on lawful grounds.[198]

E. The Relevancy Principle

14.80   Perhaps the best-known summary of the relevancy principle is that provided by Lord Greene MR in *Associated Provincial Picture Houses v Wednesbury Corp*.[199] It is worth repeating here:

> If, in the statute conferring . . . discretion, there is to be found expressly or by im-
> plication matters which the authority . . . ought to have regard to, then . . . it must
> have regard to those matters. Conversely, if the nature of the subject-matter and the
> general interpretation of the Act make it clear that certain matters would not be ger-
> mane to the matter in question, the authority must disregard those irrelevant . . .
> matters.[200]

The core of the principle is that public bodies must take account of factors that the empowering provisions expressly or implicitly *require* them to consider, and they must exclude from their deliberations factors that the legislation requires to be ex-cluded.[201] Where legislation is not prescriptive as to the factors to be considered or excluded, decision-makers may choose the factors to consider. That choice, how-ever, must be exercised in accordance with the policy and objects of the scheme and may be reviewed by the courts.[202] Relevancy issues arise in a variety of contexts, including as an aspect of rationality,[203] fairness,[204] or in the context of allegations

---

[198] 'Another approach to the same problem in such circumstances, which really reflects the same thinking is this: the grant of what may be the appropriate remedies in an application for judicial re-view is a matter for the discretion of the court. Where one is satisfied that although a reason relied on . . . may not properly be described as insubstantial, nevertheless even without it the . . . body would have been bound to come to precisely the same conclusion on valid grounds, then it would be wrong for this court to exercise its discretion to strike down one way or another, that body's con-clusion.' [1985] QB 1153, 1177 *per* May LJ.

[199] [1948] 1 KB 223.

[200] ibid 228.

[201] *R (on the application of J (a child)) v North Warwickshire BC* [2001] EWCA Civ 315; [2001] 2 PLR 59 at [20] *per* Laws LJ.

[202] See discussion of *Padfield v Minister of Agriculture, Fisheries and Food* [1968] AC 997 at para 14.68 above.

[203] As when it is alleged that the reasoning leading to a decision is inadequate because there has been a failure to consider the relevant issues. See, eg *Bugdaycay v Secretary of State for the Home Department* [1987] AC 514.

[204] eg *R (on application of Bibi) v Newham LBC* [2001] EWCA Civ 607; [2002] 1 WLR 237 (fail-ure to acknowledge that a promise that it had given—that tenants would be given secure tenan-cies—was a relevant consideration was an error of law). 'The law requires that any legitimate expectation be properly taken into account in the decision making process', *per* Schiemann LJ at [51]. If the authority then acts contrary to these expectations the authority is required to articulate its reasons so that the propriety of the action may be tested by the court (at [59]). See also Sedley J, as he then was, in *R v Islington LBC, ex p Rixon* [1997] Ed LR 66.

that a public authority has failed to comply with human rights obligations.[205] Relevancy issues may also be one of a combination of errors that together indicate that the decision-maker has acted unlawfully.[206]

(1) Establishing That a Public Body has Thwarted the Relevancy Principle

The task of claimants will be comparatively easy where an authority admits a breach of the relevancy principle, or where it has given reasons indicating that a breach has occurred.[207] In other situations the courts will have to infer the factors that have influenced the authority from the surrounding circumstances, including policy statements, correspondence and available minutes of meetings. Judges will be very reluctant to go behind the clear statement of a public body that matters were or were not considered, especially when contained in a sworn affidavit, unless independent evidence justifies doing so.[208]

14.81

Where a breach has occurred this will not necessarily mean that the decision will be unlawful. The decision may be allowed to stand where it can be justified on other grounds or where the irrelevant factor was minor,[209] peripheral,[210] immaterial or

14.82

---

[205] eg *Bugdaycay v Secretary of State for the Home Department* [1987] AC 514, 533 *per* Lord Bridge: 'I cannot escape the conclusion that the Secretary of State's decisions in relation to the appellant were taken on the basis of a confidence in Kenya's performance of its obligations under the convention which have now shown to have been . . . misplaced . . . The fact of such breaches must be very relevant to any assessment of the danger that the appellant, if returned to Kenya, would be sent home to Uganda. Since the decisions of the Secretary of State appear to have been made without taking that fact into account, they cannot, in my opinion, now stand.'

[206] eg, *R v Secretary of State for Transport, ex p Richmond upon Thames LBC (No 1)* [1994] 1 WLR 74. A ministerial decision to set new quotas for night flights from Heathrow and other airports was quashed. That the effect of the new quotas would be to increase noise levels had not been considered by the Minister. The new quotas also breached undertakings that had been given and appeared also to conflict with stated policy. The cumulative effect was to create the impression that the Minister had failed to make a rational decision or to act fairly.

[207] See *Padfield v Minister of Agriculture* [1968] AC 997, para 14.70 above; also de Smith, Woolf and Jowell (n 56 above) para 5-084.

[208] eg, in *Panjehali v City and County of Swansea*, The Times, 1 December 2000, Elias J commented that: 'In truth, it seems to me that the appellant's real grievance here was her impression that the LEA had been influenced by financial considerations when refusing to accept the Grange School. However, the LEA said categorically to the Tribunal that cost was not a factor in their decision and there is no evidence to justify my looking behind that statement.' Contrast the decision of Collins J in *R v Secretary of State for the Home Department, ex p Sultan* (C0/297/97) where the judge was highly critical of the way the Secretary of State had dealt with an application to revoke a deportation order. Collins J's judgment is peppered with criticisms of what he considered to be 'a quite extraordinary piece of administration'. Given the evident errors he was not satisfied from the affidavits that errors may not have persisted.

[209] eg *R (on the application of Vetterlein) v Hampshire CC* [2001] EWHC Admin 560; [2002] Env LR 8 at [24] *per* Sullivan J: ' It is . . . highly questionable whether an error, such as is alleged in ground 1 in respect of a particular aspect of one of the many topics considered in the report, could sensibly be said to invalidate the committee's decision to grant planning permission'.

[210] *R (on the application of Beresford) v Sunderland City Council* [2001] EWCA Civ 1218; [2002] QB 874 concerned the implied granting of permission to use an area of land as a 'village green'. Dyson J commented, at 885, that the authority in granting permission had taken irrelevant considerations into account, although they were no more than peripheral and were not material to the outcome.

insubstantial.[211] Likewise, the decision may not be impugned where the authority did not allow itself to be influenced by the irrelevant factor,[212] or where the court is of the view that in the circumstances there had been 'substantial compliance' with the legal requirements.[213]

(2) Legal and Non-Legal Relevancy

14.83   It is a basic principle that the last word on whether or not the relevancy principle has been breached lies with the courts and not the decision-taker. This will be the case however relevant or irrelevant something may seem to be to those making the decision. The Poplar councillors in *Roberts v Hopwood*[214] were almost certainly convinced of the relevance of the need to treat their male and female employees equally. The Minister in *Padfield v Ministry of Agriculture*,[215] no doubt regarded the breadth of the issues raised by the complaints of the south-eastern producers to be relevant to his assessment of whether a committee of investigation should be established. Likewise in *R v Somerset CC, ex p Fewings*,[216] the morality or otherwise of deer hunting was clearly perceived to be highly relevant to those who imposed the ban on hunting. Yet in each situation once the decision had been challenged it was for the courts to determine whether the decisions were lawful.

14.84   Like much in judicial review, what is or is not legally relevant will be determined by the courts having regard to the relevant legislation,[217] the nature of the decision being taken, the body involved,[218] and the impact of the decision, especially its impact on legitimate interests or individual rights. But, determining

---

[211] *R v Broadcasting Complaints Commission, ex p Owen* [1985] QB 1153, para 14.79 above.

[212] *R v London (Bishop)* (1890) 24 QBD 213.

[213] cf *Berkeley v Secretary of State for the Environment, Transport and the Regions (No 1)* [2001] 2 AC 603.

[214] [1925] AC 578.

[215] [1968] AC 997.

[216] [1995] 1 All ER 513, QBD, Laws J; [1995] 1 WLR 1037, CA. Cf *R v Sefton MBC, ex p British Association of Shooting and Conservation Ltd* [2001] Env LR 10. Here the Council's decision not to renew a licence to shoot wildfowl was unsuccessfully challenged not on the grounds that the Council acted because it disapproved of the sport, but on the ground that it had failed to identify the correct legal test.

[217] The provisions need not be contained in statute: *R v Criminal Injuries Compensation Board, ex p Evans* (CO/3259/93, 17 May 1995).

[218] cf for example the approach of the majority and minority to the sentencing powers of the Home Secretary in *R v Secretary of State for the Home Department, ex p Pierson* [1998] AC 539 and *R v Secretary of State for the Home Department, ex p Venables and Thompson* [1998] AC 407. While the majority equated these powers with that of a judge the minority emphasized that Parliament had conferred the powers upon the Home Secretary because he was a member of the executive. This fundamental difference of approach affected inter alia the range of factors that the judges considered were appropriate for the Home Secretary to consider. But see now *R (on the application of Anderson) v Secretary of State for the Home Department* [2002] UKHL 46; [2003] 1 AC 837.

legal relevancy may be no straightforward matter and may lead to disagreement between judges even when considering the same situation.[219]

(3) The Limitations of the Judicial Perspective

While judges are skilled at identifying what is or is not relevant to a particular decision taken in an adjudicative context, they may lack the practical skills and procedural facilities necessary to determine what may or may not be relevant in the broader context of public administration and policy-making. That judges are sensitive to these limitations is acutely illustrated by their reticence to interfere with decisions that are taken in the light of an authority's perception of its resource requirements.[220] Schiemann J summarized the situation when he noted that:

> In an area such as the provision of housing at public expense where decisions are informed by social and political value judgments as to priorities of expenditure the court will start with a recognition that such invidious choices are essentially political rather than judicial. In our judgment the appropriate body to make that choice . . . is the authority. However, it must do so in the light of the legitimate expectations of the respondents.[221]

This is an issue to which we shall return for it raises some of the most difficult and controversial issues in recent judicial review law.

(4) Legal and Factual Relevancy

To turn to a much more specific matter. It follows from what has already been said that important differences may exist between legal and factual relevancy. *Clarke v Secretary of State for Transport, Local Government and the Regions*[222] provides a recent example. Here the question arose as to whether a planning inspector, when considering an application for planning permission by a gypsy family to station a caravan on land, could take account of the fact that an offer of housing had been made to that family. Burton J held that the offer was relevant as a matter of fact because it indicated that the family had somewhere else to live if

14.85

14.86

---

[219] eg, in *R v Somerset CC, ex p Fewings* [1995] 1 WLR 1037, 1049 Simon Brown LJ disagreed with Laws J (at first instance) and the majority in the Court of Appeal in his view that the cruelty issue, far from being irrelevant, was an issue that was 'necessarily relevant' to the authority's decision.

[220] eg, in *R (on application of Bibi) v Newham LBC* [2001] EWCA Civ 607; [2002] 1 WLR 237 at [42], Schiemann LJ noted that, 'only part of the relevant material upon consideration of which any decision must be made is before the court. Because of the need to bear in mind more than the interests of the individual before the court, the relevant facts are always changing.' The judgment contains an interesting discussion of the polycentric nature of public decision-making. See also *R v Cambridge Health Authority, ex p B (No 1)* [1995] 1 WLR 898, 906 and paras 10.108–10.111 and 13.50–13.51 above.

[221] ibid at [64].

[222] [2001] EWHC Admin 800; [2002] JPL 552. For the decision of the Court of Appeal upholding Burton J, see [2002] EWCA Civ 819; [2002] JPL 1365.

the planning permission were refused.[223] However, he held that as a matter of law the offer was irrelevant because permanent housing was unsuitable for a gypsy family: 'It would be contrary to arts 8 and 14 [ECHR] to expect such a person to accept conventional housing and to hold it against him or her that he is has not accepted it, or is not prepared to accept it, even as a last resort factor'.[224]

14.87 This, however, does not mean that the courts will disregard the decision-maker's views on relevancy, unless of course, the legislative provisions are emphatic. Where choice exists, public bodies will be permitted a margin of discretion over what is or is not relevant to their deliberations. As always, the breadth of this margin will vary depending upon the nature of the powers being exercised and the rights and interests affected. A Chief Constable when making a decision how to allocate police resources, for instance, will be permitted a far broader margin of discretion as to what factors may be legitimately considered or excluded than the Home Secretary deciding an application for asylum.[225] In this context, it may be noted that the courts have traditionally drawn a distinction between relevancy and weight: the former being a matter of law for the courts and the latter being a matter of judgment and discretion for the decision-maker.[226] This distinction, however, is no longer as significant as it once was, especially where proportionality issues are involved.[227]

(5) Failure to Consider Relevant Factors

14.88 The following statement of Cooke J, as he then was, in the New Zealand case of *CREEDNZ v Governor General*[228] is accepted as a being a correct statement of principle applicable when it is alleged that a body has failed to consider relevant matters.[229]

> What has to be emphasised is that it is only when the statute expressly or impliedly identifies considerations required to be taken into account by the authority as a matter of legal obligation that the Court holds a decision invalid on the ground now invoked. It is not enough that a consideration is one that may properly be taken into account, nor even that it is one which many people, including the Court itself, would have taken into account if they had to make the decision.

---

[223] [2001] EWHC Admin 800; [2002] JPL 552 at [8].

[224] ibid at [34].

[225] See, eg, *R v Chief Constable of Sussex, ex p International Trader's Ferry Ltd* [1999] 2 AC 418 and *Bugdaycay v Secretary of State for the Home Department* [1987] AC 514.

[226] eg *R v Immigration Appeal Tribunal, ex p Singh (Bakhtaur)* [1986] 1 WLR 910.

[227] See further paras 16.01–16.09 below. Some have doubted that the distinction could ever be justified in principle, see eg TRS Allan, 'Pragmatism and Theory in Public Law' (1988) 104 LQR 422. Certainly there have been instances in the past in which the courts have been prepared to assess whether an improper purpose had 'materially' influenced an authority. See, eg, Glidewell LJ in *R v Inner London Education Authority, ex p Westminster City Council* [1986] 1 WLR 28.

[228] [1981] 1 NZLR 172, 183.

[229] See Lord Scarman in *Re Findlay* [1985] 1 AC 318, 333F.

He later added:

> I think that there will be some matters so obviously material to a decision on a particular project that anything short of direct consideration of them . . . would not be in accordance with the intention of the Act.

The obligation to consider factors will be imposed either by the specific legal provision under which the decision is taken or by general judicial review principles. In this category will fall the obligation to consider what Cooke J refers to as 'matters so obviously material to a decision on a particular project' that failure to consider them would not be 'in accordance with the intention of the Act'.[230] Obligations to consider certain matters may also be imposed by other general requirements, in particular the requirement to act in accordance with human rights obligations. It is important to emphasize, as Cooke J does, that decisions will not be impugned solely because the decision-maker has failed to consider matters that others, including, the court, would have considered. **14.89**

Challenges on the grounds of failure to consider relevant issues arise across the spectrum of public law litigation. The following are just a few examples. In *R v Immigration Appeal Tribunal, ex p Singh (Bakhtaur)*[231] the House of Lords held that the adverse effect that a person's deportation would have on third parties and the public as a whole was relevant to the decision to deport, both by virtue of the immigration rules and general public law principles.[232] In the context of local authority housing, it has been held that while a local housing authority could take account of the existence of rent arrears when allocating tenancies, it was unlawful to apply a policy precluding it from considering the existence of an unresolved dispute over the tenant's liability to pay the arrears.[233] In the planning context it has been argued that local planning authorities have an obligation, when deciding an application for planning permission, to consider the better suitability of alternative sites. It appears, however, that alternative sites will only be relevant in exceptional circumstances. Generally speaking, these would arise when the proposed development involves conspicuous adverse effects and there is an alternative site that lacks these adverse effects that a reasonable local authority would have considered.[234] **14.90**

---

[230] In *R v Immigration Appeal Tribunal, ex p Singh (Bakhtaur)* [1986] 1 WLR 910, 919 Lord Bridge referred to considerations that are 'in truth' relevant to the proper exercise of discretion: [1986] .

[231] ibid.

[232] This obligation might imply a requirement that proper investigations be undertaken into the impact that a person's deportation may have on the community: eg *R v Secretary of State for the Home Department, ex p Sultan* (CO/297/97) where there had been a failure, inter alia, to undertake inquiries into whether the applicant was needed as a teacher at a mosque.

[233] *R v Lambeth LBC, ex p Njomo* (1996) 28 HLR 737.

[234] *R (on the application of J (a child)) v North Warwickshire BC* [2001] EWCA Civ 315; [2001] 2 PLR 59 at [20].

14.91 The courts will tend to assume that expert bodies will be aware of, and will have considered matters that are obviously material, even when there is no express indication of their having done so. In *R v Criminal Injuries Compensation Board, ex p Evans*[235] the Criminal Injuries Compensation Board refused to make an award for compensation on the grounds that the applicant had been guilty of obtaining social security benefits by deception. Dyson J accepted that the Board was required to take into account the applicant's previous good character and that the offences in question were relatively trivial. He held, however, that these factors must have been considered: 'I find it incredible that three experienced Queen's Counsel would not have appreciated that those were important points to which they were required to give their consideration'. Likewise, in *R v Bristol City Council, ex p Baldock*[236] Laws LJ said that the Secretary of State or his officials must have had an important statement of government policy in mind when confirming a decision to close a school.

(6) Consideration of Irrelevant Factors

14.92 The general rule is that unless the statutory provisions provide an exhaustive list of the factors to be considered, the decision-maker may take account of other factors as a matter of discretion, provided consideration of these factors falls within the policy and objects of the scheme.[237] Among the most difficult situations raised in recent cases have been those in which the courts have been asked to determine whether public bodies may take account of factors such as their financial resources, the existence of public protest and threats of industrial action. The importance of the decisions justifies looking specifically at these situations.

(a) The relevance of resources

14.93 Financial considerations are rarely absent in public decision-making. In the context of local government, the courts have developed a number of common law principles according to which local authorities are expected to manage their finances. In particular, '[the] courts have, from time to time, invoked the principle'[238] that local authorities have a fiduciary duty to their local taxpayers analogous to that owed by trustees. This requires them to balance the interests of the recipients of any benefits

---

[235] CO/3259/93, 17 May 1995.

[236] 7 July 2000, CA.

[237] eg, s 22 of the Housing Act 1985 provides that when a local housing authority is allocating tenancies it 'shall secure that in their selection of their tenants a reasonable preference is given to: (a) persons occupying insanitary or overcrowded houses, (b) persons having large families, (c) persons living under unsatisfactory housing conditions and (d) persons towards whom the authority are subject to a duty under s 65 or 68 (persons found to be homeless)'. Sedley LJ has held that the words 'reasonable preference' permits the authority to take account of factors that are not listed, including the existence of rent arrears. See *R v Lambeth LBC, ex p Njomo* (1996) 28 HLR 737.

[238] de Smith, Woolf and Jowell (n 56 above) para 5-095.

and the local taxpayers who contribute to the cost.[239] This duty was held to be breached by Birmingham City Council when it granted a concession to pensioners allowing them to travel free on the Corporation's buses and trams.[240] A similar approach was adopted in the House of Lords when it held the Greater London Council to have acted unlawfully in levying a supplementary rate in order to finance a 25 per cent cut in London bus and underground fares.[241] The Council was under a duty to run the London transport system on ordinary business principles and this did not permit a deliberate decision to operate at a loss.[242]

These decisions show the courts being careful to require local authorities to adopt   **14.94**
an attitude akin to commercial prudence. This only permits expenditure on charitable or philanthropic purposes (to adopt the rather dusty language of the older cases) where this is specifically empowered.[243] More generally, the courts acknowledge that public bodies are obliged to exercise their powers and manage their responsibilities within finite resources and that it is unrealistic to expect such bodies to act as if resources are unlimited. Indeed, in certain discretionary situations, 'it is more likely to be unlawful to disregard financial considerations than to take account of them'.[244] On the other hand, it may be unlawful to act solely for financial reasons without considering whether the decision is fair to those adversely affected[245] or where financial and resource factors are beyond the objects and purposes of the scheme.[246] In general the courts will be reticent to interfere with resource allocation decisions and will usually allow a substantial margin of discretion in these matters. That this reticence exists even where a decision may have tragic consequences is evident from the Court of Appeal's judgment in *R v Cambridge Health Authority, ex p B (No 1)*.[247]

---

[239] Wade and Forsyth (n 33 above) 396.

[240] *Prescott v Birmingham Corp* [1955] Ch 210. Power to grant such concessions was conferred by the Public Service Vehicles (Travel Concessions) Act 1955. See also *Roberts v Hopwood* [1925] AC 578.

[241] *Bromley LBC v Greater London Council* [1983] 1 AC 768. While the Council had acted in accordance with its election mandate this was held not to be relevant to the legality of the decision to reduce fares. Cf *Secretary of State for Education and Science v Tameside MBC* [1977] AC 1014 where it was held that compliance with a mandate was relevant to the reasonableness of a decision.

[242] de Smith, Woolf and Jowell (n 56 above) para 5-95 observe that in so far as the fiduciary duty may imply a duty to act on ordinary business principles and not to be 'thriftless' with ratepayers' money it comes close to permitting the courts to decide levels of expenditure. This is something that they are not equipped to do. Cf *R v London Transport Executive, ex p Greater London Council* [1983] QB 484 where a subsequent transport scheme was held to be lawful.

[243] See also *A-G v Tynemouth Union* [1930] 1 Ch 616. The Tynemouth guardians could not cancel the debts of miners and their families following the General Strike of 1926.

[244] Wade and Forsyth (n 33 above) 383.

[245] *Tower Hamlets LBC v Chetnick Developments Ltd* [1988] AC 858. The decision not to repay overpaid rates in order to save money in the interests of ratepayers generally without regard to the unfairness caused to the company was held unlawful.

[246] *R v Broadcasting Complaints Commission, ex p Owen* [1985] QB 1153.

[247] [1995] 1 WLR 898.

14.95   One of the issues in this case was whether the Health Authority was legally justified in taking its resources into account when deciding not to pursue a course of treatment for a child with leukaemia. Laws J, at first instance, had said that, 'where the question is whether the life of a 10-year-old child might be saved by however slim a chance, the responsible authority . . . must do more than toll the bell of tight resources . . . they must explain the priorities that have led them to decline to fund the treatment'.[248] He found that they had not adequately done so in this case.

14.96   The Court of Appeal overturned this decision. Sir Thomas Bingham MR (as he then was) said that the courts had to adopt a more realistic approach:

> I have no doubt that in a perfect world any treatment which a patient, or a patient's family, sought would be provided if doctors were willing to give it, no matter how much it cost, particularly when a life was potentially at stake. It would however, in my view, be shutting one's eyes to the real world if the court were to proceed on the basis that we do live in such a world. It is common knowledge that health authorities of all kinds are constantly pressed to make ends meet. They cannot pay their nurses as much as they would like; they cannot provide all the treatments they would like; they cannot purchase all the extremely expensive medical equipment they would like; they cannot carry out all the research they would like; they cannot build all the hospitals and specialist units they would like. Difficult and agonising judgments have to be made as to how a limited budget is best allocated to the maximum advantage of the maximum number of patients. That is not a judgment which the court can make . . . I furthermore think, differing I regret from the judge, that it would be totally unrealistic to require the authority to come to the court with its accounts and seek to demonstrate that if this treatment were provided for B then there would be a patient, C, who would have to go without treatment. No major authority could run its financial affairs in a way which would permit such a demonstration.

14.97   A similar approach was adopted by the House of Lords in *R v Chief Constable of Sussex, ex p International Trader's Ferry Ltd.*[249] Following protests by animal rights groups against the export of livestock for slaughter, the major ferry operators stopped carrying livestock cargo on their cross-Channel ferries. The applicant company, an exporter of livestock, therefore, arranged to operate a regular service across the Channel from the port of Shoreham. The service attracted large numbers of demonstrators and a high level of policing was required to ensure that the service was maintained. For several months the police provided cover for five days of sailings per week. However, the Chief Constable decided that the financial and manpower resources required for this task was interfering with the efficient policing of the county as a whole. He accordingly decided that on certain days there would be no policing. On these the police would turn back livestock vehicles if it

---

[248] *R v Cambridge Health Authority, ex p B (No 1)* (n 247 above) (the quotation can be found in Lord Bingham's judgment at 906).
[249] [1999] 2 AC 418.

was considered that a breach of the peace might otherwise occur. The Divisional Court quashed the Chief Constable's decision on the ground that, while his decision was a proper exercise of his discretion under domestic law, there had been a breach of Article 34 of the EC Treaty as his decision was a measure having equivalent effect to a quantitative restriction on exports. On appeal by the Chief Constable, the Court of Appeal held that even if his decision did fall within the ambit of Article 34, it was justified on grounds of public policy under Article 36 EC. The company appealed unsuccessfully to the House of Lords. Their Lordships held that the police had a duty to uphold the law, but this was subject to a wide discretion on the part of the Chief Constable. In particular, there may be circumstances where, having regard to the manpower and financial resources available to meet the overall operational needs of the force, a decision could properly be taken not to commit all available resources to a given dispute or demonstration. The majority[250] also said that a decision might be taken to restrain a lawful activity so as to prevent a breach of the peace. It was held that the decisions to limit the number of sailings to be policed and to prevent lorries from entering the port on other occasions were within the bounds of the Chief Constable's discretion and he had not been in breach of his public law duty in domestic law.[251]

14.98 The duty of the Chief Constable was to reach a proper balance between the various conflicting interests. While the company had a right to trade lawfully this was not an absolute right that must be protected by the Chief Constable at all cost. Lord Slynn explained that while the courts will:

> readily review the way in which decisions are reached, they will respect the margin of appreciation or discretion which a chief constable has. He knows through his officers the local situation, the availability of officers and his financial resources, the other demands on the police in the area at different times . . . Where the use of limited resources has to be decided the undesirability of the court stepping in too quickly was made very clear by Sir Thomas Bingham MR [in *Ex p B*] . . . The facts here are different and the statutory obligations are different but mutatis mutandis the principle is relevant to the present case. It seems to me that it is the right principle and that, whilst the courts must be astute to condemn illegal acts by the police yet, as was said by Balcombe LJ in *Harris v Sheffield United Football Club Ltd* [1988] QB 77, 95:
>
> > The true rule, in my judgment, is as follows. In deciding how to exercise his public duty of enforcing the law, and of keeping the peace, a chief constable has a discretion, which he must exercise even-handedly. Provided he acts within his discretion, the courts will not interfere . . . In exercising that discretion a chief constable must clearly have regard to the resources available to him.

---

[250] Lord Slynn of Hadley, Lord Nolan and Lord Hope of Craighead.

[251] Distinguishing *R v Coventry City Council, ex p Phoenix Aviation* [1995] 3 All ER 37, QBD. The House doubted whether the Chief Constable's action fell within the ambit of Art 34 EC, but on the assumption that it did indicated that the Chief Constable's actions had been necessary for the maintenance of public order, were not disproportionate to the restrictions which they involved, and were therefore within the public policy exception of Art 36.

14.99   Lord Nolan, echoing the earlier approach of the House of Lord in *R v East Sussex CC, ex p Tandy*,[252] went to the nub of the matter. Denying that the case should be seen as a 'victory for the violent elements in the crowds at Shoreham over the forces of law', he said that the decision was:

> an acceptance of the plain fact that there are limits to the extent to which the police can control unlawful violence in any given situation. If those limits are felt to be too narrow, the remedy lies in increasing the resources of the police. It does not lie in the imposition of further restrictions upon the discretion which the law allows to a chief constable to decide upon the best use of the resources, which are in fact available to him.[253]

14.100   These cases illustrate that while judges are reluctant to be drawn into resource management issues, they are aware that their non-intervention may have implications for policy-makers. While this reluctance may appear close to conferring an effective immunity from judicial scrutiny in such matters, in fact it does not do so. Wide though it may appear, the breadth of the margin of discretion permitted is ultimately a matter for the courts. As the House of Lords emphasized in the *International Trader's* case, public bodies have a legal duty to balance properly the competing interests. Where rights and other important interests are at stake the modern approach is to require authorities to show that they have balanced the interests appropriately. The reluctance of the Master of Rolls, in *Ex p B*, to oblige health authorities to bring their accounts to court in order to justify their decisions not to spend money on one patient by showing how others would be affected is understandable. This, however, does not detract from the general principle that 'cogent evidence' may be needed to establish that a shortage of resources justifies decisions that impinge upon the rights and other important interests of those adversely affected.[254]

(i) Resources and duties

14.101   Up to now the discussion has concerned the relevance of resources where discretionary powers are exercised. Where duties are involved, the basic principle is that public bodies cannot escape the obligation to perform their statutory duties by seeking refuge behind arguments that they have insufficient resources to do what is required. Resource considerations will only be relevant if the statutory provisions imposing the duty provide that resources are a relevant consideration. The courts will now be careful to ensure that duties are not reduced to mere powers that only need to be performed when authorities regard themselves as having the resources that permit them to act.

---

[252] [1998] AC 714. See paras 14.102–14.104 below.
[253] [1999] AC 418, 440.
[254] In *R v Chief Immigration Officer, Dover, ex p Sari* (CO/3597/99, 5 June 2000) Silber J held that the existence of cogent evidence of limited resources, including the absence of a large enough room, justified a decision not to permit an asylum seeker representation during an interview.

In *R v Gloucestershire CC, ex p Barry*[255] an elderly disabled man had been receiving **14.102** home care under the provisions of s 2(1) of the Chronically Sick and Disabled Persons Act 1970. The majority of the House of Lords held that under that section an authority could take its resources into account when deciding to withdraw the provision of help. That decision was widely criticized and is now to be regarded as limited to the particular (and 'strange'[256]) statutory provisions with which it was concerned. It has since been distinguished by a unanimous House of Lords in *R v East Sussex CC, ex p Tandy.*[257]

Here it was held that a local education authority could not, for financial reasons, **14.103** reduce the provision of home tuition for sick children from five hours to three hours per week. The House held that the duty under s 298 of the Education Act 1993 to make arrangements for the provision of suitable education was to be performed having regard to educational considerations alone. There was nothing in the section to indicate that a local education authority could take its financial resources into account when considering the suitability of education. This interpretation was reinforced both by s 298(7) which defines suitability of education, and the fact that other provisions in the Act make specific reference to the relevance of resources. The House noted, however, that if there were more than one way of providing 'suitable education' the education authority would be entitled to take resources into account when considering which of the ways to adopt.

Lord Browne-Wilkinson, speaking for the House, was emphatic that lack of re- **14.104** sources cannot excuse the non-performance of statutory duties:

> to permit a local authority to avoid performing a statutory duty on the grounds that it prefers to spend the money in other ways is to downgrade a statutory duty to a discretionary power . . . Parliament has chosen to impose a statutory duty, as opposed to a power, requiring the local authority to do certain things. In my judgment the courts should be slow to downgrade such duties into what are, in effect, mere discretions over which the courts would have very little real control. If Parliament wishes to reduce public expenditure on meeting the needs of sick children then it is up to Parliament so to provide. It is not for the courts to adjust the order of priorities as between statutory duties and statutory discretions.[258]

---

[255] [1997] AC 584. Also *R v Gloucestershire CC, ex p Mahfood* (1995) 8 Admin LR 180
[256] *per* Lord Browne-Wilkinson in *R v East Sussex CC, ex p Tandy* [1998] AC 714, 748.
[257] ibid. *Barry* was also distinguished by the Court of Appeal in another care case, *R v Sefton BC, ex p Help the Aged* [1997] 4 All ER 532. Here it was held that once an authority had decided that an elderly person was in need of care and attention they were under a duty to make arrangements for accommodation to be made available for that person and lack of resources was no excuse. The Court of Appeal contrasted s 2(1) of the Chronically Sick and Disabled Persons Act 1970, with which the House was concerned in *Barry,* with s 21(1) of the National Assistance Act 1948.
[258] [1998] AC 714, 748–749 *per* Lord Browne-Wilkinson. See also *R v Birmingham CC, ex p Mohammed* [1999] 1 WLR 33 where Dyson J, following the approach taken in *Tandy* and distinguishing *Barry,* held that a local housing authority was not entitled to have regard to its financial resources in determining whether or not to approve an application for a disabled facilities grant for

14.105   The above decisions illustrate that while struggling with the issues raised by the resources cases the courts appear to have shifted from a position of trying to cushion the dilemma faced by local authorities caught between duties and lack of adequate resources to a position in which they will only allow authorities to take their resources into account where this is clearly permitted by the relevant statutory provisions.[259]

(b) The relevance of protest or industrial action

14.106   Is it lawful for public authorities to be influenced by the fear that their decisions may attract public protest, industrial action, or other forms of reaction, including reactions that might be unlawful? It appears that two distinctions are important when answering this question. The first is the distinction between reacting to unlawful protest on the one hand and lawful action on the other. The second distinction, both in practice and principle, is between reacting to threats and 'submitting' to them.

14.107   Where it is alleged that action of a public body should be impugned because the body has been wrongly influenced by unlawful action or threats, the courts will approach the issue by emphasizing the importance of vindicating the rule of law and subjecting decisions of public bodies that appear to threaten the rule of law to the closest scrutiny. As Simon Brown LJ said in *R v Coventry City Council, ex p Phoenix Aviation*,[260] another decision generated by the widespread protests over the export of livestock:

> One thread runs consistently throughout all the case law: the recognition that public authorities must beware of surrendering to the dictates of unlawful pressure groups . . . The implications of such surrender for the rule of law can hardly be exaggerated . . . Tempting though it may sometimes be for public authorities to yield too readily to threats of disruption, they must expect the courts to review any such

---

purposes within s 23(1) of the Housing Grants, Construction and Regeneration Act 1996. For a decision upholding a decision of the Special Educational Needs Tribunal that was taken on the basis of an authority's resources see *B v Harrow LBC (No 1)* [2000] 1 WLR 223.

[259] See generally, Elizabeth Palmer, 'Resource Allocation. Welfare Rights—Mapping the Boundaries of Judicial Control in Public Administrative Law' (2000) 20 OJLS 63 and also paras 10.106–10.136 above.

[260] [1995] All ER 37. This comment followed a survey of the case law and dicta, including statements: of Lord Denning MR in *R v Metropolitan Police Commissioner, ex p Blackburn* [1968] 2 QB 118, 138; of Sachs LJ in *R v Caird* (1970) 54 Cr App Rep 499, 506; and of Lord Bridge in *R v Immigration Appeal Tribunal, ex p Singh (Bakhtaur)* [1986] 1 WLR 910, 919. Here Lord Bridge said: 'Extraneous threats to instigate industrial action could only exert an improper pressure on the Secretary of State and if he allowed himself to be influenced by them, he would be taking into account wholly irrelevant considerations'. See also *R v Liverpool University, ex p Caesar Gordon* [1991] 1 QB 124 (decision of university to refuse permission for the holding of a meeting in the belief that the meeting would attract provoke public violence held unlawful).

decision with particular rigour—this is not an area where they can be permitted a wide measure of discretion. As when fundamental rights are in play, the courts will adopt a more interventionist role.[261]

Here it was held that decisions taken by airport and port authorities to ban flights or shipments of livestock by animal exporters were illegal. The decisions were taken without the 'least thought to the awesome implications for the rule of law';[262] nor was any thought given to the interests of those who depended on the lawful trade for their livelihood. Instead the authorities 'focused exclusively upon [their] narrow self interest'.[263]

The *Phoenix Aviation* decision may be contrasted with *R (on the application of L (a child)) v J School Governors*.[264] The question in this case was whether a headmaster could be influenced by the threat of industrial action by teachers when considering whether to reinstate a child who had been excluded. The Court of Appeal held that union-backed action by teachers would not fall into the category of case that Simon Brown LJ had in mind in *Phoenix Aviation*: **14.108**

> . . . the trade unions' threats of industrial action if their members were to be directed to teach or supervise L is not merely a relevant consideration to be taken into account, but, in a reasonable world, a mandatory one. I cannot see how the head or the Governors, owing duties as plainly they do to all the school's pupils, could fail to reflect and decide what would be a responsible position to take in light of the unions' attitude.[265]

(c) The relevance of public opinion

Whether public opinion is relevant to decision-makers in discretionary situations will depend on the nature of the powers, the decision-making function and the decision-maker. The issues were central to a line of decisions concerned with the powers of the Home Secretary in relation to sentencing. In this context a distinction must be made between having regard to opinion in general, or to such matters as the need to maintain public confidence in the criminal justice system, and more specific expressions of public opinion in relation to particular **14.109**

---

[261] [1995] All ER 37, 62e–g.
[262] ibid.
[263] ibid.
[264] [2001] EWCA Civ 1199; [2002] Ed LR 105. For the House of Lords decision in this case, principally on the meaning of reinstatement, see [2003] UKHL 9; [2003] 2 WLR 518. See also *P v National Association of Schoolmasters and Union of Women Teachers* [2003] UKHL 8; [2003] 2 WLR 545.
[265] per Laws LJ in *R (on the application of L (a child)) v J School Governors* [2001] EWCA Civ 1199; [2002] Ed LR 105 at [28]. In *Meade v Haringey LBC* [1979] 1 WLR 637 the Court of Appeal, by a majority, (Eveleigh LJ and Sir Stanley Rees, Lord Denning MR dissenting) indicated that it might not be a breach of an education authority's duty under s 8 of the Education Act 1944 to close a school in response to pressure from trade unions.

decisions such as public 'clamour' that those guilty of heinous crimes be severely punished.

14.110   In *R v Secretary of State for the Home Department, ex p Pierson*[266] the House of Lords by a majority held that in exercising the discretion conferred upon him[267] to release on licence a prisoner serving two mandatory life sentences for the murder of both his parents the Home Secretary's role was analogous to the judicial sentencing function and he was therefore bound by the same considerations of substantive common law fairness as judges. In this case this meant that he could not reach a decision that in effect retrospectively increased a sentence previously imposed. Lords Browne-Wilkinson and Lloyd dissented. In their view Parliament had deliberately conferred the discretionary powers to release a prisoner upon the Home Secretary as a member of the executive, rather than upon a judge. One reason for doing so was to enable the Home Secretary to 'take into account matters of government policy, and of public sentiment'.[268]

14.111   Similar issues also arose in *R v Secretary of State for the Home Department, ex p Venables and Thompson*[269] where the House of Lords considered whether the Home Secretary could lawfully take account of material such as public petitions when considering the release of prisoners sentenced to discretionary life terms. Venables and Thompson were convicted of the murder of Jamie Bulger when they were both ten, and sentenced to be detained during Her Majesty's pleasure.[270] The trial judge stated that in his view the minimum period of detention necessary to satisfy the requirements of retribution and deterrence was, given their youth, eight years. The Lord Chief Justice, agreeing that a shorter period was appropriate than that for an adult, recommended a tariff of ten years. The Secretary of State exercising his powers under s 35 of the Criminal Justice Act 1991 fixed a tariff of 15 years as appropriate to satisfy the requirements of retribution and deterrence. He did so after taking into account extensive material that he had received from members of the public by way of petitions and correspondence, and similar expressions of opinion supplied by a national newspaper, in support of a long or whole-life tariff. This decision was challenged in judicial review proceedings on the grounds, inter alia, that he had taken account of irrelevant considerations and had acted unfairly. The Divisional Court quashed the decisions. The Court of Appeal and the House of Lords dismissed appeals by the Secretary of State.

---

[266] [1998] AC 539.
[267] See now Criminal Justice Act 1991, s 35.
[268] [1998] AC 539, 573.
[269] [1998] AC 407.
[270] Pursuant to s 53(1) of the Children and Young Persons Act 1933, as substituted.

The majority of their Lordships[271] followed the approach of the majority in **14.112** *Pierson* and held that the Secretary of State was here exercising a function comparable to that of a sentencing judge. While a sentencing judge might take into account general considerations of public confidence in the administration of justice, natural justice would require him to ignore as irrelevant public petitions or public opinion as expressed in the media. Moreover, in giving weight to public protests about the level of the tariff to be fixed to the detriment of the applicants the Secretary of State had misdirected himself and acted unlawfully. There is, said Lord Goff:

> a distinction . . . between public concern of a general nature with regard to, for example, the prevalence of certain types of offence, and the need that those who commit such offences should be duly punished; and public clamour that a particular offender whose case is under consideration should be singled out for severe punishment. It is legitimate for a sentencing authority to take the former concern into account, but not the latter. In my opinion, by crossing the boundary from one type of public concern to the other, the Secretary of State erred in the present case.

These decisions should now be read in the light of *R (on the application of* **14.113** *Anderson) v Secretary of State for the Home Department*[272] in which the House of Lords held that the Secretary of State should play no part in fixing the tariff of a convicted murderer. This is because sentencing is a role to be performed by the independent judiciary and not by a member of the executive.[273]

F. Illegality and s 6 of the Human Rights Act

By virtue of s 6(1) of the HRA 1998 it is unlawful for a public authority[274] to act **14.114** in a way that is incompatible with a Convention right.[275] Section 6(1) may be

---

[271] Lord Goff of Chieveley, Lord Steyn and Lord Hope of Craighead. Lord Browne-Wilkinson refused to endorse the approach of the majority and Lord Lloyd expressly dissented. In Lord Browne-Wilkinson's view it was important that Parliament had entrusted the decision relating to the future of the two applicants to the executive and not to the judiciary. While the courts should ensure that the Home Secretary acted in accordance with natural justice, 'the court should be careful not to impose judicial procedures and attitudes on what Parliament has decided should be an executive function'. Lord Lloyd could see 'no reason why [the Home Secretary] could not take account of genuine public concern over a particular case. If he were to ignore such genuine concern . . . it would have direct impact on public confidence for the future.'

[272] [2002] UKHL 46; [2003] 1 AC 837.

[273] Applying the decision of the European Court of Human Rights in *Stafford v UK* (2002) 35 EHRR 32.

[274] For discussion of the meaning of 'public authority' see paras 7.131–7.150 above.

[275] 'Incompatible' in this context means 'inconsistent' and an act will be inconsistent with a Convention right if it violates that right. See Richard Clayton and Hugh Tomlinson, *The Law of Human Rights* (Oxford: OUP, 2000) vol 1, para 5.120.

enforced, or relied on,[276] in proceedings in any appropriate court or tribunal, including judicial review.[277] The ability to enforce s 6(1) in proceedings other than judicial review reflects the fact that violations of Convention rights may give rise to public law and private law claims. In other words, unlike the other heads of judicial review, failure to act compatibly with Convention rights may be both a public law wrong[278] and the basis of a cause of action in private law.[279]

14.115   The obligation not to violate human rights is general and far reaching. It applies whenever public authorities act[280] or fail to act.[281] It potentially extends to every action or inaction of a public authority whether or not that action results in a final or binding decision. Moreover, public authorities 'may neither contract out of the Act nor use their powers to stifle convention rights of others'.[282] Ultimately the core question will be whether the public authority has violated one or more of the Convention rights. In answering this question the courts will have to address the specific rights in issue taking into account the jurisprudence developed, in particular, by the European Court of Human Rights.[283]

14.116   This is not the place to embark on a discussion of the individual rights,[284] however several general comments may be offered. The first and most obvious point to make is that compliance with Convention rights requires more than simply taking rights into account when acting. In other words, satisfaction of the traditional relevancy test discussed earlier in this chapter will not, by itself, be sufficient to render action human rights compliant. Nor is the traditional *Wednesbury* test of irrationality appropriate for determining whether Convention rights have been violated.[285]

---

[276] HRA 1998, s 7(1)(b), eg as a defence in criminal or civil proceedings.

[277] ibid s 7(1)(a).

[278] cf Sedley LJ's comment that 'public law is not at base about rights . . . it is about wrongs—that is to say misuses of public power . . .' in *R v Somerset CC, ex p Dixon* [1998] Env LR 111.

[279] eg *Marcic v Thames Water Utilities Ltd* [2002] EWCA Civ 64; [2002] QB 929.

[280] In the case of 'functional' public bodies, this does not include acts of a private nature, see s 6(5).

[281] s 6(6). However, failure to act does not include a failure to (1) introduce in, or lay before Parliament a proposal for legislation; or (2) make any primary legislation or remedial order. It has been accepted that this means that a failure to lay regulations before Parliament that are subject to the affirmative resolution procedure is not an act within the meaning of s 6(1), but a failure to lay regulations that are only subject to a negative resolution procedure would be. The former is a proposal for legislation whereas the latter is not. See *R (on the application of Rose) v Secretary of State for Health* [2002] EWHC 1593; [2002] 2 FLR 962 at [51] *per* Scott Baker J. See also AW Bradley, Robin Allen QC and Philip Sales, 'The impact of the Human Rights Act 1998 upon subordinate legislation promulgated before October 2, 2000' [2000] PL 358.

[282] *per* Sedley LJ in *London Regional Transport v Mayor of London* [2001] EWCA 1491; [2003] EMLR 4 at [60].

[283] s 2(1).

[284] For discussion of specific rights see chs 8 to 12 above.

[285] Despite the need for 'anxious scrutiny' where human life or liberty is a risk: see Lord Bridge in *Bugdaycay v Secretary of State for the Home Department* [1987] AC 514, 531; *R v Ministry of Defence, ex p Smith* [1996] QB 517. See *Smith and Grady v UK* (2000) 29 EHRR 493 and *R (on the application of Daly) v Secretary of State for the Home Department* [2001] UKHL 26; [2001] 2 AC 532, esp Lord Steyn. See further paras 7.19 above and 16.08 below.

Secondly, it is clear that the prohibition against acting incompatibly with Convention rights may impose both negative and positive obligations upon public authorities. Thus an action may be unlawful and a failure to act may also be unlawful.[286] This is important because certain of the Convention rights require the performance of positive actions as well as obligations to refrain from acting. To take just a few examples, Article 2 (right to life) requires public authorities to refrain from intentionally and unlawfully taking life. But there are also situations in which it also requires the taking of positive steps to safeguard life.[287] Likewise, the right to respect for private or family life set out in Article 8 may require public authorities to take action to protect private and family life. These actions might include, for example, the provision of information concerning environmental hazards,[288] or details of a person's past life in care.[289]   **14.117**

The third general point concerns the relationship between the obligation in s 6(1) and the procedural requirements in s 7 of the HRA 1998. Section 7(1) permits those claiming that a public authority has or proposes to act unlawfully under s 6(1) to bring proceedings against the authority or to rely on their Convention rights in any proceedings. However, in order to do these things the claimant must be a victim of the unlawful act. The term victim is discussed elsewhere.[290] Important as they are in determining who can bring proceedings and in what courts, these requirements do not define the scope of the obligations in s 6(1). As Sedley LJ has put it: '. . . the illegality created by s 6 seems to me to be independent of the individualised provision for bringing or defending proceedings contained in s 7 . . .'.[291] This emphasizes the general and pervasive nature of the obligation to comply with human rights which is owed, as it were, to the general public and not just to victims in particular cases.   **14.118**

Finally, public authorities are only permitted to act incompatibly with a Convention right in two situations. The first, contained in s 6(2)(a), is where, as a result of primary legislation, public authorities cannot act differently. The second, contained in s 6(2)(b), is when they are giving effect to or enforcing primary legislation[292] which cannot be read or given effect in a way which is compatible with Convention rights.   **14.119**

These provisions reflect the general structure of the HRA 1998 by which the fundamental principle of parliamentary supremacy is retained. They must be read   **14.120**

---

[286] s 6(6).
[287] *LCB v UK* (1998) 27 EHRR 212; *X v UK* (1979) 14 DR 31.
[288] *Guerra v Italy* (1998) 26 EHRR 357.
[289] *Gaskin v UK* (1989) 12 EHRR 36.
[290] See paras 19.15–19.23 below.
[291] *London Regional Transport v Mayor of London* [2001] EWCA 1491; [2003] EMLR 4 at [60].
[292] Or provisions made under primary legislation that cannot be read or given effect in a way which is compatible with Convention rights.

together with the general interpretational duty in s 3(1), so that if legislation is capable of being interpreted compatibly with Convention rights no defence under s 6(2) will be available.[293] However, where legislation cannot be interpreted in this way public authorities remain compelled to perform their functions under that legislation and continue to be responsible for its implementation and enforcement.[294]

14.121 Since s 6(2) 'exculpates a public authority that infringes a human right, it is to be narrowly construed'.[295] In order to rely on s 6(2)(a) public authorities must be able to identify specific provisions of primary legislation that compel the action taken. It was, for example, insufficient for a hospital trust to refer to general powers of management when arguing that it was compelled to seclude a patient detained under the Mental Health Act 1983.[296] Once specific provisions have been identified it must be shown that the provisions 'dictated' the breach of the Convention right in question. In *S v Airedale NHS Trust*,[297] for example, the Administrative Court rejected the argument that the Trust could rely on s 6(2)(a) to justify action taken because it lacked the resources to deal with the matter in any other way. The issue is not whether an authority's resources compel it to breach human rights, it is whether provisions of primary legislation compel it to do so.

14.122 Likewise s 6(2)(b) will only provide a defence for an authority if it can show that primary legislation cannot be implemented or enforced without breaching Convention rights. Lord Lester QC and David Pannick QC distinguish this provision from s6(2)(a) by saying that it:

> covers the case, where primary legislation confers a choice on the public authority, but the choice is restricted to options each of which would involve a breach of Convention rights.[298]

14.123 One of the most difficult situations arises when an authority is obliged to apply regulations that conflict with Convention rights, but which are made under primary legislation that itself was not incompatible with Convention rights. In such a situation can an authority defend a claim that it has breached Convention rights

---

[293] *R (on the application of Bono) v Harlow DC* [2002] EWHC 423; [2002] 1 WLR 2475 at [34] *per* Richards J.
[294] This prevents legislation being treated as a dead letter; see further Stephen Grosz, Jack Beatson QC and Peter Duffy QC, *Human Rights: The 1998 Act and the European Convention* (London: Sweet and Maxwell, 1999) paras 4-21–4-22
[295] *per* Stanley Burnton J in *S v Airedale NHS Trust* [2002] EWHC 1780; [2003] Lloyd's Rep Med 21 at [112].
[296] ibid
[297] ibid.
[298] Lord Lester of Herne Hill and David Pannick QC, *Human Rights Law and Practice* (London: Butterworths, 1999) para 2.6.2. In *Ward v Hillingdon LBC* [2001] EWHC Admin 91; [2002] EHLR 4 at [38] Stanley Burnton J said that this interpretation was consistent with s 6(2)(a) but did not express a final view on whether it was correct.

by arguing that it is compelled to apply the regulations until their legality has been impugned? The issue arose in *R (on the application of Bono) v Harlow DC*.[299] Here the local authority sought to rely on s 6(2)(b) as a defence to the claim that its housing benefit review system breached Article 6 ECHR in that it was insufficiently independent. The authority said that it was doing no more than giving effect to regulations that set out the requirements of the system. It was held that the s 6(2)(b) defence was not available because while the authority was giving effect to regulations, the primary legislation under which these had been made was not itself human rights incompatible. Part of the reasoning of the court was that while it was the policy of the Act to preserve the validity of incompatible primary legislation, it was not its policy to preserve the validity of incompatible subordinate legislation where the incompatibility is avoidable.[300]

---

[299] [2002] EWHC 423; [2002] 1 WLR 2475.
[300] See ibid at [35] for the judge's reasoning.

15

GROUNDS FOR JUDICIAL REVIEW: DUE PROCESS, NATURAL JUSTICE AND FAIRNESS

A. Introduction

(a) Due process

This chapter addresses those grounds for judicial review that relate to the procedure adopted (or not adopted) by a decision-maker. The notion that the law should require that certain kinds of decision can only lawfully be taken and implemented if the person affected has had an effective opportunity to make representations has a long history in the common law. Whether it can be traced to Magna Carta itself is debatable, but the principle certainly finds expression in statutes from the 14th century. It appears as an element of the concept that certain actions should only be taken through 'due process of law,' which had both substantive and procedural dimensions:[1]

15.01

> in its substantive aspect, it meant that rights and liberties would not be affected except by law properly made, while in its procedural sense, it meant that suitable procedures would be available to determine whether any action was justified by law.[2]

---

[1] D Galligan, *Due Process and Fair Procedures* (Oxford: Clarendon Press, 1996) 170–178.
[2] ibid 178.

15.02   Early statements that 'due process of law' should be followed in particular contexts seem simply to require that the settled procedures of the common law should be followed in those contexts, rather than that the procedures ought themselves to have a defined content. The concept evolved over time to take on the latter dimension, particularly as it became applicable to issues arising in the course of administrative processes that clearly could not be resolved by trials in the ordinary courts. However, the path of evolution was significantly different as between the United States and England. In the United States, the phrase 'due process of law' was enshrined in the Constitution, the fifth amendment providing: 'nor shall any person . . . be deprived of life, liberty, or property, without due process of law'; and the fourteenth: 'nor shall any state deprive a person of life, liberty, or property, without due process of law'. These amendments have given rise to a considerable jurisprudence, which affirms a continued distinction between substantive and procedural due process.[3] In England the term 'due process of law' largely disappeared, the original concept having evolved into the elements that comprise the rule of law and the common law standards of natural justice and fairness, the latter being the equivalent (albeit without the status of an entrenched constitutional principle) of procedural due process.

(b) Procedural impropriety as a ground for judicial review

15.03   There is no single, accepted typology of the grounds of judicial review. Different approaches to classification have been adopted by different authors.[4] Lord Diplock's typology[5] has been widely cited. This distinguishes illegality, irrationality, procedural impropriety and (then, a possible fourth ground) proportionality. 'Procedural impropriety' covered both 'failure to observe basic rules of natural justice or failure to act with procedural fairness towards the person who will be affected by the decision' and 'failure by an administrative tribunal[6] to observe procedural rules that are expressly laid down in the legislative instrument by which its jurisdiction is conferred, even when such failure does not involve any denial of natural justice'. This chapter deals with both of these elements. While the fettering of discretion is treated by some[7] as an aspect of procedural fairness, the view taken here is that, as a matter that concerns more the intellectual process by

---

[3] D Galligan, *Due Process and Fair Procedures* (n 1 above) ch 6.

[4] Compare the approaches, for example, of Professor de Smith (*Judicial Review of Administrative Action* (4th edn, London: Sweet & Maxwell, 1980)), Lord Woolf and Professor Jowell (de Smith, Woolf and Jowell, *Judicial Review of Administrative Action* (5th edn, London: Sweet & Maxwell, 1995), and Professor Wade and CF Forsyth (*Administrative Law* (8th edn, Oxford: OUP, 2000)).

[5] *Council of Civil Service Unions v Minister for the Civil Service* [1985] AC 374, 410–411.

[6] This proposition cannot have been intended to be confined to those bodies that are formally constituted as tribunals, but must be read as applicable to any decision-maker whose procedures are enshrined in legislation, whether primary or secondary.

[7] Particularly the current authors of de Smith, Woolf and Jowell (n 4 above): see paras III-001–III-004.

which a decision is reached than procedural steps that have or have not been adopted, it is more appropriately considered under the heading of illegality.[8]

(c) Procedural fairness: overview

Where they apply, the common law requirements or rules of natural justice or procedural fairness are essentially two-fold. First, the person affected has the right to prior notice and an effective opportunity to make representations before a decision is made or implemented. Secondly, the person affected has the right to an unbiased tribunal, in the sense that the decision-maker must not have a direct pecuniary or proprietary interest in the matter under consideration and there must not be a real possibility that he or she is biased. All of these propositions require further elaboration. For much of their history these two basic rules have carried the Latin tags audi alteram partem (hear both sides) and nemo judex in causa sua (no man should be judge in his own cause). The use of Latin labels is now, of course, officially discouraged.

15.04

In any given case, two basic questions may arise: (1) do the rules of natural justice or fairness apply? (2) if they do, what is their content in the particular situation? There is then the factual issue of whether in the circumstances of the case the relevant requirements have been fulfilled and, if they have not, the question whether a remedy should be granted. Issues as to the content of natural justice or procedural fairness have naturally arisen over a number of centuries in the context of ordinary civil and criminal proceedings before courts of law, including in particular proceedings before justices of the peace. Substantive bodies of case law have refined the applicable principles. Issues concerning the applicability of analogous requirements to other kinds of decision-makers have proved more difficult to resolve. The further one moves away from the core model of the civil and criminal proceedings of courts of law, the greater the room for argument either that less can properly be required by way of procedural protection for the person affected or, indeed, that formal procedural standards should not be imposed at all. The development of the role of the state in the 19th and 20th centuries, both as regulator and as the provider of benefits, required the courts to consider the extent to which they could attach procedural requirements to the many and varied decision-making processes of the executive.[9]

15.05

Much of the case law up to 1963 that concerned the application of natural justice requirements to bodies other than the courts of law was focused on the first of two basic questions. It was accepted that natural justice requirements (and, indeed, the prerogative remedy of certiorari) extended only to those exercising 'judicial' as

15.06

---

[8] See paras 14.26–14.61 above.
[9] In particular, the Crown, central government departments, local authorities and other statutory bodies.

distinct from 'administrative' functions. There were significant differences of view over time as to whether the term 'judicial' should be interpreted flexibly or narrowly; in the 1950s and early 1960s a narrow approach prevailed. The landmark decision of the House of Lords in *Ridge v Baldwin*[10] made it clear that the former, flexible approach should be adopted. This decision has been interpreted and applied in much, although not all, of the subsequent case law concerning the right to a hearing as dispensing altogether with the need to classify a decision as administrative or judicial for these purposes,[11] and the same broad approach has been extended to the rule against bias.[12] The 20 years following the ruling in *Ridge v Baldwin* saw a spate of cases working through the consequences. The spate has since slackened, with most issues arising concerning the detailed content of the requirements of procedural fairness in particular factual situations, including the extension by the judges of requirements to give reasons. The other significant recent development has been the modification of the content of the rule against bias to ensure conformity with the requirements of Article 6(1) of the European Convention on Human Rights (ECHR).[13]

(d) Article 6(1) ECHR

15.07 The requirements of procedural due process as expressed in the ECHR are found in Article 6. The basic principles of this provision are discussed above[14] and their application as grounds of judicial review in English law below.[15]

(e) The purposes of procedural protection

15.08 Two broad purposes have been identified as providing justification for the imposition of procedural standards; these are applicable whether the standards are enshrined in primary or secondary legislation or determined by the judges.[16] The first approach is one of *instrumentalism*. Requirements may be imposed in order to maximize the chances that the decision-making process produces the 'right answer'. The nature of the criteria for judging what is the 'right' or optimal answer and, indeed, whether there is only one such answer will of course vary considerably according to the process.[17] But all decision-making processes are set up or un-

---

[10] [1964] AC 40.

[11] See further paras 15.20–15.29 below.

[12] See paras 15.73 and 15.88 below.

[13] See paras 15.82 and 15.83 below.

[14] See ch 12 above. The particular application of these requirements in the determination of criminal charges, set out in Art 6(2) and (3), are considered, where relevant, in Part IV of this work.

[15] See para 15.108 below.

[16] See G Richardson, in G Richardson and H Genn, *Administrative Law & Government Action* (Oxford: Clarendon Press, 1994) ch 5; P Craig, *Administrative Law* (4th edn, London: Sweet & Maxwell, 1999) 402–403.

[17] Whether it is ever appropriate for criteria to be employed that are solely economic is much debated: see eg Richardson (n 16 above) 111–113.

dertaken for a purpose and there will inevitably be a range of possible ways of proceeding, some of which will enhance and others reduce the chances of reaching the right answer. Human experience is replete with illustrations of the proposition that where X has the power to make a decision that specifically affects Y, Y is likely to have some relevant information or argument that will help X to reach the best decision as to whether the power should be exercised. The second approach recognizes that procedural standards may be 'designed to protect values which are independent of the direct outcome of the decision, such as participation, fairness and the protection of human dignity'.[18] Various theoretical justifications have been advanced.[19] A further point, which draws on both of these considerations is that: 'disadvantageous decisions are more likely to be accepted and observed if they are arrived at by means of a fair procedure'.[20]

Both main purposes have received judicial recognition. In *R v Secretary of State*   **15.09**
for the Home Department, ex p Doody[21] Lord Mustill said that a prisoner given a mandatory life sentence for murder would wish to know why a particular term had been determined for him by the Home Secretary as the tariff or penal element that had to be served before he could be considered for release on licence. This was:

> probably from an obvious human desire to be told the reason for a decision so gravely affecting his future and partly because he hopes that once the information is obtained he may be able to point out errors of fact and reasoning and thereby persuade the Secretary of State to change his mind, or if he fails in this to challenge the decision in the courts.

The House of Lords held that fairness did require reasons to be given. Two distinct   **15.10**
justifications were advanced. First, the position of a mandatory life sentence prisoner was contrasted with that of a prisoner given a long determinate sentence, for example for robbery, or a discretionary life sentence. The latter was given reasons for the sentence or the tariff, as the case may be. The former was not:

> He never sees the Home Secretary; he has no dialogue with him: he cannot fathom how his mind is working. There is no true tariff, or at least no tariff exposed to public view which might give the prisoner an idea of what to expect. The announcement of his first review date arrives out of thin air, wholly without explanation. The distant oracle has spoken, and that is that . . . I . . . simply ask, is it fair that the mandatory life prisoner should be wholly deprived of the information which all other prisoners receive as a matter of course. I am clearly of opinion that it is not.[22]

---

[18] Richardson (n 16 above) 113.
[19] ibid 113–114.
[20] C Rennig in KF Röhl and S Machura, *Procedural Justice* (Aldershot: Ashgate, 1997) 207, noting that 'this finding has been confirmed repeatedly . . . within a tradition of social psychological research that from the outset has focussed attention on the judicial system'.
[21] [1994] 1 AC 531, 551. Cited by Craig (n 16 above) 402.
[22] [1994] 1 AC 531, 565 *per* Lord Mustill.

15.11   The second, distinct justification was that reasons had to be given to enable the prisoner to mount an effective legal challenge by way of judicial review. It will be noted that the first of these justifications is simply an assertion that the failure to provide reasons is in the circumstances unfair. While the reasoning is non-instrumental, the detailed basis for it is opaque, particularly as Lord Mustill specifically indicated that it was not:

> very helpful to say that the Home Secretary should out of simple humanity provide reasons for the prisoner, since any society which operates a penal system is bound to treat some of its citizens in a way which would, in the general, be thought inhumane.[23]

It may be that the real concern here was not merely one requiring respect for human dignity but that the uncertainty caused by the absence of reasons would involve unnecessary psychological damage that could not be justified as part of the sentence. The language adopted by Lord Mustill also suggests that the policy not to give reasons might itself have been open to substantive challenge on the ground of irrationality.

15.12   In practice, the vast majority of the reasoning deployed in the area of the right to a fair hearing is instrumental.[24] The case law on the effect of non-compliance with express procedural requirements also reveals a strong trend in favour of instrumental reasoning.[25] The position is, however, different as regards the rule against bias, where the emphasis is on appearances,[26] although the third point made above as to the acceptability of decisions may apply with particular force here.

(f) The basis for intervention

15.13   The case law on procedural fairness provides fertile territory for the debate as to how far, if at all, the ultra vires doctrine provides the basis for intervention in proceedings for judicial review. Dicta can be found that support a variety of views.[27] This is also an area where a significant number of cases arise in non-statutory backgrounds, for example concerning clubs and trade unions. This matter is more fully explored elsewhere.[28] In principle, where a requirement to observe natural justice or act with procedural fairness is not fulfilled, and a remedy is granted, the act or decision in question is regarded as a nullity or void ab initio.[29] The court, however, retains a discretion to refuse to grant a remedy, for example where there has been no prejudice to the complainant.[30]

---

[23] *R v Secretary of State for the Home Department, ex p Doody* (n 21 above) 564.
[24] See Richardson (n 16 above) 117–118.
[25] See para 15.102 below.
[26] See para 15.79 below.
[27] Compare, eg, the statements of Byles J and Lord Steyn: paras 15.15 and 15.56 below.
[28] See paras 15.22 and 15.35–15.37 below.
[29] See further paras 15.92 and 15.99 et seq below .
[30] See paras 18.52–18.70 below .

(g) Terminology

In 19th century cases the term 'natural justice' was commonly used broadly; to say   **15.14**
that a particular proposition was contrary to natural justice was simply to say that
it was contrary to the fitness of things[31] or (sometimes) the law of nature.[32] The
audi alteram partem and nemo judex rules were first firmly associated with each
other in the late 19th century[33] and by the early 20th century it was said that: 'the
general statements in the older cases as to not enforcing judgments contrary to
natural justice seem now in practice limited to procedure contrary to natural justice'.[34] In the latter part of the 20th century, the term 'procedural fairness' has
come to be preferred,[35] and has the advantages of being clearer, more accurate, and
avoiding reference to the historically uncertain association with natural law.[36]

B. Procedural Fairness

(1) When Does a Right to a Fair Hearing Arise?

(a) The traditional approach

Under the traditional approach of the courts, legal requirements to afford prior   **15.15**
notice and a fair hearing before deciding a matter were applied to judicial bodies
such as courts of law and other bodies that were exercising judicial or quasi-judicial functions. The earliest cases involving decision-makers other than courts of
law concerned persons deprived of an office for cause,[37] or of their university degrees[38] and decisions on the regulation of the clergy.[39] Nineteenth century case law
applied the principles to decisions to remove members of professional or social
bodies or clubs,[40] and, particularly significantly, to decisions of public bodies that
interfered with property rights. The landmark case here was *Cooper v Wandsworth*

---

[31] See eg *Hammond v Vestry of St Pancras* (1874) LR 9 CP 316, 322 *per* Brett J: 'It would seem to
me to be contrary to natural justice to say that parliament intended to compose a liability for a thing
which no reasonable care and skill could obviate'.

[32] See HH Marshall, *Natural Justice* (London: Sweet & Maxwell, 1959) 6–15.

[33] *Spackman v Plumstead District Board of Works* (1885) 10 App Cas 229, 240 *per* Earl of Selborne
LC.

[34] Channell J in *Robinson v Fenner* [1913] 3 KB 835, 844, cited by Marshall (n 32 above) 15.

[35] See eg Lord Diplock in *O'Reilly v Mackman* [1983] 2 AC 237, 275.

[36] See further para 15.22 below.

[37] eg *Bagg's Case* (1615) 11 Co Rep 93b (deprivation of the privilege of being a burgess of
Plymouth following unseemly behaviour); *R v Gaskin* (1700) 8 Term Rep 209 (dismissal of a parish
clerk); *Ex p Ramshay* (1852) 18 QB 173 (removal of county court judge).

[38] *R v Chancellor of the University of Cambridge* (1723) 1 Str 557 (Dr Bentley's case).

[39] *Capel v Child* (1832) 2 Cr & J 558 (bishop required to give notice and opportunity to be heard
before requiring vicar to appoint a curate (at the vicar's expense)).

[40] *Wood v Woad* (1874) LR 9 Ex 190 (mutual insurance society); *Fisher v Keane* (1878) 11 Ch D
353 (club).

Board of Works.[41] Builders were required by statute to give seven days' notice to the Board before beginning to lay out the foundations of a new building. In default of such notice, the Board had power to secure demolition. The plaintiff claimed to have given notice in respect of a particular building (which was denied) but in any event commenced work within five days. The house had reached the second storey when the Board, without notice, sent workmen late in the evening to pull it down. The plaintiff recovered damages for trespass. The Court of Common Pleas held that while the Board's act was justified by the words of the statute read literally, the powers conferred were: 'subject to a qualification which has been repeatedly recognised, that no man is to be deprived of his property without his having an opportunity of being heard'.[42] The Board argued that this principle only applied to judicial proceedings. Willes J[43] and Byles J were clear that these were 'judicial powers'. Byles J, in an often-cited remark, stated:[44]

> I conceive they acted judicially, because they had to determine the offence, and they had to apportion the punishment as well as the remedy. That being so, a long course of decisions, beginning with Dr Bentley's case . . . establish that, although there are no positive words in a statute requiring that the party shall be heard, yet the justice of the common law will supply the omission of the legislature.

15.16   In 1911 the House of Lords in *Board of Education v Rice*[45] indicated obiter that the audi alteram partem rule was indeed one of broad application. Lord Loreburn said:[46]

> Comparatively recent statutes have extended, if they have not originated, the practice of imposing upon departments or officers of State the duty of deciding or determining questions of various kinds . . . In such cases . . . they must act in good faith and fairly listen to both sides, for that is a duty lying upon everyone who decides anything. But I do not think they are bound to treat such a question as though it were a trial . . .

This cannot, however, be taken too far as the dictum does refer to 'deciding or determining questions' and the context was that of the resolution of a dispute between a local education authority and school managers on a question of law and fact (was the authority complying with its duty to maintain the school and keep it efficient when paying lower salaries to teachers in non-provided schools than to teachers in provided schools?).[47]

---

[41]   (1863) 14 CB (ns) 180.
[42]   ibid 187 *per* Erle CJ.
[43]   ibid 191. Erle CJ was more equivocal: ibid 189.
[44]   ibid 194. Byles J was also of the view (at 195) that even if the Board's act had been 'ministerial' there was an implied obligation to give prior notice of the order.
[45]   [1911] AC 179.
[46]   ibid 182.
[47]   See de Smith, Woolf and Jowell (n 4 above) 384–385. Education Act 1902, s 7(3) expressly provided that if any 'question' arose between the authority and school managers it was to be 'determined' by the Board.

(b) The 'path of deviation'

Between the decisions of the House of Lords in *Local Government Board v* **15.17**
Arlidge[48] and in *Ridge v Baldwin*[49] the case law followed what de Smith termed a
'path of deviation' in which in a number of contexts the courts adopted an unduly
restrictive approach to the applicability of the audi alteram partem rule of natural
justice. Examples included decisions denying the applicability of that rule to the
discretionary determination of a housing appeal by a minister,[50] the deportation
of an alien on the ground that it was conducive to the public good,[51] the role of the
minister in respect of the confirmation of slum clearance and compulsory purchase orders,[52] the revocation of a textile dealer's[53] or taxi driver's[54] licence and the
disciplining of a fireman.[55] The cases concerning slum clearance and compulsory
purchase orders[56] did, however, establish that natural justice did apply to part of
the process by which an order was taken from initial proposal to ultimate confirmation; from the time that objections to an order proposed by a local authority
were received by the minister, and through the period in which an inquiry was
held into those objections by an inspector or the minister's behalf, it was unlawful
for the inspector or minister to obtain information behind the backs of one or
other of the parties to the dispute (the objectors and the local authority). However, once the minister had received the report and was considering whether or not
as a matter of policy the order should be confirmed, the legal obligation to observe
natural justice ceased.[57] This was rationalized on the basis that the minister was
acting 'administratively' at the first and last stages and 'quasi-judicially' in the
middle stage. Emphasis was laid on the point that it was only when objections
were received that the situation took on the form of a dispute between two contending parties (a lis inter partes).

---

[48] [1915] AC 120 (minister under no legal duty to disclose contents of report of inquiry held on
his behalf by an inspector concerning housing appeal ultimately determined by the minister).

[49] See para 15.19 below.

[50] *Local Government Board v Arlidge* [1915] AC 120.

[51] *R v Leman Street Police Station Inspector, ex p Venicoff* [1920] 3 KB 72.

[52] *Fredman v Minister of Health* (1935) 154 LT 240; *Errington v Minister of Health* [1935] 1 KB
249; *Johnson (B) & Co (Builders) Ltd v Minister of Health* [1947] 2 All ER 395.

[53] *Nakkuda Ali v Jayaratne* [1951] AC 66, PC, a case originating in Ceylon that concerned the
power of the Controller of Textiles to cancel a dealer's licence if he had reasonable grounds to believe
him unfit to be allowed to continue as a dealer. The Privy Council held (1) that the Controller had
to have objectively reasonable grounds (distinguishing *Liversidge v Anderson* [1942] AC 206); and
(2) that although the Controller had in fact observed natural justice, he had been under no legal
obligation to do so.

[54] *R v Metropolitan Police Commissioner, ex p Parker* [1958] 1 WLR 1150, DC.

[55] *Ex p Fry* [1954] 1 WLR 730, DC.

[56] See n 52 above.

[57] This point was underlined by the decision of the House of Lords in *Franklin v Minister of Town
and Country Planning* [1948] AC 87 that the nemo judex rule did not apply to the decision of a minister whether or not to confirm an order (that under the relevant legislation was proposed by him)
designating the area of Stevenage as a new town.

15.18 Whatever the rights and wrongs of this approach in its own context,[58] it did give rise to difficulty when adopted elsewhere. In particular, the view developed that both the obligation to observe natural justice and the availability of the remedy of certiorari were limited to situations where a body was itself a judicial body such as a court of law,[59] or, otherwise, was under an express statutory duty to consider objections or hold an inquiry or was determining a lis inter partes.[60] The defects of this approach were readily observable in the cases on revocation of licences, where the courts were unwilling to infer a duty to 'act judicially' or observe the audi alteram partem rule simply from the devastating impact of the decision on the interests (here, the livelihood) of the persons affected.[61] The authority was not 'determining a question' but 'taking executive action to withdraw a privilege'.[62] These cases were the subject of immediate adverse criticism,[63] that drew attention to the earlier decisions such as *Cooper v Wandsworth Board of Works*[64] in which the courts had been prepared to imply an obligation to observe natural justice into powers that interfered directly with property rights; the later approach of the courts was obviously inconsistent.

(c) *Ridge v Baldwin*

15.19 These criticisms were taken up by the House of Lords in *Ridge v Baldwin*,[65] one of the key decisions that developed the principles of judicial review in the second half of the 20th century. The case concerned the decision of Brighton's Watch Committee to dismiss the Chief Constable of Brighton, Charles Ridge. Ridge was tried, with two other officers and two civilians, for conspiracy to obstruct the course of justice. Ridge was acquitted but the two officers and one of the civilians

---

[58] Some of the decisions could be supported on the ground that it would be wrong to over-judicialize a process much of the detail of which was enshrined in legislation; others, such as the refusal to disclose inspectors' reports were less defensible and were ultimately changed by regulations.

[59] Certiorari would of course only lie to inferior courts of law; natural justice was and is required of both superior and inferior courts: see, eg, para 15.70 below.

[60] eg *Errington v Minister of Health* [1935] 1 KB 249; *Johnson (B) & Co (Builders) Ltd v Minister of Health* [1947] 2 All ER 395; *Franklin v Minister of Town and Country Planning* [1948] AC 87 (natural justice); *R v Electricity Commissioners* [1924] 1 KB 171, 204–205 (dictum of Atkin LJ that certiorari lay in respect of the decisions of 'any body of persons having legal authority to determine questions affecting the rights of subjects, and having the duty to act judicially'; the final phrase was interpreted as requiring a 'superadded' express duty to follow a judicial-type procedure: see *R v Legislative Committee of the Church Assembly* [1928] 1 KB 411; *Nakkuda Ali v Jayaratne* [1951] AC 66, PC.

[61] *Nakkuda Ali v Jayaratne*, ibid; *R v Metropolitan Police Commissioner, ex p Parker* [1958] 1 WLR 1150, DC.

[62] *Nakkuda Ali v Jayaratne*, n 60 above, at 78 *per* Lord Radcliffe.

[63] See HWR Wade, 'The Twilight of Natural Justice' (1951) 67 LQR 103 (considering *Nakkuda Ali*). No case earlier than 1911 was cited to the Privy Council.

[64] (1863) 14 CB (ns) 180.

[65] [1964] AC 40. See AW Bradley, 'A failure of justice and defect of police' [1964] CLJ 83, AL Goodhart, 'Ridge v Baldwin: Administration and natural justice' (1964) 80 LQR 105 and SA de Smith, 'The House of Lords on natural justice' (1963) 26 MLR 543.

were convicted; no evidence was offered on a further corruption charge against Ridge. The trial judge, Donovan J, strongly criticized the leadership that had been provided by Ridge for the force and referred to the force's need for a new leader. Ridge held his office subject to dismissal for cause. The Watch Committee resolved to dismiss him without giving him prior notice or an opportunity to make representations. At a subsequent meeting, the committee heard representations from Ridge's solicitor but gave no further particulars of the case against him. Ridge brought an action in the High Court for a declaration that the dismissal was illegal, ultra vires and void, and for damages. His main purpose was to obtain the opportunity to resign voluntarily, his pension rights thus being preserved. Streatfeild J held[66] that natural justice had to be observed and that the Watch Committee had done so; the Court of Appeal[67] held that natural justice did not have to be observed and had not been; the House of Lords by a majority[68] held that natural justice *did* have to be observed and had not been. The declaration was granted.[69] The leading speech on natural justice was delivered by Lord Reid, who showed how sight had been lost of the earlier authorities in decisions in the 20th century, stated that Atkin LJ's judgment in the *Electricity Commissioners* case had been misunderstood and held that the decision in *Nakkuda Ali* 'was given under a serious misapprehension of the effect of the older authorities and therefore cannot be regarded as authoritative'.[70] In particular, it was entirely legitimate to *infer* the judicial character of a duty from the nature of that duty. A duty to act judicially and to observe natural justice was readily to be inferred,[71] in accordance with an unbroken line of authority over some centuries, where an office-holder was dismissed for cause.

(d) The consequences of *Ridge v Baldwin*

The real significance of *Ridge v Baldwin* lies not merely in what it determined on its own facts but also in its wider effects. The context of the case was one where

15.20

---

[66] [1963] 1 QB 539.

[67] ibid.

[68] Lords Reid, Morris of Borth-y-Gest and Hodson; Lord Evershed dissented; Lord Devlin based his decision on the relevant regulations.

[69] A second ground was that the decision was void for non-compliance with the relevant police regulations.

[70] [1964] AC 40, 79.

[71] Under the discredited approach the focus of attention was whether the decision-making process in question should properly be analysed as 'judicial', 'quasi-judicial' or 'administrative', according to criteria that sought to draw a clear distinction in particular between the first two concepts and the third (see further de Smith, Woolf and Jowell (n 4 above) Appendix on 'Classification of Functions'). The obligation to observe natural justice would then apply to decisions that were analytically judicial or quasi-judicial. Under the approach of *Cooper v Wandsworth Board of Works* and *Ridge v Baldwin* the questions (1) is this decision 'judicial' or 'quasi-judicial'? and (2) does the audi alteram partem rule apply? become fused; if the court is satisfied *either* that the decision is analytically judicial *or* that there is good reason to require observance of natural justice, then a 'duty to act judicially' arises. To the extent that this is circular, the circularity is in fact not necessarily unhelpful.

there was significant older authority available to be resurrected. The task that fell to the courts in subsequent cases was how to develop and apply the flexibility in approach that *Ridge v Baldwin* had endorsed as appropriate, in situations where there were no established precedents. It should be noted that, *Ridge v Baldwin* broadened the range of situations in which a duty to act judicially (in accordance with natural justice) could be inferred; it did not hold that the audi alteram partem rule applied with full force and vigour across the whole range of judicial and administrative decision-making. The position was reached that the audi alteram partem rule had to be observed (1) by obviously judicial bodies such as courts of law; and (2) by other bodies where there was good reason for that requirement to be imposed, taking careful account of the effect of a decision on the interests of the person concerned, the wider context of the decision and other relevant considerations. The fact that a decision can properly be analysed and labelled as 'administrative' was, accordingly, no longer a bar to the applicability of natural justice requirements; it did not (and indeed should not) follow that natural justice automatically applied to all such decision-making.[72]

15.21   It also does not follow that the distinction between judicial and administrative decision-making is necessarily wholly irrelevant. A model whereby all decisions are to be analyzed and assigned to one or other of four basic classifications (judicial, quasi-judicial, administrative and legislative), with significant differences in outcome following according to the classification, is today accepted to be unworkable. However, if these are seen as points on a spectrum, consideration of at least the rough position of a decision on that spectrum may properly be helpful (although not normally determinative)[73] in addressing the question of the extent to which procedural standards ought to be imposed by the courts.

(e) The post-*Ridge v Baldwin* case law

15.22   A number of strands can be identified in the case law since *Ridge v Baldwin*. First, the courts have increasingly spoken in terms of 'fairness' rather than 'natural justice', the trend being particularly marked in cases where procedural standards have been imposed in contexts involving the exercise of administrative discretion. Secondly, in order to introduce at least a measure of certainty, the courts have sought to articulate criteria for identifying those situations where procedural standards are to be imposed, without becoming over-prescriptive. Thirdly, and perhaps more importantly, bodies of case law have developed across a wide range of

---

[72] 'At one time it was said that the principles [of natural justice] only apply to judicial proceedings and not to administrative proceedings. That heresy was scotched in *Ridge v Baldwin*': *per* Lord Denning MR in *R v Gaming Board for Great Britain, ex p Benaim and Khaida* [1970] 2 QB 417, 430. This dictum is to be interpreted in the former sense.
[73] A general principle remains that the exercise of a legislative power does not attract a duty of procedural fairness, although this is not without its critics: see para 15.67 below.

contexts which illustrate the detailed application of the requirements of procedural fairness. Fourthly, as the number of situations in which the courts have declined to impose any procedural standards have been relatively confined, the issues that have arisen have increasingly concerned the detailed content of those standards.

(f) Fairness

The use of the language of 'fairness' in administrative contexts is illustrated by the decision of the Divisional Court in *Re HK (An Infant)*.[74] Under s 2(1) of the Commonwealth Immigrants Act 1962, an immigration officer had a discretion to refuse admission to the United Kingdom to Commonwealth citizens; however, by virtue of s 2(2), that discretion could not be exercised in respect of 'any person who satisfies an immigration officer that he . . . is the child under 16 years of age, of a Commonwealth citizen who is resident in the United Kingdom . . .'. HK was interviewed by an officer, who refused admission on the ground that he was not satisfied that HK was under 16. The court refused an application for certiorari but did discuss the scope of the procedural standards to be implied. Lord Parker CJ said:[75]

15.23

> I myself think that even if an immigration officer is not in a judicial or quasi-judicial capacity, he must at any rate give the immigrant an opportunity of satisfying him of the matters in the subsection, and for that purpose let the immigrant know what his immediate impression is so that the immigrant can disabuse him. That is not, as I see it, a question of acting or being required to act judicially, but of being required to act fairly . . . [T]o the limited extent that the circumstances of any particular case allow, and within the legislative framework under which the administrator is working, only to that limited extent do the so-called rules of natural justice apply.

Lord Parker CJ's approach was expressly endorsed by Lord Denning MR in the Court of Appeal.[76] A duty to act with procedural fairness has been identified in a wide variety of contexts.[77]

---

[74] [1967] 2 QB 617.

[75] ibid 630. Salmon LJ said (at 633) that the officer 'must act, as Lord Parker LJ has said, fairly in accordance with the ordinary principles of natural justice'; the decision in such cases 'is of vital importance to the immigrants since their whole future may depend upon it' (ibid). Blain J agreed with Salmon and Parker L JJ.

[76] *R v Gaming Board for Great Britain, ex p Benaim and Khaida* [1970] 2 QB 417, 430; *Breen v Amalgamated Engineering Union* [1971] 2 QB 175 ('a statutory body, which is entrusted by statute with a discretion, must act fairly. It does not matter whether its functions are described as judicial or quasi-judicial on the one hand, or as administrative on the other hand, or what you will. Still it must act fairly. It must, *in a proper case* [our emphasis], give a party a chance to be heard').

[77] eg, the refusal of a certificate of consent that the applicants were fit to run a gaming club *(R v Gaming Board*, ibid (no unfairness on the facts)); the condemnation of food as unfit by a JP *(R v Birmingham City Justice, ex p Chris Foreign Foods (Wholesalers) Ltd* [1970] 1 WLR 1428); the investigation by inspectors into a company's affairs *(Re Pergamon Press Ltd* [1971] Ch 388); the decision of a medical practitioner which may lead to the compulsory retirement of a police officer *(R v Kent Police Authority, ex p Godden* [1971] 2 QB 662).

15.24   In some cases, it has been suggested that natural justice and fairness are distinct concepts, the former applying to judicial and quasi-judicial decision-making, the latter administrative.[78] This approach would retain a degree of unnecessary artificiality, and carries the implication that the content of the respective rules on either side of the divide is fixed, which is not the case. It has rightly not prevailed. The usual approach has been for the court simply to determine what if any procedural standards to impose as a matter of natural justice or fairness in all the circumstances of the case.

(g) Criteria for the imposition of procedural standards

15.25   Given that the courts had just discarded the proposition that the audi alteram partem rule only applied to decisions that were analytically judicial or quasi-judicial, it is unsurprising that the Privy Council expressed the view that 'outside the well-known classes of cases, no general rule can be laid down as to the application of the general [audi alteram partem] principle in addition to the language of the provision'.[79] The best that could be done was to identify considerations that should be borne in mind: the nature of the property or office held, status enjoyed or services to be performed by the complainant of injustice; the circumstances in which the decision-maker is entitled to intervene; and, when a right to intervene is established, what sanctions can be imposed.[80]

15.26   It was also made clear that protection was not limited to those whose legal rights were at stake; a framework for analysis was provided by Lord Denning MR in *Breen v Amalgamated Engineering Union*:[81]

> It all depends on what is fair in the circumstances. If a man seeks a privilege to which he has no particular claim—such as an appointment to some post or other—then he can be turned away without a word. He need not be heard. No explanation need be given . . . But if he is a man whose property is at stake, or who is being deprived of his livelihood, then reasons should be given why he is being turned down, and he should be given a chance to be heard. I go further. If he is a man who has some right or interest, or some legitimate expectation,[82] of which it would not be fair to deprive him without a hearing, or reasons given, then these should be afforded him, according as the case may demand.

---

[78]   eg, *Wiseman v Borneman* [1971] AC 297; *Pearlberg v Varty* [1972] 1 WLR 534, 547 *per* Lord Pearson.

[79]   *Durayappah v Fernando* [1967] 2 AC 337, 349 *per* Lord Upjohn. The Privy Council held that natural justice should have been observed on the exercise by a minister of a power to dissolve a municipal council on the ground of incompetence.

[80]   ibid.

[81]   [1971] 2 QB 175.

[82]   The concept of the 'legitimate expectation' was introduced by Lord Denning in *Schmidt v Secretary of State for Home Affairs* [1969] 2 Ch 149, 170.

Subsequent cases have developed an understanding of what rights, interests and legitimate expectations are worthy of what measure of procedural protection.[83]

A further typology that has proved of some assistance was provided by Sir Robert Megarry V-C in *McInnes v Onslow-Fane*.[84] The issue was whether procedural standards should be imposed on the refusal by the British Boxing Board of Control (a voluntary self-regulatory organization) to grant a boxing manager's licence to the plaintiff. Licences to act as a trainer and MC had previously been withdrawn. His Lordship, while not suggesting that there was any clear or exhaustive classification, thought that at least three categories could be discerned: (1) forfeiture cases, where a decision takes away some existing rights or position, as where a member of an organization is expelled or a licence is revoked; (2) application cases, at the other extreme, where a decision merely refuses to grant the applicant the right or position sought; (3) expectation cases, an intermediate category, which differ from the application cases only in that the applicant has some legitimate expectation from what has already happened that the application will be granted, as where an existing licence-holder applies for renewal of his or her licence, or a person already elected or appointed to some position seeks confirmation from some confirming authority. In forfeiture cases, the right to notice, a hearing and an unbiased tribunal were 'plainly apt';[85] in application cases the issue was normally one of general suitability rather than of changes to be answered and so natural justice did not have to be observed. Expectation cases might 'at least in some respects be regarded as more akin to the forfeiture cases than the application cases'.[86] The present case was an application case, and while there was a duty to act fairly, this on the facts had no procedural content; there was no need to give reasons or hold a hearing, only to 'reach an honest conclusion without bias, and not in pursuance of any capricious policy'.[87] It was emphasized that refusal of a licence did not necessarily put any slur on the plaintiff's reputation. The approach in *McInnes* has attracted some criticism as being unduly restrictive as regards the imposition of procedural standards to 'application cases'; furthermore, as Sir Robert himself acknowledged, the classification does not purport to be exhaustive and in appropriate circumstances third parties not themselves formally involved in the decision-making process as decision-maker or applicant may have interests worthy of protection.[88] Procedural standards have certainly been imposed in

15.27

---

[83] See below, paras 15.29–15.34 and 15.50–15.54.
[84] [1978] 1 WLR 1520.
[85] ibid 1529.
[86] ibid.
[87] ibid 1533.
[88] de Smith, Woolf and Jowell (n 4 above) 403–404.

other application cases where the impact on livelihood has been stronger than in *McInnes*.[89]

(h) The pattern of case law

15.28   The following propositions can be regarded as established by the case law. The courts are likely to impose procedural standards to the decisions of bodies other than courts of law in the following circumstances:

(1) Where the decision determines a question arising between contending parties, as where objections to a compulsory purchase order are submitted to the minister[90] or a local authority has to determine whether a landlord or a tenant should receive compensation for a 'well maintained' house.[91]

(2) Where a decision affects a person's liberty,[92] reputation[93] or livelihood, including situations where a licence is revoked or not renewed or even, in some circumstances not granted on an initial application.[94]

(3) Where a decision is taken to dismiss the holder from an office or employment terminable only for cause.[95]

---

[89] See para 15.28 below.

[90] See para 15.17 above.

[91] *Hoggard v Worsbrough UDC* [1962] 2 QB 93.

[92] Including the effect on the personal freedom of a prisoner: *R v Secretary of State for the Home Department, ex p Doody* [1994] 1 AC 531 (right to reasons in context of access to parole); *R v Secretary of State for the Home Department, ex p Duggan* [1984] 3 All ER 277 (classification of prisoner); but not the allocation of a prisoner to a Close Supervision Centre with a special regime designed to assist improved behaviour: *R v Secretary of State for the Home Department, ex p Mehmet* (1999) 11 Admin LR 529.

[93] *R v Wandsworth LBC, ex p P* (1988) 87 LGR 370 (decision to remove a foster parent from approved list without a hearing on suspicion of serious abuse of a child quashed); *R v Norfolk CC Social Services Department, ex p M* [1989] QB 619 (entry on council's child abuse register identifying applicant as known or suspected child abuser without prior notice or a hearing quashed). Cf *McInnes v Onslow-Fane* [1978] 1 WLR 1520.

[94] *R v Liverpool Corp, ex p Liverpool Taxi Owners Association* [1972] 2 QB 299, 307, 308 per Lord Denning MR (local authority must act fairly when considering applications for a taxi licence, being ready to hear not only the particular applicant but also any other persons or bodies whose interests are affected including existing licence holders who would be affected by a substantial increase in the number of licences granted; this position was not expressly endorsed by the other members of the court); but cf *R v Gravesham BC, ex p Gravesham Association of Licensed Hackney Carriage Owners*, The Independent, 14 January 1987; *R v Barnsley MBC, ex p Hook* [1976] 1 WLR 1052 (revocation of market trader's licence for alleged misconduct quashed for breach of the rule against bias); *R v Huntingdon DC, ex p Cowan* [1984] 1 WLR 501 (applicant for entertainment licence must be given an opportunity to make representations in respect of objections); *R v Wear Valley DC, ex p Binks* [1985] 2 All ER 699 (imposing requirements of notice of and reasons for proposed termination of contractual licence in respect of caravan selling take-away food, and opportunity to be heard); cf *McInnes v Onslow-Fane* [1978] 1 WLR 1520.

[95] *Osgood v Nelson* (1872) LR 5 HL 636 (council clerk); *Ridge v Baldwin* [1964] AC 40 (police officer); *Stevenson v United Road Transport Union* [1977] ICR 893 (union official); *R v BBC, ex p Lavelle* [1983] 1 WLR 23 (BBC employee); *R v Chief Constable of the North Wales Police, ex p Evans* [1982] 1 WLR 1155 (police officer).

(4) Where a decision affects property rights,[96] or financial interests.[97]
(5) Where a body with a discretion to regulate its own procedure adopts a procedure or takes a step which is so manifestly unfair that no reasonable body could have adopted it.[98]

The list is not exhaustive.

(i) Legitimate expectation[99]

Much attention has been paid in the case law of the last 30 years to the concept of the legitimate expectation. It has been recognized that such expectations may arise through a number of distinct routes.[100] The main variables are **15.29**

(1) whether the expectation arises out of some express or implied representation or undertaking made by or on behalf of the decision-making authority or simply arises from the surrounding circumstances;
(2) whether an expectation relates to a substantive interest or benefit on the part of the person claiming it, or that a particular procedure will be followed in the future;
(3) in the case of an expectation relating to a substantive interest or benefit, whether it is that an existing interest or benefit will be continued, or that a new interest or benefit will be accorded.

The claimant is in the strongest position where a public authority makes a clear and unambiguous undertaking or representation on which it is reasonable for him or her to rely; the authority will be bound by that undertaking or representation unless that is inconsistent with the proper performance of its statutory functions.[101] Examples include an undertaking that a limit on the numbers of taxi licences in an area would not be raised until legislation controlling private hire **15.30**

---

[96] *Cooper v Wandsworth Board of Works* (1863) 14 CB (ns) 180; *R v Secretary of State for the Environment, ex p Slot*, The Times, 11 December 1997 (right of property owner seeking order diverting a bridleway on her land entitled to be heard in response to an objector).

[97] *R (on the application of Lichfield Securities Ltd) v Lichfield DC* [2001] EWCA Civ 304, [2001] PLCR 519 (failure of council to consult developer A on contents of planning obligation being negotiated with developer B, where the outcome had a direct financial impact on A, held procedurally unfair).

[98] *R v Monopolies and Mergers Commission, ex p Matthew Brown plc* [1987] 1 WLR 1235; applied in *R v Hertfordshire CC, ex p B* (1986) 85 LGR 218.

[99] See P Elias, 'Legitimate expectation and Judicial Review' in J Jowell and D Oliver (eds), *New Directions in Judicial Review* (London: Stevens, 1988) 37–50; CF Forsyth, 'The Provenance and protection of legitimate expectations' [1988] CLJ 238; PP Craig, 'Legitimate expectations: a conceptual analysis' (1992) 108 LQR 79 and 'Substantive legitimate expectations in domestic and Community law' [1996] CLJ 289).

[100] See Simon Brown LJ in *R v Devon CC, ex p Baker; R v Durham CC, ex p Curtis* [1995] 1 All ER 73, 88–89, setting out four categories of legitimate expectation.

[101] ibid, category (1), citing, inter alia, *R v Secretary of State for the Home Department, ex p Khan (Asif Mahmood)* [1984] 1 WLR 1337; *R v Secretary of State for the Home Department, ex p Ruddock* [1987] 1 WLR 1482.

vehicles had been enacted and implemented,[102] and the publication of detailed criteria for permitting a child to enter the United Kingdom for the purposes of adoption.[103] It was held that the authority in question could not resile from that undertaking or apply different criteria without affording interested persons a hearing.[104] A legitimate expectation may also arise from a course of conduct on the part of the authority as distinct from an express representation.[105] Many cases claimed to be of this kind do, however, fall at the first hurdle, the court holding that there has been no unequivocal representation or course of conduct.[106]

15.31 A second category of case is where the applicant has an expectation of retaining (or attaining) a particular benefit. It seems that a necessary feature is that the decision must affect someone:

> by depriving him of some benefit or advantage which . . . he has in the past been permitted by the decision-maker to enjoy and which he can legitimately expect to be permitted to continue to do until there has been communicated to him some rational grounds for withdrawing it on which he has been given an opportunity to comment . . .[107]

Examples of interferences with such expectations attracting procedural protection include revocation of an existing permission for an alien to stay in the United

---

[102] *R v Liverpool Corp, ex p Liverpool Taxi Owners Association* [1972] 2 QB 299.

[103] *R v Secretary of State for the Home Department, ex p Khan (Asif Mahmood)* [1984] 1 WLR 1337.

[104] The extent to which such undertakings may in addition have substantive effects is considered elsewhere: paras 16.34–16.89 below.

[105] *R v Inland Revenue Commissioners, ex p Unilever plc* [1996] STC 681 (tax computations had been accepted for over 20 years without an express claim for a particular relief; held to be unfair and irrational to reject a claim on the basis that there had been no express claim without clear and general advance notice).

[106] See, eg, *R v Inland Revenue Commissioners, ex p MFK Underwriting Agents Ltd* [1980] 1 WLR 1545, 1569–1570; *R v Jockey Club, ex p RAM Racecourses Ltd* [1993] 2 All ER 225; *R v South Norfolk CC, ex p Pelham Homes Ltd* [2001] PLCR 125; *R v Birmingham City Council, ex p L* [2000] Ed CR 484; *Falmouth and Truro Port Health Authority v South West Water Ltd* (2000) 2 LGLR 1061.

[107] *per* Simon Brown LJ in *R v Devon CC, ex p Baker; R v Durham CC, ex p Curtis* [1995] 1 All ER 73, 88–89, 90–91, citing Lord Diplock in *Council of Civil Service Unions v Minister for the Civil Service* [1985] AC 374, 408 (category (2) in his Lordship's analysis). This is distinguished from cases where all that can be said is that all the circumstances call for fairness; here, the 'legitimate expectation' concept adds nothing and should be avoided (Simon Brown LJ's category (3)). Accordingly, in *R (on the application of Lichfield Securities Ltd) v Lichfield DC* [2001] EWCA Civ 304, [2001] PLCR 519, 529, the court, which found procedural unfairness, also held that the legitimate expectation concept added nothing; there had been 'no particular practice, and no special promise made to [the applicants], which added significantly to what fairness in any event required'. (There was also no question of the withdrawal of an existing benefit.) Cf *R v Secretary of State for Wales, ex p Emery* [1998] 4 All ER 367. Similarly, if a first-time applicant for a licence is held entitled to an opportunity to make representations this is likely to be because of the impact on future livelihood rather than on the basis of having a legitimate expectation (cf para 15.28). De Smith, Woolf and Jowell (n 4 above) 422–444 argue that a legitimate expectation 'must be induced by the conduct of the decision-maker' but acknowledge that the distinction between legitimate expectation and protectable interest may not be clear.

Kingdom,[108] the revocation or non-renewal of an existing licence needed for the pursuit of a person's livelihood,[109] forfeiture of the one-third remission of sentence granted 'not as a matter of right but of indulgence' by the Prison Rules,[110] and a failure to allow sufficient time for consultation with the residents of a residential home proposed for closure.[111]

A third category of case is where, notwithstanding that the situation is not one **15.32** that would otherwise attract procedural standards, there is an express promise that such standards will be observed in a particular of an established practice to that effect.[112] Here, the leading authority is *A-G of Hong Kong v Ng Yuen Shiu.*[113] Notwithstanding that there was no statutory provision for a hearing or inquiry before an order removing a person who had entered Hong Kong illegally was made or implemented, the relevant government office announced publicly through the media that illegal immigrants from Macau would be 'interviewed in due course' and that each case would be considered on its merits. The Privy Council quashed an order removing the applicant (an illegal immigrant from Macau) made without affording him opportunity to put all the circumstances of his case before the relevant official. It assumed that the lower courts were right to hold that applicants had no general right to a fair hearing. Nevertheless, the government announcement provided a 'reasonable basis' for a legitimate expectation on the part of Ng; the primary justification for intervention was that:

> when a public authority has promised to follow a certain procedure, it is in the interest of good administration that it should act fairly and should implement its promise, so long as implementation does not interfere with its statutory duty.[114]

It will of course be unusual for procedural as distinct from substantive limitations to be inconsistent with the proper performance of a statutory duty. Indeed, it was

---

[108] *per* Lord Denning, MR, obiter, in *Schmidt v Secretary of State for Home Affairs* [1969] 2 Ch 149, 171 (the court held that natural justice did not have to be observed before the Home Secretary decided to refuse an extension to a permit; no right or legitimate expectation was at stake).

[109] cf the 'expectation' cases discussed in *McInnes v Onslow-Fane* [1978] 1 WLR 1520.

[110] *O'Reilly v Mackman* [1983] 2 AC 237, 275 *per* Lord Diplock.

[111] *R v Devon CC, ex p Baker; R v Durham CC, ex p Curtis* [1995] 1 All ER 73 (procedural unfairness was found in *ex p Curtis* but not in *ex p Baker* itself).

[112] Simon Brown LJ's category (4) in *ex p Baker*, ibid.

[113] [1983] 2 AC 629. Other examples include *R v Liverpool Corp, ex p Liverpool Taxi Owners Association* [1972] 2 QB 299 (one basis for imposing procedural standards was an express promise of consultation, although the term 'legitimate expectation' was not used) and *Council of Civil Service Unions v Minister for the Civil Service* [1985] AC 374 (well-established practice of prior consultation with staff at GCHQ on significant changes in their conditions of service held to give rise to a legitimate expectation, albeit outweighed by considerations of national security); *R v Brent LBC, ex p Gunning* (1985) 84 LGR 168 (habitual practice of local authority to consult parents of pupils concerning proposals to amalgamate or close schools gave rise to legitimate expectation); *R v Birmingham City Council, ex p Dredger* (1993) 91 LGR 532 (practice of consulting market traders as to levels of charges gave rise to legitimate expectation; period allowed for consultation inadequate).

[114] [1983] 2 AC 629, 636, 638 *per* Lord Fraser of Tullybelton.

pointed out in *Ng Yuen Shiu* that 'when the promise was made, the authority must have considered that it would be assisted in discharging its duty fairly by any representations from interested parties and as a general rule that is correct'.[115]

15.33   In the case of the first and third of these categories, it is not essential that the applicant is aware of the representations or practice or has taken any particular step (detrimental or otherwise) in reliance on it,[116] although it is 'very much the exception, rather than the rule, that detrimental reliance will not be present when the court finds unfairness in the defeating of a legitimate expectation'.[117] This latter proposition appeared in cases concerning substantive legitimate expectations. It is submitted that the court should be less easily deterred by the absence of detrimental reliance from providing procedural protection to legitimate expectations.[118]

15.34   There is some authority for the proposition that the unmeritorious conduct of the complainant may deprive him or her of a legitimate expectation.[119] This has been criticized on the ground that as the legitimate expectation doctrine is founded on the principle of legal certainty, only a further representation by the decision-maker can cancel such an expectation.[120] However, an expectation may properly be held not to be legitimate where it arises out of an activity that is itself unlawful, even though there is a practice of non-enforcement.[121]

(2)   The Content of the Right to Procedural Fairness

(a)   Content depends on circumstances

15.35   The essence of procedural fairness is that a person who will be affected by a decision or act should be given prior notice of what is proposed and an effective opportunity to make representations before the decision is made or implemented. However, it is also clear that exactly what procedural fairness requires in a particular case will very much depend on the circumstances. In *R v Secretary of State for the Home Department, ex p Doody*[122] Lord Mustill said:[123]

---

[115] *A-G of Hong Kong v Ng Yuen Shin* (n 114 above) 638 *per* Lord Fraser.

[116] de Smith, Woolf and Jowell (n 4 above) 426–428.

[117] *R v Secretary of State for Education and Employment, ex p Begbie* [2000] 1 WLR 1115, 1123 *per* Peter Gibson LJ; *R (on the application of Bibi) v Newham LBC* [2002] 1 WLR 237.

[118] See, eg, *R (on the application of Gill) v Lord Chancellor's Department* [2003] EWHC 156 (decision to remove G as a JP quashed on the ground of non-compliance with a guidance document issued by the Lord Chancellor of which G was not aware).

[119] *Cinnamond v British Airports Authority* [1980] 1 WLR 582, 590–591 *per* Lord Denning MR.

[120] de Smith, Woolf and Jowell (n 4 above) 429–430.

[121] *R (on the application of Dinev) v Westminster City Council* (QBD, 24 October 2000) (street traders (portrait artists) had no legitimate expectation to be consulted about the introduction of a temporary licensing scheme notwithstanding the effect on their livelihood).

[122] [1994] 1 AC 531.

[123] ibid 560.

What does fairness require in the present case? My Lords, I think it unnecessary to refer by name or to quote from, any of the often-cited authorities in which the courts have explained what is essentially an intuitive judgment. They are far too well known. From them, I derive that (1) where an Act of Parliament confers an administrative power there is a presumption that it will be exercised in a manner which is fair in all the circumstances. (2) The standards of fairness are not immutable. They may change with the passage of time, both in the general and in their application to decisions of a particular type. (3) The principles of fairness are not to be applied by rote identically in every situation. What fairness demands is dependent on the context of the decision, and this is to be taken into account in all its aspects. (4) An essential feature of the context is the statute which creates the discretion, as regards both its language and the shape of the legal and administrative system within which the decision is taken. (5) Fairness will very often require that a person who may be adversely affected by the decision will have an opportunity to make representations on his own behalf either before the decision is taken with a view to producing a favourable result; or after it is taken, with a view to procuring its modification; or both. (6) Since the person affected usually cannot make worthwhile representations, without knowing what factors may weigh against his interests fairness will very often require that he is informed of the gist of the case which he has to answer. Furthermore, to label [a] ... function either 'judicial' or 'administrative' for the purpose of determining the appropriate procedural regime is to adopt too inflexible an approach.[124]

Nevertheless, it remains the case that the closer a decision approximates to the model **15.36** of a decision that determines questions affecting rights between contending parties, the more is likely to be required by way of procedural standards; conversely, the closer it is to a decision in the exercise of a broad discretion concerning the allocation of scarce resources, the less is likely to be required.[125] For example, the Army Board in determining a complaint of racial discrimination brought by a soldier was, as the forum of last resort, dealing with an individual's fundamental rights and so was to be required by its procedures to achieve a high standard of fairness. It was not sufficient that the Board should act bona fide, not capriciously or in a biased manner and should afford the complainant a chance to respond to the basic points made against him. There had to be a proper hearing (not necessarily oral) by the Board as a single adjudicating body[126] and all the material (other than documents for which public interest immunity would properly be claimed) seen by the Board should be disclosed to the complainant, not merely the gist of material adverse to his case.

---

[124] *per* Taylor LJ in *R v Army Board of the Defence Council, ex p Anderson* [1992] 1 QB 169, 185–186.

[125] cf Lord Lane CJ in *R v Commission for Racial Equality, ex p Cottrell and Rothon* [1980] 1 WLR 1580, 1587: 'there are degrees of judicial hearing, and those degrees run from the borders of pure administration to the borders of a full hearing of a criminal cause or matter in the Crown Court. It does not profit one to try to pigeon-hole the particular set of circumstances into the administrative pigeon-hole or into the judicial pigeon-hole. Each case will inevitably differ, and one must ask oneself what is the basic nature of the proceeding which was going on here.'

[126] The two members of the Board who determined the case had considered it separately.

15.37   In many cases, once it has been established that there is a duty to act with procedural fairness, breach of that duty is obvious in that there have simply been no prior notice and no opportunity to make representations at all.[127] In others, some steps have been taken towards the provision of notice and an opportunity to make representations, but it is claimed that more should have been done. It may, for example, be the case that a person is given prior notice of a decision that affects his or her interests, and of the grounds on which it is proposed to proceed, but then no proper opportunity is given to respond. It may be that an opportunity to make representations is given, but not of the details of the points that require a response; this is not an *effective* opportunity to make representations. Or it may be that an oral hearing is held, but it is claimed that there should have been a greater level of formality, with a procedure closer to that of a court of law. The following paragraphs deal with some commonly recurring issues. One final point of importance is that in a number of cases reference is made to the discretion of the decision-maker as to procedural steps to be taken. It should be emphasized that a reviewing court will intervene to ensure the appropriate level of fairness and is not confined to reviewing the exercise of discretion on *Wednesbury* grounds.[128] A procedural decision that is *Wednesbury* unreasonable will normally also constitute procedural unfairness.

(b) Supplementation of a statutory code

15.38   Where a decision-making process is regulated by a legislative code:

> the court will not only require the procedure prescribed by the statute to be followed, but will readily imply so much and no more to be introduced by way of additional procedural safeguards as will ensure the attainment of fairness.[129]

The court is accordingly not limited to supplementing such a code solely where its application produces manifest unfairness;[130] an argument that the code is exclusive will only succeed if it expressly or by necessary implication so provides.[131]

(c) Prior notice

15.39   In many contexts, including the proceedings of courts and tribunals and statutory licensing and planning procedures, notice requirements are set out in the governing

---

[127]   eg *Cooper v Wandsworth Board of Works* (1863) 14 CB (ns) 180; *Ridge v Baldwin* [1964] AC 40.
[128]   *R v Cheshire CC, ex p C*, The Times, 8 August 1996.
[129]   *per* Lord Bridge in *Lloyd v McMahon* [1987] AC 625, 702–703; cf Byles J in *Cooper v Wandsworth Board of Works* (1863) 14 CB (ns) 180, para 15.15 above.
[130]   The view of the majority of the Privy Council (Lords Morris of Borth-y-Gest, Simon of Glaisdale and Kilbrandon) in *Furnell v Whangarei High School Board* [1973] AC 660. See JM Evans, 'Some limits to the scope of natural justice' (1973) 36 MLR 439.
[131]   The view of the minority (Viscount Dilhorne and Lord Reid in *Furnell*, ibid).

primary or secondary legislation.[132] The requirements may be spelt out in some detail and the obligation may be one to take reasonable steps to serve notice. Issues may accordingly arise as to the consequence of non-compliance with a statutory requirement[133] and the extent to which a statutory code should be supplemented by the common law.[134]

(d) Oral or written representations

One of the significant features of English judicial procedure has been the empha-   **15.40**
sis on orality, both in the preference for witnesses to give oral testimony as to what they personally observed and for advocates to be able to make oral submissions concerning law and fact. The principle of orality has been subject to significant modifications, with, for example, much wider admissibility of cogent hearsay evidence, the submission of skeleton arguments by advocates and the pre-reading of documentation by judges. The process of change is continuing. Provisions may also be made enabling affected individuals to opt for a written representation procedure.[135] Nevertheless, there remains an assumption that the optimum model of a fair hearing involves the ability of the person affected to have his or her 'day in court' in the presence of both decision-maker(s) and accusers. Outside the context of the courts and tribunals, the courts have not held that procedural fairness necessarily requires an oral hearing.

For example, in *Lloyd v McMahon*[136] an auditor of a local authority's accounts,   **15.41**
under the statutory regime then applicable to local government, certified that a loss had been incurred through the wilful misconduct of members of the authority in delaying to set a rate. The certificate gave rise to an obligation to repay and disqualification from office. The auditor offered the councillors an opportunity to make written representations, which they did. The House refused to hold that this per se constituted a breach of natural justice. It should be noted, however, that an oral hearing was not requested and there was no reason to suppose that such a request would not have been granted. Lord Keith indicated[137] that there could be cases where 'an oral hearing would clearly be essential in the interests of fairness.' For example, if an objector to the accounts stated that he had personal knowledge of facts indicative of wilful misconduct by a councillor, 'justice would

---

[132] eg, Civil Procedure Rules; procedural regulations for tribunals; the town and country planning legislation (see Bailey et al, *Cross on Local Government Law* (London: Sweet & Maxwell), paras 22–32 (publicity for planning applications), 22–42 (planning appeals), 22-45–22-53 (enforcement).

[133] See paras 15.94 et seq. The statutory code may expressly require substantial prejudice to be shown if the ultimate decision is to be set aside.

[134] See para 15.38 above.

[135] This is possible, for example, in the case of Appeals Service tribunals and planning appeals.

[136] *Lloyd v McMahon* [1987] AC 625.

[137] ibid 696.

demand that the councillor be given an opportunity to depose to his own version of the facts'.[138] However, on these facts, an oral hearing would have been unlikely to have added anything to the written responses to the documentary evidence that had been submitted; in particular reiteration at an oral hearing of the sincerity of the councillors' motives would not in any event have constituted a defence.

15.42 Accordingly, in considering whether written representations will be sufficient it will be relevant to consider the extent that an oral hearing would have enabled relevant points to be made more effectively than a written procedure. An opportunity to make written representations has been held sufficient in cases involving the determination by the Army Board of a complaint of racial discrimination,[139] a case conference concerning the applicants' children,[140] a meeting of an adoption panel considering the placement of a child for adoption,[141] and representations from prisoners concerning the tariff period of a life sentence[142] or their security classification.[143] A rule never to hold an oral hearing may be held to be an unlawful fetter on discretion, relevant considerations including the subject matter and circumstances of the case and 'whether there are substantial issues of fact which cannot be satisfactorily resolved on the available written evidence'.[144]

(e) Adequate disclosure

15.43 Procedural fairness normally requires adequate disclosure to the person affected of the points adverse to his or her interests so that he or she has the opportunity to comment on them.[145] This may, depending on the circumstances, be in advance of a hearing or at the hearing, although in the latter case the decision-maker may need to exercise a discretion to adjourn the proceedings to enable the person to

---

[138] cf Lord Bridge, ibid 706: 'If any councillor had wanted to put forward his own independent and individual grounds in rebuttal of the charge of wilful misconduct against himself, I have no doubt he would have done so. If any had asked to be heard orally and the auditor had refused, there would have been clear ground for a complaint of unfairness.'

[139] *R v Army Board of the Defence Council, ex p Anderson* [1992] 1 QB 169.

[140] *R v Harrow LBC, ex p D* [1990] Fam 133.

[141] *R v North Yorkshire CC, ex p M (No 2)* [1989] 2 FLR 79 (guardian ad litem had to be consulted, but not necessarily invited to the meeting).

[142] *R v Secretary of State for the Home Department, ex p Doody* [1994] 1 AC 531.

[143] *R v Secretary of State for the Home Department, ex p Duggan* [1994] 3 All ER 277.

[144] *R v Army Board of the Defence Council, ex p Anderson* [1992] 1 QB 169, 185 *per* Taylor LJ.

[145] See, eg, *R v Secretary of State for the Home Department, ex p Hickey (No 2)* [1995] 1 WLR 734 (Home Secretary under duty to disclose fresh evidence generated by inquiries following petition by convicted prisoners for reference of their cases to the Court of Appeal; disclosure should take place prior to the decision being made and might be needed of the full reports rather than summaries, depending on the circumstances); *R v Secretary of State for the Home Department, ex p Fayed (No 1)* [1998] 1 WLR 763 (duty to give applicant for citizenship sufficient information as to the subject matter of any concern to enable him to make such representations as he could).

have adequate time to prepare.[146] The receipt of evidence or argument by a decision-maker from one party behind the back of another is likely to constitute unfairness.[147] For example, it will not normally be fair for a decision-maker in a disciplinary case to act on the evidence of an informant, while refusing to disclose that evidence to the accused in order to protect the informer's identity.[148] Where fairness would require disclosure, but the material would be covered by public interest immunity, disclosure can be refused on that ground, enabling the person affected to challenge the justification for the refusal before the courts.[149] In cases concerning less sensitive material it may be sufficient for the 'gist' to be disclosed.[150]

Where, however, there has been a full opportunity to make representations at an earlier stage of a decision-making process, and provided no new point is raised, fairness may not require the minister who makes the ultimate decision to disclose material produced from 'in-house' consultation[151] or to indicate in advance that he is minded not to accept a recommendation arising from that earlier stage in the process.[152]   **15.44**

(f) Conduct of an oral hearing

Where an oral hearing is held, procedural fairness requires that the person affected   **15.45**
has an effective opportunity to make representations. In respect of cases before an industrial injuries commissioner these were said to include the duties:

> (a) to consider such 'evidence' relevant to the question to be decided as any person entitled to be represented wishes to put before him; (b) to inform every person represented of any 'evidence' which the deputy commissioner proposes to take into consideration . . .; (c) to allow each person represented to comment upon any such 'evidence' and, where the 'evidence' is given orally by witnesses, to put questions to those witnesses; and (d) to allow each person represented to address argument to him on the whole of the case.[153]

---

[146] See *R v Kingston upon Thames JJ, ex p Martin* [1994] Imm AR 172; *R v Cheshire CC, ex p C* [1998] Ed LR 66. Where the prosecution is refused an adjournment, leading to dismissal of a case, the decision may be challenged if it caused 'substantial and substantive unfairness to the prosecution' and it was unreasonable for that result to be produced: *per* Richards J in *R (on the application of DPP) v Abergavenny JJ* [2002] EWHC 206; this is not a matter of 'a breach of natural justice in the sense in which that expression is normally used': ibid at [25].

[147] eg, *Errington v Minister of Health* [1935] 1 KB 249 (correspondence between council and minister after close of public inquiry; 'ex parte perambulation' on site by inspector and council representatives).

[148] *R v Governing Body of Dunraven School, ex p B* [2000] Ed LR 156: the choice will normally be either to proceed without that evidence or reveal the informer's identity.

[149] *R v Secretary of State for the Home Department, ex p Fayed (No 1)* [1998] 1 WLR 763, 776–777 *per* Lord Woolf MR.

[150] *R v Gaming Board of Great Britain, ex p Benaim and Khaida* [1970] 2 QB 417; cf *R v Secretary of State for the Home Department, ex p Hickey (No 2)* [1995] 1 WLR 734.

[151] *R v Secretary of State for Education and Science, ex p S* [1995] 2 FCR 225.

[152] *R v Secretary of State for the Home Department, ex p Draper* (QBD, 27 January 2000).

[153] *per* Diplock J in *R v Deputy Industrial Injuries Commissioner, ex p Moore* [1965] 1 QB 456, 490.

15.46   The right to be heard includes, in appropriate cases, the right to call evidence. Such a right arises, for example, in disciplinary cases where serious misconduct is alleged where 'a fair chance of exculpation cannot in many cases be given without hearing the accused's witnesses; eg in the case of an alibi defence'.[154] The decision-maker retains a discretion to refuse to allow witnesses to be called, but this must be exercised reasonably and on proper grounds; good grounds might include cases where there was an attempt to render the hearing virtually impracticable or where it was unnecessary to call so many witnesses on a particular point, whereas bad grounds might include the decision-maker's belief that there was ample evidence against the accused or mere administrative difficulties.[155]

(g) Cross-examination

15.47   In judicial proceedings, and generally where oral hearings are held, procedural fairness normally requires that parties be permitted to cross-examine the witnesses called by other parties.[156] The decision-maker again retains a discretion to refuse cross-examination, the use of which is more easily justified the further the matter moves from a judicial proceeding.[157] Clearly that discretion can be used where the cross-examination would not be directed to a relevant issue.[158]

(h) The rules of evidence

15.48   Procedural fairness does not require observation outside courts of law of the strict rules of evidence.[159] For example, the question as to the extent to which hearsay evidence can be relied upon turns not on technicalities of admissibility but on whether fairness in the circumstances of the case requires oral evidence to be called.[160] Nevertheless, the principles underlying aspects of the law of evidence may well be of significance when evaluating particular kinds of evidence. Accordingly, where identification is in issue, the decision-maker must be aware of

---

[154] *R v Board of Visitors of Hull Prison, ex p St Germain (No 2)* [1979] 1 WLR 1401, 1407 *per* Geoffrey Lane LJ. Or identification evidence, see para 15.48 below.

[155] ibid 1406.

[156] *per* Lord Edmund-Davies in *Bushell v Secretary of State for the Environment* [1981] AC 75, 116.

[157] cf *R v Board of Visitors of Hull Prison, ex p St Germain (No 2)* [1979] 1 WLR 1401 (refusal to permit cross-examination of prison officers whose evidence formed the basis of conviction for prison disciplinary offences held unfair) and *R v Commission for Racial Equality, ex p Cottrell and Rothon* [1980] 1 WLR 1580, 1586–1587 (no requirement to allow cross-examination of witnesses in context of CRE's formal investigation procedure).

[158] *Bushell v Secretary of State for the Environment* [1981] AC 75 (no requirement to permit cross-examination of officials concerning forecasts that had been adopted as a matter of government policy).

[159] *R v Deputy Industrial Injuries Commissioner, ex p Moore* [1965] 1 QB 456, 488 *per* Diplock J.

[160] *R v Cardinal Newman's School, Birmingham ex p S* [1998] COD 283 (usually necessary to have oral evidence from identifying witness where identification is an issue); *R (on the application of K) v Governors of the Weald School* [2001] Ed LR 311 (decision of Governors to uphold pupil's exclusion for sexual assaults, based to a significant extent on hearsay evidence of victim's psychiatrist and a police officer, held unfair).

the dangers of identification evidence and the need for safeguards; there should normally be an account of the initial description given by the witness of the culprit before the identification took place, an account of the process of identification and the steps taken to avoid any identification being tainted by suggestion.[161]

(i) Legal representation[162]

While there is a right to representation by a lawyer in proceedings before a criminal court,[163] no such absolute right is recognized in other proceedings,[164] such as disciplinary proceedings before a prison board of visitors[165] or a domestic tribunal.[166] A right to legal representation may be expressly conferred or excluded by a legislative provision[167] or the rules of a domestic tribunal.[168] Beyond that, where an oral hearing is held the decision-maker is likely to be held to have a discretion to permit legal representation, and in some circumstances fairness may require legal representation to be permitted.[169] Relevant factors in prison disciplinary cases are: the seriousness of the charge and of the potential penalty; whether any points of law are likely to arise; the personal capacity of the prisoner to present his or her own case; procedural difficulties (such as whether the prisoner had been able to interview relevant witnesses prior to the hearing); the need for reasonable speed in making an adjudication; and the need for fairness between prisoners and

15.49

---

[161] ibid.

[162] See J Alder, 'Representation before tribunals' [1972] PL 278; S Livingstone, 'Prisoners and boards of visitors' hearings; a right to legal representation after all?' (1987) 38 NILQ 144; MJ Dixon, 'Public law and prison inmates—two part disharmony' (1984) 40 NILQ 71. Arguments for recognition of a right to legal representation before Commissions of Inquiry is made by H Grant, 'Commissions of inquiry—is there a right to be legally represented?' [2001] PL 377.

[163] At common law (*per* Lord Goff in *R v Board of Visitors of HM Prison, The Maze, ex p Hone* [1988] 1 AC 379, 391); by statute (Magistrates' Courts Act 1980, s 122); by Art 6(3)(c) ECHR: see R Clayton and H Tomlinson, *The Law of Human Rights* (Oxford: OUP, 2000) vol 1, paras 11.213 and 11.350–11.351.

[164] The decision of the Court of Appeal in *R v Assessment Committee of St Mary Abbotts, Kensington* [1891] 1 QB 378 is regarded as authority for the different proposition that a person making a communication to an administrative body (here, the making by a householder of objections to a rating valuation list) is entitled to do so by an agent: see Lord Goff in *ex p Hone*, ibid 391.

[165] *Fraser v Mudge* [1975] 1 WLR 1132.

[166] *Enderby Town Football Club Ltd v Football Association Ltd* [1971] Ch 591.

[167] Regulations that expressly excluded legal representation at disciplinary hearings concerning police officers (other than chief constables and deputy and assistant chief constables) were held not to be unreasonable in *Maynard v Osmond* [1977] QB 240.

[168] In *Enderby Town Football Club Ltd v Football Association Ltd* [1971] Ch 591, 609 Cairns LJ held that it was open to an organization to make an absolute rule that a tribunal set up by it is not to hear legal representatives; Fenton Atkinson LJ held that the FA's rule excluding legal representation was not contrary to natural justice; Lord Denning MR doubted (at 607) that an absolute rule would be legitimate, but agreed that the court should not insist on legal representation on the facts of the case.

[169] *R v Secretary of State for the Home Department, ex p Tarrant* [1985] QB 251; *R v Board of Visitors of HM Prison, The Maze, ex p Hone* [1988] 1 AC 379 (proceedings before prison board of visitors). The disciplinary jurisdiction of boards of visitors has (from 1992) been abolished, and replaced by proceedings before the ordinary criminal courts.

between prisoners and prison officers.[170] In *Ex p Tarrant*, decisions were quashed because there had been no exercise of discretion; furthermore, in the case of very serious charges of mutiny, the discretion could only lawfully be exercised in favour of permitting legal representation. By contrast, in *Ex p Hone*, it was held that there was no right to legal representation where the charge was one of assault on a prison officer. A right to legal representation may arise in a prison disciplinary case by virtue of Article 6(3)(c) ECHR.[171]

(j) Reasons[172]

15.50   As we have seen, procedural fairness requires adequate disclosure to the person affected of the points to be met.[173] A distinct question is how far fairness requires the decision-maker to indicate after the event which are the points that have led to the outcome, by giving reasons.[174] Courts of law are under a general obligation to give reasons for their decisions.[175] No such general obligation, however, applies to administrative decision-making.[176]

15.51   Instead, there is a range of situations in which a duty to give reasons is imposed by legislation.[177] Furthermore, where statute confers a right of appeal against a decision, the decision-maker will be under at least an implied duty to give reasons to enable the right to be exercised effectively.[178] Even more significantly, there is an

---

[170] *per* Webster J in *ex p Tarrant*, ibid 285; endorsed by Lord Goff in *ex p Hone*, ibid 392.

[171] See *Ezeh and Connors v UK* (2002) 35 EHRR 28: see para 12.16 above.

[172] See M Akehurst, 'Statements of reasons for judicial and administrative decisions' (1970) 33 MLR 154; G Richardson, 'The duty to give reasons: potential and practice' [1986] PL 437.

[173] See para 15.43 above.

[174] The distinction is illustrated by the decision in *R v Secretary of State for the Home Department, ex p Fayed (No 1)* [1998] 1 WLR 763, where the Court of Appeal held that there was a duty of disclosure, but (by virtue of s 44(2) of the British Nationality Act 1981) no duty to give reasons. Government policy subsequently changed and reasons were given: see *R v Secretary of State for the Home Department, ex p Fayed (No 2)* [2001] Imm AR 134 (rejecting challenges on substantive grounds to a further decision to refuse citizenship to Mohammed Al-Fayed).

[175] *R v Knightsbridge Crown Court, ex p International Sporting Club* [1982] QB 304; *R v Harrow Crown Court, ex p Dave* [1994] 1 WLR 98. Justices, however, are not required to give reasons for rejecting a submission of no case: *Moran v DPP* [2002] EWHC 89; [2002] ACD 49.

[176] *R v Secretary of State for the Home Department, ex p Doody* [1994] 1 AC 531, 564 *per* Lord Mustill; *R v Kensington and Chelsea RLBC, ex p Grillo* (1995) 28 HLR 94, rejecting dictum of Sir Louis Blom-Cooper QC in *R v Lambeth LBC, ex p Walters* (1993) 26 HLR 170, 178 that there was now such a general duty.

[177] eg, Tribunals and Inquiries Act 1992, s 10 (reasons to be given on request by tribunals specified in Schd 1 and by ministers after a statutory inquiry or where a person concerned could have required such an inquiry to be held); Town and Country Planning (Inquiries Procedure) (England) Rules 2000, SI 2000/1624, r 18(1); Education Act 1996, Sch 16, para 14 (decision of appeal committee hearing appeal against exclusion of pupil and the grounds for it to be communicated to the relevant persons (eg the parents), the local education authority and the governing body). For case law on the scope of such duties and the consequences of non-compliance see para 15.106 below.

[178] *R v Civil Service Appeal Board, ex p Cunningham* [1992] ICR 817 (board under a duty to give outline reasons sufficient to show to what it has directed its mind and to indicate whether its decision is lawful; failure to do so constitutes breach of natural justice).

increasing tendency for such a duty to be imposed as a matter of fairness in the particular circumstances of the case.

In *R v Higher Education Funding Council, ex p Institute of Dental Surgery*[179] Sedley J (for the Divisional Court) held that two such classes of case were: **15.52**

(1) where the subject matter was an interest so highly regarded by the law, for example personal liberty, that fairness required that reasons, at least for particular decisions, be given as of right;
(2) where the decision appeared aberrant.

Fairness did not, however, require reasons to be given for the academic judgement through peer review of the quality of the research of a Higher Education Institution. However, the Secretary of State has been held to be under a duty to give reasons for departing from the tariff period recommended by the judiciary as the period a life sentence prisoner should serve for the purposes of retribution and deterrence;[180] the Court of Aldermen of the City of London was under a duty to give reasons for refusing to approve the election of the applicant as an Alderman;[181] and a court martial was under a duty to give reasons for finding that there was no causal connection between prescribed medication and violent conduct by a soldier and for imposing a sentence of imprisonment on the soldier (who had a long record of blameless service) that led automatically to his dismissal.[182]

Arguments in favour of requiring reasons include that this may concentrate the decision-maker's mind on the right questions, demonstrate to the recipient that this is so, show that the issues have been conscientiously addressed and how the result has been reached, or, alternatively, alert the recipient to a justiciable flaw. Arguments against are that it may place an undue burden on decision-makers, demand an appearance of unanimity where there is diversity, and call for articulation of sometimes inexpressible value judgments.[183] **15.53**

---

[179] [1994] 1 WLR 241, 263.
[180] *R v Secretary of State for the Home Department, ex p Doody* [1994] 1 AC 531; see para 15.35 above.
[181] *R v City of London Corp, ex p Matson* [1997] 1 WLR 765.
[182] *R v Ministry of Defence, ex p Murray* [1998] COD 134 (the court held that the proceedings were 'purely judicial' and had a profound effect on the soldier's career, livelihood, family and reputation; it held that a duty to give reasons arose on the 'unusual facts' and so did not need to reach the question whether reasons should always be given by a court martial). The Courts-Martial (Army) Rules 1997, SI 1997/169 now provide for reasons to be given for the sentence (r 80(2)) but not findings of fact.
[183] *R v Higher Education Funding Council, ex p Institute of Dental Surgery* [1994] 1 WLR 241, 256, 257.

15.54 As with the duty of adequate disclosure[184] a duty to give reasons that would otherwise arise may be excluded where there is a compelling public interest.[185] The strength of the public interest is balanced against the interest of the complainant.[186]

(3) Exceptions to the Requirement of Procedural Fairness

15.55 There are a number of identifiable situations where obligations of procedural fairness that would otherwise arise are excluded by statute expressly or by necessary implication, or otherwise held to be overridden by some compelling consideration, usually of the public interest.

(a) Exclusion by statute

15.56 The common law requirements of procedural fairness can be excluded by statute, expressly or by necessary implication; where that is done, and the outcome is also incompatible with a person's rights under the Human Rights Act 1998 (HRA),[187] a declaration of incompatibility on the latter ground can of course be made.[188] However, the obligation, where appropriate, to comply with natural justice or requirements of procedural fairness is one of the 'constitutional principles which are not easily displaced by a statutory text' by virtue of the principle of legality.[189] Indeed:

> unless there is the clearest provision to the contrary, Parliament must be presumed not to legislate contrary to the rule of law. And the rule of law enforces minimum standards of fairness, both substantive and procedural.[190]

15.57 Examples of express exclusion are relatively unusual.[191] A more common argument is that the expression of some procedural steps is to be taken as impliedly

---

[184] See para 15.43 above.

[185] *R (on the application of Tucker) v Director General of the National Crime Squad* [2003] EWCA Civ 57; [2003] ICR 599 (no need to give detailed reasons for the termination of a police officer's secondment to the NCS even though reasons were normally given in such cases).

[186] ibid. NCS work was highly sensitive work dealing with confidential information; T had been told that there was no longer confidence in his managerial responsibilities and advised of a need to develop his informant handling skills; while there was an effect on T's reputation, he was not disciplined and suffered no financial loss.

[187] After any available modifications to the interpretation of the provision in question have been made under the authority of HRA 1998, s 3.

[188] See paras 7.107 et seq above.

[189] J Bell and G Engle (eds), *Cross on Statutory Interpretation* (3rd edn, London: Butterworths, 1995) 165–166, cited with approval by Lord Steyn in *R v Secretary of State for the Home Department, ex p Pierson* [1998] AC 539, 590. Lord Steyn gave *R v Secretary of State for the Home Department, ex p Doody* [1994] 1 AC 531, a case on procedural fairness, as an example of the operation of the principle of legality.

[190] *per* Lord Steyn in *ex p Pierson*, ibid 591. See, to similar effect, Lord Browne-Wilkinson at 573–575: 'Parliament is presumed not to have intended to change the common law unless it has clearly indicated such intention either expressly or by necessary implication'.

[191] See, eg, *R v Secretary of State for the Home Department, ex p Fayed (No 1)* [1998] 1 WLR 763 (express exclusion of any requirement to give reasons).

excluding others.[192] The courts today are inclined to attach less weight to linguistic arguments of this kind and more to the extent to which the circumstances of the case call for fairness, the dictum of Lord Bridge in *Lloyd v McMahon*[193] commonly being cited. The code, however, will not be supplemented where that would frustrate the statutory purpose.[194]

(b) Confidential information

In a variety of contexts, it has been held that the public interest in maintaining the confidentiality of particular information overrides a duty of disclosure that would otherwise arise on the ground of procedural fairness. In a proportion of cases, disclosure is resisted by virtue of a substantiated claim of public interest immunity.[195] In others, the courts are prepared to balance the relevant interests, and exclude or limit the requirements of procedural fairness even though a formal public interest immunity claim has not or could not be made. These include cases raising issues of national security,[196] sensitive information concerning suspected terrorists,[197] and confidential reports concerning the welfare of children.[198] The balance of argument in a particular case may justify the exclusion of disclosure altogether, or a more limited extent of disclosure than would normally be appropriate.[199]

15.58

---

[192] Expressio unius exclusio alterius. This was, for example, one of a number of arguments that led the House of Lords in *Pearlberg v Varty* [1972] 1 WLR 534 to conclude that the procedure enabling a tax inspector to obtain leave from a general or special commissioner to make tax assessments for past years was intended to be ex parte.

[193] See para 15.38 above.

[194] *per* Lord Reid in *Wiseman v Borneman* [1971] AC 297, 308, followed in *R v Birmingham City Council, ex p Fernero Ltd* [1993] 1 All ER 530, and *R v Hounslow LBC, ex p Dooley and Bourke* (QBD, 29 November 1999) (no duty to consult before service of a stop notice); *Falmouth and Truro Port Health Authority v South West Water Ltd* (2000) 2 LGLR 1061 (no duty to consult before serving an abatement notice to the alleged perpetrator of a statutory nuisance).

[195] See *R v Chief Constable of the West Midlands Police, ex p Wiley* [1995] 1 AC 274; HWR Wade and CF Forsyth, *Administrative Law* (8th edn, Oxford: OUP, 2000) 825–836.

[196] *R v Secretary of State for the Home Department, ex p Hosenball* [1977] 1 WLR 766 (Secretary of State not obliged to disclose details of the case against H, who was subject to an order deporting him on the ground that this would be conducive to the public good as being in the interests of national security; sources of and nature of the information were highly confidential), followed in *R v Secretary of State for the Home Department, ex p Cheblak* [1991] 1 WLR 890; *Council of Civil Service Unions v Minister for the Civil Service* [1985] AC 374 (failure to consult trade unions at GCHQ prior to decision to ban them could be justified on national security grounds; the government had to adduce evidence that the decision not to consult was in fact based on such grounds but once that was shown the decision was not subject to *Wednesbury* review).

[197] *R v Secretary of State for the Home Department, ex p Stitt*, The Times, 3 February 1987; *R v Secretary of State for the Home Department, ex p McQuillan* [1995] 4 All ER 400.

[198] *Official Solicitor v K* [1965] AC 201; *Re B (a minor) (Disclosure of Evidence)* [1993] 1 FLR 191. However, in care proceedings, information held by the local authority needed for a fair trial should be disclosed unless a public interest immunity claim is made: *Re D (infants)* [1970] 1 WLR 599; *Re M (a minor) (Disclosure of Material)* [1990] 2 FLR 36.

[199] cf para 15.43 above.

Generalized arguments that advice to a minister should not be revealed as disclosure might inhibit candour are not likely to convince.[200]

(c) Where prompt action is needed

15.59　Officials may be authorized by statute to take action without prior notice where urgent action is needed to deal, for example, with a threat to health or safety. Provision is conventionally made for an opportunity to make representations after the event, so that, for example, it can be argued that a prohibition or suspension can be lifted. In some circumstances, compensation may be payable where action is shown not to be justified. Even in the absence of statutory authority to act urgently without prior warning, this may be held to be justified on the facts of a particular case.[201] The normal principle is, however, that the opportunity to make representation should be given before the decision is made.[202]

(d) Preliminary decisions

15.60　Any process which may culminate in action adverse to an individual's interests must start somewhere. Except in the most obvious of cases, there are likely to be some steps taken to investigate or consider the matter before a decision is taken to proceed formally. There are many variables. The conduct of an investigation may itself be structured or regulated by legislation or it may be informal. (Statutory or contractual authority will of course be needed for the exercise of coercive powers.) An investigation may or may not lead to a published report. It may be free-standing, as where the publication of the report is the ultimate objective, or it may formally be a preliminary to some other process. The question arises at what stage procedural fairness requires that the individual is notified that something is afoot and given a chance to comment. The greater the formality of the investigation process and the more significant the impact of the outcome of that process for individual interests, the greater the likelihood that some procedural standards will be imposed. There is, for example, no general duty for a prosecutor to consult the defendant before deciding to prosecute for a criminal offence; a similar principle applies in respect of the service of an abatement notice to the alleged perpetrator

---

[200] *R v Secretary of State for Health, ex p US Tobacco International Inc* [1992] QB 353 (unfair not to disclose advice of independent scientific experts that led to ban on oral snuff).

[201] *R v Secretary of State for Transport, ex p Pegasus Holdings (London) Ltd* [1988] 1 WLR 990 (suspension of Romanian airline's flight permit without notice following failure by five pilots of Civil Aviation Authority examinations held justified given the risk to air safety); *R v Birmingham City Council, ex p Ferrero Ltd* [1993] 1 All ER 530 (no duty to consult manufacturer before issuing notice prohibiting supply of chocolate eggs with a small toy, following choking incident; there was express provision for appeals and compensation).

[202] *R (on the application of Hurst) v Secretary of State for the Home Department* [2001] EWCA Civ 378 (prisoner to be given opportunity to make representations before reclassification from C to B; delay not justified by operational considerations).

of a statutory nuisance,[203] the appointment of inspectors to investigate the affairs of a company,[204] and the obtaining of leave to make a tax assessment.[205] In most of these situations a further process that will clearly comply with the requirements of procedural fairness is contemplated, such as a court or tribunal hearing. However, where the report of inspectors investigating the affairs of a company may itself have a significant effect on an individual's livelihood or reputation, more will be necessary:

> [B]efore they condemn or criticise a man, they must give him a fair opportunity for correcting or contradicting what is said against him. They need not quote chapter and verse. An outline of the charge will usually suffice.[206]

Here, damage will be done by publication of the report and the availability of an opportunity to challenge its contents more uncertain.

(e) Where defective decisions are cured by subsequent process

In some circumstances, the fact that an initial decision was procedurally flawed is regarded as 'cured' by the provision of a rehearing or an appeal that does satisfy the requirements of procedural fairness.[207] The leading case is *Calvin v Carr*[208] where the Privy Council held that, while there was no clear and absolute rule, it was possible to identify a number of typical situations. First, there are contractual cases where the rules, for example of a social club, provide for a rehearing by the same body or an enlarged form of it. Here, it is not difficult to conclude that the first hearing is superseded by the second and that the parties have accepted that arrangement.[209] At the other extreme are cases where the complainant has the right to nothing less than a fair hearing both at the original and at the appeal stage, as in trade union cases where a fair hearing at both branch and national levels might be necessary.[210] Then there is an intermediate position where the question is 'whether, at the end of the day, there has been a fair result, reached by fair methods.' There

15.61

---

[203] *Falmouth and Truro Port Health Authority v South West Water Ltd* (2000) 2 LGLR 1061.

[204] *Norwest Holst Ltd v Secretary of State for Trade* [1978] Ch 201.

[205] *Pearlberg v Varty* [1972] 1 WLR 534.

[206] *per* Lord Denning MR in *Re Pergamon Press Ltd* [1971] 1 Ch 388, 400; *Maxwell v Department of Trade and Industry* [1974] QB 523 (inspector not required to allow cross-examination of witnesses); see to similar effect: *R v Race Relations Board, ex p Selvarajan* [1975] 1 WLR 1686 (investigation into complaint of race discrimination); *Wiseman v Borneman* [1971] AC 297 (statutory process governing establishment of prima facie case concerning tax assessment required to be, and was, fair).

[207] cf the position under Art 6(1) ECHR; paras 12.30–12.34 above.

[208] [1980] AC 574. See M Elliott, 'Appeals, principles and pragmatism in natural justice' (1980) 43 MLR 66.

[209] eg, *De Verteuil v Knaggs* [1918] AC 557, 563.

[210] Megarry J in *Leary v National Union of Vehicle Builders* [1971] Ch 34. The Privy Council doubted Megarry J's view that there was a general rule (albeit subject to exceptions) that a failure of natural justice in the trial body cannot be cured by a sufficiency of natural justice in an appellate body.

may nevertheless be instances 'when the defect is so flagrant, the consequences so severe, that the most perfect of appeals or rehearings will not be sufficient to produce a just result'.[211]

15.62   Overall, it was held that the full hearing held by the Australian Jockey Club on an appeal against the decision of stewards that the applicant should be disqualified for breach of the Rules of Racing cured any defects in the proceedings before the stewards. In practice, the intermediate position is the one most commonly found, provided of course that the rehearing or appeal hearing is not itself procedurally unfair, whether by repetition of the same procedural defect as at the original hearing, or otherwise.[212]

(f) Where the decision-maker has not been at fault

15.63   The House of Lords has held firmly that where a procedural defect arises as the result of the fault of a person's own advisers, that person is not entitled to complain of the defect.[213] Furthermore, earlier criminal and disciplinary cases, where decisions had been quashed on the grounds of unfairness caused by the conduct of the prosecutor or a prosecution witness,[214] were to be explained as resting on a different principle based on a breach of the duty owed to the court, analogous to cases of fraud, collusion and perjury which provide a distinct ground for quashing a decision. It is submitted that while the former principle is understandable, the latter should be reconsidered; unfairness caused by the conduct of a public authority party towards an adversarial party would seem a sufficient basis for intervention on the ground of unfairness, without needing artificially to stretch the notion of a duty owed to the court or tribunal or to rely on a doubtful analogy.[215]

(g) Where there has been no prejudice to the complainant

15.64   The courts have demonstrated a measure of ambivalence in deciding what, if any, effect should be given to the consideration that a particular complainant does not appear to have been prejudiced by the procedural defect in question. In some cases, it is said that a decision should be quashed even though prejudice to the

---

[211] [1980] AC 574, 593 *per* Lord Wilberforce.

[212] *R v Oxfordshire Local Valuation Panel, ex p Oxford City Council* (1981) 79 LGR 432; *Lloyd v McMahon* [1987] AC 625, para above (held, obiter, that the appeal to the High Court, which constituted a full rehearing on the merits, would in principle have been sufficient to cure any breach of natural justice by the auditor; Lord Templeman indicated at 891 that the position might have been different if the court had been bound by the auditor's finding of facts); *Modahl v British Athletic Federation (No 2)* [2001] EWCA Civ 1447; [2002] 1 WLR 1192 (intermediate approach applicable in principle) where initial decision is tainted by apparent bias.

[213] *Al-Mehdawi v Secretary of State for the Home Department* [1990] 1 AC 876.

[214] *R v Leyland JJ, ex p Hawthorn* [1979] QB 283 (existence of relevant witnesses not disclosed to the defence); *R v Blundeston Prison Board of Visitors, ex p Fox Taylor* [1982] 1 All ER 646 (non-disclosure by prison authorities of existence of relevant witness in prison disciplinary case).

[215] See J Herberg, 'The right to a hearing: breach without fault?' [1990] PL 467.

complainant cannot be demonstrated.[216] In others, it is held that a decision should not be quashed, precisely because there has been no prejudice to the complainant. In some of these, it is held that there is no breach of natural justice or the requirements of procedural fairness unless there is prejudice;[217] in others a remedy is withheld in the exercise of the court's discretion.[218]

It is clear that if a procedural defect carries no risk of prejudice to the applicant, the court is entitled to decline to intervene. However, the court should be careful before concluding that this is indeed the case. The point was well made by Megarry J in an often-cited dictum:[219]

> As everybody who has anything to do with the law well knows, the path of the law is strewn with examples of open and shut cases which, somehow, were not; of unanswerable charges which, in the event, were completely answered; of inexplicable conduct which was fully explained; of fixed and unalterable determinations that, by discussion, suffered a change.

15.65

If the test is 'no substantial prejudice' rather than 'no risk of prejudice' then Megarry J's words of caution are even more apposite.[220] There is, however, another variable that may well be relevant. This is the magnitude of the alleged procedural defect. The court should be particularly sceptical of claims by a decision-maker, who has failed to provide an individual with any opportunity to make representations, that

15.66

---

[216] Lord Denning in *Annamunthodo v Oilfield Workers Trade Union* [1961] AC 945, 956 ('It is a prejudice to any man to be denied justice . . . [H]e can always ask for the decision to be set aside'); and *Kanda v Government of Malaya* [1962] AC 322, 337 ('The court will not go into the likelihood of prejudice. The risk of it is enough').

[217] *Malloch v Aberdeen Corp* [1971] 1 WLR 1578, 1595 *per* Lord Wilberforce: 'A breach of procedure, whether called a failure of natural justice, or an essential administrative fault, cannot give [the appellant] a remedy in the courts unless there is something of substance which has been lost by the failure. The court does not act in vain'; Lord Denning MR in *George v Secretary of State for the Environment* (1979) 77 LGR 689, 695 (a case concerning a statutory application to quash): 'You should not find a breach of natural justice unless there has been substantial prejudice to the applicant as a result of the mistake or error which has been made'. This proposition, stated by Lord Denning as part of the decision of the Court of Appeal in *George*, has been preferred to his Lordship's dicta in *Kanda v Government of Malaya* [1962] AC 322: Henriques J in *R (on the application of George Harrison (Whitby) Ltd) v Secretary of State for the Environment, Transport and the Regions* (QBD, 24 October 2000) at [83]–[85].

[218] *Glynn v Keele University* [1971] 1 WLR 487 (injunction refused to student suspended by the Vice-Chancellor, for appearing naked on the campus, without prior notice or an opportunity to make representations; the facts were not disputed, the penalty a 'proper' one and the loss of the opportunity to put in a plea in mitigation insufficient to prevent the judge concluding that the plaintiff had suffered no injustice).

[219] *John v Rees* [1970] Ch 345, 402.

[220] Recent cases have tended to maintain a sceptical approach: *R v Chief Constable of Thames Valley Police, ex p Cotton* [1990] IRLR 344; *R v Ealing Magistrates' Court, ex p Fanneran* (1996) 8 Admin LR 351; *R v Broxtowe BC, ex p Bradford* [2000] BLGR 386; cf *R (on the application of Wainwright) v Richmond upon Thames LBC* [2001] EWCA Civ 2062; The Times, 16 January 2002 (council failed to deliver sufficient letters to residents concerning proposed toucan crossing, but decision not quashed as there was no real possibility that the council would have reached a different decision; no one could suggest any new point of substance which might have been made).

representations would have made no difference. The position is different where many elements of procedural fairness were present but it is claimed that a particular further step should have been taken. Here it may well be legitimate for the court to conclude that this step was not a necessary requirement for procedural fairness overall.[221]

(h) Legislative action

15.67 The principles of natural justice or procedural fairness do not apply to legislative functions such as the making of a statutory instrument.[222] Similarly, a local authority need not give an opportunity to be heard before making a decision which is universal in its application such as the fixing by the authority of the rates for the year or the scale upon which fees are to be charged.[223] The boundaries of this principle are, however, a matter of degree. Where, for example, a decision to set fees or charges affects a discrete class, those persons may have a legitimate expectation that they will be afforded an opportunity to make representations.[224] It has been held that the impact of such decisions on livelihood is not itself sufficient to attract procedural obligations as a matter of fairness,[225] but it is not obvious (and was not explained) why that should be so. Where an act that is legislative in form affects only one person or company, it should not be treated as legislative for the purpose of excluding obligations of procedural fairness.[226]

(4) The Rule Against Interest and Bias

15.68 It is a well-established principle that a person exercising a judicial function will be disqualified from acting, unless the matter is waived, if he or she has a direct pecuniary interest in the outcome of the decision, or where, for some other reason, there is a real possibility of bias (nemo judex in causa sua). Many of the decisions giving effect to this principle have concerned courts of law (ranging from justices of the peace to a Lord Chancellor). Issues that have arisen include:

---

[221] See, eg, cases on whether a particular witness should have been made available for cross-examination or a particular piece of information disclosed: paras 15.43 and 15.47 above.
[222] *Bates v Lord Hailsham of St Marylebone* [1972] 1 WLR 1373 (Lord Chancellor under no general duty to consult bodies representing solicitors concerning legislative order (fixing fees for conveyancing; the order would be applied in 'numberless cases in the future'). There is commonly, however, a statutory duty to consult: para below; indeed, in *Bates*, a further reason for excluding a general duty to consult was the existence of an express duty to consult the Law Society.
[223] *R v Greater London Council, ex p The Rank Organisation*, The Times, 19 February 1982.
[224] *R v Birmingham City Council, ex p Dredger* (1993) 91 LGR 532 (para 15.32 above).
[225] *R v Manchester City Council, ex p Donald King* (1991) 89 LGR 696; *Dredger*, ibid.
[226] cf *R v Secretary of State for Helath, ex p US Tobacco International Inc* [1992] 1 QB 353 (regulations banning oral snuff that impinged almost exclusively on the applicants quashed on the ground that the statutory duty to consult representative organizations had been performed inadequately; it is to be noted that in the absence of a statutory duty, the case on these facts imposing procedural standards would have been very strong).

(1) the extent to which the principle applies outside courts of law;
(2) the definition of 'direct pecuniary interest';
(3) whether any interest other than a direct pecuniary interest will disqualify automatically;
(4) the correct formulation and scope of the rule against bias; and
(5) the existence and extent of any exceptions.

Even more markedly than in the case of the right to a fair hearing, the rule against interest and bias emphasizes the importance of appearances. The courts consistently stress that the issue is not whether the decision-maker was in fact improperly influenced by the interest or the matter giving rise to the possibility of bias. A decision that was so influenced would normally be open to challenge as an abuse of power on the ground that regard had been had to a legally irrelevant consideration. Instead, the point is that the appearance that an injustice may have been done is sufficient for a decision to be quashed: if a judge is improperly acting as judge in his or her own cause, 'such a proceeding would, without more, undermine public confidence in the integrity of the administration of justice'.[227]   **15.69**

(a) When does the rule apply?

It is clear that the rule against interest and bias applies to courts of law. Indeed,   **15.70**
the leading case on the rule against interest concerned a decision of the Lord Chancellor to affirm decrees made by the Vice-Chancellor in favour of a canal company in which the Lord Chancellor held shares. The House of Lords set aside the Lord Chancellor's decree.[228] There are many cases concerning the Crown Court, justices of the peace and tribunals. Furthermore, the rule was held to be applicable to other bodies acting judicially, the same test as governed the applicability of the audi alteram partem rule.[229] Examples of situations held to be covered by the rule included the decision of London County Council to refuse renewal of a music and dancing licence,[230] the decision of a local authority to grant permission to build under pre-1947 planning legislation,[231] and the rejection by a Watch Committee of an appeal against dismissal brought by a police sergeant.[232]

---

[227] *Locabail (UK) Ltd v Bayfield Properties Ltd* [2000] QB 451 at [7].
[228] *Dimes v Grand Junction Canal Proprietors* (1852) 3 HL Cas 759, 10 ER 301.
[229] There was no suggestion that the test should be applied differently as between the two rules of natural justice.
[230] *R v London CC, ex p Akkersdyk* [1892] 1 QB 190 (three councillors who voted against renewal of a licence in committee instructed counsel to oppose renewal before the full council, and were present at the Council meeting although they did not vote; the councillors had 'acted both as accusers and judges at the same time').
[231] *R v Hendon RDC, ex p Chorley* [1933] 2 KB 696 (the permission was granted to the potential purchaser of a site and safeguarded a right to compensation in the event of the site being affected by a town planning scheme; one of the councillors who voted for the grant was an estate agent acting for the site owner; decision quashed).
[232] *Cooper v Wilson* [1937] 2 KB 309 (chief constable both dismissed the sergeant and was present during the Watch Committee's deliberations; decision void).

15.71   By the way of contrast, the House of Lords in *Franklin v Minister of Town and Country Planning*[233] held that the decision of the minister to confirm a draft new town order, following a public local inquiry, was administrative only, and did not attract the application of the rule against bias.[234] The draft order designating Stevenage as the site of a new town had itself been made by the minister in accordance with the government's policy for the development of new towns. The minister subsequently addressed a 'lively' public meeting at which he had said, amongst other things, 'at the end, if people are fractious and unreasonable, I shall have to carry out my duty.' As the minister had no 'judicial duty' the only question was whether the minister in fact had genuinely considered the report of the public inquiry and the objections. The House accepted that on the evidence, including the minister's affidavit, he had. The approach to the applicability of natural justice accorded with the case law on the audi alteram partem rule that had previously arisen in the context of statutory inquiries into orders, schemes and the like affecting the use of land.[235] The outcome on the facts seems sensible. On the one hand, the minister had a formal decision-making role under the New Towns Act 1946. On the other, the orders he confirmed took forward matters of significant government policy. It would not have made sense to require him at the confirmation stage to act as a judge in weighing his own policy against the objections. However, it is not so obvious that if it had subsequently emerged that he had had a direct pecuniary interest that it would have been necessary to prove that he had actually been biased.

15.72   In the years following the decision in *Ridge v Baldwin*, an expansive view was taken of the applicability of the audi alteram partem rule.[236] It was not clear whether a similarly broad view was to be taken in respect of the rule against interest and bias. In a number of cases it was held that decisions were of a judicial or quasi-judicial character and so attracted the application of the rule.[237] Conversely, the rule was held not to apply to decisions of an administrative character,[238] it

---

[233] [1948] AC 87.

[234] Henn Collins J (63 TLR 143) had held that the minister had been under a duty to act judicially and had breached that duty; the Court of Appeal (63 TLR 187) that he had been under a duty to act judicially and bias had not been proved.

[235] See para 15.17 above.

[236] See paras 15.20 and 15.21 above.

[237] *Hannam v Bradford Corp* [1970] 1 WLR 937 (power of local education authority to prohibit dismissal of teacher by school governors); *R v Kent Police Authority, ex p Godden* [1971] 2 QB 662 (role of medical practitioner in determining whether a police officer was permanently disabled and so subject to compulsory retirement); *R v Barnsley MBC, ex p Hook* [1976] 1 WLR 1052 (termination of market stallholder's licence for misconduct).

[238] *R v Secretary of State for Trade, ex p Perestrello* [1981] QB 19 (conduct by inspectors of investigation into a company under Companies Act 1967, s 109; inspectors under duty to act fairly in sense of a duty not to exceed or abuse their discretion); *R v Reading BC, ex p Quietlynn Ltd* (1986) 85 LGR 387 (local authority panel determining applications for licences for sex establishments).

being suggested that the relevant test was whether the decision-maker had been so affected by predetermined views as to be unable to exercise a proper discretion.[239] There were conflicting authorities concerning the applicability of the rule to decisions under town and country planning legislation.[240] The Court of Appeal, however, seemed prepared to accept that it was so applicable, while holding that it was not necessarily improper for a builder to sit on a local authority planning committee considering applications for detailed planning permission submitted by a rival builder.[241]

An extended analysis of the authorities by Sedley J in *R v Secretary of State for the Environment, ex p Kirkstall Valley Campaign*[242] led to the conclusion that the nemo judex rule is not now confined to judicial and quasi-judicial decisions. An individual's interests may be more radically affected by administrative decisions than those of courts or tribunals. Modern public law since *Ridge v Baldwin* had 'set its face against the partitioning of proceedings into judicial, administrative and something in between', these distinctions being increasingly hard to make in the variety of adjudicative processes in the modern state. Public law had 're-turned to the broad highway of due process across the full range of justiciable decision-making'.[243]   **15.73**

Whether this step is desirable turns largely on the content of the nemo judex rule in its application to administrative decisions.[244] In any event, it is difficult to see this as anything but an extension of the law rather than its return to a pre-existing state. Sedley J's decision has been followed in a series of subsequent cases in the High Court,[245] but has yet to be considered by the Court of Appeal or House of Lords. It has been suggested that the extension to the categories of interests that disqualify automatically introduced by the House of Lords in the *Pinochet (No 2)* case[246] is confined to judicial decisions.[247]   **15.74**

---

[239] *ex p Quietlynn Ltd*, ibid.

[240] In favour: Webster J in *Steeples v Derbyshire CC* [1985] 1 WLR 256. Against: Glidewell J in *R v Sevenoaks DC, ex p W J Terry* [1985] 3 All ER 226 and Stocker J in *R v St Edmundsbury BC, ex p Investors in Industry Commerical Properties Ltd* [1985] 1 WLR 1168.

[241] *R v Holderness BC, ex p James Robert Developments Ltd* (1992) 66 P & CR 46 (Simon Brown and Butler-Sloss LJJ, Dillon LJ dissenting).

[242] [1996] 3 All ER 304. In *R v Advertising Standards Authority, ex p International Fund for Animal Welfare* (QBD, 11 November 1997), Dyson J rejected an argument that a test less stringent on the decision-maker than the *Gough* test applied in respect of administrative decisions.

[243] ibid 324.

[244] See further, para 15.75 below, on the distinction between personal and institutional interests.

[245] See, eg, *R (on the application of Cummins) v Camden LBC* [2001] EWHC Admin 1116; *Bovis Homes Ltd v New Forest DC* [2002] EWHC 483.

[246] See para 15.77 below.

[247] *per* Ouseley J in *Bovis Homes Ltd v New Forest DC* [2002] EWHC 483 at [87].

(b) Direct pecuniary interests and interests as a party

15.75   Where the nemo judex rule applies, a decision-maker who is also a party or who has a direct pecuniary interest in the outcome of the case is automatically disqualified:

> the maxim that no man is to be a judge in his own cause should be held sacred. And that is not to be confined to a cause to which he is a party, but applies to a cause in which he has an interest.[248]

To disqualify, the interest must not be too remote. The remoteness of the connection may arise as between the decision-maker and the interest or between the interest and the subject-matter of the determination.[249] A direct pecuniary interest will, however, disqualify even if it is small in amount.[250] The question whether a direct pecuniary interest could reasonably be suspected to have influenced the decision-maker is irrelevant. However, where an interest fails to lead to automatic disqualification under this rule, it may still be sufficient to invalidate the decision if it gives rise to a real possibility of bias.[251]

15.76   Disqualification is also automatic where a person is both a party and a judge.[252] The term 'party' covers a person who is a 'prosecutor'. However, where criminal or disciplinary proceedings are brought by an association the question may arise whether the fact that one or more of the decision-makers is a member of that association invalidates the decision. The normal approach is that mere membership of the association does not disqualify, but active involvement in the institution of the particular proceedings does. This is sometimes dealt with as a matter of the definition of the term 'prosecutor,' on the assumption that such a person is automatically disqualified, and sometimes as an application of the rule against bias.[253]

---

[248] *per* Lord Campbell in *Dimes v Grand Junction Canal Proprietors* (1852) 3 HL Cas 759, 793 (here, shares in a company which was a party to the litigation). Some formulations refer to disqualifying direct 'pecuniary or proprietary' interests, although the latter seems to be an example of the former.

[249] *R v Rand* (1866) LR 1 QB 230 (justices' interests as trustees too remote; the position might have been different if they had been liable to pecuniary loss or gain as trustees); *R v Mulvihill* [1990] 1 WLR 438 (no automatic disqualification (and, indeed, no reasonable suspicion of bias) where Crown Court judge presiding over trial for robberies at various banks and building societies held shares in one of the banks).

[250] *Serjeant v Dale* (1877) 2 QBD 558, 566–567. This now seems to be subject to a de minimis exception, 'if the potential effect of any decision on the judge's personal interest is so small as to be incapable of affecting his decision one way or another,' although any doubt should be resolved in favour of disqualification: *Locabail (UK) Ltd v Bayfield Properties Ltd* [2000] QB 451 at [10] (obiter dictum), applied in *Weatherill v Lloyds TSB Bank plc* [2000] CPLR 584 (in respect of the judge's shareholding of 570 out of a total of 5.5 billion shares in issue).

[251] cf *R v Rand* (1866) LR 1 QB 230 and *R v Mulvihill* [1990] 1 WLR 438 (no reasonable suspicion of bias on the facts).

[252] See *Dimes v Grand Junction Canal Proprietors* (1852) 3 HL Cas 759.

[253] Compare *Leeson v General Medical Council* (1889) 43 Ch D 366 with *Allinson v General Medical Council* [1894] 1 QB 750.

(c) Other interests that disqualify automatically

The House of Lords in the remarkable decision in *R v Bow Street Metropolitan*   **15.77**
Stipendiary Magistrate, ex p Pinochet Ugarte (No 2)[254] has identified a further situation where automatic disqualification arises. The House in earlier proceedings[255] had decided by three to two[256] that a warrant for the extradition of P to Chile, where he had formerly been head of state, was valid. Amnesty International (AI) had been given leave to intervene in the proceedings and had supported the validity of the warrant. It subsequently emerged that one of the majority, Lord Hoffmann, was a director and chair of Amnesty International Charity Ltd (AICL). This, together with Amnesty International Ltd, had been incorporated to carry out, respectively, charitable and other work of AI's international headquarters in the United Kingdom. Both were controlled by AI. The House in *Pinochet (No 2)* unanimously set aside its earlier decision. It was not suggested that Lord Hoffmann was actually biased. The House did not reach the question whether there was a real possibility of bias, but held instead that automatic disqualification followed where the judge's decision would lead to the promotion of a cause in which the judge was involved together with one of the parties. This constituted an extension to the law in that Lord Hoffmann's links were to AICL and not AI itself (an unincorporated association). It is submitted that it would have been preferable to apply the real possibility of bias test rather than adding a new category of automatic disqualification that is uncertain in scope. The test was variously formulated as follows:

> there must be a rule that automatically disqualifies a judge who is involved, whether personally or as a director of a company, in promoting the same causes in the same organisation as is a party to the suit.[257]

> AI, AIL and AICL can together be described as being, in practical terms, one organisation, of which AICL forms part . . . Lord Hoffmann, as chairperson of one member of that organisation, AICL, is so closely associated with another member of that organisation, AI, that he can properly be said to have an interest in the outcome of the proceedings to which AI has become party.[258]

---

[254] [2000] 1 AC 119. See D Woodhouse (ed), *The Pinochet Case* (Oxford: Hart, 2000) ch 2 (D Robertson), ch 3 (E Grant), ch 4 (P Catley and L Claydon); Sir David Williams, 'Bias; the judges and the separation of powers' [2000] PL 45; K Malleson, 'Judicial bias and disqualification after Pinochet (No 2)' (2000) 63 MLR 119; AA Olowofoyeku, 'The nemo judex rule: the case against automatic disqualification' [2000] PL 456.

[255] *R v Bow Street Stipendiary Magistrate, ex p Pinochet Ugarte (No 1)* [2000] 1 AC 61.

[256] Lords Nicholls, Steyn and Hoffmann, Lords Slynn and Lloyd dissenting.

[257] [2000] 1 AC 119, 135 *per* Lord Browne-Wilkinson. His Lordship emphasized that the facts were exceptional: 'only in cases where a judge is taking an active role as trustee or director of a charity which is closely allied to and acting with a party to the litigation should a judge normally be concerned either to recuse himself or disclose the position to the parties' although there may be other exceptional cases (at 136).

[258] ibid 139 *per* Lord Goff.

> In view of [Lord Hoffmann's] links with Amnesty International as the chairman and a director of Amnesty International Charity Ltd he could not be seen to be impartial . . . He had no financial or pecuniary interest in the outcome. But his relationship with Amnesty International was such that he was, in effect, acting as a judge in his own cause.[259]

15.78 It has been stated that this principle is confined to judicial bodies.[260] The Court of Appeal has indicated that any further extension of the present rule on automatic disqualification would be undesirable unless that was 'plainly required to give effect to the important underlying principles upon which the rule is based'.[261] Notwithstanding this exhortation, it has been held that a Chief Constable was automatically disqualified from hearing disciplinary proceedings where he was, as head of the force, the respondent to proceedings before an employment tribunal complaining of sex discrimination and victimization, including in relation to the initiation of the disciplinary charges.[262] However, this was reversed by the Court of Appeal[263] on the ground that the Chief Constable had no personal interest in the matters before the employment tribunal; there was neither any automatic disqualification nor a real danger of bias.

(d) The rule against bias

15.79 In the large majority of cases where the nemo judex rule is invoked, there is no question of automatic disqualification arising. In these cases, there is no need for the complainant to establish actual bias. There has, however, over time been a series of different formulations of the test the complainant must satisfy if a decision is to be held invalid. These formulations reflect divergent views as to the proper weight to be attached, respectively, to two competing considerations: first, the desirability that there should be no *appearance* that the decision-maker might have been biased; and secondly, the extent of the actual *risk on the facts* that the decision-maker was biased.

15.80 Prior to the decision of the House of Lords in *R v Gough*[264] there was support in the case law for two different formulations, each with its own small variations. Those who attached particular importance to the need for proper appearances preferred a test that there must be no *reasonable suspicion of bias*.[265] Those who

---

[259] *Pinochet (No 2)* (n 257 above) 143 *per* Lord Hope. Lords Hope and Nolan each agreed with Lords Browne-Wilkinson and Goff. Lord Hutton agreed with Lord Browne-Wilkinson, and also commented that the links between Lord Hoffmann and AI 'were so strong that public confidence in the administration of justice would be shaken if his decision were allowed to stand' (at 146).
[260] See para 15.73 above.
[261] *Locabail (UK) Ltd v Bayfield Properties Ltd* [2000] QB 451 at [14].
[262] *R v Chief Constable of Merseyside, ex p Bennion* [2000] IRLR 821.
[263] [2001] IRLR 442.
[264] [1993] AC 646.
[265] eg, *R v Sussex JJ, ex p McCarthy* [1924] 1 KB 256, 259 *per* Lord Hewart CJ: it is 'of fundamental importance that justice should not only be done, but should manifestly and undoubtedly be seen to be done'; *Metropolitan Properties Co (FGC) Ltd v Lannon* [1969] 1 QB 577.

were less concerned with appearances and more concerned with the level of the risk of actual unfairness preferred a test that there must be no *real likelihood of bias*.[266] *R v Gough*[267] broadly endorsed the latter approach, while preferring a formulation that there must be no *real danger of bias* on the part of the relevant member of the tribunal in question, in the sense that he or she might (a possibility not a probability) unfairly regard with favour or disfavour the case of a party to the issue under consideration. The House also held that the same test should be applicable to all cases of apparent bias, whether concerned with justices, tribunal members, jurors or arbitrators. Furthermore, the judgment whether or not there was on the facts a real danger of bias should be made by the court. The court 'should look at the matter through the eyes of a reasonable man, because the court in cases such as these personifies the reasonable man' and 'should first ascertain the relevant circumstances from the available evidence'.

The matter should not be examined from the viewpoint of an observer in court at the relevant time, as knowledge of the relevant circumstances would not necessarily be available to such a person.[268] In cases of apparent bias arising from the retirement of a magistrates' clerk with the magistrates, the court should ascertain whether the clerk had been invited to give the magistrates advice and, if so, whether it should infer that there was a 'real danger of the clerk's bias having infected the views of the magistrates adversely to the applicant'.[269]   **15.81**

Subsequent case law has seen a return to an approach that places more emphasis on the appearance to the reasonable onlooker and less on a full investigation into the facts of the decision-making process. The steps in this process were, first, that Commonwealth cases declined to follow *Gough*, applying instead a test whether the events in question gave rise to a reasonable apprehension or suspicion on the part of a fair-minded and informed member of the public that the judge was not impartial.[270] Secondly, the implementation of the HRA 1998 has required that the *Gough* test be modified to accord with the requirements of Article 6(1) ECHR.[271]   **15.82**

---

[266] eg, *R v Rand* (1866) LR 1 QB 230, 232 *per* Blackburn J; *R v Camborne JJ, ex p Pearce* [1955] 1 QB 41; *R v Barnsley Licensing JJ, ex p Barnsley and District Licensed Victuallers Association* [1960] 2 QB 167, 186–187 *per* Devlin LJ.

[267] [1993] AC 646.

[268] ibid 670 *per* Lord Goff.

[269] ibid 664 *per* Lord Goff. The key case here was *R v Sussex JJ, ex p McCarthy* [1924] 1 KB 256, where the court quashed the defendant's conviction for dangerous driving arising out of a collision with another vehicle; the magistrates' clerk was a solicitor whose firm was acting as solicitor for the other driver in civil proceedings against the defendant arising out of the collision; the clerk retired with the justices but was in fact not consulted by them. The House of Lords in *Gough* at least implied that this last consideration meant that the *Sussex JJ* case was wrongly decided: see Lord Woolf at 673.

[270] eg, *Webb v R* (1994) 181 CLR 41, HC Aus; *Moch v Nedtravel (Pty) Ltd* 1996 (3) SA1.

[271] See para 12.29 above.

15.83 This latter step has itself been reached in stages. Prior to implementation of the 1998 Act, the Court of Appeal in *Locabail (UK) Ltd v Bayfield Properties Ltd*[272] indicated how the *Gough* test might be applied to the decisions of judges, with a view to securing Article 6(1) compliance. It would often be appropriate to inquire whether the judge knew of the matter relied on as appearing to undermine his or her impartiality; if it was shown that that was not the case, the appearance of possible bias would be dispelled. The judge might provide a written statement on the point, which would often, but not invariably, be accepted. There would, however, be no question of cross-examining or seeking disclosure from the judge. The court would disregard any statement by the judge concerning the impact of any knowledge on his or her mind or decision. Guidance was given on the circumstances that might and might not in principle give rise to a real danger of bias, everything of course ultimately turning on the circumstances of the case.[273] The court considered the development of the case law in this area and did, however, note in passing that the reasonable suspicion test rejected in *Gough* might be 'more closely in harmony' with the ECHR jurisprudence than the test actually adopted.[274]

15.84 The issue was confronted directly by the Court of Appeal in *Re Medicaments and Related Classes of Goods (No 2)*,[275] which held that the principles laid down in *Gough* did indeed require modification in the light of the ECHR jurisprudence.[276] The difference was that when the European Court of Human Rights considers whether the material circumstances give rise to a reasonable apprehension of bias, it applies an objective test to the circumstances and does not pass judgment on the likelihood that the particular tribunal under review was biased. Accordingly, an English court should first ascertain all the circumstances which have a bearing on the suggestion that the judge was biased, and then 'ask whether those circumstances would lead a fair-minded and informed observer to conclude that there was a real possibility, or a real danger, the two being the same, that the tribunal was biased'.

15.85 The material circumstances would include any explanation given by the judge. If it was accepted, it could be treated as accurate; if not, it would become one further matter to be considered from the point of view of the fair-minded observer. The court did not have to rule on whether the explanation should be accepted or

---

[272] [2000] QB 451. The other cases heard with it were *Locabail (UK) Ltd v Waldorf Investment Corp*; *Timmins v Gormley*; *Williams v HM Inspector of Taxes*; *R v Bristol Betting and Gaming Licensing Committee, ex p O'Callaghan*.
[273] See further para 15.87 below.
[274] [2000] QB 451 at [17].
[275] [2000] 1 WLR 700.
[276] *Delcourt v Belgium* Series A No 11 (1970) 1 EHRR 355; *Piersack v Belgium* Series A No 53 (1982) 5 EHRR 169; *De Cubber v Belgium* Series A No 86 (1984) 7 EHRR 236; *Borgers v Belgium* Series A No 214 (1993) 15 EHRR 92; *Gregory v UK* Application 22299/93 (1997) 25 EHRR 577.

rejected.[277] The court held that there was a real danger of bias where a lay member of the Restrictive Practices Court, after the commencement of particular proceedings, applied for a post at a firm one of whose directors was a key expert witness for one of the parties.

The House of Lords in *Porter v Magill*[278] subsequently endorsed this approach, **15.86** with the textual modification that the 'real possibility of bias' formulation should be used, and not 'real danger'. In most cases, the outcome would be the same whatever the formulation adopted. It would seem that under the approach now adopted, the *Sussex Justices* case can be regarded as correctly decided.[279]

The circumstances that may give rise to a real possibility of bias are of course **15.87** many and various, although there are some recurring themes. They include, for example, personal hostility, friendship, family relationship or (particularly where an issue of credibility arises) close acquaintance with a party or a witness; or where a judge has previously expressed views on a question at issue in such extreme and unbalanced terms as to throw doubt on his or her ability to try the issue with an objective judicial mind. On the other hand, objections cannot be soundly based on the religion, ethnic or national origin, gender, age, class, means or sexual orientation of the judge. Nor, at least ordinarily, can an objection be soundly based on his or her social or educational, or service or employment, background or history, nor those of any member of his or her family, or previous political associations, or membership of social, or sporting or charitable bodies; or extra-curricular utterances; or previous receipt of instructions to act for or against any party, solicitor or advocate engaged in a case before him or her.[280] Accordingly, no real danger of bias arose where Lawrence Collins QC, sitting as a deputy High Court judge, had heard a case in circumstances that, unknown to him, his firm, Herbert Smith, had acted for parties to other proceedings against the applicant's husband;[281] or where Dyson J heard judicial review proceedings arising out of the applicant's objections to a renewal of a bookmaker's permit to Corals, and it emerged subsequently that he was non-executive director of a family company that (unknown to him) rented premises to Corals elsewhere in the country.[282] Conversely, there was such a danger where a personal injuries case in which insurers were the real defendants was heard by

---

[277] [2000] 1 WLR 700 at [83]–[86].

[278] [2002] 1 All ER 465 at [95]–[105] *per* Lord Hope.

[279] See para 15.80 above.

[280] *Locabail (UK) Ltd v Bayfield Properties Ltd* [2000] QB 451 at [18]–[26]. See also *Lawal v Northern Spirit Ltd* [2003] UKHL 35; The Times, 27 June 2003 (real possibility of bias where part-time EAT judge appears as advocate before EAT that includes a lay member who had previously sat with him).

[281] *Locabail,* ibid and *Locabail (UK) Ltd v Waldorf Investment Corp.*

[282] *R v Bristol Betting and Gaming Licensing Committee, ex p O'Callaghan.*

a recorder who had published articles that expressed 'pronounced pro-claimant anti-insurer views'.[283]

(e) Application of the rule against bias to administrative decisions

15.88 On the assumption that the rule against bias does apply to administrative decisions, it must be recognized that the nature of the decision will itself be one of the material circumstances to be considered in determining whether there is on the facts a real possibility of bias. This has arisen acutely in the context of the application of the rule to the decisions of planning authorities. A distinction has been drawn between two situations. First, a decision can be quashed where there is a real possibility of bias arising from a personal interest of one or more of the decision-makers. Secondly, the public support for a particular policy by an individual councillor or political group or an institutional interest arising, for example, from the authority's ownership of the land in question or involvement in the process will not be held in itself to give rise to a real possibility of bias. However, a decision will be unlawful if, through commitment to such a policy, the decision-maker has effectively predetermined the question, in which case it will have fettered its discretion.[284]

15.89 Examples of personal interests that may be held to disqualify include an indirect financial interest in the project in question[285] and close association with a body particularly affected by a decision.[286] Where a person has a potential disqualifying

---

[283] *Timmins v Gormley.* This and the *Bristol* and *Locabail* cases (above) were heard together. See also *Ealing LBC v Jan* [2002] EWCA Civ 329 (judge not to hear retrial of proceedings where he had said of the respondent in preliminary proceedings that he could not trust him 'further than he could throw [him]').

[284] *R v Secretary of State for the Environment, ex p Kirkstall Valley Campaign Ltd* [1996] 3 All ER 304.

[285] eg, *R v Hendon RDC, ex p Chorley* [1933] 2 KB 696 (under pre-1947 planning legislation, see para above); cf the *Kirkstall Valley* case, ibid (chairman of urban development corporation had had indirect financial interest in grant of planning permission by corporation, but not by the time the impugned decisions were made).

[286] eg, the *Kirkstall Valley* case, ibid (decision of urban development corporation to grant planning permission for retail development on land owned by rugby club not quashed; fact that some urban development corporation members were also members of the rugby club was not in itself sufficient to disqualify; continued presence at earlier meetings of another urban development corporation member, who had been closely involved in the rugby club's plans, did infringe the nemo judex principle but this did not taint the decision taken at subsequent meetings where he was not present); *R v Kensington and Chelsea RLBC, ex p de Rothschild* (QBD, 7 November 1997) (no real danger of bias where councillor involved in the grant of planning permission in respect of former school premises owned by a trust had been a governor of the school; he had no knowledge of or involvement with the trust's finances); *R (on the application of S (a child)) v C High School Head Teacher* [2001] EWHC Admin 513; [2002] Ed LR 73 (no real danger of bias where officer of local education authority acted as clerk to exclusion appeal panel); *Bovis Homes Ltd v New Forest DC* [2002] EWHC 483 (involvement of chair of planning committee as member of external committee influential in developing policy for the New Forest Heritage Area held to give rise to real possibility of bias in respect of approval by the council of the local plan). Cf *R v Kirklees MBC, ex p Beaumont* (2000) 3 LGLR 177 (real danger of bias where councillors who were school governors voted on a proposal to close a rival school).

interest, his or her involvement in the actual decision-making may, however, be so remote that the decision itself is not open to challenge.[287] Where a decision is made by a body with a number of members, the disqualifying personal interest of one member will be sufficient to invalidate the decision.[288]

Where the grant of planning permission will further a project in which the local authority is participating or which otherwise is supported as a matter of policy by the ruling political group, the 'real possibility of bias test' does not apply; instead, the question will be whether the political predisposition is such as to fetter the discretion of the decision-making body.[289] This will be more difficult to establish on the evidence where a distinction is maintained between councillors who are closely involved in the project in question and those charged with deciding the planning application. This, however, cannot always be achieved. For example, in *Franklin v Minister of Town and Country Planning*,[290] which remains good law, the decision as to confirmation of a new town order would inevitably and appropriately have been taken by a minister committed to the new town policy. Where a minister has a personal interest in a matter, however, there is both a very well-established practice and (probably) a legal requirement that the matter be dealt with by a different member of the ministerial team.

15.90

(f) Exceptions

Where the facts are sufficient to justify a finding that the nemo judex principle has been infringed, this ground of challenge will nevertheless not be established where it was necessary for the decision-maker to act or where the person affected, with full knowledge of the decision-maker's interest or the circumstances said to give rise to an appearance of bias, unequivocally waives any such objection. Necessity will, for example, arise where all those with statutory authority to make

15.91

---

[287] eg, the *Kirkstall Valley* case, ibid; *R v Bristol City Council, ex p Anderson* [1989] PLCR 314 (appeal allowed on other grounds: [2000] PLCR 104) (no real danger of bias where member remained on board the bus where the planning sub-committee considered a matter in which he declared an interest, but took no part in the discussion); *R v Newport County BC, ex p Avery* (1998) 1 LGLR 205 (no real danger of bias where councillor assisted applicant for planning permission but took no part in the decision-making).

[288] *Bovis Homes Ltd v New Forest DC* [2002] EWHC 483 at [103]–[106] *per* Ouseley J.

[289] See *R v Amber Valley DC, ex p Jackson* [1985] 1 WLR 298 (political predisposition to follow party line in favour of a leisure development insufficient to disqualify councillors; affidavit evidence that decision would be taken in the light of officer's report found by the judge to be detailed and balanced); *R v Sevenoaks DC, ex p Terry* [1985] 3 All ER 226 (council's discretion not fettered in respect of grant of planning permission to developer for land in which the council had an interest); *R v Hereford and Worcester CC, ex p Wellington Parish Council* [1996] JPL 573 (predisposition arising from performance of council duties in favour of proposal for a gypsy site held not to prevent members participating in grant of planning permission; it was not shown that they had closed minds); *Bovis Homes Ltd v New Forest DC* [2002] EWHC 483 (predetermination found on the facts).

[290] See para 15.70 above.

a particular decision are affected by the same interest that would otherwise disqualify.[291] Where necessity is established, but the case falls within the scope of Article 6(1) ECHR, the position is likely to be incompatible with Convention rights under the HRA 1998.[292] Waiver will need to be established by clear evidence that the person concerned acted freely and in full knowledge of the facts.[293]

(g) Consequences of breach of nemo judex rule

15.92   Notwithstanding some clear statements that breach of the nemo judex principle renders a decision voidable,[294] the better view is that, as with breach of the right to a fair hearing, the decision is void (subject to the discretion of the court whether to grant a remedy).[295]

(h) Statutory formulation of the rule against interest and bias

15.93   In some contexts rules concerning conflicts of interest have been enshrined in primary or secondary legislation.[296] Decisions made without complying with the procedural rules setting out the equivalent of the common law rule against interest and bias are likely to be held to be invalid.[297]

---

[291]   *The Judges v A-G for Saskatchewan* (1937) 53 TLR 464; RRS Tracey, 'Disqualified adjudicators: the doctrine of necessity in public law' [1982] PL 628. In the *Dimes* case (para above), the Lord Chancellor had to sign the enrolment order necessary for the case to proceed to the House of Lords; this was a matter of necessity. However, it had not been necessary for him to hear the case, which could have been referred to the Master of the Rolls.

[292]   See the discussion of *Kingsley v UK* (2001) 33 EHRR 288 by I Leigh, 'Bias, necessity and the Convention' [2002] PL 407; Leigh suggests that as a result a narrower approach to the necessity exception is likely to be adopted.

[293]   *per* Lord Browne-Wilkinson in *R v Bow Street Metropolitan Stipendiary Magistrate, ex p Pinochet Ugarte (No 2)* [2000] 1 AC 119, 137 (para 15.77 above).

[294]   See the opinion of the judges in the *Dimes* case (para above). Note, however, that the decision challenged in that case was that of a judge of a superior not an inferior court (the Lord Chancellor); the judgments of superior courts are not subject to judicial review unless such a jurisdiction were expressly to be conferred by statute.

[295]   See *Cooper v Wilson* [1937] 2 KB 309; *Anisminic Ltd v Foreign Compensation Commission* [1969] 2 AC 147, 171 *per* Lord Reid, 195 *per* Lord Pearce and 207–208 *per* Lord Wilberforce.

[296]   eg, Licensing Act 1964, s 193; see *R v Barnsley County Borough Licensing JJ, ex p Barnsley and District Licensed Victuallers Association* [1960] 2 QB 167. In some situations, non-compliance with statutory conflict of interest rules is a criminal offence: eg Local Government Act 1972, ss 94–97, now replaced by the new ethical framework established by Local Government Act 2000, Pt III.

[297]   See *Noble v Inner London Education Authority* (1983) 82 LGR 291 (express statutory requirement for withdrawal of a member of a governing body of a school where he was interested in a matter under consideration at a meeting of that body held to be mandatory). See also *Bostock v Kay* (1988) 87 LGR 583.

C. Non-Compliance with Statutory Procedural Requirements

The making of a decision under the authority of a statute may be regulated by a   **15.94**
procedural code (of varying degrees of elaboration) set out in the enabling legislation, in procedural rules or regulations, or a combination of the two. One question
that may arise is the relationship between such a code and the common law requirements of procedural fairness. As we have seen[298] the courts today are ready to
supplement such a code to ensure procedural fairness. However, a distinct question
may arise as the consequence of a failure to comply with all or part of an applicable
procedural code. The courts have never taken the view that non-compliance with
any statutory procedural requirement is automatically fatal to the validity of the decision subsequently taken. Such a formalistic approach would invalidate otherwise
perfectly proper decisions for minor technical defects, and bring the law into dis-
repute. On the other hand, the courts have struggled to identify clear criteria for
distinguishing those defects that are fatal and those that are not.

In dealing with these issues, the traditional approach of the courts has been to   **15.95**
draw a distinction between procedural requirements that are 'mandatory' and
those that are 'directory'. Mandatory requirements must be observed as a precondition to the validity of the ultimate decision; non-observance of a directory requirement does not have that effect, subject to a rider sometimes added that there
has been 'substantial compliance'. These labels, however, reflect the conclusion
the court has reached as to the consequence of non-compliance, rather than the
criteria used by the court in reaching that conclusion. Such criteria as have been
articulated have tended to be of a high level of generality:

> I believe, as far as any rule is concerned, you cannot safely go further than that in
> each case you must look to the subject-matter; consider the importance of the pro-
> vision that has been disregarded, and the relation of that provision to the general
> object intended to be secured by the Act.[299]

Statements that the question is whether Parliament intended that failure to com-   **15.96**
ply with a particular requirement deprived the decision-maker of jurisdiction
restate the problem without providing a solution.[300] While some generic categories of requirement are very likely to be held to be mandatory,[301] it has also been
emphasized that these issues turn on the construction of the particular Act in
question.[302] More recent authorities have suggested that the use of the labels

---

[298] See para 15.38 above.
[299] *per* Lord Penzance in *Howard v Bodington* (1877) LR 2 PD 203, 210–211.
[300] eg, Lord Slynn in *Wang v Inland Revenue Commissioner* [1994] 1 WLR 1286, 1296.
[301] See para 15.97 below.
[302] *Grunwick Processing Laboratories Ltd v Advisory Conciliation and Arbitration Service* [1978] AC
655, 698 *per* Lord Salmon.

'mandatory' and 'directory' is unhelpful and have favoured a more pragmatic approach that is focused more directly on the facts of the case and the practical consequences of non-compliance for the interests of those for whose protection the procedural rules were designed. However, it has also been recognized that it would be wrong to regard the consequences of non-compliance as purely a matter for the discretion of the reviewing court, with the consequent unpredictability of outcome. These should still be matters for judgment based on principle, although not detailed inflexible rules. Parliament may of course indicate what are to be the consequences of omitting a particular step,[303] but usually does not.

(a) Mandatory and directory requirements

15.97 The courts have tended to hold requirements to be mandatory where they provide an important safeguard to individual interests, such as giving prior notice or holding a hearing;[304] giving notice of rights of appeal[305] or of rights to make objections;[306] giving the prescribed period of notice for the introduction of a licensing scheme;[307] or regulating conflicts of interest.[308] There are strong analogies here with common law requirements of procedural fairness. The courts have also generally regarded as mandatory statutory requirements to consult in relation to the making of administrative decisions[309] and delegated legislation.[310] Here, common law requirements of procedural fairness would, respectively, be less likely and very unlikely to be imposed,[311] but it is entirely appropriate that such procedural safeguards as are enshrined in legislation be enforced.

15.98 By contrast, the courts have tended to hold requirements to be directory only where there has been compliance as regards the substance or main features of the matter in question and the non-compliance relates to matters of detail[312] or

---

[303] eg, Local Government Act 1972, s 82: 'The acts and proceedings of any person elected to an office under this Act . . . and acting in that office shall, notwithstanding his disqualification or want of qualification, be as valid and effectual as if he had been qualified'.

[304] eg, *Bradbury v Enfield LBC* [1967] 1 WLR 1311 (requirement where education authority intended to establish or cease to maintain a school to submit proposals to the minister and give public notice to enable objections to be made to the minister).

[305] *Rayner v Stepney Corp* [1911] 2 Ch 312; *London & Clydeside Estates Ltd v Aberdeen DC* [1980] 1 WLR 182.

[306] *R v Lambeth LBC ex p Sharp* (1988) 55 P & CR 232; *R v Tower Hamlets LBC, ex p Tower Hamlets Combined Traders Association* [1994] COD 325.

[307] *R v Swansea City Council, ex p Quietlynn Ltd,* The Times, 19 October 1983.

[308] *Noble v Inner London Education Authority* (1983) 82 LGR 291.

[309] *R v Governors of Small Heath School, ex p Birmingham City Council,* The Times, 31 May 1989 (duty of school governors to consult local education authority before seeking grant maintained status).

[310] *R v Secretary of State for Social Services, ex p Association of Metropolitan Authorities* [1986] 1 WLR 1.

[311] See paras 15.20 and 15.67 above.

[312] eg, *Bradbury v Enfield LBC* [1967] 1 WLR 1311 (requirement after approval of general proposals for a new school for minister to approve specifications and plans of the premises held directory; a default power was available to the minister under s 99 of the Education Act 1944); *R v*

timing,[313] or something that can appropriately be cured by means other than in-validating the whole decision.[314]

(b) A more flexible approach

In *London & Clydeside Estates Ltd v Aberdeen DC* Lord Hailsham LC,[315] having **15.99**
held that a requirement to give notice of rights of appeal was mandatory, drew at-tention to the dangers arising from the use of language in the case law that pre-supposed 'the existence of stark categories such as "mandatory" and "directory", "void" and "voidable", a "nullity", and "purely regulatory"'. While such language was useful, it was also misleading in so far as it suggested that the court had to fit particular cases into one or other of these mutually exclusive and starkly con-trasted compartments. What had to be determined in a particular case was:

> the legal consequences of non-compliance on the rights of the subject viewed in the
> light of a concrete state of facts and a continuing chain of events. It may be that what
> the courts are faced with is not so much a stark choice of alternatives but a spectrum
> of possibilities in which one compartment or description fades gradually into another.

At one end of the spectrum, flagrant non-compliance with a fundamental obligation **15.100**
may simply entitle the person affected to ignore the ensuing decision; at the other end, the defect in procedure may be so trivial that the authority can safely proceed. In a great number of cases, possibly the majority, it will be necessary for the matter to be resolved by the courts. The use of rigid legal classifications was not to be encouraged.

> The jurisdiction is inherently discretionary and the court is frequently in the pres-
> ence of differences of degree which merge almost imperceptibly into differences of
> kind.

Lord Hailsham's observations have been taken up by judges in subsequent **15.101**
cases,[316] most notably by Lord Woolf.[317] However, it has also been emphasized

---

Dacorum Gaming Licensing Committee, ex p EMI Cinemas and Leisure Ltd [1971] 3 All ER 666
(minor typographical error in notice of application for a licence, referring to 'ABE' Social Club
rather than 'ABC' held not to invalidate application).

[313] cf *Cullimore v Lyme Regis Corp* [1962] 1 QB 718 (council required to determine interests in
land benefited by coast protection works and the amount of charges within six months of comple-tion of the scheme; charges determined two years later held void on the ground either that the time
limit was mandatory or, even if it were directory, there had been nothing approaching substantial
compliance); *Wang v Inland Revenue Commissioner* [1994] 1 WLR 1286, PC (could not have been
intended that non-compliance with duty to make tax assessments 'within a reasonable time' ren-dered an assessment made later void).

[314] eg, duties to give reasons: see para 15.106 below.

[315] [1980] 1 WLR 182, 189–190.

[316] *R v Chester City Council, ex p Quietlynn Ltd*, The Times, 19 October 1983; *R v Secretary of State
for the Environment, ex p Leicester City Council* (1985) 25 RVR 31; *Main v Swansea City Council*
(1984) 49 P & CR 26; *R v Lambeth LBC, ex p Sharp* (1986) 55 P & CR 232; *R v Doncaster
Metropolitan DC* [1987] JPL 444.

[317] *ex p Quietlynn Ltd*, ibid; *ex p Leicester City Council*, ibid; *ex p Sharp*, ibid.

that it is important to distinguish between two separate issues when considering the judicial response to a breach of statutory procedural requirements. First, the legal consequences of non-compliance are variable but are to be determined as an exercise of judgment on legal criteria, and not an exercise of discretion ad hoc or ad hominem. Secondly, the grant of relief by the courts is discretionary.[318]

15.102   The approach that should be adopted was the subject of further extended consideration by the Court of Appeal in *R v Immigration Appeal Tribunal, ex p Jeyeanthan*.[319] Here, the Secretary of State failed substantially to comply with the rules governing applications for leave to appeal from a special adjudicator to the tribunal in an asylum case, in that the application omitted a declaration of truth. Lord Woolf MR[320] stated that the question whether a provision was mandatory or directory was only at most a first step. In the majority of cases there were other questions to be asked which were more likely to be of greater assistance. Those questions likely to arise were:

(1)   Is the statutory requirement fulfilled if there has been substantial compliance with the requirement and, if so, has there been substantial compliance in the case in issue even though there has not been strict compliance? (The substantial compliance question);

(2)   Is the non-compliance capable of being waived, and if so, has it, or can it and should it be waived in this particular case? (The discretionary question);

(3)   If it is not capable of being waived or is not waived then what is the consequence of the non-compliance? (The consequences question).

15.103   Which questions would arise would depend on the facts of the case and the nature of the particular requirement. On the facts here, omission of the declaration of truth did not constitute substantial compliance, the answer to this question being the same for the asylum seeker as for the Secretary of State. However, the applicants here had not been affected in any way by the omission and so the discretion and consequences question should be answered in the Secretary of State's favour. One applicant had taken part in the appeal effectively impliedly waiving the requirements; the other had taken the point as a matter of jurisdiction when he could have asked the tribunal to order the Secretary of State to rectify the omission

---

[318]   *per* Sedley J in *R v Tower Hamlets LBC, ex p Tower Hamlets Combined Traders Association* [1994] COD 325.

[319]   [2000] 1 WLR 354. Lord Woolf's approach was endorsed by the House of Lords in *A-G's Reference (No 3) of 1999* [2001] 2 AC 91, in holding DNA evidence admissible notwithstanding that the investigation had made use of another sample that should have been destroyed in accordance with Police and Criminal Evidence Act 1984, s 64(3B). Cf the simpler approach of a differently constituted Court of Appeal that gave judgment five days after *Jeyeanthan* in *Haringey LBC v Awaritefe* (2000) 32 HLR 517, 526–527 that it was 'necessary to assess "the substantive harm caused by the breach"', adopting the test proposed by Sedley J in *R v Solihull Metropolitan Council Housing Benefit Review Board, ex p Simpson* (1994) 26 HLR 370.

[320]   [2000] 1 WLR 354, 362.

or exercise its statutory power to cure procedural irregularities. Other than to discipline the Secretary of State, there could be no reason well after the event to treat his successful application for leave to appeal as a nullity. Judge LJ[321] agreed with Lord Woolf's 'illuminating analysis of the dangers of over-rigidly seeking to pigeon hole requirements of the kind under consideration . . . by the application of a single descriptive and apparently all embracing word'. However, he also hoped that counsel would not in future seek to reanalyse his analysis, leading to further over-elaboration. 'The true focus of attention, assisted by Lord Woolf MR's analysis, remains the relevant statutory framework considered as a whole.'

A number of points emerge. First, Lord Woolf's approach rightly emphasizes that **15.104** the legal consequence of non-compliance cannot be determined solely by reference to the nature of the requirement itself but must be considered in the factual context of a particular case. At the same time, the matter is not to be determined solely by reference to the question whether the interests of the applicant have been substantially prejudiced.[322] It also confirms that the use of the 'mandatory' and 'directory' labels are misleading to the extent that the detailed consequences of non-compliance fall into one of two fully defined categories. Finally, it does not endorse a position in which the consequences of non-compliance are determined by the court as a matter of broad discretion. Notwithstanding the strictures of Lord Woolf and others,[323] use of the terms 'mandatory' and 'directory' remains firmly entrenched in the language of the courts, particularly in the context of non-compliance with requirements in civil or criminal litigation. Provided they are only used as shorthand to describe broad consequences of non-compliance and their limitations are properly understood, then relatively little harm is likely to ensue.

(c) Particular requirements: consultation

Whatever general approach to the effect of non-compliance with procedural re- **15.105** quirements is adopted, a failure to comply with a duty to consult is likely to be fatal. In some cases, no consultation at all takes place and the point is clear. In others, attention has to be paid to the content of the duty to consult in the context in question. The essential requirements have been characterized as follows:[324]

---

[321] ibid 366

[322] Lord Woolf MR recognized (ibid 359) that there were cases where non-compliance with the duty to give notice of the right of appeal was held to be fatal notwithstanding that the particular applicant was aware of the right and chose not to exercise it: 'the draconian consequence is imposed as a deterrent against not observing the requirement'.

[323] eg, the Privy Council in *Wang v Inland Revenue Commissioner* [1994] 1 WLR 1286, 1296 *per* Lord Slynn; Lord Bingham in *Robinson v Secretary of State for Northern Ireland* [2002] UKHL 32; [2002] NI 390 at [13].

[324] *per* Hodgson J in *R v Brent LBC, ex p Gunning* (1986) 84 LGR 168, 189, adopting the submissions of Stephen Sedley QC; while the context was a case based on a legitimate expectation of rather than a statutory right to consultation, the basic principles are of general application. See also

First, that consultation must be at a time when proposals are still at a formative stage. Second, that the proposer must give sufficient reasons for any proposal to permit of intelligent consideration and response. Third, . . . that adequate time must be given for consideration and response and, finally, fourth, that the product of consultation must be conscientiously taken into account in finalising any statutory proposals.

Here, the process for consulting parents adopted by the council in respect of proposals relating to the amalgamation and closure of certain secondary schools was 'woefully deficient, both as to content and timing'.[325] A duty simply to consult is not, however, to be taken to comprise a duty to obtain the agreement or consensus of the consultees before acting.[326]

(d) Particular requirements: reasons

15.106 Failure to comply with a duty to give reasons for a decision will not itself automatically be sufficient to render the decision void or even open to challenge for error of law on the face of the record.[327] If he or she is in time, a person aggrieved by the absence of reasons may be able to obtain an order compelling reasons to be given.[328] Where reasons must be given, they must be 'proper', 'adequate' and 'reasons which will not only be intelligible, but which deal with the substantial points that have been raised'.[329] Where reasons are not given, or the reasons given are themselves unintelligible, the court may in appropriate circumstances infer that the decision-maker's process of legal reasoning was defective or, indeed, irrational, leading to the quashing of the decision.[330] Furthermore, in the context of planning inquiries there is both a duty for reasons to be given by the decision-maker and an express power on the part of the court, on a statutory application to quash, to set aside a decision where the applicant's interests have been substantially prejudiced by non-compliance with a procedural requirement. Here, many decisions

---

to similar effect, in the context of consultation in respect of delegated legislation, Webster J in *R v Secretary of State for Social Services, ex p Association of Metropolitan Authorities* [1986] 1 WLR 1, 4–5.

[325] *per* Hodgson J in *R v Brent LBC, ex p Gunning* (1986) 84 LGR 168, 192 (consultation document 'positively misleading' on the question of cost; copies of consultation document sent to schools on 17 May to be passed on to parents with public meetings to be held on 7 June and written responses to be received by 15 June).

[326] *R (on application of Smith) v East Kent Hospitals NHS Trust* [2002] EWHC 2640.

[327] *Mountview Court Properties Ltd v Devlin* (1970) 21 P & CR 689.

[328] *Brayhead (Ascot) Ltd v Berkshire CC* [1964] 2 QB 303 (failure to give reasons for planning condition did not render it void but court would normally grant mandamus to compel the reasons to be divulged.

[329] *per* Megaw J in *Re Poyser and Mills' Arbitration* [1964] 2 QB 467, 478.

[330] *Mountview Court Properties Ltd v Devlin* (1970) 21 P & CR 689; *Crake v Supplementary Benefits Commission* [1982] 1 All ER 498 (where Woolf J noted that the courts today were more prepared to infer that because of inadequate reasons there had been an error of law).

have been quashed and remitted to the decision-maker where intelligible reasons have not been given.[331]

Where reasons are given, for example in a decision letter, that are inadequate, the court may be prepared to receive further evidence as to the reasons for the decision, but will do so cautiously.[332] Relevant considerations include whether the new reasons are consistent with the original reasons; whether it is clear that the new reasons are indeed the original reasons of the decision-maker; whether there is a real risk that later reasons have been composed subsequently; the delay before the later reasons were put forward; the circumstances in which the later reasons were put forward; whether the decision-maker would have been expected to state in the decision document the reason that he or she is seeking to adduce later; and whether it would be just in all the circumstances to refuse to admit the subsequent reasons.[333] Further reasons cannot in any event be adduced in any case where the adequacy of the reasons is itself made a condition of the legality of the decision.[334]

15.107

D. The Common Law and Article 6(1) ECHR

Following implementation of the HRA 1998, it has been possible for claimants for judicial review to deploy arguments based on alleged breaches of Convention rights, for the most part under Article 6(1) ECHR, alongside arguments based on procedural unfairness. These are distinct, but overlapping grounds of challenge. The former only applies in respect of decisions that determine civil rights and obligations or criminal charges;[335] the latter applies more broadly.[336] The right to a fair hearing under Article 6(1) closely corresponds to the common law audi alteram partem principle; the right to a public hearing[337]

15.108

---

[331] The leading authority is *Save Britain's Heritage v Number 1 Poultry Ltd* [1991] 1 WLR 153, HL. See also *Givaudan & Co Ltd v Minister of Housing and Local Government* [1967] 1 WLR 250; *Bolton Metropolitan DC v Secretary of State for the Environment* (1995) 71 P & CR 309 (not necessary for every relevant, material consideration to be dealt with specifically in reasons for an ultimate decision to grant or withhold planning consent).
[332] *R v Westminster City Council, ex p Ermakov* [1996] 2 All ER 302.
[333] Stanley Burnton J in *R (on the application of Nash) v Chelsea College of Art* [2001] EWHC Admin 538; The Times, 5 July 2001; the last two factors were added by Silber J in *Leung v Imperial College of Science, Technology and Medicine* [2002] EWHC 1358; [2002] Ed LR 653.
[334] Laws J, obiter, in *R v Northamptonshire CC, ex p D* [1998] Ed CR 14, 24 (supplementary evidence accepted on the facts where there was no suggestion of any shift of ground).
[335] See paras 12.05–12.18 above.
[336] See paras 15.15–15.34, 15.70–15.74 above.
[337] See paras 12.23–12.24 above.

adds a new dimension.[338] The right to an *impartial* tribunal is equivalent to the rule against interest and bias, following the modifications to the *Gough* test effected by the Court of Appeal in *Re Medicaments* and the House of Lords in *Porter v Magill*.[339] The right to an *independent* tribunal is distinct but has now been read into the common law.[340]

---

[338] A separate principle requires that a court of law should normally hold its proceedings in public.

[339] See para 15.84 above; confirmed by Richards J, obiter, in *R (on the application of S (a child)) v C High School Head Teacher* [2001] EWHC Admin 513; [2002] Ed LR 73 and Tucker J in *R (on the application of Nicolaides) v General Medical Council* [2001] EWHC Admin 625; [2001] Lloyd's Rep Med 525.

[340] *R (on the application of Bewry) v Norwich City Council* [2001] EWHC Admin 657; [2002] HRLR 2, *per* Moses J.

16

GROUNDS FOR JUDICIAL REVIEW: SUBSTANTIVE CONTROL OVER DISCRETION

A. Irrationality and Proportionality

(1) The Limits of Judicial Intervention

The courts do not substitute their choice as to how discretion ought to have been exercised for that of the administrative authority. They do not intervene, reassess the matter afresh and decide that funds ought to be allocated in one way rather than another. Decisions as to political and social choice are made by the legislature, or by a person assigned the task by the legislature.[1] The courts accept that it is not their task to substitute judgment.[2] It is also recognized that there must be some control over the rationality of decisions made by the administration. The

16.01

---

[1] *R v Ministry of Agriculture, Fisheries and Food, ex p First City Trading* [1997] 1 CMLR 250, 278.
[2] *R v Cambridge Health Authority, ex p B (No 1)* [1995] 1 WLR 898, CA.

courts have therefore sought for a criterion that will allow judicial control, without leading to substitution of judgment or too great an intrusion on the merits.

(2) Wednesbury *Unreasonableness: The Traditional Formulation*

16.02   The traditional test for the rationality of administrative action has been the *Wednesbury* test.[3] Lord Greene MR used the word unreasonableness in two different senses. It was used to describe the various grounds of challenge that went to the legality of the public body's actions. This sense of unreasonableness was used to describe actions based on illegality, irrelevancy and the like. He also gave unreasonableness a substantive meaning in its own right. If an exercise of discretion successfully negotiated the hurdles of propriety of purpose and relevancy it could still be invalidated if it was so unreasonable that no reasonable body could reach such a decision.

16.03   The two senses of unreasonableness were designed to legitimate judicial intervention over discretionary decisions, and to establish the limits to any such intervention. The first meaning of the term allowed the courts to intervene where the decision was of a type that could not be made at all, and was therefore illegal. It was outside the four corners of the power that Parliament had given to the decision-maker. Where, however, the primary decision-maker was within the four corners of its power then the courts should be reluctant to interfere. The courts should not substitute their view for that of the public body, nor should they overturn a decision merely because they felt that there might have been some other reasonable way for the administration to have done its task. Some control over such decisions was, however, felt to be warranted. If the challenged decision really was so unreasonable that no reasonable body could have made it, then the court was justified in quashing it.

16.04   It is clear from Lord Greene MR's judgment that he conceived of it being used only in the extreme and hypothetical instance of 'dismissal for red hair type of case'. Lord Diplock was equally clear it would only apply to a 'decision which is so outrageous in its defiance of logic or of accepted moral standards that no sensible person who had applied his mind to the question could have arrived at it'.[4]

(3) Wednesbury *Unreasonableness: The Present Law*

16.05   The wording of the *Wednesbury* test, as interpreted by Lord Greene and Lord Diplock, might lead one to think that few cases would be condemned. The reality is that the courts have developed the test in a number of ways.

---

[3] *Associated Provincial Picture Houses Ltd v Wednesbury Corp* [1948] 1 KB 223, 233–234, CA.
[4] *Council of Civil Service Unions v Minister for the Civil Service* [1985] AC 374, 410, HL.

(a) Cases not concerned with rights

The courts have broadened the *Wednesbury* test, even in cases that are not concerned **16.06**
with rights. They have applied the test to discretionary decisions that could not,
whether right or wrong, be classified as of the 'red hair type'. The test has been used
in the planning sphere to invalidate conditions attached to planning permission.
An obligation on the developer to construct an ancillary road over the frontage of
the site, to which rights of passage should be given to others,[5] was struck down. So
too was an obligation that a property developer should allow those on a council
housing list to occupy the houses with security of tenure for ten years.[6] These cases
may have been correctly decided. It is, however, difficult to regard the subject matter under attack as determinations which were so unreasonable that no reasonable
authority could have made them. The test was applied in a way that made it closer
to asking whether the court believed that the exercise of discretion was reasonable.[7]

This has become more explicit in later cases. In *R v Lord Saville of Newdigate, ex p* **16.07**
B (No 2),[8] Lord Woolf MR held that to label a decision as irrational would often
not do justice to the decision-maker, who could be the most rational of persons. In
many such cases the true explanation for the decision being flawed was that although such perversity could not be established, the decision-maker had misdirected itself in law. In *R v Parliamentary Commissioner for Administration, ex p*
Balchin (No 1),[9] Sedley J held that a decision would be *Wednesbury* unreasonable if
it disclosed an error of reasoning, which robbed the decision of its logical integrity.
If such an error could be shown then it was not necessary for the applicant to
demonstrate that the decision-maker was 'temporarily unhinged'. In *R v North and*
East Devon Health Authority, ex p Coughlan,[10] the court held that rationality covered not only decisions that defied comprehension, but also those made by 'flawed
logic'.[11] The loosening of Lord Greene's test received explicit support from Lord
Cooke in *R v Chief Constable of Sussex, ex p International Trader's Ferry Ltd*.[12] He regarded the formulation used by Lord Greene as tautologous and exaggerated. It was
not, said Lord Cooke, necessary to have such an extreme formulation in order to

---

[5] *Hall & Co Ltd v Shoreham-by-Sea UDC* [1964] 1 WLR 240, CA.
[6] *R v Hillingdon LBC, ex p Royco Homes Ltd* [1974] QB 720.
[7] See also, *Niarchos (London) Ltd v Secretary of State for the Environment and Westminster City Council (No 2)* [1981] JPL 118; *West Glamorgan CC v Rafferty* [1987] 1 WLR 457, CA; *R v Bridgnorth DC, ex p Prime Time Promotions Ltd* [1999] COD 265; *R v Secretary of State for the Home Department, ex p Tawfick* [2001] ACD 28; *R v Secretary of State for Health, ex p Wagstaff* [2001] 1 WLR 292; *R (on the application of Howard) v Secretary of State for Health* [2002] EWHC 396, [2003] QB 830; *R (on the application of Von Brandenburg) v East London and the City Mental Health Trust* [2001] EWCA Civ 239, [2002] QB 235.
[8] [2000] 1 WLR 1855 at [33], CA.
[9] [1997] COD 146.
[10] [2001] QB 213, CA.
[11] ibid at [65].
[12] [1999] 2 AC 418, 452, HL.

ensure that the courts remained within their proper bounds as required by the separation of powers. He advocated a simpler and less extreme test: was the decision one that a reasonable authority could have reached? Lord Cooke returned to the topic in *R (on the application of Daly) v Secretary of State for the Home Department*.[13]

> [I] think that the day will come when it will be more widely recognised that . . . *Wednesbury* . . . was an unfortunately retrogressive decision in English administrative law, insofar as it suggested that there are degrees of unreasonableness and that only a very extreme degree can bring an administrative decision within the legitimate scope of judicial invalidation. The depth of judicial review and the deference due to administrative discretion vary with the subject matter. It may well be, however, that the law can never be satisfied in any administrative field by a finding that the decision under review is not capricious or absurd.

(b) Cases concerned with rights

16.08 The courts have varied the intensity with which they apply the *Wednesbury* test in cases concerned with rights. The courts apply the principles of judicial review, including the *Wednesbury* test, with varying degrees of intensity depending upon the nature of the subject matter.[14] Lord Bridge in *R v Secretary of State for the Home Department, ex p Brind*[15] said that, in cases concerned with rights, the court must inquire whether a reasonable Secretary of State could reasonably have made the primary decision being challenged. The court should begin its inquiry from the premise that only a compelling public interest would justify the invasion of the right. Sir Thomas Bingham MR's formulation in *R v Ministry of Defence, ex p Smith* was very similar.[16] The court was to consider whether the decision was beyond the range of responses open to a reasonable decision-maker, and the greater the interference with human rights the more the court would require by way of justification. This formulation has been adopted in many later cases.[17]

(c) Cases concerned with legitimate expectations: rationality and abuse of power

16.09 The case law on legitimate expectations will be considered below. This case law is however of more general relevance for the standard of review. In *Coughlan*,[18] the

---

[13] [2001] UKHL 26, [2001] 2 AC 532, 549; *R (on the application of Louis Farrakhan) v Secretary of State for the Home Department* [2002] EWCA Civ 606, [2002] QB 1391 at [66].

[14] Sir John Laws, '*Wednesbury*' in C Forsyth and I Hare (eds), *The Golden Metwand and the Crooked Cord, Essays in Honour of Sir William Wade* (Oxford: OUP, 1998) 185–202.

[15] [1991] 1 AC 696, 748–749, HL.

[16] [1996] QB 517, CA.

[17] *Bugdaycay v Secretary of State for the Home Department* [1987] AC 514, 531, HL; *R v Secretary of State for the Home Department, ex p Leech* [1994] QB 198, CA; *R v Secretary of State for the Home Department, ex p McQuillan* [1995] 4 All ER 400; *R v Lord Saville of Newdigate, ex p B (No 2)* [2000] 1 WLR 1855 at [34]–[37]; *R (on the application of Prolife Alliance) v BBC* [2003] UKHL 23, [2003] 2 WLR 1403.

[18] *R v North and East Devon Health Authority, ex p Coughlan* [2001] QB 213, CA.

court held that judicial intervention could be premised on bare rationality, as reflected in the *Wednesbury* test. This test was rejected as being insufficiently searching in cases where a public body sought to resile from a substantive legitimate expectation.[19] The court held that intervention could, alternatively, be premised on abuse of power.[20] The court's task was to ensure that the power to alter policy was not abused by unfairly frustrating an individual's legitimate expectations. This standard of review was more far-reaching than bare rationality.[21] While it was for the public body to decide when to change policy, the applicant's substantive legitimate expectation could not be frustrated unless there was an overriding public interest, and whether this existed or not was a matter for the court.[22] The nature of this test will be considered more fully below, in the discussion of legitimate expectations.

(4) Proportionality: Place and Meaning

It is important at the outset to ascertain the place of proportionality within the general scheme of review, and its relationship with other existing methods of control. It is clear, as a matter of principle, that to talk of proportionality assumes that the public body was entitled to pursue its desired objective. The presumption is, therefore, that the general objective was a legitimate one, and that the public body was not seeking to achieve an improper purpose. If the purpose was improper then the exercise of discretion should be struck down upon this ground, without any investigation as to whether it was disproportionate. **16.10**

In terms of meaning, it is clear that proportionality involves some idea of balance between interests or objectives, and that it embodies some sense of an appropriate relationship between means and ends. It is therefore necessary to identify the relevant interests, and ascribe some weight to them. A decision must then be made as to whether the public body's decision was proportionate or not, in the light of the above considerations. **16.11**

The most common formulation is for a three-part analysis, in which the court considers: whether the measure was necessary to achieve the desired objective; whether the measure was suitable for achieving the desired objective; whether it none the less imposed excessive burdens on the individual. The last part of this inquiry is often termed proportionality stricto sensu. **16.12**

It will be apparent from the subsequent analysis that the court will decide how intensively to apply these criteria. It should also be recognized that the criteria may **16.13**

---

[19] ibid at [66].
[20] *R v Inland Revenue Commissioners, ex p Preston* [1985] AC 835, HL was regarded as the principal authority.
[21] *R v North and East Devon Health Authority, ex p Coughlan* [2001] QB 213, CA at [74], [77].
[22] ibid at [76].

require the court to consider alternative strategies for attaining the desired end. This follows from the fact that the court will, in fundamental rights cases, consider whether there was a less restrictive method for attaining the desired objective. The need to consider alternative strategies may well also arise in other cases. Where the decision is of a technical or professional nature it may require specialist evidence as to the practicability of alternative strategies.[23]

(5) Proportionality: The Brind Decision

16.14   Discussion of proportionality in domestic law must begin with the House of Lords' decision in *R v Secretary of State for the Home Department, ex p Brind*.[24] The Home Secretary issued directives under the Broadcasting Act 1981 requiring the BBC and the IBA to refrain from broadcasting certain matters by persons who represented organizations which were proscribed under legislation concerning the prevention of terrorism. The ambit of this proscription was limited to direct statements made by the members of the organizations. The objective was to deny such organizations any appearance of political legitimacy, and to prevent intimidation. It did not prevent the broadcasting of such persons on film, provided that there was a voice-over account paraphrasing what had been said. The applicants argued, inter alia, that the directives were disproportionate.

16.15   Their Lordships rejected the argument. Lord Bridge held that the restrictions on freedom of speech were not unreasonable in scope, and did not believe that the applicants' case could be improved by invoking proportionality.[25] Lord Bridge did, however, agree with Lord Roskill that proportionality might be incorporated within our law at some future date. Lord Roskill acknowledged that Lord Diplock had, in the GCHQ case,[26] held this open as a possible development. Lord Roskill did not however think that this was an appropriate case for such a development, believing that this would lead the courts into substituting their view for that of the Home Secretary.[27] Similar concerns were apparent in the judgments of Lord Ackner and Lord Lowry. Thus Lord Ackner reasoned that if proportionality were to add something to our existing law, then it must be by imposing a more intensive standard of review than traditional *Wednesbury* unreasonableness. This would mean that an inquiry into the merits could not be avoided, in the sense that the court would have to balance the arguments for and against the decision being challenged.[28] Lord Lowry felt that the judges were not well equipped by training

---

[23]   *Southampton Port Health Authority v Seahawk Marine Foods Ltd* [2002] EWCA Civ 54; [2002] ACD 35 at [12].
[24]   [1991] 1 AC 696, HL.
[25]   ibid 748–749.
[26]   *Council of Civil Service Unions v Minister for the Civil Service* [1985] AC 374, 410, HL.
[27]   *R v Secretary of State for the Home Department, ex p Brind* [1991] 1 AC 696, 749–750, HL.
[28]   ibid 762.

or experience to 'decide the answer to an administrative problem where the scales are evenly balanced'.[29]

(6) Proportionality: Direct and Indirect Recognition

There are, notwithstanding the *Brind* decision, domestic cases where the courts have either explicitly applied proportionality, or have reasoned in an analogous manner.[30]   **16.16**

(a) Proportionality and rights

The application of a test akin to proportionality is apparent in cases where the af-   **16.17**
fected interest is a fundamental right. While the House of Lords in *Brind* denied
that proportionality was an independent ground of review, a number of their
Lordships reasoned in an analogous manner. Lord Templeman[31] held that the
court was not restricted in such cases to asking whether the governmental action
was perverse or irrational. The judge must rather inquire whether a reasonable
minister could reasonably conclude that the interference with the right in question was justifiable. Any such interference must be necessary and proportionate to
the damage that the restriction was designed to prevent. While Lord Bridge denied that proportionality could advance the applicant's claim, he none the less
made it clear that the real inquiry was whether the reasonable minister could reasonably reach the conclusion being challenged. In answering this inquiry the
court was entitled to start from the premise that any restriction of the right to freedom of expression must be justified, and that nothing less than an important competing public interest would suffice in this respect.

The same approach is evident in other cases. In *R v Secretary of State for the Home*   **16.18**
Department, ex p Leech[32] the court considered the validity of a rule allowing a prison
governor to read letters from prisoners, and stop those which were inordinately
long or objectionable. The court held that the more fundamental the right which
had been interfered with, the more difficult was it to imply any such rule-making
power in the primary legislation. The same approach is evident in *R v Ministry of*
Defence, ex p Smith,[33] where there was a challenge to the policy of prohibiting gay

---

[29] ibid 767.
[30] J Jowell and A Lester, 'Beyond Wednesbury: Substantive Principles of Administrative Law'
[1987] PL 368; J Jowell and A Lester, 'Proportionality: Neither Novel nor Dangerous' in J Jowell
and D Oliver (eds), *New Directions in Judicial Review* (London: Sweet & Maxwell, 1988) 51–73;
S Boyron, 'Proportionality in English Administrative Law: A Faulty Translation' (1992) 12 OJLS
237; P Craig, 'Unreasonableness and Proportionality in UK Law' in E Ellis (ed), *The Principle of
Proportionality in the Laws of Europe* (Oxford: Hart, 1999) 85–106; G de Burca, 'Proportionality
and Wednesbury Unreasonableness: The Influence of European Legal Concepts on U.K. Law' in M
Andenas (ed), *English Public Law and the Common Law of Europe* (London: Key Haven, 1998) ch 4.
[31] *R v Secretary of State for the Home Department, ex p Brind* [1991] 1 AC 696, 751, HL.
[32] [1994] QB 198, CA.
[33] [1996] QB 517, CA.

men and women from serving in the armed forces. Sir Thomas Bingham MR held that the more substantial the interference with human rights, the more the court would require by way of justification before it would accept that the decision was reasonable. In *R v Secretary of State for the Home Department, ex p McQuillan*,[34] the applicant challenged the legality of an exclusion order prohibiting him from entering Great Britain on the ground that he was or had been involved in acts of terrorism. He maintained that he was no longer a member of a terrorist organization and that his life was in danger if he continued to live in Northern Ireland. Sedley J recognized that freedom of movement, subject only to the general law, was a fundamental value of the common law. The court would scrutinize the minister's reasoning closely and 'draw the boundaries of rationality tightly around his judgment'.[35] There are other cases in the same vein.[36] It should nonetheless be recognized that the European Court of Human Rights did not think that this heightened scrutiny was sufficient to meet the necessity and proportionality tests under the European Convention of Human Rights (ECHR).[37]

16.19   The test for review in these cases is close to proportionality. This is justified in terms of principle. The recognition of certain interests as fundamental rights renders the application of proportionality necessary and natural. This is because the very denomination of an interest as a fundamental right means that any invasion should be kept to a minimum. There is a presumption that any inroad should interfere with the right as little as possible. It is natural therefore to ask whether the interference with the fundamental right was the least restrictive possible in the circumstances.

16.20   Proportionality is applied in this type of case in EC law, where the Community Treaties have granted rights. Thus the European Court of Justice (ECJ) has insisted that where a member state seeks to take advantage of an exception to one of the four freedoms concerning workers, goods, establishment and services, and capital, this will only be sanctioned where there is a genuine and serious threat to public policy, and then only if the measure is the least restrictive possible in the circumstances.[38] Proportionality is also used where individuals claim that Community regulations have infringed their fundamental rights.[39]

---

[34] [1995] 4 All ER 400.
[35] ibid 422.
[36] *Bugdaycay v Secretary of State for the Home Department* [1987] AC 514, 531, HL; *R v Secretary of State for the Home Department, ex p Moon* [1996] Imm AR 477; *R v Lord Saville of Newdigate, ex p B (No 2)* [2000] 1 WLR 1855 at [34]–[37], CA.
[37] *Smith and Grady v UK (No 1)* (1999) 29 EHRR 493 at [138].
[38] See, eg, Case 36/75 *Rutili v Minister of the Interior* [1975] ECR 1219; Case 30/77 *R v Bouchereau* [1977] ECR 1999; Case 33/74 *Van Binsbergen v Bestuur van de Bedrijsvereniging Metaalnijverheid* [1974] ECR 1299; Case C-390/99 *Canal Satelite Digital SL v Administracion General del Estado* [2003] 1 CMLR 27; Case 120/78 *Rewe-Zentrale AG v Bundesmonopolverwaltung fur Branntwein* [1979] ECR 649; Case C-217/99 *Commission v Belgium* [2000] ECR I-10251; Case C-473/98 *Kemikalieinspektionen v Toolex Alpha AB* [2000] ECR I-5681.
[39] Case 44/79 *Hauer v Land Rheinland-Pfalz* [1979] ECR 3727.

(b) Proportionality and penalties

There are a number of decisions where the courts have applied proportionality expressly or impliedly in the context of challenges to the penalty imposed by an administrative authority. This is exemplified by *R v Barnsley MBC, ex p Hook*,[40] where a stall-holder had his licence revoked for urinating in the street and using offensive language. Lord Denning MR struck down the decision in part because the penalty was excessive and out of proportion to the offence. There are a number of similar cases.[41]

16.21

Proportionality is well-suited to this type of case. The applicant will normally not be challenging the administrative rule itself, but simply the penalty imposed for the breach. The penalty that has been imposed is known, as is the offence, and the interest affected by the penalty. This interest may be personal liberty in the case of imprisonment, or it may be loss of livelihood as in *Hook*. It *is* a recognized principle of justice that penalties should not be excessive, as acknowledged in the Bill of Rights 1689. A court is unlikely to intervene unless the disproportionality is reasonably evident.[42]

16.22

Proportionality has often been applied in EC law in penalty cases.[43] *R v Intervention Board, ex p Man (Sugar) Ltd* provides a good example.[44] The applicant was required to give a security deposit to the Board when seeking a licence to export sugar outside the Community. The applicant was four hours late in completing the relevant paperwork. The Board, acting pursuant to a Community regulation, declared the entire deposit of £1,670,370 to be forfeit. The ECJ held that the automatic forfeiture of the entire deposit in the event of any failure to fulfil the time requirement was too drastic.[45]

16.23

(c) Proportionality and the exercise of administrative discretion

Proportionality has not yet become a general head of judicial review, such as to be applied in cases where there are no fundamental rights, and no excessive penalties. The paradigm of this type of case is where the public body decides to exercise its discretion in a particular manner, this necessitates the balancing of various interests, and a person affected argues that the balancing was disproportionate.

16.24

---

[40] [1976] 1 WLR 1052, 1057.

[41] *R v Highbury Magistrates' Court, ex p Uchendu* (1994) 158 JP 409; *Bolton v Law Society* [1994] 1 WLR 512; *R v Admiralty Board of the Defence Council, ex p Coupland* [1996] COD 147; *B v Secretary of State for the Home Department* [2000] HRLR 439, CA; *South Buckinghamshire DC v Porter* [2003] UKHL 26, [2003] 2 WLR 1547.

[42] *Commissioners of Customs and Excise v P & O Steam Navigation Co* [1993] COD 164.

[43] J Schwarze, *European Administrative Law* (London: Sweet & Maxwell, 1992) 729–746.

[44] Case 181/84 [1985] ECR 2889.

[45] See also, eg, Case 114/76 *Bela-Muhle Josef Bergman v Grows-Farm* [1977] ECR 1211; Case 240/78 *Atlanta Amsterdam BV v Produktschap voor Vee en Vlees* [1979] ECR 2137; Case 122/78 *Buitoni SA v Fonds d'Orientation et de Regularisation des Marches Agricoles* [1979] ECR 677; Case C-365/99 *Portugal v Commission* [2001] ECR I-5645.

16.25 In *R (on the application of Holding & Barnes plc) v Secretary of State for the Environment, Transport and the Regions,* Lord Slynn did however state that proportionality should be recognized as a general head of review within domestic law.[46]

> I consider that even without reference to the Human Rights Act the time has come to recognise that this principle [of proportionality] is part of English administrative law, not only when judges are dealing with Community acts but also when they are dealing with acts subject to domestic law. Trying to keep the *Wednesbury* principle and proportionality in separate compartments seems to me to be unnecessary and confusing. Reference to the Human Rights Act however makes it necessary that the court should ask whether what is done is compatible with Convention rights. That will often require that the question should be asked whether the principle of proportionality has been satisfied.

16.26 Concerns have been expressed about the application of proportionality to cases involving the exercise of administrative discretion. This is in part because many administrative decisions involve balancing, which is the essence of political determinations and many administrative choices. It cannot therefore be right for the judiciary to overturn a decision merely because the court would have balanced the conflicting interests differently. It should however be recognized that proportionality can be applied more or less intensively. Where the administration possesses a broad discretion proportionality can be applied less intensively.

16.27 This can be exemplified by the EC jurisprudence on proportionality. In *R v Minister of Agriculture, Fisheries and Food, ex p Fedesa,*[47] the applicants challenged the legality of a Council directive prohibiting the use of certain substances that had a hormonal action in livestock farming. The ECJ stressed that the Community institutions must pursue their policy by the least onerous means, and that the disadvantages must not be disproportionate to the aims of the measure. It then continued as follows.[48]

> However, with regard to judicial review of compliance with those conditions it must be stated that in matters concerning the common agricultural policy the Community legislature has a discretionary power which corresponds to the political responsibilities given to it by Articles 40 and 43[49] of the Treaty. Consequently, the legality of a measure adopted in that sphere can be affected only if the measure is manifestly inappropriate having regard to the objective which the competent institution is seeking to pursue.

16.28 There are nonetheless other areas where the ECJ is willing to intervene with a more searching form of inquiry. This is especially so where the area is one in which

---

[46] [2001] UKHL 23; [2001] 2 WLR 1389 at [51].
[47] Case C-331/88 [1990] ECR I-4023.
[48] ibid 4063; Case 265/87 *Schrader v Hauptzollamt Gronau* [1989] ECR 2237.
[49] Now Arts 34–37.

the administrative authorities possess a narrower discretionary power, or one which is more clearly circumscribed.

(7) Proportionality in Domestic Law: The Human Rights Act 1998

The authoritative interpretation of proportionality under the Human Rights **16.29** Act 1998 (HRA) is to be found in Lord Steyn's judgment in *Daly*.[50] His Lordship held that there was a material difference between a rationality test cast in terms of heightened scrutiny, and a proportionality test. He accepted that many cases would be decided the same way under either test, but acknowledged that the intensity of review would be greater under proportionality. Proportionality could require the reviewing court to assess the balance struck by the decision-maker, not merely whether it was within the range of reasonable decisions. A proportionality test could also oblige the court to pay attention to the relative weight accorded to relevant interests, in a manner not generally done under the traditional approach to review. It had to be shown that the limitation of the right was necessary in a democratic society, to meet a pressing social need, and was proportionate to the legitimate aim being pursued. Lord Steyn cast the test for review under the HRA 1998 in these terms, in part because the European Court of Human Rights had decided that a rationality test with heightened scrutiny was not sufficient to meet the necessity and proportionality tests under the ECHR.[51]

(8) Proportionality: Cases with a Community Law Component

Proportionality is a general principle of EC law, and therefore our courts are **16.30** obliged to apply it in cases with a Community law dimension.[52] These general principles have been developed by the ECJ and draw their inspiration from the laws of the member states. They can be relied upon in actions to contest the legality of Community measures, or national measures designed to implement Community law. It is clear that national courts are bound to apply EC law

---

[50] *R (on the application of Daly) v Secretary of State for the Home Department* [2001] UKHL 26, [2001] 2 AC 532, 547. See also, *Sudesh Madan v General Medical Council* [2001] EWHC Admin 577, [2001] ACD 3; *Samaroo v Secretary of State for the Home Department* [2001] EWCA Civ 1139, [2001] UKHRR 1150 at [29]–[35]; *R (on the application of L (a child)) v Manchester City Council* [2001] EWHC Admin 707, [2002] 1 FLR 43 at [21]; *Southampton Port Health Authority v Seahawk Marine Foods Ltd* [2002] EWCA Civ 54, [2002] ACD 35 at [12]; *R (on the application of Louis Farrakhan) v Secretary of State for the Home Department* [2002] EWCA Civ 606, [2002] QB 1391 at [65].

[51] *Smith and Grady v UK (No 1)* (1999) 29 EHRR 493 at [138].

[52] P Craig and G de Burca, *EU Law, Text, Cases and Materials* (3rd edn, Oxford: OUP, 2002) chs 8 and 9; G de Burca, 'The Principle of Proportionality and its Application in EC Law' (1993) 13 YBEL 105; T Tridimas, *The General Principles of EC Law* (Oxford: OUP, 1999) chs 3–4.

principles, and they have applied proportionality in cases which have a Community law element.[53]

16.31   This is exemplified by *R v Chief Constable of Sussex, ex p International Trader's Ferry Ltd*.[54] The applicants were exporters of live animals across the Channel. There were serious protests against such exports at the docks. The Chief Constable of Sussex deployed significant manpower to control the protests, but then decided that, because of his limited resources, he could only provide the requisite police cover for the exporters on two days a week. ITF argued that this decision was irrational under domestic law and that it was contrary to the EC Treaty. The domestic law argument failed: it was for the Chief Constable to decide how to use his limited resources, and that decision was not *Wednesbury* unreasonable. The EC claim was that the Chief Constable's decision constituted an export ban, which was prohibited by Article 29. The House of Lords accepted that if there had been a breach of Article 29, proportionality would be relevant in deciding on the application of Article 30. This latter article allows a defence for limitations placed on the free movement of goods for reasons of, inter alia, public security or public health, provided that the limitation is not disproportionate. The Chief Constable's decision was held to be a proportionate response. A further example is to be found in *R v International Stock Exchange of the UK and the Republic of Ireland Ltd, ex p Else*.[55] The decision of the Stock Exchange to delist the shares of a company pursuant to powers contained in a Community directive was challenged on the grounds of proportionality. The court accepted that proportionality was the appropriate standard of review, but found against the applicant. The relevant committee of the Stock Exchange had considered less drastic means of controlling the company short of delisting, and the court saw no reason to conclude that its findings were disproportionate.[56]

(9) Wednesbury *Unreasonableness and Proportionality*

16.32   It remains to be seen whether the *Wednesbury* test continues to exist together with proportionality, or whether the latter takes over as a general, independent head of review. It may be that the *Wednesbury* test will survive and continue to be used in

---

[53] See, eg, *R v Minister of Agriculture, Fisheries and Food, ex p Bell Lines* [1984] 2 CMLR 502; *R v Ministry of Agriculture, Fisheries and Food, ex p Roberts* [1990] 1 CMLR 555; *R v Secretary of State for the Home Department, ex p Adams* [1995] All ER (EC) 177; *R v Ministry of Agriculture, Fisheries and Food, ex p First City Trading* [1997] 1 CMLR 250.

[54] [1999] 2 AC 418, HL.

[55] [1993] QB 534, CA.

[56] See also, *B v Secretary of State for the Home Department* [2000] HRLR 439, CA; *R (on the application of Hoverspeed Ltd) v Customs and Excise Commissioners* [2002] EWHC 1630, [2002] 3 WLR 1219; *R (on the application of Castille Ltd) v Secretary of State for Trade and Industry* [2002] EWHC 16, [2002] ACD 52; *Gough v Chief Constable of Derbyshire* [2002] EWCA Civ 351, [2002] QB 1213.

cases where there is no link with EC law, and where there is no claim under the HRA. *Wednesbury* may however cease to operate as an independent test in its own right. It will be increasingly difficult, or impractical, for courts to apply different tests to different allegations made in an application for judicial review. It will be common for cases to feature claims under the HRA, and independent assertions of ultra vires conduct. The attractions of applying a single test, albeit one which can be applied with varying degrees of intensity, may prove difficult to resist over time. This is particularly so given that the courts will become more accustomed to applying proportionality through the HRA, and EC law. It is moreover clear that proportionality can be applied with varying degrees of intensity. The constitutional concerns about the limits of the judicial role that underpinned *Wednesbury* could, therefore, be perfectly well accommodated within a proportionality inquiry.

There are a number of advantages in having proportionality as a general standard **16.33** of review. It would, other things being equal, be advantageous for the *same test* to be used to deal with claims arising under EC law, the HRA, and other non-HRA domestic law challenges. The proportionality test provides a *structured form of inquiry*. The three-part proportionality inquiry focuses the attention of both the agency being reviewed, and the court undertaking the review. Proportionality facilitates a *reasoned inquiry* of a kind that is often lacking under the traditional *Wednesbury* approach. The experience with proportionality in EC law shows that the concept can be applied with varying degrees of intensity so as to accommodate the different types of decision subject to judicial review. It should nonetheless be recognized that there might well be cases that are unsuited to a proportionality analysis.[57] This is not, however, an argument for rejecting proportionality as a general head of review, but for ensuring that its application is subject to the same threshold principles which apply generally within administrative law. The reach of proportionality must be limited by justiciability.[58]

B. Substantive Legitimate Expectations

(1) The Nature of the Problem

The phrase procedural legitimate expectation denotes the existence of a proce- **16.34** dural right that the applicant claims to possess as the result of behaviour by the public body which generated the expectation. The phrase substantive legitimate

---

[57] Lord Hoffmann, 'The Influence of the European Principle of Proportionality upon English Law', in E Ellis (ed), *The Principle of Proportionality in the Laws of Europe* (Oxford: Hart, 1999) 107–116.

[58] W Van Gerven, 'The Effect of Proportionality on the Actions of Member States of the EC: National Viewpoints from Continental Europe', in Ellis (n 57 above) 37–64.

expectation refers to the situation in which the applicant seeks a particular benefit or commodity, such as a welfare benefit, or a licence.[59] The claim to such a benefit will be founded upon governmental action that is said to justify the existence of the relevant expectation.

16.35   The problem of substantive legitimate expectations is closely connected to legal certainty.[60] The most obvious application of legal certainty is in the context of rules or decisions that have an *actual retroactive effect.* Following Schwarze,[61] this covers the situation where a rule is introduced and applied to events that have already been concluded. Retroactivity of this nature may occur either where the date of entry into force precedes the date of publication; or where the regulation applies to circumstances which have actually been concluded before the entry into force of the measure. A basic tenet of the rule of law is that people ought to be able to plan their lives, secure in the knowledge of the legal consequences of their actions.[62] This fundamental aspect of the rule of law is violated by the application of measures that were not in force at the time that the actual events took place. There are also problems caused by cases of *apparent retroactivity.* A person may have planned his action on the basis of one policy choice made by the administration, and seeks redress when the chosen policy alters, even though this alteration is only prospective and not retrospective. The problem of apparent retroactivity can arise in relation to measures, whether individual or general, which change previous measures or representations with effect for events that have already occurred, but which have not yet been wholly concluded, or with effect for some transaction which is in the process of completion. The category of apparent retroactivity is more problematic because the administration must obviously have the power to alter its policy for the future, even though this may have implications for the conduct of private parties planned on the basis of the pre-existing legal regime.

16.36   There can be a tension between the principle of legal certainty and the principle of legality. It is important to understand that the principle of legality has two different meanings in this context.

---

[59]   C Forsyth, 'The Provenance and Protection of Legitimate Expectations' [1988] CLJ 238; P Elias, 'Legitimate Expectation and Judicial Review' in J Jowell and D Oliver (eds), *New Directions in Judicial Review* (London: Stevens, 1988) 37–50; P Craig, 'Legitimate Expectations: A Conceptual Analysis' (1992) 108 LQR 79; R Singh, 'Making Legitimate Use of Legitimate Expectations' (1994) 144 NLJ 1215; P Craig, 'Substantive Legitimate Expectations in Domestic and Community Law' [1996] CLJ 289; P Craig, 'Substantive Legitimate Expectations and the Principles of Judicial Review' in Andenas (n 30 above) ch 3; Y Dotan, 'Why Administrators should be Bound by their Policies' (1997) 17 OJLS 23; P Craig and S Schonberg, 'Substantive Legitimate Expectations after *Coughlan*' [2000] PL 684; S Schonberg, *Legitimate Expectations in Administrative Law* (Oxford: OUP, 2000).

[60]   Schwarze (n 43 above) ch 6.

[61]   ibid 1120.

[62]   J Raz, *The Authority of Law, Essays on Law and Morality* (Oxford: OUP, 1979) ch 11.

First, a public body may have made a representation that was within its power, but then seeks to depart from it. Or it may have published policy criteria for dealing with a particular issue, which criteria were intra vires, but it might now wish to adopt new tests for dealing with the same topic, these new criteria also being lawful. The individual may seek to rely on the initial representation or original statement of policy. A traditional objection to the individual being able to do so is that this would be a fetter on the discretion of the public body, which should be able to develop policy in the manner it believes to be best in the public interest. In this type of case the principle of legality is apparent in the doctrine that such a fetter on discretion would itself be ultra vires.

16.37

Secondly, the representation itself may have been outside the power of the public body or the officer who made it. The principle of legality manifests itself in the simple form that the representation was ultra vires and therefore should not bind the public body.

16.38

(2) The Types of Case

Problems of legal certainty and legitimate expectations can arise in a variety of circumstances. These may be characterized in the following manner.

16.39

- A general norm or policy choice, which an individual has relied on, has been replaced by a different policy choice.
- A general norm or policy choice has been departed from in the circumstances of a particular case. These cases also raise issues concerning consistency of treatment and equality.
- There has been an individual representation relied on by a person, which the administration seeks to resile from in the light of a shift in general policy.
- There has been an individualized representation that has been relied on. The administrative body then changes its mind and makes an individualized decision that is inconsistent with the original representation.

(3) Intra Vires Representations: The Policy Arguments

In *R v Ministry of Agriculture, Fisheries and Food, ex p Hamble (Offshore) Fisheries Ltd*,[63] Sedley J put the case *for* the recognition of substantive legitimate expectations in terms of *fairness in public administration*. The essence of the argument is contained in the following extract.

16.40

> [T]he real question is one of fairness in public administration. It is difficult to see why it is any less unfair to frustrate a legitimate expectation that something will or will not be done by the decision-maker than it is to frustrate a legitimate expectation that the applicant will be listened to before the decision-maker decides whether

---

[63] [1995] 2 All ER 714, 724.

to take a particular step. Such a doctrine does not risk fettering a public body in the discharge of public duties because no individual can legitimately expect the discharge of public duties to stand still or be distorted because of that individual's peculiar position.

16.41 This reasoning can be reinforced by considering the connection between *fairness in public administration, legality, legal certainty* and *legitimate expectations*. We are faced with situations in which a public body has made a lawful policy choice at one particular moment in time, and then seeks to change its mind and to adopt a second policy choice, which is also lawful. An individual has relied on the earlier policy and seeks the substantive benefit that would be forthcoming if this still represented the public body's chosen policy option. It is clear that a public body should not be able to fetter its discretion. It is, however, equally clear that legal certainty is of relevance in this type of situation. There will be some cases in which the considerations of legal certainty are felt to be sufficiently strong to enable the applicant to claim some substantive benefit from policy choice one, even if the public body has moved to policy choice two. This argument can be reinforced by *rule of law considerations*. The concept of legal certainty, which underlies much of continental and EC thinking in this area,[64] has self-evident connections with mainstream thinking about the formal conception of the rule of law, with its concern for the ability to plan one's life.

16.42 The central argument put *against* a doctrine of substantive legitimate expectations is that the liberty to make policy changes is inherent in government,[65] and therefore that existing policy should not be ossified or unduly fettered. It should however be recognized that a doctrine of substantive legitimate expectations does not lead to ministerial policy becoming ossified or fettered. If a minister wished to abolish home leave from prison,[66] or change it in any way, that choice remains open. Substantive legitimate expectation claims are of relevance to the time at which the new policy choice takes effect. This does not entail the courts expressing any preference as to a particular regime on home leave. The applicants in such cases are merely asking that where a new policy has implications for those who have relied upon a prior rule, that this should be of significance in determining the class of people affected by the shift in policy. Moreover, the recognition of a doctrine of substantive legitimate expectations still requires an applicant to prove the existence of the requisite expectation on the facts of the case. The mere fact that there has been some change of policy does not mean that those who operated under the old policy would be able to prove the existence of such an expectation. Even if the applicant is able to prove the existence of the substantive legitimate expectation, this does not mean that he wins. It will still be open to the public body to argue that there were sufficient reasons to depart from the expectation.

---

[64] Schwarze (n 43 above) ch 6.
[65] *Hughes v Department of Health and Social Security* [1985] 1 AC 776, 778, HL.
[66] *R v Secretary of State for the Home Department, ex p Hargreaves* [1997] 1 WLR 906, CA.

(4) Intra Vires Representations: The Case Law Prior to Coughlan[67]

There was, until recently, uncertainty as to whether a doctrine of substantive le-   **16.43**
gitimate expectations was part of UK law. In *Hamble Fisheries*,[68] Sedley J argued
strongly in favour of such a doctrine in a case where there had been a change of
policy in relation to the transfer of fishing licences between vessels. Moreover, in
R v Inland Revenue Commissioners, ex p Unilever Plc,[69] the Court of Appeal held
that the Inland Revenue could not without prior warning discontinue a practice,
applied consistently for about 25 years, of accepting annual tax refund claims after
the expiry of a statutory time limit. There was, however, another line of authority,
which cast doubt on the existence of substantive legitimate expectations in relation to changes of policy. In *R v Secretary of State for the Home Department, ex p
Hargreaves*,[70] the Home Secretary had changed policy on prisoners' home leave
with immediate effect in the light of concerns over crimes committed by prisoners on leave. The court held that it would only interfere if the administration's decision to apply a new policy was irrational, perverse, or *Wednesbury* unreasonable.

There was nonetheless authority for a concept of substantive legitimate expecta-   **16.44**
tions in cases where a general policy or practice had been departed from in the circumstances of a particular case. In *R v Secretary of State for the Home Department,
ex p Khan (Asif Mahmood)*,[71] the applicant alleged that the Home Office had departed from a policy, communicated to him in writing, concerning approval of
adoption of family members from abroad. Parker LJ held that a public authority
could only go back on a legitimate expectation generated by its own policy after
granting a hearing, and then only if the overriding public interest demanded it.[72]

There was also authority for a concept of substantive legitimate expectations in   **16.45**
cases where a public body made an individual representation, which was relied on
by a person, and the body subsequently sought to resile from the representation.
In *R v Inland Revenue Commissioners, ex p Preston*,[73] the applicant was assured by
the Revenue in 1978 that it would not raise further inquiries on certain tax affairs

---

[67] *R v North and East Devon Health Authority, ex p Coughlan* [2001] QB 213, CA.
[68] *R v Ministry of Agriculture, Fisheries and Food, ex p Hamble (Offshore) Fisheries Ltd* [1995] 2 All ER 714. See also, *R v Gaming Board of Great Britain, ex p Kingsley (No 2)* [1996] COD 241.
[69] [1996] STC 681, CA.
[70] [1997] 1 WLR 906, CA; *R v Secretary of State for Transport, ex p Richmond upon Thames LBC (No 1)* [1994] 1 WLR 74; *R v Secretary of State for Health, ex p US Tobacco International Inc* [1992] QB 353, 368–369.
[71] [1984] 1 WLR 1337, 1344. See also, *HTV v Price Commission* [1976] ICR 170, 185, CA; *Laker Airways v Department of Trade* [1977] QB 643, 707, CA; *R v Secretary of State for the Home Department, ex p Ruddock* [1987] 1 WLR 1482, 1487.
[72] [1984] 1 WLR 1337, 1344.
[73] [1985] AC 835, HL. See also, *R v Inland Revenue Commissioners, ex p MFK Underwriting Agencies Ltd* [1990] 1 WLR 1545; *Matrix Securities Ltd v Inland Revenue Commissioners* [1994] 1 WLR 334, HL.

if he agreed to forgo interest relief which he had claimed and to pay certain capital gains tax. The House of Lords held that the Revenue could not bind itself not to perform its statutory duties. It was therefore in principle entitled to go back on its assurance when it received new information about the applicant's dealings. A court could however hold the Revenue to its assurance where the unfairness to the applicant caused by exercising the statutory duty would amount to an abuse of power.

(5) Intra Vires Representations: The Present Law

(a) *Coughlan*

16.46   The law on substantive legitimate expectations must now be seen in the light of *R v North and East Devon Health Authority, ex p Coughlan*.[74] Ms Coughlan had been very seriously injured in a traffic accident in 1971, and was cared for in Newcourt Hospital. The hospital was considered to be unsuited for modern care, and therefore Ms Coughlan and other patients were moved to Mardon House in 1993. The patients were persuaded to move by representations made on behalf of the Health Authority that Mardon House would be more appropriate for their needs. The patients relied on an express assurance or promise that they could live there 'for as long as they chose'. In October 1998 the Health Authority decided to close Mardon House, and to move the patients to other facilities. A consultation paper issued in August 1998 preceded this decision, and it recognized the force of the promise made to the residents in 1993. The consultation paper was placed before the Health Authority when it made its decision in October 1998. The Health Authority recognized that it had a number of options. It could continue to support Mardon House; it could, in breach of the original promise, assist residents to move elsewhere; or it could move other NHS services into Mardon House. In October 1998 the Health Authority decided to close the facility and to move the residents elsewhere. The applicant challenged this as being in breach of the promise that she would have a home for life. The Court of Appeal distinguished between three situations.

16.47   In the first, the court might decide that the public authority was only required to bear in mind its previous policy or other representation, giving it the weight it thought fit, but no more, before deciding to change course. In such cases the court was confined to reviewing the decision on *Wednesbury* grounds.[75]

---

[74] [2001] QB 213, CA. See also, *R v Merton, Sutton and Wandsworth Health Authority, ex p P* [2001] ACD 9; *R (on the application of Theophilus) v Lewisham LBC* [2002] EWHC 1371, [2002] 3 All ER 851; *R (on the application of B) v Camden LBC* [2001] EWHC Admin 271, (2001) 4 CCLR 246.

[75] *R v North and East Devon Health Authority, ex p Coughlan* [2001] QB 213, CA at [57]. *R v Secretary of State for the Home Department, ex p Hargreaves* [1997] 1 WLR 906, CA was regarded as coming in this category.

The second situation was where the court decided that there was a legitimate ex- **16.48**
pectation of being consulted before a decision was taken. In such cases the court
would require there to be an opportunity for consultation, unless there was an
overriding reason to resile from the undertaking. The court would judge for itself
the adequacy of the reason advanced for the change of policy, taking into account
what fairness required.[76] The court would exercise 'full review' in such cases: it
would decide whether what happened was fair.[77]

The third situation was where the court considered that a lawful promise had in- **16.49**
duced a substantive legitimate expectation. In this type of case the court would decide whether the frustration of the expectation was so unfair that to take a new and
different course of action would amount to an abuse of power. When the legitimacy of the expectation had been established, the court would have the task of
'weighing the requirements of fairness against any overriding interest relied upon
for the change of policy'.[78] Most cases within this category were likely to be those
where the expectation was confined to one person, or a few people.[79] The present
case was held to come within this third category. This was because of the importance of what was promised to the applicant; because the promise was limited to
a few individuals; and because the consequences to the Health Authority of having to honour its promise were only financial.[80]

The divide between the three types of case in *Coughlan* should, nonetheless, be **16.50**
treated with some caution. It is clear that the second category, which is concerned
primarily with procedural legitimate expectations, is distinct from the other two.
The dividing between the first and third categories cannot however be regarded as
'hermetically sealed'.[81]

The House of Lords has acknowledged the concept of substantive legitimate ex- **16.51**
pectations in subsequent cases.[82]

---

[76] ibid at [57].

[77] ibid at [62]. *A-G for Hong Kong v Ng Yuen Shiu* [1983] 2 AC 629, PC was treated as coming in this category.

[78] *R v North and East Devon Health Authority, ex p Coughlan* [2001] QB 213, CA at [57].

[79] ibid at [59]. *R v Inland Revenue Commissioners, ex p Preston* [1985] AC 835, HL, *HTV v Price Commission* [1976] ICR 170, CA, *R v Inland Revenue Commissioners, ex p MFK Underwriting Agencies Ltd* [1990] 1 WLR 1545 and *R v Inland Revenue Commissioners, ex p Unilever Plc* [1996] STC 681, CA were treated as authority for cases of this kind.

[80] ibid at [60].

[81] *R v Secretary of State for Education and Employment, ex p Begbie* [2000] 1 WLR 1115, 1130, 1133–1134, CA.

[82] *R v Ministry of Defence, ex p Walker* [2000] 1 WLR 806, HL; *R (on the application of Zeqiri) v Secretary of State for the Home Department* [2002] UKHL 3, [2002] Imm AR 296 at [44] *per* Lord Hoffmann.

(b) The determination of whether an expectation is reasonable and legitimate

16.52   The court will consider a number of factors when determining whether an expectation was reasonable and legitimate.

- The most important factor is the nature of the representation itself. A clear and unambiguous promise, undertaking or representation provides the strongest foundation for a claim.[83] The representation may arise from words or conduct or from a combination of the two.[84] There is, however, authority that consistent conduct over a long period of time may give rise to an expectation, even if it was not a clear and unambiguous representation.[85]
- A representation may be based on a variety of sources, including an individual statement, a circular, a report or an agreement. It will normally be easier to establish a reasonable expectation the more specific was the representation in question.[86]
- An expectation will not be regarded as reasonable or legitimate if the applicant could have foreseen that the subject matter of the representation was likely to alter, or that it would not be respected by the relevant agency. Similarly if the person claiming the benefit knew that the representor did not intend his statements, etc, to create an expectation then this will tell against the expectation being reasonable or legitimate.[87]
- If an individual knew or ought to have known that an assurance could only be obtained in a particular way, and a purported assurance was obtained in a different way, it will not be an abuse of power to go back on the assurance.[88]
- Detrimental reliance will normally be required in order for the claimant to show that it would be unlawful to go back on a representation.[89] This is in accord with policy, since if the individual has suffered no hardship there is no reason based on

---

[83] *R v Inland Revenue Commissioners, ex p MFK Underwriting Agencies Ltd* [1990] 1 WLR 1545; *R v Independent Television Commission, ex p Flextech plc* [1999] EMLR 880. For cases where the representation was not deemed to be clear or precise enough, see, eg, *R (on the application of Godfrey) v Conwy County BC* [2001] EWHC Admin 640; *R (on the application of L) v Barking and Dagenham LBC* [2001] EWCA Civ 533, [2001] 2 FLR 763, CA; *R (on the application of Nemeth) v West Berkshire DC,* (CO/3551/2000, 8 December 2000); *R (on the application of C) v Brent, Kensington and Chelsea and Westminster Mental NHS Trust* [2002] EWHC 181, [2002] Lloyd's Rep Med 321.
[84] *R v Inland Revenue Commissioners, ex p MFK Underwriting Agencies Ltd* [1990] 1 WLR 1545; *R v Gaming Board of Great Britain, ex p Kingsley (No 2)* [1996] COD 241.
[85] *R v Inland Revenue Commissioners, ex p Unilever Plc* [1996] STC 681, CA.
[86] *R v Ministry of Agriculture, Fisheries and Food, ex p Hamble (Offshore) Fisheries Ltd* [1995] 2 All ER 714.
[87] *R v Gaming Board of Great Britain, ex p Kingsley (No 2)* [1996] COD 241.
[88] *Matrix Securities Ltd v Inland Revenue Commissioners* [1994] 1 WLR 334, HL.
[89] *R v Secretary of State for the Environment, ex p NALGO* [1992] COD 282; *R v Jockey Club, ex p RAM Racecourses* [1993] 2 All ER 225; *Matrix Securities Ltd v Inland Revenue Commissioners* [1994] 1 WLR 334, HL; *R v Ministry of Defence, ex p Walker* [2000] 1 WLR 806, HL; *R v Secretary of State for Education and Employment, ex p Begbie* [2000] 1 WLR 1115, 1123, 1131, 1133, CA; *R (on the application of Bibi) v Newham LBC* [2001] EWCA Civ 607, [2002] 1 WLR 237 at [29].

legal certainty to hold the agency to its representation. It should not, however, be necessary to show any monetary loss, or anything equivalent thereto. There may be moral detriment flowing from disappointment when an expectation is not honoured.[90] While in a strong case there will be both reliance and detriment, there may also be cases where there is reliance, without measurable detriment. It may still be unfair to thwart a legitimate expectation in such circumstances.[91]

- Where an agency seeks to depart from an established policy in relation to a particular person detrimental reliance should not be required. Consistency of treatment and equality are at stake in such cases, and these values should be protected irrespective of whether there has been any reliance as such.[92]
- An expectation will not be regarded as reasonable or legitimate if the potential beneficiary has not placed 'all cards face up on the table'.[93] All relevant issues must therefore be disclosed.
- The courts will not readily infer a legitimate expectation where it would confer an unmerited or improper benefit, which offended against considerations of fairness and justice.[94]
- Even if the expectation is reasonable and legitimate there may be good reasons why the public body needs to act so as to defeat it.

(c) The standard of review applied when the administration seeks to defeat a legitimate expectation

The distinction between the types of case was regarded as important in *Coughlan*   **16.53** for the standard of review. In the first type of case the normal *Wednesbury* test would apply. In the second, the court would engage in 'full review', deciding for itself whether the departure from a procedural legitimate expectation was fair.

The standard of review in the third type of case is of particular interest. This will   **16.54** be a live issue where, as in *Coughlan*, the public body seeks to resile from the legitimate expectation on the ground that the public interest demands that this should be so. It was accepted in *Coughlan* that public bodies must be able to change policy, and that undertakings were therefore open to modification or abandonment.[95] It followed that the court's task in such cases was 'not to impede executive activity but to reconcile its continuing need to initiate or respond to change with

---

[90] *R (on the application of Bibi) v Newham LBC* [2001] EWCA Civ 607, [2002] 1 WLR 237 at [54]–[55].

[91] ibid at [31].

[92] ibid at [29]–[30].

[93] *R v Inland Revenue Commissioners, ex p MFK Underwriting Agencies Ltd* [1990] 1 WLR 1545, 1569; *Matrix Securities Ltd v Inland Revenue Commissioners* [1994] 1 WLR 334, HL.

[94] *R v Gaming Board of Great Britain, ex p Kingsley (No 2)* [1996] COD 241, 243; *Matrix Securities Ltd v Inland Revenue Commissioners* [1994] 1 WLR 334, HL.

[95] *R v North and East Devon Health Authority, ex p Coughlan* [2001] QB 213, CA at [64].

the legitimate interests or expectations of citizens or strangers who have relied, and have been justified in relying, on a current policy or an extant promise'.[96] This was all the more so given that there were two lawful exercises of power in this type of case: the promise and the policy change.[97] It was this consideration which led the court to distinguish between two standards of judicial review of discretion.

16.55 There was, on the one hand, bare or intrinsic irrationality, which allowed the court to intervene to quash a decision which defied comprehension in the sense articulated by Lord Greene[98] and Lord Diplock.[99] Such cases were rare. Rationality also embraced decisions made on the basis of flawed logic. The court in *Coughlan* rejected this criterion. Where there were, as here, two lawful exercises of power, a 'bare rationality test would constitute the public authority judge in its own cause, for a decision to prioritise a policy change over legitimate expectations will almost always be rational from where the authority stands, even if objectively it is arbitrary or unfair'.[100]

16.56 The reasons given in *Coughlan* for rejecting the *Wednesbury* test, in the original manner conceived of by Lord Greene MR, are convincing. The test does not strike the right balance between the needs of the administration, and fairness to the individual. It would require the individual to show that the agency's decision to act in a manner inconsistent with the legitimate expectation was so unreasonable that no reasonable agency would have done it. It would, as recognized in *Coughlan*, be almost impossible for the individual to succeed on this criterion.[101]

16.57 There was, on the other hand, intervention on the grounds of abuse of power. A power which had been abused had not been lawfully exercised.[102] The court's task was to ensure that the power to alter policy was not abused by unfairly frustrating individual legitimate expectations. Abuse of power could take many forms. To renege on a lawful promise made to a limited number of individuals without adequate justification was one such type of case. There was, said the Court of Appeal, no suggestion in *Preston*,[103] or other relevant cases,[104] that the final arbiter of a decision which frustrated a substantive legitimate expectation was, rationality apart, the decision-maker rather than the court.[105] Nor was there any suggestion that judicial review in such instances was confined to the

---

[96] *R v North and East Devon Health Authority, ex p Coughlan* (n 95 above) at [65].

[97] ibid at [66].

[98] *Associated Provincial Picture Houses Ltd v Wednesbury Corp* [1948] 1 KB 223, 228–230, CA.

[99] *Council of Civil Service Unions v Minister for the Civil Service* [1985] AC 374, 410–411, HL.

[100] *R v North and East Devon Health Authority, ex p Coughlan* [2001] QB 213, CA at [66].

[101] ibid at [66].

[102] ibid at [70].

[103] *R v Inland Revenue Commissioners, ex p Preston* [1985] AC 835, HL.

[104] *R v Devon CC, ex p Baker* [1995] 1 All ER 73, CA.

[105] *R v North and East Devon Health Authority, ex p Coughlan* [2001] QB 213, CA at [69], [74].

bare rationality of the decision.[106] The court would intervene where there had been an abuse of power, and this was a matter for the court to determine.[107] Policy and the reasons for change were for the public authority. The court's task 'is then limited to asking whether the application of the policy to an individual who has been led to expect something different is a just exercise of power'.[108] The applicant's substantive legitimate expectation could not be frustrated unless there was an overriding public interest, and whether this existed or not was a matter for the court.[109] The court found in favour of the applicant on the facts of the case.

Abuse of power may well properly be regarded as the *conceptual rationale* for judicial intervention to protect substantive legitimate expectations.[110] It encapsulates the conclusion that the applicant had some normatively justified expectation, since there would otherwise be no foundation for finding such an abuse. The term abuse of power can also capture the conclusion that the court has found the public body's argument for going back on the expectation to be unconvincing. It must however also be recognized that abuse of power does not, in itself, furnish a *standard of review* for deciding whether a public body can resile from a proven substantive expectation. Abuse of power can express the conclusion reached under any such standard, but does not constitute a standard of review itself.   **16.58**

There are two possible standards of review that could be employed: a modified *Wednesbury* test, and proportionality. These will be considered in turn.   **16.59**

The *Wednesbury* test could be applied more intensively in cases of this kind.[111] The courts have varied the intensity with which they have applied the test where fundamental rights are at stake.[112] Where a substantive legitimate expectation has been found, and the public body seeks to justify action which would defeat the expectation, the courts could therefore demand more by way of justification before finding that this was reasonable. This approach would be even more tenable if the general reading given to the reasonableness test by Lord Cooke were to be adopted,[113] and the courts were to overturn a decision if it was one which a reasonable authority would not have made. The application of this test would however require the courts to specify why a decision was not reasonable in this sense, and the more particular factors taken into account would be very like those considered in proportionality.   **16.60**

---

[106] ibid at [74], [77].
[107] ibid at [81].
[108] ibid at [82].
[109] ibid at [76].
[110] ibid; *R v Inland Revenue Commissioners, ex p Unilever Plc* [1996] STC 681, CA; *R (on the application of Zeqiri) v Secretary of State for the Home Department* [2002] UKHL 3, [2002] Imm AR 296.
[111] C Forsyth, '*Wednesbury* Protection of Substantive Legitimate Expectations' [1997] PL 375.
[112] See para 16.08 above.
[113] *R v Chief Constable of Sussex, ex p International Trader's Ferry Ltd* [1999] 2 AC 418, 452, HL.

16.61   The other option would be to use proportionality. If we are willing to counte-
nance such a principle of judicial review, either generally or in specific types of
case, then those under consideration have a strong claim to be dealt with pursuant
to this principle. It is clear that the strongest cases for the application of proportionality are those concerned with fundamental rights. Indeed it can be argued
that such a test is logically demanded by the recognition of a category of fundamental rights. Cases concerned with penalties are also well suited to the application of such a principle of review. This leaves a broad category of cases where there
are no fundamental rights and no penalties. If we are to apply proportionality to
this general category then substantive legitimate expectations cases are especially
deserving. A substantive legitimate expectation, while falling short of a right
stricto sensu, nonetheless carries a moral force or weight that should not be ignored when determining the appropriate standard of review. The three-part proportionality test provides a structured analysis, which facilitates review, and forces
the agency to give a reasoned justification for its course of action. The analysis employed in *Coughlan* to decide whether the public body could resile from the applicant's substantive expectation was, in fact, very close to a proportionality
inquiry.

16.62   The way in which the standard of review is applied may well depend on the nature
of the case. The courts will be more reluctant to interfere with general changes of
policy, than with cases where a representation is made to a discrete group.[114] This
variability can however be accommodated within a proportionality inquiry.

16.63   The courts have in some instances remitted the case back to the original decision-
maker, where a legitimate expectation has been found to exist. This is exemplified
by *R (on the application of Bibi) v Newham LBC*.[115] The applicants had been provided with accommodation for the homeless. The local authority promised that it
would provide them with security of tenure. It had made this promise because it
thought, wrongly, that it was under a duty to provide permanent accommodation. The local authority sought to renege on the promise, having become aware
that it did not have a duty to give permanent accommodation. Schiemann LJ held
that the promise had created a substantive legitimate expectation.[116] He held further that when an authority, without even considering that it was in breach of a
promise that gave rise to a legitimate expectation, acted at variance with the
promise, then the authority was abusing its power.[117] The court did not however

---

[114] *R v Secretary of State for Education and Employment, ex p Begbie* [2000] 1 WLR 1115,
1130–1131, CA.
[115] [2001] EWCA Civ 607; [2002] 1 WLR 237. See also, *R (on the application of Theophilus) v
Lewisham LBC* [2002] EWHC 1371, [2002] 3 All ER 851 at [27]–[29]; *R (on the application of B)
v Camden LBC* [2001] EWHC Admin 271, (2001) 4 CCLR 246 at [32].
[116] ibid at [46].
[117] ibid at [39], [49]–[51].

order the local authority to provide the secure accommodation. It remitted the case to the local authority and imposed a duty on it to consider the applicants' housing on the basis that they had a legitimate expectation that they would be given secure accommodation. The reason for this strategy was that while the applicants had a legitimate expectation, so too did other people on the council's accommodation list, and the overall stock of housing was limited. It might also be open to the local authority to help the applicants in some other way, if it felt unable to give them secure housing.[118] The court nonetheless made it clear that the assumption was that effect should be given to the legitimate expectation. If the local authority decided not to do so, it had to provide reasons, and it would be open to the applicants to test those reasons in court.[119]

(d) The case law: changes in policy

There is no doubt that cases that fall within this category are the most problematic. They should nonetheless be capable of generating a legitimate expectation. In terms of principle, public bodies must of course be able to change their policy. A substantive legitimate expectation does not however normally prevent any such policy change, but has an impact on the time at which it is to take effect. Moreover, if the courts were to say that the doctrine could never apply in this type of case, it would create difficult boundary problems between this category and the others. The line between a general policy and an individual representation may well be difficult in cases where, for example, there is some administrative practice or representation, which affects a group of people across time. In terms of authority, the fact situations in cases such as *Hamble Fisheries*,[120] *Hargreaves*,[121] and *Godfrey*[122] provide examples of situations in which a change of policy might give rise to a substantive legitimate expectation claim. This is so notwithstanding the fact that the claims failed in these cases. The individual may nonetheless properly argue that there was a legitimate expectation based on representations flowing from things said or done under the old policy, and that this was ignored in the transition from the old policy to the new. This argument would be even stronger in circumstances where there were no transitional or 'pipeline' provisions between the two policies. Whether the individual can show the legitimate expectation will of course depend on the facts, and it will be open to the public body to argue that there was an overriding public interest to defeat any such expectation.

16.64

---

[118] ibid at [58].

[119] ibid at [59].

[120] *R v Ministry of Agriculture, Fisheries and Food, ex p Hamble (Offshore) Fisheries Ltd* [1995] 2 All ER 714.

[121] *R v Secretary of State for the Home Department, ex p Hargreaves* [1997] 1 WLR 906, CA.

[122] *R (on the application of Godfrey) v Conwy County BC* [2001] EWHC Admin 640.

(e) The case law: departure from an existing policy

16.65   There are cases where the public authority seeks to depart from an existing policy in relation to a particular applicant. Such cases are less difficult than those where there is a general change of policy for the future. Considerations of equality as well as legitimate expectations will be relevant here. Even if the applicant is unable to prove a legitimate expectation, considerations of equality should, in and of themselves, suffice as the basis of the claim, unless the agency can show convincing reasons for departure from the policy in this instance.[123] The legal rules that should apply when an agency seeks to depart from an established policy are as follows.[124]

- The legal principle of consistency in the exercise of public law powers creates a presumption that the agency or minister will follow a declared policy. This presumption flows from the very purpose of such a policy, which is to secure consistency.
- If there is a departure from the policy then reasons must be given to justify this.
- The agency should, when considering a departure from an established policy, weigh the interests of those affected by the existing policy with the need to depart from it in the instant case.
- The courts will construe the meaning of such policies. Thus where the policy is framed in ordinary English, the court will ensure that it is not given an interpretation which is inconsistent with its plain and ordinary meaning. Similarly, where the decision is predicated on the existence of certain legal categories the court will hold the agency to these. Where the policy contains specialist terms, or jargon, the court respects evidence as to its meaning, but not so as to subvert the object of the policy.
- There has been a difference of opinion as the standard of review that should be applied to determine the legality of a departure from an established policy. In *R v Secretary of State for the Home Department, ex p Urmaza*,[125] Sedley J held that the courts were not restricted to a bare rationality test in this regard. In *R v Secretary of State for the Home Department, ex p Gangadeen*,[126] Hirst LJ held that review should be limited to traditional *Wednesbury* grounds. This ruling was however given prior to *Coughlan*.[127] The argument in *Coughlan* for more intensive review than bare rationality is especially apposite here, given that it is a departure from an existing policy that is in issue.

---

[123]   *R (on the application of Bibi) v Newham LBC* [2001] EWCA Civ 607, [2002] 1 WLR 237 at [29]–[30]; *R v Secretary of State for the Home Department, ex p Ruddock* [1987] 1 WLR 1482; Dotan (n 59 above).
[124]   *R v Secretary of State for the Home Department, ex p Urmaza* [1996] COD 479; *R v Secretary of State for the Home Department, ex p Gangadeen* [1998] 1 FLR 762, CA; *R v Secretary of State for the Environment, ex p West Oxfordshire DC* [1994] COD 134.
[125]   [1996] COD 479, 483–485.
[126]   [1998] 1 FLR 762.
[127]   *R v North and East Devon Health Authority, ex p Coughlan* [2001] QB 213, CA.

(f) The case law: going back on individualized representations

It is clear that the courts will, subject to certain conditions, protect an individual **16.66** where a public body seeks to resile from a representation. In *R v Inland Revenue Commissioners, ex p Preston*,[128] P made an agreement with the Revenue in 1978 to forgo interest relief which he had claimed and he also paid some capital gains tax. In return, the inspector said that he would not raise any further inquiries on certain tax affairs. In 1982, following the receipt of new information concerning the same transaction, the Revenue decided to apply particular provisions of the tax legislation. P sought judicial review of this decision. Lord Templeman, giving the judgment, stated that P would have no remedy for breach of the representation as such, because the Revenue could not bind themselves in 1978 not to perform their statutory duty in 1982.[129] Judicial review was, however, available:[130] a court could direct the Revenue to abstain from performing its statutory duties or exercising its powers where the unfairness to the applicant of doing so rendered such insistence an abuse of power.[131] Conduct by the Revenue that was equivalent to a breach of representation could, said Lord Templeman, be one such instance of abuse of power.[132] Although the judgment was framed in terms of abuse of power, the Revenue's action could only have been regarded in this way if its prior representation gave rise to some normative expectation that was worthy of protection.

Further authority is provided by *R v Inland Revenue Commissioners, ex p MFK* **16.67** *Underwriting Agencies Ltd*.[133] The applicants had approached the Inland Revenue as to whether certain investments would be taxed as capital or income. The initial response from the Revenue convinced the applicants that the investments would be taxed as capital, but the Revenue later resolved to tax the assets as income. Bingham LJ held that the applicants must fail if the representation was in breach of the Revenue's statutory duty. No such breach was present on the facts of the case, since the Revenue were merely acting in pursuance of their proper managerial discretion. In such circumstances the Revenue could not withdraw from its representation *if* this would cause substantial unfairness to the applicant, and *if* the conditions for relying upon any such representation were present. Those conditions were that: the applicant should give full details of the transaction on which the Revenue's ruling was being sought; the applicant should make it apparent that it was seeking a considered ruling which it intended to rely upon; and the ruling itself would have to be clear and unambiguous.[134] It is, moreover, clear that the

---

[128] [1985] AC 835, HL.
[129] ibid 862.
[130] ibid 862–863.
[131] ibid 864.
[132] ibid 866–867.
[133] [1990] 1 WLR 1545.
[134] ibid 1568–1569.

courts will insist strictly on full disclosure of the relevant material, more particularly where the purported assurance has been given in relation to, for example, a tax avoidance scheme which should never have been authorized in this manner.[135]

16.68   A public body that seeks to justify going back on a proven expectation must satisfy two conditions. It must give the person who has a substantive legitimate expectation the opportunity to present arguments as to why the expectation should not be defeated by the public body's subsequent change of view.[136] The higher standard of review, going beyond bare rationality, will then be applied in this type of case.[137]

(g) The case law: final determinations

16.69   The discussion in the previous section was concerned with cases where there has been a representation, which the individual seeks to rely on. This should be distinguished from the case where there has been a final determination, which cannot be altered because it is a dispositive decision in that case. This is exemplified by *Re 56 Denton Road, Twickenham, Middlesex*.[138] The plaintiff's house was damaged during the war and later demolished by the local authority. The preliminary determination by the War Damage Commission was that the property was a total loss. This was later altered, the Commission saying that the loss was non-total. The Commission then reverted to the categorization of total loss. Greater compensation would be paid where the loss was non-total. It was held that the second determination was final, and that where Parliament had imposed a duty of deciding any question the deciding of which affected the rights of subjects, such a decision, when made and communicated in terms which were not preliminary, was final and conclusive. It could not, in the absence of express statutory power or the consent of the person affected, be withdrawn.[139] The intra vires decision was binding as a valid decision, in and of itself.[140]

16.70   The scope of the decision in this case is not, however, clear. In *Rootkin v Kent CC*,[141] the plaintiff's daughter was given a place at a school, which the local authority believed to be over three miles from her home. It was thereby obliged to provide transport or to reimburse travelling expenses, and decided upon the latter. It later measured the distance once again and, having decided that it was less than three miles, withdrew the funding. The plaintiff relied, inter alia, on the

---

[135] *Matrix Securities Ltd v Inland Revenue Commissioners* [1994] 1 WLR 334, HL.
[136] *R (on the application of Machi) v Legal Services Commission* [2001] EWHC Admin 580; [2002] ACD 8.
[137] *R v North and East Devon Health Authority, ex p Coughlan* [2001] QB 213, CA.
[138] [1953] Ch 51. See also, *Livingstone v Westminster Corp* [1904] 2 KB 109, 120; *R v Dacorum BC, ex p Walsh* [1992] COD 125.
[139] ibid 56–57.
[140] ibid 57.
[141] [1981] 1 WLR 1186.

Denton Road case. The argument was rejected, the court saying that it had no application where the citizen was receiving only a discretionary benefit as opposed to a statutory right, since this would fetter the discretion of the public body.[142]

The principle in *Denton Road* is surely correct. When a public body makes what is a lawful final decision this should be binding upon it, even in the absence of detrimental reliance. A citizen should be entitled to assume that it will not be overturned by a second decision, even if the latter is equally lawful. The principle of legal certainty has a particularly strong application in these circumstances, and the ideal that there must be an end to litigation is equally apposite here as elsewhere. This is so even where a new policy is introduced shortly after the initial decision. That decision should remain unaffected. Where the initial decision is changed because of a mistake or misinterpretation of the facts then, if there has been detrimental reliance, compensation should be granted. Provided that the applicant has not misled the public body then the onus of ensuring that the facts are correctly applied should be on the public body. It should make no difference whether the initial decision was the determination of a statutory right or the exercise of a discretion. The line between the two may well be a fine one. Moreover, once discretion is definitively concretized in its application to a particular person the argument that that person should be able to rely upon it is equally strong as in the case of a decision about rights. This is supported by the decision in *MFK*.[143] The applicant failed on the facts, but the case clearly demonstrates that a discretionary determination will not necessarily be defeated by the argument that to sanction such a result would be a fetter on the general discretion of that body.[144] Any lawful decision will perforce limit the way in which discretion can be used by ruling out other options.

16.71

(h) The case law: estoppel by record

A decision may also be final because of the doctrine of estoppel by record or, as it is often known, estoppel per rem judicatem.[145] There are two species of this estoppel. One is known as cause of action estoppel. If the same cause of action has been litigated to a final judgment between the same parties, or their privies, litigating in the same capacity, no further action is possible, the principle being that there must be an end to litigation. The other form of estoppel by record is issue estoppel. A single cause of action may contain several distinct issues. Where there is a final judgment between the same parties, or their privies, litigating in

16.72

---

[142] ibid 1195–1197, 1200.

[143] [1990] 1 WLR 1545.

[144] See also, *R v Inland Revenue Commissioners, ex p Preston* [1985] AC 835, HL; *Gillingham BC v Medway (Chatham) Dock Co Ltd* [1993] QB 343.

[145] Colin Tapper, *Cross and Tapper on Evidence* (8th edn, London: Butterworths, 1995) 83–91.

the same capacity on the same issue, then that issue cannot be reopened in subsequent proceedings.[146]

16.73   The application of the res judicata doctrine in the public law context was reaffirmed in *Thrasyvoulou v Secretary of State for the Environment*.[147] It was held that in relation to adjudication, which was subject to a comprehensive self-contained statutory code, the presumption was that where the statute had created a specific jurisdiction for the determination of any issue which established the existence of a legal right, the principle of res judicata applied to give finality to that determination, unless an intention to exclude that principle could be inferred as a matter of construction from the statutory provisions.

16.74   Res judicata expresses the binding nature of a matter litigated to final judgment. In administrative law jurisdictional matters decided by a tribunal or other public body are not final in this sense. They will be determined by the reviewing court. This is exemplified by *R v Hutchings*.[148] A local Board of Health had applied to the justices under the Public Health Act 1875 to recover the expenses of repairing a street from a person whose property was on that street. The latter contended that it was a public highway repairable by the inhabitants at large. The justices upheld this contention. Some years later the Board of Health made an application against the same person, and on this occasion the justices did order payment of expenses. The plea that the matter was res judicata because of the earlier decision was rejected. It was held that, on construction, the justices had no power to decide whether the street was or was not a public highway. This issue was only incidentally cognizable by them. Their only jurisdiction was to determine whether a sum of money should be paid or not. Even where the subject matter is clearly within the jurisdiction of the tribunal, there may be a temporal limit to the conclusiveness of that tribunal's findings which limits the application of res judicata.[149]

16.75   Provided that the issue is within the subject matter and temporal jurisdiction of the public body, res judicata will prevent the same matter being litigated before the original tribunal over again. Whether the public body is performing administrative rather than judicial tasks is not relevant for the application of res judicata, nor is the existence of a lis inter partes.[150]

---

[146] See *R (on the application of Nahar) v Social Security Commissioners* [2002] EWCA Civ 859; [2002] ACD 105, for a recent, unsuccessful, attempt to plead issue estoppel against a public body.
[147] [1990] 2 AC 273, 289, HL.
[148] [1881] 6 QBD 300, 304–305; *R v Secretary of State for the Environment, ex p Hackney LBC* [1984] 1 WLR 592.
[149] *Society of Medical Officers of Health v Hope* [1960] AC 551, HL; *Caffoor v Commissioner of Income Tax* [1961] AC 584, HL.
[150] *Caffoor v Commissioner of Income Tax* [1961] AC 584, 597–599, HL.

(6) Ultra Vires Representations: The Present Law

The discussion thus far has been concerned with intra vires representations. It is now necessary to consider the law relating to ultra vires representations.[151] A representation will be ultra vires if it is outside the power of the public body, or the officer who made it. The law in this area is based on the jurisdictional principle, which has traditionally been taken to mean that representations made by an agent who lacks authority, or representations leading to decisions which are ultra vires the public body itself, cannot be binding.   **16.76**

(a) The policy behind the jurisdictional principle

There are three main rationales for the present rule.[152] First, it is argued that if estoppel were to be allowed to run against the government the donee of a statutory power could make an ultra vires representation and then be bound by it through the medium of estoppel, or legitimate expectations. This would lead to the collapse of the ultra vires doctrine with public officers being enabled to extend their powers at will. Secondly, there is the argument that estoppel or legitimate expectations cannot be applied to a public body so as to prevent it from exercising its statutory powers or duties. Thirdly, it is argued that to allow an ultra vires representation to bind a public body would be to prejudice third parties that might be affected, who would have no opportunity of putting forward their views. The cogency of these arguments can be questioned,[153] but the analysis that follows will be based on the assumption, firmly embedded in the existing law, that ultra vires representations cannot bind a public body.   **16.77**

(b) The jurisdictional principle

Two questions may arise when a public body makes a representation. The first is whether the agent acting for the public body had authority, actual or apparent, to make the representation in question. This is dependent upon the law of agency. The second is whether the decision resulting from the representation made by the public body or agent is intra vires or ultra vires. This is dependent upon the extent of the powers given to that body.   **16.78**

---

[151] G Treitel, 'Crown Proceedings: Some Recent Developments' [1957] PL 321, 335–339; G Ganz, 'Estoppel and Res Judicata in Administrative Law' [1965] PL 237; M Fazal, 'Reliability of Official Acts and Advice' [1972] PL 43; P Craig, 'Representations By Public Bodies' (1977) 93 LQR 398; A Bradley, 'Administrative Justice and the Binding Effect of Official Acts' (1981) CLP 1.

[152] *Minister of Agriculture and Fisheries v Hulkin*, cited in *Minister of Agriculture and Fisheries v Mathews* [1950] 1 KB 148; *Maritime Electric Co Ltd v General Dairies Ltd* [1937] AC 610, 620, PC; *Inland Revenue Commissioners v Brooks* [1915] AC 478, 491, HL; *Thrasyvoulou v Secretary of State for the Environment* [1990] 2 AC 273, 289, HL; *R v Inland Revenue Commissioners, ex p MFK Underwriting Agencies Ltd* [1990] 1 WLR 1545, 1568; *R v Criminal Injuries Compensation Board, ex p M (a minor)* [1998] COD 128.

[153] P Craig, *Administrative Law* (4th edn, London: Sweet & Maxwell, 1999) ch 19.

16.79 For the jurisdictional principle to be effective a limit must be imposed upon the apparent authority of the agent. This is found in the principle that the agent's authority cannot extend to a matter that is ultra vires in either of two senses. The decision resulting from the representation may be outside the powers of the public body itself, or within its power, but incapable of being made by that public officer. Thus, in theory at least, it can be said that whenever a public official has apparent authority the decision itself must be intra vires, otherwise the agent would not have had the authority in question.[154]

16.80 The application of these principles can be seen in *A-G for Ceylon v AD Silva*.[155] The Collector of Customs in Ceylon advertised certain property for sale by auction in March 1947. He was mistaken in treating this as saleable, for in November 1946 an officer of the Ministry of Supply had taken over the goods and had contracted to sell them to a Ceylon firm in January 1947. The plaintiff was the buyer at the sale organized by the Collector of Customs. The Collector, having become aware of the earlier sale, refused to deliver the goods to the plaintiff who brought an action for breach of contract. The case turned upon whether the Collector had any authority to make the sale. The Privy Council considered first whether the Collector had actual authority to make the sale. Such authority could be derived from the Customs Ordinance, or, arguably, independently of it. The Court rejected the argument on both grounds. As to the former, the argument was dismissed because the Court found that the Customs Ordinance did not, on construction, bind the Crown.[156] As to the latter, it was said that the mere fact that the Collector was a public officer did not give him the right to act on behalf of the Crown in all matters concerning the Crown. The right to do so must be established by reference to statute or otherwise.[157] Thus even if the act of selling was intra vires, the contract could not be upheld if the agent had no authority to make it. The Privy Council then considered whether the Collector had apparent authority to sell the goods. The answer again was in the negative.[158] Such authority involved a representation by the principal as to the extent of the agent's authority. No representation by the agent could amount to a holding out by the principal. The Court went on to consider whether the defendant was bound because the Collector had authority, simply from his position qua Collector, to represent that the goods delivered were saleable even though they were not. The argument was rejected.[159] The Collector might have authority to do acts of a particular class,

---

[154] The same principles applied in company law, prior to statutory reform, *Freeman and Lockyer v Buckhurst Park Properties (Mangal) Ltd* [1964] 2 QB 480, CA. See generally, FMB Reynolds, *Bowstead and Reynolds on Agency* (16th edn, London: Sweet & Maxwell, 1996) Arts 5, 22, 74, 75.
[155] [1953] AC 461, PC.
[156] ibid 473–478.
[157] ibid 479.
[158] ibid 479–480.
[159] ibid 480–481.

namely to enter on behalf of the Crown into sales of certain goods. Such authority was, however, limited to those areas actually covered by the Ordinance. Thus, although the Collector had authority derived from his position as Collector this would not extend beyond the limits of the Ordinance: he could not have authority to commit an ultra vires act.

While the principles are clear, they have not always been applied. There has been **16.81** confusion in the use of terms such as delegation and agency. The strain placed upon legal language stemmed partly from the hardship that could be produced if the representation could not bind the public body. The courts sought to avoid such hardship by assuming that the representation was intra vires, even though it was extremely dubious whether the decision could be so regarded. Thus in *Lever (Finance) Ltd v Westminster Corp*,[160] Lord Denning MR held that if an officer acted within the scope of his ostensible authority, and made a representation on which another acted, then the public authority could be bound by it. When the statutory powers in the *Lever* case are examined it is evident that there was no power to delegate to the officer.[161] It does not therefore matter whether the language of the officer's power is expressed in terms of delegation or ostensible authority as an agent. If delegation is forbidden by a statute expressly or impliedly then a purported delegation will be ultra vires. That cannot be converted into an intra vires act by saying that what the officer does with ostensible authority will bind the principal. There cannot be ostensible or apparent authority to bind the principal where the act committed is ultra vires in either sense identified above.[162]

The decision in *Western Fish Products Ltd v Penwith DC*[163] reaffirmed orthodoxy. **16.82** The plaintiff purchased an industrial site, which had previously been used for the production of fertilizer from fish and fishmeal. The company intended to make animal fertilizer from fishmeal and also to pack fish for human consumption. It alleged that it had an established user right, which would entitle it to carry on business without the need for planning permission. The planning officer wrote a letter which, the plaintiff claimed, represented that the officer had accepted the established user right. Work on renovating the factories was begun even though no planning permission had yet been obtained. The full council subsequently refused this permission and enforcement notices were served on the plaintiff. The latter claimed, inter alia, that the statements of the planning officer estopped the council from refusing planning permission. The Court of Appeal rejected this argument. Megaw LJ stated that the planning officer, even acting within his apparent authority, could not do what the Town and Country Planning Act 1971 required

---

[160] [1971] 1 QB 222, 230, CA.
[161] See Craig (n 153 above) 405–406.
[162] *Southend-on-Sea Corp v Hodgson (Wickford) Ltd* [1962] 1 QB 416; *R v Leicester City Council, ex p Powergen UK Ltd* [2000] JPL 629.
[163] [1981] 2 All ER 204, CA.

the council itself to do. The Act required that the decision concerning planning permission be made by the council, not the officer. No representation by the planning officer could inhibit the discharge of these statutory duties. While specific functions could be delegated to the officer, the determination of planning permission had not been thus delegated.[164]

(c) Qualifications to the jurisdictional principle

16.83   *Western Fish* therefore reaffirmed the traditional view. Apparent authority cannot allow an officer to do what is assigned to the council. If the representation is ultra vires either because it is outside the powers of that body, or because, although within its powers, it cannot be delegated to this officer, then it cannot operate as an estoppel. There are three exceptions to this principle.

16.84   First, a procedural irregularity *may* be subject to estoppel. Whether it in fact is depends upon the construction of the statutory provision setting out the procedure.[165]

16.85   Secondly, it was said that where a power is delegated to an officer to determine specific questions any decision made cannot be revoked. The breadth of this exception depends upon whether the statute allowed the powers to be delegated, and whether they have in fact been delegated. The first condition must be an absolute one. If it is not then the whole force of the basic proposition, that estoppel cannot validate an ultra vires act, is negated. This still leaves open the meaning of the other condition, the extent to which the individual can assume that delegation has taken place. The answer from *Western Fish* is that it depends.[166] The individual cannot assume that any resolution necessary to delegate authority has been passed, nor is the seniority of the officer conclusive. If, however, there is some further evidence that the officer regularly deals with cases of a type which the individual might expect that official to be able to determine, this could be sufficient to entitle the individual to presume that delegation has occurred even if in fact it has not. In this residual area apparent authority can, therefore, have a validating effect in the following sense. Delegation may be lawful, but only when certain formalities have been complied with. It seems that, in certain circumstances, a decision made by an officer, even where those formalities of appointment have not occurred, may still be irrevocable. Whether this actually validates an ultra vires act or not depends upon whether the conditions setting out the means for delegation are mandatory or only directory.

16.86   Thirdly, it is open to the courts to construe the relevant statute so as to confer validity on, for example, a mistaken certificate unless and until it has been revoked.[167]

---

[164] *Western Fish Products Ltd v Penwith DC* (n 163 above) 219.
[165] ibid 221. See also, *Re L (AC) (an infant)* [1971] 3 All ER 743, 752.
[166] [1981] 2 All ER 204, 221–222.
[167] *R v Secretary of State for the Home Department, ex p Ejaz (Naheed)* [1994] QB 496.

In more general terms, if a court wishes to consider the effects of the representation on the individual, this may cause the court to categorize the representation as intra rather than ultra vires.[168]

(d) The conceptual language: estoppel or legitimate expectations

The preceding discussion used the language of estoppel, since that was the language used in the case law. This must now be revised in the light of *R (on the application of Reprotech (Pebsham) Ltd) v East Sussex CC.*[169] Lord Hoffmann, giving judgment for their Lordships, held that private law concepts of estoppel should not be introduced into planning law.[170] He acknowledged that there was an analogy between estoppel and legitimate expectations, but held that it was no more than an analogy because 'remedies against public authorities also have to take into account the interests of the general public which the authority exists to promote'.[171] Lord Hoffmann recognized that earlier cases had used the language of estoppel, but said that was explicable because public law concepts of legitimate expectations and abuse of power were under-developed at that time. Public law had now absorbed whatever was useful from the moral values underlying estoppel, and 'the time has come for it to stand upon its own two feet'.[172]

16.87

It should for the sake of clarity be noted that the shift from the language of estoppel to that of legitimate expectations does not touch the substance of the jurisdictional principle as explicated above. Representations made by an agent who lacks authority, or representations leading to decisions which are ultra vires the public body itself, will not bind that body. The consequence, prior to *Reprotech*, was to say that estoppel cannot apply in such circumstances. This result would now be expressed by saying that there was no legitimate expectation in such circumstances.

16.88

There is nonetheless a close analogy between estoppel and legitimate expectations. The foundation of both concepts is a representation, which provides the rationale for holding the representor to what had been represented, where the reliance was reasonable and legitimate in the circumstances. The fact that any remedy against a public body would have to take account of the broader public

16.89

---

[168] See, eg, the approach in *R v Inland Revenue Commissioners, ex p MFK Underwriting Agencies Ltd* [1990] 1 WLR 1545; *R (on the application of Bibi) v Newham LBC* [2001] EWCA Civ 607, [2002] 1 WLR 237.

[169] [2002] UKHL 8, [2003] 1 WLR 348. See also, *R v Leicester City Council, ex p Powergen UK Ltd* [2000] JPL 629; *Powergen UK Plc v Leicester City Council* [2000] JPL 1037, CA; *Coghurst Wood Leisure Park Ltd v Secretary of State for Transport, Local Government and the Regions* [2002] EWHC 1091, [2003] JPL 206.

[170] *R (on the application of Reprotech (Pebsham) Ltd) v East Sussex CC* [2002] UKHL 8, [2003] 1 WLR 348 at [33].

[171] ibid at [34].

[172] ibid at [35].

interest was moreover recognized by those judges who used the language of estoppel. They recognized that the application of estoppel to public bodies would have to be modified to take this into account.[173]

C. Equality

(1) Domestic Law

16.90 Equality features at a number of different levels within our own domestic jurisprudence.[174] It is important for the sake of clarity to distinguish these.

16.91 First, there is the concept of equality to be found in the rule of law: all should be subject to the same law, in the sense that officials should not be afforded special privileges. This particular statement must nonetheless be qualified. It is acceptable for there to be rational differences in the laws which apply to different groups within society. Moreover, the laws which are applicable to public bodies may have to differ in certain respects from those which apply to private individuals.

16.92 Secondly, there is the related but more sophisticated concept of equality, which demands both that like groups be treated in a like manner, and that different groups should be treated differently. These dictates can be taken into account under our existing heads of review, such as improper purpose or relevancy, but it would be beneficial if such cases were decided more openly on the basis of equality. Thus in *Kruse v Johnson*[175] the court held that a bye-law could not be partial or unequal in its operation as between different classes. Lord Denning in *Edwards v SOGAT*[176] held that the courts would not allow a power to be exercised arbitrarily or with unfair discrimination. In *R v Tower Hamlets LBC, ex p Abbas Ali*[177] the court held that the devolution of power by a local authority to neighbourhoods to decide on the allocation of property to the homeless was unfair and irrational, since variable criteria were applied. In *R v Secretary of State for the Home Department, ex p Urmaza*,[178] and *R v Secretary of State for the Home Department, ex p Gangadeen*,[179] it was held that the legal principle of consistency in the exercise of public law powers created a presumption that the agency or minister will follow a declared policy. This presumption flowed from the very purpose of such a policy, which was to secure consistency. A departure from such a policy would require the giving of reasons, and would have to be justified in substantive terms.

---

[173] See, eg, *Laker Airways v Department of Trade* [1977] QB 643, 707, CA.

[174] J Jowell, 'Is Equality a Constitutional Principle?' (1994) 7 CLP 1. The discussion of equality is brief. For more detail see the excellent analysis by Professor C McCrudden, chapter 11 above.

[175] [1898] 2 QB 91.

[176] [1971] Ch 354.

[177] (1992) 25 HLR 158, 314.

[178] [1996] COD 479.

[179] [1998] 1 FLR 762, CA.

The decision as to whether a certain group should or should not be regarded as the same or different from another inevitably requires the making of value judgments. Some guidance is provided by domestic legislation, which prohibits discrimination upon the grounds of, for example, race or gender. The very existence of these prohibitions on discrimination means that groups cannot be validly distinguished merely because of their respective ethnic backgrounds: disadvantageous treatment of one such group cannot be defended by claiming that they are different groups merely because of racial origin.

16.93

Further guidance is to be found in the ECHR. The HRA 1998 has brought Convention rights into domestic law, including Article 14 ECHR. This article does not enshrine equality as a free-standing principle. It does, however, provide that the enjoyment of the rights and freedoms set out in the Convention shall be secured without discrimination on any ground such as sex, race, colour, language, religion, political or other opinion, national or social origin, association with a national minority, property, birth or other status. It is clear that while there cannot be a violation of Article 14 in isolation,[180] there may be a breach of this article when considered together with other Convention articles, even if there would have been no breach of those other articles.[181] An example will make this clear. Article 6 ECHR does not compel states to establish appeal courts. If, however, such courts are set up then access must not be discriminatory since this would violate Article 14. The European Court of Human Rights has given important guidance on the meaning of discrimination. It made it clear that Article 14 did not prohibit every difference in treatment, but only those which had no objective and reasonable justification. This was to be assessed in relation to the aims and effects of the measure in question. The differential treatment must not only pursue a legitimate aim. It had to be proportionate: there had to be a reasonable relationship of proportionality between the means employed and the aim sought to be realized.[182]

16.94

(2) EC Law

EC law is of relevance in four ways. The first two of these are relatively well-known, the third and fourth less so.

16.95

First, Community law proscribes any discrimination on the grounds of nationality. This is a central feature of EC law and is enshrined in general terms in Article 12 of the EC Treaty.[183] It finds more specific recognition in, for example, Articles

16.96

---

[180] *Abdulaziz, Cabales and Balkandali v UK* Series A No 94 (1985) 7 EHRR 471 at [71].
[181] *Belgian Linguistic Case (No 2)* Series A, No 6 (1968) 1 EHRR 252; F Jacobs and R White, *The European Convention on Human Rights* (2nd edn, Oxford: OUP, 1996) ch 18.
[182] See also, *Lithgow v UK* Series A No 102 (1986) 8 EHRR 329.
[183] This numbering is based on the Treaty of Amsterdam. The previous number was Art 6.

39, 43 and 49,[184] which prohibit discriminatory treatment in relation to free movement of workers, freedom of establishment and freedom to provide services in another member state. These provisions have direct effect, both vertical and horizontal, and thus can be relied upon in national courts against either the state or a private individual. Other Treaty articles prohibit discrimination on grounds such as gender, Article 141.[185] Action by the state or a private party which infringes this article can be challenged via Article 234[186] in the national courts. This is exemplified by *Defrenne v Sabena*,[187] in which a Belgian air-hostess successfully argued that the terms and conditions of her contract were discriminatory as compared to those of her male colleagues who were doing the same job.

16.97   Secondly, EC law also has a more indirect impact in relation to equality. It provides a fertile source of information about how decisions are made in cases where an individual argues that like cases are not being treated alike, or that groups which are different are being treated in the same manner. One of the main areas in which this issue arises is under the Common Agricultural Policy. An individual may challenge a Community regulation on the ground that it was discriminatory under Article 34(3).[188] The ECJ has articulated a test to apply in such cases. This test combines two complementary ideas: one is that there should be similar treatment of comparable situations; the other is that it may only be possible to decide whether situations really are comparable by considering the background policy aims of the area in question.[189]

16.98   The third way in which EC law relating to equality will have an impact on domestic law stems from the addition of a new Article 13 to the EC Treaty by the Treaty of Amsterdam. It gives the Community legislative competence to take appropriate action to combat discrimination based on sex, racial or ethnic origin, religion or belief, disability, age or sexual orientation.[190] Two directives were adopted in 2000. There is a directive prohibiting discrimination on grounds of race and ethnic origin.[191] There is also the so-called Framework Directive, covering discrimination in the field of employment on the grounds listed in Article 13 (other than race, ethnic origin or sex, which are already covered by other legislation): religion, belief, disability, age

---

[184]   Ex Arts 48, 52 and 59.
[185]   Ex Art 119.
[186]   Ex Art 177.
[187]   Case 43/75, [1976] ECR 455.
[188]   Ex Art 40(3).
[189]   Case 6/71 *Rheinmullen Dusseldorf (FA) v Einfuhrund Vorratsstelle fur Getreide und Futtermittel* [1971] ECR 823; Case 79/77 *Firma Kulhaus Zentrum AG v Hauptzollamt Hamburg-Harburg* [1978] ECR 611; Case 8/82 *Wagner GmbH Agrarhandel v Bundesanstalt fur Landwirtschaftliche Marktordnung* [1983] ECR 371; Case 230/78 *Eridania* [1979] ECR 2749; Case 139/77 *Denkavit* [1978] ECR 1317.
[190]   See M Bell, *Anti-Discrimination Law and the EU* (Oxford: OUP, 2002).
[191]   Council Directive (EC) 2000/43 implementing the principle of equal treatment between persons irrespective of racial or ethnic origin [2000] OJ L180/22

and sexual orientation.[192] While the jurisdictional limitation in Article 13 specifies that the Community can only act within the limits of its powers, Article 3 of the Race Directive gives it an apparently wide scope, including a prohibition on discrimination in relation to social protection, healthcare, housing and education. Where the regulations or directives meet the normal conditions for direct effect then individuals will be able to rely on them in national courts. This means that a person aggrieved by government action may have recourse both to Convention rights concerning discrimination, and EC measures passed under Article 13. It should also be recognized that the latter are more potent in an important respect. National law that is inconsistent with Article 13 will be invalid, and even primary legislation can be declared inapplicable where it conflicts with a Community norm.

The fourth way in which EC law will be of relevance in relation to equality is through the Charter of Fundamental Rights.[193] Chapter III of the Charter deals with equality. It contains a basic equality before the law guarantee, as well as a provision similar, though not identical, to that in Article 13. There is also a reference to positive action provisions in the field of gender equality, protection for children's rights, and some weaker provisions guaranteeing 'respect' for cultural diversity, for the rights of the elderly and for persons with disabilities. The legal status of the Charter is to be formally decided at the Inter-Governmental Conference in 2004. It is however clear that a range of institutional actors has already made use of its provisions. The Commission decided to conduct a form of compatibility review with regard to the Charter. Any legislative proposal connected with the protection of fundamental rights would be considered by the Commission for its compatibility with the provisions of the Charter. The European Ombudsman has also made frequent reference to the Charter. The Charter has been mentioned in a decision of the Court of First Instance.[194] Numerous references to provisions of the Charter have also been made by various Advocates General.[195] The Charter is therefore beginning to enter into the 'constitutional practice' of the European Union. It has also been made binding in Part I of the Draft Treaty establishing a Constitution for Europe.[196]

16.99

---

[192] Council Directive (EC) 2000/78 establishing a general framework for equal treatment in employment and occupation [2000] OJ L303/16.

[193] Charter of Fundamental Rights of the European Union [2000] OJ C364/1.

[194] Case T-54/99 *Max.mobil Telekommunikation Service GmbH v Commission* [2002] 4 CMLR 32 at [48], [57].

[195] See, eg, AG Tizzano in C-173/99 *R v Secretary of State for Trade and Industry, ex p BECTU* [2001] ECR I-4881; AG Mischo in C 122P & 125/99P *D v Council* [2000] ECR I-4319; AG Jacobs in C-270/99P *Z v Parliament* [2001] ECR I-9197; AG Léger in C-353/99P *Council v Hautala* [2001] ECR I-9565.

[196] CONV 850/03, Brussels, 18 July 2003, Art 7.

Part III

REMEDIES IN PUBLIC LAW

17

ACCESS TO MECHANISMS OF ADMINISTRATIVE LAW

A. The Legal Foundations of the Judicial Review Procedure

Until recently the procedure for seeking judicial review was governed by RSC Ord **17.01**
53,[1] as revised in the light of the Law Commission's Report No 73.[2] Some of the
key provisions were incorporated into the Supreme Court Act 1981 (SCA), s 31.
The legal foundations for the public law procedures continued to be the revised
Ord 53, and the 1981 Act, for 20 years.

---

[1] SI 1977/1955.
[2] Law Com No 73 (Cmnd 6407, 1976).

17.02 These legal foundations have now changed.[3] The catalyst was the general reform of the civil justice system flowing from the Woolf Report.[4] This led to a radical revision of the rules on civil procedure. The initial impact of these reforms on judicial review was marginal, since RSC Ord 53, subject to minor change, was appended to the new Civil Procedure Rules (CPR). The position altered as a result of the Bowman Report into the Crown Office.[5] Judicial review is now governed by CPR 8, as modified by a new Pt 54. These provisions apply to all judicial review applications lodged on or after 2 October 2000.[6] The legal foundations for judicial review will henceforth be based on the CPR, SCA 1981, s 31, and relevant practice directions. The Crown Office has been renamed the Administrative Court.[7] It is clear that although the claim for judicial review is brought in the name of the Crown, the Crown's involvement is nominal. The real contest is between the claimant and the defendant.[8]

B. The Procedure for Seeking Judicial Review

(1) Introduction

(a) Permission

17.03 A claimant must seek permission to apply for judicial review (CPR 54.4), and the application must be made promptly and in any event within three months after the grounds for making it first arose (CPR 54.5). The claim for judicial review is made using the CPR 8 claim form, which must, in addition to the usual requirements, state the following information (CPR 54.6):

- The claimant must give the name and address of any person considered to be an interested party.
- The claimant must state that he is requesting permission to seek judicial review, and the remedy being claimed.
- Where the claimant is raising a point under the Human Rights Act 1998 (HRA), he must specify, inter alia, the Convention right alleged to have been infringed.

---

[3] See generally, C Lewis, *Judicial Remedies in Public Law* (2nd edn, London: Sweet & Maxwell, 2000).

[4] Lord Woolf, *Access to Justice: The Final Report to the Lord Chancellor on the Civil Justice System in England and Wales* (1997); SI 1998/3132.

[5] *Review of the Crown Office List* (LCD, 2000).

[6] SI 2000/2092; M Fordham, 'Judicial Review: The New Rules' [2001] PL 4; T Cornford and M Sunkin, 'The Bowman Report, Access and the Recent Reforms of the Judicial Review Procedure' [2001] PL 11.

[7] *Practice Direction (QBD; Admin Ct; Establishment)* [2000] 1 WLR 1654.

[8] *R (on the application of Ben-Abdelaziz) v Hackney LBC* [2001] EWCA Civ 803; [2001] 1 WLR 1485 at [29].

- A Practice Direction issued pursuant to CPR 54 stipulates that the claim form must also state, or be accompanied by, inter alia, a detailed statement of the claimant's grounds for bringing the claim, a statement of the facts relied on, copies of documents relied on by the claimant, relevant statutory material, and a copy of any order that the claimant seeks to have quashed.[9]

The claim form must be served on the defendant and other interested parties within seven days of the date of issue (CPR 54.7). If a person served with the claim form wishes to take part in the judicial review proceedings, he or she must acknowledge service within 21 days of being served (CPR 54.8(2)(a)). This acknowledgement must be served on the claimant and any other person named in the claim form (CPR 54.8(2)(b)). The acknowledgement must state whether the person intends to contest the claim, the grounds for doing so, and give the name and address of any other person considered to be an interested party (CPR 54.8(4)). A person who fails to file an acknowledgement is not allowed to take part in the permission hearing, unless the court allows him to do so (CPR 54.9(1)). **17.04**

The criterion that applies to the grant of permission will be considered below. Permission will not be granted unless the applicant has a sufficient interest in the matter to which the application relates.[10] Where permission is given the court may give directions, which may include a stay of the proceedings to which the claim relates (CPR 54.10). Permission decisions will often be made without a hearing. The court is obliged to provide reasons for its decision (CPR 54.12(2)). A claimant that is refused permission may not appeal, but may request, within seven days, for the decision to be reconsidered at a hearing (CPR. 54.12(3)). It is not, however, open to the defendant or any other person served with the claim form to apply to have the permission set aside (CPR 54.14). **17.05**

(b) The substantive hearing

It is for the defendant and any other person served with the claim form who wishes to contest the claim, or support it on additional grounds, to provide detailed grounds for doing so, together with any written evidence (CPR 54.14). This must be done within 35 days of service of the order giving permission. A claimant must seek the court's permission to rely on grounds other than those for which he has been given permission to proceed (CPR 54.15). Written evidence may not be relied on unless it has been served in accordance with a rule under CPR 54, or direction of the court, or the court gives permission (CPR 54.16). Any person may apply for permission to file evidence, or make representations at the judicial review hearing (CPR 54.17). The court may decide the claim for judicial review without a hearing where all the parties agree (CPR 54.18). **17.06**

---

[9] Practice Direction (PD) 54, paras 5.6–5.7.
[10] SCA 1981, s 31(3).

17.07 Where a quashing order is sought, the court may remit the matter to the decision-maker, directing it to reconsider the matter in the light of the court's judgment. Where the court considers that this would serve no useful purpose, it may, subject to any statutory provision, take the decision itself. This will not be possible where the statutory power is given to the initial decision-maker itself (CPR 54.19).

17.08 There are provisions allowing cases to be transferred to and from the Administrative Court (CPR 30). It is open to the court to order a claim to continue as if it had been started under CPR 54, and to give directions about the future management of the claim (CPR 54.20). It is also open to the court, where the relief sought is a declaration or injunction, and the court considers that such relief should not be granted in a claim for judicial review, to order that the case continue as a common law claim under CPR 7.

17.09 Where the parties have agreed on terms for resolving the case, an order may be obtained from the court to put the agreement into effect, without the need for a hearing. It will be for the judge to decide whether the case can be resolved in this manner.[11] If the judge decides that it would not be appropriate to make such an order, then the case will be heard in the normal manner.

(2) The Application/Claim for Judicial Review

17.10 The basis of the 1977 reform is the concept of application, or as it is now termed, claim for judicial review. The prerogative orders and declaration and injunction are subject to this mechanism, and the remedies may be sought in the alternative or cumulatively depending upon the type of case.[12] When the revised RSC Ord 53 was first passed it was thought that declaration and injunction would still be obtainable under their pre-existing procedures. It would, however, be inappropriate for those remedies to be claimed under the new procedure unless the case was of a public law nature. Section 31(2) of the SCA 1981 defines when cases will be of this kind. Declarations and injunctions can be granted pursuant to an application for judicial review if the court considers, having regard to the nature of the matters and the nature of the persons and bodies against whom a remedy may be granted by the prerogative orders, and all the circumstances of the case, that it would be just and convenient for the declaration to be made or for the injunction to be granted. The test is therefore both functional and institutional. It is clear, after some earlier doubts,[13] that a declaration or an injunction can be granted even if a prerogative order would not be available,[14] provided that the

---

[11] PD 54, para 17.
[12] SCA 1981, s 31(1).
[13] *R v Inland Revenue Commissioners, ex p National Federation of Self-Employed and Small Businesses Ltd* [1982] AC 617, 647–648, HL.
[14] *R v Secretary of State for Employment, ex p Equal Opportunities Commission* [1995] 1 AC 1, HL.

subject matter of the application is of a public law nature and hence suited to judicial review.[15]

This general approach has been retained by CPR 54. A claim for judicial review is defined in CPR 54.1(2)(a) to be a claim to review the lawfulness of an enactment, or decision, action or failure to act in the exercise of a public function. CPR 54.2 provides that the judicial review procedure must be used where the claimant is seeking a mandatory, prohibiting or quashing order,[16] or an injunction under SCA 1981, s 30. It must also be used where the claimant seeks a declaration or injunction in addition to a mandatory, prohibiting or quashing order. CPR 54.3(1) provides that the judicial review procedure may be used in a claim for judicial review where the claimant is seeking a declaration or an injunction. SCA 1981 s 31(2) continues to provide the circumstances in which a claimant can seek a declaration or injunction in a claim for judicial review. Damages can be claimed in conjunction with the other remedies, but a claim for judicial review may not seek damages alone (CPR 54.3(2)). This does not, however, create a new damages remedy where none existed before. The court must be satisfied that if the claim had been made in an ordinary action, the applicant would have been awarded damages.[17]

(3) The Special Features of the Judicial Review Procedure: Permission and Time

The judicial review procedure has two features that distinguish it from the procedure that applies in ordinary actions. The claimant must secure the permission of the court in order to proceed (what was previously termed leave), and the time limits within which the action can be brought are shorter than those applicable in ordinary actions. The rationale for these special features is to protect public bodies. The nature of this protection will be considered more fully below.

(a) Permission

Permission has only been required since 1933.[18] The rationale for requiring permission is that public bodies exist to perform public duties, which are for the benefit of the general public. In deciding whether an action should proceed this wider public interest must be taken into account, as well as that of the applicant, because the public have an interest in seeing that litigation does not unduly hamper the governmental process.[19] The corollary of this argument is that the permission requirement

17.11

17.12

17.13

---

[15] *R v BBC, ex p Lavelle* [1983] 1 WLR 23, 30–31.
[16] These are the new names for mandamus, prohibition and certiorari.
[17] SCA 1981, s 31(4).
[18] Administration of Justice (Miscellaneous Provisions) Act 1933, s 5.
[19] Sir H Woolf, 'Public Law—Private Law: Why the Divide? A Personal View' [1986] PL 220, 230; Sir H Woolf, *Protecting the Public—A New Challenge* (London: Sweet & Maxwell, 1990).

exists to protect public bodies from applicants who do not really have a chance of winning their case. It is a screening mechanism to prevent the public body from being troubled by cases that are unlikely to succeed.

17.14 This still leaves open the test to be applied at the permission stage. Lord Donaldson MR addressed this issue in *R v Secretary of State for the Home Department, ex p Doorga (Davendranath)*.[20] His Lordship gave directions to judges hearing applications for leave, and said that they should distinguish between three categories of case.

> The first is the case where there are, prima facie, reasons for granting judicial review. In such a case leave shall duly be granted. There are other cases in which the application for judicial review is wholly unarguable, in which case, quite clearly leave should be refused. However, there is an intermediate category—not very frequent but it does occur—in which the judge may say, 'Well, there is no prima facie case on the applicant's evidence but, nevertheless, the applicant's evidence leaves me with an uneasy feeling and I should like to know more about this.' Alternatively he may say, 'The applicant's case looks strong but I nevertheless have an uneasy feeling that there may be some very quick and easy explanation for this.' In either case it would be quite proper, and, indeed, reasonable for him to adjourn the application for leave in order that it may be further heard inter partes. At such a hearing it is not for the respondent to deploy his full case, but he simply has to put forward, if he can, some totally knock-out point which makes it clear that there is no basis for the application at all.

17.15 There are two possible interpretations of Lord Donaldson MR's criterion. On a literal interpretation permission should only be refused if the case is indeed 'unarguable' or 'wholly unarguable'.[21] This is strong language and it would seem prima facie unlikely that there will be a great many such cases. The other possible interpretation would be that a judge should refuse permission where he believed that there was no reasonable chance of success, or that the case was not reasonably arguable. The danger of this formulation is that the judge will have to make a difficult evaluation on fact and law, and this evaluation will, after the CPR, be based on written documentation.

17.16 Valuable empirical work has been done on the leave requirement.[22] It seems clear that even where the courts are purportedly applying the criterion of arguability

---

[20] [1990] COD 109, 110; *R v Secretary of State for the Home Department, ex p Begum (Angur)* [1990] COD 107, 108.

[21] In *R v Secretary of State for the Home Department, ex p Doorga (Davendranath)* [1990] COD 109, 110, Lord Donaldson MR used the language 'wholly unarguable', whereas in *R v Secretary of State for the Home Department, ex p Begum (Angur)* [1990] COD 107, 108, he stated that if there was no arguable case leave should be refused; in *R v Legal Aid Board, ex p Hughes* (1992) 24 HLR 698, the formulation was that there must be a clearly arguable case for leave to be granted ex parte.

[22] A Le Sueur and M Sunkin, 'Applications for Judicial Review: the Requirement of Leave' [1992] PL 102; L Bridges, G Meszaros and M Sunkin, *Judicial Review in Perspective* (London: Cavendish, 1995); L Bridges, G Meszaros and M Sunkin, 'Regulating the Judicial Review Case Load' [2001] PL 651.

they have been refusing roughly 40 per cent of cases. This could mean that the number of unarguable cases really is this high. The figures of failed applications could, alternatively, mean that the courts are in reality applying a more stringent test, and only allowing cases to proceed if there is some reasonable chance of success, or if the case really appears to be arguable on the merits. This certainly appears to be so with respect to some judges who have a very low rate of allowing leave. The dangers of this test have been adverted to above.

The new CPR have, unfortunately, not shed light on the criterion for permission. **17.17** The Bowman report, which led to the new CPR on judicial review, was in favour of retaining the permission stage, with explicit criteria as to when permission should be granted, and a presumption that it should be granted.[23] CPR 54.4 retained the leave requirement, subject to the linguistic alteration from leave to permission, but contains no criteria as to when permission should be granted.

CPR 54 has, however, modified the permission stage so that it is now more inter **17.18** partes than hitherto. The leave stage was traditionally ex parte, and the respondent might only become involved if leave was given. This has been altered by CPR 54.7–54.9, which has made the permission stage more inter partes than hitherto. The claim form must be served on the defendant, and any person the claimant considers to be an interested party. Any person served with the claim form who wishes to take part in the judicial review must file an acknowledgement of service. The acknowledgement must state, inter alia, the grounds on which the party is contesting the claim. The rationale for the change was to get defendants to think about the challenge at the outset, and to ensure that the court was well informed at the permission stage. There are, however, concerns that the inter partes procedure may disadvantage claimants. The court may regard the defendant's brief response as a knock out blow to the claimant, even where it is not fully supported by evidence.[24] There is also a concern that the court at the permission stage as modified by the CPR will be performing two roles, that of mediating access to judicial review, and managing the substantive dispute, and that it may be difficult to reconcile these roles.[25]

The gap between the judicial review procedure and that for ordinary actions has **17.19** narrowed, in part because of the increasingly inter partes nature of the review procedure, and in part because of changes in the rules governing the latter. A central theme of the Woolf reforms was to give the courts greater control over the management of civil litigation than existed hitherto. This is apparent in the general provisions of the CPR.[26] CPR 3.4(2) enables the court to strike out a case if it discloses

---

[23] *Review of the Crown Office List* (LCD, 2000) 64, para 13.
[24] Cornford and Sunkin (n 6 above) 19.
[25] ibid 15.
[26] CPR, Pts 1, 3.

no cause of action, or if it is an abuse of the court's process. CPR 24 empowers the court to give summary judgment, where it considers that the claimant has no real prospect of success. Increased judicial control over ordinary litigation is also evident in the judicial interpretation of the CPR, as exemplified by the approach in *Clark v University of Lincolnshire and Humberside*.[27] The court made it clear that the CPR relating to ordinary actions would be interpreted to prevent a party gaining unwarranted procedural advantages by proceeding via an ordinary action, as opposed to judicial review.

17.20   There are nonetheless still real differences between the judicial review procedure and that for ordinary actions. Public law applicants are not entitled to pursue a case of their own accord. They must secure permission and argue their way into court, subject to a short time limit. In an ordinary action the plaintiff is entitled to proceed without any requirement of permission. The onus is on the defendant to argue that the case should be struck out, and the time limit is considerably longer. It is questionable whether this dichotomy is justifiable. It has been argued that suitable techniques for protecting public bodies in ordinary actions could be devised when such protection was really warranted,[28] and that the CPR rules relating to striking out and summary judgment could be used to this end.[29] Many amongst the judiciary and government remained convinced that these protections were nonetheless necessary, particularly in the light of the increase in the number of applications for judicial review. It was felt that the ordinary procedures would be too cumbersome for most judicial review applications.[30]

(b) Time limits

17.21   The rules on time limits and delay are complicated.[31] Shorter time limits are said to be required in public law cases because of the greater need for certainty than in private law. There is a wider public interest involved in ensuring that the public service knows whether its actions will be valid or not. Before 1977 only certiorari was subject to a six-month time limit, albeit with a discretion to extend beyond this period which was rarely exercised. Declarations and injunctions were not subject to formal limitation periods, but delay could be a factor in the court deciding whether in its discretion to refuse relief. The rules concerning delay were altered by the 1977 reforms. RSC Ord 53, r 4 contained the provision for delay. This was

---

[27] [2000] 1 WLR 1988.

[28] S Fredman and G Morris, 'The Costs of Exclusivity' [1994] PL 69.

[29] Cornford and Sunkin (n 6 above) 15; D Oliver, 'Public Law Procedures and Remedies—Do We Need Them?' [2002] PL 91, 93.

[30] Law Commission, *Administrative Law: Judicial Review and Statutory Appeals* (Law Com No 226, HC 669, 1994) para 3.5.

[31] M Beloff, 'Time, Time, Time It's On My Side, Yes It Is' in C Forsyth and I Hare (eds), *The Golden Metwand and the Crooked Cord, Essays on Public Law in Honour of Sir William Wade* (Oxford: OUP, 1998) 267–295.

ambiguous[32] and was replaced in 1980.[33] The basic rule was that an application for permission to apply for judicial review should be made promptly, and in any event within three months from the date when grounds for the application first arose, unless the court considered that there was good reason for extending time.

RSC Ord 53, r 4 has now been replaced by CPR 54.5(1). This states that the claim **17.22** form must be filed promptly and in any event not later than three months after the grounds to make the claim first arose. This rule does not apply when any other enactment specifies a shorter time limit for making the claim for judicial review (CPR 54.5(3)). The time limit may not be extended by agreement between the parties (CPR 54.5(2)). It can, however, be extended by the court, pursuant to the general power in CPR 3.1(2)(a).[34]

SCA 1981, s 31(6) also contains provisions on delay, but is framed in somewhat **17.23** different terms. This states that where the High Court considers that there has been undue delay in making an application for judicial review, the court may refuse to grant leave for making the application, or any relief sought on the application, if it considers that the granting of the relief sought would be likely to cause substantial hardship to, or substantially prejudice the rights of, any person, or would be detrimental to good administration.

There are three key differences between the formulation in CPR 54.5 and that in **17.24** SCA 1981, s 31(6).

- s 31(6) contains no actual time limit, whereas CPR 54.5 sets a general limit of three months;
- s 31(6) provides that detriment to good administration and prejudice to a party's rights are to be taken into account when there is undue delay. These factors are not found in CPR 54.5;
- s 31(6) applies both at the permission stage, and at the substantive hearing, whereas CPR 54.5 applies at the permission stage.[35]

The continued existence of two provisions dealing with time limits, cast in differ- **17.25** ent terms, is to be regretted. The complications flowing from this duality have been apparent for over 20 years, and continue to pose problems for the courts.[36] It would be perfectly possible for there to be a single provision dealing with time limits, framed to include whatever was felt to be suitable from the existing provisions. The

---

[32] J Beatson and M Matthews, 'Reform of Administrative Law Remedies: The First Step' (1978) 41 MLR 437, 442–444.

[33] SI 1980/2000, r 3, amending RSC Ord 53, r 4.

[34] *R v Lichfield DC, ex p Lichfield Securities Ltd* [2001] EWCA Civ 304, [2001] LGLR 35 at [28]; *R (on the application of M) v School Organisation Committee* [2001] EWHC Admin 245, [2001] ACD 77 at [16].

[35] *R v Stratford-on-Avon DC, ex p Jackson* [1985] 1 WLR 1319.

[36] See, eg, *R v Lichfield DC, ex p Lichfield Securities Ltd* [2001] EWCA Civ 304, [2001] LGLR 35.

fact that this was not done pursuant to the recent CPR reforms of the judicial review procedure is all the more surprising. The rules on time limits flowing from CPR 54.5 and s 31(6) are as follows.

17.26   The initial issue concerns the point at which time begins to run.[37] This may be clear and unequivocal in some situations, but may be less certain in others, in particular where a challenge is made to a policy determination or rule.[38] The issue is of real importance, given the need to apply promptly and the brevity of the three-month period. It is possible for an applicant to be ruled out of time if the action was brought against a later act when it should have been brought against an earlier one.[39] It was, however, made clear in *R v Hammersmith and Fulham LBC, ex p Burkett*[40] that it was open to a claimant to challenge the actual grant of planning permission, notwithstanding the fact that there might have been a challenge to an earlier resolution to give the planning permission. Lord Steyn stated more generally that time limits operated to bar review where a public body might have committed an abuse of power. They should be interpreted with this in mind. Courts should not therefore engage in a broad discretionary exercise of determining when the claimant could first reasonably have made the application.[41] The same rules should moreover apply irrespective of the fact that the claimant is a public interest group.[42]

17.27   CPR 54.5(1)(a) requires that the decision be made promptly, and in any event within three months after the grounds to make the claim arose. It is clear that applications have been held not to be prompt, even if made within three months.[43]

---

[37] RSC Ord 53, r 4 stated that where an order of certiorari is sought in respect of any judgment, order, conviction or other proceeding, the date when grounds for the application first arose shall be taken to be the date of that judgment, order, conviction or proceeding. There is no such provision in CPR 54.5.

[38] In *R v Redbridge LBC, ex p G* [1991] COD 398, it was assumed that time ran from when a policy was actually made, but that the fact that the applicant had no knowledge of the policy until it was published later was regarded as a good reason for extending the time limit. However in *R v Secretary of State for Trade and Industry, ex p Greenpeace* [2000] COD 141, the court held that time did not begin to run from the date of the contested regulations, since any such claim at that date would have been made in a vacuum.

[39] *R v Avon CC, ex p Terry Adams Ltd* [1994] Env LR 442; *R v Customs and Excise Commissioners, ex p Eurotunnel plc* [1995] COD 291; *R v Secretary for Trade and Industry, ex p Greenpeace Ltd* [1998] COD 59.

[40] [2002] UKHL 23; [2002] 1 WLR 1593.

[41] ibid at [44]–[49], disapproving of *R v Secretary for Trade and Industry, ex p Greenpeace Ltd* [1998] COD 59.

[42] The suggestion, in *R v Secretary for Trade and Industry, ex p Greenpeace Ltd* [1998] COD 59, that such groups must be especially prompt was not accepted in *R v Secretary of State for Trade and Industry, ex p Greenpeace* [2000] COD 141, or in *R v Hammersmith and Fulham LBC, ex p Burkett* [2002] UKHL 23; [2002] 1 WLR 1593.

[43] *Hilditch v Westminster City Council* [1990] COD 434; *R v ITC, ex p TVNi Ltd*, The Times, 30 December 1991; *R v Minister of Agriculture, Fisheries and Food, ex p Dairy Trade Federation* [1995] COD 3; *R v Bath City Council, ex p Crombie* [1995] COD 283.

However, in *Burkett*,[44] doubts were raised as to whether the obligation to act promptly was sufficiently certain to comply with the European Convention on Human Rights (ECHR). The matter was not decided, but a number of their Lordships were concerned that the provision was too uncertain to satisfy Convention jurisprudence. These concerns are warranted. This is especially so when it is recognized that the requirement of promptitude may preclude access to court after a very short period of time. It was in any event made clear in *Burkett* that the three-month limit should not be regarded as having been judicially replaced by a period of six weeks.[45]

When an application for leave is not made promptly, and in any event within three months, the court can refuse permission on the grounds of delay, unless it considers that there is a good reason for extending the period.[46] The court, in deciding whether to extend time, will consider whether there was a reasonable objective excuse for late application, the possible impact on third party rights, and the administration, and the general importance of the point raised.[47] The issues must be of genuinely public importance, and must be such that they could be best ventilated in the public law context.[48] The courts have held that attempting to reach a negotiated solution with the respondent will not normally be a reason for extension of time,[49] although there are some instances where this has been taken into account.[50]

It is clear from *R v Dairy Produce Quota Tribunal, ex p Caswell*[51] that where the claim is not made promptly, or within three months, there is undue delay for the purposes of SCA 1981, s 31(6), even if the court extends the time for making the claim. The phrase 'undue delay' is the condition precedent for invoking s 31(6). The court may then have regard to hardship to third parties, and detriment to good administration, in deciding whether to refuse permission, or refuse relief at the substantive hearing. The court should not, however, refuse to grant permission at the substantive hearing on the basis of hardship to third parties or detriment to good administration, where permission has already been given, since it is too late to 'refuse' permission in such instances. The court should rather refuse relief under s 31(6).[52]

17.28

17.29

---

[44] *R v Hammersmith and Fulham LBC, ex p Burkett* [2002] UKHL 23; [2002] 1 WLR 1593 at [6,] [53].

[45] ibid at [53].

[46] *R v Dairy Produce Quota Tribunal, ex p Caswell* [1990] 2 AC 738, HL.

[47] *R v Secretary of State for Trade and Industry, ex p Greenpeace* [2000] COD 141.

[48] *R v Secretary of State for the Home Department, ex p Ruddock* [1987] 1 WLR 1482; *Re S (Application for judicial review)* [1998] 1 FLR 790; *R (on the application of M) v School Organization Committee* [2001] EWHC Admin 245, [2001] ACD 77 at [21]–[31].

[49] *R v Redbridge LBC, ex p G* [1991] COD 398, 400.

[50] *R v Bishop of Stafford, ex p Owen* [2001] ACD 14; A Lindsay, 'Delay in Judicial Review Cases: A Conundrum Solved?' [1995] PL 417, 425–426.

[51] [1990] 2 AC 738, HL.

[52] *R v Criminal Injuries Compensation Board, ex p A* [1999] 2 AC 330, 340–342, HL.

17.30 It is clear from *R v Lichfield DC, ex p Lichfield Securities Ltd*,[53] that the same factors will generally be relevant to promptness under CPR 54.5, and undue delay under s 31(6). It is nonetheless in principle open to a court to consider undue delay at the substantive hearing, even where promptness has been considered at the permission stage. The judge at the substantive hearing should, however, only do so where new and relevant material is introduced at the substantive hearing, or if exceptionally the issues as developed at the substantive hearing put a different aspect on promptness, or where the first judge has overlooked a relevant matter.[54]

17.31 Where there is undue delay, it will be for the court to decide whether hardship to third parties or detriment to the administration will lead to the denial of relief. Where the impact on third party interests is insufficient in this respect, it will rarely be in the interests of good administration to leave an abuse of power uncorrected.[55]

C. Standing to Seek Judicial Review

(1) The Law Prior to 1977

17.32 Locus standi is concerned with whether this particular claimant is entitled to invoke the jurisdiction of the court.[56] There was, prior to 1977, considerable diversity in the case law on standing, both within each remedy and as between them. Even when the same words, such as 'private right', 'special damage', 'person aggrieved' or 'sufficient interest' were used, it could not be assumed that they bore the same meaning. In general terms, the standing requirements for the prerogative orders were more liberal than those for declaration and injunction. Declarations and injunctions were available through RSC Ord 15, r 16 or by way of application to the High Court respectively. The plaintiff had to show either that the interference with the public right constituted an infringement of a private right, or there had to be special damage.[57] Not all cases in fact required a private law right, in the sense of a cause of action in contract or tort, before the

---

[53] [2001] EWCA Civ 304, [2001] LGLR 35 at [33].

[54] ibid at [34].

[55] ibid at [39].

[56] S Thio, *Locus Standi and Judicial Review* (Singapore: Singapore University Press, 1971); J Vining, *Legal Identity, The Coming of Age of Public Law* (New Haven: Yale University Press, 1978); P Van Dijk, *Judicial Review of Governmental Action and the Requirement of an Interest to Sue* (Alphen: Sijthoff & Noordhoff, 1980).

[57] *Boyce v Paddington BC* [1903] 1 Ch 109, 114; *Stockport District Waterworks Co v Manchester Corp* (1863) 9 Jur (ns) 266; *Pudsey Coal Gas Co v Corp of Bradford* (1872) LR 15 Eq 167; *London Passenger Transport Board v Moscrop* [1942] AC 332, 342; *Gregory v Camden LBC* [1966] 1 WLR 899.

plaintiff could proceed.[58] The prospect of broadening the standing requirement for declaration and injunction was, however, curtailed by *Gouriet v Union of Post Office Workers*.[59] The premise underpinning *Gouriet* was that individuals enforce private rights and the Attorney-General enforces public rights.

(2) The Sufficiency of Interest Test

The Law Commission proposed a test based on sufficiency of interest,[60] and this **17.33** was adopted in RSC Ord 53, r 3(7). This was incorporated in SCA 1981, s 31(3). The test for standing was not incorporated into the CPR, and continues to be governed by the 1981 Act, s 31(3), which states,

> No application for judicial review shall be made unless the leave of the High Court has been obtained in accordance with rules of court; and the court shall not grant leave to make such an application unless it considers that the applicant has a sufficient interest in the matter to which the application relates.

R v Inland Revenue Commissioners, ex p National Federation of Self-Employed and **17.34** *Small Businesses Ltd*[61] (the *IRC* case) was the first important decision on the sufficiency of interest test. Casual labour was common on Fleet Street newspapers, the workers often adopting fictitious names and paying no taxes. The IRC made a deal with the relevant unions, workers and employers whereby if the casuals would fill in tax returns for the previous two years then the period prior to that would be forgotten. The National Federation argued that this bargain was ultra vires the IRC, and sought a declaration plus mandamus to compel the IRC to collect the back taxes. The IRC argued that the National Federation had no standing. Their Lordships found for the IRC. *Gouriet*[62] was treated as referring only to standing for declaration and injunction in their private law roles, and as having nothing to say about the standing for those remedies in public law. The House of Lords in the *IRC* case considered whether there should be a uniform test for the prerogative orders and whether there should be a uniform test for all the remedies. Lord Diplock[63] and Lord Scarman[64] answered both questions affirmatively. The other judgments were less clear.[65] Lord Wilberforce was, by way of contrast, of the opinion that there should be a distinction even between the prerogative orders, with certiorari being subject to a

---

[58] See, eg, *Nicholls v Tavistock UDC* [1923] 2 Ch 18; *Prescott v Birmingham Corp* [1955] Ch 210; *Brownsea Haven Properties v Poole Corp* [1958] Ch 574; *R v Greater London Council, ex p Blackburn* [1976] 1 WLR 550; *Bradbury v Enfield LBC* [1967] 1 WLR 1311.
[59] [1978] AC 435, HL.
[60] Law Com No 73 (n 2 above) 22, 33.
[61] [1982] AC 617, HL; P Cane, 'Standing, Legality and the Limits of Public Law' [1981] PL 322.
[62] [1978] AC 435, HL.
[63] [1982] AC 617, 638, 640.
[64] ibid 649–653.
[65] ibid 645–646, 656–658.

less strict test than mandamus.[66] The general thrust of the *IRC* case was, nonetheless, that standing should be developed to meet new problems, and that there should not be an endless discussion of previous authority. This furthered the tendency towards a unified conception of standing based upon sufficiency of interest, notwithstanding the ambiguities in some of the judgments. Arguments that the test for standing should differ depending upon which particular remedy was being sought have been generally absent from the subsequent case law.

17.35 In private law, the merits and standing are not generally regarded as distinct: who can sue is determined by the definition of the cause of action. In public law, the traditional approach was to distinguish between standing and the merits. This must be revised to some extent in the light of the *IRC* case. Their Lordships agreed, albeit with differing degrees of emphasis, that standing and the merits could often not be separated in this way. This might be possible in relatively straightforward cases, but for more complex cases it would be necessary to consider the whole legal and factual context to determine whether an applicant possessed a sufficient interest. The term 'merits' here meant that the court would look to the substance of the allegation in order to determine whether the applicant had standing. This included the nature of the power or duties involved, the alleged breach, and the subject matter of the claim.

17.36 This 'fusion' of standing and the merits was to some extent driven by SCA, s 31(3). This requires the court to consider sufficiency of interest at the leave stage. This would, prior to the CPR reforms, often be ex parte, and thus the court might only be possessed of evidence from one side. A court might feel at this stage that the applicant had demonstrated a sufficient interest. The court will consider evidence from both parties at the substantive hearing. It might then form the view that the applicant did not in fact possess the interest claimed. This conclusion would be reached from an appraisal of the nature of the duty cast upon the public body, the nature of the breach, and the position of the applicant. Thus, in the *IRC* case itself the only evidence at the ex parte stage was from the National Federation. By the time of the hearing the IRC had prepared affidavits giving its view of the case. This caused the House of Lords to dismiss the case. The reasoning of their Lordships was, however, subtly different. Some[67] relied most heavily on the statutory framework and background to reach the conclusion that the applicant possessed no sufficient interest. A qualification was added that such a person or group might possess sufficient interest if the illegality were to be sufficiently grave. Other Law Lords, while referring to the statutory context, placed more emphasis on the absence of illegality. If at the

---

[66] [1982] AC 631.
[67] ibid 632–633 *per* Lord Wilberforce, 646 *per* Lord Fraser, 662–663 *per* Lord Roskill.

hearing of the application itself the applicant had established the allegations made at the leave stage then the case would have proceeded.[68]

The relationship between standing at the leave, now permission, stage and at the substantive hearing has been summarized by Lord Donaldson MR in *R v Monopolies and Mergers Commission, ex p Argyll Group plc*[69] as follows. At the leave stage an application should be refused only where the applicant has no interest whatsoever, and is a mere meddlesome busybody. Where, however, the application appears to be arguable, the applicant should be given leave and standing can then be reconsidered as a matter of discretion at the substantive hearing. At this stage the strength of the applicant's interest will be one of the factors to be weighed in the balance. More recently Sedley J in *R v Somerset CC, ex p Dixon*[70] emphasized that the criterion at the leave stage is set merely to prevent an applicant from intervening where there was no legitimate interest. This did not, however, mean that the applicant must show some pecuniary or special personal interest.

17.37

(3) Interpretation of the Sufficiency of Interest Test

(a) Challenges by individuals

There are numerous cases in which the courts have treated the *IRC* decision as a liberalization of the pre-existing standing rules. In reaching the decision to accord the applicant standing, the courts will, however, often not undertake any detailed analysis of the nature of the relevant statutory powers or provisions, apart from adverting to the seriousness of the alleged illegality. Thus in *R v HM Treasury, ex p Smedley*[71] a taxpayer who raised a serious question concerning the legality of governmental action in connection with the European Community was accorded standing. In *R v Felixstowe JJ, ex p Leigh*[72] a journalist as a 'guardian of the public interest' in open justice was held to have a sufficient interest to obtain a declaration that justices could not refuse to reveal their identity. In *R v General Council of the Bar, ex p Percival*[73] the head of a set of chambers was accorded standing to contest a decision by the Bar Council that another barrister should be charged with a more serious, rather than a less serious, charge. Attempts to argue that an applicant must possess something akin to a narrow legal right before being accorded standing have not been successful.[74] Thus in

17.38

---

[68] ibid 637, 644 *per* Lord Diplock, 654 *per* Lord Scarman.
[69] [1986] 1 WLR 763, 773, CA.
[70] [1997] COD 323.
[71] [1985] QB 657, 667, 669–670.
[72] [1987] QB 582, 595–598.
[73] [1991] 1 QB 212.
[74] *R v Secretary of Companies, ex p Central Bank of India* [1986] QB 1114, 1161–1163, CA; *R v Secretary of State for Social Services, ex p Child Poverty Action Group* [1990] 2 QB 540; *R v International Stock Exchange of the UK and the Republic of Ireland, ex p Else (1982) Ltd* [1993] QB 534, 551–552; *R v Haringey LBC, ex p Secretary of State for the Environment* [1991] COD 135.

R v Somerset CC, ex p Dixon [75] the applicant, who was a local resident, a local councillor and a member of various bodies concerned to protect the environment, sought to challenge the grant of planning permission to extend quarrying in a particular area. Sedley J held that standing at the leave stage should only be refused if it was clear that the applicant was a busybody with no legitimate interest in the matter. The applicant in the instant case was not a busybody, and he was perfectly entitled as a citizen to draw the attention of the court to what he considered to be an illegality in the grant of planning permission which was bound to have an impact on the natural environment. This more liberal approach has also been endorsed extra-judicially. [76]

17.39   The sufficiency of interest test has also been interpreted rather more narrowly in other cases. Thus, in *R v Legal Aid Board, ex p Bateman* [77] it was held, on construction of the relevant statutory provisions, that a legally-aided client did not have standing to contest an order made as to the taxation of her solicitor's costs, since she was not affected by the result of the taxation. The action could only be brought by the solicitor, and the fact that the applicant was genuinely concerned to see that her solicitor was properly remunerated did not suffice to afford her a sufficient interest for the purposes of judicial review. [78] In *R v Director of the Serious Fraud Office, ex p Johnson,* [79] it was held that the applicant did not have standing to question the validity of a notice served on his wife obliging her to answer inquiries into a fraud investigation currently under way against her husband. In *R v North West Leicestershire DC, ex p Moses,* [80] the applicant objected to the grant of planning permission for the extension of an airport runway. She had previously lived close to the end of the runway, but now lived six miles away. She argued that no environmental assessment had been made prior to the grant of planning permission. Scott Baker J considered the approach in the *Dixon* case, [81] but adopted a narrower approach. He held that standing should not be accorded where the applicant has no real or justifiable concern about a public law decision. The court's time should not be expended on cases that were bound to fail. The applicant did not, on this criterion, possess a sufficient interest. Moreover, in *R (on the application of Kides) v South Cambridgeshire DC,* [82] the claimant was refused standing to challenge the grant of planning permission. This was because she sought to challenge the permission on a ground related to the provision of affordable housing, whereas the

---

[75] [1997] COD 322.
[76] Woolf, 'Public Law—Private Law: Why the Divide? A Personal View' (n 19 above) 231.
[77] [1992] 1 WLR 711.
[78] See also, *R v LAUTRO, ex p Tee* [1993] COD 362; *R v Secretary of State for Defence, ex p Sancto* [1993] COD 144.
[79] [1993] COD 58.
[80] [2000] JPL 733.
[81] *R v Somerset CC, ex p Dixon* [1997] COD 323.
[82] [2001] EWHC Admin 839; [2003] 1 P & CR 4 at [109].

court held that she had no interest in this matter, and was rather using it to prevent the building of any housing at all. She was, therefore, said to be a mere busybody in relation to affordable housing. There may well be good policy reasons for limiting standing in certain types of case. Thus in *R (on the application of Bulger) v Secretary of State for the Home Department*,[83] the father of a murdered child sought to challenge the Lord Chief Justice's decision fixing the tariff term to be served by those who had murdered his son. Rose LJ held that in criminal cases there was no need for a third party to intervene to uphold the rule of law, since the traditional parties to criminal proceedings, the Crown and the defendant, could do so. The Lord Chief Justice when fixing the sentence had taken account of the views of the victim's family. This did not, however, amount to an invitation to indicate their views on the appropriate tariff, and the claimant could not therefore raise the matter by judicial review.

(b) Challenges by groups

It has been argued persuasively by Cane[84] that there are three kinds of group challenge: associational, surrogate and public interest. Associational standing is typified by an organization suing on behalf of its members. Standing has been accorded in such circumstances where the group consists of persons who are directly affected by the disputed decision.[85] There can equally be cases where one member of a group brings the action on behalf of the group as a whole.[86] Surrogate standing covers the case where a pressure group represents the interests of others, who may not be well placed to bring the action themselves. The courts have allowed challenges brought by the Child Poverty Action Group to decisions concerning social security that affected claimants. Woolf J reasoned that the CPAG was a body designed to represent the interests of unidentified claimants, who stood to be deprived of benefits by the Secretary of State and that it had a sufficient interest to argue the case.[87] The court also construed the Highgate Projects, a charitable body providing hostel accommodation to young offenders, as being a 'person affected' within the meaning of regulations concerning housing benefit. The young people could have acted for themselves, and were therefore competent to authorize the Project to act as their agent in review proceedings.[88] Public interest standing is asserted by those claiming to represent the wider public interest, rather

17.40

---

[83] [2001] EWHC Admin 119; [2001] 3 All ER 449.
[84] P Cane, 'Standing up for the Public' [1995] PL 276.
[85] *Royal College of Nursing of the UK v DHSS* [1981] AC 800; *R v Chief Adjudication Officer, ex p Bland*, The Times, 6 February 1985; *R (on the application of National Association of Guardians ad Litem and Reporting Officers) v Children Family Court Advisory and Support Service* [2001] EWHC Admin 693, [2002] 1 FLR 255.
[86] *R v Dyfed CC, ex p Manson* [1994] COD 366.
[87] *R v Secretary of State for Social Services, ex p Child Poverty Action Group* [1990] 2 QB 540.
[88] *R v Stoke City Council, ex p Highgate Projects* [1994] COD 414.

than merely that of a group with an identifiable membership. In this type of case the decision may affect the public generally, or a section thereof, but no one particular individual has any more immediate interest than any other, and a group seeks to contest the matter before the courts.

17.41   Special problems have been encountered with actions brought by unincorporated associations. The courts are divided as to whether such a body can bring proceedings in its own name. Auld J relied on the general principle that such bodies could not sue or be sued in their own name, and held that they could not seek review in their own name.[89] Turner J reached the opposite conclusion.[90] He reasoned that in private law a person asserted private rights, and such rights could only be enjoyed by a legal person. In public law it was the legality of the public body's actions that were of prime concern. The applicant who claimed a sufficient interest was invoking the supervisory jurisdiction of the court to control excess of power by a public body. Such actions could therefore be brought by an unincorporated association.

(c) Public interest challenges by a group or an individual

17.42   An individual or a group may bring a public interest challenge, although it is now more common for groups to advance such claims. A well-known claim that failed was *R v Secretary of State for the Environment, ex p Rose Theatre Trust Co.*[91] Developers, who had planning permission for an office block, discovered the remains of an important Elizabethan theatre. A number of people formed a company seeking to preserve the remains. They sought to persuade the Secretary of State to include the site in the list of monuments under the Ancient Monuments and Archaeological Areas Act 1979. The Secretary of State could do so if the site appeared to him to be of national importance. If the site was thus designated no work could be done without his consent. Although the Secretary of State agreed that the site was of national importance he declined to include it within the relevant legislation. Schiemann J found that there had in fact been no illegality, but he also held that the applicants had no locus standi. He accepted that a direct financial or legal interest was not necessary in order for an applicant to have standing, and that it was necessary to consider the statute to determine whether it afforded standing to these individuals in this instance. However, he approached the matter with the express view that not every person will always have sufficient interest to bring a case; that the assertion of an interest by many people did not mean that they actually possessed one; *and* that there might be certain types of governmental action which no one could challenge. On the

---

[89] *R v Darlington BC and Darlington Transport Company Ltd, ex p Association of Darlington Taxi Owners and the Darlington Owner Drivers Association* [1994] COD 424.

[90] *R v Traffic Commissioner for the North Western Traffic Area, ex p Brake* [1996] COD 248.

[91] [1990] 1 QB 504; Sir Konrad Schiemann, 'Locus Standi' [1990] PL 342; P Cane, 'Statutes, Standing and Representation' [1990] PL 307.

facts of the case he held that no individual could point to anything in the statute which would give him a greater right or interest than any other that the decision would be taken lawfully. Schiemann J concluded that while in a broad sense we could all expect that decisions be made lawfully, that was insufficient to give the applicants standing.[92]

In other cases public interest challenges have been successful. In *R v Secretary of* **17.43** *State for Employment, ex p Equal Opportunities Commission*,[93] the EOC sought locus standi to argue that certain of the rules concerning entitlement to redundancy pay and protection from unfair dismissal were discriminatory and in breach of EC law. The Sex Discrimination Act 1975, s 53(1) provided that the duties of the EOC were to include working towards the elimination of discrimination, and promoting equality of opportunity between men and women generally. The House of Lords held that the EOC had standing. Lord Keith, giving the majority judgment, reasoned that if the contested provisions were discriminatory then steps taken by the EOC to change them could reasonably be regarded as working towards the elimination of discrimination. It would, said his Lordship, be a retrograde step to hold that the EOC did not have standing to 'agitate in judicial review proceedings questions related to sex discrimination which are of public importance and affect a large section of the population'.[94] In *R v HM Inspector of Pollution, ex p Greenpeace Ltd (No 2)*[95] the applicant group challenged the regulation of the Sellafield nuclear site. Otton J made it clear that interest groups would not automatically be afforded standing merely because the members were concerned about a particular matter, but found that the group did have standing in this case, and declined to follow the *Rose Theatre* decision. He reached his conclusion by taking a number of factors into account, including: the fact that Greenpeace was a respected international organization with a large membership; that a number of its members lived in the Cumbria region; that the issues were serious and complex; that Greenpeace was well-placed to argue them; and that if it did not have standing there might not be any effective way to bring the matter before the court. A liberal attitude towards public interest challenges is also apparent in *R v Secretary of State for Foreign Affairs, ex p World Development Movement*.[96] The WDM sought to challenge the minister's decision to grant aid to fund the construction of the Pergau dam in Malaysia on the ground that it was outside the relevant statutory powers. The court accorded the group standing, taking into account the fact that no other challenger was likely to come forward,

---

[92] See also, *R v Secretary of State for the Home Department, ex p Amnesty International* (31 January 2000).
[93] [1995] 1 AC 1, HL.
[94] ibid 26.
[95] [1994] 4 All ER 329.
[96] [1995] 1 WLR 386.

and the importance of vindicating the rule of law by ensuring that the minister remained within his statutory powers.[97] It is moreover clear that the court will not readily find that the incorporation of a group is a bar to the bringing of an action for judicial review.[98]

(4) Special Cases

(a) Locus standi under the Human Rights Act 1998

17.44 HRA 1998, s 6, created a new statutory head of illegality, which can be used in judicial review actions. The criteria for standing is, however, not the normal test of sufficiency of interest. It is narrower than this, and HRA 1998, s 7(1) states that only a victim can plead this head of illegality concerned with breach of Convention rights. This is reinforced by s 7(3), which states that if proceedings are brought for judicial review the applicant is to be taken as having a sufficient interest in relation to the unlawful act only if he is, or would be, a victim of that act. HRA 1998, s 7(6) stipulates that the criterion as to whether a person is a victim is to be found in the jurisprudence under Art 34 ECHR.

17.45 This article provides that the European Court of Human Rights may receive a petition from any person, non-governmental organization or group of individuals claiming to be the victim of a violation of a Convention right. It is clear from the jurisprudence that there is no actio popularis in this area.[99] This is to be expected given the wording of the article in terms of 'victim'. Article 34 is nonetheless broader than might appear at first sight. It does expressly allow for actions to be brought by organizations such as trade unions, and it seems that such bodies can sue on behalf of their members.[100] It also expressly countenances actions by groups of individuals, provided that each member of the group can show a violation of the relevant right.[101] The term victim has been further expanded by the recognition of potential and indirect victims.[102] The idea of the potential victim has been held to cover the situation where a law has been enacted criminalizing homosexuality, and a complaint has been admitted even though the law had not been applied to the complainant.[103] The concept of the indirect victim has been

---

[97] See also, *R v Secretary of State for Foreign and Commonwealth Affairs, ex p Rees-Mogg* [1994] QB 552; *R v Somerset CC, ex p Dixon* [1997] COD 323; *R v Leicester CC, ex p Blackfordby & Boothorpe Action Group Ltd* [2000] EHLR 215.

[98] *Blackfordby*, ibid.

[99] D Gomien, D Harris and L Zwaak, *Law and Practice of the European Convention on Human Rights and the European Social Charter* (Strasbourg: Council of Europe, 1996) 42–47.

[100] ibid 44.

[101] ibid 43.

[102] ibid 44–46; *Campbell and Cosans v UK (No 2)* Series A No 48 (1982) 4 EHRR 293; *Open Door Counselling Ltd v Ireland* Series A No 246 (1993) 15 EHRR 244.

[103] *Norris v Ireland* Series A No 142 (1991) 13 EHRR 186.

used to admit cases brought by, for example, close relatives of the direct victim, and those who have had a close relationship with the direct victim.[104]

A claimant under the HRA may nonetheless have difficulty in establishing that he or she is a victim. Thus in *Director General of Fair Trading v Proprietary Association of Great Britain*[105] it was held that a trade association for manufacturers in the pharmaceutical industry was not a victim for the purposes of an action alleging a breach of Art 6 ECHR. In *Adams v Scottish Ministers*,[106] the claimant sought to challenge Scottish legislation that criminalized foxhunting, on the ground, inter alia, that it was in breach of the HRA. The court held that membership of a club that supported foxhunting was not equivalent to being actively engaged in it, and therefore the claimant was not a victim for the purposes of the HRA. If a claimant is unable to satisfy the victim test it may still be possible to bring an application for judicial review without directly using the HRA, and relying instead on the common law jurisprudence concerning fundamental rights. It should also be remembered that the test for standing under the HRA will not apply where a claimant seeks to vindicate Convention rights via EC law.

17.46

(b) Locus standi outside s 31

It is still open to a claimant to seek an injunction or a declaration independently of the judicial review procedure enshrined in CPR 54. The circumstances in which this is possible will be considered below.[107] We have already seen that the *IRC*[108] case restricted the *Gouriet*[109] test of private rights and special damage to the private law role of declaration and injunction. It appears nonetheless that the test for standing for declaration and injunction outside SCA 1981, s 31, is still private rights and special damage.[110]

17.47

(c) Attorney-General

The Attorney-General as the legal representative of the Crown represents the interests of the Crown qua Sovereign, and also qua parens patriae. The areas in which this jurisdiction was first invoked were public nuisance and the administration of charitable and public trusts. The Attorney-General may act on his own

17.48

---

[104] Gomien, Harris and Zwaak (n 99 above) 46; *Abdulaziz, Cabales and Balkandali v UK* Series A No 94 (1985) 7 EHRR 471.

[105] [2001] EWCA Civ 1217; [2002] 1 WLR 269.

[106] 2003 SLT 366.

[107] See paras. 17.61–17.68 below.

[108] [1982] AC 617.

[109] [1978] AC 435.

[110] *Barrs v Bethell* [1982] Ch 294; *Steeples v Derbyshire DC* [1985] 1 WLR 256, 290–298; *Ashby v Ebdon* [1985] Ch 394; *Stoke-on-Trent City Council v B & Q (Retail) Ltd* [1984] AC 754, 766–767, 769–771; *Mortimer v Labour Party*, The Independent, 28 February 2000.

initiative, as guardian of the public interest, to restrain public nuisances and prevent excess of power by public bodies.[111]

17.49 There can be particular problems where the Attorney-General seeks to buttress the criminal law. In *A-G v Smith*[112] an injunction was granted to prevent S from making repeated applications for planning permission for a caravan site, despite the presence of penalties in the relevant legislation. In *A-G v Harris*[113] a flower vendor who contravened police regulations many times was prevented from continuing to do so by an injunction. Their Lordships in *Gouriet*[114] felt that this power should be used sparingly, and should be reserved for cases where there were continued breaches of the law, or serious injury was threatened.

17.50 It is not entirely clear whether the Attorney-General seeking an injunction is in an especially privileged position. The law appears to be as follows. The Attorney-General has discretion to decide whether to bring an action or not.[115] If an action is brought and the breach proven the court is not bound to issue an injunction in the Attorney-General's favour, but exceptional circumstances would have to exist before the claim was refused. It will be regarded as a wrong in itself for the law to be flouted.[116]

17.51 The Attorney-General may proceed at the relation of an individual complainant where she does not possess the requisite interest to bring a case in her own name. The consent of the Attorney-General is necessary, the procedure being known as a relator action. In a relator action the Attorney-General is the plaintiff, but in practice the private litigant will instruct counsel, and will remain liable for costs.

(d) Public authorities

17.52 The courts have in the past restrictively construed the locus standi of public authorities. The public authority was required to show an interference with proprietary rights, special damage, or that it was the beneficiary of a statutory duty, in order that the action could be maintained without the Attorney-General.[117] Even where standing seemed to be accorded by a specific statute the courts tended to construe such provisions restrictively,[118] as they did with more general statutory terms.[119]

---

[111] eg, *A-G v PYA Quarries Ltd (No 1)* [1957] 2 QB 169; *A-G v Manchester Corp* [1906] 1 Ch 643; *A-G v Fulham Corp* [1921] 1 Ch 440.

[112] [1978] 2 QB 173, 185.

[113] [1961] 1 QB 74; *A-G v Premier Line Ltd* [1932] 1 Ch 303.

[114] [1978] AC 435. See also, *Stoke-on-Trent City Council v B & Q (Retail) Ltd* [1984] AC 754; *A-G v Able* [1984] QB 975.

[115] *London CC v A-G* [1902] AC 165, 169; *Gouriet v Union of Post Office Workers* [1978] AC 435.

[116] *A-G v Bastow* [1957] 1 QB 514; *A-G v Harris* [1961] 1 QB 74.

[117] *Devonport Corp v Tozer* [1903] 1 Ch 759; *A-G v Pontypridd Waterworks Co* [1909] 1 Ch 388.

[118] *Wallasey Local Board v Gracey* (1887) 36 Ch D 593.

[119] *Prestatyn UDC v Prestatyn Raceway Ltd* [1970] 1 WLR 33.

The legislature responded to the restrictive judicial approach through the enact-   **17.53**
ment of Local Government Act 1972, s 222. This allows a local authority to maintain an action in its own name where the authority considers it expedient for the
promotion and protection of the interests of the inhabitants of its area. It enables
the local authority to sue without joining the Attorney-General, and has been liberally interpreted.[120]

(e) Statutory appeals

The question of who has standing can also arise where a statute allows a 'person   **17.54**
aggrieved' to challenge a decision. One line of cases adopted a narrow, restrictive
meaning of the term 'person aggrieved', requiring the infringement of a private
right or something closely akin thereto.[121] The modern case law has, however, embraced a more liberal philosophy.[122] The House of Lords applied the more liberal
philosophy in *Arsenal Football Club Ltd v Ende*.[123] Their Lordships held that a
ratepayer living in the same borough or even in the same precepting area could
qualify as a person aggrieved so as to be able to challenge the assessment of another's rates as too low. The applicant did not have to show financial detriment,
and a fortiori the infringement of a legal right was not a necessary prerequisite in
order to be able to maintain a claim.

The law in this area has now been clarified by *Cook v Southend BC*.[124] Woolf LJ un-   **17.55**
dertook an extensive review of the authorities in this area. He recognized that
some of the earlier decisions had taken a restrictive view of the term 'person aggrieved', but pointed to the liberal approach adopted in more recent jurisprudence. Henceforth the following principles should apply whenever the phrase
'person aggrieved' appeared in any statute concerning appeal rights, subject to a
clear contrary intent in the particular statute.[125]

- A body corporate, including a local authority, was just as capable of being a person aggrieved as an individual.
- Any person who had a decision made against him, particularly in adversarial proceedings, would be a person aggrieved for the purposes of appealing against that
  decision, unless the decision amounted to an acquittal of a purely criminal case.

---

[120] *Solihull MBC v Maxfern Ltd* [1977] 1 WLR 127; *Stafford BC v Elkenford Ltd* [1977] WLR 324;
Thanet DC v Ninedrive Ltd [1978] 1 All ER 703; *Kent CC v Batchelor (No 2)* [1979] 1 WLR 213;
Stoke-on-Trent City Council v B & Q (Retail) Ltd [1984] AC 754; *Monks v East Northamptonshire DC*
[2002] EWHC 473, The Times, 15 March 2002.
[121] *Ex p Sidebotham* (1880) 14 Ch D 458; *Buxton v Minister of Housing and Local Government*
[1961] 1 QB 278.
[122] *A-G of the Gambia v N'Jie* [1961] AC 617, 634; *Maurice v London CC* [1964] 2 QB 362, 378;
Turner v Secretary of State for the Environment (1973) 28 P & CR 123, 134, 139.
[123] [1979] AC 1, HL.
[124] [1990] 2 QB 1.
[125] ibid 64–65.

- The fact that the decision against which the person wished to appeal reversed a decision which was originally taken by that person, and did not otherwise adversely affect him, did not prevent that person being a person aggrieved. To the contrary, it indicated that he was a person aggrieved who could use his appeal rights to have the original decision restored.

(5) Intervention in Judicial Review Actions

17.56 An issue that is closely related to standing is that of intervention. The rules on intervention by a third party in judicial review proceedings are as follows. RSC Ord 53, r 5(3) provided that the claim form must be served on all persons directly affected, and r 5(7) allowed the court to hear representations from those who ought to have been served. The requirement that a person be directly affected was narrowly construed to mean that the person had to be affected without the impact of any intermediate agency.[126] Ord 53, r 9(1) allowed the court to admit a person who wished to be heard in opposition to the application for review where the court considered that he was a proper person to be heard.[127]

17.57 The CPR now govern this area. CPR 54.1(2)(f) allows an interested party, other than the claimant and defendant, who is directly affected by the claim, to be served. CPR 54.17 provides that any person may apply for permission to file evidence or make representations at the hearing. The 'amicus brief' is used quite extensively in other countries such as the United States, Canada, and by the European Court of Human Rights. The recent liberalization of standing by our courts has made them more receptive to such interventions.[128]

D. Disclosure and Inspection

17.58 The 1977 reforms made improved provision for discovery, and this was regarded as part of the justification for procedural exclusivity. The reality is that discovery is rarely awarded in judicial review proceedings, because of the cost and time implications.[129] The normal criterion was that discovery would be

---

[126] *R v Rent Service Officer, ex p Muldoon* [1996] 1 WLR 1103.

[127] *R v Monopolies and Mergers Commission, ex p Milk Marque Ltd* [2000] COD 329.

[128] *R v Home Secretary, ex p Sivakumaran* [1988] AC 958; *R v Coventry City Council, ex p Phoenix Aviation* [1995] 3 All ER 37; *R v Secretary of State for the Home Department, ex p Venables* [1998] AC 407, HL; *R v Secretary of State for the Home Department, ex p Hargreaves* [1997] 1 WLR 906; *R v Lord Chancellor, ex p Witham* [1998] QB 575; *R (on the application of Northern Ireland Human Rights Commission) v Greater Belfast Coroner* [2002] UKHL 25, [2002] NI 236.

[129] *O'Reilly v Mackman* [1983] 2 AC 237, HL; *R v Secretary of State for the Home Department, ex p Khawaja* [1984] AC 74, HL; *Air Canada v Secretary of State for Trade (No 2)* [1983] 2 AC 394; *Lonrho plc v Tebbit* [1992] 4 All ER 280; *R v Inland Revenue Commissioners, ex p Taylor* [1989] 1 All ER 906; *R v Secretary of State for the Environment, ex p Doncaster BC* [1990] COD 441; *R v Secretary of State for the Home Department, ex p BH* [1990] COD 445; *R v Secretary of State for Education and*

allowed when it was necessary either for disposing fairly of the cause or for saving costs.[130]

The problem for the individual can be formidable. It can be extremely difficult to sustain certain types of challenge without discovery, and cross-examination. Allegations that an administrator has taken irrelevant considerations into account, or has acted for improper purposes, are but two such instances. The need for discovery will, moreover, be needed if the courts are to develop emerging doctrines such as proportionality.

17.59

It remains to be seen how far the CPR make any difference in this respect. It should be noted that CPR 54 is regarded as a modification of CPR 8, which deals with claims where there is no substantial dispute as to fact. CPR 31 deals with disclosure and inspection of documents. A party discloses a document by stating that the document exists or has existed.[131] A party to whom a document has been disclosed has, subject to certain exceptions, a right to inspect it.[132] An order to give disclosure is, unless the court otherwise directs, an order to give standard disclosure.[133] It is open to the court to dispense with or limit standard disclosure.[134] Where a court does make such an order then it requires a party to disclose the documents on which it relies, and the documents which adversely affect its own, or another party's, case, or support another party's case, and such documents which it is required to disclose by a relevant practice direction.[135] A party is under an obligation to make a reasonable search for such documents.[136] The court is also empowered to make an order for specific disclosure or specific inspection, requiring the party to disclose those documents specified in the order.[137] There is little doubt that these rules give the court ample powers through which to require the public body to provide the information needed for the applicant to sustain its case. It is, however, open to the court to dispense with or limit standard disclosure, and the court also has discretion in relation to requests for more specific disclosure. Much will, therefore, depend upon how the courts use the powers at their disposal. It should also be borne in mind that a premise underlying the new rules is that disclosure should be more limited or constrained as compared with the situation which existed hitherto.

17.60

Science, ex p J [1993] COD 146; *R v Secretary of State for Transport, ex p APH Road Safety Ltd (No 1)* [1993] COD 150; *R v Secretary of State for Health, ex p Hackney LBC* [1994] COD 432; *R v Arts Council of England, ex p Women's Playhouse Trust* [1998] COD 175.

[130] RSC Ord 24, r 13(1).
[131] CPR 31.2.
[132] ibid 31.3.
[133] ibid 31.5(1).
[134] ibid 31.5(2).
[135] ibid 31.6.
[136] ibid 31.7(1).
[137] ibid 31.12.

E. The Exclusivity Principle

(1) O'Reilly v Mackman

17.61   The claim for judicial review must be read in the light of the decision in *O'Reilly v Mackman*.[138] The case limited the circumstances in which a declaration or an injunction in a public law case could be sought outside the judicial review procedure. Lord Diplock gave judgment for the House of Lords, and reasoned as follows. The prerogative orders had, prior to the 1977 reforms, been subject to a number of limitations. There was no right to discovery, damages could not be claimed in conjunction with one of the orders and cross-examination upon affidavits occurred very rarely if at all. These limitations justified the use of the declaration. However, the reformed Ord 53 had removed the above defects by providing for discovery, allowing damages to be claimed, and making provision for cross-examination. The reformed procedure also provided important safeguards for the public body, including the requirement of leave and the short time limit. It would therefore normally be an abuse of process to seek a declaration outside of s 31. This was subject to two exceptions: collateral attack to protect private rights and consent.

17.62   Claimants have nonetheless sought to bring cases by ordinary action rather than the judicial review procedure. The principal reason is that if they were forced to bring their cases within s 31 they would be outside the short time limit and hence their claims would fail. A second reason for seeking to bring the claim outside s 31 is that the applicant may wish to investigate factual issues relating to the case, and to have the possibility of cross-examining those on the other side. While it is possible for this to be done within the judicial review procedure, it is not normal.

(2) Collateral Attack and Private Rights

17.63   The courts struggled with the private rights exception in the years after *O'Reilly*. Numerous cases went to the House of Lords.[139] The cases revealed the difficulty of deciding whether a particular interest should be characterized as a private right. It was also unclear whether the presence of a private right meant that the principle in *O'Reilly* should be deemed no longer applicable at all, or whether it was merely an important factor, which could lead the court to make a discretionary exception to the *O'Reilly* principle.

---

[138] [1983] 2 AC 237.
[139] *Cocks v Thanet DC* [1983] 2 AC 286, HL; *Davy v Spelthorne BC* [1984] AC 262, HL; *Wandsworth LBC v Winder* [1985] AC 461, HL.

This ambiguity was brought to the fore in *Roy v Kensington and Chelsea and* **17.64**
Westminster Family Practitioner Committee.[140] The applicant was a doctor who was
paid certain sums under National Health Service (NHS) regulations for treating
patients. The relevant regulations provided that the doctor would only be paid the
full basic rate if he devoted a substantial part of his time to treating patients on the
NHS, as opposed to private practice. The Kensington Committee decided that
the applicant was not complying with this condition and therefore reduced his allowance by 20 per cent. The applicant claimed that this was a breach of contract
by the Committee. The Committee argued that the action should have been
brought by way of judicial review. The application would then have failed since
it would have been outside the time limit. The House of Lords found for the
applicant. Lord Lowry proffered two possible interpretations of the exception in
O'Reilly v Mackman:[141]

> The 'broad approach' was that the 'rule in *O'Reilly v Mackman*' did not apply gen-
> erally against bringing actions to vindicate private rights in all circumstances in
> which those actions involved a challenge to a public law act or decision, but that it
> merely required the aggrieved person to proceed by judicial review only when pri-
> vate rights were not at stake. The 'narrow approach' assumed that the rule applied
> generally to *all* proceedings in which public law acts or decisions were challenged,
> subject to some exceptions when private law rights were involved. There was no
> need in *O'Reilly v Mackman* to choose between these approaches, but it seems clear
> that Lord Diplock considered himself to be stating a general rule with exceptions.
> For my part, I much prefer the broad approach, which is both traditionally ortho-
> dox and consistent with the *Pyx Granite* principle . . . It would also, if adopted, have
> the practical merit of getting rid of a procedural minefield. I shall, however, be con-
> tent for the purpose of this appeal to adopt the narrow approach, which avoids the
> need to discuss the proper scope of the rule, a point which has not been argued be-
> fore your Lordships and has hitherto been seriously discussed only by the academic
> writers.

It is clear that Lord Lowry preferred the broad view of the exception, the effect of
which is to render the rule in *O'Reilly* inapplicable when cases involve private
rights: applicants can proceed unencumbered by ordinary action. This view has
been generally adopted in later cases.[142]

In *Boddington v British Transport Police*,[143] the House of Lords held that it was **17.65**
open to a defendant in criminal proceedings to challenge a bye-law, or an administrative decision made thereunder, where the prosecution was premised on its validity, unless there was a clear parliamentary intent to the contrary. The challenge

---

[140] [1992] 1 AC 624.
[141] ibid 653.
[142] *Lonrho plc v Tebbit* [1991] 4 All ER 973, Ch D, [1992] 4 All ER 280, CA; *Trustees of the Dennis Rye Pension Fund v Sheffield City Council* [1998] 1 WLR 840; *British Steel plc v Customs and Excise Commissioners (No 1)* [1997] 2 All ER 366.
[143] [1999] 2 AC 143, HL.

to the measure did not have to be brought by way of judicial review. The inability to plead the invalidity of a bye-law in the course of a criminal prosecution was, said Lord Steyn, contrary to principle and precedent.[144] Lord Steyn held that procedural exclusivity would only be insisted upon where the sole object of the action was to challenge a public law act or decision. It did not apply in a civil case when an individual sought to establish private law rights, which could not be determined without an examination of the validity of the public law decision. Nor did it apply where a defendant in a civil case sought to defend himself by questioning the validity of the public law decision. Nor did it apply in a criminal case where the liberty of the subject was at stake.[145] It was accepted in *Boddington*[146] that there could be cases where a challenge to the validity of an order other than by way of judicial review could be defeated by special statutory provisions.[147]

17.66   The breadth of the exception to *O'Reilly* is also apparent from *Mercury Ltd v Director General of Telecommunications*.[148] In 1986 two companies, Mercury (M) and British Telecommunications (BT), made an agreement for the provision of services pursuant to condition 13 of BT's licence. The agreement provided for a reference to the Director General of Telecommunications (DGT) where there was a dispute between M and BT. The parties referred a matter to the DGT concerning pricing for the conveyance of calls. The DGT made his determination and M challenged this, arguing that the DGT had misinterpreted the costs to be taken into account when resolving the pricing issue. M's challenge was by way of originating summons for a declaration. The DGT and BT argued that the case should have been brought by way of RSC Ord 53. Lord Slynn gave the judgment for a unanimous House of Lords in favour of M. His Lordship acknowledged the rationale for the presumptive exclusivity of this procedure given in *O'Reilly*, but noted also that this exclusivity was only ever presumptive rather than conclusive in nature. The criterion that should be used to decide whether a case could be brought outside Ord 53, was whether 'the proceedings constitute an abuse of the process of the court'.[149] The abuse of process test does not on its face require the existence of any private right as a condition precedent for an applicant to be able to proceed by ordinary action. It would seem that if an applicant has private rights then the case will be allowed to proceed by ordinary action, even if it does involve a public law matter, and this will be deemed ipso facto not to be an abuse of process. However, even where there are no such rights it will be open to an applicant to convince the court that recourse to an ordinary action does not constitute an abuse of process.

---

[144] *Boddington v British Transport Police* (n 143 above) 172.
[145] ibid 172.
[146] ibid 173.
[147] *R v Wicks* [1998] AC 92.
[148] [1996] 1 WLR 48, HL.
[149] ibid 57.

(3) The Impact of the CPR

It is clear that the CPR will have a marked impact on the relationship between the public law procedures, and the ordinary procedures for civil action. This is because a central theme of the CPR is to accord the court more control over ordinary civil actions than previously existed. The implications for the issue of exclusivity, and the exceptions thereto, are apparent from *Clark v University of Lincolnshire and Humberside*.[150] The claimant brought a contract action against a University in relation to the classification of her degree. The University argued that the claim should have been brought by judicial review. It contended that the contract action was an abuse of process, by allowing suit well beyond the three-month time limit for judicial review. Lord Woolf MR held that the issue of exclusivity should now be seen in the light of the new CPR. This was because the CPR contained safeguards for public bodies *even where* there was an ordinary civil action. The safeguards related to the stopping of the action, and the time in which it could be brought. If proceedings involving public law issues were begun by ordinary action under CPR Pts 7 or 8, they would be subject to CPR Pt 24. This enabled the court to give summary judgment where it believed that the applicant had no real prospect of success. This restricted the inconvenience to public bodies by the pursuit of hopeless claims.[151] The normal time limit for a civil action is six years. Lord Woolf acknowledged that it would in the past not have been appropriate to regard delay within the six-year period as a reason for characterizing the action as abusive. The position was, said Lord Woolf, different under the CPR. Delay in commencing proceedings under the CPR could be a factor in deciding whether the proceedings were abusive. This was especially so where the action could have been brought by judicial review.[152]

17.67

(4) Exclusivity: A Summary

It might be helpful at this juncture to summarize the law and to state when an individual will be allowed to proceed by an ordinary action.

17.68

- The courts will only insist on a case being brought via the judicial review procedure if the sole aim is to challenge a public law act or decision.
- A civil case can be brought by ordinary action where the individual seeks to establish private rights, even if this requires an examination of the validity of the public law decision.
- A defendant in a civil case can challenge a public law decision in the course of defending the private law action. It is not absolutely certain whether it is

---

[150] [2000] 1 WLR 1988, CA.
[151] ibid at [27]–[28].
[152] ibid at [35]–[36].

enough to be the defendant or whether the defendant must also be able to assert that his rights are being infringed. Some cases have emphasized the first of these factors, without inquiring too closely whether the individual had private rights which were affected, or what the precise nature of these rights were.[153] Other cases suggested that an individual should have some private right in order to be able to raise the invalidity of a public body's action by way of defence in an ordinary action outside s 31.[154] However, the formulation by Lord Steyn in *Boddington* indicated that being a defendant was sufficient in itself.[155]

- A defendant in a criminal case will normally be able to raise the invalidity of the subordinate legislation or order on which the prosecution is based by way of defence to the criminal charge, unless there is a clear indication from the relevant statute that such a challenge can only be made via judicial review.

- A person may be able to proceed by ordinary action even where no private rights are present, provided that the court decides that to do so is not an abuse of process.

- In cases of doubt the advice of Lord Woolf[156] was that the action should be brought by way of judicial review. If the matter was raised in an ordinary action and there was an application to strike out the case on the ground that it should have been brought by way of judicial review, it was open to the court to consider whether leave would have been granted under the judicial review procedure. If the answer was in the affirmative then this was a good indication that the ordinary action should not be struck out.

- The degree of difference between bringing an ordinary civil action and a claim for judicial review has, however, diminished under the CPR, as interpreted in *Clark*.[157] The court read the CPR to provide some protection for public bodies even in ordinary civil actions, thereby diminishing to some extent the incentive to proceed outside the judicial review procedure.

F. The Scope of the Judicial Review Procedure: 'Public Law' Cases

(1) The Reasons for Wishing to Use the Judicial Review Procedure

17.69 The preceding discussion has concentrated upon cases where individuals wish to proceed by ordinary action. The traffic has not, however, been purely 'one way'.

---

[153] *West Glamorgan CC v Rafferty* [1987] 1 WLR 457; *R v Reading Crown Court, ex p Hutchinson* [1988] QB 384.
[154] *Waverley BC v Hilden* [1988] 1 WLR 246; *Avon CC v Buscott* [1988] QB 656.
[155] [1999] 2 AC 143, 172–173.
[156] *Trustees of the Dennis Rye Pension Fund v Sheffield City Council* [1998] 1 WLR 840.
[157] *Clark v University of Lincolnshire and Humberside* [2000] 1 WLR 1988, CA.

There have been many cases where individuals have sought to argue their way into the judicial review procedure. This may be because the claimant has no other cause of action.[158] It may be because the remedy will be more effective. It may in certain cases be because the scope of the obligations imposed upon the defendant body exceeds those that would be imposed in a private law cause of action.[159]

(2) Public Law: The Source and Nature of the Power[160]

An obvious test to determine whether a case is of public law nature and hence **17.70** susceptible to the judicial review procedure is to consider the source of the authority's power: if that power is derived from statute then the body is presumptively public and amenable to review. There are two difficulties with this test. First, applied literally it would bring within public law the activities of any body regulated by statute, even if the body generally operated within the private commercial sphere. The second problem is a converse of the first. A body may owe the source of its public authority to statute, but not all of its operations should nonetheless be regarded as raising public law issues. Local authorities and other public bodies frequently operate in an ordinary commercial capacity.

The difficulties of a formalistic test have inclined the courts towards a more open- **17.71** textured criterion, which requires them to consider the nature of the power wielded by the particular body. The formulation of this test has varied. In *R v Panel on Take-Overs and Mergers, ex p Datafin plc*,[161] Lloyd LJ stated that if the source of the power was statutory then the body would be subject to judicial review, but would not if the source of power were contractual. However in between these 'extremes' one had to look at the nature of the power. Thus if the body was exercising public law functions, or such functions had public law consequences, then the judicial review procedure would be applicable. This formulation appears to beg the question,[162] as do such statements that if a duty is a public duty then the body is subject to public law. Lord Donaldson MR, by way of contrast, seemed only to be concerned with the source of a body's power in order to exclude those

[158] *R v Panel on Take-Overs and Mergers, ex p Datafin plc* [1987] QB 815, CA; *R v Secretary of State for the Home Department, ex p Benwell* [1985] QB 554, 571, 572; *R v Bishop of Stafford, ex p Owen* [2001] ACD 14.
[159] *R v Disciplinary Committee of the Jockey Club, ex p Aga Khan* [1993] 1 WLR 909, CA.
[160] J Beatson, ' "Public" and "Private" in English Administrative Law' (1987) 103 LQR 34; P Cane, 'Public Law and Private Law: A Study of the Analysis of and Use of a Legal Concept' in J Eekelaar and J Bell (eds), *Oxford Essays in Jurisprudence, 3rd Series* (Oxford: OUP, 1987) ch 3; J Allison, *A Continental Distinction in the Common Law: A Historical and Comparative Perspective on English Public Law* (Oxford: OUP, 1996); N Bamforth, 'The Public Law–Private Law Distinction: A Comparative and Philosophical Approach' in P Leyland and T Woods (eds), *Administrative Law Facing the Future: Old Constraints and New Horizons* (London: Blackstone, 1997) ch 6.
[161] [1987] QB 815, 846–869.
[162] As admitted by Lloyd LJ, ibid 847, who nonetheless denied the circularity.

institutions whose power was based upon contract or consent.[163] Any other body could be subject to review if there was a sufficiently public element. How far power that is based upon contract or consent is subject to judicial review will be considered more fully below. The uncertainty of this approach is to be expected. Statements that a body must have a sufficiently 'public element', or must be exercising a public duty, cannot function as anything other than conclusory labels for what we choose to include in them.

(3) The Boundaries of Public Law

(a) Public bodies and Next Steps agencies

17.72 It is clear that traditional public bodies will be able to use the application for judicial review, and that they can be subject to such actions. In principle it is clear that Next Steps agencies must be subject to the judicial review procedure, given that they are not formally separate from their sponsoring department, and given also that most of these agencies are engaged in public service delivery.

(b) Public authorities and contracting-out

17.73 Contracting-out has been used increasingly by government as a method of service delivery. It is clear that a judicial review action may still be maintained against the public body that has contracted-out the power. This may however be of limited utility, since there may be no viable claim against the public body in such instances. Whether the private body to whom power has been contracted-out can be subject to judicial review is therefore important. This can be exemplified by *R v Servite Houses, ex p Goldsmith*.[164] The applicants were elderly residents at a home run by Servite Houses, a charitable housing association. Wandsworth Council had, pursuant to its statutory duties, assessed them as being in need of residential accommodation.[165] The Council was allowed to contract out the provision of such accommodation.[166] Servite decided to close the home in which the applicants lived. The residents objected claiming that they had been promised a home for life.[167] The court was therefore required to decide whether the private service provider was amenable to judicial review. This was all the more important, given that there was no obvious private law form of redress.[168] Moses J recognized the

---

[163] *R v Panel on Take-Overs and Mergers, ex p Datafin plc* (n 161 above) 838–839.

[164] (2000) 2 LGLR 997.

[165] National Health Service and Community Care Act 1990, s 47.

[166] National Assistance Act 1948, s 26.

[167] *R v North and East Devon Health Authority, ex p Coughlan* [2001] QB 213, CA.

[168] Servite had lawfully terminated its contract with Wandsworth, the applicants had no contract with Servite, and Wandsworth had discharged its obligation by making the initial arrangements with Servite. Wandsworth could not compel Servite to keep the house open, although the local authority would be under an obligation to find alternative accommodation for the applicants.

importance of the issue, as to how the courts should respond to the increasing contractualization of government,[169] but held that Servite itself was not amenable to judicial review.

Moses J considered whether Servite could be amenable to review because there was a statutory underpinning to its function. There must, said Moses J, be sufficient statutory penetration, which went beyond the statutory regulation of the manner in which the service is provided. This depended on whether the relevant legislation could be said to enmesh Servite's provision of residential accommodation into a statutory system of community care. Moses J denied that this was so, and held that the effect of the legislation was to create a mixed economy provision for community care services, some being provided in house, others through contracting-out. It followed that the relationship between Servite and the applicants was to be governed solely by private law.[170] Moses J held moreover that the legislation empowering the contracting-out could not constitute the statutory underpinning to enable Servite's functions to be regarded as public functions. The applicants could not successfully contend that 'because legislation permits a public authority to enter into arrangements with a private body, the functions of that body are, by dint of that legislation, to be regarded as public functions'.[171] Moses J also considered whether the functions performed by Servite could be regarded as public in the absence of any statutory underpinning. He found 'enormous attraction' in this approach,[172] but felt unable, in the light of existing precedent, to adopt it.

17.74

The conclusion that Servite was not amenable to review was regrettable.[173] There is nothing in the logic of contracting-out that dictates whether the service provider should be subject to private law or public law obligations. The conclusion that the case could not be resolved via statutory underpinning was premised on the irrelevance of the enabling legislation itself. This is unwarranted. The concept of statutory underpinning was developed in cases where there was no contracting-out. It served to identify when bodies that were not public in the strict sense of the term, should nonetheless be regarded as susceptible to judicial review. The fact that such a body was recognized directly or indirectly in legislation was relevant in determining the ambit of judicial review. It is axiomatic to this reasoning that the legislation, where it exists, is central to deciding whether the body is amenable to review. Consider then the application of this idea to situations where

17.75

---

[169] *R v Servite Houses, ex p Goldsmith* (2000) 2 LGLR 997, 1010, 1025.
[170] ibid 1018.
[171] ibid 1019.
[172] ibid 1020; M Hunt, 'Constitutionalism and the Contractualisation of Government' in M Taggart (ed), *The Province of Administrative Law* (Oxford: Hart, 1997) ch 2; Lord Steyn, *The Constitutionalisation of Public Law* (Constitution Unit, 1999).
[173] P Craig, 'Contracting-out, the Human Rights Act and the Scope of Judicial Review' (2002) 118 LQR 551.

there is contracting-out. There is a public function, the provision of care facilities for certain people. The legislation expressly provides that the function can be undertaken in house or contracted-out. It might well be felt with some justification that this is a stronger instance of statutory underpinning than that in a *Datafin*-type case. In the case of contracting-out there is legislation that explicitly and directly, not implicitly and indirectly, tells us that a private party can perform the public function cast on the local authority. However, whereas in the *Datafin* type of case it is regarded as axiomatic that the legislation is central to deciding whether the body is amenable to review, in the case of contracting-out we are told that it cannot be taken into account.

(c) Public authorities and contracting power

17.76 The traditional tendency was to see contracts, even those made by public bodies, as essentially private matters.[174] The courts have now moved away from this stance, but their attitude towards such contracts is still somewhat ambivalent. The preponderant approach has been to regard contracts made by public authorities as subject to judicial review if there is a sufficiently 'public law element' to the case.[175]

17.77 Procurement decisions have been held amenable to review. Thus the court reviewed a local authority decision not to deal with Shell because other companies in the same corporate group had contacts with South Africa.[176] Which procurement decisions will be subject to judicial review is, however, unclear. In *R v Lord Chancellor's Department, ex p Hibbit and Saunders*,[177] the Lord Chancellor's Department invited tenders for court reporting services. The unsuccessful applicant sought judicial review on the ground that it had a legitimate expectation that discussions would not be held with some of the tenderers to enable them to submit lower bids. The court, while sympathetic to this claim, held that the decision was not amenable to review, because it lacked a sufficiently public law element. It was not sufficient to create a public law obligation that the respondent was a public body carrying out governmental functions. If such a body entered a contract with a third party then the contract would define the nature of the parties' obligations, unless there was some additional element giving rise to a public law obligation. A public law element might be found either where there was some special aim being pursued by the government through the tendering process which set it apart from ordinary commercial tenders, or where there was

---

[174] S Arrowsmith, 'Judicial Review and the Contractual Powers of Public Authorities' (1990) 106 LQR 277.

[175] *R v Barnsley MBC, ex p Hook* [1976] 1 WLR 1052; *R v Birmingham City Council, ex p Dredger* [1993] COD 340; *Cannock Chase DC v Kelly* [1978] 1 WLR 1; *Sevenoaks DC v Emmott* (1979) 79 LGR 346.

[176] *R v Lewisham LBC, ex p Shell UK Ltd* [1988] 1 All ER 938; *R v Enfield LBC, ex p TF Unwin (Roydon)* [1989] COD 466.

[177] [1993] COD 326; *R v Leeds City Council, ex p Cobleigh* [1997] COD 69.

some statutory underpinning, such as where there was a statutory obligation to negotiate the contract in a particular way, and with particular terms. However in *R v Legal Aid Board, ex p Donn & Co*[178] it was held that a legal aid committee was susceptible to judicial review when deciding to award a contract for the conduct of multi-party litigation. Ognall J held that such a case might be regarded as being within public law either because there was a statutory underpinning; or because, irrespective of any connection with a statute or policy, the process might in any event have a sufficient public law element.

(d) Regulatory bodies

There are certain instances where it can be said that the business of government has been privatized.[179] This provides an apt description of regulatory bodies which are private, but which have been integrated, directly or indirectly, into a system of statutory regulation. *R v Panel on Take-Overs and Mergers, ex p Datafin plc*[180] is the seminal decision in this category. The applicants complained that the Panel on Take-Overs and Mergers had incorrectly applied their take-over rules, and had thereby allowed an advantage to be gained by the applicant's rivals who were bidding for the same company. The Panel was a self-regulating body which had no direct statutory, prerogative or common law powers, but it was supported by certain statutory powers that presupposed its existence, and its decisions could result in the imposition of penalties. The Panel opposed judicial review, arguing that it was not amenable to the prerogative orders, which had been restricted to bodies exercising powers derived from the prerogative or statute. The court rejected this view. The 'source' of a body's powers was not the only criterion for judging whether a body was amenable to public law. The absence of a statutory or prerogative base for such powers did not exclude s 31 if the 'nature' of the power rendered the body suitable for judicial review. The nature of the Panel's powers was held to satisfy this alternative criterion for a number of reasons.

17.78

First, the Panel, although self-regulating, did not operate consensually or voluntarily, but rather imposed a collective code on those within its ambit.[181] Secondly, the Panel was performing a public duty as manifested by the government's willingness to limit legislation in this area, and to use the Panel as part of its regulatory machinery.[182] There had been an 'implied devolution of power'[183] by the government to the Panel, and certain legislation presupposed its existence. Thirdly, its source of

17.79

---

[178] [1996] 3 All ER 1.
[179] The phrase was used by Hoffmann LJ in *R v Disciplinary Committee of the Jockey Club, ex p Aga Khan* [1993] 1 WLR 909, CA.
[180] [1987] QB 815, CA.
[181] ibid 825–826, 845–846.
[182] ibid 838–839, 848–849, 850–851.
[183] ibid 849.

power was only partly moral persuasion, this being reinforced by statutory powers exercisable by the government and the Bank of England.[184] Finally, the applicants did not appear to have any cause of action in contract or tort against the Panel.[185] Similar reasoning can be found in other cases.[186]

(e) Regulatory bodies, contract and control

17.80 The courts have experienced more difficulty in determining the boundaries of judicial review in a group of cases not far removed from those in the preceding section. These cases also concern regulatory bodies that exercise control over a particular industry, but there is no governmental involvement in these areas as such. These regulatory institutions are not part of a schema of statutory regulation. Whether this should make a difference will be considered in due course. The courts have on the whole been unwilling to extend judicial review to cover such cases.[187]

17.81 *R v Disciplinary Committee of the Jockey Club, ex p Aga Khan*[188] is the leading case. The applicant was an owner of racehorses and was therefore bound to register with the Jockey Club, and to enter a contractual relationship whereby he adhered to its rules of racing. The applicant's horse was disqualified after winning a major race, and he sought judicial review. The Court of Appeal found that in general the Club was not susceptible to judicial review. It rejected the argument that the decision in *Law* had been overtaken by *Datafin*. The court acknowledged that the Club regulated a national activity, and Sir Thomas Bingham MR accepted that if it did not regulate the sport then the government would in all probability be bound to do so. Notwithstanding this the court reached its conclusion because the Club was not in its origin, constitution, membership or history a public body, and its powers were not governmental. Moreover, the applicant in this particular case would have a remedy outside s 31, because he had a contract with the Jockey Club. The court did, however, leave open the possibility that some cases concerning bodies like the Jockey

---

[184] *R v Panel on Take-Overs and Mergers, ex p Datafin plc* (n 180 above) 838–839, 851–852.

[185] ibid 838–839.

[186] *R v Panel on Take-Overs and Mergers, ex p Guinness plc* [1990] 1 QB 146; *R v Advertising Standards Authority, ex p Insurance Services plc* [1990] COD 42; *Bank of Scotland v Investment Management Regulatory Organisation Ltd* 1989 SLT 432; *R v Financial Intermediaries Managers and Brokers Regulatory Association, ex p Cochrane* [1990] COD 33; *R v Code of Practice Committee of the Association of the British Pharmaceutical Industry, ex p Professional Counselling Aids Ltd* [1991] COD 228; *R v Visitors to the Inns of Court, ex p Calder* [1994] QB 1; *R v Governors of Haberdashers' Aske's Hatcham College Trust, ex p Tyrell* [1995] COD 399; *R v BBC and ITC, ex p Referendum Party* [1997] COD 459; *R v London Metal Exchange Ltd, ex p Albatross Warehousing BV* (30 March 2000); *Aston Cantlow and Wilmcote with Billesley Parochial Church Council v Wallbank* [2001] EWCA Civ 713, [2002] Ch 51.

[187] *Law v National Greyhound Racing Club Ltd* [1983] 1 WLR 1302; *R v Disciplinary Committee of the Jockey Club, ex p Massingberd-Mundy* [1993] 2 All ER 207; *R v Jockey Club, ex p RAM Racecourses Ltd* [1993] 2 All ER 225.

[188] [1993] 1 WLR 909, CA.

Club might be brought within the public law procedures, particularly where the applicant or plaintiff had no contractual relationship with the Club, or where the Club made rules which were discriminatory in nature.

A similar reluctance to subject the governing authorities' of sporting associations to judicial review is apparent in other cases.[189] The disinclination to intervene via judicial review with such bodies is not restricted to those in the sporting arena. In *R v Lloyd's of London, ex p Briggs*,[190] it was held that Lloyd's of London was not amenable to judicial review in an action brought by 'names' who had lost money in insurance syndicates which had covered asbestosis and pollution claims. The court held that Lloyd's was not a public body regulating the insurance market, but rather a body that ran one part of the market pursuant to a private Act of Parliament. The case was concerned solely with the contracts between the names and their managing agents.   **17.82**

There are a number of reasons for not regarding these as 'public law' cases. The courts recognize that these regulatory authorities exercise power over their area, but they do not necessarily accept that this should be characterized as a species of public power.[191] There is concern over the suitability of the public law controls for the types of body under discussion.[192] The courts have also been concerned that the 'stopping point' of public law would be difficult to determine if these bodies were held to be amenable to review.[193]   **17.83**

The line drawn by the cases considered within this section has, not surprisingly, been contested. Pannick has argued that the exercise of monopolistic power should serve to bring bodies within the ambit of judicial review. To speak of a consensual foundation for a body's power is largely beside the point where those who wish to partake in the activity will have no realistic choice but to accept that power.[194] Black has argued that the emphasis given to the contractual foundations for a body's power as the reason for withholding review are misplaced. She contends that the courts are confusing contract as an instrument of economic exchange, with contract as a regulatory instrument.[195]   **17.84**

---

[189] *R v Football Association Ltd, ex p Football League Ltd* [1993] 2 All ER 833; *R v Football Association of Wales, ex p Flint Town United Football Club* [1991] COD 44.

[190] [1993] 1 Lloyd's Rep 176; *R v Insurance Ombudsman Bureau, ex p Aegon Life Assurance Ltd* [1994] COD 426; *R v Panel of the Federation of Communication Services Ltd, ex p Kubis* [1998] COD 5; *R (on the application of Sunspell Ltd (t/a Superlative Travel) v Association of British Travel Agents* [2001] ACD 16; *R v British Standards Institution, ex p Dorgard Ltd* [2001] ACD 15.

[191] *R v Disciplinary Committee of the Jockey Club, ex p Aga Khan* [1993] 1 WLR 909, 932–933.

[192] *R v Football Association Ltd, ex p Football League Ltd* [1993] 2 All ER 833, 849.

[193] ibid 849.

[194] D Pannick, 'Who is Subject to Judicial Review and in Respect of What?' [1992] PL 1.

[195] J Black, 'Constitutionalising Self-Regulation' (1996) 59 MLR 24, 41.

(f) Employment relationships

17.85   Numerous cases have come before the courts concerning employment relationships, with employees seeking to argue that the case has a sufficiently public component to warrant judicial review, while employers have on the whole sought to
resist this argument. The employees have had mixed success in their attempts to
use judicial review. In *R v East Berkshire Health Authority, ex p Walsh*,[196] a senior
nursing officer was dismissed and sought judicial review for a breach of natural
justice. The defendant contested the suitability of the judicial review proceedings,
and this challenge was upheld. The court reasoned that judicial review was only
available for issues of public law. Ordinary master-servant relationships did not
involve any such issue, the only remedy being a damages action, or relief under the
relevant employment legislation. A public law issue could arise if Walsh could be
said to hold an office where the employer was operating under a statutory restriction as to the grounds of dismissal. However employment by a public authority
did not per se 'inject' a public law element; nor did the seniority of the employee;
nor did the fact that the employer was required to contract with its employees on
special terms. An employee could, however, be a 'potential candidate' for administrative law remedies where Parliament 'underpinned' the employees' position by
directly restricting the freedom of the public authority to dismiss. The preceding
case can be contrasted with *R v Secretary of State for the Home Department, ex p
Benwell*,[197] where a prison officer was allowed to seek judicial review, the court
holding that there was a sufficient statutory underpinning to inject the requisite
public law element.

17.86   In *McLaren v Home Office*[198] Woolf LJ distilled some of the more general principles which should apply in employment cases.

- The starting point was that employees of public bodies should pursue their
  cases in the normal way by ordinary action for a declaration, damages and the
  like. This was so even if the particular employee held an office from the Crown,
  which was dismissable at pleasure. Judicial review was therefore neither necessary, nor appropriate in normal cases.
- Judicial review could, however, be sought if the public employee was affected by
  a disciplinary body established under statute or the prerogative to which the
  employer or employee was required or entitled to refer disputes affecting their
  relationship. Provided that the tribunal had a sufficiently public law element
  then judicial review could be used.

---

[196] [1985] QB 152; *R v Derbyshire CC, ex p Noble* [1990] ICR 808; *R v BBC, ex p Lavelle* [1983]
1 WLR 23.
[197] [1985] QB 554.
[198] [1990] ICR 824.

- A public employee could also seek judicial review if attacking a decision of *general* application and doing so on grounds of irrationality.
- Even where review was not available because the disciplinary procedures were purely domestic in nature, it might still be possible for the employee to seek a declaration outside of the judicial review procedure to ensure that the proceedings were conducted fairly.

(g) Activities which are 'inherently private'

Some activities are regarded as inherently private, and hence unsuited to judicial review. *R v Chief Rabbi of the United Congregations of Great Britain and the Commonwealth, ex p Wachmann*[199] provides an example. The applicant sought judicial review of a disciplinary decision removing him as a Rabbi, because of conduct rendering him morally unfit to continue in the position. Simon Brown J refused the application, holding that the jurisdiction of the Chief Rabbi was not susceptible to judicial review. He held that the judicial review procedure could only be used when there was not merely a public, but a governmental interest in the decision-making power in question. The Chief Rabbi's functions were said to be essentially intimate, spiritual and religious, and the government could not and would not seek to discharge them if he were to abdicate his regulatory responsibility, nor would Parliament contemplate legislating to regulate the discharge of these functions. Moreover, the reviewing court was not in a position to regulate what was essentially a religious function, whether a person was morally fit to carry out their spiritual responsibilities. It should however be recognized that the courts have exercised their review powers on numerous occasions in relation to Church of England clergy. This jurisdiction was reaffirmed in *R v Bishop of Stafford, ex p Owen*,[200] where the court judicially reviewed the decision not to extend a clergyman's term of office.

17.87

G. The Effect of Alternative Remedies

Judicial review is not the only mechanism for seeking relief. There will often also be statutory appeal procedures or complaints mechanisms. This raises the issue as to the effect of such procedures upon the availability of judicial review.[201] It is clear that the existence of such a procedure does not operate as a jurisdictional bar to judicial review. It is less clear how far such a procedure creates a presumption that resort should be had to that procedure rather than judicial review. In *R v Inland*

17.88

---

[199] [1992] 1 WLR 1036; *R v Imam of Bury Park Mosque, Luton, ex p Ali (Sulaiman)* [1994] COD 142.
[200] [2001] ACD 14.
[201] C Lewis, 'The Exhaustion of Alternative Remedies' [1992] CLJ 138; J Beatson, 'Prematurity and Ripeness for Review' in Forsyth and Hare (n 31 above) 229–235.

Revenue Commissioners, ex p Preston,[202] the House of Lords stated that judicial review should only rarely be available if an appellate procedure existed. This may be contrasted with the more liberal approach of Lord Denning MR in *R v Paddington Valuation Officer, ex p Peachey Property Corp*,[203] where his Lordship stated that review would be available where the alternative appellate procedure was 'nowhere near so convenient, beneficial and effectual'. The courts have on the whole adopted the approach in *Preston*. Lord Woolf, writing extra-judicially,[204] has stated that judicial review should normally be a matter of last resort. Lord Woolf CJ returned to this theme in *Cowl v Plymouth City Council*.[205] He stated that litigation should be avoided wherever possible, and that maximum use should be made of alternative dispute resolution, and complaints procedures. The court could, of its own initiative, hold an inter partes hearing, at which the parties would be asked what use they had made of such procedures.

17.89 The courts have nonetheless been willing to recognize exceptions and allow the judicial review application. A number of factors can be identified which the courts will take into account in deciding whether to allow an application for judicial review, even though an alternative appellate structure exists.

- Judicial review is unlikely to be ousted where doubt exists as to whether a right of appeal exists,[206] or whether such an appellate right covers the circumstances of the case.[207]
- Judicial review will also be available where the statutory appeal mechanism is deemed inadequate as compared to judicial review. Thus in *Leech v Deputy Governor of Parkhurst Prison*,[208] a prisoner was allowed to seek judicial review of a disciplinary decision reached by a prison governor, notwithstanding the existence of a petition procedure to the Secretary of State. Their Lordships were influenced by the fact that the Secretary of State did not have the formal power to

---

[202] [1985] AC 835, 852, 862, HL. See also, *R v Poplar BC (No 1), ex p London CC* [1922] 1 KB 72, 84–85, 88, 94; *R v Epping and Harlow General Commissioners, ex p Goldstraw* [1983] 3 All ER 257, 262; *R v Chief Constable of the Merseyside Police, ex p Calveley* [1986] QB 424, 433–434; *Pasmore v Oswaldtwistle UDC* [1898] AC 387, 394; *R v Panel on Take-Overs and Mergers, ex p Guinness plc* [1990] 1 QB 146; *R v Police Complaints Authority, ex p Wells* [1991] COD 95; *R v Special Educational Needs Tribunal, ex p Fairpo* [1996] COD 180; *R v Secretary of State for the Home Department, ex p Capti-Mehmet* [1997] COD 61; *R v Secretary of State for the Home Department, ex p Watts* [1997] COD 152; *R v Falmouth and Truro Port Health Authority, ex p South West Water Ltd* [2001] QB 445, 472–473, 476, 486.
[203] [1966] 1 QB 380, 400. See also, *R v Leicester Guardians* [1899] 2 QB 632, 638–639; *R v North, ex p Oakey* [1927] 1 KB 491; *Stepney BC v John Walker and Sons Ltd* [1934] AC 365; *Ex p Jarrett* (1946) 52 TLR 230.
[204] Lord Woolf, 'Judicial Review: A Possible Programme for Reform' [1992] PL 221, 235.
[205] [2001] EWCA Civ 1935; [2002] 1 WLR 803.
[206] *R v Hounslow LBC, ex p Pizzey* [1977] 1 WLR 58, 62; *R v Board of Visitors of Hull Prison, ex p St Germain* [1979] QB 425, 456, 465.
[207] *R v Inland Revenue Commissioners, ex p Preston* [1985] AC 835, 862.
[208] [1988] AC 533.

quash the disciplinary decision reached by the governor, but merely the power to remit the punishment inflicted on the prisoner.

- In deciding whether to allow an applicant to utilize judicial review the courts will take into account more general factors concerning the nature of the appellate procedure, and consider how onerous it is for the individual to be restricted to the statutory mechanism. Thus in *R v Chief Constable of the Merseyside Police, ex p Calveley*,[209] the court took account of the fact that the alternative procedure was likely to be slow, and thus allowed police officers to seek judicial review. However, in *R v Secretary of State for the Home Department, ex p Swati*,[210] an immigrant was restricted to the statutory appeals procedure, save in exceptional circumstances, notwithstanding the fact that this entailed leaving the United Kingdom in order to avail himself of that right.

- The courts have in the past held that review is more likely to be available where the alleged error is one of law.[211] The general attitude of the courts has, however, changed somewhat. The mere existence of an alleged error of law will not in itself serve to displace the presumption that statutory appeal procedures should be used.[212]

- An applicant is likely to be restricted to the statutory appeal procedure where the case turns on mixed questions of law and fact,[213] disputed questions of fact, the appellate tribunal possesses expertise,[214] or where issues of criminal law are involved.[215]

- The long-standing supervisory jurisdiction exercised over magistrates should generally continue to be exercised notwithstanding rights of appeal to the Crown Court.[216]

---

[209] [1986] QB 424, 434, 440.

[210] [1986] 1 WLR 477.

[211] *R v Paddington Valuation Officer, ex p Peachey Property Corp* [1966] 1 QB 380; *R v Hillingdon LBC, ex p Royco Homes Ltd* [1974] QB 720; *R v Police Complaints Authority, ex p Wells* [1991] COD 95.

[212] See cases in n 202 above.

[213] *R v Epping Forest DC, ex p Green* [1993] COD 81.

[214] *Clark v Epsom RDC* [1929] 1 Ch 287; *R v Inland Revenue Commissioners, ex p Preston* [1985] AC 835; *Smeeton v A-G* [1920] 1 Ch 85; *Coney v Choyce* [1975] 1 WLR 422, 434; *Hilditch v Westminster City Council* [1990] COD 434.

[215] *R v DPP, ex p Camelot Group Ltd* [1998] COD 54.

[216] *R v Hereford Magistrates' Court, ex p Rowlands* [1998] QB 110.

18

REMEDIES AVAILABLE IN JUDICIAL REVIEW PROCEEDINGS

A. Introduction[1]

It is by means of the legal remedies available to them that the courts give **18.01** practical effect to the rule of law. This is particularly so in the English legal system where, as Lord Wilberforce commented, typically 'law fastens not upon principles but upon remedies'.[2] The spirit of this statement is nowhere more apparent than in the context of English public law where the link between

---

[1] The author would like to acknowledge the helpful comments of Professor Brigid Hadfield and Clive Lewis, Barrister.

[2] *per* Lord Wilberforce in *Davy v Spelthorne* [1984] AC 262, 276F, quoted by Sir John Laws, 'Judicial remedies and the Constitution' (1994) 57 MLR 213.

remedies and the development of substantive law has been particularly intimate.[3]

18.02   In principle the armoury of legal remedies available in public law should be sufficient to ensure full protection against the unlawful exercise of public powers, including the provision of relief to those whose rights and interests have been or will be directly adversely affected. As well as enabling the courts to respond to past illegality the armoury should also enable the courts to look forward in order to prevent illegality where necessary by providing clarification of the law and guidance as to the legal implications of future action.[4] Given the complex nature of public law issues and the competing interests involved, the remedies should also be sufficiently flexible to enable the courts to protect the interests of claimants while respecting broader public interests, including the necessary requirements of good administration. Recent reforms, largely the result of judicial creativity, have very nearly produced such an armoury of remedies. These reforms have focused upon the modernization of the prerogative orders and the adaptation of the declaration and injunction as public law remedies. The following brief historical summary will help to identify the key elements of this process.

(1) A Brief Historical Summary[5]

18.03   Prior to 1977 there existed two sets of procedurally distinct remedies available against public bodies that had abused their powers,[6] or threatened to do so. On the one hand were the prerogative orders of mandamus, prohibition and certiorari.[7] On the other were declarations and injunctions.[8] The prerogative orders could only be obtained using the precursor to the current judicial review procedure, but declaratory and injunctive relief could not be obtained in this way. This meant that while both sets of remedies had advantages that the other lacked, they could not be obtained in the same proceedings as alternatives to each other. The situation was famously summarized by Professor de Smith:

---

[3] See further C Lewis, *Judicial Remedies in Public Law* (2nd edn, London: Sweet & Maxwell, 2000) and de Smith, Woolf and Jowell, *Judicial Review of Administrative Action* (5th edn, London: Sweet & Maxwell, 1995) Pt IV; also de Smith, Woolf and Jowell, *Principles of Judicial Review* (London: Sweet & Maxwell, 1999).

[4] See further paras 18.33–18.39 below.

[5] For a more detailed survey of the historical development of the judicial review remedies, see de Smith, Woolf and Jowell, *Judicial Review* (n 3 above) ch 14.

[6] The term 'abuse' here includes excess of power and breach of the rules of natural justice or unfairness.

[7] Prior to the Administration of Justice (Miscellaneous Provisions) Act 1938, these orders were known as prerogative writs.

[8] Many of the technical distinctions between these sets of remedies grew out of jurisdictional differences between the King's Bench and the common law courts on the one hand and common law and equity on the other.

Until the Legislature intervenes, therefore, we shall continue to have two sets of remedies against the usurpation or abuse of power . . . remedies which overlap but do not coincide, which must be sought in wholly distinct forms of proceedings, which are overlaid with technicalities and fine distinctions, but which would conjointly cover a very substantial area of the existing field of judicial control. This state of affairs bears a striking resemblance to that which obtained when English civil procedure was still bedevilled by the old forms of action.[9]

The 1977 reforms substantially improved the situation by enabling injunctions and declarations to be claimed together with the prerogative orders in judicial review proceedings.[10] However, the reforms were essentially procedural and did little to change the characteristics and limitations of the individual remedies. In the language used by Professor de Smith, the reforms removed the need for two wholly distinct forms of proceedings, but overlap between the individual remedies remained as did many of the technical and fine distinctions between them. The availability of interim relief at the time of the reforms illustrates the problem. The prerogative orders were final remedies that could only be granted after a full hearing. While injunctions were available at an interlocutory stage as an interim remedy, they would not be granted against Crown servants. The result was that interim relief was effectively unavailable in proceedings against central government. Declarations did not fill this gap because, while they could be granted against the Crown, there was authority that an interim declaration could not be granted.[11]

18.04

In recent years the judges have taken great strides towards modernizing the individual remedies so that something resembling a comprehensive remedial system in public law now exists. The principal remaining gap is that damages are still not available to compensate those who have sustained loss as a consequence of an

18.05

---

[9] See Law Commission, *Report on Remedies in Administrative Law* (Law Com No 73, Cmnd 6407, 1976) para 32.

[10] In *O'Reilly v Mackman* [1983] 2 AC 237 the House of Lords attempted to streamline the system further by introducing a new general rule that it would be an abuse of the process of the court to use procedures other than judicial review when seeking to vindicate rights in public law. This effectively prevented litigants from claiming declaratory or injunctive relief in ordinary civil proceedings where private law rights were not at stake. While the decision had its supporters, most commentators regarded it as a retrograde step. The principal criticism was that it introduced a new procedural rigidity into the system and did so on the basis of a division between public and private rights that was foreign to the English system and which could not be easily accommodated. As was widely predicted the decision led to a generation of jurisdictional complexities that were typical of the very problems that the 1977 reforms were intended to eradicate. Fortunately, the worst effects of *O'Reilly* have now been eliminated. In particular CPR 30.5 and 54.20 permit easier transfer of cases between procedures. Moreover, where an issue arises as to whether claimants have used the appropriate procedure, judges will now focus on the suitability of the procedure for resolving the dispute in hand, rather than on whether public or private rights are involved: *Clark v University of Lincolnshire and Humberside* [2000] 1 WLR 1988.

[11] See para 18.50 below.

abuse of power on the part of public bodies that is not a breach of human rights or of rights conferred upon individuals by EC law.[12]

18.06   The major elements involved in the process of modernization of the remedies may be summarized as follows:

- The decision of the House of Lords in *M v Home Office*[13] established that injunctive relief is available against ministers and other officers of the Crown acting in their official capacity. From a remedial perspective the most important consequence of this decision was that it greatly improved the availability of interim relief against central government.

- Much work has been done to improve further the availability of declaratory relief. In particular, it is now clear that declaratory relief is available even where the prerogative orders would not be available, for example as when there is no decision or action to quash.[14] In addition it is now possible for the courts to give advisory or prospective declarations to provide guidance as to the legality of future action and thereby to provide remedies that are proactive as well as reactive in effect. In addition, the possibility of making an interim declaration has given judges a further element of flexibility.[15]

- The prerogative orders have also been modernized. In particular, the out-dated limitations on the availability of the old prerogative orders of certiorari (now termed quashing orders) have been removed. It is, for example, now clear that quashing orders may be obtained in relation to subordinate legislation. The utility of these orders has also been improved by rule changes enabling the courts to quash and then remit the matter back to the decision-maker or, in certain circumstances, to make a substituted decision.[16]

- Technical distinctions between the remedies, including differing standing requirements, have also been removed.[17]

---

[12] See para 18.72. This has for long been recognized as a serious gap, eg Law Commission Working Paper No 13 (1967) para 8 and Report of the Committee of the JUSTICE–All Souls Review of Administrative Law in the UK, *Administrative Justice: Some Necessary Reforms* (Oxford: Clarendon, 1988) ch 11.

[13] [1994] 1 AC 377.

[14] *Equal Opportunities Commission v Secretary of State for Employment* [1995] 1 AC 1.

[15] See further para 18.50 below.

[16] See further para 18.15 below.

[17] eg, prior to the 1977 reforms injunctions were primarily available only to vindicate private law rights and a claimant could only obtain an injunction against a public authority if its action had adversely affected a specific right or caused him damage over and above that caused to the public in general: *Boyce v Paddington BC* [1903] 1 Ch 109; *Gouriet v Union of Post Office Workers* [1978] AC 435. Declarations were also limited in this way. See, eg, *Gregory v Camden* [1966] 1 WLR 899. With the new RSC Ord 53 the court could grant a declaration or an injunction to an applicant who had a sufficient interest, even if a plaintiff would lack standing for these remedies in non judicial review proceedings.

- The old names of the prerogative orders have been replaced by titles that are intended to convey their functional purpose more clearly.[18] Instead of the Latin names certiorari, prohibition and mandamus, these remedies are now referred to as quashing, prohibitory and mandating orders.
- One result of the various reforms is that where remedies serve the same functional purpose there is now rarely any real difference between them.[19] In future the practical importance of the individual identities of the remedies is likely to decline further. In this context it has been argued by influential commentators that, sentimentality apart, there is no real reason for retaining the distinction between declarations and injunctions on the one hand and the remedies based on the prerogative orders on the other.[20]

The overall result of the above developments is that, subject to the limitations relating to damages, the judges may now in their discretion utilize whichever remedy or combination of remedies is most appropriate in the circumstances.

(2) An Overview of the Remedies Available Following a Claim for Judicial Review

In judicial review proceedings claimants may obtain all or any of the following: a **18.07** quashing order, a mandatory order, or a prohibiting order. The High Court's jurisdiction to grant these remedies stems from s 29 of the Supreme Court Act 1981 (SCA).[21] Despite the flexibility of the procedural framework provided by the Civil Procedure Rules (CPR),[22] these orders can only be obtained by claims made using the judicial review procedure.[23] If a quashing order is granted the court 'may remit the matter to the decision-maker and direct it to reconsider that matter and reach a decision in accordance with the judgment of the Court'.[24] The CPR, significantly, now also provide that 'where the court considers that there is no purpose to

---

[18] The change of name introduced by CPR 54 was originally recommended by the Law Commission in its report *Administrative Law: Judicial Review and Statutory Appeals* (Law Com No 226, 1994) paras 8.1–8.3.

[19] eg, a final injunction granted on a judicial review is normally indistinguishable in its effect from a prohibitory or mandatory order: see de Smith, Woolf and Jowell, *Principles* (n 3 above) para 15-016 citing *M v Home Office* [1994] 1 AC 377.

[20] Lord Woolf, in Mads Andenas and Duncan Fairgrieve (eds), *Judicial Review in International Perspective* (The Hague: Kluwer Law International, 2000); Dawn Oliver, 'Public Law Procedures and Remedies—Do We Need Them?' [2002] PL 91.

[21] 'The High Court shall have jurisdiction to make orders of mandamus, prohibition and certiorari in those classes of cases in which it had power to do so immediately before the commencement of this Act.' This provision re-enacts s 1 of the Administration of Justice (Miscellaneous Provisions) Act 1938. This Act recast the prerogative writs as prerogative orders, but made no change to the substantive law relating to the availability of these remedies.

[22] The flexibility of the CPR was emphasized by the Court of Appeal in *R (on the application of Heather) v Leonard Cheshire Foundation* [2002] EWCA Civ 366; [2002] 2 All ER 936 at [38]–[40].

[23] SCA 1981, s 31 and CPR 54.2.

[24] CPR 54.19(2). See also with slightly different wording SCA 1981, s 31(5).

be served in remitting the matter to the decision-maker it may, subject to any statutory provision, take the decision itself'.[25]

18.08   In addition to the above orders, in judicial review proceedings claimants may also seek an injunction[26] or a declaration. It is to be noted that unlike the orders mentioned above the judicial review procedure 'may' be used to obtain these remedies.[27] This recognizes that these remedies are available in proceedings other than judicial review. Where the judicial review procedure is used these remedies will be granted when the High Court:

> . . . considers that, having regard to—
> (a) the nature of the matters in respect of which relief may be granted by orders of mandamus, prohibition or certiorari;
> (b) the nature of the persons and bodies against whom relief may be granted by such orders; and
> (c) all the circumstances of the case, it would be just and
> convenient for the declaration to be made or the injunction to be granted, as the case may be . . .[28]

18.09   If a procedure other than judicial review is used to seek these remedies in a case where the central issues are public law in nature there is a danger that the claim may be struck out as an abuse of process under the general rule in *O'Reilly v Mackman*.[29] Today, however, it is likely that the courts will endeavour to use their case management powers, including their ability to transfer matters to the appropriate procedure, in order to avoid the summary rejection of cases that may have substantive merit.[30]

18.10   Each of the above remedies is discretionary. They will not be granted automatically and may be refused even where the court has decided that the defendant has acted, or proposes to act, unlawfully. This will be considered further below.

18.11   Damages may also be obtained on a claim for judicial review, provided they are not sought as the sole remedy.[31] In any case, damages will only be awarded where 'the court is satisfied that, if the claim had been made in an action begun by the

---

[25] This new provision was added by CPR 54.19(3). See further para 18.15 below.
[26] SCA 1981, s 37.
[27] The judicial review procedure need only be used to seek injunctive or declaratory relief if a mandatory order, prohibiting order, or quashing order is also sought (CPR 54.3) or where an injunction under SCA 1981, s 30 is wanted to restrain a person from acting in any office in which he is not entitled to act (CPR 54.2(d)).
[28] SCA 1981, s 31(2).
[29] [1983] 2 AC 237.
[30] *Clark v University of Lincolnshire and Humberside* [2000] 1 WLR 1988. Where there has been delay in bringing proceedings involving purely public law such that judicial review would be unavailable it is possible that the courts would not permit proceedings to proceed even though normal limitation periods have not expired.
[31] CPR 54.3(2).

applicant at the time of his making his application, he would have been awarded damages . . .'.[32] This effectively means that a claimant needs to establish contractual or tortious liability, or a breach of a right conferred by EC law, or that they are a victim of a violation by the respondent public authority of a human right protected under the Human Rights Act 1998 (HRA).[33]

The individual remedies will now be examined more closely, looking first at the remedies available at the conclusion of the final hearing and then at the pre-trial or interim remedies. **18.12**

B. Final Remedies

We shall deal first with quashing, prohibitory, and mandatory orders and then with injunctions and declarations. **18.13**

(1) Quashing Orders

Quashing orders (previously the prerogative orders of certiorari) quash or set aside an unlawful decision of a public authority thereby confirming that it is a nullity having no legal effect. At one time there were a large number of technical restrictions associated with the availability of certiorari and prohibition. It was thought, for example, that the orders were only available against 'judicial' and not 'administrative' bodies; that they could only protect rights and not other interests;[34] and, that they could not be used against delegated legislation.[35] Fortunately, the courts have now eroded these restrictions and it is generally accepted that certiorari is available to quash almost any unlawful action taken by public authorities,[36] including delegated legislation that has been unlawfully made.[37] Failure to comply with a quashing order may lead to contempt proceedings. **18.14**

---

[32] SCA 1981, s 31(4)(b).

[33] HRA 1998, s 8. See further para 18.72 below and paras 19.15–19.23 below.

[34] The relevance of many of the earlier limitations was removed by the decision of the House of Lords in *Ridge v Baldwin* [1964] AC 40, see in particular Lord Reid.

[35] Many of these restrictions stem from misunderstanding of Atkin LJ's statement that these remedies were only available against bodies having legal authority to determine questions affecting the rights of subjects and having the duty to act judicially: see *R v Electricity Commissioners, ex p London Electricity Joint Committee Co* [1924] 1 KB 171, 205.

[36] See Lord Diplock in *O'Reilly v Mackman* [1983] 2 AC 237. It is extremely unlikely that quashing orders would be used in relation to primary legislation, although declaratory relief may be available, see para 18.28 below.

[37] *R v Secretary of State for Social Services, ex p Association of Metropolitan Authorities* [1986] 1 WLR 1; *R v Secretary of State for Health, ex p US Tobacco International* [1992] 1 QB 353.

(2) Power to Remit and Make Substitute Decisions

18.15 Given that quashing orders do no more than quash, the usefulness of these orders has been enhanced by the court's power to remit the matter to the original decision-maker with a direction to reconsider the issue and reach a decision in accordance with the judgment of the court.[38] The CPR now also permit a possible significant departure from the accepted doctrine that the judicial review court is not concerned with the merits of decisions of public authorities. Once a decision has been quashed the court has power to take the fresh decision itself.[39] This power (which may be described as the power to make a substitute decision) is subject to any statutory provision,[40] and may only be used where there is no purpose to be served in remitting the matter to the decision-maker.

18.16 Introduction of power to make substitute decisions was first recommended by the Law Commission.[41] The Law Commission envisaged that the power should be restricted to exceptional cases, namely those in which it would be a mere formality to remit the case to the decision-maker: 'where the ground of review is error of law and the error of law is one which, once corrected, necessarily leads to an obvious outcome'.[42] It would not be appropriate, said the Law Commission, to make a substituted decision where the challenge was based on a breach of natural justice or abuse of discretion. '[I]n such cases there will often be more than one permissible answer . . . and a power of substitution would be incompatible with the court's reviewing function.' Substitution would also be inappropriate, it said, in relation to decisions of administrative authorities such as ministers and regulatory bodies. For these reasons the Law Commission recommended that the power should only exist in relation to decisions by inferior courts or tribunals and then only where 'one lawful decision could be arrived at' and the 'grounds for review arose out of an error of law'.[43]

18.17 CPR 54.19(3) is not expressly circumscribed in these ways and its scope is potentially greater than originally envisaged. In particular, the wording does not limit the power to decisions of courts or tribunals where the challenge is based on an

---

[38] SCA 1981, s 31(5)and CPR 54.19(2).

[39] CPR 54.19(3).

[40] The meaning of this phrase is uncertain. The notes to the CPR say that where a statutory power is given to a tribunal, person or other body it may be the case that the court cannot take the decision itself. It remains to be seen whether this is the case. If it is this could suggest that the power to substitute is likely to be very rarely used, given that most judicial reviews are of decisions taken by public authorities under statutory powers. An alternative view is that the courts may make a substitute decision save where legislation requires or necessarily implies the existence of special reasons why the original decision-maker should retake the decision (M Fordham, 'The New Procedure: How is it Working?', Sweet & Maxwell Conference paper 2001).

[41] Law Com No 226 (n 18 above) paras 8.15 and 8.16. The Law Commission's recommendation was endorsed by Sir Jeffrey Bowman, *Review of the Crown Office List* (March 2000) ch 7, para 45.

[42] ibid.

[43] ibid para 8.16.

error of law. However, given the nature of the CPR, limited as they are to matters of procedure, this reform cannot be regarded as representing an increase in the jurisdiction of the courts to substitute decisions of public authorities in general. In principle, the power should be used where 'only one substantive decision . . . is capable of being made and where it is a waste of time to send the thing back [sic] to the decision-making body' or possibly, where the body makes it clear that it would have reached a particular decision but for its view of the law.[44] Subject to these limitations the power may be applicable in cases involving any public authority.

(3) Prohibitory Orders

18.18 Prohibitory orders (previously prerogative orders of prohibition[45]) prohibit a public body from acting unlawfully or implementing an unlawful decision.[46] Such orders have been used, for example, to prevent a doctor who was incapable of being impartial from deciding that a chief inspector was permanently disabled[47] and to prevent a local authority granting additional taxicabs without first granting a hearing to existing taxi drivers.[48]

18.19 There appears to be doubt as to the earliest stage at which a prohibitory order may be claimed. However, it is generally accepted that the order may be sought if it is apparent that a tribunal lacks jurisdiction. Where the lack of jurisdiction is not apparent it appears that the claimant must wait until the tribunal acts unlawfully or is undoubtedly about to do so.[49] Failure to comply with a prohibitory order may lead to contempt proceedings.

(4) Mandatory Orders

18.20 Mandatory orders (previously known as prerogative orders of mandamus[50]) lie to compel the performance of 'public law' duties.[51] In one of the earliest cases, the then prerogative writ of mandamus commanded the Mayor and commonalty of Plymouth to restore Bagg as a burgess of Plymouth.[52] In recent times the courts have compelled public bodies to exercise their discretion in accordance with the law[53] and

---

[44] *R (on the application of Dhadly) v Greenwich LBC* [2001] EWCA 1822 at [16] *per* May LJ. Following post-Bowman consultations the Secretary of State has said that there would be merit in clarifying the circumstances in which the Court may make a substitute decision: see n 222 below.
[45] And prior to this the prerogative writ of prohibition.
[46] A prohibitory order has essentially the same effect as a restraining injunction.
[47] *R v Kent Police Authority, ex p Godden* [1971] 2 QB 662.
[48] *R v Liverpool Corp, ex p Liverpool Taxi Fleet Operators' Association* [1972] 2 QB 299.
[49] de Smith, Woolf and Jowell, *Principles* (n 3 above) para 5-015.
[50] And prior to this as the writ of mandamus.
[51] A mandatory order has essentially the same effect as a mandatory injunction.
[52] *Bagg's Case* (1615) 11 Co Rep 93b.
[53] *Padfield v Ministry of Agriculture* [1968] AC 997. In *R v Secretary of State for Trade and Industry, ex p Lonrho* [1989] 1 WLR 525 the House of Lords emphasized that mandamus can only force official bodies and ministers to exercise their discretionary powers lawfully, it cannot be used to dictate what decision should be reached.

to disclose information in the interests of fairness.[54] The orders are regularly sought to compel magistrates to state a case[55] and tribunals to give reasons where these are required by statute.[56] A minister may also seek a mandatory order to secure compliance with a direction issued under default powers.[57]

18.21   In so far as a mandatory order forces a public authority to undertake action it is an intrusive remedy,[58] which will only be granted with some caution. Claimants will normally be expected to show that their letter before action has brought the alleged failure to perform the duty to the defendant's attention and given the defendant an opportunity to remedy the omission or to provide an explanation.[59] Even then courts will prefer to grant a declaration that a duty is owed on the assumption that this will be sufficient to secure compliance.

18.22   The courts will only compel public authorities to perform duties that are intended to be legally enforceable. Some duties contained in statute will be regarded as being too general or vague to be enforceable by mandatory orders. In *R v Inner London Education Authority, ex p Ali*,[60] for instance, the court refused to force a local education authority to open more schools because the statutory duty to provide sufficient primary schools in its area was only a 'target duty' that was not legally enforceable. A similar approach has more recently been taken in relation to the duty owed by local authorities to children in need under s 17 of the Children Act 1989.[61]

18.23   As with the other judicial review remedies, mandatory orders may be refused as a matter of discretion.[62] Given that failure to comply with a mandatory order may lead to contempt proceedings, the courts may be more hesitant in relation to granting mandatory orders than in relation to issuing a declaration. They might, for example, decline to grant a mandatory order where they consider that the authority

---

[54] *R v Kent Police Authority, ex p Godden* [1971] 2 QB 662.
[55] *R v Watson, ex p Bretherton* [1945] KB 96.
[56] *Brayhead (Ascot) Ltd v Berkshire CC* [1964] 2 QB 303, 313–314.
[57] *Secretary of State for Education and Science v Tameside MBC* [1977] AC 1014. Note that the existence of a default power will not prevent an individual seeking a mandatory order, although it would be relevant to the exercise of the court's discretion to grant the remedy. *R v Inner London Education Authority, ex p Ali* (1990) 2 Admin LR 822.
[58] P Cane, 'The Constitutional Basis of Judicial Remedies in Public Law' in Peter Leyland and Terry Woods (eds), *Administrative Law Facing the Future* (London: Blackstone Press, 1997).
[59] *R v Horsham DC, ex p Wenman* [1995] 1 WLR 680.
[60] (1990) 2 Admin LR 822.
[61] The Court of Appeal held that s 17 did not create a duty owed to individuals but it was emphasized that in applying s 17 local authorities were subject to the normal principles of judicial review: *R (on the application of A) v Lambeth LBC* [2001] EWCA Civ 1624; [2002] 1 FLR 353. Note that the decision of the Court of Appeal in this case was held to be per incuriam in *R (on the application of W) v Lambeth LBC* [2002] EWCA Civ 613; [2002] 2 All ER 901. This finding was in relation to the question whether s 17 gave power to assist families with the provision of accommodation. Also *R v Barnet LBC, ex p B* [1994] 1 FLR 592.
[62] See para 18.52 below.

has taken reasonable steps to perform the duty.[63] In exercising discretion as to the appropriate remedy to grant the courts might also take into account the nature of the claimant's interest. In *Ex p Leigh*, for example, a journalist was granted a declaration that a policy not to disclose the names of magistrates was unlawful, but he was refused a mandamus to compel the disclosure of the names of magistrates who had heard a particular case. While he had a sufficient interest in the general policy his interest in the particular case was insufficient to justify issuing mandamus.[64]

(5) Injunctions[65]

An injunction is an order of a court addressed to a party[66] requiring that party to do or to refrain from doing a particular act. Injunctions are equitable remedies that are widely used to protect rights in private law.[67] They now also play an important role in judicial review proceedings to vindicate public law rights.[68] They may be granted against almost all public bodies[69] to restrain authorities from acting unlawfully[70] or from implementing unlawful decisions.[71] They may be granted against ministers or servants of the Crown acting in their official capacity,[72] although they are not generally available against the Crown itself.[73] The

18.24

---

[63] *per* Scarman LJ in *R v Bristol Corp, ex p Hendy* [1974] 1 WLR 498, 503: 'if there is evidence that a local authority is doing all that it honestly and honourably can to meet the statutory obligation, and that its failure . . . to meet that obligation arises really out of circumstances over which it has no control, then I would think that it would be improper for the court to make an order of mandamus . . .'. While courts may be reluctant to compel authorities to act when they claim to lack necessary resources, they will not for this reason permit duties to be reduced to mere powers. Cf *R v East Sussex CC, ex p Tandy* [1998] AC 714.

[64] *R v Felixstowe Justices, ex p Leigh* [1987] QB 582.

[65] For interim injunctions, see para 18.41 below.

[66] cf orders staying proceedings, para 18.51 below. An injunction will not be granted to restrain a non-party from acting even though the non-party has been served with the papers: *R v Environment Agency, ex p Turnbull* [2000] Env LR 715.

[67] See generally, P Birks (ed), *English Private Law* (Oxford: OUP, 2000) 875–882.

[68] With adaptations such as the introduction of a more liberal test of standing.

[69] cf Lewis (n 3 above) para 8-024 citing *R v Kensington and Chelsea RLBC, ex p Hammell* [1989] 1 QB 518; *M v Home Office* [1994] 1 AC 377. However, injunctions are not available against the Crown itself (see n 88 below regarding declarations and the Crown), nor can injunctions be used to prevent the enactment of a Bill, or prevent either House of Parliament debating or approving a Bill. This would violate Art 9 of the Bill of Rights. See *Bradlaugh v Gossett* (1884) 12 QBD 271. See further Lewis (n 3 above) paras 8-015–8-017.

[70] eg, *Lee v Enfield LBC* (1967) 11 SJ 772 (injunction restraining a local authority from implementing unlawful changes to a school); *R v Brent LBC, ex p McDonagh* [1990] COD 3 (injunction restraining a local authority from withdrawing its consent to gypsies remaining on a site without providing reasons for doing so and an opportunity to make objections).

[71] *R v North Yorkshire CC, ex p M* [1989] QB 411 (injunction granted to restrain a local authority from implementing a decision to place a child for adoption when the decision had been quashed).

[72] *M v Home Office* [1994] 1 AC 377. The liberalization introduced by the House in this decision was not followed in Scotland: *McDonald v Secretary of State for Scotland* 1994 SLT 692.

[73] It is, however, now possible to obtain an interim declaration against the Crown if this is necessary (see para 18.50 below).

traditional immunities and privileges of the Crown itself will not, however, prevent the courts granting injunctive relief to protect rights granted by EC Law.[74] Nor should these traditional immunities stand in the way of the effective protection of fundamental human rights.[75]

18.25   Like mandatory orders, injunctions may also be used to compel the performance of a duty where the court can specify precisely what needs to be done in order to perform the duty.[76] They may be granted at the final hearing or (unlike mandatory or prohibitive orders) as an interim remedy to preserve the status quo until the final hearing.[77] Another advantage that injunctions have over these orders is what has been described as their elasticity of form and content.[78] They are elastic in the sense that they may be awarded for a fixed period, that may be extendable, or for an indefinite period to last until the defendant satisfies certain conditions, subject to the claimant being able to reapply to extend the injunction.

(6) Declarations[79]

18.26   A declaratory judgment is a formal statement by a court of the legal position. The Court of Chancery exercised an inherent power to make declarations of right long before statute first conferred a limited jurisdiction to do so in 1850.[80] The common law courts did not exercise or claim a power to make declaratory judgments until this power was conferred by the Judicature Act 1873. The current jurisdiction to grant declaratory judgments stems from this legislation.[81]

---

[74] *R v Secretary of State for Transport, ex p Factortame (No 2)* [1991] 1 AC 603. An injunction might also restrain the making of subordinate legislation which is ultra vires the powers contained in the parent Act. Lewis says that while the courts could grant an injunction to restrain a minister from laying draft subordinate legislation before Parliament, in practice 'the courts are extremely unlikely to' to do so. It is, he says, more likely that they will grant a declaration indicating that the subordinate legislation is ultra vires so that Parliament is aware of the legal position when it considers the legislation. See Lewis (n 3 above) para 8-021 citing *R v HM Treasury, ex p Smedley* [1985] QB 657 (a prohibition case) and *R v Boundary Commissioners for England and Wales, ex p Foot* [1983] QB 600.

[75] cf *Gairy v A-G of Grenada* [2002] 1 AC 167, PC. Here Lord Bingham observed that: 'It is fallacious to suppose that the rights, powers and immunities of the Crown are immutable'. He went on to note that the law as stated in *M v Home Office* applied to the UK, '. . . a state, with no entrenched constitution *and at that time* no legal provision for the enhanced protection of fundamental human rights' (para 19(5)). That situation has, of course, been changed by the HRA 1998.

[76] *Meade v Haringey LBC* [1979] 1 WLR 637, see dicta of Sir Stanley Rees. They will not be granted where close supervision by the courts is required to ensure compliance.

[77] Or for a shorter period.

[78] de Smith, Woolf and Jowell, *Principles* (n 3 above) para 15-029.

[79] Birks (n 67 above) 895. See generally Zamir and Woolf, *The Declaratory Judgment* (3rd edn, London: Sweet & Maxwell, 2001).

[80] Chancery Act 1850 conferred power upon the Chancery Court to grant declaratory judgments in a limited range of situations and this power was extended by the Chancery Procedure Act 1852.

[81] For the history of the declaration see Zamir and Woolf (n 79 above) ch 2 and paras 4.021–4.028 dealing with the equitable nature of the remedy. The Rules of the Supreme Court 1883 were introduced under the Supreme Court of Judicature Acts 1873 and 1875. These rules encapsulated a power

Since the beginning of the 20th century it has been established that a declaration **18.27** may be granted in relation to 'any sort of legal relationship, whether or not a cause of action in the traditional sense exists'.[82] The most significant decision in the modern development of this remedy was *Dyson v A-G*.[83] Here the plaintiff obtained a declaration against the Attorney-General that tax notices issued by the Inland Revenue Commissioners were unlawful and that he was not liable to prosecution for not complying with them. The declaration was therefore granted against the Crown in relation to the legality of actions that the Crown proposed to take.[84] Moreover, the declaration was granted despite the Attorney-General's objections that Dyson had no cause of action in the conventional sense and was not claiming a declaration of his rights. This liberal approach towards declaratory relief was followed in later cases.[85] Indeed, the current rule, contained in CPR 40.20, unlike its predecessors, omits any reference to 'rights', merely stating: 'that the court may make binding declarations whether or not any other remedy is claimed'. The breadth of this wording is intended to permit courts to use declarations wherever it is appropriate to do so, whether or not other forms of relief are or could be sought. For example, the compatibility of primary legislation with EC law may be tested in proceedings for declaratory relief even though the prerogative orders would not be available in these circumstances.[86] The courts may also be willing to grant a declaration where there is no decision or action that could be the subject of a quashing, mandating or prohibitory order.[87] It is now probably true to say that, subject to the limitations mentioned below, the High Court may grant declaratory relief against all public bodies, including the Crown,[88] in relation to

---

to make declarations the wording of which remained essentially unchanged until CPR 40.20. The original RSC Ord 25, r 5 was re-enacted as RSC Ord 15, r 16. This provided that: 'No action or other proceeding shall be open to objection on the ground that a merely declaratory judgment or order is sought thereby, and the court may make binding declarations of right whether or not any consequential relief is or could be claimed'. See now CPR 40.20.

[82] Zamir and Woolf (n 79 above) para 2.23.

[83] *(No 1)* [1911] 1 KB 410; *(No 2)* [1912] 1 Ch 158.

[84] Lord Browne-Wilkinson in *R v Secretary of State for Employment, ex p Equal Opportunities Commission* [1995] 1 AC 1, 34.

[85] Including by the House of Lords in *A-G v Foran* [1916] 2 AC 128. The decision of the Court of Appeal in *Guaranty Trust Co of New York v Hannay & Co* [1918] 2 KB 623 is of particular significance. Here the majority clarified that a declaration need not be of a 'right' in the narrow sense of that term, but could extend to declarations of all sorts of legal relationships including declarations of non-liability. The majority also rejected the argument that RSC Ord 25, r 5 was ultra vires in so far as it purported to permit the granting of a declaration where no cause of action existed. It held that the rule did not purport to extend the jurisdiction of the court, but merely to allow the court to deal with a case in a different manner.

[86] *R v Secretary of State for Transport, ex p Factortame (No 2)* [1991] 1 AC 603.

[87] *R v Secretary of State for Employment, ex p Equal Opportunities Commission* [1995] 1 AC 1.

[88] In the past there has been uncertainty as to whether declaratory relief can be granted against the Crown in judicial review proceedings. Lewis (n 3 above) paras 7-054–7-056, for example, says that they probably cannot and de Smith, Woolf and Jowell, *Judicial Review* (n 3 above) para 2.39, say that the Crown cannot be sued for declaratory relief where proceedings have to be commenced by judicial

all matters that fall within its jurisdiction. Whether a declaration will be granted in a particular case is, however, a matter of discretion.

18.28 Declarations will not be granted in relation to matters of a purely moral or political nature where no justiciable issue arises. Nor will declarations be granted in relation to matters that fall exclusively within the jurisdiction of foreign courts, such as the validity of foreign legislation. Nor will the courts grant a declaration that a University Visitor has misconstrued the University's statutes, although not exceeding his jurisdiction.[89] While the courts may declare an Act of Parliament or its provisions to be incompatible with EC law or the European Convention on the Protection of Human Rights(ECHR),[90] the accepted doctrine is that the courts cannot declare an Act of Parliament to be illegal and void.[91] Nor will the courts grant declarations in relation to matters that fall within the absolute and exclusive jurisdiction of Parliament,[92] or in relation to matters that are purely academic or hypothetical; although the courts may accept that it is in the public interest to grant a declaration in certain cases, such as when doing so is likely to clarify the law in a way that provides practical assistance.[93] Only exceptionally may a member of the public bring proceedings against the Crown for a declaration that proposed conduct was lawful.[94]

18.29 Given the flexibility of the declaration and its widespread availability, it is impossible to provide an exhaustive classification of the situations in which the remedy may be used in public law.[95] We have already seen that declarations can

review. This latter view is partly based on the link between the availability of declarations and the availability of the prerogative remedies. This link has now been substantially weakened (see *R v Secretary of State for Employment, ex p Equal Opportunities Commission* [1995] 1 AC 1). In any case, today there seems to be no justification in principle for the availability of declarations against the Crown to be more limited in judicial review proceedings than in ordinary proceedings.

[89] *R v Visitor of the University of Hull, ex p Page* [1991] 1 WLR 1277; *R v Visitors of the Inns of Court, ex p Calder* [1994] 1 QB 1 (similar approach taken in relation to visitors to the Inns of Courts); *Thomas v University of Bradford* [1987] 1 AC 795 (no jurisdiction to grant a declaration that a dismissal was void because it was in breach of the University's statutes).

[90] Power to make a declaration that legislation is incompatible with Convention rights is expressly conferred by HRA 1998, s 4.

[91] *Pickin v British Rail Board* [1974] AC 765.

[92] *Bradlaugh v Gossett* (1884) 12 QBD 271. The courts may consider the legality of draft subordinate legislation that has been laid before the two Houses: see *R v HM Treasury, ex p Smedley* [1985] QB 657. The rules of parliamentary privilege also prevent the courts from granting injunctions to prevent the enactment of any public bill. See further Zamir and Woolf (n 79 above) 104–111; de Smith, Woolf and Jowell, *Judicial Review* (n 3 above) para 17-038 and also the comments on *R v Secretary of State for Foreign and Commonwealth Affairs, ex p Rees-Mogg* [1994] QB 552.

[93] Sir John Laws draws the distinction between an 'academic' question—which is concerned only with matters of intellectual curiosity—and 'hypothetical' questions which may need to be answered for real practical purposes: Sir John Laws, 'Judicial Remedies and the Constitution' (1994) 57 MLR 213, 214. See also *R v Secretary of State for the Home Department, ex p Salem* [1999] 1 AC 450.

[94] *R (on the application of Rusbridger) v A-G* [2003] UKHL 38; [2003] 3 WLR 232.

[95] See further Lewis (n 3 above) paras 7-009–7-034.

be used to challenge the compatibility of primary legislation with EC law. There is no doubt that declarations can be obtained as to the validity of delegated legislation.[96] By contrast, declarations may also be granted in relation to decisions or actions that have no legal consequences, such as a ministerial policy statement contained in a letter[97] or departmental circulars.[98] In such cases the issue is likely to focus on the potential legality of action taken on the basis of the letter or circular. In the *Royal College of Nursing* case, for example, the purpose of the litigation was to obtain clarity as to what would or would not be lawful conduct by nurses in relation to the procurement of an abortion. In the event, the House of Lords gave an advisory opinion as to the lawful role of nurses.[99] This readiness to give an advisory declaration is one of the most significant developments in the system of remedial relief in recent years, and it is an issue to which we shall return below.

18.30 The utility of the declaration is further enhanced by the control that the courts have over the form of any declaratory judgment. As will be seen, declarations are now available as an interim as well as a final remedy. In either situation the court is able to determine the precise form of the declaration made. The court can, for example, specify the action that is unlawful and the particular reasons for this, as well as the action that needs to be taken to ensure compliance and other consequential ancillary matters. Moreover, declarations 'can be precisely crafted to reduce to a minimum the extent to which it is necessary to interfere with the functions of a public authority'.[100]

18.31 Unlike the other remedies the declaration is noncoercive. This is generally understood to mean that a declaration has only limited effect and in strict law can change nothing. More particularly, a declaratory judgment cannot be enforced by normal forms of execution[101] and non-compliance with a declaration cannot be punished as a contempt of court. In exceptional circumstances, however, the courts do have inherent power to take action against a party who deliberately

---

[96] eg, *R v Lord Chancellor, ex p Witham* [1998] QB 575, 586H; *R v Secretary of State for the Home Department, ex p Leech* [1994] QB 198.

[97] *R v Secretary of State for Employment, ex p Equal Opportunities Commission* [1995] 1 AC 1. Here it was accepted that the real object of the challenge was to obtain a declaration that provisions in primary legislation were incompatible with Community law.

[98] *Royal College of Nursing of the UK v Department of Health and Social Security* [1981] AC 800 (declaration as to the legality of a DHSS circular purporting to explain the effect of the Abortion Act 1967). Also *Gillick v West Norfolk and Wisbech Area Health Authority* [1986] AC 112; *R v Secretary of State for the Environment, ex p Greenwich LBC* [1989] COD 530; *R v Deputy Governor, Parkhurst Prison, ex p Hague* [1992] 1 AC 58.

[99] Laws (n 93 above) 217.

[100] Woolf (n 20 above) 435. Also de Smith, Woolf and Jowell, *Judicial Review* (n 3 above) para 15-031.

[101] *St George's Healthcare NHS Trust v S* [1998] 3 WLR 936, 965; *St George's Healthcare NHS Trust v S (Guidelines)* [1999] Fam 26, 60.

flouts a declaration.[102] Moreover, according to de Smith, Woolf and Jowell it may be a contempt of court deliberately to interfere with a legal situation declared by the courts. It could, for example, be a contempt of court for the Home Office to remove a person from this country after having notice that the courts had issued a declaration that the person has a right to remain.[103]

18.32 The non-coercive nature of the declaration may appear to be a weakness of the remedy. However, in fact this is regarded as being one of its greatest strengths, particularly in public law where the courts emphasize that their relationship with government should be based on trust and co-operation rather than on force and coercion.[104] Indeed, its noncoercive nature at least partly explains why the declaration has developed as the remedy of first choice across the spectrum of public law litigation and has done so while attracting few of the technical restrictions that have in the past beset the other remedies. It is perhaps for this reason that it has been said that the courts' power to make a declaration 'has performed a crucial function in the emergence of the modern law of judicial review'.[105] It is certainly the case that the remedy has played a part in many of the most critical advances in modern public law, including the landmark decisions in *Ridge v Baldwin*,[106] *Anisminic v Foreign Compensation Commission*,[107] *Council for Civil Service Unions v Minister for the Civil Service*[108] and *R v Panel on Take-overs and Mergers, ex p Datafin*.[109]

(7) Advisory and Prospective Declarations

18.33 In most situations a declaration will concern the validity of a decision or action that has been taken. If a court declares that the decision or action is unlawful the practical effect is to invalidate that decision or action and to require the body to make a decision that is lawful.[110] There are circumstances, however, where the focus is not upon the past but upon the future; where it is in the public interest for

---

[102] In *Webster v Southwark LBC* [1983] QB 698 a writ of sequestration was issued against councillors who had disregarded a declaration that the Council had a duty under s 82(1) of the Representation of the People Act 1949 to allow a National Front candidate to hold a meeting in one of its meeting rooms.

[103] de Smith, Woolf and Jowell, *Principles* (n 3 above) para 15-030, n 95, where it is said that counsel for the Home Office accepted this to be the situation in *M v Home Office* [1994] 1 AC 377.

[104] '[T]he Crown's relationship with the courts does not depend on coercion . . .' *per* Lord Woolf in *M v Home Office* [1994] 1 AC 377, 425.

[105] *per* Lord Woolf CJ in *Bank of Scotland v A Ltd* [2001] EWCA Civ 52; [2001] 1 WLR 751 at [45].

[106] [1964] AC 40.

[107] [1969] 2 AC 147.

[108] [1985] AC 374.

[109] [1987] QB 815.

[110] Technically a declaration cannot quash a decision that is not a nullity, and nor can it compel the making of a fresh decision.

courts to give a declaratory judgment clarifying the law in advance of a situation occurring in order to prevent them having to 'pick up the pieces when something has or may have gone wrong'.[111] Two types of proactive declaration are often referred to: advisory declarations and prospective declarations.

The term 'prospective' refers to declarations that guide decision-makers as to their **18.34** future actions, but which do not seek to affect past actions.[112] These declarations may be made, for example, in cases where the court decides not to declare the challenged decision or action unlawful, but nonetheless takes the opportunity to clarify the law. This occurred in *R v Panel on Take-overs and Mergers, ex p Datafin*[113] where the Court of Appeal decided not to invalidate a decision of the Panel on Take-overs and Mergers that had been widely relied upon, but to declare the true meaning of the rule so that the Panel would act lawfully thereafter. A similar course was taken in a case in which Webster J granted a declaration that when making housing benefit regulations the minister had a mandatory duty to consult, but he refused to quash the regulations in the instant case despite a failure to consult, because of the administrative inconvenience that this would have caused.[114]

In the above situations the immediate purpose of the litigation was to challenge **18.35** the legality of particular decisions or actions. Claimants may also seek an advisory declaration in relation to the legality of a proposed course of action where no immediate issue has yet arisen.

At one time the courts were extremely reluctant to give advisory declarations. **18.36** Their reluctance was partly due to historical and constitutional considerations stemming from the way the system of obtaining advisory opinions of the judges was abused by the Stuarts in the early 17th century. At that time the judges could be dismissed at the King's pleasure and there was a real danger that the judiciary would be coerced into giving the executive the advice it wanted thereby legitimating its action and precluding later challenge.[115] While fear of dismissal and direct coercion of the judges by the executive has declined, concern over the constitutional propriety of using advisory declarations remains. There is, for example, still

---

[111] Laws (n 93 above) 219.

[112] Lewis (n 3 above) para 5-029 and C Lewis, 'Retrospective and Prospective Rulings in Administrative Law' [1988] PL 78.

[113] [1987] QB 815.

[114] *R v Secretary of State for Social Services, ex p Association of Metropolitan Authorities* [1986] 1 WLR 1. See also *R v Dairy Produce Quota Tribunal, ex p Caswell* [1990] 2 AC 738 where the court declared the true meaning of the relevant regulations but refused to upset the particular decision because of the applicant's delay. Cf *R v Secretary of State for the Home Department, ex p Bentley* [1994] QB 349. Although no declaration was granted, the Home Secretary was invited to reconsider his decision not to grant a posthumous pardon in a situation where his original refusal to do so was based on an error of law.

[115] See further Zamir and Woolf, 4.044 and the discussion of *Peacham's Case* (1615) 2 State Tr 869 and the *Shipmoney case* (1637) 3 State Tr 826

an awareness that the use of advisory declarations 'may give the appearance . . . of bringing the judges too close to the executive, making them too associated with the public bodies which may later appear as defendants before them'.[116] Today, however, judicial attention tends to focus on fear of an increase in litigation and the possibility that judges will become increasingly called upon to adjudicate on matters that are purely academic or hypothetical where a declaration will serve no practical purpose.

18.37   Despite such fears, the courts recognize that in public law advantages may be gained from the careful use of advisory declarations. We have already seen examples of the way declarations can provide guidance to doctors and nurses as to their legal liabilities in relation to future conduct.[117] Local authorities have also been able to seek declarations in relation to the legality of proposed action. In one case,[118] for example, doubt arose as to whether, in the light of an earlier decision of the House of Lords,[119] the Greater London Council could lawfully make grants to London Transport. Before implementing its proposals the GLC obtained a declaration that the new proposals were within its powers.[120] Advisory declarations have also been granted in proceedings brought by individuals. In *R v HM Treasury, ex p Smedley*,[121] for example, the Court of Appeal accepted that courts could grant a declaration as to the validity of subordinate legislation in proceedings brought before a draft Order in Council had been discussed by the House of Lords and the House of Commons. Sir John Donaldson MR said that if the legality of the subordinate legislation could only be challenged once the legislation had been made by Parliament this would cause unnecessary delay and be a potential waste of Parliament's time.

18.38   There is no doubt that ability to obtain an early clarification of the legal situation can benefit the public and public administration. As well as clarifying the law this can 'reduce the danger of administrative activities being declared illegal retrospectively'.[122] For these reasons, de Smith, Woolf and Jowell comment that it is 'desirable that courts adopt a generous approach to the grant of advisory relief'.[123] Despite this

---

[116] Zamir and Woolf (n 79 above) para 4.046.

[117] *Royal College of Nursing of the UK v Department of Health and Social Security* [1981] AC 800; *Gillick v West Norfolk and Wisbech Area Health Authority* [1986] AC 112. Note also, *Re F* [1990] 2 AC 1 (proposed sterilization of a mentally handicapped woman); *Airedale NHS Trust v Bland* [1993] AC 789 (withholding of medical treatment); *Re A (Conjoined twins: Medical treatment) (No 1)* [2001] Fam 147 (authorizing separation of conjoined twins).

[118] *R v London Transport Executive, ex p Greater London Council* [1983] QB 484.

[119] *Bromley LBC v Greater London Council* [1983] 1 AC 768.

[120] Also *R v Birmingham City Council, ex p Equal Opportunities Commission* [1989] AC 1155. Declaration that a local education authority's proposed arrangements for selective education of boys and girls would violate the provisions of the Sex Discrimination Act 1975.

[121] [1985] 1 QB 657.

[122] Zamir and Woolf (n 79 above) para 4.048.

[123] de Smith, Woolf and Jowell, *Judicial Review* (n 3 above) para 15-044. See also Laws (n 93 above).

encouragement the courts are likely to remain somewhat cautious, limiting advisory relief to situations where there are clear public interest justifications for granting this form of relief. A typical example is where there is a need to clarify the legality of a practice, or the meaning of statutory provisions, affecting substantial numbers of people, and where litigation is likely in the future if clarity is not provided.[124]

A related issue concerns judicial attitudes to academic or hypothetical issues. It now seems to be accepted that while the courts will generally refuse to adjudicate upon academic or hypothetical issues, they will do so as an exercise of discretion rather than because they lack jurisdiction to deal with such matters. Moreover, they will adopt a more flexible approach in public law situations than in private law.[125] In an analogous context the House of Lords has recently held that there may be public interest justifications for considering an appeal in a matter despite it having become academic for the parties.[126] Lord Slynn gave as an example a case where: 'a discrete point of statutory construction arises which does not involve detailed consideration of facts and where a large number of similar cases exist or are anticipated so that the issue will most likely need to be resolved in the near future'.[127]

18.39

C. Interim Remedies

Interim remedies are granted prior to the final determination of the issues at full hearing. Their purpose is normally to maintain the status quo and to prevent the defendant acting on the basis of the challenged decision or process to the claimant's disadvantage.[128] The High Court has very broad jurisdiction to grant remedies on an interim basis in any proceedings,[129] including claims for judicial review.[130] Two remedies are of particular relevance in claims for judicial review,

18.40

---

[124] The Law Commission has recommended that the power to make advisory declarations should be placed on a statutory footing and that the jurisdiction should only be used where judges are satisfied that the point concerned is one of general public importance. See Law Com No 226 (n 18 above) paras 8.9–8.14.

[125] *Sun Life Assurance v Jervis* [1944] AC 111, especially Viscount Simon LC at 113–114.

[126] *R v Secretary of State for the Home Department, ex p Salem* [1999] 1 AC 450 where the House of Lords accepted that in public law cases there may be situations where the court could grant a declaration in a matter that had become academic between the parties provided there was good reason in the public interest for doing so. Also *R v Dartmoor Prison Board of Visitors, ex p Smith* [1987] QB 106; *R v Secretary of State for the Home Department, ex p Abdi (Khalif Mohamed)* [1996] 1 WLR 298.

[127] *R v Secretary of State for the Home Department, ex p Salem* [1999] 1 AC 450, 457.

[128] Interim remedies will not be needed where the defendant gives an undertaking to the court that has the same effect as an interim remedy.

[129] For the equivalent remedies in non-judicial review proceedings, see Birks (n 67 above) paras 18.03–18.04.

[130] CPR 25.1(3). However, there are still situations where it appears that no interim relief is available. See, eg, *R (on the application of H) v Ashworth Hospital Authority* [2001] EWHC Admin 901; (2002) 5 CCL Rep 78 at [98] where Stanley Burnton J said that '. . . except possibly in the most exceptional cases, the Court has no power to grant effective interim relief in a case in which judicial

933

namely interim injunctions[131] and interim declarations.[132] When permission is granted to claim judicial review the court may also order a 'stay' of the proceedings to which the claim relates.[133] The effect of doing so is to impose a halt on the proceedings in order to preserve the position until the final hearing.

(1) Interim Injunctions

18.41 An interim injunction is an exceedingly important remedy in judicial review proceedings, not least because mandating orders, prohibiting orders and quashing orders are not available in an interim form. Interim injunctions are very widely used and may be available to restrain action or to mandate that something be done. They have, for example, been granted to: restrain a doctor from treating a claimant for judicial review using electro-convulsive therapy pending the final hearing;[134] restrain a council from entering a claimant's land to carry out land drainage work;[135] and to restrain a planning authority from demolishing a structure built without planning permission.[136] Mandatory injunctions have been granted to force a local housing authority to provide housing pending the determination of a judicial review;[137] to compel a local authority to provide assistance by way of food and accommodation under s 21 of the National Assistance Act 1948 and s 47 of the National Health Service and Community Care Act 1990;[138] and to require a school to accept an excluded child back into the school.[139] Interim injunctions may be granted against ministers of the Crown[140] and also to prevent the application of an Act of Parliament in order to protect rights granted by EC law.[141] Interim injunctive relief may be granted even where the sole final remedy sought is a declaratory judgment.[142]

---

review is sought of the decision of a Mental Health Review Tribunal to direct the immediate discharge of a patient'.

[131] CPR 25.1.(1)(a).

[132] CPR 25.1.(1)(b).

[133] CPR 54.10(1).

[134] In *R v Mental Health Review Tribunal for North Thames Region, ex p Pierce* (1996) 36 BMLR 137.

[135] *R (on the application of MWH & H Ward Estates Ltd) v Monmouthshire CC* [2002] EWHC 229; [2002] EHLR 14. For the Court of Appeal's decision on the substantive issue, see [2002] EWCA Civ 1804; [2003] 2 WLR 950.

[136] *R v Lewisham LBC, ex p Bello* (CO/2031/2000, 27 July 2000).

[137] *R v Kensington and Chelsea RLBC, ex p Hammell* [1989] 1 QB 518.

[138] *R v Southwark LBC, ex p Tafili* (CA, 28 July 1999).

[139] *R v Incorporated Froebel Educational Institute, ex p L.* The decision to grant the interim injunction, 14 January 1999, is unreported. For the decision on the substantive issue, see [1999] Ed LR 488. Here the injunction was discharged because Tucker J considered judicial review to be inappropriate given that the school was independent.

[140] Although not generally against the Crown itself: *M v Home Office* [1994] 1 AC 377.

[141] *R v Secretary of State for Transport, ex p Factortame Ltd (No 2)* [1991] 1 AC 603.

[142] eg *Re S (Hospital Patient: Court's Jurisdiction)* [1995] Fam 26.

A claim for an interim injunction will usually be made at the permission stage, al-   **18.42**
though a court may grant interim remedies 'at any time'.[143] In urgent situations,
such as when a person is about to be deported, it may be necessary to grant an interim injunction before proceedings have commenced.

The decision to grant an interim injunction is a potentially difficult one that is   **18.43**
made without the benefit of full argument on the merits of the claim and which
may have important repercussions not only for the parties but also for third parties and the general public. To take just two illustrations of the type of dilemma
with which the courts might be confronted. A person challenging the legality of a
deportation order may want to prevent the authorities putting him on a plane
until the legality of the order can be resolved;[144] but a deportee may be seeking
judicial review solely in order to prolong his stay in the United Kingdom. A
pharmaceutical company challenging the validity of a decision to ban one of its
products may lose hundreds of thousands of pounds of profit if it is prevented
from selling the product until the full hearing of its claim for judicial review. On
the other hand, the medicine may truly carry a risk of harming people who use it.

In deciding whether or not to grant an interim injunction in a claim for judicial   **18.44**
review, judges follow the general approach enunciated by the House of Lords in
American Cyanamid Co v Ethicon Ltd,[145] while making due allowance for the particular issues that may arise in public law situations. First, the court should consider whether there is a serious issue to be tried. If this threshold is crossed the
court will then address the question whether it is just or convenient to grant an injunction.[146]

(a) Is there a serious issue to be tried?

Following the *American Cyanamid* approach the court will need to be satisfied   **18.45**
that there is a serious issue to be tried and that the claim is not vexatious, frivolous
or scurrilous.[147] This test permits a lower threshold than the requirement that a
prima facie case be established.[148] In so doing it recognizes that judges may have
difficulty dealing with potentially complex legal or factual issues at the interim
stage. It cannot be stated unequivocally, however, that the burden is always less

---

[143] CPR 25.2(1) and (2). For the procedure in urgent applications for permission to seek judicial
review and claims for interim injunctions, see *Practice Statement (Administrative Court: Listing and
Urgent Cases)* [2002] 1 WLR 810. Note also practice form N461 to be used for urgent applications.
[144] See *M v Home Office* [1994] 1 AC 377.
[145] [1975] AC 396.
[146] See Lord Goff in *R v Secretary of State for Transport, ex p Factortame (No 2)* [1991] 1 AC 603,
671–674.
[147] In one case the judge considered an allegation that a hospital manager was in effect trying to
poison the claimant's father with a view to murdering him to be scurrilous and vexatious: *R v Mental
Health Review Tribunal, ex p Kalibala* (6 November 1996).
[148] Birks (n 67 above) para 19.192.

than a need to show a prima facie case. First, it has been said that where the decision to grant interim injunctive relief is taken at the permission stage the effective test will be whether permission should be granted and this approximates more to the need to show a prima facie case than a potentially arguable one.[149] While this may generally be true, unfortunately the precise criteria for obtaining permission cannot be identified with certainty and, in any case, there may be situations where permission is granted but an interim injunction is refused as when the court considers the application to be speculative and unpromising.[150] Secondly, a higher burden will be imposed upon those seeking to compel an authority to take positive steps prior to the final hearing. The Court of Appeal has said that in such a situation an interim mandatory injunction will only be granted if the claimant can show a strong prima facie case.[151]

18.46   Finally, in certain situations the courts may accept that there is a serious issue to be tried but nonetheless refuse to grant interim injunctive relief because special circumstances dictate that a prima facie case be established as one of the factors to be weighed when considering the general balance of convenience. Courts are likely to be loathe, for example, to prevent a public authority exercising its powers or performing duties owed to the public at large unless a prima facie case of illegality has been established.[152] In *Ex p Factortame (No 2)*, for example, the strength of the plaintiff's case was one of the factors weighed when deciding whether the balance of convenience favoured granting the interim injunction preventing application of provisions of the Merchant Shipping Act 1988. Lord Goff said that 'the court should not restrain a public authority by interim injunction from enforcing an apparently authentic law unless it is satisfied, having regard to all the circumstances, that the challenge to the validity of the law is, *prima facie*, so firmly based as to justify so exceptional a course being taken'.[153] Here then the strength of the

---

[149] de Smith, Woolf and Jowell, *Principles* (n 3 above) para 15-020.
[150] *R v London Borough Transport Committee, ex p Freight Transport Association* [1989] COD 572 cited in Lewis (n 3 above) para 8-028, n 45.
[151] *R v Kensington and Chelsea RLBC, ex p Hammell* [1989] 1 QB 518.
[152] cf Lord Denning MR's statement in *Smith v Inner London Education Authority* [1978] 1 All ER 411, 418: 'I am of the opinion that a local authority should not be restrained, even by an interlocutory injunction, from exercising its statutory powers or doing its duty to the public at large, unless the plaintiff shows that he has a real prospect of succeeding in his claim for a permanent injunction at the trial'. In the same case Browne LJ rejected the argument that the burden on plaintiffs is higher when seeking an interim injunction against public authorities than when doing so against private parties; although he accepted that the nature of the party may make a difference when considering the balance of convenience (at 419).
[153] *R v Secretary of State for Transport, ex p Factortame (No 2)* [1991] 1 AC 603, 674. Note that in this case the House adopted the *American Cyanamid* approach, that is to say the approach dictated by domestic law, even though the substantive issue in the case concerned the compatibility of primary legislation with EC law. The House of Lords has since indicated that exclusively domestic principles should not be adopted where a case concerns the control of a member state's power to adopt national regulations giving effect to a Community directive whose validity is challenged. In such situations Lord Slynn (Lords Nicholls and Clyde agreeing and Lords Hoffman and Millet disagreeing)

claimant's case is one of the relevant considerations for the court, albeit a consideration of particular importance where legislation is being challenged. Nonetheless, it is clear from Lord Goff's speech that a court might be prepared to hold legislation to be inoperative on an interim basis despite the absence of a strong prima facie case, but this would only be likely in a highly exceptional situation.

(b) Balance of convenience

Once the threshold has been crossed and the case is shown to have sufficient merit the court will then consider whether it is just or convenient to grant the injunction. This is normally approached in two stages. At the first stage the court will consider whether damages would be an adequate remedy for the claimant or for the defendant. If damages would be available to the claimant should he succeed at the final hearing this would normally preclude the grant of an interim injunction. If damages would not be an adequate remedy the court will consider whether damages would adequately compensate the defendant for his losses should the injunction be granted but the claimant be ultimately unsuccessful. If damages would provide adequate compensation the normal course would be to grant the injunction and require the claimant to undertake to pay damages. In private law situations many claims for interim injunctive relief will be resolved in this way. In many public law situations, however, damages will have little relevance because damages are generally unavailable to claimants[154] and because claimants are often in no position to give a worthwhile undertaking in damages to the public authority.[155] Moreover, even where damages may provide compensation for the particular defendant it is unlikely that they will deal adequately with wider public interests that may be involved.

18.47

---

said: 'It seems . . . highly undesirable that the question whether different governments should be restrained even temporarily from giving effect to a directive, should be considered on wholly different tests in different national courts'. He went on to indicate that while the test to be applied in such situations will overlap with the *American Cyanamid* tests there may be differences, especially in relation to the extent to which financial damage can be taken into account: *R (on the application of Imperial Tobacco Ltd) v Secretary of State for Health* [2001] 1 WLR 127. See also Case C-143/88 *Zuckerfabrik Suderdithmarschen AG v Hauptzollamt Itzehoe* [1991] ECR I-415. But compare *R v Secretary of State for Trade and Industry, ex p Trades Union Congress* [2001] 1 CMLR 8 where the Court of Appeal followed the *American Cyanamid* approach when considering whether to make an interim declaration to the effect that a domestic regulation was inoperative pending a preliminary ruling by the European Court of Justice. In the event the Court of Appeal declined to make the declaration.

[154] See para 18.72 below (damages).

[155] Where the Crown is seeking an injunction to enforce the law an undertaking in damages may not be imposed: *Hoffman-La Roche & Co v Secretary of State for Trade and Industry* [1975] AC 295. Likewise the courts may also dispense with the requirement where a public authority seeks an interim injunction to enforce the law: *Kirklees MBC v Wickes Building Supplies Ltd* [1993] AC 227.

18.48   In judicial review proceedings the court will therefore have to focus on the second stage, that is to say the general balance of convenience. Judges have a discretion that will require weighing factors such as the broader public interest, including the importance of upholding the law; the nature of the burdens placed on public authorities; and the impact of granting or refusing interim relief on the applicant, third parties and the general public.

18.49   The way these factors are weighed may be illustrated by the following decisions. *Sierbein v Westminster City Council*[156] concerned an application for an interim injunction suspending a decision to refuse a licence for a sex shop. Having balanced the public interest in limiting the number of sex shops in the area against the financial loss that would be suffered by the applicant, bearing in mind that damages would not be available if the judicial review ultimately succeeded, the court decided against granting the injunction. This outcome may be contrasted with that in *R v Durham CC, ex p Huddlestone (No 2)*.[157] The claimant, who lived close to the site, was given permission to challenge a decision permitting the working of a quarry without an environmental impact assessment. The claimant also sought an interim injunction to stop the work pending the final determination of the judicial review. The second respondent, The Sherburn Stone Co Ltd, argued that the granting of an injunction would delay the project and undermine its financial viability. It would also force it to lay off employees and create contractual difficulties as it had entered into agreements with third parties concerning the use of the materials that were to be excavated. Moreover, the claimant was in no position to offer an undertaking in damages. Against these factors Kay J weighed the prospect that if the work started without an environmental assessment irreversible harm might be caused to the environment. In view of this prospect he granted the interim injunction while inviting the respondent to apply with notice to have the injunction lifted should it be able to satisfy the court that the work could be undertaken without the possible adverse environmental consequences.

(2) Interim Declarations

18.50   Power to make interim declarations is given by CPR 25.1(1)(b). Prior to the introduction of this rule there was authority that interim declarations could not be made.[158] Their inclusion into the armoury of remedies available allows the courts

---

[156] (1987) 86 LGR 431 cited in Lewis (n 3 above) para 8-032.

[157] [2000] JPL 409.

[158] The notion of an interim declaration was rejected by Upjohn LJ and Diplock LJ in *International General Electric Co of New York v Customs and Excise Commissioners* [1962] Ch 784. Diplock LJ said that an interim declaration was a contradiction in terms (at 790). In *Re S (Hospital Patient: Court's Jurisdiction)* [1995] Fam 26, Hale J said that it was axiomatic that there was no such thing as an interim declaration. See also *St George's Health Care Trust v S* [1998] 3 WLR 936, 965. However, there was dicta indicating that an interim declaration could be made where there was a reference to the

freedom to provide an interim remedy in circumstances where an injunction is considered inappropriate by the parties or the court, or is unavailable as in proceedings against the Crown itself.[159] An interim declaration may also be more appropriate than a 'stay' where the claimant is seeking to halt the implementation of an administrative or executive decision.[160] The Law Commission indicated that this remedy might also be appropriate where the court desires to give temporary guidance to third parties.[161] In this connection it may be noted that the jurisdiction to make an interim declaration includes the power to make an interim advisory declaration.[162] In considering whether or not to grant interim declaratory relief the courts have so far, rather cautiously, applied the same tests as when considering applications for interim injunctions.[163]

(3) Stay of Proceedings

In addition to the above interim remedies, when granting permission to proceed   **18.51**
the court may also direct that the proceedings to which the claim for judicial review relates be stayed.[164] Where the court does so the proceedings will be halted, apart from the taking of steps allowed by the CPR or the terms of the stay.[165] Unlike injunctions, stays operate in relation to decisions and proceedings rather than parties.[166] On this basis the Court of Appeal has held that a stay may be used not only in relation to court or tribunal proceedings, but also to restrain a public body, including the Crown, from continuing an administrative process or implementing a decision pending the substantive hearing.[167] This was of obvious importance at a

---

European Court of Justice. See, eg, Lord Jauncey in *R v Secretary of State for the Environment, ex p RSPB* [1997] Env LR 431 referring to Hoffman LJ in the Court of Appeal in the same case. Interim declarations were available in other jurisdictions including New Zealand, Canada and Israel. For a discussion of the justifications given for the absence of interim declarations, see Zamir and Woolf (n 79 above) paras 3.097–3.099.

[159] For an assessment of the arguments for and against the introduction of interim declarations see Law Com No 226 (n 18 above) paras 6.21–6.22.

[160] See para 18.51 below.

[161] Law Com No 226 (n 18 above) para 6.26.

[162] *Bank of Scotland v A Ltd* [2001] EWCA Civ 52; [2001] 1 WLR 751.

[163] *R v Secretary of State for Trade and Industry, ex p Trades Union Congress* (CA, 20 July 2000); *per* Richards J in *R v Ministry of Agriculture and Fisheries, ex p British Agrochemicals* [2000] 1 CMLR 826 (interim declaration refused); *R v Independent Television Commission, ex p Danmark 1 Ltd* (CO/3036/2000, 8 September 2000, Jack Beatson QC) at [32] was one case where an interim declaration was granted.

[164] CPR 54.10(2).

[165] CPR glossary.

[166] There is uncertainty as to whether compliance with a 'stay' can be enforced by contempt proceedings, although the preferable view is that a breach of a stay is not of itself punishable by contempt: see Lewis (n 3 above) para 6-029.

[167] *R v Secretary of State for Education and Science, ex p Avon CC* [1991] QB 558, 560–562. This, however, was doubted by the Privy Council in *Minister of Foreign Affairs, Trade and Industry v Vehicles and Supplies Ltd* [1991] 1 WLR 550. *Ex p Avon* was not cited to the Privy Council.

time when it was impossible to obtain injunctive relief against ministers of the Crown but is of less importance now, particularly given the availability of interim declaratory relief. Finally, it has been said that a stay may defer the legal consequences of a decision, but not undo what has already been done. A stay will therefore be ineffective where the action to be stayed had already taken effect.[168]

D. Discretion Not to Grant Remedies

(1) Introduction

18.52 A claimant who succeeds in establishing that a public authority has acted or proposes to act unlawfully will normally be entitled to, and obtain, a remedy. However, the remedies so far considered in this chapter are discretionary[169] and will not be granted automatically. In each case the Administrative Court will balance the interests of the claimant in obtaining the remedy sought against the implications of granting the remedies for third parties, public administration and the public in general. Although it is unusual to do so, the court may decide to refuse remedies to an otherwise successful claimant, possibly allowing invalid public action to stand, because countervailing considerations justify withholding relief. More commonly the courts will exercise their discretion to grant the most appropriate form of relief in the circumstances. This may require, for example, refusing to grant a coercive remedy such as a quashing order or a prohibitory order and instead granting a non-coercive declaration of invalidity or a prospective declaration.[170] On occasion the court may find illegality but decline to grant any formal relief, trusting that the judgment will 'speak for itself' and that the relevant authority will act accordingly.[171]

18.53 Zamir and Woolf state that '... it is vital that the discretion is, and can be seen to be, exercised judicially. Thus reasons should be given which make it clear that the discretion is not being exercised in a selective and discriminatory manner, and neither arbitrarily nor idiosyncratically. Otherwise the rights of the parties could become, or at

---

[168] *R (on the application of H) v Ashworth Hospital Authority* [2001] EWHC Admin 901; (2002) 5 CCL Rep 78 at [96] *per* Stanley Burnton J.

[169] See further Sir Thomas Bingham, 'Should Public Law Remedies be Discretionary?' [1991] PL 64; Lewis (n 3 above) ch 11; in relation to declarations, see Zamir and Woolf (n 79 above) ch 4.

[170] eg, *R v Boundary Commission, ex p Foot* [1983] 1 QB 600, is cited by Zamir and Woolf (n 79 above) 123, n 1, as an example of a case where a declaration was regarded as being more appropriate than a prohibition. The declaration would enable the court to set out its views as to the legal position, these could then be taken into account by the Secretary of State and by Parliament when responding to the Boundary Commission's recommendations.

[171] *per* Brook LJ in *R (on the application of Hoverspeed Ltd) v Customs and Excise Commissioners* [2002] EWHC 1630; [2002] 3 WLR 1219 at [197]; also, *R v Secretary of State for the Home Department, ex p Bentley* [1994] QB 349.

least appear, dependent upon judicial whim.'[172] This was said in relation to declaratory relief, but it is equally applicable in relation to any of the public law remedies.

While the principles applied by the courts when exercising discretion have become clearer over the years, precise classification of the factors that may influence the way judicial discretion is exercised remains difficult. Nonetheless the following considerations may be mentioned as being of particular importance: the interests of the claimant; delay in seeking the relief; prematurity; the impact on administration; the impact of third parties; the practical utility of the relief; and the existence of alternative remedies. **18.54**

Before turning to consider these considerations the following general comments may be made. First, since we are dealing with discretion it is to be expected that decisions will be taken in the light of the particular, and possibly unique, circumstances of the individual case. While these may fall within one or more of the headings that are listed, they may not do so. Secondly, as mentioned above, the court will seek to award the remedy or remedies that are most appropriate and therefore the nature of the remedy will itself influence the way the discretion is exercised. Given that the declaration is non-coercive judges, for example, may well be more generous in their approach to granting this remedy.[173] Thirdly, the appellate courts may overturn the exercise of discretion where a decision of the judge is clearly wrong and has not been exercised in accordance with established principles.[174] Fourthly, as will be seen, several of the factors that are relevant to the discretion to refuse relief after the final hearing are also relevant at the permission stage. Where this is the case it is important to distinguish between the very different nature of the discretionary decisions being made at these two stages of the process. At the permission stage the court is concerned to establish whether the claim is sufficiently arguable and whether judicial review proceedings are appropriate, bearing in mind the importance of protecting the claimant's right of access to justice. At the remedial stage attention should be principally focused on selecting the most appropriate forms of relief in the circumstances. Fifthly, the nature of the substantive issues themselves may well affect the willingness of the courts to award particular forms of relief. There remains a reluctance, for instance, formally to declare action taken under the prerogative to be unlawful;[175] one might also **18.55**

---

[172] Zamir and Woolf (n 79 above) para 4.005.

[173] Zamir and Woolf (n 79 above) para 4.010 note that the language of CPR 40.20 is not as wide as that of SCA 1981, s 37(1) which expressly empowers the court to grant an injunction in all cases in which it appears to the court 'to be just and convenient' to do so; in practice a court will normally be prepared to grant a declaration if it would have been prepared to grant an injunction.

[174] For a statement of the principles, see *Hadmor Productions Ltd v Hamilton* [1983] 1 AC 191, 220 *per* Lord Diplock; *R v Stafford Justices, ex p Stafford Corp* [1940] 2 KB 33, 43 *per* Lord Greene MR; *Vine v National Dock Labour Board* [1957] AC 488 (House of Lords reversed Court of Appeal's decision to refuse a declaration).

[175] cf *R v Secretary of State for the Home Department, ex p Bentley* [1994] QB 349.

expect courts to tread extremely cautiously when exercising jurisdiction in areas that were in the past treated as beyond the reach of the judges.[176] Finally, a warning: it has been observed that '[w]hile today the approaches of different courts are more consistent they are still not uniform'.[177]

(2) The Claimant's Interest

18.56 The nature of the claimant's interest in relation to the matter is principally relevant at the permission stage,[178] but it may also be taken into account as one of the factors to be weighed in the balance at the remedial stage.[179] At this stage the claimant's interest is not a threshold issue determining access to judicial review and for this reason it is probably misleading to refer, in this context, to standing to sue or to a sufficiency of interest to seek judicial review.[180] Certainly, as Zamir and Woolf say: 'It is to be hoped that a litigant in public law proceedings is now unlikely, in a deserving case, ever to be refused relief because of a lack of standing'.[181]

18.57 Today it is probably true to say that the law does not require different standing requirements for the individual remedies. In *R v Inland Revenue Commissioners, ex p National Federation of Self Employed and Small Businesses Ltd*[182] Lord Diplock explained that the purpose of the reforms made to the judicial review procedure in the 1970s was to sweep away the procedural differences between the remedies 'including, in particular, differences as to locus standi . . .'.[183]

18.58 While law may no longer dictate the imposition of differing standing requirements, the courts may, nonetheless, in their discretion take the claimant's interest

---

[176] cf Sir John Laws' extra-judicial comment that 'the political nature of the case is no more a ground for refusing relief as a matter of *discretion* than it is for denying the courts *jurisdiction*': 'Law and Democracy' [1995] PL 72, 74.

[177] Zamir and Woolf (n 79 above) para 4.013.

[178] See paras 17.32–17.55 above and 19.15–19.20 below.

[179] *R v Monopolies and Mergers Commission, ex p Argyll Group* [1986] 1 WLR 763, 773–774 *per* Lord Donaldson MR.

[180] In *R v Department of Transport, ex p Presvac Engineering Ltd* [1994] 4 Admin LR 121 where Purchas LJ commented that: 'Personally I would prefer to restrict the use of the expression *locus standi* to the threshold exercise and to describe the decision at the ultimate stage as an exercise of discretion not to grant relief as the applicant has not established that he had been or would be sufficiently affected'. Also Otton J in *R v Inspectorate of Pollution, ex p Greenpeace (No 2)* [1994] 4 All ER 329.

[181] Zamir and Woolf (n 79 above) para 5.68.

[182] [1982] AC 617. He went on to explain that the old private law tests that were applied to injunctions and declarations were now inappropriate where these remedies were being used as public law remedies in judicial review proceedings (at 638).

[183] But contrast Lord Wilberforce who in the same case stated that the reforms did not 'remove the whole, and vitally important, question of locus standi into the realm of pure discretion . . . the fact that the same words are used to cover all the forms of relief . . . does not mean that the test is the same in all cases': [1982] AC 617, 631.

into account at the remedial stage. We saw above, for example, that in *Ex p Leigh*[184] a journalist was granted a declaration that a policy not to disclose the names of magistrates was unlawful, but was refused a mandamus compelling the disclosure of the names of particular magistrates because his interest was insufficient for this remedy. Had he been a party to the proceedings before the bench the decision may well have been different.

(3) Delay

SCA 1981, s 31(6) provides that where there has been undue delay[185] in making an application for judicial review: **18.59**

> The court may refuse to grant (a) [permission] for making the application, or (b) any relief sought on the application if it considers that the grant of the relief sought would be likely to cause substantial hardship to, or substantial prejudice to the rights of, any person or would be detrimental to good administration.

Delay is thus relevant both at the permission stage and to the granting of relief after the substantive merits of the case have been determined.[186] At this latter stage, however, delay will only be a reason for withholding a remedy if granting relief would be likely to cause substantial hardship, or substantially prejudice the rights of any person, or would be detrimental to good administration.

In *R v Dairy Produce Quota Tribunal, ex p Caswell*[187] dairy farmers sought to challenge the Dairy Produce Quota Tribunal's refusal to increase their dairy produce quota. Their application for judicial review was made over two years after the Tribunal's decision. Despite the delay leave to proceed (as it was then known) was granted and at the substantive hearing it was decided that the Tribunal had misconstrued its powers. However, the judge, exercising discretion under SCA 1981, s 31(6), refused to grant a remedy because there had been undue delay in making the application and the grant of the relief would likely be detrimental to good administration. The applicants appealed unsuccessfully both to the Court of Appeal and to the House of Lords. **18.60**

In the House of Lords Lord Goff, delivering the only speech, explained that the rules require claimants to institute their proceedings for judicial review promptly and in any case within three months of the decision being challenged. Where claimants fail to do so permission to proceed may nonetheless be granted if good **18.61**

---

[184] *R v Felixstowe Justices, ex p Leigh* [1987] QB 582.
[185] ie, where the claim for judicial review is not filed promptly or within three months after the grounds to make the claim first arose within the terms of CPR 54.5(1).
[186] In relation to delay at the permission stage see now *R (on the application of Burkett) v Hammersmith and Fulham LBC (No 1)* [2002] UKHL 23; [2001] 1 WLR 1593 and paras 17.21–17.31 above. On the procedure at the permission stage, see paras 17.13–17.20 above.
[187] [1990] 2 AC 738.

reason exists. If permission is given in such a situation the claim will proceed despite the 'undue delay' and will be considered on its substantive merits. If, however, the claim is successful on the substantive issue remedies may be refused if granting the relief would be likely to cause the hardship, detriment or prejudice mentioned in s 31(6)(b).

18.62   Lord Goff declined to formulate any precise definition or description of what constitutes detriment to good administration. This was 'because applications for judicial review may occur in many different situations, and the need for finality may be greater in one context than in another'. However, he went on to observe that 'section 31(6) recognises that there is an interest in good administration independently of hardship, or prejudice to the rights of third parties' or the harm suffered to the applicant by the impugned decision, and that:

> In asking the question whether the grant of such relief would be detrimental to good administration the court is at that stage looking at the interest in good administration independently of matters such as these.

In the context of the case, he said that:

> that interest lies essentially in a regular flow of consistent decisions, made and published with reasonable dispatch in citizens knowing where they stand, and how they can order their affairs in the light of the relevant decision. Matters of particular importance, apart from the length of time itself, will be the extent of the effect of the relevant decision, and the impact which would be felt if it were to be reopened.

Given that the decision of the Tribunal was concerned with allocating part of a finite quota, he thought it plain that it would be detrimental to good administration to allow this case to be reopened, leading as this would to claims that other cases should also be reopened.

(4)   Impact on Administration

18.63   Even where delay is not an issue the courts accept that remedies may be refused where their grant would be adverse to the public interest in maintaining good administration. This was emphasized by Sir John Donaldson MR in *R v Monopolies and Mergers Commission, ex p Argyll Group*.[188] Here, despite a finding that there had been unlawful delegation,[189] the Court of Appeal refused to grant a remedy after weighing the interests of the applicant (a commercial rival seeking to prevent the bidder from making a fresh bid) against the need for speedy decision-making and finality in the context of a decision that would affect the wider financial market. The likely administrative inconvenience was also the reason why Webster J refused to quash regulations in *R v Secretary of State for Social*

---

[188] [1986] 1 WLR 763.
[189] On lawful and unlawful delegation, see paras 14.27–14.41 above.

Services, ex p Association of Metropolitan Authorities[190] and instead granted a declaration that the Minister had failed to consult. As this case illustrates, courts will be extremely reluctant to refuse relief altogether simply in order to avoid administrative inconvenience.[191] In their attempt to balance the interests of the claimant and the administration they will instead endeavour to award the most appropriate relief. This will normally be the remedy that protects the interests of the claimant while causing the minimum disruption to public administration. It is in situations such as this that the flexibility of the declaration has proved to be of particular value.[192]

(5) Impact on Third Parties

Similarly, the courts will endeavour to weigh into the balance the adverse impact **18.64** the remedies may have on third parties, although the public interest in reducing or preventing such impacts may be less compelling than it is in relation to the need to maintain good administration. So, for example, when bodies such as the Monopolies and Mergers Commission or the Panel on Take-overs and Mergers have been found to have acted unlawfully the courts have taken account of the interests of dealers in the stock market when deciding what, if any, remedial relief should be granted.[193] Likewise, when a local authority challenged a minister on the status of a particular school the court considered the interests of other schools when deciding whether to grant a remedy.[194] And when considering whether to invalidate delegated legislation the courts will take into account the consequences for third parties of doing so.[195]

(6) Relief of No Practical Use

Remedies may be refused where relief would serve no practical use.[196] The courts, **18.65** for example, will normally refuse to grant remedies where the issues are purely

---

[190] [1986] 1 WLR 1. See also *R v Inland Revenue Commissioners, ex p Bishopp* [1999] STC 531 where Dyson J refused a declaration in part because of concern that the Revenue would stop giving rulings if it feared that its decisions would be challenged in the courts.
[191] See, eg, dicta of Lord Denning MR in *Bradbury v Enfield LBC* [1967] 1 WLR 1311, 1324; Salmon LJ in *R v Paddington Valuation Officer, ex p Peachey (No 2)* [1966] QB 380, 419; and *R v Governors of Small Heath School, ex p Birmingham City Council* [1990] COD 23.
[192] As in *R v Panel on Take-overs and Mergers, ex p Datafin* [1987] QB 815 where the Court of Appeal made a prospective declaration setting out the legal requirements for the future without upsetting the instant decision. See also *R v Dairy Produce Quota Tribunal ex p Caswell* [1990] 2 AC 738.
[193] See, eg, *R v Panel on Take-Overs and Mergers, ex p Datafin plc* [1987] QB 815.
[194] *R v Secretary of State for Education and Science, ex p Avon County Council* [1991] 1 QB 558.
[195] *R v Secretary of State for Social Services, ex p Association of Metropolitan Authorities* [1986] 1 WLR 1.
[196] Where a declaration would have no practical effect, the courts will not grant remedies simply to hold a public body up for 'public opprobrium': *R (on the application of Rhodes) v Kingston upon Hull City Council* [2001] Ed LR 230.

academic or hypothetical.[197] However, as was seen above, they may be prepared to grant a declaration clarifying the law in relation to future conduct even where no immediate legal issue has arisen.[198]

18.66 Judges are also unlikely to grant remedies where there is no longer a contentious issue to be decided between the parties.[199] However here too there may be good public interest reasons justifying their dealing with the legal issues raised possibly by means of a prospective declaration as to the appropriate legal principles to be applied in the future.[200] In this context it should be noted that HRA 1998, s 4 enables superior courts to grant declarations of incompatibility. Section 4(6) provides that such a declaration 'does not affect the validity continuing operation or enforcement of the provision in respect of which it is given' and 'is not binding on the parties to the proceedings in which it is made'.[201]

18.67 Remedies have also been refused when the claimant has suffered no injustice or prejudice as a consequence of the unlawful action. For instance, a grant of planning permission may not be quashed despite a failure to publicize the planning proposals if the public was nonetheless adequately informed of them and objectors had ample opportunity to make their objections known.[202] Similarly a claimant may be refused a remedy where a breach of the rules of natural justice did not prevent him having a fair hearing.[203] Today, however, it is more likely that the courts will deal with the absence of prejudice as an aspect of the substantive principles, for example by deciding that there has been no unfairness in such cases, rather than by finding a breach but withholding a remedy.[204] Likewise it is now regarded as generally inappropriate for the courts to refuse relief solely because it is believed that the decision-maker would have made the same decision irrespective of the error. Lewis, for example, concludes a careful review of the authorities by

---

[197] As was seen above, this restriction is today regarded as being a matter of discretion rather than jurisdiction.

[198] See para 18.33 above.

[199] The courts, for example, refused to declare that a special prison was unlawful when the unit had already been closed: *Williams v Home Office (No 2)* [1981] 1 All ER 1211. In *R v Ministry of Agriculture Fisheries and Food, ex p Live Sheep Traders Ltd* [1995] COD 297 relief was refused when the relevant legislation was repealed and replaced before the application for judicial review.

[200] *R v Secretary of State for the Home Department, ex p Salem* [1999] 1 AC 450. This case concerned the discretion of the House of Lords to deal with an appeal in a case in which there was no longer a dispute, but similar principles probably apply to the discretion to withhold remedies.

[201] See further paras 7.107 et seq above.

[202] *R v Lambeth LBC, ex p Sharp* (1988) 55 P & CR 232. The courts have not been persuaded by the argument that granting a remedy will enhance and underpin the rule of law, even though little practical purpose will be served. This argument was rejected when used by Gerry Adams to challenge an order excluding him from England after it had been revoked: *R v Secretary of State for the Home Department, ex p Adams* [1995] 3 CMLR 476.

[203] *R v Monopolies and Mergers Commission, ex p Matthew Brown plc* [1987] WLR 1235; *R v Secretary of State for Foreign and Commonwealth Affairs, ex p Everett* [1989] QB 811.

[204] cf *R v Secretary of State for the Home Department, ex p Jeyeanthan* [2000] 1 WLR 354.

saying that 'the courts should not refuse relief unless the same decision would undoubtedly be reached irrespective of the error, and there is a clear countervailing
public interest in not quashing the decision'.[205]

(7) The Existence of Alternative Remedies

Judicial review is a remedy of last resort normally only to be used once claimants
have exhausted alternative remedies.[206] Claimants who have failed to exhaust alternative remedies may be refused permission to proceed with claims for judicial review and in principle it is at the permission stage that the issue of
alternative remedies should be dealt with.[207] Nonetheless, the courts have taken
the existence of alternative remedies into account when considering the granting of remedial relief. In this connection it has been said that the judicial approach is 'entirely pragmatic'.[208] The existence of alternative procedures, for
example, may not inhibit the court from granting remedies in a claim for judicial review if those procedures would have been ineffective, unlikely to resolve
the issue, too slow or cumbersome, or have been otherwise unable to do full justice to the claimant.[209]

18.68

(8) Conduct of the Claimant

As with remedies in the private law context, public law remedies may be refused because of the claimant's conduct. For instance, a local authority was refused relief
when it challenged a ministerial confirmation of its own proposals for reorganizing
schools by relying on its own procedural error.[210] Applicants who claim to have
been treated unfairly may be refused a remedy if they did not object at the time[211]

18.69

---

[205] Lewis (n 3 above) para 11-029.
[206] Including ADR procedures, *R (on the application of Cowl) v Plymouth City Council* [2001]
EWCA Civ 1935; [2002] 1 WLR 803. See also *R v Secretary of State for the Home Department, ex p
Swati* [1986] 1 WLR 722; *R v Chief Constable of Merseyside Police, ex p Calveley* [1986] 1 QB 424.
For an extensive treatment of this issue, see Lewis (n 3 above) paras 11-042–11-073.
[207] The Court of Appeal may reverse a decision to review on the ground that alternative remedies
existed and judicial review was inappropriate, *R v Birmingham City Council, ex p Ferrero Ltd* [1993]
1 All ER 530. See now *R v Falmouth and Truro Port Health Authority, ex p South West Water Ltd*
[2001] QB 445.
[208] Zamir and Woolf (n 79 above) para 4.214.
[209] *R v Hillingdon LBC, ex p Royco Homes Ltd* [1974] 1 QB 720; *R v Chief Constable of Merseyside
Police, ex p Calveley* [1986] 1 QB 424; *R v Special Commissioners of Income Tax, ex p Stipplechoice
(No 1)* [1985] 2 All ER 465; *R v Deputy Governor of Parkhurst Prison, ex p Leech* [1988] AC 533 (prisoner's right to petition the Home Secretary was not a suitable alternative to judicial review
because it would not lead to a quashing of a disciplinary decision).
[210] *R v Secretary of State for Education and Science, ex p Birmingham City Council* (1985) 83 LGR
79.
[211] A remedy was refused because an applicant had not objected at the time to certain members
voting at a council meeting: *R v Governors of Small Heath School, ex p Birmingham City Council*
[1990] COD 23.

or because they have acquiesced in the action taken.[212] Failure to conduct the claim for judicial review appropriately may also lead to the court refusing to grant relief.[213]

18.70 The principal remedies available in judicial review proceedings have now been examined. In the next section brief consideration is given to certain forms of relief which, although not judicial review remedies as such, may nonetheless be sought in association with these remedies either in the same or in related proceedings.

E. Non-Judicial Review Remedies that may be Claimed in Association with Judicial Review Proceedings

18.71 The main forms of relief to be briefly considered in this section are damages, liability to make restitution and habeas corpus.

(1) Damages

18.72 Those seeking judicial review may include a claim for damages but may not seek damages alone.[214] If a claim for damages is made in proceedings for judicial review, the court may award damages if satisfied that damages would have been awarded in ordinary private law proceedings.[215] These provisions reflect the absence in English public law of any general right to indemnity for financial loss suffered as a consequence of invalid action on the part of public bodies.[216] Damages are not available to compensate those who have suffered as a consequence of actions or decisions that are unlawful in the public law senses of that term, unless one or more of the following situations arise:

- If the claimant can show that the defendant is in breach of a tortious or contractual duty owed to the claimant.[217]
- If the defendant acts contrary to an EC law rule conferring rights on the

---

[212] A person was taken to have acquiesced when he failed to object to the presence of a member of a tribunal despite believing him to be biased: *R v Nailsworth Licensing Justices, ex p Bird* [1953] 1 WLR 1046.

[213] Such as breaching the duty of candour or misstating the facts. Se further Lewis (n 3 above) para 11-008.

[214] CPR 54.3(2)

[215] SCA 1981, s 31(4).

[216] *R v Secretary of State for Transport, ex p Factortame Ltd (No 2)* [1991] 1 AC 603, 672H; *X (Minors) v Bedfordshire CC* [1995] 2 AC 633, 730G. See also Merris Amos, 'Extending the Liability of the State in Damages' (2001) 21 LS 1.

[217] See generally Birks (n 67 above) vol II, esp paras 14.98–14.106 on tort and public bodies. See also Michael Fordham and Gemma White, 'Monetary Claims Against Public Authorities' [2001] Judicial Rev 44 and [2001] Judicial Rev 109.

claimant where the breach of a rule intended to protect an individual is 'sufficiently serious' and a causal connection link exists between the breach and the harm sustained.[218]

- If the defendant public authority has acted (or proposes to act) incompatibly with the claimant's Convention rights and the court considers that the award of damages or the payment of compensation is necessary to afford just satisfaction under the provisions of HRA 1998, s 8.[219]

The absence of a right of damages for losses sustained as a consequence of public law wrongs is widely recognized as being one of the most serious of the remaining gaps in our remedial system. It is a gap that does not exist in more developed systems.[220]

(2) Liability to Make Restitution[221]

Unlike damages, CPR Pt 54 makes no express provision for including a claim for restitution (or debt) in judicial review proceedings.[222] Nonetheless a claim for restitution may be made in proceedings other than judicial review against a public authority, via an action in unjust enrichment, on the ground that money was paid to it in consequence of an ultra vires demand,[223] or under a contractual obligation which was ultra vires.[224]   **18.73**

Given the inability to claim restitution in judicial review proceedings where the legality of public authorities' actions are in issue it was in the past widely assumed   **18.74**

---

[218] Case C-6/90 *Francovich v Italian Republic* [1991] ECR I-5357; Joined cases C 46 & 48/93 *Brasserie du Pecheur SA v Germany, R v Secretary of State for Transport, ex p Factortame Ltd (No 4)* [1996] ECR I-1029; *R v Ministry of Agriculture, Fisheries and Food, ex p Hedley Lomas* [1997] QB 139 (refusal, contrary to EC law, to grant export licence for live sheep).

[219] See paras 19.42–19.53 below.

[220] Lord Wilberforce in *Hoffman-La Roche v Secretary of State for Trade* [1975] AC 295, 358–359. Sedley LJ has observed that despite the existing law, 'this does not necessarily mean that the door is closed to [damages] in principle. But the policy implications of such a step are immense, and it may be that . . . a legal entitlement to them cannot now come into being without the enactment of legislation'. *F & I Services Ltd v Customs and Excise Commissioners* [2001] EWCA Civ 762; [2001] STC 939 at [73]. Although it is not a gap that is necessarily universally deplored. Lord Woolf, for example, has commented on the discretionary nature of damages under HRA 1998, s 8 that '. . . any contribution which the HRA makes to the compensation culture is, and is likely to continue to be, small. It is my belief that we can and should ensure that this remains the situation.' Lord Woolf, 'Human Rights: Have the Public Benefited' *Thank Offering to Britain Fund Lecture*, 15 October 2002, The British Academy.

[221] For a detailed treatment of this topic see Birks (n 67 above) ch 15, esp paras 15.161–15.167.

[222] Reflecting the understanding that claims for restitution cannot be made by way of claims for judicial review, see eg dicta of Robert Goff LJ in *Wandsworth LBC v Winder* [1985] AC 461, 480. The Law Commission and the Bowman report both recommended that the court should be able to order restitution in judicial review proceedings, as did Lord Woolf in *Access to Justice* (1996): see Bowman report (n 41 above) B-9. This has now been accepted: *The Administrative Court: Proposed Changes to Primary Legislation Following Sir Jeffrey Bowman's Review of the Crown Office List: Response to Consultation, Department of Constitutional Affairs*, CP (R) 10/01, October 2003.

[223] *Woolwich Equitable Building Society v Inland Revenue Commissioners* [1993] AC 70.

[224] *Kleinwort Benson Ltd v Lincoln City Council* [1999] 2 AC 349.

that two sets of proceedings were needed, one in judicial review seeking to establish the illegality and the other in private law seeking to establish the right to restitution. Given the recent relaxation of the rule in *O'Reilly v Mackman* in principle it should now be possible for judges to deal with any public law issues in the ordinary proceedings where the claim for restitution is contingent upon their resolution.[225] In any case where two sets of proceedings are commenced the judge may order that any public matters be resolved as preliminary issues.[226]

(3) Habeas Corpus[227]

(a) Introduction

18.75 The purpose of the prerogative writ of habeas corpus ad subjiciendum[228] is to secure the release of a person who has been unlawfully detained. The remedy is widely considered to be of great constitutional significance and has been described as the 'most renowned contribution of the English common law to the protection of human liberty'.[229] In recent years habeas corpus has been principally used in extradition proceedings, in relation to deportation and illegal immigration, and to challenge detention under the mental health legislation. Despite its status, the writ's practical importance has diminished as more flexible methods for protecting liberty have been established either by specialized statutory procedures or more generally by way of judicial review. This has led to calls either for its abolition or its merger with judicial review.[230]

18.76 The chief value of habeas corpus is the speed with which it may be sought and its availability as of right, rather than as a matter of discretion. Unlike judicial review there is no time bar, no permission stage or discretionary bars to its availability.[231] Nor is there a requirement that leave be obtained to appeal to the Court of Appeal or, in a criminal case, that the case raises a point of general public importance.

---

[225] See Birks (n 67 above) para 15.167 and dicta referred to in n 325. See also paras 17.61–17.68 above.

[226] eg, as in *Carvill v Inland Revenue Commissioners (No 2)* [2002] EWHC 1488; [2002] STC 1167.

[227] See generally, RJ Sharpe, *The Law of Habeas Corpus* (2nd edn, Oxford: Clarendon, 1989); Lewis (n 3 above) ch 12. Jurisdiction to grant the writ existed at common law but has been extended by statute: Habeas Corpus Act 1679 (criminal matters) and Habeas Corpus Act 1816 (non-criminal matters).

[228] The other forms of habeas corpus: habeas corpus ad testificandum (requiring a prisoner to be called to court to give evidence) and ad respondendum (requiring a prisoner to appear for trial or examination) are now of little importance.

[229] De Smith, Woolf and Jowell, *Judicial Review* (n 3 above) para 5-039.

[230] See, eg, Simon Brown LJ, 'Habeas Corpus—A New Chapter' [2000] PL 31. AP Le Sueur, 'Should We Abolish the Writ of Habeas Corpus?' [1992] PL 13; cf M Shrimpton, 'In Defence of Habeas Corpus' [1993] PL 24.

[231] The current procedure is contained in RSC Ord 54 in Sch 1 to the CPR.

While these advantages may be important in certain situations, the procedural **18.77** differences between judicial review and habeas corpus are said to be less significant than they once were.[232] While there is no permission stage as such, an application for habeas corpus will usually be considered in two stages and will be refused at the first stage if it is without merit. If the application has merit the matter will normally be adjourned for a full hearing.[233] Moreover, while at one time habeas corpus may have offered a much speedier route to the court, claims for judicial review can be expedited especially where liberty is at stake. Lord Woolf MR has also suggested that the burden of proof in habeas corpus and judicial review is effectively the same. In both proceedings it is always for the custodian to show that detention is legally justified.[234]

(b) The scope of habeas corpus

There is powerful support for the view that habeas corpus may be claimed to question the legality of any detention by any body, public or private. Lord Wright, for **18.78** example, summarized the scope of the writ by saying that it applies to 'any case whatever in which the liberty of the subject is unlawfully interfered with'.[235] Likewise in *Khawaja* Lord Scarman cited with approval Blackstone's statement that: 'The King is at all times entitled to have an account why the liberty of any kind of his subjects is restrained, wherever that restraint may be inflicted'.[236] Lord Ackner, speaking for the Board of the Privy Council has also reiterated this broad approach.[237] Lewis is equally clear on this point.[238]

Despite this weight of authority others have sought to impose limitations on the **18.79** scope of the writ. Lawton LJ, for example, has said that habeas corpus '. . . is probably the most cherished sacred cow in the British Constitution; but the law has never allowed it to graze in all legal pastures'.[239] In particular, it is said that the writ cannot be used to question a sentence passed by a court of competent jurisdiction[240] or to

---

[232] Lord Woolf MR (as he then was) in *R v Barking Havering & Brentwood Community Health Care NHS Trust* [1999] 1 FLR 106, 114; see also *R (on the application of Sheikh) v Secretary of State for the Home Department* [2001] Imm AR 219.
[233] Interim relief may be granted, but greater flexibility for this exists in judicial review.
[234] In *R v Barking Havering & Brentwood Community Health Care NHS Trust* [1999] 1 FLR 106.
[235] *Greene v Secretary of State for Home Affairs* [1942] AC 284, 303 *per* Lord Wright. Cf Lord Maugham who in the same case said that: 'It is inaccurate to say . . . that the writ is available as a remedy in all cases of wrongful deprivation of liberty'.
[236] 3 *Blackstone's Commentaries* (12th edn, 1794) 131 quoted by Lord Scarman in *R v Secretary of State for the Home Department, ex p Khawaja* [1984] AC 74, 111. Also *Armah v Ghana (No 1)* [1968] AC 192.
[237] *Phillip v DPP* [1992] 1 AC 545, 560.
[238] Lewis (n 3 above) para 12-002.
[239] *Linnett v Coles* [1987] QB 555; also Simon Brown LJ in *R v Oldham Justices, ex p Cawley* [1997] QB 1.
[240] *Re Featherstone* (1953) 37 Cr App R 146, 147 see *per* Lord Goddard CJ; *Re Wring* [1960] 1 WLR 138.

challenge detention following a committal to prison for contempt of court.[241] These limitations reflect the reluctance of courts to permit resort to the writ of habeas corpus where specialized appeal procedures or judicial review could achieve the same result and do so more flexibly.[242] This being so, they are limitations of practice rather than of jurisdiction.[243]

(c) The grounds for obtaining habeas corpus

18.80   Turning to the grounds on which habeas corpus may be obtained. Again two approaches have been evident in the case law. The broad approach holds that on an application for habeas corpus the court may review the legality of the detention on any of the grounds available in judicial review proceedings.[244] In so doing they 'will wield whatever powers of review are necessary to give relief where it is thought that something has gone wrong'.[245] Both Lord Scarman and Lord Wilberforce in *R v Secretary of State for the Home Department, ex p Khawaja*[246] lend support for this broad approach. Any difference between habeas corpus and judicial review, said Lord Scarman, 'arises not in the law's substance but from the nature of the remedy . . .'.[247] Lord Wilberforce agreed with this, stating that he did 'not think it would be appropriate unless unavoidable to make a distinction between the two remedies'. Referring to these statements the Law Commission has concluded that 'judicial review and habeas corpus are subject to a common principle and that the scope of review of these remedies is and should be essentially the same'.[248]

18.81   The Court of Appeal, however, has said that the grounds on which habeas corpus may be granted are narrower than judicial review. In *R v Secretary of State for the Home Department, ex p Muboyayi*[249] it was held that habeas corpus could only be used to challenge an administrative decision leading to a detention on jurisdictional

---

[241] *Linnett v Coles* [1987] QB 555.

[242] See, eg, Simon Brown LJ in *R v Oldham Justices, ex p Cawley* [1997] QB 1, 19.

[243] Thus in *Linnett v Coles* [1987] QB 555 Lawton LJ accepted that in exceptional cases habeas corpus could be used to challenge committal orders in either criminal or civil cases. Also in *Re Wring* [1960] 1 WLR 138 Lord Parker CJ clearly contemplated situations where a prisoner might persist in seeking habeas corpus. On occasion habeas corpus has been sought to determine the legality of a conviction: *R v Governor of Spring Hill Prison ex p Sohi* [1988] 1 WLR 596. See Sharpe (n 227 above) 62–63.

[244] Although formally habeas corpus lies against the custodian rather than against the body responsible for ordering the detention, the courts may review the legality of the underlying decision, as if they were undertaking a judicial review.

[245] Sharpe (n 227 above) 62–63.

[246] [1984] AC 74.

[247] Lord Scarman in *R v Secretary of State for the Home Department, ex p Khawaja* [1984] AC 74, 99.

[248] Law Com No 226 (n 18 above) para 11.10.

[249] [1992] 1 QB 244. Also Lord Donaldson MR in *R v Secretary of State for the Home Department, ex Cheblak* [1991] 1 WLR 890, 894; *Re SC (Mental Patient: Habeas Corpus)* [1996] QB 599.

grounds such as an error of precedent fact. Where no such challenge was being made the underlying administrative decision could only be impugned by judicial review proceedings. This narrow approach was convincingly criticized by the Law Commission[250] which argued that it is contrary to authority[251]and resurrects the distinction between jurisdictional and non-jurisdictional review that is generally considered to have been laid to rest by the House of Lords in the late 1960s.[252] More recently Lord Woolf has acknowledged that the distinction between issues of precedent fact going to jurisdiction (where habeas corpus is appropriate) and the propriety of some prior administrative action (where habeas corpus appears to be inappropriate) 'is not always easy to distinguish'.[253]

(d) Conclusion

Given the current unsatisfactory state of the law it is hardly surprising that the re-**18.82** lationship between judicial review proceedings and habeas corpus is unclear. In many instances those seeking to challenge the legality of their detention are obliged to institute two sets of proceedings leading to unnecessary duplication. The judicial response has been to discourage the use of habeas corpus in favour of judicial review.[254] While this may appear to be a sensible practical response in most situations, there is a fundamental difference between the discretionary nature of judicial review and the principle that habeas corpus is available as of right. Hobhouse LJ summarized the current dilemma when he said:[255]

> I would like to endorse the need for further consideration and guidance to be given to when an application for the writ or for judicial review is appropriate. Whilst it is of the greatest constitutional importance that the availability of the right to apply for the writ should in no way be undermined, it may be thought that the present procedural confusion and overlap is undesirable and requires reconsideration and clarification.[256]

---

[250] See also Lewis (n 3 above) paras 12.011–12.012.
[251] cf *Armah v Government of Ghana (No 1)* [1968] AC 192.
[252] *Anisminic v Foreign Compensation Commission* [1969] 2 AC 147.
[253] *R v Barking Havering & Brentwood Community Health Care NHS Trust* [1999] 1 FLR 106, 116.
[254] In *R v Barking Havering & Brentwood Community Health Care NHS Trust* [1999] 1 FLR 106, 114–117 Lord Woolf said that the courts should discourage applications for habeas corpus unless it is clear that no other relief would be required.
[255] *R v Barking Havering & Brentwood Community Health Care NHS Trust* [1999] 1 FLR 106, 117.
[256] Following post-Bowman Consultation the Secretary of State has decided that no need exists to introduce an additional procedure for applying for habeas corpus by judicial review, CP (R) 10/01, October 2003, see above n 222.

19

REMEDIES FOR VIOLATIONS OF CONVENTION RIGHTS

A. Rights and Remedies in the Human Rights Act 1998

(1) Ways in Which Remedial Provisions of the Human Rights Act 1998 Affect Litigation

(a) Importance of remedies to Convention rights

Remedies are central to the legal protection offered to Convention rights under the Human Rights Act 1998 (HRA). The European Convention on Human Rights (ECHR) encapsulates the principle ubi ius, ibi remedium. Article 1 imposes an obligation on states to 'secure to everyone within their jurisdiction the rights and freedoms defined in Section I of this Convention'. Section I ECHR contains Articles 2 to 18, setting out each of the Convention rights and provisions relating to their application. The obligation under Article 1 is not limited to ensuring that the substance of the law and state policies respect the rights. Article 13 makes it clear that the state has an obligation to provide remedies for people whose

19.01

Convention rights have been violated, including remedies against public authorities: 'Everyone whose rights and freedoms as set forth in this Convention are violated shall have an effective remedy before a national authority notwithstanding that the violation has been committed by persons acting in an official capacity'.

(b) How this is translated into the Human Rights Act 1998

19.02 The HRA 1998, s 1, does not include Articles 1 and 13 among the Convention rights which it makes part of English law. Nevertheless, the Act contains several provisions which provide for remedies for violations of Convention rights, and control the nature of those remedies and the circumstances in which they are available. Three provisions are particularly important. First, s 6(1) of the Act provides: 'It is unlawful for a public authority to act in a way which is incompatible with a Convention right' (although this does not apply if primary legislation, or subordinate legislation made in a way that is demanded by primary legislation, requires the authority to act in an incompatible way: s 6(2)).

19.03 Secondly, s 7(1) of the Act provides:

A person who claims that a public authority has acted (or proposes to act) in a way which is made unlawful by section 6(1) may—
(a) bring proceedings against the authority under this Act in the appropriate court or tribunal, or
(b) rely on the Convention right or rights concerned in any legal proceedings, but only if he is (or would be) a victim of the unlawful act.

19.04 Thirdly, s 8(1) of the Act gives a wide discretion to a court to 'grant such relief or remedy, or make such order, within its powers as it considers just and appropriate'. Lord Irvine of Lairg, then the Lord Chancellor, explained while piloting the Human Rights Bill through its Committee stage in the House of Lords that the remedial provisions of the Act, especially s 8, were intended to meet the requirements of Article 13 by allowing courts to provide effective remedies for violations of the Convention rights.[1] If there is doubt about the meaning and effect of one of the remedial provisions of the 1998 Act, courts may have regard to the Lord Chancellor's statement in the House of Lords by virtue of the principle in *Pepper v Hart*.[2] If there is any ambiguity in the legislation, the court is also entitled to have regard to the fact that the remedial provisions in the Act, particularly s 8, are intended to give effect to the United Kingdom's obligations under Article 13.[3] The impact of Convention rights on remedies is extended further by s 6(3)(a) of the HRA 1998, which provides that courts and tribunals are public authorities for the purposes of the Act. This means that they have a duty, under s 6(1), to act

[1] See *Hansard*, HL vol 583, col 475 (18 November 1997).
[2] [1993] AC 593, HL. See paras 1.228–1.233 above.
[3] See paras 1.205 and 7.47 above.

compatibly with Convention rights, unless compelled by primary legislation to act otherwise.

(c) Effect on the relationship between remedies and the Human Rights Act 1998

The HRA 1998 may thus have an impact on remedies in one of three ways. First, **19.05** where a claimant or defendant is directly invoking the court's protection for a Convention right, the Act's remedial provisions directly affect the availability of remedies. For example, a straightforward action in tort for breach of the statutory duty of public authorities under s 6 of the HRA directly raises the question of the remedies which should be granted in the circumstances of the case. Secondly, Convention rights may be raised by way of defence to an action brought by a public authority. In such proceedings, the Act may directly affect the availability of remedies, if remedies otherwise available to the claimant public authority would threaten the defendant's Convention rights. For example, an action for possession of land may engage the right to respect for the defendant's home under Article 8 ECHR if the property is a dwelling. If the claimant is a public authority (say a local housing authority claiming possession of public sector housing from a tenant who has failed to pay rent), the defendant might raise Article 8 as a defence to the claim. Special problems arise in relation to criminal proceedings, where the defence may argue that the only effective remedy for a violation of Convention rights at an early stage in the process is to stay the proceedings or to exclude evidence at the trial. Thirdly, even if the claimant is a private individual rather than a public authority, the court determining the case is a public authority by virtue of s 6(3)(a) of the Act, and might have to make sure that it does not make an order that violates Article 8. In this way, the Act may indirectly affect remedies in ordinary private law proceedings. Thus special considerations arise when the HRA 1998 is involved, directly or indirectly, in a proportion of litigation, either because one of the parties is asserting a Convention right against a public authority or because the court or tribunal is itself a public authority.

The availability of remedies in proceedings brought to protect a Convention right is **19.06** examined in section B of this chapter. Section C considers the effect on remedies of using the Convention rights by way of defence, in civil and criminal proceedings. Section D looks at the incidental impact of the Act's provisions on judicial powers and discretion in ordinary civil litigation. First, however, we explain the background principles which guide legal decision-making in this area, and set out the special rules about locus standi which apply to proceedings to vindicate Convention rights.

(2) Ubi Ius, Ibi Remedium in English Public Law and under the ECHR

(a) The place of remedies for rights in English law

The principle ubi ius, ibi remedium is one of the main planks of the rule of law. As **19.07** such, the need for remedies in the face of legal wrongs has long been respected in

English law. Indeed, for centuries the law of remedies was at least important as the substantive law in settling the boundaries of civil liability. One could say that something was a legal wrong (as distinct from a social or moral wrong) if it could be shown that a writ was available for it. As recently as the early 1970s, much of administrative law consisted of the technicalities governing the availability of the prerogative writs (as they were then called) of certiorari, prohibition and mandamus. The bodies which had an obligation to act in accordance with the rules of natural justice were, essentially, those which were amenable to the writ of certiorari. In public law, the remedies enforced duties of public bodies. If no writ was available, there was no duty. The principle was ubi remedium, ibi obligatio.

19.08   Developments in English administrative law during the second half of the 20th century, and particularly since the 1960s (described in chapters 13 to 18 above), have steadily shifted the attention of lawyers from the technicalities of remedies to general principles, but it remains a fundamental principle of English law that there should be a remedy available for any legal wrong: ubi obligatio, ibi remedium. The HRA 1998 has added another layer to this by making the idea of Convention rights against public authorities as significant as the idea of the principled obligations of the public authorities to the public. Alongside (but not replacing) ubi obligatio, ibi remedium we now genuinely have ubi ius, ibi remedium as a fundamental principle of English law.

19.09   Although rights now have a genuine place in English public law, one element of the obligation-dominated days of public law continues to feature. Public authorities are supposed to operate in the public interest, and it might not be in the public interest to force a public authority to comply with an obligation to a particular claimant, either because of that claimant's behaviour and circumstances or because of the deleterious effect it would have on the ability of the authority to meet its obligations to other people. To allow courts to take account of such considerations, public law remedies have always been discretionary. This characteristic carries over to the remedies which are available under the HRA 1998 against public authorities. When a claimant brings judicial review proceedings to enforce a Convention right, the usual discretion under Pt 54 of the Civil Procedure Rules (CPR) operates in theory, although it ought to be the case that such remedies are less discretionary when sought in respect of a violation of a Convention right than when a public authority has, for example, acted without taking account of all relevant considerations. But the discretionary nature of the remedies applies to all litigation in which Convention rights are invoked. Even damages, which (outside judicial review proceedings) are normally available as of right when an unlawful act has been shown to have caused loss, are discretionary, for example in an action for breach of a public authority's statutory duty under s 6(1) of the Act to act compatibly with Convention rights, and s 8(3) and (4) of the Act seeks to limit the number of cases in which damages will be awarded to those in which it is necessary in order to afford just satisfaction to the claimant, taking into account the principles applied by the European Court of Human Rights (ECtHR) when awarding compensation under Article 41 ECHR.

This raises the question of how satisfactorily the remedial provisions of the HRA **19.10** 1998 give effect to the obligations of the state under Article 13. That forms one of the themes of this chapter as a whole. By way of background, it is important to set out the obligations arising under Article 13 as interpreted by the ECtHR.

(b) The requirements of Article 13 ECHR

Article 13 requires the state to provide a victim of an alleged violation of a **19.11** Convention right with an opportunity to obtain an authoritative decision from an independent body as to whether or not there has been a violation. The national authority which decides the issue need not be a court or judicial tribunal, but must be capable of providing a remedy.[4] If it makes decisions which are not legally binding (for example, those of the Parliamentary Commissioner for Administration in the United Kingdom) it does not provide an effective remedy,[5] although it has been said that a non-binding decision may be an effective remedy if there is a clear and consistent national practice of giving effect to the decision.[6] The national authority must be able to conduct a thorough inquiry into relevant matters if it is to provide an effective remedy,[7] and must be capable of making a decision on the issues raised by the Convention right in question. Judicial review was unable to satisfy these demands in cases arising before the HRA 1998 came into force, when the judges were restricted to examining the vires, procedural fairness and rationality of decisions, and could not provide a remedy for an infringement of a Convention right, because the threshold of unreasonableness was so high as to preclude judicial evaluation of the public authority's claims in relation to justifications for an infringement of the right, such as the existence of a pressing social need for the interference and its proportionality.[8] Similarly judicial review of a decision on the number of night flights allowed at Heathrow Airport could not provide an effective remedy for an alleged violation of Article 8 ECHR rights of local residents through noise disturbance, because the court could only assess the rationality of the decision and not its justification under Article 8(2).[9] Now the HRA 1998 is in force, it should usually be possible for judicial review to provide an effective remedy, unless the court is precluded from investigating certain matters

---

[4] *Silver v UK* Series A No 61 (1983) 5 EHRR 347.
[5] *Silver v UK*, ibid.
[6] See eg *Vilvarajah v UK* Series A No 215 (1992) 14 EHRR 248 (Home Office practice of not removing person once leave to apply for judicial review of the removal decision had been granted).
[7] *Aydin v Turkey* Application 23178/94 (1998) 25 EHRR 251.
[8] *Smith and Grady v UK (No 1)* Applications 33985/96 & 33986/96 (2000) 29 EHRR 493.
[9] *Hatton v UK* Application 36022/97, The Times, 10 July 2003.

relevant to the alleged violation of the Convention right (for example, because of a public interest immunity certificate) or if the violation is protected from review by primary legislation which cannot be read compatibly with the right in question. Generally, violations of Convention rights are now matters of illegality under s 6 of the HRA, rather than being issues going to rationality.

19.12   The requirement for the national authority to be independent means that it must be independent both of the government and of the body which is alleged to have violated the right. For example, the Police Complaints Authority was not sufficiently independent of the police to meet Article 13 standards when investigating unauthorized bugging of a flat,[10] and (by analogy with the duty to investigate suspicious deaths effectively under Article 2 ECHR) officers of a police force would not be sufficiently independent if asked to inquire into the failings of other officers of the same police force which are said to have led to a violation of a Convention right.[11]

19.13   Article 13 is concerned with remedies for violations of other Convention rights. The right to a remedy is thus not a free-standing right. Nevertheless, there can be a violation of Article 13 even if there is held to be no violation of substantive Convention rights. If there is an arguable case for saying that there has been a violation of one of the substantive rights, and the argument cannot be ventilated before a national authority which is sufficiently independent and capable of providing an effective remedy, there will be a violation even if there is ultimately held to have been no violation of the substantive right.[12]

19.14   The effective remedy required by Article 13 need not be provided by a single body or procedure. Where a number of forms of redress are available, the ECtHR has held that they may cumulatively amount to an effective remedy, even if no one of them provides a guarantee of effectiveness.[13] A somewhat analogous approach was taken by the House of Lords when deciding whether a variety of steps, several of which were untested, collectively available to a member of the Security Service who felt that the powers of the Service were being misused, provided non-legal means of drawing attention to his concerns sufficient to make a total ban on the member's ever publicly revealing his allegations a proportionate interference with his freedom of expression, justifiable under Article 10(2) ECHR.[14] However, this approach is questionable. It is hard to see how several untried or unreliable methods of ventilating a complaint can together provide an effective remedy. Until it is shown that the procedures are together effective, and that the effective parts are

---

[10]   *Khan v UK* Application 35394/97 (2001) 31 EHRR 45.

[11]   *Finucane v UK* Application 29177/95 (1 July 2003, ECtHR).

[12]   See, eg, *Hatton v UK* Application 36022/97, The Times, 10 July 2003 (no violation of Art 8, but violation of Art 13 because no body in England could allow the allegation of a breach of Art 8 to be ventilated in a way that would have led to an effective remedy had there been a breach).

[13]   See, eg, *Silver v UK* Series A No 61 (1983) 5 EHRR 347.

[14]   *R v Shayler* [2002] UKHL 11; [2003] 1 AC 247.

sufficiently independent to meet Article 13 requirements, the cumulative approach relies on the hope (rather than any expectation) that at least one of the inherently unreliable procedures will work well in every case. Even if one is an optimist, this strains credulity, and fails to reflect the value of the principle ubi ius, ibi remedium which Article 13 is designed to encapsulate.

(3) Who May Assert a Convention Right under the Human Rights Act 1998?

Standing to rely on a Convention right in English courts is the first of two areas under the HRA 1998 where English law depends directly, to a greater or lesser extent, on the jurisprudence of the ECtHR.[15] Section 7(1) allows a person to assert that a public authority has acted unlawfully by reason of an incompatibility with a Convention right, 'but only if he is (or would be) a victim of the unlawful act'. Section 7(7) makes the 'victim' test for standing depend directly on the case law of the Strasbourg Court:

> For the purposes of this section, a person is a victim of an unlawful act only if he would be a victim for the purposes of Article 34 of the Convention if proceedings were brought in the European Court of Human Rights.

19.15

Article 34 ECHR makes an application to the Strasbourg Court admissible only if the applicant is a 'person, non-governmental organization or group of individuals claiming to be the victim of a violation by one of the High Contracting Parties' of a Convention right. This allows a wide variety of bodies to assert Convention rights in English law, permitting class actions and litigation by unincorporated associations as well as bodies corporate and natural persons. However, this latitude applies only if the applicant is, or applicants are, claiming to be victims of a violation, and the word 'victim' has been treated by the Court as requiring the applicant to be individually and directly affected by the alleged violation.

19.16

(a) Examples of people who are victims for the purpose of Article 34 ECHR

Obviously, any act aimed directly at a person will make him or her a victim if it is alleged to violate a Convention right. But people may be directly affected by a violation which is not directly aimed at them. Much will depend on the nature of the right and of the alleged violation. A few examples will suffice. Where immigrants are refused entry to the United Kingdom in circumstances which are alleged to violate their right to respect for family life under Article 8 taken together with the right to be free from discrimination under Article 14, members of their families who are already in the United Kingdom may also be victims of the refusal if it interferes with their right to respect for family life (the right to enjoy the

19.17

---

[15] The other area is the availability of damages: see paras 19.42 et seq below.

company and support of those who have been refused entry) under Article 8.[16] Where a person is killed, allegedly in violation of Article 2, his or her spouse may also claim to be a victim of the violation.[17] If the state is performing a licensing or regulatory function, and permits activities by third parties which are said to interfere with other people's Convention rights, everyone whose rights are said to be injuriously affected is a victim, despite the decision not being aimed at them.[18] Where the violation takes the form of a failure by public authorities to provide an effective and independent investigation into a killing, other members of the deceased person's close family may also be victims, as they are affected by the failure to take adequate steps to find out what happened.[19] Where a generally applicable law is said to interfere with Convention rights, anyone who is at risk of being prosecuted or subjected to legal proceedings prejudicial to their Convention rights is a victim. Potential victims are victims for Article 34 purposes.[20]

(b) When are people not victims?

19.18   Generally, people claiming to be victims may be represented by others.[21] If the principal claimant dies in the course of proceedings, the case may be continued by a spouse or close relative with a legitimate interest in the proceedings.[22] However, that is permitted only because the person continuing the case is standing in the shoes of the victim who initiated it. The Court does not treat a person as a victim if he or she is neither directly affected by the alleged violation nor the appointed representative of someone who is directly affected. This means that there is no scope for individuals or groups who are interested and expert in an issue (for example, environmental protection or child poverty), but are not themselves directly affected by the act or omission said to give rise to a violation of a Convention right, to initiate litigation to enforce the right.

19.19   This approach to standing is similar to that which normally applies in English private law. A person seeking to enforce a private law duty, or protect a private law

---

[16]   *Abdulaziz, Cabales and Balkandali v UK* Series A No 94 (1985) 7 EHRR 471.

[17]   See, eg, *McCann v UK* Series A No 324 (1995) 21 EHRR 97.

[18]   *Hatton v UK* Application 36022/97, The Times, 10 July 2003.

[19]   *Finucane v UK* Application 29177/95 (1 July 2003, ECtHR).

[20]   *Norris v Ireland* Series A No 142 (1988) 13 EHRR 186 (self-proclaimed homosexual liable to prosecution under Irish sexual offences law was victim of violation of Art 8, despite not having been charged with any offence). In *R (on the application of Rusbridger) v A-G* [2003] UKHL 38; [2003] 3 WLR 232, it was accepted that a newspaper editor campaigning for the replacement of the monarchy with a republican form of government could claim to be a victim of s 3 of Treason Felony Act 1848, which criminalizes such publications. However, it was held that the declaration was to be refused, in exercise of the court's discretion, because there was no practical possibility of the editor ever being prosecuted; and, even if there were to be a prosecution, the section would have to be read down under s 3 of the HRA 1998 to make it compatible with Art 10.

[21]   See Rules of the ECtHR, r 45.

[22]   See eg *Lukanov v Bulgaria* Application 21915/93 (1997) 24 EHRR 121; *Dalban v Romania* Application 28114/95 (2001) 31 EHRR 39.

right, must generally be a direct beneficiary of the performance of the duty (which must have been created with a view to conferring that benefit on the claimant) or the person entitled to the right. However, the approach in public law is usually rather different.[23] As explained in chapter 17 above, the public interest in up-holding the principle of legality—the notion that public bodies must be able to justify their activities by reference to the legal rules conferring powers on them, and must stay within the limits of those powers—sometimes requires courts to permit public-spirited people and non-governmental organizations such as in-terest groups to bring public law proceedings in the public interest, even if the claimant's own personal interests are not themselves directly affected by the impugned act or omission. When bringing judicial review proceedings, such claimants may be treated as having a 'sufficient interest' in the matter to give them standing under CPR Pt 54. But they will not be treated as having a 'sufficient in-terest' to rely on a Convention right in those proceedings, because s 7(3) of the HRA provides that applicants have a sufficient interest to allege a violation of a Convention right only if they are 'victims' in the sense of Article 34 ECHR.

This may have one of two effects. Either there will be violations of Convention rights for which no effective remedy is available because the victim is unable to litigate (because of ignorance, poverty and failure to obtain legal aid and assis-tance, or economic or social pressure brought to bear by those responsible), or the English courts will tend to blur the distinction between standing to initiate judicial review proceedings generally and standing to rely on Convention rights. Section 11 of the HRA 1998 provides that a person's reliance on a Convention right 'does not restrict . . . (b) his right to make any claim or bring any proceed-ings which he could make or bring apart from sections 7 to 9'. As it is rare for a Convention rights point to be the sole ground for challenging a decision, act or omission by way of judicial review, it may be possible (for example) for a non-governmental organization to allege that the decision, etc, is irrational having regard to (among other things) the fact that it interferes with the Convention rights of a large number of people, rather than relying directly on the right itself as a ground of challenge in its own right. For this strategy to be successful, it would be necessary to give a narrow interpretation to the words 'rely on the Convention right' in s 7(1)(b) of the HRA, taking it to mean that the right pro-vides the cause of action or ground of challenge in the proceedings, rather than being an ancillary consideration supporting a different cause of action or ground of challenge. **19.20**

---

[23] See J Marriott and D Nicol, 'The Human Rights Act, representative standing and the victim culture' [1998] European Human Rights L Rev 730; J Miles, 'Standing under the Human Rights Act 1998: theories of rights enforcement and the nature of public law adjudication' [2000] CLJ 133.

(c) Limits of the 'victim' test

19.21   The 'victim' test for standing under s 7 of the HRA 1998 must be read as being subject to a number of other provisions which clearly contemplate a degree of reliance being placed on Convention rights even when the parties are not claiming to have been a victim of the violation. First, there is s 5 of the Act, which allows the Crown to intervene in any litigation where a court is considering whether to make a declaration of incompatibility under s 4 of the Act. The Crown is entitled to make any representations when intervening, and may clearly rely on Convention rights despite not being able to claim to be a victim of a violation. Secondly, CPR 54.17 allows a court to permit third-party interventions in judicial review proceedings, including those relating to alleged violations of Convention rights, provided they have been properly commenced by a person claiming to be a victim.[24] This power has been used reasonably regularly by English courts, and it has never been suggested that the third party intervenors are prevented from making submissions relating to the Convention rights. Indeed, sometimes that is the main purpose of allowing an intervention, for example when the intervenor is a non-governmental organization with a special expertise in human rights matters.

19.22   Interventions are allowed even in private law proceedings if human rights issues arise. This can reach the point at which the proceedings verge on absurdity. *Wilson v First County Trust (No 2)*,[25] a case raising important issues relating to Article 6 ECHR and the role of the courts under the HRA 1998, was decided by the House of Lords despite both the original parties having withdrawn from the proceedings: the case was argued entirely by intervenors. This is not a desirable state of affairs, but it demonstrates that there are practical limits to the scope of the victim test.

19.23   Finally, courts and tribunals always have various obligations under the HRA 1998 in relation to Convention rights regardless of the positions adopted by the parties to litigation. First, under s 3 the court must, so far as possible, read and give effect to all legislation in a manner compatible with Convention rights. Secondly, under s 12(1) and (4) a court, when considering whether to grant any relief which might affect the Convention right to freedom of expression, must have particular regard to the importance of that right. Thirdly, under s 13 a court, when determining any question arising under the Act which might affect the exercise by a religious organization or its members of the Convention right to freedom of thought, conscience and religion, must have particular regard to the importance of that right. Where a court or tribunal finds itself compelled to discharge one of these obligations, any party to the proceedings must be entitled to rely on Convention rights so far as they are relevant to the matter the court or tribunal has to decide, whether or not they

---

[24] See paras 17.56–17.57 above.
[25] [2003] UKHL 40; [2003] 3 WLR 568.

claim to be victims of a violation or potential violation of the rights. If they could not, they would be victims of a violation of the right to a fair hearing under Article 6(1) ECHR. Section 7 of the HRA cannot be interpreted as requiring such a violation. Instead, people making submissions in such circumstances should not be treated as 'relying on the Convention right or rights' under s 7(1)(b).[26]

B. The Availability of Remedies in Actions Brought to Assert Convention Rights

(1) Commencing Actions: the Appropriate Forum, Time Limits, and the Appropriate Defendant

(a) What violations are covered?

Where proceedings are brought to vindicate a Convention right, s 7(1)(a) of the HRA provides a cause of action to victims in respect of acts or omissions occurring on or after 2 October 2000 (the date when the Act came fully into effect) which are unlawful by reason of an incompatibility with a Convention right. An act or omission before that date does not constitute a violation of a Convention right for the purposes of English law, because the duty to act compatibly with Convention rights became part of English law only when s 6(1) of the Act came into effect.[27]

19.24

(b) The appropriate forum

Remedies for violations of Convention rights must be sought 'in the appropriate court or tribunal', as defined for different purposes by rules made by the Lord Chancellor (for England) or the Secretary of State for Wales (for Wales).[28] If the chosen vehicle for seeking redress is judicial review, the appropriate court is the Administrative Court of the High Court. If it is sought by way of an action for damages, it may be sought in the High Court or the county court, depending on the allocation of cases under the CPR. If the issue arises out of an employment dispute, the appropriate tribunal will generally be an employment tribunal, and so on. As these jurisdictions and remedial powers of the various courts and tribunals vary, the ability to obtain an effective remedy may depend on the court or tribunal in which proceedings have to be initiated. We return to this matter below.[29]

19.25

A special rule applies where the proceedings are brought in respect of a judicial act which is said to be incompatible with a Convention right. Section 9(1) of the HRA provides:

19.26

---

[26] See para 19.20 above.
[27] See paras 7.52 et seq above.
[28] HRA 1998, s 7(1)(a), (2), (9)(a).
[29] See paras 19.32 et seq below.

Proceedings under section 7(1)(a) in respect of a judicial act may be brought only—
(a) by exercising a right of appeal;
(b) on an application . . . for judicial review; or
(c) in such other forum as may be prescribed by rules.

Rights of appeal have been limited (as compared with earlier law) by the CPR, which made it necessary to obtain permission to appeal in virtually all cases. However, the importance of providing an effective remedy for a violation of a Convention right means that permission to appeal should normally be given where the grounds of appeal raise an arguable issue relating to an alleged incompatibility between the judicial act and a Convention right. Where no other means of obtaining a remedy is available, for instance because the challenged decision or order was made by a judge of the Supreme Court who is not amenable to judicial review,[30] and no other forum for obtaining redress has been prescribed by rules under s 9(1)(c), permission to appeal should always be given where there is an arguable case for an incompatibility, because courts are entitled to have regard to international obligations, including the right to an effective remedy under Article 13 ECHR, when deciding how to exercise a discretion.[31] Where the judicial act takes the form of an order for someone's arrest or detention in circumstances which are alleged to make it incompatible with the right not to be arbitrarily deprived of one's liberty and the various procedural rights attached to that right under Article 5 ECHR, the appropriate procedure for pursuing the enforceable right to compensation required by Article 5(5) is to bring an action in tort against the Crown (rather than the judge) for compensatory damages.[32]

(c) Limitation period for proceedings to vindicate a Convention right

19.27 There is a shorter limitation period than usual for the commencement of actions alleging a violation of a Convention right. The normal limitation period for commencing actions based on the law of obligations is six years, and 12 years for actions for possession of land. However, an action brought under s 7(1)(a) of the HRA must be brought within a year after the act complained of, although courts and tribunals have a discretion to extend the period if they consider it equitable to do so having regard to all the circumstances. If other rules of law impose a stricter time limit in relation to the particular procedure being used, that time limit applies.[33] In this context, 'stricter' could mean either 'shorter' or 'with less discretion to extend the time limit'. However, depriving the court or tribunal of any discretion to extend the time limit could deprive deserving claimants of an effective

---

[30] HRA 1998, s 9(2) makes it clear that s 9(1) does not make any court amenable to judicial review if it is prevented from being reviewable by any rule of law.
[31] See para 7.47 above.
[32] HRA 1998, s 9(3), (4). See *R (on the application of KB) v Mental Health Review Tribunal* [2003] EWHC 193; [2003] 3 WLR 185, Stanley Burnton J.
[33] ibid s 7(5).

remedy through no fault of their own. As this could lead to a violation of the obligation of the United Kingdom under Article 13 ECHR, the word 'stricter' should not be interpreted as removing discretion to extend the time limit in a case where an extension would be equitable.

The interaction of time limits can have an impact on the availability of remedies for violations of Convention rights. Judicial review, a procedure often invoked to protect Convention rights, has a strict time limit of three months, and even earlier applications may be rejected if the court decides that the claimant has unduly delayed before commencing proceedings.[34] These limits apply to claims that a public authority has acted incompatibly with a Convention right, rather than the one-year limit. An action in tort for breach of statutory duty may be brought outside the one-year time limit if the claimant is arguing that the duty arises from a statute other than the HRA 1998, even if the cause of action arises only because the other statute has to be read and given effect in a manner compatible with Convention rights as required by s 3 of the 1998 Act. However, if the court decides that it cannot give effect to the other statute in that way, the claimant will not be allowed to advance the alternative claim that the public authority breached its duty to act compatibly with Convention rights under s 6(1) of the 1998 Act. Similar effects occur in relation to land actions and other torts. The picture is not altogether rational or consistent. The interest in ensuring that effective remedies will be available for violations of Convention rights has been overridden, in this case, by the desire to protect public authorities against a large number of long-delayed claims under the Act.

19.28

(d) Finding an appropriate defendant

When a person applies to the ECtHR claiming that his or her Convention rights have been violated, it is not necessary to identify a particular public body (or bodies) as being responsible for the violation. The proceedings take place in an international law forum, and the respondent is the state, which is taken to be responsible in international law for the acts and omissions of state institutions, and sometimes for failing to control the activities of private bodies and individuals as well. The state is liable if the applicant's Convention rights have been violated as a result of the combined effect of action or inaction by a variety of actors, some or all of whom may have been behaving quite lawfully under national law.

19.29

The position is rather different when proceedings are brought in English courts under the HRA 1998. The Act provides for remedies against a public authority which is claimed to have acted in a way which is incompatible with a Convention right.[35] A remedy will be available only if the claimant shows that:

19.30

---

[34] See paras 17.21 et seq above.
[35] HRA 1998, ss 6(1), 7(1). On the meaning of 'public authority' see paras 7.135–7.150 above.

- the defendant(s) acted in a manner incompatible with the claimant's right; and
- a remedy against the defendant(s) will rectify or compensate for the violation.

In a simple case, it will be clear that an act or decision of a public authority violated the claimant's right, and that the authority has the power to rectify the violation. For instance, if a local authority exercises its statutory function of protecting children under the Children Act 1989 in such a way that children suffer harm of a kind that amounts to inhuman or degrading treatment, it is not difficult to conclude that the authority is the appropriate defendant in an action for acting incompatibly with rights under Article 3 ECHR. Similarly, if the Home Secretary exercises a statutory power to deprive certain destitute asylum-seekers of financial and other support, leaving them in conditions which amount to a violation of Article 3, the Home Secretary will be liable under the HRA 1998, and will not be allowed to shift responsibility for their welfare to charities if the charities themselves are unable or unwilling to help.[36]

19.31   However, other cases are more complicated. For example, sometimes an act of a public authority which is otherwise lawful produces a situation in which the claimant is prevented from enjoying his or her right because of surrounding social circumstances or the inactivity of other individuals or agencies. In *R (on the application of K) v Camden and Islington Health Authority*,[37] a mental patient, K, had been compulsorily detained for treatment under the Mental Health Act 1983. A mental health review tribunal decided that K could be released from hospital on condition that appropriate medical support could be provided in the community. The local health authority had a duty under s 117 of the 1983 Act to provide necessary services in the community, but only (the Court of Appeal held) so far as it could by using its best endeavours within the limits of its resources. The authority was unable to find a doctor with suitable expertise who was willing to provide services, so the condition for release could not be met and K continued to be detained. This combination of circumstances deprived K of the right to liberty under Article 5(1) ECHR, but the court held that the health authority was not responsible and no remedy could be granted against it. Where the proper protection of a Convention right depends on a number of public authorities acting together, it is important to ensure that the action is brought against the appropriate defendants. Where protection depends on a number of public and private bodies working together, there may be difficulty in providing effective remedies (as demanded by Article 13 ECHR) unless the statutory obligations of the public authorities are interpreted as including an absolute duty to ensure that everyone involved acts to

---

[36] *R (on the application of Q) v Secretary of State for the Home Department* [2003] EWCA Civ 364; [2003] 3 WLR 365,.

[37] [2001] EWCA Civ 240, [2002] QB 198; see further *R (on the application of H) v Secretary of State for the Home Department* [2002] EWCA 646, [2003] QB 220 (the House of Lords has given leave to appeal).

give effect to the Convention right. Such an interpretation is often unlikely, particularly when it would impose an undue burden on the public authority to take action.[38]

(2) The Remedial Powers of Courts and Tribunals

Section 8(1) allows the court or tribunal[39] to grant 'such relief or remedy, or make   **19.32**
such order, within its powers as it considers just and appropriate'. The very wide
terms of this power are significantly qualified by the words 'within its powers'.
Most courts and tribunals are empowered to award only a limited range of remedies. The High Court has very wide powers to award damages, issue injunctions,
make declarations, and make a variety of orders ranging from those available in
the Administrative Court (such as quashing orders) through orders for an account
of profits to propriety remedies, remedies in Admiralty cases, and equitable remedies for breach of trust. All these may be available to protect Convention rights in
cases brought in the High Court. County courts can make use of most, but not all,
of those remedies. By contrast, coroners' courts and criminal courts have no
power to grant remedies for violations of Convention rights, beyond granting
adjournments and stays of proceedings and making use of the power to control
evidence and procedure (although criminal courts also have limited powers to
order defendants to compensate victims of their crimes or restore stolen property). Magistrates' courts, when hearing civil proceedings, can make orders in relation to family and some other matters. Statutory tribunals typically have a very
limited range of remedies at their disposal, carefully drawn to allow the tribunal to
operate reasonably effectively in their specialized areas (such as employment disputes) but not going beyond that remit.

The HRA 1998 does not authorize courts or tribunals to create entirely new reme-   **19.33**
dies, or to make use of remedies which were not previously available to them, even
if that leaves people without an effective remedy for a violation of a Convention
right. For example, a mental health review tribunal cannot award compensation
to a patient who has been unlawfully detained in breach of Article 5 ECHR, or
order a local health authority to exercise its discretion to provide medical support
in the community to a discharged patient, because its powers are limited to ordering the patient's discharge, conditionally or unconditionally, in appropriate
cases.

On the other hand, courts and tribunals are free to use any of their existing pow-   **19.34**
ers (except the power to award damages, which is subject to special restrictions,
considered below, paras 19.42 et seq) as necessary in order to provide effective

---

[38] On the obligation to read and give effect to legislation in a manner compatible with
Convention rights when possible, see paras 1.216 et seq and 7.55 et seq, above.
[39] 'Court' includes 'tribunal': see HRA 1998, s 8(6).

remedies for violations of Convention rights. For instance, the county court does not normally have a jurisdiction to conduct judicial review of housing decisions by local housing authorities, but it has a limited statutory review function in those cases. When a housing decision affects a Convention right, the county court is not only entitled to review it (on normal judicial review principles), but must satisfy itself that any factual decision by the authority, necessary to justify an interference with the Convention right, is correct. When a housing decision affects a Convention right, the county court is not only entitled to review it (on normal judicial review principles), but may need to satisfy itself that any factual decision by the authority, necessary to justify an interference with the Convention right, is correct, in order that the regime of appeal and review may adequately protect the right against unjustified interference.[40]

19.35 However, even the High Court, which has inherent powers to provide equitable remedies, and the Court of Appeal on appeal from the High Court, are not allowed to use their wide powers to extend judicial oversight of other public authorities' exercise of their functions in order to protect Convention rights if that would be inconsistent with the clear policy of legislation designed to exclude courts from decision-making in those areas.[41] This is so even if there is clear evidence that the public authorities are putting children's rights under Article 8 ECHR at risk by failing to implement care plans approved by courts on previous occasions.[42] The authority may still be liable to pay damages to the children for violating their Article 8 rights,[43] but no judicial oversight to prevent the problem will be possible, because the importance of maintaining parliamentary sovereignty makes it more important to give effect to the policy of parliamentary legislation than to forestall violations of Convention rights. The primacy of the legislative supremacy of Parliament was preserved by the HRA 1998.[44]

(3) Human Rights Act 1998, s 12

19.36 When a court or tribunal is considering whether to grant a remedy which, if granted, might affect the exercise by anyone of the Convention right to freedom of expression, s 12 of the HRA imposes a number of requirements.

---

[40] *Adan v Newham LBC* [2001] EWCA Civ 1916, [2002] 1 WLR 2120; *Begum (Runa) v Tower Hamlets LBC* [2003] UKHL 5; [2003] 2 WLR 388.

[41] *Sheffield City Council v Smart* [2002] EWCA Civ 4; [2002] LGR 467 at [37]–[41].

[42] *Re S (Children) (Care Order: Implementation of Care Plan)* [2002] UKHL 10; [2002] 2 AC 291.

[43] *D v East Berkshire Community NHS Trust, MAK v Dewsbury Healthcare NHS Trust, RK v Oldham NHS Trust*, The Times, 22 August 2003, CA.

[44] See paras 2.158 et seq and 7.23 above.

(a) Respondent not present or represented

If the person against whom relief is sought (the respondent) is neither present nor represented, relief is to be refused unless the court is satisfied that the applicant has taken all reasonable steps to notify the respondent, or there are compelling reasons why the defendant should not be notified.[45] The latter alternative will apply where, for example, the claimant is seeking a freezing order (formerly known as a *Mareva* injunction) or a search order (previously called an *Anton Piller* order) on the ground that the respondent is likely to remove assets from the jurisdiction or conceal or destroy evidence if notified of the application. Where an order is sought against one party but will have effect against the world at large, such as an order restraining publication of allegedly confidential information pending the trial of an action for breach of confidence, s 12 is unlikely to require the claimant to take more than fairly general steps to draw the application to public attention.

19.37

(b) Orders restraining publication

Section 12(3) provides that no order is to be made restraining publication before trial unless the court is satisfied that the applicant is likely to succeed in establishing, at trial, that publication should not be allowed. 'Likely', here, does not mean that the claimant must show he or she is more likely than not to succeed at trial in establishing that publication should be restrained. It means, rather, that there must be a real prospect of success, convincingly established.[46] This in effect reverses the decision of the House of Lords in *A-G v Guardian Newspapers Ltd*[47] that it was virtually always proper to restrain publication of allegedly confidential information pending trial of a breach of confidence action, in order to avoid compromising the confidentiality which was the subject matter of the proceedings, and that this applied even if the information was already in the public domain. Section 12(3) brings English law back into line with the requirements of Article 10 ECHR as established in *Observer and Guardian v UK*.[48]

19.38

On an application for an interim injunction, a court must therefore consider factors relevant to the likelihood of restraint being ordered at trial. Those factors include the nature of the rights affected. Section 12(4) requires the court to have particular regard to the importance of freedom of expression. This means that freedom of expression is to be recognized as having a higher status than non-Convention rights, including the interests of a child in restraining publication, which, under s 1 of the Children Act 1989, would normally be paramount.[49]

19.39

---

[45] HRA 1998, s 12(2).

[46] *Cream Holdings Ltd v Banerjee* [2003] EWCA Civ 103; [2003] 2 All ER 318.

[47] [1987] 1 WLR 1248, HL.

[48] Series A No 216 (1992) 14 EHRR 153.

[49] *Richmond upon Thames LBC v Holmes* [2001] 1 FCR 541, Bracewell J; *Re S (a Child) (Identification: Restriction on Publication)* [2003] EWCA Civ 963; The Times, 21 July 2003.

Chapter 19: Remedies for Violations of Convention Rights

However, it does not necessarily mean that it will outweigh other Convention rights.[50] It is necessary to interpret s 12(3) in the light of s 3, which requires courts to read and give effect to legislation (including s 12(3)) in a manner compatible with all Convention rights (not just freedom of expression) so far as possible.[51] Other factors relevant to the court's discretion when considering whether to restrain publication before trial are the likelihood that a public interest in publication may override the confidentiality[52] and the extent to which the material is already in the public domain,[53] and the degree to which the claimant's own conduct (for instance in planning to exploit the confidential information commercially) would make it more appropriate to provide a remedy in damages or by way of an account of profits than to restrain publication permanently.[54]

19.40 In addition, when the proceedings relate to material which is claimed to be, or appears to the court to be, journalistic, literary or artistic material, or to conduct related to such material, s 12(4)(b) requires the court to have particular regard to 'any relevant privacy code'. This refers to the various codes of practice and codes of conduct promulgated, with or without statutory authority, by such regulatory or self-regulatory bodies as the Press Complaints Commission and the Broadcasting Standards Commission (a role shortly to be taken over in relation to broadcasting by OFCOM under the Communications Act 2003), laying down standards expected of journalists and broadcasters in relation to invasion of people's privacy. Where a defendant can show that he or she has complied with the relevant code, it will tell against the grant of remedies. When there has been a violation of the relevant code's provisions, remedies are more likely to follow.[55]

(c) **Remedies at trial**

19.41 These principles apply to final remedies in proceedings affecting freedom of expression as they do to interim proceedings for restraining publication before trial.

---

[50] See *Douglas v Hello! Ltd (No 1)* [2001] QB 967, CA; *A v B plc* [2002] EWCA Civ 337, [2003] QB 195; *Cream Holdings Ltd v Banerjee* [2003] EWCA Civ 103; [2003] 2 All ER 318.

[51] *Cream Holdings Ltd v Banerjee*, ibid (Arden LJ dissenting on this point).

[52] ibid *per* Sedley LJ.

[53] These factors are particularly important where the material is claimed, or appears, to be journalistic, literary or artistic material: HRA 1998, s 12(4)(a).

[54] *Douglas v Hello! Ltd (No 1)* [2001] QB 967, CA.

[55] See eg *Mills v News Group Newspapers Ltd* [2001] EMLR 41, Lawrence Collins J, and cf *Douglas v Hello! Ltd (No 6)* [2003] EWHC 786; The Times, 21 April 2003, Lindsay J.

(4) Damages[56]

HRA 1998, ss 8 and 9, contain special conditions for the award of damages as a remedy for violations of the duty of public authorities under s 6(1) to act in a manner which is compatible with Convention rights. These are of four kinds: a restriction on the courts and tribunals which may award damages for incompatible acts; a limitation on the circumstances in which damages may be awarded; special rules governing the quantum of such damages; and special rules restricting damages in respect of judicial acts.   **19.42**

(a) Courts and tribunals with power to award damages

Only a court or tribunal which already has 'power to award damages, or to order the payment of compensation, in civil proceedings' is permitted to award damages for an act which is incompatible with a Convention right.[57] This is less a special rule for damages than an application to the field of damages of the general rule, contained in s 8(1), that any remedy must be within the powers of the court or tribunal.   **19.43**

Many courts have the power to award damages or compensation in civil proceedings. However, magistrates' courts, which deal with more cases than any other kind of court in England and Wales, have power to order the payment of compensation only in criminal proceedings, which do not count for this purpose. They have power to order the payment of money by way of maintenance in family proceedings, and to make orders for the return or disposal of property in the hands of the police under the Police (Property) Act 1897, both of which are civil proceedings; but neither of these is a power to award compensation. Some courts with specialized jurisdictions (like coroners' courts) cannot award compensation, and so do not have the power to award damages under the HRA 1998.   **19.44**

Some tribunals, such as employment tribunals, can award compensation for wrongs which fall within their jurisdictions, but many do not. For example, mental health review tribunals have no power to award compensation for unlawful detention or treatment of mental patients, and the immigration appeal tribunal cannot award compensation to immigrants who have been wrongly denied entry to the United Kingdom. Tribunals in the social security and tax systems may have power to order the payment of money to applicants, but that is in the form of either a repayment of overpaid tax or contributions, which is restitutionary rather than compensatory in nature, or the payment of money which is due under   **19.45**

---

[56] See Lord Woolf, 'The Human Rights Act 1998 and remedies' in M Andenas and D Fairgrieve (eds), *Judicial Review in International Perspective: II* (London: Kluwer Law International, 2000) 429–436; Law Commission and Scottish Law Commission, Law Com No 266, Scot Law Com No 180, *Damages under the Human Rights Act 1998* (Cm 4853, SE/2000/182, 2000).

[57] HRA 1998, s 8(2).

statute, which is not compensatory. Such tribunals would not be allowed to award damages under the HRA 1998.

19.46 It follows that claimants will often need to commence several sets of proceedings in different courts if they want to have access to compensation alongside other forms of redress. This will often be possible, and s 11 of the Act provides:

> A person's reliance on a Convention right does not restrict—
> (a) any other right or freedom conferred on him by or under any law having effect in any part of the United Kingdom; or
> (b) his right to make any claim or bring any proceedings which could make or bring apart from sections 7 to 9.

19.47 Nevertheless, bringing additional proceedings could be difficult or impossible if, for example, statute provides that making use of one avenue to obtain redress precludes the right to pursue others. If the total package of remedies fails to provide sufficient means of redress, it could lead to a violation of the right to a fair hearing within a reasonable time by an independent and impartial tribunal in the determination of civil rights and obligations under Article 6(1) ECHR (which is one of the Convention rights forming part of English law under the HRA 1998), or to a failure to provide an effective remedy before a national authority for the violation of a Convention right contrary to Article 13. For example, when a parent seeks the assistance of the Child Support Agency to obtain maintenance from the other parent for their children, the Child Support Act 1991 precludes subsequent pursuit of other legal remedies. This does not prevent a parent from seeking judicial review of the Agency's decision, but if the Agency merely makes a mistake in the calculation of the maintenance (rather than exceeding its jurisdiction or acting wholly irrationally), judicial review may not be able to give what amounts to a fair hearing in the determination of the parent's civil rights and obligations. This will lead to a violation of Article 6, unless the parent can sue the Agency in the ordinary courts for damages for acting incompatibly with a Convention right.[58] Whether that possibility is available will depend on the matters considered next.

(b) Limits on the circumstances in which damages may be awarded

19.48 Section 8(3) of the HRA 1998 provides that the court may award damages under the Act only if it is satisfied that it is necessary to award compensation, on top of any other relief or remedy granted, 'to afford just satisfaction' to the victim. This means that the court must consider awarding damages only after deciding what other forms of relief it can award, and the extent to which those provide just satisfaction to the claimant. Damages are a last resort, not (as is usually the case in tort

---

[58] See *R (on the application of Kehoe) v Secretary of State for Work and Pensions* [2003] EWHC 1021; The Times, 21 May 2003, Wall J.

actions) an entitlement once the cause of action and injury have been established. Under s 8(3), the court must also take account of the consequences of any other decision of any court in respect of that act, and all the other circumstances of the case, in deciding whether damages are necessary to afford just satisfaction. The Law Commission and the Scottish Law Commission have suggested that s 8(3) was intended to allow the court to take account of ex gratia payments, and changes in procedure or legislation, for example following a declaration of incompatibility.[59]

'Just satisfaction' is a term derived from Article 41 ECHR, which empowers the ECtHR to afford just satisfaction to a victim. Section 8(4) of the HRA 1998 requires an English court or tribunal to 'take into account the principles applied by the European Court of Human Rights in relation to the award of compensation under Article 41 of the Convention' when deciding whether to award damages. Unfortunately, it is difficult to adopt the Strasbourg approach as a reliable guide to the availability of damages, for two reasons. First, the Strasbourg court does not have the obligation imposed on states by Article 13 ECHR to ensure that the victim has an effective remedy for any violation of a Convention right. The Strasbourg jurisdiction can be invoked only after all domestic remedies have been exhausted. It follows that the Strasbourg case law on the meaning of 'just satisfaction' under Article 41 ECHR cannot provide a safe guide to the obligations of states to provide effective remedies. As noted above, the government said, when presenting the Human Rights Bill to Parliament, that what is now s 8 of the Act was intended to meet the requirements of Article 13. Too great a concentration on Article 41 may make that impossible in some cases. Secondly, the English courts have a far wider range of remedies available to them than the ECtHR.[60] **19.49**

There are relatively few English cases so far on the award of damages, but there are indications that the courts are particularly willing to contemplate the award of damages in cases where a public authority causes loss or harm to a person in circumstances which would not previously have given rise to a claim for compensation. Where the authority acts in a way that leads to a violation of a Convention right causing loss, the court may well decide that damages should be awarded as well as a declaration or quashing order. When the authority is required to reconsider its decision, it may be appropriate to await the outcome before deciding whether an award of damages is necessary, but if there are already losses which could not be affected by a new decision the court may make an award of damages immediately. For example, damages can be awarded: **19.50**

---

[59] Law Commission and Scottish Law Commission (n 56 above) para 4.42.
[60] ibid para 4.38.

- against an agency which violates Article 6 by preventing an applicant from pursuing another remedy after it has wrongly decided the application, causing financial loss to the applicant;[61]
- against the Secretary of State for Health in respect of a practice by a mental health review tribunal which violated Article 5(4) by delaying hearings for a standard period of eight weeks;[62]
- against the Home Secretary for failing to decide an asylum claim within a reasonable time, causing the applicant to lose income support and causing a violation of Article 8;[63] and
- against the Secretary of State for Work and Pensions when he failed to make an extra-statutory ex gratia payment to a widower who had received a lower pension than he would have done as a widow, in breach of Article 14 taken together with Article 1 of Protocol 1.[64]

(c) Measure of damages

19.51 Section 8(4) of the HRA 1998 requires English courts to take account of the principles applied by the ECtHR in relation to the award of compensation under Article 41 when considering the amount of any damages to be awarded under the Act. However, it is difficult to identify consistent principles in the case law of the Court. A thorough study by the Law Commission and Scottish Law Commission noted that five factors are particularly important:

- in some circumstances, the finding of a violation may itself constitute just satisfaction;
- the degree of loss must be sufficient to justify an award of damages, and all losses must be convincingly established by evidence;
- the seriousness of the violation is significant;
- the conduct of the respondent state, in the instant case and earlier cases, will be taken into account. Where the state has been unco-operative, or the violation is part of a consistent pattern of disregard for rights, the Court will be less likely to conclude that the finding of a violation on its own amounts to just satisfaction, although the Court does not award what would in England be called exemplary damages as a special head of damages;
- the conduct of the applicant will be taken into account.[65]

---

[61] *R (on the application of Kehoe) v Secretary of State for Work and Pensions* [2003] EWHC 1021; The Times, 21 May 2003, Wall J.

[62] *R (on the application of KB) v Mental Health Review Tribunal* [2003] EWHC 193; [2003] 3 WLR 1, Stanley Burnton J.

[63] *R (on the application of N) v Secretary of State for the Home Department* [2003] EWHC 207; [2003] HRLR 20, Silber J.

[64] *R (on the application of Hooper) v Secretary of State for Work and Pensions* [2003] EWCA Civ 813; [2003] 2 FCR 504.

[65] Law Commission and Scottish Law Commission (n 56 above) paras 3.31–3.78, 4.43–4.91.

It has sometimes been suggested that damages under the HRA 1998 should be **19.52** limited in quantum to avoid placing an unreasonable burden on the scarce resources of public authorities. Lord Woolf, writing extra-judicially, took the view that awards should be moderate, 'normally on the low side compared to tortious awards'.[66] However, if it became a general principle this would be hard to reconcile with the scheme of the HRA 1998, which establishes a tortious claim for acting incompatibly with a Convention right, and with the high constitutional importance of Convention rights. As a result, English law, while accepting that all losses must be properly established before compensation for them can be awarded, takes the view that the quantum of damages under the HRA 1998 should be similar to the level of damages for comparable torts in English law where it is possible to find an analogy, and generally damages should as far as possible reflect the English level of damages.[67]

(d) Damages in respect of judicial acts

As noted in para 19.26 above, s 9(3) of the HRA 1998 provides that damages are **19.53** to be available in respect of a judicial act done in good faith only to the extent necessary to comply with the obligation under Article 5(5) ECHR to provide an enforceable right to compensation for a violation of rights under Article 5. It may be difficult to fix the appropriate quantum of damages for a failure to hear an application for discharge promptly, in contravention of Article 5(4), but the courts have found ways of dealing with the problem.[68]

(5) Remedies in Criminal Proceedings

Where a public authority is responsible for an act which is incompatible with a **19.54** Convention right in relation to a criminal investigation or prosecution, the criminal court before which the case comes may find itself required to take action to provide a remedy for the violation. A criminal court cannot award damages to a defendant who is the victim of an incompatibility with a Convention right, and in any case damages might not be appropriate. Other remedies have to suffice. Criminal courts (including the Court of Appeal (Criminal Division) on appeal from a conviction) have a number of powers which can be used to remedy a violation. Three of these powers were well established in English law before the HRA 1998, and have simply been reinforced by the Act. First, a prosecution may be stayed indefinitely, or an appeal against conviction allowed, if the effect of the

---

[66] Lord Woolf (n 56 above). See also M Amos, 'Damages for breach of the Human Rights Act 1998' [1999] European Human Rights L Rev 178, 186–187, drawing attention to the danger that a flood of damages awards might put 'a considerable strain on the public purse'.

[67] *R (on the application of KB) v Mental Health Review Tribunal* [2003] EWHC 193; [2003] 3 WLR 1, Stanley Burnton J.

[68] ibid.

violation is such as to amount to an abuse of the process of the court, for example by bringing the defendant into the jurisdiction unlawfully.[69] Secondly, a prosecution may be stayed or an appeal allowed if circumstances (such as prejudicial publicity before trial, or a failure to treat the defendants fairly in obtaining a confession) are such as to prevent the defendant receiving a fair trial, so that a prosecution would lead to a violation of Article 6(1) ECHR.[70] However, excessive delay in criminal proceedings, leading to a violation of Article 6, has been held not to lead automatically to a stay of proceedings or to the quashing of a conviction, despite a judgment of the ECtHR which suggests that proceedings should be stayed once there has been unreasonable delay.[71] Instead, it has been said that reduction of the sentence to take account of the delay will provide a sufficient remedy for the violation.[72] Thirdly, evidence obtained in breach of a Convention right may be excluded if admitting it would make the proceedings unfair.[73] Not all pre-trial violations of Convention rights will lead the trial to violate Article 6. For example, if evidence is reliable it may be admissible notwithstanding the fact that it was obtained in breach of Article 8.[74]

19.55   The English courts have, however, so far refused to stay prosecutions merely on the ground that proceeding with them would threaten a Convention right other than Article 6. Where it was alleged that prosecuting a former member of the Security Service for disclosing information contrary to s 1 of the Official Secrets Act 1989 would violate his right to freedom of expression, the House of Lords decided that the total ban on disclosures by officers and former officers of the service was justifiable under Article 10(2) ECHR because other routes for airing their grievances are open to them, but made it clear that in any case the discretion to stay proceedings would not be used so as to frustrate the clear words and purposes of criminal legislation.[75]

19.56   A violation of Article 6 itself, for example offering self-incriminating statements obtained by coercive means as evidence, ought in principle to lead to exclusion of the evidence or to allowing an appeal against conviction after the evidence was admitted. However, under the HRA 1998 the English courts have refused to quash

---

[69]   *R v Horseferry Road Magistrates' Court, ex p Bennett* [1994] 1 AC 42, HL; *R v Latif* [1996] 1 WLR 104, HL. See also *R v Hardy* [2002] EWCA Crim 3012, [2003] 1 Cr App R 30, CA.

[70]   See eg *R (on the application of U) v Commissioner of Police of the Metropolis* [2002] EWHC 2486, [2003] 1 WLR 897 (leave to appeal to the House of Lords has been granted); Contempt of Court Act 1981, s 2; *A-G v Birmingham Post and Mail Ltd* [1999] 1 WLR 361; *A-G v Guardian Newspapers Ltd* [1999] EMLR 904, DC.

[71]   *Bunkate v Netherlands* Series A No 248-B (1993) 19 EHRR 477.

[72]   *Mills v HM Advocate* [2002] UKPC D2, [2002] 3 WLR 1597; *HM Advocate v R* [2002] UKPC D3, [2003] 2 WLR 317, both appeals to the Privy Council from Scotland in devolution matters.

[73]   Police and Criminal Evidence Act 1998, s 78.

[74]   *Khan v UK* Application 35394/97 (2001) 31 EHRR 45.

[75]   *R v Shayler* [2002] UKHL 11; [2003] 1 AC 247.

convictions on this ground if the use of the material was authorized by primary legislation which was in force at the time of the trial.[76] The doctrine of the legislative sovereignty of Parliament overrides the importance of protecting Convention rights in this area, despite the fact that it may leave the United Kingdom in violation of Article 13 ECHR. If the effect of providing discretionary relief, by way of a stay or of excluding evidence, would make the legislation a dead letter, the court will read and give effect to the legislation in a manner compatible with Convention rights if possible, as required by s 3 of the HRA 1998, but will otherwise proceed with the case and, if appropriate, make a declaration of incompatibility.[77]

A further power which has been used in devolution cases from Scotland, as noted above, is to remedy a violation of the right to a trial within a reasonable time under Article 6 by reducing the sentence to reflect the delay.[78] However, the applicability of the reasoning in England is highly questionable, for two reasons. First, the cases were decided under the Scotland Act 1998, which (unlike s 2 of the HRA 1998) does not impose a duty on courts to take account of the case law of the ECtHR when interpreting Convention rights. Secondly, and more importantly, Article 6(1) makes trial within a reasonable time a sine qua non of a fair trial. As it is put in England, justice delayed is justice denied. It is hard to see how a reduced sentence following conviction can remedy the fact that the defendant ought not to have been tried. **19.57**

(6) Declarations of Incompatibility

Where one of the higher courts cannot read and give effect to a legislative provision in a way that is compatible with Convention rights, it may make a declaration that the provision is incompatible with one or more of the rights while leaving the legislation in force.[79] The declaration of incompatibility is really an admission that the court is unable to provide an effective remedy for a violation of a Convention right, because of primary legislation. It is more a recognition of the legislative supremacy of Parliament than a real part of the court's remedial armoury. The nature and effects of the declaration of incompatibility have been explained above.[80] **19.58**

---

[76] *R v Lyons* [2002] UKHL 44; [2003] 1 AC 976.

[77] See *R v DPP, ex p Kebilene* [2000] 2 AC 326, HL; *R v Shayler* [2002] UKHL 11; [2003] 1 AC 247.

[78] *Mills v HM Advocate* [2002] UKPC D2, [2002] 3 WLR 1597; *HM Advocate v R* [2002] UKPC D3, [2003] 2 WLR 317.

[79] HRA 1998, s 4.

[80] See paras 7.107 et seq above.

C. Remedies Available When Convention Rights are Used as a Defence

19.59   A violation by a public authority of a Convention right may be relied on as a defence in litigation (civil or criminal) instigated by a public authority, 'whenever the act in question took place'.[81] This allows the defendant to argue that a decision, rule, or action made or taken by a public authority, which forms the basis for a prosecution or civil action, is unlawful by virtue of s 6(1) of the HRA 1998, thus undermining the proceedings, even if it was made or taken, and the proceedings commenced, before the Act came into force. However, the courts have introduced a pragmatic limitation in the case of appeals: the retrospective effect of the provisions does not require a court to quash a conviction which occurred before the Act came into force merely on account of a violation of a Convention right which did not bind the trial court as a matter of English law at the time.[82]

19.60   As we have already seen, s 12 of the HRA 1998 confers defences on people if remedies are sought against them which would affect their Convention right to freedom of expression. Journalistic, literary and artistic materials, and conduct relating to them, are singled out for special protection.[83] In addition, public authorities will be unable to obtain remedies which interfere with Convention rights, such as orders to enforce land-use planning controls or orders for possession of property, unless:

- any interference with a Convention right is justifiable in terms of the right in question, with an opportunity being given to balance all the relevant factors at some stage in the proceedings (although not necessarily at the final hearing at which the order is made);[84] or
- the court is required to make the order by primary legislation which cannot be read and given effect in such a way as to permit the court to act compatibly with the right.

D. The Impact of Convention Rights on Remedies in Other Proceedings

19.61   Courts and tribunals are public authorities within the meaning of s 6 of the HRA 1998, and so are required to act compatibly with Convention rights unless primary

---

[81]   HRA 1998, ss 7(1)(b) and 22(4).
[82]   See paras 7.51 et seq above.
[83]   See paras 19.36 et seq above.
[84]   See eg *South Bucks DC v Porter* [2003] UKHL 26, [2003] 2 WLR 1547; *South Bucks DC v Secretary of State for Transport, Local Government and the Regions* [2003] EWCA Civ 697, The Times, 23 May 2003; *Harrow LBC v Qazi*, The Times, 1 August 2003, HL.

legislation prevents them from doing so. As they are 'pure', or all-purpose, public authorities, this duty affects all their activities. On its face, it is not limited to their work in cases involving public authorities. This has prompted the suggestion that the courts must make sure that their judgments and orders are compatible with Convention rights even in proceedings between private parties, allowing Convention rights to affect the substance of private law by virtue of the public law duty of courts, owed to litigants and others, not to act incompatibly with the rights. This effect between private parties is referred to as 'horizontal effect' (as distinct from 'vertical effect' between a private party and a state body).[85]

In certain respects, the express terms of the Act make it clear that the Convention **19.62** rights are to have some horizontal effect. Courts are required by s 3 to read and give effect to all legislation in a manner compatible with Convention rights so far as it is possible to do so, regardless of the public or private nature of the parties to the litigation. The restrictions on remedies affecting freedom of expression contained in s 12 also apply generally, whoever the parties to the litigation are.[86] The same applies to cases which engage the provisions of s 13 on freedom of thought, conscience and religion under Article 9 ECHR.[87]

However, where the Act makes no express provision for Convention rights to have **19.63** horizontal effect, the suggestion that the rights might operate in that way is controversial, and there is currently a dearth of case law on the subject. A number of types of horizontal effect, more or less far-reaching in their scope, have been suggested. They include:

- A relatively narrow duty on courts to apply procedural and evidential rules and discretion so as to secure due-process rights, such as those under Articles 5, 6 and 7 ECHR.[88] However, s 6 of the Act does not distinguish between different Convention rights: public authorities have a duty to act compatibly with all of them, so it is difficult to justify the limitation to due-process rights, unless by way of an argument such as that outlined in para 19.64 below.
- A very wide duty to give effect to all rights in all proceedings (unless otherwise provided by primary legislation which cannot be interpreted so as to allow compatible action).[89] However, this gives relatively little weight to the scheme of the Act, which seems to contemplate that Convention rights primarily bind public authorities, and do not give rise directly to rights against private parties. It also

---

[85] See Murray Hunt, 'The "horizontal effect" of the Human Rights Act' [1998] PL 423.
[86] See para 19.36 above.
[87] See paras 8.84 et seq above.
[88] Sir Sydney Kentridge QC, 'The Incorporation of the European Convention on Human Rights', in University of Cambridge Centre for Public Law (ed), *Constitutional Reform in the UK: Practice and Principles* (Oxford: Hart Publishing, 1998) 69–71.
[89] Sir William Wade QC, 'Human Rights and the Judiciary' [1998] European Human Rights L Rev 520, 524 et seq.

presents litigants with the problem of having to commence proceedings against the other party, relying on a non-Convention cause of action, before the duty of the court under s 6 of the Act can come into play.

- A duty of intermediate width to apply Convention rights only in private-law litigation commenced by a party asserting a cause of action in tort, contract, etc, using the Convention to guide the development and application of the common law as well (as the interpretation of legislation, as demanded by s 3 of the Act).

- A still narrower duty to ensure that decisions and orders made by the court during and at the conclusion of the hearing will not produce results which are incompatible with Convention rights, allowing a measure of horizontal effect in relation to discretionary orders and remedies, rather than permitting Convention rights to alter the substantive rules of private law. This would produce a type of 'remedial horizontality'.[90]

19.64 On the other side, it has been argued that the Convention rights (as distinct from particular provisions of the HRA 1998) are intrinsically incapable of producing horizontal effects. The rights in the ECHR, which s 1 of the Act makes part of English law, are creatures of public international law, and bind states, not private persons. By their nature, they cannot impose obligations on private persons, and so cannot produce horizontal effect.[91] On this approach, courts and tribunals would have a duty to act compatibly with those Convention rights which relate particularly to their activities, such as due-process rights, but would not affect substantive rules of private law.

19.65 It is respectfully submitted that two qualifications are needed to the argument outlined in the previous paragraph, powerful as it is as a matter of logic. First, English courts are not bound to interpret Convention rights in the same way as they are interpreted by the ECtHR. Section 2(1) of the HRA 1998 requires English courts to take account of the case law of the Strasbourg institutions when determining a question arising in connection with a Convention right, but the courts are not bound by that case law.[92] It seems to follow that English courts are free to take a different view from that of the Strasbourg institutions, even in relation to fundamental questions about the nature and incidence of the rights. Indeed, it is inevitable the rights will in some respects alter their characteristics on being translated from international to national legal standards, even where they bind purely public authorities, as the idea of a public authority, while related to the notion of a state, is not identical to it. Secondly, even in Strasbourg the

---

[90] See Ian Leigh, 'Horizontal rights, the Human Rights Act and privacy: lessons from the Commonwealth?' (1999) 48 ICLQ 57.
[91] Sir Richard Buxton, 'The Human Rights Act and private law' (2000) 116 LQR 48.
[92] See paras. 7.26–7.31 above.

Convention rights have been shown to be capable of imposing positive obligations on states to protect the vital interests of private individuals, if necessary by providing them with legal redress for wrongs which inflict damage of such a kind as to breach the standards required by the ECHR.[93] Where the state is required to provide protection for private people's interests, the courts may be entitled, if not bound, to provide that protection by developing the substantive rules of private law, if that can be done without overstepping the boundaries of the courts' constitutional authority.

A final way in which Convention rights may affect substantive private-law rules **19.66** is by influencing the development of the values which underpin private law. This does not depend on any specific authority for judicial action implementing Convention rights. Instead, the rights may lead to a gradual, and perhaps pervasive, adjustment of legal values, affecting the whole of English law, over a long period. EC law has slowly had this effect during the three decades since the European Communities Act 1972 made it part of a single system of norms encompassing large parts of English law. For example, it became more or less impossible to continue to refuse to allow coercive relief to be awarded against the Crown once it became clear that Community law required such relief to be available in some cases.[94] It is not at all unlikely that the Convention rights will have a similar effect over time.[95]

E. Conclusion

This chapter has demonstrated that the remedial regime established by the HRA **19.67** 1998 goes a long way towards allowing the United Kingdom to discharge its duty in international law under Articles 1 and 13 ECHR to secure the Convention rights to all within the jurisdiction of England and Wales, and to provide an effective remedy before national authorities for any violation of a Convention right. At the same time, it has shown that, to produce that effect, the remedies provided for in the Act need to operate alongside other remedies, and should be seen as complementing rather than replacing ordinary causes of action and systems of remedies. This is particularly true of damages under the Act, which are a last resort. While the discussion has revealed some difficulties arising from the way the

---

[93] See paras 7.154 et seq above.

[94] See Case C-213/89 *R v Secretary of State for Transport, ex p Factortame Ltd* [1990] ECR I-2433; *R v Secretary of State for Transport, ex p Factortame Ltd (No 2)* [1991] 1 AC 603, HL, and *M v Home Office* [1994] 1 AC 377, HL.

[95] For an argument that this should lead to the development of private law protection for privacy by way of a development from the law of breach of confidence, see Gavin Phillipson, 'Transforming breach of confidence? Towards a common law right of privacy under the Human Rights Act' (2003) 66 MLR 726.

Act is drafted, for example in the use of the idea of 'just satisfaction' in relation to damages, generally the remedial scheme can be regarded as reasonably principled and coherent, and as an evolution from pre-existing remedies rather than a revolutionary approach. Where there are difficulties in providing an effective remedy for a violation of a Convention right, the chapter has sought to show how courts and tribunals may be able to overcome them. In some areas, perhaps most notably that relating to action by people other than victims to remedy widespread violations and that concerning relief from criminal convictions in proceedings which violate Convention rights, there is still some way to go in providing a reliable system of effective remedies in accordance with public law principles. Generally, however, the remedies under the Act usefully complement the general system of public law remedies explained in chapters 17 and 18 above.

20

TRIBUNALS

A. Characteristics of Tribunals

In England and Wales tribunals form part of the judicial, rather than the ad-**20.01**
ministrative, arm of government. However the term tribunal is used to describe
a very wide range of bodies which possess few, if any, universally common features. Typically tribunals, unlike inquiries, are adjudicative bodies performing a
judicial function. Like courts they have the power to determine issues in dispute
but they are distinct from the court structure. Tribunals are commonly more accessible and less formal than courts and many have evolved in areas of specialized legislation dealing with the relationship between state and citizen in such
fields as immigration, welfare benefits and taxation. Ideally tribunals are independent of the government department responsible for the area of policy at
issue and are consciously established to reflect in their membership the relevant
areas of expertise.

20.02   In the discussion which follows these characteristics of tribunals will be described and considered at greater length but it is first necessary to provide a brief account of the development of tribunals into the system which exists today.

B. Background

20.03   Tribunals in one form or another have existed in England and Wales for centuries. The oldest extant tribunal in England is said to be the General Commissioners of Income Tax whose underlying structure, powers and principles of procedure were settled in 1799 and 1803.[1] However, although it is not possible to trace an obvious uniform pattern to the historical development of tribunals, it is clear that the Liberal reforms of the first two decades of the 20th century which introduced the basis for the welfare state also established the foundations of the modern tribunal system.[2] As Craig puts it, these Liberal reforms 'necessitated the development of an administrative and adjudicative mechanism on a scale different from that which had gone before'.[3] For reasons of cost, concern at the extent of the potential case-load, and political preference the courts were kept in the background and alternative adjudicative mechanisms were established.[4] While some of these reforms were consolidated between 1918 and 1939, the next major period of growth came after the publication of the Beveridge report in 1942 and the passing of the National Insurance Act 1946 by the post-war Labour government. The wider introduction and application of the principles of social insurance and assistance brought with it a need to provide additional mechanisms for the resolution of disputes concerning entitlement.

20.04   In the 1950s, following the immediate post-war expansion of the welfare state, there emerged a growing public concern about the need to protect individuals from increasing incursions by the state. In relation specifically to tribunals, this took the form of a growing concern about their proliferation, diversity, lack of supervision and the inconsistencies in their procedures. Matters came to a head after the celebrated Crichel Down affair which involved the sale of a piece of Dorset farmland and was commonly seen 'as an outrageous case of civil service

---

[1] C Stebbings, 'Historical Factors in Contemporary Tribunal Structure' in M Partington (ed), *Leggatt Review of Tribunals: Academic Seminar Papers* (Bristol Centre for the Study of Administrative Justice, 2001) ch 8.

[2] P Craig, *Administrative Law* (4th edn, London: Sweet & Maxwell, 1999) 62 and C Harlow and R Rawlings, *Law and Administration* (2nd edn, London: Butterworths, 1997) ch 14.

[3] ibid 63.

[4] B Abel-Smith and R Stevens, *In Search of Justice* (London: Allen Lane, 1968); H Genn, 'Tribunal Review of Administrative Decision-Making' in G Richardson and H Genn (eds), *Administrative Law and Government Action* (Oxford: Clarendon Press, 1994) ch 11, and Craig (n 2 above) 63.

maladministration'.[5] As part of the fall-out from this affair the Franks Committee was established to examine statutory tribunals and administrative processes involving inquiry procedures, which it did not interpret to include the Crichel Down procedure itself. The Committee was also required to restrict itself to further decisions, those taken after a request to confirm, cancel or vary the original decision. This focus on mechanisms for the redress of individual grievance can be seen as illustrative of a prevailing concern with individual rather than collective issues.[6]

Whatever the limitations of its remit, however, the Franks report which emerged **20.05** from the Committee's deliberations in 1957 is still commonly regarded as the most significant point in the development of tribunals in England and Wales throughout the whole of the second half of the 20th century.[7] The report was unambiguous in its view that tribunals were not 'appendages of Government', and confirmed that 'tribunals should properly be regarded as machinery provided by Parliament for adjudication rather than as part of the machinery of administration'.[8] This view, which was widely accepted although not universally welcomed,[9] continues to prevail and has exerted a considerable influence on the development of tribunals and the way in which they are perceived.[10] Reinforcing this model of tribunals as part of the machinery of adjudication the Franks report identified the three basic characteristics of openness, fairness and impartiality, against which tribunals continue to be judged.[11]

Many of the specific recommendations contained within the Franks report reflect **20.06** its view of the essential role of tribunals. Thus, ideally, tribunals were to be chaired by lawyers appointed by the Lord Chancellor, hearings were to be in public, legal representation was to be allowed and decisions were to be as fully reasoned as possible. Franks also recommended that appeal both on point of law and on the merits be introduced and that judicial review (as it now is) should remain available. Finally the Committee recommended the creation of a Council on Tribunals for England and Wales and a similar body for Scotland. These bodies would have a mainly advisory and co-ordinating role.

---

[5] Harlow and Rawlings (n 2 above) 460.
[6] Harlow and Rawlings (n 2 above) 461 and P Birkinshaw, *Grievances, Remedies and the State* (2nd edn, London: Sweet & Maxwell, 1995) 56.
[7] *Report of the Committee on Administrative Tribunals and Inquiries* (Cmnd 218, 1957) (the Franks report).
[8] ibid para 40.
[9] See, eg, J Farmer, *Tribunals and Government* (London: Weidenfeld & Nicolson, 1974) and Harlow and Rawlings (n 2 above).
[10] The conclusions of the Leggatt report, *Tribunals for Users: One System, One Service* (2001), for example, are broadly supportive of the view of tribunals adopted by Franks.
[11] Franks report (n 7 above) para 41. And see Council on Tribunals, *Framework of Standards for Tribunals* (2002) for the continuing relevance of Franks' three characteristics.

reduced total of 70 the range of subject matter, parties affected and the point within the decision-making process at which the tribunal is located varies widely. In an attempt to identify the essential characteristics of a tribunal, the factors which appear to lead to the selection of tribunals as the preferred decision-makers will be considered in relation to subject matter, parties, point in the decision-making process, and the demands of the HRA 1998.

(1) Subject Matter

20.12 Typically tribunals are established to deal with disputes arising out of the application of a specialist programme of entitlement or regulation. In relation to entitlements, for example, the Appeals Service, constituted under Social Security Act 1998, Pt I, Ch I, now provides the mechanism for the adjudication of disputes arising out of the operation of the social security system, and the Criminal Injuries Compensation Appeal Panel, appointed under Criminal Injuries Compensation Act 1995, s 5, hears appeals relating to applications for compensation for injury arising out of offences of violence. In relation to regulation, the Immigration Adjudicators and the Immigration Appeal Tribunal, established respectively under ss 57 and 56 of the Immigration and Asylum Act 1999, hear appeals against decisions by the Home Secretary to refuse a person asylum in the United Kingdom and appeals against decisions to refuse permanent residence. Similarly the Employment Tribunal and the Employment Appeal Tribunal, established under the Industrial Tribunals Act 1996, determine disputes relating to employment.

20.13 To the extent that these tribunals, and the many others like them, adjudicate disputes and reach binding determinations, they perform a function similar to that performed by the civil courts and yet they are constituted as tribunals. The nature of the subject matter involved is clearly relevant to the preference for a tribunal over a court, and the characteristics which would appear to be particularly influential here include; the detailed and specialist nature of the law, the low monetary value of the claims involved, and the relevance of non-legal expertise.

20.14 While the presence of a detailed legal framework is not sufficient on its own to dictate the need for a tribunal, there is certainly a tendency to use tribunals where the relevant law is specialized and distinct. Thus many tribunals apply legal schemes which were introduced by statute to deal with a specific aspect of public policy and which, although governed by the generally applicable legal principles, are designed to be largely self-sufficient. The tribunal members can therefore become expert in the application of the specific code. As a consequence of this close nexus between the tribunal and the statutory framework within which it is required to operate, tribunals in contrast to courts were sometimes said to be more concerned with policy than with legality.[23] However, such a distinction is now rarely made: '[i]n practice, the typical claim before an appellate tribunal raises issues of law, fact and policy no different from those regularly dealt with by courts exercising judicial review jurisdiction'.[24]

There has traditionally been a tendency to use tribunals where a high volume of claims is anticipated and the monetary value of each claim is low, as in social security. However, although the monetary value of the issues for resolution may typically be low this is not invariably the case, as in tax and property tribunals for example. Further, within certain tribunal jurisdictions, particularly immigration and mental health, the issues at stake, although not of great financial value, have a direct impact on the fundamental rights of the individual. Nonetheless some of the rationale lying behind the creation of tribunals certainly relates to the relative cheapness, speed, accessibility and informality commonly claimed for tribunal as compared to court adjudication. The views expressed by Street in relation to the administration of welfare benefits in the 1970s provide a clear example of these arguments: '[w]hat is needed above all else is a cheap and speedy settlement of disputes. For these cases we do not want a Rolls-Royce system of Justice.'[25]   **20.15**

Finally, in relation to subject matter, tribunals provide the opportunity for the inclusion of non-legal expertise within the decision-making body itself. Thus a tribunal might be the preferred mechanism where it is assumed that a specific professional expertise would provide valuable assistance in understanding the subject matter. Tribunals dealing with the health status of individuals, for example, frequently include doctors within their membership, while surveyors and valuers sit on rent assessment panels. The membership of tribunals can also be used as a means of representing relevant views or positions in areas where different interests are involved, and of providing for input from 'lay' members. Thus employment tribunals traditionally include members with employer and employee experience and school admission appeal panels include both lay members and those with educational experience. To that extent tribunals can be said to contribute significantly to a pluralist approach to administrative justice by providing an opportunity for the direct involvement of non-legal knowledge, experience and understanding.[26]   **20.16**

---

[23] See, eg, P Cane, *An Introduction to Administrative Law* (2nd edn, Oxford: Clarendon Press, 1992) 290 and Report of the Committee of the JUSTICE–All Souls Review of Administrative Law in the UK, *Administrative Justice: Some Necessary Reforms* (Oxford: Clarendon, 1988). And see the discussion in Genn (n 4 above) 254.

[24] P Cane, *An Introduction to Administrative Law* (3rd edn, Oxford: Clarendon Press, 1996) 334.

[25] H Street, *Justice in the Welfare State* (London: Stevens, 1975) 3.

[26] See Craig (n 2 above) ch 1, for a brief introduction to the notion of pluralism in the context of administrative law.

(2) Parties

20.17   The classic model of a tribunal in England and Wales is that of a mechanism for the adjudication of disputes between the citizen and the state, including local government. Thus typically the applicant or appellant will be a private individual while the respondent or defendant will be a public agency or government department. The most significant exceptions to this predominant citizen vs state model are to be found in relation to employment, land, housing and intellectual property. In these areas tribunals exist to resolve disputes between private citizens, and a case can be made for returning these disputes to the ordinary courts. However, the Leggatt report was of the view that 'the features which are common to citizen and state tribunals and party and party tribunals are much more important than those which divide them', and in relation to employment tribunals and the Copyright Tribunal at least, the report recommended that they remain within the tribunals system.[27] The positive features of tribunal decision-making which seem particularly to have influenced this conclusion included the opportunities available for users of tribunals to handle cases themselves without the intervention of lawyers and the better quality of decisions when taken 'jointly by lawyers and experts'.[28] Thus, even outside the classic citizen vs state model, the relative accessibility of tribunals and the opportunity they provide for the involvement of non-lawyers in decision-making are regarded as significant advantages.

(3) The Stage in the Decision-Making Process

20.18   Tribunals in England and Wales, as already described, are seen primarily as a mechanism for the resolution of disputes between individual citizens and the state. They still retain the individualistic model endorsed by Franks and play little part in policy formulation. If quasi-judicial bodies are employed in policy-making the inquiry model is preferred.[29]

20.19   As a review mechanism tribunals are typically located at the end of the policy implementation process. Policy, perhaps emanating originally from statute, will be refined and particularized before it is eventually applied to an individual in the form of an award, grant, licence, etc. The role of a tribunal is to provide the forum for the review of that application decision.[30] Again there are exceptions to this predominantly adjudicatory model. Mental health review tribunals in their present form are already empowered to take certain decisions effectively as a first-tier body, and under the proposed legislation the new mental health tribunal will be

---

[27] Leggatt report (n 10 above) para 3.19.
[28] ibid.
[29] See ch 22 below.
[30] G Richardson, *Law, Process and Custody: Prisoners and Patients* (London: Weidenfeld & Nicolson, 1993) ch 4.

empowered to make orders authorizing medical treatment.[31] However, whether
the tribunal is adjudicating a dispute or making a first-tier decision, it is essentially
dealing with an individual application of policy and here its status as an independent decision-maker is crucial. If independence were not deemed to be essential
the dispute could be resolved internally. While questions can properly be raised
about the degree of independence currently enjoyed by tribunals, their relative independence is one of the main reasons lying behind their use as the preferred review mechanism.[32] Tribunals may not be as independent as courts but they are
regarded as sufficiently independent to satisfy the need for external review.

(4) The Demands of the Human Rights Act

Article 6(1) ECHR provides that: 'In the determination of his civil rights and   **20.20**
obligations or of any criminal charge against him, everyone is entitled to a fair and
public hearing within a reasonable time by an independent and impartial tribunal'. This provision may have been incorporated directly as part of our law only
as recently as 2000 but, as Carol Harlow argues, the principles it enshrines closely
resemble those reflected in the Franks report.[33] The extent of the article's application and the full implications of its requirements will be discussed further below,
but the basic principle of independent and impartial adjudication which it contains matches very closely the role attributed to tribunals by Franks. Ever since
Franks, tribunals in England and Wales have been seen essentially as mechanisms
for external and independent review and have been introduced where, for whatever reason, such review was deemed necessary. Thus the recent incorporation of
Article 6 can hardly be regarded as providing entirely fresh motivation for the creation of tribunals. Nonetheless, apprehension about the implications of Article 6,
together with the need to provide adequate protection for other rights, including
the right to respect for private life and the right to freedom of expression, has led
to the creation of a small number of new tribunals where no mechanism for independent adjudication previously existed.[34]

---

[31] Draft Mental Health Bill (Cm 5538-I, 2002).
[32] The question of independence is discussed further below: see paras 20.23–20.35.
[33] C Harlow, 'The ECHR and Administrative Justice' in Partington (ed) (n 1 above) ch 2.
[34] Examples include: the Interception of Communications Tribunal established under the
Interception of Communications Act 1985, now superseded by the Regulation of Investigatory
Powers Tribunal under the Regulation of Investigatory Powers Act 2000; the Commissioners appointed to oversee authorizations allowing the police covertly to enter and bug premises under Pt III
of the Police Act 1997; the tribunal established under the Intelligence Services Act 1994 to hear
complaints about covert entry and surveillance by the intelligence and security services; the tribunal
for hearing appeals by organizations proscribed under the Terrorism Act 2000; and the Special
Immigration Appeals Commission (which, unusually, has the status of a superior court of record)
established under the Special Immigration Appeals Commission Act 1997 to hear appeals in immigration matters in cases involving national security.

(5) Discussion

20.21 From the above discussion it would appear that the alleged characteristics of tribunals which make them attractive as a mechanism for the resolution of disputes include their relative cheapness, accessibility and informality, the opportunities they provide for the involvement of non-lawyers, and their independence. As will become evident none of these claims on the part of tribunals can go unchallenged and each claim will be analysed further in the sections that follow. However, two points need to be made at the outset. First, it is relevant to draw out the value judgments which certainly used to lie behind the importance attached by some to the cheapness of tribunals. As the quote from Street given above suggests, certain types of claim were not thought to merit the full rigour of court adjudication.[35] Such sentiments would not be expressed quite so transparently today. Indeed, the Leggatt report makes no direct mention of relative costs in its three tests to determine 'whether tribunals rather than courts should decide cases'.[36] The emphasis in the report is on the question whether the subject matter is such that users can realistically be expected to prepare and present their cases themselves. Secondly, although policy-makers tend to cite the characteristics listed above in support of their decision to establish a tribunal, the political motivation behind the creation of certain tribunals is not always as simple. Tribunals may be established not in order to provide an accessible and independent mechanism for redress but rather to provide a convenient legal buffer between the responsible government department and the implementation of an unpopular policy.[37] But, as always, it is impossible to make general statements about tribunals. Other tribunals, far from being treated as convenient legal buffers between politicians and policy implementation, have only been able to wrest potentially sensitive decisions from the hands of ministers with the aid of the European Court of Human Rights (ECtHR). The mental health review tribunal, for example, was only given the power to discharge certain offender patients from hospital detention after the government's hand was forced by the judgment in *X v UK*.[38]

---

[35] See para 20.15 above, and Genn (n 4 above) 256, for further discussion.

[36] Leggatt report (n 10 above) paras 1.10–1.13.

[37] For examples of this approach, see T Prosser, 'Poverty, Ideology and Legality: Supplementary Benefit Appeal Tribunals and their Predecessors' (1977) 4 British J of L and Society 59; L Bridges, 'Legality and Immigration Control' (1975) 2 British J of L and Society 221; and M Adler and A Bradley, 'The Case for Systematic Reform and the Establishment of a Unified Administrative Tribunal' in Partington (ed) (n 1 above) ch 1.

[38] *X v UK* Series A No 46 (1981) 4 EHRR 188. Similarly the Parole Board was only granted power to order the release of prisoners serving discretionary life sentences following the ECtHR judgment in *Thynne, Wilson and Gunnell v UK* Series A No 190 (1991) 13 EHRR 666. See also the creation of SIAC by the Special Immigration Appeals Commission Act 1997 following the decision of the ECtHR in *Chahal v UK* Application 22414/93 (1996) 23 EHRR 413.

The main themes emerging from the above introduction will now be considered **20.22** further in the following five sections concerning: the relationship between tribunals and their 'sponsoring' departments, tribunal composition, the relationship between tribunals and courts, tribunal procedures, and the possible future structure of the tribunal system.

D. The Relationship Between Tribunals and 'Sponsoring' Departments

(1) The Importance of Independence

The provision of external, independent review has been regarded as central to the **20.23** role of tribunals in England and Wales since the Franks report. As part of the judicial arm of government, tribunals are designed to be formally independent of the body responsible for the implementation of the relevant policy. In the words of the Franks report: 'We consider that tribunals should properly be regarded as machinery provided by Parliament for adjudication . . . Parliament has deliberately provided for a decision outside and independent of the Department concerned'.[39]

This view has been recently re-emphasized in the Leggatt report where the principle of independence provides the driving force behind the call for a single, unified tribunal system. The precise constitutional origins of the principle, however, are hard to identify. It is clear that tribunals do not have to be seen as part of the judicial arm of government, with all the necessity for demonstrable independence that that involves. In Australia they are seen as part of the executive. Even in this country the judicial model has not met with universal approval. Some of the evidence submitted to Franks argued 'that tribunals should be properly regarded as part of the machinery of administration, for which the Government must retain a close and continuing responsibility'.[40] Although this argument was not accepted by Franks, some commentators continued to regard tribunals as working more closely with the merits of administrative policy than do the courts.[41]

Despite these lingering reservations, however, the idea of independence is now **20.25** well established. The Whyatt report in 1961 enunciated the general principle that individuals are entitled to have an impartial adjudication of their disputes with authority unless there are overriding public interest considerations against holding such an adjudication.[42] Then in 1967 the Wilson Committee argued

---

[39] Franks report (n 7 above) para 40.
[40] ibid.
[41] eg, JUSTICE–All Souls (n 23 above).
[42] For discussion, see Alder and Bradley (n 37 above) 19.

forcefully for independent appeal in the context of immigration decisions: 'it is fundamentally wrong and inconsistent with the rule of law that power to take decisions affecting a man's whole future should be vested in officers of the executive, from whose findings there is no appeal'.[43] In the Committee's view the suspicion inspired by such an unaccountable system would never be dispelled 'so long as there is no ready way of having decisions . . . subjected to an impartial review'.[44] More recently in 1997 the Council on Tribunals published a report, *Tribunals, their Organisation and Independence*, in which the Council stated: 'the principal hallmark of any tribunal is that it must be independent. Equally importantly, it must be perceived as such.'[45]

20.26   Thus by 2001 independence was so well established as an essential characteristic of tribunals in England and Wales that the Leggatt report felt able to emphasize the importance of independence without having to rely on the ECHR for support. Certainly Article 6 requires access to an independent and impartial tribunal, but the Leggatt report was not prepared to ground its insistence on independence solely on the requirements of that article. In the first place the report was concerned that not all tribunals within its scope could properly be said to determine a person's civil rights and obligations. Not all tribunal decisions, therefore, would engage Article 6. Further the report was aware of the evolving nature of the relevant case law and was reluctant to limit its recommendations simply to achieving compliance with the current jurisprudence. In the opinion of the report, a 'narrowly ECHR-based approach would . . . lead to an absurd result'.[46] The principle of independence did not need to rely on the demands of Article 6 but was implicit in the whole role and function of tribunals in England and Wales. In particular, the link between demonstrable independence and confidence in the system is an important theme throughout the whole report, and much of the support given to the principle of independence is grounded on the need to nurture public confidence. 'Tribunals were established because it was clear that the citizen needed an independent means of challenging possible mistakes and illegalities which was faster, simpler and cheaper than recourse to the courts. Tribunals are an alternative to court not administrative processes. They will keep the confidence of users only in so far as they are seen to demonstrate similar qualities of independence and impartiality to the courts.'[47]

20.27   Whatever the strength of the arguments in favour of independence, however, one possible adverse impact of enhanced independence should be mentioned. Close

---

[43] *Wilson Committee on Immigration Appeals* (Cmnd 3387, 1967) para 83.
[44] ibid para 85.
[45] Council on Tribunals, *Tribunals, their Organisation and Independence* (Cm 3744, 1997) 3. The report also refers to guidance from the Cabinet Office emphasizing the need for independence.
[46] Leggatt report (n 10 above) para 2.17.
[47] ibid para 2.18.

communication between a tribunal and its relevant policy department could be said to encourage the department to improve the quality of its first-tier decision-making.[48] On this basis any loosening of the bond between tribunal and department might threaten the easy communication between the two to the detriment of the quality of first-tier decision-making. Perhaps in anticipation of these concerns the Leggatt report emphasized the need for effective internal review procedures within departments and for the maintenance of good communication between tribunals and departments.[49]

(2) Independence and Impartiality

The ECHR and the Leggatt report refer to both independence and impartiality. **20.28** The two are not interchangeable and must be distinguished one from the other. While ideally both are required in order to meet the demands of fair procedure, full independence can sometimes be hard to achieve.[50] Impartiality must be both real and apparent. In the words of the ECtHR: 'first, the tribunal must be subjectively free of personal prejudice or bias. Secondly, it must also be impartial from an objective viewpoint, that is, it must offer sufficient guarantees to exclude any legitimate doubt in this respect.'[51] A partial decision-maker is one who possesses a predisposition to one outcome rather than another. Such a predisposition can arise from personal interest in an outcome, from preconceived conclusions of fact, or from personal feelings either for or against a particular party. Independence, on the other hand, has a more structural dimension. Independence requires the absence of control by interested parties and the absence of any conflicting function in the decision-maker. According to the Council on Tribunals, independence means 'that the tribunal should be enabled to reach decisions according to law without pressure either from the body or person whose decision is being appealed, or from anyone else.'[52] Ideally, perhaps, independence should entail full institutional separation between the initial decision-maker and the first-tier tribunal, but this can be hard to achieve in practice. It is now accepted by the English courts that the Article 6 requirement of independence can be met if the decision-making process *viewed as a whole* is compliant. Thus the availability of judicial review or

---

[48] For general consideration of the role of internal review see M Harris, 'The Place of Formal and Informal Review in the Administrative Justice System' in M Harris and M Partington (eds), *Administrative Justice in the 21ˢᵗ Century* (Oxford: Hart, 1999); T Buck, 'A Model of Independent Review?' in Partington (n 1 above) ch 9; and D Cowan and S Halliday, *The Appeal of Internal Review* (Oxford: Hart Publishing, 2003).

[49] Leggatt report (n 10 above) ch 9, where the whole issue of the relationship between tribunals and departments is discussed.

[50] See M Bayles, *Procedural Justice* (Dordrecht: Kluwer, 1990) and the discussion in Richardson (n 30 above) 60, 162. And see paras 12.29 et seq and 15.68 et seq above.

[51] *Findlay v UK* Application 22107/93 (1997) EHRR 221.

[52] Council on Tribunals (n 45 above) 3.

appeal to the county court could introduce sufficient independence to the process as a whole to meet the requirements of Article 6.[53]

(3) The Leggatt Report

20.29   The Leggatt report was concerned primarily with independence. It makes it clear that there is no question of the government improperly attempting to influence individual decisions: 'in that sense, tribunal decisions seem to us clearly impartial'.[54] In relation to independence, however, the report was much more critical. It pointed to the fact that for most tribunals the sponsoring government department provides administrative and IT support, pays the salaries and expenses of members, provides accommodation, is responsible for some appointments, and often will have promoted the legislation which prescribes the tribunal's procedures. At best, according to Leggatt, 'such arrangements result in tribunals and their departments being, or appearing to be, common enterprises'.[55]

20.30   For Leggatt the only truly satisfactory solution lay in the creation of a separate tribunal system, independent of the sponsoring departments. The details of these proposals and the government's response are considered further below. It is, however, relevant to note that the consultation document issued by the Lord Chancellor's Department in August 2001 expressed confidence that the current structure was compliant with the ECHR requirements of independence and impartiality: 'the Government has already taken steps to ensure that tribunals meet the standards of independence and impartiality required by the Human Rights Act . . . So the Government firmly believe that tribunals fully meet all human rights requirements and that no further changes should be required for that reason.'[56]

20.31   Certainly, the common law rules against bias which already govern tribunal decision-making are generally assumed to satisfy the impartiality requirement of Article 6 in most essential respects,[57] and following the Scottish case involving the appointment of part-time sheriffs, particular care is taken with the terms governing tribunal

---

[53] On the relevance of judicial review see *Bryan v UK* Series A No 335-A (1995) 21 EHRR 342 and now *R (on the application of Holding & Barnes plc) v Secretary of State for the Environment, Transport and the Regions* [2001] UKHL 23; [2001] 2 WLR 1389. On appeal to the county court see *Begum (Runa) v Tower Hamlets LBC* [2003] UKHL 5; [2003] 2 WLR 388. For a general discussion see P Craig, 'The Courts, the Human Rights Act and Judicial Review' [2001] 117 LQR 589, 596–600.

[54] Leggatt report (n 10 above) para 2.20.

[55] ibid.

[56] Consultation Paper (n 21 above) 7–8.

[57] For general discussion of the relationship between the common law and Art 6 in this regard see paras 5.108 et seq above. With reference to the Employment Appeal Tribunal see *Lawal v Northern Spirit* [2003] UKHL 35; The Times, 27 June 2003, and to the Gaming Board see *Kingsley v UK* Application 35605/97 (2002) 35 EHRR 10.

appointments.[58] However, as already explained, the case for greater independence does not rest solely on the requirements of Article 6, the maintenance of user confidence in the system is thought to demand demonstrable independence. Three areas of particular sensitivity in this regard are briefly described below.

(4) Appointments and Structure

The appointment of members by the sponsoring department can be thought to compromise a tribunal's independence. Thus the Franks report had recommended that legal chairs of tribunals should be appointed by the Lord Chancellor and lay members by the Council on Tribunals. In the event legal members are appointed either directly by the Lord Chancellor or by the relevant minister from a panel approved by the Lord Chancellor.[59] Non-legal members are usually selected by the minister. In furtherance of its desire to enhance the independence of tribunals the Leggatt report recommended that all appointments be made by the Lord Chancellor, in the same way as ordinary judicial appointments.[60] Such a development would impose a large administrative burden on the Lord Chancellor's Department (now the Department of Constitutional Affairs) but in terms of demonstrable independence the case for change is strong. **20.32**

In its 1997 report on *Organisation and Independence* the Council on Tribunals expressed the view that the independence of a tribunal structure was greatly enhanced when there was a single national president responsible for matters such as training and the maintenance of proper judicial standards.[61] In practice not all tribunals are organized nationally, some are regional, while others are the responsibility of local authorities or local health authorities. However, many, but not all, national tribunals do now adopt a presidential system of organization and have a national president who is responsible for the administration of that particular tribunal system.[62] **20.33**

(5) Funding and Administrative Support

At present tribunals are required to operate within a budget set in negotiation with their sponsoring departments. The tribunal has to submit a bid to its department and the outcome of that bid will depend on, among other things, the total amount voted to that department by Parliament. In a very direct sense, therefore, each tribunal is dependent on its sponsoring department for the overall size of its annual **20.34**

---

[58] *Starrs v Ruxton* 2000 SLT 42.

[59] Tribunals and Inquiries Act 1992, s 5.

[60] Leggatt report (n 10 above) paras 7.7–7.12. See now *Constitutional reform—a new way of appointing judges* (2003) DCA.

[61] Council on Tribunals (n 10 above) 3, where a full list of the recommended functions of such a president appears.

[62] Examples include the Appeals Service and the Immigration Appeal Tribunal.

budget. In some cases tribunals are also dependent on their departments for the level and quality of administrative support received. This has led to concern that tribunals may suffer in terms of resources at the hands of departments who may accord them little priority.[63]

(6) Responsibility for Procedural Rules

20.35   Tribunals are not bound by the Civil Procedure Rules which govern ordinary courts. Usually the statute setting up the tribunal will confer power on the relevant government department to introduce specific procedural rules to govern that tribunal. Since tribunals are designed to be less formal and more accessible to non-lawyers than courts, it is entirely appropriate that they should have their own procedures, nonetheless there is an argument that the drafting of these rules should not be the responsibility of the sponsoring department which could have an interest in cutting costs as far as possible. At present the Council on Tribunals must be consulted prior to the enactment of any new procedural rules applying to the tribunals under the Council's scrutiny.[64] The Council also produced a set of Model Rules in 1991 to guide departmental lawyers, but the ultimate responsibility resides within the department.[65] In the interests of independence there is now a suggestion that these responsibilities should be transferred to the Department of Constitutional Affairs in consultation with the Council and the relevant departments.[66]

E. Tribunal Composition

20.36   The need for special expertise is one of the traditional reasons given for the choice of a tribunal rather than a court. However, a need for expertise cannot on its own be enough to indicate the preference for a tribunal. Countless cases decided by ordinary courts in both public and private law involve issues of huge complexity, the resolution of which might well be said to require special expertise, yet that expertise is rarely obtained by placing an expert on the bench. In practice it seems the 'expertise' argument can only be understood against the overall context in which many tribunals work. As described above tribunals are often established to adjudicate disputes arising from a specific statutory scheme. They may be required to deal with a high volume of cases and to provide an informal setting in

---

[63] See comments in Council on Tribunals, *Mental Health Review Tribunals: Special Report* (Cm 4740, 2000).

[64] Tribunals and Inquiries Act 1992, s 8.

[65] Council on Tribunals, *Model Rules of Procedure for Tribunals* (Cm 1434, 1991). In 2000 the Rules were revised to take account of the obligations arising from the HRA 1998. In 2003 they were further revised: Council on Tribunals, *Guide to Drafting Tribunal Rules* (2003), see para 20.57 below.

[66] Consultation Paper (n 21 above) 19.

which private citizens will feel confident to appear without legal representation. The proper performance of this task might be thought to demand one or more of a variety of skills, characteristics, professional expertise or experience, over and above those commonly possessed by an ordinary lawyer or judge. Sometimes the scheme will be of such complexity that specialized knowledge of the regulations themselves might be called for, as in immigration or social security. In other cases where the decision in dispute has involved the exercise of professional judgment, by for example a doctor or a valuer, it might be useful for the tribunal to include a representative of the relevant profession. Not all 'experts' or non-lawyers are chosen for their professional expertise, however. In some cases non-legal members are included in order to represent specific interests, as in employment tribunals, or to introduce knowledge of local services, as in social security tribunals, or simply to represent the local community. Under the pre-1998 social security tribunal system, for example, so-called lay members played an important role in this respect.

In many cases the desire to include non-legal expertise has led to the introduction **20.37** of multi-member panels, usually but not exclusively chaired by a lawyer. The classic model, as the name tribunal would suggest, is that of a panel of three, although panels of up to seven members do exist in some jurisdictions. Health authority disciplinary committees, for example, can have a legally qualified chair and up to three professional and three lay members. On the other hand, the number of single member tribunals has increased recently, in the areas of social security, parking adjudication and immigration, for example.[67] Adjudication by one legally qualified member is thought to be cheaper and more efficient. While it is hard to find a convincing justification for seven member panels,[68] the growth of single member tribunals has not been universally welcomed either. Single person panels appear to deny one of the defining characteristics of tribunals: the ability to reflect non-legal skills and experience directly in decision-making.[69]

The question of tribunal composition and panel size was raised directly by the re- **20.38** constitution of social security tribunals under the Social Security Act 1998. The evolution of this legislation has attracted considerable criticism.[70] Before the Act social security tribunals almost invariably comprised three members, a lawyer and two lay members. Following the Act these tribunals may now be constituted by one, two or three members. The aim is to introduce sufficient flexibility to enable the appropriate panel to be constituted. In practice social security appeals are normally heard by a single legally qualified member, unless the issue involves the

---

[67] N Wikeley, 'Expertise and the Role of Members' in Partington (n 1 above) ch 5.
[68] Wikeley, ibid, and Leggatt report (n 10 above) para 7.25.
[69] See the arguments presented in the Australian Administrative Review Council Report No 39, *Better Decisions: Review of Commonwealth Review Tribunals* (1995).
[70] See Wikeley (n 67 above) and M Adler, 'Lay Tribunal Members and Administrative Justice' [1999] PL 616.

claimant's capacity or incapacity for work (lawyer and doctor) or entitlement to disability living allowance or attendance allowance (lawyer, doctor and carer or disabled member).[71] The controversy surrounding these provisions has served to raise the question of the choice of mechanism to be adopted to determine panel composition in individual cases where one, two or three person panels are available. Traditionally the Council on Tribunals has indicated that tribunal composition should be contained in primary legislation.[72] However, other possible mechanisms include secondary legislation and presidential direction, and the Leggatt report seems to favour the power to determine whether non-lawyers should sit on particular cases or classes of case being devolved to divisional presidents or regional chairs.[73]

20.39 While the opportunity for non-legal involvement has been identified as one of the defining characteristics of tribunals, it is necessary to consider further what this means in practice. As will be evident from the description of the health authority disciplinary committees, a distinction is sometimes made between professional non-legal members and lay members. The current trend, however, is to focus on the specific skill or experience sought in the non-legal, or specialist member, whether or not that skill or experience is professionally recognized.[74] Traditionally, professional members were included for their specific skills and lay members were there to reflect the community, or to bring a broader experience to the finding of fact, or to reassure unrepresented claimants. However, empirical research has cast doubt on these assumptions in relation to the role of lay members. Predictably enough lay members were found to be representative of only a rather narrow segment of the community.[75] But in addition, studies conducted in both social security and mental health have reported that lay members were easily marginalized in tribunal proceedings and often failed to participate in deliberations.[76] While many of these reservations about lay members could be addressed by better training, there is certainly an argument that both recruitment and training are made easier if the qualities and functions of 'lay' members are fully specified in advance. In practice the approach taken by the parent legislation varies widely. The new social security legislation provides for the appointment to social security appeal tribunals 'of persons appearing to the President to have knowledge or experience of conditions in the area and to be representative of persons living or working

---

[71] For an interesting discussion see Wikeley (n 67 above).

[72] Council on Tribunals 1991 (n 65 above) annex A.

[73] Leggatt report (n 10 above) para 7.23.

[74] ibid paras 7.20–7.23.

[75] M Adler and A Bradley, *Justice, Discretion and Poverty* (London: Professional Books, 1976) chs 7–11.

[76] J Baldwin, N Wikeley and R Young, *Judging Social Security Claims* (Oxford: Clarendon Press, 1992) and J Peay, 'Mental Health Review Tribunals: Just or Efficacious Safeguards' (1981) 5 Law and Human Behaviour 161.

in the area'. It also provides for the appointment to disability benefit tribunals of 'persons who are experienced in dealing with the needs of disabled persons in a professional or voluntary capacity; or because they are themselves disabled'. By contrast the Lord Chancellor has wide discretion to appoint to the Immigration Appeal Tribunal 'such number . . . of other members as he considers appropriate'.

In looking at the role of non-legal or specialist members the Leggatt report was **20.40** very clear that all tribunal members should be appointed on the basis of the particular contribution which they can make and that that contribution should be defined in the statutory criteria for appointment. The report also recommended that the statutory criteria 'should always be sufficiently explicit to form a clear basis for recruitment material and for training, by defining the main activities to be expected of a specialist member'.[77]

With regard to non-legal specialist members with a professional skill, doctors and **20.41** valuers for example, there are unlikely to be any problems with the identification of their roles within the decision-making process, as these are usually clearly defined. The difficulties lie rather in the need to accommodate their professional values and skills within what is essentially a legal process. Just as there is evidence of the dominance exercised by legal chairs over lay members,[78] so is there evidence of the significant influence exercised by other professional members such as the psychiatrist on the mental health review tribunal.[79] To an extent this is to be expected; professional members sit on tribunals precisely because their professional expertise is relevant to the understanding of the subject matter at issue. However, the introduction of another set of values beyond those reflected by the legal system can cause problems both for the individual professional and for the proper conduct of the tribunal. The dilemma is particularly well illustrated by the role of the psychiatrist on the mental health review tribunal. As a doctor the psychiatrist will be concerned with the question: is the patient well or unwell? The tribunal on the other hand is a legal actor addressing a legal question: is the detention in hospital lawful or unlawful? Unfortunately there is not always a perfect match between the answer to the legal question and the answer to the medical question.[80] Both the tribunal and the individual doctor are thus presented with difficult choices.[81] In addition to these almost inevitable dilemmas, the role of the psychiatrist on the

[77] Leggatt report (n 10 above) para 7.23.
[78] Baldwin et al (n 76 above).
[79] J Peay, *Tribunals On Trial* (Oxford: Clarendon, 1989); Council on Tribunals, *Annual Report 1982–3* (1984 HC 129); and G Richardson and D Machin, 'Judicial Review and Tribunal Decision Making' [2000] PL 494.
[80] P Taylor, E Goldberg, M Leese, M Butwell and A Reed, 'Limits to the Value of Mental Health Review Tribunals for Offender Patients' (1999) 174 British J of Psychiatry 164.
[81] A Stone, 'Revisiting the Parable: Truth without Consequences' (1994) 17 Int J of L and Psychiatry 79 and G Richardson and D Machin, 'Doctors on Tribunals: A Confusion of Roles' (2000) 176 British J of Psychiatry 110.

mental health review tribunal is made even more difficult by the specific requirements imposed by the relevant procedural rules. Those rules oblige the medical
member of the tribunal to examine the patient before the hearing in order 'to form
an opinion of the patient's mental condition'.[82] The medical member is thus required to perform the dual role of expert witness and decision-maker. This immediately presents problems in terms of procedural fairness if the medical member
takes a different view of the patient's condition to that taken by other medical
witnesses. In such circumstances the duty to act fairly would require the medical
member to reveal his or her opinion in the course of the hearing.[83] It is clear from
the results of empirical research that this rarely, if ever, occurs.[84] Indeed the extent
of the problem is now recognized by the Department of Health and the proposed
new mental health tribunal will not involve an examination of the patient by the
medical member.[85]

F. The Relationship Between Tribunals and Courts

20.42   Tribunals are not courts and are specifically designed to be different from courts.
However, they are now widely regarded as forming part of the judicial arm of government and they are empowered to make binding interpretations of the law that
can affect the rights and obligations of individuals. The basic doctrine of the rule
of law would therefore suggest that they should be answerable to the courts for the
way in which they interpret and apply the law. Thus, appeal should lie to the ordinary courts from the decisions of tribunals, at least on point of law. According
to Wade and Forsyth, 'it is of great importance that [appeal on point of law]
should be generally available, so that the courts may give guidance on the proper
interpretation of the law and so that there may not be inconsistent rulings by tribunals in different localities. It is through appeals that the courts and tribunals are
kept in touch, so that the tribunals are integrated into the machinery of justice.'[86]
Such a view cannot be accepted, however, without at least some reservations. The
very considerations that led to the setting up of a tribunal in the first place and the
desire to encourage legal pluralism might suggest that the involvement of the ordinary courts should be kept to a minimum. Whatever the relative merits of these
two sets of arguments, however, the present arrangements governing appeals cannot be said to reflect a single consistent approach. According to the Leggatt report:

---

[82] Mental Health Tribunal Rules, SI 1983/492, r 11.
[83] *Mahon v Air New Zealand* [1984] AC 808, and *R v Mental Health Review Tribunal, ex p
Clatworthy* [1985] 3 All ER 699.
[84] Richardson and Machin (n 79 and n 81 above).
[85] See n 31 above.
[86] HWR Wade and C Forsyth, *Administrative Law* (8th edn, Oxford: OUP, 2000) 919.

'the arrangements for appealing from tribunals have developed piece-meal and show little logic'.[87]

In some jurisdictions special appellate tribunals have been established. There are five such second-tier tribunals in relation to citizen vs state disputes in the areas of immigration, social security, land, transport and, in some respects, tax. One second-tier tribunal, the Employment Appeal Tribunal, exists in relation to party vs party disputes. In some cases the appeal to an appellate tribunal is limited to point of law (social security), in others it can extend to both law and fact.[88] The mechanisms provided for appealing on from the decisions of these second-tier bodies again vary, but appeals from the Employment Appeal Tribunal, the Immigration Appeal Tribunal and the Lands Tribunal go straight to the Court of Appeal. In jurisdictions where no special appellate tribunal exists and no special arrangements are made in the legislation setting up the tribunal, the Tribunals and Inquiries Act 1992 provides a right of appeal from the decision of the first-tier tribunal to the High Court.[89] Special arrangements exist, for example, in relation to the Special Immigration Appeal Commission and the Foreign Compensation Commission, appeal from both of which lies directly to the Court of Appeal. **20.43**

Typically appeals from tribunals to courts are limited to points of law only, whether they are from the appellate tribunal to the Court of Appeal or from the first tier to the High Court.[90] On the face of it this limitation reflects the appropriate role of the courts in relation to tribunals. Tribunals are established to provide expert decision-making in specific areas of public policy. They should therefore have exclusive powers in relation to the finding of fact. The courts are only required to ensure the correct and consistent interpretation of the law. Unfortunately this distinction is not easy to maintain or, sometimes, even to justify. **20.44**

In the first place, as the case law since *Edwards v Bairstow*[91] suggests, it is extremely difficult, even in conceptual terms, to maintain an absolute distinction between law and fact. Further, even if the question is one of law the court has to decide how far it wishes to impose its particular interpretation. If the question is one of law then ostensibly it is one for the courts. Under the UK constitution the courts properly provide the authoritative interpretation of the law. However, in many areas of administrative justice, and certainly in relation to specialist tribunals, the courts might feel inclined to grant some leeway in the interpretation of specialized statutory terms.[92] Such a pragmatic attitude on the part of the courts would help **20.45**

---

[87] Leggatt report (n 10 above) para 3.9.
[88] Wade and Forsyth (n 86 above) provide an excellent account, ch 24.
[89] Tribunals and Inquiries Act 1992, s 11.
[90] ibid.
[91] *Edwards v Bairstow* [1956] AC 14. See also paras 14.16–14.25 above.
[92] *Woodhouse v Peter Brotherhood Ltd* [1972] 2 QB 520, and see Craig (n 2 above) 265–268.

to maintain the pluralist approach to administrative justice which is strongly reflected in the decision to establish tribunals in the first place. Certainly, in tribunal jurisdictions where there are alternative meanings to be attributed to statutory phrases, an interpretation imposed by the courts may in practice be ignored if it does not match the meaning preferred by the tribunal. In the case of the mental health review tribunal, for example, research suggests that legal meanings delivered by the High Court through judicial review may be ignored in practice if they do not match the more medical meaning preferred by the tribunal.[93]

20.46 In addition to a right of appeal on a point of law, in relation to most tribunals the inherent right to apply to the High Court for judicial review of the tribunal's decision is retained.[94] The precise relationship between appeal on point of law and judicial review has given rise to extensive speculation, particularly since the ground for review encompassed by error of law has been expanded, as discussed in chapter 14 above, especially at para 14.15. However it is clear that the two now cover very similar grounds, even though formally appeal might be concerned with merits and review with legality. Given their similarity the question then arises of which of the two routes should be taken in any given case. In principle judicial review should not be sought until alternative remedies have been exhausted,[95] but the case law is full of conflicting opinions.[96] On the other hand there are authorities suggesting that if grounds for judicial review exist which imply that the tribunal's decision is a nullity, it would be inappropriate to seek an appeal.[97] Against this uncertain background it is at least clear that the desire to limit the resort to judicial review, particularly in relation to immigration and asylum, provided one of the political drivers behind the appointment of the Leggatt review.[98] In the event, the Leggatt report has recommended the creation of a general appellate division of the tribunal system.[99] This appellate division would hear appeals from first-tier tribunals on the ground that the decision was unlawful, and appeals would lie from it to the Court of Appeal on similar grounds. The report has also recommended that express statutory provision be used to exclude judicial review in relation to the decisions of that appellate division and in relation to decisions of first-tier tribunals where there was a right of appeal which had not been exercised.[100]

---

[93] Richardson and Machin (n 79 above).
[94] Tribunals and Inquiries Act 1992, s 12.
[95] See Leggatt report (n 10 above) para 6.29 and Law Commission, *Administrative Law: Judicial Review and Statutory Appeals* (Law Com No 226, 1994) para 5.35.
[96] See Wade and Forsyth (n 86 above) 691–696.
[97] *Metropolitan Properties Ltd v Lannon* [1968] 1 WLR 815. And see the discussion in Wade and Forsyth (n 86 above) 928.
[98] Leggatt report (n 10 above) para 6.27.
[99] ibid paras 6.9–6.11.
[100] ibid paras 6.31–6.36.

The Leggatt report recommendations, if followed, will very significantly reduce **20.47** the relevance of judicial review to tribunals. Traditionally the courts have been extremely jealous of their inherent power of review and have treated most legislative attempts to oust it with considerable disdain.[101] However, the introduction of the appellate tribunal and the growing concern felt at the increase in the judicial review case load might combine to dispel judicial doubts. Nonetheless, in some tribunal jurisdictions users might need convincing that an appellate tribunal body will provide as impartial and legally astute a forum for challenge as that provided by the High Court in judicial review.

On the other hand the Leggatt report recommendations would introduce an appellate body to deal with points of law arising from first-tier tribunals that would **20.48** have some claim to special expertise. It is not clear exactly what role non-legal, specialist members might play on such a body, but the senior legal members would build up experience and knowledge of the context of the tribunals within their jurisdiction. An appellate tribunal could therefore avoid some of the difficulties associated with the interpretation of the law by High Court judges with little experience of its operation in practice, which were alluded to above. There would still be appeal from the appellate tribunal to the Court of Appeal, but if the appellate tribunal were regarded as having sufficient authority the Court of Appeal might be reluctant to overrule it on questions of law clearly within its area of expertise.

The problems faced by any attempt to identify the ideal relationship between **20.49** courts and tribunals is perhaps just one illustration of the difficulties presented by the specific role of tribunals within administrative justice. While tribunals are part of the judicial arm of government, they are also different from courts and must maintain their distinct characteristics. This need to be 'judicial' but not too court-like immediately gives rise to the familiar tension between consistency and flexibility, rules and discretion. Court oversight of tribunal decision-making provides an external mechanism for encouraging the consistent application by tribunals of the law, and that oversight should ideally be designed to provide sufficient consistency without stifling all tribunal discretion.[102] Within the tribunal structure a similar tension is reflected in any discussion of the proper role of precedent.

Tribunals are designed to be more flexible and less technical than courts. They **20.50** have 'a remit to consider each individual case on its merits'[103] and they are designed to be accessible to users without the need for legal representation. For all

---

[101] See paras 17.01 and 17.88 et seq above. See postscript, para 20.77.
[102] For a discussion of the role of the Independent Review Service see M Sunkin and K Pick, 'The Changing Impact of Judicial Review: the Independent Review Service of the Social Fund' [2001] PL 736.
[103] Leggatt report (n 10 above) para 6.19.

these reasons first-tier tribunals do not operate a formal doctrine of precedent. Indeed ordinary principles of public law would prohibit tribunals from pursuing 'consistency at the expense of the merits of individual cases'.[104] However, some commentators doubt the practical ability of tribunals to remain entirely unfettered: 'the court-substitute tribunals are often as precedent conscious as, and may even exercise a much narrower discretion than, the ordinary courts'.[105] In reporting the results of her research Genn confirms such doubts: 'These doubts about the ability of tribunals to free themselves from the constraints of precedent are clearly supported by the views of tribunals themselves when describing their approach to decision-making.'[106]

20.51 At the appellate level of tribunal decision-making some formal notion of precedent does in fact operate within some jurisdictions. The Social Security and Child Support Commissioners and the Immigration Appeal Tribunal already designate some decisions as binding on the first-tier tribunals. Both jurisdictions have had to deal with increasingly complex law and a large and increasing number of cases.[107] Genn's research provides vivid examples of the complexities which abound within immigration.[108] In considering the question of precedent in relation to its proposed appellate tribunal, the Leggatt report discussed the various options available for introducing a 'clear and coherent system of precedent in appeal tribunals', and eventually decided in favour of recommending the introduction of a system similar to that which operates currently in social security and immigration.[109]

G. The Council on Tribunals

20.52 The Council on Tribunals provides an element of extra-judicial oversight of the tribunals within its remit. The Franks report recommended the creation of two councils, one for England and Wales and one for Scotland. Their main function was to be to suggest how the 'general principles of constitution, organisation and procedure enunciated in the [Franks] Report should be applied in detail to the various tribunals'.[110] All proposals to establish new tribunals were to be referred to the councils for their advice on the tribunal's constitution, organization and

---

[104] *Merchandise Transport Ltd v British Transport Commission* [1962] 2 QB 173, 193. See discussion in paras 14.46 et seq above.

[105] Abel-Smith and Stevens (n 4 above) 228; R Wraith and P Hutchesson, *Administrative Tribunals* (London: Allen & Unwin, 1973) ch 10; and J Farmer (n 9 above) ch 7.

[106] Genn (n 4 above) 260.

[107] Leggatt report (n 10 above) para 6.20.

[108] Genn (n 4 above) 274–275.

[109] Leggatt report (n 10 above) para 6.26.

[110] Franks report (n 7 above) para 133.

procedure. The Franks report accepted that the Council's role would primarily be advisory but did recommend the creation of certain executive powers in relation to appointment and remuneration of tribunal members and the formulation of procedural rules.[111]

In the event a single Council was established with a Scottish Committee, and with a primary remit to 'keep under review' and to report upon the constitution and working of the tribunals under its supervision.[112] The Council is also required to respond to consultations concerning procedural rules initiated under s 8 of the Tribunals and Inquiries Act 1992.[113] There is no obligation imposed on government to consult the Council prior to establishing a new tribunal and the Council has no executive powers in relation to the matters recommended by Franks. It is, therefore, a weaker body than that envisaged by Franks. **20.53**

Traditionally the Council has performed its remit by visiting tribunals and responding to the consultations presented by the various government departments. It publishes an annual report to Parliament in which it describes its current concerns and activities. It also publishes special reports both on matters of general significance, such as its report *Tribunals their Organisation and Independence*, and on specific tribunals, *Mental Health Review Tribunals—Special Report*, for example.[114] In recent years the Council has become more open in its concerns about certain tribunals and the attitude of government departments, as the above reports suggest. It has also become more proactive in the work it is doing on the revision of the Model Rules and the publication in 2002 of a *Framework of Standards for Tribunals*.[115] Given the nature of its powers, however, there are clear limits to the Council's influence. There is, for example, no obligation on government departments to inform Parliament of the Council's views on draft legislation, nor of what the department has done in response. Many commentators have remarked on the Council's relative powerlessness and have recommended a strengthening of its remit, perhaps along the lines of the Australian Administrative Review Council.[116] **20.54**

The Leggatt report considered the role of the Council within its proposed Tribunals Service and concluded that the Council should monitor the development of the **20.55**

---

[111] For discussion see Harlow and Rawlings (n 2 above) 467–471.

[112] Tribunals and Inquiries Act 1992 and see Council on Tribunals, *Annual Report 2000/2001* (2001 HC 343) for the Council's Statement of Purpose.

[113] ibid Appendix E, for an account of consultations taking place in 2000/01.

[114] Council on Tribunals (n 45 and n 63 above).

[115] Council on Tribunals, *Framework of Standards for Tribunals 2002*. For the revision of the Model Rules see para 20.57 below.

[116] Harlow and Rawlings (n 2 above); O Lomas, 'The Twenty-Fifth Annual Report of the Council on Tribunals—an opportunity sadly missed' (1985) 48 MLR 694; and B Thompson, 'Keeping the System Under Review' in Partington (n 1 above) ch 3.

new service and its compliance with the ECHR. In the report's view the Council should have a primary duty to champion the cause of users.[117] More specifically the report made certain recommendations designed to raise the profile of the Council and to increase the pressure on government departments to respond to the Council's various interventions. For example, the Council should report to an appropriate select committee such as the Home Affairs Parliamentary Select Committee and departments should be obliged to record the Council's views and their own response in the explanatory memoranda for Bills and statutory instruments. In the longer term the report recommended that 'like the Administrative Review Council in Australia, the Council should be made responsible for upholding the system of administrative justice and keeping it under review, for monitoring developments in administrative law, and for making recommendations to the Lord Chancellor about improvements that might be made to the system'.[118] These latter recommendations would constitute a major shift in the nature of the Council and it remains to be seen precisely how the government will respond.

H. Procedures

20.56   As has already frequently been emphasized, tribunals are designed to be less formal and more accessible than ordinary courts. In this section an attempt will be made to examine further what this means in practice and what model of tribunal decision-making might best be designed to achieve the appropriate balance between rigorous decision-making and accessibility, or as Genn puts it, 'between the conflicting demands of procedural simplicity and legal precision'.[119] But first it is necessary to consider briefly the various sources of procedural regulation which can apply to tribunals.

(1) Sources of Procedural Regulation

20.57   Primary legislation provides the first source of procedural regulation for most tribunals. The Tribunals and Inquiries Act 1992 imposes some general procedural requirements on all tribunals within its remit, such as the obligation to provide reasons for their decisions.[120] The primary legislation which establishes the tribunal and stipulates its composition is also likely to deal with procedural matters relating to such issues as time limits, costs, interim relief and penal sanctions, if any, for failure to comply with procedural requirements.[121] The main bulk of

---

[117] Leggatt report (n 10 above) para 7.49.
[118] ibid para 7.54.
[119] Genn (n 4 above) 286.
[120] s 10.
[121] See the list in Council on Tribunals 2003 (n 65 above) Annex A.

procedural requirements, however, are likely to be contained in specific procedural rules, usually in the form of a statutory instrument. The Franks report recommended that the Council on Tribunals be responsible for drafting these rules, but in the event the sponsoring departments have been given the responsibility with merely an obligation to consult the Council(s). The Council has, however, published a set of Model Rules to guide departmental lawyers. These Model Rules were first published in 1991, they were revised in 2000 in order to reflect the requirements of the HRA 1998, and have now undergone a thorough reformulation.[122] In addition tribunals are bound by the duty to act fairly which is imposed by the common law and can be applied to supplement any requirements introduced by statute.[123] Finally, as already explained, many tribunals will additionally be bound by the requirements of Article 6 of the ECHR, and some, in addition, will be bound by the procedural aspects of Article 5(4). The nature of all these obligations will be considered below in relation to specific procedural issues.

(2) Informality

While the nature of the procedural requirements deriving from all these sources **20.58** vary across the different tribunals, they are distinct from the rules of procedure and evidence which apply to ordinary courts and are, in many respects, less formal.[124] Any attempt at a general assessment of the operation of tribunals in practice is not, however, possible. The range is far too great. Nonetheless, most tribunals do strive to create a less formal environment than that which is common within a court. The nature of the accommodation, the presence of non-lawyers on the panel and the forms of address and language used all help to create a more relaxed atmosphere. But as Genn has shown there are both limits to the informality which can be achieved and dangers for the applicant if he or she believes the decision of the tribunal will reflect the informality of the setting.[125] The complexity of many of the issues coming before tribunals and the tendency of individual panels to be guided by past decisions both tend to render the substance of the decision-making more formal than the procedures themselves might suggest. In Genn's view this asymmetry between substance and procedure can present particular difficulties for the applicant who is not represented.[126]

---

[122] Council on Tribunals 1991 (n 65 above). For the reformulation see Council on Tribunals 2003, *Guide to Drafting Tribunal Rules*, and Council on Tribunals, *Annual Report 2002/2003*.
[123] See ch 15 above.
[124] A small minority of tribunals do follow strict rules of evidence similar to those applying in the civil courts, eg, the Lands Tribunal, and the tribunals concerned with patents.
[125] H Genn, 'Tribunals and Informal Justice' (1993) MLR 393.
[126] Genn (n 4 above).

(3) Adversarial vs Inquisitorial

20.59 Traditionally any description of tribunal procedures has tended to include a discussion of the distinction between the adversarial and the inquisitorial model of adjudication. Court adjudication in the United Kingdom and in many other common law jurisdictions has adopted a predominantly adversarial approach. Indeed, according to Fuller's classic analysis, adjudication requires full adversarial participation and a fully responsive decision-maker who bases his or her decision solely on the arguments presented by the parties.[127] The alternative inquisitorial approach recognizes a more active role for the decision-maker who might be vested with the power to call for witnesses or documents on his or her own initiative. While the Franks report appeared to give some support to the inquisitorial model and such a model has been adopted by tribunals in other common law jurisdictions,[128] there has been a general reluctance in the United Kingdom to move far beyond the classic adversarial model even for tribunals.[129] There is a concern that the principle of impartiality can be compromised by vesting tribunals with too inquisitorial a role: decision-makers who are responsible for investigating and presenting evidence might find it hard to maintain an appearance of neutrality.[130]

(4) Enabling

20.60 To some extent the Leggatt report has moved the discussion on. The importance of encouraging users to prepare and present their own cases is one of the major themes running through the whole report but, at the same time, the report is alive to the difficulties which may be faced by the unrepresented applicant in a citizen vs state tribunal when the 'state' is represented by an experienced official. It is the report's view that in 'these circumstances, tribunal chairmen may find it necessary to intervene in the proceedings more than might be thought proper in the courts in order to hold the balance between the parties, and enable the citizens to present their cases'.[131] The report is accordingly keen to encourage what it describes as an enabling approach: that is one which supports parties in such a way as to give them confidence both 'in their own abilities to participate in the process, and in the tribunal's capacity to compensate for the appellants' lack of skills or knowledge'.[132] The clearest implications of such an approach would become apparent during the hearings themselves, but an enabling approach would also have consequences for

---

[127] L Fuller, 'The Forms and Limits of Adjudication' (1978) 92 Harvard L Rev 353.
[128] Leggatt report (n 10 above) para 7.3.
[129] Craig (n 2 above) 260–261, and see the early attitude of the Council on Tribunals, *Annual Report 1964* and *Annual Report 1965*.
[130] Fuller (n 127 above) and J Thibaut and L Walker, *Procedural Justice: A Psychological Analysis* (New Jersey: Erebaum, 1975) 49.
[131] Leggatt report (n 10 above) para 7.4.
[132] ibid para 7.5.

the pre-hearing stage, especially in relation to the nature of the information made available to the parties.

(5) Pre-hearing

Essentially the legal principles and, more particularly, the procedural rules have to deal with the three stages of the tribunal process, before, during and after the hearing. The pre-hearing arrangements have to ensure that potential applicants or appellants know of their right of access to the tribunal and how to exercise it. This much flows both from the desire to make tribunals accessible to users[133] and, where Article 6 is engaged, from the right of *effective* access to an independent tribunal.[134] These pre-hearing arrangements must also provide for all parties to be informed and invited to comment.[135] The question of legal help and advice is relevant at the pre-hearing stage as well as obviously at the hearing itself. While most of the arguments concerning the appropriate role for lawyers relate specifically to the question of legal representation at the hearing,[136] the Leggatt report emphasizes the advantages of providing high quality independent advice and support to users in preparation for the hearing. The report accordingly makes a number of recommendations relating to possible improvements to the current Community Legal Service contract scheme.[137]

20.61

The procedural rules dealing with pre-hearing matters will also usually stipulate time limits within which applications must be made, responded to, etc, and it is important that the hearing itself is not subject to unjustifiable delay. Article 6 guarantees a 'fair and public hearing within a reasonable time'[138] and Article 5(4), relating to detention, imposes the obligation to provide access to a 'court' to determine 'speedily' the legality of that detention. In the context of the mental health review tribunal the delays experienced by a number of patients awaiting tribunal hearings have been found by the High Court to be in breach of Article 5(4). The court recognized the practical difficulties facing the tribunal but held that these did not justify the delays.[139]

20.62

(6) The Hearing

At the hearing itself the procedural rules may deal with issues such as representation, the calling of witnesses, the use of experts and the exclusion of persons from

20.63

---

[133] See Council on Tribunals, *Framework of Standards for Tribunals* (2002).

[134] See, eg, *Airey v Ireland (No 1)* Series A No 32 (1979–80) 2 EHRR 305.

[135] This requirement springs from the common law principles of adequate notice, see paras 15.37 and 15.39 above.

[136] See paras 20.65–20.69 below.

[137] Leggatt report (n 10 above) paras 4.15–4.28.

[138] For an account of the relevant European case law, see K Starmer, *European Human Rights Law* (London: Legal Action Group, 1999) paras 13.78–13.83. See also ch 12 above.

[139] *R (on the application of KB) v Mental Health Review Tribunal* [2002] EWHC 639; (2002) 5 CCL Rep 458.

the hearing. Procedural rules are also likely to provide the tribunal with a general power to regulate its own procedure.[140] While the details of the procedures adopted will vary depending on the nature of the tribunal and the degree of formality required, all tribunals will be governed by the general common law principles of fair process and many will be bound in addition by the requirements of Article 6. It is assumed that tribunal rules will be drafted in order to reflect these general legal requirements,[141] but four perhaps deserve particular attention; the need for an oral hearing, the meaning of a public hearing, the question of legal representation and the burden of proof.

20.64 The traditional principles of natural justice in England and Wales can be satisfied without resort to an oral hearing.[142] However, where a tribunal has been established the assumption is that an oral hearing will be held unless both parties agree to dispense with one or certain exceptional circumstances prevail. Where Article 6 applies, the right to a public hearing implies a right to an oral hearing.[143] The right to a public hearing is now widely recognized across most tribunals. Indeed the publicity of proceedings was regarded by the Franks report as an essential component of openness. The Council on Tribunals' *Guide to Drafting Tribunal Rules* now reflect the wording of Article 6 itself and require that all hearings be in public except where the Article 6 exceptions apply.[144] The jurisprudence of the Strasbourg court tends to regard the presumption in favour of a public hearing as a strong one.[145] However, there are certain tribunals involving children, mentally disordered people, or national security where the hearing might properly be held in private. On the other hand the exclusion of the applicant and/or his or her lawyer from the hearing on grounds of national security can be highly controversial.[146]

20.65 The question of legal representation at the tribunal hearing itself can be seen as touching on some sensitive issues concerning the nature of tribunal justice. There are essentially two questions: should legal representation be allowed? And if it is allowed should legal aid be available? In relation to the first question it can be argued that legal representation will lead to unnecessary formality and legalism and should therefore be prohibited, as is in practice the case before some tribunals.[147]

---

[140] Council on Tribunals 2003 (n 65 above) r 67.

[141] ibid.

[142] Compare *R v Army Board of Defence Council, ex p Anderson* [1992] QB 169, oral hearing required, and *R v Department of Health, ex p Gandhi* [1991] 1 WLR 1053, no oral hearing required.

[143] *Fischer v Austria* Series A No 312 (1995) 20 EHRR 349 at [44].

[144] Council on Tribunals 2003 (n 65 above) r 69.

[145] *Gautrin v France* (1999) 28 EHRR 196.

[146] On the question of excluding the applicant see the position of the SIAC under Special Immigration Appeals Commission Act 1997, s 5 and A Tomkins, 'Legislating against Terror: the Anti-terrorism, Crime and Security Act 2001 [2002] PL 205. For a general rule on the exclusion of any of the parties see Council on Tribunals 2003 (n 65 above) r 72.

[147] eg, health authority disciplinary committees.

Indeed the Leggatt report is very clear in its view that legal representation should be the exception. Tribunals should be so organized and their procedures should be so designed as to encourage and enable users to have the confidence to represent themselves. 'We are convinced . . . that representation not only often adds unnecessarily to cost, formality and delay, but it also works against the objective of making tribunals directly and easily accessible to the full range of potential users.'[148]

However, research conducted by Genn suggests that applicants can, in practice, be **20.66** at a severe disadvantage if they lack adequate representation. Genn concludes 'although tribunal procedures are generally more flexible and straightforward than court hearings, the nature of tribunal adjudication means that those who appear before tribunals without representation are often at a disadvantage'.[149] There is also evidence that a general prohibition on legal representation can have unfortunate consequences for the tribunal itself.[150] Thus it is arguable that the Leggatt report is being unduly optimistic in its belief that the adoption by tribunals of a genuinely enabling approach will serve to neutralize the disadvantages currently suffered by unrepresented appellants.[151]

The second question posed above relates to the funding of representation, if al- **20.67** lowed. While the Leggatt report's support for an enabling approach is, no doubt, based primarily on the report's belief in the value of direct participation,[152] by discouraging the use of legal representation it also serves to reduce claims on the legal aid budget. Once legal representation is allowed requests will be made for such representation to be publicly funded.[153] The position under the ECHR might be considered first.

Article 6(3)(c) guarantees anyone charged with a criminal offence the right 'to de- **20.68** fend himself in person or through legal assistance of his own choosing or, if he has not sufficient means to pay for legal assistance, to be given it free when the interests of justice so require'. Further, the ECtHR has ruled that 'where the deprivation of liberty is at stake, the interests of justice in principle will call for legal representation'.[154] Thus a strong case can be made under the ECHR for the provision of legal aid before tribunals having the power to impose a penalty tantamount to a criminal charge, or where personal liberty is at stake. In other contexts the argument for legal aid has to rely on the notion of effective access to court

---

[148] Leggatt report (n 10 above) para 4.21.
[149] Genn (n 4 above) 285.
[150] See Council on Tribunals, *Annual Report 2002–2003* in relation to Health Authority Discipline Committees.
[151] Leggatt report (n 10 above) para 4.21.
[152] ibid para 1.11.
[153] For examples of such requests, see Genn (n 4 above) 263.
[154] *Benham v UK* Application 19380/92 (1996) 22 EHRR 293.

under Article 6(1) and its interpretation in *Airey v Ireland*.[155] Here the complexity of the law, the importance of the decision and the ability of the applicant realistically to represent himself or herself are all likely to be influential. The 'equality of arms' principle could also be relevant where one party is regularly represented and the other is not.[156] As Harlow concludes, the approach of the ECtHR is likely to be individuated: based on the situation in a given case.[157]

20.69 At present in England and Wales legal aid is available to cover representation before mental health review tribunals, immigration adjudicators, the Immigration Appeal Tribunal and the Employment Appeal Tribunal. The Leggatt report recommended that the remit of the Community Legal Service should be extended to include representation at more tribunals, but that this should be on an exceptional basis by reference to specific cases, or classes of cases, rather than to particular tribunals.[158]

20.70 Finally, in relation to procedures at the hearing the ECHR has been used to challenge the location of the burden of proof in relation to the mental health review tribunal's power to discharge patients from hospital detention. The original provisions of the Mental Health Act 1983 were interpreted as placing the onus of proof on the patient seeking discharge and this was held to be incompatible with the rights of patients under Article 5 ECHR.[159] This finding by the Court of Appeal led to a declaration of incompatibility under HRA 1998, s 10 and the introduction of a remedial order to remedy the breach.[160]

(7) After the Hearing

20.71 After the hearing the main issues relate to the giving of reasons and to the publication of the decision. Again Article 6(1) is relevant. The article has been interpreted as obliging civil courts to provide reasons for their judgments,[161] and it expressly requires judgments to be 'pronounced publicly'. This latter obligation can be complied with either by the announcement of the decision at a public hearing or by the later publication of the decision, and steps may be taken to respect the confidentiality of the parties in cases involving children or the mentally disordered, for example. The publication of the decision is in accord with the Franks principle of openness.

---

[155] See n 134 above.
[156] See the discussion in C Harlow, 'Access to Justice as a Human Right: The European Convention and the EU' in P Alston (ed), *The EU and Human Rights* (Oxford: OUP, 1999) 187–213, and Harlow (n 33 above) 35–36.
[157] Harlow (n 33 above) 36.
[158] Leggatt report (n 10 above) para 4.22.
[159] *R (on the application of H) v Mental Health Review Tribunal for North and East London Region* [2001] EWCA Civ 415; [2002] QB 1.
[160] Mental Health Act 1983 (Remedial) Order 2001, SI 2001/3712.
[161] *Van de Hurk v Netherlands* Series A No 288 (1994) 18 EHRR 481.

The vast majority of tribunals are already under a statutory obligation to provide **20.72** reasons either through the Tribunals and Inquiries Act 1992, s 10, or through their own procedural rules. Further, in the absence of any specific obligation the common law has now developed to such a point that, save in very exceptional circumstances, the courts are likely to recognize a common law duty to provide reasons.[162] Where a duty to provide reasons applies it is well established that the reasons given must be adequate.[163] However, the precise requirements of 'adequacy' in any given context are by no means clear. The benefits thought to flow to applicants, reviewing courts, and even the first-tier tribunal themselves, from the provision of reasons are now well rehearsed, but the practical realization of these benefits will depend in large part on the quality of the reasons given. Empirical research in relation to one particular tribunal suggests both that the quality of reason-giving is not high and that reviewing courts are unlikely to be in a position themselves to give the comprehensive guidance required to introduce the necessary improvements.[164] Thus, if the giving of reasons is really to deliver the anticipated benefits, the obligation must be expressed in more detailed and precise terms in the relevant statute or rules.

I. A Tribunals System?

As will now be clear the Leggatt report has recommended the creation of a single **20.73** Tribunals System which would provide a single structure for all the disparate tribunals which currently exist in England and Wales, including those currently dealing with local government matters.[165] The report's reasoning rests on the desire to improve the structural and apparent independence of tribunals, to encourage the adoption of a more user-focused and enabling approach throughout all tribunals, and to streamline and simplify the administration. The creation of a single entity would also improve the status of tribunals, would provide a structure within which a general appellate tribunal could operate, and would provide the mechanism for improvements in the recruitment, training, deployment, supervision and career development of tribunal members.

The structure recommended by the Leggatt report for such a system owes **20.74** much to the proposed reform of the Australian tribunal system at the federal level.[166] The proposed Tribunals System would be constituted as an executive

---

[162] See discussion in paras 15.50–15.54 above.
[163] *Re Poyser and Mills Arbitration* [1964] 2 QB 467.
[164] Richardson and Machin (n 79 above).
[165] The report considers the possible implication for tribunals in Scotland and Northern Ireland, see Leggatt report (n10 above) ch 11.
[166] See Adler and Bradley (n 37 above) for an interesting discussion.

agency responsible to the Department of Constitutional Affairs. It would contain nine divisions of first-tier tribunals, grouped according to subject matter. There would be a single appellate division which would hear appeals from all first-tier tribunals, but which would retain within its structure five specialist areas reflecting, where relevant, existing appellate bodies. The Tribunals System itself would be headed by a Senior President. There would be a President of each of the five appellate areas and each first-tier tribunal would also have its own President.

20.75 In March 2003 the then Lord Chancellor's Department (now Department of Constitutional Affairs) announced its intention to create a unified tribunals service accountable to the Lord Chancellor. This service will have as its core the ten 'top' non-devolved tribunals which are currently the responsibility of various central government departments. These tribunals include, the Appeals Service, the Immigration Appellate Authority, the Employment Tribunals Service and the mental health review tribunals. According to the announcement of this initiative, the reform is designed to increase the accessibility of tribunals, to raise customer service standards and to improve administration.[167] The details of the scheme have yet to be determined and the government has promised the publication of a White Paper 'later in the year'.

20.76 Thus the government appears to have accepted the main arguments in the Leggatt report and is intending to move towards a unified tribunals service in England. The question of devolved tribunals has yet to be addressed and the scheme appears to be confined to central government tribunals, not those organized locally. More considered analysis will have to await the publication of the White Paper.

J. Postscript

20.77 Since this chapter went to the printers the Government has published its Asylum and Immigration (Treatment of Claimants, etc) Bill 2003. The Bill will abolish the two-tier system of asylum and immigration appeals, there will be no separate appellate tribunal. The Bill will also remove the right of appeal to the Court of Appeal leaving only a power in the new tribunal to refer a point of law. In addition and perhaps most controversially the Bill will seek to remove the court's inherent review jurisdiction. Thus by removing virtually all access to the courts this Bill challenges some of the most fundamental principles which govern the relationship between courts and tribunals. It remains to be seen whether these particular provisions will survive the Parliamentary process intact, and, if they do so survive, how the courts themselves will respond.

---

[167] Lord Chancellor's Department Press Notice 106/03, 11 March 2003.

21

INVESTIGATIONS BY THE PUBLIC SECTOR OMBUDSMEN

A. Introduction

(1) The Origins and Concept of an Ombudsman

The Nordic word 'ombudsman' means simply 'an entrusted person', but the origins of the concept go back to 1713 when the Swedish King appointed an officer known as the Chancellor of Justice to investigate complaints against royal officials. This idea that the ombudsman's role is to remedy injustices done to citizens by the state was made more precise when in 1809 the Swedish Constitution created a new

21.01

post of Justitieombudsman who was appointed by Parliament to investigate complaints by citizens. This office remained unique to Sweden until Finland adopted an ombudsman in 1919. It was not however until the second half of the 20th century that the world was to see a flowering of the institution with ombudsmen being set up in many different countries. Indeed, such has been the proliferation of ombudsmen that the term has been used to describe widely differing bodies.[1] In particular there are now private sector ombudsmen as well as those whose remit is the public sector, and their independence, jurisdiction and powers can be very different.

21.02   It is therefore hard to define exactly what constitutes an ombudsman and views as to the proper function of the office can vary. However it would seem to be generally accepted that to be recognized as a genuine ombudsman the institution must be independent from the sector it is investigating. The courts, of course, are independent, but the other essential feature which distinguishes ombudsmen from the courts is their method of working. Ombudsmen investigate informally the working of the state and are cost-free to the complainant. The public sector ombudsmen therefore constitute an alternative system of administrative justice to judicial review. Unlike administrative tribunals they cannot be regarded as court substitutes as, while there is clearly an overlap with judicial review, ombudsmen differ significantly from courts both as to their jurisdiction and their objectives.

(2)   The Functions of an Ombudsman

21.03   The obvious and usually overt function of an ombudsman is to investigate individual complaints of injustice by the state and to remedy any injustices that are found. The second function is to improve the general standard of administrative practice of government; what can be termed the 'quality control audit role'. The second function tends to flow from the first in that it is the experience of investigating individual complaints that reveals the general shortcomings of the administration and enables the ombudsman to suggest reforms. However, commentators have repeatedly pointed out the tensions between these two functions. The obtaining of a quick resolution of a grievance may satisfy the complainant but it could forestall the uncovering of a general problem. There is also the problem of the number of complaints. The higher the case load the more the ombudsman will resemble a cheap substitute for the courts and this will prevent the ombudsman from conducting in-depth investigations into a general problem. Conversely a long investigation can delay the remedying of the individual grievance. A third possible function is that of citizen's defender. This function would be to champion

---

[1]   The International Ombudsman Institute lists today around 200 members in its Directory of Ombudsmen.

those who, such as prisoners and the poor, may find it difficult to articulate their grievances.[2]

(3) The History of the Public Sector Ombudsmen in the United Kingdom

The first public sector ombudsman to be created was the Parliamentary Commis- **21.04** sioner for Administration (PCA), set up by the Parliamentary Commissioner Act 1967. The PCA's job is to investigate complaints of maladministration against the executive. In 1961 a report, *The Citizen and the Administration. The Redress of Grievances,*[3] had recommended that a parliamentary commissioner should be created who would investigate complaints of maladministration forwarded to him by members of the House of Commons. Although the then Conservative government rejected the proposal on the grounds that it would 'seriously interfere with the prompt and efficient dispatch of public business', the idea was implemented by the next Labour administration. The decision to make access to the PCA exclusive to MPs (the so-called 'MPs filter') was clearly made to counter the argument that the creation of the PCA would undermine Parliament's constitutional role in holding the executive accountable. The institution was therefore set up as a 'tool of parliament' and this explains the way the original complainant is virtually excluded from the investigatory process. The lack of direct access by complainants has been repeatedly criticized but it still remains a distinctive feature of the PCA.

Once the PCA had been created, instead of the fears that the office would be **21.05** swamped with complaints, the number of complaints referred by MPs proved to be quite small. In 1967 743 complaints were referred to the PCA and, after having to reject 561 because of lack of jurisdiction, he investigated only 188.[4] Over the years the numbers have steadily increased so that for 2000–01 he received 1,752 new cases.[5] This small workload enabled the first ombudsman to carry out what has been described as 'Rolls Royce' type investigations. It has also been argued that the PCA was set up on the model of the office of the Controller and Auditor General and it is certainly significant that the first PCA was Sir Edmund Compton, previously Controller and Auditor General.[6] The principal function of

---

[2] Carol Harlow has particularly pressed this function; see G Gregory, P Giddings, Victor Moore and J Pearson (eds), *Practice and Prospects for Ombudsman in the United Kingdom* (Lewiston: Edwin Mellor Press) 53.

[3] The report was issued by a committee of JUSTICE, which is the British section of the International Commission of Jurists. It was chaired by Sir John Whyatt and for that reason is generally known as the Whyatt report.

[4] See tables set out in *The Parliamentary Ombudsman after twenty-five years: Problem and solutions* 4 and 5 (1992) 70 Public Administration 469.

[5] See evidence given by Sir Michael Buckley to the Select Committee on Public Administration, 21 March 2002.

[6] See F Stacey, *Ombudsmen Compared* (Oxford: Clarendon Press, 1978) 135.

the Controller and Auditor General backed by the Public Accounts Committee is to carry out an audit of accounts of government departments and thereby to seek out financial maladministration. So although the PCA has no powers to initiate investigations, his investigations are always very thorough and do resemble an audit of government administration.

21.06 The Parliamentary Commissioner Act 1967 excludes certain matters from investigation by the PCA, including actions taken by National Health Service (NHS) hospitals. This exclusion was criticized on the grounds that the existing procedure for the internal handling of complaints was unsatisfactory. This loophole was filled by the NHS (Scotland) Act 1972 and the NHS Reorganization Act 1973. These Acts provide for separate health service commissioners (HSCs) for England, Scotland and Wales. Unlike the PCA, complaints can be made direct to a HSC and there is no need to go through an MP, though complainants must first use the internal NHS complaints procedures and give the authority an adequate opportunity to investigate the complaint. The jurisdiction is wider in that the HSC is empowered to investigate alleged failures in providing a service as well as maladministration. The HSC used to be excluded from examining matters of clinical judgment, but the HSC (Amendment) Act 1996 removed this restriction. This Act also extended the remit of the HSC to the family health services covered by general medical practitioners, community dentists, opticians and pharmacists. The HSC therefore now has the widest powers of all the public sector ombudsmen.

21.07 When the Parliamentary Commissioner Bill was introduced the government resisted including local government within the scope of the Bill on the grounds that it would be better for a system to be introduced for local government under separate legislation. This system was eventually created by the Local Government Act 1974. The Act sets up two separate Commissions of Local Administration for England and Wales. The English Commission, as required by the Act, is divided up into regions for which a named local commissioner for administration (LCA) is responsible; there have always been three regions. Wales is the responsibility of one commissioner. Originally a complainant had first to make the complaint through a member of the local authority, though if the member refused, the complaint could then be made direct. The Local Government Act 1988, however, removed this restriction on direct access. In line with the PCA and the HSC the recommendations of the LCAs are not binding and, in a small minority of the large numbers of cases investigated by the commissioners, the authority refuses to comply with the recommendation.

(4) Other Ombudsmen and Complaints Mechanisms

21.08 Since the three main public sector ombudsmen were set up in the last decades of the 20th century, a whole host of ombudsmen, quasi-ombudsmen and complaint handlers have emerged. The legal basis, jurisdiction and powers of these bodies vary considerably and this is not the place to go into the variation in any detail. It is, however, important to be aware of their existence since as well as providing a comparison to the public sector ombudsmen, they are often part of the world in which those ombudsmen work. The Legal Services Ombudsman and the Pensions Ombudsman were set up by statute[7] and mainly operate in the private sector. The Legal Services Ombudsman is unusual in that his job is to investigate the way that professional bodies such as the Law Society or the Bar Council themselves handle complaints and therefore he does not directly investigate the original complaint itself. The Pensions Ombudsman also differs from the standard ombudsman model in that his decisions are binding and enforceable in the courts. In this regard the Pensions Ombudsman resembles a tribunal and this characteristic is emphasized by the fact that there is a right of appeal to the High Court against the decisions. The Financial Services and Markets Act 2000 has created another statutory ombudsman whose remit covers companies operating in the private sector. This body replaces eight voluntary self-regulating ombudsmen schemes such as the Banking and Insurance ombudsmen. The new statutory scheme bolsters the independence of the ombudsman by creating an Ombudsman Board that includes the Financial Services Ombudsman: the Board is independent of the Financial Services Authority. There still exist voluntary schemes such as the Estate Agents and Funeral Ombudsmen. A further variation is provided by the Building Societies Ombudsman, whose remit is entirely in the private sector, but the Building Society Act 1986 requires building societies covered by the Act to set up an ombudsman scheme and sets out minimum requirements for such schemes.

21.09 Another important feature is that the public bodies that are covered by the main public sector ombudsmen often have both their own internal and external complaints mechanisms. For example, one of the features of the Charter programme is a requirement for public bodies to establish internal procedures for handling complaints. Thus in the case of the NHS, complainants can go first to what is termed local resolution and then if they are still not satisfied they can have recourse to an independent review panel. A complaint can still go to the HSC but the complainant would normally have first to exhaust these procedures. Similarly, in the case of central government departments there now exist special officers whose function is to investigate complaints. For example, the Prisons Ombudsman investigates complaints by prisoners and the Adjudicator investigates complaints about the Inland Revenue. In both cases this does not restrict the right of an MP to refer a complaint to the PCA.

---

[7] See Courts and Legal Services Act 1990 and Social Security Act 1990 respectively.

21.10 Devolution has also meant an increase in the actual number of public sector ombudsmen covering the United Kingdom. The position in Wales is that as well as the separate LCA for Wales there is also a separate HSC. The Government of Wales Act 1998 has further established a Welsh Administration Ombudsman whose jurisdiction includes the Welsh Assembly and a number of Welsh public bodies. The British PCA of course still retains his jurisdiction over the central government. In the case of Scotland the position is basically the same as for Wales except that the more radical devolution means that there is a new Scottish Parliamentary Ombudsman, created by the Scotland Act 1998, who has responsibility for the matters devolved to the Scottish Parliament. Again the British PCA retains power over reserved matters. Finally in Northern Ireland an Assembly Ombudsman has responsibility for most devolved matters but there is a Commissioner for Complaints who deals with health and local government. Once again the British PCA has jurisdiction over reserved matters.

B. The Parliamentary Commissioner for Administration

(1) Appointment, Tenure and Staffing

21.11 The PCA is appointed by the Crown.[8] This means that in practice the choice is made by the Prime Minister. There is no statutory duty to consult Parliament on the appointment even though the PCA makes an annual report to each House of Parliament.[9] In 1977 the JUSTICE Committee[10] criticized the lack of consultation in the way appointments had been made and recommended either that there should be an obligation to consult the House of Commons Select Committee on the PCA or that the select committee should be asked for nominations with the appointment being made by resolution of the House of Commons. No statutory changes have been made but the Chairman of the Select Committee on Public Administration (the Select Committee on the PCA is no longer in existence) is now in practice consulted about new appointments and the approval of the Leader of the Opposition is sought.[11] The independence of the PCA is secured by giving the office the same security as a High Court judge. The PCA holds office subject to good behaviour and can only be removed by the executive by an address from both Houses of Parliament.[12] There are also provisions for the office to be declared vacant if the current Commissioner becomes incapable of carrying out the duties because of medical reasons and for an acting Commissioner to be appointed,

---

[8] Parliamentary Commissioner Act 1967, s 2.
[9] ibid s10(4).
[10] JUSTICE, *Our Fettered Ombudsman* (1977).
[11] (1993–94 HC 33-1) para 31.
[12] Parliamentary Commissioner Act 1967, s 1(3).

who will hold office until the appointment of a new full-time Commissioner.[13] As the PCA must make an annual report to each House of Parliament,[14] he is for all practical purposes, if not technically, an officer of Parliament and is answerable to Parliament through the Select Committee on Public Administration. There has been discussion about the type of person who should be appointed. The first three PCAs were all career civil servants. This was then followed by a period when independent lawyers were appointed. The present incumbent is a lawyer but his immediate predecessor was a civil servant. So there has been no consistency. Civil servants bring with them experience of ways of government but can be seen as too close to government. Lawyers emphasize the impartiality and neutrality of the office but their appointment can also be seen to make it more adversarial as opposed to investigatory in function.[15]

It is obviously important that the PCA should have sufficient staff and resources **21.12** to carry out the functions of the office. The PCA has the power to appoint officers, who can carry out any of his functions,[16] though the costs of all expenses have to be sanctioned by the Treasury.[17] There are about 100 people employed. Most of these are career civil servants seconded from central government departments but there are a number of lawyers. It seems to be accepted that this practice is effective.[18]

(2) Jurisdiction

When the PCA was first set up in 1967 the function of the office was to investi- **21.13** gate complaints about central government. The long list of departments and authorities subject to investigation contained in Sch 2 to the 1967 Act was largely confined to departments of the Crown. At that time the structure of government in the United Kingdom was relatively simple but the proliferation of the number and nature of non-departmental public bodies or 'quangos' and the establishment of executive agencies has complicated the face of central government. A report[19] in 1984 of the Select Committee on the PCA recommended the extension

---

[13] ibid ss 1(3A) and 3A, both inserted by Parliamentary and Health Service Commissioners Act 1987.

[14] ibid s 10(4).

[15] See G Drewry and C Harlow, 'A "Cutting Edge": The Parliamentary Commissioner and MPs' (1991) 53 MLR 745.

[16] Officers of the HSCs for England, Scotland and Wales can now carry out investigations. This provision was inserted by s 3 of the Parliamentary and Health Service Commissioners Act 1997 to enable the PCA to set up joint investigations.

[17] Parliamentary Commissioner Act 1967, s 3.

[18] See C Harlow and R Rawlings, *Law and Administration* (2nd edn, London: Butterworths, 1997) 424 and D Pollard, N Parpworth and D Hughes, *Constitutional and Administrative Law* (3rd edn, London: Butterworths, 2001) 458.

[19] Select Committee on the PCA, Fourth Report, *Non-Departmental Public Bodies* (1983–84 HC 619).

of jurisdiction to certain non-departmental bodies. The government accepted that such bodies should be included where they had executive or administrative functions that directly affect citizens and are subject to some degree of ministerial accountability to Parliament.[20] As a consequence the Parliamentary and Health Service Commissioners Act 1987 added a long list of new bodies that were subject to the jurisdiction of the PCA and in addition substantially increased the number of departments. The 1987 Act also enables the list to be amended by Order in Council, but this is restricted to bodies more than half of whose running costs comes from money provided by Parliament or funds raised under legislative authority.[21] It has not, however, been necessary to add the executive agencies created under the 'next steps' initiative (such as the Benefits Agency) to the list, as s 5(1) of the 1967 Act covers actions taken on behalf of a government department or other authority to which the Act applies and these agencies are still technically part of the parent department. Section 5(1) equally enables the PCA to cover complaints about public services that have been contracted out to the private sector. The list of departments and authorities subject to the jurisdiction of the PCA is very long[22] and it has been suggested that it would be more appropriate to specify the bodies that are excluded rather than those that are included.[23] This could create confusion as to what was included and would seem to require the adoption of a generic term for what type of bodies were included unless expressly excluded.

21.14   More controversial are the functions that are excluded from the PCA's jurisdiction. Section 5(1) of the 1967 Act empowers the PCA to investigate 'actions taken in the exercise of administrative functions'. This would presumably exclude legislative and judicial functions and in any case courts and tribunals are not included in the list of authorities subject to investigation. However the PCA does in practice accept complaints about the need to keep rules under review and has investigated the operation of quasi-judicial functions such as public inquiries. More significantly the 1967 Act contains a schedule of 11 matters that are excluded.[24] These range from actions relating to foreign affairs to the grant by the Crown of honours. In 1977 JUSTICE concluded that only three of these exclusions were justified.[25] The most sweeping exclusions are contractual or commercial transactions and personnel matters.[26] This means the PCA cannot investigate complaints

---

[20] White Paper responding to the Select Committee Report (Cmnd 9563, 1985).

[21] Parliamentary Commissioner Act 1967, s 4(3), as amended by the 1987 Act.

[22] See the Cabinet Office paper, *Sweeping Extension of the Parliamentary Ombudsman's Jurisdiction* (1999).

[23] See Cabinet Office, *Review of Public Sector Ombudsmen in England* (April 2000) para 5.8.

[24] Sch 3.

[25] These were actions affecting foreign affairs (Sch 3, para 1), the prerogative of mercy and references to the courts (Sch 3, para 7) and the grant of honours (Sch 3, para 11). All these actions are done under the royal prerogative and might be regarded as non-justiciable.

[26] ibid paras 9 and 10 respectively.

about the way a department has gone about the placing of commercial orders or has treated its staff. There have been repeated calls for these exclusions to be removed.[27] The most recent review by the Cabinet Office points out that the explanation for not including such matters was that the ombudsman was there to investigate complaints against government by the governed and not the government in its role as employer or customer.[28] The exclusion of complaints by employees is perhaps understandable, as this would give such employees a special remedy not available to other employees. It is harder to understand why commercial customers of government should be treated differently from those being provided with service by government and it should be noted that the Royal Commission on Standards in Public Life considered that there was no convincing reason for the exclusion. The review by the Cabinet Office did not come to a view on whether the matters should be in or out of jurisdiction, though they did conclude that commercial matters should be within jurisdiction where the department or authority is also regulating the customer.[29] Section 5(2) of the 1967 Act also excludes an investigation where the complainant has or had an alternative remedy before a tribunal or court of law. However there is an important proviso that allows the PCA nonetheless to investigate, if satisfied that in the particular circumstances that it is not reasonable to expect the complainant to resort or have resorted to the tribunal or court. This gives the PCA a discretion but this is reviewable by the courts.[30]

(3) The Concept of 'Injustice in Consequence of Maladministration'

The PCA can only investigate claims by members of the public that they have **21.15** sustained injustice in consequence of maladministration in connection with the administrative action.[31] The terms injustice and maladministration are therefore fundamental to the process but neither are defined in the 1967 Act. In this regard Sedley J has held that the question of whether any given facts amount to maladministration is for the PCA alone to decide.[32] In *R v Local Commissioner for Administration for the North and East Area of England, ex p Bradford City Council,*[33] the first case concerning the LCA, Eveleigh LJ accepted the *Shorter Oxford English Dictionary* definition of 'maladministration' as 'faulty administration' or 'inefficient

---

[27] See, eg, *Our Fettered Ombudsman* (n 10 above) 14.

[28] Cabinet Office Review (n 23 above) para 5.11.

[29] They justified this on the grounds that this situation is similar to commercial transactions relating to the compulsory purchase and subsequent transfer of land and these matters are expressly included.

[30] See *R v Commissioner for Local Administration, ex p Croydon LBC* [1989] 1 All ER 1033 (decision concerning an identically worded provision governing the jurisdiction of the LCA).

[31] Parliamentary Commissioner Act 1976, s 5(1)(a).

[32] See *R v Parliamentary Commissioner for Administration, ex p Balchin (No 1)* [1997] JPL 917, 925–926.

[33] [1979] QB 287.

or improper management of affairs, esp. Public affairs'. He therefore concluded that the 1967 Act makes provision for investigation where a person claims to have sustained injustice as a result of inefficient or improper administration.[34] More detailed guidance as to what is 'maladministration' had been provided by Richard Crossman, the Minister responsible for introducing the Bill, who at the second reading stage of the Bill described maladministration as 'including bias, neglect, inattention, delay, incompetence, ineptitude, turpitude, arbitrariness and so on' and that the meaning could be filled out by the practical application of case work by the PCA.[35] Lord Denning adopted this approach (known as the Crossman catalogue) in the *Bradford* case and emphasized, as had Crossman, that it covered the manner in which a decision is reached or discretion is exercised but excluded its merits.[36] As to merits, s 12(3) expressly states that nothing in the 1967 Act authorizes or requires the PCA to question the merits of a decision taken without maladministration. As Lord Denning explained in the *Bradford* case, this provision makes clear that, if there is no finding of maladministration, there is no power to question the decision taken by the authorities.[37] Strictly the proviso does not itself define what can amount to maladministration but it does emphasize that the investigation is not about the merits of the decision. Lord Donaldson MR, in another decision concerning the LCA, summed up the position:

> Administration and maladministration have nothing to do with the nature, quality or reasonableness of the decision itself.[38]

21.16   In another decision concerning the LCA, Woolf LJ accepted that complaints that a decision had been taken on inadequate evidence or that a policy had been applied to the exclusion of the merits of the particular case did come within the jurisdiction of the LCA.[39] In this respect the concept of maladministration is very similar to the grounds of judicial review, in that while the PCA cannot review the merits of the decision in themselves, the PCA can examine the basis for the decision and how it

---

[34]   *Bradford* case (n 33 above) 314G.

[35]   *Hansard*, HC vol 734, col 51 (18 October 1966).

[36]   See *R v Local Commissioner for Administration for the North and East Area of England, ex p Bradford City Council* [1979] QB 287, 312B. At that time the courts had excluded themselves from looking at *Hansard* as an aid to construction. It is now permissible in certain conditions.

[37]   Despite this prohibition Stacey in 1978 pointed out that in three important reports the PCA pointed out failings by government without characterizing those failings as maladministration; see Stacey (n 6 above) 160. Stacey argues that this is justified because the PCA is not required to report whether or not he has found maladministration. However it would seem that it is implicit in the Act that there should be a formal finding whether or not there has been maladministration and if there is no finding of maladministration he should not criticize the merits of the public body's actions. However, in discussing whether there has been maladministration, in practice the PCA will always be able to make his views known about shortcomings.

[38]   See *R v Local Commissioner for Administration for England, ex p Eastleigh BC* [1988] QB 855, 863F.

[39]   See *R v Commissioner for Local Administration, ex p Croydon LBC* [1989] 1 All ER 1033, 1043j, 1044a.

was made. The courts are also increasingly willing to overturn a decision on the grounds that it is clearly unreasonable, irrational or disproportionate. The PCA has equally been willing to find maladministration based on a decision being simply 'bad'.[40] This can be termed a kind of constructive maladministration as the maladministration is inferred from the badness of the decision. Similarly the PCA is prepared to find maladministration where there has been a failure to review a 'bad' rule that is causing hardship. This fault has been described by one PCA as 'failure to mitigate the effects of rigid adherence to the letter of the law where that produces manifestly unequal treatment'.[41] Government policy can be as important as legally binding rules and the same principle should apply. So, while the PCA should not directly question the merits of the policy, he should investigate whether the policy is causing hardship.[42]

The New Zealand Ombudsman can report on actions or omissions by govern-   **21.17** ment departments that are unreasonable, unjust, based on a mistake, or merely 'wrong'.[43] The Justice Report, *Our Fettered Ombudsman*, recommended that the PCA should similarly be empowered to investigate complaints that actions, or omissions, by government departments are unreasonable, unjust or oppressive and to suggest changes in legislation and departmental rules. There is little likelihood of this ever happening and the concept of maladministration, like that of illegality, is sufficiently flexible to allow the PCA to condemn bad administration when he finds it. In 1993 the then PCA in his annual report updated the Crossman catalogue by setting out a new list of examples of maladministration.[44] All these kept to the way in which the complainant was treated (they included such things as rudeness and refusal to answer reasonable questions) and the statement was endorsed by the Select Committee on the PCA.[45] The new list, however, illustrates the elasticity of the concept.

For the PCA to be able to report adversely on a public body, maladministration   **21.18** must not only be found but there must also be a finding that injustice to the

---

[40] The Select Committee on the PCA urged him on to take this approach (1967–68 HC 350) para 14. An example of a bad decision is given in Sir William Wade and Christopher Forsyth, *Administrative Law* (8th edn, Oxford: OUP, 2000) 96, n 64, of a case where the PCA held that a refusal of Customs and Excise to refund the fee for a gaming licence did not stand up to examination; see *Annual Report* (1970 HC 261) 36.

[41] This was included in a list of examples of maladministration that was intended to update the 'Crossman catalogue', (1993–94 HC 290) para 7.

[42] In a detailed analysis of the approach of the PCA to policy guidance, Mowbray found no cases of maladministration on such a basis, though he did find many examples of the PCA challenging the interpretation and application of policy; see A Mowbray, 'The Parliamentary Commissioner and Administrative Guidance' [1987] PL 570.

[43] Parliamentary Commissioner (Ombudsman) Act 1962, s 19.

[44] See n 41 above.

[45] Select Committee on the PCA, First Report, *Maladministration and Redress* (1994–95 HC 112).

complainant has been sustained. There must also be a causal connection between the maladministration and the injustice and so the PCA must both conclude that the maladministration has caused injustice and have a reasonable basis for that conclusion.[46] There is some confusion over what amounts to injustice and whether the complainant needs to show that she has been prejudiced by the decision. As with maladministration, Sedley J in *R v Parliamentary Commissioner for Administration, ex Balchin (No 1)*[47] held that whether injustice had been caused in any particular set of circumstances was for the PCA to decide. However the PCA must not err in law in the approach taken and the courts will intervene if they consider that the decision is one that is outside the range of meaning which the English language and the statutory purpose make possible.[48] Richard Crossman in promoting the 1967 Act made clear that it was intended that injustice should be given a wide meaning. He stated:

> We have not tried to define injustice by using such terms as 'loss or damage'. These may have legal overtones which could be held to exclude one thing which I am particularly anxious shall remain—the sense of outrage aroused by unfair or incompetent administration, even where the complainant has suffered no actual loss.[49]

This flexible meaning was approved by both Sedley J in the *Balchin* case and by Dyson J in *Balchin (No 2)*.[50]

21.19   The problem arises where it is argued that, although there may have been maladministration, the outcome would have inevitably been the same and that therefore no injustice was caused. Thus in the *Balchin* litigation it was argued that, even if the Department of Transport had been guilty of maladministration by not asking the local authority to use its powers to purchase land that had been blighted by a road scheme, the fault had not caused any injustice because the council would still have refused to purchase the property. Dyson J in *Balchin (No 2)* held that the Balchins (the owners of the property) had an extremely strong case that injustice had been caused, because of outrage. The judge, however, accepted that the PCA was not bound to come to that conclusion but that he should have given reasons for holding that it did not amount to injustice.

21.20   Yet in *R v Commissioner for Local Administration, ex p S*[51] Collins J said that it was clearly not enough that the applicant feels that she has been unfairly treated and

---

[46] See *R v Local Commissioner for Administration for England, ex p Eastleigh BC* [1988] QB 855. In this decision concerning the LCA the Court of Appeal by a majority held that the LCA's conclusion that the maladministration of the council had led to the necessity for the expenditure on remedial work could not be sustained.

[47] [1997] JPL 917.

[48] ibid 925–926.

[49] *Hansard*, HC vol 734, col 51 (18 October 1966).

[50] *R v Parliamentary Commissioner for Administration, ex p Balchin (No 2)* [2000] JPL 267.

[51] [1999] 1 LGLR 633.

so has suffered an injustice. He argued that there had to be some prejudice, though this could be just the loss of an opportunity and he accepted that no particular damage had to be established. Collins J therefore found that the LCA was entitled to conclude that no injustice had been caused by the maladministration that had been found because it would have made no difference. The Judge was not referred to Sedley J's decision in *Balchin (No 1)* and the more persuasive view is that while maladministration by itself cannot automatically amount to injustice, a sense of outrage can amount to injustice even though it is clear that the maladministration would have made no difference to the outcome. Of course it will depend on the particular circumstances and whether the sense of outrage is justified.[52] In such a case the obvious remedy will be an apology for the mistake.

(4) Access to the PCA: the MP Filter

Section 5 of the 1967 Act makes it a precondition of the PCA's power to investi- **21.21**
gate a complaint that both:

- a written complaint has been made to a member of the House of Commons by a member of the public who claims to have suffered injustice in consequence of maladministration and;
- a member of the House of Commons refers the complaint to the PCA for investigation with the consent of the person who made the complaint.

The PCA cannot therefore investigate a complaint that comes to him direct from a complainant. Successive PCAs have, however, adopted the practice in suitable cases of offering to forward the complaint to her constituency MP or to some other MP,[53] so that the precondition can be satisfied by the MP then referring the complaint back to the PCA.

The Cabinet Office *Review of the Public Sector Ombudsman in England* reported **21.22**
that: 'Contributors to this review have expressed almost universal dissatisfaction with the arrangement for access to the PCA via an MP',[54] and pointed out that the MP filter had been questioned throughout the life of the PCA. The review strongly recommended, like many other previous reviews,[55] that it should be abolished. The filter was mainly put in place to avoid accusations that the ombudsman remedy would undermine MPs' constitutional role of making the executive accountable to Parliament: the PCA was to be a new weapon for MPs. As the

---

[52] It has been suggested that the test should be whether the reasonable person would consider that the complainant was entitled to feel that there had been injustice; see G Jones and M Grekos, 'Great Expectations? The Ombudsman and the Meaning of Injustice' [2001] JR 20.

[53] An MP can refer a complaint from any member of the public and so the complainant does not have to be a constituent.

[54] Cabinet Office Review (n 23 above) para 3.10

[55] See *Our Fettered Ombudsman* (n 10 above).

Cabinet Office Review argues,[56] modernization of government and constitutional change has brought many other means for citizens to seek redress against government. It seems strange that the PCA remedy should be singled out for this particular restriction. It is also significant that there is now only a small majority of MPs who favour the retention of the filter. It would also seem that the practical argument (that MPs filter out the cases that are suitable for investigation by the PCA) does not bear close examination. Many MPs automatically refer complaints to the PCA if requested and a significant number of complaints have to be rejected by the PCA following referral. The fact that the referral is made by the MP and not the complainant can also be seen to influence the actual process of the investigation. Section 10 of the 1967 Act requires the PCA to send the results of the referral to the MP and not to the complainant. The PCA does not directly communicate with the person who has actually made the complaint. Direct access would mean that there was a direct relationship between the complainant and the PCA.

(5) The Significance of Alternative Legal Remedies

21.23 Section 5(2) of the 1967 Act provides that the PCA should not investigate if the complainant has a right of appeal to a tribunal or remedy by proceeding before a court of law. There is however an important proviso that gives the PCA discretion nevertheless to conduct an investigation if satisfied that in the particular circumstances it is not reasonable to expect the complainant to resort or to have resorted to that right or remedy. A crucial factor in deciding whether to investigate must be whether the alternative remedy is as appropriate as an investigation by the PCA. In practice this will mean that if the complainant has the right to appeal to a tribunal or court, the PCA will normally refuse to investigate. In this regard in *R v Commissioner of Local Administration, ex p Croydon LBC*,[57] in the context of an identical provision concerning the LCA, Woolf LJ said:

> Section 26(6) makes it clear that where there is a remedy in the sense which I have indicated, inter alia, in a court of law, the courts do not have sole jurisdiction and the commissioner may still intervene. On the other hand the general tenor of section 26(6) is that, if there is a tribunal (whether it be an appeal tribunal, a Minister of the Crown or a court of law) which is specifically designed to deal with the issue, that is the body to whom the complainant should normally resort.[58]

21.24 The PCA is most likely to exercise his discretion and take on the case where there is the alternative remedy of seeking judicial review of the administrative action. This is because there is a large overlap between the ombudsman remedy

---

[56] Cabinet Office Review (n 23 above) para 3.43.
[57] [1989] 1 All ER 1033.
[58] ibid 1044.

and judicial review. Both are concerned with the actions or omissions of public bodies and what amounts to maladministration will often also be grounds for judicial review. If the PCA was constrained to reject referrals where the complainant might also be able to seek judicial review, his workload would be considerably reduced. Thus in *R v Local Commissioner for Administration in North and North East England, ex p Liverpool City Council*[59] Henry LJ observed in the context of the LCA that what may not have been recognized in drafting the proviso was 'the emergence of judicial review to the point where most if not almost all matters which could form the basis for a complaint of maladministration are matters for which the elastic qualities of judicial review might provide a remedy'.[60] This observation applies even more forcibly to the drafting of the Parliamentary Commissioner Act in 1967. Also, judicial review is very costly and the applicant takes the risk that if she loses she may have to pay both her own costs and those of the respondents. The great advantage of complaining to the PCA is that it is free. It will therefore often be unreasonable to expect the person of modest resources to resort to judicial review. Finally, investigation by the PCA may be the more appropriate remedy because it is more likely to get at the facts. In the *Liverpool* case Henry LJ held that:

> In my judgment this was a clear case for the application of the proviso. Serious allegations of maladministration had been made. Such allegations could best be investigated by the resources and powers of the commissioner, with her powers to compel both disclosure of documents, and the giving of assistance to the investigation. The commissioner was in a position to get to the bottom of a prima facie case of maladministration, and the ratepayers would be unlikely to have reached that goal, having regard to the weaknesses of the coercive fact finding potential of judicial review.[61]

So it is not surprising that it would seem that the potential for judicial review does **21.25** not often cause the PCA to refuse to investigate on the grounds that the complainant had or has a remedy by way of an application for judicial review. Yet there will be occasions when it will be more appropriate to seek judicial review. This was made clear in *R v Commissioner for Local Administration, ex p Croydon LBC.*[62] Woolf LJ held that, in deciding whether there was a 'remedy by way of proceeding in any court of law', the commissioner was not concerned to consider whether the proceedings would succeed but merely whether the court of law was an appropriate forum. This question obviously has to be asked at the threshold stage of deciding whether to take on the investigation. However Woolf LJ also held that, if in the course of the investigation it transpired that the issues were appropriate

---

[59] [2001] 1 All ER 462.
[60] ibid 471b.
[61] ibid 472 at [28].
[62] [1989] 1 All ER 1033.

for a court of law, the commissioner must again consider whether to continue the investigation. At each stage the crucial question will be, which is the most appropriate remedy, investigation by the ombudsman or judicial review? In this regard Woolf LJ indicated that where the essential issue was a matter of law, then judicial review would be the more appropriate forum as it was the specialist forum. He also pointed out that an important factor to be considered by the commissioner in deciding whether to exercise her discretion under the proviso was the fact that the procedures for judicial review had safeguards for the protection of public bodies and that these safeguards did not apply to the ombudsman remedy. Finally he stated that:

> Issues whether an administrative tribunal has properly understood the relevant law and the legal obligations which it is under when conducting an inquiry are more appropriate for resolution by the High Court than by a commissioner, however eminent.[63]

However, the overlap between the concepts of maladministration and illegality means that it will sometimes be difficult for the PCA to decide whether the complaint is really just a pure question of law for the courts to determine.

21.26   Section 5(1) literally only excludes investigation where a complainant 'has or had' a remedy before a tribunal or a court. It does not expressly state that investigation is excluded when the remedy has actually been exercised. However in *R v Commissioner for Local Administration, ex p H*[64] the LCA took the view that the identical provision in the Local Government Act 1974 meant that the ombudsman could not investigate a complaint if a remedy had been sought by way of proceeding in a court of law and in such a case the proviso did not apply. There was therefore no discretion to investigate where the alternative remedy had actually been exercised. In that case an application for judicial review had been taken, challenging the legality of the decision of the local authority excluding the complainant's son from a school. These proceedings were successful as the authority accepted that it had acted improperly. It was, however, argued that in these judicial review proceedings the court could not provide a remedy for the past maladministration and could only ensure that the authority acted legally in future. Turner J rejected this argument, holding that:

> The essential feature of the legislation is the creation of a legal right to complain about a grievance, but in respect of which there had been no available form of redress whether through the common law or by means of judicial review. Where a party has ventilated a grievance by means of judicial review it was not contemplated that they should enjoy an alternative, let alone an additional right by way of complaint to a local government commissioner.

---

[63] *R v Commissioner for Local Administration, ex p Croydon LBC* (n 62 above) 1045b.
[64] [1999] 1 LGLR 932.

The judgment also makes clear that it does not matter that in judicial review pro-   **21.27**
ceedings the court cannot provide a remedy for the past illegality. The crucial issue
is whether the judicial review proceedings had substantively addressed the same
complaint as was now being made to the ombudsman, ie had the court effectively
considered whether there had been injustice through maladministration. The
Court of Appeal in refusing leave to appeal affirmed the judgment of Turner J.[65]
Simon Brown LJ stated that it would be turning the legislation on its head to suggest that whenever maladministration is established in judicial review proceedings
then compensation should flow by way of a subsequent complaint to the ombudsman. The difficulty with this interpretation is that in judicial review proceedings the court does not decide whether there has been maladministration, but
whether the authority has acted unlawfully.[66] Also, in a case where the judicial
review application was unsuccessful, it would seem wrong that a complainant
should be denied the right to get the PCA to investigate the complaint just because a court has already held that the authority has not acted illegally. In such circumstances the PCA should have discretion to investigate.

In contrast the courts are not excluded from investigating the legality of a decision   **21.28**
just because the applicant has already complained to an ombudsman. In *Congreve
v Home Office*[67] complaints had already been made to the PCA about the way the
Home Secretary had dealt with persons renewing their TV licences. The PCA
found that there had been maladministration but strangely did not recommend
any remedy on the grounds that the government had been advised that it was acting legally. The Court of Appeal then subsequently held that the Home Office had
acted unlawfully. In that case the action of the Home Office was found both to
amount to maladministration and to be unlawful. This will often be the position
but equally there will be many cases where the action is lawful but nevertheless
amounts to maladministration. It may therefore be advisable for aggrieved persons first to complain to the ombudsman and then to consider going to the courts
in an appropriate case.

The jurisdiction of the PCA will not be excluded just because there has been litiga-   **21.29**
tion prior to the complaint being made, if the complaint does not cover the matters which were the subject of those proceedings. Thus in *R v Local Commissioner
for Administration for the North and East Area of England, ex p Bradford MBC*[68]
there was a complaint about the way the council had taken children into care. At

---

[65] [1999] Ed LR 314.
[66] In *R v Local Commissioner for Administration for the North and East Area of England, ex p
Bradford MBC* [1979] QB 287, 317G Eveleigh LJ appeared to lay down that the test was whether
the question of whether the complainant had suffered injustice through maladministration will be
directly at issue in the other proceedings.
[67] [1976] QB 629.
[68] [1979] QB 287.

one stage the mother had unsuccessfully taken legal proceedings to overturn care orders granted by the Juvenile Court but the LCA had made clear that he was only going to investigate the behaviour of the council before the children had formally been taken into care and the courts had been involved. The Court of Appeal therefore held that the LCA was not excluded. The different remedies were concerned with related but different events.

(6) Complaint and Investigation Procedures

(a) The person who can complain

21.30 Few restrictions are imposed as to who can complain. Any individual, body of persons or corporation can make a complaint. The only restriction is that complaints cannot be made by local authorities, public service bodies, nationalized industries or a body that is financed or appointed by the government.[69] Obviously the intention is that only private persons and not public bodies should be able to take advantage of the remedy. The individual's personal representative or some other suitable person can make the complaint where the individual has died or for any reason is unable to act for herself. So pressure groups cannot themselves make complaints unless the group itself has suffered injustice. The complainant does not have to be a citizen of the United Kingdom but must be resident in the United Kingdom or have been so at the time of death.[70] However non-residents can make complaints if the complaint relates to actions taken against the complainant when present in the United Kingdom.[71]

(b) Formalities of complaining

21.31 The complaint must be in writing[72] and must be made to any MP not later than one year after the date on which the complainant first had notice of the matters alleged in the complaint.[73] This time limit is much more generous than the time limits for applying for judicial review where the application must be made promptly and at least within three months. As with judicial review, the PCA has discretion to conduct investigations of complaints made out of time as long as he considers that there are special circumstances that make this proper.[74] The 1967 Act does not require the complaint to specify the action alleged to constitute maladministration and in *R v Local Commissioner for Administration for North and East England, ex p Bradford MBC*[75] Lord Denning approved the view of the then

---

[69] See Parliamentary Commissioner Act 1967, s 6(4).
[70] ibid s 6(1).
[71] There are special provisions for actions taken on ships and aircraft registered in the UK; see ibid s 6(4).
[72] ibid s 5(1)(a).
[73] ibid s 6(3).
[74] ibid.
[75] [1979] QB 287.

PCA that it was sufficient for the complaint to allege that injustice had been suffered. Lord Denning said:

> I must say I agree with the approach of the Parliamentary Commissioner. In the nature of things a complainant only knows or feels that he has suffered injustice. He cannot know what was the cause of the injustice. It may have been due to an erroneous decision on the merits or it may have been due to maladministration somewhere along the line leading to the decision. If the commissioner looking at the case—with all his experience—can say: 'It looks to me as if there was maladministration somewhere along the line—and not merely an erroneous decision'—then he is entitled to investigate it. It would be putting too heavy a burden on the complainant to make him specify the maladministration: since he has no knowledge of what took place behind the closed doors of the administrators' offices.[76]

(c) The decision to take up an investigation

Section 5(5) of the 1967 Act gives the PCA a discretion as to whether to initiate, **21.32** continue or discontinue an investigation and further provides that the PCA is to determine whether a complaint has been duly made. This provision gets close to holding that the PCA can decide his own jurisdiction, and in *Re Fletcher's Application*[77] the appeal committee of the House of Lords, in refusing leave to appeal, held that the courts had no jurisdiction to order the PCA to investigate a complaint. However, in *R v Parliamentary Commissioner for Administration, ex p Dyer*[78] the Divisional Court held that the courts did have the power to review decisions regarding the matters appropriate for investigation and the proper manner of their investigation. On the other hand, Simon Brown LJ (who gave the only reasoned judgment) also held that the wording of s 5(5) showed that Parliament intended to give the PCA a wide discretion and that:

> Bearing in mind too that the exercise of these particular discretions inevitably involves a high degree of subjective judgment, it follows that it will always be difficult to mount an effective challenge on what may be called the conventional ground of *Wednesbury* unreasonableness.[79]

The test of *Wednesbury*[80] unreasonableness in effect means that the decision has to **21.33** be shown to be totally unreasonable or irrational. Indeed Simon Brown appeared to put the PCA's decision almost into the category of what has been termed 'super-*Wednesbury*' where manifest absurdity has to be shown. It can be argued that the intensity of judicial review has increased in the last few years but nevertheless it is still clear that attempts to challenge decisions of the PCA simply on the quality of

---

[76] ibid 313C.
[77] [1970] 2 All ER 527.
[78] [1994] 1 WLR 621.
[79] ibid 626G.
[80] The name given to the test laid down by Lord Greene in *Associated Provincial Picture Houses Ltd v Wednesbury Corp* [1948] 1 KB 223.

the decision will be very unlikely to succeed. This does not mean that the courts would not readily intervene if they found that the PCA had misinterpreted his legal powers and responsibilities, and there is now case law to this effect.[81] It therefore follows that the courts would overturn a decision of the PCA refusing to investigate a complaint if it was proved that the PCA had made an error of law. In such a case the PCA would presumably reconsider the complaint even if technically the courts could not order him to do so by a mandatory order.

(d) The process of investigation

21.34 Section 7 of the 1967 Act gives the PCA a very free hand as to how the investigation should be conducted. The only legal constraints are that the investigation must be in private[82] and that the head of the department or authority concerned and the person who is alleged to have taken or authorized the action, should be given an opportunity to comment on any allegations contained in the complaint. This of course means that different PCAs can adopt different procedures. However it seems that certain basic practices have been established and there is continuity of approach. There exist various accounts of the basic process by the PCAs themselves.[83] The process is divided into stages. First before any investigation proper can begin, there has to be a *screening* stage at which it is decided whether the complaint is within the jurisdiction of the PCA. A large number of complaints are rejected at this stage and indeed it seems that only 24 per cent of complaints referred to the PCA are actually investigated.[84] Once it is accepted that the PCA has jurisdiction, the next step is to give the principal officer of the department or authority or other officers the opportunity to comment on the complaint. This can lead to a settlement as the department or authority may accept that they are at fault. This in effect results in a 'fast track ' procedure as there will not be any formal investigation of the department or authority and a large number of complaints are resolved simply by inquiries of the bodies complained about.[85] It seems that these cases will be recorded as being screened out. While a swift settlement is very acceptable to the complainant, it can be seen as turning the PCA into a 'small claims court' and thus undermining the PCA's purpose of identifying and publicizing systemic problems in the

---

[81] See *R v Parliamentary Commissioner for Administration, ex p Balchin (No 1)* [1997] JPL 917 and *R v Parliamentary Commissioner for Administration, ex p Balchin (No 2)* [2000] JPL 267.

[82] Parliamentary Commissioner Act 1967, s 7(2).

[83] See I Pugh, 'The Ombudsman—Jurisdiction, Powers and Practice' (1978) 56 Public Administration 127, 134–136; the Management Plans 1992/93–1994/95 quoted in P Birkinshaw, *Grievances, Remedies and the State* (2nd edn, London: Sweet & Maxwell, 1994) 195 and the booklet, *Ombudsman in Your Files* (London: Cabinet Office, 1996).

[84] See Cabinet Office Review (n 23 above) para 3.27.

[85] In a memorandum submitted to the Select Committee on Public Administration in 2002, the PCA stated that in the first 11 months of his business year 39% of complaints had been resolved in this way.

administration of government.[86] However, such settlements also free up the PCA's time to carry out a thorough investigation of complaints that cannot be so easily remedied. Where there has been no investigation, s 10(1) of the 1967 Act requires the PCA to send to the MP who made the referral,[87] a statement of the reasons for not conducting an investigation.

Section 5(5) of the 1967 Act makes clear that an investigation, once initiated, can   **21.35** be later discontinued. The Act, however, does not make clear whether in such circumstances there is simply a duty to give reasons why the investigation has been discontinued or whether s 10(1) requires a formal report of the results of the investigation. The Court of Appeal in *R (on the application of Maxhuni) v Commissioner for Local Administration*[88] has held, in the case of identical wording relating to the LCA, that where an investigation is discontinued, there is no legal requirement to produce a report. The only requirement is to explain why the investigation has been discontinued. So there is an important distinction between initiation and completion (where a report is required) and initiation and discontinuance (where only reasons for the discontinuance are required).

After the screening stage comes the formal *investigation* of the complaint. In this   **21.36** case the principal officer's reply is only the starting point of the investigation. The investigation will be conducted by examining the papers and files held by the department or authority. The staff of the PCA will also usually conduct interviews with the relevant officials and, if necessary, the complainant. Lawyers will not usually represent the parties and there is a complete absence of the adversarial approach. There is no public hearing at which the complainant can give evidence and cross-examine the evidence given by the other side. There are no rules of evidence and all the statements made can be relied upon in the final report. This results in the preparation of a draft report that sets out all the facts of the case, the investigation that has been carried out, and the conclusions and findings on the complaint. If the complaint is upheld it will also specify the remedy that is needed.

The third stage starts with the draft report being sent to the principal officer con-   **21.37** cerned, who is invited to check whether the facts have been correctly reported and to offer any comments on the presentation. The officer will also be asked to confirm whether or not the department or authority will or will not agree to the remedy where one is included in the report. If the remedy is for compensation to be paid the authority may have to seek the consent of the Treasury. The complainant is not given an opportunity to see the draft report and in *R v Parliamentary*

---

[86] Cabinet Office Review (n 23 above) para 6.9.
[87] If that MP is no longer a member of the House of Commons the statement must be sent to such member as the PCA considers appropriate.
[88] [2002] EWCA Civ 973; [2003] BLGR 113.

Commissioner for Administration, ex p Dyer[89] Miss Dyer argued that fairness required that she should also be given an opportunity to comment. Simon LJ commented that the practice of sending the draft report to the authority and not to the original complainant had been established for 25 years and was known to and acquiesced in by the Select Committee. The court concluded that fairness did not require that the complainant should be shown the draft report and justified the practice on the grounds that it was the authority who was being investigated and was liable to face public criticism for its actions. The authority might be called on to justify its actions before the Select Committee and, if on being shown the report, the authority had not disputed the facts it would then be unable to dispute these facts. Simon Brown LJ also pointed out that the practice afforded the authority an opportunity to use its power[90] to prevent the disclosure of any document or information which, in the opinion of the relevant minister, would be prejudicial to the safety of the state or otherwise contrary to the public interest.[91] This report must be sent to the referring MP[92] and the principal officer of the authority and to any other person alleged to have taken or authorized the action complained about.[93] In addition the report is also sent to the Select Committee. This report is signed personally by the PCA or by his deputy if he is absent.

(e) The investigatory powers of the PCA

21.38   The PCA is provided with wide powers to get at the truth. Section 8(1) of the 1967 Act gives the PCA, for the purpose of an investigation, the same powers as a court to require anyone to furnish information or to produce documents and to require the attendance and examination of witnesses (including the administration of oaths) and the production of documents. Any wilful obstruction of an investigation is punishable in the same way as a contempt of court and so anyone who refused to attend or produce documents can be imprisoned or fined.[94] These powers apply to civil servants and ministers alike. The only restriction is that no person can be required or authorized to furnish any document, information or answer any question relating to the proceedings of the Cabinets or a committee of the Cabinet.[95] Having obtained information, the PCA and his officers can only disclose that information for the purposes of the investigation and the subsequent report and that information is subject to the Official Secrets legislation.[96] With regard to an equivalent provision relating to the LCA, Collins J in *R*

---

[89] [1994] 1 WLR 621.
[90] Parliamentary Commissioner Act 1967, s 11(3).
[91] [1994] 1 WLR 621, 628H.
[92] This is required by Parliamentary Commissioner Act 1967, s 10(1).
[93] ibid s 10(2)
[94] ibid s 9.
[95] ibid s 8(4).
[96] ibid s 11.

(on the application of Turpin) v Commissioner for Local Administration[97] held that the provision did not prevent the disclosure of information to the complainant and that it was implicit that any disclosure considered necessary or desirable can be made. However the government can prevent the further dissemination of information once it has been acquired. Section 11(3) of the 1976 Act enables a minister of the Crown, when he considers that it would be prejudicial to the safety of the state or otherwise contrary to the public interest, to prevent the disclosure of any information by giving notice in writing to the PCA or one of his officers. This power extends to whole classes of documents as well as to particular documents.

(f) Fairness and the Human Rights Act 1998

The courts have imposed a duty on public authorities that are making decisions   **21.39** that affect the rights and interests of individuals to act fairly, though what is required by this duty will vary according to the particular function and circumstances.[98] The PCA, although he carries out his functions in private, is undoubtedly a public authority. As the findings and recommendations of the PCA are not legally binding, the decisions of the PCA do not strictly affect the rights of the complainant or the authority. However the government normally accepts the findings of the PCA and so the decisions of the PCA undoubtedly affect the interests of individuals. In *R v Parliamentary Commissioner for Administration, ex p Dyer*[99] Simon Brown LJ assumed that the PCA had made "'a decision which will affect the rights of" Miss Dyer'.[100] Further, in *R (on the application of Turpin) v Commissioner for Local Administration* Collins J had no hesitation in holding that the LCA had to conduct its investigations fairly. It would seem to follow that the PCA is not exempt from the general duty to act fairly.

The more difficult question is what is the content of the duty to act fairly as ap-   **21.40** plied to a body like the PCA that is required by statute to carry out its investigations in private. In the *Dyer* case the Divisional Court held that the PCA had not acted unfairly in showing the draft report to the authority but not to the complainant. Yet in *Turpin* Collins J stated:

> The law as to the requirements of fairness in conducting an investigation is, as it seems to me, clear. The general rule is that a person or body which has to make a decision based on an issue raised by one person against another should normally disclose the material on which it is going to rely or which comes into its possession which may influence its decision to each of the parties so that each party can know what material is available, what matters are likely to be held against them and whether it is necessary for that party to itself put forward material or to make

[97] [2001] EWHC Admin 503; [2002] JPL 326.
[98] See Lord Bridge in *Lloyd v McMahon* [1987] AC 625, 702.
[99] [1994] 1 WLR 621.
[100] ibid 629D.

representations to deal with such matters. If that is not done, it is clear that there is a risk—I put it no higher—that injustice will be occasioned to such a party.[101]

Collins J accepted that there would be circumstances where the ombudsman would be justified in refusing to disclose information as when it had been given in confidence. However if his view of law is correct it could significantly change the methodology of all the public sector ombudsmen by lengthening the process of investigation. On the other hand such procedural rights would certainly give the parties more control over the process and meet the objections that there is no opportunity to present a case, cross-examine or hear the other side's case.[102]

21.41 Article 6 of the European Convention on Human Rights (ECHR) provides that in the determination of his 'civil rights and obligations' everyone is entitled to a fair and public hearing by an independent and impartial tribunal established by law. As in the case of the legal duty to act fairly, it could be argued that the PCA and the other public sector ombudsmen do not determine civil rights and obligations, though there is clearly a 'contestation' between the complainant and the authority. Indeed the review by the Cabinet Office confidently states that: 'The non-binding nature of the English public ombudsman's recommendations has led legal opinion to conclude they are not caught by Article 6 and therefore that there is no requirement for public hearings'.[103] If, however, Article 6 does apply to the PCA, it would seem clear that the legal requirement that the PCA carry out his investigation in private is incompatible with the Convention rights. It would similarly support the argument that the PCA should involve the parties more during the process of investigation. On the other hand oral hearings would undoubtedly make the whole process more adversarial and costly.

(7) Redress and Enforcement

21.42 The 1967 Act is silent as to what should be the consequence of a finding that injustice has been caused by maladministration and does not even expressly empower the PCA to make recommendations as to how the injustice should be remedied. In practice the PCA does make recommendations to the department or authority. Such recommendations, however, are not legally binding. The only legal consequence of a finding of injustice through maladministration is that, if it appears to the PCA that the injustice has not been or will not be remedied, he may lay before the each House of Parliament a special report on the case.[104] However, it is only exceptionally that there is a refusal to implement the recommendation

---

[101] [2001] EWHC Admin 503; [2002] JPL 326 at [64].
[102] See Cabinet Office Review (n 23 above) para 6.18. The review thought this problem would generally be met by allowing the complainant to see the draft report.
[103] ibid para 6.74.
[104] Parliamentary Commissioner Act 1967, s 10(3).

and successive government ministers have accepted the conventional understanding that government operates on the basis that it accepts and implements the PCA's recommendations.[105] There seems to be little pressure to make the PCA's recommendations legally binding as it is felt that this would change the essential nature of the remedy.[106] Certainly it would seem significant that even where the government of the day has rejected the finding of maladministration, it may nevertheless concede a remedy by paying out compensation.[107]

As already indicated, a finding in favour of the complainant will almost always result in some form of redress but the type of redress can vary widely. The PCA has accepted that the guiding principle should be that so far as possible the complainant should be put back in the position she would have been in if the action complained of had not occurred.[108] So redress can take the form of solving the problem by providing the service or grant that has been withheld or delayed. This is obviously the most desirable outcome from the complainant's point of view but it may not always be legally possible, especially as the PCA has no power to affect the validity of a challenged decision. At the other end of the spectrum the redress may simply be an explanation or an apology. It appears that compensation is an increasingly used form of redress and in this regard the ombudsman remedy is close to creating an administrative tort. This is important, as the courts are reluctant to impose liability on public authorities for damage caused by them in the faulty exercise of their public responsibilities.[109] The amounts paid can vary from a few pounds to the £150 million paid out in compensation in the Barlow Clowes investigation. Compensation will be paid not only where there has been financial loss but also to compensate for inconvenience or distress. The Cabinet Office Review found no evidence that this trend is distorting the ombudsman's function but the report did recommend that the position should be monitored.[110] It is important that there should be some consistency in the level of payments, while retaining the flexibility of the remedy. **21.43**

As one PCA has acknowledged, there is more to redress than apologies or compensation, complainants need to be reassured that as far as possible the identified failings will not be repeated.[111] The need to change departmental practices relates **21.44**

---

[105] See Select Committee report (1994–95 HC 270) paras 1 and 5.

[106] See, eg, Report of the Committee of the JUSTICE–All Souls Review of Administrative Law in the UK, *Administrative Justice: Some Necessary Reforms* (Oxford: Clarendon, 1988) paras 5.36–5.39. The Cabinet Office Review (n 23 above) also concluded that the current position is acceptable; see para 6.75.

[107] This has happened in some of the most prominent investigations such as the Sachenhausen, Court Line and Barlow Clowes investigations.

[108] Cabinet Office Review (n 23 above) para 6.77.

[109] See, eg, *Alcock v Chief Constable of South Yorkshire Police* [1992] 1 AC 310.

[110] Cabinet Office Review (n 23 above) para 6.79.

[111] See statement of Mr Reid (1995–96 HC 20).

to the other function of the ombudsman of improving the quality of administration generally by identifying systematic defects. Thus in investigating an individual complaint the PCA may find that many others have suffered the same injustice and there is a particular flaw in the administrative system. Although technically the PCA is only concerned with the individual complaints, in practice he will want to be assured that others affected will be traced and provided with appropriate redress[112] and may suggest necessary changes to the system.[113] There are, however, limits as to how far the PCA can go beyond investigating the specific process that led to the complaint and in looking more widely at the general organization and management of the department or authority. The PCA has no powers to initiate investigations or to issue good practice guides.

(8) The Select Committee and the PCA's Relationship to Parliament

21.45 The 1967 Act makes the PCA directly answerable to Parliament by requiring him to lay annually a general report on the performance of his functions before each House of Parliament.[114] Also, as well as the power to lay a special report to Parliament (when he is dissatisfied with the response to one of his investigations), the PCA may at any time lay such other reports on his functions as he thinks fit.[115] The latter normally take the form of quarterly reports containing summaries of typical cases but the practice is not to reveal the names of the complainant and the individuals in the authority who were involved in the administrative action.[116] He may also make separate reports on important cases.[117] The PCA's relationship to Parliament is strengthened by the work of the House of Commons Select Committee on Public Administration. Shortly after the office of PCA was established, a Select Committee of the House of Commons was set up as the parliamentary focus for the review of his work and discussion of the issues raised. In 1997 the work of this committee (called the Select Committee on the PCA) was taken over by the Select Committee on Public Administration (both hereafter referred to as the Select Committee). It is clear that the effectiveness of the PCA has been enhanced by the support and encouragement provided by the Select Committee. The Select Committee is formally charged by standing order of the House of Commons with the examination of the reports of the PCA and the HSC

---

[112] See the case where a special report under s 10(3) criticizing the Department of Health and Social Security for not backdating an officer's disability pension resulted in several other cases being reviewed (1970–71 HC 587).

[113] See, eg, the investigations into the work of the Child Support Agency (1994–95 HC 135), (1995–96 HC 20).

[114] Parliamentary Commissioner Act 1967, s 10(4).

[115] ibid s 10(3) and (4).

[116] All these reports are given absolute privilege for the purposes of the laws of defamation; see ibid s 10(5)(a).

[117] eg, the War Pensions case (1970–71 HC 587) and the Barlow Clowes case (1989–90 HC 76).

and takes evidence from the PCA on the annual report and on other reports as it thinks fit, and in turn reports to the House. The reports of the Committee are sometimes debated on the floor of the House of Commons and the Committee therefore acts as a conduit between the PCA and Parliament.

The Select Committee therefore has a close relationship with the PCA. The **21.46** Committee meets regularly with the PCA and advises him as to how he should carry out his functions. The Select Committee has always taken on itself to find out how far the PCA's recommendations are being implemented. Where the Select Committee considers that the response of the administration is unsatisfactory it will pursue the matter, summon witnesses and issue its own report. The Select Committee, like all select committees, has the powers to call for persons and papers. As well as putting pressure on departments to provide remedies, the Select Committee is concerned to ensure that systems are improved where a complaint has revealed systematic maladministration. Finally, the Select Committee has frequently reviewed the jurisdiction and powers of the PCA and has consistently argued for it to be widened and strengthened.[118] Most commentators agree that the Select Committee's role has been beneficial and that it provides important backing to the PCA. However, it has been argued that the relationship can become too cosy and that the PCA is too subservient to Parliament.[119]

(9) Judicial Review of the PCA

In response to the question 'who guards the guardians', the PCA can point out **21.47** that he is both politically accountable to Parliament and legally accountable to the courts. However, it took 27 years from the establishment of the PCA before it was held that the PCA's decisions were susceptible to judicial review. In *R v Parliamentary Commissioner for Administration, ex p Dyer*[120] Simon Brown LJ unhesitatingly rejected the argument that the legislation had been enacted in such terms as to indicate that the PCA was answerable to Parliament alone, though he accepted that the courts should be reluctant to interfere with the way the PCA exercises his discretion. The courts also accept that whether the facts amount to injustice through maladministration is not a matter of law and the court of judicial review is only concerned to see that the PCA's decision is within the range of meaning which the English language and the statutory purpose together make possible.[121] So it would seem clear that the courts will overturn a decision of the PCA if he has misdirected himself on a point of law, or has failed to have regard to

---

[118] See, eg, the Select Committee's inquiry into the powers, work and jurisdiction of the PCA (1993–94 HC 333).

[119] See, eg, Harlow and Rawlings (n 18 above) 426–427.

[120] [1994] 1 WLR 621.

[121] *per* Sedley J in *R v Parliamentary Commissioner for Administration, ex p Balchin (No 1)* [1997] JPL 917, 925.

a relevant consideration, or has had regard to an irrelevant consideration or has in some other way abused his powers. In other words there is nothing to restrict the courts' usual power to ensure that statutory powers are exercised in accordance with the law. Most importantly the courts will overturn a finding of the PCA if his reasoning is defective. The Act does not require reasons to be given but the reports of the PCA are always reasoned. In *R v Parliamentary Commissioner for Administration, ex p Balchin (No 2)*[122] Dyson J held that, similarly to the decision of inspectors and ministers in planning appeals, there was a duty on the PCA to address the principal important controversial issues.[123] The detailed reasoning of the reports of the PCA must therefore make his findings vulnerable to reason challenges. Indeed in *Balchin (No 3)*[124] Harrison J quashed the third report of the PCA on the issue on the grounds that the PCA had made a mistake that had affected his decision that no maladministration had occurred. The fact that in the *Balchin* litigation all three decisions of the PCA were quashed emphasizes that, despite the wide areas of judgment and discretion provided, his decisions can no longer be regarded as somehow sacrosanct. Actions for judicial review may therefore become more frequent.

C. The Health Service Commissioner

(1) General

21.48 The HSC was originally set up by the NHS Reorganization Act 1973 but the present law is to be found in the Health Service Commissioners Act 1993 as amended. This consolidated the previous statutes and also attempted to clarify potential overlaps between the PCA and the HSC and to facilitate consultation between the various ombudsmen. So far the same person has always been both the PCA and the HSC (though there is no reason why a different person should not be appointed) and the office is appointable and answerable to Parliament in a similar way.[125] As with the PCA the Select Committee on Public Administration receives the annual report of the HSC and the Committee similarly makes suggestions as to how the system could be improved and puts pressure on the government to respond to criticisms made by the HSC. Again those employed by the NHS cannot complain about personnel matters, and contractual and commercial matters are also excluded except in relation to NHS contracts and to arrangements

---

[122] [2000] JPL 267.
[123] ibid 276, applying by analogy the House of Lords decision *in Bolton MBC v Secretary of State for the Environment* [1995] 1 WLR 1176.
[124] See *R (on the application of Balchin) v Parliamentary Commissioner for Administration (No 3)* [2002] EWHC 1876.
[125] Health Service Commissioners Act 1993, ss 1 and 14.

to provide services for patients.[126] Like the PCA, the HSC is excluded from investigating a complaint if the complainant has a right of appeal, reference or review to a tribunal or a remedy by way of proceedings in any court of law; though the HSC has the same discretion to take up a complaint if he considers that it is not reasonable to the complainant to take up those rights.[127] This exclusion is obviously important in the light of the number of legal actions for negligence brought against the NHS, but it seems that the PCA will rarely refuse to investigate just because there might be a possible legal cause of action.[128] The process of investigation, not surprisingly, is also very similar. Despite these similarities there are very important differences between the two offices. These differences will now be discussed.

(2) Access

The most obvious difference is that the complainant does not have to get an MP **21.49** to refer the complaint to the HSC. Under s 8 of the 1993 Act any individual[129] can make a complaint direct to the HSC. However, before commencing an investigation, the HSC must satisfy himself that any internal complaints procedure has been invoked or exhausted or in the particular circumstances it is not reasonable to expect that procedure to be either invoked or exhausted.[130] There are now revised complaints procedures for the NHS that allow for independent review. In the House of Lords the Health Minister suggested that it would not be reasonable to expect a complainant to use the internal complaints procedure, where either there had been excessive delay in dealing with the complaint or the complainant had lost all confidence in the local complaints arrangements.[131] A health service body can itself refer a complaint that it has received,[132] but this is unusual. As with the PCA the complaint should normally be made within one year after the complainant had notice of the matters alleged in the complaint.[133]

(3) The Bodies and Persons Subject to Investigation

The bodies and persons whose conduct can be investigated by the HSC are set **21.50** out in s 2 of the 1993 Act as amended by the Health Service Commissioners Amendment Acts 1996 and 2000. The first category is termed a 'health service body' and includes the regional, district and special health authorities; family

---

[126] ibid s 7.
[127] ibid s 4.
[128] See *Health Service Commissioner Annual Report 1998*.
[129] The persons who can and cannot complain are basically the same as for the PCA; see Health Service Commissioners Act 1993, s 8.
[130] NHS Reorganization Act 1973, s 4(4) and (5).
[131] *Hansard*, HL vol 569, col 1677 (29 February 1996).
[132] See Health Service Commissioners Act 1993, s 10.
[133] ibid s 9(4).

health service authorities; the Dental Practice Board and the NHS trusts.[134] The Health Service Commissioners Amendment Act 1996 extended jurisdiction to two other categories. The second category, that used to be excluded, is termed a 'family health service provider' and covers general medical practitioners, community dentists, opticians and pharmacists.[135] The services provided by these persons used to be outside the remit of the HSC and came within the jurisdiction of the NHS tribunals that have been abolished. The Health Service Commissioners (Amendment) Act 2000 has made clear that such family health service providers can be investigated even after they have retired, but the HSC must not entertain a complaint if it is made more than three years after the practitioner retired.[136] The third category is termed an 'independent provider' and covers bodies outside the NHS who are contracted to provide services for NHS patients.[137] This category will cover private hospitals and nursing homes in so far as they are providing services for the NHS.

(4) What Can be Investigated?

21.51   As with the PCA, the HSC may investigate complaints that injustice has been sustained in consequence of maladministration connected to actions taken by health service bodies and independent providers.[138] Complaints are not, however, confined to injustice through maladministration. The HSC can investigate in addition complaints of injustice or hardship in consequence of failures in the service provided by any of the three categories. This can be a complaint about a failure in the actual service provided or failure to provide the service at all.[139] The difference in wording would clearly indicate that there can be a finding that injustice or hardship has been caused by a failure in the service provided even if there has been no maladministration. Yet, as with the PCA, the HSC is expressly prevented from questioning the merits of an exercise of discretion made by a health service body.[140] So if a failure to provide a service had resulted from the exercise of a discretion, the HSC could not criticize the quality of the decision unless there had been maladministration. On the other hand, the HSC could still find that the complainant had suffered hardship through the failure to provide the service and

---

[134] Health Services Commissioners Act 1993, s 2.

[135] ibid s 2A.

[136] Health Service Commissioners (Amendment) Act 2000, ss 1–3.

[137] Health Service Commissioners Act 1993, s 2B.

[138] See ibid s 3(1)(c) (for health service bodies) and s 3(1C)(c) (for independent providers). Strangely there is no reference to maladministration in connection with family health service providers.

[139] See ibid s 3(1) for health service bodies, s 3(1A) for family health service providers and s 3(1C) for independent providers.

[140] See s 3(4). In the case of family health service providers and independent providers the HSC is excluded from questioning the merits of any decisions taken without maladministration, whether or not a discretion is involved; see s 3(5) and (6).

it would seem that because of the wider terms of reference the HSC can make broader criticism and more far-reaching recommendations.[141]

The HSC used to be expressly prohibited from investigating actions connected **21.52** with the diagnosis of illness or the care or treatment of a patient which in the opinion of the HSC was taken solely in consequence of clinical judgment.[142] The term 'clinical judgment' has never been statutorily defined but in 1996 the Minister steering the 1996 Bill gave the following explanation:

> The essence of the concept is that clinical judgment is that which a health professional makes by virtue of his or her particular skills, expertise and training, and that which a lay person could not make.[143]

This exclusion received substantial criticism as a large proportion of complaints **21.53** had to be rejected on this ground.[144] The 1996 Act not only dropped the prohibition but went further and provided that the examination of clinical judgment can include the questioning of the merits of such judgments even if the decision was taken without maladministration.[145] So now clinical judgments can be more closely scrutinized than administrative decisions. This situation creates the anomaly that while the HSC cannot question the merits of a decision to refuse a service because of resource implications, he can question a refusal to provide a treatment based on clinical judgment. The changes to the HSC's remit have not surprisingly increased his workload and in the last annual report for 2000–01 it was stated that 2,595 complaints had been received of which 241 had been accepted for investigation. Of the cases that were accepted for investigation, 77 per cent concerned matters of clinical judgment. It seems that the medical professions generally believe that the investigations into clinical decisions benefit the professions.[146]

D. The Commissions for Local Administration

(1) General

As indicated earlier, the Local Government Act 1974 created two Commissions **21.54** for Local Administration, one for England and one for Wales.[147] Each Commission consists of a number of commissioners who are known as Local

---

[141] Stacey (n 6 above) 186 gives the example of a man having to wait 18 months for nose surgery, where the major cause was a decision not to appoint an additional consultant.
[142] See Health Service Commissioners Act 1993, s 5.
[143] *Hansard*, HC vol 268, col 898 (John Horam).
[144] See 1979–80 HC 465.
[145] See Health Service Commissioners (Amendment) Act 1996, s 6, which amended ss 3 and 5 of the 1993 Act.
[146] See Cabinet Office Review (n 23 above) para 1.31.
[147] See Local Government Act 1974, s 23.

Commissioners for Administration (LCAs).[148] They are appointed by the Crown and have the same independence as the PCA and the HSC.[149] In the case of Wales only one LCA has been appointed but the PCA is a member of both Commissions in an ex officio capacity. There are three LCAs for England who deal with complaints from particular areas of the country.[150] The Commissions themselves supervise the organization, finance and accommodation of the ombudsmen but otherwise the LCAs act independently. Unlike the PCA and the HSC the LCAs have no direct connection to Parliament, though the Select Committee does from time to time take evidence from the LCAs and gives them support. The lack of direct parliamentary backing does detract from the prestige of the LCAs. Originally the Commissions were financed by and reported to 'representative bodies' who represented the local authorities.[151] This undermined the independence of the system[152] and s 25 of the Local Government and Housing Act 1989 abolished the representative bodies. The Commissions are now funded by central government out of the revenue support grant. They now publish their own reports on the discharge of their functions but the local authority associations must be consulted on the draft reports and receive the final reports.[153] As with the PCA the function of the LCAs is to investigate complaints of injustice caused by maladministration, but as with the HSC there are important differences.

(2) The Bodies Subject to Investigation and Access

21.55 Originally the bodies subject to investigation were the various local authorities, joint boards of local authorities, police, fire and water authorities. However the Local Government Act 1988 extended the remit of the LCAs to the various development corporations and to the Commission for New Towns.[154] Education appeal committees and the flood defence and drainage functions of the Environment Agency have since been added. As well as the standard exclusion of personnel, commercial and contractual matters, the LCAs cannot investigate matters relating to the internal regulation of schools and actions concerning the commencement of legal proceedings and criminal investigations.[155] The LCA is also precluded from investigating an action which, in his opinion, affects all or most of the inhabitants of the authority concerned. This exclusion would presumably prevent an investigation into a

---

[148] Advisers can also be appointed under ibid s 23 as amended by s 22 of the Local Government and Housing Act 1989.
[149] ibid s 23(4) and (6).
[150] ibid s 24(8) requires such a division.
[151] See ibid s 24.
[152] See D Widdicombe, *Report of the Committee of Inquiry into the Conduct of Local Authority Business* (Cmnd 9797, 1986) para 9.82.
[153] Local Government and Housing Act 1989, s 25.
[154] Local Government Act 1988, s 29 and Sch 3, para 4.
[155] Local Government Act 1974, s 26 and Sch 5.

general complaint into the level of council tax or the way services have been provided. As with the PCA, LCAs should not investigate if the complainant has a remedy before a court of law or tribunal but there is the same discretion to override this exclusion. Originally the complaint had to be referred to the LCA by a member of the authority but the Local Government Act 1988 removed this member filter and now complaints can be made directly in writing by the complainant to the authority, though a member can still refer complaints.[156] The right of direct access resulted in a dramatic increase in the number of complaints.[157] The complaint must be in writing and must specify the action connected with the alleged maladministration, but the courts have held that it is sufficient to allege simply that injustice has been caused.[158]

(3) The Conduct of Investigation

The process of investigation is very similar to that of the PCA. As well as determining whether the complaint is within his jurisdiction, the LCA must be satisfied that the authority has already been informed of the complaint and has been provided with a reasonable opportunity to investigate and reply to the complaint.[159] However it seems that the LCAs quite frequently attempt to achieve a 'local settlement'. This is done by sending the complaint to the chief officer for comment on the understanding that the comment may be sent to the complainant. The Cabinet Office Review reports that in 1998/99 out of 15,653 decided cases, local settlement accounted for 2,251.[160] Such local settlements will not result in a formal report. Where the LCA decides to make a formal investigation, as with the PCA the investigation must be conducted in private and those complained against given an opportunity for comment.[161] The decision of Collins J in the *Turpin*[162] case, however, means that the LCAs may have to give the complainant a chance to comment on any evidence that they receive from the authority, before coming to a decision.

21.56

The LCAs, like the PCA and HSC, have wide powers to require information to be produced and to compel the attendance and examination of witnesses. Section 32(3) of the Local Government Act 1974 gives the authorities being investigated a power to give notice that it would not be in the public interest for documents or

21.57

---

[156] Local Government Act 1988, s 29 and Sch 3, para 5.
[157] See Birkinshaw (n 83 above) 219.
[158] *R v Local Commissioner for Administration for the North and East Area of England, ex p Bradford MBC* [1979] QB 287.
[159] Local Government Act 1974, s 26(5).
[160] Cabinet Office Review (n 23 above) para 1.33.
[161] Local Government Act 1974, s 28.
[162] *R (on the application of Turpin) v Commissioner for Local Administration* [2001] EWHC Admin 503; [2002] JPL 326 (discussed above in connection with the PCA).

information to be disclosed. In *Re Complaint against Liverpool City Council*[163] the original wording was interpreted by the Divisional Court as meaning that where such a notice had been given, the authority was entitled to refuse disclosure. Section 184 of the Local Government, Planning and Land Act 1980, however, amended the wording of s 32(3) so that the LCA is in the same position as the PCA and the effect of the notice is only to prevent the LCA disclosing such information and not to excuse the authority from disclosure. Section 29(7) of the Local Government Act 1974 provides that the right to require information does not compel disclosure when the person would not be compelled to produce the information in civil proceedings before a High Court. This provision suggests that the doctrine of public interest immunity could prevent disclosure. However in *Re Subpoena (Adoption: Commissioner for Local Administration)*[164] Carnwath J made clear that, while the courts might in exceptional circumstances prevent disclosure, the balance would always be in favour of disclosure and the judgment should be primarily for the LCA to make.

(4) Remedies and Enforcement

21.58   Section 30 of the 1974 Act requires the LCA to produce a report where the LCA has decided to conduct an investigation and a statement where he has decided not to conduct an investigation.[165] The report must set out the results of the investigation and the statement the reasons for not investigating. The report or statement must be sent to the complainant (and the member if referred by a member) and to the authority (and to any other authority or person who was alleged to have taken or authorized the action).[166] Copies of the report must be made available for public inspection for three weeks but must not identify or name the persons involved.[167] Where there has been an investigation the report will either conclude that there has been no injustice caused by maladministration (or at least no injustice if there has been maladministration) or will make a finding that there has been injustice caused by maladministration. As with the PCA, the LCA is prevented from questioning the merits of a discretionary decision unless there has been maladministration.[168] Where injustice through maladministration has been found, the report has to be laid before the authority concerned. At this stage the legislation does not expressly authorize the LCA to make a recommendation as to how the injustice is to be remedied but in practice such a recommendation is always made. The standard remedy recommended is the payment of a sum of money as

---

[163] [1977] 1 WLR 995.
[164] [1996] 2 FLR 629.
[165] In *R (on the application of Maxhuni) v Commissioner for Local Administration* [2002] EWCA Civ 973; [2003] BLGR 113.
[166] Local Government Act 1974, s 30(1).
[167] ibid s 30(3).
[168] ibid s 34(3).

compensation, but where possible the LCA will want the complainant to be restored to the position she would have been if the maladministration had not taken place by providing the grant or repairing the home, etc. In order to prevent the authority risking being surcharged, the authority is now expressly authorized to incur such expenditure as appear appropriate to make a payment or confer some other benefit.[169]

Like all the public sector ombudsmen, the LCA has no power to enforce any recommendations. Originally the only way that pressure could be put on an authority that defied an adverse report was to issue a further report. The authority is under a duty to consider the first adverse report and to notify the LCA within three months of receipt[170] or any longer period specified by the LCA what action the authority has taken or proposes to take.[171] A further report must then be issued if the authority fails to respond within the three months or the period specified or its response is considered unsatisfactory. This report must make recommendations as to how the injustice should be remedied and how similar injustices can be prevented in the future.[172] The authority may, however, still fail to make an adequate response and the Local Government and Housing Act 1989 strengthened the process and has imposed a further stage. First, where a further report has been issued, the full council must consider the report and no member can vote if he has been criticized in the report.[173] Secondly, if there is no response or the response is still considered unsatisfactory, the LCA may require the authority to publish an agreed statement in a local newspaper setting out in full the recommendations of the LCA and the extent to which the authority has failed to comply.[174] The authority can, if it wishes, also set out its reasons for non-compliance in the statement. If the authority fails to publish such a statement, the LCA can do so and charge the authority the cost. The sanction for non-compliance is therefore a mixture of bad publicity and the costs of publication. **21.59**

It is difficult to assess whether the changes have had any effect but it seems that a majority of further reports do not produce compliance. Birkinshaw stated in 1994 that since 1974 302 further reports had been issued and there had been 201 cases of unsatisfactory outcomes.[175] He also found that in only one case had the publication of a statement resulted in compliance but this is perhaps not surprising since by that stage the authority has little to lose by non-compliance. The Financial Management and Policy Review of the Commission for England in **21.60**

---

[169] ibid s 31(3) as amended by Local Government Act 1988.
[170] This time limit was inserted by Local Government and Housing Act 1989, s 26(1).
[171] See Local Government Act 1974, s 31.
[172] ibid s 31(2A) and (2B) as inserted by Local Government and Housing Act 1989, s 26.
[173] ibid s 31A as inserted by Local Government and Housing Act 1989, s 28.
[174] ibid s 31(2D), (2E) and (2F) as inserted by Local Government and Housing Act 1989, s 26.
[175] See Birkinshaw (n 83 above) 224.

1996 found that over the last 20 years about 6 per cent of the recommendations had not wholly been accepted. The obvious reason for non-compliance must be that the authorities do not believe that injustice through maladministration has been suffered. In this regard the Annual Report of the Commission for England for 1995–96 advised that more care should be given to explaining why a finding of injustice through maladministration had been made and that authorities should be given advance notice of criticisms that might be included in the final report. There have been suggestions that the LCA's recommendations should be enforceable in the courts as is the case in Northern Ireland.[176] However, as with the PCA, most opinion would seem to be against making the recommendations legally enforceable.[177] The most favoured solution would appear to be for the Select Committee to take oversight of the Commissions for Local Administration so that the Committee could put pressure on authorities that refused to comply.[178]

(5) Advice and Guidance on Good Administration

21.61 As is the case with the other public sector ombudsmen, the LCAs have got no power to initiate investigations themselves. However, unlike the other ombudsmen, the two Commissions have been given a specific power to provide any of the authorities under their jurisdiction with advice and guidance about good administrative practice.[179] So they have been expressly given the function of improving the general standard of administrative practice of government as well as redressing individual injustices. Using this power the English Commission has issued a series of papers giving 'Guidance on Good Practice' on a range of matters. For example, a paper has been issued on 'Good Administrative Practice',[180] which sets out principles of good administration. Failure to abide by such principles would clearly be grounds for a finding of maladministration in a particular case but whether there had been injustice through maladministration should always depend on the particular factual circumstances. We have seen that before investigating a complaint the LCA must be satisfied that the authority has been given a reasonable opportunity to investigate the complaint. The internal complaint mechanisms of the authorities are therefore very important to the operation of the ombudsman system. However, studies have shown that the internal

---

[176] See the recommendations of the Widdicombe Committee (n 152 above) and Lord Woolf, *Access to Justice* (1996).

[177] The Financial Management and Policy Review in 1996 came to no firm conclusion

[178] The Select Committee recommended this in 1986 and so did the Financial Management and Policy Review in 1996. The Cabinet Review has also recommended that the work of the LCAs should be subsumed in a new Commission that would report to the Select Committee.

[179] See Local Government Act 1974, s 23(12A) as inserted by Local Government and Housing Act 1989, s 23.

[180] Guidance on Good Practice 2 (1995), available at www.lgo.org.uk.

complaints systems of local authorities are often very unsatisfactory.[181] The English Commission's first guidance paper, 'Devising a Complaints System', therefore tackled this problem and provides advice on how an effective system can be instituted. The guidance is not legally binding but again the absence of an effective complaints system could in itself be evidence of maladministration.

(6) The Model Code of Conduct for Members of Local Authorities

Section 31 of the Local Government and Housing Act 1989 empowered the government to issue a National Code of Local Government Conduct. This Code was not directly enforceable. However, where the LCA made a finding of maladministration involving a member of the authority and the member's conduct constituted a breach of the Code, the report had to name the member and the breach unless this was considered unjust.[182] Breach of the Code was not automatically deemed to be maladministration but it was evidence of maladministration. Further, the courts have upheld findings of maladministration based on breaches of the Code. In *R v Local Commissioner for Administration in North and North East England, ex p Liverpool City Council*[183] the Court of Appeal accepted that a finding of maladministration could be based on a breach of the Code, though the court appeared to accept that breach of the Code and maladministration were not automatically synonymous.[184]

21.62

The position has been radically changed by Pt III of the Local Government Act 2000. The effect in England is to take away the LCAs' function of enforcing ethical standards and to set up a complicated and more judicial system of enforcement. The National Code has been abolished and every authority is required to adopt its own code but this must be based on a model code and general principles laid down by central government.[185] Section 52 imposes a duty on members to make a declaration that they will observe the code. Further, a Standards Board for England has been created whose function is to enforce the codes. The Board is given the power to investigate allegations that a member has failed to comply with the authority's own code.[186] The investigation is carried out by ethical standards officers employed by the Board[187] and the process is very similar to investigations by the LCAs. The final stage is that the matters should be referred to an adjudication

21.63

---

[181] See Norman Lewis et al, *Complaint Procedures in Local Government* (University of Sheffield, 1987).

[182] See Local Government Act 1974, s 30 as amended by Local Government and Housing Act 1989, s 32.

[183] [2001] 1 All ER 462.

[184] See also *R v Commissioner for Local Administration, ex p Blakey* [1994] 1 All ER 961.

[185] See Local Government Act 2000, ss 49–51.

[186] ibid s 58.

[187] Except in Wales where the Local Commissioner for Wales carries out the investigation; see ibid s 69.

panel for adjudication by a case tribunal. The consequence can be that the member can be suspended or disqualified. The Act does not prevent the LCAs from investigating complaints of maladministration involving breaches of the code and presumably breaches of the code can still amount to maladministration. However, if a LCA in the course of an investigation forms the opinion that the complaint relates partly to a matter that could be subject to an investigation by an ethical standards officer, the Standards Board must be consulted.[188] The ethical standards officer must equally consult the LCA if in the course of an investigation he considers the matter could be the subject of an investigation by the LCA.[189] The result of this consultation can be that the person bringing the allegation or making the complaint can be informed of how he can also complain to the LCA or make an allegation to the ethical standards officer, whichever is the case. It would therefore seem that there can be two parallel investigations, one by the LCA and one by the ethical standards officer. This can be appropriate since the function of the new system is to punish the member for breach of the code and not to remedy the injustice caused by the maladministration, which is the function of the LCA. In the case of Wales the National Assembly has issued orders and regulations that give to the LCA for Wales the job of investigating allegations that members of local authorities in Wales have breached the code.

E. The Relationship Between the Public Sector Ombudsmen and the Information Commissioner

21.64   One of the PCA's tasks was to investigate complaints that information had been wrongly withheld under the Code of Practice on Access to Government Information. The Code has now been replaced by the Freedom of Information Act 2000 and an Information Commissioner has been created whose job is to promote good practice and to investigate complaints that authorities have failed to comply with the new requirement to provide information. The new Commissioner has significant enforcement powers and his decisions are enforceable by the courts.[190] As the Act extends to local authorities, the NHS and other public bodies covered by the public sector ombudsmen, it has been necessary to provide for disclosure of information between the Commissioner and these ombudsmen. Section 76 of the Freedom of Information Act 2000 permits the Commissioner to pass relevant information if it appears that the information relates to a matter that could be the subject of an investigation by that particular ombudsman. Similarly the ombudsmen are authorized to pass on information that

---

[188] Local Government Act 2000, s 67(2).
[189] ibid s 67(3).
[190] Freedom of Information Act 2000, Pt IV.

might be relevant to the Commissioner's powers of investigation and enforcement.[191] So, as with the new system of enforcement of the conduct of officers, investigation by the Information Commissioner will not prevent a separate investigation by one of the public sector ombudsmen.

F. Evaluation and Future Reform

The institution of the public sector ombudsman is now well established in **21.65**
England and is widely regarded as successful. In their submission to the Cabinet Office Review, JUSTICE emphasized the value of the ombudsmen in providing an independent investigation which was informal and free.[192] They provide an invaluable method by which individuals can have their complaints against government remedied and in several instances have discovered important instances of systematic maladministration. On the other hand there is a general concern that they have too low a profile and there are criticisms of their working methods. The Cabinet Office Review was in particular concerned that the system had failed to adapt to the new shape of modern government. The complex structure of the public sector provision of services means that a complainant often does not know who to address his complaint to in the first place. This confusion can then be made even worse by the introduction of independent complaints examiners in the public sector as, from the point of view of the complainant, it creates a multi-layered complaints process. This process must usually be gone through even before approaching one of the public sector ombudsmen. It may then be unclear which of the three public sector ombudsmen must be approached. The Cabinet Office Review gives the example of a complaint about the discharge from hospital to local authority social services. In such a case, the complaint crosses boundaries between agencies and may have to be pursued through two or more complaint processes and then to two or more ombudsmen. The Review therefore makes the central recommendation for the creation of a new Commission of Ombudsmen combining the current PCA, HSC and LCA in England. The new commission would operate as a single gateway for all complaints and the MP filter would be removed so that all complainants could deal directly with the ombudsman for the first time. The new commission would be answerable to Parliament. The Review also recommends that the new collegiate structure should have a strong customer service ethos and should be able to operate informally and achieve early resolution of complaints. In this regard the Review would seem to be emphasizing the ombudsman's function of remedying individual grievances.

---

[191] ibid Sch 7 amending the appropriate legislation.
[192] See Cabinet Office Review (n 23 above) para 2.3.

21.66 The Scottish Public Services Ombudsman Act 2002 has adopted the recommendation and created a 'one stop shop' for public service complaints in Scotland by bringing together the Scottish Parliamentary, Health, Local Government and Housing Association Ombudsmen in one collegiate body. It is led by the Scottish Public Services Ombudsman and up to three deputies, each of which is to oversee a particular public service area. The government in 2001 announced that it intended to replace existing arrangements in England and Wales with a unified and flexible ombudsman body to which the public would have direct access. At the time of writing there is no sign of legislation being brought forward.

22

PUBLIC INQUIRIES AS A PART OF PUBLIC ADMINISTRATION

A. Introduction

(1) The Origins of the Public Inquiry and its Evolution

The public inquiry is an important feature of the English administrative **22.01** process. It is a device by which both public decision-makers can be informed and those affected by the decision protected. A public inquiry is an everyday occurrence and every year thousands of public inquiries take place. However the term 'public inquiry' is imprecise in that it can apply to many different types of procedures. The most common type of public inquiry is the planning inquiry, which arises in connection with the appeal against the refusal of planning permission, but there are then various forms that a planning inquiry can take. At the other extreme is the rather misleadingly named 'tribunal of inquiry' that can be set up under the Tribunals of Inquiry (Evidence) Act 1921 to investigate matters of urgent public importance such as public scandals and disasters.

22.02   The public inquiry has its origins in the private Acts of Enclosure that were adopted between 1745 and 1845. Private legislation confers particular powers or benefits on any person or body of persons—including individuals, local authorities, companies, or corporations—in excess of or in conflict with the general law. The Bill is in effect a petition to Parliament from someone outside Parliament. From about 1700 a growing number of private Bills were concerned with the construction of works such as toll roads, canals, railways, and reservoirs as well as the local government of boroughs and other areas. The normal procedure for the enactment of a private Bill is that, at the second reading stage in each House, a small committee is set up that hears arguments and evidence put by the promoters and opponents of the Bill. The Enclosure Act 1801 provided for the appointment of a commission of inquiry to examine each individual scheme and it is in these procedures that the germ of the modern public inquiry can be discerned. The appointment of a commission or inspector to hold the inquiry obviously saved parliamentary time. The General Inclosure Act 1845 refined the procedure so that the application for what was termed 'a provisional order' was made to the government who would appoint the inspector, even though the provisional order had still to be approved by Parliament.

22.03   Subsequently this provisional order procedure was used to assist the passing of private Acts for the taking of land for the development of canals, railways, harbours, bridges and reservoirs. The procedure was then adapted for the granting of powers to public authorities to regulate the use of private property and to acquire private property to provide public services. Eventually the need for final parliamentary sanction was removed and a government department made the final decision. Indeed in the case of planning and compulsory purchase inquiries today the role of central government has become nominal and in the vast majority of cases the final decision is made by the inspector on behalf of the government. Thus in the recent decision in *R (on behalf of Alconbury Developments Ltd) v Secretary of State for the Environment*[1] Tuckey LJ in his judgment in the Divisional Court pointed out that:

> There are about 500,000 planning applications a year of which 130 are called in. There are about 13,000 appeals to the Secretary of State of which about 1000 are recovered so Inspectors decide the vast majority of appeals. Of the called-in decisions and recovered appeals, the Secretary of State follows the recommendation of the Inspector in about 95% of cases.

(2) A Classification of Public Inquiries

22.04   Most Acts of Parliament that are concerned with public administration will either impose a duty on the government to hold an inquiry in certain circumstances or

---

[1] [2001] JPL 291 at [61].

will give government a general power to hold an inquiry. On the other hand there is nothing to prevent a government department deciding to hold an inquiry without express statutory authority. There normally can be an implied statutory power to set up an inquiry and inquiries can be set up under the royal prerogative as in the case of Royal Commissions. So distinctions can be made between statutory and non-statutory inquiries and between mandatory inquiries and discretionary inquiries. However the names can sometimes be confusing as the Tribunals and Inquiries Act 1992 uses the term statutory inquiry but defines it as an inquiry or hearing held because of a statutory duty.[2] Most inquiries are held in public and there may be a statutory requirement to hold the inquiry in public. However this is not always the case and it would seem that there is no general presumption that inquiries have to be held in public.

Adopting a more functional classification, most inquiries concern a specific dispute between individuals and the state. Thus an inquiry or hearing is normally part of the process by which an applicant can appeal to government against some regulatory control, such as the refusal of planning permission to carry out development. Similarly the inquiry is part of the process under which an individual can object to a project such as a motorway or airport that may involve compulsory purchase of land and otherwise affect the interests of the individual. A rather different type of inquiry is when the inquiry is set up to investigate a particular past event such as an accident or a scandal. Into this class can also be put those inquiries which help to advise the government on future decisions, whether it be the redrawing of electoral boundaries or the level of the minimum wage. Such inquiries are a means of providing the government with information and policy advice as to future action.

22.05

(3) The Purpose of Public Inquiries

In the case of inquiries into appeals or objections, there has always been an ambivalence as to whether the primary purpose is to give rights to the individuals who will be affected by the outcome or to provide the minister with all the necessary facts and argument necessary to make a sensible and rational decision. The courts have always seen one of their responsibilities as protecting the individual against abuse of power by public authorities. One way of achieving this is to ensure that those affected by the decision are given the opportunity to test the decision before an unbiased person: this is termed today the right to a fair hearing but used to be referred to as the rules of natural justice. The courts themselves have been prepared to impose what they consider to be the minimum standards of fairness onto the administrative process. The public inquiry can therefore be seen as

22.06

---

[2] However s 16 of the Tribunals and Inquiries Act 1992 also includes within the term 'statutory inquiry' any inquiries designated by order for that purpose.

an additional statutory device for ensuring that power is exercised fairly. It is an additional safeguard in that compliance with the statutory procedures will not prevent the courts holding that the process was unfair.[3] On the other hand the courts have been ambivalent as to the extent that the process should be judicialized; especially the post-inquiry procedures. Thus in *R v Local Government Board, ex p Arlidge*[4] the House of Lords held that, where an inquiry had been held, the person affected had no right to see the report of the inspector or to appear before the civil servant who made the eventual decision. On the other hand, in *Errington v Minister of Health*[5] the Court of Appeal held that where, after the inquiry, the Minister received new evidence from the local authority seeking a slum clearance order, he should have consulted those objecting to the order.[6]

22.07   Dissatisfaction with inquiries led to the setting up of the Committee on Tribunals and Inquiries (the Franks Committee), which reported in 1957. The Franks report pointed out that there were two contrasting perceptions of the inquiry: the administrative view and the judicial view. The administrative view is that inquiries are just an extension of departmental decision-making and the main purpose is to inform the mind of the minister. The minister should therefore not be constrained by rules. In contrast the judicial view saw the inquiry as akin to a court of law with formal rules and the decision being taken directly on the evidence presented to the inquiry. Franks purported to reject both views and to adopt a balanced approach. The report stated that:

> Our general conclusion is that those procedures cannot be classified as purely administrative or purely judicial. They are not purely administrative because of the provision for a special procedure preliminary to the decision—a feature not to be found in the ordinary course of administration—and because this procedure, as we have shown, involves the testing of an issue, often partly in public. They are not on the other hand purely judicial, because the final decision cannot be reached by the application of rules and must allow the exercise of wide discretion in the balancing of public and private interest. Neither view at its extreme is tenable, nor should either be emphasied at the expense of the other.

22.08   Franks recommended that the public inquiry should be characterized by the principles of openness, fairness and impartiality and, as a result of Franks, most appeal and objection inquiries are bound by statutory rules of procedure. These rules

---

[3] See *Performance Cars Ltd v Secretary of State for the Environment* (1977) 34 P & CR 92. It has been asserted that where a breach of natural justice was alleged outside of the scope of the inquiry procedure rules, there is a heavy burden of proof of the complainant. However this argument was rejected by David Widdicombe QC (sitting as a Deputy Judge) in *Reading BC v Secretary of State for the Environment* [1986] JPL 115.

[4] [1915] AC 120.

[5] [1935] 1 KB 249.

[6] In doing this the court relied on the now discredited distinction between purely administrative and quasi-judicial functions.

govern not only the way the inquiry itself is run but also the pre- and post-inquiry stages. Although the rules still leave the eventual decision to either the inspector or his minister, in substance a quasi-judicial structure has been imposed on what was originally primarily an administrative function.

A purpose that was not discussed by Franks is public participation in policy-mak- **22.09** ing. This is because Franks was mainly concerned with protecting the rights of those directly affected by the outcome: usually the property owners who wished to develop their land or to prevent it being compulsorily purchased for a public scheme. The rules do not usually give third parties express procedural rights to participate in the inquiry but inspectors usually permit neighbours and other to take part. In the standard appeal or objection inquiry this does not cause much difficulty as the policies being applied are usually reasonably clear and uncon-tested and the inquiry will only be concerned with site-specific issues. In contrast in the case of projects of national significance such as nuclear power stations and airports, the policies behind the project may be controversial and unsettled. As a result those opposing the project (which can often include important pressure groups) will wish to challenge those policies. So as well as providing those who will be directly affected by the project with a forum at which they can attempt to pro-tect their rights, inquiries into such projects can also be seen as a move towards a more participatory democracy. In their critique of the Sizewell B inquiry,[7] O'Riordan et al argued that such a major inquiry had shifted from its origin in individual rights, resting on property rights, to become an institution of policy formulation and political decision-making in an open forum.[8] While such a painstaking and public analysis of important national policies can turn the major inquiry into a powerful instrument of accountability and legitimization, from the government point of view it makes the processing of major projects through the planning system increasingly difficult. It also places a strain on the traditional pro-cedures of the public inquiry and increases the costs and delay caused by the in-quiry procedure.

(4) Tribunals and Inquiries Contrasted

Tribunals and inquiries are often linked together. The Franks Committee was set up **22.10** to look into both and the Council on Tribunals, which was set up to keep the struc-ture of the tribunal system under constant review, also has responsibilities regarding inquiries. The traditional distinction between the two used to be that tribunals make final decisions, while inquiries result in recommendations. However this dis-tinction has become blurred by the fact that in the case of numerous inquiries the

---

[7] See T O'Riordan, R Kemp and M Purdue, *Sizewell B: An Anatomy of the Inquiry* (London: Macmillan, 1988).
[8] ibid 53.

inspector makes the final decision but it is still significant that a minister will retain the right to take the matter out of the hands of the inspector. Another distinction is independence as those presiding over a tribunal will normally be more independent than inspectors: the Planning Inspectorate, although it is now an executive agency, is still part of government. The crucial distinction lies in their work. Tribunals tend to settle disputes by applying set rules, even if those rules are infused with policy. Inspectors in the case of inquiries are much more involved with pure policy, whether it is applying policy in respect of inquiries relating to appeals or objections or coming up with policy recommendations as in the more general inquiries. So, as a generalization, tribunals carry out a judicial function, while inquiries carry out an administrative function but take on some of the techniques of the courts.

(5) Inquiries and the Human Rights Act 1998

22.11   Most of the rights listed in the European Convention on Human Rights (ECHR) can have implications about the way that inquiries go about their business. The most directly applicable is Article 6, which provides that in the determination of his civil rights everyone is entitled to a fair and public hearing within a reasonable time by an independent and impartial tribunal established by law. In *Bryan v UK*[9] the European Court of Human Rights (ECtHR) held that while a planning inspector might not have the requisite appearance of independence, the power of the High Court to review the legality of the decisions of inspectors was sufficient for compliance with Article 6. This decision left open the question of whether there was compliance when the final decision was made by the government and the person holding the inquiry only made recommendations to the minister. However in *R (on the application of Holding & Barnes plc) v Secretary of State for the Environment, Transport and the Regions*[10] the House of Lords, reversing the decision of the Divisional Court, held that, while the Secretary of State was not himself an independent and impartial tribunal, there was again sufficient power of review by the High Court to satisfy Article 6. If the decision had gone the other way it would in effect have meant that where civil rights and obligations were involved, persons holding inquiries would have to make the final decisions, turning them into tribunals.

22.12   Article 6 could also be interpreted as requiring an inquiry or at least some similar form of oral hearing when civil rights and obligations were being determined. In this regard the Court of Appeal in *Begum (Runa) v Tower Hamlets LBC*[11] held that, with regard to Article 6, administrative decisions could be divided up into those where there would generally be a need to afford persons whose civil rights and

---

[9]   Series A No 335-A (1991) 21 EHRR 342.
[10]   [2001] UKHL 23; [2001] 2 WLR 1389.
[11]   [2002] EWCA Civ 239; [2002] 1 WLR 2491.

obligations were being affected with a right to a hearing and those where no such right arose. Laws LJ laid down the following analysis to be applied, in deciding whether Article 6 had been observed:

> Where the scheme's subject matter generally or systematically involves the resolution of primary fact, the court will incline to look for procedures akin to our conventional mechanisms for finding fact: cross-examination, access to documents, a strictly independent decision-maker. To the extent that procedures of that kind are not given by the first instance approach, the court will look to see how far they are given by the appeal or review; and the judicial review jurisdiction (or its equivalent in the shape of a statutory appeal on law) may not suffice.

The Court of Appeal in *R (on the application of Adlard) v Secretary of State for the Environment, Transport and the Regions*[12] held that the statutory process of determining planning applications fell into the same category as in *Begum*. It was therefore found that Article 6 did not require there to be an oral hearing of any sort before a decision by the local planning authority granting planning permission. The House of Lords upheld the decision in *Begum* but did so on slightly different grounds.[13] Lord Hoffmann, who gave the main opinion, said that he now considered that it did not matter whether there were many or few occasions when the decision-maker had to make findings of fact. He basically found that where administrative decisions are being made, there is no need for a mechanism for independent findings of fact or a full appeal as long as the overall process is lawful and fair. Lawfulness and fairness can be ensured by judicial review. The consequence is that it will be very difficult to use Article 6 to found a right to the equivalent of a public inquiry.

22.13

B. Inquiries into Appeals and Objections: The Planning Inquiries Model

(1) Introduction

Parliament has invested public authorities with wide ranging powers to regulate activities and to provide services. Both functions involve interference with the property rights of individuals and so the statute that sets up the regulatory scheme or authorizes the compulsory purchase of land, will usually provide for a right to appeal against the refusal of permission or a right to object to the compulsory purchase order. The appeal or objection will be made to a government department and there will normally be a right to a hearing before a person appointed by the government. This can, but does not always have to, take the form of a public inquiry. For example, s 79 of the Town and Country Planning Act 1990 simply

22.14

---

[12] [2002] EWCA Civ 735; [2002] 1 WLR 2515.
[13] [2003] UKHL 5; [2003] 2 WLR 388.

states that, before determining an appeal against the refusal or conditional grant of planning permission, the Secretary of State shall give either the appellant or the local planning authority 'an opportunity of appearing before and being heard by a person appointed by the Secretary of State for the purpose'. Section 320 gives the Secretary of State a general power to cause a local inquiry to be held for the purposes of the exercise of any of his functions and he may decide to cause such an inquiry to be held into the appeal. However, he may decide that a less formal 'hearing' is more suitable to the subject matter of the appeal. Indeed the parties may agree that there is no need for a hearing of any kind and that the appeal can be decided by written representations.

22.15 Following the Franks report most inquiries have their own procedural rules. Section 9 of the Tribunals and Inquiries Act 1992 gives the Lord Chancellor (the Government is proposing to introduce legislation to abolish the Office of Lord Chancellor but we doubt the Bill will transfer his legal powers to another office) the power to make procedural rules for inquiries held by or on behalf of ministers, after consulting the Council on Tribunals. However, s 9 only applies where there is a statutory duty to hold either an inquiry or a hearing, though there is a power for the Lord Chancellor to extend the term 'statutory inquiry' to other designated inquiries held under statutory powers. Also where procedural rules are made not by the Lord Chancellor but by some other government department, the department will usually consult the Council on Tribunals anyway. Although numerous different sets of rules exist for different public inquiries, they tend to follow a standard pattern and indeed, where there are no rules, it is the practice to follow this pattern. In the section that follows the rules that apply to planning appeals will be examined in detail as a general model.

(2) Public Local Inquiries into Planning Appeals

22.16 Planning inquiries are governed by two main sets of rules.[14] One set, the Town and Country Planning (Inquiries Procedure) (England) Rules 2000,[15] apply mainly[16] to appeals recovered[17] by the Secretary of State and to applications called in for his

---

[14] There is now another set of rules for inquiries into major infrastructure projects. These are the Town and Country Planning (Major Infrastructure Project Inquiries Procedure) (England) Rules 2002, SI 2002/1223 that came into force on 7 June 2002.

[15] SI 2000/1624.

[16] They also apply to certain listed building consent and conservation consent appeals.

[17] Under Sch 6 to the Town and Country Planning Act 1990 regulations can be made transferring an appeal to be decided not by the Secretary of State but by an inspector. In fact the Town and Country Planning (Determination of Appeals by Appointed Person) (Prescribed Classes) Regulations 1997, SI 1997/420 have transferred all planning appeals to be decided by the appointed persons except for appeals by statutory undertakers relating to operational land. However para 3 allows the Secretary of State to recover the power to determine the appeal and about a hundred are recovered each year. The policy as to which appeals should be recovered is set out in the government's response to the Environment Committee's Fifth Report, *Planning: Appeals, Call-in and Major Public Inquiries* (Cm 43, 1986) para 36.

decision by the Secretary of State[18] and are referred to as the 'Secretary of State Rules'. It has already been pointed out that there are only a few hundred of these inquiries every year but by their nature they are the most important inquiries. The other set, the Town and Country Planning Appeals (Determination by Inspectors) (Inquiry Procedure) (England) Rules 2000[19] (referred to as the 'Inspector's Rules') apply to all the other planning appeals where it is decided to hold a local inquiry into the appeal. The Secretary of State's Rules are largely the same as the Inspector's Rules but there are important differences concerning the pre- and post-inquiry stages. In most cases the corresponding rule in the Inspector's Rules has the same number as the Secretary of State's Rules and so in the text that follows any reference to a rule number will refer to both sets of rules. Where the corresponding rule in the Inspector's Rules has a different number or there is no corresponding number this will be made clear.

The present Rules came into effect from 1 August 2000. They are the latest in a **22.17** series of inquiry rules going back to 1962. The Franks report in 1957 commented that, in regard to inquiries, a balance had to be found between 'private right and public advantage, between fair play for the individual and the efficiency of the administration'.[20]

Successive governments have tried to streamline and speed up the process, whilst **22.18** safeguarding public participation and fairness. Timetables have been imposed on the parties but as yet the government has not come up with a mechanism for ensuring that these timetables are kept.

(a) The pre-inquiry stage procedure

This stage can be important both as to the fairness of the process and its efficiency. **22.19** The duty to act fairly requires that there should be a right to see the opposing case and so the parties to the inquiry should set out in advance what their main submissions will be and the supporting evidence. Also the effective use of the time between the announcement that there will an inquiry and its commencement can make a crucial contribution to the speed and efficiency of the inquiry. The Rules address both objectives.

(i) The crucial dates

Because of the importance of adherence to a strict timetable, there has to be a date **22.20** fixed from which this timetable operates. This date is called the 'starting date' and is whichever is the later of the following dates; the date of the Secretary of State's

---

[18] Under Town and Country Planning Act 1990, s 77.
[19] SI 2000/1625.
[20] Report of the Committee on Administrative Tribunals and Inquiries (Franks report) (Cmnd 218, 1957) para 5.

written notice that he has received all the necessary documents to proceed with the appeal, or the date when he gave written notice that an inquiry was to be held.

22.21　The next important date is obviously the date of the commencement of the inquiry and r 10 provides that, unless the Secretary of State considers this to be impractical, this must be, in the case of cases decided by the Secretary of State, not later than 22 weeks after the starting date and in the case of cases decided by an inspector, not later than 20 weeks. Both the applicant and the planning authority must be given at least four weeks' notice of the date. Although this is not set out in the Rules, Circular 05/00 states that both parties can refuse the first date offered.[21] In *Lambeth LBC v Secretary of State for the Environment*[22] Glidewell LJ accepted that because of a similar statement in a previous circular, the two parties would have a legitimate expectation that they could refuse the first date offered. The more important question is the extent to which the Secretary of State could impose a date, which was disadvantageous to either party or even to a third party. There is a power in r 10(4) to vary the date of the start of the inquiry but Circular 05/00 states that the date will only be changed for exceptional reasons.

22.22　A decision fixing the date of the inquiry or refusing a variation can be challenged by way of an application for judicial review. In *Ostreicher v Secretary of State for the Environment*[23] Lord Denning accepted that such decisions could be challenged on the grounds that they were unfair. However, although the standard of review is unfairness rather than *Wednesbury* unreasonableness, the courts will not interfere unless the decision is clearly wrong. The difference between the two tests is obviously one of degree but the test of unfairness gives more power to the courts.[24] Also the way r 10 is drafted means that the Secretary of State could not fix a date after the deadlines unless he considered any earlier date impractical. In *R v Secretary of State for the Environment, Transport and the Regions, ex p Kirklees MBC*,[25] Kirklees objected to the date because of the non-availability of witnesses for that date but Collins J held that this was not enough in itself to make it impracticable to hold the inquiry at that date. He argued that inconvenience and even hardship was not the same as injustice. In this case the challenge was made before the inquiry had even started. The position could be different if it was clear after the inquiry was over that the overall process had been unfair.[26]

---

[21] Circular 05/00 *Planning Appeals: Procedures (including Inquiries into Called-In Planning Applications)*, Annex 3, para 25.

[22] [1990] JPL 196.

[23] [1978] 1 WLR 810.

[24] For an attempt to distinguish between procedural and substantive unfairness, see D Herling and M Purdue, 'The Divide between Procedural and Substantive Unfairness' [2000] JPL 666.

[25] [1999] JPL 882.

[26] On the problem of distinguishing between the individual decision and the overall process, see *Croydon LBC v Secretary of State for the Environment* [2000] PLCR 171.

(ii) *The appointment of the inspector/assessor*

The inspector is the person appointed to hold the inquiry.[27] Most inspectors ap- **22.23**
pointed to hold planning appeals are drawn from the Planning Inspectorate.
Since 1 April 1992 the Planning Inspectorate has been an executive agency and so
it is more independent of the department it serves. The Inspectorate's 1998 framework document describes one of its duties as being 'to decide appeals and process
casework efficiently and effectively, embracing the principles of openness, fairness
and impartiality'. The inspectors apply government policy but in the *Holding &*
Barnes case Lord Hoffmann accepted that with regard to matters of fact the inspectors acted independently.[28] The Planning Inspectorate also helps to train a
panel of independent inspectors to hold public inquiries and be available for nomination by the Lord Chancellor for inquiries into motorways and trunk road
schemes.

There is a power to appoint an assessor to sit with the inspector to advise him on **22.24**
such matters as the Secretary of State may specify.[29] This will normally only be
done when the inquiry concerns very technical matters on which the inspector
will not have sufficient expertise. The role of the assessor is to advise, not decide,
but there is provision for the assessor to make a separate report.

(iii) *The exchange of information and identification of the issues*

The present Rules try to ensure that the period between the starting date and the **22.25**
date of the commencement of the inquiry is not wasted. In particular the Rules require the parties to exchange what are termed 'statements of case'. The statement
of case is defined as 'a written statement which contains full particulars of the case
which a person proposes to put forward at an inquiry and a list of any documents
which that person intends to refer to or put in evidence'.[30] The purpose is to enable the parties to know as much as possible about each other's case at an early
stage. Advance knowledge, as well as achieving fairness, should help the parties to
focus on the matters that are in dispute. This can save inquiry time and even lead
to a settlement. The Rules do not expressly provide that a party is bound to keep
to the arguments and evidence in the statement of case. However this would appear implicit by the fact that r 15(10) (Secretary of State's Rules) and r 16(10)
(Inspector's Rules) give the Inspector the power to permit alterations or additions
to the statement of case, as long as the other parties are given an adequate opportunity of considering any fresh matter or document. No such power would be
necessary if parties could freely depart from the statement of case. However in

---

[27] r 2.
[28] [2001] UKHL 23; [2001] 2 WLR 1389 at [110].
[29] See Town and Country Planning Act, Sch 6, para 6(2).
[30] See r 2

Behrman v Secretary of State for the Environment[31] Forbes J held that where new evidence was produced by one party, it was incumbent upon the other party to the appeal to object and there was no duty on the inspector to check whether the document was covered by the r 6 statement. So a departure from the statement will not invalidate any subsequent decision unless it were to make the overall process wholly unfair. Inevitably some statements of case may be inadequate or incomplete but the Secretary of State or the inspector has the power under r 6(8) to require further information about the matters contained in the statement of case. A party that is concerned about the other party's statement of case can ask the Secretary of State or his inspector to exercise this power.

22.26   Both the local planning authority and the appellant/applicant should ensure that within six weeks of the starting date two copies of their statement of case are sent to the Secretary of State: where a pre-inquiry meeting is being held under r 5 the deadline is four weeks after the conclusion of that meeting.[32] It is the responsibility of the Inspectorate on receipt to send a copy of the statements to the other party 'as soon as practicable'.[33] There is no direct sanction for a failure to get the statement in on time; though it could be the basis for an application for costs if the delay was extreme and it caused another party financial loss.[34] Any challenge to the subsequent decision on the basis of breach of this rule would be unlikely to succeed. Again it would be incumbent on the other party to ask for the start of the inquiry to be delayed and only if refusal made the proceedings unfair would there be grounds for the decision to be overturned.[35] Normally it is only the local planning authority and the applicant/appellant who must provide statements of case but the Secretary of State does have a power to require any other person who wishes to appear at the inquiry to send in a statement of case within four weeks of being so notified.[36] There is also provision for those who produce statements of case to comment on the statement of case of another party: this should normally be done within nine weeks of the starting date.[37]

22.27   An innovation of the latest rules is that following the exchange of statements of case, the local planning authority and the applicant/appellant must together prepare an agreed statement of common ground and ensure that it is received by

---

[31] [1979] JPL 677.
[32] r 6(10) and (3).
[33] See r 6(4).
[34] The power to award costs is explained at paras 22.61 et seq.
[35] See *Barraclough v Secretary of State for the Environment* [1990] JPL 911 where the Deputy Judge suggested that it would be more appropriate to challenge directly the refusal to delay the inquiry rather than wait till the final determination. See also *Davies v Secretary of State for Wales* (1977) 33 P & C R 330.
[36] r 6(6).
[37] r 14.

the Secretary of State not less than four weeks before the date fixed for the inquiry.[38] The purpose is to save inquiry time by ensuring that the evidence presented to the inquiry concentrates on the issues in dispute. The common ground would normally cover factual matters such as the history of the site, the relevant planning policies and technical data. The statement of common ground should complement the 'proofs of evidence'. Persons giving evidence to the inquiry usually do so by reading a written statement prepared in advance. These proofs of evidence, together with any summary that is being provided, must also be received by the Secretary of State no later than four weeks before the inquiry or, if a timetable has been agreed, by the date fixed in that timetable.[39]

The Franks Committee had recommended that the minister, who will finally **22.28** make the decision, should, whenever possible, make available before the inquiry a statement of relevant policy, but this was rejected. However, where a pre-inquiry meeting is held under r 5 the Secretary of State must send out, with the notification of such a meeting, a statement of the matters he particularly wishes to be informed about. Where the inspector is making the ultimate decision he may, within 12 weeks of the starting date, send to the parties a similar statement.[40]

(iv) Pre-inquiry meetings

A 'pre-inquiry meeting' is defined in the Rules as 'a meeting held before an inquiry **22.29** to consider what may be done with a view to securing that the inquiry is conducted efficiently and expeditiously'.[41] In the case of decisions that are to be made by the Secretary of State, under r 5 (Secretary of State's Rules) he can cause a pre-inquiry meeting to be held if he thinks it necessary. Indeed there is a presumption that such a meeting will be held when he expects that the inquiry will last for eight days or more. There is the same power where the inspector is to make the decision[42] and even in the case where the Secretary of State's Rules apply, where no pre-inquiry meeting has been fixed under r 5, the inspector has a further power to hold pre-inquiry meetings.[43] The significance of a pre-inquiry meeting being held under r 5 is that it also triggers off other special procedures appropriate for major inquiries. It seems therefore that r 5 will only be invoked for major inquiries and there is a special code of practice that applies to the preparation of such inquiries.[44] There are, however, now special rules for what are termed 'major infrastructure

---

[38] r 14 (Secretary of State's Rules) and r 15 (Inspector's Rules).
[39] r 13(3) (Secretary of State's Rules) and r 14(3) (Inspector's Rules).
[40] r 7(1) (Inspector's Rules).
[41] r 2.
[42] r 7(2) (Inspector's Rules).
[43] r 7(1) (Secretary of State's Rules).
[44] See Circular 05/00, Annex 3, para 9.

projects' and these provide for pre-inquiry meetings.[45] The special nature of such inquiries is discussed below.[46] One of the tasks of the pre-inquiry meeting will be to arrange a timetable for the running of the inquiry[47] though the inspector has a general power to arrange a timetable even if there is no pre-inquiry meeting.[48] The timetable can specify a time by which proofs of evidence must be received by the Secretary of State.[49]

(b) Inquiry procedures

(i) General principles

22.30   The overriding principle is that the inspector determines the procedure at the inquiry provided the inspector keeps within the statutory Rules and the process overall is fair. This is made plain by r 15(1), and in *TA Miller Ltd v Minister of Housing and Local Government*[50] Lord Denning described the inquiry as 'master of its own procedure provided that the rules of natural justice are applied'. Despite the quasi-judicial format of an inquiry, the courts have tried to prevent an over-judicialization of the inquiry. Thus in *TA Miller Ltd* it was held that there are no formal rules of evidence and that hearsay evidence could be relied upon as long as it was logically probative.[51] The flexible nature of the Rules also enables inquiries to become investigatory or inquisitorial where necessary. The Inspectorate issues notes of guidance to inspectors as to how inquiries should be run. While these notes are not strictly binding on inspectors, they will normally follow them. The present notes encourage inspectors to be more pro-active and informal. The inspector must ensure that she is not perceived to be biased towards one of the parties and there have been numerous cases where the eventual decision has been challenged in the courts because the inspector has been alleged to be hostile or too favourably disposed to one side.[52] Today the courts would have to apply the test of whether the circumstances would lead a fair-minded and informed observer to conclude that there was a real possibility, or real danger, that the inspector was biased.[53]

---

[45] See Town and Country Planning (Major Infrastructure Project Inquiries Procedure) (England) Rules 2002, r 6.

[46] See para 22.79.

[47] r 8.

[48] r 8(2).

[49] r 8(4).

[50] [1968] 1 WLR 992.

[51] See also Lord Diplock's statement in *Bushell v Secretary of State for the Environment* [1981] AC 75, 97B that it would over-judicialize the inquiry to insist on the observance of the procedures of a court of justice.

[52] See, eg, *Halifax Building Society v Secretary of State for the Environment* [1983] JPL 816 as compared to *British Muslims Association v Secretary of State for the Environment* (1987) 55 P & CR 205.

[53] See *Porter v Magill* [2001] UKHL 67; [2002] 2 AC 357.

(ii) The parties to the inquiry and their order of appearance

22.31 Section 321 requires that at any planning inquiry oral evidence shall be heard in public and documentary evidence shall be open to public inspection,[54] so normally anyone has a right to attend. However under the Rules only certain persons are entitled to appear at the inquiry. All persons entitled to appear are also entitled to call evidence but there are restrictions on who can cross-examine other persons giving evidence.[55] It is only the appellant/applicant, local planning authority and the 'statutory parties' who have what can be termed full rights: that is the right to make submissions, present evidence and cross-examine.[56] The term 'statutory party' is defined so as to include those persons who, in response to the publicizing of the application, have made representations within the required period. Their inclusion therefore ensures a degree of public participation in the inquiry process. The Rules, however, do not open up the inquiry to the general public and it has been argued that such procedural rules are invalid in so far as they prevent interested members of the general public from having the right to present evidence and to cross-examine. This argument is based on the statement by Lord Moulton in *R v Local Government Board, ex p Arlidge* that the relevant statute, by using the word public, had intended that every member of the public should have the right to bring before the inquiry any matters relevant to the subject matter of the inquiry.[57] Section 320 of the 1990 Act does not use the word public and it is doubtful whether the courts today would imply such a general right. Rule 11(3), however, authorizes the Inspector to permit any other person to appear at the inquiry and such permission must not be unreasonably withheld. The Inspector has a general discretion to allow any other person to give evidence or cross-examine.[58] It would follow that a refusal to allow a person such rights could be challenged in the courts as unreasonable or unfair, if the third party has a genuine interest in the outcome of the inquiry. In practice inspectors readily grant rights of appearance though they are more reluctant to allow cross-examination.

22.32 The determination of a planning application may be based on either a direction issued or a view expressed by some body other than the local planning authority. In such a case r 12 provides that the applicant, the local planning authority or a person entitled to appear at the inquiry, can require a representative of the body to be made available to give the reasons for the directive or the expressed view. The

---

[54] This section derives from the Planning Inquiries (Attendance of Public) Act 1982. The Secretary of State can direct that the inquiry sit in private if he is satisfied that public disclosure would not be in the public interest.

[55] See r 15(5) (Secretary of State's Rules) and r 16(5) (Inspectors's Rules).

[56] Various statutory bodies with an interest in the subject of the inquiry have a right of appearance and to call evidence; see r 11(1).

[57] See Sir William Wade and Christopher Forsyth, *Administrative Law* (8th edn, Oxford: OUP, 2000) 953–954.

[58] r 15(5) (Secretary of State's Rules) and r 16(5) (Inspector's Rules).

representative must give evidence and be subject to cross-examination. The representative can be called as a witness for the local planning authority or the body concerned can be represented in its own right. The inspector also has the power to summon any other person to attend the inquiry and to give evidence and produce documents.[59]

22.33   The inquiry must start with the inspector identifying what are in her opinion the main issues to be considered at the inquiry and any matters on which she requires further explanation from parties appearing at the inquiry.[60] This statement is only to provide guidance to the parties and it is made clear that it does not preclude those entitled to appear from referring to issues that they consider relevant to the subject of the inquiry.[61] The local planning authority should give evidence first unless the inspector decides otherwise in a particular case.[62] The applicant has the right of final reply, but it is left to the inspector to determine the order of any other parties.

(iii)   The presentation of evidence

22.34   Any person entitled or permitted to appear at the inquiry can either do so on his own behalf or be represented by any other person. In practice lawyers will represent the developer and the local planning authority and, where much is at stake, both solicitors and Queen's Counsel will be instructed. There is no right to legal funding for representation at an inquiry under the Access to Justice Act 1999.[63] The only possibility is for the applicant to ask the Lord Chancellor to direct the Commission to provide funding or for the Commission itself to ask the Lord Chancellor to authorize funding.[64] Therefore each party must normally bear its own costs; though as we will see there is a power for the Secretary of State to order one party to pay the costs of another party. The lack of legal aid does mean that third parties may be at a disadvantage in putting their case if they cannot afford to pay for counsel and witnesses: though inspectors will try to assist parties who are not legally represented. In *R v Legal Aid Area No 8 (Northern), ex p Sendall*[65] the Court of Appeal held that there was no right to legal aid so that an objector to a proposed incinerator could get the necessary legal and scientific assistance to make her case at a public inquiry. The Court rejected as unarguable the submission that Directive (EC) 85/337 on Environmental Assessment required such legal aid as it imposed an obligation

---

[59]   See Local Government Act 1972, s 250(2) applied by s 320 of the 1990 Act to planning inquiries.
[60]   See r 15(1) (Secretary of State's Rules) and r 16(1) (Inspector's Rules).
[61]   See r 15(2) (Secretary of State's Rules) and r 16(2) (Inspector's Rules)
[62]   See r 15(4) (Secretary of State's Rules) and r 16(4) (Inspector's Rules).
[63]   Access to Justice Act 1999, s 6(6) and Sch 2.
[64]   ibid s 6(8)
[65]   [1993] Env LR 167.

on member states to give the public an opportunity of commenting on the environmental impact of certain projects before they were approved. Lord Donaldson MR commented that if the objector raised concerns, it would be for the public inquiry to pursue these concerns in scientific terms. In practice, however, if the main parties do not take up the matter, it is only rarely that the inspector will investigate the matter independently.

It was argued in *R v Secretary of State for the Environment, Transport and the Regions, ex p Challenger*[66] that the inability to be properly represented through lack of financial resources at an inquiry could be a breach of Article 6 ECHR. Harrison J did not have to decide the point as the Human Rights Act 1998 was not then in force. He did nevertheless express a view on the issue. He accepted that 'inequality of arms' could be a breach of Article 6 but that each case had to be determined on its particular facts. In essence it would depend on whether the applicant's access to the inquiry would be practical and effective and not theoretical and illusory. In deciding that the applicant would have a fair hearing he put particular emphasis on the fact that the local planning authority would be making essentially the same case as the objector to the scheme. It would seem to follow that the absence of legal funding for a third party would very rarely make the hearing a breach of Article 6.   **22.35**

There is nothing to prevent a person combining the role of advocate and witness but this is unusual. The two roles are not really compatible and in *Multi Media Productions Ltd v Secretary of State for the Environment*[67] the Judge commented that: **22.36**

> While there is no rule against somebody combining the role of advocate and expert witness at an inquiry, it is generally speaking an undesirable practice. That is why planning authorities are not represented at inquiries by planning officers. An expert witness should be trying to give his time and unbiased professional opinion to assist the Inspector. An advocate is trying to argue the best case he can for his client. Someone who combines these roles must not be surprised if an Inspector or a court approaches his evidence with a degree of caution.

Of course sometimes the combination of roles will be inevitable as when a third party is appearing in person and also has evidence to present to the inquiry.

Over the years the practice has grown up of witnesses preparing in advance written proofs of evidence. The Rules do not make this mandatory but, as has already been pointed out, where it is proposed that evidence shall be given by reading from a proof of evidence, the proof must be submitted to the Secretary of State four weeks before the start of the inquiry. The reading out of a very long proof can   **22.37**

---

[66] [2001] Env LR 12.
[67] [1989] JPL 96.

be both tedious and take up a lot of inquiry time. This is why the Rules provide for a written summary and r 13(5) (Secretary of State's Rules) and r 14(5) (Inspector's Rules) require that where a written summary has been provided, only that summary shall be read out, unless the inspector permits or requires otherwise. In fact the Rules do not expressly require a written summary to be always provided. However the Rules do state that no written summary shall be required where the proof of evidence contains no more than 1,500 words and so imply that one is required if the words exceed 1,500. There is no restriction on the size of the summary and it can be difficult to summarize complex technical evidence. Presumably the inspector could require a summary to be shortened if it was almost as long as the original proof of evidence. The restriction on the reading out of proofs of evidence can make it difficult for third parties to follow the arguments and Circular 05/00 does advise that situations can arise where the inspector would consider it necessary to use her powers to allow more than the summary to be read out. In any case the Rules state that the proof of evidence shall be treated as having been tendered as evidence and subject to cross-examination.[68]

22.38 Evidence is not restricted to the proofs of evidence and oral evidence. The inspector is expressly authorized to take into account any written representations or evidence or any other document sent to her before or during the inquiry provided she discloses it at the inquiry. Although parties, who are entitled to appear, have a right to give evidence, the inspector in turn has a power to refuse to permit the giving or production of evidence or presentations that are irrelevant or repetitious: though evidence can then be submitted to the inspector in writing.[69]

22.39 Although there are no strict rules of evidence, the reliance on worthless evidence of no probative value could result in the subsequent decision being overturned in the courts. In *French Kier Developments Ltd v Secretary of State for the Environment*[70] Willis J commented that, '. . . some limit must surely be imposed in fairness to an appellant on the scope of so-called evidence which by no stretch of the imagination can be said to have the slightest evidential value'.[71] Then in *Knights Motors v Secretary of State for the Environment*[72] the Judge had to consider the probative value of a statement by a witness that some other body had told him that a sewer was working to capacity. He was very doubtful whether an inspector could act on such evidence alone but the wealth of supporting evidence justified the inspector in concluding that there was a drainage problem.

---

[68] r 15(7) (Secretary of State's Rules) and r 16(7) (Inspector's Rules).
[69] r 15(6) (Secretary of State's Rules) and r 16(6) (Inspector's Rules).
[70] [1977] 1 All ER 296.
[71] ibid 302j.
[72] [1984] JPL 584.

(iv) Cross-examination

It has been noted that only the main parties have the right to cross-examine per- **22.40**
sons giving evidence. However the inspector can both permit other parties to
cross-examine and refuse to permit any cross-examination that he considers
to be irrelevant or repetitious. These powers must be exercised fairly. So a refusal
to permit a third party to cross-examine a witness could lead to the decision being
quashed by the courts as unfair. In *Nicholson v Secretary of State for Energy*[73] it was
held that, even where an objector did not have an express right to cross-examine,
a refusal to allow cross-examination to such an objector could be a breach of natural justice if the objection was bona fide and the questions were not repetitive or
irrelevant. *Nicholson* was a case concerning objections to a proposal to mine coal
under the Opencast Coal Act 1958 and at the time there were no procedural rules
governing inquiries under that Act. So the position could be different where the
Rules distinguish between different classes of parties, only some of which have
rights of cross-examination. Nevertheless the Judge based his judgment on the
general principle that those who would be directly injuriously affected by the decision should be able to cross-examine witnesses giving evidence contrary to their
case. Indeed the Judge endorsed the participatory function of an inquiry when he
stated:

> It used to be commonly thought that the purpose of a local inquiry was to enable
> local residents and organisations to 'blow off steam', but that no longer is the case,
> for persons and bodies opposed to a project now expect to take an active, intelligent
> and informed part in the decision-making process. If that expectation is denied, a
> sense of grievance results and public opinion is affronted. In my judgment it should
> be a primary aim of an inspector holding an inquiry to ensure that nobody leaves
> that inquiry with a reasonable cause for dissatisfaction, although I recognise that
> there are some people who can never be satisfied.[74]

However the House of Lords took a very different approach in *Bushell v Secretary* **22.41**
of State for the Environment,[75] another case where there were no procedural rules.
The ratio of the majority was basically that the inspector had acted fairly in refusing to allow cross-examination on a matter of government policy (the methodology for calculating future traffic) as this was a topic unsuitable for investigation.
Lord Diplock, who gave the leading speech, took an administrative view of the
function of the inquiry by holding that the purpose was to inform the minister.
He went on to say that:

> Whether fairness requires an inspector to permit a person who made statements on
> matters of fact or opinion, whether expert or otherwise, to be cross-examined by a
> party to the inquiry who wishes to dispute a particular statement must depend on

---

[73] (1978) 76 LGR 693.
[74] ibid 700.
[75] [1980] 3 WLR 22.

all the circumstances. In the instant case, the question arises in connection with expert opinion on a technical matter. Here the relevant circumstances in considering whether fairness requires that cross-examination should be allowed include the nature of the topic on which the opinion is expressed, the qualifications of the maker of the statement to deal with that topic, the forensic competence of the proposed cross-examiner, and, most important, the inspector's own views as to whether the likelihood that cross-examination will enable him to make a report which will be more useful to the minister in reaching his decision than it would otherwise be is sufficient to justify any expense and inconvenience to other parties to the inquiry which would be caused by any resulting prolongation of it.[76]

The whole emphasis is therefore on whether the Inspector considers that the cross-examination will assist him in carrying out his function, rather than the need to ensure that parties do not go away feeling aggrieved.

22.42   In the case where the Rules give a right to cross-examination, the discretion of the inspector must be narrower since cross-examination can only be refused if the inspector considers it to be 'irrelevant or repetitious'. It should be fairly obvious when cross-examination becomes repetitious but relevancy is more problematic. Relevancy should depend on whether the issue being examined is both legally and factually material to the subject of the inquiry. For example, the existence of an alternative site for the proposed development may or may not be material depending on the kind of development and the particular circumstances.[77] Government policy can of course be relevant to the inquiry but in *Bushell* Lord Diplock said that the merits of government policy would normally be unsuitable for investigation at an inquiry. He therefore held that it was not unfair of the inspector to refuse to allow cross-examination of a departmental witness and r 12(4) expressly provides that a representative of a minister or a government department does not have to answer questions which in the opinion of the inspector are directed at the merits of government policy. On the other hand in *R v Secretary of State for Transport, ex p Gwent CC*[78] Woolf LJ accepted that parties to an inquiry are entitled to argue that the particular circumstances justify a departure from government policy. It would seem to follow that the merits of the application of government policy are a fit subject for evidence, cross-examination and eventual judgment by the decision-maker.

22.43   If a witness refused to reply to questions, it could be an offence under s 250(3) of the Local Government Act 1972 but only if the witness had been formally summoned to give evidence. Otherwise it would seem there is little an inspector can

---

[76] *Bushell v Secretary of State for the Environment* (n 75 above) 30A.
[77] For a recent decision setting out the law on when an alternative site is material see *R (on the application of Jones) v North Warwickshire BC* [2001] PLCR 509.
[78] [1988] QB 429.

do. In *Accountancy Tuition Centre v Secretary of State for the Environment*[79] the Judge deplored a refusal to answer questions, which he said was the equivalent of contempt, but considered that it would not be grounds for overturning the decision.[80] However a refusal to answer could result in the decision being overturned if it rendered the whole process unfair.

(v) Adjournments

The Rules expressly give the inspector the power from time to time to adjourn the inquiry[81] and in any case the courts would normally imply such a power unless it had been expressly or necessarily excluded.[82] There can be various grounds for an adjournment but the standard ones would be that new evidence or issues have been raised or that a particular witness is not available. If one of the parties is aggrieved by the inspector's decision to adjourn or not to adjourn, the party can either immediately challenge the adjournment decision by way of judicial review or await the outcome of the inquiry and then challenge the legality of the whole proceedings.[83] The problem with an immediate challenge is that by the time the court hears the challenge the inspector or the Secretary of State may have made the final decision. However it would seem that if there is an immediate challenge, the legality of the adjournment decision must be considered separately from whether it did or did not prejudice the final decision. In *Croydon LBC v Secretary of State for the Environment*[84] Keene J had to consider two separate applications. First, an application for judicial review of the refusal by the inspector to adjourn the inquiry and secondly, an application under s 288 to question the validity of the ultimate decision of the inspector to allow the planning appeal. He considered that it could not be right to judge the fairness of the adjournment decision by looking at the strengths and weaknesses of the eventual decision on the merits. That would be judging the procedural decision with the benefit of hindsight, which was not available to the decision-maker. Similarly in *R v Lord Saville of Newdigate, ex p B (No 2)*,[85] in a case concerning a tribunal of inquiry set up under the Tribunal of Inquiry (Evidence) Act 1921, Lord Woolf held that the fact that the court would not quash the final decision of a tribunal on a procedural ground does not mean that a preliminary decision will not be quashed.

22.44

---

[79] [1977] JPL 792.

[80] It is unclear the extent to which the planning witness for a local planning authority can properly refuse to answer questions as to his professional judgment when he is at odds with the views of his authority; see [1977] JPL 792 and [1979] JPL 257. Where it is a matter of professional expertise rather than personal opinion it is submitted that the witness should answer the questions.

[81] r 15(13) (Secretary of State's Rules) and r 16(13) (Inspector's Rules).

[82] See *R v Panel on Take-overs and Mergers, ex p Guinness plc* [1990] 1 QB 146 where such a power appears to have been assumed.

[83] In the case of planning inquiries, s 288 of the Town and Country Planning Act 1990 provides a statutory right of challenging the decision of the Secretary of State in the High Court within six weeks of the decision.

[84] [2000] PLCR 171.

[85] [2000] 1 WLR 1855.

22.45   While it is clear that the courts themselves will determine whether the adjournment decision was unfair, it is not enough that the court itself would have come to a decision different to that of the inspector. The court must be satisfied that the decision was clearly wrong or unjust.[86] In making this evaluation the court must view the decision in the round and strike a balance between fairness to one party as against fairness to other parties and the public interest generally.[87] Thus in the *Croydon* decision Keene J found that the need to avoid delay had to be balanced against the public interest in sound decision-making. What is unclear is the weight the court will place on the judgment of the inspector. The views of the inspector are clearly relevant but they are certainly not determinative. The overriding duty of the court is to ensure that the proceedings are conducted fairly. It is submitted that Sedley J set out the correct position in *R v Cheshire CC, ex p Cherrih*,[88] a case concerning a special educational needs tribunal, when he stated:

> It follows in the ordinary case, where the power of adjournment is at large, there is no true margin of appreciation for the tribunal; the court itself will decide on the relevant material whether fairness required an adjournment.[89]

(vi) Site inspections

22.46   The Rules make a clear distinction between accompanied and unaccompanied site visits. The crucial difference is that in the case of accompanied visits the inspector must give the main parties notice of the date and time of the proposed visit so that they or their representatives have the opportunity of being present on the visit. The site visit is not the occasion for the parties to give further evidence or to make submissions to the inspector and Circular 05/200 states that the inspector will refuse to hear evidence or other submissions.[90] As the Circular states, it is legitimate for the inspector to have drawn to her attention particular features of the site and its surroundings. The fact that the inspector makes the visit accompanied also means that it can be drawn to her attention whether the conditions being observed are normal. The Rules also provide that the inspector can always make an unaccompanied inspection of the land which is the subject of the inquiry before or during the inquiry without informing any of the parties.[91] The accompanied site visit can take place during the inquiry or after the inquiry has closed. The inspector has discretion whether to make such a site visit but she must make a site visit if the applicant or the local planning authority requests it before or during the

---

[86] See Mars-Jones J in *Gill & Co (London) v Secretary of State for the Environment* [1978] JPL 373.

[87] See *R v Lord Saville of Newdigate, ex p B (No 2)* [2000] 1 WLR 1855.

[88] (1996) 95 LGR 299.

[89] ibid 308.

[90] Circular 05/200, para 46.

[91] r 16 (Secretary of State's Rules) and r 17 (Inspector's Rules). In *Kyprianou v Secretary of State for the Environment* [1991] JPL 234 it was held that the wording of the Rules means that an unaccompanied site visit cannot be made after the inquiry has closed.

inquiry.[92] While the applicant, the local planning authority and any statutory parties have the right to accompany the inspector on the visit, the inspector does not have to defer the visit if they do not turn up at the date and time fixed for the visit.[93]

The purpose of a site visit is that the inspector can receive, as it were, the evidence **22.47** of her own eyes. There is therefore nothing improper in the inspector using the site visit to make an evaluation of the evidence and submissions that have been made during the inquiry.[94] Indeed, in *Fairmount Investments Ltd v Secretary of State for the Environment*[95] the House of Lords accepted that the inspector was under a duty to use his expertise to evaluate the relevant facts. However, if in the course of the site inspection (whether accompanied or not) the inspector receives information that had not been considered at the inquiry or forms a view on an issue not considered by the inquiry, the parties should be given an opportunity to comment on the new evidence or the new issue. Failure to do this may result in the decision being quashed for unfairness.[96]

(c) Post-inquiry procedures

The procedures following the close of the inquiry diverge sharply depending on **22.48** whether it is the Secretary of State who is making the ultimate decision or his inspector. This is inevitable as in the case of decisions by the Secretary of State there is both an interplay and a gap between the report of the inspector and the Secretary of State's decision letter.

(i) The inspector's report: Secretary of States' cases

Under r 17(1) the inspector has to make a report in writing to the Secretary of **22.49** State which shall include her conclusions and recommendations or her reasons for not making any recommendations. The Rules otherwise do not specify what must be included in the report but the courts have held that the report must be proper and adequate.[97] This basically means that the inspector should give a fair account of the main evidence and arguments, including legal argument. On the other hand the report does not have to record everything and the inspector can decide in what form to present the arguments and evidence. Where an assessor has been

---

[92] r 16(2) (Secretary of State's Rules) and r 17(2) (Inspector's Rules).
[93] r 16(4) (Secretary of State's Rules) and r 17(4) (Inspector's Rules).
[94] See *Wass v Secretary of State for the Environment* [1986] JPL 120 and *Winchester City Council v Secretary of State for the Environment* (1979) 39 P & CR 1.
[95] [1976] 1 WLR 1255.
[96] See ibid; *Hibernian Property Co Ltd v Secretary of State for the Environment* (1973) 27 P & CR 197 and *Southwark LBC v Secretary of State for the Environment* [1987] JPL 36.
[97] See Slynn J in *East Hampshire DC v Secretary of State for the Environment* [1978] JPL 182 and *Preston BC v Secretary of State for the Environment* [1978] JPL 548.

appointed, the assessor may, but does not have to, produce a report. If the assessor does produce a report it must be appended to the inspector's report and the inspector must make clear if she agrees or disagrees and give the reasons for any disagreement.[98] In effect reversing the decision of the House of Lords in *Arlidge*,[99] anyone entitled to be notified of the Secretary of State's decision[100] can also ask for a copy of the inspector's report but only once the decision has been notified.[101] In practice a copy of the inspector's report is always included with the decision letter.

(ii) The emergence of new evidence and disagreements between the Secretary of State and the inspector

22.50   As the report will be disclosed, it will be clear whether there has been any disagreement between the Secretary of State and his inspector. The Secretary of State is of course entitled to disagree and indeed is required to exercise his own judgment. The result is therefore that the person who makes the final decision (who in most cases will not be the Secretary of State but a civil servant in the department) has not heard the evidence and the arguments. This power can be seen as a breach of the principle that 'the one who decides must hear'.[102] However the Rules do impose some safeguards where the Secretary of State's rejection of a recommendation of the Inspector is based on a difference over a matter of fact or the consideration of new evidence.[103]

22.51   The rule in the case of a difference over a matter of fact is that the Secretary of State must notify the main parties[104] of the reasons for the disagreement and give them the opportunity to make representations. It only applies to matters of fact mentioned in, or appearing to the Secretary of State to be material to a conclusion reached by the inspector. In an inquiry most of what can be termed primary facts, such as the physical layout of the site and the details of the proposed development, will be beyond dispute. The crucial question is therefore the extent to which the term 'matter of fact' can extend to inferences or conclusions that can be drawn from such facts.

22.52   Most of the judicial authorities are concerned with the meaning of a different term, 'finding of fact', that was used by the previous procedural rules. These authorities made a distinction between finding of fact and expressions of opinion on planning merits. Thus in *Lord Luke of Pavenham v Minister of Housing and Local Government*[105] it was held by the Court of Appeal that a conclusion that a

---

[98]   See r 17(2) and (3).

[99]   *R v Local Government Board, ex p Arlidge* [1915] AC 120.

[100]   This basically includes anyone who appeared at the inquiry; see r 18(1).

[101]   See r 18(2).

[102]   See Wade and Forsyth (n 57 above) 969.

[103]   r 17(5).

[104]   These are the persons entitled to appear and who did appear at the inquiry; see r 17(5).

[105]   [1968] 1 QB 172.

a statement of reasons for the decision, if requested, in the case of any statutory inquiry[119] and Article 6 ECHR also requires reasons for any decision to which Article 6 applies.[120] The existence of a statutory duty to give reasons undoubtedly makes it easier for the legality of the decision to be challenged in the courts and also is a means of imposing a check on the quality of decision-making by requiring the reasoning process to be spelt out and justified. This duty to give reasons has been interpreted by the courts as requiring the reasons to be 'proper, intelligible and adequate'.[121]

However in *Save Britain's Heritage v Number 1 Poultry Ltd*[122] it was held that reasons will only be considered inadequate if the applicant has been substantially prejudiced by the alleged failing. So even if there is a gap in the reasons, this will not result in the court quashing the decisions, unless that gap or inadequacy has substantially prejudiced the applicant.[123] The result is in effect that inadequacy of reasons is not in itself an error of law. Then in *Bolton MBC v Secretary of State for the Environment*[124] it was emphasized that reasoning could only be considered to be inadequate if there was a failure to address the 'principal important controversial issues'. So although the decision-maker must by law consider all the material considerations, the reasons do not have to set out the views of the decision-maker on arguments based on material considerations if they are not the principal important controversial issues. This last ruling makes life easier for the Secretary of State but leaves open the possibility that a party may be prejudiced by a failure to take into account a relevant consideration. The Secretary of State is entitled simply to adopt the reasoning contained in the inspector's report but where he adopts a different reasoning, whether he agrees or disagrees with the inspector he must make clear his own reasoning.[125]

22.58

(iv) Decisions by inspectors

The post-inquiry procedure is obviously more straightforward where the inspector has been delegated the power to make the decision as there is just one document issued, the inspector's decision letter. However, as with the Secretary of State, an inspector who proposes to take into consideration any new evidence or any new matter of fact (not being a matter of government policy) that is material to the decision, must notify the persons entitled to appear at the inquiry. Such persons can then make written representations or require the inquiry to be

22.59

---

[119] See para 22.04 above for the meaning of a statutory inquiry.
[120] See also the Privy Council decision in *Stefan v General Medical Council (No 1)* [1999] 1 WLR 1293.
[121] *Westminster City Council v Great Portland Estates plc* [1984] AC 661.
[122] [1991] 1 WLR 153.
[123] Lord Bridge in his speech gave three examples of such prejudice.
[124] [1995] JPL 1043.
[125] *London Welsh Association v Secretary of State for the Environment* [1980] JPL 745.

reopened.[126] The inspector has the same power as the Secretary of State to disregard written representations or evidence received after the inquiry.[127] The duty to give reasons for the decision also applies to the decisions of inspectors.[128] The subject matter of inspectors' decisions will inevitably tend to be less important and wide-ranging but in *MJT Securities v Secretary of State for the Environment*[129] the Court of Appeal (disagreeing with the judgment of the judge at first instance, Brooke J) held that the test of the adequacy of the reasons did not vary depending on the size of the inquiry and the number of issues. While the degree of particularity will vary according to the particular circumstances, the overall duty is still simply to deal with the 'principal, important and controversial issues'.[130]

(v) Reopening the inquiry

22.60   There is a general power for the inquiry to be reopened[131] and, as we have seen, the inquiry may have to be reopened where new evidence or matters of fact have been taken into account. The Rules also expressly provide a power for the Secretary of State to reopen an inquiry (under the same or a different inspector) where the decision has been quashed in proceedings before any court.[132] A decision to reopen or not to reopen an inquiry can be challenged in the courts by way of judicial review. It is clear that the courts will intervene if the decision is perverse or if the decision-maker has failed to take into account relevant considerations and in several cases decisions to reopen inquiries have been overturned.[133] The authorities, however, leave rather unclear whether the courts can only review such decisions on the basis of *Wednesbury* unreasonableness or whether they can substitute their own view as to whether the overall process has been fair.[134] It would, however, seem that the approach of the courts to decisions whether to reopen an inquiry is more deferential than their approach to decisions whether to adjourn made during an inquiry.[135]

---

[126] r 18(3) (Inspector's Rules).
[127] r 18(2) (Inspector's Rules). The same problems would arise concerning the exercise of this power and the possibility of a duty to take into account new evidence that has arisen since the inquiry, as apply to Secretary of State decisions.
[128] r 19(1) (Inspector's Rules).
[129] [1998] JPL 138.
[130] ibid 145 *per* Evans LJ.
[131] r 17(7) (Secretary of State's Rules) and r 18(4) (Inspector's Rules).
[132] r 19(1)(c) (Secretary of State's Rules) and r 20(1)(c) (Inspector's Rules).
[133] See *Niarchos (London) Ltd v Secretary of State for the Environment* [1981] JPL 118 and *R v Secretary of State for the Environment, ex p Fielder Estates (Canvey) Ltd* [1989] JPL 39.
[134] See *Rea v Minister of Transport and the Secretary of State for the Environment* (1984) 48 P & CR 239 and *R v Secretary of State for the Environment and John Mowlem & Co, ex p Greater London Council* [1986] JPL 32.
[135] See Herling and Purdue (n 24 above).

(vi) The costs of parties to the inquiry

The general principle is that parties must meet their own expenses and, as already **22.61** pointed out, there is no provision for legal aid. However s 250(5) of the Local Government Act 1972 confers on the Secretary of State the power to order one party to pay the costs of another party with regard to inquiries held under that Act and this power is applied by s 320 of the Town and Country Planning Act 1990 to local inquiries held under that Act and indeed to any proceedings where a party is entitled to insist on being heard, whether an inquiry is held or not.[136] The decision to award costs can now be made by the inspector holding the inquiry.[137] A power has also been introduced to award costs that have been incurred in the run-up to an inquiry where that inquiry has been cancelled.[138] The legislation itself lays down no criteria as to when an award of costs should be made and so it is entirely a matter of policy. The present criteria are set out in Department of the Environment Circular 8/93, *Awards of Costs incurred in planning and other (including compulsory purchase order) proceedings*. In the case of compulsory purchase orders and other analogous orders, where objectors are defending their rights or protecting their interests, an award of costs will normally be made against the authority who made the order, if the objection is successful. These analogous orders and proposals are set out in an appendix to annex 6 of the Circular. Otherwise the policy is to order one party to pay another's costs only if those costs have been caused by the unreasonable behaviour of the other party. So in order for there to be an award of costs, para 6 of the Circular states that the following preconditions must be normally satisfied:

(a) an application for costs has been made by one of the parties. This should be made before the inquiry has been concluded;
(b) the party against whom the application has been made has acted unreasonably;
(c) the unreasonable conduct has caused the party making the claim to incur unnecessary expense.

The Circular sets out examples of what is taken to be unreasonable behaviour and **22.62** in *R v Secretary of State for the Environment, Transport and the Regions, ex p Rochford DC*[139] Turner J accepted that unreasonable behaviour was not confined to behaviour at the inquiry. For example, unreasonable behaviour on behalf of the local planning inquiry can include making the decision without reasonable grounds, or the case of an appellant pursuing an appeal where there is no likelihood of success. An award of costs can be made against third parties but the Circular states that this

---

[136] Town and Country Planning Act 1990, Sch 6, para 6(5).
[137] ibid Sch 6, para 6(4).
[138] ibid s 322A.
[139] [2000] 3 All ER 1018.

will only be made in exceptional circumstances. In *R v Secretary of State for the Environment, ex p Reinisch*[140] the Divisional Court held that, in applying the criteria set out in the Circular, the Secretary of State was acting legally and was not fettering his discretion.

22.63   A decision awarding costs can be challenged by judicial review but in *Manchester City Council v Secretary of State for the Environment and Mercury Communications*[141] it was held that the behaviour does not have to be unreasonable in a *Wednesbury* sense and the crucial question was whether on the facts the decision-maker was entitled to conclude that the behaviour was unreasonable. However, clear and intelligible reasons must be given for an award of costs. In *R v Secretary of State for the Environment, ex p North Norfolk DC*[142] an award of costs was quashed because it was neither clear what criteria were being applied nor what was the basis for the finding.

22.64   The government obviously incurs costs in setting up an inquiry and s 42 of the Housing and Planning Act 1986 has created a power for the Secretary of State to recover staff costs from the parties to the inquiry. It is also provided that he is entitled to his costs even when the inquiry does not go ahead. So far no steps have been taken to charge parties for these costs.

C. Hearings, Written Representations and Major Inquiries

22.65   While the public local inquiry can be regarded as the standard model for inquiries, this model has been developed to cater for both minor decision-making that does not require such formality and for major infrastructure decisions that have significant national policy implications.

(1) Hearings

22.66   Where a statute gives a right to a hearing, that hearing does not have to take the form of a public local inquiry. In the case of planning appeals there has been developed the alternative of what is termed a 'hearing'. There are now statutory rules as to the procedure for hearings (it used to be left to a code of practice). These rules, the Town and Country Planning (Hearings Procedure) (England) Rules 2000,[143] make clear that the main difference between a hearing and a public inquiry is that a hearing takes the form of a discussion between the participants led

---

[140] (1971) 22 P & CR 1022.
[141] [1988] JPL 774.
[142] [1994] 2 PLR 78.
[143] SI 2000/1626.

by the inspector and there is a presumption against cross-examination.[144] Indeed, where the inspector considers that cross-examination is required to ensure a thorough examination of all the issues, the inspector must consider whether the hearing should be closed and an inquiry held instead.[145] Legal representation is not excluded but it is not encouraged. This puts a heavy responsibility on the inspector and Circular 05/00[146] states that:

> An important element of the hearings procedure is that the Inspector must be fully appraised of the relevant issues and arguments before the hearing opens so that he can properly lead the discussion.

This departure from the adversarial model means that the inspector may have to take on an inquisitorial duty. This was made clear by the Court of Appeal in *Dyason v Secretary of State for the Environment*.[147] On the facts of this case the Court concluded that the appellant's case for the proposed development (the erection of a building for ostrich breeding) had not been sufficiently tested. Pill LJ stated that: **22.67**

> The danger is that the 'more relaxed' atmosphere could lead not to a 'full and fair' hearing but to a less than thorough examination of the issues. A relaxed hearing is not necessarily a fair hearing. The hearing must not become so relaxed that the rigorous examination essential to the determination of difficult questions may be diluted. The absence of an accusatorial procedure places an inquisitorial burden upon an Inspector.

Another distinctive feature of the hearing is that the site visit can be used as an opportunity for further discussion and r 12 expressly allows the inspector to adjourn the hearing and for it to be continued on site. However the inspector can only do this if it is considered that this would enable one or more matters to be more satisfactorily resolved. The parties present at the hearing must also be given the opportunity to attend the adjourned hearing, must not be placed at a disadvantage and must not have made reasonable objections to this procedure. There is still a duty to ensure that the site inspection procedures do not cause unfairness to any of the parties.[148]   **22.68**

The policy of the Office of the Deputy Prime Minister is to promote hearings, where appropriate, as they are simpler, quicker and less daunting for unrepresented parties.[149] The Office however accepts that they are not suitable for appeals   **22.69**

---

[144] r 11(2)

[145] r 11(3). Interestingly there is now provision for enforcement notice appeals to be decided by hearings and r 11(2) of the Town and Country Planning (Enforcement) (Hearings Procedure) (England) Rules 2002, SI 2002/2684, expressly states that cross-examination shall not be permitted.

[146] Circular 05/00, Annex 2(ii), para 4.

[147] [1998] JPL 778.

[148] *Rydon Homes Ltd v Secretary of State for the Environment and Sevenoaks DC* [1997] JPL 145.

[149] Circular 05/00, para 26.

where a substantial number of parties wish to speak or which concern complex polices or technical issues. Although the appellant has a right to be heard, the appellant has no legal right to opt for a hearing rather than a public inquiry and vice versa. However, the principal parties will be asked for their preferences and it seems that, in practice, if the appellant wants an inquiry rather than a hearing, an inquiry will be held. The *Dyason* case shows that the hearing procedure must be fair. Insistence on only a hearing being held could result in the decision being quashed if, for example, the lack of cross-examination resulted in significant issues not being properly tested. This could also be a breach of Article 6 ECHR.[150]

22.70   Hearings have proved popular and more than 20 per cent of planning appeals are decided this way as opposed to 7 per cent decided by way of a public inquiry.[151] The rest of the appeals are decided without a hearing of any kind as they are decided by written representations. This procedure will be briefly explained next.

(2) Written Representations

22.71   The written representations process is strictly outside the topic of public inquiries but, as it is often used as an alternative, it needs to be explained. It involves an exchange of written submissions on the issues between the appellant and the local planning authority. The procedure is now set out in the Town and Country Planning (Appeals) (Written Representation Procedure) (England) Regulations 2000.[152] The process is commenced by a notice of appeal that will set out the grounds of appeal. The local planning authority can then simply respond by filling in a questionnaire but can also make further submissions. The appellant can then make one further written submission that can respond to the argument put forward by the authority.

22.72   There is a strict timetable for these submissions and the Secretary of State is empowered to proceed to a decision taking into account only those written representations made in time as long as he considers that he has sufficient information to come to a decision on the merits.[153] Third parties are only peripherally involved. Individuals who made representations in response to the application can submit representations. They, however, have no right to see the further representations made by the main parties or even the comments made by those parties on their

---

[150] See, however, *In the matter of an Application by James Stewart for Judicial Review* (26 June 2002) where the High Court of Justice in Northern Ireland reviewed the procedures for informal hearing and found them to be fair.

[151] See Planning Inspectorate, *Statistical Report 1999/2000*.

[152] SI 2000/1628.

[153] In *Geha v Secretary of State for the Environment* [1994] JPL 717 it was made clear that there is no duty to exclude representations made out of time. Therefore the Inspectorate would be acting unfairly if, after asking for further comments, the decision was made without those comments; see *Ball v Secretary of State for the Environment, Transport and the Regions* [2000] 3 PLCR 299.

representations. The rules do not provide for a site visit but the inspector will normally carry out a site visit and this may be an accompanied site visit. No discussion of the merits of the case will be allowed. The duty to act fairly of course applies to appeals decided by written representations. Although there is no express statutory duty to give reasons, reasons are invariably given and are almost certainly required by law.[154] Although the appellant and the local planning authority can insist on a hearing rather than written representations, they cannot insist that the appeal be decided by way of written representations if the Secretary of State considers a hearing is more appropriate.[155]

(3) Major Inquiries

There is no precise definition of the major inquiry. Apart from the actual length of the inquiry the term will normally apply to projects of national significance, such as airports, nuclear power stations and the like. The need for such projects will be controversial and contested and so the policy context will often not be settled. The evidence supporting the project will often be complicated and scientifically difficult.   **22.73**

(a) Alternative methods of determining major projects

There exist various methods for the authorization for such projects apart from the traditional planning inquiry. The Town and Country Planning Act 1968 created the device of the Planning Inquiry Commission. This mechanism is still available[156] but it has never been used. The crucial difference between the Planning Inquiry Commission and the traditional inquiry is that the Commission would do its work in two stages. In the first stage it would look at the need for the project and the alternative sites. The standard reason why it has never been used is that the outcome of the second stage (the standard inquiry) would be prejudged by the Commission's conclusions on the first stage. Another probable reason is that, although the government would still take the final decision, the authority of the Planning Inquiry Commission would effectively take matters of high policy out of the hands of government.[157]   **22.74**

Other alternatives are private and hybrid Acts of Parliament. The private Bill procedure resembles a public inquiry in that after the second reading the Bill is   **22.75**

---

[154] In *North Wiltshire DC v Secretary of State for the Environment* [1992] 3 PLR 113 Mann LJ found that s 10(1)(b)(ii) of the Tribunals and Inquiries Act 1992 applied and that a request for reasons was implicit. In any case Art 6 ECHR would today require reasons to be given.
[155] In *Shaw v Secretary of State for the Environment and Wirral MBC* [1998] JPL 962 the court commented that written representations were an inappropriate way of dealing with the appeal as it turned on the assessment of facts, that needed to be tested by cross-examination.
[156] It is now to be found in Town and Country Planning Act 1990, s 101 and Sch 8.
[157] For an analysis of the Planning Inquiry Commission see L Edwards and J Rowan-Robinson, 'Whatever Happened to the Planning Inquiry Commission' [1980] JPL 307.

committed to a small committee[158] that hears arguments and evidence put by the promoters and opponents of the Bill. The process is expensive, as the parties have to bear the expense of hiring advocates, expert witnesses and parliamentary agents and documents. It can also take up much valuable parliamentary time and the members of the committee may not have the expertise to judge the arguments. It is now rarely used as a means of approving large projects. A hybrid Bill is a public Bill that may in certain respects affect private rights and interests.[159] As with private Bills, a committee of each House is set up to hear arguments by those who allege their interests are injuriously or adversely affected by a hybrid Bill. However, unless the House has given an instruction to the contrary, the second reading of a hybrid Bill establishes its principle and removes from the promoters the onus of proving its expediency. So, as well as having the disadvantages of the private Bill procedure, it can be seen as unfair to objectors.

22.76   Finally, authorization can be made by ministerial order. Under s 59 of the Town and Country Planning Act 1990 a development order can grant permission for development of land specified in the order. This is the equivalent of an express grant of planning permission and has the advantage from the point of view of the promoters of the scheme that it obviates the need for a public inquiry. In fact the procedure has not been used to authorize major projects except when the proposal has already been considered by a public inquiry. There is authority that such an order could not be challenged on grounds of procedural fairness[160] but the better view would seem to be that such an order could be challenged for unfairness or abuse of power.[161] At the most the courts might give some deference to the fact that the decision has been debated and approved by Parliament. Part I of the Transport and Works Act 1992 also enables the approval of infrastructure projects such as railway, tramway and inland waterway schemes to be made by ministerial order. Such orders are made by statutory instrument, and do not involve any parliamentary procedure except in a case where a scheme is one of national significance. Before making the order the Secretary of State can afford objectors a hearing and this will take the form of a public inquiry; the rules for which are very similar to planning inquiries. In this regard the Department of Transport on 22 December 2003 issued consultation papers proposing changes to the procedural rules concerning both the handling of applications and objections and any subsequent public inquiries.

---

[158] The committee consists of four members in the Commons and five members in the Lords.

[159] eg, the Channel Tunnel Rail Link Bill (1994–95), which authorized the construction of a new rail link between St Pancras and the Channel Tunnel, contained powers of land acquisition. It affected the rights of property owners and communities along the length of the line and was declared hybrid.

[160] *Essex CC v Minister of Housing and Local Government* (1967) 18 P & CR 531.

[161] *Council for the Civil Service Unions v Minister for the Civil Service* [1984] AC 374.

However, under s 9 of the 1992 Act, in the case of schemes that the Secretary of **22.77** State considers to be of 'national significance', the application including the draft order, the environmental statement and the supporting documents are submitted to Parliament. Single debates are held in each House on a motion inviting the House to approve the proposals. The importance of this procedure is that, although a public local inquiry must be held in cases where a statutory objector makes a valid objection, there is a presumption that parliamentary approval has settled the case for and the location of the project. After the conclusion of the inquiry the inspector reports to the Secretary of State who then determines whether to make or reject the order, after taking into account any objections that have not been withdrawn and the inspector's report.

(b) The procedures for major inquiries

The government decided in 1986 not to draw up a binding set of rules for major **22.78** inquiries and instead to rely on codes of practice. In addition the standard rules were adapted to fit the special needs of a big inquiry. As pointed out earlier, r 5 of the Town and Country Planning (Inquiries Procedure) (England) Rules 2000 provides for pre-inquiry meetings. The pre-inquiry meeting is a very important aspect of major inquiries as it helps to fix the scope of the inquiry and to ensure that it is conducted as efficiently and as speedily as possible. The present Code of Practice, 'Preparing For Major Planning Inquiries in England', was issued on 27 June 2000 but is still in substantially the same form as the first Code that appeared in 1988. Like the pre-inquiry meeting the main purpose of the Code is to help the inspector and the parties to prepare for the inquiry and it is mainly concerned with the day to day organization of the inquiry.

The government must now consider it appropriate to lay down set rules, as in 2002 **22.79** it issued the Town and Country Planning (Major Infrastructure Project Inquiries Procedure) (England) Rules 2002 (hereinafter called the 'Major Infrastructure Rules').[162] These Rules (which came into force on 7 June 2002), as the title indicates, apply to 'major infrastructure projects'. The definition of this follows the model of the Town and Country Planning (Environmental Impact Assessment) (England and Wales) Regulations 1999[163] by listing developments of a particular type and size as being automatically major infrastructure projects. The Rules follow the model of the Secretary of State's Rules and some of the additions, such as the registration of persons who wish to participate in the inquiry and the powers to appoint technical advisers and hold meetings other than pre-inquiry meetings are already substantially covered in the Code of Practice. The most important changes are the introduction of a power to resort to mediation by appointing a mediator,

---

[162] SI 2002/1223.
[163] SI 1999/293.

the provisions on timetabling and the new power to curtail cross-examination. The power to appoint a mediator builds upon the emphasis that already exists to try to get the parties to agree statements of common ground.[164]

22.80 With regard to timetabling the Secretary of State's Rules leave the arranging and variation of the timetable to the inspector but do not provide the inspector with any express power to enforce that timetable apart from stopping irrelevant and repetitious cross-examination. Rule 8 of the Major Infrastructure Rules provides that the inspector shall propose the timetable but it has to be agreed by the Secretary of State. Further, any variation of the timetable has to be agreed by the Secretary of State. This need to get the agreement of the Secretary of State could be seen to undermine the independence of the inspector who ought to have the final say on operational matters. The fact that the Secretary of State's permission is required for a variation of the timetable raises the issue of what happens if it is clear that insufficient time has been allocated for a particular witness. Under r 17(7) the inspector *may* refuse to permit cross-examination or may require such cross-examination to cease if it appears to her that permitting such cross-examination or allowing it to continue would have the effect that the agreed timetable could not be adhered to. The 'may' must mean that the inspector does not have to stop or prevent cross-examination just because of disruption to the timetable and any exercise of the power could be challenged in the courts on the grounds of unfairness or breach of Convention rights. However the implication of the link between the timetable and cross-examination is that, if the inspector decides that cross-examination is not to be curtailed, the permission of the Secretary of State will have to be sought if this will result in the timetable not being adhered to. There is also the point that the fact that there is already a power to stop irrelevant and repetitious cross-examination clearly implies that where the timetable is threatened, cross-examination that is neither irrelevant nor repetitious can be stopped. The new Rules therefore give more power to the Secretary of State.

(c) Proposed reforms

22.81 In December 2001 the government published a Green Paper on 'New Parliamentary Procedures for Processing Major Infrastructure Projects' in which it was proposed that Parliament should take decisions on the principle of the need for and the broad location of a major infrastructure project. This proposal was severely criticized, especially by the House of Commons Select Committee on Transport, Local Government and the Regions.[165] The government has since announced that it does not intend to go ahead with this proposal. However the government is still committed to speeding up the processes for dealing with major

---

[164] See Town and Country Planning (Inquiries Procedure) (England) Rules 2000, r 14.
[165] *Thirteenth Report on the Planning Green Paper* (3 July 2002).

infrastructure projects. In addition to the recent enactment of inquiry rules for major infrastructure projects, already referred to above, it is proposed to issue clear statements of national policy on the need for specific investment and to consider further ways to make public inquiries more efficient. It is suggested that inquiries could consider issues concurrently rather than sequentially; thus saving time. It is proposed therefore to bring forward necessary legislation when parliamentary time permits and to introduce new rules as necessary.[166]

It is also possible for government policy to set out not only the need for new infra-structure but where it is to be located. It seems that this is going to be done in relation to where any new airport capacity is to be located. In *R (on the application of Medway Council) v Secretary of State for Transport*[167] Maurice Kay J stated that this would be a highly material consideration in relation to any grant or refusal but it would presumably be capable of being challenged at any subsequent public inquiry. **22.82**

D. Examinations in Public

Examinations in Public (EIPs) were introduced by the Town and Country Planning Amendment Act 1972 as a new procedure for the processing of what at that time were the new-style structure plans. The Town and Country Planning Act 1968, that had created the structure plan, had also provided for the holding of public inquiries into objections to submitted structure plans. However the government was obviously concerned that this would result in intolerable delay in processing the new structure plans. The 1972 Act therefore took away the right for objectors to appear before and have objections heard by a person appointed to hold a public inquiry. The format of the EIP is very different. Unless the Secretary of State otherwise directs, the local planning authority, who has prepared the plan, must cause an EIP to be held.[168] The local planning authority also determines the issues relating to the structure plan that the authority considers should be examined; though the Secretary of State has an overriding power to direct as to what matters should be considered.[169] No person has any right to be heard but the person or persons appointed to hold the examination can invite additional persons to take part.[170] The Secretary of State appoints the person or persons (usually an independent chairman plus at least one other expert member is appointed).[171] **22.83**

---

[166] See *Sustainable Communities—Delivering through Planning* (Office of the Deputy Prime Minister, 21 July 2002) paras 22–24. The changes are now to be found in clause 44 of the Planning and Compulsory Purchase Bill at present before Parliament.
[167] [2002] EWHC 2516; [2003] JPL 583.
[168] Town and Country Planning Act 1990, s 35B(1).
[169] ibid s 35B(1)(a) and (b).
[170] ibid s 35B(4) and (5). The local planning authority itself has a right to take part; see s 35B(5)(a).
[171] ibid s 35B(3).

22.84   There is a power to make regulations governing the procedure to be followed at any EIP[172] but this power has never been used. Instead codes of practice have been issued; the present one is to be found in a booklet called *Structure Plans: A Guide to Procedures (2000)*. The booklet makes clear that the purpose of the EIP is to inform the local planning authority and the task of the persons holding the EIP is to find out the relevant facts and arguments and to report on the merits of the evidence and make recommendations as to how the plan could be modified.[173] It therefore follows that the authority should only select issues on proposals on which it wants to be more fully informed. Again it is stated in the Code that the basic criterion in selecting participants is the significance of the contribution that they can be expected to make to the discussion of those matters.[174] The Code states that the EIP will take the form of a probing discussion involving the authority and other participants, led by the chair or another member of the panel.[175] It is therefore inquisitorial rather than adversarial in character and the conduct of the proceeding is almost entirely in the hands of the chair and the other members of the panel. In *Edwin Bradley & Sons Ltd v Secretary of State for the Environment*[176] Glidewell J commented that the procedure was not in the nature of a judicial or quasi-judicial hearing between parties. Representation is not encouraged and there is no right for participants to cross-examine each other. The EIP constitutes a statutory inquiry for the purposes of s 1(1)(c) of the Tribunals and Inquiries Act 1992 but not for any other purpose.[177] This means that the Council on Tribunals can consider and report on the EIP procedures.

22.85   The administrative nature of the EIP can be justified on the grounds of the general nature of the policies in the structure plan and its use has been extended non-statutorily to the process by which the government adopts regional planning guidance. Nevertheless there has been concern that the EIP does not provide an opportunity for effective public participation, especially when the local planning authority has the power to adopt the structure plan against the recommendations of the panel.[178] However there is the safeguard under reg 15 of the Town and Country Planning (Development Plan) (England) Regulations 1999[179] that if the planning authority rejects the recommendation it must invite objections and representations and then consider whether to hold another EIP. Finally, if it decides not to hold another EIP, reg 16 requires that it must give reasons for its decision.

---

[172]   Town and Planning Act 1990, s 35B(6).
[173]   See para 22 of the booklet.
[174]   ibid para 33.
[175]   ibid para 44.
[176]   (1983) 47 P & CR 374.
[177]   Town and Country Planning Act 1990, s 35B(7).
[178]   See M Grant, Urban Planning Law (London: Sweet & Maxwell, 1982) 107–108 and de Smith, Woolf and Jowell, *Judicial Review of Administrative Action* (5th edn, London: Sweet & Maxwell, 1995) para 22-013.
[179]   SI 1999/3289.

It is unclear the extent to which Article 6(1) ECHR applies to decisions adopting **22.86** structure plans, as the policies in such plans do not normally directly determine anyone's civil rights and obligations.[180] In any case it would now seem clear that in such a policy-dominated area, the right to seek judicial review would satisfy Article 6(1) and that the public participation provided by the EIP would be sufficient.[181] The government has announced that structure plans are to be abolished but the format of the EIP will still be retained for the examination of the proposed new Regional Spatial Strategies.[182] These changes are contained in the Planning and Compulsory Purchase Bill at present before Parliament.

E. Inquiries into Scandals, Accidents and Other Matters of Public Concern

(1) Introduction

The public inquiries examined so far have all been an integral part of a particular **22.87** regulatory scheme. There are, however, numerous inquiries that are set up to investigate past events where something has gone wrong. The role of the inquiry in such a case is normally to find out what has happened and to come up with recommendations as how the harm can be prevented from happening in the future. This objective is often termed 'the lessons to be learnt'. The emphasis can, however, vary from establishing the truth and apportioning blame to making recommendations for the future. The power to set up the inquiry can be contained in an Act of Parliament or the inquiry can be set up as a Royal Commission or just as an internal administrative investigation. It is hard to generalize about such inquiries but they tend to be inquisitorial in nature and to lack detailed procedural rules.

(2) Tribunals of Inquiry

The Tribunals of Inquiry (Evidence) Act 1921 was passed to deal with a particular **22.88** problem of allegations of misconduct by civil servants. It was considered that the previous use of a parliamentary committee to investigate such matters was unsatisfactory.[183] The Act requires a resolution of both Houses of Parliament that it is expedient for a tribunal of inquiry to be established for inquiring into a particular

---

[180] On this see Ouseley J in *Bovis Homes v New Forest DC* (25 January 2002). This case concerned a local plan but the logic would apply even more strongly to structure plans, as they should only contain general and not detailed policies.

[181] See *JS Bloor Ltd v Swindon BC* [2001] EWHC Admin 966; [2002] PLCR 22 and *Adlard v Secretary of State for the Environment, Transport and the Regions* [2002] EWCA Civ 735; [2002] 1 WLR 2515.

[182] *Sustainable Communities—Delivering through Planning* (n 166 above) paras 28–29.

[183] See Z Segal, 'Tribunals of Inquiry: A British Invention Ignored in Britain' [1984] PL 206, 207.

matter of 'urgent public importance'.[184] The Act gives little guidance otherwise as to when it should be used but the mechanism has generally been used to investigate alleged mismanagement and improprieties carried out by the state.[185] Wraith and Lamb state that their purpose is to discover what has happened and if necessary to prevent its recurrence.[186] However, they also point out that many who have been intimately concerned with tribunals of inquiry consider that the primary purpose is to restore public confidence.[187] The recommendations of the tribunal of inquiry are not binding but they will inevitably carry great weight.

22.89 The Act gives a tribunal of inquiry the powers of a High Court to compel the attendance of witnesses and the production of documents. Witnesses can then be examined on oath or affirmation. Although the tribunal of inquiry cannot itself commit for contempt, it can cite cases of disobedience or contempt to the High Court, which can then punish the offenders. The Act provides no guidance as to the membership of a tribunal of inquiry but in practice a person holding high judicial office has always chaired them.[188] As the Act is silent as to the procedures that the tribunal of inquiry should follow, this is left to the discretion of the particular tribunal. The practice has varied but they tend to be inquisitorial rather than adversarial in style. Section 2(a) of the 1921 Act, however, does make clear that the proceedings should be open to the public unless in the opinion of the tribunal it is not expedient. In this regard the Supreme Court of Ireland has interpreted the words 'any proceedings of the tribunal' as only including proceedings where evidence is being given and witnesses cross-examined. It was therefore held that the tribunal was entitled to conduct its preliminary investigations in private as to what evidence was relevant and what evidence would be given orally.[189] Section 2(b) also gives the tribunal of inquiry a specific power to allow a person appearing to be legally represented but representation can be refused.

22.90 The wide powers given to the tribunal of inquiry and the absence of any procedural checks on the way it investigates can cause unfairness to individuals who appear before it and who may be blamed in the final report. Following the Radcliffe

---

[184] Tribunals of Inquiry (Evidence) Act 1921, s 1(1).

[185] The mechanism has been used relatively sparingly as to date tribunals under the Act have only been set up some 20 times.

[186] See RE Wraith and GB Lamb, *Public Inquiries as an Instrument of Government* (London: Allen & Unwin, 1971) 212.

[187] ibid 212.

[188] The second tribunal of inquiry into the events of 'Bloody Sunday ' was chaired by a Lord of Appeal, Lord Saville of Newdigate, and serving with him was a former judge of the Court of Appeal of New Zealand and the Chief Justice of Brunswick. Hadfield has pointed out that this use of the higher judiciary can cause problems when the tribunal is itself subject to judicial review; see B Hadfield, 'R v Lord Saville of Newdigate, ex p anonymous soldiers: what is the purpose of a tribunal of inquiry?' [1999] PL 663, 676.

[189] See Case 103/98, *Haughey v Moriarty* (July 1998) and the analysis by L Blom-Cooper, 'The role and functions of tribunals of inquiry—an Irish perspective' [1999] PL 175.

Tribunal[190] a Royal Commission (the Salmon Commission) was set up in July 1965 to review the workings of the 1921 Act. The Salmon Commission[191] identified six cardinal principles that all tribunals established under the Act should observe. The six principles are:

(1) witnesses should only be called if the tribunal is satisfied that there are circumstances that affect that witness and which the tribunal proposes to investigate;

(2) witnesses should be informed in advance of any allegations against that witness and the substance of the evidence;

(3) witnesses should have an opportunity to prepare their case and to be legally represented with such costs normally being met out of public funds;

(4) witnesses should have the right to be examined by solicitor or counsel and of stating their case in public;

(5) witnesses should have the right to call any material witness if reasonably practicable;

(6) witnesses should have the opportunity of testing by cross-examination through counsel or solicitor any evidence that could affect them.

22.91 A government White Paper, published in 1973,[192] accepted these six principles but significantly qualified this acceptance by also stating that the Salmon Commission's report should be used as 'guidelines' and there would be circumstances where practicalities meant that the principles could only be observed in the spirit and not the letter. Certainly the six principles have never been made into law and subsequent tribunals of inquiry have not strictly followed them.[193] Thus the Crown Agents Tribunal concluded in its report in 1982 that:

> The subjects investigated under the 1921 Act are so disparate that we believe that each tribunal must have some flexibility to adapt its own procedure to meet its own circumstances.[194]

22.92 The Scott Inquiry into the Arms to Iraq affair (1995–96) was heavily criticized for not following the Salmon principles.[195] In particular witnesses were not represented by counsel and were given no opportunity to cross-examine other witnesses. The Scott Inquiry was not a tribunal of inquiry as it was set up on a non-statutory basis but it nevertheless illustrates the difficulty of injecting into what is primarily an investigatory process adversarial principles of procedure.

---

[190] This resulted in three journalists being found guilty of contempt for refusing to reveal their sources.

[191] Cmnd 3121, 1966.

[192] Cmnd 5313, 1973.

[193] See BK Winetrobe, 'Inquiries after Scott: the return of the tribunal of inquiry' [1997] PL 18 for a useful analysis of the way the principles have been followed.

[194] 1981–82 HC 364, para 1.06.

[195] Particularly by Lord Howe of Aberavon; see 'Procedure at the Scott Inquiry' [1996] PL 445. For Sir Richard Scott's defence of the conduct of his inquiry, see 'Procedures at inquiries—the duty to be fair' (1995) 111 LQR 596.

22.93 Tribunals of inquiry can be the subject of judicial review proceedings. This has been established by the litigation regarding the Lord Saville tribunal of inquiry into Bloody Sunday. Lord Woolf MR, giving the judgment of the Court of Appeal in *R v Lord Saville of Newdigate, ex p B (No 2)*,[196] stated:

> It is accepted on all sides that the tribunal is subject to the supervisory role of the courts. The courts have to perform that role even though they are naturally loath to do anything which would interfere with or complicate the extraordinarily difficult task of the tribunal.

It must equally follow that the normal grounds of review apply subject to their adaptation to the particular context of the tribunal of inquiry. In *Saville* Lord Woolf set out the position:[197]

> It is only where the decision is unlawful in the broadest sense that the courts can intervene. The courts have the final responsibility of deciding (whether a decision is unlawful) and not the body being reviewed. The courts therefore can and do intervene when unlawfulness is established. This can only be because a body such as a tribunal has misdirected itself in law, has not taken into account a consideration it is required to take into account or taken into account a consideration that it is not entitled to take into account when exercising its discretion. A court can also decide a decision was unlawful because it was reached in an unfair or unjust manner.

22.94 It is therefore clear that the procedures must be fair and whether the procedures are fair or not is ultimately to be decided by the courts.[198] Also, as was pointed out earlier in relation to the issue of granting adjournments for planning inquiries, the *Saville* decision established that the courts will intervene to overturn a preliminary decision even though they might not have quashed the final decision on a preliminary ground.[199] So while the courts will only intervene where there is some good reason to do so, they will review the exercise of discretion in such cases. The exact approach in such circumstances is rather unclear but *Saville* makes clear that where the decision interferes with Convention rights, the courts will require a compelling justification.[200] The Court of Appeal in *Saville* went on to hold that the tribunal had acted unlawfully in refusing to give anonymity to the soldiers who had fired live rounds, as the grant of anonymity was the only possible decision open to the tribunal.[201]

---

[196] [2000] 1 WLR 1855 at [31].

[197] ibid at [32].

[198] See Lord Woolf in the *Saville* decision; ibid at [38]. See also the Privy Council decision in *Lloyd v McMahon* [1987] AC 625, 702. For an analysis of the implications of this decision for tribunals of inquiry, see C Crawford, 'Tribunals of Inquiry: The Privy Council Contribution' [1984] PL 50.

[199] ibid at [43]

[200] ibid at [33].

[201] For a criticism of this reasoning; see Hadfield (n 188 above) 679.

(3) Other Inquiries into Past Events

Tribunals of inquiry are rare events but many other types of inquiry are set up to investigate matters of public concern such as accidents, improprieties and other matters of public concern. Such inquiries can be set up under non-statutory powers, as when a Royal Commission is set up under the royal prerogative or when a government department simply sets up an investigation. There are also numerous statutes that give ministers very general powers to cause inquiries to be held. For example, s 84(1) of the National Health Service Act 1977 provides that the Secretary of State may cause an inquiry to be held in any case where he deems it is advisable to do so in connection with any matter arising under this Act. Alternatively s 1(2)(b) also gives the Secretary of State authority to do any thing whatsoever calculated to facilitate, or be conducive or incidental to the discharge of any of his duties under the Act and it has been held that this section can be used to set up an inquiry.[202] The main difference is that if s 84 is used, the person appointed to hold the inquiry is given express powers, as in the case of a tribunal of inquiry, to compel the attendance of witnesses, obtain production of documents, take evidence on oath and so forth. However, as Simon Brown LJ has observed, such inquiries come in all shapes and sizes and it is wrong to try to fit them into one model.

(a) The determination whether to set up an inquiry

The fact that a power exists for an inquiry to be set up does not give anyone the right to an inquiry,[203] though a decision not to hold an inquiry could be challenged by an application for judicial review if it was based on an error of law. However, in the decision of the ECtHR in *Edwards v UK*[204] it was held that the right to life under Article 2 ECHR should be read as imposing a positive duty on member states to provide some form of effective official investigation when individuals have been killed as a result of the use of force. Such an investigation does not have to take the form of a public local inquiry but it must be independent from those implicated in the event and have sufficient powers to ensure an effective investigation. It was therefore held that where a prisoner under the care and responsibility of the state dies from an act of violence of another prisoner, the state was under an obligation to carry out an effective investigation. On the other hand in another case concerning a death of a prisoner at the hands of another prisoner, *R (on the application of Amin (Imtiaz)) v Secretary of State for the Home*

22.95

22.96

---

[202] See *R v Secretary of State for Health, ex p Wagstaff* [2000] 1 WLR 292, 307D-E and *R (on the application of Howard) v Secretary of State for Health* [2002] EWHC 396; [2003] QB 830 at [67].

[203] See the observation of Clarke LJ at para 5.1 of his Final Report into whether there was a case for further investigation into the circumstances surrounding the Marchioness disaster; the Thames Safety Inquiry (Cm 4558, 2000).

[204] Application 46477/99 (2002) 35 EHRR 19.

Department[205] Lord Woolf, giving the judgment of the Court of Appeal, held that this duty to investigate had been created by the ECtHR to ensure that the substantive rights under Article 2 were not rendered nugatory. Therefore it only had 'life case by case' and was contingent upon what was required in any individual instance for the substantive right's protection.[206]

22.97 However the House of Lords (overturning the decision of the Court of Appeal) has held that this is not the correct approach.[207] The House basically held that while there is a measure of flexibility in selecting the means of investigation, there are minimum standards that must be met. These minimum standards apply both to the situation where the person in custody has been killed by agents of the state and to the situation where it is alleged that the negligence of the state has caused the death. Lord Bingham of Cornhill, in an opinion with which their other Lordships agreed, approved of the approach taken by Jackson J in *R (on the application of Wright) v Secretary of State for the Home Department*[208] who set out the minimum requirements. Lord Bingham stated:[209]

> In a succinct and accurate judgment Jackson J reviewed the domestic and Strasbourg case law, deriving from *Jordan v United Kingdom (2001) 37 EHRR 52* the requirement that an investigation to satisfy article 2 must satisfy the following features:—
> (1) The investigation must be independent.
> (2) The investigation must be effective.
> (3) The investigation must be reasonably prompt.
> (4) There must be a sufficient element of public scrutiny.
> (5) The next of kin must be involved to an appropriate extent.

(b) The remit of the inquiry

22.98 Where the inquiry is set up by a specific Act of Parliament it is clearly possible for the scope fixed for the inquiry to be outside the powers of the Act. In this regard in the *Wagstaff* decision the Divisional Court considered that the inquiry could not make recommendations as to how other agencies apart from the National Health Service should do their jobs.

(c) The need for coercive powers

22.99 Many inquiries have no powers to require the attendance of witnesses or the production of documents; the Scott Inquiry is a good example. The inquiry must therefore rely on the co-operation of those from whom it seeks evidence. The lack of such powers could in very special circumstances render the procedures unfair,

---

[205] [2002] EWCA Civ 390; [2003] QB 581.
[206] ibid at [32].
[207] *R v Secretary of State for the Home Department, ex p Amin* [2003] UKHL 51.
[208] [2001] EWHC Admin 520; [2001] UKHRR 1399.
[209] ibid at [25].

but it is very unlikely. However it is worth noting that in *Edwards v UK*[210] the ECtHR held that the lack of a power to compel witnesses had diminished the effectiveness of the inquiry and helped to establish a breach of Article 2 ECHR.

(d) The need for legal representation and rights of cross-examination

There will usually be no right to legal representation or to cross-examine but the inquiry will have discretion to allow such rights. Whether a refusal to allow such rights will make the procedures unfair will undoubtedly depend on the particular inquiry and its subject matter. Where an inquiry is set up to investigate serious allegations of misconduct, there must be a strong case for holding that a refusal to allow legal representation would be unfair.[211]　　**22.100**

(e) The need for the inquiry to sit in public

Unless there is a statutory presumption for the hearing to be in public, as in the case of tribunals of inquiry, it will be up to the person setting up the inquiry to decide whether it should be held in public. However in *R v Secretary of State for Health, ex p Wagstaff*[212] the Divisional Court stated that:　　**22.101**

> Where, as here, an inquiry purports to be a public inquiry, as opposed to an internal domestic inquiry,[213] there is now in law what really amounts to a presumption that it will proceed in public unless there are persuasive reasons for taking some other course.

In fact in the *Wagstaff* case the minister, in setting up the inquiry, did not expressly state that the inquiry would be public; though he did fail to correct early assumptions that the inquiry would be in public. Further, the approach taken in *Wagstaff* has since been repudiated in two High Court decisions both handed down on the same day. In *R (on the application of Howard) v Secretary of State for Health*[214] Scott Baker J held that, with regard to a decision to set up an inquiry under the National Health Service Act 1977, there was no presumption either way and so the person setting up the inquiry had a discretion as to whether it should be held in public. In coming to that decision the decision-maker had of course to have regard to all the relevant considerations and the court can, as the Divisional Court did in *Wagstaff*, hold that the decision to exclude the press and the general public is invalid for irrationality. Yet Scott Baker J emphasized that the facts of *Wagstaff* were very special and unusual and that it was, so far as he was aware, the only instance　　**22.102**

---

[210] Application 46477/99 (2002) 35 EHRR 19.
[211] For an analysis of the issue; see H Grant, 'Commissions of inquiry—is there a right to be legally represented?' [2001] PL 377.
[212] [2001] 1 WLR 292.
[213] By an internal domestic inquiry the court presumably meant an inquiry into matters internal to the department or body setting up the inquiry; the results of which would not be published to the public.
[214] [2002] EWHC 396; [2003] QB 830.

of a court concluding that a minister's decision to hold an inquiry in private was unlawful.[215] The same approach was taken in the case of *R (on the application of Persey) v Secretary of State for Environment, Food and Rural Affairs*[216] where Simon Brown LJ and Scott Baker J upheld a decision by the Minister to hold three closed inquiries rather than one single open one into the outbreak of foot and mouth disease that occurred in 2001. Simon Brown LJ confessed that he found *Wagstaff* a puzzling decision and confined it to its particular facts. The only Court of Appeal authority on the issue is *Crampton v Secretary of State for Health*.[217] In this decision, in rejecting a challenge to a decision setting up a private investigatory inquiry rather than a public adversarial inquiry, Sir Thomas Bingham MR made clear that a decision as to the form an inquiry will take will be very hard to challenge as long as the decision-maker is alive to all the relevant considerations.

22.103 Simon Brown LJ in the *Persey* decision emphasized that each case will turn on its particular context. So, while the court in *Wagstaff* was wrong to argue that there is a general presumption in favour of an inquiry being public, there will be circumstances where the case for the inquiry being held in public will be overwhelming. Thus Simon Brown LJ accepted that, where some awful evil or misconduct has been committed and the purpose of the inquiry is to establish the truth, it will be imperative that the inquiry is held in public.[218] The case law also reveals that there can be disagreement among both those who practice in the area and the judges as to the respective advantages and disadvantages of holding inquiries in public. Thus there can be differences of opinion as to whether taking evidence in public will inevitably extend the length and cost of the inquiry and discourage candour on the part of the witnesses.

22.104 The Divisional Court in *Wagstaff* took the view that the decision to hold the inquiry in private was an infringement of the applicant's right to freedom of expression under Article 10 ECHR. The court considered that Article 10 gave a right for a witness to an inquiry to receive information being given to the inquiry by another witness. The court therefore concluded that a ban on reporting would be an interference with Article 10. The judges in *Persey* and *Howard* fundamentally disagreed. Simon Brown LJ, who gave the main judgment in *Persey*, argued that Article 10 only prevents restrictions on the giving and receiving of information, it does not give a right to access to information. Furthermore it does not require a particular forum to be set up for the transmission of information. He stated:

> It is not a corollary of the right to freedom of expression that public authorities can be required to put in place additional opportunities for its exercise. Article 10 imposes no

---

[215] *R (on the application of Howard) v Secretary of State for Health* (n 214 above) at [79].
[216] [2002] EWHC 371; [2003] QB 794.
[217] 9 July 1993.
[218] [2002] EWHC 371; [2003] QB 794 at [39].

positive obligation on government to provide in addition to existing means of communication, an open forum to achieve the yet wider dissemination of views.

On the other hand, it would appear undeniable that the holding of an inquiry in public will help to ensure a more effective transmission of information by all the parties that may have information on the issues raised by the inquiry. This could justify a wider reading of Article 10. Also the decision of the ECtHR in *Edwards v UK*[219] shows that in the case of investigations into deaths by the use of force, Article 2 ECHR may require the inquiry to be conducted in public in order to secure the requisite degree of public scrutiny.   **22.105**

F. Complaints about Inquiries

Section 1(1)(c) of the Tribunals and Inquiries Act 1992 gives the Council on Tribunals the general function of considering and reporting on matters that the Council determines to be of special importance with respect to the administrative procedures involving statutory inquiries. The Council has used this power to carry out what can be termed an ombudsman role by both investigating individual complaints and issuing special reports on certain subjects. The Council can only make recommendations and has no powers to enforce such recommendations. The Parliamentary Commissioner for Administration is an ex officio member of the Council but he also investigates complaints concerning the administration of inquiries. So there exists an overlap between the two bodies.   **22.106**

---

[219] Application 46477/99 (2002) 35 EHRR 19 at [82]–[84].

PART IV

CRIMINAL LAW, PROCEDURE AND SENTENCING

23

ENGLISH CRIMINAL PROCEDURE

A. Introduction

The English system of criminal procedure is adversarial and accusatorial. The term 'accusatorial' is something of a term of art. It signifies that the procedure is controlled by the parties: a prosecutor and an accused with the state providing for trial in an open and impartial court and deciding the case on the evidence brought before it. Such evidence is, for the most part, brought before the court and developed by the prosecution and the defence with the court occupying at best a subordinate role in the development of the case. **23.01**

The accusatorial label owes something to history: it does not entirely describe the contemporary system of procedure. The contemporary system involves state organs acting in the investigation of crime (an inquisitorial procedure albeit one in which the defence has extensive rights), in the prosecution of crime (through one or other prosecutorial organs), and where the right of private prosecution is exercised in only a small number of cases. Nor do historic labels or descriptions reflect the extent to which the trial process is managed by the court, for example by way of plea and directions hearings. **23.02**

23.03   Certain assumptions owe more to history and even mythology than to contemporary arrangements. Historically the parties secured evidence which supported their side of the case. Advance disclosure was limited. An acceptable outcome was the product of the clash of forensic adversaries, a process which has been characterized as a dialectical process of proof.[1] To this process the pursuit of truth was occasionally described as incidental. Today the search for truth may be regarded as a primary aim of the system. Furthermore, modern English criminal procedure depends upon investigation, disclosure, and a modicum of co-operation between the parties in which the state organs seek the truth, albeit in ways limited by civil liberties considerations, while the defence is limited in the impediments which it can put in the way of this process.[2]

23.04   Three great principles deriving from the common law and latterly from the Human Rights Act 1998 (HRA) may be said to underlie English criminal procedure. The first of these is the principle of legality which implies that procedures are fixed by law, and that limitations and restrictions applicable to procedural as well as substantive law in the interests of human rights shall be sufficiently clear and precise to exclude arbitrary executive action. Persons subjected to the criminal law should be treated equally without regard to rank or wealth. Procedures which restrict individual freedom must be ordered by law. The second great principle is that of the protection of persons caught up in the criminal process. This implies that procedures shall respect human dignity and thus that measures such as torture and inhuman and degrading treatment are impermissible. The third principle specifies that a just system must ensure the quality of the criminal process, effectively ensuring to the suspect equality of arms through such institutions as the right to legal assistance, the right to disclosure of the prosecution case, and the right to influence the conduct of the investigation. None of these are, however, absolute, nor do they favour only the defence. They compete with values such as speed and efficiency and the balance struck varies with time and circumstance.

23.05   English criminal procedure is today in a state of flux. At the time of writing an extensive White Paper has been issued which envisages fundamental changes to hallowed rules, procedures and practices.[3] This has been followed by a Criminal Justice Bill which may or may not survive the legislative process unscathed but which, in any event, will bring about extensive change to institutions and practice. This follows major amending legislation in virtually every year of the past decade. The reader must note that no account of the topic, however contemporary it may seem, can be trusted to be wholly accurate.

---

[1] G Goodpaster, 'On The Theory of American Adversary Criminal Trial' (1987) 78 J of Criminal L and Criminology 118, 184.

[2] An illustration of this is afforded by *R v Langford*, The Times, 12 January 2001 which holds that both the defence and the prosecution must bring relevant authorities to the attention of the court whether or not the authority supports their case.

[3] *Justice for All* (Cm 5563, 2002).

B. The Organs of Criminal Justice

(1) The Police

The police in England and Wales are locally organized and administered but sub-   **23.06**
ject to standards set by central government after consultation. For the most part
the investigation of crime, the choice whether to take no action, to caution an
offender or to bring charges, is in the first instance for the police. A considerable
number of investigations are, however, conducted by other bodies which also
have the power to prosecute. Prosecutions for smuggling and for VAT evasion are
brought by HM Customs and Excise. The Inland Revenue prosecutes cases of income and corporation tax evasion.[4] The Serious Fraud Office has both investigative and prosecutorial functions.

The police, as will be seen, have very wide autonomous powers in the investiga-   **23.07**
tion of crime.

(2) The Prosecution Structure

Most cases are prosecuted by the Crown Prosecution Service, a central govern-   **23.08**
ment service organized on a regional basis.[5] The functions of the Crown
Prosecution Service are to review and to prosecute cases emanating from the
police. About one-quarter of all prosecutions are brought by other government
bodies. Some few prosecutions are brought privately, by individuals or by special
interest groups.[6]

The Crown Prosecution Service, as will be seen, operates a system of structured   **23.09**
discretion embodied in a Code for Crown prosecutors which is periodically revised.[7] The Code is organized around the two principles of evidential sufficiency
and public interest. The aim is to apply consistent standards in determining
whether to prosecute while avoiding rigid uniformity. The principles stated in the
Code have not been universally adopted. Other government bodies adopt policies
which suit their own regulatory purposes. The Inland Revenue is a striking example of this. The result is that no uniform set of prosecution standards applies
throughout the criminal process.

---

[4] On the power of the Inland Revenue to prosecute see *R (on the application of Hunt) v Criminal Cases Review Commission* [2001] QB 1108.
[5] Prosecution of Offences Act 1985.
[6] An example is the Campaign Against Drunk Driving which instructs prosecutions for such offences where it feels that official prosecution action fails to reflect the gravity of the case.
[7] For the text see P Murphy (ed), *Blackstone's Criminal Practice* (14th edn, Oxford: OUP, 2004)
Appendix 4.

(3) The Courts

23.10 Criminal cases are tried either in the magistrates' courts or in the Crown Court. Magistrates' courts are composed either by lay justices sitting in panels of three who are advised on matters of law and evidence by a clerk or, increasingly in major centres, by district judges (formerly known as stipendiary magistrates). Most cases are tried in the magistrates' courts which have exclusive jurisdiction over a wide range of offences including many motoring offences. These are known as summary conviction offences.

23.11 More serious offences, known as indictable offences, are tried in the Crown Court by a judge and jury. Some indictable offences are known as offences triable either way. Such offences may be tried by a magistrates' court provided that the accused consents and the court accepts jurisdiction.

23.12 Judges in the Crown Court may be justices of the High Court, circuit judges, and part-time judges known as recorders and assistant recorders, A practice direction specifies the gravity of cases which may be heard by circuit judges, recorders and assistant recorders.[8] They are not, however, to be confused with such judicial officers as, for example, the Recorder of Birmingham who is a full-time judge and the senior presiding judge at that Crown Court.

23.13 Two further points may be noted. Crown Courts act in an appellate capacity in respect of magistrates' courts. This point is developed further in relation to appeals.[9] Some few convictions for civil offences are made by courts sitting under military jurisdiction, known as standing civilian courts. No account of them is taken in this book.

23.14 Finally, mention must be made of the Court of Appeal to which applications for leave are brought from convictions and sentences made in the Crown Court, and the House of Lords which hears appeals only in matters felt to be of public interest and importance.

C. Pre-Trial Procedure

(1) The Apprehension of Offenders

(a) Introduction

23.15 A suspected person may be brought before the courts either by way of summons or arrest. In either event reasonable grounds for doing so will be required. Such

---

[8] *Practice Direction (Criminal Proceedings: Consolidations)* [2002] 1 WLR 2870.
[9] See paras 23.443 et seq below.

grounds may be provided by other procedures, for example stop and search. The discussion which follows is directed to the use of powers of stop and search and arrest as a means of bringing offenders before the courts. It does not take account of other purposes of such procedures, for example to preserve public order, save incidentally.[10]

(b) Stop and search

A primary purpose of powers to stop and search is to search suspected individuals for evidence of crime, that is, the discovery of something clandestine or concealed.[11] A constable, whether in uniform or plain clothes may, on reasonable grounds, search any person or vehicle for stolen or prohibited articles, the latter term including all offensive weapons and articles made or adapted for use in respect of such offences as burglary, theft, or taking and driving away a motor vehicle, and obtaining property by deception.[12] A constable who discovers such an article may seize it.   **23.16**

'Reasonable grounds' or 'reasonable cause' conveys an objective standard. The officer conducting the search must himself have reasonable grounds for doing so: he may not rely on the unparticularized assertion of other officers.[13]   **23.17**

Powers to stop and search are conferred under other, specific legislation, such as the Misuse of Drugs Act 1971. Such powers are intended for use in the investigation of crime but it by no means follows that an exercise of a power to stop and search will be followed by an arrest.   **23.18**

(c) Arrest

Arrest, in Lord Simonds' striking phrase, is the beginning of imprisonment.[14] With certain exceptions, for example the power to arrest a mentally ill person for his own protection, the police should not arrest a person unless they propose to charge him with a criminal offence should evidence justifying that course emerge. Arrest is thus a means of ensuring the custody of an offender with a view to bringing him before a court. An arrested person may, however, be released on bail without charge and later required to appear before a court by summons. Furthermore, not every arrest, even where there is evidence to prosecute, will result in a charge: the offender may be diverted out of the criminal justice system by caution.   **23.19**

---

[10] See further on these points *Blackstone's Criminal Practice* (n 7 above) para D.1.

[11] *DPP v Avery* [2001] EWHC Admin 748; [2002] 1 Cr App R 31: eg, a power to require a person to remove a mask is not a search.

[12] Police and Criminal Evidence Act 1984, ss 1 and 8A, and see Criminal Justice Act 1988, s 139.

[13] *French v DPP* [1997] COD 174.

[14] *Christie v Leachinsky* [1947] AC 573, 600.

23.20   The use of arrest enables the police to utilize other powers without recourse to the courts, for example the power to enter and search premises and persons found therein and the power to question suspects under caution.

(i) Elements of arrest

23.21   An arrest occurs when the person arresting states in terms that a person is arrested, when he uses force to restrain the individual concerned, or when by words or conduct he makes it clear that he will, if necessary, use force to prevent the individual from going where he wants to go.[15] The essence of arrest is that the person has been deprived, by the exercise of lawful powers of arrest, of his liberty to go where he pleases.[16]

23.22   Only reasonable force may be used in making an arrest.[17] What is reasonable will depend on the circumstances including the nature and degree of the force used, the gravity of the offence in question, the harm that would accrue to the suspect from the use of force, and the possibility of effecting the arrest or preventing harm by other means. The use of excessive force will not, it seems, render the arrest unlawful.[18]

(ii) Reasonable cause

23.23   Police powers to arrest are, in general, premised upon there being reasonable cause to do so. The standard is objective, but it is a lower standard than that required to prove a prima facie case. Reasonable cause or reasonable suspicion may rely upon matters which are not admissible in evidence or matters which, while admissible, could not form part of a prima facie case.[19]

23.24   Reasonable cause must be determined by what the constable knew or perceived at the time.[20] A constable may act on hearsay provided that it is reasonable and that the constable believed in it.[21] This can include a computer entry in the police national computer provided that the circumstances were not such as to suggest that further inquiry was called for.[22] A constable may not, however, rely simply upon an instruction by his superior officer to make an arrest.[23]

23.25   A constable in determining whether to arrest a suspected offender is required to act objectively and reasonably. He is not obliged to follow up every suggestion

---

[15]   *Murray v Ministry of Defence* [1988] 1 WLR 692.
[16]   *Lewis v Chief Constable of the South Wales Constabulary* [1991] 1 All ER 206.
[17]   Police and Criminal Evidence Act 1984, s 117; Criminal Law Act 1967, s 3.
[18]   *Simpson v Chief Constable of South Yorkshire Police*, The Times, 7 March 1991.
[19]   *Hussein v Chong Fook Kam* [1970] AC 942.
[20]   *Redmond-Bate v DPP* (1999) 163 JP 789.
[21]   *Clarke v Chief Constable of North Wales Police*, The Independent, 22 May 2000.
[22]   *Hough v Chief Constable of Staffordshire Police* [2001] EWCA Civ 39; The Times, 14 February 2001.
[23]   *O'Hara v Chief Constable of the Royal Ulster Constabulary* [1997] AC 286.

made to him by the suspected person before arresting him.[24] Failure to follow an obvious course of inquiry may, however, form grounds for impeaching an arrest as an abuse of power.[25] English law, in these respects, appears to be fully in conformity with the European Convention on Human Rights (ECHR),[26] Article 5(1) of which requires reasonable suspicion for an arrest for a criminal offence: see paras 8.52 to 8.54 above.

(iii) Reasons for arrest

23.26 Every person arresting another must inform the arrested person of the reason for the arrest either at the time or as soon as is practicable thereafter. In the case of a constable this applies even though the reason for the arrest is obvious.[27] The arresting person is not entitled to keep the reason to himself or to give a reason which is not the true reason.[28] This complies with similar requirements in Article 5(2) ECHR.

(iv) Use of force

23.27 Only such force as is reasonable in the circumstances may be used to effect an arrest.[29] It must be proportionate to the gravity of the offence or the harm to be averted and necessary to secure and subdue the arrested person.[30] Regard must be had to the consequences of escape. Lethal force cannot be used simply because the person will otherwise escape: Article 2 ECHR, the common law and statute all restrict the degree of force which can lawfully be used.[31]

(v) Resisting arrest

23.28 While a person has an unqualified right at common law to resist an unlawful arrest, he may not use gross or lethal force to do so where the only consequence which he apprehends from the arrest is a period of unlawful detention.[32]

---

[24] *Ward v Chief Constable of Avon and Somerset Constabulary*, The Times, 26 June 1986; *McCarrick v Oxford* [1983] RTR 117.

[25] *Castorina v Chief Constable of Surrey* (1988) 138 NLJ 180.

[26] *O'Hara v UK* Application 37555/97 (2002) 34 EHRR 32.

[27] Police and Criminal Evidence Act 1984, s 28.

[28] *Christie v Leachinsky* [1947] AC 573, 587–588 *per* Viscount Simon; *Wilson v Chief Constable of Lancashire Constabulary* [2000] All ER (D) 949.

[29] Police and Criminal Evidence Act 1984, s 117.

[30] *Allen v Metropolitan Police Commissioner* [1980] Crim LR 441. Handcuffs should only be used where they are necessary to prevent escape or a violent breach of the peace by the prisoner: *R v Lockley* (1864) 4 F & F 155 and see *Bibby v Chief Constable of Essex* (2000) 164 JP 297.

[31] *A-G for Northern Ireland's Reference (No 1 of 1975)* [1977] AC 105, 137 *per* Lord Diplock. For further discussion of the use of lethal force under Art 2 ECHR and the HRA 1998, see paras 8.04–8.14 above.

[32] *Christie v Leachinsky* [1947] AC 573; *Palmer v The Queen* [1971] AC 814, 825.

(vi) Search on arrest

23.29 A constable who arrests a person elsewhere than at a police station may search that person, if he believes that he may present a danger to himself or others, and seize and retain any object which the person may use to that end.[33] He may also search the person for evidence and may enter and search premises where the person was at or immediately before the time of arrest.[34] Search is only permitted to the extent necessary for discovering any injurious thing or item of evidentiary value.[35] Material having apparent evidentiary value may be kept by police until trial.[36]

(vii) Disposition after arrest

23.30 A person who is arrested elsewhere than at a police station must be taken to a designated police station as soon as is practicable.[37] It may in some circumstances be appropriate to detain the person at the scene if to do so is reasonable in deciding whether or not to take further proceedings against him.[38] A constable may delay taking an arrested person to a police station if the person's presence is required elsewhere in aid of such investigations as may be carried out immediately.[39] An example is taking a suspect from place to place to check his alibi.[40] He may also be taken to his lodgings with a view to searching them.[41]

(viii) Arrest without warrant

23.31 English law distinguishes between arrestable offences for which plenary powers of arrest are provided, other offences for which the offender may be arrested under a necessity principle, and preserved powers of arrest.[42]

23.32 Arrestable offences are those which bear a fixed penalty, offences for which an adult offender may be sentenced to five years' or more imprisonment (in effect the bulk of serious offences), and an expanding catalogue of offences which are specially listed, for example certain motoring and sexual offences.[43] Any person may arrest without warrant a person who is in the act of committing an arrestable offence or whom he has reasonable grounds for suspecting to be committing such an offence.[44] Where such an offence has been committed a person may arrest

---

[33] Police and Criminal Evidence Act 1984, s 32.
[34] ibid s 32(2)(b).
[35] *R v Beckford* (1991) 94 Cr App R 43.
[36] *R v Uxbridge Justices, ex p Metropolitan Police Commissioner* [1981] 1 QB 829.
[37] Police and Criminal Evidence Act 1984, s 30.
[38] *John Lewis & Co v Tims* [1952] AC 676.
[39] Police and Criminal Evidence Act 1984, s 30(10) and (11); *R v Kerawalla* [1991] Crim LR 451.
[40] *Dallison v Caffery* [1965] 1 QB 348.
[41] Police and Criminal Evidence Act 1984, s 18.
[42] These latter are contained in ibid Sch 2.
[43] ibid s 24 and Sch 1A.
[44] ibid s 24(4)(a)–(b).

someone who is or who he reasonably believes to be, guilty of committing it.[45] A constable may arrest someone who he has reasonable grounds for suspecting of having committed such an offence whether it has been committed or not.[46] A constable may, furthermore, arrest anyone who is or whom he reasonably suspects of being about to commit an arrestable offence.[47] These powers of arrest also extend to inchoate offences connected to the arrestable offence such as conspiracy.

A constable may enter premises to arrest any person for an arrestable offence.[48] A constable may arrest a person who he reasonably suspects of having committed or attempted to commit an offence falling outside the category of arrestable offences. Any one of a list of arrest conditions must be satisfied before he can do so. These include an inability to verify the person's name and address, possible injury to person or property, or for protective persons in respect of a child or vulnerable person.[49]   **23.33**

Extensive provision is made for cross-border powers of arrest so that a constable in one part of the United Kingdom may arrest a suspected person in another part of the United Kingdom.[50]   **23.34**

(ix) Arrest under warrant

A justice may issue a warrant on the basis of a written information substantiated by oath.[51] Such a warrant may or may not be endorsed for bail. If bail is granted, with or without sureties, the person is bailed to appear at a magistrates' court at the time and place specified in the recognizance.[52] In the case of a person aged 17 or over the offence concerned must be indictable or punishable with imprisonment or the person's address must be unknown so that a summons cannot be served on him.[53] The Crown Court may issue a warrant for the arrest of a person who has been charged with or convicted of an offence and who has failed to appear before the Crown Court pursuant to his recognizance.[54] Similar powers apply in relation to the Court of Appeal.[55] Warrants may also issue to ensure the attendance of witnesses.[56] Warrants of arrest, whether definitive or provisional, may issue in extradition cases.[57]   **23.35**

---

[45] ibid s 24(5)(a)–(b).
[46] ibid s 24(6) and see *R v Self* [1992] 1 WLR 657.
[47] ibid s 24(7).
[48] ibid s 17.
[49] ibid s 25.
[50] Criminal Justice and Public Order Act 1994, ss 136–140.
[51] Magistrates' Courts Act 1980, s 1.
[52] ibid s 117.
[53] ibid s 1(4).
[54] Supreme Court Act 1981, s 81.
[55] Criminal Appeal Rules 1968, rr 3 and 23.
[56] Magistrates' Courts Act 1980, s 97; Criminal Procedure (Attendance of Witnesses) Act 1965, s 4.
[57] Extradition Act 1989, s 8(5).

23.36 Finally, extensive provision is made for the execution of warrants from the Republic of Ireland[58] and for the execution of warrants emanating from elsewhere in the United Kingdom[59] and from the Isle of Man and the Channel Islands.[60]

23.37 A warrant of arrest remains valid until it is executed or withdrawn.[61]A constable may execute such a warrant anywhere in England and Wales.[62] Certain arrest warrants (but not search warrants) may be executed by a constable even though the warrant is not in his possession at the time.[63] A constable who arrests a person under warrant must inform the person both of the reason for arrest and that he is acting under a warrant.[64]

(2) Detention and Treatment of Suspects

23.38 The Police and Criminal Evidence Act 1984 and codes made under it provide for the questioning and treatment of detained persons and for procedures for investigation in respect of them. Detention may be used, in the case of a person properly arrested on reasonable grounds, as an aid to questioning.[65] It follows from this that in such circumstances a person may be arrested on a holding charge as an aid to questioning in respect of a more serious charge. However, s 6 of the HRA 1998 requires officers to exercise their discretion in a manner compatible with Article 5(3) ECHR, which gives to arrested and detained persons the right to be brought promptly before a judge or other officer authorized to exercise judicial power. Furthermore, Article 5(4) entitles detainees to have the lawfulness of their detention decided speedily by a court, and to have an order made for their release if the detention is found to be unlawful. A detainee who has been unlawfully detained also has a right to compensation under Article 5(5), considered in paras 8.52 and 8.56 above.

23.39 A person who attends voluntarily at a police station is free to leave at will unless he is arrested. A person who is not arrested but is cautioned as a prelude to questioning must be informed that he is free to leave and that he is entitled to legal advice.[66] The supervision of detention and the circumstances which apply to it are the responsibility of the custody officer.[67]

---

[58] Backing of Warrants (Republic of Ireland) Act 1965, ss 1 and 4.
[59] Criminal Justice and Public Order Act 1994, s 136.
[60] Indictable Offences Act 1848, s 13 and see as to form *R v Metropolitan Police Commissioner, ex p Melia* [1957] 1 WLR 1065.
[61] Magistrates' Courts Act 1980, s 125.
[62] Police Act 1996, s 30.
[63] *R v Purdy* [1975] QB 288.
[64] Police and Criminal Evidence Act 1984, s 28.
[65] *Holgate-Mohammed v Duke* [1984] AC 437.
[66] Police and Criminal Evidence Act 1984, s 29 and Code C, para 3.15.
[67] ibid ss 34 and 36.

(a) Detention, charge and release

The custody officer must determine, as soon as is practicable, whether or not an ar-   **23.40**
rested person is to be charged.[68] This procedure involves opening a custody record
which may later be inspected by the person arrested or his legal representative.[69] At
this stage the arrested person is advised both orally and in writing of his rights and in
particular his right to be privately advised by a solicitor.[70] The duty solicitor scheme
ensures that a person may be so advised at an early stage, free of charge.

Special provision is made for particularly vulnerable individuals, and in particular   **23.41**
juveniles, and those who are mentally ill or mentally handicapped.[71] In particular,
an appropriate adult must be informed.[72] Such a person performs the functions of
advising, observing for fairness, and helping in communication with the detained
person. The detainee is informed of his right to consult privately with the appropriate adult. The latter may decide that the detained person should be legally advised.

(b) Detention or release

A person may be released either without bail or, if further investigations appear to   **23.42**
be warranted, on bail to appear at a police station at a specified future time.[73] A
custody officer who believes that it is necessary to detain a person without charge
in order to secure or preserve evidence relating to an offence for which the person
is detained or to obtain such evidence by questioning him, may authorize his detention in police custody.[74] If, however, the custody officer believes that he has sufficient evidence to charge the person he must either charge him or release him
with or without bail.

(c) Calculating time of detention

In the case of a serious arrestable offence prolonged detention may be authorized.   **23.43**
Otherwise, a suspect may not be held in detention for more than 24 hours. He
must then be released either on bail or without bail.[75] He may then not be re-ar-
rested for the same offence unless further evidence of the offence comes to light.[76]
This is intended to guard against the use of cat and mouse tactics by the police.

---

[68] ibid s 37.
[69] Code C, paras 2.1 and 2.5.
[70] ibid para. 3.1
[71] The question is whether the person appears to be mentally ill or mentally handicapped and not
whether he exhibits acute symptoms: *R v Ali (Haroon)* (24 November 1998).
[72] For definition see Code C, para 1.7.
[73] Police and Criminal Evidence Act 1984, s 34.
[74] ibid s 37.
[75] ibid s 41.
[76] ibid s 41(9).

23.44 Complicated rules relate to the calculation of the period of detention but in essence the scheme is intended to ensure that the time clock runs from the moment when the suspect is taken to the police station where he is to be questioned and that it does not run in the case where he is held elsewhere provided that he is not questioned there.[77] Detention is periodically reviewed by a review officer.[78]

23.45 While, hitherto, pre-charge reviews have been carried out at the relevant station by the review officer, provision is now made for reviews by video link where the review officer is at a different station, and by telephone.[79]

(d) Extended detention

23.46 A person may normally not be detained at a police station for more than 24 hours. This period may be extended to 36 hours provided that a superintendent or above has reasonable grounds for believing this to be necessary to the investigation of the offence, that the investigation is being conducted expeditiously, and that the offence is a serious arrestable offence.[80]

23.47 Further detention up to a maximum of 96 hours may be ordered, if sufficient grounds are shown, by a magistrates' court.[81] Application must be made before the expiry of the 36-hour period.[82] A first extension may be granted up to 72 hours and yet a further extension up to but not beyond 96 hours.[83]

(e) Remands to police custody

23.48 A magistrates' court may remand a suspect into police custody for not more than three days where this is necessary for the purposes of inquiring into other offences. At the end of the period he must be brought back before the magistrates' court.[84]

(f) Detention after charge

23.49 A person in custody, once charged, must be brought before a magistrates' court not later than the first sitting after he is charged with the offence.[85]

---

[77] For details see ibid s 41(2).

[78] ibid s 40: failure to do so may result in an action for false imprisonment: *Roberts v Chief Constable of the Cheshire Constabulary* [1999] 1 WLR 662.

[79] Police and Criminal Evidence Act 1984, ss 40A and 45A.

[80] ibid s 42(1). For definition of 'serious arrestable offence' see s 116 and Sch 5, the terms of which are amended from time to time.

[81] ibid s 45(1). The justices do not sit as an open court.

[82] ibid s 43(4)(a): this may be extended where a court cannot sit in time but no extension is permitted where the police act unreasonably in delaying the application: *R v Slough Justices, ex p Stirling* (1987) 151 JP 603.

[83] ibid s 44.

[84] Magistrates' Courts Act 1980, s 128.

[85] Police and Criminal Evidence Act 1984, s 46.

(g) Notification of arrest

An arrested person who is being held in custody at a police station has the right to **23.50** have a friend, relative or other person known to him told of his arrest and the place where he is being detained.[86] An inspector may authorize delay in notification where the person is being held in a police station for a serious arrestable offence. Such delay cannot extend beyond 36 hours from the inception of detention.[87] The officer must have reasonable grounds for believing that notification will lead to the destruction of evidence, hinder the recovery of property, or harm to witnesses.[88]

(h) Access to solicitor

An arrested person who is held in custody at a police station has a right to consult **23.51** and communicate privately with a solicitor at any time.[89] Such an interview must take place out of the hearing of a third person and in particular a constable. A violation of this right contravenes the HRA 1998 and *may* render any subsequent conviction unsafe.[90] A person who is held in custody in a magistrates' court has a right at common law to see a solicitor as soon as is reasonably practicable.[91] No attempt should be made to dissuade a person from obtaining legal advice and the police may not refuse access simply because they believe that the solicitor will advise his client not to answer questions.[92]

The right of access to a solicitor is a right of the first importance. As well as being **23.52** necessary if a detainee is to be able to test the legality of the detention effectively, as stipulated by Article 5(4) ECHR, access to legal advice is an important element of the fairness of the criminal process as a whole, guaranteed by Article 6(1). Article 6(3)(c) expressly provides that everyone charged with a criminal offence has the right to defend himself through legal assistance of his own choosing. The right of access is linked to a duty solicitor scheme which ensures that the suspect will be able to take effective advantage of it by consulting a solicitor free of charge. Furthermore, Code C permits the suspect to have a solicitor present during interview and the solicitor is expected to protect his client against unfair questioning by the police. While the police may exclude a solicitor this may only be done if there is reasonable cause to think that the solicitor will impede the inquiry by, for example, passing on information to the suspect's criminal associates.[93] In turn the

---

[86] ibid s 56. This is to be done as soon as practicable. Elaborate provisions for notifying responsible persons apply to the case of juveniles.

[87] See Criminal Justice and Police Act 2001, s 74.

[88] Police and Criminal Evidence Act 1984, s 56: powers also apply in the case of drug trafficking to aid in the recovery of the proceeds of trading: s 56(5A).

[89] ibid s 58; Code C, para 6.1.

[90] *Brennan v UK* Application 39846/98 (2002) 34 EHRR 18.

[91] *R v Chief Constable of South Wales, ex p Merrick* [1994] 1 WLR 663.

[92] *R v Alladice* (1988) 87 Cr App R 380.

[93] *R v Samuel* [1988] QB 615.

right to legal advice is tied into the power of a court to draw adverse inferences against a person who fails to mention to the police matters relevant to his defence. Such inferences would not appear proper if the person was denied legal advice.

23.53   Access to a solicitor may be delayed on the same grounds as notification of detention. Access must be granted as soon as the reason for delaying it ceases to subsist.[94] The effect of the statute is that access may be delayed for 36 or 48 hours. Where the effect of such a delay is to cause irretrievable damage to the defence, for example because adverse inferences can be drawn at trial from silence under pre-trial questioning, the accused may be held to have been denied a fair trial with consequential effect on the admissibility of evidence or the safety of the conviction.[95]

(i)   Search of the person

23.54   A person in detention at a police station may be searched for articles likely to cause harm to himself or others or to impede the inquiry. These articles may be seized.[96]

23.55   A custody officer may authorize a strip search of the person. An intimate search may only be allowed on the authority of an inspector or above. An intimate search is not a search for evidence but rather a search for articles which the prisoner may use to cause injury or escape.[97] An additional ground concerns concealment of class A drugs.[98] The conditions of such searches are regulated by Code C.

(3)   Search of Premises

(a)   Entry of premises: under warrant

23.56   Legal protection against arbitrary or unjustified searches is an essential element in the right to respect for private life, home and correspondence guaranteed by Article 8 ECHR and the HRA 1998. Article 8 has helped in important ways to strengthen English law on search, seizure and surveillance, as discussed at paras 8.58–8.60, 8.74 and 8.77 above. Extensive provision is made for the issue of warrants to search for evidence. The conditions surrounding the issue of such warrants concern what may be searched for and seized. Material is divided into categories and, in the case of categories of special procedure and excluded materials, a warrant or order to produce may only be made, subject to stringent conditions, by a circuit judge. These powers do not limit or supplant powers to search contained in other legislation, for example powers under the Theft Act 1968 to search for stolen goods.[99]

---

[94] Police and Criminal Evidence Act 1984, s 58 and see *R v Kerawalla* [1991] Crim LR 451.
[95] *Murray (John) v UK* Application 18731/91 (1996) 22 EHRR 29.
[96] Police and Criminal Evidence Act 1984, s 54.
[97] ibid s 58 and see Criminal Justice and Police Act 2001, s 79.
[98] ibid s 55.
[99] Theft Act 1968, s 26.

A justice of the peace may issue a warrant to a constable to enter and search **23.57** premises if the justice has reasonable grounds for believing that a serious arrestable offence has been committed and that there is material on the premises which is likely to be of substantial value (whether by itself or taken with other material) to the investigation of the offence. Such material must be likely to be admissible in evidence at the trial of the offence.[100] Certain conditions must apply, the effect of which may be subsumed under a principle of necessity: that entry cannot otherwise be obtained and that failure to do so would stultify the inquiry as, for example, by permitting property to be secreted or destroyed.[101]

A magistrate is not prevented from issuing such a warrant simply because there **23.58** may be special procedure or excluded material on the premises provided that such material is not part of the subject matter of the application.[102]

(b) Excluded and special procedure material

Briefly, excluded material means certain material such as personal records, human **23.59** tissue and journalistic records if these are held in confidence.[103] Special procedure material includes material other than items subject to legal professional privilege or excluded material where it is held in confidence under an express or implied undertaking to do so or a statutory requirement to restrict disclosure.[104]

An order for access to such material may be made by a circuit judge whose powers **23.60** to do so are constrained by statutory conditions which may be thought of as necessity conditions. The circuit judge must be provided with such material as is necessary to enable him to be satisfied before making the order. He must not allow the police to engage in a fishing expedition. He must be told of any factor which might militate against making the order.[105] A judge may make an access order only if he is satisfied that one of the sets of access conditions is made out.[106]

A circuit judge may, in a proper case, issue a search warrant. He may do so on the **23.61** footing that an order for access has been made and has not been complied with. He may, furthermore, issue a warrant where either set of access conditions is fulfilled and that, additionally, unless such a warrant is issued entry cannot be granted or the service of notice of application for an access order would seriously prejudice the investigation.[107]

---

[100] Police and Criminal Evidence Act 1984, s 8.
[101] ibid s 8(3).
[102] *R v Chief Constable of Warwickshire Constabulary, ex p Fitzpatrick* [1999] 1 WLR 564.
[103] Police and Criminal Evidence Act 1984, s 11(1).
[104] ibid s 14.
[105] *R v Lewes Crown Court, ex p Hill* (1991) 93 Cr App R 60.
[106] For these see Police and Criminal Evidence Act 1984, Sch 1
[107] ibid Sch 1, para 12.

(c) Enforcement

23.62 The Police and Criminal Evidence Act 1984 lays down conditions which apply to a search of premises under any enactment. The material to be seized must fall within the terms of the warrant. The constable must have reasonable grounds for believing it to have evidential value, and it must be thought likely to be of substantial value to the investigation. Complex rules govern the seizure of material alleged to be legally privileged. A warrant may be executed by any constable and may authorize another person to accompany him.[108] Such a person may for example be a lawyer brought along to assist in relation to problems of material for which legal privilege is claimed.[109]

23.63 Detailed provisions surround the execution of search warrants for which reference should be made to one of the standard practitioner works on the subject.[110]

(d) Entry without warrant

23.64 A constable may enter and search premises in order to effect an arrest or to save life and limb or prevent serious damage to property.[111] A constable may also enter and search property occupied or controlled by a person who is under arrest for an arrestable offence if the constable has reasonable grounds for suspecting that there is on the premises evidence relating to that or another arrestable offence. The constable may seize and detain anything for which he may search. The scope of the search is restricted to that which is reasonably required for the purpose of discovering such evidence.[112]

(e) Seizure of, access to and retention of materials

23.65 A constable who is lawfully on premises has power to seize anything which he has reasonable grounds to believe has been obtained in consequence of the commission of an offence or is evidence in relation to an offence and which it is necessary to seize to preserve it.[113]

23.66 Sweeping new powers enable material to be removed from premises in order to determine whether it is subject to seizure. The essence of these powers is to facilitate seizures by allowing material to be seized subject to a procedure by way of later verification for determining whether the material should have been seized and whether, therefore, it is to be returned. The only permitted use of seized articles is

---

[108] Police and Criminal Evidence Act 1984, s 16.
[109] *R v Middlesex Guildhall Crown Court, ex p Tamosius & Partners* [2001] 1 WLR 453.
[110] eg, *Blackstone's Criminal Practice* (n 7 above) or *Stone's Justices Manual* (London: Butterworths Tolley, 2002).
[111] Police and Criminal Evidence Act 1984, s 17.
[112] ibid s 18.
[113] ibid s19.

for the purpose of investigating and prosecuting crime. Specific provision is made for the return of legally privileged material.[114]

(4) Other Investigative Procedures

(a) Interception of communications

In cases other than interception by consent, the interception of messages passing by a postal or telecommunications system requires a warrant from the Secretary of State or, in cases of emergency, by an official. Authorizations for intrusive surveillance may be granted on grounds of necessity and proportionality. These powers are intended for use in cases of national security, prevention and detection of serious crime, and safeguarding the economic well-being of the United Kingdom.[115]   **23.67**

(b) Interrogation of suspects

The interrogation of suspects is governed by common law, by the Police and Criminal Evidence Act 1984 and by Code C made thereunder. The most recent version came into force on 1 April 2003. The resulting scheme which balances the rights of the suspect and the community may be thought of as the modern settlement of police powers.   **23.68**

Code C, which applies to interviews, must be followed not only by constables but also by other enforcement agencies such as the Inland Revenue when conducting *Hansard* interviews and even store detectives, since the latter are charged with the investigation of crime.[116] 'Interview' is defined in purposive terms as the questioning of a person concerning his involvement or suspected involvement in a crime or criminal offences.[117] It is irrelevant to the definition where an interview takes place: conversations in the back of a police car may amount to an interview.[118] Questions asked of a person to ascertain his identity do not, but questions directed to obtaining admissions do, amount to an interview.[119]   **23.69**

Save where necessity requires otherwise, interviews should be held at a police station. A suspect is entitled to legal advice before he is interviewed and to have his solicitor present during the interview. An officer should inform the suspect of the offence for which he is being questioned.[120] A person who requests legal advice   **23.70**

---

[114] Criminal Justice and Public Order Act 2001, ss 50–56.
[115] Regulation of Investigatory Powers Act 2000.
[116] Police and Criminal Evidence Act 1984, s 67(9) and see *R v Bayliss* (1994) 98 Cr App R 235; *R v Gill*, The Times, 29 August 2003. The test is, however, somewhat elusive: Code C does not apply where a head teacher interviews a teacher who is thought to have assaulted a pupil: *DPP v Goodfellow* [1998] COD 94.
[117] Code C, para 11.1A.
[118] *R v Parchment* [1989] Crim LR 290.
[119] *R v Cox* (1993) 96 Cr App R 464.
[120] *R v Kirk* [2000] 1 WLR 567.

may not be interviewed until it is provided unless the person is being held incommunicado or there is reason to believe that delay will involve an immediate risk of harm to persons or serious loss of or damage to property.[121] The compatibility of this scheme with the HRA 1998 has not been tested but, in the light of the duty solicitor scheme, there will be few instances in which delay of access to legal advice would be justified. If an immediate interview must take place before advice has been obtained any resulting admissions might well be held to be inadmissible.

23.71 No police officer should attempt to secure admissions by oppression.[122] Interviews must be preceded by a caution which, in the current approved form informs a suspect that inferences may be drawn against him if he fails to mention matters relevant to his defence. Interviews are recorded on audio tape. Special protections are provided for juveniles or mentally ill or handicapped persons.

23.72 A constable who has sufficient evidence to charge the individual with an offence should ask the person whether he has anything more to say. If the person replies in the negative the constable should not question him further about that offence.[123] After a charge has been laid the accused person may no longer be questioned. This rule is subject to three exceptions. First, a police officer may bring to the person's attention a statement made by another person and he must then caution him but he must not do anything to invite a reply. Secondly, questions may be put where they are necessary to prevent harm or loss to another person or to the public. The third exception relates to the power of the Director of the Serious Fraud Office to require a person under investigation to produce documents and to provide explanations because this power permits a person to be re-interviewed even after production of a defence case statement.[124] The use of this latter power risks conflict with the privilege against self-incrimination, which is one of the elements of a fair hearing in criminal cases under Article 6 ECHR and the HRA 1998. The trial judge may cater for this contingency by deciding in his discretion to exclude evidence.[125]

(c) Fingerprints and samples

23.73 The taking of fingerprints or other samples is permitted where the person is in custody. Furthermore, a person not in custody who has been charged with or informed that he will be reported for a recordable offence may be required to attend

---

[121] See Police and Criminal Evidence Act 1984, s 58 and Code C, para 6.
[122] Code C, para 11.5.
[123] ibid para 11.6 and see *R v Osbourne* [1973] QB 678.
[124] Criminal Justice Act 1987, s 2.
[125] *R v Hertfordshire CC, ex p Green Environmental Industries Ltd* [2000] 2 AC 412. See further A Ashworth, *Human Rights, Serious Crime and Criminal Procedure* (London: Sweet & Maxwell, 2002) ch 2, and D Feldman, *Civil Liberties and Human Rights in England and Wales* (2nd edn, Oxford: OUP, 2002) 384–398.

at a police station to have a sample taken. This should facilitate the use of summons to bring a person before the court and should also facilitate liberty before trial simply because a person will not need to be held in custody for investigative steps to be taken.[126]

(i) Fingerprints

A person's fingerprints or palm prints may be taken freely provided that he consents.[127] Fingerprints may be taken without consent if an officer of at least the rank of inspector so orders, or if the person has been charged with a recordable offence or informed that he will be reported for such an offence and if his fingerprints have not been taken in the course of the investigation.[128] Fingerprints may also be taken compulsorily where a previous set is incomplete or unsatisfactory. They may be taken for the purposes of detecting personation by a person answering to bail. Fingerprints may also be taken from someone who has been convicted of a recordable offence, or cautioned ,warned or reprimanded for such an offence.[129]

23.74

Provision has also been made for taking footprints and skin impressions generally.[130]

23.75

(ii) Intimate and non-intimate samples

Intimate samples, that is, blood, semen, or other tissue fluid, urine, saliva or pubic hair or a swab taken from a person's body orifices other than from the mouth may be taken from a person if an officer of the rank of inspector authorizes this and the suspect consents. The person must be suspected, on reasonable grounds, of involvement in a recordable offence. It must reasonably be believed that a sample will tend to prove or disprove his involvement.[131] If a person refuses to consent the trial court may draw an adverse inference against him.

23.76

Non-intimate samples may be taken compulsorily or by consent. The offence must be a recordable offence.[132] Dental impressions may be taken by a registered dental practitioner. Other intimate samples may be taken by a registered medical practitioner or registered nurse.[133] Fingerprints or samples may be checked against an appropriate database. A person who is detained at a police station may be photographed with or without consent. Such a photograph may be used in the investigation of crime.[134]

23.77

---

[126] Police and Criminal Evidence Act 1984, s 63A.
[127] ibid s 61(1)
[128] ibid s 61(3).
[129] ibid s 61(4A)–8(A).
[130] Criminal Justice and Police Act 2001, s 80.
[131] Police and Criminal Evidence Act 1984, ss 61 and 65.
[132] ibid s 63
[133] ibid s 62(9).
[134] ibid s 64A

(d) Ascertaining identity

23.78 An officer of the rank of inspector may authorize the search and examination of a person detained at a police station for the purpose of ascertaining whether he has a mark which would tend to identify him as a person involved in the commission of an offence or for the purpose of facilitating the ascertainment of his identity. A photograph may be taken of any such mark.[135]

23.79 Further powers apply to terrorist suspects under the Terrorism Act 2000. No account is taken of them here.

D. The Decision to Prosecute

23.80 English procedure permits the bringing of a private prosecution. While such prosecutions are rare they are sometimes brought by aggrieved persons in respect of matters which the authorities do not propose to take forward, and sometimes by pressure groups who feel that particular categories of offences, for example driving offences, are not being pursued with sufficient vigour. The discussion which follows deals, however, with prosecutions brought by public authorities and primarily by the police.

(a) The role of the police

23.81 The police in the first instance determine whether proceedings should be brought; that is, the police have authority to divert matters out of the criminal justice system or to charge the offender. The police may, in the case of an adult offender, formally caution the offender.[136] For this to be done there must be sufficient evidence to prosecute, the offender must admit his guilt, and the offender must agree to be cautioned. While a caution does not amount to a conviction it may be brought to the attention of the court when considering sentence if the offender re-offends in future.

23.82 Cautioning procedure is or may be used in the case of vulnerable offenders, for example those who are elderly and infirm or suffering from mental or severe physical illness.

23.83 The issue of a caution does not preclude a prosecution for the matter in question. The Director of Public Prosecutions may prosecute notwithstanding a discontinuance letter though he should take account of it.[137] Furthermore, a caution cannot preclude a private prosecution. There can, in particular, be no abuse of process

---

[135] Police and Criminal Evidence Act 1984, s 54A.
[136] See Home Office Circulars 1990/59 and 1994/18.
[137] *R v DPP, ex p Burke* [1997] COD 169.

where the suspect is told by the police officer administering the caution that the cautioning procedure does not preclude a private prosecution.[138]

The Crime and Disorder Act 1998 contains a procedure for the reprimand and warning of children and young persons. There must be evidence that the person committed the offence. The offender must admit guilt. The constable must be satisfied that a prosecution would not be in the public interest. A constable may then reprimand an offender who has not previously been reprimanded or warned. Alternatively he may warn an offender who has not previously been warned.[139]   **23.84**

(b) Public prosecutions

Most prosecutions are brought by the Crown Prosecution Service whose duty it is to take over all prosecutions brought by the police.[140] Common to all prosecuting authorities which include other government departments and agencies is the principle of discretion to prosecute. That discretion may not, however, take the form of a decision not to prosecute all prosecutions for a particular statutory or, indeed, common law offence. Discretion may only be exercised for or against prosecution in the light of the circumstances of a particular offence.[141]   **23.85**

The Crown Prosecution Service may, on reviewing the case papers, decide that no prosecution should be brought or, as not infrequently happens, that a different or lesser charge than that proposed by the police should be proceeded with.   **23.86**

Decisions by the Crown Prosecution Service whether or not to prosecute are taken in the light of the Code for Crown Prosecutors.[142] The Code is organized according to two principles. The first is that of evidential sufficiency according to which no prosecution should be brought unless there is enough evidence to provide a realistic prospect of conviction. The prosecutor must have regard to the likely nature of the defence case. The test is objective and means that the trier of fact, properly directed in accordance with the law, is more likely than not to convict the defendant of the charge alleged.[143]   **23.87**

The Crown prosecutor must, if there is sufficient evidence to justify proceedings, consider whether it is in the public interest to continue proceedings either for the charge as laid by the police or for a different charge. The factors to be taken into account are set out in the Code for Crown Prosecutors. They include such questions as whether vulnerable persons need to be protected, the significance of the   **23.88**

---

[138] *Hayter v L* [1997] 1 WLR 854.
[139] Crime and Disorder Act 1998, ss 65 and 66.
[140] Prosecution of Offences Act 1985, s 39(2)(a).
[141] *R (on the application of Pretty) v DPP* [2001] UKHL 61; [2002] 1 AC 800.
[142] The current text is reproduced in *Blackstone's Criminal Practice* (n 7 above) Appendix 4.
[143] Code for Crown Prosecutors, para 5.2. The factors to be applied in assessing the case are contained in paras 5.3 and 5.4 of the Code.

offender's participation in the offence, whether the offence was motivated by racial or religious factors, the defendant's previous record, the penalty likely to be imposed in the event of conviction , and whether the defendant is elderly or in ill-health.

23.89   The Code provides that Crown prosecutors should select charges which are commensurate with the gravity of the offending. Crown prosecutors should not over-charge in order to provoke a guilty plea. Charges should, conversely, not be reduced simply because that will bring the matter within the exclusive jurisdiction of the magistrates' court. These principles together with the principle, also enshrined in the Code, that Crown prosecutors should accept a plea arrangement only if they think that such an arrangement will enable the court to pass a sentence commensurate with the gravity of the offending, should militate against improvident plea bargaining. Whether they do so in all cases is doubtful.

23.90   A decision not to prosecute may be subject to judicial review but there must be present bad faith, dishonesty or some exceptional circumstance.[144] The prosecution may, for example, bring a charge of indecent assault even though the time limit for another, apt offence, has expired provided that the prosecution was not at fault in failing to bring charges earlier, and did not act in bad faith.[145] A decision to caution may, for example, be quashed where there has been a failure to investigate the matter fully, or to consult the victim, or irrelevant circumstances have been taken into account.[146]

23.91   It is doubtful whether judicial review applies to decisions to prosecute. Other remedies are available, for example a stay on grounds of abuse of process.[147]

E. Jurisdiction of English Courts

(a) Introduction

23.92   The general principle, subject to statutory exceptions, is that English courts do not have jurisdiction to try offences committed abroad even if the accused is a British subject.[148]

23.93   The first difficulty is to know when an offence occurred abroad. In determining this question courts have asked where the offence terminated. If the terminatory

---

[144] *R v DPP, ex p Kebilene* [2000] 2 AC 326.
[145] *R v Jones* [2002] EWCA Crim 2983; [2003] 1 WLR 1590.
[146] *R (on the application of Omar) v Chief Constable of Bedfordshire Police* [2002] All ER (D) 295 (Dec).
[147] ibid; *R v DPP, ex p Kebilene* [1999] 3 WLR 972, 983 *per* Lord Steyn, 1006 *per* Lord Hobhouse; but see *R v Chief Constable of Kent , ex p L* [1993] 1 All ER 756.
[148] *Treacy v DPP* [1971] AC 357.

element of a substantive offence occurred in England and Wales the offence is held to have been committed here.[149] It follows that English courts have jurisdiction over it.

Where inchoate offences are concerned the rules differ according to the type of **23.94** offence concerned. Attempts are triable in England, even though none of the physical acts constituting the offence occurred here provided that the completed offence would have been triable in England had it succeeded. The accused need thus not have been in England at the time of the alleged attempt.[150] A conspiracy entered into abroad to commit an offence in England and Wales may be tried here even though no overt act is performed in England and Wales. Such a conspiracy may be to commit a crime in England and Wales or, more broadly, within the English jurisdiction.[151] It will, of course, be necessary to establish the link between the conspiracy and England and Wales or the English jurisdiction or possibly to show that the conspiracy is continuing, but this may, in any given case, be established otherwise than by showing an overt act.[152]

(b) Statutory extensions: fraud and dishonesty

The common law rule that it is not an offence to conspire in England and Wales **23.95** to do something in a foreign country has been modified by statute. It is an offence to pursue a course of conduct that would amount to an offence in the foreign state provided that the conduct in question would also amount to an offence in England and Wales. The accused must have done some act in relation to the agreement before it was formed here, or have joined it here, or have done or omitted to do something here in pursuance of the agreement.[153]

Major statutory extensions concern offences of fraud and dishonesty. The relevant **23.96** offences are designated as group A offences—the major substantive offences of fraud and dishonesty) and group B offences (inchoate offences relating to them). Jurisdiction over group A offences depends upon a relevant event having occurred here: that is, any act or omission or other event proof of which is required for commission of the offence.[154] A person may be guilty of attempting to commit a group A offence whether or not the attempt took place or had an effect in England and Wales.[155]

---

[149] *R v Manning* [1999] QB 980.
[150] *DPP v Stonehouse* [1978] AC 55.
[151] *R v Bow Street Metropolitan Stipendiary Magistrate, ex p Pinochet Ugarte (No 3)* [2000] 1 AC 147; *R (on the application of Al Fawwaz) v Governor of Brixton Prison* [2001] UKHL 69, [2002] 1 AC 556.
[152] *DPP v Doot* [1973] AC 807; *Liangsiriprasert v US* [1991] AC 225.
[153] Criminal Justice (Terrorism and Conspiracy) Act 1998.
[154] Criminal Justice Act 1993, s 2
[155] ibid s 3(3)(a) and (b).

23.97   In respect of conspiracy to defraud there must have been a conspiracy to defraud someone in England and Wales but the person to be tried need not himself have become party to the conspiracy in England and Wales nor need any act or omission have been done here pursuant to it.[156] Similarly, incitement becomes triable here if the incitement takes place here even though it is to commit an offence abroad. If the purpose of the inchoate offence is to commit a crime abroad it must be shown that the act or omission intended would constitute an offence in the place where the act or event was intended to occur. This applies to common law offences of conspiracy to cheat and defraud as well.[157]

(c) Other statutory exceptions

23.98   British courts have jurisdiction in respect of certain offences of incitement to commit sexual acts abroad against infants.[158] Furthermore, British courts now have jurisdiction over certain sexual offences committed abroad.[159] These provision are aimed at 'sex tourists' who debauch children abroad.

23.99   Murder, manslaughter, bigamy and offences under the Official Secrets Act 1911 committed by a British subject are triable in England.[160] So too are war crimes in certain limited circumstances.[161]

23.100   Offences committed at sea in territorial waters or on board any UK ship on the high seas are triable here[162] as are offences committed on the high seas by a British subject on a vessel to which he does not belong.[163] To these instances may be added offences on British aircraft, and certain terrorist offences, piracy (at common law) and aircraft hijacking.[164]

(d) Consents to prosecution

23.101   Certain offences require consent to prosecution by one or other of the Law Officers or by the Director of Public Prosecutions. The list is heterogeneous simply because it is not clear what the public policy which underlies certain of these instances may be though it is fair to say that in many of them the decision to prosecute may be of some delicacy.[165]

---

[156] Criminal Justice Act 1993, s 3(2).
[157] ibid s 6
[158] Sexual Offences (Conspiracy and Incitement) Act 1996.
[159] Sexual Offences Act 1997, s 7.
[160] Offences Against the Person Act 1861, ss 9, 10, and 57; Official Secrets Act 1911, s 10.
[161] War Crimes Act 1991, s 1.
[162] Territorial Waters Jurisdiction Act 1878; *R v Liverpool Justices, ex p Molyneux* [1972] 2 QB 384.
[163] *R v Kelly* [1982] AC 665; *R v Cumberworth* (1989) 89 Cr App R 187.
[164] Respectively, Civil Aviation Act 1982, s 92; Suppression of Terrorism Act 1978, s 4; Aviation Security Act 1982, s 1.
[165] See, eg, Law Reform (Year and a Day) Act 1996; War Crimes Act 1991.

Consent to prosecution is normally given in writing but may be given orally.[166] **23.102**
The consent may be in general terms to prosecution under a particular enactment.
The Director of Public Prosecutions' consent to prosecution may be given on his
behalf by a Crown prosecutor.[167]

(e) Time limits

In general time does not run against the Crown. An information for a summary **23.103**
offence must, however, be laid within six months of the offence.[168] Time limits
also apply to certain sexual offences.[169] Even where there is no statutory time limit,
Article 6(1) ECHR and the HRA 1998 guarantee a right to a fair hearing within
a reasonable time.

(f) Immunity

Children under ten are irrebuttably presumed not to be capable of crime. The pre- **23.104**
sumption against criminal capacity is rebuttable in the case of children aged between ten and 13.

Sovereign immunity applies to Her Majesty or to foreign heads of state and their en- **23.105**
tourage.[170] Immunity is also conferred upon diplomatic agents of foreign states.[171]

F. Classification of Offences and Mode of Trial

(a) Classification of offences

Offences are divided into three classes, those triable only on indictment, offences **23.106**
triable either on indictment or summarily (offences triable either way), and offences triable only summarily. The classification of statutory offences is determined either by the statute creating the offence, or by virtue of being listed in
Sch I to the Magistrates' Courts Act 1980. All common law offences are indictable.
Some are listed in Sch 1 and so are triable either way. In effect most indictable offences are triable either way: the most serious are triable only on indictment.

(b) Mode of trial

Mode of trial must be determined where a person over the age of 18 is charged **23.107**
with an offence triable either way. A person who is brought before a magistrates'

---

[166] *R v Cain* [1976] QB 496.
[167] Prosecution of Offences Act 1985, s 7.
[168] Magistrates' Courts Act 1980, s 127.
[169] Sexual Offences Act 1956, Sch 2, para 10; Sexual Offences Act 1967, s 7.
[170] State Immunity Act 1978, s 20.
[171] Diplomatic Privileges Act 1964.

court charged with an 'either way' offence will be asked to intimate a plea were the case to go to trial. If he intimates that he will plead guilty the proceedings are treated as a summary trial at which he pleaded guilty. He may, however, be remitted to the Crown Court for sentence if the magistrates' court considers that its sentencing powers are insufficient.[172] The purpose of this procedure is to limit the number of 'cracked' cases being brought before the Crown Court.

23.108　If the accused intimates that he proposes to plead guilty the magistrates will, after hearing representations by the prosecution and the defence, determine whether the case is more suitable for summary trial or for trial on indictment The court has regard to such matters as the gravity of the offence, its nature, and whether it has adequate powers of punishment. In the case of criminal damage the value of the property concerned is relevant and may deprive the accused of his election.[173]

23.109　If the case appears suitable for summary trial the court puts the accused to his election as to whether he wishes the case to be tried summarily or on indictment. The court informs the accused that if he elects summary trial he may be sent to the Crown Court for sentence if he is convicted and if the court concludes that its sentencing powers are inadequate.[174]

23.110　A magistrates' court should not take account of the accused's character and antecedents when determining mode of trial.[175] These matters are relevant when the court comes to consider sentence.

23.111　If the accused chooses to be tried on indictment the matter proceeds by way of committal proceedings. If the court concludes that the case is suitable for trial on indictment only, the court proceeds to committal proceedings.[176] The prosecution may not prevent summary trial save in the special case when one of the Law Officers is conducting the prosecution and requires that the matter be tried on indictment.[177]

23.112　The accused must be present at the mode of trial procedure unless his disorderly behaviour makes it impracticable for proceedings to be conducted in his presence or he is legally represented and consents to the proceedings being conducted in his absence. The court must, in addition, consider that there is good reason for so doing.[178]

---

[172] Magistrates' Courts Act 1980, s 17A.

[173] ibid s 22. See further *Practice Direction (Criminal Proceedings: Consolidation)* [2002] 1 WLR 2870, Pt V.

[174] ibid s 20(2)(b).

[175] *R v Colchester Justices, ex p North Essex Building Co* [1977] 1 WLR 1109; *R v Warley Magistrates' Court, ex p DPP* [1999] 1 WLR 216.

[176] ibid s.20(3)(b).

[177] Magistrates' Courts Act 1980, s 19.

[178] ibid s 23(2)(a).

(c) Variation of mode of trial decision

A summary trial may be converted into committal proceedings by the magistrates' **23.113** court at any time before the conclusion of the evidence for the prosecution.[179] Conversely, a magistrates' court which has commenced committal proceedings in respect of an either way offence may, if it considers that the offence is more suitable for summary proceedings, switch to summary trial.[180] The accused must consent and he is warned that the matter may be remitted to the Crown Court if the magistrates' powers of sentencing are inadequate.

(d) Withdrawal of election

The magistrates have a discretion to permit the accused to withdraw his elec-   **23.114** tion.[181] Such an election should be permitted when it appears that the accused did not properly understand the nature of the choice put to him, or is allowed to change his plea or where the justice of the case otherwise requires it.

(e) Reducing charges and mode of trial

Save in a case of blatant abuse the prosecution can reduce a charge from an offence **23.115** triable either way to one triable only summarily, so depriving the accused of his election.[182] The prosecution should not, however, reduce such a charge if the case is too serious for summary trial.[183] Nor should the prosecution gratuitously increase charges to avoid summary trial or generally.[184]

(f) From first court appearance to committal

The accused may be brought before a magistrates' court from police detention fol-   **23.116** lowing arrest, or following bail granted by the police after arrest, or by summons.

A magistrate may issue either a summons or a warrant for arrest on the basis of an **23.117** information laid before him. An information may be laid orally or in writing by the prosecutor, by counsel or solicitor, or in the case of a police force laid on behalf of a named officer or the chief constable.[185]

A justice before whom an information has been laid may issue a summons to at-   **23.118** tend.[186] The information must allege an offence known to the law, be within any specified time limits, disclose any necessary consents, and be within the jurisdiction

---

[179] ibid s 25(1). 'Evidence' means evidence to establish the guilt of the accused: *Chief Constable of West Midlands v Gillard* [1986] AC 442.
[180] ibid s 25(3).
[181] *R v Birmingham Justices, ex p Hodgson* [1985] QB 1131.
[182] *R v Canterbury and St Augustine Justices, ex p Klisiak* [1982] QB 398.
[183] *R v Bodmin Justices, ex p McEwen* [1947] KB 321. The principles refer to accepting summary jurisdiction but apply in the context of reduction.
[184] See generally Code for Crown Prosecutors, para 7.3
[185] Magistrates' Courts Rules 1981, SI 1981/552, r 4(2); *Rubin v DPP* [1990] 2 QB 80.
[186] Magistrates' Courts Act 1980, s 1(2).

of the court.[187] The decision to issue a summons is judicial. The magistrates may refuse a summons which appears to be frivolous or vexatious or otherwise to be an abuse of process.[188]

23.119 Alternatively, a justice may issue a warrant for the arrest of the offender provided that the information be in writing and substantiated on oath and that the offence be indictable or punishable with imprisonment or the accused's address be insufficiently established for a summons to be served.[189] Such a warrant may be endorsed for bail.

(g) Jurisdiction

23.120 The jurisdiction of the court does not depend upon the manner in which the accused is brought before it. Even if he is brought before the court on an invalid warrant the magistrates' court will have jurisdiction to try him. If, however, he has been brought before the court as a result of a blatant abuse the accused may be able to secure a stay of proceedings on the basis of abuse of process.[190]

(h) Adjournments and remands

23.121 A magistrates' court may, before beginning to inquire into the offence as examining justices or at any time thereafter, adjourn the hearing and remand the accused. It has the like power whether before or after beginning to try an information.[191] An adjournment should not be unreasonably refused either to the defence or the prosecution.[192]

23.122 The accused may be remanded in custody or on bail. The general rule is that a magistrates' court may not remand an accused in custody for more than eight clear days.[193] Following summary conviction an accused may, however, be remanded for up to three weeks in custody for reports.[194] A similar period applies to obtain medical examinations and reports where the accused, being under a disability, is found to have made the act or omission charged.[195] Where a court is not so constituted as to proceed immediately to summary trial the accused may be remanded in custody to a day when the court will be properly constituted.[196]

---

[187] *R v Gateshead Justices, ex p Tesco Stores Ltd* [1981] QB 470.

[188] *R v Bury Justices, ex p Anderton* (1987) 137 NLJ 410.

[189] Magistrates' Courts Act 1980, s 1(1)(b).

[190] *R v Manchester Stipendiary Magistrate, ex p Hill* [1981] 1 AC 328; *R v Horseferry Road Magistrates' Court, ex p Bennett (No 1)* [1994] 1 AC 42.

[191] Magistrates' Courts Act 1980, ss 5, 10 and 18.

[192] *R v Neath and Port Talbot Justices, ex p DPP* [2000] 1 WLR 1376; *R v Thames Magistrates' Court, ex p Polemis* [1974] 1 WLR 1371 where the effect of the refusal was to disable the defence from preparing the case.

[193] Magistrates' Courts Act 1980, s 128.

[194] ibid s 10(3).

[195] Powers of Criminal Courts (Sentencing) Act 2000, s 11(1).

[196] Magistrates' Courts Act 1980, s 128(6)(c).

A remand in custody for a longer period will also be allowed where the accused has **23.123** previously been remanded in custody for the same offence, is before the court, and the court has fixed a date on which it expects the next effective hearing to take place.[197] The maximum period is 28 days or the date of the next effective hearing, whichever is the shorter. The same period applies to an accused who is already in custody under a custodial sentence.[198]

An accused who has consented not to be present at future remands, whose consent **23.124** is still subsisting, and who is legally represented, may be remanded in his absence but this cannot be done on more than three consecutive occasions. The period of remand is eight clear days.[199] The intent is to expedite court procedures when the matter is not yet ready to be dealt with.

(i) Advance information

An accused who is charged with an offence triable either way is entitled to advance **23.125** information of the prosecution case and no mode of trial hearing may take place until either such information has been provided or the accused has waived his right to it.[200] Where the defence requires such information the prosecution must either serve its witness statements or a summary of the case. The accused is entitled to see any document on which the prosecution proposes to rely which includes a video tape.[201]

G. Bail

In the interests of individual liberty English law has long stressed two distinct, but **23.126** complementary, values. The first is represented by bail which permits a person to be released provisionally during the proceedings. The second is that of speedy trial itself. Both these values are now bolstered by Article 5(4) and Article 6(1) ECHR, and the HRA 1998.

Bail was defined by Blackstone, thus:[202] **23.127**

> . . . a delivery or bailment, of a person to his sureties, upon their giving (together with himself) sufficient security for his appearance: he being supposed to continue in their friendly custody instead of going to gaol.

---

[197] ibid s 128A.
[198] ibid s 131.
[199] ibid s 128(3A)–(3E).
[200] Magistrates' Courts (Advance Information) Rules 1985, SI 1985/601.
[201] *R (on the application of Donahue) v Calderdale Magistrates' Court* [2001] Crim LR 141.
[202] *Blackstone's Commentaries*, vol IV, 294: on the surety as custodian see *Foxall v Barnett* (1853) 2 E & B 928.

This is no longer an accurate description of the bail system for most bail orders do not require sureties and where they are required do not hold the accused in their custody. Blackstone's definition does, nonetheless, serve to explain the strictness with which sureties are held to their obligation.

23.128 Historically, again, the law struck both at the wrongful refusal of bail and at demanding excessive bail.[203] The modern statute governing bail, the Bail Act 1976, emphasizes the value which English law places upon freedom before trial.

(a) Who may grant bail

23.129 In the great majority of cases the police grant bail. A person who is arrested without warrant for an offence, or under a warrant not endorsed for bail, or a person who returns to a police station to answer to bail, may be released either with or without sureties either to appear before a magistrates' court or at a police station at a designated time and place.[204] A person whose further detention cannot be justified must be released with or without bail.[205] A person who is charged may, again, be released either unconditionally or on bail.[206]

(b) Magistrates' court

23.130 A magistrates' court may grant bail to a person who appears or is brought before it in the course of or in connection with proceedings other than treason.[207] A prisoner will usually make a bail application on first appearance. If bail is refused he may reapply on successive remands. The right to make repeated bail applications is, however, subject to restriction. At the first hearing after that at which the court decided not to grant bail, the accused may support his bail application with any argument as to fact or law that he desires whether or not he has advanced that argument previously. At subsequent hearings the court need not hear arguments as to fact or law which it has heard previously.[208] Thus, an accused cannot renew a bail application before the magistrates unless he has something new to say. A magistrates' court which declines bail after fully hearing the matter must issue a certificate to that effect. The accused may then appeal against a refusal of bail to the Crown Court.[209]

23.131 Magistrates may commit an accused for trial either in custody or on bail. This affords another occasion for a fully argued bail hearing. The fact of committal is not,

---

[203] *Blackstone's Commentaries*, vol IV, 294, and see Bill of Rights 1688 on excessive bail.
[204] Police and Criminal Evidence Act 1984, ss 37 , 43 and 47.
[205] ibid s 40.
[206] ibid s 38.
[207] Bail Act 1976, s 4(2)(a)–(b); as to treason, Magistrates' Courts Act 1980, s 2.
[208] Bail Act 1976, Sch 1, Pt IIA.
[209] ibid s 6A, and see *Practice Direction (Criminal Proceeedings: Consolidation)* [2002] 1 WLR 2870, paras 53.1–53.2.

however, a new argument for the purpose.[210] Magistrates may also consider bail when committing a person to the Crown Court for sentence.[211]

A person, summarily convicted, who has been sentenced to a custodial sentence may be granted bail pending appeal.[212] So too may a person who has been remanded for reports.[213]   **23.132**

(c) Crown Court

The Crown Court may grant bail to a person committed for trial or whose case has been transferred to the Crown Court or who has been sent to the Crown Court without committal proceedings for an offence triable only on indictment.[214] Similarly, bail may be granted to a person summarily convicted, who appeals a custodial sentence; to a person in the custody of the Crown Court pending disposal of his case; to any person who is applying for case stated or for judicial review to quash the decision; to any person to whom the Crown Court has granted a certificate that his case is fit for appeal to the Court of Appeal; and any person who has been remanded in custody by a magistrates' court.[215]   **23.133**

(d) High Court

The High Court may grant bail to any person who has been refused bail by a magistrates' court.[216] It may grant bail after sentence in respect of summary conviction offence where the applicant applies to the High Court to state a case or for judicial review.[217]   **23.134**

The jurisdiction of the High Court to grant bail is distinct from that of the Crown Court being founded both upon statute and the inherent jurisdiction of the court.[218] Bail applications are, however, usually made to the Crown Court for reasons pertaining to legal aid.   **23.135**

(e) Court of Appeal

The powers of the Court of Appeal are considered at paras 23.142–23.413 below.   **23.136**

---

[210] *R v Reading Crown Court, ex p Malik* [1981] QB 451.
[211] Magistrates' Courts Act 1980, ss 37 and 38.
[212] ibid s 113.
[213] ibid s 10(3); Powers of Criminal Courts (Sentencing) Act 2000, s 11.
[214] Supreme Court Act 1981, s 81(1)(a).
[215] ibid s 81(b)–(g) and see *Practice Direction (Criminal Proceedings: Consolidation)* [2002] 1 WLR 2870, para 50.
[216] Criminal Justice Act 1967, s 22(1).
[217] Criminal Justice Act 1948, s 37.
[218] *R v Reading Crown Court, ex p Malik* [1981] QB 451. Habeas Corpus Act 1679, s 2 also empowers the judges to grant bail, at any rate in vacation, but it is obscurely expressed and appears to be in desuetude.

(f) Prosecution appeal against bail

23.137   The prosecution has a right to appeal to the Crown Court against a grant of bail where the offence carries a maximum of five years' imprisonment or is an offence of taking a motor vehicle without consent. The prosecution must be conducted by the Director of Public Prosecutions or a person prescribed in an order by the Home Secretary. The prosecution must have made representations opposing bail before it was granted. Written notice must have been given and served within two hours of the decision.

23.138   The prosecution may also, in the case of an offence triable either way or on indictment only, apply on the basis of information not available to the court or the police officer granting bail for a grant of bail to be reconsidered. The court may withhold bail or impose or vary bail conditions.[219]

(g) Principles relating to grant of bail

23.139   Section 4 of the Bail Act 1976 creates a presumption in favour of bail in favour of the following classes of persons: first, an accused person other than a fugitive; secondly, an offender who is being dealt with for breach of a community based punishment order; and thirdly to a convicted person whose case is being adjourned for reports. The court may not, in the absence of exceptional circumstances, grant bail to a person who is charged with or who has been convicted by a UK court of murder, attempted murder, culpable homicide, rape or attempted rape.[220]

23.140   The right to, or presumption in favour of, bail is far from absolute. The court, when dealing with an imprisonable offence, need not grant bail where there are substantial grounds for believing that the accused, if released, would abscond, or commit another offence while on bail, or interfere with witnesses or otherwise obstruct the course of justice.[221] In addition a person may be denied bail where the court considers this necessary for his own protection. A person in custody pursuant to the sentence of a court need not be granted bail. Nor need bail be granted to a person in breach of bail conditions; or a person remanded for reports where these can best be done in custody. Finally, a court can deny bail where it does not have the information necessary for it to make a decision.[222]

23.141   Courts, in deciding bail applications where there is a danger of abscondence, the commission of further offences, or interference with proceedings must have regard

---

[219] Bail Act 1976, s 5B.

[220] Criminal Justice and Public Order Act 1994, s 25. This provision is compatible with Art 5 ECHR: *R (on the application of O) v Harrow Crown Court* [2003] EWHC 868; The Times, 29 May 2003. Assuming that the provision is worth having, the limitation to convictions by UK courts seems strange. In any event the courts are not powerless, where a person has a prior overseas conviction for such an offence, to refuse bail.

[221] Bail Act 1976, Sch 1, Pt I, para 2.

[222] ibid Sch 1, paras 3–7.

to any of four relevant considerations each of which may have an effect upon the accused's actions. The first is the nature and seriousness of the offence and the way in which it will probably be dealt with. Secondly, it must consider the accused's character, antecedents, and family ties. Thirdly, the accused's previous bail history is relevant, as is, fourthly, the strength of the case against him.[223]

The task of the court is to weigh up the relevant circumstances. It may on balance, for example, grant bail to a person who proposes to emigrate if to refuse to do so would cause disproportionate hardship.[224]

23.142

Bail may only be refused to a person accused or convicted of a non-imprisonable offence on narrow grounds. These are: failure to appear to bail previously which leads the court to fear a possibility of abscondence; for protective reasons; in the case of offenders in custody; and where there is a breach of bail conditions.[225] In addition, where a custody time limit has expired the accused has an absolute right to bail. In such a case the court may impose conditions which must be complied with after release.[226]

23.143

Bail does not involve the accused either in depositing money or entering into a recognizance.[227] Failure to appear or to abide by conditions is instead created an offence subject to a power of arrest.[228] The accused may, however, be required to provide a surety or sureties for his surrender to custody and if it appears likely that he will not remain in the United Kingdom until the time appointed for his surrender he may be required to give security for his appearance.[229]

23.144

A court granting bail may impose conditions upon it so as to ensure against abscondence, the commission of further offences, or interference with witnesses and the investigation of the offence. The only prerequisite for lawfully imposing a condition on bail is that its imposition be necessary to achieve the aims of the section.[230] Commonly imposed conditions relate to residence, notification of change of address, periodic reporting to the police, the surrender of passports, a curfew, and a requirement not to approach or be in the vicinity of the victim or witnesses. A requirement may also be imposed requiring the accused to co-operate in the making of reports for the purpose of dealing with him.[231]

23.145

---

[223] Bail Act 1976, Sch 1, para 9.
[224] *R v Edwards* [1976] Crim LR 122.
[225] Bail Act 1976, Pt II, Sch 1.
[226] ibid s 4(1) as read with Prosecution of Offences (Custody Time Limits) Regulations 1987, SI 1987/299, reg 8.
[227] On the impropriety of demanding money see *R v Harrow Justices, ex p Morris* [1973] 1 QB 672.
[228] Bail Act 1976, s 6.
[229] ibid s 3. The court or the police must consider whether the surety, if any, will be good for the obligation assumed.
[230] *R (on the application of CPS) v Chorley Justices* [2002] EWHC 2162; (2002) 166 JP 764.
[231] Bail Act 1976, s 3(6)(d) and see Powers of Criminal Courts (Sentencing) Act 2000, ss 11(1), 3(6A) and 6(B) (re murder).

23.146 A court may vary the conditions of bail. Conversely it may impose conditions upon bail originally granted unconditionally.[232]

23.147 An absconder or a person who, having surrendered, absents himself from the court without leave may be arrested.[233] A constable may arrest a person who he believes, on reasonable grounds, will breach his bail conditions. A surety may protect himself by notifying a constable in writing that the accused is unlikely to attend trial so enabling a constable to arrest the person.[234] The fact of arrest relieves the surety of his obligations. A person so arrested may be held in custody or be granted bail.

(h) Continuous bail

23.148 Magistrates' courts and the Crown Court may, in effect, make bail continuous. This obviates the necessity of requiring sureties to enter into a fresh recognizance every time the accused's case is adjourned. Continuous bail is useful where the accused is granted bail for the overnight adjournments of his case and should be granted unless there is an apparent risk that the accused will abscond. The surety will, however, be liable if at any further stage the accused fails to appear.[235]

23.149 It should be noted that while bail may be continued after the summing up has started, the power is used sparingly.[236]

(i) Estreat

23.150 Estreat is the procedure by which a person may be made to forfeit all or part of the sum represented by the recognizance into which he entered. Estreat may be ordered in full, in part, or not at all.[237] The purpose of estreat is not to punish the surety but marks the fact that he has failed in his obligation to ensure that the accused will be present to stand his trial.[238] Fault is, however, relevant to the question of estreat.[239]

23.151 It is for the surety to satisfy the court that it would be unfair to order estreat of the recognizance, whether in whole or in part.[240] The courts have refused or limited estreat where the surety was not at fault and where he used all due diligence to ensure the presence of the accused.[241] He may be treated leniently by the court when

---

[232] Bail Act 1976, s 3(8).
[233] For the meaning of surrender see *R v Central Criminal Court, ex p Guney* [1996] AC 616.
[234] Bail Act 1976, s 7(3)–(5).
[235] Magistrates' Courts Act 1980, s 128(4).
[236] *Practice Direction (Criminal Proceedings: Consolidation)* [2002] 1 WLR 2870, para 25.
[237] eg, Crown Court Rules 1982, r 21; Magistrates' Courts Act 1980, s 120; Criminal Appeal Rules, r 6.
[238] *R v Maidstone Crown Court, ex p Lever* [1995] 1 WLR 928.
[239] *R v Southampton Justices, ex p Green* [1976] 1 QB 11.
[240] *Re Cheesman, Adams and Wright* [1993] COD 369.
[241] *R v York Crown Court, ex p Coleman* [1987] Crim LR 761; *R v Reading Crown Court, ex p Bello* [1992] 3 All ER 353.

he was not notified of the dates of adjourned hearings even though the court is under no obligation to do this. The practice of making bail continuous could otherwise prove unworkable because the surety would have to be present and consent at each hearing.[242] A surety cannot, however, expect mercy where he has not exercised due diligence or where he has misled the court by misstating his assets in the first place.[243]

Estreat of the security posted by an accused who absconds may also be ordered.[244]   **23.152**

H. Speedy Trial and Custody Time Limits

(a) Introduction

We have noted that the values of liberty before trial and speedy trial are complementary. Both were originally ensured by the Habeas Corpus Act 1679. Today speedy trial is vindicated by the power to stay proceedings for abuse of power where culpable delay causes grave prejudice to the defence.[245] In addition r 24 of the Crown Court Rules 1982 provides that the minimum and maximum periods between committal or the giving of a notice of transfer and arraignment shall be 14 days and eight weeks respectively. This rule is, however, directory only, and so does not afford a strong guarantee of speedy trial.[246] The principal guarantee for speedy trial is thus to be found in the scheme of custody time limits.   **23.153**

(b) Custody time limits

The Home Secretary may make regulations fixing a maximum period within which the prosecution may complete the preliminary stages of proceedings as a whole.[247] No overall time limit has, however, been set. Time limits do apply to limit the time during which a person may be kept in custody while awaiting completion of particular stages in the procedure. Each offence attracts its own time limit.[248]   **23.154**

The time limits are:[249]   **23.155**

- In the case of an indictable offence. 70 days between the first appearance of the accused and committal proceedings or, if the court decides to hear the case

---

[242] *R v Warwick Crown Court, ex p Smalley* [1987] 1 WLR 237.
[243] *R v Wood Green Crown Court, ex p Howe* [1992] 1 WLR 702.
[244] Bail Act 1976, ss 3(5) and 5(7) and see *R v Thayne* [1970] 1 QB 141.
[245] See para 23.261 below.
[246] *R v Urbanowski* [1976] 1 WLR 455.
[247] Prosecution of Offences Act 1985, s 22.
[248] *R v Wirral District Magistrates' Court, ex p Meikle* (1990) 154 JP 1035.
[249] Prosecution of Offences (Custody Time Limits) Regulations 1987, rr 4 and 5.

summarily, between first appearance and the court beginning to hear the evidence unless the decision for summary trial is taken within 56 days in which case that is the applicable limit.

- An accused committed for trial in the Crown Court must be tried within 112 days after committal.
- These procedures also apply to proceedings by way of bill of indictment or transfer but the time limits in the latter case differ as the maximum period between the date on which a person is sent to Crown Court for an indictable only offence is 182 days until the start of the trial.[250]
- In certain parts of the country modified time limits apply to proceedings in the Youth Courts.[251]

(c) Extensions

23.156   A time limit may, before it expires, be extended if the court is satisfied that there is good and sufficient cause for doing so and that the prosecution has acted with due expedition and diligently.[252] These are distinct criteria. What may be good and sufficient cause is partially capitulated by statute and includes illness or absence of the accused, a necessary witness, judge or magistrate, or a postponement caused by ordering separate trials.[253] Furthermore, such matters as the nature and complexity of the case are relevant.[254] On the other hand neither the seriousness of the offence nor the need to protect the public are in themselves good and sufficient cause for extending time, nor is the shortness of the extension requested.[255] Most importantly, such matters as staff shortages or inadequate administrative arrangements cannot modify the requirement that the matter proceed with due expedition.[256]

23.157   It is for the prosecution to satisfy the court that an extension is required.

(d) Expiry

23.158   On expiry of a custody time limit the accused must be granted bail. On the other hand, where an accused is committed for trial justices may order his detention notwithstanding the expiry of an earlier time limit (after which he had been held unlawfully in custody).[257] Each stage is thus distinct for the purpose of the scheme.

---

[250] Prosecution of Offences (Custody Time Limits) Regulations 1987, r 5(6B) and see Crime and Disorder Act 1998, s 51.

[251] Prosecution of Offences (Youth Courts Time Limits) Regulations 1999, SI 1999/2743.

[252] Prosecution of Offences Act 1985, s 22.

[253] ibid s 22(3).

[254] *R v Manchester Crown Court, ex p McDonald* [1999] 1 WLR 841.

[255] *R v Sheffield Crown Court, ex p Headley* [2000] Crim LR 374; *R (on the application of Eliot) v Reading Crown Court* [2001] EWHC Admin 464, [2001] 4 All ER 625.

[256] *R v Governor of Winchester Prison, ex p Roddie* [1991] 1 WLR 303.

[257] *R v Sheffield Justices, ex p Turner* [1991] 2 QB 472.

Sureties may not be required but the grant of bail may be subject to conditions and **23.159** a power of arrest applies where it is feared that such conditions may be breached or where they have been breached.[258]

(e) Appeals

Both the prosecution and the defence may appeal against an adverse decision in **23.160** respect of an application to extend.[259]

I. Disclosure

The prosecution is under stringent duties to disclose relevant material in its pos- **23.161** session to the defence. The prosecution thus owes a duty to disclose to the defence the evidence upon which it proposes to rely at trial. The duty differs in its extent depending upon whether the case is to be tried in the Crown Court or summarily (where the submission of a case statement is voluntary).[260]

In addition to the material upon which it proposes to rely the Crown also owes du- **23.162** ties of disclosure in relation to unused material. Disclosure of unused material is regulated by the Criminal Procedure and Investigation Act 1996 and a code of practice made thereunder. The statute distinguishes between primary and sec- ondary disclosure.

Duties in relation to disclosure arise from the commencement of a criminal in- **23.163** vestigation.[261] A police officer investigating an offence comes under a duty to record and retain material gathered or generated during the investigation and which may be relevant to it. He must prepare a schedule for the prosecutor listing material which does not form part of the case against the accused. Sensitive mate- rial should be set out in a separate schedule.

The prosecutor must, as a matter of primary disclosure, disclose any prosecution **23.164** material which has not already been disclosed and which, in the prosecutor's opin- ion, might undermine the prosecution's case against the accused.[262] The test is a subjective one. Material can be said potentially to undermine the prosecution case if it has an adverse effect on the strength of that case. If there is no such material the defence is given a written notice to this effect.

---

[258] Bail Act 1976, ss 3(6) and 7(3)(b).
[259] Prosecution of Offences Act 1985, s 22(7) and (8). On the relationship between disclosure rules and the right to a fair hearing under Art 6(1) ECHR, see Ashworth (n 125 above) 32–33.
[260] Criminal Procedure and Investigations Act 1996, s 1(1).
[261] For definition see Criminal Procedure and Investigations Act 1996, s 22(1)(a)–(b). See Code of Practice, para 2.1.
[262] ibid s 3.

23.165 In some cases it may be appropriate to make disclosure before committal albeit there is no statutory obligation to do so. Examples are material such as a witness' previous convictions which might assist the accused to obtain bail, or material which might facilitate an early application to quash proceedings for abuse of process, material which suggests that a lesser charge should have been preferred, and material the early disclosure of which is essential to the preparation of the defence case.[263]

(a) Defence disclosure

23.166 Once primary disclosure has been made the defence must give a defence statement to the prosecutor.[264] This is a written statement setting out in general terms the nature of the accused's defence, the matters on which he takes issue with the prosecution, and setting out, in the case of each such matter, why he takes issue with the prosecution. Particulars of any alibi must be given including information in the accused's possession which might be of material assistance in finding any such witness.

23.167 The importance of the defence case statement is two-fold. First, it triggers a duty of secondary disclosure in respect of previously undisclosed prosecution material which might reasonably be expected to assist the defence in the light of that statement.[265] Secondly, failure to mention a defence, or putting forward a different defence at trial or to disclose information concerning an alibi witness may be the subject of adverse comment by the trial court.[266]

23.168 The test for secondary disclosure is objective: the prosecutor's duty is to disclose such previously undisclosed prosecution material as might reasonably be expected to assist the accused's defence or to give the accused a written statement that there is no such material.[267]

(b) Material not to be disclosed

23.169 Material must not be disclosed under the Act to the extent that the court, on an application by the prosecutor, concludes that it is not in the public interest to disclose it.[268] Nor may material be disclosed the disclosure of which is prohibited by legislation concerning surveillance.[269]

23.170 Material may be safeguarded from disclosure on grounds of public interest immunity and here the common law rules apply.[270] Under the statute as at common

---

[263] *R v DPP, ex p Lee* [1999] 1 WLR 1950, 1962 *per* Kennedy LJ.
[264] Criminal Procedure and Investigations Act 1996, s 5.
[265] ibid s 7.
[266] ibid s 11. A person cannot, however, be convicted on the basis of an adverse inference alone.
[267] ibid s 7.
[268] ibid s 7(5).
[269] ibid s 7(6).
[270] ibid s 22(1).

The Crown Court will, however, only be able to deal with the charge so committed if the accused pleads guilty to it. Otherwise, it will have to be remitted to the magistrates' court for trial.

(e) Publicity

A report of committal proceedings is restricted to certain formal matters before the court and does not permit an account of the evidence to be given unless either the court has decided not to commit, or trials consequential on committal have all been held, or the court has made an order on application by the accused or any of them that restrictions on reporting shall not apply.[285]   **23.181**

(f) Consequential matters

The court will specify the location of the Crown Court where trial is to take place.[286]   **23.182**
Committal will be on bail or in custody. The better practice, if bail has previously been refused, is to leave the matter to the discretion of the Crown Court.

Committal proceedings are susceptible to judicial review.[287] Judicial review, save   **23.183**
perhaps for abuse of process, will be rare given that committal proceedings are on paper and normally do not involve consideration of the evidence.

Where a person has been committed for trial the bill of indictment is not re-   **23.184**
stricted to the charges on which he was committed but may include, either in substitution for or in addition to counts charging those offences, any counts founded on facts or evidence before the committing justices.[288]

(g) Voluntary bills of indictment

As an alternative to committal proceedings charges may be brought by way of bill   **23.185**
of indictment by the direction or with the consent of a justice of the High Court.[289] This procedure may be used where magistrates have refused to commit an accused or, commonly, where it is desired to add an accused in respect of whom there is no time to conduct committal proceedings to an indictment charging others who have been properly committed. In the former case the magistrates' decision is entitled to respect and there will have to be exceptional circumstances to warrant prosecuting a defendant after it has been found in committal proceedings that he has no case to answer.[290]

---

[285] Magistrates' Courts Act 1980, s 8(2)–(3).
[286] ibid s 7.
[287] *Neill v North Antrim Magistrates' Court* [1992] 1 WLR 1220.
[288] Administration of Justice (Miscellaneous Provisions) Act 1933, s 2.
[289] ibid s 2(2)(b).
[290] *Brooks (Lloyd) v DPP for Jamaica* [1994] 1 AC 568.

23.186   Modern practice contains safeguards for the accused. Voluntary bill procedure is exceptional in character. Consent should only be granted where there is good reason to depart from the ordinary procedure. Prosecutors must give notice to the prospective defendant that an application is to be made. Copies of the documents to be sent to the judge must be served on him. He must be informed that he can make submissions in writing to the judge. The judge may invite or may accede to a request for oral submissions.[291] The issue of a voluntary bill is not subject to judicial review.[292]

(h) Notices of transfer

23.187   In cases of serious or complex fraud a case may be transferred, on the application of a designated authority, usually the Director of the Serious Fraud Office, from the magistrates' court to the Crown Court by way of a notice of transfer.[293] The jurisdiction of the magistrates' court then ceases save for matters of legal aid and bail.

23.188   The accused may then apply to the Crown Court, before arraignment, orally or in writing, for the charges to be dismissed.[294] The judge must dismiss the charge or charges if it appears to him that the evidence is not such that a jury could properly convict on it.[295] Such a decision is in principle subject to judicial review but this jurisdiction should only be exercised in extremely limited circumstances. Normally, the assessment of the judge of the merits of the proceedings should be regarded as conclusive.[296] Alternatively the prosecution may seek to prefer a voluntary bill.

(i) Child witness cases

23.189   The notice of transfer system has been extended to cover specified offences of a violent or sexual nature where there is a child witness.[297] The evidence must be such as would justify committal. The child, whether victim or witness, is to be called at trial. The Director of Public Prosecutions must be of opinion that the case should, for the purpose of avoiding any prejudice to the child, be taken over by the Crown Court. Where the defendant is a juvenile the transfer system should not be used unless the case is such as to call for long-term detention.[298]

---

[291] *Practice Direction (Criminal Proceedings: Consolidation)* [2002] 1 WLR 2870, para 35.
[292] *R v Rothfield* (1937) 26 Cr App R 103.
[293] Criminal Justice Act 1987, s 4. For 'designated authority' see s 4(2).
[294] ibid s 6.
[295] ibid s 6(1).
[296] *R v Central Criminal Court and Nadir, ex p Director of Serious Fraud Office* [1993] 1 WLR 949, 958 *per* Woolf LJ.
[297] Criminal Justice Act 1991, s 53.
[298] As to this see Magistrates' Courts Act 1980, s 24 and Powers of Criminal Courts (Sentencing) Act 2000, s 91.

(i) Offences triable only on indictment

Where an adult is charged with an offence triable only on indictment, or is to be **23.190**
tried for such an offence and a related offence triable either way or an imprisonable related summary only offence, the case must be sent for trial without committal proceedings. This also applies to an adult co-defendant charged on the
same occasion with an offence triable either way.[299] The effect is that where an offence triable only on indictment is, as it were, in the frame, committal proceedings will not be held.[300]

In addition magistrates may send cases immediately to the Crown Court for trial **23.191**
where a defendant having been sent to the Crown Court for an indictable only offence is to be tried for a related offence triable either way or summarily. There are
variations on this theme for co-defendants who appear subsequently to a defendant sent to the Crown Court for an indictable only offence, to juveniles jointly
charged with an adult offender facing an indictable only charge, and to juveniles
sent to the Crown Court in respect of related triable either way or summary offences.[301]

The papers sent to the court are akin to those on committal proceedings. They **23.192**
must be served on the defendant within 42 days but this may be extended by the
Crown Court judge in the light of all the circumstances.[302] Provision is made for
the defendant to apply, before arraignment, to have the charges dismissed.[303]

K. Criminal Pleadings

(a) Introductory

The prosecution sets out the substance of its case either by way of an information **23.193**
which is tried in a magistrates' court or by an indictment which is tried by a judge
and jury in the Crown Court. While there is no system of criminal pleadings by
the defence the accused will have to give advance notice of reliance on alibi or expert evidence. The nature of his defence will doubtless become obvious as a result
of the disclosure requirements and the institution of the defence case statement.[304]
Formally, however, the defendant, unless he relies on a double jeopardy plea, will
simply plead guilty or not guilty.

---

[299] Crime and Disorder Act 1998, s 51.
[300] For transitional problems and their resolution, see *R (on the application of Salubi) v Bow Street
Magistrates' Court* [2002] EWHC 919; [2002] 1 WLR 3073.
[301] Crime and Disorder Act 1998, s 51(2), (3), (5) and (6).
[302] *Fehily v Governor of Wandsworth Prison* [2002] EWHC 1295; [2003] 1 Cr App R 10.
[303] Crime and Disorder Act 1998, Sch 3.
[304] See para 23.166.

23.194   Criminal pleadings were, until quite recent times, marked by an absurd formalism.[305] Today, they are brief to the point of being laconic. The modern emphasis is upon clarity, simplicity and flexibility. Despite the fact that faults are generally curable and amendments freely allowable, so long as they do not produce injustice to the accused, a considerable body of difficult and uncertain case law remains.

23.195   The basic rules relating to informations and indictments are the same. The discussion which follows is directed primarily towards indictments.

(b)   Formulating the indictment

23.196   Every indictment shall contain and shall be sufficient if it contains a statement of the specific offence or offences with which the accused is charged together with such particulars as may be necessary for giving reasonable information as to the nature of the charge.[306] Failure to disclose an essential element of the offence in the particulars will not be fatal to conviction provided that the accused was not prejudiced thereby.[307] The statement of offence need not negative an exception, proviso, excuse or qualification to the offence. It must disclose the reference to an offence created by legislation.[308]

23.197   Where more than one offence is charged each offence is set out in a separate count.[309] Both offences and offenders may be joined in the same indictment.[310] A count for a summary offence may be added to an indictment provided that it is founded upon the same facts or evidence as a count in the indictment charging an indictable offence or is part of a series of offences of the same or similar character as an indictable offence which is also charged. This power relates to a restricted range of offences and includes driving while disqualified and taking a motor vehicle without consent.[311]

(c)   New counts

23.198   The indictment may contain counts for which the magistrates have not committed and, indeed, counts for which they have refused to commit. Added counts need not be similar to those for which the magistrates committed the accused. The power to add new counts is, furthermore, not limited to cases in which the facts or evidence were before the magistrates. General considerations of fairness apply, however, and an attempt to introduce any quite separate material to that before the magistrates might well be rejected on this ground.[312]

---

[305] Note the strictures of Lord Hale CJ in 2 Hale PC 193 and T Starkie, *A Treatise on Criminal Pleading* (London: 1814) vol 1, 229.

[306] Indictments Act 1915, s 3.

[307] *R v McVitie* [1960] 2 QB 483.

[308] Indictments Rules 1971, r 6.

[309] ibid r 4.

[310] Indictments Act 1915, s 4; Indictments Rules 1971, r 9.

[311] Criminal Justice Act 1988, s 40.

[312] See *R v Mehmet* [2002] EWCA Crim 514 affirming *R v Osieh* [1996] 1 WLR 1260

(d) Overloading the indictment

There is, in law, no upper limit to the number of counts which an indictment may **23.199**
contain. The courts, however, deprecate overloading indictments.[313] No more
counts should be joined in an indictment than is necessary to give a true picture
of the accused's criminality.[314]

The prosecution may split the counts into different indictments. It may seek to meet **23.200**
problems of manageability and fairness by charging offences in specimen counts but
if, after conviction, the accused does not admit offences with which he has not specifically been charged, the court may not sentence him on the basis that he is guilty of
them. The prosecution must, therefore, ensure that enough counts are charged to enable the court to sentence the accused on the basis of his true criminality.

(e) Particularizing the charge

In some cases particulars will be needed so that the accused will know the case he **23.201**
has to meet.[315] Furthermore, particulars may be necessary so that the record of any
resulting conviction will show the true significance of the crime.[316] In some few
cases, for example obtaining credit by a bankrupt, the specification of value may
be fundamental to the offence.

The accused must be described in a manner sufficient to identify him.[317] The date **23.202**
of commission of the offence should be given but it has never been regarded as a
material matter unless it is actually an essential part of the alleged offence.[318] An
error as to date may require amendment. Specification of the place of commission
is regarded as surplusage save where the accused raises an alibi.[319] Again, the remedy for error or omission is by way of amendment.

(f) Duplicity

The rule against duplicity is easier to state than to apply. A count in an indictment **23.203**
may contain only one offence. Each information again must charge one offence
but more than one information may be set out in the same document.[320] The rule
which renders a count bad for duplicity applies to a count which charges two offences. It applies also to a count which charges the commission of one offence on

---

[313] See *Practice Direction (Criminal Proceedings: Consolidation)* [2002] 1 WLR 2870, para 34.3.
[314] *R v Novac* (1976) 65 Cr App R 107, 118–119 *per* Bridge LJ; *R v Thorne* (1977) 66 Cr App R
6, 13 *per* Lawton LJ; *R v Kidd* [1998] 1 WLR 604.
[315] *R v Gregory* [1972] 1 WLR 991.
[316] *R v Young* (1923) 17 Cr App R 131.
[317] *Archbold: Criminal Pleading, Evidence and Practice* (London: Sweet & Maxwell, 2003), para 1-124.
[318] *R v Dossi* (1918) 13 Cr App R 158.
[319] *R v Allamby* [1974] 1 WLR 1494.
[320] Magistrates' Courts Rules 1981, SI 1981/552, r 12.

more than one occasion.[321] The rule is a formal rule of pleading. The court in determining whether there is duplicity looks at the count itself, any particulars supplied by the prosecution and, where the prosecution has refused to supply particulars or further particulars, the depositions.[322]

(g) Applying the rule

23.204 The courts seek to determine questions of duplicity by applying common sense and deciding what is fair in the circumstances. This approach cannot, however, resolve all the problems encountered.[323]

23.205 The first and basic difficulty is to know when an enactment creates two or more offences in the same section or sub-section because if it does a count which follows the wording of the section will be duplicitous. Rule 7 of the Indictments Rules 1971 assists by providing that where an offence is stated to be the doing of or omission to do different acts in the alternative or in any one of different capacities or with any one of different intentions or some part of the offence in the alternative, the acts, omissions, capacities, intentions or other matters stated in the relevant statute or statutory instrument may be stated in the alternative in an indictment charging the offence. Thus the Incitement to Disaffection Act 1934 creates a single offence: to seduce a member of the armed forces from his duty or allegiance.[324]

23.206 Separate offences may not, however, be alleged in the alternative in a single count and it is sometimes difficult to determine whether a statute creates one offence which may be committed in separate modes, or two or more distinct offences.[325] The fundamental principle appears to be that adjectival phrases used to describe behaviour which are phrased disjunctively are consistent with the view that only a single offence is created.[326]Having regard to the gravamen of the offence charged, the manner of its commission may be specified disjunctively without necessarily vitiating the indictment.[327]

23.207 A further problem occurs when the indictment charges an activity rather than individual acts comprehended in it. Given that it would be possible to charge each component act as a separate offence, the puzzle is to know when the court will take an holistic rather than an atomistic approach to the problem. The courts again

---

[321] *DPP v Merriman* [1973] AC 584, 599 *per* Viscount Dilhorne.
[322] *R v Greenfield* [1973] 1 WLR 1151.
[323] *DPP v Merriman* [1973] AC 584, 593 *per* Lord Morris of Borth-y-Gest.
[324] *R v Arrowsmith* [1975] QB 678.
[325] Compare *Ware v Fox* [1967] 1 WLR 379 with *Thompson v Knights* [1947] KB 116 (being in charge of a motor vehicle while under the influence of drink or drugs discloses one offence: having control while in a state of incapacity).
[326] *Vernon v Paddon* [1973] 1 WLR 663.
[327] *R v Inman* [1967] 1 QB 140.

stress a common sense approach to the problem. The fundamental question appears to be whether a series of acts can reasonably be characterized as a transaction or as part of an activity prohibited by the criminal law. In determining this question there is a good deal of judicial discretion involved but it is clear that the fact that each action could be charged separately does not necessarily mean that a count charging an activity as a single offence will be bad for duplicity.[328]

(h) Effect of duplicity

A duplicitous indictment may be cured by a timely amendment. Furthermore, a conviction returned on a duplicitous indictment will not be treated as a nullity provided that the defendant was not embarrassed or prejudiced in his defence.[329]   **23.208**

(i) Joinder and severance

Joinder is permitted of two or more accused in one count, of different accused in separate counts, of several offences in different counts in one indictment, and of persons separately committed for trial. There is an emphasis in favour of joint trials because these enable the trial court to dispose of a series of connected matters at the same time thus saving expense, and facilitating the defence where one co-accused desires to cross-examine others, as is the case in so-called 'cut-throat' defences.[330] Joint trials guard against potential future problems of double jeopardy and abuse of process.[331] They also minimize the risks of inconsistent verdicts and inconsistent sentences.[332]   **23.209**

(i) Joinder of offenders

Two or more accused may be tried together in the same indictment.[333] The prosecution may be permitted to prefer a consolidated indictment against two or more offenders.[334] There can be no joint trial of separate indictments.[335] The remedy is to prefer a new, consolidated indictment, and then withdraw the original indictments. Magistrates can order a joint trial of separate informations against different accused where the facts are connected and it is fair to do so.[336]   **23.210**

---

[328] *Jemmison v Priddle* [1972] 1 QB 489; *Anderton v Cooper* (1980) 72 Cr App R 232; but cf *R v Ballysingh* (1953) 37 Cr App R 28, 31.

[329] *R v Levantiz* [1999] 1 Cr App R 465.

[330] *R v Grondkowski and Malinowski* [1946] KB 369.

[331] *Connelly v DPP* [1964] AC 1280, 1296 *per* Lord Reid; *R v Josephs and Christie* (1977) 65 Cr App R 253.

[332] *R v Lake* (1976) 64 Cr App R 172.

[333] *R v Hooley* (1922) 16 Cr App R 171; Indictments Rules, r 9.

[334] *R v Bell* (1984) 78 Cr App R 305.

[335] *R v Assim* [1966] QB 249; *Crane v DPP* [1922] 2 AC 299 and see *Practice Direction (Criminal Proceedings: Consolidation)* [2002] 1 WLR 2870 para 34(2).

[336] *Chief Constable of Norfolk v Clayton* [1983] 2 AC 473.

23.211   Although accused persons may be charged jointly their responsibility is several.[337] It is thus possible for one accused to be convicted and the other acquitted without there being any logical inconsistency in the verdicts. In some circumstances, however, it must be shown that the accused named in the indictment were animated by a common design, for example to utter counterfeit coins where these are uttered by the several accused at different times and places.[338]

(ii) Joinder of offences

23.212   Rule 9 of the Indictments Rules 1971 provides that charges for any offence may be joined in the same indictment where such charges are founded on the same facts or form or are part of a series of offences of the same or a similar character.

23.213   The simplest example of charges founded on the same facts is where a single act by the accused, for example arson, produces several deaths.[339] The fundamental issue is whether the charges have their origin in the same facts: they may be quite distinct in their legal description. A charge of perverting the course of justice may thus be joined to affray where the attempt consisted of inducing witnesses to the affray to change their story.[340]

23.214   In determining whether offences form or are part of a series of offences of the same or a similar character it is not enough that the offences be similar in their legal definition or in terms of the conduct to which they relate.[341] They must form part of a series and be connected by a nexus.

23.215   It is settled that two offences can amount to a series. In the leading case, *Ludlow v Metropolitan Police Commissioner*,[342] nexus is defined as 'a feature of similarity which in all the circumstances of the case enables the offence to be described as "series"'. The fact that offences are widely separated in time will not prevent them from being part of a series but a clear nexus must be shown. There must be a historical continuum between them.[343]

23.216   Nexus will certainly be made out where the evidence in respect of one count is probative on another by way of exception to the rule against admitting similar fact evidence.[344] Such cross-admissibility is not a pre-condition to the joint trial of counts relating to more than one complainant.[345] Where, however, the evidence is not admissible under the similar fact rule it may be appropriate,

---

[337]   *DPP v Merriman* [1973] AC 584.
[338]   ibid 603 *per* Viscount Dilhorne.
[339]   *R v Mansfield* [1977] 1 WLR 1102.
[340]   *R v Barrell and Wilson* (1979) 69 Cr App R 250 and see *R v Conti* (1973) 58 Cr App R 387.
[341]   *R v Muir* (1938) 26 Cr App R 164.
[342]   [1971] AC 29.
[343]   *R v O'Brien*, The Times, 23 March 2000.
[344]   *DPP v P* [1991] 2 AC 447 and see *R v Middleditch* [2001] EWCA Crim 3014.
[345]   *R v Christou* [1997] AC 117.

even where the case for joinder is made out, to order severance on the grounds of prejudice.

(iii) Severance

The question of severance arises only if counts are properly joined. The decision whether or not to order severance is within the discretion of the trial judge and that discretion will not be interfered with unless the judge has exercised it unreasonably.[346] The judge must exercise his discretion not on the basis of speculation concerning what may happen at trial but on the basis of the factual material available to him and in particular the witness statements.[347] **23.217**

The fundamental question is whether holding a joint trial would prejudice or embarrass the accused in making his defence. As, however, there is often an element of prejudice in joint trials the judge must weigh the prejudice against other relevant factors.[348] Strong prejudice is needed.[349] Where, for example, evidence admissible on one count of a multiple count indictment was inadmissible on other counts, the Court of Appeal held that the one count should have been tried separately because the effect of admitting the evidence in a joint trial would simply have been prejudicial making it more likely for the jury to convict on those counts.[350] **23.218**

It is also relevant to consider whether a co-accused objects to severance because he wishes to cross-examine another co-accused. In this respect it must be remembered that an accused cannot give evidence of ex cathedra admissions made by another perpetrator because to do so infringes the hearsay rule.[351] **23.219**

(iv) Effect of misjoinder

The basic rule is that a misjoinder cannot be cured if the offences pass into verdict. In relation to joined summary offences, however, the rule appears to be that misjoinder of the summary offence will not render convictions on the counts for indictable offences nullities provided that they are properly joined.[352] The topic is not free from difficulty. **23.220**

(j) Defects and amendments

Section 5 of the Indictments Act 1915 enables the court to amend the indictment or to order severance before or at any stage during the trial. An application to **23.221**

---

[346] *Ludlow v Metropolitan Police Commissioner* [1971] AC 29.
[347] *R v Scarrott* [1978] QB 1016.
[348] *R v Josephs and Christie* (1977) 65 Cr App R 253, 255.
[349] *R v Stead and Lawlor* [2002] EWCA Crim 1697.
[350] *R v Trew* [1996] 2 Cr App R 138.
[351] *Myers v DPP* [1998] AC 124.
[352] *R v Lockley* [1997] Crim LR 455.

amend should preferably be made at the start of the trial though not necessarily before plea.[353] This is particularly so where the accused moves to quash the indictment for want of jurisdiction.[354] Purely technical amendments are likely to be acceded to at any stage in the trial. Otherwise, the farther along the trial progresses, the more difficult it may be to allow an amendment without prejudice to the defence.[355]

23.222 Courts have adopted an expansive approach to amendments. Perhaps the most striking example of this is the willingness, noted above, of the courts to allow an amendment to a charge not founded on facts or evidence disclosed at committal.[356] An indictment may be amended as though it were defective where the intention was to add a new defendant and no injustice was likely to accrue.[357] Furthermore, on a new trial the judge may permit an amendment even if it resulted in the accused being tried for offences for which the Court of Appeal had no power to order a retrial.[358]

23.223 While most defects in criminal pleading can be cured, some flaws may be regarded as more grave than others, and this may affect the time at which an amendment may be sought and the status of a conviction made on a flawed indictment. A verdict based on an indictment which does not charge an offence known to the law is a nullity. Where, however, the indictment essentially pleads an offence in inaccurate, incomplete or imperfect terms, a conviction under it will be upheld provided that the conviction is otherwise safe.[359]

23.224 The court will, likewise, treat other defects as curable or, if a conviction is pronounced upon them, as safe, provided that no prejudice appears to have been caused to the accused. This, as noted above, applies to misjoinder and to duplicity.

L. Trial

(a) Introductory

23.225 This chapter deals primarily with trials on indictment. Summary trials and trials of juveniles differ in several respects. For reasons of space it is not possible to do more than to allude to some of the significant differences in the course of this chapter.

---

[353] *R v Grondkowski and Malinowski* [1946] KB 369.
[354] *R v Maywhort* [1955] 1 WLR 848.
[355] *R v Johal and Ram* [1973] QB 475.
[356] *R v Osieh* [1996] 1 WLR 1260; followed in *R v Mehmet* [2002] EWCA Crim 514.
[357] *R v Palmer*, The Times, 18 April 2002.
[358] *R v Hemmings* [2000] 1 WLR 661.
[359] *R v Ayres* [1984] AC 447.

(b) Place of trial

Indictable offences when tried on indictment are tried in the Crown Court. The **23.226**
committing magistrates' court must send the case to the most convenient location
of the Crown Court. In so doing the magistrates' court must have regard to practice directions given by the Lord Chief Justice concerning the competence to try
cases of justices of the High Court, Crown Court judges, recorders and assistant
recorders.[360] In brief, the most serious cases, those designated in class 1 which includes murder, may only be tried by a High Court judge or an approved Crown
Court judge and must thus be sent to a court where such a judge regularly sits.
There is greater flexibility in choice of courts with respect to lesser offences.

The Crown Court may give directions altering the place of any trial on indict- **23.227**
ment. Either party, if dissatisfied, may apply to the Crown Court for a variation.[361]
An application for change of venue may be made on the basis of prejudicial publicity, but the durability of prejudicial publicity must be balanced against the undesirability of delaying the commencement of trial.[362]

(c) Pre-trial hearings

Pre-trial hearings are part of a trial on indictment although they take place before **23.228**
a jury is empanelled and the trial proper gets under way. A pre-trial hearing is held
after the accused has been committed for trial, or has been sent for trial for an offence under s 51 of the Crime and Disorder Act 1998 or after proceedings have
been transferred to the Crown Court.[363] Such a hearing is also a pre-trial hearing
in relation to proceedings commenced by bill of indictment.

Pre-trial hearings afford an opportunity to make rulings concerning questions of **23.229**
law, evidence and procedure relating to the trial. Their purpose is to identify the
key issues at trial including whether issues of admissibility of evidence are likely to
arise. In indictable cases other than serious fraud cases they take the form of plea
and directions hearings.[364] At this stage the defendant will be arraigned and will
plead. The defence will give notice of the prosecution witnesses they require to attend trial. In serious cases the prosecution supplies the defence with a case summary which assists in identifying the issues.

In long and complex cases provision is made for preparatory hearings.[365] The trial be- **23.230**
gins with such a hearing which enables issues to be canvassed in the absence of the

---

[360] Supreme Court Act 1981, s 75 and *Practice Direction (Criminal Proceedings: Consolidation)*
[2002] 1 WLR 2870.
[361] Supreme Court Act 1981, s 76.
[362] *R v Oliver* [1958] 1 QB 250.
[363] Criminal Procedure and Investigations Act 1996, s 39.
[364] *Practice Direction (Criminal Proceedings: Consolidation)* [2002] 1 WLR 2870.
[365] Criminal Procedure and Investigations Act 1996, ss 28–36.

jury. In the absence of exceptional circumstances the judge who presides at the preparatory hearing should conduct the trial. Administrative convenience is not a good reason for changing the judge mid-trial.[366] Similar provision for preparatory hearings is made for serious fraud cases. Such a hearing marks the beginning of trial.[367]

23.231 Such hearings are designed to ensure that the issues to be tried will be indicated in advance. A defence case statement may take the form of a simple denial. In fact, however, the issues to be litigated will be manifest to counsel and the judge and the opportunities for an ambush defence are thus reduced.

(d) Plea

23.232 The defendant will be arraigned and plead at the pre-trial hearing. The defendant may plead guilty, not guilty, or enter a plea in bar of trial. If he is absent and the judge decides to continue with the trial a plea of not guilty will be entered on his behalf. The same procedure is followed if he refuses to plead.

(i) Fitness to plead

23.233 An accused may fail to plead on arraignment. He may be mentally or physically incapable of doing so or he may simply decline to plead. An accused who is fit to plead but who wilfully refuses to do so is regarded as mute of malice. A plea of not guilty is entered on his behalf and trial proceeds.

23.234 The issue of unfitness to plead usually arises where the accused is severely mentally ill or mentally defective. The principle is, however, wider and encompasses all cases where the accused is unable to follow the proceedings or to instruct counsel.[368] The classic example is of a deaf mute who could not read or write or communicate by sign language.[369] Mental abnormality will not lead to a finding of unfit to plead unless it is such that the accused cannot follow the trial.[370] Hysterical amnesia does not amount to unfitness where the accused is normal at the time of trial.[371]

23.235 The issue of fitness may be raised either by the defence or the prosecution. The issue should be raised before arraignment but may be raised later. If, having regard to the nature of the supposed disability, the court is of opinion that it is expedient to do so and in the interests of the accused, it may postpone consideration of the question of fitness up to the time of defence opening.[372]

---

[366] *R v Southwark Crown Court, ex p Customs and Excise Commissioners* [1993] 1 WLR 764.
[367] Criminal Justice Act 1987, s 7.
[368] The classic statement of principle is to be found in *R v Pritchard* (1836) 7 C & P 303.
[369] *R v Stafford Prison Governor, ex p Emery* [1909] 2 KB 81.
[370] *R v Berry* (1977) 66 Cr App R 156.
[371] *R v Podola* [1960] 1 QB 325.
[372] Criminal Procedure (Insanity) Act 1964, s 4(2).

If the matter is raised on arraignment, it is tried by a jury empanelled for the pur- **23.236**
pose.[373] If the matter arises at a separate time it may be determined by the trial jury
or by a specially empanelled jury as the court may direct.[374] A jury shall not determine fitness except on the written or oral evidence of two medical practitioners
one of whom must be approved for the purpose under the Mental Health Act
1983.[375]

If the jury decides that the accused is under a disability the trial shall not proceed **23.237**
or further proceed. Instead the jury decides on the evidence already given, or on
further evidence by the prosecution or by a person appointed to put the case for
the defence, whether they are satisfied that the accused did the act or made the
omission charged against him.[376] The jury are not concerned with any mental element of the offence and so are not required to determine whether the accused did
the act or made the omission with mens rea. Thus the jury is not to consider issues
of diminished responsibility or provocation on a trial of the facts.[377] If there is objective evidence to raise the issue of mistake, accident, self-defence or involuntariness the jury should not find that the defendant did the act or made the omission
unless it is satisfied that the Crown has negatived that defence.[378]

A finding that the accused did the act or made the omission charged against him **23.238**
is not a verdict of guilty. It is a finding, however, upon which orders for hospital
treatment, for other treatment, or for an absolute discharge may be made.[379]

The foregoing describes the procedure in the Crown Court. In the case of of- **23.239**
fences tried summarily in the magistrates' court and punishable with imprisonment, if the court is satisfied that the accused did the act or made the omission
charged, but is of the opinion that an inquiry should be made into his physical or
mental condition before the method of dealing with him is determined, the
court must adjourn the case for a medical examination or report.[380] If the court
concludes that the accused did the act or made the omission and that it would
have power if he were convicted to make a hospital or guardianship order, the
court may make such an order without convicting him.[381] These provisions represent a complete and flexible statutory framework for determination of fitness

---

[373] ibid s 4(5)(a).
[374] ibid s 4(5)(b).
[375] ibid s 4(6).
[376] ibid s 4A(2).
[377] *R v Antoine* [2001] 1 AC 340; *R v Grant* [2002] Crim LR 57. In some circumstances, however,
a defendant's intention particularized in a count may be a material fact, eg in relation to facts actually represented to an investor: *R (on the application of Young) v Central Criminal Court* [2002]
EWHC 548; [2002] 2 Cr App R 12 considering Financial Services Act 1986, s 47(1).
[378] *R v Antoine* [2001] 1 AC 340.
[379] Criminal Procedure (Insanity) Act 1964, s 5.
[380] Powers of Criminal Courts (Sentencing) Act 2000, s 11(1).
[381] Mental Health Act 1981, s 37(3).

to be tried in the magistrates' court.[382] There is, however, an unresolved question whether a person unfit to be tried can make a valid election for trial in the magistrates' court.[383]

(ii) Effect of plea

23.240   Where an accused pleads not guilty to an indictment, the whole of the issues on which his guilt depends are joined between the prosecution and the defence.[384] The issues to be actively litigated will of course have been indicated at the pre-trial hearing.

23.241   A guilty plea is a confession of fact on the basis of which the court may convict the defendant.[385] It must be entered personally by the defendant. In order for a guilty plea to have that effect it must be free, unequivocal, and informed.[386] A court, before accepting a plea of guilty, is under a duty to ensure that these requisites are satisfied.[387] The court's inquiry is into the integrity of the plea rather than the existence of facts which, once a plea is entered, is presumed.

23.242   A plea will be considered to be free unless there is reason to think that it was obtained by pressure which the law forbids. An example of such pressure is conduct by the trial judge which leads the accused to think that he will be sentenced more heavily if he pleads not guilty and is convicted than if he pleads guilty.[388] This proposition sits uneasily with the rule that a defendant who enters a timely plea of guilty may receive a substantial sentence discount. The fundamental principle is, however, that the defendant must not be placed under such pressure as to vitiate the voluntary character of the guilty plea. That does not exclude strong advice from counsel concerning sentence in the event of a not guilty plea and subsequent conviction.[389]

23.243   Pressure sufficient to vitiate a plea may arise from other sources. Judicial error rather than coercion may vitiate a plea, for example as a result of an erroneous statement of law by a judge when ruling on a motion of no case which leads the defendant to conclude that the judge is denying the validity of his defence.[390] Similarly, a ruling by the judge which leaves no legal basis for a plea of not guilty may be treated as not precluding appeal and a wider irregularity may have that

---

[382] *R (on the application of P) v Barking Youth Court* [2002] 2 Cr App R 294.

[383] *R v Lincoln (Kestevan) Justices, ex p O'Connor* [1983] 1 WLR 355.

[384] See discussion in *Maher v The Queen* (1987) 61 ALJR 432 which contains a useful discussion of English procedure.

[385] *R v Rimmer* [1972] 1 WLR 268.

[386] *R v Courtie* [1984] AC 463.

[387] *R v Rochdale Justices, ex p Allwork* [1981] 3 All ER 434.

[388] *R v Hall (Michael)* [1968] 2 QB 788; *R v Inns* (1974) 60 Cr App R 231.

[389] *R v Peace* [1976] Crim LR 119; *R v Herbert* (1991) 94 Cr App R 233.

[390] *R v Whitefield* (1983) 79 Cr App R 36.

effect.[391] A plea may be vitiated by reason of pressure upon a wife by her husband.[392] These are but examples of the application of the principle.

The application of the principle does not depend upon the proposition that the defendant was ignorant of the nature of the charge or that he did not intend to admit the facts alleged but upon the proposition that a plea coerced by improper pressure cannot be allowed to stand.   **23.244**

A plea must be informed. The court must, therefore, satisfy itself that the defendant understands the nature of the charge. This may well involve making extensive explanations to him, particularly if he is young, or of low intelligence, or a foreigner.[393] Where an accused is represented by solicitor or counsel the court will usually not inquire into the defendant's understanding of the charge but where it is shown that the legal representative misunderstood the law a change of plea may be permitted.[394]   **23.245**

The plea must be unequivocal. If it is ambiguous the court must decline to receive it. The classic example of an equivocal plea is one in which the defendant admits guilt but then, or at the stage of mitigation, advances an explanation which is inconsistent with guilt.[395]   **23.246**

(iii) Plea bargain

The essence of plea bargaining is: 'a discussion aimed at an agreement by the defence to plead guilty in exchange for some perceived benefit'.[396] It is dealt with in this context because, while plea negotiations commonly occur between prosecution and defence at or before the stage of pre-trial hearing and are often seen as mutually beneficial, they may involve an element of coercion. They may, conversely, lead to the defendant's criminality being understated.   **23.247**

Plea negotiation frequently takes place at or before plea and directions hearings. Such discussions concern charge rather than sentence bargains and typically concern whether a charge should be reduced or a charge or charges dropped. In determining whether to drop or reduce charges the Crown Prosecution Service and prosecuting counsel act as guardians of the public interest.   **23.248**

---

[391] *R v Togher* [2001] 3 All ER 463; cf *R v Chalkley* [1998] QB 848 which recognizes only the narrower ground.

[392] *R v Huntingdon Justices, ex p Jordan* [1981] QB 857.

[393] *R v Rochdale Justices, ex p Allwork* [1981] 3 All ER 434.

[394] *P Foster (Haulage) Ltd v Roberts* [1978] 2 All ER 751.

[395] *R v Durham Quarter Sessions, ex p Virgo* [1952] 2 QB 1; *R v Drew* [1985] 1 WLR 914; on the court's duty to make inquiries see *R v South Tameside Magistrates' Court, ex p Rowland* [1983] 3 All ER 689.

[396] R Ericson and P Baranek, *The Ordering of Justice* (Toronto: University of Toronto Press, 1982) 112.

23.249   Counsel may in some cases seek the view of the judge before agreeing to drop charges but he is not obliged to do so. If he does, however, he will be bound by the judge's view.[397] Where counsel does not seek approval in advance he will nonetheless explain his reasons for accepting the pleas in open court. While the judge cannot then require counsel to prosecute he may make his disapproval of any such arrangement manifest. In a case where the judge manifests strong disapproval which counsel cannot dispel, the judge may require an officer of the Crown Prosecution Service to attend to justify a decision not to proceed. In the final analysis a decision by the prosecution not to enter evidence will prevail because the judge cannot himself conduct the proceedings.[398]

23.250   A judge may not, save in the most exceptional circumstances, engage in a private interview with counsel in which the disposition of the accused is discussed. The judge may thus not lend himself to a bargain between the prosecution and the defence concerning what sentence the accused will receive if he pleads guilty. Even in an exceptional case the most that a judge can do is to indicate what type of sentence he is minded to impose.[399] The result of strong criticism by the Court of Appeal of judicial involvement in sentence discussions has been the virtual elimination of judicial involvement in sentence bargaining.[400] Non-observance of the rule against such judicial involvement may result in a successful appeal by the defendant.[401]

23.251   In those exceptional cases where counsel may properly approach the judge in private, a shorthand writer or a recording device should always be present.[402]

(iv) Withdrawal of plea

23.252   The judge may allow the defendant to change his plea from not guilty to guilty at any time before verdict. The procedure is for the defence to ask for the indictment to be put again. On such a plea of guilty the judge need not invite the jury to enter a verdict of guilty but may instead treat the matter as if the plea had been entered on arraignment.[403]

23.253   A court has a discretion to allow a defendant to change his plea of guilty to one of not guilty at any time before sentence. Lord Macdermott explained the discretion thus:[404]

---

[397]   *R v Broad* (1978) 68 Cr App R 281.
[398]   *R v Grafton* [1993] QB 101.
[399]   *R v Turner* [1970] 2 QB 321.
[400]   *R v Llewellyn* (1978) 67 Cr App R 149; *R v Winterflood* (1979) 69 Cr App R 249.
[401]   *R v Smith* [1990] 1 WLR 1311 where counsel told his client that the judge, following a private hearing, had agreed to deal with the case by way of a non-custodial sentence.
[402]   ibid.
[403]   *R v Poole* [2002] 1 WLR 1528.
[404]   *S (An infant) v Manchester City Recorder* [1971] AC 481, 493.

Every experienced judge knows that, even in uncontested matters, the truth has a habit of emerging in bits and pieces, and that the legal ingredients of the offence charged may not be fully understood by the accused.

A Crown Court to which a matter is remitted for sentence may permit a change of plea in which case the matter is remitted to a magistrates' court for trial.[405] The court's discretion is exercised sparingly and only in clear cases. Only rarely will a defendant who has been advised by experienced counsel be allowed to change his plea.[406] An application to change a plea of guilty arising from the defendant's fear that he is likely to be sentenced to imprisonment will fail.[407] **23.254**

(v) Review of plea

If, on an appeal from the magistrates' court to the Crown Court, the defendant raises the question whether an unequivocal plea of guilty was entered in the court below, the Crown Court should only entertain the matter if it has real grounds based on adequate evidence for doubting the unequivocal character of the plea in the magistrates' court.[408] If the Crown Court concludes that the plea was equivocal it has a right to direct the justices to rehear the case.[409] **23.255**

A defendant tried on indictment may appeal against a conviction based on a guilty plea whenever he has grounds for establishing a vitiating factor.[410] **23.256**

(vi) Guilty plea to lesser offence

An accused may plead guilty to a lesser offence provided that it is such as a jury could convict him as an alternative to that charged against him.[411] If the plea is accepted he will be treated as having been acquitted of the greater offence and will be sentenced for the offence to which he has pleaded. The prosecution may refuse to accept a plea to a lesser offence. The plea is deemed to be withdrawn and trial proceeds upon the offence charged.[412] The judge may, however, direct specifically on both the charge laid and lesser offences in which case the accused may be convicted of the same offence as that to which he was prepared to plead guilty. Where the withdrawn plea is inconsistent with the defence offered the prosecution may cross-examine the defendant upon that plea.[413] **23.257**

---

[405] *R v Mutford and Lothingland Justices, ex p Harber* [1971] 2 QB 291.
[406] *R v Drew* [1985] 1 WLR 914; *P Foster (Haulage) Ltd v Roberts* [1978] 2 All ER 751.
[407] *R v South Tameside Magistrates' Court, ex p Rowland* [1983] 3 All ER 689; *R v Bow Street Metropolitan Stipendiary Magistrate, ex p Roche and Riley*, The Times, 5 February 1987.
[408] *R v Plymouth Justices, ex p Whitton* (1980) 71 Cr App R 322.
[409] *R v Plymouth Justices, ex p Hart* [1986] 1 QB 950.
[410] See paras 23.378–23.380 below.
[411] Criminal Law Act 1967, s 6.
[412] *R v Hazeltine* [1967] 2 QB 857.
[413] ibid.

23.258 There is authority for the proposition that the judge may refuse to accept a plea to a lesser offence.[414] While doubts expressed about that proposition may be valid, counsel would wish to be on strong ground before taking issue with the judge's view of the dictates of public interest on such a matter.

(vii) Pleas and motions in bar of trial

23.259 **Abuse of process.**   Three principles are common to applications to stay proceedings for abuse of process. First, such applications should be made at the commencement of the trial.[415] Secondly, the burden of showing that an abuse of process has taken place and that a stay is appropriate lies on the defence on a balance of probabilities. Thirdly, the purpose of the jurisdiction is to prevent the accused from being prosecuted when it is seriously unjust to do so.[416]

23.260 A magistrates' court should show restraint in dealing with such motions. The power to stay is strictly confined to matters directly affecting the fairness of the trial before the magistrates' court such as delay or unfair manipulation of court procedures. Where the point is complex or novel the magistrates' court should normally leave it for resolution to the Crown Court or the High Court.[417]

23.261 **Delay.**   Delay between charging an individual and bringing him to trial may breach the right to trial within a reasonable time guaranteed by Article 6(1) ECHR. A stay of proceedings will be an appropriate remedy where it is no longer possible for a defendant to have a fair trial bearing in mind the ability to exclude evidence or to take other action to achieve a fair trial.[418] In such circumstances an order staying proceedings would, in any event, have been ordered at common law.[419]

23.262 In *A-G's Reference (No 2 of 2001)* the Court of Appeal intimated that situations might arise where it would simply be unfair to try the accused. The Privy Council, under s 57(2) of the Scotland Act 1998, has now held that undue delay between charge and trial, even where the accused can defend himself, may lead the court to order the discontinuance of proceedings where to hold the trial at all would violate the Convention right. In less extreme instances a different remedy, for example a reduction in sentence, may be appropriate. In determining whether to make an order and, if so, of what character the court will have regard to the complexity

---

[414] *R v Soanes* [1948] 1 All ER 289. This was done in the famous 'Yorkshire Ripper' case.

[415] *Practice Direction (Criminal Proceedings: Consolidation)* [2002] 1 WLR 2870, para 36; but see *R v Loosely* [2001] UKHL 53, [2001] 1 WLR 2060; in some instances the point may not fully be appreciated until later in the trial and may give rise to a motion to exclude evidence. That motion will then be dealt with according to the principles noted above.

[416] *R v Martin* [2001] EWCA Crim 342.

[417] *R (on the application of Salubi) v Bow Street Magistrates' Court* [2002] EWHC 919; [2002] 1 WLR 3073.

[418] *A-G's Reference (No 2 of 2001)* [2001] EWCA Crim 1568, [2001] 1 WLR 1869; *R v Ashton*, The Times, 6 December 2002.

[419] *A-G's Reference (No 1 of 1990)* [1992] QB 630.

of the case, the conduct of the defendant, and the manner in which the case was dealt with by the administrative and judicial authorities.[420] While this represents the position in Scotland, ss 6(1) and 8(1) of the HRA 1998 could lead to the same result. At present there are conflicting dicta in the Privy Council and the House of Lords has yet to rule on the matter.[421]

Conduct shocking justice.   Here, the approach taken by the courts is one of bal-   **23.263**
ancing the competing requirements that those who commit crimes should be convicted and punished against the principle that the courts should not condone an
abuse of process which would amount to an affront to the public conscience. An
example would be a case in which law enforcement officers instigate the commission of an offence.[422]

Conduct denying fair trial.   Conduct by the prosecution which results in the   **23.264**
accused being unable to defend himself may also give rise to abuse of process even
though the prosecution's conduct, for example in improperly storing exhibits
which then deteriorated, is negligent rather than intentional.[423]

Pleas in bar of trial.   These are pleas of autrefois acquit, autrefois convict, or par-   **23.265**
don.[424] The first two raise the principle against placing an accused in double jeopardy and, though seldom encountered, they are of fundamental importance. The
third refers to a grant which has the force of an acquittal though is not an acquittal
strictly speaking. These pleas are seldom encountered, not least because the procedural system has rules, for example those permitting joinder of counts in an indictment, which seek to ensure that double jeopardy problems will not arise in
practice.[425] The essence of double jeopardy is that a person is not to be placed in
peril twice for the same offence. The principle thus applies to offences, not to facts.
It prevents the unwonted harassment of persons by multiple prosecutions.[426]

---

[420] *Dyer v Watson* [2002] UKPC D1; [2002] 3 WLR 1488. Note that the case was one where the accused was a juvenile aged 13 at the time of charge, but would have attained the age of 16 at the time of trial.

[421] In *HM Advocate v R* [2002] UKPC D3; [2003] 2 WLR 317, Lord Hope suggests that the law of England may not as yet be settled. Lords Steyn and Walker (dissenting) suggest that there should be no stay where prejudice is not shown. To the same effect see Lord Steyn in *Mills v HM Advocate* [2002] UKPC D2; [2002] 3 WLR 1597. The House of Lords has not yet ruled on the issue which may turn on differences in wording between HRA 1998, s 6 and Scotland Act 1998, s 57(2).

[422] *R v Loosely* [2001] UKHL 53, [2001] 1 WLR 2060; *R v Chalkley* [1998] QB 848; *R v Latif* [1996] 1 WLR 104; *R v Mullen* [2000] QB 520.

[423] *R v Boyd* [2002] All ER (D) 252 (Nov); *R v Early* [2002] EWCA Crim 1904, [2003] 1 Cr App R 288.

[424] While the double jeopardy pleas strictly speaking are entered in trials on indictment the same result is achieved in magistrates' courts by virtue of the maxim nemo debet bis vexari pro uno et eadem causa: *Flatman v Light* [1946] 1 KB 414; *R v Campbell, ex p Hay* [1953] 1 QB 585.

[425] As early as 1827 it was said that a double jeopardy plea rarely succeeded: see reporter's note to *R v Sheen* (1827) 2 C & P 634.

[426] See further J Sigler, *Double Jeopardy: The Development of A Legal and Social Policy* (Ithaca: Cornell University Press, 1969) and M Freedland, *Double Jeopardy* (Oxford: Clarendon Press, 1969).

23.266   A plea in bar of trial should be entered on arraignment and should be reduced to writing.[427] In an exceptional case it may, however, be raised at any time during trial.[428] Such a plea is tried by the judge alone.[429] It is for the defendant to prove that he is entitled to the benefit of the principle which he may do by, for example, producing a certified copy of the record of previous proceedings.[430] An accused who unsuccessfully pleads autrefois acquit or convict may then plead not guilty.[431]

(viii) Requisites of pleas

23.267   In order to raise a special plea the accused must show that he was placed in peril on a previous occasion. This means that he must show that he was previously acquitted or convicted for the same offence.[432] This implies that the procedure on the former occasion was not such as to render any verdict a nullity nor the verdict so ambiguous as to be no verdict at all.[433] Where, therefore, a court lacking jurisdiction purports to decide a matter the result is regarded as a nullity and does not preclude a subsequent trial.[434] A double jeopardy plea may be raised in respect of an acquittal or conviction before a foreign court of competent jurisdiction.[435]

23.268   The trial must have resulted in a valid verdict. Where the prosecution offers no evidence on summary proceedings the result is an acquittal.[436] On indictment the judge may enter an acquittal under such circumstances.[437] In both these cases the accused may raise a double jeopardy plea to a later prosecution. The same result must follow where the Court of Appeal quashes a conviction and does not order a new trial.[438]

23.269   Once the jury has given a verdict the accused may take the benefit of it. The judge may not order a retrial of the count to which it relates.[439]

---

[427]   Such a plea may as a matter of law be entered orally: Criminal Procedure Act 1851, s 28.

[428]   *Connelly v DPP* [1964] AC 1254 *per* Lord Devlin.

[429]   Criminal Justice Act 1988, s 120.

[430]   *R v Coughlan* (1976) 63 Cr App R 33.

[431]   Criminal Law Act 1967, s 6(1).

[432]   *DPP v Nasralla* [1967] 2 AC 238, 250–251 *per* Lord Devlin.

[433]   *R v Campbell, ex p Hay* [1953] 1 QB 585; *Halstead v Clark* [1944] 1 KB 250; *R v Drury* (1849) 18 LJMC 189.

[434]   *R v Marsham, ex p Pethick-Lawrence* [1964] 1 QB 15.

[435]   *Treacy v DPP* [1971] AC 537, 562 *per* Lord Diplock. Note, however, that the principle will not apply where the person was found guilty in absentia and is not likely to return to serve his sentence: *R v Thomas* [1985] QB 604.

[436]   *Metropolitan Police Commissioner v Meller* [1963] Crim LR 856.

[437]   Criminal Justice Act 1967, s 17.

[438]   See *Conlon v Patterson* [1915] 2 IR 169; cf where the conviction is quashed on judicial review because the original decision is considered a nullity; *R v Drury* (1849) 18 LJMC 189.

[439]   *R v Lester* (1938) 27 Cr App R 8. On the limited circumstances in which a verdict may be corrected see *Igwemma v Chief Constable of Greater Manchester Police* [2001] EWCA Civ 593; [2002] QB 1012.

It is not, however, enough that the matter has passed into verdict: it must have been the subject of complete adjudication including the passing of sentence.[440] **23.270**

In relation to sentence there is a practice known as taking offences into consideration. Where an accused intimates that he will admit to further offences when sentenced for a crime for which he is convicted, no later double jeopardy plea could be raised in respect of them because they have not passed into verdict. The device is, however, intended to ensure that proceedings will not later be taken in respect of such offences and the court has ample discretion to prevent such a result.[441] **23.271**

(e) Same offence

Any given set of facts may give rise to a number of distinct criminal offences. The double jeopardy pleas are concerned with identity of offences, not facts. In *Connelly v DPP*[442] Lord Morris of Borth-y-Gest stated the law in the following propositions all of which, save for (3) and (8), are generally accepted: **23.272**

(1) A person cannot be tried for a crime in respect of which he has previously been acquitted or convicted.

(2) A person cannot be tried for a crime in respect of which he could on some previous indictment have been convicted.

(3) The same rule applies if the crime in respect of which he is being charged is in effect the same or is substantially the same as either the principal or a different crime in respect of which he has been acquitted or could have been convicted or has been convicted.

(4) One test whether the rule applies is whether the evidence which is necessary to support the second indictment or offence would have been sufficient to procure a legal conviction on the first indictment either as to the offence charged or as to an offence of which, on the indictment, the accused could have been found guilty.

(5) This test is subject to the provision that the offence charged in the second indictment had in fact been committed at the time of the first charge; thus, if there is an assault and a prosecution in respect of it, there is no bar to a charge of murder if the victim later dies.

(6) On a plea of autrefois convict or autrefois acquit a person is not restricted to a comparison between the later indictment and some previous indictment or record of the court, 'but that he may prove by evidence all such questions as to the identity of persons, dates and facts as to show that he is being charged with an offence which is either the same or substantially the same as one of

---

[440] *Richards v The Queen* [1993] AC 217, PC, which contains a full discussion of the relevant English authorities.
[441] *R v Nicholson* [1947] 2 All ER 535.
[442] [1964] AC 1254, 1311–1312.

which he has been acquitted or convicted or as one in respect of which he could have been convicted'.

(7) The court must consider whether the offence charged in the later indictment is the same or substantially the same as the crime charged in the earlier indictment. Where the charges are distinct it does not matter the facts being examined or the witnesses called are the same as in earlier proceedings.

(8) Apart from cases where pleas in bar may be entered a person may be able to show that a matter has been decided by a competent court so that the principle of res judicata applies.

(9) The double jeopardy principle applies to summary trials as well as trials on indictment.

23.273 Despite doubts expressed in the same case by Lord Devlin it would seem that one offence may be substantially similar to another, that is, that there is no real difference in their legal characteristics.[443] On the other hand, the suggestion by an Australian court that the double jeopardy pleas should be available where the gist and gravamen of the first offence is the same as that of the second seems less well founded.[444] First, at least one English authority seems to have been misunderstood.[445] Secondly, the notion of gist and gravamen invites a descent into policy rather than an essentially technical inquiry into identity of offences.

23.274 Even where a person can show that proof of the facts alleged in a second indictment were such as to lead to his conviction on the former indictment, the defendant will not be able to set up a double jeopardy plea where the second offence is not merely an aggravated form of the first offence but involves a further consequence which is not reflected in the definition of the first offence. A conviction for assault does not bar a charge of homicide if the victim later dies.[446] On the other hand an accused who has been acquitted of common assault cannot later be charged with assault occasioning actual bodily harm because both the mens rea and the actus reus of the two offences are the same.[447] The same reasoning suggests that a person having been convicted of a greater offence could not thereafter be prosecuted for a lesser included offence.

(i) Statutory provisions

23.275 Sections 44 and 45 of the Offences Against the Person Act 1861 provide in respect of a hearing by justices on the merits of offences of assault and battery for the issue

---

[443] eg, compare the offences of false accounting under the Theft Act 1968 with the offence of making false statements and records under the Agriculture Act 1957.

[444] *R v O'Loughlin, ex p Ralphs* [1971] 1 SASR 219 *per* Wells J.

[445] *Wemyss v Hopkins* (1875) LR 10 QB 378, 381 *per* Blackburn J.

[446] *R v Thomas* [1950] 1 KB 26.

[447] *R v FG (Autrefois Acquit)* [2001] EWCA Crim 1215; [2001] 1 WLR 1727. It does not matter that the original acquittal was entered by the judge rather than by verdict of the jury.

of a certificate to the defendant. This operates as a bar to civil or criminal proceedings for the same cause. It operates only where the prosecution is brought by the aggrieved person or on his behalf and thus not where the prosecution is brought by the Crown Prosecution Service.

Section 18 of the Interpretation Act 1978 provides that where an act or omission constitutes an offence under two or more Acts or under both an Act and at common law, the accused is not liable to suffer double punishment.   **23.276**

(ii) Tainted acquittals

The statutory provisions relating to tainted acquittals constitute a major exception to the double jeopardy principle. In summary the High Court may quash an acquittal where a person has been convicted for an administration of justice offence involving interference with or intimidation of a juror, witness or potential witness, in any proceedings which led to the acquittal.[448] The court must be satisfied that there is a real possibility that the acquitted person would not have been acquitted but for the interference of intimidation.   **23.277**

Four conditions must be satisfied. First, it must appear to the court likely that the accused would not have been acquitted had the administration of justice offence not occurred. Secondly, it must not appear to the court that lapse of time or other considerations would render the possibility of further proceedings against the acquitted person contrary to the interests of justice. Thirdly, the acquitted person must be given a reasonable opportunity to make written representations to the court, and fourthly it must appear that the conviction for the administration of justice offence will stand. It follows that no order should be made if the time allowed for giving notice of appeal has not expired or an appeal is pending.[449]   **23.278**

(iii) Demurrer

An accused may enter a plea of demurrer. This is an objection to the form or substance of the indictment apparent on its face.[450] The scope of the remedy is no different from a motion to quash and its continued invocation has been deprecated by the courts. It may have utility where the demurrer is to the jurisdiction of the court in respect of an offence allegedly arising abroad but it is hard to see why this should be so since the essence of the plea is to a defect patent on the face of the indictment.[451] It is submitted, with respect, that the plea is rightly in desuetude.   **23.279**

---

[448] Criminal Procedure and Investigations Act 1996, s 54. For definition of such offences see s 54(6).
[449] ibid s 55.
[450] *R v Inner London Quarter Sessions, ex p Metropolitan Police Commissioner* [1970] 2 QB 80.
[451] A suggestion advanced in *R v Cumberworth* (1989) 89 Cr App R 187.

(iv) Issue estoppel

23.280 In *Connolly v DPP* Lord Morris alludes to the possibility of issue estoppel barring a prosecution for a particular offence where the verdict of the jury is such as to negate the accused's guilt in respect of an essential element of the charge which it is desired to bring.

23.281 Issue estoppel treats an issue of fact or law as settled once and for all between the parties if it is distinctly raised and if the judgment pronounced implies its determination necessarily as a matter of law.[452] The principle has been rejected in criminal procedure partly because it could not apply mutually against the accused as well as the Crown and partly because it is usually not possible to determine whether the jury has pronounced on any particular issue.[453] Nonetheless, the underlying principle may have some application in relation to trial, first because as a matter of discretion the Court of Appeal in ordering a new trial may be able to intimate, but not at present to order, that the trial should be on a lesser or different charge where the verdict in fact does show that a jury was not satisfied that a particular element was proven, and secondly because the Crown Prosecution Service may take such a consideration into account in determining whether to amend the indictment to reduce the charge in such a case.[454]

(v) Abuse of process

23.282 In *Connolly v DPP* the House of Lords intimated that an accused might further be protected against multiple prosecutions by invocation of the discretion to halt proceedings as an abuse of process. This would seem now to be an established principle.

(f) Empanelling the jury

23.283 All persons, save those rendered ineligible by statute, who are between the ages of 18 and 70 and are registered voters are eligible for jury service.[455] The list is extensive and is now under review. In addition certain groups, while eligible, are entitled as of right to be excused from jury service. These include persons who have served on a jury within the previous two years or who have been excused from jury service by the Crown Court for a period which has not yet terminated.[456]

23.284 A person who has been summoned for jury service may be excused in the discretion of the court if he can show that there is good reason for the court to do so.

---

[452] *Connelly v DPP* [1964] AC 1254, *per* Lord Morris.
[453] *DPP v Humphrys* [1977] AC 1.
[454] For further discussion of these points see LH Leigh, 'New Trials in Criminal Cases' [1977] Crim LR 525 and see *R v Hemmings* [2000] 1 WLR 661.
[455] Juries Act 1974, s 1.
[456] ibid s 8 and Sch 1, Pt III.

Personal hardship or conscientious objection are relevant.[457] Religious belief itself is not a good reason for excusal from jury service unless a person's belief would stand in the way of his properly performing the functions of a juror.[458]

The court has power to defer attendance for jury service.[459] A person summoned **23.285** for jury service may be referred to a judge for excusal if it appears to the appropriate officer of the court that he may, by reason of physical disability or an insufficient understanding of English, be unable to act effectively as a juror.[460]

Jurors are selected in any given case from among those persons named in a panel **23.286** and summoned for jury service.[461]

Jury challenges have been much reduced by recent legislation. In particular, there **23.287** is no longer any right of peremptory challenge by the defence. Either the prosecution or the defence may challenge for cause. Such a challenge may be either to a particular juror or to the whole panel, the latter on the basis that the person who composed the panel was biased.[462] In the absence of bias or impropriety an allegation of racial imbalance in the panel is not a sufficient ground for challenge. There is no principle that a jury should be racially balanced.[463]

Individual jurors may be challenged for cause on the ground that they are ineligi- **23.288** ble or disqualified. A juror may also be challenged on the ground of bias, actual or presumed, which makes him unsuitable to try the case. A juror may be challenged if he has expressed hostility to one side or the other, or a wish as to the outcome of the case, or is related to or has a connection with a party. The principles generally applicable to allegations of judicial bias would seem to apply where juror bias is alleged, namely, whether the circumstances which bear on bias would lead a fair minded and informed observer to conclude that there was a real possibility or a real danger that the proposed juror is or may be biased.[464]

The Crown also has the right to ask that a juror stand by for the Crown. The ef- **23.289** fect of this is that such a juror will not be sworn unless the panel has otherwise been exhausted. This is unlikely to occur. Counsel may stand by a juror in a case involving national security or terrorism or where the juror is unsuitable and the

---

[457] *Practice Direction (Criminal Proceedings: Consolidation)* [2002] 1 WLR 2870.
[458] *R v Guildford Crown Court, ex p Siderfin* [1990] 2 QB 683.
[459] Juries Act 1974, s 9A.
[460] ibid s 10 and see *R v Osman* [1995] 1 WLR 1327.
[461] ibid ss 5 and 11.
[462] ibid s 12.
[463] *R v Ford* [1989] QB 868, 874.
[464] *Porter v Magill* [2001] UKHL 67, [2002] 2 AC 357; *R v Mason* [2002] EWCA Crim 385, [2002] 2 Cr App R 38; *Hawkin's Pleas of the Crown* (1834) vol 2, c 43, s 31 amusingly notes that the Crown was allowed to challenge for cause on the ground that the prospective juror 'hath given his dogs the names of the King's witnesses'.

defence agrees.[465] Furthermore, the trial judge may himself, in such circumstances, stand the juror by.[466]

(g) Presence of accused at trial

23.290 The accused person has a right and an obligation to be present at trial. He may waive his right by his own conduct. A judge may embark upon trial in the absence of the accused where the absence of the accused is attributable to his desire to frustrate proceedings. The discretion to commence a trial in the absence of the defendant is, however, to be exercised with great caution and if the defendant's absence is attributable to involuntary illness or incapacity it will rarely if ever be right to do so.[467]

23.291 Among the relevant factors in the exercise of discretion are: whether the defendant's absence is voluntary or not; whether an adjournment might result in his being caught or attending voluntarily and/or not disrupting the proceedings; the likely length of such an adjournment; the extent of the disadvantage to the defendant in not being able to give his account of events having regard to the nature of the evidence against him; the risk of the jury reaching an improper conclusion about his absence; the general public interest and the particular interests of victims and witnesses that a trial should take place within a reasonable time of the events to which it relates; and where there is more than one defendant and not all have absconded, the undesirability of separate trials and the prospects of a fair trial for those defendants who are present.[468]

23.292 The judge's overriding concern is to ensure that the trial will be as fair as circumstances permit and lead to a just decision. It is generally desirable that a defendant be represented even though he voluntarily absconded. Counsel is thus routinely asked to continue despite the absence of his client and in general does so. These principles are compatible with the fair trial principles of the ECHR.[469]

23.293 Similar principles apply where a defendant who, having been present at the commencement of his trial, is absent during it. The judge's discretion is not limited to cases where the accused voluntarily absents himself: he may permit trial to continue where the defendant is absent through illness, but in such case the discretion is to be used sparingly and never if the defendant's defence could be prejudiced by his absence.[470] The judge must determine whether to continue with trial or dis-

---

[465] A-G's Guidelines. The text may be found in *Blackstone's Criminal Practice* (n 7 above) para 2433.
[466] *R v Chandler (No 2)* [1964] 2 QB 322, 327.
[467] *R v Jones (Anthony William)* [2002] UKHL 5; [2003] 1 AC 1.
[468] ibid, considering the list of relevant factors in *R v Hayward* [2001] 3 WLR 125 at [22(5)].
[469] *R v Jones (Anthony William)* [2002] UKHL 5; [2003] 1 AC 1.
[470] *R v Hayward* [2001] 3 WLR 125 at [6].

charge the jury from giving a verdict. The longer the trial has continued the greater is the likelihood that the judge will permit the trial to continue.[471]

The judge may also continue with a trial where the defendant, by his misconduct, **23.294** has abused his right to be present. A defendant may do so by misconducting himself in such a way that it becomes impracticable to conduct proceedings with him present.[472]

(h) Presence of witnesses

It is for the prosecution and the defence to ensure that witnesses required at trial **23.295** attend. Witness orders are made in respect of those prosecution witnesses to the reading of whose statements the defence will not consent.

In a case where the Crown Court is satisfied that a witness who is likely to be able **23.296** to give material evidence will not voluntarily attend or will not voluntarily produce a document or thing, the court may issue a witness summons requiring the person to attend and to produce any specified document or thing.[473] Such a requirement may specify that the person is to produce a specified document or thing for inspection at a time preceding the actual trial.[474] A witness summons may be set aside on application by a person who satisfies the court that he cannot give material evidence or produce a document or thing likely to be material evidence.[475]

In certain circumstances evidence may be given by live video link. The witness **23.297** must be outside the United Kingdom, or a child, or to be cross-examined in respect of offences of assault or injury, or sexual offences or offences involving indecency. Leave of the court is required.[476]

(i) Vulnerable witnesses

The Youth Justice and Criminal Evidence Act 1999 makes provision for measures **23.298** protecting certain classes of witnesses the quality of whose evidence might otherwise be diminished; those who are under 17 years of age, or suffering from mental disorder or having otherwise a significant impairment of intelligence and social functioning or physical disability or disorder.[477] These include screening the witness from the accused, allowing evidence by live link, excluding persons other than the accused and those directly engaged in the trial from court while evidence is being given, or the use of a video recording as evidence in chief. Wigs and gowns

---

[471] *R v Jones (No 2)* [19782] 1 WLR 887.
[472] *R v Lee Kun* [1916] 1 KB 337; *R v Howson* (1981) 74 Cr App R 172.
[473] Criminal Procedure (Attendance of Witnesses) Act 1965, s 2.
[474] ibid s 2A.
[475] ibid ss 2B–2D.
[476] Criminal Justice Act 1988, s 32.
[477] Youth Justice and Criminal Evidence Act 1999, s 16.

may also be dispensed with.[478] Furthermore, at common law the trial judge may allow a defendant with learning difficulties to be assisted by an interpreter who understands that person's language difficulties.[479]

(i) Prosecution case

23.299 Prosecuting counsel are to regard themselves as ministers of justice. They are to present the case fairly but not to strive for a conviction.[480] This affects the manner in which prosecution counsel opens the case.

23.300 Counsel's opening address provides a sketch of the facts which the prosecution proposes to prove together with a brief account of the law including the burden and standard of proof.[481] Counsel should not make assertions which he does not propose to prove.[482] Where inadmissible material is referred to in opening, the judge has a discretion to discharge the jury.[483]

23.301 Doubtfully admissible confessions should not be mentioned by prosecuting counsel in opening. Defence counsel should notify prosecuting counsel that he proposes to object.

23.302 Where two or more persons are indicted together and one pleads guilty the general practice is to tell the jury that comments made about the individual are not a matter of concern for them.[484] If such evidence becomes relevant the jury will be instructed about it in the normal way.

(i) Calling and tendering witnesses

23.303 The prosecution should call or tender those witnesses whose evidence is served on the defence on committal or transfer.[485] No such obligation applies in respect of witnesses whose statements were served as part of the bundle of unused material. The prosecution's obligation to call a witness is not absolute: the prosecution

---

[478] Youth Justice and Criminal Evidence Act 1999, ss 16–30.

[479] *R v H (Special measures)*, The Times, 15 April 2003.

[480] *Randall v The Queen* [2002] UKPC 19, [2002] 1 WLR 2237: *R v Banks* (1916) 12 Cr App R 73, 76. Where counsel's address is improper the trial judge should check it at once: *R v House* (1921) 16 Cr App R 49.

[481] *R v Peckham* (1935) 25 Cr App R 125; *R v Olivo* (1942) 28 Cr App R 173.

[482] Rarely, unsupported assertions could provide a ground for appeal, but problems of this sort will usually be dealt with in the summing up: see *R v Jackson* [1953] 1 WLR 591.

[483] *R v Thatcher* (1968) 53 Cr App R 201.

[484] See *Blackstone's Criminal Practice* (n 7 above) para D.14.4. The wording suggested is obviously sensible but will not always be dictated, as the text seems to suggest, by s 74 of the Police and Criminal Evidence Act 1984. The older wording informed the jury that the co-accused had pleaded guilty but that the jury must not pay any attention to the fact: *R v Moore* (1956) 40 Cr App R 50, 53–54.

[485] Older cases refer to the former practice of listing witnesses on the back of the indictment: see *El Dabbah v A-G for Palestine* [1944] AC 156.

should not put such a person forward at trial as a witness of truth if his evidence is not capable of belief. There is, however, no rule of law which prevents the prosecution from calling a witness only part of whose evidence the Crown relies upon as credible.[486] Subject to that the Crown should call the witness even though his evidence may not entirely favour the prosecution's case.[487] The prosecution may not simply close its case and refuse to call such witnesses.[488] Witnesses whose evidence may be relevant but who the prosecution does not intend to call should be notified as unused material.

The prosecution should ensure that a witness whose statement is served on committal or transfer but who they do not propose to call or whose statement is not to be read should be present in court so that the defence may call that witness.[489] If, however, it is not possible for the prosecution to do so the judge may allow the trial to proceed provided that the prosecution has witnesses available to prove its case and that the defence will not be disadvantaged thereby.[490]   **23.304**

In a proper case the judge may invite the prosecution to call a witness whom the prosecution is reluctant to call. This is subject to the qualification that the witness not be rightly regarded as unreliable.[491] In the final analysis the judge may call the witness himself.[492] In that case the judge has a discretion to allow either side to cross-examine the witness in the interests of justice.[493]   **23.305**

Prosecution counsel may simply call a witness and tender him for cross-examination. This may be done where there are ample other witnesses for the Crown or where the Crown is prepared to oblige the defence who hope to extract a favourable nuance from a witness whose evidence generally favours the prosecution.   **23.306**

The prosecution has a duty to supply to the defence inconsistent statements by prosecution witnesses. Such statements may arise after committal. The test is whether they disclose material which might undermine the prosecution's case.[494]   **23.307**

(ii) Reading statements in at trial

Statements of prosecution witnesses tendered at committal or transfer may be read in evidence at the Crown Court trial.[495] A similar provision applies to trials   **23.308**

---

[486] *R v Cairns* [2002] EWCA Crim 2838; [2003] 1 WLR 796.
[487] *R v Oliva* (1965) 49 Cr App R 698; *R v Nugent* [1977] 1 WLR 789..
[488] *R v Wellingborough Justices, ex p Francois*, 1994, Times 1 July and see further C Tapper, *Cross and Tapper on Evidence* (8th edn, London: Butterworths, 1995) 278–279.
[489] *R v Oliva* (1965) 49 Cr App R 698.
[490] *R v Cavanagh* [1972] 1 WLR 676.
[491] ibid.
[492] *R v Holden* (1838) 8 C & P 606.
[493] *Coulson v Desborough* [1894] 2 QB 316.
[494] Criminal Procedure and Investigations Act 1996, ss 3 and 9.
[495] ibid Sch 2

in the magistrates' court.[496] These provisions are subject to objection by the defence. Section 9 of the Criminal Justice Act 1967 provides for the admissibility of witness statements, by agreement, at the instance either of the prosecution or the defence. Such statements are commonly read in where witnesses are giving purely formal evidence. Provision is also made for the admission in certain circumstances of the deposition of a juvenile.[497]

(iii) Objections to prosecution evidence

23.309 The defence, if it proposes to object to prosecution evidence, should make this known before prosecution counsel opens to the jury. That the defence proposes to raise such an issue will normally be mentioned at the plea and directions hearing or other pre-trial hearing.

23.310 Where an issue arises concerning how evidence was obtained, for example that the circumstances were such as to raise doubts about the voluntary character of a confession or whether the evidence was fairly obtained or whether requirements of the Police and Criminal Evidence Act 1984 and its constellation of accompanying codes of practice which seek to ensure the accuracy of evidence may have been breached, the issue will be dealt with by holding a voire dire.

23.311 No discussion of an intended objection may take place in the presence of the jury. When the voire dire has been completed, and the judge has given his ruling, the judge should give no explanation of the outcome of the voire dire to the jury.[498]

23.312 It is submitted, with deference to contrary views, that questions of the voluntariness of confessions and alleged unfairness in admitting other evidence ought always to be dealt with by voire dire.[499] The court can, in any event, order that a voire dire be held where the voluntariness of a confession is in issue.[500]

23.313 Normally objections to admissibility are heard immediately prior to the evidence being called but this is not an invariable rule. If the prosecution feels it necessary to refer to evidence in opening and it is known that the defence objects to admissibility the question may be dealt with as a preliminary matter provided that it is convenient to do so and that no harm will be done thereby.[501]

---

[496] Magistrates' Courts Act 1980, s 97A.
[497] Children and Young Persons Act 1933, s 42.
[498] *Mitchell v The Queen* [1998] AC 695, 703. While this case seems to intimate that the defence may require the voire dire to take place in the presence of the jury, the practice noted in the text above is not consistent with any such right. In any event any exercise of it would seem quixotic. See, however, *Blackstone's Criminal Practice* (n 7 above) para 1323 approved by the Privy Council.
[499] *R v Sat Bhambra* (1988) 88 Cr App R 55, 62; as to summary trial see *R v Liverpool Juvenile Court, ex p R* [1988] QB 1.
[500] Police and Criminal Evidence Act 1984, s 76(3).
[501] *R v Hammond* [1941] 3 All ER 318, 320.

(iv) Editing statements

In cases where prosecution evidence is admissible, but the committal statements contain matter which is plainly prejudicial so that the jury ought not to hear it, the accepted practice is for counsel to edit the material out.[502] An example is the case where police questioning suggests that a story contrary to that given by the accused in interview is supported by other witnesses who it is not proposed to call.[503] Provision is made by practice direction for the editing of written statements which it is proposed to offer in evidence.[504]

23.314

The prosecution may use evidence additional to that relied upon at committal. The prosecution must, in such case, notify the defence of their intention and supply a copy of any additional witness statement.[505]

23.315

(j) No case

The defence may, at the close of the prosecution case, submit that the accused has no case to answer. Such a submission may be made in respect of all or any of the counts in the indictment.[506] It is made in the absence of the jury and is not alluded to before the jury if it fails.[507]

23.316

If the submission of no case succeeds the jury is formally asked to return a verdict of not guilty. If the submission succeeds on one or several but not all counts the jury will be informed that the accused is no longer to be regarded as being tried on those counts. A formal verdict will then be taken at the end of the trial.[508]

23.317

The leading authority, *R v Galbraith*,[509] holds that the judge should stop the trial either if there is no evidence that the accused committed the crime or where there is some evidence, but it is of a tenuous character, for example because of inherent weakness or because it conflicts with other evidence. Where the judge considers that the Crown's evidence, taken at its highest, is such that a properly directed jury could not properly convict on it, it is his duty on a submission being made, to stop the case. Indeed, the judge should do so whether or not a formal submission of no case has been made where it is apparent to him that the interests of justice so demand.[510] Where, however, the Crown's evidence is such that its strength or

23.318

---

[502] *R v Weaver* [1968] 1 QB 353.
[503] See *R v Mills and Poole* (CA, 1996): the point is not alluded to in the judgment of the House of Lords [1998] AC 382.
[504] *Practice Direction (Criminal Proceedings: Consolidation)* [2002] 1 WLR 2870.
[505] See *R v Wright* (1934) 25 Cr App R 35.
[506] *R v Bellman* [1989] AC 836.
[507] *Crosdale v The Queen* [1995] 1 WLR 864, PC; *R v Falconer-Atlee* (1973) 58 Cr App R 348. On a motion of no case the Crown is not entitled to change the basis upon which it has presented its case.
[508] *R v Plain* [1967] 1 WLR 565.
[509] [1981] 1 WLR 1039.
[510] *Daley v The Queen* [1994] 1 AC 117, 123, PC.

weakness depends on the view to be taken of a witness' reliability or other matters generally within the province of the jury and where on one view of the facts there is evidence on which a jury could properly come to the conclusion that the accused is guilty, the judge should leave the matter to the jury.

23.319 The emphasis thus is on leaving the case to the jury unless either there is no evidence as to a material part of the case or the only evidence is so inherently incredible that no reasonable person could accept it as being true.[511] In identification cases the principle is that a case should be withdrawn from the jury not where the judge considers the witness to be lying but where the evidence, even if taken to be honest, has a base which is so slender that it is unreliable and therefore not sufficient to found a conviction.[512]

23.320 The judge may also withdraw the case from the jury where the prosecution case depends only on a confession, the defendant is significantly mentally handicapped, and the confession was so unconvincing that no properly directed jury could properly convict on it.[513]

23.321 Such a motion is also possible in summary trials. Justices, even after the coming into force of the HRA 1998, are under no obligation to give reasons for their decision.[514]

(k) Mutually exclusive counts

23.322 The question whether it is proper for two mutually exclusive counts in an indictment to be left to the jury for them to decide which, if either, count has been proven, or whether the prosecution should be obliged to elect upon which count they wish to proceed arose in *R v Bellman*.[515] 'Mutually exclusive' in this sense signifies that the counts are mutually contradictory so that a conviction on the one count necessarily involves an acquittal on the other. Their Lordships held that in some circumstances it may be necessary in the interests of justice to charge mutually contradictory counts in the indictment. If at the end of the prosecution case the evidence establishes a prima facie case on both counts, the matter should be left to the jury to determine the question of guilt.

(l) Prima facie case against two accused

23.323 If the evidence shows that the offence must have been committed by one of two or more accused but it is impossible to say which, the case must be stopped.[516]

---

[511] *Haw Tua Tua v Public Prosecutor* [1982] AC 136: see further *R v Shippey* [1988] Crim LR 767.
[512] *Daley v The Queen* [1994] 1 AC 117, 129. Note that the Board refers to *R v Heffernan* (23 May 1896) with approval.
[513] *R v McKenzie* [1993] 1 WLR 453; *R v Wood* [1994] Crim LR 222.
[514] *Moran v DPP* [2002] EWHC 89; (2002) 166 JP 467.
[515] [1989] AC 836.
[516] *R v Bellman* [1989] AC 836.

(m) Evidence after wrong ruling on no case

23.324 Where a submission of no case has been made but has (wrongly) failed, and the accused has continued to take part in the trial, the court, on appeal, will be required to allow the appeal unless it is able to conclude that had the judge not committed an error of law the jury would nevertheless have convicted the accused on the rest of the evidence.[517] This applies even though the accused admitted his guilt in cross-examination.[518]

23.325 Where experienced counsel fails to raise the issue it would seem that the Court of Appeal will not interfere even though had such a motion been made it would have succeeded.[519] So broad a statement is, however, inconsistent with a strong statement to the contrary in the Privy Council which states that the judge has both a right and a duty to raise the issue.[520]

(n) Jury stopping case

23.326 At common law the jury, at any time after the close of the prosecution case, may indicate that they do not wish to hear further evidence and desire to acquit forthwith. Furthermore, the judge may himself raise the matter with counsel at the close of the evidence and should withdraw the case from the jury if, after hearing submissions, he regards this as the appropriate course to take.[521]

(o) The defence case

(i) Opening speech

23.327 Defence counsel has the right to make an opening speech where he proposes to call evidence as to the facts of the case other than that of the accused. He may, in the course of so doing, criticize evidence already given by the prosecution.[522]

(ii) Order of evidence

23.328 Where the only witness as to the facts of the case is the accused he shall be called as a witness immediately after the close of the evidence for the prosecution.[523] Where the defence proposes to call two or more witnesses as to the facts of the case and those witnesses include the accused, the accused shall be called before those other witnesses unless the court otherwise directs.[524]

---

[517] *R v Garside* (1967) 52 Cr App R 85.
[518] *R v Smith* [1999] 2 Cr App R 28.
[519] *R v Juett* [1988] 1 Crim LR 113.
[520] *Daley v The Queen* [1994] 1 AC 117, 123.
[521] *R v Brown* [2001] EWCA Crim 961; [2001] Crim LR 675.
[522] *R v Hill* (1911) 7 Cr App R 1 and see *R v Randall*, The Times, 11 July 1973.
[523] Criminal Evidence Act 1898, s 2.
[524] Police and Criminal Evidence Act 1984, s 79

23.329   Counsel is entitled to and indeed obliged to advise the accused whether he should give evidence but the decision is for the accused alone.[525] If the accused does not give evidence he may be the subject of an adverse inference.[526]

(iii) Alibi evidence

23.330   The accused must in his defence statement give particulars of the alibi and the name and address of any alibi witness or, if these are not known, any information which might assist in finding such a witness.[527] Counsel is under a duty to consult the accused before deciding whether or not alibi witnesses should be called. [528]

(iv) Expert evidence

23.331   In respect of Crown Court trials any party to the proceedings must furnish to the other party or parties particulars of any expert evidence on which he proposes to rely.[529] A party may demand to see a copy of the record of tests, observations and calculations carried out for the purpose.

(v) After close of defence evidence

23.332   In general, once the prosecution case has been closed counsel may not adduce any further evidence in support of it. This rule is required in the interests of orderly procedure; the jury must not be confused by introducing prosecution evidence at random throughout the trial.[530] The judge has, however, a discretion to permit further evidence to be adduced in support of the prosecution case where the interests of justice so require. The applicable principles are: (1) that the prosecution must in general call the whole of their evidence before closing their case; (2) evidence may be called in rebuttal to deal with matters which have arisen ex improviso; (3) the prosecution do not have to foresee every eventuality but are entitled to make reasonable assumptions; (4) where what has been omitted is a mere formality as distinct from a central issue in the case. In these latter two situations the judge has a discretion to allow evidence to be admitted. It must be exercised reasonably. It would appear that there is a wider discretion which may be exercised where the principles of justice so require.[531]

23.333   Application should be made to call such evidence as soon as possible. In one reported case evidence was allowed after the close of speeches to rebut an alibi defence raised ex improviso, a situation against which modern procedure offers safeguards by way of advance disclosure.[532]

---

[525] *R v Bevan* (1994) 98 Cr App R 354.
[526] Criminal Justice and Public Order Act 1994, s 35.
[527] ibid s 5.
[528] *R v Irwin* [1987] 1 WLR 902.
[529] Crown Court (Advance Notice of Expert Evidence) Rules, SI 1987/716.
[530] *R v Day* [1940] 1 All ER 402.
[531] *R v Munnery* (1992) 94 Cr App R 164 affirming *R v Francis* [1990] 1 WLR 1264.
[532] *R v Flynn* (1957) 42 Cr App R 15.

(vi) Re-opening defence case

The judge may allow evidence to be called where it favours the defence at any time **23.334** up to the point where the jury has retired to consider its verdict. There appears to be a strict rule against allowing such evidence to be called after the jury has retired.[533] It may be, however, that the rule will be relaxed in the light of the Criminal Law Revision Committee's conclusion that it is too strict and authorities elsewhere which take the same view.[534] The overriding consideration must be whether the interests of justice would be served by admitting the evidence.

(p) Judge calling witness

It has long been recognized that the judge has a power to call a witness where the **23.335** interests of justice so require.[535] This power may be exercised on appeal as well. The power should be used most sparingly and it is rarely exercised.[536] The guiding principle is whether the interests of justice so require.[537] The procedure is not free from difficulty. Under the former practice where witnesses were named on the back of the indictment the judge could call a witness present in court where he considered that the prosecution acted wrongly in not so doing.[538] The same must be true today of a witness summoned to appear. It is submitted, on the basis it must be admitted of no authority, that where a witness, about whom there are doubts, may give evidence which favours the prosecution's case but where he may be of some use to the defence when cross-examined, the better procedure is for the prosecution to ensure his attendance at court and either to tender him for cross-examination or invite the judge to call him in the exercise of his discretion. A witness called by the judge may be cross-examined by the defence.[539]

(q) Questioning by judge and jury

The trial judge has a discretion to question witnesses. This discretion should be **23.336** exercised sparingly in order to prevent points from going by default. The trial judge must not act as an advocate. He may ask questions of the accused but he must not comment on the replies.[540]

The jury may ask a question but should not be encouraged to do so. Jurors are not **23.337** familiar with the rules of evidence and might ask embarrassing questions which

---

[533] *R v Owen* [1952] 2 QB 362.
[534] See Cross and Tapper (n 488 above) 280 and *People (AG) v O'Brien* [1963] IR 65 cited therein.
[535] *R v Harris (Dora)* (1927) 2 KB 587.
[536] *R v Grafton* [1993] QB 101, 107.
[537] *R v Wallwork* (1958) 42 Cr App R 153; *R v Roberts* (1984) 80 Cr App R 89.
[538] *R v Holden* (1838) 8 C & P 606.
[539] *R v Howarth* (1918) 13 Cr App R 99.
[540] *R v Barnes* (1991) 155 JP 417: the full transcript of the judgment should be consulted.

could not be answered or would be difficult to deal with.[541] It follows that such questions should be put by the judge on due consideration.

(r) Closing speeches

23.338 The prosecution speech is made immediately after the close of defence evidence.[542] The defence speech follows that of the prosecution. Where the accused is unrepresented and does not call evidence the prosecution may not make a closing speech. Both prosecution and defence speeches should be brief.[543] Such speeches should not refer to matters which have not been dealt with by evidence.

23.339 Prosecution counsel should not allude to the potentially serious consequences to police officers of being disbelieved.[544] Defence counsel should not refer to the likely consequences of conviction.[545]

(s) Summing up

23.340 It is customary for the judge, before summing up, to canvass with counsel any points which they wish to be included in the summing up or to be dealt with in any particular way.

23.341 The summing up is a survey of the case. It consists of a direction on the law and a summary of the facts. There is no regular pattern to the summing up because that depends on the course of the trial. The judge must direct the jury accurately on the law. In so doing he is assisted by specimen directions contained in guidance published by the Judicial Studies Board, but the sample directions are not comprehensive and may require adaptation.

23.342 The summing up normally begins with a statement by the judge that he is the judge of law while the jury are judges of fact. While they must apply the law as stated by the judge they are free to and indeed must form their own conclusions on the evidence. The judge may in a complex case assist the jury by supplying them with a written list of questions or directions. These are usually discussed with counsel in advance.[546] The judge is not, however, obliged to do so.[547]

23.343 Every summing up must contain a direction on the standard and burden of proof.[548] The form of such a direction is contained in the Judicial Studies Board's

---

[541] *R v Barnes,* ibid. The authority sometimes cited for the practice, *R v Lillyman* [1896] 2 QB 167, seems barely to do so.
[542] Criminal Procedure Act 1865, s 2.
[543] *R v Bryant* [1979] QB 108.
[544] *R v Gale* [1994] Crim LR 208.
[545] *A-G of South Australia v Brown* [1960] AC 432.
[546] *R v McKechnie* (1991) 94 Cr App R 51.
[547] *R v Lawson* [1998] Crim LR 883.
[548] *R v Edwards* (1983) 77 Cr App R 5.

guidance and it is usually unhelpful to gloss it.[549] The summing up must also contain a direction outlining the ingredients of the offence or offences which the prosecution is obliged to prove.

The summing up must present a fair picture of the prosecution and defence cases, analysing the evidence and relating it to the issues in the case.[550] The judge in reviewing the evidence is entitled to be selective provided that the case is fairly put to the jury. He is obliged to mention a defence, however weak, provided that there is evidence to support it and this applies even though the defence has not expressly relied on it.[551]   **23.344**

The judge may comment even in strong terms, about the strength of the defence, the demeanour and credibility of witnesses, and the weight to be attached to their evidence. The judge must not, however, sum up in such a way as to make the summing up as a whole unbalanced. He must not sum up intemperately or unfairly, and he must not use language which is so strong that the jury derives the impression that they must decide the case in any one sense.[552]   **23.345**

Both counsel are obliged to advise the judge of an error in the summing up. This applies equally to prosecution and defence counsel.[553]   **23.346**

(t) The jury

(i) Unanimity

The ideal is that of a unanimous verdict. The judge in summing up will advise the jury to retire and endeavour to reach a unanimous verdict. He will inform the jury that while it is possible for the court to accept a majority verdict the time has not yet arisen when this may be done.[554]   **23.347**

In a proper case, where there is a danger that the jury might find the accused guilty because some jurors found that one ingredient was proved and others found another ingredient proved, the judge must direct the jury that they must be unanimous as to the proof of the ingredient that proved that offence.[555]   **23.348**

(ii) Jury retirement

Once the jury retires they are in the custody of the jury bailiff. They must not leave the precincts of the court without leave of the judge. Modern practice is not to   **23.349**

---

[549] *R v Stephens* [2002] EWCA Crim 1529; The Times, 27 June 2002.
[550] *R v Lawrence* [1982] AC 510 *per* Lord Hailsham.
[551] *Mancini v DPP* [1942] AC 1.
[552] *R v Wood* [1996] 1 Cr App R 202. D Karlen, *Anglo-American Criminal Justice* (Oxford: Clarendon Press, 1967) 190 notes that judicial comment on these matters is usually temperate.
[553] *R v Langford*, The Times, 12 January 2001.
[554] The form of words used is that suggested by the Judicial Studies Board specimen direction.
[555] *R v D* [2001] 1 Cr App R 194.

commence a summing up in a long case late in the day and not to prolong a summing up beyond normal hours. Jurors are no longer kept together overnight.

23.350 The prohibition upon jurors hearing evidence after they have retired has as a consequence that the jury may not have items which were not exhibited in evidence. On the other hand, the tape of an interview may be supplied to the jury even though at trial the evidence was adduced by way of a transcript.[556]

23.351 Juries not infrequently communicate with the court after retirement, for example to ask for clarification, or an exhibit. Any such communication, provided that it is not unconnected with the trial, must be read out in open court and the answer given in the presence of the prosecution and the accused.[557] It is not always necessary, however, for the jury to be brought back into court to hear the answer.

(iii) *Confidentiality of jury deliberations*

23.352 The principle is well established that the court will not admit the evidence of a juryman as to what took place in the jury room, either by way of explanation of the grounds upon which the verdict was given or by way of statement as to what he believed its effect to be. Where a verdict is given in the sight and hearing of the entire jury without any dissent by any member of it there is a presumption that all assented to it.[558] The reasons for this rule are to ensure the finality of verdicts and to protect jurors from inducement or pressure to reveal what happened in the jury room or to alter their view.[559] The prohibition does not apply to events occurring outside the jury room. The celebrated case of *Young* is an example: there evidence was received that certain jurors at the hotel consulted a ouija board on the question of guilt or innocence.[560]

(u) **The verdict**

(i) *Returning the verdict*

23.353 The verdict is given in open court. The jury foreman is asked whether the jury have reached a verdict on which they are all agreed.[561] If the jury are not unanimous they should be sent out again for further deliberation with a further direction to arrive, if possible, at a unanimous verdict. If the jury return after a period of time which the judge thinks reasonable they may be directed in terms of a majority verdict.[562]

---

[556] *R v Riaz* (1991) 94 Cr App R 339.
[557] *R v Green* [1950] 1 All ER 38; *R v Gorman* [1987] 1 WLR 545.
[558] *R v Austin* [2002] All ER (D) 192 (June).
[559] *Noonan v The State* (1986) 83 Cr App R 292, PC. See further Contempt of Court Act 1981, s 8.
[560] *R v Young* [1995] QB 324.
[561] *Practice Direction (Criminal Proceedings: Consolidation)* [2002] 1 WLR 2870, para 46.1.
[562] ibid paras 46.2–46.4.

If the indictment is a multi-count indictment the question is put in respect of each **23.354**
count. It not infrequently happens that the jury is able to reach unanimous verdicts on some but not all counts. It is proper for the court to receive the verdicts arrived at and to remit the others to the jury with a direction that a majority verdict may be received.

Where counts are laid in the alternative the practice is to take a verdict on one **23.355**
count and discharge the jury from taking a verdict on the other. This enables the Court of Appeal to substitute a verdict for the alternative count if an appeal against conviction on the primary count succeeds. Where the counts are not, strictly, alternatives but are for example of the same genre but of different gravity, the judge will direct the jury to consider the more serious count first. The jury will then only consider the lesser count if they cannot agree on a verdict on the greater. The jury should not, however, be invited to convict of both since that may give a misleading impression of the accused's criminality at a later time.[563]

(ii) Correcting the verdict

Once the judge has discharged the jury he is functus officio. If the jury have been dis- **23.356**
charged accidentally without being invited to deliver their verdicts the judge is entitled to set aside the discharge and accept the verdict already reached. Similarly, where the court has made a procedural error in taking a majority verdict and even such a verdict of guilty, the discharge may be set aside and the jury invited to give the precise figures on which the verdict was based. The jury, once discharged, may not, in general, return a verdict which is the subject of further debate.[564] In a recent civil case in which the criminal law authorities were reviewed the court intimated, however, that there may be cases where a verdict which has been the subject of further debate may be received. If there may have been a misunderstanding and that misunderstanding was raised before the jury separated and before they heard anything they should not have heard, it may be proper for the judge to allow them to continue to debate. Jurors must raise the question of a misunderstanding or mistake as promptly as possible. The court will not accede to a request to re-open matters if it is satisfied that what is sought is an opportunity to debate matters already decided.[565]

(iii) Refusing the verdict

While in general the judge must accept the jury's verdict, he may refuse to do so **23.357**
where a single verdict is ambiguous, or two verdicts are inconsistent, or the verdict is one which on the indictment cannot be returned.[566] The jury will be invited to

---

[563] *R v Harris* [1969] 1 WLR 745.
[564] *R v Alowi* (8 March 1999).
[565] *Igwemma v Chief Constable of Greater Manchester Police* [2001] EWCA Civ 953; [2002] QB 1012.
[566] *R v Harris* [1964] Crim LR 54.

return a second verdict and that verdict will prevail. Presumably, if the jury refuse to return an unambiguous verdict, for example, they may be discharged.

(iv) Questions about the verdict

23.358 While the jury should not in general be asked questions about the basis of their verdict, it is accepted that the judge may do so where the accused is found guilty of manslaughter for that affects the question of sentence.[567]

(v) Majority verdicts

23.359 The ideal remains a unanimous verdict. A majority verdict may not be accepted until the jury has considered its verdict for such time as the court considers reasonable and, in any event, for not less than two hours. No court may accept a majority verdict unless the court considers that the jury have had such time for deliberation as the court thinks reasonable having regard to the nature and complexity of the case.[568]

23.360 Where there are not less than 11 jurors ten of them must agree on the verdict. In a case where there are ten jurors, nine must agree on a verdict.[569] A verdict of guilty shall not be accepted unless the foreman of the jury has stated in open court the number of jurors who respectively agreed to and dissented from the verdict.[570] Failure to comply with this requirement will, if the circumstances are such that the number for and against is not immediately apparent, result in the conviction being quashed.[571] The practice directions which prescribe the mode of taking the verdict are, however, directory so that a failure to comply with them may not render the conviction a nullity.[572]

(vi) Alternative verdicts

23.361 The law concerning when a court may receive an alternative verdict is complex. What follows is a brief sketch.[573]

23.362 For the most part the availability of an alternative verdict depends on statute. Section 6(3) of the Criminal Law Act 1967 provides that, save in cases of treason or murder, a person found not guilty of the offence charged in the indictment may be found guilty of another offence. This requires that the allegations in the

---

[567] *R v Matheson* [1958] 1 WLR 474 and see further *Blackstone's Criminal Practice* (n 7 above) para D17.11.

[568] Juries Act 1974, s 17(4).

[569] ibid s 17(1)(a)–(b).

[570] ibid s 17(3).

[571] *R v Barry* [1975] 1 WLR 1190; *R v Austin* [2002] All ER (D) 192 (June).

[572] *R v Georgiou* (1969) 53 Cr App R 428.

[573] Reference may be made to the standard practitioner texts: see, eg, *Blackstone's Criminal Practice* (n 7 above) paras D17.18–17.30.

indictment include, expressly or by implication, an allegation falling within the jurisdiction of the trial court. A count which alleges burglary may be held to state expressly an allegation of theft where the particulars relating to burglary, if excised, nonetheless leave an allegation of theft.[574] The same result followed where, on an indictment alleging inflicting grievous bodily harm, a verdict of assault occasioning actual bodily harm was returned.[575] An offence may be impliedly alleged where commission of the offence charged may or will involve the commission of another offence.[576]

A number of statutory provisions make explicit provision for alternative verdicts. **23.363**
A person found not guilty of murder may be convicted of manslaughter, infanticide, child destruction, causing grievous bodily harm with intent to do so, or attempted murder or an attempt to commit any of the other offences of which he might be convicted.[577]

Of the further provisions relating to the topic, the offences of assisting offend- **23.364**
ers,[578] attempts,[579] offences against the Public Order Act 1986[580] and common assault[581] may be noted.

The judge has a discretion whether or not to direct the jury concerning a possible **23.365**
alternative verdict. The trial judge must ensure, before leaving such a possible verdict to the jury, that by doing so he will not expose the accused to any risk of injustice.[582] Furthermore, an alternative verdict should only be left to the jury where it is in the interests of justice to do so.[583] Where, for example, the principal offence is grave and the alternative trifling, the judge is entitled not to distract the jury by forcing them to consider something which is remote from the real point of the case. The Court of Appeal, before interfering with the verdict in a case where the judge refused to leave an alternative verdict to the jury, must be satisfied that the jury convicted out of reluctance to allow the accused to get clean away with what on any view was disgraceful conduct.[584]

---

[574] *R v Lillis* [1972] 2 QB 236.
[575] *Metropolitan Police Commissioner v Wilson* [1984] AC 482. Attempting to cause grievous bodily harm with intent is a verdict implied within attempted murder: *R v Morrison* [2003] 1 WLR 1859.
[576] ibid *per* Lord Roskill and see the discussion in *Blackstone's Criminal Practice* (n 7 above) para D17.21.
[577] Criminal Law Act 1967, s 6(2).
[578] ibid s 4(2).
[579] ibid s 6(4)
[580] Public Order Act 1986, s 7.
[581] Criminal Justice Act 1988, s 40 provided that a specific count for the offence (which is otherwise summary) is added to the indictment.
[582] *Metropolitan Police Commissioner v Wilson* [1984] AC 242, 261 *per* Lord Roskill.
[583] *R v Fairbanks* [1986] 1 WLR 1202.
[584] *R v Maxwell* [1990] 1 WLR 401, 408 *per* Lord Ackner.

23.366 The jury may only convict the accused of an alternative offence if they find him not guilty of the offence charged.[585] Where the jury cannot agree upon a verdict the practice is to add a count to the indictment expressly charging the alternative offence.[586] Where, however, the charge is murder and the jury cannot agree on a verdict the court may, at common law, receive a verdict of manslaughter.[587]

(vii) Jury unable to agree

23.367 Where the jury cannot agree upon a verdict they will be discharged from doing so. The accused may then be retried by a different jury. While in general a person will not be retried where the jury has twice been unable to agree, in some cases, for example where a jury has been tampered with or fresh evidence discovered, it may be proper to do so.[588]

(viii) Pressure on jury

23.368 The jury must be free to deliberate without any form of pressure being imposed upon them. They must be given reasonable time in which to reach their verdict. The jury should not be led to believe that they must reach a verdict within any given time.[589] The jury may, however, be asked whether there is any reasonable prospect of their reaching agreement and be told that if there is not the judge will discharge them. This must be done in open court.[590]

23.369 Another instance of pressure comes where the judge uses a form of words which makes the jury feel that it is incumbent upon them to express a view which they do not truly hold simply because it might be inconvenient, tiresome or expensive for all parties if they did not do so. The jury may be directed to take their individual experience and pool it with others and that agreement may be reached by a process of give and take. They should also be told that if at least ten of them cannot agree they must say so.[591]

23.370 In most cases there will be no need for such a direction. If given it should be given either during the summing up or after the jury have had a reasonable time to consider a majority direction. It should never be combined with a majority direction.[592]

---

[585] Criminal Law Act 1967, ss 4(2), 6(2) and (3).
[586] *R v Collison* (1980) 71 Cr App R 249.
[587] *R v Saunders* [1988] AC 148.
[588] *R v Henworth* [2001] EWCA Crim 120; [2001] 2 Cr App R 4.
[589] *R v McKenna* [1960] 1 QB 411.
[590] *R v Wharton* [1990] Crim LR 877.
[591] *R v Watson* [1988] QB 690 disapproving *R v Walhein* (1952) 36 Cr App R 167.
[592] *R v Buono* (1992) 95 Cr App R 338.

M. Appeals

(1) Appeals to the Court of Appeal

By s 1 of the Criminal Appeal Act 1968 a person convicted of an offence on in-   **23.371**
dictment may appeal to the Court of Appeal against his conviction. Such an appeal requires leave which may be granted by the Court of Appeal or by certificate
of the trial judge that the case is fit for appeal.[593] The 1968 Act as amended by the
Criminal Appeal Act 1995 sets out the circumstances in which appeals may be
made (against conviction or sentence) and the power of the court to determine
them. The court's procedures are set out in the Criminal Appeal Rules 1968.[594]

The trial judge may grant a certificate of his own motion or he may do so on coun-   **23.372**
sel's application. In the latter case counsel will draft the question. The application
will then be made in chambers.[595] Such a certificate should be granted only when
exceptional circumstances are present.[596] The general practice is that leave to appeal is granted either by the single judge or by the full court.

The Registrar may refer an application for leave to appeal to the court for summary   **23.373**
determination. If the court then determines that the appeal is frivolous or vexatious
and may be determined without full hearing they may dismiss it summarily.[597]

The court has power to direct that an applicant for leave to appeal be subject to a   **23.374**
direction for loss of time if his application is unsuccessful.[598] This power may not,
however, be exercised if counsel has advised in writing that there are good grounds
for appeal and if, following a refusal by the single judge the applicant does not
renew his application to the full court.[599] While the Court of Appeal is reluctant
to make such directions it has from time to time done so where an unmeritorious
application has been renewed to the full court.

(a) Appeal against conviction with leave

The general practice is for an application for leave to be sent to the single judge.   **23.375**
The papers available to the judge will include the grounds of appeal, a short transcript giving the summing up, any explanations by counsel which may be needed
if his competence in handling the case at trial has been questioned by the applicant, details of witnesses to be called, and a summary prepared by the Registrar's
office. This latter is also made available to counsel in the case.

---

[593] Criminal Appeal Act 1968, s 1(2)(a)–(b).
[594] SI 1968/1262.
[595] *Practice Direction (Criminal Proceedings: Consolidation)* [2002] 1 WLR 1292, para 50.
[596] *R v Bansal* [1999] Crim LR 484.
[597] Criminal Appeal Act 1968, s 20.
[598] ibid s 29.
[599] *Practice Direction (Criminal Proceedings: Consolidation)* [2002] 1 WLR 2870.

23.376　The single judge will decide the leave application on the papers without oral representation. He will have the applicant's grounds of appeal which may have been drafted by counsel or by the applicant himself.[600] If the single judge refuses the application the applicant is entitled to have the application determined by the Court of Appeal.[601]

23.377　The Registrar has a discretion, to be exercised in an apparently meritorious case, to list an application for leave without first going through the single judge. A two judge court may refuse an application for leave to appeal but only the full court may refuse an application which has previously been refused by a single judge.[602]

(b) Appeal: guilty plea

23.378　Only rarely will the Court of Appeal grant an application for leave to appeal on behalf of a person convicted on his plea of guilty. The leading principle is whether, having regard to the circumstances, the conviction on a guilty plea is unsafe.[603]

23.379　In *R v Forde*[604] two grounds only were indicated: first, that the appellant did not appreciate the nature of the charge or did not intend to admit that he was guilty of it, and secondly that upon the admitted facts he could not in law have been convicted of the offence charged. These grounds include the case where a person pleads guilty as a result of improper pressure by the judge[605] or where a wrong ruling on law which deprives the accused of any defence provokes such a plea.[606] Wrong advice by counsel which persuades a person that he has no valid defence permits the court to entertain an application for leave to appeal because the applicant did not appreciate the nature of the charge.[607] Similarly, non-disclosure by the prosecution which induces the accused to plead guilty may result in a successful appeal.[608]

23.380　From this it follows that the categories in *R v Forde* are not exclusive. The facts that a person is fit to plead, knew what he was doing, and pleaded guilty without equivocation after receiving expert advice, while highly relevant to whether a conviction was unsafe cannot of themselves deprive the court of the jurisdiction to hear an application.[609]

---

[600] See Criminal Appeal Act 1968, s 31.
[601] ibid s 31(3).
[602] Supreme Court Act 1981, s 55(4)(c).
[603] *R v Boal* [1992] QB 591.
[604] [1923] 2 KB 400.
[605] Plea bargaining affords a classic context for such cases; see *R v Turner* [1970] 2 QB 321.
[606] *R v Clark* [1972] 1 All ER 219.
[607] *R v Boal* [1992] QB 591, 599.
[608] *R v Early* [2002] EWCA Crim 1904; [2003] 1 Cr App R 288.
[609] *R v Lee* [1984] 1 WLR 578, 583.

Cases on incorrect rulings of law which provoke guilty pleas fall into two cate-   **23.381**
gories only the first of which results in an unsafe conviction. Where an incorrect
ruling of law on admitted facts leaves the accused with no legal escape from a verdict of guilty, the conviction will be unsafe. This is not the case where an accused
is influenced to change his plea to guilty because he recognizes that as a result of a
ruling to admit strong evidence against him the case has become factually overwhelming. Such a ruling does not make it impossible for him to maintain his innocence as a matter of law or of fact; it merely makes it harder.[610] In the latter
circumstances a change of plea to guilty will normally be regarded as an acknow-
ledgment of the truth of the facts constituting the offence charged.

Appeal from a plea of guilty may also be possible where to have proceeded with the trial   **23.382**
may be regarded as so grave an abuse of process that no trial should have been held.[611]
This is to construe a want of safety as referring not to guilt in fact but to whether the
abuse is such that to allow the trial would amount to an affront to justice.[612]

(c) Single right of appeal

An appellant is restricted to a single appeal in respect of any matter even though   **23.383**
the applicant seeks to raise fresh grounds.[613] The rule also applies where the applicant has abandoned his application save where this was brought about by a procedural irregularity of substance or where the abandonment can be treated as a
nullity. Otherwise, the matter may only reach the Court of Appeal on reference by
the Criminal Cases Review Commission. For this reason it is desirable that the
court deal with all grounds of appeal put before it.

(d) Who may appeal

Only a person convicted on indictment may appeal to the Court of Appeal.[614]   **23.384**
Where a person convicted has died, however, an appeal which might have been
brought by him may be brought by a person approved by the Court of Appeal.[615]
Such approval may only be granted to the person's widow or widower, to a legal
personal representative, or to any other person who appears to the court to have,
by reason of a family or similar relationship to the deceased, a substantial financial
or other interest in the determination of an appeal brought by him.[616] This latter
phrase comprehends a close emotional relationship.[617]

---

[610] *R v Chalkley* [1998] QB 848, 860–861 *per* Auld LJ.
[611] *R v Mullen* [2000] QB 520.
[612] *R v Togher* [2001] 1 Cr App R 457, and see further *R v Loosely* [2001] UKHL 53; [2001] 1
WLR 2060.
[613] *R v Pinfold* [1988] QB 462.
[614] Criminal Appeal Act 1968, s 1(1).
[615] ibid s 44A
[616] ibid s 44A(3).
[617] *R v Bentley* [1999] Crim LR 330.

23.385   Such an appeal must, save in the case of a reference by the Criminal Cases Review Commission, be brought within one year of the person's death.[618]

(e) Determination of appeals

23.386   Section 2(1) of the Criminal Appeal Act 1968 contains a single test. The Court of Appeal is to allow the appeal if it thinks the conviction is unsafe and otherwise shall dismiss the appeal. This test, as stated, covers both a want of factual safety and abuse of process such that no trial should have taken place and no conviction should be allowed to stand.[619] In addition the test covers the case where the judge wrongly refused a motion of no case after which the accused, in evidence, admitted his guilt.[620]

23.387   The interrelation between the test of 'unsafe' contained in s 2 of the Criminal Appeal Act 1968 and the test of fairness contained in the ECHR and the HRA 1998 has produced a difficult body of case law. The result appears to be that where the accused has been denied a fair trial it is almost inevitable that his conviction will be said to be unsafe.[621] A breach of Article 6 ECHR will, however, not necessarily have this effect. While the right to a fair trial is absolute, subsidiary rights contained within Article 6 are not absolute. Regard must be had to the significance of any breach in relation to the case taken as a whole.[622] There may come a point, however, and this principle is not restricted to the ECHR, when the departure from good practice was so gross, or so persistent, or so prejudicial or irremediable that the appellate court must regard the verdict as unsafe however strong the grounds for believing the appellant to be guilty.[623]

(f) Effect of appeal

23.388   If the Court of Appeal allows an appeal against conviction it shall quash the conviction. This operates as a direction to the trial court to enter a judgment and verdict of acquittal.[624] The Court of Appeal may, however, instead order the appellant to be retried.[625] The retrial may be for the offence in respect of which the appeal was brought, or an included offence, or an offence charged in the alternative in respect of which the jury were discharged from giving a verdict. [626] The power is sparingly exercised.

---

[618] Criminal Appeal Act 1968, s 44A(4).
[619] *R v Mullen* [2000] QB 520 and see *R v Martin* [2001] EWCA Crim 342.
[620] *R v Smith* [2000] 1 All ER 263.
[621] *R v Togher* [2001] 1 Cr App R 457.
[622] *R v Lyons (No 3)* [2002] UKHL 44, [2003] 1 AC 976; *R v Forbes* [2001] 1 AC 473, HL and see *R (on the application of M (a child) v Metropolitan Police Commissioner* [2001] EWHC Admin 553; [2002] Crim LR 215.
[623] *Randall v The Queen* [2002] UKPC 19; [2002] 1 WLR 2237.
[624] Criminal Appeal Act 1968, s 2.
[625] ibid s 7(1).
[626] ibid.

(g) Venire de novo

Where there has been a mistrial such that the procedure may be considered a nullity, the Court of Appeal may issue a writ of venire de novo.[627] The irregularity may result in no trial having been validly commenced. The trial may have come to an end without a properly constituted jury having returned a valid verdict.[628] The verdict may have been ambiguous. The effect of venire de novo is to remit the matter back to the point where the fundamental error occurred.

23.389

(h) Substitution of verdict

The Court of Appeal may quash a conviction and substitute a verdict for another offence. Three conditions must be satisfied. The first is that the conviction resulted from a jury verdict of guilty. No substitution is possible where there was a guilty plea.[629] The second is that the jury could on the indictment have found him guilty of some other offence. The third is that the jury must have been satisfied of facts which proved him guilty of the other offence.[630] It follows that where the Crown's case proceeded on a basis of evidence which the Court of Appeal concludes ought to have been excluded, and there is not enough evidence otherwise to justify a conclusion that the jury must have convicted, no substitution is possible.[631]

23.390

The power to substitute does not, however, apply where the accused has been arraigned on alternative counts and where the offence to be substituted is one on which the jury has entered a verdict of not guilty. The better practice in such cases is for the jury to convict on one count but to be discharged from giving a verdict on the alternative count.[632]

23.391

The Court of Appeal may, when substituting a verdict of guilty, pass such sentence as may be authorized for the substituted offence but such a sentence may not be more severe than that originally passed.[633]

23.392

(i) Appeal against sentence

A person convicted on indictment may appeal with leave to the Court of Appeal against any sentence passed on him for the offence other than one fixed by law.[634] He may also appeal against a sentence passed in respect of a summary offence which was joined to the indictment and to which he pleaded guilty.[635] Such an

23.393

---

[627] *R v Rose* [1982] AC 822.

[628] ibid; an example of a case in which a valid trial never commenced is *R v Baker* (1912) 7 Cr App R 217.

[629] *R v Horsman* [1998] QB 531.

[630] Criminal Appeal Act 1968, s 3.

[631] *R v Deacon* [1973] 1 WLR 696; *R v Spratt* [1980] 1 WLR 554.

[632] *R v Seymour* [1954] 1 WLR 678.

[633] Criminal Appeal Act 1968, s 3(2).

[634] ibid s 9

[635] ibid s 9(2) and see Criminal Justice Act 1988, s 41.

appeal may be brought whether the sentence was passed immediately on conviction or subsequently.[636]

23.394   For the purposes of appeal, 'sentence' bears a wide meaning.[637] It includes any order made by a court when dealing with an offender and thus includes hospital orders under Pt III of the Mental Health Act 1983, deportation orders, orders for costs, compensation and forfeiture orders. A conditional or absolute discharge may also be appealed.[638]

23.395   In the case of discretionary, but not mandatory, life sentences, the accused may appeal against any recommendation by the court that he should spend a minimum time in prison before becoming eligible for parole or any failure to specify such a period.[639]

(j) Summary conviction and Crown Court disposal

23.396   As will be seen, an offender may under certain circumstances be remitted by the magistrates' court which convicted him to the Crown Court, for sentence.[640] In such a case he may appeal against sentence to the Court of Appeal provided that he was sentenced to six months' or more imprisonment (or to detention in a young offenders institution) whether for that offence alone or for that offence and other offences for which sentence was passed in the same proceedings.[641]

23.397   Appeal also lies where the sentence imposed was not one which the court had jurisdiction to pass.[642]

23.398   The offender may appeal where, having been made the subject of a conditional discharge or community order, he is brought before the Crown Court to be further dealt with for his offence (essentially where he is in breach of the earlier order).[643]

23.399   Similarly, an appeal lies where a person has been released under Pt II of the Criminal Justice Act 1991 after serving part of a sentence of imprisonment or detention and is ordered by the Crown Court to be returned to prison or detention.[644]

23.400   Appeal also lies against a recommendation for deportation, an order disqualifying the offender from driving, and sundry other orders.[645] The thrust of the legislation

---

[636] *R v Neal* [1999] Crim LR 509.
[637] Criminal Appeal Act 1968, s 50.
[638] ibid s 50(1A).
[639] On life sentences see *Blackstone's Criminal Practice* (n 7 above) paras E1.23 et seq. This part of the law relating to sentencing is in a state of flux.
[640] In particular see Powers of Criminal Courts (Sentencing) Act 2000, ss 3, 4 and 6.
[641] Criminal Appeal Act 1968, s 10.
[642] ibid s 10(3)(b).
[643] ibid s 10(2)(b).
[644] ibid s 10(2)(c).
[645] ibid s 10(3).

is to permit appeal to rectify substantial injustices but not to interfere with lawful sentences by way of minute variation of their terms.

(k) Leave to appeal against sentence

No appeal lies against sentence unless either the Court of Appeal grants leave to appeal or the sentencing judge grants a certificate that the case is fit for appeal against sentence.[646] The former is the approved course; the latter should be resorted to only exceptionally.[647]   **23.401**

The court may quash any sentence or order which is the subject of the appeal and in place of it pass such sentence or order as it thinks appropriate. The court may not, on an appeal against sentence, taking the case as a whole, deal more severely with the appellant than he was dealt with at trial.[648]   **23.402**

(l) Not guilty by reason of insanity: unfitness to plead

A person in whose case there is returned a verdict of not guilty by reason of insanity may appeal to the Court of Appeal against the verdict either with leave of the court or by certificate of the trial judge.[649] The court may allow the appeal if it thinks that the verdict is unsafe.[650] If, in such case, the court concludes that, but for the insanity the proper verdict would have been guilty of the offence charged or an included offence, it may substitute such a verdict and pass an appropriate sentence.[651] If an appeal brought under this provision would fall to be allowed on grounds that do not relate to the finding of insanity, the court may dismiss the appeal if it is of the opinion that, but for the insanity of the accused, the proper verdict would have been that he was guilty of an offence other than the offence charged.[652]   **23.403**

An appeal also lies against a finding of unfitness to plead. If the court considers that before the issue was determined the accused should have been acquitted it will enter a verdict of not guilty. Otherwise the matter is remitted to the Crown Court for trial.[653] If on an appeal against conviction the appellant successfully contends that he should have been found unfit to plead, or not guilty by reason of insanity, the court will quash the conviction and make such order as the trial court could have made.[654]   **23.404**

---

[646] ibid s 11.
[647] *R v Grant* (1990) 12 Cr App R (S) 441.
[648] Criminal Appeal Act 1968, s 11(3).
[649] ibid s 12.
[650] ibid s 12. If the appeal fails the court has consequential powers of disposition under Criminal Appeal Rules 1968, r 14.
[651] Criminal Appeal Act 1968, s 13(4).
[652] ibid s 13.
[653] ibid s 15.
[654] ibid s 6.

(m) Appeals against orders restricting publicity

23.405 Section 159 of the Criminal Justice Act 1988 creates a right of appeal where the trial court has made an order restricting publicity or an order restricting access to the proceedings. An order lifting reporting restrictions may not be appealed against but may be made the subject of an application for judicial review.[655]

(n) Procedure on appeal

23.406 Notice of appeal (where the trial judge has granted a certificate) or of application for leave to appeal must be given within 28 days of the conviction, if it is desired to appeal against conviction, or sentence if it is desired to appeal against sentence. An application for leave to appeal against conviction must not be delayed until sentence is passed.[656]

23.407 The notice must be accompanied by grounds of appeal. These may be in tentative form to be perfected later when, for example, a transcript of the summing up or of the hearing of an application for an order is received.[657] The required notice shall, where the applicant has been convicted of more than one offence, specify the convictions or sentences in respect of which the application is brought.[658]

23.408 The application must be signed by the applicant or by someone authorized to act on his behalf.[659] If counsel has advised that there are grounds for appeal he will prepare and submit them. Such grounds must be reasonable, have some real prospect of success, and be such as counsel is prepared to argue before the court. If the applicant is unrepresented he will draft and submit grounds. It not infrequently happens that an applicant submits additional grounds even though counsel has already done so. The court will normally indicate whether or not it has considered these, usually at the leave stage.

23.409 Leave to appeal may be granted by a single judge.[660] The Registrar may, however, submit the papers direct to the full court. If the single judge refuses the application, the applicant may renew his application before the full court.[661] He will usually be given 14 days in which to do so, failing which the appeal is treated as having been refused.[662]

23.410 The single judge may grant leave in respect of one or more points. If he expressly refuses leave on a point the applicant may not argue it without leave of the full court.[663]

---

[655] *R v Lee* [1993] 1 WLR 103.
[656] Criminal Appeal Act 1968, s 18 and see *R v Long* (1997) 161 JP 769.
[657] The usual period allowed for this is 14 days.
[658] Criminal Appeal Rules 1968, r 2(2)(b).
[659] ibid r 2(5).
[660] Criminal Appeal Act 1968, s 31.
[661] ibid s 31(3).
[662] Criminal Appeal Rules 1968, r 12(4).
[663] *R v Cox and Thomas* [1999] 2 Cr App R 6.

(o) Leave to appeal out of time

While the court has a discretion to grant leave to appeal out of time it is in general **23.411**
reluctant to do so. A clutch of difficult cases concerns applications of this nature
where the conviction has been founded upon what has since been shown to be an
erroneous interpretation of a statutory offence. The court states that it deals with
these matters on a broad basis, inquiring whether the accused has actually suffered
a miscarriage of justice.[664] Save in those cases where the applicant has simply slept
on his rights this is simplistic. In determining whether an applicant has suffered a
miscarriage the court inquires, where there has been the verdict of a jury, whether
substitution would be possible.[665] Where there has been a plea of guilty it asks the
question whether, had a timely amendment been made, the accused would have
been convicted of another, like offence.[666] In either case resolution of the problem
depends upon an analysis both of the evidence and of the legal characteristics of
offences.

(p) Bail pending appeal

The Court of Appeal may grant bail pending appeal subject to the restrictions in **23.412**
s 25 of the Criminal Justice and Public Order Act 1994.[667] The decision is usually
made by a single judge on the papers.

The court exercises this power sparingly. There must be a particular and cogent **23.413**
ground of appeal.[668] The court considers whether prima facie the appeal is likely
to be successful or whether there is a risk that the sentence will be served before the
appeal is heard.[669] Courts dislike returning a bailed applicant to gaol and this
clearly serves as a disincentive to granting bail.[670] Where, exceptionally, bail is
granted and delay follows in the hearing of the appeal, the applicant may not rely
on such delay as a ground for not being returned to prison.[671]

The Crown Court may also grant bail pending appeal.[672] The Court of Appeal **23.414**
may vary or revoke the terms of bail so granted.[673]

---

[664] *R v Hawkins* [1997] 1 Cr App R 234.
[665] ibid.
[666] *R v Horsman* [1997] 2 Cr App R 118; *R v Richardson* (15 October 1998).
[667] Criminal Appeal Act 1968, s 19(1)(a). The restrictions are those which apply where a
person has previously been convicted of one or more serious listed offences, eg offences of
homicide.
[668] *Practice Direction* (1983) 77 Cr App R 138.
[669] *R v Watton* (1979) 68 Cr App R 293 but see *Practice Direction (Crown Court: Bail Pending
Appeal)* [1983] 1 WLR 1292, para 6.
[670] *R v Rowe* (1968) 118 NLJ 1149; *R v Fisher* (1969) 113 SJ 70.
[671] *R v Kalia* (1974) 60 Cr App R 200.
[672] Supreme Court Act 1981, s 81(1)(f).
[673] Criminal Appeal Act 1968, s 19(1)(b) and (c).

(q) Suspension of sentences

23.415   In general an application for leave to appeal does not suspend the execution of punishment. The court may, however, suspend a disqualification from driving.[674] An order for compensation or for the restitution of property will be suspended unless the court otherwise directs.[675]

(r) Presence of appellant

23.416   An appellant who is at liberty has a right to be present at his appeal. An appellant in custody is not entitled to be present on an application for leave to appeal, or on any proceedings preliminary or incidental to an appeal, or where his appeal involves a ground of law alone. He is not entitled to be present where he is in custody by virtue of a finding of not guilty by reason of insanity or a finding of disability. In the above cases the court may give leave.[676] The court may pass sentence upon a person who is not before the court.[677]

(s) Hearing

23.417   A few points may be noted. Adequate advance notice of the appeal will be given.[678] A summary of the case for the use of the judges is prepared by the Criminal Appeal Office and supplied to counsel unless the court otherwise directs.[679] Skeleton arguments must be lodged with the Registrar within 14 days of receipt by the advocate of leave to appeal.[680]

(t) Power to receive new evidence

23.418   Section 23(1) of the Criminal Appeal Act 1968 gives the Court of Appeal power to receive evidence if it thinks it necessary or expedient to do so in the interests of justice. The power extends to ordering the production of documents or things, ordering any witness who would have been a compellable witness at trial to attend and be examined before the Court of Appeal whether or not he was called at trial, and to receive any evidence which was not adduced in the court below.

23.419   This is a general discretionary power. In exercising the power the court must have regard to the following considerations:[681]

---

[674] Road Traffic Offenders Act 1988, s 40(2).

[675] Criminal Appeal Act 1968, s 30(1); Powers of Criminal Courts (Sentencing) Act 2000, s 148.

[676] Criminal Appeal Act 1968, s 22(1) and (2).

[677] ibid s 22(3).

[678] Criminal Appeal Rules 1968, r 22(2).

[679] *Practice Direction (Criminal Proceedings: Consolidation)* [2002] 1 WLR 2870, para 18. Summaries may be shown by counsel to the applicant but not copied without permission which will normally be withheld in cases involving children or sexual offences.

[680] ibid para 17.

[681] ibid s 23(2).

- whether the evidence appears to the court to be capable of belief;
- whether it appears to the court that the evidence may afford any ground for allowing the appeal;
- whether the evidence would have been admissible in the proceedings from which the appeal lies on an issue which is the subject of the appeal; and
- whether there is a reasonable explanation for the failure to adduce the evidence in those proceedings.

The power to receive evidence of any witness if tendered extends to the evidence **23.420** of a witness (including the appellant) who is competent but not compellable and applies also to the appellant's husband or wife where the appellant makes an application for that purpose and the evidence of the spouse could not have been given in proceedings from which the appeal lies except on such application.[682]

The court may appoint a judge or officer of the court or other person to examine **23.421** a witness and take a deposition from him.[683] It may order the Criminal Cases Review Commission to investigate a matter and report to the court.[684]

The capitulations noted above are factors which the court must take into consideration in determining whether it is necessary or expedient in the interests of justice to receive evidence. The court may, nonetheless, receive evidence even though one or more is not made out. In certain exceptional cases evidence has been received which was directly contrary to an accused's confession or plea of guilty. These were, however, unusual cases in which the appellants were young, of subnormal intelligence or both, and imperfectly protected at the stage of police investigations.[685]

The general rule is that an accused must adduce any available defence at trial. The **23.423** court is in general unwilling to allow a defence to be raised in the appellate proceedings where it could have been raised at trial but was not for tactical reasons.[686] There have, nonetheless, been striking instances where the court has allowed evidence of an alternative defence to be led, for example where the accused was mentally unstable which affected the instructions which he gave for his defence and where a medical expert gave evidence to this effect.[687]

The question for the Court of Appeal, in receiving evidence, is to determine **23.424** whether the conviction is unsafe. It is undesirable that that word be glossed. The court may, when it is desired to bring fresh evidence before it, refuse to do so if it

---

[682] Criminal Appeal Act 1968, s 23(3).
[683] ibid s 23(4).
[684] Criminal Appeal Act 1995, s 15.
[685] *R v Lee* [1984] 1 WLR 578; *R v Lattimore* (1975) 62 Cr App R 53.
[686] *R v Ahluwalia* [1992] 4 All ER 889.
[687] *R v Richardson* (CA 1991 May 9, unrep).

thinks it neither credible nor relevant to an issue before it. If it thinks it credible and relevant it may receive the evidence either orally or in the form of a written statement. If the court is doubtful about these matters it may receive the evidence de bene esse in the first instance.

23.425   The court, in determining whether to allow the appeal, must assess the new evidence in relation to an issue or issues in the case. Its approach to the task is exemplified in *R v Pendleton*.[688] In this case the appellant was convicted of murder some 14 years after the event on the basis of admissions which he made to the police.

23.426   Pendleton was interviewed over a number of hours concerning the offence. After initial denials and assertions of inability to remember what happened on the night in question he admitted being in the company of one Thorpe and in the vicinity of the crime. Pendleton denied that he had inflicted violence on the deceased alleging that Thorpe alone had inflicted violence. At trial Pendleton asserted that he had not been in the vicinity of the offence. When arrested he had been so upset and distressed that he could not stop shaking. He had made a statement to get the police 'off his back' and in doing so he tried to recite what the police had said even though it was a pack of lies. He was unable to call evidence to show that at the time of the murder he was not in the vicinity. Pendleton and Thorpe were convicted of the murder.

23.427   The Criminal Cases Review Commission referred Pendleton's conviction to the Court of Appeal on the basis of new psychiatric evidence which suggested that the appellant was vulnerable to suggestion and had been placed under considerable pressure to confess.

23.428   The Court of Appeal upheld Pendleton's conviction relying on the formula in *Stafford* according to which, if the members of the court are not left with a 'lurking doubt' concerning the safety of the conviction. they are entitled to hold that a jury would not entertain such a doubt either.[689]

23.429   In *Pendleton* the House of Lords declined to adhere to any particular formula for the assessment of fresh evidence. While the primary fact-finding function must be that of the jury, their Lordships pointed out that the structure of the Criminal Appeal Act 1968, as of its predecessors, assumed that the Court of Appeal would on occasions have to grapple with disputed issues of fact. The court may hear evidence pursuant to its own decision or by agreement or de bene esse. Such evidence will, on paper, have appeared capable of belief and to afford a possible ground for allowing the appeal.

---

[688] [2001] UKHL 66; [2002] 1 WLR 72.
[689] [1974] AC 878.

If, having heard the evidence and submissions on it the court may conclude with- **23.430** out doubt that the evidence cannot be accepted or cannot afford a ground for allowing the appeal, the appeal will then be dismissed. Conversely, the court may judge the fresh evidence to be conclusive in favour of the appeal. In any such case it will be allowed. The difficult cases are those which fall between the extreme ends of the spectrum.

Their Lordships concluded that the Court of Appeal, in determining the appeal, **23.431** should not be constrained by words not found in the statute. Adherence to a particular thought process should not be required by judicial decision. The issue for the court is whether the conviction is unsafe. *Stafford* does not lay down any incorrect principle 'so long as the Court of Appeal bears very clearly in mind that the question for its consideration is whether the conviction is safe and not whether the accused is guilty'. In *Pendleton* no one could be sure what would have happened had the psychiatric expert's evidence been available at trial. It was plainly relevant to the accused's defence. It followed that the House could not be sure that Pendleton's conviction was safe and the appeal was allowed.

It is possible to argue that *Pendleton* does not lay down any new principle. It **23.432** does, nonetheless, afford an important emphasis on the role of the jury as the primary finder of fact. Its effect may be to make the Court of Appeal cautious in its approach to cases where new evidence is in issue and in particular where such evidence relates to an issue which was not before the jury at trial. In *R v McMillan* such considerations induced the court to allow an appeal even though the fresh evidence, of a possible tumour, was weak in relation to diminished responsibility.[690]

Pendleton does not, however, deprive the court of its power to evaluate evidence **23.433** and the effect of new evidence must be assessed in the light of the defence adduced at trial and all the evidence in the case.[691]

(u) Abandonment

The effect of abandonment is that the appeal or application for leave to appeal is **23.434** treated as having been dismissed or refused by the court.[692] Such abandonment may be by prior notice or orally before the court before the appeal is called on. Once commenced, an appeal may only be abandoned with leave.[693] An appellant who has given notice of abandonment may only reinstate his appeal if the court concludes that his notice of abandonment can be treated as a nullity.[694]

---

[690] [2002] EWCA Crim 114.
[691] *R v Hakala* [2002] EWCA Crim 730.
[692] Criminal Appeal Rules 1968, r 10(4).
[693] *R v Spicer* (1987) 87 Cr App R 297.
[694] *R v Medway* [1976] QB 779.

(v) References by the Criminal Cases Review Commission

23.435   The Commission was created to assume the review of alleged miscarriages of justice formerly conducted by the Home Office.[695] The Commission may refer a conviction on indictment to the Court of Appeal.[696] This includes the power to refer a verdict of not guilty by reason of insanity or a finding that the person was under a disability.[697] It may also refer a sentence whether or not it refers the conviction to which it relates.[698] The Commission has the like powers in respect of a conviction or sentence passed by a magistrates' court.[699]

23.436   A reference to the Court of Appeal is treated as an appeal so that leave is not required.[700] The appellant may thus argue any grounds he pleases whether the Commission has referred on the basis of them or not and however unmeritorious they may appear to be.[701]

23.437   The conditions for making a reference are carefully circumscribed. The Commission must consider that there is a real possibility that the conviction, verdict, finding or sentence would not be upheld were a reference to be made.[702] This is obviously not a closely defined formula. Save in exceptional circumstances, in the case of a conviction, verdict or finding the Commission must base the finding of a real possibility on the basis of argument or evidence not raised in the original proceedings or any appeal from them.[703] In the case of sentence there must be a new argument on point of law or information not raised earlier.[704]

23.438   An application may be brought by the convicted person or by an approved person in respect of a dead person.[705] The Commission may, in addition, undertake the review of a matter of its own motion.[706]

23.439   The Commission has wide powers to call for information from public bodies.[707] It may appoint an investigating officer to assist it with its inquiries and it may call upon others to assist in making inquiries or obtaining opinions, statements or reports.[708]

---

[695] For a brief account of its workings see LH Leigh, 'Correcting Miscarriages of Justice: The Role of the Criminal Cases Review Commission' (2000) 38 Alberta L Rev 365.

[696] Criminal Appeal Act 1995, s 9(1)(a).

[697] ibid s 9(5) and (6).

[698] ibid s 9(1)(b).

[699] ibid s 11(1).

[700] ibid s 9(2).

[701] ibid s 14(5).

[702] ibid s 13(1).

[703] ibid s 13(1)(b)(i).

[704] ibid s 13(b)(ii) and see *R v Smith (Wallace Duncan) (No 3)* [2002] EWCA Crim 2907; [2003] 1 WLR 1647.

[705] Criminal Appeal Act 1968, s 44A(1)(b).

[706] Criminal Appeal Act 1995, s 14(1).

[707] ibid s 17.

[708] ibid ss 19, 20 and 21.

(w) References by the Attorney-General

Two procedures are involved. The first is a reference by the Attorney-General fol- **23.440**
lowing a person's acquittal in the Crown Court to determine the correctness of a
ruling on law by the trial judge. The acquitted person may have counsel present to
put argument on the reference but the reference does not affect the acquittal.[709]
The name of the person acquitted is treated as confidential. The Court of Appeal's
opinion may be referred by the court to the House of Lords.[710]

The second procedure is a reference for review of sentence.[711] This is being in- **23.441**
creasingly used and it does have an effect on the sentence passed. The offence must
be one which is triable only on indictment or one which is triable either way and
specified by order of the Home Secretary.[712] The Attorney-General must conclude
that the sentence passed in the Crown Court was unduly lenient. A s 35(2) further
reference may be made to the House of Lords.[713]

The court's power is discretionary. It must conclude that the sentence was unduly **23.442**
lenient. The court may and very often does mitigate the increased sentence by reason of the fact that the defendant has twice been placed in jeopardy.[714]

(2) Appeals to Other Courts

(a) Appeals, etc: summary conviction

An appeal may be taken to the Crown Court by way of trial de novo. It may be **23.443**
taken to the Divisional Court on the basis of case stated. It is also possible to apply
to the Administrative Division of the High Court for judicial review.

(b) New trial

A person may appeal to the Crown Court against conviction or sentence or **23.444**
against a binding over order,[715] but if he pleaded guilty he may appeal against sentence alone.[716] It follows that a person who pleaded guilty may not appeal unless
that plea can properly be considered to be a nullity. An accused may raise a plea of
double jeopardy notwithstanding his earlier plea of guilty.[717] Furthermore, where
the Criminal Cases Review Commission refers a conviction to the Crown Court

---

[709] Criminal Justice Act 1972, s 36.
[710] ibid s 36(3).
[711] Criminal Justice Act 1988, ss 35 and 36.
[712] ibid s 35(2) and see Criminal Justice Act 1988 (Reviews of Sentencing) Orders, SI 1994/119,
SI 1995/10 and SI 2000/1924.
[713] ibid s 36(5).
[714] eg, *A-G's Reference (No 22 of 2002)* [2002] All ER (D) 250.
[715] Magistrates' Courts (Appeals From Binding-Over Orders) Act 1956, s 1.
[716] Magistrates' Courts Act 1980, s 108. For the meaning of sentence see s 108(3): it does not include an order for costs.
[717] *Cooper v New Forest DC* [1992] Crim LR 877.

such a reference is treated as an appeal notwithstanding that the person pleaded guilty.[718] As a matter of practice, however, the Commission requires as a condition of making a reference that the guilty plea be open to challenge.

23.445 If, however, the person pleaded guilty and is then committed for sentence the Crown Court may refer the matter back to the magistrates' court on terms that the case should be reheard on the basis of a plea of not guilty.[719]

23.446 Notice of appeal must be given within 21 days of sentence even though the person is appealing only against conviction.[720] Grounds of appeal need not be given and very often are not. If the accused has been sentenced to imprisonment he may be granted bail either by the magistrates' court or by the Crown Court or by a High Court judge in chambers.[721]

23.447 The appeal is heard by a circuit judge or recorder assisted by two lay magistrates who were not concerned with the original case.[722] The defence should, on request, be given a copy of the clerk's notes of the original hearing.[723] The parties may adduce evidence not led at the original hearing. The Crown Court may not, however, amend the information.[724]

23.448 As a matter of common law the Crown Court, when sitting in its appellate capacity, should give sufficient reasons for its decision to demonstrate that it has identified and resolved the main contentious issues in the case. A refusal to do so may amount to a denial of natural justice.[725] This obligation may be thought the stronger in the light of the HRA 1998 in that a failure to give reasons may detract from the right to a fair trial.

23.449 The Crown Court may confirm, reverse or vary any part of the decision appealed against including a determination not to impose a separate penalty. It may remit the matter with its opinion to the magistrates' court. It may make such other order as it thinks just and by such order exercise any power which the magistrates' court might have exercised.[726] The Crown Court may, thus, increase penalty but not above the maximum which the magistrates' court could have awarded.[727]

---

[718] Criminal Appeal Act 1995, s 11.

[719] The Crown Court must satisfy itself that the plea was, for example, equivocal: see *R v Rochdale Justices, ex p Allwork* [1981] 3 All ER 484.

[720] Crown Court Rules 1982, r 7.

[721] Magistrates' Courts Act 1980, s 113(1); Supreme Court Act 1981, s 81(1)(b).

[722] Supreme Court Act 1981, s 74.

[723] *R v Highbury Corner Justices' Clerk, ex p Hussein* [1986] 1 WLR 1266.

[724] *R v Norwich Crown Court, ex p Russell* [1993] Crim LR 518.

[725] *R v Harrow Crown Court, ex p Dave* [1994] 1 WLR 98, 105–106.

[726] Supreme Court Act 1981, s 48(2). The Crown Court may, for example, have to express an opinion on the status of a plea of guilty or a procedural irregularity.

[727] ibid s 48(4).

An appellant may abandon his appeal. The effect of this is that any decision made **23.450**
by the magistrates' court may be enforced and costs incurred to the time of abandonment may be awarded against the appellant.[728]

Where neither party appears the appeal should be dismissed. Where the appellant **23.451**
fails to appear but has not given notice of abandonment the court has a discretion
whether to allow the appeal to proceed. The nature of the appeal, the question
whether disputed issues of fact require to be resolved, and the reasons for non-
appearance are all relevant.[729]

(c) Appeal by case stated

This is an appeal to the Divisional Court on a point of law either from the magis- **23.452**
trates' court or from the Crown Court acting in its appellate capacity. The points
concerned are identified in a case drawn up either by the clerk where the appeal is
from the magistrates' court or the party desiring to appeal where it is from the
Crown Court. The very act of making an application for case stated causes the
right of a person to appeal to the Crown Court to cease.[730]

Appeal by case stated may be brought either by the prosecution or defence. It is **23.453**
limited to decisions which are alleged to be wrong in law or in excess of jurisdiction.[731] The appellant must specify the issue of law or jurisdiction on which the
Divisional Court's opinion is sought. Case stated is not a forum for challenging
the facts as stated save that a finding of fact which cannot be supported on the evidence is treated as amounting to an error of law.[732]

Case stated procedure applies to sentence where the magistrates can be shown to **23.454**
have erred in law or acted in excess of jurisdiction. A sentence which is unreasonably harsh may be thought to have proceeded from an error of law.[733] Procedure
by case stated applies to final decisions rather than to preliminary rulings. This
may be regarded as a matter of jurisdiction or of invariable practice.[734]

The Divisional Court may reverse, affirm or amend the decision appealed from, **23.455**
or remit it to the magistrates with its opinion thereon, or make any other order as

---

[728] Magistrates' Courts Act 1980, s 109.

[729] *R v Guildford Crown Court, ex p Brewer* (1987) 87 Cr App R 265.

[730] Magistrates' Courts Act 1980, s 111(1). Note, however, that where the appeal by case stated results in remitting the case to magistrates to be further dealt with as, for example, where the procedure corrects procedural unfairness, a right to appeal to the Crown Court exists in respect of the
ensuing decision by magistrates on the merits: see *R v Hereford Magistrates' Court, ex p Rowlands*
[1998] QB 110, 125.

[731] Magistrates' Courts Act 1980, s 111(1).

[732] *Bracegirdle v Oxley* [1947] KB 349. See further R Pattenden, *Judicial Discretion and Criminal
Litigation* (Oxford: Clarendon, 1990) 397.

[733] *R v Truro Crown Court, ex p Adair* [1997] COD 296.

[734] *Loade v DPP* [1990] 1 QB 1052, 1064. The jurisdiction in civil cases is wider but should be
used sparingly.

it thinks fit, including an order as to costs.[735] It may substitute an acquittal for the defendant's conviction. On a prosecution appeal the Divisional Court may remit the matter to the magistrates with a direction to convict and proceed to sentence. Alternatively, the court may replace the acquittal and pass the appropriate sentence. The court may replace a sentence appealed against with one which is appropriate. The Divisional Court may, furthermore, order a rehearing before a different bench. This power is particularly useful where the case stated reveals manifest inconsistencies by the justices in their findings of fact.[736]

23.456 Similar principles apply to challenging decisions of the Crown Court in summary matters. Either party may appeal by way of case stated . It is for the appellant to draft the desired case.[737] The judge then states the case. The appellant may be granted bail pending appeal.[738]

(d) Judicial review

23.457 While there is considerable overlap between appeal by case stated and judicial review, the appropriate procedure for referring a point of law which has arisen in the magistrates' court to the High Court is by way of case stated.[739] Nonetheless, where a challenge to a decision of a magistrates' court is made on grounds of procedural impropriety, unfairness or bias, an applicant may challenge a decision by way of judicial review even if he has a right of appeal to the Crown Court or the right to apply to the justices to state a case.[740]An order to quash is the usual means of pursuing challenges based on unfairness, bias or procedural irregularity in magistrates' courts.

23.458 The courts emphasize the use of the supervisory jurisdiction in guaranteeing the integrity of proceedings in magistrates' courts. The principle that an order for judicial review should not be granted until the applicant has exhausted the other remedies open to him does not apply in this context: an applicant is not expected first to have invoked the appeal procedure to the Crown Court before applying for judicial review. Leave to move should not, however, be granted unless the applicant advances an apparently plausible complaint which, if made good, might arguably be held to vitiate the proceedings in the magistrates' court. The decision whether to grant relief is discretionary. The courts cannot anticipate all the factors which may be relevant to the exercise of discretion.[741]

---

[735] Supreme Court Act 1981, s 28A.
[736] *Griffith v Jenkins* [1992] 2 AC 76.
[737] See Crown Court Rules 1982, r 26.
[738] Supreme Court Act 1981, s 81(1)(d.
[739] *R v Morpeth Ward Justices, ex p Ward* (1992) 95 Cr App R 215.
[740] *R v Hereford Magistrates' Court, ex p Rowlands* [1998] QB 110.
[741] ibid 125.

The orders available are orders to quash where there has been an excess of juris- **23.459**
diction[742] or a violation of the rules of natural justice and extends to cases analogous to fraud which deny the defendant an opportunity to enter an informed plea
or to defend the case.[743] An order may also issue where there is an error of law on
the face of the record.[744] Mandatory and prohibitory orders are also available.

---

[742] *R v Truro Crown Court, ex p Adair* [1997] COD 296.
[743] *R v Bolton Magistrates' Court, ex p Scally* [1991] 1 QB 537.
[744] *R v Southampton Justices, ex p Green* [1976] QB 11.

24

GENERAL PRINCIPLES OF CRIMINAL LAW

A. Origins, Structure and Sources

(a) Common law, statutes and possible codification

24.01   The criminal law is still dominated by judge-made doctrines of the common law. Much of the systematization and doctrinal development of the criminal law can be traced to the institutional writers of the 17th and 18th centuries.[1] The 19th century saw various proposals for and attempts at the codification of the criminal law, but they all came to nothing.[2] However, during that century the amount of legislation on criminal law did increase markedly: to some extent this is evidenced by the great consolidating statutes of the year 1861, such as the Malicious Damage Act and the Offences Against the Person Act (much of which is still in force), but a large amount of the new legislation was directed at the regulation of shops, businesses, railways and the like. The amount of legislation continued to increase through the 20th century, so that there are probably more than 8,000 criminal offences in English law. The vast bulk of these are statutory, usually not requiring proof of fault and often carrying relatively low penalties.[3] However, significant

---

[1] eg, Sir Edward Coke, *Institutes* (1628–24); Sir Matthew Hale, *Pleas of the Crown* (1678); Sir Michael Foster, *Crown Law* (1762); Sir William Blackstone, *Commentaries on the Laws of England*, Book IV (1769); and Sir Edward Hyde East, *A Treatise of the Pleas of the Crown* (1803).

[2] For a concise introduction, see R Cross, 'The Reports of the Criminal Law Commissioners (1833–1849) and the Abortive Bills of 1853' in PR Glazebrook (ed), *Reshaping the Criminal Law* (London: Stevens, 1978).

[3] For further discussion of these offences see paras 24.11–24.13 and 24.21 below.

parts of the criminal law remain creatures of the common law: for example, much of the law of murder and manslaughter and the law of common assault, and almost all of the 'general part' of the criminal law considered in this chapter. Moreover, even where legislation has 'intervened,' it often provides little more than a skeletal framework which assumes that further development will take place judicially.

24.02   A concerted effort at reform started again in the second half of the 20th century. The Criminal Law Revision Committee was appointed in 1959, and produced some 18 reports until its demise in 1985. Major reports on offences against the person and sexual offences were not taken up by the government, but others were, including that which led to the enactment of the Theft Act 1968.[4] Shortly after its creation in 1965 the Law Commission set out on a programme of codification of the criminal law, but thus far the programme has met with little more success than the various attempts in the 19th century. The greatest achievements were the codification of the law on damage to property in the Criminal Damage Act 1971 and the law of attempts in the Criminal Attempts Act 1981. Some of the most far-reaching of the Law Commission's subsequent reports on the criminal law have not been acted on by governments. A team of academic lawyers produced a draft criminal code for the Law Commission in 1985,[5] and after consultation with judges, practitioners and others the Law Commission produced a revised *Criminal Code for England and Wales* in 1989.[6] The 1990s produced much further discussion about codification but no legislative activity. In 2002 the Law Commission started work on a further revision of the draft criminal code, but there is still no government commitment to allocate the considerable parliamentary time necessary for enactment.[7]

(b) The judicial role and the Human Rights Act 1998

24.03   Judicial decisions continue to play a major part in the development of the criminal law. This is not merely because much of the 'general part' is still undisturbed common law, but also because the appellate courts have frequently been called upon to interpret leading statutes in criminal law. Thus the contemporary meaning of the major offences under the Offences Against the Person Act 1861 is to be found in the judgments of appellate courts, as is the meaning given to certain sections of legislation as recent as the Theft Act 1968. Judicial activism in the criminal law, particularly in the second half of the 20th century, suggests that the

---

[4] Amended by the Theft Act 1978.

[5] *Codification of the Criminal Law: a Report to the Law Commission* (Law Com No 143, 1985), prepared by Professors JC Smith, E Griew and I Dennis.

[6] *A Criminal Code for England and Wales* (Law Com No 177, 1989).

[7] For the arguments in favour of codifying English criminal law, see ATH Smith, 'The Case for a Code' [1986] Crim LR 285, and Sir Henry Brooke, 'The Law Commission and Criminal Law Reform' [1995] Crim LR 911.

higher judiciary places relatively few constraints on its powers of interpretation,[8] despite occasional references to the principle that penal statutes are to be construed strictly.[9] The House of Lords has articulated some constraints on the development of the common law through judicial decisions,[10] although it is not clear that these are always applied.

Section 6 of the Human Rights Act 1998 requires courts to decide cases in conformity with rights under the European Convention on Human Rights (ECHR), and enjoins courts to interpret statutes, if possible, in such a way as to protect Convention rights. It is doubtful whether the Human Rights Act will bring major changes in the substantive criminal law:[11] possible changes will be mentioned at appropriate places in the text below. **24.04**

(c) Sources for the study of English criminal law

The two most extensive works on serious criminal offences are *Archbold*[12] and **24.05** *Blackstone*,[13] both of which have a new edition each year. There is now a proliferation of academic texts on the criminal law, of which three—Smith and Hogan's *Criminal Law*,[14] Simester and Sullivan's *Criminal Law: Theory and Doctrine*,[15] and Ashworth's *Principles of Criminal Law*[16]—might be regarded as leading the field. The *Oxford Monographs on Criminal Law and Justice* series now has over 20 titles offering detailed examination of particular aspects of criminal law, and there has been a significant increase in recent years in writings on the philosophy of criminal law. There is one set of law reports devoted entirely to criminal cases, *Criminal Appeal Reports*, and for the last 50 years the *Criminal Law Review* has published both articles and case reports with commentaries.

B. Criminal Capacity

(a) Infancy

At common law the minimum age for criminal responsibility was seven, but it was **24.06** raised by statute and since 1963 has stood at ten.[17] There was also a common law

---

[8] cf ATH Smith, 'Judicial Lawmaking in the Criminal Law' (1984) 100 LQR 46.
[9] J Bell, 'Sources of Law' in P Birks (ed), *English Private Law* (Oxford: OUP, 2000) para 1.59.
[10] Lord Lowry in *C v DPP* [1996] AC 1, 28.
[11] For analysis, see B Emmerson and A Ashworth, *Human Rights and Criminal Justice* (London: Sweet & Maxwell, 2001) esp chs 8, 10 and 11.
[12] *Archbold's Criminal Pleading, Evidence and Practice* (London: Sweet & Maxwell).
[13] *Blackstone's Criminal Practice* (Oxford: OUP).
[14] JC Smith, *Smith & Hogan: Criminal Law* (10th edn, London: Butterworths, 2002).
[15] AP Simester and GR Sullivan, *Criminal Law: Theory and Doctrine* (2nd edn, Oxford: Hart, 2003).
[16] A Ashworth, *Principles of Criminal Law* (4th edn, Oxford: OUP, 2003).
[17] Children and Young Persons Act 1963, s 16.

presumption that any child under 14 was doli incapax, which meant that the prosecution had to rebut that presumption by adducing evidence that the child knew that the conduct was seriously wrong. Many judges criticized the presumption as anachronistic, but the House of Lords held that it could only be abolished by legislation.[18] Parliament moved to abolish the presumption in 1998,[19] but there remains uncertainty whether a defendant under 14 can rely on the doctrine of doli incapax, as distinct from the presumption, by adducing evidence to raise a doubt about his understanding of the serious wrongness of the conduct. This has not been tested; but questions must be raised about the appropriateness of the English approach when most other European jurisdictions have 14 or 15 as the minimum age of criminal responsibility.

24.07   In the procedural context, however, the decision of the European Court of Human Rights in *T and V v UK*[20] has enforced recognition of the need to adapt ordinary Crown Court processes in order to 'assist the young defendant to understand and participate in the proceedings'.[21] Thus where a young defendant is tried in the Crown Court for a serious crime, the emphasis should be on informality and both the judge and counsel should make special efforts to ensure that everything is understandable by or explained to the young defendant, who may be 'very young and very immature'.

(b) Insanity[22]

24.08   As a matter of criminal procedure, the first issue to be raised where a defendant is seriously mentally disordered may be one of fitness to plead. If this issue is raised by the defence, the jury must decide whether the defendant has the mental capacity to give, receive and understand communications relating to the trial.[23] If the defendant is found to be fit, the trial proceeds. If the defendant is found unfit to plead, perhaps because he is thought incapable of giving instructions to counsel on key questions, the court must then hold a 'trial of the facts' to determine whether he did the acts complained of.[24] Only if the court is satisfied that the defendant did the acts may it proceed to make an order under the Criminal Procedure (Insanity and Unfitness to Plead) Act 1991.

24.09   About 20 to 30 defendants a year are found unfit to plead. Fewer defendants plead insanity as a defence to the charge, around a dozen each year.[25] This is probably because

---

[18]   *C v DPP* [1996] AC 1.

[19]   Crime and Disorder Act 1998, s 34.

[20]   Applications 24724/94 & 24888/94 (2000) 30 EHRR 121.

[21]   *Practice Direction (Crown Court: Trial of Children and Young Persons)* [2000] 1 WLR 659.

[22]   The leading work is RD Mackay, *Mental Condition Defences in the Criminal Law* (Oxford: Clarendon Press, 1995).

[23]   *R v Robertson* [1968] 1 WLR 1767.

[24]   In *R v H* [2003] UKHL 1 the House of Lords held that the 'trial of the facts' does not amount to the determination of a criminal charge within Art 6 ECHR.

[25]   R Mackay and G Kearns, 'More Facts about the Insanity Defence' [1999] Crim LR 714.

the defence of insanity is very narrow in some respects (although, as will appear from the next paragraph, broad in other respects), and because it may have coercive consequences. Until 1991 the consequences were very severe, inasmuch as either a finding of unfitness to plead or a verdict of 'not guilty by reason of insanity' led to indefinite commitment to mental hospital. The Criminal Procedure (Insanity and Unfitness to Plead) Act 1991 retains mandatory commitment where the charge is murder, but in all other cases allows the court to select a treatment order based either in hospital or in the community, or even to grant an absolute discharge.

The scope of the insanity defence is entirely a creature of the common law. It stems **24.10** from *M'Naghten's Case* in 1843,[26] and requires the defendant to establish that he was suffering from such a 'defect of reason', arising from a 'disease of the mind', as not to know the nature and quality of the act or, if he did know, not to know that it was against the law. This definition is narrow in the sense that it excludes any form of serious mental disorder that does not affect the defendant's cognition, even though that condition might be thought to affect moral responsibility. On the other hand, the definition was broadened considerably by the courts during the last century, in order to ensure that defendants thought to be dangerous are subjected to the 'special verdict' (with the power to impose a coercive order) rather than acquitted entirely. Thus the phrase 'defect of reason' has been interpreted as applying to a loss of the ordinary powers of reasoning and understanding;[27] and the phrase 'from disease of the mind' has been interpreted so as to encompass any disease that affects the functioning of the mind, even though that 'disease' has a physical origin not normally associated with mental disorder,[28] so long as its origins are 'internal' and not caused by some external factor. The internal/external distinction has been taken to extraordinary lengths, sweeping into the insanity doctrine cases of epilepsy,[29] sleepwalking,[30] and diabetes leading to hyperglycaemia.[31] In the result, the division between mental conditions falling inside or outside the defence of insanity bears little relation to medical opinion or to moral responsibility. This gross divergence from received medical opinion may lead to successful challenges under the Human Rights Act,[32] but more fundamental reform is called for.[33]

---

[26] (1843) 10 Cl & Fin 200.

[27] *R v Clarke* [1972] 1 All ER 219.

[28] *R v Kemp* [1957] 1 QB 399 (arteriosclerosis).

[29] *R v Sullivan* [1984] 1 AC 156.

[30] *R v Burgess* [1991] 2 QB 92.

[31] *R v Hennessy* [1989] 1 WLR 287; where diabetes leads to hypoglycaemia, however, it is classified as automatism and treated differently (see para 24.15 below).

[32] See *Winterwerp v Netherlands* Series A No 33 (1979) 2 EHRR 387, stating that compliance with Art 5 requires inter alia a close correspondence between the grounds of detention and 'expert medical opinion'.

[33] Proposals may be found in Law Com No 177 (n 6 above) clauses 34–40.

(c) Corporate liability[34]

24.11   The criminal liability of corporations is an example of the development of doctrine by the judiciary through statutory interpretation. In the mid-19th century the courts had little difficulty in convicting companies of offences in the form of 'failing to do *x*', such as failing to construct bridges to connect land severed by a new railway line.[35] Similarly, the courts showed no reluctance in convicting an employer of selling meat which was wrongly labelled, when the sale was carried out by an employee, on the basis that the meat was owned by the employer and in law only he could contract to sell it[36]—in effect, a conviction amounting to vicarious liability, a doctrine that the courts have been slow to recognize as such in criminal law.[37]

24.12   Those two developments were confined to offences of strict liability, but in 1944 the courts took the next, bold step and began to hold companies criminally liable for offences requiring proof of fault. Companies could now be convicted of offences requiring proof of 'knowledge' or of an 'intent to deceive', on the basis of imputing to the company the knowledge or intention of any officer who could be regarded as the 'directing mind and will' of the company.[38] The restricted application of the doctrine became apparent in *Tesco Supermarkets Ltd v Nattrass*,[39] where the House of Lords confirmed the rule that a company can be identified with its controlling officers for the purposes of imposing criminal liability, but held that the manager of a local supermarket is not sufficiently high in the corporate hierarchy for the identification principle to apply. In its subsequent decision in *Meridian Global Funds v Management Asia Ltd*[40] the House of Lords suggested that corporate criminal liability might be developed more widely, but that has not yet occurred.

24.13   Particular attention has been focused on the possibility of convicting companies of manslaughter, following major transport disasters in which corporations have been at fault. English courts have accepted that a company may be convicted of manslaughter,[41] although in the prosecution of large companies it remains difficult to establish that company officials high enough to be regarded as 'the directing mind and will' of the corporation had the requisite knowledge or fault. In many of these cases the company can be successfully prosecuted for an offence under the

---

[34] The leading work is C Wells, *Corporations and Criminal Responsibility* (2nd edn, Oxford: OUP, 2001).

[35] *R v Birmingham and Gloucester Rly Co* (1842) 3 QB 223.

[36] *Coppen v Moore (No 2)* [1898] 2 QB 306.

[37] For vicarious liability in tort, see JW Davies, 'Tort' in Birks (n 9 above) paras 14.356–14.382.

[38] *DPP v Kent and Sussex Contractors Ltd* [1944] KB 146

[39] [1972] AC 153; see also *A-G's Reference (No 2 of 1999)* [2000] QB 796.

[40] [1995] 2 AC 500.

[41] Notably in the case arising from the sinking of the *Herald of Free Enterprise*, although the prosecution actually failed: *R v P & O European Ferries (Dover) Ltd* (1990) 93 Cr App R 72.

Health and Safety at Work Act 1974, but there are now proposals for a new, more serious offence of corporate killing which would depend on proof of a general 'management failure' rather than upon the present identification doctrine.[42]

C. Criminal Conduct

(a) The involuntariness doctrine

The involuntariness doctrine concerns perhaps the most fundamental element in criminal liability. It has become traditional to divide the components of criminal offences in English law into actus reus (conduct elements) and mens rea (fault elements), but the involuntariness doctrine is usually situated within actus reus since it concerns the very connection between the defendant and the specified conduct. If there is an insufficient link between the defendant's bodily movements and conscious direction by him or her, then in principle there can be no conviction of any criminal offence. The doctrine has developed at common law, and there is no complete statement of the situations in which the required link is regarded as absent. A case of physical compulsion by virtue of being overpowered by another would surely suffice, but most of the decided cases concern impaired consciousness. It seems that if the defendant was totally or partly unconscious, to the extent of being unable to exert any control over bodily movements, this will amount to involuntariness (automatism).[43] Conditions such as concussion or a hypoglycaemic state may therefore suffice, so long as the loss of bodily control was complete and not merely partial or intermittent.[44]

24.14

Not surprisingly, since the effect of a finding of involuntariness is a complete acquittal (it is often termed a 'defence of automatism'), the courts have sought to restrict its application. It is apparent from para 24.10 above that certain conditions that might otherwise be regarded as involuntary have been classified as insanity—epilepsy, sleepwalking and diabetes leading to hyperglycaemia (but not hypoglycaemia).[45] Thus, wherever the origin of a condition of involuntariness can be classified as a 'disease of the mind', a prosecution may result in a special verdict of insanity rather than a complete acquittal.[46] A further restriction stems from the

24.15

---

[42] *Legislating the Criminal Code: Involuntary Manslaughter* (Law Com No 237, 1996) pts VI, VII and VIII; Home Office, *Reforming the Law on Involuntary Manslaughter: the Government's Proposals* (2000).

[43] *A-G's Reference (No 2 of 1992)* [1994] QB 91.

[44] *Broome v Perkins* (1987) 85 Cr App R 321.

[45] See nn 29–31 above for references.

[46] In practice, many defendants would change their plea to guilty in the event of a judicial ruling that their condition amounted to insanity: for an example, see the leading case of *R v Sullivan* [1984] AC 156.

doctrine of prior fault: if the involuntary state arose from the defendant's own fault, it will not be possible to obtain an acquittal on the basis of automatism.[47]

(b) Acts and omissions

24.16 Most criminal offences require some action by the defendant, or at least the causing of a result, but this is not invariable. There are many offences of possession, notably under the Misuse of Drugs Act 1971; and there may also be criminal liability for a state of affairs, such as the vicarious liability of an employer[48] or the offence of being drunk in charge of a motor vehicle. Offences that do not require proof of non-involuntary conduct by the defendant may be thought objectionable, in so far as they hold people liable for matters outside their control, but much turns on whether a fault element is required (see paras 24.23 et seq below).

24.17 The common law has adopted an ambivalent attitude towards criminal liability for omissions. The general principle is that an omission should not render a person criminally liable unless there is a duty to act. There are many statutory offences of 'failing to do *x*', such as failing to stop after a road accident and failing to report a road accident. The law also recognizes certain general duties to act, which the courts have taken as the basis for omissions liability for serious offences such as murder and manslaughter. Five of these may be enumerated, the first being statutory and the others having been developed through common law: (1) a parent's statutory duty to ensure the health and welfare of her or his child;[49] (2) a voluntarily assumed duty to care for a relative or other vulnerable person;[50] (3) a duty undertaken by contract;[51] (4) the duty of a property owner not to acquiesce in the commission of offences with or on the property;[52] and (5) the duty of a person who causes a dangerous situation to prevent it from causing further harm.[53] However, the breach of such a duty may not be sufficient for liability if the offence is held to be incapable of commission by omission: there is some judicial authority to the effect that assault and battery cannot be committed by omission,[54] and courts may take the same approach to other offences.

24.18 There is also uncertainty about the very distinction between an act and an omission, which comes to the fore when considering a sixth category of duty—the duty of a doctor or nurse to ensure that a patient is appropriately treated. In

---

[47] *R v Quick* [1973] QB 910; *R v Bailey* [1983] 1 WLR 760.

[48] See nn 36–37 above, and text.

[49] Children and Young Persons Act 1933, s 1; *R v Gibbons and Proctor* (1918) 13 Cr App R 134.

[50] *R v Stone and Dobinson* [1977] QB 354.

[51] *R v Pittwood* (1902) 19 TLR 37; *R v Instan* [1893] 1 QB 450.

[52] *DuCros v Lambourne* [1907] 1 KB 40.

[53] *R v Miller* [1983] 2 AC 161: this duty arises even if the causation of the danger was inadvertent, but the necessary degree of fault in relation to the causing of further harm would have to be proved.

[54] *Fagan v Metropolitan Police Commissioner* [1969] 1 QB 439.

Airedale NHS Trust v Bland[55] the House of Lords held that it would not be murder to discontinue the artificial feeding of a patient who was in a persistent vegetative state without hope of recovery, since this amounted to an omission rather than an act, and there was no duty to prolong a patient's treatment when that would not be in his best interests. The Court of Appeal declined thus to distort the act/omission distinction in *Re A (Conjoined twins: surgical separation) (No 1)*,[56] holding that the surgical separation of the twins would undoubtedly be an act, and subsequently deciding that carrying out an operation which would result in the death of one twin, in order to save the life of the other, could be justified on grounds of necessity.

(c) Causation[57]

Where the definition of an offence specifies the occurrence of a certain consequence, it must be established that the defendant caused that consequence. In most cases this will be unproblematic, but where some unexpected event or intervention occurs the question of causal responsibility will be raised. The law has developed case by case, and so there is no authoritative statement of the relevant principles of causation. In general, a defendant will be held to have caused a result if his voluntary conduct was the last significant contributory act, but for which the result would not have occurred.[58] In this way the law treats individuals as autonomous and responsible beings. The assumption is that if, after the defendant's voluntary act, a completely unpredictable event intervenes (for example, the ambulance taking the victim to hospital crashes, or the hospital has an outbreak of a deadly virus), that will relieve the defendant from liability for a homicide offence—although he may still be liable for an attempt, or for a non-fatal offence.

24.19

Most of the decided cases tackle the question of when an intervening human act will *not* be treated as relieving the defendant of causal responsibility, and three major propositions may be distilled from the judgments. First, if the intervening act cannot be described as 'voluntary', it will not be held to have severed the causal connection between the defendant's act and the prohibited consequence. Non-voluntary conduct would include the acts of persons deceived by the defendant, or the acts of a child or insane person,[59] or acts done in necessary self-defence.[60] On this principle the deliberate act of a trespasser (being a voluntary

24.20

---

[55] [1993] AC 789.

[56] [2001] Fam 147.

[57] The leading treatise is HLA Hart and T Honoré, *Causation in the Law* (2nd edn, Oxford: Clarendon Press, 1985).

[58] The word 'significant' is interposed because there are several judicial statements purporting to rule out minimal contributions; eg *R v Cato* [1976] 1 WLR 110, more than a 'de minimis' contribution.

[59] *R v Michael* (1840) 9 C & P 356.

[60] *R v Pagett* (1983) 76 Cr App R 279.

act)[61] should have relieved the owners of an oil tank of liability for causing pollution in *Environment Agency v Empress Cars Ltd*,[62] but the House of Lords held otherwise, largely on the ground that the trespasser's act could not be regarded as 'abnormal and extraordinary'. Secondly, if the intervening act is bona fide and non-culpable medical treatment which occurs before the original wound has ceased to be life-threatening, it will not sever the causal chain. The decisions distinguish between cases where the original wound has begun to heal and grossly negligent treatment is then administered which causes death,[63] and others where the original wound was still life-threatening when wrong treatment was administered,[64] cases in the latter group being held not to break the causal chain. Thirdly, if the intervening conduct is that of the victim, this should not relieve the defendant of causal responsibility unless wholly abnormal. Thus where a driver begins to make sexual advances to his passenger and she jumps out of the moving car, injuring herself, her conduct may not be considered so abnormal as to remove the driver's responsibility for causing her injury.[65] However, in *R v Blaue*[66] the victim of a stabbing refused to have a blood transfusion, because of her religion, even though advised that she would die without one. The Court of Appeal upheld the defendant's conviction for murder, stating the principle that a wrongdoer must 'take his victim as he finds her', both physically and spiritually. This brief discussion of the cases shows that the courts are often more concerned with moral judgments and public policy outcomes than with strict causal principles, and it is doubtful whether codification,[67] important as it would be for other reasons, would stifle this tendency.

(d) Proof

24.21 In *Woolmington v DPP*[68] Lord Sankey LC declared that 'throughout the web of English criminal law one golden thread is always to be seen—that it is the duty of the prosecution to prove the prisoner's guilt'. He acknowledged two exceptions. The first is the defence of insanity (see para 22.10 above), which the defence bears the burden of proving. The second consists of statutory exceptions, and these have burgeoned since 1935 to the extent that it became normal for Parliament to place the burden of proving any exception, proviso or defence to a crime on the defendant.[69] However the courts, inspired by Article 6(2) ECHR, have now begun to

---

[61] Assuming an adult of sound mind, not a child or a mentally disordered person.
[62] [1999] 2 AC 22.
[63] *R v Jordan* (1956) 40 Cr App R 152, causal link severed; cf *R v Cheshire* [1991] 1 WLR 844, causal link not severed because medical mistreatment not grossly negligent.
[64] *R v Smith* [1959] 2 QB 35.
[65] *R v Roberts* (1971) 56 Cr App R 95.
[66] [1975] 1 WLR 1411.
[67] On causation, see Law Com No 177 (n 6 above) clause 17.
[68] [1935] AC 462.
[69] Magistrates' Courts Act 1980, s 101 requires this in all summary proceedings.

question the justifications for 'reverse onus' provisions, and in some cases have reinterpreted such a provision so as to impose on the defendant only the burden of adducing sufficient evidence to raise an issue for the prosecution to disprove.[70]

D. Fault Requirements

Probably a majority of the 8,000 or so offences in English criminal law do not **24.22** have an explicit fault requirement (see para 24.28 below). Of the remainder, some have fault requirements that are stated in archaic language ('maliciously', 'wilfully') and others use special terms ('fraudulently', 'dishonestly'). In this short discussion, the emphasis is on four general categories of fault requirement, rather than attempting a survey of the many variations that can be found in English law.

(a) Intention and knowledge

The highest and most demanding fault requirement is 'with intent' or 'knowingly'. **24.23** The prosecution is required to prove intention in offences such as murder, wounding with intent to cause grievous bodily harm, all attempted crimes, and many others. It now seems settled that a requirement of intention may be satisfied in one of two ways. First, a person intends a result if he desires it, either in its own right or as a means to some other end. Secondly, a person is regarded as intending a result if he is aware that that result is virtually certain to follow from what he is doing (even though he cannot be said to desire it).[71] The inclusion of this second category, sometimes termed 'oblique intent', is now established, but its boundaries appear to have been left deliberately vague by the courts. Thus in *R v Woollin* the House of Lords held that a jury is 'not entitled to find the necessary intention' unless it is satisfied that the defendant foresaw the virtual certainty of it occurring;[72] that formulation may be taken to suggest that the jury does not always have to treat such foresight as intention, and there are scattered judicial decisions along those lines.[73]

Whereas intention relates to the bringing about of results, knowledge relates to **24.24** awareness of facts or circumstances specified in the definition of the crime. For example, the criminal law contains many offences penalizing a person who 'knowingly permits' another person to drive a vehicle in certain circumstances; and a

---

[70] Notably in *R v Lambert* [2001] UKHL 37, [2002] 2 AC 545 and *R v Carass* [2001] EWCA Crim 2845, [2002] 1 WLR 1714; but cf *Lynch v DPP* [2002] Crim LR 320 and *R v Drummond* [2002] EWCA Crim 527, [2002] 2 Cr App R 25.

[71] *R v Nedrick* [1986] 1 WLR 1025; *R v Woollin* [1999] 1 AC 82.

[72] ibid 96 *per* Lord Steyn, followed in *R v Matthews and Alleyne* [2003] EWCA Crim 192; The Times, 18 February 2003.

[73] Compare *R v Steane* [1947] KB 997 and *Gillick v West Norfolk and Wisbech Area Health Authority* [1986] AC 122.

person commits an offence by acting as an auditor 'at a time when he knows that he is disqualified for appointment to that office'.[74] The prosecution has to prove the necessary knowledge. In the first place, one can only know that a fact or circumstance exists if it does exist. And secondly, knowledge includes both actual awareness or (on an analogy with oblique intention) belief that the fact or circumstance is virtually certain to exist[75]—as where a defendant refrains from asking about the provenance of goods because, the court is satisfied, he had no real doubt that they were stolen.

(b) Recklessness and reckless knowledge

24.25   Recklessness as to the prohibited consequence is a sufficient fault element for many serious offences, either as an alternative to intention or knowledge (as in criminal damage or assault) or as the sole fault requirement (as in the offence of unlawfully wounding or inflicting grievous bodily harm, a less serious crime than wounding with intent). The standard definition is that a person is reckless if he 'has foreseen that the particular kind of harm might be done, and yet has gone on to take the risk of it'.[76] This requires the court to be satisfied that the defendant actually (subjectively) foresaw the risk of the harm resulting, and the judgments indicate that any degree of risk will suffice. It appears that only unreasonable risks count,[77] a qualification which ensures that surgeons justifiably undertaking dangerous operations do not attract criminal liability. An alternative and broader definition of recklessness was introduced into the law by the House of Lords in *R v Caldwell*,[78] which included not only advertent risk-takers but also those who create an obvious risk without giving any thought to it. However, in *R v G*[79] the House of Lords has now overruled *Caldwell* and has reinstated the subjective (*Cunningham*) test, concluding that it is a fairer approach, especially in relation to young people.

24.26   There are also offences for which recklessness as to the existence of a fact or circumstances (sometimes called 'reckless knowledge') is a sufficient fault element. The offence of rape is committed if a man has sexual intercourse with a non-consenting victim and 'at the time he knows that the person does not consent to the intercourse or is reckless as to whether that person consents to it'.[80] If the standard definition of recklessness as to consequences were applied, the man would be reckless only if he realized there was a risk that the victim was not consenting.[81] There

---

[74] See *Secretary of State for Trade and Industry v Hart* [1982] 1 WLR 481.
[75] *Westminster City Council v Croyalgrange Ltd* [1986] 1 WLR 674.
[76] *R v Cunningham* [1957] 2 QB 396, 399.
[77] See *R v Renouf* [1986] 1 WLR 522.
[78] [1982] AC 341.
[79] [2003] UKHL 50.
[80] See the discussion of rape at paras 25.104 below.
[81] *R v S (Satnam) and S (Kewal)* (1983) 78 Cr App R 149.

is, however, some authority for the proposition that a man may be regarded as reckless if he 'could not care less' about consent or non-consent, without establishing actual awareness of the risk of non-consent.[82]

(c) Negligence

When English criminal lawyers refer to mens rea, they normally mean intention, knowledge or recklessness—all of those being fault elements that require proof of advertence to the relevant consequence, fact or circumstance. Some offences require fault only in the more objective sense of negligence, ie the culpable failure to attain the proper standard of care. The degree of negligence varies from crime to crime. The Health and Safety at Work Act 1974 imposes on employers a duty to ensure 'so far as is reasonably practicable' that a site is safe, a closely circumscribed test. The offence of driving without due care and attention penalizes the taking of any unreasonable risk, whereas the more serious offence of dangerous driving is only committed where a person's driving 'falls far below what would be expected of a competent and careful driver'.[83] Thus the fault requirement for dangerous driving comes closer to the concept of gross negligence, which is a sufficient fault element for manslaughter.[84] Finally, there are some offences for which, in effect, negligence as to knowledge is sufficient: several offences incorporate a fault element such as 'knowing or having reason to suspect'.[85]

24.27

(d) Strict liability

There are many statutory offences which appear to penalize simply the doing of *x*, without stipulating any fault requirement. Sometimes the absence of a stated fault requirement relates merely to one element of an offence, sometimes it relates to the very essence of the crime. Since it is often unclear whether or not Parliament intended to impose strict liability (ie liability without proof of fault), the courts have had to develop an approach to the interpretation of statutory offences which are silent on this issue. The most prominent principle is the presumption of mens rea: that Parliament is to be assumed to have recognized the common law's preference for requiring proof of either intention or recklessness, unless it is clear that the particular statutory offence was drafted so as to dispense with such requirements.[86] This principle has not been given primacy in all cases, and there are also at least two factors that have been held capable of outweighing it. One is where the offence is not regarded as a 'real crime' and carries only a small penalty.[87] Another

24.28

---

[82] *R v Kimber* [1983] 1 WLR 1118.
[83] Road Traffic Act 1988, ss 3 and 2A.
[84] *R v Adomako* [1995] 1 AC 171, discussed at para 25.23 below.
[85] eg, Trade Marks Act 1994, s 92.
[86] *Sweet v Parsley* [1970] AC 132; *B v DPP* [2000] 2 AC 428; *R v K* [2002] 1 Cr App R 121.
[87] eg, *Alphacell Ltd v Woodward* [1972] AC 824.

factor, which tends to contradict the first, is where the statute deals with 'an issue of social concern' such as 'public safety' in the regulation of the construction industry.[88] It is evident from this brief summary that there is no consistent approach to the interpretation of statutory offences which are silent as to fault,[89] but recent decisions of the House of Lords[90] suggest increasing recognition that, at least for imprisonable offences, strict liability should be regarded as exceptional. There remain many statutory offences, however, which have been held to impose strict liability.

(e) Relating fault to conduct

24.29 Also relevant is constructive criminal liability, whereby the fault element does not correspond to the prohibited conduct or result, but relates only to some lesser harm. Two clear examples are murder, for which an intent to cause really serious harm is sufficient fault, and manslaughter, for which the intentional or reckless commission of a crime likely to cause harm may be sufficient.[91] Constructive liability of this kind is to be found in several offences: it does not result in conviction without fault, since a degree of fault is required, but it contains an element of strict liability (ie liability without corresponding fault) and there is much debate in academic writings about the justifications for this.[92]

24.30 All of this demonstrates that there may be variations in the way in which the mens rea element in an offence relates to the actus reus element. At common law further variations have been held immaterial to liability. In general, it does not matter if a foreseen result (such as killing or wounding) is caused by an unforeseen method, or if another person is mistaken for the intended victim when committing an offence. Moreover, the common law doctrine of transferred fault still applies, so that where a defendant sets out to commit an offence against a particular person or item of property but the harm unexpectedly falls on a different person or object, English law treats the assailant's fault as transferred to the eventual victim, so long as the other elements of the offence are the same.[93]

E. Justificatory Defences

24.31 There is a wide range of defences at common law and under statute, and their rationales vary. However, one basic distinction which is helpful in understanding

---

[88] *Gammon v A-G for Hong Kong* [1985] AC 1.

[89] cf also *R v Howells* [1977] QB 614, and *Pharmaceutical Society of Great Britain v Storkwain Ltd* [1986] 1 WLR 903.

[90] See n 86 above.

[91] See paras 25.05 and 25.22 below.

[92] For references, see Ashworth (n 16 above) 86–92; Simester and Sullivan (n 15 above) 176–181.

[93] cf *A-G's Reference (No 3 of 1994)* [1998] AC 245.

many defences—even though it no longer has any procedural consequences—is that between justifications and excuses. Conduct is justified if it is something that a person has a right to do, whereas a person may be excused because he or she was not responsible or could not fairly be expected to act otherwise. Justifications are discussed here, and excusatory defences are outlined at paras 24.37 et seq.

(a) Offence and defence

There is no satisfactory distinction between the elements of an offence and defences to that offence: much depends on the drafting, and on the way in which the courts interpret a provision. For example, the actus reus of battery could be described as the use of force against another, or as the unjustifiable use of force against another. The difference in formulation may have consequences. Thus since the mid-1980s the English courts have held that the latter formulation is accurate,[94] and therefore that the absence of justification is an element of the actus reus or prohibited conduct, with the consequence that a defendant must be proved to have mens rea as to both the use of force and the absence of justification. A person who believed that it was necessary to use the force may be acquitted, not so much because he had 'raised a defence' but rather because the prosecution has failed to prove the offence. There may be other circumstances in which the categorization of an element as a defence rather than as a part of the offence has consequences for the burden of proof,[95] but the general position in trials on indictment is that the defendant has the burden of adducing sufficient evidence to 'raise' a defence (such as duress or necessity) and the prosecution then bears the burden of disproving it beyond reasonable doubt.

24.32

(b) Self-defence

The common law has long respected an individual's right to use force in defence against attack. In former times there were elaborate rules about the permissibility of force, but recent decisions suggest that there are now two principal elements in justified force: the use of force must be necessary, and the amount of force must be reasonable. As to necessity, the common law formerly insisted that a person had a duty to retreat before using force, but the possibility of avoiding conflict is now described merely as a factor in deciding whether the force was truly defensive or merely retaliatory.[96] The right to make a pre-emptive strike is recognized, in situations where an attack is imminent.[97] As to reasonableness, the law requires some degree of proportion between the force used and the attack received or apprehended, but the courts are indulgent to citizens

24.33

---

[94] *R v Williams (Gladstone)* [1987] 3 All ER 411; *Beckford v The Queen* [1988] 1 AC 130.
[95] See para 24.21 above.
[96] *R v Bird* [1985] 1 WLR 816.
[97] *Beckford v The Queen* [1988] 1 AC 130. Cf *A-G's Reference (No 2 of 1983)* [1984] QB 456.

who react 'honestly and instinctively' to a sudden attack.[98] In cases where the defensive force is fatal, Article 2 ECHR has been held to require that the use of force was 'absolutely necessary' to preserve an individual's safety, and 'strictly proportionate' to the (threatened) attack.[99] The effect of this Strasbourg jurisprudence has not yet been assessed by an appellate court, and some tightening of English law may be required. Moreover the Strasbourg authorities appear to require that any mistake be based on reasonable grounds, whereas the common law insists that a defendant should be judged on the facts as he believed them to be.[100]

(c) Prevention of crime

24.34   Section 3 of the Criminal Law Act 1967 provides that 'a person may use such force as is reasonable in the prevention of crime . . .'. The section could be interpreted as supplanting the common law relating to self-defence in most cases, since all attacks are crimes unless carried out by someone who is insane or under ten, or who has a good defence such as duress or mistake of fact. But the courts have not so interpreted it, and therefore self-defence (or the defence of another) remains a common law justification, whereas the prevention of crime and the carrying out of an arrest are justifications under s 3. It is doubtful whether this will lead to different results, even though s 3 mentions 'reasonableness' and not 'necessity'. If fatal force is used, however, it should be noted that Article 2 ECHR permits this only 'to effect a lawful arrest or to prevent the escape of a person lawfully detained', as well as 'in defence of any person from unlawful violence', and therefore does not extend to the use of fatal force in defence of property or in order to prevent a non-violent crime.

(d) Parental chastisement

24.35   The common law has long permitted a parent to use reasonable and moderate force when chastising a child, but this approach was found to be in breach of Article 3 ECHR in *A v UK*.[101] The state has a duty under Article 3 to protect children from inhuman and degrading treatment, and in this case the common law defence proved to be so broad that the child's stepfather was acquitted after striking him with a cane in such a way as to cause bruising which lasted for days. In *R v H (Assault of child: reasonable chastisement)*[102] the Court of Appeal purported to apply this by approving the course of directing the jury to consider the context and duration of the defendant's conduct, its physical and mental consequences to

---

[98] *Palmer v The Queen* [1971] AC 814.

[99] *McCann v UK* Series A No 324 (1996) 21 EHRR 97; *Andronicou v Cyprus* Application 25052/94 (1998) 25 EHRR 491.

[100] See the two Privy Council decisions, in *Beckford v The Queen* [1988] 1 AC 130 and *Shaw v The Queen* [2001] UKPC 26; [2001] 1 WLR 1519.

[101] (1999) 27 EHRR 611.

[102] [2001] EWCA Crim 1024; [2002] 1 Cr App R 7.

the child, and the age and personal characteristics of the child. However, this fails
to cure the vagueness of the standard of 'reasonableness', and fails to ensure that
the prohibitions of Article 3 are taken sufficiently seriously.

(e) Necessity and the balance of evils

It is not clear in English law whether the causing of harm can be justified by refer-   **24.36**
ence to the 'balance of evils', that is, the argument that to cause certain harm is
likely to have less deleterious consequences than merely allowing events to take
their course. Such a justification appears to have been rejected in *R v Dudley and
Stephens*,[103] where three people had been adrift in a boat for many days and the
two men decided to kill and eat the cabin boy in order to preserve their own lives.
This particular decision seems to tell against any defence based on a net saving of
lives, but it is unclear whether (for example) a decision to make a small breach in
a dam, foreseeably killing two or three people, could not be held justifiable if it
succeeded in saving the lives of many more. In *Re A (Children) (Conjoined Twins:
Separation)*,[104] a majority of the Court of Appeal adopted this kind of 'balance of
evils' doctrine in holding justifiable a surgical operation which separated two conjoined twins and caused the death of the weaker twin so as to save the life of the
stronger, in the knowledge that both would have died soon if events had been allowed to take their course. The courts are understandably anxious to treat such decisions as confined to their particular facts, but the principles they invoke may
well be applied in other extreme cases.

F. Excusatory and Other Defences

(a) Mistake of fact

At common law it was long assumed that, where an accused's defence was that he   **24.37**
was mistaken about a material fact, that mistake must have been based on reasonable grounds if it was to excuse. However, in *DPP v Morgan*[105] the House of Lords
held that, where the prosecution has to prove knowledge of certain facts or circumstances in order to obtain a conviction, an accused who claims a mistake as to
one of those material elements is merely challenging the prosecution to prove the
required knowledge. Not only are reasonable grounds not required, but also the
claim of mistake is not a defence, as such. This 'logical' analytical approach has
now been applied to mistaken beliefs which relate to facts grounding a justifica-
tory defence (for example, mistaken belief that one was about to be attacked),[106]

---

[103] (1884) LR 14 QBD 273.
[104] [2001] Fam 147.
[105] [1976] AC 182.
[106] See para 24.32 above, and n 94.

and its application to sexual offences with an age limit has also been confirmed, so that the prosecution must prove knowledge or reckless knowledge that the victim was under-age.[107] However, there are several statutory provisions that explicitly require any mistake to be reasonable, and the Sexual Offences Act 2003 will introduce further such requirements.[108]

(b) Intoxication

24.38 If the 'logical' approach adopted in mistake cases were applied to intoxication cases, prosecutors would frequently have to disprove claims that defendants lacked the required mens rea because they were intoxicated. However, the courts have long declined to adopt this approach, and have constructed a restrictive doctrine that leaves little room for 'defences' based on acute intoxication. The leading case is *DPP v Majewski*,[109] which holds that evidence of intoxication is simply not admissible in relation to offences of 'basic intent' but that it may be adduced to show an absence of mens rea for a crime of 'specific intent'. The distinction between crimes of specific and basic intent is elusive,[110] and the few violent crimes of specific intent have, beneath them, lesser offences of basic intent (for example, manslaughter, unlawfully and maliciously inflicting grievous bodily harm) to which intoxication cannot be a defence. Even in crimes of specific intent the degree of intoxication must be so acute as to negative the minimum intent or awareness required. The cause of the intoxication may be alcohol, drugs or a combination; but where drugs such as valium are taken for their calming effect, and are generally known for their tranquillizing properties rather than being associated with disinhibition and aggression, it appears that the 'logical' approach will be adopted and their effect on mens rea taken into account.[111]

24.39 Where the claim of intoxication relates not to intent but to knowledge, the judicial approach has been inconsistent. On at least two occasions it has been assumed that the 'logical' approach in mistake cases should also apply to intoxicated mistakes,[112] whereas in *R v O'Grady*[113] the Court of Appeal not only held that an intoxicated mistake should not be allowed to lead to acquittal of an offence of basic intent, but also suggested that the same should apply in offences of specific intent.[114] There is thus no clear position on whether cases of intoxicated mistake are to be decided by reference to the mistake approach or the intoxication approach.

---

[107] *B v DPP* [2000] 2 AC 428; *R v K* [2002] 1 Cr App R 121, and para 24.28 above.
[108] eg, insider dealing contrary to ss 52–53 of the Criminal Justice Act 1993.
[109] [1977] AC 443.
[110] Offences such as murder, causing grievous bodily harm with intent, theft, burglary and handling stolen goods have so far been held to be offences of 'specific intent' for this purpose.
[111] *R v Hardie* [1985] 1 WLR 64.
[112] *Jaggard v Dickinson* [1981] QB 417; *R v Richardson* [1999] 1 Cr App R 392.
[113] [1987] QB 995.
[114] See also *R v O'Connor* [1991] Crim LR 135.

All the above remarks assume that the state of intoxication was voluntarily induced.   **24.40**
Where a person has been surreptitiously (and therefore involuntarily) intoxicated
by the act of another,[115] there might be reasons in favour of a wider defence.
However, in *R v Kingston*[116] the House of Lords held that such a defence could only
be created by Parliament, and it confirmed that the same distinction between offences of specific and basic intent applies to involuntary intoxication, with mitigation of sentence as the only means of reflecting an absence of culpability.

(c) Duress and necessity

In para 24.36 above there was brief discussion of those rare circumstances in which   **24.41**
otherwise criminal conduct might be justified on grounds of necessity, by reference
to the avoidance of a greater evil. We turn here to the apparently more common
type of case, where there is no question of justifying what the defendant did but
where circumstances of either duress or necessity might excuse the defendant from
criminal liability. The foundations for defences of this kind are not entirely secure:
even allowing for the unusual circumstances in *R v Dudley and Stephens*,[117] there are
few English decisions which unambiguously accept necessity as an excusatory defence. However, it is well established that duress by threats may afford a defence to
all crimes other than murder and attempted murder,[118] if the defendant was threatened with death or serious bodily harm unless he committed the offence.[119] And in
the late 1980s the Court of Appeal recognized a related defence known as 'duress of
circumstances', where the defendant committed the offence because he had good
cause to believe that there was a danger of death or serious harm to him or to another if he did not do so.[120] The requirements of the two defences of duress by
threats and duress of circumstances are carefully circumscribed.

The threat must be imminent: there is no need for it to be immediate,[121] but there   **24.42**
must be no reasonable opportunity for the defendant to neutralize the threat as,
for example, by notifying the police.[122] It appears that no threat of consequences
less than death or serious bodily harm will suffice, but the threat may be against
another rather than against the defendant.[123] Additionally, the circumstances
must have been such that the defendant responded as a 'sober person of reasonable
firmness sharing the characteristics of the defendant would have done':[124] this

---

[115] Intoxication is classed as voluntary if the defendant knew it was alcohol but was misinformed
as to its strength: *R v Allen* [1988] Crim LR 698.
[116] [1995] 2 AC 355.
[117] See para 24.36 above.
[118] *R v Howe* [1987] AC 417; *R v Gotts* [1992] 2 AC 412.
[119] *R v Hudson and Taylor* [1971] 2 QB 202; *R v Howe* [1987] AC 417.
[120] *R v Willer* (1986) 83 Cr App R 225; *R v Conway* (1988) 89 Cr App R 159.
[121] *R v Abdul-Hussain et al* [1999] CrimLR 570.
[122] *R v Hudson and Taylor* [1971] 2 QB 202.
[123] *R v Hudson and Taylor* [1971] 2 QB 202, *R v Conway* [1989] QB 290.
[124] *R v Bowen* [1997] 1 WLR 372, developing *R v Graham* [1982] 1 WLR 294.

seems to allow account to be taken of age, sex, pregnancy, and any recognized physical or psychiatric condition. There is also a further objective requirement: the defendant is not judged on the facts as he believed them to be, as is generally the approach in English law (see para 24.37 above), but on the facts as he *reasonably* believed them to be.[125] Lastly, the defences will not be available if the defendant is found to have exposed himself voluntarily to the risk of being threatened to force him to commit this kind of offence, as, for example, by joining a criminal enterprise in which violence is used.[126]

24.43 The rationale of the duress defences is that the law should recognize that acts done under the pressure of extreme threats or danger should not result in criminal conviction. A similarly demanding standard would be applied to necessity, if ever it were recognized as an excusing defence. But a more flexible approach appears to apply to the rare defence of marital coercion, where it need only be shown that the defendant's will was overborne by her husband, in whose presence she committed the crime,[127] and not that any dire threats were made.

(d) Other possible defences

24.44 It was noted in para 24.40 above that the House of Lords in *R v Kingston*[128] held that it is not for the courts to create new defences, whereas it is apparent from para 24.41 above that the courts did just this when recognizing the defence of duress of circumstances. This uncertainty about the limits of the judicial role make it worth mentioning briefly a number of defences and possible defences that lie on the margins of English criminal law. Various attempts have been made to persuade the courts to follow the American example and recognize a defence of entrapment, in cases where a person has been enticed or lured into committing an offence by the police or others acting on the state's behalf, but the House of Lords has now settled on a procedural remedy for entrapment— a prosecution will be stayed, for abuse of process, if the defendant was entrapped rather than simply provided with an unexceptional opportunity to commit the offence.[129] Much less has been heard of a possible defence of superior orders, applicable when a person in the military has apparently committed an offence during the course of duty, and the prevailing view is that no such defence will be recognized.[130] There is considerable confusion over whether English law admits a defence based on the defendant's intention to expose an

---

[125] *R v Graham* [1982] 1 WLR 294.

[126] Compare *R v Shepherd* (1987) 86 Cr App R 47, *R v Sharp* [1987] QB 853 and *Z* [2003] Crim LR 721.

[127] *R v Shortland* [1996] 1 Cr App R 116, interpreting s 47 of the Criminal Justice Act 1925.

[128] [1995] 2 AC 355.

[129] *A-G's Reference (No 3 of 2000)* [2001] UKHL 53; [2001] 1 WLR 2060, effectively overruling the previous decision in *R v Sang* [1980] AC 402.

[130] *R v Clegg* [1995] 2 AC 355.

offence by someone else or otherwise to pursue a law-abiding purpose. A few statutory provisions allow such a justification,[131] but the courts have allowed the defence on some occasions and then denied its existence on others.[132]

Perhaps the most substantial of these defences 'on the margins' is mistake of law. **24.45** Whereas some legal systems, particularly in Scandinavia, have long recognized ignorance or mistake of law as a possible defence, the leading English maxim has been that 'ignorance of the law is no excuse'. The maxim has not prevented courts from effectively allowing a defence of this kind where the wording of a statutory offence requires the prosecution to prove knowledge of a legal matter,[133] but beyond that the courts have not pursued a consistent path. Even where it appears that the defendant's mistake about the law has been implanted or encouraged by state officials there has been a reluctance to approve an acquittal,[134] but, as with entrapment, there now seems to be the possibility that the equivalent of a criminal law defence may be provided through the procedural doctrine of abuse of process.[135]

G. Inchoate Offences

(a) Attempt

The inchoate offences are those which penalize people before a substantive offence **24.46** has been completed, and the crime of attempt is probably the clearest example of this type of liability. An attempted crime is committed when, in the words of the Criminal Attempts Act 1981, 'with intent to commit the offence . . . a person does an act which is more than merely preparatory to the commission of the offence'.

The first question arising in the law of attempts is how close the defendant needs **24.47** to have come to committing the intended offence. The 1981 Act replaced a rather confused common law with the 'more than merely preparatory' formula, and s 4(3) of the Act states that the determination of this issue is a question of fact. However, a trial judge still has to decide whether there is sufficient evidence to be left to the jury, and should direct the jury how to interpret the formula. Half a dozen Court of Appeal judgments have tackled this question, but the line between

---

[131] eg, s 5(4) of the Misuse of Drugs Act 1971, allowing a person to argue that the purpose of keeping possession of a drug was to prevent another from committing an offence or to hand it over to the authorities; see also s 31 of the Criminal Justice and Police Act 2001.

[132] Compare *R v Clarke* (1984) 79 Cr App R 344 and *R v Pommell* [1995] 2 Cr App R 607 with *R v Smith* [1960] 2 QB 423 and *Yip Chiu-Cheung v The Queen* [1995] 1 AC 111.

[133] *Secretary of State for Trade and Industry v Hart* [1982] 1 WLR 481; cf the approach in *Grant v Borg* [1982] 1 WLR 638.

[134] Notably in *Cambridgeshire and Isle of Ely CC v Rust* [1972] 1 QB 426 and in *R v Bowsher* [1973] RTR 202.

[135] *Postermobile Ltd v Brent LBC*, The Times, 8 December 1997.

'merely preparatory' acts and 'more than merely preparatory' acts remains hard to identify. In *R v Campbell*[136] the defendant had in his possession a demanding note, dark glasses and an imitation firearm, and he had been seen walking up and down past the post office; but he was arrested before he entered the post office, and it was held that he had not yet passed the point of preparation because he had not 'gained the place' where the offence was to be perpetrated. He had not yet attempted to rob. The distinction, as put by Lord Bingham CJ in *R v Geddes*,[137] falls between doing an act 'which shows that he has actually tried to commit the offence' and doing something that suggests that 'he has only got ready or put himself in a position or equipped himself to do so'. Applying this distinction to different sets of facts is problematic, but the courts have resisted the temptation to expand the ambit of attempted crime so as to leave people with no opportunity to change their mind and withdraw.

24.48   The fault element in criminal attempts seems plain on the face of the statute: 'with intent to commit the offence'. It has been confirmed that 'intent' is to be interpreted as elsewhere in criminal law, so that it includes both direct and oblique intention (see para 24.23 above).[138] More difficult is the question whether any element of recklessness may be relied upon in attempts. It seems possible to keep faith with the statutory wording where the prosecution proves intention as to consequences but only reckless knowledge of a required circumstance: a person who intended to have sexual intercourse with another, reckless as to whether or not she consented, was held to have been rightly convicted of attempted rape.[139] Surprisingly, however, the Court of Appeal has also taken a broader view by holding that a person may be convicted of attempted arson being reckless whether life be endangered, contrary to s 1(2) of the Criminal Damage Act 1971,[140] rather than requiring the prosecution to prove attempted arson with intent to endanger life. Although recklessness as to this consequence is one form of mens rea for the full offence, it might have been expected that only the 'with intent' version would be available where the charge was an attempt. These extensions to the 'with intent' requirement call for further examination.

24.49   If it appears that it was impossible to commit the offence in the circumstances obtaining, does this prevent a conviction for attempt? The Criminal Attempts Act 1981 was intended to answer this in the negative, but it was drafted so obscurely that it took two decisions of the House of Lords, the second reversing the first, to confirm that there is now no defence of factual impossibility.[141]

---

[136] (1990) 93 Cr App R 350; cf *R v Tosti* [1997] Crim LR 746.
[137] [1996] Crim LR 894.
[138] *R v Pearman* (1985) 80 Cr App R 259.
[139] *R v Khan* [1990] 1 WLR 813.
[140] *A-G's Reference (No 3 of 1992)* [1994] 1 WLR 409.
[141] *R v Shivpuri* [1987] AC 1, overruling *Anderton v Ryan* [1985] 1 AC 560.

(b) Conspiracy

English law on criminal conspiracies, like the law of attempts, has a lengthy his- **24.50**
tory. But, whereas the law of attempts is now entirely cast in statutory form, the
statutory law of conspiracy co-exists with certain elements of common law conspiracy (to be discussed presently). The primary purpose behind Pt I of the
Criminal Law Act 1977 was to replace as much as possible of the ill-defined common law with a clear legislative definition. Statutory conspiracy under s 1 of the
1977 Act covers any agreement to commit a statutory or common law offence.
Although the offence is inchoate inasmuch as there can be a conviction based on
the mere agreement, it is possible (and not infrequent) to charge conspiracy when
the planned acts have already been carried out, a charge which is said to enable the
prosecution better to convey the essence of the conduct of those involved.

Under s 1 of the 1977 Act there must be an agreement between two or more **24.51**
people that a 'course of conduct will be pursued which, if the agreement is carried
out in accordance with their intentions, will necessarily amount to or involve the
commission of an offence'. For an agreement there must be some commonality of
purpose among the parties: it is immaterial that the agreement may be subject to
conditions, but if it is possible to do everything agreed upon without committing
the offence it seems that this is insufficient.[142] The wording of s 1 seems very demanding, in its requirement that the parties should agree on a course of conduct
that will 'necessarily' involve the commission of an offence, but the courts have
not adopted a strict interpretation. In a case where the defendants agreed to shoot
in the leg a man who was on trial for burglary, in order to provide him with mitigation if he were convicted, the Court of Appeal upheld the conviction for conspiracy to pervert the course of justice on the basis that the agreement would
necessarily have led to the commission of the offence if the contingency (the conviction for burglary) had occurred.[143]

Section 1(2) of the 1977 Act establishes that the fault element for conspiracy is full **24.52**
intention as to consequences and full knowledge of circumstances, even where the
offence agreed upon is one of strict liability. However, the House of Lords in *R v
Anderson*[144] was confronted with two questions not covered on the face of the Act,
and its answers were surprising and problematic. First, the defendant had argued
that he had no part in planning the offence (a prison break-out), and merely
agreed to play a small role by supplying certain equipment. The House resisted
this line of defence by holding that it was unnecessary to prove that each defendant intended the whole conspiracy to be carried out, so long as each agreed to
play a part. However, this might be taken to suggest that a conspiracy could take

---

[142] *R v Reed* [1982] Crim LR 819.
[143] *R v Jackson, Golding and Jackson* [1985] Crim LR 442.
[144] [1986] AC 27.

place without any one person intending that it be carried out; the better view is that each co-conspirator must be shown to intend the offence to be carried out.[145] Secondly, the House of Lords went on to hold that it should be shown that the defendant intended to play some part in the agreed course of conduct. This, too, was a requirement with no foundation in common law or statute, and a subsequent Court of Appeal decision interpreted it almost out of existence.[146]

24.53 Impossibility is no more a defence to conspiracy than it is to an attempt.[147] However, s 2 of the Criminal Law Act 1977 establishes that certain configurations cannot amount to a conspiracy: where a husband and wife are the only parties, where the only other party is under the age of ten, and where the only other party is someone whom the law regards as a victim of the agreed offence.

24.54 Three forms of common law conspiracy may still exist. The offence of conspiracy to corrupt public morals, an ill-defined crime controversially created by the House of Lords in *Shaw v DPP*,[148] still exists. This offence penalizes an agreement to do acts which are not in themselves crimes (so long as a jury regards them as tending to corrupt public morals); this is objectionable because the boundaries of the crime are therefore too uncertain to give citizens fair warning of its reach. A second surviving form of common law conspiracy, which is open to the same objections, is conspiracy to outrage public decency.[149] The Court of Appeal has held that the offence of outraging public decency may be committed by one person,[150] and so conspiracies to outrage public decency (and possibly also conspiracies to corrupt public morals) may now be statutory.[151] But this does not affect the third member of this common law trio, conspiracy to defraud, which is again characterized by a broad and flexible definition capable of penalizing agreements to do things that would not be criminal if done by one person.[152] Conspiracy to defraud is used, in effect, as an auxiliary to the various Theft Act offences, and it is discussed in that context at paras 26.124–24.126 below.

(c) Incitement

24.55 The incitement of another to commit a crime is also an inchoate offence but, unlike attempt and conspiracy, it has not been the subject of statutory restatement.

---

[145] *Yip Chiu-Cheung v The Queen* [1995] 1 AC 111.

[146] *R v Siracusa* (1989) 90 Cr App R 340, holding that any failure to stop the course of conduct was sufficient participation.

[147] Criminal Attempts Act 1981, s 5.

[148] [1962] AC 220.

[149] *Knuller v DPP* [1973] AC 435.

[150] *R v Gibson* [1990] 2 QB 619.

[151] Criminal Law Act 1977, s 5(3) provides that these conspiracies would be classed as statutory conspiracies if the courts decided that either corrupting public morals or outraging public decency were a substantive offence, capable of commission by one person.

[152] *Scott v Metropolitan Police Commissioner* [1975] AC 819.

The concept of incitement is capable of encompassing any encouragement of another, perhaps including threats.[153] The essence is that one person seeks to persuade another to do acts which would, if done, amount to a criminal offence. The inciter must also know or believe that the other would do the acts with the required fault element:[154] merely inciting an actus reus would not suffice. It appears that factual impossibility may afford a defence to incitement, since the common law still governs the matter.[155]

(d) Threats

Attempt, conspiracy and incitement are the only three inchoate offences known to the common law. However, there are some other general forms of offence that might be described as inchoate in nature. English law contains several offences of making threats to do certain acts: threatening to kill another is an offence,[156] and many threats are covered by the offence of blackmail,[157] but there is no general crime of threatening to commit an offence against another.   **24.56**

(e) Possession

English law also contains a wide range of offences of possession, including possession of an offensive weapon,[158] possessing any article for use in connection with burglary, theft or cheat,[159] and the various offences of possessing drugs under the Misuse of Drugs Act 1971. Most of these offences are created because the possession of certain items is thought to imply that the possessor intends to use them for a nefarious purpose, but proof of such a purpose is rarely required. Indeed, the concept of possession is relatively broad and undemanding: a defendant may be convicted if he knows he has a certain object or container, even if he is ignorant of its properties or contents.[160]   **24.57**

H. Complicity

(a) Principals and accomplices

The law of criminal complicity is riddled with obscurities and difficulties. It is almost entirely governed by the common law, and contains a fairly high proportion   **24.58**

---

[153] *Race Relations Board v Applin* [1973] QB 815.
[154] *R v Curr* [1968] 2 QB 944.
[155] *R v Fitzmaurice* [1983] QB 1083.
[156] Offences Against the Person Act 1861, s 16.
[157] Theft Act 1968, s 21; paras 26.99 et seq below.
[158] Prevention of Crime Act 1953, s 1; see also the Knives Act 1996.
[159] Theft Act 1968, s 25.
[160] *Warner v Metropolitan Police Commissioner* [1969] 2 AC 256; cf *R v Jolie* [2003] EWCA Crim 1543, (2003) 167 JP 313.

of opportunistic judicial decisions that lend no coherence to the rules. There is no settled name for this branch of the law: actual perpetrators of the offence itself are termed 'principals', but others who are liable to conviction as parties to the crime may be termed accomplices, accessories, or secondary parties. There is also a fundamental doctrinal obscurity: are there simply two forms of liability, that of principals and of accomplices, or is there a third and separate doctrine of 'joint enterprise'? Judicial and academic opinions are divided,[161] but this branch of criminal law is so malleable that it is unlikely that the outcome of any case would be held to depend on whether or not 'joint enterprise' exists as a separate set of rules.

24.59 The only general statutory provision in this field is s 8 of the Accessories and Abettors Act 1861, which lays down that any person who 'shall aid, abet, counsel or procure the commission' of an offence 'shall be liable to be tried, indicted, and punished as a principal offender'. This means not only that a convicted accomplice is described as having committed the full offence, but also that accomplices face the same maximum penalty as principals. The section has also been interpreted as permitting the prosecution to obtain a conviction on the basis that the defendant was either the principal or an accomplice, even though they cannot prove which.[162] Generally speaking, it must be established that there was a principal offender before the defendant can be convicted as an accomplice. The basic distinction is that a principal is someone who is engaged in the commission of the actus reus of the offence with the required mens rea, whereas an accomplice does not engage in the actus reus of the offence itself. Thus there can be two or more co-principals if they all fulfil the definition of principal (for example, where three people deliver blows to a victim, they will usually be co-principals).

(b) Accomplice liability: conduct

24.60 The older decisions on the meaning of 'aid, abet, counsel or procure' have now been overtaken by a decision that these four words should be given their meaning in ordinary language,[163] an approach that preserves considerable flexibility. The term 'aiding' would appear to cover many forms of help, for example by supplying an instrument or information. To abet is to give encouragement. A person counsels by inciting another to commit an offence or by giving advice in relation to it. 'To procure means to produce by endeavour',[164] and this implies some causal effect in taking steps to bring the offence about. Only procurement has this element of causation: for the other three forms of complicity, it need only be shown

---

[161] For different reviews of the authorities, see Smith (n 14 above) 160–168 and Simester and Sullivan (n 15 above) 210–219.
[162] eg, *R v Giannetto* [1997] 1 Cr App R 1.
[163] *A-G's Reference (No 1 of 1975)* [1975] 1 QB 773.
[164] ibid.

that the accomplice made some actual contribution to the principal's offence, however slight.

A person may be liable as an accomplice on the basis of an omission, but it is not clear exactly under what conditions this will be so. In principle a duty must be established, and therefore a parent who takes no steps to avoid a child being killed or injured by another would be liable as an accomplice. An unrelated citizen who happens upon a crime being committed by one person against another has no duty to intervene in English law, and therefore would not be liable unless he or she does something else amounting to complicity (for example, by encouraging the offence rather than watching passively).[165] In some decisions the courts have gone further, and have held that where a person has the power to prevent the commission of an offence and fails to exercise that power, he or she becomes an accomplice.[166] These decisions transform a power to prevent into a duty to prevent, whereas others insist that a power alone may not be sufficient.[167]

24.61

(c) Accomplice liability: fault

The fault element for accomplice liability must be found in two different dimensions—first, the accomplice must intend to aid, abet, counsel or procure; and secondly, the accomplice must have sufficient awareness of what the principal goes on to do. On the first point, the requirement of intention is satisfied by foresight that the acts of the accomplice are virtually certain to aid, abet, counsel or procure the commission of the offence. It does not matter that a person was simply 'doing his job' if he does acts that amount to aiding and if he realizes that this is virtually certain to help a customer to commit a particular offence.[168]

24.62

There is much greater complexity on the second point, the accomplice's awareness of what the principal goes on to do. Fifty years ago it was declared that the accomplice must 'at least know the essential matters which constitute' the principal's offence,[169] but this statement contains much indeterminacy. Is full knowledge required, or may reckless knowledge suffice in some circumstances? There is some authority that it is enough for the accomplice to know that the principal will probably or possibly commit the offence,[170] even though the general principle is that knowledge to the level of foresight of virtual certainty should be proved. What are the 'essential matters' of the principal's offence? It is

24.63

---

[165] *R v Clarkson* [1971] 1 WLR 1402.

[166] eg, *Du Cros v Lambourne* [1907] 1 KB 40 (owner of car failing to prevent driver from driving dangerously); *Tuck v Robson* [1970] 1 WLR 741 (owner of public house failing to prevent drinkers from remaining beyond licensing hours).

[167] eg, *Cassady v Morris (Reg) Transport Ltd* [1975] RTR 470.

[168] *National Coal Board v Gamble* [1959] 1 QB 11.

[169] *Johnson v Youden* [1950] 1 KB 544, 546 *per* Lord Goddard CJ.

[170] *Carter v Richardson* [1974] RTR 314; *Blakely and Sutton v DPP* [1991] RTR 405.

not required that the accomplice should know the legal category of the offence, let alone its time and place, but on the other hand mere knowledge that the principal plans to commit some crime is insufficient for liability. The prosecution must prove that the accomplice knew what 'type' of crime the principal was going to commit,[171] or at least that he was going to commit one of a number of known offences,[172] two tests which offer considerable flexibility.

24.64   If the principal deviates from what the accomplice envisaged, under what circumstances might the accomplice's liability be negatived? The courts have drawn some unexpected distinctions in answer to this question. Where the accomplice realizes that there is a possibility that the principal might intentionally commit a more serious offence—as where one of a group is known to be carrying a knife or gun, even though they have agreed not to use actual violence—this has been held sufficient to render the person liable as accomplice to the higher offence.[173] But where parties are committing an offence and one of them produces a weapon that the others did not know about, it seems that the others will only be accomplices if the weapon was dangerous to the same degree as any weapons they had agreed to use, and not where the weapon is much more dangerous—for example, where a knife is used when the understanding was that the victim would be attacked with blunt instruments.[174] And where the principal deviates from the plan without the accomplice's knowledge or foresight, allowing a different victim to be killed, the accomplice is no longer liable.[175] These two decisions are surprising, as in both cases the same crime (murder) was committed and the law normally takes no notice of different means of committing the offence or of the identity of the victim. If the principal deviates by committing a less serious offence, it appears that the accomplice can be convicted of aiding and abetting the more serious offence, even though it was not committed[176]—a ruling that departs from the general doctrine of complicity that the liability of the accomplice must derive from that of the principal.

(d) Original liability and special defences

24.65   One exception to the general approach that the accomplice's liability derives from that of the principal has just been noticed. Further strain has been placed on that approach by cases in which the conduct and fault of the accomplice would lead to liability if it were not for the fact that there is a bar to convicting the principal. Courts have upheld the accomplice's conviction even though the principal had a

---

[171] *R v Bainbridge* [1960] 1 QB 129.
[172] *DPP for Northern Ireland v Maxwell* [1978] 1 WLR 1350.
[173] *R v Powell* [1999] AC 1 (described as a case of joint enterprise: see para 24.58 above).
[174] *R v English* [1999] AC 1, a 'joint enterprise' appeal conjoined with *Powell*, ibid.
[175] *R v Saunders and Archer* (1573) 2 Plowd 473.
[176] *R v Howe* [1987] AC 417.

defence of duress, mistake or non-age.[177] It therefore seems that it is criminal to aid, abet, counsel or procure an act which would otherwise amount to the actus reus of an offence.

There are various special defences available to accomplices. A person may not be convicted as an accomplice if he or she falls into the category of persons for whose protection the offence was created: thus, no matter if she is the clear instigator, a girl under 16 cannot be convicted as an accomplice to an offence of unlawful sexual intercourse committed with her.[178] An accomplice who wishes to withdraw, even though a contribution to the offence has already been made, may do so effectively but only by taking some steps to counteract any previous assistance or, if the offence is already taking place, by actively trying to prevent its continuation.[179] There is some authority in favour of granting a defence to an accomplice whose involvement in the offence is solely in order to assist the police and to ensure the recovery of the victim's property.[180]

24.66

---

[177] *R v Bourne* (1952) 36 Cr App R 125; *R v Cogan and Leak* [1976] 1 QB 217; *DPP v K and B* [1997] 1 Cr App R 36.

[178] *R v Tyrell* [1894] 1 QB 710.

[179] *R v Becerra and Cooper* (1976) 62 Cr App R 212; *R v Whitefield* (1984) 79 Cr App R 36.

[180] *R v Clarke* (1985) 80 Cr App R 344.

25

OFFENCES AGAINST THE PERSON

A. Homicide

(1) Murder

25.01   The English law of homicide contains a number of offences, including the broad crime of manslaughter and more specific statutory crimes such as causing death by dangerous driving. The crime of murder is traditionally located at the apex of the criminal law, and it is unique in English law because it carries a mandatory sentence of life imprisonment, the presence of which may sometimes lead juries to reduce to manslaughter offences which strictly fall within the definition of murder. The minimum term of the mandatory sentence of life imprisonment is now set judicially, the Home Secretary having lost the power to alter the minimum term set by the courts as a result of judicial decisions in Strasbourg and London interpreting Articles 5 and 6 of the European

Convention on Human Rights (ECHR).[1] Schedule 19 of the Criminal Justice Act 2003 now requires judges to take account of certain statutory starting points when setting the minimum term: these starting points, which are considerably higher than previous levels, reassert some political control over the minimum length of sentences for murder. After the expiry of the minimum term, the date of release is determined on grounds of risk and public protection by the Parole Board.

(a) The conduct requirement

25.02 Murder remains a common law offence, without a statutory definition. The essence of the crime, according to Sir Edward Coke, is that a person unlawfully kills 'any reasonable creature *in rerum natura* under the King's peace, with malice aforethought'.[2] At common law the death must have resulted within a year and a day of the attack, but that rule has been abrogated for killings after 1996.[3] The general principles of causation in criminal law apply in homicide cases—indeed, many of the leading decisions arose in the context of murder or manslaughter[4]—but certain specific issues have arisen. One is the liability of a doctor who administers pain-relieving drugs which have the effect of shortening a patient's life: the basic principle, that to hasten death by hours or minutes amounts to causing death just as surely as does hastening death by weeks or years, seems not to be applied rigorously in medical cases, and the acceleration of death by administering pain-relieving drugs might not be regarded as 'significant'.[5]

25.03 The definition of death seems likely to include cases of irreversible 'brain death', although that is not yet authoritatively settled.[6] As to the reach of Coke's phrase, 'any reasonable creature *in rerum natura*', this does not extend to a foetus, and so a baby does not come within the protection of the law of homicide until it is capable of breathing independently of its mother.[7] However, if the child dies subsequently from injuries inflicted before birth, this has been held to amount to criminal homicide if the requisite fault element is present.[8] In a case where twins were born conjoined and would both die within months if left conjoined, but the

---

[1] *Stafford v UK* (2002) 35 EHRR 32; *R v Secretary of State for the Home Department, ex p Anderson* [2002] UKHL 46, [2003] 1 AC 837.

[2] 3 Co Inst 47.

[3] Law Reform (Year and a Day Rule) Act 1996.

[4] See paras 24.19–24.20 above.

[5] These points were originally made by Devlin J in his direction to the jury in *R v Bodkin Adams* [1957] Crim LR 365; for subsequent trial directions, see A Arlidge, 'The Trial of Dr David Moor' [2000] Crim LR 31.

[6] cf *R v Malcherek and Steel* [1981] 1 WLR 690; *Airedale NHS Trust v Bland* [1993] AC 789.

[7] There are certain other offences relating to unborn children, including that of child destruction contrary to the Infant Life (Preservation) Act 1929.

[8] *A-G's Reference (No 3 of 1994)* [1998] AC 245, strangely holding that the killing could be manslaughter but not murder, even though the mens rea of murder was present.

stronger twin had good prospects of survival if the weaker twin were separated, the Court of Appeal held that the weaker twin was sufficiently capable of independent breathing to count as a 'human being', and that the operation to separate the twins would amount to the actus reus of murder in relation to the weaker twin (who would die quickly afterwards).[9] The Court went on to hold that the killing was justifiable on grounds of necessity.[10]

(b) The fault requirement

For many centuries the mens rea of murder has been expressed as 'malice afore-thought', but that is now a confusing term if interpreted literally. There are two forms of sufficient fault for murder, an intent to kill and an intent to cause griev-ous bodily harm. As noted earlier,[11] the meaning of intention in English criminal law embraces both killings that are desired and cases where the defendant realizes that death or grievous bodily harm is virtually certain to result from the act or omission. However, the courts appear to have preserved some room for moral as-sessments by declining to state clearly that a person who is virtually certain that death or grievous bodily harm will result is always taken to intend such a result: by stating that in such circumstances the jury is 'entitled to infer' or 'entitled to find' intention, the judges appear to have left open the possibility that there are cir-cumstances in which intention may properly not be found in such a case.[12]   **25.04**

More controversial is the established common law rule that an intent to cause 're-ally serious harm', where death in fact results, is sufficient to constitute murder.[13] This means that a verdict of murder should follow if a defendant deliberately broke the arm of another and this happened to cause death.[14] There have been many claims that this rule renders the fault element for murder too wide,[15] a crit-icism that is even stronger so long as the mandatory life sentence remains.   **25.05**

Neither mercy killing nor euthanasia has any formal standing as the basis for a de-fence or qualified defence in English criminal law, but in medico-socially contro-versial cases the courts have occasionally stated the law in questionable terms. Whereas in the case of the conjoined twins (para 25.03 above) the Court of   **25.06**

---

[9] *Re A (Children) (Conjoined twins: surgical separation) (No 1)* [2001] Fam 147.
[10] See para 24.36 above.
[11] See paras 24.23–24.24 above.
[12] See the discussion of *R v Nedrick* [1986] 1 WLR 1025 and *R v Woollin* [1999] 1 AC 82 in para 24.23 above; A Norrie, 'After *Woollin*' [1999] Crim LR 532; and now *R v Matthews and Alleyne* [2003] EWCA Crim 192, The Times, 18 February 2003.
[13] Confirmed in *R v Cunningham* [1982] AC 566.
[14] ibid 582 *per* Lord Edmund-Davies.
[15] Among judicial criticisms are those of Lord Mustill in *A-G's Reference (No 3 of 1994)* [1998] AC 245, 258, and Lord Steyn in *R v Powell and Daniels* [1999] 1 AC 1, 15. Cf also A Ashworth, *Principles of Criminal Law* (4th edn, Oxford: OUP, 2003) ch 7.3(c) with W Wilson, 'Murder and the Structure of Homicide' in A Ashworth and B Mitchell (eds), *Rethinking English Homicide Law* (Oxford: OUP, 2000).

Appeal accepted that the constituent elements of murder were present and sought a special defence, in other cases where a doctor administered treatment that shortened life, and did so in order to relieve suffering, there has been a tendency to suggest that this should not be classed as an intended killing.[16] However, any suggestion that a doctor does not intend to kill if her or his primary purpose is to relieve pain contradicts the courts' general insistence that a person who does an act knowing that it is virtually certain that it will cause death or really serious harm fulfils the requirement of intention.[17] A person who assists another to commit suicide, even at the other's request or entreaty, commits an offence.[18] The case of Mrs Diane Pretty, who suffered from motor neurone disease and wished her husband to help her to die in the way and at the time of her choice, confirmed that there is no defence of consent to the offence of assisting suicide, and that neither Article 2 ECHR (right to life) nor Article 3 (right not to be subjected to inhuman or degrading treatment) is engaged in such a case.[19]

(2) Voluntary Manslaughter

25.07 Where a case fulfils the requirements for murder, it may still be reduced to manslaughter if one of the partial defences applies, such as provocation, diminished responsibility, or a suicide pact. These cases are often classified as 'voluntary manslaughter', in order to distinguish them from other cases in which the basis for the verdict of manslaughter is that the defendant lacked the fault element for murder. Life imprisonment is the maximum penalty, but the courts have discretion as to sentence. The offence of infanticide is also discussed in this section.

(a) Manslaughter upon provocation

25.08 At common law, provocation has developed over several centuries as a partial defence to murder. Aspects of the provocation doctrine were superseded by s 3 of the Homicide Act 1957, which provides:

> Where on a charge of murder there is evidence on which the jury can find that the person charged was provoked (whether by things done or by things said or by both together) to lose his self-control, the question whether the provocation was enough to make a reasonable man do as he did shall be left to be determined by the jury.

---

[16] Compare *R v Bodkin Adams* [1957] Crim LR 365, and *Airedale NHS Trust v Bland* [1993] AC 789, *per* Lord Goff, with the direction of Hooper J in *Moor*, which appears to allow to doctors a limited defence to murder where their primary purpose was to administer proper pain-relieving treatment: see Arlidge (n 5 above).

[17] Unless these are cases in which a court would not 'find' intention where a doctor is virtually certain that death or serious harm would result: see n 12 above.

[18] Suicide Act 1961, a statute that abolished the offence of attempted suicide but retained the offence of aiding and abetting suicide.

[19] *R (on application of Pretty) v DPP* [2001] UKHL 61; [2002] 1 AC 800 (no judicial review of DPP's refusal to give an undertaking not to prosecute the husband if he assisted her suicide), and *Pretty v UK* Application 2346/02 (2002) 35 EHRR 1 (no breach of Convention involved).

One effect of that section is that, wherever a judge finds that there is evidence that the defendant was provoked to lose self-control, the provocation defence (as it is often called, although it merely reduces the offence from murder to manslaughter) must be left for the jury to decide upon. Thus s 3 ensures that judges leave provocation to the jury in a considerable range of cases where the victim (or another)[20] has done or said something that appeared to provoke the defendant. Typically the provocation will be a perceived insult, but it has been held that any potentially provocative human act, including the crying of a 17-day-old baby, can satisfy this part of the statutory test.[21] It is not clear what constitutes a 'loss of self-control', but various forms of unsuppressed anger seem sufficient. One formulation of the common law requires a 'sudden and temporary loss of self-control, rendering the accused so subject to passion as to make him or her not master of his mind',[22] but it is not clear that this is truly the rule. Whereas there are some decisions insisting that the loss of self-control must follow reasonably swiftly after the provocation, so that there is no time for passions to cool,[23] the more recent trend is to accept that a delay between provocation and retaliation is not inconsistent with s 3 and that killing a sleeping or recumbent victim may be compatible with the partial defence.[24]

Once sufficient evidence has emerged that the defendant was thus provoked to lose self-control, the judge must leave the evaluative questions to the jury. Section 3 not only propounds the objective test of whether the provocation was 'enough to make a reasonable man do as he did' but also states that 'in determining that question the jury shall take into account everything both done and said according to the effect which, in their opinion, it would have on a reasonable man'. This was intended to effect a transfer of power from judge to jury, and the key question now concerns the extent to which the judge may direct the jury on the meaning of the term, 'a reasonable man'. There is a plethora of appellate decisions, but three House of Lords cases are pre-eminent. In *R v Camplin*[25] a boy aged 15 had been provoked to lose his self-control when an older man committed sodomy on him and then jeered at him. The House of Lords held that the appropriate test was to consider the effect of the provocation on a 'person having the power of self-control to be expected of an ordinary person of the sex and age of the accused, but in other respects sharing such of the accused's characteristics as they think would affect the gravity of the provocation to him'. This not only established that the standard should be modified to allow for

25.09

---

[20] The provoking act may be that of someone other than the victim: see *R v Davies* [1975] QB 691.

[21] *R v Doughty* (1986) 83 Cr App R 319, where the judge was wrong not to leave provocation to the jury.

[22] *per* Devlin J in *R v Duffy* [1949] 1 All ER 932.

[23] eg, *R v Ibrams* (1982) 74 Cr App R 154.

[24] eg, *R v Pearson* [1992] Crim LR 193, and most clearly *R v Ahluwahlia* [1992] 4 All ER 889.

[25] [1978] AC 705.

reduced self-control among the young, but also accepted that, although the standard of self-control is that of an 'ordinary' person, those individual characteristics which explain the force of the provocation should be taken into account. In *R v Morhall*[26] the defendant, a glue-sniffer, had killed someone who taunted him about his addiction. The House of Lords held that the jury should have been directed to consider the effect of the provocation on a glue-sniffer with ordinary powers of self-control. Whereas the Court of Appeal had held that certain discreditable characteristics should be excluded because they are inconsistent with the concept of a reasonable man (alcoholism, drug addiction, paedophilia and glue-sniffing were mentioned), the House of Lords held that any discredit associated with being addicted to solvents should not rule that characteristic out of consideration when a jury was assessing the gravity of the provocation.

25.10   The most recent decision of the House of Lords appears to broaden the scope of the provocation defence considerably. In *Camplin* the House had distinguished between the general standard of self-control expected of persons of the age and sex of the accused, and individual characteristics that have a bearing on the gravity of the provocation. This apparently logical division led to controversy when applied in cases where provocation was raised by a woman suffering from 'battered woman's syndrome' or from a psychological condition: on a strict application of the *Camplin* distinction these conditions should be left out of account, but the Court of Appeal showed itself increasingly willing to allow them to be considered by juries as explanations of why the woman reacted as she did.[27] The general issue came before the House of Lords in *R v Smith (Morgan)*,[28] and the decision was that any characteristics of the defendant that might affect powers of self-control (in this case, clinical depression) may be taken into account. This extends the provocation defence and blurs the line between it and diminished responsibility as partial defences to murder, but goes some way towards ensuring that abused women who retaliate may fall within the provocation doctrine rather than being labelled 'mentally abnormal'. However, the majority in the House of Lords emphasized that their decision does not obliterate the normative element in provocation. As Lord Hoffmann put it:

> The law expects people to exercise control over their emotions. A tendency to violent rages or childish tantrums is a defect in character rather than an excuse. The jury must think that the circumstances were such as to make the loss of self-control sufficiently *excusable* to reduce the gravity of the offence from murder to manslaughter.[29]

---

[26] [1996] 1 AC 90.
[27] eg, *R v Ahluwahlia* [1992] 4 All ER 889; *R v Humphreys* [1995] 4 All ER 1008.
[28] [2001] 1 AC 146, departing (by a majority of 3–2) from the decision of the Privy Council (by a majority of 3–1) in *Luc Thiet-Thuan v The Queen* [1997] AC 131.
[29] ibid 173.

The jury should be allowed to take account of all aspects of the defendant's personality and condition—excluding intoxication, one assumes[30]—and should then decide whether he or she exercised the level of self-control that society could reasonably expect in the circumstances. **25.11**

The subsequent decision of the Court of Appeal in *R v Weller*[31] makes it clear that juries should be instructed to take account of everything and ignore nothing when applying the test in s 3 of the Homicide Act. Although in *Smith* Lord Hoffmann mentioned 'male possessiveness and jealousy' as unacceptable, the jury cannot be so directed. Those characteristics were said to form part of the defendant's nature in *Weller*, and the jury was rightly left to decide 'what society expects of a man like this defendant in his position'. Thus there is still a normative element in the test for provocation, but (apart from any element of intoxication, which must presumably be left out of account) it is for the jury to determine it. They may take account of any psychiatric or psychological condition of which evidence has been given,[32] and presumably also of addiction to glue-sniffing, racism, homophobia, etc. The jury sets the standard. **25.12**

The effect of one final element in s 3 of the 1957 Act also remains uncertain. Another evaluative question for the jury is whether 'the provocation was enough to make a reasonable man do as he did'. The last four words might be interpreted with varying degrees of specificity, but they appear to have caused little difficulty in practice. Their import seems to be to require some fairly loose correspondence between the perceived gravity of the provocation and the degree of loss of self-control, and subsequent killing.[33] **25.13**

It will be evident that the place of provocation in the law of homicide remains controversial. Some argue that its objective element must be re-asserted, because the whole purpose of the doctrine is to mark out those killings stemming from understandable (even, justifiable) anger; on this view, the decision of the House of Lords in *Smith* blurs important distinctions by allowing the standard to be lowered for those with mental disturbance or personality disorders.[34] Others see the blurring as inevitable because of the conflicting principles and policies with which the law has to deal.[35] A more radical view—that the provocation doctrine is so flawed and unworkable that it should be abolished as a **25.14**

---

[30] The courts have consistently held that intoxication does not lower the standard of self-control to be expected: see, eg, Lord Goff in *R v Morhall* [1996] 1 AC 90.

[31] [2003] EWCA Crim 815.

[32] cf *Paria v The State* [2003] UKPC 36, where the Privy Council held that insufficient evidence of the alleged condition had been adduced.

[33] *Phillips v The Queen* [1969] 2 AC 130.

[34] For a forceful view, see J Gardner and T Macklem, 'Compassion without Respect? Nine Fallacies in *R v Smith*' [2001] Crim LR 623.

[35] A Norrie, 'The Structure of Provocation' (2001) 54 CLP 307.

qualified defence[36]—now seems to have some support from the government, which has referred to the Law Commission the doctrine of provocation and the other qualified defences to murder. One particular concern is that the provocation defence is more widely available to men who kill out of sexual jealousy or in response to infidelity, than to women who kill in response to prolonged violence or other abuse. The Law Commission has put forward various options for reform, including a merger of provocation and diminished responsibility (below) and, more radically, the abolition of both the provocation defence and the mandatory sentence for murder.[37]

(b) Manslaughter by reason of diminished responsibility

25.15 Section 2 of the Homicide Act 1957 introduced a partial defence of diminished responsibility with no basis in English common law,[38] and did so largely because the penalty for murder is mandatory and the defence of insanity is so narrow.[39] Under s 2, the defendant bears the burden of proving that he was 'suffering from such abnormality of mind . . . as substantially impaired his mental responsibility for his acts or omissions in doing or being a party to the killing'. In most cases in which psychiatric evidence falling within s 2 is offered by the defence, the prosecution will accept it, and the judge will then proceed to pass sentence for diminished responsibility manslaughter. But the small minority of contested cases has given the courts the opportunity to interpret the statutory provision.

25.16 Section 2 specifies that the mental disorder may arise 'from a condition of arrested or retarded development of mind or any inherent causes or induced by disease or injury', terms that are broad enough to include psychopathy and other mental disorders in which control rather than cognition is impaired.[40] Alcoholism may fall within s 2 if it amounts to a 'disease or injury',[41] but the mere excessive consumption of alcohol or drugs is insufficient. Where there are elements of intoxication and mental abnormality in a case, the House of Lords in *R v Dietschmann*[42] has decided that the jury should be asked: 'has the defendant satisfied you that, despite the drink, his mental abnormality substantially impaired his mental responsibility for his fatal acts?' This remains a difficult question for the jury, requiring them to separate the defendant's underlying condition from the effect of drink or drugs on the particular occasion.

25.17 It is well known that the qualified defence of diminished responsibility is, on occasion, interpreted generously so as to accommodate those such as mercy killers

---

[36] C Wells, 'Provocation: the Case for Abolition' in Ashworth and Mitchell (n 15 above).
[37] Law Commission Consultation Paper 173 Partial Defences to Murder (2003).
[38] The doctrine had existed in Scots law for some years.
[39] See para 24.08 above.
[40] *R v Byrne* [1960] 2 QB 396.
[41] *R v Tandy* [1989] 1 WLR 350.
[42] [2003] UKHL 10; [2003] 2 WLR 613.

who do not fall within any other defence.[43] On the other hand, there are some decisions that construe the terms of s 2 even more narrowly than the common law
defence of insanity.[44] It remains possible for a defendant to raise this partial defence as well as provocation (although the burden of proof is upon the defendant
in diminished responsibility), but after the decision in *R v Smith (Morgan)*[45] to the
effect that mental abnormality can be taken into account in provocation cases,
this might become less common.

(c) Manslaughter as a result of a suicide pact

Section 4 of the Homicide Act 1957 provides that the killing of another is **25.18**
manslaughter, not murder, if a defendant can prove that he was 'acting in pursuance of a suicide pact between him and another to kill the other or be party to
the other being killed by a third person'. As stated earlier, the Suicide Act 1961
preserves the offence of aiding and abetting suicide. Whilst this enables the conviction of those who seek to take advantage of a vulnerable relative, for example,[46]
it leaves no room for the exculpation of those who through compassion respond
to a request to help another to die with dignity.[47]

(d) Infanticide

This statutory offence is discussed here because, according to s 1 of the Infanticide **25.19**
Act 1938, its essence is that an offence that would otherwise be murder is reduced to
infanticide where a woman kills her child when it is under the age of 12 months, and
does so at a time when her mind was disturbed as a result of the birth. The section
refers to the mother 'not having fully recovered from the effect of giving birth to the
child' and to 'the effect of lactation', but in most cases the medical details are not disputed and the prosecution either charges or accepts a plea of guilty to infanticide.

(e) Extending voluntary manslaughter?

In the absence of legislative activity in the field of homicide, the courts have been **25.20**
called upon to extend the heads of voluntary manslaughter. In *R v Howe*[48] the
House of Lords held that duress cannot be a defence to murder, and also declined
to hold that it could reduce murder to manslaughter. In *R v Clegg*[49] the House of
Lords declined to hold that the use of excessive force on an occasion that justified
some force could reduce murder to manslaughter. In the latter case the House

---

[43] For discussion, see Ashworth (n 15 above) ch 7.4(e).
[44] Notably *R v Sanderson (No 2)* (1994) 98 Cr App R 325; for critique and more general discussion, see R Mackay, 'Diminished Responsibility and Mentally Disordered Killers' in Ashworth and
Mitchell (n 15 above).
[45] [2001] 1 AC 146.
[46] *R v McShane* (1977) 66 Cr App R 97.
[47] See the case of *Pretty*, n 19 above.
[48] [1987] AC 417.
[49] [1996] 1 AC 482.

made it clear that it regarded such fundamental decisions as lying within the province of the legislature, and outside that of judicial development of the common law. The draft criminal code would provide for a qualified defence of excessive force in self-defence,[50] and the Law Commission's current review of qualified defences to murder may produce recommendations along these lines.

(3) Involuntary Manslaughter

25.21   The same verdict, guilty of manslaughter, may be handed down where the defendant lacks the mens rea of murder and so falls outside that offence and outside the categories of voluntary manslaughter. Thus 'involuntary' manslaughter[51] ranges from those offences where the defendant almost satisfies the fault element for murder (for example, where he was reckless as to death or serious harm, but cannot be proved to have intended either consequence), down to cases in which death might almost be described as accidental. Most of the decisions—for this branch of manslaughter is governed entirely by the common law—are concerned to define the lower boundaries of involuntary manslaughter. What, then, must the prosecution prove in order to obtain a conviction of manslaughter by an unlawful and dangerous act, or manslaughter by gross negligence?

(a) Manslaughter by an unlawful and dangerous act

25.22   Where death is caused by the defendant's criminal and dangerous act, the offence of manslaughter may be committed, even though the defendant's act was essentially nothing more than a battery upon the victim which led unexpectedly to death. The prosecution must first establish that the defendant committed a crime against another: often this will be an assault or battery,[52] and it seems that an offence of supplying drugs might suffice, although mere possession of drugs should not.[53] Certain types of crime have been held insufficient to form the basis for this kind of manslaughter, notably crimes of omission[54] and crimes of negligence:[55] on such facts the case must be brought on the alternative ground of gross negligence (below). Once the prosecution have established the commission of a sufficient criminal act, they must further show that this act caused the death[56] and that it was

---

[50]   *A Criminal Code for England and Wales* (Law Com No 177, 1989) cl 57.

[51]   It may be noted that this is an aberrant use of the term 'involuntary', which otherwise denotes a fundamental lack of consciousness or control over actions: see para 24.14 above.

[52]   *R v Lamb* [1967] 2 QB 981, where all the elements of assault were not present.

[53]   *R v Dias* [2001] EWCA 2986, [2002] 2 Cr App R 5, disapproving *R v Kennedy* [1999] Crim LR 65; however, if D supplies drugs to V, who then (being adult and of sound mind and capacity) voluntarily takes them, V's voluntary intervening act breaks any causal connection with D's act of supply.

[54]   *R v Lowe* [1973] QB 702.

[55]   *Andrews v DPP* [1937] AC 576.

[56]   ie, that there was no voluntary intervening act: cf *A Criminal Code for England and Wales* (n 50 above) and paras 24.19–24.20 above.

a dangerous act. The restriction to dangerous acts was introduced in *R v Church*,[57] where it was held that the defendant's criminal act must be 'such as all sober and reasonable people would inevitably recognise must subject the other person to, at least, the risk of some harm resulting therefrom, albeit not serious harm'. This is clearly an objective test, requiring the foreseeability of some harm but not death, and discounting intoxication and any other individual impairment. The *Church* test is not satisfied merely by showing that it was foreseeable that shock would be caused to another, unless it is also proved that the shock might foreseeably cause injury.[58] It should be added that the Law Commission has recommended the abolition of this form of manslaughter, largely on the ground that the element of fault involved is often too small to justify conviction for such a serious crime carrying a maximum of life imprisonment.[59]

(b) Manslaughter by gross negligence

The common law relating to this form of the offence was authoritatively revised **25.23** and restated by the House of Lords in *R v Adomako*.[60] The prosecution must show that the defendant breached a duty of care recognized by the tort of negligence,[61] and that this breach caused the death. It is then for the jury to decide whether the defendant was grossly negligent as to the risk of death: they should convict if they conclude that, 'having regard to the risk of death involved, the conduct of the defendant . . . [was] so bad in all the circumstances as to amount to a criminal act or omission'. Those final few words emphasize that the jury's judgment of degree is crucial, but the words actually understate their task—which is to decide whether the conduct was so bad as to justify a conviction for manslaughter. The test of negligence is that of the reasonably prudent person in the defendant's position, and negligence is 'gross' if it falls far below the standard to be expected. Thus on the facts of *Adomako* itself the test was whether a reasonably competent anaesthetist working in a hospital would have noticed that the oxygen tube has become disconnected and would have reconnected it so as to save the patient's life; in *R v Holloway*[62] the test was whether a reasonably competent electrician would have discovered why the occupants of a house were receiving electric shocks after he

---

[57] [1966] 1 QB 59, approved in *DPP v Newbury and Jones* [1977] AC 500.
[58] *R v Dawson* (1985) 81 Cr App R 150.
[59] *Involuntary Manslaughter* (Law Com No 237, 1996); for criticism, see CMV Clarkson, 'Context and Culpability in Involuntary Manslaughter: Principle or Instinct?' in Ashworth and Mitchell (n 15 above).
[60] [1995] 1 AC 171.
[61] In *R v Wacker* [2002] EWCA Crim 1944; [2003] 2 WLR 374 the Court of Appeal held that, even if the maxim 'ex turpi causa non oritur ius' might apply to defeat a claim in tort, that doctrine should have no application in criminal law where the victims accepted a degree of risk as part of their involvement in a joint unlawful enterprise.
[62] (1994) 98 Cr App R 262, 279–283.

had worked on the central heating system, and thus would have prevented the subsequent electrocution of a person who touched the kitchen sink whilst not wearing rubber-soled footwear.

25.24 Cases in which the prosecution allege that an omission by the defendant caused death would now be dealt with under the *Adomako* test. In *R v Stone and Dobinson*[63] the defendants were charged with manslaughter when a sick relative, whom they had allowed to stay in their house and to whom they had given some care, died in circumstances where proper medical care could have prolonged her life. If a duty of care is recognized on these facts,[64] it seems that the proper standard for liability would now be gross negligence, and not the test of recklessness enunciated by the Court of Appeal in that case.

(c) Corporate killing

25.25 It is now accepted that a company can be convicted of homicide (usually, involuntary manslaughter) so long as a sufficiently high-ranking officer can be proved to have had the requisite fault.[65] There are proposals, not yet put before Parliament, to create a distinct offence of corporate killing where death is caused as a result of a 'management failure' in which the conduct of the management falls far below the standard reasonably to be expected in ensuring the health and safety of those affected by the company's activities.[66]

(4) Causing Death on the Roads

25.26 Beneath the offence of manslaughter by gross negligence, and carrying a maximum penalty of 10 years' imprisonment, lie the two statutory offences of causing death by dangerous driving and causing death by careless driving whilst intoxicated. It is perfectly possible to prosecute a driver for manslaughter or even murder, but it is more common to select one of the statutory offences. The essence of the offence of causing death by dangerous driving is that the defendant caused death by driving in a way that fell 'far below what would be expected of a competent and careful driver', and in circumstances where it would be 'obvious' to such a driver 'that driving in that way would be dangerous'.[67] The offence of causing death by careless or inconsiderate driving while under the influence of drink or drugs was introduced in 1991[68] and is prosecuted frequently. There is also an offence of causing death by

---

[63] [1977] QB 354; where the fault element for murder is present, of course, then killing by omission may amount to murder: *R v Gibbons and Proctor* (1918) 13 Cr App R 134.

[64] See the discussion of omissions liability at paras 24.16–24.18 above.

[65] *A-G's Reference (No 2 of 1999)* [2000] QB 796; on corporate criminal liability generally, see paras 24.11–24.13 above.

[66] *Involuntary Manslaughter* (n 59 above), and Home Office, *Reforming the Law on Involuntary Manslaughter: the Government's Proposals* (2000).

[67] Road Traffic Act 1988, ss 1 and 2A.

[68] ibid ss 3 and 3A.

aggravated vehicle-taking, with a lower maximum penalty of five years' imprisonment.[69] Sentencing levels for the offences of causing death by dangerous driving or by careless driving while intoxicated are increasing,[70] and the government seems likely to introduce legislation to increase the maximum penalty for those offences to 14 years.

(5) Genocide

The Genocide Act 1969, passed in order to fulfil the government's obligations under the Genocide Convention, creates several offences committed 'with intent to destroy, in whole or in part, a national, ethnical, racial or religious group'. One form of genocide, killing members of such a group, carries the mandatory sentence of life imprisonment.

25.27

B. The Assaults

That the criminal law should be employed to protect bodily integrity hardly requires argument or justification. It is a prime example of the sort of harm that is central to the functioning of the criminal law. The problematic questions arise at the margins; to what extent should a person be permitted to consent to the infliction of harm upon him or herself? This is an issue upon which social attitudes have changed markedly through the years; it was not so very long ago that Lord Denning was wondering whether the law would permit a man to undergo a vasectomy.[71] What society will tolerate in the name of sporting diversion, by contrast, has progressively been narrowed as first duelling then bare knuckle fighting were criminally outlawed. How far force may be used in the chastisement of children either by schoolteachers or by their own parents is another matter about which views have changed over time.[72]

25.28

(1) General Conceptions

(a) Distinction between assault and battery

Although the penalties for the offences against the person are laid down by statute, there is no statutory definition of what amounts to either an assault or a battery. At common law a distinction is drawn between the two concepts, which were (and still are) regarded as being separate offences.[73] That the offences remain separate was

25.29

---

[69] Theft Act 1968, s 12A(4), inserted by the Aggravated Vehicle-Taking Act 1992.
[70] See *A-G's Reference (No 152 of 2002)* [2003] EWCA Crim 996; [2003] 3 All ER 40.
[71] *Bravery v Bravery* [1954] 1 WLR 1169.
[72] J Rogers, 'A Criminal Lawyer's Response to Chastisement in the European Court of Human Rights' [2002] Crim LR 98.
[73] By virtue of Criminal Justice Act 1988, s 39.

confirmed by the Divisional Court in *DPP v Taylor and Little*,[74] but there are great difficulties with that conclusion. An 'assault' as technically understood is 'any act by which a person intentionally or recklessly causes another to apprehend immediate unlawful violence'.[75] A battery is any act by which a person intentionally or recklessly inflicts unlawful personal violence upon another. An assault in the technical sense is rarely going to occasion actual bodily harm. Yet the actus reus of the offence referred to in s 47 of the Offences Against the Person Act 1861 (OAPA) is defined in terms of an assault occasioning actual bodily harm.[76] The conclusion that 'common assault' can be construed to include 'battery'[77] is practically convenient but does little to re-inforce the sense that this branch of the law is in any sense rational.

(b) Requirement of a positive act

25.30 The traditional view is that assault (or battery) requires some positive act (as opposed to an omission), but in *Fagan v Metropolitan Police Commissioner*[78] the Divisional Court nevertheless held that driving on to a policeman's foot acciden-tally and then intentionally leaving it there was sufficient, since this was a contin-uing act rather than a 'pure' omission. Similarly in *Smith v Chief Superintendent of Woking Police Station*[79] the conduct element of assault was satisfied where a tres-passer in enclosed grounds looked through a bedroom window where a woman was undressing—she was terrified when she saw him standing there.

(c) Wide definition of 'violence'

25.31 The use of the word 'violence' in the context of assault and battery is misleading, since the degree of force used may be minimal. Any intentional touching of another per-son without the consent of that person and without lawful authority or excuse will amount to a battery. In *R v Lynsey*,[80] for example, it was held that spitting on someone might constitute a battery. Similarly in *R v Thomas*[81] it was held that rubbing the hem of a woman's skirt could constitute a battery. If the victim apprehends an immediate threat of such unlawful touching the actus reus of assault will be satisfied.

(d) Mens rea

25.32 It is tolerably clear that the mens rea for assault is that the defendant should be proved to have acted with the intention that the victim should be caused to fear

---

[74] [1992] QB 645, DC.
[75] *R v Ireland and Burstow* [1998] AC 147, 165 *per* Lord Hope of Craighead; see further J Horder, 'Reconsidering Psychic Assault' [1998] Crim LR 392.
[76] On the details of the s 47 offence see further para 25.60 below.
[77] *R v Lynsey* [1995] 3 All ER 654.
[78] [1969] 1 QB 439.
[79] (1983) 76 Cr App R 234.
[80] [1995] 3 All ER 654.
[81] (1985) 81 Cr App R 331.

the possibility of immediate unlawful violence or being subjectively reckless as to that result.[82] The same mens rea applies with respect to the application of unlawful violence for battery.

(e) Assault by spoken or written words, or by silence

In former times, it was said that words alone could not constitute an assault, and that some gesture was required in addition. However, in *R v Ireland and Burstow*,[83] the House of Lords clearly proceeded on the basis that this was no longer the law, and held that, in principle, the conduct element of the offence could be satisfied by the making of silent telephone calls, so long as they cause actual harm or cause the victim to fear the immediate infliction of harm. This means, a fortiori, that spoken or written[84] words may constitute an assault. The meaning and context of the words used must be carefully analysed. In the old case of *Tuberville v Savage*,[85] for example, the defendant had placed his hand on his sword. This would prima facie amount to an assault. However the gesture was accompanied by words to the effect that he would have attacked the victim if it had not been assize time. This negated the threat of the defendant's gesture.   25.33

(f) The requirement of immediacy

Assault requires the victim to apprehend immediate unlawful violence. The immediacy requirement was satisfied in *Logdon v DPP*[86] where the defendant showed the victim a gun in a drawer and told her that she was to be held hostage. The victim perceived a threat of violence which could occur at any time. In *Smith v Chief Superintendent of Woking Police Station*,[87] the threat posed by a trespasser outside looking in through a window was sufficiently immediate. This would presumably not be the case, however, if the defendant could not possibly get close enough to the victim to inflict unlawful violence and the victim knows this to be so.   25.34

The 'immediacy' requirement proved to be problematic in *R v Constanza*,[88] because the threat was contained in a letter. The Court of Appeal held that the sending of threatening letters could amount to an assault where this caused a fear of violence at some time not excluding the immediate future. It is sufficient that the victim fears a possible imminent attack. This relaxation of the immediacy requirement was also necessary to allow silent telephone calls to amount to an assault as in *R v Ireland and Burstow*.[89] The silent caller may have been many   25.35

---

[82] *R v Spratt* [1990] 1 WLR 1073; *R v Savage* [1992] 1 AC 699.
[83] [1998] AC 147.
[84] *R v Constanza* (1997) 2 Cr App R 492.
[85] (1669) 1 Mod Rep 3, 86 ER 684.
[86] [1976] Crim LR 121.
[87] (1983) 76 Cr App R 234.
[88] (1997) 2 Cr App R 492.
[89] [1998] AC 147.

miles away but he equally may have been very close. The victim had no way of knowing.

(g) Is there a direct application of force requirement for battery? [90]

25.36 It is clear that person-to-person contact or the application of force through the medium of any weapon will suffice for battery. There is, however, still dispute over the precise extent of directness which is required. In *DPP v K*[91] a schoolboy decanted a test tube full of acid into the upturned nozzle of a drying machine in such a way that a later user of the machine was injured when the acid was injected into his face. The boy had intended to remove the acid before this might happen. It was held by the Divisional Court that the boy had in principle committed the actus reus of battery. More recently the Divisional Court has had an opportunity to reconsider the extent of the directness requirement for battery in *Haystead v Chief Constable of Derbyshire*.[92] In that case the defendant had been convicted of battery of a child. The child was being held by its mother when the defendant punched the mother twice in the face, as a result of which the mother dropped the baby and injured it. The Divisional Court concluded that there was no requirement of directness for battery. The crucial consideration was instead whether the mother dropping the child was the immediate result of the defendant's having punched her. It held that there was no logical or reasonable distinction between the present case and a case where the defendant had attacked the baby using a weapon, except that this case was a reckless (as opposed to intentional) battery. To all intents and purposes the mother was a 'weapon' through which the defendant had applied force to the baby.

(h) A hostility requirement for battery?

25.37 In *Wilson v Pringle*,[93] the Civil Division of the Court of Appeal held that a requirement of a 'hostile' contact was necessary to found a conviction for battery. This requirement was endorsed by the House of Lords in *R v Brown*,[94] but the status and import of the requirement are problematic. To begin with, it is difficult to classify the need for hostility as being either a part of the actus reus or the mens rea. Indeed given the view of the majority of their Lordships in *Brown* that the hostility requirement was satisfied in that case notwithstanding that the sado-masochistic activities impugned were entirely consensual, it appears a rather hollow requirement. It seems that the intentional infliction of actual bodily harm or worse for a purpose not recognized as being acceptable will automatically be

---

[90] See further M Hirst, 'Assault, Battery and Indirect Violence' [1999] Crim LR 557.
[91] [1990] 1 WLR 1067.
[92] [2000] 3 All ER 890.
[93] [1987] QB 237.
[94] [1994] 1 AC 212.

deemed hostile. If this is so the requirement would seem to be little more than a disguised policy hurdle. The hostility requirement has been widely criticized, inter alia, by Goff LJ in *Collins v Wilcock*.[95] He felt that, rather than seek to add an additional element requiring to be satisfied as part of the actus reus of battery it could serve a limiting purpose. The definition of battery was better restricted by excluding the 'physical contacts of ordinary life' from its scope. This exclusion is based on implied consent. Thus if the victim makes clear that he or she does not consent to being touched in the way contemplated (for example, by refusing to shake hands) and it is reasonably possible for the defendant to desist, he may still be guilty of battery.

(i) Consent

There is some doubt over whether the absence of consent is a part of the actus reus of the offence, or whether it is a defence. In principle the distinction is of relevance to the burden of proof. If absence of consent is part of the actus reus, it would follow that the prosecution must prove as part of their case that the victim did not consent. If consent is a defence, by contrast, the prosecution need only prove the absence of consent if the defendant succeeds in discharging an evidential burden in respect of consent. In practice however the distinction is of limited practical importance. In many cases the lack of consent will be readily inferred from the circumstances. The issue will only become live if the defendant establishes a prima facie case. In *R v Kimber*[96] the Court of Appeal clearly considered the absence of consent to be an element of the offences of assault and battery which rendered the conduct 'unlawful'. In *R v Brown*, however, a bare majority considered consent to be a defence to assault or battery.[97] If this latter view is to prevail, it could still be confined to assaults which cause actual bodily harm, since that was the subject matter of the *Brown* case itself. **25.38**

The question of consent is one of fact to be determined by the jury in the light of all the evidence. Consent nevertheless raises fundamental normative issues and difficult analytical questions. The victim's apparent consent may be vitiated by factors such as duress or mistake. There are a number of recurring situations in which the courts have given guidance as to the meaning of consent. **25.39**

(i) Submission is not consent

In *R v Olugboja*,[98] the Court of Appeal drew a distinction between reluctant consent and submission. Little guidance was given, however, as to how we should go **25.40**

---

[95] [1984] 1 WLR 1172.
[96] [1983] 1 WLR 1118.
[97] [1994] 1 AC 212.
[98] [1982] QB 320.

about drawing the dividing line between these two concepts. Consent will not be valid if it is obtained as a result of violence or the threat of violence. Apparent consent in such circumstances will constitute submission and not consent. Where the victim gives in to non-physical coercion the position is less clear. It has been suggested that pressure falling short of threats of violence cannot vitiate consent[99] but this position is difficult to maintain following *Olugboja*. In that case the victim had been driven to a house and raped by a third party. The defendant then told the victim that he was going to have sex with her and told her to remove her trousers, which she did. The Court of Appeal stated that consent could be vitiated in the absence of the threat of force. This statement must remain obiter since the actual situation in which the victim found herself might easily have carried a threat of force. A wider approach to the vitiation of consent was unambiguously taken in the Rhodesian case of *McCoy*.[100] In that case the victim, an air stewardess, was subject to a grounding order which would cause her to lose pay. The defendant, her manager, asked her to permit him to cane her in return for cancelling the grounding order. He was convicted of indecent assault on the basis that the victim's consent was vitiated by coercion.

(ii) Mistakes regarding the defendant's conduct or its consequences

25.41   If the victim gives an apparent consent to the defendant's otherwise criminal conduct by virtue of a mistake, the consent may be vitiated. There is no requirement that the mistake be induced by the defendant's misrepresentation or fraud.[101]

25.42   Not all mistakes will vitiate consent. A distinction that is drawn is that a mistake will negate consent only if it is made in relation to the 'nature' of the act rather than its 'attributes'. This categorization is rather more difficult to operate in practice than it is to state. In *R v Clarence*[102] it was held that the victim's consent to sexual intercourse with the defendant was valid, even though she was unaware that the defendant was infected with gonorrhoea. Whether or not the defendant was suffering from a sexually transmitted disease was merely an attribute of the sexual act. Similarly in *R v Linekar*[103] consent was not vitiated when the defendant had sex with a prostitute and then made off without making payment. The nature of sexual intercourse is not altered by the fact that it is paid for. Conversely the defendant in the old case of *R v Rosinki*[104] was rightly convicted of assault after he had obtained the victim's consent to an unnecessary intimate 'medical procedure'.[105] In *R v Williams*[106] a young woman's consent to sexual intercourse was held to be

---

[99] *Latter v Bradell* (1881) 50 LJQB 166.
[100] 1953 (2) SA 4.
[101] *R v Linekar* [1995] QB 250.
[102] (1888) 28 QBD 23.
[103] [1995] QB 250.
[104] (1824) 1 Lew CC 11, 168 ER 941.
[105] See also *R v Flattery* (1877) Cox CC 388.
[106] [1923] 1 KB 340.

invalid when the defendant, a music teacher, had persuaded her that the intercourse was an essential aspect of her singing lessons.

The operation of the nature/attributes distinction depends crucially on how the **25.43** criminal act is defined. The case of *R v Clarence*[107] is an obvious example. The victim's consent to sexual intercourse was unaffected by her ignorance of the defendant's infection with gonorrhoea. Few would argue that such a mistake should render the defendant's conduct rape on the grounds that she would not have consented had she known about his condition. Whether or not the defendant has a sexually transmitted disease does not impinge on the victim's sexual autonomy. The consent in *Clarence* was, however, also deemed to negate an assault and thus prevent liability arising under s 20 of the OAPA 1861.[108] The question whether or not the victim knows that a person has a sexually transmitted disease is relevant to whether the victim has given valid consent to an activity which gives rise to a risk of being infected. Offences against the person protect the victim's physical integrity and autonomy and the validity of consent should be determined with this in mind.

In *R v Tabassum*[109] the Court of Appeal appears to have created a new category of **25.44** mistake as to 'quality' which is capable of vitiating consent. A man had falsely claimed to be a medical researcher and had persuaded his victims to allow him to examine their breasts. The defendant claimed that he had been compiling statistics and that his motive was not sexual. It was held that they had consented to acts of the same 'nature' as the compilation of statistics.

Nevertheless, it was held that they were labouring under a mistake as to 'quality' of **25.45** the act which negated their consent. The basis, meaning and utility of this concept of 'quality' is unclear.[110] It seems likely that the Court of Appeal was influenced by the fact that there are no lesser 'procurement' offences[111] related to indecent assault. Consequently if they had found the victims' consent to be valid there would be no offence of which the defendant could have been convicted. If this is the case, the reasoning should not be extended to rape cases where such situations are adequately catered for by ss 2 and 3 of the Sexual Offences Act 1956 (SOA).

(iii) Mistakes regarding the defendant's identity

Mistaken identity will be relevant to the validity of the victim's consent only if one **25.46** would ordinarily consider identity to be of crucial importance. The most obvious

---

[107] (1888) 28 QBD 23.
[108] There is no longer a requirement of assault or battery for OAPA 1861, s 20: see paras 23.65 et seq below.
[109] [2000] 2 Cr App R 328.
[110] Sir John Smith has taken the view that the case is inconsistent with *Richardson* and 'wrongly decided'; *Smith and Hogan: Criminal Law* (10th edn, London: Butterworths, 2002) 420, n 5.
[111] cf procurement of sexual intercourse with a woman by force (SOA 1956, s 2); procurement of sexual intercourse with a woman by false pretences (SOA 1956, s 3).

context in which identity is relevant is sexual activity. The choice of sexual partner will usually be influenced profoundly by the victim's perception of identity. If a man obtains the consent of a woman to sexual intercourse by impersonating her husband he will commit the actus reus of rape.[112] In *R v Elbekkay*[113] it was held that identity was crucial to consent to sexual relations even outside the context of marriage. Indeed, it could be argued that the *Elbekkay* decision may have been impliedly overruled by the subsequent re-enactment in 1994 of s 1(3) of the SOA 1956.[114] Alternatively s 1(3) may be explained as simply one particular example of a broader common law rule.

25.47   The same nature/attributes distinction is employed in determining whether mistakes as to something other than identity can negate consent. Thus in *R v Richardson*[115] a dentist who continued to practise despite the revocation of her licence was not guilty of assault occasioning actual bodily harm. Her patients had consented to dental treatment and the defendant had provided perfectly adequate treatment. The fact that they were unaware that the defendant was operating without a licence was a mistake as to attributes only.

(iv) Capacity to consent

25.48   A person's consent will only be valid if that person is deemed to be capable of giving consent. Children, for example, are sometimes considered to be insufficiently mature to understand the nature of the act to which they are supposed to have consented .[116] The consent of a 16-year-old to medical treatment is generally considered to be valid. It appears from *Gillick v West Norfolk and Wisbech Area Health Authority*[117] that a sufficiently mature younger child can give consent to beneficent treatment. Similar considerations apply to the consent of a mentally incapacitated person.

(v) Limitations on the right to consent

25.49   It is clear that valid and genuine consent by the 'victim', whether express or implied, generally negatives the criminality of the act. There are limits, however, as to the extent of consensual harm that the law will permit. In *R v Brown*,[118] the House of Lords held (by a narrow majority) that consent was no defence where the

---

[112] SOA 1956, s 1(3).

[113] [1995] Crim LR 163.

[114] Criminal Justice and Public Order Act 1994, s 142(3).

[115] [1999] QB 444.

[116] *Burrell v Harmer* [1967] Crim LR 169 (consent to tattooing for payment by 13-year-old invalid).

[117] [1986] AC 112; cf *Re R (A Minor) (Wardship: Consent to Treatment)* [1992] Fam 11 *per* Sir John Donaldson MR, suggesting that the same would not be true if the same child refused potentially beneficial treatment.

[118] [1994] 1 AC 212.

willing participants had injured one another in the course of consensual sado-masochistic acts. If actual bodily harm or worse is either caused or intended, the 'victim's' consent to that harm will be immaterial unless there are special considerations of public policy which demand the recognition of that consent.[119] It was suggested in *R v Boyea*[120] however that where actual bodily harm was caused (but not intended), consent would be recognized provided that actual bodily harm was not objectively likely to have occurred.

Determining whether special considerations of policy exist which demand the recognition of consent can be difficult. Consent should be recognized when it would be in the public interest to do so.[121] In *Brown*, however, no such special considerations were found. The majority noted that the sexual activity in question was potentially harmful, creating the risk of HIV infection and the corruption of young people. The House of Lords adopted a paternalistic approach to consent. The arguments of the majority are, however, speculative rather than concrete. The participants had taken steps to guard against these risks by employing code-words to prevent harm becoming too severe and the HIV-infected participants took extra care. Moreover there was no evidence that children were involved. It is difficult to resist the conclusion therefore that the majority were heavily influenced by moralistic factors. Lord Templeman expressly states that 'pleasure derived from the infliction of pain is an evil thing. Cruelty is uncivilised.'[122]   **25.50**

The minority view in *Brown* deals with consent in a substantially different way. Lord Mustill noted that the use of the OAPA 1861 was adventitious. The offences of violence were not intended to sanction sexual conduct. He emphasized that for an offence to be against the person it must in some way be adverse to that person's wishes. His Lordship's default position was that consent should be recognized unless there are pressing grounds of policy which justify the imposition of criminal sanctions.   **25.51**

The 'victim's' consent to the risk of sustaining physical harm which occurs in the ordinary course of 'organized sport' will be recognized. Intentionally inflicted injuries caused on the sports field will nevertheless fall outside the scope of 'organized sport'.[123] 'Organized sport' includes boxing,[124] but prize fighting[125] and street fighting[126] are unlawful. It is also accepted that consent to so-called 'horseplay' will be valid. Thus in *R v Aitken*[127] no offence was committed when air force   **25.52**

---

[119] *A-G's Reference (No 6 of 1980)* [1981] QB 715; *R v Brown* [1994] 1 AC 212.

[120] (1992) 156 JP 505.

[121] *A-G's Reference (No 6 of 1980)* [1981] QB 715.

[122] [1994] 1 AC 212, 237.

[123] *R v Bradshaw* (1878) Cox CC 83.

[124] See further D Ormerod and M Gunn, 'The Legality of Boxing' (1995) 15 LS 181.

[125] *R v Coney* (1882) 8 QBD 534.

[126] *A-G's Reference (No 6 of 1980)* [1981] QB 715.

[127] [1992] 1 WLR 1006.

officers played an 'after dinner game' which involved dousing each other in petrol and setting each other alight. The victim suffered severe burns. The aim of this exercise was apparently to test the fire-retardant properties of their flying-suits.[128] Other cases where consent to actual bodily harm or worse is permitted include therapeutic and cosmetic surgery, body piercing and tattooing.

25.53 It is difficult in terms of principle to draw a sensible distinction between the 'public interest' in rough horseplay and risky unconventional sexual activity.[129] Attempts to draw such a distinction may be thought to provide further evidence that the majority decision in *Brown* was based on moral disapproval of the defendants' behaviour.

25.54 The Court of Appeal decision in *R v Wilson*[130] is difficult to reconcile with the clear statement of the law by the majority of the House of Lords in *Brown*. The defendant's wife had encouraged him to brand his initials on her buttocks with a red hot poker. The court sought to distinguish *Brown* on a number of grounds and consequently quashed the defendant's conviction under s 47 of the OAPA 1861. None of these grounds of distinction is particularly convincing. The wife's encouragement of the defendant, the fact that the acts were not aggressive or that the acts were committed in private do not permit any relevant distinctions to be drawn between the facts of *Wilson* and *Brown*. Moreover it seems far-fetched to describe *Wilson* as a case of 'personal adornment' akin to tattooing rather than as a case of sexual gratification.[131] The court finally argued that there was no valid public policy reason to deny the validity of the wife's consent. This is identical to the approach proposed by Lord Mustill in his dissenting judgment in *Brown*. At the same time, however, it is inconsistent with the binding majority decision.

25.55 In the light of the enactment of the Human Rights Act 1998, it is pertinent to consider whether a different approach may now be required. The courts are now under an obligation, in so far as possible, to interpret and develop the common law in accordance with the European Convention on Human Rights and Fundamental Freedoms (ECHR).[132] The relevant article of the ECHR in the case of *Brown* was Article 8, which accords individuals a right to respect for private and family life. The law's refusal to recognize the consent of willing participants in sexual activity which causes actual bodily harm arguably represents a prima facie infringement of this right. The right to respect for private and family life is not, however, absolute. Restrictions on the right may be justified as a

---

[128] See also *R v Jones* (1986) 83 Cr App R 375.
[129] See further M Giles, 'R v Brown: Consensual Harm and the Public Interest' (1994) 57 MLR 101.
[130] [1996] QB 47.
[131] This was how *Wilson* was reconciled with *Brown* in *R v Emmett*, The Times, 15 October 1999.
[132] Human Rights Act 1998, s 3.

proportionate response to a legitimate aim laid down in Article 8(2). The derogation based on 'public health and morals' is of particular significance. The contracting states are given a wide 'margin of appreciation' in determining their own standards of morality. Thus when the defendants in *Brown* took their case before the European Court of Human Rights, no infringement of the ECHR was found.[133] Whilst the defendants' human rights were not infringed in *Brown* it is suggested, however, that the structure of the ECHR supports the adoption of Lord Mustill's approach to consent. Any prima facie restriction of a right guaranteed by the ECHR must be justified by the state which seeks to impose the restriction. Unless the state can show that there are grounds of public policy to justify denying effective consent, it should be recognized.

(j) Racial or religious aggravation[134]

Part II of the Crime and Disorder Act 1998 created various racially aggravated offences against the person. By virtue of the Anti-Terrorism, Crime and Security Act 2001, the element of religious aggravation was added.[135] These offences are charged separately, and allow longer prison sentences to be imposed on offenders whose crimes are racially motivated. Racial aggravation is defined in two ways by s 28 of the 1998 Act (as amended). The defendant may have demonstrated hostility based on the victim's membership (or presumed membership) of a racial or religious group at or around the time of the alleged offence.[136] Alternatively the defendant may have been motivated (wholly or partly) by hostility towards the victim on grounds of race or religion.[137]   **25.56**

In *DPP v Pal*[138] the Divisional Court asserted strongly that the racially aggravated   **25.57**
offences must genuinely relate to offending with a race element. In that case an Asian man assaulted another Asian man after the latter had asked him and three other youths to leave a community centre. The magistrates acquitted the defendant on the basis that his use of the words 'white man's arse licker' and 'brown Englishman' did not make the offence racially aggravated. The Director of Public Prosecutions appealed but the Divisional Court dismissed the appeal. The defendant had not shown hostility towards his victim because of the victim's race. The

---

[133] *Laskey v UK* (1997) 24 EHRR 39.
[134] See further F Brennan, 'Crime and Disorder Act 1998: Racially Motivated Crime: The Response of the Criminal Justice System [1999] Crim LR 17.
[135] Pt 5.
[136] Crime and Disorder Act 1998, s 28(1)(a). Under this sub-section it is immaterial that the initial attack was not motivated by racial hostility. It is arguable that an outburst in the heat of the moment which does not give a real insight into the motivations of the defendant should not be treated as a relevant aggravating factor.
[137] ibid s 28(1)(b).
[138] [2000] Crim LR 756.

hostile attitude was not aimed at Asians. It reflected his annoyance with the conduct of his victim on that occasion. It was unrealistic to argue conversely that the defendant had displayed racial hostility towards white men generally since he was part of a gang including white youths immediately prior to the attack.

25.58 The special racially aggravated offences are assault,[139] assault occasioning actual bodily harm,[140] malicious wounding or infliction of grievous bodily harm,[141] criminal damage,[142] public order offences under ss 4, 4A and 5 of the Public Order Act 1986,[143] harassment,[144] and putting a person in fear of violence.[145] But there is no racially aggravated version of wounding or causing grievous bodily harm with intent since the maximum sentence under s 18 of the OAPA 1861 is already life imprisonment.

25.59 In addition to these separate offences, s 153 of the Powers of Criminal Courts (Sentencing) Act 2000 provides that racial motivation is an aggravating factor in sentencing for all offences. Under s 82 the trial judge must also state in open court at the time of sentencing that the offence was racially motivated.

(2) Assault Occasioning Actual Bodily Harm: OAPA 1861, s 47

25.60 Section 47 of the OAPA 1861 provides:

> Whosoever shall be convicted on indictment of any assault occasioning actual bodily harm shall be liable . . . to imprisonment for not more than five years.

(a) Actus reus

25.61 The actus reus of the offence consists of both an assault and the causation of actual bodily harm. The assault may either be a technical 'pure' assault or a battery.[146] It may not be immediately obvious how a threat of immediate unlawful violence can cause actual bodily harm. An assault (in the technical sense) may cause actual bodily harm in one of two ways. The unlawful threats may cause the victim to suffer from a recognized psychiatric condition. Psychiatric injury (although not mere distress or other ordinary emotions) is within the broad scope of the concept of 'bodily harm'.[147] Alternatively the threat of immediate unlawful violence may cause the victim to hurt himself in making an escape. If the victim's act

---

[139] Crime and Disorder Act 1998, s 29(1)(c).
[140] ibid s 29(1)(b).
[141] ibid s 29(1)(a).
[142] ibid s 30(1).
[143] ibid s 31(1).
[144] ibid s 32(1)(a).
[145] ibid s 32(1)(b).
[146] *R v Lynsey* [1995] 3 All ER 654.
[147] *R v Chan-Fook* [1994] 1 WLR 689; *R v Ireland and Burstow* [1998] AC 147.

is a reasonable response to the defendant's assault it will not constitute a *novus actus interveniens*,[148] and the person uttering the threat commits the offence.

Actual bodily harm is a vague concept. In *R v Donovan* it was described as phys‐   **25.62**
ical injury which is 'calculated to interfere with the health or comfort' of the
victim in a manner which, albeit not necessarily permanent, is not 'transient or
trifling'.[149] This gives wide scope for the exercise of prosecutorial discretion in
determining which offence(s) should be charged.[150] The threshold of actual
bodily harm has a normative dimension. In, for example, the context of sexual
activity the acceptable level of harm may be greater to reflect changing social
attitudes.[151]

(b) Mens rea

The mens rea under s 47 is the same as for assault or battery. The defendant must   **25.63**
intend that the victim apprehend or be subjected to unlawful violence or be sub‐
jectively reckless as to the same.[152] No mental element is required in respect of the
aggravating feature of actual bodily harm. The offence is thus one of constructive
liability.

(3) *Maliciously Inflicting Wounds or Grievous Bodily Harm: OAPA 1861, s 20*

Section 20 of the OAPA 1861 provides: **25.64**

> Whosoever shall unlawfully and maliciously wound or inflict any grievous bodily
> harm upon any other person, either with or without any weapon or instrument,
> shall be guilty of a misdemeanour, and being convicted thereof shall be liable . . . to
> imprisonment . . . for not more than five years.

It may be noted at the outset that the maximum sentence under ss 47 and 20 is the
same. By common accord, however, s 20 is the more serious offence. A defendant
who is convicted under s 20 can on average expect to receive a greater sentence
than one who is convicted under s 47.

(a) Actus reus

The actus reus of s 20 can be committed either by wounding, or by inflicting   **25.65**
grievous bodily harm.

---

[148] *R v Lewis* [1970] Crim LR 647; *R v Roberts* (1972) 56 Cr App R 95.
[149] [1934] 2 KB 498, 509.
[150] The Joint Charging Standards agreed between the police and the Crown Prosecution Service
state that OAPA 1861, s 47 (as opposed to Criminal Justice Act 1988, s 39) should be charged where
there is, for example, loss or breakage of teeth, extensive bruising, minor fractures, cuts requiring
stitches or a broken nose.
[151] *R v Boyea* (1992) 156 JP 505. This is of most significance in determining whether or not con‐
sent to physical injury is legally relevant.
[152] *R v Savage* [1992] 1 AC 699.

25.66   A wound requires all the layers of the skin to be pierced. Purely internal injuries will not suffice.[153] Grievous bodily harm is described as 'really serious harm'[154] taking account of the victim's injuries in their entirety.[155] In *DPP v Smith*[156] the House of Lords held that it was not desirable to attempt a more precise formulation. The concept of grievous bodily harm is thus broad and flexible.

25.67   The most problematic area of s 20 has proved to be the meaning of the word 'inflict'. Originally it was thought that s 20 required an assault or battery[157] but the House of Lords decided in *R v Wilson*[158] that this was unnecessary. 'Inflict' meant an intentional act which 'though it is not itself a direct application of force to the body of the victim, it does directly result in force being directly applied violently to the body of the victim so that he suffers grievous bodily harm'.[159] The decision in *Wilson* was endorsed by the House of Lords in *R v Mandair*.[160] The case concerned a procedural matter since the defendant had been charged with maliciously causing (rather than inflicting) grievous bodily harm contrary to s 20. The defendant argued that his conviction was for an offence not known to the law. The majority of the House of Lords (Lord Mustill dissenting) sustained the defendant's conviction on the basis that the word 'causing' is wide enough to include 'inflicting'. This is clearly true. It does not, however, follow from this proposition that a conviction for causing harm also entails a finding that the defendant inflicted harm. The word causing has a wider scope than inflicting. It is unrealistic to suppose that the majority concluded that causing was synonymous with inflicting since this would have represented a departure from the settled authority of *Wilson*. There is nothing in the speeches of the majority which demonstrates that they considered themselves to be changing the law. Lord Mustill recognized the logical fallacy of the majority's approach.[161] He argued that inflicting required the 'direct and immediate doing of harm'.[162] It must be said that this approach is difficult to reconcile with *Wilson*. The House of Lords has recently had the opportunity to reconsider the meaning of 'inflict' in the context of psychiatric harm. In *R v Ireland and Burstow*[163] Lord Hope argued that 'cause' and 'inflict' bear the same meaning, save that inflict has connotations of an unpleasant or harmful act.[164] Lord Steyn (whose speech forms the majority opinion) took a narrower approach.

[153] *C (a minor) v Eisenhower* [1984] QB 331.
[154] *R v Metharam* [1961] 3 All ER 200.
[155] *R v Grundy* [1977] Crim LR 543.
[156] [1961] AC 290.
[157] *R v Clarence* (1888) 22 QBD 23.
[158] [1984] AC 242.
[159] ibid 260 *per* Lord Roskill.
[160] [1995] 1 AC 208.
[161] ibid 230.
[162] ibid 229.
[163] [1998] AC 147.
[164] ibid 164.

The words cause and inflict do have different meanings. It is, however, perfectly natural to talk of inflicting psychiatric harm without making reference to direct or indirect violent contact.[165] It appears that there is little if any divergence between the meanings of cause and inflict if psychiatric injury has been caused. It is unclear whether the decision in *Ireland and Burstow* will have a wider impact on the application of s 20 more generally.

(b) Mens rea

The mens rea requirement for s 20 is intention or subjective recklessness in respect of some, albeit not necessarily serious, harm.[166]

25.68

(4) Wounding or Causing Grievous Bodily Harm with Intent: OAPA 1861, s 18

Section 18 of the OAPA 1861 provides that:

25.69

> Whosoever shall unlawfully and maliciously by any means whatsoever wound or cause grievous bodily harm to any person . . . with intent . . . to do some grievous bodily harm to any person, or with intent to resist or prevent the lawful apprehension or detainer of any person shall be guilty of an offence, and being convicted thereof shall be liable . . . to imprisonment for life.

There are four ways in which the s 18 offence can be committed:

25.70

- wounding with intent to cause grievous bodily harm;
- causing grievous bodily harm with intent to cause grievous bodily harm;
- wounding with intent to resist or prevent lawful arrest;
- causing grievous bodily harm with intent to resist or prevent lawful arrest.

The meanings of 'wounding' and 'grievous bodily harm' are the same as in relation to s 20.

The mental element is intention with respect to either causing grievous bodily harm or resisting/preventing lawful arrest. For three of the variant forms of the offence this is an ulterior intention.[167] Where the defendant is charged with causing grievous bodily harm with intent to cause grievous bodily harm the actus reus and mens rea correspond exactly. It has been suggested that the word 'maliciously' is superfluous.[168] This must be correct where the defendant has been charged with causing grievous bodily harm with intent to cause grievous bodily harm. As far as the other variants are concerned, the word 'maliciously' imports a requirement of intention or subjective recklessness in relation to the harm actually caused.[169] It is

25.71

---

[165] ibid 160–161.
[166] *R v Savage* [1992] 1 AC 699.
[167] This refers to a mental element which relates to an act, circumstance or consequence which does not form part of the actus reus.
[168] *R v Mowatt* [1968] 1 QB 421.
[169] *R v Morrison* (1989) 89 Cr App R 17.

unclear whether 'malice' is required in respect of some (but not necessarily serious) harm[170] or in respect of wounding or grievous bodily harm (as appropriate).

(5) *Maliciously Administering Poison or Other Destructive or Noxious Thing*

25.72 Several offences are concerned with the administration of poison. Section 23 of the OAPA 1861 provides:

> Whosoever shall unlawfully and maliciously administer to, or cause to be administered to or taken by any other person any poison, or other destructive or noxious thing, so as thereby to endanger the life of such person, or so as thereby to inflict upon such person any grievous bodily harm, shall be guilty of an offence . . .

(a) So as to endanger life or inflict grievous bodily harm

25.73 There are three elements of the actus reus of the offence under s 23.

25.74 The expression 'poison or other destructive or noxious thing' must be considered both in terms of the quantity and the nature of the substance in question. If a substance is harmless in small doses it may still be considered 'noxious' if it is administered in a harmful larger dose.[171] A substance is 'noxious' if it is dangerous, unpleasant or unwholesome. This is determined objectively. It is immaterial that the victim has developed tolerance to a substance as a result of, for example, addiction.[172]

25.75 'Administration' is given a broad definition. In *R v Gillard*[173] this requirement was held to be satisfied by the defendant's spraying CS gas from a canister at the victim. The victim's consent to administration is immaterial.[174] The act of administration cannot, however, be made out by a voluntary act of the victim (such as self-injection) provided that the victim knew what he was injecting.[175] Such an act will constitute a novus actus interveniens on ordinary principles of causation.

25.76 The final element of the actus reus distinguishes the s 23 offence from the s 24 offence. The defendant's act must endanger life or inflict grievous bodily harm. The use of the word 'inflict' has the potential to raise the same difficulties as discussed in relation to s 20. It is suggested, however, that in this context 'inflict' is best viewed as being synonymous with 'cause'. This demonstrates further the inconsistent use of terminology within the OAPA 1861. The offences do not together form a coherent and rational body of law.

---

[170] This would accord with the mental element for s 20.

[171] *R v Marcus* [1981] 1 WLR 774.

[172] *R v Cato* [1976] 1 WLR 110.

[173] (1988) 87 Cr App R 189.

[174] *R v Cato* [1976] 1 WLR 110.

[175] *R v Dias* [2001] EWCA Crim 2986, [2002] 2 Cr App R 5; noted by G Virgo, 'Constructing manslaughter in drug abuse cases' [2003] 62 CLJ 12.

The mens rea requirement for s 23 is that the defendant administer the substance   **25.77**
'maliciously'.[176] It seems, however, that there is no need for there to be any intention or recklessness in respect of the possibility that administering a noxious substance might cause injury. In *R v Cato*[177] it was held that there was no requirement of mens rea in respect of the endangerment of life or infliction of grievous bodily harm. The offence is one of constructive liability in respect of the feature of the actus reus which distinguishes s 23 from s 24. Moreover the mens rea requirements of the lesser offence under s 24 are in fact more onerous than for s 23.

(b) With intent to injure, aggrieve or annoy: OAPA 1861, s 24

The offence under s 24 (which is less serious than the previous offence, carry-   **25.78**
ing as it does five years' as opposed to ten years' imprisonment) requires the administration of a poison or other destructive or noxious thing. The meaning of these actus reus terms is as for s 23. The mens rea requirement of malice in respect of administration is also applicable. There is, however, also the requirement of an ulterior intent to injure, aggrieve or annoy. It was established in *R v Hill*[178] that it need not be the defendant's subjective purpose to injure, aggrieve or annoy the victim. The defendant was a paedophile who administered a slimming drug to some boys. The drug had the side effect of keeping the boys awake so that he could perform indecent acts with them. The defendant claimed that he believed his actions would make the boys happy. It was held, however, that it was sufficient that the object which the defendant intended would objectively injure, aggrieve or annoy the victim.

(6) Harassment

In response to high-profile 'stalker' cases Parliament enacted two new offences   **25.79**
under the Protection from Harassment Act 1997 (PHA). Section 2 creates an offence of 'harassment'. Section 4 sanctions conduct which puts a person in fear of unlawful violence.[179] Before legislative action could be taken, however, the scope of the OAPA 1861 was enlarged by the courts in an attempt to combat harassment. Consequently liability may follow under ss 47, 20 or 18 for psychiatric injury provided that the other elements of the actus reus and the mens rea are satisfied. It was not originally contemplated that the 1861 Act would cover such situations, and the result has been the distortion of a group of offences which were already renowned for their inconsistency, lack of coherence and illogicality.

---

[176] It was established in *R v Cunningham* [1957] 2 QB 396, that this would be satisfied by either intention or subjective recklessness.

[177] [1976] 1 WLR 110.

[178] (1986) 83 Cr App R 386.

[179] See further C Wells, 'Stalking: The Criminal Law Response' [1997] Crim LR 463; J Herring, 'The Criminalisation of Harassment' (1998) 57 CLJ 10; S Gardner, 'Stalking' (1998) 114 LQR 33.

(a) Harassment: PHA 1997, s 2

(i) Actus reus

25.80 The PHA Act 1997 provides no statutory definition of 'harassment'.[180] It includes causing alarm or distress.[181] Harassing conduct will only constitute an offence if it forms part of a course of conduct which occurs on at least two occasions.[182] In *Lau v DPP*[183] it was held that there must be some sort of causal link between the separate incidents of harassment to constitute a 'course of conduct'. The smaller the number of incidents and the greater the separation of the incidents in point of time, the less likely they are to constitute a course of conduct.

(ii) Mens rea

25.81 The mens rea of the s 2 offence is that the defendant must know or should know that his conduct constitutes harassment.[184] The defendant ought to know that his conduct amounts to harassment if a reasonable person in the defendant's position with the same information as the defendant would think that the conduct amounted to harassment. This objective mens rea element is not relaxed to take account of the special characteristics of the defendant. In *R v Colohan*[185] the defendant had inundated his Member of Parliament with vast amounts of correspondence on various matters. Some of these concerns were genuine but others were fictitious. The Court of Appeal ruled that expert evidence which showed the defendant to be a schizophrenic who genuinely believed his complaints to be real was irrelevant to the issue of mens rea.

(iii) Defences

25.82 The statute provides[186] three defences for which the defendant bears the burden of proof on the balance of probabilities. These defences are that the course of conduct was being pursued for the purpose of the prevention or detection of crime; that it was pursued in compliance with statutory obligation and that the conduct was reasonable for the protection of himself or another, or that in the particular

---

[180] This is perhaps not surprising given the breadth of the concept of harassment. The law would be unduly constrained by a rigid statutory definition. It has been noted that the PHA 1997 captures the essence of harassment. It sanctions conduct which causes the victim to feel 'harassed' and which occurs as part of a 'course of conduct'.

[181] See further, E Finch, 'Stalking the Perfect Stalking Law: Evaluating the Efficacy of the Protection from Harassment Act 1997' [2002] Crim LR 703.

[182] PHA 1997, s 7(2).

[183] [2000] Crim LR 580.

[184] PHA 1997, s 1(1)(b).

[185] [2001] EWCA Crim 1251; [2001] Crim LR 845.

[186] PHA 1997, s 1(3).

circumstances the pursuit of the course of conduct was reasonable.[187] No criteria are afforded by which the reasonableness or otherwise of the conduct is to be assessed.

(b) Putting another in fear of violence: PHA 1997, s 4

It is an offence to pursue a course of conduct which causes a person to fear on at least two occasions[188] that violence will be used against him.[189] It will not suffice that the victim was seriously frightened about what might happen to him if he does not specifically fear violence.[190] Similarly a fear that violence will be used against other people, such as members of the victim's family, is insufficient.[191] **25.83**

The mens rea requirement for s 4 is that the defendant knew or ought to have known that his conduct would cause the victim to fear that violence would be used against him.[192] **25.84**

The same basic three defences are applicable to s 4 as for s 2.[193] The reasonableness defence is, however, more narrowly drawn to include only conduct which is necessary for self-defence or the protection of property.[194] **25.85**

The maximum sentence for the s 4 offence is five years' imprisonment. It is thus to be considered on a par with offences under ss 47 and 20 of the OAPA 1861. It could be argued that the mens rea requirement is insufficiently subjective for such a serious offence. It would have been more satisfactory to enact a series of harassment offences with gradually more subjective mens rea and correspondingly increased maximum sentences. **25.86**

The requirement of fear that violence will be used has been considered too stringent to deal with, for example, silent telephone calls which cause severe distress but do not contain specific threats.[195] Lord Steyn noted in *R v Ireland and Burstow*[196] that the sentences available under s 2 of the PHA 1997 would be inadequate to deal with the most serious cases of offending. Where psychiatric injury has been caused these cases have been rather unconvincingly dealt with through the offences of the OAPA 1861. **25.87**

---

[187] ibid s 1(3).
[188] ibid s 7(3).
[189] ibid s 4(1).
[190] *R v Henley* [2000] Crim LR 582.
[191] ibid.
[192] PHA 1997, s 4(1)–(2).
[193] ibid s 4(3).
[194] ibid s 4(3)(c).
[195] *R v Ireland and Burstow* [1998] AC 147, 153 *per* Lord Steyn.
[196] ibid.

(7) False Imprisonment

25.88   It is an offence at common law to imprison any person without lawful excuse. A person may be falsely imprisoned without knowing of their unlawful detention.[197] It is not, however, false imprisonment to block someone's path if they are free to turn around and walk another way.[198] Restraint of a child's freedom only amounts to false imprisonment if that imprisonment is unlawful. If the detention falls outside the bounds of reasonable chastisement criminal liability may follow.[199] In determining the gravity of a false imprisonment (for the purpose of sentencing) it is important to bear in mind the purpose for which the defendant detained the victim. In *R v Willoughby*[200] the Court of Appeal considered that a life sentence was too harsh a sentence where the purpose of the imprisonment had been indecent assault. In *R v Sullivan*,[201] a sentence of 18 years for false imprisonment (concurrent with a life sentence) was upheld in a case where the defendant had kidnapped and tortured and murdered the victim.

(8) Kidnapping

(a) Common law

25.89   The House of Lords has held that the common law offence of kidnapping has four ingredients:[202] there must be a taking or carrying away of one person by another; this must be by use of force or fraud; the absence of consent of the person taken or carried away must be established and there must be an absence of lawful excuse.

25.90   In *R v D*[203] the House of Lords indicated in particular that statutory provisions on child stealing did not have the effect of abolishing the common law offence of kidnapping. The offence of kidnapping can be committed against a child under the age of 14. A parent can kidnap his own unmarried child even if the child has not yet reached the age of majority.

25.91   Lord Brandon emphasized[204] that when considering the kidnap of a child it is the consent of the child (rather than the parent or guardian) that is relevant. Where the child is too young to have capacity to consent a lack of consent will be inferred. Where the child is older the question of consent is one of fact for the jury. If the defendant argues that the parent or guardian of the child consented to the child's being taken away this may be highly relevant to the question of lawful excuse.

---

[197] *Meering v Graham-White Aviation Co Ltd* (1919) 122 LT 44.
[198] *Bird v Jones* (1845) 7 QB 742.
[199] *R v Rahman* (1985) 81 Cr App R 349.
[200] [1999] Crim LR 244.
[201] [2003] EWCA Crim 764; The Times, 18 March 2003.
[202] *R v D* [1984] AC 778, 801 *per* Lord Brandon of Oakbrook.
[203] ibid.
[204] ibid 806.

(b) Child abduction: Child Abduction Act 1984, ss 1 and 2

The Child Abduction Act 1984 creates the two distinct offences of child abduc- **25.92**
tion by a parent,[205] and child abduction by other persons.[206] Each will be considered in turn.

(i) Child abduction by a parent

A parent[207] commits an offence if he takes or sends a child under the age of 16 out **25.93**
of the United Kingdom without 'appropriate consent'.[208] No offence is committed (even without appropriate consent) if the defendant is a person in whose
favour a residence order is in force in respect of the child and the child is outside
of the United Kingdom for less than a month.[209]

Section 1(5) of the Child Abduction Act 1984 provides defences for which the **25.94**
burden of proof lies on the prosecution. There will be a defence if the defendant
believes that the other person has consented, or believes that the other person
would consent if he was aware of all relevant circumstances; where the defendant
has taken all reasonable steps to communicate with the other person but has been
unable to do so, or where the other person has unreasonably withheld consent.[210]

(ii) Child abduction by other persons

Any person (apart from those specifically excepted)[211] commits an offence if with- **25.95**
out lawful authority or reasonable excuse he takes or detains a child under 16 so as
to take or keep him away from persons having lawful control of the child.

It is a defence for the defendant to prove that[212] he is the father of the illegitimate **25.96**
child or at the time of the alleged offence he reasonably believed that he was the
father of the illegitimate child or that at the time of the alleged offence he believed
that the child had reached the age of 16.

---

[205] Child Abduction Act 1984, s 1.
[206] ibid s 2.
[207] ibid s 1(2) defines the scope of the Act as including a parent, a person who reasonably believes that he is the father of an illegitimate child, a guardian of the child, a person in whose favour a residence order in respect of the child is in force and a person who has custody of the child.
[208] ibid s 1(3) defines 'appropriate consent' as: consent of each of child's mother, child's father (if he has parental responsibility), any guardian of the child, any person in whose favour a residence order in respect of the child is in force and any person who has custody of the child; leave of the court granted under a provision of the Children Act 1989; or leave of court which awarded custody to an individual.
[209] ibid s 1(4).
[210] Unless the 'other person' is a person in whose favour a residence order in respect of the child is in force or who has custody of the child, or taking/sending the child outside the UK is in breach of a court order: ibid s 1(5A).
[211] The father or mother of a legitimate child, the mother of an illegitimate child, the guardian of the child, a person in whose favour a residence order in respect of the child is in force and a person who has custody of the child are all excepted: ibid s 2(2).
[212] ibid s 2(3).

(c) Taking of hostages

25.97 Section 1 of the Taking of Hostages Act 1982[213] creates an offence, punishable with life imprisonment, of 'hostage-taking'. A person who takes a hostage or hostages and threatens to kill, injure or continue to detain the hostage(s) in order to make the state or an international governmental organization or another person do or not do an act commits an offence.

(9) Road Traffic Offences

(a) Causing death by dangerous driving[214]

25.98 'Dangerous' driving is defined as a standard of driving which falls 'far below what would be expected of a competent and careful driver' and which would be obviously dangerous to a competent and careful driver.[215] The defendant's driving may also be dangerous if it would be obvious to a competent and careful driver that driving the vehicle in its current state would be dangerous.[216] 'Danger' refers to the risk of either injury to any person or damage to property.[217] When determining what would be obvious to a competent and careful driver the court should consider what the defendant actually knew as well as what he could reasonably be expected to have been aware of.[218]

25.99 The defendant commits an offence if he causes death whilst driving a 'mechanically propelled vehicle' dangerously on a road or other public place.

(b) Dangerous driving: Road Traffic Act 1988, s 2

25.100 Even if a dangerous driver does not cause death he will still be guilty of an offence. The definition of dangerous is the same as that adopted for s 1.

(c) Careless and inconsiderate driving: Road Traffic Act 1988, s 3

25.101 It is an offence to drive a mechanically propelled vehicle on a road or other public place without 'due care or attention' or 'reasonable consideration of other persons'.

(d) Causing death by careless driving under the influence of drink or drugs: Road Traffic Act 1988, s 3A

25.102 The definition of 'careless' is the same as that adopted for the s 3 offence. The aggravated offence for causing death by careless driving is engaged where the defendant is

---

[213] The Act implements the International Convention against the Taking of Hostages.
[214] Road Traffic Act 1988, s 1. This replaces the offence of causing death by reckless driving on which see *R v Lawrence* [1982] AC 510.
[215] ibid s 2A(1).
[216] ibid s 2A(2).
[217] ibid s 2A(3).
[218] ibid.

unfit to drive through drink or drugs;[219] or is over the prescribed 'drink-driving'
limit; or fails to provide a specimen without reasonable excuse when required to
do so.[220]

C. Sexual Offences

The sexual offences operate to protect a wide range of values which are considered   **25.103**
important for the well-being of society. The most obvious function of sexual offences is to protect the sexual integrity of individuals against unwanted advances.
As a consequence, the absence of consent is ordinarily a crucial feature of the actus
reus of any sexual offence. Some offences demonstrate the law's commitment
to paternalistic values by protecting vulnerable individuals such as children and
the mentally deficient. The sexual offences may also be used to enforce moral
norms.[221]

(1) Rape

(a) Actus reus

Until Parliament enacted s 1(1) of the Sexual Offences Amendment Act 1976, the   **25.104**
definition of rape was a matter for the common law. Earlier legislation laid down
that it was an offence for a man to rape a woman, but the precise ingredients of the
offence had to be culled from the decisions of the judges. At common law, the
actus reus of rape was constituted by non-consensual vaginal sexual intercourse
between a man and a woman. The statutory definition of rape, however, extended
the definition of rape to include anal intercourse, and to extend the protection of
the law to male victims.[222] It is still the case, however, that only a man may commit rape as a principal.[223] The common law presumption that a boy under the age
of 14 is incapable of sexual intercourse was abolished by s 1 of the SOA 1993.

(i) Marital rape

At common law a husband could not be convicted of raping his wife.[224] The basis   **25.105**
for this rule was the fiction that man and wife should be regarded as a single in-
separable entity represented by the man. Over the course of the 20th century,
with the changing position of women in society, this exception began to appear

---

[219] 'Unfit' means that the defendant's ability to drive properly is impaired: ibid s 3A(2).
[220] Provided that the request for the specimen was made within 18 hours of the alleged driving.
[221] At the time of writing, a Sexual Offences Bill was before Parliament, intended to rid the law of
some of its deficiencies. These are considered at paras 25.144 et seq below.
[222] See Criminal Justice and Public Order Act 1994, s 142.
[223] A woman may be an accomplice to rape: *R v Ram and Ram* (1893) 17 Cox CC 609.
[224] See, eg, *R v Miller* [1954] 2 QB 282.

increasingly anachronistic. It was widely thought, however, that the statutory description of the necessary sexual intercourse as 'unlawful' incorporated the marital rape exception into the definition of rape. In *R v R*,[225] the House of Lords
controversially abolished the ancient rule that a husband could not be guilty of
raping his wife, an outcome that necessarily involved regarding the word 'unlawful' in the statutory definition as being superfluous. Although it may be difficult
to dissent from the outcome achieved in *R v R*, the decision was an illegitimate
usurpation of legislative powers by the judiciary. In the case of the particular defendant in *R v R*, the principles of 'fair warning' and non-retrospectivity appeared
to have been breached because he was convicted of a criminal offence for an act
which was not punishable as rape[226] when it was done. It may well be that, as some
would argue in a legal system based on a body of common law, the most senior
judges must have a power (or even the duty) to ensure that the criminal law is kept
up to date and that it mirrors current social norms. The doctrine of parliamentary
sovereignty requires the judiciary to accept their subordination to the will of the
legislature, as currently expressed in applicable statutes. It is not open to the courts
to ignore the words of a statute. It is nevertheless clear that Parliament clearly
adopted this decision in the new definition of rape (to be found in the SOA 1956,
as amended by the Criminal Justice and Public Order Act 1994), which omitted
the word 'unlawful' from the previous definition. That Act also redefined the act
of rape to include male victims and anal intercourse.

(ii) Sexual intercourse as a 'continuing act'

25.106 The ordinary understanding of what constitutes 'sexual intercourse' is altered and
supplemented by s 44 of the SOA 1956 which provides that:

> It shall not be necessary to prove the completion of intercourse by emission of seed,
> but the intercourse shall be deemed complete upon proof of penetration only.

The use of the word 'complete' has caused controversy because of the requirement
of temporal coincidence of actus reus and mens rea. In *R v Kaitamaki*,[227] the defendant appealed against his conviction for rape on the basis that he formed the
required mens rea only after the moment of penetration. This might have arisen
either because, at the moment of penetration the defendant mistakenly believed
that the woman was consenting or that, having given her permission at the outset,
the woman withdrew consent. If the act of sexual intercourse was complete on
penetration, the logical consequence was that mens rea could not be seen to coincide with actus reus. The Judicial Committee of the Privy Council were unper-
suaded by this essentially technical argument. The purpose of s 44 was solely to

[225] [1992] AC 599.
[226] The conduct would have been punishable as indecent assault, and the victim was not therefore
wholly outside the protection of the criminal law.
[227] [1985] AC 147, PC.

establish that it was unnecessary to prove ejaculation in order to bring a rape charge. The act of sexual intercourse commences upon penetration but is a continuing act.[228] The outcome of the decision would appear to be that, if a woman withdraws consent in the course of the sexual act, a man who is aware of this fact and declines to desist is guilty of rape. Whether that is a satisfactory state for the law to be in is a matter of some difficulty and debate.

(iii) Absence of consent

The required absence of consent is determined by reference to the same principles discussed above in relation to the non-fatal offences against the person. It is not proposed to repeat them here, but the discussions of submission to threats and mistake as to the nature of the act and as to identity of the defendant are particularly relevant in this context. It will be remembered that the defendant cannot be convicted of rape unless the victim is in fact not consenting. If the 'victim' is a consenting participant the accused may only be convicted (if at all) of attempted rape.[229] It is, however, possible for the defendant to be convicted of rape even if the victim has not manifested a lack of consent.[230] The victim's failure to resist or protest may, however, be of evidential significance to the claim of non-consensual intercourse, as well as to the defendant's mens rea.

25.107

(b) Mens rea

The mens rea of rape requires either the intention to have sexual intercourse with the victim, whilst knowing that that person is not consenting or being reckless as to whether or not there is consent. This simple statement belies the complexities and controversies surrounding, in particular, mistaken belief in consent and the meaning of 'recklessness' in this context.

25.108

(i) Honest belief in consent

Parliament acted in 1976 because of widespread public concern following the controversial decision of the House of Lords in *Morgan v DPP*[231] in which the House held that, as a matter of 'inexorable logic',[232] a man was not guilty of rape if he had intercourse with a non-consenting woman, acting in the honest but mistaken belief that the woman had consented. And that was true, according to the House, even though the mistake was an unreasonable one. Whether or not

25.109

---

[228] This analysis was approved and followed in *R v Schaub and Cooper* [1994] Crim LR 531 and is adopted by clause 81(1) of the Sexual Offences Bill 2003.

[229] See discussion of general mens rea requirements for attempts liability and liability for impossible attempts at para 24.48 above.

[230] *R v Malone* [1998] 2 Cr App R 447.

[231] [1976] AC 182.

[232] ibid 218 *per* Lord Hailsham.

the defendant had reasonable grounds for his mistaken belief is, however, of evidential significance. The more unreasonable the mistake, the less likely that it was genuine. Parliament subsequently confirmed the decision in s 1(2) of the Sexual Offences (Amendment) Act 1976[233] where it stated that:

> the presence or absence of reasonable grounds for such a belief is a matter to which the jury is to have regard, in conjunction with any other relevant matters, in considering whether he so believed.

25.110 When the criminal law exculpates a defendant on the basis of his mistaken assumptions, it does so on the basis of negation of mens rea. In this respect the *Morgan* decision is a strongly subjectivist ruling. It would be hypocritical for the law to impose strict liability in respect of mistakes and convict a person of rape who reasonably, but mistakenly, believed that the victim was consenting. Some commentators, however, question whether the law should allow a defendant who makes an unreasonable mistake to escape criminal liability.[234] The relevance of unreasonable mistakes is justified on the basis of logic. A person who has a positive honest belief in consent must lack the requisite subjective mens rea.[235] Dr Horder, for example, argues that this fails to take account of the need to provide a moral justification for exculpating a defendant on the basis of an unreasonable mistake. Everybody agrees that no one should be convicted of an offence if they lack mens rea but the law should not adopt such a formalistic definition of mens rea that it is unable to catch unreasonable mistakes where this is appropriate. Horder's analysis provides a sophisticated and nuanced approach to different circumstances where the defendant may make a relevant mistake.

25.111 Whether or not an unreasonable mistake can exculpate the defendant depends on the circumstances of the case. Thus in the context of consent to sexual activity it is not unreasonable for the law to demand that a person, who is driven by sexual desires, takes all reasonable steps to ensure that the victim is consenting.[236] On the other hand where the accused acted quickly in self-defence or in the defence of others it is not possible to expect the same level of rational behaviour.

---

[233] Following the recommendations of the Heilbron report (Cmnd 6352, 1975).

[234] See further C Wells, 'Swatting the Subjectivist Bug' [1982] Crim LR 209; J Horder, 'Cognition, Emotion and Criminal Culpability' (1990) 106 LQR 469.

[235] *Morgan v DPP* [1976] AC 182, 218 *per* Lord Hailsham; *Beckford v R* [1988] 1 AC 130, 142, PC, *per* Lord Griffiths.

[236] This is especially so given that the definition of recklessness for the purposes of rape has a strongly objective element (see para 25.112 below). See further S Gardner, 'Reckless and Inconsiderate Rape' [1991] Crim LR 172, 176.

(ii) The meaning of recklessness

The recklessness requirement has been variously described as 'not caring'[237] or 'in-   **25.112**
difference'[238] or 'lack of honest belief'.[239] In *B (a child) v DPP*,[240] the House of
Lords confirmed the 'lack of honest belief' formulation for requirements of recklessness as to circumstances generally. It is, however, difficult to reconcile these descriptions with the proposition that objective recklessness[241] as to the absence of
consent is not sufficient for rape.[242] A defendant can be convicted of rape without
having given any consideration to whether or not the victim was consenting. This
form of recklessness stands out alongside the remarkably subjectivist position
when the accused makes an honest mistake in relation to the victim's consent.

(2) Procurement of Sexual Intercourse with a Woman

Sections 2 and 3 of the SOA 1956 create 'procurement' offences which fill in the   **25.113**
gaps between some of the other sexual offences. The procurement offences may be
committed by both males and females but the victim must be a woman. Section 2
creates an offence of procuring a woman to have sexual intercourse by using
threats or intimidation. Under s 3 it is an offence to procure a woman to have sexual intercourse by false pretences or misrepresentation. Where the defendant is
also the person who has sexual intercourse with the victim it seems that the
threats/intimidation or false pretences/misrepresentation must fall short of that
required to vitiate the victim's consent.[243]

(3) Buggery and Bestiality

Until 1967, homosexuality was treated as criminal irrespective of the fact that the   **25.114**
participants were consenting adults acting in private. The law was changed in that
year, following protracted debate.[244] Initially, the age of consent was set at 21, but
it was successively reduced, first to 18, and then, as the result of a successful challenge to the European Court of Human Rights in *Sutherland v UK*,[245] to 16.

---

[237] *Morgan v DPP* [1976] AC 182.
[238] *R v Breckenridge* (1984) 79 Cr App R 244.
[239] *R v S (Satnam) and S (Kewal)* (1983) 78 Cr App R 149.
[240] [2000] 2 AC 428.
[241] See earlier discussion of the House of Lords decisions in *R v Caldwell* [1982] AC 341 and *R v Lawrence* [1982] AC 510 at para 24.25 above. *R v Caldwell* was 'departed from' by the House of Lords in *R v G* [2003] UKHL 50, [2003] 3 WLR 1060.
[242] *R v S (Satnam) and S (Kewal)* (1983) 78 Cr App R 149.
[243] See discussion of consent at para 25.38 above.
[244] Stimulated in particular by the Wolfenden report, *Report of the Committee on Homosexual Offences and Prostitution* (Cmnd 247, 1957).
[245] (1997) EHRR CD22.

25.115   Section 12(1) of the SOA 1956 makes it an offence to commit consensual buggery[246] with another person except where:

- the act takes place in private and both parties are at least 16 years old;[247]
- the defendant is aged under 16 and the other person has attained that age.[248]

A homosexual act of buggery will not be deemed to take place in 'private' if more than two people are present or the act takes place in a public lavatory.[249] Anal intercourse between heterosexual partners need only be 'private' in the everyday sense.

25.116   It is always an offence for a man to commit an act of buggery with an animal.[250]

(4) *Indecent Assault*

25.117   The offence of indecent assault is created by ss 14 and 15 of the SOA 1956. Section 14 makes it an offence for a person (either male or female) to commit an indecent assault against a woman. The equivalent offence for male victims is created by s 15 of the SOA 1956.

(a) **Actus reus**

(i) *Assault or battery*

25.118   The meaning of 'assault' in this context is broadly the same as for the non-fatal offences against the person.[251] Thus in *R v Rolfe*[252] the defendant was correctly convicted of indecent assault after having moved towards the victim, whilst exposing himself and asking her to have sex with him.

25.119   Conversely in *Fairclough v Whipp*,[253] where the defendant had invited the victim to touch his penis, there was no indecent assault since there was not an immediate threat of non-consensual touching by the defendant. In *Faulkner v Talbot*[254] a boy, aged under 16 years,[255] had sexual intercourse with the female defendant. It was held that no assault would be committed during the act of sexual intercourse unless the defendant actively touched the boy. If she had remained entirely passive she could not be convicted of indecent assault. Nevertheless touching as a prelude to the sexual act could constitute an indecent assault irrespective of whether the defendant remained entirely passive during intercourse itself.

---

[246] Non-consensual buggery should now be charged as rape.
[247] SOA 1956, s 12(1A).
[248] ibid s 12(lAA).
[249] The law on homosexual buggery was amended by SOA 1967, s 1.
[250] SOA 1956, s 12(1).
[251] See general discussion at para 25.29 above.
[252] (1952) 36 Cr App R 4.
[253] [1951] 2 All ER 834.
[254] [1981] 1 WLR 1528.
[255] See para 25.127 below on the relevance of age to the capacity to consent to an indecent assault.

Since the offence is based on the concepts of assault and battery it follows that no **25.120** offence is committed where the defendant consents to the act.[256] If, however, the harm caused reaches the threshold of actual bodily harm the victim's consent will be regarded as legally irrelevant.[257] Consent to the element of indecency in itself (rather than the assault) is always regarded as immaterial.

(ii) Indecency

The concept of indecency is left undefined by statute. English law avoids this de- **25.121** finitional problem by leaving the matter to the jury as a question of fact. The jury must decide whether 'right minded persons would consider the conduct indecent or not'. In applying this test the jury should bear in mind whether the conduct so offends against contemporary standards of modesty and privacy as to be indecent. This is an objective test. There is no need that the victim should apprehend the circumstances of indecency.

An assault will not be an indecent assault only because it takes place in indecent **25.122** circumstances. The assault must itself contribute to the indecency. In *R v Sutton*,[258] for example, the defendant took photographs of naked boys for paedophilic magazines. The defendant only touched the boys in order to arrange the poses. There was no indecent assault because the defendant's touching of the boys did not contribute to the indecency of the situation.

Most indecent assaults will be unambiguously of a sexual nature. In such a case **25.123** there arises an irresistible inference of indecency which cannot be rebutted by evidence of the defendant's non-sexual motive. Other assaults may be incapable of being regarded as indecent in any circumstance. In this case the undisclosed sexual motive of the accused is irrelevant to determining whether the act was indecent. Therefore in *R v George*[259] the defendant's foot fetish did not render his attempt to steal the victim's shoe from her feet an indecent assault because his conduct was not unambiguously indecent in an objective sense.

The difficult cases arise where the defendant's conduct is capable of being re- **25.124** garded as indecent but analysis of the act by itself leaves some ambiguity. In *R v Court*,[260] the defendant, a shop assistant, had smacked a young girl's bottom. As the girl was clothed the House of Lords concluded that the act was of an ambiguous nature. The defendant might have been administering a form of punishment

---

[256] *R v Kimber* [1983] 1 WLR 1118.
[257] *R v Brown* [1994] 1 AC 212, HL; see general discussion of consent at para 25.38 above.
[258] [1977] 1 WLR 1086.
[259] [1956] Crim LR 52.
[260] [1989] AC 28.

or taking part in a rough game rather than fulfilling any sexual motive. The majority of their Lordships[261] decided that once the court held the conduct to be ambiguously indecent the jury could have regard to evidence of the defendant's motive in determining whether right-minded persons would actually consider the act indecent. Since the defendant in *Court* had admitted to having a bottom fetish his motive was clearly sexual and the circumstances of indecency were made out against him.

25.125 Glanville Williams has attacked the reasoning of the House of Lords in *Court*.[262] It is very difficult to distinguish *Court* from the earlier case of *George*. Evidence of sexual motive was admissible in *Court* because it illustrated the 'true nature' of the assault. A similar argument could easily be made for the admissibility of evidence of sexual motive in *George*. It also appears to find that the assault in *Court* was capable of being indecent without also considering the possible evidence of motive. If this is so the court's argument becomes dangerously circular and self-validating. If the court concludes that the assault is capable of being indecent the conclusive evidence of sexual motive is admitted and almost inevitably the defendant will be convicted of indecent assault. If the court reaches the opposite conclusion the jury has no evidence on which to find indecency and the defendant is acquitted. It is suggested that the defendant's sexual motive should either always be relevant or never be relevant. Lord Goff argued in *Court* that evidence of sexual motive confused the actus reus with the mens rea. This overstates the use of sexual motive to determine whether an act is indecent.

25.126 The defendant's subjective motivations will influence how we evaluate a particular set of objective facts. The better position, it is suggested, is that evidence of sexual motive should always be admissible since it will always shed light on the nature of the assault in question.

(iii) Persons whose consent to indecent acts is ineffective

25.127 Children under the age of 16[263] cannot give valid consent which would prevent an indecent assault being committed. Similarly so-called 'defectives' are unable to give valid consent to an otherwise indecent assault.[264] 'Defective' is defined in s 45 of the SOA 1956 as 'a person suffering from a state of arrested or incomplete development of mind which includes severe impairment of intelligence and social functioning'.

---

[261] *R v Court* (n 260 above) 36 et seq, *per* Lord Ackner (Lord Goff of Chieveley dissenting).
[262] See 'The Meaning of Indecency' (1992) LS 20.
[263] SOA 1956, ss 14(2) and 15(2).
[264] ibid ss 14(4) and 15(3).

(b) Mens rea

(i) Assault and indecency

The general mens rea requirement is that the defendant intended to assault the **25.128** victim in a way which is objectively indecent.[265] It appears from *R v C*,[266] however, that in unambiguously indecent cases subjective recklessness as to indecency will suffice.

(ii) Consent

The mens rea in respect of consent is the same as that for rape. An honest belief in **25.129** consent, even if based on unreasonable grounds, will be sufficient to negate mens rea.[267] It is, however, sufficient to ground liability that the defendant lacks an honest belief in consent.

(iii) Defectives

Although 'defectives' are unable to give valid consent, the defendant will only com- **25.130** mit an offence if he knew or had reason to suspect that the victim was a defective.[268]

(iv) Age of victim

In *R v K*[269] the House of Lords controversially held that no indecent assault **25.131** was committed if the defendant held an honest belief that the victim was aged 16 or over, provided that the victim consented or the defendant lacked mens rea in respect of the absence of consent. The burden of proof in respect of this rests with the prosecution.[270] This is a strongly subjectivist approach to the interpretation of the relevant sections of the SOA 1956. Lord Millett acknowledged that Parliament had probably intended to create an offence of strict liability in respect of age. An express mens rea term was inserted in respect of the consent of 'defectives' but no such term was included for the consent of children under the age of 16. Its omission is unlikely to have been a careless oversight. The House of Lords nevertheless affirmed that the presumption of mens rea principle should only be rebutted where Parliament's intention is made 'compellingly clear'.

(5) Unlawful Sexual Intercourse with Girls

Children may still have the legal capacity to consent to sexual intercourse. Sexual **25.132** intercourse with children under the age of 16 is thus not automatically rape. In

---

[265] *R v Court* [1989] AC 28.
[266] [1992] Crim LR 642.
[267] *R v Kimber* [1983] 1 WLR 1118.
[268] SOA 1956, ss 14(4) and 15(3).
[269] [2001] UKHL 41; [2002] 1 AC 462.
[270] *R v Fernandez* [2002] EWCA Crim 1318; The Times, 26 June 2002.

addition to the special protection provided by the offence of indecent assault there are several offences specifically aimed at the protection of children. This section deals with the offences of unlawful sexual intercourse with girls. Reference should be made to the section on buggery above for the law on anal intercourse with girls and boys under the age of 16. Subsequent sections will also deal with acts of gross indecency with a child and sexual activity in breach of a position of trust.

(a) Unlawful sexual intercourse with a girl under the age of 13

25.133   Under s 5 of the SOA 1956 it is an offence punishable with life imprisonment for a man to have unlawful sexual intercourse with a girl under the age of 13, even if the girl is in fact and in law consenting.

(b) Unlawful sexual intercourse with a girl under the age of 16

25.134   Section 6 of the SOA 1956 provides that it is an offence for a man to have unlawful sexual intercourse with a girl under the age of 16 regardless of whether or not the girl consents. Section 6(3) provides a man under the age of 24 with a 'young man's defence' provided that he has not previously been charged with a 'like offence' and provided that he reasonably believed the girl to be aged 16 or over. 'Like offence' is defined as an offence (or an attempt to commit an offence) under s 6 of the SOA 1956. The burden of proof for this defence is on the accused. The compatibility of the limitation of this defence to men aged under 24 with the ECHR was challenged recently in *R v Kirk*.[271] The Court of Appeal concluded that there was no violation of Article 14, which prohibits discrimination within the ratione materiae of the Convention, because the imposition of an age limit had a legitimate aim and was proportionate.

(6) Acts of Gross Indecency with Children

25.135   Under s 1 of the Indecency with Children Act 1960 it is an offence for a person (either male or female) to commit an act of gross indecency with or towards a child under the age of 16. It is also an offence to incite a child under 16 to a grossly indecent act with himself or another. This offence closes a loophole in indecent assault exposed by *Fairclough v Whipp*,[272] because there is no need to establish an assault or battery.

25.136   The question of gross indecency is one of fact for the jury. Just like the concept of 'indecency', an act will be 'grossly indecent' if right-minded persons would think it so according to accepted contemporary standards of modesty and privacy.

---

[271] [2002] EWCA 1580; [2002] Crim LR 756.
[272] [1951] 2 All ER 834.

The House of Lords recently applied the presumption of mens rea in *B v DPP*[273] **25.137**
to impose an obligation on the prosecution to prove that the defendant did not
have an honest belief that the victim was aged 16 years or above. Lord Nicholls
stated that 'the common law presumes that, unless Parliament indicated otherwise, the appropriate mental element is an unexpressed ingredient of every statutory offence'. The presence or absence of reasonable grounds for the defendant's
belief goes only towards the jury's evaluation of whether such a belief was genuinely held.

(7) Sexual Activity in Breach of a Position of Trust[274]

It is an offence for a person aged 18 years or above to engage in any form of 'sex- **25.138**
ual activity' with a person under 18 years if he is in a 'position of trust' in relation
to that person.[275] It is irrelevant that the victim consents to the sexual activity.

(a) 'Sexual activity'

'Sexual activity' is defined objectively as that which would reasonably be regarded **25.139**
as sexual, without regard to the intentions, motives or feelings of the parties.[276]

(b) 'Position of trust'

The offence seeks to prevent individuals taking advantage of young people who **25.140**
form a relationship of dependence with them. The concept of 'position of trust' is
exhaustively defined by s 4 of the Sexual Offences (Amendment) Act 2000. An individual aged over 18 cannot engage in sexual activity with a child under the age
of 18 who they care for or supervise at an institution where the victim is detained
under a court order or enactment, or at a children's home or accommodation provided by a voluntary organization, or at a hospital, residential care home, community home or voluntary home, or at an educational institution where the
victim receives full-time education.

(c) Defences

It is a defence for the defendant to prove that they did not know nor could rea- **25.141**
sonably be expected to know that[277] the victim was under 18, or that they were in
a position of trust in relation to the victim. The defendant will also have a defence
if he can prove that he was lawfully married to the victim at the time of the alleged

---

[273] [2000] 2 AC 428, HL.
[274] Sexual Offences (Amendment) Act 2000, ss 3 and 4; see further J Burnside, 'The Sexual
Offences (Amendment) Act 2000: the head of a "kiddy-libber" and the torso of a "child-saver"?'
[2001] Crim LR 425.
[275] ibid s 3(1).
[276] ibid s 3(5).
[277] ibid s 3(2)(a)–(b).

sexual activity.[278] Additionally it is not an offence if a sexual relationship and the position of trust both existed between the defendant and victim immediately prior to the commencement of the Sexual Offences (Amendment) Act 2000.[279]

(8) Incest

25.142 Incest is a highly stigmatic offence which attracts a great deal of social, cultural and moral condemnation. A man commits incest if he has sexual intercourse with a woman whom he knows to be his grand-daughter, daughter, sister (including half-sister) or mother.[280] A woman over the age of 16 commits incest if she consents to having sexual intercourse with a man whom she knows to be her grandfather, father, brother (including half-brother) or son.[281] In either case it is immaterial that the relationship between the parties cannot be traced through 'lawful wedlock'.[282]

25.143 Incest cannot be committed by women under the age of 16. The provision was enacted in order to protect girls who are exploited by oppressive relatives. Since the provision was enacted for their protection, it followed that it was not possible at common law for a person to incite a girl under 16 to incest.[283] Parliament reacted to this clear loophole in the law by enacting s 54 of the Criminal Law Act 1977 which creates an offence of inciting a girl under 16 to 'incestuous sexual intercourse'.

(9) The Sexual Offences Act 2003

(a) Introduction

25.144 In recent years the Home Office has been undertaking a review of the sexual offences.[284] This culminated in the Sexual Offences Act 2003 which, at the time of writing, was making its way through Parliament.[285] It is thus appropriate to consider in some detail the substantial changes that this piece of legislation has made to the sexual offences.

---

[278] Sexual Offences (Amendment) Act 2000, s 3(2)(c).

[279] ibid s 3(3).

[280] SOA 1956, s 10.

[281] ibid s 11.

[282] ibid ss 10(2), 11(2).

[283] *R v Whitehouse* [1977] QB 868, applying the exception that arises from the case to that effect, *R v Tyrell* [1894] 1 QB 710.

[284] Home Office Sex Offences Review, *Setting the Boundaries: Reforming the law on sex offences* (2000); see further N Lacey, 'Beset by boundaries: the Home Office review of sex offences' [2001] Crim LR 3. Home Office White Paper, *Protecting the Public: strengthening protection and reforming the law on sexual offences* (Cm 5668, 2002).

[285] The Bill received the Royal Assent on 20 November 2003. It will come into force on days to be appointed: see s 141.

(b) Consent

The victim will be presumed not to have consented in six discrete situations.[286] **25.145**
The prosecution need only prove that the case falls within one of the six categories, and that the defendant knew of these circumstances, before the burden of
proof 'shifts'. The defendant must discharge an evidential burden in respect of the
victim's consent. The drafting of the section appears to place the evidential burden
on the defendant to show on the balance of probabilities that he had an honest belief that the victim was consenting. If, for example, the victim was asleep or unconscious there will be a presumption of lack of consent. Similarly if the victim
was subjected, at the time of the alleged offence, to force or the threat of immediate violence the prosecution will be relieved of the burden of proving the lack of
consent unless the defendant puts the question at issue. The presumption would
also be engaged if the victim had been (but the defendant was not) unlawfully detained at the time of the alleged offence. Finally the section would apply if the victim suffered from a physical disability which would prevent him or her from
communicating lack of consent to the defendant at the time of the relevant act.

In addition to these rebuttable presumptions, there is provision for absence of **25.146**
consent to be conclusively presumed in two situations; namely, where the defendant intentionally deceived the complainant as to the nature and purpose of the
act[287] or where the defendant intentionally induced the complainant to consent
through impersonation.[288]

(c) Rape

Under the Sexual Offences Act only male defendants can be charged with rape. **25.147**
The Home Office concluded that the definition of rape as 'non-consensual sexual
intercourse by a man' was so deeply embedded in the public consciousness that it
would be unfair to extend its application to female defendants. It is not entirely
clear why this should be the case. The public currently associate rape with male defendants because that represents the present state of the law. There is no reason to
suppose that the public would carry this perception over to female defendants
charged with a new form of rape. Nevertheless the additional offence of 'causing a
person to engage in sexual activity without his or her consent' included in the
Sexual Offences Act[289] does criminalize situations which would fall within a definition of 'female rape'. The maximum sentence for sexual intercourse falling
within this offence is life imprisonment (corresponding with sentence for rape)

---

[286] Sexual Offences Act 2003, s 75(2).
[287] ibid s 76(2)(a).
[288] ibid s 76(2)(b).
[289] ibid s 4. See also the offence of 'assault by penetration'; s 2.

and ten years for other sexual acts. At the same time this offence succeeds in labelling 'female rape' offences more precisely and fairly.

25.148 The legislation extends the definition of rape to include non-consensual penile penetration of the mouth.[290] Additionally any sexual intercourse with a child under the age of 13 will automatically constitute rape irrespective of whether the child understands what is happening and gives informed consent.[291] The Sexual Offences Act removes the capacity of children under 13 to consent to sexual activity. There is no express mens rea term in relation to the victim's age in the Act. It appears that the draftsman's intention was to create an offence of strict liability. This conclusion is supported by a comparison with the proposed offences against children aged between 13 and 15. It nevertheless remains to be seen how the courts will interpret this section in the light of the subjectivist approach previously demonstrated in *B v DPP* and *R v K*.

(d) Indecent assault

25.149 The proposed abolition of indecent assault is to be welcomed. It has been seen that the concept of 'indecency' has proved highly problematic. The new offence of 'assault by penetration' will apply to non-consensual penetration with objects.[292] The proposed offence of 'sexual assault' will be of more general application.[293] An assault will be considered 'sexual' if a reasonable person might consider it so taking into account its nature and circumstances and the motivations of any person in relation to the act.[294]

(e) Sexual offences against children

25.150 Children under the age of 13 will lack capacity to consent to any sexual activity. Sexual intercourse with a child under 13 will automatically be rape. Other sexual activity will be a sexual assault. Section 5 of the SOA 1956 imposed strict liability for the offence of unlawful sexual intercourse in respect of the victim's age. It is presently unclear how far there is to be a mens rea requirement under the new regime.

25.151 The Sexual Offences Act proposes to create a new offence of 'sexual activity with a child'[295] to cover all sexual conduct between a person aged 18 or over and children aged between 13 and 15. This offence appears to replace the offences of unlawful sexual intercourse with a child under 16, acts of gross indecency with a

---

[290] Sexual Offences Act 2003, s 1(1)(a).
[291] ibid s 5.
[292] ibid s 2.
[293] ibid s 3.
[294] ibid s 78.
[295] ibid s 9.

child and indecent assault. In addition there will be related offences of causing and inciting a child to engage in sexual activity and an offence of engaging in sexual activity in the presence of a child.[296] Similar, but lesser, offences will apply when the defendant is aged under 18.[297]

The reforms enacted here also expanded the scope of relationships to which the 'abuse of trust' offence created by s 3 of the Sexual Offences (Amendment) Act 2000 apply.[298] New 'abuse of trust' offences of causing/inciting a child to engage in sexual activity[299] and offences committed if the child is present when the defendant engages in sexual activity[300] are also created by the Act. **25.152**

The present offence of incest is believed to focus on too narrow a range of relationships to protect children against predatory members of the modern family. The scope of the current law of incest is influenced largely by genetic considerations, such as the risk of birth defects in children conceived by close blood relatives. By switching the centre of attention to the risk of exploitation of vulnerable children, the law is extended to a much broader range of relationships. With this in mind the Sexual Offences Act 2003 creates two offences of 'sexual activity with a child family member'[301] and 'inciting a child family member to engage in sexual activity'.[302] A child under the age of 18 will be protected from parents, grandparents, siblings (including half-brothers and half sisters), aunts and uncles and current or previous step-parents and foster parents. Additionally the offences will apply if the defendant lives/lived in the same household as the victim or is/was regularly involved in the care or supervision of the victim and in either case the defendant is the partner of one of the victim's parents, uncles or aunts or the victim's cousin or the parent of the defendant or victim has been the other's step-parent or foster-parent.[303] Finally the 'familial sexual offences' are engaged without any formal relationship if the defendant and victim live in the same household and the defendant is regularly involved in caring for the victim.[304] The legislation also seeks to overturn the decisions of the House of Lords in *R v K* and *B v DPP* concerning the mens rea requirements regarding the age of the child. Whereas the House would allow a defendant who held an honest yet unreasonable belief that the victim was aged over 16 to escape conviction for indecent assault or acts of gross indecency, under the new measures only reasonable mistakes would entitle the defendant to an acquittal. **25.153**

---

[296] ibid ss 10–13.
[297] ibid s 13.
[298] ibid s 21.
[299] ibid s 17.
[300] ibid ss 18–19.
[301] ibid s 25.
[302] ibid s 26. See also ss 65 and 66—sex with an adult-relative.
[303] ibid s 27(2).
[304] ibid s 27(4).

26

OFFENCES AGAINST PROPERTY

26.01
Although it is customary to speak of the 'offences against property',[1] the term in truth refers to the protection of human beings (and other legal persons) in respect of their property; the protection of proprietary rights through the criminal law. A layman might suppose that this involves a relationship between persons and things; but things cannot have rights and duties, and the concept of property denotes a highly complex set of relationships between people.

26.02
'The great and *Chief end* therefore, of Mens uniting into Commonwealths, and putting themselves under Government, *is the preservation of their property*.' These words, uttered by philosopher John Locke in the 18th century,[2] were written at a time when the institution of property was under threat. They were echoed by Lord Camden CJ in the landmark case of *Entick v Carrington*,[3] which emphasized that property should be secure even as against agencies of the state itself. Historically, the protection of property through the criminal law, has evolved through the law of larceny. As that offence was less and less

---

[1] Specialist monographs include ATH Smith, *Property Offences* (London: Sweet & Maxwell, 1994); JC Smith, *The Law of Theft* (8th edn, London: Butterworths, 1997), though both are somewhat dated, and should be supplemented by reference to AJ Ashworth, *Principles of Criminal Law* (4th edn, Oxford: OUP, 2003) and AP Simester and GR Sullivan, *Criminal Law: Theory and Doctrine* (2nd edn, Oxford: Hart, 2003).

[2] *Two Treatises of Government*, Second Treatise (P Laslett (ed), Cambridge: CUP, 1960) s 124.

[3] (1765) 19 St Tr 1029.

able to offer protection to proprietary interests, it was supplemented by the judges[4] and increasingly by Parliament.

26.03 The Larceny Acts of 1861 and 1916 were essentially legislative consolidations of the pre-existing law. It was not until the Theft Act 1968 that a major conceptual shift forward was taken, when the protection of property was explicitly shifted from possessory rights to proprietary rights. That Act effected major changes, but it has not itself been without difficulties of interpretation since enacted, especially as to the meaning of 'appropriation'. Financial transactions, particularly those effected by electronic means, have also caused particular difficulties, and the Act has been amended on a number of occasions subsequently. The 1968 Act and its progeny do not even now contain all of the offences against property, the Criminal Damage Act 1971 and the Forgery and Counterfeiting Act 1981 being two obvious additional measures. And even now, the common law rears its head, with the offences of bribery,[5] conspiracy to defraud[6] and cheating the Revenue[7] being hangovers from the past.

A. Theft

(a) History

26.04 In origin, the offence of theft (originally called 'larceny') protected a person's possessory interests in property, rather than ownership. As the concepts of ownership and possession became more distinct, the courts and the legislature devised a variety of stratagems for protecting ownership, but without abandoning the fiction that the subject of larceny was possession rather than ownership.

26.05 The history of the law of theft charts the extension of the concept of possession in order to protect ownership. For example, a person was said to be in possession of something even though he was not in its presence (for example, when he was at work), so that he had a protected interest so far as the law of theft was concerned.

26.06 Anomalies in the law caused Lord Goddard CJ to call for reform. In *Moynes v Coopper*,[8] the defendant had received an advance on his pay. The pay clerk did not know this, and put the full amount into an employee's pay packet. The employee discovered this when he arrived home, at which point he decided to spend the money. To Lord Goddard's considerable indignation, this could not be held to be

---

[4] Although not always enthusiastically, as in the case of persons who had been defrauded by false pretences. The initial response was Lord Holt CJ in *R v Jones* (1704) 1 Salk 379. 'Shall we indict one man for making a fool of another? . . . Let him bring his action.'

[5] See para 26.121 below.

[6] See para 26.124 below.

[7] See para 26.128 below.

[8] [1956] 1 QB 439.

larceny, because the defendant had acquired possession innocently, and he recommended that the law be amended. The matter was referred to the Criminal Law Revision Committee in 1959, which produced a report[9] on which most of the Act is based.

The protection of possession rather than ownership gave rise to anomalies. A person who came by property innocently (ie, without intending to steal it) could not be guilty of theft, because he did not interfere with the owner's right to possession. Thus, where a person took a bicycle when drunk, he did not commit theft when he sobered up and merely failed to return it.[10]

26.07

The position of the employee caused particular difficulties. If the employee was already in possession, he could not steal from the employer—so it was held that the employee was not in possession at all. He was said to have mere 'custody', and if having been entrusted with custody of his employer's property, he decided to keep it (or dispose of it) as his own, he could be convicted of larceny. But this caused a further complication where somebody took from the employee; since the employee had custody only, his possessory rights could not logically be the subject of theft or robbery. Yet the courts held that they could be. So for the purposes of convicting the servant, he was not in possession, but for the purposes of convicting a stranger, he was.

26.08

Ideally, of course, it should have been possible to charge the thief with stealing from the employer, because it was his ownership that the law of theft ought to have been protecting; but larceny protected possession and not ownership.

26.09

Eventually, the law could stretch no further, and it became necessary for Parliament to enact the Theft Act 1968,[11] which (as modified by the Theft Act 1978) now contains the principal offences designed to protect property interests.

26.10

(b) The Theft Act 1968

The Theft Act 1968 was explicitly based upon the need to protect ownership directly, rather than as historically, at second hand.

26.11

Section 1(1) of the Theft Act 1968 provides:

26.12

> A person is guilty of theft if he dishonestly appropriates property belonging to another with intent to deprive the other permanently of it.

It is proposed to deal first with the actus reus of the offence, appropriating property belonging to another, before turning to the mental elements, dishonesty and the intent permanently to deprive. The offence was originally punishable with

---

[9] Eighth Report, *Theft and Related Offences* (Cmnd 2977, 1966).
[10] *R v Kindon* (1957) 41 Cr App R 208.
[11] Following the report of the Criminal Law Revision Committee (n 9 above).

imprisonment for ten years but this was reduced to seven years some years later.[12]

(c) The controversial case of *R v Hinks*

26.13 Not long after the Act was passed, a case occurred in which the question whether a person might be guilty of theft notwithstanding that the transaction in the course of which the theft was alleged to have occurred was a valid one. The case was *Lawrence v Metropolitan Police Commissioner*,[13] where a taxi driver took from a recently-arrived foreign student a sum of money far in excess of the prescribed taxi fare. Notwithstanding that the student was almost certainly the victim of deception, it was held that the taxi driver was guilty of theft, as charged, a decision affirmed by the House of Lords.

26.14 The precise ambit of the decision was always controversial,[14] since it was not clear whether or not the transaction impugned was a valid or voidable one. The same question, in one guise or another, has been considered by the House of Lords[15] on no fewer than three subsequent occasions,[16] most recently in *R v Hinks*.[17] The defendant was a woman who persuaded a somewhat simple-minded man to make gifts to her of considerable sums of money. The House of Lords took the view that it was irrelevant that the transaction in question might have been a perfectly valid one, and upheld the conviction of theft. This means that the actus reus of theft is potentially enormously wide.[18] A person might, apparently, be committing theft by the very act of becoming the owner of the disputed property. This sets the criminal law and the civil speaking with two distinct voices, which is an unsatisfactory state of affairs.

26.25 The questions posed on appeal to the House of Lords were:

> When theft is alleged and that which is alleged to be stolen passes to the defendant with the consent of the owner, but that consent has been obtained by a false representation, has (a) an appropriation within the meaning of section 1(1) of the Theft Act 1968 taken place, or (b) must such a passing of property necessarily involve an

---

[12] By Criminal Justice Act 1991, s 26. The offence is triable either way.

[13] [1972] AC 626.

[14] See G Williams, 'Theft, Consent and Illegality: Some Problems' [1977] Crim LR 127, 205, 327; see also S Gardner, 'Property and Theft' [1998] Crim LR 35 and the reply by Sir JC Smith [1998] Crim LR 80.

[15] The same issue has troubled the Court of Appeal, apart from those cases that went to the House: in the Civil Division, *Dobson v General Accident Fire and Life Assurance* [1990] QB 274, and in the Criminal Division, *R v Gallasso* [1993] Crim LR 459; *R v Mazo* [1997] 2 Cr App R 518; *R v Hopkins and Kendrick* [1997] 2 Cr App R 524.

[16] *R v Morris* [1984] AC 320; *R v Gomez* [1993] AC 442 in addition to *R v Hinks* [2001] AC 241.

[17] [2001] 2 AC 241.

[18] For the objections of principle, see ATH Smith, 'Gifts and the law of theft' (1999) 58 CLJ 10; J Beatson and AP Simester, 'Stealing one's own property' (1999) 115 LQR 372; Sir John Smith [1993] Crim LR 304, [1998] Crim LR 904, [2001] Crim LR 162.

element of adverse interference with or some usurpation of some right of the owner.

The questions were answered, in effect, (a) yes and (b) no. That is to say, a person might now be guilty of theft notwithstanding that she becomes the owner of the property alleged to be the subject matter of the theft. The answer to the second question means that, in effect, a person might now be guilty of theft even though, apart from the state of mind by which it is accompanied, a person can be guilty of theft by doing an otherwise lawful act. A person buys a painting offered for sale at a very low price. The buyer knows that the painting is by an important artist and is worth a good deal more than is being asked for it. If a jury were prepared to call such conduct dishonest, this would be theft.

(d) The overlap between theft and deception[19]

The 1968 Act was premised upon a decision that the offences of theft and deception should both be retained. There may well have been an overlap between the two. But there was also an important distinction to be drawn. If no ownership passed in the course of the transaction alleged to constitute the theft (as will usually be the case), there was to be no great difficulty, and the miscreant could be convicted of either theft or deception, whichever was the more appropriate. But if ownership actually passed, then unless there had been a deception there was to be no offence at all, according to the framers of the Act. All of this may well have become water under the bridge because of the decisions on the matter in the House of Lords in *Hinks* and the earlier cases, since the House of Lords has held that not only does it not matter whether or not ownership has passed, but that there can be liability even if ownership has passed validly, so long as a jury is prepared to account the defendant dishonest. In the course of his judgment in *R v Gomez*, Lord Lowry through the medium of the Criminal Law Revision Committee's report, showed how the framers of the Act had intended that it should work in this respect.

26.16

(e) What can be stolen?

Whereas the law of larceny was concerned only with tangible things, the subject matter of theft is 'property' which is a much broader notion. Section 4(1) provides that:

26.17

> 'Property' includes money and all other property, real or personal, including things in action and other intangible property.

Property itself is not, however, further defined; what constitutes property is a matter for the civil law. More or less any physical thing is capable of being property, but an exception is the human body. The body is not capable of being owned

26.18

---

[19] See Russell Heaton, 'Deceiving without Thieving?' [2001] Crim LR 712.

when alive, and the logic of this was historically followed into the dead body.[20] But the body may become property by the application of skill such as dissection and preservation techniques for teaching and exhibition purposes, as in *R v Kelly*[21] where a sculptor persuaded a technician to take anatomical specimens from the Royal College of Surgeons. Their convictions were upheld by the Court of Appeal.

26.19 It has been held that export quotas are capable of being stolen, principally because they were capable of being bought and sold.[22] But electricity can be bought and sold, and it does not count as property.[23]

26.20 Particular difficulties have been experienced with the protection that should be afforded to intangible property—so-called 'things in action',[24] a conception that includes the position of the parties inter se in the use of bank accounts. Where a bank account is in credit, the bank is a debtor of the customer, and the position is reversed when the account is in debit. The debt can then be stolen by the fraudulent manipulation of the account, but only as against the party in whose favour it is in credit.[25] For example, in *R v Williams*,[26] it was confirmed that a person who had received payment by cheque could be convicted of stealing the thing in action in the account of the drawer by paying in the cheque and causing the debt owed to the drawer by the bank to be extinguished to the extent of the amount for which the cheque was drawn.

26.21 Special provision is made for land, which is in general incapable of being stolen, unless by a person not in possession of the land who can be guilty of stealing it by severing anything forming part of the land.[27] Special provision is also made for wild mushrooms and fruit or foliage from a plant growing wild, which are not stealable unless picked for reward, sale or other commercial purpose.[28] Wild animals are regarded as property but cannot be stolen unless tamed or ordinarily kept in captivity (or the carcass of any such creature). Where such a creature has been reduced into possession by or on behalf of another and possession has not been lost or abandoned, or another person is in the course of reducing it into possession, then it can be stolen.[29]

---

[20] See ATH Smith, 'Stealing the Human Body and its Parts' [1976] Crim LR 622.
[21] [1999] QB 621.
[22] *A-G for Hong Kong v Nai-Keung* [1987] 1 WLR 1339.
[23] Which explains the existence of s 13 of the Theft Act 1968, which penalizes the dishonest abstraction of electricity as an offence in its own right.
[24] In *R v Hallam* [1995] Crim LR 323, the Court of Appeal expressed some vexation that it should have to be untangling the difficulties of 'choses in action', but that is not a term used in the Act.
[25] *R v Kohn* (1979) 69 Cr App R 395.
[26] [2001] 1 Cr App R 23.
[27] Theft Act 1968, s 4(2).
[28] ibid s 4(3).
[29] ibid s 4(4).

(f) The act of stealing: appropriation

Most thefts are, no doubt, committed by taking tangible things, but the concept of appropriation goes far wider than that. **26.22**

Section 3(1) provides that: **26.23**

> Any assumption by a person of the rights of an owner amounts to an appropriation, and this includes, where he has come by the property (innocently or not) without stealing it, any later assumption of a right to it by keeping or dealing with it as owner.

(i) Theft by keeping

It is clear that a person who comes innocently into possession of property can be convicted of stealing it. Given that this area was one of the difficulties that prompted reform of the law of larceny, there has been surprisingly little authority on the circumstances in which the possessor might be guilty of theft. A question arises as to whether any keeping can amount to theft, or whether, in the words of the Act, the person who appropriates must do something that indicates his intention to keep the property 'as owner'. There is no real authority on the point, which could have been considered (but was not) in *Broom v Crowther*,[30] where a young man bought a theodolite from a friend, and was later told by the friend that it was stolen. He then placed it under his bed, and had not decided what to do about it at the time when he was apprehended. It was decided that there had been no appropriation in those circumstances; although the court does not explicitly say so, there had been no decision to keep the property 'as owner' in those circumstances (as opposed to a rather unlucky purchaser who was going to have to make good the loss). If it were otherwise, the offence would become one of theft by omission and there is a risk that mere inactivity, pardonable inertia, might be treated as theft. **26.24**

Section 3(2) would have avoided the difficulties in *Broom v Crowther* itself since it makes provision for the non-liability of a person who purchases in good faith.[31] No later assumption of 'rights which he believed himself to be acquiring shall, by reason of any defect in the transferor's title, amount to theft of the property'. **26.25**

(ii) Appropriation by the non-possessor

The most common form of theft is undoubtedly the non-consensual taking of one person's property by another. But appropriation is plainly much wider than the taking and carrying away which was at the heart of the law of larceny. It can be committed by destroying property, by giving it away or selling it or even, it would **26.26**

---

[30] (1984) 148 JP 592.
[31] *R v Wheeler* (1991) 92 Cr App R 279.

appear, by offering it for sale.[32] In each of these cases, the person appropriating does something that only the owner or a person deriving authority from the owner, has a right to do, and a right to prevent others from doing.

(g) Belonging to another

(i) The standard rule

26.27   Whereas for the law of larceny, the protected interest was essentially possessory, the new law of theft sought to protect a very wide range of proprietary interests. This is reflected in the language of the Act, s 5(1) of which provides:

> (1) Property shall be regarded as belonging to any person having possession or control of it, or having in it any proprietary right or interest (not being an equitable interest arising only from an agreement to transfer or grant an interest).

26.28   It might be supposed that, where property has been abandoned, it would be free for any third party to appropriate at will. That is not so, however, since the ownership of abandoned property, both as a matter of the civil law, and for the purposes of the law of theft, may be transferred in somewhat unexpected ways. A good example is afforded by *R v Woodman*,[33] where the alleged stolen property consisted of scrap metal left in a factory by the previous owners of the factory who had taken as much of the metal as they wanted to remove. There was a fence around the property, and it was held that this was sufficient to give an interest in the metal to the purchasers of the factory, an interest that existed even though the new owners might be unaware of the property alleged to have been stolen.

26.29   It is clear that a person may even be guilty of stealing his own property in appropriate circumstances. Where property is held in partnership with another, for example, it would be theft for one of the partners to deal with the property in such a way as to defeat the interests of the other partner.[34] It may be in the hands of another in circumstances where that other has a better right to possess it than does the true owner. The Court of Appeal in *R v Turner (No 2)*,[35] an early decision under the Act, went even further, saying that there was no reason why the plain language of the Act should be qualified in any way. But in that case, the person in possession of the property, a car upon which he had done some repair work at the request of the owner, had a repairer's lien. The difficulty with which the Court of Appeal was faced was that the trial judge had advised the jury that they could safely ignore the lien. But in the absence of the lien, the owner had a

---

[32] *R v Pitham and Hehl* (1976) 65 Cr App R 45. The case for saying that this should not, without more, be accounted theft is that it does not affect the legal status of the property at all—it is a matter of mere words.

[33] [1974] QB 754.

[34] *R v Bonner* [1970] 1 WLR 838.

[35] [1971] 1 WLR 901.

better right to the car, as a matter of law. Although the decision has never been expressly disavowed, it appears to have been overlooked in *R v Meredith*,[36] in which it was held that a man did not commit theft by taking his car from the police yard where it had been impounded, the police having had no right to impound the car as they did. The decision seems to accord altogether better with the underlying principle that a person should not be guilty of theft when he does no more than the civil law gives him a perfect right to do.

(ii) Property received from or on account of another: s 5(3)

A situation that has historically caused difficulties is that in which one person has **26.30** been entrusted with the care of another's property, often acting as an agent or trustee or having a power of attorney. In such situations, the person entrusted with the property may be no more than a bailee or have only a limited financial interest in the property in question. This should cause no difficulty for the law of theft, since the person who acts in a way that shows that he has appropriated the proprietary interest belonging to another is plainly guilty of theft for that reason. But the property may have been transferred in circumstances of trust such that ownership has passed and, in such circumstances it is difficult to see how the ordinary law of theft might bite. To deal with this sort of situation, s 5(3) provides that:

> Where a person receives property from or on account of another, and is under an obligation to the other to retain and deal with that property or its proceeds in a particular way, the property or proceeds shall be regarded (as against him) as belonging to the other.

The operation of the section is illustrated by the decision of the Court of Appeal **26.31** in *R v Hall*.[37] A travel agent was prosecuted because, having taken the money from prospective travellers, he was unable either to fulfil his contractual obligations or to refund the money. His defence was that he was no more than an unlucky businessman in charge of a failed venture. When he had taken the money, he had had every intention of providing the travel as required. But when the business had collapsed through circumstances beyond his control, he could not be made liable. The Court agreed; there was no evidence that the customers expected him to retain and/or deal with the property in a particular way, and no evidence that Hall had undertaken to do so, and the conviction was quashed.

The obligation must be a legal one. Although initially the courts gave this sec- **26.32** tion a rather wide interpretation, reading the word 'obligation' in the section as extending to moral obligations,[38] it was eventually settled that the obligation referred to in the Act must be a legal one.[39] This must be right, since the alternative

---

[36] [1973] Crim LR 253.
[37] [1973] QB 126.
[38] *R v Meech* [1974] QB 549.
[39] *R v Huskinson* [1988] Crim LR 620.

would be that the civil law and the criminal law might be found to be speaking with different voices. A person might be held to be under an obligation because he believed himself to be so bound, or because a court (or worse, a jury) thought that he ought to be. But even though the principle is clear, its application can be a matter of some difficulty, since it is the civil law that must be applied in these situations. A comparison might be made between *R v Brewster*,[40] where insurance premiums were collected but then dissipated by an agent, and it was held that there was an obligation to keep the moneys separate because his contract with the insurance company required him to do so, and *R v Robertson*,[41] where it was held that the agent was no more than a debtor of the insurance company on whose behalf he had collected the premiums. Charity collections have proved to be another fruitful source of confusion. In *Lewis v Lethbridge*,[42] for example, a man collected money from people who had sponsored his run, but he did not then hand it over to the charity as expected. His conviction was quashed by a Divisional Court which agreed that, whatever he had done, the runner had not appropriated a debt as between himself and the charity, since there were no rules requiring him to hand the money over to the charity. But had the case been properly presented, it is suggested, he could have been convicted on the footing that it was the intention of the sponsor that the money should go to the charity, and that would have been sufficient to impress the money with an obligation on the runner in a particular way, sufficient to attract the operation of s 5(3).

26.33 This line of reasoning appealed to the Court of Appeal in *R v Wain*,[43] which upheld the conviction of a person in possession of money that had been subscribed by sponsors and which he then used for his own purposes. Where the trustees of a charity themselves appropriated the money, by contrast, and the property in the money had been laid as belonging to 'persons unknown', it was held that the convictions must be quashed, since the money must have belonged to the charity.[44] It may be wondered whether the outcome is correct, since by s 5(2) of the Act, money belonging to a trust is to be treated as belonging to the person entitled to enforce the trust, which, in the case of a charitable trust is the Attorney-General. So the prosecutor's fear that he was unable to charge the trustees with theft from the trust was imaginary. The conviction was quashed nevertheless, since that is not the way in which the case had been put to the jury.

26.34 **Profits and bribes.**[45] A person who receives a bribe does not receive it 'on account of 'another, and the language of the section is therefore unable to convert his

---

[40] (1979) 69 Cr App R 375.
[41] [1977] Crim LR 629.
[42] [1987] Crim LR 59.
[43] [1995] 2 Cr App R 660.
[44] *R v Dyke and Munro* [2001] EWCA Crim 2184; [2002] Crim LR 153.
[45] See ATH Smith, 'Constructive Trusts in the Law of Theft' [1977] Crim LR 395.

corrupt act into theft. This was the situation before the Theft Act,[46] and the 1968 legislation was not intended to change the law. The courts were persuaded to plug the gap in part by holding that where an employee makes a secret profit by the use of his employers' goods, he is guilty of the offence of going equipped to cheat.[47] How far the civil law has developed since the enactment of the Theft Act is a matter of some uncertainty, but it would seem that in certain circumstances there is a proprietary interest in the property that is the subject of the bribe, in favour of the person whose trust has been abused.[48] If that is so, the later appropriation of that interest would be theft, even though that may not be what Parliament had intended. But that would have been as a result of a change in the civil law, and the development is unobjectionable; the criminal law would have changed to reflect the change in the civil law, and not the other way round.

(iii) Property got by mistake: s 5(4)

Getting property (and in particular money) by another's mistake caused particular difficulties at common law.[49] It will be recalled that it was the mistake on the part of the employer in *Moynes v Coopper*[50] that excited Lord Goddard's indignation and caused the law of theft to be referred to the reformers.   **26.35**

Section 5(4) of the Theft Act 1968 provides: **26.36**

> Where a person gets property by another's mistake, and is under an obligation to make restoration (in whole or in part) of the property or its proceeds or of the value thereof, then to the extent of that obligation the property or proceeds shall be regarded (as against him) as belonging to the person entitled to restoration, and an intention not to make restoration shall be regarded accordingly as an intention to deprive that person of the property or proceeds.

At first the section was believed to be a deeming provision. That is, it was thought   **26.37** that it provided that, whatever the position might be as a matter of the civil law, where a person received property by the mistake of another, that property would be deemed to belong to the person who was entitled to the restoration. In *Chase Manhattan Bank NA v Israel British Bank*,[51] however, it was held that as a matter of civil law, where a person receives money from another as a result of a mistake, there remains in the transferor an equitable proprietary interest in the money. Since equitable interests (other than those arising solely from an agreement to

---

[46] *R v Cullum* (1873) LR 2 CCR 28.
[47] *R v Rashid* [1977] 1 WLR 298; *R v Doukas* [1978] 1 WLR 372.
[48] *A-G for Hong Kong v Reid* [1994] 1 AC 324. For a discussion of the implications of the decision for the law of theft, see JC Smith, '*Lister v Stubbs* and the Criminal Law' (1994) 110 LQR 180.
[49] The cases of *R v Ashwell* (1885) 16 QBD 190 and *R v Middleton* (1873) LR 2 CCR 38 puzzled generations of students—in both cases, a coin passed to the recipient, a mistake having been made as to the denomination of the coin in question.
[50] [1956] 1 QB 439; see para 26.06 above.
[51] [1981] Ch 105.

transfer an interest) are protected by the Act it seems clear that there can be a conviction of theft even without the assistance of s 5(4). In *R v Shadrokh-Cigari*,[52] therefore, a man was convicted when he withdrew from his nephew's bank account (he being the guardian of the nephew) large parts of the sum of $286,000 that had been mistakenly credited to the account, on the basis that the crediting bank retained an interest in the amount mistakenly credited.

26.38 As with the preceding section, it may be supposed that the 'obligation' referred to in the section is a legal one. This was stated to be the law in *R v Gilks*,[53] although the actual decision of the Court of Appeal may appear to have been to the opposite effect. A punter had made a bet on a horse that was unplaced, but was paid as though the horse had won. His own view that the bookmaker's mistake was the latter's 'hard luck' which, as a matter of the civil law, it would have been, since the bookmaker could not claim to recover his loss, because he would have to plead the Gaming Acts. But the Court said that he was under an obligation notwithstanding this. That case was, however, decided without reliance upon s 5(4), so the point may be regarded as being strictly without binding authority.

(h) The mental element in theft

26.39 To be guilty of theft, the perpetrator must be shown to have acted dishonestly, and with the intention of permanently depriving the other of the goods. Each element can be considered separately. It may also be noted that the offence may be committed even without a view to gain. This represented the law of larceny, but to make the point that the law was not changed, the legislation makes the point explicit (s 1(2)).

(i) Dishonesty [54]

26.40 The concept of 'dishonesty' underlies many of the offences against property. It is not given a general definition by the statute, although the section identifies a certain number of situations where conduct is said to be not dishonest, at least for the purposes of the law of theft.

(i) Dishonesty under the statute

26.41 Section 2 of the Theft Act provides:

(1) A person's appropriation of property belonging to another is not to be regarded as dishonest—

(a) if he appropriates the property in the belief that he has in law the right to deprive the other of it, on behalf of himself or of a third person: or

(b) if he appropriates the property in the belief that he would have the other's consent if the other knew of the appropriation and the circumstances of it; or

---

[52] [1988] Crim LR 465.
[53] [1972] 1 WLR 1341.
[54] A Halpin, 'The Test for Dishonesty' [1996] Crim LR 283.

    (c) (except where the property came to him as trustee or personal representative) if he appropriates the property in the belief that the person to whom the property belongs cannot be discovered by taking reasonable steps.

 (2) A person's appropriation of property belonging to another may be dishonest notwithstanding that he is willing to pay for the property.

(ii) Liability subjective

The test established by s 2(1)(a) is a highly subjective one. The belief need not be   **26.42** a reasonable one, and it would be a misdirection to tell the jury that reasonableness of belief is required.[55] The highly subjective nature of the test is illustrated by *R v Robinson*,[56] where it was held that a man was not guilty of theft where he took property at knife point on the basis that at the time when he acted, he believed that he had a legal right to the property in question. It did not matter that he knew that he was not entitled to repossess his property in the manner chosen.

Paragraphs (b) and (c) are equally subjective in their orientation. The question is   **26.43** not, in either case, whether the belief held by the defendant was a reasonable one, but whether or not it was an actual one, that the owner would consent (in the case of para (b))[57] or that it would not be possible to find the owner by taking reasonable steps—the question of reasonableness refers to the steps to be taken and not to the belief of the defendant.

(iii) Willingness to pay

The mere fact that a person who appropriates is prepared to pay for what he   **26.44** takes does not necessarily prevent the conduct from being dishonest. The point may be obvious, but it is stated in the Act (s 2(2)) just in case it may be overlooked. The provision may interact with the more general proposition, however, that a person who is prepared to pay may well think that the owner would not object to the appropriation. A person who 'buys' a newspaper and leaves the money on the counter in a busy shop is not dishonest, not just because of his willingness to pay, but because his conduct will ordinarily come within the terms of s 2(1)(b).

(j) Dishonesty apart from the section

Whereas larceny was committed 'fraudulently', the framers of the Theft Act   **26.45** chose the word 'dishonestly'. The reasons given for this were that '[t]he question "was this dishonest?" is easier for a jury to answer than the question "Was this fraudulent?" "Dishonesty" is something which laymen can easily recognise

---

[55] *R v Holden* [1991] Crim LR 478.
[56] [1977] Crim LR 173.
[57] *R v Kell* [1985] Crim LR 239.

when they see it, whereas "fraud" may seem to involve technicalities which have to be explained by a lawyer.'[58] Fraud might also have certain fixed legal meanings. Thus, taking another's money, even with the intention of returning it, was to be regarded as theft.[59] Yet the precise function of the concept of dishonesty in this context was unclear and to a certain degree contested.[60] It is quite possible that it was used by the framers of the Act in a defeasible way— that (apart from s 2), where a person appropriated another's property with the intention of permanently depriving the other of it, the conduct was to be regarded as dishonest unless the actor was able to point to an aspect of the conduct that may afford an innocent explanation for the behaviour. The Court of Appeal in *R v Feely*[61] took a different line, saying that no person should be convicted of theft on account of an act to which no moral obloquy attaches. A person to whom money was owed and who took money leaving an indication of what he had done (an IOU) was not necessarily (subject to the decision of a jury) to be automatically guilty of theft, even though he knew that his employers would object to what he was doing.

26.46 The leading decision now as to the meaning of dishonesty is to be found in *R v Ghosh*,[62] where Lord Lane CJ stated the law in the following terms:

> In determining whether the prosecution has proved that the defendant was acting dishonestly, a jury must first of all decide whether, according to the ordinary standards of reasonable and honest people what was done was dishonest. If it was not dishonest by those standards, that is the end of the matter and the prosecution fails.
>
> If it was dishonest by those standards, then the jury must consider whether the defendant himself must have realised that what he was doing was by those standards dishonest.
>
> In most cases, where the actions are obviously dishonest by ordinary standards, there will be no doubt about it. It will be obvious that the defendant himself knew that he was acting dishonestly. It is dishonest for a defendant to act in a way which he knows ordinary people consider to be dishonest, even if he asserts or genuinely believes that he is morally justified in acting as he did. For example, Robin Hood or those ardent anti-vivisectionists who remove animals from vivisection laboratories are acting dishonestly, even though they may consider themselves to be morally justified in doing what they do, because they know that ordinary people would consider these actions to be dishonest.

---

[58] Eighth Report (n 9 above) para 39.

[59] As in the case of the fraudulent sub-postmistress, *R v Williams* [1953] 1 QB 660.

[60] See K Campbell, 'The Test of Dishonesty in *Ghosh*' [1984] 43 CLJ 349; E Griew, 'Dishonesty —the Objections to Feely and Ghosh' [1985] Crim LR 341; DW Elliott, 'Dishonesty in Theft: A Dispensable Concept' [1982] Crim LR 341.

[61] [1973] QB 530. The decision was not followed in the Australian state of Victoria, which has legislation very similar to the Theft Act 1968. See *R v Salvo* [1982] VR 401, 423 where Murphy J voiced objections as follows: 'I cannot believe that conviction of a crime carrying a sentence of 10 years' imprisonment may be dependent upon an answer dictated by the uninstructed intuitive reaction of a jury to what more and more judges are finding to be a quite difficult question'.

[62] [1982] QB 1053.

(i) When is a Ghosh direction called for?

It will be observed that the statement of the law is heavily directed towards what the **26.47** judge should say when he directs the jury. But a question arises as to whether the judge should give a *Ghosh* direction in every case where dishonesty is in issue. It is plain that the answer is that he need not. In *R v Price*,[63] the defendant, who had passed a series of cheques which were returned by the bank unpaid, claimed that he believed that he was about to be the beneficiary of a large trust fund. The trial judge declined to direct in *Ghosh* terms, taking the view that if the defendant's story were (or might have been) true, he would be entitled to an acquittal, and that a direction in *Ghosh* terms would be unnecessary and potentially misleading.[64] The law would seem to be that a direction in *Ghosh* terms should be given where it can plausibly be said that honest and ordinary people might think that whatever the defendant was doing was not dishonest. Since there is room for doubt as to what ordinary people might think dishonest or otherwise, it might be argued that the benefit of any such doubt should be given to the defendant.

Where a judge does decide that it is necessary to give a *Ghosh* direction, it is better **26.48** to use the language employed by Lord Lane rather than seek to put the effect of the decision into language of his own.[65]

(ii) The significance of the defendant's own belief

In a prosecution concerning the dishonest abstraction of electricity, *Boggeln v* **26.49** *Williams*,[66] the Court of Appeal took the view that the defendant's own belief as to whether or not his conduct was dishonest was not only relevant to liability, but 'crucial' thereto, and the conviction was quashed. It may be thought that this is to take a very subjective view, and later in *R v Landy*,[67] Lawton LJ said:

> . . . an assertion by a defendant that throughout a transaction he acted honestly does not have to be accepted but has to be weighed like any other piece of evidence. If that was the defendant's state of mind, or may have been, he is entitled to be acquitted.

It is suggested that this is, with respect, the better view. Were it otherwise, a person whose standards were warped would be able to assert his innocence of theft. One of the functions of the concept of dishonesty is to maintain certain standards of respect for the property rights of others.

---

[63] (1989) 90 Cr App R 409.
[64] In *R v O'Connell* [1991] Crim LR 771, it was held that a failure to give the *Ghosh* direction might not be fatal to a conviction even where, technically, the defendant should have been given the benefit of such an instruction.
[65] See *R v Hyam* [1997] Crim LR 439; *R v Green* [1992] Crim LR 292.
[66] [1978] 1 WLR 873.
[67] [1981] 1 WLR 355.

(k) The intention permanently to deprive

26.50   The question whether, in addition to dishonesty, the law of theft ought to contain a further requirement as to mens rea is controversial. Glanville Williams took the view that nothing further was required.[68] Parliament disagreed, but it watered down[69] the requirement by enacting s 6 of the Act which, it has been pithily observed, 'sprouts obscurity at every phrase'.[70] It would be unprofitable in the course of an exercise such as this to explore those obscurities. Suffice to say that the purpose of the section was to provide for those situations where the defendant is able to assert that he lacked the intention to deprive. A person might be guilty of theft even though he intended the owner to have the thing itself back, as where, for example, a shop-lifter takes a thing back to the shop and asks for a refund. In those circumstances, he is said to have stolen the thing itself.[71]

26.51   Section 6 of the Theft Act 1968 provides:

> (1) A person appropriating property belonging to another without meaning the other permanently to lose the thing itself is nevertheless to be regarded as having the intention of permanently depriving the other of it if his intention is to treat the thing as his own to dispose of regardless of the other's rights; and a borrowing or lending of it may amount to so treating it if, but only if, the borrowing or lending is for a period and in circumstances making it equivalent to an outright taking or disposal.
>
> (2) Without prejudice to the generality of subsection (1) above, where a person, having possession or control (lawfully or not) of property belonging to another, parts with the property under a condition as to its return which he may not be able to perform, this (if done for purposes of his own and without the other's authority) amounts to treating the property as his own to dispose of regardless of the other's rights.

(i) Conditional intent

26.52   In *R v Easom*,[72] the Court of Appeal somewhat incautiously remarked that what may loosely described as a 'conditional appropriation' will not do. The appellant had been charged with stealing the itemized contents of a woman's handbag that he had picked up and rummaged through in a darkened cinema. The bag belonged to a plain-clothed policewoman. Since the appellant did not want to take any of the itemized objects, according to the Court, the appeal had to be allowed. The decision overlooks the point that all intention, since it necessarily relates to the future, is the subject of many more and less articulated conditions. The truth

---

[68] 'Temporary Appropriation Should be Theft' [1981] Crim LR 129.

[69] The Court in *R v Warner* (1970) 55 Cr App R 93 took exception to this phraseology, but it is difficult to see what else might be the purpose of the section. In *R v Lloyd* [1985] QB 829, 834B Lord Lane CJ notes that the provision was, and was intended to be, a deeming provision.

[70] JR Spencer, 'The Metamorphosis of Section 6 of the Theft Act' [1977] Crim LR 653.

[71] *R v Scott* [1984] Crim LR 235.

[72] [1971] 2 QB 315. Followed in *R v Hussein* (1978) 67 Cr App R 131.

is that, in the situation in *Easom*, the defendant has decided to steal, and the only question to be resolved (and one largely beyond his control) is whether the receptacle contains anything that is worth keeping. Not without some extraordinary decisions having occurred in the interim,[73] the Court of Appeal eventually accepted this view of the law.[74]

B. Robbery

Robbery is in essence an aggravated form of theft. It is theft accompanied by violence which is used for the purpose of committing the theft. The offence is regarded as being particularly serious, carrying as it does the possibility of life imprisonment.   **26.53**

Section 8 of the Theft Act provides: **26.54**

> (1) A person is guilty of robbery if he steals, and immediately before or at the time of doing so, and in order to do so, he uses force on any person or puts or seeks to put any person in fear of being then and there subjected to force.

Force must be used 'on' the person, but the Court of Appeal has construed this to include the situation where a man approached his victim from behind and grabbed her bag, running off with it. It was held that, notwithstanding that the framers of the Act would not have accounted this robbery, the trial judge did not err in leaving the question of whether or not there was appropriate force to constitute robbery.[75]

Since robbery requires proof of a theft, it requires proof of dishonesty, and s 2 of   **26.55**
the Act applies. This may have the result that a person is not guilty of robbery when he uses force to take property, even though he may well realize that the use of force is not permissible, if he has a genuine belief in his right to deprive the other of the property.[76]

C. Deception

Historically, there has never been a general offence of fraud. Rather, there have   **26.56**
been fraud-like offences (such as obtaining property by false pretences, and obtaining credit by fraud). Conspiracy to defraud[77] is a partial exception to the

---

[73] *R v Greenhof* [1979] Crim LR 108; *R v Walkington* [1979] 1 WLR 1169.
[74] *A-G's Reference (Nos 1 and 2 of 1979)* [1980] QB 180.
[75] *R v Clouden* [1987] Crim LR 56.
[76] *R v Robertson* [1977] Crim LR 629; *R v Forrester* [1992] Crim LR 792.
[77] Discussed further at para 26.124 below.

general proposition, but that offence preserves the anomalous position that it makes criminal when done by two or more people, conduct that would not be criminalized when committed by a single person acting on his or her own.

26.57 When the framers of the Theft Act were deliberating, they came to the conclusion that it was not possible to do without the deception offence, as a supplement to the offences of theft, and as a substitute for the fraud-like offences already mentioned. Developments since the Theft Act came into force have falsified some of the premises of those conclusions. The decisions of the House of Lords in *R v Gomez*[78] and *R v Hinks*[79] have had the effect that virtually all acts constituting the offence of obtaining property by deception are also theft.

26.58 One provision of the 1968 Act[80] caused particular difficulty, since it appeared to criminalize the person who used deception to put off paying debts even when there was an intention to make good the obligation eventually. This was considered to be socially objectionable, being not far short of criminalizing for failure to pay one's debts, and that had been decriminalized by the Victorians.[81]

(a) What is deception? [82]

26.59 To replace the old concept of obtaining by false pretences and obtaining by fraud, the Criminal Law Revision Committee fastened on the concept of deception, a word chosen because it concentrated on the mind of the victim rather than the conduct of the defendant. 'Deception' was familiar, particularly as a civil law notion; in the words of Buckley LJ in *Re London and Globe Finance Corp*:[83] 'to deceive is, I apprehend, to induce a man to *believe* that a thing is true which is false'. That certainly captured the essence of what the framers of the Act had intended, and it was augmented by s 15(4) of the Theft Act 1968 which provides:

> For the purposes of this section 'deception' means any deception (whether deliberate or reckless) by words or conduct as to fact or as to law, including a deception as to the present intentions of the person using the deception or any other person.

26.60 False pretences by conduct was known to the common law. In *R v Barnard*,[84] it was held that a young man who passed himself off as an undergraduate member of an Oxford college was thereby asserting that he was a person of some financial substance (and could afford the lavish clothing that he was ordering). But

---

[78] Discussed at paras 26.13 et seq above.
[79] Discussed at paras 26.13 et seq above.
[80] s 16(1)(a), as interpreted by the House of Lords in *R v Turner* [1974] AC 357.
[81] Debtors Act 1869. See further paras 26.77 et seq below.
[82] ATH Smith, 'The Idea of Criminal Deception' [1982] Crim LR 721.
[83] [1903] 1 Ch 728, 732.
[84] (1837) 7 C & P 784.

concentrating on the mind of the victim has brought its own difficulties. How, for example, can one be said to deceive a company or a machine? One can,[85] and one can't, respectively.[86] And what of the situation where the person to whom the deception is addressed never adverts to the alleged untruth, or is quite simply indifferent to it? This may well be the practical reality in cases where a cheque card or a credit card is used; the person who accepts the cheque card is entitled to ignore the fact that its user may not in fact have the funds to meet the cheques since it is precisely the purpose of the cheque card scheme to protect the person who accepts the cheque in such circumstances. The House of Lords did its best to save the legislation in *R v Charles*[87] and *R v Lambie*,[88] by holding, apparently contrary to the evidence presented in the cases themselves, that the casino manager and shop assistant who had accepted the cards in the respective cases had been deceived. But the reasoning employed in those decisions has not generally been found to be persuasive, and was distinguished in *R v Nabina*,[89] where the card user had employed deception to enable himself to be issued with cards which he subsequently used. The court took the view, correctly it is submitted, that it may be doubted whether a jury could infer that the person accepting the card might concern himself with the details of how the card had been obtained in the first place, and quashed convictions secured on the basis that the judge had allowed such inferences to be drawn.

A difficult question arises as to how far the victim of the offence must consciously advert to the representation addressed to him. In the cases of *R v Rashid*[90] and *R v Doukas*,[91] cases in which British Rail sandwich stewards were convicted of going equipped to cheat when they had sold, using their employers' premises and facilities, their own sandwiches, it was concluded that there could be a deception in such a situation. But the truth would seem to be that the victim does not advert to the question of the ownership at all; he makes an assumption of which the steward (or as in *Doukas* the wine waiter) takes advantage. It is perfectly true that he would in all likelihood have done otherwise had he known the truth, since the food and drink with which he was being presented would not come with the guarantees that the proper supplier would afford. But anybody who has been at the wrong end of a bad bargain might say the same thing, and that is not the same as being deceived.   **26.61**

The courts have held that a person might count as deceived when he or she has paid too much as part of a contract, but only in very limited circumstances, such as where it was clear that the buyer was relying upon the expert knowledge of the   **26.62**

---

85 *R v Rozeik* [1996] 1 WLR 159.
86 *Davies v Flackett* [1973] RTR 8.
87 [1977] AC 177.
88 [1981] AC 449.
89 [2000] Crim LR 481.
90 [1977] 1 WLR 298.
91 [1978] 1 WLR 372.

seller. In *R v Silverman*,[92] for example, the defendant had charged two elderly sisters grossly excessive prices for work done. He was known to the sisters, having previously done work for the family, and it was held that the situation of mutual trust that had been built up over a long time permitted an inference of deception. Nor is it difficult to permit the inference of deception where a fare in excess of the statutorily regulated one is charged.[93]

26.63 For these reasons, it would seem the Law Commission has recommended that the reliance of the Theft Act on the whole concept of deception should be abandoned in favour of more generalized fraud offences.[94]

(b) Mens rea

(i) Dishonesty

26.64 The offences of deception require proof of dishonesty, but technically, s 2 of the Act does not apply to them.[95] A person who tells lies in order to secure some sort of advantage over another will usually be accounted dishonest. But if an explanation is offered that might lead a jury to conclude that the conduct may have been without dishonesty, a *Ghosh* direction should be given. A person who told lies in order to get back his own property, for example, might well be able to evoke the sympathy of a jury.[96]

26.65 It has been held that the intention to give valuable consideration does not negate dishonesty. In *R v Potger*,[97] a student sold magazines, telling prospective purchasers that he was involved in a competition and that every subscription that he sold increased his chances of winning the competition. This was untrue, and he was convicted of obtaining property by deception, even though full value was given for the money paid.

26.66 The deception must also be shown to be made deliberately or with recklessness as to its truth. Although there is no authority directly on the point, it is contended that recklessness in this context means subjective, *Cunningham*-type recklessness, discussed by Professor Ashworth at paras 24.25 to 24.26 above. That is, the defendant must be shown to have realized that his statement might not be true, but obtained the advantage or property nevertheless. It has been emphasized that this is a quite separate element from the requirement of dishonesty. Each must be considered separately.[98]

---

[92] *R v Silverman* (1987) 86 Cr App R 213. See also *R v King and Stockwell* [1987] QB 547.
[93] *R v Miller* [1992] Crim LR 744 (causation in deception a matter of fact).
[94] See the Law Commission, *Fraud* (Law Com No 276, 2002), summarized by I Dennis at [2002] Crim LR 769.
[95] *R v Woolven* (1983) 77 Cr App R 231.
[96] As in the Australian case of *R v Salvo* [1980] VR 401.
[97] (1970) 55 Cr App R 42.
[98] *R v Feeny* [1991] Crim LR 561.

(ii) Intent permanently to deprive

This aspect of mens rea has the same significance in this context as it has in the law   **26.67**
of theft, and s 6 applies 'with the necessary adaptation of the reference to appropriation'.

(c) Obtaining property

The types of property that can be obtained by deception are very similar to those   **26.68**
that can be stolen although the overlap is not complete. In particular, real property can be obtained by deception, but not stolen.

(i) Cheques

The property must be in existence before the deception occurs, which causes dif-   **26.69**
ficulties where, as a result of a deception, a victim writes out a cheque. This can be
prosecuted as the very serious offence of securing the execution of a valuable security contrary to s 20. But prosecutors frequently charged theft of the thing in action that the cheque form represents, over the frequently voiced objections of the
commentators. The principal objection was that, as that species of property, the
thing in action, it never belonged to the person who drew the cheque. The point
was eventually accepted by the House of Lords in *R v Preddy*.[99] Indeed, Lord Goff
went so far as to say in that case that even the cheque form on which the cheque
was written did not count as property, and in *R v Clark*,[100] the Court of Appeal
took the view that it had no option but to treat this ruling as being binding upon
them, quashing a conviction as a result.

(ii) Money transfers

The House of Lords caused consternation when it decided in *R v Preddy*[101] that   **26.70**
where a person deceives another into making a payment by way of telegraphic
transfer, through the Clearing Houses Automatic Payment System or by transferring property in the form of a cheque drawn for that purpose, no offence is committed under s 15 of the Theft Act 1968, since the thing in action that the cheque
represented had never belonged to the drawer of it. It was not, as a thing in action,
property belonging to another. This prompted Parliament[102] to enact legislation
to close the loophole and create the offence of obtaining a money transfer by deception contrary to s 15A inserted by s 1 of the Theft (Amendment) Act 1996.

---

[99] [1996] AC 815.
[100] [2002] 1 Cr App R 14. The Court expressed itself in agreement with the criticisms of this aspect of the decision made by Professor JC Smith, 'Obtaining Cheques by Deception or Theft' [1997] Crim LR 396, and indicated that it would probably have followed his advice had it been free to do so.
[101] [1996] AC 815.
[102] Following consultation with the Law Commission: *Offences of Dishonesty: Money Transfers* (Law Com No 243, 1996).

The Act creates the new offence (punishable with ten years' imprisonment) of obtaining a money transfer by deception.

(d) Obtaining pecuniary advantages

26.71   The original s 16(2)(a) of the Theft Act was repealed by the Theft Act 1978, and replaced by a range of offences whose scope can only be sketched here.

26.72   Section 16(1) of the Theft Act 1968 makes it an offence to obtain a 'pecuniary advantage' by deception and a person is said by s 16(2) to obtain a pecuniary advantage where:

> (b) he is allowed to borrow by way of overdraft, or to take out any policy of insurance or annuity contract, or obtains an improvement of the terms on which he is allowed to do so;
> (c) he is given the opportunity to earn remuneration or greater remuneration in an office or employment, or to win money by betting.

(i) Overdrafts

26.73   This offence is complete as soon as the overdraft has been granted, and even before it has been exercised.[103] The appellant in *Charles* was charged with the offence of obtaining an overdraft by deception through the use of a cheque guarantee card. This reading of the Act was not challenged until the decision in *R v Waites*,[104] where it was argued that a person could hardly be said to be 'permitted to borrow by way of overdraft' when at the time that the bank honoured the cheque, it knew (or certainly had the means of knowing) that meeting the cheque would take the account into overdraft. The court held that 'allowed' effectively meant enable rather than permitted.

(ii) Insurance contracts

26.74   Where a person is permitted to take out an insurance contract, and the insured event materializes, it is possible to argue that the insurance money has been received because of the fact that the insured event has occurred and that this is too remote from the deception that gave rise to the creation of the contract. The Act makes it impossible to deploy this argument, and the courts have held subsequently that the section applies even where the contract in question is a void one.[105]

(iii) Opportunity to earn money in employment

26.75   Section 16(2)(b) can be explained as being the result of the intention to reverse the effect of the old decision in *R v Lewis*[106] where a school teacher was able to evade

---

[103] *R v Watkins* [1976] 1 All ER 578.
[104] [1982] Crim LR 369. The decision was affirmed in *R v Bevan* (1986) 84 Cr App R 143.
[105] *R v Alexander* [1981] Crim LR 183.
[106] (1922) reported only in JWC Turner (ed), *Russell on Crime* (12th edn, London: Stevens, 1964) ii, 1186.

criminal liability for taking payment of her salary, her argument that her deception in obtaining the teaching post in the first place was too remote from the obtaining. That argument succeeded, and it was clearly the intention of the framers of the Theft Act 1968 to reverse that finding. It would seem that the framers of the Act have gone further, since in *R v Callender*[107] it was held that a man who performed accountancy services on a freelance basis was guilty of the offence, the argument that he did not hold an 'office' or an 'employment' falling on deaf ears.

(iv) Betting

The remoteness argument was also successful in *R v Clucas*,[108] where the defendant had used a false name in which to place a bet, because the bookmakers would not have accepted a bet from him had they known his true identity. Again, the effect of the section is to reverse the decision.   **26.76**

D. Fraudulent Debtors

(a) The social policy

It was decided in England as long ago as 1869 that it was no longer socially desirable to pursue through the criminal law those who did not pay their debts. Persons might become unable to pay what was due for a whole host of perfectly acceptable reasons—through ill health, unemployment or other circumstances leading to financial misfortune. Those who contracted debts dishonestly (as by buying goods with no intention of paying for them) obtained those goods by a false pretence, and could be criminalized for that reason. But if at the time the contract was made, there had been an intention to pay, later inability should not be visited by the use of the criminal law. What might be frowned upon, however, was the use of deception or false pretences to secure time to pay, with the intention of making permanent default upon the obligation. Section 16 of the Theft Act 1968 attempted to steer a course between these two positions, making it an offence to obtain a pecuniary advantage by deception. But the provision in s 16(2)(a) as interpreted by the House of Lords in *DPP v Turner*[109] rapidly proved unworkable, since it penalized those who used deception in order to buy time in which to pay—the temporizing debtor, rather than the person who intended never to pay. This was thought to be socially unacceptable. The legislative decision to reverse the effect of *Turner* has led to the creation of a considerable number of offences. The primary offence to be found in s 1 makes it an offence to obtain services by deception. Section 2 deals with persons who are, in effect, fraudulent debtors who either contract a debt   **26.77**

---

[107] [1993] QB 303.
[108] [1949] 2 KB 226.
[109] [1974] AC 357.

dishonestly at the outset (and thereby secure advantages to which they would not, but for the deception, be entitled) or who contract a debt and then behave dishonestly in such a way as to avoid paying, intending never to pay.

(b) Obtaining services by deception

26.78 Until 1978, the criminal law did not directly protect those who were deceived into providing services. This was not as great a gap in the law as might be supposed, since persons who provide services often also provide property in the process. But there were some gaps. A person who induced another to hire a car would not be guilty of the offence under s 15, since there was no intention permanently to deprive of the car. A person who obtains the services of an auctioneer or a solicitor intending never to pay does not obtain property, but he certainly obtains an advantage at another's expense, and the view was taken that this gap in the law should be plugged by legislation for that purpose.

26.79 Accordingly, the Theft Act 1978, s 1 provides as follows:

> (1) A person who by any deception dishonestly obtains services from another shall be guilty of an offence.
> (2) It is an obtaining of services where the other is induced to confer a benefit by doing some act, or causing or permitting some act to be done, on the understanding that the benefit has been or will be paid for.

It is still not an offence to steal services—the offence can be committed only by employing deception.

26.80 It has been held that a person who deceives another into making him a loan (in the case in question, a mortgage loan) does not commit the service offence.[110] This interpretation was always doubtful,[111] but Parliament took the opportunity of reaffirming its original intention in the Theft (Amendment) Act 1996 that the use of deception to induce another to make a loan is to be treated as criminal in character.[112]

> (3) Without prejudice to the generality of subsection (2) above, it is an obtaining of services where the other is induced to make a loan, or to cause or permit a loan to be made, on the understanding that any payment (whether by way of interest or otherwise) will be or has been made in respect of the loan.

(c) Evasion of liability by deception

26.81 Failure to pay one's debts does not normally give rise to criminal liability. But where certain steps are taken to impede the creditor in pursuing his legal remedy,

---

[110] *R v Halai* [1983] Crim LR 624.

[111] In *R v Chuah* [1991] Crim LR 463, the Court of Appeal said that it had 'all the hallmarks of a decision *per incuriam*'. See ATH Smith (n 1 above) para 18-11. The decision appears to have been treated as having been decided per incuriam in *R v Graham* [1997] 1 Cr App R 302; *R v Nathan* [1997] Crim LR 835, and *R v Naviede* [1997] Crim LR 662.

[112] s 4.

liability might arise. In particular, where deception is employed in such a way as to make the task of the creditor in pursuing what is his more difficult, the law intervenes. That was the view taken by the Criminal Law Revision Committee,[113] whose recommendations gave rise to s 2 of the Theft Act 1978. The Act creates three offences which overlap. The first two of these only relate to an existing liability: ie, the person has contracted a debt and only then decides to renege on the deal. Obtaining exemption, by contrast, relates to dishonesty at the outset of the transaction.

(i) Securing the remission of liability[114]

The conduct covered by this aspect of the offence is the use of deception to persuade a creditor to agree to let the debtor off the whole or part of an existing debt. It need not be shown that there was an intention to make permanent default, but it would be most unusual were a debtor to act in such a way without having such an intent. **26.82**

(ii) Inducing the creditor to wait for or forego payment[115]

This offence too is committed in relation to an existing liability. The important thing to be noted in this context being that there is no liability unless there is an intention to make permanent default. But whereas the previous offence requires proof of some agreement on the part of the creditor, the offence created by s 2(1)(b) does not. A person who gave a dud cheque intending to evade payment altogether is caught by the terms of this provision. **26.83**

(iii) Obtaining exemption from or abatement of liability to make a payment116

Whereas the previous two offences just considered apply to existing debts, the third of the trio relates to the use of deception at the outset of the transaction. The cheat persuades the potential creditor to charge too little, or perhaps to charge nothing at all. **26.84**

(iv) Failing to alert another to the fact that a debt is due

The appellant in *R v Firth*[117] was a doctor providing obstetric services both through the National Health Service and privately. He was supposed to alert the hospital to the status of private patients, but in the case for which he was charged, he had failed to do so, his explanation being that he had been muddled in his paperwork. It was held that he was guilty of the offence. This looks rather like liability for an omission. **26.85**

---

[113] Thirteenth Report, *Section 16 of the Theft Act 1968* (Cmnd 6733, 1977). For comment upon the 1978 Act, see generally JR Spencer, 'The Theft Act 1978' [1979] Crim LR 24.
[114] Theft Act 1978, s 2(1)(a).
[115] ibid s 2(1)(b).
[116] ibid s 2(1)(c).
[117] (1989) 91 Cr App R 217.

(v) Inducing another to wait for payment by giving a false cheque

26.86   Section 2(3) says:

> For purposes of ss.1(*b*) a person induced to take in payment a cheque or other security for money by way of conditional satisfaction of a pre-existing liability is not to be treated as being paid but as being induced to wait for payment.

26.87   In *R v Andrews and Hedges*,[118] the Court held that since the course of dealing between the parties established that the suppliers were happy to accept a cheque by way of satisfaction, they had not been induced to accept it (in preference to cash). This rather suggests that the use of 'inducement' in s 2(3) was unfortunate. They meant to say no more than if a person accepts a cheque, he is induced to wait for payment. Now it seems an offence will only be committed where the trader says something like that no 'cheques are accepted'.

(d) Making off without payment

26.88   One particular form of wrongdoing that was said to be prevalent when the reform of the law was in contemplation was conduct described as 'bilking'. This describes the situation of the person who obtains the benefit of goods or services (at a petrol station, for example, or at a restaurant)[119] and then who simply disappears without trying to pay. This is in essence a form of failing to pay one's debts, and the principle is that failing to pay one's debts should not be criminalized, but its prevalence was thought to be such that it warranted the creation of a separate and special offence.

26.89   Section 3 of the Theft Act 1978 accordingly provides:

> . . . a person who, knowing that payment on the spot for any goods supplied or service done is required or expected from him, dishonestly makes off without having paid as required or expected and with intent to avoid payment of the amount due shall be guilty of an offence.

(i) Making off

26.90   The essence of the offence is that the defaulter should 'make off' from the particular place where the payment is required or expected. It denotes a sudden and unexpected departure from a particular physical locality such as the petrol station after petrol has been taken. There is some irony in the fact that if a person owes a large sum of money and leaves for foreign parts intending never to meet his commitments, he commits no offence, but where a relatively small sum is involved, and the debtor makes off from the spot where payment is expected, we use the majesty of the criminal law.

---

[118] [1981] Crim LR 106, 276.

[119] *Ray v Sempers* [1974] AC 370 is a reported example of this phenomenon, where the House of Lords held that a student, having decided not to pay half-way through the meal, was guilty of deception by remaining in the restaurant.

The offence is not made out where there has been an arrangement to defer pay-   **26.91**
ment, even if the 'arrangement' has been secured by fraud on the part of the
debtor.[120] Such conduct would, however, amount to the offence of inducing another to wait for payment, and so long as there was an intention never to pay, the
fraudster could be convicted of that.

(ii) Consensual departures

It is slightly unclear whether a person can be said to 'make off' when the other per-   **26.92**
mits him to leave. In *R v Hammond*,[121] a Crown Court judge ruled that there could
be no offence under s 3 when the defendant had given a false cheque before leaving.
But if the victim were to consent to a departure for a purely temporary purpose (to go
next door to a cash machine, perhaps) and the person securing the agreement were
then to decamp, that would amount to a making off for the purposes of the section.

(iii) The mental element

It is clear that there must be proved an intention never to pay. The language of the   **26.93**
Act is unclear, but in *R v Allen*,[122] the House of Lords, having consulted the report
of the Criminal Law Revision Committee,[123] concluded that this further element
was required.

E. Burglary

The existence of an offence of burglary requires little by way of justification,   **26.94**
whether the building invaded is a dwelling, a business premises or a church. But
the law prior to the Theft Act 1968 was complicated. It drew numerous distinctions making liability turn on such questions as the time of day when the burglary
occurred, the nature of the building and the property stolen. Under the 1968 Act,
the law is altogether wider in its scope.

Section 9 of the Theft Act 1968 provides: **26.95**

> (1) A person is guilty of burglary if–
>   (a) he enters any building or part of a building as a trespasser and with intent to
>   commit any such offence as is mentioned in subsection (2) below; or
>   (b) having entered any building or part of a building as a trespasser he steals or
>   attempts to steal anything in the building or that part of it or inflicts or at-
>   tempts to inflict on any person therein any grievous bodily harm.

---

[120] *R v Vincent* [2001] EWCA Crim 295; [2001] 1 WLR 1172.
[121] [1982] Crim LR 611.
[122] [1985] AC 1029.
[123] Which the Court of Appeal had declined to do on the grounds that it should look only at the language of the statute to determine its meaning, and the intention of Parliament. Recent developments
in the law of statutory interpretation make it plainer than ever that such recourse is permissible.

(2) The offences referred to in subsection (1)(a) above are offences of stealing anything in the building or part of a building in question, of inflicting on any person therein any grievous bodily harm or raping any woman therein, and of doing unlawful damage to the building or anything therein.

(a) Who is a trespasser?

26.96   The question whether or not a person is a trespasser is governed by the civil law. Technically, a trespass is any unauthorized interference with land in the possession of another. This will for present purposes generally be committed by entering onto another's land, although entry is an independent requirement in the law of burglary.

26.97   In *R v Jones and Smith*,[124] a man was convicted of stealing television sets from his father's house, where he had a general licence to be. This was held to be a trespass (and hence burglary) since he had knowingly exceeded the permission granted to him to enter and remain on the property. The decision potentially has the effect of casting the law very wide. A person who enters a shop with the intention of shoplifting would appear, on this analysis, to be guilty of burglary.

(b) Aggravated burglary

26.98   Section 10(1) of the Act provides that a person is guilty of the offence of aggravated burglary if he commits burglary and at the time has with him any firearm or imitation firearm, any weapon of offence or any explosive. The offence is regarded as serious, carrying as it does the penalty of life imprisonment.

F. Blackmail[125]

26.99   Blackmail, the making of an unwarranted demand with menaces, is sometimes said to be murder of the soul. But it can contain the paradox that a person who threatens to do something entirely lawful may commit the offence if the demand can be said to be unwarranted and he acts with menaces. To take a homely example: suppose that a person discovers that a wealthy business associate is behaving discreditably. The newspapers would be very interested in buying a story with the sordid details. The would-be story teller approaches the associate and says that he intends to sell the story to the press. If the associate says that he will pay the same

---

[124] [1976] 1 WLR 672. See also *R v Collins* [1973] QB 100, where the question was whether or not a man who had mistakenly been invited to enter in the middle of the night by the daughter of the householder was guilty of burglary; it was held that he was not, principally because he lacked any intention to trespass, but also because the daughter would have been authorized to permit him to enter.

[125] P Alldridge, 'Attempted Murder of the Soul: Blackmail, Piracy and Secrets' (1993) 13 OJLS 368.

amount as the newspapers provided that the original actor promises not to go to the press, the first person could be found guilty of blackmail.

The offence, which is punishable with imprisonment for 14 years, is defined by s 21(1) of the Theft Act 1968 as follows: **26.100**

> A person is guilty of blackmail if, with a view to gain for himself or another or with intent to cause loss to another, he makes any unwarranted demand with menaces; and for this purpose a demand with menaces is unwarranted unless the person making it does so in the belief—
> (a) that he has reasonable grounds for making the demand; and
> (b) that the use of the menaces is a proper means of reinforcing the demand.

Consistently with the view that the meaning of 'ordinary' English words should be left as far as possible to the jury, the Court of Appeal has held in *R v Garwood*[126] that the interpretation of 'menaces' will not usually need to be explained to the jury. Instead, the court said, it is necessary for the judge to tell the jury what is meant in two situations only: **26.101**

- where the words used did not actually cause the person to whom they were addressed to feel that he was being menaced thereby, although they would have constituted a menace so far as ordinary people were concerned, that can count as a menace, and
- where the menace would not have affected the mind of a person of normal stability, although it did in fact affect the mind of the victim. 'In our judgment the existence of menaces is proved providing that the accused man was aware of the likely effect of his actions upon the victim.'

The Court has also said that a 'view to gain' does not necessarily involve economic gain, as is graphically illustrated by the decision in *R v Bevans*.[127] The appellant had summoned a doctor, pulled a handgun and demanded that he be given an injection of morphine. The doctor injected pethedine (with the appellant's approval). On appeal he argued that he should not have been convicted, because the words 'with a view to gain for himself' related to financial or economic gain. The Court of Appeal held, however, (1) that the substance injected into him was undoubtedly property and (2) the demand involved gain to the appellant. The fact that his ultimate motive was the relief of pain was irrelevant.   **26.102**

G. Documents Offences

A fraud of any significance will almost invariably involve commission of one of the many documents offences with which the law is cluttered. No attempt has ever   **26.103**

---

[126] [1987] 1 WLR 319.
[127] [1988] Crim LR 236.

been made to rationalize the law regulating the use (and misuse) of documents, and it is common for general legislation (relating to taxation, for example, or company accounting procedures) to make it an offence to produce documents that are false in a material particular. The Theft Act 1968 contains four provisions. False accounting,[128] the suppression and destruction of certain documents (valuable securities, wills or other testamentary documents and court and governmental documents),[129] or procuring the execution of a valuable security by deception.[130] There is also an offence of using false documents to mislead principals.[131]

H. Handling Stolen Property

26.104 'Without handlers', runs the old adage, 'there would be no thieves.' Whatever the truth of this folk wisdom, Parliament preserved its spirit by enacting a wide-ranging offence of handling stolen goods to replace the pre-Act law of receiving stolen goods.

26.105 Section 22 of the Theft Act 1968 provides:

> (1) A person handles stolen goods if (otherwise than in the course of the stealing) knowing or believing them to be stolen goods he dishonestly receives the goods, or dishonestly assists in their retention, removal, disposal or realisation by or for the benefit of another person, or if he arranges to do so.

(a) The actus reus

26.106 In order to secure a conviction for handling, the prosecution must prove that the goods were stolen, and that the defendant handled the goods in question. If the goods were not in fact stolen, but the handler believed that they were, he can be convicted of attempting to handle stolen goods.[132] Goods are 'stolen' for the purposes of this offence not simply when they have been the object of an offence of theft, but also where the goods have been obtained by blackmail or by deception.[133]

26.107 By comparison with the offence which it replaced, receiving stolen goods, the actus reus of the offence of handling is both far wider and more complex. In addition to receiving, the offence can be committed by retention, removal, disposal or realization or by arranging to do any of these things. For example, where the wife of a thief told lies to the police who were searching her house about the origins of

---

[128] s 17, which is a successor to the Falsification of Accounts Act 1875.
[129] s 20(1).
[130] s 20(2).
[131] Prevention of Corruption Act 1906, s 1(1).
[132] *Anderton v Ryan* [1985] AC 560.
[133] Theft Act 1968, s 24(4).

some stolen property, it was held that she was guilty of assisting her husband.[134] One significant limit on the scope of the offence is that the person for whose benefit the handling was undertaken must be somebody other than the defendant himself. It was necessary to take the matter to the House of Lords before this apparently obvious point was established.[135] Goods having once been stolen do not retain the status as stolen property forever thereafter, and provision is made for when they cease to be 'stolen' for the purposes of the law of handling.

Section 24(3) provides: **26.108**

> But no goods shall be regarded as having continued to be stolen goods after they have been restored to the person from whom they were stolen or to other lawful possession or custody, or after that person and any other person claiming through him have otherwise ceased as regards those goods to have any right to restitution in respect of the theft.

(b) Mens rea

The offence requires proof of dishonesty, which means the same in this context as   **26.109** it does in the law of theft. It requires in addition, however, knowledge or belief that the goods in question were stolen. On a number of occasions, the courts have insisted that mere suspicion that the goods were stolen is insufficient.[136] The putative handler must not only have suspected that the goods were stolen, but come to a (correct) conclusion that they were actually stolen.

I. Criminal Damage

The modern law of criminal damage is a result of the work of the Law   **26.110** Commission's project to codify the criminal law. Its report[137] was rapidly implemented as the Criminal Damage Act 1971, s 1 of which provides as follows:

> (1) a person who without lawful excuse destroys or damages any property belonging to another intending to destroy or damage any such property or being reckless as to whether any such property would be destroyed or damaged shall be guilty of an offence.
> (2) A person who without lawful excuse destroys or damages any property, whether belonging to himself or another–
>   (a) intending to destroy or damage any property or being reckless as to whether any property would be destroyed or damaged; and

---

[134] *R v Kanwar* [1982] 1 WLR 845. Cf, however, *R v Sanders* (1982) 75 Cr App R 84, where it was held that the mere use of property stolen by another did not meet the requirements of the Act.
[135] *R v Bloxham* [1983] 1 AC 109.
[136] *R v Griffiths* (1974) 60 Cr App R 14. The position is criticized by JR Spencer, 'Theft, Handling and the *Mala Fide* Purchaser' [1985] Crim LR 92, but it is a position to which the courts have consistently adhered. *R v Grainge* [1984] 1 WLR 619; *R v Moys* (1984) 79 Cr App R 72; *R v Hall* (1985) 81 Cr App R 260; *R v Toor* (1987) 85 Cr App R 116.
[137] Law Commission, *Offences of Damage to Property* (Law Com No 29, 1970).

(b) intending by the destruction to endanger the life of another or being reckless as to whether the life of another would be thereby endangered;
shall be guilty of an offence.

(3) An offence committed under this section by destroying or damaging property by fire shall be charged as arson.

(a) Simple and dangerous damage distinguished

26.111 The offences under s 1(2) are particularly serious, carrying as they do the potential penalty of imprisonment for life. The essence of the offences is that they are committed by causing damage to property with the accompanying mental element of recklessness or intention as to endangering the life of another. It is immaterial that life is not in fact endangered; what matters is the defendant's state of mind. But it must be shown that the defendant must intend to cause the harm to the person (or be reckless thereto) through the medium of damage to the property. The point is illustrated in the decision of the House of Lords in *R v Steer*,[138] in which the defendant had fired several shots at the victim's house, one of which went through the window. The trial judge had ruled that it was sufficient for the prosecutor to establish that the defendant had caused damage and had at the same time acted with the relevant intention or recklessness. The House of Lords ruled that this was a misdirection, and that what must be shown is that the defendant intended to endanger life through the damage, most obviously in cases such as arson, or the use of explosives—since life is likely to be damaged by smoke or flames, or the disintegration of the building, the causal link is established.

(b) What constitutes damage?

26.112 A thing is physically damaged when is sustains some physical harm, impairment or deterioration, depending on the circumstances, and the nature of the object. A person may be guilty of causing damage even of a minimal kind, eg where long grass is damaged by two persons walking abreast through it.[139] It may be, however, that some sort of de minimis principle operates in practice, as in *R v Woolcock*,[140] where it was held that nails fastening a piece of iron used to block a doorway were not damaged upon their removal, even though they had been bent in the process. But daubing a wall with graffiti using paint is clearly caught.[141]

26.113 Although the Act says that '"property" means property of a tangible nature . . .' it does not follow that the damage caused must itself be tangible. Thus, where a computer hacker altered the magnetic particles on the disks in such a way as to

---

[138] [1988] AC 111.
[139] *Gayford v Chouler* [1898] 1 QB 316.
[140] [1977] Crim LR 104, 161.
[141] *Roe v Kingerlee* [1986] Crim LR 735.

impair the value or usefulness of the disk, that was held to amount to causing damage for these purposes.[142]

(c) Belonging to another

It is not a criminal offence to damage one's own property, except where fire is used, and there is a danger to others (when the conduct is classified as arson). Similarly one would not be entitled to damage property belonging to a company, even if one is the director of a private company. The point appears to have been overlooked in *R v Denton*,[143] where an employee set fire to a company's property at the suggestion of his employer. He was acquitted, it being accepted apparently that the employer was the person entitled to authorize the employee to behave in such a way. A different view on very similar facts was taken in *R v Appleyard*,[144] where the managing director of a company was convicted of arson when he set fire to a store belonging to the company.

26.114

(d) Damage by omission

It has been held that a person might be guilty of causing damage by omission as in *R v Miller*,[145] where a defendant accidentally set fire to a mattress (having fallen asleep with a lighted cigarette). When he awoke, he did nothing to extinguish the flames. It was held that, having unintentionally set the chain of causation in motion, he was nevertheless responsible for the resulting damage once he had become aware of what he had done, and had then done nothing further to prevent the harm in question from occurring. The effect is that the actor has a duty to take reasonable steps to prevent the harm and is responsible for the omission if he fails to do so.

26.115

(e) Lawful excuse

The Act provides[146] that it is a lawful excuse—

  (a) if at the time of the act or acts alleged to constitute the offence the actor believed that the person or persons whom he believed to be entitled to consent to the destruction of or damage to the property in question had so consented, or would have so consented to it if he or they had known of the destruction or damage and its circumstances; or

  (b) if he destroyed or damaged or threatened to destroy or damage the property in question in order to protect property belonging to himself or another or a right or interest in property which was or which he believed to be vested in himself or another, and at the time of the act or acts alleged to constitute the offence he believed—

---

[142] *R v Whiteley* (1991) 93 Cr App R 25.
[143] [1981] 1 WLR 1446.
[144] [1985] Crim LR 723.
[145] [1983] 2 AC 161.
[146] s 5.

(i) that the property, right or interest was in immediate need of protection; and

(ii) that the means of protection adopted or proposed to be adopted were or would be reasonable having regard to all the circumstances.

(3) For the purposes of this section it is immaterial whether a belief is justified or not if it is honestly held.

It has been held[147] that in order to apply the section, the court has to decide first what is subjectively in the actor's mind, and then whether, objectively on those facts as believed by him, that act could amount to something done to protect that right or interest.

26.116   The threat which it is sought to avert must be an imminent one, and it would be no defence to damage a perimeter fence at an American air base in the hope that this would encourage the US authorities to withdraw from the base and that this would reduce the risk of nuclear attack and hence protect their homes. Such a threat would be altogether too remote.[148]

26.117   It may be that in addition to the statutory defences, a person has a defence available at common law. The point has not been decided. In *Lloyd v DPP*[149] such an assertion was put forward in a case in which the defendant had been charged with damaging two padlocks holding a clamp by which his car had been immobilized. The court held that he had no defence on the facts since he had given his consent to being clamped when he had parked in a place where the notices (which he had seen) warned that clamping was in operation.

(f) The mental element

26.118   The much criticized decision of the House of Lords in *R v Caldwell*[150] was concerned with the meaning of recklessness in the interpretation of the Criminal Damage Act 1971. A person is said to be reckless under the Act '(1) if he does an act which in fact creates an obvious risk that property will be destroyed or damaged, and (2) when he does the act he either has not given any thought to there being any such risk or has recognised that there was some risk involved and has none the less gone on to do it'.

26.119   The decision was eventually 'departed from' by the House of Lords itself in *R v G*[151] where it was held that the defendant could be said to be reckless only where there is actual, subjective, awareness of the risk involved.

---

[147] *Chamberlain v Lindon* [1998] 1 WLR 1252.
[148] *R v Hill and Hall* (1989) 89 Cr App R 74. And see *R v Blake* [1993] Crim LR 586.
[149] [1992] 1 All ER 982.
[150] [1982] AC 341. Discussed at para 24.25 above.
[151] [2003] UKHL 50, [2003] 3 WLR 1060.

J. Computer Misuse

The pervasiveness of the computer in business and domestic life, and the vulner-   **26.120**
ability of computing systems to fraud and other forms of abuse was an increasing
social menace throughout the 1980s. Computer 'hacking' could not be penalized
through the ordinary processes of the criminal law, although attempts were made
to use the ordinary law for this purpose.[152] Some indeed sought to argue that hacking was a harmless, or even positively beneficial activity. These attitudes could not
prevail in the light of the increasing evidence that computers were an integral part
of not merely business and commercial transactions such as banking and trading on the stock markets, but also institutions where safety might be compromised, such as hospitals and air traffic control. Not without some hesitation, then,
Parliament enacted the Computer Misuse Act 1991, which creates three offences:
obtaining unauthorized access to computer material, doing so with the intent to
commit or facilitate further offences, and thirdly, causing the unauthorized modification of computer material. The first of the offences is aimed clearly at the
'hacker', the person who without necessarily having any sinister purpose, gains
unauthorized access to another's files. The time, trouble and expense to which the
true owner of the files might be put is seen to be a sufficient justification for the
use of the criminal law.

K. Corruption

The law governing bribery and corruption is a tangled web of statute and com-   **26.121**
mon law. At common law, it is an offence for any person to offer or to give a reward to a public officer as an inducement to act contrary to his duty, or to show
favour or to forbear to show disfavour in the discharge of his duty.

As a result of deficiencies in the common law, and a reluctance on the part of   **26.122**
prosecuting authorities to use what powers were available, Parliament enacted a
series of overlapping and interconnecting measures in the Public Bodies
Corrupt Practices Act 1889, supplemented by the Prevention of Corruption
Acts of 1906 and 1916. The first of these Acts was concerned principally with
public corruption, and the principles evolved in that context were then extended further to private transactions and extended the public element further,
by defining 'agents' to include Crown servants. The law is in a plainly unsatisfactory state, and after an extensive programme of consultation,[153] a draft Bill to

---

[152] See eg *R v Whitely* (1991) 93 Cr App R 25.
[153] See in particular the White Paper, *Raising Standards and Upholding Integrity: The Prevention of Corruption* (Cm 4759, 2000) and the Law Commission Report, *Legislating the Criminal Code: Corruption* (Law Com No 248, 1998).

reform the law of bribery and corruption was published by the Home Office on 24 March 2003.[154]

L. Forgery

26.123   Forgery is in essence the creation of false documents that tell lies about themselves; and in particular the circumstances in which, and by whom, they were created. Although the creation of a forgery will often be undertaken as a preliminary to fraud of some kind, the underpinning of a separate offence is seen to be the need to preserve confidence in the authenticity of documents upon which reliance might be placed. The modern law is to be found in the Forgery and Counterfeiting Act 1981, which formed part of the Law Commission's codification project.[155]

M. Conspiracy to Defraud[156]

26.124   When the general law of conspiracy was reformed in 1977, several aspects of the common law were left untouched. The principal reform effected by that legislation was aimed at the fact that the 'unlawful act' which made criminal an agreement by two or more persons might not necessarily be a criminal one. To take a simple example. For the most part, trespass is not a criminal offence when committed by a single person—it is no more than a civil wrong. But when two or more conspired to trespass, it magically became criminal, for no very obvious reason.[157] It was feared that, if conspiracy to defraud were to be reformed in accordance with a general principle that avoided this absurd result, it was possible that various forms of fraud that were not otherwise criminal would escape punishment, and conspiracy to defraud was thus preserved.[158] It is probable too that a prosecution for conspiracy to defraud has certain presentation advantages for the prosecutor (and it may be for the jury) since it enables the Crown to present a fraud as it were 'in the round', showing a pattern of wrongdoing that might be

---

[154] Cm 5777. The law was extended in certain respects by the Anti-terrorism, Crime and Security Act 2001, Pt XII.

[155] *Report on Forgery and Counterfeit Currency* (Law Com No 55, 1973).

[156] For the relationship between this form of conspiracy, and the offence of conspiracy more generally, see paras 24.50–24.54 above.

[157] For a discussion of the unreformed law, see IH Dennis, 'The Rationale of Criminal Conspiracy' (1997) 93 LQR 39.

[158] Criminal Law Act 1977, s 5(2). The section was regrettably ambiguous, and in *R v Ayres* [1984] AC 447, the House of Lords interpreted it in such a way that, if any substantive offence had been committed in the course of the alleged conspiracy, the conspiracy charge was no longer available. Parliament quickly remedied the damage: Criminal Justice Act 1987.

difficult to demonstrate were it necessary to present the case through the use of separate counts against a large number of different defendants. However satisfactory for the prosecutor this might be, it has the adverse qualities inherent in the common law of vagueness and uncertainty. It also means that impossibility is a defence to a charge of conspiracy to defraud, since it is governed by the unreformed common law in this respect, a situation that Parliament has implicitly said to be unsatisfactory in relation to other conspiracies.[159]

26.125 The leading statement of the current law is to be found in the language of the House of Lords in *Scott v Metropolitan Police Commissioner*:[160]

> . . . it is clearly the law that an agreement by two or more by dishonesty to deprive a person of something which is his or to which he is or would be or might be entitled and an agreement by two or more by dishonesty to injure some proprietary right of his, suffices to constitute the offence of conspiracy to defraud.

The definition is remarkably broad, and in *R v Withers*[161] the House of Lords expressed the view that conspiring to cause a person to act contrary to his public duty might come within the ambit of the offence. The language in which the definition is couched ('something to which he is or would be *or might be* entitled') raises such questions as: 'who might be the victim of such behaviour?', and more pertinently, 'might be entitled' in what circumstances? The potential of this is such that a challenge under Article 7 of the European Convention on Human Rights might well be appropriate.

26.126 So far as the mens rea of the offence is concerned, it is clear that it requires proof of dishonesty.[162] Some doubt about what this might entail in the conspiracy context was raised in *R v Landy*,[163] where the view was expressed that the defendant's own view of the honesty or otherwise of his conduct was paramount. But the opportunity was taken by Lord Lane CJ in *R v Ghosh*[164] to set the matter straight. It is now clear that, on a charge of conspiracy to defraud, the jury should be directed in exactly the same terms as they would on a charge of theft. That is, where the possibility that the defendant might have been acting honestly arises, the jury must decide first what the defendant actually thought, and then consider whether or not that was dishonest according to the ordinary community standards of right or wrong. They must then determine whether or not the defendant was aware that the community regarded the conduct as dishonest.

---

[159] See paras 24.50 et seq above.
[160] [1975] AC 819.
[161] [1975] AC 842.
[162] *R v Allsop* (1976) 64 Cr App R 29.
[163] [1981] 1 WLR 355.
[164] [1982] QB 1053.

N. Miscellaneous Offences

26.127   The Theft Act preserves a miscellany of offences whose presence is often explicable purely by reference to history. As the Theft Bill was going through Parliament, for example, there was an incident involving the taking of a famous Goya painting from the National Gallery—the taker being acquitted of theft. This provoked a national outcry, and the result was that Parliament enacted a specific offence of taking articles from places open to the public. Notwithstanding the extremely broad definition of property generally, it is thought that electricity does not fall within it, and there is in consequence a separate offence of dishonestly abstracting electricity.[165] The strict liability offence of advertising for reward has its ancient origins in the activities of the notorious thief-taker Jonathan Wild, who would arrange for articles to be stolen, and then advertise them as being available for return to the owner who agreed to pay for them 'no questions asked'.[166]

26.128   One particular form of fraud deserves special mention, since the common law version of it was expressly preserved by the Theft Act 1968, namely cheating the public revenue.[167] The penalty being at large, far greater sentences can be imposed than those that would be available under statute for fraudulent tax evasion.[168] The Criminal Law Revision Committee had recommended the abolition of the offence, and the recommendation was accepted except in relation to the revenue. It is suggested that the recommendation might be revisited in the light of the reforms currently in contemplation by the Law Commission.[169]

---

[165]   Theft Act 1968, s 13.
[166]   See L Radzinowicz, *A History of English Criminal Law* (London: Stevens, 1948–56) vol 1 at 682, vol 3 at 25.
[167]   See D Ormerod, 'Cheating the Public Revenue' [1998] Crim LR 627.
[168]   As in *R v Mavji* [1987] 1 WLR 1388, [1987] 2 All ER 758.
[169]   See n 94 above.

27

OFFENCES AGAINST THE STATE, PUBLIC ORDER, PUBLIC MORALITY AND DECENCY

A. The State

In one sense, all offences are offences against the state, in that citizens look to the state to take action on their behalf when they have been aggrieved by the criminal misconduct of others. The violation of the Queen's Peace that occurs when a crime is committed justifies the state conducting the prosecution rather than leaving the matter to the self help of the aggrieved individual. This section, however, is concerned with the state as victim. Historically, much of the criminal law in this sphere has been utilized to preserve the established order, and many of the offences were directed at the expression of sentiments that would undermine that order. Seditious and blasphemous libel were clear examples of this phenomenon. As attitudes towards participatory democracy and freedom of speech have

27.01

altered, so the criminal law has found itself correspondingly relegated to the legal margins.[1]

27.02 When the head that wore the Crown was more uneasy than it is today, the crimes of treason[2] and sedition were employed to preserve society from (or punish after the event) widespread outbreaks of disorder.[3] Here, we are at the borderline between riots and revolutions. Today, the remnants of both offences continue to exist, though they are in practical terms dead letters. On 19 May 1986, the Attorney-General explained to Parliament the legal difficulties of employing the charge of treason in modern conditions in response to a question demanding to know why treason was not employed in cases of terrorism.[4] 'One must realize that the 600-year-old statute is couched in such archaic language that it would be difficult to prove all the necessary ingredients of the crime and for a modern jury to come to grips with the terminology', he said. Since the common law has displayed over the years a remarkable ability to reassert itself, it may be a mistake to suppose that the law will never be employed. The Attorney-General had cautiously prefaced his remarks with the observation that 'treason remains available for an appropriate case'.

(1) Treason

27.03 Originally, treason was (along with felonies and misdemeanours) a category of offence. The classification was rendered more or less meaningless when the distinction between felonies and misdemeanours was abolished in 1967.

(a) High treason: Treason Act 1351

27.04 There are a number of outstanding heads of treason, including high treason under the Treason Act 1351, the 600-year-old statute to which the Attorney-General was referring.[5] The Act makes it an offence to:

---

[1] As Lord Bridge put it when speaking in the Privy Council in *Hector v A-G of Antigua and Baruda* [1990] 2 AC 312, 318: '. . . their Lordships cannot help viewing a statutory provision which criminalises statements likely to undermine confidence in the conduct of public affairs with the utmost suspicion'.

[2] The Law Commission issued a working paper on the reform of this area of the law *Treason, Sedition and Allied Offences* (Working Paper No 72, 1977), but there has been no attempt to implement the changes suggested. And see LH Leigh, 'Law Reform and the Law of Treason and Sedition' [1977] PL 128; E Barendt, *Freedom of Speech* (Oxford: Clarendon, 1985) 155. And see A Wharam, (1976) 126 NLJ 428. See also L Lustgarten and I Leigh, *In From the Cold* (Oxford: Clarendon, 1994) 205–210.

[3] Riot was initially limited to situations where the rioting was for a private purpose, the reason being that riots with a public purpose were punishable as treason: *R v Vincent* (1839) 9 C & P 91. The 19th century Criminal Code Commissioners were highly critical of this, saying that the distinction between public and private purposes was 'wholly inapplicable to the present state of society'. It was founded on a 'fundamentally erroneous' principle of 'constructive treason in its most obnoxious shape' in a way that was 'repugnant to all just notions of criminal law': Fifth Report (1840) 90. See Lord Leary CJ in *O'Brien v Friel* [1974] NILR 29, 43.

[4] See *Hansard*, HC vol 98, col 14.

[5] This account is based substantially upon JC Smith and B Hogan, *Criminal Law* (6th edn, London: Butterworths, 1988) ch 21. See also *Archbold: Criminal Pleading, Evidence and Practice* (London: Sweet & Maxwell) ch 25.

- 'compass or imagine the death of our lord the King or our lady his Queen or of their eldest son and heir';
- 'violate the King's companion [wife] or the King's eldest daughter unmarried or the wife [of] the King's eldest sone and heir';
- 'levy war against our lord the King in his realm';
- 'be adherent to the King's enemies in his realm giving to them aid and comfort in the realm, or elsewhere';
- slay 'the chancellor, treasurer, or the King's justices . . . being in their places, doing their offices';
- 'by overt act to attempt to deprive or hinder the person next in succession to the Crown from succeeding'.[6]

Although historically a capital offence, the death penalty for all forms of treason was abolished by the Crime and Disorder Act 1998, s 36.

(b) Who may be guilty of treason

Since the offence of treason rests upon a link between allegiance and protection,[7] only persons who owe allegiance to the Crown may commit the act of treason. This turns primarily upon citizenship of the United Kingdom but others may owe the relevant allegiance. Thus, aliens can be guilty of treason where they have adopted the protection of the Crown, as by being voluntarily on British territory or, it has been held, if having been within British territory he leaves with a British passport which is still within his possession at the time of the treasonable act.[8]

27.05

(c) Treason Felony Act 1848

In addition to the 1351 legislation, possibly out of fear that 'the contagion of revolution, with its associations with the Terror after 1789, might spread to Britain'[9], the Treason Felony Act was passed in 1848. Its provisions may be summarized as providing that it is treason to:

27.06

(1) deprive the Sovereign of the Crown;
(2) levy war against the Sovereign; and
(3) encourage foreigners to invade the United Kingdom.

An attempt to clarify the state of the law through the use of the declaratory process was rejected by the House of Lords in *R (on the application of Rusbridger) v A-G*.[10]

27.07

---

[6] Treason Act 1702, s 3.

[7] See Glanville Williams, 'The Correlation of Allegiance and Protection' (1948) 10 CLP 54.

[8] This is the effect of the decision in *Joyce v DPP* [1946] AC 347. See also *R v Casement* [1917] 1 KB 98.

[9] See Lord Steyn in *R (on the application of Rusbridger) v A-G* [2003] UKHL 38; [2003] 3 WLR 232 at [2].

[10] ibid.

The editor of The Guardian published a series of articles advocating the replacement of the Crown by republicanism. The Attorney-General had declined to give any undertaking not to prosecute for the possible breach of s 3 of the Treason Felony Act 1848. The supposed point of concern was that whereas heads (2) and (3) expressly require that the prohibited objective be secured by use of force, the offence in part (1) is not so qualified. This made it appear, on its face, to prohibit the advocacy of republicanism. The House was unsympathetic to the attempt to secure a declaration, both on the constitutional grounds that the courts will not in general grant declarations in criminal proceedings, but also because the Act would now have to be construed in accordance with the Human Rights Act 1998 (HRA), and in particular with the free speech guarantees contained within Article 10 of the European Convention on Human Rights (ECHR). That being so, there was no realistic possibility of a prosecution under the Act, and no need to grant a declaration.[11] The sooner Parliament acts to rid us of this unnecessary legislation, the better.

(2) Sedition[12]

27.08 Sedition, which was committed by, inter alia, inciting hostility or ill-will between different classes of Her Majesty's subjects,[13] is rarely if ever prosecuted in modern Britain. The principal modern form of the offence is incitement to racial hatred. Historically, there was a strong link with the offences against public order so that, for example, a meeting of more than 50 people organized to make speeches critical of the established institutions of the state was an unlawful assembly unless advertised in accordance with the statutory requirements as to notice.[14] Originally, seditious libel was used to stifle criticism of the government. Any formulation of the ingredients of the offence today would have to bear in mind that an offence that so plainly inhibits freedom of speech, and particularly speech critical of the established order, must be justified as necessary in a democratic society before it could be regarded as compatible with the free speech guarantees of the HRA 1998.[15] The uncertainty of scope generated by the fact that the offence is common

---

[11] The decision of the European Court of Human Rights in *Johnston v Ireland* Series A No 112 (1986) 9 EHRR 203, which is to the effect that a person may be a victim of a law which breaches the Convention even if never personally charged or threatened with proceedings and the state organs have announced a decision not to prosecute, appears not to have been cited to their Lordships.

[12] See generally D Feldman, *Civil Liberties and Human Rights in England and Wales* (2nd edn, Oxford: OUP, 2002) 897 et seq.

[13] JF Stephen, *A History of the Criminal Law of England* (London: Macmillan, 1883) vol 2, 298 et seq.

[14] The Seditious Meetings Act 1817, though long passed into desuetude, was not repealed until the Public Order Act 1986.

[15] Technically, s 3 of the HRA 1998 does not apply in this situation, since the offences are creatures of the common law rather than statute, to which the section pertains. But the Convention is applicable to determine the scope of the common law in much the same way as it informs statutory interpretation; *R v Secretary of State for the Home Department, ex p Brind* [1991] 1 AC 696.

law rather than statutory is highly unsatisfactory where freedom of speech is at stake.

(a) The actus reus of seditious libel

The publication (whether orally or in writing) of words with a seditious intent was a misdemeanour at common law. But the better view would seem to be that such words must be shown to have a tendency to incite public disorder involving physical violence.[16] If the tendency of the words is to incite violence, it has been held to be no defence to the charge that the particular audience addressed was not incited.[17] 'Thus words are seditious (i) if they are likely to incite ordinary men whether likely to incite the audience actually addressed or not: or (ii) if, though not likely to incite ordinary men, they are likely to incite the audience actually addressed.'[18]

27.09

(b) The mens rea of seditious libel

It is tolerably clear that the prosecution is required to prove that the person prosecuted must be shown to have acted with the intention to produce public disorders, as opposed to having an intention to utter the words said to give rise to the risk of disorder.[19]

27.10

An unsuccessful attempt to resuscitate the offence was made in *R v Bow Street Magistrates' Court, ex p Choudhury*[20] which was an attempt to prosecute for sedition the author and publisher of Salman Rushdie's book *The Satanic Verses*. The Divisional Court upheld the decision of the magistrates to refuse to issue a summons. The court held that:

27.11

> . . . the seditious intention on which a prosecution for seditious libel must be founded is an intention to incite to violence or to create public disturbance or disorder against His Majesty or the institutions of government. Proof of an intention to promote feelings of ill-will and hostility between different classes of subjects does not alone establish a seditious intention. Not only must there be proof of an incitement to violence in this connection but it must be violence or resistance or defiance for the purpose of disturbing constituted authority.

What amounted to 'constituted authority' for these purposes was further said to extend to 'some person or body holding public office or discharging some public

---

[16] See JC Smith, *Smith and Hogan: Criminal Law* (10th edn, London: Butterworths, 2002) 759, citing *R v Aldred* (1909) 22 Cox CC 1.

[17] *R v Burns* (1886) 16 Cox CC 355.

[18] Smith and Hogan (n 16 above) 760.

[19] *R v Caunt* (unreported, but discussed by ECS Wade in (1948) LQR 203. See also *R v Burns* (1886) 16 Cox CC 355 at 364.

[20] [1991] 1 QB 429. *R v Messenger* (1668) Kel 70; *R v Dammaree* (1709) 15 St Tr 521; *R v Frost* (1839) 9 C & P 129. *Foster's Crown Cases and Discourses* (Oxford: Clarendon Press, 1762) 210. See LW Maher, 'The Use and Abuse of Sedition' (1992) 14 Sydney L Rev 261.

function of the state'. These remarks were obiter only in the case itself, and it is suggested that taken literally they take the offence far wider than is to be found in previous authorities and wider than is necessary for the purposes of the criminal law.

(3) Terrorism

(a) Background

27.12 It would be a mistake to suppose that the UK law devoted to the suppression of terrorism is particularly modern, let alone a reaction to the events that convulsed the world following the attacks in the United States in September 2001. Continuing problems in Northern Ireland meant that the statute books were replete with offences directed against terrorist groups and their activities.[21] Some time before the American events and in the light of a continued improvement of the situation in Northern Ireland, it had been decided to replace the legislation hitherto designated as 'temporary' with a revised framework. The opportunity was to be taken at the same time to acknowledge that there was an increasingly international dimension to terrorism, and the result was the Terrorism Act 2000.[22] Further initiatives were taken in response to the American atrocities, in the Anti-terrorism, Crime and Security Act 2001.[23] These confirm and extend the measures relating to, for example, proscribed organizations, ie organizations (including Irish and other domestic or foreign groups) membership of or support for which is a criminal offence. The jurisdiction of the courts was extended to cover inciting terrorism overseas, and to deal with bribery and corruption outside this country. The law was also extended in certain respects to cater for the situation where the motivation for the commission of offences against the person or public order offences was religious hatred. The Acts additionally offer extended police powers, including powers to set up cordons, compulsory obtaining of testimony and evidence, additional disclosure powers in connection with financial organizations, account monitoring information, arrest without warrant, stop and search, search of premises, search of persons, parking restrictions, port and border controls, retention of communications data, electronic surveillance, curtailment of access to legal advice and the right to silence, and prohibitions on torture.

(b) The offences

27.13 Many of the offences are familiar, originating as they do in the earlier terrorism legislation relating to Northern Ireland. Some of the offences are broadened by the 2001 legislation.

---

[21] One might instance in particular the Explosive Substances Act 1883 as an example of this.
[22] For the criminal law aspects of which, see JJ Rowe, 'The Terrorism Act 2000' [2001] Crim LR 527.
[23] The best overview is C Walker, *Blackstone's Guide to the Anti-Terrorism Legislation* (Oxford: OUP, 2002) ch 6.

(i) Weapons training

A person commits an offence under s 54(1) of the Terrorism Act 2000 (as amen-   **27.14**
ded), punishable with ten years' imprisonment, if he provides instruction or training in the making or use of:

(a) firearms,
(aa) radioactive material or weapons designed or adapted for the discharge of any
       radioactive material;
(b) explosives or
(c) chemical,[24] biological[25] or nuclear weapons.

It is also an offence to receive such training, or to invite another to undergo such
training whether in this country or abroad.

(ii) Noxious substances

Sections 113 to 115 of the Anti-terrorism, Crime and Security Act 2001 extend   **27.15**
the offences relating to the use of weapons, and threats and hoaxes concerning
such weapons, to chemical, biological and nuclear weapons and materials. Specific intentions are required, such as that the conduct be 'designed to influence the
government or to intimidate the public or a section of the public'.[26] The action
must also have the effect of causing serious violence to a person, serious damage to
property, endangering human life, creating a serious risk to health or safety or inducing public fear that there is a danger to life or a serious health or safety risk.

(iii) Directing a terrorist organization[27]

Section 56(1) of the Terrorism Act 2000 makes it an offence to direct at any level   **27.16**
the activities of an organization which is concerned in the commission of acts of
terrorism. The offence is regarded as extremely serious, carrying as it does the
mandatory penalty of life imprisonment.

(iv) Possessing materials for terrorist purposes

Section 57(1) of the Terrorism Act 2000 makes it an offence to possess an article   **27.17**
in circumstances which give rise to a reasonable suspicion that the possession is
for a purpose connected with the commission, preparation or instigation of an
act of terrorism. Possession of the article(s) may be in itself inherently perfectly
lawful, for example rubber gloves, wires, batteries, overalls and balaclavas. Their
possession in conjunction with one another is what gives rise to the suspicion of

---

[24] Chemical Weapons Act 1996, s 1.
[25] Within the meaning of the Biological Weapons Act 1974.
[26] Anti-terrorism, Crime and Security Act 2001, s 113(1)(c).
[27] See C Walker and K Reid, 'The Offence of Directing Terrorist Organisations' [1993] Crim LR
669.

a terrorist purpose. It is a defence for the person charged to prove that his possession of the article was not for one of the designated purposes, or that the possessor did not know of the presence of the item on the premises or had no control of it. A question has arisen in connection with these two defences as to whether or not they breach Article 6(2) ECHR by placing a burden of proof upon the defendant.[28]

(v) Collecting information

27.18 It is an offence to collect, record or possess information of a kind likely to be useful to a person committing or preparing an act of terrorism.[29] The offence is of considerable breadth, and could easily sweep within its scope those who are collecting information for perfectly legitimate reasons, such as the journalist.[30] That they have a defence of reasonable excuse does not entirely allay the concerns that arise from such catch-all drafting.

(4) Piracy[31]

27.19 Notwithstanding the general rule that international law is not part of English law unless it has been incorporated by statute or by judicial decision, piracy iure gentium occupies a special position, and the English courts will exercise jurisdiction over persons who commit piracy as defined by international law. From time to time, statutes were enacted which added to and modified the law thus created, but the usefulness of these was questioned in the light of the fact that the criminal law generally applies to British ships afloat and in territorial waters, so that persons (whether or not British nationals) who commit offences on board or within the territorial sea were subject to the jurisdiction of the ordinary criminal law. The statutes were therefore repealed.[32] The death penalty for piracy was abolished by the Crime and Disorder Act 1998, s 36.

(5) Hijacking

27.20 A modern form of piracy involves the hijacking of aeroplanes. This is dealt with in the Aviation Security Act 1982, ss 1–4 of which create offences of hijacking, destroying, damaging or endangering safety of aircraft and offences in relation to certain dangerous articles. Since the offence is not infrequently committed by persons fleeing their own countries, and from fear of persecution, it is important to note that it has been held that the defences of duress of circumstances and/or necessity may be available. Thus, in *R v Abdul-Hussain*,[33] it was held that the judge

---

[28] *R v DPP, ex p Kebilene* [2000] 2 AC 326.
[29] Terrorism Act 2000, s 58.
[30] See L Hickman, 'Press Freedom and the New Legislation' (2001) 151 NLJ 716.
[31] See Smith and Hogan (n 5 above) 815 et seq.
[32] Statute Law (Repeals) Act 1993, s 1(1), Sch 1, Pt 1.
[33] [1999] Crim LR 570.

had erred in withdrawing the defence from the jury on the grounds that it was available only where the threat was sufficiently close and immediate as to give rise to a virtually spontaneous reaction to the physical risk arising. He should instead have asked himself whether there was evidence of such fear in the minds of the appellants at the time of the hijacking as to impel them to act as they did and whether, if so, there was evidence that the danger they feared objectively existed and that hijacking was a reasonable and proportionate response to it. More recently in *R v Safi*,[34] the test was restated to make it plain that what was required was not a threat in fact, but a reasonable belief that such a threat existed. Evidence as to whether or not there was an actual threat is, on this view, technically relevant only on the question as to the reasonableness or otherwise of the defendant's belief.

(6) *Official Secrets*[35]

(a) History

The Official Secrets Act 1911 was passed through the House of Commons in a single day, in response to scares about spies. Section 1 of the Act, which remains law, is concerned with spying, although it has been held that the marginal note to the section which reads 'penalties for spying' cannot be used to limit the language in which the Act is couched. In *Chandler v DPP*,[36] anti-nuclear protesters who had trespassed on an airfield were held to have committed an offence under s 1(1)(a), which makes it an offence: **27.21**

> If any person for any purpose prejudicial to the safety or interests of the State–
> (a) approaches, inspects, passes over or is in the neighbourhood of, or enters any prohibited place within the meaning of this Act . . .

(b) Section 2

Section 2 of the 1911 Act, which was concerned with the wrongful communication of information was regularly criticized, principally because it applied where the information had been obtained 'owing to his position as a person who holds or has held office under Her Majesty'. There was no need for the information to be of a sensitive or secret character, and in the *Sunday Telegraph* case[37] Caulfield J was severely critical of the section and its catchall nature, and he said that the trial: **27.22**

---

[34] [2003] EWCA Crim 1809; The Times, 10 June 2003.

[35] See Feldman (n 12 above) 889 et seq; SH Bailey, DJ Harris and BL Jones, *Civil Liberties: Cases and Materials* (5th edn, London: Butterworths, 2000) ch 8. See also DGT Williams, *Not in the Public Interest* (London: Hutchinson, 1965), which is the best historical account, and DGT Williams, 'Official Secrecy in the Courts' in P Glazebrook (ed), *Reshaping the Criminal Law* (London: Stevens, 1978) 154.

[36] [1964] AC 763.

[37] Unreported, but see Jonathan Aitken, *Officially Secret* (London: Weidenfeld & Nicolson, 1971).

. . . may well alert those who govern us to at least to consider whether or not section 2 had reached retirement age and should be pensioned off.

Another defect was that the section was riddled with obscurities—who could authorize the disclosure or receipt of information?

27.23   The Act also gave rise to the charge of selective prosecution—those who embarrassed the government were more likely to be prosecuted.[38] Following a report[39] and a great deal of subsequent consultation,[40] legislation was eventually enacted that became the Official Secrets Act 1989.

(c) Official Secrets Act 1989[41]

27.24   The new Act was said to be intended to 'replace the blunderbuss of section 2 with the armalite rifle' of the new law. The Act is based in essence upon a concept of harm or 'damage' to the interests of the state, those interests being identified as: security and intelligence[42] (a clear reaction to the defeat in *Spycatcher*), defence,[43] international relations,[44] information 'likely to be useful to criminals,'[45] 'unauthorised disclosure of confidential information'[46] and information entrusted in confidence to other states or international organizations.[47]

(i) The tests of damage

27.25   Liability arises under several sections of the Act only where the leaker makes a 'damaging disclosure' to the identified interest,[48] a notion that is then further identified in the Act itself in relation to that interest. A disclosure is damaging to defence, for example, if it damages the capability of any part of the armed forces of the Crown to carry out their tasks or leads to loss of life or injury to members of those forces or serious damage to the equipment or installations of those forces or inter alia 'endangers the interests of the United Kingdom abroad'.[49] This is

---

[38] As in the *ABC* case (1977–78); see A Nicol [1979] Crim LR 284. See also *R v Ponting* [1985] Crim LR 318 (as to which see R Thomas, 'The British Official Secrets Act 1911–1939 and the Ponting Case' [1986] Crim LR 491).

[39] *Report of the Departmental Committee on Section 2 of the Official Secrets Act 1911* (The Franks report) (Cmnd 5104, 1972).

[40] Which culminated in the White Paper, *Reform of Section 2 of the Official Secrets Act 1911* (Cm 408, 1988).

[41] S Palmer, 'Tightening Secrecy Law: The Official Secrets Act 1989' [1990] PL 243; J Griffith, 'The Official Secrets Act 1989' (1989) 16 JLS 273.

[42] s 1.

[43] s 2.

[44] s 3.

[45] s 4.

[46] s 5.

[47] s 6.

[48] See ss 1(4), 2(2), 3(2), 4(2)–(3), 5(3), 6(4).

[49] s 2(2).

remarkably broad language to be found in a criminal statute, a consideration only partly tempered by the fact that it will be for theprosecution to prove beyond reasonable doubt that the terms of the Act are satisfied.

(ii) Defences

In several sections of the Act,[50] it is provided that: 27.26

> . . . it is a defence to prove that at the time of the alleged offence he did not know and had no reasonable cause to believe that the information, document or article in question was such as is mentioned (in the relevant subsection) or that its disclosure would be damaging with the meaning of that subsection.

(iii) No defence of 'public interest'

Another (unsuccessful) argument in the *R v Ponting*[51] proceedings was that the   27.27
disclosure was in the public interest. Attempts to insert such a defence into the new legislation were resisted by the government, which argued that, since the whole Act was premised upon the test of damage, it could not be argued that it was in the public interest to disclose that which was, by definition, 'damaging'. An exception to the 'damaging disclosure' is, however, made in s 1 of the Act, which forbids members and former members of the security services from making any disclosures, damaging or otherwise. An attempt was made in *R v Shayler*[52] to persuade the courts, and ultimately the House of Lords, that this was a violation of Article 10 ECHR. The House noted that Article 10(2) acknowledged that the rights of free speech affirmed in Article 10(1) were not absolute but permitted the member states to act in the protection of their national security interests, and concluded that it is no defence that one was publishing information in the public interest.

(iv) Authorization[53]

A disclosure is 'authorized' under the Act only if it is made by the individual   27.28
concerned 'in accordance with his official duty'. This harks back to the arguments in the *Ponting* case, where it was argued (unsuccessfully) that the word 'duty' might include a moral or social duty to inform the public. The wording of the Act makes it clear that these arguments are not available under the 1989 legislation.

---

[50] See ss 1(5), 2(3), 3(4), 4(4)–(5), 5(2)–(4), 6(2)–(3).
[51] [1985] Crim LR 318.
[52] [2002] UKHL 11; [2003] 1 AC 247.
[53] s 7.

B. Public Order[54]

(1) Introduction[55]

(a) Background

27.29   Historically, the most serious of the offences against public order (riot) had a public dispersal rationale. Where there was an unlawful assembly, it was open to magistrates to 'read the Riot Act',[56] requiring the crowd to disperse in the course of the following hour. A failure to leave the spot meant that the unlawful assembly (a misdemeanour) became a riot (a felony) whose commission could be prevented by fatal force if necessary. The Riot Act was repealed in 1967, when the distinction between felonies and misdemeanours was abolished, and with it (unreplaced) went the dispersal rationale. Subsequent suggestions that some modified version of the Riot Act might be enacted requiring an unruly mob to disperse have never borne fruit.

27.30   Why, then, should we have such offences now? There are two possibilities that might be advanced. The first is to be found in the remote harms[57] attendant in incipient public disorder, which carry inchoate danger to persons and property. Related to this is the fear that is caused to the public by riotous behaviour (and even by affrays).

27.31   A second explanation of the public order offences is that they can be used to supplement and make up for the deficiencies of the laws of complicity. It may often be the case, in the sorts of situations with which these offences are concerned, that it will not be possible to identify the person whom the perpetrator has assaulted, or possible to prove that he has encouraged another person to commit an assault. It is enough to establish liability that the participants encourage others to use violence, even though they cannot be shown to have used it themselves. It is not necessary to prove precisely who has done what to whom, and with exactly what consequences as is required by the law of assault[58] or criminal damage.

---

[54]   This section will not be considering the practically important aspects of public order law such as the powers of the police to arrest for 'breach of the peace' which, though arrestable, is not strictly speaking a criminal offence. Nor will it deal with the powers of the courts to bind a person over to keep the peace. Minor offences may be committed by persons who organize marches and demonstrations under the Public Order Act 1986, but there is not space to consider them in the course of this work.

[55]   R Card, *Public Order Law* (Bristol: Jordans, 2000); ATH Smith, *The Offences Against Public Order* (London: Sweet & Maxwell, 1987); Smith and Hogan (n 16 above).

[56]   The Riot Act 1714 (now repealed) provided: 'Our Sovereign Lord the King chargeth and commandeth all Persons, being assembled, immediately to disperse themselves, and peaceably to depart to their Habitations, or to their lawful Business, upon the Pains contained in the Act made in the first year of King George, for preventing Tumults and riotous Assemblies. God Save the King.'

[57]   See A von Hirsch, 'Extending the Harm Principle: "Remote" Harms and Fair Imputation' in AP Simester and ATH Smith (eds), *Harm and Culpability* (Oxford: OUP, 1996) 259–276.

[58]   The courts have insisted that the public order offences should not be automatically charged in cases of disorder, where offences against the person are the more obvious choice of charge; see *R v Plavecz* [2002] EWCA Crim 1802; [2002] Crim LR 837.

(b) Public Order Act 1986

Two of the principal offences in this area (riot and affray) are in origin the crea-   **27.32**
tures of the common law. But the modern source of the law is to be found in the
work of Parliament, the Public Order Act 1986.[59] This Act is not a code of public
order law in the sense that it is a comprehensive restatement of all of the relevant
applicable law. It does not deal with obstruction of the highway or obstruction of
constables, and it expressly preserves the powers of the police to preserve the
peace. Nevertheless, it does abolish the common law public order offences,[60] repeal certain ancient statutes,[61] and create a number of new statutory offences.

The Act creates a hierarchical structure of offences graded in terms of available   **27.33**
penalty and procedure. The new offences are riot, violent disorder and affray.
There are two lesser offences of using threats, abuse or insults, and disorderly conduct. Each will be examined in turn.

(2) Violent Disorder

(a) Background

This is the innovative offence, and was envisaged by Parliament as the mainstay of   **27.34**
the new public order law. Riot is essentially an aggravated form of violent disorder. The offence is intended to deal with groups of persons participating in public
disorder whose conduct has gone beyond the stage of mere insults or abuse, and
amounts to the threat or use of violence.

(b) The offence defined

Section 2 provides: **27.35**

> (1) Where 3 or more persons who are present together use or threaten unlawful vio-
> lence and the conduct of them (taken together) is such as would cause a person of
> reasonable firmness present at the scene to fear for his personal safety, each of the
> persons using or threatening unlawful violence is guilty of violence disorder.
> (2) It is immaterial whether or not the 3 or more use or threaten unlawful violence
> simultaneously.

The offence is punishable with imprisonment for five years, and is triable either
way.

---

[59] House of Commons, Fifth Report from the Home Affairs Committee, *The Law Relating to
Public Order* (1979–80 HC 756–1); Lord Scarman, *The Brixton Disorders* (Cmnd 8427, 1981) Pt
VI; Home Office White Paper, *Review of Public Order Law* (Cmnd 9510, 1985), ATH Smith,
'Public Order Law: The Government's Proposals' [1985] PL 533; Law Commission, *Offences
Relating to Public Order* (Law Com No 123, 1983).
[60] s 9.
[61] Including the Tumultuous Petitioning Act 1661, the Shipping Offences Act 1793 and the
Seditious Meetings Act 1817.

(c) Elements of the offence

27.36 To give effect to the element of group action that is the essence of violent disorder, the Act provides that there must be three or more persons present together using or threatening unlawful violence before the offence can be committed. A number of points may be made. It is not necessary that three people should be convicted of the offence; if some of those present have managed to escape detection or capture, there could still be a conviction. It is sufficient that three are present using or threatening unlawful violence. The point is made by *R v Mahroof.* [62] The appellant had been charged, along with two others, with the offence of violent disorder. He had gone to the house of one of the co-defendants (and with two others, X and Y who were not named in the indictment, nor charged). There was an argument about money and M claimed that money was owing to him. Failing to obtain satisfaction, he went and obtained a can of petrol, returned and threatened to set fire to the victim and the victim's house.

27.37 The two named co-defendants were acquitted, and the question was then whether the prosecutor could allege that other people (X and Y) in addition to those identified in the indictment could make up the threesome. The trial judge had told the jury that they could convict in spite of the acquittal of one of the three defendants. The Court held that technically this could be done in a case like the present one, because of the proved presence at the scene of X and Y. But if such a step were to be taken, this should have been done by the prosecution early in the proceedings so that the defendants knew what charge they had to meet. In the circumstances, the Court quashed the conviction, but substituted a conviction for the lesser offence created by s 4.

27.38 The court in *Mahroof* does not appear to have considered s 6(2) and (7), the effect of which is this: if a co-defendant had been acquitted because of a lack of mens rea, he might still count towards the quorum for the purposes of violent disorder. But he would not count if he had been acting in self-defence, because what he was doing was not then unlawful.

(d) The meaning of 'violence'

27.39 The element of 'violence' in violent disorder is common to the offences of riot, affray and s 4 and its meaning is critical to a proper understanding of the scope of

---

[62] (1989) 88 Cr App R 317. Followed in *R v Worton* (1990) 154 JP 201. See, however, *R v Turpin* [1990] Crim LR 514, where it was held that such a direction is not always required. Where, as here, the defendant had admitted that the offence of violent disorder had been committed by those present, his own defence being that he was not present, it was open to the jury to convict even in the absence of a direction.

the law.[63] But the Act does not define what the concept entails. In *R v Brodie*,[64] it was held that the term covered a situation where three men followed another along a path for some three-quarters of a mile and three-quarters of an hour in the middle of the night. This was said to create 'an aura of violence'.

(i) Brutus v Cozens: *an excursus*

Parliamentary draftsmen often use words without further explaining or defining their meaning in the context of the legislation. This is a perfectly defensible legislative technique, but it has the difficulty for the commentator that it may be difficult to say with certainty how the Act will apply in any given situation. This decision is exacerbated by the tendency in the courts to say that when the legislator has used 'ordinary' English language, its meaning is a matter of fact for the jury or other tribunal of fact. The high water mark of this approach is to be found in the decision of the House of Lords in *Brutus v Cozens*,[65] a prosecution under the Public Order Act 1936 for conduct that was threatening, abusive or insulting. Given that these words are being used to describe the use of language, they plainly frequently involve important free-speech issues, and it is possible to discern in recent case law a tendency to have far greater regard to the importance of freedom of speech issues than was apparent in the earlier decisions.[66] **27.40**

(e) Violence

According to the *Oxford English Dictionary*, violence means 'the exercise of physical force so as to inflict injury or damage to persons or property', and the Law Commission accepted that this is its primary meaning.[67] **27.41**

In addition to this primary meaning, the Act clarifies what violence connotes in this context,[68] and makes it plain that it includes violent conduct towards **27.42**

---

[63] And decisions on the law of riot, violent disorder and affray might be used to illustrate the scope of the Act. The common elements of the offence may not be precisely interchangeable, but it would be most unsatisfactory if the same expression used in the different sections of the Act were accorded a different meaning from one context to another.

[64] [2000] Crim LR 775.

[65] [1973] AC 834. See also *R v Dawson* (1976) 64 Cr App R 170 where it was held that the meaning to be attributed to 'force' in robbery is, as an ordinary word, for the jury to decide, and *Chambers and Edwards v DPP* [1995] Crim LR 896, where the technique was applied to the meaning of 'disorderly' in s 5 of the Public Order Act 1986. In *R v White* [2001] EWCA Crim 216; [2001] 1 WLR 1352, it was held that the language of the legislation creating racially aggravated offences was to be given a broad and non-technical meaning.

[66] See, eg, *R v Percy* [2001] EWHC Admin 1125; [2002] Crim LR 835 and *Norwood v DPP* [2003] EWHC 1564, where the question whether a particular expression was threatening, abusive or insulting is said by Auld LJ to be a 'value judgment'. In *DPP v Stoke-on-Trent Magistrates' Court* [2003] EWHC 1593; The Times, 23 June 2003, Auld LJ ruled that the derogatory use of the word 'Paki' was insulting for the purposes of the Football (Offences) Act 1991 and that it was 'of a racialist nature' for the purposes of that legislation.

[67] Law Com No 123 (n 59 above) para 5.31.

[68] s 8.

property as well as towards persons, and can include missile throwing, where the missile is capable of causing injury but does not hit or falls short. This was included at the suggestion of the Law Commission largely to cover the missile hurler, who is difficult to catch under the offences against the person or criminal damage. When a person hurls a brick over the picket line, it may be difficult to prove that he hit any body or thing. Even if that can be proved, he can then say (when charged with criminal damage) that he meant to hit a person or conversely that he meant to damage property if charged with an offence against the person. It is then for the prosecutor to prove that he intended to cause one or other type of damage (or was reckless thereto). This extended definition of violence means that he is guilty if he can be shown to have intended to hurl the brick.

(f) The presence or absence of bystanders

27.43 Although the Act creates 'public order' offences, it makes it clear at several points in the Act that no person of reasonable firmness need actually be, or be likely to be, present at the scene.[69] Rather, the requirement that the violence should be such as would cause a person of reasonable firmness present at the scene to fear for his personal safety is a measure of the violence used. It does not denote a requirement that any person should actually be present at the scene. Instead, the matter is to be measured by asking whether, if a reasonable bystander were present, he would be frightened for his personal safety. The notional bystander must be an objectively reasonable one, and not a person of peculiar timidity, nor a person of exceptional courage.

27.44 There must be an explicit direction to the jury as to how they should assess this element of the offence. The point was apparently overlooked in *R v Sanchez*.[70] The defendant had been sitting drunk in a car outside her boyfriend's house. When he joined her, she attacked him with a knife, saying that if she could not have him, then nobody else could. She was convicted of affray.

27.45 On appeal, it was contended that the trial judge had failed to direct the jury that they needed to have regard not only to those immediately involved in the violence, but also to the 'hypothetical reasonable bystander' who would have to be put in fear for his personal safety if the offence was to be made out. The Criminal Division of the Court of Appeal agreed that there had been a misdirection of the kind suggested.

27.46 The Court added that it was not really sure that this was a public order case at all. The violence used had been solely between the appellant and her boyfriend, personal to them and it took place in the car park of a block of flats, with every

[69] ss 1(4), 2(3), 3(4), relating to riot, violent disorder and affray respectively.
[70] [1996] Crim LR 572.

opportunity for the hypothetical bystander to distance himself. Even if there had been a proper direction, the Court said that it could not have been sure that the offence was made out.

(g) Public or private?

Several provisions of the Act are to the effect that the offences 'may be committed in private as well as in public places'.[71] It is surprising to find that, in a statute concerned with offences against public order, the offences may be committed in private as well as in public. The reasoning here was as follows: riots might well take place on private premises. Gatecrashers at a party or in a private club, who cause untold havoc, should not be exempt from liability merely because they could assert that they were causing their mayhem on somebody else's private property. Bystanders were quite as likely to be terrified whether the location was a public or a private place. The logic of the point having been made in connection with the law of riot, the point was then carried through the first three sections of the Act creating the serious offences of riot, violent disorder and affray.

27.47

(h) Illegality

The word 'unlawful' imports all of the common law defences: self defence, private defence, duress of circumstances and so forth. A direction that overlooked this point was given in *R v Rothwell and Barton*.[72] The appellants had gone to a nightclub where one of their number had had a previous altercation with a doorman. Violence ensued and the police were called. Counsel for the appellants addressed the jury on the basis that what was done was either self-defence, reasonable defence of a friend or prevention of a breach of the peace. The Recorder directed the jury that these were not defences to the charge. It was held that the Recorder was wrong to have done this. The word 'unlawful' was included in the Act to ensure that those concepts were preserved under the new Act.

27.48

(i) Mens rea

Section 6(2) provides that

27.49

> a person is guilty of violent disorder or affray only if he intends[73] to use or threaten violence or is aware that his conduct may be violent or threaten violence.

Partly because of uncertainties surrounding the notion of violence, it is not entirely easy to say what 'awareness' might denote in this context. In what circumstances (other than those involving intoxication, for which separate provision is

---

[71] ss 2(4), 1(5) and 3(5) dealing with violent disorder, riot and affray respectively.
[72] [1993] Crim LR 626. See also *R v Hughes* [1995] Crim LR 957.
[73] As to the meaning of intention, see para 24.23 above.

made) might a person be able plausibly to say that he lacked an awareness that his own conduct may be violent? A reflex reaction might qualify, or accident.

(j) Intoxication as a defence

27.50 Section 6(5) of the Public Order Act spells out the exculpating effect of drunkenness in this context as follows:

> a person whose awareness is impaired by intoxication[74] shall be taken to be aware of that of which he would be aware if not intoxicated, unless he shows either that his intoxication was not self-induced or that it was caused solely by the taking or administration of a substance in the course of medical treatment.

This effectively spells out the common law rule for the offences of 'basic intent'.[75] Somewhat surprisingly, perhaps, there is no reported authority on the effect of the section. The Act appears to place a burden of proof upon the defendant to permit him to show that the intoxication was involuntary or that the substance was being taken for medicinal purposes.

(3) Riot

(a) The offence defined

27.51 The most serious of the public order offences is riot, which is punishable with imprisonment for ten years and is indictable only. It is defined in s 1, which provides:

> (1) Where 12 or more persons who are present together use or threaten unlawful violence for a common purpose and the conduct of them (taken together) is such as would cause a person of reasonable firmness present at the scene to fear for his personal safety, each of the persons using unlawful violence for the common purpose is guilty of riot.

It is immaterial whether or not the 12 or more use or threaten unlawful violence simultaneously, and the common purpose may be inferred from conduct.

(b) The distinctive features of riot

27.52 The distinctive features of riot, as opposed to violent disorder and affray, are that there must be 12 or more people present together, they must have a common purpose, and only the person who actually 'uses' violence is guilty of the offence. The latter point is to a certain extent undermined by the decision in *R v Jefferson*[76] where it was held that the ordinary rules of aiding and abetting are applicable to the serious public order offences. In context this means that a person is guilty if he himself actually uses violence, or if he aids, abets, counsels or procures another to

---

[74] Which may be the result of drink, drugs or other means; Public Order Act 1986, s 6(6).
[75] As to which, see para 24.38 above.
[76] [1994] 1 All ER 270.

do so. A further point of distinction is that the element of purpose makes the offence one of specific intent for the purpose of the rules relating to the exculpating effects of intoxication. The common purpose may be either lawful or unlawful, so long as the participants intend to accomplish their objective through the use of unlawful means. In *Jefferson*, for example, the participants were intending to celebrate the victory of the English football team in a match with Egypt, the allegation being that they intended to do this through unlawful violence.

(4) Affray

Affray was an ancient offence, deriving its title from the Norman French effrayer, 'to frighten'. It had more or less disappeared from the prosecutor's armoury until it was revived in the late 1950s, and the vitality of the offence was affirmed by the House of Lords in *Button v Swain*.[77] It is now an offence punishable with imprisonment for three years, triable either way.

27.53

Section 3(1) of the Public Order Act 1986 provides that:

27.54

> a person is guilty of affray if he uses or threatens unlawful violence towards another and his conduct is such as would cause a person of reasonable firmness present at the scene to fear for his personal safety.

The relatively low penalty represents something of a change in the law. The common law offence was technically punishable with life imprisonment, but in sentencing and prosecuting practice two forms of it emerged. It was used against those who engaged in staged, pitched battles and organized gang fights. As such it was a rather serious offence, punishable in practice with imprisonment for seven to ten years. It was also used to prosecute spontaneous fights, especially pub brawls. In such situations, the offence was a useful supplement to the offences against the person, in situations where a victim was hurt, but it was not possible to say (because of the poor quality of identification evidence or something of the sort) who had actually caused the harm to the person. It is difficult to justify the continued existence of a serious form of the offence when little more could be proved than that the defendant had been present at the fight threatening violence, and the penalty available is thus now only three years.

27.55

(a) 'Uses towards another'

Since the offence requires proof that the violence has been used 'towards another', it follows that there must be at least one person present towards whom the threat must be uttered. Where a group were carrying primed petrol bombs, none of which were lit or brandished, the House of Lords held that this element was missing since, when the police arrived at the scene, the defendants had all immediately dispersed.[78]

27.56

---

[77] [1996] AC 591. See ID Brownlie, 'The Renovation of Affray' [1965] Crim LR 479.
[78] See *I v DPP* [2002] UKHL 10; [2002] 1 AC 285.

(b) Public or private

27.57 As explained above, the serious public order offences may be committed both in public and in private.[79] The cumulative effects of s 3(4) (which provides that no bystander need be or be likely to be present) and s 3(5) (which says that affray is capable of commission in both public and private places) complete the march of logic, with the result that if a person assaults another in private (for example in a domestic assault) and uses violence of such a degree that the other members of the household would be frightened if they were there, there is technically an affray. The public order essence of the offence has been wholly lost, and affray has become a form of aggravated assault.[80] The courts have on several occasions protested against the use of the public order offences when it would have been possible for the prosecutors to have charged with a different offence, such as the offences against the person,[81] or the possession of explosives.[82] That the proper application of prosecutorial charging practices will usually rescue the offence from this unsatisfactory situation is no real substitute for such catchall drafting.

27.58 The particularly odd effect of this filleting of the law is illustrated by *R v Davison,*[83] where the offence was committed by an attack on a policeman in a private house. When the police arrived to deal with a domestic dispute, they were told that the disagreement between the parties had been settled. They nevertheless decided that it would be prudent to check. The policeman walked into the flat, and noticed that the defendant had an eight-inch blade, which he told the defendant to put down. Instead of doing as instructed, the defendant made threatening gestures towards the policeman who backed away until he was up against an open window. The officer jumped over the settee and joined his colleagues, whereupon the defendant threw the knife out of the window and was arrested. On appeal, it appears to have been contended only that care must be taken to avoid extending the ambit of the offence, so that it covered every case of common assault, a consequence not intended by Parliament. The Court dismissed the appeal—looking at the Law Commission Report, it came to the conclusion that it was within the mischief intended. But affray was intended to be used, according to the Law Commission, 'in cases of pitched street battles between rival gangs, spontaneous fights in public houses, clubs and at seaside resorts and revenge attacks on individuals'. The circumstances of this case were very far removed from that. Furthermore, there could not have been an identification problem of the kind that justifies the retention of public order offences, in the sense that it was difficult to ascertain that the defendant committed the act towards a particular person.

---

[79] See para 24.74 above.
[80] See ATH Smith, 'The Metamorphosis of Affray' (1986) 136 NLJ 521.
[81] *R v Davison* [1992] Crim LR 31; *R v Plavecz* [2002] EWCA 1802, [2002] Crim LR 837.
[82] *I v DPP* [2001] UKHL 10; [2002] 1 AC 285.
[83] [1992] Crim LR 31.

(c) Words alone as affray

In an earlier section, the question whether words alone could constitute an assault **27.59**
was considered.[84] The same issue arises in the context of affray, but the statute says
that so far as the offence of affray is concerned, 'a threat cannot be made by the use
of words alone'.[85] The correct interpretation of the provision arose in *R v Dixon*,[86]
where the appellant had been convicted of affray. He was being pursued by two police officers after a fracas between himself and his wife. The police chased him and
cornered him in the driveway. He was accompanied by an 'alsatian-type' dog,
which was said to be in an excitable state, snarling and dashing about. The officers
asked him to take hold of the dog, but he kept saying 'go, go' to it, whereupon it ran
forward and bit both of the officers. The appellant restrained the animal, but then
again let it go, saying 'go, kill', at which point the officers retreated to await rein-
forcements. The appellant claimed that this was an accident, that he was simply out
walking the dog, that there had been no domestic incident and that the dog was an
ordinary family pet, not trained to attack or respond to orders to attack.

Before the Court of Appeal, it was argued (1) that words alone could not suffice **27.60**
for affray; (2) that there was insufficient evidence from which it could be inferred
that the dog had responded to words of encouragement; and (3) that the judge in
his summing up had failed to define the actus reus on which the prosecution
sought to rely. The prosecution case was that what happened in context should
not be treated as words alone. The appellant was in truth treating the dog as a
weapon; it was as though he were actually brandishing a weapon, at the same time
as he was uttering words intended to instil fear in to the officers. The court agreed,
emphasizing the presence of the dog in an excitable state. But it may be asked
whether the presence of the dog amounts to anything done by the owner. He still
merely utters words, and the Act says that these are not enough, however aggressive his language or manner.

(5) Public Order Act 1986, ss 4 and 5

(a) The constitutional significance of ss 4 and 5[87]

Although they are relatively low level,[88] the offences under ss 4 and 5 of the Public **27.61**
Order Act are of considerable constitutional significance, since they represent one

---

[84] See para 25.33 above.
[85] Public Order Act 1986, s 3(3).
[86] [1993] Crim LR 579. See also *R v Robinson* [1993] Crim LR 581 where the defendant was alleged by the prosecution to have created a menacing atmosphere by the language that he used. It was
held that merely uttering a threat in an aggressive tone of voice would not raise a sufficient case
within s 3 since that was no more than words alone, and the appeal was allowed.
[87] DGT Williams, 'Threats, Abuses, Insults' [1967] Crim LR 385.
[88] D Brown and T Ellis, *Policing low-level disorder: Police use of the Public Order Act 1986* (Home
Office research study, HMSO, 1994) 38.

of the limits to freedom of expression in public places. As the reported case law since 1986 will attest, they are frequently used in the context of political demonstrations, where those intending to make a political point are brought within the ambit of the law. The full significance of this has not always been appreciated by the courts, at least in part because of the operation of the *Brutus v Cozens* doctrine that the meaning of words is a matter of fact for the jury or other tribunal of fact.[89] The enactment of the HRA 1998 has enabled the courts to look with a fresh eye to the appropriate limits to this area of the law.

27.62 The change in approach is well illustrated by a comparison of *Brutus v Cozens* with the decision in *R v Percy*[90] where the appellant had been demonstrating against American military policy at an American air base, and 'desecrated' the American flag (by writing 'stop the war' across it) to the annoyance of American service personnel and families. She was charged with and convicted of the offence under s 5 of the Public Order Act 1986—insulting behaviour giving rise to harassment, alarm and distress. The District Judge had held that there was a pressing social need in a multicultural society to prevent denigration of objects of veneration and symbolic importance, and found the offence proved.

27.63 The Divisional Court allowed the appeal, saying that since the exceptions to the Article 10 guarantees of freedom of expression were to be narrowly construed, the court had to presume that the appellant's conduct was protected unless it was established that any restriction on her freedom of expression was strictly necessary. The court took the view that the District Judge had placed too much reliance on the factor that the appellant's insulting behaviour could have been avoided, which gave insufficient weight to the presumption in the appellant's favour, and failed to address the question of proportionality. There can be little doubt that, in the absence of the HRA arguments, the appeal would have failed; the court would have said that the question whether or not any particular conduct was or was not 'insulting' was one of fact for the tribunal.

27.64 It is as well that this was the outcome, since the case raised an issue that famously went to the US Supreme Court in 1989,[91] where it was held that convictions for flag desecration breached the first amendment free speech guarantees. It would have seemed odd, to say the least, that it might be an offence to desecrate the American flag in England, but not in America itself.

(b) Section 4: fear or provocation of violence

27.65 Section 4(1) of the Act provides that a person is guilty of an offence if he:

---

[89] Discussed at para 27.40 above.
[90] [2001] EWHC Admin 1125; [2002] Crim LR 835. See also *Norwood v DPP* [2003] EWHC 1564.
[91] *Texas v Johnson* 109 S Ct 2533 (1989).

(a) uses towards another person threatening, abusive or insulting words or behaviour, or

(b) distributes or displays to another person any writing, sign or other visible representation which is threatening, abusive or insulting,

with intent to cause that person to believe that immediate unlawful violence will be used against him or another by any person, or to provoke the immediate use of unlawful violence by that person or another, or whereby that person is likely to believe that such violence will be used or it is likely that such violence will be provoked.

This is, with one or two exceptions in its drafting, the successor of the old s 5 of the Public Order Act 1936. It sets very important (and to some extent controversial) limits to what it is permissible to say in public. To proscribe the use of threats is one thing; setting constraints upon abuse and insults is another matter. As Sedley LJ has said in the analogous context of arrest for breach of the peace:[92]

> Free speech includes not only the inoffensive but the irritating, the contentious, the eccentric, the heretical, the unwelcome and the provocative provided it does not tend to provoke violence. Freedom only to speak inoffensively is not worth having.

The penalty for commission of the offence is three months, but where the offence can be shown to have been committed intentionally, the penalty is enhanced to six months.[93] Both s 4 and s 5 (to be considered below) are offences of racial or religious aggravation.[94]

The section essentially creates two[95] quite different offences: **27.66**

- the threats, abuse and insults are used in such a way as to cause a person to fear that he is, in effect, about to be assaulted; or
- the conduct is such as to provoke another to behave in a violent way.

That the two offences are quite distinct is emphasized in *Winn v DPP*.[96] An attempt was being made to serve a court summons upon the defendant at his home. As soon as the process server announced who he was, the defendant struck him, and the process server withdrew to a distance. The appellant (as he became) emerged from his house holding an object in a threatening manner, swearing and shouting, saying 'if you come back here, you'll get this'.   **27.67**

He was charged with two offences; assault (to which he pleaded guilty) and s 4, the charge being framed in such a way that its essence was such that the appellant's   **27.68**

---

[92] *Redmond-Bate v DPP* [2000] HRLR 249. On the human rights implications, see ch 9 above, especially para 9.72.

[93] Public Order Act 1986, s 4A.

[94] Crime and Disorder Act 1998, s 31, as amended by the Anti-terrorism, Crime and Security Act 2001, ss 39(5), 39(6), 42.

[95] In *Winn v DPP* (1992) 156 JP 881, the court said that there were (once the different mentes reae were taken into account) four separate offences, but the additional two are simply variants of the two basic offences.

[96] ibid.

conduct was such as to provoke the process server to unlawful violence, because he had used such words or behaviour that it was likely that such behaviour would be provoked.

27.69 The court took the view that the charge was badly framed; the difficulty with putting the prosecution on that basis was that there was no evidence that the process server was likely to react violently. If by any chance he did, he would in all likelihood be acting in self defence. The variation between what was charged, and what had actually happened was such that the appeal had to be allowed.

(i) The presence of a victim

27.70 In both situations, the drafting of the section contemplates that there is a person present at whom the conduct is directed.[97] By contrast with the more serious offences under the Act (riot and violent disorder) which do not require the presence of an actual victim, there must here be present a person at whom the conduct is directed, and who suffers, or may suffer, the harassment, alarm or distress. That person may be a policeman,[98] though the courts may take rather more persuasion that the requirement is fulfilled when the victim is a person who is routinely subject to abuse as part of his job.

(ii) The immediacy of the violence threatened or feared

27.71 It will be observed that s 4 refers to the requirement of immediacy. The effect of the requirement was considered in *R v Horseferry Road Magistrates' Court, ex p Siadatan*.[99] The applicant had laid an information against Salman Rushdie and his publishers, accusing them of committing an offence under s 4 of the Public Order Act 1986, namely that he had written and published a book (*The Satanic Verses*) that was 'threatening, abusive or insulting with intent . . . to provoke immediate use of unlawful violence . . . or whereby . . . it is likely that such violence will be provoked'. The book was offensive to many Muslims, and a shop owned by the publishers (in the King's Road, London) was actually fire-bombed while the book was on sale there.

27.72 The magistrate refused to issue a summons, on the grounds that the requirements of immediacy in the Act were not satisfied. The Act refers to 'immediate unlawful violence', but the use of the words 'such violence' in the section appears on its face to refer back only to the words 'unlawful violence' earlier in the statute, and not to

---

[97] Although it is not necessary to call the person as a witness to establish that he did suffer as the section describes; *R v Swanston* (1997) 161 JP 203.

[98] *R v Orum* [1989] 1 WLR 88. See ATH Smith, 'Assaulting and Abusing the Police' [1988] Crim LR 600; for a different view, see C Gearty, 'Trusting the Judges: Public Order' [1989] CLJ 168.

[99] [1991] 1 QB 280. See T Modood, 'British Asian Muslims and the Rushdie Affair' (1990) 61 Political Q 143.

be qualified by the word 'immediate'. There was certainly an argument, therefore, on the construction of the statute, and its history, that the section should be construed in the way contended for by the applicant.

The court looked at the language used by the Law Commission in its prelimi-   **27.73**
nary report, and found that it made reference to 'immediate unlawful violence' and 'immediate use of unlawful violence'. It was regrettable that the draftsman had not achieved the same clarity and precision, but it was possible to read the Act in the way in which the Law Commission had intended, so that an offence was committed only if another was provoked to the immediate use of unlawful violence.

As reasons of policy, the court advanced the considerations that the section was   **27.74**
in the middle of other provisions concerned with immediate violence—riot and violent disorder. The court considered it most unlikely that Parliament could have intended to include, among sections which undoubtedly deal with conduct having an immediate impact on bystanders, a section creating an offence for conduct which is likely to lead to violence at some unspecified time in the future. Additionally, the court said that this was a literal reading of the section and that, since this was a penal statute, the courts should interpret it restrictively. It has been held that the question of immediacy is to be judged from the perspective of the victim.[100] Thus, where a person sent threatening letters to an organization assisting the Asian community stating that a bombing campaign was to be arranged, it was held that the Stipendiary Magistrate was wrong to have ruled that since the letter was silent as to when the threat would be carried out, there was insufficient evidence of immediacy to support the charge. The Divisional Court held that so long as the victims believed and were likely to believe that something could happen at any time there was a case to answer.

(iii) The exemption for conduct in a 'dwelling'

Consistently with the policy consideration that the Act is concerned with public   **27.75**
order, there is an exemption from liability for the situation where the conduct complained of takes place inside a dwelling.[101] But that exemption does not apply where the conduct complained of can be seen outside the dwelling. An offensive poster in a window, for example, is caught by the Act if it can be read from the street.[102]

---

[100] *DPP v Ramos* [2000] Crim LR 768. See in particular the commentary of Sir John Smith, who questions whether this is a correct application of the law's requirement that there should be a fear of immediate violence, which is not, as he points out, the same thing as an immediate fear of violence. See also *Atkin v DPP* (1989) 89 Cr App R 199.
[101] Public Order Act 1986, s 4(2).
[102] As in *Norwood v DPP* [2003] EWHC 1564.

(iv) Illegality

27.76   As with the earlier sections in the Act, an offence is committed only where the use or threat of violence is 'unlawful', and this has the effect of preserving the common law defences such as self-defence.[103]

(v) The mental element

27.77   The mens rea for the offence is rather complicated, consisting as it does of both the intention or awareness used in relation to the unlawful violence or fear thereof referred to in s 4(1), and the additional requirement, to be found in s 4(3) which stipulates that a person is guilty of the offence only if he intends his words or behaviour to be threatening, abusive or insulting or is aware that they may be.

(c) Section 5: disorderly conduct

27.78   Even more controversial than s 4 was the succeeding provision, which deals with, inter alia, 'disorderly conduct'. The provision was stated in the report[104] to be aimed at:

> . . . hooligans on housing estates causing disturbances in the common parts of blocks of flats, blockading entrances, throwing things down stairs, banging on doors, peering in at windows,[105] and knocking over dustbins;
> groups of youths persistently shouting abuse and obscenities or pestering people waiting to catch public transport or to enter a hall or cinema;
> someone turning out the light in a crowded dance hall, in a way likely to cause panic;
> rowdy behaviour[106] in the streets late at night which alarms local residents.

(i) The offence defined

> (1) A person is guilty of an offence if he–
>   (a) uses threatening, abusive or insulting words or behaviour, or disorderly behaviour, or
>   (b) displays any writing, sign or other visible representation which is threatening, abusive or insulting
>   within the hearing or sight of a person likely to be caused harassment, alarm or distress thereby.

---

[103] *R v Afzal* [1993] Crim LR 791 (self-defence).
[104] Law Com No 123 (n 59 above) para 3.22.
[105] In *Smith v Chief Superintendent of Woking Police Station* (1983) 76 Cr App R 234, it was held that such conduct might amount to an assault where the person spied upon saw the Peeping Tom, and was frightened by him, so long as the defendant intended to frighten.
[106] In *Vigon v DPP* [1998] Crim LR 289, it was held that the section applied to the conduct of a man who operated a market stall where he sold women's swim-wear. He placed a partially concealed video camera in the changing area so that when customers tried on the garments, they would be filmed. It did not seem to the Divisional Court that the words of s 5 were meant to be limited to rowdy behaviour. It was open to the justices to say that the actus in setting up the camera, switching it on and then letting it run amounted to disorderly behaviour.

The principal differences between s 5 and s 4 are that the former can be committed by the commission of 'disorderly'[107] conduct, the language and conduct need not be proved to have been directed at another person, and effect of the conduct is not that it causes a fear of violence, but that the audience might suffer harassment, alarm or distress. **27.79**

(ii) What constitutes harassment?

It has been held that no element of apprehension about one's personal safety is necessary for there to be harassment. In *Chambers and Edwards v DPP*[108] the appellants were demonstrators who persistently prevented a surveyor from using his theodolite by blocking its infra red beam with parts of their body, or a placard. The Crown Court found that the behaviour caused harassment to the surveyor, but that there was no threat or fear of violence; the surveyor was inconvenienced or annoyed by the appellant's behaviour, and this was such as to be likely to cause harassment to the surveyor. The Divisional Court concluded that there was quite sufficient evidence for the Crown Court to have arrived at this conclusion. **27.80**

(iii) The presence of a victim

Unlike s 4, there is no requirement that the objectionable language or conduct is directed at another. But it is clear that there must be another within whose sight or hearing the objectionable conduct takes place and who may suffer the harassment, alarm or distress. **27.81**

(iv) Public or private

As with the s 4 offence, there is a private dwelling exception,[109] with the added difference that in relation to s 5, the exception is more clearly cast as a 'defence' with whatever consequences this might produce for the burden of proof being placed upon the defendant. In *R v Chappell*,[110] the appellant was alleged to have committed the offence on four occasions by putting offensive (threatening, abusive and insulting) letters through the letter box of his victim. He was charged with offences under both paras (a) and (b). This was held to be an inappropriate use of the Act. These provisions plainly contemplate offences with a requisite public element. That is why the dwelling exception was enacted. Its purpose was to make clear the intention to exclude conduct taking place within the dwelling house. **27.82**

---

[107] In *Chambers and Edwards v DPP* [1995] Crim LR 896, it was said that the approach adopted in *Brutus v Cozens* [1973] AC 854 was the correct one to adopt as to the meaning of 'disorderly' in this context, namely the question whether any particular conduct is disorderly is a question of fact for the trial court to determine.
[108] ibid.
[109] Public Order Act 1968, s 5(2) and (3)(b).
[110] (1988) 89 Cr App R 82.

(v) The mental element

27.83 It must be shown that the actors intended that their words or conduct be threatening, abusive or insulting or at least that they were aware that this may be so (and similarly with disorderly conduct).[111] This has on occasion afforded a surprisingly high degree of protection. In *R v Clarke, Lewis, O'Connell and O'Keefe*,[112] the respondents were demonstrating outside an abortion clinic, each carrying a picture of an aborted foetus which they displayed to the police on uniform patrol duty, and which they declined to put away when requested to do so. The magistrates concluded that the pictures were abusive and insulting giving the words their ordinary everyday meaning, and that they were displayed in the sight of a person likely to be caused harassment, alarm or distress and did in fact do so, causing distress to the police officer concerned. However, they dismissed the prosecutions on the basis that none of the respondents intended that the pictures should be threatening, abusive or insulting, nor was any of them aware that they might be.

27.84 The prosecutor appealed by way of case stated, but the Divisional Court refused to interfere, taking the view that it had to be said that they were at least aware that the display or continuing display of the pictures might be abusive or insulting. On that the court held that this was a question of fact for the magistrates, who had simply accepted the defendants' evidence on the point. The court was not prepared to upset that ruling.

(vi) Defences—that the conduct was 'reasonable'

27.85 It is a defence, to be found in s 5(3)(c), that the conduct was reasonable. This is a quite remarkable provision,[113] since it provokes the question, reasonable having regard to what factors? The Act is silent as to that question. In *DPP v Morrow, Geach and Thomas*[114] demonstrators outside an abortion clinic were shouting slogans, waving banners and preventing staff and patients from entering the clinic. Some of the patients had become distressed as a result. The appellants argued in their defence that it was their belief there were unlawful abortions being conducted inside the clinic, and that their conduct was reasonable when viewed in that light. The Divisional Court said that there was ample evidence that, even allowing for the appellants' view, the conduct was not justified.

27.86 Whether such a result would be arrived at after the enactment of the HRA 1998 is perhaps questionable. It is clear that the fact that the appellants were exercising

---

[111] Public Order Act 1986, s 6(4).

[112] [1992] Crim LR 60.

[113] In *R v Marylebone Magistrates' Court, ex p Perry* [1992] Crim LR 514, a conviction was quashed on the grounds that the magistrate declined to listen to the evidence as to the evils of the apartheid system in South Africa that the defendants wished to advance in support of their claim that their trespass was in all the circumstances reasonable under the Act.

[114] [1994] Crim LR 58.

rights to freedom of expression would be more explicitly addressed. In *Norwood v DPP*,[115] Auld LJ said that 'the question whether a defendant's conduct is objectively reasonable necessarily included consideration of his right to freedom of expression under Article 10'.[116] His Lordship also made the point that this included all the circumstances, including those for which Article 10(2) makes provision for restrictions in the interests of others. The conclusion to which his Lordship came, in the light of those permissible restrictions, was that the poster displayed in the appellant's window ('Islam out of Britain' and a picture of the World Trade Centre in flames) was correctly treated by the District Judge in that case as justifying a conviction.

(vii) Illegality

Unlike the offence under s 4, there is no express provision to the effect that the conduct must be unlawful. But the illegality or otherwise of the behaviour can be considered under s 5(3)(c), that the conduct was reasonable. Thus, in *Kwasi-Poku v DPP*,[117] where the defendant had used force to resist the unlawful seizure of his property, it was held by the Divisional Court that the defence should have been considered by the magistrates.

27.87

(6) Incitement to Racial Hatred

Legislation making the utterance of racialist sentiments a criminal offence was first introduced in Britain by the Race Relations Act 1965. The common law offence of sedition, which consists of stirring hatred amongst different classes of Her Majesty's subjects, had fallen into disuse. An unsuccessful attempt to use it to prosecute for making anti-Semitic remarks[118] proved unsuccessful. Part III of the Public Order Act 1986 is now in effect a code of the various offences concerned with racial hatred.

27.88

The Act creates six offences,[119] all of which involve the use of language or material that is 'threatening, abusive or insulting', and each of which will be considered in turn. These are the use of words or behaviour, or the display of inflammatory written material,[120] the publication or distribution of racially inflammatory written

27.89

---

[115] [2003] EWHC 1564.
[116] ibid at [35].
[117] [1993] Crim LR 705.
[118] *R v Caunt* (1947), discussed in (1948) 64 LQR 203. In *R v Edwards* (1983) 5 Cr App R (S) 145, Lawton LJ describes incitement to racial hatred as the modern form of sedition.
[119] Although there may be alternative modes of committing the one offence. Section 27(2) provides that for the purposes of the rule against duplicity, each of ss 18–23 creates one offence. But if the prosecutor wishes to have the material that is the subject of a charge under s 18 forfeited, he must particularize the offence as being one of display; see s 25(1)(a).
[120] s 18.

material,[121] publicly performing a play containing inflammatory material,[122] distributing, playing or showing a recording containing such material,[123] broadcasting or including inflammatory material in a cable programme service[124] and possessing it with a view to publishing or distributing it.[125]

27.90 Underlying the offences now found in Pt III is the assumption that a serious threat to public order is inherent in certain forms of expression. But the assumption is controversial,[126] and there are obvious dangers that freedom of expression will be unnecessarily curtailed. Where speech is made criminal by direct reference to its contents, the way is opened for those in authority to censor minority or officially deprecated opinions. The legislature has sought to steer a course between these conflicting considerations by building public order elements into the definitions of the offences in the requirement that the conduct be threatening, abusive or insulting, and in the requirement that 'hatred' should be an intended or likely outcome of the expression impugned. The difficulty then is that the law does not reach those persons who couch their racialist sentiments in moderate terms rather than virulently abusive ones, whereas—so the argument runs—this propaganda is equally insidious. The fear is that, as Lawton LJ put it in *R v Relf,*[127] 'in this class of case constant repetition of lies might in the end lead some people into thinking that the lies are true. It is a matter of recent history that the constant repetition of lies in Central Europe led to the tragedy which came about in the years 1939 to 1945.'

27.91 The stance adopted by the Act does not concede the full force of the argument that 'there may be a need for a clear legislative recognition that expression of unashamedly racist sentiments, as such, is an aspect of freedom of speech too costly in terms of long-term social disharmony to be tolerated in a pluralistic society where ultimately the possibility of democracy and civil liberty may depend on wholehearted public commitment to the fostering of social solidarity'.[128] Instead, it compromises: expressions of opinion, however distasteful or offensive

---

[121] s 19.
[122] s 20.
[123] s 21.
[124] s 22.
[125] s 23.
[126] Discussed in greater detail in Barendt (n 2 above) 161-167. And see G Hughes, 'Prohibiting Incitement to Racial Hatred' (1966) 16 U of Toronto L Rev 361; I Hare, 'Legislating against hate: the legal response to bias crimes' (1997) 17 OJLS 414; and also paras 9.40 and 9.53–9.54 above. In *Glimmerveen v Netherlands* Application 8348/78 (1979) 4 EHRR 260, it was held that comparable Dutch legislation was not in breach of Art 10 ECHR, which guarantees freedom of speech. For a balanced discussion of the issues, see the Australian Human Rights Commission Report No 7, *Proposals for Amendments to the Racial Discrimination Act to Cover Incitement to Racial Hatred and Racial Defamation* (1984).
[127] (1979) 1 Cr App R (S) 111.
[128] R Cotterrell, 'Prosecuting Incitement to Racial Hatred' [1982] PL 379.

they may be, are not within the ambit of the legislation without the additional public order elements.

(7) Firearms

The control and licensing of firearms is a legal subject of considerable complexity well beyond the scope of this work.[129] The seven Firearms Acts 1968 to 1997 regulate (and penalize by serious penalty failures to comply with their requirements) such detailed matters as carrying firearms and imitation firearms in public places, dealing in firearms, possession, both generally and with intent to cause fear of violence and with intent to endanger life. **27.92**

(8) Offensive Weapons

A number of statutory provisions criminalize the carrying and use of offensive weapons. The principal offence is created by the Prevention of Crime Act 1953, s 1 of which provides that any person who 'without lawful authority or reasonable excuse' has with him in any public place any offensive weapon, is guilty of an offence punishable on indictment for up to four years. Supplementing this are the Criminal Justice Act 1988, s 139 (having an article with blade or point in a public place) and the Knives Act 1997. **27.93**

(9) Explosives

The Explosive Substances Act 1883 makes it an offence to cause an explosion likely to endanger life or to cause serious injury to property,[130] or to possess explosives with intent to endanger life or cause serious injury to property.[131] There is a considerable overlap with the Criminal Damage Act 1971,[132] and the Law Commission contemplated advocating[133] the repeal of these older Acts, desisting from doing so largely because it was felt that the explosives legislation belonged to the area of public order offences and should be considered in the context of a review of the offences relating to public order. **27.94**

(10) Trespass

(a) Statutory trespass offences

There is in English law no general offence of trespass, either in statute or at common law. However, the statutory and regulatory exceptions to this proposition are **27.95**

---

[129] Readers wishing to know more are referred to *Archbold* (n 5 above) ch 24.
[130] s 2.
[131] s 3.
[132] Considered at paras 26.110 et seq above.
[133] Law Commission, *Report on Offences of Damage to Property* (Law Com No 29, 1970).

now such that they virtually swallow up the general rule. Thus, it has long been a statutory offence to trespass on the railway,[134] on a ship,[135] an aircraft,[136] a licensed aerodrome,[137] military lands,[138] the premises of a foreign mission[139] and numerous other offences besides. A controversial addition to this catalogue is the creation of an offence of aggravated trespass[140] which was designed to be used against protesters such as hunt saboteurs who disrupt the lawful activities of others, of which they disapprove.

(b) Trespass on the highway

27.96 One feature of English law that requires special mention relates to the offence of obstructing the highway, contrary to s 137 of the Highways Act 1980. At common law, users of the highway were permitted to occupy the highway for purposes of passing and re-passing, and other uses reasonably incidental thereto. This meant that a static assembly on the highway was prima facie a trespass and as such an unlawful obstruction.[141] In *DPP v Jones*,[142] however, the House of Lords modified the common law position considerably; the public right to use the highway was not henceforth to be restricted to passing and re-passing, and the highway was to be regarded as a 'public place, on which all manner of reasonable activities may go on'. Lord Irvine LC said that users were entitled to undertake such activities as 'making a sketch, taking a photograph, handing out leaflets, collecting money for charity, singing carols, playing in a Salvation Army band, children playing a game on the pavement, having a picnic, or reading a book'. The question in each case is whether the actual user of the highway was reasonable in the circumstances, and the circumstances might include the fact that one was engaged in the exercise of one's rights to freedom of expression and freedom of association.

(11) Defamatory Libel

27.97 Although reputation is protected in English law through the processes of the civil law, there remains an offence, of uncertain ambit, of criminal libel.[143] Recently,

---

[134] Railways Regulation Act 1840, s 16.
[135] Merchant Shipping Act 1970, ss 77 (stowaways) and 78 (ships in port).
[136] Air Navigation Order, SI 1974/1114, art 48.
[137] Civil Aviation Act 1949, s 38. See also the Official Secrets Act 1911, s 11.
[138] Military Lands Act 1892, ss 14, 17(2).
[139] Criminal Law Act 1977, s 9.
[140] Criminal Justice and Public Order Act 1984, s 68. For discussion, see ATH Smith, 'The Criminal Justice and Public Order Act 1994—the public order elements' [1995] Crim LR 19.
[141] *Hubbard v Pitt* [1976] QB 142.
[142] [1999] 2 AC 240. The case involved a prosecution for trespassory assembly, contrary to s 14B(2) of the Public Order Act 1986, as inserted by s 70 of the Criminal Justice and Public Order Act 1994.
[143] For very thorough (and amusing) accounts of the law, see JR Spencer, 'Criminal Libel—A Skeleton in the Cupboard' [1977] Crim LR 383 and 465 and by the same author, 'The Press and the Reform of Criminal Libel' in Glazebrook (n 35 above) 266.

the law has diminished the attractiveness to claimants by placing caps on the amounts of damages that juries should be free to award,[144] and it is not impossible that the criminal law will be resuscitated.[145] But prosecutions against newspapers require the consent of a High Court judge.[146] A statement is defamatory for these purposes when published of and concerning a person in a way that is calculated to expose him to hatred, contempt or ridicule, or to damage him in his trade, business, profession, calling or office. The libel must be shown to be serious and not trivial, but does not have to be such as is likely to cause a breach of the peace,[147] and must be in a permanent form. The defences of privilege (absolute and qualified) and (probably) fair comment are available.

(12) Public Nuisance

There is a common law offence,[148] triable either way, which consists of committing 'an act not warranted by law or an omission to discharge a legal duty, which act or omission obstructs or causes inconvenience or damage to the public in the exercise of rights common to all His Majesty's subjects'.   **27.98**

The ambit of the offence thus described seems extraordinarily broad, and it must be seriously open to question whether the limits of the offence are sufficiently clear and certain as to escape condemnation under the terms of Article 7 ECHR. Many of the cases still cited as to the scope of the law date from the early years of the 19th century.   **27.99**

C. Public Morality and Decency

Arguments as to whether or not there is any such notion as a shared morality in modern Britain, and as to whether, if so, it was the province of the criminal law to proscribe immorality as such, were at the heart of the debate[149] sparked by the   **27.100**

---

[144] See, eg, *Campbell v News Group Newspapers* [2002] EWCA Civ 1143; [2002] EMLR 43 and *Lillie and Reed v Newcastle City Council* [2002] EWHC 1600; (2002) 146 SJLB 225, QBD: the courts were responding to the decision of the European Court of Human Rights in *Tolstoy Miloslavsky v UK* Series A No 323 (1995) 20 EHRR 442. See further paras 9.36–9.37 above.

[145] In 1991, the Supreme Court Procedure Committee, *Report on Practice and Procedure in Defamation* (Neill report) recommended that the criminal offence should be abolished, but the suggestion was not taken up when the Defamation Act 1996 was enacted.

[146] Law of Libel Amendment Act 1888, s 8.

[147] *Gleaves v Deakin* [1980] AC 477, HL; *Desmond v Thorn* [1983] 1 WLR 163. It may be noted that the current *Archbold* (n 5 above) directs readers to its pre-1994 editions for fuller treatment of the offence.

[148] Public nuisance is also a tort, actionable at the suit of a person who has suffered particular damage caused by the nuisance. See AM Dugdale (ed), *Clerk & Lindsell on Torts* (18th edn, London: Sweet & Maxwell, 2000).

[149] Two of the most prominent contributions to the debate were HLA Hart, *Law, Liberty and Morality* (London: OUP, 1963) and P Devlin, *The Enforcement of Morals* (London: OUP, 1965).

publication of Lord Wolfenden's *Report of the Committee on Homosexual Offences and Prostitution.*[150] That report had been commissioned as part of a drive to clear the streets (and in particular the streets of Soho in London) of soliciting prostitutes.[151] How far harm to self, and offence to others should be the subject of the criminal law remain controversial questions[152] in areas as diverse as sexual conduct, drug use and the publication (whether in written form, or graphically as in film, video and otherwise) of obscene and pornographic material. Lord Wolfenden's stance that many areas of private life were 'not the law's business' has certainly mitigated the harshness of the law that prevailed when he reported. But there is still a good deal of law that is restrictive of what may be published.

(1) Blasphemy[153]

27.101   It is a common law offence of somewhat uncertain ambit[154] to publish blasphemous matter, both orally, and in writing. Matter is said to be blasphemous when the publication of anti-Christian material is couched in terms of ridicule and vilification. The continued existence of the offence is controversial, and the Law Commission has recommended that consideration be given to abolishing it.[155] A different view has been taken by such experienced commentators as Lord Scarman who said, in *Whitehouse v Gay News and Lemon,*[156] that in a multicultural community such as modern Britain now is, there was an argument in favour of extending it to religions other than the Christian religion. A suggestion that the law might be judicially so extended was rejected by the Divisional Court in *R v Chief Metropolitan Stipendiary Magistrate, ex p Choudhury,*[157] the court taking the view that, if the law were to be extended in any way, that must be a matter for Parliament.

27.102   It has been held by the House of Lords that the only mens rea required is the intention to publish the words that were in fact blasphemous.[158] This makes the

---

[150] Cmnd 247, 1957.

[151] Prostitution is not as such a criminal offence in England. But the conduct of the business of prostitution is made very difficult by the existence of such offences as a prohibition of soliciting (Street Offences Act 1959, s 1), living off immoral earnings (Sexual Offences Act 1956, s 30) and brothel keeping (Sexual Offences Act 1956, ss 33–35).

[152] Explored by J Feinberg, *Offense to Others* (New York: OUP, 1985).

[153] For extended treatment, see Feldman (n 12 above) 907 et seq; Bailey, Harris and Jones (n 12 above) 1045 et seq.

[154] But not so uncertain as to be in breach of the certainty requirement of Art 10(2) that a restriction on freedom of expression must be 'prescribed by law': *Wingrove v UK* Application 17419/90 (1996) 24 EHRR 1. See by contrast the decision of the Irish Supreme Court in *Corway v Independent Newspapers (Ireland) Ltd* [1999] 4 IR 485.

[155] *Offences against Religion and Public Worship* (Law Com No 145, 1985).

[156] [1979] AC 617.

[157] [1991] 1 QB 429.

[158] *Whitehouse v Gay News and Lemon* [1979] AC 617.

offence one of strict liability so far as the effect on its audience is concerned. The defendant need not be proved to have intended or even known that his language might be regarded as blasphemous.

Successive attempts to challenge the law before the European Court of Human Rights have proved to be unsuccessful, partly because of the stance adopted by the Court in *Otto-Preminger Institute v Austria*[159] which took the view that since it is not possible to find in the legal and social orders of the contracting states a uniform conception of morals,[160] such matters were best left to the national authorities.[161] **27.103**

(2) Obscenity[162]

(a) Background

Although the criminal law affords some protection against the dissemination of pornography, there are in addition a great many other mechanisms through which such material is censored. Obscene articles may be made the subject of forfeiture proceedings,[163] and many of the leading cases on the interpretation of the legislation date from a time at which public tolerance of smutty material was a good deal less liberal than obtains at the beginnings of the 21st century, and it may well be that (partly through the judicious exercise of the discretion to prosecute) there is a considerable gap between the letter of the law, and its application in practice.[164] **27.104**

Obscene libel was at common law a misdemeanour, and the common law offence of obscene libel has not, technically, been abolished.[165] But the modern law is to be found in the Obscene Publications Act 1959 and 1964. An article is said to be obscene if its effect is such as to 'tend to deprave and corrupt persons who are likely, having regard to all the relevant circumstances, to read, see or hear the matter contained or embodied in it'.[166] The depravity and corruption is not confined to matters of a sexual nature. In *John Calder (Publications) Ltd v Powell*[167] it was **27.105**

---

[159] Series A No 295-A (1994) 19 EHRR 34.

[160] The point was articulated in *Handyside v UK* Series A No 24 (1976) 1 EHRR 737.

[161] See S Ghandhi and J James, 'The English Law of Blasphemy and the ECHR' [1998] European Human Rights L Rev 430; P Kearns, 'Uncultural God: Blasphemy Law's Reprieve and the Art Matrix' [2000] European Human Rights L Rev 512.

[162] See generally G Robertson, *Obscenity* (London: Weidenfeld & Nicolson, 1979).

[163] Under the Obscene Publications Act 1959, s 3.

[164] *R v Goring* [1999] Crim LR 670 is a relatively recent report of the application of the Act to films.

[165] Obscene Publications Act 1959, s 2(4) provides that no offence shall be prosecuted at common law where the essence of the offence is that the matter published is obscene. But in *R v Gibson* [1990] 2 QB 619, this did not protect the organizers of an exhibition at which one of the exhibits was the display of a head adorned with earrings made from freeze-dried foetuses. Since the prosecution was brought at common law, the defence of public good was not available.

[166] Obscene Publications Act 1959, s 1(1). This is essentially the test that was laid down in the common law in *R v Hicklin* (1868) LR 3 QB 360.

[167] [1965] 1 QB 509.

held to extend to the situation where drug-taking was portrayed in a favourable light. How literally the test of depravity and corruption is to be applied is problematic. For example, it has been held that it would be no defence that the persons to whom the article was published were already depraved and corrupted.[168]

(b) The offences

27.106   It is an offence to publish an obscene article, whether for gain or not;[169] or to have an obscene article for publication for gain (whether gain to himself or gain to another).

(c) The defence of public good

27.107   It is a defence to each of the offences that the publication of the article in question is justified as being for the public good on the ground that it is in the interests of science, literature, art or learning, or other objects of general concern.

27.108   It has been held that the exceptions provided for in Article 10(2) ECHR permit restrictions of the kind imposed by the obscenity laws.[170]

(3) Conspiracy to Corrupt Public Morals and Conspiracy to Outrage Public Decency

27.109   When the law of conspiracy was reformed in the Criminal Law Act 1977,[171] certain common law conspiracies were intended to be preserved. One area was that of conspiracy to corrupt public morals, an offence whose existence had been controversially affirmed by the House of Lords in *Shaw v DPP*.[172] In precisely what conduct the offence consists, it is much more difficult to say. In *Shaw* itself, it was held to extend to the publication of the *Ladies Directory* offering the services of prostitutes, and in *Knuller v DPP*[173] the logic of this was extended to convict the publishers of a homosexual contact magazine of a kind that is now utterly commonplace. The offence is a candidate for challenge under Article 7 ECHR because of its hopeless indeterminacy, but in the cognate area of obscenity, the European Court has proved itself to be willing to leave a considerable margin to individual states for the protection of public morals, and it may well take the same approach in this context were challenge to be issued.

---

[168]   *DPP v Whyte* [1972] AC 849.

[169]   Obscene Publications Act 1959, as amended by the Broadcasting Act 1990, s 162(1)(b) and by the Criminal Justice and Public Order Act 1994, s 168(1) and Sched 9.

[170]   *R v Perrin* [2002] EWCA 747. See also *R v Smethurst* [2001] EWCA Crim 772; [2002] 1 Cr App R 6.

[171]   See para 24.50 above.

[172]   [1962] AC 220.

[173]   [1973] AC 435.

It is also clear that there is an offence of outraging public decency, where the con- **27.110**
duct in question takes place where two members of the public might see it, and it
outrages and disgusts those who witness it. It has been held that it is not necessary
to lead direct evidence that witnesses were outraged and disgusted by what they
saw,[174] if this can be inferred from the evidence. The act itself must be such as to
outrage or disgust, and it is not permissible to seek to establish the offensive nature of the otherwise ambiguous act by reference to material to be found in, for example, private diaries.[175] Where two or more agree to do the act in question,
therefore, they can be convicted of a conspiracy to outrage public decency.

(4) Bigamy

It is, by statute, an offence for a person who, 'being married, shall marry any other **27.111**
person during the life of the former husband or wife . . . .'.[176] Whether, at a time
when the divorce and remarriage rates are as high as they are, the offence is properly classified as an offence against public morals and policy[177] is perhaps a moot
point.[178] The offence is likely to be treated as being serious for sentencing purposes
when another person is deceived,[179] or where it is done for money, or to enable the
evasion of immigration controls.[180]

---

[174] *R v Lunderbech* [1991] Crim LR 784. See also *R v May* (1989) 91 Cr App R 157.
[175] *R v Rowley* [1991] 1 WLR 1020.
[176] Offences Against the Person Act 1861, s 57.
[177] As it still is in, eg, *Archbold* (n 5 above) ch 31.
[178] In 'Bigamy and the Third Marriage' (1950) 13 MLR 417, Glanville Williams argued that the
law of bigamy should be recast in a 'secular' form saying that at least where no fraud was involved,
bigamy was little more than 'a minor offence of falsification of public records'.
[179] *R v Smith* (1994) 15 Cr App R (S) 407.
[180] *R v Cairns* [1997] 1 Cr App R (S) 118.

28

PRINCIPLES OF SENTENCING

A. Introduction

This chapter is concerned with an exploration of the principles of sentencing, and **28.01** how those principles currently operate within English law. It does not provide a detailed description of the wide range of sentencing powers which are currently available to the courts. Nor does it deal in any depth with those parts of criminal procedure which impact upon sentencing, such as committal for sentence, the presentation of pre-sentence and other reports to the sentencer, or appeals against sentence. For these, a specialist practitioner work on sentencing should be consulted.[1]

---

[1] The standard works are *Archbold: Criminal Evidence, Pleading and Practice* (London: Sweet & Maxwell, 2004) ch 5, and *Blackstone's Criminal Practice* (14th edn, Oxford: OUP, 2004) Pt E. The

Furthermore, the main emphasis in this chapter is on the sentencing of offenders aged 18 and over, although the rather different operation of sentencing principles as they affect juvenile offenders is referred to where appropriate.

28.02 The principles which govern sentencing are derived from a number of different sources. At the broadest level the principles reflect, and serve to constrain, the philosophical justifications for the imposition of punishment upon offenders. While these justifications are discussed at length in the academic literature on sentencing,[2] they are infrequently referred to directly by practitioners. An exception is the decision of the Court of Appeal in *R v Sargeant*,[3] in which Lawton LJ expounded what he took to be the 'classical principles' of sentencing: 'retribution', 'deterrence', 'prevention' and 'rehabilitation'. More recently, in *R v Howells*,[4] Lord Bingham CJ observed that '. . . sentences are in almost every case intended to protect the public, whether by punishing the offender or reforming him, or deterring him and others, or all of these things'. Modern legislation has declared the overriding aim of the youth justice system, including the sentencing of juveniles, to be 'the prevention of offending'.[5] Although there has been no stated aim for the sentencing of adults, the government now proposes that a list of aims, comprising punishment, crime reduction, public protection and reparation, should be specified and set out in statute.[6]

28.03 A list of aims or aspirations of this sort, which contains no clear set of priorities or hierarchy within it, offers little of practical value to sentencers. In sentencing cases such aims often conflict with one another, and point the sentencer in different directions. Sentencers will be required to make choices among these objectives. To some degree this can be dealt with by the exercise of discretion in individual cases, and nobody doubts that judicial discretion must remain an important element in sentencing practice. But wide and unprincipled discretion inevitably leads to disparity in sentencing, with very different outcomes arrived at in factually similar cases. Disparity is clearly objectionable, since it is a basic requirement of justice that like cases be treated alike, and different cases differently.[7] A recognition of the

---

four-volume encyclopedia *Current Sentencing Practice* (London: Sweet & Maxwell) contains extracts from many reported and unreported appellate sentencing decisions. All three works are used and regularly cited in the Crown Court and magistrates' courts. The leading book-length treatments of sentencing principles and practice are A Ashworth, *Sentencing and Criminal Justice* (3rd edn, London: Butterworths, 2000) and M Wasik, *Emmins on Sentencing* (4th edn, London: Blackstone, 2001).

[2] See A von Hirsch and A Ashworth, *Principled Sentencing; Readings on Theory and Policy* (2nd edn, Oxford: Hart, 1998).
[3] (1974) 60 Cr App R 74.
[4] [1999] 1 WLR 307.
[5] Crime and Disorder Act 1998, s 37.
[6] *Justice for All* (Cm 5563, 2002) para 5.8. Criminal Justice Act 2003, s 135.
[7] See further A Ashworth, 'Disentangling disparity' in D Pennington and S Lloyd-Bostock (eds), *The Psychology of Sentencing* (Oxford: Centre for Social-Legal Studies, 1987) 24.

importance of consistency should be the first step towards prioritizing sentencing aims and developing sentencing principles of general application. The priorities and principles in English law are given effect though a number of different mechanisms, the most important of which are the general legislative framework for sentencing, and the body of appellate guidance on sentencing principles developed through case law.[8]

The practice of sentencing (as well as the criminal process which precedes sentencing, and the executive functions which are consequent upon it) must first of all comply with the requirements of the European Convention for the Protection of Human Rights and Fundamental Freedoms (ECHR). **28.04**

B. Compliance with Human Rights Requirements

(1) Inhuman or Degrading Treatment or Punishment

At the most fundamental level, sentences created by Parliament or imposed by the courts must not infringe Article 3 ECHR, which prohibits 'inhuman or degrading treatment or punishment'. For example, the European Court of Human Rights (ECtHR) held in 1968 that corporal punishment of young offenders (a practice at that time carried out on the Isle of Man) contravened Article 3.[9] It is not now thought that a serious argument could be raised for breach of Article 3 in respect of any of the existing sentencing options in English law. Strasbourg case law on Article 3 establishes, however, that the characteristics of offenders subjected to the particular treatment or punishment must be taken into account.[10] It may be, therefore, that a punishment regarded as appropriate for a healthy adult could be found to be inhuman or degrading if used on a juvenile, or on a person suffering from a serious physical or mental condition.[11] **28.05**

In the important case of *V v UK*,[12] the ECtHR held that imposition of a mandatory indeterminate custodial sentence (of detention during Her Majesty's pleasure), on offenders aged ten at the time of the killing and 11 at the time of sentence, who were convicted of the murder of a young child, did not contravene Article 3. There had, however, been breach of Article 6 in the manner in which the defendants had been tried in an adult court. Section 109 of the Powers of Criminal Courts (Sentencing) Act 2000, which occasioned much discussion in **28.06**

---

[8] See paras 28.11 and 28.15 below.
[9] *Tyrer v UK* Series A No 26 (1979–80) 2 EHRR 1.
[10] See, eg, *Ireland v UK* Series A No 25 (1978) 2 EHRR 25.
[11] Especially where there is evidence that the condition will deteriorate more quickly as a result of incarceration: *Aerts v Belgium* (2000) 29 EHRR 50.
[12] (2000) 30 EHRR 121.

the human rights context, required the imposition of an 'automatic' life sentence on an offender convicted for the second time of a 'serious offence'. The section permitted no exception where the offender is mentally disordered and a hospital order would be a more appropriate disposal than a prison sentence.[13] The Court of Appeal in *R v Drew*[14] held, however, that s 109 did not breach Article 3, since the Secretary of State had power (exercised in this case) to transfer a life prisoner after sentence to receive treatment in a hospital. Applications to the European Commission brought by prisoners suffering from life-threatening medical conditions, such as AIDS, have not been successful.[15]

28.07 The above examples relate to the nature and content of particular sentences. The ECHR appears to offer less scope for constraining disproportionate sentencing more generally.[16] The existence of sentencing schemes of differing severity across contracting states cannot in itself form the basis for a challenge under Article 3[17] nor, it seems, can a change in the sentencing policy of a particular contracting state over a period of time. In the case of *Weeks v UK*[18] the ECtHR stated that the imposition of a life sentence for a relatively minor offence could be such a disproportionate penalty as to infringe Article 3, but added that this argument is more difficult to make if the purpose of custody is to provide public protection, or to rehabilitate, rather than simply to punish. The mix of sentencing aims referred to in para 28.02 above suggests that there will rarely if ever be a single purpose to a custodial sentence.[19] An argument that s 109, referred to above, contravened Article 3 on this ground was rejected by the Court of Appeal in *R v Offen (No 2)*,[20] because the section did permit the sentencing court to find 'exceptional circumstances' in any particular case, and thereby to avoid imposing the life sentence, where the offender was found not to represent a danger to the public.

28.08 There is an unresolved query as to whether community punishment orders (formerly known as community service orders) infringe Article 4(2) ECHR, which states that 'no-one shall be required to perform forced or compulsory labour'. Such an order, which requires the offender to perform unpaid work in the

---

[13] *R v Newman* [2000] 2 Cr App R (S) 227.
[14] [2003] UKHL 25; [2003] 1 WLR 1213.
[15] eg, the defendant in *R v Moore* (1993) 15 Cr App R (S) 97. See also *B v UK* (1995) 45 DR 41, an unsuccessful application to the Commission by a prisoner suffering from AIDS, arguing discriminatory treatment under Art 14.
[16] See A Ashworth, 'Sentencing and the Human Rights Act' (1999) 163 JP 64.
[17] See *R v Alden and Wright*, The Times, 27 February 2001.
[18] Series A No 114 (1987) 10 EHRR 293 at [47].
[19] Though there is a doubtful decision by the Commission in *Mansell v UK* [1997] EHRLR 666 to the effect that longer than commensurate custodial sentences imposed on violent or sexual offenders are entirely punitive. See para 28.12 below.
[20] [2001] 1 WLR 253.

community for up to a maximum 240 hours, may now[21] be imposed on an offender without consent. In practice, however, courts tend to assure themselves that offenders are minded to comply, since the imposition of a community sentence on an unwilling person is generally counter-productive.

(2) *Vagueness and Uncertainty*

English sentencing provisions may be found to contravene rights under the ECHR because of their vague and uncertain scope. In *Hashman and Harrup v UK*[22] the offenders, who disrupted a fox hunt as part of a noisy protest against blood sports, were bound over by a magistrates' court for a specified period 'to be of good behaviour'. It was held by the ECtHR that this form of sentence infringed Article 10 ECHR, which requires that state restrictions imposed on a citizen's freedom of expression must be such as are 'prescribed by law'. This form of sentence was so vague as to the conditions which it imposed upon those bound over, that it failed to satisfy the requirement of reasonable legal certainty.

28.09

(3) *Contravention of International Agreements*[23]

In addition to the requirements of the ECHR, sentencing laws must not contravene other international agreements to which the United Kingdom is a signatory, such as the European Communities Treaty. This is recognized in provisions of the Immigration Act 1971 relating to a court's power to recommend deportation of an offender.[24] It has been held that a power to ban an offender convicted of football-related violence from travelling abroad to attend football matches, as an order ancillary to sentence, is a lawful and proportionate restriction on a UK citizen's freedom of movement under EC law.[25] A recent provision to restrict overseas travel of offenders convicted of drug trafficking offences[26] has been criticized on the ground that it is incompatible with the International Covenant on Civil and Political Rights.[27] It may be questioned whether long-standing common law powers, such as the bind over to come up for judgment,[28] occasionally exercised by the Crown Court to order non-UK citizens to leave the country indefinitely or for a stated period,[29] are compatible with EC law and international agreements.

28.10

---

[21] Pre-existing general requirements of consent to a number of community sentences were abolished by the Crime (Sentences) Act 1997, s 38.

[22] Application 25594/94 (2000) 30 EHRR 241.

[23] See L Kurki, 'International standards for sentencing and punishment' in M Tonry and R Frase (eds), *Sentencing and Sanctions in Western Countries* (Oxford: OUP, 2001) ch 9.

[24] Art 48 EC; Directive 64/221 [1936–64] OJ Spec Ed 99, Arts 3 and 9. See *R v Escauriaza* (1987) 87 Cr App R 344.

[25] *Gough v Chief Constable of Derbyshire* [2002] EWCA Civ 351; [2002] QB 1213.

[26] Criminal Justice and Police Act 2001, s 33.

[27] Joint Committee on Human Rights, *First Special Report* (2001) para 36.

[28] See *R v Spratling* [1911] 1 KB 77.

[29] *R v Williams* [1982] 1 WLR 1398; *R v Gonzalez-Baillon* (11 July 1997). The point may never be tested, since the defendant must consent to be bound over.

C. Parliament and the Courts

(1) The General Legislative Framework

28.11 A general legislative framework for sentencing was established by the Criminal Justice Act 1991. This Act, now part of the consolidation statute, the Powers of Criminal Courts (Sentencing) Act 2000, set out governing principles for sentencing which are still applicable to the Crown Court and to magistrates' courts. Foremost among these is the requirement of proportionality (or desert)[30] as the predominant principle in sentence selection. Some critics have suggested that the 1991 Act merely restated the principles which the judges applied before the Act,[31] but this is to underestimate the effect of the legislation. In so far as there was a general justifying aim in English criminal sentencing before the 1991 Act, it was probably that of deterrence. The 1991 Act, in contrast, made offence seriousness the key driver in sentencing. Sentencers are required, under the 2000 Act consolidation, to determine whether the offence is 'serious enough to warrant [a community] sentence',[32] or is 'so serious that only [a custodial] sentence can be justified'.[33] Seriousness is also the key second order question in determining (where a community sentence is selected) the form and extent of restriction of liberty,[34] or (where custody is inevitable) its duration.[35] When a fine is the appropriate penalty, the amount of the fine should reflect primarily the seriousness of the offence.[36] The key concept of seriousness is not further defined in the legislation, but the writings on desert indicate that the principal elements are the degree of harm caused (or risked) by the offender, and the degree of the offender's culpability.[37]

28.12 Although desert is predominant in English sentencing, other important principles are also in play. In particular, if the offender has committed a violent offence or a sexual offence (as defined in the Act[38]), the sentencer may justify the imposition of custody on the basis of public protection rather than desert,[39] and may fix

---

[30] In fact the statute uses neither of these terms, but it is clear from the White Paper which preceded it that this was the theoretical basis for the Act. See Home Office, *Crime, Justice and Protecting the Public* (Cm 965, 1990) and, for detailed analysis of the Act's provisions, M Wasik and R Taylor, *Blackstone's Guide to the Criminal Justice Act 1991* (2nd edn, London: Blackstone, 1993).

[31] As to which see DA Thomas, *Principles of Sentencing* (2nd edn, London: Heinemann Educational, 1979).

[32] Powers of Criminal Courts (Sentencing) Act 2000, s 35(1).

[33] ibid s 79(2)(a).

[34] ibid s 35(3)(b).

[35] ibid s 80(2)(a).

[36] ibid s 128(2).

[37] See A von Hirsch, *Past or Future Crimes* (Manchester: Manchester University Press, 1986) ch 6 for the clearest exposition. This form of words is adopted by the government in *Justice for All* (n 6 above) para 5.10.

[38] Powers of Criminal Courts (Sentencing) Act 2000, s 161.

[39] ibid s 79(2)(b).

the duration of custody on the basis of the risk to the public posed by that offender.[40] It is important to appreciate, however, that the general rule in sentencing (violent and sexual offences included) is that the sentence should be proportionate to the offence committed. A longer-than-commensurate sentence for a violent or sexual offence can be imposed only where special risk to the public is made out and where the imposition of a proportionate sentence would not provide adequate protection.[41] To take a different example, in the selection of community sentences, the sentencer is always required to consider, alongside the degree of restriction of liberty involved, which of the available orders would be the most 'suitable' for the offender.[42]

The relatively clear statutory framework originating in the 1991 Act has been significantly compromised, by selective repeal[43] and by subsequent legislative developments. Many new non-custodial sentences have been introduced, and Parliament has encouraged the mixing and stacking of these sentences in a way which obscures proportionality.[44] The provision on the relevance to sentence of the offender's previous convictions has been amended in an obscure and unsatisfactory manner. Most significantly, however, in the Crime (Sentences) Act 1997, Parliament bolted on to the legislative scheme two special presumptive custodial sentences, requiring imprisonment for at least three years for third-time domestic burglars,[45] and imprisonment for at least seven years for third-time traffickers in Class A drugs.[46] In the same Act the 'automatic' life sentence[47] for those convicted of a second 'serious offence' (as defined in the Act[48]) was introduced. These provisions represent a clear departure from the proportionality principle of the 1991 Act, since they are based upon goals of deterrence and incapacitation of repeat offenders. **28.13**

At the time of writing, the legislative sentencing framework is under review. The Halliday report,[49] published in July 2001, recommended a number of changes. A White Paper[50] issued in July 2002 proposed that a revised statutory framework should list the purposes of sentencing.[51] It also clearly stated that, while sentence **28.14**

---

[40] ibid s 80(2)(b).
[41] *R v Christie* (1995) 16 Cr App R (S) 469.
[42] Powers of Criminal Courts (Sentencing) Act 2000, s 35(3)(a).
[43] Especially in the Criminal Justice Act 1993.
[44] See M Wasik and A von Hirsch, 'Non-custodial penalties and the principles of desert' [1988] Crim LR 555.
[45] Now Powers of Criminal Courts (Sentencing) Act 2000, s 111.
[46] ibid s 110.
[47] ibid s 109
[48] ibid s 109(5).
[49] Home Office, *Making Punishments Work*, Report of a Review of the Sentencing Framework for England and Wales (July 2001).
[50] *Justice for All* (n 6 above).
[51] See para 28.02 above.

severity should continue to reflect the seriousness of the offence committed, 'persistent offending should also justify a more severe view and more intensive efforts at preventing reoffending'.[52] This wording endorses the primacy of proportionality in sentencing, but with greater severity for repeat offending. Provisions in the Criminal Justice Act 2003 are designed to effect this policy change, but it will take some time before the full implications for sentencing practice become clear.

(2) Sentencing Guidelines

28.15 As we have seen, Parliament has provided a general legislative framework for sentencing. Maximum penalties for individual offences have also been laid down in statute.[53] Within these parameters, sentencing courts retain a fair degree of discretion over selection of sentence in individual cases. Their exercise of that discretion has been controlled in two main ways.

28.16 First, the Court of Appeal (Criminal Division), which is in practice the senior appellate court in sentencing matters, has over the years developed a series of sentencing principles of general application across the range of criminal offences. These principles govern such matters as sentencing at or near the statutory maximum for the offence, the circumstances in which consecutive or concurrent sentences may properly be imposed, the appropriate level of discount for a guilty plea, and so on. Some of these areas, such as the last mentioned, have also received legislative attention, but most of them remain case law constructs. These important general principles are considered individually, in more detail, below.

28.17 Secondly, concern over sentencing disparity has prompted the development of sentencing guidelines. In England guidelines are expressed in words rather than numbers, and there is nothing resembling the 'grid' systems prominent in the United States.[54] In the magistrates' courts guidelines have been produced by the Magistrates' Association, with the support and encouragement of the senior judiciary. The latest edition of the *Magistrates' Courts' Sentencing Guidelines* was issued in 2003. In earlier editions the Guidelines were confined to motoring offences, but they now cover just about all the offences which come regularly before the lower courts. The Guidelines are set out with one offence to each page. They indicate various features of a case which might be regarded as making the particular offence before the court more or less serious than an 'average' case. The court is

---

[52] *Justice for All* (n 6 above) para 5.10. For detailed criticism see A von Hirsch, 'Record-enhanced sentencing in England and Wales' in S Rex and M Tonry (eds), *Reform and Punishment* (Cullompton: Willan, 2002) ch 10.

[53] See further Ashworth (n 1 above) ch 2.

[54] See A von Hirsch, 'Guidance by numbers or words? Numerical versus narrative guidelines for sentencing' in M Wasik and K Pease (eds), *Sentencing Reform: Guidance or Guidelines* (Manchester: Manchester University Press, 1986) 46.

then reminded to look for matters of personal mitigation, and a starting point or 'guideline' is then suggested.[55]

For Crown Court sentencers the Court of Appeal has produced, from the early **28.18** 1980s onwards, a series of appellate guideline judgments. These judgments have always been issued in the context of a particular sentencing appeal, but the appeal itself provides a vehicle for the Lord Chief Justice or a senior Lord Justice of Appeal to issue general guidance in sentencing offences of the type in question. Such judgments typically indicate a range of mitigating and aggravating features, and often also indicate sentencing 'brackets' or 'starting points'. Leading guideline judgments are *R v Aramah*[56] on drugs, *R v Barrick*[57] on theft in breach of trust, *R v Millberry*[58] on rape, *R v McInerney*[59] on domestic burglary, *R v Oliver*[60] on child pornography, and *R v Webbe*[61] on handling stolen goods. Since 1998 the Court of Appeal has been assisted in this task by the Sentencing Advisory Panel, a broadly-based body which consults widely before submitting its advice to the Court.[62] The government has proposed further reform of these arrangements,[63] with guidelines henceforth to be issued by a new Sentencing Guidelines Council chaired by the Lord Chief Justice. It is envisaged that the Council would then be advised and assisted by the Panel.

D. Over-Arching Principles of Sentencing

(1) Non-Retroactivity of Penalty

There is a long-established judicial presumption against retroactivity in English **28.19** sentencing, but the old cases were always careful to allow for the possibility that Parliament might choose expressly to increase penalties with retrospective effect.[64] It is now clear, however, that any such legislative provision would be incompatible with the ECHR. Article 7(1) ECHR states that 'a heavier penalty' shall not be imposed on an offender 'than the one that was applicable at the time the offence was

---

[55] For further information see Ashworth (n 1 above) 122.
[56] (1982) 4 Cr App R (S) 407, modified and updated in later cases including *R v Warren* [1996] 1 Cr App R (S) 233, *R v Hurley* [1998] 1 Cr App R (S) 299, *R v Mashaollahi* [2001] 1 Cr App R (S) 96, and *R v Morris* [2001] 1 Cr App R (S) 87.
[57] (1985) 7 Cr App R (S) 143, updated in *R v Clark* [1998] 2 Cr App R 137.
[58] [2002] EWCA Crim 2891; [2003] 1 WLR 546.
[59] [2002] EWCA Crim 3003; [2003] 1 All ER 1089.
[60] [2002] EWCA Crim 2766; [2003] 2 Cr App R (S) 15.
[61] [2001] EWCA Crim 1217; [2002] 1 Cr App R (S) 22.
[62] Established under the Crime and Disorder Act 1998. See Sentencing Advisory Panel, *Fourth Annual Report* (June 2003).
[63] *Justice for All* (n 6 above) paras 5.13–5.18.
[64] *R v Chandra Dharma* (1905) 16 Cr App R 109; *DPP v Lamb* [1941] 2 KB 89; *Penwith Justices, ex p Hay, Pender and Perkes* (1979) 1 Cr App R (S) 265.

committed'. The case law on Article 7 shows that it is concerned with two types of case. The first is that, where a *new form* of penalty is created by Parliament as a means of dealing with a particular kind of offence, such penalty cannot be used in respect of an offence committed before it was made available.[65] The second is that, where Parliament has increased the *maximum* penalty for an offence, an offender sentenced now for an offence committed before that increase must be sentenced on the basis of the old maximum.[66] It is unclear whether Article 7 protection extends to an offender sentenced now for a crime committed years ago, but where *general sentencing levels* for that offence have increased over that time.

28.20   A sentencing provision which states that a penal consequence will follow if an offender with a previous conviction of a particular type is convicted of a further offence, will not infringe Article 7 as long as the further offence is committed after that provision comes into effect. This is because the offender is on notice of what the consequences will be of conviction for that further offence. Thus, in *R v Offen (No 2)*,[67] the Court of Appeal held that s 109 of the Powers of Criminal Courts (Sentencing) Act 2000[68] did not infringe Article 7, even though the first 'serious offence' was committed before that provision became law. The offender had been on notice of what would happen if a further 'serious offence' was committed. The same reasoning was applied in *Taylor v UK*,[69] a decision on the retrospective effect of confiscation orders in relation to drug trafficking offences.

28.21   Article 7 uses the term 'penalty', which has an autonomous meaning. It follows that Article 7 will not apply to a measure which, by its nature and purpose, is not properly to be regarded as a penalty. One example is the football banning order. The Divisional Court has held that a football banning order[70] is not a 'penalty', and so when a sentencer imposed a ban of six years (which was twice the maximum period permissible at the time the offence was committed) there was no breach of Article 7. Similar reasoning was applied in respect of an order disqualifying an offender from working with children in the future.[71] Another example is the requirement of registration for sex offenders under the Sex Offenders Act 1997. These obligations were held by the European Commission to be preventative rather than punitive in scope, and so the retrospective registration requirements of that Act did not infringe the ECHR.[72] On the other hand, in *Welch v*

---

[65] *Welch v UK* Series A No 307-A (1995) 20 EHRR 247.

[66] If it is unclear whether the offence was committed before or after the date when the maximum sentence was increased, the lower maximum applies: *R v Street* [1997] 2 Cr App R (S) 309; *R v Cairns* [1998] 1 Cr App R (S) 434.

[67] [2001] 1 WLR 253.

[68] See para 28.06 above.

[69] [1998] EHRLR 90.

[70] See para 28.10 above.

[71] *R v Field and Young* [2002] EWCA Crim 2912; [2003] 1 WLR 882.

[72] *Ibbotson v UK* [1999] Crim LR 153.

UK,[73] the ECtHR held that an order made to confiscate the proceeds of an offender convicted of a drug trafficking offence had punitive as well as preventative aims and so the retrospective provisions of the relevant statute did infringe Article 7. These decisions leave a degree of uncertainty over how the courts should treat sentencing measures which have both punitive and preventative aims.

(2) Sentencing Only for Offences Proved or Admitted

One of the most fundamental principles of sentencing is that the offender should be sentenced only for an offence (or offences) which have been proved against him following a contested trial, or admitted by him either by way of a guilty plea or by asking for such offences to be taken into consideration on sentence. A number of implications flow from this point. The first is that the judge should never assume, for sentencing purposes, that the offender is guilty of something more than the offence for which he has been convicted or to which he has pleaded guilty.[74] A person should not, for example, be sentenced for possession of drugs with intent to supply where he has been convicted of, or pleaded guilty to, simple possession. Even though there may have been evidence of supply, and had a charge for supply been brought it might have succeeded, the offender cannot be sentenced for a crime which has not formally been proved or admitted by him. The second is that a sentencer should not go behind what he or she regards as a perplexing finding by the jury, such as that the offender is guilty of unlawful wounding rather than wounding with intent, and pass sentence on the basis that the jury has fallen into error, and the offender is actually guilty of the greater offence.[75] A contrary approach, adopted in some other jurisdictions, is to permit the sentencer to go behind the formal returns on convictions and pass sentence for the 'real offence'.[76] Such an approach is objectionable for any system which takes seriously the formal requirements of proof of guilt.

28.22

The examples given in the last paragraph are relatively straightforward and clear, but the principle described there can give rise to real practical difficulties. Sometimes an offender is charged with a number of offences which are represented by the prosecution as 'sample counts', reflecting more extensive offending by the offender of a closely similar kind. This approach is common in cases involving repetitive thefts or deceptions, and can be found in other contexts too.[77] The prosecutor adopts this course quite properly in order to avoid bringing too many charges, thereby overloading the indictment, lengthening proceedings and

28.23

---

[73] Series A No 307-A (1995) 20 EHRR 247.

[74] *R v Lawrence* (1983) 5 Cr App R (S) 220; *R v O'Prey* (1999) 2 Cr App R (S) 83.

[75] *R v Hazelwood* (1984) 6 Cr App R (S) 52; *R v Baldwin* (1989) 11 Cr App R (S) 139.

[76] M Tonry, 'Real offense sentencing' (1981) 72 J of Crim L and Criminology 1550.

[77] Law Commission, *Effective prosecution of multiple offences: background and proposals for debate* (February 2002).

perhaps confusing the jury. It is now clearly established, however, that when sentencing an offender convicted on the basis of sample counts, the wider alleged offending must be disregarded for sentencing purposes unless the offender admits it.[78]

28.24 While this is consistent with the principle that sentence should be passed only for offences proved or admitted, it can result in sentence being passed on an artificial basis. In *R v Huchison*,[79] a case of incest, the victim's statement to the police alleged that sexual intercourse with the defendant had occurred regularly over a period of time, but the offender pleaded guilty to only one count of incest, the defence denying the other occasions. A sentence of four years, imposed by the trial judge on the basis that the offence had been repeated, was reduced by the Court of Appeal to two years. The judge was bound to sentence only on the basis of the single offence admitted. The main lesson seems to be that a sufficient number of instances of the alleged offending should be prosecuted in order that, on conviction, sentencing on the basis solely of those offences will permit the sentencer to pass a sentence which is appropriate to the overall seriousness of the offending.

(3) Sentencing Only on the Established Factual Basis

28.25 The Court of Appeal established through a series of decisions starting in the 1980s, that where there are important differences between the prosecution and defence versions of the facts of the offence, it is the responsibility of the sentencing judge to determine the factual basis on which the offender is to be sentenced. In such a case the judge (or magistrates in a summary case) will need to determine that issue by using a procedure known as a '*Newton* hearing'. The name derives from the leading decision, which is considered next.

(a) Establishing the facts after a guilty plea

28.26 In *R v Newton*[80] the offender pleaded guilty to an offence of buggery, committed on his wife. As the law then stood, the offence was committed if the act was proved, irrespective of the wife's consent. Clearly, however, a case involving consent was less serious for sentencing purposes than one where the sexual act had been forced. The defence lawyer made it clear in the plea in mitigation that, according to his client, the victim had consented. The judge passed a sentence of eight years' imprisonment without hearing any evidence on this issue. A sentence of that magnitude clearly reflected the judge's acceptance of the prosecution version of the facts. On appeal, the Court of Appeal cut the sentence to one year, to allow Newton's immediate release from prison (he had by the time of the appeal

---

[78] *R v Canavan* [1998] 1 Cr App R 79.
[79] [1972] 1 WLR 398, a decision approved in *Canavan*.
[80] (1982) 4 Cr App R (S) 388.

served ten months). Lord Lane CJ explained that in such a case there were three ways in which a judge could 'approach his difficult task'. In some circumstances it may be possible to obtain the answer from the jury. More usually, the judge should either hear evidence from each side and come to his own conclusion, or he could simply listen to submissions from counsel and then reach a view. On the facts of *Newton*, of course, the first option was not possible, since this was a guilty plea rather than a trial, but the judge had failed to adopt either of the other recommended courses of action. The basic propositions set out by Lord Lane CJ in this case have been developed in a number of later decisions of the Court of Appeal. The main points which have emerged are now considered.

It is not in every case where there is a factual dispute that it is necessary to conduct a *Newton* hearing. As Lord Lane CJ recognized in that case, the requirement arises only where there is 'a substantial conflict' between the two sides. If the factual difference is insignificant and would make no difference to the sentencing outcome, then it is not necessary to embark on the procedure.[81] Even so, it would be good sentencing practice for the judge to make it clear that he is sentencing on the defence version of the facts.[82] Alternatively, the sentencer may conclude that a *Newton* hearing is unnecessary, because the defence version of the facts is so implausible that it can be dismissed out of hand. While this course has on occasion been supported by the Court of Appeal,[83] a decision to reject the defence version in this way should not be taken lightly.[84] **28.27**

The initiative to request a *Newton* hearing will generally come from the defence, which should draw the relevant issue to the attention of the prosecution and the sentencer.[85] It will then be necessary to make arrangements to call relevant witnesses, and the defence must be aware that to initiate a factual dispute at the sentencing stage may well result in the loss of some of the discount which the defendant would expect to receive for pleading guilty.[86] This may be important in a sexual case if the victim, despite the offender's guilty plea, is still required to give evidence.[87] Whether to hold a *Newton* hearing or not is a matter for the sentencer and, indeed, it is open to the judge to decide to hold one, quite irrespective of the requests or wishes of the parties.[88] Occasionally, a sentencer has required an investigation into the facts, even though prosecution and defence have presented an agreed version of what happened. In *R v Beswick*[89] the judge was not prepared to **28.28**

---

[81] An example is *R v Bent* (1986) 8 Cr App R (S) 19.
[82] As recommended in *R v Hall* (1984) 6 Cr App R (S) 321, 324 *per* Lincoln J.
[83] An example is *R v Hawkins* (1985) 7 Cr App R (S) 351.
[84] See *R v Costley* (1989) 11 Cr App R (S) 357.
[85] *R v Tolera* [1988] Crim LR 425.
[86] *R v Satchell* [1997] 2 Cr App R (S) 258 and see para 28.59 below.
[87] *R v Williams* (1991) 12 Cr App R (S) 415.
[88] *R v Williams* (1983) 5 Cr App R (S) 134.
[89] [1996] 1 Cr App R (S) 343.

accept what had been agreed between the parties, and the Court of Appeal, in supporting the holding of a *Newton* hearing by the sentencer, commented that the prosecution should never lend its support to the defence in a factual basis which was unreal.

28.29   In *Newton* cases the burden of proof rests on the prosecution to establish the facts to the normal criminal standard of proof.[90] A *Newton* hearing bears a number of other similarities to trial procedure. The parties have the opportunity to call witnesses, and may cross-examine the witnesses for the other side. The defendant is a competent witness for the defence, but cannot be called by the prosecution. The hearing follows adversarial lines, and the sentencer should not intervene directly to cross-examine the defendant on the facts.[91] The judge should preside over the matter and, in effect, direct himself on the issue as if directing a jury.[92]

(b)   Establishing the facts after a guilty verdict

28.30   So far, the discussion in this section has centred upon defendants who plead guilty, and this is the circumstance in which the need for a *Newton* hearing is most likely to arise. Since there has been no trial, and no evidence heard at that stage from witnesses, there has been no opportunity to test the opposing versions of the facts. If there has been a trial, it is for the judge at the sentencing stage to form his own view of the facts on the evidence which has been heard. Sometimes, however, an issue of importance to sentence will not have been fully explored at trial because it was not relevant to liability. As we have seen, the sentence must be faithful to the jury's verdict, but sometimes that verdict does not make clear the factual basis on which it was reached. There is authority that the sentencer is not bound to accept the version of the facts which is most favourable to the defendant,[93] but general principles clearly dictate that the benefit of the doubt should normally be given.[94]

28.31   Lord Lane CJ said in *Newton* that it might be proper for the sentencer to ask the jury to explain the reasoning behind their verdict, but other cases suggest that this is an exceptional course for a judge to take.[95] One example is *R v McGlade*,[96] where the issue was the same as that which arose in *Newton* itself. The judge resolved it here by inviting the jury to indicate, in a rider to its verdict, whether they found the sexual act to have been consensual or not. Problems also arise in

---

[90]   *R v Kerrigan* (1993) 14 Cr App R (S) 179.
[91]   *R v McGrath and Casey* (1983) 5 Cr App R (S) 460, 463 *per* May LJ.
[92]   *R v Gandy* (1989) 11 Cr App R (S) 564.
[93]   *R v Triumph* (1984) 6 Cr App R (S) 120.
[94]   See *R v Stosiek* (1982) 4 Cr App R (S) 205.
[95]   *R v Larkin* [1943] KB 174; *R v Stosiek* (1982) 4 Cr App R (S) 205. In *R v Cranston* (1993) 14 Cr App R (S) 103, seeking advice from the jury was 'not necessarily wrong', according to the Court of Appeal.
[96]   (1990) 12 Cr App R (S) 105.

manslaughter, an offence which can be legally established in several different ways. If the defence has argued in a murder trial that the offender lacked the requisite intent or, alternatively, that he was suffering from diminished responsibility, the jury's verdict of guilty of manslaughter affords the judge little help in selecting the proper disposal.[97] The Court of Appeal has on occasion approved the judge asking further questions of the jury in such cases.[98]

(4) *Proportionality in Punishment*

The statutory sentencing framework described in para above requires that similarly situated offenders who have committed offences of comparable seriousness ought to receive similar sentences. This is a basic principle of natural justice, reflecting the importance of equality before the law. Proportionality, according to von Hirsch,[99] has two elements. First, *ordinal proportionality* provides that persons convicted of similar crimes should receive punishments of comparable severity (save for special aggravating or mitigating circumstances) and persons convicted of crimes of differing gravity should receive punishments correspondingly differentiated. Secondly, *cardinal proportionality* provides that there should be a proportionate relationship between the range of offences and the range of penalties, such that the use of the most severe sanction (ie, imprisonment) is confined in its use to the most serious examples of lawbreaking, and that less severe penalties are used for less serious cases. Here we are concerned with ordinal proportionality, and the issue of the overall severity of the penalty scale is considered in para 28.39 below. **28.32**

The basic premise of ordinal proportionality is reflected in the statutory sentencing framework, which requires that each upward step in the sentencing range which might be taken by the sentencer can only be justified by reference to the seriousness of the offence being sentenced. Thus, the question to be asked is whether the offence is 'serious enough' to justify a community sentence (or whether a discharge or fine would do instead), or whether the offence is 'so serious' that only a custodial sentence is justified. A key decision is whether the particular case before the court has crossed the custody threshold. The leading decision on this issue is *R v Howells*,[100] although the case in fact does little more than reiterate familiar considerations of seriousness, such as the 'nature and extent of the defendant's criminal intention, and the nature and extent of any injury or damage caused to the victim'. **28.33**

One can see the principles of ordinal proportionality at work most clearly when considering the sentencing of two or more offenders being dealt with for participation **28.34**

[97] See M Wasik, 'Form and function in the law of involuntary manslaughter' [1994] Crim LR 883.
[98] *R v Frankum* [1984] Crim LR 434; *R v Baldwin* (1989) 11 Cr App R (S) 139.
[99] von Hirsch (n 37 above) ch 4.
[100] [1999] 1 WLR 307.

in the same offence. It has long been established by the appellate courts that the nature and duration of the sentences passed on co-offenders must reflect their differing responsibilities for the offence, any aggravating or mitigating factors relevant to one and not the other, and their respective criminal records. Where there is an unacceptable difference in the sentencing of co-offenders, or where the imposition of similar sentences has failed to take into account relevant differences between them, the higher sentence may be reduced on appeal where 'right-thinking members of the public, with full knowledge of the facts and circumstances, learning of this sentence [would] consider that something had gone wrong with the administration of justice'.[101]

28.35 Sentencers should generally draw a distinction between offenders who had different degrees of involvement in the offence,[102] or where one is also being sentenced for an additional offence,[103] or where one has committed the offence while on bail.[104] Exceptionally, however, relevant differences between offenders can cancel themselves out, such as in *R v McClurkin*,[105] where sentences of three years' imprisonment for importation of cannabis were upheld on two offenders, one of whom played the main role in the offence but pleaded guilty and gave considerable assistance to the prosecuting authorities and the other played a lesser role but contested the case. This example shows that sentencing distinctions may be drawn for reasons other than the intrinsic seriousness of the case, or the degree of offender culpability. A timely guilty plea, entered by one offender but not the other, should normally be reflected in the sentence.[106] The relevance and weight of other personal mitigation is a matter for the sentencer's discretion, but will usually be reflected in the final outcome. A clean record is one of the most effective mitigating factors.[107]

28.36 At one time it was said that arguments based upon disparity of sentence would only be entertained on appeal if they related to co-offenders.[108] This line is untenable, however, since the disposal of similar cases in a disparate way by different courts is surely no more acceptable than disparity within a single case. The Court of Appeal is now regularly presented with sentencing appeals which proceed on the basis that a particular offender has been unfairly dealt with by comparison with other offenders sentenced for similar offences on other occasions. While members of the Court often stress that combinations of factors hardly ever arise

---

[101] *R v Fawcett* (1983) 5 Cr App R (S) 158, *per* Lawton LJ.
[102] An example is *R v Beard* (1992) 14 Cr App R (S) 302.
[103] An example is *R v Belton* [1997] 1 Cr App R (S) 215.
[104] An example is *R v Whitehead* (1995) 16 Cr App R (S) 395.
[105] (1979) 1 Cr App R (S) 67.
[106] See para 28.59 below.
[107] See para 28.83 below.
[108] See, eg, *R v Large* (1981) 3 Cr App R (S) 80.

twice in quite the same way, and so comparisons are difficult to make, there is now more willingness to consider a range of earlier appellate decisions as a background against which to judge the appropriateness of the sentence passed on the particular offender.[109]

A major exception to the principles of proportionality discussed in this paragraph arises where an offender is convicted of a violent offence or a sexual offence (as defined in the relevant legislation) and the sentencer is of the opinion that the public requires protection from the offender. Then, under the provisions of ss 79(2)(b) and 80(2)(b) of the Powers of Criminal Courts (Sentencing) Act 2000, the court may (not must) impose a longer than commensurate custodial sentence. Such a sentence is justified by the nature and degree of the risk posed by the offender, and so the proportionality restraints more usually evident in sentencing are of less importance here. A stark example is *R v Bestwick and Huddleston*[110] where two offenders had been involved in a series of offences of arson (which qualifies as a violent offence under the statute[111]). One was given a proportionate sentence of 30 months' detention in a young offenders institution, but the other received a sentence of five years' imprisonment, passed as a longer than commensurate sentence. An appeal on the basis of disparity was rejected, the Court of Appeal noting that the offender who received the longer sentence had a seriously disturbed personality and an obsession with lighting fires, and represented a real risk to the public. The other offender had a normal personality, and hence fell to be sentenced in accordance with the seriousness of the offence. In so far as this case might be seen as an example of sentencing disparity, that disparity derives from a distinction drawn within the legislative sentencing framework itself. **28.37**

The Court of Appeal has generally taken the view that where differential sentencing of co-offenders arises as a result of the legislative provisions, there is nothing that the sentencer can do. If one of the co-offenders is eligible for an automatic sentence of life imprisonment under s 109 of the Powers of Criminal Courts (Sentencing) Act 2000, but the other is not, no disparity arises.[112] Or, where an offender aged 24 receives an appropriate sentence of two years' imprisonment, there is no disparity because his 17-year-old co-offender is not eligible for a custodial sentence of that length by virtue of his age.[113] There is, it seems, no disparity in the sentencing of two offenders, one of whom is 21 and eligible for suspension of his **28.38**

---

[109] See, eg, *R v France* [2002] EWCA Crim 1419; [2003] 1 Cr App R (S) 25, in which the Court of Appeal referred to a dozen or so earlier decisions to determine the appropriate sentencing bracket for a case of causing death by dangerous driving where multiple deaths had resulted, and *R v Archer* [2002] EWCA Crim 1996; [2003] 1 Cr App R (S) 86, in which nine earlier decisions on sentencing in perjury or perverting the course of justice were considered.

[110] (1995) 16 Cr App R (S) 168.

[111] Powers of Criminal Courts Act 2000, s 161(3).

[112] *A-G's Reference (No 71 of 1999)* [1999] 2 Cr App R (S) 369.

[113] *R v Harper* (1995) 16 Cr App R (S) 639.

prison sentence, and the other of whom is not quite 21, for whom no suspension is possible,[114] nor where co-defendants receive sentences which fall either side of the four-year mark, which renders them subject to different provisions for early release.[115]

(5) Limiting the Severity of Punishment

28.39 Punishment should be only as severe as is required to meet the purpose of imposing it in the first place. Thus if punishment is imposed on a retributive basis, the amount imposed for an offence should reflect the seriousness of that offence, and no more. If punishment is imposed to achieve one or more utilitarian goals, then the amount should be no more than is thought to be required to achieve that goal, or goals. Additional punishment would be gratuitous. It might well constitute a form of institutional revenge, rather than proper state punishment, and contravene Article 3 ECHR. We are usually talking about the use of custodial sentences here but, in principle, the principle of limiting the severity of punishment applies to community orders and fines as well.[116]

28.40 Ashworth[117] has shown that this principle, which he calls the 'parsimony' principle, operates at two different levels. One level is that of overall sentencing policy, where endorsement of the principle by the legislature could produce an incremental reduction over time in the levels of sentences imposed. Parliament has, however, shown little inclination to scale down punishments in recent years. The trend has been very much in the opposite direction.[118] The other level is application of the principle to individual sentencing cases. The appellate courts, proceeding as they do on a case-by-case basis, are not well placed to make adjustments to overall sentencing levels. The judiciary has not managed to find a sustained and consistent message on severity of sentence.

28.41 From time to time the Court of Appeal has taken the opportunity, in the course of dealing with an appeal against sentence, to make a general statement about the overall severity of sentencing. These statements have mainly been prompted by an impending crisis in the sentenced custodial population. They have also reflected an acceptance of research evidence that there is little difference in effectiveness of

---

[114] cf *R v Horney* (1990) 12 Cr App R (S) 20.

[115] *R v Ensley* [1996] 1 Cr App R (S) 294; a sentencer may, however, adjust for an unusual adverse effect on early release eligibility: *R v Cozens* [1996] 2 Cr App R (S) 321; *R v Brown* [1999] 1 Cr App R (S) 47.

[116] For discussion of the relevance of proportionality restraints on the imposition of disqualification on sentence see A von Hirsch and M Wasik, 'Civil disqualifications attending conviction: a suggested conceptual framework' (1997) 56 CLJ 599.

[117] Ashworth (n 1 above) 83–84.

[118] See A Ashworth, 'Sentencing' in M Maguire, R Morgan and R Reiner (eds), *The Oxford Handbook of Criminology* (3rd edn, Oxford: OUP, 2002) ch 29.

sentence (certainly in terms of measured reconviction rates), between custodial and non-custodial sentences, or between custodial sentences of a few weeks as compared to those of a few months.[119] The message in these judgments has, then, been consistently to the effect that custody should be reserved for those cases which really require it, and that when custody is imposed the sentence should be as short as possible, consistent with the aims for which sentence was imposed. Thus in the landmark case of *R v Bibi*[120] in 1981, Lord Lane CJ stated that 'many offenders can be dealt with equally justly and effectively by a sentence of six or nine months' imprisonment as by one of 18 months or three years', and in *R v Upton*[121] the Court of Appeal reduced from six months to two months a prison sentence imposed on a supermarket manager for theft, commenting that 'non-violent petty offenders should not be allowed to take up what has become valuable space in prison . . . overcrowding in many of the penal establishments of this country is such that a prison sentence, however short, is a very unpleasant experience indeed'.

28.42 Twenty years later, the tenor of *Bibi* has been restated in a number of decisions, prompted by a sentenced custodial population currently at record levels. In *R v Ollerenshaw*[122] in 1999 the Court of Appeal said that the comments in *Bibi* were no less relevant now than they had been then. A major restatement by Lord Woolf CJ came in *R v Kefford*,[123] a case of theft in breach of trust by a building society cashier with no previous record who committed a total of 21 offences of theft and false accounting, amounting to a loss of over £11,000. His Lordship pointed out that the prison population, at 71,000 (as compared to 45,000 in 1990) was significantly in excess of the certified normal accommodation of the prison estate, and the courts 'must accept the realities of the situation'. When prisons were overcrowded the ability of the prison service to tackle the offender's behaviour was adversely affected, and in the case of economic crimes prison was not the only appropriate form of punishment. The offender's custodial sentence, taking account of his clean record, immediate admissions and guilty plea, was reduced from 12 months to four months, effective to ensure his immediate release.[124]

(6) Non-Discrimination

28.43 English law has no specific statutory provision declaring the illegality of discriminatory practices in sentencing,[125] but Article 14 ECHR, which is clearly applicable

---

[119] *Making Punishments Work* (2001) Appendix 6.
[120] [1980] 1 WLR 1193, 1195.
[121] (1980) 2 Cr App R (S) 132, 133–134.
[122] [1999] 1 Cr App R (S) 65. See also *R v Howells* [1999] 1 WLR 307.
[123] [2002] EWCA Crim 519; [2002] 2 Cr App R (S) 106.
[124] See also *R v Mills* [2002] 2 Cr App R (S) 229, discussed in para 28.45 below.
[125] There is an indirect reference to these principles in the Criminal Justice Act 1991, s 95, which requires the Secretary of State to publish information from time to time in relation to the 'duty to avoid discriminating against any persons on the ground of race or sex or any other improper ground'.

in this context, states that enjoyment of Convention rights shall be secured 'without discrimination on any ground such as sex, race, colour, language, religion, political or other opinion, national or social origin, association with a national minority, property, birth or other status'. Discrimination may take two forms: direct and indirect. While there are many who claim to have experienced or observed direct discrimination in sentencing practice, the empirical evidence for this is not compelling. In the most comprehensive study of racial discrimination in sentencing, Hood[126] found that apparent differences in sentencing outcomes between black, Asian and white offenders sentenced in West Midland courts were largely but not wholly explicable by reference to legally relevant variables, such as differences in the nature of offences committed, and the seriousness of respective criminal histories. The issue of discrimination in sentencing can only properly be considered within a discussion of bias within the criminal justice system as a whole, and that issue lies outside the scope of this chapter.[127] Our subject is the principles of sentencing, and it is not seriously suggested that any of the existing principles have a *direct* discriminatory effect. An important, but somewhat neglected question, however, is the extent to which the practical operation of particular sentencing principles may have an *indirect* discriminatory impact.

28.44   The principle of proportionality in punishment was discussed earlier.[128] It underpins the basic legislative framework in the 1991 Act, now consolidated into the 2000 Act. This principle is, however, cut across by the operation of other sentencing principles, such as the sentencing discount normally available for offenders who enter a timely guilty plea.[129] A key finding of Hood's study was that black offenders were significantly more likely than white offenders to contest the prosecution case, and go to trial. Black offenders who are ultimately convicted after a trial thereby lose the discount which they would have received if they had entered a timely guilty plea.[130] In a system which places as much emphasis on the guilty plea discount as does that of England and Wales, the inevitable effect of this demographic difference is that, overall, black offenders will receive heavier sentences than white offenders.

28.45   Further, as we shall see in a moment, sentencers always retain a discretion to take into account in mitigation matters relevant to the personal circumstances of the individual offender.[131] Although the Court of Appeal has on occasion said that

---

[126]   R Hood, *Race and Sentencing* (1992).

[127]   See C Phillips and M Bowling, 'Racism, ethnicity, crime and criminal justice' in Maguire, Morgan and Reiner (n 118 above) ch 17.

[128]   See para 28.32 below.

[129]   See 28.59 below.

[130]   Hood (n 126 above) 125 states that two-thirds of the observed differential in sentencing between blacks and whites stems from forfeiture of the discount.

[131]   See para 28.77 below.

sentencing should be even-handed as between men and women who have committed the same offence,[132] it is well known that the pattern of sentencing disposals of men and women differs markedly. One reason for this is the availability to women of certain matters of personal mitigation which are generally less open to men. In *R v Mills*,[133] for example, the Court of Appeal observed that when sentencing, for an offence of dishonesty, a woman of previous good character who was the mother of two young children, the court must bear in mind the consequences to those children if the sole carer was sent to prison. The remarks were made in the context of a crisis of overcrowding in women's prisons, but the point has independent weight. Decisions to the same effect, made at less acute times, can be found.[134] These cases create a situation of indirect discrimination, since women are more likely to find themselves in the situation of sole carer of children.[135]

Loss of employment is another factor sometimes urged in mitigation of sentence, **28.46** particularly as a reason for avoiding a custodial sentence. The argument may be that the offender's good employment record is in itself a reason for passing a more lenient sentence, or it may be that the imprisonment of the owner of a small business would cause other people to lose their jobs.[136] To the extent that unemployment rates are higher among black offenders than white offenders,[137] this sentencing principle inevitably has some indirect discriminatory effect.

E. General Principles

(1) Maximum Sentences to be Reserved for the Worst Cases

The principle of sentencing that the courts should reserve the imposition of the **28.47** maximum sentence prescribed by Parliament for the very worst examples of that offence was one of the first to be clearly established by the appellate criminal courts.[138] At a time when there was very little legislative intervention in the sphere of sentencing discretion, the Court of Criminal Appeal required the sentencing courts to use the full range provided, and to 'steer by the maximum'. These comments have subsequently been qualified in *R v Ambler*,[139] where Lawton LJ explained that when a sentencer was considering whether a particular offence is one

---

[132] eg, *R v Okuya* (1984) 6 Cr App R (S) 253; *R v Hancock* [1986] Crim LR 697.
[133] [2002] 2 Cr App R (S) 229.
[134] *R v Vaughan* (1982) 4 Cr App R (S) 83; *R v Whitehead* [1996] 1 Cr App R (S) 111.
[135] Though not always. *R v Franklyn* (1981) 3 Cr App R (S) 65 is an example of sentence being reduced on the ground that the offender was a widower responsible for the care of four children.
[136] An example is *R v Olliver* (1989) 11 Cr App R (S) 10, 13.
[137] The research is discussed in Ashworth (n 1 above) 206–208.
[138] Thomas (n 31 above) 29 et seq.
[139] (1975) *Current Sentencing Practice*, para A1-4C01.

of the worst examples, they should ask themselves whether the particular case falls within a broad band of such cases, rather than 'conjur[ing] up unlikely worst possible kinds of case'. In fact, the guidance provided for sentencers by the available maximum sentences is not very helpful. Maxima have been set by the legislature at different times, for different purposes, and in very different penological climates. Many anomalies exist,[140] and for some offences the maximum sentence is set so high, to allow for the occasional very serious case, that it provides no useful guidance in more run of the mill cases.[141]

28.48   Some aspects of the principle outlined here can, however, have important implications for sentencers. First, it is well established that a sentencer should not impose the maximum sentence for an offence in a case where there are important countervailing features. A good example is the reduction in sentence which is generally accorded to an offender who pleads guilty. It follows that the maximum sentence should not normally be imposed on a guilty plea.[142] Secondly, if there is significant mitigation, the maximum sentence should not be passed simply because the sentencer believes the maximum set by Parliament is too low.[143] Almost all the case law relates to maximum custodial sentences, but the same principles apply to maximum fines, and maximum permitted obligations under community sentences, such as the total number of hours unpaid work required under a community punishment order.

(2)   Concurrent and Consecutive Sentences

28.49   Where an offender is to be sentenced on one occasion for more than one offence, the court should normally pass a separate sentence for each of the offences,[144] making it clear which sentence relates to which count. Then the court should determine whether the sentences passed are to be served by the offender concurrently (at the same time) or consecutively (one after the other). There may, in a complex case, be a mixture of concurrent and consecutive sentences. If the court fails to explain that particular sentences are to be served consecutively, then it will be presumed that they are concurrent. However the sentencer reaches the final sentence, its overall effect is subject to the totality principle,[145] which requires that the total sentence should fairly reflect the overall nature of the offending. If the sentencing court is imposing a new custodial sentence on an offender who is

---

[140] One example is the maximum of five years for aggravated vehicle-taking where death has resulted, compared to the maximum of ten years for causing death by dangerous driving.
[141] An example is the maximum of 14 years for handling stolen goods.
[142] *R v Greene* (1993) 14 Cr App R (S) 682; *R v Barnes* (1983) 5 Cr App R (S) 368.
[143] *R v Carroll* (1995) 16 Cr App R (S) 488.
[144] Sometimes sentencers dealing with several offences impose 'no separate penalty' for some of them, but this practice has no statutory authority.
[145] See para 28.53 below.

currently serving such a sentence, it must again be made clear whether the new sentence is to be served concurrently with, or consecutively to, the existing term. The rules on concurrent and consecutive sentences are of particular importance in relation to custodial terms, but similar arise in other contexts, such as where two community punishment orders are imposed on the same occasion,[146] or where additional hours for a new offence are imposed on an offender who is already subject to such an order.[147]

The general principle is that sentences should be concurrent where the offences **28.50** for which they are imposed arose out of the same incident, such as where an offender is convicted of dangerous driving and driving while disqualified on the same occasion.[148] Sometimes, however, a different line is taken in such cases, with consecutive sentences being passed on the basis that concurrent sentences offer no disincentive against the commission of additional offences.[149] So, for example, it has been said that consecutive sentences should be imposed where an offender has carried a firearm when committing another offence,[150] or has used violence to make good his escape from the scene of another offence.[151] If concurrent sentences are passed here, the reasoning goes, there is no deterrent against carrying a firearm or using violence. One issue here is that in these examples the prosecutor might well have chosen to bring just one charge, relying on the sentencer to take account of the carrying of the firearm, or the use of the violence, as an aggravating feature of the main offence.

On balance, it seems preferable in these cases for the sentencer to select a sentence **28.51** for the main offence which reflects its full seriousness, including the aggravating circumstances in which it was committed. If additional charges have in fact been brought then these should be sentenced concurrently, to avoid double counting. A striking example is *R v Noble*,[152] where the offender was convicted of six offences of causing death by dangerous driving, arising from a single incident. The sentencer had imposed three sentences of five years' imprisonment concurrent on each of three counts, to run consecutively to three sentences of ten years' imprisonment concurrent, making a total of 15 years. The Court of Appeal adjusted the sentence such that all the sentences ran concurrently, making a total sentence of ten years.

There are a number of particular situations where the imposition of consecutive **28.52** custodial sentences has been endorsed by the Court of Appeal. Examples are

---

[146] Powers of Criminal Courts (Sentencing) Act 2000, s 46(8).
[147] *R v Evans* [1977] 1 WLR 27; *R v Siha* (1992) 13 Cr App R (S) 588.
[148] *R v Skinner* (1986) 8 Cr App R (S) 166.
[149] *R v Jordan* [1996] 1 Cr App R (S) 181.
[150] *R v French* (1982) 4 Cr App R (S) 57; *R v McGrath* (1986) 8 Cr App R (S) 372.
[151] *R v Bunch* (1971) *Current Sentencing Practice*, para A5-2C01.
[152] [2002] EWCA Crim 1713; [2003] 1 Cr App R (S) 65.

where an offender receives a custodial sentence for escape from lawful custody,[153] or for an offence committed within prison by a serving prisoner,[154] where an offender has attempted to pervert the course of justice in relation to an offence committed by him,[155] or where an offender has committed a second offence while on bail for the first.[156] These examples differ from those discussed in the previous paragraph because they do not arise out of the same incident, being distinct in time and context. It should be remembered, however, that consecutive sentences are always subject to the totality principle and there may be occasions where, to avoid a disproportionate overall sentence, the penalty for offences which are distinct in time and context may properly be ordered to run concurrently. The totality principle is considered next.

(3) The Totality Principle

28.53 Section 158(2)(b) of the Powers of Criminal Courts (Sentencing) Act 2000 states that nothing shall prevent a court 'in a case of an offender who is convicted of one or more other offences, from mitigating his sentence by applying any rule of law as to the totality of sentences'. This provision is an oblique reference to the 'totality principle', long established by the appellate courts,[157] that a sentencer dealing with an offender on one occasion for more than one offence must always have regard to the total penalty imposed, to ensure that this does not become wholly disproportionate to the seriousness of the offending behaviour. An offender being sentenced for several instances of theft from shops, or for a series of frauds, will receive a stiffer sentence than if he had been convicted of just one such offence but, for example, three shopliftings do not attract three times the sentence appropriate for one. Put another way, the totality principle is a discount for bulk offending.[158]

28.54 It may be thought that this approach is hard to square with the normal requirements of proportionality. It is difficult to see why an offender should receive a lower sentence for three thefts sentenced on a single occasion than he would receive if sentenced for these on three different occasions. On the other hand, in the context of a single sentencing decision, it is important to retain a sense of proportion between the sentence passed and the *kind* of offending which is being sentenced. To adopt a simple additive formula for sentencing multiple offences would mean that the prolific shoplifter will receive a sentence on a par with a serious violent or sexual offender which, in itself, offends proportionality requirements. The totality

---

[153] *R v Clarke* (1994) 15 Cr App R (S) 825.
[154] *R v Ali* [1998] 2 Cr App R (S) 123.
[155] *A-G's Reference (No 1 of 1990)* (1990) 12 Cr App R (S) 245.
[156] *R v Young* (1973) *Current Sentencing Practice*, para A5-2F01.
[157] Thomas (n 31 above) 56 et seq.
[158] N Jareborg, 'Why bulk discounts for multiple offence sentencing?', in A Ashworth and M Wasik (eds), *Fundamentals of Sentencing Theory* (Oxford: Clarendon, 1998) ch 5.

principle, while well known, is applied by the courts in a very flexible manner, and hardly merits the status of 'rule of law' accorded to it by the subsection. It is most frequently encountered in the context of imposing consecutive custodial sentences,[159] including cases where a suspended sentence has been activated to run consecutively to an immediate prison sentence, but it also applies to other forms of disposal, such as consecutive community punishment orders,[160] or cumulative fines.[161]

(4) *Financial Penalties and Economic Circumstances*

According to the statutory sentencing framework, a fine may be imposed on sentence where the offence comes below the custody threshold. It has sometimes been said that fines come below the community sentence threshold as well,[162] but that is not strictly true. An offence must be 'serious enough' to justify a community sentence, but that does not exclude the use of the fine in an appropriate case.[163] If the circumstances indicate that the offender has committed an offence falling below the custody threshold, and it is one for which a simple punishment is required rather than efforts being made towards rehabilitation, then there is no need to trouble the probation service by imposing a community sentence. The proportionality principles in the statutory framework entail that there are some offences which are too serious for a fine to be an appropriate response,[164] and it may be that there are some offences which are too trivial to justify even a small fine, where a conditional or absolute discharge should be used instead.[165] It is also clear from the statutory framework that, where a fine is selected as the appropriate penalty for the offence, the amount of the fine should reflect the seriousness of the offence.[166]

28.55

When imposing a fine, however, economic circumstances, especially the offender's ability to pay, must always be borne in mind.[167] What is clear beyond doubt is that an offender who cannot afford to pay the fine must not be dealt with in a more severe way instead, such as by imposing a custodial sentence (whether

28.56

---

[159] *R v Jones* [1996] 1 Cr App R (S) 153.

[160] Powers of Criminal Courts (Sentencing) Act 2000, s 46(8); *R v Siha* (1992) 13 Cr App R (S) 588.

[161] *Chelmsford Crown Court, ex p Birchall* (1989) 11 Cr App R (S) 510.

[162] *Making Punishments Work* (2001) paras 1.31–1.33.

[163] See the diagram 'Outline of the sentencing system' in Wasik (n 1 above) 52.

[164] See, eg, *A-G's Reference (No 41 of 1994)* (1995) 16 Cr App R (S) 792: fine of £350 imposed for an offence of wounding with intent held to be unduly lenient.

[165] eg, *R v Jamieson* (1975) 60 Cr App R (S) 318.

[166] Powers of Criminal Courts (Sentencing) Act 2000, s 128(2). See also *R v Messana* (1981) 3 Cr App R (S) 88: the 'first duty' of the sentencer is to 'measure [the] fine against the gravity of the offence', *per* Kenneth Jones LJ.

[167] ibid s 128(3).

immediate[168] or suspended[169]). This is to punish someone more harshly than they deserve, because they are poor. It has long been accepted, therefore, that if an offender has very limited means, the amount of the fine should be reduced to a level which they can manage to pay.[170] The court should investigate the offender's ability to pay, and select a fine which is in accord with this requirement.[171] Then, it may also be possible to allow the payment of the fine over a period of time, by instalments.

28.57 If the offender is financially well off, and paying the standard fine would occasion no difficulty to him, it is contrary to principle to impose a more severe sentence, such as a custodial term, instead.[172] Statute, by s 128(4) of the Powers of Criminal Courts (Sentencing) Act 2000, however, permits that the amount of the fine may be increased in such a case, so as to increase its impact on the offender.[173] This remains a controversial approach, and the Court of Appeal has warned that it should not be taken too far,[174] but the present law can be supported on the basis of the putative principle of 'equal impact' of punishments.[175] This is a persuasive idea, but it has not so far been developed beyond the context of financial penalties.[176] Section 128(4) does not, of course, affect the principle that, if the offence is over the custody threshold, an offender who is financially well off cannot avoid prison by paying a fine instead. To allow this would permit a rich man to 'buy his way out of the penalty for the crime', and would be quite wrong.[177]

28.58 Compensation orders are not financial *penalties*, but are ancillary orders designed to require the offender to compensate the victim of the crime. The sentencing principles applicable to such orders are considered below.[178]

(5) Discount for Guilty Plea

28.59 It is a very well established principle of sentencing that the length of a custodial sentence should normally be reduced for an offender who pleads guilty and that, depending on the circumstances of the case, such 'discount' for guilty plea could normally be expected to be in the range of one quarter to one third of the sentence

---

[168] *R v Reeves* (1972) 56 Cr App R 366.
[169] *R v Whitehead* (1979) 1 Cr App R (S) 187.
[170] A degree of hardship is appropriate (that is part of the punishment), but a fine beyond the means of the offender is wrong in principle: *R v Olliver* (1989) 11 Cr App R (S) 10.
[171] Powers of Criminal Courts (Sentencing) Act 2000, s 128(1).
[172] *R v Gillies* [1965] Crim LR 664.
[173] Powers of Criminal Courts (Sentencing) Act 2000, s 128(4).
[174] *R v Jerome* [2001] 1 Cr App R (S) 92.
[175] See Ashworth (n 1 above) 82–83 and ch 7.
[176] For an attempt to do so see A Ashworth and E Player, 'Sentencing, equal treatment and the impact of sanctions' in Ashworth and Wasik (n 158 above) ch 10.
[177] *R v Markwick* (1953) 37 Cr App R (S) 125.
[178] See para 28.106 below.

which would have been imposed on conviction following a contested trial.[179] The reason for the existence of this sentencing principle is to provide a strong incentive to defendants to admit their guilt, and thereby save the time and considerable expense of a contested trial. This argument is perhaps at its strongest in sexual cases, where an admission of guilt will save the victim of the offence from having to give evidence in court, a point recognized in *R v Millberry*,[180] the guideline case on sentencing for rape. While the principle was clear from the case law, Parliament has made specific provision for reductions in sentences for guilty pleas in the Powers of Criminal Courts (Sentencing) Act 2000, s 152.[181] That section states that 'in determining what sentence to pass on an offender who has pleaded guilty . . . a court shall take into account . . . the stage in the proceedings for the offence at which the offender indicated his intention to plead guilty' and 'the circumstances in which this indication was given'. Section 152 further requires the court, whenever it has adjusted sentence by virtue of the offender's guilty plea, to 'state in open court that it has done so'.[182]

A number of points emerge from this provision. The first is that the discount is **28.60** clearly intended to apply to other forms of sentence as well as custodial ones. The traditional form of proportionate reduction in a custodial sentence can also be reflected in the amount of a fine, or the number of hours of unpaid work required of the offender under a community punishment order. There is little guidance, however, on whether a guilty plea can make the difference between a community sentence and a discharge, or a custodial sentence and a community one.[183] There is authority, however, that a guilty plea per se cannot justify the suspension of a sentence of imprisonment.[184] This is because a suspended sentence may be passed only where there are 'exceptional circumstances' to justify that course,[185] and pleas of guilty are commonplace rather than exceptional. The wording of s 152 also makes it clear that the granting of a discount, and its extent, is dependent upon the stage of the proceedings at which it was tendered. A 'timely' guilty plea is what is required and, in principle, the earlier the stage at which guilt is admitted the greater the discount which can be expected. If the defendant admits guilt before venue is determined a discount of a third, and in some cases even more than a third, may be appropriate.[186] If somewhat later, then less than a full discount

---

[179] *R v Buffery* (1992) 14 Cr App R (S) 511.

[180] [2002] EWCA Crim 2891; [2003] 1 WLR 546.

[181] A provision originally found in the Criminal Justice and Public Order Act 1994, s 48.

[182] See further *R v Aroride* [1999] 2 Cr App R (S) 406; *R v Bishop* [2000] 1 Cr App R (S) 432.

[183] In *R v Howells* [1999] 1 WLR 307, it was said that a timely guilty plea, particularly where associated with other mitigation, might form the basis for passing a community sentence rather than a custodial one.

[184] *R v Okinikan* [1993] 1 WLR 173.

[185] Powers of Criminal Courts (Sentencing) Act 2000, s 118(4)(b).

[186] *R v Barber* [2001] EWCA Crim 2267; [2002] 1 Cr App R (S) 130.

should be given.[187] If the admission comes very late, even at the 'door of the court', the discount should be much less but it is appropriate still to give some reduction.

28.61 The statute, and the case law, recognize that the timing of the plea, although very important, is not the only thing which matters. The 'circumstances' in which the admission of guilt is made are also important. The strength of the case against the defendant can make a difference. A defendant who voluntarily surrenders to the police and admits a crime which could not otherwise have been proved against him may be entitled to more than the usual discount,[188] while a defendant who has been caught red-handed at the scene of the crime has little option but to plead guilty, and should thereby receive little credit for doing so.[189] The guilty plea discount may be refused or reduced for other reasons, such as where the defendant delays his plea in an attempt to secure some tactical advantage,[190] or pleads guilty but adduces a version of the facts so different from that contended by the prosecution that a *Newton* hearing[191] is required to determine the factual basis for sentence.[192]

28.62 The authorities maintain that while an offender who pleads guilty should normally receive a discount from sentence for so doing, an offender should not be penalized for pleading not guilty.[193] This position, although it may strike some as odd, is logically defensible, since it assumes that there is a normally appropriate sentence for the offence, from which there can be a reduction for a guilty plea but no enhancement for contesting the case. It is hard to be sure that this principle is always followed in practice, however, since sentencing brackets and starting points are rarely precise enough to measure compliance with it.

(6) Discount for Assisting the Authorities

28.63 Closely related to the discount for guilty plea is the further discount which may accrue where an offender renders substantial assistance to the police, customs, or other investigating authorities. Such assistance usually takes the form of providing information about other lawbreaking, or about other individuals involved with the offender, and sometimes by giving evidence for the prosecution against those named. The leading authority is *R v A and B*,[194] in which Lord Bingham said that an enhanced discount would follow in two main situations. The first is where, as a result of the assistance by the offender, a co-offender is convicted or pleads guilty. The second is where the offender pleads guilty and assists the authorities by

---

[187] *R v Rafferty* [1998] 2 Cr App R (S) 449.
[188] *R v Claydon* (1993) 15 Cr App R (S) 526.
[189] *R v Scarley* [2001] 1 Cr App R (S) 24.
[190] *R v Costen* (1989) 11 Cr App R (S) 182.
[191] See para 28.26 above.
[192] *R v Williams* (1990) 12 Cr App R (S) 415.
[193] *R v Spinks* (1980) 2 Cr App R (S) 335.
[194] [1999] 1 Cr App R (S) 52.

supplying information, where the extent of the discount will depend on the quality and quantity of the intelligence supplied.[195] No discount is appropriate if the information is vague, unreliable, or already known to the authorities. A substantial discount may be given if the information is accurate, particularized, useful in practice and hitherto unknown to the authorities, enabling serious criminal activity to be stopped and serious criminals to be brought to book. In some cases, an offender who supplies information to the authorities will thereby expose himself and his family to personal jeopardy, perhaps for a considerable period of time and, where appropriate, that should be recognized in the discount given.

The extent of the discount is a matter within the sentencer's discretion, bearing in mind the considerations mentioned above, but it would appear from the decision in *R v Guy*[196] that where an offender has both pleaded guilty and given assistance to the authorities the extent of the discount will be between one half and two thirds of the sentence which would otherwise have been imposed.   **28.64**

(7) Relevance of Previous Convictions

The relevance of the offender's previous convictions to the sentence to be passed is an area of some complexity. Everyone accepts that the offender's record is often of considerable importance in sentence selection, but there is very little appellate discussion of the general issue, and it is not clear precisely what aspects of an offender's record are to be regarded as relevant. One relatively straightforward point is that offenders with a clean record generally receive a lighter sentence than would otherwise be the case. This is part of the sentencer's general discretion to take into account matters of personal mitigation, considered further below.[197] The more serious the offence for which the offender is being sentenced, however, the less effective such mitigation is likely to be.   **28.65**

There are some situations where the presence of particular previous convictions on an offender's record will have a triggering effect on a subsequent sentence. An offender convicted of a second 'serious offence' must receive an automatic life sentence unless there are exceptional circumstances,[198] and an offender convicted for the third time for an offence of domestic burglary must receive a sentence of at least three years' imprisonment, unless there are particular circumstances which would render such a sentence unjust.[199] The effect of these   **28.66**

---

[195] If the offender contests the case and is convicted, a subsequent disclosure of information to the authorities is not relevant to sentence exercise, but it may influence later decisions to be made by the executive over early release: *R v Waddingham* (1983) 5 Cr App R (S) 66.

[196] [1999] 2 Cr App R (S) 24, applying *R v King* (1986) 82 Cr App R 120.

[197] See para 28.77 below.

[198] Powers of Criminal Courts (Sentencing) Act 2000, s 109.

[199] ibid s 111.

statutory rules is to enhance significantly the usual role of criminal record in sentencing.[200] A second point is that when a sentencer is considering whether to impose a longer than commensurate custodial sentence on an offender convicted of a violent or sexual offence, the court will always have regard to the offender's criminal record, amongst other information,[201] in assessing whether he poses a sufficient degree of risk to the public so as to justify such a sentence. In this context the record provides the sentencer with material on which a judgment of risk can be made. The court must ensure that the information being relied upon is accurate,[202] and sometimes it may be necessary to investigate the circumstances of the earlier offence(s) to see whether the offender really does represent a grave risk, or whether he can properly be sentenced on a proportionate basis.[203]

28.67 Leaving aside these special cases, however, the great bulk of sentencing decisions are driven by requirements of proportionality and offence seriousness. In this context, s 151(1) of the Powers of Criminal Courts (Sentencing) Act 2000 simply states that: 'In considering the seriousness of any offence, the court may take into account any previous convictions or any failure of his to respond to previous sentences'.[204] This sub-section gives sentencers a power to take previous convictions into account, but provides no guidance as to when or how that should be done. There is no useful modern appellate guidance. Some cases which pre-date the statutory provision had indicated that 'no [offender] is to be sentenced for the offences which he has committed in the past and for which he has already been punished'[205] and that a poor record should not in itself be regarded as an aggravating feature.

28.68 On the other hand, more recent decisions of the Court of Appeal clearly accept that a bad record can be a significant aggravating feature. In *R v Brewster*,[206] an important case on sentencing for domestic burglary, Lord Bingham CJ remarked that[207] 'the record of the offender is of more significance . . . than in the case of some other crimes' and added that 'domestic burglaries are the more serious . . . if they are committed by persistent offenders [or] . . . if there is a pattern of repeat offending'. The 'very severe' sentence of nine years' imprisonment which had been imposed on Brewster was upheld by the Court of Appeal, taking into account the

---

[200] See M Wasik, 'The vital importance of certain previous convictions' [2001] Crim LR 363.

[201] The court may 'take into account *any* information about the offender which is before it': Powers of Criminal Courts (Sentencing) Act 2000, s 81(4)(b) (emphasis added). A medical report will generally be required: *R v Crow and Pennington* (1995) 16 Cr App R (S) 409.

[202] *R v Oudkerk* (1995) 16 Cr App R (S) 172.

[203] *R v Samuels* (1995) 16 Cr App R (S) 856.

[204] For discussion of this provision see M Wasik and A von Hirsch, 'Section 29 revised: Previous convictions in sentencing' [1994] Crim LR 409.

[205] *R v Queen* (1981) 3 Cr App R (S) 245.

[206] [1998] 1 Cr App R (S) 181. See now *R v McInerney* [2002] EWCA Crim 3003; [2003] 1 All ER 1089.

[207] ibid 186.

offender's 'appalling record as aggravating the seriousness of the offences'.[208] The *Magistrates' Courts' Sentencing Guidelines* clearly treat 'relevant previous convictions' as an aggravating factor in sentence.

The Halliday report identified a 'muddled approach' to persistent offenders,[209] and proposed that 'sentencing severity should increase as a consequence of sufficiently recent and relevant previous convictions'.[210] Although this would, it is claimed, 'serve to target resources on the offenders who commit a disproportionate amount of crime and are most likely to re-offend', the proposed new approach must be 'governed by the proportionality principle to avoid excessively severe and therefore unjust punishments'. It is not apparent that this policy would be an improvement over the current regime, and there are powerful arguments against moving to a model of 'sentencing on the record'.[211] The indications are, however, that the government intends to adjust the sentencing framework in such a way as to give increased weight to previous convictions. The relevant section of the Criminal Justice Act 2003 states that 'the court must treat each previous conviction as an aggravating factor . . . if it can reasonably be so treated'.[212] **28.69**

F. Mitigation and Aggravation[213]

Mitigating factors are features of a case which tend to cause the sentencer to reduce the sentence for the offence. This may be by reducing the quantum of punishment, such as by shortening a prison sentence, or reducing a fine, or it may by persuading the sentencer to change the form of the sentence, such as by eschewing an immediate sentence of imprisonment, and suspending it, or by imposing a community sentence instead. The forms of mitigation vary widely, almost infinitely, in their detail and combinations, but it is helpful to draw some basic distinctions. Mitigating factors tend to fall into one of two categories: those which mitigate offence seriousness, and those which reflect personal characteristics of the offender, although sometimes the boundary between the two is not entirely clear. The sentencing discounts available for a timely guilty plea or when an offender provides assistance to the authorities, do not properly fall into either category. Although commonly referred to as mitigating matters, they have a different rationale, and so they were dealt with earlier.[214] **28.70**

---

[208] ibid 187.
[209] *Making Punishments Work* (2001) paras 1.11–1.14.
[210] ibid para 2.7.
[211] See von Hirsch (n 52 above) ch 10.
[212] s 136(2). It further provides that the court may have regard to the nature of any previous conviction, its relevance to the current offence, and the time that has elapsed since the conviction.
[213] See generally, N Walker, *Aggravation, Mitigation and Mercy in English Criminal Justice* (London: Blackstone, 1999).
[214] See paras 28.59 and 28.63 above

(1) Factors Which Mitigate Offence Seriousness

28.71   The statutory sentencing framework, by s 81(4) of the Powers of Criminal Courts (Sentencing) Act 2000 tells us that, when determining the seriousness of an offence, the sentencer is obliged to 'take into account all such information as is available to him about the circumstances of the offence (including any aggravating or mitigating factors)'. There are several mitigating factors which impinge upon the culpability of the offender for the offence, and so are relevant when assessing the seriousness of that offence. If the prosecution disputes the defence claim on such a matter, then it may be necessary to invoke a *Newton* hearing to resolve the matter.[215]

(a) Provocation, duress, and mistake of law

28.72   It is well accepted that if the offender acted under provocation, or under duress, or was labouring under mistake or ignorance of the law, these may be accepted as significant mitigating factors.[216] In English law provocation is recognized as a partial defence to murder, reducing that crime to manslaughter, but in respect of all other offences it is relevant solely as a matter in mitigation. The weight to be attached to the provocation varies from case to case, but a sudden and impulsive reaction is generally regarded as being less blameworthy than a planned retaliation.[217] Indeed the taking of revenge against the initial aggressor is thought to be incompatible with the notion of provocation, and may instead be regarded as an aggravating feature on sentence.

28.73   Duress is recognized as a full defence to liability, but it is tightly circumscribed. If an offender is unable to found the defence at trial it may still prove possible to take the duress into account in mitigation.[218] As with provocation, at the sentencing stage duress can be treated more flexibly, shading into other circumstances where the offender has succumbed to significant pressures.

28.74   Neither mistake nor ignorance of the law constitutes a defence in English law, but some circumstances of legal mistake or ignorance entail that culpability is virtually non-existent, and this can be reflected by the passing of a lenient sentence. In *Universal Salvage v Boothby*[219] a fine imposed on a company for breach of regulations was reduced to take account of the fact that company officers had reasonably, but mistakenly, relied on official advice that the company was exempt.

---

[215] See para 28.26 above.
[216] See M Wasik, 'Excuses at the sentencing stage' [1983] Crim LR 450.
[217] An example is *R v Brookin* (1995) 16 Cr App R (S) 78, where the victim had attacked the offender's girlfriend and taunted him before the offender struck him.
[218] An example is *R v Taonis* (1974) 59 Cr App R 160.
[219] (1983) 5 Cr App R (S) 428.

(b) Lack of planning/temptation

In some cases where the offence was committed 'on the spur of the moment' or **28.75** 'after temptation' the sentencer may regard this as reflecting a lesser degree of culpability than a planned offence, but neither is a particularly strong basis for mitigation. Entrapment is a special form of temptation, where the offender has committed the offence after being tricked into doing so by an undercover police officer. While entrapment does not provide a defence to liability in criminal law, it is relevant in mitigation, where the passing of a lenient sentence may in part reflect reduced culpability of the offender's part (that he would not otherwise have committed the offence) but also provide a measure of the court's disapproval of underhanded tactics of law enforcement.[220]

(c) Intoxication[221]

A controversial issue is the relevance to culpability of the offender's intoxication at **28.76** the time of the offence. Intoxication can negative criminal liability only in very limited situations, and there are several statements in appellate judgments that intoxication is largely irrelevant on sentence.[222] On the other hand, some cases recognize that the offender would not have behaved like that had he been sober. Of course intoxication is a serious aggravating factor in relation to some offences, such as careless driving or dangerous driving.

(2) Matters of Personal Mitigation

In contrast to mitigating factors which impinge on the seriousness of the offence, **28.77** other mitigating factors relate to the individual's personal, financial, or domestic situation, inviting the sentencer to exercise a degree of mercy, or to make a more favourable assessment of the offender, seen in the context of his general moral character, or in the light of other aspects of the offender's life. Section 158(1) of the Powers of Criminal Courts (Sentencing) Act 2000 states that 'nothing shall prevent a court from mitigating an offender's sentence by taking into account any such matters as, in the opinion of the court, are relevant in mitigation of sentence'. It will be seen that while there is a *duty* on the part of the sentencer to take into account mitigation which impinges on offence seriousness, there is merely a *discretion* over whether to take account of personal mitigation.[223] Often sentencers will do so, but there are some occasions on which the word of the offender may be doubted and, according to the important decision in *R v Guppy and Marsh*,[224] in

---

[220] *R v Underhill* (1979) 1 Cr App R (S) 270; *R v Tonnessen* [1998] 2 Cr App R (S) 328.
[221] See M Wasik, 'Is intoxication a mitigating factor in sentencing?' (1999) 163 JP 724.
[222] *R v Bradley* (1980) 2 Cr App R (S) 12.
[223] Consistent with the pre-Act authorities. See, eg, *R v Inwood* (1974) 60 Cr App R (S) 70.
[224] (1995) 16 Cr App R (S) 25.

such cases the burden is on the defence to satisfy the sentencer on the balance of probability.[225]

28.78   Personal mitigation may, in an appropriate case, have a powerful effect on sentence. As was shown in the case of *R v Cox*,[226] where the offender pleaded guilty to reckless driving and theft, even though the offence is so serious that only custody can be justified, personal mitigation available to the offender (in that case his youth, and the fact that he had only one previous court appearance) can rescue the offender and pull the case back from the custody threshold. Personal mitigation may sometimes permit suspension of an otherwise well deserved prison sentence, but in that context the statute requires that the relevant circumstances be 'exceptional'.[227] Youth and good character are not exceptional, so they should not result in suspension of sentence,[228] but of course they might still have an impact on the length of the term imposed. Cases in which 'exceptional circumstances' have been accepted include *R v Bellikli*,[229] where a two-year prison term was suspended on the basis that the offender's child was very ill and would soon require major surgery. Matters of personal mitigation may, on the other hand, be ignored for reasons of public policy. For the most serious offences, such as rape,[230] there is clearly little scope for arguments based on personal mitigation. Two of the most important matters of personal mitigation, good character and clean record, were said in the leading decision in *R v Aramah*[231] to be largely irrelevant when sentencing drug couriers, since it is generally such people who are targeted and recruited to perform that role.

28.79   The details of personal mitigation vary considerably from case to case and, since their relevance and weight is very much a matter of judicial discretion, this is an area of sentencing in which general principles are hard to discern. The main categories of personal mitigation have been touched upon already: the offender's age, good character, and remorse. It is appropriate to say a little more about each of these, and to consider briefly some other matters relating to personal circumstances which are occasionally urged on sentencers in mitigation.

(a) Youth and age

28.80   Walker[232] has observed that '[y]outh must be the oldest reason for leniency', yet the effect of youth as a mitigating factor in sentencing is not altogether clear. On

---

[225] In such cases a *Newton* hearing will rarely be an option, since the prosecution may have no basis on which to challenge what the defendant says.
[226] [1993] 1 WLR 188.
[227] Powers of Criminal Courts (Sentencing) Act 2000, s 118(4)(b).
[228] According to Lord Taylor CJ in *R v Okinikan* [1993] 1 WLR 173.
[229] [1998] 1 Cr App R (S) 135.
[230] According to Lord Lane CJ in *R v Billam* (1986) 8 Cr App R (S) 48, 50: 'Previous good character is of only minor relevance'.
[231] (1982) 4 Cr App R (S) 407.
[232] Walker (n 213 above) 135.

some occasions it may tend to show reduced culpability, in which case it belongs in the category of cases discussed earlier, where offence seriousness is reduced. Lower maximum custodial sentences are generally applicable for offenders aged under 18. For certain grave offences the maximum is the same as for an adult,[233] but the courts will still tend to scale down the sentence if it can.[234] Even if convicted of murder, the Court of Appeal has said[235] that when passing the mandatory life sentence a significantly lower minimum term recommendation will normally be appropriate for a juvenile as against an adult.[236]

In the majority of cases, however, the youth of the offender will sound as a matter of personal mitigation. In *R v Howells*[237] Lord Bingham CJ said that it will often be right to pass a shorter custodial sentence on a young offender than would be passed on an adult for the same offence. Youth gathers extra strength as a mitigating factor when found in combination with other features, such as good character and remorse. In *R v Dodds*,[238] however, the Court of Appeal said that the importance of youth as a mitigating factor had been overstated in some earlier cases. Where the offender is very young, and bearing in mind that the age of criminal responsibility in English law is ten, the court should have regard to the principle contained in s 44(1) of the Children and Young Persons Act 1933, which states that when dealing with a child or young person every court 'shall have regard to [his or her] welfare'. **28.81**

At the other end of the scale, the fact that the offender is relatively old can have some mitigating effect, and this effect can start to be seen from about the age of 60.[239] The older the offender is, the more persuasive the mitigation is likely to be, since sentencers are reluctant to impose a sentence which will mean that much of the remainder of the offender's life will be spent in prison, but this always has to be set against the seriousness of the offending. The Court of Appeal in *R v Adams*[240] reduced a sentence on a man aged 67 for soliciting murder from ten years to eight years mainly for this reason, but the nature of the offence prevented any further reduction. In *R v Anderson*,[241] the offender was aged 77 and had been convicted in 1999 of a number of serious sexual offences against children. These **28.82**

---

[233] Generally for offences attracting a maximum penalty of at least 14 years on indictment: Powers of Criminal Courts (Sentencing) Act 2000, s 91.

[234] *R v M* [1998] 1 WLR 363.

[235] *Practice Statement (Crime: Life Sentences)* [2002] 1 WLR 1789.

[236] See A von Hirsch, 'Proportionate sentences for juveniles: how different than for adults?' (2001) 3 Punishment and Society 221.

[237] [1999] 1 WLR 307.

[238] The Times, 28 January 1997.

[239] See *R v Wilkinson* (1974) *Current Sentencing Practice*, para C2-2B01, where Roskill LJ said that 'no court willingly sentences a man of sixty to spend a large part of the remainder of his life in prison'.

[240] (1995) 16 Cr App R (S) 307.

[241] [1999] 1 Cr App R (S) 273.

offences took place between 1972 and 1982 and none was reported until 1997. A sentence of eight years' imprisonment was said to be appropriate for the nature and scale of the offending but was reduced 'as a merciful course' to six years. While normally a matter of personal mitigation, old age can occasionally reflect reduced culpability, where there is evidence of senility or disordered thinking.

(b) Good character

28.83   The matter of the offender's good character will be urged upon the sentencing court wherever possible. 'Good character' basically means an absence of previous convictions. A clean record mitigates because it suggests that the offence was an isolated lapse rather than part of a pattern of law-breaking, and because in many such cases the fact of conviction itself may be a sufficient penalty. Even if the offence is so serious that only a custodial sentence can be justified, the 'clang of the gates' is likely to have a salutary effect on a first offender such that the custodial term can be shorter than it otherwise would have been. Sometimes sentencers will stretch a point, and treat offenders as being of good character if they are only lightly convicted. Conviction for minor offences, or those incurred some years ago, which are likely to be 'spent',[242] may be disregarded for this purpose. Even an offender with an objectively poor record may scrape some credit from the fact that he has not reoffended for a number of years.[243]

28.84   Mitigation will be stronger, according to Lord Bingham CJ in *R v Howells*, 'if there is evidence of positive good character (such as a solid employment record or faithful discharge of family duties) as opposed to a mere absence of previous convictions'. In *R v Clark*,[244] a six month sentence for a series of frauds was reduced to one week because of the offender's voluntary service to the local community and the fact that she had brought up four motherless nephews and nieces. In *A-G's Reference (No 22 of 2002)*,[245] the Court of Appeal accepted that the sentencer had been right to have regard to an offender's 'quite outstanding career of public service' as well as to his relatively advanced age, clean record and timely guilty plea, when dealing with a man who had subjected his wife to a violent assault from which she suffered rib fractures and a collapsed lung. Sentence was, nonetheless, increased from a community rehabilitation order to a prison term of six months.

28.85   Related to the influence of good character, but going beyond it, is the occasional example of a case where the sentencer reduces sentence having heard in mitigation of some wholly unrelated incident of meritorious conduct performed by the offender. There are examples in the law reports of custodial sentences being reduced

---

[242] Under the provisions of the Rehabilitation of Offenders Act 1974.
[243] An example is *R v Bleasdale* (1984) 6 Cr App R (S) 177.
[244] The Times, 27 January 1999, quoted in Walker (n 213 above)110.
[245] [2002] EWCA Crim 1500.

because the offender has saved a child from drowning,[246] has put himself at risk in trying to rescue three children from a burning house,[247] or has gone to the assistance of a wounded police officer.[248]

(c) Remorse

There are many cases which show that the offender's remorse for the crime and its **28.86** consequences can properly sound in mitigation of sentence. Of course it is easy to express regret, and its genuineness may be difficult for the sentencer to assess. In *R v Howells*[249] Lord Bingham CJ said that admission of responsibility for the offence might tip the balance between a custodial and a non-custodial sentence, but there had to be 'hard evidence of genuine remorse' as well as an early guilty plea. The offender can normally expect a significant discount for a timely guilty plea,[250] so there is some overlap between the guilty plea discount and mitigation for remorse. They are not the same thing, however. An offender may be advised to plead guilty for good strategic reasons, but express no particular regret for his offending.

A case which illustrates the distinct mitigating power of remorse is *R v Claydon*,[251] **28.87** where the crime had been on the offender's conscience and he had gone to the police to confess at a time when he had not even been suspected of committing it. Remorse is a relevant factor in some cases of causing death by dangerous driving. Sometimes the victim will have been a relative or close friend of the offender, who will have experienced great emotional shock at the outcome.[252] Occasionally a voluntary payment of compensation by the offender to the victim ahead of sentence will demonstrate remorse, but there is some risk in giving credit for this since it is a form of mitigation which is available only to the better off.[253]

(d) Addiction

The courts often encounter cases where the background to the offence is the of- **28.88** fender's dependency on drink or drugs. While this will not be regarded as a matter making the offence itself less serious,[254] it may found the basis of an argument that a non-custodial sentence designed to address that underlying condition, such as a drug treatment and testing order, might be preferred. In *R v Howells*,[255] Lord Bingham CJ said that in such cases, 'the court will be inclined to look more favourably on an

---

[246] *R v Keightley* [1972] Crim LR 262.
[247] *R v Reid* (1982) 4 Cr App R (S) 280.
[248] *R v Playfair* [1972] Crim LR 387.
[249] [1999] 1 WLR 307.
[250] See para 28.59 above.
[251] (1994) 15 Cr App R (S) 526. Another example is *R v Hoult* (1990) 12 Cr App R (S) 180.
[252] See *R v Cooksley* [2003] EWCA Crim 996 (the guideline case).
[253] A point noted by the Court of Appeal in *R v Crosby* (1974) 60 Cr App R 234.
[254] See *R v Lawrence* (1988) 10 Cr App R (S) 463.
[255] [1999] 1 WLR 307.

offender who has already demonstrated . . . a genuine, self-motivated determination to address his addiction'. In a case at the custody threshold, a court may be persuaded for this reason to pass a community sentence rather than a custodial one.

(e) Collateral effects of the offence, or the sentence

28.89 Not infrequently the basis for personal mitigation is the collateral impact of that sentence on the offender's life, or the lives of close family members. The passing of a custodial sentence usually has such effects, and sentencers generally say that they cannot be taken into account.[256] The fact that an offender is finding prison very hard to cope with physically or psychologically, has not been regarded as a sufficient reason for adjustment of sentence on appeal,[257] nor is the fact that the offender is required to serve his sentence in segregation because of concerns over threats of violence from other inmates.[258] Even in the case of an offender suffering from serious illness which will affect his life expectancy, the Court of Appeal has generally stuck to this line, indicating that prisoners should petition the Home Office for the exercise of mercy, rather than expecting adjustment through the sentencing process.[259] Occasionally, however, the courts have relented and adjusted sentence on appeal in such cases.[260]

28.90 A special example of the collateral impact on the offence is where the offender has sustained serious injury in the course of committing the offence. This has been treated as a mitigating factor in a number of cases. These include *R v Barbery*,[261] where the offender's hand was severed in the course of the affray in which he had been involved, and *R v Mallone*,[262] where an offender who pleaded guilty to causing death by dangerous driving had himself sustained severe injuries in the collision in which the driver of the other car had been killed.

28.91 As far as impact on the family is concerned, again the general line is that offenders should realize that 'imprisonment of the father inevitably causes hardship to the rest of the family . . . [That] is part of the price to pay . . .'.[263] We saw earlier, however, that sentence may be adjusted, when sentencing a female offender, to take account of the effect of sentence on the children of the family.[264] In other exceptional cases, where the collateral consequences are unusual or extreme, the courts will sometimes adjust the sentence. In *R v Richards*,[265] a 57-year-old doctor was

---

[256] *R v Ingham* (1974) *Current Sentencing Practice*, para C4-2A01.
[257] *R v Kay* (1980) 2 Cr App R (S) 284.
[258] *R v Parker* [1996] 2 Cr App R (S) 275.
[259] *R v Bernard* [1997] 1 Cr App R (S) 135.
[260] An example is *R v Green* (1992) 13 Cr App R (S) 613.
[261] (1975) 62 Cr App R 248.
[262] [1996] 1 Cr App R (S) 221.
[263] According to Lord Widgery CJ in *R v Ingham* (1974) *Current Sentencing Practice*, para C4-2A01.
[264] See para 28.45 above.
[265] (1980) 2 Cr App R (S) 119.

convicted of obtaining the sum of £600 from the health authority by submitting false expenses claims. He was sentenced to imprisonment for 30 months. On appeal, it was argued that the sentence was too severe, given that the offender now faced professional disciplinary action, and would almost certainly be struck off, with no chance of obtaining future employment. Since the offence his wife had committed suicide. In light of these factors, sentence was reduced to 12 months. On the other hand, in *R v Lowery*,[266] where a police officer with 20 years' service in the force was convicted of false accounting, the Court of Appeal felt unable to adjust or suspend the prison sentence of three months despite evidence that the offender had, in consequence of his offence, lost his job and the police house in which he lived with his disabled wife, and that following discovery of the offence the offender had twice tried to commit suicide.

28.92 This is an area of sentencing practice where the exercise of judicial discretion is all-pervasive, and it is very difficult to discern any general principles being applied consistently.

(f) Lifestyle

28.93 Occasionally a court will be impressed by personal mitigation based upon a pending change in the offender's lifestyle, such as that he is now in a settled relationship, or has found employment. A good example is *R v Killen*,[267] an offender with an 'absolutely appalling record' of burglaries, where the Court of Appeal varied a sentence of 12 months' imprisonment to a community service order[268] on the basis that the offender had now formed a relationship with 'a sensible level-headed girl', offering him a real chance to mend his ways. Of course it is difficult to know whether such mitigation is truth or fabrication. Sometimes sentencers will defer the passing of sentence, for up to the maximum permissible period of six months,[269] to see whether the promised change materializes or not.

(3) Factors Which Aggravate Offence Seriousness

28.94 The sentencing framework, by s 81(4) of the Powers of Criminal Courts (Sentencing) Act 2000, requires the sentencer, when determining the seriousness of the offence, to 'take into account all such information as is available to him about the circumstances of the offence (including any aggravating or mitigating factors)'. Aggravating features are matters which tend to cause the sentencer to increase the sentence, and for convenience they can be classified in two groups.

---

[266] (1993) 14 Cr App R (S) 485.
[267] (1982) 4 Cr App R (S) 251.
[268] Now known as a community punishment order.
[269] Powers of Criminal Courts (Sentencing) Act 2000, s 1.

28.95 Some aggravating factors are narrow and offence-specific. In the guideline case on handling stolen goods,[270] for example, the following specific aggravating features are noted: (1) the closeness of the handler to the original offence, (2) a high level of seriousness of the original offence, (3) high value of the goods to the loser (including sentimental value), (4) the fact that the goods handled were the product of a domestic burglary, (5) a high degree of sophistication in the commission or organization of the handling, (6) a high level of profit made, or expected to be made, by the handler, (7) the fact that the handler provided a regular outlet for stolen goods, and (8) threats of violence or abuse of power by the handler over others. These are all matters of fact and degree, for detailed assessment by the sentencer. They can have considerable impact when sentencing a particular example of the offence in question, and they form an important element in the offence-specific sentencing guidelines.[271]

28.96 Other aggravating factors are applicable more generally in sentencing, being relevant across all, or a wide range of, offences. Examples, considered further below, include racial aggravation, the commission of an offence while on bail, commission of an offence in breach of trust, and offences involving a vulnerable victim. Whichever of the two forms they take, however, aggravating features will impinge in some way on offence seriousness, either by affecting the degree of harm caused (or risked) by the offender, or the degree of the offender's culpability. There should be no scope for arguing that, in contrast to personal mitigation, that matters personal to the offender, such as his bad character or disorganized lifestyle, may reflect badly on him and justify an increase in the sentence. So, it has been said that a sentencer must deal with the offender on the facts of the offence, and not on the basis of his 'feckless character and general behaviour'.[272] Courts must not impose a prison sentence on a persistent petty offender just because he is a social nuisance.[273] Occasionally, however, sentencers do come close to doing just that, when they impose a custodial sentence on a petty offender who has continued to offend in the face of one sentencing appearance after another.

(a) Racial or religious aggravation

28.97 It is a long-standing principle of sentencing that where an offence is shown to have been racially motivated, it is a significant aggravating feature.[274] This is the clearest example in English law of an offender's bad motive being directly relevant to sentence outcome, but the enhancement also reflects the additional insult and

---

[270] *R v Webbe* [2001] EWCA Crim 1217; [2002] 1 Cr App R (S) 22, and see Sentencing Advisory Panel, *Advice to the Court of Appeal 5—Handling Stolen Goods* (2001).
[271] See para 28.18 above.
[272] *R v Loosemore* (1980) 2 Cr App R (S) 72.
[273] See Thomas (n 31 above) 39 et seq.
[274] Clear examples are *A-G's References (Nos 29, 30 and 31 of 1994)* (1994) 16 Cr App R (S) 698, and *R v Craney* [1996] 2 Cr App R (S) 336.

harm which is done to the victim in such cases. Parliament has placed the principle on a statutory footing, and extended it to cover religious as well as racial aggravation.[275] In this context 'racial or religious aggravation' may take the form either of racial or religious motivation, or the demonstration towards the victim of hostility based on their membership of a racial or religious group.[276] Parliament has also created a number of special 'racially or religiously aggravated offences' (for example, certain aggravated assaults, aggravated criminal damage, aggravated public order offences, and aggravated harassment), all of which carry higher maximum penalties than the equivalent offence in its non-aggravated form.

The Court of Appeal in *R v Kelly and Donnelly*[277] said that whenever an offence is **28.98** shown to have been racially aggravated, the sentencer should indicate in open court what the sentence would have been without the racial element, and then add a further term, bearing in mind the enhanced penalties which Parliament has provided. In a case where the basic offence might not have crossed the custody threshold, the aggravated version might well do so. The Court of Appeal in that case also listed various matters likely to affect the degree of racial aggravation from case to case.

(b) Offending on bail

Section 152(2) of the Powers of Criminal Courts (Sentencing) Act 2000 confers a **28.99** duty on the sentencer to regard the commission of an offence while the offender is on bail as an aggravating feature of that offence. The rationale is that the offender's culpability is increased by the clear contravention of the court's requirement of bail. Bail is an expression of trust reposed in the offender to comply with its terms and, while breach of bail conditions is itself an offence, the commission of a further offence in breach of that trust is regarded as a serious aggravating feature of the case. Although Ashworth states[278] that breach of bail has always been so regarded, there are few authorities specifically on the point. The cases tend to take account of breach of bail as one among a number of aggravating features justifying a more severe sentence, or as a reason for distinguishing sentences passed on co-defendants, only one of whom committed their offence while on bail.[279] It can perhaps be assumed that the most aggravating circumstances will be where the offender has committed the new offence very soon after being released on bail, and it may be relevant that the new offence is similar to the offence for which the defendant was bailed.

While s 152(2) is expressed in mandatory terms, it has to be set against the sen- **28.100** tencing principle mentioned above,[280] that consecutive sentences are appropriate

---

[275] Powers of Criminal Courts (Sentencing) Act 2000, s 153(1).
[276] Crime and Disorder Act 1998, s 28.
[277] [2001] 2 Cr App R (S) 341, building on the decision in *R v Saunders* [2000] 2 Cr App R (S) 71.
[278] See also Ashworth (n 1 above) 28, 48.
[279] See *R v Whitehead* (1995) 16 Cr App R (S) 395.
[280] See para 28.52 above.

where one offence is committed while the offender is on bail in respect of another. The problem is that operation of these two rules together might result in a disproportionately severe sentence. There appears to be no modern authority on this issue.

(c) Breach of trust

28.101   This is one of the most important aggravating features, and it operates in a number of distinct areas of sentencing. In sexual offences, it arises in cases where an offender has taken advantage of a position of authority or power to perpetrate the offence. In *R v B*,[281] the Court of Appeal said that the sexual offences, two rapes and one indecent assault committed by a father on his teenage daughter, had been committed 'in gross breach of trust'. The same phrase was used in *R v Upfield*[282] where a family friend had unlawful sexual intercourse with the 12-year-old daughter of the family, while acting as a babysitter. Other examples are *R v Taylor*,[283] where a volunteer worker indecently assaulted four disabled women, and *R v Pike*,[284] where the offender pretended to be a hypnotherapist and conducted vaginal examinations on patients. This form of 'breach of trust' overlaps substantially with the category of 'vulnerable victim', considered below.

28.102   There is a different category of offender, whose job is to enforce and uphold the law, for whom commission of an offence in itself can be regarded as a breach of trust reposed in them by the public. Police officers[285] are obvious examples. The Court of Appeal issued a guideline judgment on 'theft in breach of trust' in *R v Barrick*,[286] which deals with cases where a person in a position of trust has used that opportunity to defraud his partners, clients, employers or the public of substantial sums of money. While a typical *Barrick* case might involve a solicitor, an accountant, or a bank employee, it is the element of trust rather than the precise role which matters. In *R v Clark*[287] the offender was bursar of the Royal Academy and he also acted as treasurer of his local church. He abused his position to steal just under £400,000 from his employer and £29,000 from the church. The offences were said to be aggravated by the four-year period over which they took place, and the fact that the money was spent on personal items regarded by the court as extravagant. Consecutive sentences of three years and one year were imposed.

---

[281] [1997] 2 Cr App R (S) 96.
[282] (1984) 6 Cr App R (S) 63.
[283] [1997] 1 Cr App R (S) 36.
[284] [1996] 1 Cr App R (S) 4.
[285] See, eg, *R v Keyte* [1998] 2 Cr App R (S) 165.
[286] (1985) 7 Cr App R (S) 142.
[287] [1998] 2 Cr App R 137.

(d) Vulnerable victim[288]

Vulnerable victims include those who are very young, elderly or handicapped,[289] and some others who through their office or employment place themselves at relatively greater risk of becoming victims, such as late-night bus drivers,[290] taxi drivers,[291] and traffic wardens.[292] Victim vulnerability is an aggravating feature in sentencing for two reasons. The first is that some such victims (especially the very young, or the elderly) may well suffer a greater degree of physical or psychological damage from the offence than the 'average' victim would. This greater harm makes the offence more serious.[293] The second is that in many cases involving vulnerable victims, the offender has *selected* the victim because they are less likely to be able to resist, or to defend themselves, and this displays a higher degree of culpability on the offender's part. Particular cases may display one or both of these features. The worst cases are surely those where a vulnerable victim has been deliberately targeted, and has suffered disproportionately as a result. The *Magistrates' Courts Sentencing Guidelines* are defective in this respect, by referring simply to 'vulnerable victim' as a general aggravating feature, without specifying any degree of culpability on the offender's part. Although the case law is not as clear on this point as it might be, the guideline case on domestic burglary, *R v McInerney*,[294] does draw a distinction between more than usually harmful consequences which are foreseen by the offender, and those which are not.

28.103

G. The Role of the Victim in Sentencing

(1) Representations From the Victim[295]

It is clear from the legislative sentencing framework that a key dimension in the seriousness of offences is the nature and extent of injury occasioned to the victim, and it was said in *R v Nunn*[296] to be an 'elementary principle of sentencing' that particularly damaging or distressing effects on the victim should be made known to, and be taken into account by, the sentencer. The court will require clear and accurate information on that matter, and should not make assumptions about the

28.104

---

[288] See further M Wasik, 'Crime seriousness and the offender-victim relationship in sentencing' in Ashworth and Wasik (n 158 above) ch 4.

[289] See *R v Goodwin* (1995) 16 Cr App R (S) 144, a case of 'gross and deliberate breach of trust' where a psychiatric nurse was convicted of unlawful sexual intercourse with patients in his care.

[290] An example is *R v Tremlett* (1983) 5 Cr App R (S) 199.

[291] *R v Rankin* (1993) 14 Cr App R (S) 636.

[292] *R v Robertson* (1990) 12 Cr App R (S) 278.

[293] See para 28.104 below.

[294] [2002] EWCA Crim 3003; [2003] 1 All ER 1089.

[295] A Ashworth, 'Victim impact statements and sentencing' [1993] Crim LR 498.

[296] [1996] 2 Cr App R (S) 136.

victim which are unsupported by evidence.[297] Until recently such information was provided by the prosecution in their statement of the facts of the case, but the practice has now developed whereby the victim of the offence (or the next relative if the victim is deceased) may, if they wish, prepare a victim personal statement for consideration by the sentencer.[298] Such statement will contain information as to the impact of the crime on the victim (or their surviving close family). The courts have said that such statements must be approached with care, especially where they relate to matters which the defence cannot be expected to investigate.

28.105 On the other hand, the opinion of the victim (or close relatives) on the appropriate sentence for the offender should *not* be taken into account.[299] The court must pass what it believes to be the correct sentence and it should not accede to a plea for vengeance by the victim. It should also be cautious about giving weight to a plea for mercy, although case law recognizes some exceptions to this. Occasionally, where the victim and the offender are close friends or relations, a severe sentence may aggravate the victim's distress, and so may be moderated to some degree.[300] Also, there can be cases where the victim's forgiveness of the offender may indicate resilience on their part, or that the harm done to them has turned out to be rather less than might have been expected.[301]

(2) Compensation Orders[302]

28.106 A compensation order is an order made by a criminal court that the offender should pay a sum of money to the victim in compensation for 'any personal injury, loss or damage'[303] occasioned by the offence. Compensation orders are the most important form of *ancillary* order made on sentence. This means that orders for compensation are made at the time of sentence, but do not form part of the punishment for the offence. They can be added to any form of disposal. The courts are under a duty to consider making a compensation order in every case, and must give reasons if they do not make one. The victim does not have to apply to the court. A court may, however, decide that a compensation order cannot be made because the offender cannot afford to pay. If, for example, a custodial sentence has been imposed for the offence, this will often mean that the offender is effectively deprived of the means to pay.[304]

---

[297] *R v Hobstaff* (1993) 14 Cr App R (S) 605.
[298] *Practice Statement (CA (Crim Div): Victim Personal Statements)* [2001] 1 WLR 2038.
[299] ibid para 3(b); *R v Perks* [2001] 1 Cr App R (S) 19.
[300] An example is *R v Roche* [1999] 2 Cr App R (S) 105.
[301] An example is *R v Hutchinson* (1994) 15 Cr App R (S) 134.
[302] M Wasik, 'The compensation order on sentence' (1999) 163 JP 564.
[303] Powers of Criminal Courts (Sentencing) Act 2000, s 130(1).
[304] *R v Love* [1999] 1 Cr App R (S) 484.

Compensation orders are designed as a speedy and effective remedy in straight-forward cases.[305] Criminal courts are discouraged from making compensation orders in cases likely to involve protracted dispute over the extent of the damage or loss. In such cases the victim should be left to pursue a remedy through the civil courts.[306]   **28.107**

Since a compensation order is ancillary to sentence, a decision to make such an order should not affect the disposal itself. In particular, an expression of willingness by the offender to pay money to the victim should not justify the suspension of an otherwise deserved custodial sentence. As Scarman LJ said in *R v Inwood*,[307] 'compensation orders were not introduced into our law to enable the convicted to buy themselves out of the penalties for crime'. This important sentencing principle is, however, subject to a modification where the sentence selected is a fine. Here, statute provides that where a compensation order is made in addition to a fine, and the offender has limited means, priority should be given to the compensation order ahead of the fine.[308]   **28.108**

---

[305] *R v White* [1996] 2 Cr App R (S) 58.
[306] *R v Donovan* (1981) 3 Cr App R (S) 192.
[307] (1974) 60 Cr App R 70. The principle was restated in *A-G's Reference (No 5 of 1993)* (1994) 15 Cr App R (S) 201.
[308] Powers of Criminal Courts (Sentencing) Act 2000, s 130(12).

Evans, P, *Handbook of House of Commons Procedure* (3rd edn, London: Vacher Dod, 2002)
Oliver, D, and Drewry, G (eds), *The Law and Parliament* (London: Butterworths, 1998)
Shell, D, *The House of Lords* (2nd edn, Hemel Hempstead: Wheatsheaf, 1992)

The Legislative Supremacy of Parliament and its Limits
Dicey, AV, *Law of the Constitution* (10th edn, London: Macmillan, 1959)
Hood Phillips, O, *Reform of the Constitution* (London: Chatto and Windus, 1970)
Le Sueur, A, and Sunkin, M, *Public Law* (London: Longman, 1997)
Wade, HWR, 'The Basis of Legal Sovereignty' [1955] CLJ 172
—— 'Sovereignty—Revolution or Evolution?' (1996) 112 LQR 568

Chapter 3: The Nature, Powers and Accountability of Central Government

Daintith, T, and Page, A, *The Executive in the Constitution: Structure, Autonomy and Internal Control* (Oxford: OUP, 1999)
Hennessy, P, *Cabinet* (Oxford: Basil Blackwell, 1996)
—— *Whitehall* (London: Fontana Press, 1990)
Oliver, D, *Government in the UK: The Search for Accountability, Effectiveness and Citizenship* (Oxford: OUP, 2003)
Woodhouse, D, *Ministers and Parliament: Accountability in Theory and Practice* (Oxford: Clarendon Press, 1994)

Chapter 4: The Structure, Powers and Accountability of Local Government

Arden, A, Manning, J, and Collins, S, *Local Government Constitutional and Administrative Law* (London: Sweet & Maxwell, 1999)
Bailey, SH, et al, *Cross on Local Government Law* (London: Sweet & Maxwell)
Elias, P, and Goudie, J, (eds), *Butterworths Local Government Law* (London: Butterworths)
Leigh, I, *Law, Politics and Local Democracy* (Oxford: OUP, 2000)
Loughlin, M, *Legality and Locality : The role of Law in Central-Local Government Relations* (Oxford: Clarendon Press, 1996)

Chapter 5: The Powers and Accountability of Agencies and Regulators

Baldwin, R, *Rules and Government* (Oxford: Clarendon Press, 1995)
Ferran, E, and Goodhart, C (eds), *Regulating Financial Services and Markets in the 21st Century* (Oxford: Hart Publishing, 2001)
Majone, G, *Regulating Europe* (London: Routledge, 1996)
Prosser, T, *Law and the Regulators* (Oxford: Clarendon Press, 1997)
Rodger, B, and MacCulloch, A (eds), *The UK Competition Act: A New Era for UK Competition Law* (Oxford: Hart, 2000)

Chapter 6: The Constitutional Position of the Judiciary

Le Sueur, A, and Cornes, R, *The Future of the UK's Highest Courts* (London: UCL Constitution Unit, 2001)
Olowofoyeku, A, *Suing Judges: A Study of Judicial Immunity* (Oxford: Clarendon Press, 1993)

Stevens, RB, *The English Judges: Their Role in the Changing Constitution* (Oxford: Hart Publishing, 2002)

Chapter 7: Standards of Review and Human Rights in English Law

Cane, P, *An Introduction to Adminstrative Law* (3rd edn, Oxford: Clarendon Press, 1996)

Clayton, R, and Tomlinson, H, *The Law of Human Rights* (Oxford: OUP, 2000)

Feldman, D, *Civil Liberties and Human Rights in English Law* (2nd edn, Oxford: OUP, 2002)

Fenwick, H, *Civil Rights: New Labour, Freedom and the Human Rights Act* (London: Longman, 2000)

Grosz, S, Beatson, J, and Duffy, P, *Human Rights: The 1998 Act and the European Convention* (London: Sweet & Maxwell, 1999)

Lester, Lord, and Pannick, D, *Human Rights Law and Practice* 2/e (London: Butterworths, 2004)

Starmer, K, *European Human Rights Law* (London: Legal Action Group, 1999)

Chapter 8: Rights to Life, Physical and Moral Integrity, Freedom of Lifestyle and Religion or Belief

Bradney, A, *Religions, Rights and Laws* (Leicester: Leicester University Press, 1993)

Clayton, R, and Tomlinson, H, *The Law of Human Rights* (Oxford: OUP, 2000), chapters 7–10 and 11–14

Colvin, M (ed), *Developing Key Privacy Rights: The Impact of the Human Rights Act 1998* (Oxford: Hart Publishing, 2002)

Evans, C, *Freedom of Religion under the European Convention on Human Rights* (Oxford: OUP, 2001)

Chapter 9: Political Rights

Beatson, J, and Cripps, Y (eds), *Freedom of Expression and Freedom of Information: Essays in Honour of Sir David Williams* (Oxford: OUP, 2000)

Clayton, R, and Tomlinson, H, *The Law of Human Rights* (Oxford: OUP, 2000), chapters 15, 16 and 20

Feldman, D, *Civil Liberties and Human Rights in English Law* (2nd edn, Oxford: OUP, 2002), Part IV

Chapter 10: Social, Economic and Cultural Rights

Steiner, HJ, and Alston, P, *International Human Rights in Context: Law, Politics, Morals* (2nd edn, Oxford: OUP, 2000), chapter 4

Chapter 11: Equality and Non-Discrimination

Bell, M, *Anti-Discrimination Law and the EU* (Oxford: OUP, 2002)

Fredman, S, *Discrimination Law* (Oxford: OUP, 2001)

Hepple, B, Coussey, M, and Choudhury, T, *Equality: A New Framework* (Oxford: Hart Publishing, 2000)

McColgan, A, *Discrimination Law: Text, Cases and Materials* (Oxford: Hart Publishing, 2000)

McCrudden, C, *Anti-Discrimination Law* (2nd edn, Aldershot: Ashgate, 2004)

Chapter 12: Due Process Rights

Mowbray, AR, *Cases and Materials on the European Convention on Human Rights* (London: Butterworths, 2001)

Simor, J, and Emmerson , B (eds), *Human Rights Practice* (London: Sweet & Maxwell, 2000)

Stavros, S, *The Guarantees for Accused Persons Under Article 6 of the European Convention on Human Rights* (Dordrecht: Martinus Nijhoff, 1993)

Chapter 13: Fundamental Principles of Administrative Law

Elliott, M, *The Constitutional Foundations of Judicial Review* (Oxford: Hart Publishing, 2001)

Forsyth, C (ed), *Judicial Review and the Constitution* (Oxford: Hart Publishing, 2000)

Harlow, C, and Rawlings, R, *Law and Administration* (2nd edn, London: Butterworths, 1997)

Taggart, M (ed), *The Province of Administrative Law* (Oxford: Hart Publishing, 1997)

Chapter 14: Grounds for Judicial Review: Illegality in the Strict Sense

Craig, PP, *Administrative Law* (5th edn, London: Sweet & Maxwell, 2003), especially chapters 16, 17 and 18.

De Smith, SA, Woolf, Lord, and Jowell, J, *Judicial Review of Administrative Action* (5th edn, London: Sweet & Maxwell, 1995), chapter 6

——— ——— and ——— *Principles of Judicial Review of Administrative Action* (London: Sweet & Maxwell, 1999), chapter 5

Wade, Sir W, and Forsyth, CF, *Administrative Law* (8th edn, Oxford: OUP, 2000), Part IV.

Chapter 15: Grounds for Judicial Review: Due Process, Natural Justice and Fairness

Craig, PP, *Administrative Law* (5th edn, London: Sweet & Maxwell, 2003)

de Smith, SA, Woolf, Lord, and Jowell, J, *Judicial Review of Administrative Action* (5th edn, London: Sweet & Maxwell, 1995)

Galligan, D, *Due Process and Fair Procedures* (Oxford: Clarendon Press, 1996)

Wade, Sir W, and Forsyth, CF, *Administrative Law* (8th edn, Oxford: OUP, 2000)

Chapter 16: Grounds for Judicial Review: Substantive Control over Discretion

Craig, PP, *Administrative Law* (5th edn, London: Sweet & Maxwell, 2003), chapters 18 and 19

Ellis, E (ed), *The Principle of Proportionality in the Laws of Europe* (Oxford: Hart Publishing, 1999)

Laws, Sir J, 'Wednesbury' in Hare, I, and Forsyth, CF (eds), *The Golden Metwand and the Crooked Cord: Essays in Honour of Sir William Wade* (Oxford: OUP, 1998)

Schonberg, S, *Legitimate Expectations in English Law* (Oxford: OUP, 2000)
Wade, Sir W, and Forsyth, CF, *Administrative Law* (8th edn, Oxford: OUP, 2000), chapter 12

Chapter 17: Access to Mechanisms of Administrative Law

Birkinshaw, P, *Grievances, Remedies and the State* (2nd edn, London: Sweet & Maxwell, 1994)
Bridges, L, Meszaros, G, and Sunkin, M, *Judicial Review in Perspective* (2nd edn, London: Cavendish Publishing, 1995)
Cane, P, 'Standing, Legality and the Limits of Public Law' [1981] PL 322
Wade, Sir W, and Forsyth, CF, *Administrative Law* (8th edn, Oxford: OUP, 2000), chapters 18 and 20

Chapter 18: Remedies Available in Judicial Review Proceedings

Craig, PP, *Administrative Law* (5th edn, London: Sweet & Maxwell, 2003), Part 3
Lewis, C, *Judicial Remedies in Public Law* (2nd edn, London: Sweet & Maxwell, 2000)
de Smith, SA, Woolf, Lord, and Jowell, J, *Judicial Review of Administrative Action* (5th edn, London: Sweet & Maxwell 1995), Part IV
—— —— and —— *Principles of Judicial Review of Administrative Action* (London: Sweet & Maxwell, 1999), Part III
Wade, Sir W, and Forsyth, CF, *Administrative Law* (8th edn, Oxford: OUP, 2000), Part VII

Chapter 19: Remedies for Violations of Convention Rights

Clayton, R, and Tomlinson, H, *The Law of Human Rights* (Oxford: OUP, 2000), chapters 21 and 22
Marriott, J, and Nicol, D, 'The Human Rights Act, Representative Standing and the Victim Culture' [1998] EHRLR 730
Miles, J, 'Standing under the Human Rights Act 1998: Theories of Rights Enforcement and the Nature of Public Law Adjudication' [2000] CLJ 133
Simor, J, and Emmerson, B (eds), *Human Rights Practice* (London: Sweet & Maxwell, 2000)
Woolf, Lord, 'The Human Rights Act 1998 and Remedies' in Andenas, M, and Fairgrieve, D (eds), *Judicial Review in International Perspective: II* (London: BIICL, 2000)

Chapter 20: Tribunals

Genn, H, 'Tribunal Review of Administrative Decision-Making' in Richardson, G, and Genn, H, *Administrative Law and Government Action* (Oxford: Clarendon Press, 1994)
Report of the Committee on Administrative Tribunals and Inquiries (the Franks Report), Cmnd 218 (London: HMSO, 1957)
Tribunal for Users: One System, One Service (the Leggatt Report) (London: Stationery Office, 2001)

Chapter 21: Investigations by the Public Sector Ombudsmen

Gregory, R, and Pearson, J, 'The Parliamentary Ombudsman after Twenty-Five Years' (1992) 70 *Public Administration* 469

Rawlings, R, 'The MPs' Complaints Service—Parts I and II' (1990) 53 MLR 22 and 149

Chapter 22: Public Inquiries as a Part of Public Administration

Wade, Sir W, and Forsyth, CF, *Administrative Law* (8th edn, Oxford: OUP, 2000), chapter 25

Winetrobe, BK, 'Inquiries after Scott: the Return of the Tribunal of Inquiry' [1997] PL 18

Wraith, RE, and Lamb, GB, *Public Inquiries as an Instrument of Government* (London: Allen & Unwin, 1972)

Chapter 23: English Criminal Procedure

Archbold's Criminal Pleadings, Evidence and Practice, 2004 (London: Sweet & Maxwell, 2004)

Murphy, P (ed), *Blackstone's Criminal Practice 2004* (Oxford: OUP, 2004)

Pattenden, R, *Judicial Discretion and Criminal Litigation* (2nd edn, Oxford: Clarendon Press, 1990)

Stone's Justices Manual, 2003 (London: Shaw & Sons Ltd, 2003)

Taylor, P, *Taylor on Appeals* (London: Sweet & Maxwell, 2000)

Chapter 24: General Principles of Criminal Law

Duff, RA (ed), *Philosophy and the Criminal Law: Principle and Critique* (Cambridge: CUP, 1998)

Shute, S, Gardner, J, and Horder, J (eds), *Action and Value in Criminal Law* (Oxford: OUP, 1993)

Shute, S, and Simester, AP (eds), *Criminal Law Theory: Doctrines of the General Part* (Oxford: OUP, 2002)

Simester, AP, and Smith, ATH (eds), *Harm and Culpability* (Oxford: OUP, 1996)

Chapter 25: Offences Against the Person

Ashworth, A, *Principles of Criminal Law* (4th edn, Oxford: OUP, 2003)

Ashworth, A, and Mitchell, B (eds), *Rethinking English Homicide Law* (Oxford: OUP, 2000)

Simester, AP, and Sullivan, GR, *Criminal Law: Theory and Doctrine* (2nd edn, Oxford: Hart Publishing, 2003)

Smith, JC, *Smith and Hogan: Criminal Law* (10th edn, London: Butterworths, 2002)

Chapter 26: Offences Against Property

Simester, AP, and Sullivan, GR, *Criminal Law Theory and Doctrine* (2nd edn, Oxford: Hart Publishing, 2003), chapters 13-15

Smith, ATH, *Property Offences* (London: Sweet & Maxwell, 1994)

Smith, JC, *The Law of Theft* (8th edn, London: Butterworths, 1997)

Smith, JC, *Smith and Hogan: Criminal Law* (10th edn, London: Butterworths, 2002), chapters 16-19

Chapter 27: Offences Against the State, Public Order, Public Morality and Decency

Feldman, D, *Civil Liberties and Human Rights in English Law* (2nd edn, Oxford: OUP, 2002), chapters 15, 16 and 18
Smith, JC, *Smith and Hogan: Criminal Law* (10th edn, London: Butterworths, 2002), chapters 20 and 21

Chapter 28: Principles of Sentencing

Ashworth, A, *Sentencing and Criminal Justice* (3rd edn, London: Butterworths, 2000)
Thomas, DA, *Principles of Sentencing* (2nd edn, London: Heinemann, 1979)
von Hirsch, A, and Ashworth, A, *Principled Sentencing: Readings on Theory and Policy* (2nd edn, Oxford: Hart Publishing, 1998)
Walker, N, *Aggravation, Mitigation and Mercy in English Criminal Justice* (London: Blackstone, 1999)
Wasik, M, *Emmins on Sentencing* (4th edn, London: Blackstone, 2001)

B. Comprehensive List of all Books and Articles referred to in *English Public Law*

(1) Books and looseleafs

Abel-Smith, B, and Stevens, R, *In Search of Justice* (London: Allen Lane, 1968)
Ackner, Lord, 'The Erosion of Judicial Independence' (John Stuart Mill Institute, 1997)
Adams, J, and Robinson, P, *Devolution in Practice: Public Policy Differences within the UK* (London: IPPR, 2002)
Adler, M, and Bradley, A, *Justice, Discretion and Poverty* (London: Professional Books, 1976)
Aitken, J, *Officially Secret* (London: Weidenfeld & Nicolson, 1971)
Allan, TRS, *Law, Liberty, and Justice: the Legal Foundations of British Constitutionalism* (Oxford: Clarendon Press, 1993)
—— *Constitutional Justice: a Liberal Theory of the Rule of Law* (Oxford: OUP, 2001)
Allison, J, *A Continental Distinction in the Common Law: A Historical and Comparative Perspective on English Public Law* (Oxford: OUP, 1996)
—— *A Continental Distinction in the Common Law: a Historical and Comparative Perspective on English Public Law* (rev edn, New York: OUP, 2000)
Amery, LS, *Thoughts on the Constitution* (Oxford: OUP, 1947)
Amos, Sir M, *The English Constitution* (London: Longman, 1930)
Andenas, M (ed), *English Public Law and the Common Law of Europe* (London: Key Haven, 1998)
—— and Fairgrieve, D (eds), *Judicial Review in International Perspective* (The Hague: Kluwer Law International, 2000)
Anson, Sir WR, *The Law and Custom of the Constitution* (4th edn, Oxford: Clarendon Press, 1935)

Archbold: Criminal Pleading, Evidence and Practice (London: Sweet & Maxwell)

Arden, A, Manning, J, and Collins, S, *Local Government Constitutional and Administrative Law* (London: Sweet & Maxwell, 1999)

Arnull, A, *The General Principles of EEC Law and the Individual* (London: Leicester University Press, 1990)

—— *The European Union and Its Court of Justice* (Oxford: OUP, 1999)

Arthurs, HW, *'Without the Law': Administrative Justice and Legal Pluralism in Nineteenth-Century England* (Toronto: University of Toronto Press, 1985)

Ashworth, A, *Sentencing and Criminal Justice* (3rd edn, London: Butterworths, 2000)

—— *Principles of Criminal Law* (4th edn, Oxford: OUP, 2003)

Austin, J, *The Province of Jurisprudence Determined* (London: Weidenfeld and Nicholson, 1954)

Ayres, I, and Braithwaite, J, *Responsive Regulation: Transcending the Deregulation Debate* (Oxford: OUP, 1992)

Bagehot, W, *The English Constitution* (London: Collins, 1963)

Bailey, SH (ed), *Encyclopedia of Local Government Law* (London: Sweet & Maxwell)

—— et al, *Cross on Local Government Law* (London: Sweet & Maxwell)

Bailey (ed), Ching, JPL, Gunn, MJ, and Ormerod, DC, *Smith, Bailey and Gunn on the Modern English Legal System* (4th edn, London: Sweet & Maxwell, 2002)

—— Harris, DJ, and Jones, BL, *Civil Liberties: Cases and Materials* (5th edn, London: Butterworths, 2000)

Baldwin, J, Wikeley, N, and Young, R, *Judging Social Security Claims* (Oxford: Clarendon Press, 1992)

Baldwin, R, *Rules and Government* (Oxford: Clarendon Press, 1995)

Barendt, E, *Freedom of Speech* (Oxford: Clarendon Press, 1985)

—— *An Introduction to Constitutional Law* (Oxford: OUP, 1998)

Bayles, M, *Procedural Justice* (Dordrecht: Kluwer, 1990)

Beatson, J, and Cripps, Y (eds), *Freedom of Expression and Freedom of Information: Essays in Honour of Sir David Williams* (Oxford: OUP, 2000)

Bell, J, and Engle, G (eds), *Cross on Statutory Interpretation* (3rd edn, London: Butterworths, 1995)

Bell, M, *Anti-Discrimination Law and the EU* (Oxford: OUP, 2002)

Benn, T, *Arguments for Democracy* (London: Cape, 1981)

—— and Hood, A, *Common Sense: A New Constitution for Britain* (London: Hutchinson, 1993)

Bennett, J, and Cirell, S, *Municipal Trading* (London: Longman, 1992)

Bennion, F, *Bennion on Statute Law* (3rd edn, London: Longman, 1990)

—— *Statutory Interpretation* (3rd edn, London: Butterworths, 1997)

—— *Statutory Interpretation* (4th edn, London: Butterworths, 2002)

Birkinshaw, P, *Grievances, Remedies and the State* (2nd edn, London: Sweet & Maxwell, 1994)

Birks, P (ed), *English Private Law* (Oxford: OUP, 2000)

Blackburn, R, *The Meeting of Parliament: The Law and Practice Relating to the Frequency and Duration of the UK Parliament* (Aldershot: Dartmouth, 1990)

—— and Polakiewicz, Jörg (eds), *Fundamental Rights in Europe: The ECHR and its Member States, 1950–2000* (Oxford: OUP, 2001)

—— , Kennon, K, and Wheeler-Booth, Sir M, *Griffith and Ryle on Parliament. Functions, Practice and Procedures* (2nd edn, London: Sweet & Maxwell, 2003)

Blackstone, Sir William, *Commentaries on the Laws of England*, Book IV (1769)
—— *Commentaries on the Law of England* (16th edn, 1825)
Bogdanor, V, *The Monarchy and the Constitution* (Oxford: Clarendon Press, 1995)
Bonner, D, *Emergency Powers in Peacetime* (London: Sweet & Maxwell, 1985)
Bossuyt, M, *L'interdiction de la discrimination dans le droit international des droits de l'homme* (Bruxelles: Bruylant, 1976)
Bradley, AW, and Ewing, KD, *Constitutional and Administrative Law* (12th edn, London: Longman, 1997)
—— and —— *Constitutional and Administrative Law* (13th edn, Harlow: Longman, 2001)
Brazier, M, and Murphy J (eds), *Street on Torts* (10th edn, London: Butterworths, 1999)
Brazier, R, *Constitutional Practice* (Oxford: Clarendon Press, 1988)
—— *Constitutional Practice* (2nd edn, Oxford: Clarendon Press, 1994)
Bridges, L, Meszaros, G, and Sunkin, M, *Judicial Review in Perspective* (2nd edn, London: Cavendish Publishing, 1995)
Brown, D, and Ellis, T, *Policing low-level disorder: Police use of the Public Order Act 1986* (Home Office research study, HMSO, 1994)
Browning AR (ed), *House of Representative Practice* (2nd edn, Canberra: Australian Government Publishing Service, 1989)
Bryce, J, *Studies in History and Jurisprudence* (Oxford: Clarendon Press, 1901)
Burrows, N, *Devolution* (London: Sweet & Maxwell, 2000)

Cane, P, *An Introduction to Administrative Law* (2nd edn, Oxford: Clarendon Press, 1992)
—— *An Introduction to Administrative Law* (3rd edn, Oxford: Clarendon Press, 1996)
Card, R, *Public Order Law* (Bristol: Jordans, 2000)
Chayes, A, and Chayes, AH, *The new sovereignty: compliance with international regulatory regimes* (Cambridge, Massachusetts: Harvard University Press, 1995)
Clayton, R, and Tomlinson, H, *The Law of Human Rights* (Oxford: OUP, 2000)
Coke, Sir E, *Institutes* (1628–24)
Cowan, D, and Halliday, S, *The Appeal of Internal Review* (Oxford: Hart Publishing, 2003)
Craig, P, *Administrative Law* (4th edn, London: Sweet & Maxwell, 1999)
—— and de Burca, G, *EU Law, Text, Cases and Materials* (3rd edn, Oxford: OUP, 2002)
Craufurd-Smith, R, *Broadcasting Law and Fundamental Rights* (Oxford: OUP, 1997)
Crawford, C, and Grace, C (eds), *'Conducive or Incidental To?' Local Authority Discretionary Powers in the Modern Era* (University of Birmingham, 1992)
Creighton, WB, *Working Women and the Law* (London: Mansell, 1979)
Cygan, AJ, *National Parliaments in an Integrated Europe: An Anglo-German Perspective* (The Hague: Kluwer International, 2001)

Daintith, T, and Page, A, *The Executive in the Constitution: Structure, Autonomy and Internal Control* (Oxford: OUP, 1999)
Davis, KC, *Discretionary Justice* (Urbana: University of Illinois Press, 1971)
de Smith, SA, Woolf, Lord, and Jowell, J, *Judicial Review of Administrative Action* (5th edn, London: Sweet & Maxwell, 1995)
—— —— and —— *Principles of Judicial Review* (London: Sweet & Maxwell, 1999)
Deakin, S, and Morris, G, *Labour Law* (3rd edn, London: Butterworths, 2001)
Devlin, P, *The Enforcement of Morals* (London: OUP, 1965)
Dicey, AV, *Lectures Introductory to the Study of the Law of the Constitution* (London: Macmillan, 1885)

—— *Lectures on the Relation between Law & Public Opinion in England during the Nineteenth Century* (London: Macmillan, 1908)

—— *Law of the Constitution* (10th edn, London: Macmillan, 1959)

Douglas Lewis, N, *Law and Governance* (London: Cavendish, 2001)

Douglas-Scott, S, *Constitutional Law of the European Union* (Harlow: Longman, 2002)

Drewry, G, *The New Select Committees* (2nd edn, Oxford: OUP, 1989)

Dugdale, AM (ed), *Clerk & Lindsell on Torts* (18th edn, London: Sweet & Maxwell, 2000)

Dworkin, R, *Taking Rights Seriously* (London: Duckworth, 1977)

—— *A Matter of Principle* (Cambridge, Mass: Harvard University Press, 1985)

—— *Law's Empire* (London: Fontana, 1986)

Eady, D, and Smith, ATH, *Eady and Smith on Contempt* (London: Sweet & Maxwell, 2000)

East, Sir Edward Hyde, *A Treatise of the Pleas of the Crown* (1803)

Elias, P, and Goudie, J (eds), *Butterworths Local Government Law* (London: Butterworths)

Elliott, M, *The Constitutional Foundations of Judicial Review* (Oxford: Hart Publishing, 2001)

Emmerson, B, and Ashworth, A, *Human Rights and Criminal Justice* (London: Sweet & Maxwell, 2001)

Ericson, R, and Baranek, P, *The Ordering of Justice* (Toronto: University of Toronto Press, 1982)

Erskine May, Sir T, *Treatise on the Law, Privileges, Proceedings and Usage of Parliament* (22nd edn, London: Butterworths, 1997)

Eskridge, WN, *Dynamic Statutory Interpretation* (Cambridge, Massachusetts: Harvard University Press, 1994)

Estella, A, *The EU principle of subsidiarity and its critique* (Oxford: OUP, 2002)

Ewing, KD, *The EU Charter of Fundamental Rights: Waste of Time or Wasted Opportunity?* (London: Institute of Employment Rights, 2002)

—— and Gearty, CA, *The Struggle for Civil Liberties: Political Freedom and the Rule of Law in Britain, 1914–1945* (Oxford: OUP, 2000)

Fabian Society Commission on the Future of the Monarchy, *The Future of the Monarchy* (London: Fabian Society, 2003)

Farmer, J, *Tribunals and Government* (London: Weidenfeld & Nicolson, 1974)

Fawcett, Sir JES, *The Application of the European Convention on Human Rights* (2nd edn, Oxford: Clarendon Press, 1987)

Feinberg, J, *Offense to Others* (New York: OUP, 1985)

Feldman, D, *Civil Liberties and Human Rights in England and Wales* (2nd edn, Oxford: OUP, 2002)

Fenwick, H, *Civil Rights: New Labour, Freedom and the Human Rights Act* (London: Longman, 2000)

Finer, SE, Bogdanor, V, and Rudden, B, *Comparing Constitutions* (Oxford: OUP, 1995)

Forsyth, C (ed), *Judicial Review and the Constitution* (Oxford: Hart Publishing, 2000)

Foster, Sir M, *Crown Law* (1762)

Foster's Crown Cases and Discourses (Oxford: Clarendon Press, 1762) 27.11

Fredman, S, *Women and the Law* (Oxford: Clarendon Press, 1997)

—— and Morris, G, *The State as Employer: Labour Law in the Public Services* (London: Mansell, 1989)

Galligan, DJ, *Discretionary Powers* (Oxford: Clarendon Press, 1986)

Le Sueur, A, and Sunkin, M, *Public Law* (London: Longman, 1997)

—— and Cornes, R, *The Future of the UK's Highest Courts* (London: UCL Constitution Unit, 2001)

Lewis, C, *Judicial Remedies in Public Law* (2nd edn, London: Sweet & Maxwell, 2000)

Lewis, D, *Hidden Agendas: Politics, Law and Disorder* (London: Hamish Hamilton, 1997)

Lewis, N, et al, *Complaint Procedures in Local Government* (University of Sheffield, 1987)

Liberty, *A People's Charter: Liberty's Bill of Rights* (London: Liberty, 1991)

Littlechild, S, *Regulation of British Telecommunications Profitability* (London: Department of Industry, 1983)

Locke, John, *Two Treatises of Government*, Second Treatise (P Laslett (ed), Cambridge: CUP, 1960)

Loughlin, M, *Legality and Locality: The Role of Law in Central-Local Government Relations* (Oxford: Clarendon Press, 1996)

Lowe, NV, and Sufrin, BE, *Borrie and Lowe: The Law of Contempt* (3rd edn, London: Butterworths, 1995)

Lustgarten, L, and Leigh, I, *In From the Cold* (Oxford: Clarendon, 1994)

Mackay, RD, *Mental Condition Defences in the Criminal Law* (Oxford: Clarendon Press, 1995)

Mahajan, VD, *Constitutional Law of India* (7th edn, Lucknow: Eastern Book Company, 1991)

Majone, G, *Regulating Europe* (London: Routledge, 1996)

Manchester, C, Salter, D, Moodie, P, and Lynch, B, *Exploring the Law: The Dynamics of Precedent and Statutory Interpretation* (2nd edn, London: Sweet & Maxwell, 2000)

Marshall, G, *Constitutional Theory* (Oxford: Clarendon, 1971)

—— *Constitutional Conventions* (Oxford: Clarendon, 1984)

—— *Ministerial Responsibility* (Oxford: OUP, 1989)

Marshall, HH, *Natural Justice* (London: Sweet & Maxwell, 1959)

McCrudden, C, and Chambers, G, *Individual Rights and the Law in Britain* (Oxford: Clarendon Press, 1994)

Michael, J, *Privacy and Human Rights* (Aldershot: Dartmouth, 1994)

Miller, CJ, *Contempt of Court* (3rd edn, Oxford: OUP, 2000)

Mitchell, JDB, *The Contracts of Public Authorities* (London: G Bell & Sons, 1954)

Mount, F, *The British Constitution Now* (London: Heinemann, 1992)

Mowbray, AR, *Cases and Materials on the European Convention of Human Rights* (London: Butterworths, 2001)

Munro, CR, *Studies in Constitutional Law* (2nd edn, London: Butterworths, 1999)

Murphy, P (ed), *Blackstone's Criminal Practice* (13th edn, Oxford: OUP, 2003)

O'Donovan, K, and Rubin, G, *Human Rights and Legal History* (Oxford: OUP, 2000)

Oliver, D, *Common Values and the Public–Private Divide* (London: Butterworths, 1999)

—— *Government in the UK: The Search for Accountability, Effectiveness and Citizenship* (Oxford: OUP, 2003)

Oliver, D, and Drewry, G, *Public Service Reforms: Issues of Accountability and Public Law* (London: Pinter, 1996)

Olowofoyeku, A, *Suing Judges: A Study of Judicial Immunity* (Oxford: Clarendon Press, 1993)

O'Riordan, T, Kemp, R, and Purdue, M, *Sizewell B: An Anatomy of the Inquiry* (London: Macmillan, 1988)

Ovey, C, and White, RCA, *Jacobs & White, European Convention on Human Rights* (3rd edn, Oxford: OUP, 2002)

Paine, Thomas, *Rights of Man* (1791–92, Penguin Classics edn, 1985)

Pattenden, R, *Judicial Discretion and Criminal Litigation* (2nd edn, Oxford: Clarendon Press, 1990)

Peay, J, *Tribunals On Trial* (Oxford: Clarendon Press, 1989)

Plucknett, TFT, *Taswell-Langmead's English Constitutional History* (11th edn, London: Sweet & Maxwell, 1960)

Prosser, T, *Nationalised Industries and Public Control* (Oxford: Blackwell, 1986)

—— *Law and the Regulators* (Oxford: Clarendon Press, 1997)

Pyper, R (ed), *Aspects of Accountability in the British System of Government* (Eastham: Tudor, 1996)

Radzinowicz, L, *A History of English Criminal Law* (London: Stevens, 1948–56)

Raz, J, *The Authority of Law, Essays on Law and Morality* (Oxford: OUP, 1979)

—— *Ethics in the Public Domain, Essays on the Morality of Law and Politics* (Oxford: OUP, 1994)

Reynolds, FMB, *Bowstead and Reynolds on Agency* (16th edn, London: Sweet & Maxwell, 1996)

Richardson, G, *Law, Process and Custody: Prisoners and Patients* (London: Weidenfeld & Nicolson, 1993)

—— and Genn, H, *Administrative Law & Government Action* (Oxford: Clarendon Press, 1994)

Robertson, G, *Obscenity* (London: Weidenfeld & Nicolson, 1979)

Robson, WA, *The Development of Local Government* (3rd edn, London: George Allen & Unwin, 1954)

Röhl, KF, and Machura, S, *Procedural Justice* (Aldershot: Ashgate, 1997)

Russell, PH, and O'Brien, DM (eds) *Judicial Independence in the Age of Democracy: Critical Perspectives from around the World* (Charlottesville: University Press of Virginia, 2001)

Schonberg, S, *Legitimate Expectations in Administrative Law* (Oxford: OUP, 2000)

Schwarze, J, *European Administrative Law* (London: Sweet & Maxwell, 1992)

Sharpe, RJ, *The Law of Habeas Corpus* (2nd edn, Oxford: Clarendon Press, 1989)

Shetreet, S, and Deschênes, J (eds), *Judicial Independence: the Contemporary Debate* (Dordercht: Nijhoff, 1985)

Shue, H, *Basic Rights: Subsistence, Affluence, and US Foreign Policy* (2nd edn, Princeton: Princeton University Press, 1996)

Simester, AP, and Sullivan, GR, *Criminal Law: Theory and Doctrine* (Oxford: Hart Publishing, 2000)

—— and —— *Criminal Law: Theory and Doctrine* (2nd edn, Oxford: Hart Publishing, 2003)

Simor, J, and Emmerson, B (eds), *Human Rights Practice* (London: Sweet & Maxwell, 2000)

Simpson, AW, *Human Rights and the End of Empire* (Oxford: OUP, 2001)

Smith, ATH, *The Offences Against Public Order* (London: Sweet & Maxwell, 1987)

—— *Property Offences* (London: Sweet & Maxwell, 1994)

Smith, JC, *The Law of Theft* (8th edn, London: Butterworths, 1997)

—— *Smith & Hogan: Criminal Law* (10th edn, London: Butterworths, 2002)
—— and Hogan, B, *Criminal Law* (6th edn, London: Butterworths, 1988)
Smith, Marsh, and Richards, *The Changing Role of Central Government Departments* (Basingstoke: Macmillan, 2001)
Stacey, F, *Ombudsmen Compared* (Oxford: Clarendon Press, 1978)
Starkie, T, *A Treatise on Criminal Pleading* (London: 1814)
Starmer, K, *European Human Rights Law* (London: Legal Action Group, 1999)
Stavros, S, *The Guarantees for Accused Persons Under Article 6 of the European Convention on Human Rights* (Dordrecht: Martinus Nijhoff, 1993)
Steiner, H, and Alston, P, *International Human Rights in Context* (2nd edn, Oxford: OUP, 2000)
Stephen, JF, *A History of the Criminal Law of England* (London: Macmillan, 1883)
Stevens, RB, *The Independence of the Judiciary: the View from the Lord Chancellor's Office* (Oxford: Clarendon Press, 1993)
—— *The English Judges: Their Role in the Changing Constitution* (Oxford: Hart Publishing, 2002)
Steyn, Lord, *The Constitutionalisation of Public Law* (Constitution Unit, 1999)
Street, H, *Justice in the Welfare State* (London: Stevens, 1975)
Sunkin, M, and Payne, S (eds), *The Nature of the Crown: A Legal and Political Analysis* (Oxford: OUP, 1999)
Supperstone, M (ed), *Brownlie's Law of Public Order and National Security* (2nd edn, London: Butterworths, 1981)

Tapper, C, *Cross and Tapper on Evidence* (8th edn, London: Butterworths, 1995)
Thibaut, J, and Walker, L, *Procedural Justice: A Psychological Analysis* (New Jersey: Erebaum, 1975)
Thio, S, *Locus Standi and Judicial Review* (Singapore: Singapore University Press, 1971)
Thomas, DA, *Principles of Sentencing* (2nd edn, London: Heinemann Educational, 1979)
Tomkins, A, *The Constitution After Scott: Government Unwrapped* (Oxford: Clarendon Press, 1998)
Toth, AG, *The Oxford Encyclopaedia of European Community Law* (Oxford: Clarendon Press, 1990)
Tridimas, T, *The General Principles of EC Law* (Oxford: OUP, 1999)
Turner, JWC (ed), *Russell on Crime* (12th edn, London: Stevens, 1964)

Van Dijk, P, *Judicial Review of Governmental Action and the Requirement of an Interest to Sue* (Alphen: Sijthoff & Noordhoff, 1980)
—— and van Hoof, GJH, *Theory and Practice of the European Convention on Human Rights* (3rd edn, The Hague: Kluwer, 1998)
Vile, MJC, *Constitutionalism and the Separation of Powers* (Oxford: Clarendon Press, 1967)
Vincenzi, C, *Crown Powers, Subjects and Citizens* (London: Pinter, 1998)
Vining, J, *Legal Identity, The Coming of Age of Public Law* (New Haven: Yale University Press, 1978)
von Hirsch, A, *Past or Future Crimes* (Manchester: Manchester University Press, 1986)
—— and Ashworth, A, *Principled Sentencing: Readings on Theory and Policy* (2nd edn, Oxford: Hart Publishing, 1998)

Wade, Sir W, *Administrative Law* (7th edn, Oxford: Clarendon, 1994)

Wade, Sir W, and Forsyth, C, *Administrative Law* (8th edn, Oxford: OUP, 2000)

Wade, HWR, *Constitutional Fundamentals* (Oxford: OUP, 1980)

Wadham, J, and Mountfield, H, *Blackstone's Guide to the Human Rights Act 1998* (2nd edn, London: Blackstone Press, 2000)

Walker, C, *Blackstone's Guide to the Anti-Terrorism Legislation* (Oxford: OUP, 2002)

Walker, N, *Aggravation, Mitigation and Mercy in English Criminal Justice* (London: Blackstone, 1999)

Wasik, M, *Emmins on Sentencing* (4th edn, London: Blackstone, 2001)

—— and Taylor, R, *Blackstone's Guide to the Criminal Justice Act 1991* (2nd edn, London: Blackstone, 1993)

Weir, S, and Hall, W, *Behind Closed Doors: Advisory Quangos in the Corridors of Power* (London: Channel 4, 1995)

Wells, C, *Corporations and Criminal Responsibility* (2nd edn, Oxford: OUP, 2001)

Whitty, N, Murphy, T, and Livingstone, S, *Civil Liberties Law: The Human Rights Act Era* (London: Butterworths, 2001)

Wilks, S, *In the Public Interest: Competition Policy and the Monopolies and Mergers Commission* (Manchester: Manchester University Press, 1999)

Williams, DGT, *Not in the Public Interest* (London: Hutchinson, 1965)

—— *Keeping the Peace* (London: Hutchinson, 1967)

Wilson, D, and Game, C, *Local Government in the United Kingdom* (3rd edn, Basingstoke: Palgrave, 2002)

Woodhouse, D, *Ministers and Parliament. Accountability in Theory and Practice* (Oxford: Clarendon Press, 1994)

—— *In Pursuit of Good Administration: Ministers, Civil Servants, and Judges* (Oxford: OUP, 1997)

—— (ed), *The Pinochet Case* (Oxford: Hart Publishing, 2000)

Woodhouse, D, *The Office of Lord Chancellor* (Oxford: Hart Publishing, 2001)

Woolf, Sir H, *Protecting the Public—A New Challenge* (London: Sweet & Maxwell, 1990)

Wraith, R, and Hutchesson, P, *Administrative Tribunals* (London: Allen & Unwin, 1973)

—— and Lamb, GB, *Public Inquiries as an Instrument of Government* (London: Allen & Unwin, 1971)

Zamir, and Woolf, *The Declaratory Judgment* (3rd edn, London: Sweet & Maxwell, 2001)

Zander, M, *Cases and Materials on the English Legal System* (7th edn, London: Butterworths, 1996)

—— *A Bill of Rights?* (4th edn, London: Sweet & Maxwell, 1997)

—— *The Law-Making Process* (5th edn, London: Butterworths, 1999)

(2) Articles in books

Adler, M, and Bradley, A, 'The Case for Systematic Reform and the Establishment of a Unified Administrative Tribunal' in M Partington (ed), *Leggatt Review of Tribunals: Academic Seminar Papers* (Bristol Centre for the Study of Administrative Justice, 2001)

Ashworth, A, 'Disentangling disparity' in D Pennington and S Lloyd-Bostock (eds), *The Psychology of Sentencing* (Oxford: Centre for Social-Legal Studies, 1987)

—— 'Sentencing' in M Maguire, R Morgan and R Reiner (eds), *The Oxford Handbook of Criminology* (3rd edn, Oxford: OUP, 2002)

—— and Player, E, 'Sentencing, equal treatment and the impact of sanctions' in

A Ashworth and M Wasik (eds), *Fundamentals of Sentencing Theory* (Oxford: Clarendon, 1998)

Bamforth, N, 'The Public Law–Private Law Distinction: A Comparative and Philosophical Approach' in P Leyland and T Woods (eds), *Administrative Law Facing the Future: Old Constraints and New Horizons* (London: Blackstone, 1997)

Beloff, M, 'Time, Time, Time It's On My Side, Yes It Is' in C Forsyth and I Hare (eds), *The Golden Metwand and the Crooked Cord, Essays on Public Law in Honour of Sir William Wade* (Oxford: OUP, 1998)

Blackburn, R, and Plant, R, 'Monarchy and the Royal Prerogative' in R Blackburn and R Plant (eds), *Constitutional Reform: the Labour Government's Constitutional Reform Agenda* (London: Longman, 1999)

Buck, T, 'A Model of Independent Review?' in M Partington (ed), *Leggatt Review of Tribunals: Academic Seminar Papers* (Bristol Centre for the Study of Administrative Justice, 2001)

Cane, P, 'Public Law and Private Law: A Study of the Analysis of and Use of a Legal Concept' in J Eekelaar and J Bell (eds), *Oxford Essays in Jurisprudence, 3rd Series* (Oxford: OUP, 1987)

—— 'The Constitutional Basis of Judicial Remedies in Public Law' in Peter Leyland and Terry Woods (eds), *Administrative Law Facing the Future* (London: Blackstone Press, 1997)

Clarkson, CMV, 'Context and Culpability in Involuntary Manslaughter: Principle or Instinct?' in A Ashworth and B Mitchell (eds), *Rethinking English Homicide Law* (Oxford: OUP, 2000)

Craig, P, 'Unreasonableness and Proportionality in UK Law' in E Ellis (ed), *The Principle of Proportionality in the Laws of Europe* (Oxford: Hart Publishing, 1999)

Cross, R, 'The Reports of the Criminal Law Commissioners (1833–1849) and the Abortive Bills of 1853' in PR Glazebrook (ed), *Reshaping the Criminal Law* (London: Stevens, 1978)

Drewry, Gavin, 'The Civil Service' in R Blackburn and R Plant (eds), *Constitutional Reform: the Labour Government's Constitutional Reform Agenda* (London: Longman, 1999)

Dyzenhaus, D, 'The Politics of Deference: Judicial Review and Democracy' in M Taggart (ed), *The Province of Administrative Law* (Oxford: Hart Publishing, 1997)

—— 'Form and Substance in the Rule of Law: A Democratic Justification for Judicial Review' in C Forsyth (ed), *Judicial Review and the Constitution* (Oxford: Hart Publishing, 2000)

Elias, P, 'Legitimate expectation and Judicial Review' in J Jowell and D Oliver (eds), *New Directions in Judical Review* (London: Stevens, 1988)

Feldman, D, 'Proportionality and the Human Rights Act 1998' in E Ellis (ed), *The Principle of Proportionality in the Laws of Europe* (Oxford: Hart Publishing, 1999)

—— 'Civil Liberties' in V Bogdanor (ed), *The British Constitution in the Twentieth Century* (Oxford: OUP, 2003)

Fredman, S, 'Equality Issues' in Basil S Markesinis, *The Impact of the Human Rights Bill on English Law: The Clifford Chance Lectures Vol 3* (Oxford: OUP, 1998)

Freedland, M, 'The Crown and the Changing Nature of Government' in Sunkin, M, and Payne, S (eds) *The Nature of the Crown* (Oxford: OUP, 1999)

Gardiner, R, 'Interpreting Treaties in the United Kingdom' in M Freeman (ed), *Legislation and the Courts* (Aldershot: Dartmouth, 1997)

Genn, H, 'Tribunal Review of Administrative Decision-Making' in G Richardson and H Genn (eds), *Administrative Law and Government Action* (Oxford: Clarendon Press, 1994)

Harlow, C, 'Access to Justice as a Human Right: The European Convention and the EU' in P Alston (ed), *The EU and Human Rights* (Oxford: OUP, 1999)

Harris, M, 'The Place of Formal and Informal Review in the Administrative Justice System' in M Harris and M Partington (eds), *Administrative Justice in the 21ˢᵗ Century* (Oxford: Hart Publishing, 1999)

Hepple and Fredman, 'Great Britain' in Blanpain (ed), *International Encyclopaedia of Labour Law* (Deventer: Kluwer)

Himma, K, 'Inclusive Legal Positivism' in J Coleman and S Shapiro (eds), *The Oxford Handbook of Jurisprudence and the Philosophy of Law* (Oxford: OUP, 2002)

Hoffmann, Lord, 'The Influence of the European Principle of Proportionality upon English Law', in E Ellis (ed), *The Principle of Proportionality in the Laws of Europe* (Oxford: Hart Publishing, 1999)

Hunt, M, 'Constitutionalism and the Contractualisation of Government' in M Taggart (ed), *The Province of Administrative Law* (Oxford: Hart Publishing, 1997)

Jareborg, N, 'Why bulk discounts for multiple offence sentencing?', in A Ashworth and M Wasik (eds), *Fundamentals of Sentencing Theory* (Oxford: Clarendon Press, 1998)

Jowell, J, 'The Rule of Law' in Jowell and Oliver (eds), *The Changing Constitution* (Oxford: OUP, 2000)

—— 'Judicial Deference and Human Rights: A Question of Competence' in P Craig and R Rawlings (eds), *Law and Administration in Europe, Essays in Honour of Carol Harlow* (Oxford: OUP, 2003)

—— and Lester, A, 'Proportionality: Neither Novel nor Dangerous' in J Jowell and D Oliver (eds), *New Directions in Judicial Review* (London: Sweet & Maxwell, 1988)

Kahn Freund, O, 'The European Social Charter' in FG Jacobs (ed), *European Law and the Individual* (Amsterdam: North-Holland Publishing Co, 1976)

Kentridge, Sir S, 'The Incorporation of the European Convention on Human Rights', in University of Cambridge Centre for Public Law (ed), *Constitutional Reform in the UK: Practice and Principles* (Oxford: Hart Publishing, 1998)

Kurki, L, 'International standards for sentencing and punishment' in M Tonry and R Frase (eds), *Sentencing and Sanctions in Western Countries* (Oxford: OUP, 2001)

Laws, Sir J, '*Wednesbury*' in C Forsyth and I Hare (eds), *The Golden Metwand and the Crooked Cord, Essays in Honour of Sir William Wade* (Oxford: OUP, 1998)

Mackay, R, 'Diminished Responsibility and Mentally Disordered Killers' in A Ashworth and B Mitchell (eds), *Rethinking English Homicide Law* (Oxford: OUP, 2000)

MacNeil, I, 'Investigations Under the Competition Act 1998' in B Rodger and A MacCulloch, *The UK Competition Act: A New Era for UK Competition Law* (Oxford: Hart Publishing, 2000)

Maduro, M, 'Striking the Elusive Balance Between Economic Freedom and Social Rights in the EU' in P Alston (ed), *The EU and Human Rights* (Oxford: OUP, 1999)

Manson, A and Mullan, D (eds), *Commissions of Inquiry—Praise or Reappraise?* (Toronto: Irwin Law, 2003)

Marmor, A, 'Exclusive Legal Positivism' in J Coleman and S Shapiro (eds), *The Oxford Handbook of Jurisprudence and the Philosophy of Law* (Oxford: OUP, 2002)

McBride, J, 'Proportionality and the European Convention on Human Rights', in Evelyn Ellis (ed), *The Principle of Proportionality in the Laws of Europe* (Oxford: Hart Publishing, 1999)

McCrudden, C, 'The Commission for Racial Equality: Formal Investigations in the Shadow of Judicial Review' in Robert Baldwin and Christopher McCrudden, *Regulation and Public Law* (London: Weidenfeld & Nicolson, 1987)

—— 'Editor's Introduction: Theorizing About Anti-Discrimination Law: A review of Recent Literature' in Christopher McCrudden (ed), *Anti-Discrimination Law* (2nd edn, The International Library of Essays in Law and Legal Theory, Ashgate Publishing Ltd, forthcoming)

Page, A, 'Regulating the Regulator—A Lawyer's Perspective on Accountability and Control' in E Ferran and C Goodhart (eds), *Regulating Financial Services and Markets in the 21ˢᵗ Century* (Oxford: Hart Publishing, 2001)

Phillips, C, and Bowling, M, 'Racism, ethnicity, crime and criminal justice' in M Maguire, R Morgan and R Reiber (eds), *The Oxford Handbook of Criminology* (3rd edn, Oxford: OUP, 2002)

Prosser, T, 'Competition, Regulators and Public Service' in B Rodger and A MacCulloch, *The UK Competition Act: A New Era for UK Competition Law* (Oxford: Hart Publishing, 2000)

Ramsay, I, 'The Office of Fair Trading: Policing the Consumer Marketplace' in R Baldwin and C McCrudden (eds), *Regulation and Public Law* (London: Weidenfeld & Nicolson, 1987)

Reichman, A, 'Property Rights, Public Policy and the Limits of the Legal Power to Discriminate' in D Friedman and D Barak-Erez, *Human Rights in Private Law* (Oxford: Hart Publishing, 2001)

Scott, C, 'The Juridification of Relations in the UK Utilities Sector' in J Black, P Muchlinski and P Walker (eds), *Commercial Regulation and Judicial Review* (Oxford: Hart Publishing, 1998)

Sedley, S, 'The Common Law and the Constitution' in Lord Nolan and Sir Stephen Sedley (eds), *The Making & Remaking of the British Constitution* (London: Blackstone, 1997)

Stebbings, C, 'Historical Factors in Contemporary Tribunal Structure' in M Partington (ed), *Leggatt Review of Tribunals: Academic Seminar Papers* (Bristol Centre for the Study of Administrative Justice, 2001)

Stoker, G, 'Normative Theories of Local Government and Democracy' in D King and G Stoker (eds), *Rethinking Local Democracy* (Basingstoke: Macmillan/ESRC, 1996)

Taggart, M, 'Public Utilities and Public Law', in Philip A Joseph (ed), *Essays on the Constitution* (Wellington, NZ: Brookers, 1995)

Thompson, B, 'Keeping the System Under Review' in M Partington (ed), *Leggatt Review of Tribunals: Academic Seminar Papers* (Bristol Centre for the Study of Administrative Justice, 2001)

Van Gerven, W, 'The Effect of Proportionality on the Actions of Member States of the EC: National Viewpoints from Continental Europe', in E Ellis (ed), *The Principle of Proportionality in the Laws of Europe* (Oxford: Hart Publishing, 1999)

von Hirsch, A, 'Guidance by numbers or words? Numerical versus narrative guidelines for sentencing' in M Wasik and K Pease (eds), *Sentencing Reform: Guidance or Guidelines* (Manchester: Manchester University Press, 1986)

—— 'Extending the Harm Principle: "Remote" Harms and Fair Imputation' in AP Simester and ATH Smith (eds), *Harm and Culpability* (Oxford: OUP, 1996)

—— 'The Ethics of Public Television Surveillance' in Andrew von Hirsch, David Garland and Alison Wakefield (eds), *Ethical and Social Perspectives on Situational Crime Prevention* (Oxford: Hart Publishing, 2000)

—— 'Record-enhanced sentencing in England and Wales' in S Rex and M Tonry (eds), *Reform and Punishment* (Cullompton: Willan, 2002)

Ward, AJ, 'Devolution: Labour's Strange Constitutional "Design"' in J Jowell and D Oliver (eds), *The Changing Constitution* (4th edn, Oxford: Clarendon Press, 2000)

Wells, C, 'Provocation: the Case for Abolition' in A Ashworth and B Mitchell (eds), *Rethinking English Homicide Law* (Oxford: OUP, 2000)

Williams, DGT, 'Official Secrecy in the Courts' in P Glazebrook (ed), *Reshaping the Criminal Law* (London: Stevens, 1978)

Williams, KS, Johnstone, C, and Goodwin, M, 'Closed Circuit Television (CCTV) Surveillance in Urban Britain: Beyond the Rhetoric of Crime Prevention' in J Gold and G Revill (eds), *Landscapes of Defence* (London: Longman, 2000)

Wilson, W, 'Murder and the Structure of Homicide' in A Ashworth and B Mitchell (eds), *Rethinking English Homicide Law* (Oxford: OUP, 2000)

Woolf, Lord, 'The Human Rights Act 1998 and remedies' in M Andenas and D Fairgrieve (eds), *Judicial Review in International Perspective: II* (London: BIICL, 2000)

Young, K, 'The Justification of Local Government' in M Goldsmith (ed), *Essays on the Future of Local Government* (West Yorkshire Metropolitan County Council, 1986)

(3) Articles in Journals

Adler, M, 'Lay Tribunal Members and Administrative Justice' [1999] PL 616

Akehurst, M, 'Statements of reasons for judicial and administrative decisions' (1970) 33 MLR 154

Alder, J, 'Representation before tribunals' [1972] PL 278

Alderman, G, 'The Parliamentary Delegated Legislation' [1989] PL 38

Allan, TRS, 'Parliamentary sovereignty: Lord Denning's Dexterous Revolution' (1983) 3 OJLS 22

—— 'Legislative Supremacy and the Rule of Law: Democracy and Constitutionalism' (1985) 44 CLJ 111

—— 'Pragmatism and Theory in Public Law' (1988) 104 LQR 422

—— 'Parliament, ministers, courts and prerogative: criminal injuries compensation and the dormant statute' (1995) 54 CLJ 481

—— 'The Rule of Law as the Rule of Reason: Consent and Constitutionalism' (1999) 115 LQR 221

—— 'The Constitutional Foundations of Judicial Review: Constitutional Conundrum or Interpretative Inquiry' [2002] CLJ 87

Alldridge, P, 'Attempted Murder of the Soul: Blackmail, Piracy and Secrets' (1993) 13 OJLS 368

Alston, P, 'Resisting the Merger and Acquisition of Human Rights by Trade Law' (2002) 13 European J of International L 815

Amos, M, 'Damages for breach of the Human Rights Act 1998' [1999] European Human Rights L Rev 178

—— 'Extending the Liability of the State in Damages' (2001) 21 LS 1

Andenas, Mads, and Fairgrieve, Duncan, 'Misfeasance in Public Office, Governmental Liability and European Influences' (2002) 51 ICLQ 757

Arden, A, and Cirell, S, 'Safe harbours for some; others still at sea? The Local Government (Contracts) Act 1997 and indemnities for officers and members' [1998] J of Local Government L 13

Arlidge, A, 'The Trial of Dr David Moor' [2000] Crim LR 31

Arrowsmith, S, 'Judicial Review and the Contractual Powers of Public Authorities' (1990) 106 LQR 277

Ashworth, A, 'Interpreting Criminal Statutes: A Crisis of Legality?' (1991) 107 LQR 419

—— 'Victim impact statements and sentencing' [1993] Crim LR 498

—— 'Sentencing and the Human Rights Act' (1999) 163 JP 64

Baldwin, R, and Houghton, J, 'Circular Arguments: The Status and Legitimacy of Administrative Rules' [1986] PL 239

Barber, N, 'The Academic Mythologians' (2001) 22 OJLS 369

Barberis, P, 'The New Public Management and a New Accountability' (1998) 76 Public Administration 451

Barendt, E, 'Separation of Powers and Constitutional Government' [1995] PL 599

Barnard, C, and Hare, I, 'Police Discretion and the Rule of Law: Economic Community Rights versus Civil Rights' (2000) 63 MLR 581

Bates, T St J N, 'The Future of Parliamentary Scrutiny of Delegated Legislation: Some Judicial Perspectives' (1998) 19 Statute L Rev 155

Baxi, U, 'Judicial Discourse: The Dialectics of the Face and the Mask' (1993) 35 J of the Indian Law Institute 1

Beatson, J, ' "Public" and "Private" in English Administrative Law' (1987) 103 LQR 34

—— 'Crown Service: Contract or Status?' (1988) 104 LQR 182

—— and Matthews, M, 'Reform of Administrative Law Remedies: The First Step' (1978) 41 MLR 437

Beer, SH, 'Strong Government and Democratic Control' (1999) 70 Political Q 146

Bell, M, 'The New Article 13 EC Treaty: A Sound Basis for European Anti-Discrimination Law?' (1999) 6 Maastricht J of European L 5

—— 'Art 13 EC: The European Commission's Anti-discrimination Proposals' (2000) 29 ILJ 79

—— and Waddington, L, 'The 1996 Intergovernmental Conference and the Prospects of a Non-discrimination Treaty Article' (1996) 25 ILJ 320

Bennion, F, 'What Interpretation is "Possible" under Section 3(1) of the Human Rights Act 1998?' [2000] PL 77

Bingham, Sir T, 'Should Public Law Remedies be Discretionary?' [1991] PL 64

Birks, P, 'Harassment and Hubris: The Right to an Equality of Respect' [1997] Irish Jurist 1

Black, J, 'Constitutionalising Self-Regulation' (1996) 59 MLR 24

Blackburn, R, 'The dissolution of Parliament: the Crown Prerogatives (House of Commons Control) Bill 1988' (1989) 52 MLR 837

—— 'The Royal Assent to legislation and the monarch's fundamental human rights' [2003] PL 205

Blom-Cooper, L, 'The role and functions of tribunals of inquiry—an Irish perspective' [1999] PL 175

Bogdanor, V, 'Civil Service Reform: A Critique' (2001) 72 Political Q 291

Born, G, and Prosser, T, 'Culture and Consumerism: Citizenship, Public Service Broadcasting and the BBC's Fair Trading Obligations' (2001) 64 MLR 657

Bowers, J, and Moran, E, 'Justification in Direct Sex Discrimination Law: Breaking the Taboo' (2002) 31 ILJ 307

Boyron, S, 'Proportionality in English Administrative Law: A Faulty Translation' (1992) 12 OJLS 237

Bradley, AW, 'A failure of justice and defect of police' [1964] CLJ 83

—— 'Administrative Justice and the Binding Effect of Official Acts' (1981) CLP 1

—— 'Police Powers and the Prerogative' [1988] PL 298

—— Allen QC, Robin, and Sales, Philip, 'The impact of the Human Rights Act 1998 upon subordinate legislation promulgated before October 2, 2000' [2000] PL 358

—— 'Judicial Independence Under Attack' [2003] PL 397

Brady, C, 'Collective responsibility of the Cabinet: an ethical, constitutional or managerial tool?' (1999) 53 Parliamentary Affairs 214

Brazier, M, 'Judicial Immunity and the Independence of the Judiciary' [1976] PL 397

Brazier, R, 'It is a constitutional issue: fitness for ministerial office in the 1990s' [1994] PL 431

—— 'The Constitutional Position of the Prince of Wales' [1995] PL 501

—— 'The Constitution of the United Kingdom' [1999] CLJ 96

—— 'Skipping a Generation in the Line of Succession' [2000] PL 568

—— 'A British Republic' (2002) 61 CLJ 351

Brennan, F, 'Crime and Disorder Act 1998: Racially Motivated Crime: The Response of the Criminal Justice System [1999] Crim LR 17

Brest, P, 'The Substance of Process' (1981) 42 Ohio State LJ 131

Bridges, L, 'Legality and Immigration Control' (1975) 2 British J of L and Society 221

—— Meszaros, G, and Sunkin, M, 'Regulating the Judicial Review Case Load' [2001] PL 651

Brooke, Sir H, 'The Law Commission and Criminal Law Reform' [1995] Crim LR 911

Browne-Wilkinson, Lord, 'The Independence of the Judiciary in the 1980s' [1988] PL 44

Brownlie, ID, 'The Renovation of Affray' [1965] Crim LR 479

Burch, M, and Holliday, I, 'The Prime Minister's and Cabinet Office: an Executive Office in all but Name' (1999) 52 Parliamentary Affairs 32

Burney, E, 'Using the Law on Racially Aggravated Offences' [2003] Crim LR 28

Burnside, J, 'The Sexual Offences (Amendment) Act 2000: the head of a "kiddy-libber" and the torso of a "child-saver"?' [2001] Crim LR 425

Buxton, Sir R, 'The Human Rights Act and private law' (2000) 116 LQR 48

Campbell, E, and Groves, M, 'Attacks on judges under parliamentary privilege: a sorry Australian episode' [2002] PL 626

Campbell, K, 'The Test of Dishonesty in *Ghosh*' [1984] 43 CLJ 349

Cane, P, 'Standing, Legality and the Limits of Public Law' [1981] PL 322
—— 'Statutes, Standing and Representation' [1990] PL 307
—— 'Standing up for the Public' [1995] PL 276
Carnwath, Sir R, 'The reasonable limits of local authority powers' [1996] PL 244
Chapman, A, 'A New Approach to Monitoring the ICESCR', Review of the International Commission of Jurists, No 55, December 1995, 23
Clayton, R, 'The Limits of What's "Possible": Statutory Construction under the Human Rights Act' [2002] European Human Rights L Rev 559
Coleman, J, 'Negative and Positive Positivism' (1982) 11 J of Legal Studies 139
Collins, L, 'Foreign relations and the judiciary' (2002) 51 ICLQ 485
Cooke of Thorndon, Lord, 'The Law Lords: an Endangered Heritage' (2003) 119 LQR 49
Coppel, J, 'Horizontal Effect of Directives' (1997) 26 ILJ 69
Cornes, R, '*McGonnell v United Kingdom*, the Lord Chancellor and the Law Lords' [2000] PL 166
Cornford, T, and Sunkin, M, 'The Bowman Report, Access and the Recent Reforms of the Judicial Review Procedure' [2001] PL 11
Cotterrell, R, 'Prosecuting Incitement to Racial Hatred' [1982] PL 379
Craig, P, 'Representations By Public Bodies' (1977) 93 LQR 398
—— 'Sovereignty of the United Kingdom Parliament after *Factortame*' (1991) 11 Ybk of Eur L 221
—— 'Legitimate expectations: a conceptual analysis' (1992) 108 LQR 79
—— 'Substantive legitimate expectations in domestic and Community law' [1996] CLJ 289
—— 'Formal and Substantive Conceptions of the Rule of Law: an Analytical Framework' [1997] PL 467
—— 'Public Law, Political Theory and Legal Theory' [2000] PL 211
—— 'The Courts, the Human Rights Act and Judicial Review' (2001) 117 LQR 589
—— 'Contracting-out, the Human Rights Act and the Scope of Judicial Review' (2002) 118 LQR 551
—— 'Constitutional Foundations, the Rule of Law and Supremacy' [2003] PL 92
—— and Bamforth, N, 'Constitutional analysis, constitutional principle and judicial review' [2001] PL 763
—— and Schonberg, S, 'Substantive Legitimate Expectations after *Coughlan*' [2000] PL 684
Crawford, C, 'Rule of law, lawyers or ombudsmen?' [2001] J of Local Government L 73
Cullen, H, 'The Collective Complaints Mechanism of the European Social Charter' [2000] ELR 25

Dandeker, C, and Freedman, L, 'The British Armed Services' (2002) 73 Political Q 465
Davies, P, 'Market Integration and Social Policy in the Court of Justice' (1995) 24 ILJ 49
de Burca, G, 'The Principle of Proportionality and its Application in EC Law' (1993) 13 YBEL 105
de Smith, SA, 'The House of Lords on natural justice' (1963) 26 MLR 543
Dennis, IH, 'The Rationale of Criminal Conspiracy' (1997) 93 LQR 39
Dixon, MJ, 'Public law and prison inmates—two part disharmony' (1984) 40 NILQ 71
Dixon, O, 'The Common Law as an Ultimate Constitutional Foundation' (1957) 31 Australian LJ 240
Docksey, C, 'The Principle of Equality between Women and Men as Fundamental Right under Community Law' (1991) 20 ILJ 258

Doig, A, 'Sleaze Fatigue: An Inauspicious Year for Democracy' (2002) 55 Parliamentary Affairs 389

Dotan, Y, 'Why Administrators should be Bound by their Policies' (1997) 17 OJLS 23

Drewry, G, 'The civil service: from the 1940s to "Next Steps" and beyond' (1994) 47 Parliamentary Affairs 583

—— 'Whatever happened to the Citizen's Charter?' [2002] PL 9

—— and Harlow, C, 'A "Cutting Edge": The Parliamentary Commissioner and MPs' (1991) 53 MLR 745

Dunleavy, P, 'The Architecture of the British Central State, Part I: Framework for Analysis' (1989) 67 Public Administration 249

Dworkin, R, 'The Forum of Principle' (1981) 56 New York U L Rev 469

Edwards, L, and Rowan-Robinson, J, 'Whatever Happened to the Planning Inquiry Commission' [1980] JPL 307

Edwards, RA, 'Generosity and the HRA: the Right Interpretation?' [1999] PL 400

—— 'Judicial deference under the Human Rights Act' (2002) 65 MLR 859

Eekelaar, J, 'The Death of Parliamentary Sovereignty—A Comment' (1997) 113 LQR 185

Elder, N, and Page, EC, 'Culture and Agency: Fragmentation and Agency Structures in Germany and Sweden' 13 Public Policy and Administration J 28

Elliott, DW, 'Dishonesty in Theft: A Dispensable Concept' [1982] Crim LR 341

Elliott, M, 'Appeals, principles and pragmatism in natural justice' (1980) 43 MLR 66

—— 'The Human Rights Act 1998 and the Standard of Substantive Review' (2001) 60 CLJ 301

—— 'Human Rights Review: Raising the Standard' (2001) 60 CLJ 455

Ellis, DL, 'Collective Ministerial Responsibility and Collective Solidarity' [1980] PL 367

Ellis, E, 'Supremacy of Parliament and European law' (1980) 96 LQR 511

Evans, JM, 'Some limits to the scope of natural justice' (1973) 36 MLR 439

Ewing, KD, 'The Human Rights Act and Parliamentary Democracy' (1999) 62 MLR 79

—— 'Transparency, Accountability and Equality: The Political Parties, Elections and Referendums Act 2000' [2001] PL 542

Fazal, M, 'Reliability of Official Acts and Advice' [1972] PL 43

Feldman, D, 'The King's peace, the royal prerogative and public order: the roots and early development of binding over powers' (1988) 47 CLJ 101

—— 'The Human Rights Act 1998 and Constitutional Principles' (1999) 19 LS 186

—— 'Parliamentary Scrutiny of Legislation and Human Rights' [2002] PL 323

Finch, E, 'Stalking the Perfect Stalking Law: Evaluating the Efficacy of the Protection from Harassment Act 1997' [2002] Crim LR 703

Finer, SE, 'The Individual Responsibility of Ministers' (1956) 34 Public Administration 377

Flinders, M, 'Shifting the Balance? Parliament, the Executive and the British Constitution' (2002) 50 Political Studies 23

—— 'Governance in Whitehall' (2002) 80 Public Administration 51

Fordham, M, 'Judicial Review: The New Rules' [2001] PL 4

—— and White, G, 'Monetary Claims Against Public Authorities' [2001] Judicial Rev 44 and [2001] Judicial Rev 109

Forsyth, CF, 'The Provenance and Protection of Legitimate Expectations' [1988] CLJ 238

—— '*Wednesbury* Protection of Substantive Legitimate Expectations' [1997] PL 375

Fox, HM, 'Judicial Control of the Spending Powers of Local Authorities' (1956) 72 LQR 237

Fredman, S, 'Equality: A New Generation?' (2001) 30 ILJ 145
—— and Morris, G, 'The Costs of Exclusivity [1994] PL 69
—— , McCrudden, C, and Freedland, M, 'An EU Charter of Fundamental Rights' [2000] PL 178

Freedland, M, 'Contracting the Employment of Civil Services—a Transparent Exercise?' [1995] PL 224
—— 'The rule against delegation and the Carltona doctrine in an agency context' [1996] PL 19

Fuller, L, 'The Forms and Limits of Adjudication' (1978) 92 Harvard L Rev 353

Galligan, DJ, 'The Nature and Functions of Policy Within Discretionary Power' [1976] PL 332

Ganz, G, 'Estoppel and Res Judicata in Administrative Law' [1965] PL 237

Gardner, J, and Macklem, T, 'Compassion without Respect? Nine Fallacies in *R v Smith*' [2001] Crim LR 623

Gardner, S, 'Reckless and Inconsiderate Rape' [1991] Crim LR 172
—— 'Stalking' (1998) 114 LQR 33
—— 'Property and Theft' [1998] Crim LR 35

Gay, O, 'The fall of Canada's privacy czar: institutionalising officers of Parliament' [2003] PL 632

Gearty, C, 'Trusting the Judges: Public Order' [1989] CLJ 168
—— 'How We Declare War' (2002) 24 London Review of Books, 3 October

Genn, H, 'Tribunals and Informal Justice' (1993) MLR 393

Ghandhi, S, and James, J, 'The English Law of Blasphemy and the ECHR' [1998] European Human Rights L Rev 430

Giles, M, 'R v Brown: Consensual Harm and the Public Interest' (1994) 57 MLR 101

Goodhart, AL, 'Thomas v Sawkins: A Constitutional Innovation' (1936) 6 CLJ 22
—— 'Ridge v Baldwin: Administration and natural justice' (1964) 80 LQR 105

Goodpaster, G, 'On The Theory of American Adversary Criminal Trial' (1987) 78 J of Criminal L and Criminology 118

Grant, H, 'Commissions of inquiry—is there a right to be legally represented?' [2001] PL 377

Grant, M, 'Progress and transition: the work of the Local Government Commission for England' [1999] J of Local Government L 23

Gray, K, and Gray, SF, 'Civil Rights, Civil Wrongs and Quasi-Public Space' [1999] European Human Rights L Rev 46

Greenbaum, 'Toward a Common Law of Employment Discrimination' (1985) 58 Temple LQ 65

Griew, E, 'Dishonesty—the Objections to Feely and Ghosh' [1985] Crim LR 341

Griffith, J, 'The Official Secrets Act 1989' (1989) 16 JLS 273

Hadfield, B, 'R v Lord Saville of Newdigate, ex p anonymous soldiers: what is the purpose of a tribunal of inquiry?' [1999] PL 663

Halpin, A, 'The Test for Dishonesty' [1996] Crim LR 283

Hare, I, 'Legislating against hate: the legal response to bias crimes' (1997) 17 OJLS 414

Harlow, C, 'Accountability, New Public Management, and the Problems of the Child Support Agency' (1999) 26 J of L and Society 150

Hayhurst, JD, and Wallington, P, 'The Parliamentary Scrutiny of Delegated Legislation' [1988] PL 547

Hazell, R, 'Merger, what merger? Scotland, Wales and the Department for Constitutional Affairs' [2003] PL 650

Heaton, R, 'Deceiving without Thieving?' [2001] Crim LR 712

Hennessey, P, 'The Blair Style of Government: An Historical Perspective and an Interim Audit' (1998) 33 *Government and Opposition* 3

Herberg, J, 'The right to a hearing: breach without fault?' [1990] PL 467

Herling, D, and Purdue, M, 'The Divide between Procedural and Substantive Unfairness' [2000] JPL 666

Herring, J, 'The Criminalisation of Harassment' (1998) 57 CLJ 10

Hickman, L, 'Press Freedom and the New Legislation' (2001) 151 NLJ 716

Hilson, C, 'Judicial Review, Policies and the Fettering of Discretion' [2002] PL 111

Hirst, M, 'Assault, Battery and Indirect Violence' [1999] Crim LR 557

Hoffmeister, F, 'German Bundesverfassungsgericht: Alcan Decision of 17 February 2000; Constitutional Review of EC Regulation on Bananas, Decision of 7 June 2000' (2001) 38 CML Rev 791

Holliday, I, 'Is the British State Hollowing Out?' (2000) 71 Political Q 167

Hood Phillips, O, 'Has the incoming tide reached the Palace of Westminster?' (1979) 95 LQR 167

—— 'High tide in the Strand? Post-1972 Acts and Community law' (1980) 96 LQR 31

Hooper, Sir A, 'The Impact of the HRA on Judicial Decision-making' [1998] European Human Rights L Rev 676

Horder, J, 'Cognition, Emotion and Criminal Culpability' (1990) 106 LQR 469

—— 'Reconsidering Psychic Assault' [1998] Crim LR 392

Hough, B, 'Ministerial responses to parliamentary questions' [2003] PL 211

Howe of Aberavon, Lord, 'Procedure at the Scott Inquiry' [1996] PL 445

Howell, J, 'Public duties and resources: "Won't pay—Won't do"' [1998] J of Local Government L 49

Howse, R, 'Human Rights in the WTO' (2002) 13 European J of International L 651

Hughes, G, 'Prohibiting Incitement to Racial Hatred' (1966) 16 U of Toronto L Rev 361

Hunt, M, 'The "horizontal effect" of the Human Rights Act' [1998] PL 423

Irvine of Lairg, Lord, 'Activism and Restraint: Human Rights and the Interpretative Process' [1999] European Human Rights L Rev 350

—— 'The Spirit of Magna Carta continues to resonate in modern law' (2003) 119 LQR 227

Issacharoff, S, and Nelson, J, 'Discrimination with a Difference: Can Employment Discrimination Law Accommodate the American With Disabilities Act?' (2001) 79 North Carolina L Rev 307

Jaconelli, J, 'Regency and Parliamentary Sovereignty' [2002] PL 449

Jolls, C, 'Accommodation Mandates and Anti-discrimination Law' (2000) 53 *Stanford L Rev* 223

Jones, G, and Grekos, M, 'Great Expectations? The Ombudsman and the Meaning of Injustice' [2001] JR 20

Joseph, PA, 'The demise of ultra vires—judicial review in the New Zealand courts' [2001] PL 354

Jowell, J, 'The Legal Control of Administrative Discretion' [1973] PL 178
—— 'Is Equality a Constitutional Principle?' (1994) 47 CLP 1
—— 'Beyond the Rule of Law: Towards Constitutional Judicial Review' [2000] PL 671
—— and Lester, A, 'Beyond Wednesbury: Substantive Principles of Administrative Law' [1987] PL 368
Jurgens, E, 'Parliaments and Treaty-Making' (1995) 1 J of Legislative Studies 175

Karlen, P and Rutherglen, G, 'Disabilities, Discrimination, and Reasonable Accommodation' (1996) 46 Duke LJ 1
Kavanagh, D, and Richards, D, 'Departmentalism and Joined-Up Government: Back to the Future' (2001) 54 Parliamentary Affairs 1
Kearns, P, 'Uncultural God: Blasphemy Law's Reprieve and the Art Matrix' [2000] European Human Rights L Rev 512
Kentridge, Sir S, 'The Highest Court: Selecting the Judges' [2003] CLJ 55
Klug, F, and Starmer, K, 'Incorporation through the "front door": the first year of the Human Rights Act' [2001] PL 654

Lacey, N, 'Beset by boundaries: the Home Office review of sex offences' [2001] Crim LR 3
Lanham, 'Delegation and the Alter Ego Principle' (1984) 100 LQR 587
Laws, Sir J, 'Is the High Court the guardian of fundamental constitutional rights?' [1993] PL 59
—— 'Judicial Remedies and the Constitution' (1994) 57 MLR 213
—— 'Law and Democracy' [1995] PL 72
Leigh, I, 'The prerogative, legislative power, and the democratic deficit: the Fire Brigades Union case' [1995] Web JCLI 3
—— 'Horizontal rights, the Human Rights Act and privacy: lessons from the Commonwealth?' (1999) 48 ICLQ 57
—— 'Bias, necessity and the Convention' [2002] PL 407
—— and Lustgarten, Laurence, 'Making Rights Real: The Courts, Remedies and the Human Rights Act' [1999] CLJ 509
Leigh, LH, 'New Trials in Criminal Cases' [1977] Crim LR 525
—— 'Law Reform and the Law of Treason and Sedition' [1977] PL 128
—— 'Correcting Miscarriages of Justice: The Role of the Criminal Cases Review Commission' (2000) 38 Alberta L Rev 365
Leopold, PM, 'Report of the Joint Committee on Parliamentary Privilege' [1999] PL 604
Leopold, PN, 'Letters to and from "next steps" agency chief executives' [1994] PL 214
Lester, A, 'Parliamentary Scrutiny of Legislation under the HRA 1998' [2002] European Human Rights L Rev 432
Lester of Herne Hill, Lord, 'The mouse that roared: the Human Rights Bill 1995' [1995] PL 198
—— 'Government Compliance with International Human Rights Law: A New Year's Legitimate Expectation' [1996] PL 187
—— 'First steps towards a constitutional bill of rights' [1997] European Human Rights L Rev 124
—— 'The Art of the Possible—Interpreting Statutes under the Human Rights Act 1998' [1998] European Human Rights L Rev 665
—— and Weait, Matthew, 'The use of ministerial powers without parliamentary authority: the Ram doctrine [2003] PL 415

Le Sueur, A, 'Should We Abolish the Writ of Habeas Corpus?' [1992] PL 13

—— 'The Judicial Reivew Debate: from Partnership to Friction' (1996) 31 Government and Opposition 8

Lester of Herne Hill, Lord, 'New Labour's next (surprisingly quick) steps in constitutional reform' [2003] PL 368

—— and Sunkin, M, 'Applications for Judicial Review: the Requirement of Leave' [1992] PL 102

Lewis, C, 'Retrospective and Prospective Rulings in Administrative Law' [1988] PL 78

—— 'The Exhaustion of Alternative Remedies' [1992] CLJ 138

Lewis, N, 'IBA Programme Contract Awards' [1975] PL 317

Lewis, N, 'Reviewing change in government: new public management and next steps' [1994] PL 105

—— and Longley, Diane, 'Ministerial responsibility: the next steps' [1996] PL 490

Leyland, P, and Donati, D, 'Executive accountability and the changing face of government: UK and Italy compared' (2001) 7 European Public L 217

Lindsay, A, 'Delay in Judicial Review Cases: A Conundrum Solved?' [1995] PL 417

Ling, T, 'Delivering Joined-Up Government in the UK: Dimensions, Issues and Problems' (2002) 80 Public Administration 615

Livingstone, S, 'Prisoners and boards of visitors' hearings; a right to legal representation after all?' (1987) 38 NILQ 144

Lomas, O, 'The Twenty-Fifth Annual Report of the Council on Tribunals—an opportunity sadly missed' (1985) 48 MLR 694

MacCormick, N, 'Does the United Kingdom Have a Constitution? Reflections on MacCormick v Lord Advocate' (1978) 29 Northern Ireland Legal Q 1

—— 'Beyond the Sovereign State' (1993) 56 MLR 1

Mackay, R, and Kearns, G, 'More Facts about the Insanity Defence' [1999] Crim LR 714

Maher, LW, 'The Use and Abuse of Sedition' (1992) 14 Sydney L Rev 261

Malleson, K, 'Judicial bias and disqualification after Pinochet (No 2)' (2000) 63 MLR 119

Marriott, J, and Nicol, D, 'The Human Rights Act, representative standing and the victim culture' [1998] European Human Rights L Rev 730

Marsh, D, Richards, D, and Smith, MJ, 'Re-Assessing the Role of Departmental Cabinet Ministers' (2000) 78 Public Administration 305

Marshall, G, 'Two Kinds of Compatibility: More about Section 3 of the Human Rights Act 1998' [1999] PL 377

Mastroianni, R, 'On the Distinction Between Vertical and Horizontal Direct Effects of Community Directives: What Role for the Principle of Equality?' (1999) 5 European Public L 417

McCrudden, C, 'Affirmative Action and Fair Participation: Interpreting the Fair Employment Act 1989' (1992) 21 ILJ 170

—— 'A Common Law of Human Rights? Transnational Judicial Conversations on Constitutional Rights' (2000) 20 OJLS 499

McHarg, A, 'A Duty to be Consistent' [1998] MLR 93

McInerney, S, 'Equal treatment between persons irrespective of racial or ethnic origin: a comment' (2000) 25 ELR 317

Michelman, F, 'Traces of Self-Government' (1986–87) 100 Harvard L Rev 4

Middleton, KWB, 'New Thoughts on the Union' (1954) 66 Juridical Rev 37

Miers, D, 'The deregulation procedure: An expanding role' [1999] PL 477

Miles, J, 'Standing under the Human Rights Act 1998: theories of rights enforcement and the nature of public law adjudication' [2000] CLJ 133

Mitchell, JDB, 'Sovereignty of Parliament—Yet Again' (1963) 79 LQR 196

—— 'The Causes and Effects of the Absence of a System of Public Law in the United Kingdom' [1965] PL 95

Mirfield, P, 'Can the House of Lords Lawfully be Abolished?' (1979) 95 LQR 36

Modood, T, 'British Asian Muslims and the Rushdie Affair' (1990) 61 Political Q 143

Molot, HL, 'The Duty of Business to Serve the Public: Analogy to the Innkeeper's Obligation' (1968) 46 Canadian Bar Rev 612

Morris, GS, 'Local government workers and rights of political participation: time for a change' [1998] PL 25

Mowbray, A, 'The Parliamentary Commissioner and Administrative Guidance' [1987] PL 570

—— 'The Role of the European Court of Human Rights in the Promotion of Democracy' [1999] PL 703

Mulgan, R, '"Accountability": an Ever-expanding Concept?' (2000) 78 Public Administration 555

Munro, C, 'The Separation of Powers: Not such a Myth' [1981] PL 19

Norrie, A, 'After *Woollin*' [1999] Crim LR 532

—— 'The Structure of Provocation' (2001) 54 CLP 307

Norton, P, 'Government Defeats in the House of Commons: Myth and Reality' [1978] PL 360

Note, 'The Antidiscrimination Principle in the Common Law' (1993) 102 Harvard L Rev 1994

Nowicki, MA, 'Perspectives on Equal Protection—Part II: The European Convention of Human Rights: Prohibition on Discrimination' [1999] St Louis-Warsaw Transatlantic LJ 17

O'Cinneide, C, 'The Race Relations (Amendment) Act 2000' [2001] PL 220

Oliver, D, 'Public Law Procedures and Remedies—Do We Need Them?' [2002] PL 91

Olowofoyeku, A, 'State Liability for the Exercise of Judicial Power' [1998] PL 444

—— 'The nemo judex rule: the case against automatic disqualification' [2000] PL 456

O'Neill QC, A, 'Judicial Politics and the Judicial Committee: the Devolution Jurisprudence of the Privy Council' (2001) 64 MLR 603

Ormerod, D, 'Cheating the Public Revenue' [1998] Crim LR 627

—— and Gunn, M, 'The Legality of Boxing' (1995) 15 LS 181

Page, EC, 'The Impact of European Legislation on British Public Policy Making: A Research Note' (1998) 76 Public Administration 803

Palmer, E, 'Resource Allocation. Welfare Rights—Mapping the Boundaries of Judicial Control in Public Administrative Law' (2000) 20 OJLS 63

Palmer, S, 'Tightening Secrecy Law: The Official Secrets Act 1989' [1990] PL 243

—— '"They made a desert and called it peace": banishment and the royal prerogative' (2001) 60 CLJ 234

Pannick, D, 'Who is Subject to Judicial Review and in Respect of What?' [1992] PL 1

—— 'Principles of Interpretation of the HRA and the Discretionary Area of Judgment' [1998] PL 545

Peay, J, 'Mental Health Review Tribunals: Just or Efficacious Safeguards' (1981) 5 Law and Human Behaviour 161

Petersmann, E, 'Time for a United Nations Global Compact' (2002) 13 European J of International L 621

Petersmann, E, 'Taking Human Dignity, Poverty and Empowerment of Individuals More Seriously' (2002) 13 European J of International L 845

Phillipson, G, 'Transforming breach of confidence? Towards a common law right of privacy under the Human Rights Act' (2003) 66 MLR 726

Plucknett, TFT, 'Bonham's Case and Judicial Review' (1926) 40 Harvard L Rev 30

Prosser, T, 'Poverty, Ideology and Legality: Supplementary Benefit Appeal Tribunals and their Predecessors' (1977) 4 British J of L and Society 59

Pugh, I, 'The Ombudsman—Jurisdiction, Powers and Practice' (1978) 56 Public Administration 127

Purchas, F, 'Lord Mackay and the judiciary' [1994] NLJ 527

Rawlings, R, 'Legal politics: the United Kingdom and ratification of the Treaty on European Union: Part 2' [1994] PL 367

—— 'Concordats and the Constitution' (2000) 11 LQR 257

Raz, J, 'The Rule of Law and its Virtue' (1977) 93 LQR 195

Reichman, A, 'Professional Status and the Freedom to Contract: Towards a Common Law Duty of Non-Discrimination' (2001) 14 Canadian J of L and Jurisprudence 79

Rhodes, RAW, 'The Hollowing Out of the State: The Changing Nature of the Public Service in Britain' (1994) 65 Political Q 138

—— 'New Labour's civil service: summing-up joining-up' (2000) 71 Political Q 151

Richards, S, 'New Labour(New Civil Service' (1997) 67 Political Q 311

Richardson, G, 'The duty to give reasons: potential and practice' [1986] PL 437

—— and Machin, D, 'Judicial Review and Tribunal Decision Making' [2000] PL 494

—— and —— 'Doctors on Tribunals: A Confusion of Roles' (2000) 176 British J of Psychiatry 110

Ridley, FF, 'There is no British Constitution: A Dangerous Case of the Emperor's Clothes' (1988) 41 Parliamentary Affairs 340

Rogers, J, 'A Criminal Lawyer's Response to Chastisement in the European Court of Human Rights' [2002] Crim LR 98

Rogerson, P, 'On Fettering of Public Power' [1971] PL 300

Rowe, JJ, 'The Terrorism Act 2000' [2001] Crim LR 527

Rubin, GR, 'UK military law: autonomy, civilianisation, juridification' (2000) 65 MLR 36

Schaffer, B, 'The Idea of the Ministerial Department: Bentham, Mill and Bagehot' (1957) 3 The Australian J of Politics and History 60

Schiek, D, 'Positive Action before the European Court of Justice—New Conceptions of Equality in Community Law? From Kalanke and Marschall to Badeck' (2000) 16 Int J of Comparative Labour L and Industrial Relations 251

Schiemann, Sir K, 'Locus Standi' [1990] PL 342

Scott, Sir R, 'Procedures at inquiries—the duty to be fair' (1995) 111 LQR 596

Sedley, S, 'The Sound of Silence: Constitutional Law without a Constitution' (1994) 110 LQR 270

—— 'Human Rights: A Twenty-First Century Agenda' [1995] PL 386

Sharpe, LJ, 'Theories and Values of Local Government' (1970) 18 Political Studies 153

Shrimpton, M, 'In Defence of Habeas Corpus' [1993] PL 24

Silkin, A, 'The "Agreement to Differ" of 1975' (1977) 46 Political Q 65

Simcock, AJC, 'One and Many—The Office of Secretary of State' (1992) 70 Public Administration 535

Simon Brown LJ, 'Habeas Corpus—A New Chapter' [2000] PL 31

Singer, JW, 'No Right to Exclude: Public Accomodations and Private Property' (1996) 90 Northwestern U L Rev 1283

Singh, R, 'Making Legitimate Use of Legitimate Expectations' (1994) 144 NLJ 1215

Skidmore, P, 'EC Framework Directive on Equal Treatment in Employment: Towards a Comprehensive Community Anti-Discrimination Policy?' (2001) 30 ILJ 126

Smith, ATH, 'Stealing the Human Body and its Parts' [1976] Crim LR 622

—— 'Constructive Trusts in the Law of Theft' [1977] Crim LR 395

—— 'The Idea of Criminal Deception' [1982] Crim LR 721

—— 'Breaching the Peace and Disturbing the Quiet' [1982] PL 212

—— 'Judicial Lawmaking in the Criminal Law' (1984) 100 LQR 46

—— 'Public Order Law: The Government's Proposals' [1985] PL 533

—— 'The Case for a Code' [1986] Crim LR 285

—— 'The Metamorphosis of Affray' (1986) 136 NLJ 521

—— 'Assaulting and Abusing the Police' [1988] Crim LR 600

—— 'The Criminal Justice and Public Order Act 1994—the public order elements' [1995] Crim LR 19

Smith, J, 'The European Charter of Local Self-Government: Does the UK Government Comply?' [2002] J of Local Government L 90

Smith, JC, '*Lister v Stubbs* and the Criminal Law' (1994) 110 LQR 180

—— 'Obtaining Cheques by Deception or Theft' [1997] Crim LR 396

—— 'Property and Theft' [1998] Crim LR 80

Smith, MJ, 'Reconceptualizing the British State: Theoretical and Empirical Challenges to Central Government' (1998) 76 Public Administration 45

Smith, TB, 'The Union of 1707 as Fundamental Law' [1957] PL 99

Soper, P, 'Legal Theory and the Obligation of the Judge: The Hart/Dworkin Dispute' (1977) 75 Michigan L Rev 511

Spencer, JR, 'The Metamorphosis of Section 6 of the Theft Act' [1977] Crim LR 653

—— 'Criminal Libel—A Skeleton in the Cupboard (1)' [1977] Crim LR 383

—— 'Criminal Libel—A Skeleton in the Cupboard (2)' [1977] Crim LR 465

—— 'The Theft Act 1978' [1979] Crim LR 24

—— 'Theft, Handling and the *Mala Fide* Purchaser' [1985] Crim LR 92

Spigelman, JJ, 'Judicial accountability and performance indicators' (2002) 21 CJQ 18

Stanton-Ife, J, 'Should Equality be a Constitutional Principle?' (2000) 11 Kings College LJ 132

Steyn, J, '*Pepper v Hart*: A Re-Examination' (2001) 21 OJLS 59

Steyn, Lord, 'The Case for a Supreme Court' (2002) 118 LQR 382

—— 'Human rights: the legacy of Mrs. Roosevelt' [2002] PL 473

Stone, A, 'Revisiting the Parable: Truth without Consequences' (1994) 17 Int J of L and Psychiatry 79

Sunkin, M, and Pick, K, 'The Changing Impact of Judicial Review: the Independent Review Service of the Social Fund' [2001] PL 736

Swadling, WJ, 'Liability for Negligent Refusal of Unemployment Benefit' [1988] PL 328

Tanworth, Lord Hunt of, 'Access to a Previous Government's Papers' [1982] PL 514

Taylor, GDS, 'Judicial Review of Improper Purposes and Irrelevant Considerations' [1976] CLJ 272

Taylor, P, Goldberg, E, Leese, M, Butwell, M, and Reed, A, 'Limits to the Value of Mental Health Review Tribunals for Offender Patients' (1999) 174 British J of Psychiatry 164

Thomas, R, 'The British Official Secrets Act 1911–1939 and the Ponting Case' [1986] Crim LR 491

Thomson, JM, 'Community Law, the Act of Union and the Supremacy of Parliament' (1976) 92 LQR 36

Thorne, SE, 'Dr Bonham's Case' (1938) 54 LQR 543

Tomkins, A, 'Magna Carta, Crown and colonies' [2001] PL 571

—— 'Legislating against Terror: the Anti-terrorism, Crime and Security Act 2001 [2002] PL 205

Tonry, M, 'Real offense sentencing' (1981) 72 J of Crim L and Criminology 1550

Tracey, RRS, 'Disqualified adjudicators: the doctrine of necessity in public law' [1982] PL 628

Treitel, G, 'Crown Proceedings: Some Recent Developments' [1957] PL 321

Tribe, L, 'The Puzzling Persistence of Process-Based Constitutional Theories' (1980) 89 Yale LJ 1063

Tridimas, T, 'Horizontal Effect of Directives: A Missed Opportunity?' (1994) 19 ELR 621

Trinidade, FA, 'Parliamentary Sovereignty and the Primacy of European Community Law' (1972) 35 MLR 375

Vincent-Jones, P, 'Central-local relations under the Local Government Act 1999: a new consensus?' (2000) 63 MLR 84

Virgo, G, 'Constructing manslaughter in drug abuse cases' [2003] 62 CLJ 12

Vizkelety, B, 'Discrimination, the Right to Seek Redress and the Common Law: A Century Old Debate' (1992) 15 Dalhousie LJ 306

von Hirsch, A, 'Proportionate sentences for juveniles: how different than for adults?' (2001) 3 Punishment and Society 221

—— and Wasik, M, 'Civil disqualifications attending conviction: a suggested conceptual framework' (1997) 56 CLJ 599

Waddington, L, 'Testing the Limits of the EC Treaty Art on Non-discrimination' (1999) 28 ILJ 133

—— 'Art 13 EC: Setting Priorities in the Proposal for a Horizontal Employment Directive' (2000) 29 ILJ 176

Wade, HWR, 'The Twilight of Natural Justice' (1951) 67 LQR 103

—— 'The Basis of Legal Sovereignty' [1955] CLJ 172

—— 'Sovereignty and the European Communities' (1972) 88 LQR 1

—— 'Sovereignty—Revolution or Evolution?' (1996) 112 LQR 568

Wade, Sir W, 'Human Rights and the Judiciary' [1998] European Human Rights L Rev 520

Walker, C, and Reid, K, 'The Offence of Directing Terrorist Organisations' [1993] Crim LR 669

Warbrick, C, 'International law and domestic law: ministerial powers' (1989) 38 ICLQ 965

Wasik, M, 'Excuses at the sentencing stage' [1983] Crim LR 450

—— 'Form and function in the law of involuntary manslaughter' [1994] Crim LR 883

—— 'The compensation order on sentence' (1999) 163 JP 564

—— 'Is intoxication a mitigating factor in sentencing?' (1999) 163 JP 724

Wasik, M, 'The vital importance of certain previous convictions' [2001] Crim LR 363
—— and von Hirsch, A, 'Non-custodial penalties and the principles of desert' [1988] Crim LR 555
—— and —— 'Section 29 revised: Previous convictions in sentencing' [1994] Crim LR 409
Weatherill, S, 'After *Keck*' [1996] CML Rev 885
Wells, C, 'Swatting the Subjectivist Bug' [1982] Crim LR 209
—— 'Stalking: The Criminal Law Response' [1997] Crim LR 463
Williams, Sir D, 'Bias; the judges and the separation of powers' [2000] PL 45
Williams, DGT, 'Threats, Abuses, Insults' [1967] Crim LR 385
Williams, G, 'The Correlation of Allegiance and Protection' (1948) 10 CLP 54
—— 'Bigamy and the Third Marriage' (1950) 13 MLR 417
—— 'Theft, Consent and Illegality: Some Problems' [1977] Crim LR 127
—— 'Temporary Appropriation Should be Theft' [1981] Crim LR 129
—— 'The Meaning of Literal Interpretation—I' [1981] NLJ 1128
—— 'The Meaning of Literal Interpretation—II' [1981] NLJ 1149
—— 'The Meaning of Indecency' (1992) LS 20
Williams, NG, 'Offer, Acceptance and Improper Considerations: A Common Law Model for the Prohibition of Racial Discrimination in the Contracting Process' (1994) 62 George Washington L Rev 183
Winetrobe, BK, 'Inquiries after Scott: the return of the tribunal of inquiry' [1997] PL 18
—— 'Collective responsibility in devolved Scotland' [2002] PL 24
Winterton, G, 'The British Grundnorm: Parliamentary Supremacy Re-examined' (1976) 92 LQR 591
Woodhouse, D, 'Ministerial responsibility in the 1990s: when do ministers resign? (1993) 46 Parliamentary Affairs 297
—— 'Ministerial Responsibility: Something Old, Something New' [1997] PL 262
—— 'The Office of Lord Chancellor' [1998] PL 617
—— 'The Reconstruction of Constitutional Accountability' [2002] PL 73
Woolf, Sir H, 'Public Law–Private Law: Why the Divide? A Personal View' [1986] PL 220
—— 'Judicial Review: A Possible Programme for Reform' [1992] PL 221
—— '*Droit Public*—English Style' [1995] PL 57

INDEX

conspiracy (*cont.*):
definition 24.50
defraud, to 24.54, 26.124–26.126
deprave and corrupt, conspiracy to 27.105
fault 24.52
impossibility 24.53
intention 24.52
outrage public decency, to 9.45, 24.54,
  27.109–27.110
statutory law 24.50, 24.52–24.54
strict liability 24.52
constituencies 1.75–1.77, 2.10, 2.13–2.15, 9.10
constitutional conventions 1.32–1.39
binding nature of 1.36
Cabinet 1.33, 1.36, 3.45
constitutional law 1.04, 1.05, 1.34, 1.38–1.39
Crown 1.18–1.19, 1.32, 3.05, 3.91
Crown model of central government 3.04–3.05
definition, 1.32
establishing 1.34–1.37
executive 2.40–2.41
hung parliaments 1.18–1.19
ministers 1.23
  collective responsibility of 1.33, 1.39, 1.113
  Crown acting on the advice of 1.33
  individual responsibility of 1.37, 2.80,
    3.132–3.139
  resignation of 1.37
parliamentary democracy 1.33
Prime Minister 1.18–1.19, 1.33, 2.85
purpose of 1.33
Royal Assent 1.17
royal prerogative, 1.32
scope of 1.34
significance of, 1.32–1.33
sources of 1.34
UK Constitution 1.17, 1.33
constitutional law 1.05–1.08
administrative law distinguished from 1.07
Church of England legislation 7.99
civil liberties 1.115, 1.120
constitutional conventions 1.04, 1.05, 1.34,
  1.38–1.39
constitutional framework 1.118–1.119
devolution 1.62–1.65, 1.116
Dicey, AV 1.04–1.05
EC law 1.67, 1.75–1.78
European Union 1.76–1.77
flexibility 1.120
freedom of expression 9.07
human rights 7.08
Human Rights Act 1998 1.78, 1.100, 1.116
judiciary 6.01–6.54
local authorities 4.24–4.37

meaning 1.03–1.07
Northern Ireland 1.52
parliamentary supremacy 1.05, 1.78–1.87,
  1.114–1.115
prerogative powers 1.05, 1.78–1.117
primary legislation 2.55
proportionality 7.167
public order 27.61–27.64
rule of law 1.78, 1.88–1.100, 1.114, 1.115
Scotland 1.52
separation of powers 1.78, 1.101–1.115
tribunals 6.07
UK Constitution 1.03, 1.11
constitutions 1.01–1.02 *see also* **UK Constitution**
amendments 1.01, 1.14–1.15
case law 1.176
central government, division of powers in 3.16
constitutional conventions 1.33
federal 1.40
form of 1.01
judicial review 1.01
meaning of 1.01
states 1.40
consumer credit 13.11
contempt
civil 9.46
criminal 9.47–9.48
declarations 18.31
face of the court, in the 9.47
fair trials 9.47, 9.49
freedom of expression 9.46–9.49
independent and impartial tribunal 9.47
journalists' sources 9.21
judges 9.47–9.48
law officers 3.96
legal proceedings, prejudicing or impeding
  9.49
mandatory orders 18.23
national security 9.44
parliament and 2.118–2.123
penalties 9.46
public authorities 9.48
scandalizing the court 9.48
strict liability 9.49
tribunals of inquiry 22.89
contempt, Parliament and
allowances, claims for 2.121–2.122
bribery 2.123
Committee on Standards and Privileges in
  Public Life 2.120–2.121
Committee on Standards in Public Life 2.120
definition of contempt 2.118
examples of 2.119
fines 2.120